A Statistical History
of the
American Electorate

A Statistical History
of the
American Electorate

Jerrold G. Rusk

University of Illinois at Chicago

CQ PRESS

A Division of Congressional Quarterly Inc.
Washington, D.C.

CQ Press
A Division of Congressional Quarterly Inc.
1255 22nd Street, N.W., Suite 400
Washington, D.C. 20037

(202) 822-1475; (800) 638-1710

www.cqpress.com

Cover design by Rich Pottern

Printed and bound in the United States of America

05 04 03 02 01   5 4 3 2 1

Ref.
JK
1967
.R87
2001

Library of Congress Cataloging-in-Publication Data

Rusk, Jerrold G., 1941–
   A statistical history of the American electorate / Jerrold G. Rusk.
     p. cm.
   Includes bibliographical references and index.
   ISBN 1-56802-364-2 (cloth)—ISBN 1-56802-363-4 (paper)
    1. Elections—United States—Statistics. 2. Voting—United States—Statistics. I. Title.

JK1967.R87 2001
324.973—dc21

00-067453

To Lyn and Sally,
who helped make this book possible

Contents

List of Tables   ix

Preface   xxi

1   The Accuracy and Inaccuracy of Election Data   1

2   Who Is Allowed to Vote: Suffrage and Election Laws   13

3   Who Goes to the Polls   37

4   The Familiarity of Presidential Elections   118

5   The Obscurity of House Elections   198

6   The Notoriety of Senate Elections   369

7   The Isolation of Gubernatorial Elections?   434

8   Party Winners and Losers Across Multiple Elections   510

Appendix

A   Major-Party Labels   690

B   Additional House Election Data   694

Bibliography   698

Index   701

List of Tables

Chapter 1   The Accuracy and Inaccuracy of Election Data

Table 1-1   National Discrepancy Between ICPSR Data Set and Current Data Set for the House of Representatives, 1824–1972 (Percentages)   9

Table 1-2   National Discrepancy Between ICPSR Data Set and Current Data Set for the House of Representatives, 1824–1972 (Raw Differences)   10

Table 1-3   Alternative Party Codings for All Races, 1788–1999   12

Chapter 2   Who Is Allowed to Vote: Suffrage and Election Laws

Table 2-1   Dates of Constitutions Applicable to States Upon Entry into the Union and Dates of Statehood Entry   21

Table 2-2   Freehold, Landed Property, and Other Economic Qualifications for Voting in the British Colonies, 1650–1776   22

Table 2-3   Various Property Qualifications Immediately After the Revolutionary War   22

Table 2-4   Economic Requirements for Voting, 1788–1932   23

Table 2-5   Dates for Economic Requirements for Voting, 1788–1932   24

Table 2-6   Economic Law Combinations for Voting, 1788–1932   24

Table 2-7   Residence Requirement Combinations for the States, 1788–1970   25

Table 2-8   State Residence Requirements for Voting, 1788–1970   26

Table 2-9   County Residence Requirements for Voting, 1788–1970   28

Table 2-10   City or Town Residence Requirements for Voting, 1788–1970   29

Table 2-11   Precinct or Ward Residence Requirements for Voting, 1788–1970   30

Table 2-12   Citizenship Requirements for Voting, 1788–Present   31

Table 2-13   Alien Voting Laws, 1848–1926   32

Table 2-14   White-Only Requirements for Voting, 1788–1870   33

Table 2-15   Poll Tax Laws in Southern States, 1801–1964   33

Table 2-16   Descriptive Characteristics of Poll Tax Laws in Southern States, 1890–1918   34

Table 2-17   Literacy Test Laws in Southern States, 1890–1965   34

Table 2-18   Grandfather and Old Soldier Clauses to Southern Literacy Tests, 1900–1915   35

Table 2-19   Literacy Test Laws in Nonsouthern States, 1855–1970   35

Table 2-20   Female Suffrage Acts (Prior to Passage of 19th Amendment)   36

Table 2-21   Federal Amendments on Voting, 1870–1971   36

Chapter 3   Who Goes to the Polls

Table 3-1   National and Regional Voter Eligibility Percentages for Presidential Elections, 1788–1996   50

Table 3-2   National and Regional Voter Mobilization Percentages for Presidential Elections, 1788–1996   51

Table 3-3   National and Regional Voter Turnout Percentages for Presidential Elections, 1788–1996   52

Table 3-4   National and Regional Voter Mobilization Percentages for Congressional Elections, 1788–1998   53

Table 3-5   National and Regional Voter Turnout Percentages for Congressional Elections, 1788–1998   54

Table 3-6   Percentage Differences in National Voter Turnout Between the Presidential Races and House Races Held in Presidential and Midterm Election Years, 1788–1996   55

Table 3-7	National and Regional Voter Mobilization Percentages for Senate Elections, 1912–1998	55
Table 3-8	National and Regional Voter Turnout Percentages for Senate Elections, 1912–1998	56
Table 3-9	Percentage Differences in National Turnout Between Presidential, Senate, and House Elections, 1912–1998	57
Table 3-10	State Eligibility Percentages in Presidential Elections, 1788–1816	58
Table 3-11	State Eligibility Percentages in Presidential Elections, 1820–1856	59
Table 3-12	State Eligibility Percentages in Presidential Elections, 1860–1896	60
Table 3-13	State Eligibility Percentages in Presidential Elections, 1900–1936	61
Table 3-14	State Eligibility Percentages in Presidential Elections, 1940–1976	62
Table 3-15	State Eligibility Percentages in Presidential Elections, 1980–1996	63
Table 3-16	State Voter Mobilization Percentages in Presidential Elections, 1788–1816	64
Table 3-17	State Voter Mobilization Percentages in Presidential Elections, 1820–1856	65
Table 3-18	State Voter Mobilization Percentages in Presidential Elections, 1860–1896	66
Table 3-19	State Voter Mobilization Percentages in Presidential Elections, 1900–1936	67
Table 3-20	State Voter Mobilization Percentages in Presidential Elections, 1940–1976	68
Table 3-21	State Voter Mobilization Percentages in Presidential Elections, 1980–1996	69
Table 3-22	State Voter Turnout Percentages in Presidential Elections, 1788–1816	70
Table 3-23	State Voter Turnout Percentages in Presidential Elections, 1820–1856	71
Table 3-24	State Voter Turnout Percentages in Presidential Elections, 1860–1896	72
Table 3-25	State Voter Turnout Percentages in Presidential Elections, 1900–1936	73
Table 3-26	State Voter Turnout Percentages in Presidential Elections, 1940–1976	74
Table 3-27	State Voter Turnout Percentages in Presidential Elections, 1980–1996	75
Table 3-28	State Voter Mobilization Percentages for Congressional Elections Using Two-Year Election Cycles, 1788–1799	76
Table 3-29	State Voter Mobilization Percentages for Congressional Elections Using Two-Year Election Cycles, 1800–1819	77
Table 3-30	State Voter Mobilization Percentages for Congressional Elections Using Two-Year Election Cycles, 1820–1839	78
Table 3-31	State Voter Mobilization Percentages for Congressional Elections Using Two-Year Election Cycles, 1840–1859	79
Table 3-32	State Voter Mobilization Percentages for Congressional Elections Using Two-Year Election Cycles, 1860–1879	80
Table 3-33	State Voter Mobilization Percentages for Congressional Elections Using Two-Year Election Cycles, 1880–1898	81
Table 3-34	State Voter Mobilization Percentages for Congressional Elections Using Two-Year Election Cycles, 1900–1918	82
Table 3-35	State Voter Mobilization Percentages for Congressional Elections Using Two-Year Election Cycles, 1920–1938	83
Table 3-36	State Voter Mobilization Percentages for Congressional Elections Using Two-Year Election Cycles, 1940–1959	84
Table 3-37	State Voter Mobilization Percentages for Congressional Elections Using Two-Year Election Cycles, 1960–1978	85
Table 3-38	State Voter Mobilization Percentages for Congressional Elections Using Two-Year Election Cycles, 1980–1998	86
Table 3-39	State Voter Mobilization Percentages for Congressional Elections in Odd-Numbered Years Only, 1789–1809	87
Table 3-40	State Voter Mobilization Percentages for Congressional Elections in Odd-Numbered Years Only, 1811–1829	88
Table 3-41	State Voter Mobilization Percentages for Congressional Elections in Odd-Numbered Years Only, 1831–1849	89
Table 3-42	State Voter Mobilization Percentages for Congressional Elections in Odd-Numbered Years Only, 1851–1869	90
Table 3-43	State Voter Mobilization Percentages for Congressional Elections in Odd-Numbered Years Only, 1871–1959	91
Table 3-44	State Voter Turnout Percentages for Congressional Elections Using Two-Year Election Cycles, 1788–1799	92

Table 3-45   State Voter Turnout Percentages for Congressional Elections Using Two-Year Election
Cycles, 1800–1819   93
Table 3-46   State Voter Turnout Percentages for Congressional Elections Using Two-Year Election
Cycles, 1820–1839   94
Table 3-47   State Voter Turnout Percentages for Congressional Elections Using Two-Year Election
Cycles, 1840–1859   95
Table 3-48   State Voter Turnout Percentages for Congressional Elections Using Two-Year Election
Cycles, 1860–1879   96
Table 3-49   State Voter Turnout Percentages for Congressional Elections Using Two-Year Election
Cycles, 1880–1898   97
Table 3-50   State Voter Turnout Percentages for Congressional Elections Using Two-Year Election
Cycles, 1900–1918   98
Table 3-51   State Voter Turnout Percentages for Congressional Elections Using Two-Year Election
Cycles, 1920–1938   99
Table 3-52   State Voter Turnout Percentages for Congressional Elections Using Two-Year Election
Cycles, 1940–1959   100
Table 3-53   State Voter Turnout Percentages for Congressional Elections Using Two-Year Election
Cycles, 1960–1978   101
Table 3-54   State Voter Turnout Percentages for Congressional Elections Using Two-Year Election
Cycles, 1980–1998   102
Table 3-55   State Voter Turnout Percentages for Congressional Elections in Odd-Numbered Years
Only, 1789–1809   103
Table 3-56   State Voter Turnout Percentages for Congressional Elections in Odd-Numbered Years
Only, 1811–1829   104
Table 3-57   State Voter Turnout Percentages for Congressional Elections in Odd-Numbered Years
Only, 1831–1849   105
Table 3-58   State Voter Turnout Percentages for Congressional Elections in Odd-Numbered Years
Only, 1851–1869   106
Table 3-59   State Voter Turnout Percentages for Congressional Elections in Odd-Numbered Years
Only, 1871–1959   107
Table 3-60   State Voter Mobilization Percentages for Senate Elections, 1912–1928   108
Table 3-61   State Voter Mobilization Percentages for Senate Elections, 1930–1948   109
Table 3-62   State Voter Mobilization Percentages for Senate Elections, 1950–1968   110
Table 3-63   State Voter Mobilization Percentages for Senate Elections, 1970–1988   111
Table 3-64   State Voter Mobilization Percentages for Senate Elections, 1990–1998   112
Table 3-65   State Voter Turnout Percentages for Senate Elections, 1912–1928   113
Table 3-66   State Voter Turnout Percentages for Senate Elections, 1930–1948   114
Table 3-67   State Voter Turnout Percentages for Senate Elections, 1950–1968   115
Table 3-68   State Voter Turnout Percentages for Senate Elections, 1970–1988   116
Table 3-69   State Voter Turnout Percentages for Senate Elections, 1990–1998   117

Chapter 4   The Familiarity of Presidential Elections

Table 4-1   Method of Choosing Presidential Electors, 1788–1832   131
Table 4-2   Comparison of Popular and Electoral Vote Mandates, 1824–1996   132
Table 4-3   Electoral Vote for President, 1788–1996   133
Table 4-4   Popular Vote for President, 1788–1996   134
Table 4-5   Popular Vote for President, by Region, 1788–1996   135
Table 4-6   Popular Vote for President, by Non-South and South, 1788–1996   139
Table 4-7   Electoral Vote for President, by Non-South and South, 1856–1996   141
Table 4-8   Party Winning Presidential Election, by State, in Regions, 1788–1996   142
Table 4-9   Vote Shifts Needed to Change Presidential Election Outcome   143
Table 4-10   Presidential Election Results, by State, 1788–1792 (Percentages)   144
Table 4-11   Presidential Election Results, by State, 1796–1800 (Percentages)   145
Table 4-12   Presidential Election Results, by State, 1804–1808 (Percentages)   146
Table 4-13   Presidential Election Results, by State, 1812–1816 (Percentages)   147

Table 4-14	Presidential Election Results, by State, 1820–1824 (Percentages)	148
Table 4-15	Presidential Election Results, by State, 1828–1832 (Percentages)	149
Table 4-16	Presidential Election Results, by State, 1836–1840 (Percentages)	150
Table 4-17	Presidential Election Results, by State, 1844–1848 (Percentages)	151
Table 4-18	Presidential Election Results, by State, 1852–1856 (Percentages)	152
Table 4-19	Presidential Election Results, by State, 1860–1864 (Percentages)	153
Table 4-20	Presidential Election Results, by State, 1868–1872 (Percentages)	154
Table 4-21	Presidential Election Results, by State, 1876–1880 (Percentages)	155
Table 4-22	Presidential Election Results, by State, 1884–1888 (Percentages)	156
Table 4-23	Presidential Election Results, by State, 1892–1896 (Percentages)	157
Table 4-24	Presidential Election Results, by State, 1900–1904 (Percentages)	158
Table 4-25	Presidential Election Results, by State, 1908–1912 (Percentages)	159
Table 4-26	Presidential Election Results, by State, 1916–1920 (Percentages)	160
Table 4-27	Presidential Election Results, by State, 1924–1928 (Percentages)	161
Table 4-28	Presidential Election Results, by State, 1932–1936 (Percentages)	162
Table 4-29	Presidential Election Results, by State, 1940–1944 (Percentages)	163
Table 4-30	Presidential Election Results, by State, 1948–1952 (Percentages)	164
Table 4-31	Presidential Election Results, by State, 1956–1960 (Percentages)	165
Table 4-32	Presidential Election Results, by State, 1964–1968 (Percentages)	166
Table 4-33	Presidential Election Results, by State, 1972–1976 (Percentages)	167
Table 4-34	Presidential Election Results, by State, 1980–1984 (Percentages)	168
Table 4-35	Presidential Election Results, by State, 1988–1992 (Percentages)	169
Table 4-36	Presidential Election Results, by State, 1996 (Percentages)	170
Table 4-37	Raw Popular Vote for President, by State, 1788–1792	171
Table 4-38	Raw Popular Vote for President, by State, 1796–1800	172
Table 4-39	Raw Popular Vote for President, by State, 1804–1808	173
Table 4-40	Raw Popular Vote for President, by State, 1812–1816	174
Table 4-41	Raw Popular Vote for President, by State, 1820–1824	175
Table 4-42	Raw Popular Vote for President, by State, 1828–1832	176
Table 4-43	Raw Popular Vote for President, by State, 1836–1840	177
Table 4-44	Raw Popular Vote for President, by State, 1844–1848	178
Table 4-45	Raw Popular Vote for President, by State, 1852–1856	179
Table 4-46	Raw Popular Vote for President, by State, 1860–1864	180
Table 4-47	Raw Popular Vote for President, by State, 1868–1872	181
Table 4-48	Raw Popular Vote for President, by State, 1876–1880	182
Table 4-49	Raw Popular Vote for President, by State, 1884–1888	183
Table 4-50	Raw Popular Vote for President, by State, 1892–1896	184
Table 4-51	Raw Popular Vote for President, by State, 1900–1904	185
Table 4-52	Raw Popular Vote for President, by State, 1908–1912	186
Table 4-53	Raw Popular Vote for President, by State, 1916–1920	187
Table 4-54	Raw Popular Vote for President, by State, 1924–1928	188
Table 4-55	Raw Popular Vote for President, by State, 1932–1936	189
Table 4-56	Raw Popular Vote for President, by State, 1940–1944	190
Table 4-57	Raw Popular Vote for President, by State, 1948–1952	191
Table 4-58	Raw Popular Vote for President, by State, 1956–1960	192
Table 4-59	Raw Popular Vote for President, by State, 1964–1968	193
Table 4-60	Raw Popular Vote for President, by State, 1972–1976	194
Table 4-61	Raw Popular Vote for President, by State, 1980–1984	195
Table 4-62	Raw Popular Vote for President, by State, 1988–1992	196
Table 4-63	Raw Popular Vote for President, by State, 1996	197

Chapter 5   The Obscurity of House Elections

Table 5-1	Alternative Party Coding for House of Representatives, 1788–1998	213
Table 5-2	Methods of Apportioning Seats for the House of Representatives, 1788–1998	214
Table 5-3	Political Composition of the House of Representatives, 1789–2001	215

Table 5-4	National Results of House Elections, by Two-Year Election Cycle, 1788–1998	217
Table 5-5	National Results of House Elections, Annually, 1788–1998	219
Table 5-6	Comparison of National Seats and Votes in House Elections, 1794–1998	222
Table 5-7	Votes in House Elections, by Region, 1788–1998	224
Table 5-8	Votes in House Elections, by Non-South and South, 1788–1998	232
Table 5-9	Party Victories in House Elections, by State, in Regions, 1788–1822	235
Table 5-10	Party Victories in House Elections, by State, in Regions, 1824–1852	238
Table 5-11	Party Victories in House Elections, by State, in Regions, 1854–1892	241
Table 5-12	Party Victories in House Elections, by State, in Regions, 1894–1928	245
Table 5-13	Party Victories in House Elections, by State, in Regions, 1930–1964	250
Table 5-14	Party Victories in House Elections, by State, in Regions, 1966–1998	255
Table 5-15	Party Victories in House Elections, by Non-South and South, 1856–1998	260
Table 5-16	Reelection Rates of House Incumbents, 1791–2001	261
Table 5-17	House Election Results, by State, 1788–1791 (Percentages)	262
Table 5-18	House Election Results, by State, 1792–1795 (Percentages)	263
Table 5-19	House Election Results, by State, 1796–1799 (Percentages)	264
Table 5-20	House Election Results, by State, 1800–1803 (Percentages)	265
Table 5-21	House Election Results, by State, 1804–1807 (Percentages)	266
Table 5-22	House Election Results, by State, 1808–1811 (Percentages)	267
Table 5-23	House Election Results, by State, 1812–1815 (Percentages)	268
Table 5-24	House Election Results, by State, 1816–1819 (Percentages)	269
Table 5-25	House Election Results, by State, 1820–1823 (Percentages)	270
Table 5-26	House Election Results, by State, 1824–1827 (Percentages)	271
Table 5-27	House Election Results, by State, 1828–1831 (Percentages)	272
Table 5-28	House Election Results, by State, 1832–1835 (Percentages)	273
Table 5-29	House Election Results, by State, 1836–1839 (Percentages)	274
Table 5-30	House Election Results, by State, 1840–1843 (Percentages)	275
Table 5-31	House Election Results, by State, 1844–1847 (Percentages)	276
Table 5-32	House Election Results, by State, 1848–1851 (Percentages)	277
Table 5-33	House Election Results, by State, 1852–1855 (Percentages)	278
Table 5-34	House Election Results, by State, 1856–1859 (Percentages)	279
Table 5-35	House Election Results, by State, 1860–1863 (Percentages)	280
Table 5-36	House Election Results, by State, 1864–1867 (Percentages)	281
Table 5-37	House Election Results, by State, 1868–1871 (Percentages)	282
Table 5-38	House Election Results, by State, 1872–1875 (Percentages)	283
Table 5-39	House Election Results, by State, 1876–1879 (Percentages)	284
Table 5-40	House Election Results, by State, 1880–1882 (Percentages)	285
Table 5-41	House Election Results, by State, 1884–1886 (Percentages)	286
Table 5-42	House Election Results, by State, 1888–1890 (Percentages)	287
Table 5-43	House Election Results, by State, 1892–1895 (Percentages)	288
Table 5-44	House Election Results, by State, 1896–1898 (Percentages)	289
Table 5-45	House Election Results, by State, 1900–1902 (Percentages)	291
Table 5-46	House Election Results, by State, 1904–1907 (Percentages)	292
Table 5-47	House Election Results, by State, 1908–1911 (Percentages)	293
Table 5-48	House Election Results, by State, 1912–1914 (Percentages)	294
Table 5-49	House Election Results, by State, 1916–1918 (Percentages)	295
Table 5-50	House Election Results, by State, 1920–1922 (Percentages)	296
Table 5-51	House Election Results, by State, 1924–1926 (Percentages)	297
Table 5-52	House Election Results, by State, 1928–1930 (Percentages)	298
Table 5-53	House Election Results, by State, 1932–1934 (Percentages)	299
Table 5-54	House Election Results, by State, 1936–1938 (Percentages)	300
Table 5-55	House Election Results, by State, 1940–1942 (Percentages)	301
Table 5-56	House Election Results, by State, 1944–1946 (Percentages)	302
Table 5-57	House Election Results, by State, 1948–1950 (Percentages)	303
Table 5-58	House Election Results, by State, 1952–1954 (Percentages)	304
Table 5-59	House Election Results, by State, 1956–1959 (Percentages)	305

Table 5-60	House Election Results, by State, 1960–1962 (Percentages)	306
Table 5-61	House Election Results, by State, 1964–1966 (Percentages)	307
Table 5-62	House Election Results, by State, 1968–1970 (Percentages)	308
Table 5-63	House Election Results, by State, 1972–1974 (Percentages)	309
Table 5-64	House Election Results, by State, 1976–1978 (Percentages)	310
Table 5-65	House Election Results, by State, 1980–1982 (Percentages)	311
Table 5-66	House Election Results, by State, 1984–1986 (Percentages)	312
Table 5-67	House Election Results, by State, 1988–1990 (Percentages)	313
Table 5-68	House Election Results, by State, 1992–1994 (Percentages)	314
Table 5-69	House Election Results, by State, 1996–1998 (Percentages)	315
Table 5-70	House Election Results, by State, 1788–1791 (Raw Count)	316
Table 5-71	House Election Results, by State, 1792–1795 (Raw Count)	317
Table 5-72	House Election Results, by State, 1796–1799 (Raw Count)	318
Table 5-73	House Election Results, by State, 1800–1803 (Raw Count)	319
Table 5-74	House Election Results, by State, 1804–1807 (Raw Count)	320
Table 5-75	House Election Results, by State, 1808–1811 (Raw Count)	321
Table 5-76	House Election Results, by State, 1812–1815 (Raw Count)	322
Table 5-77	House Election Results, by State, 1816–1819 (Raw Count)	323
Table 5-78	House Election Results, by State, 1820–1823 (Raw Count)	324
Table 5-79	House Election Results, by State, 1824–1827 (Raw Count)	325
Table 5-80	House Election Results, by State, 1828–1831 (Raw Count)	326
Table 5-81	House Election Results, by State, 1832–1835 (Raw Count)	327
Table 5-82	House Election Results, by State, 1836–1839 (Raw Count)	328
Table 5-83	House Election Results, by State, 1840–1843 (Raw Count)	329
Table 5-84	House Election Results, by State, 1844–1847 (Raw Count)	330
Table 5-85	House Election Results, by State, 1848–1851 (Raw Count)	331
Table 5-86	House Election Results, by State, 1852–1855 (Raw Count)	332
Table 5-87	House Election Results, by State, 1856–1859 (Raw Count)	333
Table 5-88	House Election Results, by State, 1860–1863 (Raw Count)	334
Table 5-89	House Election Results, by State, 1864–1867 (Raw Count)	335
Table 5-90	House Election Results, by State, 1868–1871 (Raw Count)	336
Table 5-91	House Election Results, by State, 1872–1875 (Raw Count)	337
Table 5-92	House Election Results, by State, 1876–1879 (Raw Count)	338
Table 5-93	House Election Results, by State, 1880–1882 (Raw Count)	339
Table 5-94	House Election Results, by State, 1884–1886 (Raw Count)	340
Table 5-95	House Election Results, by State, 1888–1890 (Raw Count)	341
Table 5-96	House Election Results, by State, 1892–1895 (Raw Count)	342
Table 5-97	House Election Results, by State, 1896–1898 (Raw Count)	343
Table 5-98	House Election Results, by State, 1900–1902 (Raw Count)	344
Table 5-99	House Election Results, by State, 1904–1907 (Raw Count)	345
Table 5-100	House Election Results, by State, 1908–1911 (Raw Count)	346
Table 5-101	House Election Results, by State, 1912–1914 (Raw Count)	347
Table 5-102	House Election Results, by State, 1916–1918 (Raw Count)	348
Table 5-103	House Election Results, by State, 1920–1922 (Raw Count)	349
Table 5-104	House Election Results, by State, 1924–1926 (Raw Count)	350
Table 5-105	House Election Results, by State, 1928–1930 (Raw Count)	351
Table 5-106	House Election Results, by State, 1932–1934 (Raw Count)	352
Table 5-107	House Election Results, by State, 1936–1938 (Raw Count)	353
Table 5-108	House Election Results, by State, 1940–1942 (Raw Count)	354
Table 5-109	House Election Results, by State, 1944–1946 (Raw Count)	355
Table 5-110	House Election Results, by State, 1948–1950 (Raw Count)	356
Table 5-111	House Election Results, by State, 1952–1954 (Raw Count)	357
Table 5-112	House Election Results, by State, 1956–1959 (Raw Count)	358
Table 5-113	House Election Results, by State, 1960–1962 (Raw Count)	359
Table 5-114	House Election Results, by State, 1964–1966 (Raw Count)	360
Table 5-115	House Election Results, by State, 1968–1970 (Raw Count)	361

Table 5-116   House Election Results, by State, 1972–1974 (Raw Count)   362
Table 5-117   House Election Results, by State, 1976–1978 (Raw Count)   363
Table 5-118   House Election Results, by State, 1980–1982 (Raw Count)   364
Table 5-119   House Election Results, by State, 1984–1986 (Raw Count)   365
Table 5-120   House Election Results, by State, 1988–1990 (Raw Count)   366
Table 5-121   House Election Results, by State, 1992–1994 (Raw Count)   367
Table 5-122   House Election Results, by State, 1996–1998 (Raw Count)   368

Chapter 6   The Notoriety of Senate Elections

Table 6-1   Senate Election Classes   376
Table 6-2   Political Composition of the Senate, 1788–1998   377
Table 6-3   National Results of Senate Elections, 1912–1998   378
Table 6-4   Comparison of National Seats and Votes in Senate Elections, 1912–1998   379
Table 6-5   Votes in Senate Elections, by Region, 1912–1998   380
Table 6-6   Votes in Senate Elections, by Non-South and South, 1912–1998   384
Table 6-7   Party Victories in Senate Elections, by State, in Regions, 1912–1998   386
Table 6-8   Party Victories in Senate Elections, by Non-South and South, 1912–1998   387
Table 6-9   Reelection Rates of Senate Incumbents, 1914–1998   388
Table 6-10   Alternative Party Coding for Senate Elections, 1912–1998   389
Table 6-11   Senate Election Results, by State, 1912–1914 (Percentages)   390
Table 6-12   Senate Election Results, by State, 1916–1918 (Percentages)   391
Table 6-13   Senate Election Results, by State, 1920–1922 (Percentages)   392
Table 6-14   Senate Election Results, by State, 1924–1926 (Percentages)   393
Table 6-15   Senate Election Results, by State, 1928–1930 (Percentages)   394
Table 6-16   Senate Election Results, by State, 1932–1934 (Percentages)   395
Table 6-17   Senate Election Results, by State, 1936–1938 (Percentages)   396
Table 6-18   Senate Election Results, by State, 1940–1942 (Percentages)   397
Table 6-19   Senate Election Results, by State, 1944–1946 (Percentages)   398
Table 6-20   Senate Election Results, by State, 1948–1950 (Percentages)   399
Table 6-21   Senate Election Results, by State, 1952–1954 (Percentages)   400
Table 6-22   Senate Election Results, by State, 1956–1959 (Percentages)   401
Table 6-23   Senate Election Results, by State, 1960–1962 (Percentages)   402
Table 6-24   Senate Election Results, by State, 1964–1966 (Percentages)   403
Table 6-25   Senate Election Results, by State, 1968–1970 (Percentages)   404
Table 6-26   Senate Election Results, by State, 1972–1974 (Percentages)   405
Table 6-27   Senate Election Results, by State, 1976–1978 (Percentages)   406
Table 6-28   Senate Election Results, by State, 1980–1982 (Percentages)   407
Table 6-29   Senate Election Results, by State, 1984–1986 (Percentages)   408
Table 6-30   Senate Election Results, by State, 1988–1990 (Percentages)   409
Table 6-31   Senate Election Results, by State, 1992–1994 (Percentages)   410
Table 6-32   Senate Election Results, by State, 1996–1998 (Percentages)   411
Table 6-33   Senate Election Results, by State, 1912–1914 (Raw Count)   412
Table 6-34   Senate Election Results, by State, 1916–1918 (Raw Count)   413
Table 6-35   Senate Election Results, by State, 1920–1922 (Raw Count)   414
Table 6-36   Senate Election Results, by State, 1924–1926 (Raw Count)   415
Table 6-37   Senate Election Results, by State, 1928–1930 (Raw Count)   416
Table 6-38   Senate Election Results, by State, 1932–1934 (Raw Count)   417
Table 6-39   Senate Election Results, by State, 1936–1938 (Raw Count)   418
Table 6-40   Senate Election Results, by State, 1940–1942 (Raw Count)   419
Table 6-41   Senate Election Results, by State, 1944–1946 (Raw Count)   420
Table 6-42   Senate Election Results, by State, 1948–1950 (Raw Count)   421
Table 6-43   Senate Election Results, by State, 1952–1954 (Raw Count)   422
Table 6-44   Senate Election Results, by State, 1956–1959 (Raw Count)   423
Table 6-45   Senate Election Results, by State, 1960–1962 (Raw Count)   424
Table 6-46   Senate Election Results, by State, 1964–1966 (Raw Count)   425

Table 6-47   Senate Election Results, by State, 1968–1970 (Raw Count)   426
Table 6-48   Senate Election Results, by State, 1972–1974 (Raw Count)   427
Table 6-49   Senate Election Results, by State, 1976–1978 (Raw Count)   428
Table 6-50   Senate Election Results, by State, 1980–1982 (Raw Count)   429
Table 6-51   Senate Election Results, by State, 1984–1986 (Raw Count)   430
Table 6-52   Senate Election Results, by State, 1988–1990 (Raw Count)   431
Table 6-53   Senate Election Results, by State, 1992–1994 (Raw Count)   432
Table 6-54   Senate Election Results, by State, 1996–1998 (Raw Count)   433

Chapter 7   The Isolation of Gubernatorial Elections?

Table 7-1   Selection and Terms of American State Governors, 1788–1999   441
Table 7-2   Election Victories for Governor, 1788–1999   442
Table 7-3   National Results for Gubernatorial Elections, by Election Year, 1788–1999
              (Percentages)   444
Table 7-4   National Results for Gubernatorial Elections, by Two-Year Election Cycle,
              1788–1999 (Percentages)   446
Table 7-5   Party Control of Statehouses, 1788–1998   447
Table 7-6   Votes in Gubernatorial Elections, by Region, 1788–1999 (Percentages)   448
Table 7-7   Votes in Gubernatorial Elections, by Non-South and South, 1788–1999 (Percentages) 453
Table 7-8   Alternative Party Codings for Governor, 1788–1999   455
Table 7-9   Governor Election Results, by State, 1788–1791 (Percentages)   456
Table 7-10   Governor Election Results, by State, 1792–1795 (Percentages)   457
Table 7-11   Governor Election Results, by State, 1796–1799 (Percentages)   458
Table 7-12   Governor Election Results, by State, 1800–1803 (Percentages)   459
Table 7-13   Governor Election Results, by State, 1804–1807 (Percentages)   460
Table 7-14   Governor Election Results, by State, 1808–1811 (Percentages)   461
Table 7-15   Governor Election Results, by State, 1812–1815 (Percentages)   462
Table 7-16   Governor Election Results, by State, 1816–1819 (Percentages)   463
Table 7-17   Governor Election Results, by State, 1820–1823 (Percentages)   464
Table 7-18   Governor Election Results, by State, 1824–1827 (Percentages)   465
Table 7-19   Governor Election Results, by State, 1828–1831 (Percentages)   466
Table 7-20   Governor Election Results, by State, 1832–1835 (Percentages)   467
Table 7-21   Governor Election Results, by State, 1836–1839 (Percentages)   468
Table 7-22   Governor Election Results, by State, 1840–1843 (Percentages)   469
Table 7-23   Governor Election Results, by State, 1844–1847 (Percentages)   470
Table 7-24   Governor Election Results, by State, 1848–1851 (Percentages)   471
Table 7-25   Governor Election Results, by State, 1852–1855 (Percentages)   472
Table 7-26   Governor Election Results, by State, 1856–1859 (Percentages)   473
Table 7-27   Governor Election Results, by State, 1860–1863 (Percentages)   474
Table 7-28   Governor Election Results, by State, 1864–1867 (Percentages)   475
Table 7-29   Governor Election Results, by State, 1868–1871 (Percentages)   476
Table 7-30   Governor Election Results, by State, 1872–1875 (Percentages)   477
Table 7-31   Governor Election Results, by State, 1876–1879 (Percentages)   478
Table 7-32   Governor Election Results, by State, 1880–1883 (Percentages)   479
Table 7-33   Governor Election Results, by State, 1884–1887 (Percentages)   480
Table 7-34   Governor Election Results, by State, 1888–1891 (Percentages)   481
Table 7-35   Governor Election Results, by State, 1892–1895 (Percentages)   482
Table 7-36   Governor Election Results, by State, 1896–1899 (Percentages)   483
Table 7-37   Governor Election Results, by State, 1900–1903 (Percentages)   485
Table 7-38   Governor Election Results, by State, 1904–1907 (Percentages)   486
Table 7-39   Governor Election Results, by State, 1908–1911 (Percentages)   487
Table 7-40   Governor Election Results, by State, 1912–1915 (Percentages)   488
Table 7-41   Governor Election Results, by State, 1916–1919 (Percentages)   489
Table 7-42   Governor Election Results, by State, 1920–1923 (Percentages)   490
Table 7-43   Governor Election Results, by State, 1924–1927 (Percentages)   491

Table 7-44   Governor Election Results, by State, 1928–1931 (Percentages)   492
Table 7-45   Governor Election Results, by State, 1932–1935 (Percentages)   493
Table 7-46   Governor Election Results, by State, 1936–1939 (Percentages)   494
Table 7-47   Governor Election Results, by State, 1940–1943 (Percentages)   495
Table 7-48   Governor Election Results, by State, 1944–1947 (Percentages)   496
Table 7-49   Governor Election Results, by State, 1948–1951 (Percentages)   497
Table 7-50   Governor Election Results, by State, 1952–1955 (Percentages)   498
Table 7-51   Governor Election Results, by State, 1956–1959 (Percentages)   499
Table 7-52   Governor Election Results, by State, 1960–1963 (Percentages)   500
Table 7-53   Governor Election Results, by State, 1964–1967 (Percentages)   501
Table 7-54   Governor Election Results, by State, 1968–1971 (Percentages)   502
Table 7-55   Governor Election Results, by State, 1972–1975 (Percentages)   503
Table 7-56   Governor Election Results, by State, 1976–1979 (Percentages)   504
Table 7-57   Governor Election Results, by State, 1980–1983 (Percentages)   505
Table 7-58   Governor Election Results, by State, 1984–1987 (Percentages)   506
Table 7-59   Governor Election Results, by State, 1988–1991 (Percentages)   507
Table 7-60   Governor Election Results, by State, 1992–1995 (Percentages)   508
Table 7-61   Governor Election Results, by State, 1996–1999 (Percentages)   509

Chapter 8   Party Winners and Losers Across Multiple Elections

Table 8-1   National Composite Competition Index, by Election Year, 1788–1999   516
Table 8-2   National Composite Competition Index, by Two-Year Election Cycle, 1788–1999   517
Table 8-3   National Competition Measures, by Election Year, 1788–1999   518
Table 8-4   National Competition Measures, by Two-Year Election Cycle, 1788–1999   523
Table 8-5   Composite Competition Index, by Region, by Two-Year Election Cycle, 1788–1999   527
Table 8-6   Competition Measures, by Region, by Two-Year Election Cycle, 1788–1999   530
Table 8-7   Composite Competition Index for Non-South and South, by Two-Year Election Cycle, 1788–1999   549
Table 8-8   Competition Measures for Non-South and South, by Two-Year Election Cycle, 1788–1999   551
Table 8-9   Composite Competition Index, by State, by Election Year, 1788–1795 (Percentages)   558
Table 8-10   Composite Competition Index, by State, by Election Year, 1796–1803 (Percentages)   559
Table 8-11   Composite Competition Index, by State, by Election Year, 1804–1811 (Percentages)   560
Table 8-12   Composite Competition Index, by State, by Election Year, 1812–1819 (Percentages)   561
Table 8-13   Composite Competition Index, by State, by Election Year, 1820–1827 (Percentages)   562
Table 8-14   Composite Competition Index, by State, by Election Year, 1828–1835 (Percentages)   563
Table 8-15   Composite Competition Index, by State, by Election Year, 1836–1843 (Percentages)   564
Table 8-16   Composite Competition Index, by State, by Election Year, 1844–1851 (Percentages)   565
Table 8-17   Composite Competition Index, by State, by Election Year, 1852–1859 (Percentages)   566
Table 8-18   Composite Competition Index, by State, by Election Year, 1860–1867 (Percentages)   567
Table 8-19   Composite Competition Index, by State, by Election Year, 1868–1875 (Percentages)   568
Table 8-20   Composite Competition Index, by State, by Election Year, 1876–1883 (Percentages)   569
Table 8-21   Composite Competition Index, by State, by Election Year, 1884–1891 (Percentages)   570
Table 8-22   Composite Competition Index, by State, by Election Year, 1892–1899 (Percentages)   571
Table 8-23   Composite Competition Index, by State, by Election Year, 1900–1907 (Percentages)   572
Table 8-24   Composite Competition Index, by State, by Election Year, 1908–1915 (Percentages)   573
Table 8-25   Composite Competition Index, by State, by Election Year, 1916–1923 (Percentages)   574
Table 8-26   Composite Competition Index, by State, by Election Year, 1924–1931 (Percentages)   575
Table 8-27   Composite Competition Index, by State, by Election Year, 1932–1939 (Percentages)   576
Table 8-28   Composite Competition Index, by State, by Election Year, 1940–1947 (Percentages)   577
Table 8-29   Composite Competition Index, by State, by Election Year, 1948–1955 (Percentages)   578
Table 8-30   Composite Competition Index, by State, by Election Year, 1956–1963 (Percentages)   579
Table 8-31   Composite Competition Index, by State, by Election Year, 1964–1971 (Percentages)   580
Table 8-32   Composite Competition Index, by State, by Election Year, 1972–1979 (Percentages)   581
Table 8-33   Composite Competition Index, by State, by Election Year, 1980–1987 (Percentages)   582
Table 8-34   Composite Competition Index, by State, by Election Year, 1988–1995 (Percentages)   583

Table 8-35   Composite Competition Index, by State, by Election Year, 1996–1999 (Percentages)   584
Table 8-36   Presidential Competition Measures, by State, by Election Year, 1788–1796 (Percentages)   585
Table 8-37   Presidential Competition Measures, by State, by Election Year, 1800–1808 (Percentages)   586
Table 8-38   Presidential Competition Measures, by State, by Election Year, 1812–1820 (Percentages)   587
Table 8-39   Presidential Competition Measures, by State, by Election Year, 1824–1832 (Percentages)   588
Table 8-40   Presidential Competition Measures, by State, by Election Year, 1836–1844 (Percentages)   589
Table 8-41   Presidential Competition Measures, by State, by Election Year, 1848–1856 (Percentages)   590
Table 8-42   Presidential Competition Measures, by State, by Election Year, 1860–1868 (Percentages)   591
Table 8-43   Presidential Competition Measures, by State, by Election Year, 1872–1880 (Percentages)   592
Table 8-44   Presidential Competition Measures, by State, by Election Year, 1884–1892 (Percentages)   593
Table 8-45   Presidential Competition Measures, by State, by Election Year, 1896–1904 (Percentages)   594
Table 8-46   Presidential Competition Measures, by State, by Election Year, 1908–1916 (Percentages)   595
Table 8-47   Presidential Competition Measures, by State, by Election Year, 1920–1928 (Percentages)   596
Table 8-48   Presidential Competition Measures, by State, by Election Year, 1932–1940 (Percentages)   597
Table 8-49   Presidential Competition Measures, by State, by Election Year, 1944–1952 (Percentages)   598
Table 8-50   Presidential Competition Measures, by State, by Election Year, 1956–1964 (Percentages)   599
Table 8-51   Presidential Competition Measures, by State, by Election Year, 1968–1976 (Percentages)   600
Table 8-52   Presidential Competition Measures, by State, by Election Year, 1980–1988 (Percentages)   601
Table 8-53   Presidential Competition Measures, by State, by Election Year, 1992–1996 (Percentages)   602
Table 8-54   House Competition Measures, by State, by Two-Year Election Cycle, 1788–1793 (Percentages)   603
Table 8-55   House Competition Measures, by State, by Two-Year Election Cycle, 1794–1799 (Percentages)   604
Table 8-56   House Competition Measures, by State, by Two-Year Election Cycle, 1800–1805 (Percentages)   605
Table 8-57   House Competition Measures, by State, by Two-Year Election Cycle, 1806–1811 (Percentages)   606
Table 8-58   House Competition Measures, by State, by Two-Year Election Cycle, 1812–1817 (Percentages)   607
Table 8-59   House Competition Measures, by State, by Two-Year Election Cycle, 1818–1823 (Percentages)   608
Table 8-60   House Competition Measures, by State, by Two-Year Election Cycle, 1824–1829 (Percentages)   609
Table 8-61   House Competition Measures, by State, by Two-Year Election Cycle, 1830–1835 (Percentages)   610
Table 8-62   House Competition Measures, by State, by Two-Year Election Cycle, 1836–1841 (Percentages)   611
Table 8-63   House Competition Measures, by State, by Two-Year Election Cycle, 1842–1847 (Percentages)   612
Table 8-64   House Competition Measures, by State, by Two-Year Election Cycle, 1848–1853 (Percentages)   613
Table 8-65   House Competition Measures, by State, by Two-Year Election Cycle, 1854–1859 (Percentages)   614
Table 8-66   House Competition Measures, by State, by Two-Year Election Cycle, 1860–1865 (Percentages)   615
Table 8-67   House Competition Measures, by State, by Two-Year Election Cycle, 1866–1871 (Percentages)   616
Table 8-68   House Competition Measures, by State, by Two-Year Election Cycle, 1872–1877 (Percentages)   617
Table 8-69   House Competition Measures, by State, by Two-Year Election Cycle, 1878–1882 (Percentages)   618
Table 8-70   House Competition Measures, by State, by Two-Year Election Cycle, 1884–1889 (Percentages)   619
Table 8-71   House Competition Measures, by State, by Two-Year Election Cycle, 1890–1895 (Percentages)   620
Table 8-72   House Competition Measures, by State, by Election Year, 1896–1900 (Percentages)   621
Table 8-73   House Competition Measures, by State, by Two-Year Election Cycle, 1902–1907 (Percentages)   622
Table 8-74   House Competition Measures, by State, by Two-Year Election Cycle, 1908–1912 (Percentages)   623
Table 8-75   House Competition Measures, by State, by Election Year, 1914–1918 (Percentages)   624
Table 8-76   House Competition Measures, by State, by Election Year, 1920–1924 (Percentages)   625
Table 8-77   House Competition Measures, by State, by Election Year, 1926–1930 (Percentages)   626
Table 8-78   House Competition Measures, by State, by Election Year, 1932–1936 (Percentages)   627
Table 8-79   House Competition Measures, by State, by Election Year, 1938–1942 (Percentages)   628
Table 8-80   House Competition Measures, by State, by Election Year, 1944–1948 (Percentages)   629
Table 8-81   House Competition Measures, by State, by Election Year, 1950–1954 (Percentages)   630
Table 8-82   House Competition Measures, by State, by Two-Year Election Cycle, 1956–1960 (Percentages)   631
Table 8-83   House Competition Measures, by State, by Election Year, 1962–1966 (Percentages)   632
Table 8-84   House Competition Measures, by State, by Election Year, 1968–1972 (Percentages)   633
Table 8-85   House Competition Measures, by State, by Election Year, 1974–1978 (Percentages)   634
Table 8-86   House Competition Measures, by State, by Election Year, 1980–1984 (Percentages)   635
Table 8-87   House Competition Measures, by State, by Election Year, 1986–1990 (Percentages)   636
Table 8-88   House Competition Measures, by State, by Election Year, 1992–1996 (Percentages)   637
Table 8-89   House Competition Measures, by State, by Election Year, 1998 (Percentages)   638
Table 8-90   Senate Competition Measures, by State, by Election Year, 1912–1916 (Percentages)   639

Table 8-91	Senate Competition Measures, by State, by Election Year, 1918–1922 (Percentages)	640
Table 8-92	Senate Competition Measures, by State, by Election Year, 1924–1928 (Percentages)	641
Table 8-93	Senate Competition Measures, by State, by Election Year, 1930–1934 (Percentages)	642
Table 8-94	Senate Competition Measures, by State, by Election Year, 1936–1940 (Percentages)	643
Table 8-95	Senate Competition Measures, by State, by Election Year, 1942–1946 (Percentages)	644
Table 8-96	Senate Competition Measures, by State, by Election Year, 1948–1952 (Percentages)	645
Table 8-97	Senate Competition Measures, by State, by Election Year, 1954–1959 (Percentages)	646
Table 8-98	Senate Competition Measures, by State, by Election Year, 1960–1964 (Percentages)	647
Table 8-99	Senate Competition Measures, by State, by Election Year, 1966–1970 (Percentages)	648
Table 8-100	Senate Competition Measures, by State, by Election Year, 1972–1976 (Percentages)	649
Table 8-101	Senate Competition Measures, by State, by Election Year, 1978–1982 (Percentages)	650
Table 8-102	Senate Competition Measures, by State, by Election Year, 1984–1988 (Percentages)	651
Table 8-103	Senate Competition Measures, by State, by Election Year, 1990–1994 (Percentages)	652
Table 8-104	Senate Competition Measures, by State, by Election Year, 1996–1998 (Percentages)	653
Table 8-105	Governor Competition Measures, by State, by Two-Year Election Cycle, 1788–1793 (Percentages)	654
Table 8-106	Governor Competition Measures, by State, by Two-Year Election Cycle, 1794–1799 (Percentages)	655
Table 8-107	Governor Competition Measures, by State, by Two-Year Election Cycle, 1800–1805 (Percentages)	656
Table 8-108	Governor Competition Measures, by State, by Two-Year Election Cycle, 1806–1811 (Percentages)	657
Table 8-109	Governor Competition Measures, by State, by Two-Year Election Cycle, 1812–1817 (Percentages)	658
Table 8-110	Governor Competition Measures, by State, by Two-Year Election Cycle, 1818–1823 (Percentages)	659
Table 8-111	Governor Competition Measures, by State, by Two-Year Election Cycle, 1824–1829 (Percentages)	660
Table 8-112	Governor Competition Measures, by State, by Two-Year Election Cycle, 1830–1835 (Percentages)	661
Table 8-113	Governor Competition Measures, by State, by Two-Year Election Cycle, 1836–1841 (Percentages)	662
Table 8-114	Governor Competition Measures, by State, by Two-Year Election Cycle, 1842–1847 (Percentages)	663
Table 8-115	Governor Competition Measures, by State, by Two-Year Election Cycle, 1848–1853 (Percentages)	664
Table 8-116	Governor Competition Measures, by State, by Two-Year Election Cycle, 1854–1859 (Percentages)	665
Table 8-117	Governor Competition Measures, by State, by Two-Year Election Cycle, 1860–1865 (Percentages)	666
Table 8-118	Governor Competition Measures, by State, by Two-Year Election Cycle, 1866–1871 (Percentages)	667
Table 8-119	Governor Competition Measures, by State, by Two-Year Election Cycle, 1872–1877 (Percentages)	668
Table 8-120	Governor Competition Measures, by State, by Two-Year Election Cycle, 1878–1883 (Percentages)	669
Table 8-121	Governor Competition Measures, by State, by Two-Year Election Cycle, 1884–1889 (Percentages)	670
Table 8-122	Governor Competition Measures, by State, by Two-Year Election Cycle, 1890–1895 (Percentages)	671
Table 8-123	Governor Competition Measures, by State, by Two-Year Election Cycle, 1896–1901 (Percentages)	672
Table 8-124	Governor Competition Measures, by State, by Two-Year Election Cycle, 1902–1907 (Percentages)	673
Table 8-125	Governor Competition Measures, by State, by Two-Year Election Cycle, 1908–1913 (Percentages)	674

Table 8-126   Governor Competition Measures, by State, by Two-Year Election Cycle, 1914–1919
(Percentages)   675

Table 8-127   Governor Competition Measures, by State, by Two-Year Election Cycle, 1920–1925
(Percentages)   676

Table 8-128   Governor Competition Measures, by State, by Two-Year Election Cycle, 1926–1931
(Percentages)   677

Table 8-129   Governor Competition Measures, by State, by Two-Year Election Cycle, 1932–1937
(Percentages)   678

Table 8-130   Governor Competition Measures, by State, by Two-Year Election Cycle, 1938–1943
(Percentages)   679

Table 8-131   Governor Competition Measures, by State, by Two-Year Election Cycle, 1944–1949
(Percentages)   680

Table 8-132   Governor Competition Measures, by State, by Two-Year Election Cycle, 1950–1955
(Percentages)   681

Table 8-133   Governor Competition Measures, by State, by Two-Year Election Cycle, 1956–1961
(Percentages)   682

Table 8-134   Governor Competition Measures, by State, by Two-Year Election Cycle, 1962–1967
(Percentages)   683

Table 8-135   Governor Competition Measures, by State, by Two-Year Election Cycle, 1968–1973
(Percentages)   684

Table 8-136   Governor Competition Measures, by State, by Two-Year Election Cycle, 1974–1979
(Percentages)   685

Table 8-137   Governor Competition Measures, by State, by Two-Year Election Cycle, 1980–1985
(Percentages)   686

Table 8-138   Governor Competition Measures, by State, by Two-Year Election Cycle, 1986–1991
(Percentages)   687

Table 8-139   Governor Competition Measures, by State, by Two-Year Election Cycle, 1992–1997
(Percentages)   688

Table 8-140   Governor Competition Measures, by State, by Two-Year Election Cycle, 1998–1999
(Percentages)   689

Appendix A   Major-Party Labels

Table A-1   Major-Party Labels Used on State Ballots, 1788–1999   693

Appendix B   Additional House Election Data

Table B-1   State House Vote Based Only on District Results for States Having Combination Systems for
Selecting Members to the House of Representatives, 1788–1998   695

Preface

This volume has three purposes: to achieve accuracy, comprehensiveness, and analytic insight into the behavior of the American electorate from 1788 to 1999. Regarding accuracy, my goal was to create the most accurate reference work to date on the history of the American electorate for the data presented here, whether on suffrage election laws; voting participation rates; votes for president, House, Senate, or governor; or party competition rates for the votes of the American electorate. This book uncovers significant errors in the election results reported in previous works and data archives, including the election data sets of the Inter-university Consortium for Political and Social Research (ICPSR). These errors raise questions of data reliability for the multitude of research studies using this material in the past. Errors include both those of commission (vote count errors) and omission (failure to report voting data that exist). Significant errors in reporting the party labels candidates used on the ballot also exist. Reference to primary sources and the ballot itself is the only recourse to correcting these errors. Further mistakes result from incorrectly distinguishing major-party candidates from minor- and other-party candidates once their true party labels have been determined. Other errors occur in the dates ascribed to the introduction, passage, and repeal of suffrage laws in the states. Recourse to state statute volumes and constitutions is needed to ascertain the correct dates for these crucial election laws defining the American electorate across time. These activities have been undertaken in this volume with the goal of presenting the most accurate data possible on American electoral history.

Regarding comprehensiveness, this is the only volume that presents the electorate's vote for the four most important races contested—president, House, Senate, and governor—across the span of American history from 1788 to 1999. As discussed in greater detail below, I did not include the 2000 election data because they were not considered accurate when this book went to press. Furthermore, the book presents election results for these four races at the state, regional, and national levels for analytic comparison. Most election guides and data sets provide the vote for president and House only since 1824, the conventionally accepted starting date for mass popular elections for the presidency in America. This volume includes, where the data are available, the crucial 1788–1823 presidential and congressional races, presenting parallel data sets for president, House, and governor from 1788 to 1999 and increasing scholars' options for data analysis on the vote for that period for all three races. The book also includes data on the competitiveness of the vote for these same three races across this entire time period at the state, regional, and national levels. Of course, direct election of senators occurred later—starting in 1912—so the complete vote for the Senate extends from 1912 to the present. Data on the vote are also recorded for races occurring in even- and odd-numbered years, an important distinction for congressional and gubernatorial races across much of America's electoral history.

Most important, I code the vote for the four political races covered in this book in two different ways: a pure or conventional coding system, also used by most other scholars, that defines major-party candidates (as distinct from "other" candidates) as those who use on the ballot only the label Democrat or Republican or the labels of their historical antecedents (see Appendix A for a list of the historical antecedents to the Democratic and Republican Parties) without other designations, labels, or party names; and an alternative coding system I devised that defines major-party candidates as those who use on the ballot the major-party label in association with other designations, labels, or party names. The latter is a novel coding that I believe better represents the partisan nature and competitiveness of the vote across time. The reader is at liberty to choose either coding result, since the two coding systems are clearly distinguished in the state vote tables in this book (main entries in these tables being the conventional coding of the vote and bold italicized entries representing my alternative coding system). Additional tables delineate the particular reasons for using my alternative coding system and the exact dates and instances when it was employed.

The book also includes voting data for any of the four races that were only partially reported or recovered at the state level. I have added these data to the state vote tables with an appropriate superscript notation to distinguish these results from the large majority of results for the four races in which complete data were reported or recovered. While ensuring comprehensiveness in covering all the vote data available in America's history, partial-data vote states are obviously not included in vote aggregation efforts to depict regional and national voting trends. I also present voter participation rates for the entire time period for the presidential and congressional races and, since 1912, for the Senate race. Comprehensiveness is again the rule since all three recognized voter participation measures are used in the book, not just voter turnout. The book includes voter mobilization and eligibility data, along with voter turnout, and all three indices of voter participation at the state, regional, and national level (for states with complete voting data only). Finally, I have listed all relevant suffrage laws in America's history and their dates of introduction, passage, or repeal. This is the only data set completely listing the dates for these laws that were so crucial in defining who was included (or not included) as part of the electorate at any particular time in America's electoral history. In addition to these vote and suffrage tables, each chapter includes other tables pertaining to the topic at hand. For example, the presidential vote chapter contains tables comparing the popular vote results for president with the electoral college vote results, and the House vote chapter presents tables comparing congressional seats won by the two major parties with actual popular votes received by these parties. The upshot is that this volume attempts to cover the complete range of topics, and the data available for these topics, on the key political characteristics of the historical American electorate: vote choice, vote participation, vote competitiveness, and the election laws shaping the electorate and its vote.

Regarding analytic insight, I present an introductory textual analysis of the data in each chapter that highlights some relevant facts, often unknown or highly neglected, about the American electorate. Important insights into the role of state politics, the condition of state party competition, the strength of state party organizations, and the changes in party realignments result. Probably the most important lesson gained from the vote data in this book is the central place of state and local politics across America's political history. Often eclipsed by the celebrity and hoopla of the more colorful national contest for the presidency, state traditions, demography, economic characteristics, and political culture are actually better explanations of state, regional, and national voting patterns than are the so-called national influences and the supposedly countrywide impact of the presidential race. Closely allied is the important role that party organization plays in each state. Analysis of the vote across all four races (including the presidential race) shows that most states are not very competitive. National aggregation of the vote appears to suggest otherwise, but it largely disguises the fact that one-party states for one major party offset one-party states for the other major party, with only a few states being truly competitive. State tradition, political culture, and party organization figure prominently in producing such voting patterns. Even in periods of acknowledged party and voting realignment—such as during the Civil War, the 1890s economic crisis, and the Great Depression—only a few states had major shifts in their votes; most largely adhered to their traditional partisan ways. For states that did shift their vote significantly, it was usually local races—congressional and gubernatorial contests preceding the presidential election—that demonstrated the partisan shifts that subsequently would occur in the presidential race. In short, for these states, House and gubernatorial races were the harbingers signaling the coming party realignment and not the more researched and colorful presidential race occurring later. Former House Speaker Tip O'Neill once said, "All politics is local." The data in this book place renewed emphasis on state and local politics in explaining the voting patterns of the American electorate over three centuries.

Analysis of historical voting patterns also pinpoints the crucial breakpoints between different political eras in American politics when realignment actually did occur. While they have often been labeled by historians according to who occupied the White House—for instance, the Jacksonian period, the Lincoln era, or the Franklin Roosevelt era—the crucial breakpoints, as mentioned above, often occurred with partisan swings in earlier congressional and gubernatorial races, giving new importance to these races in understanding the general intent of the American electorate. The political eras and their breakpoints emphasized in this book are: (1) the Federalist/Democratic-Republican era (1788–1823), (2) the Democratic/National Republican–Whig era (1824–1853), (3) the Civil War–Reconstruction Republican/Democratic era (1854–1893), (4) the conservative Republican/Democratic era (1894–1929), (5) the New Deal Democratic/Republican era (1930–1965), and (6) the competitive Democratic/Republican era (1966–present). Each of these eras started with a significant change in voter sentiment, resulting in a party realignment. However, as important as the defining characteristics of each of these periods were for subsequent election years, it must be remembered that the most important pattern of voting across over two hundred years of American history remained the persistence and stability of most states' voting patterns—ones that were mainly noncompetitive and one-party in nature.

The first goal of this book—accuracy in the data collection reported—was achieved through several stages. Chief among them was ensuring that the presidential vote (Chapter 4), House vote (Chapter 5), Senate vote (Chapter 6), and gubernatorial vote (Chapter 7) were as accurate as possible. These data provided the foundation for calculating the vote participation data in Chapter 3 and the vote competition data in Chapter 8. If the former data were inaccurate, then the latter would also be. The house of cards would fall in Chapters 3 and 8 if the data foundation on which they were based (Chapters 4 through 7) was faulty. Ensuring accuracy in the data was extremely time consuming, especially for the House and gubernatorial races. Almost everything was done by hand. Reliance on primary sources (election archives, newspapers, ballots, state statute volumes, and official reports, for example) is an intense research activity. The determination of proper party labels alone for House and gubernatorial candidates was troublesome. Calculation of the House vote to the state level for each state over two hundred years of electoral history was both demanding and tedious. However, it was extremely important to derive the partisan composition of state delegations to the House of Representatives—and, especially, to offer a parallel data set for comparative analytic purposes at the state level to those for the presidency, Senate, and governorship in assessing partisan and political trends in the states. As an illustration of the time-consuming nature of compiling such data, consider calculating the state-level vote for the House for just three states—New York, Ohio, and Pennsylvania—from their entrance into the Union to 1998 and arriving at the correct totals for the Democratic, Republican, and Other vote in each instance. This gives a small indication of the overall, rather massive task. These calculations for the House were checked repeatedly until complete correspondence was found for all three numerical values (Democrat, Republican, and Other vote) in any given election year for a state. Despite the work involved, it is my firm belief that one has to inspect by hand each district of each state in each election year to fully understand what was happening politically in each district contest, and only in this way are the correct vote count and party labels of House candidates ascertained for each state. In essence, there is no easy, computer-generated way to shortcut this process without incurring both vote count and party label error.

Also in the interest of accuracy, I have chosen not to report the 2000 vote results. A complete and fully accurate vote count for president and the other races was still not available when this book went to press. For people who may think the contrary (beyond the obvious controversy surrounding the Florida vote result for president and the difference in vote reports for president in several other states that did recounts during this controversial period), a simple illustration from the 1996 elections is instructive. Three sources—Congressional Quarterly, the Federal Election Commission, and the Elections Research Center—reported three different sets of results for president, House, Senate, and governor for the 1996 elections. Admittedly, the first set of election results was released just after the 1996 elections and was labeled "preliminary." But the second set was published by the Federal Election Commission, and the third offered by Richard Scammon and his staff for the *America Votes* series. As it turned out, the third set was almost completely accurate, but it was not published until 1998. Scammon and his staff had taken over two years after the 1996 elections to check with the individual secretaries of state (and others) from the fifty states to get the proper set of election results for president, House, Senate, and governor. Given the even more controversial vote counts in the

election year 2000, the true vote count for each state is only now beginning to be known.

This volume raises an important yet perplexing methodological question for the future. Given the impetus from political scientist Gary King and others, a current concern of political science has focused on the question of data and researcher reliability. The gist of this argument is that, in order to build a cumulative body of knowledge that is valid, political scientists should be able to replicate the data research findings of other political scientists, using the exact same data sets. If replication results are found wanting (or the same findings are not achieved), then this research becomes questionable in building up such a cumulative body of knowledge. In short, political science cannot truly be a science unless it uses replication as a standard procedure in its research activities. However, the methodological problem observed in this book poses a different question about reliability that precedes and is ultimately more crucial than the replication criterion expressed in the current debate. If the data relied on are riddled with error, replicating the findings of researchers using such data adds little to political science as a science. This especially is the case for the congressional and gubernatorial races. Also the miscoding of party labels associated with candidates for these two races adds further errors to the errors already existing with the vote count itself. Maybe the same data patterns and interpretations of the vote will occur after replication of past studies are made using correct vote counts and correct party labels of candidates. But currently this remains an open question.

The scope of this project involved approximately five years of concentrated activity and the equivalent of two further years pieced across an earlier time. In some ways, the topics of historical voting and political change have always been of interest to me. A double major in political science and history in my undergraduate days partially explains this interest in the political analysis of the historical vote. In graduate school, my mentor, Philip E. Converse, renewed my interest in this area with fresh insights into the political history of the American electorate. To some, political science is mainly contemporary history, as history is the politics of the past. Certainly, the two disciplines are complementary, if not completely intertwined.

I owe a debt of gratitude to several institutions and individuals who helped me in my work on this book. The staff and facilities of the libraries at the University of Michigan, the University of Arizona (especially Atifa Rawan), and the Los Angeles County Law Library (especially Director Richard Iamele) must be noted. Also, the staff and facilities of the Library of Congress, the New York City Public Library, the Harvard University Library, and the Bowdoin University Library were very helpful. Special thanks must go to Michael J. Dubin of Sun City, Arizona, for allowing me access to the election materials he has collected over thirty-some years, and for answering my many questions on the vote in particular races and years. I also am grateful to Philip Lampi and the American Antiquarian Society, through the efforts of Dubin, for providing me with important voting data. Certainly the ICPSR's initial data collection efforts on the vote were very useful to me, as was the help of one of its staff members, Erik Austin. Even if supporters of the ICPSR may wince at the flaws in its data collection, all later data collection efforts on the vote, including this one, are indebted to ICPSR for these initial efforts. Acknowledgments are also due to Cam Gibson of the U.S. Census Bureau for providing census information about adult population counts for the states and related material that helped me estimate voter turnout, voter mobilization, and voter eligibility in Chapter 3. Grant money for this project was obtained from the National Science Foundation and the Social and Behavioral Sciences Institute at the University of Arizona. I would also like to acknowledge Professor Bill Mishler, head of my former department at the University of Arizona, for his encouragement and support for this project. Several graduate and undergraduate students helped to collect data or check data proofs, and their help is appreciated: Hung der Fu, Sylvia Manzano, Yanbo Wang, and Peter Yacobucci among the graduate students, and Nick Jaskolski, Kimberly Johnson, Teresa Krpata, Valerie Silverman, and Brian Utsey among the undergraduates. All the staff at CQ Press have been wonderful: Kerry Kern for her editing work that made much of my prose intelligible; Talia Greenberg for her overall supervision of the book project and for keeping it on track; Kelly Galla and her staff for their excellent work in setting the book into type; and, most of all, Dave Tarr, for his faith in this project and his patience. Finally, and most importantly, I would like to thank two people without whose help this book would not have been completed: my wife, Lyn Ragsdale, and my computer programmer, Sally Garnaat, at the University of Arizona. This book is dedicated to them for their invaluable contributions. I would also like to thank my son, Matthew, for allowing me to give him "quality time" instead of "real time" during this book's duration.

Jerrold G. Rusk

A Statistical History
of the
American Electorate

1

The Accuracy and Inaccuracy of Election Data

A number is a number. Researchers treat numbers as concrete, determinative, and true. Political science's claims of being a science have been steeped in numbers that permit theories to be confirmed, hypotheses to be contradicted, and generalizations to be asserted. Many students of American elections consider election returns to be among the most incontrovertible numbers in political science. Analysts presume that these election numbers are accurate; they take at face value that the election results represent, at least at a descriptive level, empirical reality. Over the past fifty years, as the field of elections and voting behavior has moved from a cottage industry to a large capital company, little attention has been given to the raw materials upon which the theoretically driven variables, the carefully designed models, and the complicated statistical techniques have been based. This inattention is partly the result of the public nature of elections. Election results are posted in official state records and documents, and so few questions are raised about the translation from these official references to the election volumes and data sets on which most researchers rely. This inattention also rests on the sheer number of scholars in the field. Since everyone is using the same data, there is little reason to question its validity.

Yet, a number can be misleading, imprecise, and even false. Imagine a situation in which for decades scores of researchers have used data that are commonly shared and commonly presumed to be accurate, but that are, in fact, riddled with errors. A half-century of data analyses, each one more methodologically sophisticated than the next, becomes a house of cards, all but ready to fall. This volume is about these data errors and their correction. This book corrects mistakes that have been made, offers data that have not previously been presented, and shows new ways of considering the party labels under which candidates ran.

This volume covers the sweep of electoral history in America from 1788 to the present, detailing the statistical framework of elections and electorates for this entire time period. It also attempts to do this more accurately than any other data presentations currently available for the state, regional, and national levels. The main unit of analysis in this book is the state vote, with aggregations to key regions and the nation. American electoral history is fundamentally a tale of politics at the state level and how these state patterns determine regional and national electoral outcomes. The tale of

American politics across two hundred years of history has never been one of county politics; state politics has been the stuff from which U.S. political history books are written. The way historical and contemporary electorates vote at the state level has consequences for the political system at large. Elections produce outcomes—winners and losers—that provide the basis for the organization of the executive and legislative branches at the national and state levels. These consequences are part of the electoral map used by voters as they make their choices in the polling booth. They are also the data used by researchers to explore various interpretations of the American electorate. In considering these outcomes, this book offers the most accurate presentation of election data currently available on three dimensions of the vote—legal-institutional structure, participation, and vote choice—at three levels of voting—state, regional, and national.

Dimensions of the Vote

Among the three dimensions of the vote, the first pertains to the legal-institutional structure of elections and how voting laws permit or exclude people from the franchise. Chapter 2 presents the first complete analysis of suffrage laws from 1788 to the present, including enactment, ratification, and repeal dates. Heretofore, there have been studies of one or more suffrage laws with partial coverage of relevant legislative dates in limited historical time periods. But until now no study has covered the entire sweep of suffrage history.

The second dimension involves participation: who votes among those who are permitted to vote. Participation data do not exist de novo but instead must be derived from the number of votes cast for all candidates in a given race and a determination of the size of the adult population that is eligible to vote. This means that who votes must be compiled from a tally of how the votes were cast. Those tallies can be offered only when the raw vote counts are accurate for all candidates running for a given office. This may seem straightforward, but it is not because of the failure, in some cases, to report the "other" vote, including the "scatter" vote—those few votes for marginal and write-in candidates. The other vote, no matter how small, is a part of participation data for a considerable portion of the time period studied. Studies also compound these vote-count problems by deriving data from sources that misreport the vote for major-party candidates. In addition, the eligible electorate and adult population must be accurately calculated in order to compute turnout and mobilization rates, respectively, for state electorates. Chapter 3 presents the most accurate voter turnout and mobilization figures available because they rest on precise tallies of the presidential, House, and Senate contests. These figures also rely on the most accurate counts and estimates for both the "eligible electorate" and the adult population, including previously unreported figures for these two variables in the pre-1824 period.

The third dimension pertains to vote choice: the aggregate raw vote and corresponding percentages for presidential, House, Senate, and gubernatorial elections. Errors found here encompass the actual miscalculation or misreporting of raw vote counts, the presumed absence of data that actually exists, and the questionable coding of the party labels of the candidates. These problems are corrected in Chapters 4 through 7 for president, House, Senate, and governor, respectively. Chapter 8 offers a series of various competition measures for these offices, based on the corrected data from the preceding chapters. Taken together these chapters offer the most precise vote counts available over the full sweep of two centuries of U.S. elections.

Levels of the Vote

The three levels of voting involve state, regional, and national patterns. The principal focus of this book is the state. The import of the state as a unit of analysis is threefold. First, it provides the ability to offer parallel data sets from 1788 to the present for president, House, and governor and from 1912 to the present for these three offices and the Senate.

Second, the state is the most appropriate unit of analysis for presidential, senatorial, and gubernatorial races, which are decided by the state. Although House races are typically decided at the district level, important indicators of party competition can be obtained from how state House delegations shape up and from how the state as a whole votes for the House in contrast to, for example, how it votes for governor or senator.

Third, although each of the dimensions analyzed—legal-institutional structures, participation, and vote choice—has consequences for national politics, each dimension originates within the states. Aggregation to the national level may play tricks on researchers who do not also consider the state-level origins of these national results. For instance, in the chapters for president, House, and Senate, it is clear that the Democrats and Republicans are *nationally* quite competitive. One party holds the White House about as often as the other. Also, one party wins about the same percentage of seats in the House and in the Senate as the other. But when examining the states individually, one-partyism is rampant across these three offices. One party dominates one set of states, while the other party controls another set of states. These one-party states tend to cancel each another out and, in combination

with a few truly competitive states, produce what appears to be a national competitive result. But if researchers were to presume that national competition between the parties stemmed from the sum of state-by-state competition, they would be wrong. Also, as will become clear in the later chapters of this book, national trends are, first of all, state trends. Several states may shift support from one party to the other in a key election year, which can produce a national trend in favor of that party in later years. Thus state-level data provide researchers with the ability to analyze the nature of competition by using complementary election time-series figures.

Plan of the Chapter

This chapter is divided into two parts. The first part considers errors that occur when collecting data on the vote. This can lead to inaccurate vote choice tallies. To the extent this happens, any estimates of voter participation (for example, turnout, mobilization) will also be in error since these estimates depend on the accurate reporting of the vote. The second part examines problems in the proper determination of party labels associated with the candidates who contest elections.

Errors in Data Gathering

How does a researcher know what is a correct number and what is not? To resolve this dilemma involves searching for clues like in a Sherlock Holmes mystery. On a particular electoral data point, discrepancies are observed across the most commonly used sources. This occurs most frequently in situations where it is impossible to tell how a source counted a particular aspect of the variable of interest. Researchers present vague documentation or no documentation at all. The problem is often made worse by researchers' reliance on earlier secondary sources; many authors merely quote each other and presume that the data used by an earlier source were gathered accurately and completely. The problem is further compounded when authors do not use primary data, settling instead for the use of these earlier secondary data.

For any given race in a given state in a given election year, especially in the 1700s and 1800s (and even in the 1900s, although to a much lesser extent), there is a significant lack of correspondence among data sources on the reported vote. While this lack of correspondence is much more frequent for House and gubernatorial races, even the more prominent races for president and Senate have errors in vote reporting.

Presidential Data Problems

For example, the vote collection efforts for president done by Robinson (1934), Burnham (1955), Petersen (1963), Congressional Quarterly (1994), and the Inter-university

Consortium for Political and Social Research (ICPSR data sets 0001 and 0019) show differences in the vote reported for president on certain occasions. One would expect virtual unanimity for a race where state vote totals are reported to the U.S. government every four years.

Congressional Quarterly's Guide to U.S. Elections (1994) is certainly the most accurate source for presidential election data. It uses data from Burnham (1955), as reported in the ICPSR data sets, Petersen (1963), Scammon (1965, and various other dates), and original ICPSR archival efforts when they are correct and ignores other portions of the data from these data collection efforts when they seem inaccurate or list data as missing. The result is that the effort by Congressional Quarterly (CQ) is the most accurate reporting of the presidential vote in the literature today, with only a few minor discrepancies. However, CQ does not offer presidential election data prior to the 1824 election. As discussed in greater detail in Chapter 4, these data, long assumed to be either unavailable or so inaccurate as not to be worthy of report, are presented here for the first time. They were obtained by drawing upon original archival sources heretofore not examined. For the most part, the 1788–1820 presidential vote results have been added to those presented from 1824 on in *Congressional Quarterly's Guide to U.S. Elections*.

House Data Discrepancies

House discrepancies are by far the most prevalent among presidential, congressional, and gubernatorial vote counts. There is considerable disagreement among the main ICPSR House data sets (0001 compiled by Howard Allen, Jerome Clubb, and ICPSR staff; 0075 compiled by Walter Dean Burnham, Jerome Clubb, William Flanigan, and ICPSR staff; and subsequently published in Erik Austin and Jerome Clubb's 1986 book, *Political Facts of the United States Since 1789*) and the archival efforts of Cox (1972), and Dubin (1998). In addition, some of these sources do not denote that the data reported are only partial returns, rather than complete vote tallies. In these instances, some counties and congressional districts are missing from the vote counts, but no mention is made that these counties and districts are not part of the state results. In this volume, states with partial data are included but notations are provided in order to clearly distinguish them from states reporting complete data from all districts for the House vote. Only the latter states are used when aggregating the House vote to state, regional, and national levels (see Chapter 5).

To ascertain the correct raw vote counts for House races requires a thorough search of primary sources—manuscript returns (mostly handwritten accountings of the votes for individual candidates), newspaper reporting of the final returns, legislative manuals, and other sources. What was uncovered in primary data sources and ultimately confirmed as an accurate vote count for a given House race was usually found in at least one of the data collections or archival

sources mentioned above. However, the correct source could change from candidate to candidate, year to year, and state to state.

Michael J. Dubin's book, *United States Congressional Elections, 1788–1997* (1998), is by far the most complete and accurate accounting of the House vote to date. Spending more than thirty years collecting and archiving House data and using mainly primary sources (original manuscript vote returns, newspapers, and others), Dubin has compiled a monumental research work. His volume is particularly important for the 1700s and 1800s, when so many inaccuracies in House vote counts exist in the literature. Dubin's accuracy rests on an election archive of primary source material dating from 1788. These are data meticulously gathered through the help of the Massachusetts Antiquarian Society (with the aid of employee Philip Lampi), the New York Public Library, the Library of Congress, and various state sources. Dubin generously provided the author access to this extensive election archive and the current House data set was constructed from it and other primary sources obtained by the author from the Library of Congress and elsewhere. In general, the primary source searches upon which the data presented in this volume are based match the results reported in Dubin. In only a few instances were sources at odds with Dubin found to be correct, the differences largely centering on the minuscule scatter vote for the House in the twentieth century. Of course, the focus of attention in this book is on the state-level House vote, and various aggregations to regional and national levels, while Dubin's archive is solely on the House vote at the district level.

An Analysis of House Vote Count Errors

To understand the depth of the data discrepancy problem, it is illuminating to compare the data used in the ICPSR's state-level data set 0075 and the data presented in this volume in Chapter 5. Since so many states are in error at the district and state levels throughout much of the 1800s in the ICPSR data set, a full accounting of these errors would comprise a volume in itself. A more concise yet conservative estimate of this rather large error pattern would be to look at the aggregation of state differences between the two data sets (0075 and Chapter 5) at the national level. Table 1-1 presents the absolute mean difference for states between the two data sets for the Democratic percent of the House vote, the Republican percent of the House vote, and the Other percent of the House vote aggregated to the national level for the period 1824–1972 (the years covered in ICPSR data set 0075). Thus the national mean for any given election year is taken from the differences observed in each individual state between the two data sets for that year. Hence, data are available in 1824 for seventeen states, and so the national mean difference is calculated on 17 as the number of cases. Table 1-2 records the national mean differences in the raw vote for the Democratic vote, Republican vote, Other vote, and total vote across all states for which data were available. (See the notes to Tables 1-1 and 1-2 for further detail on the procedures used to compute these House data differences.)

The most striking observation gained from these two tables is the often wide gaps that exist between the data reported in this volume and the ICPSR data on the House vote. This is especially true in the nineteenth century, before the introduction of the official Australian ballot, when greater errors in the ICPSR data might be expected (the Australian ballot reform occurred mainly in the 1890s in America, replacing a nonsecret party strip ballot with a state-prepared secret ballot). However, errors still occur with some frequency throughout the twentieth century, when there would be less reason to anticipate any errors because of the far greater accuracy in the government's reporting of the vote and in the legitimacy of such reporting efforts. It is also striking that these wide gaps between the two data sets are seen using a very conservative approach of averaging House errors at the national level. Reporting each state separately in an election year—without aggregating to the national level—would show a large number of states to be in error, especially in the nineteenth century, and thereby present an even more dramatic picture of data discrepancies.

Several examples from Tables 1-1 and 1-2 show the extent of the House vote reporting error. For example, in 1824, in Table 1-1, the mean national voting error for Democratic, Republican, and Other tallies for the House between the two data sets is 56.6 percent, 10.9 percent, and 61.7 percent, respectively, and the average error in the total vote reported in Table 1-2 for the seventeen states is 23,067. Of course, one cannot simply add up these respective vote percent errors, since an error in one vote category (say, Democratic) may be caused by an error in another vote category (say, Other). Coding voting data in the wrong vote category or misreporting the vote in a particular vote category can produce changes in the other vote categories, and this is later reflected in the percentages computed on these data. This is important for the researcher and analyst to know since such changes can lead to misleading interpretations for all three vote categories. However, overall these tables show sizable errors in the ICPSR data.

The period from 1824 to the end of the Civil War is particularly rampant with voting error. Rarely does an election in this period fail to have at least one voting category showing a double-digit percentage error in the House vote. The raw vote difference values in Table 1-2 are similarly striking. From 1866 to 1900, the percentage difference values are less in magnitude but still worrisome. For example, in 1872 the Democratic, Republican, and Other vote errors, averaged at the national level, are 4.9, 6.1, and 7.7 percent, respectively. This is followed by the midterm election of 1874, with percentage voting errors of 6.8, 3.6, and 6.6, respectively. Even the crucial election of 1896 shows an error pattern of 8.0, 6.4, and 13.1 percent, respectively. In the twentieth century, the percentage errors are generally in the 1 to 4 percent range—still an unacceptable range for a period using the official Australian ballot and having governmental reporting of the vote. Also, throughout the entire 1824–1972 time

period the total vote differences in Table 1-2 are never zero or usually not even close to zero, which is an unacceptable result. Even if vote errors occur in particular vote categories, sources should be able to agree on the total number of votes cast in House elections. According to Table 1-2, they do not, and this is a constant source of error throughout America's electoral history.

Large standard deviation values, which indicate that states varied widely in their vote error for the House in any given election year, can be seen in Tables 1-1 and 1-2. Some states had small data errors, while others had moderate and large errors; some had no errors. Visual inspection of these individual state difference values within election years fails to reveal a situation of a few extreme values unduly influencing the final standard deviation results, which lends more confidence in these results and in the fact that Tables 1-1 and 1-2 generally reflect well-behaved statistical patterns of error distribution in the vote. Why the accuracy of the vote reported by the ICPSR varied so much among the states, particularly in the earlier years in U.S. history, remains a subject to be researched and explained.

National mean values, national standard deviation values, and visual inspection of the vote data patterns of the individual states all convey the same general message: vote discrepancies in House elections are widespread across America's history and often are quite sizable. The lesson here is that earlier collected vote data for the House are not reliable and should no longer be used for data analysis. As mentioned before, errors occur in these data for several reasons: failure to accurately retrieve or correctly count the House vote; failure to distinguish partial data states from states reporting complete data; failure to accurately record or interpret the party labels candidates use on the ballot; and failure to identify and record the names of candidates correctly, which can lead to other errors in reporting the vote.

Two last points need to be made. First, the ICPSR does not include vote returns in the pre-1824 period; this volume does. This is an important addition to the House data collection, enabling this volume to offer parallel data sets for House, president, and governor from 1788 to the present. Second, the ICPSR data set does not distinguish election years in a given election cycle for a particular Congress (for example, it does not distinguish 1824 House elections held in certain states from 1825 House races held in other states); this volume does. This omission by the ICPSR is unfortunate since different election years have different electoral stimuli: a candidate running in a House race in 1824 runs in a year dominated by presidential campaigning, while a candidate running in 1825 does not. ICPSR's practice of collapsing the 1824 and 1825 state House vote results into one category contributes to problems in the proper interpretation of House elections. In essence, this decision constitutes a serious data error, although a data error very different in nature from the other types of data errors considered in this chapter. House elections reported in Chapter 5 of this volume list vote results for states at the state level in the actual election years in which they occurred. As it turns out, states using odd-numbered years for their House elections tended to phase out this practice shortly after the Civil War.

Corruption and the Vote

A discussion of data accuracy and vote counts is not complete without recognition of an underlying problem in these vote counts, even when they are collected from the most accurate primary sources. These sources record the vote as it was counted; they do not, and cannot, reflect on how well these vote counts capture the legitimate vote that was cast. The issue of vote corruption at the polls was a serious problem in America, especially in the nineteenth century, as strong party organizations attempted to manipulate and control the vote result for their benefit.

Much of the problem of vote corruption arose from the type of ballot used in the first one hundred years in America. During this time, states and local communities used what often was called an "unofficial" or "party strip" ballot (Evans, 1917; Rusk, 1970). Other voting methods, such as voice voting or corn and beans voting (corn kernels designating one candidate, beans the other), were also used, particularly in the earliest years. The unofficial ballot was distinguished by being prepared by the parties themselves, usually with only their slate of candidates on it, and being voted in public. Often the ballot was printed in a particular color and size to distinguish it from other parties' ballots. Finally, party workers often distributed the ballots to voters on their way to the polls or even gave them to voters before election day in some states and communities.

The key was that the ballot was "unofficial"—not state-prepared or distributed. Without the state being directly involved, record keeping was often haphazard. With the introduction of the Australian secret ballot in 1888 in Massachusetts and the subsequent adoption of one or more of its provisions by approximately 90 percent of the states by 1896, record keeping became more accurate since the state was now directly involved in the balloting process (Evans, 1917; Fredman, 1968; Rusk, 1970). This new ballot system was state-prepared and distributed, consolidated (candidates from all parties had to be listed on the same ballot), secret, and available only at the polling station on election day. With the state now running the election process, record keeping became more accurate. As Seymour and Frary put it:

> The Australian ballot is prepared by the state at public expense, so that in a sense the state guarantees the authenticity of the nominations on it. As it is necessary to restrict its size, the law provides that only names proposed by parties of a certain numerical strength, or by petition by a large number of electors, shall appear. In effect this is a state recognition of parties, or of the party machine (1918, p. 250).

The Australian ballot reform also counteracted significant corruption and intimidation of the voter fostered by the ear-

lier ballot systems (Rusk, 1970, 1974). Just as Australia passed a secret ballot act in the 1850s to stem electoral corruption, so did the American states in the late 1880s and 1890s. While some would argue that voter intimidation and corruption were modest in the 1800s (for example, see Burnham, 1970; Allen and Allen, 1981), the institutional environment surrounding the vote would indicate otherwise (Rusk, 1970, 1974; Converse, 1972). Political party organizations were very strong, unlike the 1900s; voter partisanship was high; and the parties were able to control the election process by making sure there were no personal voter registration systems or consolidated, secret ballots. Without personal registration systems, repeat voting could easily occur. Without a secret ballot, voters were faced with voting in public on a party strip ticket with only one party's candidates listed. If votes were bought, the lack of a secret ballot would ensure that they were delivered as promised. If an employer intimidated employees to vote a certain way, party representatives at the polls could see if the workers voted as they had been instructed. For a party's purposes, the most important element of the party strip ballot other than its public nature was the absence of a consolidation feature. With only one party's slate on a ballot, the prevailing norm was to vote a straight party ticket, as the parties, indeed, intended. While voting a split ticket was possible, usually there were no instructions on how to do this on the party ticket. States varied on the procedure for such voting: some states made a person cross out a given candidate's name on the party ticket and write in another, while others made a voter get both party tickets and vote for different candidates on the two ballots. What the parties intended, however, was usually what happened. Straight-ticket voting was statistically associated with the unofficial party strip ballot period, and increases in split-ticket voting more often occurred in the states after they had adopted the consolidated, secret Australian ballot that made this type of voting easier (Rusk, 1970, 1974). This is an important piece of evidence supporting the relevance of a legal-institutional theory of voting that suggests that the institutional arrangements of elections written into law—the types of ballots, registration systems, and legal restrictions on the franchise—influence voting behavior and electoral outcomes (Rusk, 1970, 1974; Rusk and Stucker, 1973, 1991).

Parties were strong in other ways in the 1800s, which could also have led to voter intimidation and corruption. Patronage, at least since the age of Andrew Jackson, was a strong element in rewarding party workers and voters to be sure the vote count came in as intended. The parties' use of social welfare in the large cities was another way to control the vote, especially among immigrants, newer voters, and lower-class denizens down on their luck. The parties' complete control of the nomination process through party caucuses and conventions ensured party worker loyalty and the hard work and motivation required of party workers by the political machine to mobilize and control the vote. Coupled with the party organization's almost complete control of the election process through the unofficial ballot and the absence of personal voter registration systems, the political machine had little to deter it from achieving power through incentive and rewards, on the one hand, and intimidation and corruption, on the other.

What is often overlooked in this environment is that strong party organizations could control the governmental apparatus itself and, with it, the counting and recording of votes. Allusions to "ballot box stuffing" in historical accounts of the day mentioned by such authors as Wigmore (1889), Evans (1917), and Seymour and Frary (1918) hardly seem exaggerated. The parties' express purpose was to control the political process, encourage partisan vote patterns, and ensure winning—at almost any cost. State governments did not usually take an active role in preventing voter intimidation and corruption; indeed, strong party organizations usually controlled the governmental apparatus to be sure reform did not occur. Only after a century of corruption and intimidation was public pressure for reform acquiesced to and then only begrudgingly. With secret ballot reform also came personal registration systems, direct primaries, civil service and merit exams, and the government's entry into the social welfare field. From 1888 on these reforms eroded political parties' once strong monopolies of the nomination, general election, patronage, and social welfare functions. With these reforms would also come a more honest vote and a more accurate counting of the vote.

The Determination of Party Label Errors

Achieving an accurate vote count hinges not only on the proper primary sources for electoral data but also on the appropriate designation of party labels for specific candidates. The principal election data sources are rife with instances of the miscoding of party labels. For example, ICPSR election data often list "Opposition Republican" candidates in House elections in the early 1800s when this particular party label never seemed to be in use. Similarly, the party label "States Rights Whigs" was apparently not used in southern House elections in the 1800s. (Dubin separately confirmed both of these points in communications with the author on September 2, 1999, and June 19, 2000.) As late as 1920 in Oregon (candidate Lovejoy), 1926 in Nebraska (candidate Shallenberger), and 1944 in North Dakota (candidate Burdick), ICPSR lists these respective House candidates as Prohibition, Democrat-LaFollette fusion, and Independent Republican when their actual party labels on the ballot were Democrat, Democrat (only), and Independent (only), respectively (Dubin communication of May 8, 2000). Thus, what appears to be "hard" data that can be taken at face value are anything but.

In this book, the ballot itself was the point of reference for deciding what party label a candidate used. While this decision seems both simple and obvious, the execution of this decision rule was neither. The problem was not as severe for winners, since other documentation of party labels usu-

ally could be obtained, such as in the *Biographical Directory of the U.S. Congress,* the *Congressional Directory,* newspaper reports, almanacs, and state histories. The problem was more acute for the losers of state election campaigns, especially for the House of Representatives and governor, since little, if any, mention is made of them in state histories. This obstacle was compounded by the difficulties, discussed above, during the period when states and communities used the unofficial or party strip ballot.

Sources for Party Labels

As discussed more thoroughly in Chapter 5, original manuscript returns—the handwritten poll books that recorded election results—were in some cases attainable. For instance, even in the first congressional elections in 1788–1789, manuscript returns were available for seven of the thirteen states.

When manuscript returns were not available, other sources that routinely recorded election results in the early period, such as newspapers and almanacs, were obtained. Newspapers were an important source because they usually listed the election returns with candidates' names and party labels. Many of these early newspapers are available in various archives, such as the American Antiquarian Society in Worchester, Massachusetts, the State Historical Society of Wisconsin at the Madison campus of the University of Wisconsin, and the Library of Congress. As useful as these sources are, sometimes they misidentify the party label of a candidate (for instance, a newspaper using more its notion of what a party label was for a given candidate than the actual label contained on the ballot itself). Other times the newspapers could not be faulted for errors since, for example, different branches or wings of a given party existed in the same legislative district and used alternate "party slates" for such offices as the state assembly and the House of Representatives. Correspondence of party label names among two or more separate sources (often two or more newspapers) was often needed to resolve these cases.

Alternative sources for party labels included various almanacs published in the 1800s and early 1900s, such as the *Whig/Tribune Almanac* (1838–1914), the *Evening Journal Almanac* (1858–1892, 1895–1896), the *World Almanac* (1868–1876, 1884–present), the *American Almanac* (1878–1889), and the *Daily News Almanac* (1885–1937). Parts of the ICPSR election archive collection were also useful, since they obtained party names from some of these same sources, as well as from various manuscript returns and newspapers. Obviously, almanacs varied in their accuracy and quality. Typically, ambiguities were resolved by a simple decision rule—when there was correspondence among two or more credible sources on a candidate's party affiliation, then this was the label recorded for that candidate. Of the almanacs used, the *Whig/Tribune Almanac* was the most helpful because it documented its entries more thoroughly than the other almanacs.

Analysis of Party Codings

Once candidates' party labels were determined as accurately as possible, a second level of analysis took place to determine whether major-party candidates running under their primary party designation were also aligned with a faction or independent movement within their party or if their candidacies were also associated with another, usually minor, party. In these situations questions arose as to whether the candidates' vote counts should be included in the major-party or in the Other column. A novel feature of the presentations in this volume is the use of two different coding systems to address this dilemma and to give different perspectives on what constituted the "partisan vote" at any given moment in American history. A conventional or pure system of party coding, often used in the ICPSR state-level data sets for House, Senate, and governor, only lists candidates in the Democratic or Republican categories if this is the sole designation these candidates used on the ballot. (For a list of the historical antecedents of the Democratic and Republican party labels, see Appendix A.) In situations where a candidate ran from a faction or wing of the major party, or as an independent within the major party, or was associated with another, usually minor, party, the conventional or pure coding system places these candidates and their vote counts in the Other category. An alternative coding system, devised by the author, places these major-party candidates and their vote counts in the major-party column—Democrat or Republican—instead of the Other column.

More specifically, the author's alternative party coding scheme encompasses five different instances where candidates may be associated with a major-party label but not in the straightforward fashion of a candidate running on a major-party label alone. The first instance is when candidates ran from wings or factions of the major party, with different qualifying labels (such as the "Benton Democrats" and "Anti-Benton Democrats" in Missouri in the nineteenth century). In such cases, often two or more candidates from the same party would contest a House or gubernatorial election, a situation particularly common in the 1800s. These factional candidates are coded as Other in the ICPSR data sets, as well as in the conventional coding system used in this book; however, it seems more appropriate to consider these individuals as candidates from their own parties, as is done in the author's alternative coding scheme.

A second instance is when candidates ran as independent members of their own parties, often attempting to move their party in one direction or another. Designated as Independent Democrats and Independent Republicans (or their historical antecedents), the ICPSR's coding system and the conventional coding system used here list these candidates in the Other category. These candidates, however, were party-affiliated individuals who usually had not left the party and, hence, are coded as major-party candidates in the author's alternative coding scheme.

A third situation is when a major-party candidate ran on a fusion ticket with a minor party, such as the Democrat-Greenback and Republican-Greenback fusion tickets in the late 1800s. Minor parties wanted to be in such fusion tickets, backing the major-party candidate in order to gain legitimacy with the electorate, increase their vote share, and get their issue positions across to a broader public. In addition, major-party candidates sometimes found such fusions useful, especially if this would increase their following and vote count. Fusion tickets occurred in different periods of American history, often when the major parties, for whatever reason, seemed less well established and more fluid. Periods of intense political controversy and crisis were often catalysts for the appearance of fusion candidacies. ICPSR state-level data sets sometimes code these fusion candidacies as Other and sometimes not; there is no consistent coding pattern evident. This book's conventional coding system always codes these candidacies as Other, while the alternative coding system always codes these candidates with the major party with which they are affiliated.

A similar situation—that of joint party endorsements—constitutes the fourth instance of party coding. In this case, the minor party also endorses a major-party candidate but has a separate place on the ballot to list this endorsement. In the case of a fusion candidacy, the minor party is listed only with the major-party name and only beside the name of the major-party candidate. The situation of joint party endorsements, as distinct from fusion candidacies, occurred frequently in the 1900s, particularly in New York, Pennsylvania, and, to a much lesser extent, in a few other states, such as Vermont. For example, in New York's 10th Congressional District in 1938, Emanuel Celler, the mainstream Democratic candidate, was also listed under both the American Labor Party and the City Fusion Party columns on the ballot, where he received additional votes as a result of these separate minor party endorsements. Coding for joint party endorsements follows the logic of the coding definitions used above for fusion tickets.

The last instance involves the situation where a candidate is endorsed by both major parties and is listed on the ballot as such. This can occur either informally, pending the outcome of both parties' nominating procedures, or formally in states such as California, which passed a law allowing cross-filing (that is, allowing a candidate to run in both major parties' primary elections). In the ICPSR and conventional coding systems, these candidates are coded as Other; in the author's alternative scheme, they are coded with the major party with which they were principally affiliated.

The importance of the alternative coding scheme is to provide the most accurate assessment of the partisan vote and, hence, party strength across the entire history of American elections. The conventional coding system biases codings toward the contemporary pattern, where the two major-party candidates are easily identified and their vote counts quickly recorded as the major two-party vote, with all other candidates and their votes neatly placed in the Other category. Researchers can determine for themselves the relative merits of the two coding systems by comparing their values for various elections across time. Tables presented in the chapters that follow show which years the alternative coding system is used for a given race and the specific reason why it is used is noted in each case. This provides researchers with considerable flexibility, as they can use the alternative coding system when they feel it is appropriate and use the conventional coding system when they do not. For instance, analysts can screen out cases of Independent Democrat and Independent Republican candidacies while retaining other alternative party codings if this seems appropriate to their research purposes. (For a complete discussion of these coding differences and the reasons for them, see the discussion in Chapter 5.)

Table 1-3 displays the number of times that these alternative party codings—party wings, independent party candidacies, fusion tickets, joint endorsements, and dual major-party endorsements—existed across races for the House, Senate, and governor from 1788 to the present. There were numerous instances across the full time period when major-party candidates campaigned with these other designations. The alternative coding system was used 715 times for House races, 276 times for gubernatorial races, and 76 times for Senate races. Factional and fusion candidates for the House and governor were frequent in the 1800s. House candidates running as independents tied to a party label were frequent throughout most of the 1788–1998 time period. Many candidates also received joint endorse-

ments by a major and a minor party, especially beginning in the twentieth century for the House, Senate, and governor. The extent to which these alternative party codings occur across these races, especially those for the House and governor, is another piece of evidence supporting the contention that major data errors exist in the ICPSR data sets and other data compilations. (The alternative coding system seemed less useful for the presidential race and so was not used here; historians generally agree on who were the major-party candidates for president across time.) It also calls into question the party assumptions underlying the coding of the ICPSR data sets, particularly the state-level voting data for House, Senate, and governor contained in ICPSR study 0075.

Conclusion

Much has been made recently of the need to replicate existing studies to test the reliability of their data analyses. But unless these studies are based on accurate data, there is little to be gained from their replication. If data are missing or incorrect, or party labels inappropriately coded, then it is difficult to rely on these data analyses or the conclusions drawn from them. As the chapters of this book make clear, many of the central hypotheses which studies have addressed now require careful reexamination based on the proper data.

Table 1-1 National Discrepancy Between ICPSR Data Set and Current Data Set for the House of Representatives, 1824–1972 (Percentages)

Year	Democrat Percent Mean Difference	Standard Deviation	Republican Percent Mean Difference	Standard Deviation	Other Percent Mean Difference	Standard Deviation	Number of States
1824	56.6	35.8	10.9	18.2	61.7	35.1	17
1826	24.6	27.8	24.4	25.5	48.6	36.4	19
1828	25.0	28.2	27.2	26.8	36.3	36.7	20
1830	26.4	26.0	18.0	20.4	41.0	104.8	19
1832	27.0	28.6	27.4	26.0	70.9	174.7	21
1834	16.4	30.0	12.3	24.8	5.7	9.8	23
1836	21.8	29.0	16.0	20.5	12.3	22.6	23
1838	10.4	22.7	15.3	27.6	19.6	93.4	24
1840	6.4	15.9	14.7	29.4	8.1	26.9	25
1842	14.8	30.2	19.8	33.2	20.6	74.9	25
1844	7.9	16.9	15.2	28.2	6.0	15.2	26
1846	15.3	24.9	9.6	17.5	7.3	19.5	27
1848	8.1	17.0	13.2	23.4	8.8	16.5	31
1850	7.3	14.8	11.7	23.8	12.3	22.5	29
1852	12.3	20.4	10.6	21.7	7.6	15.4	29
1854	10.0	17.9	15.5	22.7	24.7	36.2	30
1856	4.5	11.6	4.9	12.5	12.5	26.0	32
1858	11.4	22.7	5.2	13.3	13.2	23.5	33
1860	6.2	14.2	6.7	19.0	14.7	31.9	27
1862	3.6	15.4	6.9	22.9	8.4	26.5	27
1864	1.1	2.8	6.5	17.6	16.6	33.9	29
1866	5.2	13.7	9.9	22.5	1.6	4.9	27
1868	4.4	10.7	8.9	18.1	4.2	12.8	37
1870	2.8	7.2	6.4	16.4	8.6	24.8	36
1872	4.9	13.6	6.1	14.3	7.7	20.4	37
1874	6.8	16.4	3.6	9.1	6.6	14.6	37
1876	3.3	9.4	1.7	7.5	1.8	3.9	38
1878	5.1	9.0	3.0	5.7	7.2	10.1	38
1880	3.8	9.4	1.1	4.2	4.8	10.0	38
1882	1.3	2.4	3.3	6.7	4.1	7.1	38
1884	1.5	3.5	2.4	7.1	2.9	7.2	38
1886	2.4	6.9	0.9	1.8	3.0	8.0	38
1888	1.1	2.8	0.4	1.0	1.4	3.5	42
1890	1.2	3.0	1.6	3.8	2.6	5.0	44
1892	6.0	14.0	1.1	3.3	6.4	14.0	44
1894	3.3	9.4	1.9	7.6	3.0	6.7	45
1896	8.0	15.1	6.4	16.2	13.1	21.5	45
1898	5.7	12.5	2.9	9.2	7.0	13.5	45
1900	3.1	10.3	0.2	0.4	3.1	10.3	45
1902	2.1	8.2	1.1	5.1	3.1	9.5	45
1904	2.0	8.5	0.2	0.4	2.1	8.5	45
1906	2.4	8.3	1.5	7.5	3.9	14.5	46
1908	0.3	0.9	0.4	1.3	0.3	1.1	46
1910	3.1	10.7	2.3	9.0	1.5	4.4	48
1912	0.3	0.8	2.2	7.2	2.3	7.3	48
1914	1.9	7.2	2.5	6.8	4.3	10.4	48
1916	3.5	14.6	3.1	10.0	4.5	14.5	48
1918	1.3	5.3	2.2	8.6	3.5	12.1	48
1920	1.8	5.4	3.2	8.9	3.7	11.6	48
1922	1.2	4.2	2.5	9.4	3.7	12.1	48
1924	2.2	7.2	1.8	7.5	2.3	8.4	48
1926	1.1	3.0	1.8	6.9	2.4	8.7	48
1928	0.7	2.1	1.6	8.5	1.7	9.1	48
1930	0.5	1.7	1.8	8.4	2.0	9.5	48
1932	0.4	1.0	0.7	2.1	0.6	2.6	48
1934	0.8	2.8	0.9	3.0	1.4	5.6	48
1936	2.6	14.5	0.6	2.2	1.0	5.0	48
1938	0.6	2.4	0.8	3.7	0.9	5.7	48
1940	0.5	2.9	0.8	5.2	1.2	8.1	48
1942	0.6	3.3	1.3	5.4	1.6	7.9	48
1944	0.4	1.9	0.8	3.5	1.2	4.8	48
1946	1.0	3.5	0.8	2.9	1.3	5.8	48
1948	1.5	5.7	1.1	5.0	2.1	9.5	48
1950	0.7	3.3	0.9	4.1	1.0	6.5	48
1952	0.9	4.2	0.9	4.4	0.8	5.5	48
1954	0.5	1.6	0.3	1.3	0.3	1.1	48
1956	0.3	1.4	0.1	0.5	0.3	1.4	48
1958	1.8	9.8	0.7	4.4	2.3	14.2	49
1960	1.8	11.7	0.4	2.4	0.1	0.4	49
1962	0.1	0.7	2.0	14.1	0.2	0.9	49
1964	0.3	1.5	2.5	14.2	0.4	1.4	49
1966	0.2	0.8	2.2	14.1	0.0	0.2	49
1968	1.1	5.8	3.2	15.1	0.1	0.4	49
1970	0.3	1.5	0.1	0.6	0.4	1.9	48
1972	1.7	8.2	2.6	12.6	0.1	0.7	48

Notes: This table assesses data discrepancies in the House vote for Democratic, Republican, and Other percent of total vote between ICPSR data set 0075, which covers the 1824–1972 period, and the author's vote percent data for the House. The ICPSR House vote percents are computed for each state for each election year

(Notes continue)

Table 1-1 *(Continued)*

available in this data set from the raw vote numbers given at the state-level for each of the states. The corresponding vote percentage data for the author are found in Tables 5-26 through 5-63 in Chapter 5. If a state has two sets of vote values for House races in any of Tables 5-26 through 5-63—known as the conventionally coded values and the author's alternative coded values—the latter are always used. They are designated in Tables 5-26 through 5-63 as bold italicized entries. If no italicized entries exist for a given state in a given year, the conventionally coded vote values for the House are used. Absolute difference values for each state are then computed by comparing the House percent data calculated from the ICPSR data file and the vote percents shown in Tables 5-26 through 5-63 for Democrat, Republican, and Other categories of the vote separately. Difference values take into consideration the possibility of data errors occurring by either commission or omission. If the ICPSR reports inaccurate vote values, this constitutes an error. If the ICPSR data set has no vote values and the author's data set has values, this constitutes an error. If the ICPSR data set has values for only certain vote categories but not others, this constitutes an error. (These states are regarded as states with data if these values are not zero, and difference values, therefore, are computed, which usually result in data error values being produced.) If the ICPSR data set purports to have complete data for House races in a state when only partial vote data for the House actually exist, this is a data error. After the computation of data difference values for all states in a given election year, means and standard deviations are calculated across all states' data difference values for this year and reported in this table. The number of states having difference values in any given election year is given in the last column of this table.

Sources: ICPSR data set 0075 and Tables 5-26 through 5-63 in this book.

Table 1-2 National Discrepancy Between ICPSR Data Set and Current Data Set for the House of Representatives, 1824–1972 (Raw Differences)

Year	Democrat Raw Mean Difference	Democrat Standard Deviation	Republican Raw Mean Difference	Republican Standard Deviation	Other Raw Mean Difference	Other Standard Deviation	Total Vote Raw Mean Difference	Total Vote Standard Deviation	Number of States
1824	18,675	43,273	2,342	4,457	34,059	49,879	23,067	28,718	17
1826	9,815	21,423	10,959	21,216	20,738	42,431	14,681	24,856	19
1828	13,885	31,969	10,287	23,612	15,393	37,668	17,990	25,258	20
1830	18,201	23,672	11,315	13,932	17,592	50,659	22,491	38,272	19
1832	14,264	24,283	12,580	24,074	41,172	93,936	19,406	38,161	21
1834	4,761	8,969	4,259	8,030	3,505	7,166	7,759	14,436	23
1836	11,520	19,825	10,880	16,508	6,983	17,722	18,078	36,100	23
1838	5,399	9,927	6,948	10,404	12,314	59,074	11,174	18,774	24
1840	6,557	25,875	6,786	15,564	215	424	10,106	33,304	25
1842	5,813	10,719	5,833	8,355	7,590	26,238	9,755	14,434	25
1844	9,675	30,734	10,962	28,779	5,378	11,355	17,385	61,630	26
1846	11,559	31,807	5,394	8,598	3,131	5,299	14,305	34,180	27
1848	4,913	7,900	7,413	10,120	4,858	7,969	8,586	15,263	31
1850	5,767	11,967	6,876	12,260	6,108	10,514	7,274	20,069	29
1852	7,335	9,697	5,666	7,831	6,124	10,694	13,114	19,889	29
1854	15,826	43,045	27,758	59,433	32,303	83,703	9,887	38,198	30
1856	4,735	10,590	7,474	29,008	11,310	30,270	3,089	7,902	32
1858	7,817	16,373	5,428	20,737	10,320	21,783	7,949	19,522	33
1860	5,804	15,155	2,760	9,846	9,652	17,212	6,861	16,171	27
1862	3,458	13,207	3,881	12,510	1,596	4,059	1,984	3,897	27
1864	2,972	10,690	5,532	15,873	9,837	20,733	3,743	11,255	29
1866	2,860	8,828	7,218	18,611	2,037	5,749	9,512	27,513	27
1868	4,115	12,155	9,436	25,545	6,435	23,404	16,328	48,106	37
1870	3,621	7,706	6,929	16,835	9,675	24,075	11,572	30,566	36
1872	2,934	7,446	3,753	8,367	5,685	15,795	1,842	4,882	37
1874	9,645	22,983	5,263	12,663	9,553	20,612	4,902	23,787	37
1876	7,124	21,259	3,859	16,941	4,155	9,410	6,419	36,593	38
1878	11,824	24,228	4,700	7,822	13,685	28,206	2,017	4,731	38
1880	8,773	18,238	4,236	16,130	11,776	23,520	1,183	2,693	38
1882	4,884	11,096	4,586	8,078	6,970	10,353	2,884	10,021	38
1884	4,830	14,478	8,415	30,620	11,581	33,731	859	2,246	38
1886	8,236	24,422	2,215	4,724	9,314	27,268	1,070	4,773	38
1888	6,922	24,604	2,187	7,585	9,331	32,647	619	1,452	42
1890	2,562	6,614	2,031	4,738	4,558	8,297	1,476	4,310	44
1892	11,401	30,752	1,224	3,563	12,588	30,683	702	2,292	44
1894	6,510	16,917	2,207	6,906	8,044	17,460	1,337	6,207	45
1896	15,857	35,094	8,442	22,888	21,148	38,430	1,039	4,362	45
1898	11,460	34,399	4,410	18,892	13,780	36,829	931	3,093	45
1900	5,651	24,311	491	1,641	5,845	24,240	570	1,743	45
1902	6,403	24,053	991	3,374	4,023	11,647	3,692	22,559	45
1904	3,414	14,067	372	1,145	3,253	13,945	503	2,716	45
1906	6,462	24,010	2,117	8,984	8,498	26,750	200	575	46
1908	446	1,924	1,194	3,680	592	2,111	1,077	3,769	46
1910	7,415	32,769	4,221	15,550	9,509	46,085	2,533	9,744	48
1912	965	4,184	12,020	51,863	12,435	52,077	1,159	3,761	48
1914	7,583	28,544	11,211	34,801	20,753	62,960	2,698	13,803	48
1916	13,573	58,077	20,828	92,352	32,538	149,424	2,218	11,402	48
1918	6,548	29,244	14,660	66,443	21,752	94,663	719	3,705	48
1920	9,709	34,382	26,277	116,132	28,911	125,010	3,281	20,808	48
1922	9,814	29,261	20,138	87,340	27,809	114,221	2,197	12,854	48
1924	28,697	125,044	29,186	132,418	19,418	77,852	3,422	22,916	48
1926	4,568	18,602	14,439	64,486	18,040	81,347	934	4,362	48
1928	16,287	79,242	20,300	112,942	21,443	120,364	11,349	77,929	48
1930	2,893	12,546	14,561	89,433	16,692	100,740	1,530	5,470	48
1932	5,638	20,133	10,075	40,315	8,660	47,442	4,908	20,283	48

Table 1-2 *(Continued)*

Year	Democrat		Republican		Other		Total Vote		Number of States
	Raw Mean Difference	*Standard Deviation*	*Raw Mean Difference*	*Standard Deviation*	*Raw Mean Difference*	*Standard Deviation*	*Raw Mean Difference*	*Standard Deviation*	
1934	9,843	50,492	13,428	58,346	18,572	102,265	3,190	13,086	48
1936	14,215	68,515	8,158	46,383	19,124	112,299	4,045	21,497	48
1938	7,816	50,998	13,884	84,022	19,714	135,249	2,219	7,207	48
1940	14,338	80,776	20,979	144,295	32,880	224,326	3,063	14,603	48
1942	8,992	60,436	12,315	73,159	20,351	133,773	1,078	5,101	48
1944	10,959	57,371	10,485	57,993	22,137	115,133	1,515	9,317	48
1946	14,992	74,717	10,677	62,415	23,839	132,656	1,943	8,376	48
1948	58,127	302,789	31,639	174,488	87,503	419,952	1,471	8,705	48
1950	16,015	92,034	18,499	125,140	33,290	217,060	1,268	5,974	48
1952	28,841	134,145	28,727	145,962	38,303	248,830	152	599	48
1954	8,196	33,160	1,405	5,221	8,097	33,882	640	2,743	48
1956	11,700	70,555	737	3,437	12,015	70,638	412	1,608	48
1958	17,680	101,676	2,589	10,843	16,352	100,995	5,231	24,625	49
1960	7,864	27,491	1,134	3,944	5,765	26,635	4,011	14,756	49
1962	2,490	13,907	1,137	6,798	2,706	14,146	973	6,763	49
1964	2,385	13,271	5,628	21,897	5,812	24,052	2,304	9,973	49
1966	2,249	13,738	5,304	24,755	601	3,384	2,862	18,488	49
1968	4,893	19,045	13,498	45,881	5,309	25,222	3,777	22,533	49
1970	8,631	44,371	6,161	33,881	12,627	76,860	512	1,701	48
1972	28,347	150,622	22,928	128,550	7,552	49,024	43,928	273,761	48

Notes: This table assesses data discrepancies in the House vote for Democratic, Republican, Other, and total vote count between ICPSR data set 0075 and the author's vote data for the House. The ICPSR vote data are taken from the state-level vote for the House contained in data set 0075 for each of the states for the 1824–1972 period. The corresponding House vote for the states are found in the author's Tables 5-79 through 5-116 in Chapter 5. If a state has two sets of vote counts for House races in any of Tables 5-79 through 5-116—known as the conventionally coded values and the author's alternative coded values—the latter are always used. They are designated in Tables 5-79 through 5-116 as bold italicized entries. If no italicized entries exist for a given state in a given year, the conventionally coded vote values for the House are used. Absolute difference values for the House are then computed by comparing the House vote data from the ICPSR data file and the vote data shown in Tables 5-79 through 5-116 for Democratic, Republican, Other, and total vote categories of the vote separately. Difference values take into consideration the possibility of data errors occurring by either commission or omission. If the ICPSR reports inaccurate vote values, this constitutes an error. If the ICPSR data set has no vote values and the author's data set has values, this constitutes an error. If the ICPSR data set has values for only certain vote categories but not others, this constitutes an error. (These states are regarded as states with data if these values are not zero, and difference values, therefore, are computed, which usually result in data error values being produced.) If the ICPSR data set purports to have complete data for House races in a state when only partial vote data for the House actually exist, this is a data error. After the computation of data difference values for all states in a given election year, means and standard deviations are calculated across all states' data difference values for this year and reported in this table. The number of states having difference values in any given election year is given in the last column of this table.

Sources: ICPSR data set 0075 and Tables 5-79 through 5-116 in this book.

Table 1-3 Alternative Party Codings for All Races,
1788–1999

	Wing	Fusion	Joint	Independent	Both Major	Total
1805–1820						
House	1	9	0	8	3	21
Governor	4	0	0	0	1	5
1821–1840						
House	15	8	0	6	1	30
Governor	12	2	0	1	1	16
1841–1860						
House	36	27	0	44	1	108
Governor	28	14	0	8	0	50
1861–1880						
House	15	22	0	68	4	109
Governor	17	10	0	8	1	36
1881–1900						
House	30	67	0	75	8	180
Governor	28	26	0	10	3	67
1901–1920						
House	8	44	13	21	10	96
Governor	7	20	14	6	0	47
Senate	1	6	4	0	0	11
1921–1940						
House	8	14	16	14	22	74
Governor	4	3	9	6	0	22
Senate	2	3	7	12	2	26
1941–1960						
House	5	2	13	7	20	47
Governor	4	0	4	8	2	18
Senate	2	0	5	8	2	17
1961–1980						
House	7	0	12	3	9	31
Governor	1	0	6	3	0	10
Senate	2	0	9	1	1	13
1981–1999						
House	0	0	8	0	11	19
Governor	0	0	4	1	0	5
Senate	0	0	9	0	0	9

Notes: No alternate party coding examples were found for the 1788–1804 period.

Direct election of Senators began in 1912 for six states, which explains why alternative party codings first appear for the Senate race in the 1901–1920 category in this table. Wing = candidate affiliated with a major party running as a splinter, wing, or factional candidate from that party (e.g., Benton Democrat, Anti-Benton Democrat, Union Democrat; Fusion = candidate of a major party running on a fusion ticket with one or more minor parties (e.g., Democrat-Greenback fusion, Republican-Greenback fusion) or on the "fusion" label itself (if parties in a fusion ticket can be identified); Joint = candidate of a major party also endorsed by a minor party under the latter's own slate of candidates on the ballot (e.g., Liberal Party endorsement of a Democratic candidate in New York under the Liberal Party's own slate of candidates on the ballot); Independent = major party candidate also running as an independennt (e.g., using the Independent Democrat label or the Democrat Independent label); Both Major = candidate running on both major party tickets (e.g., listed on both Democratic and Republican tickets on the ballot, as successful crossfiling candidates were in California up to 1960). For a further explanation of these categories, see the notes to Table 5-1, 6-10, and 7-8.

Sources: For House, Table 5-1; for Governor, Table 7-8; for Senate, Table 6-10.

2

Who Is Allowed to Vote: Suffrage and Election Laws

One of the foundations of elections is the franchise: who is entitled to vote. The degree to which elections serve democratic government rests on the right to participate or, in Robert Dahl's words, the "inclusiveness" of a government—"the proportion of the population entitled to participate on a more or less equal plane in controlling and contesting the conduct of government" (1971, p. 4). The Framers of the Constitution gave decisions regarding inclusiveness to the states as an indication of the strength of federalism. Article I, section 2 of the U.S. Constitution states: "The House of Representatives shall be composed of Members chosen every second Year by the People of the several States, and the Electors in each State shall have the Qualifications requisite for Electors of the most numerous Branch of the State Legislature." Despite the fact that these were national offices, states were allowed to define their eligible electorate upon entrance into the Union for state and national offices and define the qualifications for individuals running, for example, for the House and governor. Yet the strength of federalism often had the effect of denying inclusiveness, as some states overtly blocked large groups of citizens from voting. National intervention occurred in dramatic fashion when states discriminated against certain classes of people for voting. The response was a set of constitutional amendments on voting rights—the 15th Amendment in 1870, allowing black, male adults to vote; the 19th Amendment in 1920, allowing female adults to vote; and the 24th Amendment in 1964, repealing the poll tax requirement for voting.

This chapter is organized in five parts. The economic and property requirements for voting that were initially established in early state constitutions are discussed in the first section. The use of residency requirements to restrict the electorate is considered next. The ways in which citizenship was used as a barrier to voting are outlined in the third section. How literacy tests and poll taxes were used to curtail blacks' voting rights is examined in the fourth section. Women's suffrage is discussed in the final section. The presentation of the legal requirements to vote in this chapter is the most thorough and accurate available. While certain legal requirements have previously been analyzed for finite time periods, this chapter offers the only full accounting of all legal requirements, when they were in effect, and how they differed from state to state.

Economic Voting Requirements

Despite the democratic flavor of the American Revolution, states defined their early electorates and officeholders in the spirit of earlier colonial voting laws: an upper-class, white, male background was necessary to vote and hold office. The definitions of these electorates and officeholders were usually contained in the early constitutions of the states or earlier colonial constitutions, charters, and laws, since some states—Connecticut, Delaware, Georgia, Maryland, Massachusetts, New Hampshire, New Jersey, New York, North Carolina, Pennsylvania, Rhode Island, Vermont, and Virginia—did not feel it necessary to draft new constitutions upon entering the Union. Table 2-1 lists the passage dates of the constitutions applicable to states upon entry into the Union and also the dates when states officially achieved statehood. Passage dates of these constitutions, charters, or laws involved one, two, or even three steps: adoption of the constitution by a constitutional convention (or a law or charter by legislative assembly or royal decree); ratification by the people in a general election; and selection of a separate date from the preceding to declare the constitution in full force as law.

Property Requirements

Initially the American colonies borrowed their ideas of suffrage from the country they revolted against. Landed property or freehold was a crucial prerequisite for office holding and voting in England, where only the propertied upper class was deemed to have the wisdom, virtue, and economic stake in society necessary to vote and govern. The stability, prosperity, and direction of society depended on the propertied upper class having political power. Sir William Blackstone defined *freehold* as an estate (that is, landed property) for life or otherwise of indefinite duration, not to be confused with a leasehold in land for a definite length of time, even ninety-nine years (as paraphrased in McGovney, 1949, p. 12). These were the people who had the greatest stake in society and government or, to use Charles Beard's (1913) and Carl Becker's (1922) logic, the ones who had the most to protect and gain from exercising political power. Table 2-2 shows the freehold or landed property qualifications to vote in the colonial period, 1650–1776, along with other economic requirements. All thirteen colonies required landed property in order to vote. After the Revolutionary War, most of them still did (see Table 2-3).

Obviously America's independence did not bring immediate electoral democracy. People with power do not easily relinquish it. Whether from noble motives, tradition, English influence, economic self-interest, or a simple fear of giving the masses the vote, the propertied upper classes were not easily pressured into diffusing political power. However, the revolutionary spirit and corresponding democratic sentiment did, in time, influence the spread of suffrage to the middle- and lower-class male. Indeed, most Western democracies today have pursued suffrage extension chronologically from the upper-class male to the middle-class male, lower-class male, and, finally, women. America is no exception, but, in its unique culture, the ingredient of race also has played an important role in the chronology of suffrage.

Table 2-4 details the landed property and other economic requirements that states used to define their early eligible electorates. Listed with each economic requirement are the inclusive dates, month and year, for the period that a given requirement was used by a state. The month/year dates for a period indicate when the law first took effect and when it was repealed. This exact pinpointing of dates is important to political researchers who wish to see if the laws have had any effect historically on voting behavior. The extent to which legal requirements historically affect the voting behavior of the electorate is the central premise of the "legal-institutional theory of voting" (Rusk, 1970, 1973, 1974; Converse, 1972). This theory maintains that legal-institutional structures, including economic restrictions, poll taxes, literacy tests, and female and black suffrage, directly affect who votes and for whom they vote. Empirical support for the theory indicates that turnout levels and vote choices are directly affected by the laws guiding elections (Rusk, 1970, 1974; Rusk and Stucker, 1973, 1991).

Other Economic Requirements

States used one or more of three distinct types of economic requirements for voting: landed property or freehold requirements, personal property alternatives, and taxpaying requirements. First, borrowing from colonial days and English tradition, Connecticut, Delaware, Georgia, Maryland, Massachusetts, New Jersey, New York, Rhode Island, South Carolina, Tennessee, and Virginia were among the first states to use freehold requirements for voting after the Union was formed (see Table 2-4). Usually these freehold requirements were expressed in one of three ways: number of acres owned, value produced by the land (such as in rental income, sale of agricultural goods), or value of the land (as assessed for taxation). For example, Maryland stipulated ownership of a 50-acre freehold (1777–1810); Connecticut, a freehold producing an annual income of 40 shillings (1784–1818); and New Jersey, a freehold valued for annual taxation purposes at 50 pounds or more (1776–1844).

Second, while some states like New York, Rhode Island, Tennessee, and Virginia only allowed ownership of landed property for voting, reflecting colonial tradition, other states were already showing the influence of revolutionary and democratic ideas. Upon entry into the Union, states like Connecticut, Delaware, Georgia, Maryland, Massachusetts, and New Jersey extended the vote to the middle-class male by allowing a personal property alternative to landed property for voting. According to William Blackstone, personal property was "chattels personal," such as "animals, household stuff, money, jewels, corn, garments, and everything else that can properly be put in motion, and transferred from place to place" (as quoted in Williamson, 1960, p. 14). This definition, written during colonial times, was expanded to include the store and inventory of goods of the urban shopkeeper and related possessions of the urban middle class. Indeed, the political pressure of this kind of wealth—the growing bourgeoisie—more than democratic ideas may have been the main reason for allowing other people of means into the electorate. The landed wealthy viewed these people as rational and stable in character with a vested interest in the community.

Taxpaying was the third economic criteria for voting. In true democratic fashion, some states such as Ohio, Louisiana, and Mississippi entered the Union with only a taxpaying requirement for voting (in 1803, 1812, and 1817, respectively). Even three of the original colonies—New Hampshire, North Carolina, and Pennsylvania—required only taxpaying. However, several of the other states, such as Massachusetts, Virginia, and Rhode Island substituted the more lenient taxpaying requirement for landed or personal property later in their history (in 1821, 1830, and 1843, respectively). States such as these followed a logical progression from stringent to lenient economic qualifications for voting, which correlates well with different social classes getting the vote at different times. Unfortunately not all states followed this orderly progression from less to more democratic suffrage. Taxpaying was sometimes used as an additional, rather than alternate, requirement for voting. For instance, New York in the 1788–1822 period required taxpaying as well as freehold ownership in order to vote. South Carolina (1788–1810) also used taxpaying in a more stringent way: requiring a white male to have paid taxes equal to the tax on 50 acres of land to gain the franchise if he did not possess a freehold of 50 acres.

Taxpaying requirements were written quite generally. Usually the requirement was to pay a certain tax (for example, state or county tax) or pay a state tax of a certain amount. While this may remind the reader of the southern poll taxes at the end of the nineteenth century (see Table 2-15 for poll tax laws in southern states), few states in the early period of American history had poll tax (head tax) requirements for voting. Poll tax laws had required that everyone pay a fee of a certain amount in order to register and be eligible to vote, which distinguished them from taxpaying laws where everyone either pay a minimum amount of tax or a certain kind of tax in order to vote. Notable instances in our early history where poll taxes were actually used as requirements for voting include Georgia (1801–1945; see poll tax table), Massachusetts (1786–1891), New Hampshire (1784–1792), Pennsylvania (1799–1832 for propertyless single males), and Rhode Island (1843–1888 for propertyless native-born citizens). Some of these laws, like those in Georgia and Massachusetts, usually required payment of other taxes besides the poll tax to vote (although Georgia ended the other tax requirement in 1932, while retaining the poll tax stipulation until 1945).

Taxpaying requirements, at least the less stringent ones, provided the opportunity for lower-class white males to vote. With their introduction, particularly as alternatives to or replacements for property tests, the objective of universal white male suffrage was closer to being realized. By 1860, if not before, this goal was achieved. While a few states still had taxpaying qualifications (such as Rhode Island until 1888, Delaware until 1897, and Pennsylvania until 1932), these taxes were small and, in practice, served more as a registry fee than as a tax payment (Porter, 1918, p. 111). (For a summary of these various economic criteria for voting, the economic combinations involved, and their dates of applicability for the states, see Tables 2-5 and 2-6.)

Residency Requirements

Stringent economic requirements for voting were not the only election laws limiting the eligible electorate. Early in their history many states also imposed strict residency requirements for voting. Residency could be required in any or all of the following four geographic areas: state, county, city, and precinct. Table 2-7 lists the various residency combinations that the states used from their entry into the Union until 1970. Tables 2-8 through 2-11 list the actual residency requirements for state, county, city and precinct for the fifty states up to 1970. With the passage of the Voting Rights Act of 1970, which imposed a thirty-day residency for voting in presidential elections, and the subsequent Supreme Court decision in *Dunn v. Blumstein* (1972), which suggested a similar residency rule for other elections, most of the variation in residency restrictions has been reduced to a minimum. As Wolfinger and Rosenstone observe:

> The result was that relatively few people were still affected by residency requirements. Our estimates indicate that the probability of voting in the 1972 general election was not affected by existing residency requirements anywhere. Further relaxation of residency requirements (below the thirty-day level) would produce no appreciable increase in voting (1980, p. 76).

As shown in Tables 2-8 through 2-11, a large majority of the states when entering the Union had 12 or 24 months as their state residency requirements for voting. County and city residency requirements were often substantial as well. Six states had 365-day requirements in the county for voting when they entered the Union and another eight had 180-day

requirements. One state had a 365-day residency requirement in the city, and two had 180-day requirements. Over time, the length of residency required for voting tended to decline from the steep levels imposed at the time of statehood. Still, these initial steep levels persisted for long periods of time and, in the South, often increased after the "Compromise of 1876" allowed Rutherford Hayes to be president in exchange for the removal of Union troops from the South after the Civil War. Coupled with poll taxes and literacy tests, residency was a potent weapon to eliminate carpetbaggers (northern politicians who tried to take advantage of the unsettled conditions in the South after the Civil War) and blacks from the electorate. In earlier times, strict residency requirements ensured that only stable, permanent citizens of the state and local community were permitted to vote. Having a vested interest in the community was crucial to deciding who would be the political leaders in the community and the state. The concept of residence was intertwined with economic criteria for voting and both ideas were borrowed from England. Implicit in freehold and taxpaying criteria for voting was the assumption that one could not own substantial landed property or pay state taxes unless one had already resided in the state for some time.

Reading the residency tables is somewhat complicated because of the multiple layers of requirements. For example, Table 2-7 shows Alabama having a state and a county or city residency requirement from 1819 to 1868; a state and a county requirement from 1868 to 1875; and a state, county, and precinct requirement from 1875 to 1970. Looking at Tables 2-8 through 2-11 explains these different residency combinations. The first point to recognize is that both the enactment date (when the residency law was proposed) and ratification date (when the law was ratified and, afterwards, became effective) are given. The latter date is more crucial for the researcher; the former is perhaps more interesting to the historian or general reader. Often a constitutional convention proposed the requirement and the people ratified it at a general election. Sometimes there was no vote of the people and the requirement immediately became law when the constitutional convention ended its labors, unless an alternate date was specified in the constitution. The main exception to this logic is that the first ratification date given in the table for each state is often not the effective date of its constitution and, hence, its residency law since the state had not yet entered the Union at that time. Recourse to Table 2-1 is necessary to note the actual date of statehood in such cases.

To continue the example, Alabama had a 12-month state residency requirement for voting from September 1819 to July 1868. During that time, a white male also had to satisfy a 90-day residency requirement in the county or the city. From July 1868 to December 1875 a person had to satisfy a 6-month residency requirement in the state and a 180-day county residency. From December 1875 to 1970 an individual had to meet a state, county, and precinct residency stipulation, but while this residency combination remained the same through 1970, the actual time of residency required did not. From December 1875 to November 1901 state residency was 12 months, county 90 days, and precinct 30 days. From November 1901 through 1970, it was 24 months, 365 days, and 90 days, respectively. This reflected Alabama's move to create a one-party state by imposing more stringent residence requirements as well as a poll tax and literacy test. The "Solid Democratic South" was molded from legislation such as this (see Rusk and Stucker, 1973; Rusk, 1974, esp. pp. 1042–1043; also see Kousser, 1974).

A caution should be noted for the political researcher who uses these residency tables: the ratification dates in Tables 2-8 through 2-11 must be compared with the dates for elections in Alabama for state assembly, governor, Congress, and the presidency. For example, if Alabama had a general election on November 1901, this would probably mean that the people ratified the constitution and, hence, the new residency law contained within it at that time; therefore, such a law could not have an impact on voting turnout until the next regularly scheduled general election. The researcher can easily refer to Dubin (1998) for the month and year of House and Senate elections in each state and to Kallenbach and Kallenbach (1977) for similar information on gubernatorial elections. A congressional act was passed in 1845 stipulating that presidential elections must be held in November 1848 and at the same time each four years thereafter.

Citizenship Requirements and Alien Voting Laws

Citizenship requirements for voting were a natural corollary to suffrage laws requiring lengthy residences and substantial economic means. They also were intended to restrict the electorate to those considered worthy of exercising the franchise. While some states failed to mention "citizenship" as a requirement in their early suffrage provisions, their practice was often to allow only citizens to vote at the polls. Some of these states continued to use their old colonial charters or laws upon entering the Union, and these older documents often failed to mention the word *citizenship* for obvious reasons: the overwhelming portion of the population was English in colonial days, which made it unnecessary to insist on such a qualification for voting. Table 2-12 lists the dates when states actually mentioned the requirement of citizenship for voting in their constitutions. A clear majority of states mentioned citizenship as a suffrage provision upon entry into the Union. Those that did not mention it tended to be among the original thirteen colonies, which had not written new constitutions at the time of statehood. However, these states followed suit not too long thereafter by writing new constitutions with citizenship explicitly stated as a suffrage requirement.

Several decades later, some states weakened the citizenship requirement by allowing immigrants from other countries who had declared their intention to become citizens the right to vote before actually attaining citizenship. Table 2-13 shows the nineteen states that enacted alien

voting laws. Most were in the Mideast, Midwest, and the South; none were in the East. This highlights the differences between these regions and their political and economic philosophies. If class and material interests produced more of an elitist society in New England and New York, then the movement and settlement of territories west of this may have produced more egalitarian and democratic values. Juxtaposing the economic and political theories of Charles Beard (1913) for the East with Frederick Jackson Turner (1920) for the "West" may explain the rise of alien voting in the latter. The newer states needed to encourage people to move westward to help build communities and provide a labor force for them. Offering immigrants the vote immediately was one such enticement, which fit with the new democratic spirit of the West, but the opportunity of a new life, cheap land, and a relatively classless society (in contrast to the class-oriented East) were probably greater incentives to move West.

The alien voting movement in the South sprung from narrower motives, most notably the building of the white population to support the Democratic Party and, at the same time, adding to the lower-class work force after the tremendous casualties suffered by this region in the Civil War.

Around the turn of the century, the Progressive movement advocated a series of reforms designed to "clean up" corruption in elections and government. Many of these reform proposals are well known, such as the direct primary, initiative, referendum, and recall. Progressives also believed that only those loyal to and involved in the government of their community, state, and nation should be allowed to vote. Aliens were perceived as uninvolved, ignorant, and easy to manipulate, particularly by corrupt politicians and political machines. This reform movement created the impetus leading to the repeal of all alien voting laws by 1926 (see Table 2-13). Alien voting laws had served their purpose to help settle the "West"; reform-minded society now needed to return to the civic virtues in voters praised by statesmen in the early part of our history.

Like the residency tables, reading the citizenship and alien vote tables (Tables 2-12 and 2-13) takes some practice. Providing a few examples may help the reader. For instance, Wisconsin ratified its constitution in March 1848 with an alien voting clause that it used until November 1908, when the Progressive Movement influenced the state to switch to a "citizen-only" clause that is still operative today. On the other hand, Connecticut never had an alien voting law. It entered the Union using its 1663 charter and a variety of other laws, including a 1784 suffrage law that failed to mention citizenship as a requirement for voting. Since the law was silent on the subject, recourse to historical narratives of the period suggests that only citizens, in actual practice, could vote. Connecticut rectified this ambiguous situation by proposing a "citizen-only" voting requirement in September 1818 when a constitutional convention drafted a constitution for Connecticut. This constitution was ratified in a general election in October 1818 and, hence, after this date, the citizen-only clause went into effect and remains so today. A more complicated example is Texas. Its first constitution, ratified in October 1845, allowed only citizens to vote; in February 1876 the state also allowed aliens to vote; and, finally, in July 1921 Texas went back to the citizen-only voting provision that is still in effect today. This action made Texas one of the last states to repeal its alien voting act; Arkansas was the last state to do so, in 1926. After 1926 only citizens could vote in the forty-eight states.

Blacks, Poor Whites, and the Restricted Franchise

Far more sweeping than citizenship restrictions were restrictions regarding race. Most states did not allow black males to vote and, of those states that were silent on the subject, the actual practice was usually not to extend the privilege. Table 2-14 shows the states with "white-only" voting provisions prior to the 1870 ratification of the 15th Amendment which was a product of the Civil War that gave black males the franchise. (Actually, the Reconstruction Acts of March 2, 1867, and March 28, 1867, were the first acts to eliminate racial barriers to voting in the former Confederate states, requiring that these states end "white only" suffrage as a precondition to being readmitted to the Union.) The 15th Amendment and the 1867 Reconstruction Acts followed closely on the heels of several states granting the right of aliens to vote in the 1850s and 1860s. However, what had been conceded legally was not as easily obtainable in practice. Initially, blacks often formed voting coalitions with poor white males and carpetbaggers to support non-Democratic candidate slates, much to the dismay of Bourbon Democrats (a southern alliance of upper- and middle-class Democrats, former Confederate military leaders, and politicians), who had lost both their vote and their right to run for office during Reconstruction when Union troops were stationed in the South. This completely changed with the "Compromise of 1876," which brought disputed southern votes to the Republican presidential candidate, Rutherford Hayes, in exchange for his promise to remove federal troops from the region. After 1876 Bourbon Democrats routed carpetbaggers from the region, intimidated the black vote, and systematically set about to eliminate it completely from elections. Some believe that this strategy, at least in some southern states, also included eliminating the poor white vote, as much as possible, since it had failed to support the Democratic Party.

The Poll Tax

An important part of this strategy was the passage of poll tax and literacy test requirements for voting. Tables 2-15 through 2-17 show the provisions of these laws and the dates of their passage. Obviously Bourbon Democrats thought these laws were needed as late as the 1890s and early 1900s to eliminate the black vote and, possibly, much of the poor white vote (Key, 1949; Rusk and Stucker, 1973; Kousser,

1974). Indeed, Bourbon Democrats risked constitutional challenge in the U.S. Supreme Court; knowing this, they still decided to enact these laws. Court challenges were mounted shortly after the passage of these restrictive laws but, for the moment, the U.S. Supreme Court decided that these laws were constitutional.

The poll tax requirement was more onerous than it might first appear. The amount of money, while seemingly small, was considerable for poor whites and especially onerous for blacks. Often these poll tax clauses were cumulative in nature, stipulating payment for past election years when an individual had not voted. Just as burdensome, as Table 2-16 shows, was following the rules: registering and paying the poll tax when required (often many months to a year before the general election) and remembering to bring the poll tax receipt to the polls (if not presented a person's vote would be denied). It is telling that all eleven Confederate states passed a poll tax requirement for voting, most doing so in the 1890s and early 1900s.

Literacy Tests

Seven Confederate states (Alabama, Georgia, Louisiana, Mississippi, North Carolina, South Carolina, and Virginia) and one Border State (Oklahoma) also passed literacy tests for voting. These states erected a formidable double barrier to the vote. As shown in Table 2-17, it is hardly a coincidence that most of these states passed literacy tests at exactly the same time as they passed poll tax laws. The literacy tests were also formidable, usually requiring that a person be able to read and write in English. The less educated and ignorant were screened out by such requirements. The "understanding clause" of these laws is often misunderstood. States usually mentioned this clause as an alternate way to pass the literacy test if one could not read and write in English. Ostensibly, this was to allow poor whites to meet the literacy requirement. However, it was up to the discretion of the election registrar whether one gave a "reasonable" interpretation of a clause from the state or federal constitution when the registrar read it aloud. While this discretion obviously was biased against any black's interpretation of a constitutional clause, such discretion could be used in the same manner to prevent poor whites from voting.

The contrary view to the "poor white argument" is that southern states passed alternatives to the literacy test (see notes to Table 2-17), including "grandfather" and "old soldier" clauses (see Table 2-18), expressly to help poor white males overcome the literacy obstacle to voting. Supposedly these laws worked like this: if a person had fought in certain wars, such as the Civil War, or was a descendant of such an individual, he could waive the literacy requirement for voting. On the surface, such laws seemed to help the southern poor white to qualify to vote. But the language in these laws for the applicable registration periods to take advantage of the "grandfather" and "old soldier" options tells another story. The registration time to take advantage of these options was brief for the states offering them (the only exception being North Carolina). For example, Louisiana's literacy test law went into effect in May 1898, but to use the "grandfather" option, one had to register by September 1 of that year. A further point is that only five Confederate states even bothered to pass literacy test options for the franchise. In addition, poor whites still faced the onerous poll tax provisions in all eleven Confederate states.

While common knowledge usually ascribes the literacy test strategy to the South, in fact some nonsouthern states also had literacy tests for voting, several passing such a law long before the "southern system" of election laws was enacted at the end of the nineteenth century. The motives attached to these laws varied. In the earlier days, when Connecticut (1855) and Massachusetts (1857) passed such laws, it was a reaction against the alien immigration waves from Europe, comprised largely of Irish and German immigrants (see Table 2-19). Fostered by anti-immigrant sentiment expressed politically by such groups as the Native American Party (also known as the "Know Nothings"), these movements disliked the immigrants for religious reasons (for example, the Irish were usually Catholics), political reasons (for example, ignorant voters reportedly supported corrupt politicians), and ethnic reasons (for example, prejudice was expressed against the Irish for their rampant "hooliganism"). What was repulsive to New Englanders was attractive to Midwesterners who passed alien voting laws (described earlier) to lure these people to the "West." In Porter's words (1918, p. 114): "Most of the immigrants were hopelessly ignorant, but illiteracy did not have much to do with one's capacity to grow a field of wheat."

Other states passed literacy laws around the turn of the century, probably as a result of the reform movements of this period, especially the Progressive Movement, which demanded that voters be informed and responsible citizens. The assumption was that a person could hardly be an informed and responsible voter if he or she were illiterate.

Data analysis of the effects of southern poll tax and literacy test laws by Rusk and Stucker (1973), Rusk (1974), and Kousser (1974) all reveal massive declines in voter turnout at the polls after these laws were enacted. These declines were sufficiently large that they had to encompass vote casualties among both poor whites and blacks. Ecological estimation techniques used by Kousser (1974) further verify this. Such data findings lend credibility to the "legal-institutional theory of voting" and point to how it can serve as a useful explanation of how the Bourbon Democrats were able to create the one-party "Solid South" around the turn of the century, an important feature of American regional politics until the 1950s (see Rusk and Stucker, 1973).

White Primaries

Adding further insult to injury, Bourbon Democrats established white primary laws for the Democratic Party in the early 1900s. This enabled the dominant party in the region to also eliminate black voting in its primary elections. The success of poll tax and literacy test laws in the general election motivated the Democrats to employ this restrictive vote strategy in their nomination process. Initial constitutional challenges to eliminate the all-white primary failed. However, over time federal decisions (court decisions, legislative acts, and proposals for constitutional amendments) would eliminate the entire "Southern System" of restrictive laws, although long after their goal of creating a one-party South had been achieved.

An End to the Requirements

The death knell for grandfather and similar clauses was the U.S. Supreme Court decision in *Guinn v. U.S.* (1915), which invalidated Oklahoma's grandfather clause. However, the practical effect of this decision was minimal, since the registration periods for most states having grandfather and old soldier clauses had long since expired. A more important U.S. Supreme Court decision came in *Smith v. Allwright* (1944), when the Court declared the southern Democratic all-white primary unconstitutional. In 1964 a constitutional amendment proposed by the U.S. Congress was ratified by the requisite number of states, thereby becoming the 24th Amendment, which outlawed the poll tax. The related 1965 Voting Rights Act also mentioned the elimination of the poll tax requirement for voting in any federal election and banned literacy tests in certain defined areas that referred to the South. The constitutionality of this act was upheld by the Supreme Court in *South Carolina v. Katzenbach* (1966). The Voting Rights Act of 1970 went further and banned literacy tests for voting in those nonsouthern states that also had this requirement, and this action was held to be constitutional in the same year by the U.S. Supreme Court in *Oregon v. Mitchell*.

Women's Suffrage

If having literacy test and poll tax requirements around the turn of the century while repealing alien voting laws presents a picture of the United States countenancing restrictive suffrage at the time, the movement for women's suffrage counterbalances this. Women, representing approximately half the adult population, did not have the vote for federal offices until Wyoming's experimental legislation in 1889. Prior to that time, a few states had allowed women to vote only in city and school elections.

The arguments against female suffrage were several. First, women were thought to be ignorant of politics and, if given the vote, would use it irresponsibly. Second, and somewhat contradictory to the first argument, it was believed that women, if given the vote, would only vote the way their husbands did. Third, some concluded that women would only use the suffrage to close down the saloons, and male imbibers and saloon owners wanted to prevent Prohibition at any cost. Fourth, it was predicted that women, given their moralistic nature, would use their vote in an attempt to "clean up" politics, which was anathema to male politicians and various corrupt political machines. When Wyoming and other early western experiments in female suffrage (for example, Colorado in 1893, Utah in 1895, and Idaho in 1896) failed to confirm these various theories, other states followed the West's lead (see Table 2-20). A second impetus for female suffrage came from the activity of women in World War I.

In all, twenty-seven states passed female suffrage laws prior to the ratification of the 19th Amendment on August 18, 1920. However, several of these laws were passed in the 1917–1920 period, which meant their passage was unnecessary for women to vote in the November 1920 presidential election. Twelve of the twenty-seven states actually passed laws that were operative in presidential elections before 1920 (and New York passed a law in 1917 that was first applicable to the 1918 midterm election). In 1920 the 19th Amendment achieved universal suffrage in America, just as in 1870 the 15th Amendment, in theory, had achieved universal male suffrage (before the "Southern System" of election laws undermined this effort). The earlier effort to achieve universal white male suffrage had been accomplished prior to the Civil War. (For a list of the most important federal amendments affecting the suffrage, see Table 2-21.)

The entrance of almost half of the adult population to the eligible electorate raises questions about how they voted or whether they voted at all. While empirical answers have not been forthcoming for the first question, Rusk and Stucker (Rusk and Stucker, 1991; Stucker, 1973) have empirically analyzed the second question and found a statistical relationship between when states adopted women's suffrage laws and a decline in overall state voting turnout. Further, when looking at the two election years before and after passage in 1920 of the 19th Amendment, which guaranteed universal female suffrage, the average decline in states' overall voting turnout in this period was 9.7 percent for presidential elections and 10.4 percent for midterm elections. This seems to confirm the importance of the "legal-institutional theory" in explaining significant changes in historical voting patterns. However, historian Paul Kleppner (1982) disagrees. He maintains that the voting declines in this period were instead due to the fact that "politics generally lacked its earlier intensity and strong voter stimulus." Yet this fails to explain the earlier voting declines in states that adopted women's suffrage considerably before the ratification of the 19th Amendment. While this controversy is ongoing, the fact that women gained the vote changed the way politics would be conducted in the future. Male politicians now had to adapt their appeals to a much larger and potentially different issue constituency.

Conclusion

The history of suffrage and election laws has taken the United States from an elitist political society to a democra-

tic one, with a lot of detours along the way. For simplicity's sake, the first suffrage period (1788–1860) might be described as very restrictive at the start, with suffrage for only upper-class white males, but the vote was over time extended by the states, first to middle-class white males and, later, to lower-class white males. Loosely speaking, this first period achieved the goal of universal white male suffrage.

The second period (1860–1920) is not easily categorized: it was a "mixed bag," dealing with the suffrage problems of three distinct groups in the country—blacks, aliens, and women. Technically, in the first part of this period, attempts at inclusiveness were made for blacks with the Reconstruction Acts in 1867 and the 15th Amendment in 1870 giving them the vote, but the latter part of this period saw the South effectively remove the vote from this group through the use of several clever election devices. The first part of the period also extended the franchise to aliens, with several midwestern and southern states allowing aliens to vote. But, like the situation with blacks, the latter part of this period saw states taking back the vote from aliens. The suffrage movement of women, however, moved in the opposite direction in this period: from extremely restrictive to more liberalizing as some states allowed female suffrage, at least for certain political races.

It was not until the third suffrage period (1920–2000) that universal suffrage was achieved, both in theory and in practice. The voting problems of blacks were resolved and the suffrage movement for women was finalized. All women received the vote in 1920, and all the restrictions that had been hindering blacks from voting were removed in the 1960s. Legality is a necessary, but not sufficient, condition for universal suffrage. The law must be executed faithfully in the actual election situation for universal suffrage to be achieved. This last period saw this occur for blacks. The 26th Amendment, allowing eighteen-year-olds to vote, only added to the liberalizing nature of this third period.

It is interesting to note that the early liberalizing trends in the first period were initiated at the state level, while the liberalizing trends in this last period were initiated at the federal level. Placed in between these two periods was a mixed era from 1860 to 1920 when states, more often than not, reversed their liberalizing tendencies of the first period, especially in the areas of black and alien suffrage.

Changes in suffrage laws and institutional electoral procedures and the breakpoints for these three suffrage periods should be viewed in the context of the different strength and role of political parties in the nineteenth and twentieth centuries. Political parties were much stronger in the 1800s than in the present century (Rusk, 1970, 1974), but for reasons other than simply economic and issue factors (Burnham, 1965, 1970); social, ethnic, and religious factors (Jensen, 1971; Kleppner, 1970); or regional factors (Kleppner, 1982). Parties were more powerful because they had virtually complete control over the (1) nomination process, (2) election process, (3) patronage, and (4) social welfare.

Around the turn of the twentieth century, direct primary laws eroded parties' control of the nomination process, and secret ballot and personal registration laws similarly eroded their control over the voter and the voting process. Starting with the Pendleton Act of 1883, civil service reform eroded parties' control over patronage and its usefulness in rewarding party workers for mobilizing the vote at election time. With the federal government taking over the responsibility of social welfare, starting in Woodrow Wilson's presidency and accelerating in the New Deal days of Franklin Roosevelt, parties lost their social welfare advantage with voters. In essence, the passing of key legislation by state and federal governments ended the major parties' monopoly of the nomination, general election, patronage, and social welfare functions.

When the parties were in control, it was easier to add or delete groups in the electorate for partisan advantage. Much of the restrictive suffrage legislation was passed, in part, because of the powerful nature of party organizations before the twentieth century. Conversely, many of the most important extensions of suffrage occurred in the twentieth century when parties were losing much of their power and responsibilities and also when the federal government was increasingly intervening in suffrage matters, especially to thwart discriminatory practices at the polls. Thus, in the course of history, partly because of the lessening of parties' powers, partly because of national intervention in state excesses, Americans achieved what many thought the Revolutionary War had been fought for—equal rights for all people, including the right of all to vote and, hence, choose their representatives to government.

Table 2-1 Dates of Constitutions Applicable to States Upon Entry into the Union and Dates of Statehood Entry

State	Constitutional Convention[1]	Other[2]	People's Vote[3]	In Force[4]	Statehood[5]
Alabama	8/1819		9/1819		12/14/1819
Alaska	2/1956	8/1958 (R)	4/1956		1/3/1959
Arizona	10/1910		2/1911		2/14/1912
Arkansas	1/1836				6/15/1836
California	10/1849		11/1849		9/9/1850
Colorado	3/1876		7/1876		8/1/1876
Connecticut		NA/1784 (L)			1/9/1788
Delaware	9/1776				12/7/1787
Florida	1/1839		5/1839		3/3/1845
Georgia	2/1777				1/2/1788
Hawaii	NA/1949		11/1950		8/21/1959
Idaho	8/1889		11/1889		7/3/1890
Illinois	8/1818				12/3/1818
Indiana	6/1816				12/11/1816
Iowa	5/1846		8/1846		12/28/1846
Kansas	7/1859		10/1859		1/29/1861
Kentucky	4/1792				6/1/1792
Louisiana	1/1812				4/30/1812
Maine	10/1819		12/1819		3/15/1820
Maryland	11/1776			2/1777	4/28/1788
Massachusetts	3/1780		5/1780		2/6/1788
Michigan	6/1835		11/1835		1/26/1837
Minnesota	7/1857		10/1857		5/11/1858
Mississippi	8/1817		9/1817		12/10/1817
Missouri	7/1820	6/1821 (L)	8/1820		8/10/1821
Montana	8/1889		10/1889		11/8/1889
Nebraska		2/1866 (L)	6/1866	2/1867	3/1/1867
Nevada	7/1864		9/1864		10/31/1864
New Hampshire	10/1783		NA/1783	6/1784	6/21/1788
New Jersey	7/1776				12/18/1787
New Mexico	9/1910		1/1911		1/6/1912
New York	4/1777				7/26/1788
North Carolina	12/1776				11/21/1789
North Dakota	8/1889		10/1889		11/2/1889
Ohio[6]	11/1802				3/1/1803
Oklahoma	7/1907		9/1907		11/16/1907
Oregon	9/1857		11/1857		2/14/1859
Pennsylvania	9/1776				12/12/1787
Rhode Island		NA/1767 (L)			5/29/1790
South Carolina	3/1778			11/1778	5/23/1788
South Dakota	7/1889		10/1889		11/2/1889
Tennessee	2/1796				6/1/1796
Texas	8/1845		10/1845		12/29/1845
Utah	5/1895		11/1895		1/4/1896
Vermont	7/1777			3/1778	3/4/1791
Virginia	6/1776				6/25/1788
Washington	8/1889		10/1889		11/11/1889
West Virginia	2/1862		4/1862		6/20/1863
Wisconsin	2/1848		3/1848		5/29/1848
Wyoming	9/1889		11/1889		7/10/1890

Notes: NA = month of constitution or charter not available; L = legislative law; R = referendum.

[1]States in this category had a constitutional convention draft their first constitution.

[2]Alaska had a referendum to be allowed entry into the Union. Connecticut and Rhode Island operated under earlier colonial laws or charters. Missouri had its legislature pass an act to gain entry into the Union. Nebraska had its territorial legislature draft its constitution.

[3]States in this category had voters ratify their constitutions at a general election.

[4]States in this category specified in their constitutions that they would take effect at a date later than the adjournment of their constitutional convention or the date of the people's vote on that constitution.

[5]Statehood is the month, day, and year that a state was admitted into the Union by the federal government. In the case of the first thirteen states, the date given is that of ratification of the U.S. Constitution.

[6]No formal act admitting Ohio to the Union was ever passed by the U.S. Congress. Tacit recognition was first given by Congress on 2/19/1803, and official termination of territorial offices by act of Congress became effective 3/1/1803.

Sources: State constitutions and relevant state statute volumes; also certain colonial laws and colonial charters.

Table 2-2 Freehold, Landed Property, and Other Economic Qualifications for Voting in the British Colonies, 1650–1776

Connecticut[1]
    1658 30L personal property
    1662 20L personal property
    1672 20L freehold or personal property
    1689 freehold income of 40S
    1702 40S freehold income or 40L personal property
Delaware
    1701 50 acres (12 cultivated) or 50L in personal property
Georgia
    1761 50 acres
Maryland
    1670 50 acres or 40L personal property
Massachusetts[1]
    1665 householder with income of 10S
    1691 40S freehold or 40L personal property
New Hampshire
    1680 estate of 20L
    1699 40S freehold or 50L personal property
    1728 50L realty
New Jersey
    1683 50 acres (10 cultivated)
    1704 freeholder
    1709 100 acres or 50L real or personal property

New York
    1691 freehold income of 40S
    1699 40L freehold
    1700 40L realty
North Carolina
    1669 50 acres freehold
Pennsylvania
    1683 100 acres (10 cultivated), 50 acres (20 cultivated), or taxes
    1696 50 acres (10 cultivated) or 50L property
    1700 same, except 12 cultivated
Rhode Island[1]
    1665 competent estates
    1724 100L freehold or 40S income
    1729 200L freehold or 10L income
    1746 400L freehold or 20L freehold income
    1767 40L freehold property or 40S freehold income
South Carolina[2]
    1669 50 acres freehold
    1704 50 acres or 10L personal property
    1716 30L personal property
    1717 500 acres or tax of 50L
    1721 50 acres or tax of 20S
    1745 farm, 300 acres, or 60L town lot and taxes
    1759 settled freehold
Virginia
    1655 householder
    1656 freeman and taxpayer
    1670 freeholder and housekeeper
    1676 freeman
    1699 freeholder
    1736 100 acres or 25 acres and a house
    1762 50 acres or 25 acres and a house 12' by 12' or a town lot with a 12' by 12' house

Notes: Listed are the years colonies enacted various landed property or freehold requirements for voting, and personal property alternatives to freehold requirements for voting. In some cases taxpaying was also required to vote and these taxpaying requirements are listed. Freehold or landed property stipulations for voting were usually expressed either in landed property being worth or assessed for taxation purposes at a certain value, with a certain acreage, or yielding a certain amount of rental income each year. L = pounds; S = shillings. Personal property was usually considered to be "chattels personal," such as household stuff, money, jewels, garments, and animals; in later years it could refer to shops and stores and their inventories. The years listed refer to colonial charters, colonial laws, or early colonial constitutions.

[1]The 1672 Connecticut, 1665 Massachusetts, and 1767 Rhode Island charters or laws offered a religious alternative for voting in place of the freehold requirement.
[2]South Carolina's 1759 law offered an alternative of 60L in a house, 100 acres, or pay a tax of 10S.

Sources: Relevant colonial charters, laws, and early constitutions and adaptations from McCulloch (1929) Table 1, pp. 20–21.

Table 2-3 Various Property Qualifications Immediately After the Revolutionary War

State	Property Qualifications
Connecticut	Freehold income of 40S per year or 40L personal property
Delaware	Freehold 50 acres (12 cultivated) or 40L personal property
Georgia	10L landed or personal property
Maryland	Freehold 50 acres or personal property worth 30L in money
Massachusetts	Freehold income of 3L per year or 60L personal property
New Hampshire	Landed property worth 50L
New Jersey	Inhabitants who possess or are worth 50L proclamation money
New York	20L freehold or property yielding 40S of rent per year (must also pay state tax)
North Carolina[1]	Payment of state taxes
Pennsylvania	Payment of public taxes
Rhode Island	40L freehold or yielding 40S of rent per year
South Carolina	Freehold of 50 acres or a town lot or payment of a tax equal to the tax on 50 acres of land
Virginia	50 acres vacant, or 25 acres cultivated with a house 12' by 12', or a town lot with a house 12' by 12'

Notes: Descriptions were taken from the relevant colonial charters, colonial laws, and early colonial constitutions as interpreted by references to Porter (1918) and McGovney (1949). Freehold or landed property stipulations for voting were usually expressed either in landed property being worth or assessed for taxation purposes at a certain value, with a certain acreage, or yielding a certain amount of rental income each year. L = pounds; S = shillings. Personal property was usually considered to be "chattels personal," such as household stuff, money, jewels, garments, and animals; in later years it could refer to shops and stores and their inventories.

[1]North Carolina only required one to be a state taxpayer to vote for the lower house in the state assembly; the state required a freehold of 50 acres of land to vote for the upper house of the state assembly.

Sources: Relevant colonial charters, laws, and early constitutions. Also see Porter (1918, p. 13) and McGovney (1949, pp. 11–17).

Table 2-4 Economic Requirements for Voting, 1788–1932

State	Landed	Personal Property	Tax
Connecticut	freehold producing annual income of 40 shillings (NA/1784–10/1818) freehold estate of a yearly value of $7 (10/1818–10/1845) (Note: this was actually a poll or head tax as it was applied.)	personal property valued for tax assessment at 40 pounds (NA/1784–10/1818) (Note: a 1795 law converted 40 pounds to $134.)	pay a state tax (10/1818–10/1845)
Delaware	freehold with 50 well-settled acres (that is, an occupied house) with 12 of these acres clear and improved (NA/1733–6/1792)	personal property worth 40 pounds (NA/1733–6/1792)	pay a state or a county tax (6/1792–12/1831) pay a county tax (12/1831–6/1897)
Georgia[1]	land valued at 10 pounds (2/1777–5/1789)	personal property valued at 10 pounds (2/1777–5/1789)	liable to pay tax in this state (2/1777–5/1789) pay tax (5/1789–10/1798) pay all public taxes (10/1798–8/1877) pay all taxes hereafter that may be required (8/1877–11/1908) pay all taxes that hereafter may be required, or satisfy one of six other alternatives (11/1908–11/1932)
Louisiana[2]	none	none	pay a state tax (1/1812–11/1845)
Maryland	freehold of 50 acres (2/1777–11/1810)	personal property valued above 30 pounds (2/1777–11/1810)	none
Massachusetts[3]	freehold producing annual income of 3 pounds (3/1780–4/1821)	any (personal) estate valued at 60 pounds (3/1780–4/1821)	pay any state or county tax (4/1821–11/1891)
Mississippi[4]	none	none	pay state or county tax (9/1817–12/1832)
New Hampshire	none	none	pay a poll tax (6/1784–9/1792)
New Jersey[5]	land valued at 50 pounds (7/1776–10/1844)	personal property valued at 50 pounds (7/1776–10/1844)	pay state or county taxes (NA/1807–10/1844)
New York[6]	freehold worth 20 pounds or yielding 40 shillings annual income (4/1777–2/1822)	none	pay a state tax (4/1777–2/1822) pay a state or county tax (2/1822–9/1826)
North Carolina[7]	none	none	pay public taxes (12/1776–4/1868)
Ohio	none	none	pay state or county tax (11/1802–9/1851)
Pennsylvania[8]	none	none	pay public taxes (9/1776–9/1790) pay state or county tax (9/1790–11/1932)
Rhode Island	freehold valued at 40 pounds or yields rent of 40 shillings per year (NA/1767–5/1843)	none	pay a tax on real estate up to one dollar for propertied native-born male citizens; for nonpropertied native citizens, voluntarily pay a poll tax of one dollar; if a foreign-born male citizen, the requirement was to live one year in the state and six months in the county and possess real estate of a value of $134 or which rents for $7 a year; for male natives the residence requirement was two years state and six months county (5/1843–4/1888)
South Carolina[9]	freehold of at least 50 acres or a town lot (3/1778–9/1865)	none	pay tax equal to tax on 50 acres of land (3/1778–6/1790) pay a tax of 3 shillings (6/1790–12/1810)
Tennessee	possessor of a freehold (2/1796–3/1835)	none	none
Virginia[10]	50 acres of unimproved land, 25 acres cultivated and occupied by a house 12' by 12', or a town lot with a 12' by 12' house (NA/1762–4/1830) estate or freehold in land assessed at a value $25 or more (4/1830–10/1851)	none	a housekeeper and head of family who pays state taxes, or a person who has a leasehold estate with annual rent of $20 (4/1830–10/1851) pay all taxes assessed after the adoption of the 1864 constitution (4/1864–7/1869)

Notes: Landed property refers to real estate. According to McGovney (1949, p. 12), "Technically, a freehold is an estate for life or otherwise of indefinite duration, but a leasehold in land is for a definite term of years. . . ." According to Blackstone, personal property means "chattel's personal," such as animals, household stuff, money, jewels, corn, or garments (as noted in Williamson, 1960, p. 14). Taxpaying is paying some kind of state or county tax or in some cases paying a poll tax in the non-South to satisfy the vote requirement. For poll tax requirements to vote in the South, see Table 2-15. Any state having an applicable economic requirement for voting before entry into the Union that was also operative after statehood has the date of such earlier constitution, charter, or law mentioned in the table as the beginning date. Some states did not draft a new constitution upon entry into the Union but used earlier constitutions or charters. Dates are when a constitution, law, or charter was ratified or when a popular vote of the people at a general election ratified a particular economic requirement. The law became effective after the ratification date. NA = month of suffrage law not available.

[1]Georgia's 1777 constitution specified "being of any mechanic trade" as an alternative to a landed or personal property requirement. From 2/1777 to 5/1789, Georgia's constitution merely said for the taxpaying qualification: "liable to pay tax in this state." From 5/1789 to 10/1798, the law said one must have "paid a tax." From 10/1798–8/1877, the law stated that one must have "paid all public taxes." From 8/1877 to 11/1908, the law became onerous and said one must have "paid all taxes which may hereafter be required of him." This meant, for example, if a person wanted to vote in 1890, he could not do so unless he had paid all his taxes from 1877 to 1890. From 11/1908 to 11/1932, several alternatives were proposed as a way to avoid this onerous tax requirement. The alternatives were being a soldier in some war between 1776 and 1900, being a descendant of such a person, being of good character and understanding the duties of citizenship, or being able to read and write in English. Interestingly, there was also a property alternative of either owning 40 acres of land or possessing $500 in personal property. Finally, the 1930 law ratified in 1932 did not strike out the poll tax but did strike out "all taxes being required . . . since the adoption of the 1877 constitution."
[2]An alternative to being a taxpayer in Louisiana was to be a buyer of U.S. government land.
[3]Massachusetts had a 1786 law that also allowed anyone to vote who was a freeholder who had paid one and two-thirds of his poll.
[4]Mississippi's 1817 law offered service in the state militia as an alternative to paying a tax to vote.

(Notes continue)

Table 2-4 *(Continued)*

[5]Williamson (1960, p. 29) comments that there were numerous and often conflicting suffrage laws in New Jersey with vague, if any, definitions of a freeholder. Because of this, some scholars believe that New Jersey never had a personal property alternative for voting. Some also believe that the landed requirement that it had prior to 1776 was voided by New Jersey's 1776 constitution. However, McKinley (1905, pp. 251–255) shows that the early colonial documents in New Jersey specified both real and personal property alternatives for voting. New Jersey's 1807 law could not be satisfied by paying a poll tax (see McGovney, 1949, p. 119).
[6]New York's 1822 law specified the following alternatives instead of taxpaying in order to vote: serve in the state militia, serve as a fireman who is exempt from the militia, or serve as a laborer working on the public highways.
[7]North Carolina's 1776 provision applied to voting for the state lower house and, hence, for federal offices. However, North Carolina had a more strict requirement for voting for the state senate. From 12/1776 to 12/1856, one had to own landed property of 50 acres to vote for the state senate; from 12/1856 to 4/1868, the taxpaying requirement listed in the table was sufficient to vote for the state senate.
[8]Pennsylvania's 1790 provision states that the tax must be paid six months before an election in order to vote; an 1838 law said it must be paid ten days before an election, and this was the requirement until 11/1932. A direct state tax was never collected until 1832; prior to that a poll tax was required for single men to vote from 1799 to 1832. For propertied males, payment of a small county tax from 1776 to 1832 qualified these people to vote. See, for example, Williamson (1960, p. 136).
[9]South Carolina's 1790 provision for tax paying also required six months residency in the precinct. An 1810 law deleted the taxpaying requirement but still required six months residency in the precinct.
[10]Virginia's 1864 constitution had a particularly onerous tax requirement that, in essence, meant one had to pay all taxes due between 1864 and 1869 in order to vote in 1869.

Sources: State constitutions and relevant state statute volumes.

Table 2-5 Dates for Economic Requirements for Voting, 1788–1932

State	Landed	Personal Property	Taxpaying	No Requirement
Connecticut	NA/1784–10/1818	NA/1784–10/1818	10/1818–10/1845	10/1845–present
Delaware	NA/1733–6/1792	NA/1733–6/1792	6/1792–6/1897	6/1897–present
Georgia	2/1777–5/1789	2/1777–5/1789	2/1777–11/1932	11/1932–present
Louisiana	none	none	1/1812–11/1845	11/1845–present
Maryland	2/1777–11/1810	2/1777–11/1810	none	11/1810–present
Massachusetts	3/1780–4/1821	3/1780–4/1821	4/1821–11/1891	11/1891–present
Mississippi	none	none	9/1817–12/1832	12/1832–present
New Hampshire	none	none	6/1784–9/1792	9/1792–present
New Jersey	7/1776–10/1844	7/1776–10/1844	NA/1807–10/1844	10/1844–present
New York	4/1777–2/1822	none	4/1777–9/1826	9/1826–present
North Carolina	none	none	12/1776–4/1868	4/1868–present
Ohio	none	none	11/1802–9/1851	9/1851–present
Pennsylvania	none	none	9/1776–11/1932	11/1932–present
Rhode Island	NA/1767–5/1843	none	5/1843–4/1888	4/1888–present
South Carolina	3/1778–9/1865	none	3/1778–12/1810	9/1865–present
Tennessee	2/1796–3/1835	none	none	3/1835–present
Virginia	NA/1762–10/1851	none	4/1830–10/1851; 4/1864–7/1869	7/1869–present

Notes: For a description of these economic requirements, see notes to Table 2-4. NA = month of suffrage law not available. Dates are when a constitution, law, or charter was ratified or when a popular vote of the people at a general election ratified a particular economic requirement. The law became effective after the ratification date. The relevant economic law for a state at the time it entered the Union could have a ratification date prior to its official statehood date since its constitution usually was proposed and approved before this time. In the case of the original thirteen states, some had ratification dates for relevant economic laws for voting in colonial laws or charters prior to 1788 when the Union was formed.

Sources: State constitutions and relevant state statute volumes.

Table 2-6 Economic Law Combinations for Voting, 1788–1932

State	Economic Combinations
Connecticut	landed or personal (NA/1784–10/1818)
Delaware	landed or personal (NA/ 1733–6/1792)
Georgia	landed or personal and taxpaying (2/1777–5/1789)
Louisiana	none
Maryland	landed or personal (2/1777–11/1810)
Massachusetts	landed or personal (3/1780–4/1821)
Mississippi	none
New Hampshire	none
New Jersey	landed or personal (7/1776–NA/1807); landed or personal or taxpaying (NA/1807–10/1844)
New York	landed and taxpaying (4/1777–2/1822)
North Carolina	none
Ohio	none
Pennsylvania	none
Rhode Island	none
South Carolina	landed or taxpaying (3/1778–12/1810)
Tennessee	none
Virginia	landed or taxpaying (4/1830–10/1851)

Notes: For a description of these economic requirements, see notes to Table 2-4. NA = month of suffrage law not available. Dates are when a constitution, law, or charter was ratified or when a popular vote of the people at a general election ratified a particular economic requirement. The law became effective after the ratification date. The relevant economic law for a state at the time it entered the Union could have a ratification date prior to its official statehood date since its constitution usually was proposed and approved before this time. In the case of the original thirteen states, some had ratification dates for relevant economic laws for voting in colonial laws or charters prior to 1788 when the Union was formed.

Sources: State constitutions and relevant state statute volumes.

Table 2-7 Residence Requirement Combinations for the States, 1788–1970

State	Residency Combinations
Alabama	9/1819–7/1868 S and C or T; 7/1868–12/1875 S and C; 12/1875–1970 S, C, and P
Alaska	8/1958–1970 S and P
Arizona	2/1911–6/1912 S only; 6/1912–1970 S, C, and P
Arkansas	1/1836–10/1874 S only; 10/1874–1970 S, C, and P
California	11/1849–5/1879 S and C or P; 5/1879–1970 S, C, and P
Colorado	3/1876–2/1881 S and C; 2/1881–4/1903 S, C, and P; 4/1903–4/1963 S, C, T, and P; 4/1963–1970 S, C, and P
Connecticut	NA/1784–10/1818 none; 10/1818–10/1845 T only; 10/1845–1970 S and C
Delaware	9/1776–12/1831 S only; 12/1831–6/1897 S and C; 6/1897–1970 S, C, and P
Florida	5/1839–1970 S and C
Georgia	2/1777–5/1789 S only; 5/1789–10/1865 C only; 10/1865–1970 S and C
Hawaii	11/1950–1970 S only
Idaho	11/1889–1970 S and C
Illinois	8/1818–8/1870 S only; 8/1870–1970 S, C, and P
Indiana	6/1816–2/1851 S only; 2/1851–1970 S, T, and P
Iowa	5/1846–1970 S and C
Kansas	10/1859–1970 S and T or P
Kentucky	4/1792–1/1800 S or C; 1/1800–6/1850 S, C, or T; 6/1850–9/1891 S, C, or T and P; 9/1891–1970 S, C, and P
Louisiana	1/1812–11/1845 C only; 11/1845–12/1879 S and C; 12/1879–1970 S, C, and P
Maine	12/1819–10/1938 S only; 10/1938–1970 S and T
Maryland[1]	2/1777–1/1810 S and C; 1/1810–1970 S and C or T
Massachusetts	5/1780–4/1821 T only; 4/1821–1970 S and T or P
Michigan	11/1835–11/1850 S only; 11/1850–11/1932 S and T or P; 11/1932–1970 S and T
Minnesota	10/1857–1970 S and P
Mississippi	9/1817–12/1868 S and C or T; 12/1868–11/1890 S and C; 11/1890–6/1968 S and T or P; 6/1968–1970 S, C, and T or P
Missouri	6/1821–6/1865 S and C; 6/1865–1970 S and C or T
Montana	10/1889–3/1897 S only; 3/1897–1970 S and C
Nebraska[2]	2/1864–3/1879 S, C, and P; 3/1879–1970 S, C, and T or P
Nevada	9/1864–3/1917 S and C; 3/1917–1970 S, C, and P
New Hampshire	6/1784–7/1831 none; 7/1831–7/1838 T only; 7/1838–7/1860 S and T; 7/1860–NA/1867 T or P; NA/1867–1970 T only
New Jersey	7/1776–8/1844 C only; 8/1844–1970 S and C
New Mexico	1/1911–1970 S, C, and P
New York	4/1777–2/1822 C only; 2/1822–9/1826 S and C or T; 9/1826–3/1944 S, C, and P; 3/1944–1970 S and C or T and P
North Carolina	12/1776–4/1868 C only; 4/1868–7/1902 S and C; 7/1902–11/1920 S, C, and P; 11/1920–1970 S and P
North Dakota	10/1889–1970 S, C, and P
Ohio	11/1802–NA/1858 S only; NA/1858–5/1915 S, C, and T or P; 5/1915–4/1923 S, C, and P; 4/1923–1/1930 S, C and T or P; 1/1930–1970 S, C, and P
Oklahoma	9/1907–1970 S, C, and P
Oregon	11/1857–1970 S only
Pennsylvania	10/1776–1/1839 S only; 1/1839–1970 S and P
Rhode Island	NA/1767–5/1843 none; 5/1843–1970 S and T
South Carolina	11/1778–6/1790 S only; 6/1790–4/1868 S and P; 4/1868–1/1896 S and C; 1/1896–1970 S, C, and P
South Dakota	10/1889–1970 S, C, and P
Tennessee	2/1796–5/1870 C only; 5/1870–1970 S and C
Texas	10/1845–12/1869 S and C or T; 12/1869–1970 S and C
Utah	11/1895–1970; S, C, and P
Vermont	7/1777–1970 S only
Virginia[3]	6/1776–11/1788 none; 11/1788–4/1830 C only; 4/1830–10/1851 C only for landed people, C, T or P for unlanded people; 10/1851–2/1928 S and C or T; 2/1928–1970 S and C or T and P
Washington	10/1889–1970 S, C, and T or P
West Virginia	4/1862–1970 S and C
Wisconsin	3/1848–NA/1883 S only; NA 1883–1970 S and P
Wyoming	11/1889–NA/1911 S and P; NA/1911–1970 S, C, and P

Notes: This table ends in 1970, since the Voting Rights Act of that year required all states to have a fair and reasonable residency requirement, which was interpreted to mean 0–60 days, but most usually resulted in states having a 0–30-day requirement. In effect, this 1970 law almost completely eliminated variation in state residency requirements for voting. Dates reflect the month and year when the residency requirement became effective. Usually this was when the state's constitution was ratified by a constitutional convention without a popular vote, a popular vote of the people was called to ratify the constitution, or the state legislature passed a law without asking for a popular vote of the people. Residency provisions would actually go into effect after the date of ratification. The first dates listed in the table may, in some cases, predate a state's official entry into the Union because a state constitution was usually ratified in either the state constitutional convention or a popular vote of the people before the U.S. government officially granted statehood. Also, some states did not write new constitutions upon entry into the Union but instead used earlier colonial charters, laws, or constitutions. NA = month of suffrage law not available; S = state residence requirement; C = county residence requirement; T = town or city residence requirement; P = precinct, ward, or election district residence requirement.

[1]Maryland's 1810 residence law specified a six-month requirement only for the cities of Baltimore and Annapolis. The 1851 law deleted mention of Annapolis but retained the six-month requirement for Baltimore.

[2]Nebraska's 1866 constitution specified that residency would be provided by law. Since no immediate law was passed, Nebraska used its 1864 territorial law, which is found in this table.

[3]In 1830 Virginia specified for those without landed property who were housekeepers and heads of family that they must satisfy a one-year residency requirement for county, city, and precinct. For landed property owners, the only residency requirement was a one-year county requirement. The later 1851 residence law applied its requirements equally to both propertied and nonpropertied males.

Sources: State constitutions and relevant state statute volumes.

Table 2-8 State Residence Requirements for Voting, 1788–1970

State	Enactment	Ratification	Length	Enactment	Ratification	Length
Alabama	8/1819	9/1819	12	12/1867	7/1868	6
	10/1875	12/1875	12	9/1901	11/1901	24
	NA/1961	11/1962	12			
Alaska	2/1956	8/1958	12			
Arizona	10/1910	2/1911	12			
Arkansas	1/1836	1/1836	6	7/1874	10/1874	12
California	10/1849	11/1849	6	3/1879	5/1879	12
Colorado	3/1876	7/1876	6	3/1901	11/1902	12
Connecticut	NA/1784	NA/1784	0	10/1845	10/1845	12
Delaware	NA/1733	NA/1733	24	12/1831	12/1831	12
Florida	1/1839	5/1839	24	12/1847	12/1847	12
Georgia	2/1777	2/1777	6	5/1789	5/1789	0
	10/1865	11/1865	24	12/1867	3/1868	6
	8/1877	12/1877	12			
Hawaii	NA/1949	11/1950	12			
Idaho	8/1889	11/1889	6			
Illinois	8/1818	8/1818	6	8/1847	3/1848	12
Indiana	6/1816	6/1816	12	2/1851	2/1851	6
Iowa	5/1846	8/1846	6			
Kansas	6/1859	10/1859	6			
Kentucky	4/1792	4/1792	24	9/1891	9/1891	12
Louisiana	1/1812	1/1812	0	5/1845	11/1845	24
	7/1852	11/1852	12	5/1898	5/1898	24
	7/1960	11/1960	12			
Maine	10/1819	12/1819	3	3/1935	10/1935	6
Maryland	11/1776	2/1777	0	11/1809	1/1810	12
Massachusetts[1]	3/1780	5/1780	0	11/1820	4/1821	12
Michigan[2]	6/1835	11/1835	6	8/1850	11/1850	3
	NA/1893	11/1894	6			
Minnesota	7/1857	10/1857	4	NA/1896	11/1896	6
Mississippi	8/1817	9/1817	12	5/1868	12/1868	6
	11/1890	11/1890	24	3/1968	6/1968	12
Missouri	7/1820	6/1821	12			
Montana	8/1889	10/1889	12			
Nebraska[3]	2/1864	2/1864	6			
Nevada	7/1864	9/1864	6			
New Hampshire[4]	NA/1783	6/1784	0	7/1838	7/1838	6
	7/1860	7/1860	0			
New Jersey	7/1776	7/1776	0	6/1844	8/1844	12
	NA/1957	11/1957	6			
New Mexico	9/1910	1/1911	12			
New York[5]	4/1777	4/1777	0	11/1821	2/1822	12
North Carolina[6]	12/1776	12/1776	0	3/1868	4/1868	12
	3/1901	7/1902	24	3/1919	11/1920	12
North Dakota	8/1889	10/1889	12			
Ohio	11/1802	11/1802	12			
Oklahoma	7/1907	9/1907	12	5/1963	5/1964	6
Oregon	9/1857	11/1857	6			
Pennsylvania	10/1776	10/1776	12	2/1790	9/1790	24
	2/1838	1/1839	12			
Rhode Island[7]	NA/1767	NA/1767	0	NA/1841	5/1843	12
	NA/1888	4/1888	24	NA/1951	11/1952	12
South Carolina	3/1778	11/1778	12	6/1790	6/1790	24
	4/1868	4/1868	12	12/1895	1/1896	24
	5/1963	5/1963	12			
South Dakota	7/1889	10/1889	6			
Tennessee	2/1796	2/1796	0	3/1870	5/1870	12
Texas	8/1845	10/1845	12			
Utah	5/1895	11/1895	12			
Vermont	7/1777	3/1778	12			
Virginia[8]	NA/1788	11/1788	0	8/1851	10/1851	24
	4/1864	4/1864	12	7/1902	7/1902	24
	2/1928	2/1928	12			
Washington	8/1889	10/1889	12			
West Virginia	2/1862	4/1862	12			
Wisconsin	2/1848	3/1848	12			
Wyoming	9/1889	11/1889	12			

Notes: This table ends in 1970, since the Voting Rights Act of that year required all states to have a fair and reasonable residency requirement, which was interpreted to mean 0–60-day requirement, but most usually resulted in states having a 0–30-day requirement. In effect, this 1970 law almost completely eliminated variation in state residency requirements for voting. Enactment = date that constitutional convention or other entity proposed voting residence laws. Ratification = date that constitutional convention or people's vote at an election ratified state residence laws and, hence, after this date, these laws went into effect. Length = length of residence expressed in months. NA = month of suffrage law not available. The relevant residency law for a state at the time it entered the Union could have a ratification date prior to its official statehood date since its constitution was usually proposed and approved before this time. In the case of the original thirteen states, some had ratification dates for relevant residency laws for voting in colonial laws or charters prior to 1788 when the Union was formed.

[1]Massachusetts had a two-year state requirement from 1859 to 1863 for foreigners.
[2]Michigan's constitution of 1835 said that any white male who was a resident at the time of the signing of the Michigan constitution did not have to meet the six-month residence requirement for voting. Michigan's 1850 constitution had two alternatives to the residence requirement listed in this table. The first alternative was the same as the one stated in the 1835 constitution as listed in this footnote. The second applied to aliens who declared their intent to become citizens and had resided in the state for two years and six months. Michigan's 1894 constitution also mentioned two alternatives to the residency requirement listed in this table. If

Table 2-8 *(Continued)*

one were a male inhabitant residing in the state either in 6/1835 or 6/1850, the state allowed one to vote without meeting the residence requirement. If a person was an alien who had resided in the state two years and six months prior to 11/1894 and had declared his intent to become a citizen by that time, he could vote.
[3]Nebraska's 1866 constitution specified that residency would be provided by law. Since no immediate law was passed, Nebraska used its 1864 territorial law, which is found in this table.
[4]Even though New Hampshire had no state residency requirement in 1788, its constitution implies that a person must pay taxes for one year in order to vote. This implication continued into the nineteenth century. On another matter, the 1860 residency law did not apply to the presidential race in 11/1860, but it did apply to all other races on the ballot in that year.
[5]New York implied a three-month residency requirement by allowing only freeholders to vote who had held land for three months in the state.
[6]In 1856 North Carolina passed a one-year state requirement that only applied to elections for the state senate, not elections for the state house of representatives.
[7]The Dorr Rebellion in Rhode Island led to an illegal constitutional convention that was approved by the voters. The reference in this table is to the other convention, which was considered legal and whose constitution was also approved by the voters. This constitution specified a two-year residency requirement for native-born males but a one-year residency requirement for foreign-born naturalized citizens. While this seems strange, the property requirements for foreign born were onerous compared to those for native born who simply had to pay a tax of $1.
[8]Virginia's 1762 law did not specify a residency requirement but said that freeholds must be held for one year before qualifying a person to vote. This implied a one-year residency requirement that Virginia used until it got rid of the freehold stipulation in 1851. In 1830 Virginia specified for those without landed property who were housekeepers and heads of family that they must satisfy a one-year residency requirement for county, city, and precinct. For landed property owners, the only residency requirement was a one-year county requirement. The later 1851 residency law applied its requirements equally to both propertied and nonpropertied males.

Sources: State constitutions and relevant state statute volumes.

Table 2-9 County Residence Requirements for Voting, 1788–1970

State	Enactment	Ratification	Length	Enactment	Ratification	Length
Alabama	8/1819	9/1819	90	12/1867	7/1868	180
	10/1875	12/1875	90	9/1901	11/1901	365
	NA/1961	11/1962	180			
Alaska	2/1956	8/1958	0			
Arizona	6/1912	6/1912	30			
Arkansas	1/1836	1/1836	0	3/1873	4/1873	10
	7/1874	10/1874	180			
California	10/1849	11/1849	90			
Colorado	3/1876	7/1876	90			
Connecticut	NA/1784	NA/1784	0			
Delaware	NA/1733	NA/1733	0	12/1831	12/1831	30
	6/1897	6/1897	90			
Florida	1/1839	5/1839	180			
Georgia	2/1777	2/1777	0	5/1789	5/1789	180
	12/1867	3/1868	30	8/1877	12/1877	180
Hawaii	NA/1949	11/1950	0			
Idaho	8/1889	11/1889	30			
Illinois	8/1818	8/1818	0	7/1870	8/1870	90
Indiana	6/1816	6/1816	0			
Iowa	5/1846	8/1846	20	3/1857	3/1857	60
Kansas	6/1859	10/1859	0			
Kentucky	4/1792	4/1792	365	9/1891	9/1891	180
Louisiana	1/1812	1/1812	365	7/1852	11/1852	180
	7/1864	9/1864	90	3/1868	8/1868	10
	7/1879	12/1879	180	5/1898	5/1898	365
	7/1960	11/1960	180			
Maine	10/1819	12/1819	0			
Maryland	11/1776	2/1777	365	11/1809	1/1810	180
Massachusetts	3/1780	5/1780	0			
Michigan	6/1835	11/1835	0			
Minnesota	7/1857	10/1857	0			
Mississippi	8/1817	9/1817	180	10/1832	12/1832	120
	5/1868	12/1868	30	11/1890	11/1890	0
	3/1968	6/1968	365			
Missouri	7/1820	6/1821	90	4/1865	6/1865	60
Montana	8/1889	10/1889	0	3/1897	3/1897	30
Nebraska[1]	2/1864	2/1864	20	2/1869	2/1869	40
Nevada	7/1864	9/1864	30			
New Hampshire	10/1783	6/1784	0			
New Jersey	7/1776	7/1776	365	6/1844	8/1844	150
	NA/1957	11/1957	60	1/1963	11/1963	40
New Mexico	9/1910	1/1911	90			
New York	4/1777	4/1777	180	10/1846	11/1846	120
North Carolina	12/1776	12/1776	365	3/1868	4/1868	30
	3/1901	7/1902	180	3/1919	11/1920	0
North Dakota	8/1889	10/1889	180	NA 1920	11/1920	90
Ohio	11/1802	11/1802	0	NA/1858	NA/1858	30
	6/1947	1/1948	40			
Oklahoma	7/1907	9/1907	180	5/1963	5/1964	60
Oregon	9/1857	11/1857	0			
Pennsylvania	10/1776	10/1776	0			
Rhode Island	NA/1767	NA/1767	0			
South Carolina	3/1778	11/1778	0	4/1868	4/1868	60
	12/1895	1/1896	365	5/1963	5/1963	180
South Dakota	7/1889	10/1889	30			
Tennessee	2/1796	2/1796	180	NA/1953	11/1953	90
Texas	8/1845	10/1845	180			
Utah	5/1895	11/1895	120			
Vermont	7/1777	3/1778	0			
Virginia[2]	NA/1788	11/1788	365	1/1830	4/1830	365
	8/1851	10/1851	365	4/1864	4/1864	180
	4/1868	7/1869	90	7/1902	7/1902	365
	2/1928	2/1928	180			
Washington	8/1889	10/1889	90			
West Virginia	2/1862	4/1862	30	4/1872	8/1872	60
Wisconsin	2/1848	3/1848	0			
Wyoming	9/1889	11/1889	60			

Notes: This table ends in 1970, since the Voting Rights Act of that year required all states to have a fair and reasonable residency requirement, which was interpreted to mean 0–60 days, but most usually resulted in states having a 0–30-day requirement. In effect, this 1970 law almost completely eliminated variation in county residency requirements for voting. Enactment = date that constitutional convention or other entity proposed voting residence laws. Ratification = date that constitutional convention or people's vote at an election ratified county residence laws and, hence, after this date, these laws went into effect. Length = length of residency expressed in days. NA = month of suffrage law not available. The relevant residency law for a state at the time it entered the Union could have a ratification date prior to its official statehood date since its constitution was usually proposed and approved before this time. In the case of the original thirteen states, some had ratification dates for relevant residency laws for voting in colonial laws or charters prior to 1788 when the Union was formed.

[1] Nebraska's 1866 constitution specified that residency would be provided by law. Since no immediate law was passed, Nebraska used its 1864 territorial law, which is found in this table.

[2] In 1830 Virginia specified for those without landed property who were housekeepers and heads of family that they must have a one-year residency requirement for county, city, and precinct. For landed property owners, the only residency requirement was a one-year county requirement. The later 1851 residence law applied its requirements equally to both propertied and nonpropertied males.

Sources: State constitutions and relevant state statute volumes.

Table 2-10 City or Town Residence Requirements for Voting, 1788–1970

State	Enactment	Ratification	Length	Enactment	Ratification	Length
Alabama	8/1819	9/1819	90	12/1867	7/1868	0
Alaska	2/1956	8/1958	0			
Arizona	10/1910	2/1911	0			
Arkansas	1/1836	1/1836	0			
California	10/1849	11/1849	0			
Colorado	3/1876	7/1876	0	4/1903	4/1903	60
	3/1937	3/1937	30	4/1963	4/1963	0
Connecticut	NA/1784	NA/1784	0	9/1818	10/1818	180
Delaware	NA/1733	NA/1733	0			
Florida	1/1839	5/1839	0			
Georgia	2/1777	2/1777	0			
Hawaii	NA/1949	11/1950	0			
Idaho	8/1889	11/1889	0			
Illinois	8/1818	8/1818	0			
Indiana	6/1816	6/1816	0	2/1851	2/1851	60
Iowa	5/1846	8/1846	0			
Kansas	6/1859	10/1859	30			
Kentucky	4/1792	4/1792	0	8/1799	1/1800	365
	9/1891	9/1891	0			
Louisiana	1/1812	1/1812	0			
Maine	10/1819	12/1819	0	NA/1938	10/1938	90
Maryland[1]	11/1776	2/1777	0	11/1809	1/1810	180
Massachusetts	3/1780	5/1780	365	11/1820	4/1821	180
Michigan	6/1835	11/1835	0	8/1850	11/1850	10
	NA/1893	11/1894	20	NA/1949	11/1950	30
Minnesota	7/1857	10/1857	0			
Mississippi	8/1817	9/1817	180	10/1832	12/1832	120
	5/1868	12/1868	0	11/1890	11/1890	365
	3/1968	6/1968	180			
Missouri	7/1820	6/1821	0	4/1865	6/1865	60
Montana	8/1889	10/1889	0			
Nebraska[2]	2/1864	2/1864	0	3/1879	3/1879	10
Nevada	7/1864	9/1864	0			
New Hampshire[3]	NA/1783	6/1784	0	7/1831	7/1831	30
	12/1842	12/1842	0	7/1860	7/1860	180
New Jersey	7/1776	7/1776	0			
New Mexico	9/1910	1/1911	0			
New York	4/1777	4/1777	0	11/1821	2/1822	180
	NA/1826	9/1826	0	3/1944	3/1944	120
North Carolina[4]	12/1776	12/1776	0	NA/1837	NA/1837	365
	3/1868	4/1868	0			
North Dakota	8/1889	10/1889	0			
Ohio	11/1802	11/1802	0	NA/1858	NA/1858	10
	1/1878	1/1878	20	5/1915	5/1915	0
	4/1923	4/1923	20	4/1929	1/1930	0
Oklahoma	7/1907	9/1907	0			
Oregon	9/1857	11/1857	0			
Pennsylvania	10/1776	10/1776	0			
Rhode Island[5]	NA/1767	NA/1767	0	NA/1841	5/1843	180
South Carolina	3/1778	11/1778	0			
South Dakota	7/1889	10/1889	0			
Tennessee	2/1796	2/1796	0			
Texas	8/1845	10/1845	180	12/1868	12/1869	0
Utah	5/1895	11/1895	0			
Vermont	7/1777	3/1778	0			
Virginia[6]	NA/1788	11/1788	0	1/1830	4/1830	365
	8/1851	10/1851	365	4/1864	4/1864	180
	4/1868	7/1869	90	7/1902	7/1902	365
	2/1928	2/1928	180			
Washington	8/1889	10/1889	30			
West Virginia	2/1862	4/1862	0			
Wisconsin	2/1848	3/1848	0			
Wyoming	9/1889	11/1889	0			

Notes: This table ends in 1970 since the Voting Rights Act of that year required all states to have a fair and reasonable residency requirement that was interpreted to mean 0–60 days, but most usually resulted in states having a 0–30-day requirement. In effect, this 1970 law almost completely eliminated variation in city or town residency requirements for voting. Enactment = date that constitutional convention or other entity proposed voting residence laws. Ratification = date that constitutional convention or people's vote ratified city or town residence laws and, hence, after this date, these laws went into effect. Length = length of residency expressed in days. NA = month of suffrage law not available. The relevant residency law for a state at the time it entered the Union could have a ratification date prior to its official statehood date since its constitution was usually proposed and approved before this time. In the case of the original thirteen states, some had ratification dates for relevant residency laws for voting in colonial laws or charters prior to 1788 when the Union was formed.

[1]Maryland's 1810 law applied only to the cities of Baltimore and Annapolis. Maryland ratified a law in 1851 that dropped the six-month requirement for the city of Annapolis but kept it for Baltimore. Maryland's constitutions of 1864 and 1867 referred to one's residency in the "legislative district" of Baltimore instead of the city as a whole. The residency requirement, however, remained six months.

[2]Nebraska's 1866 constitution specified that residency would be provided by law. Since no immediate law was passed, Nebraska used its 1864 territorial law, which is found in this table.

[3]New Hampshire's 1860 residency law did not apply to the presidential race in 11/1860, but it did apply to all other races on the ballot in that year.

[4]North Carolina's 1837 law specifically said that inhabitants of any town for twelve months who paid public taxes could vote. However, the 1837 law specified that persons possessing a freehold in a town did not have to meet the twelve-month requirement.

[5]The Dorr Rebellion in Rhode Island led to an illegal constitutional convention that was approved by the voters. The reference in this table is to the other convention, which was considered legal and whose constitution was also approved by the voters.

[6]In 1830 Virginia specified for those without landed property who were housekeepers and heads of family that they must have a one-year residency requirement for county, city, and precinct. For landed property owners, the only residency requirement was a one-year county requirement. The later 1851 residence law applied its requirements equally to both propertied and nonpropertied males.

Sources: State constitutions and relevant state statute volumes.

Table 2-11 Precinct or Ward Residence Requirements for Voting, 1788–1970

State	Enactment	Ratification	Length	Enactment	Ratification	Length
Alabama	8/1819	9/1819	0	10/1875	12/1875	30
	9/1901	11/1901	90			
Alaska	2/1956	8/1958	30			
Arizona	6/1912	6/1912	30			
Arkansas	1/1836	1/1836	0	7/1874	10/1874	30
California	10/1849	11/1849	30			
	NA/1930	11/1932	40	1/1949	6/1949	54
Colorado	3/1876	7/1876	0	2/1881	2/1881	10
	NA/1963	NA/1963	15	5/1965	5/1965	20
Connecticut	NA/1784	NA/1784	0			
Delaware	NA/1733	NA/1733	0	6/1897	6/1897	30
Florida	1/1839	5/1839	0			
Georgia	2/1777	2/1777	0			
Hawaii	NA/1949	11/1950	0			
Idaho	8/1889	11/1889	0			
Illinois	8/1818	8/1818	0	7/1870	8/1870	30
Indiana	6/1816	6/1816	0	2/1851	2/1851	30
Iowa	5/1846	8/1846	0			
Kansas	6/1859	10/1859	30			
Kentucky	4/1792	4/1792	0	6/1850	6/1850	60
Louisiana	1/1812	1/1812	0	7/1879	12/1879	90
	5/1898	5/1898	180	NA/1921	1/1922	90
Maine	10/1819	12/1819	0			
Maryland	11/1776	2/1777	0			
Massachusetts	3/1780	5/1780	0	11/1820	4/1821	180
	6/1874	6/1874	0			
Michigan	6/1835	11/1835	0	8/1850	11/1850	10
	NA/1893	11/1894	20	NA/1931	11/1932	0
Minnesota	7/1857	10/1857	10	NA/1896	11/1896	30
Mississippi	8/1817	9/1817	0	5/1868	12/1868	30
	11/1890	11/1890	365	3/1968	6/1968	180
Missouri	7/1820	6/1821	0			
Montana	8/1889	10/1889	0			
Nebraska[1]	2/1864	2/1864	10			
Nevada	7/1864	9/1864	0	3/1917	3/1917	10
New Hampshire[2]	NA/1783	6/1784	0	7/1860	7/1860	180
	NA/1867	NA/1867	0			
New Jersey	7/1776	7/1776	0			
New Mexico	9/1910	1/1911	30			
New York	4/1777	4/1777	0	9/1894	11/1894	30
North Carolina	12/1776	12/1776	0	3/1901	7/1902	120
	4/1953	11/1954	30			
North Dakota	8/1889	10/1889	90	NA/1920	11/1920	30
Ohio	11/1802	11/1802	0	NA/1858	NA/1858	20
	NA/1939	NA/1939	28	6/1947	1/1948	40
Oklahoma	7/1907	9/1907	30	5/1963	5/1964	20
Oregon	9/1857	11/1857	0			
Pennsylvania	10/1776	10/1776	0	2/1838	1/1839	10
	12/1873	1/1874	60	12/1959	12/1959	60
Rhode Island[3]	NA/1767	NA/1767	0			
South Carolina[4]	3/1778	11/1778	0	6/1790	6/1790	180
	12/1895	1/1896	120	5/1963	5/1963	90
South Dakota	7/1889	10/1889	10			
Tennessee	2/1796	2/1796	0			
Texas	8/1845	10/1845	0			
Utah	5/1895	11/1895	60			
Vermont	7/1777	3/1778	0			
Virginia[5]	NA/1788	11/1788	0	1/1830	4/1830	365
	8/1851	10/1851	0	7/1902	7/1902	30
Washington	8/1889	10/1889	30			
West Virginia	2/1862	4/1862	0			
Wisconsin	2/1848	3/1848	0	NA/1883	NA/1883	10
Wyoming	9/1889	11/1889	0	2/1911	2/1911	10

Notes: This table ends in 1970 since the Voting Rights Act of that year required all states to have a fair and reasonable residency requirement that was interpreted to mean 0–60-days, but most usually resulted in states having a 0–30-day requirement. In effect, this 1970 law almost completely eliminated variation in precinct or ward residency requirements for voting. Enactment = date that constitutional convention or other entity proposed voting residence laws. Ratification = date that constitutional convention or people's vote at an election ratified precinct or ward residency laws and, hence, after this date, these laws went into effect. Length = length of residency expressed in days. Also the term *election district* was usually used to specify ward or precinct in early constitutions and has been used here in that context. NA = month of suffrage law not available.

[1]Nebraska's 1866 constitution specified that residency would be provided by law. Since no immediate law was passed, Nebraska used its 1864 territorial law, which is found in this table.

[2]Even though New Hampshire had no precinct or ward residency requirement in 1788, its constitution implied that a person must pay taxes for one year in order to vote. This implication continued into the nineteenth century. On another matter, the 1860 residency law did not apply to the presidential race in 11/1860, but it did apply to all other races on the ballot in that year.

[3]The Dorr Rebellion in Rhode Island led to an illegal constitutional convention that was approved by the voters. The reference in the table is to the other convention, which was considered legal and whose constitution was also approved by the voters.

[4]South Carolina's 1790 law requiring a 180-day residency in the ward applied only if a person had no freehold of a specified size.

[5]In 1830 Virginia specified for those without landed property who were housekeepers and heads of family that they must have a one-year residency requirement for county, city, and precinct. For landed property owners, the only residency requirement was a one-year county requirement. The later 1851 residence law applied its requirements equally to both propertied and nonpropertied males.

Sources: State constitutions and relevant state statute volumes.

Table 2-12 Citizenship Requirements for Voting, 1788–Present

State	The Word citizen Not Mentioned in Constitution	U.S. or State Citizenship Required: Period 1	U.S. or State Citizenship Status	End of Period 1 Citizenship Requirement	U.S. or State Citizenship Required: Period 2	U.S. or State Citizenship Status
Alabama[1]		8/1819; 9/1819	U.S.	2/1868	9/1901; 11/1901	U.S. and state
Alaska		2/1956; 8/1958	U.S.			
Arizona		10/1910; 2/1911	U.S.			
Arkansas[2]		1/1836; 1/1836	U.S.	3/1868	4/1926; 4/1926	U.S.
California		10/1849; 11/1849	U.S.			
Colorado[3]		4/1901; 11/1902	U.S.			
Connecticut	NA/1784; NA/1784	9/1818; 10/1818	U.S.			
Delaware	NA/1733; NA/1733	12/1831; 12/1831	state			
Florida		1/1839; 5/1839	U.S.	6/1868	NA/1894; 11/1894	U.S.
Georgia[4]	2/1777; 2/1777	8/1877; 12/1877	U.S.			
Hawaii		NA/1949; 11/1950	U.S.			
Idaho		8/1889; 11/1889	U.S.			
Illinois		8/1818; 8/1818	state			
Indiana		6/1816; 8/1816	U.S.	11/1851	3/1921; 3/1921	U.S.
Iowa		5/1846; 8/1846	U.S.			
Kansas[3]		3/1917; 11/1917	U.S.			
Kentucky		4/1792; 4/1792	state			
Louisiana		1/1812; 1/1812	U.S.	12/1879	5/1898; 5/1898	U.S. and state
Maine		10/1819; 12/1819	U.S.			
Maryland	11/1776; 2/1777	5/1851; 6/1851	U.S.			
Massachusetts	3/1780; 5/1780	11/1820; 4/1821	state			
Michigan[5]		6/1835; 8/1835	state	11/1850	11/1894; 11/1894	U.S.
Minnesota[3,6]		4/1896; 11/1896	U.S.			
Mississippi		8/1817; 9/1817	U.S.			
Missouri		7/1820; 6/1821	U.S.	6/1865	NA/1922; 11/1922	U.S.
Montana		8/1889; 10/1889	U.S.			
Nebraska[3]		NA/1917; 11/1918	U.S.			
Nevada		7/1864; 9/1864	U.S.			
New Hampshire[7]	10/1783; 6/1784					
New Jersey	7/1776; 7/1776	NA/1820; NA/1820	U.S.			
New Mexico		9/1910; 1/1911	state (NA/1927: U.S.)			
New York	4/1777; 4/1777	11/1821; 2/1822	state			
North Carolina[8]	12/1776; 12/1776	3/1868; 4/1868	state			
North Dakota[3]		NA/1897; 11/1898	U.S.			
Ohio	11/1802; 11/1802	3/1851; 9/1851	U.S.			
Oklahoma		7/1907; 9/1907	U.S.			
Oregon[3]		NA/1914; NA/1914	U.S.			
Pennsylvania	9/1776; 9/1776	8/1790; 9/1790	state			
Rhode Island	NA/1767; NA/1767	11/1842; 5/1843	U.S.			
South Carolina	3/1778; 11/1778	3/1868; 4/1868	U.S.			
South Dakota[3,9]		11/1918; 11/1918	U.S.			
Tennessee	2/1796; 2/1796	8/1834; 3/1835	U.S. and county			
Texas[10]		8/1845; 10/1845	U.S.	2/1876	NA/1921; 7/1921	U.S.
Utah[11]		5/1895; 11/1895	U.S.			
Vermont[12]	7/1777; 3/1778	6/1828; 6/1828	state			
Virginia	NA/1788; 11/1788	1/1818; 1/1818	state			
Washington		8/1889; 10/1889	U.S.			
West Virginia		2/1862; 4/1862	state			
Wisconsin[3,13]		NA/1907; 11/1908	U.S.			
Wyoming[3,14]		9/1889; 1/1894	U.S. and state			

Notes: First column refers to the fact that the word *citizen* or *citizenship* failed to be mentioned in a state's constitution. This usually occurs in those states that were former colonies who relied on their colonial charters, etc., when entering the Union rather than drafting a new constitution upon statehood. What this meant was that technically one did not have to a be a citizen in order to vote; what it may actually have meant was the failure of the colony to draft a state constitution upon entering the Union, which specifically would have mentioned the word *citizen* as part of a suffrage provision. The second column refers to the date when a state used the word *citizen* in its constitution as a requirement for voting. Obviously these states were "citizen-only" states, that is, states that allowed only citizens to vote. The first date listed is the date the constitutional provision or legislative act was proposed. The second date was when this provision was ratified and after that date would go into effect. The third column refers to whether U.S. or state citizenship or both were required to vote. For those states that did not clearly specify which, a close reading of the state constitution usually indicated that the state was referring to state, not U.S., citizenship, which is what is coded in this table. The fourth column refers to whether a state repealed its "citizenship" requirement for voting and the date that this law was ratified and went into effect. Usually a repeal of such a law meant that aliens, as well as citizens, were allowed to vote. (See also Table 2-13, on alien voting laws.) The fifth column refers to whether a state proposed a second citizenship requirement, usually after an alien voting law was repealed, and the proposed date and ratification date for such a law. The sixth column refers again to whether the requirement was for U.S. and/or state citizenship. For those states that did not clearly specify either, a close reading of the state constitution usually indicated that the states were referring to state, not U.S., citizenship, which is what is coded in this table. NA = month of suffrage law not available. Mention or lack of mention of a citizenship requirement for voting in a state at the time it entered the Union could have a ratification date prior to a state's official statehood date since its constitution was usually proposed and approved before this time. In the case of the original thirteen states, some had ratification dates that either mentioned "citizenship" or failed to mention this requirement for voting in colonial laws or charters prior to 1788 when the Union was formed.

[1]In Alabama, under the 1901 law, an alien could still vote if he had declared his intention to become a citizen before ratification of the 1901 constitution.
[2]In Arkansas the attorney general on 4/26/1926 stated that alien voting was no longer the law and, retroactively, should not have been in force since 11/2/1920.
[3]Colorado, Kansas, Minnesota, Nebraska, North Dakota, Oregon, South Dakota, Wisconsin, and Wyoming were all states that entered the Union with alien voting laws; hence, the first citizen laws mentioned in this table for these states came later, sometimes much later, after a state entered the Union.
[4]In Georgia its first reconstruction constitution, which was proposed in 10/1865 and ratified by the people in 11/1865, specified one had to be a citizen of the state to vote, but this constitution was quickly superseded by another reconstruction constitution in 1867, which allowed aliens to vote.
[5]Michigan's 1894 law still allowed some aliens to vote, but it was limited to those who had lived two years and six months in the state before 11/1894, that is, before passage of this 1894 law, and who must have declared their intent to become citizens before that date. Apparently, if they had declared their intent before 11/1894, these people had until 1924 to actually become citizens. In the meantime, they could vote.
[6]Minnesota's 1896 law specified that one had to be a U.S. citizen for a period of three months.
[7]New Hampshire's law was unique in American history and continued this way until 1970. From 6/1784 to 11/1902, New Hampshire specified that one had to be an "inhabitant" in a town in the state. From 11/1902 to 1970, New Hampshire specified that one had to be an "inhabitant of the state." Although not specified, New Hampshire's government possibly construed "inhabitant" to mean something similar to "citizenship."

(Notes continue)

Table 2-12 (Continued)

[8]On 12/11/1856, North Carolina ratified a constitutional amendment that required one to be a U.S. citizen in order to vote for the state senate, but this amendment imposed no such requirement for voting for the state house. The actual citizenship requirement for voting for the lower house was ratified in 4/1868 but implied citizenship by its language rather than specifically stating it as such.

[9]South Dakota's 1918 law said that one had to be a U.S. citizen for the unusually long period of five years in order to vote.

[10]Texas's 1845 constitution actually said that one could either be a U.S. citizen or at the time of the ratification of this constitution, a citizen of the Republic of Texas in order to vote.

[11]Utah's 1895 constitution specified that one had to be a U.S. citizen for a period of ninety days in order to vote.

[12]Vermont's 1828 law actually stated that one could either be a citizen of Vermont or a citizen of another state in order to vote.

[13]Wisconsin's 1908 law said alien voting was allowed in a very narrow sense for those who had declared their intention to become citizens before 12/1/1908, with such individuals having to be fully naturalized by 12/1/1912.

[14]Wyoming mentions "citizenship" in its 1889 constitution but also states: "Nothing herein contained shall be construed to deprive any person of the right to vote, who has such right at the time of the adoption of this constitution. . . . After the expiration of 5 years from the time of the adoption of this constitution, none but citizens of the United States shall have the right to vote."

Sources: State constitutions and relevant state statute volumes.

Table 2-13 Alien Voting Laws, 1848–1926

State	Legislative Enactment	Ratification	Legislative Repeal	Repeal Ratification
Alabama[1]	12/1867	2/1868	9/1901	11/1901
Arkansas[2]	2/1868	3/1868	4/1926	4/1926
Colorado	3/1876	7/1876	4/1901	11/1902
Florida	1/1868	6/1868	NA/1894	11/1894
Georgia	12/1867	3/1868	8/1877	12/1877
Indiana	2/1851	11/1851	3/1921	3/1921
Kansas	1/1859	10/1859	3/1917	11/1917
Louisiana	7/1879	12/1879	5/1898	5/1898
Michigan	8/1850	11/1850	11/1894	11/1894
Minnesota	7/1857	10/1857	4/1896	11/1896
Missouri	4/1865	6/1865	NA/1922	11/1922
Nebraska	1/1866	6/1866	NA/1917	11/1918
North Dakota	8/1889	10/1889	NA/1897	11/1898
Oregon	9/1857	11/1857	1/1913	12/1914
South Carolina	9/1865	9/1865	3/1868	4/1868
South Dakota	7/1889	10/1889	11/1918	11/1918
Texas	11/1875	2/1876	NA/1921	7/1921
Wisconsin	2/1848	3/1848	NA/1907	11/1908
Wyoming[3]	7/1868	7/1868	9/1889	1/1895

Notes: Legislative Enactment = date state legislature or state constitutional convention proposed an alien voting law or a people's initiative was certified for signatures. Ratification = date when an alien voting law was ratified by action of state legislature, a state constitutional convention, a people's vote at a general election, or a governor's proclamation. This voting provision goes into effect after the ratification date. Note that if the ratification date is the date of a general election (that is, a people's vote at a general election), then the alien voting law goes into effect after that election and hence has its first effect on suffrage at the next regularly scheduled election in that state. Legislative Repeal = date legislature or other entity proposed a repeal of an alien voting act. Repeal Ratification = date that a repeal of an alien voting provision was ratified by action of a state legislature, a state constitutional convention, a people's vote at a general election, or a governor's proclamation. After that date, the repeal of the alien voting law goes into effect. NA = month of suffrage law not available. Dates for alien voting laws could precede the official date of a state's entry into the Union since state constitutions usually were proposed and approved before a state entered the Union.

[1]Alabama stated in its 1901 constitution that any alien who shall have legally declared his intent to become a citizen prior to the ratification of this constitution could vote, but if he failed to be naturalized by the time set by federal law, he would lose his vote.

[2]The attorney general of Arkansas ruled on 4/26/1926, that the state's alien voting law was no longer in force and, also, should not have been considered effective since 11/2/1920.

[3]The first dates in the table for Wyoming refer to territorial law that extended into the state's entry into the Union. The last dates in the table refer to the odd situation that Wyoming's 1889 constitution stipulated that aliens could vote until five years after the adoption of this constitution; after that, only citizens could vote. Thus, starting in 1895, aliens were deprived of the vote in Wyoming.

Sources: State constitutions and relevant state statute volumes.

Table 2-14 White-Only Requirements for Voting, 1788–1870

State	Legislative Enactment	Ratification	Legislative Repeal	Repeal Ratification
Alabama	8/1819	9/1819	12/1867	2/1868
Alaska	none	none	none	none
Arizona	none	none	none	none
Arkansas	1/1836	1/1836	2/1868	3/1868
California	10/1849	11/1849	2/1870	2/1870
Colorado	none	none	none	none
Connecticut	9/1818	10/1818	2/1870	2/1870
Delaware	6/1792	6/1792	2/1870	2/1870
Florida	1/1839	5/1839	2/1868	5/1868
Georgia	2/1777	2/1777	12/1867	3/1868
Hawaii	none	none	none	none
Idaho	none	none	none	none
Illinois	8/1818	8/1818	2/1870	2/1870
Indiana	6/1816	6/1816	2/1870	2/1870
Iowa	5/1846	8/1846	11/1868	12/1868
Kansas	7/1859	10/1859	2/1870	2/1870
Kentucky	8/1799	1/1800	2/1870	2/1870
Louisiana	1/1812	1/1812	3/1868	8/1868
Maine	none	none	none	none
Maryland	NA/1809	NA/1810	2/1870	2/1870
Massachusetts	none	none	none	none
Michigan	6/1835	11/1835	2/1870	2/1870
Minnesota	7/1857	10/1857	NA/1868	11/1868
Mississippi	8/1817	9/1817	5/1868	12/1868
Missouri	7/1820	6/1821	2/1870	2/1870
Montana	none	none	none	none
Nebraska	2/1866	2/1867	2/1870	2/1870
Nevada	7/1864	9/1864	2/1870	2/1870
New Hampshire	none	none	none	none
New Jersey	NA/1807	NA/1807	2/1870	2/1870
New Mexico	none	none	none	none
New York[1]	none	none	none	none
North Carolina	7/1835	8/1835	3/1868	4/1868
North Dakota	none	none	none	none
Ohio	11/1802	11/1802	2/1870	2/1870
Oklahoma	none	none	none	none
Oregon	9/1857	11/1857	2/1870	2/1870
Pennsylvania[2]	2/1838	NA/1838	2/1870	2/1870
Rhode Island	none	none	none	none
South Carolina	3/1778	11/1778	3/1868	4/1868
South Dakota	none	none	none	none
Tennessee	8/1834	3/1835	2/1870	2/1870
Texas	8/1845	10/1845	4/1866	6/1866
Utah	none	none	none	none
Vermont	none	none	none	none
Virginia	NA/1785	NA/1785	4/1868	7/1869
Washington	none	none	none	none
West Virginia	2/1862	4/1862	2/1870	2/1870
Wisconsin	2/1848	3/1848	2/1870	2/1870
Wyoming	none	none	none	none

Notes: Legislative Enactment = date when a state legislature, a constitutional convention, or a people's initiative certified by the state proposed a "white-only" requirement for voting. Ratification = date when a white-only requirement for voting was ratified by action of a state legislature, a state constitutional convention, a people's vote at a general election, or a governor's proclamation. This voting requirement goes into effect after the ratification date. If the ratification date is the date of a general election (that is, a people's vote at a general election), the white-only voting law goes into effect after this election and hence has its first effect on suffrage at the next regularly scheduled general election in that state. Legislative Repeal = date when a state legislature or a state constitutional convention proposed a repeal of the white-only voting requirement. Repeal Ratification = date when a white-only voting requirement was repealed by action of a state legislature, a state constitutional convention, a people's vote at a general election, or a governor's proclamation. NA = month of suffrage law not available. This table ends in 1870, since, on 2/3/1870, the 15th Amendment to the U.S. Constitution was ratified, disallowing "white-only" voting provisions. However, two acts preceded this which affected 10 of the 11 ex-Confederate states. The Reconstruction Act of 3/2/1867 along with the Supplemental Act of 3/28/1867 required that the 10 ex-Confederate states still without federal representation must eliminate all racial barriers to the suffrage as a precondition for readmission to the Union. In practice, this meant that all Confederate states except Tennessee had to write new state constitutions eliminating racial requirements for voting. The relevant white-only voting law for a state at the time it entered the Union could have a ratification date prior to its official statehood date since its constitution was usually proposed and approved before this time. In the case of the original thirteen states, some had ratification dates for relevant white-only voting provisions in colonial laws or charters prior to 1788 when the Union was formed.

[1]New York's 1821 constitution allowed selected blacks to vote if they satisfied certain qualifications: they had a $250 freehold on which they had paid taxes and they had resided in the state for three years. This is a limited definition of the idea that all males in New York could vote.

[2]According to McGovney (1949, p. 17): "In Pennsylvania, the voting status of Negroes was dubious. According to a decision of the Supreme Court of that State, which, however, was not rendered until 1837, Negroes had been legally ineligible to vote since 1776, although in the interval Negroes had sometimes voted."

Sources: State constitutions and relevant state statute volumes.

Table 2-15 Poll Tax Laws in Southern States, 1801–1964

State	Legislative Enactment	Ratification	Legislative Repeal	Repeal Ratification
Alabama	9/1901	11/1901	—	1964
Arkansas[1]				
1892–1905	11/1892	1/1893	12/1905	12/1905
1908–1964	NA/1907	9/1908	—	1964
Florida	8/3/1885	6/1889	5/1937	1/1938
Georgia[2]				
1801–1877	NA/1801	NA/1801	8/1877	8/1877
1877–1908	8/1877	8/1877	8/1908	8/1908
1908–1945	8/1908	11/1908	2/1945	2/1945
Louisiana[3]	5/1898	1/1899	7/1934	11/1934
Mississippi	11/1890	1/1891	—	1964
North Carolina[4]	6/1900	7/1902	3/1919	11/1920
South Carolina[5]	12/1895	12/1895	3/1949	2/1951
Tennessee[6]	5/1870	3/1890	NA/1953	11/1953
Texas	NA/1901	11/1902	—	1964
Virginia[7]				
1876–1882	NA/1876	NA/1876	3/1882	3/1882
1902—1964	7/1902	7/1902	—	1964

Notes: Legislative Enactment = date when a state legislature or state constitutional convention proposed a poll tax voting law, or a people's initiative was certified for signatures. Ratification = date when a poll tax voting law was ratified by action of a state legislature, a state constitutional convention, or a people's vote at a general election or a governor's proclamation. This voting provision goes into effect after the ratification date. If the ratification date is the date of a general election (that is, a people's vote at a general election), the poll tax voting law goes into effect after that election and hence has its first effect on suffrage at the next regularly scheduled election in that state. Legislative Repeal = date legislature or other entity proposed the repeal of a poll tax law. Repeal Ratification = date that a repeal of a poll tax voting provision was ratified by action of the state legislature, a state constitutional convention, a people's vote at a general election, or a governor's proclamation. After that date, the repeal of the poll tax voting law goes into effect. The 24th Amendment to the U.S. Constitution ratified on 1/23/1964 repealed the remaining poll tax laws in existence. NA = month of suffrage law not available.

[1]The Speaker of the Arkansas House of Representatives declared the poll tax amendment enforceable in 1/1893. However, a U.S. Circuit Court declared it invalid on an election technicality in 12/1905. In 1907 the state legislature proposed another poll tax amendment, which the voters passed by a sufficient margin in 1908.

[2]Georgia's early poll tax (1801–1877) only applied to propertyless white males. In 1877 Georgia applied its poll tax to all males. In 1908 Georgia changed its poll tax law to require that all poll taxes (and other taxes) owed by an individual since the adoption of the 1877 constitution must be completely paid in order to vote. In 1932 Georgia specified only all poll taxes (not other taxes) must be paid since 1877 in order to vote.

[3]Louisiana passed an earlier poll tax law in 1880, but it was not stipulated as a requirement for voting.

[4]The electorate of North Carolina passed the poll tax amendment proposed by the state legislature in the general election in 12/1900 but it did not go into effect until 7/1902.

[5]The 1895 South Carolina constitution and some of its stipulations for the period between 1895–1898 and the period after 1898 list other alternatives for voting. Between 1895 and 1898 South Carolina allowed passing a literacy test or using the grandfather clause to avoid the poll tax. After 1898 South Carolina allowed the alternative of a property test of $300 valuation in place of the literacy test but a voter still had to pay the poll tax. In South Carolina women never had to pay the poll tax after they received the vote (1920–1951). The people voted on the 1949 South Carolina legislative amendment to repeal the poll tax in the 11/1950 general election. However, the state legislature had to ratify this vote on 2/1951, when the repeal became effective.

[6]Tennessee's constitution in 1870 stated that the legislature could prescribe a poll tax requirement for voting, but effective legislative action to do so did not occur until 1890. For a contrary interpretation of Tennessee history, see Porter (1918, p. 202). In 1943 Tennessee's legislature repealed the poll tax but the state supreme court reinstated it in the same year on a technicality. A Tennessee law passed in 2/1951, in essence, eliminated any effect of the poll tax on voting, but the official constitutional amendment was approved by the voters in 11/1953.

[7]In 1904 and later Virginia allowed an old soldier alternative to paying the poll tax. For a description of old soldier clauses, see Table 2-18.

Sources: State constitutions and relevant state statute volumes.

Table 2-16 Descriptive Characteristics of Poll Tax Laws in Southern States, 1890–1918

States	Age Liability[1]	Annual Rate	Cumulative Provision	Maximum State Cumulation	Proof of Tax Payment	Payment Dates
Solid South						
Alabama	over 21, under 45	$1.50	entire period of liability	$36.00	state	Oct. 1–Feb. 1 before election
Arkansas[2]	over 21	$1.00	none	none	voter	Jan. 1–July 1 of year before election
Florida[3]	over 21	$1.00	two years preceding election	$2.00	unknown	at least 30 days before election
Georgia	over 21, under 60	$1.00	entire period of liability	none	unknown	by April 1 before election
Louisiana	over 21	$1.00	two years preceding election	$2.00	voter	by Dec. 31 before election
Mississippi	over 21	$2.00	two years preceding election	$4.00	voter	by Feb. 1 before election
North Carolina	over 21, under 50	$1.29	none	none	unknown	by March 1 before election
South Carolina[4]	over 21, under 60	$1.00	none	none	voter	at least six months before election
Texas	over 21, under 60	$1.50	none	none	voter	by Feb. 1 before election
Virginia	over 21	$1.50	three years preceding election	$4.50	state	at least six months before election
Border States						
Tennessee	over 21	$1.00	none	none	either	at least 30 days before election

[1]The "Age Liability" category refers only to males because women's suffrage was not enacted in the South until 1920.

[2]Arkansas's poll tax was inoperative in the 1906 and 1908 elections.

[3]Florida changed to a noncumulative law in 1896. It defined the age liability as males over 21 and under 55.

[4]The law listed for South Carolina was the one used in the 1898–1918 period. In 1896 South Carolina had a slightly different law, defining the age liability as males over 21 and under 55.

Sources: State constitutions and relevant state statute volumes.

Table 2-17 Literacy Test Laws in Southern States, 1890–1965

State	Legislative Enactment	Ratification	Reading Requirement	Writing Requirement	Understanding Clause	Property Requirement	Other Requirements	Repeal
Alabama[1]								
1903–1946	9/1901	1/1903	X	X		X		11/1946
1946–1965	NA/1946	11/1946	X	X	(X)	X	X	1965
Georgia[2]								
1908–1945	8/1908	11/1908	X	X	X	X	X	8/1945
1945–1965	3/1945	8/1945	X	X	X	X		1965
Louisiana	5/1898	5/1898	X	X		X		1965
Mississippi[3]	11/1890	1/1892	X		X			1965
North Carolina[4]	6/1900	7/1902	X	X				1965
Oklahoma	8/1910	3/1911	X	X				1915
South Carolina[5]								
1895–1898	12/1895	12/1895	X		X	X		1/1898
1898–1965	12/1895	1/1898	X	X		X		1965
Virginia[6]								
1902–1904	7/1902	7/1902	X		(X)			NA/1904
1904–1965	NA/1904	NA/1904		X				1965

Notes: NA = month of suffrage law not available. Legislative Enactment = date a state legislature or a state constitutional convention proposed a literacy test voting law. Ratification = date when a literacy test voting law was ratified by action of a state legislature, a state constitutional convention, a people's vote at a general election, or a governor's proclamation. This voting provision goes into effect after this ratification date. If the ratification date is also a general election (that is, a people's vote at a general election), the literacy test law goes into effect after this election and hence has its first effect on suffrage at the next regularly scheduled election in that state. Reading Requirement "X" = denotes state stipulated an ability to read English in order to vote. Writing Requirement "X" = denotes state stipulated an ability to write in English in order to vote. Understanding Clause "X" = denotes state allowed an understanding requirement as an alternative to reading and writing in English in order to vote. Usually "understanding" meant being able to interpret a clause of the state or federal constitution when the registrar read it to the prospective voter. (X) denotes state required an understanding test, instead of offering it as an alternative, to the reading or writing requirements in English in order to vote. Property Requirement "X" = denotes state allowed a (land or personal) property alternative to the literacy test in order to vote. Other Requirements "X" = denotes state allowed other alternatives to the literacy test in order to vote. Georgia (1908 on) mentioned "be of good character and understanding the duties and obligations of citizenship under a republican government." Alabama (1946 on) also mentioned this or employment for the past twelve months as an alternative. Some states also offered a grandfather clause alternative or an old soldier clause as an alternative; see Table 2-18 for these alternatives. Repeal = date when ratification was repealed. Oklahoma's literacy test was ruled invalid in an U.S. Supreme Court case (*Guinn v. U.S.*, 238 U.S. 347) in 1915 (see McGovney, 1949, p. 60). Other literacy test laws in the South were voided by the 8/1965 U.S. Voting Rights Act and in nonsouthern states by the 6/1970 U.S. Voting Rights Act. The Voting Rights Act in 1965 eliminated the literacy test for voting in 40 counties in North Carolina rather than in all counties. The U.S. Supreme Court upheld the 1970 ban on literacy tests in *Oregon v. Mitchell* (1970).

[1]Alabama's ratification date for its constitution was 11/1901 but the actual enforcement date for literacy tests was 1/1903.

[2]Georgia (1945 on) restricted its "understanding" alternative to only those who were unable to read and write because of physical disability.

[3]Mississippi's constitution went into effect in 1/1891 but the constitution specified that the literacy test would be in force on 1/1892.

[4]North Carolina's electorate voted for a literacy test on 11/1900 but the wording of the law stated it would not go into effect until 7/1902.

[5]After 1898 South Carolina provided a tax or property alternative to the literacy test. The voter must show that he had paid all taxes on property he owned that was assessed at $300 or more.

[6]Under the 1902–1903 law, Virginia allowed voters to register for life. From 1904 on, only periodic registration was allowed under the new literacy requirements.

Sources: State constitutions and relevant state statute volumes.

Table 2-18 Grandfather and Old Soldier Clauses to Southern Literacy Tests, 1900–1915

State	Legislative Enactment	Ratification	Registration	Repeal
Grandfather Clauses				
Alabama[1]	9/1901	11/1901	up to 12/20/1902	1915
Georgia	8/1908	11/1908	unspecified	1915
Louisiana	5/1898	5/1898	up to 9/1/1898	1915
North Carolina[2]	6/1900	7/1902	up to 12/1/1908	1915
Oklahoma	8/1910	3/1911	unspecified	1915
Virginia[3]	7/1902	7/1902	up to 12/31/1903	1915
Old Soldier Clauses				
Alabama	9/1901	11/1901	up to 12/20/1902	1915
Georgia	8/1908	11/1908	unspecified	1915
Virginia	7/1902	7/1902	up to 12/31/1903	1915

Notes: Old Soldier clauses allowed people to vote who had served in the Civil War or certain other specified wars without having to take a literacy test. Grandfather clauses had a similar logic but applied to anybody who had lived during a certain period, like during the Civil War, or was a descendant of such people. Legislative Enactment = date a state legislature voted for a grandfather or old soldier law, or a state constitutional convention proposed such laws. Ratification = date when a grandfather or old soldier voting law was ratified by action of a state legislature, a state constitutional convention, a people's vote at a general election, or a governor's proclamation. This voting provision goes into effect after the ratification date. If the ratification date is the date of a general election (that is, a people's vote at a general election), the grandfather or old soldier law goes into effect after that election and hence has its first effect on suffrage at the next regularly scheduled election in that state. Registration = period allowed to register under the grandfather or old soldier alternative without having to take a literacy test. Repeal = date when the U.S. Supreme Court in 1915 (*Guinn v. U.S.*, 238 U.S. 347) declared Oklahoma's grandfather clause unconstitutional, which effectively eliminated it in the other southern states (Key, 1949, p. 556). The effective end of the grandfather laws and also the old soldier laws in all the other states, except Georgia, was the date these states set as the deadline for registration under these laws.

[1]Alabama allowed the grandfather alternative for voter registration before the literacy test went into effect on 1/1/1903.
[2]North Carolina's electorate voted for the grandfather clause in 11/1900, but the wording of the law stated it would not go into effect until 7/1902.
[3]In 1902–1903, Virginia allowed both an old soldier alternative and a grandfather alternative to taking the literacy test. In registration taking place after 1/1904, Virginia allowed an old soldier clause alternative to paying the poll tax.

Sources: State constitutions and relevant state statute volumes.

Table 2-19 Literacy Test Laws in Nonsouthern States, 1855–1970

State	Legislative Enactment	Ratification	Reading Requirement	Writing Requirement	Repeal
Alaska[1]	2/1956	3/1959	X		1965
Arizona	6/1912	6/1912	X	X	1970
California	2/1893	11/1894	X	X	1970
Connecticut[2]	NA/1855	10/1855	X		1970
Delaware	6/1897	6/1897	X	X	1970
Hawaii[3]	NA/1949	11/1950	X	X	1970
Maine[4]	4/1891	1/1893	X	X	1970
Massachusetts[5]	NA/1856	5/1857	X	X	1970
New Hampshire[6]	NA/1902	11/1902	X	X	1970
New York[7,8]	4/1921	1/1922	X	X	1970
Oregon	2/1923	12/1924	X	X	1970
Washington[8,9]	NA/1895	11/1896	X		1970
Wyoming[10]	9/1889	11/1889	X		1970

Notes: NA = month of suffrage law not available. Legislative Enactment = date a state legislature or a state constitutional convention proposed a literacy test voting law. Ratification = date when a literacy test voting law was ratified by action of a state legislature, a state constitutional convention, a people's vote at a general election, or a governor's proclamation. This voting provision goes into effect after this ratification date. If the ratification date is also a general election (that is, a people's vote at a general election), the literacy test law goes into effect after this election and hence has its first effect on suffrage at the next regularly scheduled general election in the state. Reading Requirement "X" = state stipulated an ability to read English in order to vote. Writing Requirement "X" = denotes state stipulated an ability to write in English in order to vote. Repeal = when the literacy tests for voting in the non-South were voided completely by the 6/1970 U.S. Voting Rights Act. The United States Supreme Court upheld this ban on literacy tests in *Oregon v. Mitchell* (1970).

[1]Alaska had a "speaking in English" alternative to the reading requirement. Its literacy test was eliminated in 1965 by the original Voting Rights Act of that year.
[2]Connecticut's 1855 provision failed to mention the words "in English." The 10/1897 provision stated this clearly: "be able to read in the English language any article of the constitution or any section of the statutes of this state."
[3]Hawaii also had a requirement for "speaking in English" in addition to its reading and writing requirements for voting.
[4]The complicated chronology of Maine's literacy test act was as follows: legislative proposal in 4/1891; people's vote in 10/1892; governor's proclamation in 12/1892 to take effect on 1/1/1893.
[5]Massachusetts's literacy test law did not affect people who already had the right to vote prior to 5/1/1857.
[6]New Hampshire's literacy test law did not affect people who already had the right to vote prior to 1/1/1904.
[7]New York's literacy test law did not affect people who had the right to vote prior to 1/1/1922. It went into effect on 1/1/1922, but was voted on by the people at the general election in 1921.
[8]New York and Washington, at times in their history, had one read prose rather than a clause of the state or U.S. constitution. New York also mentioned that one must read whatever was given to the applicant with "understanding."
[9]Washington's literacy provision had two unique features: (1) it had a "speech requirement" (in English); and (2) qualified voters prior to 11/1896 never had to take the literacy test.
[10]Wyoming's 1889 constitution stated that the literacy test law did not apply to Wyoming residents who had voted prior to 11/1889 (that is, when they were residents of the territory of Wyoming).

Sources: State constitutions and relevant state statute volumes.

Table 2-20 Female Suffrage Acts (Prior to Passage of 19th Amendment)

State	Legislative Enactment	Ratification	Political Applicability
Arizona	7/1912	11/1912	All races
California	1/1911	12/1911	All races
Colorado	4/1893	7/1893	All races
Idaho	1/1894	11/1896	All races
Illinois	6/1913	6/1913	President only
Indiana	2/1919	2/1919	President only
Iowa	4/1919	4/1919	President only
Kansas	2/1911	11/1913	All races
Kentucky	3/1920	3/1920	President only
Michigan	NA/1917	11/1918	All races
Minnesota	3/1919	3/1919	President only
Missouri	4/1919	4/1919	President only
Montana	1/1913	11/1914	All races
Nebraska	4/1913	4/1917	President only
Nevada	1/1913	11/1914	All races
New York	3/1917	11/1917	All races
North Dakota	2/1919	3/1920	All races
Ohio	2/1917	2/1917	President only
Oklahoma	3/1917	11/1918	All races
Oregon	11/1912	11/1912	All races
Rhode Island	4/1917	4/1917	President only
South Dakota	3/1918	11/1918	All races
Tennessee	4/1919	4/1919	President only
Utah	5/1895	5/1895	All races
Washington	2/1909	11/1910	All races
Wisconsin	2/1919	2/1919	President only
Wyoming	9/1889	11/1889	All races

Notes: All laws listed were proposed and ratified prior to the 19th Amendment of the U.S. Constitution on 8/18/1920. Legislative Enactment = date a state legislature or a state constitutional convention proposed a female voting law or a people's initiative was certified for signatures. Ratification = date when a female voting law was ratified by action of a state legislature, a state constitutional convention, a people's vote at a general election, or a governor's proclamation. This voting provision goes into effect after the ratification date. If the ratification date is the date of a general election (that is, a people's vote at a general election), then the female voting law goes into effect after that election and hence has its first effect on suffrage at the next regularly scheduled election in that state. Political Applicability = political races women could vote in, usually either "all races" or the "presidential race only." NA = month of suffrage law not available.

Sources: State constitutions and relevant state statute volumes.

Table 2-21 Federal Amendments on Voting, 1870–1971

Amendment	Ratification	Title	Text
15th Amendment	2/3/1870	Black Male Suffrage	"The right of citizens of the United States to vote shall not be denied or abridged by the United States or by any State on account of race, color, or previous condition of servitude."
17th Amendment	4/8/1913	Direct Election of Senators	"The Senate of the United States shall be composed of two Senators from each State, elected by the people thereof, for six years; and each Senator shall have one vote. The electors in each State shall have the qualifications requisite for electors of the most numerous branch of the State legislatures."
19th Amendment	8/18/1920	Women's Suffrage	"The right of citizens of the United States to vote shall not be denied or abridged by the United States or by any State on account of sex. "
24th Amendment	1/23/1964	The Anti-Poll Tax Amendment	"The right of citizens of the United States to vote in any primary or other election for President or Vice President for electors for President or Vice President, or for Senator or Representative in Congress, shall not be denied or abridged by the Untied States or any State by reason of failure to pay any poll tax or other tax."
26th Amendment	7/1/1971	Eighteen-Year-Old-Vote	"The right of citizens of the United States, who are eighteen years of age or older, to vote shall not be denied or abridged by the United States or by any State on account of age."

Source: U.S. Constitution.

3

Who Goes to the Polls

Chapter 2 discussed the ways in which who is entitled to vote serves as one of the foundations of elections and, ultimately, democracy. Following from the discussion of who is entitled to vote is the question of who actually votes. Even if election laws are written with the broadest possible inclusiveness so that all adults are allowed to vote, one of the key barometers of democracy is how many people actually choose to vote. This chapter demonstrates that determining how many people vote is not as simple or straightforward as it would seem. Several measures of voting participation shed distinctly different light on the subject. In addition, numerous factors—including socioeconomic shifts, political reforms, and the intensity of party organization—prompt levels of participation to rise and fall historically. As this chapter makes clear, there are more questions than answers to what scholars simplistically call the "turnout problem."

This examination of voting participation is organized in seven parts. The first section discusses three key measures of voting participation that tap different dimensions of voting: *voter eligibility* (the number of people legally eligible to vote), *voter mobilization* (the number of people who vote among the total adult population), and *voter turnout* (the number of people who vote among those who are eligible by law to vote). The next three sections consider the history of voter eligibility, mobilization, and turnout, respectively, in presidential elections. Sections five and six examine voting participation in House and then Senate elections. In the final section, voting participation at the state level is analyzed.

Three Measures of Voting Participation

The notion of voting participation encompasses much more than the phenomenon of voter turnout, although many believe the two terms to be synonymous. In a pioneering article, Przeworski and Sprague (1971) distinguish three types of voting participation: (1) the well-known voter turnout phenomenon but also (2) voting eligibility and (3) voting mobilization. This is not simply a play on words; each term involves a separate, but meaningful, aspect of voter participation. *Eligibility* is a term used to indicate the percentage of a state's adult population that is legally allowed to vote according to a state's suffrage laws at any given point

in time. Empirically, its formula is E/A, where E refers to the number legally eligible to vote and A refers to the total number of adults in a state in a particular year. This eligibility measure best tracks a state's progress toward full voter democracy and corresponds most closely to the discussion of the suffrage law history of the states in Chapter 2.

Mobilization is a term used to indicate the percentage of people who actually voted in a particular political race (for example, the presidential race) in a state in any given year compared to the state's entire adult population. The emphasis here is different: this measure is focusing on the ability of party organizations and other interested groups to get out the vote on election day. Mobilization efforts are rated according to their relative success by computing a time-series of mobilization values for a state across its history. Empirically, the formula for voter mobilization is V/A, where V refers to the number of people who actually voted in a given political race in a particular election year and A, again, is the number of adults in the total population in a state in that year.

The last measure of voter participation is *turnout*, a term used to indicate the number of people who vote among those who are eligible by law to vote. The familiar turnout index is defined conventionally as V/E. Most frequently used, it is tracking those who actually voted in a given political race (V) as a proportion of those who were legally eligible to vote according to a state's suffrage laws (E).

Issues of Measurement

All three of these voter participation measures are discussed in this chapter. They are computed not only for the American states over the preceding 200 years, but also aggregated in order to observe longitudinal trends at the national and regional levels. As mentioned elsewhere (Rusk and Stucker, 1984), each of these indices of voting has measurement problems. The easiest and most accurate index to use is mobilization if one has correct vote totals for political races and correct numbers for adults in each state. Hopefully, this book provides the former for national government offices (president, House, Senate) in Chapters 4, 5, and 6, respectively. The U.S. Census provides the latter, usually accurately.

Eligibility and turnout measures are more complicated, since both involve knowing E (the number of people legally eligible to vote in a state at a particular time). Knowing the dates when suffrage laws were passed or repealed is often not sufficient to ascertain E at any particular time. For example, in order to ascertain E correctly for most of the original thirteen states, one would have to know with certainty how many white males lived in each state who had landed or personal property of a certain value, acreage, or rental income. Figures like these are very difficult to find, and, if found, it is equally difficult to validate their accuracy. For states using only taxpaying requirements for voting in the early days, one would have to know how many white males had paid their taxes, a lesser but not necessarily an easier data recovery task. One would also need to know who were citizens at this early date and who were not and whether these white male propertied citizens had met the necessary residency requirements of their states in order to vote. Sometimes tax records provide residency information, if they, in turn, can be recovered.

Because of the problems with finding accurate records corresponding to definitions of the legally eligible electorate, scholars have had widely varying estimates of the vote for colonial and early state electorates. For example, Dinkin (1982, p. 39) believes 50 to 80 percent of males were eligible to vote in the provincial period (1689–1776) and 60 to 90 percent at the close of the Revolutionary War. McGovney (1949, p. 16), instead, says that "not over half of the adult white men in the United States were eligible to vote in 1787." Of course, since women were ineligible, only 25 percent of white adults were eligible to vote in 1787 if McGovney's estimate is correct. The upshot is that accurate figures do not exist for voter eligibility in the early period of American history.

The best possible eligibility and turnout indices are derived from the suffrage laws defining a state's eligible electorate for which accurate factual data corresponding to these laws are available. These data, if they exist, are recorded in U.S. Census reports. The author provided information on state suffrage laws dealing with citizenship, race, sex, and age to a colleague, John Stucker (1973), who used these laws and corresponding census data for the states to calculate estimates of voter eligibility at different points in time for each state. (For further details on the construction of these estimates, see Stucker, 1973, Appendix B.) While these estimates are more accurate for the turnout and eligibility indices, as defined above, than those that currently exist in the literature, there should be no illusion that they are in any way perfect. Without accurate knowledge of economic criteria for voting (landed and personal property, taxpaying), the definitive history of the eligibility and vote turnout of early American state electorates is missing. There are good estimates for eligibility and voting turnout after this period. For the early period, however, recourse to mobilization values and comparison of these values across time in a state's history may be the best way to gauge voter participation trends longitudinally, especially for the original thirteen states.

Historical Eras of Participation

In any discussion of voting participation—eligibility, mobilization, and turnout—it is important to consider the political context within which this participation took place. People do not go to the polls without good reasons; parties, their organizations, campaign tactics, and specific candidates provide these reasons. Moreover, people are not permitted to go to the polls unless these same parties find it advantageous to offer large segments of the populace the opportunity to vote and pass laws that enlarge the eligible electorate. Or, under other circumstances, the parties find it advantageous to deny large numbers of people the opportunity to vote and constrict the eligible electorate accordingly.

This political context can be analyzed within the framework of historical eras that chart the development of party organizations, party competition, and party power in both the presidency and Congress. All too typically, political eras are cast as presidential time periods that begin and end with a colorful president or key presidential election. The names of the eras are often the names of these chief executives—Jefferson, Jackson, Lincoln, and Franklin Roosevelt. Even more simplistically, the names reflect only the political winner of the period and do not consider that the eras reflect competition, sometimes quite intense, between two major parties across a series of races. In fact, eras in American politics emerge in congressional as well as presidential politics. Political shifts that mark the end of one era and the beginning of another often occur first in midterm congressional elections and then solidify during the next presidential election. As thoroughly discussed in Chapter 5, House elections, in particular, are more revealing of the breakpoints in political eras than presidential elections. For example, before Lincoln's presidential victory in 1860, Republicans had achieved striking victories in House elections, first in 1854, again in 1856, and then took the House majority in 1858. Before Franklin Roosevelt swept into office in 1932, the Democrats had captured a narrow House majority in 1930.

There are six political eras that capture party development and competition. The first, the Federalist/ Democratic-Republican era from 1788 through 1823, marks a time when two-partyism took hold in Congress and the presidency. The second, the Jacksonian/National Republican-Whig era from 1824 through 1853, involves attempts to cast a concerted opposition to the Jacksonian Democrats, who were first challenged by the National Republicans and then opposed by the Whigs. The third, the Civil War-Reconstruction Republican/Democratic era from 1854 through 1893, occurred as the Republican Party, upon the demise of the Whigs, emerged as the central and durable opponent to the Democrats. In the fourth era, the conservative Republican/Democratic era from 1894 through 1929, the Republicans became the dominant party in both presidential and congressional races, but the Democrats continued to compete and were never in danger of being replaced by another party. In the fifth era, the New Deal Democratic/Republican era from 1930 through 1965, the parties' fortunes reversed; the Democrats became the dominant party, while the Republicans continued to compete. The final competitive Democratic/Republican era, from 1966 to the present, marks a period of relatively balanced support and keen competition between the two major parties in congressional and presidential elections. It is within these eras that American political participation has taken place. The historical battles between the parties have determined who has been allowed to vote and who has gone to the polls.

The History of Voter Eligibility

Table 3-1 presents national and regional values for voter eligibility in presidential election years. The progression of values shows an increase over time as America approaches the goal of universal suffrage in a democracy. However, the goal is only approximated since America's considerable population of immigrants and aliens does not have the vote in contemporary America (nor do those incarcerated in prisons and psychiatric institutions).

Early Republic Era

In the early Republic era (1788–1823), the eligibility figures are optimistic since in Table 3-1 legal eligibility to vote is based only on the four criteria for which data are available—citizenship, race, sex, and age—and not on crucial economic criteria (landed property, personal property, taxpaying) or residency requirements for voting. If the economic and residency characteristics of the early American population were known, then the suffrage requirements in these areas (see Tables 2-4 through 2-11) could be used to revise voter eligibility figures downward, possibly significantly so, in the 1788–1823 period when several states, for the only time in American history, used the combination of strict economic and residency requirements to curtail the vote. Even after this period a number of states continued to use some combination of less stringent economic and residency laws to ensure that the vote did not progress to universal white male suffrage too easily or quickly. On average, 43.4 percent of adult Americans were eligible to vote in presidential election years during this era according to the criteria used in Table 3-1. This is consistent with the parties' views of the day that the electorate should be elite and restricted.

The Jacksonian Era

During the Jacksonian/National Republican-Whig era (1824–1853), eligibility rates remained the same, with 43.4 percent of adult Americans eligible to vote in presidential election years. In an era characterized by scholars as one of democratization, the similarity of this figure to the preceding eligibility rate of the Republic era may seem strange. This is less puzzling when one recalls that the determination

of voter eligibility in both eras was based on the same four criteria and that these criteria fail to include economic requirements for the vote, the most active area of suffrage legislation during the Jacksonian and Republic periods.

The data in Table 3-1 cast doubt on the exact time that universal male suffrage was achieved. Historians often argue that universal male suffrage was achieved by 1860, when most states had eliminated their economic criteria for voting, but was it, indeed, achieved at that time? At first glance, Table 3-1 seems to indicate that the historians are correct: roughly half of the adult population (45 percent) is seen as eligible to vote in 1860. However, Table 3-1 also shows that eligibility values approximating 45 percent occurred for some time prior to 1860, suggesting that, in practice, universal white male suffrage may have been achieved well before the Civil War.

Unfortunately, what is suggested by these data cannot be confirmed without the possession of accurate data on the economic characteristics of the white male population in this period. Several states in the Jacksonian period, and just prior to it, were abandoning their stringent economic requirements in favor of less stringent economic alternatives for voting. This probably enabled white males of lower social status to become part of the eligible electorate. Porter (1918), for example, believes that these later economic laws had the effect of expanding the electorate rather than constricting it. Taxpaying, for instance, demanded little of the individual compared to having to own a large parcel of land. If this is true, then new people were being added to the eligible electorate in the Jacksonian period, and universal male suffrage was being achieved before 1860, possibly much before. Although the data here are unable to pinpoint the exact date that white male suffrage was achieved, it was certainly a pre-Civil War development. It definitely was not something that led up to the Civil War or that the war itself precipitated. The Democratic Party and newly formed Republican Party were too preoccupied with defining positions on slavery and territorial expansion to address other underlying issues of voter participation.

Civil War-Reconstruction Era

The next period involving the Civil War and Reconstruction is a particularly complex one for analyzing voter eligibility. Across this period (1854–1893), eligibility was 46.5 percent. This figure takes into account that more than 550,000 died in the Civil War conflict (359,528 in the North; 198,524 in the South) and another 412,000 were wounded (U.S. Civil War Center, 2001). Casualties from the war eliminated many eligible voters from the electorate. On the other hand, the Reconstruction Acts of 1867 and the subsequent ratification of the 15th Amendment in 1870 legally allowed more than 860,000 black male adults who were former slaves into the electorate (U.S. Census Bureau, 1860 census).[1] Further complicating matters were the sizable immigrant flows to America in the 1870s. Also, the U.S. Census Bureau decided to count aliens for the first time in the 1870 census, recording both pre-1870 aliens living in America as well as the large influxes of aliens after that. This was an important occurrence since citizenship is one of the four criteria used in Table 3-1 to determine voter eligibility.

Despite the ratification of the 15th Amendment in 1870, the crucial legislation affecting black male suffrage was passed in 1867 by the U.S. Congress. The two Reconstruction Acts passed that year required that former Confederate states eliminate their racial barriers to the vote before being readmitted to the Union. Most southern states complied by writing new constitutions in 1868 that allowed blacks into the electorate before the presidential and congressional elections were held that year. Thus Table 3-1 shows voter eligibility increased nationally from 45.9 percent in 1864 to 48.5 percent in 1868 and, even more crucially, in the South, from 32.2 percent to 44.3 percent.

However, by 1872, eligibility receded to 45.8 percent nationally as Civil War deaths, the influx of aliens, and the decision by the U.S. Census to count aliens caused the eligible electorate to contract. Nonslave states in the North were losing eligible voters through Civil War deaths, while significantly increasing their adult population between 1868 and 1872 due to the influx of aliens and the inclusion of aliens by the census for the first time. (Only eight northern states allowed aliens to vote at this time.) Nationally, there were 8,503,492 eligible voters in 1868; this only increased to 8,953,577 in 1872, while the number of adults jumped from 17,542,622 in 1868 to a massive 19,531,831 in 1872. In the South, the initial increase in black male voters was, to some extent, counterbalanced by Civil War deaths in that region. The upshot of this complicated period is that eligibility initially increased as universal male suffrage was achieved in the South, largely in 1868, but receded due to Civil War casualties and the recording of aliens shortly thereafter. On paper, universal male suffrage was achieved nationally in 1870 by ratification of the 15th Amendment.

Conservative Republican/Democratic Era

In the conservative Republican era (1894–1929), voting eligibility jumped to a 62.5 percent average in presidential election years. Although the period was dominated by conservative Republican pro-business policies and "normalcy," it also held undercurrents of Progressive reforms from within the Republican Party. Among these reforms was female suffrage. The era started out with small increases in eligibility in the 1890s and progressed to larger increases in the early part of the twentieth century even before ratification of the 19th Amendment, reaching levels of 48.1 percent in 1912 and 52.6 percent in 1916. These increases reflected a scattering of states, mainly in the West and later in the Midwest, experimenting with female suffrage. However, counteracting this trend at the turn of the century was the decision by those states previously allowing alien suffrage to revert back to "citizen-only" voting laws (see Chapter 2).

The dominant trend of increases in voting eligibility was reaffirmed with the ratification of the 19th Amendment in 1920—the formal national granting of women's suffrage—when, according to Table 3-1, approximately 90 percent of all adults were legally eligible to vote. On paper, at least, universal suffrage seems to have been achieved in that year. Four years later, the percentage of eligible voters was slightly higher at 91.2 percent and has never dropped below this level since.

New Deal Democratic/Republican Era

In the New Deal era (1930–1965), eligibility averaged 96.5 percent in presidential elections. In this era, as well as the eras adjacent to it, the ratio of eligible voters to adults was mainly affected by the number of immigrants and aliens in the country. It is particularly instructive to note these effects after female suffrage was achieved. The index has, in essence, been stuck in the 90–97 percent range since 1920 because aliens have comprised a significant 3–10 percent of the adult population during this period. If anything, this 3–10 percent range in numbers of aliens since 1920 is an underestimate given the acknowledged difficulty of the U.S. Census Bureau in documenting the alien population. Using census figures from the 1990 decennial census, one discovers approximately 10 million (9,878,155) adult aliens in an overall adult population of 185,095,950 for the fifty states and the District of Columbia. This shows that 5.3 percent of America's adult population was alien in 1990, and the percentage of eligible voters, therefore, was 94.7 percent. (Table 3-1 shows similar figures for 1988: 5.1 and 94.9 percent, respectively; after 1990, the eligibility figures are more suspect, being based on U.S. Census projections of eligible voters for this decade.) Many Americans find it difficult to believe that 5.3 percent of this country's adult population is alien. In fact, the percentage is even higher given the well-known undercount of minorities in the census.

Competitive Democratic/Republican Era

In the current period (1966 to the present), voter eligibility has been legally redefined by the passage of the 26th Amendment in 1971. This changed the age criteria for voting in federal elections to eighteen. Reflecting the competitiveness of the two parties during this era, both Democrats in Congress and Republican president Richard Nixon sponsored this amendment in an attempt to bring into the electorate young people who had felt left out of the decisions surrounding the Vietnam War.

However, the introduction of eighteen-year-olds into the electorate shows only a miniscule increase in eligibility—97.8 percent of adults were eligible to vote in 1972 as compared to 97.7 in 1968. This is because the number of persons from eighteen to twenty years old is incorporated into both the numerator (eligible voters) and denominator (adults) of the eligibility index. Further complicating any attempts of the index to increase at this time is the well-known problem in statistics of encountering "ceiling effects" whenever improvement is sought in an index that already has extremely high values—in this case, values in the 90th percentile at the national level from 1920 to the present.

In sum, the voter eligibility figures in Table 3-1 tell two stories and omit two others. The first story recounts a restrictive franchise generally becoming more expansive over time. The second is that universal suffrage has only been approximated in our democracy, since not all of America's adult population is legally entitled to vote. If either residency or registration requirements for voters were added to the mix of criteria in Table 3-1, this approximation would be slightly lower than the 94.7 percent figure mentioned above.

The first story not revealed in Table 3-1 is that America started out with an even more restrictive suffrage than the eligibility values in this table would indicate. As noted in Chapter 2, despite the democratic spirit of the Declaration of Independence and the subsequent Revolutionary War, the first states entering the Union imposed stringent economic and residency requirements on who could vote. States entering the Union after that also imposed economic requirements for voting. Universal white male suffrage may not have seemed a major accomplishment coming several decades later, but, given the backdrop of very restrictive suffrage laws in the beginning, it can be seen as quite an achievement for the short period involved to realize it. The second story missing in Table 3-1 is one of restrictive suffrage laws in the South, particularly around the turn of the century. Poll taxes and literacy tests passed in the 1890s and early 1900s placed a large roadblock in this region to the national pattern of suffrage expansion at this time (Rusk and Stucker, 1973). However, the criteria for voter eligibility in Table 3-1 do not include poll taxes and literacy tests since, according to the wording of these laws, no actual mention is made of "racial" qualifications for voting. Eligibility figures, therefore, do not reflect the disfranchising effect these laws actually had on those blacks (and poor whites) legally entitled to vote.

The History of Voter Mobilization

Table 3-2 extends the voter participation picture by showing national and regional voter mobilization values in presidential election years from 1788 to 1996. The ebb and flow of voter mobilization values across time coincide nicely with well-known facts about the different historical eras in American politics.

Early Republic Era

The first era in American politics—the Republic era—occurred between 1788 and 1823 and involved uneven competition between the Federalists and the Democratic-Republicans. Voter mobilization values in early America were

low, averaging just 11 percent in the presidential election years in this period. Parties largely were not organized outside of government at that time to mobilize voters to the polls. The age of grass-roots party organizations was yet to come. The Federalists, with their elitist views and constituency, faded as a credible opponent to the Democratic-Republicans in the presidential elections of 1816 and 1820, not even bothering to contest these two elections. Lack of party competition usually leads to voter apathy. The high point for mobilization in this rather lackluster era of voter activity was the election of 1812, when the Federalists attempted to mount opposition to James Madison and the Democratic-Republicans over the War of 1812, which many considered to be unnecessary.

The Jacksonian Era

The Jacksonian era with National Republican and Whig opposition (1824–1853) involved an expansion of the electorate from upper- and middle-class white males to lower-class white males at the same time party politics was becoming more popularized and more well organized. Andrew Jackson's presence on the national political scene occurred as early as 1824, when he received more popular votes than the other candidates for president but failed to win the electoral college. In 1828 and 1832, his twin victories for the presidency would enable him to place his unique stamp on the Democratic Party. His competitors, the National Republicans, moved to the fore after the collapse of the Federalist Party between 1816 and 1820 but were in turn replaced in 1834 by the Whigs, who become a more national, rather than regional, party opposing the Democrats. Mobilization rates increased over time during this era as more Americans were allowed to vote and political parties were organized outside of government to recruit these new voters to the party fold. The growth of grass-roots party organizations from the Jacksonian period onward was hardly a coincidence in a period characterized by the emergence of a larger and more diverse electorate. Mobilization was the name of the game, especially in the more urban non-South, where the existence of political machines in cities like New York, Boston, and Philadelphia became a commonplace in nineteenth-century politics. The political machines were fueled by patronage to reward party workers for their recruitment efforts and the use of social welfare to woo the lower-class vote. Mobilization more than doubled between Jackson's first presidential attempt in 1824 (11.4 percent) and his successful bid for the presidency in 1828 (24.0 percent).

Further increases in mobilization occurred in the crucial 1840 election, an election much ignored by scholars, in which mobilization rose to 34 percent from 24 percent in the 1836 election. This was the first presidential election in which symbols and imagery played a crucial role in voter mobilization, much as they do in American politics today. William Henry Harrison, the Whig candidate for president, was presented as the candidate of log-cabin and hard-cider origins, neither of which was true. Combined with stories of his wartime vigor in the frontier and apocryphal images of common-man roots, Harrison and his party mobilized a significant new constituency of voters to presidential politics. This effective approach to campaign techniques would not go unnoticed by politicians in later elections.

Civil War-Reconstruction Era

The Civil War and Reconstruction era (1854–1893) involved crisis politics. The controversial slavery issue, emergence of a new major party—the Republican Party—and the inevitable Civil War and its Reconstruction aftermath sustained the voter mobilization levels that Harrison had achieved in the 1840 election into the succeeding decades of the century. During this Civil War-Reconstruction era, mobilization rates averaged 35 percent.

The pivotal elements in this period were the realigning election of 1860 and the Civil War itself. Periods with major crises and party realignments like this are generally associated with intense voter mobilization efforts. After the war, Republicans in Congress devised a political strategy to make the South a "Republican region" by using military troops to occupy the South while Republican candidates campaigned for election by appealing for votes from carpetbaggers, blacks, and poor whites.

However, the harsh Reconstruction policies imposed on the South had a backlash effect. The death knell to Republican plans for the South came in the 1876 election when Republican candidate Rutherford B. Hayes agreed to remove federal troops from the region in exchange for much needed electoral votes to become president. With the troops gone, southern Confederate and Democratic leaders pursued their own political strategy to return the region to the Democratic fold by eliminating carpetbaggers, blacks, and poor whites from the electorate by force, intimidation, and, later, by poll tax and literacy test laws. As Table 3-2 shows, this strategy worked. Mobilization figures decline in the South in presidential election years after 1876. In fact, this decline continued through 1948, testifying to the establishment of the noncompetitive "Solid South," a region completely dominated by the Democratic Party during this period.

Conservative Republican/Democratic Era

The fourth political era (1894–1929) encompassed the period when conservative Republicans dominated party politics and yet Democrats still remained active challengers. This period saw national voter mobilization increase slightly during the realigning election of 1896 and then fall back to a somewhat lower but relatively constant pattern through World War I. From 1896 through 1916, average voter mobilization was 32 percent, slightly lower than the 35 percent rate from the Civil War-Reconstruction period.

Reforms such as female suffrage dominated participatory politics in the latter part of the conservative Republican era, fueled by progressive strains in the party, and this provided the opportunity for voter mobilization to increase. On paper, the female suffrage movement was completed in 1920 with the national ratification of the 19th Amendment. In actual practice, the voter mobilization rate did not double overnight. The initial increase in voter mobilization nationally went from 32.6 percent in 1916 to 44.2 percent in 1920, suggesting that women were not being mobilized to vote at the same rate as men in the first election in which all women in America were legally entitled to vote. However, over time, the mobilization figures picked up, starting in 1928, as women became more engaged in politics and more socialized into the belief that politics was no longer solely "a man's business" (Rusk and Stucker, 1991).

New Deal Democratic/Republican Era

The New Deal era (1930–1965) encompassed the Great Depression, World War II, and the emergence of the United States as a military and economic superpower. The increase in mobilization posted in the 1920s continued in the 1930s and 1940s, as America confronted economic crisis and international chaos. The pivotal election in this era was the realigning election of 1932, which brought the Democrats to power under Franklin Roosevelt for an unprecedented four terms and for one term for his former vice president, Harry S. Truman. This crisis-laden realigning era kept voter mobilization rates high, as one would expect from the earlier example of the 1860s realignment. Massive government intervention in the economic life of Americans to overcome the depression was the initial catalyst for voter mobilization; World War II played the role of the second catalyst, as national effort and national unity would be tested in a completely different crisis situation. During the early part of this era, in presidential elections from 1932 to 1948, mobilization averaged 55.3 percent.

Mobilization rates also increased during the remainder of this era, averaging 62.0 percent in presidential election years. The 1950s witnessed the birth of new campaign strategies and techniques that mobilized Americans to vote at even higher levels than the 1930s and 1940s. The advent of television and the introduction of the airplane changed campaigning forever. Now the symbols and imagery so imaginatively used by Harrison in the 1840 election could be employed on television. Political television commercials and television news were the new media for creating images and symbols for the presidential race (and House and Senate races). Use of the airplane ensured the "personal touch" in campaigning—seeing presidential candidates in one's state as they attempted to mobilize the vote with the grass-roots approach and related imagery. Without airplane transportation, it would be difficult, if not impossible, for candidates to be able to see potential voters in all the states. The days of Harry Truman's "whistle-stop" railway campaign in 1948 were over.

Competitive Democratic/Republican Era

In the final era (1966 to the present), the two parties have been highly competitive and well funded. They have battled with each other for the White House and Congress as seemingly intractable problems such as Vietnam, civil rights, Watergate, stagflation, terrorism, and a large budget deficit created minefields for both parties.

The beginning of this era saw the continuation of the high levels of voter mobilization observed in the 1950s and early 1960s. In 1968 mobilization was 61.1 percent (as compared to 62 percent from 1952 through 1964). The successive crises of Vietnam, race riots, and issues related to civil rights and law and order dominated the early part of this period. Mass demonstrations were also an important part of this period, reflecting a different kind of voter mobilization.

However, voter survey data (Converse et al., 1969; Weisberg and Rusk, 1970; Abramson, 1975; Norpoth and Rusk, 1982) indicate that these overlapping crises did not produce realignment but instead dealignment—an increase in independents and a movement away from party, instead of a conversion to the party out of power, which characterizes realignments. Coinciding with dealignment was an increased public distrust of government furthered compounded by the Watergate scandal in the early 1970s. The crises in the 1960s spurred voter mobilization, while their aftermath in the 1970s—dealignment, public distrust, and Watergate—worked in the opposite direction. Mobilization dropped from 61.1 percent in 1968 to 55.2 percent in 1972 and 53.7 percent in 1976. The 50 percent range in which mobilization found itself in presidential elections during the 1970s continues to the present day, still accompanied by significant numbers distrusting government and declaring themselves to be independents.

The History of Voter Turnout

Table 3-3 displays national and regional voter turnout values in presidential election years from 1788 to 1996. These figures vary somewhat from other turnout compilations (such as Burnham, 1975, and Austin and Clubb, 1986) because of better data retrieval here of the components making up the turnout measure (that is, total presidential vote and number of eligible voters). Also, since the 1950s there has been a tendency among scholars (Burnham, 1975; Austin and Clubb, 1986; Scammon, various publication dates) to calculate voter mobilization values but to mistakenly call them "voter turnout" values. This error, in practice, results from using adults in the denominator for voter turnout instead of eligible voters. In essence, the compilations for what these scholars call "voter turnout" ignore or seriously underestimate the alien adult population in America.

The voter turnout values in Table 3-3, while different in magnitude from the voter mobilization values in Table 3-2, manifest some of the general patterns seen earlier in the mobilization data. For example, turnout tends to increase during periods when grass-roots party organizations are first established, when fundamental changes in campaign techniques occur, when competition is intense between the two major parties, and when major crises and party realignments are occurring. Conversely, turnout tends to decline when there is less party competition (or no party competition during the period of the "Solid South" or the era of "good feelings" surrounding the noncompetitive presidential elections of 1816 and 1820, when the Federalist Party was no longer a credible contender for the presidency); when dealignment, rather than realignment, occurs in the electorate; and when massive public distrust of government is evident.

The turnout index, however, is not as accurate in measuring voter turnout as the mobilization index is in measuring voter mobilization, especially during the early part of America's history. The turnout index depends on an exact accounting of eligible voters, which, as the discussion above on eligibility revealed, is not available for the early American electorate. Determining the number of adults in the states is much easier and more reliable during this period. The inability to collect eligibility data on the economic and class composition of the early American electorate, in essence, ignores crucial suffrage laws stipulating landed property, personal property, and taxpaying requirements for voting. If this demographic information was available, possibly the national voter turnout figures in Table 3-3 would be higher, rather than lower, reflecting the upper-class bias in voting so well documented in contemporary survey research (Campbell et al., 1960; Verba and Nie, 1972).

Political Eras of Turnout

With the limits of the turnout measure in mind, the six political eras can be examined. In the early Republic era (1788–1823), turnout was low, as the Federalist Party failed to establish itself as a permanent competitor against the Democratic-Republicans. On average, during the presidential elections in this period, 25 percent of eligible adult males went to the polls. As with mobilization, turnout was highest as the controversies surrounding the War of 1812 swirled around the election that year; turnout rose to nearly 40 percent, only to fall to 16 percent in the 1816 election.

In the Jacksonian era (1824–1853), turnout rose to 59.2 percent in presidential election years. Two pivotal elections boosted turnout. First, in the 1828 election, turnout of eligible white males was 55.2 percent—more than double the rate of the 1824 election (26.7 percent) and more than five times the rate of the 1820 election (10.2 percent). In the 1840 election, turnout of eligible males was 77.5 percent, increasing from 54.4 percent in the 1836 election. This was the highest level of turnout achieved during the era as William Henry Harrison's popular campaign captured the public imagination.

In the Civil War-Reconstruction era (1854–1893), turnout rose to an average of 75.3 percent in the presidential elections of this period. The war, its aftermath, and rapid industrialization may well account for this increase, but, as discussed in greater detail below, part of the high turnout rates of the latter half of the nineteenth century was artificial, a result of political parties engaging in voter corruption and intimidation to keep voting rates high.

In the conservative Republican era (1894–1929), turnout moved downward to 62.2 percent. The decline was most obvious in 1920 with the introduction of universal women suffrage when turnout fell to 49.2 percent from 61.9 percent in 1916.

In the New Deal era, turnout rose in the first three presidential elections defining the realigning period of the 1930s, dipped as World War II came to a close, only to increase again in the early television age of the 1950s. For the entire period (1930–1965), voter mobilization averaged 60.4 percent in presidential election years, with all but three elections in this period showing turnout rates above 60 percent, as Americans reacted to economic crisis, world war, and a new media age in politics.

In the final era (1966 to the present), turnout dropped to 56.2 percent during presidential election years of this period. Consistent with the drop in mobilization, turnout went from 62.5 percent in 1968 to 56.4 percent in 1972 and has not risen above that except in 1992, when it was at a slightly higher 58.6 percent—still well under the 60 percent range of values in the 1960s. The lowest point was the 1996 election, when turnout was 52.1 percent of the eligible electorate and the corresponding mobilization value among adults was 48.9 percent.

Suffrage Laws and Turnout

Suffrage laws obviously play a role in shaping the turnout values in Table 3-3. Suffrage laws that have corresponding demographic information available in the census records on the composition of the electorate can reveal the impact that legal changes in the electorate have on voter turnout and also on voter eligibility and mobilization. The most important example of this is female suffrage, where census records can tell us the number of female adults in each of the states. Using this information, one can determine the fall off in voting when the 19th Amendment was ratified in 1920. As mentioned above, voter turnout in the presidential race declined from 61.9 percent in 1916 to 49.2 percent in 1920, although it revived shortly thereafter as women became accustomed to voting and showed a greater interest in politics. A similar decline in voting turnout occurred in House and Senate races in this time period (see Tables 3-5 and 3-8). However, while turnout was initially declining after the ratification of the 19th Amendment, the voter eligibility and voter mobilization indices were behaving quite differently— they were increasing in value. What, on the surface, seems to be puzzling trends for these voting measures actually follows a logical pattern that probably characterizes the initial stages of any legal expansion of the suffrage to a very large

group. In this example, large numbers of women were added to the ranks of legally eligible voters; this increased the numerator of the eligibility index, while the denominator of this index—the number of adults in the country—remained largely stationary. This movement of women to the ranks of eligible voters also increased the values of the mobilization index, since some of these newly enfranchised women would vote, adding to the numerator of this index while the denominator—the number of adults in the county—would again remain largely stationary. On the other hand, the addition of large numbers of women to the ranks of eligible voters meant that they would have to vote initially at the same rate as men in order for national voter turnout not to decline. Adding women to the denominator of the turnout measure (eligible voters) without being able to add the same number of women to the numerator (those actually voting) results in a decline in voter turnout nationally.

The more usual pattern of interaction between voter turnout and mobilization indices occurs in situations where there is not a large expansion of the electorate overnight. In these more common situations, the values of turnout and mobilization will generally increase at the same time, since whatever political stimuli are motivating voters (for example, crises, realigning elections, and new campaign techniques) will result in increases in the numerators of both measures (those voting) against the backdrop of relatively stationary denominators (number of eligible voters and adults, respectively). Of course, both measures will decline in value in the absence of motivating political stimuli. Eligibility will act more independently of these two voting measures—varying much less in the absence of major legislation by the states (or federal government) to significantly increase or decrease the number of people who can legally exercise the franchise. Interaction with the voting turnout measure will mainly occur at times when the eligibility index shows substantial changes in value, reflecting large expansions or contractions of the legal suffrage.

Regions and Turnout

Another area of interest is how the regional composition of the electorate affects vote turnout. Regional differences in voting might be expected, given the well-known political and socioeconomic differences between the North and South. Table 3-3 shows that the South, as a region, has generally tended to vote less than the non-South—regardless of the time period or election being considered. This happens in competitive and noncompetitive eras, slavery and nonslavery eras, and realigning and nonrealigning periods. Turnout was higher in the South when the slavery issue was intense, but it fails to surpass the nonsouthern turnout rate except in 1848 and 1860. In earlier years, it does not succumb as much to Harrison's new style of campaigning nor to Jeffersonian and Jacksonian party appeals to the common man.

Obviously, turnout comparisons are even less favorable to the South as it develops into a noncompetitive one-party region after 1876. The low values for southern voter turnout in the twentieth century are likely the product of both the lack of party competition in the region over long periods and the socioeconomic characteristics of the southern electorate (that is, lower education and lower income). Even with the Republican Party making inroads in the South since the 1950s, the South still lags in voter turnout compared to the non-South.

Historical Changes in Turnout

The most interesting yet least understood vote turnout pattern in Table 3-3 is the seemingly higher vote turnout values nationally in the nineteenth century as compared with those in the twentieth century. More than any other vote turnout pattern observed historically, this particular pattern has caused the most controversy and scholarly debate. The debate largely centers on whether the higher vote turnout in the 1800s was genuine and what specific factors influenced voter turnout in this century. As Table 3-3 shows, the higher vote turnout in the nineteenth century is actually confined to a sixty-year period in that century: 1840–1900. Still, even allowing for this, the turnout values from 1840 to 1900 initially seem quite impressive, ranging from 63.2 to 82.9 percent. By contrast, turnout values fail to reach the 70 percent level in the twentieth century.

While scholars agree that voter turnout was high in the 1800s, particularly from 1840 to 1900, and that voting decline occurred after the turn of the century, what factors were contributing to this puzzling pattern in American politics is more in doubt. Burnham (1965; also see Lane, 1959) attributes the higher voter turnout in the 1800s to greater public interest in politics. According to Burnham, the nineteenth century was a golden age in American politics, when people were more inclined to view politics as interesting business. This changed as the political and economic landscape changed, and greater class divisions dampened voting among those with lower incomes and less education. Burnham believes that a decline in the quality of politics and engagement in politics occurred in America in the twentieth century associated with a public less interested in issues, less attached to party, and seemingly more alienated from the political process. This notion of a deteriorating state in the American electorate and in American politics more generally is complemented by Burnham's later prognosis of an "end to (political) parties" as we know them in contemporary America (Burnham, 1969).

In contrast, Jensen (1971) believes that religious issues and affiliations were at the core of the early interest in politics that dissipated as cities grew, industrialization flourished, and secularization, in general, increased. Kleppner (1970) gives the argument a slightly different twist and maintains that ethnic issues and affiliations created strong turnout in the nineteenth century. Of course, all these authors believe their theories explain not only vote turnout, the subject of this chapter, but also partisan vote choice, the subject of the remaining chapters in this book (Chapters 4–8).

Yet another competing explanation involves the legal-institutional theory discussed in Chapter 2 (Rusk, 1970, 1974). The key to this argument is that election laws implemented different procedures for the vote and defined different electorates that caused historical changes in the vote. Put simply, as the laws changed, voting participation changed. Some laws, most notably personal voter registration and the introduction of the state-sponsored, secret ballot in the crucial elections around the turn of the century, dampened turnout because the parties no longer controlled the vote. Jensen (1971) writes of the "militaristic" way political parties mobilized voters to the polls. In the absence of personal registration systems and secret ballots, parties had the ability to control the general election process and, therefore, the vote, ensuring high turnout. Part of the strength of party organizations emerged in the form of vote corruption. Unfortunately, the extent to which turnout figures should be adjusted for the corruption factor can never be known with any precision, but reports of corruption throughout the period were commonplace (Converse, 1972; Rusk, 1970, 1974). In the absence of secret ballots and personal registration systems, parties—often in urban political machines—bribed people to the polls or intimidated them (for example, employers often pressured their employees to vote the "right" way). While these votes counted as legitimate in the final vote tallies, the corruption upon which they were based artificially inflated turnout levels, creating an impression of an enlightened electorate and a golden political age that may never have existed.

Personal registration laws and Australian secret ballot acts were passed to end both vote corruption and voter intimidation, which was their intended consequence; however, the unintended effect of these reforms was to lower voter turnout as the "cost" of voting, in a Downsian (1957) sense, increased with the implementation of new and formidable barriers to the vote. When Australians initiated the secret ballot reform in the 1850s to end vote corruption in their country, they probably never imagined that this reform would lead to lower voter turnout among those legally eligible to vote (Fredman, 1968; Kousser, 1974). They also probably never imagined that the introduction of this new ballot would lead to increases in split-ticket voting in countries, like America, where party competition was so important (Rusk, 1970; also Roscoe, 2001). The opportunity provided by a consolidated secret ballot to exercise voting options other than the straight-ticket option most stressed in the earlier unofficial party strip ballot days in America would lead to a further weakening of party power in this country. Australia, on the other hand, viewed its secret ballot as a reform mainly to end the manipulating and buying of votes at the polling place; with the new ballot's secrecy provision, there was no longer a way for the parties to verify that the goods had been delivered on election day. The intended purpose of ballot and registration reforms to eliminate vote corruption was realized in both Australia and America, but very important yet unintended declines in legitimate voting were also created. Ridding the electorate of both corrupt voters and legitimate but marginally interested voters would produce significant drops in voter turnout rates. (For a more detailed discussion of these general arguments, see Rusk, 1974.)

Political reform of a different nature came later: the passage of state laws and a federal amendment to expand the suffrage to women. This also produced declines in voter turnout in the twentieth century, as mentioned earlier (Rusk and Stucker, 1991). Suddenly giving the vote to almost half the adult population, which was largely unsocialized politically and also probably unaffiliated with political parties to any real extent, led to a decline in state and national indices of voting, until women became more accustomed to the new norm of politics that they should be just as interested in politics as men. Today, vote turnout rates of women and men are virtually identical.

Changes in suffrage laws also affected the class and economic composition of the American electorate. In the early years of the Union, suffrage laws largely defined an upper-class and, then, a middle-class (white male) electorate. As more adult men were allowed into the electorate in the 1800s, the upper-class tendency toward higher voting rates was displaced by lower-class workers and laborers who probably were less likely to vote. Also, as discussed in Chapter 2, many states allowed newly arrived immigrants to vote (alien voting laws), which further exaggerated the lower-class bias toward nonvoting. Parties initially mobilized many of these men to vote in the late nineteenth century with strong political machines, but this does not mean that their presence in the electorate defined a golden age of politics.

Indeed, the notion that higher voter turnout necessarily means a more involved electorate is questionable. Usually "more involved" or "more interested" are phrases alluding to issue awareness, issue knowledge, and issue voting. Yet, high vote turnout figures do not necessarily indicate high issue saliency on the part of voters, especially after the Civil War, which is the period of most interest to scholars like Burnham (1965). Issues of business, monopolies, tariffs, and trade are not usually the issues that most excite voters. Yet what is more likely is that strong party organizations, employing various militaristic mobilizing methods, corruption, and "party strip" unofficial ballots got the growing number of lower-class men to the polls. If Jensen is correct, the resulting voters, so mobilized, were hardly the involved, issue-conscious voters usually associated with a golden age in politics. They were more likely to be less involved voters, with less knowledge, who were voting simply and solely for the party that mobilized them.

When reforms ended the parties' firm control of mobilization, it became more difficult for parties to get these voters to the polls, and voting participation declined. The power of party organizations also declined. In addition to losing their control over the election process, the introduction of primary elections in 1901 seriously eroded the parties' monopoly over the nomination process. Civil service reforms eroded the parties' patronage functions, and Woodrow Wilson's and especially Franklin Roosevelt's involvement of the government in social welfare rendered useless the parties' social welfare advantage with voters. The combination of these various reforms reduced the rewards available to party workers for mobilizing the vote and also reduced the incentives of voters to be so mobilized. Instead of a deteriorating political situation, the twentieth century witnessed voters less responsive to the party's heavy-handed recruitment methods and its attempts to trade votes for political and economic favors. Political reform had led to a cleaning up of the system. Thus the golden age of American politics may well have been after the turn of the century rather than before.

Voting Participation in House Elections

Tables 3-4 and 3-5 display voter participation figures for House elections in two-year election cycles. (Tables 3-28 through 3-59 distinguish House elections in even-numbered years from those in odd-numbered years.) A quick glance shows similar patterns for House mobilization and turnout indices to those for the presidential race in presidential election years. While the House indices generally follow similar patterns, the House values are usually lower, as one might expect. Also, House elections in midterm elections (off years) have lower values than their presidential counterparts and reveal, for the most part, the familiar sawtooth pattern between higher voter activity in presidential races than in off-year House races. Lower voter activity in congressional races in both presidential and midterm elections is usually attributed to less voter interest in House races than in the more colorful, more publicized, more prestigious, and usually more exciting national contest for president.

A better way to contrast voter activity in presidential and House races is to compare their nationally aggregated outcomes (see Table 3-6). The first column in this table documents the differences in voter turnout in the two races in presidential election years. One can see that the difference values computed are generally positive, especially since 1840. For example, in 1840, national presidential vote turnout was 77.5 percent while national House vote turnout was 69.9 percent, resulting in a positive difference value of 7.6 percent that indicates greater voter turnout in the presidential race. Forty-two of the fifty-three election years in the table—approximately 80 percent—show this pattern, which is often called "roll-off," since it reveals the tendency of voters not to vote for offices on the lower part of the ballot with the same frequency as the presidential race.

The second column in this table compares the greater tendency for people to vote in the presidential race than in the midterm House races. An example of this familiar sawtooth pattern, which is often labeled "drop-off," can be seen by comparing the 1840 presidential race with the 1842 House races. National turnout in the presidential race in 1840 was 77.5 percent, while national turnout in midterm House races in 1842 was 62.1 percent, resulting in a difference value of 15.4 percent in the predicted direction (positive). Comparisons show that turnout is greater for presidential rather than House elections 83 percent of the time, and, once again, this trend begins with the 1840 election year.

The consistency of this sawtooth or drop-off pattern since 1840 is particularly important for two reasons. First, Walter Dean Burnham (1965) and others maintain that such a pattern often ran in the opposite direction after the Civil War, helping to confirm a golden age in politics where the electorate's interest in politics extended far beyond the more glamorous presidential race to the supposedly dull House elections in the off years. Table 3-6 fails to confirm this scenario; indeed, the pattern in the post-Civil War period (and even before it, from 1840 to 1864) is just the opposite of what Burnham presumed and instead is more in keeping with the familiar sawtooth pattern that also characterizes voter activity in the twentieth century. Second, the consistency of this sawtooth pattern is an important ingredient for the "surge and decline" theory that attempts to explain why the winning presidential party usually loses House seats in the next midterm election, that is, a surge in House seats for the party winning the presidency is followed by a decline in House seats for this party in the midterm House elections two years later (see Angus Campbell, 1960; James Campbell, 1993). The surge-and-decline theory attributes this to two movements in the electorate: lower interest in the midterm election causes voters swayed to the House candidates of the winning presidential party in a presidential election year to either not vote in the subsequent midterm election or, if voting, to return home to their party in House races in the absence of any presidential race influencing their vote. The crux of this theory lies in voters' lower interest in House races in midterm elections, which leads to lower voter turnout in these races. The end result is that the presidential party is usually doomed to this electoral fate in midterm elections. Since 1860, when the current Republican Party first successfully contested the presidency against the Democratic Party, thirty-three of thirty-five midterm elections have followed the predictions of the surge-and-decline theory. Only in two midterm elections—1934 and 1998—has the winning presidential party countered this trend by winning, instead of losing, House seats in the midterm election. In all, 95 percent of midterm elections in the 1862–1998 period follow the contours of the familiar sawtooth pattern in voter turnout.

This sawtooth pattern reveals another important point. If House voter turnout in midterm elections is less than presidential voter turnout in the preceding election, this also probably means that House voter turnout in midterm election years is less than House voter turnout in presidential election years. In general, Table 3-6 shows this pattern. What this also indicates is that the researcher should not compare "apples" with "oranges" when attempting to analyze congressional voter participation across time. Longitudinal analysis within the earlier congressional participation tables (Tables 3-4 and 3-5) requires comparing House vote values in presidential election years to each other, on the one hand,

and comparing House vote values in midterm elections to each other, on the other. Otherwise, misleading conclusions result. Different political stimuli are usually associated with presidential and off-year elections, which can lead to different congressional values between presidential years and off years. For example, the congressional turnout values for 1916, 1918, 1920, and 1922 in Table 3-5, when viewed consecutively, do not clearly delineate the effect in 1920 of the 19th Amendment dampening voter turnout in elections. Comparing the 1918 House value of 40.0 percent to the 1920 House value of 47.0 percent appears to tell a story of increasing turnout when the female suffrage amendment was adopted. However, the correct comparison of House values in presidential election years (1916 value of 59.0 percent compared to the 1920 value of 47.0 percent) and in off years (1918 value of 40.0 percent compared to the 1922 value of 35.8 percent) tells the same story of voter decline after women receive the suffrage.

Voting Participation in Senate Elections

Tables 3-7 and 3-8 on Senate voter participation also reflect some of the patterns observed in the presidential and House voter participation tables for the period in which the Senate has been directly elected by the people. (The 17th Amendment providing for direct election of senators was ratified on April 8, 1913, although six states had elections for U.S. senators in 1912.) For example, there is evidence of an increase in voter mobilization and a corresponding decline in voter turnout at the time of the 19th Amendment in 1920. There is also the expected increase in voter turnout in Senate races in the realigning election of 1932 and in subsequent years.

However, Senate elections have certain unique features that also play a role in differentiating their vote patterns, to some extent, from those of the president and the House. National trends affecting the presidential and House races in presidential election years will not affect all one hundred senators since only approximately one-third of these races are contested in a presidential election year. Also, the Senate race falls midway between the presidential and House race in prestige and media coverage, suggesting somewhat different roll-off values for this race. It especially receives more publicity as a statewide race than House races do at the district level. Table 3-8 suggests these possible effects on voter participation, but Table 3-9 summarizes them more clearly by presenting difference values for president-Senate, president-House, and Senate-House vote turnout comparisons. The mean roll-off in voter turnout nationally between presidential and Senate races is a relatively low 2.5 percent, compared to the average 3.7 percent roll-off in voter turnout between presidential and House races.

This confirms that the Senate race is midway between the presidential and House races in terms of voter activity. The average roll-off value nationally between Senate and House races in presidential years is 1.2 percent, in off years is 1.6 percent, and in all elections between 1912 and 1998 is

1.4 percent. Again, these statistics place the Senate race in between the presidential and House races in voter interest, which is expected given the greater publicity and prestige this race receives compared to House races but the lesser publicity and prestige it receives compared to the more colorful and exciting presidential contest.

Voting Participation in the American States

Presented in Tables 3-10 through 3-69 are states' voter participation values for president, House, and Senate races. One can discern individual state patterns in voter activity longitudinally by using these tables. Of particular interest are Tables 3-28 through 3-59 for House races. Tables 3-28 through 3-38 and 3-44 through 3-54 within this set of House tables present voter mobilization and turnout values, respectively, for congressional races in two-year election cycles, using data for the denominator of these measures (number of adults and eligible voters, respectively) for the even-numbered years, which is the conventional way of computing these values. For example, whether a state held its House races in 1840 or 1841, its mobilization value would be based on the number of adults in that state in 1840, not 1841. However, Tables 3-39 through 3-43 and 3-55 through 3-59 list mobilization and turnout values, respectively, for states that had House elections in odd-numbered years, using data for the odd-numbered years for adults and eligible voters to compute these two measures. In this case, if a state held House elections in 1841, data for the denominator of the mobilization measure (that is, adults) would be based on the number of adults in that state in 1841, not 1840. This practice of holding House elections in odd-numbered years was phased out approximately fifteen years after the Civil War, although new states entering the Union after that time were sometimes forced to hold their first House elections in an odd-numbered year, depending on when Congress decided to set their legal date for entry into the Union.

Both approaches to computing voter participation values for House races have advantages and disadvantages. The first approach employs a common base for calculating voter mobilization and turnout measures that can be seen as either an advantage or a disadvantage. Using adult and eligible voter data for even-numbered years to compute these measures provides a common frame of reference by which to compare all states' House races with one another. In doing this, it also follows the custom of regarding the even-numbered year as the year in which federal elections are (supposed to be) held. However, some degree of inaccuracy occurs in using this approach since not all states followed the convention of holding elections for federal office in even-numbered years. The second approach remedies this and, hence, provides greater accuracy in estimating actual House voter participation for those states holding House elections in odd-numbered years. This approach also recognizes that House elections in odd-numbered years have different political stimuli associated with them than House elections contested in conventional midterm and presidential election years. But recognition of this fact is an argument against combining the two sets of House elections together—a disadvantage if one wishes to analytically treat all House races electing a given Congress in the same way. The assumption underlying the second approach is that all House elections for a given Congress cannot be treated as a single entity.

Tables 3-28 through 3-59 have been set up in such a way that the researcher can use either of the two approaches. If the first approach is seen as more useful, the researcher simply uses the voter data in Tables 3-28 through 3-38 for mobilization and 3-44 through 3-54 for turnout, ignoring table series 3-39 through 3-43 and 3-55 through 3-59. If the second approach is seen as more legitimate, the researcher will use the even-numbered election year states in Tables 3-28 through 3-38 (the entries without superscript 1) with the odd-numbered election year states in Tables 3-39 through 3-43 for mobilization and a similar selection procedure for Tables 3-44 through 3-59 for turnout. An actual comparison of these various sets of tables reveals some differences in mobilization and turnout values for states holding House races in odd-numbered years. Whether these differences are sufficiently important to account for is a question the researcher must decide.

Conclusion

Overall, voting participation has been shaped historically by a variety of factors: suffrage law and election procedures, party organization and competition, major issues and crises, party and voter realignments, important changes in campaign techniques, and differences in the type of political offices being contested and the type of political stimuli associated with the election years in which they are contested. Regional differences and associated demographic factors have also been important. Obviously, the presidential race is at the top of the pecking order in terms of voter activity, followed by the Senate and then the House race, and this ordering has been true historically for some time. The difference in voter activity in presidential and House races also has led to the surge-and-decline phenomenon where the winning presidential party almost always loses House seats in the next midterm election.

America started as an elitist political society, allowing only a few to participate in the political process; over time it evolved into a democratic one as middle-class white males, lower-class white males, black males, and women were, in turn, granted the franchise. At certain points in time, aliens were also allowed to vote in some states, while blacks were discouraged from exercising their legal right to vote in the South through intimidation and the use of such legal devices as the poll tax and literacy test. All these developments had some effect on voter participation rates historically. At first glance, voter participation seemed high in the 1800s, especially after 1840, only to decline after the turn of the century. Whether the 1800s was essentially a unique age in American politics with a more involved and interested electorate or mainly a corrupt age with strong party organizations mobilizing and controlling the vote is up for debate, as voter mobilization and turnout data are only partially able to comment on the credibility of these alternative explanations.

With electoral reform occurring around the turn of the century, the quality of American politics picked up as the system was cleaned up. The state took responsibility for the election process. Parties lost their monopolies on nominations, elections, patronage, and social welfare. People started exercising their right to split their vote on a new consolidated secret ballot and to be educated on the issues through new channels of mass communication. This seems to have led to a better age in politics and a more responsible electorate compared to the preceding century. With the advent of female suffrage in 1920 and the eighteen-year-old vote in 1971, this age also achieved virtual universal suffrage. Today, approximately 95 percent of America's adult population has the right to vote, with only aliens being denied the franchise. Political reform has enabled America to become a full-fledged democracy in the twentieth century.

Note

1. The number of black male slaves twenty-one years of age and over was taken from the 1860 census. The 1870 census no longer collected information on "slaves," since the 15th Amendment had been ratified in that year.

Table 3-1 National and Regional Voter Eligibility Percentages for Presidential Elections, 1788–1996

Year	National	Non-South	South	Year	National	Non-South	South
1788	42.5	49.0	32.8	1908	46.4	45.5	50.0
1792	42.9	49.3	32.1	1912	48.1	47.6	49.9
1796	43.1	49.7	31.9	1916	52.6	53.4	49.8
1800	43.3	49.9	32.4	1920	89.7	87.6	97.8
1804	44.0	50.4	32.5	1924	91.2	89.3	98.4
1808	44.4	50.7	32.6	1928	92.5	90.8	99.1
1812	44.0	50.2	32.6	1932	93.6	92.0	99.3
1816	43.2	49.3	31.7	1936	94.4	93.1	99.1
1820	42.8	48.6	31.3	1940	95.1	94.0	98.9
1824	42.3	48.2	30.5	1944	96.4	95.7	99.0
1828	42.3	48.2	30.4	1948	97.6	97.1	99.1
1832	42.6	48.5	30.4	1952	98.0	97.7	99.1
1836	43.1	48.9	30.4	1956	97.9	97.6	98.9
1840	43.3	49.0	30.5	1960	97.8	97.5	98.8
1844	43.7	49.3	30.7	1964	97.8	97.5	98.7
1848	44.2	49.7	31.0	1968	97.7	97.5	98.7
1852	44.9	50.3	31.3	1972	97.8	97.6	98.7
1856	45.1	50.4	31.5	1976	97.1	96.8	98.1
1860	45.5	50.5	31.7	1980	96.5	96.1	97.6
1864	45.9	50.2	32.2	1984	95.7	95.2	96.9
1868	48.5	49.7	44.3	1988	94.9	94.4	96.3
1872	45.8	45.3	47.6	1992	94.3	93.7	95.7
1876	46.2	45.7	48.0	1996	93.7	93.1	95.2
1880	46.5	45.9	48.4				
1884	46.8	46.1	49.0				
1888	47.0	46.3	49.6				
1892	47.2	46.5	49.9				
1896	47.5	46.8	49.9				
1900	47.4	46.7	49.9				
1904	46.8	45.9	50.0				

Notes: Eligibility is the ratio E/A, where E is the number of people eligible by law to vote in a state according to the criteria of citizenship, race, sex, and age laws on suffrage, where race has two dimensions: color (black/white) and bondage (slave/free); and A is the total number of adults in that state. These raw data—number of eligibles and adults in the states—are then aggregated to the national and regional levels to produce the entries, where the South refers to the 11 original Confederate states (Alabama, Arkansas, Florida, Georgia, Louisiana, Mississippi, North Carolina, South Carolina, Tennessee, Texas, and Virginia) and the Non-South refers to the remainder of the states. The data for eligibles in each state are taken from John J. Stucker's data archive for the 1824–1948 period, as amended and corrected by the author. The author has supplemented these data for the 1788–1824 and 1948–1996 periods using the same criteria. More detailed notes for the data recovery for the 1788–1824 period can be obtained from the author. Adjustments for citizenship in the eligibles data could only be made from 1870 on, since this was the first year the U.S. Census collected data on aliens. Data were also not available on aliens in 1960, requiring a linear interpolation of alien data from the 1950 and 1970 censuses. Linear interpolation is used in general between decennial censuses to derive information for intercensus years as adjusted for dates when suffrage laws were passed on the four criteria mentioned above. See Stucker (1973), Appendix B, for a detailed discussion of these procedures. Adult data for the states (including slaves) were also obtained from the decennial censuses and linear interpolation was used to derive values for intercensus years. When the U.S. Census collected data on age intervals not beginning with 21 (largely before 1870), linear adjustments were made to derive the number of adults 21 years of age and older. The starting age of 21 for voting was kept as a constant for data comparison purposes longitudinally for both eligibles and adults until 1971, when the 26th Amendment was ratified to allow the 18-year-old vote, although four states (Alaska, Georgia, Hawaii, and Kentucky) had actually lowered the voting age prior to this time. Only states with data on both variables (eligibles and adults) were used in the aggregation process to the national and regional levels.

Sources: Decennial censuses (1790–1990) of the U.S. Census Bureau; Bureau of U.S. Census P Series pamphlets for estimated eligibles in 1972 and the 1990s; *Statistical Abstracts* for estimated eligibles in 1972; Richard Scammon's book series, *America Votes* (various publication dates); the data archive of John J. Stucker; and relevant state constitutions and statute volumes. Also see Stucker (1973), Appendix B.

Table 3-2 National and Regional Voter Mobilization Percentages for Presidential Elections, 1788–1996

Year	National	Non-South	South	Year	National	Non-South	South
1788	8.4	8.4	—	1908	30.4	34.5	15.3
1792	14.1	14.1	—	1912	28.3	32.1	13.9
1796	11.7	11.7	—	1916	32.6	37.0	15.8
1800	9.9	14.5	7.6	1920	44.2	50.2	21.2
1804	10.9	13.9	3.6	1924	44.5	51.3	18.5
1808	15.0	19.5	5.5	1928	52.4	60.2	23.1
1812	18.4	23.4	5.4	1932	53.2	61.0	24.0
1816	6.8	9.5	2.6	1936	57.7	66.8	24.6
1820	4.4	5.8	1.2	1940	59.8	69.2	26.0
1824	11.4	12.6	8.7	1944	54.0	62.5	24.1
1828	24.0	28.5	13.4	1948	51.8	59.6	24.8
1832	23.7	29.6	9.4	1952	62.2	69.2	38.2
1836	23.9	27.3	15.5	1956	60.1	67.2	36.3
1840	34.1	38.2	23.8	1960	63.8	70.7	40.9
1844	33.1	36.8	23.6	1964	61.9	66.9	45.7
1848	30.2	33.3	22.0	1968	61.1	64.2	51.4
1852	28.8	32.3	19.1	1972	55.2	58.9	44.0
1856	32.4	35.8	22.6	1976	53.7	56.2	46.6
1860	33.1	36.2	24.0	1980	53.1	55.2	47.4
1864	33.2	33.2	—	1984	54.0	55.7	49.5
1868	35.2	36.2	30.4	1988	50.7	52.6	45.9
1872	33.1	33.5	31.8	1992	55.2	57.0	50.8
1876	38.2	38.9	36.0	1996	48.9	50.3	45.5
1880	37.4	39.3	31.3				
1884	36.9	38.5	31.4				
1888	38.0	39.9	31.6				
1892	36.0	37.8	29.4				
1896	37.8	40.4	28.6				
1900	34.9	38.5	21.0				
1904	30.6	35.1	14.5				

Notes: Mobilization is the ratio V/A, where V is the total vote cast in the presidential race in a given election year in a state, and A is the total number of adults in that state. These raw data—number of presidential votes cast and adults in the states—are then aggregated to the national and regional levels to produce the entries, where the South refers to the 11 original Confederate states (Alabama, Arkansas, Florida, Georgia, Louisiana, Mississippi, North Carolina, South Carolina, Tennessee, Texas, and Virginia) and the Non-South refers to the remainder of the states. The sources for locating the presidential vote are given in Tables 4-37 through 4-63 in Chapter 4, as are the raw data for the presidential vote for each state from 1788 to 1996. Adult data for the states (including slaves) were obtained from decennial censuses and linear interpolation was used to derive values for intercensus years. When the U.S. Census collected data on age intervals not beginning with 21 (largely before 1870), linear adjustments were made to derive the number of adults 21 years of age and older. The starting age of 21 for voting was kept as a constant for data comparison purposes longitudinally for adults until 1971, when the 26th Amendment was ratified to allow the 18-year-old vote, although four states (Alaska, Georgia, Hawaii, and Kentucky) had actually lowered the voting age prior to this time. Only states with data on both variables (presidential vote and adults) were used in the aggregation process to the national and regional levels. States with only partial data reported for the presidential race were not included in the aggregation process.

Sources: Adults—decennial censuses (1790–1990) of the U.S. Census Bureau; Bureau of U.S. Census P pamphlets for 1972 and the 1990s; and Richard Scammon's book series, *America Votes* (various publication dates). Presidential vote—Tables 4-37 through 4-63. Also see the national presidential vote totals reported in Table 4-4.

Table 3-3 National and Regional Voter Turnout Percentages for Presidential Elections, 1788–1996

Year	National	Non-South	South	Year	National	Non-South	South
1788	17.2	17.2	—	1908	65.5	75.8	30.7
1792	28.4	28.4	—	1912	58.8	67.4	27.8
1796	23.1	23.1	—	1916	61.9	69.3	31.7
1800	29.9	38.4	24.9	1920	49.2	57.3	21.7
1804	23.8	26.9	11.3	1924	48.8	57.5	18.8
1808	35.0	40.9	16.9	1928	56.7	66.3	23.3
1812	39.7	45.3	16.7	1932	56.8	66.2	24.2
1816	16.1	19.6	8.2	1936	61.1	71.7	24.8
1820	10.2	11.9	3.9	1940	62.9	73.6	26.3
1824	26.7	26.7	26.7	1944	56.0	65.3	24.4
1828	55.2	59.0	42.0	1948	53.1	61.4	25.1
1832	54.4	61.1	29.8	1952	63.5	70.8	38.6
1836	54.4	55.8	49.1	1956	61.4	68.8	36.7
1840	77.5	78.1	75.3	1960	65.2	72.5	41.4
1844	74.5	74.6	74.5	1964	63.3	68.6	46.3
1848	67.3	66.9	68.7	1968	62.5	65.8	52.1
1852	63.2	64.1	59.1	1972	56.4	60.4	44.6
1856	70.9	71.1	69.8	1976	55.3	58.1	47.5
1860	72.1	71.7	73.7	1980	55.1	57.5	48.6
1864	66.2	66.2	—	1984	56.4	58.4	51.1
1868	71.8	72.9	66.2	1988	53.4	55.7	47.7
1872	72.2	73.9	66.9	1992	58.6	60.8	53.1
1876	82.9	85.3	75.0	1996	52.1	54.0	47.8
1880	80.5	85.6	64.7				
1884	78.8	83.4	64.1				
1888	80.9	86.2	63.8				
1892	76.2	81.3	58.9				
1896	79.7	86.2	57.4				
1900	73.6	82.6	43.3				
1904	65.4	76.3	29.0				

Notes: Turnout is the ratio V/E, where V is the total vote cast in the presidential race in a given election year in a state, and E is the number of people eligible by law to vote in that state according to the criteria of citizenship, race, sex, and age laws on suffrage, where race has two dimensions: color (black/white) and bondage (slave/free). These raw data—number of presidential votes cast and eligibles in the states—are then aggregated to the national and regional levels to produce the entries, where the South refers to the 11 original Confederate states (Alabama, Arkansas, Florida, Georgia, Louisiana, Mississippi, North Carolina, South Carolina, Tennessee, Texas, and Virginia) and the Non-South refers to the remainder of the states. The sources for locating the presidential vote are given in Tables 4-37 through 4-63, as are the raw data for the presidential vote for each state from 1788 to 1996. The data for eligibles in each state are taken from John J. Stucker's data archive for the 1824–1948 period, as amended and corrected by the author. The author has supplemented these data for the 1788–1824 and 1948–1996 periods using the same criteria. More detailed notes for the data recovery for the 1788–1824 period can be obtained from the author. Adjustments for citizenship in the eligibles data could only be made from 1870 on, since this was the first year the U.S. Census collected data on aliens. Data were also not available on aliens in 1960, requiring a linear interpolation of alien data from the 1950 and 1970 censuses. Linear interpolation is used in general between decennial censuses to derive information for inter-census years as adjusted for dates when suffrage laws were passed on the four criteria mentioned above. When the U.S. Census collected data on age intervals not beginning with 21 (largely before 1870), linear adjustments were made to derive the number of eligibles 21 years of age and older. The starting age of 21 for voting was kept as a constant for data comparison purposes longitudinally for eligibles until 1971, when the 26th Amendment was ratified to allow the 18-year-old vote, although four states (Alaska, Georgia, Hawaii, and Kentucky) had actually lowered the voting age prior to this time. See Stucker (1973), Appendix B, for a detailed discussion of many of these procedures. Only states with data on both variables (presidential vote and eligibles) were used in the aggregation process to the national and regional levels. States with only partial data reported for the presidential race were not included in the aggregation process.

Sources: Eligibles—decennial censuses (1790–1990) of the U.S. Census Bureau; Bureau of U.S. Census Series P pamphlets for estimated eligibles in 1972 and the 1990s; *Statistical Abstracts* for estimated eligibles in 1972; Richard Scammon's book series, *America Votes* (various publication dates); the data archive of John J. Stucker; and relevant state constitutions and statute volumes. Also see Stucker (1973), Appendix B. Presidential vote—Tables 4-37 through 4-63. Also see the national presidential vote totals reported in Table 4-4.

Table 3-4 National and Regional Voter Mobilization Percentages for Congressional Elections, 1788–1998

Year	National	Non-South	South	Year	National	Non-South	South
1788–1789	8.4	8.3	9.0	1898	28.5	31.7	16.8
1790–1791	7.8	7.9	6.1	1900	34.2	37.9	20.9
1792–1793	12.3	12.2	14.3	1902	26.1	30.0	11.9
1794–1795	10.1	10.2	8.5	1904	29.8	34.1	14.1
1796–1797	10.4	10.4	10.3	1906–1907	23.9	27.8	9.3
1798–1799	15.7	15.9	12.5	1908	29.5	33.6	14.5
1800–1801	17.2	17.1	17.9	1910–1911	23.8	27.4	10.2
1802–1803	14.3	15.5	10.1	1912	26.8	30.5	12.9
1804–1805	19.2	19.3	18.5	1914	24.8	28.9	9.2
1806–1807	16.4	17.8	10.5	1916	29.4	33.2	15.0
1808–1809	28.1	28.3	26.2	1918	21.7	25.5	7.3
1810–1811	20.3	20.2	21.0	1920	42.1	47.7	20.8
1812–1813	23.5	24.5	11.5	1922	32.4	37.7	12.2
1814–1815	22.9	24.5	11.9	1924	41.1	47.3	17.5
1816–1817	20.3	20.3	20.4	1926	30.1	35.9	8.2
1818–1819	15.9	15.5	17.5	1928	48.7	56.1	20.9
1820–1821	19.9	20.6	14.7	1930	34.2	39.9	12.3
1822–1823	18.8	19.8	14.2	1932	50.2	57.3	23.5
1824–1825	19.7	20.7	8.2	1934	41.9	49.8	12.9
1826–1827	21.6	21.7	19.7	1936	54.3	63.0	22.8
1828–1829	25.6	26.1	22.5	1938	44.4	53.7	11.1
1830–1831	25.8	25.2	29.5	1940	55.9	65.0	23.3
1832–1833	27.8	28.0	26.2	1942	32.6	39.8	7.0
1834–1835	29.5	30.5	24.2	1944	50.7	59.0	21.5
1836–1837	27.0	27.8	23.0	1946	37.6	45.3	10.4
1838–1839	32.7	34.0	25.8	1948	48.7	56.7	21.1
1840–1841	32.1	34.6	21.2	1950	41.6	50.0	12.5
1842–1843	28.7	30.4	22.4	1952	58.5	66.2	32.1
1844–1845	33.0	35.3	23.8	1954	42.1	49.9	16.0
1846–1847	27.7	28.6	23.2	1956	56.4	64.5	29.0
1848–1849	29.4	31.1	22.7	1958–1959	43.7	52.1	14.5
1850–1851	27.1	27.8	22.2	1960	59.9	67.7	33.2
1852–1853	29.6	30.7	23.1	1962	46.6	53.3	23.8
1854–1855	27.9	29.1	23.7	1964	58.3	64.1	38.9
1856–1857	31.5	34.3	21.5	1966	45.6	50.8	28.3
1858–1859	29.2	31.0	21.6	1968	55.8	60.2	41.3
1860–1861	35.4	35.5	31.5	1970	45.3	49.2	30.5
1862–1863	28.3	28.3	—	1972	51.8	55.9	36.5
1864–1865	30.8	31.6	11.9	1974	37.1	40.4	23.7
1866–1867	31.0	31.5	18.8	1976	50.1	52.9	40.1
1868–1869	33.8	36.0	25.3	1978	36.1	38.9	25.2
1870–1871	30.5	30.4	30.9	1980	49.1	51.5	39.8
1872–1873	33.9	34.3	32.7	1982	39.6	42.1	30.7
1874–1875	29.9	29.8	30.1	1984	50.3	52.4	42.4
1876–1877	37.6	38.4	34.7	1986	34.8	36.4	29.3
1878–1879	30.3	32.2	23.7	1988	46.9	48.7	40.4
1880	36.9	38.8	30.5	1990	34.3	36.0	28.6
1882	30.8	32.5	25.2	1992	51.6	53.1	46.7
1884	36.3	38.1	30.2	1994	37.4	38.9	32.8
1886	30.0	32.6	21.1	1996	46.3	47.8	41.7
1888–1889	37.7	39.6	30.9	1998	34.7	36.9	27.4
1890	30.7	32.9	22.6				
1892	35.4	37.2	28.7				
1894–1895	32.0	34.3	23.4				
1896	37.1	39.5	28.4				

Notes: Mobilization is the ratio V/A, where V is the total vote cast in congressional (House) races in a given election year in a state, and A is the total number of adults in that state. These raw data—number of House votes cast and adults in the states—are then aggregated to the national and regional levels to produce the entries, where the South refers to the 11 original Confederate states (Alabama, Arkansas, Florida, Georgia, Louisiana, Mississippi, North Carolina, South Carolina, Tennessee, Texas, and Virginia) and the Non-South refers to the remainder of the states. The sources for locating the House vote are given in Tables 5-70 through 5-122, as are the raw data for the House vote for each state from 1788 to 1998. Adult data for the states (including slaves) were obtained from decennial censuses and linear interpolation was used to derive values for intercensus years. When the U.S. Census collected data on age intervals not beginning with 21 (largely before 1870), linear adjustments were made to derive the number of adults 21 years of age and older. The starting age of 21 for voting was kept as a constant for data comparison purposes longitudinally for adults until 1971, when the 26th Amendment was ratified to allow the 18-year-old vote, although four states (Alaska, Georgia, Hawaii, and Kentucky) had actually lowered the voting age prior to this time. Only states with data on both variables (congressional vote and adults) were used in the aggregation process to the national and regional levels. States with partial data reported for House races (less than 100 percent of districts reporting the vote) in a given year were not included in the aggregation process for that year, nor were states with special House elections. Regardless of whether a state held its House races in an even- or odd-numbered year, its congressional vote was divided by the number of adults in that state in the even-numbered year, which served as a common base by which to compare states' congressional votes in any given two-year cycle for House elections. The rarity of a state holding House elections in both even- and odd-numbered years in a two-year election cycle saw only its congressional vote in the even-numbered year used in the aggregation process.

Sources: Adults—decennial censuses (1790–1990) of the U.S. Census Bureau; Bureau of U.S. Census Series P pamphlets for 1972 and the 1990s; and Richard Scammon's book series, *America Votes* (various publication dates). House vote—Tables 5-70 through 5-122. Also see the national congressional vote totals reported in Table 5-4.

Table 3-5 National and Regional Voter Turnout Percentages for Congressional Elections, 1788–1998

Year	National	Non-South	South	Year	National	Non-South	South
1788–1789	17.2	16.9	26.9	1898	60.0	67.8	33.7
1790–1791	16.4	16.3	18.3	1900	72.2	81.2	41.8
1792–1793	26.2	25.7	42.8	1902	55.4	64.9	23.8
1794–1795	20.9	20.7	25.3	1904	63.7	74.3	28.3
1796–1797	22.9	21.1	38.2	1906–1907	51.1	60.7	18.6
1798–1799	30.8	30.5	37.4	1908	63.6	73.8	28.9
1800–1801	35.5	34.7	47.0	1910–1911	51.3	60.4	20.4
1802–1803	29.8	29.4	31.9	1912	55.7	64.0	25.8
1804–1805	39.0	38.0	49.7	1914	50.1	58.5	18.5
1806–1807	35.0	34.6	38.0	1916	59.0	66.0	30.0
1808–1809	55.8	54.6	86.2	1918	40.0	46.0	14.8
1810–1811	40.8	39.3	57.4	1920	47.0	54.5	21.3
1812–1813	47.5	48.2	35.6	1922	35.8	42.6	12.4
1814–1815	48.1	49.0	37.7	1924	45.0	53.0	17.8
1816–1817	42.3	39.9	57.0	1926	32.8	39.8	8.3
1818–1819	33.2	30.7	49.7	1928	52.7	61.8	21.1
1820–1821	41.8	41.4	46.6	1930	36.7	43.7	12.4
1822–1823	42.0	40.6	55.0	1932	53.6	62.3	23.6
1824–1825	42.1	43.0	27.6	1934	44.6	53.8	13.0
1826–1827	46.5	45.5	66.2	1936	57.6	67.7	23.0
1828–1829	57.1	55.0	74.9	1938	46.9	57.4	11.2
1830–1831	54.4	51.2	83.1	1940	58.8	69.2	23.6
1832–1833	59.1	57.0	77.4	1942	34.0	42.0	7.0
1834–1835	62.1	60.6	73.7	1944	52.6	61.7	21.7
1836–1837	57.5	56.0	69.3	1946	38.7	47.0	10.5
1838–1839	69.9	68.8	78.0	1948	50.0	58.4	21.3
1840–1841	69.9	70.6	65.1	1950	42.5	51.2	12.6
1842–1843	62.1	60.9	69.0	1952	59.6	67.7	32.4
1844–1845	71.8	71.6	73.4	1954	43.0	51.0	16.2
1846–1847	58.9	57.2	69.8	1956	57.5	66.1	29.4
1848–1849	63.5	62.4	69.9	1958–1959	44.6	53.4	14.7
1850–1851	56.6	55.2	71.3	1960	61.3	69.4	33.6
1852–1853	62.0	60.9	72.7	1962	47.6	54.6	24.1
1854–1855	60.2	57.8	73.6	1964	59.6	65.7	39.5
1856–1857	67.9	68.1	66.6	1966	46.6	52.1	28.7
1858–1859	62.1	61.6	65.8	1968	57.1	61.8	41.8
1860–1861	70.4	70.2	82.6	1970	46.3	50.5	30.8
1862–1863	56.3	56.3	—	1972	52.9	57.3	36.9
1864–1865	61.9	62.9	30.3	1974	38.0	41.6	24.0
1866–1867	62.4	62.8	48.1	1976	51.5	54.7	40.6
1868–1869	69.6	72.4	57.6	1978	37.3	40.4	25.7
1870–1871	66.8	67.2	64.9	1980	50.8	53.6	40.6
1872–1873	74.0	75.7	68.7	1982	41.1	44.0	31.3
1874–1875	65.0	65.6	63.0	1984	52.5	55.1	43.5
1876–1877	81.3	84.0	71.9	1986	36.5	38.4	30.1
1878–1879	65.3	70.3	49.3	1988	49.3	51.6	41.6
1880	79.3	84.5	63.2	1990	36.2	38.3	29.6
1882	66.1	70.6	51.8	1992	54.7	56.7	48.3
1884	77.6	82.6	61.5	1994	39.8	41.6	34.0
1886	64.0	70.5	42.9	1996	49.4	51.3	43.3
1888–1889	79.9	85.1	62.3	1998	37.1	39.8	28.5
1890	64.9	70.6	45.3				
1892	74.9	79.9	57.6				
1894–1895	67.4	73.4	46.9				
1896	78.1	84.3	56.9				

Notes: Turnout is the ratio V/E, where V is the total vote cast in congressional (House) races in a given election year in a state, and E is the number of people eligible by law to vote in that state according to the criteria of citizenship, race, sex, and age laws on suffrage, where race has two dimensions: color (black/white) and bondage (slave/free). These raw data—number of House votes cast and eligibles in the states—are then aggregated to the national and regional levels to produce the entries, where the South refers to the 11 original Confederate states (Alabama, Arkansas, Florida, Georgia, Louisiana, Mississippi, North Carolina, South Carolina, Tennessee, Texas, and Virginia) and the Non-South refers to the remainder of the states. The sources for locating the House vote are given in Tables 5-70 through 5-122, as are the raw data for the House vote for each state from 1788 to 1998. The data for eligibles in each state are taken from John J. Stucker's data archive for the 1824–1948 period, as amended and corrected by the author. The author has supplemented these data for the 1788–1824 and 1948–1998 periods using the same criteria. More detailed notes for the data recovery for the 1788–1824 period can be obtained from the author. Adjustments for citizenship in the eligibles data could only be made from 1870 on, since this was the first year the U. S. Census collected data on aliens. Data were also not available on aliens in 1960, requiring a linear interpolation of alien data from the 1950 and 1970 censuses. Linear interpolation is used in general between decennial censuses to derive information for intercensus years as adjusted for dates when suffrage laws were passed on the four criteria mentioned above. When the U.S. Census collected data on age intervals not beginning with 21 (largely before 1870), linear adjustments were made to derive the number of eligibles 21 years of age and older. The starting age of 21 for voting was kept as a constant for data comparison purposes longitudinally for eligibles until 1971 when the 26th Amendment was ratified to allow the 18-year-old vote, although four states (Alaska, Georgia, Hawaii, and Kentucky) had actually lowered the voting age prior to this time. See Stucker (1973), Appendix B, for a detailed discussion of many of these procedures. Only states with data on both variables (congressional vote and eligibles) were used in the aggregation process to the national and regional levels. States with partial data reported for House races (less than 100 percent of districts reporting the vote) in a given year were not included in the aggregation process for that year, nor were states with special House elections. Regardless of whether a state held its House races in an even- or odd-numbered year, its congressional vote was divided by the number of eligibles in that state in the even-numbered year, which served as a common base by which to compare states' congressional votes in any given two-year cycle for House elections. The rarity of a state holding House elections in both even- and odd-numbered years in a two-year election cycle saw only its congressional vote in the even-numbered year used in the aggregation process.

Sources: Eligibles—decennial censuses (1790–1990) of the U.S. Census Bureau; Bureau of U.S. Census Series P pamphlets for 1972 and the 1990s; Richard Scammon's book series, *America Votes* (various publication dates); the data archive of John J. Stucker; and relevant state constitutions and statute volumes. Also see Stucker (1973), Appendix B. House vote—Tables 5-70 through 5-122. Also see the national congressional vote totals reported in Table 5-4.

Table 3-6 Percentage Differences in National Voter Turnout Between the Presidential Races and House Races Held in Presidential and Midterm Election Years, 1788–1996

| Presidential Year | National Turnout Difference | | Presidential Year | National Turnout Difference | |
	Presidential Election Years (Roll-Off)	Midterm Election Years (Drop-Off)		Presidential Election Years (Roll-Off)	Midterm Election Years (Drop-Off)
1788	0.0	0.8	1908	1.9	14.2
1792	2.2	7.5	1912	3.1	8.7
1796	0.2	−7.7	1916	2.9	19.0
1800	−5.6	0.1	1920	2.2	13.4
1804	−15.2	−11.2	1924	3.8	16.0
1808	−20.8	−5.8	1928	4.0	20.0
1812	−7.8	−8.4	1932	3.2	12.2
1816	−26.2	−17.1	1936	3.5	14.2
1820	−31.6	−31.8	1940	4.1	28.9
1824	−15.4	−19.8	1944	3.4	17.3
1828	−1.9	0.8	1948	3.1	10.6
1832	−5.3	−7.7	1952	3.9	20.5
1836	−3.1	−15.5	1956	3.9	16.8
1840	7.6	15.4	1960	3.9	17.6
1844	2.7	15.6	1964	3.7	16.7
1848	3.8	10.7	1968	5.4	16.2
1852	4.2	3.1	1972	3.5	18.4
1856	3.0	8.8	1976	3.8	18.0
1860	1.7	15.8	1980	4.3	14.0
1864	4.2	3.8	1984	3.9	19.9
1868	3.0	5.0	1988	4.1	17.2
1872	−1.8	7.2	1992	3.9	18.8
1876	1.6	17.6	1996	2.7	15.0
1880	1.2	14.4			
1884	1.2	14.8			
1888	1.0	16.0			
1892	1.3	8.8			
1896	1.6	19.7			
1900	1.4	18.2			
1904	1.7	14.3			

Notes: Difference values are computed from national vote turnout values in Tables 3-3 and 3-5. Roll-off is the difference between values for national presidential turnout and national House turnout in presidential election years. Drop-off is the difference between values for national presidential turnout in presidential election years and national House turnout in midterm elections. A positive difference value indicates that presidential turnout was higher; a negative value indicates that House turnout was higher.

Sources: Tables 3-3 and 3-5.

Table 3-7 National and Regional Voter Mobilization Percentages for Senate Elections, 1912–1998

Year	National	Non-South	South	Year	National	Non-South	South
1912	31.6	31.6	—	1960	56.7	70.9	34.7
1914	27.9	30.9	8.8	1962	48.5	53.8	24.1
1916	29.5	31.8	15.6	1964	61.5	65.8	42.1
1918	19.2	25.6	7.8	1966	43.8	53.1	29.2
1920	44.5	49.0	20.1	1968	58.3	61.4	45.0
1922	34.4	37.9	13.6	1970	48.9	51.6	36.2
1924	40.2	52.7	18.0	1972	52.3	59.0	42.8
1926	33.0	37.4	9.0	1974	38.5	41.4	27.1
1928	51.0	56.1	21.3	1976	51.6	53.6	44.0
1930	32.7	43.9	12.8	1978	36.2	42.0	27.6
1932	52.7	58.3	23.0	1980	50.8	52.2	45.0
1934	44.7	50.5	12.8	1982	41.0	43.3	33.1
1936	49.4	65.3	22.2	1984	53.3	57.4	47.7
1938	47.6	54.4	12.6	1986	37.6	37.9	36.6
1940	58.6	65.1	23.4	1988	49.4	50.7	44.9
1942	29.0	42.2	7.2	1990	36.3	41.8	29.2
1944	54.1	60.5	22.1	1992	51.9	53.9	44.5
1946	40.3	46.1	10.1	1994	38.9	39.8	36.1
1948	44.8	59.2	21.5	1996	48.5	52.4	44.0
1950	46.0	52.0	16.1	1998	36.8	37.5	34.4
1952	60.8	66.4	32.8				
1954	38.5	52.5	16.4				
1956	58.5	65.0	27.8				
1958	47.3	53.8	16.4				
1959	46.7	46.7	—				

Notes: Mobilization is the ratio V/A, where V is the total vote cast in a Senate race (or races) in a given election year in a state, and A is the total number of adults in that state. These raw data—number of Senate votes cast and adults in the states—are then aggregated to the national and regional levels to produce the entries, where the South refers to the 11 original Confederate states (Alabama, Arkansas, Florida, Georgia, Louisiana, Mississippi, North Carolina, South Carolina, Tennessee, Texas, and Virginia), and the Non-South refers to the remainder of the states. The sources for locating the Senate vote are given in Tables 6-33 through 6-54, as are the raw data for the Senate vote for each state from 1912 to 1998. Adult data for the states (including slaves) were obtained from decennial censuses and linear interpolation was used to derive values for intercensus years. When the U.S. Census collected data on age intervals not beginning with 21 (largely before 1870), linear adjustments were made to derive the number of adults 21 years of age and older. The starting age of 21 for voting was kept as a constant for data comparison purposes longitudinally for adults until 1971, when the 26th Amendment was ratified to allow the 18-year-old vote, although four states (Alaska, Georgia, Hawaii, and Kentucky) had actually lowered the voting age prior to this time. Only states with data on both variables (Senate vote and adults) were used in the aggregation process to the national and regional levels. States with only partial data reported for Senate races in a given election year were not included in the aggregation process for that year, nor were states with special Senate elections.

Sources: Adults—decennial censuses (1910–1990) of the U.S. Census Bureau; Bureau of U.S. Census Series P pamphlets for 1972 and the 1990s; and Richard Scammon's book series, *America Votes* (various publication dates). Senate vote—Tables 6-33 through 6-54. Also see the national Senate vote totals reported in Table 6-3.

Table 3-8 National and Regional Voter Turnout Percentages for Senate Elections, 1912–1998

Year	National	Non-South	South	Year	National	Non-South	South
1912	57.5	57.5	—	1960	57.5	72.2	35.0
1914	54.6	60.4	17.6	1962	49.6	55.2	24.3
1916	61.4	66.6	31.4	1964	63.2	67.7	42.9
1918	37.9	50.0	15.6	1966	44.5	54.1	29.5
1920	49.4	55.4	20.3	1968	59.7	63.0	45.6
1922	38.9	43.5	14.1	1970	50.2	53.0	37.0
1924	43.2	58.4	18.3	1972	53.0	60.0	43.1
1926	35.8	41.2	9.1	1974	39.6	42.6	27.5
1928	56.1	62.6	21.6	1976	53.4	55.6	45.3
1930	34.6	47.7	12.9	1978	36.9	43.0	28.1
1932	56.3	62.9	23.1	1980	52.8	54.5	46.1
1934	48.3	55.1	12.9	1982	43.0	45.4	34.5
1936	51.5	69.6	22.4	1984	54.8	59.1	48.9
1938	50.2	57.9	12.7	1986	39.6	40.2	37.8
1940	62.3	69.8	23.8	1988	52.5	54.0	47.4
1942	29.9	44.1	7.2	1990	37.6	43.2	30.2
1944	56.1	63.1	22.2	1992	55.4	57.9	46.3
1946	41.8	48.1	10.2	1994	41.9	42.9	38.6
1948	45.6	60.7	21.7	1996	50.4	54.5	45.7
1950	46.8	53.1	16.2	1998	39.6	40.7	36.1
1952	62.3	68.1	33.3				
1954	39.0	53.5	16.5				
1956	59.7	66.6	28.0				
1958	48.5	55.3	16.7				
1959	54.7	54.7	—				

Notes: Turnout is the ratio V/E, where V is the total vote cast in a Senate race (or races) in a given election year in a state, and E is the number of people eligible by law to vote in that state according to the criteria of citizenship, race, sex, and age laws on suffrage, where race has two dimensions: color (black/white) and bondage (slave/free). These raw data—number of Senate votes cast and eligibles in the states—are then aggregated to the national and regional levels to produce the entries, where the South refers to the 11 original Confederate states (Alabama, Arkansas, Florida, Georgia, Louisiana, Mississippi, North Carolina, South Carolina, Tennessee, Texas, and Virginia) and the Non-South refers to the remainder of the states. The sources for locating the Senate vote are given in Tables 6-33 to 6-54, as are the raw data for the Senate vote for each state from 1912 to 1998. The data for eligibles in each state is taken from John J. Stucker's data archive for the 1912–1948 period, as amended and corrected by the author. The author has supplemented these data for the 1948–1998 period using the same criteria. Adjustments for citizenship in the eligibles data could only be made from 1870 on, since this was the first year the U.S. Census collected data on aliens. Data were also not available on aliens in 1960, requiring a linear interpolation of alien data from the 1950 and 1970 censuses. Linear interpolation is used in general between decennial censuses to derive information for intercensus years as adjusted for dates when suffrage laws were passed on the four criteria mentioned above. When the U.S. Census collected data on age intervals not beginning with 21 (largely before 1870), linear adjustments were made to derive the number of eligibles 21 years of age and older. The starting age of 21 for voting was kept as a constant for data comparison purposes longitudinally for eligibles until 1971, when the 26th Amendment was ratified to allow the 18-year-old vote, although four states (Alaska, Georgia, Hawaii, and Kentucky) had actually lowered the voting age prior to this time. See Stucker (1973), Appendix B, for a detailed discussion of many of these procedures. Only states with data on both variables (Senate vote and eligibles) were used in the aggregation process to the national and regional levels. States with only partial data reported for Senate races in a given election year were not included in the aggregation process for that year, nor were states with special Senate elections.

Sources: Eligibles—decennial censuses (1910–1990) of the U.S. Census Bureau; Bureau of U.S. Census Series P pamphlets for 1972 and the 1990s; Richard Scammon's book series, *America Votes* (various publication dates); the data archive of John J. Stucker; and relevant state constitutions and statute volumes. Also see Stucker (1973), Appendix B. Senate vote—Tables 6-33 through 6-54. Also see the national Senate vote totals in Table 6-3.

Table 3-9 Percentage Differences in National Turnout Between Presidential, Senate, and House Elections, 1912–1998

Election Year	National Turnout Difference			
	Between President and Senate in Presidential Election Years (Roll-Off)	Between President and House in Presidential Election Years (Roll-Off)	Between Senate and House in Presidential Election Years (Roll-Off)	Between Senate and House in Mid-Term Election Years (Roll-Off)
1912	1.3	3.1	1.8	
1914				4.5
1916	0.5	2.9	2.4	
1918				−2.1
1920	−0.2	2.2	2.4	
1922				3.1
1924	5.6	3.8	−1.8	
1926				3.0
1928	0.6	4.0	3.4	
1930				−2.1
1932	0.5	3.2	2.7	
1934				3.7
1936	9.6	3.5	−6.1	
1938				3.3
1940	0.6	4.1	3.5	
1942				−4.1
1944	−0.1	3.4	3.5	
1946				3.1
1948	7.5	3.1	−4.4	
1950				4.3
1952	1.2	3.9	2.7	
1954				−4.0
1956	1.7	3.9	2.2	
1958				3.9
1960	7.7	3.9	−3.8	
1962				2.0
1964	0.1	3.7	3.6	
1966				−2.1
1968	2.8	5.4	2.6	
1970				3.9
1972	3.4	3.5	0.1	
1974				1.6
1976	1.9	3.8	1.9	
1978				−0.4
1980	2.3	4.3	2.0	
1982				1.9
1984	1.6	3.9	2.3	
1986				3.1
1988	0.9	4.1	3.2	
1990				1.4
1992	3.2	3.9	0.7	
1994				2.1
1996	1.7	2.7	1.0	
1998				2.5
Grand Means =	2.5	3.7	1.2	1.6

Notes: Difference values are computed from national vote turnout values in Tables 3-3, 3-5, and 3-8. Roll-off is the difference in national turnout for the two races being compared in any given column in Table 3-9. A positive difference value indicates that national presidential turnout was higher in the political race comparisons with Senate and House in columns 1 and 2, respectively, and that national Senate turnout was higher than national House turnout in columns 3 and 4 of the table. Negative difference values indicate that national Senate turnout was higher than national presidential turnout in column 1, that national House turnout was higher than national presidential turnout in column 2, and that national House turnout was higher than national Senate turnout in columns 3 and 4.

Sources: Tables 3-3, 3-5, and 3-8.

Table 3-10 State Voter Eligibility Percentages in Presidential Elections, 1788–1816

	1788	1792	1796	1800	1804	1808	1812	1816
Alabama	—	—	—	—	—	—	—	—
Alaska	—	—	—	—	—	—	—	—
Arizona	—	—	—	—	—	—	—	—
Arkansas	—	—	—	—	—	—	—	—
California	—	—	—	—	—	—	—	—
Colorado	—	—	—	—	—	—	—	—
Connecticut	47.3	47.3	47.5	47.7	47.7	47.7	47.6	47.4
Delaware	44.3	44.5	44.9	45.3	46.5	47.6	48.0	47.8
Dist. of Columbia	—	—	—	—	—	—	—	—
Florida	—	—	—	—	—	—	—	—
Georgia	33.4	33.4	33.5	33.5	31.7	30.4	29.6	29.2
Hawaii	—	—	—	—	—	—	—	—
Idaho	—	—	—	—	—	—	—	—
Illinois	—	—	—	—	—	—	—	—
Indiana	—	—	—	—	—	—	—	54.2
Iowa	—	—	—	—	—	—	—	—
Kansas	—	—	—	—	—	—	—	—
Kentucky	—	44.6	44.2	44.0	43.3	42.9	42.2	41.3
Louisiana	—	—	—	—	—	—	39.4	35.0
Maine	—	—	—	—	—	—	—	—
Maryland	35.6	35.6	35.8	35.9	36.3	36.7	37.2	37.7
Massachusetts	58.6	59.6	61.5	63.2	65.6	67.8	64.1	55.3
Michigan	—	—	—	—	—	—	—	—
Minnesota	—	—	—	—	—	—	—	—
Mississippi	—	—	—	—	—	—	—	—
Missouri	—	—	—	—	—	—	—	—
Montana	—	—	—	—	—	—	—	—
Nebraska	—	—	—	—	—	—	—	—
Nevada	—	—	—	—	—	—	—	—
New Hampshire	49.7	49.5	49.2	48.9	48.7	48.4	48.2	48.0
New Jersey	49.0	48.8	48.3	47.8	48.0	48.3	47.6	47.9
New Mexico	—	—	—	—	—	—	—	—
New York	49.0	49.2	49.6	49.9	50.6	51.1	51.2	51.1
North Carolina	37.7	37.3	36.7	36.2	35.6	35.0	34.4	33.9
North Dakota	—	—	—	—	—	—	—	—
Ohio	—	—	—	—	55.0	54.2	53.9	53.7
Oklahoma	—	—	—	—	—	—	—	—
Oregon	—	—	—	—	—	—	—	—
Pennsylvania	51.9	52.0	52.1	52.1	51.8	51.5	51.3	51.1
Rhode Island	45.6	45.7	45.9	46.1	46.5	46.9	46.8	46.4
South Carolina	28.3	28.1	27.8	27.5	26.3	25.3	24.4	23.6
South Dakota	—	—	—	—	—	—	—	—
Tennessee	—	—	—	46.0	44.7	44.1	43.2	42.2
Texas	—	—	—	—	—	—	—	—
Utah	—	—	—	—	—	—	—	—
Vermont	—	54.1	52.9	52.2	51.4	50.8	50.3	49.9
Virginia	32.0	30.8	30.7	30.7	31.7	32.7	32.5	31.3
Washington	—	—	—	—	—	—	—	—
West Virginia	—	—	—	—	—	—	—	—
Wisconsin	—	—	—	—	—	—	—	—
Wyoming	—	—	—	—	—	—	—	—

Notes: Eligibility is the ratio E/A, where E is the number of people eligible by law to vote in a state according to the criteria of citizenship, race, sex, and age laws on suffrage; where race has two dimensions; color (black/white) and bondage (slave/free); and A is the total number of adults in that state. These raw data—number of eligibles and adults in each state—are used to produce the entries. For a more detailed discussion of the methodology used, see the notes to Table 3-1.

Sources: Decennial censuses (1790–1990) of the U.S. Census Bureau; Bureau of U.S. Census Series P pamphlets for 1972 and the 1990s; Richard Scammon's book series, *America Votes* (various publication dates); the data archive of John J. Stucker; and relevant state constitutions and statute volumes. Also see Stucker (1973), Appendix B.

Table 3-11 State Voter Eligibility Percentages in Presidential Elections, 1820–1856

	1820	1824	1828	1832	1836	1840	1844	1848	1852	1856
Alabama	38.0	37.4	35.0	33.1	31.5	30.6	29.7	29.1	28.7	28.6
Alaska	—	—	—	—	—	—	—	—	—	—
Arizona	—	—	—	—	—	—	—	—	—	—
Arkansas	—	—	—	—	48.0	47.3	44.6	43.2	42.0	41.2
California	—	—	—	—	—	—	—	—	90.1	85.2
Colorado	—	—	—	—	—	—	—	—	—	—
Connecticut	47.2	46.0	46.2	46.3	46.2	46.2	47.0	47.7	47.9	47.8
Delaware	47.6	37.8	37.6	37.5	37.6	37.6	38.5	39.3	40.1	40.8
Dist. of Columbia	—	—	—	—	—	—	—	—	—	—
Florida	—	—	—	—	—	—	33.4	32.1	31.3	30.9
Georgia	28.9	29.5	29.8	30.1	30.3	30.4	30.1	29.9	29.7	29.4
Hawaii	—	—	—	—	—	—	—	—	—	—
Idaho	—	—	—	—	—	—	—	—	—	—
Illinois	56.7	55.0	54.6	55.5	56.4	56.8	55.4	54.6	54.4	54.6
Indiana	54.2	52.8	52.4	52.4	52.4	52.4	52.4	52.4	52.5	52.6
Iowa	—	—	—	—	—	—	—	55.1	54.6	54.6
Kansas	—	—	—	—	—	—	—	—	—	—
Kentucky	40.7	40.1	40.0	40.0	40.1	40.2	40.8	41.2	41.7	42.3
Louisiana	32.3	28.0	24.9	25.3	26.9	27.9	28.7	29.3	29.0	28.2
Maine	49.6	49.7	49.7	49.8	50.0	50.1	50.7	51.1	51.0	50.6
Maryland	38.3	35.9	33.7	33.9	34.1	34.2	35.8	37.0	37.7	37.9
Massachusetts	47.5	47.4	47.4	47.8	48.5	49.1	49.0	48.9	48.6	48.1
Michigan	—	—	—	—	56.8	56.1	55.2	54.6	54.4	54.3
Minnesota	—	—	—	—	—	—	—	—	—	—
Mississippi	32.7	30.8	29.9	28.6	27.6	27.2	26.8	26.6	26.1	25.4
Missouri	50.8	48.4	47.3	47.7	48.4	48.8	48.8	48.8	49.4	50.1
Montana	—	—	—	—	—	—	—	—	—	—
Nebraska	—	—	—	—	—	—	—	—	—	—
Nevada	—	—	—	—	—	—	—	—	—	—
New Hampshire	47.8	47.2	46.8	46.7	46.9	47.1	47.8	48.3	48.4	48.2
New Jersey	48.2	46.4	46.7	46.8	46.8	46.7	47.1	47.5	47.7	47.8
New Mexico	—	—	—	—	—	—	—	—	—	—
New York	51.0	51.2	51.3	51.3	51.2	51.1	51.2	51.3	51.0	50.3
North Carolina	33.5	33.3	33.0	32.9	31.4	31.3	31.5	31.6	31.8	32.1
North Dakota	—	—	—	—	—	—	—	—	—	—
Ohio	53.6	52.6	52.3	52.2	52.1	52.1	52.0	51.9	51.6	51.1
Oklahoma	—	—	—	—	—	—	—	—	—	—
Oregon	—	—	—	—	—	—	—	—	—	—
Pennsylvania	51.0	50.9	51.0	50.8	50.6	48.9	49.3	49.6	49.6	49.4
Rhode Island	46.1	44.3	44.5	44.8	45.1	45.3	47.5	48.1	48.1	47.6
South Carolina	23.0	22.2	22.2	22.1	22.0	21.8	21.7	21.6	21.7	21.9
South Dakota	—	—	—	—	—	—	—	—	—	—
Tennessee	41.4	40.6	41.2	40.8	39.7	39.1	38.8	38.5	38.6	39.0
Texas	—	—	—	—	—	—	—	44.3	43.1	42.0
Utah	—	—	—	—	—	—	—	—	—	—
Vermont	49.5	49.5	49.4	49.3	49.3	49.3	50.0	50.6	50.8	50.5
Virginia	30.3	28.5	28.5	28.7	29.3	29.8	30.8	31.7	32.4	33.0
Washington	—	—	—	—	—	—	—	—	—	—
West Virginia	—	—	—	—	—	—	—	—	—	—
Wisconsin	—	—	—	—	—	—	—	57.1	55.9	55.0
Wyoming	—	—	—	—	—	—	—	—	—	—

Notes: Eligibility is the ratio E/A, where E is the number of people eligible by law to vote in a state according to the criteria of citizenship, race, sex, and age laws on suffrage; where race has two dimensions; color (black/white) and bondage (slave/free); and A is the total number of adults in that state. These raw data—number of eligibles and adults in each state—are used to produce the entries. For a more detailed discussion of the methodology used, see the notes to Table 3-1.

Sources: Decennial censuses (1790–1990) of the U.S. Census Bureau; Bureau of U.S. Census Series P pamphlets for 1972 and the 1990s; Richard Scammon's book series, *America Votes* (various publication dates); the data archive of John J. Stucker; and relevant state constitutions and statute volumes. Also see Stucker (1973), Appendix B.

Table 3-12 State Voter Eligibility Percentages in Presidential Elections, 1860–1896

	1860	1864	1868	1872	1876	1880	1884	1888	1892	1896
Alabama	28.4	30.1	48.0	47.4	47.3	47.2	48.1	48.8	49.3	49.5
Alaska	—	—	—	—	—	—	—	—	—	—
Arizona	—	—	—	—	—	—	—	—	—	—
Arkansas	40.7	46.4	51.6	50.7	51.5	52.0	52.7	53.3	53.3	52.8
California	82.7	69.4	60.6	44.4	44.1	43.9	44.5	44.9	45.3	45.8
Colorado	—	—	—	—	66.1	65.9	62.1	59.9	57.7	92.8
Connecticut	47.7	47.8	47.9	41.3	41.3	41.3	41.0	40.7	40.6	40.5
Delaware	41.4	41.2	41.1	46.8	47.2	47.4	48.1	48.6	48.8	48.8
Dist. of Columbia	—	—	—	—	—	—	—	—	—	—
Florida	30.6	30.5	51.7	49.1	49.4	49.6	50.1	50.5	50.9	51.1
Georgia	29.2	29.3	47.9	46.9	47.2	47.5	48.3	49.1	49.4	49.5
Hawaii	—	—	—	—	—	—	—	—	—	—
Idaho	—	—	—	—	—	—	—	—	56.9	56.1
Illinois	54.7	53.7	53.0	46.3	46.1	46.0	45.8	45.7	45.9	46.5
Indiana	52.6	51.8	51.1	50.4	50.4	50.4	50.5	50.5	50.5	50.3
Iowa	54.5	54.2	54.3	47.8	47.9	47.9	48.1	48.2	48.6	49.1
Kansas	58.7	58.4	58.0	56.1	54.8	54.2	53.2	52.4	52.0	51.6
Kentucky	42.7	43.2	43.7	49.1	49.3	49.3	53.7	58.2	57.8	53.6
Louisiana	27.6	29.6	46.2	46.4	46.7	47.3	47.5	47.8	48.1	48.5
Maine	50.3	49.9	49.5	44.6	44.6	44.7	45.0	45.3	45.3	45.0
Maryland	38.0	38.2	38.3	45.2	45.7	46.1	46.2	46.3	46.6	47.0
Massachusetts	47.8	47.7	47.6	37.3	37.1	37.0	37.4	37.7	37.6	37.3
Michigan	54.3	53.6	53.1	48.1	48.1	48.1	47.5	47.0	46.8	44.7
Minnesota	57.5	56.9	56.9	44.3	45.4	46.0	47.2	48.0	48.5	48.9
Mississippi	24.8	25.6	47.8	48.3	48.7	49.0	49.4	49.8	50.1	50.2
Missouri	50.6	50.4	50.3	50.5	50.6	50.7	50.7	50.7	50.7	50.6
Montana	—	—	—	—	—	—	—	—	57.6	56.8
Nebraska	—	—	62.5	57.3	55.7	55.0	53.5	52.7	52.2	51.6
Nevada	—	68.5	76.0	56.5	54.1	52.1	52.9	53.8	54.1	53.3
New Hampshire	48.0	48.0	47.9	43.8	43.7	43.6	43.3	43.0	42.7	42.3
New Jersey	47.9	47.8	47.7	41.4	41.6	41.7	42.4	43.0	43.0	42.6
New Mexico	—	—	—	—	—	—	—	—	—	—
New York	49.8	49.5	49.3	41.7	41.6	41.5	41.9	42.2	42.2	41.9
North Carolina	32.3	33.0	46.2	45.7	46.2	46.7	47.3	47.9	48.3	48.5
North Dakota	—	—	—	—	—	—	—	—	49.1	50.5
Ohio	50.8	50.0	49.4	46.7	47.1	47.4	47.5	47.6	47.7	47.8
Oklahoma	—	—	—	—	—	—	—	—	—	—
Oregon	70.0	64.4	61.0	57.5	56.2	55.4	54.8	54.5	54.1	53.6
Pennsylvania	49.2	49.1	49.0	45.3	46.2	46.9	45.9	45.1	44.6	44.4
Rhode Island	47.2	47.2	47.2	35.4	35.4	35.4	35.9	36.2	36.9	37.9
South Carolina	22.2	22.8	47.1	47.1	47.2	47.3	47.9	48.4	48.7	48.9
South Dakota	—	—	—	—	—	—	—	—	52.9	51.9
Tennessee	39.3	39.1	39.0	47.8	48.0	48.2	49.0	49.6	50.0	50.0
Texas	41.5	44.9	47.5	49.7	50.8	51.2	51.7	52.1	51.9	51.4
Utah	—	—	—	—	—	—	—	—	—	84.7
Vermont	50.2	49.9	29.7	41.3	42.0	42.7	43.8	44.9	45.5	45.6
Virginia	33.5	29.4	31.1	47.2	47.5	47.7	48.2	48.6	48.9	49.1
Washington	—	—	—	—	—	—	—	—	55.9	54.8
West Virginia	—	50.0	50.0	49.2	49.5	49.8	50.4	50.8	51.2	51.5
Wisconsin	54.5	53.8	53.2	46.0	46.2	46.3	46.5	46.6	46.8	47.1
Wyoming	—	—	—	—	—	—	—	—	89.0	87.8

Notes: Eligibility is the ratio E/A, where E is the number of people eligible by law to vote in a state according to the criteria of citizenship, race, sex, and age laws on suffrage; where race has two dimensions; color (black/white) and bondage (slave/free); and A is the total number of adults in that state. These raw data—number of eligibles and adults in each state—are used to produce the entries. For a more detailed discussion of the methodology used, see the notes to Table 3-1.

Sources: Decennial censuses (1790–1990) of the U.S. Census Bureau; Bureau of U.S. Census Series P pamphlets for 1972 and the 1990s; Richard Scammon's book series, *America Votes* (various publication dates); the data archive of John J. Stucker; and relevant state constitutions and statute volumes. Also see Stucker (1973), Appendix B.

Table 3-13 State Voter Eligibility Percentages in Presidential Elections, 1900–1936

	1900	1904	1908	1912	1916	1920	1924	1928	1932	1936
Alabama	49.7	49.8	49.9	50.0	49.9	99.3	99.5	99.6	99.6	99.7
Alaska	—	—	—	—	—	—	—	—	—	—
Arizona	—	—	—	45.3	76.0	75.9	86.1	94.3	96.3	93.7
Arkansas	52.5	52.4	52.4	52.3	52.0	99.5	99.6	99.6	99.7	99.7
California	46.2	47.0	47.6	87.4	86.7	86.2	88.8	90.6	91.2	91.2
Colorado	92.6	89.9	89.7	90.2	91.4	92.4	93.9	95.2	96.0	96.2
Connecticut	40.4	39.0	37.9	37.3	37.2	75.4	77.9	80.0	82.4	85.0
Delaware	48.7	48.1	47.5	47.2	47.1	92.5	93.8	95.0	95.8	96.3
Dist. of Columbia	—	—	—	—	—	—	—	—	—	—
Florida	51.6	51.6	51.6	51.1	50.4	95.8	96.5	97.0	97.2	97.4
Georgia	49.5	49.7	49.9	49.9	49.8	99.5	99.6	99.7	99.7	99.7
Hawaii	—	—	—	—	—	—	—	—	—	—
Idaho	90.7	91.0	91.2	92.1	93.6	94.8	95.6	96.4	96.9	97.3
Illinois	47.0	45.6	44.5	44.1	87.0	87.9	89.7	91.2	92.6	93.9
Indiana	50.2	49.9	49.7	49.6	49.6	97.1	96.4	97.1	97.6	98.0
Iowa	49.5	48.9	48.2	48.2	48.6	95.7	96.6	97.5	97.9	98.1
Kansas	51.3	51.0	50.7	50.6	96.2	96.1	97.2	98.1	98.6	98.6
Kentucky	50.5	50.4	50.4	50.4	50.5	99.1	99.3	99.5	99.6	99.7
Louisiana	48.5	48.8	49.1	49.2	49.2	97.2	97.9	98.5	98.9	99.1
Maine	44.7	44.4	44.0	43.9	44.1	88.7	89.3	89.9	90.7	91.7
Maryland	47.3	46.9	46.6	46.7	47.1	94.9	95.5	96.0	96.5	96.9
Massachusetts	37.1	36.6	36.3	36.3	36.7	77.3	79.3	81.2	83.4	86.0
Michigan	44.6	44.5	44.5	44.4	44.5	85.0	86.4	87.5	89.0	91.0
Minnesota	45.3	45.3	45.3	45.7	46.4	89.6	92.0	94.1	95.4	95.9
Mississippi	50.4	50.4	50.5	50.4	50.3	99.6	99.7	99.7	99.8	99.8
Missouri	50.6	50.1	49.8	49.6	49.6	97.3	97.2	97.7	98.1	98.3
Montana	56.2	54.1	52.7	51.9	88.6	90.9	92.4	93.9	95.0	95.7
Nebraska	51.0	50.6	50.3	50.2	50.4	93.1	94.7	96.2	97.1	97.4
Nevada	52.5	54.9	56.1	55.7	86.3	85.3	88.1	90.5	92.0	92.7
New Hampshire	42.0	41.5	41.1	41.0	41.1	83.8	85.4	86.9	88.3	89.7
New Jersey	42.3	40.9	39.7	39.4	39.7	80.5	83.5	85.9	87.9	89.8
New Mexico	—	—	—	51.2	50.6	91.3	94.6	97.4	98.3	97.5
New York	41.8	40.0	38.5	38.1	38.6	78.9	81.2	83.1	85.1	87.2
North Carolina	48.6	48.9	49.1	49.3	49.5	99.7	99.8	99.8	99.8	99.8
North Dakota	44.7	46.3	47.2	47.9	48.7	90.8	92.7	94.4	95.4	95.7
Ohio	47.9	46.9	46.1	45.8	46.0	90.8	92.2	93.5	94.5	95.3
Oklahoma	—	—	51.7	53.9	53.2	98.4	98.9	99.3	99.5	99.5
Oregon	53.2	53.7	54.1	53.6	91.5	92.0	93.0	93.7	94.4	95.2
Pennsylvania	44.2	42.8	41.6	41.5	42.2	86.0	88.7	91.2	92.9	94.0
Rhode Island	38.7	37.6	36.7	36.7	37.3	78.6	81.5	84.0	86.1	87.9
South Carolina	49.0	49.0	49.1	49.2	49.4	99.6	99.7	99.8	99.8	99.8
South Dakota	51.1	51.8	52.4	52.5	52.5	93.4	95.0	96.4	97.2	97.3
Tennessee	50.1	50.1	50.0	50.0	49.9	99.5	99.6	99.6	99.7	99.7
Texas	51.0	50.5	50.0	49.5	49.0	92.4	95.4	98.1	98.5	97.2
Utah	86.1	85.6	85.3	86.7	89.3	91.7	93.3	94.7	95.7	96.2
Vermont	45.7	45.7	45.7	45.7	45.7	91.5	91.8	92.1	92.6	93.3
Virginia	49.2	49.3	49.4	49.6	49.9	98.8	99.1	99.3	99.8	99.8
Washington	54.1	51.9	50.8	86.9	87.9	88.7	90.1	91.3	92.3	93.3
West Virginia	51.7	50.9	50.2	49.8	49.7	94.5	95.6	96.6	97.3	97.7
Wisconsin	47.3	47.0	46.8	43.5	44.4	87.9	90.4	92.6	94.2	95.3
Wyoming	88.9	87.2	86.0	86.8	88.8	90.5	92.7	94.8	95.9	96.2

Notes: Eligibility is the ratio E/A, where E is the number of people eligible by law to vote in a state according to the criteria of citizenship, race, sex, and age laws on suffrage; where race has two dimensions; color (black/white) and bondage (slave/free); and A is the total number of adults in that state. These raw data—number of eligibles and adults in each state—are used to produce the entries. For a more detailed discussion of the methodology used, see the notes to Table 3-1.

Sources: Decennial censuses (1790–1990) of the U.S. Census Bureau; Bureau of U.S. Census Series P pamphlets for 1972 and the 1990s; Richard Scammon's book series, *America Votes* (various publication dates); the data archive of John J. Stucker; and relevant state constitutions and statute volumes. Also see Stucker (1973), Appendix B.

Table 3-14 State Voter Eligibility Percentages in Presidential Elections, 1940–1976

	1940	1944	1948	1952	1956	1960	1964	1968	1972	1976
Alabama	99.7	99.8	99.9	99.8	99.8	99.8	99.8	99.7	99.7	99.6
Alaska	—	—	—	—	—	98.7	98.6	98.6	98.8	98.3
Arizona	91.4	93.7	95.4	96.4	96.9	97.2	97.5	97.7	98.0	97.2
Arkansas	99.8	99.8	99.8	99.8	99.8	99.8	99.8	99.8	99.8	99.6
California	91.2	93.5	95.2	95.7	95.4	95.1	95.0	94.8	94.8	91.9
Colorado	96.4	97.3	98.1	98.5	98.5	98.5	98.6	98.7	98.8	98.4
Connecticut	87.2	90.9	94.0	95.6	95.8	95.9	96.1	96.3	96.6	96.4
Delaware	96.8	97.7	98.5	98.9	98.9	98.8	98.8	98.8	98.9	98.8
Dist. of Columbia	—	—	—	—	—	—	97.1	96.7	96.8	96.3
Florida	97.5	98.1	98.5	98.0	97.1	96.5	96.1	95.7	96.0	95.1
Georgia	99.8	99.8	99.9	99.8	99.7	99.7	99.7	99.6	99.6	99.4
Hawaii	—	—	—	—	—	86.1	88.7	91.0	93.0	91.9
Idaho	97.6	98.2	98.8	99.0	99.0	99.0	99.0	99.0	99.1	98.8
Illinois	95.1	96.5	97.8	98.3	98.1	97.9	97.8	97.6	97.6	96.7
Indiana	98.4	98.8	99.2	99.4	99.3	99.3	99.3	99.3	99.3	99.2
Iowa	98.2	98.7	99.2	99.5	99.5	99.5	99.5	99.5	99.6	99.4
Kansas	98.5	98.9	99.3	99.5	99.5	99.5	99.4	99.4	99.4	99.1
Kentucky	99.7	99.8	99.8	99.8	99.8	99.8	99.8	99.8	99.8	99.6
Louisiana	99.3	99.4	99.5	99.5	99.5	99.5	99.4	99.4	99.4	99.1
Maine	92.5	94.3	95.9	96.8	97.0	97.3	97.6	97.8	98.2	98.4
Maryland	97.3	98.0	98.5	98.7	98.5	98.4	98.3	98.3	98.4	97.9
Massachusetts	88.3	91.6	94.7	96.1	96.2	96.3	96.5	96.6	96.9	96.5
Michigan	92.8	94.9	96.8	97.6	97.7	97.8	97.9	98.0	98.2	98.1
Minnesota	96.3	97.4	98.5	99.0	99.0	99.1	99.1	99.2	99.2	99.1
Mississippi	99.8	99.8	99.8	99.8	99.8	99.8	99.8	99.8	99.8	99.7
Missouri	98.5	98.9	99.4	99.5	99.5	99.5	99.5	99.4	99.5	99.4
Montana	96.4	97.4	98.3	98.9	99.0	99.1	99.2	99.3	99.4	99.4
Nebraska	97.7	98.4	99.0	99.3	99.3	99.3	99.4	99.4	99.4	99.3
Nevada	93.3	95.4	97.0	97.5	97.4	97.4	97.6	97.8	98.0	96.8
New Hampshire	91.0	93.4	95.8	96.9	97.1	97.2	97.5	97.7	98.1	98.3
New Jersey	91.5	93.9	96.1	96.9	96.8	96.7	96.6	96.5	96.8	96.0
New Mexico	96.8	97.5	98.1	98.4	98.5	98.6	98.6	98.7	98.7	98.2
New York	89.1	91.9	94.6	95.7	95.5	95.3	95.2	95.0	95.2	94.2
North Carolina	99.8	99.8	99.8	99.8	99.8	99.7	99.7	99.7	99.7	99.5
North Dakota	96.0	97.2	98.5	99.2	99.3	99.3	99.4	99.5	99.6	99.5
Ohio	96.1	97.2	98.2	98.7	98.8	98.8	98.8	98.9	99.0	98.9
Oklahoma	99.5	99.6	99.7	99.7	99.7	99.6	99.6	99.6	99.6	99.2
Oregon	95.8	97.1	98.1	98.5	98.5	98.5	98.6	98.7	98.8	98.3
Pennsylvania	95.0	96.5	97.9	98.6	98.6	98.7	98.8	98.8	99.0	98.9
Rhode Island	89.6	92.7	95.4	96.7	96.8	96.9	97.1	97.3	97.5	96.6
South Carolina	99.8	99.8	99.9	99.8	99.8	99.7	99.7	99.6	99.6	99.5
South Dakota	97.5	98.3	99.1	99.5	99.5	99.6	99.7	99.7	99.8	99.7
Tennessee	99.8	99.8	99.8	99.8	99.8	99.7	99.7	99.7	99.7	99.6
Texas	96.1	96.6	97.1	97.4	97.5	97.7	97.8	97.9	98.0	96.8
Utah	96.7	97.5	98.1	98.4	98.4	98.3	98.3	98.4	98.5	98.2
Vermont	93.9	95.3	96.7	97.3	97.4	97.5	97.7	97.9	98.2	98.2
Virginia	99.8	99.8	99.8	99.5	99.4	99.3	99.2	99.1	99.1	98.5
Washington	94.2	95.8	97.1	97.7	97.7	97.7	97.8	97.8	98.0	97.5
West Virginia	98.1	98.6	99.1	99.3	99.4	99.4	99.5	99.6	99.7	99.6
Wisconsin	96.2	97.4	98.6	99.1	99.1	99.0	99.1	99.1	99.1	99.1
Wyoming	96.5	97.5	98.3	98.8	98.8	99.0	99.0	99.1	99.2	99.1

Notes: Eligibility is the ratio E/A, where E is the number of people eligible by law to vote in a state according to the criteria of citizenship, race, sex, and age laws on suffrage; where race has two dimensions; color (black/white) and bondage (slave/free); and A is the total number of adults in that state. These raw data—number of eligibles and adults in each state—are used to produce the entries. For a more detailed discussion of the methodology used, see the notes to Table 3-1.

Sources: Decennial censuses (1790–1990) of the U.S. Census Bureau; Bureau of U.S. Census Series P pamphlets for 1972 and the 1990s; Richard Scammon's book series, *America Votes* (various publication dates); the data archive of John J. Stucker; and relevant state constitutions and statute volumes. Also see Stucker (1973), Appendix B.

Table 3-15 State Voter Eligibility Percentages in Presidential Elections, 1980–1996

	1980	1984	1988	1992	1996
Alabama	99.5	99.5	99.4	99.3	99.3
Alaska	97.9	97.6	97.4	97.4	97.6
Arizona	96.7	95.7	95.1	93.4	91.1
Arkansas	99.5	99.5	99.4	99.3	99.1
California	89.5	86.6	84.2	82.4	81.1
Colorado	98.0	97.7	97.5	96.6	95.4
Connecticut	96.2	95.8	95.5	95.4	95.6
Delaware	98.7	98.5	98.3	98.1	97.7
Dist. of Columbia	95.7	94.3	93.0	92.4	92.4
Florida	94.4	93.2	92.2	91.3	90.2
Georgia	99.2	98.7	98.3	98.1	98.0
Hawaii	91.1	91.6	92.0	91.8	90.9
Idaho	98.6	98.3	98.0	97.6	97.1
Illinois	95.9	95.4	94.8	94.4	94.1
Indiana	99.1	99.1	99.1	99.0	98.8
Iowa	99.3	99.2	99.1	98.9	98.5
Kansas	98.9	98.7	98.5	98.1	97.6
Kentucky	99.5	99.5	99.4	99.4	99.3
Louisiana	98.9	98.8	98.6	98.5	98.4
Maine	98.5	98.5	98.5	98.6	98.8
Maryland	97.4	96.6	95.9	95.2	94.5
Massachusetts	96.1	95.3	94.6	94.4	94.9
Michigan	98.0	98.0	98.0	97.9	97.7
Minnesota	98.9	98.7	98.5	98.1	97.6
Mississippi	99.6	99.5	99.5	99.3	98.9
Missouri	99.3	99.2	99.2	99.1	98.9
Montana	99.3	99.3	99.2	99.3	99.5
Nebraska	99.2	99.1	99.1	98.8	98.4
Nevada	96.1	95.1	94.5	93.8	93.3
New Hampshire	98.4	98.2	98.1	98.1	98.2
New Jersey	95.3	94.2	93.2	92.4	91.6
New Mexico	97.7	97.1	96.5	95.9	95.2
New York	93.2	92.0	90.8	89.5	88.1
North Carolina	99.4	99.1	99.0	98.5	98.0
North Dakota	99.4	99.3	99.3	99.3	99.5
Ohio	98.9	98.9	98.9	98.8	98.8
Oklahoma	98.9	98.8	98.7	98.6	98.7
Oregon	97.9	97.4	97.0	96.0	94.7
Pennsylvania	98.8	98.7	98.6	98.5	98.5
Rhode Island	95.8	95.2	94.6	94.1	93.7
South Carolina	99.3	99.3	99.2	99.2	99.3
South Dakota	99.6	99.5	99.5	99.5	99.5
Tennessee	99.5	99.4	99.3	99.2	99.2
Texas	95.8	94.6	93.5	92.6	91.9
Utah	97.9	97.7	97.5	97.0	96.3
Vermont	98.3	98.4	98.4	98.5	98.5
Virginia	98.1	97.4	96.9	96.4	96.0
Washington	97.1	96.6	96.2	96.0	96.0
West Virginia	99.5	99.5	99.6	99.6	99.5
Wisconsin	99.0	98.9	98.7	98.6	98.5
Wyoming	99.0	99.0	99.0	99.0	99.0

Notes: Eligibility is the ratio E/A, where E is the number of people eligible by law to vote in a state according to the criteria of citizenship, race, sex, and age laws on suffrage; where race has two dimensions; color (black/white) and bondage (slave/free); and A is the total number of adults in that state. These raw data—number of eligibles and adults in each state—are used to produce the entries. For a more detailed discussion of the methodology used, see the notes to Table 3-1.

Sources: Decennial censuses (1790–1990) of the U.S. Census Bureau; Bureau of U.S. Census Series P pamphlets for 1972 and the 1990s; Richard Scammon's book series, *America Votes* (various publication dates); the data archive of John J. Stucker; and relevant state constitutions and statute volumes. Also see Stucker (1973), Appendix B.

Table 3-16 State Voter Mobilization Percentages in Presidential Elections, 1788–1816

	1788	1792	1796	1800	1804	1808	1812	1816
Alabama	—	—	—	—	—	—	—	—
Alaska	—	—	—	—	—	—	—	—
Arizona	—	—	—	—	—	—	—	—
Arkansas	—	—	—	—	—	—	—	—
California	—	—	—	—	—	—	—	—
Colorado	—	—	—	—	—	—	—	—
Connecticut	—	—	—	—	—	—	—	—
Delaware	—	—	—	—	—	—	—	—
Dist. of Columbia	—	—	—	—	—	—	—	—
Florida	—	—	—	—	—	—	—	—
Georgia	—	—	—	—	—	—	—	—
Hawaii	—	—	—	—	—	—	—	—
Idaho	—	—	—	—	—	—	—	—
Illinois	—	—	—	—	—	—	—	—
Indiana	—	—	—	—	—	—	—	—
Iowa	—	—	—	—	—	—	—	—
Kansas	—	—	—	—	—	—	—	—
Kentucky	—	—	—	—	—	—	—	—
Louisiana	—	—	—	—	—	—	—	—
Maine	—	—	—	—	—	—	—	—
Maryland	7.4	—	9.7	14.5	6.5	15.4	17.8	6.2
Massachusetts	8.5	—	8.4	—	27.2	—	34.6	—
Michigan	—	—	—	—	—	—	—	—
Minnesota	—	—	—	—	—	—	—	—
Mississippi	—	—	—	—	—	—	—	—
Missouri	—	—	—	—	—	—	—	—
Montana	—	—	—	—	—	—	—	—
Nebraska	—	—	—	—	—	—	—	—
Nevada	—	—	—	—	—	—	—	—
New Hampshire	9.9	14.1	26.0	—	21.0	29.9	27.8	27.5
New Jersey	—	—	—	—	14.1	33.4	—	4.8
New Mexico	—	—	—	—	—	—	—	—
New York	—	—	—	—	—	—	—	—
North Carolina	—	—	—	—	—	—	—	4.3
North Dakota	—	—	—	—	—	—	—	—
Ohio	—	—	—	—	6.7	6.9	9.7	2.4
Oklahoma	—	—	—	—	—	—	—	—
Oregon	—	—	—	—	—	—	—	—
Pennsylvania	—	—	11.3	—	8.3	17.3	22.5	11.0
Rhode Island	—	—	—	14.3	4.0	16.9	16.8	3.3
South Carolina	—	—	—	—	—	—	—	—
South Dakota	—	—	—	—	—	—	—	—
Tennessee	—	—	—	—	—	—	—	—
Texas	—	—	—	—	—	—	—	—
Utah	—	—	—	—	—	—	—	—
Vermont	—	—	—	—	—	—	—	—
Virginia	—	—	—	7.6	3.6	5.5	5.4	1.7
Washington	—	—	—	—	—	—	—	—
West Virginia	—	—	—	—	—	—	—	—
Wisconsin	—	—	—	—	—	—	—	—
Wyoming	—	—	—	—	—	—	—	—

Notes: Mobilization is the ratio V/A, where V is the total vote cast in the presidential race in a given election year in a state, and A is the total number of adults in that state. These raw data—number of presidential votes cast and adults in each state—are used to produce the entries. States with partial presidential vote data are not included. For a more detailed discussion of the methodology used, see the notes to Table 3-2.

Sources: Adults—decennial censuses (1790–1990) of the U.S. Census Bureau; Bureau of U.S. Census Series P pamphlets for 1972 and the 1990s; and Richard Scammon's book series, *America Votes* (various publication dates). Presidential vote—Tables 4-37 through 4-63.

Table 3-17 State Voter Mobilization Percentages in Presidential Elections, 1820–1856

	1820	1824	1828	1832	1836	1840	1844	1848	1852	1856
Alabama	—	18.4	18.4	10.4	20.4	27.4	24.2	20.8	13.3	20.6
Alaska	—	—	—	—	—	—	—	—	—	—
Arizona	—	—	—	—	—	—	—	—	—	—
Arkansas	—	—	—	—	13.9	32.0	27.7	23.4	19.7	23.9
California	—	—	—	—	—	—	—	—	76.3	73.1
Colorado	—	—	—	—	—	—	—	—	—	—
Connecticut	2.9	7.7	13.3	21.6	24.2	34.9	35.9	31.6	30.8	33.7
Delaware	—	—	—	25.1	26.1	31.2	32.7	30.9	29.0	30.5
Dist. of Columbia	—	—	—	—	—	—	—	—	—	—
Florida	—	—	—	—	—	—	—	20.4	17.1	22.2
Georgia	—	—	10.6	9.6	19.5	26.8	28.1	26.8	16.6	24.3
Hawaii	—	—	—	—	—	—	—	—	—	—
Idaho	—	—	—	—	—	—	—	—	—	—
Illinois	7.0	13.3	28.5	25.6	24.4	48.8	42.4	38.6	35.3	39.5
Indiana	—	19.6	36.1	38.1	36.3	45.3	44.4	41.0	42.1	46.4
Iowa	—	—	—	—	—	—	—	33.6	29.3	44.9
Kansas	—	—	—	—	—	—	—	—	—	—
Kentucky	—	10.2	28.3	29.6	24.4	29.9	32.8	30.3	26.4	31.1
Louisiana	—	—	9.0	5.4	5.1	11.0	12.9	13.9	12.9	13.8
Maine	4.4	8.8	21.2	33.6	18.8	41.0	34.1	32.2	28.2	35.7
Maryland	2.9	18.0	23.5	18.9	23.0	28.9	28.7	27.6	26.4	28.4
Massachusetts	9.5	15.3	13.1	20.7	20.8	32.2	28.9	25.9	21.9	26.8
Michigan	—	—	—	—	19.7	47.6	43.8	40.3	38.8	44.1
Minnesota	—	—	—	—	—	—	—	—	—	—
Mississippi	—	12.3	16.9	7.8	17.8	24.0	23.6	23.0	16.9	20.4
Missouri	—	9.6	25.3	7.4	16.9	36.1	36.3	28.7	21.1	25.5
Montana	—	—	—	—	—	—	—	—	—	—
Nebraska	—	—	—	—	—	—	—	—	—	—
Nevada	—	—	—	—	—	—	—	—	—	—
New Hampshire	8.5	8.5	34.8	32.8	17.9	41.2	31.3	29.7	28.5	38.4
New Jersey	3.6	15.4	33.1	32.3	32.4	37.6	38.4	34.6	32.5	33.4
New Mexico	—	—	—	—	—	—	—	—	—	—
New York	—	—	34.6	36.1	30.0	38.8	37.0	30.6	31.4	32.4
North Carolina	1.3	13.4	18.1	10.0	16.6	26.2	24.9	22.5	20.8	21.1
North Dakota	—	—	—	—	—	—	—	—	—	—
Ohio	3.3	18.3	39.7	38.5	39.4	44.0	43.5	40.2	38.9	39.1
Oklahoma	—	—	—	—	—	—	—	—	—	—
Oregon	—	—	—	—	—	—	—	—	—	—
Pennsylvania	7.4	9.6	27.8	25.8	26.1	37.9	37.4	36.3	34.0	36.6
Rhode Island	1.8	5.5	7.8	11.6	10.7	15.2	18.4	14.5	20.2	21.9
South Carolina	—	—	—	—	—	—	—	—	—	—
South Dakota	—	—	—	—	—	—	—	—	—	—
Tennessee	—	11.0	20.5	11.4	21.9	35.1	34.9	32.3	28.2	30.6
Texas	—	—	—	—	—	—	—	32.0	16.9	26.3
Utah	—	—	—	—	—	—	—	—	—	—
Vermont	—	—	26.7	24.8	26.0	36.3	32.8	30.3	26.7	30.4
Virginia	1.2	3.3	7.9	8.9	10.4	16.3	16.8	15.2	20.7	22.3
Washington	—	—	—	—	—	—	—	—	—	—
West Virginia	—	—	—	—	—	—	—	—	—	—
Wisconsin	—	—	—	—	—	—	—	33.3	35.0	44.8
Wyoming	—	—	—	—	—	—	—	—	—	—

Notes: Mobilization is the ratio V/A, where V is the total vote cast in the presidential race in a given election year in a state, and A is the total number of adults in that state. These raw data—number of presidential votes cast and adults in each state—are used to produce the entries. States with partial presidential vote data are not included. For a more detailed discussion of the methodology used, see the notes to Table 3-2.

Sources: Adults—decennial censuses (1790–1990) of the U.S. Census Bureau; Bureau of U.S. Census Series P pamphlets for 1972 and the 1990s; and Richard Scammon's book series, *America Votes* (various publication dates). Presidential vote—Tables 4-37 through 4-63.

Table 3-18 State Voter Mobilization Percentages in Presidential Elections, 1860–1896

	1860	1864	1868	1872	1876	1880	1884	1888	1892	1896
Alabama	22.5	—	35.5	37.7	34.4	27.8	26.1	27.7	33.7	25.6
Alaska	—	—	—	—	—	—	—	—	—	—
Arizona	—	—	—	—	—	—	—	—	—	—
Arkansas	31.2	—	21.1	34.5	33.8	31.3	31.7	34.9	29.6	27.4
California	59.6	42.1	36.0	26.5	36.0	32.6	33.1	36.5	34.8	34.8
Colorado	—	—	—	—	—	42.4	37.9	40.9	35.5	64.7
Connecticut	28.8	31.2	33.0	30.0	35.6	36.2	34.2	35.3	34.7	33.7
Delaware	30.9	30.5	31.6	34.3	34.6	38.7	36.4	33.5	39.4	38.5
Dist. of Columbia	—	—	—	—	—	—	—	—	—	—
Florida	22.7	—	—	37.8	44.9	42.8	41.5	39.5	18.1	20.5
Georgia	24.4	—	32.6	25.8	29.9	23.4	19.9	18.5	26.5	17.6
Hawaii	—	—	—	—	—	—	—	—	—	—
Idaho	—	—	—	—	—	—	—	—	36.3	42.7
Illinois	44.0	37.4	41.2	34.7	40.3	41.1	39.1	38.8	40.5	45.1
Indiana	47.0	43.3	47.9	44.1	49.0	48.8	47.4	48.3	46.2	49.1
Iowa	44.3	34.2	39.9	37.0	43.1	41.6	45.9	43.2	43.3	46.9
Kansas	—	21.6	29.1	43.0	35.4	43.0	44.7	50.6	45.3	45.2
Kentucky	29.8	17.6	27.8	31.4	38.4	35.8	37.1	47.0	42.7	47.9
Louisiana	14.7	—	33.0	35.5	36.6	24.1	24.6	23.8	21.7	17.2
Maine	31.2	34.6	33.2	25.8	32.1	38.0	32.8	32.4	28.7	28.3
Maryland	28.4	21.0	25.2	33.8	37.6	36.3	41.6	39.5	37.5	41.0
Massachusetts	24.6	23.4	24.2	21.8	26.6	26.5	27.0	26.2	26.9	25.1
Michigan	43.5	36.8	41.6	34.4	42.3	41.0	37.3	43.6	39.2	42.6
Minnesota	43.1	32.8	40.3	38.5	40.5	40.1	37.9	43.3	37.5	42.1
Mississippi	21.5	—	—	34.2	38.4	24.4	24.0	22.0	9.2	11.1
Missouri	32.6	17.1	21.5	33.7	38.5	39.3	38.9	41.4	39.1	44.6
Montana	—	—	—	—	—	—	—	—	44.8	42.7
Nebraska	—	—	29.0	27.8	31.7	40.1	39.4	43.7	37.8	41.5
Nevada	—	61.0	43.4	43.0	52.0	44.1	34.8	39.5	37.4	36.6
New Hampshire	35.4	37.1	36.1	35.3	38.9	39.9	37.5	38.8	36.7	33.1
New Jersey	35.9	33.0	36.8	33.8	39.7	40.2	37.5	38.9	38.4	37.4
New Mexico	—	—	—	—	—	—	—	—	—	—
New York	33.4	33.9	37.2	33.7	38.1	38.4	37.1	38.7	36.0	35.2
North Carolina	22.7	—	39.2	32.8	41.5	38.6	40.7	41.2	37.9	41.5
North Dakota	—	—	—	—	—	—	—	—	34.0	35.8
Ohio	41.4	41.0	42.1	39.4	44.2	44.4	44.1	43.6	41.0	45.5
Oklahoma	—	—	—	—	—	—	—	—	—	—
Oregon	60.7	57.8	56.3	38.3	41.7	45.0	42.4	39.3	41.8	45.6
Pennsylvania	34.5	37.7	39.4	30.7	37.6	39.7	36.5	36.6	33.6	36.6
Rhode Island	20.5	21.3	16.4	14.4	18.0	17.9	18.1	20.6	24.4	22.9
South Carolina	—	—	34.6	28.4	47.6	39.3	20.5	17.0	14.1	12.8
South Dakota	—	—	—	—	—	—	—	—	40.9	44.7
Tennessee	31.6	—	15.7	31.4	35.7	35.9	35.8	39.3	32.0	35.7
Texas	25.6	—	—	27.9	27.3	33.7	40.0	38.8	39.1	44.5
Utah	—	—	—	—	—	—	—	—	—	67.5
Vermont	26.3	31.8	31.2	28.3	34.1	33.8	30.3	31.9	27.5	30.6
Virginia	23.6	—	—	31.2	36.7	30.4	39.3	40.4	36.8	34.8
Washington	—	—	—	—	—	—	—	—	38.4	34.9
West Virginia	—	19.0	26.2	30.1	41.4	41.1	43.5	47.8	45.9	48.1
Wisconsin	43.1	37.0	42.6	37.5	44.5	41.6	43.7	43.2	40.9	45.0
Wyoming	—	—	—	—	—	—	—	—	41.3	44.4

Notes: Mobilization is the ratio V/A, where V is the total vote cast in the presidential race in a given election year in a state, and A is the total number of adults in that state. These raw data—number of presidential votes cast and adults in each state—are used to produce the entries. States with partial presidential vote data are not included. For a more detailed discussion of the methodology used, see the notes to Table 3-2.

Sources: Adults—decennial censuses (1790–1990) of the U.S. Census Bureau; Bureau of U.S. Census Series P pamphlets for 1972 and the 1990s; and Richard Scammon's book series, *America Votes* (various publication dates). Presidential vote—Tables 4-37 through 4-63.

Table 3-19 State Voter Mobilization Percentages in Presidential Elections, 1900–1936

	1900	1904	1908	1912	1916	1920	1924	1928	1932	1936
Alabama	19.3	12.0	10.8	11.3	11.9	20.5	13.4	19.0	17.6	18.7
Alaska	—	—	—	—	—	—	—	—	—	—
Arizona	—	—	—	18.0	36.3	35.5	35.2	39.2	46.7	45.9
Arkansas	21.6	17.8	21.2	16.2	20.8	21.2	15.3	20.9	21.8	17.1
California	32.2	27.6	26.5	39.0	49.3	40.7	43.6	50.5	55.7	58.9
Colorado	68.6	62.9	58.3	53.1	54.8	51.7	58.2	64.1	71.3	72.1
Connecticut	32.2	31.4	28.9	26.7	27.6	43.6	44.6	57.8	58.2	63.4
Delaware	39.9	39.4	40.9	39.4	39.8	69.5	64.3	71.5	73.0	76.8
Dist. of Columbia	—	—	—	—	—	—	—	—	—	—
Florida	15.4	12.4	13.5	12.1	16.9	27.1	16.3	31.5	29.6	30.4
Georgia	12.1	11.9	11.2	9.6	11.9	10.5	11.5	15.6	16.5	17.6
Hawaii	—	—	—	—	—	—	—	—	—	—
Idaho	68.0	58.8	60.2	55.3	63.3	59.1	61.8	62.0	71.7	69.7
Illinois	42.2	36.7	36.3	33.3	59.4	53.1	57.4	66.7	68.8	76.6
Indiana	47.5	46.2	46.4	40.1	42.2	71.0	68.1	72.6	76.9	77.1
Iowa	44.2	39.6	39.5	37.9	38.0	62.6	66.9	67.7	67.6	72.1
Kansas	45.9	39.1	41.2	38.0	63.4	55.7	62.1	64.3	69.7	75.3
Kentucky	44.0	39.2	42.3	37.6	41.7	71.2	60.6	67.4	67.1	59.7
Louisiana	10.5	7.6	9.7	9.5	10.6	13.7	12.1	19.8	22.7	25.8
Maine	24.6	21.9	23.4	27.9	29.0	41.6	40.0	54.1	60.1	59.1
Maryland	40.6	32.6	33.0	30.3	32.2	49.7	39.1	54.5	49.4	56.3
Massachusetts	23.8	23.6	22.6	22.6	23.3	41.2	44.8	60.0	57.8	65.2
Michigan	39.7	35.1	33.6	31.0	32.5	47.3	46.3	49.1	55.0	56.4
Minnesota	34.8	29.1	29.9	27.8	30.0	53.3	56.9	64.5	63.1	66.7
Mississippi	8.6	7.8	8.3	7.6	10.1	9.4	12.0	15.1	13.7	14.3
Missouri	41.8	37.2	39.3	36.7	39.9	65.3	61.5	67.5	69.5	75.9
Montana	42.4	34.4	31.5	31.7	62.0	55.8	54.5	60.8	66.4	67.6
Nebraska	44.2	38.4	42.3	37.3	40.8	51.8	60.4	68.6	69.8	73.5
Nevada	37.5	30.6	47.2	35.3	61.0	52.1	48.4	54.9	65.0	63.1
New Hampshire	35.2	33.9	33.2	32.1	32.1	56.6	57.6	67.5	68.4	69.7
New Jersey	36.3	34.1	32.7	27.3	28.4	48.0	50.8	64.8	63.3	67.3
New Mexico	—	—	—	28.5	37.5	56.9	57.0	56.1	65.8	65.7
New York	35.4	33.3	30.6	27.5	27.8	44.5	45.5	56.4	55.9	63.1
North Carolina	34.2	22.5	25.5	22.9	25.5	44.5	35.9	43.0	43.9	47.3
North Dakota	36.4	32.8	35.2	28.7	37.0	63.7	59.1	68.3	71.0	74.5
Ohio	43.6	38.8	40.3	34.4	35.4	56.8	53.2	62.4	61.8	68.4
Oklahoma	—	—	35.5	29.9	31.3	47.5	46.8	50.1	54.1	56.1
Oregon	34.8	28.6	28.5	31.2	56.0	48.2	51.2	53.7	57.0	59.4
Pennsylvania	33.1	31.8	29.8	26.8	27.1	36.7	40.6	56.9	49.3	68.1
Rhode Island	21.7	23.8	22.9	23.1	24.9	45.6	53.9	57.8	61.6	68.5
South Carolina	8.8	9.1	10.1	7.2	8.6	8.6	6.4	8.5	12.2	12.5
South Dakota	48.3	41.5	39.6	36.5	38.9	52.8	56.4	69.3	74.7	76.6
Tennessee	28.4	23.9	24.1	22.5	23.3	35.2	23.2	25.6	26.4	30.0
Texas	30.7	14.8	16.4	15.1	16.9	20.0	23.9	23.4	26.1	23.6
Utah	72.5	66.4	61.3	56.8	67.2	63.8	64.6	68.6	75.6	74.5
Vermont	26.5	24.1	24.1	28.6	29.5	41.4	47.1	61.5	61.7	63.9
Virginia	29.3	13.6	13.5	12.7	13.3	19.1	18.0	23.8	22.0	23.0
Washington	35.1	30.8	28.8	43.2	47.5	46.5	45.9	51.1	58.7	61.8
West Virginia	47.3	45.3	43.6	41.4	41.3	67.8	71.9	73.8	79.6	83.0
Wisconsin	40.9	38.0	36.3	29.8	31.2	45.9	51.8	59.1	61.3	65.6
Wyoming	45.3	44.0	44.5	43.7	48.8	48.6	65.2	64.0	70.5	70.6

Notes: Mobilization is the ratio V/A, where V is the total vote cast in the presidential race in a given election year in a state, and A is the total number of adults in that state. These raw data—number of presidential votes cast and adults in each state—are used to produce the entries. States with partial presidential vote data are not included. For a more detailed discussion of the methodology used, see the notes to Table 3-2.

Sources: Adults—decennial censuses (1790–1990) of the U.S. Census Bureau; Bureau of U.S. Census Series P pamphlets for 1972 and the 1990s; and Richard Scammon's book series, *America Votes* (various publication dates). Presidential vote—Tables 4-37 through 4-63.

Table 3-20 State Voter Mobilization Percentages in Presidential Elections, 1940–1976

	1940	1944	1948	1952	1956	1960	1964	1968	1972	1976
Alabama	18.9	15.0	12.6	24.1	27.6	31.1	36.1	52.9	43.3	46.8
Alaska	—	—	—	—	—	45.5	46.2	52.8	46.9	52.1
Arizona	52.0	39.4	43.1	52.1	47.1	54.5	56.5	50.2	47.4	45.8
Arkansas	18.2	19.2	21.8	36.8	38.0	41.1	51.3	54.2	48.1	51.7
California	66.9	60.5	59.6	66.8	63.0	67.4	66.0	61.8	59.5	50.2
Colorado	76.9	65.9	62.9	71.4	68.7	71.4	68.2	65.0	59.5	58.7
Connecticut	67.4	66.6	66.0	77.0	74.1	76.8	71.6	69.3	66.2	63.1
Delaware	76.8	65.7	68.1	78.3	72.7	73.6	69.6	68.8	62.1	58.5
Dist. of Columbia	—	—	—	—	—	—	40.3	35.8	30.4	32.7
Florida	39.9	33.1	33.9	47.6	43.6	50.0	51.6	53.4	48.6	49.6
Georgia	17.6	17.6	21.4	31.4	29.8	30.4	45.2	47.5	37.3	42.1
Hawaii	—	—	—	—	—	51.3	52.3	54.7	49.4	47.1
Idaho	75.1	63.6	62.8	78.1	75.2	80.7	75.4	72.6	63.3	61.0
Illinois	78.4	71.9	68.2	74.4	71.6	75.7	72.7	69.3	62.3	59.9
Indiana	79.8	70.7	66.5	75.2	73.4	76.9	72.2	70.5	60.8	60.3
Iowa	74.1	63.4	61.7	75.1	73.6	76.5	70.6	69.0	64.0	63.9
Kansas	74.0	61.4	64.3	71.2	67.1	70.3	63.9	64.1	59.5	58.9
Kentucky	59.3	51.7	47.8	56.0	57.4	59.2	54.9	55.2	48.0	48.6
Louisiana	27.1	23.9	27.0	40.0	36.0	44.8	47.2	55.1	44.0	48.6
Maine	60.2	53.8	46.6	60.9	60.7	72.6	64.9	66.3	60.3	64.6
Maryland	55.7	46.0	40.9	56.7	54.3	57.2	54.6	55.1	49.8	49.9
Massachusetts	69.5	64.7	66.9	74.2	72.7	76.1	70.0	67.5	62.0	62.1
Michigan	61.8	60.1	53.3	66.6	70.2	72.4	66.6	65.7	59.4	59.0
Minnesota	69.6	61.1	64.2	71.5	68.2	77.0	74.4	73.0	68.7	71.7
Mississippi	14.7	15.0	15.9	23.8	20.9	25.5	34.1	53.3	44.2	48.6
Missouri	73.3	61.4	60.4	71.3	68.5	71.8	65.6	63.6	57.3	57.5
Montana	69.6	57.2	60.8	70.6	71.0	71.4	70.5	68.3	67.6	64.2
Nebraska	73.6	66.6	57.1	70.9	67.2	71.4	66.9	60.5	56.4	56.7
Nevada	70.6	61.6	61.6	68.0	65.3	61.2	60.4	56.5	49.5	42.4
New Hampshire	72.4	68.3	66.6	76.5	73.2	79.4	71.9	69.3	63.6	57.2
New Jersey	69.6	64.5	60.0	70.0	67.9	71.8	69.4	66.2	59.8	58.1
New Mexico	64.5	47.5	52.4	59.6	56.4	62.1	62.9	60.2	57.7	53.8
New York	67.4	64.7	60.7	68.0	66.5	67.0	64.5	59.8	56.3	51.1
North Carolina	42.6	38.0	35.4	51.3	47.4	53.5	52.1	54.5	42.8	43.2
North Dakota	75.2	59.4	60.0	74.2	70.6	78.5	72.7	69.7	68.3	68.1
Ohio	72.4	64.8	57.1	68.6	65.9	71.3	65.6	63.3	57.3	55.4
Oklahoma	60.3	52.6	52.3	68.3	61.3	63.8	62.9	60.9	56.7	54.8
Oregon	64.3	56.5	55.1	68.4	70.5	72.3	67.9	66.0	62.1	60.5
Pennsylvania	64.2	57.4	54.4	65.3	64.8	70.5	66.9	65.0	56.0	54.5
Rhode Island	67.7	59.9	62.4	77.0	71.9	75.1	69.6	66.3	61.0	59.3
South Carolina	10.1	9.8	12.7	29.1	24.6	30.5	39.0	46.7	38.2	40.7
South Dakota	79.5	59.0	62.8	73.7	74.3	78.3	75.3	72.6	69.4	64.8
Tennessee	30.6	28.1	28.6	44.6	45.9	50.3	51.8	53.8	43.5	48.8
Texas	29.1	27.3	27.4	42.4	37.5	41.8	44.2	48.4	45.0	46.2
Utah	80.3	72.8	74.0	81.3	76.5	80.1	78.9	76.9	69.4	67.2
Vermont	62.7	54.1	52.4	65.0	65.5	72.5	67.2	63.4	60.7	55.7
Virginia	22.3	22.3	21.7	29.8	31.8	33.4	41.6	50.5	44.7	47.6
Washington	66.5	63.9	60.9	69.3	69.6	72.3	67.9	65.6	63.1	58.4
West Virginia	81.4	64.5	65.1	75.7	74.3	77.3	73.5	70.4	62.5	57.6
Wisconsin	69.6	63.8	58.5	71.5	67.4	73.4	69.1	66.5	62.5	66.7
Wyoming	72.2	61.5	58.3	71.4	66.9	74.0	74.2	65.5	64.4	56.9

Notes: Mobilization is the ratio V/A, where V is the total vote cast in the presidential race in a given election year in a state, and A is the total number of adults in that state. These raw data—number of presidential votes cast and adults in each state—are used to produce the entries. States with partial presidential vote data are not included. For a more detailed discussion of the methodology used, see the notes to Table 3-2.

Sources: Adults—decennial censuses (1790–1990) of the U.S. Census Bureau; Bureau of U.S. Census Series P pamphlets for 1972 and the 1990s; and Richard Scammon's book series, *America Votes* (various publication dates). Presidential vote—Tables 4-37 through 4-63.

Table 3-21 State Voter Mobilization Percentages in Presidential Elections, 1980–1996

	1980	1984	1988	1992	1996
Alabama	49.1	50.9	47.0	55.2	47.7
Alaska	58.4	66.2	56.2	65.9	57.2
Arizona	45.4	46.0	46.3	51.3	42.2
Arkansas	51.9	53.2	48.5	53.8	48.0
California	49.7	49.6	46.9	49.6	43.1
Colorado	56.9	58.3	58.1	61.2	53.4
Connecticut	61.6	61.5	58.0	64.2	56.1
Delaware	55.1	55.6	51.2	55.8	49.1
Dist. of Columbia	35.4	42.9	39.3	48.1	42.1
Florida	49.9	49.4	45.1	51.1	48.0
Georgia	41.8	42.4	39.6	46.6	42.2
Hawaii	44.0	45.1	44.3	44.4	41.6
Idaho	68.6	62.1	59.6	64.7	58.5
Illinois	58.0	58.0	54.1	59.1	49.6
Indiana	57.9	56.4	53.6	55.3	49.3
Iowa	63.1	63.6	59.4	65.0	57.9
Kansas	57.1	58.2	55.3	62.8	56.6
Kentucky	50.2	51.9	49.0	53.4	47.5
Louisiana	53.9	58.4	54.8	59.0	57.4
Maine	65.1	65.1	62.0	73.2	63.9
Maryland	50.5	51.1	48.9	54.1	47.2
Massachusetts	59.4	58.0	57.5	59.3	54.2
Michigan	60.1	57.2	54.2	61.6	53.8
Minnesota	70.7	68.9	66.6	71.6	64.2
Mississippi	52.3	53.6	51.7	52.4	45.4
Missouri	59.1	58.1	55.8	61.9	54.2
Montana	65.6	68.2	63.9	68.8	63.9
Nebraska	57.1	57.5	57.8	63.0	56.0
Nevada	42.4	40.2	41.6	50.3	38.3
New Hampshire	58.0	53.3	56.6	63.6	57.0
New Jersey	55.4	57.5	53.3	56.0	50.9
New Mexico	51.6	53.6	50.5	51.1	46.2
New York	48.2	51.5	47.8	50.6	46.4
North Carolina	43.9	47.9	43.9	50.3	45.6
North Dakota	65.3	66.8	64.2	66.0	56.3
Ohio	55.6	58.0	55.1	60.7	54.5
Oklahoma	53.0	56.4	51.3	59.2	49.8
Oregon	61.9	61.5	57.9	66.2	57.6
Pennsylvania	52.2	54.6	50.3	54.5	49.5
Rhode Island	59.1	55.9	53.0	58.8	51.5
South Carolina	41.0	41.5	39.6	45.4	41.0
South Dakota	67.5	64.9	63.2	66.2	61.3
Tennessee	49.1	49.8	45.6	52.5	47.3
Texas	45.8	49.9	46.4	48.5	40.8
Utah	65.6	63.6	61.0	63.1	49.4
Vermont	58.3	60.5	59.5	67.9	58.6
Virginia	48.2	51.2	48.5	53.3	47.9
Washington	58.2	58.2	53.6	60.7	55.1
West Virginia	53.1	53.5	48.1	50.1	45.7
Wisconsin	67.9	64.1	61.7	68.9	57.7
Wyoming	54.5	58.8	55.3	61.3	61.3

Notes: Mobilization is the ratio V/A, where V is the total vote cast in the presidential race in a given election year in a state, and A is the total number of adults in that state. These raw data—number of presidential votes cast and adults in each state—are used to produce the entries. States with partial presidential vote data are not included. For a more detailed discussion of the methodology used, see the notes to Table 3-2.

Sources: Adults—decennial censuses (1790–1990) of the U.S. Census Bureau; Bureau of U.S. Census Series P pamphlets for 1972 and the 1990s; and Richard Scammon's book series, *America Votes* (various publication dates). Presidential vote—Tables 4-37 through 4-63.

Table 3-22 State Voter Turnout Percentages in Presidential Elections, 1788–1816

	1788	1792	1796	1800	1804	1808	1812	1816
Alabama	—	—	—	—	—	—	—	—
Alaska	—	—	—	—	—	—	—	—
Arizona	—	—	—	—	—	—	—	—
Arkansas	—	—	—	—	—	—	—	—
California	—	—	—	—	—	—	—	—
Colorado	—	—	—	—	—	—	—	—
Connecticut	—	—	—	—	—	—	—	—
Delaware	—	—	—	—	—	—	—	—
Dist. of Columbia	—	—	—	—	—	—	—	—
Florida	—	—	—	—	—	—	—	—
Georgia	—	—	—	—	—	—	—	—
Hawaii	—	—	—	—	—	—	—	—
Idaho	—	—	—	—	—	—	—	—
Illinois	—	—	—	—	—	—	—	—
Indiana	—	—	—	—	—	—	—	—
Iowa	—	—	—	—	—	—	—	—
Kansas	—	—	—	—	—	—	—	—
Kentucky	—	—	—	—	—	—	—	—
Louisiana	—	—	—	—	—	—	—	—
Maine	—	—	—	—	—	—	—	—
Maryland	20.9	—	27.1	40.4	18.0	42.1	47.8	16.4
Massachusetts	14.6	—	13.6	—	41.4	—	54.1	
Michigan	—	—	—	—	—	—	—	—
Minnesota	—	—	—	—	—	—	—	—
Mississippi	—	—	—	—	—	—	—	—
Missouri	—	—	—	—	—	—	—	—
Montana	—	—	—	—	—	—	—	—
Nebraska	—	—	—	—	—	—	—	—
Nevada	—	—	—	—	—	—	—	—
New Hampshire	19.8	28.4	52.9	—	43.1	61.8	57.7	57.4
New Jersey	—	—	—	—	29.3	69.2	—	10.0
New Mexico	—	—	—	—	—	—	—	—
New York	—	—	—	—	—	—	—	—
North Carolina	—	—	—	—	—	—	—	12.6
North Dakota	—	—	—	—	—	—	—	—
Ohio	—	—	—	—	12.1	12.7	18.1	4.5
Oklahoma	—	—	—	—	—	—	—	—
Oregon	—	—	—	—	—	—	—	—
Pennsylvania	—	—	21.6	—	16.1	33.7	44.0	21.6
Rhode Island	—	—	—	31.1	8.5	36.0	36.0	7.0
South Carolina	—	—	—	—	—	—	—	—
South Dakota	—	—	—	—	—	—	—	—
Tennessee	—	—	—	—	—	—	—	—
Texas	—	—	—	—	—	—	—	—
Utah	—	—	—	—	—	—	—	—
Vermont	—	—	—	—	—	—	—	—
Virginia	—	—	—	24.9	11.3	16.9	16.7	5.4
Washington	—	—	—	—	—	—	—	—
West Virginia	—	—	—	—	—	—	—	—
Wisconsin	—	—	—	—	—	—	—	—
Wyoming	—	—	—	—	—	—	—	—

Notes: Turnout is the ratio V/E, where V is the total vote cast in the presidential race in a given election year in a state, and E is the number of people eligible by law to vote in that state according to the criteria of citizenship, race, sex, and age laws on suffrage, where race has two dimensions: color (black/white) and bondage (slave/free). These raw data—number of presidential votes cast and eligibles in a state—are used to produce the entries. States with partial presidential vote data are not included. For a more detailed discussion of the methodology used, see the notes to Table 3-3.

Sources: Eligibles—decennial censuses (1790–1990) of the U.S. Census Bureau; Bureau of U.S. Census Series P Pamphlets for 1972 and the 1990s; Richard Scammon's book series, *America Votes* (various publication dates); the data archive of John J. Stucker; and relevant state constitutions and statute volumes. See also Stucker (1973), Appendix B. Presidential vote—Tables 4-37 through 4-63.

Table 3-23 State Voter Turnout Percentages in Presidential Elections, 1820–1856

	1820	1824	1828	1832	1836	1840	1844	1848	1852	1856
Alabama	—	49.1	52.6	31.5	64.9	89.7	81.3	71.5	46.5	72.1
Alaska	—	—	—	—	—	—	—	—	—	—
Arizona	—	—	—	—	—	—	—	—	—	—
Arkansas	—	—	—	—	28.8	67.7	62.2	54.1	46.8	58.1
California	—	—	—	—	—	—	—	—	84.7	85.8
Colorado	—	—	—	—	—	—	—	—	—	—
Connecticut	6.2	16.7	28.7	46.6	52.3	75.6	.76.3	66.2	64.3	70.5
Delaware	—	—	—	67.1	69.5	82.8	84.7	78.7	72.4	74.7
Dist. of Columbia	—	—	—	—	—	—	—	—	—	—
Florida	—	—	—	—	—	—	—	63.5	54.6	71.9
Georgia	—	—	35.6	32.0	64.3	88.2	93.2	89.6	55.8	82.5
Hawaii	—	—	—	—	—	—	—	—	—	—
Idaho	—	—	—	—	—	—	—	—	—	—
Illinois	12.3	24.1	52.2	46.1	43.3	85.9	76.6	70.7	64.8	72.4
Indiana	—	37.1	68.9	72.8	69.4	86.4	84.7	78.2	80.2	88.3
Iowa	—	—	—	—	—	—	—	61.0	53.7	82.2
Kansas	—	—	—	—	—	—	—	—	—	—
Kentucky	—	25.4	70.7	74.0	60.8	74.3	80.4	73.6	63.3	73.7
Louisiana	—	—	36.3	21.5	19.2	39.4	44.9	47.3	44.4	48.9
Maine	8.9	17.6	42.6	67.5	37.7	81.7	67.3	63.1	55.3	70.5
Maryland	7.6	50.1	69.7	55.7	67.5	84.5	80.4	74.4	70.0	75.1
Massachusetts	20.1	32.2	27.7	43.4	42.8	65.6	59.0	53.0	45.1	55.6
Michigan	—	—	—	—	34.8	84.9	79.4	73.8	71.3	81.1
Minnesota	—	—	—	—	—	—	—	—	—	—
Mississippi	—	40.0	56.5	27.2	64.2	88.2	88.1	86.3	64.9	80.5
Missouri	—	19.8	53.5	15.5	34.9	74.1	74.3	58.8	42.8	51.0
Montana	—	—	—	—	—	—	—	—	—	—
Nebraska	—	—	—	—	—	—	—	—	—	—
Nevada	—	—	—	—	—	—	—	—	—	—
New Hampshire	17.8	17.9	74.5	70.3	38.1	87.4	65.5	61.4	58.9	79.7
New Jersey	7.5	33.2	70.8	68.9	69.2	80.5	81.4	73.0	68.3	69.8
New Mexico	—	—	—	—	—	—	—	—	—	—
New York	—	—	67.4	70.3	58.7	76.0	72.2	59.7	61.5	64.3
North Carolina	3.9	40.3	54.7	30.5	52.7	83.7	79.2	71.3	65.6	65.8
North Dakota	—	—	—	—	—	—	—	—	—	—
Ohio	6.2	34.8	75.9	73.9	75.5	84.5	83.6	77.6	75.4	76.5
Oklahoma	—	—	—	—	—	—	—	—	—	—
Oregon	—	—	—	—	—	—	—	—	—	—
Pennsylvania	14.6	18.9	54.6	50.7	51.5	77.5	75.7	73.2	68.6	74.1
Rhode Island	4.0	12.4	17.5	26.0	23.8	33.6	38.7	30.2	42.1	45.9
South Carolina	—	—	—	—	—	—	—	—	—	—
South Dakota	—	—	—	—	—	—	—	—	—	—
Tennessee	—	27.0	49.7	27.9	55.3	89.6	89.9	83.8	73.0	78.6
Texas	—	—	—	—	—	—	—	72.3	39.1	62.5
Utah	—	—	—	—	—	—	—	—	—	—
Vermont	—	—	54.0	50.2	52.7	73.7	65.5	59.9	52.7	60.2
Virginia	3.9	11.6	27.7	31.1	35.4	54.7	54.6	48.0	63.9	67.6
Washington	—	—	—	—	—	—	—	—	—	—
West Virginia	—	—	—	—	—	—	—	—	—	—
Wisconsin	—	—	—	—	—	—	—	58.4	62.6	81.5
Wyoming	—	—	—	—	—	—	—	—	—	—

Notes: Turnout is the ratio V/E, where V is the total vote cast in the presidential race in a given election year in a state, and E is the number of people eligible by law to vote in that state according to the criteria of citizenship, race, sex, and age laws on suffrage, where race has two dimensions: color (black/white) and bondage (slave/free). These raw data—number of presidential votes cast and eligibles in a state—are used to produce the entries. States with partial presidential vote data are not included. For a more detailed discussion of the methodology used, see the notes to Table 3-3.

Sources: Eligibles—decennial censuses (1790–1990) of the U.S. Census Bureau; Bureau of U.S. Census Series P Pamphlets for 1972 and the 1990s; Richard Scammon's book series, *America Votes* (various publication dates); the data archive of John J. Stucker; and relevant state constitutions and statute volumes. See also Stucker (1973), Appendix B. Presidential vote—Tables 4-37 through 4-63.

Table 3-24 State Voter Turnout Percentages in Presidential Elections, 1860–1896

	1860	1864	1868	1872	1876	1880	1884	1888	1892	1896
Alabama	79.2	—	74.0	79.5	72.9	58.9	54.2	56.6	68.4	51.8
Alaska	—	—	—	—	—	—	—	—	—	—
Arizona	—	—	—	—	—	—	—	—	—	—
Arkansas	76.7	—	40.9	68.1	65.6	60.2	60.0	65.4	55.6	51.8
California	72.1	60.7	59.5	59.6	81.6	74.4	74.4	81.4	76.7	76.1
Colorado	—	—	—	—	—	64.3	61.0	68.2	61.6	69.7
Connecticut	60.4	65.2	69.0	72.6	86.1	87.7	83.3	86.6	85.4	83.3
Delaware	74.6	74.0	76.8	73.3	73.3	81.7	75.7	69.0	80.6	78.9
Dist. of Columbia	—	—	—	—	—	—	—	—	—	—
Florida	74.1	—	—	76.9	90.8	86.3	82.8	78.2	35.5	40.0
Georgia	83.5	—	68.0	55.1	63.3	49.3	41.1	37.6	53.7	35.6
Hawaii	—	—	—	—	—	—	—	—	—	—
Idaho	—	—	—	—	—	—	—	—	63.7	76.2
Illinois	80.5	69.6	77.7	75.0	87.3	89.4	85.4	85.1	88.1	96.9
Indiana	89.4	83.5	93.7	87.3	97.2	96.8	93.8	95.6	91.5	97.6
Iowa	81.2	63.1	73.6	77.5	90.1	86.8	95.5	89.5	89.3	95.6
Kansas	—	37.0	50.1	76.7	64.6	79.3	84.1	96.5	87.1	87.6
Kentucky	69.8	40.6	63.8	63.8	78.0	72.5	69.1	80.7	73.9	89.3
Louisiana	53.4	—	71.4	76.6	78.4	50.9	51.7	49.7	45.1	35.5
Maine	62.0	69.4	67.1	57.9	71.9	85.1	73.0	71.5	63.3	63.0
Maryland	74.6	55.0	65.8	74.9	82.3	78.8	90.1	85.3	80.4	87.3
Massachusetts	51.4	49.1	50.8	58.5	71.7	71.6	72.2	69.5	71.6	67.3
Michigan	80.1	68.7	78.3	71.6	87.9	85.2	78.6	92.7	83.6	95.3
Minnesota	75.0	57.7	70.8	87.1	89.4	87.2	80.2	90.2	77.3	86.0
Mississippi	86.6	—	—	70.8	78.8	49.7	48.5	44.1	18.4	22.0
Missouri	64.4	34.0	42.7	66.8	76.1	77.6	76.7	81.7	77.2	88.1
Montana	—	—	—	—	—	—	—	—	77.7	75.2
Nebraska	—	—	46.5	48.5	56.8	72.9	73.6	82.8	72.4	80.4
Nevada	—	89.1	57.1	76.0	96.1	84.5	65.8	73.3	69.1	68.7
New Hampshire	73.8	77.3	75.3	80.5	89.1	91.5	86.8	90.2	86.1	78.2
New Jersey	74.9	69.0	77.1	81.5	95.4	96.3	88.3	90.4	89.2	87.8
New Mexico	—	—	—	—	—	—	—	—	—	—
New York	67.1	68.5	75.3	80.9	91.6	92.5	88.7	91.7	85.4	83.9
North Carolina	70.2	—	84.7	71.9	89.7	82.6	86.1	86.0	78.5	85.7
North Dakota	—	—	—	—	—	—	—	—	69.3	71.0
Ohio	81.6	81.9	85.2	84.2	93.8	93.6	92.8	91.6	85.9	95.1
Oklahoma	—	—	—	—	—	—	—	—	—	—
Oregon	86.8	89.7	92.4	66.6	74.2	81.2	77.3	72.0	77.4	85.1
Pennsylvania	70.3	76.9	80.5	67.8	81.5	84.6	79.6	81.3	75.2	82.4
Rhode Island	43.5	45.2	34.7	40.6	50.8	50.7	50.6	56.7	66.1	60.5
South Carolina	—	—	73.4	60.4	89.4	83.1	42.9	35.0	28.9	26.2
South Dakota	—	—	—	—	—	—	—	—	77.2	86.1
Tennessee	80.5	—	40.2	65.7	74.3	74.4	73.2	79.2	64.0	71.4
Texas	61.7	—	—	56.2	53.8	65.8	77.3	74.5	75.3	86.6
Utah	—	—	—	—	—	—	—	—	—	79.6
Vermont	52.5	63.8	67.2	68.6	81.2	79.1	69.2	71.0	60.4	67.1
Virginia	70.5	—	—	66.2	77.2	63.7	81.7	83.1	75.3	70.9
Washington	—	—	—	—	—	—	—	—	68.7	63.7
West Virginia	—	38.1	52.4	61.2	83.5	82.5	86.3	94.0	89.7	93.4
Wisconsin	79.0	68.8	80.0	81.6	96.4	89.7	94.0	92.7	87.3	95.5
Wyoming	—	—	—	—	—	—	—	—	46.4	50.6

Notes: Turnout is the ratio V/E, where V is the total vote cast in the presidential race in a given election year in a state, and E is the number of people eligible by law to vote in that state according to the criteria of citizenship, race, sex, and age laws on suffrage, where race has two dimensions: color (black/white) and bondage (slave/free). These raw data—number of presidential votes cast and eligibles in a state—are used to produce the entries. States with partial presidential vote data are not included. For a more detailed discussion of the methodology used, see the notes to Table 3-3.

Sources: Eligibles—decennial censuses (1790–1990) of the U.S. Census Bureau; Bureau of U.S. Census Series P Pamphlets for 1972 and the 1990s; Richard Scammon's book series, *America Votes* (various publication dates); the data archive of John J. Stucker; and relevant state constitutions and statute volumes. See also Stucker (1973), Appendix B. Presidential vote—Tables 4-37 through 4-63.

Table 3-25 State Voter Turnout Percentages in Presidential Elections, 1900–1936

	1900	1904	1908	1912	1916	1920	1924	1928	1932	1936
Alabama	38.8	24.2	21.6	22.7	24.0	20.6	13.5	19.1	17.7	18.8
Alaska	—	—	—	—	—	—	—	—	—	—
Arizona	—	—	—	39.6	47.7	46.8	40.8	41.6	48.5	49.0
Arkansas	41.2	33.9	40.4	31.0	39.9	21.3	15.3	20.9	21.8	17.2
California	69.8	58.8	55.6	44.7	56.9	47.2	49.1	55.8	61.1	64.6
Colorado	74.0	70.0	65.0	58.8	60.0	56.0	62.0	67.4	74.3	74.9
Connecticut	79.7	80.4	76.2	71.5	74.2	57.8	57.3	72.3	70.7	74.6
Delaware	81.8	81.9	86.2	83.5	84.5	75.1	68.5	75.3	76.3	79.8
Dist. of Columbia	—	—	—	—	—	—	—	—	—	—
Florida	29.8	24.0	26.1	23.6	33.4	28.3	16.9	32.5	30.4	31.2
Georgia	24.4	24.0	22.4	19.1	23.9	10.6	11.5	15.7	16.5	17.7
Hawaii	—	—	—	—	—	—	—	—	—	—
Idaho	75.0	64.6	66.0	60.0	67.6	62.3	64.6	64.4	74.0	71.6
Illinois	89.9	80.5	81.5	75.6	68.3	60.4	64.0	73.1	74.4	81.6
Indiana	94.7	92.6	93.4	81.0	84.9	73.1	70.6	74.7	78.8	78.6
Iowa	89.2	81.0	81.8	78.7	78.2	65.4	69.3	69.5	69.1	73.5
Kansas	89.5	76.7	81.3	75.1	65.9	58.0	63.9	65.5	70.7	76.4
Kentucky	87.1	77.7	84.0	74.6	82.6	71.9	61.0	67.7	67.4	59.9
Louisiana	21.7	15.5	19.7	19.3	21.5	14.1	12.4	20.1	23.0	26.0
Maine	55.0	49.4	53.1	63.6	65.8	47.0	44.8	60.2	66.3	64.5
Maryland	85.9	69.6	70.8	64.9	68.3	52.3	41.0	56.7	51.2	58.1
Massachusetts	64.1	64.4	62.2	62.2	63.3	53.3	56.5	73.8	69.3	75.8
Michigan	89.0	78.7	75.7	69.7	73.0	55.7	53.6	56.1	61.8	62.0
Minnesota	76.7	64.1	65.9	60.9	64.7	59.5	61.9	68.5	66.1	69.6
Mississippi	17.0	15.5	16.4	15.1	20.0	9.4	12.0	15.2	13.7	14.4
Missouri	82.6	74.2	78.9	74.0	80.4	67.1	63.2	69.1	70.9	77.2
Montana	75.5	63.5	59.9	61.0	70.0	61.4	59.0	64.8	69.9	70.6
Nebraska	86.6	75.8	84.2	74.3	81.0	55.7	63.7	71.3	71.8	75.5
Nevada	71.4	55.8	84.1	63.4	70.7	61.0	54.9	60.6	70.7	68.0
New Hampshire	83.9	81.5	80.8	78.4	78.1	67.5	67.4	77.7	77.5	77.7
New Jersey	85.9	83.5	82.2	69.2	71.4	59.6	60.8	75.5	72.0	74.9
New Mexico	—	—	—	55.7	74.2	62.3	60.3	57.5	67.0	67.4
New York	84.6	83.2	79.5	72.1	71.9	56.4	56.1	67.8	65.7	72.4
North Carolina	70.2	46.0	51.9	46.5	51.5	44.6	35.9	43.1	44.0	47.4
North Dakota	81.5	70.8	74.5	59.8	75.9	70.2	63.7	72.3	74.4	77.9
Ohio	91.0	82.8	87.4	75.0	77.1	62.6	57.7	66.8	65.4	71.8
Oklahoma	—	—	68.7	55.6	58.8	48.3	47.3	50.5	54.3	56.4
Oregon	65.4	53.2	52.7	58.2	61.2	52.4	55.1	57.3	60.4	62.4
Pennsylvania	75.0	74.3	71.8	64.6	64.1	42.7	45.8	62.5	53.1	72.5
Rhode Island	56.2	63.3	62.3	62.8	66.6	57.9	66.2	68.8	71.6	77.9
South Carolina	18.0	18.5	20.5	14.7	17.5	8.6	6.4	8.5	12.3	12.5
South Dakota	94.5	80.0	75.7	69.4	74.0	56.6	59.4	71.9	76.8	78.7
Tennessee	56.6	47.7	48.1	45.0	46.7	35.4	23.3	25.7	26.5	30.1
Texas	60.3	29.2	32.8	30.4	34.4	21.6	25.1	23.9	26.5	24.3
Utah	84.2	77.6	71.8	65.5	75.2	69.6	69.3	72.5	79.0	77.4
Vermont	57.9	52.7	52.7	62.6	64.5	45.3	51.3	66.8	66.6	68.4
Virginia	59.6	27.6	27.4	25.7	26.7	19.4	18.1	24.0	22.1	22.9
Washington	64.9	59.3	56.7	49.8	54.1	52.4	51.0	56.0	63.6	66.2
West Virginia	91.4	89.1	86.9	83.1	83.1	71.7	75.2	76.4	81.8	84.9
Wisconsin	86.5	80.8	77.5	68.5	70.3	52.2	57.3	63.8	65.0	68.9
Wyoming	51.0	50.5	51.7	50.3	55.0	53.7	70.3	67.5	73.6	73.4

Notes: Turnout is the ratio V/E, where V is the total vote cast in the presidential race in a given election year in a state, and E is the number of people eligible by law to vote in that state according to the criteria of citizenship, race, sex, and age laws on suffrage, where race has two dimensions: color (black/white) and bondage (slave/free). These raw data—number of presidential votes cast and eligibles in a state—are used to produce the entries. States with partial presidential vote data are not included. For a more detailed discussion of the methodology used, see the notes to Table 3-3.

Sources: Eligibles—decennial censuses (1790–1990) of the U.S. Census Bureau; Bureau of U.S. Census Series P Pamphlets for 1972 and the 1990s; Richard Scammon's book series, *America Votes* (various publication dates); the data archive of John J. Stucker; and relevant state constitutions and statute volumes. See also Stucker (1973), Appendix B. Presidential vote—Tables 4-37 through 4-63.

Table 3-26 State Voter Turnout Percentages in Presidential Elections, 1940–1976

	1940	1944	1948	1952	1956	1960	1964	1968	1972	1976
Alabama	18.9	15.0	12.6	24.2	27.7	31.2	36.2	53.1	43.4	47.0
Alaska	—	—	—	—	—	46.1	46.8	53.5	47.5	53.0
Arizona	57.0	42.0	45.1	54.1	48.6	56.0	57.9	51.4	48.3	47.1
Arkansas	18.2	19.3	21.9	36.9	38.0	41.2	51.4	54.3	48.2	51.9
California	73.4	64.7	62.6	69.8	66.0	70.8	69.5	65.2	62.8	54.6
Colorado	79.7	67.7	64.2	72.6	69.7	72.5	69.2	65.9	60.2	59.7
Connecticut	77.2	73.3	70.2	80.6	77.4	80.1	74.5	71.9	68.5	65.5
Delaware	79.4	67.2	69.1	79.2	73.6	74.5	70.4	69.7	62.8	59.2
Dist. of Columbia	—	—	—	—	—	—	41.5	37.0	31.4	34.0
Florida	40.9	33.7	34.4	48.6	44.9	51.8	53.7	55.7	50.6	52.2
Georgia	17.7	17.6	21.4	31.5	29.8	30.5	45.4	47.7	37.4	42.4
Hawaii	—	—	—	—	—	59.6	59.0	60.1	53.2	51.3
Idaho	77.0	64.8	63.6	78.9	75.9	81.5	76.2	73.0	63.9	61.8
Illinois	82.4	74.5	69.7	75.7	73.0	77.4	74.3	71.1	63.9	61.9
Indiana	81.1	71.6	67.0	75.7	73.9	77.4	72.7	71.0	61.2	60.7
Iowa	75.5	64.2	62.2	75.5	74.0	76.9	70.9	69.3	64.2	64.3
Kansas	75.1	62.1	64.8	71.6	67.5	70.6	64.3	64.4	59.9	59.4
Kentucky	59.5	51.8	47.9	56.1	57.5	59.4	55.0	55.3	48.1	48.8
Louisiana	27.3	24.1	27.1	40.2	36.1	45.0	47.5	55.4	44.3	49.0
Maine	65.0	57.1	48.6	62.9	62.6	74.6	66.5	67.7	61.4	65.7
Maryland	57.2	47.0	41.5	57.5	55.1	58.1	55.5	56.0	50.6	51.0
Massachusetts	78.7	70.6	70.7	77.1	75.6	79.0	72.6	69.8	64.0	64.3
Michigan	66.6	63.3	55.1	68.2	71.8	74.1	68.1	67.0	60.5	60.1
Minnesota	72.3	62.7	65.2	72.2	68.9	77.8	75.1	73.6	69.2	72.3
Mississippi	14.7	15.0	16.0	23.8	21.0	25.5	34.2	53.4	44.3	48.7
Missouri	74.4	62.1	60.8	71.6	68.9	72.1	66.0	64.0	57.6	57.9
Montana	72.2	58.7	61.8	71.4	71.7	72.1	71.1	68.8	68.0	64.6
Nebraska	75.4	67.7	57.7	71.4	67.6	71.9	67.4	60.9	56.8	57.1
Nevada	75.6	64.5	63.5	69.8	67.0	62.8	61.9	57.8	50.6	43.8
New Hampshire	79.6	73.1	69.6	78.9	75.4	81.6	73.7	70.9	64.9	58.2
New Jersey	76.1	68.7	62.4	72.2	70.2	74.3	71.9	68.6	61.8	60.5
New Mexico	66.6	48.7	53.4	60.6	57.2	63.0	63.8	61.0	58.5	54.9
New York	75.7	70.4	64.2	71.1	69.6	70.3	67.7	62.9	59.2	54.2
North Carolina	42.7	38.0	35.5	51.4	47.5	53.7	52.3	54.7	42.9	43.4
North Dakota	78.4	61.1	60.9	74.8	71.2	79.0	73.2	70.1	68.6	68.5
Ohio	75.4	66.7	58.1	69.5	66.8	72.1	66.4	64.1	57.9	56.0
Oklahoma	60.6	52.8	52.5	68.5	61.5	64.0	63.1	61.1	56.9	55.2
Oregon	67.1	58.2	56.2	69.5	71.5	73.4	68.9	66.9	62.8	61.6
Pennsylvania	67.6	59.5	55.6	66.2	65.7	71.4	67.8	65.7	56.5	55.1
Rhode Island	75.6	64.6	65.4	79.6	74.2	77.5	71.7	68.1	62.5	61.4
South Carolina	10.1	9.8	12.8	29.1	24.7	30.6	39.1	46.9	38.4	40.9
South Dakota	81.5	60.0	63.3	74.1	74.7	78.6	75.5	72.8	69.5	65.0
Tennessee	30.7	28.2	28.7	44.7	46.0	50.4	52.0	54.0	43.6	49.0
Texas	30.3	28.3	28.2	43.5	38.4	42.8	45.2	49.4	45.9	47.7
Utah	83.1	74.7	75.4	82.6	77.8	81.5	80.2	78.1	70.5	68.5
Vermont	66.8	56.7	54.2	66.8	67.3	74.4	68.8	64.8	61.8	56.7
Virginia	22.1	22.2	21.8	29.9	32.0	33.6	42.0	51.0	45.1	48.3
Washington	70.6	66.7	62.7	71.0	71.2	74.0	69.4	67.0	64.4	60.0
West Virginia	83.0	65.5	65.7	76.2	74.7	77.8	73.9	70.7	62.8	57.8
Wisconsin	72.4	65.5	59.4	72.1	68.0	74.1	69.7	67.1	63.0	67.3
Wyoming	74.8	63.1	59.3	72.3	67.6	74.7	74.9	66.1	64.9	57.4

Notes: Turnout is the ratio V/E, where V is the total vote cast in the presidential race in a given election year in a state, and E is the number of people eligible by law to vote in that state according to the criteria of citizenship, race, sex, and age laws on suffrage, where race has two dimensions: color (black/white) and bondage (slave/free). These raw data—number of presidential votes cast and eligibles in a state—are used to produce the entries. States with partial presidential vote data are not included. For a more detailed discussion of the methodology used, see the notes to Table 3-3.

Sources: Eligibles—decennial censuses (1790–1990) of the U.S. Census Bureau; Bureau of U.S. Census Series P Pamphlets for 1972 and the 1990s; Richard Scammon's book series, *America Votes* (various publication dates); the data archive of John J. Stucker; and relevant state constitutions and statute volumes. See also Stucker (1973), Appendix B. Presidential vote—Tables 4-37 through 4-63.

Table 3-27 State Voter Turnout Percentages in Presidential Elections, 1980–1996

	1980	1984	1988	1992	1996
Alabama	49.3	51.2	47.3	55.5	48.1
Alaska	59.7	67.8	57.7	67.6	58.7
Arizona	46.9	48.1	48.7	54.9	46.3
Arkansas	52.1	53.5	48.8	54.2	48.4
California	55.5	57.3	55.7	60.2	53.2
Colorado	58.1	59.7	59.6	63.3	56.0
Connecticut	64.0	64.1	60.8	67.2	58.7
Delaware	55.9	56.5	52.1	56.9	50.3
Dist. of Columbia	37.0	45.4	42.2	52.0	45.6
Florida	52.9	53.0	48.9	56.0	53.2
Georgia	42.2	43.0	40.3	47.5	43.1
Hawaii	48.3	49.2	48.1	48.3	45.8
Idaho	69.6	63.2	60.8	66.2	60.3
Illinois	60.5	60.9	57.1	62.5	52.7
Indiana	58.4	56.9	54.1	55.9	49.9
Iowa	63.5	64.1	59.9	65.8	58.7
Kansas	57.8	59.0	56.2	64.0	58.0
Kentucky	50.4	52.1	49.2	53.7	47.8
Louisiana	54.5	59.1	55.6	59.9	58.3
Maine	66.1	66.1	62.9	74.2	64.7
Maryland	51.9	52.9	51.0	56.8	50.0
Massachusetts	61.9	60.9	60.8	62.8	57.2
Michigan	61.3	58.4	55.3	62.9	55.0
Minnesota	71.4	69.8	67.6	73.0	65.8
Mississippi	52.5	53.9	51.9	52.8	45.9
Missouri	59.5	58.6	56.3	62.5	54.8
Montana	66.1	68.7	64.4	69.2	64.2
Nebraska	57.5	58.0	58.4	63.8	56.9
Nevada	44.1	42.3	44.1	53.6	41.1
New Hampshire	58.9	54.3	57.7	64.9	58.1
New Jersey	58.1	61.0	57.1	60.7	55.6
New Mexico	52.8	55.3	52.3	53.3	48.5
New York	51.7	56.0	52.7	56.5	52.6
North Carolina	44.2	48.3	44.4	51.1	46.5
North Dakota	65.7	67.3	64.7	66.5	56.6
Ohio	56.2	58.7	55.7	61.4	55.2
Oklahoma	53.6	57.1	52.0	60.1	50.4
Oregon	63.2	63.2	59.7	68.9	60.8
Pennsylvania	52.8	55.3	51.0	55.3	50.2
Rhode Island	61.7	58.8	56.1	62.5	54.9
South Carolina	41.3	41.8	39.9	45.8	41.3
South Dakota	67.8	65.2	63.5	66.6	61.6
Tennessee	49.4	50.1	45.9	52.9	47.7
Texas	47.8	52.8	49.6	52.4	44.4
Utah	67.0	65.0	62.6	65.0	51.3
Vermont	59.3	61.5	60.4	68.9	59.5
Virginia	49.1	52.5	50.0	55.3	49.9
Washington	60.0	60.2	55.7	63.3	57.3
West Virginia	53.3	53.8	48.3	50.4	45.9
Wisconsin	68.6	64.8	62.5	69.9	58.6
Wyoming	55.1	59.3	55.9	62.0	61.9

Notes: Turnout is the ratio V/E, where V is the total vote cast in the presidential race in a given election year in a state, and E is the number of people eligible by law to vote in that state according to the criteria of citizenship, race, sex, and age laws on suffrage, where race has two dimensions: color (black/white) and bondage (slave/free). These raw data—number of presidential votes cast and eligibles in a state—are used to produce the entries. States with partial presidential vote data are not included. For a more detailed discussion of the methodology used, see the notes to Table 3-3.

Sources: Eligibles—decennial censuses (1790–1990) of the U.S. Census Bureau; Bureau of U.S. Census Series P Pamphlets for 1972 and the 1990s; Richard Scammon's book series, *America Votes* (various publication dates); the data archive of John J. Stucker; and relevant state constitutions and statute volumes. See also Stucker (1973), Appendix B. Presidential vote—Tables 4-37 through 4-63.

Table 3-28 State Voter Mobilization Percentages for Congressional Elections Using Two-Year Election Cycles, 1788–1799

	1788–1789	1790–1791	1792–1793	1794–1795	1796–1797	1798–1799
Alabama	—	—	—	—	—	—
Alaska	—	—	—	—	—	—
Arizona	—	—	—	—	—	—
Arkansas	—	—	—	—	—	—
California	—	—	—	—	—	—
Colorado	—	—	—	—	—	—
Connecticut	—	2.8	3.0	3.2	2.6	4.4
Delaware	8.9[1]	—	19.1	19.5	16.5	18.2
Florida	—	—	—	—	—	—
Georgia	9.0[1]	6.1[1]	14.3	8.5	20.1	12.5
Hawaii	—	—	—	—	—	—
Idaho	—	—	—	—	—	—
Illinois	—	—	—	—	—	—
Indiana	—	—	—	—	—	—
Iowa	—	—	—	—	—	—
Kansas	—	—	—	—	—	—
Kentucky	—	—	—	—	—	—
Louisiana	—	—	—	—	—	—
Maine	—	—	—	—	—	—
Maryland	5.9[1]	12.9	12.4	11.7	9.0	—
Massachusetts	6.7	8.3	—	8.9	9.4	12.1
Michigan	—	—	—	—	—	—
Minnesota	—	—	—	—	—	—
Mississippi	—	—	—	—	—	—
Missouri	—	—	—	—	—	—
Montana	—	—	—	—	—	—
Nebraska	—	—	—	—	—	—
Nevada	—	—	—	—	—	—
New Hampshire	4.0	6.0	6.8	10.4	10.4	9.7
New Jersey	17.7[1]	8.3[1]	8.8	10.7	13.4 [1]	22.5
New Mexico	—	—	—	—	—	—
New York	—	7.4	14.8[1]	12.9	13.4	16.6
North Carolina	—	—	—	—	—	—
North Dakota	—	—	—	—	—	—
Ohio	—	—	—	—	—	—
Oklahoma	—	—	—	—	—	—
Oregon	—	—	—	—	—	—
Pennsylvania	9.0	—	18.4	—	—	22.7
Rhode Island	—	—	—	10.0	12.0	13.1
South Carolina	—	—	—	—	7.7	—
South Dakota	—	—	—	—	—	—
Tennessee	—	—	—	—	4.2	—
Texas	—	—	—	—	—	—
Utah	—	—	—	—	—	—
Vermont	—	—	7.2[1]	10.5	14.8	19.6
Virginia	—	—	—	—	—	—
Washington	—	—	—	—	—	—
West Virginia	—	—	—	—	—	—
Wisconsin	—	—	—	—	—	—
Wyoming	—	—	—	—	—	—

Notes: Mobilization is the ratio V/A, where V is the total vote cast in congressional (House) races in a given election year in a state, and A is the total number of adults in that state. These raw data—number of House votes cast and adults in each state—are used to produce the entries in this table. Both states with even-numbered year House races and states with odd-numbered year House races in a given two-year election cycle have their congressional vote divided by the number of adults in the state in the even-numbered year, which serves as a common base by which to compare congressional votes in any given two-year cycle for House elections. States with partial data (less than 100 percent of districts reporting the vote) are not included. States with special House elections are also not included. The few states having House elections in both even- and odd-numbered years in the same two-year election cycle only have the even-numbered election included in this table. For a more detailed discussion of the methodology used, see the notes to Table 3-4.

[1]Election held in odd-numbered year.

Sources: Adults—decennial censuses (1790–1990) of the U.S. Census Bureau; Bureau of U.S. Census Series P pamphlets for 1972 and the 1990s; and Richard Scammon's book series, *America Votes* (various publication dates). House vote—Tables 5-70 through 5-122.

Table 3-29 State Voter Mobilization Percentages for Congressional Elections Using Two-Year Election Cycles, 1800–1819

	1800–1801	1802–1803	1804–1805	1806–1807	1808–1809	1810–1811	1812–1813	1814–1815	1816–1817	1818–1819
Alabama	—	—	—	—	—	—	—	—	—	32.6[1]
Alaska	—	—	—	—	—	—	—	—	—	—
Arizona	—	—	—	—	—	—	—	—	—	—
Arkansas	—	—	—	—	—	—	—	—	—	—
California	—	—	—	—	—	—	—	—	—	—
Colorado	—	—	—	—	—	—	—	—	—	—
Connecticut	8.2	7.6	8.5	—	—	3.9	8.6	—	7.5	7.1
Delaware	19.6	25.8	30.9	13.8	21.0	24.4	24.8	21.7	23.5	20.1
Florida	—	—	—	—	—	—	—	—	—	—
Georgia	13.6	15.2	12.8	11.1	26.2	20.7	13.8	14.6	15.3	5.8
Hawaii	—	—	—	—	—	—	—	—	—	—
Idaho	—	—	—	—	—	—	—	—	—	—
Illinois	—	—	—	—	—	—	—	—	—	24.2
Indiana	—	—	—	—	—	—	—	—	19.3	—
Iowa	—	—	—	—	—	—	—	—	—	—
Kansas	—	—	—	—	—	—	—	—	—	—
Kentucky	27.5[1]	—	—	—	—	—	—	—	—	—
Louisiana	—	—	—	—	—	—	5.8	6.0	4.7	6.5
Maine	—	—	—	—	—	—	—	—	—	—
Maryland	10.5[1]	—	11.6	20.1	23.2	11.7	20.9	19.4	—	—
Massachusetts	15.7	16.5	25.9	18.4	31.9	20.1	30.9	22.9	18.4	14.0
Michigan	—	—	—	—	—	—	—	—	—	—
Minnesota	—	—	—	—	—	—	—	—	—	—
Mississippi	—	—	—	—	—	—	—	—	12.5[1]	—
Missouri	—	—	—	—	—	—	—	—	—	—
Montana	—	—	—	—	—	—	—	—	—	—
Nebraska	—	—	—	—	—	—	—	—	—	—
Nevada	—	—	—	—	—	—	—	—	—	—
New Hampshire	11.8	14.4	25.5	11.8	30.5	26.0	36.0	34.8	28.3	22.1[1]
New Jersey	33.2	15.9[1]	14.3	21.2	33.6	13.7	24.5[1]	31.2	5.0	12.6
New Mexico	—	—	—	—	—	—	—	—	—	—
New York	19.3	16.7	23.2	18.4	23.1	28.1	22.2	24.0	24.9	14.9
North Carolina	—	—	—	—	—	—	—	—	—	—
North Dakota	—	—	—	—	—	—	—	—	—	—
Ohio	—	25.4[1]	13.5	16.1	21.1	—	20.8	—	—	21.6
Oklahoma	—	—	—	—	—	—	—	—	—	—
Oregon	—	—	—	—	—	—	—	—	—	—
Pennsylvania	—	—	—	—	35.3	19.7	26.0	—	—	—
Rhode Island	12.0	13.2	4.9	10.6	17.9	20.0	21.0	18.1	5.9	5.0
South Carolina	—	4.4[1]	—	10.2	—	—	—	—	—	—
South Dakota	—	—	—	—	—	—	—	—	—	—
Tennessee	25.5[1]	20.4[1]	26.1[1]	—	—	21.4[1]	—	—	32.1[1]	33.4[1]
Texas	—	—	—	—	—	—	—	—	—	—
Utah	—	—	—	—	—	—	—	—	—	—
Vermont	17.6	14.5	22.4	—	—	26.1	35.3	—	32.1	19.3
Virginia	—	—	—	—	—	—	—	—	—	—
Washington	—	—	—	—	—	—	—	—	—	—
West Virginia	—	—	—	—	—	—	—	—	—	—
Wisconsin	—	—	—	—	—	—	—	—	—	—
Wyoming	—	—	—	—	—	—	—	—	—	—

Notes: Mobilization is the ratio V/A, where V is the total vote cast in congressional (House) races in a given election year in a state, and A is the total number of adults in that state. These raw data—number of House votes cast and adults in each state—are used to produce the entries in this table. Both states with even-numbered year House races and states with odd-numbered year House races in a given two-year election cycle have their congressional vote divided by the number of adults in the state in the even-numbered year, which serves as a common base by which to compare congressional votes in any given two-year cycle for House elections. States with partial data (less than 100 percent of districts reporting the vote) are not included. States with special House elections are also not included. The few states having House elections in both even- and odd-numbered years in the same two-year election cycle only have the even-numbered election included in this table. For a more detailed discussion of the methodology used, see the notes to Table 3-4.

[1] Election held in odd-numbered year.

Sources: Adults—decennial censuses (1790–1990) of the U.S. Census Bureau; Bureau of U.S. Census Series P pamphlets for 1972 and the 1990s; and Richard Scammon's book series, *America Votes* (various publication dates). House vote—Tables 5-70 through 5-122.

Table 3-30 State Voter Mobilization Percentages for Congressional Elections Using Two-Year Election Cycles, 1820–1839

	1820–1821	1822–1823	1824–1825	1826–1827	1828–1829	1830–1831	1832–1833	1834–1835	1836–1837	1838–1839
Alabama	36.0[1]	—	—	—	30.9[1]	—	—	—	—	—
Alaska	—	—	—	—	—	—	—	—	—	—
Arizona	—	—	—	—	—	—	—	—	—	—
Arkansas	—	—	—	—	—	—	—	—	31.6	34.1
California	—	—	—	—	—	—	—	—	—	—
Colorado	—	—	—	—	—	—	—	—	—	—
Connecticut	5.6[1]	3.9[1]	5.7[1]	10.4[1]	10.3[1]	11.9[1]	13.3[1]	26.4[1]	28.4[1]	31.7[1]
Delaware	26.0	24.4	20.8	26.7	28.1	24.6	25.2	27.9	26.3	25.6
Florida	—	—	—	—	—	—	—	—	—	—
Georgia	11.6	21.2	6.5	19.3	25.5	27.7	28.5	26.8	24.1	25.2
Hawaii	—	—	—	—	—	—	—	—	—	—
Idaho	—	—	—	—	—	—	—	—	—	—
Illinois	37.4	30.8	34.1	30.0	33.3	42.2[1]	30.5	29.3	32.0	35.6
Indiana	34.0	—	—	32.8	—	42.1[1]	40.8[1]	38.7[1]	40.4[1]	43.3[1]
Iowa	—	—	—	—	—	—	—	—	—	—
Kansas	—	—	—	—	—	—	—	—	—	—
Kentucky	—	—	—	31.5[1]	—	—	—	—	—	—
Louisiana	6.5	—	—	—	7.8	—	6.8	7.4	5.4	8.4
Maine	7.8	19.8[1]	11.6	13.9	17.0	28.8	25.9[1]	35.2	26.6	40.7
Maryland	—	16.4	23.7	20.5	20.2[1]	20.2[1]	23.4[1]	—	18.8[1]	25.5[1]
Massachusetts	10.5	—	13.1	7.4	11.9	11.2	13.0[1]	20.3	20.4	23.2
Michigan	—	—	—	—	—	—	—	16.4[1]	35.5[1]	42.1
Minnesota	—	—	—	—	—	—	—	—	—	—
Mississippi	—	21.5	15.0	21.4	—	21.5	—	19.7[1]	16.2[1]	26.2[1]
Missouri	—	32.4	29.9	26.4	28.2	25.0[1]	18.9[1]	26.5[1]	24.7	31.9
Montana	—	—	—	—	—	—	—	—	—	—
Nebraska	—	—	—	—	—	—	—	—	—	—
Nevada	—	—	—	—	—	—	—	—	—	—
New Hampshire	10.4	13.6	14.4	24.1[1]	31.7[1]	31.3[1]	23.8[1]	28.1[1]	16.6[1]	39.0[1]
New Jersey	4.6	—	13.7	19.8	33.2	20.8	32.5	35.0	32.2	34.4
New Mexico	—	—	—	—	—	—	—	—	—	—
New York	25.9[1]	21.6	27.5	24.6	35.9	30.0	35.7	36.6	29.7	34.8
North Carolina	—	—	—	—	—	—	—	—	—	—
North Dakota	—	—	—	—	—	—	—	—	—	—
Ohio	—	—	27.7	28.4	—	27.7	32.7	29.3	34.4	36.4
Oklahoma	—	—	—	—	—	—	—	—	—	—
Oregon	—	—	—	—	—	—	—	—	—	—
Pennsylvania	32.3	23.1	—	—	—	24.8	28.8	28.4	24.7	35.2
Rhode Island	16.4	3.5	7.2[1]	5.1[1]	12.2[1]	7.3[1]	10.3[1]	15.0[1]	14.4[1]	14.1[1]
South Carolina	—	8.3[1]	—	—	—	—	—	—	—	—
South Dakota	—	—	—	—	—	—	—	—	—	—
Tennessee	—	—	—	—	—	32.7[1]	32.9[1]	31.7[1]	32.8[1]	34.5[1]
Texas	—	—	—	—	—	—	—	—	—	—
Utah	—	—	—	—	—	—	—	—	—	—
Vermont	20.9	25.9	19.7	17.9	—	22.7	17.4[1]	27.3	25.1	31.3
Virginia	—	—	—	—	—	—	—	—	—	—
Washington	—	—	—	—	—	—	—	—	—	—
West Virginia	—	—	—	—	—	—	—	—	—	—
Wisconsin	—	—	—	—	—	—	—	—	—	—
Wyoming	—	—	—	—	—	—	—	—	—	—

Notes: Mobilization is the ratio V/A, where V is the total vote cast in congressional (House) races in a given election year in a state, and A is the total number of adults in that state. These raw data—number of House votes cast and adults in each state—are used to produce the entries in this table. Both states with even-numbered year House races and states with odd-numbered year House races in a given two-year election cycle have their congressional vote divided by the number of adults in the state in the even-numbered year, which serves as a common base by which to compare congressional votes in any given two-year cycle for House elections. States with partial data (less than 100 percent of districts reporting the vote) are not included. States with special House elections are also not included. The few states having House elections in both even- and odd-numbered years in the same two-year election cycle only have the even-numbered election included in this table. For a more detailed discussion of the methodology used, see the notes to Table 3-4.

[1] Election held in odd-numbered year.

Sources: Adults—decennial censuses (1790–1990) of the U.S. Census Bureau; Bureau of U.S. Census Series P pamphlets for 1972 and the 1990s; and Richard Scammon's book series, *America Votes* (various publication dates). House vote—Tables 5-70 through 5-122.

Table 3-31 State Voter Mobilization Percentages for Congressional Elections Using Two-Year Election Cycles, 1840–1859

	1840–1841	1842–1843	1844–1845	1846–1847	1848–1849	1850–1851	1852–1853	1854–1855	1856–1857	1858–1859
Alabama	17.8[1]	—	—	—	23.7[1]	—	—	20.9[1]	20.3[1]	—
Alaska	—	—	—	—	—	—	—	—	—	—
Arizona	—	—	—	—	—	—	—	—	—	—
Arkansas	37.0	35.9	34.3	26.1	32.9	25.7[1]	17.4[1]	25.3	30.8	28.4
California	—	—	—	—	17.0[1]	60.6[1]	73.6	64.8	71.7	56.2[1]
Colorado	—	—	—	—	—	—	—	—	—	—
Connecticut	29.4[1]	31.8[1]	32.1[1]	31.5[1]	28.4[1]	29.3[1]	27.6[1]	27.8[1]	26.3[1]	31.4[1]
Delaware	31.2	30.2	32.7	31.6	30.9	29.6	30.5	28.7	30.2	30.6
Florida	—	—	19.8[1]	17.9	23.2	22.6	21.8	22.1	23.9	17.9
Georgia	27.8	23.9	25.5	18.1	22.5	25.8[1]	24.3[1]	26.1[1]	24.5[1]	23.2[1]
Hawaii	—	—	—	—	—	—	—	—	—	—
Idaho	—	—	—	—	—	—	—	—	—	—
Illinois	36.5[1]	41.9[1]	38.5	34.3	32.1	29.3	34.5	27.0	38.1	36.6
Indiana	34.1[1]	41.7[1]	39.8[1]	39.4[1]	37.8[1]	37.2[1]	38.4	40.4	45.3	39.9
Iowa	—	—	—	28.4	36.6	32.5	26.9	26.8	35.9	38.2
Kansas	—	—	—	—	—	—	—	—	—	26.6[1]
Kentucky	13.1[1]	31.6[1]	32.0[1]	33.3[1]	26.9[1]	25.0[1]	28.0[1]	30.8[1]	28.5[1]	29.8[1]
Louisiana	9.4	7.7[1]	7.1	—	—	13.8[1]	—	14.1[1]	12.2[1]	11.5[1]
Maine	39.9	26.8[1]	36.7	28.4	30.1	28.0	30.6	29.7	39.0	35.7
Maryland	18.9[1]	—	20.5	—	21.8[1]	19.6[1]	25.2[1]	27.7[1]	28.0[1]	23.9[1]
Massachusetts	31.7	27.2	28.8	20.5	23.8	21.1	22.3	20.0	25.4	17.5
Michigan	47.9	35.4[1]	43.9	33.1	40.4	33.7	38.3	32.8	43.9	37.9
Minnesota	—	—	—	—	—	—	—	—	70.9[1]	59.8[1]
Mississippi	23.4[1]	22.5[1]	26.0[1]	22.6[1]	24.2[1]	23.4[1]	24.3[1]	21.7[1]	12.9[1]	12.9[1]
Missouri	34.9	15.2	32.6	29.7	32.3	27.9	24.9	28.0	26.7	27.5
Montana	—	—	—	—	—	—	—	—	—	—
Nebraska	—	—	—	—	—	—	—	—	—	—
Nevada	—	—	—	—	—	—	—	—	—	—
New Hampshire	35.0[1]	29.2[1]	33.8[1]	36.7[1]	32.9[1]	29.9[1]	29.1[1]	35.7[1]	35.1[1]	37.4[1]
New Jersey	37.7	—	35.1	26.4	33.2	31.0	32.4	28.3	33.2	30.0
New Mexico	—	—	—	—	—	—	—	—	—	—
New York	38.7	31.8	36.8	28.4	30.6	27.0	31.1	26.2	32.0	27.8
North Carolina	—	18.0[1]	23.4[1]	18.6[1]	21.3[1]	—	21.4[1]	23.3[1]	19.4[1]	19.7[1]
North Dakota	—	—	—	—	—	—	—	—	—	—
Ohio	44.1	32.6[1]	42.0	31.7	35.1	29.3	32.7	30.8	35.9	33.5
Oklahoma	—	—	—	—	—	—	—	—	—	—
Oregon	—	—	—	—	—	—	—	—	—	54.3[1]
Pennsylvania	33.6	24.3[1]	35.4	21.7	32.8	25.8	28.7	29.5	33.4	28.0
Rhode Island	4.9[1]	18.8[1]	17.1[1]	15.7[1]	11.3[1]	15.9[1]	18.7[1]	—	16.3[1]	13.5[1]
South Carolina	—	—	—	—	—	—	—	—	—	—
South Dakota	—	—	—	—	—	—	—	—	—	—
Tennessee	21.3[1]	32.0[1]	30.3[1]	31.6[1]	18.6[1]	—	—	29.9[1]	28.3[1]	30.7[1]
Texas	—	—	—	37.7	37.4[1]	26.0[1]	27.8[1]	29.6[1]	27.4[1]	27.3[1]
Utah	—	—	—	—	—	—	—	—	—	—
Vermont	38.5	33.6[1]	34.3	30.2	29.7	27.6	25.6	24.3	25.7	23.9
Virginia	—	—	—	—	—	—	—	—	—	—
Washington	—	—	—	—	—	—	—	—	—	—
West Virginia	—	—	—	—	—	—	—	—	—	—
Wisconsin	—	—	—	—	32.7	30.1	34.9	26.2	44.6	37.5
Wyoming	—	—	—	—	—	—	—	—	—	—

Notes: Mobilization is the ratio V/A, where V is the total vote cast in congressional (House) races in a given election year in a state, and A is the total number of adults in that state. These raw data—number of House votes cast and adults in each state—are used to produce the entries in this table. Both states with even-numbered year House races and states with odd-numbered year House races in a given two-year election cycle have their congressional vote divided by the number of adults in the state in the even-numbered year, which serves as a common base by which to compare congressional votes in any given two-year cycle for House elections. States with partial data (less than 100 percent of districts reporting the vote) are not included. States with special House elections are also not included. The few states having House elections in both even- and odd-numbered years in the same two-year election cycle only have the even-numbered election included in this table. For a more detailed discussion of the methodology used, see the notes to Table 3-4.

[1] Election held in odd-numbered year.

Sources: Adults—decennial censuses (1790–1990) of the U.S. Census Bureau; Bureau of U.S. Census Series P pamphlets for 1972 and the 1990s; and Richard Scammon's book series, *America Votes* (various publication dates). House vote—Tables 5-70 through 5-122.

Table 3-32 State Voter Mobilization Percentages for Congressional Elections Using Two-Year Election Cycles, 1860–1879

	1860–1861	1862–1863	1864–1865	1866–1867	1868–1869	1870–1871	1872–1873	1874–1875	1876–1877	1878–1879
Alabama	—	—	—	—	15.7	35.9	38.0	41.3	31.7	16.9
Alaska	—	—	—	—	—	—	—	—	—	—
Arizona	—	—	—	—	—	—	—	—	—	—
Arkansas	34.7	—	—	—	21.0	26.2	34.7	24.8	29.8	24.7
California	59.1[1]	48.2[1]	41.8	33.6[1]	36.0	36.6[1]	26.5	30.8[1]	35.9	33.5[1]
Colorado	—	—	—	—	—	—	—	—	30.6	27.1
Connecticut	32.3[1]	29.7[1]	26.2[1]	32.5[1]	29.9[1]	30.5[1]	27.0[1]	30.3[1]	35.4	29.4
Delaware	30.6	29.8	30.7	32.3	31.6	37.1	—	35.4	34.4	18.6
Florida	22.0	—	—	—	22.9	30.5	38.1	36.5	46.9	35.2
Georgia	—	—	—	—	29.6	33.6	27.2	22.2	28.6	19.7
Hawaii	—	—	—	—	—	—	—	—	—	—
Idaho	—	—	—	—	—	—	—	—	—	—
Illinois	43.3	30.1	37.5	34.6	41.2	27.1	35.1	28.1	40.0	31.1
Indiana	45.3	39.9	43.4	47.5	47.6	41.9	47.5	43.2	49.1	44.2
Iowa	44.1	33.9	35.6	33.8	39.9	30.3	35.4	29.2	42.9	35.7
Kansas	—	20.4	20.6	21.9	28.8	35.0	43.5	29.8	34.7	33.7
Kentucky	26.5[1]	16.6[1]	21.3[1]	20.9[1]	26.6	25.7	26.4	19.5	37.3	22.5
Louisiana	—	—	—	—	20.5	30.3	35.4	38.1	40.4	28.2
Maine	38.1	26.2	33.8	32.9	38.6	28.9	36.0	26.4	37.3	33.5
Maryland	20.6[1]	14.9[1]	20.9	19.1	24.9	35.5	33.9	29.0	37.3	26.8
Massachusetts	24.2	18.6	23.3	15.0	23.9	16.5	21.8	19.6	26.0	24.7
Michigan	43.5	32.2	36.5	33.2	41.6	31.3	34.6	31.1	42.1	34.8
Minnesota	43.7	23.5	32.6	27.2	40.1	32.7	37.8	33.8	40.2	29.4
Mississippi	—	—	—	—	32.7[1]	—	32.9	39.2[1]	38.3	11.6
Missouri	30.7	15.5	15.7	16.0	20.3	23.2	33.9	29.5	37.6	33.5
Montana	—	—	—	—	—	—	—	—	—	—
Nebraska	—	—	—	20.7	28.6	32.7	29.5	28.9	33.2	26.8
Nevada	—	—	60.7	42.8	43.0	41.3	44.0	49.7	51.7	47.3
New Hampshire	36.0[1]	35.2[1]	35.3[1]	36.4[1]	35.4[1]	36.5[1]	34.5[1]	39.3[1]	37.8[1]	35.7
New Jersey	36.0	29.5	33.1	31.1	36.7	33.5	34.3	34.3	39.5	33.6
New Mexico	—	—	—	—	—	—	—	—	—	—
New York	33.1	28.8	33.2	32.1	36.7	32.3	34.1	30.5	37.1	29.9
North Carolina	—	—	—	—	—	—	38.8	35.8	—	21.9
North Dakota	—	—	—	—	—	—	—	—	—	—
Ohio	38.3	32.6	36.3	39.3	41.8	33.5	38.5	32.7	42.3	37.5
Oklahoma	—	—	—	—	—	—	—	—	—	—
Oregon	17.5	37.2	46.6	56.8	76.4	53.2	48.5	40.8	41.3	41.3
Pennsylvania	34.9	29.8	32.7	37.5	39.2	30.9	36.7	28.7	37.3	33.0
Rhode Island	22.6[1]	18.1[1]	9.0[1]	7.5[1]	15.7	9.8	14.3	4.8	17.7	11.8
South Carolina	—	—	—	—	34.5	38.6	26.7	39.2	47.6	39.7
South Dakota	—	—	—	—	—	—	—	—	—	—
Tennessee	—	—	11.9[1]	18.8[1]	10.6	22.2	32.3	25.9	34.8	22.5
Texas	—	—	—	—	23.4[1]	31.0[1]	28.0	10.1	26.2	34.9
Utah	—	—	—	—	—	—	—	—	—	—
Vermont	24.9	22.5[1]	24.4	24.5	30.2	22.8	26.6	22.4	31.3	28.8
Virginia	—	—	—	—	39.0[1]	—	32.1	28.8	36.5	18.8
Washington	—	—	—	—	—	—	—	—	—	—
West Virginia	—	10.9[1]	12.0	—	26.0	28.9	21.6	29.8	41.3	36.9
Wisconsin	43.0	33.3	35.5	31.4	42.5	30.7	37.7	34.2	44.1	33.8
Wyoming	—	—	—	—	—	—	—	—	—	—

Notes: Mobilization is the ratio V/A, where V is the total vote cast in congressional (House) races in a given election year in a state, and A is the total number of adults in that state. These raw data—number of House votes cast and adults in each state—are used to produce the entries in this table. Both states with even-numbered year House races and states with odd-numbered year House races in a given two-year election cycle have their congressional vote divided by the number of adults in the state in the even-numbered year, which serves as a common base by which to compare congressional votes in any given two-year cycle for House elections. States with partial data (less than 100 percent of districts reporting the vote) are not included. States with special House elections are also not included. The few states having House elections in both even- and odd-numbered years in the same two-year election cycle only have the even-numbered election included in this table. For a more detailed discussion of the methodology used, see the notes to Table 3-4.

[1]Election held in odd-numbered year.

Sources: Adults—decennial censuses (1790–1990) of the U.S. Census Bureau; Bureau of U.S. Census Series P pamphlets for 1972 and the 1990s; and Richard Scammon's book series, *America Votes* (various publication dates). House vote—Tables 5-70 through 5-122.

Table 3-33 State Voter Mobilization Percentages for Congressional Elections Using Two-Year Election Cycles, 1880–1898

	1880	1882	1884	1886	1888–1889	1890	1892	1894–1895	1896	1898
Alabama	25.9	21.2	24.0	14.2	27.4	18.1	33.7	17.6	24.4	11.4
Alaska	—	—	—	—	—	—	—	—	—	—
Arizona	—	—	—	—	—	—	—	—	—	—
Arkansas	30.7	17.5	31.4	13.1	34.7	23.6	27.4	10.0	27.7	4.8
California	32.5	30.0	32.8	30.2	36.2	34.2	31.0	32.9	32.4	30.4
Colorado	42.1	40.5	37.9	29.1	40.9	33.7	35.0	64.1	61.2	47.0
Connecticut	36.1	30.0	34.2	29.4	35.2	29.7	34.5	31.1	33.7	27.7
Delaware	38.7	39.4	36.3	26.0	33.5	38.4	39.3	40.0	35.0	32.2
Florida	42.5	36.0	41.4	36.4	39.8	24.7	18.1	12.3	18.6	13.6
Georgia	22.0	15.2	17.5	3.7	16.8	13.4	25.7	22.9	18.5	7.1
Hawaii	—	—	—	—	—	—	—	—	—	—
Idaho	—	—	—	—	—	39.8	36.2	39.0	41.6	50.6
Illinois	41.0	32.6	39.6	31.0	38.7	33.3	40.4	37.2	44.7	34.3
Indiana	48.7	43.9	47.4	43.6	48.2	41.0	45.9	44.8	48.6	42.0
Iowa	41.2	35.4	43.8	38.4	43.0	39.8	43.2	39.3	46.5	36.3
Kansas	42.9	40.8	46.3	44.9	50.1	41.5	45.4	40.2	44.2	37.1
Kentucky	34.4	25.7	34.1	28.3	46.4	26.7	40.3	39.3	46.9	27.4
Louisiana	23.4	17.4	23.1	17.9	23.3	14.8	21.5	20.4	16.6	5.4
Maine	38.8	36.1	36.5	32.8	36.6	28.0	31.4	26.2	29.7	19.8
Maryland	36.4	32.1	36.6	28.1	39.4	33.1	37.2	34.7	40.8	34.4
Massachusetts	26.3	22.7	25.4	19.4	26.0	20.3	25.7	21.5	23.4	18.7
Michigan	40.9	34.0	40.9	36.7	43.4	34.4	39.1	33.0	41.7	31.4
Minnesota	39.9	33.6	38.4	39.2	43.0	35.4	36.3	37.6	41.8	29.0
Mississippi	23.8	16.1	22.2	9.1	21.9	11.5	8.9	6.6	10.6	4.1
Missouri	37.2	34.2	38.5	35.0	41.0	35.1	38.5	34.5	44.0	35.0
Montana	—	—	—	—	51.2[1]	35.9	43.6	43.9	34.8	36.2
Nebraska	38.7	31.5	38.9	33.9	43.5	40.2	37.1	37.2	40.2	34.8
Nevada	44.2	36.2	34.8	36.1	39.6	42.0	34.2	35.5	34.5	32.1
New Hampshire	39.9	34.8	36.6	33.5	38.7	35.8	35.2	33.0	32.5	31.5
New Jersey	40.1	31.5	37.4	31.3	38.8	30.6	38.1	31.7	37.2	31.7
New Mexico	—	—	—	—	—	—	—	—	—	—
New York	37.6	30.7	35.9	28.4	37.1	27.2	35.0	31.4	33.8	31.4
North Carolina	36.7	34.8	39.5	31.4	40.3	36.0	36.6	36.1	41.1	40.1
North Dakota	—	—	—	—	51.3[1]	38.9	34.1	32.7	35.3	31.4
Ohio	43.5	36.9	43.9	37.4	43.6	37.0	40.6	35.1	45.0	33.4
Oklahoma	—	—	—	—	—	—	—	—	—	—
Oregon	41.9	38.8	39.7	38.3	38.2	42.0	40.4	43.0	41.9	36.6
Pennsylvania	39.3	31.8	36.5	31.5	36.1	32.4	33.1	30.1	35.5	27.7
Rhode Island	17.7	5.9	17.9	9.4	20.3	17.7	23.2	16.8	22.3	15.2
South Carolina	41.2	27.5	19.8	8.4	16.2	15.2	13.7	12.2	12.7	5.7
South Dakota	—	—	—	—	59.3[1]	46.9	42.8	43.1	44.6	37.4
Tennessee	34.7	31.3	34.8	31.0	38.7	24.4	30.9	26.4	35.1	19.0
Texas	35.9	32.5	38.0	33.6	37.2	33.0	39.4	38.1	44.0	31.4
Utah	—	—	—	—	—	—	—	37.8[1]	67.0	55.8
Vermont	34.3	24.2	27.8	24.5	34.3	26.3	26.8	27.0	32.2	24.8
Virginia	27.8	27.9	39.5	30.5	40.3	24.6	35.8	26.2	35.6	19.9
Washington	—	—	—	—	33.3[1]	26.1	38.7	31.1	33.9	27.3
West Virginia	40.6	31.6	43.2	41.2	45.3	34.8	42.9	42.9	47.6	39.3
Wisconsin	41.2	31.5	43.5	36.5	43.1	34.8	40.4	38.7	44.0	32.9
Wyoming	—	—	—	—	—	42.3	42.7	43.5	44.2	38.6

Notes: Mobilization is the ratio V/A, where V is the total vote cast in congressional (House) races in a given election year in a state, and A is the total number of adults in that state. These raw data—number of House votes cast and adults in each state—are used to produce the entries in this table. Both states with even-numbered year House races and states with odd-numbered year House races in a given two-year election cycle have their congressional vote divided by the number of adults in the state in the even-numbered year, which serves as a common base by which to compare congressional votes in any given two-year cycle for House elections. States with partial data (less than 100 percent of districts reporting the vote) are not included. States with special House elections are also not included. The few states having House elections in both even- and odd-numbered years in the same two-year election cycle only have the even-numbered election included in this table. For a more detailed discussion of the methodology used, see the notes to Table 3-4.

[1] Election held in odd-numbered year.

Sources: Adults—decennial censuses (1790–1990) of the U.S. Census Bureau; Bureau of U.S. Census Series P pamphlets for 1972 and the 1990s; and Richard Scammon's book series, *America Votes* (various publication dates). House vote—Tables 5-70 through 5-122.

Table 3-34 State Voter Mobilization Percentages for Congressional Elections Using Two-Year Election Cycles, 1900–1918

	1900	1902	1904	1906–1907	1908	1910–1911	1912	1914	1916	1918
Alabama	17.0	10.6	11.4	7.0	10.3	9.6	9.6	7.6	11.3	5.6
Alaska	—	—	—	—	—	—	—	—	—	—
Arizona	—	—	—	—	—	18.1[1]	17.8	30.6	32.7	25.5
Arkansas	21.4	6.3	16.8	7.4	21.3	5.5	15.1	5.4	21.1	9.3
California	31.1	27.2	27.3	21.4	25.4	22.8	35.9	45.5	43.5	28.8
Colorado	67.4	52.2	62.4	46.7	58.0	45.5	53.0	47.9	48.8	39.2
Connecticut	32.4	27.2	31.4	25.4	28.9	24.3	26.5	24.3	27.5	20.7
Delaware	40.0	35.3	39.4	33.5	40.9	36.6	39.4	36.1	39.4	31.0
Florida	12.3	5.9	10.5	6.8	10.7	9.6	10.5	5.3	14.0	6.3
Georgia	10.5	3.9	10.6	2.9	8.1	3.7	9.2	6.2	10.0	4.3
Hawaii	—	—	—	—	—	—	—	—	—	—
Idaho	64.4	57.2	57.0	50.5	59.4	46.3	56.6	50.9	60.4	42.0
Illinois	41.7	29.0	36.1	27.0	35.8	27.3	33.3	26.1	35.6	23.7
Indiana	46.9	40.8	45.5	38.5	45.8	39.0	39.3	37.8	41.4	32.6
Iowa	43.7	32.4	38.9	32.7	37.0	29.6	33.1	30.7	35.1	25.0
Kansas	44.7	35.0	37.0	34.8	41.9	31.2	36.4	49.4	57.2	42.5
Kentucky	43.5	26.8	38.6	25.4	41.3	27.8	33.3	26.4	40.9	28.1
Louisiana	10.4	3.9	7.4	5.0	9.1	6.3	7.9	5.9	9.8	5.0
Maine	27.3	24.6	29.2	29.7	31.3	30.5	30.5	30.2	32.2	25.8
Maryland	40.5	29.5	30.3	28.2	29.3	27.6	23.5	27.5	27.6	19.1
Massachusetts	22.5	21.5	21.8	20.6	20.8	20.3	21.7	20.1	22.1	16.8
Michigan	39.5	27.5	34.7	21.2	33.2	22.6	30.6	22.9	32.3	19.3
Minnesota	34.9	27.6	28.2	23.9	28.2	23.0	23.3	25.9	29.5	24.9
Mississippi	7.5	2.5	7.1	2.6	7.4	2.8	5.8	4.3	9.1	3.7
Missouri	41.1	30.3	36.5	33.0	39.0	35.9	36.1	31.0	39.5	27.5
Montana	40.8	31.8	34.4	27.8	30.6	27.8	30.1	30.4	59.4	34.2
Nebraska	41.7	34.0	38.1	30.8	41.9	36.0	37.4	34.0	40.2	30.1
Nevada	37.4	32.7	28.8	31.1	45.8	34.7	34.7	38.1	59.2	46.3
New Hampshire	34.4	29.1	32.7	29.5	32.1	29.7	30.0	29.4	30.8	25.1
New Jersey	36.2	30.4	34.0	26.6	32.3	28.5	22.5	23.4	25.2	19.2
New Mexico	—	—	—	—	—	37.0[1]	28.4	26.6	37.4	25.9
New York	34.6	29.5	32.2	28.4	30.5	25.4	26.7	22.6	24.8	32.2
North Carolina	34.1	22.1	22.6	21.2	25.5	23.0	21.3	18.4	25.2	20.0
North Dakota	36.1	26.3	31.6	25.5	32.5	27.2	26.5	27.4	31.0	26.4
Ohio	43.1	32.6	38.1	28.7	40.1	31.3	33.7	33.9	34.0	26.5
Oklahoma	—	—	—	38.7[1]	35.3	29.2	29.5	27.6	30.9	19.4
Oregon	34.6	31.9	29.9	26.6	28.4	26.6	29.6	52.1	48.1	29.5
Pennsylvania	31.9	27.0	28.4	23.6	26.1	21.3	24.2	22.8	26.0	17.9
Rhode Island	20.3	21.2	22.1	21.7	23.0	20.4	22.2	22.5	24.6	22.1
South Carolina	8.9	5.4	9.3	4.6	9.9	4.6	7.1	4.6	8.5	3.4
South Dakota	48.1	33.6	40.9	27.6	39.0	33.0	36.1	29.7	38.1	25.8
Tennessee	27.5	15.4	22.5	19.2	21.7	20.7	20.6	18.8	20.8	10.1
Texas	29.8	23.1	15.8	10.4	16.1	11.0	15.0	10.0	16.5	7.1
Utah	72.3	60.3	66.5	50.9	62.8	53.9	56.8	55.3	66.7	39.4
Vermont	30.2	20.6	30.1	27.4	28.1	23.8	22.2	28.1	28.6	19.8
Virginia	29.9	13.3	13.8	8.7	13.8	9.7	12.5	7.7	13.7	3.6
Washington	34.6	25.9	30.2	20.7	26.4	19.2	40.7	43.3	44.6	24.3
West Virginia	47.1	38.6	45.2	32.6	43.5	33.6	41.1	34.9	40.4	29.4
Wisconsin	40.7	31.6	37.4	25.7	35.1	23.9	28.4	22.3	29.1	20.6
Wyoming	45.0	39.8	44.2	35.1	44.4	40.3	42.6	41.0	47.4	36.8

Notes: Mobilization is the ratio V/A, where V is the total vote cast in congressional (House) races in a given election year in a state, and A is the total number of adults in that state. These raw data—number of House votes cast and adults in each state—are used to produce the entries in this table. Both states with even-numbered year House races and states with odd-numbered year House races in a given two-year election cycle have their congressional vote divided by the number of adults in the state in the even-numbered year, which serves as a common base by which to compare congressional votes in any given two-year cycle for House elections. States with partial data (less than 100 percent of districts reporting the vote) are not included. States with special House elections are also not included. The few states having House elections in both even- and odd-numbered years in the same two-year election cycle only have the even-numbered election included in this table. For a more detailed discussion of the methodology used, see the notes to Table 3-4.

[1]Election held in odd-numbered year.

Sources: Adults—decennial censuses (1790–1990) of the U.S. Census Bureau; Bureau of U.S. Census Series P pamphlets for 1972 and the 1990s; and Richard Scammon's book series, *America Votes* (various publication dates). House vote—Tables 5-70 through 5-122.

Table 3-35 State Voter Mobilization Percentages for Congressional Elections Using Two-Year Election Cycles, 1920–1938

	1920	1922	1924	1926	1928	1930	1932	1934	1936	1938
Alabama	19.6	11.8	12.4	8.5	15.3	14.7	16.7	11.5	17.3	8.2
Alaska	—	—	—	—	—	—	—	—	—	—
Arizona	32.6	26.0	23.3	30.8	35.0	21.4	42.1	36.7	40.2	37.2
Arkansas	21.9	3.9	15.0	3.6	21.1	15.0	21.9	13.7	16.6	13.4
California	35.0	29.8	34.0	29.4	37.3	28.4	46.1	47.5	50.0	51.0
Colorado	49.1	46.1	54.3	48.6	57.7	50.5	66.9	60.0	67.5	64.6
Connecticut	43.3	37.3	41.6	32.5	57.7	43.4	58.1	52.3	63.3	56.0
Delaware	68.6	52.2	62.2	47.5	71.3	58.5	72.5	61.7	76.3	63.2
Florida	22.9	8.4	14.5	8.8	27.2	11.1	26.4	12.4	26.4	13.3
Georgia	19.6	5.5	10.9	3.2	13.5	3.8	15.9	3.3	16.6	4.0
Hawaii	—	—	—	—	—	—	—	—	—	—
Idaho	58.6	51.2	56.5	47.5	60.0	51.3	70.6	59.8	68.1	59.6
Illinois	53.0	40.7	51.4	36.4	62.2	42.7	63.6	54.4	72.2	57.9
Indiana	70.3	59.3	66.7	53.7	72.2	60.6	75.5	69.5	76.0	71.8
Iowa	50.2	40.5	56.6	34.2	54.4	35.2	61.4	53.2	66.5	49.8
Kansas	51.5	50.2	55.7	44.1	53.5	50.0	63.3	66.3	69.6	63.8
Kentucky	66.1	26.8	51.7	36.8	67.3	38.6	66.2	31.1	59.2	33.5
Louisiana	10.0	4.6	9.3	5.2	15.3	11.7	20.7	15.1	22.8	11.5
Maine	42.7	36.7	51.3	35.9	42.9	29.5	47.4	55.2	58.5	53.7
Maryland	43.8	34.2	34.0	35.6	47.8	46.7	43.9	42.5	48.9	42.4
Massachusetts	38.8	33.4	42.7	36.2	54.9	43.8	54.9	49.7	63.0	59.9
Michigan	45.6	23.1	44.5	21.2	47.9	25.3	52.1	38.9	53.1	47.1
Minnesota	54.1	45.1	56.3	44.7	64.5	49.4	72.1	60.7	64.4	61.4
Mississippi	8.0	7.5	10.6	2.8	11.2	3.4	12.6	5.2	13.1	3.0
Missouri	64.7	46.8	60.0	45.4	68.2	41.7	70.6	55.9	75.2	50.7
Montana	54.6	46.8	49.7	48.0	57.0	53.4	64.0	59.0	61.1	59.9
Nebraska	48.8	49.9	57.0	49.7	65.6	51.2	66.8	63.2	68.8	57.4
Nevada	51.5	52.1	46.7	53.2	54.3	55.3	64.5	62.6	62.9	62.7
New Hampshire	55.0	44.8	55.4	43.0	63.2	42.1	64.3	55.5	65.1	56.8
New Jersey	44.1	39.2	45.4	34.9	60.1	39.4	58.3	50.3	62.4	55.3
New Mexico	56.9	57.3	57.0	52.8	55.7	54.1	64.9	60.8	65.4	57.3
New York	41.6	35.5	43.0	37.2	53.9	37.2	52.2	41.9	59.4	49.5
North Carolina	44.0	28.5	34.9	25.5	43.7	34.5	43.6	29.1	45.0	25.9
North Dakota	64.7	45.6	50.6	42.5	57.1	51.0	60.3	76.0	64.2	58.4
Ohio	54.5	43.3	49.1	33.0	59.1	45.5	55.6	45.9	63.3	50.0
Oklahoma	47.5	43.7	44.7	30.7	48.0	35.5	49.3	40.2	50.3	33.0
Oregon	40.3	34.7	47.0	36.5	49.2	36.8	53.8	42.5	55.9	50.6
Pennsylvania	35.6	28.0	38.0	27.2	54.3	35.7	48.1	49.3	67.0	60.9
Rhode Island	45.3	41.0	53.2	41.0	57.2	52.1	60.4	55.3	67.4	64.8
South Carolina	8.4	4.5	6.2	1.8	7.6	2.0	12.5	2.5	12.5	4.8
South Dakota	52.8	45.3	54.2	45.5	65.9	44.1	70.8	71.8	74.0	70.8
Tennessee	32.6	17.5	17.4	7.7	21.4	14.0	23.1	17.9	24.7	16.0
Texas	16.7	15.5	24.5	8.2	21.2	9.1	25.6	12.8	22.7	9.8
Utah	63.1	50.7	61.1	56.6	68.4	58.5	75.2	63.8	74.2	60.9
Vermont	40.8	32.3	44.6	33.1	58.9	33.0	60.3	58.0	62.4	50.5
Virginia	20.4	13.6	18.5	8.5	23.9	12.7	27.0	10.6	22.2	8.4
Washington	43.8	29.3	37.9	28.5	43.7	28.6	52.9	44.3	57.8	50.7
West Virginia	66.4	48.8	69.2	50.8	73.4	59.7	78.8	64.1	82.5	60.3
Wisconsin	40.9	28.7	44.2	28.8	52.1	28.8	57.4	47.4	58.5	46.3
Wyoming	48.7	48.6	58.4	51.4	58.1	51.5	65.6	64.4	67.1	62.6

Notes: Mobilization is the ratio V/A, where V is the total vote cast in congressional (House) races in a given election year in a state, and A is the total number of adults in that state. These raw data—number of House votes cast and adults in each state—are used to produce the entries in this table. Both states with even-numbered year House races and states with odd-numbered year House races in a given two-year election cycle have their congressional vote divided by the number of adults in the state in the even-numbered year, which serves as a common base by which to compare congressional votes in any given two-year cycle for House elections. States with partial data (less than 100 percent of districts reporting the vote) are not included. States with special House elections are also not included. The few states having House elections in both even- and odd-numbered years in the same two-year election cycle only have the even-numbered election included in this table. For a more detailed discussion of the methodology used, see the notes to Table 3-4.

Sources: Adults—decennial censuses (1790–1990) of the U.S. Census Bureau; Bureau of U.S. Census Series P pamphlets for 1972 and the 1990s; and Richard Scammon's book series, *America Votes* (various publication dates). House vote—Tables 5-70 through 5-122.

Table 3-36 State Voter Mobilization Percentages for Congressional Elections Using Two-Year Election Cycles, 1940–1959

	1940	1942	1944	1946	1948	1950	1952	1954	1956	1958–1959
Alabama	17.3	4.3	13.6	10.7	11.5	8.7	19.4	15.7	21.3	13.1
Alaska	—	—	—	—	—	—	—	—	—	39.6
Arizona	48.5	25.0	36.6	29.7	38.7	40.2	49.7	40.1	45.6	41.2
Arkansas	19.0	8.9	19.6	13.7	22.6	26.6	32.9	25.8	24.3	—
California	56.7	35.5	51.7	37.2	52.7	46.6	59.2	47.3	59.6	54.0
Colorado	73.5	46.3	64.4	41.9	60.8	52.4	68.8	52.2	65.7	53.7
Connecticut	67.5	47.3	66.3	52.6	65.7	63.5	76.8	63.6	73.8	62.5
Delaware	75.9	46.0	66.2	57.0	68.8	61.4	76.5	61.8	72.0	59.7
Florida	31.2	6.8	28.3	11.8	20.6	13.9	35.7	14.0	36.5	17.4
Georgia	15.3	3.4	14.7	8.4	18.6	14.4	26.2	16.3	26.3	6.8
Hawaii	—	—	—	—	—	—	—	—	—	47.3[1]
Idaho	74.0	43.5	62.8	53.4	62.1	57.3	74.8	63.1	71.7	65.0
Illinois	74.9	52.5	69.2	60.4	65.9	58.9	72.3	53.5	68.9	52.0
Indiana	78.8	56.0	69.9	54.9	65.5	62.1	74.4	60.0	72.9	63.0
Iowa	68.0	40.3	58.6	35.5	56.4	48.4	67.7	48.6	69.8	49.7
Kansas	67.9	41.9	55.6	45.8	57.4	48.7	65.5	48.3	64.1	55.0
Kentucky	54.6	20.7	50.3	34.3	43.0	28.0	53.6	37.0	52.6	25.5
Louisiana	23.3	6.0	19.4	7.1	20.8	14.3	25.5	12.9	22.6	10.3
Maine	46.3	29.7	33.4	31.1	37.6	41.2	40.5	41.7	50.5	47.4
Maryland	49.4	26.9	41.7	32.0	36.6	37.5	52.9	38.6	50.4	40.0
Massachusetts	67.0	44.6	62.3	52.3	61.8	58.0	71.2	55.3	69.7	54.9
Michigan	58.9	33.3	59.0	42.1	52.1	43.9	66.2	49.7	68.2	50.2
Minnesota	67.1	41.8	60.2	46.9	62.6	53.3	72.0	58.1	70.7	57.0
Mississippi	12.2	4.3	12.7	4.1	12.6	7.3	20.1	8.3	17.3	5.2
Missouri	72.6	36.6	59.5	41.9	59.7	47.3	70.1	44.5	63.3	43.5
Montana	66.8	47.2	54.4	52.0	58.1	56.5	68.2	59.3	68.9	59.3
Nebraska	68.8	42.5	60.8	43.7	53.8	50.7	65.8	47.3	63.6	48.4
Nevada	67.3	48.2	58.7	51.9	58.2	56.3	66.7	57.7	63.6	50.9
New Hampshire	67.1	47.2	64.2	47.1	63.5	52.5	72.2	53.2	69.4	53.6
New Jersey	65.7	41.0	61.1	43.9	57.0	46.8	67.0	50.2	65.3	50.7
New Mexico	64.0	35.0	47.3	37.5	52.1	46.0	58.4	44.4	54.2	41.6
New York	64.5	41.4	61.7	47.3	59.0	48.7	66.0	47.3	64.5	51.2
North Carolina	41.3	15.7	36.2	21.0	34.2	22.6	47.5	25.1	41.7	24.3
North Dakota	63.0	49.0	54.2	39.1	51.9	49.5	63.4	52.2	63.8	55.3
Ohio	65.5	35.2	59.8	43.1	54.4	50.8	62.7	45.4	60.2	54.3
Oklahoma	53.3	25.6	49.8	35.7	49.3	43.9	67.2	39.1	57.9	37.6
Oregon	61.7	34.6	52.1	37.2	51.6	49.9	65.6	54.8	68.8	56.2
Pennsylvania	60.6	38.4	56.2	46.2	53.2	50.2	64.4	52.5	64.0	56.0
Rhode Island	66.3	48.6	58.7	53.2	60.6	54.9	75.6	60.5	69.7	63.1
South Carolina	10.1	2.3	9.6	2.4	12.6	4.4	24.2	17.8	21.5	6.2
South Dakota	76.9	45.6	57.4	41.1	60.4	61.9	72.0	58.2	72.8	65.6
Tennessee	24.4	8.9	22.0	10.3	23.3	13.3	35.0	17.0	33.3	18.0
Texas	26.6	6.9	25.2	8.0	23.1	7.6	40.4	12.5	28.0	14.3
Utah	80.0	46.3	72.6	55.0	73.4	67.7	80.6	62.5	75.4	63.3
Vermont	61.6	25.3	53.1	31.3	51.8	37.4	64.8	48.7	66.2	52.9
Virginia	20.4	5.5	19.7	13.8	19.8	10.5	21.5	16.0	31.7	19.1
Washington	62.4	33.8	60.0	45.7	55.0	46.4	64.1	49.9	64.1	52.0
West Virginia	81.6	42.3	64.8	47.6	65.9	56.6	75.8	52.0	72.1	55.9
Wisconsin	62.9	36.4	55.4	45.9	55.5	49.9	69.7	50.1	66.1	50.7
Wyoming	68.8	46.8	58.4	46.9	56.0	52.3	70.0	59.3	64.7	59.5

Notes: Mobilization is the ratio V/A, where V is the total vote cast in congressional (House) races in a given election year in a state, and A is the total number of adults in that state. These raw data—number of House votes cast and adults in each state—are used to produce the entries in this table. Both states with even-numbered year House races and states with odd-numbered year House races in a given two-year election cycle have their congressional vote divided by the number of adults in the state in the even-numbered year, which serves as a common base by which to compare congressional votes in any given two-year cycle for House elections. States with partial data (less than 100 percent of districts reporting the vote) are not included. States with special House elections are also not included. The few states having House elections in both even- and odd-numbered years in the same two-year election cycle only have the even-numbered election included in this table. For a more detailed discussion of the methodology used, see the notes to Table 3-4.

[1]Election held in odd-numbered year.

Sources: Adults—decennial censuses (1790–1990) of the U.S. Census Bureau; Bureau of U.S. Census Series P pamphlets for 1972 and the 1990s; and Richard Scammon's book series, *America Votes* (various publication dates). House vote—Tables 5-70 through 5-122.

Table 3-37 State Voter Mobilization Percentages for Congressional Elections Using Two-Year Election Cycles, 1960–1978

	1960	1962	1964	1966	1968	1970	1972	1974	1976	1978
Alabama	23.9	24.8	32.3	36.3	45.9	36.7	41.8	23.1	38.9	24.4
Alaska	44.2	42.0	46.1	43.5	51.1	49.0	47.0	43.6	49.9	48.9
Arizona	51.5	44.1	54.1	40.0	47.8	39.0	45.2	37.0	45.0	29.3
Arkansas	—	—	—	—	—	—	—	—	—	—
California	64.1	54.8	63.8	56.0	59.7	51.6	57.7	39.4	47.6	39.6
Colorado	69.4	55.0	66.5	53.7	62.6	49.0	56.9	45.5	55.5	40.0
Connecticut	76.6	62.6	71.1	57.1	66.6	57.3	64.6	50.4	61.6	45.7
Delaware	72.8	55.1	68.7	54.3	64.5	49.7	59.6	41.0	53.3	37.9
Florida	40.4	28.2	39.4	27.4	43.2	—	—	—	—	—
Georgia	23.8	13.5	33.2	33.0	35.9	32.8	28.3	24.8	36.0	16.1
Hawaii	50.7	51.5	58.0	50.3	56.3	46.3	50.2	44.5	47.5	38.8
Idaho	77.9	66.9	73.4	62.8	68.7	57.1	61.5	47.5	60.7	47.5
Illinois	73.3	56.9	70.7	56.9	66.4	51.7	57.9	36.8	55.4	37.9
Indiana	76.4	63.1	71.6	56.8	67.7	56.2	60.3	48.2	57.1	38.3
Iowa	73.7	48.0	68.0	52.2	66.3	45.9	62.4	46.1	62.0	39.7
Kansas	65.9	46.9	60.6	48.8	60.0	52.4	57.1	49.0	55.9	40.5
Kentucky	48.1	33.2	50.1	35.5	45.2	24.7	44.4	29.4	41.2	19.2
Louisiana	28.8	18.7	31.6	28.1	31.6	17.8	28.4	—	38.5	—
Maine	70.4	48.9	63.0	53.0	64.8	53.4	59.7	49.1	63.3	47.7
Maryland	53.2	35.8	48.2	35.7	45.5	37.8	44.8	31.2	45.6	31.1
Massachusetts	69.6	59.8	62.9	53.2	59.5	51.3	54.5	42.1	57.1	43.3
Michigan	70.1	57.1	63.6	48.1	60.5	49.8	55.7	41.8	55.4	42.6
Minnesota	75.7	58.9	72.7	57.2	70.5	60.4	66.6	46.4	66.0	54.3
Mississippi	22.0	13.6	30.1	31.5	36.5	25.1	40.2	20.1	40.2	31.5
Missouri	68.4	44.4	64.0	37.2	60.5	41.6	56.6	36.4	56.1	44.5
Montana	70.0	63.4	70.0	64.9	65.6	61.6	67.0	51.7	62.6	53.1
Nebraska	67.5	51.4	64.3	53.5	58.9	50.1	55.7	42.8	56.1	45.1
Nevada	59.1	46.7	58.4	51.5	52.9	46.3	49.2	39.9	42.0	36.0
New Hampshire	76.4	57.2	69.6	55.1	65.9	48.2	60.4	39.2	54.8	41.1
New Jersey	68.9	49.2	66.3	49.7	62.2	47.1	56.5	40.8	54.1	36.6
New Mexico	60.1	47.9	61.2	47.2	57.0	51.5	55.8	43.8	51.6	34.3
New York	64.8	50.5	60.8	49.1	53.9	47.5	52.0	38.4	46.8	34.1
North Carolina	50.9	30.9	47.7	32.5	48.0	31.0	38.1	26.6	40.4	25.2
North Dakota	72.2	60.9	70.1	55.6	67.0	59.1	65.4	55.2	66.4	49.1
Ohio	65.9	49.7	59.4	45.5	58.1	47.9	53.7	40.4	51.7	36.7
Oklahoma	59.2	43.1	56.7	42.0	52.3	42.7	44.9	26.6	53.6	28.3
Oregon	71.0	56.6	66.3	55.4	63.4	50.8	58.2	47.1	54.4	48.4
Pennsylvania	69.8	60.9	64.9	54.7	62.6	49.1	54.4	40.5	52.3	41.1
Rhode Island	72.7	57.9	66.6	56.5	62.8	55.1	56.9	44.2	56.1	44.1
South Carolina	25.9	20.1	33.2	26.3	44.0	29.1	35.8	27.7	39.8	27.8
South Dakota	76.9	64.7	73.9	57.9	70.1	60.8	67.9	60.1	63.6	53.8
Tennessee	30.7	28.2	46.9	35.3	43.6	41.6	39.9	31.1	41.3	33.6
Texas	36.8	27.0	42.5	20.5	37.7	27.9	37.4	18.0	41.5	23.3
Utah	79.0	64.9	77.8	58.1	75.6	65.4	68.7	55.3	67.6	43.9
Vermont	72.0	51.3	67.4	54.6	61.7	58.5	60.4	43.7	54.8	34.3
Virginia	27.7	18.6	37.1	26.3	47.1	32.5	39.0	27.1	41.0	28.4
Washington	65.5	49.3	64.6	48.9	60.5	49.7	55.9	39.3	53.6	34.6
West Virginia	75.7	56.7	71.5	46.0	66.5	41.1	61.7	32.9	50.8	32.9
Wisconsin	70.6	51.8	67.3	46.2	64.5	51.1	60.7	39.1	62.2	44.6
Wyoming	70.6	60.9	72.4	62.3	63.5	59.6	64.7	50.7	55.2	43.2

Notes: Mobilization is the ratio V/A, where V is the total vote cast in congressional (House) races in a given election year in a state, and A is the total number of adults in that state. These raw data—number of House votes cast and adults in each state—are used to produce the entries in this table. Both states with even-numbered year House races and states with odd-numbered year House races in a given two-year election cycle have their congressional vote divided by the number of adults in the state in the even-numbered year, which serves as a common base by which to compare congressional votes in any given two-year cycle for House elections. States with partial data (less than 100 percent of districts reporting the vote) are not included. States with special House elections are also not included. The few states having House elections in both even- and odd-numbered years in the same two-year election cycle only have the even-numbered election included in this table. For a more detailed discussion of the methodology used, see the notes to Table 3-4.

Sources: Adults—decennial censuses (1790–1990) of the U.S. Census Bureau; Bureau of U.S. Census Series P pamphlets for 1972 and the 1990s; and Richard Scammon's book series, *America Votes* (various publication dates). House vote—Tables 5-70 through 5-122.

Table 3-38 State Voter Mobilization Percentages for Congressional Elections Using Two-Year Election Cycles, 1980–1998

	1980	1982	1984	1986	1988	1990	1992	1994	1996	1998
Alabama	37.0	34.5	40.6	38.7	40.2	34.1	52.4	35.5	45.7	36.9
Alaska	57.0	61.9	65.8	53.8	54.1	50.7	60.9	51.1	55.4	51.1
Arizona	44.3	34.2	42.3	33.8	44.4	36.0	48.6	35.3	40.7	28.3
Arkansas	—	46.4	—	39.5	—	38.5	50.3	39.3	46.8	—
California	47.3	41.6	46.7	35.8	44.5	33.1	47.0	36.5	40.8	33.8
Colorado	55.3	44.0	56.2	44.4	55.7	41.1	57.7	39.1	51.7	43.0
Connecticut	58.6	45.8	60.0	40.2	53.9	40.9	57.0	42.8	52.1	38.7
Delaware	50.6	42.5	53.1	34.0	48.1	35.3	53.2	36.4	48.4	31.8
Florida	—	—	—	—	—	—	—	—	—	—
Georgia	35.5	22.6	36.3	24.3	36.6	29.3	44.4	28.7	39.7	28.7
Hawaii	40.7	41.6	37.0	42.9	42.5	41.2	42.6	41.5	40.8	45.3
Idaho	65.1	49.4	61.2	55.8	59.4	45.0	63.4	49.6	58.8	42.7
Illinois	54.7	43.8	55.1	36.1	51.6	36.3	56.5	35.3	47.5	36.7
Indiana	56.5	45.9	55.1	38.9	52.4	37.0	53.2	36.4	48.6	35.7
Iowa	60.2	48.3	61.1	43.0	57.6	38.5	59.7	46.4	56.3	41.8
Kansas	54.4	43.6	56.7	44.3	51.9	43.0	61.0	43.7	55.3	37.8
Kentucky	41.0	26.8	45.0	23.6	40.9	28.0	48.7	27.4	42.3	36.8
Louisiana	—	—	—	—	—	—	—	—	—	—
Maine	63.9	54.7	63.7	48.3	61.9	56.3	72.1	53.6	63.3	43.3
Maryland	46.0	34.5	45.6	31.3	44.5	30.1	49.3	36.1	43.4	38.8
Massachusetts	53.1	43.7	53.2	33.4	51.8	44.0	55.9	42.1	51.1	36.8
Michigan	55.1	42.7	52.0	34.7	51.0	35.6	55.9	42.6	51.7	41.1
Minnesota	65.6	59.0	65.3	45.1	62.6	55.5	69.4	52.3	62.7	58.6
Mississippi	46.2	37.1	49.5	29.4	50.9	20.2	51.5	32.3	46.0	27.4
Missouri	57.7	42.4	55.8	38.6	55.2	35.6	60.8	45.0	53.1	38.9
Montana	61.0	56.6	65.8	56.0	63.8	55.0	67.6	57.0	63.4	50.4
Nebraska	55.7	46.0	57.4	48.8	57.4	51.0	60.8	48.0	54.7	42.7
Nevada	41.8	36.1	38.0	33.1	40.9	34.6	48.8	33.9	37.1	31.2
New Hampshire	55.0	38.6	51.1	31.5	53.9	35.0	60.5	36.0	56.1	35.7
New Jersey	51.0	39.1	53.5	27.2	47.7	30.8	50.1	33.4	46.7	29.9
New Mexico	46.2	42.8	52.1	38.7	43.5	33.6	49.8	39.8	45.5	39.8
New York	43.6	35.9	47.1	29.2	40.6	26.7	43.3	33.8	40.7	31.4
North Carolina	41.1	30.1	47.5	33.4	40.8	40.0	48.7	29.7	45.5	33.5
North Dakota	63.5	56.4	66.8	61.9	64.8	50.5	63.8	50.1	55.6	44.7
Ohio	51.3	42.8	55.3	38.8	52.1	42.5	56.3	40.1	52.8	40.2
Oklahoma	38.5	39.0	49.9	32.2	33.6	37.1	54.4	40.6	48.7	34.9
Oregon	57.9	52.0	60.4	50.7	49.3	49.7	62.9	51.8	55.8	43.9
Pennsylvania	49.4	41.2	52.5	36.9	46.5	31.4	50.5	37.0	47.4	31.8
Rhode Island	54.9	46.3	53.2	40.8	51.2	44.6	51.7	44.7	47.5	39.0
South Carolina	38.1	29.1	39.7	29.7	39.8	26.1	42.2	31.8	37.7	33.7
South Dakota	65.9	56.5	64.5	58.8	63.0	51.7	65.6	59.1	61.2	48.1
Tennessee	39.6	34.9	38.3	31.5	39.3	19.6	45.7	36.4	44.5	22.2
Texas	41.0	27.5	43.3	26.7	39.9	27.0	44.3	31.2	37.9	24.2
Utah	64.3	51.2	60.7	41.8	57.4	40.4	61.7	39.9	49.2	32.9
Vermont	53.2	43.8	58.4	47.4	58.7	50.0	66.0	48.7	57.8	48.0
Virginia	40.1	33.1	43.8	23.9	41.8	24.6	49.3	38.8	43.6	22.2
Washington	54.3	42.0	55.8	38.5	49.7	36.4	59.0	42.9	53.1	43.6
West Virginia	49.3	39.5	51.3	29.0	41.9	27.8	41.2	29.5	37.5	25.0
Wisconsin	63.8	42.7	60.2	39.5	57.3	34.9	65.0	39.0	56.5	43.2
Wyoming	52.4	49.3	58.4	49.9	55.6	49.7	60.2	58.4	60.9	49.2

Notes: Mobilization is the ratio V/A, where V is the total vote cast in congressional (House) races in a given election year in a state, and A is the total number of adults in that state. These raw data—number of House votes cast and adults in each state—are used to produce the entries in this table. Both states with even-numbered year House races and states with odd-numbered year House races in a given two-year election cycle have their congressional vote divided by the number of adults in the state in the even-numbered year, which serves as a common base by which to compare congressional votes in any given two-year cycle for House elections. States with partial data (less than 100 percent of districts reporting the vote) are not included. States with special House elections are also not included. The few states having House elections in both even- and odd-numbered years in the same two-year election cycle only have the even-numbered election included in this table. For a more detailed discussion of the methodology used, see the notes to Table 3-4.

Sources: Adults—decennial censuses (1790–1990) of the U.S. Census Bureau; Bureau of U.S. Census Series P pamphlets for 1972 and the 1990s; and Richard Scammon's book series, *America Votes* (various publication dates). House vote—Tables 5-70 through 5-122.

Table 3-39 State Voter Mobilization Percentages for Congressional Elections in Odd-Numbered Years Only, 1789–1809

	1789	1791	1793	1795	1797	1799	1801	1803	1805	1807	1809
Alabama	—	—	—	—	—	—	—	—	—	—	—
Alaska	—	—	—	—	—	—	—	—	—	—	—
Arizona	—	—	—	—	—	—	—	—	—	—	—
Arkansas	—	—	—	—	—	—	—	—	—	—	—
California	—	—	—	—	—	—	—	—	—	—	—
Colorado	—	—	—	—	—	—	—	—	—	—	—
Connecticut	—	—	—	—	—	—	—	—	—	—	—
Delaware	8.9	—	—	—	—	—	—	—	—	—	—
Florida	—	—	—	—	—	—	—	—	—	—	—
Georgia	9.0	5.6	—	—	—	—	—	—	—	—	—
Hawaii	—	—	—	—	—	—	—	—	—	—	—
Idaho	—	—	—	—	—	—	—	—	—	—	—
Illinois	—	—	—	—	—	—	—	—	—	—	—
Indiana	—	—	—	—	—	—	—	—	—	—	—
Iowa	—	—	—	—	—	—	—	—	—	—	—
Kansas	—	—	—	—	—	—	—	—	—	—	—
Kentucky	—	—	—	—	—	—	25.4	—	—	—	—
Louisiana	—	—	—	—	—	—	—	—	—	—	—
Maine	—	—	—	—	—	—	—	—	—	—	—
Maryland	5.9	—	—	—	—	—	10.3	—	—	—	—
Massachusetts	—	—	—	—	—	—	—	—	—	—	—
Michigan	—	—	—	—	—	—	—	—	—	—	—
Minnesota	—	—	—	—	—	—	—	—	—	—	—
Mississippi	—	—	—	—	—	—	—	—	—	—	—
Missouri	—	—	—	—	—	—	—	—	—	—	—
Montana	—	—	—	—	—	—	—	—	—	—	—
Nebraska	—	—	—	—	—	—	—	—	—	—	—
Nevada	—	—	—	—	—	—	—	—	—	—	—
New Hampshire	—	—	—	—	—	—	—	—	—	—	—
New Jersey	17.7	8.2	—	—	13.3	—	—	15.6	—	—	—
New Mexico	—	—	—	—	—	—	—	—	—	—	—
New York	—	—	13.9	—	—	—	—	—	—	—	—
North Carolina	—	—	—	—	—	—	—	—	—	—	—
North Dakota	—	—	—	—	—	—	—	—	—	—	—
Ohio	—	—	—	—	—	—	—	20.6	—	—	—
Oklahoma	—	—	—	—	—	—	—	—	—	—	—
Oregon	—	—	—	—	—	—	—	—	—	—	—
Pennsylvania	—	—	—	—	—	—	—	—	—	—	—
Rhode Island	—	—	—	—	—	—	—	—	—	—	—
South Carolina	—	—	—	—	—	—	—	4.3	—	—	—
South Dakota	—	—	—	—	—	—	—	—	—	—	—
Tennessee	—	—	—	—	—	—	22.0	18.2	23.8	—	—
Texas	—	—	—	—	—	—	—	—	—	—	—
Utah	—	—	—	—	—	—	—	—	—	—	—
Vermont	—	—	6.8	—	—	—	—	—	—	—	—
Virginia	—	—	—	—	—	—	—	—	—	—	—
Washington	—	—	—	—	—	—	—	—	—	—	—
West Virginia	—	—	—	—	—	—	—	—	—	—	—
Wisconsin	—	—	—	—	—	—	—	—	—	—	—
Wyoming	—	—	—	—	—	—	—	—	—	—	—

Notes: The entries are states that held their House elections in odd-numbered years. Mobilization is defined here as the ratio V/A, where V is the total vote cast in congressional (House) races in an odd-numbered election year in a state, and A is the total number of adults in that state in the odd-numbered year. These raw data—number of House votes cast in an odd-numbered year and number of adults in that state in the odd-numbered year—are used to produce the entries. States with partial data (less than 100 percent of districts reporting the vote) are not included. States with special House elections are also not included. For a more detailed discussion of the general methodology used to obtain congressional vote and adult data, see the notes to Table 3-4.

Sources: Adults—decennial censuses (1790–1990) of the U.S. Census Bureau; Bureau of U.S. Census Series P pamphlets for 1972 and the 1990s; and Richard Scammon's book series, *America Votes* (various publication dates). House vote—Tables 5-70 through 5-122.

Table 3-40 State Voter Mobilization Percentages for Congressional Elections in Odd-Numbered Years Only, 1811–1829

	1811	1813	1815	1817	1819	1821	1823	1825	1827	1829
Alabama	—	—	—	—	32.6	31.6	—	—	—	28.9
Alaska	—	—	—	—	—	—	—	—	—	—
Arizona	—	—	—	—	—	—	—	—	—	—
Arkansas	—	—	—	—	—	—	—	—	—	—
California	—	—	—	—	—	—	—	—	—	—
Colorado	—	—	—	—	—	—	—	—	—	—
Connecticut	—	—	—	—	—	5.5	3.9	5.7	10.3	10.1
Delaware	—	—	—	—	—	—	—	—	—	—
Florida	—	—	—	—	—	—	—	—	—	—
Georgia	—	—	—	—	—	—	—	—	—	—
Hawaii	—	—	—	—	—	—	—	—	—	—
Idaho	—	—	—	—	—	—	—	—	—	—
Illinois	—	—	—	—	—	—	—	—	—	—
Indiana	—	—	—	23.9	—	—	—	—	—	—
Iowa	—	—	—	—	—	—	—	—	—	—
Kansas	—	—	—	—	—	—	—	—	—	—
Kentucky	—	—	—	—	—	—	—	—	30.8	—
Louisiana	—	—	—	—	—	—	—	—	—	—
Maine	—	—	—	—	—	—	19.1	—	—	—
Maryland	—	—	—	—	—	—	—	—	—	20.0
Massachusetts	—	—	—	—	—	—	—	—	—	—
Michigan	—	—	—	—	—	—	—	—	—	—
Minnesota	—	—	—	—	—	—	—	—	—	—
Mississippi	—	—	—	12.5	—	—	—	—	—	—
Missouri	—	—	—	—	—	—	—	—	—	—
Montana	—	—	—	—	—	—	—	—	—	—
Nebraska	—	—	—	—	—	—	—	—	—	—
Nevada	—	—	—	—	—	—	—	—	—	—
New Hampshire	—	—	—	—	21.8	—	—	—	23.8	31.3
New Jersey	—	24.1	—	—	—	—	—	—	—	—
New Mexico	—	—	—	—	—	—	—	—	—	—
New York	—	—	—	—	—	24.8	—	—	—	—
North Carolina	—	—	—	—	—	—	—	—	—	—
North Dakota	—	—	—	—	—	—	—	—	—	—
Ohio	—	—	—	—	—	—	—	—	—	—
Oklahoma	—	—	—	—	—	—	—	—	—	—
Oregon	—	—	—	—	—	—	—	—	—	—
Pennsylvania	—	—	—	—	—	—	—	—	—	—
Rhode Island	—	—	—	—	—	—	—	7.1	5.0	11.9
South Carolina	—	—	—	—	—	—	8.1	—	—	—
South Dakota	—	—	—	—	—	—	—	—	—	—
Tennessee	20.2	—	—	30.7	32.0	—	—	—	—	—
Texas	—	—	—	—	—	—	—	—	—	—
Utah	—	—	—	—	—	—	—	—	—	—
Vermont	—	—	—	—	—	—	—	—	—	—
Virginia	—	—	—	—	—	—	—	—	—	—
Washington	—	—	—	—	—	—	—	—	—	—
West Virginia	—	—	—	—	—	—	—	—	—	—
Wisconsin	—	—	—	—	—	—	—	—	—	—
Wyoming	—	—	—	—	—	—	—	—	—	—

Notes: The entries are states that held their House elections in odd-numbered years. Mobilization is defined here as the ratio V/A, where V is the total vote cast in congressional (House) races in an odd-numbered election year in a state, and A is the total number of adults in that state in the odd-numbered year. These raw data—number of House votes cast in an odd-numbered year and number of adults in that state in the odd-numbered year—are used to produce the entries. States with partial data (less than 100 percent of districts reporting the vote) are not included. States with special House elections are also not included. For a more detailed discussion of the general methodology used to obtain congressional vote and adult data, see the notes to Table 3-4.

Sources: Adults—decennial censuses (1790–1990) of the U.S. Census Bureau; Bureau of U.S. Census Series P pamphlets for 1972 and the 1990s; and Richard Scammon's book series, *America Votes* (various publication dates). House vote—Tables 5-70 through 5-122.

Table 3-41 State Voter Mobilization Percentages for Congressional Elections in Odd-Numbered Years Only, 1831–1849

	1831	1833	1835	1837	1839	1841	1843	1845	1847	1849
Alabama	—	—	—	—	—	17.2	—	—	—	23.1
Alaska	—	—	—	—	—	—	—	—	—	—
Arizona	—	—	—	—	—	—	—	—	—	—
Arkansas	—	—	—	14.8	—	—	—	—	—	—
California	—	—	—	—	—	—	—	—	—	17.0
Colorado	—	—	—	—	—	—	—	—	—	—
Connecticut	11.8	13.1	26.2	28.2	31.4	28.7	31.0	31.4	30.7	27.8
Delaware	—	—	—	—	—	—	—	—	—	—
Florida	—	—	—	—	—	—	—	19.0	—	—
Georgia	—	—	—	—	—	—	—	—	—	—
Hawaii	—	—	—	—	—	—	—	—	—	—
Idaho	—	—	—	—	—	—	—	—	—	—
Illinois	34.2	—	—	—	—	33.6	39.0	—	—	—
Indiana	37.9	37.4	35.9	37.8	40.9	32.3	39.8	38.1	37.8	36.4
Iowa	—	—	—	—	—	—	—	—	34.1	—
Kansas	—	—	—	—	—	—	—	—	—	—
Kentucky	—	—	—	—	—	12.7	30.6	31.1	32.4	26.3
Louisiana	—	—	—	—	—	—	7.4	—	—	—
Maine	—	25.2	—	—	—	—	26.2	—	—	—
Maryland	20.1	23.3	—	18.7	25.3	18.4	—	24.7	—	21.3
Massachusetts	—	12.7	—	—	—	—	—	—	—	—
Michigan	—	—	14.0	31.5	—	—	32.8	—	—	—
Minnesota	—	—	—	—	—	—	—	—	—	—
Mississippi	—	—	17.9	14.9	24.4	22.0	21.3	24.7	21.6	23.3
Missouri	21.1	16.6	24.0	—	—	—	—	—	—	—
Montana	—	—	—	—	—	—	—	—	—	—
Nebraska	—	—	—	—	—	—	—	—	—	—
Nevada	—	—	—	—	—	—	—	—	—	—
New Hampshire	30.9	23.5	27.8	16.4	38.6	34.3	28.7	33.2	36.1	32.3
New Jersey	—	—	—	—	—	—	—	—	—	—
New Mexico	—	—	—	—	—	—	—	—	—	—
New York	—	—	—	—	—	—	—	—	—	—
North Carolina	—	—	—	—	—	—	17.7	22.9	18.3	20.9
North Dakota	—	—	—	—	—	—	—	—	—	—
Ohio	—	—	—	—	—	—	31.4	—	—	—
Oklahoma	—	—	—	—	—	—	—	—	—	—
Oregon	—	—	—	—	—	—	—	—	—	—
Pennsylvania	—	—	—	—	—	—	23.4	—	—	—
Rhode Island	7.1	10.1	14.8	14.1	13.8	4.7	18.1	16.5	15.2	11.0
South Carolina	—	—	—	—	—	—	—	—	—	—
South Dakota	—	—	—	—	—	—	—	—	—	—
Tennessee	31.9	32.2	31.0	32.1	33.8	20.7	31.2	29.5	30.8	18.2
Texas	—	—	—	—	—	—	—	—	—	28.1
Utah	—	—	—	—	—	—	—	—	—	—
Vermont	—	17.3	—	—	—	—	33.0	—	—	—
Virginia	—	—	—	—	—	—	—	—	—	—
Washington	—	—	—	—	—	—	—	—	—	—
West Virginia	—	—	—	—	—	—	—	—	—	—
Wisconsin	—	—	—	—	—	—	—	—	—	—
Wyoming	—	—	—	—	—	—	—	—	—	—

Notes: The entries are states that held their House elections in odd-numbered years. Mobilization is defined here as the ratio V/A, where V is the total vote cast in congressional (House) races in an odd-numbered election year in a state, and A is the total number of adults in that state in the odd-numbered year. These raw data—number of House votes cast in an odd-numbered year and number of adults in that state in the odd-numbered year—are used to produce the entries. States with partial data (less than 100 percent of districts reporting the vote) are not included. States with special House elections are also not included. For a more detailed discussion of the general methodology used to obtain congressional vote and adult data, see the notes to Table 3-4.

Sources: Adults—decennial censuses (1790–1990) of the U.S. Census Bureau; Bureau of U.S. Census Series P pamphlets for 1972 and the 1990s; and Richard Scammon's book series, *America Votes* (various publication dates). House vote—Tables 5-70 through 5-122.

Table 3-42 State Voter Mobilization Percentages for Congressional Elections in Odd-Numbered Years Only, 1851–1869

	1851	1853	1855	1857	1859	1861	1863	1865	1867	1869
Alabama	—	—	20.4	19.9	—	—	—	—	—	27.2
Alaska	—	—	—	—	—	—	—	—	—	—
Arizona	—	—	—	—	—	—	—	—	—	—
Arkansas	23.1	15.9	—	—	—	—	—	—	—	—
California	52.0	—	—	—	52.5	55.6	45.7	—	32.1	—
Colorado	—	—	—	—	—	—	—	—	—	—
Connecticut	28.6	26.9	27.2	25.7	30.8	31.7	29.1	25.8	32.0	29.4
Delaware	—	—	—	—	—	—	—	—	—	—
Florida	—	—	—	—	—	—	—	—	—	—
Georgia	25.3	23.8	25.6	24.1	22.8	—	—	—	—	—
Hawaii	—	—	—	—	—	—	—	—	—	—
Idaho	—	—	—	—	—	—	—	—	—	—
Illinois	—	—	—	—	—	—	—	—	—	—
Indiana	35.6	—	—	—	—	—	—	—	—	—
Iowa	—	—	—	—	—	—	—	—	—	—
Kansas	—	—	—	—	26.6	—	—	—	—	—
Kentucky	24.5	27.4	30.3	28.0	29.3	26.1	16.3	21.0	20.5	—
Louisiana	13.4	—	13.7	11.9	11.2	—	—	—	—	—
Maine	—	—	—	—	—	—	—	—	—	—
Maryland	19.2	24.7	27.2	27.5	23.5	20.3	14.7	—	—	—
Massachusetts	—	—	—	—	—	—	—	—	—	—
Michigan	—	—	—	—	—	—	—	—	—	—
Minnesota	—	—	—	61.3	53.5	—	—	—	—	—
Mississippi	22.7	23.6	21.2	12.6	12.6	—	—	—	—	32.4
Missouri	—	—	—	—	—	—	—	—	—	—
Montana	—	—	—	—	—	—	—	—	—	—
Nebraska	—	—	—	—	—	—	—	—	—	—
Nevada	—	—	—	—	—	—	—	31.1	—	—
New Hampshire	29.7	28.9	35.4	34.9	37.2	35.9	35.1	35.2	36.3	35.3
New Jersey	—	—	—	—	—	—	—	—	—	—
New Mexico	—	—	—	—	—	—	—	—	—	—
New York	—	—	—	—	—	—	—	—	—	—
North Carolina	—	21.1	23.0	19.1	19.4	—	—	—	—	—
North Dakota	—	—	—	—	—	—	—	—	—	—
Ohio	—	—	—	—	—	—	—	—	—	—
Oklahoma	—	—	—	—	—	—	—	—	—	—
Oregon	—	—	—	—	49.8	—	—	—	—	—
Pennsylvania	—	—	—	—	—	—	—	—	—	—
Rhode Island	15.5	18.4	—	16.0	13.2	22.0	17.6	8.8	7.4	—
South Carolina	—	—	—	—	—	—	—	—	—	—
South Dakota	—	—	—	—	—	—	—	—	—	—
Tennessee	—	—	29.5	27.9	30.3	—	—	11.7	18.5	—
Texas	22.1	24.6	26.8	25.3	25.4	—	—	—	—	22.7
Utah	—	—	—	—	—	—	—	—	—	—
Vermont	—	—	—	—	—	—	22.4	—	—	—
Virginia	—	—	—	—	—	—	—	—	—	38.7
Washington	—	—	—	—	—	—	—	—	—	—
West Virginia	—	—	—	—	—	—	10.9	—	—	—
Wisconsin	—	—	—	—	—	—	—	—	—	—
Wyoming	—	—	—	—	—	—	—	—	—	—

Notes: The entries are states that held their House elections in odd-numbered years. Mobilization is defined here as the ratio V/A, where V is the total vote cast in congressional (House) races in an odd-numbered election year in a state, and A is the total number of adults in that state in the odd-numbered year. These raw data—number of House votes cast in an odd-numbered year and number of adults in that state in the odd-numbered year—are used to produce the entries. States with partial data (less than 100 percent of districts reporting the vote) are not included. States with special House elections are also not included. For a more detailed discussion of the general methodology used to obtain congressional vote and adult data, see the notes to Table 3-4.

Sources: Adults—decennial censuses (1790–1990) of the U.S. Census Bureau; Bureau of U.S. Census Series P pamphlets for 1972 and the 1990s; and Richard Scammon's book series, *America Votes* (various publication dates). House vote—Tables 5-70 through 5-122.

Table 3-43 State Voter Mobilization Percentages for Congressional Elections in Odd-Numbered Years Only, 1871–1959

	1871	1873	1875	1877	1879	1889	1895	1907	1911	1959
Alabama	—	—	—	—	—	—	—	—	—	—
Alaska	—	—	—	—	—	—	—	—	—	—
Arizona	—	—	—	—	—	—	—	—	17.1	—
Arkansas	—	—	—	—	—	—	—	—	—	—
California	34.7	—	29.5	—	32.3	—	—	—	—	—
Colorado	—	—	—	—	—	—	—	—	—	—
Connecticut	29.9	26.5	29.8	—	—	—	—	—	—	—
Delaware	—	—	—	—	—	—	—	—	—	—
Florida	—	—	—	—	—	—	—	—	—	—
Georgia	—	—	—	—	—	—	—	—	—	—
Hawaii	—	—	—	—	—	—	—	—	—	46.4
Idaho	—	—	—	—	—	—	—	—	—	—
Illinois	—	—	—	—	—	—	—	—	—	—
Indiana	—	—	—	—	—	—	—	—	—	—
Iowa	—	—	—	—	—	—	—	—	—	—
Kansas	—	—	—	—	—	—	—	—	—	—
Kentucky	—	—	—	—	—	—	—	—	—	—
Louisiana	—	—	—	—	—	—	—	—	—	—
Maine	—	—	—	—	—	—	—	—	—	—
Maryland	—	—	—	—	—	—	—	—	—	—
Massachusetts	—	—	—	—	—	—	—	—	—	—
Michigan	—	—	—	—	—	—	—	—	—	—
Minnesota	—	—	—	—	—	—	—	—	—	—
Mississippi	—	—	38.0	—	—	—	—	—	—	—
Missouri	—	—	—	—	—	—	—	—	—	—
Montana	—	—	—	—	—	47.4	—	—	—	—
Nebraska	—	—	—	—	—	—	—	—	—	—
Nevada	—	—	—	—	—	—	—	—	—	—
New Hampshire	36.0	34.0	38.8	37.3	—	—	—	—	—	—
New Jersey	—	—	—	—	—	—	—	—	—	—
New Mexico	—	—	—	—	—	—	—	—	36.6	—
New York	—	—	—	—	—	—	—	—	—	—
North Carolina	—	—	—	—	—	—	—	—	—	—
North Dakota	—	—	—	—	—	45.6	—	—	—	—
Ohio	—	—	—	—	—	—	—	—	—	—
Oklahoma	—	—	—	—	—	—	—	36.1	—	—
Oregon	—	—	—	—	—	—	—	—	—	—
Pennsylvania	—	—	—	—	—	—	—	—	—	—
Rhode Island	—	—	—	—	—	—	—	—	—	—
South Carolina	—	—	—	—	—	—	—	—	—	—
South Dakota	—	—	—	—	—	52.7	—	—	—	—
Tennessee	—	—	—	—	—	—	—	—	—	—
Texas	28.1	—	—	—	—	—	—	—	—	—
Utah	—	—	—	—	—	—	36.7	—	—	—
Vermont	—	—	—	—	—	—	—	—	—	—
Virginia	—	—	—	—	—	—	—	—	—	—
Washington	—	—	—	—	—	30.4	—	—	—	—
West Virginia	—	—	—	—	—	—	—	—	—	—
Wisconsin	—	—	—	—	—	—	—	—	—	—
Wyoming	—	—	—	—	—	—	—	—	—	—

Notes: The entries are states that held their House elections in odd-numbered years. Mobilization is defined here as the ratio V/A, where V is the total vote cast in congressional (House) races in an odd-numbered election year in a state, and A is the total number of adults in that state in the odd-numbered year. These raw data—number of House votes cast in an odd-numbered year and number of adults in that state in the odd-numbered year—are used to produce the entries. States with partial data (less than 100 percent of districts reporting the vote) are not included. States with special House elections are also not included. For a more detailed discussion of the general methodology used to obtain congressional vote and adult data, see the notes to Table 3-4.

Sources: Adults—decennial censuses (1790–1990) of the U.S. Census Bureau; Bureau of U.S. Census Series P pamphlets for 1972 and the 1990s; and Richard Scammon's book series, *America Votes* (various publication dates). House vote—Tables 5-70 through 5-122.

Table 3-44 State Voter Turnout Percentages for Congressional Elections Using Two-Year Election Cycles, 1788–1799

	1788–1789	1790–1791	1792–1793	1794–1795	1796–1797	1798–1799
Alabama	—	—	—	—	—	—
Alaska	—	—	—	—	—	—
Arizona	—	—	—	—	—	—
Arkansas	—	—	—	—	—	—
California	—	—	—	—	—	—
Colorado	—	—	—	—	—	—
Connecticut	—	5.8	6.4	6.8	5.5	9.3
Delaware	20.1[1]	—	43.0	43.5	36.8	40.3
Florida	—	—	—	—	—	—
Georgia	26.9[1]	18.3[1]	42.8	25.3	60.1	37.4
Hawaii	—	—	—	—	—	—
Idaho	—	—	—	—	—	—
Illinois	—	—	—	—	—	—
Indiana	—	—	—	—	—	—
Iowa	—	—	—	—	—	—
Kansas	—	—	—	—	—	—
Kentucky	—	—	—	—	—	—
Louisiana	—	—	—	—	—	—
Maine	—	—	—	—	—	—
Maryland	16.6[1]	36.1	34.7	32.8	25.3	—
Massachusetts	11.4	14.2	—	14.7	15.2	19.4
Michigan	—	—	—	—	—	—
Minnesota	—	—	—	—	—	—
Mississippi	—	—	—	—	—	—
Missouri	—	—	—	—	—	—
Montana	—	—	—	—	—	—
Nebraska	—	—	—	—	—	—
Nevada	—	—	—	—	—	—
New Hampshire	8.0	12.0	13.7	21.1	21.1	19.8
New Jersey	36.1[1]	16.8[1]	18.0	22.1	27.8[1]	46.8
New Mexico	—	—	—	—	—	—
New York	—	15.2	30.0[1]	26.1	27.0	33.3
North Carolina	—	—	—	—	—	—
North Dakota	—	—	—	—	—	—
Ohio	—	—	—	—	—	—
Oklahoma	—	—	—	—	—	—
Oregon	—	—	—	—	—	—
Pennsylvania	17.4	—	35.4	—	—	43.7
Rhode Island	—	—	—	21.8	26.1	28.5
South Carolina	—	—	—	—	27.6	—
South Dakota	—	—	—	—	—	—
Tennessee	—	—	—	—	—	—
Texas	—	—	—	—	—	—
Utah	—	—	—	—	—	—
Vermont	—	—	13.3[1]	19.7	28.0	37.3
Virginia	—	—	—	—	—	—
Washington	—	—	—	—	—	—
West Virginia	—	—	—	—	—	—
Wisconsin	—	—	—	—	—	—
Wyoming	—	—	—	—	—	—

Notes: Turnout is the ratio V/E, where V is the total vote cast in congressional (House) races in a given election year in a state, and E is the number of people eligible by law to vote in that state according to the criteria of citizenship, race, sex, and age laws on suffrage, where race has two dimensions: color (black/white) and bondage (slave/free). These raw data—number of House votes cast and eligibles in each state—are used to produce the entries. Both states with even-numbered year House races and states with odd-numbered year House races in a given two-year election cycle have their congressional vote divided by the number of eligibles in the state in the even-numbered year, which serves as a common base by which to compare congressional votes in any given two-year cycle for House elections. States with partial data (less than 100 percent of districts reporting the vote) are not included. States with special House elections are also not included. The few states having House elections in both even- and odd-numbered years in the same two-year election cycle only have the even-numbered election included in this table. For a more detailed discussion of the methodology used, see the notes to Table 3-5.

[1]House election held in odd-numbered year.

Sources: Eligibles—decennial censuses (1790–1990) of the U.S. Census Bureau; Bureau of U.S. Census Series P pamphlets for 1972 and the 1990s; Richard Scammon's book series, *America Votes* (various publication dates); the data archive of John J. Stucker; and relevant state constitutions and statute volumes. Also see Stucker (1973), Appendix B. House vote—Tables 5-70 through 5-122.

Table 3-45 State Voter Turnout Percentages for Congressional Elections Using Two-Year Election Cycles, 1800–1819

	1800–1801	1802–1803	1804–1805	1806–1807	1808–1809	1810–1811	1812–1813	1814–1815	1816–1817	1818–1819
Alabama	—	—	—	—	—	—	—	—	—	85.7[1]
Alaska	—	—	—	—	—	—	—	—	—	—
Arizona	—	—	—	—	—	—	—	—	—	—
Arkansas	—	—	—	—	—	—	—	—	—	—
California	—	—	—	—	—	—	—	—	—	—
Colorado	—	—	—	—	—	—	—	—	—	—
Connecticut	17.1	15.9	17.9	—	—	8.2	18.1	—	15.9	15.0
Delaware	43.2	56.2	66.5	29.4	44.2	50.7	51.7	45.3	49.3	42.2
Florida	—	—	—	—	—	—	—	—	—	—
Georgia	40.5	46.7	40.4	35.8	86.2	69.2	46.7	49.5	52.2	19.9
Hawaii	—	—	—	—	—	—	—	—	—	—
Idaho	—	—	—	—	—	—	—	—	—	—
Illinois	—	—	—	—	—	—	—	—	—	40.4
Indiana	—	—	—	—	—	—	—	—	35.6	—
Iowa	—	—	—	—	—	—	—	—	—	—
Kansas	—	—	—	—	—	—	—	—	—	—
Kentucky	62.5[1]	—	—	—	—	—	—	—	—	—
Louisiana	—	—	—	—	—	—	14.8	16.2	13.4	19.4
Maine	—	—	—	—	—	—	—	—	—	—
Maryland	29.2[1]	—	32.0	55.1	63.3	31.7	56.3	51.7	—	—
Massachusetts	24.9	25.7	39.5	27.6	47.1	29.2	48.3	38.5	33.3	27.3
Michigan	—	—	—	—	—	—	—	—	—	—
Minnesota	—	—	—	—	—	—	—	—	—	—
Mississippi	—	—	—	—	—	—	—	—	37.1[1]	—
Missouri	—	—	—	—	—	—	—	—	—	—
Montana	—	—	—	—	—	—	—	—	—	—
Nebraska	—	—	—	—	—	—	—	—	—	—
Nevada	—	—	—	—	—	—	—	—	—	—
New Hampshire	24.2	29.6	52.3	24.3	63.0	53.8	74.8	72.3	58.9	46.2[1]
New Jersey	69.5	33.1[1]	29.9	44.1	69.7	28.8	51.5[1]	65.4	10.4	26.2
New Mexico	—	—	—	—	—	—	—	—	—	—
New York	38.6	33.1	45.9	36.2	45.2	54.8	43.3	47.0	48.6	29.1
North Carolina	—	—	—	—	—	—	—	—	—	—
North Dakota	—	—	—	—	—	—	—	—	—	—
Ohio	—	45.4[1]	24.6	29.5	38.9	—	38.7	—	—	40.3
Oklahoma	—	—	—	—	—	—	—	—	—	—
Oregon	—	—	—	—	—	—	—	—	—	—
Pennsylvania	—	—	—	—	68.6	38.3	50.8	—	—	—
Rhode Island	26.0	28.5	10.5	22.7	38.1	42.6	44.8	38.9	12.8	10.9
South Carolina	—	16.3[1]	—	39.4	—	—	—	—	—	—
South Dakota	—	—	—	—	—	—	—	—	—	—
Tennessee	55.4[1]	45.1[1]	58.4[1]	—	—	48.8[1]	—	—	76.3[1]	79.9[1]
Texas	—	—	—	—	—	—	—	—	—	—
Utah	—	—	—	—	—	—	—	—	—	—
Vermont	33.7	28.0	43.5	—	—	51.7	70.2	—	64.3	38.8
Virginia	—	—	—	—	—	—	—	—	—	—
Washington	—	—	—	—	—	—	—	—	—	—
West Virginia	—	—	—	—	—	—	—	—	—	—
Wisconsin	—	—	—	—	—	—	—	—	—	—
Wyoming	—	—	—	—	—	—	—	—	—	—

Notes: Turnout is the ratio V/E, where V is the total vote cast in congressional (House) races in a given election year in a state, and E is the number of people eligible by law to vote in that state according to the criteria of citizenship, race, sex, and age laws on suffrage, where race has two dimensions: color (black/white) and bondage (slave/free). These raw data—number of House votes cast and eligibles in each state—are used to produce the entries. Both states with even-numbered year House races and states with odd-numbered year House races in a given two-year election cycle have their congressional vote divided by the number of eligibles in the state in the even-numbered year, which serves as a common base by which to compare congressional votes in any given two-year cycle for House elections. States with partial data (less than 100 percent of districts reporting the vote) are not included. States with special House elections are also not included. The few states having House elections in both even- and odd-numbered years in the same two-year election cycle only have the even-numbered election included in this table. For a more detailed discussion of the methodology used, see the notes to Table 3-5.

[1]House election held in odd-numbered year.

Sources: Eligibles—decennial censuses (1790–1990) of the U.S. Census Bureau; Bureau of U.S. Census Series P pamphlets for 1972 and the 1990s; Richard Scammon's book series, *America Votes* (various publication dates); the data archive of John J. Stucker; and relevant state constitutions and statute volumes. Also see Stucker (1973), Appendix B. House vote—Tables 5-70 through 5-122.

Table 3-46 State Voter Turnout Percentages for Congressional Elections Using Two-Year Election Cycles, 1820–1839

	1820–1821	1822–1823	1824–1825	1826–1827	1828–1829	1830–1831	1832–1833	1834–1835	1836–1837	1838–1839
Alabama	94.8[1]	—	—	—	88.0[1]	—	—	—	—	—
Alaska	—	—	—	—	—	—	—	—	—	—
Arizona	—	—	—	—	—	—	—	—	—	—
Arkansas	—	—	—	—	—	—	—	—	65.8	71.7
California	—	—	—	—	—	—	—	—	—	—
Colorado	—	—	—	—	—	—	—	—	—	—
Connecticut	11.8[1]	8.4[1]	12.5[1]	22.6[1]	22.2[1]	25.7[1]	28.7[1]	57.1[1]	61.5[1]	68.5[1]
Delaware	54.7	57.3	55.0	71.0	74.7	65.6	67.2	74.3	69.9	68.1
Florida	—	—	—	—	—	—	—	—	—	—
Georgia	40.1	72.5	22.2	65.0	85.4	92.1	94.9	88.6	79.7	83.0
Hawaii	—	—	—	—	—	—	—	—	—	—
Idaho	—	—	—	—	—	—	—	—	—	—
Illinois	65.9	55.3	62.0	54.7	60.9	77.3[1]	54.9	52.3	56.7	62.9
Indiana	62.7	—	—	62.4	—	80.5[1]	78.0[1]	73.9[1]	77.0[1]	82.6[1]
Iowa	—	—	—	—	—	—	—	—	—	—
Kansas	—	—	—	—	—	—	—	—	—	—
Kentucky	—	—	—	78.6[1]	—	—	—	—	—	—
Louisiana	20.1	—	—	—	31.1	—	26.7	28.4	20.1	30.7
Maine	15.8	39.9[1]	23.5	28.0	34.1	57.8	52.0[1]	70.5	53.2	81.3
Maryland	—	44.3	66.1	59.1	60.0[1]	59.9[1]	69.2[1]	—	55.3[1]	74.7[1]
Massachusetts	22.0	—	27.5	15.6	25.0	23.6	27.2[1]	42.2	42.2	47.6
Michigan	—	—	—	—	—	—	—	24.6[1]	62.6[1]	74.7
Minnesota	—	—	—	—	—	—	—	—	—	—
Mississippi	—	67.8	48.8	70.7	—	72.8	—	70.4[1]	58.7[1]	95.8[1]
Missouri	—	65.6	61.8	55.2	59.7	53.3[1]	39.5[1]	55.1[1]	51.0	65.5
Montana	—	—	—	—	—	—	—	—	—	—
Nebraska	—	—	—	—	—	—	—	—	—	—
Nevada	—	—	—	—	—	—	—	—	—	—
New Hampshire	21.7	28.7	30.5	51.4[1]	67.9[1]	67.2[1]	50.9[1]	60.1[1]	35.3[1]	82.9[1]
New Jersey	9.5	—	29.6	42.6	71.1	44.3	69.3	74.7	68.9	73.6
New Mexico	—	—	—	—	—	—	—	—	—	—
New York	50.8[1]	42.2	53.7	48.0	70.1	58.4	69.6	71.3	58.1	68.1
North Carolina	—	—	—	—	—	—	—	—	—	—
North Dakota	—	—	—	—	—	—	—	—	—	—
Ohio	—	—	52.7	54.2	—	51.4	62.7	56.2	66.0	69.9
Oklahoma	—	—	—	—	—	—	—	—	—	—
Oregon	—	—	—	—	—	—	—	—	—	—
Pennsylvania	63.3	45.2	—	—	—	48.4	56.6	56.1	48.7	72.0
Rhode Island	35.6	7.8	16.3[1]	11.5[1]	27.3[1]	16.3[1]	22.9[1]	33.5[1]	31.9[1]	31.1[1]
South Carolina	—	36.7[1]	—	—	—	—	—	—	—	—
South Dakota	—	—	—	—	—	—	—	—	—	—
Tennessee	—	—	—	—	—	79.3[1]	80.7[1]	79.2[1]	82.7[1]	87.5[1]
Texas	—	—	—	—	—	—	—	—	—	—
Utah	—	—	—	—	—	—	—	—	—	—
Vermont	42.1	52.3	39.9	36.2	—	46.1	35.3[1]	55.3	50.9	63.4
Virginia	—	—	—	—	—	—	—	—	—	—
Washington	—	—	—	—	—	—	—	—	—	—
West Virginia	—	—	—	—	—	—	—	—	—	—
Wisconsin	—	—	—	—	—	—	—	—	—	—
Wyoming	—	—	—	—	—	—	—	—	—	—

Notes: Turnout is the ratio V/E, where V is the total vote cast in congressional (House) races in a given election year in a state, and E is the number of people eligible by law to vote in that state according to the criteria of citizenship, race, sex, and age laws on suffrage, where race has two dimensions: color (black/white) and bondage (slave/free). These raw data—number of House votes cast and eligibles in each state—are used to produce the entries. Both states with even-numbered year House races and states with odd-numbered year House races in a given two-year election cycle have their congressional vote divided by the number of eligibles in the state in the even-numbered year, which serves as a common base by which to compare congressional votes in any given two-year cycle for House elections. States with partial data (less than 100 percent of districts reporting the vote) are not included. States with special House elections are also not included. The few states having House elections in both even- and odd-numbered years in the same two-year election cycle only have the even-numbered election included in this table. For a more detailed discussion of the methodology used, see the notes to Table 3-5.

[1]House election held in odd-numbered year.

Sources: Eligibles—decennial censuses (1790–1990) of the U.S. Census Bureau; Bureau of U.S. Census Series P pamphlets for 1972 and the 1990s; Richard Scammon's book series, *America Votes* (various publication dates); the data archive of John J. Stucker; and relevant state constitutions and statute volumes. Also see Stucker (1973), Appendix B. House vote—Tables 5-70 through 5-122.

Table 3-47 State Voter Turnout Percentages for Congressional Elections Using Two-Year Election Cycles, 1840–1859

	1840–1841	1842–1843	1844–1845	1846–1847	1848–1849	1850–1851	1852–1853	1854–1855	1856–1857	1858–1859
Alabama	58.3[1]	—	—	—	81.7[1]	—	—	73.0[1]	71.2[1]	—
Alaska	—	—	—	—	—	—	—	—	—	—
Arizona	—	—	—	—	—	—	—	—	—	—
Arkansas	78.2	78.5	77.0	59.5	76.3	60.2[1]	41.5[1]	61.0	74.9	69.3
California	—	—	—	—	17.9[1]	63.8[1]	81.7	74.9	84.2	67.1[1]
Colorado	—	—	—	—	—	—	—	—	—	—
Connecticut	63.7[1]	68.1[1]	68.3[1]	66.4[1]	59.5[1]	61.1[1]	57.5[1]	58.2[1]	55.0[1]	65.9[1]
Delaware	82.9	79.2	84.7	81.0	78.4	74.6	76.1	71.0	74.0	74.5
Florida	—	—	59.4[1]	54.9	72.2	71.6	69.5	71.0	77.4	58.2
Georgia	91.7	79.1	84.8	60.4	75.3	86.5[1]	81.7[1]	88.4[1]	83.3[1]	79.0[1]
Hawaii	—	—	—	—	—	—	—	—	—	—
Idaho	—	—	—	—	—	—	—	—	—	—
Illinois	64.2[1]	74.8[1]	69.5	62.4	58.8	53.9	63.3	49.4	69.8	67.0
Indiana	65.0[1]	79.5[1]	75.9[1]	75.1[1]	72.1[1]	70.9[1]	73.3	76.9	86.2	75.8
Iowa	—	—	—	51.0	66.4	59.3	49.3	49.1	65.7	69.9
Kansas	—	—	—	—	—	—	—	—	—	45.2[1]
Kentucky	32.6[1]	77.9[1]	78.4[1]	81.2[1]	65.4[1]	60.4[1]	67.1[1]	73.4[1]	67.5[1]	70.2[1]
Louisiana	33.7	27.3[1]	24.6	—	—	47.0[1]	—	49.4[1]	43.2[1]	41.1[1]
Maine	79.5	53.1[1]	72.5	55.8	58.9	54.6	60.0	58.5	77.0	70.8
Maryland	55.2[1]	—	57.4	—	58.7[1]	52.5[1]	66.8[1]	73.3[1]	73.9[1]	62.9[1]
Massachusetts	64.6	55.6	58.8	41.9	48.6	43.2	45.9	41.3	52.7	36.5
Michigan	85.3	63.6[1]	79.5	60.3	74.0	61.9	70.5	60.4	80.9	69.8
Minnesota	—	—	—	—	—	—	—	—	75.9[1]	84.1[1]
Mississippi	86.2[1]	83.4[1]	96.8[1]	84.5[1]	91.0[1]	88.0[1]	93.0[1]	84.6[1]	50.9[1]	51.5[1]
Missouri	71.5	31.2	66.9	60.8	66.1	57.2	50.5	56.2	53.4	54.6
Montana	—	—	—	—	—	—	—	—	—	—
Nebraska	—	—	—	—	—	—	—	—	—	—
Nevada	—	—	—	—	—	—	—	—	—	—
New Hampshire	74.3[1]	61.5[1]	70.8[1]	76.5[1]	68.2[1]	61.6[1]	60.0[1]	73.8[1]	72.7[1]	77.7[1]
New Jersey	80.6	—	74.5	55.8	69.9	65.2	68.1	59.3	69.4	62.7
New Mexico	—	—	—	—	—	—	—	—	—	—
New York	75.7	62.1	71.7	55.4	59.7	52.6	61.0	51.7	63.6	55.6
North Carolina	—	57.3[1]	74.2[1]	59.1[1]	67.4[1]	—	67.4[1]	73.1[1]	60.4[1]	61.3[1]
North Dakota	—	—	—	—	—	—	—	—	—	—
Ohio	84.8	62.7[1]	80.7	61.0	67.6	56.5	63.3	60.0	70.3	65.8
Oklahoma	—	—	—	—	—	—	—	—	—	—
Oregon	—	—	—	—	—	—	—	—	—	78.3[1]
Pennsylvania	68.7	49.6[1]	71.9	43.8	66.0	51.9	57.9	59.6	67.7	56.9
Rhode Island	10.8[1]	39.9[1]	36.1[1]	32.8[1]	23.6[1]	32.8[1]	39.0[1]	—	34.2[1]	28.4[1]
South Carolina	—	—	—	—	—	—	—	—	—	—
South Dakota	—	—	—	—	—	—	—	—	—	—
Tennessee	54.5[1]	82.2[1]	78.0[1]	81.6[1]	48.3[1]	—	—	77.2[1]	72.6[1]	78.5[1]
Texas	—	—	—	77.1	84.5[1]	58.8[1]	64.6[1]	69.6[1]	65.3[1]	65.3[1]
Utah	—	—	—	—	—	—	—	—	—	—
Vermont	78.1	67.6[1]	68.6	60.0	58.7	54.3	50.5	48.1	51.0	47.6
Virginia	—	—	—	—	—	—	—	—	—	—
Washington	—	—	—	—	—	—	—	—	—	—
West Virginia	—	—	—	—	—	—	—	—	—	—
Wisconsin	—	—	—	—	57.2	53.0	62.3	47.3	81.1	68.5
Wyoming	—	—	—	—	—	—	—	—	—	—

Notes: Turnout is the ratio V/E, where V is the total vote cast in congressional (House) races in a given election year in a state, and E is the number of people eligible by law to vote in that state according to the criteria of citizenship, race, sex, and age laws on suffrage, where race has two dimensions: color (black/white) and bondage (slave/free). These raw data—number of House votes cast and eligibles in each state—are used to produce the entries. Both states with even-numbered year House races and states with odd-numbered year House races in a given two-year election cycle have their congressional vote divided by the number of eligibles in the state in the even-numbered year, which serves as a common base by which to compare congressional votes in any given two-year cycle for House elections. States with partial data (less than 100 percent of districts reporting the vote) are not included. States with special House elections are also not included. The few states having House elections in both even- and odd-numbered years in the same two-year election cycle only have the even-numbered election included in this table. For a more detailed discussion of the methodology used, see the notes to Table 3-5.

[1]House election held in odd-numbered year.

Sources: Eligibles—decennial censuses (1790–1990) of the U.S. Census Bureau; Bureau of U.S. Census Series P pamphlets for 1972 and the 1990s; Richard Scammon's book series, *America Votes* (various publication dates); the data archive of John J. Stucker; and relevant state constitutions and statute volumes. Also see Stucker (1973), Appendix B. House vote—Tables 5-70 through 5-122.

Table 3-48 State Voter Turnout Percentages for Congressional Elections Using Two-Year Election Cycles, 1860–1879

	1860–1861	1862–1863	1864–1865	1866–1867	1868–1869	1870–1871	1872–1873	1874–1875	1876–1877	1878–1879
Alabama	—	—	—	—	32.7	75.6	80.2	87.3	67.1	35.7
Alaska	—	—	—	—	—	—	—	—	—	—
Arizona	—	—	—	—	—	—	—	—	—	—
Arkansas	85.3	—	—	—	40.8	52.3	68.4	48.4	57.9	47.6
California	71.4[1]	64.0[1]	60.2	51.9[1]	59.3	82.0[1]	59.7	69.5[1]	81.3	76.2[1]
Colorado	—	—	—	—	—	—	—	—	46.3	41.0
Connecticut	67.6[1]	62.1[1]	54.9[1]	68.0[1]	62.5[1]	73.7[1]	65.2[1]	73.4[1]	85.6	71.1
Delaware	74.0	72.2	74.4	78.6	76.9	79.5	—	75.4	72.9	39.3
Florida	71.8	—	—	—	44.3	62.2	77.4	74.1	94.9	71.1
Georgia	—	—	—	—	61.8	72.0	58.0	47.1	60.6	41.6
Hawaii	—	—	—	—	—	—	—	—	—	—
Idaho	—	—	—	—	—	—	—	—	—	—
Illinois	79.2	55.5	69.8	65.0	77.7	58.4	75.9	60.9	86.7	67.6
Indiana	86.1	76.5	83.8	92.3	93.1	83.1	94.2	85.7	97.4	87.6
Iowa	80.8	62.5	65.6	62.4	73.5	63.4	74.1	61.1	89.7	74.6
Kansas	—	34.7	35.2	37.7	49.7	61.0	77.7	53.9	63.4	61.8
Kentucky	62.1[1]	38.6[1]	49.3[1]	48.0[1]	60.8	52.4	53.8	39.6	75.8	45.6
Louisiana	—	—	—	—	44.4	65.5	76.2	81.9	86.4	60.2
Maine	75.8	52.3	67.7	66.1	77.9	64.8	80.8	59.3	83.5	75.1
Maryland	54.2[1]	39.2[1]	54.6	49.9	65.1	79.1	75.0	63.9	81.7	58.3
Massachusetts	50.7	38.9	48.8	31.5	50.3	44.1	58.6	52.7	70.2	66.7
Michigan	80.1	59.7	68.2	62.2	78.3	65.1	72.0	64.5	87.4	72.4
Minnesota	76.0	41.1	57.3	47.9	70.5	75.2	85.5	75.2	88.7	64.2
Mississippi	—	—	—	—	68.3[1]	—	67.9	80.6[1]	78.7	23.6
Missouri	60.7	30.7	31.1	31.9	40.3	46.1	67.2	58.3	74.3	66.2
Montana	—	—	—	—	—	—	—	—	—	—
Nebraska	—	—	—	33.1	45.7	55.2	51.5	51.3	59.6	48.5
Nevada	—	—	88.6	55.4	56.6	71.4	77.8	89.9	95.6	89.1
New Hampshire	74.9[1]	73.4[1]	73.6[1]	75.9[1]	73.9[1]	78.8[1]	78.8[1]	89.8[1]	86.6[1]	81.9
New Jersey	75.3	61.7	69.3	65.1	76.8	81.1	82.7	82.6	95.0	80.6
New Mexico	—	—	—	—	—	—	—	—	—	—
New York	66.6	57.9	67.0	65.0	74.5	77.4	81.9	73.2	89.3	71.9
North Carolina	—	—	—	—	—	—	84.9	77.9	—	47.0
North Dakota	—	—	—	—	—	—	—	—	—	—
Ohio	75.5	64.8	72.5	79.1	84.6	72.1	82.4	69.7	89.7	79.4
Oklahoma	—	—	—	—	—	—	—	—	—	—
Oregon	25.0	55.7	72.4	90.9	90.8	90.8	84.4	71.9	73.5	74.0
Pennsylvania	71.0	60.7	66.7	76.4	80.0	68.9	81.1	62.7	80.9	70.9
Rhode Island	47.8[1]	38.3[1]	19.0[1]	16.0[1]	33.3	27.7	40.5	13.7	50.1	33.3
South Carolina	—	—	—	—	73.3	82.1	56.7	83.2	85.2	84.0
South Dakota	—	—	—	—	—	—	—	—	—	—
Tennessee	—	—	30.3[1]	48.1[1]	27.2	46.6	67.5	54.0	72.4	46.7
Texas	—	—	—	—	49.4[1]	63.0[1]	56.5	20.1	51.6	68.3
Utah	—	—	—	—	—	—	—	—	—	—
Vermont	49.6	45.0[1]	48.8	49.3	66.6	55.9	64.5	53.9	74.4	68.1
Virginia	—	—	—	—	82.1[1]	—	68.1	60.9	77.0	39.6
Washington	—	—	—	—	—	—	—	—	—	—
West Virginia	—	21.6[1]	23.9	—	52.0	56.3	44.0	60.3	83.4	74.2
Wisconsin	78.9	61.5	66.1	58.7	79.9	66.9	82.0	74.3	95.5	73.1
Wyoming	—	—	—	—	—	—	—	—	—	—

Notes: Turnout is the ratio V/E, where V is the total vote cast in congressional (House) races in a given election year in a state, and E is the number of people eligible by law to vote in that state according to the criteria of citizenship, race, sex, and age laws on suffrage, where race has two dimensions: color (black/white) and bondage (slave/free). These raw data—number of House votes cast and eligibles in each state—are used to produce the entries. Both states with even-numbered year House races and states with odd-numbered year House races in a given two-year election cycle have their congressional vote divided by the number of eligibles in the state in the even-numbered year, which serves as a common base by which to compare congressional votes in any given two-year cycle for House elections. States with partial data (less than 100 percent of districts reporting the vote) are not included. States with special House elections are also not included. The few states having House elections in both even- and odd-numbered years in the same two-year election cycle only have the even-numbered election included in this table. For a more detailed discussion of the methodology used, see the notes to Table 3-5.

[1] House election held in odd-numbered year.

Sources: Eligibles—decennial censuses (1790–1990) of the U.S. Census Bureau; Bureau of U.S. Census Series P pamphlets for 1972 and the 1990s; Richard Scammon's book series, *America Votes* (various publication dates); the data archive of John J. Stucker; and relevant state constitutions and statute volumes. Also see Stucker (1973), Appendix B. House vote—Tables 5-70 through 5-122.

Table 3-49 State Voter Turnout Percentages for Congressional Elections Using Two-Year Election Cycles, 1880–1898

	1880	1882	1884	1886	1888–1889	1890	1892	1894–1895	1896	1898
Alabama	54.8	44.6	49.8	29.2	56.0	36.8	68.4	35.7	49.4	23.1
Alaska	—	—	—	—	—	—	—	—	—	—
Arizona	—	—	—	—	—	—	—	—	—	—
Arkansas	59.0	33.5	59.4	24.7	65.2	44.2	51.5	18.9	52.5	9.1
California	74.1	67.9	73.8	67.6	80.7	76.1	68.4	72.2	70.9	66.1
Colorado	63.9	63.6	61.1	47.8	68.2	57.0	60.7	69.0	65.9	50.7
Connecticut	87.5	72.8	83.5	71.8	86.4	73.1	85.1	76.8	83.3	68.5
Delaware	81.6	82.5	75.6	53.7	68.9	78.6	80.4	82.0	71.8	66.1
Florida	85.7	72.1	82.6	72.3	78.7	48.7	35.6	24.1	36.5	26.5
Georgia	46.3	31.8	36.2	7.6	34.2	27.1	52.0	46.3	37.4	14.4
Hawaii	—	—	—	—	—	—	—	—	—	—
Idaho	—	—	—	—	—	69.2	63.6	69.0	74.2	55.9
Illinois	89.1	70.9	86.4	67.7	84.8	73.1	88.0	80.4	96.0	73.3
Indiana	96.5	86.9	93.9	86.4	95.3	81.1	90.9	88.9	96.6	83.6
Iowa	86.1	73.7	91.2	79.9	89.1	82.4	88.9	80.5	94.8	73.7
Kansas	79.2	76.1	87.0	85.2	95.6	79.5	87.3	77.7	85.5	72.2
Kentucky	69.7	49.8	63.6	50.6	79.7	44.1	69.8	70.8	87.5	52.8
Louisiana	49.6	36.7	48.6	37.4	48.7	30.9	44.6	42.3	34.2	11.2
Maine	86.9	80.5	81.1	72.6	80.8	61.6	69.4	58.0	66.1	44.0
Maryland	78.8	69.6	79.1	60.8	85.0	71.4	79.9	74.1	86.7	72.9
Massachusetts	71.1	61.1	67.9	51.7	69.1	53.8	68.2	57.3	62.7	50.3
Michigan	84.9	71.1	86.1	77.7	92.4	73.5	83.4	72.2	93.3	70.3
Minnesota	86.8	72.0	81.3	82.2	89.8	73.3	74.9	77.3	85.5	61.7
Mississippi	48.6	32.7	44.9	18.3	44.1	23.1	17.8	13.2	21.0	8.3
Missouri	73.3	67.6	75.9	69.0	80.9	69.1	75.9	68.0	86.9	69.2
Montana	—	—	—	—	81.3[1]	61.7	75.7	76.9	61.2	64.1
Nebraska	70.4	58.3	72.7	63.9	82.6	76.7	71.0	71.7	78.0	67.8
Nevada	84.8	69.0	65.9	67.7	73.5	77.2	63.1	66.0	64.8	60.7
New Hampshire	91.5	80.2	84.7	77.8	90.1	83.6	82.4	77.7	76.9	74.8
New Jersey	96.1	74.8	88.0	73.3	90.3	70.7	88.6	74.0	87.3	74.7
New Mexico	—	—	—	—	—	—	—	—	—	—
New York	90.4	73.6	85.8	67.5	87.9	64.3	83.0	74.7	80.7	75.1
North Carolina	78.7	73.9	83.5	66.0	84.1	74.7	75.9	74.6	84.8	82.6
North Dakota	—	—	—	—	95.5[1]	80.9	69.4	65.6	70.0	66.3
Ohio	91.8	77.7	92.4	78.7	91.5	77.7	85.0	73.5	94.2	69.7
Oklahoma	—	—	—	—	—	—	—	—	—	—
Oregon	75.6	70.4	72.5	70.1	70.1	77.3	74.7	79.9	78.2	68.6
Pennsylvania	83.8	68.5	79.5	69.4	80.1	72.4	74.2	67.8	80.1	62.5
Rhode Island	50.1	16.6	49.8	26.2	56.1	48.7	62.9	45.0	59.0	39.8
South Carolina	87.1	57.7	41.4	17.5	33.4	31.3	28.1	25.1	26.1	11.7
South Dakota	—	—	—	—	94.3[1]	93.2	80.8	82.3	86.0	72.7
Tennessee	71.9	64.4	71.1	62.9	78.0	49.0	61.8	52.7	70.1	37.9
Texas	70.1	63.1	73.6	64.8	71.5	63.2	76.0	73.9	85.7	61.3
Utah	—	—	—	—	—	—	—	42.2[1]	79.0	65.3
Vermont	80.2	56.0	63.3	55.2	76.3	57.9	58.8	59.3	70.7	54.3
Virginia	58.3	58.3	81.9	63.0	82.9	50.4	73.2	53.4	72.6	40.4
Washington	—	—	—	—	53.6[1]	47.5	69.2	56.2	61.9	50.7
West Virginia	81.4	63.1	85.8	81.5	89.1	84.0	89.4	83.6	92.3	76.2
Wisconsin	89.0	68.0	93.6	78.4	92.4	74.6	86.3	82.4	93.4	69.7
Wyoming	—	—	—	—	—	47.9	47.9	48.6	50.4	43.7

Notes: Turnout is the ratio V/E, where V is the total vote cast in congressional (House) races in a given election year in a state, and E is the number of people eligible by law to vote in that state according to the criteria of citizenship, race, sex, and age laws on suffrage, where race has two dimensions: color (black/white) and bondage (slave/free). These raw data—number of House votes cast and eligibles in each state—are used to produce the entries. Both states with even-numbered year House races and states with odd-numbered year House races in a given two-year election cycle have their congressional vote divided by the number of eligibles in the state in the even-numbered year, which serves as a common base by which to compare congressional votes in any given two-year cycle for House elections. States with partial data (less than 100 percent of districts reporting the vote) are not included. States with special House elections are also not included. The few states having House elections in both even- and odd-numbered years in the same two-year election cycle only have the even-numbered election included in this table. For a more detailed discussion of the methodology used, see the notes to Table 3-5.

[1] House election held in odd-numbered year.

Sources: Eligibles—decennial censuses (1790–1990) of the U.S. Census Bureau; Bureau of U.S. Census Series P pamphlets for 1972 and the 1990s; Richard Scammon's book series, *America Votes* (various publication dates); the data archive of John J. Stucker; and relevant state constitutions and statute volumes. Also see Stucker (1973), Appendix B. House vote—Tables 5-70 through 5-122.

Table 3-50 State Voter Turnout Percentages for Congressional Elections Using Two-Year Election Cycles, 1900–1918

	1900	1902	1904	1906–1907	1908	1910–1911	1912	1914	1916	1918
Alabama	34.3	21.3	22.9	14.0	20.7	19.2	19.2	15.1	22.6	11.2
Alaska	—	—	—	—	—	—	—	—	—	—
Arizona	—	—	—	—	—	37.8[1]	39.4	40.2	43.1	33.6
Arkansas	40.9	12.0	32.0	14.2	40.7	10.5	28.8	10.4	40.6	18.0
California	67.4	58.4	58.2	45.3	53.5	47.7	41.0	52.2	50.2	33.4
Colorado	72.8	56.6	69.3	52.0	64.7	50.8	58.8	52.7	53.4	42.7
Connecticut	80.1	68.7	80.3	66.1	76.3	65.1	71.2	65.4	74.0	55.8
Delaware	82.1	72.9	81.9	70.0	86.1	77.5	83.5	76.4	83.5	65.8
Florida	23.8	11.4	20.3	13.1	20.7	18.5	20.6	10.5	27.9	12.5
Georgia	21.2	7.9	21.4	5.9	16.3	7.4	18.3	12.4	20.0	8.7
Hawaii	—	—	—	—	—	—	—	—	—	—
Idaho	71.0	62.9	62.7	55.4	65.2	50.8	61.5	54.8	64.6	44.6
Illinois	88.8	62.8	79.2	60.0	80.6	62.0	75.5	59.0	80.4	53.1
Indiana	93.5	81.5	91.1	77.3	92.2	78.7	79.3	76.2	83.4	65.5
Iowa	88.3	65.9	79.6	67.4	76.8	61.7	68.7	63.4	72.1	51.1
Kansas	87.2	68.4	72.6	68.5	82.5	61.5	72.0	51.6	59.5	44.1
Kentucky	86.2	53.1	76.6	50.4	81.9	55.2	66.0	52.3	81.0	55.7
Louisiana	21.5	8.0	15.1	10.2	18.6	12.8	16.0	12.1	20.0	10.1
Maine	61.1	55.2	65.8	67.3	71.2	69.5	69.5	68.5	73.0	58.3
Maryland	85.6	62.6	64.5	60.4	63.0	59.4	50.4	58.6	58.6	40.4
Massachusetts	60.6	58.3	59.6	56.5	57.5	56.3	59.8	55.1	60.1	45.5
Michigan	88.6	61.8	77.9	47.8	74.7	50.9	68.9	51.4	72.6	43.5
Minnesota	77.1	61.0	62.2	52.8	62.1	50.7	51.0	56.3	63.5	53.4
Mississippi	14.8	5.0	14.1	5.2	14.6	5.6	11.5	8.6	18.1	7.4
Missouri	81.3	60.2	72.8	66.0	78.4	72.3	72.7	62.5	79.7	55.4
Montana	72.6	57.8	63.7	52.1	58.1	53.3	58.0	58.7	67.0	38.0
Nebraska	81.7	66.9	75.3	61.0	83.3	71.8	74.5	67.7	79.9	59.6
Nevada	71.2	60.7	52.5	56.0	81.6	66.2	62.3	64.3	68.6	53.9
New Hampshire	81.9	69.8	78.8	71.4	78.2	72.8	73.4	71.7	74.9	60.8
New Jersey	85.5	73.3	83.2	66.0	81.4	72.5	57.2	59.1	63.5	48.1
New Mexico	—	—	—	—	—	71.5[1]	55.4	52.2	74.0	51.5
New York	82.7	72.3	80.6	72.4	79.2	67.1	70.2	59.0	64.4	41.1
North Carolina	70.0	45.3	46.2	43.2	52.0	46.8	43.1	37.3	50.9	40.3
North Dakota	80.7	57.7	68.2	54.4	68.9	57.3	55.3	56.7	63.7	53.9
Ohio	90.0	68.7	81.2	61.8	87.1	68.5	73.5	73.8	74.0	57.5
Oklahoma	—	—	—	65.7[1]	68.4	53.8	54.8	51.5	58.1	36.6
Oregon	65.1	59.6	55.7	49.4	52.5	49.1	55.2	55.9	52.6	32.1
Pennsylvania	72.1	62.1	66.4	55.9	62.7	51.6	58.4	54.4	61.6	42.0
Rhode Island	52.6	55.7	58.7	58.3	62.6	56.2	60.4	60.8	65.9	58.6
South Carolina	18.1	11.0	18.9	9.4	20.2	9.3	14.4	9.4	17.3	6.8
South Dakota	94.1	65.3	79.0	53.0	74.4	62.9	68.7	56.6	72.5	49.2
Tennessee	55.0	30.7	44.9	38.3	43.4	41.3	41.2	37.6	41.7	20.3
Texas	58.5	45.6	31.3	20.8	32.1	22.0	30.3	20.2	33.7	14.6
Utah	84.0	70.3	77.7	59.5	73.6	63.2	65.5	62.8	74.6	43.5
Vermont	66.1	45.2	65.8	60.0	61.5	52.1	48.7	61.4	62.5	43.3
Virginia	60.8	26.9	28.0	17.7	28.0	19.6	25.3	15.4	27.4	7.2
Washington	63.9	49.2	58.2	40.4	51.9	38.1	46.8	49.5	50.8	27.5
West Virginia	91.0	75.2	88.8	64.5	86.7	67.4	82.5	70.1	81.2	59.2
Wisconsin	86.0	66.9	79.6	54.8	74.9	51.1	65.2	50.6	65.5	46.1
Wyoming	50.7	45.3	50.7	40.6	51.6	47.1	49.1	46.7	53.4	41.1

Notes: Turnout is the ratio V/E, where V is the total vote cast in congressional (House) races in a given election year in a state, and E is the number of people eligible by law to vote in that state according to the criteria of citizenship, race, sex, and age laws on suffrage, where race has two dimensions: color (black/white) and bondage (slave/free). These raw data—number of House votes cast and eligibles in each state—are used to produce the entries. Both states with even-numbered year House races and states with odd-numbered year House races in a given two-year election cycle have their congressional vote divided by the number of eligibles in the state in the even-numbered year, which serves as a common base by which to compare congressional votes in any given two-year cycle for House elections. States with partial data (less than 100 percent of districts reporting the vote) are not included. States with special House elections are also not included. The few states having House elections in both even- and odd-numbered years in the same two-year election cycle only have the even-numbered election included in this table. For a more detailed discussion of the methodology used, see the notes to Table 3-5.

[1]House election held in odd-numbered year.

Sources: Eligibles—decennial censuses (1790–1990) of the U.S. Census Bureau; Bureau of U.S. Census Series P pamphlets for 1972 and the 1990s; Richard Scammon's book series, *America Votes* (various publication dates); the data archive of John J. Stucker; and relevant state constitutions and statute volumes. Also see Stucker (1973), Appendix B. House vote—Tables 5-70 through 5-122.

Table 3-51 State Voter Turnout Percentages for Congressional Elections Using Two-Year Election Cycles, 1920–1938

	1920	1922	1924	1926	1928	1930	1932	1934	1936	1938
Alabama	19.7	11.9	12.4	8.5	15.4	14.8	16.7	11.5	17.3	8.2
Alaska	—	—	—	—	—	—	—	—	—	—
Arizona	42.9	32.0	27.0	34.0	37.2	21.9	43.7	38.6	42.9	40.3
Arkansas	22.0	3.9	15.1	3.6	21.2	15.0	22.0	13.7	16.7	13.4
California	40.6	33.9	38.2	32.7	41.2	31.1	50.5	52.0	54.9	56.0
Colorado	53.1	49.5	57.8	51.3	60.6	52.7	69.8	62.4	70.2	67.1
Connecticut	57.4	48.6	53.4	41.2	72.1	53.6	70.5	62.5	74.4	65.0
Delaware	74.1	56.1	66.3	50.3	75.1	61.2	75.7	64.2	79.2	65.4
Florida	23.9	8.8	15.0	9.1	28.1	11.4	27.2	12.8	27.2	13.7
Georgia	19.7	5.5	11.0	3.2	13.5	3.8	15.9	3.3	16.7	4.0
Hawaii	—	—	—	—	—	—	—	—	—	—
Idaho	61.9	53.8	59.1	49.5	62.3	53.0	72.8	61.6	70.0	61.2
Illinois	60.3	45.9	57.3	40.2	68.2	46.8	68.7	58.3	76.9	61.3
Indiana	72.4	61.3	69.2	55.5	74.3	62.2	77.3	71.0	77.6	73.2
Iowa	52.5	42.2	58.6	35.3	55.8	36.0	62.7	54.3	67.8	50.7
Kansas	53.6	52.0	57.3	45.2	54.5	50.7	64.2	67.2	70.6	64.7
Kentucky	66.7	27.0	52.1	37.0	67.6	38.7	66.5	31.3	59.4	33.6
Louisiana	10.3	4.7	9.5	5.3	15.6	11.8	20.9	15.3	23.0	11.6
Maine	48.1	41.3	57.5	40.0	47.7	32.7	52.3	60.6	63.8	58.3
Maryland	46.1	35.9	35.6	37.2	49.7	48.6	45.5	43.9	50.5	43.6
Massachusetts	50.3	42.7	53.8	45.1	67.6	53.3	65.8	58.7	73.3	68.7
Michigan	53.6	27.0	51.6	24.4	54.8	28.8	58.5	43.2	58.3	51.2
Minnesota	60.4	49.7	61.2	48.0	68.5	51.9	75.6	63.4	67.2	63.9
Mississippi	8.1	7.5	10.6	2.8	11.3	3.4	12.7	5.2	13.1	3.0
Missouri	66.5	48.0	61.7	46.5	69.8	42.6	72.0	56.9	76.5	51.5
Montana	60.0	51.0	53.8	51.6	60.7	56.4	67.4	61.8	63.8	62.3
Nebraska	52.4	53.1	60.2	52.1	68.1	52.8	68.8	65.0	70.7	58.9
Nevada	60.3	60.0	53.0	59.5	60.0	60.3	70.1	67.7	67.9	67.4
New Hampshire	65.6	52.9	64.9	49.9	72.8	48.1	72.8	62.4	72.6	62.9
New Jersey	54.8	47.8	54.4	41.2	70.0	45.4	66.3	56.6	69.5	61.0
New Mexico	62.3	61.6	60.3	55.0	57.1	54.8	66.1	62.1	67.1	59.0
New York	52.7	44.3	52.9	45.3	64.8	44.3	61.3	48.6	68.1	56.2
North Carolina	44.1	28.6	35.0	25.5	43.8	34.6	43.7	29.1	45.1	25.9
North Dakota	71.3	49.7	54.7	45.4	60.5	53.5	63.2	79.5	67.1	61.0
Ohio	60.0	47.3	53.3	35.5	63.3	48.6	58.8	48.4	66.4	52.2
Oklahoma	48.3	44.3	45.2	31.0	48.4	35.7	49.5	40.4	50.6	33.1
Oregon	43.8	37.5	50.6	39.1	52.6	39.1	56.9	44.8	58.7	53.0
Pennsylvania	41.4	32.1	42.9	30.2	59.6	38.7	51.7	52.8	71.3	64.5
Rhode Island	57.6	51.2	65.3	49.5	68.1	61.2	70.1	63.5	76.7	72.9
South Carolina	8.5	4.5	6.2	1.8	7.6	2.0	12.5	2.5	12.5	4.8
South Dakota	56.5	48.1	57.1	47.5	68.3	45.4	72.8	73.8	76.0	72.7
Tennessee	32.8	17.6	17.5	7.7	21.5	14.0	23.1	18.0	24.7	16.1
Texas	18.1	16.5	25.7	8.4	21.6	9.2	26.0	13.1	23.4	10.2
Utah	68.9	54.8	65.5	60.2	72.2	61.4	78.6	66.5	77.1	63.2
Vermont	44.5	35.2	48.5	35.9	63.9	35.8	65.1	62.4	66.9	54.0
Virginia	20.7	13.7	18.6	8.6	24.0	12.7	27.0	10.6	22.1	8.3
Washington	49.3	32.8	42.1	31.5	47.8	31.2	57.3	47.7	61.9	54.1
West Virginia	70.2	51.3	72.4	52.8	75.9	61.5	81.0	65.7	84.5	61.6
Wisconsin	46.5	32.2	48.8	31.4	56.3	30.7	60.9	50.0	61.4	48.4
Wyoming	53.9	53.0	62.9	54.8	61.3	53.8	68.4	67.0	69.8	65.0

Notes: Turnout is the ratio V/E, where V is the total vote cast in congressional (House) races in a given election year in a state, and E is the number of people eligible by law to vote in that state according to the criteria of citizenship, race, sex, and age laws on suffrage, where race has two dimensions: color (black/white) and bondage (slave/free). These raw data—number of House votes cast and eligibles in each state—are used to produce the entries. Both states with even-numbered year House races and states with odd-numbered year House races in a given two-year election cycle have their congressional vote divided by the number of eligibles in the state in the even-numbered year, which serves as a common base by which to compare congressional votes in any given two-year cycle for House elections. States with partial data (less than 100 percent of districts reporting the vote) are not included. States with special House elections are also not included. The few states having House elections in both even- and odd-numbered years in the same two-year election cycle only have the even-numbered election included in this table. For a more detailed discussion of the methodology used, see the notes to Table 3-5.

Sources: Eligibles—decennial censuses (1790–1990) of the U.S. Census Bureau; Bureau of U.S. Census Series P pamphlets for 1972 and the 1990s; Richard Scammon's book series, *America Votes* (various publication dates); the data archive of John J. Stucker; and relevant state constitutions and statute volumes. Also see Stucker (1973), Appendix B. House vote—Tables 5-70 through 5-122.

Table 3-52 State Voter Turnout Percentages for Congressional Elections Using Two-Year Election Cycles, 1940–1959

	1940	1942	1944	1946	1948	1950	1952	1954	1956	1958–1959
Alabama	17.3	4.3	13.6	10.8	11.5	8.7	19.5	15.7	21.3	13.1
Alaska	—	—	—	—	—	—	—	—	—	40.2
Arizona	53.1	27.0	39.1	31.3	40.5	41.8	51.5	41.4	47.0	42.4
Arkansas	19.0	8.9	19.7	13.7	22.6	26.6	33.0	25.9	24.3	—
California	62.2	38.4	55.2	39.4	55.4	48.5	61.9	49.5	62.5	56.7
Colorado	76.3	47.7	66.2	42.9	61.9	53.3	69.8	53.0	66.7	54.5
Connecticut	77.4	53.0	72.9	56.8	69.9	66.6	80.4	66.5	77.0	65.2
Delaware	78.4	47.3	67.8	58.1	69.8	62.0	77.4	62.5	72.8	60.4
Florida	32.0	7.0	28.8	12.0	20.9	14.1	36.4	14.4	37.6	18.0
Georgia	15.3	3.4	14.8	8.5	18.7	14.5	26.3	16.3	26.4	6.8
Hawaii	—	—	—	—	—	—	—	—	—	55.9[1]
Idaho	75.9	44.4	64.0	54.3	62.9	57.9	75.5	63.7	72.4	65.6
Illinois	78.8	54.8	71.7	62.1	67.3	59.8	73.5	54.5	70.3	53.0
Indiana	80.1	56.8	70.7	55.4	66.1	62.5	74.9	60.4	73.4	63.4
Iowa	69.3	40.9	59.3	35.8	56.9	48.6	68.1	48.8	70.2	49.9
Kansas	68.9	42.4	56.2	46.2	57.8	48.9	65.8	48.5	64.5	55.2
Kentucky	54.8	20.7	50.4	34.4	43.1	28.1	53.7	37.1	52.7	25.5
Louisiana	23.5	6.0	19.5	7.1	20.9	14.4	25.7	13.0	22.7	10.4
Maine	50.0	31.8	35.4	32.8	39.3	42.6	41.9	43.1	52.0	48.8
Maryland	50.8	27.6	42.5	32.6	37.2	38.0	53.6	39.2	51.2	40.6
Massachusetts	75.9	49.6	68.0	56.2	65.3	60.3	74.1	57.5	72.4	57.0
Michigan	63.5	35.4	62.1	43.9	53.9	45.0	67.8	50.8	69.8	51.4
Minnesota	69.7	43.2	61.8	47.9	63.6	53.8	72.7	58.7	71.3	57.6
Mississippi	12.2	4.3	12.7	4.2	12.7	7.3	20.1	8.3	17.4	5.2
Missouri	73.7	37.1	60.1	42.3	60.1	47.5	70.5	44.7	63.6	43.7
Montana	69.3	48.7	55.9	53.1	59.1	57.2	69.0	59.9	69.6	59.9
Nebraska	70.4	43.4	61.8	44.3	54.3	51.1	66.3	47.6	64.0	48.7
Nevada	72.2	51.0	61.6	54.0	60.1	57.7	68.4	59.2	65.3	52.3
New Hampshire	73.7	51.2	68.7	49.8	66.3	54.2	74.5	54.8	71.5	55.1
New Jersey	71.8	44.2	65.1	46.2	59.4	48.3	69.1	51.9	67.4	52.4
New Mexico	66.1	36.0	48.4	38.3	53.1	46.8	59.3	45.1	55.0	42.2
New York	72.5	45.7	67.1	50.7	62.4	50.8	68.9	49.5	67.5	53.7
North Carolina	41.4	15.7	36.3	21.0	34.2	22.6	47.6	25.1	41.8	24.3
North Dakota	65.7	50.8	55.7	40.0	52.6	49.9	64.0	52.6	64.2	55.7
Ohio	68.2	36.4	61.5	44.1	55.4	51.5	63.5	46.0	61.0	55.0
Oklahoma	53.6	25.8	50.0	35.9	49.4	44.0	67.4	39.2	58.1	37.7
Oregon	64.4	35.9	53.6	38.1	52.7	50.6	66.6	55.6	69.8	57.0
Pennsylvania	63.8	40.1	58.2	47.5	54.4	50.9	65.3	53.2	64.9	56.7
Rhode Island	74.0	53.3	63.4	56.5	63.5	56.8	78.2	62.5	71.9	65.2
South Carolina	10.1	2.3	9.6	2.4	12.6	4.4	24.2	17.9	21.5	6.2
South Dakota	78.9	46.6	58.4	41.7	61.0	62.3	72.4	58.5	73.2	65.8
Tennessee	24.5	8.9	22.0	10.4	23.4	13.3	35.1	17.1	33.4	18.0
Texas	27.7	7.2	26.1	8.2	23.7	7.8	41.5	12.8	28.7	14.7
Utah	82.8	47.7	74.5	56.3	74.8	68.8	81.9	63.5	76.7	64.4
Vermont	65.6	26.7	55.7	32.6	53.5	38.4	66.6	50.0	68.0	54.3
Virginia	20.2	5.4	19.6	13.8	19.9	10.5	21.6	16.1	31.9	19.3
Washington	66.2	35.6	62.6	47.3	56.7	47.5	65.7	51.1	65.7	53.2
West Virginia	83.2	43.0	65.7	48.1	66.6	57.0	76.3	52.4	72.5	56.3
Wisconsin	65.4	37.6	56.8	46.9	56.3	50.4	70.4	50.6	66.8	51.2
Wyoming	71.2	48.2	59.9	47.9	57.0	53.0	70.9	60.1	65.5	60.1

Notes: Turnout is the ratio V/E, where V is the total vote cast in congressional (House) races in a given election year in a state, and E is the number of people eligible by law to vote in that state according to the criteria of citizenship, race, sex, and age laws on suffrage, where race has two dimensions: color (black/white) and bondage (slave/free). These raw data—number of House votes cast and eligibles in each state—are used to produce the entries. Both states with even-numbered year House races and states with odd-numbered year House races in a given two-year election cycle have their congressional vote divided by the number of eligibles in the state in the even-numbered year, which serves as a common base by which to compare congressional votes in any given two-year cycle for House elections. States with partial data (less than 100 percent of districts reporting the vote) are not included. States with special House elections are also not included. The few states having House elections in both even- and odd-numbered years in the same two-year election cycle only have the even-numbered election included in this table. For a more detailed discussion of the methodology used, see the notes to Table 3-5.

[1] House election held in odd-numbered year.

Sources: Eligibles—decennial censuses (1790–1990) of the U.S. Census Bureau; Bureau of U.S. Census Series P pamphlets for 1972 and the 1990s; Richard Scammon's book series, *America Votes* (various publication dates); the data archive of John J. Stucker; and relevant state constitutions and statute volumes. Also see Stucker (1973), Appendix B. House vote—Tables 5-70 through 5-122.

Table 3-53 State Voter Turnout Percentages for Congressional Elections Using Two-Year Election Cycles, 1960–1978

	1960	1962	1964	1966	1968	1970	1972	1974	1976	1978
Alabama	23.9	24.9	32.4	36.4	46.1	36.8	41.9	23.2	39.1	24.5
Alaska	44.8	42.5	46.8	44.1	51.8	49.7	47.6	44.3	50.7	49.8
Arizona	52.9	45.3	55.5	41.0	48.9	39.9	46.1	38.0	46.3	30.2
Arkansas	—	—	—	—	—	—	—	—	—	—
California	67.4	57.6	67.2	59.0	62.9	54.5	60.9	42.3	51.8	43.7
Colorado	70.4	55.8	67.4	54.4	63.4	49.6	57.6	46.2	56.4	40.8
Connecticut	79.8	65.2	73.9	59.3	69.1	59.4	66.9	52.2	63.9	47.4
Delaware	73.7	55.8	69.5	55.0	65.3	50.3	60.3	41.5	53.9	38.4
Florida	41.9	29.3	41.0	28.6	45.1	—	—	—	—	—
Georgia	23.9	13.6	33.3	33.2	36.1	32.9	28.4	24.9	36.2	16.2
Hawaii	58.9	58.8	65.4	56.0	61.9	50.4	54.1	48.2	51.7	42.4
Idaho	78.7	67.6	74.1	63.4	69.3	57.7	62.1	48.0	61.4	48.1
Illinois	74.9	58.1	72.3	58.2	68.0	53.0	59.3	37.9	57.3	39.4
Indiana	76.9	63.6	72.1	57.2	68.2	56.6	60.7	48.5	57.5	38.7
Iowa	74.0	48.3	68.4	52.4	66.6	46.1	62.6	46.3	62.4	39.9
Kansas	66.2	47.2	61.0	49.1	60.3	52.8	57.4	49.4	56.4	40.9
Kentucky	48.2	33.3	50.2	35.5	45.3	24.8	44.5	29.5	41.3	19.3
Louisiana	29.0	18.8	31.8	28.2	31.7	17.9	28.6	—	38.9	—
Maine	72.3	50.2	64.5	54.3	66.2	54.5	60.8	49.9	64.4	48.4
Maryland	54.0	36.4	49.0	36.3	46.2	38.5	45.5	31.8	46.6	31.9
Massachusetts	72.3	62.0	65.2	55.1	61.6	53.1	56.2	43.6	59.2	45.0
Michigan	71.7	58.3	65.0	49.1	61.7	50.8	56.7	42.5	56.5	43.5
Minnesota	76.4	59.4	73.4	57.7	71.1	60.9	67.1	46.8	66.6	54.8
Mississippi	22.1	13.7	30.2	31.6	36.6	25.2	40.3	20.1	40.3	31.7
Missouri	68.7	44.6	64.3	37.5	60.9	41.8	56.9	36.6	56.4	44.8
Montana	70.7	63.9	70.6	65.3	66.1	62.0	67.4	52.1	63.0	53.5
Nebraska	67.9	51.7	64.7	53.9	59.2	50.4	56.0	43.1	56.5	45.4
Nevada	60.7	47.9	59.8	52.7	54.1	47.4	50.2	41.0	43.4	37.3
New Hampshire	78.5	58.7	71.4	56.5	67.4	49.3	61.6	40.0	55.7	41.8
New Jersey	71.2	50.9	68.7	51.5	64.4	48.8	58.4	42.4	56.4	38.3
New Mexico	61.0	48.6	62.1	47.8	57.8	52.2	56.6	44.5	52.6	35.0
New York	68.0	53.1	63.9	51.6	56.7	50.0	54.6	40.5	49.7	36.4
North Carolina	51.1	31.0	47.8	32.6	48.2	31.1	38.2	26.7	40.6	25.3
North Dakota	72.7	61.3	70.5	55.9	67.3	59.4	65.7	55.4	66.8	49.4
Ohio	66.7	50.3	60.1	46.0	58.8	48.4	54.2	40.8	52.3	37.2
Oklahoma	59.4	43.3	56.9	42.1	52.5	42.9	45.1	26.7	54.0	28.6
Oregon	72.0	57.4	67.3	56.2	64.2	51.5	58.9	47.8	55.4	49.3
Pennsylvania	70.7	61.7	65.7	55.3	63.4	49.7	55.0	40.9	52.9	41.6
Rhode Island	75.0	59.7	68.6	58.1	64.6	56.6	58.3	45.5	58.1	45.8
South Carolina	26.0	20.2	33.3	26.4	44.2	29.2	35.9	27.8	40.0	28.0
South Dakota	77.2	64.9	74.1	58.1	70.3	60.9	68.1	60.2	63.8	54.0
Tennessee	30.8	28.3	47.0	35.5	43.8	41.7	40.0	31.3	41.5	33.8
Texas	37.7	27.7	43.4	20.9	38.5	28.5	38.1	18.5	42.9	24.2
Utah	80.3	66.0	79.1	59.1	76.9	66.5	69.7	56.2	68.8	44.8
Vermont	73.9	52.6	69.0	55.8	63.1	59.8	61.5	44.5	55.8	34.9
Virginia	27.9	18.8	37.4	26.5	47.5	32.8	39.4	27.4	41.6	28.9
Washington	67.0	50.5	66.1	50.0	61.8	50.7	57.0	40.2	54.9	35.6
West Virginia	76.2	57.1	71.9	46.2	66.8	41.3	61.9	33.1	51.0	33.0
Wisconsin	71.3	52.3	67.9	46.6	65.1	51.6	61.3	39.4	62.8	45.0
Wyoming	71.3	61.5	73.1	62.9	64.1	60.1	65.2	51.1	55.7	43.6

Notes: Turnout is the ratio V/E, where V is the total vote cast in congressional (House) races in a given election year in a state, and E is the number of people eligible by law to vote in that state according to the criteria of citizenship, race, sex, and age laws on suffrage, where race has two dimensions: color (black/white) and bondage (slave/free). These raw data—number of House votes cast and eligibles in each state—are used to produce the entries. Both states with even-numbered year House races and states with odd-numbered year House races in a given two-year election cycle have their congressional vote divided by the number of eligibles in the state in the even-numbered year, which serves as a common base by which to compare congressional votes in any given two-year cycle for House elections. States with partial data (less than 100 percent of districts reporting the vote) are not included. States with special House elections are also not included. The few states having House elections in both even- and odd-numbered years in the same two-year election cycle only have the even-numbered election included in this table. For a more detailed discussion of the methodology used, see the notes to Table 3-5.

Sources: Eligibles—decennial censuses (1790–1990) of the U.S. Census Bureau; Bureau of U.S. Census Series P pamphlets for 1972 and the 1990s; Richard Scammon's book series, *America Votes* (various publication dates); the data archive of John J. Stucker; and relevant state constitutions and statute volumes. Also see Stucker (1973), Appendix B. House vote—Tables 5-70 through 5-122.

Table 3-54 State Voter Turnout Percentages for Congressional Elections Using Two-Year Election Cycles, 1980–1998

	1980	1982	1984	1986	1988	1990	1992	1994	1996	1998
Alabama	37.2	34.7	40.8	38.9	40.4	34.3	52.7	35.8	46.0	37.2
Alaska	58.3	63.4	67.4	55.2	55.6	52.2	62.6	52.4	56.7	52.3
Arizona	45.9	35.6	44.2	35.4	46.7	38.0	52.0	38.3	44.7	31.4
Arkansas	—	46.6	—	39.8	—	38.7	50.6	39.6	47.2	—
California	52.9	47.3	54.0	41.9	52.9	39.8	57.0	44.7	50.3	42.0
Colorado	56.4	45.0	57.5	45.5	57.1	42.2	59.7	40.8	54.2	45.4
Connecticut	60.9	47.7	62.6	42.0	56.4	42.9	59.7	44.8	54.5	40.5
Delaware	51.3	43.1	53.9	34.5	48.9	35.9	54.3	37.2	49.5	32.6
Florida	—	—	—	—	—	—	—	—	—	—
Georgia	35.8	22.8	36.8	24.6	37.3	29.9	45.3	29.3	40.5	29.3
Hawaii	44.7	45.5	40.4	46.7	46.1	44.6	46.5	45.5	44.9	50.1
Idaho	66.1	50.2	62.3	56.8	60.6	46.0	65.0	50.9	60.6	44.1
Illinois	57.0	45.8	57.8	37.9	54.4	38.3	59.8	37.5	50.5	39.1
Indiana	57.0	46.3	55.6	39.2	52.9	37.4	53.8	36.8	49.2	36.2
Iowa	60.6	48.6	61.6	43.3	58.1	38.9	60.3	47.0	57.2	42.5
Kansas	55.0	44.1	57.4	45.0	52.7	43.7	62.2	44.7	56.6	38.8
Kentucky	41.2	27.0	45.2	23.7	41.1	28.1	49.0	27.6	42.6	37.0
Louisiana	—	—	—	—	—	—	—	—	—	—
Maine	64.9	55.6	64.7	49.1	62.9	57.2	73.1	54.3	64.1	43.8
Maryland	47.2	35.6	47.2	32.6	46.4	31.5	51.8	38.1	46.0	41.2
Massachusetts	55.3	45.6	55.8	35.2	54.7	46.7	59.2	44.4	53.9	38.7
Michigan	56.2	43.6	53.1	35.4	52.1	36.3	57.2	43.5	52.9	42.1
Minnesota	66.3	59.7	66.1	45.8	63.5	56.4	70.7	53.4	64.3	60.2
Mississippi	46.4	37.2	49.7	29.6	51.2	20.3	51.9	32.6	46.5	27.7
Missouri	58.1	42.7	56.3	38.9	55.6	35.9	61.4	45.5	53.7	39.3
Montana	61.5	57.0	66.3	56.4	64.3	55.5	68.1	57.4	63.8	50.6
Nebraska	56.1	46.4	57.9	49.2	57.9	51.5	61.5	48.7	55.6	43.5
Nevada	43.5	37.8	39.9	34.9	43.3	36.7	52.0	36.2	39.8	33.5
New Hampshire	55.9	39.3	52.0	32.1	55.0	35.7	61.6	36.6	57.2	36.3
New Jersey	53.5	41.3	56.7	29.0	51.2	33.2	54.3	36.3	51.0	32.8
New Mexico	47.3	44.0	53.7	40.0	45.1	34.9	52.0	41.7	47.8	41.9
New York	46.8	38.8	51.2	31.9	44.7	29.6	48.3	38.0	46.2	35.9
North Carolina	41.4	30.4	47.9	33.8	41.2	40.5	49.4	30.2	46.5	34.3
North Dakota	63.9	56.8	67.2	62.3	65.3	50.9	64.3	50.4	55.9	44.9
Ohio	51.9	43.3	55.9	39.2	52.7	43.0	56.9	40.6	53.4	40.6
Oklahoma	38.9	39.4	50.5	32.6	34.1	37.6	55.1	41.2	49.3	35.3
Oregon	59.2	53.3	62.0	52.2	50.8	51.4	65.6	54.4	58.9	46.7
Pennsylvania	50.0	41.7	53.2	37.5	47.2	31.8	51.2	37.6	48.1	32.2
Rhode Island	57.3	48.5	55.9	43.1	54.2	47.3	54.9	47.6	50.6	41.7
South Carolina	38.3	29.3	40.0	30.0	40.2	26.3	42.5	32.1	37.9	34.0
South Dakota	66.1	56.8	64.8	59.1	63.3	52.0	65.9	59.4	61.5	48.3
Tennessee	39.8	35.1	38.5	31.7	39.6	19.7	46.1	36.7	44.9	22.3
Texas	42.8	28.9	45.8	28.4	42.7	29.0	47.9	33.8	41.3	26.4
Utah	65.7	52.4	62.1	42.8	58.9	41.4	63.6	41.3	51.1	34.2
Vermont	54.1	44.5	59.4	48.2	59.6	50.8	67.0	49.5	58.6	48.7
Virginia	40.9	33.9	44.9	24.6	43.2	25.5	51.1	40.3	45.4	23.2
Washington	56.0	43.3	57.8	40.0	51.7	38.0	61.5	44.7	55.3	45.5
West Virginia	49.6	39.7	51.5	29.1	42.1	27.9	41.4	29.6	37.7	25.1
Wisconsin	64.4	43.1	60.8	40.0	58.0	35.3	66.0	39.6	57.3	43.9
Wyoming	52.9	49.8	59.0	50.4	56.2	50.2	60.8	59.0	61.5	49.7

Notes: Turnout is the ratio V/E, where V is the total vote cast in congressional (House) races in a given election year in a state, and E is the number of people eligible by law to vote in that state according to the criteria of citizenship, race, sex, and age laws on suffrage, where race has two dimensions: color (black/white) and bondage (slave/free). These raw data—number of House votes cast and eligibles in each state—are used to produce the entries. Both states with even-numbered year House races and states with odd-numbered year House races in a given two-year election cycle have their congressional vote divided by the number of eligibles in the state in the even-numbered year, which serves as a common base by which to compare congressional votes in any given two-year cycle for House elections. States with partial data (less than 100 percent of districts reporting the vote) are not included. States with special House elections are also not included. The few states having House elections in both even- and odd-numbered years in the same two-year election cycle only have the even-numbered election included in this table. For a more detailed discussion of the methodology used, see the notes to Table 3-5.

Sources: Eligibles—decennial censuses (1790–1990) of the U.S. Census Bureau; Bureau of U.S. Census Series P pamphlets for 1972 and the 1990s; Richard Scammon's book series, *America Votes* (various publication dates); the data archive of John J. Stucker; and relevant state constitutions and statute volumes. Also see Stucker (1973), Appendix B. House vote—Tables 5-70 through 5-122.

Table 3-55 State Voter Turnout Percentages for Congressional Elections in Odd-Numbered Years Only, 1789–1809

	1789	1791	1793	1795	1797	1799	1801	1803	1805	1807	1809
Alabama	—	—	—	—	—	—	—	—	—	—	—
Alaska	—	—	—	—	—	—	—	—	—	—	—
Arizona	—	—	—	—	—	—	—	—	—	—	—
Arkansas	—	—	—	—	—	—	—	—	—	—	—
California	—	—	—	—	—	—	—	—	—	—	—
Colorado	—	—	—	—	—	—	—	—	—	—	—
Connecticut	—	—	—	—	—	—	—	—	—	—	—
Delaware	20.1	—	—	—	—	—	—	—	—	—	—
Florida	—	—	—	—	—	—	—	—	—	—	—
Georgia	26.9	16.6	—	—	—	—	—	—	—	—	—
Hawaii	—	—	—	—	—	—	—	—	—	—	—
Idaho	—	—	—	—	—	—	—	—	—	—	—
Illinois	—	—	—	—	—	—	—	—	—	—	—
Indiana	—	—	—	—	—	—	—	—	—	—	—
Iowa	—	—	—	—	—	—	—	—	—	—	—
Kansas	—	—	—	—	—	—	—	—	—	—	—
Kentucky	—	—	—	—	—	—	58.0	—	—	—	—
Louisiana	—	—	—	—	—	—	—	—	—	—	—
Maine	—	—	—	—	—	—	—	—	—	—	—
Maryland	16.6	—	—	—	—	—	28.7	—	—	—	—
Massachusetts	—	—	—	—	—	—	—	—	—	—	—
Michigan	—	—	—	—	—	—	—	—	—	—	—
Minnesota	—	—	—	—	—	—	—	—	—	—	—
Mississippi	—	—	—	—	—	—	—	—	—	—	—
Missouri	—	—	—	—	—	—	—	—	—	—	—
Montana	—	—	—	—	—	—	—	—	—	—	—
Nebraska	—	—	—	—	—	—	—	—	—	—	—
Nevada	—	—	—	—	—	—	—	—	—	—	—
New Hampshire	—	—	—	—	—	—	—	—	—	—	—
New Jersey	36.1	16.7	—	—	27.5	—	—	32.5	—	—	—
New Mexico	—	—	—	—	—	—	—	—	—	—	—
New York	—	—	28.3	—	—	—	—	—	—	—	—
North Carolina	—	—	—	—	—	—	—	—	—	—	—
North Dakota	—	—	—	—	—	—	—	—	—	—	—
Ohio	—	—	—	—	—	—	—	37.3	—	—	—
Oklahoma	—	—	—	—	—	—	—	—	—	—	—
Oregon	—	—	—	—	—	—	—	—	—	—	—
Pennsylvania	—	—	—	—	—	—	—	—	—	—	—
Rhode Island	—	—	—	—	—	—	—	—	—	—	—
South Carolina	—	—	—	—	—	—	—	16.2	—	—	—
South Dakota	—	—	—	—	—	—	—	—	—	—	—
Tennessee	—	—	—	—	—	—	48.4	40.6	53.5	—	—
Texas	—	—	—	—	—	—	—	—	—	—	—
Utah	—	—	—	—	—	—	—	—	—	—	—
Vermont	—	—	12.6	—	—	—	—	—	—	—	—
Virginia	—	—	—	—	—	—	—	—	—	—	—
Washington	—	—	—	—	—	—	—	—	—	—	—
West Virginia	—	—	—	—	—	—	—	—	—	—	—
Wisconsin	—	—	—	—	—	—	—	—	—	—	—
Wyoming	—	—	—	—	—	—	—	—	—	—	—

Notes: The entries are states that held their House elections in odd-numbered years. Turnout is the ratio V/E, where V is the total vote cast in congressional (House) races in an odd-numbered election year in a state, and E is the total number of eligibles in that state in the odd-numbered year. These raw data—number of House votes cast in an odd-numbered year and number of eligibles in that state in that odd-numbered year—are used to produce the entries. States with partial data (less than 100 percent of districts reporting the vote) are not included. States with special House elections are also not included. For a more detailed discussion of the general methodology used to obtain congressional vote and eligibles data, see the notes to Table 3-5.

Sources: Eligibles—decennial censuses (1790–1990) of the U.S. Census Bureau; Bureau of U.S. Census Series P pamphlets for 1972 and the 1990s; Richard Scammon's book series, *America Votes* (various publication dates); the data archive of John J. Stucker; and relevant state constitutions and statute volumes. Also see Stucker (1973), Appendix B. House vote—Tables 5-70 through 5-122.

Table 3-56 State Voter Turnout Percentages for Congressional Elections in Odd-Numbered Years Only, 1811–1829

	1811	1813	1815	1817	1819	1821	1823	1825	1827	1829
Alabama	—	—	—	—	85.7	83.5	—	—	—	83.5
Alaska	—	—	—	—	—	—	—	—	—	—
Arizona	—	—	—	—	—	—	—	—	—	—
Arkansas	—	—	—	—	—	—	—	—	—	—
California	—	—	—	—	—	—	—	—	—	—
Colorado	—	—	—	—	—	—	—	—	—	—
Connecticut	—	—	—	—	—	11.7	8.4	12.3	22.3	22.0
Delaware	—	—	—	—	—	—	—	—	—	—
Florida	—	—	—	—	—	—	—	—	—	—
Georgia	—	—	—	—	—	—	—	—	—	—
Hawaii	—	—	—	—	—	—	—	—	—	—
Idaho	—	—	—	—	—	—	—	—	—	—
Illinois	—	—	—	—	—	—	—	—	—	—
Indiana	—	—	—	44.1	—	—	—	—	—	—
Iowa	—	—	—	—	—	—	—	—	—	—
Kansas	—	—	—	—	—	—	—	—	—	—
Kentucky	—	—	—	—	—	—	—	—	77.0	—
Louisiana	—	—	—	—	—	—	—	—	—	—
Maine	—	—	—	—	—	—	38.4	—	—	—
Maryland	—	—	—	—	—	—	—	—	—	59.2
Massachusetts	—	—	—	—	—	—	—	—	—	—
Michigan	—	—	—	—	—	—	—	—	—	—
Minnesota	—	—	—	—	—	—	—	—	—	—
Mississippi	—	—	—	37.6	—	—	—	—	—	—
Missouri	—	—	—	—	—	—	—	—	—	—
Montana	—	—	—	—	—	—	—	—	—	—
Nebraska	—	—	—	—	—	—	—	—	—	—
Nevada	—	—	—	—	—	—	—	—	—	—
New Hampshire	—	—	—	—	45.5	—	—	—	50.7	67.0
New Jersey	—	50.6	—	—	—	—	—	—	—	—
New Mexico	—	—	—	—	—	—	—	—	—	—
New York	—	—	—	—	—	48.5	—	—	—	—
North Carolina	—	—	—	—	—	—	—	—	—	—
North Dakota	—	—	—	—	—	—	—	—	—	—
Ohio	—	—	—	—	—	—	—	—	—	—
Oklahoma	—	—	—	—	—	—	—	—	—	—
Oregon	—	—	—	—	—	—	—	—	—	—
Pennsylvania	—	—	—	—	—	—	—	—	—	—
Rhode Island	—	—	—	—	—	—	—	15.9	11.3	26.8
South Carolina	—	—	—	—	—	—	36.4	—	—	—
South Dakota	—	—	—	—	—	—	—	—	—	—
Tennessee	46.3	—	—	73.3	77.0	—	—	—	—	—
Texas	—	—	—	—	—	—	—	—	—	—
Utah	—	—	—	—	—	—	—	—	—	—
Vermont	—	—	—	—	—	—	—	—	—	—
Virginia	—	—	—	—	—	—	—	—	—	—
Washington	—	—	—	—	—	—	—	—	—	—
West Virginia	—	—	—	—	—	—	—	—	—	—
Wisconsin	—	—	—	—	—	—	—	—	—	—
Wyoming	—	—	—	—	—	—	—	—	—	—

Notes: The entries are states that held their House elections in odd-numbered years. Turnout is the ratio V/E, where V is the total vote cast in congressional (House) races in an odd-numbered election year in a state, and E is the total number of eligibles in that state in the odd-numbered year. These raw data—number of House votes cast in an odd-numbered year and number of eligibles in that state in that odd-numbered year—are used to produce the entries. States with partial data (less than 100 percent of districts reporting the vote) are not included. States with special House elections are also not included. For a more detailed discussion of the general methodology used to obtain congressional vote and eligibles data, see the notes to Table 3-5.

Sources: Eligibles—decennial censuses (1790–1990) of the U.S. Census Bureau; Bureau of U.S. Census Series P pamphlets for 1972 and the 1990s; Richard Scammon's book series, *America Votes* (various publication dates); the data archive of John J. Stucker; and relevant state constitutions and statute volumes. Also see Stucker (1973), Appendix B. House vote—Tables 5-70 through 5-122.

Table 3-57 State Voter Turnout Percentages for Congressional Elections in Odd-Numbered Years Only, 1831–1849

	1831	1833	1835	1837	1839	1841	1843	1845	1847	1849
Alabama	—	—	—	—	—	56.6	—	—	—	79.6
Alaska	—	—	—	—	—	—	—	—	—	—
Arizona	—	—	—	—	—	—	—	—	—	—
Arkansas	—	—	—	31.0	—	—	—	—	—	—
California	—	—	—	—	—	—	—	—	—	17.9
Colorado	—	—	—	—	—	—	—	—	—	—
Connecticut	25.5	28.4	56.6	61.0	68.0	61.8	66.2	66.5	64.7	58.1
Delaware	—	—	—	—	—	—	—	—	—	—
Florida	—	—	—	—	—	—	—	57.6	—	—
Georgia	—	—	—	—	—	—	—	—	—	—
Hawaii	—	—	—	—	—	—	—	—	—	—
Idaho	—	—	—	—	—	—	—	—	—	—
Illinois	62.0	—	—	—	—	59.6	70.1	—	—	—
Indiana	72.4	71.4	68.6	72.2	78.0	61.6	75.8	72.7	72.2	69.5
Iowa	—	—	—	—	—	—	—	—	61.6	—
Kansas	—	—	—	—	—	—	—	—	—	—
Kentucky	—	—	—	—	—	31.5	75.3	76.0	78.8	63.5
Louisiana	—	—	—	—	—	—	25.9	—	—	—
Maine	—	50.5	—	—	—	—	51.8	—	—	—
Maryland	59.3	68.5	—	54.8	74.1	53.1	—	68.4	—	57.3
Massachusetts	—	26.4	—	—	—	—	—	—	—	—
Michigan	—	—	24.6	55.7	—	—	59.2	—	—	—
Minnesota	—	—	—	—	—	—	—	—	—	—
Mississippi	—	—	64.2	54.3	89.6	81.4	79.2	92.4	81.0	87.6
Missouri	44.5	34.6	49.6	—	—	—	—	—	—	—
Montana	—	—	—	—	—	—	—	—	—	—
Nebraska	—	—	—	—	—	—	—	—	—	—
Nevada	—	—	—	—	—	—	—	—	—	—
New Hampshire	66.3	50.3	59.3	34.9	81.9	72.6	60.2	69.3	74.9	66.8
New Jersey	—	—	—	—	—	—	—	—	—	—
New Mexico	—	—	—	—	—	—	—	—	—	—
New York	—	—	—	—	—	—	—	—	—	—
North Carolina	—	—	—	—	—	—	56.2	72.9	58.0	66.1
North Dakota	—	—	—	—	—	—	—	—	—	—
Ohio	—	—	—	—	—	—	60.5	—	—	—
Oklahoma	—	—	—	—	—	—	—	—	—	—
Oregon	—	—	—	—	—	—	—	—	—	—
Pennsylvania	—	—	—	—	—	—	47.6	—	—	—
Rhode Island	15.9	22.5	32.8	31.3	30.6	10.1	38.3	34.7	31.6	22.8
South Carolina	—	—	—	—	—	—	—	—	—	—
South Dakota	—	—	—	—	—	—	—	—	—	—
Tennessee	77.7	79.6	77.8	81.2	86.0	53.1	80.2	76.2	79.8	47.2
Texas	—	—	—	—	—	—	—	—	—	63.4
Utah	—	—	—	—	—	—	—	—	—	—
Vermont	—	35.0	—	—	—	—	66.3	—	—	—
Virginia	—	—	—	—	—	—	—	—	—	—
Washington	—	—	—	—	—	—	—	—	—	—
West Virginia	—	—	—	—	—	—	—	—	—	—
Wisconsin	—	—	—	—	—	—	—	—	—	—
Wyoming	—	—	—	—	—	—	—	—	—	—

Notes: The entries are states that held their House elections in odd-numbered years. Turnout is the ratio V/E, where V is the total vote cast in congressional (House) races in an odd-numbered election year in a state, and E is the total number of eligibles in that state in the odd-numbered year. These raw data—number of House votes cast in an odd-numbered year and number of eligibles in that state in that odd-numbered year—are used to produce the entries. States with partial data (less than 100 percent of districts reporting the vote) are not included. States with special House elections are also not included. For a more detailed discussion of the general methodology used to obtain congressional vote and eligibles data, see the notes to Table 3-5.

Sources: Eligibles—decennial censuses (1790–1990) of the U.S. Census Bureau; Bureau of U.S. Census Series P pamphlets for 1972 and the 1990s; Richard Scammon's book series, *America Votes* (various publication dates); the data archive of John J. Stucker; and relevant state constitutions and statute volumes. Also see Stucker (1973), Appendix B. House vote—Tables 5-70 through 5-122.

Table 3-58 State Voter Turnout Percentages for Congressional Elections in Odd-Numbered Years Only, 1851–1869

	1851	1853	1855	1857	1859	1861	1863	1865	1867	1869
Alabama	—	—	71.3	69.6	—	—	—	—	—	57.0
Alaska	—	—	—	—	—	—	—	—	—	—
Arizona	—	—	—	—	—	—	—	—	—	—
Arkansas	54.5	38.2	—	—	—	—	—	—	—	—
California	56.4	—	—	—	63.1	70.6	63.2	—	51.3	—
Colorado	—	—	—	—	—	—	—	—	—	—
Connecticut	59.6	56.2	56.9	53.8	64.5	66.3	61.0	53.9	66.8	66.0
Delaware	—	—	—	—	—	—	—	—	—	—
Florida	—	—	—	—	—	—	—	—	—	—
Georgia	85.0	80.3	86.9	81.9	77.8	—	—	—	—	—
Hawaii	—	—	—	—	—	—	—	—	—	—
Idaho	—	—	—	—	—	—	—	—	—	—
Illinois	—	—	—	—	—	—	—	—	—	—
Indiana	67.9	—	—	—	—	—	—	—	—	—
Iowa	—	—	—	—	—	—	—	—	—	—
Kansas	—	—	—	—	45.2	—	—	—	—	—
Kentucky	58.9	65.5	71.8	66.1	68.8	60.9	37.8	48.4	47.2	—
Louisiana	45.9	—	48.4	42.4	40.4	—	—	—	—	—
Maine	—	—	—	—	—	—	—	—	—	—
Maryland	51.2	65.5	72.0	72.6	61.8	53.3	38.6	—	—	—
Massachusetts	—	—	—	—	—	—	—	—	—	—
Michigan	—	—	—	—	—	—	—	—	—	—
Minnesota	—	—	—	75.9	84.1	—	—	—	—	—
Mississippi	86.2	91.1	82.9	49.9	50.6	—	—	—	—	68.3
Missouri	—	—	—	—	—	—	—	—	—	—
Montana	—	—	—	—	—	—	—	—	—	—
Nebraska	—	—	—	—	—	—	—	—	—	—
Nevada	—	—	—	—	—	—	—	33.6	—	—
New Hampshire	61.2	59.7	73.4	72.4	77.4	74.8	73.2	73.5	75.8	74.9
New Jersey	—	—	—	—	—	—	—	—	—	—
New Mexico	—	—	—	—	—	—	—	—	—	—
New York	—	—	—	—	—	—	—	—	—	—
North Carolina	—	66.2	71.8	59.4	60.3	—	—	—	—	—
North Dakota	—	—	—	—	—	—	—	—	—	—
Ohio	—	—	—	—	—	—	—	—	—	—
Oklahoma	—	—	—	—	—	—	—	—	—	—
Oregon	—	—	—	—	71.8	—	—	—	—	—
Pennsylvania	—	—	—	—	—	—	—	—	—	—
Rhode Island	32.2	38.3	—	33.7	28.0	46.5	37.3	18.6	15.6	—
South Carolina	—	—	—	—	—	—	—	—	—	—
South Dakota	—	—	—	—	—	—	—	—	—	—
Tennessee	—	—	75.8	71.4	77.2	—	—	29.8	47.4	—
Texas	50.7	57.6	63.4	60.3	61.0	—	—	—	—	47.3
Utah	—	—	—	—	—	—	—	—	—	—
Vermont	—	—	—	—	—	—	44.8	—	—	—
Virginia	—	—	—	—	—	—	—	—	—	81.9
Washington	—	—	—	—	—	—	—	—	—	—
West Virginia	—	—	—	—	—	—	21.6	—	—	—
Wisconsin	—	—	—	—	—	—	—	—	—	—
Wyoming	—	—	—	—	—	—	—	—	—	—

Notes: The entries are states that held their House elections in odd-numbered years. Turnout is the ratio V/E, where V is the total vote cast in congressional (House) races in an odd-numbered election year in a state, and E is the total number of eligibles in that state in the odd-numbered year. These raw data—number of House votes cast in an odd-numbered year and number of eligibles in that state in that odd-numbered year—are used to produce the entries. States with partial data (less than 100 percent of districts reporting the vote) are not included. States with special House elections are also not included. For a more detailed discussion of the general methodology used to obtain congressional vote and eligibles data, see the notes to Table 3-5.

Sources: Eligibles—decennial censuses (1790–1990) of the U.S. Census Bureau; Bureau of U.S. Census Series P pamphlets for 1972 and the 1990s; Richard Scammon's book series, *America Votes* (various publication dates); the data archive of John J. Stucker; and relevant state constitutions and statute volumes. Also see Stucker (1973), Appendix B. House vote—Tables 5-70 through 5-122.

Table 3-59 State Voter Turnout Percentages for Congressional Elections in Odd-Numbered Years Only, 1871–1959

	1871	1873	1875	1877	1879	1889	1895	1907	1911	1959
Alabama	—	—	—	—	—	—	—	—	—	—
Alaska	—	—	—	—	—	—	—	—	—	—
Arizona	—	—	—	—	—	—	—	—	37.8	—
Arkansas	—	—	—	—	—	—	—	—	—	—
California	78.0	—	66.7	—	73.5	—	—	—	—	—
Colorado	—	—	—	—	—	—	—	—	—	—
Connecticut	72.4	64.1	72.1	—	—	—	—	—	—	—
Delaware	—	—	—	—	—	—	—	—	—	—
Florida	—	—	—	—	—	—	—	—	—	—
Georgia	—	—	—	—	—	—	—	—	—	—
Hawaii	—	—	—	—	—	—	—	—	—	54.3
Idaho	—	—	—	—	—	—	—	—	—	—
Illinois	—	—	—	—	—	—	—	—	—	—
Indiana	—	—	—	—	—	—	—	—	—	—
Iowa	—	—	—	—	—	—	—	—	—	—
Kansas	—	—	—	—	—	—	—	—	—	—
Kentucky	—	—	—	—	—	—	—	—	—	—
Louisiana	—	—	—	—	—	—	—	—	—	—
Maine	—	—	—	—	—	—	—	—	—	—
Maryland	—	—	—	—	—	—	—	—	—	—
Massachusetts	—	—	—	—	—	—	—	—	—	—
Michigan	—	—	—	—	—	—	—	—	—	—
Minnesota	—	—	—	—	—	—	—	—	—	—
Mississippi	—	—	78.0	—	—	—	—	—	—	—
Missouri	—	—	—	—	—	—	—	—	—	—
Montana	—	—	—	—	—	81.3	—	—	—	—
Nebraska	—	—	—	—	—	—	—	—	—	—
Nevada	—	—	—	—	—	—	—	—	—	—
New Hampshire	80.0	77.8	88.7	85.6	—	—	—	—	—	—
New Jersey	—	—	—	—	—	—	—	—	—	—
New Mexico	—	—	—	—	—	—	—	—	71.5	—
New York	—	—	—	—	—	—	—	—	—	—
North Carolina	—	—	—	—	—	—	—	—	—	—
North Dakota	—	—	—	—	—	95.5	—	—	—	—
Ohio	—	—	—	—	—	—	—	—	—	—
Oklahoma	—	—	—	—	—	—	—	65.7	—	—
Oregon	—	—	—	—	—	—	—	—	—	—
Pennsylvania	—	—	—	—	—	—	—	—	—	—
Rhode Island	—	—	—	—	—	—	—	—	—	—
South Carolina	—	—	—	—	—	—	—	—	—	—
South Dakota	—	—	—	—	—	94.3	—	—	—	—
Tennessee	—	—	—	—	—	—	—	—	—	—
Texas	56.9	—	—	—	—	—	—	—	—	—
Utah	—	—	—	—	—	—	42.2	—	—	—
Vermont	—	—	—	—	—	—	—	—	—	—
Virginia	—	—	—	—	—	—	—	—	—	—
Washington	—	—	—	—	—	53.6	—	—	—	—
West Virginia	—	—	—	—	—	—	—	—	—	—
Wisconsin	—	—	—	—	—	—	—	—	—	—
Wyoming	—	—	—	—	—	—	—	—	—	—

Notes: The entries are states that held their House elections in odd-numbered years. Turnout is the ratio V/E, where V is the total vote cast in congressional (House) races in an odd-numbered election year in a state, and E is the total number of eligibles in that state in the odd-numbered year. These raw data—number of House votes cast in an odd-numbered year and number of eligibles in that state in that odd-numbered year—are used to produce the entries. States with partial data (less than 100 percent of districts reporting the vote) are not included. States with special House elections are also not included. For a more detailed discussion of the general methodology used to obtain congressional vote and eligibles data, see the notes to Table 3-5.

Sources: Eligibles—decennial censuses (1790–1990) of the U.S. Census Bureau; Bureau of U.S. Census Series P pamphlets for 1972 and the 1990s; Richard Scammon's book series, *America Votes* (various publication dates); the data archive of John J. Stucker; and relevant state constitutions and statute volumes. Also see Stucker (1973), Appendix B. House vote—Tables 5-70 through 5-122.

Table 3-60 State Voter Mobilization Percentages for Senate Elections, 1912–1928

	1912	1914	1916	1918	1920	1922	1924	1926	1928
Alabama	—	7.6	—	4.9	20.0	—	13.0	9.0	—
Alaska	—	—	—	—	—	—	—	—	—
Arizona	—	33.2	33.7	—	34.6	30.7	—	34.5	37.2
Arkansas	—	5.6	—	9.3	22.1	—	15.0	3.7	—
California	—	47.1	46.4	—	39.4	34.6	—	32.7	43.6
Colorado	49.9	49.0	—	39.7	50.9	—	54.1	49.6	—
Connecticut	—	24.3	27.5	—	43.6	37.3	—	32.6	57.7
Delaware	—	—	39.4	31.6	—	53.9	62.8	—	71.4
Florida	—	5.1	14.7	—	24.8	8.6	—	8.9	28.0
Georgia	—	6.9	—	4.4	9.2	—	10.7	3.2	—
Hawaii	—	—	—	—	—	—	—	—	—
Idaho	—	53.6	—	42.3	60.0	—	52.5	51.8	—
Illinois	—	28.5	—	24.9	52.4	—	53.0	40.1	—
Indiana	—	38.7	41.4	—	70.2	60.1	—	54.6	72.2
Iowa	—	32.1	—	25.2	60.2	—	61.3	38.8	—
Kansas	36.4	52.0	—	43.9	49.9	—	57.3	44.6	—
Kentucky	—	27.7	—	28.6	70.1	—	58.7	40.4	—
Louisiana	—	—	—	4.9	10.3	—	9.4	5.2	—
Maine	—	—	32.2	25.5	—	36.8	51.3	—	43.1
Maryland	—	27.4	28.3	—	45.4	34.4	—	36.0	48.9
Massachusetts	—	—	22.6	17.8	—	35.3	44.7	—	58.0
Michigan	—	—	32.5	20.8	—	24.7	46.2	—	48.7
Minnesota	23.0	—	29.5	25.8	—	48.9	57.9	—	67.5
Mississippi	—	—	8.6	3.6	—	7.5	10.4	—	11.1
Missouri	—	31.9	39.8	—	65.0	46.8	—	45.3	68.2
Montana	27.2	—	58.4	37.0	—	49.7	53.1	—	61.1
Nebraska	—	—	40.7	30.4	—	51.5	57.3	—	66.3
Nevada	—	38.7	60.2	—	52.5	53.7	—	54.5	55.7
New Hampshire	—	29.6	—	25.3	55.6	—	55.2	44.0	—
New Jersey	—	—	25.1	19.5	—	40.7	45.9	—	60.9
New Mexico	—	—	37.5	26.0	—	57.7	58.1	—	56.0
New York	—	22.8	25.1	—	42.0	35.5	—	37.9	54.3
North Carolina	—	19.0	—	20.2	44.6	—	35.7	25.7	—
North Dakota	—	28.4	34.3	—	67.6	58.7	—	45.1	57.2
Ohio	—	33.9	35.3	—	54.0	42.5	—	34.3	57.9
Oklahoma	29.6	28.0	—	19.4	47.9	—	49.1	30.2	—
Oregon	30.4	54.2	—	31.6	46.5	—	48.5	39.2	—
Pennsylvania	—	23.8	25.2	—	35.4	27.7	—	27.8	54.7
Rhode Island	—	—	25.2	22.5	—	41.9	53.8	—	57.4
South Carolina	—	4.6	—	3.4	8.3	—	6.2	1.8	—
South Dakota	—	30.5	—	27.5	53.4	—	50.7	48.1	—
Tennessee	—	—	22.6	13.3	—	17.7	19.9	—	21.5
Texas	—	—	16.8	7.7	—	15.1	25.2	—	22.8
Utah	—	55.8	66.8	—	63.8	51.2	—	57.3	68.2
Vermont	—	28.6	29.2	—	41.1	30.6	—	32.5	59.2
Virginia	—	—	11.7	3.5	—	13.2	16.6	—	21.5
Washington	—	44.6	45.5	—	44.9	33.2	—	33.7	50.0
West Virginia	—	—	41.1	29.6	—	49.7	70.2	—	74.1
Wisconsin	—	22.9	29.5	—	44.3	29.9	—	32.7	43.2
Wyoming	—	—	48.1	37.4	—	52.8	63.5	—	62.1

Notes: Mobilization is the ratio V/A, where V is the total vote cast in a Senate race (or races) in a given election year in a state, and A is the total number of adults in that state. These raw data—number of Senate votes cast and adults in each state—are used to produce the entries. States with partial Senate vote data are not included. States with special Senate elections are also not included. For a more detailed discussion of the methodology used, see the notes to Table 3-7.

Sources: Adults—decennial censuses (1910–1990) of the U.S. Census Bureau; Bureau of U.S. Census Series P pamphlets for 1972 and the 1990s; and Richard Scammon's book series, *America Votes* (various publication dates). Senate vote—Tables 6-33 through 6-54.

Table 3-61 State Voter Mobilization Percentages for Senate Elections, 1930–1948

	1930	1932	1934	1936	1938	1940	1942	1944	1946	1948
Alabama	18.8	17.5	—	18.7	8.7	—	4.3	15.2	—	12.9
Alaska	—	—	—	—	—	—	—	—	—	—
Arizona	—	44.1	35.9	—	38.7	49.2	—	37.2	30.6	—
Arkansas	14.6	20.6	—	18.1	12.8	—	9.0	19.4	—	20.9
California	—	53.4	48.2	—	53.9	55.5	—	56.8	42.0	—
Colorado	51.7	68.0	—	69.6	64.8	—	47.0	64.6	—	62.3
Connecticut	—	58.2	52.0	—	56.0	67.6	—	66.3	52.8	—
Delaware	59.1	—	61.9	76.3	—	75.9	46.3	—	57.4	69.2
Florida	—	21.9	13.1	—	15.4	26.5	—	32.2	12.6	—
Georgia	3.7	16.3	—	15.8	4.1	—	3.4	14.6	—	18.5
Hawaii	—	—	—	—	—	—	—	—	—	—
Idaho	53.1	71.2	—	70.9	60.9	—	44.5	64.0	—	62.7
Illinois	46.2	64.6	—	73.5	60.5	—	54.1	69.7	—	66.7
Indiana	—	76.4	70.4	—	72.3	78.7	—	69.9	55.5	—
Iowa	36.3	64.9	—	67.6	51.6	—	42.9	61.5	—	59.4
Kansas	52.8	63.4	—	71.3	64.6	—	42.2	56.0	—	58.4
Kentucky	45.4	66.4	—	59.2	35.1	—	23.7	50.4	—	46.1
Louisiana	11.5	21.1	—	22.9	11.4	—	6.0	19.6	—	21.4
Maine	29.7	—	55.1	60.5	—	48.0	30.9	—	31.3	39.3
Maryland	—	42.8	43.9	—	45.6	51.4	—	42.2	34.0	—
Massachusetts	44.9	—	51.7	63.9	—	67.1	46.2	—	53.8	65.3
Michigan	27.6	—	39.2	53.4	—	59.3	33.8	—	42.4	52.1
Minnesota	50.8	—	61.5	62.9	—	67.3	41.7	—	47.1	64.6
Mississippi	3.3	—	4.7	12.4	—	12.0	4.3	—	3.9	12.6
Missouri	—	69.5	56.0	—	50.8	72.7	—	60.9	42.0	—
Montana	55.3	—	61.0	64.9	—	67.6	47.5	—	52.1	59.9
Nebraska	53.5	—	67.3	71.4	—	71.3	45.2	—	45.0	55.2
Nevada	—	64.5	64.2	—	64.2	68.8	—	59.5	53.3	—
New Hampshire	42.4	65.3	—	66.5	58.2	—	49.1	64.6	—	64.2
New Jersey	40.9	—	51.4	61.7	—	65.9	41.6	—	43.5	57.5
New Mexico	54.5	—	62.3	65.8	—	64.9	35.4	—	39.3	53.0
New York	—	54.2	42.9	—	50.3	65.8	—	63.6	48.8	—
North Carolina	34.7	43.1	—	44.9	26.8	—	17.4	36.5	—	34.2
North Dakota	—	66.1	71.3	—	71.1	70.8	—	56.8	44.8	—
Ohio	—	58.2	49.4	—	52.2	66.8	—	61.4	44.7	—
Oklahoma	38.0	49.8	—	54.3	34.8	—	27.1	51.1	—	51.4
Oregon	38.0	54.6	—	57.5	51.2	—	34.9	52.2	—	52.4
Pennsylvania	—	48.0	49.6	—	61.4	62.9	—	56.4	46.4	—
Rhode Island	53.0	—	55.7	67.7	—	66.5	49.0	—	53.4	61.1
South Carolina	2.0	12.5	—	12.5	4.8	—	2.3	9.6	—	12.6
South Dakota	53.4	73.0	—	74.8	72.2	—	46.5	57.8	—	60.9
Tennessee	15.2	—	20.1	22.5	—	24.4	9.1	—	11.7	25.9
Texas	9.5	—	13.0	23.2	—	27.3	6.8	—	8.7	23.3
Utah	—	75.5	64.1	—	61.2	80.2	—	72.8	55.3	—
Vermont	—	60.7	58.9	—	49.7	61.6	—	53.2	31.4	—
Virginia	11.2	—	10.3	18.4	—	18.9	5.3	—	13.8	20.0
Washington	—	57.7	45.8	—	51.3	62.6	—	61.2	46.7	—
West Virginia	61.4	—	65.6	82.9	—	82.0	42.6	—	48.0	66.4
Wisconsin	—	58.9	49.3	—	47.6	66.3	—	59.8	47.3	—
Wyoming	55.6	—	66.9	68.4	—	71.2	47.5	—	48.2	58.3

Notes: Mobilization is the ratio V/A, where V is the total vote cast in a Senate race (or races) in a given election year in a state, and A is the total number of adults in that state. These raw data—number of Senate votes cast and adults in each state—are used to produce the entries. States with partial Senate vote data are not included. States with special Senate elections are also not included. For a more detailed discussion of the methodology used, see the notes to Table 3-7.

Sources: Adults—decennial censuses (1910–1990) of the U.S. Census Bureau; Bureau of U.S. Census Series P pamphlets for 1972 and the 1990s; and Richard Scammon's book series, *America Votes* (various publication dates). Senate vote—Tables 6-33 through 6-54.

Table 3-62 State Voter Mobilization Percentages for Senate Elections, 1950–1968

	1950	1952	1954	1956	1958	1959	1960	1962	1964	1966	1968
Alabama	9.4	—	17.6	18.3	—	—	30.2	21.2	—	41.2	46.0
Alaska	—	—	—	—	40.4	—	44.9	41.7	—	43.1	51.4
Arizona	41.9	51.5	—	45.2	43.6	—	—	45.8	55.1	—	49.4
Arkansas	27.2	—	26.8	37.3	—	—	36.2	29.3	—	—	51.8
California	51.1	59.0	—	61.8	56.0	—	—	55.5	65.8	—	60.5
Colorado	53.3	—	52.7	66.6	—	—	70.6	56.5	—	53.2	63.0
Connecticut	63.5	76.8	—	73.9	62.5	—	—	62.5	71.0	—	66.6
Delaware	—	76.8	62.1	—	60.3	—	73.0	—	69.4	54.8	—
Florida	17.2	29.8	—	25.4	19.1	—	—	28.1	43.4	—	49.4
Georgia	13.0	—	15.4	24.1	—	—	23.9	12.4	—	24.5	43.4
Hawaii	—	—	—	—	—	46.7	—	51.9	52.7	—	52.6
Idaho	57.7	—	63.2	73.1	—	—	78.4	68.1	—	63.9	71.5
Illinois	60.8	—	55.3	69.3	—	—	73.8	58.2	—	58.2	66.8
Indiana	62.5	74.8	—	73.0	63.1	—	—	63.5	71.7	—	68.1
Iowa	50.7	—	50.4	70.3	—	—	74.4	48.3	—	50.9	67.6
Kansas	49.8	—	48.5	64.0	—	—	67.2	46.7	—	49.6	60.0
Kentucky	35.4	—	44.2	54.8	—	—	57.3	43.1	—	39.3	49.3
Louisiana	15.9	—	12.4	19.5	—	—	30.0	22.8	—	22.5	26.0
Maine	—	41.1	42.6	—	49.0	—	71.7	—	64.8	54.2	—
Maryland	40.3	53.8	—	51.9	42.1	—	—	36.5	52.9	—	50.5
Massachusetts	—	73.4	58.7	—	57.5	—	74.5	—	69.0	58.8	—
Michigan	—	67.1	49.9	—	50.6	—	70.4	—	64.5	49.6	—
Minnesota	—	71.9	58.5	—	58.0	—	76.8	—	73.9	59.6	—
Mississippi	—	19.5	8.8	—	5.2	—	22.7	—	28.6	32.5	—
Missouri	48.4	70.4	—	67.3	43.7	—	—	44.7	64.4	—	61.1
Montana	—	69.8	60.0	—	59.5	—	71.2	—	70.9	65.2	—
Nebraska	—	68.8	48.7	—	48.6	—	69.8	—	64.6	55.0	—
Nevada	57.6	67.1	—	65.1	52.2	—	—	48.7	60.1	—	56.0
New Hampshire	54.0	—	53.9	69.1	—	—	77.1	58.0	—	55.2	66.9
New Jersey	—	67.1	49.8	—	50.0	—	69.0	—	66.1	50.5	—
New Mexico	—	59.9	45.7	—	42.7	—	60.0	—	62.4	48.4	—
New York	50.4	66.6	—	65.5	52.0	—	—	51.8	64.3	—	58.0
North Carolina	23.7	—	25.7	44.7	—	—	50.5	30.7	—	31.9	49.3
North Dakota	50.9	65.3	—	67.9	57.3	—	—	63.0	72.9	—	67.4
Ohio	54.2	63.8	—	62.8	55.0	—	—	50.4	63.4	—	59.9
Oklahoma	45.7	—	43.0	59.3	—	—	61.0	45.9	—	42.1	58.7
Oregon	50.3	—	55.2	70.1	—	—	70.4	57.1	—	57.1	65.6
Pennsylvania	50.7	64.4	—	64.2	56.3	—	—	61.3	66.7	—	63.3
Rhode Island	—	76.3	60.6	—	63.9	—	74.1	—	69.0	56.8	—
South Carolina	4.4	—	19.0	22.9	—	—	26.1	23.9	—	31.5	45.7
South Dakota	62.7	—	59.3	73.5	—	—	78.0	65.1	—	58.5	72.3
Tennessee	—	36.7	17.6	—	19.4	—	39.6	—	48.2	38.3	—
Texas	—	38.7	12.6	—	14.6	—	40.7	—	43.8	24.3	—
Utah	67.8	80.7	—	75.7	64.4	—	—	65.2	78.1	—	76.3
Vermont	37.5	65.2	—	66.5	53.6	—	—	51.3	67.7	—	61.8
Virginia	—	26.1	14.3	—	20.3	—	26.9	—	37.1	28.2	—
Washington	47.8	66.5	—	67.8	52.6	—	—	52.8	65.4	—	62.1
West Virginia	—	75.9	52.2	—	58.6	—	76.5	—	70.7	45.7	—
Wisconsin	50.2	71.4	—	66.2	51.3	—	—	52.5	68.3	—	65.0
Wyoming	—	71.9	61.2	—	60.7	—	72.8	—	73.7	63.5	—

Notes: Mobilization is the ratio V/A, where V is the total vote cast in a Senate race (or races) in a given election year in a state, and A is the total number of adults in that state. These raw data—number of Senate votes cast and adults in each state—are used to produce the entries. States with partial Senate vote data are not included. States with special Senate elections are also not included. For a more detailed discussion of the methodology used, see the notes to Table 3-7.

Sources: Adults—decennial censuses (1910–1990) of the U.S. Census Bureau; Bureau of U.S. Census Series P pamphlets for 1972 and the 1990s; and Richard Scammon's book series, *America Votes* (various publication dates). Senate vote—Tables 6-33 through 6-54.

Table 3-63 State Voter Mobilization Percentages for Senate Elections, 1970–1988

	1970	1972	1974	1976	1978	1980	1982	1984	1986	1988
Alabama	—	45.2	21.6	—	22.1	47.5	—	48.4	42.1	—
Alaska	—	47.3	42.4	—	48.3	57.8	—	65.8	54.0	—
Arizona	39.6	—	37.5	45.7	—	45.4	34.8	—	36.2	46.0
Arkansas	—	46.9	38.3	—	33.7	50.1	—	52.7	41.3	—
California	53.0	—	41.0	47.7	—	48.2	42.8	—	36.8	46.3
Colorado	—	57.7	47.8	—	41.8	56.4	—	58.4	46.3	—
Connecticut	58.3	—	50.7	62.2	—	59.4	46.4	—	40.1	55.6
Delaware	50.1	60.6	—	55.7	39.0	—	43.1	53.7	—	49.9
Florida	38.5	—	30.9	45.0	—	47.8	33.5	—	38.1	42.7
Georgia	—	37.4	26.4	—	17.7	41.4	—	40.1	28.0	—
Hawaii	53.6	—	43.0	48.9	—	41.8	42.7	—	42.6	40.5
Idaho	—	63.2	49.1	—	47.3	69.0	—	61.4	56.7	—
Illinois	53.3	60.8	37.7	—	39.7	56.0	—	57.7	37.3	—
Indiana	56.6	—	48.8	58.9	—	56.8	46.4	—	38.6	51.9
Iowa	—	62.8	45.4	—	40.3	61.2	—	62.3	43.1	—
Kansas	—	56.6	50.2	—	44.8	54.8	—	56.8	46.4	—
Kentucky	—	46.7	32.3	—	19.2	42.9	—	49.0	25.4	—
Louisiana	—	45.4	17.3	—	—	—	—	—	46.5	—
Maine	54.3	60.9	—	65.0	48.4	—	55.6	64.9	—	62.2
Maryland	40.8	—	31.3	47.3	—	42.2	35.2	—	32.8	46.1
Massachusetts	55.2	59.8	—	60.7	47.6	—	47.4	57.3	—	56.9
Michigan	50.7	58.0	—	56.4	44.8	—	45.5	55.7	—	51.8
Minnesota	61.5	68.3	—	70.3	56.2	—	60.9	68.3	—	66.5
Mississippi	26.1	44.2	—	35.0	35.5	—	37.3	54.3	—	52.5
Missouri	44.6	—	36.9	56.4	—	58.2	42.8	—	39.9	55.4
Montana	61.2	67.0	—	62.7	54.0	—	57.4	67.3	—	63.8
Nebraska	51.3	55.7	—	55.8	45.1	—	48.4	56.4	—	58.4
Nevada	49.7	—	40.2	42.4	—	42.1	37.1	—	33.7	41.6
New Hampshire	—	61.8	39.9	—	42.0	56.6	—	52.7	32.1	—
New Jersey	48.0	55.7	—	53.4	37.1	—	40.0	55.3	—	51.3
New Mexico	52.3	56.6	—	53.2	41.3	—	43.9	52.4	—	49.2
New York	51.5	—	40.5	49.4	—	46.7	38.1	—	31.2	44.6
North Carolina	—	41.5	27.5	—	28.0	42.6	—	49.3	33.8	—
North Dakota	61.7	—	55.6	64.9	—	64.8	56.8	—	62.5	62.4
Ohio	49.6	—	41.0	52.8	—	52.3	43.7	—	39.5	54.6
Oklahoma	—	55.3	41.5	—	36.2	50.6	—	53.8	39.7	—
Oregon	—	61.6	47.9	—	49.4	59.7	—	60.9	51.2	—
Pennsylvania	49.5	—	41.7	53.7	—	50.5	40.9	—	37.8	48.4
Rhode Island	57.7	60.6	—	57.5	43.7	—	47.7	53.9	—	52.2
South Carolina	—	38.2	27.5	—	30.5	39.9	—	41.3	30.6	—
South Dakota	—	69.2	61.5	—	53.9	67.5	—	64.4	60.1	—
Tennessee	46.2	42.1	—	47.3	36.6	—	37.4	47.9	—	43.7
Texas	34.0	44.2	—	43.9	24.7	—	29.9	49.1	—	45.5
Utah	65.6	—	56.3	67.1	—	64.5	55.5	—	42.4	60.4
Vermont	59.4	—	44.3	56.1	—	57.1	44.6	—	49.3	58.7
Virginia	33.9	42.9	—	43.7	32.9	—	35.1	47.8	—	45.8
Washington	51.8	—	40.4	56.0	—	57.8	43.9	—	39.8	53.1
West Virginia	41.7	60.0	—	43.4	36.6	—	40.9	52.6	—	46.7
Wisconsin	51.6	—	39.2	61.3	—	65.8	45.5	—	42.4	61.0
Wyoming	61.8	62.9	—	56.5	44.5	—	51.8	58.1	—	56.7

Notes: Mobilization is the ratio V/A, where V is the total vote cast in a Senate race (or races) in a given election year in a state, and A is the total number of adults in that state. These raw data—number of Senate votes cast and adults in each state—are used to produce the entries. States with partial Senate vote data are not included. States with special Senate elections are also not included. For a more detailed discussion of the methodology used, see the notes to Table 3-7.

Sources: Adults—decennial censuses (1910–1990) of the U.S. Census Bureau; Bureau of U.S. Census Series P pamphlets for 1972 and the 1990s; and Richard Scammon's book series, *America Votes* (various publication dates). Senate vote—Tables 6-33 through 6-54.

Table 3-64 State Voter Mobilization Percentages for Senate Elections, 1990–1998

	1990	1992	1994	1996	1998
Alabama	39.8	51.6	—	46.6	39.3
Alaska	50.3	61.1	—	54.9	50.8
Arizona	—	47.7	35.9	—	28.6
Arkansas	28.6	52.0	—	45.9	37.2
California	—	48.2	37.3	—	35.1
Colorado	42.0	60.5	—	51.9	44.8
Connecticut	—	59.6	43.2	—	39.1
Delaware	35.8	—	37.2	50.0	—
Florida	—	47.7	38.3	—	34.3
Georgia	21.8	25.2	—	41.5	30.9
Hawaii	—	43.3	41.8	—	45.3
Idaho	45.2	64.2	—	59.2	42.6
Illinois	38.3	57.8	—	48.9	38.8
Indiana	—	53.0	36.3	—	36.0
Iowa	47.8	62.1	—	57.4	43.9
Kansas	43.3	61.1	—	55.5	37.8
Kentucky	33.5	47.6	—	44.7	38.3
Louisiana	—	—	—	54.7	30.8
Maine	56.6	—	54.6	64.0	—
Maryland	—	50.2	36.8	—	39.4
Massachusetts	49.7	—	46.4	54.2	—
Michigan	37.5	—	43.2	52.6	—
Minnesota	56.4	—	53.0	63.9	—
Mississippi	15.0	—	31.7	44.7	—
Missouri	—	61.0	45.3	—	39.0
Montana	55.3	—	56.7	63.9	—
Nebraska	51.7	—	48.7	55.9	—
Nevada	—	49.2	34.3	—	33.2
New Hampshire	35.1	61.3	—	56.3	35.4
New Jersey	32.7	—	34.2	47.8	—
New Mexico	38.0	—	39.9	45.8	—
New York	—	47.2	35.1	—	34.4
North Carolina	41.2	49.7	—	46.3	35.4
North Dakota	—	65.1	50.4	—	44.8
Ohio	—	58.9	41.8	—	40.5
Oklahoma	38.3	55.1	—	48.8	34.9
Oregon	51.9	62.3	—	56.9	45.0
Pennsylvania	—	52.8	38.6	—	32.4
Rhode Island	46.8	—	45.2	48.0	—
South Carolina	29.3	44.6	—	41.4	37.0
South Dakota	52.1	65.9	—	61.5	48.7
Tennessee	21.4	—	38.1	44.4	—
Texas	31.5	—	32.4	40.2	—
Utah	—	64.3	41.1	—	34.6
Vermont	—	67.0	48.8	—	47.8
Virginia	23.1	—	41.8	46.7	—
Washington	—	58.9	43.2	—	44.4
West Virginia	30.0	—	30.5	42.8	—
Wisconsin	—	66.9	41.9	—	45.4
Wyoming	49.6	—	60.0	61.2	—

Notes: Mobilization is the ratio V/A, where V is the total vote cast in a Senate race (or races) in a given election year in a state, and A is the total number of adults in that state. These raw data—number of Senate votes cast and adults in each state—are used to produce the entries. States with partial Senate vote data are not included. States with special Senate elections are also not included. For a more detailed discussion of the methodology used, see the notes to Table 3-7.

Sources: Adults—decennial censuses (1910–1990) of the U.S. Census Bureau; Bureau of U.S. Census Series P pamphlets for 1972 and the 1990s; and Richard Scammon's book series, *America Votes* (various publication dates). Senate vote—Tables 6-33 through 6-54.

Table 3-65 State Voter Turnout Percentages for Senate Elections, 1912–1928

	1912	1914	1916	1918	1920	1922	1924	1926	1928
Alabama	—	15.2	—	9.9	20.2	—	13.1	9.0	—
Alaska	—	—	—	—	—	—	—	—	—
Arizona	—	43.7	44.4	—	45.6	37.7	—	38.1	39.5
Arkansas	—	10.8	—	17.9	22.3	—	15.1	3.7	—
California	—	54.1	53.5	—	45.8	39.4	—	36.4	48.1
Colorado	55.3	53.9	—	43.2	55.0	—	57.6	52.5	—
Connecticut	—	65.2	74.0	—	57.8	48.7	—	41.3	72.1
Delaware	—	—	83.5	67.0	—	57.8	67.0	—	75.2
Florida	—	10.0	29.2	—	25.9	9.0	—	9.2	28.9
Georgia	—	13.8	—	8.8	9.3	—	10.8	3.2	—
Hawaii	—	—	—	—	—	—	—	—	—
Idaho	—	57.7	—	45.0	63.3	—	54.9	54.0	—
Illinois	—	64.4	—	55.9	59.6	—	59.1	44.3	—
Indiana	—	78.1	83.4	—	72.3	62.2	—	56.4	74.4
Iowa	—	66.2	—	51.6	62.9	—	63.4	40.0	—
Kansas	71.9	54.3	—	45.5	51.9	—	59.0	45.6	—
Kentucky	—	54.9	—	56.7	70.7	—	59.1	40.7	—
Louisiana	—	—	—	10.0	10.6	—	9.6	5.3	—
Maine	—	—	72.9	57.6	—	41.3	57.5	—	47.9
Maryland	—	58.4	60.1	—	47.8	36.1	—	37.5	50.9
Massachusetts	—	—	61.6	48.2	—	45.0	56.3	—	71.3
Michigan	—	—	73.0	46.8	—	28.8	53.4	—	55.7
Minnesota	50.3	—	63.7	55.1	—	53.9	63.0	—	71.8
Mississippi	—	—	17.2	7.3	—	7.6	10.4	—	11.1
Missouri	—	64.3	80.1	—	66.8	48.0	—	46.5	69.8
Montana	52.5	—	65.9	41.2	—	54.3	57.5	—	65.0
Nebraska	—	—	80.7	60.2	—	54.8	60.5	—	68.9
Nevada	—	65.3	69.8	—	61.6	61.9	—	61.0	61.6
New Hampshire	—	72.0	—	61.3	66.3	—	64.7	51.1	—
New Jersey	—	—	63.1	49.0	—	49.6	54.9	—	70.9
New Mexico	—	—	74.1	51.8	—	62.0	61.5	—	57.5
New York	—	59.4	65.1	—	53.3	44.3	—	46.2	65.4
North Carolina	—	38.5	—	40.8	44.7	—	35.8	25.7	—
North Dakota	—	58.9	70.5	—	74.5	64.0	—	48.2	60.6
Ohio	—	74.0	76.7	—	59.5	46.4	—	36.9	62.0
Oklahoma	54.9	52.2	—	36.6	48.7	—	49.7	30.5	—
Oregon	56.7	58.0	—	34.4	50.5	—	52.2	42.0	—
Pennsylvania	—	56.9	59.7	—	41.2	31.7	—	30.9	60.0
Rhode Island	—	—	67.4	59.8	—	52.3	66.0	—	68.4
South Carolina	—	9.3	—	6.9	8.3	—	6.2	1.8	—
South Dakota	—	58.0	—	52.4	57.2	—	53.4	50.3	—
Tennessee	—	—	45.3	26.7	—	17.8	20.0	—	21.5
Texas	—	—	34.4	15.8	—	16.1	26.5	—	23.2
Utah	—	63.4	74.8	—	69.6	55.4	—	60.9	72.0
Vermont	—	62.6	63.9	—	44.9	33.4	—	35.3	64.3
Virginia	—	—	23.4	6.9	—	13.3	16.8	—	21.7
Washington	—	51.0	51.8	—	50.6	37.1	—	37.2	54.8
West Virginia	—	—	82.6	59.6	—	52.3	73.4	—	76.7
Wisconsin	—	52.0	66.6	—	50.4	33.5	—	35.7	46.6
Wyoming	—	—	54.2	41.7	—	57.7	68.5	—	65.5

Notes: Turnout is the ratio V/E, where V is the total vote cast in a Senate race (or races) in a given election year in a state, and E is the number of people eligible by law to vote in that state according to the criteria of citizenship, race, sex, and age laws on suffrage, where race has two dimensions: color (black/white) and bondage (slave/free). These raw data—number of Senate votes cast and eligibles in each state—are used to produce the entries. States with partial Senate vote data are not included. States with special Senate elections are also not included. For a more detailed discussion of the methodology used, see the notes to Table 3-8.

Sources: Eligibles—decennial censuses (1910–1990) of the U.S. Census Bureau; Bureau of U.S. Census Series P pamphlets for 1972 and the 1990s; Richard Scammon's book series, *America Votes* (various publication dates); the data archive of John J. Stucker; and relevant state constitutions and statute volumes. Also see Stucker (1973), Appendix B. Senate vote—Tables 6-33 through 6-54.

Table 3-66 State Voter Turnout Percentages for Senate Elections, 1930–1948

	1930	1932	1934	1936	1938	1940	1942	1944	1946	1948
Alabama	18.8	17.5	—	18.7	8.7	—	4.3	15.2	—	12.9
Alaska	—	—	—	—	—	—	—	—	—	—
Arizona	—	45.7	37.8	—	41.8	53.8	—	39.7	32.3	—
Arkansas	14.7	20.7	—	18.1	12.8	—	9.0	19.4	—	20.9
California	—	58.6	52.8	—	59.1	60.9	—	60.8	44.5	—
Colorado	53.9	70.9	—	72.4	67.3	—	48.5	66.4	—	63.5
Connecticut	—	70.7	62.1	—	65.1	77.5	—	73.0	57.1	—
Delaware	61.9	—	64.4	79.2	—	78.5	47.6	—	58.5	70.2
Florida	—	22.5	13.4	—	15.8	27.2	—	32.9	12.8	—
Georgia	3.7	16.3	—	15.9	4.1	—	3.4	14.6	—	18.5
Hawaii	—	—	—	—	—	—	—	—	—	—
Idaho	54.9	73.4	—	72.9	62.5	—	45.4	65.2	—	63.5
Illinois	50.6	69.8	—	78.2	64.0	—	56.4	72.2	—	68.2
Indiana	—	78.3	71.9	—	73.6	80.0	—	70.7	56.1	—
Iowa	37.1	66.2	—	68.9	52.6	—	43.6	62.3	—	59.9
Kansas	53.5	64.3	—	72.3	65.5	—	42.8	56.6	—	58.8
Kentucky	45.6	66.6	—	59.4	35.2	—	23.7	50.6	—	46.2
Louisiana	11.7	21.3	—	23.1	11.5	—	6.1	19.7	—	21.5
Maine	33.0	—	60.5	66.0	—	51.9	33.0	—	32.9	41.0
Maryland	—	44.4	45.4	—	46.9	52.8	—	43.1	34.6	—
Massachusetts	54.7	—	61.0	74.3	—	76.0	51.4	—	57.7	69.0
Michigan	31.4	—	43.5	58.7	—	63.9	36.0	—	44.3	53.8
Minnesota	53.4	—	64.3	65.6	—	69.9	43.0	—	48.1	65.6
Mississippi	3.3	—	4.7	12.5	—	12.0	4.3	—	3.9	12.6
Missouri	—	70.8	57.0	—	51.7	73.8	—	61.6	42.4	—
Montana	58.4	—	64.0	67.8	—	70.1	49.0	—	53.2	60.9
Nebraska	55.2	—	69.2	73.3	—	73.0	46.1	—	45.6	55.7
Nevada	—	70.1	69.5	—	69.0	73.7	—	62.4	55.4	—
New Hampshire	48.5	74.0	—	74.2	64.4	—	53.2	69.1	—	67.0
New Jersey	47.1	—	57.8	68.7	—	72.0	44.8	—	45.7	59.9
New Mexico	55.2	—	63.6	67.6	—	67.0	36.4	—	40.2	54.0
New York	—	63.7	49.7	—	57.1	73.8	—	69.2	52.4	—
North Carolina	34.8	43.1	—	45.0	26.8	—	17.5	36.6	—	34.3
North Dakota	—	69.3	74.6	—	74.2	73.7	—	58.4	45.8	—
Ohio	—	61.6	52.0	—	54.5	69.5	—	63.1	45.8	—
Oklahoma	38.2	50.1	—	54.6	35.0	—	27.3	51.3	—	51.5
Oregon	40.5	57.8	—	60.4	53.6	—	36.1	53.7	—	53.5
Pennsylvania	—	51.6	53.1	—	65.0	66.3	—	58.5	47.8	—
Rhode Island	62.2	—	64.0	77.0	—	74.2	53.7	—	56.7	64.0
South Carolina	2.0	12.5	—	12.5	4.8	—	2.3	9.7	—	12.6
South Dakota	55.0	75.1	—	76.9	74.1	—	47.5	58.8	—	61.5
Tennessee	15.3	—	20.2	22.5	—	24.5	9.1	—	11.7	26.0
Texas	9.6	—	13.3	23.9	—	28.4	7.1	—	9.0	24.0
Utah	—	78.9	66.8	—	63.5	83.0	—	74.7	56.5	—
Vermont	—	65.6	63.3	—	53.1	65.5	—	55.8	32.7	—
Virginia	11.3	—	10.3	18.3	—	18.7	5.3	—	13.8	20.1
Washington	—	62.5	49.4	—	54.7	66.5	—	63.9	48.4	—
West Virginia	63.3	—	67.3	84.8	—	83.6	43.4	—	48.6	67.0
Wisconsin	—	62.5	52.1	—	49.7	68.9	—	61.4	48.3	—
Wyoming	58.1	—	69.7	71.1	—	73.8	48.9	—	49.2	59.3

Notes: Turnout is the ratio V/E, where V is the total vote cast in a Senate race (or races) in a given election year in a state, and E is the number of people eligible by law to vote in that state according to the criteria of citizenship, race, sex, and age laws on suffrage, where race has two dimensions: color (black/white) and bondage (slave/free). These raw data—number of Senate votes cast and eligibles in each state—are used to produce the entries. States with partial Senate vote data are not included. States with special Senate elections are also not included. For a more detailed discussion of the methodology used, see the notes to Table 3-8.

Sources: Eligibles—decennial censuses (1910–1990) of the U.S. Census Bureau; Bureau of U.S. Census Series P pamphlets for 1972 and the 1990s; Richard Scammon's book series, *America Votes* (various publication dates); the data archive of John J. Stucker; and relevant state constitutions and statute volumes. Also see Stucker (1973), Appendix B. Senate vote—Tables 6-33 through 6-54.

Table 3-67 State Voter Turnout Percentages for Senate Elections, 1950–1968

	1950	1952	1954	1956	1958	1959	1960	1962	1964	1966	1968
Alabama	9.4	—	17.7	18.4	—	—	30.3	21.3	—	41.4	46.1
Alaska	—	—	—	—	40.9	—	45.5	42.2	—	43.7	52.1
Arizona	43.6	53.4	—	46.6	44.9	—	—	47.0	56.5	—	50.6
Arkansas	27.2	—	26.9	37.4	—	—	36.3	29.3	—	—	51.9
California	53.3	61.6	—	64.7	58.8	—	—	58.4	69.3	—	63.9
Colorado	54.1	—	53.5	67.6	—	—	71.6	57.3	—	53.9	63.8
Connecticut	66.5	80.3	—	77.1	65.2	—	—	65.1	73.8	—	69.1
Delaware	—	77.7	62.8	—	61.0	—	73.8	—	70.2	55.4	—
Florida	17.4	30.3	—	26.1	19.8	—	—	29.2	45.2	—	51.6
Georgia	13.0	—	15.4	24.1	—	—	24.0	12.5	—	24.6	43.6
Hawaii	—	—	—	—	—	54.7	—	59.4	59.4	—	57.8
Idaho	58.3	—	63.8	73.8	—	—	79.2	68.8	—	64.5	72.2
Illinois	61.8	—	56.3	70.7	—	—	75.3	59.5	—	59.6	68.4
Indiana	62.9	75.3	—	73.5	63.5	—	—	63.9	72.2	—	68.6
Iowa	50.9	—	50.6	70.7	—	—	74.7	48.6	—	51.1	67.9
Kansas	50.1	—	48.7	64.3	—	—	67.6	47.0	—	49.9	60.3
Kentucky	35.5	—	44.2	54.9	—	—	57.5	43.2	—	39.4	49.4
Louisiana	15.9	—	12.4	19.6	—	—	30.2	22.9	—	22.6	26.2
Maine	—	42.4	44.0	—	50.5	—	73.7	—	66.5	55.4	—
Maryland	40.8	54.6	—	52.7	42.7	—	—	37.1	53.8	—	51.4
Massachusetts	—	76.4	61.1	—	59.8	—	77.4	—	71.5	60.9	—
Michigan	—	68.8	51.1	—	51.8	—	72.0	—	65.9	50.6	—
Minnesota	—	72.7	59.1	—	58.6	—	77.5	—	74.5	60.1	—
Mississippi	—	19.5	8.9	—	5.2	—	22.8	—	28.7	32.6	—
Missouri	48.6	70.7	—	67.7	43.9	—	—	45.0	64.7	—	61.5
Montana	—	70.6	60.7	—	60.1	—	71.8	—	71.4	65.7	—
Nebraska	—	69.3	49.0	—	48.9	—	70.2	—	65.0	55.4	—
Nevada	59.1	68.8	—	66.8	53.6	—	—	49.9	61.6	—	57.3
New Hampshire	55.8	—	55.6	71.1	—	—	79.3	59.6	—	56.6	68.4
New Jersey	—	69.2	51.4	—	51.7	—	71.4	—	68.4	52.3	—
New Mexico	—	60.8	46.4	—	43.4	—	60.9	—	63.2	49.1	—
New York	52.6	69.6	—	68.5	54.5	—	—	54.4	67.6	—	61.0
North Carolina	23.8	—	25.8	44.8	—	—	50.7	30.8	—	32.0	49.5
North Dakota	51.4	65.9	—	68.4	57.7	—	—	63.4	73.3	—	67.8
Ohio	54.9	64.7	—	63.6	55.7	—	—	51.0	64.1	—	60.6
Oklahoma	45.8	—	43.1	59.5	—	—	61.3	46.0	—	42.3	58.9
Oregon	51.0	—	56.1	71.2	—	—	71.5	57.9	—	57.9	66.4
Pennsylvania	51.5	65.3	—	65.1	57.1	—	—	62.1	67.5	—	64.0
Rhode Island	—	78.9	62.6	—	65.9	—	76.4	—	71.0	58.4	—
South Carolina	4.4	—	19.0	23.0	—	—	26.2	24.0	—	31.6	45.9
South Dakota	63.0	—	59.6	73.8	—	—	78.3	65.3	—	58.6	72.4
Tennessee	—	36.8	17.6	—	19.5	—	39.7	—	48.4	38.4	—
Texas	—	39.7	12.9	—	15.0	—	41.7	—	44.8	24.8	—
Utah	68.9	82.0	—	76.9	65.5	—	—	66.3	79.4	—	77.5
Vermont	38.6	67.0	—	68.3	55.0	—	—	52.6	69.4	—	63.2
Virginia	—	26.2	14.4	—	20.4	—	27.1	—	37.4	28.5	—
Washington	48.9	68.1	—	69.5	53.9	—	—	54.1	66.9	—	63.5
West Virginia	—	76.5	52.6	—	58.9	—	76.9	—	71.0	45.9	—
Wisconsin	50.7	72.0	—	66.8	51.8	—	—	53.0	69.0	—	65.6
Wyoming	—	72.8	62.0	—	61.4	—	73.6	—	74.4	64.1	—

Notes: Turnout is the ratio V/E, where V is the total vote cast in a Senate race (or races) in a given election year in a state, and E is the number of people eligible by law to vote in that state according to the criteria of citizenship, race, sex, and age laws on suffrage, where race has two dimensions: color (black/white) and bondage (slave/free). These raw data—number of Senate votes cast and eligibles in each state—are used to produce the entries. States with partial Senate vote data are not included. States with special Senate elections are also not included. For a more detailed discussion of the methodology used, see the notes to Table 3-8.

Sources: Eligibles—decennial censuses (1910–1990) of the U.S. Census Bureau; Bureau of U.S. Census Series P pamphlets for 1972 and the 1990s; Richard Scammon's book series, *America Votes* (various publication dates); the data archive of John J. Stucker; and relevant state constitutions and statute volumes. Also see Stucker (1973), Appendix B. Senate vote—Tables 6-33 through 6-54.

Table 3-68 State Voter Turnout Percentages for Senate Elections, 1970–1988

	1970	1972	1974	1976	1978	1980	1982	1984	1986	1988
Alabama	—	45.3	21.6	—	22.2	47.7	—	48.7	42.3	—
Alaska	—	47.9	43.0	—	49.3	59.1	—	67.4	55.4	—
Arizona	40.5	—	38.4	47.0	—	46.9	36.2	—	38.0	48.4
Arkansas	—	47.0	38.4	—	33.8	50.3	—	53.0	41.5	—
California	55.9	—	44.0	51.9	—	53.8	48.7	—	43.1	54.9
Colorado	—	58.4	48.5	—	42.5	57.5	—	59.8	47.4	—
Connecticut	60.5	—	52.5	64.6	—	61.7	48.3	—	41.9	58.2
Delaware	50.7	61.3	—	56.4	39.5	—	43.7	54.5	—	50.8
Florida	40.3	—	32.3	47.3	—	50.6	35.7	—	41.1	46.3
Georgia	—	37.5	26.5	—	17.8	41.8	—	40.7	28.4	—
Hawaii	58.2	—	46.5	53.2	—	45.9	46.8	—	46.4	44.0
Idaho	—	63.8	49.7	—	47.9	70.0	—	62.4	57.7	—
Illinois	54.6	62.3	38.8	—	41.2	58.4	—	60.5	39.3	—
Indiana	57.0	—	49.2	59.4	—	57.3	46.8	—	39.0	52.4
Iowa	—	63.0	45.6	—	40.6	61.6	—	62.8	43.5	—
Kansas	—	57.0	50.6	—	45.3	55.4	—	57.6	47.1	—
Kentucky	—	46.8	32.4	—	19.2	43.1	—	49.2	25.5	—
Louisiana	—	45.7	17.4	—	—	—	—	—	47.1	—
Maine	55.5	62.0	—	66.1	49.2	—	56.5	65.9	—	63.2
Maryland	41.5	—	31.9	48.4	—	43.3	36.3	—	34.1	48.1
Massachusetts	57.1	61.7	—	62.9	49.4	—	49.5	60.2	—	60.2
Michigan	51.7	59.0	—	57.5	45.7	—	46.5	56.9	—	52.9
Minnesota	62.0	68.8	—	70.9	56.8	—	61.6	69.2	—	67.5
Mississippi	26.1	44.3	—	35.1	35.6	—	37.4	54.5	—	52.8
Missouri	44.8	—	37.1	56.7	—	58.6	43.2	—	40.2	55.9
Montana	61.6	67.4	—	63.1	54.3	—	57.8	67.8	—	64.3
Nebraska	51.6	56.0	—	56.2	45.4	—	48.8	56.9	—	58.9
Nevada	50.9	—	41.3	43.8	—	43.9	38.8	—	35.6	44.0
New Hampshire	—	63.0	40.7	—	42.7	57.5	—	53.6	32.7	—
New Jersey	49.8	57.6	—	55.6	38.7	—	42.2	58.7	—	55.1
New Mexico	53.0	57.3	—	54.2	42.2	—	45.1	54.0	—	51.0
New York	54.2	—	42.8	52.4	—	50.1	41.1	—	34.2	49.1
North Carolina	—	41.6	27.6	—	28.2	42.8	—	49.7	34.2	—
North Dakota	62.0	—	55.9	65.2	—	65.2	57.2	—	62.9	62.9
Ohio	50.1	—	41.4	53.4	—	52.9	44.2	—	39.9	55.2
Oklahoma	—	55.5	41.8	—	36.6	51.2	—	54.5	40.2	—
Oregon	—	62.4	48.7	—	50.4	61.0	—	62.6	52.7	—
Pennsylvania	50.1	—	42.2	54.3	—	51.2	41.4	—	38.3	49.1
Rhode Island	59.3	62.2	—	59.6	45.5	—	49.9	56.6	—	55.1
South Carolina	—	38.3	27.6	—	30.7	40.2	—	41.6	30.8	—
South Dakota	—	69.3	61.6	—	54.0	67.8	—	64.7	60.4	—
Tennessee	46.3	42.3	—	47.5	36.8	—	37.6	48.2	—	44.0
Texas	34.7	45.1	—	45.4	25.6	—	31.5	52.0	—	48.6
Utah	66.7	—	57.3	68.3	—	65.9	56.8	—	43.5	62.0
Vermont	60.7	—	45.1	57.1	—	58.1	45.3	—	50.1	59.6
Virginia	34.3	43.3	—	44.3	33.4	—	35.9	49.1	—	47.2
Washington	53.0	—	41.3	57.5	—	59.5	45.4	—	41.3	55.2
West Virginia	41.9	60.2	—	43.6	36.8	—	41.1	52.8	—	46.9
Wisconsin	52.1	—	39.5	61.9	—	66.5	45.9	—	42.9	61.8
Wyoming	62.3	63.3	—	57.0	44.9	—	52.3	58.7	—	57.3

Notes: Turnout is the ratio V/E, where V is the total vote cast in a Senate race (or races) in a given election year in a state, and E is the number of people eligible by law to vote in that state according to the criteria of citizenship, race, sex, and age laws on suffrage, where race has two dimensions: color (black/white) and bondage (slave/free). These raw data—number of Senate votes cast and eligibles in each state—are used to produce the entries. States with partial Senate vote data are not included. States with special Senate elections are also not included. For a more detailed discussion of the methodology used, see the notes to Table 3-8.

Sources: Eligibles—decennial censuses (1910–1990) of the U.S. Census Bureau; Bureau of U.S. Census Series P pamphlets for 1972 and the 1990s; Richard Scammon's book series, *America Votes* (various publication dates); the data archive of John J. Stucker; and relevant state constitutions and statute volumes. Also see Stucker (1973), Appendix B. Senate vote—Tables 6-33 through 6-54.

Table 3-69 State Voter Turnout Percentages for Senate Elections, 1990–1998

	1990	1992	1994	1996	1998
Alabama	40.0	51.9	—	47.0	39.6
Alaska	51.7	62.7	—	56.3	52.0
Arizona	—	51.0	39.0	—	31.7
Arkansas	28.8	52.4	—	46.3	37.6
California	—	58.4	45.6	—	43.7
Colorado	43.2	62.6	—	54.5	47.3
Connecticut	—	62.4	45.2	—	40.9
Delaware	36.5	—	38.0	51.1	—
Florida	—	52.3	42.2	—	38.2
Georgia	22.2	25.7	—	42.3	31.5
Hawaii	—	47.1	45.8	—	50.1
Idaho	46.2	65.7	—	60.9	44.0
Illinois	40.5	61.2	—	52.0	41.3
Indiana	—	53.6	36.7	—	36.5
Iowa	48.3	62.8	—	58.3	44.7
Kansas	44.0	62.3	—	56.8	38.8
Kentucky	33.7	47.9	—	45.0	38.6
Louisiana	—	—	—	55.5	31.3
Maine	57.5	—	55.3	64.8	—
Maryland	—	52.7	38.8	—	41.9
Massachusetts	52.7	—	49.0	57.1	—
Michigan	38.2	—	44.1	53.8	—
Minnesota	57.2	—	54.2	65.5	—
Mississippi	15.1	—	32.0	45.2	—
Missouri	—	61.6	45.7	—	39.5
Montana	55.8	—	57.1	64.2	—
Nebraska	52.2	—	49.4	56.8	—
Nevada	—	52.5	36.7	—	35.6
New Hampshire	35.8	62.5	—	57.3	36.0
New Jersey	35.2	—	37.2	52.1	—
New Mexico	39.5	—	41.8	48.1	—
New York	—	52.7	39.5	—	39.3
North Carolina	41.7	50.4	—	47.3	36.2
North Dakota	—	65.6	50.7	—	45.0
Ohio	—	59.6	42.3	—	41.0
Oklahoma	38.8	55.9	—	49.5	35.4
Oregon	53.6	64.9	—	60.1	47.8
Pennsylvania	—	53.6	39.2	—	32.9
Rhode Island	49.6	—	48.1	51.2	—
South Carolina	29.5	45.0	—	41.7	37.3
South Dakota	52.3	66.2	—	61.8	48.9
Tennessee	21.6	—	38.3	44.8	—
Texas	33.8	—	35.1	43.7	—
Utah	—	66.3	42.5	—	36.0
Vermont	—	68.0	49.5	—	48.5
Virginia	24.0	—	43.5	48.6	—
Washington	—	61.4	45.1	—	46.2
West Virginia	30.1	—	30.7	43.0	—
Wisconsin	—	67.8	42.5	—	46.1
Wyoming	50.1	—	60.6	61.8	—

Notes: Turnout is the ratio V/E, where V is the total vote cast in a Senate race (or races) in a given election year in a state, and E is the number of people eligible by law to vote in that state according to the criteria of citizenship, race, sex, and age laws on suffrage, where race has two dimensions: color (black/white) and bondage (slave/free). These raw data—number of Senate votes cast and eligibles in each state—are used to produce the entries. States with partial Senate vote data are not included. States with special Senate elections are also not included. For a more detailed discussion of the methodology used, see the notes to Table 3-8.

Sources: Eligibles—decennial censuses (1910–1990) of the U.S. Census Bureau; Bureau of U.S. Census Series P pamphlets for 1972 and the 1990s; Richard Scammon's book series, *America Votes* (various publication dates); the data archive of John J. Stucker; and relevant state constitutions and statute volumes. Also see Stucker (1973), Appendix B. Senate vote—Tables 6-33 through 6-54.

4

The Familiarity of Presidential Elections

Presidential election results are the most familiar outcomes of contemporary American politics. Pollsters predict the results well in advance of election day. Television news reporters tally the returns minute by minute and long into the night. Political analysts comment on the mandate the election does or does not afford the winner. With this familiarity often goes a decided lack of attention to historical patterns and change. Students of presidential elections, while deeply familiar with the specific results of a given election and those immediately before it, are much less knowledgeable about the results of an array of presidential elections. They often eagerly offer sweeping generalizations about the presidency based on those elections with which they are familiar.

For instance, prior to Bill Clinton's election in 1992, many analysts wrote of a Republican presidential ascendancy, noting that from 1968 to 1988 only one Democrat (Jimmy Carter) had won the White House. The Republican Party's domination of the presidency seemed to many an unalterable fact of political life. With the Clinton victories in 1992 and 1996, talk of Republican presidential prowess vanished, as the tally since 1968 was now three Democratic wins versus five Republican wins. Familiarity with immediate results and attempts to build patterns from what were only six data points—the presidential election results from 1968 to 1988—gave Republican strategists too much credit and left their Democratic counterparts overwrought. Had the analysts focused on a longer historical record, they would have recognized that the so-called Republican ascendancy during this period existed primarily because the data were taken out of historical context. If the period from 1960 to 1996 is considered, there were five Democratic presidential winners (Kennedy, Johnson, Carter, and Clinton twice), five Republican presidential winners (Nixon twice, Reagan twice, and Bush), and no Republican ascendancy. If the time line is pushed back to include all post–World War II presidential elections from 1948 to 1996, a balance between seven Republican victories and six Democratic ones is evident. These simple, yet less familiar, patterns are essential to fully understand the nature of presidential elections.

This chapter is divided into five sections. The availability and accuracy of data for the early federal period during which popular election results have been assumed to be missing or incorrect are discussed in the first section. The legal structure of presidential elections is examined next. National party competition in presidential elections is considered in section three, followed by a discussion of the historical eras within which national and regional patterns of party support developed. The final section examines the basis for presidential elections—the federal system of state returns and the autonomy of state politics.

Data Accuracy and Availability

To move away from familiarity with the last several races and to consider the full historical time frame of presidential elections, new data are brought to bear on the subject. Data for the presidential popular vote cast prior to 1824 have long been missing. Because of problems with the "availability, accessibility, and quality of the returns," the major sources for early presidential elections—data sets 0001 and 0019 from the Inter-university Consortium for Political and Social Research (ICPSR)—report returns only since 1824 (*CQ Guide,* 1994, p. 428). The ICPSR archives a data set named "U.S. Historical Election Returns, 1788–1832" (ICPSR 0079) but stresses that these data are "only approximately half of the possible returns for elections in this period."

Scholars have accepted these limitations and have not probed the degree to which other data are available and reliable. Improving on the existing data sets, then, hinges on finding original election returns for the early period. These original returns compose the most accurate data available for the period before 1824. Extensive searches of sources other than the ICPSR data set, including the exhaustive American election archive compiled by Michael J. Dubin, have yielded data that provide a new look at America's oldest elections. In many cases, these data are from the original manuscript returns for a state or its counties. Some of these returns are housed in the state's hall of records, others are at the National Archives, and still others are taken from collations provided at state historical libraries. Many of these original returns have been checked against major state newspapers' reports of vote returns. The tables for this chapter provide data for presidential returns beginning in 1788. Indeed, the very year of this election reveals how little has previously been considered about America's first presidential election. Typically, this election is cited as the presidential election of

1789. While it is correct that the electoral college met in February 1789 to ratify Washington's victory, several state legislatures and state electorates actually made their choice for president in 1788.

To be sure, there are limitations to these data. For instance, of the twenty-one counties in Pennsylvania, returns for two of them could not be located for 1788 and returns for six of them could not be retrieved in 1792. In this instance, the data that are available give a clear indication of the state's early voting patterns and are not rendered useless by missing data. More usually when data are found, they are typically found for the entire state; when they are missing, they are typically missing for the entire state. The presence of data for an entire state provides a high level of confidence in those returns. Of course, reliability issues will always plague the early period to some degree because of the lack of official reporting requirements and the nature of the ballots used at that time. Nonetheless, useful presidential election data that were presumed to be unattainable for the 1788–1820 period are now available.

Legal Structure of Presidential Elections

A thorough look at the historical patterns of presidential elections begins with the electoral college as the defining legal characteristic of presidential elections. Difficult to devise, explain, and operate, the electoral college nevertheless decides presidential winners and losers. As provided in the Constitution, the electoral college system mandates that the candidate who receives a majority of electoral votes becomes president. If no such majority exists, then the House of Representatives determines the race by a majority vote of its members voting, not as individuals but as state delegations. The Constitution also calculates the number of electoral votes to which each state is entitled as the total number of its seats in the House and Senate. State legislatures are given the discretion to determine the method of choosing electors.

Several questions arise regarding this complicated and indirect system of election for chief executive. First, what method have state legislatures chosen in selecting electors? Second, what is the connection between the popular vote for president and the electoral vote? Third, under what circumstances is a race likely to be settled in the House?

Method of Selection

Observers of presidential elections are familiar with the current method of selecting electors used in most states: a statewide, winner-take-all popular vote. This means that the candidate winning a plurality of the popular vote wins all the state's electoral votes. Observers may not know that states did not always follow this approach. In early presidential elections, notably from 1788 to 1832, the states used nine different methods to select electors (see Table 4-1). The

methods ranged from where the legislature chose the electors to a two-step process whereby the voters chose the electors by congressional districts and then the legislature made the final choice from the top two districtwide popular vote getters. Three methods (and their variations) were most often used: statewide direct popular election, district-based direct popular election, and selection by the legislature.

As shown in Table 4-1, four of the ten states held direct popular elections to choose their electors in the first presidential election in 1788: Pennsylvania and Maryland held a statewide popular vote contest, while Virginia and Delaware had popular elections for electors in congressional districts. The legislatures of four states—Connecticut, Georgia, New Jersey, and South Carolina—selected electors. Massachusetts and New Hampshire adopted hybrid systems. Massachusetts voters in congressional districts chose two people for presidential electors; the legislature, by joint ballot of both houses, then chose one elector from the two district electoral candidates receiving the highest number of votes. The Massachusetts legislature also chose two electors at large. In New Hampshire, a simpler system provided that electors would be chosen by a statewide majority popular vote; if a majority was not obtained, then the legislature chose the electors (see *Historical Statistics of the United States, Colonial Times to 1970,* Chapter Y).

The low point for popular election of electors was in 1800 when only five of the sixteen states (31 percent) had some form of popular vote. The heated competition between Federalists and Democratic-Republicans prompted several legislatures dominated by one of the parties to reassert control over electors in an attempt to deliver the state's entire electoral slate to the preferred candidate. The Federalists did this to assure John Adams's victory in Massachusetts and New Hampshire; the Democratic-Republicans followed a similar strategy in Georgia to guarantee the state to Jefferson.

By 1820, however, fifteen of twenty-four states had popular election of electors. Three more states adopted popular elections in 1824 and four more in 1828. By 1836 all states except South Carolina had adopted the statewide winner-take-all method. All new states entering the Union after that followed suit. In 1868 South Carolina also moved to this method. Today only Maine has a hybrid statewide-district system, adopted in 1972, in which voters elect two electors statewide and then choose the remaining electors from congressional districts.

The fairly rapid evolution of the statewide winner-take-all popular vote underscores two features of American politics. The popular vote component reflects early interests in the democratization of the presidential vote. Despite the Framers' anxieties about the knowledge and interests of voters, state legislatures responded to demands for public input on choosing the president. Indeed, one of the most revealing aspects of Table 4-1 is that the trend toward democratization was not only fast, but it took place several years before the Jacksonian period, which has long been touted as a pivotal democratic era. The winner-take-all component also points to the development of political parties and their abilities to dominate states. Many legislatures adopted the winner-take-all popular ballot for electors as the best way to capitalize on statewide party strength. A party with a firm statewide base could count on sweeping all the state's electoral votes with the at-large winner-take-all approach. This foreclosed any opportunity for the opposition party with some local or regional areas of strength to gain electoral votes, which could have resulted under a district system.

Popular Vote-Electoral Vote Connection

The winner-take-all approach combined with the popular vote create an odd hybrid that inflates the value of the votes of those citizens who choose the statewide winner and discounts the votes of citizens who choose any other candidate. The winner-take-all approach skews the electoral college vote in favor of the winner and creates a disparity, sometimes quite large, between the popular vote in a particular state and the electoral vote. Candidates who win in a highly competitive state by small margins still win all the state's electoral votes. Thus, as shown in Table 4-2, presidents' popular vote mandates are typically much smaller than their electoral vote mandates. The largest electoral vote skew occurred in 1912 when Woodrow Wilson received 80 percent of the electoral vote but a minority of the popular vote: 42 percent.

This also raises the possibility that a candidate will receive a majority of the electoral vote but fewer popular votes than the opposing candidate. This has occurred three times. In 1876 Republican Rutherford B. Hayes won the electoral vote as decided by a specially appointed electoral commission, but his opponent Democrat Samuel Tilden carried the popular vote. In 1888 Republican Benjamin Harrison won the electoral vote while Democrat Grover Cleveland won the popular vote. In 2000 Republican George W. Bush won by one electoral college vote while Democrat Al Gore won the popular vote by a margin of more than 300,000 votes.

The House Decides

The mismatch between the popular vote and the electoral vote can create a situation in which no candidate receives a majority of electoral votes and, as required by the Constitution, the House must decide the presidential race. This has occurred only once, in 1824, in a four-way race among Andrew Jackson, John Quincy Adams, Henry Clay, and William Crawford, where Jackson received more popular and electoral votes than his nearest rival and eventual winner, John Quincy Adams, but did not receive a majority of either vote. As shown in Table 4-2, Jackson received 41 percent of the popular vote to Adams's 31 percent and Jackson won 38 percent of the electoral vote to Adams's 32 percent. In other elections, most notably 1856, 1860, and

1968, a shift of a few votes from the winner in one or more pivotal states could have required House action (see the discussion of Table 4-9). While the Framers thought that the House would decide most presidential races, and some candidates have adopted strategies designed to throw the race into the House, neither the Framers nor the candidates would likely be very good at predicting House outcomes. Voting by state delegations, rather than as individuals, in the House suggests that there would be considerable intrastate strategizing in addition to pressure from the political parties, the Senate, and the presidential candidates themselves.

National Patterns of Party Competition

While the electoral college structures presidential election results in specific ways, these outcomes first rest on how the presidential campaign unfolds. Although contemporary analyses of presidential elections center on the personal images and messages of candidates, presidential elections have been and continue to be statements about American political parties and their campaigns for office. Table 4-3 presents the national electoral college results of presidential elections from 1788 to 1996; Table 4-4 presents the comparable popular vote results. There are three notable national patterns of presidential elections, each of which reflects the role of party: strong two-party competition; increases in victory margins over time; and the limited, but at times pivotal, role of third parties.

Two-Party Competition

Looking down the columns of Table 4-4 reveals the extent to which the presidency has been a strongly competitive two-party office. Since 1824, when a preponderance of states cast popular votes for president, chief executives have won with an average of 51.4 percent of the vote. This competitiveness has occurred through the strength of only a handful of major parties. Throughout the entire history of the country, presidents have been elected from only six parties: Federalists, Democratic-Republicans, Democrats, National Republicans, Whigs, and Republicans. Only in one election, 1856, did three, rather than two, of these main parties—Democrats, Whigs, and the newly formed Republicans—vie for the presidency. Otherwise, two-party competition has been the norm in presidential contests. While this norm has characterized the struggle for the presidency throughout America's history, obviously the names of the players have changed over time. It is generally acknowledged that historical precursors to the Republican Party have been the Federalists, National Republicans, and Whigs, while historical antecedents to the Democratic Party have usually been considered to be the Anti-Federalists, Democratic-Republicans, and Jacksonian Democrats. (For a full list of the party labels used by the precursors of the Democratic and Republican parties, see Appendix A.)

Table 4-4 reveals the remarkable longevity of the two-party system. Even if one starts with dates when the two major parties were called only "Democrat" and "Republican," one can see the emergence of the Democrats in the 1828–1832 period contesting the presidency and House races, and the emergence of the Republicans in 1854 contesting House races and, two years later, the presidency as well. From 1856 to 1996, the Republicans won twenty-one presidential elections; the Democrats won fifteen. The White House swung from one party to the other fourteen times in this period. In presidential races in the twentieth century, from 1904 to 1996 (excluding 1900, since this election is more similar to nineteenth century elections), the Republican and Democratic parties each garnered twelve victories and the White House changed hands nine times.[1] Finally, as noted at the beginning of the chapter, in the most recent era, even with the introduction of television and its potential for volatility, the stability of the two-party system has continued as Democrats and Republicans have evenly split control of the White House five times from 1960 through 1996.

What is remarkable in viewing this table is the virtually continuous pattern of two-partyism, regardless of the two parties involved. Scholars often refer to the *two-party system* without detailing what the term means. In the context of this book, the system involves the regular, relatively seamless fight between two parties that have organizations in at least some states and field candidates for several offices in most states. So defined, this two-party system makes a strong statement about the nature of American politics. In part, two-partyism is a function of the winner-take-all system of the electoral college, the single-member district system, and, since the 17th Amendment, the statewide direct election of senators. The probability of victory is at its highest for any one party when competition is built around two—and only two—parties. However, there has been a more fundamental set of philosophical and policy issues (discussed in greater depth below) upon which regions and economic sectors of the nation have been at odds: matters of the strength of the national government; the role of the government in domestic and foreign affairs; the power of the states; and the relative economic interests of agrarian, manufacturing, commercial, and technological pursuits over which the parties have divided. A void created by the organizational collapse of one party creates a demand for a successor because the issues are ongoing and difficult to resolve.

Increases in Victory Margins

In addition to close two-party competition, a second pattern of the level of party competitiveness is apparent in Tables 4-3 and 4-4, when read in conjunction with Table 4-2. Specifically, the level of competitiveness between the two major parties has declined from the nineteenth to the twentieth century. While parties continue to rotate the presidential office, they do so with more convincing victories than they did before.

Popularly elected nineteenth-century presidents (those elected in the twenty elections from 1824 to 1900) won with an average of 49 percent of the popular vote and 64 percent of the electoral vote. They held on average a 5 percentage-point popular vote advantage over their nearest rival and a 34 percentage-point electoral vote advantage. While no nineteenth-century candidate captured more than 56 percent of the popular vote, the *average* popular vote tally in the twentieth century (the twenty-four elections from 1904 to 1996) has been 53 percent. Victorious twentieth-century candidates have held nearly a 13 percentage-point popular vote advantage over their chief opponent and approximately a 55 percentage-point electoral vote advantage. Indeed, as amplified in Table 4-4, in ten of twenty elections from 1824 to 1900, presidents were elected with less than 50 percent of the popular vote. The oft-cited period of Republican dominance after the Civil War looks much less robust when considered in relation to the popular election results during that period: Rutherford B. Hayes, James A. Garfield, and Benjamin Harrison were all minority presidents; and Grover Cleveland, who purportedly stole the office from the Republicans on two separate occasions, did so with a minority of the popular vote. In contrast, only seven of the twenty-four elections in the twentieth century (1904–1996) have seen presidential candidates win with a minority of the popular vote.

Incumbent presidents' electoral strength is also somewhat stronger in the twentieth century as compared with the nineteenth century. On average, the four presidents who successfully sought reelection in the nineteenth century since 1824 (Jackson, Lincoln, Grant, and McKinley) captured 54 percent of the vote; on nine occasions in the twentieth century incumbent presidents were reelected by 56 percent of the vote. Indeed, one of the principal reasons for the enlarged victories in the twentieth century is the success of Presidents Roosevelt, Eisenhower, Nixon, and Reagan in their reelection bids. Despite the complexities of the modern presidency, it is easier to run for reelection today than it was when the office was less powerful and less highly contested. In large measure this is accounted for by the years surrounding the Civil War when presidents had difficulty seeking their party's nomination for a second term, let alone actually running and winning a second time. In the twentieth century it is more difficult for the parties to field credible opponents against popular incumbents who appear to have mastered a complex and demanding office.

Third-Party Chances

There have been many minor parties in American history—the Liberty Party, Equal Rights Party, Liberal Republican Party of Colored Men, Industrial Reform Party, National Silver Party, Continental Party, United Christian Party, Jobless Party, Theocratic Party, Universal Party, Third World Assembly Party, Down with Lawyers Party, and Looking Back Party, to name only a few. As many of these names suggest, minor parties have typically not been pivotal forces in American presidential politics. There have been few true "third" parties that were organized to field candidates for several offices in several states. In only four instances have organized third parties fielded presidential candidates and candidates for other offices in the same election: the Republicans in 1856 (before they became a major party), the Populists in 1892, and the Progressives in 1912 and 1924.[2]

In seven instances there have been third (and fourth) candidates running for president who received significant votes but were either not tied to any new party organization or were not accompanied by candidates running for other offices under the same banner. Votes in 1824 were split among four candidates, but they were all considered at the time to represent factions of the same major party, the Democratic-Republican Party. In 1860 John Breckinridge ran as a Southern Democrat and John Bell as a Constitutional Unionist, but these party designations were little more than labels. Strom Thurmond, in a break with President Harry S. Truman over civil rights, captured electoral votes in five southern states in 1948 running as a States' Rights Democrat or "Dixiecrat." Thurmond's attempt, however, came as a splinter movement within the Democratic Party, not as a new party effort. (In fact, Thurmond ran under the Democrat Party label in four of these five states.) In 1968 Governor George Wallace of Alabama ran under the American Independent Party label and captured five states in the South. Wallace's candidacy, like John Anderson's in 1980 and H. Ross Perot's in 1992 and again in 1996, were personal candidacies. None were true attempts to erect a third-party organization as a viable, long-term competitor to the Democratic and Republican parties.

Historical Development of Presidential Elections

As introduced in Chapter 3, the longevity of a relatively balanced two-party system has emerged in six eras that reflect the politics of both presidential and congressional elections. In many historical accounts, it is commonplace to refer to these party eras by the names of the victors: the Jeffersonian period; the Jacksonian period; the Radical Republican period after the Civil War; the period of Republican normalcy during the 1920s; the New Deal era; and the most recent, erroneously named, era of Republican ascendancy. It is more accurate to consider the eras as reflections of the competition between the two major parties—sometimes ragged, other times quite keen. As will become evident, underlying what appears to be a striking victory for a party during an election or series of elections is actually the considerable strength of both parties, often in separate regions of the country. Within the regions, it is often specific states that ultimately decide the election. With the shift of a modest number of popular votes in a few key states, the dominant party could well have lost the White House on

more than one occasion, wrecking havoc on the broad generalizations about the winners and labels of a given era.

Tables 4-3 and 4-4 reveal the six political eras discussed in Chapter 3. In the current chapter, the focus is on the presidential elections within these eras, realizing that these eras are more generally defined by the outcomes of congressional as well as presidential elections. These eras tell the story of how the two-party system creates and recreates itself to changing political conditions across more than 200 years of American history. The six eras are: a Federalist/Democratic-Republican era from 1788 to 1823, a Democratic/National Republican-Whig era from 1824 to 1853, a Civil War and Reconstruction Republican/Democratic era from 1854 to 1893, a conservative Republican/Democratic era from 1894 to 1929, a New Deal Democratic/Republican era from 1930 to 1965, and a competitive Democratic/Republican era from 1966 to the present.

Federalist/Democratic-Republican Era

The earliest period of party competition (1788–1823) saw the Federalist Party of George Washington, Alexander Hamilton, and John Adams vie against the Democratic-Republicans, led by Thomas Jefferson and James Madison. Federalist tenets included asserting the national government over the states, which Washington proceeded to do by suppressing the Whiskey Rebellion in 1794, and a policy of national economic strength, which took the form of Secretary of the Treasury Hamilton's plan for a national bank. Jefferson led the campaign against Hamilton's bank plan and worked to develop a party press in various state newspapers and a strong party in Congress (see Rubin, 1981). Jefferson wrote: "The party division in this country is certainly not among its pleasant features. To a certain degree, it will always exist" (quoted in Hoadley, 1986, p. 191).

The Federalists won the White House in 1788, 1792, and 1796 but lost it in 1800 to the Democrat-Republicans. Although the Federalists fielded presidential candidates until 1816, they never regained the presidency, nor did they hold a majority of seats in Congress. In the election of 1816 the Federalists were so weak that they were unable to convene a nominating caucus. Three states' electors supported Rufus King for president, but it could hardly be said that King was a Federalist Party presidential candidate. The collapse of the Federalist Party at the presidential level ensured the preeminence of the Democratic-Republican Party, which ran James Monroe all but unopposed in the election of 1820.

As shown in Tables 4-5 and 4-6, the first era (1788–1823) reflected parties of strong regional bases. As seen most clearly in Table 4-5, the Federalists (who appear in the Republican column as a historical antecedent of that party) appealed to the urban and commercial interests of New England, where they gained an average of 65 percent of the popular vote in the presidential elections of this period. In contrast, the Jeffersonians were strongest among the agrarian interests of the South, where they claimed an average of 85 percent of the popular vote across the presidential elections of the period. The two parties were more competitive in the Mid-Atlantic and Border South states. Their regional competitiveness ebbed swiftly in the 1816 election when the Jeffersonians began to dominate the presidential vote in most regions of the country. Federalist support, however, remained strong in New England until 1820.

Despite the weaknesses of the Federalist Party, this first party era set the stage for national party competition in three ways. First, both parties adopted regularized methods of selecting presidential nominees through the use of the congressional caucus. Although by 1832 the caucus broke down in favor of the national nominating convention, it established that parties could meet with the strategic objective of selecting a single candidate who presumably had the best chance of winning the presidential race. Second, both parties also asserted national party positions, although they would not be considered formal platforms in the way they existed later. Finally, both parties fielded candidates for office at the state and national levels, each party showing strength in different regions of the country. Even when the Democratic-Republican Party dominated the presidency and won a great many of the other races in the late 1810s and 1820s, Federalists continued to run candidates, particularly in the New England area. Their success, however, at the congressional level was diminishing, with only thirty House victories in 1818, thirty-one in 1820, twenty-four in 1822, and twenty-two in 1824. In 1826, although continuing to field candidates, the Federalists were not able to win a single seat in the House.

Democratic/National Republican-Whig Era

The success of the Democratic-Republican Party in the latter years of the Federalist/Democratic-Republican era exacerbated intraparty factions and competition, which led to the emergence of a second era of competition between the Democratic-Republicans and two other parties that sprang from this party—first, the National Republicans and, then, their successors, the Whigs. The crucial election that prompted these developments was the first election in this era: the 1824 presidential election. This particular election, while seemingly demonstrating the one-party strength of the Democratic-Republican Party at the time, also revealed its inherent regional fault lines. Sectional issues focusing on governmental power, states rights, slavery, business, and economic growth were stimulating rifts within the Democratic-Republican Party. In 1824 five Democratic-Republicans from different regions of the country with different political views sought the presidency: from the West, Senator Andrew Jackson of Tennessee and House Speaker Henry Clay of Kentucky; from the East, Secretary of State John Quincy Adams of Massachusetts; and from the South, Secretary of the Treasury William Crawford of Georgia and Secretary of War John C. Calhoun of South Carolina, who soon dropped out in favor of Crawford. These regional and issue divisions would later lead political observers to view

Adams as the precursor of the Republican Party (later confirmed by Adams, establishing the National Republican Party) and Jackson as the precursor of the mainstream Democratic Party.

As shown in Table 4-5, Adams claimed his home base of New England in the 1824 presidential election with 77 percent of the popular vote; Jackson did well in the South and Mid-Atlantic states, receiving 62 and 69 percent of the popular vote, respectively. With Clay in the race, the Border states split between Clay and Jackson, as did the Midwest. The 1824 election was then a four-way race among regional candidates, none of whom captured a majority of electoral college votes. As noted above, this forced the decision into the House of Representatives, which ultimately supported Adams.

After the 1824 election, disarray persisted. The factionalized Democratic-Republican Party split into two wings. Sorely defeated presidential candidate Jackson led one group that continued to be known formally as the "Democratic-Republicans" and informally as the "Jackson Democrats" until 1830 when the name was shortened to "Democrat." The Jackson Party favored a large role for the states, a limited national government, and offered a democratic message to many who were voting for the first time. The newly elected president, John Quincy Adams, led the other wing, which adopted the name National Republicans. This party supported a strong national government and federally directed internal improvements, such as roads and canals. Although the National Republicans ran presidential candidates in 1828 and 1832, losing both times to the Jacksonians, the early years of the age of Jackson still reflected party competition. As shown in Table 4-5, the Democratic-Republicans and the National Republicans maintained strong regional bases—the National Republicans in New England and the Jacksonians in the South. In the Mid-Atlantic, Border South, and the Midwest, the parties were relatively competitive, even though the Jacksonians typically captured a majority of the popular vote in these regions.

By 1834 the Whigs, expressly formed as an opposition party to Jackson, entered the void left by the losses of the National Republicans. As Jackson's new opponent, the Whig Party embodied a number of inherently contradictory interests. The Whig Party appealed to southerners furious over Jackson's stand on the nullification of states rights, a change in position for both parties. Another part of the party, more reminiscent of the early National Republican Party, opposed Jackson's attack on the Bank of the United States and favored a plan of national economic expansion designed to unite sections of the country. Yet another faction came from the collapse of a minor party, the Anti-Mason Party, which had among its supporters poor farmers and laborers in New York and New England. Being this diverse, it was almost impossible for the Whigs to resolve the internal tension between those party members interested in a national economic plan and commercial prosperity and those who advocated states rights and the rights of workers.

Partly because of these internal tensions, the party named no national candidate in 1836. Instead, three candidates from different parts of the country—William Henry Harrison, Hugh White, and Daniel Webster—ran and lost against the Democrats. Each had hoped to carry a region of the country with sufficient electoral college votes to throw the election into the House. In Table 4-5, the Whig vote among the three candidates is added together and presented in the Republican column, revealing how strong the Whigs might have been had they fielded only one candidate. The Whigs followed the latter strategy in 1840 by running Harrison, who had made the best showing in 1836 against Democratic winner Martin Van Buren. As displayed in Table 4-5, in each region of the country, the Whigs secured a majority of the popular votes. Although the Whigs did not adopt a party platform, Harrison won with stories of his wartime vigor and apocryphal images of common man roots, revealing he was born in a log cabin and partial to hard cider. The Whigs continued to field candidates through the election of 1856, almost winning the presidency in 1844 and winning with another military general, Zachary Taylor, in 1848. But the sectional tensions between antislavery Whigs from New England and southern slave-owning Whigs precipitated the breakup of the party. Many northern Whigs were attracted to parties, including the Republicans, who expressly addressed the slavery issue. Many southern Whigs drifted to the Democrats, who they felt best protected states' rights interests (Holt, 1999).

During this era, even with the difficulties of the National Republicans and the Whigs in maintaining organizations and fielding candidates, these parties nonetheless provided concerted opposition to the Jackson Democrats. Party competition between the two major parties continued in three ways that had not occurred even two decades before. First, the Whigs advanced techniques of modern campaign imagery. Without a well-developed policy plan, the party relied on the images of its candidates and the associated props, such as hard cider and log cabins. These images, no matter how misleading, sent powerful visual messages to the many "average voters" who had once found the Democrats so appealing. Consequently, the parties' appeals were more national and less regional than they had been in the previous era. Table 4-5 reveals the striking competitiveness between the Whigs and Democrats in the elections from 1840 through 1852. The prevailing party in a particular region often captured little more than 50 percent of the vote. The Whigs' appeal in the South, as well as New England, moved it away from the limited appeal of the Federalists and National Republicans. On the other side, Jackson promoted his own image of "democracy" and the representation of the "common man." Like the Whig Harrison, Jackson was adept at identifying with "drink" and the agrarian and frontier life. The term *Jacksonian democracy* became embedded in the electorate's mind. Unfortunately, for the party, Democratic candidates after Jackson were not as skilled as "Old Hickory" in using this imagery.

The Democrats and Whigs also established a firm connection between the party in elections and the party in government through the spoils system—whereby party regulars were awarded jobs in the federal government via patronage. Begun by Jefferson and expanded by Jackson, the spoils system was continued by the Whigs, who would not permit Jacksonians to stay in government offices that could be filled by loyal Whigs.

Finally, the two parties showed clear signs of political practicality in their policy positions. On the central issues of the time, parties' positions were fluid and it was not uncommon to see one party adopt the position of the other party if it appeared to be strategic politically. Jackson promoted states rights but also took a strong stand on the integrity of the Union. The Whigs advocated a national economic plan but earlier one of their leaders, Henry Clay, pushed the states' rights Missouri Compromise of 1820, which offered westward expansion while simultaneously continuing and limiting slavery.[3] Many touted Clay's next Compromise of 1850 as the "final solution" to western movement and slavery. The 1850 compromise admitted California as a free state, permitted residents of the New Mexico and Utah territories to decide slavery on their own, and left intact the Missouri Compromise. During the decades before the Civil War, adopting umbrella positions that were often vaguely presented or purposely blurry became one of the hallmarks of American parties running presidential campaigns.

The Civil War and Reconstruction Republican/Democratic Era

This abruptly changed in the years immediately leading up to the Civil War. The parties' popular, nationally based campaigns and practical policy positions fell by the wayside. The Civil War and Reconstruction Republican/Democratic era (1854–1893) renewed the sectional quality of party campaigns that was more typical of the Jeffersonian-Federalist era than it was of the Democratic-Whig era. As shown in Table 4-6, in the prewar elections of 1856 and 1860 the Democrats had a stronghold in the South; the Republicans had absolutely no appeal in the South. Table 4-7 offers a companion South/non-South breakdown for the electoral votes for president received since 1856.[4]

In addition, notions of compromise, practicality, and mutual respect for the ideas of contesting parties all but vanished. The only issue that counted by 1856—slavery—replaced the broader array of issues on which presidential candidates had campaigned before: tariffs, banks, currency, transportation, industrial development, and western expansion. On the issue of slavery, forty years of compromises—one more clever then the next, each presumed to be the last—ended with four quick successive blasts. The first was the passage of the Kansas-Nebraska Act in 1854, which divided the Nebraska territory into two parts, each of which would determine by its state constitution whether slavery would be permitted. The "finality" of the Compromise of 1850 was gone in four short years; slavery could now be introduced into northern states.

The second burst occurred in 1857 with the Supreme Court's *Dred Scott v. Sanford* decision, which held that Congress did not have the authority to regulate slavery in the territories. No matter how many members of Congress might wish to offer another compromise, the Court had derailed such efforts.

The third rupture came in 1856 with the strong, although ultimately unsuccessful, showing of the emergent Republican Party's first presidential candidate—General John C. Fremont. Despite Fremont's defeat by Democrat James Buchanan, the Republicans won a crucial victory. As seen in Table 4-5, they showed strength in New England, garnering 61 percent of the popular vote, and were competitive in the Mid-Atlantic and Midwest, capturing 39 percent and 43 percent of the popular vote, respectively. Their presence forced the demise of the Whigs and also showed that the slavery issue was no longer a matter of compromise.

The fourth, and final, volley occurred in 1860 with the election of the first Republican president, Abraham Lincoln. Lincoln's victory was little in doubt in a four-way race that left the Democrats splintered between Stephen Douglas, the author of the Kansas-Nebraska Act and the official Democratic candidate, and John Breckinridge, the southern Democratic candidate. John Bell of the Constitutional Union Party opposed Breckinridge in the South. As displayed in Table 4-5, Lincoln did well in New England, the Mid-Atlantic, and the Midwest. A few weeks after Lincoln's victory, South Carolina became the first of the southern states to secede from the Union.

Obviously, the South did not vote in federal elections for president (or House) during the Civil War. With the victory of the North, the aftermath of the Civil War revealed a further regionalization of politics, leaving the Democrats in control of the emergent "Solid South." This began with the election of 1876 between Republican Rutherford Hayes and Democrat Samuel Tilden. With disputed electoral college votes in Florida, Louisiana, and South Carolina, the Republican Congress established a bipartisan election commission to investigate the three states' vote tallies. Weeks of bargaining produced the Compromise of 1876 in which Hayes was deemed the victor, but, in turn, Republicans agreed to pull out federal troops from the South. This permitted white Southern Democrats to regain control of the state governments and construct racial barriers that did not begin to ease until federal intervention in the 1950s and 1960s. The Civil War settled the issue of slavery, yet the Compromise of 1876 established the practice of segregation. Thus the North's victory over the South seemed much less clear than it had at Appomattox.

Strangely, this regionalized pattern of politics had the effect of promoting sharp two-party competition at the national level. As shown in Table 4-6, from 1876 through 1892 Democrats captured approximately 60 percent of the popular vote in the South. As displayed in Table 4-7, during the same period they captured all the electoral votes of the South, except in the transition election of 1876. The rest of the nation, however, posed a roughly equal battleground between the two parties. In each of the presidential elections from 1876 to 1888, the winning party won by only 50 per-

cent of the popular vote in the non-South, although the electoral votes tipped decidedly in favor of the Republicans except in 1892 (see Tables 4-6 and 4-7). The Republicans built a strategy from 1860 to 1960 of running for and, in sixteen instances, winning the White House with only scattered electoral college votes from the South.[5]

What is perhaps most surprising about the years surrounding the Civil War is the extent to which two parties—Republicans and Democrats—continued to control elections to office. Even though the election of 1860 was a frenzied breakdown of the principles of two-party politics, this was the only year in which candidates other than those from the two main parties captured any electoral college votes until the Populists won a scant 22 electoral college votes in 1892. One could hardly have predicted, with the volatility of party politics before the Civil War, that two parties would emerge at the onset of the war and maintain themselves for the next 140 years. In terms of issues, the party of Lincoln is not necessarily the party of Reagan or Bush, nor is the party of Cleveland necessarily the party of Clinton. Changing economic interests and regional strengths have shaped and reshaped the constituents of the parties over time. Nonetheless, since the Civil War the two parties have organized campaigns at all levels of government and maintained continuous party organizations. A relatively stable two-party system has thus existed.

Conservative Republican/Democratic Era

It is typical to describe the period from 1894 to 1929 as one of Republican domination of presidential politics. In the nine elections for president during this era, only one Democrat, Woodrow Wilson, won the White House. Yet as Table 4-5 indicates, the parties continued to be very competitive in some regions while dominant in others. Even though Democrat William Jennings Bryan (who also was allied with the Populists) had back-to-back losses in 1896 and 1900, regional breakdowns reveal that his candidacy was competitive in the Border South and the Midwest and dominant in the South and West in 1896. In 1900, although slipping in the West (dropping from 64 percent of the popular vote to 47 percent), Bryan remained competitive in this region and also continued to be competitive in the Border South and Midwest.

The Republicans assumed preeminence during the 1920s, garnering 57–63 percent of the popular vote and virtually all the electoral votes outside the South in 1920, 1924, and 1928 (see Tables 4-6 and 4-7). Indeed, Warren Harding captured the single largest percentage of the popular vote of *any* presidential candidate outside the South, winning 63 percent of the non-South popular vote. For the first time since Grant and Hayes, Republicans captured southern electoral votes in 1920 in Tennessee and 1928 in North Carolina, Tennessee, Texas, Virginia, and Florida. Although the Democratic Party was not victorious at the presidential level during much of this period, it remained a credible political opponent against the Republicans. As made clear in Chapters 5 and 6, Democrats continued to fare well in congressional races during this period, and there was no talk that the Democrats might go the way of the Whigs, the National Republicans, and the long-forgotten Federalists.

The pivotal election of 1896 was as important for the campaign message of reform that lost as for the contrasting message of industrial expansion that won. During the 1870s and 1880s both parties took positions in support of strong economic expansion. Neither party addressed the various problems that accompanied U.S. industrialization, the most pressing of which were in the cities and on the farms. None of the major parties attempted to discuss reforms necessary to alleviate the plights of farmers and industrial workers until Democrat Bryan's first candidacy in 1896. Bryan's solution was the free coinage of silver, which would help farmers by easing currency swings, high interest rates, and low crop prices and help workers who, he argued, were being exploited by eastern bankers and business owners who benefited from the gold standard. While the appeal to workers against management would later become the fulcrum of Democratic Party strength, in 1896 the message backfired in the industrial cities of the East and Midwest. Workers felt that they had more to gain by keeping business strong and voted for Bryan's opponent, William McKinley (see Schlesinger and Israel, 1971, vol. 2, pp. 1787–1825). This left the populist movement within the Democratic Party as largely an agrarian and western phenomenon, insufficient to win the White House.

Reform messages from the Populists and later the Progressives continued to be heard in American politics. The fact that a nonreform candidate had won did not diminish the conditions that required reform. With the assassination of William McKinley, Theodore Roosevelt, who had espoused Progressive beliefs as governor of New York, became president. Roosevelt's Progressive message growing out of the Republican Party was more broad-based than that of the Populists within the Democratic Party. Under Roosevelt's banner, antitrust legislation, conservation, civil service reform, and regulation became the issues of the day rather than free silver reforms. This was followed by the programs of Woodrow Wilson, who offered tariff reform, bank restructuring, antimonopoly action, and attacks on unfair business practices. Roosevelt and Wilson shifted the main theme in presidential election politics. The old question had been how best to promote economic expansion. The new question became: What is the role of government, not only in the economy, but also in society? Yet these reform initiatives ended as World War I came to a close. The question of governmental activism produced different answers from Presidents Harding, Coolidge, and Hoover than those offered by Roosevelt and Wilson. Harkening back to the 1880s, the use of these conservative principles in the 1920s promoted both a smaller governmental role and a broader support of business. Nevertheless, the issue of governmental activism and intervention became the new standard upon which most presidential elections would be contested during the rest of the twentieth century.

New Deal Democratic/Republican Era

The Roosevelt New Deal years from 1932 to 1944 were as strongly Democratic at the presidential level as the 1920s had been Republican. As shown in Table 4-6, in each of the four presidential elections Franklin Roosevelt ran in he won decisively, even capturing 81 percent of the popular vote in the South in 1932 and 1936, 78 percent in 1940, and 72 percent in 1944. In the non-South, he also received at least a majority of the popular vote in each of the four elections, his highest percentage being 59 percent in 1936 and his lowest being 51 percent in 1944.

By 1948 a fundamental shift in American regional politics began. As noted earlier, Strom Thurmond left the mainstream Democratic Party to challenge President Truman over civil rights. As displayed in Table 4-6, Truman won only 50 percent of the southern vote, the lowest percentage won by a Democratic candidate (winner or loser) since Horace Greeley in 1872. Some analysts might have considered this an anomaly, easily explained by the Thurmond Dixiecrat candidacy. But matters improved little in 1952 with Thurmond gone. Democratic candidate Adlai Stevenson won only 52 percent of the southern vote against Eisenhower; in the 1956 rematch, Eisenhower beat Stevenson in the South, capturing 49 percent of the southern vote against Stevenson's 48 percent. Eisenhower also tallied 45 percent of the southern electoral vote in 1952 and 53 percent in 1956. Problems for the Democrats continued beyond Eisenhower. Kennedy barely received a majority of the southern popular vote in 1960 and Carter, a southerner, only received 54 percent in 1976. In the nine other presidential elections after Kennedy, the Democratic candidate did not gain a majority of the popular vote in the South. The solid Democratic South was gone.

During the period that encompassed the Great Depression, the New Deal, World War II, the release of the atomic bomb, communist barricades to parts of the world, and the United States embroiled in a war in Korea, the level of governmental activism continued to be a central question of presidential campaigns. During the Progressive era, the initial answer was government regulation—direct intervention of government in the market to end unfair practices. The second answer in the 1930's New Deal was more sweeping—governmental redistribution of income, through social security, unemployment compensation, and welfare. This activism also manifested itself on the world stage as the United States entered World War II as a principal player and exited the war as a global superpower with nuclear capabilities. By the end of the period, presidential politics had entered a different stage of activism when Lyndon Johnson campaigned for his Great Society. The activism of Roosevelt, as sweeping as it was, nonetheless took place during extraordinary times of economic crisis and world war. The activism of Johnson was not a response to crisis but rather to curing societal ills that existed in the midst of booming prosperity. The war that Johnson waged in Vietnam was a statement about the presumed abilities and responsibilities of the United States as a superpower when the United States and traditional allies were not threatened. Thus the end of this period revealed a new brand of governmental activism different in nature and scope from the activism of the earlier part of this period. The question of governmental activism established a new degree of ideological clarity in the differences between the two parties that would typify the next era.

Competitive Democratic/Republican Era

In many ways, the Vietnam War ended the New Deal Democratic/Republican era. Lyndon Johnson campaigned in the 1964 election saying that "the only real issue in this campaign, the only one you ought to be concerned about is who can best keep the peace" (Barber, 1972, p. 34). Yet as the campaign proceeded, so too did Johnson's plans to significantly increase U.S. involvement in Vietnam. Although Johnson decided to hold back his secret plans to escalate the war until after the election, this escalation took full form in 1965 and 1966, involving America in what became an unwinnable war. In the 1968 election Republicans capitalized on discontent over the war, civil rights, fear about riots, and a backlash against some Great Society programs. As shown in Table 4-5, this message appealed particularly to voters in the South, Border South, Midwest, and West. Even in a three-way race among Republican candidate Richard Nixon, Democratic nominee Hubert Humphrey, and independent George Wallace, Nixon tied with Wallace in the South, both receiving approximately 35 percent of the popular vote. Nixon tied with Humphrey in the Border states and bested him in the Midwest and West. Humphrey ran strong in New England and the Mid-Atlantic.

The role of governmental activism continued as the central issue of presidential election politics. Questions were now being raised about the limits to this activism, which had been considered useful to boost prosperity in the economy and protect against the worst societal ills. In domestic affairs, an effective response to this activism came in the candidacy of Ronald Reagan, who sharpened the ideological debate between liberal government programs and the conservative determination to dismantle such programs and return responsibilities to the states. While many Republicans, including Nixon, had accepted the idea that the government should play some role in stimulating the economy and addressing social ills, Reagan attempted to eclipse this government role in domestic programs—although, in contradictory fashion, he promoted an increase in the government's role in military affairs. Reagan's election in 1980, reelection in 1984, and Bush's election in 1988 continued to show the new strength of the Republican Party in the South. Reagan in 1984 and Bush in 1988 did better in the South than in any other region. As seen in Table 4-7, the Republicans captured virtually all southern electoral votes in 1980, 1984, and 1988. Even Democrat Bill Clinton's candidacy in 1992, specifically designed to attract the South, gained electoral votes in only Arkansas, Georgia, Louisiana, and Tennessee. In seeking reelection in 1996, Clinton fared no

better, still capturing only 40 of the 147 southern electoral votes (in Arkansas, Florida, and Louisiana). In other regions during this period, competition rather than one-partyism prevailed. New England was keenly competitive between the two parties during the Reagan-Bush years, although strongly Democratic for Clinton. In contrast, the West was strongly Republican during the Reagan-Bush years, but two-party competitive in both Clinton victories. The Midwest and Border South were also competitive between the two parties during this period. Thus, while regional differences existed during this era, they were less dramatic than in the past.

The Autonomy of State Politics

The national and regional patterns of two-party competitiveness are misleading without considering the state results that yielded them. Presidential politics has always been state—not national or regional—politics. American voters have always been federal—not national—voters. V. O. Key was incorrect when he wrote that "while the governmental system may be federal the voter in the polling booth usually is not" (Key, 1956, p. 33). The constitutional system of the electoral college forces people to be federal voters. Although voters may respond to certain national messages, especially in the modern period, the votes are cast and tallied locally. Thus, while the national results announce who wins the presidency, the state-by-state results disclose how the candidates win. Table 4-8 displays the number of times a party won a state in presidential races for a given period. Table 4-9 considers how shifts in certain states would have produced a victory for the losing presidential candidate. Tables 4-10 through 4-36 provide the corresponding state analyses of the popular vote percentages by election year. Tables 4-37 through 4-63 provide the raw vote totals upon which these vote percentages are based.

One-Party Politics and Two-Party Competition

In considering these data, there are two main state presidential election patterns: one-party domination and two-party competition, the former being more typical than the latter. As shown in Table 4-8, the most striking feature of the first historical era (1788–1823) is the strong one-party patterns for the states. Connecticut, Delaware, Massachusetts, and New Hampshire were predominantly or exclusively Federalist, with the Federalists winning at least six of nine races in each of these states during this period. Georgia, Kentucky, Maryland, North Carolina, Ohio, Pennsylvania, South Carolina, Tennessee, Vermont, and Virginia were solidly Jeffersonian. Only New Jersey, New York, and Rhode Island were relatively competitive, with the Jeffersonians winning four of nine elections in New Jersey, five of eight elections in New York, and three of eight elections in Rhode Island.[6] Table 4-8 also reveals the degree of support the two parties had in states within specific regions. The Federalists were prominent in New England, except in Vermont where the Jeffersonians won six of the nine elections during this period. There was also competition in Rhode Island, where the Jeffersonians won three elections while the Federalists won five. The Jeffersonians were well entrenched in all, not just some, southern states, where the Federalists made few inroads. Table 4-8 also clarifies that the Federalists' strength extended outside New England to the Mid-Atlantic region in Delaware, where they won eight of nine elections; in New Jersey, where they won five of nine elections; and in New York, where they won three of eight elections.

As detailed in Table 4-8, the second historical era from 1824 to 1853 shows continued signs of one-party regionalism, although not as intense as in the earlier period. The Democrats dominated Alabama, Arkansas, Georgia, Illinois, Indiana, Louisiana, Michigan, Mississippi, Missouri, Pennsylvania, South Carolina, Vermont, and Virginia. The National Republicans and Whigs prevailed in Connecticut, Delaware, Kentucky, Maryland, and Massachusetts. There was some degree of competition in Maine, New Hampshire, New York, North Carolina, and Ohio, which nonetheless tipped in favor of the Democrats, and in New Jersey, Rhode Island, and Tennessee, which tipped in favor of the National Republicans and Whigs. These results clarify the much broader appeal of the Whigs. It extended into the Border South in Maryland and Kentucky. The Whigs won Maryland in all years from 1828 through 1848 and Kentucky from 1832 through 1852. The Whigs' strength in New England hinged on wins in Connecticut, Massachusetts, Rhode Island, and, to a lesser extent, New Hampshire. The Democrats continued to do well in the Deep South. Table 4-8 also shows, for the new states of the Midwest, the early Democratic leanings of Illinois, Indiana, and Michigan, but the stronger competition between the two parties in Ohio. Tables 4-15 through 4-18 show how competitive Ohio was, with only an average 4.5 percentage-point vote difference between the two major parties from 1828 to 1852.

Table 4-8 reveals that, in the Civil War-Reconstruction period from 1854 to 1893 only six states—Connecticut, Florida, Indiana, New York, South Carolina, and West Virginia—were fairly competitive, although the competitiveness in Florida and South Carolina ended after 1872 and did not return. The remaining thirty-two states that had at least two elections in this period were dominated by one party—fourteen states by Democrats, eighteen by Republicans. The period presents some striking reversals from the previous period. Delaware, Kentucky, and Maryland, which had been supportive of Whig candidates, now became heavily Democratic. In the Midwest three former Democratic states—Illinois, Michigan, and, to a lesser extent Indiana—swung to the Republicans. In New England, Maine, New Hampshire, and Vermont, which had supported Democrats, now were strongly Republican. Only the South continued as a Democratic stronghold. Tables 4-18 through 4-23 show the remarkable disappearance of the Republican Party in the South, except in the Grant elections of 1868 and 1872.

The degree of competitiveness within the states was roughly similar in the presidential election years from 1896 to 1928. As shown in Table 4-8, nine states, mostly in the West, were competitive: Arizona, Colorado, Idaho, Montana, Nebraska, Nevada, New Mexico, Missouri, and Oklahoma; twelve states were Democratic-dominant; and twenty-seven were Republican-dominant. Excluding Nebraska and Missouri, individual states in the Midwest were as strongly Republican as individual states in the South were Democratic. As Tables 4-23 through 4-27 indicate, if one excludes the three-way presidential race in 1912, the Republican percentages in the Midwest generally increased across this time period. For instance, in Michigan, Republicans won with only 54 percent of the vote in 1896 and 58 percent in 1900, but with a much larger 70 percent of the vote in 1904. This vote margin subsequently increased to 73 percent Republican in 1920 and 75 percent in 1924, when there was a huge 62 percentage-point advantage for Coolidge in Michigan over his Democratic opponent. As the tables show, other midwestern states were more competitive than Michigan but still posted significant Republican gains during these elections. This era also shows some key partisan changes in states. For example, while New Jersey and West Virginia were solidly Democratic in the Civil War era, they became solidly Republican in the conservative Republican/Democratic era (1894–1929).

Party competition was sharper during the New Deal era (1930–1965), when thirteen states were two-party competitive—Alaska, Arizona, Colorado, Connecticut, Delaware, Iowa, Michigan, New Hampshire, Ohio, Oregon, Pennsylvania, Wisconsin, and Wyoming. Of the remaining states, seven were Republican-dominant and thirty were Democratic-dominant. Competition increased in the Midwest in states like Iowa, Michigan, and Ohio, where Democrats made in-roads into what had been highly Republican states, and in the Mid-Atlantic, where former Republican states Delaware and Pennsylvania became more Democratic. What is also apparent in Table 4-8 is that one-party domination of a specific state can go through several permutations. For instance, Illinois, Massachusetts, New Jersey, New York, Rhode Island, Utah, and Washington were Republican strongholds in the 1896–1928 presidential elections, but were Democratic-dominant in the 1932–1964 elections. Illinois, New Jersey, and Utah then swung back to Republican dominance in the last period (1968–1996). Often the key for the out-party to take the White House is to be able to swing states like these against the incumbent party.

The competitiveness of the final era (1966 to the present)—greater than any of the other eras—is evident in Table 4-8. Both parties virtually traded victories in seventeen states in all regions of the country—Arkansas, Connecticut, Delaware, Georgia, Iowa, Kentucky, Louisiana, Maine, Maryland, Missouri, New York, Ohio, Oregon, Pennsylvania, Tennessee, Washington, and Wisconsin. Twenty-seven states were dominated by Republican presidential victories, while the remaining six were primarily Democratic. Table 4-8 clarifies the Republican gains in the South, which were most dramatic in Alabama, Mississippi, North Carolina, South Carolina, and Virginia. Each state, heavily Democratic during the New Deal era, became Republican states in the current era. The vote percentage results in Tables 4-32 through 4-36 show that Democrats remain competitive in several southern states, falling only a few percentage points behind the Republicans, but with the winner-take-all electoral system, the Republican presidential candidate consistently wins.

Losers Become Winners

Another feature of state races that national results do not reveal is the way in which small shifts in state results could turn the election in favor of the losing presidential candidate. These potential vote shifts turn attention away from the prevalence of one-party states in American elections and toward competitive two-party states that can decide close elections. The combination of these two types of states creates patterns in which the Republican-controlled states cancel out the Democratic-controlled states, leaving the election to be decided by voters in the handful of states with true two-party competition. Although it is tempting to merely file these possible outcomes away in the heap of political "what ifs," they are significant barometers of the competition between the two major parties throughout American history.

As documented in Table 4-9, of the fifty-three presidential elections from 1788 to 1996, fully twenty-one races could have gone the other way with a shift of one percent or less of the total vote; in seven instances a shift in only one state would have been necessary to change the electoral outcome. In another three races—1856, 1860, 1968—a small shift would have thrown the race into the House of Representatives. Thus a considerable number of races for president would have had a different outcome with a slight shift in the votes in key states, frequently California, Illinois, New York, Ohio, and Pennsylvania. As seen in Table 4-9, what is often cast as the dramatic beginnings of the age of Jackson in 1828 rested on Jackson garnering just 12,779 more votes than Adams in the five states of Indiana, Louisiana, Kentucky, New York, and Ohio—a scant 1.11 percent of the total national popular vote. Had these votes switched, Adams would have narrowly won a second term and American history books would have been rewritten.

Table 4-9 also reveals the close competition between Whigs and Democrats before the Civil War and Republicans and Democrats after the Civil War. In 1840 a switch of only 8,184 votes in the four states of New York, Pennsylvania, Maine, and New Jersey would have resulted in Van Buren's reelection. A switch of 2,554 votes in New York would have made Henry Clay president in 1844 rather than James K. Polk. Zachary Taylor would have lost in 1848 if 3,229 votes in Georgia, Maryland, and Delaware had changed. After the Civil War, in the elections of 1876, 1880, and 1888, a shift of a small number of voters in only one state would have

yielded a Democratic victory.[7] In 1884 a shift of just 525 votes in New York would have produced a Republican victory. Also as shown in Table 4-9, although William Jennings Bryan's populist Democratic candidacies were often depicted as predestined to failure, Bryan would have won in 1896 if 0.13 percent of the total national vote had switched in six states; he would have won in 1900 if 0.53 percent of the total national vote had switched in seven states; and he would have won in 1908 if 0.50 percent of the total national vote had switched in eight states. The most recent example of a highly competitive election occurred in 1976. Despite economic problems and his pardon of Richard Nixon, Gerald Ford would have won his own presidential term if just 9,246 votes had shifted in Ohio and Hawaii.

There is a nagging aggregation problem in understanding national presidential election results. Although national party organizations and campaigns can be found in all states, some states are more equal than others in their support for specific candidates and, in the longer term, for a specific party. Often one group of one-party states cancels out another group of one-party states, leaving the presidential race highly competitive. This national competitiveness results from a heavy dose of the uncompetitiveness of certain states as parties build strategies that place a number of states safely in their column. Often only a handful of states with sufficient competition between the two parties determines the national winner.

Conclusion

American politics has shifted radically since the days of Washington, Adams, and Jefferson. The population has burgeoned, the economy has transformed, and the role of the United States in the world has become preeminent. Universal suffrage is taken for granted; presidential primaries, rather than King Caucus (party members in Congress selecting their presidential candidates), direct the nomination process; campaigns are waged over television rather than in the newspapers. Yet in many ways, presidential elections remain the same. Two parties continue to prevail. While many current analyses downplay the importance of parties in the contemporary period, parties remain critical to presidential elections. In the time of Jefferson the role of the party press was critical; today the role of the parties' "party-building" media campaigns designed to get voters to the polls has taken the place of partisan newspapers. In the time of Jackson, wealthy citizens donated money to both parties and the parties dispensed the money to win elections. Today, parties' fund-raising mechanisms, while limited by federal law and overshadowed by the funds directly raised by candidates, are still at the heart of parties' efforts to win presidential elections. Despite the ability of certain third parties and third candidates to enter races and conduct well-publicized campaigns, they rarely do well at the polls. The structure of the electoral college further weakens their chances. Regionalism still remains a key part of American presidential elections, although with much less intensity. The role of governmental activism that Washington, Adams, and Jefferson grappled with continues to be the prevailing theme in American political contests today, although the scope of this activism has expanded well beyond debates about national banks and internal improvement projects in the country.

A clearer understanding of parties, voting, issues, and state and regional politics is brought to bear when contemporary elections are placed in historical context. Observing continuities and changes in politics over two centuries brings insight into not only what has happened in the past but also into what may happen in the future.

Notes

1. The election of 1900 is excluded from the twentieth century because of its traditional issues of trade and industrial strength and the reelection of William McKinley. This makes it more akin to nineteenth-century elections. It is especially similar to the 1896 election. However, if the election of 1900 is considered as part of the twentieth century, conclusions change little with Republicans winning thirteen presidential elections and Democrats capturing twelve.
2. In 1912 Theodore Roosevelt broke with the Republican Party and President William Howard Taft to run as a Progressive. It is not clear, however, if Roosevelt had won the election whether he would have returned to being a Republican or whether the Progressives would have become a credible new party.
3. The Compromise of 1820 permitted slavery in incoming states below the 36° 30' parallel and prohibited it in states above this line, except Missouri, which entered the Union as a slave state.
4. Most of the southern "Democratic vote" in 1860 went to "Southern Democrat" candidate John Breckinridge, who is coded as "other" in Tables 4-6 and 4-7, since historians agree that Stephen Douglas was the primary Democratic candidate for president in this election.
5. The record of the Republican Party in the South in the 1860–1960 period is as follows. Grant won some southern states in 1868 (Alabama, Arkansas, Florida, North Carolina, South Carolina, and Tennessee) and again in 1872 (Alabama, Arkansas, Florida, Louisiana, Mississippi, North Carolina, South Carolina, and Virginia). In 1876 Hayes won disputed electoral votes in Florida, Louisiana, and South Carolina. In 1920 Harding took Tennessee. In 1928 Hoover won Florida, North Carolina, Tennessee, Texas, and Virginia. Eisenhower won Florida, Tennessee, Texas, and Virginia in 1952 and these four states plus Louisiana in 1956. In 1960 Nixon won Florida, Tennessee, and Virginia.
6. Competitiveness is measured by the net difference in the number of victories achieved by the two parties during the era in a state (for example, Democratic wins − Republican wins). A net difference of 2 or less is considered a competitive state, while a net difference of 3 or more is considered a party-dominant state. Those states that had just entered the Union and did not have elections for most of a given political era are not evaluated.
7. In 1876 had Florida shifted 462 disputed votes to Democrat Tilden, he would have won the electoral college. In 1880, had New Yorkers given Democrat Hancock 10,517 more votes, he would have won the election. In 1888, had New York given home state candidate Cleveland 7,187 more votes, he would have been reelected to a second term.

Table 4-1 Method of Choosing Presidential Electors, 1788–1832

State	1788	1792	1796	1800	1804	1808	1812	1816	1820	1824	1828	1832
Connecticut	L	L	L	L	L	L	L	L	PV-S	PV-S	PV-S	PV-S
Delaware	PV-D	L	L	L	L	L	L	L	L	L	L	PV-S
Georgia	L	L	PV-S	L	L	L	L	L	L	L	PV-S	PV-S
Maryland	PV-S	PV-S	PV-D	PV-D	PV-D	PV-D	PV-D	PV-D	PV-D	PV-D	PV-D	PV-D
Massachusetts	L-PV-d	PV-d-L	PV-d-L+	L	PV-S	L	PV-D	L	PV-S	PV-S	PV-S	PV-S
New Hampshire	PV-s-L	PV-S	PV-s-L	L	PV-S	PV-S	PV-S	PV-S	PV-S	PV-S	PV-S	PV-S
New Jersey	L	L	L	L	PV-S	PV-S	L	PV-S	PV-S	PV-S	PV-S	PV-S
Pennsylvania	PV-S	PV-S	PV-S	L	PV-S	PV-S	PV-S	PV-S	PV-S	PV-S	PV-S	PV-S
South Carolina	L	L	L	L	L	L	L	L	L	L	L	L
Virginia	PV-D	PV-D	PV-D	PV-S	PV-S	PV-S	PV-S	PV-S	PV-S	PV-S	PV-S	PV-S
New York		L	L	L	L	L	L	L	L	L	PV-D+	PV-S
North Carolina		L	PV-D	PV-D	PV-D	PV-D	L	PV-S	PV-S	PV-S	PV-S	PV-S
Rhode Island		L	L	PV-S	PV-S	PV-S	PV-S	PV-S	PV-S	PV-S	PV-S	PV-S
Vermont		L	L	L	L	L	L	L	L	L	PV-S	PV-S
Kentucky		PV-D	PV-D	PV-D	PV-D	PV-D	PV-D	PV-D	PV-D	PV-D	PV-S	PV-S
Tennessee			L	L-e	PV-D	PV-D	PV-D	PV-D	PV-D	PV-D	PV-D	PV-S
Ohio					PV-S	PV-S	PV-S	PV-S	PV-S	PV-S	PV-S	PV-S
Louisiana							L	L	L	L	PV-S	PV-S
Indiana								L	L	PV-S	PV-S	PV-S
Alabama									L	PV-S	PV-S	PV-S
Illinois									PV-D	PV-S	PV-S	PV-S
Maine									PV-D,S	PV-D,S	PV-D,S	PV-D
Mississippi									PV-S	PV-S	PV-S	PV-S
Missouri									L	PV-D	PV-S	PV-S
States with popular elections (%)	60	40	50	31	65	59	50	53	63	75	92	96

Notes: By 1832 all states chose electors by statewide vote except South Carolina, where the legislature chose the electors. In 1868 South Carolina adopted statewide vote for presidential electors.

Legend:
L = electors chosen by the legislature; L-e = legislature appointed individuals who then chose electors; L-PV-d = electors chosen first by voters by congressional district, legislature made final choice from top two; PV-D = popular vote by congressional district; PV-D,S = popular vote by congressional district plus two elected statewide; PV-D+ = popular vote by congressional district; electors then chose two remaining electors; PV-d-L+ = popular vote by congressional district, but legislature chose where there was no majority and also chose two additional electors; PV-S = popular vote for all electors chosen statewide; PV-s-L = popular vote statewide, but legislature made choice where there was no majority.

Sources: Adapted from *Historical Statistics of the United States, Colonial Times to 1970* (Washington, D.C.: U.S. Government Printing Office, 1975), Table 41–26.

Table 4-2 Comparison of Popular and Electoral Vote Mandates, 1824–1996

Year	Winning Candidate	% of Popular Vote Received	Popular Vote Advantage[1]	% of Electoral Vote Received	Electoral Vote Advantage[1]	% Difference Between Electoral and Popular Votes
1824	J. Q. Adams (NR)	30.92	−10.43	32.18	−5.75	1.26
1828	Jackson (DR)	55.97	12.34	68.20	36.40	12.23
1832	Jackson (D)	54.23	16.81	76.04	59.03	21.81
1836	Van Buren (D)	50.83	1.74	57.82	32.99	6.99
1840	W. Harrison (W)	52.88	6.07	79.59	59.18	26.71
1844	Polk (D)	49.54	1.46	61.82	23.64	12.28
1848	Taylor (W)	47.28	4.79	56.21	12.42	8.93
1852	Pierce (D)	50.84	6.97	85.81	71.62	34.97
1856	Buchanan (D)	45.28	12.17	58.78	20.27	13.50
1860	Lincoln (R)	39.82	10.36	59.41	55.45	19.59
1864	Lincoln (R)	55.02	10.06	90.60	81.63	35.58
1868	Grant (R)	52.66	5.32	72.79	45.58	20.13
1872	Grant (R)	55.63	11.80	78.14	66.66	22.51
1876	Hayes (R)	47.95	−3.02	50.14	0.28	2.19
1880	Garfield (R)	48.27	0.02	57.99	15.98	9.72
1884	Cleveland (D)	48.50	0.25	54.61	9.22	6.11
1888	B. Harrison (R)	47.82	−0.80	58.10	16.20	10.28
1892	Cleveland (D)	46.05	3.09	62.39	29.73	16.34
1896	McKinley (R)	51.01	4.28	60.63	21.26	9.62
1900	McKinley (R)	51.67	6.16	65.32	30.64	13.65
1904	T. Roosevelt (R)	56.41	18.81	70.59	41.18	14.18
1908	Taft (R)	51.58	8.53	66.46	32.92	14.88
1912	Wilson (D)	41.84	18.66	81.92	80.41	40.08
1916	Wilson (D)	49.24	3.13	52.17	4.34	2.93
1920	Harding (R)	60.34	26.22	76.08	52.16	15.74
1924	Coolidge (R)	54.03	25.20	71.94	46.33	17.91
1928	Hoover (R)	58.24	17.46	83.62	67.24	25.38
1932	F. Roosevelt (D)	57.42	17.78	88.89	77.78	31.47
1936	F. Roosevelt (D)	60.80	24.26	98.49	96.98	37.69
1940	F. Roosevelt (D)	54.74	9.95	84.56	69.12	29.82
1944	F. Roosevelt (D)	53.39	7.50	81.36	62.72	27.97
1948	Truman (D)	49.55	4.48	57.06	21.47	7.51
1952	Eisenhower (R)	55.14	10.76	83.24	66.48	28.10
1956	Eisenhower (R)	57.38	15.43	86.06	72.31	28.68
1960	Kennedy (D)	49.72	0.17	56.42	15.64	6.70
1964	L. Johnson (D)	61.05	22.58	90.33	80.66	29.28
1968	Nixon (R)	43.42	0.70	55.95	20.45	12.53
1972	Nixon (R)	60.69	23.16	96.65	93.49	35.96
1976	Carter (D)	50.06	2.06	55.20	10.59	5.14
1980	Reagan (R)	50.75	9.74	90.89	81.78	40.14
1984	Reagan (R)	58.77	18.21	97.58	95.16	38.81
1988	Bush (R)	53.37	7.72	79.18	58.55	25.81
1992	Clinton (D)	43.01	5.56	68.77	37.54	25.76
1996	Clinton (D)	49.23	8.52	70.45	40.90	21.22

Notes: NR = National Republican; DR = Democratic-Republican; W = Whig; D = Democrat; R = Republican. J.Q. Adams is considered a Republican in this table although, technically, he ran as a Democratic-Republican in 1824.

[1]Percentage point difference between winner and nearest rival.

Sources: *Congressional Quarterly's Guide to U.S. Elections,* 3rd ed. (Washington, D.C.: Congressional Quarterly, 1994); corrected and updated by the author.

Table 4-3 Electoral Vote for President, 1788–1996

Year	Number of States	Total Electoral Votes	Winning Candidate	Losing Candidate	Winner (N)	Winner (%)	Loser (N)	Loser (%)	Other (N)	Other (%)
1788	10	69	Washington (F)	Unopposed	69	100.00	—	—	—	—
1792	15	135	Washington (F)	Unopposed	132[1]	97.78	—	—	—	—
1796	16	138	J. Adams (F)	Jefferson (DR)	71	51.45	67	48.55	0	0.00
1800	16	138	Jefferson (DR)	J. Adams (F)	73	52.90	65	47.10	0	0.00
1804	17	176	Jefferson (DR)	Pinckney (F)	162	92.05	14	7.95	0	0.00
1808	17	176	Madison (DR)	Pinckney (F)	122[1]	69.32	47	26.70	6	3.41
1812	18	218	Madison (DR)	Clinton (F)	128[1]	58.72	89	40.83	0	0.00
1816	19	221	Monroe (DR)	King (F)	183[1]	82.81	34	15.38	0	0.00
1820	24	235	Monroe (DR)	Unopposed	231[1]	98.30	—	—	1	0.43
1824	24	261	J.Q. Adams (NR)	Jackson (DR)	84	32.18	99	37.93	78	29.89
1828	24	261	Jackson (DR)	J.Q. Adams (NR)	178	68.20	83	31.80	0	0.00
1832	24	288	Jackson (D)	Clay (NR)	219[1]	76.04	49	17.01	18	6.25
1836	26	294	Van Buren (D)	W. Harrison (W)	170	57.82	73	24.83	51	17.35
1840	26	294	W. Harrison (W)	Van Buren (D)	234	79.59	60	20.41	0	0.00
1844	26	275	Polk (D)	Clay (W)	170	61.82	105	38.18	0	0.00
1848	30	290	Taylor (W)	Cass (D)	163	56.21	127	43.79	0	0.00
1852	31	296	Pierce (D)	Scott (W)	254	85.81	42	14.19	0	0.00
1856	31	296	Buchanan (D)	Fremont (R)	174	58.78	114	38.51	8	2.70
1860	33	303	Lincoln (R)	Douglas (D)	180	59.41	12	3.96	111	36.63
1864	36	234	Lincoln (R)	McClellan (D)	212[1]	90.60	21	8.97	0	0.00
1868	37	294	Grant (R)	Seymour (D)	214	72.79	80	27.21	0	0.00
1872	37	366	Grant (R)	Greeley (D)	286	78.14	42[2]	11.48	21	5.74
1876	38	369	Hayes (R)	Tilden (D)	185	50.14	184	49.86	0	0.00
1880	38	369	Garfield (R)	Hancock (D)	214	57.99	155	42.01	0	0.00
1884	38	401	Cleveland (D)	Blaine (R)	219	54.61	182	45.39	0	0.00
1888	38	401	B. Harrison (R)	Cleveland (D)	233	58.10	168	41.90	0	0.00
1892	44	444	Cleveland (D)	B. Harrison (R)	277	62.39	145	32.66	22	4.95
1896	45	447	McKinley (R)	Bryan (D)	271	60.63	176	39.37	0	0.00
1900	45	447	McKinley (R)	Bryan (D)	292	65.32	155	34.68	0	0.00
1904	45	476	T. Roosevelt (R)	Parker (D)	336	70.59	140	29.41	0	0.00
1908	46	483	Taft (R)	Bryan (D)	321	66.46	162	33.54	0	0.00
1912	48	531	Wilson (D)	Taft (R)	435	81.92	8	1.51	88	16.57
1916	48	531	Wilson (D)	Hughes (R)	277	52.17	254	47.83	0	0.00
1920	48	531	Harding (R)	Cox (D)	404	76.08	127	23.92	0	0.00
1924	48	531	Coolidge (R)	David (D)	382	71.94	136	25.61	13	2.45
1928	48	531	Hoover (R)	Smith (D)	444	83.62	87	16.38	0	0.00
1932	48	531	F. Roosevelt (D)	Hoover (R)	472	88.89	59	11.11	0	0.00
1936	48	531	F. Roosevelt (D)	Landon (R)	523	98.49	8	1.51	0	0.00
1940	48	531	F. Roosevelt (D)	Wilkes (R)	449	84.56	82	15.44	0	0.00
1944	48	531	F. Roosevelt (D)	Dewey (R)	432	81.36	99	18.64	0	0.00
1948	48	531	Truman (D)	Dewey (R)	303	57.06	189	35.59	39	7.35
1952	48	531	Eisenhower (R)	Stevenson (D)	442	83.24	89	16.76	0	0.00
1956	48	531	Eisenhower (R)	Stevenson (D)	457	86.06	73	13.75	1	0.19
1960	50	537	Kennedy (D)	Nixon (R)	303	56.42	219	40.78	15	2.79
1964[3]	50	538	Johnson (D)	Goldwater (R)	486	90.33	52	9.67	0	0.00
1968	50	538	Nixon (R)	Humphrey (D)	301	55.95	191	35.50	46	8.55
1972	50	538	Nixon (R)	McGovern (D)	520	96.65	17	3.16	1	0.19
1976	50	538	Carter (D)	Ford (R)	297	55.20	240	44.61	1	0.19
1980	50	538	Reagan (R)	Carter (D)	489	90.89	49	9.11	0	0.00
1984	50	538	Reagan (R)	Mondale (D)	525	97.58	13	2.42	0	0.00
1988	50	538	Bush (R)	Dukakis (D)	426	79.18	111	20.63	1	0.19
1992	50	538	Clinton (D)	Bush (R)	370	68.77	168	31.23	0	0.00
1996	50	538	Clinton (D)	Dole (R)	379	70.45	159	29.55	0	0.00

Notes: Only the top two vote-getters are listed. F = Federalist; DR = Democratic-Republican; NR = National Republican; W = Whig; D = Democrat; R = Republican. See Table 4-2 notes for an explanation of J.Q. Adams's party designation in the 1824 election.

[1]Candidates' electoral votes do not add to the total electoral votes: 1808, 1812, 1864—1 elector did not vote, 1832—2 electors did not vote, 1792, 1820—3 electors did not vote, 1816—4 electors did not vote.

[2]Horace Greeley, the Democratic candidate, died between the popular vote and the casting of the electoral votes; 42 electors voted for the replacement Democratic candidate, Thomas Hendricks; 21 for several other candidates, and three chose to vote for Greeley, which Congress refused to count.

[3]The Twenty-Third Amendment provided for three electoral votes for the District of Columbia beginning in 1964.

Sources: (1788–1992) *Congressional Quarterly's Guide to U.S. Elections,* 3rd ed. (Washington, D.C.: Congressional Quarterly, 1994), updated by the author; (1996) *Congressional Quarterly Weekly Report,* January 18, 1997, pp. 185–188.

Table 4-4 Popular Vote for President, 1788–1996

| Year | National Raw Vote | | | | National % of Raw Vote | | | Democratic % of Two-Party Vote |
	Democratic	Republican	Other	Total Vote	Democratic	Republican	Other	
1788	2,280	28,242	0	30,522	7.47	92.53	0.00	7.47
1792	0	8,924	0	8,924	0.00	100.00	0.00	0.00
1796	18,956	37,532	15,438	71,926	26.35	52.18	21.46	33.56
1800	33,976	18,345	0	52,321	64.94	35.06	0.00	64.94
1804	97,795	38,259	0	136,054	71.88	28.12	0.00	71.88
1808	111,105	54,402	3,504	169,011	65.74	32.19	2.07	67.13
1812	129,996	120,331	0	250,327	51.93	48.07	0.00	51.93
1816	74,696	17,611	17,589	109,896	67.97	16.03	16.01	80.92
1820	82,444	16,727	3,147	102,318	80.58	16.35	3.08	83.13
1824	151,271	113,122	101,440	365,833	41.35	30.92	27.73	57.21
1828	642,553	500,897	4,568	1,148,018	55.97	43.63	0.40	56.19
1832	701,780	484,205	107,988	1,293,973	54.23	37.42	8.35	59.17
1836	764,176	738,124	1,234	1,503,534	50.83	49.09	0.08	50.87
1840	1,128,854	1,275,390	7,564	2,411,808	46.81	52.88	0.31	46.95
1844	1,339,494	1,300,004	64,161	2,703,659	49.54	48.08	2.37	50.75
1848	1,223,460	1,361,393	294,331	2,879,184	42.49	47.28	10.22	47.33
1852	1,607,510	1,386,942	167,378	3,161,830	50.84	43.87	5.29	53.68
1856	1,836,072	1,342,345	876,230	4,054,647	45.28	33.11	21.61	57.77
1860	1,380,202	1,865,908	1,439,451	4,685,561	29.46	39.82	30.72	42.52
1864	1,812,807	2,218,388	692	4,031,887	44.96	55.02	0.02	44.97
1868	2,708,744	3,013,650	46	5,722,440	47.34	52.66	0.00	47.34
1872	2,834,761	3,598,235	34,683	6,467,679	43.83	55.63	0.54	44.07
1876	4,288,546	4,034,311	90,244	8,413,101	50.97	47.95	1.07	51.53
1880	4,444,260	4,446,158	320,002	9,210,420	48.25	48.27	3.47	49.99
1884	4,874,621	4,848,936	326,197	10,049,754	48.50	48.25	3.25	50.13
1888	5,534,488	5,443,892	404,940	11,383,320	48.62	47.82	3.56	50.41
1892	5,551,883	5,179,244	1,324,970	12,056,097	46.05	42.96	10.99	51.74
1896	6,511,495	7,108,480	315,763	13,935,738	46.73	51.01	2.27	47.81
1900	6,358,345	7,218,039	394,086	13,970,470	45.51	51.67	2.82	46.83
1904	5,082,898	7,626,593	809,473	13,518,964	37.60	56.41	5.99	39.99
1908	6,406,801	7,676,258	799,675	14,882,734	43.05	51.58	5.37	45.49
1912	6,293,152	3,486,333	5,261,478	15,040,963	41.84	23.18	34.98	64.35
1916	9,126,300	8,546,789	861,933	18,535,022	49.24	46.11	4.65	51.64
1920	9,133,092	16,153,115	1,482,406	26,768,613	34.12	60.34	5.54	36.12
1924	8,386,704	15,719,921	4,988,398	29,095,023	28.83	54.03	17.15	34.79
1928	15,007,698	21,437,277	360,976	36,805,951	40.78	58.24	0.98	41.18
1932	22,829,501	15,760,684	1,168,574	39,758,759	57.42	39.64	2.94	59.16
1936	27,757,333	16,684,231	1,213,199	45,654,763	60.80	36.54	2.66	62.46
1940	27,313,041	22,348,480	238,897	49,900,418	54.74	44.79	0.48	55.00
1944	25,612,610	22,017,617	346,443	47,976,670	53.39	45.89	0.72	53.77
1948	24,179,345	21,991,291	2,623,190	48,793,826	49.55	45.07	5.38	52.37
1952	27,314,992	33,936,234	299,692	61,550,918	44.38	55.14	0.49	44.60
1956	26,022,752	35,590,472	413,684	62,026,908	41.95	57.38	0.67	42.24
1960	34,226,731	34,108,157	503,331	68,838,219	49.72	49.55	0.73	50.09
1964	43,129,566	27,178,188	336,838	70,644,592	61.05	38.47	0.48	61.34
1968	31,275,166	31,785,480	10,151,229	73,211,875	42.72	43.42	13.87	49.60
1972	29,170,383	47,169,911	1,378,260	77,718,554	37.53	60.69	1.77	38.21
1976	40,830,763	39,147,793	1,577,333	81,555,889	50.06	48.00	1.93	51.05
1980	35,483,883	43,904,153	7,127,185	86,515,221	41.01	50.75	8.24	44.70
1984	37,577,185	54,455,075	620,582	92,652,842	40.56	58.77	0.67	40.83
1988	41,809,074	48,886,097	899,638	91,594,809	45.65	53.37	0.98	46.10
1992	44,909,326	39,103,882	20,411,806	104,425,014	43.01	37.45	19.55	53.46
1996	47,402,357	39,198,755	9,676,760	96,277,872	49.23	40.71	10.05	54.74

Notes: Entries for the major parties (Democratic, Republican, or their historical antecedents listed in Appendix A) are votes gained by those candidates that historical records show are the primary candidates of the two major parties, except in 1836 when the three Whig candidates are tallied for the total Whig vote. When aggregating state votes for the national result, any states reporting only partial data for the presidential race are deleted. Democratic = Anti-Federalists (1788–1796), Democratic-Republicans (1796–1828), Jacksonian Democrats (1824–1828), and Democrats (since 1832). Republicans = Federalists (1788–1816), National Republicans (1828–1832), Whigs (1836–1852), and Republicans (since 1856). Other = other third parties. J.Q. Adams is considered a Republican in this table in the 1824 election.

Sources: Adapted from the election archive of Michael J. Dubin, *Congressional Quarterly's Guide to U.S. Elections* (1994), ICPSR data sets 0001 and 0019, *A Statistical History of the American Presidential Elections* (1963), *America at the Polls* (1965), *America Votes* (various publication dates), and independent search of state sources by the author. For the state data used from these sources to get the national values in this table, see Tables 4-37 through 4-63.

Table 4-5 Popular Vote for President by Region, 1788–1996

Year/Region[1]	Regional Raw Vote				Regional % of Raw Vote			Democratic % of Two-Party Vote
	Democratic	Republican	Other	Total Vote	Democratic	Republican	Other	
1788 NEng	0	20,577	0	20,577	0.00	100.00	0.00	0.00
1788 South	—	—	—	—	—	—	—	—
1788 MAtl	—	—	—	—	—	—	—	—
1788 BdrS	2,280	7,665	0	9,945	22.93	77.07	0.00	22.93
1788 MidW	—	—	—	—	—	—	—	—
1788 West	—	—	—	—	—	—	—	—
1792 NEng	0	8,924	0	8,924	0.00	100.00	0.00	0.00
1792 South	—	—	—	—	—	—	—	—
1792 MAtl	—	—	—	—	—	—	—	—
1792 BdrS	—	—	—	—	—	—	—	—
1792 MidW	—	—	—	—	—	—	—	—
1792 West	—	—	—	—	—	—	—	—
1796 NEng	0	18,274	15,438	33,712	0.00	54.21	45.79	0.00
1796 South	—	—	—	—	—	—	—	—
1796 MAtl	12,516	12,229	0	24,745	50.58	49.42	0	50.58
1796 BdrS	6,440	7,029	0	13,469	47.81	52.19	0	47.81
1796 MidW	—	—	—	—	—	—	—	—
1796 West	—	—	—	—	—	—	—	—
1800 NEng	2,345	2,149	0	4,494	52.18	47.82	0.00	52.18
1800 South	21,002	6,178	0	27,180	77.27	22.73	0.00	77.27
1800 MAtl	—	—	—	—	—	—	—	—
1800 BdrS	10,629	10,018	0	20,647	51.48	48.52	0.00	51.48
1800 MidW	—	—	—	—	—	—	—	—
1800 West	—	—	—	—	—	—	—	—
1804 NEng	39,913	34,196	0	74,109	53.86	46.14	0.00	53.86
1804 South	12,879	0	0	12,879	100.00	0.00	0.00	100.00
1804 MAtl	35,200	1,238	0	36,438	96.60	3.40	0.00	96.60
1804 BdrS	7,301	2,461	0	9,762	74.79	25.21	0.00	74.79
1804 MidW	2,502	364	0	2,866	87.30	12.70	0.00	87.30
1804 West	—	—	—	—	—	—	—	—
1808 NEng	15,436	17,178	0	32,614	47.33	52.67	0.00	47.33
1808 South	15,682	758	3,504	19,944	78.63	3.80	17.57	95.39
1808 MAtl	60,996	26,419	0	87,415	69.78	30.22	0.00	69.78
1808 BdrS	15,346	8,873	0	24,219	63.36	36.64	0.00	63.36
1808 MidW	3,645	1,174	0	4,819	75.64	24.36	0.00	75.64
1808 West	—	—	—	—	—	—	—	—
1812 NEng	43,448	67,668	0	111,116	39.10	60.90	0.00	39.10
1812 South	14,980	5,573	0	20,553	72.88	27.12	0.00	72.88
1812 MAtl	49,397	29,509	0	78,906	62.60	37.40	0.00	62.60
1812 BdrS	14,751	14,280	0	29,031	50.81	49.19	0.00	50.81
1812 MidW	7,420	3,301	0	10,721	69.21	30.79	0.00	69.21
1812 West	—	—	—	—	—	—	—	—
1816 NEng	16,433	13,330	0	29,763	55.21	44.79	0.00	55.21
1816 South	16,408	640	0	17,048	96.25	3.75	0.00	96.25
1816 MAtl	31,094	0	17,589	48,683	63.87	0.00	36.13	100.00
1816 BdrS	7,435	3,048	0	10,483	70.92	29.08	0.00	70.92
1816 MidW	3,326	593	0	3,919	84.87	15.13	0.00	84.87
1816 West	—	—	—	—	—	—	—	—
1820 NEng	26,617	16,341	587	43,545	61.13	37.53	1.35	61.96
1820 South	8,547	0	0	8,547	100.00	0.00	0.00	100.00
1820 MAtl	34,634	0	1,893	36,527	94.82	0.00	5.18	100.00
1820 BdrS	4,544	386	175	5,105	89.01	7.56	3.43	92.17
1820 MidW	8,102	0	492	8,594	94.28	0.00	5.72	100.00
1820 West	—	—	—	—	—	—	—	—
1824 NEng	0	60,003	17,701	77,704	0.00	77.22	22.78	0.00
1824 South	55,953	7,711	27,038	90,702	61.69	8.50	29.81	87.89
1824 MAtl	46,068	13,750	7,092	66,910	68.85	20.55	10.60	77.01
1824 BdrS	20,879	14,632	21,041	56,552	36.92	25.87	37.21	58.80
1824 MidW	28,371	17,026	28,568	73,965	38.36	23.02	38.62	62.50
1824 West	—	—	—	—	—	—	—	—
1828 NEng	53,769	115,379	4,541	173,689	30.96	66.43	2.61	31.79
1828 South	156,427	36,411	19	192,857	81.11	18.88	0.01	81.12
1828 MAtl	262,678	206,079	8	468,765	56.04	43.96	0.00	56.04
1828 BdrS	62,090	54,482	0	116,572	53.26	46.74	0.00	53.26
1828 MidW	107,589	88,546	0	196,135	54.85	45.15	0.00	54.85
1828 West	—	—	—	—	—	—	—	—
1832 NEng	93,951	110,419	40,119	244,489	38.43	45.16	16.41	45.97
1832 South	132,276	19,755	3	152,034	87.01	12.99	0.00	87.01
1832 MAtl	287,406	182,638	67,174	537,218	53.50	34.00	12.50	61.14
1832 BdrS	55,448	62,609	0	118,057	46.97	53.03	0.00	46.97
1832 MidW	132,699	108,784	692	242,175	54.79	44.92	0.29	54.95
1832 West	—	—	—	—	—	—	—	—
1836 NEng	111,304	104,735	1,223	217,262	51.23	48.21	0.56	51.52
1836 South	143,292	138,770	6	282,068	50.80	49.20	0.00	50.80
1836 MAtl	288,007	256,656	5	544,668	52.88	47.12	0.00	52.88
1836 BdrS	55,496	62,713	0	118,209	46.95	53.05	0.00	46.95
1836 MidW	166,077	175,250	0	341,327	48.66	51.34	0.00	48.66
1836 West	—	—	—	—	—	—	—	—
1840 NEng	177,869	215,025	2,981	395,875	44.93	54.32	0.75	45.27
1840 South	223,160	254,223	0	477,383	46.75	53.25	0.00	46.75
1840 MAtl	392,311	409,342	2,891	804,544	48.76	50.88	0.36	48.94
1840 BdrS	61,368	92,016	0	153,384	40.01	59.99	0.00	40.01
1840 MidW	274,146	304,784	1,692	580,622	47.22	52.49	0.29	47.35
1840 West	—	—	—	—	—	—	—	—

(Table continues)

Table 4-5 *(Continued)*

Year/Region[1]	Regional Raw Vote				Regional % of Raw Vote			Democratic % of Two-Party Vote
	Democratic	Republican	Other	Total Vote	Democratic	Republican	Other	
1844 NEng	178,667	186,230	26,835	391,732	45.61	47.54	6.85	48.96
1844 South	280,605	254,079	2	534,686	52.48	47.52	0.00	52.48
1844 MAtl	448,364	438,266	19,088	905,718	49.50	48.39	2.11	50.57
1844 BdrS	84,694	97,233	0	181,927	46.55	53.45	0.00	46.55
1844 MidW	347,164	324,196	18,236	689,596	50.34	47.01	2.64	51.71
1844 West	—	—	—	—	—	—	—	—
1848 NEng	144,846	171,266	77,709	393,821	36.78	43.49	19.73	45.82
1848 South	282,563	293,040	79	575,682	49.08	50.90	0.01	49.09
1848 MAtl	329,316	450,768	135,129	915,213	35.98	49.25	14.76	42.22
1848 BdrS	84,248	104,847	129	189,224	44.52	55.41	0.07	44.55
1848 MidW	382,487	341,472	81,285	805,244	47.50	42.41	10.09	52.83
1848 West	—	—	—	—	—	—	—	—
1852 NEng	169,709	160,870	56,865	387,444	43.80	41.52	14.68	51.34
1852 South	314,848	238,530	7,725	561,103	56.11	42.51	1.38	56.90
1852 MAtl	511,270	458,908	36,635	1,006,813	50.78	45.58	3.64	52.70
1852 BdrS	93,971	92,505	287	186,763	50.32	49.53	0.15	50.39
1852 MidW	476,991	400,157	65,749	942,897	50.59	42.44	6.97	54.38
1852 West	40,721	35,972	117	76,810	53.02	46.83	0.15	53.10
1856 NEng	162,552	306,669	31,147	500,368	32.49	61.29	6.22	34.64
1856 South	429,233	0	308,214	737,447	58.21	0.00	41.79	100.00
1856 MAtl	481,597	452,615	237,205	1,171,417	41.11	38.64	20.25	51.55
1856 BdrS	113,765	285	114,868	228,918	49.70	0.12	50.18	99.75
1856 MidW	595,583	562,072	148,587	1,306,242	45.60	43.03	11.38	51.45
1856 West	53,342	20,704	36,209	110,255	48.38	18.78	32.84	72.04
1860 NEng	121,737	296,554	57,860	476,151	25.57	62.28	12.15	29.10
1860 South	71,920	1,887	782,654	856,461	8.40	0.22	91.38	97.44
1860 MAtl	393,210	692,844	202,874	1,288,928	30.51	53.75	15.74	36.21
1860 BdrS	31,617	3,658	203,443	238,718	13.24	1.53	85.22	89.63
1860 MidW	719,583	826,903	144,232	1,690,718	42.56	48.91	8.53	46.53
1860 West	42,135	44,062	48,388	134,585	31.31	32.74	35.95	48.88
1864 NEng	193,095	332,584	6	525,685	36.73	63.27	0.00	36.73
1864 South	—	—	—	—	—	—	—	—
1864 MAtl	716,216	733,906	0	1,450,122	49.39	50.61	0.00	49.39
1864 BdrS	108,118	91,739	0	199,857	54.10	45.90	0.00	54.10
1864 MidW	736,490	978,392	681	1,715,563	42.93	57.03	0.04	42.95
1864 West	58,888	81,767	5	140,660	41.87	58.13	0.00	41.87
1868 NEng	198,464	352,578	37	551,079	36.01	63.98	0.01	36.02
1868 South	430,856	405,019	6	835,881	51.55	48.45	0.00	51.55
1868 MAtl	837,223	849,914	0	1,687,137	49.62	50.38	0.00	49.62
1868 BdrS	198,552	99,019	0	297,571	66.72	33.28	0.00	66.72
1868 MidW	973,241	1,235,097	3	2,208,341	44.07	55.93	0.00	44.07
1868 West	70,408	72,023	0	142,431	49.43	50.57	0.00	49.43
1872 NEng	181,658	337,502	313	519,473	34.97	64.97	0.06	34.99
1872 South	659,007	759,886	924	1,419,817	46.41	53.52	0.07	46.45
1872 MAtl	685,983	893,112	488	1,579,583	43.43	56.54	0.03	43.44
1872 BdrS	197,214	187,846	2,989	388,049	50.82	48.41	0.77	51.22
1872 MidW	1,056,204	1,345,651	28,361	2,430,216	43.46	55.37	1.17	43.97
1872 West	54,695	74,238	1,608	130,541	41.90	56.87	1.23	42.42
1876 NEng	290,097	376,815	2,988	669,900	43.30	56.25	0.45	43.50
1876 South	1,093,483	740,024	259	1,833,766	59.63	40.36	0.01	59.64
1876 MAtl	1,017,496	987,633	13,673	2,018,802	50.40	48.92	0.68	50.74
1876 BdrS	308,385	211,545	4,102	524,032	58.85	40.37	0.78	59.31
1876 MidW	1,479,160	1,613,446	68,647	3,161,253	46.79	51.04	2.17	47.83
1876 West	99,925	104,848	575	205,348	48.66	51.06	0.28	48.80
1880 NEng	311,474	414,939	13,487	739,900	42.10	56.08	1.82	42.88
1880 South	1,072,463	664,954	52,106	1,789,523	59.93	37.16	2.91	61.73
1880 MAtl	1,079,685	1,134,951	39,478	2,254,114	47.90	50.35	1.75	48.75
1880 BdrS	299,971	231,248	20,747	551,966	54.35	41.90	3.76	56.47
1880 MidW	1,546,028	1,862,983	188,958	3,597,969	42.97	51.78	5.25	45.35
1880 West	134,639	137,083	5,226	276,948	48.62	49.50	1.89	49.55
1884 NEng	310,592	386,618	65,144	762,354	40.74	50.71	8.55	44.55
1884 South	1,147,373	778,100	18,817	1,944,290	59.01	40.02	0.97	59.59
1884 MAtl	1,102,524	1,171,182	83,844	2,357,550	46.77	49.68	3.56	48.49
1884 BdrS	317,138	267,534	32,206	616,878	51.41	43.37	5.22	54.24
1884 MidW	1,849,808	2,073,028	116,877	4,039,713	45.79	51.32	2.89	47.15
1884 West	147,186	172,474	9,309	328,969	44.74	52.43	2.83	46.04
1888 NEng	354,682	445,102	21,711	821,495	43.18	54.18	2.64	44.35
1888 South	1,270,527	771,213	59,269	2,101,009	60.47	36.71	2.82	62.23
1888 MAtl	1,250,505	1,333,726	66,483	2,650,714	47.18	50.32	2.51	48.39
1888 BdrS	368,695	333,295	13,259	715,249	51.55	46.60	1.85	52.52
1888 MidW	2,102,980	2,344,448	229,678	4,677,106	44.96	50.13	4.91	47.29
1888 West	187,099	216,108	14,540	417,747	44.79	51.73	3.48	46.40
1892 NEng	389,999	453,405	26,985	870,389	44.81	52.09	3.10	46.24
1892 South	1,238,738	531,333	356,198	2,126,269	58.26	24.99	16.75	69.98
1892 MAtl	1,296,700	1,299,497	118,316	2,714,513	47.77	47.87	4.36	49.95
1892 BdrS	373,794	308,490	42,934	725,218	51.54	42.54	5.92	54.79
1892 MidW	2,072,063	2,319,676	606,760	4,998,499	41.45	46.41	12.14	47.18
1892 West	180,589	266,843	173,777	621,209	29.07	42.96	27.97	40.36
1896 NEng	243,217	615,672	37,216	896,105	27.14	68.71	4.15	28.32
1896 South	1,432,965	803,125	44,361	2,280,451	62.84	35.22	1.95	64.08
1896 MAtl	1,134,846	1,789,955	102,900	3,027,701	37.48	59.12	3.40	38.80
1896 BdrS	416,524	460,509	20,901	897,934	46.39	51.29	2.33	47.49
1896 MidW	2,728,428	3,136,005	97,647	5,962,080	45.76	52.60	1.64	46.53
1896 West	555,515	303,214	12,738	871,467	63.74	34.79	1.46	64.69

(Table continues)

Table 4-5 *(Continued)*

Year/Region[1]	Regional Raw Vote			Total Vote	Regional % of Raw Vote			Democratic % of Two-Party Vote
	Democratic	Republican	Other		Democratic	Republican	Other	
1900 NEng	335,983	538,002	31,831	905,816	37.09	59.39	3.51	38.44
1900 South	1,157,368	668,541	55,387	1,881,296	61.52	35.54	2.94	63.39
1900 MAtl	1,286,354	1,778,920	99,018	3,164,292	40.65	56.22	3.13	41.97
1900 BdrS	456,170	483,112	14,165	953,447	47.84	50.67	1.49	48.57
1900 MidW	2,668,882	3,270,354	162,581	6,101,817	43.74	53.60	2.66	44.94
1900 West	453,588	479,110	31,104	963,802	47.06	49.71	3.23	48.63
1904 NEng	334,984	570,555	38,415	943,954	35.49	60.44	4.07	36.99
1904 South	912,135	399,897	65,878	1,377,910	66.20	29.02	4.78	69.52
1904 MAtl	1,205,892	1,969,351	155,363	3,330,606	36.21	59.13	4.66	37.98
1904 BdrS	427,471	447,574	25,116	900,161	47.49	49.72	2.79	48.85
1904 MidW	1,880,971	3,565,904	428,716	5,875,591	32.01	60.69	7.30	34.53
1904 West	321,445	673,312	95,985	1,090,742	29.47	61.73	8.80	32.31
1908 NEng	329,048	582,406	56,281	967,735	34.00	60.18	5.82	36.10
1908 South	1,023,152	502,561	61,260	1,586,973	64.47	31.67	3.86	67.06
1908 MAtl	1,320,827	1,906,161	193,930	3,420,918	38.61	55.72	5.67	40.93
1908 BdrS	593,772	600,566	47,270	1,241,608	47.82	48.37	3.81	49.72
1908 MidW	2,655,278	3,400,079	328,134	6,383,491	41.60	53.26	5.14	43.85
1908 West	484,724	684,485	112,800	1,282,009	37.81	53.39	8.80	41.46
1912 NEng	379,568	334,750	322,442	1,036,760	36.61	32.29	31.10	53.14
1912 South	1,032,913	191,993	318,243	1,543,149	66.94	12.44	20.62	84.33
1912 MAtl	1,252,479	833,910	1,202,015	3,288,404	38.09	25.36	36.55	60.03
1912 BdrS	564,398	317,946	324,773	1,207,117	46.76	26.34	26.90	63.97
1912 MidW	2,379,859	1,509,079	2,239,751	6,128,689	38.83	24.62	36.55	61.20
1912 West	683,935	298,655	854,254	1,836,844	37.23	16.26	46.51	69.61
1916 NEng	518,587	573,639	31,202	1,123,428	46.16	51.06	2.78	47.48
1916 South	1,328,125	466,211	78,583	1,872,919	70.91	24.89	4.20	74.02
1916 MAtl	1,516,981	1,878,054	154,711	3,549,746	42.73	52.91	4.36	44.68
1916 BdrS	696,875	599,558	67,682	1,364,115	51.09	43.95	4.96	53.75
1916 MidW	3,750,507	3,909,520	364,969	8,024,996	46.74	48.72	4.55	48.96
1916 West	1,315,225	1,119,807	164,786	2,599,818	50.59	43.07	6.34	54.01
1920 NEng	595,016	1,317,617	61,477	1,974,110	30.14	66.74	3.11	31.11
1920 South	1,621,458	941,756	109,200	2,672,414	60.67	35.24	4.09	63.26
1920 MAtl	1,583,112	3,757,573	414,202	5,754,887	27.51	65.29	7.20	29.64
1920 BdrS	1,074,030	1,214,444	54,219	2,342,693	45.85	51.84	2.31	46.93
1920 MidW	3,496,597	7,329,200	607,182	11,432,979	30.58	64.11	5.31	32.30
1920 West	762,879	1,592,525	236,126	2,591,530	29.44	61.45	9.11	32.39
1924 NEng	582,910	1,392,597	224,719	2,200,226	26.49	63.29	10.21	29.51
1924 South	1,692,600	704,333	130,406	2,527,339	66.97	27.87	5.16	70.62
1924 MAtl	1,691,476	3,950,257	945,995	6,587,728	25.68	59.96	14.36	29.98
1924 BdrS	1,036,695	1,073,563	173,705	2,283,963	45.39	47.00	7.61	49.13
1924 MidW	2,893,529	6,948,329	2,556,116	12,397,974	23.34	56.04	20.62	29.40
1924 West	489,494	1,650,842	957,457	3,097,793	15.80	53.29	30.91	22.87
1928 NEng	1,370,150	1,575,460	16,643	2,962,253	46.25	53.18	0.56	46.51
1928 South	1,758,311	1,611,461	8,040	3,377,812	52.05	47.71	0.24	52.18
1928 MAtl	3,809,320	5,243,636	157,265	9,210,221	41.36	56.93	1.71	42.08
1928 BdrS	1,087,654	1,629,140	13,254	2,730,048	39.84	59.67	0.49	40.03
1928 MidW	5,626,146	8,921,644	121,312	14,669,102	38.35	60.82	0.83	38.67
1928 West	1,356,117	2,455,936	44,462	3,856,515	35.16	63.68	1.15	35.57
1932 NEng	1,514,237	1,489,889	77,285	3,081,411	49.14	48.35	2.51	50.41
1932 South	3,059,224	700,135	28,386	3,787,745	80.77	18.48	0.75	81.38
1932 MAtl	4,691,856	4,224,260	374,483	9,290,599	50.50	45.47	4.03	52.62
1932 BdrS	1,816,480	1,097,796	28,244	2,942,520	61.73	37.31	0.96	62.33
1932 MidW	8,994,545	6,489,658	446,222	15,930,425	56.46	40.74	2.80	58.09
1932 West	2,753,159	1,758,946	213,954	4,726,059	58.25	37.22	4.53	61.02
1936 NEng	1,786,100	1,526,817	194,484	3,507,401	50.92	43.53	5.54	53.91
1936 South	3,372,615	798,848	12,527	4,183,990	80.61	19.09	0.30	80.85
1936 MAtl	6,800,562	4,648,528	233,453	11,682,543	58.21	39.79	2.00	59.40
1936 BdrS	1,935,207	1,171,617	23,971	3,130,795	61.81	37.42	0.77	62.29
1936 MidW	10,351,751	6,850,894	626,137	17,828,782	58.06	38.43	3.51	60.18
1936 West	3,511,098	1,687,527	122,627	5,321,252	65.98	31.71	2.30	67.54
1940 NEng	2,022,363	1,792,622	13,983	3,828,968	52.82	46.82	0.37	53.01
1940 South	3,722,506	1,025,970	8,973	4,757,449	78.25	21.57	0.19	78.39
1940 MAtl	6,514,360	5,924,241	50,635	12,489,236	52.16	47.43	0.41	52.37
1940 BdrS	1,911,843	1,401,204	11,508	3,324,555	57.51	42.15	0.35	57.71
1940 MidW	9,560,222	9,525,280	92,269	19,177,771	49.85	49.67	0.48	50.09
1940 West	3,581,747	2,679,163	61,529	6,322,439	56.65	42.38	0.97	57.21
1944 NEng	1,959,912	1,772,241	11,164	3,743,317	52.36	47.34	0.30	52.51
1944 South	3,396,220	1,195,318	150,155	4,741,693	71.62	25.21	3.17	73.97
1944 MAtl	6,300,757	5,840,783	59,165	12,200,705	51.64	47.87	0.48	51.89
1944 BdrS	1,582,405	1,327,640	4,550	2,914,595	54.29	45.55	0.16	54.38
1944 MidW	8,803,612	9,018,187	82,744	17,904,543	49.17	50.37	0.46	49.40
1944 West	3,569,704	2,863,448	38,665	6,471,817	55.16	44.24	0.60	55.49
1948 NEng	2,029,289	1,830,370	78,316	3,937,975	51.53	46.48	1.99	52.58
1948 South	2,630,937	1,382,969	1,201,458	5,215,364	50.45	26.52	23.04	65.55
1948 MAtl	5,495,898	5,794,072	711,343	12,001,313	45.79	48.28	5.93	48.68
1948 BdrS	1,635,247	1,221,092	33,416	2,889,755	56.59	42.26	1.16	57.25
1948 MidW	8,828,288	8,422,697	289,451	17,540,436	50.33	48.02	1.65	51.18
1948 West	3,559,686	3,340,091	309,206	7,208,983	49.38	46.33	4.29	51.59
1952 NEng	2,037,291	2,622,629	13,180	4,673,100	43.60	56.12	0.28	43.72
1952 South	4,428,163	4,113,525	12,023	8,553,711	51.77	48.09	0.14	51.84
1952 MAtl	6,350,087	7,832,274	119,426	14,301,787	44.40	54.76	0.84	44.77
1952 BdrS	1,775,583	1,932,468	9,703	3,717,754	47.76	51.98	0.26	47.88
1952 MidW	8,886,923	12,190,270	76,188	21,153,381	42.01	57.63	0.36	42.16
1952 West	3,836,945	5,245,068	69,172	9,151,185	41.93	57.32	0.76	42.25

(Table continues)

Table 4-5 *(Continued)*

Year/Region[1]	Regional Raw Vote				Regional % of Raw Vote			Democratic % of Two-Party Vote
	Democratic	Republican	Other	Total Vote	Democratic	Republican	Other	
1956 NEng	1,750,440	2,867,000	7,474	4,624,914	37.85	61.99	0.16	37.91
1956 South	4,118,737	4,218,468	286,018	8,623,223	47.76	48.92	3.32	49.40
1956 MAtl	5,659,471	8,635,757	39,546	14,334,774	39.48	60.24	0.28	39.59
1956 BdrS	1,616,181	2,054,996	5,636	3,676,813	43.96	55.89	0.15	44.02
1956 MidW	8,697,943	12,373,338	42,383	21,113,664	41.20	58.60	0.20	41.28
1956 West	4,179,980	5,440,913	32,627	9,653,520	43.30	56.36	0.34	43.45
1960 NEng	2,790,378	2,186,793	5,579	4,982,750	56.00	43.89	0.11	56.06
1960 South	5,184,750	4,723,364	363,776	10,271,890	50.48	45.98	3.54	52.33
1960 MAtl	7,871,372	7,346,072	49,970	15,267,414	51.56	48.12	0.33	51.73
1960 BdrS	1,899,560	2,021,179	3	3,920,742	48.45	51.55	0.00	48.45
1960 MidW	10,943,013	11,994,593	41,158	22,978,764	47.62	52.20	0.18	47.71
1960 West	5,537,658	5,836,156	42,845	11,416,659	48.51	51.12	0.38	48.69
1964 NEng	3,482,609	1,293,010	9,995	4,785,614	72.77	27.02	0.21	72.92
1964 South	6,097,011	5,993,384	221,890	12,312,285	49.52	48.68	1.80	50.43
1964 MAtl	10,034,991	4,959,468	43,489	15,037,948	66.73	32.98	0.29	66.92
1964 BdrS	2,628,288	1,453,891	3,519	4,085,698	64.33	35.58	0.09	64.38
1964 MidW	13,625,671	8,550,624	32,707	22,209,002	61.35	38.50	0.15	61.44
1964 West	7,260,996	4,927,811	25,238	12,214,045	59.45	40.35	0.21	59.57
1968 NEng	2,755,453	1,855,223	213,946	4,824,622	57.11	38.45	4.43	59.76
1968 South	4,578,323	5,122,657	5,102,736	14,803,716	30.93	34.60	34.47	47.19
1968 MAtl	6,991,275	6,520,130	1,117,973	14,629,378	47.79	44.57	7.64	51.74
1968 BdrS	1,751,166	1,768,670	638,966	4,158,802	42.11	42.53	15.36	49.75
1968 MidW	9,701,398	10,392,363	2,111,790	22,205,551	43.69	46.80	9.51	48.28
1968 West	5,497,551	6,126,437	965,818	12,589,806	43.67	48.66	7.67	47.29
1972 NEng	2,427,876	2,730,555	38,454	5,196,885	46.72	52.54	0.74	47.07
1972 South	4,465,383	10,740,943	228,668	15,434,994	28.93	69.59	1.48	29.37
1972 MAtl	5,942,529	8,893,158	155,083	14,990,770	39.64	59.32	1.03	40.06
1972 BdrS	1,529,149	2,784,966	62,916	4,377,031	34.94	63.63	1.44	35.45
1972 MidW	9,126,844	13,711,334	351,703	23,189,881	39.36	59.13	1.52	39.96
1972 West	5,678,602	8,308,955	541,436	14,528,993	39.08	57.19	3.73	40.60
1976 NEng	2,765,874	2,455,126	129,853	5,350,853	51.69	45.88	2.43	52.98
1976 South	9,916,123	8,191,471	235,500	18,343,094	54.06	44.66	1.28	54.76
1976 MAtl	7,285,484	6,925,914	193,865	14,405,263	50.58	48.08	1.35	51.27
1976 BdrS	2,481,503	2,092,854	44,727	4,619,084	53.72	45.31	0.97	54.25
1976 MidW	11,670,593	11,994,594	490,102	24,155,289	48.31	49.66	2.03	49.32
1976 West	6,711,186	7,487,834	483,286	14,682,306	45.71	51.00	3.29	47.27
1980 NEng	2,205,666	2,444,489	816,800	5,466,955	40.35	44.71	14.94	47.43
1980 South	9,205,105	10,637,351	837,079	20,679,535	44.51	51.44	4.05	46.39
1980 MAtl	5,919,030	6,813,512	1,242,502	13,975,044	42.35	48.75	8.89	46.49
1980 BdrS	2,243,179	2,369,201	285,403	4,897,783	45.80	48.37	5.83	48.63
1980 MidW	10,291,213	12,826,582	2,059,870	25,177,665	40.87	50.94	8.18	44.52
1980 West	5,619,690	8,813,018	1,885,531	16,318,239	34.44	54.01	11.55	38.94
1984 NEng	2,436,949	3,153,309	23,358	5,613,616	43.41	56.17	0.42	43.59
1984 South	8,675,753	14,549,109	105,444	23,330,306	37.19	62.36	0.45	37.36
1984 MAtl	6,710,719	8,334,906	78,522	15,124,147	44.37	55.11	0.52	44.60
1984 BdrS	2,221,087	2,997,642	29,195	5,247,924	42.32	57.12	0.56	42.56
1984 MidW	10,510,922	14,760,880	169,277	25,441,079	41.31	58.02	0.67	41.59
1984 West	7,021,755	10,659,229	214,786	17,895,770	39.24	59.56	1.20	39.71
1988 NEng	2,826,162	2,835,636	68,458	5,730,256	49.32	49.49	1.19	49.92
1988 South	9,504,679	13,560,887	188,010	23,253,576	40.87	58.32	0.81	41.21
1988 MAtl	6,971,825	7,264,789	134,764	14,371,378	48.51	50.55	0.94	48.97
1988 BdrS	2,390,518	2,626,470	37,111	5,054,099	47.30	51.97	0.73	47.65
1988 MidW	11,555,606	12,914,860	192,623	24,663,089	46.85	52.37	0.78	47.22
1988 West	8,560,284	9,683,455	278,672	18,522,411	46.22	52.28	1.50	46.92
1992 NEng	2,820,331	2,012,073	1,518,248	6,350,652	44.41	31.68	23.91	58.36
1992 South	11,341,338	11,731,404	4,482,996	27,555,738	41.16	42.57	16.27	49.15
1992 MAtl	7,245,874	5,597,668	2,676,522	15,520,064	46.69	36.07	17.25	56.42
1992 BdrS	2,650,361	2,179,873	949,405	5,779,639	45.86	37.72	16.43	54.87
1992 MidW	11,691,537	10,234,058	5,809,575	27,735,170	42.15	36.90	20.95	53.32
1992 West	9,159,885	7,348,806	4,975,060	21,483,751	42.64	34.21	23.16	55.49
1996 NEng	3,237,449	1,769,161	696,594	5,703,204	56.77	31.02	12.21	64.66
1996 South	12,133,935	12,109,706	2,045,538	26,289,179	46.16	46.06	7.78	50.05
1996 MAtl	7,764,680	4,936,801	1,467,657	14,169,138	54.80	34.84	10.36	61.13
1996 BdrS	2,576,958	2,138,413	483,105	5,198,476	49.57	41.14	9.29	54.65
1996 MidW	12,076,303	10,151,279	2,725,830	24,953,412	48.40	40.68	10.92	54.33
1996 West	9,613,032	8,093,395	2,258,036	19,964,463	48.15	40.54	11.31	54.29

Notes: Entries for the major parties (Democratic, Republican, or their historical antecedents listed in Appendix A) are votes gained by those candidates that historical records show are the primary candidates of the two major parties, except in 1836 when the three Whig candidates are tallied for the total Whig vote. When aggregating state votes for the national result, any states reporting only partial data for the presidential race are deleted. Democratic = Anti-Federalists (1788–1796), Democratic-Republicans (1796–1828), Jacksonian Democrats (1824–1828), and Democrats (since 1832). Republicans = Federalists (1788–1816), National Republicans (1828–1832), Whigs (1836–1852), and Republicans (since 1856). Other = other third parties. J.Q. Adams is considered a Republican in this table in the 1824 election. — indicates that the state had no data, either because no vote data were found for the state in question or the state had not yet entered the Union.

[1]The regional categorizations are adapted from the ICPSR regional codings. In the current analysis, Tennessee is categorized in the South, since it was part of the Confederacy, although the ICPSR treats it as a Border South state. The regional categories are: New England (NEng)—Connecticut, Maine, Massachusetts, New Hampshire, Rhode Island, Vermont; Mid-Atlantic (MAtl)—Delaware, New Jersey, New York, Pennsylvania; South—Alabama, Arkansas, Florida, Georgia, Louisiana, Mississippi, North Carolina, South Carolina, Tennessee, Texas, Virginia; Border South (BdrS)— Kentucky, Maryland, Oklahoma, West Virginia; Midwest (MidW)—Illinois, Indiana, Iowa, Kansas, Michigan, Minnesota, Missouri, Nebraska, North Dakota, Ohio, South Dakota, Wisconsin; West—Alaska, Arizona, California, Colorado, Hawaii, Idaho, Montana, Nevada, New Mexico, Oregon, Utah, Washington, Wyoming.

Sources: Adapted from the election archive of Michael J. Dubin, *Congressional Quarterly's Guide to U.S. Elections* (1994), ICPSR data sets 0001 and 0019, *A Statistical History of the American Presidential Elections* (1963), *America at the Polls* (1965), *America Votes* (various publication dates), and independent search of state sources by the author. For the state vote data used from these sources to get the regional values in this table, see Tables 4-37 through 4-63.

Table 4-6 Popular Vote for President, by Non-South and South, 1788–1996

Year/Region[1]	Regional Raw Vote			Total Vote	Regional % of Raw Vote			Democratic % of Two-Party Vote
	Democratic	Republican	Other		Democratic	Republican	Other	
1788 N-S	2,280	28,242	0	30,522	7.47	92.53	0.00	7.47
1788 S	—	—	—	—	—	—	—	—
1792 N-S	0	8,924	0	8,924	0.00	100.00	0.00	0.00
1792 S	—	—	—	—	—	—	—	—
1796 N-S	18,956	37,532	15,438	71,926	26.35	52.18	21.46	33.56
1796 S	—	—	—	—	—	—	—	—
1800 N-S	12,974	12,167	0	25,141	51.60	48.40	0.00	51.60
1800 S	21,002	6,178	0	27,180	77.27	22.73	0.00	77.27
1804 N-S	84,916	38,259	0	123,175	68.94	31.06	0.00	68.94
1804 S	12,879	0	0	12,879	100.00	0.00	0.00	100.00
1808 N-S	95,423	53,644	0	149,067	64.01	35.99	0.00	64.01
1808 S	15,682	758	3,504	19,944	78.63	3.80	17.57	95.39
1812 N-S	115,016	114,758	0	229,774	50.06	49.94	0.00	50.06
1812 S	14,980	5,573	0	20,553	72.88	27.12	0.00	72.88
1816 N-S	58,288	16,971	17,589	92,848	62.78	18.28	18.94	77.45
1816 S	16,408	640	0	17,048	96.25	3.75	0.00	96.25
1820 N-S	73,897	16,727	3,147	93,771	78.81	17.84	3.36	81.54
1820 S	8,547	0	0	8,547	100.00	0.00	0.00	100.00
1824 N-S	95,318	105,411	74,402	275,131	34.64	38.31	27.04	47.49
1824 S	55,953	7,711	27,038	90,702	61.69	8.50	29.81	87.89
1828 N-S	486,126	464,486	4,549	955,161	50.89	48.63	0.48	51.14
1828 S	156,427	36,411	19	192,857	81.11	18.88	0.01	81.12
1832 N-S	569,504	464,450	107,985	1,141,939	49.87	40.67	9.46	55.08
1832 S	132,276	19,755	3	152,034	87.01	12.99	0.00	87.01
1836 N-S	620,884	599,354	1,228	1,221,466	50.83	49.07	0.10	50.88
1836 S	143,292	138,770	6	282,068	50.80	49.20	0.00	50.80
1840 N-S	905,694	1,021,167	7,564	1,934,425	46.82	52.79	0.39	47.00
1840 S	223,160	254,223	0	477,383	46.75	53.25	0.00	46.75
1844 N-S	1,058,889	1,045,925	64,159	2,168,973	48.82	48.22	2.96	50.31
1844 S	280,605	254,079	2	534,686	52.48	47.52	0.00	52.48
1848 N-S	940,897	1,068,353	294,252	2,303,502	40.85	46.38	12.77	46.83
1848 S	282,563	293,040	79	575,682	49.08	50.90	0.01	49.09
1852 N-S	1,292,662	1,148,412	159,653	2,600,727	49.70	44.16	6.14	52.95
1852 S	314,848	238,530	7,725	561,103	56.11	42.51	1.38	56.90
1856 N-S	1,406,839	1,342,345	568,016	3,317,200	42.41	40.47	17.12	51.17
1856 S	429,233	0	308,214	737,447	58.21	0.00	41.79	100.00
1860 N-S	1,308,282	1,864,021	656,797	3,829,100	34.17	48.68	17.15	41.24
1860 S	71,920	1,887	782,654	856,461	8.40	0.22	91.38	97.44
1864 N-S	1,812,807	2,218,388	692	4,031,887	44.96	55.02	0.02	44.97
1864 S	—	—	—	—	—	—	—	—
1868 N-S	2,277,888	2,608,631	40	4,886,559	46.62	53.38	0.00	46.62
1868 S	430,856	405,019	6	835,881	51.55	48.45	0.00	51.55
1872 N-S	2,175,754	2,838,349	33,759	5,047,862	43.10	56.23	0.67	43.39
1872 S	659,007	759,886	924	1,419,817	46.41	53.52	0.07	46.45
1876 N-S	3,195,063	3,294,287	89,985	6,579,335	48.56	50.07	1.37	49.24
1876 S	1,093,483	740,024	259	1,833,766	59.63	40.36	0.01	59.64
1880 N-S	3,371,797	3,781,204	267,896	7,420,897	45.44	50.95	3.61	47.14
1880 S	1,072,463	664,954	52,106	1,789,523	59.93	37.16	2.91	61.73
1884 N-S	3,727,248	4,070,836	307,380	8,105,464	45.98	50.22	3.79	47.80
1884 S	1,147,373	778,100	18,817	1,944,290	59.01	40.02	0.97	59.59
1888 N-S	4,263,961	4,672,679	345,671	9,282,311	45.94	50.34	3.72	47.71
1888 S	1,270,527	771,213	59,269	2,101,009	60.47	36.71	2.82	62.23
1892 N-S	4,313,145	4,647,911	968,772	9,929,828	43.44	46.81	9.76	48.13
1892 S	1,238,738	531,333	356,198	2,126,269	58.26	24.99	16.75	69.98
1896 N-S	5,078,530	6,305,355	271,402	11,655,287	43.57	54.10	2.33	44.61
1896 S	1,432,965	803,125	44,361	2,280,451	62.84	35.22	1.95	64.08
1900 N-S	5,200,977	6,549,498	338,699	12,089,174	43.02	54.18	2.80	44.26
1900 S	1,157,368	668,541	55,387	1,881,296	61.52	35.54	2.94	63.39
1904 N-S	4,170,763	7,226,696	743,595	12,141,054	34.35	59.52	6.12	36.59
1904 S	912,135	399,897	65,878	1,377,910	66.20	29.02	4.78	69.52
1908 N-S	5,383,649	7,173,697	738,415	13,295,761	40.49	53.95	5.55	42.87
1908 S	1,023,152	502,561	61,260	1,586,973	64.47	31.67	3.86	67.06
1912 N-S	5,260,239	3,294,340	4,943,235	13,497,814	38.97	24.41	36.62	61.49
1912 S	1,032,913	191,993	318,243	1,543,149	66.94	12.44	20.62	84.33
1916 N-S	7,798,175	8,080,578	783,350	16,662,103	46.80	48.50	4.70	49.11
1916 S	1,328,125	466,211	78,583	1,872,919	70.91	24.89	4.20	74.02
1920 N-S	7,511,634	15,211,359	1,373,206	24,096,199	31.17	63.13	5.70	33.06
1920 S	1,621,458	941,756	109,200	2,672,414	60.67	35.24	4.09	63.26
1924 N-S	6,694,104	15,015,588	4,857,992	26,567,684	25.20	56.52	18.29	30.83
1924 S	1,692,600	704,333	130,406	2,527,339	66.97	27.87	5.16	70.62
1928 N-S	13,249,387	19,825,816	352,936	33,428,139	39.64	59.31	1.06	40.06
1928 S	1,758,311	1,611,461	8,040	3,377,812	52.05	47.71	0.24	52.18
1932 N-S	19,770,277	15,060,549	1,140,188	35,971,014	54.96	41.87	3.17	56.76
1932 S	3,059,224	700,135	28,386	3,787,745	80.77	18.48	0.75	81.38
1936 N-S	24,384,718	15,885,383	1,200,672	41,470,773	58.80	38.31	2.90	60.55
1936 S	3,372,615	798,848	12,527	4,183,990	80.61	19.09	0.30	80.85

(Table continues)

Table 4-6 (Continued)

Year/Region[1]	Regional Raw Vote				Regional % of Raw Vote			Democratic % of
	Democratic	Republican	Other	Total Vote	Democratic	Republican	Other	Two-Party Vote
1940 N-S	23,590,535	21,322,510	229,924	45,142,969	52.26	47.23	0.51	52.52
1940 S	3,722,506	1,025,970	8,973	4,757,449	78.25	21.57	0.19	78.39
1944 N-S	22,216,390	20,822,299	196,288	43,234,977	51.39	48.16	0.45	51.62
1944 S	3,396,220	1,195,318	150,155	4,741,693	71.62	25.21	3.17	73.97
1948 N-S	21,548,408	20,608,322	1,421,732	43,578,462	49.45	47.29	3.26	51.11
1948 S	2,630,937	1,382,969	1,201,458	5,215,364	50.45	26.52	23.04	65.55
1952 N-S	22,886,829	29,822,709	287,669	52,997,207	43.18	56.27	0.54	43.42
1952 S	4,428,163	4,113,525	12,023	8,553,711	51.77	48.09	0.14	51.84
1956 N-S	21,904,015	31,372,004	127,666	53,403,685	41.02	58.75	0.24	41.11
1956 S	4,118,737	4,218,468	286,018	8,623,223	47.76	48.92	3.32	49.40
1960 N-S	29,041,981	29,384,793	139,555	58,566,329	49.59	50.17	0.24	49.71
1960 S	5,184,750	4,723,364	363,776	10,271,890	50.48	45.98	3.54	52.33
1964 N-S	37,032,555	21,184,804	114,948	58,332,307	63.49	36.32	0.20	63.61
1964 S	6,097,011	5,993,384	221,890	12,312,285	49.52	48.68	1.80	50.43
1968 N-S	26,696,843	26,662,823	5,048,493	58,408,159	45.71	45.65	8.64	50.03
1968 S	4,578,323	5,122,657	5,102,736	14,803,716	30.93	34.60	34.47	47.19
1972 N-S	24,705,000	36,428,968	1,149,592	62,283,560	39.67	58.49	1.85	40.41
1972 S	4,465,383	10,740,943	228,668	15,434,994	28.93	69.59	1.48	29.37
1976 N-S	30,914,640	30,956,322	1,341,833	63,212,795	48.91	48.97	2.12	49.97
1976 S	9,916,123	8,191,471	235,500	18,343,094	54.06	44.66	1.28	54.76
1980 N-S	26,278,778	33,266,802	6,290,106	65,835,686	39.92	50.53	9.55	44.13
1980 S	9,205,105	10,637,351	837,079	20,679,535	44.51	51.44	4.05	46.39
1984 N-S	28,901,432	39,905,966	515,138	69,322,536	41.69	57.57	0.74	42.00
1984 S	8,675,753	14,549,109	105,444	23,330,306	37.19	62.36	0.45	37.36
1988 N-S	32,304,395	35,325,210	711,628	68,341,233	47.27	51.69	1.04	47.77
1988 S	9,504,679	13,560,887	188,010	23,253,576	40.87	58.32	0.81	41.21
1992 N-S	33,567,988	27,372,478	15,928,810	76,869,276	43.67	35.61	20.72	55.08
1992 S	11,341,338	11,731,404	4,482,996	27,555,738	41.16	42.57	16.27	49.15
1996 N-S	35,268,422	27,089,049	7,631,222	69,988,693	50.39	38.70	10.90	56.56
1996 S	12,133,935	12,109,706	2,045,538	26,289,179	46.16	46.06	7.78	50.05

Notes: Entries for the major parties (Democratic, Republican, or their historical antecedents listed in Appendix A) are votes gained by those candidates that historical records show are the primary candidates of the two major parties, except in 1836 when the three Whig candidates are tallied for the total Whig vote. When aggregating state votes for the national result, any states reporting only partial data for the presidential race are deleted. Democratic = Anti-Federalists (1788–1796), Democratic-Republicans (1796–1828), Jacksonian Democrats (1824–1828), and Democrats (since 1832). Republicans = Federalists (1788–1816), National Republicans (1828–1832), Whigs (1836–1852), and Republicans (since 1856). Other = other third parties. J.Q. Adams is considered a Republican in this table in the 1824 election. — indicates that the state had no data, either because no vote data were found for the state in question or the state had not yet entered the Union.

[1]The regional categorization follows that of the ICPSR except that in the current analysis Tennessee is categorized in the South since it was part of the Confederacy, whereas the ICPSR codes it as a Border South state. Thus the South (S) includes Alabama, Arkansas, Florida, Georgia, Louisiana, Mississippi, North Carolina, South Carolina, Tennessee, Texas, and Virginia. All other states make up the Non-South (N-S).

Sources: Adapted from the election archive of Michael J. Dubin, *Congressional Quarterly's Guide to U.S. Elections* (1994), ICPSR data sets 0001 and 0019, *A Statistical History of the American Presidential Elections* (1963), *America at the Polls* (1965), *America Votes* (various publication dates), and independent search of state sources by the author. For the state vote data used from these sources to get the regional values in this table, see Tables 4-37 through 4-63.

Table 4-7 Electoral Vote for President, by Non-South and South, 1856–1996

	Nation				Non-South				South			
Year	Dem.	Rep.	Dem. %	Rep.%	Dem.	Rep.	Dem.%	Rep. %	Dem.	Rep.	Dem. %	Rep. %
1856	174	114	60.42	39.58	86	114	43.00	57.00	88	0	100.00	0.00
1860	12	180	6.25	93.75	12	180	6.25	93.75	0	0	0.00	0.00
1864	21	212	9.01	90.89	21	212	9.01	90.89	—	—	—	—
1868	80	214	27.21	72.79	64	173	27.00	73.00	16	41	28.07	71.93
1872	63	286	18.05	81.95	43	247	14.83	85.17	20	39	33.90	66.10
1876	184	185	49.86	50.14	108	166	39.42	60.58	76	19	80.00	20.00
1880	155	214	42.00	58.00	60	214	21.90	78.10	95	0	100.00	0.00
1884	219	182	54.61	45.39	112	182	38.10	61.90	107	0	100.00	0.00
1888	168	233	41.90	58.10	61	233	20.75	79.25	107	0	100.00	0.00
1892	277	145	65.64	34.36	165	145	53.22	46.77	112	0	100.00	0.00
1896	176	271	39.37	60.63	64	271	19.10	80.90	112	0	100.00	0.00
1900	155	292	34.68	65.32	43	292	87.16	12.84	112	0	100.00	0.00
1904	140	336	29.41	70.59	20	336	5.62	94.38	120	0	100.00	0.00
1908	162	321	11.57	88.43	42	321	11.57	88.43	120	0	100.00	0.00
1912	435	8	98.19	1.81	309	8	97.48	2.52	126	0	100.00	0.00
1916	277	254	52.17	47.83	151	254	37.28	62.72	126	0	100.00	0.00
1920	127	404	23.92	76.08	13	392	3.21	96.79	114	12	90.48	9.52
1924	136	382	26.25	73.75	10	382	2.55	97.45	126	0	100.00	0.00
1928	87	444	16.38	83.62	23	382	5.68	94.32	64	62	50.79	49.21
1932	472	59	88.89	11.11	348	59	85.50	14.50	124	0	100.00	0.00
1936	523	8	98.49	1.51	399	8	98.03	1.96	124	0	100.00	0.00
1940	449	82	84.56	15.44	325	82	79.85	20.15	124	0	100.00	0.00
1944	432	99	81.36	18.64	305	99	75.50	24.50	127	0	100.00	0.00
1948	303	189	61.59	38.41	215	189	53.22	46.78	88	0	100.00	0.00
1952	89	442	16.76	83.24	18	385	4.47	95.53	71	57	55.47	44.53
1956	73	457	13.77	86.23	13	390	3.23	96.77	60	67	47.24	52.76
1960	303	219	58.05	41.95	222	186	54.41	45.59	81	33	71.05	28.95
1964	486	52	90.33	9.67	395	15	96.34	3.66	91	37	71.09	28.91
1968	191	301	38.82	61.18	154	256	37.56	62.44	37	45	45.12	54.88
1972	17	520	3.17	96.83	17	391	4.17	95.83	0	129	0.00	100.00
1976	297	240	55.31	44.70	179	228	43.98	56.10	118	12	90.77	9.23
1980	49	489	9.11	90.89	37	371	9.07	90.93	12	118	9.23	90.77
1984	13	525	2.41	97.58	13	387	3.25	96.75	0	138	0.00	100.00
1988	111	426	20.67	79.33	111	288	27.82	72.18	0	138	0.00	100.00
1992	370	168	68.77	31.23	331	68	82.96	17.04	39	100	28.06	71.94
1996	379	159	70.45	29.55	339	52	86.70	13.30	40	107	27.21	72.79

Notes: Excludes any third-party votes. The South includes Alabama, Arkansas, Florida, Georgia, Louisiana, Mississippi, North Carolina, South Carolina, Tennessee, Texas, and Virginia. This follows the regional categorization from the ICPSR except that in the current analysis Tennessee is considered a southern state since it was a part of the Confederacy whereas the ICPSR categorizes it as a Border South state. Dem. = Democratic; Rep. = Republican. — indicates that no state in that particular region had voting data for that election year (that is, by 1864 all southern states had seceded from the Union and, therefore, did not vote for president). J.Q. Adams is considered a Republican in this table in the 1824 election.

Sources: Adapted from *Congressional Quarterly's Guide to U.S. Elections,* 3rd ed. (1994); corrected and updated by the author.

Table 4-8 Party Winning Presidential Election, by State in Regions, 1788–1996

State[2]	1788–1820[1] D	R	O	1824–1852 D	R	O	1856–1892 D	R	O	1896–1928 D	R	O	1932–1964 D	R	O	1968–1996 D	R	O
New England																		
Connecticut	1	8	0	2	6	0	4	6	0	1	8	0	5	4	0	3	5	0
Maine	1	0	0	5	3	0	0	10	0	1	8	0	1	8	0	3	5	0
Massachusetts	2	7	0	0	7	1	0	10	0	2	7	0	7	2	0	6	2	0
New Hampshire	3	6	0	5	3	0	0	10	0	2	7	0	4	5	0	2	6	0
Rhode Island	3	5	0	3	5	0	0	10	0	2	7	0	7	2	0	6	2	0
Vermont	6	3	0	7	1	0	0	10	0	0	9	0	1	8	0	2	6	0
Mid-Atlantic																		
Delaware	1	8	0	1	6	1	8	1	1	1	8	0	5	4	0	3	5	0
New Jersey	4	5	0	3	5	0	8	2	0	1	8	0	6	3	0	2	6	0
New York	5	3	0	5	3	0	4	6	0	1	8	0	6	3	0	5	3	0
Pennsylvania	7	2	0	6	2	0	1	9	0	0	8	1	5	4	0	4	4	0
South																		
Alabama	1	0	0	8	0	0	6	2	1	9	0	0	7	1	1	1	6	1
Arkansas	—	—	—	5	0	0	6	1	1	9	0	0	9	0	0	3	4	1
Florida	—	—	—	1	1	0	5	3	1	8	1	0	6	3	0	2	6	0
Georgia	7	2	0	5	2	1	7	0	2	9	0	0	8	1	0	3	4	1
Louisiana	3	0	0	6	2	0	6	1	1	9	0	0	6	2	1	3	4	1
Mississippi	1	0	0	7	1	0	6	1	1	9	0	0	6	1	2	1	6	1
North Carolina	7	1	0	5	3	0	6	2	1	8	1	0	9	0	0	1	7	0
South Carolina	7	2	0	6	1	1	5	3	1	9	0	0	7	1	1	1	7	0
Tennessee	7	0	0	3	4	1	7	1	1	7	2	0	6	3	0	3	5	0
Texas	—	—	—	2	0	0	7	0	1	8	1	0	7	2	0	2	6	0
Virginia	8	2	0	7	0	1	6	1	1	8	1	0	6	3	0	0	8	0
Border South																		
Dist. of Columbia[3]	—	—	—	—	—	—	—	—	—	—	—	—	1	0	0	8	0	0
Kentucky	7	1	0	1	6	1	9	0	1	6	3	0	7	2	0	3	5	0
Maryland	6	3	0	2	6	0	7	1	2	3	6	0	6	3	0	5	3	0
Oklahoma	—	—	—	—	—	—	—	—	—	4	2	0	6	3	0	0	8	0
West Virginia	—	—	—	—	—	—	5	3	0	1	8	0	8	1	0	6	2	0
Midwest																		
Illinois	1	0	0	8	0	0	2	8	0	1	8	0	7	2	0	2	6	0
Indiana	2	0	0	6	2	0	4	6	0	1	8	0	3	6	0	0	8	0
Iowa	—	—	—	1	1	0	0	10	0	1	8	0	4	5	0	3	5	0
Kansas	—	—	—	—	—	—	0	7	1	3	6	0	3	6	0	0	8	0
Michigan	—	—	—	4	1	0	0	10	0	0	8	1	5	4	0	6	2	0
Minnesota	—	—	—	—	—	—	0	9	0	0	8	1	7	2	0	7	1	0
Missouri	1	—	—	7	0	1	8	2	0	4	5	0	8	1	0	3	5	0
Nebraska	—	—	—	—	—	—	0	7	0	4	5	0	3	6	0	0	8	0
North Dakota	—	—	—	—	—	—	—	—	1	2	7	0	3	6	0	0	8	0
Ohio	5	0	0	4	3	1	0	10	0	2	7	0	5	4	0	3	5	0
South Dakota	—	—	—	—	—	—	0	1	0	1	7	1	3	6	0	0	8	0
Wisconsin	—	—	—	2	0	0	1	9	0	1	7	1	5	4	0	4	4	0
West																		
Alaska	—	—	—	—	—	—	—	—	—	—	—	—	1	1	0	0	8	0
Arizona	—	—	—	—	—	—	—	—	—	2	3	0	5	4	0	1	7	0
California	—	—	—	1	0	0	3	7	0	1	7	1	6	3	0	2	6	0
Colorado	—	—	—	—	—	—	0	5	1	5	4	0	4	5	0	1	7	0
Hawaii	—	—	—	—	—	—	—	—	—	—	—	—	2	0	0	6	2	0
Idaho	—	—	—	—	—	—	—	—	1	4	5	0	6	3	0	0	8	0
Montana	—	—	—	—	—	—	0	1	0	4	5	0	6	3	0	1	7	0
Nevada	—	—	—	—	—	—	1	6	1	5	4	0	7	2	0	2	6	0
New Mexico	—	—	—	—	—	—	—	—	—	2	3	0	7	2	0	2	6	0
Oregon	—	—	—	—	—	—	2	8	0	1	8	0	5	4	0	3	5	0
Utah	—	—	—	—	—	—	—	—	—	2	7	0	6	3	0	0	8	0
Washington	—	—	—	—	—	—	0	1	0	2	6	1	6	3	0	4	4	0
Wyoming	—	—	—	—	—	—	0	1	0	3	6	0	5	4	0	0	8	0
Total[4]	113 (65%)	61 (35%)	0 (0%)	136 (62%)	79 (36%)	3 (1%)	118 (37%)	189 (59%)	15 (5%)	170 (40%)	244 (58%)	7 (2%)	274 (62%)	158 (36%)	5 (1%)	128 (31%)	275 (67%)	5 (1%)

Notes: States with split electoral votes are assigned to the Democratic or Republican winner column depending on which party received the most electoral votes in those states. D = Anti-Federalists (1788–1796), Democratic-Republicans (1796–1828), Jacksonian Democrats (1824–1828), and Democrats (since 1832). R = Federalists (1788–1816), National Republicans (1828–1832), Whigs (1836–1852), and Republicans (since 1856). Other = other third parties. J.Q. Adams in 1824 is considered a Republican. Southern Democrats in 1860 are counted as Democratic in this particular table. — indicates that the state had no data, either because no vote data were found for the state in question or the state had not yet entered the Union.

[1]This first period has been extended to the election of 1820, even though the Democratic-Republican Party had no (Federalist) opposition in this particular presidential election.

[2]The regional categorizations are adapted from the ICPSR, except that in the current analysis Tennessee is categorized in the South because it was a member state of the Confederacy while the ICPSR categorizes it as a Border South state.

[3]Residents of the District of Columbia received the presidential vote beginning in the 1964 election.

[4]Fewer total votes for a given state within a given era indicate admission of the state into the Union during this period or nonvoting in certain southern states in 1864, 1868, and 1872.

Sources: Adapted from Lyn Ragsdale, *Vital Statistics on the Presidency,* rev. ed. (Washington D.C.: CQ Press, 1998), pp. 109–110.

Table 4-9 Vote Shifts Needed to Change Presidential
Election Outcome

Year	Number of States	Vote Shift	% of Total Vote Accomplish Shift	Outcome
1828	5	12,779	1.110	Adams (NR)
1840	4	8,184	0.340	Van Buren (D)
1844	1	2,554	0.097	Clay (W)
1848	3	3,229	0.011	Cass (D)
1856	3	20,625	0.510	House of Rep.
1860	1	25,069	0.540	House of Rep.
1864	7	37,040	0.920	McClellan (D)
1868	7	29,697	0.520	Seymour (D)
1876	1	462	0.001	Tilden (D)
1880	1	10,518	0.110	Hancock (D)
1884	1	525	0.006	Blaine (D)
1888	1	7,188	0.070	Cleveland (D)
1892	5	36,965	0.310	Harrison (R)
1896	6	18,562	0.130	Bryan (D)
1900	7	73,539	0.530	Bryan (D)
1908	8	75,032	0.500	Bryan (D)
1916	1	1,983	0.010	Hughes (D)
1948	3	29,296	0.060	Dewey (R)
1960	5	11,876	0.001	Nixon (R)
1968	3	86,072	0.120	House of Rep.
1976	2	9,246	0.010	Ford (R)

Notes: NR = National Republican; D= Democrat; W = Whig; and R = Republican. Table denotes the number of votes in a specific number of states that would have been needed to change the electoral college results, producing a different winner or a race decided by the House of Representatives. The specific states are: 1828—Indiana, Kentucky, Louisiana, New York, Ohio; 1840—Maine, New Jersey, New York, Pennsylvania; 1844—New York; 1848—Georgia, Maryland, Delaware; 1856—Delaware, Illinois, Indiana; 1860—New York; 1864—Connecticut, Indiana, Maryland, New York, Pennsylvania, Oregon, Wisconsin; 1868—Alabama, California, Connecticut, Nevada, North Carolina, Pennsylvania; 1876—Florida; 1880—New York; 1884—New York; 1888—New York; 1892—California, Indiana, New Jersey, New York; Wisconsin; 1896—California, Delaware, Indiana, Kentucky, Oregon, West Virginia; 1900: Indiana, Kansas, Maryland, Nebraska, Ohio, Utah, Wyoming; 1908—Delaware, Indiana, Kansas, Maryland, Missouri, Montana, Ohio, West Virginia; 1916—California; 1948—California, Illinois, Ohio; 1960—Hawaii, Illinois, Missouri, Nevada, New Mexico; 1968—Missouri, New Jersey, Ohio; 1976—Hawaii, Ohio.

Sources: Tables 4-37 through 4-63 as conceived by Svend Petersen, *A Statistical History of the American Presidential Elections.* New York: Frederick Unger, 1963.

Table 4-10 Presidential Election Results, by State, 1788–1792 (Percentages)

State	1788				1792			
	Democratic	Republican	Other	Democratic % of Two-Party Vote	Democratic	Republican	Other	Democratic % of Two-Party Vote
Alabama	—	—	—	—	—	—	—	—
Alaska	—	—	—	—	—	—	—	—
Arizona	—	—	—	—	—	—	—	—
Arkansas	—	—	—	—	—	—	—	—
California	—	—	—	—	—	—	—	—
Colorado	—	—	—	—	—	—	—	—
Connecticut	—	—	—	—	—	—	—	—
Delaware	0.0[1]	0.0[1]	100.0[1]	—	—	—	—	—
Dist. of Columbia	—	—	—	—	—	—	—	—
Florida	—	—	—	—	—	—	—	—
Georgia	—	—	—	—	—	—	—	—
Hawaii	—	—	—	—	—	—	—	—
Idaho	—	—	—	—	—	—	—	—
Illinois	—	—	—	—	—	—	—	—
Indiana	—	—	—	—	—	—	—	—
Iowa	—	—	—	—	—	—	—	—
Kansas	—	—	—	—	—	—	—	—
Kentucky	—	—	—	—	—	—	—	—
Louisiana	—	—	—	—	—	—	—	—
Maine	—	—	—	—	—	—	—	—
Maryland	22.9	77.1	0.0	22.9	—	—	—	—
Massachusetts	0.0	100.0	0.0	0.0	0.0[1]	100.0[1]	0.0[1]	0.0[1]
Michigan	—	—	—	—	—	—	—	—
Minnesota	—	—	—	—	—	—	—	—
Mississippi	—	—	—	—	—	—	—	—
Missouri	—	—	—	—	—	—	—	—
Montana	—	—	—	—	—	—	—	—
Nebraska	—	—	—	—	—	—	—	—
Nevada	—	—	—	—	—	—	—	—
New Hampshire	0.0	100.0	0.0	0.0	0.0	100.0	0.0	0.0
New Jersey	—	—	—	—	—	—	—	—
New Mexico	—	—	—	—	—	—	—	—
New York	—	—	—	—	—	—	—	—
North Carolina	—	—	—	—	—	—	—	—
North Dakota	—	—	—	—	—	—	—	—
Ohio	—	—	—	—	—	—	—	—
Oklahoma	—	—	—	—	—	—	—	—
Oregon	—	—	—	—	—	—	—	—
Pennsylvania	9.1[1]	90.9[1]	0.0[1]	9.1[1]	0.0[1]	72.7[1]	27.3[1]	0.01[1]
Rhode Island	—	—	—	—	—	—	—	—
South Carolina	—	—	—	—	—	—	—	—
South Dakota	—	—	—	—	—	—	—	—
Tennessee	—	—	—	—	—	—	—	—
Texas	—	—	—	—	—	—	—	—
Utah	—	—	—	—	—	—	—	—
Vermont	—	—	—	—	—	—	—	—
Virginia	0.0[1]	0.0[1]	100.0[1]	—	—	—	—	—
Washington	—	—	—	—	—	—	—	—
West Virginia	—	—	—	—	—	—	—	—
Wisconsin	—	—	—	—	—	—	—	—
Wyoming	—	—	—	—	—	—	—	—

Notes: Entries for the major parties (Democratic, Republican, or their historical antecedents listed in Appendix A) are votes gained by those candidates that historical records show are the primary candidates of the two major parties, except in 1836 when the three Whig candidates are tallied for the total Whig vote. Democratic = Anti-Federalists (1788–1796), Democratic-Republicans (1796–1828), Jacksonian Democrats (1824–1828), and Democrats (since 1832). Republicans = Federalists (1788–1816), National Republicans (1828–1832), Whigs (1836–1852), and Republicans (since 1856). Other = other third parties. — indicates that the state had no data, either because no vote data were found for the state in question or the state had not yet entered the Union. Residents of the District of Columbia received the presidential vote beginning in the 1964 election.

[1]Partial data.

Sources: From the election archive collection of Michael J. Dubin.

Table 4-11 Presidential Election Results, by State, 1796–1800 (Percentages)

State	1796				1800			
	Democratic	Republican	Other	Democratic % of Two-Party Vote	Democratic	Republican	Other	Democratic % of Two-Party Vote
Alabama	—	—	—	—	—	—	—	—
Alaska	—	—	—	—	—	—	—	—
Arizona	—	—	—	—	—	—	—	—
Arkansas	—	—	—	—	—	—	—	—
California	—	—	—	—	—	—	—	—
Colorado	—	—	—	—	—	—	—	—
Connecticut	—	—	—	—	—	—	—	—
Delaware	—	—	—	—	—	—	—	—
Dist. of Columbia	—	—	—	—	—	—	—	—
Florida	—	—	—	—	—	—	—	—
Georgia	69.4[1]	29.8[1]	0.8[1]	70.0[1]	—	—	—	—
Hawaii	—	—	—	—	—	—	—	—
Idaho	—	—	—	—	—	—	—	—
Illinois	—	—	—	—	—	—	—	—
Indiana	—	—	—	—	—	—	—	—
Iowa	—	—	—	—	—	—	—	—
Kansas	—	—	—	—	—	—	—	—
Kentucky	—	—	—	—	—	—	—	—
Louisiana	—	—	—	—	—	—	—	—
Maine	—	—	—	—	—	—	—	—
Maryland	47.8	52.2	0.0	47.8	51.5	48.5	0.0	51.5
Massachusetts	0.0	0.0	100.0	—	—	—	—	—
Michigan	—	—	—	—	—	—	—	—
Minnesota	—	—	—	—	—	—	—	—
Mississippi	—	—	—	—	—	—	—	—
Missouri	—	—	—	—	—	—	—	—
Montana	—	—	—	—	—	—	—	—
Nebraska	—	—	—	—	—	—	—	—
Nevada	—	—	—	—	—	—	—	—
New Hampshire	0.0	100.0	0.0	0.0	—	—	—	—
New Jersey	—	—	—	—	—	—	—	—
New Mexico	—	—	—	—	—	—	—	—
New York	—	—	—	—	—	—	—	—
North Carolina	—	—	—	—	49.8[1]	50.2[1]	0.0[1]	49.8[1]
North Dakota	—	—	—	—	—	—	—	—
Ohio	—	—	—	—	—	—	—	—
Oklahoma	—	—	—	—	—	—	—	—
Oregon	—	—	—	—	—	—	—	—
Pennsylvania	50.6	49.4	0.0	50.6	—	—	—	—
Rhode Island	—	—	—	—	52.2	47.8	0.0	52.2
South Carolina	—	—	—	—	—	—	—	—
South Dakota	—	—	—	—	—	—	—	—
Tennessee	—	—	—	—	—	—	—	—
Texas	—	—	—	—	—	—	—	—
Utah	—	—	—	—	—	—	—	—
Vermont	—	—	—	—	—	—	—	—
Virginia	—	—	—	—	77.3	22.7	0.0	77.3
Washington	—	—	—	—	—	—	—	—
West Virginia	—	—	—	—	—	—	—	—
Wisconsin	—	—	—	—	—	—	—	—
Wyoming	—	—	—	—	—	—	—	—

Notes: Entries for the major parties (Democratic, Republican, or their historical antecedents listed in Appendix A) are votes gained by those candidates that historical records show are the primary candidates of the two major parties, except in 1836 when the three Whig candidates are tallied for the total Whig vote. Democratic = Anti-Federalists (1788–1796), Democratic-Republicans (1796–1828), Jacksonian Democrats (1824–1828), and Democrats (since 1832). Republicans = Federalists (1788–1816), National Republicans (1828–1832), Whigs (1836–1852), and Republicans (since 1856). Other = other third parties. — indicates that the state had no data, either because no vote data were found for the state in question or the state had not yet entered the Union. Residents of the District of Columbia received the presidential vote beginning in the 1964 election.

[1]Partial data.

Sources: From the election archive collection of Michael J. Dubin.

Table 4-12 Presidential Election Results, by State, 1804–1808 (Percentages)

State	1804				1808			
	Democratic	Republican	Other	Democratic % of Two-Party Vote	Democratic	Republican	Other	Democratic % of Two-Party Vote
Alabama	—	—	—	—	—	—	—	—
Alaska	—	—	—	—	—	—	—	—
Arizona	—	—	—	—	—	—	—	—
Arkansas	—	—	—	—	—	—	—	—
California	—	—	—	—	—	—	—	—
Colorado	—	—	—	—	—	—	—	—
Connecticut	—	—	—	—	—	—	—	—
Delaware	—	—	—	—	—	—	—	—
Dist. of Columbia	—	—	—	—	—	—	—	—
Florida	—	—	—	—	—	—	—	—
Georgia	—	—	—	—	—	—	—	—
Hawaii	—	—	—	—	—	—	—	—
Idaho	—	—	—	—	—	—	—	—
Illinois	—	—	—	—	—	—	—	—
Indiana	—	—	—	—	—	—	—	—
Iowa	—	—	—	—	—	—	—	—
Kansas	—	—	—	—	—	—	—	—
Kentucky	100.0[1]	0.0[1]	0.0[1]	100.0[1]	98.0[1]	2.0[1]	0.0[1]	98.0[1]
Louisiana	—	—	—	—	—	—	—	—
Maine	—	—	—	—	—	—	—	—
Maryland	74.8	25.2	0.0	74.8	63.4	36.6	0.0	63.4
Massachusetts	53.3	46.7	0.0	53.3	—	—	—	—
Michigan	—	—	—	—	—	—	—	—
Minnesota	—	—	—	—	—	—	—	—
Mississippi	—	—	—	—	—	—	—	—
Missouri	—	—	—	—	—	—	—	—
Montana	—	—	—	—	—	—	—	—
Nebraska	—	—	—	—	—	—	—	—
Nevada	—	—	—	—	—	—	—	—
New Hampshire	52.1	47.9	0.0	52.1	47.6	52.4	0.0	47.6
New Jersey	100.0	0.0	0.0	100.0	55.7	44.3	0.0	55.7
New Mexico	—	—	—	—	—	—	—	—
New York	—	—	—	—	—	—	—	—
North Carolina	71.0[1]	29.0[1]	0.0[1]	71.0[1]	52.1[1]	41.8[1]	6.1[1]	55.5[1]
North Dakota	—	—	—	—	—	—	—	—
Ohio	87.3	12.7	0.0	87.3	75.6	24.4	0.0	75.6
Oklahoma	—	—	—	—	—	—	—	—
Oregon	—	—	—	—	—	—	—	—
Pennsylvania	94.7	5.3	0.0	94.7	78.4	21.6	0.0	78.4
Rhode Island	100.0	0.0	0.0	100.0	45.9	54.1	0.0	45.9
South Carolina	—	—	—	—	—	—	—	—
South Dakota	—	—	—	—	—	—	—	—
Tennessee	—	—	—	—	—	—	—	—
Texas	—	—	—	—	—	—	—	—
Utah	—	—	—	—	—	—	—	—
Vermont	—	—	—	—	—	—	—	—
Virginia	100.0	0.0	0.0	100.0	78.6	3.8	17.6	95.4
Washington	—	—	—	—	—	—	—	—
West Virginia	—	—	—	—	—	—	—	—
Wisconsin	—	—	—	—	—	—	—	—
Wyoming	—	—	—	—	—	—	—	—

Notes: Entries for the major parties (Democratic, Republican, or their historical antecedents listed in Appendix A) are votes gained by those candidates that historical records show are the primary candidates of the two major parties, except in 1836 when the three Whig candidates are tallied for the total Whig vote. Democratic = Anti-Federalists (1788–1796), Democratic-Republicans (1796–1828), Jacksonian Democrats (1824–1828), and Democrats (since 1832). Republicans = Federalists (1788–1816), National Republicans (1828–1832), Whigs (1836–1852), and Republicans (since 1856). Other = other third parties. — indicates that the state had no data, either because no vote data were found for the state in question or the state had not yet entered the Union. Residents of the District of Columbia received the presidential vote beginning in the 1964 election.

[1] Partial data.

Sources: From the election archive collection of Michael J. Dubin.

Table 4-13 Presidential Election Results, by State, 1812–1816 (Percentages)

| | 1812 | | | | 1816 | | | |
State	Democratic	Republican	Other	Democratic % of Two-Party Vote	Democratic	Republican	Other	Democratic % of Two-Party Vote
Alabama	—	—	—	—	—	—	—	—
Alaska	—	—	—	—	—	—	—	—
Arizona	—	—	—	—	—	—	—	—
Arkansas	—	—	—	—	—	—	—	—
California	—	—	—	—	—	—	—	—
Colorado	—	—	—	—	—	—	—	—
Connecticut	—	—	—	—	—	—	—	—
Delaware	—	—	—	—	—	—	—	—
Dist. of Columbia	—	—	—	—	—	—	—	—
Florida	—	—	—	—	—	—	—	—
Georgia	—	—	—	—	—	—	—	—
Hawaii	—	—	—	—	—	—	—	—
Idaho	—	—	—	—	—	—	—	—
Illinois	—	—	—	—	—	—	—	—
Indiana	—	—	—	—	—	—	—	—
Iowa	—	—	—	—	—	—	—	—
Kansas	—	—	—	—	—	—	—	—
Kentucky	98.3[1]	1.7[1]	0.0[1]	98.3[1]	—	—	—	—
Louisiana	—	—	—	—	—	—	—	—
Maine	—	—	—	—	—	—	—	—
Maryland	50.8	49.2	0.0	50.8	70.9	29.1	0.0	70.9
Massachusetts	36.6	63.4	0.0	36.6	—	—	—	—
Michigan	—	—	—	—	—	—	—	—
Minnesota	—	—	—	—	—	—	—	—
Mississippi	—	—	—	—	—	—	—	—
Missouri	—	—	—	—	—	—	—	—
Montana	—	—	—	—	—	—	—	—
Nebraska	—	—	—	—	—	—	—	—
Nevada	—	—	—	—	—	—	—	—
New Hampshire	47.6	52.4	0.0	47.6	53.3	46.7	0.0	53.3
New Jersey	—	—	—	—	100.0	0.0	0.0	100.0
New Mexico	—	—	—	—	—	—	—	—
New York	—	—	—	—	—	—	—	—
North Carolina	—	—	—	—	93.7	6.3	0.0	93.7
North Dakota	—	—	—	—	—	—	—	—
Ohio	69.2	30.8	0.0	69.2	84.9	15.1	0.0	84.9
Oklahoma	—	—	—	—	—	—	—	—
Oregon	—	—	—	—	—	—	—	—
Pennsylvania	62.6	37.4	0.0	62.6	59.3	0.0	40.7	100.0
Rhode Island	34.1	65.9	0.0	34.1	100.0	0.0	0.0	100.0
South Carolina	—	—	—	—	—	—	—	—
South Dakota	—	—	—	—	—	—	—	—
Tennessee	—	—	—	—	—	—	—	—
Texas	—	—	—	—	—	—	—	—
Utah	—	—	—	—	—	—	—	—
Vermont	—	—	—	—	—	—	—	—
Virginia	72.9	27.1	0.0	72.9	100.0	0.0	0.0	100.0
Washington	—	—	—	—	—	—	—	—
West Virginia	—	—	—	—	—	—	—	—
Wisconsin	—	—	—	—	—	—	—	—
Wyoming	—	—	—	—	—	—	—	—

Notes: Entries for the major parties (Democratic, Republican, or their historical antecedents listed in Appendix A) are votes gained by those candidates that historical records show are the primary candidates of the two major parties, except in 1836 when the three Whig candidates are tallied for the total Whig vote. Democratic = Anti-Federalists (1788–1796), Democratic-Republicans (1796–1828), Jacksonian Democrats (1824–1828), and Democrats (since 1832). Republicans = Federalists (1788–1816), National Republicans (1828–1832), Whigs (1836–1852), and Republicans (since 1856). Other = other third parties. — indicates that the state had no data, either because no vote data were found for the state in question or the state had not yet entered the Union. Residents of the District of Columbia received the presidential vote beginning in the 1964 election.

[1] Partial data.

Sources: From the election archive collection of Michael J. Dubin.

Table 4-14 Presidential Election Results, by State, 1820–1824 (Percentages)

State	1820				1824			
	Democratic	Republican	Other	Democratic % of Two-Party Vote	Democratic	Republican	Other	Democratic % of Two-Party Vote
Alabama	—	—	—	—	69.3	17.8	12.9	79.6
Alaska	—	—	—	—	—	—	—	—
Arizona	—	—	—	—	—	—	—	—
Arkansas	—	—	—	—	—	—	—	—
California	—	—	—	—	—	—	—	—
Colorado	—	—	—	—	—	—	—	—
Connecticut	100.0	0.0	0.0	100.0	0.0	70.4	29.6	0.0
Delaware	—	—	—	—	—	—	—	—
Dist. of Columbia	—	—	—	—	—	—	—	—
Florida	—	—	—	—	—	—	—	—
Georgia	—	—	—	—	—	—	—	—
Hawaii	—	—	—	—	—	—	—	—
Idaho	—	—	—	—	—	—	—	—
Illinois	65.6	0.0	34.4	100.0	27.2	32.5	40.3	45.6
Indiana	—	—	—	—	47.0	19.4	33.6	70.8
Iowa	—	—	—	—	—	—	—	—
Kansas	—	—	—	—	—	—	—	—
Kentucky	100.0[1]	0.0[1]	0.0[1]	100.0[1]	27.2	0.0	72.8	100.0
Louisiana	—	—	—	—	—	—	—	—
Maine	89.2	0.0	10.8	100.0	0.0	81.5	18.5	0.0
Maryland	89.0	7.6	3.4	92.2	43.7	44.1	12.2	49.8
Massachusetts	32.0	68.0	0.0	32.0	0.0	73.0	27.0	0.0
Michigan	—	—	—	—	—	—	—	—
Minnesota	—	—	—	—	—	—	—	—
Mississippi	—	—	—	—	63.8	33.8	2.4	65.4
Missouri	—	—	—	—	34.0	4.6	61.4	88.0
Montana	—	—	—	—	—	—	—	—
Nebraska	—	—	—	—	—	—	—	—
Nevada	—	—	—	—	—	—	—	—
New Hampshire	100.0	0.0	0.0	100.0	0.0	93.6	6.4	0.0
New Jersey	100.0	0.0	0.0	100.0	52.1	41.9	6.0	55.4
New Mexico	—	—	—	—	—	—	—	—
New York	—	—	—	—	—	—	—	—
North Carolina	100.0	0.0	0.0	100.0	56.0	0.0	44.0	100.0
North Dakota	—	—	—	—	—	—	—	—
Ohio	100.0	0.0	0.0	100.0	37.0	24.5	38.5	60.1
Oklahoma	—	—	—	—	—	—	—	—
Oregon	—	—	—	—	—	—	—	—
Pennsylvania	94.1	0.0	5.9	100.0	75.9	11.6	12.5	86.8
Rhode Island	100.0	0.0	0.0	100.0	0.0	91.5	8.5	0.0
South Carolina	—	—	—	—	—	—	—	—
South Dakota	—	—	—	—	—	—	—	—
Tennessee	—	—	—	—	97.5	1.0	1.5	98.9
Texas	—	—	—	—	—	—	—	—
Utah	—	—	—	—	—	—	—	—
Vermont	—	—	—	—	—	—	—	—
Virginia	100.0	0.0	0.0	100.0	19.4	22.2	58.4	46.5
Washington	—	—	—	—	—	—	—	—
West Virginia	—	—	—	—	—	—	—	—
Wisconsin	—	—	—	—	—	—	—	—
Wyoming	—	—	—	—	—	—	—	—

Notes: Entries for the major parties (Democratic, Republican, or their historical antecedents listed in Appendix A) are votes gained by those candidates that historical records show are the primary candidates of the two major parties, except in 1836 when the three Whig candidates are tallied for the total Whig vote. Democratic = Anti-Federalists (1788–1796), Democratic-Republicans (1796–1828), Jacksonian Democrats (1824–1828), and Democrats (since 1832). Republicans = Federalists (1788–1816), National Republicans (1828–1832), Whigs (1836–1852), and Republicans (since 1856). Other = other third parties. — indicates that the state had no data, either because no vote data were found for the state in question or the state had not yet entered the Union. Residents of the District of Columbia received the presidential vote beginning in the 1964 election. J.Q. Adams is considered a Republican in this table in the 1824 election.

[1] Partial data.

Sources: From the election archive collection of Michael J. Dubin, *Congressional Quarterly's Guide to U.S. Elections* (1994), ICPSR data sets 0001 and 0019, *A Statistical History of the American Presidential Elections* (1963), and independent search of state sources by the author.

Table 4-15 Presidential Election Results, by State, 1828–1832 (Percentages)

State	1828				1832			
	Democratic	Republican	Other	Democratic % of Two-Party Vote	Democratic	Republican	Other	Democratic % of Two-Party Vote
Alabama	89.9	10.1	0.0	89.9	100.0	0.0	0.0	100.0
Alaska	—	—	—	—	—	—	—	—
Arizona	—	—	—	—	—	—	—	—
Arkansas	—	—	—	—	—	—	—	—
California	—	—	—	—	—	—	—	—
Colorado	—	—	—	—	—	—	—	—
Connecticut	23.0	71.4	5.7	24.3	34.3	55.3	10.4	38.3
Delaware	—	—	—	—	49.0	51.0	0.0	49.0
Dist. of Columbia	—	—	—	—	—	—	—	—
Florida	—	—	—	—	—	—	—	—
Georgia	96.8	3.2	0.0	96.8	100.0	0.0	0.0	100.0
Hawaii	—	—	—	—	—	—	—	—
Idaho	—	—	—	—	—	—	—	—
Illinois	67.2	32.8	0.0	67.2	68.0	31.4	0.6	68.4
Indiana	56.6	43.4	0.0	56.6	55.4	44.6	0.0	55.4
Iowa	—	—	—	—	—	—	—	—
Kansas	—	—	—	—	—	—	—	—
Kentucky	55.5	44.5	0.0	55.5	45.5	54.5	0.0	45.5
Louisiana	53.0	47.0	0.0	53.0	61.7	38.3	0.0	61.7
Maine	40.0	59.7	0.3	40.1	54.7	44.0	1.4	55.4
Maryland	49.7	50.3	0.0	49.7	50.0	50.0	0.0	50.0
Massachusetts	15.4	76.4	8.3	16.8	20.6	47.3	32.1	30.4
Michigan	—	—	—	—	—	—	—	—
Minnesota	—	—	—	—	—	—	—	—
Mississippi	81.1	18.9	0.0	81.1	100.0	0.0	0.0	100.0
Missouri	70.6	29.4	0.0	70.6	100.0	0.0	0.0	100.0
Montana	—	—	—	—	—	—	—	—
Nebraska	—	—	—	—	—	—	—	—
Nevada	—	—	—	—	—	—	—	—
New Hampshire	45.9	54.1	0.0	45.9	56.8	43.2	0.0	56.8
New Jersey	47.9	52.1	0.0	47.9	49.9	49.1	1.0	50.4
New Mexico	—	—	—	—	—	—	—	—
New York	51.4	48.6	0.0	51.4	52.1	47.9	0.0	52.1
North Carolina	73.1	26.9	0.0	73.1	84.8	15.2	0.0	84.8
North Dakota	—	—	—	—	—	—	—	—
Ohio	51.6	48.4	0.0	51.6	51.3	48.4	0.3	51.5
Oklahoma	—	—	—	—	—	—	—	—
Oregon	—	—	—	—	—	—	—	—
Pennsylvania	66.7	33.3	0.0	66.7	57.7	0.0	42.3	100.0
Rhode Island	22.9	77.0	0.1	22.9	35.7	50.0	14.4	41.7
South Carolina	—	—	—	—	—	—	—	—
South Dakota	—	—	—	—	—	—	—	—
Tennessee	95.2	4.8	0.0	95.2	95.4	4.6	0.0	95.4
Texas	—	—	—	—	—	—	—	—
Utah	—	—	—	—	—	—	—	—
Vermont	25.4	74.2	0.4	25.5	24.3	34.5	41.2	41.3
Virginia	69.0	31.0	0.0	69.0	75.0	25.0	0.0	75.0
Washington	—	—	—	—	—	—	—	—
West Virginia	—	—	—	—	—	—	—	—
Wisconsin	—	—	—	—	—	—	—	—
Wyoming	—	—	—	—	—	—	—	—

Notes: Entries for the major parties (Democratic, Republican, or their historical antecedents listed in Appendix A) are votes gained by those candidates that historical records show are the primary candidates of the two major parties, except in 1836 when the three Whig candidates are tallied for the total Whig vote. Democratic = Anti-Federalists (1788–1796), Democratic-Republicans (1796–1828), Jacksonian Democrats (1824–1828), and Democrats (since 1832). Republicans = Federalists (1788–1816), National Republicans (1828–1832), Whigs (1836–1852), and Republicans (since 1856). Other = other third parties. — indicates that the state had no data, either because no vote data were found for the state in question or the state had not yet entered the Union. Residents of the District of Columbia received the presidential vote beginning in the 1964 election.

Sources: *Congressional Quarterly's Guide to U.S. Elections* (1994), ICPSR data sets 0001 and 0019, *A Statistical History of the American Presidential Elections* (1963), and independent search of state sources by the author.

Table 4-16 Presidential Election Results, by State, 1836–1840 (Percentages)

State	1836				1840			
	Democratic	Republican	Other	Democratic % of Two-Party Vote	Democratic	Republican	Other	Democratic % of Two-Party Vote
Alabama	55.3	44.7	0.0	55.3	54.4	45.6	0.0	54.4
Alaska	—	—	—	—	—	—	—	—
Arizona	—	—	—	—	—	—	—	—
Arkansas	64.1	35.9	0.0	64.1	56.4	43.6	0.0	56.4
California	—	—	—	—	—	—	—	—
Colorado	—	—	—	—	—	—	—	—
Connecticut	50.6	49.4	0.0	50.6	44.4	55.6	0.0	44.4
Delaware	46.7	53.2	0.1	46.7	44.9	55.0	0.1	44.9
Dist. of Columbia	—	—	—	—	—	—	—	—
Florida	—	—	—	—	—	—	—	—
Georgia	48.2	51.8	0.0	48.2	44.2	55.8	0.0	44.2
Hawaii	—	—	—	—	—	—	—	—
Idaho	—	—	—	—	—	—	—	—
Illinois	54.7	45.3	0.0	54.7	50.9	48.9	0.2	51.0
Indiana	44.5	55.5	0.0	44.5	44.0	55.5	0.5	44.2
Iowa	—	—	—	—	—	—	—	—
Kansas	—	—	—	—	—	—	—	—
Kentucky	47.4	52.6	0.0	47.4	35.8	64.2	0.0	35.8
Louisiana	51.7	48.3	0.0	51.7	40.3	59.7	0.0	40.3
Maine	58.9	38.2	2.9	60.7	49.8	50.2	0.0	49.8
Maryland	46.3	53.7	0.0	46.3	46.2	53.8	0.0	46.2
Massachusetts	44.8	55.1	0.1	44.8	41.3	57.4	1.3	41.8
Michigan	54.0	46.0	0.0	54.0	47.9	52.1	0.0	47.9
Minnesota	—	—	—	—	—	—	—	—
Mississippi	51.3	48.7	0.0	51.3	46.6	53.4	0.0	46.6
Missouri	60.0	40.0	0.0	60.0	56.6	43.4	0.0	56.6
Montana	—	—	—	—	—	—	—	—
Nebraska	—	—	—	—	—	—	—	—
Nevada	—	—	—	—	—	—	—	—
New Hampshire	75.0	25.0	0.0	75.0	54.7	43.9	1.5	55.5
New Jersey	49.5	50.5	0.0	49.5	48.1	51.7	0.1	48.2
New Mexico	—	—	—	—	—	—	—	—
New York	54.6	45.4	0.0	54.6	48.2	51.2	0.6	48.5
North Carolina	53.1	46.9	0.0	53.1	42.3	57.7	0.0	42.3
North Dakota	—	—	—	—	—	—	—	—
Ohio	47.9	52.1	0.0	47.9	45.4	54.3	0.3	45.6
Oklahoma	—	—	—	—	—	—	—	—
Oregon	—	—	—	—	—	—	—	—
Pennsylvania	51.2	48.8	0.0	51.2	49.9	50.1	0.0	49.9
Rhode Island	52.2	47.8	0.0	52.2	37.8	60.4	1.8	38.5
South Carolina	—	—	—	—	—	—	—	—
South Dakota	—	—	—	—	—	—	—	—
Tennessee	42.1	57.9	0.0	42.1	44.3	55.7	0.0	44.3
Texas	—	—	—	—	—	—	—	—
Utah	—	—	—	—	—	—	—	—
Vermont	40.0	59.8	0.2	40.1	35.5	63.9	0.7	35.7
Virginia	56.6	43.3	0.0	56.6	50.6	49.4	0.0	50.6
Washington	—	—	—	—	—	—	—	—
West Virginia	—	—	—	—	—	—	—	—
Wisconsin	—	—	—	—	—	—	—	—
Wyoming	—	—	—	—	—	—	—	—

Notes: Entries for the major parties (Democratic, Republican, or their historical antecedents listed in Appendix A) are votes gained by those candidates that historical records show are the primary candidates of the two major parties, except in 1836 when the three Whig candidates are tallied for the total Whig vote. Democratic = Anti-Federalists (1788–1796), Democratic-Republicans (1796–1828), Jacksonian Democrats (1824–1828), and Democrats (since 1832). Republicans = Federalists (1788–1816), National Republicans (1828–1832), Whigs (1836–1852), and Republicans (since 1856). Other = other third parties. — indicates that the state had no data, either because no vote data were found for the state in question or the state had not yet entered the Union. Residents of the District of Columbia received the presidential vote beginning in the 1964 election.

Sources: *Congressional Quarterly's Guide to U.S. Elections* (1994), ICPSR data sets 0001 and 0019, *A Statistical History of the American Presidential Elections* (1963), and independent search of state sources by the author.

Table 4-17 Presidential Election Results, by State, 1844–1848 (Percentages)

State	1844				1848			
	Democratic	Republican	Other	Democratic % of Two-Party Vote	Democratic	Republican	Other	Democratic % of Two-Party Vote
Alabama	59.0	41.0	0.0	59.0	50.6	49.4	0.0	50.6
Alaska	—	—	—	—	—	—	—	—
Arizona	—	—	—	—	—	—	—	—
Arkansas	63.0	37.0	0.0	63.0	55.1	44.9	0.0	55.1
California	—	—	—	—	—	—	—	—
Colorado	—	—	—	—	—	—	—	—
Connecticut	46.2	50.8	3.0	47.6	43.4	48.6	8.1	47.2
Delaware	48.8	51.2	0.0	48.8	47.5	51.8	0.7	47.9
Dist. of Columbia	—	—	—	—				
Florida	—	—	—	—	42.8	57.2	0.0	42.8
Georgia	51.2	48.8	0.0	51.2	48.5	51.5	0.0	48.5
Hawaii	—	—	—	—	—	—	—	—
Idaho	—	—	—	—	—	—	—	—
Illinois	53.9	42.0	4.0	56.2	44.9	42.4	12.7	51.4
Indiana	50.1	48.4	1.5	50.8	49.0	45.7	5.3	51.7
Iowa	—	—	—	—	50.5	44.6	5.0	53.1
Kansas	—	—	—	—	—	—	—	—
Kentucky	45.9	54.1	0.0	45.9	42.5	57.5	0.0	42.5
Louisiana	51.3	48.7	0.0	51.3	45.4	54.6	0.0	45.4
Maine	53.8	40.5	5.7	57.1	45.9	40.3	13.9	53.3
Maryland	47.6	52.4	0.0	47.6	47.7	52.1	0.2	47.8
Massachusetts	40.2	50.8	9.0	44.2	26.2	45.3	28.5	36.6
Michigan	49.9	43.5	6.5	53.4	47.2	36.8	16.0	56.2
Minnesota	—	—	—	—	—	—	—	—
Mississippi	57.4	42.6	0.0	57.4	50.6	49.4	0.0	50.6
Missouri	57.0	43.0	0.0	57.0	55.1	44.9	0.0	55.1
Montana	—	—	—	—	—	—	—	—
Nebraska	—	—	—	—	—	—	—	—
Nevada	—	—	—	—	—	—	—	—
New Hampshire	55.2	36.3	8.5	60.3	55.4	29.5	15.1	65.3
New Jersey	49.4	50.5	0.2	49.5	47.5	51.5	1.1	48.0
New Mexico	—	—	—	—	—	—	—	—
New York	48.9	47.8	3.3	50.5	25.1	47.9	27.0	34.3
North Carolina	47.6	52.4	0.0	47.6	44.8	55.2	0.0	44.8
North Dakota	—	—	—	—	—	—	—	—
Ohio	47.8	49.7	2.6	49.0	47.0	42.1	10.8	52.7
Oklahoma	—	—	—	—	—	—	—	—
Oregon	—	—	—	—	—	—	—	—
Pennsylvania	50.4	48.6	0.9	50.9	46.7	50.3	3.0	48.1
Rhode Island	39.9	60.0	0.0	39.9	32.7	60.7	6.6	35.0
South Carolina	—	—	—	—	—	—	—	—
South Dakota	—	—	—	—	—	—	—	—
Tennessee	49.9	50.1	0.0	49.9	47.5	52.5	0.0	47.5
Texas	—	—	—	—	68.5	31.1	0.4	68.8
Utah	—	—	—	—	—	—	—	—
Vermont	37.0	54.9	8.1	40.3	22.8	48.3	28.9	32.1
Virginia	53.0	47.0	0.0	53.0	50.8	49.2	0.0	50.8
Washington	—	—	—	—	—	—	—	—
West Virginia	—	—	—	—	—	—	—	—
Wisconsin	—	—	—	—	38.3	35.1	26.6	52.2
Wyoming	—	—	—	—	—	—	—	—

Notes: Entries for the major parties (Democratic, Republican, or their historical antecedents listed in Appendix A) are votes gained by those candidates that historical records show are the primary candidates of the two major parties, except in 1836 when the three Whig candidates are tallied for the total Whig vote. Democratic = Anti-Federalists (1788–1796), Democratic-Republicans (1796–1828), Jacksonian Democrats (1824–1828), and Democrats (since 1832). Republicans = Federalists (1788–1816), National Republicans (1828–1832), Whigs (1836–1852), and Republicans (since 1856). Other = other third parties. — indicates that the state had no data, either because no vote data were found for the state in question or the state had not yet entered the Union. Residents of the District of Columbia received the presidential vote beginning in the 1964 election.

Sources: *Congressional Quarterly's Guide to U.S. Elections* (1994), ICPSR data sets 0001 and 0019, *A Statistical History of the American Presidential Elections* (1963), and independent search of state sources by the author.

Table 4-18 Presidential Election Results, by State, 1852–1856 (Percentages)

State	1852 Democratic	1852 Republican	1852 Other	1852 Democratic % of Two-Party Vote	1856 Democratic	1856 Republican	1856 Other	1856 Democratic % of Two-Party Vote
Alabama	60.9	34.1	5.0	64.1	62.1	0.0	37.9	100.0
Alaska	—	—	—	—				
Arizona	—	—	—	—	—	—	—	—
Arkansas	62.2	37.8	0.0	62.2	67.1	0.0	32.9	100.0
California	53.0	46.8	0.2	53.1	48.4	18.8	32.8	72.0
Colorado	—	—	—	—	—	—	—	—
Connecticut	49.8	45.5	4.8	52.3	43.6	53.2	3.3	45.1
Delaware	49.9	49.7	0.5	50.1	54.8	2.1	43.0	96.3
Dist. of Columbia	—	—	—	—	—	—	—	—
Florida	60.0	40.0	0.0	60.0	56.8	0.0	43.2	100.0
Georgia	64.7	26.6	8.7	70.9	57.1	0.0	42.9	100.0
Hawaii	—	—	—	—	—	—	—	—
Idaho	—	—	—	—	—	—	—	—
Illinois	51.9	41.8	6.4	55.4	44.1	40.2	15.7	52.3
Indiana	52.0	44.2	3.8	54.1	50.4	40.1	9.5	55.7
Iowa	50.2	44.8	4.9	52.8	40.7	48.8	10.5	45.5
Kansas	—	—	—	—	—	—	—	—
Kentucky	48.3	51.4	0.2	48.4	52.5	0.0	47.5	100.0
Louisiana	51.9	48.1	0.0	51.9	51.7	0.0	48.3	100.0
Maine	50.6	39.6	9.8	56.1	35.7	61.3	3.0	36.8
Maryland	53.3	46.7	0.0	53.3	45.0	0.3	54.6	99.3
Massachusetts	35.1	41.4	23.5	45.8	23.1	63.6	13.3	26.6
Michigan	50.4	40.8	8.7	55.3	41.5	57.2	1.3	42.1
Minnesota	—	—	—	—	—	—	—	—
Mississippi	60.5	39.5	0.0	60.5	59.4	0.0	40.6	100.0
Missouri	56.4	43.6	0.0	56.4	54.4	0.0	45.6	100.0
Montana	—	—	—	—	—	—	—	—
Nebraska	—	—	—	—	—	—	—	—
Nevada	—	—	—	—	—	—	—	—
New Hampshire	56.4	30.6	13.0	64.8	45.7	53.7	0.6	46.0
New Jersey	52.8	45.9	1.3	53.5	47.2	28.5	24.3	62.4
New Mexico	—	—	—	—	—	—	—	—
New York	50.2	45.0	4.8	52.7	32.8	46.3	20.9	41.5
North Carolina	50.4	49.5	0.1	50.5	56.8	0.0	43.2	100.0
North Dakota	—	—	—	—	—	—	—	—
Ohio	47.9	43.2	8.8	52.6	44.2	48.5	7.3	47.7
Oklahoma	—	—	—	—	—	—	—	—
Oregon	—	—	—	—	—	—	—	—
Pennsylvania	51.2	46.2	2.6	52.6	50.1	32.1	17.8	60.9
Rhode Island	51.4	44.8	3.8	53.4	33.7	57.8	8.5	36.8
South Carolina	—	—	—	—	—	—	—	—
South Dakota	—	—	—	—	—	—	—	—
Tennessee	49.3	50.7	0.0	49.3	52.2	0.0	47.8	100.0
Texas	73.5	26.5	0.0	73.5	66.6	0.0	33.4	100.0
Utah	—	—	—	—	—	—	—	—
Vermont	29.8	50.6	19.7	37.0	20.9	78.1	1.1	21.1
Virginia	55.7	44.3	0.0	55.7	60.0	0.0	40.0	100.0
Washington	—	—	—	—	—	—	—	—
West Virginia	—	—	—	—	—	—	—	—
Wisconsin	52.0	34.4	13.7	60.2	43.8	55.7	0.5	44.1
Wyoming	—	—	—	—	—	—	—	—

Notes: Entries for the major parties (Democratic, Republican, or their historical antecedents listed in Appendix A) are votes gained by those candidates that historical records show are the primary candidates of the two major parties, except in 1836 when the three Whig candidates are tallied for the total Whig vote. Democratic = Anti-Federalists (1788–1796), Democratic-Republicans (1796–1828), Jacksonian Democrats (1824–1828), and Democrats (since 1832). Republicans = Federalists (1788–1816), National Republicans (1828–1832), Whigs (1836–1852), and Republicans (since 1856). Other = other third parties. — indicates that the state had no data, either because no vote data were found for the state in question or the state had not yet entered the Union. Residents of the District of Columbia received the presidential vote beginning in the 1964 election.

Sources: *Congressional Quarterly's Guide to U.S. Elections* (1994), ICPSR data sets 0001 and 0019, *A Statistical History of the American Presidential Elections* (1963), and independent search of state sources by the author.

Table 4-19 Presidential Election Results, by State, 1860–1864 (Percentages)

	1860				1864			
State	Democratic	Republican	Other	Democratic % of Two-Party Vote	Democratic	Republican	Other	Democratic % of Two-Party Vote
Alabama	15.1	0.0	84.9	100.0	—	—	—	—
Alaska	—	—	—	—	—	—	—	—
Arizona	—	—	—	—	—	—	—	—
Arkansas	9.9	0.0	90.1	100.0	—	—	—	—
California	31.7	32.3	36.0	49.5	41.4	58.6	0.0	41.4
Colorado	—	—	—	—	—	—	—	—
Connecticut	20.6	58.1	21.3	26.2	48.6	51.4	0.0	48.6
Delaware	6.6	23.7	69.7	21.8	51.8	48.2	0.0	51.8
Dist. of Columbia	—	—	—	—	—	—	—	—
Florida	1.7	0.0	98.3	100.0	—	—	—	—
Georgia	10.9	0.0	89.1	100.0	—	—	—	—
Hawaii	—	—	—	—	—	—	—	—
Idaho	—	—	—	—	—	—	—	—
Illinois	47.2	50.7	2.1	48.2	45.6	54.4	0.0	45.6
Indiana	42.4	51.1	6.5	45.4	46.5	53.5	0.0	46.5
Iowa	43.2	54.6	2.2	44.2	36.9	63.1	0.0	36.9
Kansas	—	—	—	—	17.8	79.2	3.0	18.3
Kentucky	17.5	0.9	81.5	95.0	69.8	30.2	0.0	69.8
Louisiana	15.1	0.0	84.9	100.0	—	—	—	—
Maine	29.4	62.2	8.3	32.1	40.9	59.1	0.0	40.9
Maryland	6.4	2.5	91.1	72.2	44.9	55.1	0.0	44.9
Massachusetts	20.2	62.8	17.0	24.4	27.8	72.2	0.0	27.8
Michigan	42.0	57.2	0.8	42.4	44.9	55.1	0.0	44.9
Minnesota	34.2	63.4	2.3	35.1	40.9	59.0	0.1	41.0
Mississippi	4.7	0.0	95.3	100.0	—	—	—	—
Missouri	35.5	10.3	54.2	77.5	30.3	69.7	0.0	30.3
Montana	—	—	—	—	—	—	—	—
Nebraska	—	—	—	—	—	—	—	—
Nevada	—	—	—	—	40.2	59.8	0.0	40.2
New Hampshire	39.3	56.9	3.8	40.8	47.4	52.6	0.0	47.4
New Jersey	51.9	48.1	0.0	51.9	52.8	47.2	0.0	52.8
New Mexico	—	—	—	—	—	—	—	—
New York	46.3	53.7	0.0	46.3	49.5	50.5	0.0	49.5
North Carolina	2.8	0.0	97.2	100.0	—	—	—	—
North Dakota	—	—	—	—	—	—	—	—
Ohio	42.3	52.3	5.4	44.7	43.6	56.4	0.0	43.6
Oklahoma	—	—	—	—	—	—	—	—
Oregon	28.0	36.1	35.9	43.7	46.1	53.9	0.0	46.1
Pennsylvania	3.5	56.3	40.2	5.9	48.4	51.6	0.0	48.4
Rhode Island	38.6	61.4	0.0	38.6	37.8	62.2	0.0	37.8
South Carolina	—	—	—	—	—	—	—	—
South Dakota	—	—	—	—	—	—	—	—
Tennessee	7.7	0.0	92.3	100.0	—	—	—	—
Texas	0.0	0.0	100.0	—	—	—	—	—
Utah	—	—	—	—	—	—	—	—
Vermont	19.4	75.7	4.9	20.4	23.9	76.1	0.0	23.9
Virginia	9.7	1.1	89.2	89.6	—	—	—	—
Washington	—	—	—	—	—	—	—	—
West Virginia	—	—	—	—	31.8	68.2	0.0	31.8
Wisconsin	42.7	56.6	0.7	43.0	44.1	55.9	0.0	44.1
Wyoming	—	—	—	—	—	—	—	—

Notes: Entries for the major parties (Democratic, Republican, or their historical antecedents listed in Appendix A) are votes gained by those candidates that historical records show are the primary candidates of the two major parties, except in 1836 when the three Whig candidates are tallied for the total Whig vote. Democratic = Anti-Federalists (1788–1796), Democratic-Republicans (1796–1828), Jacksonian Democrats (1824–1828), and Democrats (since 1832). Republicans = Federalists (1788–1816), National Republicans (1828–1832), Whigs (1836–1852), and Republicans (since 1856). Other = other third parties. — indicates that the state had no data, either because no vote data were found for the state in question or the state had not yet entered the Union. Residents of the District of Columbia received the presidential vote beginning in the 1964 election. Stephen Douglas is considered the Democrat in this table in the 1860 election.

Sources: *Congressional Quarterly's Guide to U.S. Elections* (1994), ICPSR data sets 0001 and 0019, *A Statistical History of the American Presidential Elections* (1963), and independent search of state sources by the author.

Table 4-20 Presidential Election Results, by State, 1868–1872 (Percentages)

State	1868				1872			
	Democratic	Republican	Other	Democratic % of Two-Party Vote	Democratic	Republican	Other	Democratic % of Two-Party Vote
Alabama	48.7	51.3	0.0	48.7	46.8	53.2	0.0	46.8
Alaska	—	—	—	—	—	—	—	—
Arizona	—	—	—	—	—	—	—	—
Arkansas	46.3	53.7	0.0	46.3	47.8	52.2	0.0	47.8
California	49.8	50.2	0.0	49.8	42.5	56.4	1.1	43.0
Colorado	—	—	—	—	—	—	—	—
Connecticut	48.5	51.5	0.0	48.5	47.6	52.4	0.0	47.6
Delaware	59.0	41.0	0.0	59.0	46.8	51.0	2.2	47.8
Dist. of Columbia	—	—	—	—	—	—	—	—
Florida	—	—	—	—	46.5	53.5	0.0	46.5
Georgia	64.3	35.7	0.0	64.3	55.0	45.0	0.0	55.0
Hawaii	—	—	—	—	—	—	—	—
Idaho	—	—	—	—	—	—	—	—
Illinois	44.3	55.7	0.0	44.3	43.0	56.3	0.7	43.3
Indiana	48.6	51.4	0.0	48.6	46.8	53.2	0.0	46.8
Iowa	38.1	61.9	0.0	38.1	32.9	60.8	6.3	35.1
Kansas	31.2	68.8	0.0	31.2	32.8	66.5	0.7	33.0
Kentucky	74.5	25.5	0.0	74.5	52.3	46.4	1.2	53.0
Louisiana	70.7	29.3	0.0	70.7	44.3	55.7	0.0	44.3
Maine	37.6	62.4	0.0	37.6	32.1	67.9	0.0	32.1
Maryland	67.2	32.8	0.0	67.2	50.3	49.7	0.0	50.3
Massachusetts	30.2	69.8	0.0	30.2	30.7	69.3	0.0	30.7
Michigan	43.0	57.0	0.0	43.0	35.5	62.6	1.9	36.2
Minnesota	39.2	60.8	0.0	39.2	38.5	61.4	0.2	38.5
Mississippi	—	—	—	—	36.5	63.5	0.0	36.5
Missouri	43.0	57.0	0.0	43.0	55.5	43.7	0.9	56.0
Montana	—	—	—	—	—	—	—	—
Nebraska	36.1	63.9	0.0	36.1	29.3	70.7	0.0	29.3
Nevada	44.6	55.4	0.0	44.6	42.6	57.4	0.0	42.6
New Hampshire	44.8	55.2	0.0	44.8	45.6	53.9	0.5	45.8
New Jersey	50.9	49.1	0.0	50.9	45.5	54.5	0.0	45.5
New Mexico	—	—	—	—	—	—	—	—
New York	50.6	49.4	0.0	50.6	46.8	53.2	0.0	46.8
North Carolina	46.6	53.4	0.0	46.6	42.5	57.4	0.2	42.5
North Dakota	—	—	—	—	—	—	—	—
Ohio	46.0	54.0	0.0	46.0	46.1	53.2	0.6	46.4
Oklahoma	—	—	—	—	—	—	—	—
Oregon	50.4	49.6	0.0	50.4	38.5	58.8	2.7	39.6
Pennsylvania	47.8	52.2	0.0	47.8	37.8	62.2	0.0	37.8
Rhode Island	33.3	66.7	0.0	33.3	28.1	71.9	0.0	28.1
South Carolina	42.1	57.9	0.0	42.1	23.8	75.7	0.5	23.9
South Dakota	—	—	—	—	—	—	—	—
Tennessee	31.6	68.4	0.0	31.6	52.2	47.8	0.0	52.2
Texas	—	—	—	—	58.5	41.4	0.1	58.5
Utah	—	—	—	—	—	—	—	—
Vermont	21.4	78.6	0.0	21.4	20.8	79.2	0.0	20.8
Virginia	—	—	—	—	49.5	50.5	0.0	49.5
Washington	—	—	—	—	—	—	—	—
West Virginia	41.2	58.8	0.0	41.2	47.3	51.7	1.0	47.7
Wisconsin	43.7	56.3	0.0	43.7	44.9	54.6	0.4	45.1
Wyoming	—	—	—	—	—	—	—	—

Notes: Entries for the major parties (Democratic, Republican, or their historical antecedents listed in Appendix A) are votes gained by those candidates that historical records show are the primary candidates of the two major parties, except in 1836 when the three Whig candidates are tallied for the total Whig vote. Democratic = Anti-Federalists (1788–1796), Democratic-Republicans (1796–1828), Jacksonian Democrats (1824–1828), and Democrats (since 1832). Republicans = Federalists (1788–1816), National Republicans (1828–1832), Whigs (1836–1852), and Republicans (since 1856). Other = other third parties. — indicates that the state had no data, either because no vote data were found for the state in question or the state had not yet entered the Union. Residents of the District of Columbia received the presidential vote beginning in the 1964 election.

Sources: *Congressional Quarterly's Guide to U.S. Elections* (1994), ICPSR data sets 0001 and 0019, *A Statistical History of the American Presidential Elections* (1963), and independent search of state sources by the author.

Table 4-21 Presidential Election Results, by State, 1876–1880 (Percentages)

State	1876				1880			
	Democratic	Republican	Other	Democratic % of Two-Party Vote	Democratic	Republican	Other	Democratic % of Two-Party Vote
Alabama	60.0	40.0	0.0	60.0	60.0	37.1	2.9	61.8
Alaska	—	—	—	—	—	—	—	—
Arizona	—	—	—	—	—	—	—	—
Arkansas	59.9	39.9	0.2	60.0	56.1	38.7	5.2	59.2
California	49.1	50.9	0.0	49.1	49.0	48.9	2.1	50.0
Colorado	—	—	—	—	46.0	51.3	2.7	47.3
Connecticut	50.7	48.3	1.0	51.2	48.5	50.5	1.0	49.0
Delaware	55.4	44.6	0.0	55.4	51.5	48.0	0.4	51.8
Dist. of Columbia	—	—	—	—	—	—	—	—
Florida	49.0	51.0	0.0	49.0	54.2	45.8	0.0	54.2
Georgia	72.0	28.0	0.0	72.0	65.4	34.6	0.0	65.4
Hawaii	—	—	—	—	—	—	—	—
Idaho	—	—	—	—	—	—	—	—
Illinois	46.6	50.2	3.2	48.2	44.6	51.1	4.3	46.6
Indiana	49.5	48.3	2.2	50.7	47.9	49.3	2.8	49.3
Iowa	38.2	58.4	3.4	39.6	32.8	56.9	10.3	36.5
Kansas	30.5	63.1	6.4	32.6	29.7	60.4	9.8	33.0
Kentucky	61.4	37.4	1.2	62.1	55.7	39.9	4.4	58.3
Louisiana	48.4	51.6	0.0	48.4	62.3	37.3	0.4	62.5
Maine	42.6	56.6	0.7	43.0	45.3	51.5	3.2	46.8
Maryland	56.0	44.0	0.0	56.0	54.4	45.6	0.0	54.4
Massachusetts	41.9	57.8	0.3	42.0	39.6	58.5	1.9	40.4
Michigan	44.5	52.4	3.1	45.9	37.3	52.5	10.2	41.5
Minnesota	39.3	58.8	1.9	40.1	35.4	62.3	2.4	36.2
Mississippi	68.1	31.9	0.0	68.1	64.7	29.8	5.5	68.5
Missouri	57.6	41.4	1.0	58.2	52.5	38.7	8.8	57.6
Montana	—	—	—	—	—	—	—	—
Nebraska	35.2	64.8	0.0	35.2	32.7	62.9	4.4	34.2
Nevada	47.3	52.7	0.0	47.3	52.4	47.6	0.0	52.4
New Hampshire	48.1	51.8	0.1	48.1	47.2	51.9	0.8	47.6
New Jersey	52.7	47.0	0.3	52.8	49.8	49.0	1.1	50.4
New Mexico	—	—	—	—	—	—	—	—
New York	51.4	48.2	0.4	51.6	48.4	50.3	1.3	49.0
North Carolina	53.6	46.4	0.0	53.6	51.5	48.0	0.5	51.8
North Dakota	—	—	—	—	—	—	—	—
Ohio	49.1	50.2	0.7	49.4	47.0	51.7	1.3	47.6
Oklahoma	—	—	—	—	—	—	—	—
Oregon	47.4	50.9	1.7	48.2	48.9	50.5	0.7	49.2
Pennsylvania	48.2	50.6	1.1	48.8	46.6	50.8	2.6	47.8
Rhode Island	40.4	59.6	0.0	40.4	36.9	62.2	0.9	37.2
South Carolina	49.8	50.2	0.0	49.8	65.5	34.1	0.4	65.7
South Dakota	—	—	—	—	—	—	—	—
Tennessee	59.8	40.2	0.0	59.8	53.3	44.3	2.5	54.6
Texas	70.3	29.7	0.0	70.3	66.8	21.5	11.7	75.6
Utah	—	—	—	—	—	—	—	—
Vermont	31.4	68.4	0.2	31.5	28.1	70.0	1.9	28.7
Virginia	59.6	40.4	0.0	59.6	60.5	39.5	0.0	60.5
Washington	—	—	—	—	—	—	—	—
West Virginia	56.7	42.1	1.1	57.4	50.9	41.1	8.0	55.4
Wisconsin	48.2	50.6	1.2	48.8	42.9	54.0	3.0	44.3
Wyoming	—	—	—	—	—	—	—	—

Notes: Entries for the major parties (Democratic, Republican, or their historical antecedents listed in Appendix A) are votes gained by those candidates that historical records show are the primary candidates of the two major parties, except in 1836 when the three Whig candidates are tallied for the total Whig vote. Democratic = Anti-Federalists (1788–1796), Democratic-Republicans (1796–1828), Jacksonian Democrats (1824–1828), and Democrats (since 1832). Republicans = Federalists (1788–1816), National Republicans (1828–1832), Whigs (1836–1852), and Republicans (since 1856). Other = other third parties. — indicates that the state had no data, either because no vote data were found for the state in question or the state had not yet entered the Union. Residents of the District of Columbia received the presidential vote beginning in the 1964 election.

Sources: *Congressional Quarterly's Guide to U.S. Elections* (1994), ICPSR data sets 0001 and 0019, *A Statistical History of the American Presidential Elections* (1963), and independent search of state sources by the author.

Table 4-22 Presidential Election Results, by State, 1884–1888 (Percentages)

State	1884				1888			
	Democratic	Republican	Other	Democratic % of Two-Party Vote	Democratic	Republican	Other	Democratic % of Two-Party Vote
Alabama	60.4	38.7	0.9	60.9	67.0	32.7	0.3	67.2
Alaska	—	—	—	—	—	—	—	—
Arizona	—	—	—	—	—	—	—	—
Arkansas	57.8	40.7	1.5	58.7	54.8	38.0	7.2	59.0
California	45.3	52.0	2.7	46.6	46.8	49.7	3.5	48.5
Colorado	41.7	54.2	4.1	43.4	40.8	55.2	3.9	42.5
Connecticut	48.9	48.0	3.0	50.5	48.7	48.4	2.9	50.1
Delaware	56.6	43.2	0.2	56.7	55.1	43.5	1.3	55.9
Dist. of Columbia	—	—	—	—	—	—	—	—
Florida	53.0	46.7	0.3	53.1	59.5	39.9	0.6	59.9
Georgia	65.9	33.8	0.2	66.1	70.3	28.3	1.4	71.3
Hawaii	—	—	—	—	—	—	—	—
Idaho	—	—	—	—	—	—	—	—
Illinois	46.4	50.2	3.4	48.1	46.6	49.5	3.9	48.5
Indiana	49.8	48.5	1.7	50.7	48.6	49.0	2.4	49.8
Iowa	45.1	50.1	4.9	47.4	44.4	52.3	3.3	45.9
Kansas	35.9	61.5	2.6	36.9	31.0	55.2	13.8	36.0
Kentucky	55.6	43.2	1.2	56.3	53.3	45.0	1.7	54.2
Louisiana	55.3	40.9	3.8	57.5	73.4	26.5	0.2	73.5
Maine	41.0	56.8	2.2	41.9	39.4	57.5	3.2	40.6
Maryland	46.2	40.9	13.0	53.0	50.3	47.4	2.3	51.5
Massachusetts	38.1	45.7	16.2	45.5	44.0	53.4	2.5	45.2
Michigan	41.1	52.9	6.0	43.7	44.9	49.7	5.4	47.5
Minnesota	37.6	59.9	2.5	38.6	39.7	54.1	6.2	42.3
Mississippi	64.3	35.7	0.0	64.3	73.8	26.0	0.2	74.0
Missouri	53.5	46.0	0.5	53.8	50.2	45.3	4.4	52.6
Montana	—	—	—	—	—	—	—	—
Nebraska	40.5	57.3	2.2	41.4	39.8	53.5	6.7	42.6
Nevada	43.6	56.2	0.2	43.7	42.2	57.5	0.3	42.3
New Hampshire	46.3	51.1	2.5	47.5	47.8	50.4	1.8	48.7
New Jersey	49.0	47.3	3.7	50.9	49.9	47.5	2.6	51.2
New Mexico	—	—	—	—	—	—	—	—
New York	48.2	48.2	3.6	50.0	48.2	49.3	2.5	49.4
North Carolina	53.3	46.6	0.2	53.3	51.8	47.2	1.0	52.3
North Dakota	—	—	—	—	—	—	—	—
Ohio	46.9	51.0	2.1	47.9	47.1	49.6	3.3	48.7
Oklahoma	—	—	—	—	—	—	—	—
Oregon	46.7	51.0	2.4	47.8	42.8	53.8	3.4	44.3
Pennsylvania	43.9	52.5	3.6	45.5	44.8	52.7	2.5	45.9
Rhode Island	37.8	58.1	4.1	39.4	43.0	53.9	3.1	44.4
South Carolina	75.3	23.4	1.3	76.3	82.3	17.2	0.5	82.7
South Dakota	—	—	—	—	—	—	—	—
Tennessee	51.5	47.7	0.8	51.9	52.3	45.8	2.0	53.3
Texas	69.5	28.4	2.1	71.0	65.5	25.0	9.5	72.4
Utah	—	—	—	—	—	—	—	—
Vermont	29.2	66.5	4.3	30.5	26.4	71.2	2.4	27.1
Virginia	51.1	48.9	0.0	51.1	50.0	49.5	0.6	50.3
Washington	—	—	—	—	—	—	—	—
West Virginia	50.9	47.7	1.3	51.6	49.3	49.0	1.6	50.2
Wisconsin	45.8	50.4	3.8	47.6	43.8	49.8	6.4	46.8
Wyoming	—	—	—	—	—	—	—	—

Notes: Entries for the major parties (Democratic, Republican, or their historical antecedents listed in Appendix A) are votes gained by those candidates that historical records show are the primary candidates of the two major parties, except in 1836 when the three Whig candidates are tallied for the total Whig vote. Democratic = Anti-Federalists (1788–1796), Democratic-Republicans (1796–1828), Jacksonian Democrats (1824–1828), and Democrats (since 1832). Republicans = Federalists (1788–1816), National Republicans (1828–1832), Whigs (1836–1852), and Republicans (since 1856). Other = other third parties. — indicates that the state had no data, either because no vote data were found for the state in question or the state had not yet entered the Union. Residents of the District of Columbia received the presidential vote beginning in the 1964 election.

Sources: *Congressional Quarterly's Guide to U.S. Elections* (1994), ICPSR data sets 0001 and 0019, *A Statistical History of the American Presidential Elections* (1963), and independent search of state sources by the author.

Table 4-23 Presidential Election Results, by State, 1892–1896 (Percentages)

State	1892				1896			
	Democratic	Republican	Other	Democratic % of Two-Party Vote	Democratic	Republican	Other	Democratic % of Two-Party Vote
Alabama	59.4	3.9	36.6	93.8	67.0	28.6	4.4	70.1
Alaska	—	—	—	—	—	—	—	—
Arizona	—	—	—	—	—	—	—	—
Arkansas	59.3	31.8	8.9	65.1	73.7	25.1	1.2	74.6
California	43.8	43.8	12.4	50.0	48.5	49.1	2.3	49.7
Colorado	0.0	41.1	58.9	0.0	84.9	13.9	1.2	86.0
Connecticut	50.1	46.8	3.1	51.7	32.5	63.2	4.2	34.0
Delaware	49.9	48.5	1.5	50.7	43.1	53.2	3.7	44.8
Dist. of Columbia	—	—	—	—	—	—	—	—
Florida	85.0	0.0	15.0	100.0	70.5	24.3	5.2	74.4
Georgia	58.0	21.7	20.3	72.8	57.8	36.6	5.7	61.3
Hawaii	—	—	—	—	—	—	—	—
Idaho	0.0	44.3	55.7	0.0	78.1	21.3	0.6	78.5
Illinois	48.8	45.7	5.5	51.6	42.7	55.7	1.7	43.4
Indiana	47.5	46.2	6.4	50.7	48.0	50.8	1.2	48.6
Iowa	44.3	49.6	6.1	47.2	42.9	55.5	1.6	43.6
Kansas	0.0	48.3	51.7	0.0	51.5	47.5	1.1	52.0
Kentucky	51.5	39.7	8.8	56.4	48.9	48.9	2.2	50.0
Louisiana	76.5	23.5	0.0	76.5	76.4	21.8	1.8	77.8
Maine	41.3	54.0	4.7	43.3	29.2	67.9	2.9	30.1
Maryland	53.4	43.5	3.1	55.1	41.6	54.7	3.7	43.2
Massachusetts	45.2	51.9	2.9	46.6	26.3	69.5	4.2	27.4
Michigan	43.3	47.7	9.0	47.6	43.5	53.8	2.8	44.7
Minnesota	37.6	45.8	16.6	45.0	40.9	56.6	2.5	41.9
Mississippi	76.2	2.7	21.1	96.6	91.0	6.9	2.0	92.9
Missouri	49.6	42.0	8.4	54.1	54.0	45.2	0.8	54.4
Montana	39.8	42.4	17.8	48.4	79.9	19.7	0.4	80.2
Nebraska	12.5	43.6	44.0	22.2	51.5	46.2	2.3	52.7
Nevada	6.5	26.0	67.5	20.0	81.2	18.8	0.0	81.2
New Hampshire	47.1	51.1	1.8	48.0	25.9	68.7	5.5	27.4
New Jersey	50.7	46.2	3.1	52.3	36.0	59.7	4.3	37.7
New Mexico	—	—	—	—	—	—	—	—
New York	49.0	45.6	5.4	51.8	38.7	57.6	3.7	40.2
North Carolina	47.4	35.8	16.8	57.0	52.6	46.8	0.5	52.9
North Dakota	0.0	48.5	51.5	0.0	43.6	55.6	0.8	44.0
Ohio	47.5	47.7	4.8	49.9	47.1	51.9	1.1	47.6
Oklahoma	—	—	—	—	—	—	—	—
Oregon	18.2	44.7	37.2	28.9	48.0	50.0	1.9	49.0
Pennsylvania	45.1	51.4	3.5	46.7	36.3	61.0	2.7	37.3
Rhode Island	45.7	50.7	3.5	47.4	26.4	68.3	5.3	27.9
South Carolina	77.6	18.9	3.5	80.4	85.3	13.5	1.2	86.3
South Dakota	12.7	49.5	37.8	20.4	49.7	49.5	0.8	50.1
Tennessee	51.4	37.8	10.8	57.6	52.1	46.3	1.6	52.9
Texas	57.7	17.3	25.0	77.0	68.4	30.3	1.3	69.3
Utah	—	—	—	—	82.7	17.3	0.0	82.7
Vermont	29.3	68.1	2.6	30.1	16.3	80.4	3.3	16.9
Virginia	56.2	38.7	5.1	59.2	52.5	45.9	1.6	53.3
Washington	33.9	41.4	24.7	45.0	57.0	41.8	1.2	57.7
West Virginia	49.4	46.9	3.7	51.3	46.8	52.2	0.9	47.3
Wisconsin	47.7	46.1	6.2	50.9	37.0	59.9	3.1	38.2
Wyoming	0.0	50.6	49.4	0.0	51.6	47.8	0.6	51.9

Notes: Entries for the major parties (Democratic, Republican, or their historical antecedents listed in Appendix A) are votes gained by those candidates that historical records show are the primary candidates of the two major parties, except in 1836 when the three Whig candidates are tallied for the total Whig vote. Democratic = Anti-Federalists (1788–1796), Democratic-Republicans (1796–1828), Jacksonian Democrats (1824–1828), and Democrats (since 1832). Republicans = Federalists (1788–1816), National Republicans (1828–1832), Whigs (1836–1852), and Republicans (since 1856). Other = other third parties. — indicates that the state had no data, either because no vote data were found for the state in question or the state had not yet entered the Union. Residents of the District of Columbia received the presidential vote beginning in the 1964 election.

Sources: *Congressional Quarterly's Guide to U.S. Elections* (1994), ICPSR data sets 0001 and 0019, *A Statistical History of the American Presidential Elections* (1963), and independent search of state sources by the author.

Table 4-24 Presidential Election Results, by State, 1900–1904 (Percentages)

State	1900				1904			
	Democratic	Republican	Other	Democratic % of Two-Party Vote	Democratic	Republican	Other	Democratic % of Two-Party Vote
Alabama	60.8	34.8	4.4	63.6	73.4	20.7	6.0	78.0
Alaska	—	—	—	—	—	—	—	—
Arizona	—	—	—	—	—	—	—	—
Arkansas	63.5	35.0	1.5	64.5	55.4	40.2	4.4	57.9
California	41.3	54.5	4.2	43.1	26.9	61.9	11.2	30.3
Colorado	55.5	42.0	2.5	57.0	41.1	55.3	3.7	42.6
Connecticut	41.1	56.9	2.0	41.9	38.1	58.1	3.7	39.6
Delaware	44.9	53.7	1.4	45.6	44.1	54.1	1.8	44.9
Dist. of Columbia	—	—	—	—	—	—	—	—
Florida	71.3	18.6	10.1	79.4	68.3	21.5	10.2	76.1
Georgia	66.9	28.2	4.9	70.3	63.7	18.3	18.0	77.7
Hawaii	—	—	—	—	—	—	—	—
Idaho	50.8	46.9	2.2	52.0	25.5	65.8	8.7	27.9
Illinois	44.4	52.8	2.7	45.7	30.4	58.8	10.8	34.1
Indiana	46.6	50.6	2.8	47.9	40.2	54.0	5.8	42.7
Iowa	39.5	58.0	2.5	40.5	30.7	63.4	5.9	32.6
Kansas	46.0	52.6	1.5	46.6	26.2	64.9	8.9	28.8
Kentucky	50.2	48.5	1.3	50.9	49.8	47.1	3.1	51.4
Louisiana	79.0	21.0	0.0	79.0	88.5	9.7	1.8	90.2
Maine	34.8	61.9	3.3	36.0	28.5	67.4	4.1	29.7
Maryland	46.2	51.5	2.3	47.3	48.8	48.8	2.4	50.0
Massachusetts	37.8	57.6	4.6	39.7	37.2	57.9	4.8	39.1
Michigan	38.9	58.1	3.0	40.1	25.8	69.5	4.7	27.0
Minnesota	35.7	60.2	4.1	37.2	18.8	74.0	7.2	20.3
Mississippi	87.6	9.7	2.8	90.1	91.1	5.6	3.3	94.2
Missouri	51.5	45.9	2.6	52.8	46.0	49.9	4.1	48.0
Montana	58.4	39.8	1.8	59.5	34.3	53.5	12.2	39.1
Nebraska	47.2	50.5	2.3	48.3	23.4	61.4	15.2	27.6
Nevada	62.2	37.8	0.0	62.2	32.9	56.7	10.5	36.7
New Hampshire	38.4	59.3	2.2	39.3	37.8	60.1	2.1	38.6
New Jersey	41.1	55.3	3.6	42.6	38.1	56.7	5.2	40.2
New Mexico	—	—	—	—	—	—	—	—
New York	43.8	53.1	3.1	45.2	42.3	53.1	4.6	44.3
North Carolina	53.9	45.5	0.6	54.3	59.7	39.7	0.6	60.1
North Dakota	35.5	62.1	2.4	36.4	20.4	75.1	4.5	21.3
Ohio	45.7	52.3	2.0	46.6	34.3	59.7	5.9	36.5
Oklahoma	—	—	—	—	—	—	—	—
Oregon	39.4	55.5	5.1	41.5	19.3	67.3	13.4	22.3
Pennsylvania	36.2	60.7	3.1	37.3	27.3	68.0	4.7	28.7
Rhode Island	35.0	59.7	5.2	37.0	36.2	60.6	3.2	37.4
South Carolina	93.0	7.0	0.0	93.0	95.4	4.6	0.0	95.4
South Dakota	41.1	56.7	2.1	42.0	21.7	71.1	7.2	23.4
Tennessee	53.0	45.0	2.0	54.1	54.2	43.4	2.4	55.5
Texas	63.1	30.9	5.9	67.1	71.5	22.0	6.5	76.5
Utah	48.3	50.6	1.1	48.8	32.9	61.4	5.7	34.9
Vermont	22.9	75.7	1.4	23.2	18.8	78.0	3.2	19.5
Virginia	55.3	43.8	0.9	55.8	61.8	36.9	1.2	62.6
Washington	41.7	53.4	4.9	43.8	19.4	70.0	10.7	21.7
West Virginia	44.8	54.3	1.0	45.2	42.0	55.3	2.7	43.2
Wisconsin	36.0	60.1	4.0	37.5	28.0	63.2	8.8	30.7
Wyoming	41.1	58.6	0.3	41.2	29.2	66.9	3.9	30.4

Notes: Entries for the major parties (Democratic, Republican, or their historical antecedents listed in Appendix A) are votes gained by those candidates that historical records show are the primary candidates of the two major parties, except in 1836 when the three Whig candidates are tallied for the total Whig vote. Democratic = Anti-Federalists (1788–1796), Democratic-Republicans (1796–1828), Jacksonian Democrats (1824–1828), and Democrats (since 1832). Republicans = Federalists (1788–1816), National Republicans (1828–1832), Whigs (1836–1852), and Republicans (since 1856). Other = other third parties. — indicates that the state had no data, either because no vote data were found for the state in question or the state had not yet entered the Union. Residents of the District of Columbia received the presidential vote beginning in the 1964 election.

Sources: *Congressional Quarterly's Guide to U.S. Elections* (1994), ICPSR data sets 0001 and 0019, *A Statistical History of the American Presidential Elections* (1963), and independent search of state sources by the author.

Table 4-25 Presidential Election Results, by State, 1908–1912 (Percentages)

State	1908 Democratic	1908 Republican	1908 Other	1908 Democratic % of Two-Party Vote	1912 Democratic	1912 Republican	1912 Other	1912 Democratic % of Two-Party Vote
Alabama	70.7	24.3	4.9	74.4	69.9	8.3	21.8	89.4
Alaska	—	—	—	—	—	—	—	—
Arizona	—	—	—	—	43.6	12.6	43.8	77.6
Arkansas	57.3	37.3	5.4	60.6	55.0	20.5	24.5	72.9
California	33.0	55.5	11.6	37.3	41.8	0.6	57.6	98.7
Colorado	48.0	46.9	5.1	50.6	42.8	22.0	35.2	66.1
Connecticut	35.9	59.4	4.7	37.7	39.2	35.9	25.0	52.2
Delaware	45.9	52.1	2.0	46.9	46.5	32.9	20.7	58.6
Dist. of Columbia	—	—	—	—	—	—	—	—
Florida	63.0	21.6	15.4	74.5	69.5	8.4	22.1	89.2
Georgia	54.6	31.2	14.2	63.6	76.6	4.3	19.1	94.7
Hawaii	—	—	—	—	—	—	—	—
Idaho	37.2	54.1	8.7	40.7	32.1	31.0	36.9	50.8
Illinois	39.0	54.5	6.4	41.7	35.3	22.1	42.5	61.5
Indiana	46.9	48.4	4.7	49.2	43.1	23.1	33.8	65.1
Iowa	40.6	55.6	3.8	42.2	37.6	24.3	38.0	60.7
Kansas	42.9	52.5	4.7	45.0	39.3	20.5	40.2	65.7
Kentucky	49.7	48.0	2.2	50.9	48.5	25.5	26.0	65.5
Louisiana	84.6	11.9	3.4	87.6	76.8	4.8	18.4	94.1
Maine	33.3	63.0	3.7	34.6	39.4	20.5	40.1	65.8
Maryland	48.6	48.8	2.6	49.9	48.6	23.7	27.7	67.2
Massachusetts	34.0	58.2	7.7	36.9	35.5	32.0	32.5	52.7
Michigan	32.4	61.9	5.6	34.4	27.4	27.6	45.0	49.8
Minnesota	33.1	59.3	7.6	35.8	31.8	19.2	48.9	62.3
Mississippi	90.1	6.5	3.4	93.3	88.9	2.4	8.7	97.4
Missouri	48.4	48.5	3.1	50.0	47.3	29.7	22.9	61.4
Montana	42.6	46.9	10.5	47.6	35.0	23.1	41.8	60.2
Nebraska	49.1	47.6	3.3	50.8	43.7	21.7	34.6	66.8
Nevada	45.7	43.9	10.4	51.0	39.7	15.9	44.4	71.4
New Hampshire	37.6	59.3	3.1	38.8	39.5	37.4	23.1	51.3
New Jersey	39.1	56.8	4.1	40.8	41.2	20.5	38.3	66.7
New Mexico	—	—	—	—	41.9	35.2	23.0	54.4
New York	40.7	53.1	6.2	43.4	41.3	28.7	30.0	59.0
North Carolina	54.2	45.5	0.3	54.4	59.2	11.9	28.8	83.2
North Dakota	34.8	61.0	4.2	36.3	34.2	26.6	39.2	56.2
Ohio	44.8	51.0	4.1	46.8	41.0	26.8	32.2	60.4
Oklahoma	48.1	43.4	8.4	52.6	47.0	35.8	17.3	56.8
Oregon	34.2	56.5	9.3	37.7	34.3	25.3	40.4	57.6
Pennsylvania	35.4	58.8	5.8	37.6	32.5	22.4	45.1	59.1
Rhode Island	34.2	60.8	5.1	36.0	39.0	35.6	25.4	52.3
South Carolina	93.8	5.9	0.2	94.0	95.9	1.1	3.0	98.9
South Dakota	35.1	58.8	6.1	37.4	42.1	0.0	57.9	100.0
Tennessee	52.7	45.9	1.4	53.5	52.8	24.0	23.2	68.7
Texas	74.0	22.4	3.6	76.8	72.7	9.4	17.9	88.5
Utah	39.2	56.2	4.6	41.1	32.6	37.4	30.0	46.5
Vermont	21.8	75.1	3.1	22.5	24.4	37.1	38.5	39.7
Virginia	60.5	38.4	1.1	61.2	65.9	17.0	17.1	79.5
Washington	31.8	57.8	10.4	35.5	26.9	21.8	51.3	55.2
West Virginia	43.2	53.4	3.4	44.7	42.1	21.1	36.8	66.6
Wisconsin	36.7	54.5	8.8	40.2	41.1	32.7	26.3	55.7
Wyoming	39.7	55.4	4.9	41.7	36.2	34.4	29.4	51.3

Notes: Entries for the major parties (Democratic, Republican, or their historical antecedents listed in Appendix A) are votes gained by those candidates that historical records show are the primary candidates of the two major parties, except in 1836 when the three Whig candidates are tallied for the total Whig vote. Democratic = Anti-Federalists (1788–1796), Democratic-Republicans (1796–1828), Jacksonian Democrats (1824–1828), and Democrats (since 1832). Republicans = Federalists (1788–1816), National Republicans (1828–1832), Whigs (1836–1852), and Republicans (since 1856). Other = other third parties. — indicates that the state had no data, either because no vote data were found for the state in question or the state had not yet entered the Union. Residents of the District of Columbia received the presidential vote beginning in the 1964 election.

Sources: *Congressional Quarterly's Guide to U.S. Elections* (1994), ICPSR data sets 0001 and 0019, *A Statistical History of the American Presidential Elections* (1963), and independent search of state sources by the author.

Table 4-26 Presidential Election Results, by State, 1916–1920 (Percentages)

	1916				1920			
State	Democratic	Republican	Other	Democratic % of Two-Party Vote	Democratic	Republican	Other	Democratic % of Two-Party Vote
Alabama	76.0	22.0	2.0	77.6	66.7	31.9	1.4	67.6
Alaska	—	—	—	—	—	—	—	—
Arizona	57.2	35.4	7.5	61.8	44.2	55.4	0.4	44.4
Arkansas	66.0	28.7	5.3	69.7	57.9	39.3	2.8	59.5
California	46.6	46.3	7.1	50.2	24.3	66.2	9.5	26.8
Colorado	60.8	34.7	4.5	63.6	35.9	59.3	4.7	37.7
Connecticut	46.7	49.8	3.5	48.4	33.0	62.7	4.3	34.5
Delaware	47.8	50.2	2.0	48.8	42.1	55.7	2.2	43.0
Dist. of Columbia	—	—	—	—	—	—	—	—
Florida	69.3	18.1	12.6	79.3	62.1	30.8	7.1	66.9
Georgia	79.5	7.0	13.5	91.9	71.0	28.7	0.3	71.2
Hawaii	—	—	—	—	—	—	—	—
Idaho	52.0	41.1	6.8	55.9	33.9	66.1	0.0	33.9
Illinois	43.3	52.6	4.1	45.2	25.5	67.8	6.7	27.3
Indiana	46.5	47.4	6.1	49.5	40.5	55.1	4.4	42.3
Iowa	42.7	54.1	3.2	44.2	25.5	70.9	3.6	26.4
Kansas	49.9	44.1	6.0	53.1	32.5	64.8	2.7	33.4
Kentucky	51.9	46.5	1.6	52.7	49.7	49.3	1.1	50.2
Louisiana	85.9	7.0	7.1	92.5	69.2	30.5	0.3	69.4
Maine	47.0	51.0	2.0	48.0	29.8	68.9	1.3	30.2
Maryland	52.8	44.8	2.4	54.1	42.2	55.1	2.7	43.3
Massachusetts	46.6	50.5	2.8	48.0	27.8	68.5	3.6	28.9
Michigan	43.9	52.2	3.9	45.7	22.3	72.8	5.0	23.4
Minnesota	46.2	46.3	7.4	49.9	19.4	70.6	10.0	21.6
Mississippi	92.8	4.9	2.3	95.0	84.0	14.1	2.0	85.7
Missouri	50.6	46.9	2.5	51.9	43.1	54.6	2.3	44.1
Montana	56.8	37.6	5.6	60.2	32.1	61.1	6.8	34.4
Nebraska	55.3	41.0	3.7	57.4	31.3	64.7	4.1	32.6
Nevada	53.4	36.4	10.2	59.4	36.2	56.9	6.9	38.9
New Hampshire	49.1	49.1	1.8	50.0	39.4	59.8	0.8	39.7
New Jersey	42.7	54.4	2.9	44.0	28.4	67.6	4.0	29.6
New Mexico	50.4	46.5	3.1	52.0	44.3	54.7	1.1	44.7
New York	44.5	51.5	4.0	46.3	27.0	64.6	8.5	29.5
North Carolina	58.1	41.7	0.2	58.2	56.7	43.2	0.1	56.7
North Dakota	47.8	46.3	5.8	50.8	18.2	77.8	4.0	18.9
Ohio	51.9	44.2	4.0	54.0	38.6	58.5	2.9	39.8
Oklahoma	50.7	33.3	16.1	60.4	44.5	50.2	5.3	47.0
Oregon	45.9	48.5	5.6	48.6	33.5	60.2	6.3	35.8
Pennsylvania	40.2	54.3	5.5	42.6	27.2	65.8	7.0	29.2
Rhode Island	46.0	51.1	2.9	47.4	32.8	64.0	3.2	33.9
South Carolina	96.7	2.4	0.9	97.6	96.1	3.9	0.0	96.1
South Dakota	45.9	49.8	4.3	48.0	19.7	60.7	19.5	24.5
Tennessee	56.3	42.7	1.0	56.9	48.3	51.2	0.5	48.5
Texas	77.0	17.4	5.6	81.6	59.2	23.6	17.2	71.5
Utah	58.8	37.8	3.4	60.9	38.8	55.9	5.2	41.0
Vermont	35.2	62.4	2.4	36.1	23.3	75.8	0.9	23.5
Virginia	67.0	31.8	1.2	67.8	61.3	37.9	0.8	61.8
Washington	48.1	43.9	8.0	52.3	21.1	56.0	22.9	27.4
West Virginia	48.5	49.4	2.1	49.5	43.3	55.3	1.4	43.9
Wisconsin	42.8	49.4	7.8	46.4	16.2	71.1	12.7	18.5
Wyoming	54.7	41.8	3.5	56.7	31.0	62.4	6.6	33.2

Notes: Entries for the major parties (Democratic, Republican, or their historical antecedents listed in Appendix A) are votes gained by those candidates that historical records show are the primary candidates of the two major parties, except in 1836 when the three Whig candidates are tallied for the total Whig vote. Democratic = Anti-Federalists (1788–1796), Democratic-Republicans (1796–1828), Jacksonian Democrats (1824–1828), and Democrats (since 1832). Republican = Federalists (1788–1816), National Republicans (1828–1832), Whigs (1836–1852), and Republicans (since 1856). Other = other third parties. — indicates that the state had no data, either because no vote data were found for the state in question or the state had not yet entered the Union. Residents of the District of Columbia received the presidential vote beginning in the 1964 election.

Sources: *Congressional Quarterly's Guide to U.S. Elections* (1994), ICPSR data sets 0001 and 0019, *America at the Polls: 1920–1964* (1965); *A Statistical History of the American Presidential Elections* (1963), and independent search of state sources by the author.

Table 4-27 Presidential Election Results, by State, 1924–1928 (Percentages)

	1924				1928			
State	Democratic	Republican	Other	Democratic % of Two-Party Vote	Democratic	Republican	Other	Democratic % of Two-Party Vote
Alabama	68.8	26.0	5.2	72.5	51.3	48.5	0.2	51.4
Alaska	—	—	—	—	—	—	—	—
Arizona	35.5	41.3	23.3	46.2	42.2	57.6	0.2	42.3
Arkansas	61.2	29.3	9.5	67.6	60.3	39.3	0.4	60.5
California	8.2	57.2	34.6	12.6	34.2	64.7	1.1	34.6
Colorado	22.0	57.0	21.0	27.8	33.9	64.7	1.3	34.4
Connecticut	27.5	61.5	11.0	30.9	45.6	53.6	0.8	45.9
Delaware	36.8	57.7	5.5	38.9	33.8	65.8	0.4	33.9
Dist. of Columbia	—	—	—	—	—	—	—	—
Florida	56.9	28.1	15.1	67.0	40.4	57.9	1.8	41.1
Georgia	74.0	18.2	7.8	80.3	56.0	44.0	0.1	56.0
Hawaii	—	—	—	—	—	—	—	—
Idaho	16.2	47.3	36.5	25.5	34.9	64.2	0.9	35.2
Illinois	23.4	58.8	17.8	28.4	42.3	56.9	0.8	42.6
Indiana	38.7	55.3	6.1	41.2	39.6	59.7	0.7	39.9
Iowa	16.4	55.0	28.6	23.0	37.6	61.8	0.7	37.8
Kansas	23.6	61.5	14.9	27.7	27.1	72.0	0.9	27.3
Kentucky	46.2	48.8	5.1	48.6	40.5	59.3	0.1	40.6
Louisiana	76.4	20.2	3.3	79.1	76.3	23.7	0.0	76.3
Maine	21.8	72.0	6.1	23.3	31.0	68.6	0.4	31.1
Maryland	41.3	45.3	13.4	47.7	42.3	57.1	0.6	42.6
Massachusetts	24.9	62.3	12.9	28.5	50.2	49.2	0.6	50.5
Michigan	13.1	75.4	11.5	14.8	28.9	70.4	0.7	29.1
Minnesota	6.8	51.2	42.0	11.7	40.8	57.8	1.4	41.4
Mississippi	89.4	7.6	3.1	92.2	82.2	17.8	0.0	82.2
Missouri	43.9	49.5	6.6	47.0	44.2	55.6	0.3	44.3
Montana	19.4	42.5	38.1	31.3	40.5	58.4	1.1	41.0
Nebraska	29.6	47.2	23.1	38.5	36.2	63.2	0.6	36.4
Nevada	21.9	41.8	36.3	34.5	43.5	56.5	0.0	43.5
New Hampshire	34.7	59.8	5.5	36.7	41.0	58.7	0.3	41.2
New Jersey	27.4	62.2	10.5	30.6	39.8	59.8	0.4	40.0
New Mexico	43.0	48.5	8.5	47.0	40.8	59.0	0.1	40.9
New York	29.1	55.8	15.1	34.3	47.4	49.8	2.8	48.8
North Carolina	59.0	39.6	1.4	59.8	45.1	54.9	0.0	45.1
North Dakota	7.0	47.7	45.4	12.7	44.5	54.8	0.7	44.8
Ohio	23.7	58.3	18.0	28.9	34.5	64.9	0.7	34.7
Oklahoma	48.5	42.8	8.8	53.1	35.4	63.7	0.8	35.7
Oregon	24.2	51.0	24.8	32.2	34.1	64.2	1.7	34.7
Pennsylvania	19.1	65.3	15.6	22.6	33.9	65.2	0.9	34.2
Rhode Island	36.5	59.6	3.9	37.9	50.2	49.5	0.3	50.3
South Carolina	96.6	2.2	1.2	97.8	91.4	8.5	0.1	91.5
South Dakota	13.3	49.7	37.0	21.2	39.2	60.2	0.6	39.4
Tennessee	52.9	43.5	3.6	54.9	44.5	55.3	0.2	44.6
Texas	73.6	19.9	6.5	78.7	48.0	51.9	0.1	48.1
Utah	29.9	49.3	20.8	37.8	45.9	53.6	0.6	46.1
Vermont	15.7	78.2	6.1	16.7	32.9	66.9	0.3	33.0
Virginia	62.5	32.8	4.7	65.6	45.9	53.9	0.2	46.0
Washington	10.2	52.2	37.6	16.3	31.3	67.1	1.6	31.8
West Virginia	44.1	49.5	6.5	47.1	41.0	58.4	0.5	41.3
Wisconsin	8.1	37.1	54.8	17.9	44.3	53.5	2.2	45.3
Wyoming	16.1	52.4	31.5	23.5	35.4	63.7	1.0	35.7

Notes: Entries for the major parties (Democratic, Republican, or their historical antecedents listed in Appendix A) are votes gained by those candidates that historical records show are the primary candidates of the two major parties, except in 1836 when the three Whig candidates are tallied for the total Whig vote. Democratic = Anti-Federalists (1788–1796), Democratic-Republicans (1796–1828), Jacksonian Democrats (1824–1828), and Democrats (since 1832). Republicans = Federalists (1788–1816), National Republicans (1828–1832), Whigs (1836–1852), and Republicans (since 1856). Other = other third parties. — indicates that the state had no data, either because no vote data were found for the state in question or the state had not yet entered the Union. Residents of the District of Columbia received the presidential vote beginning in the 1964 election.

Sources: *Congressional Quarterly's Guide to U.S. Elections* (1994), ICPSR data sets 0001 and 0019, *America at the Polls: 1920–1964* (1965); *A Statistical History of the American Presidential Elections* (1963), and independent search of state sources by the author.

Table 4-28 Presidential Election Results, by State, 1932–1936 (Percentages)

State	1932				1936			
	Democratic	Republican	Other	Democratic % of Two-Party Vote	Democratic	Republican	Other	Democratic % of Two-Party Vote
Alabama	84.8	14.1	1.1	85.7	86.4	12.8	0.8	87.1
Alaska	—	—	—	—	—	—	—	—
Arizona	67.0	30.5	2.4	68.7	69.8	26.9	3.2	72.2
Arkansas	86.3	12.7	1.1	87.2	81.8	17.9	0.3	82.1
California	58.4	37.4	4.2	61.0	67.0	31.7	1.3	67.9
Colorado	54.8	41.4	3.8	57.0	60.4	37.1	2.5	61.9
Connecticut	47.4	48.5	4.1	49.4	55.3	40.3	4.3	57.8
Delaware	48.1	50.6	1.3	48.8	54.6	44.9	0.5	54.9
Dist. of Columbia	—	—	—	—	—	—	—	—
Florida	74.5	25.0	0.5	74.9	76.1	23.9	0.0	76.1
Georgia	91.6	7.8	0.6	92.2	87.1	12.6	0.3	87.4
Hawaii	—	—	—	—	—	—	—	—
Idaho	58.7	38.2	3.1	60.6	63.0	33.2	3.8	65.5
Illinois	55.2	42.0	2.7	56.8	57.7	39.7	2.6	59.2
Indiana	54.7	42.9	2.4	56.0	56.6	41.9	1.5	57.5
Iowa	57.7	40.0	2.3	59.1	54.4	42.7	2.9	56.0
Kansas	53.6	44.1	2.3	54.8	53.7	46.0	0.4	53.9
Kentucky	59.1	40.2	0.8	59.5	58.5	39.9	1.6	59.4
Louisiana	92.8	7.0	0.2	93.0	88.8	11.2	0.0	88.8
Maine	43.2	55.8	1.0	43.6	41.5	55.5	3.0	42.8
Maryland	61.5	36.0	2.5	63.1	62.3	37.0	0.6	62.7
Massachusetts	50.6	46.6	2.7	52.1	51.2	41.8	7.0	55.1
Michigan	52.4	44.4	3.2	54.1	56.3	38.8	4.9	59.2
Minnesota	59.9	36.3	3.8	62.3	61.8	31.0	7.1	66.6
Mississippi	96.0	3.5	0.5	96.4	97.0	2.8	0.2	97.2
Missouri	63.7	35.1	1.2	64.5	60.8	38.2	1.1	61.4
Montana	58.8	36.1	5.1	62.0	69.3	27.6	3.1	71.5
Nebraska	63.0	35.3	1.7	64.1	57.1	40.7	2.1	58.4
Nevada	69.4	30.6	0.0	69.4	72.8	27.2	0.0	72.8
New Hampshire	49.0	50.4	0.6	49.3	49.7	48.0	2.3	50.9
New Jersey	49.5	47.6	2.9	51.0	59.5	39.6	0.9	60.1
New Mexico	62.7	35.8	1.5	63.7	62.7	36.5	0.8	63.2
New York	54.1	41.3	4.6	56.7	58.8	39.0	2.2	60.2
North Carolina	69.9	29.3	0.8	70.5	73.4	26.6	0.0	73.4
North Dakota	69.6	28.0	2.4	71.3	59.6	26.6	13.8	69.2
Ohio	49.9	47.0	3.1	51.5	58.0	37.4	4.6	60.8
Oklahoma	73.3	26.7	0.0	73.3	66.8	32.7	0.5	67.2
Oregon	58.0	36.9	5.1	61.1	64.4	29.6	5.9	68.5
Pennsylvania	45.3	50.8	3.8	47.1	56.9	40.8	2.3	58.2
Rhode Island	55.1	43.3	1.6	56.0	53.0	40.3	6.7	56.8
South Carolina	98.0	1.9	0.1	98.1	98.6	1.4	0.0	98.6
South Dakota	63.6	34.4	2.0	64.9	54.0	42.5	3.5	56.0
Tennessee	66.5	32.5	1.0	67.2	68.8	30.8	0.4	69.1
Texas	88.2	11.2	0.6	88.7	87.1	12.3	0.6	87.6
Utah	56.5	41.0	2.4	57.9	69.3	29.8	0.9	69.9
Vermont	41.1	57.7	1.3	41.6	43.2	56.4	0.4	43.4
Virginia	68.5	30.1	1.5	69.5	70.2	29.4	0.4	70.5
Washington	57.5	33.9	8.6	62.9	66.4	29.9	3.7	69.0
West Virginia	54.5	44.5	1.1	55.1	60.6	39.2	0.2	60.7
Wisconsin	63.5	31.2	5.4	67.0	63.8	30.3	5.9	67.8
Wyoming	56.1	40.8	3.1	57.9	60.6	37.5	2.0	61.8

Notes: Entries for the major parties (Democratic, Republican, or their historical antecedents listed in Appendix A) are votes gained by those candidates that historical records show are the primary candidates of the two major parties, except in 1836 when the three Whig candidates are tallied for the total Whig vote. Democratic = Anti-Federalists (1788–1796), Democratic-Republicans (1796–1828), Jacksonian Democrats (1824–1828), and Democrats (since 1832). Republicans = Federalists (1788–1816), National Republicans (1828–1832), Whigs (1836–1852), and Republicans (since 1856). Other = other third parties. — indicates that the state had no data, either because no vote data were found for the state in question or the state had not yet entered the Union. Residents of the District of Columbia received the presidential vote beginning in the 1964 election.

Sources: *Congressional Quarterly's Guide to U.S. Elections* (1994), ICPSR data sets 0001 and 0019, *America at the Polls: 1920–1964* (1965); *A Statistical History of the American Presidential Elections* (1963), and independent search of state sources by the author.

Table 4-29 Presidential Election Results, by State, 1940–1944 (Percentages)

State	1940				1944			
	Democratic	Republican	Other	Democratic % of Two-Party Vote	Democratic	Republican	Other	Democratic % of Two-Party Vote
Alabama	85.2	14.3	0.4	85.6	81.3	18.2	0.5	81.7
Alaska	—	—	—	—	—	—	—	—
Arizona	63.5	36.0	0.5	63.8	58.8	40.9	0.3	59.0
Arkansas	78.4	21.0	0.5	78.9	70.0	29.8	0.2	70.1
California	57.4	41.3	1.2	58.1	56.5	43.0	0.5	56.8
Colorado	48.4	50.9	0.7	48.7	46.4	53.2	0.4	46.6
Connecticut	53.4	46.3	0.3	53.6	52.3	46.9	0.8	52.7
Delaware	54.7	45.1	0.2	54.8	54.4	45.3	0.4	54.6
Dist. of Columbia	—	—	—	—	—	—	—	—
Florida	74.0	26.0	0.0	74.0	70.3	29.7	0.0	70.3
Georgia	84.8	14.9	0.3	85.1	81.7	18.3	0.0	81.7
Hawaii	—	—	—	—	—	—	—	—
Idaho	54.4	45.3	0.3	54.5	51.6	48.1	0.4	51.7
Illinois	51.0	48.5	0.5	51.2	51.5	48.0	0.4	51.7
Indiana	49.0	50.5	0.5	49.3	46.7	52.4	0.9	47.1
Iowa	47.6	52.0	0.4	47.8	47.5	52.0	0.5	47.7
Kansas	42.4	56.9	0.7	42.7	39.2	60.2	0.6	39.4
Kentucky	57.4	42.3	0.3	57.6	54.5	45.2	0.3	54.6
Louisiana	85.9	14.1	0.0	85.9	80.6	19.4	0.0	80.6
Maine	48.8	51.1	0.1	48.8	47.4	52.4	0.1	47.5
Maryland	58.3	40.8	0.9	58.8	51.9	48.1	0.0	51.9
Massachusetts	53.1	46.4	0.5	53.4	52.8	47.0	0.2	52.9
Michigan	49.5	49.9	0.6	49.8	50.2	49.2	0.6	50.5
Minnesota	51.5	47.7	0.9	51.9	52.4	46.9	0.7	52.8
Mississippi	95.7	4.2	0.1	95.8	93.6	6.4	0.0	93.6
Missouri	52.3	47.5	0.2	52.4	51.4	48.4	0.2	51.5
Montana	58.8	40.2	1.0	59.4	54.3	44.9	0.8	54.7
Nebraska	42.8	57.2	0.0	42.8	41.4	58.6	0.0	41.4
Nevada	60.1	39.9	0.0	60.1	54.6	45.4	0.0	54.6
New Hampshire	53.2	46.8	0.0	53.2	52.1	47.9	0.0	52.1
New Jersey	51.5	47.9	0.5	51.8	50.3	49.0	0.7	50.7
New Mexico	56.6	43.3	0.1	56.7	53.5	46.4	0.1	53.5
New York	51.6	48.0	0.4	51.8	52.3	47.3	0.4	52.5
North Carolina	74.0	26.0	0.0	74.0	66.7	33.3	0.0	66.7
North Dakota	44.2	55.1	0.8	44.5	45.5	53.8	0.7	45.8
Ohio	52.2	47.8	0.0	52.2	49.8	50.2	0.0	49.8
Oklahoma	57.4	42.2	0.4	57.6	55.6	44.2	0.2	55.7
Oregon	53.7	45.6	0.7	54.1	51.8	46.9	1.3	52.5
Pennsylvania	53.2	46.3	0.4	53.5	51.1	48.4	0.5	51.4
Rhode Island	56.7	43.2	0.1	56.8	58.6	41.3	0.1	58.7
South Carolina	95.6	4.4	0.0	95.6	87.6	4.5	7.9	95.2
South Dakota	42.6	57.4	0.0	42.6	41.7	58.3	0.0	41.7
Tennessee	67.3	32.4	0.4	67.5	60.4	39.2	0.3	60.6
Texas	80.9	18.9	0.2	81.1	71.4	16.6	11.9	81.1
Utah	62.3	37.6	0.2	62.4	60.4	39.4	0.1	60.5
Vermont	44.9	54.8	0.3	45.1	42.9	57.1	0.0	42.9
Virginia	68.1	31.6	0.4	68.3	62.4	37.4	0.2	62.5
Washington	58.2	40.6	1.2	58.9	56.8	42.2	0.9	57.4
West Virginia	57.1	42.9	0.0	57.1	54.9	45.1	0.0	54.9
Wisconsin	50.1	48.3	1.5	50.9	48.6	50.4	1.1	49.1
Wyoming	52.8	46.9	0.3	53.0	48.8	51.2	0.0	48.8

Notes: Entries for the major parties (Democratic, Republican, or their historical antecedents listed in Appendix A) are votes gained by those candidates that historical records show are the primary candidates of the two major parties, except in 1836 when the three Whig candidates are tallied for the total Whig vote. Democratic = Anti-Federalists (1788–1796), Democratic-Republicans (1796–1828), Jacksonian Democrats (1824–1828), and Democrats (since 1832). Republicans = Federalists (1788–1816), National Republicans (1828–1832), Whigs (1836–1852), and Republicans (since 1856). Other = other third parties. — indicates that the state had no data, either because no vote data were found for the state in question or the state had not yet entered the Union. Residents of the District of Columbia received the presidential vote beginning in the 1964 election.

Sources: *Congressional Quarterly's Guide to U.S. Elections* (1994), ICPSR data sets 0001 and 0019, *America at the Polls: 1920–1964* (1965); *A Statistical History of the American Presidential Elections* (1963), and independent search of state sources by the author.

Table 4-30 Presidential Election Results, by State, 1948–1952 (Percentages)

State	1948 Democratic	1948 Republican	1948 Other	1948 Democratic % of Two-Party Vote	1952 Democratic	1952 Republican	1952 Other	1952 Democratic % of Two-Party Vote
Alabama	0.0	19.0	81.0	0.0	64.6	35.0	0.4	64.8
Alaska	—	—	—	—	—	—	—	—
Arizona	53.8	43.8	2.4	55.1	41.7	58.3	0.0	41.7
Arkansas	61.7	21.0	17.3	74.6	55.9	43.8	0.3	56.1
California	47.6	47.1	5.3	50.2	42.7	56.3	0.9	43.1
Colorado	51.9	46.5	1.6	52.7	39.0	60.3	0.8	39.3
Connecticut	47.9	49.5	2.5	49.2	43.9	55.7	0.4	44.1
Delaware	48.8	50.0	1.2	49.4	47.9	51.8	0.4	48.1
Dist. of Columbia	—	—	—	—	—	—	—	—
Florida	48.8	33.6	17.5	59.2	45.0	55.0	0.0	45.0
Georgia	60.8	18.3	20.9	76.9	69.7	30.3	0.0	69.7
Hawaii	—	—	—	—	—	—	—	—
Idaho	50.0	47.3	2.8	51.4	34.4	65.4	0.2	34.5
Illinois	50.1	49.2	0.7	50.4	44.9	54.8	0.2	45.0
Indiana	48.8	49.6	1.6	49.6	41.0	58.1	0.9	41.4
Iowa	50.3	47.6	2.1	51.4	35.6	63.8	0.7	35.8
Kansas	44.6	53.6	1.8	45.4	30.5	68.8	0.7	30.7
Kentucky	56.7	41.5	1.8	57.8	49.9	49.8	0.2	50.0
Louisiana	32.7	17.5	49.8	65.2	52.9	47.1	0.0	52.9
Maine	42.3	56.7	1.0	42.7	33.8	66.0	0.2	33.8
Maryland	48.0	49.4	2.6	49.3	43.8	55.4	0.8	44.2
Massachusetts	54.7	43.2	2.2	55.9	45.5	54.2	0.3	45.6
Michigan	47.6	49.2	3.2	49.1	44.0	55.4	0.6	44.2
Minnesota	57.2	39.9	2.9	58.9	44.1	55.3	0.6	44.4
Mississippi	10.1	2.6	87.3	79.4	60.4	39.6	0.0	60.4
Missouri	58.1	41.5	0.4	58.3	49.1	50.7	0.1	49.2
Montana	53.1	43.1	3.8	55.2	40.1	59.4	0.5	40.3
Nebraska	45.8	54.2	0.0	45.8	30.8	69.2	0.0	30.8
Nevada	50.4	47.3	2.4	51.6	38.6	61.4	0.0	38.6
New Hampshire	46.7	52.4	0.9	47.1	39.1	60.9	0.0	39.1
New Jersey	45.9	50.3	3.7	47.7	42.0	56.8	1.2	42.5
New Mexico	56.4	42.9	0.7	56.8	44.3	55.4	0.3	44.4
New York	45.0	46.0	9.0	49.5	43.6	55.5	1.0	44.0
North Carolina	58.0	32.7	9.3	64.0	53.9	46.1	0.0	53.9
North Dakota	43.4	52.2	4.4	45.4	28.4	71.0	0.6	28.6
Ohio	49.5	49.2	1.3	50.1	43.2	56.8	0.0	43.2
Oklahoma	62.7	37.3	0.0	62.7	45.4	54.6	0.0	45.4
Oregon	46.4	49.8	3.8	48.2	38.9	60.5	0.5	39.1
Pennsylvania	46.9	50.9	2.2	48.0	46.9	52.7	0.4	47.0
Rhode Island	57.6	41.4	1.0	58.2	49.0	50.9	0.1	49.1
South Carolina	24.1	3.8	72.1	86.5	50.7	49.3	0.0	50.7
South Dakota	47.0	51.8	1.1	47.6	30.7	69.3	0.0	30.7
Tennessee	49.1	36.9	14.0	57.1	49.7	50.0	0.3	49.9
Texas	66.0	24.3	9.8	73.1	46.7	53.1	0.2	46.8
Utah	54.0	45.0	1.0	54.5	41.1	58.9	0.0	41.1
Vermont	36.9	61.5	1.5	37.5	28.2	71.5	0.3	28.3
Virginia	47.9	41.0	11.1	53.9	43.4	56.3	0.3	43.5
Washington	52.6	42.7	4.7	55.2	44.7	54.3	1.0	45.1
West Virginia	57.3	42.2	0.4	57.6	51.9	48.1	0.0	51.9
Wisconsin	50.7	46.3	3.0	52.3	38.7	61.0	0.3	38.8
Wyoming	51.6	47.3	1.1	52.2	37.1	62.7	0.2	37.2

Notes: Entries for the major parties (Democratic, Republican, or their historical antecedents listed in Appendix A) are votes gained by those candidates that historical records show are the primary candidates of the two major parties, except in 1836 when the three Whig candidates are tallied for the total Whig vote. Democratic = Anti-Federalists (1788–1796), Democratic-Republicans (1796–1828), Jacksonian Democrats (1824–1828), and Democrats (since 1832). Republicans = Federalists (1788–1816), National Republicans (1828–1832), Whigs (1836–1852), and Republicans (since 1856). Other = other third parties. — indicates that the state had no data, either because no vote data were found for the state in question or the state had not yet entered the Union. Residents of the District of Columbia received the presidential vote beginning in the 1964 election.

Sources: *Congressional Quarterly's Guide to U.S. Elections* (1994), ICPSR data sets 0001 and 0019, *America at the Polls: 1920–1964* (1965), *America Votes* (various publication dates), *A Statistical History of the American Presidential Elections* (1963), and independent search of state sources by the author.

Table 4-31 Presidential Election Results, by State, 1956–1960 (Percentages)

State	1956				1960			
	Democratic	Republican	Other	Democratic % of Two-Party Vote	Democratic	Republican	Other	Democratic % of Two-Party Vote
Alabama	56.5	39.4	4.1	58.9	56.8	41.7	1.4	57.7
Alaska	—	—	—	—	49.1	50.9	0.0	49.1
Arizona	38.9	61.0	0.1	38.9	44.4	55.5	0.1	44.4
Arkansas	52.5	45.8	1.7	53.4	50.2	43.1	6.8	53.8
California	44.3	55.4	0.3	44.4	49.6	50.1	0.3	49.7
Colorado	39.3	60.0	0.7	39.5	44.9	54.6	0.5	45.1
Connecticut	36.3	63.7	0.0	36.3	53.7	46.3	0.0	53.7
Delaware	44.6	55.1	0.3	44.7	50.6	49.0	0.4	50.8
Dist. of Columbia	—	—	—	—	—	—	—	—
Florida	42.7	57.2	0.1	42.7	48.5	51.5	0.0	48.5
Georgia	66.4	33.3	0.3	66.6	62.5	37.4	0.0	62.6
Hawaii	—	—	—	—	50.0	50.0	0.0	50.0
Idaho	38.8	61.2	0.1	38.8	46.2	53.8	0.0	46.2
Illinois	40.3	59.5	0.2	40.4	50.0	49.8	0.2	50.1
Indiana	39.7	59.9	0.4	39.9	44.6	55.0	0.4	44.8
Iowa	40.7	59.1	0.3	40.8	43.2	56.7	0.1	43.3
Kansas	34.2	65.4	0.4	34.3	39.1	60.4	0.4	39.3
Kentucky	45.2	54.3	0.5	45.4	46.4	53.6	0.0	46.4
Louisiana	39.5	53.3	7.2	42.6	50.4	28.6	21.0	63.8
Maine	29.1	70.9	0.0	29.1	43.0	57.0	0.0	43.0
Maryland	39.9	60.0	0.1	40.0	53.6	46.4	0.0	53.6
Massachusetts	40.4	59.3	0.3	40.5	60.2	39.6	0.2	60.4
Michigan	44.1	55.6	0.2	44.2	50.9	48.8	0.3	51.0
Minnesota	46.1	53.7	0.2	46.2	50.6	49.2	0.3	50.7
Mississippi	58.2	24.5	17.3	70.4	36.3	24.7	39.0	59.6
Missouri	50.1	49.9	0.0	50.1	50.3	49.7	0.0	50.3
Montana	42.9	57.1	0.0	42.9	48.6	51.1	0.3	48.7
Nebraska	34.5	65.5	0.0	34.5	37.9	62.1	0.0	37.9
Nevada	42.0	58.0	0.0	42.0	51.2	48.8	0.0	51.2
New Hampshire	33.9	66.1	0.0	33.9	46.6	53.4	0.0	46.6
New Jersey	34.2	64.7	1.1	34.6	50.0	49.2	0.9	50.4
New Mexico	41.8	57.8	0.4	42.0	50.2	49.4	0.4	50.4
New York	38.7	61.2	0.0	38.7	52.5	47.3	0.2	52.6
North Carolina	50.7	49.3	0.0	50.7	52.1	47.9	0.0	52.1
North Dakota	38.1	61.7	0.2	38.2	44.5	55.4	0.1	44.5
Ohio	38.9	61.1	0.0	38.9	46.7	53.3	0.0	46.7
Oklahoma	44.9	55.1	0.0	44.9	41.0	59.0	0.0	41.0
Oregon	44.7	55.2	0.1	44.8	47.3	52.6	0.1	47.4
Pennsylvania	43.3	56.5	0.2	43.4	51.1	48.7	0.2	51.2
Rhode Island	41.7	58.3	0.0	41.7	63.6	36.4	0.0	63.6
South Carolina	45.4	25.2	29.4	64.3	51.2	48.8	0.0	51.2
South Dakota	41.6	58.4	0.0	41.6	41.8	58.2	0.0	41.8
Tennessee	48.6	49.2	2.2	49.7	45.8	52.9	1.3	46.4
Texas	44.0	55.3	0.7	44.3	50.5	48.5	1.0	51.0
Utah	35.4	64.6	0.0	35.4	45.2	54.8	0.0	45.2
Vermont	27.8	72.2	0.0	27.8	41.4	58.6	0.0	41.4
Virginia	38.4	55.4	6.3	40.9	47.0	52.4	0.6	47.2
Washington	45.4	53.9	0.6	45.7	48.3	50.7	1.0	48.8
West Virginia	45.9	54.1	0.0	45.9	52.7	47.3	0.0	52.7
Wisconsin	37.8	61.6	0.6	38.1	48.0	51.8	0.2	48.1
Wyoming	39.9	60.1	0.0	39.9	45.0	55.0	0.0	45.0

Notes: Entries for the major parties (Democratic, Republican, or their historical antecedents listed in Appendix A) are votes gained by those candidates that historical records show are the primary candidates of the two major parties, except in 1836 when the three Whig candidates are tallied for the total Whig vote. Democratic = Anti-Federalists (1788–1796), Democratic-Republicans (1796–1828), Jacksonian Democrats (1824–1828), and Democrats (since 1832). Republicans = Federalists (1788–1816), National Republicans (1828–1832), Whigs (1836–1852), and Republicans (since 1856). Other = other third parties. — indicates that the state had no data, either because no vote data were found for the state in question or the state had not yet entered the Union. Residents of the District of Columbia received the presidential vote beginning in the 1964 election.

Sources: *Congressional Quarterly's Guide to U.S. Elections* (1994), ICPSR data sets 0001 and 0019, *America at the Polls: 1920–1964* (1965), *America Votes* (various publication dates), *A Statistical History of the American Presidential Elections* (1963), and independent search of state sources by the author.

Table 4-32 Presidential Election Results, by State, 1964–1968 (Percentages)

State	1964				1968			
	Democratic	Republican	Other	Democratic % of Two-Party Vote	Democratic	Republican	Other	Democratic % of Two-Party Vote
Alabama	0.0	69.5	30.5	0.0	18.7	14.0	67.3	57.2
Alaska	65.9	34.1	0.0	65.9	42.6	45.3	12.1	48.5
Arizona	49.5	50.4	0.1	49.5	35.0	54.8	10.2	39.0
Arkansas	56.1	43.4	0.5	56.4	30.4	30.8	38.9	49.7
California	59.1	40.8	0.1	59.2	44.7	47.8	7.4	48.3
Colorado	61.3	38.2	0.5	61.6	41.3	50.5	8.2	45.0
Connecticut	67.8	32.1	0.1	67.9	49.5	44.3	6.2	52.8
Delaware	60.9	38.8	0.3	61.1	41.6	45.1	13.3	48.0
Dist. of Columbia	85.5	14.5	0.0	85.5	81.8	18.2	0.0	81.8
Florida	51.1	48.9	0.0	51.1	30.9	40.5	28.5	43.3
Georgia	45.9	54.1	0.0	45.9	26.7	30.4	42.8	46.8
Hawaii	78.8	21.2	0.0	78.8	59.8	38.7	1.5	60.7
Idaho	50.9	49.1	0.0	50.9	30.7	56.8	12.5	35.1
Illinois	59.5	40.5	0.0	59.5	44.2	47.1	8.8	48.4
Indiana	56.0	43.6	0.5	56.2	38.0	50.3	11.7	43.0
Iowa	61.9	37.9	0.2	62.0	40.8	53.0	6.2	43.5
Kansas	54.1	45.1	0.9	54.6	34.7	54.8	10.4	38.8
Kentucky	64.0	35.7	0.3	64.2	37.6	43.8	18.6	46.2
Louisiana	43.2	56.8	0.0	43.2	28.2	23.5	48.3	54.6
Maine	68.8	31.2	0.0	68.8	55.3	43.1	1.6	56.2
Maryland	65.5	34.5	0.0	65.5	43.6	41.9	14.5	51.0
Massachusetts	76.2	23.4	0.4	76.5	63.0	32.9	4.1	65.7
Michigan	66.7	33.1	0.2	66.8	48.2	41.5	10.4	53.8
Minnesota	63.8	36.0	0.2	63.9	54.0	41.5	4.5	56.6
Mississippi	12.9	87.1	0.0	12.9	23.0	13.5	63.5	63.0
Missouri	64.0	36.0	0.0	64.0	43.7	44.9	11.4	49.4
Montana	58.9	40.6	0.5	59.2	41.6	50.6	7.8	45.1
Nebraska	52.6	47.4	0.0	52.6	31.8	59.8	8.4	34.7
Nevada	58.6	41.4	0.0	58.6	39.3	47.5	13.2	45.3
New Hampshire	63.9	36.1	0.0	63.9	43.9	52.1	4.0	45.7
New Jersey	65.6	33.9	0.5	66.0	44.0	46.1	9.9	48.8
New Mexico	59.0	40.4	0.5	59.4	39.7	51.8	8.4	43.4
New York	68.6	31.3	0.1	68.7	49.7	44.3	6.0	52.9
North Carolina	56.2	43.8	0.0	56.2	29.2	39.5	31.3	42.5
North Dakota	58.0	41.9	0.2	58.1	38.2	55.9	5.8	40.6
Ohio	62.9	37.1	0.0	62.9	42.9	45.2	11.8	48.7
Oklahoma	55.7	44.3	0.0	55.7	32.0	47.7	20.3	40.1
Oregon	63.7	36.0	0.3	63.9	43.8	49.8	6.4	46.8
Pennsylvania	64.9	34.7	0.4	65.2	47.6	44.0	8.4	51.9
Rhode Island	80.9	19.1	0.0	80.9	64.0	31.8	4.2	66.8
South Carolina	41.1	58.9	0.0	41.1	29.6	38.1	32.3	43.7
South Dakota	55.6	44.4	0.0	55.6	42.0	53.3	4.8	44.1
Tennessee	55.5	44.5	0.0	55.5	28.1	37.8	34.0	42.6
Texas	63.3	36.5	0.2	63.4	41.1	39.9	19.0	50.8
Utah	54.7	45.3	0.0	54.7	37.1	56.5	6.4	39.6
Vermont	66.3	33.7	0.0	66.3	43.5	52.8	3.7	45.2
Virginia	53.5	46.2	0.3	53.7	32.5	43.4	24.1	42.8
Washington	62.0	37.4	0.7	62.4	47.2	45.1	7.6	51.1
West Virginia	67.9	32.1	0.0	67.9	49.6	40.8	9.6	54.9
Wisconsin	62.1	37.7	0.2	62.2	44.3	47.9	7.8	48.0
Wyoming	56.6	43.4	0.0	56.6	35.5	55.8	8.7	38.9

Notes: Entries for the major parties (Democratic, Republican, or their historical antecedents listed in Appendix A) are votes gained by those candidates that historical records show are the primary candidates of the two major parties, except in 1836 when the three Whig candidates are tallied for the total Whig vote. Democratic = Anti-Federalists (1788–1796), Democratic-Republicans (1796–1828), Jacksonian Democrats (1824–1828), and Democrats (since 1832). Republicans = Federalists (1788–1816), National Republicans (1828–1832), Whigs (1836–1852), and Republicans (since 1856). Other = other third parties. Residents of the District of Columbia received the presidential vote beginning in the 1964 election.

Sources: *Congressional Quarterly's Guide to U.S. Elections* (1994), ICPSR data sets 0001 and 0019, *America at the Polls: 1920–1964* (1965), *America Votes* (various publication dates), and independent search of state sources by the author.

Table 4-33 Presidential Election Results, by State, 1972–1976 (Percentages)

	1972				1976			
State	Democratic	Republican	Other	Democratic % of Two-Party Vote	Democratic	Republican	Other	Democratic % of Two-Party Vote
Alabama	25.5	72.4	2.0	26.1	55.7	42.6	1.7	56.7
Alaska	34.6	58.1	7.2	37.3	35.7	57.9	6.4	38.1
Arizona	31.9	64.7	3.5	33.0	39.8	56.4	3.8	41.4
Arkansas	30.7	68.9	0.4	30.8	65.0	34.9	0.1	65.0
California	41.5	55.0	3.5	43.0	47.6	49.3	3.1	49.1
Colorado	34.6	62.6	2.8	35.6	42.6	54.0	3.4	44.1
Connecticut	40.1	58.6	1.3	40.7	46.9	52.1	1.0	47.4
Delaware	39.2	59.6	1.2	39.7	52.0	46.6	1.4	52.7
Dist. of Columbia	78.1	21.6	0.3	78.4	81.6	16.5	1.9	83.2
Florida	27.8	71.9	0.3	27.9	51.9	46.6	1.4	52.7
Georgia	24.6	75.0	0.3	24.7	66.7	33.0	0.3	66.9
Hawaii	37.5	62.5	0.0	37.5	50.6	48.1	1.3	51.3
Idaho	26.0	64.2	9.7	28.8	36.8	59.3	3.9	38.3
Illinois	40.5	59.0	0.5	40.7	48.1	50.1	1.8	49.0
Indiana	33.3	66.1	0.6	33.5	45.7	53.3	1.0	46.2
Iowa	40.5	57.6	1.9	41.3	48.5	49.5	2.1	49.5
Kansas	29.5	67.7	2.8	30.4	44.9	52.5	2.6	46.1
Kentucky	34.8	63.4	1.9	35.4	52.8	45.6	1.7	53.7
Louisiana	28.4	65.3	6.3	30.3	51.7	46.0	2.3	53.0
Maine	38.5	61.5	0.0	38.5	48.1	48.9	3.0	49.6
Maryland	37.4	61.3	1.4	37.9	52.8	46.7	0.5	53.0
Massachusetts	54.2	45.2	0.6	54.5	56.1	40.4	3.4	58.1
Michigan	41.8	56.2	2.0	42.7	46.4	51.8	1.7	47.3
Minnesota	46.1	51.6	2.4	47.2	54.9	42.0	3.1	56.6
Mississippi	19.6	78.2	2.2	20.1	49.6	47.7	2.8	51.0
Missouri	37.6	62.2	0.3	37.7	51.1	47.5	1.4	51.8
Montana	37.8	57.9	4.2	39.5	45.4	52.8	1.8	46.2
Nebraska	29.5	70.5	0.0	29.5	38.5	59.2	2.3	39.4
Nevada	36.3	63.7	0.0	36.3	45.8	50.2	4.0	47.7
New Hampshire	34.9	64.0	1.2	35.3	43.5	54.7	1.8	44.3
New Jersey	36.8	61.6	1.7	37.4	47.9	50.1	2.0	48.9
New Mexico	36.5	61.0	2.5	37.5	48.1	50.5	1.4	48.8
New York	41.2	58.5	0.3	41.3	51.9	47.5	0.7	52.2
North Carolina	28.9	69.5	1.6	29.4	55.2	44.2	0.6	55.6
North Dakota	35.8	62.1	2.1	36.6	45.8	51.6	2.6	47.0
Ohio	38.1	59.6	2.3	39.0	48.9	48.7	2.4	50.1
Oklahoma	24.0	73.7	2.3	24.6	48.7	50.0	1.3	49.4
Oregon	42.3	52.4	5.2	44.7	47.6	47.8	4.6	49.9
Pennsylvania	39.1	59.1	1.8	39.8	50.4	47.7	1.9	51.4
Rhode Island	46.8	53.0	0.2	46.9	55.4	44.1	0.6	55.7
South Carolina	27.7	70.8	1.5	28.1	56.2	43.1	0.7	56.6
South Dakota	45.5	54.2	0.3	45.7	48.9	50.4	0.7	49.3
Tennessee	29.7	67.7	2.6	30.5	55.9	42.9	1.1	56.6
Texas	33.3	66.2	0.5	33.4	51.1	48.0	0.9	51.6
Utah	26.4	67.6	6.0	28.1	33.6	62.4	3.9	35.0
Vermont	36.5	62.7	0.9	36.8	43.1	54.4	2.5	44.2
Virginia	30.1	67.8	2.0	30.7	48.0	49.3	2.7	49.3
Washington	38.6	56.9	4.4	40.4	46.1	50.0	3.9	48.0
West Virginia	36.4	63.6	0.0	36.4	58.0	41.9	0.0	58.1
Wisconsin	43.7	53.4	2.9	45.0	49.4	47.8	2.8	50.9
Wyoming	30.5	69.0	0.5	30.6	39.8	59.3	0.9	40.2

Notes: Entries for the major parties (Democratic, Republican, or their historical antecedents listed in Appendix A) are votes gained by those candidates that historical records show are the primary candidates of the two major parties, except in 1836 when the three Whig candidates are tallied for the total Whig vote. Democratic = Anti-Federalists (1788–1796), Democratic-Republicans (1796–1828), Jacksonian Democrats (1824–1828), and Democrats (since 1832). Republicans = Federalists (1788–1816), National Republicans (1828–1832), Whigs (1836–1852), and Republicans (since 1856). Other = other third parties. Residents of the District of Columbia received the presidential vote beginning in the 1964 election.

Sources: *Congressional Quarterly's Guide to U.S. Elections* (1994), ICPSR data sets 0001 and 0019, *America Votes* (various publication dates), and independent search of state sources by the author.

Table 4-34 Presidential Election Results, by State, 1980–1984 (Percentages)

	1980				1984			
State	Democratic	Republican	Other	Democratic % of Two-Party Vote	Democratic	Republican	Other	Democratic % of Two-Party Vote
Alabama	47.4	48.8	3.8	49.3	38.3	60.5	1.2	38.7
Alaska	26.4	54.3	19.2	32.7	29.9	66.7	3.5	30.9
Arizona	28.2	60.6	11.1	31.8	32.5	66.4	1.0	32.9
Arkansas	47.5	48.1	4.3	49.7	38.3	60.5	1.2	38.8
California	35.9	52.7	11.4	40.5	41.3	57.5	1.2	41.8
Colorado	31.1	55.1	13.9	36.1	35.1	63.4	1.4	35.6
Connecticut	38.5	48.2	13.3	44.4	38.8	60.7	0.4	39.0
Delaware	44.8	47.2	8.0	48.7	39.9	59.8	0.3	40.0
Dist. of Columbia	74.8	13.4	11.7	84.8	85.4	13.7	0.9	86.1
Florida	38.5	55.5	6.0	40.9	34.7	65.3	0.0	34.7
Georgia	55.8	41.0	3.2	57.7	39.8	60.2	0.0	39.8
Hawaii	44.8	42.9	12.3	51.1	43.8	55.1	1.1	44.3
Idaho	25.2	66.5	8.4	27.5	26.4	72.4	1.2	26.7
Illinois	41.7	49.6	8.6	45.7	43.3	56.2	0.5	43.5
Indiana	37.7	56.0	6.3	40.2	37.7	61.7	0.6	37.9
Iowa	38.6	51.3	10.1	42.9	45.9	53.3	0.8	46.3
Kansas	33.3	57.9	8.9	36.5	32.6	66.3	1.1	33.0
Kentucky	47.6	49.1	3.3	49.2	39.4	60.0	0.6	39.6
Louisiana	45.7	51.2	3.1	47.2	38.2	60.8	1.1	38.6
Maine	42.3	45.6	12.1	48.1	38.8	60.8	0.4	38.9
Maryland	47.1	44.2	8.7	51.6	47.0	52.5	0.5	47.2
Massachusetts	41.7	41.9	16.4	49.9	48.4	51.2	0.3	48.6
Michigan	42.5	49.0	8.5	46.5	40.2	59.2	0.5	40.5
Minnesota	46.5	42.6	10.9	52.2	49.7	49.5	0.7	50.1
Mississippi	48.1	49.4	2.5	49.3	37.4	61.9	0.7	37.7
Missouri	44.3	51.2	4.5	46.4	40.0	60.0	0.0	40.0
Montana	32.4	56.8	10.7	36.3	38.2	60.5	1.3	38.7
Nebraska	26.0	65.5	8.4	28.4	28.8	70.6	0.6	29.0
Nevada	26.9	62.5	10.6	30.1	32.0	65.8	2.2	32.7
New Hampshire	28.4	57.7	13.9	32.9	30.9	68.6	0.4	31.1
New Jersey	38.6	52.0	9.5	42.6	39.2	60.1	0.7	39.5
New Mexico	36.7	54.9	8.4	40.1	39.2	59.7	1.1	39.7
New York	44.0	46.7	9.3	48.5	45.8	53.8	0.3	46.0
North Carolina	47.2	49.3	3.5	48.9	37.9	61.9	0.2	38.0
North Dakota	26.3	64.2	9.5	29.0	33.8	64.8	1.4	34.3
Ohio	40.9	51.5	7.6	44.3	40.1	58.9	1.0	40.5
Oklahoma	35.0	60.5	4.5	36.6	30.7	68.6	0.7	30.9
Oregon	38.7	48.3	13.0	44.4	43.7	55.9	0.4	43.9
Pennsylvania	42.5	49.6	7.9	46.1	46.0	53.3	0.7	46.3
Rhode Island	47.7	37.2	15.1	56.2	48.0	51.7	0.3	48.2
South Carolina	48.1	49.4	2.4	49.3	35.6	63.6	0.9	35.9
South Dakota	31.7	60.5	7.8	34.4	36.5	63.0	0.5	36.7
Tennessee	48.4	48.7	2.9	49.9	41.6	57.8	0.6	41.8
Texas	41.4	55.3	3.3	42.8	36.1	63.6	0.3	36.2
Utah	20.6	72.8	6.7	22.0	24.7	74.5	0.8	24.9
Vermont	38.4	44.4	17.2	46.4	40.8	57.9	1.3	41.3
Virginia	40.3	53.0	6.7	43.2	37.1	62.3	0.6	37.3
Washington	37.3	49.7	13.0	42.9	42.9	55.8	1.3	43.4
West Virginia	49.8	45.3	4.9	52.4	44.6	55.1	0.3	44.7
Wisconsin	43.2	47.9	8.9	47.4	45.0	54.2	0.8	45.4
Wyoming	28.0	62.6	9.4	30.9	28.2	70.5	1.2	28.6

Notes: Entries for the major parties (Democratic, Republican, or their historical antecedents listed in Appendix A) are votes gained by those candidates that historical records show are the primary candidates of the two major parties, except in 1836 when the three Whig candidates are tallied for the total Whig vote. Democratic = Anti-Federalists (1788–1796), Democratic-Republicans (1796–1828), Jacksonian Democrats (1824–1828), and Democrats (since 1832). Republicans = Federalists (1788–1816), National Republicans (1828–1832), Whigs (1836–1852), and Republicans (since 1856). Other = other third parties. Residents of the District of Columbia received the presidential vote beginning in the 1964 election.

Sources: *Congressional Quarterly's Guide to U.S. Elections* (1994), *America Votes* (various publication dates), and independent search of state sources by the author.

Table 4-35 Presidential Election Results, by State, 1988–1992 (Percentages)

State	1988 Democratic	1988 Republican	1988 Other	1988 Democratic % of Two-Party Vote	1992 Democratic	1992 Republican	1992 Other	1992 Democratic % of Two-Party Vote
Alabama	39.9	59.2	1.0	40.3	40.9	47.6	11.5	46.2
Alaska	36.3	59.6	4.1	37.8	30.3	39.5	30.3	43.4
Arizona	38.7	60.0	1.3	39.3	36.5	38.5	25.0	48.7
Arkansas	42.2	56.4	1.4	42.8	53.2	35.5	11.3	60.0
California	47.6	51.1	1.3	48.2	46.0	32.6	21.4	58.5
Colorado	45.3	53.1	1.7	46.0	40.1	35.9	24.0	52.8
Connecticut	46.9	52.0	1.1	47.4	42.2	35.8	22.0	54.1
Delaware	43.5	55.9	0.6	43.8	43.5	35.3	21.2	55.2
Dist. of Columbia	82.6	14.3	3.0	85.2	84.6	9.1	6.3	90.3
Florida	38.5	60.9	0.6	38.7	39.0	40.9	20.1	48.8
Georgia	39.5	59.8	0.7	39.8	43.5	42.9	13.7	50.3
Hawaii	54.3	44.8	1.0	54.8	48.1	36.7	15.2	56.7
Idaho	36.0	62.1	1.9	36.7	28.4	42.0	29.6	40.3
Illinois	48.6	50.7	0.7	49.0	48.6	34.3	17.1	58.6
Indiana	39.7	59.8	0.5	39.9	36.8	42.9	20.3	46.2
Iowa	54.7	44.5	0.8	55.1	43.3	37.3	19.4	53.7
Kansas	42.6	55.8	1.6	43.3	33.7	38.9	27.4	46.5
Kentucky	43.9	55.5	0.6	44.1	44.6	41.3	14.1	51.9
Louisiana	44.1	54.3	1.7	44.8	45.6	41.0	13.4	52.7
Maine	43.9	55.3	0.8	44.2	38.8	30.4	30.8	56.1
Maryland	48.2	51.1	0.7	48.5	49.8	35.6	14.6	58.3
Massachusetts	53.2	45.4	1.4	54.0	47.5	29.0	23.4	62.1
Michigan	45.7	53.6	0.8	46.0	43.8	36.4	19.9	54.6
Minnesota	52.9	45.9	1.2	53.6	43.5	31.9	24.7	57.7
Mississippi	39.1	59.9	1.0	39.5	40.8	49.7	9.5	45.1
Missouri	47.8	51.8	0.3	48.0	44.1	33.9	22.0	56.5
Montana	46.2	52.1	1.7	47.0	37.6	35.1	27.3	51.7
Nebraska	39.2	60.2	0.6	39.4	29.4	46.6	24.0	38.7
Nevada	37.9	58.9	3.2	39.2	37.4	34.7	27.9	51.8
New Hampshire	36.3	62.4	1.3	36.8	38.9	37.6	23.5	50.8
New Jersey	42.6	56.2	1.2	43.1	43.0	40.6	16.5	51.4
New Mexico	46.9	51.9	1.2	47.5	45.9	37.3	16.8	55.1
New York	51.6	47.5	0.9	52.1	49.7	33.9	16.4	59.5
North Carolina	41.7	58.0	0.3	41.8	42.7	43.4	13.9	49.5
North Dakota	43.0	56.0	1.0	43.4	32.2	44.2	23.6	42.1
Ohio	44.1	55.0	0.9	44.5	40.2	38.3	21.5	51.2
Oklahoma	41.3	57.9	0.8	41.6	34.0	42.6	23.3	44.4
Oregon	51.3	46.6	2.1	52.4	42.5	32.5	25.0	56.6
Pennsylvania	48.4	50.7	0.9	48.8	45.1	36.1	18.7	55.5
Rhode Island	55.6	43.9	0.4	55.9	47.0	29.0	23.9	61.8
South Carolina	37.6	61.5	0.9	37.9	39.9	48.0	12.1	45.4
South Dakota	46.5	52.8	0.6	46.8	37.1	40.7	22.2	47.7
Tennessee	41.5	57.9	0.6	41.8	47.1	42.4	10.5	52.6
Texas	43.3	56.0	0.7	43.7	37.1	40.6	22.4	47.8
Utah	32.0	66.2	1.7	32.6	24.7	43.4	32.0	36.2
Vermont	47.6	51.1	1.3	48.2	46.1	30.4	23.5	60.3
Virginia	39.2	59.7	1.0	39.6	40.6	45.0	14.4	47.4
Washington	50.0	48.5	1.5	50.8	43.4	32.0	24.6	57.6
West Virginia	52.2	47.5	0.3	52.4	48.4	35.4	16.2	57.8
Wisconsin	51.4	47.8	0.8	51.8	41.1	36.8	22.1	52.8
Wyoming	38.0	60.5	1.5	38.6	34.0	39.6	26.5	46.2

Notes: Entries for the major parties (Democratic, Republican, or their historical antecedents listed in Appendix A) are votes gained by those candidates that historical records show are the primary candidates of the two major parties, except in 1836 when the three Whig candidates are tallied for the total Whig vote. Democratic = Anti-Federalists (1788–1796), Democratic-Republicans (1796–1828), Jacksonian Democrats (1824–1828), and Democrats (since 1832). Republicans = Federalists (1788–1816), National Republicans (1828–1832), Whigs (1836–1852), and Republicans (since 1856). Other = other third parties. Residents of the District of Columbia received the presidential vote beginning in the 1964 election.

Sources: *Congressional Quarterly's Guide to U.S. Elections* (1994), *America Votes* (various publication dates), and independent search of state sources by the author.

Table 4-36 Presidential Election Results, by State, 1996 (Percentages)

State	1996 Democratic	Republican	Other	Democratic % of Two-Party Vote
Alabama	43.2	50.1	6.7	46.3
Alaska	33.3	50.8	15.9	39.6
Arizona	46.5	44.3	9.2	51.2
Arkansas	53.7	36.8	9.5	59.4
California	51.1	38.2	10.7	57.2
Colorado	44.4	45.8	9.8	49.2
Connecticut	52.8	34.7	12.5	60.4
Delaware	51.8	36.5	11.7	58.6
Dist. of Columbia	85.2	9.3	5.5	90.1
Florida	48.0	42.3	9.7	53.2
Georgia	45.8	47.0	7.1	49.4
Hawaii	56.9	31.6	11.4	64.3
Idaho	33.6	52.2	14.2	39.2
Illinois	54.3	36.8	8.9	59.6
Indiana	41.5	47.1	11.3	46.9
Iowa	50.3	39.9	9.8	55.7
Kansas	36.1	54.3	9.6	39.9
Kentucky	45.8	44.9	9.3	50.5
Louisiana	52.0	39.9	8.0	56.6
Maine	51.6	30.8	17.6	62.7
Maryland	54.3	38.3	7.5	58.6
Massachusetts	61.5	28.1	10.4	68.6
Michigan	51.7	38.5	9.8	57.3
Minnesota	51.1	35.0	13.9	59.4
Mississippi	44.1	49.2	6.7	47.3
Missouri	47.5	41.2	11.2	53.5
Montana	41.2	44.1	14.7	48.3
Nebraska	35.0	53.7	11.4	39.4
Nevada	43.9	42.9	13.2	50.6
New Hampshire	49.3	39.4	11.3	55.6
New Jersey	53.7	35.9	10.4	60.0
New Mexico	49.2	41.9	9.0	54.0
New York	59.5	30.6	9.9	66.0
North Carolina	44.0	48.7	7.2	47.5
North Dakota	40.1	46.9	12.9	46.1
Ohio	47.4	41.0	11.6	53.6
Oklahoma	40.4	48.3	11.3	45.6
Oregon	47.2	39.1	13.8	54.7
Pennsylvania	49.2	40.0	10.9	55.2
Rhode Island	59.7	26.8	13.5	69.0
South Carolina	44.0	49.8	6.2	46.9
South Dakota	43.0	46.5	10.5	48.1
Tennessee	48.0	45.6	6.4	51.3
Texas	43.8	48.8	7.4	47.3
Utah	33.3	54.4	12.3	38.0
Vermont	53.4	31.1	15.6	63.2
Virginia	45.1	47.1	7.7	48.9
Washington	49.8	37.3	12.9	57.2
West Virginia	51.5	36.8	11.7	58.4
Wisconsin	48.8	38.5	12.7	55.9
Wyoming	36.8	49.8	13.4	42.5

Notes: Entries for the major parties (Democratic, Republican, or their historical antecedents listed in Appendix A) are votes gained by those candidates that historical records show are the primary candidates of the two major parties, except in 1836 when the three Whig candidates are tallied for the total Whig vote. Democratic = Anti-Federalists (1788–1796), Democratic-Republicans (1796–1828), Jacksonian Democrats (1824–1828), and Democrats (since 1832). Republicans = Federalists (1788–1816), National Republicans (1828–1832), Whigs (1836–1852), and Republicans (since 1856). Other = other third parties. Residents of the District of Columbia received the presidential vote beginning in the 1964 election.

Sources: *America Votes* (various publication dates) and independent search of state sources by the author.

Table 4-37 Raw Popular Vote for President, by State, 1788–1792

State	1788				1792			
	Democratic	Republican	Other	Total Vote	Democratic	Republican	Other	Total Vote
Alabama	—	—	—	—	—	—	—	—
Alaska	—	—	—	—	—	—	—	—
Arizona	—	—	—	—	—	—	—	—
Arkansas	—	—	—	—	—	—	—	—
California	—	—	—	—	—	—	—	—
Colorado	—	—	—	—	—	—	—	—
Connecticut	—	—	—	—	—	—	—	—
Delaware	0[1]	0[1]	685[1]	685[1]	—	—	—	—
Dist. of Columbia	—	—	—	—	—	—	—	—
Florida	—	—	—	—	—	—	—	—
Georgia	—	—	—	—	—	—	—	—
Hawaii	—	—	—	—	—	—	—	—
Idaho	—	—	—	—	—	—	—	—
Illinois	—	—	—	—	—	—	—	—
Indiana	—	—	—	—	—	—	—	—
Iowa	—	—	—	—	—	—	—	—
Kansas	—	—	—	—	—	—	—	—
Kentucky	—	—	—	—	—	—	—	—
Louisiana	—	—	—	—	—	—	—	—
Maine	—	—	—	—	—	—	—	—
Maryland	2,280	7,665	0	9,945	—	—	—	—
Massachusetts	0	14,668	0	14,668	0[1]	19,929[1]	0[1]	19,929[1]
Michigan	—	—	—	—	—	—	—	—
Minnesota	—	—	—	—	—	—	—	—
Mississippi	—	—	—	—	—	—	—	—
Missouri	—	—	—	—	—	—	—	—
Montana	—	—	—	—	—	—	—	—
Nebraska	—	—	—	—	—	—	—	—
Nevada	—	—	—	—	—	—	—	—
New Hampshire	0	5,909	0	5,909	0	8,924	0	8,924
New Jersey	—	—	—	—	—	—	—	—
New Mexico	—	—	—	—	—	—	—	—
New York	—	—	—	—	—	—	—	—
North Carolina	—	—	—	—	—	—	—	—
North Dakota	—	—	—	—	—	—	—	—
Ohio	—	—	—	—	—	—	—	—
Oklahoma	—	—	—	—	—	—	—	—
Oregon	—	—	—	—	—	—	—	—
Pennsylvania	672[1]	6,711[1]	0[1]	7,383[1]	0[1]	3,358[1]	1,261[1]	4,619[1]
Rhode Island	—	—	—	—	—	—	—	—
South Carolina	—	—	—	—	—	—	—	—
South Dakota	—	—	—	—	—	—	—	—
Tennessee	—	—	—	—	—	—	—	—
Texas	—	—	—	—	—	—	—	—
Utah	—	—	—	—	—	—	—	—
Vermont	—	—	—	—	—	—	—	—
Virginia	0[1]	0[1]	2,453[1]	2,453[1]	—	—	—	—
Washington	—	—	—	—	—	—	—	—
West Virginia	—	—	—	—	—	—	—	—
Wisconsin	—	—	—	—	—	—	—	—
Wyoming	—	—	—	—	—	—	—	—

Notes: Entries for the major parties (Democratic, Republican, or their historical antecedents listed in Appendix A) are votes gained by those candidates that historical records show are the primary candidates of the two major parties, except in 1836 when the three Whig candidates are tallied for the total Whig vote. Democratic = Anti-Federalists (1788–1796), Democratic-Republicans (1796–1828), Jacksonian Democrats (1824–1828), and Democrats (since 1832). Republicans = Federalists (1788–1816), National Republicans (1828–1832), Whigs (1836–1852), and Republicans (since 1856). Other = other third parties. — indicates that the state had no data, either because no vote data were found for the state in question or the state had not yet entered the Union. Residents of the District of Columbia received the presidential vote beginning in the 1964 election.

[1]Partial data.

Sources: From the election archive collection of Michael J. Dubin.

Table 4-38 Raw Popular Vote for President, by State, 1796–1800

	1796				1800			
State	Democratic	Republican	Other	Total Vote	Democratic	Republican	Other	Total Vote
Alabama	—	—	—	—	—	—	—	—
Alaska	—	—	—	—	—	—	—	—
Arizona	—	—	—	—	—	—	—	—
Arkansas	—	—	—	—	—	—	—	—
California	—	—	—	—	—	—	—	—
Colorado	—	—	—	—	—	—	—	—
Connecticut	—	—	—	—	—	—	—	—
Delaware	—	—	—	—	—	—	—	—
Dist. of Columbia	—	—	—	—	—	—	—	—
Florida	—	—	—	—	—	—	—	—
Georgia	19,132[1]	8,202[1]	230[1]	27,564[1]	—	—	—	—
Hawaii	—	—	—	—	—	—	—	—
Idaho	—	—	—	—	—	—	—	—
Illinois	—	—	—	—	—	—	—	—
Indiana	—	—	—	—	—	—	—	—
Iowa	—	—	—	—	—	—	—	—
Kansas	—	—	—	—	—	—	—	—
Kentucky	—	—	—	—	—	—	—	—
Louisiana	—	—	—	—	—	—	—	—
Maine	—	—	—	—	—	—	—	—
Maryland	6,440	7,029	0	13,469	10,629	10,018	0	20,647
Massachusetts	0	0	15,438	15,438	—	—	—	—
Michigan	—	—	—	—	—	—	—	—
Minnesota	—	—	—	—	—	—	—	—
Mississippi	—	—	—	—	—	—	—	—
Missouri	—	—	—	—	—	—	—	—
Montana	—	—	—	—	—	—	—	—
Nebraska	—	—	—	—	—	—	—	—
Nevada	—	—	—	—	—	—	—	—
New Hampshire	0	18,274	0	18,274	—	—	—	—
New Jersey	—	—	—	—	—	—	—	—
New Mexico	—	—	—	—	—	—	—	—
New York	—	—	—	—	—	—	—	—
North Carolina	—	—	—	—	7,540[1]	7,588[1]	0[1]	15,128[1]
North Dakota	—	—	—	—	—	—	—	—
Ohio	—	—	—	—	—	—	—	—
Oklahoma	—	—	—	—	—	—	—	—
Oregon	—	—	—	—	—	—	—	—
Pennsylvania	12,516	12,229	0	24,745	—	—	—	—
Rhode Island	—	—	—	—	2,345	2,149	0	4,494
South Carolina	—	—	—	—	—	—	—	—
South Dakota	—	—	—	—	—	—	—	—
Tennessee	—	—	—	—	—	—	—	—
Texas	—	—	—	—	—	—	—	—
Utah	—	—	—	—	—	—	—	—
Vermont	—	—	—	—	—	—	—	—
Virginia	—	—	—	—	21,002	6,178	0	27,180
Washington	—	—	—	—	—	—	—	—
West Virginia	—	—	—	—	—	—	—	—
Wisconsin	—	—	—	—	—	—	—	—
Wyoming	—	—	—	—	—	—	—	—

Notes: Entries for the major parties (Democratic, Republican, or their historical antecedents listed in Appendix A) are votes gained by those candidates that historical records show are the primary candidates of the two major parties, except in 1836 when the three Whig candidates are tallied for the total Whig vote. Democratic = Anti-Federalists (1788–1796), Democratic-Republicans (1796–1828), Jacksonian Democrats (1824–1828), and Democrats (since 1832). Republicans = Federalists (1788–1816), National Republicans (1828–1832), Whigs (1836–1852), and Republicans (since 1856). Other = other third parties. — indicates that the state had no data, either because no vote data were found for the state in question or the state had not yet entered the Union. Residents of the District of Columbia received the presidential vote beginning in the 1964 election.

[1]Partial data.

Sources: From the election archive collection of Michael J. Dubin.

Table 4-39 Raw Popular Vote for President by State, 1804–1808

State	1804				1808			
	Democratic	Republican	Other	Total Vote	Democratic	Republican	Other	Total Vote
Alabama	—	—	—	—	—	—	—	—
Alaska	—	—	—	—	—	—	—	—
Arizona	—	—	—	—	—	—	—	—
Arkansas	—	—	—	—	—	—	—	—
California	—	—	—	—	—	—	—	—
Colorado	—	—	—	—	—	—	—	—
Connecticut	—	—	—	—	—	—	—	—
Delaware	—	—	—	—	—	—	—	—
Dist. of Columbia	—	—	—	—	—	—	—	—
Florida	—	—	—	—	—	—	—	—
Georgia	—	—	—	—	—	—	—	—
Hawaii	—	—	—	—	—	—	—	—
Idaho	—	—	—	—	—	—	—	—
Illinois	—	—	—	—	—	—	—	—
Indiana	—	—	—	—	—	—	—	—
Iowa	—	—	—	—	—	—	—	—
Kansas	—	—	—	—	—	—	—	—
Kentucky	5,080[1]	0[1]	0[1]	5,080[1]	2,679[1]	54[1]	0[1]	2,733[1]
Louisiana	—	—	—	—	—	—	—	—
Maine	—	—	—	—	—	—	—	—
Maryland	7,301	2,461	0	9,762	15,346	8,873	0	24,219
Massachusetts	29,514	25,832	0	55,346	—	—	—	—
Michigan	—	—	—	—	—	—	—	—
Minnesota	—	—	—	—	—	—	—	—
Mississippi	—	—	—	—	—	—	—	—
Missouri	—	—	—	—	—	—	—	—
Montana	—	—	—	—	—	—	—	—
Nebraska	—	—	—	—	—	—	—	—
Nevada	—	—	—	—	—	—	—	—
New Hampshire	9,088	8,364	0	17,452	12,744	14,006	0	26,750
New Jersey	13,119	0	0	13,119	18,488	14,684	0	33,172
New Mexico	—	—	—	—	—	—	—	—
New York	—	—	—	—	—	—	—	—
North Carolina	1,056[1]	431[1]	0[1]	1,487[1]	9,733[1]	7,798[1]	1,139[1]	18,670[1]
North Dakota	—	—	—	—	—	—	—	—
Ohio	2,502	364	0	2,866	3,645	1,174	0	4,819
Oklahoma	—	—	—	—	—	—	—	—
Oregon	—	—	—	—	—	—	—	—
Pennsylvania	22,081	1,238	0	23,319	42,508	11,735	0	54,243
Rhode Island	1,311	0	0	1,311	2,692	3,172	0	5,864
South Carolina	—	—	—	—	—	—	—	—
South Dakota	—	—	—	—	—	—	—	—
Tennessee	—	—	—	—	—	—	—	—
Texas	—	—	—	—	—	—	—	—
Utah	—	—	—	—	—	—	—	—
Vermont	—	—	—	—	—	—	—	—
Virginia	12,879	0	0	12,879	15,682	758	3,504	19,944
Washington	—	—	—	—	—	—	—	—
West Virginia	—	—	—	—	—	—	—	—
Wisconsin	—	—	—	—	—	—	—	—
Wyoming	—	—	—	—	—	—	—	—

Notes: Entries for the major parties (Democratic, Republican, or their historical antecedents listed in Appendix A) are votes gained by those candidates that historical records show are the primary candidates of the two major parties, except in 1836 when the three Whig candidates are tallied for the total Whig vote. Democratic = Anti-Federalists (1788–1796), Democratic-Republicans (1796–1828), Jacksonian Democrats (1824–1828), and Democrats (since 1832). Republicans = Federalists (1788–1816), National Republicans (1828–1832), Whigs (1836–1852), and Republicans (since 1856). Other = other third parties. — indicates that the state had no data, either because no vote data were found for the state in question or the state had not yet entered the Union. Residents of the District of Columbia received the presidential vote beginning in the 1964 election.

[1]Partial data.

Sources: From the election archive collection of Michael J. Dubin.

Table 4-40 Raw Popular Vote for President, by State, 1812–1816

State	1812				1816			
	Democratic	Republican	Other	Total Vote	Democratic	Republican	Other	Total Vote
Alabama	—	—	—	—	—	—	—	—
Alaska	—	—	—	—	—	—	—	—
Arizona	—	—	—	—	—	—	—	—
Arkansas	—	—	—	—	—	—	—	—
California	—	—	—	—	—	—	—	—
Colorado	—	—	—	—	—	—	—	—
Connecticut	—	—	—	—	—	—	—	—
Delaware	—	—	—	—	—	—	—	—
Dist. of Columbia	—	—	—	—	—	—	—	—
Florida	—	—	—	—	—	—	—	—
Georgia	—	—	—	—	—	—	—	—
Hawaii	—	—	—	—	—	—	—	—
Idaho	—	—	—	—	—	—	—	—
Illinois	—	—	—	—	—	—	—	—
Indiana	—	—	—	—	—	—	—	—
Iowa	—	—	—	—	—	—	—	—
Kansas	—	—	—	—	—	—	—	—
Kentucky	8,501[1]	144[1]	0[1]	8,645[1]	—	—	—	—
Louisiana	—	—	—	—	—	—	—	—
Maine	—	—	—	—	—	—	—	—
Maryland	14,751	14,280	0	29,031	7,435	3,048	0	10,483
Massachusetts	28,620	49,630	0	78,250	—	—	—	—
Michigan	—	—	—	—	—	—	—	—
Minnesota	—	—	—	—	—	—	—	—
Mississippi	—	—	—	—	—	—	—	—
Missouri	—	—	—	—	—	—	—	—
Montana	—	—	—	—	—	—	—	—
Nebraska	—	—	—	—	—	—	—	—
Nevada	—	—	—	—	—	—	—	—
New Hampshire	12,744	14,006	0	26,750	15,197	13,330	0	28,527
New Jersey	—	—	—	—	5,441	0	0	5,441
New Mexico	—	—	—	—	—	—	—	—
New York	—	—	—	—	—	—	—	—
North Carolina	—	—	—	—	9,549	640	0	10,189
North Dakota	—	—	—	—	—	—	—	—
Ohio	7,420	3,301	0	10,721	3,326	593	0	3,919
Oklahoma	—	—	—	—	—	—	—	—
Oregon	—	—	—	—	—	—	—	—
Pennsylvania	49,397	29,509	0	78,906	25,653	0	17,589	43,242
Rhode Island	2,084	4,032	0	6,116	1,236	0	0	1,236
South Carolina	—	—	—	—	—	—	—	—
South Dakota	—	—	—	—	—	—	—	—
Tennessee	—	—	—	—	—	—	—	—
Texas	—	—	—	—	—	—	—	—
Utah	—	—	—	—	—	—	—	—
Vermont	—	—	—	—	—	—	—	—
Virginia	14,980	5,573	0	20,553	6,859	0	0	6,859
Washington	—	—	—	—	—	—	—	—
West Virginia	—	—	—	—	—	—	—	—
Wisconsin	—	—	—	—	—	—	—	—
Wyoming	—	—	—	—	—	—	—	—

Notes: Entries for the major parties (Democratic, Republican, or their historical antecedents listed in Appendix A) are votes gained by those candidates that historical records show are the primary candidates of the two major parties, except in 1836 when the three Whig candidates are tallied for the total Whig vote. Democratic = Anti-Federalists (1788–1796), Democratic-Republicans (1796–1828), Jacksonian Democrats (1824–1828), and Democrats (since 1832). Republicans = Federalists (1788–1816), National Republicans (1828–1832), Whigs (1836–1852), and Republicans (since 1856). Other = other third parties. — indicates that the state had no data, either because no vote data were found for the state in question or the state had not yet entered the Union. Residents of the District of Columbia received the presidential vote beginning in the 1964 election.

[1]Partial data.

Sources: From the election archive collection of Michael J. Dubin.

Table 4-41 Raw Popular Vote for President by State, 1820–1824

State	1820				1824			
	Democratic	Republican	Other	Total Vote	Democratic	Republican	Other	Total Vote
Alabama	—	—	—	—	9,429	2,422	1,752	13,603
Alaska	—	—	—	—	—	—	—	—
Arizona	—	—	—	—	—	—	—	—
Arkansas	—	—	—	—	—	—	—	—
California	—	—	—	—	—	—	—	—
Colorado	—	—	—	—	—	—	—	—
Connecticut	3,889	0	0	3,889	0	7,494	3,153	10,647
Delaware	—	—	—	—	—	—	—	—
Dist. of Columbia	—	—	—	—	—	—	—	—
Florida	—	—	—	—	—	—	—	—
Georgia	—	—	—	—	—	—	—	—
Hawaii	—	—	—	—	—	—	—	—
Idaho	—	—	—	—	—	—	—	—
Illinois	938	0	492	1,430	1,272	1,516	1,883	4,671
Indiana	—	—	—	—	7,444	3,071	5,323	15,838
Iowa	—	—	—	—	—	—	—	—
Kansas	—	—	—	—	—	—	—	—
Kentucky	3,169[1]	0[1]	0[1]	3,169[1]	6,356	0	16,982	23,338
Louisiana	—	—	—	—	—	—	—	—
Maine	4,867	0	587	5,454	0	10,289	2,336	12,625
Maryland	4,544	386	175	5,105	14,523	14,632	4,059	33,214
Massachusetts	7,689	16,341	0	24,030	0	30,687	11,369	42,056
Michigan	—	—	—	—	—	—	—	—
Minnesota	—	—	—	—	—	—	—	—
Mississippi	—	—	—	—	3,121	1,654	119	4,894
Missouri	—	—	—	—	1,166	159	2,107	3,432
Montana	—	—	—	—	—	—	—	—
Nebraska	—	—	—	—	—	—	—	—
Nevada	—	—	—	—	—	—	—	—
New Hampshire	9,448	0	0	9,448	0	9,389	643	10,032
New Jersey	4,321	0	0	4,321	10,332	8,309	1,196	19,837
New Mexico	—	—	—	—	—	—	—	—
New York	—	—	—	—	—	—	—	—
North Carolina	3,300	0	0	3,300	20,231	0	15,878	36,109
North Dakota	—	—	—	—	—	—	—	—
Ohio	7,164	0	0	7,164	18,489	12,280	19,255	50,024
Oklahoma	—	—	—	—	—	—	—	—
Oregon	—	—	—	—	—	—	—	—
Pennsylvania	30,313	0	1,893	32,206	35,736	5,441	5,896	47,073
Rhode Island	724	0	0	724	0	2,144	200	2,344
South Carolina	—	—	—	—	—	—	—	—
South Dakota	—	—	—	—	—	—	—	—
Tennessee	—	—	—	—	20,197	216	312	20,725
Texas	—	—	—	—	—	—	—	—
Utah	—	—	—	—	—	—	—	—
Vermont	—	—	—	—	—	—	—	—
Virginia	5,247	0	0	5,247	2,975	3,419	8,977	15,371
Washington	—	—	—	—	—	—	—	—
West Virginia	—	—	—	—	—	—	—	—
Wisconsin	—	—	—	—	—	—	—	—
Wyoming	—	—	—	—	—	—	—	—

Notes: Entries for the major parties (Democratic, Republican, or their historical antecedents listed in Appendix A) are votes gained by those candidates that historical records show are the primary candidates of the two major parties, except in 1836 when the three Whig candidates are tallied for the total Whig vote. Democratic = Anti-Federalists (1788–1796), Democratic-Republicans (1796–1828), Jacksonian Democrats (1824–1828), and Democrats (since 1832). Republicans = Federalists (1788–1816), National Republicans (1828–1832), Whigs (1836–1852), and Republicans (since 1856). Other = other third parties. — indicates that the state had no data, either because no vote data were found for the state in question or the state had not yet entered the Union. Residents of the District of Columbia received the presidential vote beginning in the 1964 election. J.Q. Adams is considered a Republican in this table in the 1824 election.

[1]Partial data.

Sources: From the election archive collection of Michael J. Dubin, *Congressional Quarterly's Guide to U.S. Elections* (1994), ICPSR data sets 0001 and 0019, *A Statistical History of the American Presidential Elections* (1963), and independent search of state sources by the author.

Table 4-42 Raw Popular Vote for President, by State, 1828–1832

State	1828				1832			
	Democratic	Republican	Other	Total Vote	Democratic	Republican	Other	Total Vote
Alabama	16,736	1,878	4	18,618	14,286	5	0	14,291
Alaska	—	—	—	—	—	—	—	—
Arizona	—	—	—	—	—	—	—	—
Arkansas	—	—	—	—	—	—	—	—
California	—	—	—	—	—	—	—	—
Colorado	—	—	—	—	—	—	—	—
Connecticut	4,448	13,829	1,101	19,378	11,269	18,155	3,409	32,833
Delaware	—	—	—	—	4,110	4,276	0	8,386
Dist. of Columbia	—	—	—	—	—	—	—	—
Florida	—	—	—	—	—	—	—	—
Georgia	19,362	642	0	20,004	20,750	0	0	20,750
Hawaii	—	—	—	—	—	—	—	—
Idaho	—	—	—	—	—	—	—	—
Illinois	9,560	4,662	0	14,222	14,609	6,745	127	21,481
Indiana	22,201	17,009	0	39,210	31,652	25,473	27	57,152
Iowa	—	—	—	—	—	—	—	—
Kansas	—	—	—	—	—	—	—	—
Kentucky	39,308	31,468	0	70,776	36,292	43,449	0	79,741
Louisiana	4,605	4,082	0	8,687	3,908	2,429	0	6,337
Maine	13,927	20,773	89	34,789	33,978	27,331	844	62,153
Maryland	22,782	23,014	0	45,796	19,156	19,160	0	38,316
Massachusetts	6,012	29,836	3,226	39,074	13,933	31,963	21,723	67,619
Michigan	—	—	—	—	—	—	—	—
Minnesota	—	—	—	—	—	—	—	—
Mississippi	6,763	1,581	0	8,344	5,750	0	0	5,750
Missouri	8,232	3,422	0	11,654	5,192	0	0	5,192
Montana	—	—	—	—	—	—	—	—
Nebraska	—	—	—	—	—	—	—	—
Nevada	—	—	—	—	—	—	—	—
New Hampshire	20,212	23,823	0	44,035	24,855	18,938	0	43,793
New Jersey	21,809	23,753	8	45,570	23,826	23,466	468	47,760
New Mexico	—	—	—	—	—	—	—	—
New York	139,412	131,563	0	270,975	168,497	154,896	0	323,393
North Carolina	37,814	13,918	15	51,747	25,261	4,538	0	29,799
North Dakota	—	—	—	—	—	—	—	—
Ohio	67,596	63,453	0	131,049	81,246	76,566	538	158,350
Oklahoma	—	—	—	—	—	—	—	—
Oregon	—	—	—	—	—	—	—	—
Pennsylvania	101,457	50,763	0	152,220	90,973	0	66,706	157,679
Rhode Island	820	2,755	5	3,580	2,051	2,871	825	5,747
South Carolina	—	—	—	—	—	—	—	—
South Dakota	—	—	—	—	—	—	—	—
Tennessee	44,293	2,240	0	46,533	28,078	1,347	0	29,425
Texas	—	—	—	—	—	—	—	—
Utah	—	—	—	—	—	—	—	—
Vermont	8,350	24,363	120	32,833	7,865	11,161	13,318	32,344
Virginia	26,854	12,070	0	38,924	34,243	11,436	3	45,682
Washington	—	—	—	—	—	—	—	—
West Virginia	—	—	—	—	—	—	—	—
Wisconsin	—	—	—	—	—	—	—	—
Wyoming	—	—	—	—	—	—	—	—

Notes: Entries for the major parties (Democratic, Republican, or their historical antecedents listed in Appendix A) are votes gained by those candidates that historical records show are the primary candidates of the two major parties, except in 1836 when the three Whig candidates are tallied for the total Whig vote. Democratic = Anti-Federalists (1788–1796), Democratic-Republicans (1796–1828), Jacksonian Democrats (1824–1828), and Democrats (since 1832). Republicans = Federalists (1788–1816), National Republicans (1828–1832), Whigs (1836–1852), and Republicans (since 1856). Other = other third parties. — indicates that the state had no data, either because no vote data were found for the state in question or the state had not yet entered the Union. Residents of the District of Columbia received the presidential vote beginning in the 1964 election.

Sources: *Congressional Quarterly's Guide to U.S. Elections* (1994), ICPSR data sets 0001 and 0019, *A Statistical History of the American Presidential Elections* (1963), and independent search of state sources by the author.

Table 4-43 Raw Popular Vote for President, by State, 1836–1840

State	1836				1840			
	Democratic	Republican	Other	Total Vote	Democratic	Republican	Other	Total Vote
Alabama	20,638	16,658	0	37,296	33,996	28,515	0	62,511
Alaska	—	—	—	—	—	—	—	—
Arizona	—	—	—	—	—	—	—	—
Arkansas	2,380	1,334	0	3,714	6,679	5,160	0	11,839
California	—	—	—	—	—	—	—	—
Colorado	—	—	—	—	—	—	—	—
Connecticut	19,294	18,799	0	38,093	25,281	31,598	0	56,879
Delaware	4,154	4,736	5	8,895	4,872	5,967	13	10,852
Dist. of Columbia	—	—	—	—	—	—	—	—
Florida	—	—	—	—	—	—	—	—
Georgia	22,778	24,481	0	47,259	31,983	40,339	0	72,322
Hawaii	—	—	—	—	—	—	—	—
Idaho	—	—	—	—	—	—	—	—
Illinois	18,369	15,220	0	33,589	47,441	45,574	160	93,175
Indiana	33,084	41,339	0	74,423	51,696	65,280	629	117,605
Iowa	—	—	—	—	—	—	—	—
Kansas	—	—	—	—	—	—	—	—
Kentucky	33,229	36,861	0	70,090	32,616	58,488	0	91,104
Louisiana	3,842	3,583	0	7,425	7,616	11,296	0	18,912
Maine	22,825	14,803	1,112	38,740	46,190	46,612	0	92,802
Maryland	22,267	25,852	0	48,119	28,752	33,528	0	62,280
Massachusetts	33,486	41,201	45	74,732	52,355	72,852	1,618	126,825
Michigan	6,507	5,545	0	12,052	21,096	22,933	0	44,029
Minnesota	—	—	—	—	—	—	—	—
Mississippi	10,297	9,782	0	20,079	17,010	19,515	0	36,525
Missouri	10,995	7,337	0	18,332	29,969	22,954	0	52,923
Montana	—	—	—	—	—	—	—	—
Nebraska	—	—	—	—	—	—	—	—
Nevada	—	—	—	—	—	—	—	—
New Hampshire	18,697	6,228	0	24,925	32,774	26,310	872	59,956
New Jersey	25,592	26,137	0	51,729	31,034	33,351	69	64,454
New Mexico	—	—	—	—	—	—	—	—
New York	166,795	138,548	0	305,343	212,733	226,001	2,809	441,543
North Carolina	26,631	23,521	1	50,153	34,168	46,567	0	80,735
North Dakota	—	—	—	—	—	—	—	—
Ohio	97,122	105,809	0	202,931	123,944	148,043	903	272,890
Oklahoma	—	—	—	—	—	—	—	—
Oregon	—	—	—	—	—	—	—	—
Pennsylvania	91,466	87,235	0	178,701	143,672	144,023	0	287,695
Rhode Island	2,962	2,710	1	5,673	3,263	5,213	155	8,631
South Carolina	—	—	—	—	—	—	—	—
South Dakota	—	—	—	—	—	—	—	—
Tennessee	26,170	36,027	0	62,197	47,951	60,194	0	108,145
Texas	—	—	—	—	—	—	—	—
Utah	—	—	—	—	—	—	—	—
Vermont	14,040	20,994	65	35,099	18,006	32,440	336	50,782
Virginia	30,556	23,384	5	53,945	43,757	42,637	0	86,394
Washington	—	—	—	—	—	—	—	—
West Virginia	—	—	—	—	—	—	—	—
Wisconsin	—	—	—	—	—	—	—	—
Wyoming	—	—	—	—	—	—	—	—

Notes: Entries for the major parties (Democratic, Republican, or their historical antecedents listed in Appendix A) are votes gained by those candidates that historical records show are the primary candidates of the two major parties, except in 1836 when the three Whig candidates are tallied for the total Whig vote. Democratic = Anti-Federalists (1788–1796), Democratic-Republicans (1796–1828), Jacksonian Democrats (1824–1828), and Democrats (since 1832). Republicans = Federalists (1788–1816), National Republicans (1828–1832), Whigs (1836–1852), and Republicans (since 1856). Other = other third parties. — indicates that the state had no data, either because no vote data were found for the state in question or the state had not yet entered the Union. Residents of the District of Columbia received the presidential vote beginning in the 1964 election.

Sources: *Congressional Quarterly's Guide to U.S. Elections* (1994), ICPSR data sets 0001 and 0019, *A Statistical History of the American Presidential Elections* (1963), and independent search of state sources by the author.

Table 4-44 Raw Popular Vote for President, by State, 1844–1848

	1844				1848			
State	Democratic	Republican	Other	Total Vote	Democratic	Republican	Other	Total Vote
Alabama	37,401	26,002	0	63,403	31,173	30,482	4	61,659
Alaska	—	—	—	—	—	—	—	—
Arizona	—	—	—	—	—	—	—	—
Arkansas	9,546	5,604	0	15,150	9,301	7,587	0	16,888
California	—	—	—	—	—	—	—	—
Colorado	—	—	—	—	—	—	—	—
Connecticut	29,841	32,832	1,943	64,616	27,051	30,318	5,029	62,398
Delaware	5,970	6,271	6	12,247	5,910	6,440	82	12,432
Dist. of Columbia	—	—	—	—	—	—	—	—
Florida	—	—	—	—	3,083	4,120	0	7,203
Georgia	44,147	42,100	0	86,247	44,785	47,532	0	92,317
Hawaii	—	—	—	—	—	—	—	—
Idaho	—	—	—	—	—	—	—	—
Illinois	58,795	45,854	4,408	109,057	55,952	52,853	15,791	124,596
Indiana	70,183	67,866	2,108	140,157	74,695	69,668	8,031	152,394
Iowa	—	—	—	—	11,238	9,930	1,103	22,271
Kansas	—	—	—	—	—	—	—	—
Kentucky	51,988	61,249	0	113,237	49,720	67,145	0	116,865
Louisiana	13,782	13,083	0	26,865	15,379	18,487	0	33,866
Maine	45,719	34,378	4,836	84,933	40,195	35,273	12,157	87,625
Maryland	32,706	35,984	0	68,690	34,528	37,702	129	72,359
Massachusetts	53,039	67,062	11,936	132,037	35,281	61,072	38,395	134,748
Michigan	27,737	24,185	3,638	55,560	30,742	23,947	10,393	65,082
Minnesota	—	—	—	—	—	—	—	—
Mississippi	25,846	19,158	0	45,004	26,545	25,911	0	52,456
Missouri	41,322	31,200	0	72,522	40,077	32,671	0	72,748
Montana	—	—	—	—	—	—	—	—
Nebraska	—	—	—	—	—	—	—	—
Nevada	—	—	—	—	—	—	—	—
New Hampshire	27,160	17,866	4,161	49,187	27,763	14,781	7,560	50,104
New Jersey	37,495	38,318	131	75,944	36,901	40,015	829	77,745
New Mexico	—	—	—	—	—	—	—	—
New York	237,588	232,482	15,812	485,882	114,319	218,583	123,042	455,944
North Carolina	39,287	43,232	2	82,521	35,772	44,054	0	79,826
North Dakota	—	—	—	—	—	—	—	—
Ohio	149,127	155,091	8,082	312,300	154,782	138,656	35,549	328,987
Oklahoma	—	—	—	—	—	—	—	—
Oregon	—	—	—	—	—	—	—	—
Pennsylvania	167,311	161,195	3,139	331,645	172,186	185,730	11,176	369,092
Rhode Island	4,867	7,322	5	12,194	3,613	6,705	731	11,049
South Carolina	—	—	—	—	—	—	—	—
South Dakota	—	—	—	—	—	—	—	—
Tennessee	59,917	60,040	0	119,957	58,142	64,321	0	122,463
Texas	—	—	—	—	11,644	5,281	75	17,000
Utah	—	—	—	—	—	—	—	—
Vermont	18,041	26,770	3,954	48,765	10,943	23,117	13,837	47,897
Virginia	50,679	44,860	0	95,539	46,739	45,265	0	92,004
Washington	—	—	—	—	—	—	—	—
West Virginia	—	—	—	—	—	—	—	—
Wisconsin	—	—	—	—	15,001	13,747	10,418	39,166
Wyoming	—	—	—	—	—	—	—	—

Notes: Entries for the major parties (Democratic, Republican, or their historical antecedents listed in Appendix A) are votes gained by those candidates that historical records show are the primary candidates of the two major parties, except in 1836 when the three Whig candidates are tallied for the total Whig vote. Democratic = Anti-Federalists (1788–1796), Democratic-Republicans (1796–1828), Jacksonian Democrats (1824–1828), and Democrats (since 1832). Republicans = Federalists (1788–1816), National Republicans (1828–1832), Whigs (1836–1852), and Republicans (since 1856). Other = other third parties. — indicates that the state had no data, either because no vote data were found for the state in question or the state had not yet entered the Union. Residents of the District of Columbia received the presidential vote beginning in the 1964 election.

Sources: *Congressional Quarterly's Guide to U.S. Elections* (1994), ICPSR data sets 0001 and 0019, *A Statistical History of the American Presidential Elections* (1963), and independent search of state sources by the author.

Table 4-45 Raw Popular Vote for President, by State, 1852–1856

State	1852 Democratic	Republican	Other	Total Vote	1856 Democratic	Republican	Other	Total Vote
Alabama	26,881	15,061	2,205	44,147	46,739	0	28,552	75,291
Alaska	—	—	—	—	—	—	—	—
Arizona	—	—	—	—	—	—	—	—
Arkansas	12,173	7,404	0	19,577	21,910	0	10,732	32,642
California	40,721	35,972	117	76,810	53,342	20,704	36,209	110,255
Colorado	—	—	—	—	—	—	—	—
Connecticut	33,249	30,359	3,173	66,781	35,028	42,717	2,615	80,360
Delaware	6,318	6,293	62	12,673	8,004	310	6,284	14,598
Dist. of Columbia	—	—	—	—	—	—	—	—
Florida	4,318	2,875	0	7,193	6,358	0	4,833	11,191
Georgia	40,516	16,660	5,450	62,626	56,581	0	42,439	99,020
Hawaii	—	—	—	—	—	—	—	—
Idaho	—	—	—	—	—	—	—	—
Illinois	80,378	64,733	9,863	154,974	105,528	96,275	37,531	239,334
Indiana	95,340	80,907	6,929	183,176	118,670	94,375	22,356	235,401
Iowa	17,763	15,856	1,745	35,364	37,568	45,073	9,669	92,310
Kansas	—	—	—	—	—	—	—	—
Kentucky	53,949	57,428	266	111,643	74,642	0	67,416	142,058
Louisiana	18,647	17,255	0	35,902	22,164	0	20,709	42,873
Maine	41,609	32,543	8,030	82,182	39,140	67,279	3,270	109,689
Maryland	40,022	35,077	21	75,120	39,123	285	47,452	86,860
Massachusetts	44,569	52,683	29,851	127,103	39,244	108,172	22,632	170,048
Michigan	41,842	33,860	7,237	82,939	52,136	71,762	1,660	125,558
Minnesota	—	—	—	—	—	—	—	—
Mississippi	26,896	17,558	0	44,454	35,456	0	24,191	59,647
Missouri	38,817	29,984	0	68,801	57,964	0	48,522	106,486
Montana	—	—	—	—	—	—	—	—
Nebraska	—	—	—	—	—	—	—	—
Nevada	—	—	—	—	—	—	—	—
New Hampshire	28,503	15,486	6,546	50,535	31,891	37,473	410	69,774
New Jersey	44,301	38,551	1,074	83,926	46,943	28,338	24,115	99,396
New Mexico	—	—	—	—	—	—	—	—
New York	262,083	234,882	25,329	522,294	195,878	276,004	124,604	596,486
North Carolina	39,788	39,043	60	78,891	48,243	0	36,720	84,963
North Dakota	—	—	—	—	—	—	—	—
Ohio	169,193	152,577	31,133	352,903	170,874	187,497	28,269	386,640
Oklahoma	—	—	—	—	—	—	—	—
Oregon	—	—	—	—	—	—	—	—
Pennsylvania	198,568	179,182	10,170	387,920	230,772	147,963	82,202	460,937
Rhode Island	8,735	7,626	644	17,005	6,680	11,467	1,675	19,822
South Carolina	—	—	—	—	—	—	—	—
South Dakota	—	—	—	—	—	—	—	—
Tennessee	56,900	58,586	0	115,486	69,704	0	63,878	133,582
Texas	14,857	5,356	10	20,223	31,995	0	16,010	48,005
Utah	—	—	—	—	—	—	—	—
Vermont	13,044	22,173	8,621	43,838	10,569	39,561	545	50,675
Virginia	73,872	58,732	0	132,604	90,083	0	60,150	150,233
Washington	—	—	—	—	—	—	—	—
West Virginia	—	—	—	—	—	—	—	—
Wisconsin	33,658	22,240	8,842	64,740	52,843	67,090	580	120,513
Wyoming	—	—	—	—	—	—	—	—

Notes: Entries for the major parties (Democratic, Republican, or their historical antecedents listed in Appendix A) are votes gained by those candidates that historical records show are the primary candidates of the two major parties, except in 1836 when the three Whig candidates are tallied for the total Whig vote. Democratic = Anti-Federalists (1788–1796), Democratic-Republicans (1796–1828), Jacksonian Democrats (1824–1828), and Democrats (since 1832). Republicans = Federalists (1788–1816), National Republicans (1828–1832), Whigs (1836–1852), and Republicans (since 1856). Other = other third parties. — indicates that the state had no data, either because no vote data were found for the state in question or the state had not yet entered the Union. Residents of the District of Columbia received the presidential vote beginning in the 1964 election.

Sources: *Congressional Quarterly's Guide to U.S. Elections* (1994), ICPSR data sets 0001 and 0019, *A Statistical History of the American Presidential Elections* (1963), and independent search of state sources by the author.

Table 4-46 Raw Popular Vote for President, by State, 1860–1864

State	1860				1864			
	Democratic	Republican	Other	Total Vote	Democratic	Republican	Other	Total Vote
Alabama	13,618	0	76,504	90,122	—	—	—	—
Alaska	—	—	—	—	—	—	—	—
Arizona	—	—	—	—	—	—	—	—
Arkansas	5,357	0	48,795	54,152	—	—	—	—
California	37,999	38,733	43,095	119,827	43,837	62,053	0	105,890
Colorado	—	—	—	—	—	—	—	—
Connecticut	15,431	43,488	15,900	74,819	42,285	44,673	0	86,958
Delaware	1,066	3,822	11,227	16,115	8,767	8,155	0	16,922
Dist. of Columbia	—	—	—	—	—	—	—	—
Florida	223	0	13,078	13,301	—	—	—	—
Georgia	11,581	0	95,136	106,717	—	—	—	—
Hawaii	—	—	—	—	—	—	—	—
Idaho	—	—	—	—	—	—	—	—
Illinois	160,215	172,171	7,280	339,666	158,724	189,512	0	348,236
Indiana	115,509	139,033	17,601	272,143	130,230	149,887	0	280,117
Iowa	55,639	70,302	2,798	128,739	49,089	83,858	0	132,947
Kansas	—	—	—	—	3,836	17,089	655	21,580
Kentucky	25,651	1,364	119,201	146,216	64,301	27,787	0	92,088
Louisiana	7,625	0	42,885	50,510	—	—	—	—
Maine	29,693	62,811	8,414	100,918	46,992	67,805	0	114,797
Maryland	5,966	2,294	84,242	92,502	32,739	40,153	0	72,892
Massachusetts	34,370	106,684	28,822	169,876	48,745	126,742	6	175,493
Michigan	65,057	88,481	1,220	154,758	74,146	91,133	0	165,279
Minnesota	11,920	22,069	815	34,804	17,376	25,031	26	42,433
Mississippi	3,282	0	65,813	69,095	—	—	—	—
Missouri	58,801	17,028	89,734	165,563	31,596	72,750	0	104,346
Montana	—	—	—	—	—	—	—	—
Nebraska	—	—	—	—	—	—	—	—
Nevada	—	—	—	—	6,594	9,826	0	16,420
New Hampshire	25,887	37,519	2,537	65,943	33,034	36,596	0	69,630
New Jersey	62,869	58,346	0	121,215	68,020	60,724	0	128,744
New Mexico	—	—	—	—	—	—	—	—
New York	312,510	362,646	0	675,156	361,986	368,735	0	730,721
North Carolina	2,737	0	93,975	96,712	—	—	—	—
North Dakota	—	—	—	—	—	—	—	—
Ohio	187,421	231,709	23,736	442,866	205,609	265,674	0	471,283
Oklahoma	—	—	—	—	—	—	—	—
Oregon	4,136	5,329	5,293	14,758	8,457	9,888	5	18,350
Pennsylvania	16,765	268,030	191,647	476,442	277,443	296,292	0	573,735
Rhode Island	7,707	12,244	0	19,951	8,718	14,349	0	23,067
South Carolina	—	—	—	—	—	—	—	—
South Dakota	—	—	—	—	—	—	—	—
Tennessee	11,281	0	134,825	146,106	—	—	—	—
Texas	18	0	62,837	62,855	—	—	—	—
Utah	—	—	—	—	—	—	—	—
Vermont	8,649	33,808	2,187	44,644	13,321	42,419	0	55,740
Virginia	16,198	1,887	148,806	166,891	—	—	—	—
Washington	—	—	—	—	—	—	—	—
West Virginia	—	—	—	—	11,078	23,799	0	34,877
Wisconsin	65,021	86,110	1,048	152,179	65,884	83,458	0	149,342
Wyoming	—	—	—	—	—	—	—	—

Notes: Entries for the major parties (Democratic, Republican, or their historical antecedents listed in Appendix A) are votes gained by those candidates that historical records show are the primary candidates of the two major parties, except in 1836 when the three Whig candidates are tallied for the total Whig vote. Democratic = Anti-Federalists (1788–1796), Democratic-Republicans (1796–1828), Jacksonian Democrats (1824–1828), and Democrats (since 1832). Republicans = Federalists (1788–1816), National Republicans (1828–1832), Whigs (1836–1852), and Republicans (since 1856). Other = other third parties. — indicates that the state had no data, either because no vote data were found for the state in question or the state had not yet entered the Union. Residents of the District of Columbia received the presidential vote beginning in the 1964 election. Stephen Douglas is considered a Democrat in this table in the 1860 election.

Sources: *Congressional Quarterly's Guide to U.S. Elections* (1994), ICPSR data sets 0001 and 0019, *A Statistical History of the American Presidential Elections* (1963), and independent search of state sources by the author.

Table 4-47 Raw Popular Vote for President, by State, 1868–1872

	1868				1872			
State	Democratic	Republican	Other	Total Vote	Democratic	Republican	Other	Total Vote
Alabama	72,921	76,667	6	149,594	79,444	90,272	0	169,716
Alaska	—	—	—	—	—	—	—	—
Arizona	—	—	—	—	—	—	—	—
Arkansas	19,078	22,112	0	41,190	37,927	41,373	0	79,300
California	54,068	54,588	0	108,656	40,717	54,007	1,061	95,785
Colorado	—	—	—	—	—	—	—	—
Connecticut	47,781	50,789	0	98,570	45,685	50,307	0	95,992
Delaware	10,957	7,614	0	18,571	10,205	11,129	488	21,822
Dist. of Columbia	—	—	—	—	—	—	—	—
Florida	—	—	—	—	15,427	17,763	0	33,190
Georgia	102,707	57,109	0	159,816	76,356	62,550	0	138,906
Hawaii	—	—	—	—	—	—	—	—
Idaho	—	—	—	—	—	—	—	—
Illinois	199,116	250,304	0	449,420	184,884	241,936	3,151	429,971
Indiana	166,980	176,548	0	343,528	163,632	186,147	0	349,779
Iowa	74,040	120,399	0	194,439	71,189	131,566	13,610	216,365
Kansas	13,600	30,027	3	43,630	32,970	66,805	737	100,512
Kentucky	115,889	39,566	0	155,455	99,995	88,766	2,374	191,135
Louisiana	80,225	33,263	0	113,488	57,029	71,663	0	128,692
Maine	42,460	70,502	0	112,962	29,097	61,426	0	90,523
Maryland	62,357	30,438	0	92,795	67,687	66,760	0	134,447
Massachusetts	59,103	136,379	26	195,508	59,195	133,455	0	192,650
Michigan	97,069	128,563	0	225,632	78,651	138,768	4,150	221,569
Minnesota	28,075	43,545	0	71,620	35,131	56,040	168	91,339
Mississippi	—	—	—	—	47,282	82,175	0	129,457
Missouri	65,628	86,860	0	152,488	151,434	119,196	2,429	273,059
Montana	—	—	—	—	—	—	—	—
Nebraska	5,519	9,772	0	15,291	7,603	18,329	0	25,932
Nevada	5,215	6,474	0	11,689	6,236	8,413	0	14,649
New Hampshire	30,575	37,718	11	68,304	31,425	37,168	313	68,906
New Jersey	83,001	80,132	0	163,133	76,456	91,656	0	168,112
New Mexico	—	—	—	—	—	—	—	—
New York	429,883	419,888	0	849,771	387,282	440,738	0	828,020
North Carolina	84,559	96,939	0	181,498	70,130	94,772	261	165,163
North Dakota	—	—	—	—	—	—	—	—
Ohio	238,506	280,159	0	518,665	244,320	281,852	3,263	529,435
Oklahoma	—	—	—	—	—	—	—	—
Oregon	11,125	10,961	0	22,086	7,742	11,818	547	20,107
Pennsylvania	313,382	342,280	0	655,662	212,040	349,589	0	561,629
Rhode Island	6,494	13,017	0	19,511	5,329	13,665	0	18,994
South Carolina	45,237	62,301	0	107,538	22,699	72,290	463	95,452
South Dakota	—	—	—	—	—	—	—	—
Tennessee	26,129	56,628	0	82,757	93,391	85,655	0	179,046
Texas	—	—	—	—	67,675	47,910	115	115,700
Utah	—	—	—	—	—	—	—	—
Vermont	12,051	44,173	0	56,224	10,927	41,481	0	52,408
Virginia	—	—	—	—	91,647	93,463	85	185,195
Washington	—	—	—	—	—	—	—	—
West Virginia	20,306	29,015	0	49,321	29,532	32,320	615	62,467
Wisconsin	84,708	108,920	0	193,628	86,390	105,012	853	192,255
Wyoming	—	—	—	—	—	—	—	—

Notes: Entries for the major parties (Democratic, Republican, or their historical antecedents listed in Appendix A) are votes gained by those candidates that historical records show are the primary candidates of the two major parties, except in 1836 when the three Whig candidates are tallied for the total Whig vote. Democratic = Anti-Federalists (1788–1796), Democratic-Republicans (1796–1828), Jacksonian Democrats (1824–1828), and Democrats (since 1832). Republicans = Federalists (1788–1816), National Republicans (1828–1832), Whigs (1836–1852), and Republicans (since 1856). Other = other third parties. — indicates that the state had no data, either because no vote data were found for the state in question or the state had not yet entered the Union. Residents of the District of Columbia received the presidential vote beginning in the 1964 election.

Sources: *Congressional Quarterly's Guide to U.S. Elections* (1994), ICPSR data sets 0001 and 0019, *A Statistical History of the American Presidential Elections* (1963), and independent search of state sources by the author.

Table 4-48 Raw Popular Vote for President, by State, 1876–1880

State	1876				1880			
	Democratic	Republican	Other	Total Vote	Democratic	Republican	Other	Total Vote
Alabama	102,989	68,708	2	171,699	91,130	56,350	4,422	151,902
Alaska	—	—	—	—	—	—	—	—
Arizona	—	—	—	—	—	—	—	—
Arkansas	58,086	38,649	211	96,946	60,489	41,661	5,622	107,772
California	76,460	79,258	66	155,784	80,426	80,282	3,510	164,218
Colorado	—	—	—	—	24,647	27,450	1,449	53,546
Connecticut	61,927	59,033	1,174	122,134	64,411	67,071	1,316	132,798
Delaware	13,381	10,752	0	24,133	15,181	14,148	129	29,458
Dist. of Columbia	—	—	—	—	—	—	—	—
Florida	22,927	23,849	0	46,776	27,964	23,654	0	51,618
Georgia	130,157	50,533	0	180,690	102,981	54,470	0	157,451
Hawaii	—	—	—	—	—	—	—	—
Idaho	—	—	—	—	—	—	—	—
Illinois	258,611	278,232	17,525	554,368	277,321	318,036	26,948	622,305
Indiana	213,529	208,011	9,533	431,073	225,523	232,169	13,066	470,758
Iowa	112,121	171,326	9,951	293,398	105,845	183,904	33,391	323,140
Kansas	37,902	78,324	7,908	124,134	59,789	121,520	19,745	201,054
Kentucky	160,060	97,568	2,998	260,626	148,875	106,490	11,739	267,104
Louisiana	70,508	75,315	0	145,823	65,047	38,978	437	104,462
Maine	49,917	66,300	828	117,045	65,211	74,052	4,640	143,903
Maryland	91,779	71,980	0	163,759	93,706	78,515	0	172,221
Massachusetts	108,777	150,063	779	259,619	111,960	165,198	5,347	282,505
Michigan	141,665	166,901	9,860	318,426	131,596	185,335	36,145	353,076
Minnesota	48,799	72,962	2,399	124,160	53,314	93,939	3,553	150,806
Mississippi	112,173	52,603	0	164,776	75,750	34,844	6,474	117,068
Missouri	202,086	145,027	3,497	350,610	208,600	153,647	35,042	397,289
Montana	—	—	—	—	—	—	—	—
Nebraska	17,343	31,915	0	49,258	28,523	54,979	3,853	87,355
Nevada	9,308	10,383	0	19,691	9,611	8,732	0	18,343
New Hampshire	38,510	41,540	93	80,143	40,797	44,856	708	86,361
New Jersey	115,962	103,517	714	220,193	122,565	120,555	2,808	245,928
New Mexico	—	—	—	—	—	—	—	—
New York	521,949	489,207	4,347	1,015,503	534,511	555,544	13,890	1,103,945
North Carolina	125,427	108,484	0	233,911	124,204	115,616	1,126	240,946
North Dakota	—	—	—	—	—	—	—	—
Ohio	323,182	330,698	4,770	658,650	340,867	375,048	9,069	724,984
Oklahoma	—	—	—	—	—	—	—	—
Oregon	14,157	15,207	509	29,873	19,955	20,619	267	40,841
Pennsylvania	366,204	384,157	8,612	758,973	407,428	444,704	22,651	874,783
Rhode Island	10,712	15,787	0	26,499	10,779	18,195	261	29,235
South Carolina	90,897	91,786	0	182,683	111,236	57,954	603	169,793
South Dakota	—	—	—	—	—	—	—	—
Tennessee	133,177	89,566	0	222,743	129,569	107,677	6,017	243,263
Texas	106,372	45,013	46	151,431	156,010	50,217	27,405	233,632
Utah	—	—	—	—	—	—	—	—
Vermont	20,254	44,092	114	64,460	18,316	45,567	1,215	65,098
Virginia	140,770	95,518	0	236,288	128,083	83,533	0	211,616
Washington	—	—	—	—	—	—	—	—
West Virginia	56,546	41,997	1,104	99,647	57,390	46,243	9,008	112,641
Wisconsin	123,922	130,050	3,204	257,176	114,650	144,406	8,146	267,202
Wyoming	—	—	—	—	—	—	—	—

Notes: Entries for the major parties (Democratic, Republican, or their historical antecedents listed in Appendix A) are votes gained by those candidates that historical records show are the primary candidates of the two major parties, except in 1836 when the three Whig candidates are tallied for the total Whig vote. Democratic = Anti-Federalists (1788–1796), Democratic-Republicans (1796–1828), Jacksonian Democrats (1824–1828), and Democrats (since 1832). Republicans = Federalists (1788–1816), National Republicans (1828–1832), Whigs (1836–1852), and Republicans (since 1856). Other = other third parties. — indicates that the state had no data, either because no vote data were found for the state in question or the state had not yet entered the Union. Residents of the District of Columbia received the presidential vote beginning in the 1964 election.

Sources: *Congressional Quarterly's Guide to U.S. Elections* (1994), ICPSR data sets 0001 and 0019, *A Statistical History of the American Presidential Elections* (1963), and independent search of state sources by the author.

Table 4-49 Raw Popular Vote for President, by State, 1884–1888

State	1884				1888			
	Democratic	Republican	Other	Total Vote	Democratic	Republican	Other	Total Vote
Alabama	92,736	59,444	1,444	153,624	117,314	57,177	594	175,085
Alaska	—	—	—	—	—	—	—	—
Arizona	—	—	—	—	—	—	—	—
Arkansas	72,734	51,198	1,847	125,779	86,062	59,752	11,244	157,058
California	89,288	102,369	5,331	196,988	117,729	124,816	8,794	251,339
Colorado	27,723	36,084	2,712	66,519	37,549	50,772	3,625	91,946
Connecticut	67,167	65,879	4,175	137,221	74,920	74,584	4,474	153,978
Delaware	16,957	12,953	74	29,984	16,414	12,950	400	29,764
Dist. of Columbia	—	—	—	—	—	—	—	—
Florida	31,769	28,031	190	59,990	39,557	26,529	414	66,500
Georgia	94,667	48,603	340	143,610	100,493	40,499	1,944	142,936
Hawaii	—	—	—	—	—	—	—	—
Idaho	—	—	—	—	—	—	—	—
Illinois	312,351	337,469	22,850	672,670	348,351	370,475	28,987	747,813
Indiana	244,989	238,466	8,194	491,649	260,990	263,366	12,632	536,988
Iowa	177,316	197,089	19,137	393,542	179,876	211,607	13,211	404,694
Kansas	90,111	154,410	6,470	250,991	102,739	182,845	45,549	331,133
Kentucky	152,961	118,690	3,259	274,910	183,830	155,138	5,900	344,868
Louisiana	62,594	46,347	4,293	113,234	85,032	30,660	199	115,891
Maine	52,153	72,217	2,744	127,114	50,472	73,730	4,051	128,253
Maryland	96,866	85,748	27,209	209,823	106,188	99,986	4,767	210,941
Massachusetts	122,352	146,724	52,177	321,253	151,590	183,892	8,761	344,243
Michigan	149,835	192,669	21,986	364,490	213,469	236,387	25,500	475,356
Minnesota	70,065	111,685	4,684	186,434	104,372	142,492	16,298	263,162
Mississippi	77,653	43,035	0	120,688	85,451	30,095	240	115,786
Missouri	236,023	203,081	2,164	441,268	261,943	236,252	23,164	521,359
Montana	—	—	—	—	—	—	—	—
Nebraska	54,391	76,912	2,899	134,202	80,552	108,417	13,661	202,630
Nevada	5,577	7,176	26	12,779	5,303	7,229	41	12,573
New Hampshire	39,198	43,254	2,134	84,586	43,382	45,734	1,654	90,770
New Jersey	127,747	123,436	9,670	260,853	151,493	144,347	7,794	303,634
New Mexico	—	—	—	—	—	—	—	—
New York	563,048	562,001	41,954	1,167,003	635,965	650,338	33,445	1,319,748
North Carolina	142,905	125,021	430	268,356	147,902	134,784	2,877	285,563
North Dakota	—	—	—	—	—	—	—	—
Ohio	368,280	400,092	16,248	784,620	395,456	416,054	27,847	839,357
Oklahoma	—	—	—	—	—	—	—	—
Oregon	24,598	26,845	1,240	52,683	26,518	33,291	2,080	61,889
Pennsylvania	394,772	472,792	32,146	899,710	446,633	526,091	24,844	997,568
Rhode Island	12,391	19,030	1,350	32,771	17,530	21,969	1,276	40,775
South Carolina	69,845	21,730	1,237	92,812	65,824	13,736	437	79,997
South Dakota	—	—	—	—	—	—	—	—
Tennessee	133,770	124,101	2,107	259,978	158,699	138,978	6,017	303,694
Texas	223,209	91,234	6,799	321,242	232,189	88,604	33,619	354,412
Utah	—	—	—	—	—	—	—	—
Vermont	17,331	39,514	2,564	59,409	16,788	45,193	1,495	63,476
Virginia	145,491	139,356	130	284,977	152,004	150,399	1,684	304,087
Washington	—	—	—	—	—	—	—	—
West Virginia	67,311	63,096	1,738	132,145	78,677	78,171	2,592	159,440
Wisconsin	146,447	161,155	12,245	319,847	155,232	176,553	22,829	354,614
Wyoming	—	—	—	—	—	—	—	—

Notes: Entries for the major parties (Democratic, Republican, or their historical antecedents listed in Appendix A) are votes gained by those candidates that historical records show are the primary candidates of the two major parties, except in 1836 when the three Whig candidates are tallied for the total Whig vote. Democratic = Anti-Federalists (1788–1796), Democratic-Republicans (1796–1828), Jacksonian Democrats (1824–1828), and Democrats (since 1832). Republicans = Federalists (1788–1816), National Republicans (1828–1832), Whigs (1836–1852), and Republicans (since 1856). Other = other third parties. — indicates that the state had no data, either because no vote data were found for the state in question or the state had not yet entered the Union. Residents of the District of Columbia received the presidential vote beginning in the 1964 election.

Sources: *Congressional Quarterly's Guide to U.S. Elections* (1994), ICPSR data sets 0001 and 0019, *A Statistical History of the American Presidential Elections* (1963), and independent search of state sources by the author.

Table 4-50 Raw Popular Vote for President, by State, 1892–1896

State	1892				1896			
	Democratic	Republican	Other	Total Vote	Democratic	Republican	Other	Total Vote
Alabama	138,135	9,184	85,224	232,543	130,298	55,673	8,609	194,580
Alaska	—	—	—	—	—	—	—	—
Arizona	—	—	—	—	—	—	—	—
Arkansas	87,834	47,072	13,211	148,117	110,103	37,512	1,781	149,396
California	118,151	118,027	33,407	269,585	144,877	146,756	6,965	298,598
Colorado	0	38,620	55,261	93,881	161,005	26,271	2,263	189,539
Connecticut	82,395	77,030	5,168	164,593	56,740	110,285	7,369	174,394
Delaware	18,581	18,077	577	37,235	16,574	20,450	1,432	38,456
Dist. of Columbia	—	—	—	—	—	—	—	—
Florida	30,153	0	5,318	35,471	32,756	11,298	2,434	46,488
Georgia	129,446	48,408	45,272	223,126	93,885	59,395	9,200	162,480
Hawaii	—	—	—	—	—	—	—	—
Idaho	0	8,599	10,808	19,407	23,135	6,324	172	29,631
Illinois	426,281	399,308	48,078	873,667	465,593	607,130	18,043	1,090,766
Indiana	262,740	255,615	35,258	553,613	305,538	323,754	7,797	637,089
Iowa	196,367	219,795	26,997	443,159	223,744	289,293	8,513	521,550
Kansas	0	156,134	167,457	323,591	173,049	159,484	3,552	336,085
Kentucky	175,461	135,462	29,941	340,864	217,894	218,171	9,863	445,928
Louisiana	87,926	26,963	0	114,889	77,175	22,037	1,834	101,046
Maine	48,049	62,936	5,466	116,451	34,587	80,403	3,429	118,419
Maryland	113,866	92,736	6,673	213,275	104,150	136,959	9,140	250,249
Massachusetts	176,813	202,814	11,401	391,028	105,414	278,976	16,879	401,269
Michigan	202,396	222,708	41,813	466,917	237,164	293,336	15,083	545,583
Minnesota	100,589	122,736	44,516	267,841	139,735	193,503	8,524	341,762
Mississippi	40,030	1,398	11,091	52,519	63,355	4,819	1,417	69,591
Missouri	268,400	227,646	45,537	541,583	363,667	304,940	5,425	674,032
Montana	17,690	18,871	7,900	44,461	42,628	10,509	193	53,330
Nebraska	24,956	87,213	88,036	200,205	115,007	103,064	5,110	223,181
Nevada	703	2,811	7,312	10,826	8,348	1,938	0	10,286
New Hampshire	42,081	45,658	1,589	89,328	21,650	57,444	4,576	83,670
New Jersey	170,987	156,059	10,439	337,485	133,675	221,367	15,972	371,014
New Mexico	—	—	—	—	—	—	—	—
New York	654,868	609,350	72,575	1,336,793	551,369	819,838	52,669	1,423,876
North Carolina	132,951	100,346	46,973	280,270	174,408	155,122	1,807	331,337
North Dakota	0	17,519	18,599	36,118	20,686	26,335	370	47,391
Ohio	404,115	405,187	40,862	850,164	477,497	525,991	10,807	1,014,295
Oklahoma	—	—	—	—	—	—	—	—
Oregon	14,243	35,002	29,133	78,378	46,739	48,700	1,896	97,335
Pennsylvania	452,264	516,011	34,725	1,003,000	433,228	728,300	32,827	1,194,355
Rhode Island	24,336	26,975	1,885	53,196	14,459	37,437	2,889	54,785
South Carolina	54,680	13,345	2,479	70,504	58,801	9,313	824	68,938
South Dakota	8,894	34,714	26,552	70,160	41,225	41,040	672	82,937
Tennessee	136,468	100,537	28,727	265,732	167,168	148,683	5,052	320,903
Texas	236,979	70,982	102,899	410,860	370,308	163,894	6,816	541,018
Utah	—	—	—	—	64,607	13,491	0	78,098
Vermont	16,325	37,992	1,476	55,793	10,367	51,127	2,074	63,568
Virginia	164,136	113,098	15,004	292,238	154,708	135,379	4,587	294,674
Washington	29,802	36,459	21,707	87,968	53,314	39,153	1,116	93,583
West Virginia	84,467	80,292	6,320	171,079	94,480	105,379	1,898	201,757
Wisconsin	177,325	171,101	23,055	371,481	165,523	268,135	13,751	447,409
Wyoming	0	8,454	8,249	16,703	10,862	10,072	133	21,067

Notes: Entries for the major parties (Democratic, Republican, or their historical antecedents listed in Appendix A) are votes gained by those candidates that historical records show are the primary candidates of the two major parties, except in 1836 when the three Whig candidates are tallied for the total Whig vote. Democratic = Anti-Federalists (1788–1796), Democratic-Republicans (1796–1828), Jacksonian Democrats (1824–1828), and Democrats (since 1832). Republicans = Federalists (1788–1816), National Republicans (1828–1832), Whigs (1836–1852), and Republicans (since 1856). Other = other third parties. — indicates that the state had no data, either because no vote data were found for the state in question or the state had not yet entered the Union. Residents of the District of Columbia received the presidential vote beginning in the 1964 election.

Sources: *Congressional Quarterly's Guide to U.S. Elections* (1994), ICPSR data sets 0001 and 0019, *A Statistical History of the American Presidential Elections* (1963), and independent search of state sources by the author.

Table 4-51 Raw Popular Vote for President, by State, 1900–1904

State	1900 Democratic	1900 Republican	1900 Other	1900 Total Vote	1904 Democratic	1904 Republican	1904 Other	1904 Total Vote
Alabama	97,129	55,612	6,951	159,692	79,797	22,472	6,516	108,785
Alaska	—	—	—	—	—	—	—	—
Arizona	—	—	—	—	—	—	—	—
Arkansas	81,242	44,800	1,924	127,966	64,434	46,760	5,134	116,328
California	124,985	164,755	12,578	302,318	89,294	205,226	37,248	331,768
Colorado	122,705	92,701	5,489	220,895	100,105	134,661	8,901	243,667
Connecticut	74,014	102,572	3,609	180,195	72,909	111,089	7,138	191,136
Delaware	18,852	22,535	602	41,989	19,347	23,705	804	43,856
Dist. of Columbia	—	—	—	—	—	—	—	—
Florida	28,273	7,355	4,021	39,649	26,449	8,314	3,942	38,705
Georgia	81,180	34,260	5,970	121,410	83,466	24,004	23,516	130,986
Hawaii	—	—	—	—	—	—	—	—
Idaho	29,484	27,198	1,302	57,984	18,480	47,783	6,314	72,577
Illinois	503,061	597,985	30,852	1,131,898	327,606	632,645	116,244	1,076,495
Indiana	309,584	336,063	18,447	664,094	274,356	368,289	39,561	682,206
Iowa	209,261	307,799	13,285	530,345	149,141	307,907	28,655	485,703
Kansas	162,601	185,955	5,210	353,766	86,164	213,455	29,428	329,047
Kentucky	235,126	227,132	6,007	468,265	217,170	205,457	13,319	435,946
Louisiana	53,668	14,234	4	67,906	47,708	5,205	995	53,908
Maine	36,822	65,412	3,459	105,693	27,642	65,432	3,949	97,023
Maryland	122,237	136,151	5,998	264,386	109,446	109,497	5,286	224,229
Massachusetts	156,997	238,866	18,941	414,804	165,746	257,813	21,541	445,100
Michigan	211,432	316,014	16,343	543,789	134,163	361,863	24,417	520,443
Minnesota	112,901	190,461	12,949	316,311	55,187	216,651	21,022	292,860
Mississippi	51,706	5,707	1,642	59,055	53,480	3,280	1,961	58,721
Missouri	351,922	314,092	17,644	683,658	296,312	321,449	26,100	643,861
Montana	37,311	25,409	1,136	63,856	21,816	33,994	7,758	63,568
Nebraska	114,013	121,835	5,582	241,430	52,921	138,558	34,253	225,732
Nevada	6,347	3,849	0	10,196	3,982	6,864	1,269	12,115
New Hampshire	35,489	54,799	2,076	92,364	34,071	54,157	1,923	90,151
New Jersey	164,808	221,707	14,535	401,050	164,566	245,164	22,517	432,247
New Mexico	—	—	—	—	—	—	—	—
New York	678,462	822,013	47,568	1,548,043	683,981	859,533	74,251	1,617,765
North Carolina	157,733	132,997	1,788	292,518	124,091	82,442	1,285	207,818
North Dakota	20,524	35,898	1,361	57,783	14,273	52,595	3,146	70,014
Ohio	474,882	543,918	21,273	1,040,073	344,674	600,095	59,626	1,004,395
Oklahoma	—	—	—	—	—	—	—	—
Oregon	32,810	46,172	4,269	83,251	17,327	60,309	12,020	89,656
Pennsylvania	424,232	712,665	36,313	1,173,210	337,998	840,949	57,791	1,236,738
Rhode Island	19,812	33,784	2,952	56,548	24,839	41,605	2,212	68,656
South Carolina	47,173	3,525	0	50,698	53,320	2,570	0	55,890
South Dakota	39,538	54,574	2,057	96,169	21,969	72,083	7,343	101,395
Tennessee	145,240	123,108	5,512	273,860	131,653	105,363	5,734	242,750
Texas	267,945	131,174	25,215	424,334	167,088	51,307	15,214	233,609
Utah	44,949	47,089	1,033	93,071	33,413	62,446	5,767	101,626
Vermont	12,849	42,569	794	56,212	9,777	40,459	1,652	51,888
Virginia	146,079	115,769	2,360	264,208	80,649	48,180	1,581	130,410
Washington	44,833	57,455	5,235	107,523	28,098	101,540	15,513	145,151
West Virginia	98,807	119,829	2,160	220,796	100,855	132,620	6,511	239,986
Wisconsin	159,163	265,760	17,578	442,501	124,205	280,314	38,921	443,440
Wyoming	10,164	14,482	62	24,708	8,930	20,489	1,195	30,614

Notes: Entries for the major parties (Democratic, Republican, or their historical antecedents listed in Appendix A) are votes gained by those candidates that historical records show are the primary candidates of the two major parties, except in 1836 when the three Whig candidates are tallied for the total Whig vote. Democratic = Anti-Federalists (1788–1796), Democratic-Republicans (1796–1828), Jacksonian Democrats (1824–1828), and Democrats (since 1832). Republicans = Federalists (1788–1816), National Republicans (1828–1832), Whigs (1836–1852), and Republicans (since 1856). Other = other third parties. — indicates that the state had no data, either because no vote data were found for the state in question or the state had not yet entered the Union. Residents of the District of Columbia received the presidential vote beginning in the 1964 election.

Sources: *Congressional Quarterly's Guide to U.S. Elections* (1994), ICPSR data sets 0001 and 0019, *A Statistical History of the American Presidential Elections* (1963), and independent search of state sources by the author.

Table 4-52 Raw Popular Vote for President, by State, 1908–1912

State	1908				1912			
	Democratic	Republican	Other	Total Vote	Democratic	Republican	Other	Total Vote
Alabama	74,391	25,561	5,200	105,152	82,438	9,807	25,714	117,959
Alaska	—	—	—	—				
Arizona	—	—	—	—	10,324	2,986	10,377	23,687
Arkansas	87,020	56,684	8,141	151,845	68,814	25,585	30,705	125,104
California	127,492	214,398	44,735	386,625	283,436	3,847	390,594	677,877
Colorado	126,644	123,693	13,521	263,858	113,912	58,386	93,656	265,954
Connecticut	68,255	112,815	8,833	189,903	74,561	68,324	47,519	190,404
Delaware	22,055	25,014	938	48,007	22,631	15,997	10,062	48,690
Dist. of Columbia	—	—	—	—	—	—	—	—
Florida	31,104	10,654	7,602	49,360	35,343	4,279	11,215	50,837
Georgia	72,350	41,355	18,799	132,504	93,087	5,191	23,192	121,470
Hawaii	—	—	—	—				
Idaho	36,162	52,621	8,510	97,293	33,921	32,810	39,023	105,754
Illinois	450,810	629,932	74,512	1,155,254	405,048	253,593	487,532	1,146,173
Indiana	338,262	348,993	33,862	721,117	281,890	151,267	221,317	654,474
Iowa	200,771	275,210	18,789	494,770	185,322	119,805	187,226	492,353
Kansas	161,209	197,316	17,518	376,043	143,663	74,845	147,052	365,560
Kentucky	244,092	235,711	10,916	490,719	219,484	115,510	117,720	452,714
Louisiana	63,568	8,958	2,591	75,117	60,871	3,833	14,544	79,248
Maine	35,403	66,987	3,945	106,335	51,113	26,545	51,983	129,641
Maryland	115,908	116,513	6,110	238,531	112,674	54,956	64,351	231,981
Massachusetts	155,533	265,966	35,406	456,905	173,408	155,948	158,700	488,056
Michigan	174,619	333,313	30,192	538,124	150,201	151,434	246,336	547,971
Minnesota	109,401	195,843	25,010	330,254	106,426	64,334	163,459	334,219
Mississippi	60,287	4,363	2,254	66,904	57,324	1,560	5,599	64,483
Missouri	346,574	347,203	22,064	715,841	330,746	207,821	159,999	698,566
Montana	29,511	32,471	7,251	69,233	28,129	18,575	33,552	80,256
Nebraska	131,099	126,997	8,703	266,799	109,008	54,226	86,249	249,483
Nevada	11,212	10,775	2,539	24,526	7,986	3,196	8,933	20,115
New Hampshire	33,655	53,144	2,796	89,595	34,724	32,927	20,310	87,961
New Jersey	182,522	265,298	19,291	467,111	178,638	89,066	165,959	433,663
New Mexico	—	—	—	—	20,437	17,164	11,206	48,807
New York	667,468	870,070	100,812	1,638,350	655,573	455,487	477,255	1,588,315
North Carolina	136,928	114,887	739	252,554	144,407	29,129	70,240	243,776
North Dakota	32,884	57,680	3,960	94,524	29,549	22,990	33,935	86,474
Ohio	502,721	572,312	46,519	1,121,552	424,834	278,168	334,112	1,037,114
Oklahoma	122,362	110,473	21,425	254,260	119,143	90,726	43,825	253,694
Oregon	37,792	62,454	10,293	110,539	47,064	34,673	55,303	137,040
Pennsylvania	448,782	745,779	72,889	1,267,450	395,637	273,360	548,739	1,217,736
Rhode Island	24,706	43,942	3,669	72,317	30,412	27,703	19,779	77,894
South Carolina	62,288	3,945	146	66,379	48,355	536	1,512	50,403
South Dakota	40,266	67,536	6,973	114,775	48,942	0	67,385	116,327
Tennessee	135,608	117,977	3,595	257,180	133,021	60,475	58,437	251,933
Texas	216,662	65,605	10,646	292,913	218,921	28,310	53,730	300,961
Utah	42,610	61,165	4,982	108,757	36,576	42,013	33,683	112,272
Vermont	11,496	39,552	1,632	52,680	15,350	23,303	24,151	62,804
Virginia	82,946	52,572	1,547	137,065	90,332	23,288	23,355	136,975
Washington	58,383	106,062	19,125	183,570	86,840	70,445	165,514	322,799
West Virginia	111,410	137,869	8,819	258,098	113,097	56,754	98,877	268,728
Wisconsin	166,662	247,744	40,032	454,438	164,230	130,596	105,149	399,975
Wyoming	14,918	20,846	1,844	37,608	15,310	14,560	12,413	42,283

Notes: Entries for the major parties (Democratic, Republican, or their historical antecedents listed in Appendix A) are votes gained by those candidates that historical records show are the primary candidates of the two major parties, except in 1836 when the three Whig candidates are tallied for the total Whig vote. Democratic = Anti-Federalists (1788–1796), Democratic-Republicans (1796–1828), Jacksonian Democrats (1824–1828), and Democrats (since 1832). Republicans = Federalists (1788–1816), National Republicans (1828–1832), Whigs (1836–1852), and Republicans (since 1856). Other = other third parties. — indicates that the state had no data, either because no vote data were found for the state in question or the state had not yet entered the Union. Residents of the District of Columbia received the presidential vote beginning in the 1964 election.

Sources: *Congressional Quarterly's Guide to U.S. Elections* (1994), ICPSR data sets 0001 and 0019, *A Statistical History of the American Presidential Elections* (1963), and independent search of state sources by the author.

Table 4-53 Raw Popular Vote for President, by State, 1916–1920

State	1916 Democratic	Republican	Other	Total Vote	1920 Democratic	Republican	Other	Total Vote
Alabama	99,116	28,662	2,657	130,435	156,064	74,719	3,168	233,951
Alaska	—	—	—	—	—	—	—	—
Arizona	33,170	20,522	4,327	58,019	29,546	37,016	241	66,803
Arkansas	112,211	48,879	9,014	170,104	106,427	72,316	5,128	183,871
California	465,936	462,516	70,798	999,250	229,191	624,992	89,280	943,463
Colorado	177,496	101,388	13,153	292,037	104,936	173,248	13,869	292,053
Connecticut	99,786	106,514	7,574	213,874	120,721	229,238	15,559	365,518
Delaware	24,753	26,011	1,046	51,810	39,911	52,858	2,106	94,875
Dist. of Columbia	—	—	—	—	—	—	—	—
Florida	55,984	14,611	10,139	80,734	90,515	44,853	10,316	145,684
Georgia	127,754	11,294	21,633	160,681	106,112	42,981	465	149,558
Hawaii	—	—	—	—	—	—	—	—
Idaho	70,054	55,368	9,193	134,615	46,930	91,351	0	138,281
Illinois	950,229	1,152,549	89,929	2,192,707	534,395	1,420,480	139,839	2,094,714
Indiana	334,063	341,005	43,785	718,853	511,364	696,370	55,240	1,262,974
Iowa	221,699	280,439	16,600	518,738	227,804	634,674	32,481	894,959
Kansas	314,588	277,658	37,567	629,813	185,464	369,268	15,511	570,243
Kentucky	269,990	241,854	8,234	520,078	456,497	452,480	9,659	918,636
Louisiana	79,875	6,466	6,633	92,974	87,519	38,539	339	126,397
Maine	64,033	69,508	2,773	136,314	58,961	136,355	2,524	197,840
Maryland	138,359	117,347	6,333	262,039	180,626	236,117	11,700	428,443
Massachusetts	247,885	268,784	15,153	531,822	276,691	681,153	35,874	993,718
Michigan	283,993	337,952	24,928	646,873	233,450	762,865	52,096	1,048,411
Minnesota	179,155	179,544	28,668	387,367	142,994	519,421	73,423	735,838
Mississippi	80,422	4,253	2,004	86,679	69,136	11,576	1,639	82,351
Missouri	398,032	369,339	19,402	786,773	574,699	727,252	30,189	1,332,140
Montana	101,104	66,933	9,972	178,009	57,372	109,430	12,204	179,006
Nebraska	158,827	117,771	10,717	287,315	119,608	247,498	15,637	382,743
Nevada	17,776	12,127	3,411	33,314	9,851	15,479	1,864	27,194
New Hampshire	43,781	43,725	1,621	89,127	62,662	95,196	1,234	159,092
New Jersey	211,018	268,982	14,442	494,442	258,761	615,333	36,157	910,251
New Mexico	33,693	31,097	2,089	66,879	46,668	57,634	1,110	105,412
New York	759,426	879,238	67,641	1,706,305	781,238	1,871,167	246,108	2,898,513
North Carolina	168,383	120,890	564	289,837	305,367	232,819	463	538,649
North Dakota	55,206	53,471	6,713	115,390	37,422	160,082	8,282	205,786
Ohio	604,161	514,753	46,177	1,165,091	780,037	1,182,022	59,594	2,021,653
Oklahoma	148,123	97,233	46,971	292,327	216,122	243,840	25,716	485,678
Oregon	120,087	126,813	14,750	261,650	80,019	143,592	14,911	238,522
Pennsylvania	521,784	703,823	71,582	1,297,189	503,202	1,218,215	129,831	1,851,248
Rhode Island	40,394	44,858	2,564	87,816	55,062	107,463	5,456	167,981
South Carolina	61,845	1,550	555	63,950	64,170	2,610	28	66,808
South Dakota	59,191	64,217	5,534	128,942	35,938	110,692	35,607	182,237
Tennessee	153,280	116,223	2,687	272,190	206,558	219,229	2,249	428,036
Texas	287,415	64,999	20,896	373,310	287,920	114,658	83,531	486,109
Utah	84,145	54,137	4,863	143,145	56,639	81,555	7,634	145,828
Vermont	22,708	40,250	1,517	64,475	20,919	68,212	830	89,961
Virginia	101,840	48,384	1,801	152,025	141,670	87,456	1,874	231,000
Washington	183,388	167,208	30,398	380,994	84,298	223,137	91,280	398,715
West Virginia	140,403	143,124	6,144	289,671	220,785	282,007	7,144	509,936
Wisconsin	191,363	220,822	34,949	447,134	113,422	498,576	89,283	701,281
Wyoming	28,376	21,698	1,832	51,906	17,429	35,091	3,733	56,253

Notes: Entries for the major parties (Democratic, Republican, or their historical antecedents listed in Appendix A) are votes gained by those candidates that historical records show are the primary candidates of the two major parties, except in 1836 when the three Whig candidates are tallied for the total Whig vote. Democratic = Anti-Federalists (1788–1796), Democratic-Republicans (1796–1828), Jacksonian Democrats (1824–1828), and Democrats (since 1832). Republicans = Federalists (1788–1816), National Republicans (1828–1832), Whigs (1836–1852), and Republicans (since 1856). Other = other third parties. — indicates that the state had no data, either because no vote data were found for the state in question or the state had not yet entered the Union. Residents of the District of Columbia received the presidential vote beginning in the 1964 election.

Sources: *Congressional Quarterly's Guide to U.S. Elections* (1994), ICPSR data sets 0001 and 0019, *America at the Polls: 1920–1964* (1965), *A Statistical History of the American Presidential Elections* (1963), and independent search of state sources by the author.

Table 4-54 Raw Popular Vote for President, by State, 1924–1928

	1924				1928			
State	Democratic	Republican	Other	Total Vote	Democratic	Republican	Other	Total Vote
Alabama	113,138	42,823	8,602	164,563	127,796	120,725	460	248,981
Alaska	—	—	—	—	—	—	—	—
Arizona	26,235	30,516	17,210	73,961	38,537	52,533	184	91,254
Arkansas	84,790	40,583	13,167	138,540	119,196	77,784	746	197,726
California	105,514	733,250	443,014	1,281,778	614,365	1,162,323	19,968	1,796,656
Colorado	75,238	195,171	71,852	342,261	133,131	253,872	5,239	392,242
Connecticut	110,184	246,322	43,890	400,396	252,085	296,641	4,392	553,118
Delaware	33,445	52,441	4,999	90,885	35,354	68,860	388	104,602
Dist. of Columbia	—	—	—	—	—	—	—	—
Florida	62,083	30,633	16,442	109,158	101,764	145,860	4,444	252,068
Georgia	123,262	30,300	13,073	166,635	129,604	101,800	188	231,592
Hawaii	—	—	—	—	—	—	—	—
Idaho	23,951	69,791	53,948	147,690	52,926	97,322	1,293	151,541
Illinois	576,975	1,453,321	439,771	2,470,067	1,313,817	1,769,141	24,531	3,107,489
Indiana	492,245	703,042	77,103	1,272,390	562,691	848,290	10,333	1,421,314
Iowa	160,382	537,458	278,930	976,770	379,011	623,570	6,608	1,009,189
Kansas	156,320	407,671	98,465	662,456	193,003	513,672	6,525	713,200
Kentucky	375,593	396,758	41,492	813,843	381,070	558,064	1,387	940,521
Louisiana	93,218	24,670	4,063	121,951	164,655	51,160	18	215,833
Maine	41,964	138,440	11,788	192,192	81,179	179,923	1,068	262,170
Maryland	148,072	162,414	48,144	358,630	223,626	301,479	3,243	528,348
Massachusetts	280,831	703,476	145,530	1,129,837	792,758	775,566	9,499	1,577,823
Michigan	152,359	874,631	133,429	1,160,419	396,762	965,396	9,924	1,372,082
Minnesota	55,913	420,759	345,474	822,146	396,451	560,977	13,548	970,976
Mississippi	100,474	8,494	3,474	112,442	124,538	27,030	0	151,568
Missouri	574,962	648,488	86,645	1,310,095	662,684	834,080	4,081	1,500,845
Montana	33,805	74,138	66,482	174,425	78,578	113,300	2,230	194,108
Nebraska	137,299	218,985	107,275	463,559	197,950	345,745	3,433	547,128
Nevada	5,909	11,243	9,769	26,921	14,090	18,327	0	32,417
New Hampshire	57,201	98,575	8,993	164,769	80,715	115,404	638	196,757
New Jersey	298,043	676,277	113,734	1,088,054	616,517	926,050	6,814	1,549,381
New Mexico	48,542	54,745	9,543	112,830	48,211	69,708	158	118,077
New York	950,796	1,820,058	493,085	3,263,939	2,089,863	2,193,344	122,419	4,405,626
North Carolina	284,190	190,754	6,664	481,608	286,227	348,923	0	635,150
North Dakota	13,858	94,931	90,292	199,081	106,648	131,419	1,778	239,845
Ohio	477,887	1,176,130	362,279	2,016,296	864,210	1,627,546	16,590	2,508,346
Oklahoma	255,798	225,756	46,274	527,828	219,174	394,046	5,207	618,427
Oregon	67,589	142,579	69,320	279,488	109,223	205,341	5,378	319,942
Pennsylvania	409,192	1,401,481	334,177	2,144,850	1,067,586	2,055,382	27,644	3,150,612
Rhode Island	76,606	125,286	8,223	210,115	118,973	117,522	699	237,194
South Carolina	49,008	1,123	624	50,755	62,700	5,858	47	68,605
South Dakota	27,214	101,299	75,355	203,868	102,660	157,603	1,594	261,857
Tennessee	159,339	130,831	10,860	301,030	157,143	195,388	661	353,192
Texas	483,381	130,794	42,879	657,054	344,542	372,324	867	717,733
Utah	47,001	77,327	32,662	156,990	80,985	94,618	1,000	176,603
Vermont	16,124	80,498	6,295	102,917	44,440	90,404	347	135,191
Virginia	139,717	73,328	10,558	223,603	140,146	164,609	609	305,364
Washington	42,842	220,224	158,483	421,549	156,772	335,844	8,224	500,840
West Virginia	257,232	288,635	37,795	583,662	263,784	375,551	3,417	642,752
Wisconsin	68,115	311,614	461,098	840,827	450,259	544,205	22,367	1,016,831
Wyoming	12,868	41,858	25,174	79,900	29,299	52,748	788	82,835

Notes: Entries for the major parties (Democratic, Republican, or their historical antecedents listed in Appendix A) are votes gained by those candidates that historical records show are the primary candidates of the two major parties, except in 1836 when the three Whig candidates are tallied for the total Whig vote. Democratic = Anti-Federalists (1788–1796), Democratic-Republicans (1796–1828), Jacksonian Democrats (1824–1828), and Democrats (since 1832). Republicans = Federalists (1788–1816), National Republicans (1828–1832), Whigs (1836–1852), and Republicans (since 1856). Other = other third parties. — indicates that the state had no data, either because no vote data were found for the state in question or the state had not yet entered the Union. Residents of the District of Columbia received the presidential vote beginning in the 1964 election.

Sources: *Congressional Quarterly's Guide to U.S. Elections* (1994), ICPSR data sets 0001 and 0019, *America at the Polls: 1920–1964* (1965), *A Statistical History of the American Presidential Elections* (1963), and independent search of state sources by the author.

Table 4-55 Raw Popular Vote for President, by State, 1932–1936

| | 1932 | | | | 1936 | | | |
State	Democratic	Republican	Other	Total Vote	Democratic	Republican	Other	Total Vote
Alabama	207,910	34,675	2,718	245,303	238,196	35,358	2,190	275,744
Alaska	—	—	—	—	—	—	—	—
Arizona	79,264	36,104	2,883	118,251	86,722	33,433	4,008	124,163
Arkansas	186,829	27,465	2,275	216,569	146,765	32,049	617	179,431
California	1,324,157	847,902	94,913	2,266,972	1,766,836	836,431	35,615	2,638,882
Colorado	250,877	189,617	17,202	457,696	295,021	181,267	12,397	488,685
Connecticut	281,632	288,420	24,131	594,183	382,129	278,685	29,909	690,723
Delaware	54,319	57,073	1,509	112,901	69,702	57,236	665	127,603
Dist. of Columbia	—	—	—	—	—	—	—	—
Florida	206,307	69,170	1,466	276,943	249,117	78,248	71	327,436
Georgia	234,118	19,863	1,609	255,590	255,363	36,943	864	293,170
Hawaii	—	—	—	—	—	—	—	—
Idaho	109,479	71,312	5,729	186,520	125,683	66,256	7,678	199,617
Illinois	1,882,304	1,432,756	92,866	3,407,926	2,282,999	1,570,393	103,130	3,956,522
Indiana	862,054	677,184	37,689	1,576,927	934,974	691,570	24,353	1,650,897
Iowa	598,019	414,433	24,235	1,036,687	621,756	487,977	33,004	1,142,737
Kansas	424,204	349,498	18,276	791,978	464,520	397,727	3,260	865,507
Kentucky	580,574	394,716	7,769	983,059	541,944	369,702	14,568	926,214
Louisiana	249,418	18,853	533	268,804	292,894	36,791	93	329,778
Maine	128,907	166,631	2,906	298,444	126,333	168,823	9,084	304,240
Maryland	314,314	184,184	12,556	511,054	389,612	231,435	3,849	624,896
Massachusetts	800,148	736,959	43,007	1,580,114	942,716	768,613	129,028	1,840,357
Michigan	871,700	739,894	53,171	1,664,765	1,016,794	699,733	88,571	1,805,098
Minnesota	600,806	363,959	38,078	1,002,843	698,811	350,461	80,703	1,129,975
Mississippi	140,168	5,180	686	146,034	157,333	4,467	342	162,142
Missouri	1,025,406	564,713	19,775	1,609,894	1,111,043	697,891	19,701	1,828,635
Montana	127,286	78,078	11,115	216,479	159,690	63,598	7,214	230,502
Nebraska	359,082	201,177	9,876	570,135	347,445	247,731	12,847	608,023
Nevada	28,756	12,674	0	41,430	31,925	11,923	0	43,848
New Hampshire	100,680	103,629	1,211	205,520	108,460	104,642	5,012	218,114
New Jersey	806,630	775,684	47,749	1,630,063	1,083,850	720,322	16,265	1,820,437
New Mexico	95,089	54,217	2,300	151,606	106,037	61,727	1,371	169,135
New York	2,534,959	1,937,963	215,692	4,688,614	3,293,222	2,180,670	122,506	5,596,398
North Carolina	497,566	208,344	5,588	711,498	616,141	223,294	40	839,475
North Dakota	178,350	71,772	6,168	256,290	163,148	72,751	37,817	273,716
Ohio	1,301,695	1,227,319	80,714	2,609,728	1,747,140	1,127,855	137,665	3,012,660
Oklahoma	516,468	188,165	0	704,633	501,069	245,122	3,549	749,740
Oregon	213,871	136,019	18,861	368,751	266,733	122,706	24,582	414,021
Pennsylvania	1,295,948	1,453,540	109,533	2,859,021	2,353,788	1,690,300	94,017	4,138,105
Rhode Island	146,604	115,266	4,300	266,170	164,338	125,031	20,909	310,278
South Carolina	102,347	1,978	82	104,407	113,791	1,646	0	115,437
South Dakota	183,515	99,212	5,711	288,438	160,137	125,977	10,338	296,452
Tennessee	259,473	126,752	4,048	390,273	328,083	147,055	1,948	477,086
Texas	771,109	98,218	5,055	874,382	739,952	104,661	5,088	849,701
Utah	116,750	84,795	5,033	206,578	150,248	64,555	1,876	216,679
Vermont	56,266	78,984	1,730	136,980	62,124	81,023	542	143,689
Virginia	203,979	89,637	4,326	297,942	234,980	98,336	1,274	334,590
Washington	353,260	208,645	52,909	614,814	459,579	206,892	25,867	692,338
West Virginia	405,124	330,731	7,919	743,774	502,582	325,358	2,005	829,945
Wisconsin	707,410	347,741	59,663	1,114,814	802,984	380,828	74,748	1,258,560
Wyoming	54,370	39,583	3,009	96,962	62,624	38,739	2,019	103,382

Notes: Entries for the major parties (Democratic, Republican, or their historical antecedents listed in Appendix A) are votes gained by those candidates that historical records show are the primary candidates of the two major parties, except in 1836 when the three Whig candidates are tallied for the total Whig vote. Democratic = Anti-Federalists (1788–1796), Democratic-Republicans (1796–1828), Jacksonian Democrats (1824–1828), and Democrats (since 1832). Republicans = Federalists (1788–1816), National Republicans (1828–1832), Whigs (1836–1852), and Republicans (since 1856). Other = other third parties. — indicates that the state had no data, either because no vote data were found for the state in question or the state had not yet entered the Union. Residents of the District of Columbia received the presidential vote beginning in the 1964 election.

Sources: *Congressional Quarterly's Guide to U.S. Elections* (1994), ICPSR data sets 0001 and 0019, *America at the Polls: 1920–1964* (1965), *A Statistical History of the American Presidential Elections* (1963), and independent search of state sources by the author.

Table 4-56 Raw Popular Vote for President, by State, 1940–1944

State	1940 Democratic	Republican	Other	Total Vote	1944 Democratic	Republican	Other	Total Vote
Alabama	250,726	42,184	1,309	294,219	198,918	44,540	1,285	244,743
Alaska	—	—	—	—	—	—	—	—
Arizona	95,267	54,030	742	150,039	80,926	56,287	421	137,634
Arkansas	157,213	42,122	1,094	200,429	148,965	63,551	438	212,954
California	1,877,618	1,351,419	39,754	3,268,791	1,988,564	1,512,965	19,346	3,520,875
Colorado	265,554	279,576	3,874	549,004	234,331	268,731	1,977	505,039
Connecticut	417,621	361,819	2,062	781,502	435,146	390,527	6,317	831,990
Delaware	74,599	61,440	335	136,374	68,166	56,747	448	125,361
Dist. of Columbia	—	—	—	—	—	—	—	—
Florida	359,334	126,158	148	485,640	339,377	143,215	211	482,803
Georgia	265,194	46,495	997	312,686	268,187	59,900	42	328,129
Hawaii	—	—	—	—	—	—	—	—
Idaho	127,842	106,553	773	235,168	107,399	100,137	785	208,321
Illinois	2,149,934	2,047,240	20,761	4,217,935	2,079,479	1,939,314	17,268	4,036,061
Indiana	874,063	899,466	9,218	1,782,747	781,403	875,891	14,797	1,672,091
Iowa	578,802	632,370	4,260	1,215,432	499,876	547,267	5,456	1,052,599
Kansas	364,725	489,169	6,403	860,297	287,458	442,096	4,222	733,776
Kentucky	557,322	410,384	2,457	970,163	472,589	392,448	2,887	867,924
Louisiana	319,751	52,446	108	372,305	281,564	67,750	69	349,383
Maine	156,478	163,951	411	320,840	140,631	155,434	335	296,400
Maryland	384,546	269,534	6,024	660,104	315,490	292,949	0	608,439
Massachusetts	1,076,522	939,700	10,771	2,026,993	1,035,296	921,350	4,019	1,960,665
Michigan	1,032,991	1,039,917	13,021	2,085,929	1,106,899	1,084,423	13,901	2,205,223
Minnesota	644,196	596,274	10,718	1,251,188	589,864	527,416	8,224	1,125,504
Mississippi	168,267	7,364	193	175,824	168,621	11,613	0	180,234
Missouri	958,476	871,009	4,244	1,833,729	807,356	761,175	3,166	1,571,697
Montana	145,698	99,579	2,596	247,873	112,556	93,163	1,636	207,355
Nebraska	263,677	352,201	0	615,878	233,246	329,880	0	563,126
Nevada	31,945	21,229	0	53,174	29,623	24,611	0	54,234
New Hampshire	125,292	110,127	0	235,419	119,663	109,916	46	229,625
New Jersey	1,016,808	945,475	10,269	1,972,552	987,874	961,335	14,552	1,963,761
New Mexico	103,699	79,315	244	183,258	81,389	70,688	148	152,225
New York	3,251,918	3,027,478	22,200	6,301,596	3,304,238	2,987,647	24,905	6,316,790
North Carolina	609,015	213,633	0	822,648	527,399	263,155	0	790,554
North Dakota	124,036	154,590	2,149	280,775	100,144	118,535	1,503	220,182
Ohio	1,733,139	1,586,773	0	3,319,912	1,570,763	1,582,293	0	3,153,056
Oklahoma	474,313	348,872	3,027	826,212	401,549	319,424	1,663	722,636
Oregon	258,415	219,555	3,270	481,240	248,635	225,365	6,147	480,147
Pennsylvania	2,171,035	1,889,848	17,831	4,078,714	1,940,479	1,835,054	19,260	3,794,793
Rhode Island	182,181	138,654	317	321,152	175,356	123,487	433	299,276
South Carolina	95,470	4,360	0	99,830	90,601	4,617	8,164	103,382
South Dakota	131,362	177,065	0	308,427	96,711	135,365	0	232,076
Tennessee	351,601	169,153	2,069	522,823	308,707	200,311	1,674	510,692
Texas	909,974	212,692	1,771	1,124,437	821,605	191,423	137,306	1,150,334
Utah	154,277	93,151	391	247,819	150,088	97,891	340	248,319
Vermont	64,269	78,371	422	143,062	53,820	71,527	14	125,361
Virginia	235,961	109,363	1,284	346,608	242,276	145,243	966	388,485
Washington	462,145	322,123	9,565	793,833	486,774	361,689	7,865	856,328
West Virginia	495,662	372,414	0	868,076	392,777	322,819	0	715,596
Wisconsin	704,821	679,206	21,495	1,405,522	650,413	674,532	14,207	1,339,152
Wyoming	59,287	52,633	320	112,240	49,419	51,921	0	101,340

Notes: Entries for the major parties (Democratic, Republican, or their historical antecedents listed in Appendix A) are votes gained by those candidates that historical records show are the primary candidates of the two major parties, except in 1836 when the three Whig candidates are tallied for the total Whig vote. Democratic = Anti-Federalists (1788–1796), Democratic-Republicans (1796–1828), Jacksonian Democrats (1824–1828), and Democrats (since 1832). Republicans = Federalists (1788–1816), National Republicans (1828–1832), Whigs (1836–1852), and Republicans (since 1856). Other = other third parties. — indicates that the state had no data, either because no vote data were found for the state in question or the state had not yet entered the Union. Residents of the District of Columbia received the presidential vote beginning in the 1964 election.

Sources: *Congressional Quarterly's Guide to U.S. Elections* (1994), ICPSR data sets 0001 and 0019, *America at the Polls: 1920–1964* (1965), *A Statistical History of the American Presidential Elections* (1963), and independent search of state sources by the author.

Table 4-57 Raw Popular Vote for President, by State, 1948–1952

State	1948				1952			
	Democratic	Republican	Other	Total Vote	Democratic	Republican	Other	Total Vote
Alabama	0	40,930	174,050	214,980	275,075	149,231	1,814	426,120
Alaska	—	—	—	—	—	—	—	—
Arizona	95,251	77,597	4,217	177,065	108,528	152,042	0	260,570
Arkansas	149,659	50,959	41,857	242,475	226,300	177,155	1,345	404,800
California	1,913,134	1,895,269	213,135	4,021,538	2,197,548	2,897,310	46,991	5,141,849
Colorado	267,288	239,714	8,235	515,237	245,504	379,782	4,817	630,103
Connecticut	423,297	437,754	22,467	883,518	481,649	611,012	4,250	1,096,911
Delaware	67,813	69,588	1,672	139,073	83,315	90,059	651	174,025
Dist. of Columbia	—	—	—	—	—	—	—	—
Florida	281,988	194,280	101,375	577,643	444,950	544,036	351	989,337
Georgia	254,646	76,691	87,507	418,844	456,823	198,961	1	655,785
Hawaii	—	—	—	—	—	—	—	—
Idaho	107,370	101,514	5,932	214,816	95,081	180,707	466	276,254
Illinois	1,994,715	1,961,103	28,228	3,984,046	2,013,920	2,457,327	9,811	4,481,058
Indiana	807,831	821,079	27,302	1,656,212	801,530	1,136,259	17,260	1,955,049
Iowa	522,380	494,018	21,866	1,038,264	451,513	808,906	8,354	1,268,773
Kansas	351,902	423,039	13,878	788,819	273,296	616,302	6,568	896,166
Kentucky	466,756	341,210	14,692	822,658	495,729	495,029	2,390	993,148
Louisiana	136,344	72,657	207,335	416,336	345,027	306,925	0	651,952
Maine	111,916	150,234	2,637	264,787	118,806	232,353	627	351,786
Maryland	286,521	294,814	15,413	596,748	395,337	499,424	7,313	902,074
Massachusetts	1,151,788	909,370	45,988	2,107,146	1,083,525	1,292,325	7,548	2,383,398
Michigan	1,003,448	1,038,595	67,566	2,109,609	1,230,657	1,551,529	16,406	2,798,592
Minnesota	692,966	483,617	35,643	1,212,226	608,458	763,211	7,814	1,379,483
Mississippi	19,384	5,043	167,763	192,190	172,566	112,966	0	285,532
Missouri	917,315	655,039	6,274	1,578,628	929,830	959,429	2,803	1,892,062
Montana	119,071	96,770	8,437	224,278	106,213	157,394	1,430	265,037
Nebraska	224,165	264,774	1	488,940	188,057	421,603	0	609,660
Nevada	31,291	29,357	1,469	62,117	31,688	50,502	0	82,190
New Hampshire	107,995	121,299	2,146	231,440	106,663	166,287	0	272,950
New Jersey	895,455	981,124	72,976	1,949,555	1,015,902	1,373,613	29,039	2,418,554
New Mexico	105,464	80,303	1,296	187,063	105,661	132,170	777	238,608
New York	2,780,204	2,841,163	555,970	6,177,337	3,104,601	3,952,813	70,825	7,128,239
North Carolina	459,070	258,572	73,567	791,209	652,803	558,107	0	1,210,910
North Dakota	95,812	115,139	9,765	220,716	76,694	191,712	1,721	270,127
Ohio	1,452,791	1,445,684	37,596	2,936,071	1,600,367	2,100,391	0	3,700,758
Oklahoma	452,782	268,817	0	721,599	430,939	518,045	0	948,984
Oregon	243,147	260,904	20,029	524,080	270,579	420,815	3,665	695,059
Pennsylvania	1,752,426	1,902,197	80,725	3,735,348	2,146,269	2,415,789	18,911	4,580,969
Rhode Island	188,736	135,787	3,179	327,702	203,293	210,935	270	414,498
South Carolina	34,423	5,386	102,762	142,571	173,004	168,082	1	341,087
South Dakota	117,653	129,651	2,801	250,105	90,426	203,857	0	294,283
Tennessee	270,402	202,914	76,967	550,283	443,710	446,147	2,696	892,553
Texas	824,235	303,467	121,875	1,249,577	969,228	1,102,878	3,840	2,075,946
Utah	149,151	124,402	2,753	276,306	135,364	194,190	0	329,554
Vermont	45,557	75,926	1,899	123,382	43,355	109,717	485	153,557
Virginia	200,786	172,070	46,400	419,256	268,677	349,037	1,975	619,689
Washington	476,165	386,314	42,579	905,058	492,845	599,107	10,756	1,102,708
West Virginia	429,188	316,251	3,311	748,750	453,578	419,970	0	873,548
Wisconsin	647,310	590,959	38,531	1,276,800	622,175	979,744	5,451	1,607,370
Wyoming	52,354	47,947	1,124	101,425	47,934	81,049	270	129,253

Notes: Entries for the major parties (Democratic, Republican, or their historical antecedents listed in Appendix A) are votes gained by those candidates that historical records show are the primary candidates of the two major parties, except in 1836 when the three Whig candidates are tallied for the total Whig vote. Democratic = Anti-Federalists (1788–1796), Democratic-Republicans (1796–1828), Jacksonian Democrats (1824–1828), and Democrats (since 1832). Republicans = Federalists (1788–1816), National Republicans (1828–1832), Whigs (1836–1852), and Republicans (since 1856). Other = other third parties. — indicates that the state had no data, either because no vote data were found for the state in question or the state had not yet entered the Union. Residents of the District of Columbia received the presidential vote beginning in the 1964 election.

Sources: *Congressional Quarterly's Guide to U.S. Elections* (1994), ICPSR data sets 0001 and 0019, *America at the Polls: 1920–1964* (1965), *America Votes* (various publication dates), *A Statistical History of the American Presidential Elections* (1963), and independent search of state sources by the author.

Table 4-58 Raw Popular Vote for President, by State, 1956–1960

State	1956				1960			
	Democratic	Republican	Other	Total Vote	Democratic	Republican	Other	Total Vote
Alabama	280,844	195,694	20,323	496,861	324,050	237,981	8,194	570,225
Alaska	—	—	—	—	29,809	30,953	0	60,762
Arizona	112,880	176,990	303	290,173	176,781	221,241	469	398,491
Arkansas	213,277	186,287	7,008	406,572	215,049	184,508	28,952	428,509
California	2,420,135	3,027,668	18,552	5,466,355	3,224,099	3,259,722	22,757	6,506,578
Colorado	257,997	394,479	4,598	657,074	330,629	402,242	3,365	736,236
Connecticut	405,079	711,837	205	1,117,121	657,055	565,813	15	1,222,883
Delaware	79,421	98,057	510	177,988	99,590	96,373	720	196,683
Dist. of Columbia	—	—	—	—	—	—	—	—
Florida	480,371	643,849	1,542	1,125,762	748,700	795,476	0	1,544,176
Georgia	444,688	222,778	2,189	669,655	458,638	274,472	239	733,349
Hawaii	—	—	—	—	92,410	92,295	0	184,705
Idaho	105,868	166,979	142	272,989	138,853	161,597	0	300,450
Illinois	1,775,682	2,623,327	8,398	4,407,407	2,377,846	2,368,988	10,575	4,757,409
Indiana	783,908	1,182,811	7,888	1,974,607	952,358	1,175,120	7,882	2,135,360
Iowa	501,858	729,187	3,519	1,234,564	550,565	722,381	864	1,273,810
Kansas	296,317	566,878	3,048	866,243	363,213	561,474	4,138	928,825
Kentucky	476,453	572,192	5,160	1,053,805	521,855	602,607	0	1,124,462
Louisiana	243,977	329,047	44,520	617,544	407,339	230,980	169,572	807,891
Maine	102,468	249,238	0	351,706	181,159	240,608	0	421,767
Maryland	372,613	559,738	476	932,827	565,808	489,538	3	1,055,349
Massachusetts	948,190	1,393,197	7,119	2,348,506	1,487,174	976,750	5,556	2,469,480
Michigan	1,359,898	1,713,647	6,923	3,080,468	1,687,269	1,620,428	10,400	3,318,097
Minnesota	617,525	719,302	3,178	1,340,005	779,933	757,915	4,039	1,541,887
Mississippi	144,453	60,685	42,966	248,104	108,362	73,561	116,248	298,171
Missouri	918,273	914,289	0	1,832,562	972,201	962,221	0	1,934,422
Montana	116,238	154,933	0	271,171	134,891	141,841	847	277,579
Nebraska	199,029	378,108	0	577,137	232,542	380,553	0	613,095
Nevada	40,640	56,049	0	96,689	54,880	52,387	0	107,267
New Hampshire	90,364	176,519	111	266,994	137,772	157,989	0	295,761
New Jersey	850,337	1,606,942	27,033	2,484,312	1,385,415	1,363,324	24,372	2,773,111
New Mexico	106,098	146,788	1,040	253,926	156,027	153,733	1,347	311,107
New York	2,747,944	4,345,506	2,521	7,095,971	3,830,085	3,446,419	14,575	7,291,079
North Carolina	590,530	575,062	0	1,165,592	713,136	655,420	0	1,368,556
North Dakota	96,742	156,766	483	253,991	123,963	154,310	158	278,431
Ohio	1,439,655	2,262,610	0	3,702,265	1,944,248	2,217,611	0	4,161,859
Oklahoma	385,581	473,769	0	859,350	370,111	533,039	0	903,150
Oregon	329,204	406,393	535	736,132	367,402	408,060	959	776,421
Pennsylvania	1,981,769	2,585,252	9,482	4,576,503	2,556,282	2,439,956	10,303	5,006,541
Rhode Island	161,790	225,819	0	387,609	258,032	147,502	1	405,535
South Carolina	136,372	75,700	88,511	300,583	198,129	188,558	1	386,688
South Dakota	122,288	171,569	0	293,857	128,070	178,417	0	306,487
Tennessee	456,507	462,288	20,609	939,404	481,453	556,577	13,762	1,051,792
Texas	859,958	1,080,619	14,591	1,955,168	1,167,567	1,121,310	22,207	2,311,084
Utah	118,364	215,631	0	333,995	169,248	205,361	100	374,709
Vermont	42,549	110,390	39	152,978	69,186	98,131	7	167,324
Virginia	267,760	386,459	43,759	697,978	362,327	404,521	4,601	771,449
Washington	523,002	620,430	7,457	1,150,889	599,298	629,273	13,001	1,241,572
West Virginia	381,534	449,297	0	830,831	441,786	395,995	0	837,781
Wisconsin	586,768	954,844	8,946	1,550,558	830,805	895,175	3,102	1,729,082
Wyoming	49,554	74,573	0	124,127	63,331	77,451	0	140,782

Notes: Entries for the major parties (Democratic, Republican, or their historical antecedents listed in Appendix A) are votes gained by those candidates that historical records show are the primary candidates of the two major parties, except in 1836 when the three Whig candidates are tallied for the total Whig vote. Democratic = Anti-Federalists (1788–1796), Democratic-Republicans (1796–1828), Jacksonian Democrats (1824–1828), and Democrats (since 1832). Republicans = Federalists (1788–1816), National Republicans (1828–1832), Whigs (1836–1852), and Republicans (since 1856). Other = other third parties. — indicates that the state had no data, either because no vote data were found for the state in question or the state had not yet entered the Union. Residents of the District of Columbia received the presidential vote beginning in the 1964 election.

Sources: *Congressional Quarterly's Guide to U.S. Elections* (1994), ICPSR data sets 0001 and 0019, *America at the Polls: 1920–1964* (1965), *America Votes* (various publication dates), *A Statistical History of the American Presidential Elections* (1963), and independent search of state sources by the author.

Table 4-59 Raw Popular Vote for President, by State, 1964–1968

	1964				1968			
State	Democratic	Republican	Other	Total Vote	Democratic	Republican	Other	Total Vote
Alabama	0	479,085	210,733	689,818	196,579	146,923	706,420	1,049,922
Alaska	44,329	22,930	0	67,259	35,411	37,600	10,024	83,035
Arizona	237,753	242,535	482	480,770	170,514	266,721	49,701	486,936
Arkansas	314,197	243,264	2,965	560,426	188,228	190,759	240,982	619,969
California	4,171,877	2,879,108	6,601	7,057,586	3,244,318	3,467,664	539,605	7,251,587
Colorado	476,024	296,767	4,195	776,986	335,174	409,345	66,680	811,199
Connecticut	826,269	390,996	1,313	1,218,578	621,561	556,721	77,950	1,256,232
Delaware	122,704	78,078	538	201,320	89,194	96,714	28,459	214,367
Dist. of Columbia	169,796	28,801	0	198,597	139,566	31,012	0	170,578
Florida	948,540	905,941	0	1,854,481	676,794	886,804	624,207	2,187,805
Georgia	522,556	616,584	195	1,139,335	334,440	380,111	535,715	1,250,266
Hawaii	163,249	44,022	0	207,271	141,324	91,425	3,469	236,218
Idaho	148,920	143,557	0	292,477	89,273	165,369	36,541	291,183
Illinois	2,796,833	1,905,946	62	4,702,841	2,039,814	2,174,774	405,161	4,619,749
Indiana	1,170,848	911,118	9,640	2,091,606	806,659	1,067,885	249,053	2,123,597
Iowa	733,030	449,148	2,361	1,184,539	476,699	619,106	72,126	1,167,931
Kansas	464,028	386,579	7,294	857,901	302,996	478,674	91,113	872,783
Kentucky	669,659	372,977	3,469	1,046,105	397,541	462,411	195,941	1,055,893
Louisiana	387,068	509,225	0	896,293	309,615	257,535	530,300	1,097,450
Maine	262,264	118,701	0	380,965	217,312	169,254	6,370	392,936
Maryland	730,912	385,495	50	1,116,457	538,310	517,995	178,734	1,235,039
Massachusetts	1,786,422	549,727	8,649	2,344,798	1,469,218	766,844	95,690	2,331,752
Michigan	2,136,615	1,060,152	6,335	3,203,102	1,593,082	1,370,665	342,503	3,306,250
Minnesota	991,117	559,624	3,721	1,554,462	857,738	658,643	72,125	1,588,506
Mississippi	52,618	356,528	0	409,146	150,644	88,516	415,349	654,509
Missouri	1,164,344	653,535	0	1,817,879	791,444	811,932	206,126	1,809,502
Montana	164,246	113,032	1,350	278,628	114,117	138,835	21,452	274,404
Nebraska	307,307	276,847	0	584,154	170,784	321,163	44,904	536,851
Nevada	79,339	56,094	0	135,433	60,598	73,188	20,432	154,218
New Hampshire	184,064	104,029	0	288,093	130,589	154,903	11,806	297,298
New Jersey	1,868,231	964,174	15,258	2,847,663	1,264,206	1,325,467	285,722	2,875,395
New Mexico	194,015	132,838	1,792	328,645	130,081	169,692	27,577	327,350
New York	4,913,102	2,243,559	9,614	7,166,275	3,378,470	3,007,932	405,286	6,791,688
North Carolina	800,139	624,844	0	1,424,983	464,113	627,192	496,188	1,587,493
North Dakota	149,784	108,207	398	258,389	94,769	138,669	14,444	247,882
Ohio	2,498,331	1,470,865	0	3,969,196	1,700,586	1,791,014	468,098	3,959,698
Oklahoma	519,834	412,665	0	932,499	301,658	449,697	191,731	943,086
Oregon	501,017	282,779	2,509	786,305	358,866	408,433	52,323	819,622
Pennsylvania	3,130,954	1,673,657	18,079	4,822,690	2,259,405	2,090,017	398,506	4,747,928
Rhode Island	315,463	74,615	13	390,091	246,518	122,359	16,123	385,000
South Carolina	215,723	309,048	8	524,779	197,486	254,062	215,430	666,978
South Dakota	163,010	130,108	0	293,118	118,023	149,841	13,400	281,264
Tennessee	634,947	508,965	34	1,143,946	351,233	472,592	424,792	1,248,617
Texas	1,663,185	958,566	5,060	2,626,811	1,266,804	1,227,844	584,568	3,079,216
Utah	219,628	181,785	0	401,413	156,665	238,728	27,175	422,568
Vermont	108,127	54,942	20	163,089	70,255	85,142	6,007	161,404
Virginia	558,038	481,334	2,895	1,042,267	442,387	590,319	328,785	1,361,491
Washington	779,881	470,366	8,309	1,258,556	616,037	588,510	99,734	1,304,281
West Virginia	538,087	253,953	0	792,040	374,091	307,555	72,560	754,206
Wisconsin	1,050,424	638,495	2,896	1,691,815	748,804	809,997	132,737	1,691,538
Wyoming	80,718	61,998	0	142,716	45,173	70,927	11,105	127,205

Notes: Entries for the major parties (Democratic, Republican, or their historical antecedents listed in Appendix A) are votes gained by those candidates that historical records show are the primary candidates of the two major parties, except in 1836 when the three Whig candidates are tallied for the total Whig vote. Democratic = Anti-Federalists (1788–1796), Democratic-Republicans (1796–1828), Jacksonian Democrats (1824–1828), and Democrats (since 1832). Republicans = Federalists (1788–1816), National Republicans (1828–1832), Whigs (1836–1852), and Republicans (since 1856). Other = other third parties. Residents of the District of Columbia received the presidential vote beginning in the 1964 election.

Sources: *Congressional Quarterly's Guide to U.S. Elections* (1994), ICPSR data sets 0001 and 0019, *America at the Polls: 1920–1964* (1965), *America Votes* (various publication dates), and independent search of state sources by the author.

Table 4-60 Raw Popular Vote for President, by State, 1972–1976

State	1972				1976			
	Democratic	Republican	Other	Total Vote	Democratic	Republican	Other	Total Vote
Alabama	256,923	728,701	20,487	1,006,111	659,170	504,070	19,610	1,182,850
Alaska	32,967	55,349	6,903	95,219	44,058	71,555	7,961	123,574
Arizona	198,540	402,812	21,574	622,926	295,602	418,642	28,475	742,719
Arkansas	199,892	448,541	2,887	651,320	498,604	267,903	1,028	767,535
California	3,475,847	4,602,096	289,919	8,367,862	3,742,284	3,882,244	242,589	7,867,117
Colorado	329,980	597,189	26,715	953,884	460,353	584,367	36,834	1,081,554
Connecticut	555,498	810,763	18,016	1,384,277	647,895	719,261	14,370	1,381,526
Delaware	92,283	140,357	2,876	235,516	122,596	109,831	3,407	235,834
Dist. of Columbia	127,627	35,226	568	163,421	137,818	27,873	3,139	168,830
Florida	718,117	1,857,759	7,407	2,583,283	1,636,000	1,469,531	45,100	3,150,631
Georgia	289,529	881,496	3,747	1,174,772	979,409	483,743	4,306	1,467,458
Hawaii	101,409	168,865	0	270,274	147,375	140,003	3,923	291,301
Idaho	80,826	199,384	30,169	310,379	126,549	204,151	13,371	344,071
Illinois	1,913,472	2,788,179	21,585	4,723,236	2,271,295	2,364,269	83,350	4,718,914
Indiana	708,568	1,405,154	11,807	2,125,529	1,014,714	1,183,958	21,690	2,220,362
Iowa	496,206	706,207	23,531	1,225,944	619,931	632,863	26,512	1,279,306
Kansas	270,287	619,812	25,996	916,095	430,421	502,752	24,672	957,845
Kentucky	371,159	676,446	19,894	1,067,499	615,717	531,852	19,573	1,167,142
Louisiana	298,142	686,852	66,497	1,051,491	661,365	587,446	29,628	1,278,439
Maine	160,584	256,458	0	417,042	232,279	236,320	14,617	483,216
Maryland	505,781	829,305	18,726	1,353,812	759,612	672,661	7,624	1,439,897
Massachusetts	1,332,540	1,112,078	14,138	2,458,756	1,429,475	1,030,276	87,807	2,547,558
Michigan	1,459,435	1,961,721	68,571	3,489,727	1,696,714	1,893,742	63,293	3,653,749
Minnesota	802,346	898,269	41,037	1,741,652	1,070,440	819,395	60,096	1,949,931
Mississippi	126,782	505,125	14,056	645,963	381,309	366,846	21,206	769,361
Missouri	697,147	1,153,852	4,804	1,855,803	998,387	927,443	27,770	1,953,600
Montana	120,197	183,976	13,430	317,603	149,259	173,703	5,772	328,734
Nebraska	169,991	406,298	0	576,289	233,692	359,705	14,271	607,668
Nevada	66,016	115,750	0	181,766	92,479	101,273	8,124	201,876
New Hampshire	116,435	213,724	3,896	334,055	147,635	185,935	6,048	339,618
New Jersey	1,102,211	1,845,502	49,516	2,997,229	1,444,653	1,509,688	60,131	3,014,472
New Mexico	141,084	235,606	9,551	386,241	201,148	211,419	5,842	418,409
New York	2,951,084	4,192,778	22,057	7,165,919	3,389,558	3,100,791	43,821	6,534,170
North Carolina	438,705	1,054,889	25,018	1,518,612	927,365	741,960	9,589	1,678,914
North Dakota	100,384	174,109	6,021	280,514	136,078	153,470	7,640	297,188
Ohio	1,558,889	2,441,827	94,071	4,094,787	2,011,621	2,000,505	99,747	4,111,873
Oklahoma	247,147	759,025	23,728	1,029,900	532,442	545,708	14,101	1,092,251
Oregon	392,760	486,686	48,500	927,946	490,407	492,120	47,349	1,029,876
Pennsylvania	1,796,951	2,714,521	80,634	4,592,106	2,328,677	2,205,604	86,506	4,620,787
Rhode Island	194,645	220,383	780	415,808	227,636	181,249	2,285	411,170
South Carolina	186,824	477,044	10,092	673,960	450,807	346,149	5,627	802,583
South Dakota	139,945	166,476	994	307,415	147,068	151,505	2,105	300,678
Tennessee	357,293	813,147	30,742	1,201,182	825,879	633,969	16,497	1,476,345
Texas	1,154,289	2,298,896	18,096	3,471,281	2,082,319	1,953,300	36,265	4,071,884
Utah	126,284	323,643	28,549	478,476	182,110	337,908	21,180	541,198
Vermont	68,174	117,149	1,624	186,947	80,954	102,085	4,726	187,765
Virginia	438,887	988,493	29,639	1,457,019	813,896	836,554	46,644	1,697,094
Washington	568,334	837,135	65,378	1,470,847	717,323	777,732	60,479	1,555,534
West Virginia	277,435	484,964	0	762,399	435,914	314,760	290	750,964
Wisconsin	810,174	989,430	53,286	1,852,890	1,040,232	1,004,987	58,956	2,104,175
Wyoming	44,358	100,464	748	145,570	62,239	92,717	1,387	156,343

Notes: Entries for the major parties (Democratic, Republican, or their historical antecedents listed in Appendix A) are votes gained by those candidates that historical records show are the primary candidates of the two major parties, except in 1836 when the three Whig candidates are tallied for the total Whig vote. Democratic = Anti-Federalists (1788–1796), Democratic-Republicans (1796–1828), Jacksonian Democrats (1824–1828), and Democrats (since 1832). Republicans = Federalists (1788–1816), National Republicans (1828–1832), Whigs (1836–1852), and Republicans (since 1856). Other = other third parties. Residents of the District of Columbia received the presidential vote beginning in the 1964 election.

Sources: *Congressional Quarterly's Guide to U.S. Elections* (1994), ICPSR data sets 0001 and 0019, *America Votes* (various publication dates), and independent search of state sources by the author.

Table 4-61 Raw Popular Vote for President, by State, 1980–1984

	1980				1984			
State	Democratic	Republican	Other	Total Vote	Democratic	Republican	Other	Total Vote
Alabama	636,730	654,192	51,007	1,341,929	551,899	872,849	16,965	1,441,713
Alaska	41,842	86,112	30,491	158,445	62,007	138,377	7,221	207,605
Arizona	246,843	529,688	97,414	873,945	333,854	681,416	10,627	1,025,897
Arkansas	398,041	403,164	36,377	837,582	338,646	534,774	10,986	884,406
California	3,083,661	4,524,858	978,544	8,587,063	3,922,519	5,467,009	115,895	9,505,423
Colorado	367,973	652,264	164,178	1,184,415	454,975	821,817	18,588	1,295,380
Connecticut	541,732	677,210	187,343	1,406,285	569,597	890,877	6,426	1,466,900
Delaware	105,754	111,252	18,894	235,900	101,656	152,190	726	254,572
Dist. of Columbia	131,113	23,545	20,579	175,237	180,408	29,009	1,871	211,288
Florida	1,419,475	2,046,951	220,504	3,686,930	1,448,816	2,730,350	885	4,180,051
Georgia	890,733	654,168	51,794	1,596,695	706,628	1,068,722	770	1,776,120
Hawaii	135,879	130,112	37,296	303,287	147,154	185,050	3,642	335,846
Idaho	110,192	290,699	36,540	437,431	108,510	297,523	5,111	411,144
Illinois	1,981,413	2,358,049	410,259	4,749,721	2,086,499	2,707,103	25,486	4,819,088
Indiana	844,197	1,255,656	142,180	2,242,033	841,481	1,377,230	14,358	2,233,069
Iowa	508,672	676,026	132,963	1,317,661	605,620	703,088	11,097	1,319,805
Kansas	326,150	566,812	86,833	979,795	333,149	677,296	11,546	1,021,991
Kentucky	616,417	635,274	42,936	1,294,627	539,539	821,702	8,104	1,369,345
Louisiana	708,453	792,853	47,285	1,548,591	651,586	1,037,299	17,937	1,706,822
Maine	220,974	238,522	63,515	523,011	214,515	336,500	2,129	553,144
Maryland	726,161	680,606	133,729	1,540,496	787,935	879,918	8,020	1,675,873
Massachusetts	1,053,802	1,057,631	412,865	2,524,298	1,239,606	1,310,936	8,911	2,559,453
Michigan	1,661,532	1,915,225	332,968	3,909,725	1,529,638	2,251,571	20,449	3,801,658
Minnesota	954,174	873,268	224,538	2,051,980	1,036,364	1,032,603	15,482	2,084,449
Mississippi	429,281	441,089	22,250	892,620	352,192	582,377	6,535	941,104
Missouri	931,182	1,074,181	94,461	2,099,824	848,583	1,274,188	12	2,122,783
Montana	118,032	206,814	39,106	363,952	146,742	232,450	5,185	384,377
Nebraska	166,851	419,937	54,066	640,854	187,866	460,054	4,170	652,090
Nevada	66,666	155,017	26,202	247,885	91,655	188,770	6,242	286,667
New Hampshire	108,864	221,705	53,421	383,990	120,395	267,051	1,620	389,066
New Jersey	1,147,364	1,546,557	281,763	2,975,684	1,261,323	1,933,630	22,909	3,217,862
New Mexico	167,826	250,779	38,366	456,971	201,769	307,101	5,500	514,370
New York	2,728,372	2,893,831	579,756	6,201,959	3,119,609	3,664,763	22,438	6,806,810
North Carolina	875,635	915,018	65,180	1,855,833	824,287	1,346,481	4,593	2,175,361
North Dakota	79,189	193,695	28,661	301,545	104,429	200,336	4,206	308,971
Ohio	1,752,414	2,206,545	324,644	4,283,603	1,825,440	2,678,560	43,619	4,547,619
Oklahoma	402,026	695,570	52,112	1,149,708	385,080	861,530	9,066	1,255,676
Oregon	456,890	571,044	153,582	1,181,516	536,479	685,700	4,348	1,226,527
Pennsylvania	1,937,540	2,261,872	362,089	4,561,501	2,228,131	2,584,323	32,449	4,844,903
Rhode Island	198,342	154,793	62,937	416,072	197,106	212,080	1,306	410,492
South Carolina	430,385	441,841	21,845	894,071	344,459	615,539	8,531	968,529
South Dakota	103,855	198,343	25,505	327,703	116,113	200,267	1,487	317,867
Tennessee	783,051	787,761	46,804	1,617,616	711,714	990,212	10,068	1,711,994
Texas	1,881,147	2,510,705	149,784	4,541,636	1,949,276	3,433,428	14,867	5,397,571
Utah	124,266	439,687	40,269	604,222	155,369	469,105	5,182	629,656
Vermont	81,952	94,628	36,719	213,299	95,730	135,865	2,966	234,561
Virginia	752,174	989,609	124,249	1,866,032	796,250	1,337,078	13,307	2,146,635
Washington	650,193	865,244	226,957	1,742,394	807,352	1,051,670	24,888	1,883,910
West Virginia	367,462	334,206	36,047	737,715	328,125	405,483	2,134	735,742
Wisconsin	981,584	1,088,845	202,792	2,273,221	995,740	1,198,584	17,365	2,211,689
Wyoming	49,427	110,700	16,586	176,713	53,370	133,241	2,357	188,968

Notes: Entries for the major parties (Democratic, Republican, or their historical antecedents listed in Appendix A) are votes gained by those candidates that historical records show are the primary candidates of the two major parties, except in 1836 when the three Whig candidates are tallied for the total Whig vote. Democratic = Anti-Federalists (1788–1796), Democratic-Republicans (1796–1828), Jacksonian Democrats (1824–1828), and Democrats (since 1832). Republicans = Federalists (1788–1816), National Republicans (1828–1832), Whigs (1836–1852), and Republicans (since 1856). Other = other third parties. Residents of the District of Columbia received the presidential vote beginning in the 1964 election.

Sources: *Congressional Quarterly's Guide to U.S. Elections* (1994), *America Votes* (various publication dates), and independent search of state sources by the author.

Table 4-62 Raw Popular Vote for President, by State, 1988–1992

State	1988				1992			
	Democratic	Republican	Other	Total Vote	Democratic	Republican	Other	Total Vote
Alabama	549,506	815,576	13,394	1,378,476	690,080	804,283	193,697	1,688,060
Alaska	72,584	119,251	8,281	200,116	78,294	102,000	78,212	258,506
Arizona	454,029	702,541	15,303	1,171,873	543,050	572,086	371,839	1,486,975
Arkansas	349,237	466,578	11,923	827,738	505,823	337,324	107,506	950,653
California	4,702,233	5,054,917	129,915	9,887,065	5,121,325	3,630,574	2,379,822	11,131,721
Colorado	621,453	728,177	22,764	1,372,394	629,681	562,850	376,649	1,569,180
Connecticut	676,584	750,241	16,569	1,443,394	682,318	578,313	355,701	1,616,332
Delaware	108,647	139,639	1,605	249,891	126,054	102,313	61,368	289,735
Dist. of Columbia	159,407	27,590	5,880	192,877	192,619	20,698	14,255	227,572
Florida	1,656,701	2,618,885	26,727	4,302,313	2,072,698	2,173,310	1,068,384	5,314,392
Georgia	714,792	1,081,331	13,549	1,809,672	1,008,966	995,252	316,907	2,321,125
Hawaii	192,364	158,625	3,472	354,461	179,310	136,822	56,710	372,842
Idaho	147,272	253,881	7,815	408,968	137,013	202,645	142,484	482,142
Illinois	2,215,940	2,310,939	32,241	4,559,120	2,453,350	1,734,096	862,711	5,050,157
Indiana	860,643	1,297,763	10,215	2,168,621	848,420	989,375	468,076	2,305,871
Iowa	670,557	545,355	9,702	1,225,614	586,353	504,891	263,363	1,354,607
Kansas	422,636	554,049	16,359	993,044	390,434	449,951	316,950	1,157,335
Kentucky	580,368	734,281	7,868	1,322,517	665,104	617,178	210,618	1,492,900
Louisiana	717,460	883,702	27,040	1,628,202	815,971	733,386	240,660	1,790,017
Maine	243,569	307,131	4,335	555,035	263,420	206,504	209,575	679,499
Maryland	826,304	876,167	11,887	1,714,358	988,571	707,094	289,381	1,985,046
Massachusetts	1,401,415	1,194,635	36,755	2,632,805	1,318,662	805,049	649,989	2,773,700
Michigan	1,675,783	1,965,486	27,894	3,669,163	1,871,182	1,554,940	848,551	4,274,673
Minnesota	1,109,471	962,337	24,982	2,096,790	1,020,997	747,841	579,110	2,347,948
Mississippi	363,921	557,890	9,716	931,527	400,258	487,793	93,742	981,793
Missouri	1,001,619	1,084,953	7,141	2,093,713	1,053,873	811,159	526,533	2,391,565
Montana	168,936	190,412	6,326	365,674	154,507	144,207	111,897	410,611
Nebraska	259,235	397,956	4,274	661,465	216,864	343,678	177,004	737,546
Nevada	132,738	206,040	11,289	350,067	189,148	175,828	141,342	506,318
New Hampshire	163,696	281,537	5,841	451,074	209,040	202,484	126,419	537,943
New Jersey	1,320,352	1,743,192	36,009	3,099,553	1,436,206	1,356,865	550,523	3,343,594
New Mexico	244,497	270,341	6,449	521,287	261,617	212,824	95,545	569,986
New York	3,347,882	3,081,871	55,930	6,485,683	3,444,450	2,346,649	1,135,826	6,926,925
North Carolina	890,167	1,237,258	6,945	2,134,370	1,114,042	1,134,661	363,147	2,611,850
North Dakota	127,739	166,559	2,963	297,261	99,168	136,244	72,721	308,133
Ohio	1,939,629	2,416,549	37,521	4,393,699	1,984,942	1,894,310	1,060,715	4,939,967
Oklahoma	483,423	678,367	9,246	1,171,036	473,066	592,929	324,364	1,390,359
Oregon	616,206	560,126	25,362	1,201,694	621,314	475,757	365,572	1,462,643
Pennsylvania	2,194,944	2,300,087	41,220	4,536,251	2,239,164	1,791,841	928,805	4,959,810
Rhode Island	225,123	177,761	1,736	404,620	213,299	131,601	108,577	453,477
South Carolina	370,554	606,443	9,012	986,009	479,514	577,507	145,506	1,202,527
South Dakota	145,560	165,415	2,016	312,991	124,888	136,718	74,648	336,254
Tennessee	679,794	947,233	9,223	1,636,250	933,521	841,300	207,817	1,982,638
Texas	2,352,748	3,036,829	37,833	5,427,410	2,281,815	2,496,071	1,376,132	6,154,018
Utah	207,343	428,442	11,223	647,008	183,429	322,632	237,938	743,999
Vermont	115,775	124,331	3,222	243,328	133,592	88,122	67,987	289,701
Virginia	859,799	1,309,162	22,648	2,191,609	1,038,650	1,150,517	369,498	2,558,665
Washington	933,516	903,835	27,902	1,865,253	993,037	731,234	563,959	2,288,230
West Virginia	341,016	310,065	2,230	653,311	331,001	241,974	110,787	683,762
Wisconsin	1,126,794	1,047,499	17,315	2,191,608	1,041,066	930,855	559,193	2,531,114
Wyoming	67,113	106,867	2,571	176,551	68,160	79,347	53,091	200,598

Notes: Entries for the major parties (Democratic, Republican, or their historical antecedents listed in Appendix A) are votes gained by those candidates that historical records show are the primary candidates of the two major parties, except in 1836 when the three Whig candidates are tallied for the total Whig vote. Democratic = Anti-Federalists (1788–1796), Democratic-Republicans (1796–1828), Jacksonian Democrats (1824–1828), and Democrats (since 1832). Republicans = Federalists (1788–1816), National Republicans (1828–1832), Whigs (1836–1852), and Republicans (since 1856). Other = other third parties. Residents of the District of Columbia received the presidential vote beginning in the 1964 election.

Sources: *Congressional Quarterly's Guide to U.S. Elections* (1994), *America Votes* (various publication dates), and independent search of state sources by the author.

Table 4-63 Raw Popular Vote for President, by State, 1996

State	1996 Democratic	Republican	Other	Total Vote
Alabama	662,165	769,044	103,140	1,534,349
Alaska	80,380	122,746	38,494	241,620
Arizona	653,288	622,073	129,044	1,404,405
Arkansas	475,171	325,416	83,675	884,262
California	5,119,835	3,828,380	1,071,269	10,019,484
Colorado	671,152	691,848	147,704	1,510,704
Connecticut	735,740	483,109	173,765	1,392,614
Delaware	140,355	99,062	31,667	271,084
Dist. of Columbia	158,220	17,339	10,167	185,726
Florida	2,546,870	2,244,536	512,388	5,303,794
Georgia	1,053,849	1,080,843	164,379	2,299,071
Hawaii	205,012	113,943	41,165	360,120
Idaho	165,443	256,595	69,681	491,719
Illinois	2,341,744	1,587,021	382,626	4,311,391
Indiana	887,424	1,006,693	241,725	2,135,842
Iowa	620,258	492,644	121,173	1,234,075
Kansas	387,659	583,245	103,396	1,074,300
Kentucky	636,614	623,283	128,811	1,388,708
Louisiana	927,837	712,586	143,536	1,783,959
Maine	312,788	186,378	106,731	605,897
Maryland	966,207	681,530	133,133	1,780,870
Massachusetts	1,571,763	718,107	266,915	2,556,785
Michigan	1,989,653	1,481,212	377,979	3,848,844
Minnesota	1,120,438	766,476	305,726	2,192,640
Mississippi	394,022	439,838	59,997	893,857
Missouri	1,025,935	890,016	242,114	2,158,065
Montana	167,922	179,652	59,687	407,261
Nebraska	236,761	363,467	77,187	677,415
Nevada	203,974	199,244	61,061	464,279
New Hampshire	246,214	196,532	56,429	499,175
New Jersey	1,652,329	1,103,078	320,400	3,075,807
New Mexico	273,495	232,751	49,828	556,074
New York	3,756,177	1,933,492	626,460	6,316,129
North Carolina	1,107,849	1,225,938	182,020	2,515,807
North Dakota	106,905	125,050	34,456	266,411
Ohio	2,148,222	1,859,883	526,329	4,534,434
Oklahoma	488,105	582,315	136,293	1,206,713
Oregon	649,641	538,152	189,967	1,377,760
Pennsylvania	2,215,819	1,801,169	489,130	4,506,118
Rhode Island	233,050	104,683	52,551	390,284
South Carolina	506,283	573,458	71,948	1,151,689
South Dakota	139,333	150,543	33,950	323,826
Tennessee	909,146	863,530	121,429	1,894,105
Texas	2,459,683	2,736,167	415,794	5,611,644
Utah	221,633	361,911	82,085	665,629
Vermont	137,894	80,352	40,203	258,449
Virginia	1,091,060	1,138,350	187,232	2,416,642
Washington	1,123,323	840,712	289,802	2,253,837
West Virginia	327,812	233,946	74,701	636,459
Wisconsin	1,071,971	845,029	279,169	2,196,169
Wyoming	77,934	105,388	28,249	211,571

Notes: Entries for the major parties (Democratic, Republican, or their historical antecedents listed in Appendix A) are votes gained by those candidates that historical records show are the primary candidates of the two major parties, except in 1836 when the three Whig candidates are tallied for the total Whig vote. Democratic = Anti-Federalists (1788–1796), Democratic-Republicans (1796–1828), Jacksonian Democrats (1824–1828), and Democrats (since 1832). Republicans = Federalists (1788–1816), National Republicans (1828–1832), Whigs (1836–1852), and Republicans (since 1856). Other = other third parties. Residents of the District of Columbia received the presidential vote beginning in the 1964 election.

Sources: *America Votes* (various publication dates) and independent search of state sources by the author.

5

The Obscurity of House Elections

While presidential elections are the most familiar elections in American politics, congressional elections are among the more obscure. Little attention generally is given to these races in newspapers or on television. Many candidates run with little money and slight visibility. People often enter the voting booth unfamiliar with the names of the people they select for the House of Representatives. Yet despite this immediate obscurity, House elections are pivotal to the understanding of American politics. The Framers of the Constitution saw biennial House elections as the ultimate expression of republican government. It was the only direct electoral link they were willing to entrust to "the people." Roger Sherman, a Constitutional Convention delegate from Connecticut, summed up the views of many of the Framers: "The people should have as little to do as may be about the government" (Byrd, 1988, p. 389). So the Framers rested the selection of presidents and senators in the hands of other bodies—the electoral college and state legislatures, respectively. The House stood as the radical experiment, especially because of the decision to opt for frequent elections. Although the frequency of elections was to constrain House members, it also worried some delegates, like Eldridge Gerry of Massachusetts, who felt that "the people do not lack virtue, but are the dupes of pretended patriots" (Byrd, 1988, p. 389). Despite Gerry's foreboding, House elections are the longest standing indicator of popular control of the U.S. national government.

This popular control has taken place through American political parties. As much as presidential elections are statements about parties, House elections are far more detailed and comprehensive treatises about them. Historically, a party's inception, survival, and dissolution have depended as much, if not more, on its winning House seats as its vying for the White House. As will become apparent in the tables in this chapter, the emergence of a new political party is typically first seen in House races, not presidential ones. The demise of a party also usually manifests itself first at the House, not the presidential, level. Critical realignments and other major shifts in party fortunes typically begin in House midterm races, the results of which become significant predictors of the changes about to occur in the next presidential contest (see also Ewing, 1947). House elections tell a more complex story about the nature of party alliances and third parties. As noted in Chapter 4, presidential elections have

been successfully contested by only a handful of historically visible parties. House elections, however, are not only fertile battlegrounds for these main parties, but they also reflect the influence of smaller parties, splinters and factions of existing parties, and the fusions of several parties. Finally, House elections have a good deal to say about the nature of state party politics. While it is important to discuss the national results of House elections—the net wins and losses of a party—it is equally critical to view House elections as state political races. How the trends in state politics shift across time and across states become the basis for understanding the aggregate national result and parties' national fortunes.

In this chapter House elections are considered as reflections of party development in the American states. This chapter proceeds in four parts. Issues of data accuracy and party labels are considered first, followed by a discussion of the district and at-large methods of assigning House seats. The history of House election results are then examined and compared with presidential elections. Finally, regional patterns of party development and strength are considered using state House election results.

Data Errors

As discussed in Chapter 1, the data that have heretofore been available and most widely used to study U.S. House elections have been rife with errors. These errors are of three types: miscalculations, omissions, and interpretive errors. The first type— miscalculations of the raw vote for a candidate, district, or state—was considered in detail in Chapter 1.

Errors of omission are created when data are indicated as missing but, in fact, are available. In some years the principal data sets used by scholars to analyze House elections—data sets 0001 and 0075 from the Inter-university Consortium for Political and Social Research (ICPSR)—fail to report data for a race or a state when those data are, in fact, available. A larger omission involves the absence of data before 1824. It is common to consider House and presidential election data as beginning in 1824. Data prior to that time are presumed to be unavailable or inaccurate. One of the reasons for this presumed lack of availability is that, unlike presidential results that are conveyed to Congress, there has never been a legal requirement that the states submit their House (or Senate) election tallies to Congress. It was not until the elections of 1866–1867 that Congress began to publish returns in the *Congressional Directory.* In addition, it was not until the 1860s that the states began to routinely publish their election returns in some form of official state document—such as a *Blue Book, Register,* report of the secretary of state, or legislative manual (see Dubin, 1998, p. xiii).

Exhaustive searches of individual state archives, the National Archives, and newspapers have uncovered official returns that have not been previously reported. These searches were conducted by Michael J. Dubin, Philip Lampi of the Massachusetts Antiquarian Society, and, to a lesser extent, by the author. In many cases prior to the 1860s the data were in the form of manuscript returns—the handwritten documentation of the election results. In other cases the official returns were published in a state newspaper. For instance, in the first congressional elections in 1788–1789, manuscript returns were available and collected for Georgia, Massachusetts, Maryland, New Jersey, and Pennsylvania. Newspapers recorded the official returns in Delaware, New Hampshire, and New York. The returns for Virginia were found in both official poll books and newspapers. Although data are missing from some counties or districts in some states, the record for seven of the original thirteen states is complete and substantial, but partial data exist for two other states.[1] In the second election, 1790–1791, seven of the thirteen states again have complete data and four others have partial data. These data, presented later in this chapter, fill an important gap in the chronicle of congressional elections.

The third type of error—interpretive error—has been generated most often in coding party labels, as analysts grapple with the multiple banners under which certain candidates ran, notably in the nineteenth century. Data offered in this chapter present a more factual accounting of candidates' party labels than previously available in the political science literature. As noted in Chapter 1, this is a crucial aspect of electoral data accuracy, especially at the House level. Data in this chapter offer two coding schemes based on what exactly was listed on the ballot as party labels. This is the main information upon which these codings are based, except in the unofficial ballot period, when recourse to original sources (such as manuscript returns, state records, or newspapers) is required to ascertain these party labels. The two coding systems, then, use this party label information in different ways to count and record the vote for each state. Both coding systems are incorporated in the House vote tables, whether the House vote is expressed as vote percent values (Tables 5-17 through 5-69) or as raw vote numbers (Tables 5-70 through 5-122), with the former being computed from the latter.

Conventional and Alternative Coding Schemes

The primary party coding system used is the conventionally accepted one. Only candidates who carry the sole designation "Democrat" or "Republican," or their historical antecedents, on the ballot are coded as Democratic or Republican votes. Democratic ancestors mainly included the Anti-Federalists, Democratic-Republicans, and Jacksonian Democrats; Republican predecessors mainly included Federalists, National Republicans, and Whigs. (For a full list of these earlier parties, see Appendix A.) Under this conventional coding, all candidates with party labels of any other kind are coded as "Other." This is also the coding system used with some consistency in the state-level data set for the House compiled by Walter Dean Burnham, Jerome Clubb, and William Flanigan for the Inter-university Consortium for Political and Social Research (data set 0075) and printed in *Political Facts of the United States Since 1789* (Austin and Clubb, 1986). Since many readers are familiar with these labels and the data set from which they are taken, they are presented in this volume as the conventional codings.

However, the House vote tables also present, in bold italics, alternative party codings that in many instances reveal quite different vote balances among parties running in a state. These alternative codings are necessary in instances when a state ballot lists a candidate with a major-party name in association with other designations or party names. In all instances, however, when only the name of a major party is listed next to a candidate's name on the ballot, the conventional coding prevails. Table 5-1 outlines the five specific types of alternative codings and the House election years and states for which they were appropriate.

Party Factions. The first type of alternative coding encompasses splinters, wings, or factions of a major party. Many of these instances reflected tensions within one of the major parties in a given state. For instance, in New York in the 1820s, the supporters and opponents of Governor De Witt Clinton became the Clinton Democratic-Republicans and the Anti-Clinton or Bucktail Democratic-Republicans. These groups were two factions within the Democratic-Republican Party, not two separate parties. Similarly, in the 1850s. Missouri Democrats split between those who were supporters of Senator Thomas Hart Benton and those who were not—the Benton Democrats and the anti-Benton Democrats. In the 1848 House elections in South Carolina, the Democratic Party was badly splintered among the Cass Democrats (who supported Senator Lewis Cass of Michigan, the Democratic presidential candidate), Taylor Democrats (who abandoned Cass in favor of the Whig presidential candidate, Zachary Taylor), and Conservative Democrats (who favored Cass but did not use the name).

A faction or wing of a party can also oppose its parent party. In the 1896 House elections in Idaho, a "Silver Republican" candidate ran against the establishment Republican candidate who favored the gold standard. Similarly, as late as the 1970s, the "National Democratic Party of Alabama" label was used by a candidate opposing the main Democratic Party candidate in that state.

Under conventional coding, each of these candidates is placed in the "Other" category. Using alternative coding, they are considered part of the vote total for the major party. For example, each of the candidates in South Carolina in 1848 mentioned above is coded as Democrat rather than Other. This alternative coding recognizes that these candidates were indeed major-party candidates. They had not left the party in an attempt to set up a new party, but they were attempting to move the major party in a particular direction. In addition, the study of voting psychology indicates that voters likely see the label "Democrat" or "Republican" (or their historical antecedents) before they judge any adjectives attached to the label. Thus voters likely associate the candidates with the main political parties.

Fusion Tickets. The second type of alternative party coding involves the fusion of the major party with a minor party. In this case, the minor party usually does not have a separate column on the ballot; instead, its name appears in association with the major party. Fusion tickets, for example, occurred prior to the Civil War, as the Whig Party began to falter and new parties attempted to take its place. In the 1850s Whig-American fusion tickets appeared when the American Party attempted to replace the Whigs because of the Whigs' split over the Kansas-Nebraska Act, which divided the Nebraska territory into two parts, allowing each territory to determine the status of slavery and thereby opening the possibility of slavery in the North. Another ambitious party was the Free Soil Party, which was interested in stopping the spread of slavery. The new party fused with the Whigs in many states, backing several Whig-Free Soil candidacies. (There were also several Democrat-Free Soil candidacies at the time.)

After the Civil War, the fight over the use of silver or gold as a monetary standard led to the rise of the Greenback Party, which also fused with both the Republicans and Democrats. These fusions were useful for the Greenbacks in promoting their cause of cheap money (that is, retaining inflationary paper money instead of returning to the gold standard) to aid small farmers and urban laborers. During the Progressive period, several candidates ran on a Republican-Progressive fusion ticket, following the lead of Theodore Roosevelt's Bullmoose Progressive Party in 1912. In election reference guides, fusion tickets such as the Republican-Progressives are symbolized as (R & Prog) in *Congressional Quarterly's Guide to U.S. Elections* (1994) or as (R, Prog) in *United States Congressional Elections, 1788–1997* (Dubin, 1998).

Using conventional coding, these candidates are coded in the "Other" category. Using alternative coding, they are coded as major-party candidates. The major party is often, although not always, the dominant element in these fusions. To the extent that issue positions of the smaller and major party coincide, it is typically through the larger party that these issues will enjoy any degree of success. In addition, emerging parties desire to fuse with a major party to give them a better chance to win elections. Finally, voters likely see the label of the major party first while in the voting booth before evaluating the smaller party.

Joint Endorsements. The third type of alternate coding is the joint endorsement of a candidate by both the major party and a minor party. While this is similar to the fusion ticket, in this case the minor party also appears on the ballot in a separate row or column and lists the main party candidate as its choice as well. This has only occurred in this century and only in a few states, especially New York, Pennsylvania, and, to a lesser extent, Vermont. For instance, in 1916 several Republican candidates in Pennsylvania were also endorsed by the Personal Liberty Party. The Democrats and the Liberals often jointly endorse the Democratic candidate in New York. These joint endorsements are usually denoted in election reference guides with a comma (D, L) rather than the ampersand or plus signs commonly used to symbolize fusion tickets.

Using conventional coding, these candidates are considered as "Other." Using alternative coding, they are coded under the major party since, like the fusion situation, these individuals are most usually the candidates of the main parties who merely receive endorsements from the minor parties.

Independent Candidates. The fourth type of alternative coding involves candidates who use the label "Independent" as well as a major-party label on the ballot. There are several variations of this, the most common being Independent Democrat and Independent Republican, often symbolized in election reference guides as (ID) and (IR). Less common are fusions and joint endorsements using the Independent label (D & I, or D, I; R & I or R, I). The first Independent Democratic-Republican candidates ran in the House elections of 1812–1813 when a few candidates attempted to distinguish themselves from President James Madison and the Democratic-Republicans in Congress, especially regarding the events surrounding the War of 1812. In the 1820s there were a few other Independent Democratic-Republican candidates who were attempting to steer away from the growing split between the National Republicans and the followers of Andrew Jackson in the party. From these humble beginnings, the phenomenon of independent major-party candidacies would substantially grow, as Table 1-3 in Chapter 1 indicates. In these instances, candidates are usually running against the parent party. In a sense, this phenomenon is similar to a faction or wing of a major party except that the label "Independent" is used instead of some other descriptor, such as "silver," "Benton," or "Cass." Conventional coding assigns these independents to the "Other" category. Alternative coding assigns them to the tallies for the main party, whether Republican or Democrat, because they are usually members of that party, not members of an independent party. In addition, voters are likely to recognize the major-party labels before interpreting how an independent party candidate differs from an establishment party candidate.

Dual Major-Party Endorsements. The final type of alternative coding involves candidates who receive the endorsement of both major parties—Democrats and Republicans—and are listed either under both parties' columns on the ballot or have both party designations beside their names on the ballot. In some states this is a matter of cross-filing, when state law permits a candidate to go on the ballot for both parties. California permitted cross-filing from 1911 to 1960. The California law allowed a candidate to enter both major-party primaries and, if successful, to be listed on the general election ballot with both party names. In certain other states without an actual cross-filing law, candidates could go through their states' normal procedures to secure the nominations of both parties and therefore appear on the ballot affiliated with both. In conventional coding these candidates are treated as "Other." In alternative coding, they are listed according to the party with which they are primarily associated. As an example, George Miller, a longtime Democratic member of the House from California, ran his first race in 1944 as a Democrat, but in 1946 through 1952, and also in 1958, he ran as a candidate endorsed by both the Republican and Democratic parties. In 1954, 1956, and after 1958, he ran only as a Democrat. Election reference guides usually symbolize such dual major-party candidacies as (D-R) and (R-D) or as (D, R) and (R, D).

Under conventional coding, Representative Miller is coded as a Democrat in 1944, 1954, 1956, and after 1958; he is coded as Other in 1946–1952 and in 1958. With alternative coding, he is coded as a Democrat for the entire period. In general, then, the alternative party codings are designed to offer a more exact accounting of the major parties' strengths in a state than conventional coding.

Matters of Interpretation

Even with these two coding schemes, questions of interpretation can arise. In one state a House race may have a Greenback Democrat (GD) running against a regular Democrat, while in another state a Democrat-Greenback fusion candidate (D & G) may be on the ballot with no other Democratic competitors. In the first instance, alternate coding designates the candidate as part of a faction or wing (W) in Table 5-1; in the second example, as a fusion candidate (F). In both cases, however, alternative coding considers these candidates "Democratic," while conventional coding considers them "Other."

Another case of interpretation involves a House fusion ticket that mimics a presidential fusion ticket. This occurred only when in 1896 William Jennings Bryan ran on a Democratic-Populist ticket for president. Here, there is an exception to the normal fusion coding from 1896 through 1900 for those House candidates who were emulating Bryan in also running as Democratic-Populists. Since Bryan himself was mainly considered a Democrat in 1896 and since he also ran only as a Democrat in 1900, these House candidates were also treated as Democrats in the conventional sense since they were following in Bryan's footsteps and these footsteps were largely Democratic. Thus there was no alternative coding necessary for House candidates in this unique situation when House fusion labels exactly mimic the presidential ticket.

Another question of interpretation can arise. What if a district has two or more Republicans (or two or more Democrats) running without additional designations or labels? As it turns out, this was a customary practice before the official Australian ballot[2] was enacted by most states close to the turn of the century and, surprisingly, even after that time, although to a much lesser extent. As Dubin notes, "the absence of legislation regulating the nomination process or the use of party names made it possible for more than one candidate to claim to be the nominee of a particular party or for committees in different counties of a district to nominate different candidates" (1998, p. xxiv). In these cases, having no other designations to distinguish, for example, two Republicans was purposive. Both candidates were considered mainstream Republican nominees (not splinters or fusions). Hence, no alternative coding is necessary. What is coded conventionally is exactly what is listed on the ballot. If both candidates are listed solely as Republicans or Democrats (or Whigs, Federalists, etc.), then both are considered in conventional coding to be Republican and their votes are aggregated to accurately reflect the partisan and competitive character of their House district.

In essence, the conventional coding system used here is a "pure" coding system that can easily be understood by layman and politician alike. The alternative coding system is just that—an alternative way of looking at the partisan and competitive nature of the House vote. This latter coding system is meant not only to give a different perspective on the House vote but also, and most importantly, to provide a better way by which to accurately measure the partisan composition of this vote. It is for this reason that the national and regional tables in this chapter (Tables 5-4 through 5-8) use these alternative coding values when they occur as part of the process of aggregating votes to the national and regional levels.

Presenting the two coding systems together offers researchers a unique opportunity. For those who believe, for example, that the alternative coding scheme best captures the partisan vote by employing the information provided by political faction, fusion, joint endorsement, cross-file, and main party independent candidacies, these vote values from this coding scheme are reported in the state vote tables in this chapter (Tables 5-17 through 5-122). For those who may feel, for example, that main party independent candidacies are more accurately considered in the "Other" category, they can rely on the conventional coding system in these particular instances. Using Table 5-1 in connection with *Congressional Quarterly's Guide to U.S. Elections* (1994) and *United States Congressional Elections, 1788–1997* (1988), can, for the most part, pinpoint the exact candidates (that is, their names, districts, and votes) who have this particular designation on their state ballots. Of course, for the researcher who only believes in a "pure" system of coding the partisan vote where partisan candidates are only those solely using a major party label on the ballot, the conventional coding system provides these values as the main entries in the state vote tables in this chapter (Tables 5-17 through 5-122).

A last question occurs. One might wonder if joint endorsements (for example, D, L) and major two-party endorsements (for example, D-R) might be better served in a conventional coding scheme if the vote counts of the separate parties could be distinguished for the same candidate. ICPSR data set 0075 at times attempts to do just that but at other times does not. The reason for the coding inconsistency in ICPSR 0075 is very simple: it is difficult, if not impossible, to ascertain the separate vote counts for joint endorsements and major two-party candidacies in every election in which they occur. Without complete data recovery, using a conventional coding system here would be inconsistent and, hence, useless.

The House Data Set

In summary, the data offered in this chapter attempt to accomplish three objectives. First, they attempt to remedy the errors reported in the House vote by the ICPSR and other sources at the state level. (For most of the district-level correction of errors in the House vote, see Dubin, 1998). The ICPSR errors run the gamut from vote omissions to vote miscounts. Second, the data attempt to correct errors regarding the party labels used by House candidates on their state ballots. Third, the data attempt to place the resulting correct party label information for the candidate into two separate coding systems, each with different purposes.

In reaching these objectives, the data in this chapter represent the single most accurate data set on House elections available at the state level. The data are largely presented at the state, rather than district, level in order to capture how states voted for specific parties. This state-level analysis is pivotal in the early decades during which the first state party organizations evolved, mobilized voters, controlled patronage, and later developed well-run political machines. Although it is crucial which party wins a specific district, it is of equal importance how the party fares across a state in order to understand patterns of state partisanship. This permits directly comparable measures across the presidency, the House, the Senate, and the governorships at the state level that are analyzed in Chapter 8.

Legal Structure of House Elections

It is common to think of the structure of House elections as it exists today: single-member districts holding elections simultaneously across all states on the first Tuesday after the first Monday in November in even-numbered years. Yet through the eighteenth and much of the nineteenth century, House elections were anything but uniform. Many states held elections in odd-numbered years because Congress did not convene until December of the odd-numbered year after

House elections. By 1880 most of the states had moved to even-numbered year elections, but prior to this there was, in effect, a two-year House election cycle.

In addition, states had various district, district-state, and state-only combinations they used in apportioning their number of House seats. Parties used these approaches to accentuate their strength in a state. Table 5-2 displays the several types of configurations other than the single-member district that have been used by the states. The first type, still employed today, is the at-large method in which the entire state is treated as one district. This applies to those states that have only one representative, such as Alaska, Delaware, Montana, North Dakota, South Dakota, Vermont, and Wyoming currently. More populated states adopted a variant of this method by having multiple at-large contests for the House. Although primarily used before the Civil War, some states adopted this practice in the twentieth century. For instance, as late as 1968, Hawaii had two statewide races for the House, rather than races in two single-member districts. A third method combines one or more at-large seats with conventional single-member districts. Many of these existed after the Civil War and into the early twentieth century. As an example, as late as 1964, Ohio elected one at-large member and twenty-three House members in districts. The at-large seats, whether multiple seats or in combination with single-member districts, benefit the party that holds a strong statewide base, effectively giving it some "free" seats. Finally, a few states adopted multimember/single-member combinations. In the multimember districts, the top vote getters were sent to Congress for the number of seats allocated to these districts. In 1813, New Jersey adopted multimember districts alone. Congress outlawed all multimember district voting schemes in 1842, but states are not prevented from adopting any of the at-large configurations listed above.

In developing the House election data set, questions arose regarding how to handle those states that used something other than the normal single-member district system. For states with only multiple at-large seats, the decision was to use the vote count of the highest vote getter for the Democratic and Republican parties and for each of the separately identified third parties. If, in addition, there were one or more independent or unidentified candidates in a House race without a specific third-party label, the decision was to use the highest voter getter among all these unaffiliated candidacies. For states with a single at-large race, the decision was obvious: to use the vote count as it was reported for any (and all) Democrat, Republican, and other party candidacies. For states with one or more at-large race with a single-member district system, the decision was to use only the at-large vote in the manner described above. This decision was based on the assumption that the at-large race represents the purest expression of the House vote at the state level. For those who instead prefer the aggregation of the House vote across single-member districts for these states, refer to Appendix 2 for these vote results. For states with single-member/multimember district combinations, the decision was to treat this similarly to states with multiple at-large seats: to use the vote of the highest vote getter for each specific party in the multimember districts and aggregate these votes with the normal single-member district votes to get House results at the state level. For the sole state with a multimember district arrangement (New Jersey in 1813), the decision was to handle this like any other case of a multi-member district: to use the highest vote getter from each party for each district and aggregate across districts for statewide vote totals.

An Overview of House Elections

This chapter now turns to a historical account of House elections. Table 5-3 presents the composition of the House of Representatives from 1789 to the present. Table 5-4 presents the aggregated national House vote from 1788 to 1998 presented in two-year election cycles. This combines the even- and odd-year elections largely held before 1880 to provide an indicator of House election results for the entire nation. Table 5-5 permits a separate examination of the House election results for those states that had even- and odd-year races.[3] These tables reveal, like the presidential tables, the dominance of a handful of major parties in House elections. Only five parties have held a majority of House seats: Federalists, Democratic-Republicans, Democrats, Whigs, and Republicans. The majority has shifted among these parties twenty-two times, with the majority party holding the House an average of almost ten years. Yet these figures belie the considerable longevity that the majority party has had in six instances totaling 124 years. The Democratic-Republicans held the House for twenty-four years (1800–1824). The Jacksonian Democrats held the House for sixteen years (1824–1840). The Republicans were in the majority for thirty-two years (1858–1874, 1894–1910). The Democrats were the House majority party for fourteen years (1932–1946). Finally, the Democrats held the longest consecutive majority for forty years (1954–1994).

Across the entire time frame since parties were formally organized (1794–1998),[4] the majority party has held an average of 60.4 percent of the two-party seats in the House. The strength of the majority party, however, has declined somewhat over time. In elections in the eighteenth and nineteenth centuries (1794–1900), the majority party in the House captured 62.6 percent of House seats. In the twentieth century (1902–1998), this edge has slipped to 59.2 percent of the two-party seats in the House. This 3.4 percentage-point difference, while not large, points to the growing exposure of House races to the public in a century where mass media institutions were being developed (mass circulation newspapers and magazines, radio, and television). This growing exposure has led to some increase in competition between the two main parties for House votes and, hence, for control of the House.

Overall, these various indicators suggest that House elections are less competitive than presidential elections at the national level. While House and presidential parties have changed hands about the same number of times in the 1794–1998 time span (twenty-one times for the presidential race and twenty-two times for House races), only twice in American politics has a major party held the White House for as long as six consecutive elections, while, in the House, continuous periods of one-party control have happened more often and, on average, for a longer time span (the average period of House control being 9.6 years).[5] Also, in House elections not only do certain parties retain a majority of seats for significant periods of time, but also their majorities, whether in the nineteenth or twentieth century, tend to be well above the 50 percent plus one additional seat needed to organize the House. By contrast, presidential victors have won with only an average of 51 percent of the vote across America's history (see Chapter 4). The end story is, while two-party politics dominates House elections like presidential elections, the party out of power in the House is typically less competitive than the party out of power seeking the presidency.

The Eras of House Elections

Tables 5-3 and 5-4 also reveal the presence of the six political eras in House elections: the Federalist/Democratic-Republican era (1788–1823), the Democratic/National Republican-Whig era (1824–1853), a Civil War and Reconstruction Republican/Democratic era (1854–1893), a conservative Republican/Democratic era (1894–1929), the New Deal Democratic/Republican era (1930–1965), and the competitive Democratic/Republican era (1966–present). Indeed, despite the typical focus on presidential elections as the defining events for the beginnings and endings of political eras, these tables indicate that House elections are usually more revealing of these political breakpoints for two reasons: the tendency of congressional parties to maintain some competitiveness in House elections after their national parties are no longer viable contenders for the presidency and the tendency of congressional elections to signal changes in party dominance in advance of presidential elections.

An example of the first tendency for a congressional party to outlast its presidential party is found in the Federalist/Democratic-Republican period. Although the Federalist/Democratic-Republican era ended at the presidential level in 1816, the Federalists continued to field congressional candidates until 1826. The congressional remnants of the Federalist Party may have laid the foundations for John Quincy Adams's later National Republican Party. As an example of the second tendency, before Lincoln's presidential victory in 1860, Republicans had captured considerable numbers of seats in Congress in 1854 and 1856 and achieved a House majority in 1858. Scholars frequently mark the election of 1896 as the pivotal election leading to early twentieth-century Republican ascendancy, but the Republicans actually regained the House in 1894 in one of the largest turnarounds in House history—a 115-seat Republican gain. Also, before Franklin Roosevelt swept into office in the pivotal New Deal election of 1932, the Democrats had organized the House by a narrow majority in 1930.

The Federalist/Democratic-Republican Era

During the Federalist/Democratic-Republican years (1788–1823), two partyism took root in the House as it did in the presidency. Beginning with the 4th Congress (1795–1797), party lines between the Federalists and Jefferson's Democratic-Republicans were clearly drawn.[6] The Federalists advocated a strong national government intervening to direct the country's growth with roads, canals, and a national bank. The Jeffersonians responded with the power of the states and agrarianism. As seen in Table 5-3, the Democratic-Republicans took control of the House in the 1795–1797 Congress, while the Federalists gained the majority in the 1797–1799 and 1799–1801 Congresses. In the 1801–1803 Congress, the Democratic-Republicans regained the majority and never lost it again in this era. Still, the Federalists continued as a viable minority party, picking up 29 seats in the 1809–1811 Congress and 31 seats in the 1813–1815 Congress in the midst of the War of 1812, which many Federalists did not support. Table 5-4 also shows the viability of the Federalists. While the two parties held distinct regional advantages (as examined below), the Federalists held an average 58 percent of the national House vote from the 1794–1795 to 1798–1799 elections, even though they did not control the House in the 1794–1795 election period. The Jeffersonians won 59 percent of the national House vote from 1800–1801 through 1810–1811. From 1812–1813 through 1816–1817 the two parties' vote percentages were roughly equal—the Democratic-Republicans gained just 51 percent of the national vote. Somewhat surprisingly, even in the 1816–1817 House elections in the midst of the Federalist debacle at the presidential level, with the party unable to nominate a candidate, Democratic-Republicans attained only 54 percent of the vote. It was not until the remaining elections in this era that they began to widen the gap between themselves and the Federalists, receiving an average of 71 percent of the vote up to 1824. (Also see Table 5-5 for an annual breakdown of these vote statistics for the House).

A note of caution is in order in interpreting the data in Tables 5-4 and 5-5 since the single-member district vote structure of House races (used in a majority of districts even at this time) creates an imbalance between votes and seats in favor of the majority party. The majority party wins far more seats than votes when calculated nationally. Table 5-6 offers a comparison of House seat and vote percentages. As an example, the table shows that from 1812–1813 through 1816–1817 the Democratic-Republicans claimed 66 percent of House seats with 51 percent of the national vote.

The regional analyses of Tables 5-7 through 5-9 shed more light on the early federal period. Beginning with the 1794 election, the Federalists and Democratic-Republicans were reasonably competitive across the several regions of the country. As can be seen in Tables 5-7 and 5-9, although the Federalists always did well in New England, they also were competitive in the Mid-Atlantic and Border South states. Also, even though the Jeffersonians were always strongest in the South, they performed well in the Mid-Atlantic and Border South and made inroads into Massachusetts. Unlike the largely regional support given Federalist presidential candidates, appealing mostly to John Adams's New England region, the Federalists' success in House races was actually much broader and longer lived.

The demise of the Federalist Party began in the 1818 House elections. As shown in Tables 5-7 and 5-9, for only the second time in this era, the Federalists did not win a majority of either House votes or seats in New England and the Democratic-Republicans tallied lop-sided advantages in the other regions. Part of this collapse was foreshadowed in the years before with the rapid expansion of the House. What was a 106-seat House in 1800 more than doubled in size to a 213-seat body by 1824, as eight new states—Ohio (1803), Louisiana (1812), Indiana (1816), Mississippi (1817), Illinois (1818), Alabama (1819), Maine (1820), and Missouri (1821)—were admitted to the Union (see Table 2-1). The Federalists were unable to make inroads into these states, except Maine, as the Democratic-Republican message of western expansion, states rights, and agrarian development appealed to these new voters. In addition, unlike the Jeffersonians, the Federalists did not establish a set of state and local party organizations nor a well-developed national party in Congress necessary to sustain a durable party. From 1818 onward, national support for the Democratic-Republican House candidates increased, Federalist candidate support dwindled, and office seekers began to run under factional and independent labels from within the Democratic-Republican Party, especially in New York and Pennsylvania (see Table 5-1).

The death knell of the Federalist Party, and the subsequent end of the first party era, can be traced to the House—not presidential—elections. To be sure, the Federalists were on their way out in the presidential elections of 1816 and 1820, but they remained the only viable opposition to the Jeffersonians in House races in the three elections of 1816, 1818, and 1820. But, by 1822, the Federalists' seats had diminished to just 24. Their base in New England became frayed and disorganized. One by one Federalists joined the Democratic-Republican Party.

Democratic/National Republican-Whig Era

The election cycles of 1824–1825 and 1826–1827 brought about an all but full realignment of the House. The Democratic-Republicans began to split into two parties—Jacksonian Democrats and National Republicans. When Andrew Jackson gained the White House in 1828, the party divisions were clear: the Jackson Democrats held a 57-seat advantage over John Quincy Adams's National Republicans (Table 5-3). They also held a twelve percentage-point national vote advantage (Table 5-4). These vote imbalances grew even larger in the elections of 1830–1831 and 1832–1833. Indeed, the National Republicans were even less competitive and less organized than the ill-fated Federalists. Nor did their message of strong national government, emerging from the older Federalist profile, suit the prevailing mood of states' rights and agrarianism. In contrast to their opponents, the Jacksonians had a much stronger national base and were a well-organized political party, running candidates in all states and leveraging loyalty through patronage. As seen in Tables 5-7 through 5-10, like the Jeffersonians, the Jacksonians dominated the South but also did well in the other regions, including New England.

Despite the atrophy of the National Republicans, two threads of popular opinion remained woven into American politics. First, a significant number of voters and politicians favored nationalism. They felt that the country's economy should be diversified, involving commerce, finance, and industry as well as farming and small mercantilism. To achieve this, they advanced notions of protective tariffs, national improvements, and a national bank. Second, a significant number of voters and politicians disliked the policies and the presence of Andrew Jackson. Some of these people were nationalists who opposed Jackson's efforts to dismantle the Bank of the United States; some were not, instead resisting his efforts against nullification in the South. Still others who disliked Jackson formed the Anti-Mason Party in Massachusetts, New York, Pennsylvania, Vermont, and Rhode Island, objecting to money, privilege, and elitism in society and appealing to poor farmers and laborers. Although this anti-elite message had in part put Jackson in the White House, the Anti-Masons opposed Jackson, who himself was a Mason.[7] These groups combined to form the Whig Party, which began running House candidates in 1834 (Holt, 1999).

In that midterm election, the National Republicans did not run any candidates, while the Whigs ran candidates in all states and virtually all districts. The Whigs captured 81 seats (Table 5-3) and 43 percent of the national congressional vote (Table 5-4) in their first electoral effort. One of the keys to the Whigs' early success was their ability to compete in the South, which the National Republicans had not been able to do. Indeed, they beat the Jacksonians in the South, capturing 52 percent of the southern House vote to the Jacksonians' 43 percent of the vote (Table 5-8). As seen in Table 5-10, which examines the House seats won by parties in states, the Whigs also captured fully 32 percent of southern seats in their first outing. They also did well in pockets in the Mid-Atlantic, notably New York and Pennsylvania, and in Ohio in the Midwest. In 1840 the Whigs captured the House for the first time, as their presidential standard-bearer William Henry Harrison entered the White House. They captured a majority of House seats in all regions of the country, except the South, where they virtually tied with the Jacksonians. This was the first time that a party opposing either the Jeffersonian Democratic-Republicans or the Jacksonian Democrats had done so well in the South since the Federalists in 1798. The Whigs made significant inroads in states where the National Republicans had scarcely ventured: Georgia, North Carolina, Tennessee, and Virginia. Although the Whigs promptly lost their majority to the Democrats in 1842, they regained it in 1846.

The Whig Party in Congress was not dependent on the common man images of hard cider and log cabins that had led Harrison to victory in the White House. Instead, it existed as a series of regional parties, loosely tied together. This lack of unity within the Whig Party produced the Compromise of 1850, the central legislation on slavery and western expansion in Congress, which left intact the Missouri Compromise of 1820 (permitting slavery in the territories below the 36°30' parallel and prohibiting slavery above it), admitted California as a free state, and permitted Utah and New Mexico to determine the status of slavery. The regional differences within the Whig Party allowed it to offer such major legislation but prevented it from sustaining itself as a national party. What had first tied the party together was members' opposition to Andrew Jackson. But with Jackson gone, the party struggled to keep its uncertain confederation together. Creating further difficulties for the Whigs and Democrats alike, the House continued to expand as Arkansas (1836), Michigan (1837), Florida (1845), Texas (1845), Iowa (1846), Wisconsin (1848), California (1850), Minnesota (1858), and Oregon (1859) entered the Union, adding important seats to this body and a new party to the political landscape—the Republicans who had their origins in the Midwest (see Table 2-1).

The Civil War and Reconstruction Republican/Democratic Era

The beginnings of the Republican Party occurred in the House elections of 1854. Never before or since were the established parties so unable to construct majority politics. Although President Franklin Pierce campaigned in favor of the Compromise of 1850, in the 1852 election he abandoned it in favor of Stephen A. Douglas's Kansas-Nebraska Act, which dominated attention in the 1854–1855 elections. This act opened the possibility of slavery in the North and set off a political firestorm among northerners, many of whom interpreted the act as the latest evidence of the power of "slavocracy."

This protest took the form of numerous anti-Democratic parties. Many were simply referred to as Anti-Nebraska men, but others included the People's, Fusion, Union, Know-Nothing, American, Free Soil, and Republican parties (Dubin, 1998, p. 174). Because the Whigs had split over the bill in Congress—northern Whigs voting against the bill and southern Whigs voting in favor—the Whig Party was no longer a credible force in opposition to the Democrats. Although candidates contested elections under the Whig name in the 1854 portion of the House election cycle, the label disappeared in those states that balloted in 1855. Quiet on slavery, opposed to sectionalism, and stressing the love of the Union, the American Party attempted to fill the void left by the fractured Whigs. Indeed, the Whig leadership was ensconced in the new American Party, with former president Millard Fillmore running again for president in 1856 partly as a Whig, partly as an American Party candidate. But taking no position on slavery left the American Party unable to capitalize on the Kansas furor (Holt, 1999). The other wing of the Whig Party, known as the Conscience Whigs, were antislavery people who promoted fusion tickets with other anti-Nebraska groups that became the core of the Republicans (Table 5-1). The Republicans, who were the only party taking a consistent position against slavery, stood to gain most from the backlash against the Kansas-Nebraska Act. The several parties that made up the opposition to the Democrats were far from stable, but, as seen in Table 5-3, they were significant as the Democrats lost 74 seats in a body of 234 in the 1854–1855 elections and, therefore, were unable to organize the 34th Congress.

Before Fort Sumter. In some ways, the elections after 1854 were anticlimactic. Even though the Whigs chose Fillmore as their presidential candidate in 1856, no one ran as a Whig in any congressional races. Fillmore himself was more a third-party candidate than a major-party candidate, taking only the state of Maryland. Instead, John C. Fremont, the first Republican presidential candidate, ran in a strong showing against the ultimate winner, Democrat James Buchanan. In the House elections of 1856–1857, the solidification of those opposing the Democrats around the Republican banner was complete as the Republicans won 93 seats (Table 5-3). They ran well in all regions, except the South and Border South, claiming 56 percent of House seats outside the South (Tables 5-7, 5-8, 5-11, and 5-15). The Democrats took all the Border South seats and all but one of the southern seats as part of their voting coalition, claiming the House majority alongside Buchanan's presidential victory, but few Democrats could overlook the rising strength of the Republican Party and the looming slavery issue upon which the party had risen.

The Civil War period permanently reoriented American party politics. At all levels, the Republican Party emerged as the central opponent of the Democrats. The Republicans succeeded where the Federalists and Whigs had failed—in offering an enduring, viable alternative to the Democrats. The party's origins were as an authentic grass-roots movement focusing on the slavery issue about which most people had strong opinions and drawing supporters from almost every party and group in American politics—from Whigs, Abolitionists, Free-Soilers, Know-Nothings, local third parties, and the temperance movement. In 1858 the Republicans captured a majority of House seats, which they maintained until 1874 (Table 5-3). Their success was built on stark regionalism. They claimed only four seats in the South in 1858 (all in North Carolina), but held nearly all the seats in New England and the Mid-Atlantic and a majority in the Midwest (Table 5-11). Just four years after entering party politics, the Republicans had taken control of the House.

Just as House races—not presidential races—dictated the collapse of the Federalist Party and the National Republicans, House races also signaled the collapse of the Whig Party, which disintegrated as a party in the 1855 midterm House election cycle, not in the presidential election of 1856. Voters defected from its disjointed platform of nationalism and national compromise on slavery. House races in 1854 through 1858, rather than the presidential election of 1860, cast the Republican Party as not simply a new contending party but as a new majority party. The Republicans could not have done well at the presidential level in 1860 without having solidified a base of party organizations and House seats outside the South in the years prior to that.

After Appomattox. The post–Civil War period often saw a rough balance between the parties at both the presidential and congressional levels. Although there were efforts from other parties throughout the remainder of the nineteenth and early twentieth century as populism and progressivism came and went, the Republicans and Democrats structured the national debate. As discussed in Chapter 4, presidential races were keenly competitive. Even though the Republicans won all but two presidential contests between 1860 and 1892, their victory margins were paper-thin and a few vote shifts in a single state would have produced Democratic victories in 1876, 1880, and 1888. The balance between Democrats and Republicans in the House was equally striking. From the elections of 1868–1869 through the elections of 1892, the Democrats gained 49 percent of the national House vote and 52 percent of the seats, while the Republicans held 46 percent of the national vote and 47 percent of the seats. Majority status switched back and forth between the parties in Congress. In 1874 the Democrats regained the House majority for the first time since 1856 and kept it until 1880, when the Republicans regained control; the Democrats won a majority again in 1882 that was maintained until the election of 1888 and then won again in 1890.

An examination of regional patterns indicates the extent to which this national competitiveness rested on strong one-party regionalism. In 1874 the Democrats returned to control the South in House races. As seen in Table 5-11, in 1872 Republicans held 60 percent of southern House seats; two years later the Democrats captured 77 percent of southern seats. In focusing on presidential races, analysts point to the election of 1876 and the Compromise of 1876 certifying Republican Rutherford B. Hayes as president and the removal of Union troops from the South as pivotal events that brought about the post-war return of the "Solid South" (see Chapter 4). Yet House data tables make clear that the pattern was already established in 1874 before Hayes and Samuel J. Tilden contested the presidency. After winning 77 percent of southern seats in 1874, Democrats never held less than 80 percent of the southern House seats from 1876 through 1964. The Border South was also heavily Democratic. On the other side, Republicans held 77 percent of the House seats in states in New England from 1872 through 1892. States in the Mid-Atlantic and Midwest were more competitive but tipped in favor of the Republicans, who held 57 percent and 56 percent of the seats, respectively, from 1872 through 1892. Thus the Democrats' strength in the South and Border South states offset the Republicans' strength in other regions. In years when Republicans lost their two-to-one advantage in the Mid-Atlantic and Midwest regions, the Democrats captured the House; in years when Republicans maintained this base, the Democrats served as the minority party in the House of Representatives.

The Conservative Republican/Democratic Era

This pattern continued until 1894 when an overall shift toward the Republican Party occurred first at the congressional and then the presidential level. As seen in Table 5-3, the 53d Congress elected in 1892 was composed of 221 Democrats and 130 Republicans. The 54th Congress elected in 1894 was its mirror opposite: 245 Republicans and 107 Democrats. The Democrats won only 11 percent of the seats (Table 5-15) and 37 percent of the votes (Table 5-8) outside the South. The Panic of 1893 radically shifted party fortunes as farm prices dropped, thousands of businesses closed, unemployment mounted, and labor unrest surged. Although President Grover Cleveland and congressional Democrats were not necessarily responsible for the panic or the ensuing depression, people nevertheless blamed them. Cleveland summarized Democrats' fears as they faced the 1894 elections: "I am very much depressed. I find that I am looking full in the face a loss of popular faith in the Democratic Party which means its relegation to the rear again for many years if not its destruction" (quoted in Schlesinger and Israel, 1971, p. 1791).

The central issues of the 1894 elections were money and economic power, which left the Democrats splintered and their message confused. Cleveland and many Democrats in Congress unequivocally felt that the proper road to economic recovery was to save the gold standard, and they advocated the repeal of the Sherman Silver Purchase Act of 1890, which provided for the issuance of treasury notes to pay for silver bullion. But western and southern Democrats abandoned the party's position and rallied with the reform-oriented Populist Party, which ran candidates in most congressional districts who demanded an abandonment of the gold standard and the free coinage of silver. The Populists and wayward Democrats believed that eastern financial and business interests were exploiting agricultural sections of the country by propping up a depreciating currency. The Democrats also suffered over Cleveland's attempts to lower tariff rates. Eastern and southern Democrats wanted to maintain high rates on specific items to protect local economies. Matters worsened as issues of economic power spilled into fears about domestic instability. Worker strikes erupted into violence, the most malignant of which was the Pullman strike in June–July 1894, just months before the congressional elections. Although Cleveland ordered troops to quell the violence and the strike, many Americans were left wondering why workers felt the need to resort to violence (Schlesinger and Israel, 1971, pp. 1787–1826).

The disunity in the Democratic Party made Republican victories in House elections a virtual certainty. For their part, Republicans campaigned as "gold bugs" and favored high tariffs. In the minds of millions of voters, the Democratic Party had become the party of depression, hard times, and disorder. The Populists gained 1,471,000 votes nationally, although only 7 House seats. The Republicans emerged as the country's strongest political force approaching the twentieth century.

Thus it was the 1894 House elections—not its more well-studied 1896 presidential counterpart—that first signaled a crossroads in American politics. While in the first twenty years after the Civil War the parties differed little in their support of economic expansion and industrialization as the primary goals of the country, by the end of the century the parties offered two different futures for America. The Republicans envisioned the United States as a major industrial power; the Democrats foresaw industrialization alongside a petit bourgeois and agricultural nation (Brady, 1988). The Republicans' vision won out. House seats turned decisively Republican in 1894 and remained so until the election of 1910. As shown in Table 5-12, the solid Democratic South remained intact, but it was contradicted by the now solidly Republican regions of New England (89 percent of seats Republican), the Midwest (77 percent), the Mid-Atlantic (76 percent), and the West (75 percent). Only the Border South was relatively two-party competitive. The presidential elections in 1896 and 1900 further strengthened the Republican direction with William McKinley's victories over William Jennings Bryan and his call for "free silver." Cleveland's fears about the deterioration of the Democratic Party proved well founded.

The grand industrialization sponsored by the Republicans did not proceed without calls for reform. With McKinley's assassination, Theodore Roosevelt focused on the curtailment of monopolies and the protection of natural resources. After Roosevelt left the White House, Republicans returned to their conservative message of protecting business and expanding economic growth under William Howard Taft, whose political views were similar to McKinley's. But Republicans had difficulty maintaining this conservative stance to the exclusion of progressive ideas when they depended on support in a rapidly urbanizing East and an agrarian, independent-minded West. In both regions, insurgent Progressives in the Republican ranks ran against the conservatives. This growing split in the Republican Party permitted Democrats to take the House in 1910. They made key inroads in the Mid-Atlantic region, especially New Jersey and New York, and in Ohio (Table 5-12). The Republican Party split even wider in 1912, with Roosevelt leaving the party to run as a Progressive, virtually assuring that the Democratic candidate, Woodrow Wilson, would win the presidency. President Wilson and congressional Democrats continued Roosevelt's spirit of Progressivism by instituting the following reforms: the establishment of the income tax, Federal Reserve, and Federal Trade Commission; the revision of tariff laws; and the adoption of female suffrage and Prohibition. This Reform Era was powerful but brief. The Republicans took a one-seat House majority from the Democrats in 1916, despite Wilson's reelection as president, and did not relinquish control of the House until 1930.

The 1916 Republican congressional victories foreshadowed a return to conservative Republican domination of politics in both Congress and the White House after World War I. The peak of Republican control occurred in the election of 1920. Republican Warren Harding scored the largest victory of any presidential candidate since James Monroe in 1820 (see Chapter 4). Republicans held 69 percent of the seats in the 67th Congress (1921–1923) and won 58 percent of the national House vote. As displayed in Table 5-15, the regional division in the country was never more acute: Democrats held 93 percent of two-party seats in the South, while Republicans held 90 percent of seats outside the South. As shown in Table 5-12, Republicans dominated California and New Jersey, which had been more competitive during the war, and continued to hold the Midwest (Illinois, Indiana, Iowa, Kansas, Michigan, Minnesota, Wisconsin, and the Dakotas) as tightly as the Democrats held the South. After Woodrow Wilson, the Democratic Party was badly disorganized; its two main groups of supporters could not have been more different: southerners and Irish-Catholic workers in the North. They held safe seats in segregated Alabama and in New York City, in rural Mississippi and in Chicago.

The New Deal Democratic/Republican Era

Political fortunes again shifted in 1930 as the American economy fell into depression and President Herbert Hoover and the Republican Congress were blamed for reticence to invoke plans for governmental relief. Calls for governmental activism to alleviate the crisis mounted and the Democrats gained 51 seats in 1930, 48 from outside the South. Although the initial returns gave Republicans a narrow 217–216 edge in seats, from the time of the elections in November 1930 to the actual convening of Congress in December 1931, three special elections and one vacant seat previously held by Republicans gave the Democrats a majority of 219 to 213 seats (Dubin, 1998, p. 487). Democrats had gained 45 percent of the national congressional vote in 1930 (Table 5-4). Democratic victories were even more striking in 1932 with a gain of 97 more seats, 96 of them in the non-South (Table 5-15).

The 1930 House elections stand as pivotal elections, foreshadowing the start of the New Deal era in 1932 when Franklin Roosevelt began his campaign for the White House. The period from 1930 through 1965 marks one of the most stable and predictable periods of party politics at both the congressional and presidential levels. The Democrats held the majority in Congress through the entire period except for two Republican terms, the 80th Congress (1947–1949) and the 83d Congress (1953–1955), and the presidency except for the two Eisenhower terms (1953–1961).

A comparison of Tables 5-12 and 5-13 shows that four elements established this new Democratic majority. First, the Democrats continued to count on the South to give them a solid core of voters for House seats. Second, they bolstered this with additional votes and seats in the Border South. While the Democrats held only 39 percent of House seats in the Border states in 1928, they held 77 percent in 1930 and 100 percent in 1932. Third, they captured seats in the heavily Republican Midwest—in Illinois, Indiana, and Nebraska in 1930, and by 1932 in Iowa, Michigan, Ohio, and Wisconsin. Fourth, they took seats in the East, which they had not done before. In 1930 they won seats in Connecticut and, in 1932, New York and Pennsylvania. In fact, the turnaround in Pennsylvania could not have been more striking. Democrats held 1 of 36 seats in 1928, 3 of 36 in 1930, 11 of 34 in 1932, and a majority of 23 of 34 by 1934. This amounted to 28.4 and 30.6 percent of the two-party vote in the 1928–1930 period, rising to 41.9 percent in 1932 and 56.2 percent in 1934 (Tables 5-52 and 5-53). From these various movements in the vote, the Democrats were able to capture a majority of votes and seats in 1932 in both the South *and* the non-South. With this majority they passed the New Deal—a series of governmental programs, including Social Security; unemployment compensation; welfare; agricultural relief; reorganization of the banking system; wages, hours, and price agreements; and public works projects. The New Deal placed governmental activism in the forefront of efforts to combat the economic collapse and reversed the laissez-faire approach that Republicans had offered in the 1920s.

The New Deal Democrats' early electoral success should not leave the impression, however, that they were invincible in House elections after 1932. As shown in Tables 5-7 and 5-13, even before the economy had improved much, the Republicans regained New England in 1936. By 1938 they had reclaimed their majority in the Midwest and Mid-Atlantic, as some people opposed the New Deal as too expensive and ineffective. Beginning in 1942 and lasting through 1956 and again in 1960 and 1962, Republicans captured a majority of House seats *outside* the South in both midterm and presidential election years (Table 5-15). The Democrats continued their hold on the South and Border South and did well in the West (Table 5-13). In particular, the South and its strong Democratic voting patterns obscured the strength of the Republican Party elsewhere. But the age of Roosevelt was not as long-lasting or as monolithic in the House as it might have appeared from the other end of Pennsylvania Avenue with Roosevelt's four presidential victories.

The Competitive Democratic/Republican Era

In some ways it is difficult to call the most recent period a political era. There have been no massive swings in elections from one party to the other that mark the end of one era and the beginning of another. In short, there has been no evidence of a dramatic breakpoint. Instead, the features of the New Deal period that assured a Democratic hold on the House began to shift over time toward national competition between the two parties in House elections. At the height of the New Deal era during Franklin Roosevelt's four terms (1932–1948), Democrats controlled an average of 62.5 percent of the two-party seats in the House, and throughout the entire 1930–1965 period they never lost two House elections in a row. The current period (1966–1998) has seen this Democratic edge fall by approximately 5 percentage points and, most recently, seen the Republicans win three close House elections to take control of the House in the 1995–2001 period. (As this book went to press, another close House election in 2000 favored the Republicans, extending their control of the House until 2003.) While changes in control of the House have not been as often or as publicized by the media as changes in control of the Senate in the current political period, the trend toward greater party competition for both chambers is definitely in evidence.

Several factors have contributed to the greater competitiveness of the two parties in the current period. First, there were gains by the Republican Party in House elections in the South associated with the party's more conservative appeal. The Solid South was finally manifesting cracks in its political foundation. Second, beginning in 1980, Republicans also made gains in the West, notably in California. Third, offsetting these new Republican strengths, Democrats continued inroads into the Midwest and took over New England, a former Republican stronghold. As depicted in Table 5-14, Democrats captured a majority of midwestern seats in 1974, which they had last done in 1958; they held this majority for the remainder of the time period, except in 1980 and the post-1994 period. Fourth, the Mid-Atlantic states were tightly competitive during the entire period, with Democrats winning 52 percent of the two-party vote (Table 5-7).

These increases in party competition occurred slowly. The first indication came in the 1960s when southern states that had not elected Republicans to the House since Reconstruction began to do so. White southerners protested national Democratic efforts on civil rights during the Kennedy and Johnson administrations. In many instances, Republicans claimed only one or two seats in a particular state, but, given the history of Democratic one-partyism in the region, these shifts were difficult to ignore. In the 1960s Alabama, Arkansas, Georgia, Mississippi, and South Carolina elected Republican members for the first time since Reconstruction. Florida, North Carolina, and Texas had done so in the 1950s and Louisiana did so in the 1970s. In 1964 Alabama elected five Republicans and consistently elected three during the remainder of the 1960s and 1970s, and two or more since then. By 1996 Republicans had become a majority in the Alabama congressional delegation. Georgia and Mississippi elected their first Republican House member in 1964, as did South Carolina in 1966. Each state continued to elect some Republicans to Congress since then. South Carolina became a Republican majority delegation in 1980

and again in 1996 and 1998. Georgia and North Carolina tipped to a Republican majority in 1994, and Mississippi did so in 1996. Florida had first elected a Republican House member in 1954, but consistently since 1966 elected three or more. In 1990 the Republicans held a majority of the Florida delegation, which they have maintained to date. Arkansas and Texas remain the only southern states that have not at some point become majority Republican delegations, although exactly 50 percent of Arkansas seats and roughly 40 percent of Texas seats are now Republican. In 1994 Republicans captured a majority of the southern House vote (Table 5-8) and a majority of southern House seats (Tables 5-14 and 5-15) for the first time since 1872. Although Republican House victories in the South were not as striking as Republican vote gains for president in this region (discussed in Chapter 4), the solid Democratic South was gone.

Yet, as Republicans were making strides in the South, Democrats were building larger bases outside the South. Table 5-15 indicates that in 1964 Democrats achieved a majority of House seats outside the South, which they kept, for the most part, until 1994. This nonsouthern majority did not result from universal shifts to the Democratic Party, but instead resulted from specific, but long-term, changes in six states. Strong increases in Democratic seats from the 1960s on took place in California and New Jersey; this was maintained until 1994. Republican Party reversals occurred in Indiana and Michigan, where majority Democratic delegations replaced majority Republican delegations in 1974. This continued through 1992 in Indiana and through 1998 in Michigan. Ohio, which had been dominated by the Republicans in the 1960s, became a highly competitive state by the late 1970s and this continued until 1994, when the Republicans regained their former edge (see Table 5-14). In addition, the Illinois congressional delegation entered a period of partisan switches from one election to the next. A majority Republican delegation in 1972 became a majority Democratic delegation in 1974, a tied delegation in 1976, and a majority Republican delegation in 1978 and 1980. In 1982 Illinois returned a majority of Democratic House members; this time Democrats kept their majority until 1992. The Democratic totals are impressive; for example, Democrats held 169 seats outside the South in 1972 and claimed 41 additional seats in this region in 1974 (Table 5-15). Of these new seats, 27 were from California, Illinois, Indiana, Michigan, New Jersey, and New York. The remainder were largely one- or two-seat increases in other states.

This started a difficult trend for Republican congressional candidates to counter. As seen in Table 5-16, during the 1970s and 1980s incumbents of both parties were highly successful in winning reelection. But with Democrats holding more seats, this made it even more difficult for Republican challengers to gain seats. Also, there were few open seats available where competition might be more even. This Democratic incumbency advantage was not weakened until the 1990s, when the Republican Party targeted pivotal House races and, hence, created more competitive districts.

In the so-called Republican Revolution of 1994, Republicans gained a majority of House seats (228–206) for the first time since 1952. As shown in Table 5-15, they did so by winning a majority of seats in the South (63–62) for the first time ever in the twentieth century. Despite Republican gains in the House since the 1960s, the party was unable to command a majority of seats until 1994. The Republicans also won a majority of seats outside the South (165–144). In 1996 and 1998 competition mounted as the Republican Party again captured a majority of seats in the South, but the Democrats slightly increased their seats in the non-South in both elections, actually capturing a majority of seats outside the South in 1998.

The 1994 House results had their antecedents in the 1992 House elections. One of the most significant features of the 1992 House races was the increase in competitive or marginal races—those won by 55 percent of the total vote or less. In 1988 only 12 percent of House races nationwide were won by less than 55 percent of the vote; in 1992 this nearly doubled to 23 percent. This increase was especially noteworthy outside the South. In nonsouthern districts, the number of marginal races rose from 10 percent in 1988 to 26 percent in 1992. This meant that many of the Democrats who lost in 1992 only lost by a little. More importantly, many of the freshman Democrats who won in 1992 won by only a little. The number of marginal districts remained similarly high in 1994—24 percent of the districts nationally were won by 55 percent of the vote or less (28 percent of the districts in the non-South). Of the marginal districts won by Democrats in 1992, all were recaptured by Republicans in 1994 (Ragsdale, 1996).

The "revolution" was far from a national phenomenon. In some states, there were startling reversals; in other states, nothing happened. As shown in Table 5-14, little occurred in some of the largest states—California, Florida, Illinois, Michigan, New York, and Texas. In California the Republicans only picked up three seats, and in Florida and Texas they only picked up two seats. However, House delegations shifted from Democrat to Republican in Arizona, Georgia, Indiana, Kansas, Kentucky, Ohio, Oklahoma, Utah, and Washington. As one example, Washington's delegation had eight Democrats and one Republican in 1992 but two Democrats and seven Republicans in 1994. Yet with Democrats increasing their majority of nonsouthern House seats since 1994, it is unclear how long the Republican majority will last. What is clear is that this latest period of American politics reflects a sharp competition between the two parties in vying for key House seats.

One-Party State Politics

If voters are supposedly federal voters in presidential elections, they are even more keenly state and district voters in House elections. National party trends rest on the partisan makeup of individual states. Regional generalizations may or may not apply to a specific state or district. Thus, to ade-

quately understand House elections, statewide percentage results for House races from 1788 to 1998 are presented in Tables 5-17 through 5-69. The raw votes for those years are presented in Tables 5-70 through 5-122.

In considering this wealth of data, three points tie these results to the national and regional patterns that unfold across historical eras. First, like in national presidential races, there are numerous one-party states in House races. These states stick to the same party across most if not all their congressional districts, and they do so for long periods of time. The origins of the Democrats' long-time domination of the South are seen in the congressional elections of 1800 and thereafter in such states as Georgia, South Carolina, Tennessee, and Virginia (Table 5-20 and succeeding tables). This is not only true of the Democrats who dominated southern voting patterns for nearly two hundred years. For instance, Massachusetts began as a strongly Federalist state. Federalist candidates continued to win in Massachusetts when they no longer contested House seats in other states, even in New England. By 1828, when the Jacksonians prevailed across the country, Massachusetts—with its strong ties to John Quincy Adams—emerged as a leading anti-Jackson state. The successor to the Federalists, the National Republicans, claimed 84 percent of the statewide House vote (see Table 5-27). National Republicans later became Whigs, who commanded more than 50 percent of the House vote in most House elections in the 1830s and 1840s. By the 1850s Whigs had become Republicans, who were also strong in Massachusetts, capturing 61 percent of the statewide vote in 1856 and 60 percent in 1858 (see Table 5-34). Republicans have continued to dominate the state since then, even through the New Deal era until 1958, when the state became Democratic just before its favorite son, John Kennedy, would ascend to the presidency. Other states, such as Kansas, Nebraska, North Dakota, and South Dakota, became Republican at statehood and stayed with the party through the 1970s in the case of the Dakotas and to the present day in Kansas and Nebraska.

These one-party states tend to cancel each other out at the national level in House elections. As an example, Tables 5-39 through 5-44 show one-party Democratic states canceling out one-party Republican states during the entire period from the mid-1870s until the 1896 realignment. One-party Democratic states included Alabama, Arkansas, Delaware, Florida, Georgia, Kentucky, Louisiana, Mississippi, Missouri, South Carolina, and Texas. Thus the Democrats, who had dominated the deep South and Border states since before the Civil War, added Delaware, which had been Whig before the war, and also Kentucky, which had fought on the side of the Union. The Republicans held Kansas, Maine, Massachusetts, Minnesota, Nebraska, New Hampshire, Oregon, and Vermont during most of this period.

Second, in contrast, only a few states are truly competitive and their competitiveness does not necessarily last. Several states have been competitive throughout much of their history, notably New York, Pennsylvania, California, Indiana, and Colorado. Other states, such as Ohio and Illinois, have had periods of two-party competition bracketed by periods of one-party domination. Illinois was two-party competitive before the 1890s, when it emerged as a solidly Republican state; its House delegation stayed Republican until the New Deal, when it returned to a more competitive profile that has continued to the present.

Third, historic shifts in party competition at the national level do not typically result from large shifts in many states. Instead, these national partisan realignments typically result from shifts in only a few states. The two largest shifts in state voting patterns in the history of House elections were during the elections of 1894 and 1932. Yet even these dramatic shifts only occurred in a handful of states. The 1894 shift to the Republican Party largely occurred in five states—New Jersey, New York, Maryland, Illinois, and Indiana. In each case, delegations that had been primarily Democratic switched to being primarily Republican, and this switch lasted for several elections. Seemingly overnight, Illinois— which in 1892 had 11 Democratic seats, 11 Republican seats, and a statewide Democratic percentage of two-party vote of 51.6 percent—emerged after the 1894 House elections with 20 Republican seats, 2 Democratic seats, and a statewide Democratic vote of only 41.1 percent (see Table 5-43). In Indiana, the change was even more stark: the 11 Democratic and 2 Republican seat tally in 1892 became 13 Republican seats in 1894. The Republicans garnered 55.1 percent of the two-party vote, the first time they had received a majority of House votes since 1872. The remainder of the country in 1894 was relatively unaffected. In 1932 six states mainly created the New Deal majority—Illinois, Indiana, Michigan, Ohio, California, and Washington; each delegation shifted from Republican to Democratic and this shift lasted over several elections. In other states, the party makeup of congressional delegations largely continued as though the New Deal had not taken place.

These state-level patterns suggest that states' interests, economic bases, demographic breakdowns, social traditions, and political pasts are more likely to be supportive of one party than the other. This permits one party to build and maintain a well-run organization, while the other has difficulty raising money, fielding candidates, and attracting voters. Unless money is funneled to the state from the national party organization, for particularly promising House candidates, the opposing party's deficit in the state is unlikely to change. Even when large political shocks hit the national landscape, many states' party politics are left relatively untouched. What is also clear in examining House elections since the end of the Civil War is that, in order to survive, the Democratic and Republican parties have become adaptable political institutions that have adjusted their messages, images, and tactics to meet political changes at both the national and state levels. Unlike the instability and disorganization faced by the Federalists and Whigs, the Democrats during the Republicans' period of normalcy and the Republicans during the New Deal were not likely to go out of business. While the Democrats had difficulty fielding credible presidential candidates during the 1920s, they con-

tinued to run well in Congress. The Republicans had similarly bad luck contesting the presidency against Franklin Roosevelt, but they nonetheless made strides in congressional races, especially outside the South. The Democrats and Republicans were able to sustain their parties in these bad times by the power of incumbency and by having well-entrenched party organizations in specific states.

Conclusion

Why are House elections, especially those at the midterm, critical indicators of rapidly shifting fortunes of political parties? Part of the answer lies in happenstance. The Kansas-Nebraska Act of 1854 was passed in a midterm year. The Panic of 1893 and the collapse of the stock market in 1929 occurred just before midterm elections. Another part of the answer lies in the interrelationships between congressional results and presidential results that political scientists have grappled with for decades. The loss of House seats by the president's party in midterm elections has been variously examined as "surge and decline," the result of less involved voters entering and then leaving the electorate; as a plebiscite on the president's performance in office, which is typically judged harshly at midterm time; and as a referendum on the economy (for a review of these issues, see Campbell, 1993). Yet data presented in this chapter suggest that these often searing losses for the president's party may have less to do with national explanations centering on the presidency than regional and state explanations of party strength and competition.

State parties operate and survive as distinct and relatively autonomous entities shaped by local economic conditions, social cleavages, and political legacies. They acquire organizational effectiveness and deficiencies in *each* state. They have established leaders, interests, and patronage in some states but do not have these resources or the wherewithal to attain them in other states. As Gimpel writes, "state history is not merely a carbon copy of national history, nor are state elections simply second-rate versions of national elections" (1993, p. 3). These state histories are unique and may insulate a party from national conditions that prevail against it. Also, states are differentially affected by such national matters as a national bank, slavery, the gold standard, and economic depressions. Local conditions, not national messages, dictate if, when, and how a state responds to the changing fortunes of the national political parties.

Thus the overlay between state and national politics creates a two-stage dynamic in party politics that begins fundamentally at the grass-roots level and culminates nationally at the presidential level. In the first stage, parties offer appeals at the local level in efforts to capitalize on political and economic cleavages. The local political environment and makeup of the electorate become the critical features at this stage. As Speaker of the House Thomas "Tip" O'Neill was fond of saying, "All politics is local." Voters make their choices with local conditions in mind, even if they are reflecting on national issues. In addition, a local base is far easier to build than a national one. It is easier to win a House seat or many House seats than the presidency. These local appeals permit the party to build a base from which to succeed at the second level—the national level. Parties do not build from the top down.

This two-stage dynamic exists for a new party or for a major party with minority status in a given area seeking to take new ground. As an example of the former, the Whigs rapidly emerged on the scene in 1834 in New England and the Mid-Atlantic, claiming old Federalist roots, with a familiar message of national growth and economic expansion. They made strides in the South in North Carolina and Tennessee by offering a national compromise on slavery that would protect southern interests. Other states in the South, such as Alabama, Mississippi, and South Carolina, were less receptive to the Whigs because their political leaders were far more interested in southern states' autonomy and less inclined toward any national solutions on slavery. In states in the Midwest, the Whigs were less successful because neither of their primary messages—national growth or national compromise—were of special interest to this region. But, overall, the Whigs' attractiveness in certain states was sufficient for them to win 81 of 241 seats in 1834. This provided the Whigs a congressional base from which to run for the presidency in 1836.

One example of an established party penetrating one-party areas occurred in 1930, when the Democrats made some of their first appeals to the lower class in Illinois, Indiana, Missouri, and Ohio. Republicans had captured these voters decades before during the growth and prosperity of the 1890s, when the Democrats' free silver appeal to workers and farmers had failed. But in 1930 the good times were gone, as unemployment mounted and long hours prevailed for those who still had jobs. Democratic House candidates targeted the local economic and political landscapes and captured 24 new House seats in these four important states. Thus the Democrats started to create new state bases in 1930 that would permit them to run a successful presidential campaign in 1932.

Since the 1850s state histories have directly commented on the development of one-partyism for the Democratic and Republican parties and why these patterns are important for understanding the two parties' fortunes nationally. One-partyism continues, even today, through the tailoring of partisan messages to local interests. When a national crisis hits, its political impact depends on how each state party responds to the crisis and how bad the crisis is locally—not nationally.

States are often able to insulate themselves from such shocks. Double-digit national vote swings away from the party blamed for the crisis often are not paralleled at the state level, where single-digit shifts at best are more commonplace. Often the underlying story of American politics lies in the interactions between local conditions and voting behavior in House elections. In this context, House elections take on a renewed importance in our attempts to understand the American political condition across time.

Notes

1. Returns by state and year are presented in Tables 5-17 through 5-122. States with complete House voting returns comprise the main entries in these tables and the data that should be used to trace a state's electoral development across time. States with partial voting data (less than 100 percent of the districts reporting) are indicated by a superscript.

2. The official Australian ballot is discussed in Chapters 1 and 3. Basically, it is a state-prepared and state-distributed ballot that is also secret and consolidated. American states adopted the idea for this ballot from Australia, which first used it in the 1850s. In America, the ballot system in use before the Australian ballot was the single party-strip ballot prepared and distributed by the party and voted in public, not in the privacy of the polling booth.

3. The national and regional aggregations of the vote are calculated using the alternative party codings for the statewide House vote when they occur. Hence, where bold italicized entries appear in Tables 5-70 through 5-122, these data points are used in the calculation of the statewide House vote and in the subsequent calculations of regional votes, national votes, and the parties' victories in House seats.

4. Historians acknowledge that the Federalists and Anti-Federalists in Congress prior to 1794 were more loose groupings than formally organized parties recognized as such (see Dubin, 1998, p. xxv).

5. At the presidential level, two parties have held the office a maximum of six consecutive elections: the Democratic-Republicans (1800, 1804, 1808, 1812, 1816, 1820) and the Republicans (1860, 1864, 1868, 1872, 1876, 1880).

6. Prior to that time, it is difficult to consider partisan divisions in the House because party affiliations were just beginning to take hold. Party tendencies, however, have been coded before then for Federalist tendencies and Anti-Federalist tendencies using Dubin (1998) but are not used here in the text discussion of this period. Also see note 4.

7. The Anti-Masons contested 44 districts and won 16 seats in 1830 and contested 66 districts and won 24 of them in 1832 (Dubin, 1998, pp. 101, 108). However, Masonry itself declined rapidly by 1832 and robbed the Anti-Masons of their principal issue.

Table 5-1 Alternative Party Coding for House of Representatives, 1788–1998

State	Year
Alabama	1849 (I); 1851 (W); 1853 (W); 1857 (F); 1859 (I); 1869 (I); 1876 (W,I); 1882 (F,I); 1884 (I); 1886 (I); 1892 (F); 1896 (W,F); 1898 (W); 1900 (F); 1902 (I); 1968 (W); 1970 (W); 1972 (W); 1974 (W); 1976 (W); 1980 (W)
Alaska	
Arizona	
Arkansas	1858 (I); 1876 (I); 1878 (I); 1880 (I); 1890 (F); 1946 (I); 1958 (I)
California	1854 (W); 1859 (W,M); 1861 (W); 1880 (F); 1886 (F); 1890 (W,F); 1892 (F); 1894 (I); 1898 (I); 1902 (F); 1904 (F); 1906 (F); 1910 (M); 1914 (F,M); 1916 (F,M); 1918 (F,M); 1920 (F,M); 1922 (F,M); 1924 (M); 1926 (F,M); 1928 (M); 1930 (M); 1932 (M); 1934 (F,M); 1936 (F,M); 1938 (F,M); 1940 (F,M); 1942 (J,M); 1944 (M); 1946 (F,M); 1948 (F,M); 1950 (M); 1952 (M); 1954 (M); 1956 (J,M); 1958 (M); 1960 (M); 1968 (W,M)
Colorado	1892 (F); 1896 (F); 1898 (F); 1900 (F); 1914 (F)
Connecticut	1818 (M); 1827 (F); 1849 (F); 1896 (W); 1920 (F); 1924 (F); 1932 (I)
Delaware	1860 (W); 1896 (W); 1902 (W); 1930 (F); 1936 (I); 1938 (I); 1940 (W)
Florida	1858 (I); 1878 (I); 1882 (I); 1884 (I); 1896 (W); 1920 (W); 1926 (W)
Georgia	1828 (F); 1830 (W); 1832 (W); 1846 (I); 1857 (I); 1870 (I); 1872 (W); 1874 (I); 1876 (I); 1878 (I); 1880 (I); 1884 (I); 1890 (I); 1892 (F); 1910 (I); 1940 (I,M); 1962 (I)
Hawaii	
Idaho	1896 (W); 1898 (M); 1900 (M); 1926 (F)
Illinois	1841 (I); 1846 (I); 1852 (I); 1854 (W); 1858 (W); 1874 (I); 1876 (I); 1882 (F,I), 1884 (F); 1886 (F); 1888 (F); 1896 (W); 1904 (I); 1924 (I)
Indiana	1851 (F); 1858 (W); 1870 (I); 1874 (I); 1878 (F); 1886 (I); 1888 (F); 1894 (F); 1896 (W)
Iowa	1850 (W); 1878 (F); 1880 (F); 1882 (F); 1884 (F); 1886 (F,I); 1888 (F); 1892 (F); 1894 (F); 1950 (W)
Kansas	1886 (I); 1892 (F)
Kentucky	1816 (F); 1847 (I); 1851 (I); 1863 (W,I); 1870 (I); 1872 (I); 1874 (I); 1876 (I); 1878 (I); 1882 (I); 1884 (I); 1886 (I); 1890 (F); 1894 (I); 1896 (W,M); 1898 (I)
Louisiana	1830 (W); 1832 (W); 1857 (I); 1878 (I); 1882 (I); 1884 (I); 1886 (I); 1892 (F,I); 1896 (W)
Maine	1862 (W); 1878 (F); 1880 (F); 1882 (F,I); 1892 (I); 1898 (W); 1900 (I); 1932 (I); 1952 (W); 1960 (W)
Maryland	1851 (I); 1861 (F); 1878 (I); 1882 (I); 1886 (I); 1898 (W); 1900 (I); 1904 (I)
Massachusetts	1814 (M); 1833 (F); 1848 (F); 1854 (W); 1856 (F); 1860 (W,F); 1868 (I); 1876 (I); 1878 (F); 1882 (F); 1888 (F); 1890 (I); 1892 (F); 1894 (F,I); 1896 (W); 1898 (W,I); 1902 (W); 1910 (I); 1914 (F); 1920 (F); 1926 (M); 1928 (M); 1934 (M); 1936 (F); 1942 (M); 1954 (M); 1968 (M)
Michigan	1848 (F); 1850 (F); 1852 (F); 1872 (I); 1874 (F); 1876 (F); 1882 (F); 1884 (F); 1888 (F); 1892 (F); 1894 (F); 1916 (F); 1938 (W)
Minnesota	1860 (I); 1868 (I); 1878 (F); 1880 (I); 1882 (I); 1890 (F); 1940 (I); 1942 (W)
Mississippi	1843 (W); 1847 (I); 1859 (W); 1875 (I); 1880 (I); 1882 (I); 1896 (W); 1898 (W,I); 1932 (W)
Missouri	1833 (W); 1850 (W,I); 1852 (W); 1854 (W); 1856 (W); 1858 (W,I); 1862 (I); 1864 (I); 1866 (F); 1872 (I); 1876 (I); 1878 (I); 1880 (W,F,I); 1882 (I); 1886 (I); 1898 (I); 1910 (F); 1912 (F)
Montana	1896 (W); 1898 (F); 1900 (F); 1904 (F); 1906 (F)
Nebraska	1878 (F); 1890 (F); 1892 (F); 1894 (F); 1898 (F); 1900 (F); 1902 (F); 1904 (F); 1906 (F); 1908 (F); 1910 (F); 1912 (F); 1914 (F); 1916 (F)
Nevada	1902 (F); 1904 (F); 1906 (F)
New Hampshire	1849 (F); 1851 (F); 1853 (F)
New Jersey	1843 (I); 1856 (F); 1858 (W); 1870 (W); 1876 (I); 1878 (F,I); 1882 (F); 1886 (I); 1888 (I); 1896 (W,M); 1906 (F); 1912 (F); 1914 (W,I)
New Mexico	
New York	1806 (F); 1812 (I); 1818 (W,I); 1821 (W); 1822 (W); 1824 (W,I); 1830 (F); 1844 (I); 1846 (W,I); 1848 (W,F,I); 1850 (I); 1852 (I); 1854 (W,F,I); 1856 (I); 1858 (W,F,I); 1860 (W,I); 1864 (W); 1866 (F,I); 1868 (I); 1870 (W,I,M); 1874 (W,I,M); 1876 (W,F,I); 1878 (W,F,I,M); 1880 (F,I,M); 1884 (W,F,I); 1886 (F,I,M); 1888 (W); 1890 (W,I); 1894 (W); 1896 (W,I,M); 1898 (W); 1902 (W); 1906 (J); 1910 (J); 1912 (J); 1914 (J); 1916 (J); 1918 (F,M); 1920 (J); 1922 (J); 1924 (J); 1926 (J,M); 1928 (J); 1930 (J); 1938 (J); 1940 (J); 1942 (J); 1944 (J,M); 1946 (J); 1948 (J,M); 1950 (J,M); 1952 (J,M); 1954 (J,M); 1956 (J,M); 1958 (J,M); 1960 (J); 1962 (J); 1964 (J); 1966 (J); 1968 (J); 1970 (J,M); 1972 (J,M); 1974 (J,M); 1976 (J,M); 1978 (J,M); 1980 (J,M); 1982 (J,M); 1984 (J,M); 1986 (J,M); 1988 (M); 1990 (J,M); 1992 (J,M); 1994 (J); 1996 (J); 1998 (J)
North Carolina	1835 (W); 1847 (I); 1851 (W); 1853 (W,I); 1859 (I); 1878 (F,I); 1886 (I); 1890 (I); 1894 (F); 1896 (F,I); 1898 (F,I); 1900 (I)
North Dakota	1896 (F); 1898 (F); 1942 (I); 1944 (I)
Ohio	1806 (F); 1843 (I); 1846 (I); 1848 (F,I); 1850 (I); 1862 (I); 1872 (W); 1874 (I); 1892 (I); 1900 (I); 1906 (I); 1908 (I)
Oklahoma	
Oregon	1898 (F); 1900 (F,I); 1912 (F); 1914 (F); 1916 (F); 1918 (M); 1920 (M); 1926 (F); 1948 (F)
Pennsylvania	1806 (F); 1808 (F); 1810 (F); 1812 (I); 1816 (F,I); 1818 (F,I); 1820 (M); 1822 (I); 1824 (W,I); 1826 (W,I); 1830 (F,I,M); 1832 (W,F,I); 1843 (F,I); 1846 (W); 1848 (W,F,I); 1850 (F); 1854 (F,I); 1858 (W); 1860 (I); 1864 (W); 1870 (I); 1874 (I); 1878 (F,I); 1880 (F); 1888 (F); 1890 (I); 1894 (F); 1902 (F,I); 1904 (F,I); 1906 (I); 1908 (I); 1910 (J,M); 1912 (J); 1914 (I); 1916 (J); 1922 (J,M); 1924 (J,M); 1926 (J,M); 1928 (J,M); 1930 (J,M); 1932 (J,M); 1934 (J,I,M); 1936 (J); 1938 (J); 1944 (I); 1948 (J); 1968 (J); 1988 (M); 1990 (M); 1992 (M); 1994 (M); 1998 (M)
Rhode Island	1833 (F); 1843 (W); 1859 (F); 1938 (F)
South Carolina	1848 (W); 1870 (I); 1872 (I); 1874 (I); 1882 (F,I); 1888 (I); 1890 (I); 1894 (I); 1896 (W,I); 1936 (W)
South Dakota	1898 (F); 1900 (F)
Tennessee	1827 (W); 1829 (W); 1833 (W); 1845 (I); 1851 (I); 1859 (I); 1867 (I); 1870 (I); 1874 (I); 1876 (I); 1878 (I); 1880 (I); 1882 (I); 1884 (I); 1886 (I); 1890 (I); 1892 (F,I); 1894 (M); 1896 (W,I,M); 1902 (I); 1906 (I); 1908 (I); 1910 (I); 1912 (W); 1914 (I); 1920 (I); 1930 (I); 1950 (I); 1958 (W); 1962 (I)
Texas	1859 (I); 1876 (I); 1886 (F); 1888 (I); 1892 (F); 1894 (F); 1896 (W); 1906 (W); 1920 (F); 1952 (M)
Utah	1896 (F); 1914 (F); 1916 (F); 1918 (F)
Vermont	1818 (F); 1830 (F); 1848 (F); 1850 (F); 1852 (W,F); 1854 (F); 1860 (W); 1874 (I); 1878 (I); 1880 (I); 1914 (F); 1916 (F); 1918 (F); 1920 (F); 1922 (F); 1924 (F); 1964 (I); 1968 (M); 1976 (J)
Virginia	1809 (I); 1811 (I); 1813 (I); 1849 (I); 1853 (I); 1859 (I); 1874 (I); 1876 (I); 1878 (I); 1884 (I); 1886 (I); 1888 (I); 1890 (I); 1892 (I); 1896 (W,I); 1898 (W,I); 1902 (I); 1904 (I); 1908 (I); 1920 (W,I); 1930 (W,I); 1944 (I)
Washington	
West Virginia	1872 (I); 1884 (F); 1912 (F)
Wisconsin	1850 (W,F); 1874 (F); 1882 (I); 1884 (F); 1888 (F); 1894 (F); 1906 (I); 1922 (W,I); 1926 (W,I); 1930 (I); 1932 (I)
Wyoming	

Notes: Wing (W) = candidate affiliated with a major party running as a splinter, wing, or factional candidate from that party (e.g., Benton Democrat, Anti-Benton Democrat, Union Democrat); Fusion (F) = candidate of a major party running on a fusion ticket with one or more minor parties (e.g., Democrat-Greenback fusion, Republican-Greenback fusion) or on the "fusion" label itself (if parties in a fusion ticket can be identified); Joint (J) = candidate of a major party also endorsed by a minor party under the latter's own slate of candidates on the ballot (e.g., Liberal Party endorsement of a Democratic candidate in New York under the Liberal Party's own slate of candidates on the ballot); Independent (I) = major party candidate also running as an independent (e.g., using the Independent Democrat label or the Democrat Independent label); Both major (M) = candidate running on both major party tickets (e.g., listed on both Democratic and Republican tickets on the ballot, as successful crossfiling candidates were in California up to 1960. For a further explanation of these categories, see the text discussion of this table in Chapter 5 and also the text discussion of Table 1-3 in Chapter 1.

Sources: *U.S. Congressional Elections, 1788–1997* (1998), *Congressional Quarterly's Guide to U.S. Elections* (1994), ICPSR data sets 0001 and 0075, and independent search for state sources by the author.

Table 5-2 Methods of Apportioning Seats for the House of Representatives, 1788–1998

State	At Large, One Seat	At Large, Multiple Seats	Single Member + At Large
Alabama	1819; 1821	1841 (5)	1872–1874; 1912–1914
Alaska	1958–1998		
Arizona	1912–1940	1942–1946 (2)	
Arkansas	1836–1851		1872; 1882
California		1849–1861 (2); 1863 (3)	1882
Colorado	1876–1890		1902–1912
Connecticut		1788–1790 (5); 1792–1821 (7); 1823–1835 (6)	1902–1910; 1932–1962
Delaware	1789–1998		
Florida	1845–1860; 1868–1870	1872 (2)	1912; 1932–1934; 1942
Georgia		1792–1800 (2); 1802–1810 (4); 1812–1820 (6); 1822–1830 (7); 1832–1840 (9); 1842 (8)	1882
Hawaii	1959–1960	1962–1968 (2)	
Idaho	1890–1910	1912–1916 (2)	
Illinois	1819–1831		1862–1870; 1912–1946
Indiana	1816–1820		1872
Iowa		1846 (2)	
Kansas	1861–1870	1872 (3)	1882; 1892–1904
Kentucky		1932 (9)	
Louisiana	1812–1820		
Maine		1882 (4)	
Maryland			1962–1964
Massachusetts			1792
Michigan	1835–1840		1912; 1962
Minnesota		1857–1860 (2)	1912
Mississippi	1817–1831	1832–1841 (2); 1843–1845 (4)	1853
Missouri	1820–1833	1835–1840 (2); 1842–1844 (5); 1932 (13)	
Montana	1890–1910; 1992–1998	1912–1916 (2)	
Nebraska	1866–1880		
Nevada	1864–1980		
New Hampshire		1788–1790 (3); 1792–1800 (4); 1802–1810 (5); 1812–1831 (6); 1833–1841 (5); 1843–1845 (4)	
New Jersey		1789–1791 (4); 1792–1797 (5); 1800 (5); 1803–1810 (6); 1814–1840 (6)	
New Mexico	1911–1940	1942–1966 (2)	
New York			1872; 1882; 1932–1942
North Carolina			
North Dakota	1889–1900; 1972–1998	1902–1910 (2); 1932–1960 (2)	
Ohio	1803–1810		1912; 1932–1950, 1962–1964
Oklahoma			1912; 1932–1940
Oregon	1858–1890		
Pennsylvania		1788 (8); 1792 (13); 1816 (4)	1882–1886; 1892–1900; 1912–1920; 1942
Rhode Island	1790	1792–1841 (2)	
South Carolina			1868–1872
South Dakota	1982–1998	1889–1910 (2)	
Tennessee	1796–1801	1803 (3)	1872
Texas			1872; 1912–1916; 1932; 1952–1956; 1962–1964
Utah	1896–1910	1912 (2)	
Vermont	1932–1998	1812–1818 (6); 1822 (5)	
Virginia		1932 (9)	1869–1870; 1882
Washington	1889–1890	1892–1900 (2); 1902–1906 (3)	1912; 1952–1956
West Virginia			1912–1914
Wisconsin			
Wyoming	1890–1998		

State	Single-Member + Multimember	Multimember Only
Maryland	1803–1831; 1835–1841	
New Jersey		1813
New York	1808–1840	
Pennsylvania	1794–1840	

Notes: All other states and years used the standard single-member district method. Numbers in parentheses are the number of seats elected statewide.

Sources: Compiled by the author from state constitutions, state statute books, *United States Congressional Elections, 1788–1997* (1998), and *Congressional Quarterly's Guide to U.S. Elections,* 3d ed., (1994).

Table 5-3 Political Composition of the House of Representatives, 1789–2001

Congress	Years	Number of Representatives	Federalists	National Republicans/ Whigs	Republicans	Democrats	Others	Majority Party Gain/Loss
1st	1789–1791	65	18			6	41	—
2d	1791–1793	69	5			1	63	—
3d	1793–1795	105	22			18	65	—
4th	1795–1797	105	49			56	0	—
5th	1797–1799	106	58			48	0	+9
6th	1799–1801	106	64			42	0	+6
7th	1801–1803	106	43			63	0	−21
8th	1803–1805	142	41			101	0	+38
9th	1805–1807	142	30			111	1	+10
10th	1807–1809	142	26			111	5	−1
11th	1809–1811	142	55			87	0	−24
12th	1811–1813	142	41			100	1	+14
13th	1813–1815	182	72			110	0	+10
14th	1815–1817	182	71			111	0	+1
15th	1817–1819	184	43			141	0	+30
16th	1819–1821	186	30			156	0	+15
17th	1821–1823	187	31			154	2	−2
18th	1823–1825	213	24			149	40	+22
19th	1825–1827	213	22			127	64	−22
20th	1827–1829	213		80		92	41	−35
21st	1829–1831	213		75		132	6	+41
22d	1831–1833	213		68		120	25	−12
23d	1833–1835	240		62		144	34	+24
24th	1835–1837	241		81		145	15	+6
25th	1837–1839	242		104		131	7	−14
26th	1839–1841	242		118		124	0	−7
27th	1841–1843	242		142		99	1	−25
28th	1843–1845	223		70		150	3	−72
29th	1845–1847	223		81		136	6	−14
30th	1847–1849	228		118		108	2	−29
31st	1849–1851	232		107		117	8	−11
32d	1851–1853	233		89		129	15	+12
33d	1853–1855	234		72		158	4	+29
34th	1855–1857	234		58	13	84	79	−74
35th	1857–1859	236			93	130	13	+46
36th	1859–1861	238			119	99	20	−31
37th	1861–1863	171			114	52	5	−5
38th	1863–1865	183			108	75	0	−6
39th	1865–1867	192			145	35	12	+37
40th	1867–1869	193			143	50	0	−2
41st	1869–1871	244			165	72	7	+22
42d	1871–1873	244			138	95	11	−27
43d	1873–1875	292			202	86	4	+64
44th	1875–1877	292			108	179	5	−94
45th	1877–1879	293			141	152	0	−27
46th	1879–1881	293			136	152	5	0
47th	1881–1883	293			152	138	3	−14
48th	1883–1885	325			120	197	8	−32
49th	1885–1887	325			142	183	0	−14
50th	1887–1889	325			152	170	3	−13
51st	1889–1891	326			164	162	0	−8
52d	1891–1893	332			87	238	7	−77
53d	1893–1895	356			130	221	5	−17
54th	1895–1897	357			245	107	5	−114
55th	1897–1899	357			211	142	4	−34
56th	1899–1901	357			184	172	1	−25
57th	1901–1903	357			198	159	0	+14
58th	1903–1905	386			205	180	1	+7
59th	1905–1907	386			251	135	0	+46
60th	1907–1909	391			224	167	0	−27
61st	1909–1911	391			219	172	0	−4
62d	1911–1913	393			167	226	0	−52
63d	1913–1915	435			145	279	11	+53
64th	1915–1917	435			191	236	8	−43
65th	1917–1919	435			216	215	4	−21
66th	1919–1921	435			243	190	2	+27
67th	1921–1923	435			302	131	2	+59
68th	1923–1925	435			225	207	3	−77
69th	1925–1927	435			247	183	5	+22
70th	1927–1929	435			237	195	3	−10
71st	1929–1931	435			269	165	1	+32
72d	1931–1933[1]	435			217	216	2	−52
73d	1933–1935	435			117	313	5	−100
74th	1935–1937	435			103	322	10	+8
75th	1937–1939	435			89	335	11	+13

(Table continues)

Table 5-3 *(Continued)*

Congress	Years	Number of Representatives	Federalists	National Republicans/ Whigs	Republicans	Democrats	Others	Majority Party Gain/Loss
76th	1939–1941	435			170	262	3	−73
77th	1941–1943	435			163	267	5	+5
78th	1943–1945	435			210	222	3	−45
79th	1945–1947	435			191	242	2	+20
80th	1947–1949	435			246	188	1	−54
81st	1949–1951	435			171	263	1	−75
82d	1951–1953	435			199	235	1	−28
83d	1953–1955	435			221	213	1	−22
84th	1955–1957	435			203	232	0	−18
85th	1957–1959	435			201	234	0	+2
86th	1959–1961	436			153	283	0	+49
87th	1961–1963	437			174	263	0	−20
88th	1963–1965	435			176	259	0	−4
89th	1965–1967	435			140	295	0	+36
90th	1967–1969	435			187	248	0	−47
91st	1969–1971	435			192	243	0	−5
92d	1971–1973	435			180	255	0	+12
93d	1973–1975	435			192	243	0	−12
94th	1975–1977	435			144	291	0	+48
95th	1977–1979	435			143	292	0	+1
96th	1979–1981	435			158	277	0	−15
97th	1981–1983	435			192	243	0	−34
98th	1983–1985	435			166	269	0	+26
99th	1985–1987	435			182	253	0	−16
100th	1987–1989	435			177	258	0	+5
101st	1989–1991	435			175	260	0	+2
102d	1991–1993	435			166	268	1	+8
103d	1993–1995	435			176	258	1	−10
104th	1995–1997	435			228	206	1	−52
105th	1997–1999	435			226	207	2	−2
106th	1999–2001	435			223	211	1	−3

Notes: Entries reflect winners from the actual vote result and are not adjusted for contested seats, runoffs, inaccuracies of other types in reporting party labels or winners, or gubernatorial and legislative proclamations of different winners. For these reasons, the figures may not completely correspond to the most recent reports of the Clerk of the House of Representatives regarding the composition of the House over time. No entries were made in the first three Congresses in the "Majority Party Gain/Loss" column since historians acknowledge that the Federalists and Anti-Federalists were more loosely organized groupings in Congress than formal parties prior to 1794. Republicans = Republican Party since 1854. Federalists, National Republicans, and Whigs are considered historical precursors to the Republican Party in this table. Democrats = Democratic Party since 1830. Anti-Federalists, Democratic-Republicans, and Jackson Democrats are considered historical antecedents to the Democratic Party in this table. Also see Appendix A for a list of the various labels and designations used by historical antecedents of the Republican and Democratic parties.

[1]Democrats organized the House of Representatives after the 1930 election despite the vote result, since Republican seat vacancies occurred shortly after the election due to deaths and the contesting of one House election.

Sources: Data from Tables 5-9 through 5-14.

Table 5-4 National Results of House Elections by Two-Year Election Cycle, 1788–1998

Year	National Raw Vote				National Percent			Democratic % of Two-Party Vote
	Democratic	Republican	Other	Total	Democratic	Republican	Other	
1788–1789	10,148	13,861	32,631	56,640	17.92	24.47	57.61	42.27
1790–1791	3,132	7,154	46,750	57,036	5.49	12.54	81.97	30.44
1792–1793	35,095	40,962	27,685	103,742	33.83	39.48	26.69	46.14
1794–1795	35,738	50,571	5,051	91,360	39.12	55.35	5.53	41.41
1796–1797	40,721	69,688	4,295	114,704	35.50	60.75	3.74	36.88
1798–1799	67,405	99,433	3,782	170,620	39.51	58.28	2.22	40.40
1800–1801	111,711	79,700	6,884	198,295	56.34	40.19	3.47	58.36
1802–1803	96,398	68,129	3,041	167,568	57.53	40.66	1.81	58.59
1804–1805	151,203	88,838	1,336	241,377	62.64	36.80	0.55	62.99
1806–1807	129,656	68,367	4,759	202,782	63.94	33.71	2.35	65.48
1808–1809	219,879	182,100	7,543	409,522	53.69	44.47	1.84	54.70
1810–1811	217,878	128,523	10,133	356,534	61.11	36.05	2.84	62.90
1812–1813	223,309	218,045	6,408	447,762	49.87	48.70	1.43	50.60
1814–1815	148,080	149,777	484	298,341	49.63	50.20	0.16	49.72
1816–1817	180,570	122,330	31,301	334,201	54.03	36.60	9.37	59.61
1818–1819	211,070	61,836	34,110	307,016	68.75	20.14	11.11	77.34
1820–1821	329,415	92,734	25,510	447,659	73.59	20.72	5.70	78.03
1822–1823	327,493	50,559	52,631	430,683	76.04	11.74	12.22	86.63
1824–1825	317,841	39,812	115,169	472,822	67.22	8.42	24.36	88.87
1826–1827	233,119	255,025	135,506	623,650	37.38	40.89	21.73	47.76
1828–1829	317,213	243,282	55,744	616,239	51.48	39.48	9.05	56.60
1830–1831	505,776	311,220	166,499	983,495	51.43	31.64	16.93	61.91
1832–1833	595,771	297,246	266,099	1,159,116	51.40	25.64	22.96	66.71
1834–1835	650,139	561,802	90,547	1,302,488	49.92	43.13	6.95	53.64
1836–1837	668,662	641,191	42,192	1,352,045	49.46	47.42	3.12	51.05
1838–1839	868,851	870,603	7,027	1,746,481	49.75	49.85	0.40	49.95
1840–1841	957,480	1,029,612	9,403	1,996,495	47.96	51.57	0.47	48.18
1842–1843	940,561	824,387	74,444	1,839,392	51.13	44.82	4.05	53.29
1844–1845	1,214,293	1,189,562	87,345	2,491,200	48.74	47.75	3.51	50.51
1846–1847	1,155,687	960,112	119,464	2,235,263	51.70	42.95	5.34	54.62
1848–1849	1,137,376	1,183,768	239,989	2,561,133	44.41	46.22	9.37	49.00
1850–1851	1,082,727	996,046	232,520	2,311,293	46.85	43.09	10.06	52.08
1852–1853	1,402,819	1,209,081	153,568	2,765,468	50.73	43.72	5.55	53.71
1854–1855	1,421,899	791,021	859,890	3,072,810	46.27	25.74	27.98	64.25
1856–1857	1,771,273	1,421,301	557,232	3,749,806	47.24	37.90	14.86	55.48
1858–1859	1,818,744	1,267,464	519,669	3,605,877	50.44	35.15	14.41	58.93
1860–1861	1,650,435	1,987,871	182,484	3,820,790	43.20	52.03	4.78	45.36
1862–1863	1,546,915	1,610,452	56,430	3,213,797	48.13	50.11	1.76	48.99
1864–1865	1,645,716	2,096,655	153,699	3,896,070	42.24	53.81	3.94	43.98
1866–1867	1,809,747	2,265,155	38,369	4,113,271	44.00	55.07	0.93	44.41
1868–1869	2,605,134	3,147,981	131,505	5,884,620	44.27	53.50	2.23	45.28
1870–1871	2,481,531	2,591,797	77,702	5,151,030	48.18	50.32	1.51	48.91
1872–1873	2,927,921	3,491,873	184,911	6,604,705	44.33	52.87	2.80	45.61
1874–1875	3,099,918	2,817,263	289,839	6,207,020	49.94	45.39	4.67	52.39
1876–1877	4,322,100	3,905,401	90,081	8,317,582	51.96	46.95	1.08	52.53
1878–1879	3,313,147	2,862,571	887,109	7,062,827	46.91	40.53	12.56	53.65
1880	4,440,239	4,220,865	412,051	9,073,155	48.94	46.52	4.54	51.27
1882	4,062,716	3,336,406	596,152	7,995,274	50.81	41.73	7.46	54.91
1884	5,016,423	4,682,168	193,118	9,891,709	50.71	47.33	1.95	51.72
1886	4,233,021	3,906,416	438,610	8,578,047	49.35	45.54	5.11	52.01
1888–1889	5,579,308	5,468,975	413,448	11,461,731	48.68	47.72	3.61	50.50
1890	5,029,443	4,212,903	540,032	9,782,378	51.41	43.07	5.52	54.42
1892	5,946,971	4,902,506	998,532	11,848,009	50.19	41.38	8.43	54.81
1894–1895	4,438,515	5,454,350	1,370,990	11,263,855	39.40	48.42	12.17	44.87
1896	6,218,664	6,893,934	544,431	13,657,029	45.53	50.48	3.99	47.43
1898	5,149,719	5,380,574	423,452	10,953,745	47.01	49.12	3.87	48.90
1900	6,434,532	6,948,459	326,304	13,709,295	46.94	50.68	2.38	48.08
1902	5,088,122	5,478,660	421,139	10,987,921	46.31	49.86	3.83	48.15
1904	5,400,170	7,172,968	589,899	13,163,037	41.03	54.49	4.48	42.95
1906–1907	4,891,691	5,708,031	579,367	11,179,089	43.76	51.06	5.18	46.15
1908	6,551,965	7,237,227	656,332	14,445,524	45.36	50.10	4.54	47.52
1910–1911	5,750,691	5,682,268	777,825	12,210,784	47.10	46.53	6.37	50.30
1912	6,233,325	5,012,684	3,012,030	14,258,039	43.72	35.16	21.13	55.43
1914	5,806,505	5,832,617	2,006,978	13,646,100	42.55	42.74	14.71	49.89
1916	7,709,350	8,025,364	998,077	16,732,791	46.07	47.96	5.96	49.00
1918	5,568,265	6,610,510	589,307	12,768,082	43.61	51.77	4.62	45.72
1920	9,150,957	14,874,251	1,503,303	25,528,511	35.85	58.27	5.89	38.09
1922	9,062,740	10,633,303	714,785	20,410,828	44.40	52.10	3.50	46.01
1924	10,746,697	15,009,086	1,098,383	26,854,166	40.02	55.89	4.09	41.73
1926	8,271,764	11,610,611	516,454	20,398,829	40.55	56.92	2.53	41.60

(Table continues)

Table 5-4 *(Continued)*

	National Raw Vote				National Percent			Democratic % of Two-Party Vote
Year	Democratic	Republican	Other	Total	Democratic	Republican	Other	
1928	14,216,500	19,369,186	616,272	34,201,958	41.57	56.63	1.80	42.33
1930	11,087,763	13,051,778	661,299	24,800,840	44.71	52.63	2.67	45.93
1932	20,267,306	15,726,307	1,532,449	37,526,062	54.01	41.91	4.08	56.31
1934	17,457,671	13,185,721	1,636,592	32,279,984	54.08	40.85	5.07	56.97
1936	24,196,344	17,025,266	1,774,968	42,996,578	56.28	39.60	4.13	58.70
1938	17,927,403	16,972,061	1,229,004	36,128,468	49.62	46.98	3.40	51.37
1940	24,266,432	21,346,565	1,046,162	46,659,159	52.01	45.75	2.24	53.20
1942	13,239,668	14,253,793	583,786	28,077,247	47.15	50.77	2.08	48.16
1944	23,458,538	21,183,304	431,802	45,073,644	52.04	47.00	0.96	52.55
1946	15,496,218	18,409,852	458,884	34,364,954	45.09	53.57	1.34	45.70
1948	22,025,949	20,697,755	3,175,598	45,899,302	47.99	45.09	6.92	51.55
1950	19,998,288	19,763,965	549,525	40,311,778	49.61	49.03	1.36	50.29
1952	28,994,253	28,320,766	530,478	57,845,497	50.12	48.96	0.92	50.59
1954	22,490,589	19,895,605	198,878	42,585,072	52.81	46.72	0.47	53.06
1956	29,956,895	28,074,609	139,619	58,171,123	51.50	48.26	0.24	51.62
1958–1959	25,727,794	19,875,549	152,984	45,756,327	56.23	43.44	0.33	56.42
1960	35,059,315	28,738,811	260,047	64,058,173	54.73	44.86	0.41	54.95
1962	26,424,880	24,461,879	196,134	51,082,893	51.73	47.89	0.38	51.93
1964	37,633,283	27,665,266	325,552	65,624,101	57.35	42.16	0.50	57.63
1966	26,742,798	25,394,956	455,086	52,592,840	50.85	48.29	0.87	51.29
1968	33,180,963	32,030,978	751,339	65,963,280	50.30	48.56	1.14	50.88
1970	28,361,957	23,730,423	767,771	52,860,151	53.65	44.89	1.45	54.45
1972	36,084,414	32,146,173	954,136	69,184,723	52.16	46.46	1.38	52.89
1974	29,050,981	20,408,393	937,805	50,397,179	57.64	40.50	1.86	58.74
1976	40,358,475	30,229,202	1,259,152	71,846,829	56.17	42.07	1.75	57.17
1978	28,093,358	23,679,754	779,766	52,552,878	53.46	45.06	1.48	54.26
1980	36,934,769	35,623,558	1,260,264	73,818,591	50.03	48.26	1.71	50.90
1982	33,954,496	26,739,456	979,440	61,673,392	55.06	43.36	1.59	55.94
1984	41,395,632	37,436,165	696,405	79,528,202	52.05	47.07	0.88	52.51
1986	30,996,645	25,425,142	538,024	56,959,811	54.42	44.64	0.94	54.94
1988	41,668,053	35,167,206	922,376	77,757,635	53.59	45.23	1.19	54.23
1990	31,148,060	26,442,421	1,278,943	58,869,424	52.91	44.92	2.17	54.09
1992	46,257,050	40,903,585	3,284,744	90,445,379	51.14	45.22	3.63	53.07
1994	30,544,369	34,900,685	1,483,559	66,928,613	45.64	52.15	2.22	46.67
1996	41,327,666	40,864,430	2,318,264	84,510,360	48.90	48.35	2.74	50.28
1998	30,519,753	31,279,825	2,048,440	63,848,018	47.80	48.99	3.21	49.39

Notes: Entries are calculated from the raw vote values in Tables 5-70 through 5-122. Whenever bold italicized values occur in Tables 5-70 through 5-122, denoting the author's alternate party coding system, they are used instead of the conventionally coded main entries in these tables in the aggregation process to the national level for Table 5-4. See text and Table 5-1 for a more complete discussion of the conventional and alternate party coding systems. Also see Table 1-3 for a similar discussion. Entries in Table 5-4 are based on candidates who use the designation "Democrat" or "Republican" (or their historical antecedents listed in Appendix A) either solely or with other labels or parties (often minor parties) on the ballot. In general, historical antecedents to the Democratic Party were Anti-Federalists, Democratic-Republicans, and Jackson Democrats; historical precursors of the Republican Party were Federalists, National Republicans, and Whigs. Other = candidates who use third-party names only on the ballot or are listed as independent or unidentified. Odd-numbered year House elections were held in several states prior to 1880 but only rarely thereafter. States with partial House vote data are not included in the aggregation process. Special House elections are also not included.

Sources: Data in Tables 5-70 through 5-122 as adapted from *United States Congressional Elections, 1788–1997* (1998), *Congressional Quarterly's Guide to U.S. Elections* (1994), ICPSR data sets 0001 and 0075, *America Votes* (various publication dates), and independent search of state sources by the author.

Table 5-5 National Results of House Elections, Annually, 1788–1998

Year	National Raw Vote				National Percent			Democratic % of Two-Party Vote
	Democratic	Republican	Other	Total	Democratic	Republican	Other	
1788	7,417	8,707	13,883	30,007	24.72	29.02	46.27	46.00
1789	2,731	5,154	18,748	26,633	10.25	19.35	70.39	34.64
1790	3,132	7,154	38,361	48,647	6.44	14.71	78.86	30.44
1791	0	0	8,389	8,389	0.00	0.00	100.00	—
1792	24,068	28,011	24,629	76,708	31.38	36.52	32.11	46.21
1793	11,027	12,951	3,056	27,034	40.79	47.91	11.30	45.99
1794	35,738	50,571	5,051	91,360	39.12	55.35	5.53	41.41
1795	—	—	—	—	—	—	—	—
1796	36,861	62,588	4,077	103,526	35.61	60.46	3.94	37.07
1797	3,860	7,100	218	11,178	34.53	63.52	1.95	35.22
1798	67,405	99,433	3,782	170,620	39.51	58.28	2.22	40.40
1799	—	—	—	—	—	—	—	—
1800	75,077	74,069	3,132	152,278	49.30	48.64	2.06	50.34
1801	36,634	5,631	3,752	46,017	79.61	12.24	8.15	86.68
1802	63,051	63,464	3,041	129,556	48.67	48.99	2.35	49.84
1803	33,347	4,665	0	38,012	87.73	12.27	0.00	87.73
1804	135,857	88,838	1,336	226,031	60.11	39.30	0.59	60.46
1805	15,346	0	0	15,346	100.00	0.00	0.00	100.00
1806	129,656	68,367	4,759	202,782	63.94	33.71	2.35	65.48
1807	—	—	—	—	—	—	—	—
1808	219,879	182,100	7,543	409,522	53.69	44.47	1.84	54.70
1809	—	—	—	—	—	—	—	—
1810	203,204	128,523	4,973	336,700	60.35	38.17	1.48	61.26
1811	14,674	0	5,160	19,834	73.98	0.00	26.02	100.00
1812	210,866	204,237	6,334	421,437	50.03	48.46	1.50	50.80
1813	12,443	13,808	74	26,325	47.27	52.45	0.28	47.40
1814	148,080	149,777	484	298,341	49.63	50.20	0.16	49.72
1815	—	—	—	—	—	—	—	—
1816	147,418	122,330	10,864	280,612	52.53	43.59	3.87	54.65
1817	33,152	0	20,437	53,589	61.86	0.00	38.14	100.00
1818	163,815	54,743	3,034	221,592	73.93	24.70	1.37	74.95
1819	47,255	7,093	31,076	85,424	55.32	8.30	36.38	86.95
1820	163,352	92,270	18,813	274,435	59.52	33.62	6.86	63.90
1821	166,063	464	6,697	173,224	95.87	0.27	3.87	99.72
1822	293,853	43,430	43,519	380,802	77.17	11.40	11.43	87.12
1823	33,640	7,129	9,112	49,881	67.44	14.29	18.27	82.51
1824	308,646	38,519	114,618	461,783	66.84	8.34	24.82	88.90
1825	9,195	1,293	551	11,039	83.30	11.71	4.99	87.67
1826	181,268	222,130	98,040	501,438	36.15	44.30	19.55	44.94
1827	51,851	32,895	37,466	122,212	42.43	26.92	30.66	61.18
1828	251,630	190,065	43,294	484,989	51.88	39.19	8.93	56.97
1829	65,583	53,217	12,450	131,250	49.97	40.55	9.49	55.20
1830	355,200	213,051	143,932	712,183	49.87	29.92	20.21	62.51
1831	150,576	98,169	22,567	271,312	55.50	36.18	8.32	60.53
1832	432,614	166,581	182,709	781,904	55.33	21.30	23.37	72.70
1833	163,157	130,665	83,390	377,212	43.25	34.64	22.11	55.53
1834	502,191	444,198	65,039	1,011,428	49.65	43.92	6.43	53.06
1835	147,948	117,604	25,508	291,060	50.83	40.41	8.76	55.71
1836	520,223	454,969	41,912	1,017,104	51.15	44.73	4.12	53.35
1837	148,439	186,222	280	334,941	44.32	55.60	0.08	44.36
1838	664,575	673,908	2,430	1,340,913	49.56	50.26	0.18	49.65
1839	204,276	196,695	4,597	405,568	50.37	48.50	1.13	50.95
1840	729,177	782,073	2,751	1,514,001	48.16	51.66	0.18	48.25
1841	228,303	247,539	6,652	482,494	47.32	51.30	1.38	47.98
1842	326,772	284,684	16,625	628,081	52.03	45.33	2.65	53.44
1843	613,789	539,703	57,819	1,211,311	50.67	44.56	4.77	53.21
1844	891,074	882,127	62,273	1,835,474	48.55	48.06	3.39	50.25
1845	323,219	307,435	25,072	655,726	49.29	46.88	3.82	51.25
1846	841,839	655,857	104,438	1,602,134	52.54	40.94	6.52	56.21
1847	313,848	304,255	15,026	633,129	49.57	48.06	2.37	50.78
1848	782,203	840,181	214,700	1,837,084	42.58	45.73	11.69	48.21
1849	355,173	343,587	25,289	724,049	49.05	47.45	3.49	50.83
1850	802,176	738,773	63,772	1,604,721	49.99	46.04	3.97	52.06
1851	280,551	257,273	168,748	706,572	39.71	36.41	23.88	52.16
1852	1,074,437	964,859	122,107	2,161,403	49.71	44.64	5.65	52.69
1853	328,382	244,222	31,461	604,065	54.36	40.43	5.21	57.35
1854	977,055	787,265	424,149	2,188,469	44.65	35.97	19.38	55.38
1855	444,844	3,756	435,741	884,341	50.30	0.42	49.27	99.16
1856	1,247,674	1,329,375	279,416	2,856,465	43.68	46.54	9.78	48.41
1857	523,599	91,926	277,816	893,341	58.61	10.29	31.10	85.07
1858	1,250,795	1,073,367	289,780	2,613,942	47.85	41.06	11.09	53.82
1859	567,949	194,097	229,889	991,935	57.26	19.57	23.18	74.53
1860	1,510,613	1,693,022	128,361	3,331,996	45.34	50.81	3.85	47.15
1861	139,822	294,849	54,123	488,794	28.61	60.32	11.07	32.17
1862	1,318,426	1,375,128	53,874	2,747,428	47.99	50.05	1.96	48.95

(Table continues)

Table 5-5 *(Continued)*

Year	National Raw Vote				National Percent			Democratic % of Two-Party Vote
	Democratic	*Republican*	*Other*	*Total*	*Democratic*	*Republican*	*Other*	
1863	228,489	235,324	2,556	466,369	48.99	50.46	0.55	49.26
1864	1,581,015	1,982,797	6,884	3,570,696	44.28	55.53	0.19	44.36
1865	64,701	113,858	146,815	325,374	19.89	34.99	45.12	36.24
1866	1,601,850	2,029,211	9,332	3,640,393	44.00	55.74	0.26	44.12
1867	207,897	235,944	29,037	472,878	43.96	49.90	6.14	46.84
1868	2,414,830	2,781,286	9,778	5,205,894	46.39	53.43	0.19	46.47
1869	190,304	366,695	121,727	678,726	28.04	54.03	17.93	34.17
1870	2,280,125	2,404,457	76,672	4,761,254	47.89	50.50	1.61	48.67
1871	201,406	187,340	1,030	389,776	51.67	48.06	0.26	51.81
1872	2,853,292	3,415,343	182,355	6,450,990	44.23	52.94	2.83	45.52
1873	74,629	76,530	2,556	153,715	48.55	49.79	1.66	49.37
1874	2,866,836	2,617,011	263,409	5,747,256	49.88	45.53	4.58	52.28
1875	233,082	200,252	26,430	459,764	50.70	43.56	5.75	53.79
1876	4,284,234	3,865,630	89,828	8,239,692	52.00	46.91	1.09	52.57
1877	37,866	39,771	253	77,890	48.61	51.06	0.32	48.77
1878	3,265,232	2,787,920	852,901	6,906,053	47.28	40.37	12.35	53.94
1879	47,915	74,651	34,208	156,774	30.56	47.62	21.82	39.09
1880	4,440,239	4,220,865	412,051	9,073,155	48.94	46.52	4.54	51.27
1882	4,062,716	3,336,406	596,152	7,995,274	50.81	41.73	7.46	54.91
1884	5,016,423	4,682,168	193,118	9,891,709	50.71	47.33	1.95	51.72
1886	4,233,021	3,906,416	438,610	8,578,047	49.35	45.54	5.11	52.01
1888	5,501,257	5,333,964	413,448	11,248,669	48.91	47.42	3.68	50.77
1889	78,051	135,011	0	213,062	36.63	63.37	0.00	36.63
1890	5,029,443	4,212,903	540,032	9,782,378	51.41	43.07	5.52	54.42
1892	5,946,971	4,902,506	998,532	11,848,009	50.19	41.38	8.43	54.81
1894	4,418,849	5,433,787	1,369,840	11,222,476	39.37	48.42	12.21	44.85
1895	19,666	20,563	1,150	41,379	47.53	49.69	2.78	48.89
1896	6,218,664	6,893,934	544,431	13,657,029	45.53	50.48	3.99	47.43
1898	5,149,719	5,380,574	423,452	10,953,745	47.01	49.12	3.87	48.90
1900	6,434,532	6,948,459	326,304	13,709,295	46.94	50.68	2.38	48.08
1902	5,088,122	5,478,660	421,139	10,987,921	46.31	49.86	3.83	48.15
1904	5,400,170	7,172,968	589,899	13,163,037	41.03	54.49	4.48	42.95
1906	4,755,595	5,606,363	574,284	10,936,242	43.48	51.26	5.25	45.89
1907	136,096	101,668	5,083	242,847	56.04	41.87	2.09	57.24
1908	6,551,965	7,237,227	656,332	14,445,524	45.36	50.10	4.54	47.52
1910	5,709,136	5,643,621	774,640	12,127,397	47.08	46.54	6.39	50.29
1911	41,555	38,647	3,185	83,387	49.83	46.35	3.82	51.81
1912	6,233,325	5,012,684	3,012,030	14,258,039	43.72	35.16	21.13	55.43
1914	5,806,505	5,832,617	2,006,978	13,646,100	42.55	42.74	14.71	49.89
1916	7,709,350	8,025,364	998,077	16,732,791	46.07	47.96	5.96	49.00
1918	5,568,265	6,610,510	589,307	12,768,082	43.61	51.77	4.62	45.72
1920	9,150,957	14,874,251	1,503,303	25,528,511	35.85	58.27	5.89	38.09
1922	9,062,740	10,633,303	714,785	20,410,828	44.40	52.10	3.50	46.01
1924	10,746,697	15,009,086	1,098,383	26,854,166	40.02	55.89	4.09	41.73
1926	8,271,764	11,610,611	516,454	20,398,829	40.55	56.92	2.53	41.60
1928	14,216,500	19,369,186	616,272	34,201,958	41.57	56.63	1.80	42.33
1930	11,087,763	13,051,778	661,299	24,800,840	44.71	52.63	2.67	45.93
1932	20,267,306	15,726,307	1,532,449	37,526,062	54.01	41.91	4.08	56.31
1934	17,457,671	13,185,721	1,636,592	32,279,984	54.08	40.85	5.07	56.97
1936	24,196,344	17,025,266	1,774,968	42,996,578	56.28	39.60	4.13	58.70
1938	17,927,403	16,972,061	1,229,004	36,128,468	49.62	46.98	3.40	51.37
1940	24,266,432	21,346,565	1,046,162	46,659,159	52.01	45.75	2.24	53.20
1942	13,239,668	14,253,793	583,786	28,077,247	47.15	50.77	2.08	48.16
1944	23,458,538	21,183,304	431,802	45,073,644	52.04	47.00	0.96	52.55
1946	15,496,218	18,409,852	458,884	34,364,954	45.09	53.57	1.34	45.70
1948	22,025,949	20,697,755	3,175,598	45,899,302	47.99	45.09	6.92	51.55
1950	19,998,288	19,763,965	549,525	40,311,778	49.61	49.03	1.36	50.29
1952	28,994,253	28,320,766	530,478	57,845,497	50.12	48.96	0.92	50.59
1954	22,490,589	19,895,605	198,878	42,585,072	52.81	46.72	0.47	53.06
1956	29,956,895	28,074,609	139,619	58,171,123	51.50	48.26	0.24	51.62
1958	25,616,067	19,824,491	152,052	45,592,610	56.18	43.48	0.33	56.37
1959	111,727	51,058	932	163,717	68.24	31.19	0.57	68.63
1960	35,059,315	28,738,811	260,047	64,058,173	54.73	44.86	0.41	54.95
1962	26,424,880	24,461,879	196,134	51,082,893	51.73	47.89	0.38	51.93
1964	37,633,283	27,665,266	325,552	65,624,101	57.35	42.16	0.50	57.63
1966	26,742,798	25,394,956	455,086	52,592,840	50.85	48.29	0.87	51.29
1968	33,180,963	32,030,978	751,339	65,963,280	50.30	48.56	1.14	50.88
1970	28,361,957	23,730,423	767,771	52,860,151	53.65	44.89	1.45	54.45
1972	36,084,414	32,146,173	954,136	69,184,723	52.16	46.46	1.38	52.89
1974	29,050,981	20,408,393	937,805	50,397,179	57.64	40.50	1.86	58.74
1976	40,358,475	30,229,202	1,259,152	71,846,829	56.17	42.07	1.75	57.17
1978	28,093,358	23,679,754	779,766	52,552,878	53.46	45.06	1.48	54.26
1980	36,934,769	35,623,558	1,260,264	73,818,591	50.03	48.26	1.71	50.90
1982	33,954,496	26,739,456	979,440	61,673,392	55.06	43.36	1.59	55.94
1984	41,395,632	37,436,165	696,405	79,528,202	52.05	47.07	0.88	52.51

Table 5-5 (*Continued*)

| Year | National Raw Vote | | | | National Percent | | | Democratic % of Two-Party Vote |
	Democratic	Republican	Other	Total	Democratic	Republican	Other	
1986	30,996,645	25,425,142	538,024	56,959,811	54.42	44.64	0.94	54.94
1988	41,668,053	35,167,206	922,376	77,757,635	53.59	45.23	1.19	54.23
1990	31,148,060	26,442,421	1,278,943	58,869,424	52.91	44.92	2.17	54.09
1992	46,257,050	40,903,585	3,284,744	90,445,379	51.14	45.22	3.63	53.07
1994	30,544,369	34,900,685	1,483,559	66,928,613	45.64	52.15	2.22	46.67
1996	41,327,666	40,864,430	2,318,264	84,510,360	48.90	48.35	2.74	50.28
1998	30,519,753	31,279,825	2,048,440	63,848,018	47.80	48.99	3.21	49.39

Notes: Entries are calculated from the raw vote values in Tables 5-70 through 5-122. Whenever bold italicized values occur in Tables 5-70 through 5-122, denoting the author's alternate party coding system, they are used instead of the conventionally coded main entries in these tables in the aggregation process to the national level for Table 5-5. See text and Table 5-1 for a more complete discussion of the conventional and alternate party coding systems. Also see Table 1-3 for a similar discussion. Entries in Table 5-5 are based on candidates who use the designation "Democrat" or "Republican" (or their historical antecedents listed in Appendix A) either solely or with other labels or parties (often minor parties) on the ballot. In general, historical antecedents to the Democratic Party were Anti-Federalists, Democratic-Republicans, and Jackson Democrats; historical precursors of the Republican Party were Federalists, National Republicans, and Whigs. Other = candidates who use third-party names only on the ballot or are listed as independent or unidentified. Odd-numbered year House elections were held in several states prior to 1880 but only rarely thereafter. States with partial House vote data are not included in the aggregation process. Special House elections are also not included.

Sources: Data in Tables 5-70 through 5-122 as adapted from *United States Congressional Elections, 1788–1997* (1998), *Congressional Quarterly's Guide to U.S. Elections* (1994), ICPSR data sets 0001 and 0075, *America Votes* (various publication dates), and independent search of state sources by the author.

Table 5-6 Comparison of National Seats and Votes in House Elections, 1794–1998

Election	Congress	Democratic % of Total Seats	Republican % of Total Seats	Democratic % of Total Votes	Republican % of Total Votes	Difference Dem. Seats to Dem. Votes	Difference Rep. Seats to Rep. Votes
1794–1795	4th	53.33	46.67	39.12	55.35	14.21	−8.68
1796–1797	5th	45.28	54.72	35.50	60.75	9.78	−6.03
1798–1799	6th	39.62	60.38	39.51	58.28	0.11	2.10
1800–1801	7th	59.43	40.57	56.34	40.19	3.09	0.38
1802–1803	8th	71.13	28.87	57.53	40.66	13.60	−11.79
1804–1805	9th	78.17	21.13	62.64	36.80	15.53	−15.67
1806–1807	10th	78.17	18.31	63.94	33.71	14.23	−15.40
1808–1809	11th	61.27	38.73	53.69	44.47	7.58	−5.74
1810–1811	12th	70.42	28.87	61.11	36.05	9.31	−7.18
1812–1813	13th	60.44	39.56	49.87	48.70	10.57	−9.14
1814–1815	14th	60.99	39.01	49.63	50.20	11.36	−11.19
1816–1817	15th	76.63	23.37	54.03	36.60	22.60	−13.23
1818–1819	16th	83.87	16.13	68.75	20.14	15.12	−4.01
1820–1821	17th	82.35	16.58	73.59	20.72	8.76	−4.14
1822–1823	18th	69.95	11.27	76.04	11.74	−6.09	−0.47
1824–1825	19th	59.62	10.33	67.22	8.42	−7.60	1.91
1826–1827	20th	43.19	37.56	37.38	40.89	5.81	−3.33
1828–1829	21st	61.97	35.21	51.48	39.48	10.49	−4.27
1830–1831	22d	56.34	31.92	51.43	31.64	4.91	1.09
1832–1833	23d	60.00	25.83	51.40	25.64	8.60	0.23
1834–1835	24th	60.17	33.61	49.92	43.13	10.25	−9.52
1836–1837	25th	54.13	42.98	49.46	47.42	4.67	−4.44
1838–1839	26th	51.24	48.76	49.75	49.85	1.49	−1.09
1840–1841	27th	40.91	58.68	47.96	51.57	−7.05	7.11
1842–1843	28th	67.26	31.39	51.13	44.82	16.13	−13.43
1844–1845	29th	60.99	36.32	48.74	47.75	12.25	−11.43
1846–1847	30th	47.37	51.75	51.70	42.95	−4.33	8.80
1848–1849	31st	50.43	46.12	44.41	46.22	6.02	−0.10
1850–1851	32d	55.36	38.20	46.85	43.09	8.51	−4.89
1852–1853	33d	67.52	30.77	50.73	43.72	16.79	−12.95
1854–1855	34th	35.90	30.34	46.27	25.74	−10.37	4.60
1856–1857	35th	55.08	39.41	47.24	37.90	7.84	1.51
1858–1859	36th	41.60	50.00	50.44	35.15	−8.84	14.85
1860–1861	37th	30.41	66.67	43.20	52.03	−12.79	14.64
1862–1863	38th	40.98	59.02	48.13	50.11	−7.15	8.91
1864–1865	39th	18.23	75.52	42.24	53.81	−24.01	21.71
1866–1867	40th	25.91	74.09	44.00	55.07	−18.09	19.02
1868–1869	41st	29.51	67.62	44.27	53.50	−14.76	14.12
1870–1871	42d	38.93	56.56	48.18	50.32	−9.25	6.24
1872–1873	43d	29.45	69.18	44.33	52.87	−14.88	16.31
1874–1874	44th	61.30	36.99	49.94	45.39	11.36	−8.40
1876–1877	45th	51.88	48.12	51.96	46.95	−0.08	1.17
1878–1879	46th	51.88	46.42	46.91	40.53	4.97	5.89
1880	47th	47.10	51.88	48.94	46.52	−1.84	5.36
1882	48th	60.62	36.92	50.81	41.73	9.81	−4.81
1884	49th	56.31	43.69	50.71	47.33	5.60	−3.64
1886	50th	52.31	46.77	49.35	45.54	2.96	1.23
1888–1889	51st	49.69	50.31	48.68	47.72	1.01	2.59
1890	52d	71.69	26.20	51.41	43.07	20.28	−16.87
1892	53d	62.08	36.52	50.19	41.38	11.89	−4.86
1894–1895	54th	29.97	68.63	39.40	48.42	−9.43	20.21
1896	55th	39.78	59.10	45.53	50.48	−5.75	8.62
1898	56th	48.18	51.54	47.01	49.12	1.17	2.42
1900	57th	44.54	55.46	46.94	50.68	−2.40	4.78
1902	58th	46.63	53.11	46.31	49.86	0.32	3.25
1904	59th	34.97	65.03	41.03	54.49	−6.06	10.54
1906–1907	60th	42.71	57.29	43.76	51.06	−1.05	6.23
1908	61st	43.99	56.01	45.36	50.10	−1.37	5.91
1910–1911	62d	57.51	42.49	47.10	46.53	10.41	−4.04
1912	63d	64.14	33.33	43.72	35.16	20.42	−1.83
1914	64th	54.25	43.91	42.55	42.74	11.70	1.17
1916	65th	49.43	49.66	46.07	47.96	3.36	1.70
1918	66th	43.68	55.86	43.61	51.77	0.07	4.09
1920	67th	30.11	69.43	35.85	58.27	−5.74	11.16
1922	68th	47.59	51.72	44.40	52.10	3.19	−0.38
1924	69th	42.07	56.78	40.02	55.89	2.05	0.89
1926	70th	44.83	54.48	40.55	56.92	4.28	−2.44
1928	71st	37.93	61.84	41.57	56.63	−3.64	5.21
1930	72d	49.65	49.89	44.71	52.63	4.94	−2.74
1932	73d	71.95	26.90	54.01	41.91	17.94	−15.01
1934	74th	74.02	23.68	54.08	40.85	19.94	−17.17
1936	75th	77.01	20.46	56.28	39.60	20.73	−19.14
1938	76th	60.23	39.08	49.62	46.98	10.61	−7.90
1940	77th	61.38	37.47	52.01	45.75	9.37	−8.28
1942	78th	51.03	48.28	47.15	50.77	3.88	−2.49
1944	79th	55.63	43.91	52.04	47.00	3.59	−3.09
1946	80th	43.22	56.55	45.09	53.57	−1.87	2.98
1948	81st	60.46	39.31	47.99	45.09	12.47	−5.78
1950	82d	54.02	45.75	49.61	49.03	4.41	−3.28
1952	83d	48.97	50.80	50.12	48.96	−1.15	1.84
1954	84th	53.33	46.67	52.81	46.72	0.52	−0.05
1956	85th	53.79	46.21	51.50	48.26	2.29	−2.05
1958–1959	86th	64.91	35.09	56.23	43.44	8.68	−8.35
1960	87th	60.18	39.82	54.73	44.86	5.45	−5.04
1962	88th	59.54	40.46	51.73	47.89	7.81	−7.43

Table 5-6 *(Continued)*

Election	Congress	Democratic % of Total Seats	Republican % of Total Seats	Democratic % of Total Votes	Republican % of Total Votes	Difference Dem. Seats to Dem. Votes	Difference Rep. Seats to Rep. Votes
1964	89th	67.82	32.18	57.35	42.16	10.47	−9.98
1966	90th	57.01	42.99	50.85	48.29	6.16	−5.30
1968	91st	55.86	44.14	50.30	48.56	5.56	−4.42
1970	92d	58.62	41.38	53.65	44.89	4.97	−3.51
1972	93d	55.86	44.14	52.16	46.46	3.70	−2.32
1974	94th	66.90	33.10	57.64	40.50	9.26	−7.40
1976	95th	67.13	32.87	56.17	42.07	10.96	−9.20
1978	96th	63.68	36.32	53.46	45.06	10.22	−8.74
1980	97th	55.86	44.14	50.03	48.26	5.83	−4.12
1982	98th	61.84	38.16	55.06	43.36	6.78	−5.20
1984	99th	58.16	41.84	52.05	47.07	6.11	−5.23
1986	100th	59.31	40.69	54.42	44.64	4.89	−3.95
1988	101st	59.77	40.23	53.59	45.23	6.18	−5.00
1990	102d	61.61	38.16	52.91	44.92	8.70	−6.76
1992	103d	59.31	40.46	51.14	45.22	8.17	−4.76
1994	104th	47.36	52.41	45.64	52.15	1.72	0.26
1996	105th	47.59	51.95	48.90	48.35	−1.31	3.60
1998	106th	48.51	51.26	47.80	48.99	0.71	2.27

Notes: Vote results in columns 5 and 6 are taken from Table 5-4; seat allocations in columns 3 and 4 are derived from Table 5-3. Odd-numbered year House elections were largely not held in the states in the post-1880 period. For information on party affiliations, see notes to Table 5-3 and also Appendix A. This table starts with the 4th Congress (1794–1795) since political parties were neither formally established nor organized as such in the House prior to that date.

Sources: Data from Tables 5-3 and 5-4.

Table 5-7 Votes in House Elections, by Region, 1788–1998

Year/Region[1]	Regional Raw Vote				Regional Percent			Democratic % of Two-Party Vote
	Democratic	Republican	Other	Total	Democratic	Republican	Other	
1788–1789 NEng	0	0	13,883	13,883	0.00	0.00	100.00	—
1788–1789 South	0	0	2,878	2,878	0.00	0.00	100.00	—
1788–1789 MAtl	7,417	8,707	15,870	31,994	23.18	27.21	49.60	46.00
1788–1789 BdrS	2,731	5,154	0	7,885	34.64	65.36	0.00	34.64
1788–1789 MidW	—	—	—	—	—	—	—	—
1788–1789 West	—	—	—	—	—	—	—	—
1790–1791 NEng	0	0	20,789	20,789	0.00	0.00	100.00	—
1790–1791 South	0	0	1,954	1,954	0.00	0.00	100.00	—
1790–1791 MAtl	3,132	7,154	6,834	17,120	18.29	41.79	39.92	30.45
1790–1791 BdrS	0	0	17,173	17,173	0.00	0.00	100.0	—
1790–1791 MidW	—	—	—	—	—	—	—	—
1790–1791 West	—	—	—	—	—	—	—	—
1792–1793 NEng	0	0	10,468	10,468	0.00	0.00	100.00	—
1792–1793 South	0	0	5,488	5,488	0.00	0.00	100.00	—
1792–1793 MAtl	28,399	30,948	11,706	71,053	39.97	43.56	16.48	47.85
1792–1793 BdrS	6,696	10,014	23	16,733	40.02	59.85	0.14	40.07
1792–1793 MidW	—	—	—	—	—	—	—	—
1792–1793 West	—	—	—	—	—	—	—	—
1794–1795 NEng	13,918	19,849	664	34,431	40.42	57.65	1.93	41.22
1794–1795 South	1,487	1,150	1,143	3,780	39.34	30.42	30.24	56.39
1794–1795 MAtl	13,800	20,039	3,244	37,083	37.21	54.04	8.75	40.78
1794–1795 BdrS	6,533	9,533	0	16,066	40.66	59.34	0.00	40.66
1794–1795 MidW	—	—	—	—	—	—	—	—
1794–1795 West	—	—	—	—	—	—	—	—
1796–1797 NEng	9,275	27,239	2,093	38,607	24.02	70.55	5.42	25.40
1796–1797 South	10,818	8,539	1,757	21,114	51.24	40.44	8.32	55.89
1796–1797 MAtl	15,894	26,084	445	42,423	37.47	61.49	1.05	37.86
1796–1797 BdrS	4,734	7,826	0	12,560	37.69	62.31	0.00	37.69
1796–1797 MidW	—	—	—	—	—	—	—	—
1796–1797 West	—	—	—	—	—	—	—	—
1798–1799 NEng	11,132	34,938	3,773	49,843	22.33	70.10	7.57	24.16
1798–1799 South	3,111	4,055	0	7,166	43.41	56.59	0.00	43.41
1798–1799 MAtl	53,162	60,440	9	113,611	46.79	53.20	0.01	46.80
1798–1799 BdrS	—	—	—	—	—	—	—	—
1798–1799 MidW	—	—	—	—	—	—	—	—
1798–1799 West	—	—	—	—	—	—	—	—
1800–1801 NEng	26,353	33,817	2,943	63,113	41.76	53.58	4.66	43.80
1800–1801 South	17,854	0	0	17,854	100.00	0.00	0.00	100.00
1800–1801 MAtl	40,108	40,252	189	80,549	49.79	49.97	0.23	49.91
1800–1801 BdrS	27,396	5,631	3,752	36,779	74.49	15.31	10.20	82.95
1800–1801 MidW	—	—	—	—	—	—	—	—
1800–1801 West	—	—	—	—	—	—	—	—
1802–1803 NEng	25,546	39,680	1,659	66,885	38.19	59.33	2.48	39.17
1802–1803 South	22,047	4,863	0	26,910	81.93	18.07	0.00	81.93
1802–1803 MAtl	43,274	21,626	1,382	66,282	65.29	32.63	2.09	66.68
1802–1803 BdrS	—	—	—	—	—	—	—	—
1802–1803 MidW	5,531	1,960	0	7,491	73.84	26.16	0.00	73.84
1802–1803 West	—	—	—	—	—	—	—	—
1804–1805 NEng	47,875	52,687	880	101,442	47.19	51.94	0.87	47.61
1804–1805 South	25,249	0	0	25,249	100.00	0.00	0.00	100.00
1804–1805 MAtl	61,200	29,919	396	91,515	66.87	32.69	0.43	67.16
1804–1805 BdrS	12,778	4,514	60	17,352	73.64	26.01	0.35	73.90
1804–1805 MidW	4,101	1,718	0	5,819	70.48	29.52	0.00	70.48
1804–1805 West	—	—	—	—	—	—	—	—
1806–1807 NEng	27,618	23,468	1,123	52,209	52.90	44.95	2.15	54.06
1806–1807 South	22,799	2,993	0	25,792	88.40	11.60	0.00	88.40
1806–1807 MAtl	50,261	31,302	3,283	84,846	59.24	36.89	3.87	61.62
1806–1807 BdrS	22,243	8,240	353	30,836	72.13	26.72	1.14	72.97
1806–1807 MidW	6,735	2,364	0	9,099	74.02	25.98	0.00	74.02
1806–1807 West	—	—	—	—	—	—	—	—
1808–1809 NEng	47,611	54,204	79	101,894	46.73	53.20	0.08	46.76
1808–1809 South	12,805	4,838	6,240	23,883	53.62	20.26	26.13	72.58
1808–1809 MAtl	128,912	102,364	1,224	232,500	55.45	44.03	0.53	55.74
1808–1809 BdrS	20,242	16,209	0	36,451	55.53	44.47	0.00	55.53
1808–1809 MidW	10,309	4,485	0	14,794	69.68	30.32	0.00	69.68
1808–1809 West	—	—	—	—	—	—	—	—
1810–1811 NEng	48,725	51,942	1,966	102,633	47.47	50.61	1.92	48.40
1810–1811 South	32,368	2,591	5,160	40,119	80.68	6.46	12.86	92.59
1810–1811 MAtl	122,853	69,237	2,961	195,051	62.99	35.50	1.52	63.96
1810–1811 BdrS	13,932	4,753	46	18,731	74.38	25.38	0.25	74.56
1810–1811 MidW	—	—	—	—	—	—	—	—
1810–1811 West	—	—	—	—	—	—	—	—
1812–1813 NEng	62,338	91,714	492	154,544	40.34	59.34	0.32	40.47
1812–1813 South	12,761	2,699	1,592	17,052	74.84	15.83	9.34	82.54
1812–1813 MAtl	112,264	105,675	1,119	219,058	51.25	48.24	0.51	51.51
1812–1813 BdrS	21,090	13,074	0	34,164	61.73	38.27	0.00	61.73
1812–1813 MidW	14,856	4,883	3,205	22,944	64.75	21.28	13.97	75.26
1812–1813 West	—	—	—	—	—	—	—	—
1814–1815 NEng	37,469	57,190	107	94,766	39.54	60.34	0.11	39.58
1814–1815 South	19,073	242	29	19,344	98.60	1.25	0.15	98.75
1814–1815 MAtl	79,543	72,133	348	152,024	52.32	47.45	0.23	52.44
1814–1815 BdrS	11,995	20,212	0	32,207	37.24	62.76	0.00	37.24
1814–1815 MidW	—	—	—	—	—	—	—	—
1814–1815 West	—	—	—	—	—	—	—	—

Table 5-7 (Continued)

Year/Region[1]	Regional Raw Vote				Regional Percent			Democratic % of Two-Party Vote
	Democratic	Republican	Other	Total	Democratic	Republican	Other	
1816–1817 NEng	51,171	63,225	1,563	115,959	44.13	54.52	1.35	44.73
1816–1817 South	41,064	0	23,981	65,045	63.13	0.00	36.87	100.00
1816–1817 MAtl	77,482	59,105	350	136,937	56.58	43.16	0.26	56.73
1816–1817 BdrS	—	—	—	—	—	—	—	—
1816–1817 MidW	10,853	0	5,407	16,260	66.75	0.00	33.25	100.00
1816–1817 West	—							
1818–1819 NEng	50,836	33,032	4,416	88,284	57.58	37.42	5.00	60.61
1818–1819 South	44,069	0	29,118	73,187	60.21	0.00	39.79	100.00
1818–1819 MAtl	77,591	22,985	0	100,576	77.15	22.85	0.00	77.15
1818–1819 BdrS	—	—	—	—	—	—	—	—
1818–1819 MidW	38,574	5,819	576	44,969	85.78	12.94	1.28	86.89
1818–1819 West	—							
1820–1821 NEng	47,798	25,943	8,911	82,652	57.83	31.39	10.78	64.82
1820–1821 South	26,081	0	11,115	37,196	70.12	0.00	29.88	100.00
1820–1821 MAtl	233,883	66,791	1,503	302,177	77.40	22.10	0.50	77.79
1820–1821 BdrS	—	—	—	—	—	—	—	—
1820–1821 MidW	21,653	0	3,981	25,634	84.47	0.00	15.53	100.00
1820–1821 West	—							
1822–1823 NEng	50,597	12,734	13,353	76,684	65.98	16.61	17.41	79.89
1822–1823 South	31,735	1,167	23,944	56,846	55.83	2.05	42.12	96.45
1822–1823 MAtl	202,042	46,351	771	249,164	81.09	18.60	0.31	81.34
1822–1823 BdrS	21,481	7,181	846	29,508	72.80	24.34	2.87	74.95
1822–1823 MidW	4,764	0	13,717	18,481	25.78	0.00	74.22	100.00
1822–1823 West	—							
1824–1825 NEng	61,282	20,965	20,762	103,009	59.49	20.35	20.16	74.51
1824–1825 South	16,504	0	0	16,504	100.00	0.00	0.00	100.00
1824–1825 MAtl	205,343	3,387	2,321	211,051	97.30	1.60	1.10	98.38
1824–1825 BdrS	25,153	15,460	3,217	43,830	57.39	35.27	7.34	61.93
1824–1825 MidW	9,559	0	88,869	98,428	9.71	0.00	90.29	100.00
1824–1825 West	—							
1826–1827 NEng	28,808	50,898	30,740	110,446	26.08	46.08	27.83	36.14
1826–1827 South	24,021	1,451	17,859	43,331	55.44	3.35	41.22	94.30
1826–1827 MAtl	107,036	105,982	2,014	215,032	49.78	49.29	0.94	50.25
1826–1827 BdrS	37,931	25,658	50,947	114,536	33.12	22.40	44.48	59.65
1826–1827 MidW	35,323	71,036	33,946	140,305	25.18	50.63	24.19	33.21
1826–1827 West	—							
1828–1829 NEng	42,682	70,747	10,478	123,907	34.45	57.10	8.46	37.63
1828–1829 South	67,991	7,837	10,763	86,591	78.52	9.05	12.43	89.66
1828–1829 MAtl	167,437	135,051	34,232	336,720	49.73	40.11	10.17	55.35
1828–1829 BdrS	20,788	18,362	271	39,421	52.73	46.58	0.69	53.10
1828–1829 MidW	18,315	11,285	0	29,600	61.88	38.13	0.00	61.88
1828–1829 West	—							
1830–1831 NEng	66,143	96,311	13,418	175,872	37.61	54.76	7.63	40.71
1830–1831 South	116,074	19,715	12,188	147,977	78.44	13.32	8.24	85.48
1830–1831 MAtl	211,320	97,344	122,502	431,166	49.01	22.58	28.41	68.46
1830–1831 BdrS	17,424	22,757	266	40,447	43.08	56.26	0.66	43.36
1830–1831 MidW	94,815	75,093	18,125	188,033	50.42	39.94	9.64	55.80
1830–1831 West	—							
1832–1833 NEng	72,109	70,234	27,700	170,043	42.41	41.30	16.29	50.66
1832–1833 South	94,880	34,817	24,893	154,590	61.38	22.52	16.10	73.16
1832–1833 MAtl	285,700	98,640	168,177	552,517	51.71	17.85	30.44	74.34
1832–1833 BdrS	23,971	23,591	0	47,562	50.40	49.60	0.00	50.40
1832–1833 MidW	119,111	69,964	45,329	234,404	50.81	29.85	19.34	63.00
1832–1833 West	—							
1834–1835 NEng	116,766	124,777	20,030	261,573	44.64	47.70	7.66	48.34
1834–1835 South	76,058	90,412	8,934	175,404	43.36	51.55	5.09	45.69
1834–1835 MAtl	314,588	254,173	28,758	597,519	52.65	42.54	4.81	55.31
1834–1835 BdrS	—	—	—	—	—	—	—	—
1834–1835 MidW	142,727	92,440	32,825	267,992	53.26	34.49	12.25	60.69
1834–1835 West	—							
1836–1837 NEng	119,978	110,801	6,963	237,742	50.47	46.61	2.93	51.99
1836–1837 South	81,405	107,913	1,268	190,586	42.71	56.62	0.67	43.00
1836–1837 MAtl	281,594	217,227	33,228	532,049	52.93	40.83	6.25	56.45
1836–1837 BdrS	16,071	23,097	208	39,376	40.81	58.66	0.53	41.03
1836–1837 MidW	169,614	182,153	525	352,292	48.15	51.71	0.15	48.22
1836–1837 West	—							
1838–1839 NEng	157,476	170,870	4,220	332,566	47.35	51.38	1.27	47.96
1838–1839 South	110,122	115,050	422	225,594	48.81	51.00	0.19	48.91
1838–1839 MAtl	344,963	350,564	0	695,527	49.60	50.40	0.00	49.60
1838–1839 BdrS	27,553	24,196	2,385	54,134	50.90	44.70	4.41	53.24
1838–1839 MidW	228,737	209,923	0	438,660	52.14	47.86	0.00	52.14
1838–1839 West	—							
1840–1841 NEng	168,888	199,434	2,345	370,667	45.56	53.80	0.63	45.85
1840–1841 South	122,929	123,191	939	247,059	49.76	49.86	0.38	49.95
1840–1841 MAtl	380,488	388,596	1,918	771,002	49.35	50.40	0.25	49.47
1840–1841 BdrS	25,100	52,204	3,418	80,722	31.09	64.67	4.23	32.47
1840–1841 MidW	260,075	266,187	783	527,045	49.35	50.51	0.15	49.42
1840–1841 West	—							
1842–1843 NEng	161,272	144,429	32,540	338,241	47.68	42.70	9.62	52.75
1842–1843 South	166,690	132,311	1,686	300,687	55.44	44.00	0.56	55.75
1842–1843 MAtl	305,480	278,375	17,050	600,905	50.84	46.33	2.84	52.32
1842–1843 BdrS	42,623	52,268	7,657	102,548	41.56	50.97	7.47	44.92
1842–1843 MidW	264,496	217,004	15,511	497,011	53.22	43.66	3.12	54.93
1842–1843 West	—	—	—	—	—	—	—	—

(Table continues)

Table 5-7 *(Continued)*

| | Regional Raw Vote | | | | Regional Percent | | | Democratic % of |
Year/Region[1]	Democratic	Republican	Other	Total	Democratic	Republican	Other	Two-Party Vote
1844–1845 NEng	166,288	187,597	42,583	396,468	41.94	47.32	10.74	46.99
1844–1845 South	182,940	162,115	3,730	348,785	52.45	46.48	1.07	53.02
1844–1845 MAtl	422,088	434,201	22,843	879,132	48.01	49.39	2.60	49.29
1844–1845 BdrS	107,806	110,603	1,542	219,951	49.01	50.29	0.70	49.36
1844–1845 MidW	335,171	295,046	16,647	646,864	51.81	45.61	2.57	53.18
1844–1845 West	—	—	—	—	—	—	—	—
1846–1847 NEng	144,048	163,435	43,369	350,852	41.06	46.58	12.36	46.85
1846–1847 South	321,330	135,746	4,337	461,413	69.64	29.42	0.94	70.30
1846–1847 MAtl	308,142	314,036	50,394	672,572	45.82	46.69	7.49	49.53
1846–1847 BdrS	53,949	64,553	3,143	121,645	44.35	53.07	2.58	45.53
1846–1847 MidW	328,218	282,342	18,221	628,781	52.20	44.90	2.90	53.76
1846–1847 West	—	—	—	—	—	—	—	—
1848–1849 NEng	151,821	172,891	47,825	372,537	40.75	46.41	12.84	46.76
1848–1849 South	208,703	182,403	9,998	401,104	52.03	45.48	2.49	53.36
1848–1849 MAtl	316,498	428,922	129,973	875,393	36.15	49.00	14.85	42.46
1848–1849 BdrS	67,895	87,947	5,137	160,979	42.18	54.63	3.19	43.57
1848–1849 MidW	387,159	311,605	41,605	740,369	52.29	42.09	5.62	55.41
1848–1849 West	5,300	0	5,451	10,751	49.30	0.00	50.70	100.00
1850–1851 NEng	159,227	173,358	33,422	366,007	43.50	47.36	9.13	47.88
1850–1851 South	50,983	31,729	157,534	240,246	21.22	13.21	65.57	61.64
1850–1851 MAtl	397,596	382,303	10,990	790,889	50.27	48.34	1.39	50.98
1850–1851 BdrS	70,395	81,788	2,894	155,077	45.39	52.74	1.87	46.26
1850–1851 MidW	380,053	305,511	27,680	713,244	53.29	42.83	3.88	55.44
1850–1851 West	24,473	21,357	0	45,830	53.40	46.60	0.00	53.40
1852–1853 NEng	172,190	170,668	44,760	387,618	44.42	44.03	11.55	50.22
1852–1853 South	178,257	112,753	5,267	296,277	60.17	38.06	1.78	61.25
1852–1853 MAtl	474,483	431,025	36,982	942,490	50.34	45.73	3.92	52.40
1852–1853 BdrS	84,295	84,827	20,812	189,934	44.38	44.66	10.96	49.84
1852–1853 MidW	453,858	375,450	45,747	875,055	51.87	42.91	5.23	54.73
1852–1853 West	39,736	34,358	0	74,094	53.63	46.37	0.00	53.63
1854–1855 NEng	112,899	110,609	154,313	377,821	29.88	29.28	40.84	50.51
1854–1855 South	315,284	13,162	251,399	579,845	54.37	2.27	43.36	95.99
1854–1855 MAtl	436,179	419,415	48,770	904,364	48.23	46.38	5.39	50.98
1854–1855 BdrS	105,631	0	111,631	217,262	48.62	0.00	51.38	100.00
1854–1855 MidW	405,081	213,094	293,777	911,952	44.42	23.37	32.21	65.53
1854–1855 West	46,825	34,741	0	81,566	57.41	42.59	0.00	57.41
1856–1857 NEng	169,548	276,778	18,741	465,067	36.46	59.51	4.03	37.99
1856–1857 South	361,888	0	193,552	555,440	65.15	0.00	34.85	100.00
1856–1857 MAtl	470,493	518,642	135,705	1,124,840	41.83	46.11	12.06	47.57
1856–1857 BdrS	110,933	0	104,776	215,709	51.43	0.00	48.57	100.00
1856–1857 MidW	607,519	603,896	69,133	1,280,548	47.44	47.16	5.40	50.15
1856–1857 West	50,892	21,985	35,325	108,202	47.03	20.32	32.65	69.83
1858–1859 NEng	176,971	244,300	7,729	429,000	41.25	56.95	1.80	42.01
1858–1859 South	349,973	33,073	123,864	506,910	69.04	6.52	24.44	91.37
1858–1859 MAtl	456,767	320,647	240,842	1,018,256	44.86	31.49	23.65	58.75
1858–1859 BdrS	105,067	0	111,483	216,550	48.52	0.00	51.48	100.00
1858–1859 MidW	666,812	622,357	35,751	1,324,920	50.33	46.97	2.70	51.72
1858–1859 West	63,154	47,087	0	110,241	57.29	42.71	0.00	57.29
1860–1861 NEng	186,286	303,942	15,469	505,697	36.84	60.10	3.06	38.00
1860–1861 South	40,780	0	32,331	73,111	55.78	0.00	44.22	100.00
1860–1861 MAtl	593,489	680,467	15,400	1,289,356	46.03	52.78	1.19	46.59
1860–1861 BdrS	0	143,186	54,123	197,309	0.00	72.57	27.43	0.00
1860–1861 MidW	758,489	808,625	65,141	1,632,255	46.47	49.54	3.99	48.40
1860–1861 West	71,391	51,651	20	123,062	58.01	41.97	0.02	58.02
1862–1863 NEng	130,409	244,994	47,436	422,839	30.84	57.94	11.22	34.74
1862–1863 South	—	—	—	—	—	—	—	—
1862–1863 MAtl	600,336	552,976	3,572	1,156,884	51.89	47.80	0.31	52.05
1862–1863 BdrS	94,347	57,275	2,556	154,178	61.19	37.15	1.66	62.23
1862–1863 MidW	674,275	683,258	2,866	1,360,399	49.56	50.22	0.21	49.67
1862–1863 West	47,548	71,949	0	119,497	39.79	60.21	0.00	39.79
1864–1865 NEng	169,321	308,493	553	478,367	35.40	64.49	0.12	35.44
1864–1865 South	0	24,043	34,579	58,632	0.00	41.01	58.99	0.00
1864–1865 MAtl	683,004	675,996	311	1,359,311	50.25	49.73	0.02	50.26
1864–1865 BdrS	31,922	55,755	118,256	205,933	15.50	27.07	57.42	36.41
1864–1865 MidW	703,601	948,103	0	1,651,704	42.60	57.40	0.00	42.60
1864–1865 West	57,868	84,265	0	142,133	40.71	59.29	0.00	40.71
1866–1867 NEng	160,691	280,754	564	442,009	36.35	63.52	0.13	36.40
1866–1867 South	0	73,617	22,506	96,123	0.00	76.59	23.41	0.00
1866–1867 MAtl	689,596	767,997	217	1,457,810	47.30	52.68	0.01	47.31
1866–1867 BdrS	136,827	78,063	6,452	221,342	61.82	35.27	2.91	63.67
1866–1867 MidW	760,283	1,004,879	8,630	1,773,792	42.86	56.65	0.49	43.07
1866–1867 West	62,350	59,845	0	122,195	51.03	48.97	0.00	51.03
1868–1869 NEng	211,419	342,495	0	553,914	38.17	61.83	0.00	38.17
1868–1869 South	293,431	604,408	128,480	1,026,319	28.59	58.89	12.52	32.68
1868–1869 MAtl	841,587	829,015	2,583	1,673,185	50.30	49.55	0.15	50.38
1868–1869 BdrS	195,744	92,931	293	288,968	67.74	32.16	0.10	67.81
1868–1869 MidW	993,297	1,198,842	149	2,192,288	45.31	54.68	0.01	45.31
1868–1869 West	69,656	80,290	0	149,946	46.45	53.55	0.00	46.45
1870–1871 NEng	188,319	255,673	10,665	454,657	41.42	56.23	2.35	42.41
1870–1871 South	429,568	419,667	1,739	850,974	50.48	49.32	0.20	50.58
1870–1871 MAtl	739,180	730,098	5,477	1,474,755	50.12	49.51	0.37	50.31
1870–1871 BdrS	195,405	142,047	0	337,452	57.91	42.09	0.00	57.91
1870–1871 MidW	853,585	964,037	59,821	1,877,443	45.47	51.35	3.19	46.96
1870–1871 West	75,474	80,275	0	155,749	48.46	51.54	0.00	48.46

Table 5-7 (Continued)

Year/Region[1]	Regional Raw Vote				Regional Percent			Democratic % of Two-Party Vote
	Democratic	Republican	Other	Total	Democratic	Republican	Other	
1872–1873 NEng	202,441	333,178	5,499	541,118	37.41	61.57	1.02	37.80
1872–1873 South	535,885	752,444	169,561	1,457,890	36.76	51.61	11.63	41.60
1872–1873 MAtl	788,041	892,282	919	1,681,242	46.87	53.07	0.05	46.90
1872–1873 BdrS	198,455	135,960	6,379	340,794	58.23	39.90	1.87	59.34
1872–1873 MidW	1,136,192	1,308,458	2,553	2,447,203	46.43	53.47	0.10	46.48
1872–1873 West	66,907	69,551	0	136,458	49.03	50.97	0.00	49.03
1874–1875 NEng	214,802	265,649	24,316	504,767	42.55	52.63	4.82	44.71
1874–1875 South	789,073	629,539	19,750	1,438,362	54.86	43.77	1.37	55.62
1874–1875 MAtl	804,897	698,754	32,095	1,535,746	52.41	45.50	2.09	53.53
1874–1875 BdrS	187,975	109,945	15,086	313,006	60.05	35.13	4.82	63.10
1874–1875 MidW	1,026,214	1,055,007	168,446	2,249,667	45.62	46.90	7.49	49.31
1874–1875 West	76,957	58,369	30,146	165,472	46.51	35.27	18.22	56.87
1876–1877 NEng	298,691	374,081	1,500	674,272	44.30	55.48	0.22	44.40
1876–1877 South	1,123,732	672,052	1,523	1,797,307	62.52	37.39	0.08	62.58
1876–1877 MAtl	1,017,372	960,243	8,961	1,986,576	51.21	48.34	0.45	51.44
1876–1877 BdrS	304,784	209,521	709	515,014	59.18	40.68	0.14	59.26
1876–1877 MidW	1,467,140	1,569,435	77,388	3,113,963	47.11	50.40	2.49	48.32
1876–1877 West	110,381	120,069	0	230,450	47.90	52.10	0.00	47.90
1878–1879 NEng	223,784	334,590	71,693	630,067	35.52	53.10	11.38	40.08
1878–1879 South	872,225	259,022	152,192	1,283,439	67.96	20.18	11.86	77.10
1878–1879 MAtl	734,149	796,346	202,845	1,733,340	42.35	45.94	11.70	47.97
1878–1879 BdrS	223,178	127,824	25,751	376,753	59.24	33.93	6.83	63.58
1878–1879 MidW	1,174,102	1,230,504	396,905	2,801,511	41.91	43.92	14.17	48.83
1878–1879 West	85,709	114,285	37,723	237,717	36.06	48.08	15.87	42.86
1880 NEng	319,639	413,057	8,554	741,250	43.12	55.72	1.15	43.63
1880 South	1,082,432	503,709	161,466	1,747,607	61.94	28.82	9.24	68.24
1880 MAtl	1,057,715	1,124,933	38,748	2,221,396	47.61	50.64	1.74	48.46
1880 BdrS	296,163	227,069	16,837	540,069	54.84	42.04	3.12	56.60
1880 MidW	1,552,634	1,817,076	179,833	3,549,543	43.74	51.19	5.07	46.08
1880 West	131,656	135,021	6,613	273,290	48.17	49.41	2.42	49.37
1882 NEng	291,931	340,468	11,486	643,885	45.34	52.88	1.78	46.16
1882 South	873,535	350,060	279,212	1,502,807	58.13	23.29	18.58	71.39
1882 MAtl	973,426	829,996	99,373	1,902,795	51.16	43.62	5.22	53.98
1882 BdrS	238,273	194,827	6,122	439,222	54.25	44.36	1.39	55.02
1882 MidW	1,542,340	1,487,582	194,849	3,224,771	47.83	46.13	6.04	50.90
1882 West	143,211	133,473	5,110	281,794	50.82	47.37	1.81	51.76
1884 NEng	307,080	402,665	40,463	750,208	40.93	53.67	5.39	43.27
1884 South	1,189,110	660,015	15,566	1,864,691	63.77	35.40	0.83	64.31
1884 MAtl	1,122,104	1,140,920	56,074	2,319,098	48.39	49.20	2.42	49.58
1884 BdrS	319,305	247,348	1,837	568,490	56.17	43.51	0.32	56.35
1884 MidW	1,929,496	2,061,706	73,787	4,064,989	47.47	50.72	1.82	48.34
1884 West	149,328	169,514	5,391	324,233	46.06	52.28	1.66	46.83
1886 NEng	283,945	326,242	27,646	637,833	44.52	51.15	4.33	46.53
1886 South	873,184	390,831	91,416	1,355,431	64.42	28.83	6.74	69.08
1886 MAtl	932,557	958,847	110,297	2,001,701	46.59	47.90	5.51	49.31
1886 BdrS	273,520	199,710	12,925	486,155	56.26	41.08	2.66	57.80
1886 MidW	1,720,285	1,876,415	181,641	3,778,341	45.53	49.66	4.81	47.83
1886 West	149,530	154,371	14,685	318,586	46.94	48.46	4.61	49.20
1888–1889 NEng	366,546	450,128	23,090	839,764	43.65	53.60	2.75	44.88
1888–1889 South	1,283,761	667,923	102,131	2,053,815	62.51	32.52	4.97	65.78
1888–1889 MAtl	1,188,534	1,325,524	67,579	2,581,637	46.04	51.34	2.62	47.28
1888–1889 BdrS	363,616	328,186	10,149	701,951	51.80	46.75	1.45	52.56
1888–1889 MidW	2,149,206	2,426,256	198,493	4,773,955	45.02	50.82	4.16	46.97
1888–1889 West	227,645	270,958	12,006	510,609	44.58	53.07	2.35	45.66
1890 NEng	329,421	353,850	18,701	701,972	46.93	50.41	2.66	48.21
1890 South	1,082,432	419,832	48,623	1,550,886	69.79	27.07	3.14	72.05
1890 MAtl	1,087,339	1,026,731	62,764	2,176,834	49.95	47.17	2.88	51.43
1890 BdrS	303,033	215,454	7,602	526,089	57.60	40.95	1.45	58.45
1890 MidW	1,987,341	1,915,573	382,715	4,285,629	46.37	44.70	8.93	50.92
1890 West	239,878	281,463	19,627	540,968	44.34	52.03	3.63	46.01
1892 NEng	394,934	432,253	27,225	854,412	46.22	50.59	3.19	47.74
1892 South	1,351,349	339,669	389,206	2,080,224	64.96	16.33	18.71	79.91
1892 MAtl	1,267,685	1,293,849	100,237	2,661,771	47.63	48.61	3.77	49.49
1892 BdrS	374,098	294,260	35,419	703,777	53.16	41.81	5.03	55.97
1892 MidW	2,298,856	2,297,020	364,944	4,960,820	46.34	46.30	7.36	50.02
1892 West	260,049	245,455	81,501	587,005	44.30	41.81	13.88	51.44
1894–1895 NEng	278,744	454,684	31,931	765,359	36.42	59.41	4.17	38.01
1894–1895 South	970,568	391,821	414,888	1,777,277	54.61	22.05	23.34	71.24
1894–1895 MAtl	966,713	1,418,580	110,987	2,496,280	38.73	56.83	4.45	40.53
1894–1895 BdrS	333,092	347,137	34,215	714,444	46.62	48.59	4.79	48.97
1894–1895 MidW	1,667,270	2,497,458	591,637	4,756,365	35.05	52.51	12.44	40.03
1894–1895 West	222,128	344,670	187,332	754,130	29.45	45.70	24.84	39.19
1896 NEng	278,115	581,639	15,388	875,142	31.78	66.46	1.76	32.35
1896 South	1,324,384	711,989	225,272	2,261,645	58.56	31.48	9.96	65.04
1896 MAtl	1,112,761	1,736,416	84,436	2,933,613	37.93	59.19	2.88	39.06
1896 BdrS	425,352	433,544	25,726	884,622	48.08	49.01	2.91	49.52
1896 MidW	2,703,429	3,109,539	70,666	5,883,634	45.95	52.85	1.20	46.51
1896 West	374,623	320,807	122,943	818,373	45.78	39.20	15.02	53.87
1898 NEng	281,415	416,557	18,923	716,895	39.25	58.11	2.64	40.32
1898 South	895,428	388,406	117,234	1,401,068	63.91	27.72	8.37	69.75
1898 MAtl	1,141,570	1,374,518	114,974	2,631,062	43.39	52.24	4.37	45.37
1898 BdrS	325,199	326,052	13,372	664,623	48.93	49.06	2.01	49.93
1898 MidW	2,174,774	2,509,495	91,536	4,775,805	45.54	52.55	1.92	46.43
1898 West	331,333	365,546	67,413	764,292	43.35	47.83	8.82	47.55

(Table continues)

Table 5-7 (Continued)

Year/Region[1]	Regional Raw Vote				Regional Percent			Democratic % of Two-Party Vote
	Democratic	Republican	Other	Total	Democratic	Republican	Other	
1900 NEng	337,253	528,386	32,237	897,876	37.56	58.85	3.59	38.96
1900 South	1,226,500	523,040	65,172	1,814,712	67.59	28.82	3.59	70.10
1900 MAtl	1,263,022	1,732,218	87,124	3,082,364	40.98	56.20	2.83	42.17
1900 BdrS	456,925	482,445	7,116	946,486	48.28	50.97	0.75	48.64
1900 MidW	2,701,507	3,218,456	105,845	6,025,808	44.83	53.41	1.76	45.63
1900 West	449,325	463,914	28,810	942,049	47.70	49.25	3.06	49.20
1902 NEng	335,888	447,310	52,293	835,491	40.20	53.54	6.26	42.89
1902 South	831,284	242,803	6,358	1,080,445	76.94	22.47	0.59	77.39
1902 MAtl	1,167,527	1,485,598	113,074	2,766,199	42.21	53.71	4.09	44.01
1902 BdrS	337,367	325,363	18,402	681,132	49.53	47.77	2.70	50.91
1902 MidW	2,041,899	2,512,047	172,024	4,725,970	43.21	53.15	3.64	44.84
1902 West	374,157	465,539	58,988	898,684	41.63	51.80	6.56	44.56
1904 NEng	355,860	553,565	37,754	947,179	37.57	58.44	3.99	39.13
1904 South	986,336	351,481	6,360	1,344,177	73.38	26.15	0.47	73.73
1904 MAtl	1,174,312	1,830,908	141,824	3,147,044	37.31	58.18	4.51	39.08
1904 BdrS	423,825	437,356	15,608	876,789	48.34	49.88	1.78	49.21
1904 MidW	2,069,501	3,391,963	302,426	5,763,890	35.90	58.85	5.25	37.89
1904 West	390,336	607,695	85,927	1,083,958	36.01	56.06	7.93	39.11
1906–1907 NEng	368,148	506,854	26,478	901,480	40.84	56.22	2.94	42.07
1906–1907 South	677,346	240,206	6,536	924,088	73.30	25.99	0.71	73.82
1906–1907 MAtl	1,156,835	1,453,561	195,600	2,805,996	41.23	51.80	6.97	44.32
1906–1907 BdrS	461,434	423,253	28,539	913,226	50.53	46.35	3.13	52.16
1906–1907 MidW	1,896,256	2,562,933	231,941	4,691,130	40.42	54.63	4.94	42.52
1906–1907 West	331,672	521,224	90,273	943,169	35.17	55.26	9.57	38.89
1908 NEng	362,083	571,144	42,896	976,123	37.09	58.51	4.39	38.80
1908 South	1,095,896	390,137	11,653	1,497,686	73.17	26.05	0.78	73.75
1908 MAtl	1,339,963	1,735,499	172,889	3,248,351	41.25	53.43	5.32	43.57
1908 BdrS	585,764	576,686	39,248	1,201,698	48.74	47.99	3.27	50.39
1908 MidW	2,694,084	3,295,528	283,816	6,273,428	42.94	52.53	4.52	44.98
1908 West	474,175	668,233	105,830	1,248,238	37.99	53.53	8.48	41.51
1910–1911 NEng	440,102	464,664	28,910	933,676	47.14	49.77	3.10	48.64
1910–1911 South	827,575	249,053	21,300	1,097,928	75.38	22.68	1.94	76.87
1910–1911 MAtl	1,254,444	1,338,862	244,803	2,838,109	44.20	47.17	8.63	48.37
1910–1911 BdrS	498,878	430,265	48,427	977,570	51.03	44.01	4.95	53.69
1910–1911 MidW	2,273,301	2,559,940	302,739	5,135,980	44.26	49.84	5.89	47.03
1910–1911 West	456,391	639,484	131,646	1,227,521	37.18	52.10	10.72	41.65
1912 NEng	423,405	418,573	164,786	1,006,764	42.06	41.58	16.37	50.29
1912 South	1,113,511	236,782	81,726	1,432,019	77.76	16.53	5.71	82.46
1912 MAtl	1,197,222	1,230,650	626,204	3,054,076	39.20	40.30	20.50	49.31
1912 BdrS	553,941	369,499	173,815	1,097,255	50.48	33.67	15.84	59.99
1912 MidW	2,376,261	2,092,110	1,447,562	5,915,933	40.17	35.36	24.47	53.18
1912 West	568,985	665,070	517,937	1,751,992	32.48	37.96	29.56	46.11
1914 NEng	412,072	490,545	87,670	990,287	41.61	49.54	8.85	45.65
1914 South	822,720	179,597	59,907	1,062,224	77.45	16.91	5.64	82.08
1914 MAtl	1,019,356	1,340,317	488,327	2,848,000	35.79	47.06	17.15	43.20
1914 BdrS	499,168	405,408	116,535	1,021,111	48.88	39.70	11.41	55.18
1914 MidW	2,342,506	2,518,108	736,517	5,597,131	41.85	44.99	13.16	48.19
1914 West	710,683	898,642	518,022	2,127,347	33.41	42.24	24.35	44.16
1916 NEng	462,529	601,577	40,014	1,104,120	41.89	54.48	3.62	43.47
1916 South	1,347,860	384,085	44,000	1,775,945	75.90	21.63	2.48	77.82
1916 MAtl	1,309,408	1,724,457	230,308	3,264,173	40.11	52.83	7.06	43.16
1916 BdrS	658,830	583,515	64,259	1,306,604	50.42	44.66	4.92	53.03
1916 MidW	2,991,392	3,583,786	338,448	6,913,626	43.27	51.84	4.90	45.50
1916 West	939,331	1,147,944	281,048	2,368,323	39.66	48.47	11.87	45.00
1918 NEng	360,310	498,525	17,219	876,054	41.13	56.91	1.97	41.95
1918 South	750,353	146,960	891	898,204	83.54	16.36	0.10	83.62
1918 MAtl	1,325,623	1,726,787	255,612	3,308,022	40.07	52.20	7.73	43.43
1918 BdrS	471,854	436,668	11,417	919,939	51.29	47.47	1.24	51.94
1918 MidW	2,032,905	2,901,863	204,415	5,139,183	39.56	56.47	3.98	41.20
1918 West	627,220	899,707	99,753	1,626,680	38.56	55.31	6.13	41.08
1920 NEng	621,820	1,247,906	42,829	1,912,555	32.51	65.25	2.24	33.26
1920 South	1,742,624	840,156	42,255	2,625,035	66.38	32.01	1.61	67.47
1920 MAtl	1,701,228	3,276,845	453,508	5,431,581	31.32	60.33	8.35	34.17
1920 BdrS	1,049,492	1,104,696	60,084	2,214,272	47.40	49.89	2.71	48.72
1920 MidW	3,380,946	6,917,399	676,491	10,974,836	30.81	63.03	6.16	32.83
1920 West	654,847	1,487,249	228,136	2,370,232	27.63	62.75	9.63	30.57
1922 NEng	740,774	928,492	7,226	1,676,492	44.19	55.38	0.43	44.38
1922 South	1,231,049	370,413	527	1,601,989	76.85	23.12	0.03	76.87
1922 MAtl	2,128,346	2,404,219	206,683	4,739,248	44.91	50.73	4.36	46.96
1922 BdrS	826,655	648,846	32,533	1,508,034	54.82	43.03	2.16	56.03
1922 MidW	3,439,336	4,964,013	355,663	8,759,012	39.27	56.67	4.06	40.93
1922 West	696,580	1,317,320	112,153	2,126,053	32.76	61.96	5.28	34.59
1924 NEng	808,006	1,333,467	17,725	2,159,198	37.42	61.76	0.82	37.73
1924 South	1,876,396	498,688	8,602	2,383,686	78.72	20.92	0.36	79.00
1924 MAtl	2,275,973	3,600,396	271,673	6,148,042	37.02	58.56	4.42	38.73
1924 BdrS	1,101,555	930,210	40,331	2,072,096	53.16	44.89	1.95	54.22
1924 MidW	3,833,415	7,058,872	575,648	11,467,935	33.43	61.55	5.02	35.19
1924 West	851,352	1,587,453	184,404	2,623,209	32.45	60.52	7.03	34.91
1926 NEng	685,209	1,080,182	2,854	1,768,245	38.75	61.09	0.16	38.81
1926 South	907,168	246,542	730	1,154,440	78.58	21.36	0.06	78.63
1926 MAtl	2,076,958	2,903,185	138,232	5,118,375	40.58	56.72	2.70	41.70
1926 BdrS	860,816	764,929	3,576	1,629,321	52.83	46.95	0.22	52.95
1926 MidW	3,008,488	4,999,396	314,803	8,322,687	36.15	60.07	3.78	37.57
1926 West	733,125	1,616,377	56,259	2,405,761	30.47	67.19	2.34	31.20

Table 5-7 *(Continued)*

Year/Region[1]	Regional Raw Vote				Regional Percent			Democratic % of Two-Party Vote
	Democratic	Republican	Other	Total	Democratic	Republican	Other	
1928 NEng	1,225,864	1,516,865	10,243	2,752,972	44.53	55.10	0.37	44.70
1928 South	2,306,635	747,073	1,798	3,055,506	75.49	24.45	0.06	75.54
1928 MAtl	3,504,397	5,078,452	176,270	8,759,119	40.01	57.98	2.01	40.83
1928 BdrS	1,227,172	1,402,003	4,985	2,634,160	46.59	53.22	0.19	46.68
1928 MidW	5,078,787	8,349,565	360,898	13,789,250	36.83	60.55	2.62	37.82
1928 West	873,645	2,275,228	62,078	3,210,951	27.21	70.86	1.93	27.74
1930 NEng	974,973	1,168,243	21,062	2,164,278	45.05	53.98	0.97	45.49
1930 South	1,445,760	420,154	2,518	1,868,432	77.38	22.49	0.13	77.48
1930 MAtl	2,563,994	3,341,103	217,237	6,122,334	41.88	54.57	3.55	43.42
1930 BdrS	1,118,414	883,519	7,271	2,009,204	55.66	43.97	0.36	55.87
1930 MidW	4,174,221	5,424,853	385,174	9,984,248	41.81	54.33	3.86	43.49
1930 West	810,401	1,813,906	28,037	2,652,344	30.55	68.39	1.06	30.88
1932 NEng	1,403,927	1,475,869	36,497	2,916,293	48.14	50.61	1.25	48.75
1932 South	3,031,264	564,212	103,572	3,699,048	81.95	15.25	2.80	84.31
1932 MAtl	4,249,033	4,093,105	430,679	8,772,817	48.43	46.66	4.91	50.93
1932 BdrS	1,735,713	1,055,005	11,581	2,802,299	61.94	37.65	0.41	62.20
1932 MidW	7,706,344	6,668,341	770,406	15,145,091	50.88	44.03	5.09	53.61
1932 West	2,141,025	1,869,775	179,714	4,190,514	51.09	44.62	4.29	53.38
1934 NEng	1,330,150	1,376,484	50,362	2,756,996	48.25	49.93	1.83	49.14
1934 South	1,784,153	303,374	23,751	2,111,278	84.51	14.37	1.12	85.47
1934 MAtl	4,292,229	3,350,264	325,082	7,967,575	53.87	42.05	4.08	56.16
1934 BdrS	1,221,474	821,613	32,316	2,075,403	58.85	39.59	1.56	59.79
1934 MidW	6,586,839	5,712,372	962,941	13,262,152	49.67	43.07	7.26	53.55
1934 West	2,242,826	1,621,614	242,140	4,106,580	54.62	39.49	5.90	58.04
1936 NEng	1,609,996	1,660,089	150,298	3,420,383	47.07	48.54	4.39	49.23
1936 South	3,293,839	575,435	10,325	3,879,599	84.90	14.83	0.27	85.13
1936 MAtl	6,232,879	4,625,025	291,802	11,149,706	55.90	41.48	2.62	57.40
1936 BdrS	1,832,245	1,107,132	19,477	2,958,854	61.92	37.42	0.66	62.33
1936 MidW	8,451,983	7,177,697	1,184,881	16,814,561	50.27	42.69	7.05	54.08
1936 West	2,775,402	1,879,888	118,185	4,773,475	58.14	39.38	2.48	59.62
1938 NEng	1,418,143	1,699,485	109,766	3,227,394	43.94	52.66	3.40	45.49
1938 South	1,654,950	271,067	33,235	1,959,252	84.47	13.84	1.70	85.93
1938 MAtl	4,885,910	4,871,136	177,402	9,934,448	49.18	49.03	1.79	50.08
1938 BdrS	1,255,344	827,719	6,023	2,089,086	60.09	39.62	0.29	60.26
1938 MidW	6,273,367	7,157,863	726,776	14,158,006	44.31	50.56	5.13	46.71
1938 West	2,439,689	2,144,791	175,802	4,760,282	51.25	45.06	3.69	53.22
1940 NEng	1,750,976	1,892,659	13,440	3,657,075	47.88	51.75	0.37	48.06
1940 South	3,726,944	498,276	30,834	4,256,054	87.57	11.71	0.72	88.21
1940 MAtl	6,133,365	5,708,143	38,539	11,880,047	51.63	48.05	0.32	51.80
1940 BdrS	1,894,104	1,179,473	4,912	3,078,489	61.53	38.31	0.16	61.63
1940 MidW	7,970,898	9,285,892	832,973	18,089,763	44.06	51.33	4.60	46.19
1940 West	2,790,145	2,782,122	125,464	5,697,731	48.97	48.83	2.20	50.07
1942 NEng	1,143,751	1,334,322	29,904	2,507,977	45.60	53.20	1.19	46.15
1942 South	1,159,894	153,556	6,538	1,319,988	87.87	11.63	0.50	88.31
1942 MAtl	3,603,031	4,021,617	106,679	7,731,327	46.60	52.02	1.38	47.26
1942 BdrS	813,822	672,521	5,712	1,492,055	54.54	45.07	0.38	54.75
1942 MidW	4,712,540	6,234,603	373,413	11,320,556	41.63	55.07	3.30	43.05
1942 West	1,806,630	1,837,174	61,540	3,705,344	48.76	49.58	1.66	49.58
1944 NEng	1,689,926	1,837,576	6,128	3,533,630	47.82	52.00	0.17	47.91
1944 South	3,585,550	616,264	21,144	4,222,958	84.91	14.59	0.50	85.33
1944 MAtl	5,856,930	5,657,579	208,636	11,723,145	49.96	48.26	1.78	50.87
1944 BdrS	1,561,717	1,232,731	3,404	2,797,852	55.82	44.06	0.12	55.89
1944 MidW	7,816,097	8,977,050	180,627	16,973,774	46.05	52.89	1.06	46.54
1944 West	2,948,318	2,862,104	11,863	5,822,285	50.64	49.16	0.20	50.74
1946 NEng	1,322,446	1,621,378	34,112	2,977,936	44.41	54.45	1.15	44.92
1946 South	1,682,487	394,332	33,808	2,110,627	79.72	18.68	1.60	81.01
1946 MAtl	3,851,958	5,214,855	252,198	9,319,011	41.33	55.96	2.71	42.48
1946 BdrS	1,061,262	996,173	320	2,057,755	51.57	48.41	0.02	51.58
1946 MidW	5,476,166	7,736,227	107,355	13,319,748	41.11	58.08	0.81	41.45
1946 West	2,101,899	2,446,887	31,091	4,579,877	45.89	53.43	0.68	46.21
1948 NEng	1,813,652	1,868,526	18,385	3,700,563	49.01	50.49	0.50	49.25
1948 South	3,731,908	668,549	26,495	4,426,952	84.30	15.10	0.60	84.81
1948 MAtl	3,587,178	5,306,103	2,755,245	11,648,526	30.80	45.55	23.65	40.34
1948 BdrS	1,606,950	1,089,891	15,994	2,712,835	59.24	40.18	0.59	59.59
1948 MidW	8,416,771	8,342,324	84,476	16,843,571	49.97	49.53	0.50	50.22
1948 West	2,869,490	3,422,362	275,003	6,566,855	43.70	52.12	4.19	45.61
1950 NEng	1,726,776	1,791,316	26,984	3,545,076	48.71	50.53	0.76	49.08
1950 South	2,338,410	367,716	7,236	2,713,362	86.18	13.55	0.27	86.41
1950 MAtl	4,786,914	5,135,768	341,763	10,264,445	46.64	50.03	3.33	48.24
1950 BdrS	1,329,936	997,984	3,243	2,331,163	57.05	42.81	0.14	57.13
1950 MidW	6,952,953	8,273,333	29,321	15,255,607	45.58	54.23	0.19	45.66
1950 West	2,863,299	3,197,848	140,978	6,202,125	46.17	51.56	2.27	47.24
1952 NEng	1,990,264	2,426,956	17,586	4,434,806	44.88	54.73	0.40	45.06
1952 South	6,144,417	1,011,151	28,361	7,183,929	85.53	14.08	0.39	85.87
1952 MAtl	6,297,153	7,382,009	234,543	13,913,705	45.26	53.06	1.69	46.03
1952 BdrS	1,917,533	1,678,201	4,337	3,600,071	53.26	46.62	0.12	53.33
1952 MidW	8,868,420	11,358,010	96,249	20,322,679	43.64	55.89	0.47	43.85
1952 West	3,776,466	4,464,439	149,402	8,390,307	45.01	53.21	1.78	45.83
1954 NEng	1,838,183	1,748,552	1,938	3,588,673	51.22	48.72	0.05	51.25
1954 South	3,022,316	653,282	14,732	3,690,330	81.90	17.70	0.40	82.23
1954 MAtl	5,230,171	5,282,335	116,674	10,629,180	49.21	49.70	1.10	49.75
1954 BdrS	1,468,404	974,514	1,636	2,444,554	60.07	39.86	0.07	60.11
1954 MidW	7,326,918	7,811,153	54,542	15,192,613	48.23	51.41	0.36	48.40
1954 West	3,604,597	3,425,769	9,356	7,039,722	51.20	48.66	0.13	51.27

(Table continues)

Table 5-7 (Continued)

Year/Region[1]	Regional Raw Vote				Regional Percent			Democratic % of Two-Party Vote
	Democratic	Republican	Other	Total	Democratic	Republican	Other	
1956 NEng	2,014,402	2,422,172	672	4,437,246	45.40	54.59	0.02	45.40
1956 South	5,434,899	1,425,548	34,488	6,894,935	78.82	20.68	0.50	79.22
1956 MAtl	6,261,957	7,615,351	91,866	13,969,174	44.83	54.52	0.66	45.12
1956 BdrS	1,861,298	1,588,149	514	3,449,961	53.95	46.03	0.01	53.96
1956 MidW	9,559,540	10,670,441	12,078	20,242,059	47.23	52.71	0.06	47.25
1956 West	4,824,799	4,352,948	1	9,177,748	52.57	47.43	0.00	52.57
1958–1959 NEng	2,069,170	1,608,860	1,727	3,679,757	56.23	43.72	0.05	56.26
1958–1959 South	2,763,049	597,777	30,682	3,391,508	81.47	17.63	0.90	82.21
1958–1959 MAtl	5,799,277	5,647,932	96,253	11,543,462	50.24	48.93	0.83	50.66
1958–1959 BdrS	1,523,913	806,635	2,958	2,333,506	65.31	34.57	0.13	65.39
1958–1959 MidW	8,621,625	7,575,370	16,304	16,213,299	53.18	46.72	0.10	53.23
1958–1959 West	4,950,760	3,638,975	5,060	8,594,795	57.60	42.34	0.06	57.64
1960 NEng	2,672,551	2,055,972	570	4,729,093	56.51	43.47	0.01	56.52
1960 South	6,141,609	1,757,067	91,144	7,989,820	76.87	21.99	1.14	77.75
1960 MAtl	7,577,341	7,135,711	150,519	14,863,571	50.98	48.01	1.01	51.50
1960 BdrS	2,049,158	1,502,747	0	3,551,905	57.69	42.31	0.00	57.69
1960 MidW	10,910,580	11,113,448	16,158	22,040,186	49.50	50.42	0.07	49.54
1960 West	5,708,076	5,173,866	1,656	10,883,598	52.45	47.54	0.02	52.45
1962 NEng	2,177,097	1,755,794	15,396	3,948,287	55.14	44.47	0.39	55.36
1962 South	3,838,028	2,045,198	51,039	5,934,265	64.68	34.46	0.86	65.24
1962 MAtl	5,975,497	5,939,959	110,818	12,026,274	49.69	49.39	0.92	50.15
1962 BdrS	1,485,506	1,079,594	860	2,565,960	57.89	42.07	0.03	57.91
1962 MidW	8,125,423	8,908,325	15,770	17,049,518	47.66	52.25	0.09	47.70
1962 West	4,823,329	4,733,009	2,251	9,558,589	50.46	49.52	0.02	50.47
1964 NEng	2,763,659	1,731,429	7,614	4,502,702	61.38	38.45	0.17	61.48
1964 South	6,599,291	3,300,393	171,716	10,071,400	65.53	32.77	1.70	66.66
1964 MAtl	8,128,450	6,094,915	135,582	14,358,947	56.61	42.45	0.94	57.15
1964 BdrS	2,281,562	1,268,692	0	3,550,254	64.26	35.74	0.00	64.26
1964 MidW	11,525,900	9,756,485	7,505	21,289,890	54.14	45.83	0.04	54.16
1964 West	6,334,421	5,513,352	3,135	11,850,908	53.45	46.52	0.03	53.47
1966 NEng	2,141,957	1,647,636	25,009	3,814,602	56.15	43.19	0.66	56.52
1966 South	4,950,443	2,494,679	116,456	7,561,578	65.47	32.99	1.54	66.49
1966 MAtl	5,752,369	5,701,459	285,541	11,739,369	49.00	48.57	2.43	50.22
1966 BdrS	1,382,488	1,190,793	0	2,573,281	53.72	46.28	0.00	53.72
1966 MidW	7,517,956	8,904,055	6,270	16,428,281	45.76	54.20	0.04	45.78
1966 West	4,997,585	5,456,334	21,810	10,475,729	47.71	52.09	0.21	47.81
1968 NEng	2,189,769	2,196,224	66,444	4,452,437	49.18	49.33	1.49	49.93
1968 South	7,327,959	3,972,160	106,284	11,406,403	64.24	34.82	0.93	64.85
1968 MAtl	6,656,242	6,525,177	413,734	13,595,153	48.96	48.00	3.04	50.50
1968 BdrS	1,855,928	1,547,630	3,256	3,406,814	54.48	45.43	0.10	54.53
1968 MidW	9,629,167	11,359,745	19,418	21,008,330	45.83	54.07	0.09	45.88
1968 West	5,521,898	6,430,042	142,203	12,094,143	45.66	53.17	1.18	46.20
1970 NEng	2,066,556	1,730,294	83,998	3,880,848	53.25	44.59	2.16	54.43
1970 South	5,003,098	2,283,837	94,158	7,381,093	67.78	30.94	1.28	68.66
1970 MAtl	5,836,915	5,130,224	353,854	11,320,993	51.56	45.32	3.13	53.22
1970 BdrS	1,414,846	1,051,206	7,494	2,473,546	57.20	42.50	0.30	57.37
1970 MidW	8,544,491	8,443,717	95,472	17,083,680	50.02	49.43	0.56	50.30
1970 West	5,496,051	5,091,145	132,795	10,719,991	51.27	47.49	1.24	51.91
1972 NEng	2,522,322	2,176,564	115,281	4,814,167	52.39	45.21	2.39	53.68
1972 South	6,409,630	3,833,380	128,662	10,371,672	61.80	36.96	1.24	62.58
1972 MAtl	6,987,755	6,819,396	322,776	14,129,927	49.45	48.26	2.28	50.61
1972 BdrS	2,101,823	1,657,215	14,606	3,773,644	55.70	43.92	0.39	55.91
1972 MidW	10,666,001	11,274,159	199,954	22,140,114	48.18	50.92	0.90	48.61
1972 West	7,396,883	6,385,459	172,857	13,955,199	53.00	45.76	1.24	53.67
1974 NEng	2,312,444	1,324,927	157,455	3,794,826	60.94	34.91	4.15	63.57
1974 South	4,181,984	2,226,116	102,018	6,510,118	64.24	34.19	1.57	65.26
1974 MAtl	6,049,049	4,240,451	226,014	10,515,514	57.52	40.33	2.15	58.79
1974 BdrS	1,536,931	919,528	18,681	2,475,140	62.09	37.15	0.75	62.57
1974 MidW	8,872,544	7,195,102	227,167	16,294,831	54.45	44.16	1.39	55.22
1974 West	6,098,029	4,502,251	206,470	10,806,750	56.43	41.66	1.91	57.53
1976 NEng	2,847,433	2,076,158	142,343	5,065,934	56.21	40.98	2.81	57.83
1976 South	7,920,285	4,487,313	213,020	12,620,618	62.76	35.56	1.69	63.83
1976 MAtl	7,552,795	5,677,390	220,399	13,450,584	56.15	42.21	1.64	57.09
1976 BdrS	2,524,566	1,376,685	134,585	4,035,836	62.55	34.11	3.33	64.71
1976 MidW	11,887,695	10,627,516	229,515	22,744,726	52.27	46.73	1.01	52.80
1976 West	7,625,701	5,984,140	319,290	13,929,131	54.75	42.96	2.29	56.03
1978 NEng	2,302,382	1,461,950	122,255	3,886,587	59.24	37.62	3.15	61.16
1978 South	4,459,558	3,071,133	117,433	7,648,124	58.31	40.16	1.54	59.22
1978 MAtl	5,188,074	4,623,297	200,804	10,012,175	51.82	46.18	2.01	52.88
1978 BdrS	1,491,134	930,620	11,721	2,433,475	61.28	38.24	0.48	61.57
1978 MidW	8,556,474	8,284,014	120,012	16,960,500	50.45	48.84	0.71	50.81
1978 West	6,095,736	5,308,740	207,541	11,612,017	52.50	45.72	1.79	53.45
1980 NEng	2,697,526	2,287,032	69,473	5,054,031	53.37	45.25	1.37	54.12
1980 South	6,958,884	5,440,837	247,706	12,647,427	55.02	43.02	1.96	56.12
1980 MAtl	6,224,344	6,371,122	300,680	12,896,146	48.27	49.40	2.33	49.42
1980 BdrS	2,307,017	1,665,442	8,094	3,980,553	57.96	41.84	0.20	58.08
1980 MidW	11,443,870	12,147,190	128,655	23,719,715	48.25	51.21	0.54	48.51
1980 West	7,303,128	7,711,935	505,656	15,520,719	47.05	49.69	3.26	48.64
1982 NEng	2,391,160	1,733,207	55,866	4,180,233	57.20	41.46	1.34	57.98
1982 South	6,348,480	4,088,584	167,421	10,604,485	59.87	38.56	1.58	60.83
1982 MAtl	5,832,690	4,594,651	216,903	10,644,244	54.80	43.17	2.04	55.94
1982 BdrS	2,038,535	1,141,479	14,196	3,194,210	63.82	35.74	0.44	64.10
1982 MidW	10,368,122	8,550,546	170,580	19,089,248	54.31	44.79	0.89	54.80
1982 West	6,975,509	6,630,989	354,474	13,960,972	49.96	47.50	2.54	51.27

Table 5-7 *(Continued)*

Year/Region[1]	Regional Raw Vote				Regional Percent			Democratic % of Two-Party Vote
	Democratic	Republican	Other	Total	Democratic	Republican	Other	
1984 NEng	2,822,531	2,434,247	52,371	5,309,149	53.16	45.85	0.99	53.69
1984 South	8,253,661	6,106,950	96,673	14,457,284	57.09	42.24	0.67	57.47
1984 MAtl	7,436,745	6,582,238	94,603	14,113,586	52.69	46.64	0.67	53.05
1984 BdrS	2,686,280	1,797,990	13,985	4,498,255	59.72	39.97	0.31	59.90
1984 MidW	12,231,318	11,812,710	128,754	24,172,782	50.60	48.87	0.53	50.87
1984 West	7,965,097	8,702,030	310,019	16,977,146	46.92	51.26	1.83	47.79
1986 NEng	2,122,681	1,434,013	83,123	3,639,817	58.32	39.40	2.28	59.68
1986 South	6,395,493	4,324,836	95,219	10,815,548	59.13	39.99	0.88	59.66
1986 MAtl	4,803,793	3,983,075	137,422	8,924,290	53.83	44.63	1.54	54.67
1986 BdrS	1,772,821	1,035,204	5,663	2,813,688	63.01	36.79	0.20	63.13
1986 MidW	8,954,713	7,967,955	58,724	16,981,392	52.73	46.92	0.35	52.92
1986 West	6,947,144	6,680,059	157,873	13,785,076	50.40	48.46	1.15	50.98
1988 NEng	3,086,083	2,065,755	175,185	5,327,023	57.93	38.78	3.29	59.90
1988 South	8,484,202	6,059,958	170,325	14,714,485	57.66	41.18	1.16	58.33
1988 MAtl	6,561,769	5,999,044	152,880	12,713,693	51.61	47.19	1.20	52.24
1988 BdrS	2,313,557	1,681,955	6,205	4,001,717	57.81	42.03	0.16	57.90
1988 MidW	12,270,201	11,205,034	64,025	23,539,260	52.13	47.60	0.27	52.27
1988 West	8,952,241	8,155,460	353,756	17,461,457	51.27	46.71	2.03	52.33
1990 NEng	2,523,355	1,741,977	187,477	4,452,809	56.67	39.12	4.21	59.16
1990 South	6,468,056	4,626,067	179,410	11,273,533	57.37	41.03	1.59	58.30
1990 MAtl	4,075,443	4,183,649	257,739	8,516,831	47.85	49.12	3.03	49.34
1990 BdrS	1,689,453	1,375,675	20,367	3,085,495	54.75	44.59	0.66	55.12
1990 MidW	9,370,068	7,970,300	143,494	17,483,862	53.59	45.59	0.82	54.04
1990 West	7,021,685	6,544,753	490,456	14,056,894	49.95	46.56	3.49	51.76
1992 NEng	3,006,889	2,333,932	569,049	5,909,870	50.88	39.49	9.63	56.30
1992 South	9,931,020	8,623,920	474,103	19,029,043	52.19	45.32	2.49	53.52
1992 MAtl	6,677,451	6,690,245	415,574	13,783,270	48.45	48.54	3.02	49.95
1992 BdrS	2,883,139	2,108,202	17,078	5,008,419	57.57	42.09	0.34	57.76
1992 MidW	13,260,038	12,237,704	734,080	26,231,822	50.55	46.65	2.80	52.00
1992 West	10,498,513	8,909,582	1,074,860	20,482,955	51.25	43.50	5.25	54.09
1994 NEng	2,431,047	1,754,040	225,511	4,410,598	55.12	39.77	5.11	58.09
1994 South	6,021,298	7,622,719	198,968	13,842,985	43.50	55.07	1.44	44.13
1994 MAtl	4,636,703	5,310,681	235,412	10,182,796	45.53	52.15	2.31	46.61
1994 BdrS	1,615,313	1,825,681	63,988	3,504,982	46.09	52.09	1.83	46.94
1994 MidW	8,413,802	10,146,772	211,096	18,771,670	44.82	54.05	1.12	45.33
1994 West	7,426,206	8,240,792	548,584	16,215,582	45.80	50.82	3.38	47.40
1996 NEng	3,173,829	1,976,641	258,796	5,409,266	58.67	36.54	4.78	61.62
1996 South	8,147,130	9,694,213	330,921	18,172,264	44.83	53.35	1.82	45.66
1996 MAtl	6,688,730	5,979,525	289,196	12,957,451	51.62	46.15	2.23	52.80
1996 BdrS	2,273,004	2,279,833	27,101	4,579,938	49.63	49.78	0.59	49.93
1996 MidW	11,923,047	11,642,176	660,417	24,225,640	49.22	48.06	2.73	50.60
1996 West	9,121,926	9,292,042	751,833	19,165,801	47.59	48.48	3.92	49.54
1998 NEng	2,410,080	1,316,948	209,563	3,936,591	61.22	33.45	5.32	64.66
1998 South	5,055,242	6,330,287	414,051	11,799,580	42.84	53.65	3.51	44.40
1998 MAtl	4,619,061	4,307,911	232,316	9,159,288	50.43	47.03	2.54	51.74
1998 BdrS	1,846,128	1,893,953	50,651	3,790,732	48.70	49.96	1.34	49.36
1998 MidW	8,841,600	9,845,155	375,333	19,062,088	46.38	51.65	1.97	47.31
1998 West	7,747,642	7,585,571	766,526	16,099,739	48.12	47.12	4.76	50.53

Notes: Entries are calculated from the raw vote values in Tables 5-70 through 5-122. Whenever bold italicized values occur in Tables 5-70 through 5-122, denoting the author's alternate party coding system, they are used instead of the conventionally coded main entries in these tables in the aggregation process to the regional level for Table 5-7. See text and Table 5-1 for a more complete discussion of the conventional and alternate party coding systems. Also see Table 1-3 for a similar discussion. Entries in Table 5-7 are, therefore, based on candidates who use the designation "Democrat" or "Republican" (or their historical antecedents listed in Appendix A) either solely or with other labels or parties (often minor parties) on the ballot. In general, historical antecedents to the Democratic Party were Anti-Federalists, Democratic-Republicans, and Jackson Democrats; historical precursors of the Republican Party were Federalists, National Republicans, and Whigs. Other = candidates who use third-party names only on the ballot or are listed as independent or unidentified. Odd-numbered year House elections were held in several states prior to 1880 but only rarely thereafter. States with partial House vote data are not included in the aggregation process. Special House elections are also not included.

[1]Regional categories are adapted from the ICPSR regional codings. In the current analysis, Tennessee is categorized in the South, since it was part of the Confederacy, although the ICPSR treats it as a Border South state. The regional categories are: New England (NEng)—Connecticut, Maine, Massachusetts, New Hampshire, Rhode Island, Vermont; Mid-Atlantic (MAtl)—Delaware, New Jersey, New York, Pennsylvania; South—Alabama, Arkansas, Florida, Georgia, Louisiana, Mississippi, North Carolina, South Carolina, Tennessee, Texas, Virginia; Border South (BdrS)—Maryland, Kentucky, Oklahoma, West Virginia; Midwest (MidW)—Illinois, Indiana, Iowa, Kansas, Michigan, Minnesota, Missouri, Nebraska, North Dakota, Ohio, South Dakota, Wisconsin; West—Alaska, Arizona, California, Colorado, Hawaii, Idaho, Montana, Nevada, New Mexico, Oregon, Utah, Washington, Wyoming.

Sources: Data in Tables 5-70 through 5-122 as adapted from *United States Congressional Elections, 1788–1997* (1998), *Congressional Quarterly's Guide to U.S. Elections* (1994), ICPSR data sets 0001 and 0075, *America Votes* (various publication dates), and independent search of state sources by the author.

Table 5-8 Votes in House Elections, by Non-South and South, 1788–1998

Year/Region[1]	Regional Raw Vote				Regional Percent			Democratic % of Two-Party Vote
	Democratic	Republican	Other	Total	Democratic	Republican	Other	
1788–1789 N-S	10,148	13,861	29,753	53,762	18.88	25.78	55.34	42.27
1788–1789 S	0	0	2,878	2,878	0.00	0.00	100.00	—
1790–1791 N-S	3,132	7,154	44,796	55,082	5.69	12.99	81.33	30.45
1790–1791 S	0	0	1,954	1,954	0.00	0.00	100.00	—
1792–1793 N-S	35,095	40,962	22,197	98,254	35.72	41.69	22.59	46.14
1792–1793 S	0	0	5,488	5,488	0.00	0.00	100.00	—
1794–1795 N-S	34,251	49,421	3,908	87,580	39.11	56.43	4.46	40.93
1794–1795 S	1,487	1,150	1,143	3,780	39.34	30.42	30.24	56.39
1796–1797 N-S	29,903	61,149	2,538	93,590	31.95	65.34	2.71	32.84
1796–1797 S	10,818	8,539	1,757	21,114	51.24	40.44	8.32	55.89
1798–1799 N-S	64,294	95,378	3,782	163,454	39.33	58.35	2.31	40.27
1798–1799 S	3,111	4,055	0	7,166	43.41	56.59	0.00	43.41
1800–1801 N-S	93,857	79,700	6,884	180,441	52.02	44.17	3.82	54.08
1800–1801 S	17,854	0	0	17,854	100.00	0.00	0.00	100.00
1802–1803 N-S	74,351	63,266	3,041	140,658	52.86	44.98	2.16	54.03
1802–1803 S	22,047	4,863	0	26,910	81.93	18.07	0.00	81.93
1804–1805 N-S	125,954	88,838	1,336	216,128	58.28	41.10	0.62	58.64
1804–1805 S	25,249	0	0	25,249	100.00	0.00	0.00	100.00
1806–1807 N-S	106,857	65,374	4,759	176,990	60.37	36.94	2.69	62.04
1806–1807 S	22,799	2,993	0	25,792	88.40	11.60	0.00	88.40
1808–1809 N-S	207,074	177,262	1,303	385,639	53.70	45.97	0.34	53.88
1808–1809 S	12,805	4,838	6,240	23,883	53.62	20.26	26.13	72.58
1810–1811 N-S	185,510	125,932	4,973	316,415	58.63	39.80	1.57	59.56
1810–1811 S	32,368	2,591	5,160	40,119	80.68	6.46	12.86	92.59
1812–1813 N-S	210,548	215,346	4,816	430,710	48.88	50.00	1.12	49.44
1812–1813 S	12,761	2,699	1,592	17,052	74.84	15.83	9.34	82.54
1814–1815 N-S	129,007	149,535	455	278,997	46.24	53.60	0.16	46.32
1814–1815 S	19,073	242	29	19,344	98.60	1.25	0.15	98.75
1816–1817 N-S	139,506	122,330	7,320	269,156	51.83	45.45	2.72	53.28
1816–1817 S	41,064	0	23,981	65,045	63.13	0.00	36.87	100.00
1818–1819 N-S	167,001	61,836	4,992	233,829	71.42	26.44	2.13	72.98
1818–1819 S	44,069	0	29,118	73,187	60.21	0.00	39.79	100.00
1820–1821 N-S	303,334	92,734	14,395	410,463	73.90	22.59	3.51	76.59
1820–1821 S	26,081	0	11,115	37,196	70.12	0.00	29.88	100.00
1822–1823 N-S	295,758	49,392	28,687	373,837	79.11	13.21	7.67	85.69
1822–1823 S	31,735	1,167	23,944	56,846	55.83	2.05	42.12	96.45
1824–1825 N-S	301,337	39,812	115,169	456,318	66.04	8.72	25.24	88.33
1824–1825 S	16,504	0	0	16,504	100.00	0.00	0.00	100.00
1826–1827 N-S	209,098	253,574	117,647	580,319	36.03	43.70	20.27	45.19
1826–1827 S	24,021	1,451	17,859	43,331	55.44	3.35	41.22	94.30
1828–1829 N-S	249,222	235,445	44,981	529,648	47.05	44.45	8.49	51.42
1828–1829 S	67,991	7,837	10,763	86,591	78.52	9.05	12.43	89.66
1830–1831 N-S	389,702	291,505	154,311	835,518	46.64	34.89	18.47	57.21
1830–1831 S	116,074	19,715	12,188	147,977	78.44	13.32	8.24	85.48
1832–1833 N-S	500,891	262,429	241,206	1,004,526	49.86	26.12	24.01	65.62
1832–1833 S	94,880	34,817	24,893	154,590	61.38	22.52	16.10	73.16
1834–1835 N-S	574,081	471,390	81,613	1,127,084	50.94	41.82	7.24	54.91
1834–1835 S	76,058	90,412	8,934	175,404	43.36	51.55	5.09	45.69
1836–1837 N-S	587,257	533,278	40,924	1,161,459	50.56	45.91	3.52	52.41
1836–1837 S	81,405	107,913	1,268	190,586	42.71	56.62	0.67	43.00
1838–1839 N-S	758,729	755,553	6,605	1,520,887	49.89	49.68	0.43	50.10
1838–1839 S	110,122	115,050	422	225,594	48.81	51.00	0.19	48.91
1840–1841 N-S	834,551	906,421	8,464	1,749,436	47.70	51.81	0.48	47.94
1840–1841 S	122,929	123,191	939	247,059	49.76	49.86	0.38	49.95
1842–1843 N-S	773,871	692,076	72,758	1,538,705	50.29	44.98	4.73	52.79
1842–1843 S	166,690	132,311	1,686	300,687	55.44	44.00	0.56	55.75
1844–1845 N-S	1,031,353	1,027,447	83,615	2,142,415	48.14	47.96	3.90	50.09
1844–1845 S	182,940	162,115	3,730	348,785	52.45	46.48	1.07	53.02
1846–1847 N-S	834,357	824,366	115,127	1,773,850	47.04	46.47	6.49	50.30
1846–1847 S	321,330	135,746	4,337	461,413	69.64	29.42	0.94	70.30
1848–1849 N-S	928,673	1,001,365	229,991	2,160,029	42.99	46.36	10.65	48.12
1848–1849 S	208,703	182,403	9,998	401,104	52.03	45.48	2.49	53.36
1850–1851 N-S	1,031,744	964,317	74,986	2,071,047	49.82	46.56	3.62	51.69
1850–1851 S	50,983	31,729	157,534	240,246	21.22	13.21	65.57	61.64
1852–1853 N-S	1,224,562	1,096,328	148,301	2,469,191	49.59	44.40	6.01	52.76
1852–1853 S	178,257	112,753	5,267	296,277	60.17	38.06	1.78	61.25
1854–1855 N-S	1,106,615	777,859	608,491	2,492,965	44.39	31.20	24.41	58.72
1854–1855 S	315,284	13,162	251,399	579,845	54.37	2.27	43.36	95.99
1856–1857 N-S	1,409,385	1,421,301	363,680	3,194,366	44.12	44.49	11.39	49.79
1856–1857 S	361,888	0	193,552	555,440	65.15	0.00	34.85	100.00
1858–1859 N-S	1,468,771	1,234,391	395,805	3,098,967	47.40	39.83	12.77	54.34
1858–1859 S	349,973	33,073	123,864	506,910	69.04	6.52	24.44	91.37
1860–1861 N-S	1,609,655	1,987,871	150,153	3,747,679	42.95	53.04	4.01	44.74
1860–1861 S	40,780	0	32,331	73,111	55.78	0.00	44.22	100.00
1862–1863 N-S	1,546,915	1,610,452	56,430	3,213,797	48.13	50.11	1.76	48.99
1862–1863 S	—	—	—	—	—	—	—	—

Table 5-8 *(Continued)*

	Regional Raw Vote				Regional Percent			Democratic % of
Year/Region[1]	Democratic	Republican	Other	Total	Democratic	Republican	Other	Two-Party Vote
1864–1865 N-S	1,645,716	2,072,612	119,120	3,837,448	42.89	54.01	3.10	44.26
1864–1865 S	0	24,043	34,579	58,622	0.00	41.01	58.99	0.00
1866–1867 N-S	1,809,747	2,191,538	15,863	4,017,148	45.05	54.55	0.39	45.23
1866–1867 S	0	73,617	22,506	96,123	0.00	76.59	23.41	0.00
1868–1869 N-S	2,311,703	2,543,573	3,025	4,858,301	47.58	52.36	0.06	47.61
1868–1869 S	293,431	604,408	128,480	1,026,319	28.59	58.89	12.52	32.68
1870–1871 N-S	2,051,963	2,172,130	75,963	4,300,056	47.72	50.51	1.77	48.58
1870–1871 S	429,568	419,667	1,739	850,974	50.48	49.32	0.20	50.58
1872–1873 N-S	2,392,036	2,739,429	15,350	5,146,815	46.48	53.23	0.30	46.62
1872–1873 S	535,885	752,444	169,561	1,457,890	36.76	51.61	11.63	41.60
1874–1875 N-S	2,310,845	2,187,724	270,089	4,768,658	48.46	45.88	5.66	51.37
1874–1875 S	789,073	629,539	19,750	1,438,362	54.86	43.77	1.37	55.62
1876–1877 N-S	3,198,368	3,233,349	88,558	6,520,275	49.05	49.59	1.36	49.73
1876–1877 S	1,123,732	672,052	1,523	1,797,307	62.52	37.39	0.08	62.58
1878–1879 N-S	2,440,922	2,603,549	734,917	5,779,388	42.23	45.05	12.72	48.39
1878–1879 S	872,225	259,022	152,192	1,283,439	67.96	20.18	11.86	77.10
1880 N-S	3,357,807	3,717,156	250,585	7,325,548	45.84	50.74	3.42	47.46
1880 S	1,082,432	503,709	161,466	1,747,607	61.94	28.82	9.24	68.24
1882 N-S	3,189,181	2,986,346	316,940	6,492,467	49.12	46.00	4.88	51.64
1882 S	873,535	350,060	279,212	1,502,807	58.13	23.29	18.58	71.39
1884 N-S	3,827,313	4,022,153	177,552	8,027,018	47.68	50.11	2.21	48.76
1884 S	1,189,110	660,015	15,566	1,864,691	63.77	35.40	0.83	64.31
1886 N-S	3,359,837	3,515,585	347,194	7,222,616	46.52	48.67	4.81	48.87
1886 S	873,184	390,831	91,416	1,355,431	64.42	28.83	6.74	69.08
1888–1889 N-S	4,295,547	4,801,052	311,317	9,407,916	45.66	51.03	3.31	47.22
1888–1889 S	1,283,761	667,923	102,131	2,053,815	62.51	32.52	4.97	65.78
1890 N-S	3,947,012	3,793,071	491,409	8,231,492	47.95	46.08	5.97	50.99
1890 S	1,082,431	419,832	48,623	1,550,886	69.79	27.07	3.14	72.05
1892 N-S	4,595,622	4,562,837	609,326	9,767,785	47.05	46.71	6.24	50.18
1892 S	1,351,349	339,669	389,206	2,080,224	64.96	16.33	18.71	79.91
1894–1895 N-S	3,467,947	5,062,529	956,102	9,486,578	36.56	53.37	10.08	40.65
1894–1895 S	970,568	391,821	414,888	1,777,277	54.61	22.05	23.34	71.24
1896 N-S	4,894,280	6,181,945	319,159	11,395,384	42.95	54.25	2.80	44.19
1896 S	1,324,384	711,989	225,272	2,261,645	58.56	31.48	9.96	65.04
1898 N-S	4,254,291	4,992,168	306,218	9,552,677	44.54	52.26	3.21	46.01
1898 S	895,428	388,406	117,234	1,401,068	63.91	27.72	8.37	69.75
1900 N-S	5,208,032	6,425,419	261,132	11,894,583	43.78	54.02	2.20	44.77
1900 S	1,226,500	523,040	65,172	1,814,712	67.59	28.82	3.59	70.10
1902 N-S	4,256,838	5,235,857	414,781	9,907,476	42.97	52.85	4.19	44.84
1902 S	831,284	242,803	6,358	1,080,445	76.94	22.47	0.59	77.39
1904 N-S	4,413,834	6,821,487	583,539	11,818,860	37.35	57.72	4.94	39.29
1904 S	986,336	351,481	6,360	1,344,177	73.38	26.15	0.47	73.73
1906–1907 N-S	4,214,345	5,467,825	572,831	10,255,001	41.10	53.32	5.59	43.53
1906–1907 S	677,346	240,206	6,536	924,088	73.30	25.99	0.71	73.82
1908 N-S	5,456,069	6,847,090	644,679	12,947,838	42.14	52.88	4.98	44.35
1908 S	1,095,896	390,137	11,653	1,497,686	73.17	26.05	0.78	73.75
1910–1911 N-S	4,923,116	5,433,215	756,525	11,112,856	44.30	48.89	6.81	47.54
1910–1911 S	827,575	249,053	21,300	1,097,928	75.38	22.68	1.94	76.87
1912 N-S	5,119,814	4,775,902	2,930,304	12,826,020	39.92	37.24	22.85	51.74
1912 S	1,113,511	236,782	81,726	1,432,019	77.76	16.53	5.71	82.46
1914 N-S	4,983,785	5,653,020	1,947,071	12,583,876	39.60	44.92	15.47	46.85
1914 S	822,720	179,597	59,907	1,062,224	77.45	16.91	5.64	82.08
1916 N-S	6,361,490	7,641,279	954,077	14,956,846	42.53	51.09	6.38	45.43
1916 S	1,347,860	384,085	44,000	1,775,945	75.90	21.63	2.48	77.82
1918 N-S	4,817,912	6,463,550	588,416	11,869,878	40.59	54.45	4.96	42.71
1918 S	750,353	146,960	891	898,204	83.54	16.36	0.10	83.62
1920 N-S	7,408,333	14,034,095	1,461,048	22,903,476	32.35	61.27	6.38	34.55
1920 S	1,742,624	840,156	42,255	2,625,035	66.38	32.01	1.61	67.47
1922 N-S	7,831,691	10,262,890	714,258	18,808,839	41.64	54.56	3.80	43.28
1922 S	1,231,049	370,413	527	1,601,989	76.85	23.12	0.03	76.87
1924 N-S	8,870,301	14,510,398	1,089,781	24,470,480	36.25	59.30	4.45	37.94
1924 S	1,876,396	498,688	8,602	2,383,686	78.72	20.92	0.36	79.00
1926 N-S	7,364,596	11,364,069	515,724	19,244,389	38.27	59.05	2.68	39.32
1926 S	907,168	246,542	730	1,154,440	78.58	21.36	0.06	78.63
1928 N-S	11,909,865	18,622,113	614,474	31,146,452	38.24	59.79	1.97	39.01
1928 S	2,306,635	747,073	1,798	3,055,506	75.49	24.45	0.06	75.54
1930 N-S	9,642,003	12,631,624	658,781	22,932,408	42.05	55.08	2.87	43.29
1930 S	1,445,760	420,154	2,518	1,868,432	77.38	22.49	0.13	77.48
1932 N-S	17,236,042	15,162,095	1,428,877	33,827,014	50.95	44.82	4.22	53.20
1932 S	3,031,264	564,212	103,572	3,699,048	81.95	15.25	2.80	84.31
1934 N-S	15,673,518	12,882,347	1,612,841	30,168,706	51.95	42.70	5.35	54.89
1934 S	1,784,153	303,374	23,751	2,111,278	84.51	14.37	1.12	85.47
1936 N-S	20,902,505	16,449,831	1,764,643	39,116,979	53.44	42.05	4.51	55.96
1936 S	3,293,839	575,435	10,325	3,879,599	84.90	14.83	0.27	85.13

(Table continues)

Table 5-8 *(Continued)*

Year/Region[1]	Regional Raw Vote				Regional Percent			Democratic % of Two-Party Vote
	Democratic	Republican	Other	Total	Democratic	Republican	Other	
1938 N-S	16,272,453	16,700,994	1,195,769	34,169,216	47.62	48.88	3.50	49.35
1938 S	1,654,950	271,067	33,235	1,959,252	84.47	13.84	1.70	85.93
1940 N-S	20,539,488	20,848,289	1,015,328	42,403,105	48.44	49.17	2.39	49.63
1940 S	3,726,944	498,276	30,834	4,256,054	87.57	11.71	0.72	88.21
1942 N-S	12,079,774	14,100,237	577,248	26,757,259	45.15	52.70	2.16	46.14
1942 S	1,159,894	153,556	6,538	1,319,988	87.87	11.63	0.50	88.31
1944 N-S	19,872,988	20,567,040	410,658	40,850,686	48.65	50.35	1.01	49.14
1944 S	3,585,550	616,264	21,144	4,222,958	84.91	14.59	0.50	85.33
1946 N-S	13,813,731	18,015,520	425,076	32,254,327	42.83	55.85	1.32	43.40
1946 S	1,682,487	394,332	33,808	2,110,627	79.72	18.68	1.60	81.01
1948 N-S	18,294,041	20,029,206	3,149,103	41,472,350	44.11	48.30	7.59	47.74
1948 S	3,731,908	668,549	26,495	4,426,952	84.30	15.10	0.60	84.81
1950 N-S	17,659,878	19,396,249	542,289	37,598,416	46.97	51.59	1.44	47.66
1950 S	2,338,410	367,716	7,236	2,713,362	86.18	13.55	0.27	86.41
1952 N-S	22,849,836	27,309,615	502,117	50,661,568	45.10	53.91	0.99	45.55
1952 S	6,144,417	1,011,151	28,361	7,183,929	85.53	14.08	0.39	85.87
1954 N-S	19,468,273	19,242,323	184,146	38,894,742	50.05	49.47	0.47	50.29
1954 S	3,022,316	653,282	14,732	3,690,330	81.90	17.70	0.40	82.23
1956 N-S	24,521,996	26,649,061	105,131	51,276,188	47.82	51.97	0.21	47.92
1956 S	5,434,899	1,425,548	34,488	6,894,935	78.82	20.68	0.50	79.22
1958–1959 N-S	22,964,745	19,277,772	122,302	42,364,819	54.21	45.50	0.29	54.36
1958–1959 S	2,763,049	597,777	30,682	3,391,508	81.47	17.63	0.90	82.21
1960 N-S	28,917,706	26,981,744	168,903	56,068,353	51.58	48.12	0.30	51.73
1960 S	6,141,609	1,757,067	91,144	7,989,820	76.87	21.99	1.14	77.75
1962 N-S	22,586,852	22,416,681	145,095	45,148,628	50.03	49.65	0.32	50.19
1962 S	3,838,028	2,045,198	51,039	5,934,265	64.68	34.46	0.86	65.24
1964 N-S	31,033,992	24,364,873	153,836	55,552,701	55.86	43.86	0.28	56.02
1964 S	6,599,291	3,300,393	171,716	10,071,400	65.53	32.77	1.70	66.66
1966 N-S	21,792,355	22,900,277	338,630	45,031,262	48.39	50.85	0.75	48.76
1966 S	4,950,443	2,494,679	116,456	7,561,578	65.47	32.99	1.54	66.49
1968 N-S	25,853,004	28,058,818	645,055	54,556,877	47.39	51.43	1.18	47.95
1968 S	7,327,959	3,972,160	106,284	11,406,403	64.24	34.82	0.93	64.85
1970 N-S	23,358,859	21,446,586	673,613	45,479,058	51.36	47.16	1.48	52.13
1970 S	5,003,098	2,283,837	94,158	7,381,093	67.78	30.94	1.28	68.66
1972 N-S	29,674,784	28,312,793	825,474	58,813,051	50.46	48.14	1.40	51.17
1972 S	6,409,630	3,833,380	128,662	10,371,672	61.80	36.96	1.24	62.58
1974 N-S	24,868,997	18,182,277	835,787	43,887,061	56.67	41.43	1.90	57.77
1974 S	4,181,984	2,226,116	102,018	6,510,118	64.24	34.19	1.57	65.26
1976 N-S	32,438,190	25,741,889	1,046,132	59,226,211	54.77	43.46	1.77	55.75
1976 S	7,920,285	4,487,313	213,020	12,620,618	62.76	35.56	1.69	63.83
1978 N-S	23,633,800	20,608,621	662,333	44,904,754	52.63	45.89	1.47	53.42
1978 S	4,459,558	3,071,133	117,433	7,648,124	58.31	40.16	1.54	59.22
1980 N-S	29,975,885	30,182,721	1,012,558	61,171,164	49.00	49.34	1.66	49.83
1980 S	6,958,884	5,440,837	247,706	12,647,427	55.02	43.02	1.96	56.12
1982 N-S	27,606,016	22,650,872	812,019	51,068,907	54.06	44.35	1.59	54.93
1982 S	6,348,480	4,088,584	167,421	10,604,485	59.87	38.56	1.58	60.83
1984 N-S	33,141,971	31,329,215	599,732	65,070,918	50.93	48.15	0.92	51.41
1984 S	8,253,661	6,106,950	96,673	14,457,284	57.09	42.24	0.67	57.47
1986 N-S	24,601,152	21,100,306	442,805	46,144,263	53.31	45.73	0.96	53.83
1986 S	6,395,493	4,324,836	95,219	10,815,548	59.13	39.99	0.88	59.66
1988 N-S	33,183,851	29,107,248	752,051	63,043,150	52.64	46.17	1.19	53.27
1988 S	8,484,202	6,059,958	170,325	14,714,485	57.66	41.18	1.16	58.33
1990 N-S	24,680,004	21,816,354	1,099,533	47,595,891	51.85	45.84	2.31	53.08
1990 S	6,468,056	4,626,067	179,410	11,273,533	57.37	41.03	1.59	58.30
1992 N-S	36,326,030	32,279,665	2,810,641	71,416,336	50.87	45.20	3.94	52.95
1992 S	9,931,020	8,623,920	474,103	19,029,043	52.19	45.32	2.49	53.52
1994 N-S	24,523,071	27,277,966	1,284,591	53,085,628	46.20	51.38	2.42	47.34
1994 S	6,021,298	7,622,719	198,968	13,842,985	43.50	55.07	1.44	44.13
1996 N-S	33,180,536	31,170,217	1,987,343	66,338,096	50.02	46.99	3.00	51.56
1996 S	8,147,130	9,694,213	330,921	18,172,264	44.83	53.35	1.82	45.66
1998 N-S	25,464,511	24,949,538	1,634,389	52,048,438	48.92	47.94	3.14	50.51
1998 S	5,055,242	6,330,287	414,051	11,799,580	42.84	53.65	3.51	44.40

Notes: Entries are calculated from the raw vote values in Tables 5-70 through 5-122. Whenever bold italicized values occur in Tables 5-70 through 5-122, denoting the author's alternate party coding system, they are used instead of the conventionally coded main entries in these tables in the aggregation process to the regional level for Table 5-8. See text and Table 5-1 for a more complete discussion of the conventional and alternate party coding systems. Also see Table 1-3 for a similar dis-cussion. Entries in Table 5-8 are, therefore, based on candidates who use the designation "Democrat" or "Republican" (or their historical antecedents listed in Appendix A) either solely or with other labels or parties (often minor parties) on the ballot. In general, historical antecedents to the Democratic Party were Anti-Fed-eralists, Democratic-Republicans, and Jackson Democrats; historical precursors of the Republican Party were Federalists, National Republicans, and Whigs. Other = candidates who use third-party names only on the ballot or are listed as independent or unidentified. Odd-numbered year House elections were held in several states prior to 1880 but only rarely thereafter. States with partial House vote data are not included in the aggregation process. Special House elections are also not included.

[1]Regional categories are adapted from the ICPSR, except that in the current analysis Tennessee is categorized in the South since it was part of the Confederacy, whereas the ICPSR codes it as a Border South state. Thus, the South includes Alabama, Arkansas, Florida, Georgia, Louisiana, Mississippi, North Carolina, South Car-olina, Tennessee, Texas, and Virginia. All other states make up the non-South.

Sources: Data in Tables 5-70 through 5-122 as adapted from *United States Congressional Elections, 1788–1997* (1998), *Congressional Quarterly's Guide to U.S. Elec-tions* (1994), ICPSR data sets 0001 and 0075, *America Votes* (various publication dates), and independent search of state sources by the author.

Table 5-9 Party Victories in House Elections, by State, in Regions, 1788–1822

Region/State	1788	1790	1792	1794	1796	1798	1800	1802	1804	1806	1808	1810	1812	1814	1816	1818	1820	1822	Total Wins	% of Wins
NEW ENGLAND																				
Democratic	0	0	0	5	3	2	8	11	13	20	8	13	10	2	21	33	27	30	206	34.4
Republican	0	0	0	24	26	27	21	24	22	15	27	22	31	39	20	8	12	9	327	54.6
Other	16	19	29	0	0	0	0	0	0	0	0	0	0	0	0	0	2	0	66	11.0
Democratic %	0.0	0.0	0.0	17.2	10.3	6.9	27.6	31.4	37.1	57.1	22.9	37.1	24.4	4.9	51.2	80.5	65.9	76.9	—	—
Republican %	0.0	0.0	0.0	82.8	89.7	93.1	72.4	68.6	62.9	42.9	77.1	62.9	75.6	95.1	48.8	19.5	29.3	23.1	—	—
Other %	100.0	100.0	100.0	0.0	0.0	0.0	0.0	0.0	0.0	0.0	0.0	0.0	0.0	0.0	0.0	0.0	4.9	0.0	—	—
Connecticut																				
Democratic	0	0	0	0	0	0	0	0	0	0	0	0	0	0	0	6	7	6	19	18.3
Republican	0	0	0	7	7	7	7	7	7	7	7	7	7	7	7	1	0	0	85	81.7
Other	5	5	7	0	0	0	0	0	0	0	0	0	0	0	0	0	0	0	0	0.0
Maine																				
Democratic	—	—	—	—	—	—	—	—	—	—	—	—	—	—	—	—	5	5	10	71.4
Republican	—	—	—	—	—	—	—	—	—	—	—	—	—	—	—	—	2	2	4	28.6
Other	—	—	—	—	—	—	—	—	—	—	—	—	—	—	—	—	0	0	0	0.0
Massachusetts																				
Democratic	0	0	0	2	2	1	5	7	10	11	7	8	4	2	9	13	4	6	91	32.9
Republican	0	0	0	12	12	13	9	10	7	6	10	9	16	18	11	7	8	7	155	56.0
Other	8	8	14	0	0	0	0	0	0	0	0	0	0	0	0	0	1	0	31	11.2
New Hampshire																				
Democratic	0	0	0	1	0	0	0	0	0	5	0	2	0	0	6	6	6	6	32	36.8
Republican	0	0	0	3	4	4	4	5	5	0	5	3	6	6	0	0	0	0	45	51.7
Other	3	3	4	0	0	0	0	0	0	0	0	0	0	0	0	0	0	0	10	11.5
Rhode Island																				
Democratic	—	0	0	0	0	0	2	2	2	2	0	0	0	0	0	2	1	2	13	39.4
Republican	—	0	0	2	2	2	0	0	0	0	2	2	2	2	2	0	0	0	16	48.5
Other	—	1	2	0	0	0	0	0	0	0	0	0	0	0	0	0	1	0	4	12.1
Vermont																				
Democratic	—	0	0	2	1	1	1	2	1	2	1	3	6	0	6	6	4	5	41	61.2
Republican	—	0	0	0	1	1	1	2	3	2	3	1	0	6	0	0	2	0	22	32.8
Other	—	2	2	0	0	0	0	0	0	0	0	0	0	0	0	0	0	0	4	6.0
MID-ATLANTIC																				
Democratic	4	1	8	14	11	17	21	36	38	32	27	34	32	41	47	47	46	61	517	69.4
Republican	10	5	14	15	18	12	8	6	4	5	15	7	26	17	11	11	12	6	202	27.1
Other	5	13	7	0	0	0	0	0	0	0	0	1	0	0	0	0	0	0	26	3.5
Democratic %	21.1	5.3	27.6	48.3	37.9	58.6	72.4	85.7	90.5	86.5	64.3	80.9	55.2	70.7	81.0	81.0	79.3	91.0	—	—
Republican %	52.6	26.3	48.3	51.7	62.1	41.4	27.6	14.3	9.5	13.5	35.7	16.7	44.8	29.3	19.0	19.0	20.7	9.0	—	—
Other %	26.3	68.4	24.1	0.0	0.0	0.0	0.0	0.0	0.0	0.0	0.0	2.4	0.0	0.0	0.0	0.0	0.0	0.0	—	—
Delaware																				
Democratic	0	0	0	1	0	0	0	1	0	0	0	0	0	0	1	1	1	0	5	21.7
Republican	0	0	0	0	1	1	1	0	1	1	1	1	2	2	1	1	1	1	15	65.2
Other	1	1	1	0	0	0	0	0	0	0	0	0	0	0	0	0	0	0	3	13.1
New Jersey																				
Democratic	0	0	0	0	0	3	5	6	6	6	6	6	2	6	6	6	6	6	70	70.7
Republican	0	0	0	5	5	2	0	0	0	0	0	0	4	0	0	0	0	0	16	16.2
Other	4	4	5	0	0	0	0	0	0	0	0	0	0	0	0	0	0	0	13	13.1
New York																				
Democratic	2	1	3	5	4	6	6	11	15	14	9	12	8	19	22	22	27	34	220	69.6
Republican	4	5	7	5	6	4	4	6	2	3	8	5	19	8	5	5	0	0	96	30.4
Other	0	0	0	0	0	0	0	0	0	0	0	0	0	0	0	0	0	0	0	0.0

(Table continues)

Table 5-9 (Continued)

Region/State	1788	1790	1792	1794	1796	1798	1800	1802	1804	1806	1808	1810	1812	1814	1816	1818	1820	1822	Total Wins	% of Wins
Pennsylvania																				
Democratic	2	0	5	8	7	8	10	18	17	12	12	16	22	16	18	18	12	21	222	72.5
Republican	6	0	7	5	6	5	3	0	1	1	6	1	1	7	5	5	11	5	75	24.5
Other	0	8	1	0	0	0	0	0	0	5	0	1	0	0	0	0	0	0	9	3.0
SOUTH																				
Democratic	0	0	7	32	30	18	27	41	46	46	39	40	47	48	53	53	56	47	630	75.4
Republican	0	0	3	5	8	20	11	8	2	3	10	9	11	10	6	7	4	5	122	14.6
Other	18	23	27	0	0	0	0	0	1	0	0	0	0	0	0	0	0	15	84	10.0
Democratic %	0.0	0.0	18.9	86.5	78.9	47.4	71.1	83.7	93.9	93.9	79.6	81.6	81.0	82.8	89.8	88.3	93.3	70.1	—	—
Republican %	0.0	0.0	8.1	13.5	21.1	52.6	28.9	16.3	4.1	6.1	20.4	18.4	19.0	17.2	10.2	11.7	6.7	7.5	—	—
Other %	100.0	100.0	73.0	0.0	0.0	0.0	0.0	0.0	2.0	0.0	0.0	0.0	0.0	0.0	0.0	0.0	0.0	22.4	—	—
Alabama																				
Democratic	—	—	—	—	—	—	—	—	—	—	—	—	—	—	1	1	1	3	5	100.0
Republican	—	—	—	—	—	—	—	—	—	—	—	—	—	—	0	0	0	0	0	0.0
Other	—	—	—	—	—	—	—	—	—	—	—	—	—	—	0	0	0	0	0	0.0
Georgia																				
Democratic	0	0	0	2	2	0	2	4	4	4	4	4	6	6	6	6	6	7	63	86.3
Republican	0	0	0	0	0	2	0	0	0	0	0	0	0	0	0	0	0	0	2	2.7
Other	3	3	2	0	0	0	0	0	0	0	0	0	0	0	0	0	0	0	8	10.9
Louisiana																				
Democratic	—	—	—	—	—	—	—	—	—	—	—	—	1	1	1	1	1	0	5	62.5
Republican	—	—	—	—	—	—	—	—	—	—	—	—	0	0	0	0	0	0	0	0.0
Other	—	—	—	—	—	—	—	—	—	—	—	—	0	0	0	0	0	3	3	37.5
Mississippi																				
Democratic	—	—	—	—	—	—	—	—	—	—	—	—	—	—	1	1	1	0	3	75.0
Republican	—	—	—	—	—	—	—	—	—	—	—	—	—	—	0	0	0	0	0	0.0
Other	—	—	—	—	—	—	—	—	—	—	—	—	—	—	0	0	0	1	1	25.0
North Carolina																				
Democratic	—	0	7	9	9	5	5	10	12	11	8	10	9	9	10	9	11	10	144	74.6
Republican	—	0	3	1	1	5	5	2	0	1	4	2	4	4	3	4	2	3	44	22.8
Other	—	5	0	0	0	0	0	0	0	0	0	0	0	0	0	0	0	0	5	2.6
South Carolina																				
Democratic	0	0	3	5	3	1	2	6	8	8	8	8	9	8	9	9	9	7	98	74.2
Republican	0	0	5	5	3	5	4	2	0	0	0	0	0	1	0	0	0	0	18	13.6
Other	5	8	2	0	0	0	0	0	0	0	0	0	0	0	0	0	0	2	16	12.1
Tennessee																				
Democratic	—	—	—	—	1	1	1	3	3	3	3	3	6	6	6	6	6	0	39	81.3
Republican	—	—	—	—	0	0	0	0	0	0	0	0	0	0	0	0	0	0	0	0.0
Other	—	—	—	—	0	0	0	0	0	0	0	0	0	0	0	0	0	9	9	18.7
Virginia																				
Democratic	0	0	0	18	15	11	17	18	19	20	16	15	16	18	20	20	21	20	264	73.1
Republican	0	0	0	1	4	8	2	4	2	2	6	7	7	5	3	3	2	2	58	16.1
Other	10	10	19	0	0	0	0	0	1	0	0	0	0	0	0	0	0	0	39	10.8
BORDER SOUTH																				
Democratic	0	0	3	5	4	5	7	12	13	12	12	12	16	14	14	16	16	6	167	65.5
Republican	5	0	5	5	6	5	3	3	2	3	3	3	3	5	5	3	3	3	65	25.5
Other	1	8	2	0	0	0	0	0	0	0	0	0	0	0	0	0	0	12	23	9.0
Democratic %	0.0	0.0	30.0	50.0	40.0	50.0	70.0	80.0	86.7	80.0	80.0	80.0	84.2	73.7	73.7	84.2	84.2	28.6	—	—
Republican %	83.3	0.0	50.0	50.0	60.0	50.0	30.0	20.0	13.3	20.0	20.0	20.0	15.8	26.3	26.3	15.8	15.8	14.3	—	—
Other %	16.7	100.0	20.0	0.0	0.0	0.0	0.0	0.0	0.0	0.0	0.0	0.0	0.0	0.0	0.0	0.0	0.0	57.1	—	—
Kentucky																				
Democratic	—	0	0	2	2	2	2	6	6	6	6	6	10	10	10	10	10	0	88	84.6
Republican	—	0	0	0	0	0	0	0	0	0	0	0	0	0	0	0	0	0	0	0.0
Other	—	2	2	0	0	0	0	0	0	0	0	0	0	0	0	0	0	12	16	15.4

Table 5-9 (Continued)

Region/State	1788	1790	1792	1794	1796	1798	1800	1802	1804	1806	1808	1810	1812	1814	1816	1818	1820	1822	Total Wins	% of Wins
Maryland																				
Democratic	0	0	3	3	2	3	5	6	7	6	6	6	6	4	4	6	6	6	79	52.3
Republican	5	0	5	5	6	5	3	3	2	3	3	3	3	5	5	3	3	3	65	43.0
Other	1	6	0	0	0	0	0	0	0	0	0	0	0	0	0	0	0	0	7	4.6
MIDWEST																				
Democratic	—	—	—	—	—	—	—	1	1	1	1	1	5	6	6	7	9	5	43	71.7
Republican	—	—	—	—	—	—	—	0	0	0	0	0	1	0	1	1	0	1	4	6.7
Other	—	—	—	—	—	—	—	0	0	0	0	0	0	0	0	0	0	13	13	21.7
Democratic %	—	—	—	—	—	—	—	100.0	100.0	100.0	100.0	100.0	83.3	100.0	85.7	87.5	100.0	26.3	—	—
Republican %	—	—	—	—	—	—	—	0.0	0.0	0.0	0.0	0.0	16.7	0.0	14.3	12.5	0.0	5.3	—	—
Other %	—	—	—	—	—	—	—	0.0	0.0	0.0	0.0	0.0	0.0	0.0	0.0	0.0	0.0	68.4	—	—
Illinois																				
Democratic	—	—	—	—	—	—	—	—	—	—	—	—	—	—	—	1	1	1	3	100.0
Republican	—	—	—	—	—	—	—	—	—	—	—	—	—	—	—	0	0	0	0	0.0
Other	—	—	—	—	—	—	—	—	—	—	—	—	—	—	—	0	0	0	0	0.0
Indiana																				
Democratic	—	—	—	—	—	—	—	—	—	—	—	—	—	—	1	1	1	0	3	100.0
Republican	—	—	—	—	—	—	—	—	—	—	—	—	—	—	0	0	0	0	0	0.0
Other	—	—	—	—	—	—	—	—	—	—	—	—	—	—	0	0	0	3	3	0.0
Missouri																				
Democratic	—	—	—	—	—	—	—	—	—	—	—	—	—	—	—	—	1	0	1	50.0
Republican	—	—	—	—	—	—	—	—	—	—	—	—	—	—	—	—	0	0	0	0.0
Other	—	—	—	—	—	—	—	—	—	—	—	—	—	—	—	—	0	1	1	50.0
Ohio																				
Democratic	—	—	—	—	—	—	—	1	1	1	1	1	5	6	5	5	6	4	36	73.5
Republican	—	—	—	—	—	—	—	0	0	0	0	0	1	0	1	1	0	1	4	8.2
Other	—	—	—	—	—	—	—	0	0	0	0	0	0	0	0	0	0	9	9	18.4

Notes: Entries reflect winners from the actual vote results and are not adjusted for contested seats, runoffs, inaccuracies of other types in reporting party labels or winners, or gubernatorial and legislative proclamations of different winners. For these reasons, these figures may not completely correspond to the most recent reports of the Clerk of the House of Representatives regarding the composition of the House over time. The regional categories are adapted from the ICPSR, except that in the current analysis Tennessee is coded in the South, because it was part of the Confederacy, whereas the ICPSR places Tennessee in the Border South. House elections were generally held in both even- and odd-numbered years prior to 1880 (that is, in two-year election cycles). Although only the even-numbered years of these two-year election cycles are used as column headings in this table, the House election results for both the even- and odd-numbered years in these two-year election cycles are reported as data in the table. —indicates state not yet in Union or data unavailable for that state. North Carolina and Rhode Island had elections in 1790 for the first Congress; as a result, they are not included in the table for either the 1788–1789 elections (1st Congress) or the 1790–1791 elections (2d Congress).

Sources: Data adapted from *United States Congressional Elections, 1788–1997* (1998), *Congressional Quarterly's Guide to U.S. Elections* (1994), Report of the Clerk of the House of Representatives (various dates), and independent search of state sources by the author.

Table 5-10 Party Victories in House Elections, by State, in Regions, 1824–1852

Region/State	1824	1826	1828	1830	1832	1834	1836	1838	1840	1842	1844	1846	1848	1850	1852	Total Wins	% of Wins
NEW ENGLAND Democratic	27	8	9	12	12	21	19	15	9	19	11	10	12	13	12	209	39.4
Republican	9	27	30	25	21	15	19	23	29	10	20	21	17	17	16	299	56.4
Other	3	4	0	2	5	2	0	0	0	2	0	0	2	1	1	22	4.2
Democratic %	69.2	20.5	23.1	30.8	31.6	55.3	50.0	39.5	23.7	61.3	35.5	32.2	38.7	41.9	41.4	—	—
Republican %	23.1	69.2	76.9	64.1	55.3	39.5	50.0	60.5	76.3	32.2	64.5	67.8	54.8	54.8	55.2	—	—
Other %	7.7	10.3	0.0	5.1	13.2	5.3	0.0	0.0	0.0	6.5	0.0	0.0	6.5	3.2	3.4	—	—
Connecticut Democratic	6	0	0	0	0	6	6	0	0	4	0	0	3	3	4	32	41.0
Republican	0	6	6	6	6	0	0	6	6	0	4	4	1	1	0	46	59.0
Other	0	0	0	0	0	0	0	0	0	0	0	0	0	0	0	0	0.0
Maine Democratic	5	2	3	6	7	6	5	6	2	5	5	5	5	5	3	70	64.2
Republican	1	4	4	1	1	2	3	2	6	2	2	2	2	2	3	37	33.9
Other	1	1	0	0	0	0	0	0	0	0	0	0	0	0	0	2	1.8
Massachusetts Democratic	4	0	0	0	0	1	2	2	2	5	1	0	0	1	0	18	10.4
Republican	8	12	13	12	11	10	10	10	10	5	9	10	8	8	10	146	84.4
Other	1	1	0	1	1	1	0	0	0	0	0	0	2	1	1	9	5.2
New Hampshire Democratic	6	6	6	6	5	5	5	5	5	4	4	4	2	2	3	68	94.4
Republican	0	0	0	0	0	0	0	0	0	0	0	0	2	2	0	4	5.6
Other	0	0	0	0	0	0	0	0	0	0	0	0	0	0	0	0	0.0
Rhode Island Democratic	2	0	0	0	0	2	0	0	0	0	0	0	1	1	2	8	26.7
Republican	0	2	2	2	1	0	2	2	2	0	2	2	1	1	0	19	63.3
Other	0	0	0	0	1	0	0	0	0	2	0	0	0	0	0	3	10.0
Vermont Democratic	4	0	0	0	0	1	1	2	0	1	1	1	1	1	0	13	19.1
Republican	0	3	5	4	2	3	4	3	5	3	3	3	3	3	3	47	69.1
Other	1	2	0	1	3	1	0	0	0	0	0	0	0	0	0	8	11.8
MID-ATLANTIC Democratic	60	43	41	39	53	54	48	42	36	39	34	18	11	37	43	598	58.2
Republican	7	23	20	14	4	18	23	33	39	24	24	44	51	27	20	371	36.1
Other	0	1	6	14	18	3	4	0	0	1	6	2	2	0	1	58	5.6
Democratic %	89.6	64.2	61.2	58.2	70.7	72.0	64.0	56.0	48.0	60.9	53.1	28.1	17.2	57.8	67.2	—	—
Republican %	10.4	34.3	29.9	20.9	5.3	24.0	30.7	44.0	52.0	37.5	37.5	68.8	79.7	42.2	31.3	—	—
Other %	0.0	1.5	8.9	20.9	24.0	4.0	5.3	0.0	0.0	1.6	9.4	3.1	3.1	0.0	1.6	—	—
Delaware Democratic	0	0	0	0	0	0	0	1	0	0	0	0	0	1	1	3	20.0
Republican	1	1	1	1	1	1	1	0	1	1	1	1	1	0	0	12	80.0
Other	0	0	0	0	0	0	0	0	0	0	0	0	0	0	0	0	0.0
New Jersey Democratic	0	1	0	0	6	6	0	5	0	4	1	1	1	4	4	33	39.3
Republican	6	5	6	6	0	0	6	1	6	1	4	4	4	1	1	51	60.7
Other	0	0	0	0	0	0	0	0	0	0	0	0	0	0	0	0	0.0
New York Democratic	34	20	18	23	32	31	30	19	21	24	21	10	1	17	21	322	59.7
Republican	0	14	12	3	0	9	10	21	19	10	9	23	32	17	11	190	35.3
Other	0	0	4	8	8	0	0	0	0	0	4	1	1	0	1	27	5.0
Pennsylvania Democratic	26	22	23	16	15	17	18	17	15	11	12	7	9	15	17	240	61.7
Republican	0	3	1	4	3	8	6	11	13	12	10	16	14	9	8	118	30.3
Other	0	1	2	6	10	3	4	0	0	1	2	1	1	0	0	31	8.0
SOUTH Democratic	20	28	55	47	49	42	44	40	38	53	50	43	50	39	52	650	62.0
Republican	3	8	12	11	17	24	30	36	37	13	15	26	19	18	12	281	26.8
Other	44	31	0	9	9	9	2	0	1	0	0	0	0	12	0	117	11.2
Democratic %	29.9	41.8	82.1	70.1	65.3	56.0	57.9	52.6	50.0	80.3	76.9	62.3	72.5	56.5	81.3	—	—
Republican %	4.5	11.9	17.9	16.4	22.7	32.0	39.5	47.4	48.7	19.7	23.1	37.7	27.5	26.1	18.7	—	—
Other %	65.7	46.3	0.0	13.4	12.0	12.0	2.6	0.0	1.3	0.0	0.0	0.0	0.0	17.4	0.0	—	—

Table 5-10 *(Continued)*

Region/State	*1824*	*1826*	*1828*	*1830*	*1832*	*1834*	*1836*	*1838*	*1840*	*1842*	*1844*	*1846*	*1848*	*1850*	*1852*	*Total Wins*	*% of Wins*
Alabama																	
Democratic	3	3	3	3	5	3	3	3	5	6	1	5	5	4	6	58	79.5
Republican	0	0	0	0	0	2	2	2	0	1	0	2	2	3	1	15	20.5
Other	0	0	0	0	0	0	0	0	0	0	0	0	0	0	0	0	0.0
Arkansas																	
Democratic	—	—	—	—	—	—	1	1	1	1	1	1	1	1	2	0	0.0
Republican	—	—	—	—	—	—	0	0	0	0	0	0	0	0	0	10	100.0
Other	—	—	—	—	—	—	0	0	0	0	0	0	0	0	0	0	0.0
Florida																	
Democratic	—	—	—	—	—	—	—	—	—	—	—	0	0	0	1	1	50.0
Republican	—	—	—	—	—	—	—	—	—	—	—	1	1	1	0	1	50.0
Other	—	—	—	—	—	—	—	—	—	—	—	0	0	0	0	0	0.0
Georgia																	
Democratic	7	7	7	7	9	9	8	0	0	8	4	4	4	0	6	80	66.1
Republican	0	0	0	0	0	0	1	9	9	0	4	4	4	0	2	33	27.3
Other	0	0	0	0	0	0	0	0	0	0	0	0	0	8	0	8	6.6
Louisiana																	
Democratic	1	1	1	0	1	1	1	0	1	4	3	3	3	2	3	25	49.0
Republican	0	2	2	3	2	2	2	3	2	0	1	1	1	2	1	24	47.1
Other	2	0	0	0	0	0	0	0	0	0	0	0	0	0	0	2	3.9
Mississippi																	
Democratic	1	1	1	1	2	2	2	2	2	4	4	3	4	0	5	34	87.2
Republican	0	0	0	0	0	0	0	0	0	0	0	1	0	0	0	1	2.6
Other	0	0	0	0	0	0	0	0	0	0	0	0	0	4	0	4	10.3
North Carolina																	
Democratic	5	0	10	11	7	6	6	9	6	5	6	3	3	3	5	85	50.0
Republican	0	3	3	2	6	7	7	4	7	4	3	6	6	6	3	67	39.4
Other	8	10	0	0	0	0	0	0	0	0	0	0	0	0	0	18	10.6
South Carolina																	
Democratic	3	9	9	0	0	0	5	7	8	7	7	7	7	7	6	82	67.2
Republican	0	0	0	0	0	0	2	2	1	0	0	0	0	0	0	5	4.1
Other	6	0	0	9	9	9	2	0	0	0	0	0	0	0	0	35	28.7
Tennessee																	
Democratic	0	5	8	8	12	5	3	6	5	6	6	6	7	7	5	89	53.6
Republican	0	0	1	1	1	8	10	7	8	5	5	5	4	4	5	64	38.6
Other	9	4	0	0	0	0	0	0	0	0	0	0	0	0	0	13	7.8
Texas																	
Democratic	—	—	—	—	—	—	—	—	—	—	—	2	2	2	2	8	100.0
Republican	—	—	—	—	—	—	—	—	—	—	—	0	0	0	0	0	0.0
Other	—	—	—	—	—	—	—	—	—	—	—	0	0	0	0	0	0.0
Virginia																	
Democratic	0	2	16	17	13	16	15	12	10	12	13	9	14	13	13	175	62.3
Republican	3	3	6	5	8	5	6	9	10	3	2	6	1	2	0	69	24.6
Other	19	17	0	0	0	0	0	0	1	0	0	0	0	0	0	37	13.2
BORDER SOUTH																	
Democratic	16	9	16	12	10	7	5	7	4	5	7	6	7	7	9	127	44.6
Republican	3	8	5	9	11	14	15	14	17	11	9	10	9	9	7	151	53.0
Other	2	4	0	0	0	0	1	0	0	0	0	0	0	0	0	7	2.5
Democratic %	76.2	42.9	76.2	57.1	47.6	33.3	23.8	33.3	19.0	31.3	43.7	37.5	43.7	43.7	56.3	—	—
Republican %	14.3	38.1	23.8	42.9	52.4	66.7	71.4	66.7	81.0	68.8	56.3	62.5	56.3	56.3	43.7	—	—
Other %	9.5	19.0	0.0	0.0	0.0	0.0	4.8	0.0	0.0	0.0	0.0	0.0	0.0	0.0	0.0	—	—
Kentucky																	
Democratic	10	7	10	8	6	4	1	2	2	5	3	4	4	5	5	76	43.9
Republican	0	5	2	4	7	9	11	11	11	5	7	6	6	5	5	94	54.3
Other	2	0	0	0	0	0	1	0	0	0	0	0	0	0	0	3	1.7
Maryland																	
Democratic	6	2	6	4	4	3	4	5	2	0	4	2	3	2	4	51	45.5
Republican	3	3	3	5	4	5	4	3	6	6	2	4	3	4	2	57	50.9
Other	0	4	0	0	0	0	0	0	0	0	0	0	0	0	0	4	3.6

(Table continues)

Table 5-10 (Continued)

Region/State	1824	1826	1828	1830	1832	1834	1836	1838	1840	1842	1844	1846	1848	1850	1852	Total Wins	% of Wins
MIDWEST																	
Democratic	4	4	11	10	20	21	15	20	12	34	34	31	36	31	29	312	59.8
Republican	0	14	8	9	9	10	17	12	20	12	12	17	11	18	16	185	35.4
Other	15	1	0	0	2	1	0	0	0	0	0	0	3	1	2	25	4.8
Democratic %	21.1	21.1	57.9	52.6	64.5	65.6	46.9	62.5	37.5	73.9	73.9	64.6	72.0	62.0	61.7	—	—
Republican %	0.0	73.7	42.1	47.4	29.0	31.3	53.1	37.5	62.5	26.1	26.1	35.4	22.0	36.0	34.0	—	—
Other %	78.9	5.3	0.0	0.0	6.5	3.1	0.0	0.0	0.0	0.0	0.0	0.0	6.0	2.0	4.3	—	—
Illinois																	
Democratic	0	1	1	1	3	3	3	2	2	6	6	6	6	6	5	51	81.0
Republican	0	0	0	0	0	0	0	1	1	1	1	1	1	1	4	11	17.5
Other	1	0	0	0	0	0	0	0	0	0	0	0	0	0	0	1	1.6
Indiana																	
Democratic	3	1	1	3	6	7	1	4	1	8	8	5	8	8	0	64	65.3
Republican	0	2	2	0	1	0	6	3	6	2	2	5	1	2	1	33	33.7
Other	0	0	0	0	0	0	0	0	0	0	0	0	1	0	0	1	1.0
Iowa																	
Democratic	—	—	—	—	—	—	—	—	—	—	—	2	2	2	1	7	87.5
Republican	—	—	—	—	—	—	—	—	—	—	—	0	0	0	1	1	12.5
Other	—	—	—	—	—	—	—	—	—	—	—	0	0	0	0	0	0.0
Michigan																	
Democratic	—	—	—	—	—	1	1	1	0	3	3	3	2	1	4	19	82.6
Republican	—	—	—	—	—	0	0	0	1	0	0	0	1	2	0	4	17.4
Other	—	—	—	—	—	0	0	0	0	0	0	0	0	0	0	0	0.0
Missouri																	
Democratic	1	0	1	1	0	1	2	2	2	5	4	5	5	2	3	34	73.9
Republican	0	0	0	0	2	0	0	0	0	0	1	0	0	3	4	10	21.7
Other	0	1	0	0	0	1	0	0	0	0	0	0	0	0	0	2	4.3
Ohio																	
Democratic	0	2	8	5	11	9	8	11	7	12	13	10	11	11	12	130	46.9
Republican	0	12	6	9	6	10	11	8	12	9	8	11	8	9	7	126	45.5
Other	14	0	0	0	2	0	0	0	0	0	0	0	2	1	2	21	7.6
Wisconsin																	
Democratic	—	—	—	—	—	—	—	—	—	—	—	—	2	1	3	6	85.7
Republican	—	—	—	—	—	—	—	—	—	—	—	—	0	1	0	1	14.3
Other	—	—	—	—	—	—	—	—	—	—	—	—	0	0	0	0	0.0
WEST																	
Democratic	—	—	—	—	—	—	—	—	—	—	—	—	1	2	2	5	83.3
Republican	—	—	—	—	—	—	—	—	—	—	—	—	0	0	0	0	0.0
Other	—	—	—	—	—	—	—	—	—	—	—	—	1	0	0	1	16.7
Democratic %	—	—	—	—	—	—	—	—	—	—	—	—	50.0	100.0	100.0	—	—
Republican %	—	—	—	—	—	—	—	—	—	—	—	—	0.0	0.0	0.0	—	—
Other %	—	—	—	—	—	—	—	—	—	—	—	—	50.0	0.0	0.0	—	—
California																	
Democratic	—	—	—	—	—	—	—	—	—	—	—	—	1	2	2	5	83.3
Republican	—	—	—	—	—	—	—	—	—	—	—	—	0	0	0	0	0.0
Other	—	—	—	—	—	—	—	—	—	—	—	—	1	0	0	1	16.7

Notes: Entries reflect winners from the actual vote results and are not adjusted for contested seats, runoffs, inaccuracies of other types in reporting party labels or winners, or gubernatorial and legislative proclamations of different winners. For these reasons, these figures may not completely correspond to the most recent reports of the Clerk of the House of Representatives regarding the composition of the House over time. The regional categories are adapted from the ICPSR, except that in the current analysis Tennessee is coded in the South, because it was part of the Confederacy, whereas the ICPSR places Tennessee in the Border South. House elections were generally held in both even- and odd-numbered years prior to 1880 (that is, in two-year election cycles). Although only the even-numbered years of these two-year election cycles are used as column headings in this table, the House election results for both the even- and odd-numbered years in these two-year election cycles are reported as data in the table. —indicates state not yet in Union or data unavailable for that state.

Sources: Data adapted from *United States Congressional Elections, 1788–1997* (1998), *Congressional Quarterly's Guide to U.S. Elections* (1994), Report of the Clerk of the House of Representatives (various dates), and independent search of state sources by the author.

Table 5-11 Party Victories in House Elections, by State, in Regions, 1854–1892

Region/State	1854	1856	1858	1860	1862	1864	1866	1868	1870	1872	1874	1876	1878	1880	1882	1884	1886	1888	1890	1892	Total Wins	% of Wins
NEW ENGLAND																						
Democratic	1	2	2	3	3	0	3	1	4	2	9	5	3	4	7	4	9	3	14	6	85	15.5
Republican	8	27	27	26	24	27	24	26	23	26	17	23	24	24	19	22	17	23	12	21	440	80.3
Other	20	0	0	0	0	0	0	0	0	0	2	0	1	0	0	0	0	0	0	0	23	4.2
Democratic %	3.4	6.9	6.9	10.3	11.1	0.0	11.1	3.7	14.8	7.1	32.1	17.9	10.7	14.3	26.9	15.4	34.6	11.5	53.8	22.2	—	—
Republican %	27.6	93.1	93.1	89.7	88.9	100.0	88.9	96.3	85.2	92.9	60.7	82.1	85.7	85.7	73.1	84.6	65.4	88.5	46.2	77.8	—	—
Other %	69.0	0.0	0.0	0.0	0.0	0.0	0.0	0.0	0.0	0.0	7.1	0.0	3.6	0.0	0.0	0.0	0.0	0.0	0.0	0.0	—	—
Connecticut																						
Democratic	0	2	0	2	1	0	3	3	1	1	3	3	1	1	3	2	3	1	3	3	34	42.5
Republican	0	2	4	2	3	4	1	1	3	3	1	1	3	3	1	2	1	3	1	1	42	52.5
Other	4	0	0	0	0	0	0	0	0	0	0	0	0	0	0	0	0	0	0	0	4	5.0
Maine																						
Democratic	1	0	0	0	1	0	0	0	0	0	0	0	1	2	0	0	0	0	0	0	5	5.1
Republican	5	6	6	6	4	5	5	5	5	5	5	5	3	3	4	4	4	4	4	4	92	93.9
Other	0	0	0	0	0	0	0	0	0	0	0	0	1	0	0	0	0	0	0	0	1	1.0
Massachusetts																						
Democratic	0	0	0	1	0	0	0	0	0	0	4	1	1	1	4	2	4	2	7	3	30	13.5
Republican	0	11	11	10	10	10	10	10	10	11	5	10	10	10	8	10	8	10	5	10	179	80.6
Other	11	0	0	0	0	0	0	0	0	0	2	0	0	0	0	0	0	0	0	0	13	5.9
New Hampshire																						
Democratic	0	0	0	0	1	0	0	0	3	1	2	1	0	0	0	0	1	0	2	0	11	20.4
Republican	0	3	3	3	2	3	3	3	0	2	1	2	3	3	2	2	1	2	0	2	40	74.1
Other	3	0	0	0	0	0	0	0	0	0	0	0	0	0	0	0	0	0	0	0	3	5.6
Rhode Island																						
Democratic	0	0	2	0	0	0	0	0	0	0	0	0	0	0	0	0	0	0	2	0	5	12.5
Republican	0	2	0	2	2	2	2	2	2	2	2	2	2	2	2	2	1	2	0	2	33	82.5
Other	2	0	0	0	0	0	0	0	0	0	0	0	0	0	0	0	0	0	0	0	2	5.0
Vermont																						
Democratic	0	0	0	0	0	0	0	0	0	0	0	0	0	0	0	0	0	0	0	0	0	0.0
Republican	3	3	3	3	3	3	3	3	3	3	3	3	3	3	2	2	2	2	2	2	54	100.0
Other	0	0	0	0	0	0	0	0	0	0	0	0	0	0	0	0	0	0	0	0	0	0.0
MID-ATLANTIC																						
Democratic	14	30	12	19	34	23	21	26	30	15	41	31	20	25	37	29	27	27	39	37	537	40.6
Republican	47	34	52	44	27	38	40	35	31	53	27	37	48	43	33	41	43	43	31	36	783	59.1
Other	3	0	0	1	0	0	0	0	0	0	0	0	0	0	0	0	0	0	0	0	4	0.3
Democratic %	21.9	46.9	18.8	29.7	55.7	37.7	34.4	42.6	49.2	22.1	60.3	45.6	29.4	36.8	52.9	41.4	38.6	38.6	55.7	50.7	—	—
Republican %	73.4	53.1	81.3	68.8	44.3	62.3	65.6	57.4	50.8	77.9	39.7	54.4	70.6	63.2	47.1	58.6	61.4	61.4	44.3	49.3	—	—
Other %	4.7	0.0	0.0	1.6	0.0	0.0	0.0	0.0	0.0	0.0	0.0	0.0	0.0	0.0	0.0	0.0	0.0	0.0	0.0	0.0	—	—
Delaware																						
Democratic	0	1	1	0	1	1	1	1	1	0	1	1	1	1	1	1	1	1	1	1	17	85.0
Republican	0	0	0	0	0	0	0	0	0	1	0	0	0	0	0	0	0	0	0	0	1	5.0
Other	1	0	0	1	0	0	0	0	0	0	0	0	0	0	0	0	0	0	0	0	2	10.0
New Jersey																						
Democratic	1	3	2	3	4	3	2	3	2	1	5	4	3	3	3	3	3	3	5	6	62	50.4
Republican	4	2	3	2	1	2	3	2	3	6	2	3	4	4	4	4	4	4	2	2	61	49.6
Other	0	0	0	0	0	0	0	0	0	0	0	0	0	0	0	0	0	0	0	0	0	0.0
New York																						
Democratic	5	11	4	10	17	11	12	13	16	9	18	16	7	13	21	17	15	16	23	20	274	41.8
Republican	27	22	29	23	14	20	19	18	15	24	15	17	26	20	13	17	19	18	11	14	381	58.1
Other	1	0	0	0	0	0	0	0	0	0	0	0	0	0	0	0	0	0	0	0	1	0.2
Pennsylvania																						
Democratic	8	15	5	6	12	8	6	9	11	5	17	10	9	8	12	8	8	7	10	10	184	35.0
Republican	16	10	20	19	12	16	18	15	13	22	10	17	18	19	16	20	20	21	18	20	340	64.8
Other	1	0	0	0	0	0	0	0	0	0	0	0	0	0	0	0	0	0	0	0	1	0.2

(Table continues)

Table 5-11 (Continued)

Region/State	1854	1856	1858	1860	1862	1864	1866	1868	1870	1872	1874	1876	1878	1880	1882	1884	1886	1888	1890	1892	Total Wins	% of Wins
SOUTH																						
Democratic	50	59	51	n/a	n/a	n/a	n/a	10	18	25	56	63	67	62	70	77	74	76	82	86	926	77.5
Republican	0	1	4	n/a	n/a	n/a	n/a	42	30	44	17	10	4	7	7	8	9	9	3	4	199	16.7
Other	16	6	11	n/a	n/a	n/a	n/a	7	11	4	0	0	2	3	8	0	2	0	0	0	70	5.9
Democratic %	75.8	89.4	77.3	n/a	n/a	n/a	n/a	16.9	30.5	34.2	76.7	86.3	91.8	86.1	82.4	90.6	87.1	89.4	96.5	95.6	—	—
Republican %	0.0	1.5	6.1	n/a	n/a	n/a	n/a	71.2	50.8	60.3	23.3	13.7	5.5	9.7	8.2	9.4	10.6	10.6	3.5	4.4	—	—
Other %	24.2	9.1	16.7	n/a	n/a	n/a	n/a	11.9	18.6	5.5	0.0	0.0	2.7	4.2	9.4	0.0	2.4	0.0	0.0	0.0	—	—
Alabama																						
Democratic	5	7	7	n/a	n/a	n/a	n/a	2	3	3	6	8	7	8	8	8	8	8	8	9	105	86.1
Republican	0	0	0	n/a	n/a	n/a	n/a	4	3	5	2	0	0	0	0	0	0	0	0	0	14	11.5
Other	2	0	0	n/a	n/a	n/a	n/a	0	0	0	0	0	1	0	0	0	0	0	0	0	3	2.5
Arkansas																						
Democratic	2	2	2	1	n/a	n/a	n/a	1	2	0	4	4	4	4	5	5	5	5	5	6	50	86.2
Republican	0	0	0	0	n/a	n/a	n/a	2	1	4	0	0	0	0	0	0	0	0	0	0	7	12.1
Other	0	0	0	1	n/a	n/a	n/a	0	0	0	0	0	0	0	0	0	0	0	0	0	1	1.7
Florida																						
Democratic	1	1	1	1	n/a	n/a	n/a	0	0	0	0	1	2	2	1	2	2	2	2	2	16	69.6
Republican	0	0	0	0	n/a	n/a	n/a	1	1	2	2	1	0	0	0	0	0	0	0	0	7	30.4
Other	0	0	0	0	n/a	n/a	n/a	0	0	0	0	0	0	0	0	0	0	0	0	0	0	0.0
Georgia																						
Democratic	6	6	6	n/a	n/a	n/a	n/a	3	4	7	9	9	9	9	9	10	10	10	10	11	110	88.0
Republican	0	0	0	n/a	n/a	n/a	n/a	4	3	2	0	0	0	0	0	0	0	0	0	0	9	7.2
Other	2	2	2	n/a	n/a	n/a	n/a	0	0	0	0	0	0	0	0	0	0	0	0	0	6	4.8
Louisiana																						
Democratic	3	3	3	n/a	n/a	n/a	n/a	1	0	0	3	4	6	5	5	5	6	5	6	6	52	65.8
Republican	0	0	0	n/a	n/a	n/a	n/a	4	5	6	3	2	0	1	1	1	0	1	0	0	24	30.4
Other	1	1	1	n/a	n/a	n/a	n/a	0	0	0	0	0	0	0	0	0	0	0	0	0	3	3.8
Mississippi																						
Democratic	4	5	5	n/a	n/a	n/a	n/a	0	0	1	4	6	6	6	6	7	7	7	7	7	64	76.2
Republican	0	0	0	n/a	n/a	n/a	n/a	5	5	5	2	0	0	0	2	0	0	0	0	0	19	22.6
Other	1	0	0	n/a	n/a	n/a	n/a	0	0	0	0	0	0	0	0	0	0	0	0	0	1	1.2
North Carolina																						
Democratic	5	7	4	4	n/a	n/a	n/a	0	0	5	7	7	6	7	5	8	7	6	8	8	74	67.3
Republican	0	1	4	4	n/a	n/a	n/a	6	2	3	1	1	2	1	2	1	1	3	1	1	25	22.7
Other	3	0	0	0	n/a	n/a	n/a	1	5	0	0	0	0	0	1	0	1	0	0	0	11	10.0
South Carolina																						
Democratic	6	6	6	5	n/a	n/a	n/a	0	0	0	0	2	5	5	6	6	7	7	7	6	53	69.7
Republican	0	0	0	0	n/a	n/a	n/a	2	4	5	5	3	0	0	1	1	0	0	0	1	22	28.9
Other	0	0	0	1	n/a	n/a	n/a	0	0	0	0	0	0	0	0	0	0	0	0	0	1	1.3
Tennessee																						
Democratic	5	7	3	0	n/a	0	0	0	6	3	9	8	9	7	8	7	8	7	8	8	88	56.1
Republican	0	0	0	4	n/a	5	8	8	2	7	1	2	1	3	2	3	2	3	2	2	51	32.5
Other	5	3	7	0	n/a	3	0	0	0	0	0	0	0	0	0	0	0	0	0	0	18	11.5
Texas																						
Democratic	1	2	2	n/a	n/a	n/a	n/a	1	3	6	9	8	5	5	10	11	11	11	11	13	104	92.9
Republican	0	0	0	n/a	n/a	n/a	n/a	3	1	0	1	2	0	0	0	0	0	0	0	0	4	3.6
Other	1	0	0	n/a	n/a	n/a	n/a	0	0	0	0	0	1	1	1	0	0	0	0	0	4	3.6
Virginia																						
Democratic	12	13	12	n/a	n/a	n/a	n/a	0	0	0	8	8	8	5	4	8	3	8	10	10	108	67.1
Republican	0	0	0	n/a	n/a	n/a	n/a	3	3	5	1	1	1	2	0	2	6	2	0	0	26	16.1
Other	1	0	1	n/a	n/a	n/a	n/a	6	6	4	0	0	0	2	6	0	1	0	0	0	27	16.8
BORDER SOUTH																						
Democratic	6	11	8	0	1	2	13	14	16	16	18	19	18	17	16	18	16	17	20	20	266	71.9
Republican	0	0	0	15	16	6	4	3	1	3	1	0	0	2	5	3	5	4	1	1	71	19.2
Other	10	5	8	1	0	9	0	0	0	0	0	0	0	0	0	0	0	0	1	1	33	8.9
Democratic %	37.5	68.8	50.0	0.0	5.9	11.8	76.5	82.4	94.1	84.2	94.7	100.0	94.7	89.5	76.2	85.7	76.2	81.0	90.9	90.9	—	—
Republican %	0.0	0.0	0.0	93.7	94.1	35.3	23.5	17.6	5.9	15.8	5.3	0.0	5.3	10.5	23.8	14.3	23.8	19.0	4.5	4.5	—	—
Other %	62.5	31.3	50.0	6.3	0.0	52.9	0.0	0.0	0.0	0.0	0.0	0.0	0.0	0.0	0.0	0.0	0.0	0.0	4.5	4.5	—	—

Table 5-11 (Continued)

Region/State	1854	1856	1858	1860	1862	1864	1866	1868	1870	1872	1874	1876	1878	1880	1882	1884	1886	1888	1890	1892	Total Wins	% of Wins
Kentucky																						
Democratic	4	8	5	0	0	0	9	9	9	10	9	10	10	9	9	10	8	9	10	10	148	73.6
Republican	0	0	0	9	9	0	0	0	0	0	1	0	0	1	2	1	3	2	1	1	30	14.9
Other	6	2	5	1	0	9	0	0	0	0	0	0	0	0	0	0	0	0	0	0	23	11.4
Maryland																						
Democratic	2	3	3	0	1	2	4	5	5	4	6	6	5	5	4	5	5	4	6	6	81	70.4
Republican	0	0	0	6	4	3	1	0	0	2	0	0	1	1	2	1	1	2	0	0	24	20.9
Other	4	3	3	0	0	0	0	0	0	0	0	0	0	0	0	0	0	0	0	0	10	8.7
West Virginia																						
Democratic	—	—	—	—	0	0	0	0	2	2	3	3	3	3	3	3	3	4	4	4	37	68.5
Republican	—	—	—	—	3	3	3	3	1	1	0	0	0	0	1	0	1	0	0	0	17	31.5
Other	—	—	—	—	0	0	0	0	0	0	0	0	0	0	0	0	0	0	0	0	0	0.0
MIDWEST																						
Democratic	11	26	22	23	37	10	11	18	25	26	51	33	42	26	60	54	42	37	80	65	699	38.8
Republican	16	31	36	37	37	64	64	57	50	72	44	65	54	72	54	60	71	80	30	59	1053	58.4
Other	30	2	1	1	0	0	0	0	0	0	3	0	2	0	0	0	1	0	7	4	51	2.8
Democratic %	19.3	44.1	37.3	37.7	50.0	13.5	14.7	24.0	33.3	26.5	52.0	33.7	42.9	26.5	52.6	47.4	36.8	31.6	68.4	50.8	—	—
Republican %	28.1	52.5	61.0	60.7	50.0	86.5	85.3	76.0	66.7	73.5	44.9	66.3	55.1	73.5	47.4	52.6	62.3	68.4	25.6	46.1	—	—
Other %	52.6	3.4	1.7	1.6	0.0	0.0	0.0	0.0	0.0	0.0	3.1	0.0	2.0	0.0	0.0	0.0	0.9	0.0	6.0	3.1	—	—
Illinois																						
Democratic	5	5	5	5	9	3	3	4	6	5	11	8	6	6	9	9	6	7	14	11	137	42.4
Republican	4	4	4	4	5	11	11	10	8	14	7	11	12	13	11	11	14	13	6	11	184	57.0
Other	0	0	0	0	0	0	0	0	0	0	1	0	1	0	0	0	0	0	0	0	2	0.6
Indiana																						
Democratic	2	6	4	4	7	3	3	4	5	3	8	4	7	5	9	9	6	10	11	11	121	50.0
Republican	0	5	7	7	4	8	8	7	6	10	5	9	6	8	4	4	7	3	2	2	112	46.3
Other	9	0	0	0	0	0	0	0	0	0	0	0	0	0	0	0	0	0	0	0	9	3.7
Iowa																						
Democratic	1	0	0	0	0	0	0	0	0	0	0	0	2	0	3	4	2	1	6	1	20	13.4
Republican	1	2	2	2	6	6	6	6	6	9	8	9	7	9	8	7	9	10	5	10	128	85.9
Other	0	0	0	0	0	0	0	0	0	0	1	0	0	0	0	0	0	0	0	0	1	0.7
Kansas																						
Democratic	—	—	—	0	0	0	0	0	0	0	0	0	0	0	0	0	0	0	0	3	3	4.6
Republican	—	—	—	1	1	1	1	1	1	3	2	3	3	3	7	7	7	7	2	3	54	83.1
Other	—	—	—	0	0	0	0	0	0	0	1	0	0	0	0	0	0	0	5	2	8	12.3
Michigan																						
Democratic	1	0	1	0	1	0	0	0	1	0	3	1	0	0	6	7	5	2	8	5	41	25.9
Republican	3	4	3	4	5	6	6	6	5	9	6	8	9	9	5	4	6	9	3	7	117	74.1
Other	0	0	0	0	0	0	0	0	0	0	0	0	0	0	0	0	0	0	0	0	0	0.0
Minnesota																						
Democratic	—	2	0	0	0	0	0	0	0	0	0	0	1	0	0	0	3	0	3	2	12	19.0
Republican	—	0	2	2	2	2	2	2	2	3	3	3	2	3	5	5	2	5	1	4	49	77.8
Other	—	0	0	0	0	0	0	0	0	0	0	0	0	0	0	0	0	0	1	1	2	3.2
Missouri																						
Democratic	1	5	6	5	3	1	1	2	6	9	13	9	12	8	14	12	12	10	14	13	156	70.0
Republican	6	0	0	1	6	8	8	7	3	4	0	4	0	5	0	2	2	4	0	2	62	27.8
Other	0	2	1	1	0	0	0	0	0	0	0	0	1	0	0	0	0	0	0	0	5	2.2
Nebraska																						
Democratic	—	—	—	—	—	—	0	0	0	0	0	0	0	0	0	0	1	0	2	2	5	17.9
Republican	—	—	—	—	—	—	1	1	1	1	1	1	1	1	3	3	2	3	0	3	21	75.0
Other	—	—	—	—	—	—	0	0	0	0	0	0	0	0	0	0	0	0	1	1	2	7.1
North Dakota																						
Democratic	—	—	—	—	—	—	—	—	—	—	—	—	—	—	—	—	—	0	0	0	0	0.0
Republican	—	—	—	—	—	—	—	—	—	—	—	—	—	—	—	—	—	1	1	1	3	100.0
Other	—	—	—	—	—	—	—	—	—	—	—	—	—	—	—	—	—	0	0	0	0	0.0

(Table continues)

Table 5-11 (Continued)

Region/State	1854	1856	1858	1860	1862	1864	1866	1868	1870	1872	1874	1876	1878	1880	1882	1884	1886	1888	1890	1892	Total Wins	% of Wins
Ohio																						
Democratic	0	8	6	8	14	2	3	6	5	7	13	8	11	5	13	11	6	5	14	11	156	38.5
Republican	0	13	15	13	5	17	16	13	14	13	7	12	9	15	8	10	15	16	7	10	228	56.3
Other	21	0	0	0	0	0	0	0	0	0	0	0	0	0	0	0	0	0	0	0	21	5.2
South Dakota																						
Democratic	—	—	—	—	—	—	—	—	—	—	—	—	—	—	—	—	—	0	0	0	0	0.0
Republican	—	—	—	—	—	—	—	—	—	—	—	—	—	—	—	—	—	2	2	2	6	100.0
Other	—	—	—	—	—	—	—	—	—	—	—	—	—	—	—	—	—	0	0	0	0	0.0
Wisconsin																						
Democratic	1	0	1	0	3	1	1	1	2	2	3	3	3	2	6	2	1	2	8	6	48	35.0
Republican	2	3	2	3	3	5	5	5	4	6	5	5	5	6	3	7	7	7	1	4	88	64.2
Other	0	0	0	0	0	0	0	0	0	0	0	0	0	0	0	0	1	0	0	0	1	0.7
WEST																						
Democratic %	100.0	100.0	100.0	25.0	0.0	0.0	40.0	60.0	40.0	33.3	66.7	14.3	28.6	42.9	77.8	11.1	22.2	18.8	23.1	41.2	—	—
Republican %	0.0	0.0	0.0	75.0	100.0	100.0	60.0	40.0	60.0	66.7	33.3	85.7	71.4	57.1	22.2	88.9	77.8	81.2	76.9	52.9	—	—
Other %	0.0	0.0	0.0	0.0	0.0	0.0	0.0	0.0	0.0	0.0	0.0	0.0	0.0	0.0	0.0	0.0	0.0	0.0	0.0	5.9	—	—
California																						
Democratic	2	2	2	0	0	0	2	2	0	1	3	1	1	2	6	1	2	2	2	4	35	43.2
Republican	0	0	0	3	3	3	1	1	3	3	1	3	3	2	0	5	4	4	4	3	46	56.8
Other	0	0	0	0	0	0	0	0	0	0	0	0	0	0	0	0	0	0	0	0	0	0
Colorado																						
Democratic	—	—	—	—	—	—	—	—	—	—	—	0	0	0	0	0	0	0	0	2	2	20.0
Republican	—	—	—	—	—	—	—	—	—	—	—	1	1	1	1	1	1	1	1	0	8	80.0
Other	—	—	—	—	—	—	—	—	—	—	—	0	0	0	0	0	0	0	0	0	0	0.0
Idaho																						
Democratic	—	—	—	—	—	—	—	—	—	—	—	—	—	—	—	—	—	—	0	0	0	0.0
Republican	—	—	—	—	—	—	—	—	—	—	—	—	—	—	—	—	—	—	1	1	2	100.0
Other	—	—	—	—	—	—	—	—	—	—	—	—	—	—	—	—	—	—	0	0	0	0.0
Montana																						
Democratic	—	—	—	—	—	—	—	—	—	—	—	—	—	—	—	—	—	0	1	0	1	33.3
Republican	—	—	—	—	—	—	—	—	—	—	—	—	—	—	—	—	—	1	0	1	2	66.7
Other	—	—	—	—	—	—	—	—	—	—	—	—	—	—	—	—	—	0	0	0	0	0.0
Nevada																						
Democratic	—	—	—	—	—	—	0	0	1	1	0	0	0	1	1	0	0	0	0	0	4	25.0
Republican	—	—	—	—	—	—	1	1	0	0	1	1	1	0	0	1	1	1	1	0	11	68.8
Other	—	—	—	—	—	—	0	0	0	0	0	0	0	0	0	0	0	0	0	1	1	6.3
Oregon																						
Democratic	—	—	1	1	0	0	0	1	1	0	1	0	1	0	0	0	0	0	0	0	6	31.6
Republican	—	—	0	0	1	1	1	0	0	1	0	1	0	1	1	1	1	1	1	2	13	68.4
Other	—	—	0	0	0	0	0	0	0	0	0	0	0	0	0	0	0	0	0	0	0	0.0
Washington																						
Democratic	—	—	—	—	—	—	—	—	—	—	—	—	—	—	—	—	—	0	0	0	0	0.0
Republican	—	—	—	—	—	—	—	—	—	—	—	—	—	—	—	—	—	1	1	2	4	100.0
Other	—	—	—	—	—	—	—	—	—	—	—	—	—	—	—	—	—	0	0	0	0	0.0
Wyoming																						
Democratic	—	—	—	—	—	—	—	—	—	—	—	—	—	—	—	—	—	—	0	1	1	50.0
Republican	—	—	—	—	—	—	—	—	—	—	—	—	—	—	—	—	—	—	1	0	1	50.0
Other	—	—	—	—	—	—	—	—	—	—	—	—	—	—	—	—	—	—	0	0	0	0.0

Notes: Entries reflect winners from the actual vote results and are not adjusted for contested seats, runoffs, inaccuracies of other types in reporting party labels or winners, or gubernatorial and legislative proclamations of different natures. For these reasons, these figures may not completely correspond to the most recent reports of the Clerk of the House of Representatives regarding the composition of the House over time. The regional categories are adapted from the ICPSR, except that in the current analysis Tennessee is coded in the South, because it was part of the Confederacy, whereas the ICPSR places Tennessee in the Border South. House elections were generally held in both even- and odd-numbered years prior to 1880 (that is, in two-year election cycles). Although only the even-numbered years of these two-year election cycles are used as column headings in this table, the House election results for both the even- and odd-numbered years in these two-year election cycles are reported as data in the table. —indicates state not yet in Union or data unavailable for that state. n/a indicates state seceded from the Union during the Civil War.

Sources: Data adapted from *United States Congressional Elections, 1788–1997* (1998), Report of the Clerk of the House of Representatives (various dates), and *Congressional Quarterly's Guide to U.S. Elections* (1994), Congressional Quarterly's Guide to U.S. Elections (1994), and independent search of state sources by the author.

Table 5-12 Party Victories in House Elections, by State, in Regions, 1894-1928

Region/State	1894	1896	1898	1900	1902	1904	1906	1908	1910	1912	1914	1916	1918	1920	1922	1924	1926	1928	Total Wins	% of Wins
NEW ENGLAND																				
Democratic	1	1	3	3	5	4	4	3	8	17	11	6	5	2	6	4	3	4	90	16.6
Republican	26	26	24	24	24	25	25	26	21	15	21	25	27	30	26	28	29	28	450	83.2
Other	0	0	1	0	0	0	0	0	0	0	0	1	0	0	0	0	0	0	1	0.2
Democratic %	3.7	3.7	11.1	11.1	17.2	13.8	13.8	10.3	27.6	53.1	34.4	18.8	15.6	6.2	18.7	12.5	9.4	12.5	—	
Republican %	96.3	96.3	88.9	88.9	82.8	86.2	86.2	89.7	72.4	46.9	65.6	78.1	84.4	93.8	81.3	87.5	90.6	87.5	—	
Other %	0.0	0.0	0.0	0.0	0.0	0.0	0.0	0.0	0.0	0.0	0.0	3.1	0.0	0.0	0.0	0.0	0.0	0.0	—	
Connecticut																				
Democratic	0	0	0	0	0	0	0	0	1	5	5	1	1	0	1	0	0	0	14	16.3
Republican	4	4	4	4	5	5	5	5	4	0	0	4	4	5	4	5	5	5	72	83.7
Other	0	0	1	0	0	0	0	0	0	0	0	0	0	0	0	0	0	0	0	0.0
Maine																				
Democratic	0	0	0	0	0	0	0	0	2	1	1	0	0	0	0	0	0	0	4	5.6
Republican	4	4	4	4	4	4	4	4	2	3	3	4	4	4	4	4	4	4	68	94.4
Other	0	0	0	0	0	0	0	0	0	0	0	0	0	0	0	0	0	0	0	0.0
Massachusetts																				
Democratic	1	1	3	3	4	3	3	3	4	7	4	4	4	2	3	3	3	3	58	21.8
Republican	12	12	10	10	10	11	11	11	10	9	12	11	12	14	13	13	13	13	207	77.8
Other	0	0	0	0	0	0	0	0	0	0	0	1	0	0	0	0	0	0	1	0.4
New Hampshire																				
Democratic	0	0	0	0	0	0	0	0	0	2	0	0	0	0	1	0	0	0	3	8.3
Republican	2	2	2	2	2	2	2	2	2	0	2	2	2	2	1	2	2	2	33	91.7
Other	0	0	0	0	0	0	0	0	0	0	0	0	0	0	0	0	0	0	0	0.0
Rhode Island																				
Democratic	0	0	0	0	1	1	1	0	1	2	1	1	0	0	1	1	0	1	11	24.4
Republican	2	2	2	2	1	1	1	2	1	1	2	2	3	3	2	2	3	2	34	75.6
Other	0	0	0	0	0	0	0	0	0	0	0	0	0	0	0	0	0	0	0	0.0
Vermont																				
Democratic	0	0	0	0	0	0	0	0	0	0	0	0	0	0	0	0	0	0	0	0.0
Republican	2	2	2	2	2	2	2	2	2	2	2	2	2	2	2	2	2	2	36	100.0
Other	0	0	0	0	0	0	0	0	0	0	0	0	0	0	0	0	0	0	0	0.0
MID-ATLANTIC																				
Democratic	8	9	30	19	26	13	23	19	39	55	29	26	26	10	36	24	31	26	449	29.5
Republican	65	63	42	54	53	67	57	61	41	33	61	65	66	80	56	67	61	66	1058	69.6
Other	0	1	1	0	1	0	0	0	0	4	2	1	0	2	0	1	0	0	13	0.9
Democratic %	11.0	12.3	41.1	26.0	32.5	16.2	28.7	23.7	48.7	59.8	31.5	28.3	28.3	10.9	39.1	26.1	33.7	28.3	—	
Republican %	89.0	86.3	57.5	74.0	66.3	83.8	71.3	76.3	51.3	35.9	66.3	70.7	71.7	87.0	60.9	72.8	66.3	71.7	—	
Other %	0.0	1.4	1.4	0.0	1.3	0.0	0.0	0.0	0.0	4.3	2.2	1.1	0.0	2.2	0.0	1.1	0.0	0.0	—	
Delaware																				
Democratic	1	1	0	0	1	0	0	0	0	1	0	1	0	0	1	0	0	0	6	33.3
Republican	0	0	1	1	0	1	1	1	1	0	1	0	1	1	0	1	1	1	12	66.7
Other	0	0	0	0	0	0	0	0	0	0	0	0	0	0	0	0	0	0	0	0.0
New Jersey																				
Democratic	0	0	2	2	3	1	4	3	7	11	4	3	5	1	6	2	3	2	59	31.1
Republican	8	8	6	6	7	9	6	7	3	1	8	9	7	11	6	10	9	10	131	68.9
Other	0	0	0	0	0	0	0	0	0	0	0	0	0	0	0	0	0	0	0	0.0
New York																				
Democratic	5	5	18	13	17	11	12	11	23	31	19	16	16	9	23	22	26	23	300	42.4
Republican	29	29	16	21	20	26	25	26	14	11	22	26	27	33	20	20	17	20	402	56.8
Other	0	0	0	0	0	0	0	0	0	1	2	1	0	1	0	1	0	0	6	0.8

(Table continues)

Table 5-12 (Continued)

Region/State	1894	1896	1898	1900	1902	1904	1906	1908	1910	1912	1914	1916	1918	1920	1922	1924	1926	1928	Total Wins	% of Wins
Pennsylvania																				
Democratic	2	3	10	4	5	1	7	5	9	12	6	6	5	0	6	0	2	1	84	13.9
Republican	28	26	19	26	26	31	25	27	23	21	30	30	31	35	30	36	34	35	513	84.9
Other	0	1	1	0	1	0	0	0	0	3	0	0	0	1	0	0	0	0	7	1.2
SOUTH																				
Democratic	77	76	85	86	95	94	95	92	95	101	99	100	101	97	101	101	101	97	1693	94.8
Republican	10	13	5	4	3	4	3	6	3	3	4	3	3	7	3	3	3	7	87	4.9
Other	3	1	0	0	0	0	0	0	0	0	1	1	0	0	0	0	0	0	6	0.3
Democratic %	85.6	84.4	94.4	95.6	96.9	95.9	96.9	93.9	96.9	97.1	95.2	96.2	97.1	93.3	97.1	97.1	97.1	93.3	—	—
Republican %	11.1	14.4	5.6	4.4	3.1	4.1	3.1	6.1	3.1	2.9	3.8	2.9	2.9	6.7	2.9	2.9	2.9	6.7	—	—
Other %	3.3	1.1	0.0	0.0	0.0	0.0	0.0	0.0	0.0	0.0	1.0	1.0	0.0	0.0	0.0	0.0	0.0	0.0	—	—
Alabama																				
Democratic	8	8	9	9	9	9	9	9	9	10	10	10	10	10	10	10	10	10	169	98.8
Republican	0	0	0	0	0	0	0	0	0	0	0	0	0	0	0	0	0	0	0	0.0
Other	1	1	1	0	0	0	0	0	0	0	0	0	0	0	0	0	0	0	2	1.2
Arkansas																				
Democratic	6	6	6	6	7	7	7	7	7	7	7	7	7	7	7	7	7	7	122	100.0
Republican	0	0	0	0	0	0	0	0	0	0	0	0	0	0	0	0	0	0	0	0.0
Other	0	0	0	0	0	0	0	0	0	0	0	0	0	0	0	0	0	0	0	0.0
Florida																				
Democratic	2	2	2	2	3	3	3	3	3	4	4	4	4	4	4	4	4	4	59	100.0
Republican	0	0	0	0	0	0	0	0	0	0	0	0	0	0	0	0	0	0	0	0.0
Other	0	0	0	0	0	0	0	0	0	0	0	0	0	0	0	0	0	0	0	0.0
Georgia																				
Democratic	11	11	11	11	11	11	11	11	11	12	12	12	12	12	12	12	12	12	207	100.0
Republican	0	0	0	0	0	0	0	0	0	0	0	0	0	0	0	0	0	0	0	0.0
Other	0	0	0	0	0	0	0	0	0	0	0	0	0	0	0	0	0	0	0	0.0
Louisiana																				
Democratic	6	6	6	6	7	7	7	7	7	8	7	7	8	8	8	8	8	8	129	98.5
Republican	0	0	0	0	0	0	0	0	0	0	1	0	0	0	0	0	0	0	0	0.0
Other	0	0	0	0	0	0	0	0	0	0	1	1	0	0	0	0	0	0	2	1.5
Mississippi																				
Democratic	7	7	7	7	8	8	8	8	8	8	8	8	8	8	8	8	8	8	140	100.0
Republican	0	0	0	0	0	0	0	0	0	0	0	0	0	0	0	0	0	0	0	0.0
Other	0	0	0	0	0	0	0	0	0	0	0	0	0	0	0	0	0	0	0	0.0
North Carolina																				
Democratic	3	1	7	7	10	9	10	7	10	10	9	10	10	10	10	10	10	8	151	85.8
Republican	4	8	2	2	0	1	0	3	0	0	1	0	0	0	0	0	0	2	23	13.1
Other	2	0	0	0	0	0	0	0	0	0	0	0	0	0	0	0	0	0	2	1.1
South Carolina																				
Democratic	7	7	7	7	7	7	7	7	7	7	7	7	7	7	7	7	7	7	126	100.0
Republican	0	0	0	0	0	0	0	0	0	0	0	0	0	0	0	0	0	0	0	0.0
Other	0	0	0	0	0	0	0	0	0	0	0	0	0	0	0	0	0	0	0	0.0
Tennessee																				
Democratic	6	8	8	8	8	8	8	8	8	8	8	8	8	5	8	8	8	8	139	77.2
Republican	4	2	2	2	2	2	2	2	2	2	2	2	2	5	2	2	2	2	41	22.8
Other	0	0	0	0	0	0	0	0	0	0	0	0	0	0	0	0	0	0	0	0.0
Texas																				
Democratic	12	12	12	13	16	16	16	16	16	18	18	18	18	17	17	17	17	18	287	97.6
Republican	1	1	1	0	0	0	0	0	0	0	0	0	0	1	1	1	1	0	7	2.4
Other	0	0	0	0	0	0	0	0	0	0	0	0	0	0	0	0	0	0	0	0.0

Table 5-12 (Continued)

Region/State	1894	1896	1898	1900	1902	1904	1906	1908	1910	1912	1914	1916	1918	1920	1922	1924	1926	1928	Total Wins	% of Wins
Virginia																				
Democratic	9	8	10	10	9	9	9	9	9	9	9	9	9	9	10	10	10	7	164	91.1
Republican	1	2	0	0	1	1	1	1	1	1	1	1	1	1	0	0	0	3	16	8.9
Other	0	0	0	0	0	0	0	0	0	0	0	0	0	0	0	0	0	0	0	0.0
BORDER SOUTH																				
Democratic	9	7	12	9	12	12	14	13	21	23	24	21	19	13	22	19	21	12	283	58.0
Republican	12	14	9	12	10	10	13	14	6	8	7	10	12	18	9	12	10	19	205	42.0
Other	0	0	0	0	0	0	0	0	0	0	0	0	0	0	0	0	0	0	0	0.0
Democratic %	42.9	33.3	57.1	42.9	54.5	54.5	51.9	48.1	77.8	74.2	77.4	67.7	61.3	41.9	71.0	61.3	67.7	38.7	—	—
Republican %	57.1	66.7	42.9	57.1	45.5	45.5	48.1	51.9	22.2	25.8	22.6	32.3	38.7	58.1	29.0	38.7	32.3	61.3	—	—
Other %	0.0	0.0	0.0	0.0	0.0	0.0	0.0	0.0	0.0	0.0	0.0	0.0	0.0	0.0	0.0	0.0	0.0	0.0	—	—
Kentucky																				
Democratic	6	7	9	9	10	9	7	8	9	9	9	9	8	8	8	8	8	2	143	72.2
Republican	5	4	2	2	1	2	4	3	2	2	2	2	3	3	3	3	3	9	55	27.8
Other	0	0	0	0	0	0	0	0	0	0	0	0	0	0	0	0	0	0	0	0.0
Maryland																				
Democratic	3	0	2	0	2	3	3	3	5	6	5	4	3	2	3	4	5	4	57	52.8
Republican	3	6	4	6	4	3	3	3	1	0	1	2	3	4	3	2	1	2	51	47.2
Other	0	0	0	0	0	0	0	0	0	0	0	0	0	0	0	0	0	0	0	0.0
Oklahoma																				
Democratic	—	—	—	—	—	—	4	2	3	6	7	6	7	3	7	6	7	5	63	72.4
Republican	—	—	—	—	—	—	1	3	2	2	1	2	1	5	1	2	1	3	24	27.6
Other	—	—	—	—	—	—	0	0	0	0	0	0	0	0	0	0	0	0	0	0.0
West Virginia																				
Democratic	0	0	1	0	0	0	0	0	4	2	3	2	1	0	4	1	1	1	20	21.1
Republican	4	4	3	4	5	5	5	5	1	4	3	4	5	6	2	5	5	5	75	78.9
Other	0	0	0	0	0	0	0	0	0	0	0	0	0	0	0	0	0	0	0	0.0
MIDWEST																				
Democratic	10	39	35	37	37	11	30	41	57	76	61	48	28	5	34	28	33	21	631	25.5
Republican	117	89	93	91	99	125	106	95	79	63	80	94	113	138	106	111	107	121	1827	73.7
Other	1	0	0	0	0	0	0	0	0	4	2	1	2	0	0	1	3	1	21	0.8
Democratic %	7.8	30.5	27.3	28.9	27.2	8.1	22.1	30.1	41.9	53.1	42.7	33.6	19.6	3.5	23.8	19.6	23.1	14.7	—	—
Republican %	91.4	69.5	72.7	71.1	72.8	91.9	77.9	69.9	58.1	44.1	55.9	65.7	79.0	96.5	74.1	77.6	74.8	84.6	—	—
Other %	0.8	0.0	0.0	0.0	0.0	0.0	0.0	0.0	0.0	2.8	1.4	0.7	1.4	0.0	2.1	2.8	2.1	0.7	—	—
Illinois																				
Democratic	2	5	8	11	8	1	5	6	6	11	10	6	5	3	7	5	7	6	112	24.6
Republican	20	17	14	11	17	24	20	19	19	14	16	21	22	24	20	22	20	21	341	74.8
Other	0	0	0	0	0	0	0	0	0	2	1	0	0	0	0	0	0	0	3	0.7
Indiana																				
Democratic	0	4	4	4	5	2	4	11	12	13	11	4	0	0	5	3	3	3	88	37.6
Republican	13	9	9	9	8	11	9	2	1	0	2	9	13	13	8	10	10	10	146	62.4
Other	0	0	0	0	0	0	0	0	0	0	0	0	0	0	0	0	0	0	0	0.0
Iowa																				
Democratic	0	0	0	0	1	0	1	1	1	3	1	0	0	0	0	0	0	0	8	4.0
Republican	11	11	11	11	10	11	10	10	10	8	10	11	11	11	11	11	11	11	190	96.0
Other	0	0	0	0	0	0	0	0	0	0	0	0	0	0	0	0	0	0	0	0.0
Kansas																				
Democratic	0	6	1	1	0	0	0	0	0	5	6	5	1	0	1	2	1	1	30	20.8
Republican	7	2	7	7	8	8	8	8	8	3	2	3	7	8	7	6	7	7	113	78.5
Other	1	0	0	0	0	0	0	0	0	0	0	0	0	0	0	0	0	0	1	0.7

(Table continues)

Table 5-12 (Continued)

Region/State	1894	1896	1898	1900	1902	1904	1906	1908	1910	1912	1914	1916	1918	1920	1922	1924	1926	1928	Total Wins	% of Wins
Michigan																				
Democratic	0	2	0	0	1	0	0	0	2	2	2	1	1	0	1	0	0	0	12	5.3
Republican	12	10	12	12	11	12	12	12	10	9	11	12	12	13	12	13	13	13	211	93.8
Other	0	0	0	0	0	0	0	0	0	2	0	0	0	0	0	0	0	0	2	0.9
Minnesota																				
Democratic	0	0	0	0	1	0	1	1	1	1	1	1	1	0	0	0	0	0	8	4.9
Republican	7	7	7	7	8	9	8	8	8	9	8	8	8	10	8	7	8	9	144	88.3
Other	0	0	0	0	0	0	0	0	0	0	1	1	1	0	2	3	2	1	11	6.7
Missouri																				
Democratic	5	12	12	13	15	6	12	10	13	14	14	14	11	2	11	9	12	6	191	67.3
Republican	10	3	3	2	1	10	4	6	3	2	2	2	5	14	5	7	4	10	93	32.7
Other	0	0	0	0	0	0	0	0	0	0	0	0	0	0	0	0	0	0	0	0.0
Nebraska																				
Democratic	1	4	4	4	1	0	1	3	3	3	3	3	0	0	3	3	4	2	42	38.9
Republican	5	2	2	2	5	6	5	3	3	3	3	3	6	6	3	3	2	4	66	61.1
Other	0	0	0	0	0	0	0	0	0	0	0	0	0	0	0	0	0	0	0	0.0
North Dakota																				
Democratic	0	0	0	0	0	0	0	0	0	0	0	0	0	0	0	0	0	0	0	0.0
Republican	1	1	1	1	2	2	2	2	2	3	3	3	3	3	3	3	3	3	41	100.0
Other	0	0	0	0	0	0	0	0	0	0	0	0	0	0	0	0	0	0	0	0.0
Ohio																				
Democratic	2	6	6	4	4	1	5	8	16	19	9	13	8	0	6	6	6	3	122	31.5
Republican	19	15	15	17	17	20	16	13	5	3	13	9	14	22	16	16	16	19	265	68.5
Other	0	0	0	0	0	0	0	0	0	0	0	0	0	0	0	0	0	0	0	0.0
South Dakota																				
Democratic	0	0	0	0	0	0	0	0	0	0	1	1	1	0	0	0	0	0	3	6.7
Republican	2	2	2	2	2	2	2	2	2	3	2	2	2	3	3	3	3	3	42	93.3
Other	0	0	0	0	0	0	0	0	0	0	0	0	0	0	0	0	0	0	0	0.0
Wisconsin																				
Democratic	0	0	0	0	1	1	1	1	3	5	3	0	0	0	0	0	0	0	15	7.7
Republican	10	10	10	10	10	10	10	10	8	6	8	11	10	11	10	10	10	11	175	90.2
Other	0	0	0	0	0	0	0	0	0	0	0	0	1	0	1	1	1	0	4	2.1
WEST																				
Democratic %	11.1	55.6	38.9	27.8	23.8	4.8	4.8	19.0	28.0	21.2	36.4	42.4	33.3	12.1	24.2	21.2	18.2	15.2	116	24.3
Republican %	83.3	33.3	61.1	72.2	76.2	95.2	95.2	81.0	72.0	69.7	54.5	57.6	66.7	87.9	75.8	78.8	81.8	84.8	353	73.8
Other %	5.6	11.1	0.0	0.0	0.0	0.0	0.0	0.0	0.0	9.1	9.1	0.0	0.0	0.0	0.0	0.0	0.0	0.0	9	1.9
Arizona																				
Democratic	—	—	—	—	—	—	—	—	1	1	1	1	1	1	1	1	1	1	10	100.0
Republican	—	—	—	—	—	—	—	—	0	0	0	0	0	0	0	0	0	0	0	0.0
Other	—	—	—	—	—	—	—	—	0	0	0	0	0	0	0	0	0	0	0	0.0
California																				
Democratic	1	4	1	0	3	0	0	0	1	3	4	5	5	2	2	2	1	1	35	21.0
Republican	6	3	6	7	5	8	8	8	7	7	4	6	6	9	9	9	10	10	128	76.6
Other	0	0	0	0	0	0	0	0	0	1	3	0	0	0	0	0	0	0	4	2.4
Colorado																				
Democratic	1	2	2	2	1	0	0	3	3	0	3	3	1	1	1	1	1	1	26	44.1
Republican	1	0	0	0	2	3	3	0	0	4	1	1	3	3	3	3	3	3	33	55.9
Other	0	0	0	0	0	0	0	0	0	0	0	0	0	0	0	0	0	0	0	0.0

Table 5-12 (Continued)

Region/State	1894	1896	1898	1900	1902	1904	1906	1908	1910	1912	1914	1916	1918	1920	1922	1924	1926	1928	Total Wins	% of Wins
Idaho																				
Democratic	0	1	1	1	0	0	0	0	0	0	0	0	0	0	0	0	0	0	3	11.1
Republican	1	0	0	0	1	1	1	1	1	2	2	2	2	2	2	2	2	2	24	88.9
Other	0	0	0	0	0	0	0	0	0	0	0	0	0	0	0	0	0	0	0	0.0
Montana																				
Democratic	0	0	1	1	0	0	0	0	0	2	2	1	1	0	1	1	1	1	12	44.4
Republican	1	1	0	0	1	1	1	1	1	0	0	1	1	2	1	1	1	1	15	55.6
Other	0	0	0	0	0	0	0	0	0	0	0	0	0	0	0	0	0	0	0	0.0
Nevada																				
Democratic	0	1	1	1	1	1	1	1	0	0	0	0	1	0	1	0	0	0	9	50.0
Republican	0	0	0	0	0	0	0	0	1	1	1	1	0	1	0	1	1	1	8	44.4
Other	1	0	0	0	0	0	0	0	0	0	0	0	0	0	0	0	0	0	1	5.6
New Mexico																				
Democratic	—	—	—	—	—	—	—	—	1	1	0	1	0	0	1	1	1	0	6	54.5
Republican	—	—	—	—	—	—	—	—	1	0	1	0	1	1	0	0	0	1	5	45.5
Other	—	—	—	—	—	—	—	—	0	0	0	0	0	0	0	0	0	0	0	0.0
Oregon																				
Democratic	0	0	0	0	0	0	0	0	0	0	0	0	0	0	1	0	0	0	1	2.2
Republican	2	2	2	2	2	2	2	2	2	3	3	3	3	3	2	3	3	3	44	97.8
Other	0	0	0	0	0	0	0	0	0	0	0	0	0	0	0	0	0	0	0	0.0
Utah																				
Democratic	0	1	1	0	0	0	0	0	0	0	1	2	2	0	0	0	0	0	7	25.9
Republican	1	0	0	1	1	1	1	1	1	2	1	0	0	2	2	2	2	2	20	74.1
Other	0	0	0	0	0	0	0	0	0	0	0	0	0	0	0	0	0	0	0	0.0
Washington																				
Democratic	0	0	0	0	0	0	0	0	0	0	1	1	0	0	0	1	1	1	5	7.4
Republican	2	0	2	2	3	3	3	3	3	3	4	4	5	5	5	4	4	4	59	86.8
Other	0	2	0	0	0	0	0	0	0	2	0	0	0	0	0	0	0	0	4	5.9
Wyoming																				
Democratic	0	1	0	0	0	0	0	0	0	0	0	0	0	0	0	0	0	0	1	5.6
Republican	1	0	1	1	1	1	1	1	1	1	1	1	1	1	1	1	1	1	17	94.4
Other	0	0	0	0	0	0	0	0	0	0	0	0	0	0	0	0	0	0	0	0.0

Notes: Entries reflect winners from the actual vote results and are not adjusted for contested seats, runoffs, inaccuracies of other types in reporting party labels or winners, or gubernatorial and legislative proclamations of different winners. For these reasons, these figures may not completely correspond to the most recent reports of the Clerk of the House of Representatives regarding the composition of the House over time. The regional categories are adapted from the ICPSR, except that in the current analysis Tennessee is coded in the South, because it was part of the Confederacy, whereas the ICPSR places Tennessee in the Border South. House elections were generally held in both even- and odd-numbered years prior to 1880 (that is, in two-year election cycles). Although only the even-numbered years of these two-year election cycles are used as column headings in this table, the House election results for both the even- and odd-numbered years in these two-year election cycles are reported as data in the table. —indicates state not yet in Union or data unavailable for that state.

Sources: Data adapted from *United States Congressional Elections, 1788–1997* (1998), *Congressional Quarterly's Guide to U.S. Elections* (1994), Report of the Clerk of the House of Representatives (various dates), and independent search of state sources by the author.

Table 5-13 Party Victories in House Elections, by State, in Regions, 1930–1964

Region/State	1930	1932	1934	1936	1938	1940	1942	1944	1946	1948	1950	1952	1954	1956	1958	1960	1962	1964	Total Wins	% of Wins
NEW ENGLAND																				
Democratic	7	12	16	14	7	14	6	10	7	11	10	9	10	10	19	14	14	17	207	40.8
Republican	25	17	13	15	22	15	22	18	21	17	18	19	18	18	9	14	11	8	300	59.2
Other	0	0	0	0	0	0	0	0	0	0	0	0	0	0	0	0	0	0	0	0.0
Democratic %	21.9	41.4	55.2	48.3	24.1	48.3	21.4	35.7	25.0	39.3	35.7	32.1	35.7	35.7	67.9	50.0	56.0	68.0	—	—
Republican %	78.1	58.6	44.8	51.7	75.9	51.7	78.6	64.3	75.0	60.7	64.3	67.9	64.3	64.3	32.1	50.0	44.0	32.0	—	—
Other %	0.0	0.0	0.0	0.0	0.0	0.0	0.0	0.0	0.0	0.0	0.0	0.0	0.0	0.0	0.0	0.0	0.0	0.0	—	—
Connecticut																				
Democratic	2	2	4	6	2	6	0	4	0	3	2	1	1	0	6	4	5	6	54	50.5
Republican	3	4	2	0	4	0	6	2	6	3	4	5	5	6	0	2	1	0	53	49.5
Other	0	0	0	0	0	0	0	0	0	0	0	0	0	0	0	0	0	0	0	0.0
Maine																				
Democratic	0	2	2	0	0	0	0	0	0	0	0	0	0	1	2	0	0	1	8	15.1
Republican	4	1	1	3	3	3	3	3	3	3	3	3	3	2	1	3	2	1	45	84.9
Other	0	0	0	0	0	0	0	0	0	0	0	0	0	0	0	0	0	0	0	0.0
Massachusetts																				
Democratic	4	5	7	5	5	6	4	4	5	6	6	6	7	7	8	8	7	7	107	42.0
Republican	12	10	8	10	10	9	10	10	9	8	8	8	7	7	6	6	5	5	148	58.0
Other	0	0	0	0	0	0	0	0	0	0	0	0	0	0	0	0	0	0	0	0.0
New Hampshire																				
Democratic	0	1	1	1	0	0	0	0	0	0	0	0	0	0	0	0	0	1	4	11.1
Republican	2	1	1	1	2	2	2	2	2	2	2	2	2	2	2	2	2	1	32	88.9
Other	0	0	0	0	0	0	0	0	0	0	0	0	0	0	0	0	0	0	0	0.0
Rhode Island																				
Democratic	1	2	2	2	0	2	2	2	2	2	2	2	2	2	2	2	2	2	33	89.2
Republican	2	0	0	0	2	0	0	0	0	0	0	0	0	0	0	0	0	0	4	10.8
Other	0	0	0	0	0	0	0	0	0	0	0	0	0	0	0	0	0	0	0	0.0
Vermont																				
Democratic	0	0	0	0	0	0	0	0	0	0	0	0	0	0	1	0	0	0	1	5.3
Republican	2	1	1	1	1	1	1	1	1	1	1	1	1	1	0	1	1	1	18	94.7
Other	0	0	0	0	0	0	0	0	0	0	0	0	0	0	0	0	0	0	0	0.0
MID-ATLANTIC																				
Democratic	29	45	56	64	43	49	40	40	23	45	41	32	38	34	41	43	41	54	758	46.4
Republican	63	49	38	30	51	45	53	52	69	47	52	56	50	54	47	45	43	30	874	53.5
Other	0	0	0	0	0	0	0	1	1	1	0	0	0	0	0	0	0	0	3	0.2
Democratic %	31.5	47.9	59.6	68.1	45.7	52.1	43.0	43.0	24.7	48.4	44.1	36.4	43.2	38.6	46.6	48.9	48.8	64.3	—	—
Republican %	68.5	52.1	40.4	31.9	54.3	47.9	57.0	55.9	74.2	50.5	55.9	63.6	56.8	61.4	53.4	51.1	51.2	35.7	—	—
Other %	0.0	0.0	0.0	0.0	0.0	0.0	0.0	1.1	1.1	1.1	0.0	0.0	0.0	0.0	0.0	0.0	0.0	0.0	—	—
Delaware																				
Democratic	0	1	0	1	0	1	0	1	0	0	0	0	1	0	1	1	1	1	9	50.0
Republican	1	0	1	0	1	0	1	0	1	1	1	1	0	1	0	0	0	0	9	50.0
Other	0	0	0	0	0	0	0	0	0	0	0	0	0	0	0	0	0	0	0	0.0
New Jersey																				
Democratic	3	4	4	7	3	4	3	2	2	5	5	5	6	4	5	6	7	11	86	34.1
Republican	9	10	10	7	11	10	11	12	12	9	9	9	8	10	9	8	8	4	166	65.9
Other	0	0	0	0	0	0	0	0	0	0	0	0	0	0	0	0	0	0	0	0.0
New York																				
Democratic	23	29	29	29	25	25	23	22	16	24	23	16	17	17	19	22	20	27	406	51.4
Republican	20	16	16	16	20	20	22	22	28	20	22	27	26	26	24	21	21	14	381	48.2
Other	0	0	0	0	0	0	0	1	1	1	0	0	0	0	0	0	0	0	3	0.4
Pennsylvania																				
Democratic	3	11	23	27	15	19	14	15	5	16	13	11	14	13	16	14	13	15	257	44.7
Republican	33	23	11	7	19	15	19	18	28	17	20	19	16	17	14	16	14	12	318	55.3
Other	0	0	0	0	0	0	0	0	0	0	0	0	0	0	0	0	0	0	0	0.0

Table 5-13 *(Continued)*

Region/State	1930	1932	1934	1936	1938	1940	1942	1944	1946	1948	1950	1952	1954	1956	1958	1960	1962	1964	Total Wins	% of Wins
SOUTH																				
Democratic	99	100	100	100	100	99	103	103	103	103	103	99	99	99	99	99	95	90	1793	95.4
Republican	4	2	2	2	2	2	2	2	2	2	2	6	7	7	7	7	11	16	85	4.5
Other	0	0	0	0	0	1	0	0	0	0	0	0	0	0	0	0	0	0	1	0.1
Democratic %	96.1	98.0	98.0	98.0	98.0	97.1	98.1	98.1	98.1	98.1	98.1	94.3	93.4	93.4	93.4	93.4	89.6	84.9	—	—
Republican %	3.9	2.0	2.0	2.0	2.0	2.0	1.9	1.9	1.9	1.9	1.9	5.7	6.6	6.6	6.6	6.6	10.4	15.1	—	—
Other %	0.0	0.0	0.0	0.0	0.0	1.0	0.0	0.0	0.0	0.0	0.0	0.0	0.0	0.0	0.0	0.0	0.0	0.0	—	—
Alabama																				
Democratic	9	9	9	9	9	9	9	9	9	9	9	9	9	9	9	9	8	3	155	96.9
Republican	0	0	0	0	0	0	0	0	0	0	0	0	0	0	0	0	0	5	5	3.1
Other	0	0	0	0	0	0	0	0	0	0	0	0	0	0	0	0	0	0	0	0.0
Arkansas																				
Democratic	7	7	7	7	7	7	7	7	7	7	7	6	6	6	6	6	4	4	115	100.0
Republican	0	0	0	0	0	0	0	0	0	0	0	0	0	0	0	0	0	0	0	0.0
Other	0	0	0	0	0	0	0	0	0	0	0	0	0	0	0	0	0	0	0	0.0
Florida																				
Democratic	4	5	5	5	5	5	6	6	6	6	6	8	7	7	7	7	10	10	115	93.5
Republican	0	0	0	0	0	0	0	0	0	0	0	0	1	1	1	1	2	2	8	6.5
Other	0	0	0	0	0	0	0	0	0	0	0	0	0	0	0	0	0	0	0	0.0
Georgia																				
Democratic	12	10	10	10	10	10	10	10	10	10	10	10	10	10	10	10	10	9	181	99.5
Republican	0	0	0	0	0	0	0	0	0	0	0	0	0	0	0	0	0	1	1	0.5
Other	0	0	0	0	0	0	0	0	0	0	0	0	0	0	0	0	0	0	0	0.0
Louisiana																				
Democratic	8	8	8	8	8	8	8	8	8	8	8	8	8	8	8	8	8	8	144	100.0
Republican	0	0	0	0	0	0	0	0	0	0	0	0	0	0	0	0	0	0	0	0.0
Other	0	0	0	0	0	0	0	0	0	0	0	0	0	0	0	0	0	0	0	0.0
Mississippi																				
Democratic	8	7	7	7	7	7	7	7	7	7	7	6	6	6	6	6	5	4	117	99.2
Republican	0	0	0	0	0	0	0	0	0	0	0	0	0	0	0	0	0	1	1	0.8
Other	0	0	0	0	0	0	0	0	0	0	0	0	0	0	0	0	0	0	0	0.0
North Carolina																				
Democratic	10	11	11	11	11	11	12	12	12	12	12	11	11	11	11	11	9	9	198	95.7
Republican	0	0	0	0	0	0	0	0	0	0	0	1	1	1	1	1	2	2	9	4.3
Other	0	0	0	0	0	0	0	0	0	0	0	0	0	0	0	0	0	0	0	0.0
South Carolina																				
Democratic	7	6	6	6	6	6	6	6	6	6	6	6	6	6	6	6	6	6	109	100.0
Republican	0	0	0	0	0	0	0	0	0	0	0	0	0	0	0	0	0	0	0	0.0
Other	0	0	0	0	0	0	0	0	0	0	0	0	0	0	0	0	0	0	0	0.0
Tennessee																				
Democratic	8	7	7	7	7	6	8	8	8	8	8	7	7	7	7	7	6	6	129	76.8
Republican	2	2	2	2	2	2	2	2	2	2	2	2	2	2	2	2	3	3	38	22.6
Other	0	0	0	0	0	1	0	0	0	0	0	0	0	0	0	0	0	0	1	0.6
Texas																				
Democratic	17	21	21	21	21	21	21	21	21	21	21	21	21	21	21	21	21	23	376	98.2
Republican	1	0	0	0	0	0	0	0	0	0	0	0	1	1	1	1	2	0	7	1.8
Other	0	0	0	0	0	0	0	0	0	0	0	0	0	0	0	0	0	0	0	0.0
Virginia																				
Democratic	9	9	9	9	9	9	9	9	9	9	9	7	8	8	8	8	8	8	154	90.6
Republican	1	0	0	0	0	0	0	0	0	0	0	3	2	2	2	2	2	2	16	9.4
Other	0	0	0	0	0	0	0	0	0	0	0	0	0	0	0	0	0	0	0	0.0

(Table continues)

Table 5-13 (Continued)

Region/State	1930	1932	1934	1936	1938	1940	1942	1944	1946	1948	1950	1952	1954	1956	1958	1960	1962	1964	Total Wins	% of Wins
BORDER SOUTH																				
Democratic	24	30	29	29	28	28	22	24	18	25	22	19	21	19	24	23	20	21	426	83.0
Republican	7	0	1	1	2	2	7	5	11	4	7	8	6	8	3	4	6	5	87	17.0
Other	0	0	0	0	0	0	0	0	0	0	0	0	0	0	0	0	0	0	0	0.0
Democratic %	77.4	100.0	96.7	96.7	93.3	93.3	75.9	82.8	62.1	86.2	75.9	70.4	77.8	70.4	88.9	85.2	76.9	80.8	—	—
Republican %	22.6	0.0	3.3	3.3	6.7	6.7	24.1	17.2	37.9	13.8	24.1	29.6	22.2	29.6	11.1	14.8	23.1	19.2	—	—
Other %	0.0	0.0	0.0	0.0	0.0	0.0	0.0	0.0	0.0	0.0	0.0	0.0	0.0	0.0	0.0	0.0	0.0	0.0	—	—
Kentucky																				
Democratic	9	9	8	8	8	8	8	8	6	7	7	6	6	6	7	7	5	6	129	83.2
Republican	2	0	1	1	1	1	1	1	3	2	2	2	2	2	1	1	2	1	26	16.8
Other	0	0	0	0	0	0	0	0	0	0	0	0	0	0	0	0	0	0	0	0.0
Maryland																				
Democratic	6	6	6	6	6	6	4	5	4	4	3	3	4	4	7	6	6	6	92	78.6
Republican	0	0	0	0	0	0	2	1	2	2	3	4	3	3	0	1	2	2	25	21.4
Other	0	0	0	0	0	0	0	0	0	0	0	0	0	0	0	0	0	0	0	0.0
Oklahoma																				
Democratic	7	9	9	9	9	8	7	6	6	8	6	5	5	5	5	5	5	5	119	88.1
Republican	1	0	0	0	0	1	1	2	2	0	2	1	0	1	0	0	0	1	16	11.9
Other	0	0	0	0	0	0	0	0	0	0	0	0	0	0	0	0	0	0	0	0.0
West Virginia																				
Democratic	2	6	6	6	5	6	3	5	2	6	6	5	6	4	5	5	4	4	86	81.1
Republican	4	0	0	0	1	0	3	1	4	0	0	1	0	2	1	1	1	1	20	18.9
Other	0	0	0	0	0	0	0	0	0	0	0	0	0	0	0	0	0	0	0	0.0
MIDWEST																				
Democratic	49	94	87	90	54	49	25	36	20	55	37	34	44	46	68	51	47	66	952	40.0
Republican	93	38	40	36	80	84	103	94	111	76	93	94	85	83	61	78	78	59	1386	58.3
Other	1	5	10	11	3	4	3	1	0	0	1	1	0	0	0	0	0	0	40	1.7
Democratic %	34.3	68.6	63.5	65.7	39.4	35.8	19.1	27.5	15.3	42.0	28.2	26.4	34.1	35.7	52.7	39.5	37.6	52.8	—	—
Republican %	65.0	27.7	29.2	26.3	58.4	61.3	78.6	71.8	84.7	58.0	71.0	72.9	65.9	64.3	47.3	60.5	62.4	47.2	—	—
Other %	0.7	3.6	7.3	8.0	2.2	2.9	2.3	0.8	0.0	0.0	0.8	0.8	0.0	0.0	0.0	0.0	0.0	0.0	—	—
Illinois																				
Democratic	12	19	21	21	17	11	7	11	6	12	8	9	12	11	14	14	12	13	230	49.5
Republican	15	8	6	6	10	16	19	15	20	14	18	16	13	14	11	11	12	11	235	50.5
Other	0	0	0	0	0	0	0	0	0	0	0	0	0	0	0	0	0	0	0	0.0
Indiana																				
Democratic	9	12	11	11	5	4	2	2	2	7	2	1	2	2	8	4	4	6	94	45.9
Republican	4	0	1	1	7	8	9	9	9	4	9	10	9	9	3	7	7	5	111	54.1
Other	0	0	0	0	0	0	0	0	0	0	0	0	0	0	0	0	0	0	0	0.0
Iowa																				
Democratic	1	6	6	5	2	2	0	0	0	0	0	0	0	1	4	2	1	6	36	24.0
Republican	10	3	3	4	7	7	8	8	8	8	8	8	8	7	4	6	6	1	114	76.0
Other	0	0	0	0	0	0	0	0	0	0	0	0	0	0	0	0	0	0	0	0.0
Kansas																				
Democratic	1	3	3	2	1	1	0	0	0	0	0	1	0	1	3	1	0	0	17	15.0
Republican	7	4	4	5	6	6	6	6	6	6	6	5	6	5	3	5	5	5	96	85.0
Other	0	0	0	0	0	0	0	0	0	0	0	0	0	0	0	0	0	0	0	0.0
Michigan																				
Democratic	0	10	6	8	5	6	5	6	3	5	5	5	7	6	7	7	8	12	111	35.7
Republican	13	7	11	9	12	11	12	11	14	12	12	13	11	12	11	11	11	7	200	64.3
Other	0	0	0	0	0	0	0	0	0	0	0	0	0	0	0	0	0	0	0	0.0
Minnesota																				
Democratic	0	1	1	1	1	0	0	2	1	4	4	4	5	5	4	3	4	4	44	27.3
Republican	9	3	5	3	7	8	8	7	8	5	5	5	4	4	5	6	4	4	100	62.1
Other	1	5	3	5	1	1	1	0	0	0	0	0	0	0	0	0	0	0	17	10.6

Table 5-13 (Continued)

Region/State	1930	1932	1934	1936	1938	1940	1942	1944	1946	1948	1950	1952	1954	1956	1958	1960	1962	1964	Total Wins	% of Wins
Missouri																				
Democratic	12	13	12	12	12	10	5	7	4	12	10	7	9	10	10	9	8	8	170	76.9
Republican	4	0	1	1	1	3	8	6	9	1	3	4	2	1	1	2	2	2	51	23.1
Other	0	0	0	0	0	0	0	0	0	0	0	0	0	0	0	0	0	0	0	0.0
Nebraska																				
Democratic	4	5	4	4	2	2	0	0	0	1	0	0	0	0	2	0	0	1	25	32.5
Republican	2	0	1	1	3	3	4	4	4	3	4	4	4	4	2	4	3	2	52	67.5
Other	0	0	0	0	0	0	0	0	0	0	0	0	0	0	0	0	0	0	0	0.0
North Dakota																				
Democratic	0	0	0	0	0	0	0	0	0	0	0	0	0	0	1	0	0	1	2	5.4
Republican	3	2	2	2	2	2	2	2	2	2	2	2	2	2	1	2	2	1	35	94.6
Other	0	0	0	0	0	0	0	0	0	0	0	0	0	0	0	0	0	0	0	0.0
Ohio																				
Democratic	9	18	18	22	9	12	3	6	4	12	7	6	6	6	9	7	6	10	170	40.5
Republican	13	6	6	2	15	12	20	17	19	11	15	16	17	17	14	16	18	14	248	59.0
Other	0	0	0	0	0	0	0	0	0	0	1	1	0	0	0	0	0	0	2	0.5
South Dakota																				
Democratic	0	2	2	1	0	0	0	0	0	0	0	0	0	1	1	0	0	0	7	18.9
Republican	3	0	0	1	2	2	2	2	2	2	2	2	2	1	1	2	2	2	30	81.1
Other	0	0	0	0	0	0	0	0	0	0	0	0	0	0	0	0	0	0	0	0.0
Wisconsin																				
Democratic	1	5	3	3	0	1	3	2	0	2	1	1	3	3	5	4	4	5	46	25.4
Republican	10	5	0	1	8	6	5	7	10	8	9	9	7	7	5	6	6	5	114	63.0
Other	0	0	7	6	2	3	2	1	0	0	0	0	0	0	0	0	0	0	21	11.6
WEST																				
Democratic	7	32	34	38	30	28	26	29	17	24	22	19	20	26	33	33	42	47	507	55.1
Republican	26	11	9	5	13	15	23	20	32	25	27	38	37	31	26	26	27	22	413	44.8
Other	1	0	0	0	0	0	0	0	0	0	0	0	0	0	0	0	0	0	1	0.1
Democratic %	20.6	74.4	79.1	88.4	69.8	65.1	53.1	59.2	34.7	49.0	44.9	33.3	35.1	45.6	55.9	55.9	60.9	68.1	—	—
Republican %	76.5	25.6	20.9	11.6	30.2	34.9	46.9	40.8	65.3	51.0	55.1	66.7	64.9	54.4	44.1	44.1	39.1	31.9	—	—
Other %	2.9	0.0	0.0	0.0	0.0	0.0	0.0	0.0	0.0	0.0	0.0	0.0	0.0	0.0	0.0	0.0	0.0	0.0	—	—
Alaska																				
Democratic	—	—	—	—	—	—	—	—	—	—	—	—	—	—	1	1	1	1	4	100.0
Republican	—	—	—	—	—	—	—	—	—	—	—	—	—	—	0	0	0	0	0	0.0
Other	—	—	—	—	—	—	—	—	—	—	—	—	—	—	0	0	0	0	0	0.0
Arizona																				
Democratic	1	1	1	1	1	1	2	2	2	2	2	1	1	1	1	1	2	2	25	78.1
Republican	0	0	0	0	0	0	0	0	0	0	0	1	1	1	1	1	1	1	7	21.9
Other	0	0	0	0	0	0	0	0	0	0	0	0	0	0	0	0	0	0	0	0.0
California																				
Democratic	1	11	13	16	12	11	12	16	9	10	10	11	11	13	16	16	25	23	236	52.2
Republican	10	9	7	4	8	9	11	7	14	13	13	19	19	17	14	14	13	15	216	47.8
Other	0	0	0	0	0	0	0	0	0	0	0	0	0	0	0	0	0	0	0	0.0
Colorado																				
Democratic	1	4	4	4	4	2	1	0	1	3	2	2	2	2	3	2	2	4	43	59.7
Republican	3	0	0	0	0	2	3	4	3	1	2	2	2	2	1	2	2	0	29	40.3
Other	0	0	0	0	0	0	0	0	0	0	0	0	0	0	0	0	0	0	0	0.0
Hawaii																				
Democratic	—	—	—	—	—	—	—	—	—	—	—	—	—	—	1	1	2	2	6	100.0
Republican	—	—	—	—	—	—	—	—	—	—	—	—	—	—	0	0	0	0	0	0.0
Other	—	—	—	—	—	—	—	—	—	—	—	—	—	—	0	0	0	0	0	0.0

(Table continues)

Table 5-13 (Continued)

Region/State	1930	1932	1934	1936	1938	1940	1942	1944	1946	1948	1950	1952	1954	1956	1958	1960	1962	1964	Total Wins	% of Wins
Idaho																				
Democratic	0	2	2	2	1	1	1	1	0	1	0	1	1	1	1	2	2	1	20	55.6
Republican	2	0	0	0	1	1	1	1	2	1	2	1	1	1	1	0	0	1	16	44.4
Other	0	0	0	0	0	0	0	0	0	0	0	0	0	0	0	0	0	0	0	0.0
Montana																				
Democratic	1	2	2	2	1	1	2	1	1	1	1	1	1	2	2	1	1	1	24	66.7
Republican	1	0	0	0	1	1	0	1	1	1	1	1	1	0	0	1	1	1	12	33.3
Other	0	0	0	0	0	0	0	0	0	0	0	0	0	0	0	0	0	0	0	0.0
Nevada																				
Democratic	0	1	1	1	1	1	1	1	0	1	1	0	0	1	1	1	1	1	14	73.7
Republican	1	0	0	0	0	0	0	0	1	0	0	1	1	0	0	0	0	0	4	21.1
Other	1	0	0	0	0	0	0	0	0	0	0	0	0	0	0	0	0	0	1	5.3
New Mexico																				
Democratic	1	1	1	1	1	1	2	2	2	2	2	2	2	2	2	2	2	2	30	100.0
Republican	0	0	0	0	0	0	0	0	0	0	0	0	0	0	0	0	0	0	0	0.0
Other	0	0	0	0	0	0	0	0	0	0	0	0	0	0	0	0	0	0	0	0.0
Oregon																				
Democratic	1	2	1	2	1	1	0	0	0	0	0	0	1	3	3	2	3	3	23	34.8
Republican	2	1	2	1	2	2	4	4	4	4	4	4	3	1	1	2	1	1	43	65.2
Other	0	0	0	0	0	0	0	0	0	0	0	0	0	0	0	0	0	0	0	0.0
Utah																				
Democratic	0	2	2	2	2	2	2	2	1	2	2	0	0	0	1	2	0	1	23	63.9
Republican	2	0	0	0	0	0	0	0	1	0	0	2	2	2	1	0	2	1	13	36.1
Other	0	0	0	0	0	0	0	0	0	0	0	0	0	0	0	0	0	0	0	0.0
Washington																				
Democratic	1	6	6	6	6	6	3	4	1	2	2	1	1	1	1	2	1	5	55	48.2
Republican	4	0	0	0	0	0	3	2	5	4	4	6	6	6	6	5	6	2	59	51.8
Other	0	0	0	0	0	0	0	0	0	0	0	0	0	0	0	0	0	0	0	0.0
Wyoming																				
Democratic	0	0	1	1	0	1	0	0	0	0	0	0	0	0	0	0	0	1	4	22.2
Republican	1	1	0	0	1	0	1	1	1	1	1	1	1	1	1	1	1	0	14	77.8
Other	0	0	0	0	0	0	0	0	0	0	0	0	0	0	0	0	0	0	0	0.0

Notes: Entries reflect winners from the actual vote results and are not adjusted for contested seats, runoffs, inaccuracies of other types in reporting party labels or winners, or gubernatorial and legislative proclamations of different winners. For these reasons, these figures may not completely correspond to the most recent reports of the Clerk of the House of Representatives regarding the composition of the House over time. The regional categories are adapted from the ICPSR, except that in the current analysis Tennessee is coded in the South, because it was part of the Confederacy, whereas the ICPSR places Tennessee in the Border South. House elections were generally held in both even- and odd-numbered years prior to 1880 (that is, in two-year election cycles). Although only the even-numbered years of these two-year election cycles are used as column headings in this table, the House election results for both the even- and odd-numbered years in these two-year election cycles are reported as data in the table. —indicates state not yet in Union or data unavailable for that state.

Sources: Data adapted from *United States Congressional Elections, 1788–1997* (1998), *Congressional Quarterly's Guide to U.S. Elections* (1994), Report of the Clerk of the House of Representatives (various dates), and independent search of state sources by the author.

Table 5-14 Party Victories in House Elections, by State, in Regions, 1966–1998

Region/State	1966	1968	1970	1972	1974	1976	1978	1980	1982	1984	1986	1988	1990	1992	1994	1996	1998	Total Wins	% of Wins
NEW ENGLAND																			
Democratic	16	15	16	15	17	18	16	16	14	16	15	14	16	14	14	18	18	268	65.2
Republican	9	10	9	10	8	8	7	9	8	10	9	10	7	8	8	4	4	138	33.6
Other	0	0	0	0	0	0	0	0	0	0	0	0	1	1	1	1	1	5	1.2
Democratic %	64.0	60.0	64.0	60.0	68.0	69.2	69.6	64.0	63.6	61.5	62.5	58.3	66.7	60.9	60.9	78.3	78.3	—	—
Republican %	36.0	40.0	36.0	40.0	32.0	30.8	30.4	36.0	36.4	38.5	37.5	41.7	29.2	34.8	34.8	17.4	17.4	—	—
Other %	0.0	0.0	0.0	0.0	0.0	0.0	0.0	0.0	0.0	0.0	0.0	0.0	4.2	4.3	4.3	4.3	4.3	—	—
Connecticut																			
Democratic	5	4	4	3	4	4	5	4	4	3	3	3	3	3	3	4	4	63	61.8
Republican	1	2	2	3	2	2	1	2	2	3	3	3	3	3	3	2	2	39	38.2
Other	0	0	0	0	0	0	0	0	0	0	0	0	0	0	0	0	0	0	0.0
Maine																			
Democratic	2	2	2	1	0	0	0	0	0	0	1	1	1	1	1	2	2	16	47.1
Republican	0	0	0	1	2	2	2	2	2	2	1	1	1	1	1	0	0	18	52.9
Other	0	0	0	0	0	0	0	0	0	0	0	0	0	0	0	0	0	0	0.0
Massachusetts																			
Democratic	7	7	8	9	10	10	10	10	10	10	10	10	10	8	8	10	10	157	82.2
Republican	5	5	4	3	2	2	2	1	1	1	1	1	1	2	2	0	0	34	17.8
Other	0	0	0	0	0	0	0	0	0	0	0	0	0	0	0	0	0	0	0.0
New Hampshire																			
Democratic	0	0	0	0	1	1	1	1	1	0	0	0	1	1	0	0	0	7	20.6
Republican	2	2	2	2	1	1	1	1	1	2	2	2	1	1	2	2	2	27	79.4
Other	0	0	0	0	0	0	0	0	0	0	0	0	0	0	0	0	0	0	0.0
Rhode Island																			
Democratic	2	2	2	2	2	2	2	1	1	1	1	0	1	1	2	2	2	26	76.5
Republican	0	0	0	0	0	0	0	1	1	1	1	2	0	0	0	0	0	8	23.5
Other	0	0	0	0	0	0	0	0	0	0	0	0	0	0	0	0	0	0	0.0
Vermont																			
Democratic	0	0	0	0	0	0	0	0	0	0	0	0	0	0	0	0	0	0	0.0
Republican	1	1	1	1	1	1	1	1	1	1	1	1	0	0	0	0	0	12	70.6
Other	0	0	0	0	0	0	0	0	0	0	0	0	1	1	1	1	1	5	29.4
MID-ATLANTIC																			
Democratic	49	49	47	43	53	56	51	43	43	41	41	42	41	36	33	35	36	739	57.9
Republican	35	35	37	37	27	24	29	37	29	31	31	30	31	30	33	31	30	537	42.1
Other	0	0	0	0	0	0	0	0	0	0	0	0	0	0	0	0	0	0	0.0
Democratic %	58.3	58.3	56.0	53.8	66.3	70.0	63.8	53.8	59.7	56.9	56.9	58.3	56.9	54.5	50.0	53.0	54.5	—	—
Republican %	41.7	41.7	44.0	46.2	33.7	30.0	36.2	46.2	40.3	43.1	43.1	41.7	43.1	45.5	50.0	47.0	45.5	—	—
Other %	0.0	0.0	0.0	0.0	0.0	0.0	0.0	0.0	0.0	0.0	0.0	0.0	0.0	0.0	0.0	0.0	0.0	—	—
Delaware																			
Democratic	0	0	0	0	0	0	0	0	1	1	1	1	1	0	0	0	0	5	29.4
Republican	1	1	1	1	1	1	1	1	0	0	0	0	0	1	1	1	1	12	70.6
Other	0	0	0	0	0	0	0	0	0	0	0	0	0	0	0	0	0	0	0.0
New Jersey																			
Democratic	9	9	9	8	12	11	10	8	9	8	8	8	8	7	5	6	7	142	58.7
Republican	6	6	6	7	3	4	5	7	5	6	6	6	6	6	8	7	6	100	41.3
Other	0	0	0	0	0	0	0	0	0	0	0	0	0	0	0	0	0	0	0.0
New York																			
Democratic	26	26	24	22	27	28	26	22	20	19	20	21	21	18	17	18	18	373	60.9
Republican	15	15	17	17	12	11	13	17	14	15	14	13	13	13	14	13	13	239	39.1
Other	0	0	0	0	0	0	0	0	0	0	0	0	0	0	0	0	0	0	0.0

(Table continues)

Table 5-14 (Continued)

Region/State	1966	1968	1970	1972	1974	1976	1978	1980	1982	1984	1986	1988	1990	1992	1994	1996	1998	Total Wins	% of Wins
Pennsylvania																			
Democratic	14	14	14	13	14	17	15	13	13	13	12	12	11	11	11	11	11	219	54.1
Republican	13	13	13	12	11	8	10	12	10	10	11	11	12	10	10	10	10	186	45.9
Other	0	0	0	0	0	0	0	0	0	0	0	0	0	0	0	0	0	0	0.0
SOUTH																			
Democratic	83	80	79	74	81	81	77	69	82	73	77	77	78	77	62	54	54	1258	64.9
Republican	23	26	27	34	27	27	31	39	34	43	39	39	38	48	63	71	71	680	35.1
Other	0	0	0	0	0	0	0	0	0	0	0	0	0	0	0	0	0	0	0.0
Democratic %	78.3	75.5	74.5	68.5	75.0	75.0	71.3	63.9	70.7	62.9	66.4	66.4	67.2	61.6	49.6	43.2	43.2	—	—
Republican %	21.7	24.5	25.5	31.5	25.0	25.0	28.7	36.1	29.3	37.1	33.6	33.6	32.8	38.4	50.4	56.8	56.8	—	—
Other %	0.0	0.0	0.0	0.0	0.0	0.0	0.0	0.0	0.0	0.0	0.0	0.0	0.0	0.0	0.0	0.0	0.0	—	—
Alabama																			
Democratic	5	5	5	4	4	4	4	4	5	5	5	5	5	4	4	2	2	72	59.0
Republican	3	3	3	3	3	3	3	3	2	2	2	2	2	3	3	5	5	50	41.0
Other	0	0	0	0	0	0	0	0	0	0	0	0	0	0	0	0	0	0	0.0
Arkansas																			
Democratic	3	3	3	3	3	3	2	2	2	3	3	3	3	2	2	2	2	44	64.7
Republican	1	1	1	1	1	1	2	2	2	1	1	1	1	2	2	2	2	24	35.3
Other	0	0	0	0	0	0	0	0	0	0	0	0	0	0	0	0	0	0	0.0
Florida																			
Democratic	9	9	9	11	10	10	12	11	13	12	12	10	9	10	8	8	8	171	57.4
Republican	3	3	3	4	5	5	3	4	6	7	7	9	10	13	15	15	15	127	42.6
Other	0	0	0	0	0	0	0	0	0	0	0	0	0	0	0	0	0	0	0.0
Georgia																			
Democratic	8	8	8	9	10	10	9	9	9	8	8	9	9	7	4	3	3	131	75.3
Republican	2	2	2	1	0	0	1	1	1	2	2	1	1	4	7	8	8	43	24.7
Other	0	0	0	0	0	0	0	0	0	0	0	0	0	0	0	0	0	0	0.0
Louisiana																			
Democratic	8	8	8	7	6	6	5	6	6	6	5	4	4	4	4	2	2	91	68.9
Republican	0	0	0	1	2	2	3	2	2	2	3	4	4	3	3	5	5	41	31.1
Other	0	0	0	0	0	0	0	0	0	0	0	0	0	0	0	0	0	0	0.0
Mississippi																			
Democratic	5	5	5	3	3	3	3	3	3	3	4	4	5	5	4	2	3	63	74.1
Republican	0	0	0	2	2	2	2	2	2	2	1	1	0	0	1	3	2	22	25.9
Other	0	0	0	0	0	0	0	0	0	0	0	0	0	0	0	0	0	0	0.0
North Carolina																			
Democratic	8	7	7	7	9	9	9	7	9	6	8	8	7	8	4	6	5	124	64.9
Republican	3	4	4	4	2	2	2	4	2	5	3	3	4	4	8	6	7	67	35.1
Other	0	0	0	0	0	0	0	0	0	0	0	0	0	0	0	0	0	0	0.0
South Carolina																			
Democratic	5	5	5	4	5	5	4	2	3	3	4	4	4	3	3	2	2	63	61.8
Republican	1	1	1	2	1	1	2	4	3	3	2	2	2	3	3	4	4	39	38.2
Other	0	0	0	0	0	0	0	0	0	0	0	0	0	0	0	0	0	0	0.0
Tennessee																			
Democratic	5	5	5	3	5	5	5	5	6	6	6	6	6	6	4	4	4	86	58.1
Republican	4	4	4	5	3	3	3	3	3	3	3	3	3	3	5	5	5	62	41.9
Other	0	0	0	0	0	0	0	0	0	0	0	0	0	0	0	0	0	0	0.0
Texas																			
Democratic	21	20	20	20	21	22	20	19	22	17	17	19	20	21	19	17	17	332	74.8
Republican	2	3	3	4	3	2	4	5	5	10	10	8	7	9	11	13	13	112	25.2
Other	0	0	0	0	0	0	0	0	0	0	0	0	0	0	0	0	0	0	0.0
Virginia																			
Democratic	6	5	4	3	5	4	4	1	4	4	5	5	6	7	6	6	6	81	46.6
Republican	4	5	6	7	5	6	6	9	6	6	5	5	4	4	5	5	5	93	53.4
Other	0	0	0	0	0	0	0	0	0	0	0	0	0	0	0	0	0	0	0.0

Table 5-14 (Continued)

Region/State	1966	1968	1970	1972	1974	1976	1978	1980	1982	1984	1986	1988	1990	1992	1994	1996	1998	Total Wins	% of Wins
BORDER SOUTH																			
Democratic	17	17	19	18	20	19	19	18	20	19	18	18	17	15	10	8	8	280	66.7
Republican	9	9	7	7	5	6	6	7	5	6	7	7	8	8	13	15	15	140	33.3
Other	0	0	0	0	0	0	0	0	0	0	0	0	0	0	0	0	0	0	0.0
Democratic %	65.4	65.4	73.1	72.0	80.0	76.0	76.0	72.0	80.0	76.0	72.0	72.0	68.0	65.2	43.5	34.8	34.8	—	—
Republican %	34.6	34.6	26.9	28.0	20.0	24.0	24.0	28.0	20.0	24.0	28.0	28.0	32.0	34.8	56.5	65.2	65.2	—	—
Other %	0.0	0.0	0.0	0.0	0.0	0.0	0.0	0.0	0.0	0.0	0.0	0.0	0.0	0.0	0.0	0.0	0.0	—	—
Kentucky																			
Democratic	4	4	5	5	5	5	4	4	4	4	4	4	4	4	2	1	1	64	55.7
Republican	3	3	2	2	2	2	3	3	3	3	3	3	3	2	4	5	5	51	44.3
Other	0	0	0	0	0	0	0	0	0	0	0	0	0	0	0	0	0	0	0.0
Maryland																			
Democratic	5	4	5	4	5	5	6	7	7	6	6	6	5	4	4	4	4	87	64.0
Republican	3	4	3	4	3	3	2	1	1	2	2	2	3	4	4	4	4	49	36.0
Other	0	0	0	0	0	0	0	0	0	0	0	0	0	0	0	0	0	0	0.0
Oklahoma																			
Democratic	4	4	4	5	6	5	5	5	5	5	4	4	4	4	1	0	0	65	63.7
Republican	2	2	2	1	0	1	1	1	1	1	2	2	2	2	5	6	6	37	36.3
Other	0	0	0	0	0	0	0	0	0	0	0	0	0	0	0	0	0	0	0.0
West Virginia																			
Democratic	4	5	5	4	4	4	4	2	4	4	4	4	4	3	3	3	3	64	95.5
Republican	1	0	0	0	0	0	0	2	0	0	0	0	0	0	0	0	0	3	4.5
Other	0	0	0	0	0	0	0	0	0	0	0	0	0	0	0	0	0	0	0.0
MIDWEST																			
Democratic	45	46	55	51	69	68	65	58	62	62	62	64	68	61	47	50	51	984	50.1
Republican	80	79	70	70	52	53	56	63	51	51	51	49	45	44	58	54	54	980	49.9
Other	0	0	0	0	0	0	0	0	0	0	0	0	0	0	0	1	0	1	0.1
Democratic %	36.0	36.8	44.0	42.1	57.0	56.2	53.7	47.9	54.9	54.9	54.9	56.6	60.2	58.1	44.8	47.6	48.6	—	—
Republican %	64.0	63.2	56.0	57.9	43.0	43.8	46.3	52.1	45.1	45.1	45.1	43.4	39.8	41.9	55.2	51.4	51.4	—	—
Other %	0.0	0.0	0.0	0.0	0.0	0.0	0.0	0.0	0.0	0.0	0.0	0.0	0.0	0.0	0.0	1.0	0.0	—	—
Illinois																			
Democratic	12	12	12	10	13	12	11	10	12	13	13	14	15	12	10	10	10	201	52.6
Republican	12	12	12	14	11	12	13	14	10	9	9	8	7	8	10	10	10	181	47.4
Other	0	0	0	0	0	0	0	0	0	0	0	0	0	0	0	0	0	0	0.0
Indiana																			
Democratic	5	4	5	4	9	8	7	6	5	5	6	6	8	7	4	4	4	97	54.5
Republican	6	7	6	7	2	3	4	5	5	5	4	4	2	3	6	6	6	81	45.5
Other	0	0	0	0	0	0	0	0	0	0	0	0	0	0	0	0	0	0	0.0
Iowa																			
Democratic	2	2	2	3	5	4	3	3	3	2	2	2	2	1	0	1	1	38	37.6
Republican	5	5	5	3	1	2	3	3	3	4	4	4	4	4	5	4	4	63	62.4
Other	0	0	0	0	0	0	0	0	0	0	0	0	0	0	0	0	0	0	0.0
Kansas																			
Democratic	0	0	1	1	1	2	1	1	2	2	2	2	2	2	0	0	1	20	24.7
Republican	5	5	4	4	4	3	4	4	3	3	3	3	3	2	4	4	3	61	75.3
Other	0	0	0	0	0	0	0	0	0	0	0	0	0	0	0	0	0	0	0.0
Michigan																			
Democratic	7	7	7	7	12	11	13	12	12	11	11	11	11	10	9	10	10	171	55.9
Republican	12	12	12	12	7	8	6	7	6	7	7	7	7	6	7	6	6	135	44.1
Other	0	0	0	0	0	0	0	0	0	0	0	0	0	0	0	0	0	0	0.0

(Table continues)

Table 5-14 (Continued)

Region/State	1966	1968	1970	1972	1974	1976	1978	1980	1982	1984	1986	1988	1990	1992	1994	1996	1998	Total Wins	% of Wins
Minnesota																			
Democratic	3	3	4	4	5	5	4	3	5	5	5	5	6	6	6	6	6	81	59.6
Republican	5	5	4	4	3	3	4	5	3	3	3	3	2	2	2	2	2	55	40.4
Other	0	0	0	0	0	0	0	0	0	0	0	0	0	0	0	0	0	0	0.0
Missouri																			
Democratic	8	9	9	9	9	8	8	6	6	6	5	5	6	6	6	5	5	116	72.0
Republican	2	1	1	1	1	2	2	4	3	3	4	4	3	3	3	3	4	44	27.3
Other	0	0	0	0	0	0	0	0	0	0	0	0	0	0	1	1	0	1	0.6
Nebraska																			
Democratic	0	0	0	0	0	1	1	0	0	0	0	1	1	1	0	0	0	5	9.8
Republican	3	3	3	3	3	2	2	3	3	3	3	2	2	2	3	3	3	46	90.2
Other	0	0	0	0	0	0	0	0	0	0	0	0	0	0	0	0	0	0	0.0
North Dakota																			
Democratic	0	0	1	0	0	0	0	1	1	1	1	1	1	1	1	1	1	11	55.0
Republican	2	2	1	1	1	1	1	0	0	0	0	0	0	0	0	0	0	9	45.0
Other	0	0	0	0	0	0	0	0	0	0	0	0	0	0	0	0	0	0	0.0
Ohio																			
Democratic	5	6	7	7	8	10	10	10	10	11	11	11	11	10	7	8	8	150	40.8
Republican	19	18	17	16	15	13	13	13	11	10	10	10	10	9	12	11	11	218	59.2
Other	0	0	0	0	0	0	0	0	0	0	0	0	0	0	0	0	0	0	0.0
South Dakota																			
Democratic	0	0	2	1	0	0	1	1	1	1	1	1	1	1	1	0	0	12	48.0
Republican	2	2	0	1	2	2	1	1	0	0	0	0	0	0	0	1	1	13	52.0
Other	0	0	0	0	0	0	0	0	0	0	0	0	0	0	0	0	0	0	0.0
Wisconsin																			
Democratic	3	3	5	5	7	7	6	5	5	5	5	5	4	4	3	5	5	82	52.6
Republican	7	7	5	4	2	2	3	4	4	4	4	4	5	5	6	4	4	74	47.4
Other	0	0	0	0	0	0	0	0	0	0	0	0	0	0	0	0	0	0	0.0
WEST																			
Democratic	**38**	**36**	**39**	**42**	**51**	**51**	**47**	**39**	**46**	**44**	**45**	**45**	**48**	**55**	**40**	**42**	**44**	**752**	**54.3**
Republican	**31**	**33**	**30**	**34**	**25**	**25**	**29**	**37**	**39**	**41**	**40**	**40**	**37**	**38**	**53**	**51**	**49**	**632**	**45.7**
Other	**0**	**0**	**0**	**0**	**0**	**0**	**0**	**0**	**0**	**0**	**0**	**0**	**0**	**0**	**0**	**0**	**0**	**0**	**0.0**
Democratic %	**55.1**	**52.2**	**56.5**	**55.3**	**67.1**	**67.1**	**61.8**	**51.3**	**54.1**	**51.8**	**52.9**	**52.9**	**56.5**	**59.1**	**43.0**	**45.2**	**47.3**		
Republican %	**44.9**	**47.8**	**43.5**	**44.7**	**32.9**	**32.9**	**38.2**	**48.7**	**45.9**	**48.2**	**47.1**	**47.1**	**43.5**	**40.9**	**57.0**	**54.8**	**52.7**		
Other %	**0.0**	**0.0**	**0.0**	**0.0**	**0.0**	**0.0**	**0.0**	**0.0**	**0.0**	**0.0**	**0.0**	**0.0**	**0.0**	**0.0**	**0.0**	**0.0**	**0.0**		
Alaska																			
Democratic	0	0	1	1	0	0	0	0	0	0	0	0	0	0	0	0	0	2	11.8
Republican	1	1	0	0	1	1	1	1	1	1	1	1	1	1	1	1	1	15	88.2
Other	0	0	0	0	0	0	0	0	0	0	0	0	0	0	0	0	0	0	0.0
Arizona																			
Democratic	1	1	1	1	1	3	2	2	2	1	1	1	1	3	1	1	1	23	29.5
Republican	2	2	2	3	3	2	2	2	3	4	4	4	4	3	5	5	5	55	70.5
Other	0	0	0	0	0	0	0	0	0	0	0	0	0	0	0	0	0	0	0.0
California																			
Democratic	21	21	20	23	28	29	26	22	28	27	27	27	26	30	27	29	28	439	57.6
Republican	17	17	18	20	15	14	17	21	17	18	18	18	19	22	25	23	24	323	42.4
Other	0	0	0	0	0	0	0	0	0	0	0	0	0	0	0	0	0	0	0.0
Colorado																			
Democratic	3	3	2	2	3	3	3	3	3	2	3	3	3	2	2	2	2	44	48.4
Republican	1	1	2	3	2	2	2	2	3	4	3	3	3	4	4	4	4	47	51.6
Other	0	0	0	0	0	0	0	0	0	0	0	0	0	0	0	0	0	0	0.0
Hawaii																			
Democratic	2	2	2	2	2	2	2	2	2	2	1	1	2	2	2	2	2	32	94.1
Republican	0	0	0	0	0	0	0	0	0	0	1	1	0	0	0	0	0	2	5.9
Other	0	0	0	0	0	0	0	0	0	0	0	0	0	0	0	0	0	0	0.0

Table 5-14 (Continued)

Region/State	1966	1968	1970	1972	1974	1976	1978	1980	1982	1984	1986	1988	1990	1992	1994	1996	1998	Total Wins	% of Wins
Idaho																			
Democratic	0	0	0	0	0	0	0	0	0	1	1	1	2	1	0	0	0	6	17.6
Republican	2	2	2	2	2	2	2	2	2	1	1	1	0	1	2	2	2	28	82.4
Other	0	0	0	0	0	0	0	0	0	0	0	0	0	0	0	0	0	0	0.0
Montana																			
Democratic	1	1	1	1	2	1	1	1	1	1	1	1	1	1	1	0	0	16	53.3
Republican	1	1	1	1	0	1	1	1	1	1	1	1	1	0	0	1	1	14	46.7
Other	0	0	0	0	0	0	0	0	0	0	0	0	0	0	0	0	0	0	0.0
Nevada																			
Democratic	1	1	1	0	1	1	1	1	1	1	1	1	1	1	0	0	1	14	53.8
Republican	0	0	0	1	0	0	0	0	1	1	1	1	1	1	2	2	1	12	46.2
Other	0	0	0	0	0	0	0	0	0	0	0	0	0	0	0	0	0	0	0.0
New Mexico																			
Democratic	2	0	1	1	1	1	1	0	1	1	1	1	1	1	1	1	1	16	37.2
Republican	0	2	1	1	1	1	1	2	2	2	2	2	2	2	2	2	2	27	62.8
Other	0	0	0	0	0	0	0	0	0	0	0	0	0	0	0	0	0	0	0.0
Oregon																			
Democratic	2	2	2	2	4	4	4	3	3	3	3	3	4	4	3	4	4	54	70.1
Republican	2	2	2	2	0	0	0	1	2	2	2	2	1	1	2	1	1	23	29.9
Other	0	0	0	0	0	0	0	0	0	0	0	0	0	0	0	0	0	0	0.0
Utah																			
Democratic	0	0	1	2	2	1	1	0	0	0	1	1	2	2	1	0	0	14	32.6
Republican	2	2	1	0	0	1	1	2	3	3	2	2	1	1	2	3	3	29	67.4
Other	0	0	0	0	0	0	0	0	0	0	0	0	0	0	0	0	0	0	0.0
Washington																			
Democratic	5	5	6	6	6	6	6	5	5	5	5	5	5	8	2	3	5	88	66.7
Republican	2	2	1	1	1	1	1	2	3	3	3	3	3	1	7	6	4	44	33.3
Other	0	0	0	0	0	0	0	0	0	0	0	0	0	0	0	0	0	0	0.0
Wyoming																			
Democratic	0	0	1	1	1	1	0	0	0	0	0	0	0	0	0	0	0	4	23.5
Republican	1	1	0	0	0	0	1	1	1	1	1	1	1	1	1	1	1	13	76.5
Other	0	0	0	0	0	0	0	0	0	0	0	0	0	0	0	0	0	0	0.0

Notes: Entries reflect winners from the actual vote results and are not adjusted for contested seats, runoffs, inaccuracies of other types in reporting party labels or winners, or gubernatorial and legislative proclamations of different winners. For these reasons, these figures may not completely correspond to the most recent reports of the Clerk of the House of Representatives regarding the composition of the House over time. The regional categories are adapted from the ICPSR, except that in the current analysis Tennessee is coded in the South, because it was part of the Confederacy, whereas the ICPSR places Tennessee in the Border South. House elections were generally held in both even- and odd-numbered years prior to 1880 (that is, in two-year election cycles). Although only the even-numbered years of these two-year election cycles are used as column headings in this table, the House election results for both the even- and odd-numbered years in these two-year election cycles are reported as data in the table. —indicates state not yet in Union or data unavailable for that state.

Sources: Data adapted from *United States Congressional Elections, 1788–1997* (1998), Report of the Clerk of the House of Representatives (various dates), and independent search of state sources by the author.

Table 5-15 Party Victories in House Elections by Non-South and South, 1856–1998

Year	Nation				Non-South				South			
	Dem.	Rep.	Dem. %	Rep. %	Dem.	Rep.	Dem. %	Rep. %	Dem.	Rep.	Dem. %	Rep. %
1856	130	93	58.30	41.70	71	92	43.56	56.44	59	1	98.33	1.67
1858	99	119	45.41	54.59	48	115	29.45	70.55	51	4	92.73	7.27
1860	52	114	31.33	68.67	52	114	31.33	68.67	—	—	—	—
1862	75	108	40.98	59.02	75	108	40.98	59.02	—	—	—	—
1864	35	140	20.00	80.00	35	140	20.00	80.00	—	—	—	—
1866	50	143	25.91	74.09	50	143	25.91	74.09	—	—	—	—
1868	72	165	30.38	69.62	62	123	33.51	66.49	10	42	19.23	80.77
1870	95	138	40.77	59.23	77	108	41.62	58.38	18	30	37.50	62.50
1872	86	202	29.86	70.14	61	158	27.85	72.15	25	44	36.23	63.77
1874	179	108	62.37	37.63	123	91	57.48	42.52	56	17	76.71	23.29
1876	152	141	51.88	48.12	89	131	40.45	59.55	63	10	86.30	13.70
1878	152	136	52.78	47.22	85	132	39.17	60.83	67	4	94.37	5.63
1880	138	152	47.59	52.41	76	145	34.39	65.61	62	7	89.86	10.14
1882	197	120	62.15	37.85	127	113	52.92	47.08	70	7	90.91	9.09
1884	183	142	56.31	43.69	106	134	44.17	55.83	77	8	90.59	9.41
1886	170	152	52.80	47.20	96	143	40.17	59.83	74	9	89.16	10.84
1888	162	164	49.69	50.31	86	155	35.68	64.32	76	9	89.41	10.59
1890	238	87	73.23	26.77	156	84	65.00	35.00	82	3	96.47	3.53
1892	221	130	62.96	37.04	135	126	51.72	48.28	86	4	95.56	4.44
1894	107	245	30.40	69.60	30	235	11.32	88.68	77	10	88.51	11.49
1896	142	211	40.23	59.77	66	198	25.00	75.00	76	13	85.39	14.61
1898	172	184	48.31	51.69	87	179	32.71	67.29	85	5	94.44	5.56
1900	159	198	44.54	55.46	73	194	27.34	72.66	86	4	95.56	4.44
1902	180	205	46.75	53.25	85	202	29.62	70.38	95	3	96.94	3.06
1904	135	251	34.97	65.03	41	247	14.24	85.76	94	4	95.92	4.08
1906	167	224	42.71	57.29	72	221	24.57	75.43	95	3	96.94	3.06
1908	172	219	43.99	56.01	80	213	27.30	72.70	92	6	93.88	6.12
1910	226	167	57.51	42.49	131	164	44.41	55.59	95	3	96.94	3.06
1912	279	145	65.80	34.20	178	142	55.63	44.38	101	3	97.12	2.88
1914	236	191	55.27	44.73	137	187	42.28	57.72	99	4	96.12	3.88
1916	215	216	49.88	50.12	115	213	35.06	64.94	100	3	97.09	2.91
1918	190	243	43.88	56.12	89	240	27.05	72.95	101	3	97.12	2.88
1920	131	302	30.25	69.75	34	295	10.33	89.67	97	7	93.27	6.73
1922	207	225	47.92	52.08	106	222	32.32	67.68	101	3	97.12	2.88
1924	183	247	42.56	57.44	82	244	25.15	74.85	101	3	97.12	2.88
1926	195	237	45.14	54.86	99	234	28.66	71.34	101	3	97.12	2.88
1928	165	269	38.02	61.98	68	262	20.61	79.39	97	7	93.27	6.73
1930	216	217	49.88	50.12	117	213	35.45	64.55	99	4	96.12	3.88
1932	313	117	72.79	27.21	213	115	64.94	35.06	100	2	98.04	1.96
1934	322	103	75.76	24.24	222	101	68.73	31.27	100	2	98.04	1.96
1936	335	89	79.01	20.99	235	87	72.98	27.02	100	2	98.04	1.96
1938	262	170	60.65	39.35	162	168	49.09	50.91	100	2	98.04	1.96
1940	267	163	62.09	37.91	168	161	51.06	48.94	99	2	98.02	1.98
1942	222	210	51.39	48.61	119	208	36.39	63.61	103	2	98.10	1.90
1944	242	191	55.89	44.11	139	189	42.38	57.62	103	2	98.10	1.90
1946	188	246	43.32	56.68	85	244	25.84	74.16	103	2	98.10	1.90
1948	263	171	60.60	39.40	160	169	48.63	51.37	103	2	98.10	1.90
1950	235	199	54.15	45.85	132	197	40.12	59.88	103	2	98.10	1.90
1952	213	221	49.08	50.92	113	215	34.45	65.55	100	6	94.34	5.66
1954	232	203	53.33	46.67	133	196	40.43	59.57	99	7	93.40	6.60
1956	234	201	53.79	46.21	135	194	41.03	58.97	99	7	93.40	6.60
1958	283	153	64.91	35.09	184	146	55.76	44.24	99	7	93.40	6.60
1960	263	174	60.18	39.82	164	167	49.55	50.45	99	7	93.40	6.60
1962	259	176	59.54	40.46	164	165	49.85	50.15	95	11	89.62	10.38
1964	295	140	67.82	32.18	205	124	62.31	37.69	90	16	84.91	15.09
1966	246	187	56.81	43.19	163	164	49.85	50.15	83	23	78.30	21.70
1968	243	192	55.86	44.14	163	166	49.54	50.46	80	26	75.47	24.53
1970	255	180	58.62	41.38	176	153	53.50	46.50	79	27	74.53	25.47
1972	243	191	55.99	44.01	169	157	51.84	48.16	74	34	68.52	31.48
1974	291	144	66.90	33.10	210	117	64.22	35.78	81	27	75.00	25.00
1976	292	143	67.13	32.87	211	116	64.53	35.47	81	27	75.00	25.00
1978	277	158	63.68	36.32	200	127	61.16	38.84	77	31	71.30	28.70
1980	243	192	55.86	44.14	174	153	53.21	46.79	69	39	63.89	36.11
1982	269	166	61.84	38.16	187	132	58.62	41.38	82	34	70.69	29.31
1984	253	182	58.16	41.84	180	139	56.43	43.57	73	43	62.93	37.07
1986	258	177	59.31	40.69	181	138	56.74	43.26	77	39	66.38	33.62
1988	260	175	59.77	40.23	183	136	59.37	42.63	77	39	66.38	33.62
1990	268	166	61.75	38.25	190	128	59.75	40.25	78	38	67.24	32.76
1992	258	176	59.45	40.55	181	128	58.58	41.42	77	48	61.60	38.40
1994	206	228	47.47	52.53	144	165	46.60	53.40	62	63	49.60	50.40
1996	207	226	47.81	52.19	153	155	49.68	50.32	54	71	43.20	56.80
1998	211	223	48.62	51.38	155	154	50.16	49.84	54	71	43.20	56.80

Notes: Excludes seats held by other parties. The South includes Alabama, Arkansas, Florida, Georgia, Louisiana, Mississippi, North Carolina, South Carolina, Tennessee, Texas, and Virginia. This is consistent with the ICPSR regional categorization except that in the current analysis Tennessee is included in the South because it was in the Confederacy, whereas the ICPSR codes it as a Border South state. —indicates data not available for that region (that is, southern states seceding from the Union during the Civil War period).

Sources: Data from Tables 5-11 through 5-14.

Table 5-16 Reelection Rates of House Incumbents, 1791–2001

Congress	Years	Seeking Reelection Number	%	Reelected Number	%	Defeated	Congress	Years	Seeking Reelection Number	%	Reelected Number	%	Defeated
2d	1791–1793	56	86.2	41	73.2	15	54th	1895–1897	249	69.9	177	71.1	72
3d	1793–1795	50	72.5	44	88.0	6	55th	1897–1899	225	71.7	198	88.0	27
4th	1795–1797	83	79.0	67	80.7	16	56th	1899–1901	290	81.2	252	86.9	38
5th	1797–1799	75	70.1	60	80.0	15	57th	1901–1903	290	81.2	274	94.5	16
6th	1799–1801	78	73.6	60	76.9	18	58th	1903–1905	284	73.6	257	90.5	27
7th	1801–1803	63	59.4	59	93.7	4	59th	1905–1907	322	83.4	299	92.9	23
8th	1803–1805	80	75.5	70	87.5	10	60th	1907–1909	323	83.7	296	91.6	27
9th	1805–1807	106	74.6	95	89.6	11	61st	1909–1911	340	87.0	311	91.5	29
10th	1807–1809	111	76.8	91	82.0	20	62d	1911–1913	308	78.8	261	84.7	47
11th	1809–1811	104	73.2	85	81.7	19	63d	1913–1915	324	74.5	281	86.7	43
12th	1811–1813	94	66.2	83	88.3	11	64th	1915–1917	361	83.0	298	82.5	63
13th	1813–1815	100	69.9	79	79.0	21	65th	1917–1919	387	89.0	351	90.7	36
14th	1815–1817	127	69.8	95	74.8	32	66th	1919–1921	375	86.2	331	88.3	44
15th	1817–1819	100	54.6	56	56.0	44	67th	1921–1923	365	83.9	314	86.0	51
16th	1819–1821	116	62.7	96	82.8	20	68th	1923–1925	365	83.9	301	82.5	64
17th	1821–1823	129	69.4	100	77.5	29	69th	1925–1927	381	87.6	352	92.4	29
18th	1823–1825	126	67.4	99	78.6	27	70th	1927–1929	389	89.4	373	95.9	16
19th	1825–1827	160	75.1	126	78.8	34	71st	1929–1931	396	91.0	365	92.2	31
20th	1827–1829	166	73.2	128	77.1	38	72d	1931–1933	397	91.3	355	89.4	42
21st	1829–1831	151	70.9	117	77.5	34	73d	1933–1935	345	79.3	272	78.8	73
22d	1831–1833	153	71.8	125	81.7	28	74th	1935–1937	371	85.3	329	88.7	42
23d	1833–1835	129	60.6	101	78.3	28	75th	1937–1939	373	85.7	344	92.2	29
24th	1835–1837	177	73.8	143	80.8	34	76th	1939–1941	393	90.3	322	81.9	71
25th	1837–1839	148	61.2	121	81.8	27	77th	1941–1943	399	91.7	363	91.0	36
26th	1839–1841	157	64.9	119	75.8	38	78th	1943–1945	372	85.5	327	87.9	45
27th	1841–1843	153	63.2	124	81.0	29	79th	1945–1947	392	90.1	359	91.6	33
28th	1843–1845	85	35.1	52	61.2	33	80th	1947–1949	383	88.0	332	86.7	51
29th	1845–1847	141	63.2	105	74.5	36	81st	1949–1951	383	88.0	316	82.5	67
30th	1847–1849	115	50.7	98	85.2	17	82d	1951–1953	397	89.1	364	91.7	33
31st	1849–1851	117	51.1	94	80.3	23	83d	1953–1955	379	87.1	353	93.1	26
32d	1851–1853	132	56.7	102	77.3	30	84th	1955–1957	400	92.0	378	94.5	22
33d	1853–1855	109	46.8	87	79.8	22	85th	1957–1959	402	92.4	387	96.3	15
34th	1855–1857	145	62.0	91	62.8	54	86th	1959–1961	390	89.7	354	90.8	36
35th	1857–1859	156	66.7	117	75.0	39	87th	1961–1963	404	92.9	378	93.6	26
36th	1859–1861	155	65.4	118	76.1	37	88th	1963–1965	390	89.7	368	94.4	22
37th	1861–1863	104	56.2	85	81.7	19	89th	1965–1967	389	89.4	344	88.4	45
38th	1863–1865	94	53.7	67	71.3	27	90th	1967–1969	401	92.2	362	90.3	39
39th	1865–1867	131	71.7	96	73.3	35	91st	1969–1971	403	92.6	395	98.0	8
40th	1867–1869	124	64.2	109	87.9	15	92d	1971–1973	397	91.3	384	96.7	13
41st	1869–1871	127	56.2	108	85.0	19	93d	1973–1975	374	86.0	360	96.3	14
42d	1871–1873	134	58.0	112	83.6	22	94th	1975–1977	382	87.8	343	89.8	39
43d	1873–1875	143	58.8	115	80.4	28	95th	1977–1979	380	87.4	367	96.6	13
44th	1875–1877	172	58.7	113	65.7	59	96th	1979–1981	376	56.4	358	95.2	18
45th	1877–1879	191	65.4	152	79.6	39	97th	1981–1983	392	90.1	360	91.8	32
46th	1879–1881	186	63.5	154	82.8	32	98th	1983–1985	382	87.8	355	92.9	27
47th	1881–1883	214	73.7	185	86.4	29	99th	1985–1987	407	93.6	394	96.8	13
48th	1883–1885	182	62.1	137	75.3	45	100th	1987–1989	391	89.9	385	98.5	6
49th	1885–1887	222	68.3	182	82.0	40	101st	1989–1991	410	94.3	404	98.5	6
50th	1887–1889	227	69.8	201	88.5	26	102d	1991–1993	407	93.6	392	96.3	15
51st	1889–1891	236	72.6	205	86.9	31	103d	1993–1995	351	80.7	327	93.2	24
52d	1891–1893	226	68.3	167	73.9	59	104th	1995–1997	383	88.0	349	91.1	34
53d	1893–1895	242	72.9	206	85.1	36	105th	1997–1999	381	87.6	362	95.0	19
							106th	1999–2001	404	92.9	395	97.8	7

Source: Adapted from author's data set.

Table 5-17 House Election Results by State, 1788–1791 (Percentages)

	1788–1789				1790–1791			
State	Democratic	Republican	Other	Democratic % of Two-Party Vote	Democratic	Republican	Other	Democratic % of Two-Party Vote
Alabama	—	—	—	—	—	—	—	—
Alaska	—	—	—	—	—	—	—	—
Arizona	—	—	—	—	—	—	—	—
Arkansas	—	—	—	—	—	—	—	—
California	—	—	—	—	—	—	—	—
Colorado	—	—	—	—	—	—	—	—
Connecticut	—	—	—	—	0.0	0.0	100.0	—
Delaware	0.0[1]	0.0[1]	100.0[1]	—	—	—	—	—
Florida	—	—	—	—	—	—	—	—
Georgia	0.0[1]	0.0[1]	100.0[1]	—	0.0[1]	0.0[1]	100.0[1]	—
Hawaii	—	—	—	—	—	—	—	—
Idaho	—	—	—	—	—	—	—	—
Illinois	—	—	—	—	—	—	—	—
Indiana	—	—	—	—	—	—	—	—
Iowa	—	—	—	—	—	—	—	—
Kansas	—	—	—	—	—	—	—	—
Kentucky	—	—	—	—	—	—	—	—
Louisiana	—	—	—	—	—	—	—	—
Maine	—	—	—	—	—	—	—	—
Maryland	34.6[1]	65.4[1]	0.0[1]	34.6[1]	0.0	0.0	100.0	—
Massachusetts	0.0	0.0	100.0	—	0.0	0.0	100.0	—
Michigan	—	—	—	—	—	—	—	—
Minnesota	—	—	—	—	—	—	—	—
Mississippi	—	—	—	—	—	—	—	—
Missouri	—	—	—	—	—	—	—	—
Montana	—	—	—	—	—	—	—	—
Nebraska	—	—	—	—	—	—	—	—
Nevada	—	—	—	—	—	—	—	—
New Hampshire	0.0	0.0	100.0	—	0.0	0.0	100.0	—
New Jersey	0.0[1]	0.0[1]	100.0[1]	—	0.0[1]	0.0[1]	100.0[1]	—
New Mexico	—	—	—	—	—	—	—	—
New York	35.9[1,2]	59.5[1,2]	4.6[1,2]	37.7[1,2]	29.3	67.0	3.7	30.4
North Carolina	—	—	—	—	43.8[2]	51.6[2]	4.6[2]	45.9[2]
North Dakota	—	—	—	—	—	—	—	—
Ohio	—	—	—	—	—	—	—	—
Oklahoma	—	—	—	—	—	—	—	—
Oregon	—	—	—	—	—	—	—	—
Pennsylvania	46.0	54.0	0.0	46.0	0.0[1,2]	0.0[1,2]	100.0[1,2]	—
Rhode Island	—	—	—	—	—	—	—	—
South Carolina	—	—	—	—	—	—	—	—
South Dakota	—	—	—	—	—	—	—	—
Tennessee	—	—	—	—	—	—	—	—
Texas	—	—	—	—	—	—	—	—
Utah	—	—	—	—	—	—	—	—
Vermont	—	—	—	—	0.0[1,2]	0.0[1,2]	100.0[1,2]	—
Virginia	0.0[1,2]	0.0[1,2]	100.0[1,2]	—	0.0[2]	0.0[2]	100.0[2]	—
Washington	—	—	—	—	—	—	—	—
West Virginia	—	—	—	—	—	—	—	—
Wisconsin	—	—	—	—	—	—	—	—
Wyoming	—	—	—	—	—	—	—	—
North Carolina	—	—	—	—	0.0[2,3]	0.0[2,3]	100.0[2,3]	—

Notes: Main entries are calculated from the raw vote values in table series 5-70 to 5-122 for the appropriate years based on candidates who used the sole designation "Democrat" or "Republican" (or their historical antecedents listed in Appendix A) on the ballot. In general, historical antecedents to the Democratic Party were Anti-Federalists, Democratic-Republicans, and Jacksonian Democrats; historical precursors of the Republican Party were Federalists, National Republicans, and Whigs. Other = candidates who used third-party names on the ballot or were listed as independent, unidentified, or scatter vote. —indicates that the state had no data, either because no vote data were found for the state in question or the state had not yet entered the Union. No special House elections are included in the table. The table only lists at-large vote values for states having both at-large and district House races; see Appendix B for these states' district results aggregated to the state level.

[1] Election held in odd-numbered year.
[2] Partial data (less than 100% of the districts reporting).
[3] 1791 election when a state had annual elections in both 1790 and 1791.

Sources: Adapted from *United States Congressional Elections, 1788–1997* (1998), independent search for state sources by the author, and personal communications with Michael J. Dubin (various dates).

Table 5-18 House Election Results, by State, 1792–1795 (Percentages)

	1792–1793				1794–1795			
State	Democratic	Republican	Other	Democratic % of Two-Party Vote	Democratic	Republican	Other	Democratic % of Two-Party Vote
Alabama	—	—	—	—	—	—	—	—
Alaska	—	—	—	—	—	—	—	—
Arizona	—	—	—	—	—	—	—	—
Arkansas	—	—	—	—	—	—	—	—
California	—	—	—	—	—	—	—	—
Colorado	—	—	—	—	—	—	—	—
Connecticut	0.0	0.0	100.0	—	0.0	100.0	0.0	0.0
Delaware	0.0	0.0	100.0	—	51.3	48.7	0.0	51.3
Florida	—	—	—	—	—	—	—	—
Georgia	0.0	0.0	100.0	—	39.3	30.4	30.2	56.4
Hawaii	—	—	—	—	—	—	—	—
Idaho	—	—	—	—	—	—	—	—
Illinois	—	—	—	—	—	—	—	—
Indiana	—	—	—	—	—	—	—	—
Iowa	—	—	—	—	—	—	—	—
Kansas	—	—	—	—	—	—	—	—
Kentucky	—	—	—	—	—	—	—	—
Louisiana	—	—	—	—	—	—	—	—
Maine	—	—	—	—	—	—	—	—
Maryland	40.0	59.8	0.1	40.1	40.7	59.3	0.0	40.7
Massachusetts	—	—	—	—	41.4	58.6	0.0	41.4
Michigan	—	—	—	—	—	—	—	—
Minnesota	—	—	—	—	—	—	—	—
Mississippi	—	—	—	—	—	—	—	—
Missouri	—	—	—	—	—	—	—	—
Montana	—	—	—	—	—	—	—	—
Nebraska	—	—	—	—	—	—	—	—
Nevada	—	—	—	—	—	—	—	—
New Hampshire	0.0	0.0	100.0	—	45.6	54.4	0.0	45.6
New Jersey	0.0	0.0	100.0	—	0.0	64.4	35.6	0.0
New Mexico	—	—	—	—	—	—	—	—
New York	45.6[1]	53.6[1]	0.8[1]	46.0[1]	48.2	51.3	0.5	48.4
North Carolina	61.0[1,2]	39.0[1,2]	0.0[1,2]	61.0[1,2]	61.0[1,2]	29.6[1,2]	9.4[1,2]	67.3[1,2]
North Dakota	—	—	—	—	—	—	—	—
Ohio	—	—	—	—	—	—	—	—
Oklahoma	—	—	—	—	—	—	—	—
Oregon	—	—	—	—	—	—	—	—
Pennsylvania	49.1	50.9	0.0	49.1	68.7[2]	31.3[2]	0.0[2]	68.7[2]
Rhode Island	—	—	—	—	38.1	61.9	0.0	38.1
South Carolina	—	—	—	—	0.0[2]	69.4[2]	30.6[2]	0.0[2]
South Dakota	—	—	—	—	—	—	—	—
Tennessee	—	—	—	—	—	—	—	—
Texas	—	—	—	—	—	—	—	—
Utah	—	—	—	—	—	—	—	—
Vermont	0.0[1]	0.0[1]	100.0[1]	—	61.4	24.5	14.1	71.5
Virginia	0.0[1,2]	0.0[1,2]	100.0[1,2]	—	—	—	—	—
Washington	—	—	—	—	—	—	—	—
West Virginia	—	—	—	—	—	—	—	—
Wisconsin	—	—	—	—	—	—	—	—
Wyoming	—	—	—	—	—	—	—	—

Notes: Main entries are calculated from the raw vote values in table series 5-70 to 5-122 for the appropriate years based on candidates who used the sole designation "Democrat" or "Republican" (or their historical antecedents listed in Appendix A) on the ballot. In general, historical antecedents to the Democratic Party were Anti-Federalists, Democratic-Republicans, and Jacksonian Democrats; historical precursors of the Republican Party were Federalists, National Republicans, and Whigs. Other = candidates who used third-party names on the ballot or were listed as independent, unidentified, or scatter vote. —indicates that the state had no data, either because no vote data were found for the state in question or the state had not yet entered the Union. No special House elections are included in the table. The table only lists at-large vote values for states having both at-large and district House races; see Appendix B for these states' district results aggregated to the state level.

[1]Election held in odd-numbered year.
[2]Partial data (less than 100% of the districts reporting).

Sources: Adapted from *United States Congressional Elections, 1788–1997* (1998), independent search for state sources by the author, and personal communications with Michael J. Dubin (various dates).

Table 5-19 House Election Results, by State, 1796–1799 (Percentages)

State	1796–1797				1798–1799			
	Democratic	Republican	Other	Democratic % of Two-Party Vote	Democratic	Republican	Other	Democratic % of Two-Party Vote
Alabama	—	—	—	—	—	—	—	—
Alaska	—	—	—	—	—	—	—	—
Arizona	—	—	—	—	—	—	—	—
Arkansas	—	—	—	—	—	—	—	—
California	—	—	—	—	—	—	—	—
Colorado	—	—	—	—	—	—	—	—
Connecticut	13.9	86.1	0.0	13.9	0.0	100.0	0.0	0.0
Delaware	43.7	56.3	0.0	43.7	38.8	61.2	0.0	38.8
Florida	—	—	—	—	—	—	—	—
Georgia	52.7	30.3	17.0	63.5	43.4	56.6	0.0	43.4
Hawaii	—	—	—	—	—	—	—	—
Idaho	—	—	—	—	—	—	—	—
Illinois	—	—	—	—	—	—	—	—
Indiana	—	—	—	—	—	—	—	—
Iowa	—	—	—	—	—	—	—	—
Kansas	—	—	—	—	—	—	—	—
Kentucky	—	—	—	—	55.3[1,2]	0.0[1,2]	44.7[1,2]	100.0[1,2]
Louisiana	—	—	—	—	—	—	—	—
Maine	—	—	—	—	—	—	—	—
Maryland	37.7	62.3	0.0	37.7	47.8[2]	52.2[2]	0.0[2]	47.8[2]
Massachusetts	27.7	64.8	7.4	30.0	25.5	66.2	8.3	27.8
Michigan	—	—	—	—	—	—	—	—
Minnesota	—	—	—	—	—	—	—	—
Mississippi	—	—	—	—	—	—	—	—
Missouri	—	—	—	—	—	—	—	—
Montana	—	—	—	—	—	—	—	—
Nebraska	—	—	—	—	—	—	—	—
Nevada	—	—	—	—	—	—	—	—
New Hampshire	13.4	79.9	6.7	14.4	2.3	80.7	17.0	2.8
New Jersey	34.5[1]	63.5[1]	2.0[1]	35.2[1]	52.4	47.6	0.0	52.4
New Mexico	—	—	—	—	—	—	—	—
New York	37.7	61.4	0.8	38.1	45.6	54.4	0.0	45.6
North Carolina	53.0[2]	47.0[2]	0.0[2]	53.0[2]	45.1[2]	54.9[2]	0.0[2]	45.1[2]
North Dakota	—	—	—	—	—	—	—	—
Ohio	—	—	—	—	—	—	—	—
Oklahoma	—	—	—	—	—	—	—	—
Oregon	—	—	—	—	—	—	—	—
Pennsylvania	51.7[2]	48.0[2]	0.3[2]	51.8[2]	46.3	53.7	0.0	46.3
Rhode Island	0.0	100.0	0.0	0.0	34.6	65.4	0.0	34.6
South Carolina	44.2	55.8	0.0	44.2	43.4[2]	56.6[2]	0.0[2]	43.4[2]
South Dakota	—	—	—	—	—	—	—	—
Tennessee	98.9	0.0	1.1	100.0	—	—	—	—
Texas	—	—	—	—	—	—	—	—
Utah	—	—	—	—	—	—	—	—
Vermont	41.8	53.9	4.3	43.7	34.5	59.4	6.1	36.7
Virginia	64.7[1,2]	29.2[1,2]	6.1[1,2]	68.9[1,2]	50.3[1,2]	49.7[1,2]	0.0[1,2]	50.3[1,2]
Washington	—	—	—	—	—	—	—	—
West Virginia	—	—	—	—	—	—	—	—
Wisconsin	—	—	—	—	—	—	—	—
Wyoming	—	—	—	—	—	—	—	—

Notes: Main entries are calculated from the raw vote values in table series 5-70 to 5-122 for the appropriate years based on candidates who used the sole designation "Democrat" or "Republican" (or their historical antecedents listed in Appendix A) on the ballot. In general, historical antecedents to the Democratic Party were Anti-Federalists, Democratic-Republicans, and Jacksonian Democrats; historical precursors of the Republican Party were Federalists, National Republicans, and Whigs. Other = candidates who used third-party names on the ballot or were listed as independent, unidentified, or scatter vote. —indicates that the state had no data, either because no vote data were found for the state in question or the state had not yet entered the Union. No special House elections are included in the table. The table only lists at-large vote values for states having both at-large and district House races; see Appendix B for these states' district results aggregated to the state level.

[1] Election held in odd-numbered year.
[2] Partial data (less than 100% of the districts reporting).

Sources: Adapted from *United States Congressional Elections, 1788–1997* (1998), independent search for state sources by the author, and personal communications with Michael J. Dubin (various dates).

Table 5-20 House Election Results, by State, 1800–1803 (Percentages)

State	1800–1801				1802–1803			
	Democratic	Republican	Other	Democratic % of Two-Party Vote	Democratic	Republican	Other	Democratic % of Two-Party Vote
Alabama	—	—	—	—	—	—	—	—
Alaska	—	—	—	—	—	—	—	—
Arizona	—	—	—	—	—	—	—	—
Arkansas	—	—	—	—	—	—	—	—
California	—	—	—	—	—	—	—	—
Colorado	—	—	—	—	—	—	—	—
Connecticut	32.4	67.6	0.0	32.4	0.0	100.0	0.0	0.0
Delaware	46.7	53.3	0.0	46.7	50.1	49.9	0.0	50.1
Florida	—	—	—	—	—	—	—	—
Georgia	100.0	0.0	0.0	100.0	76.2	23.8	0.0	76.2
Hawaii	—	—	—	—	—	—	—	—
Idaho	—	—	—	—	—	—	—	—
Illinois	—	—	—	—	—	—	—	—
Indiana	—	—	—	—	—	—	—	—
Iowa	—	—	—	—	—	—	—	—
Kansas	—	—	—	—	—	—	—	—
Kentucky	82.8[1]	0.0[1]	17.2[1]	100.0[1]	98.4[1,2]	1.6[1,2]	0.0[1,2]	98.4[1,2]
Louisiana	—	—	—	—	—	—	—	—
Maine	—	—	—	—	—	—	—	—
Maryland	62.2[1]	37.8[1]	0.0[1]	62.2[1]	61.9[1,2]	38.1[1,2]	0.0[1,2]	61.9[1,2]
Massachusetts	44.9	52.5	2.6	46.1	45.4	54.2	0.4	45.6
Michigan	—	—	—	—	—	—	—	—
Minnesota	—	—	—	—	—	—	—	—
Mississippi	—	—	—	—	—	—	—	—
Missouri	—	—	—	—	—	—	—	—
Montana	—	—	—	—	—	—	—	—
Nebraska	—	—	—	—	—	—	—	—
Nevada	—	—	—	—	—	—	—	—
New Hampshire	19.5	59.9	20.6	24.5	35.5	53.0	11.5	40.1
New Jersey	50.9	49.1	0.0	50.9	97.3[1]	2.7[1]	0.0[1]	97.3[1]
New Mexico	—	—	—	—	—	—	—	—
New York	49.4	50.2	0.4	49.6	57.4	39.5	3.1	59.3
North Carolina	47.7[2]	52.3[2]	0.0[2]	47.7[2]	69.0[1,2]	31.0[1,2]	0.0[1,2]	69.0[1,2]
North Dakota	—	—	—	—	—	—	—	—
Ohio	—	—	—	—	73.8[1]	26.2[1]	0.0[1]	73.8[1]
Oklahoma	—	—	—	—	—	—	—	—
Oregon	—	—	—	—	—	—	—	—
Pennsylvania	66.7[2]	33.3[2]	0.0[2]	66.7[2]	72.5[2]	27.5[2]	0.0[2]	72.5[2]
Rhode Island	66.8	33.2	0.0	66.8	61.3	38.7	0.0	61.3
South Carolina	55.3[2]	44.7[2]	0.0[2]	55.3[2]	64.5[1]	35.5[1]	0.0[1]	64.5[1]
South Dakota	—	—	—	—	—	—	—	—
Tennessee	100.0[1]	0.0[1]	0.0[1]	100.0[1]	100.0[1]	0.0[1]	0.0[1]	100.0[1]
Texas	—	—	—	—	—	—	—	—
Utah	—	—	—	—	—	—	—	—
Vermont	51.3	46.2	2.4	52.6	41.6	56.6	1.8	42.4
Virginia	61.4[1,2]	38.6[1,2]	0.0[1,2]	61.4[1,2]	69.6[1,2]	30.4[1,2]	0.0[1,2]	69.6[1,2]
Washington	—	—	—	—	—	—	—	—
West Virginia	—	—	—	—	—	—	—	—
Wisconsin	—	—	—	—	—	—	—	—
Wyoming	—	—	—	—	—	—	—	—

Notes: Main entries are calculated from the raw vote values in table series 5-70 to 5-122 for the appropriate years based on candidates who used the sole designation "Democrat" or "Republican" (or their historical antecedents listed in Appendix A) on the ballot. In general, historical antecedents to the Democratic Party were Anti-Federalists, Democratic-Republicans, and Jacksonian Democrats; historical precursors of the Republican Party were Federalists, National Republicans, and Whigs. Other = candidates who used third-party names on the ballot or were listed as independent, unidentified, or scatter vote. —indicates that the state had no data, either because no vote data were found for the state in question or the state had not yet entered the Union. No special House elections are included in the table. The table only lists at-large vote values for states having both at-large and district House races; see Appendix B for these states' district results aggregated to the state level.

[1] Election held in odd-numbered year.
[2] Partial data (less than 100% of the districts reporting).

Sources: Adapted from *United States Congressional Elections, 1788–1997* (1998), independent search for state sources by the author, and personal communications with Michael J. Dubin (various dates).

Table 5-21 House Election Results, by State, 1804–1807 (Percentages)

	1804–1805				1806–1807			
State	Democratic	Republican	Other	Democratic % of Two-Party Vote	Democratic	Republican	Other	Democratic % of Two-Party Vote
Alabama	—	—	—	—	—	—	—	—
Alaska	—	—	—	—	—	—	—	—
Arizona	—	—	—	—	—	—	—	—
Arkansas	—	—	—	—	—	—	—	—
California	—	—	—	—	—	—	—	—
Colorado	—	—	—	—	—	—	—	—
Connecticut	0.0	100.0	0.0	0.0	—	—	—	—
Delaware	47.9	52.1	0.0	47.9	31.2	60.5	8.3	34.0
Florida	—	—	—	—	—	—	—	—
Georgia	100.0	0.0	0.0	100.0	100.0	0.0	0.0	100.0
Hawaii	—	—	—	—	—	—	—	—
Idaho	—	—	—	—	—	—	—	—
Illinois	—	—	—	—	—	—	—	—
Indiana	—	—	—	—	—	—	—	—
Iowa	—	—	—	—	—	—	—	—
Kansas	—	—	—	—	—	—	—	—
Kentucky	—	—	—	—	85.5[2]	0.0[2]	14.5[2]	100.0[2]
Louisiana	—	—	—	—	—	—	—	—
Maine	—	—	—	—	—	—	—	—
Maryland	73.6	26.0	0.3	73.9	72.1	26.7	1.1	73.0
Massachusetts	52.7	46.5	0.9	53.1	52.2	47.6	0.2	52.3
Michigan	—	—	—	—	—	—	—	—
Minnesota	—	—	—	—	—	—	—	—
Mississippi	—	—	—	—	—	—	—	—
Missouri	—	—	—	—	—	—	—	—
Montana	—	—	—	—	—	—	—	—
Nebraska	—	—	—	—	—	—	—	—
Nevada	—	—	—	—	—	—	—	—
New Hampshire	48.2	51.8	0.0	48.2	56.7	36.2	7.1	61.0
New Jersey	99.0	1.0	0.0	99.0	71.7	28.3	0.0	71.7
New Mexico	—	—	—	—	—	—	—	—
New York	63.0	36.4	0.6	63.4	56.8	34.2	9.0	62.5
New York	—	—	—	—	***56.8***	***38.3***	***4.9***	***59.8***
North Carolina	71.0[2]	29.0[2]	0.0[2]	71.0[2]	85.8[2]	13.5[2]	0.6[2]	86.4[2]
North Dakota	—	—	—	—	—	—	—	—
Ohio	70.5	29.5	0.0	70.5	74.0	0.0	26.0	100.0
Ohio	—	—	—	—	***74.0***	***26.0***	***0.0***	***74.0***
Oklahoma	—	—	—	—	—	—	—	—
Oregon	—	—	—	—	—	—	—	—
Pennsylvania	76.0[2]	16.6[2]	7.5[2]	82.1[2]	54.4[2]	8.4[2]	37.2[2]	86.6[2]
Pennsylvania	—	—	—	—	***54.4[2]***	***18.9[2]***	***26.7[2]***	***74.3[2]***
Rhode Island	100.0	0.0	0.0	100.0	50.0	41.3	8.6	54.7
South Carolina	84.6[2]	15.4[2]	0.0[2]	84.6[2]	81.8	18.2	0.0	81.8
South Dakota	—	—	—	—	—	—	—	—
Tennessee	100.0[1]	0.0[1]	0.0[1]	100.0[1]	100.0[1,2]	0.0[1,2]	0.0[1,2]	100.0[1,2]
Texas	—	—	—	—	—	—	—	—
Utah	—	—	—	—	—	—	—	—
Vermont	52.0	45.4	2.6	53.4	43.1[2]	47.0[2]	9.9[2]	47.8[2]
Virginia	81.7[1,2]	18.3[1,2]	0.0[1,2]	81.7[1,2]	84.0[1,2]	16.0[1,2]	0.0[1,2]	84.0[1,2]
Washington	—	—	—	—	—	—	—	—
West Virginia	—	—	—	—	—	—	—	—
Wisconsin	—	—	—	—	—	—	—	—
Wyoming	—	—	—	—	—	—	—	—

Notes: Main entries are calculated from the raw vote values in table series 5-70 to 5-122 for the appropriate years based on candidates who used the sole designation "Democrat" or "Republican" (or their historical antecedents listed in Appendix A) on the ballot. In general, historical antecedents to the Democratic Party were Anti-Federalists, Democratic-Republicans, and Jacksonian Democrats; historical precursors of the Republican party were Federalists, National Republicans, and Whigs. Other = candidates who used third-party names on the ballot or were listed as independent, unidentified, or scatter vote. Bold italicized entries in the table are the author's alternative party coding, which is used when a candidate listed a major party name (Democrat, Republican, or their historical antecedents) on the ballot with other party names or labels. These values are computed from the bold italicized raw vote values in table series 5-70 to 5-122 for the appropriate states and years. For a more detailed explanation of this alternate coding system, see Tables 5-1 and 1-3. —indicates that the state had no data, either because no vote data were found for the state in question or the state had not yet entered the Union. No special House elections are included in the table. The table only lists at-large vote values for states having both at-large and district House races; see Appendix B for these states' district results aggregated to the state level.

[1] Election held in odd-numbered year.
[2] Partial data (less than 100% of the districts reporting).

Sources: Adapted from *United States Congressional Elections, 1788–1997* (1998), independent search for state sources by the author, and personal communications with Michael J. Dubin (various dates).

Table 5-22 House Election Results, by State, 1808–1811 (Percentages)

State	1808–1809				1810–1811			
	Democratic	Republican	Other	Democratic % of Two-Party Vote	Democratic	Republican	Other	Democratic % of Two-Party Vote
Alabama	—	—	—	—	—	—	—	—
Alaska	—	—	—	—	—	—	—	—
Arizona	—	—	—	—	—	—	—	—
Arkansas	—	—	—	—	—	—	—	—
California	—	—	—	—	—	—	—	—
Colorado	—	—	—	—	—	—	—	—
Connecticut	—	—	—	—	0.0	100.0	0.0	0.0
Delaware	46.7	53.3	0.0	46.7	49.9	50.1	0.0	49.9
Florida	—	—	—	—	—	—	—	—
Georgia	53.6	20.3	26.1	72.6	87.2	12.8	0.0	87.2
Hawaii	—	—	—	—	—	—	—	—
Idaho	—	—	—	—	—	—	—	—
Illinois	—	—	—	—	—	—	—	—
Indiana	—	—	—	—	—	—	—	—
Iowa	—	—	—	—	—	—	—	—
Kansas	—	—	—	—	—	—	—	—
Kentucky	—	—	—	—	100.0 [2]	0.0 [2]	0.0 [2]	100.0 [2]
Louisiana	—	—	—	—	—	—	—	—
Maine	—	—	—	—	—	—	—	—
Maryland	55.5	44.5	0.0	55.5	74.4	25.4	0.2	74.6
Massachusetts	47.4	52.5	0.1	47.5	47.9	51.0	1.1	48.5
Michigan	—	—	—	—	—	—	—	—
Minnesota	—	—	—	—	—	—	—	—
Mississippi	—	—	—	—	—	—	—	—
Missouri	—	—	—	—	—	—	—	—
Montana	—	—	—	—	—	—	—	—
Nebraska	—	—	—	—	—	—	—	—
Nevada	—	—	—	—	—	—	—	—
New Hampshire	45.0	55.0	0.0	45.0	48.0	47.7	4.3	50.2
New Jersey	56.0	44.0	0.0	56.0	96.3	3.7	0.0	96.3
New Mexico	—	—	—	—	—	—	—	—
New York	50.0	48.5	1.5	50.7	55.2	44.6	0.2	55.3
North Carolina	56.6 [2]	43.4 [2]	0.0 [2]	56.6 [2]	65.3 [2]	34.7 [2]	0.0 [2]	65.3 [2]
North Dakota	—	—	—	—	—	—	—	—
Ohio	69.7	30.3	0.0	69.7	—	—	—	—
Oklahoma	—	—	—	—	—	—	—	—
Oregon	—	—	—	—	—	—	—	—
Pennsylvania	59.9	18.8	21.4	76.1	55.6	25.6	18.7	68.4
Pennsylvania	*59.9*	*40.1*	*0.0*	*59.9*	*70.1*	*25.6*	*4.2*	*73.2*
Rhode Island	47.0	53.0	0.0	47.0	48.8	51.2	0.0	48.8
South Carolina	—	—	—	—	58.0 [2]	42.0 [2]	0.0 [2]	58.0 [2]
South Dakota	—	—	—	—	—	—	—	—
Tennessee	96.0 [1,2]	0.0 [1,2]	4.0 [1,2]	100.0 [1,2]	74.0 [1]	0.0 [1]	26.0 [1]	100.0 [1]
Texas	—	—	—	—	—	—	—	—
Utah	—	—	—	—	—	—	—	—
Vermont	45.6 [2]	51.5 [2]	2.9 [2]	46.9 [2]	55.5	42.5	2.0	56.6
Virginia	49.9 [1,2]	43.8 [1,2]	6.4 [1,2]	53.3 [1,2]	39.0 [1,2]	40.4 [1,2]	20.6 [1,2]	49.1 [1,2]
Virginia	*56.2 [1,2]*	*43.8 [1,2]*	*0.0 [1,2]*	*56.2 [1,2]*	*59.6 [1,2]*	*40.4 [1,2]*	*0.0 [1,2]*	*59.6 [1,2]*
Washington	—	—	—	—	—	—	—	—
West Virginia	—	—	—	—	—	—	—	—
Wisconsin	—	—	—	—	—	—	—	—
Wyoming	—	—	—	—	—	—	—	—

Notes: Main entries are calculated from the raw vote values in table series 5-70 to 5-122 for the appropriate years based on candidates who used the sole designation "Democrat" or "Republican" (or their historical antecedents listed in Appendix A) on the ballot. In general, historical antecedents to the Democratic Party were Anti-Federalists, Democratic-Republicans, and Jacksonian Democrats; historical precursors of the Republican party were Federalists, National Republicans, and Whigs. Other = candidates who used third-party names on the ballot or were listed as independent, unidentified, or scatter vote. Bold italicized entries in the table are the author's alternative party coding, which is used when a candidate listed a major party name (Democrat, Republican, or their historical antecedents) on the ballot with other party names or labels. These values are computed from the bold italicized raw vote values in table series 5-70 to 5-122 for the appropriate states and years. For a more detailed explanation of this alternate coding system, see Tables 5-1 and 1-3. —indicates that the state had no data, either because no vote data were found for the state in question or the state had not yet entered the Union. No special House elections are included in the table. The table only lists at-large vote values for states having both at-large and district House races; see Appendix B for these states' district results aggregated to the state level.

[1] Election held in odd-numbered year.
[2] Partial data (less than 100% of the districts reporting).

Sources: Adapted from *United States Congressional Elections, 1788–1997* (1998), independent search for state sources by the author, and personal communications with Michael J. Dubin (various dates).

Table 5-23 House Election Results, by State, 1812–1815 (Percentages)

State	1812–1813				1814–1815			
	Democratic	Republican	Other	Democratic % of Two-Party Vote	Democratic	Republican	Other	Democratic % of Two-Party Vote
Alabama	—	—	—	—	—	—	—	—
Alaska	—	—	—	—	—	—	—	—
Arizona	—	—	—	—	—	—	—	—
Arkansas	—	—	—	—	—	—	—	—
California	—	—	—	—	—	—	—	—
Colorado	—	—	—	—	—	—	—	—
Connecticut	0.0	100.0	0.0	0.0	—	—	—	—
Delaware	43.4	56.6	0.0	43.4	39.1	60.9	0.0	39.1
Florida	—	—	—	—	—	—	—	—
Georgia	81.5	18.5	0.0	81.5	100.0	0.0	0.0	100.0
Hawaii	—	—	—	—	—	—	—	—
Idaho	—	—	—	—	—	—	—	—
Illinois	—	—	—	—	—	—	—	—
Indiana	—	—	—	—	—	—	—	—
Iowa	—	—	—	—	—	—	—	—
Kansas	—	—	—	—	—	—	—	—
Kentucky	89.9[2]	0[2]	10.1[2]	100.0[2]	81.3[2]	0[2]	18.7[2]	100.0[2]
Louisiana	35.6	0.0	64.4	100.0	90.8	8.2	1.0	91.7
Maine	—	—	—	—	—	—	—	—
Maryland	61.7	38.3	0.0	61.7	37.2	62.8	0.0	37.2
Massachusetts	38.8	60.5	0.7	39.1	33.6	64.7	1.7	34.2
Massachusetts	—	—	—	—	***33.6***	***66.2***	***0.2***	***33.7***
Michigan	—	—	—	—	—	—	—	—
Minnesota	—	—	—	—	—	—	—	—
Mississippi	—	—	—	—	—	—	—	—
Missouri	—	—	—	—	—	—	—	—
Montana	—	—	—	—	—	—	—	—
Nebraska	—	—	—	—	—	—	—	—
Nevada	—	—	—	—	—	—	—	—
New Hampshire	46.3	53.7	0.0	46.3	47.8	52.2	0.0	47.8
New Jersey	47.3[1]	52.5[1]	0.3[1]	47.4[1]	51.7	48.3	0.0	51.7
New Mexico	—	—	—	—	—	—	—	—
New York	44.5	53.8	1.7	45.2	53.3	46.4	0.3	53.5
New York	***45.1***	***53.8***	***1.1***	***45.6***	—	—	—	—
North Carolina	44.8[1,2]	55.2[1,2]	0.0[1,2]	44.8[1,2]	59.5[1,2]	40.5[1,2]	0.0[1,2]	59.5[1,2]
North Dakota	—	—	—	—	—	—	—	—
Ohio	64.7	21.3	14.0	75.3	66.0[2]	21.7[2]	12.4[2]	75.3[2]
Oklahoma	—	—	—	—	—	—	—	—
Oregon	—	—	—	—	—	—	—	—
Pennsylvania	59.0	40.6	0.4	59.2	57.1[2]	42.9[2]	0.0[2]	57.1[2]
Pennsylvania	***59.4***	***40.6***	***0.0***	***59.4***	—	—	—	—
Rhode Island	41.5	58.5	0.0	41.5	43.9	56.1	0.0	43.9
South Carolina	64.2[2]	17.0[2]	18.8[2]	79.0[2]	73.1[2]	26.9[2]	0.0[2]	73.1[2]
South Dakota	—	—	—	—	—	—	—	—
Tennessee	83.1[1,2]	0.0[1,2]	16.9[1,2]	100.0[1,2]	74.9[1,2]	0.0[1,2]	25.1[1,2]	100.0[1,2]
Texas	—	—	—	—	—	—	—	—
Utah	—	—	—	—	—	—	—	—
Vermont	50.4	49.6	0.0	50.4	48.9[2]	51.1[2]	0.0[2]	48.9[2]
Virginia	54.5[1,2]	40.0[1,2]	5.5[1,2]	57.6[1,2]	59.4[1,2]	40.6[1,2]	0.1[1,2]	59.4[1,2]
Virginia	***60.0***[1,2]	***40.0***[1,2]	***0.0***[1,2]	***60.0***[1,2]	—	—	—	—
Washington	—	—	—	—	—	—	—	—
West Virginia	—	—	—	—	—	—	—	—
Wisconsin	—	—	—	—	—	—	—	—
Wyoming	—	—	—	—	—	—	—	—

Notes: Main entries are calculated from the raw vote values in table series 5-70 to 5-122 for the appropriate years based on candidates who used the sole designation "Democrat" or "Republican" (or their historical antecedents listed in Appendix A) on the ballot. In general, historical antecedents to the Democratic Party were Anti-Federalists, Democratic-Republicans, and Jacksonian Democrats; historical precursors of the Republican party were Federalists, National Republicans, and Whigs. Other = candidates who used third-party names on the ballot or were listed as independent, unidentified, or scatter vote. Bold italicized entries in the table are the author's alternative party coding, which is used when a candidate listed a major party name (Democrat, Republican, or their historical antecedents) on the ballot with other party names or labels. These values are computed from the bold italicized raw vote values in table series 5-70 to 5-122 for the appropriate states and years. For a more detailed explanation of this alternate coding system, see Tables 5-1 and 1-3. —indicates that the state had no data, either because no vote data were found for the state in question or the state had not yet entered the Union. No special House elections are included in the table. The table only lists at-large vote values for states having both at-large and district House races; see Appendix B for these states' district results aggregated to the state level.

[1]Election held in odd-numbered year.
[2]Partial data (less than 100% of the districts reporting).

Sources: Adapted from *United States Congressional Elections, 1788–1997* (1998), independent search for state sources by the author, and personal communications with Michael J. Dubin (various dates).

Table 5-24 House Election Results, by State, 1816–1819 (Percentages)

State	1816–1817				1818–1819			
	Democratic	Republican	Other	Democratic % of Two-Party Vote	Democratic	Republican	Other	Democratic % of Two-Party Vote
Alabama	—	—	—	—	53.2[1]	0.0[1]	46.8[1]	100.0[1]
Alaska	—	—	—	—	—	—	—	—
Arizona	—	—	—	—	—	—	—	—
Arkansas	—	—	—	—	—	—	—	—
California	—	—	—	—	—	—	—	—
Colorado	—	—	—	—	—	—	—	—
Connecticut	0.0	100.0	0.0	0.0	51.2	0.0	48.8	100.0
Connecticut	—	—	—	—	*51.2*	*48.8*	*0.0*	*51.2*
Delaware	49.7	50.3	0.0	49.7	49.3	50.7	0.0	49.3
Florida	—	—	—	—	—	—	—	—
Georgia	60.0	0.0	40.0	100.0	100.0	0.0	0.0	100.0
Hawaii	—	—	—	—	—	—	—	—
Idaho	—	—	—	—	—	—	—	—
Illinois	—	—	—	—	100.0	0.0	0.0	100.0
Indiana	76.0	0.0	24.0	100.0	—	—	—	—
Iowa	—	—	—	—	—	—	—	—
Kansas	—	—	—	—	—	—	—	—
Kentucky	31.4[2]	0.0[2]	68.6[2]	100.0[2]	51.2[2]	11.1[2]	37.7[2]	82.2[2]
Kentucky	*57.9[2]*	*9.2[2]*	*32.9[2]*	*86.3[2]*	—	—	—	—
Louisiana	100.0	0.0	0.0	100.0	78.9	0.0	21.1	100.0
Maine	—	—	—	—	—	—	—	—
Maryland	36.0[2]	63.7[2]	0.3[2]	36.1[2]	42.5[2]	57.5[2]	0.0[2]	42.5[2]
Massachusetts	42.6	54.1	3.3	44.0	48.8	48.7	2.5	50.0
Michigan	—	—	—	—	—	—	—	—
Minnesota	—	—	—	—	—	—	—	—
Mississippi	100.0[1]	0.0[1]	0.0[1]	100.0[1]	—	—	—	—
Missouri	—	—	—	—	—	—	—	—
Montana	—	—	—	—	—	—	—	—
Nebraska	—	—	—	—	—	—	—	—
Nevada	—	—	—	—	—	—	—	—
New Hampshire	53.2	46.5	0.3	53.4	58.2[1]	29.9[1]	11.9[1]	66.1[1]
New Jersey	100.0	0.0	0.0	100.0	94.8	5.2	0.0	94.8
New Mexico	—	—	—	—	—	—	—	—
New York	55.0	44.7	0.3	55.1	58.2	24.0	17.9	70.8
New York	—	—	—	—	*76.0*	*24.0*	*0.0*	*76.0*
North Carolina	60.7[1,2]	39.3[1,2]	0.0[1,2]	60.7[1,2]	66.1[1,2]	33.9[1,2]	0.0[1,2]	66.1[1,2]
North Dakota	—	—	—	—	—	—	—	—
Ohio	73.1[2]	4.5[2]	22.4[2]	94.2[2]	84.4	14.2	1.4	85.6
Oklahoma	—	—	—	—	—	—	—	—
Oregon	—	—	—	—	—	—	—	—
Pennsylvania	52.8[2]	28.9[2]	18.4[2]	64.6[2]	59.7[2]	28.2[2]	12.1[2]	67.9[2]
Pennsylvania	*64.5[2]*	*32.6[2]*	*2.9[2]*	*66.4[2]*	*63.1[2]*	*31.7[2]*	*5.2[2]*	*66.6[2]*
Rhode Island	0.0	100.0	0.0	0.0	100.0	0.0	0.0	100.0
South Carolina	81.8[2]	18.2[2]	0.0[2]	81.8[2]	89.6[2]	10.4[2]	0.0[2]	89.6[2]
South Dakota	—	—	—	—	—	—	—	—
Tennessee	59.3[1]	0.0[1]	40.7[1]	100.0[1]	54.6[1]	0.0[1]	45.4[1]	100.0[1]
Texas	—	—	—	—	—	—	—	—
Utah	—	—	—	—	—	—	—	—
Vermont	54.7	45.3	0.0	54.7	71.5	0.0	28.5	100.0
Vermont	—	—	—	—	*71.5*	*24.7*	*3.8*	*74.3*
Virginia	75.5[1,2]	24.5[1,2]	0.0[1,2]	75.5[1,2]	68.0[1,2]	32.0[1,2]	0.0[1,2]	68.0[1,2]
Washington	—	—	—	—	—	—	—	—
West Virginia	—	—	—	—	—	—	—	—
Wisconsin	—	—	—	—	—	—	—	—
Wyoming	—	—	—	—	—	—	—	—
Indiana	60.1[3]	0.0[3]	39.9[3]	100.0[3]	—	—	—	—

Notes: Main entries are calculated from the raw vote values in table series 5-70 to 5-122 for the appropriate years based on candidates who used the sole designation "Democrat" or "Republican" (or their historical antecedents listed in Appendix A) on the ballot. In general, historical antecedents to the Democratic Party were Anti-Federalists, Democratic-Republicans, and Jacksonian Democrats; historical precursors of the Republican party were Federalists, National Republicans, and Whigs. Other = candidates who used third-party names on the ballot or were listed as independent, unidentified, or scatter vote. Bold italicized entries in the table are the author's alternative party coding, which is used when a candidate listed a major party name (Democrat, Republican, or their historical antecedents) on the ballot with other party names or labels. These values are computed from the bold italicized raw vote values in table series 5-70 to 5-122 for the appropriate states and years. For a more detailed explanation of this alternate coding system, see Tables 5-1 and 1-3. —indicates that the state had no data, either because no vote data were found for the state in question or the state had not yet entered the Union. No special House elections are included in the table. The table only lists at-large vote values for states having both at-large and district House races; see Appendix B for these states' district results aggregated to the state level.

[1]Election held in odd-numbered year.
[2]Partial data (less than 100% of the districts reporting).
[3]1817 election when a state had annual elections in both 1816 and 1817.

Sources: Adapted from *United States Congressional Elections, 1788–1997* (1998), independent search for state sources by the author, and personal communications with Michael J. Dubin (various dates).

Table 5-25 House Election Results, by State, 1820–1823 (Percentages)

	1820–1821				1822–1823			
State	Democratic	Republican	Other	Democratic % of Two-Party Vote	Democratic	Republican	Other	Democratic % of Two-Party Vote
Alabama	64.6[1]	0.0[1]	35.4[1]	100.0[1]	24.7[1,2]	0.0[1,2]	75.3[1,2]	100.0[1,2]
Alaska	—	—	—	—	—	—	—	—
Arizona	—	—	—	—	—	—	—	—
Arkansas	—	—	—	—	—	—	—	—
California	—	—	—	—	—	—	—	—
Colorado	—	—	—	—	—	—	—	—
Connecticut	89.7[1]	6.3[1]	4.0[1]	93.4[1]	100.0[1]	0.0[1]	0.0[1]	100.0[1]
Delaware	50.7	49.3	0.0	50.7	45.7	54.3	0.0	45.7
Florida	—	—	—	—	—	—	—	—
Georgia	67.3	0.0	32.7	100.0	58.6	0.0	41.4	100.0
Hawaii	—	—	—	—	—	—	—	—
Idaho	—	—	—	—	—	—	—	—
Illinois	69.3	0.0	30.7	100.0	55.6	0.0	44.4	100.0
Indiana	91.0	0.0	9.0	100.0	0.0[2]	0.0[2]	100.0[2]	—
Iowa	—	—	—	—	—	—	—	—
Kansas	—	—	—	—	—	—	—	—
Kentucky	59.4[2]	37.8[2]	2.8[2]	61.1[2]	0.0[2]	0.0[2]	100.0[2]	—
Louisiana	100.0	0.0	0.0	100.0	0.0[2]	0.0[2]	100.0[2]	—
Maine	61.2	22.6	16.3	73.1	56.4[1]	22.5[1]	21.1[1]	71.5[1]
Maryland	50.6[2]	49.4[2]	0.0[2]	50.6[2]	72.8	24.3	2.9	74.9
Massachusetts	35.9	53.0	11.1	40.4	—	—	—	—
Michigan	—	—	—	—	—	—	—	—
Minnesota	—	—	—	—	—	—	—	—
Mississippi	—	—	—	—	0.0	0.0	100.0	—
Missouri	100.0[2]	0.0[2]	0.0[2]	100.0[2]	0.0	0.0	100.0	—
Montana	—	—	—	—	—	—	—	—
Nebraska	—	—	—	—	—	—	—	—
Nevada	—	—	—	—	—	—	—	—
New Hampshire	86.0	14.0	0.0	86.0	74.4	0.0	25.6	100.0
New Jersey	85.7	7.6	6.7	91.9	—	—	—	—
New Mexico	—	—	—	—	—	—	—	—
New York	0.0[1]	0.0[1]	100.0[1]	—	0.0	0.0	100.0	—
New York	**99.7[1]**	**0.0[1]**	**0.3[1]**	**100.0[1]**	**99.5**	**0.0**	**0.5**	**100.0**
North Carolina	54.1[1,2]	44.3[1,2]	1.7[1,2]	55.0[1,2]	65.3[1,2]	34.7[1,2]	0.0[1,2]	65.3[1,2]
North Dakota	—	—	—	—	—	—	—	—
Ohio	100.0[2]	0.0[2]	0.0[2]	100.0[2]	17.4[2]	7.6[2]	75.0[2]	69.5[2]
Oklahoma	—	—	—	—	—	—	—	—
Oregon	—	—	—	—	—	—	—	—
Pennsylvania	54.8	35.7	9.5	60.5	60.2	23.8	15.9	71.6
Pennsylvania	**54.8**	**44.6**	**0.5**	**55.1**	**76.1**	**23.8**	**0.1**	**76.1**
Rhode Island	44.8	0.0	55.2	100.0	100.0	0.0	0.0	100.0
South Carolina	85.7[2]	14.3[2]	0.0[2]	85.7[2]	74.1[1]	6.5[1]	19.5[1]	92.0[1]
South Dakota	—	—	—	—	—	—	—	—
Tennessee	70.3[1,2]	0.0[1,2]	29.7[1,2]	100.0[1,2]	0.0[1,2]	0.0[1,2]	100.0[1,2]	—
Texas	—	—	—	—	—	—	—	—
Utah	—	—	—	—	—	—	—	—
Vermont	61.2	36.1	2.6	62.9	62.1	24.4	13.5	71.8
Virginia	74.8[1,2]	22.6[1,2]	2.6[1,2]	76.8[1,2]	71.8[1,2]	27.1[1,2]	1.1[1,2]	72.6[1,2]
Washington	—	—	—	—	—	—	—	—
West Virginia	—	—	—	—	—	—	—	—
Wisconsin	—	—	—	—	—	—	—	—
Wyoming	—	—	—	—	—	—	—	—

Notes: Main entries are calculated from the raw vote values in table series 5-70 to 5-122 for the appropriate years based on candidates who used the sole designation "Democrat" or "Republican" (or their historical antecedents listed in Appendix A) on the ballot. In general, historical antecedents to the Democratic Party were Anti-Federalists, Democratic-Republicans, and Jacksonian Democrats; historical precursors of the Republican party were Federalists, National Republicans, and Whigs. Other = candidates who used third-party names on the ballot or were listed as independent, unidentified, or scatter vote. Bold italicized entries in the table are the author's alternative party coding, which is used when a candidate listed a major party name (Democrat, Republican, or their historical antecedents) on the ballot with other party names or labels. These values are computed from the bold italicized raw vote values in table series 5-70 to 5-122 for the appropriate states and years. For a more detailed explanation of this alternate coding system, see Tables 5-1 and 1-3. —indicates that the state had no data, either because no vote data were found for the state in question or the state had not yet entered the Union. No special House elections are included in the table. The table only lists at-large vote values for states having both at-large and district House races; see Appendix B for these states' district results aggregated to the state level.

[1]Election held in odd-numbered year.
[2]Partial data (less than 100% of the districts reporting).

Sources: Adapted from *United States Congressional Elections, 1788–1997* (1998), independent search for state sources by the author, and personal communications with Michael J. Dubin (various dates).

Table 5-26 House Election Results, by State, 1824–1827 (Percentages)

| | 1824–1825 | | | | 1826–1827 | | | |
State	Democratic	Republican	Other	Democratic % of Two-Party Vote	Democratic	Republican	Other	Democratic % of Two-Party Vote
Alabama	40.9[1,2]	0.0[1,2]	59.1[1,2]	100.0[1,2]	67.5[1,2]	0.0[1,2]	32.5[1,2]	100.0[1,2]
Alaska	—	—	—	—	—	—	—	—
Arizona	—	—	—	—	—	—	—	—
Arkansas	—	—	—	—	—	—	—	—
California	—	—	—	—	—	—	—	—
Colorado	—	—	—	—	—	—	—	—
Connecticut	78.6[1]	16.2[1]	5.2[1]	82.9[1]	0.0[1]	8.8[1]	91.2[1]	0.0[1]
Connecticut	—	—	—	—	**0.0[1]**	**91.8[1]**	**8.2[1]**	**0.0[1]**
Delaware	48.3	51.7	0.0	48.3	45.9	54.1	0.0	45.9
Florida	—	—	—	—	—	—	—	—
Georgia	100.0	0.0	0.0	100.0	61.5	0.0	38.5	100.0
Hawaii	—	—	—	—	—	—	—	—
Idaho	—	—	—	—	—	—	—	—
Illinois	0.0	0.0	100.0	—	49.5	44.0	6.5	52.9
Indiana	47.3[2]	0.0[2]	52.7[2]	100.0[2]	36.1	58.2	5.7	38.3
Iowa	—	—	—	—	—	—	—	—
Kansas	—	—	—	—	—	—	—	—
Kentucky	66.6[2]	0.0[2]	33.4[2]	100.0[2]	38.6[1]	22.6[1]	38.8[1]	63.1[1]
Louisiana	—	—	—	—	36.0[2]	25.6[2]	38.4[2]	58.4[2]
Maine	62.0	17.2	20.8	78.3	28.6	40.7	30.7	41.2
Maryland	57.4	35.3	7.3	61.9	22.5	22.1	55.5	50.4
Massachusetts	41.1	42.7	16.3	49.0	0.0	59.9	40.1	0.0
Michigan	—	—	—	—	—	—	—	—
Minnesota	—	—	—	—	—	—	—	—
Mississippi	100.0	0.0	0.0	100.0	33.9	15.2	50.9	69.0
Missouri	89.5	0.0	10.5	100.0	0.0	0.0	100.0	—
Montana	—	—	—	—	—	—	—	—
Nebraska	—	—	—	—	—	—	—	—
Nevada	—	—	—	—	—	—	—	—
New Hampshire	67.9	0.0	32.1	100.0	76.7[1]	0.0[1]	23.3[1]	100.0[1]
New Jersey	100.0	0.0	0.0	100.0	38.4	59.1	2.4	39.4
New Mexico	—	—	—	—	—	—	—	—
New York	0.0	0.0	100.0	—	51.6	47.6	0.8	52.0
New York	**98.8**	**0.0**	**1.2**	**100.0**	—	—	—	—
North Carolina	44.7[1,2]	10.4[1,2]	44.9[1,2]	81.1[1,2]	0.0[1,2]	12.5[1,2]	87.5[1,2]	0.0[1,2]
North Dakota	—	—	—	—	—	—	—	—
Ohio	0.0	0.0	100.0	—	20.8	55.2	24.0	27.3
Oklahoma	—	—	—	—	—	—	—	—
Oregon	—	—	—	—	—	—	—	—
Pennsylvania	68.1[2]	18.2[2]	13.8[2]	78.9[2]	58.4[2]	30.2[2]	11.4[2]	66.0[2]
Pennsylvania	**68.1[2]**	**29.7[2]**	**2.3[2]**	**69.6[2]**	**58.4[2]**	**33.7[2]**	**7.8[2]**	**63.4[2]**
Rhode Island	95.6[1]	0.0[1]	4.4[1]	100.0[1]	0.0[1]	98.7[1]	1.3[1]	0.0[1]
South Carolina	28.6[2]	0.0[2]	71.4[2]	100.0[2]	50.3[2]	0.0[2]	49.7[2]	100.0[2]
South Dakota	—	—	—	—	—	—	—	—
Tennessee	0.0[1,2]	0.0[1,2]	100.0[1,2]	—	36.6[1,2]	0.0[1,2]	63.4[1,2]	100.0[1,2]
Tennessee	—	—	—	—	**36.6[1,2]**	**6.7[1,2]**	**56.7[1,2]**	**84.6[1,2]**
Texas	—	—	—	—	—	—	—	—
Utah	—	—	—	—	—	—	—	—
Vermont	69.1	6.6	24.3	91.3	0.0	64.4	35.6	0.0
Virginia	0.0[1,2]	21.6[1,2]	78.4[1,2]	0.0[1,2]	7.0[1,2]	28.2[1,2]	64.8[1,2]	19.9[1,2]
Washington	—	—	—	—	—	—	—	—
West Virginia	—	—	—	—	—	—	—	—
Wisconsin	—	—	—	—	—	—	—	—
Wyoming	—	—	—	—	—	—	—	—

Notes: Main entries are calculated from the raw vote values in table series 5-70 to 5-122 for the appropriate years based on candidates who used the sole designation "Democrat" or "Republican" (or their historical antecedents listed in Appendix A) on the ballot. In general, historical antecedents to the Democratic Party were Anti-Federalists, Democratic-Republicans, and Jacksonian Democrats; historical precursors of the Republican party were Federalists, National Republicans, and Whigs. Other = candidates who used third-party names on the ballot or were listed as independent, unidentified, or scatter vote. Bold italicized entries in the table are the author's alternative party coding, which is used when a candidate listed a major party name (Democrat, Republican, or their historical antecedents) on the ballot with other party names or labels. These values are computed from the bold italicized raw vote values in table series 5-70 to 5-122 for the appropriate states and years. For a more detailed explanation of this alternate coding system, see Tables 5-1 and 1-3. —indicates that the state had no data, either because no vote data were found for the state in question or the state had not yet entered the Union. No special House elections are included in the table. The table only lists at-large vote values for states having both at-large and district House races; see Appendix B for these states' district results aggregated to the state level.

[1]Election held in odd-numbered year.
[2]Partial data (less than 100% of the districts reporting).

Sources: Adapted from *United States Congressional Elections, 1788–1997* (1998), *Congressional Quarterly's Guide to U.S. Elections* (1994), Inter-university Consortium for Political and Social Research (ICPSR) data sets 0001 and 0075, independent search for state sources by the author, and personal communications with Michael J. Dubin (various dates).

Table 5-27 House Election Results, by State, 1828–1831 (Percentages)

State	1828–1829 Democratic	Republican	Other	Democratic % of Two-Party Vote	1830–1831 Democratic	Republican	Other	Democratic % of Two-Party Vote
Alabama	56.4[1]	12.7[1]	30.9[1]	81.6[1]	79.6[1,2]	20.4[1,2]	0.0[1,2]	79.6[1,2]
Alaska	—	—	—	—	—	—	—	—
Arizona	—	—	—	—	—	—	—	—
Arkansas	—	—	—	—	—	—	—	—
California	—	—	—	—	—	—	—	—
Colorado	—	—	—	—	—	—	—	—
Connecticut	36.1[1]	55.3[1]	8.7[1]	39.5[1]	32.6[1]	67.4[1]	0.0[1]	32.6[1]
Delaware	47.7	52.3	0.0	47.7	47.3	52.7	0.0	47.3
Florida	—	—	—	—	—	—	—	—
Georgia	35.1	0.0	64.9	100.0	0.0	0.0	100.0	—
Georgia	*100.0*	*0.0*	*0.0*	*100.0*	*90.08*	*0.0*	*9.2*	*100.0*
Hawaii	—	—	—	—	—	—	—	—
Idaho	—	—	—	—	—	—	—	—
Illinois	62.9	37.1	0.0	62.9	54.1[1]	0.0[1]	45.9[1]	100.0[1]
Indiana	47.5[2]	52.5[2]	0.0[2]	47.5[2]	53.6[1]	39.3[1]	7.1[1]	57.7[1]
Iowa	—	—	—	—	—	—	—	—
Kansas	—	—	—	—	—	—	—	—
Kentucky	59.1[1,2]	14.1[1,2]	26.8[1,2]	80.7[1,2]	51.3[1,2]	48.7[1,2]	0.0[1,2]	51.3[1,2]
Louisiana	32.8	52.0	15.2	38.7	0.0[2]	0.0[2]	100.0[2]	—
Louisiana	—	—	—	—	*0.0[2]*	*48.0[2]*	*52.0[2]*	*0.0[2]*
Maine	40.1	36.7	23.2	52.2	51.2	46.4	2.4	52.4
Maryland	52.7[1]	46.6[1]	0.7[1]	53.1[1]	43.1[1]	56.3[1]	0.7[1]	43.4[1]
Massachusetts	12.1	83.8	4.1	12.6	13.1	65.7	21.3	16.6
Michigan	—	—	—	—	—	—	—	—
Minnesota	—	—	—	—	—	—	—	—
Mississippi	—	—	—	—	76.4	23.6	0.0	76.4
Missouri	60.5	39.5	0.0	60.5	62.3[1]	37.7[1]	0.0[1]	62.3[1]
Montana	—	—	—	—	—	—	—	—
Nebraska	—	—	—	—	—	—	—	—
Nevada	—	—	—	—	—	—	—	—
New Hampshire	54.4[1]	45.6[1]	0.0[1]	54.4[1]	54.7[1]	45.3[1]	0.0[1]	54.7[1]
New Jersey	48.1	51.9	0.0	48.1	48.3	51.7	0.0	48.3
New Mexico	—	—	—	—	—	—	—	—
New York	50.1	37.8	12.1	57.0	48.4	14.9	36.6	76.4
New York	—	—	—	—	*48.4*	*16.6*	*34.9*	*74.4*
North Carolina	75.6[1,2]	17.2[1,2]	7.2[1,2]	81.5[1,2]	49.8[1,2]	10.6[1,2]	39.6[1,2]	82.5[1,2]
North Dakota	—	—	—	—	—	—	—	—
Ohio	48.8[2]	47.7[2]	3.5[2]	50.5[2]	46.3	50.3	3.4	48.0
Oklahoma	—	—	—	—	—	—	—	—
Oregon	—	—	—	—	—	—	—	—
Pennsylvania	56.8[2]	34.0[2]	9.1[2]	62.6[2]	50.3	20.9	28.9	70.7
Pennsylvania	—	—	—	—	*50.3*	*25.3*	*24.5*	*66.5*
Rhode Island	0.0[1]	77.6[1]	22.4[1]	0.0[1]	0.0[1]	85.0[1]	15.0[1]	0.0[1]
South Carolina	41.4[2]	0.0[2]	58.6[2]	100.0[2]	0.0[2]	0.0[2]	100.0[2]	—
South Dakota	—	—	—	—	—	—	—	—
Tennessee	62.5[1,2]	0.0[1,2]	37.5[1,2]	100.0[1,2]	70.1[1]	21.1[1]	8.8[1]	76.9[1]
Tennessee	*62.5[1,2]*	*10.2[1,2]*	*27.3[1,2]*	*86.0[1,2]*	—	—	—	—
Texas	—	—	—	—	—	—	—	—
Utah	—	—	—	—	—	—	—	—
Vermont	17.5[2]	71.4[2]	11.0[2]	19.7[2]	26.9	44.0	29.1	38.0
Vermont	—	—	—	—	*26.9*	*58.2*	*14.9*	*31.6*
Virginia	35.3[1,2]	24.9[1,2]	39.8[1,2]	58.7[1,2]	36.4[1,2]	46.2[1,2]	17.4[1,2]	44.1[1,2]
Washington	—	—	—	—	—	—	—	—
West Virginia	—	—	—	—	—	—	—	—
Wisconsin	—	—	—	—	—	—	—	—
Wyoming	—	—	—	—	—	—	—	—

Notes: Main entries are calculated from the raw vote values in table series 5-70 to 5-122 for the appropriate years based on candidates who used the sole designation "Democrat" or "Republican" (or their historical antecedents listed in Appendix A) on the ballot. In general, historical antecedents to the Democratic Party were Anti-Federalists, Democratic-Republicans, and Jacksonian Democrats; historical precursors of the Republican party were Federalists, National Republicans, and Whigs. Other = candidates who used third-party names on the ballot or were listed as independent, unidentified, or scatter vote. Bold italicized entries in the table are the author's alternative party coding, which is used when a candidate listed a major party name (Democrat, Republican, or their historical antecedents) on the ballot with other party names or labels. These values are computed from the bold italicized raw vote values in table series 5-70 to 5-122 for the appropriate states and years. For a more detailed explanation of this alternate coding system, see Tables 5-1 and 1-3. —indicates that the state had no data, either because no vote data were found for the state in question or the state had not yet entered the Union. No special House elections are included in the table. The table only lists at-large vote values for states having both at-large and district House races; see Appendix B for these states' district results aggregated to the state level.

[1] Election held in odd-numbered year.
[2] Partial data (less than 100% of the districts reporting).

Sources: Adapted from *United States Congressional Elections, 1788–1997* (1998), *Congressional Quarterly's Guide to U.S. Elections* (1994), ICPSR data sets 0001 and 0075, independent search for state sources by the author, and personal communications with Michael J. Dubin (various dates).

Table 5-28 House Election Results, by State, 1832–1835 (Percentages)

	1832–1833				1834–1835			
State	Democratic	Republican	Other	Democratic % of Two-Party Vote	Democratic	Republican	Other	Democratic % of Two-Party Vote
Alabama	64.9[1,2]	9.2[1,2]	25.9[1,2]	87.6[1,2]	100.0[1,2]	0.0[1,2]	0.0[1,2]	100.0[1,2]
Alaska	—	—	—	—	—	—	—	—
Arizona	—	—	—	—	—	—	—	—
Arkansas	—	—	—	—	—	—	—	—
California	—	—	—	—	—	—	—	—
Colorado	—	—	—	—	—	—	—	—
Connecticut	37.0[1]	50.2[1]	12.8[1]	42.5[1]	52.1[1]	46.9[1]	1.0[1]	52.6[1]
Delaware	49.3	50.7	0.0	49.3	49.2	50.8	0.0	49.2
Florida	—	—	—	—	—	—	—	—
Georgia	0.0	0.0	100.0	—	53.7	46.3	0.0	53.7
Georgia	*100.0*	*0.0*	*0.0*	*100.0*	—	—	—	—
Hawaii	—	—	—	—	—	—	—	—
Idaho	—	—	—	—	—	—	—	—
Illinois	71.9	8.1	19.9	89.9	62.6	0.0	37.4	100.0
Indiana	48.2[1]	5.0[1]	46.9[1]	90.6[1]	56.2[1]	33.6[1]	10.2[1]	62.5[1]
Iowa	—	—	—	—	—	—	—	—
Kansas	—	—	—	—	—	—	—	—
Kentucky	45.1[1,2]	46.8[1,2]	8.1[1,2]	49.1[1,2]	41.3[1,2]	54.7[1,2]	3.9[1,2]	43.0[1,2]
Louisiana	35.5	0.0	64.5	100.0	9.8	49.2	41.1	16.6
Louisiana	*35.5*	*64.5*	*0.0*	*35.5*	—	—	—	—
Maine	55.7[1]	35.9[1]	8.4[1]	60.8[1]	52.4	46.7	0.9	52.9
Maryland	50.4[1]	49.6[1]	0.0[1]	50.4[1]	48.9[1,2]	50.5[1,2]	0.6[1,2]	49.2[1,2]
Massachusetts	15.6[1]	52.8[1]	31.6[1]	22.9[1]	29.8	59.0	11.2	33.6
Massachusetts	*15.6[1]*	*57.9[1]*	*26.5[1]*	*21.3[1]*	—	—	—	—
Michigan	—	—	—	—	95.9[1]	0.0[1]	4.1[1]	100.0[1]
Minnesota	—	—	—	—	—	—	—	—
Mississippi	—	—	—	—	53.8[1]	45.0[1]	1.3[1]	54.5[1]
Missouri	53.3[1]	0.0[1]	46.7[1]	100.0[1]	45.8[1]	0.0[1]	54.2[1]	100.0[1]
Missouri	*53.3[1]*	*30.7[1]*	*16.1[1]*	*63.5[1]*	—	—	—	—
Montana	—	—	—	—	—	—	—	—
Nebraska	—	—	—	—	—	—	—	—
Nevada	—	—	—	—	—	—	—	—
New Hampshire	73.0[1]	21.1[1]	5.9[1]	77.6[1]	62.6[1]	37.4[1]	0.0[1]	62.6[1]
New Jersey	50.5	49.5	0.0	50.5	50.9	49.1	0.0	50.9
New Mexico	—	—	—	—	—	—	—	—
New York	51.9	16.2	31.9	76.2	52.2	47.8	0.0	52.2
North Carolina	48.2[1,2]	24.7[1,2]	27.1[1,2]	66.1[1,2]	37.4[1,2]	57.5[1,2]	5.1[1,2]	39.4[1,2]
North Carolina	—	—	—	—	*37.4[1,2]*	*62.6[1,2]*	*0.0[1,2]*	*37.4[1,2]*
North Dakota	—	—	—	—	—	—	—	—
Ohio	47.8	45.2	7.0	51.4	48.5	51.1	0.4	48.7
Oklahoma	—	—	—	—	—	—	—	—
Oregon	—	—	—	—	—	—	—	—
Pennsylvania	50.0	4.7	45.3	91.5	54.2	30.2	15.6	64.2
Pennsylvania	*51.8*	*10.7*	*37.5*	*82.9*	—	—	—	—
Rhode Island	37.6[1]	0.0[1]	62.4[1]	100.0[1]	51.0[1]	49.0[1]	0.0[1]	51.0[1]
Rhode Island	*37.6[1]*	*62.4[1]*	*0.0[1]*	*37.6[1]*	—	—	—	—
South Carolina	0.0[1,2]	0.0[1,2]	100.0[1,2]	—	0.0[2]	0.0[2]	100.0[2]	—
South Dakota	—	—	—	—	—	—	—	—
Tennessee	31.7[1]	34.9[1]	33.3[1]	47.6[1]	37.5[1]	57.0[1]	5.5[1]	39.7[1]
Tennessee	*35.9[1]*	*34.9[1]*	*29.2[1]*	*50.7[1]*	—	—	—	—
Texas	—	—	—	—	—	—	—	—
Utah	—	—	—	—	—	—	—	—
Vermont	27.4[1]	37.4[1]	35.2[1]	42.3[1]	29.7	39.3	31.0	43.0
Virginia	53.2[1,2]	32.3[1,2]	14.6[1,2]	62.2[1,2]	54.9[1,2]	44.5[1,2]	0.6[1,2]	55.2[1,2]
Washington	—	—	—	—	—	—	—	—
West Virginia	—	—	—	—	—	—	—	—
Wisconsin	—	—	—	—	—	—	—	—
Wyoming	—	—	—	—	—	—	—	—

Notes: Main entries are calculated from the raw vote values in table series 5-70 to 5-122 for the appropriate years based on candidates who used the sole designation "Democrat" or "Republican" (or their historical antecedents listed in Appendix A) on the ballot. In general, historical antecedents to the Democratic Party were Anti-Federalists, Democratic-Republicans, and Jacksonian Democrats; historical precursors of the Republican party were Federalists, National Republicans, and Whigs. Other = candidates who used third-party names on the ballot or were listed as independent, unidentified, or scatter vote. Bold italicized entries in the table are the author's alternative party coding, which is used when a candidate listed a major party name (Democrat, Republican, or their historical antecedents) on the ballot with other party names or labels. These values are computed from the bold italicized raw vote values in table series 5-70 to 5-122 for the appropriate states and years. For a more detailed explanation of this alternate coding system, see Tables 5-1 and 1-3. —indicates that the state had no data, either because no vote data were found for the state in question or the state had not yet entered the Union. No special House elections are included in the table. The table only lists at-large vote values for states having both at-large and district House races; see Appendix B for these states' district results aggregated to the state level.

[1]Election held in odd-numbered year.
[2]Partial data (less than 100% of the districts reporting).

Sources: Adapted from *United States Congressional Elections, 1788–1997* (1998), *Congressional Quarterly's Guide to U.S. Elections* (1994), ICPSR data sets 0001 and 0075, independent search for state sources by the author, and personal communications with Michael J. Dubin (various dates).

Table 5-29 House Election Results, by State, 1836–1839 (Percentages)

State	1836–1837 Democratic	Republican	Other	Democratic % of Two-Party Vote	1838–1839 Democratic	Republican	Other	Democratic % of Two-Party Vote
Alabama	59.2[1,2]	40.8[1,2]	0.0[1,2]	59.2[1,2]	60.5[1,2]	39.5[1,2]	0.0[1,2]	60.5[1,2]
Alaska	—	—	—	—	—	—	—	—
Arizona	—	—	—	—	—	—	—	—
Arkansas	71.9	28.1	0.0	71.9	61.8	38.2	0.0	61.8
California	—	—	—	—	—	—	—	—
Colorado	—	—	—	—	—	—	—	—
Connecticut	52.4[1]	47.6[1]	0.0[1]	52.4[1]	47.0[1]	52.2[1]	0.9[1]	47.4[1]
Delaware	47.4	52.6	0.0	47.4	50.3	49.7	0.0	50.3
Florida	—	—	—	—	—	—	—	—
Georgia	50.5	49.5	0.0	50.5	48.4	51.6	0.0	48.4
Hawaii	—	—	—	—	—	—	—	—
Idaho	—	—	—	—	—	—	—	—
Illinois	63.4	36.2	0.3	63.6	59.2	40.8	0.0	59.2
Indiana	34.5[1]	65.5[1]	0.0[1]	34.5[1]	50.7[1]	49.3[1]	0.0[1]	50.7[1]
Iowa	—	—	—	—	—	—	—	—
Kansas	—	—	—	—	—	—	—	—
Kentucky	34.2[1,2]	58.5[1,2]	7.3[1,2]	36.9[1,2]	48.1[1,2]	51.9[1,2]	0.0[1,2]	48.1[1,2]
Louisiana	23.1	60.6	16.3	27.6	28.5	68.3	3.2	29.5
Maine	48.2	42.7	9.1	53.0	51.8	47.9	0.3	52.0
Maryland	40.8[1]	58.7[1]	0.5[1]	41.0[1]	50.9[1]	44.7[1]	4.4[1]	53.2[1]
Massachusetts	42.6	56.9	0.5	42.8	40.9	57.6	1.5	41.5
Michigan	52.6[1]	47.4[1]	0.0[1]	52.6[1]	50.3	49.7	0.0	50.3
Minnesota	—	—	—	—	—	—	—	—
Mississippi	61.1[1]	38.9[1]	0.0[1]	61.1[1]	53.4[1]	46.6[1]	0.0[1]	53.4[1]
Missouri	61.6	37.4	1.0	62.2	57.7	42.3	0.0	57.7
Montana	—	—	—	—	—	—	—	—
Nebraska	—	—	—	—	—	—	—	—
Nevada	—	—	—	—	—	—	—	—
New Hampshire	94.2[1]	5.8[1]	0.0[1]	94.2[1]	53.8[1]	43.0[1]	3.2[1]	55.6[1]
New Jersey	49.5	50.5	0.0	49.5	50.1	49.9	0.0	50.1
New Mexico	—	—	—	—	—	—	—	—
New York	53.1	43.9	2.9	54.7	48.4	51.6	0.0	48.4
North Carolina	54.6[1,2]	44.1[1,2]	1.4[1,2]	55.3[1,2]	51.8[1,2]	48.2[1,2]	0.0[1,2]	51.8[1,2]
North Dakota	—	—	—	—	—	—	—	—
Ohio	48.1	51.8	0.1	48.2	50.1	49.9	0.0	50.1
Oklahoma	—	—	—	—	—	—	—	—
Oregon	—	—	—	—	—	—	—	—
Pennsylvania	53.9	31.7	14.4	63.0	51.2	48.8	0.0	51.2
Rhode Island	42.8[1]	56.2[1]	0.9[1]	43.2[1]	47.5[1]	52.5[1]	0.0[1]	47.5[1]
South Carolina	0.0[2]	0.0[2]	100.0[2]	—	29.4[2]	41.6[2]	29.0[2]	41.4[2]
South Dakota	—	—	—	—	—	—	—	—
Tennessee	32.2[1]	67.8[1]	0.0[1]	32.2[1]	48.7[1]	51.3[1]	0.0[1]	48.7[1]
Texas	—	—	—	—	—	—	—	—
Utah	—	—	—	—	—	—	—	—
Vermont	40.5	54.9	4.5	42.5	43.4	55.5	1.2	43.9
Virginia	56.3[1,2]	38.8[1,2]	4.9[1,2]	59.2[1,2]	51.2[1,2]	48.5[1,2]	0.2[1,2]	51.4[1,2]
Washington	—	—	—	—	—	—	—	—
West Virginia	—	—	—	—	—	—	—	—
Wisconsin	—	—	—	—	—	—	—	—
Wyoming	—	—	—	—	—	—	—	—
Arkansas	62.4[3]	37.6[3]	0.0[3]	62.4[3]	—	—	—	—

Notes: Main entries are calculated from the raw vote values in table series 5-70 to 5-122 for the appropriate years based on candidates who used the sole designation "Democrat" or "Republican" (or their historical antecedents listed in Appendix A) on the ballot. In general, historical antecedents to the Democratic Party were Anti-Federalists, Democratic-Republicans, and Jacksonian Democrats; historical precursors of the Republican Party were Federalists, National Republicans, and Whigs. Other = candidates who used third-party names on the ballot or were listed as independent, unidentified, or scatter vote. —indicates that the state had no data, either because no vote data were found for the state in question or the state had not yet entered the Union. No special elections are included in the table. The table only lists at-large vote values for states having both at-large and district House races; see Appendix B for these states' district results aggregated to the state level.

[1]Election held in odd-numbered year.
[2]Partial data (less than 100% of the districts reporting).
[3]1837 election when a state had annual elections in both 1836 and 1837.

Sources: Adapted from *United States Congressional Elections, 1788–1997* (1998), *Congressional Quarterly's Guide to U.S. Elections* (1994), ICPSR data sets 0001 and 0075, independent search for state sources by the author, and personal communications with Michael J. Dubin (various dates).

Table 5-30 House Election Results, by State, 1840–1843 (Percentages)

	1840–1841				1842–1843			
State	Democratic	Republican	Other	Democratic % of Two-Party Vote	Democratic	Republican	Other	Democratic % of Two-Party Vote
Alabama	57.0[1]	43.0[1]	0.0[1]	57.0[1]	51.0[1,2]	48.2[1,2]	0.7[1,2]	51.4[1,2]
Alaska	—	—	—	—	—	—	—	—
Arizona	—	—	—	—	—	—	—	—
Arkansas	57.6	42.4	0.0	57.6	57.3	32.4	10.3	63.9
California	—	—	—	—	—	—	—	—
Colorado	—	—	—	—	—	—	—	—
Connecticut	44.1[1]	55.9[1]	0.0[1]	44.1[1]	50.0[1]	47.1[1]	3.0[1]	51.5[1]
Delaware	45.8	54.2	0.0	45.8	50.0	50.0	0.0	50.0
Florida	—	—	—	—	—	—	—	—
Georgia	47.3	52.7	0.0	47.3	51.4	48.6	0.0	51.4
Hawaii	—	—	—	—	—	—	—	—
Idaho	—	—	—	—	—	—	—	—
Illinois	49.8[1]	39.1[1]	11.1[1]	56.0[1]	52.7[1]	45.1[1]	2.2[1]	53.9[1]
Illinois	*60.0[1]*	*39.1[1]*	*0.9[1]*	*60.5[1]*	—	—	—	—
Indiana	44.1[1]	55.7[1]	0.2[1]	44.1[1]	51.1[1]	48.2[1]	0.7[1]	51.5[1]
Iowa	—	—	—	—	—	—	—	—
Kansas	—	—	—	—	—	—	—	—
Kentucky	23.9[1]	71.0[1]	5.1[1]	25.2[1]	41.6[1]	51.0[1]	7.5[1]	44.9[1]
Louisiana	43.5	56.5	0.0	43.5	55.3[1]	44.7[1]	0.0[1]	55.3[1]
Maine	49.3	50.1	0.6	49.6	48.7[1]	32.8[1]	18.5[1]	59.8[1]
Maryland	38.2[1]	58.4[1]	3.4[1]	39.5[1]	—	—	—	—
Massachusetts	42.2	57.7	0.2	42.2	47.4	46.5	6.1	50.5
Michigan	48.5	51.5	0.0	48.5	54.8[1]	37.9[1]	7.3[1]	59.1[1]
Minnesota	—	—	—	—	—	—	—	—
Mississippi	53.5[1]	46.5[1]	0.0[1]	53.5[1]	0.0[1]	0.0[1]	100.0[1]	—
Mississippi	—	—	—	—	*100.0[1]*	*0.0[1]*	*0.0[1]*	*100.0[1]*
Missouri	57.9	42.1	0.0	57.9	97.4	0.0	2.6	100.0
Montana	—	—	—	—	—	—	—	—
Nebraska	—	—	—	—	—	—	—	—
Nevada	—	—	—	—	—	—	—	—
New Hampshire	56.6[1]	40.9[1]	2.5[1]	58.1[1]	51.8[1]	29.2[1]	19.0[1]	64.0[1]
New Jersey	48.2	51.7	0.1	48.3	40.6[1,2]	48.3[1,2]	11.1[1,2]	45.7[1,2]
New Jersey	—	—	—	—	*40.6[1,2]*	*59.4[1,2]*	*0.0[1,2]*	*40.6[1,2]*
New Mexico	—	—	—	—	—	—	—	—
New York	48.7	50.9	0.4	48.9	50.3	47.9	1.8	51.2
North Carolina	48.9[1,2]	50.8[1,2]	0.3[1,2]	49.0[1,2]	45.3[1]	54.7[1]	0.0[1]	45.3[1]
North Dakota	—	—	—	—	—	—	—	—
Ohio	46.9	53.1	0.0	46.9	49.0[1]	44.6[1]	6.5[1]	52.4[1]
Ohio	—	—	—	—	*49.0[1]*	*46.9[1]*	*4.2[1]*	*51.1[1]*
Oklahoma	—	—	—	—	—	—	—	—
Oregon	—	—	—	—	—	—	—	—
Pennsylvania	50.9	49.1	0.0	50.9	51.4[1]	43.1[1]	5.5[1]	54.4[1]
Pennsylvania	—	—	—	—	*52.0[1]*	*43.1[1]*	*4.9[1]*	*54.6[1]*
Rhode Island	0.0[1]	91.1[1]	8.9[1]	0.0[1]	38.2[1]	0.0[1]	61.8[1]	100.0[1]
Rhode Island	—	—	—	—	*38.2[1]*	*61.8[1]*	*0.0[1]*	*38.2[1]*
South Carolina	61.8[2]	36.5[2]	1.7[2]	62.8[2]	67.0[1,2]	21.6[1,2]	11.4[1,2]	75.6[1,2]
South Dakota	—	—	—	—	—	—	—	—
Tennessee	45.9[1]	52.6[1]	1.4[1]	46.6[1]	47.0[1]	53.0[1]	0.0[1]	47.0[1]
Texas	—	—	—	—	—	—	—	—
Utah	—	—	—	—	—	—	—	—
Vermont	40.3	59.5	0.2	40.4	42.9[1]	49.5[1]	7.6[1]	46.4[1]
Virginia	42.8[1,2]	42.5[1,2]	14.7[1,2]	50.1[1,2]	51.3[1,2]	48.7[1,2]	0.0[1,2]	51.3[1,2]
Washington	—	—	—	—	—	—	—	—
West Virginia	—	—	—	—	—	—	—	—
Wisconsin	—	—	—	—	—	—	—	—
Wyoming	—	—	—	—	—	—	—	—

Notes: Main entries are calculated from the raw vote values in table series 5-70 to 5-122 for the appropriate years based on candidates who used the sole designation "Democrat" or "Republican" (or their historical antecedents listed in Appendix A) on the ballot. In general, historical antecedents to the Democratic Party were Anti-Federalists, Democratic-Republicans, and Jacksonian Democrats; historical precursors of the Republican party were Federalists, National Republicans, and Whigs. Other = candidates who used third-party names on the ballot or were listed as independent, unidentified, or scatter vote. Bold italicized entries in the table are the author's alternative party coding, which is used when a candidate listed a major party name (Democrat, Republican, or their historical antecedents) on the ballot with other party names or labels. These values are computed from the bold italicized raw vote values in table series 5-70 to 5-122 for the appropriate states and years. For a more detailed explanation of this alternate coding system, see Tables 5-1 and 1-3. —indicates that the state had no data, either because no vote data were found for the state in question or the state had not yet entered the Union. No special House elections are included in the table. The table only lists at-large vote values for states having both at-large and district House races; see Appendix B for these states' district results aggregated to the state level.

[1]Election held in odd-numbered year.
[2]Partial data (less than 100% of the districts reporting).

Sources: Adapted from *United States Congressional Elections, 1788–1997* (1998), *Congressional Quarterly's Guide to U.S. Elections* (1994), ICPSR data sets 0001 and 0075, independent search for state sources by the author, and personal communications with Michael J. Dubin (various dates).

Table 5-31 House Election Results, by State, 1844–1847 (Percentages)

State	1844–1845				1846–1847			
	Democratic	Republican	Other	Democratic % of Two-Party Vote	Democratic	Republican	Other	Democratic % of Two-Party Vote
Alabama	76.5[1,2]	22.5[1,2]	0.9[1,2]	77.2[1,2]	73.4[1,2]	21.4[1,2]	5.2[1,2]	77.5[1,2]
Alaska	—	—	—	—	—	—	—	—
Arizona	—	—	—	—	—	—	—	—
Arkansas	59.3	40.1	0.6	59.7	99.4	0.0	0.6	100.0
California	—	—	—	—	—	—	—	—
Colorado	—	—	—	—	—	—	—	—
Connecticut	45.2[1]	51.1[1]	3.7[1]	47.0[1]	46.1[1]	50.8[1]	3.1[1]	47.6[1]
Delaware	49.2	50.8	0.0	49.2	49.0	51.0	0.0	49.0
Florida	60.3[1]	39.7[1]	0.0[1]	60.3[1]	49.1	50.9	0.0	49.1
Georgia	51.4	48.6	0.0	51.4	51.4	46.3	2.3	52.6
Georgia	—	—	—	—	*53.5*	*46.3*	*0.2*	*53.6*
Hawaii	—	—	—	—	—	—	—	—
Idaho	—	—	—	—	—	—	—	—
Illinois	63.0	33.9	3.1	65.0	54.6	28.0	17.4	66.1
Illinois	—	—	—	—	*61.7*	*28.0*	*10.3*	*68.8*
Indiana	51.8[1]	46.8[1]	1.4[1]	52.5[1]	49.7[1]	49.9[1]	0.4[1]	49.9[1]
Iowa	—	—	—	—	52.6	47.4	0.0	52.6
Kansas	—	—	—	—	—	—	—	—
Kentucky	49.9[1]	49.9[1]	0.2[1]	50.0[1]	44.3[1]	48.7[1]	6.9[1]	47.7[1]
Kentucky	—	—	—	—	*44.3[1]*	*53.1[1]*	*2.6[1]*	*45.5[1]*
Louisiana	69.2	30.8	0.0	69.2	51.0[1,2]	47.3[1,2]	1.8[1,2]	51.9[1,2]
Maine	47.2	43.0	9.8	52.3	44.4	40.1	15.5	52.5
Maryland	44.8	54.8	0.4	45.0	50.7[1,2]	49.3[1,2]	0.0[1,2]	50.7[1,2]
Massachusetts	40.2	52.1	7.8	43.5	32.3	54.0	13.7	37.4
Michigan	50.1	44.2	5.7	53.1	50.1	43.8	6.1	53.3
Minnesota	—	—	—	—	—	—	—	—
Mississippi	56.5[1]	37.1[1]	6.4[1]	60.3[1]	60.6[1]	26.5[1]	12.9[1]	69.6[1]
Mississippi	—	—	—	—	*73.4[1]*	*26.5[1]*	*0.1[1]*	*73.5[1]*
Missouri	55.2	44.8	0.0	55.2	60.0	37.7	2.3	61.4
Montana	—	—	—	—	—	—	—	—
Nebraska	—	—	—	—	—	—	—	—
Nevada	—	—	—	—	—	—	—	—
New Hampshire	46.9[1]	28.6[1]	24.6[1]	62.1[1]	51.0[1]	35.1[1]	14.0[1]	59.3[1]
New Jersey	43.7	56.3	0.0	43.7	46.0	51.5	2.6	47.2
New Mexico	—	—	—	—	—	—	—	—
New York	48.2	41.5	10.4	53.7	41.9	47.1	11.0	47.1
New York	*48.2*	*51.6*	*0.2*	*48.3*	*45.1*	*47.1*	*7.8*	*48.9*
North Carolina	44.1[1]	55.9[1]	0.0[1]	44.1[1]	35.7[1]	53.0[1]	11.3[1]	40.2[1]
North Carolina	—	—	—	—	*42.3[1]*	*57.7[1]*	*0.0[1]*	*42.3[1]*
North Dakota	—	—	—	—	—	—	—	—
Ohio	47.7	49.4	2.9	49.2	47.9	46.8	5.3	50.6
Ohio	—	—	—	—	*47.9*	*50.9*	*1.2*	*48.5*
Oklahoma	—	—	—	—	—	—	—	—
Oregon	—	—	—	—	—	—	—	—
Pennsylvania	48.7	44.3	7.0	52.3	44.5	44.4	11.1	50.1
Pennsylvania	—	—	—	—	*46.9*	*44.4*	*8.8*	*51.4*
Rhode Island	0.0[1]	72.0[1]	28.0[1]	0.0[1]	39.1[1]	52.0[1]	8.9[1]	42.9[1]
South Carolina	78.0[2]	22.0[2]	0.0[2]	78.0[2]	—	—	—	—
South Dakota	—	—	—	—	—	—	—	—
Tennessee	53.5[1]	44.1[1]	2.5[1]	54.8[1]	50.8[1]	49.1[1]	0.1[1]	50.9[1]
Tennessee	*53.5[1]*	*46.1[1]*	*0.4[1]*	*53.7[1]*	—	—	—	—
Texas	—	—	—	—	40.4	0.0	59.6	100.0
Utah	—	—	—	—	—	—	—	—
Vermont	37.6	52.6	9.9	41.7	35.9	49.0	15.0	42.3
Virginia	50.8[1,2]	36.8[1,2]	12.5[1,2]	58.0[1,2]	53.1[1,2]	46.9[1,2]	0.0[1,2]	53.1[1,2]
Washington	—	—	—	—	—	—	—	—
West Virginia	—	—	—	—	—	—	—	—
Wisconsin	—	—	—	—	—	—	—	—
Wyoming	—	—	—	—	—	—	—	—
Iowa	—	—	—	—	52.0[4]	48.0[4]	0.0[4]	52.0[4]
Maryland	50.8[3]	47.3[3]	1.9[3]	51.8[3]	—	—	—	—

Notes: Main entries are calculated from the raw vote values in table series 5-70 to 5-122 for the appropriate years based on candidates who used the sole designation "Democrat" or "Republican" (or their historical antecedents listed in Appendix A) on the ballot. In general, historical antecedents to the Democratic Party were Anti-Federalists, Democratic-Republicans, and Jacksonian Democrats; historical precursors of the Republican party were Federalists, National Republicans, and Whigs. Other = candidates who used third-party names on the ballot or were listed as independent, unidentified, or scatter vote. Bold italicized entries in the table are the author's alternative party coding, which is used when a candidate listed a major party name (Democrat, Republican, or their historical antecedents) on the ballot with other party names or labels. These values are computed from the bold italicized raw vote values in table series 5-70 to 5-122 for the appropriate states and years. For a more detailed explanation of this alternate coding system, see Tables 5-1 and 1-3. —indicates that the state had no data, either because no vote data were found for the state in question or the state had not yet entered the Union. No special House elections are included in the table. The table only lists at-large vote values for states having both at-large and district House races; see Appendix B for these states' district results aggregated to the state level.

[1]Election held in odd-numbered year.
[2]Partial data (less than 100% of the districts reporting).
[3]1845 election when a state had annual elections in both 1844 and 1845.
[4]1847 election when a state had annual elections in both 1846 and 1847.

Sources: Adapted from *United States Congressional Elections, 1788–1997* (1998), *Congressional Quarterly's Guide to U.S. Elections* (1994), ICPSR data sets 0001 and 0075, independent search for state sources by the author, and personal communications with Michael J. Dubin (various dates).

Table 5-32 House Election Results, by State, 1848–1851 (Percentages)

State	1848–1849				1850–1851			
	Democratic	Republican	Other	Democratic % of Two-Party Vote	Democratic	Republican	Other	Democratic % of Two-Party Vote
Alabama	45.0[1]	46.6[1]	8.5[1]	49.1[1]	0.0[1,2]	0.0[1,2]	100.0[1,2]	—
Alabama	*45.0[1]*	*55.0[1]*	*0.0[1]*	*45.0[1]*	*58.0[1,2]*	*42.0[1,2]*	*0.0[1,2]*	*58.0[1,2]*
Alaska	—	—	—	—	—	—	—	—
Arizona	—	—	—	—	—	—	—	—
Arkansas	60.8	39.2	0.0	60.8	57.4[1]	42.6[1]	0.0[1]	57.4[1]
California	49.3[1]	0.0[1]	50.7[1]	100.0[1]	53.4[1]	46.6[1]	0.0[1]	53.4[1]
Colorado	—	—	—	—	—	—	—	—
Connecticut	36.7[1]	50.0[1]	13.3[1]	42.4[1]	49.6[1]	47.8[1]	2.6[1]	50.9[1]
Connecticut	*48.6[1]*	*50.0[1]*	*1.4[1]*	*49.3[1]*	—	—	—	—
Delaware	48.6	51.4	0.0	48.6	49.3	48.2	2.5	50.5
Florida	46.5	53.5	0.0	46.5	47.2	52.8	0.0	47.2
Georgia	50.2	49.8	0.0	50.2	0.0[1]	0.0[1]	100.0[1]	—
Hawaii	—	—	—	—	—	—	—	—
Idaho	—	—	—	—	—	—	—	—
Illinois	62.2	33.2	4.6	65.2	57.4	41.5	1.1	58.1
Indiana	49.8[1]	50.2[1]	0.0[1]	49.8[1]	50.2[1]	40.9[1]	9.0[1]	55.1[1]
Indiana	—	—	—	—	*50.2[1]*	*46.8[1]*	*3.1[1]*	*51.7[1]*
Iowa	50.6	47.4	2.0	51.6	52.0	46.2	1.9	53.0
Iowa	—	—	—	—	*53.6*	*46.2*	*0.3*	*53.7*
Kansas	—	—	—	—	—	—	—	—
Kentucky	40.4[1]	55.1[1]	4.5[1]	42.3[1]	46.8[1]	49.9[1]	3.3[1]	48.4[1]
Kentucky	—	—	—	—	*46.8[1]*	*53.2[1]*	*0.0[1]*	*46.8[1]*
Louisiana	53.1[1,2]	46.9[1,2]	0.0[1,2]	53.1[1,2]	49.6[1]	50.4[1]	0.0[1]	49.6[1]
Maine	47.1	39.9	13.1	54.1	49.5	46.7	3.8	51.4
Maryland	45.5[1]	53.7[1]	0.8[1]	45.8[1]	42.7[1]	42.7[1]	14.6[1]	50.0[1]
Maryland	—	—	—	—	*42.7[1]*	*51.9[1]*	*5.4[1]*	*45.2[1]*
Massachusetts	21.7	43.1	35.2	33.5	29.9	47.3	22.9	38.7
Massachusetts	*21.7*	*52.0*	*26.3*	*29.4*	—	—	—	—
Michigan	47.9	24.3	27.8	66.4	48.6	0.0	51.4	100.0
Michigan	*47.9*	*45.1*	*7.0*	*51.5*	*48.6*	*51.3*	*0.1*	*48.7*
Minnesota	—	—	—	—	—	—	—	—
Mississippi	57.3[1]	42.7[1]	0.0[1]	57.3[1]	0.0[1]	0.0[1]	100.0[1]	—
Missouri	61.6	38.4	0.0	61.6	7.5	40.7	51.8	15.6
Missouri	—	—	—	—	*59.3*	*40.7*	*0.0*	*59.3*
Montana	—	—	—	—	—	—	—	—
Nebraska	—	—	—	—	—	—	—	—
Nevada	—	—	—	—	—	—	—	—
New Hampshire	53.9[1]	27.2[1]	18.9[1]	66.5[1]	52.7[1]	11.8[1]	35.6[1]	81.7[1]
New Hampshire	*53.9[1]*	*39.7[1]*	*6.4[1]*	*57.6[1]*	*52.7[1]*	*43.4[1]*	*3.9[1]*	*54.8[1]*
New Jersey	48.8	49.2	2.0	49.8	53.3	45.1	1.5	54.2
New Mexico	—	—	—	—	—	—	—	—
New York	22.0	47.7	30.3	31.5	48.8	50.1	1.1	49.4
New York	*23.4*	*49.9*	*26.7*	*31.9*	*49.0*	*50.1*	*0.9*	*49.4*
North Carolina	49.6[1]	48.2[1]	2.1[1]	50.7[1]	25.2[1,2]	43.1[1,2]	31.6[1,2]	36.9[1,2]
North Carolina	—	—	—	—	*40.8[1,2]*	*58.3[1,2]*	*0.9[1,2]*	*41.2[1,2]*
North Dakota	—	—	—	—	—	—	—	—
Ohio	49.6	39.7	10.6	55.5	52.3	41.4	6.2	55.8
Ohio	*49.9*	*42.3*	*7.9*	*54.1*	*54.5*	*41.4*	*4.1*	*56.8*
Oklahoma	—	—	—	—	—	—	—	—
Oregon	—	—	—	—	—	—	—	—
Pennsylvania	46.8	47.6	5.6	49.6	49.0	44.2	6.8	52.6
Pennsylvania	*50.4*	*47.6*	*2.1*	*51.4*	*51.5*	*46.5*	*2.0*	*52.6*
Rhode Island	37.6[1]	58.1[1]	4.3[1]	39.3[1]	52.8[1]	46.0[1]	1.2[1]	53.4[1]
South Carolina	66.6[2]	0.0[2]	33.4[2]	100.0[2]	—	—	—	—
South Carolina	*80.7[2]*	*0.0[2]*	*19.3[2]*	*100.0[2]*	—	—	—	—
South Dakota	—	—	—	—	—	—	—	—
Tennessee	49.9[1]	44.3[1]	5.8[1]	52.9[1]	44.2[1,2]	49.7[1,2]	6.1[1,2]	47.0[1,2]
Tennessee	—	—	—	—	*50.3[1,2]*	*49.7[1,2]*	*0.0[1,2]*	*50.3[1,2]*
Texas	78.2[1]	0.0[1]	21.8[1]	100.0[1]	73.6[1]	0.0[1]	26.4[1]	100.0[1]
Utah	—	—	—	—	—	—	—	—
Vermont	31.2	44.5	24.2	41.2	21.9	53.2	24.9	29.2
Vermont	*55.5*	*44.5*	*0.0*	*55.5*	*46.8*	*53.2*	*0.0*	*46.8*
Virginia	48.8[1,2]	45.6[1,2]	5.6[1,2]	51.7[1,2]	53.7[1,2]	46.3[1,2]	0.0[1,2]	53.7[1,2]
Virginia	*48.8[1,2]*	*50.6[1,2]*	*0.6[1,2]*	*49.1[1,2]*	—	—	—	—
Washington	—	—	—	—	—	—	—	—
West Virginia	—	—	—	—	—	—	—	—
Wisconsin	41.3	34.5	24.2	54.5	42.4	13.4	44.3	76.0
Wisconsin	—	—	—	—	*42.4*	*30.9*	*26.8*	*57.9*
Wyoming	—	—	—	—	—	—	—	—

Notes: Main entries are calculated from the raw vote values in table series 5-70 to 5-122 for the appropriate years based on candidates who used the sole designation "Democrat" or "Republican" (or their historical antecedents listed in Appendix A) on the ballot. In general, historical antecedents to the Democratic Party were Anti-Federalists, Democratic-Republicans, and Jacksonian Democrats; historical precursors of the Republican party were Federalists, National Republicans, and Whigs. Other = candidates who used third-party names on the ballot or were listed as independent, unidentified, or scatter vote. Bold italicized entries in the table are the author's alternative party coding, which is used when a candidate listed a major party name (Democrat, Republican, or their historical antecedents) on the ballot with other party names or labels. These values are computed from the bold italicized raw vote values in table series 5-70 to 5-122 for the appropriate states and years. For a more detailed explanation of this alternate coding system, see Tables 5-1 and 1-3. —indicates that the state had no data, either because no vote data were found for the state in question or the state had not yet entered the Union. No special House elections are included in the table. The table only lists at-large vote values for states having both at-large and district House races; see Appendix B for these states' district results aggregated to the state level.

[1] Election held in odd-numbered year.
[2] Partial data (less than 100% of the districts reporting).

Sources: Adapted from *United States Congressional Elections, 1788–1997* (1998), *Congressional Quarterly's Guide to U.S. Elections* (1994), ICPSR data sets 0001 and 0075, independent search for state sources by the author, and personal communications with Michael J. Dubin (various dates).

Table 5-33 House Election Results, by State, 1852–1855 (Percentages)

State	1852–1853 Democratic	Republican	Other	Democratic % of Two-Party Vote	1854–1855 Democratic	Republican	Other	Democratic % of Two-Party Vote
Alabama	19.7[1,2]	5.7[1,2]	74.7[1,2]	77.6[1,2]	56.5[1]	0.0[1]	43.5[1]	100.0[1]
Alabama	*65.9[1,2]*	*34.1[1,2]*	*0.0[1,2]*	*65.9[1,2]*	—	—	—	—
Alaska	—	—	—	—	—	—	—	—
Arizona	—	—	—	—	—	—	—	—
Arkansas	76.1[1]	23.9[1]	0.0[1]	76.1[1]	82.8	16.2	1.1	83.6
California	53.6	46.4	0.0	53.6	0.0	42.6	57.4	0.0
California	—	—	—	—	*57.4*	*42.6*	*0.0*	*57.4*
Colorado	—	—	—	—	—	—	—	—
Connecticut	52.9[1]	41.7[1]	5.4[1]	55.9[1]	43.0[1]	0.0[1]	57.0[1]	100.0[1]
Delaware	50.2	49.8	0.0	50.2	48.2	0.0	51.8	100.0
Florida	50.1	49.9	0.0	50.1	55.3	44.7	0.0	55.3
Georgia	50.2[1]	44.3[1]	5.6[1]	53.1[1]	55.5[1]	0.0[1]	44.5[1]	100.0[1]
Hawaii	—	—	—	—	—	—	—	—
Idaho	—	—	—	—	—	—	—	—
Illinois	50.1	41.1	8.8	54.9	42.9	48.2	8.9	47.1
Illinois	*54.0*	*41.1*	*4.9*	*56.8*	*49.9*	*48.2*	*1.9*	*50.9*
Indiana	53.6	45.4	0.9	54.1	46.1	0.0	53.9	100.0
Iowa	51.8	48.2	0.0	51.8	48.2	51.4	0.4	48.4
Kansas	—	—	—	—	—	—	—	—
Kentucky	48.1[1]	51.9[1]	0.0[1]	48.1[1]	48.6[1]	0.0[1]	51.4[1]	100.0[1]
Louisiana	—	—	—	—	53.2[1]	0.0[1]	46.8[1]	100.0[1]
Maine	48.6	45.6	5.8	51.6	35.8	63.9	0.3	35.9
Maryland	38.3[1]	32.7[1]	29.0[1]	54.0[1]	48.7[1]	0.0[1]	51.3[1]	100.0[1]
Massachusetts	29.2	44.3	26.5	39.7	8.8	23.8	67.5	26.9
Massachusetts	—	—	—	—	*9.4*	*23.8*	*66.9*	*28.2*
Michigan	50.8	34.5	14.7	59.6	46.7	53.3	0.0	46.7
Michigan	*50.8*	*45.9*	*3.3*	*52.5*	—	—	—	—
Minnesota	—	—	—	—	—	—	—	—
Mississippi	54.3[1]	45.7[1]	0.0[1]	54.3[1]	54.3[1]	0.0[1]	45.7[1]	100.0[1]
Missouri	32.4	43.4	24.3	42.7	12.5	44.3	43.1	22.0
Missouri	*56.6*	*43.4*	*0.0*	*56.6*	*55.0*	*45.0*	*0.0*	*55.0*
Montana	—	—	—	—	—	—	—	—
Nebraska	—	—	—	—	—	—	—	—
Nevada	—	—	—	—	—	—	—	—
New Hampshire	56.1[1]	23.1[1]	20.8[1]	70.8[1]	42.4[1]	0.0[1]	57.6[1]	100.0[1]
New Hampshire	*56.1[1]*	*40.6[1]*	*3.4[1]*	*58.0[1]*	—	—	—	—
New Jersey	53.0	45.8	1.2	53.7	43.1	43.2	13.7	49.9
New Mexico	—	—	—	—	—	—	—	—
New York	47.5	46.1	6.4	50.7	5.8	39.6	54.6	12.8
New York	*47.5*	*48.2*	*4.3*	*49.6*	*47.7*	*47.3*	*5.0*	*50.2*
North Carolina	43.8[1]	39.5[1]	16.7[1]	52.6[1]	49.7[1]	4.1[1]	46.1[1]	92.3[1]
North Carolina	*60.5[1]*	*39.5[1]*	*0.0[1]*	*60.5[1]*	—	—	—	—
North Dakota	—	—	—	—	—	—	—	—
Ohio	48.6	43.0	8.3	53.0	36.2	0.0	63.8	100.0
Oklahoma	—	—	—	—	—	—	—	—
Oregon	—	—	—	—	—	—	—	—
Pennsylvania	54.2	41.7	4.1	56.5	45.3	44.6	10.1	50.4
Pennsylvania	—	—	—	—	*50.1*	*47.6*	*2.3*	*51.3*
Rhode Island	63.2[1]	34.2[1]	2.5[1]	64.9[1]	—	—	—	—
South Carolina	52.1[1,2]	0.0[1,2]	47.9[1,2]	100.0[1,2]	67.1[2]	0.0[2]	32.9[2]	100.0[2]
South Dakota	—	—	—	—	—	—	—	—
Tennessee	52.4[1,2]	47.6[1,2]	0.0[1,2]	52.4[1,2]	48.8[1]	0.0[1]	51.2[1]	100.0[1]
Texas	92.5[1]	7.0[1]	0.5[1]	93.0[1]	55.7[1]	0.0[1]	44.3[1]	100.0[1]
Utah	—	—	—	—	—	—	—	—
Vermont	20.8	50.9	28.3	29.0	32.1	61.8	6.1	34.2
Vermont	*49.1*	*50.9*	*0.0*	*49.1*	*38.2*	*61.8*	*0.0*	*38.2*
Virginia	50.4[1,2]	39.7[1,2]	9.9[1,2]	55.9[1,2]	52.7[1,2]	0.0[1,2]	47.3[1,2]	100.0[1,2]
Virginia	*59.5[1,2]*	*39.7[1,2]*	*0.8[1,2]*	*60.0[1,2]*	—	—	—	—
Washington	—	—	—	—	—	—	—	—
West Virginia	—	—	—	—	—	—	—	—
Wisconsin	52.5	32.9	14.6	61.5	42.1	54.4	3.5	43.6
Wyoming	—	—	—	—	—	—	—	—

Notes: Main entries are calculated from the raw vote values in table series 5-70 to 5-122 for the appropriate years based on candidates who used the sole designation "Democrat" or "Republican" (or their historical antecedents listed in Appendix A) on the ballot. In general, historical antecedents to the Democratic Party were Anti-Federalists, Democratic-Republicans, and Jacksonian Democrats; historical precursors of the Republican party were Federalists, National Republicans, and Whigs. Other = candidates who used third-party names on the ballot or were listed as independent, unidentified, or scatter vote. Bold italicized entries in the table are the author's alternative party coding, which is used when a candidate listed a major party name (Democrat, Republican, or their historical antecedents) on the ballot with other party names or labels. These values are computed from the bold italicized raw vote values in table series 5-70 to 5-122 for the appropriate states and years. For a more detailed explanation of this alternate coding system, see Tables 5-1 and 1-3. —indicates that the state had no data, either because no vote data were found for the state in question or the state had not yet entered the Union. No special House elections are included in the table. The table only lists at-large vote values for states having both at-large and district House races; see Appendix B for these states' district results aggregated to the state level.

[1]Election held in odd-numbered year.
[2]Partial data (less than 100% of the districts reporting).

Sources: Adapted from *United States Congressional Elections, 1788–1997* (1998), *Congressional Quarterly's Guide to U.S. Elections* (1994), ICPSR data sets 0001 and 0075, independent search for state sources by the author, and personal communications with Michael J. Dubin (various dates).

Table 5-34 House Election Results, by State, 1856–1859 (Percentages)

	1856–1857				1858–1859			
State	Democratic	Republican	Other	Democratic % of Two-Party Vote	Democratic	Republican	Other	Democratic % of Two-Party Vote
Alabama	67.4[1]	0.0[1]	32.6[1]	100.0[1]	66.8[1,2]	0.0[1,2]	33.2[1,2]	100.0[1,2]
Alabama	*72.7[1]*	*0.0[1]*	*27.3[1]*	*100.0[1]*	*76.2[1,2]*	*0.0[1,2]*	*23.8[1,2]*	*100.0[1,2]*
Alaska	—	—	—	—	—	—	—	—
Arizona	—	—	—	—	—	—	—	—
Arkansas	64.7	0.0	35.3	100.0	78.6	0.0	21.4	100.0
Arkansas	—	—	—	—	*86.5*	*0.0*	*13.5*	*100.0*
California	47.0	20.3	32.6	69.8	0.0[1]	0.0[1]	100.0[1]	—
California	—	—	—	—	*58.1[1]*	*41.9[1]*	*0.0[1]*	*58.1[1]*
Colorado	—	—	—	—	—	—	—	—
Connecticut	49.2[1]	50.8[1]	0.0[1]	49.2[1]	48.6[1]	50.7[1]	0.6[1]	48.9[1]
Delaware	56.1	0.0	43.9	100.0	51.4	0.0	48.6	100.0
Florida	53.1	0.0	46.9	100.0	62.4	0.0	37.6	100.0
Florida	—	—	—	—	*100.0*	*0.0*	*0.0*	*100.0*
Georgia	54.5[1]	0.0[1]	45.5[1]	100.0[1]	62.4[1]	0.0[1]	37.6[1]	100.0[1]
Georgia	*66.7[1]*	*0.0[1]*	*33.3[1]*	*100.0[1]*	—	—	—	—
Hawaii	—	—	—	—	—	—	—	—
Idaho	—	—	—	—	—	—	—	—
Illinois	47.7	51.3	1.0	48.2	48.5	49.9	1.6	49.3
Illinois	—	—	—	—	*50.1*	*49.9*	*0.0*	*50.1*
Indiana	51.4	48.6	0.0	51.4	47.7	46.6	5.7	50.6
Indiana	—	—	—	—	*53.4*	*46.6*	*0.0*	*53.4*
Iowa	44.7	54.2	1.1	45.2	48.2	51.8	0.0	48.2
Kansas	—	—	—	—	42.3[1]	57.7[1]	0.0[1]	42.3[1]
Kentucky	55.8[1]	0.0[1]	44.2[1]	100.0[1]	54.2[1]	0.0[1]	45.8[1]	100.0[1]
Louisiana	52.3[1]	0.0[1]	47.7[1]	100.0[1]	68.5[1]	0.0[1]	31.5[1]	100.0[1]
Louisiana	*57.9[1]*	*0.0[1]*	*42.1[1]*	*100.0[1]*	—	—	—	—
Maine	41.7	58.3	0.0	41.7	46.2	53.8	0.0	46.2
Maryland	44.7[1]	0.0[1]	55.3[1]	100.0[1]	37.9[1]	0.0[1]	62.1[1]	100.0[1]
Massachusetts	20.8	61.2	18.0	25.4	33.5	60.3	6.2	35.7
Massachusetts	*27.4*	*61.2*	*11.4*	*30.9*	—	—	—	—
Michigan	42.7	57.3	0.0	42.7	45.8	54.2	0.0	45.8
Minnesota	51.7[1]	48.3[1]	0.0[1]	51.7[1]	45.3[1]	54.7[1]	0.0[1]	45.3[1]
Mississippi	71.7[1]	0.0[1]	28.3[1]	100.0[1]	92.9[1]	0.0[1]	7.1[1]	100.0[1]
Mississippi	—	—	—	—	*98.9[1]*	*0.0[1]*	*1.1[1]*	*100.0[1]*
Missouri	46.6	0.0	53.4	100.0	57.6	5.2	37.2	91.7
Missouri	*58.1*	*0.0*	*41.9*	*100.0*	*67.4*	*5.2*	*27.3*	*92.8*
Montana	—	—	—	—	—	—	—	—
Nebraska	—	—	—	—	—	—	—	—
Nevada	—	—	—	—	—	—	—	—
New Hampshire	47.2[1]	52.8[1]	0.0[1]	47.2[1]	47.9[1]	52.1[1]	0.0[1]	47.9[1]
New Jersey	47.7	12.5	39.8	79.2	43.5	33.1	23.4	56.8
New Jersey	*47.7*	*44.1*	*8.2*	*52.0*	*63.0*	*33.1*	*3.9*	*65.6*
New Mexico	—	—	—	—	—	—	—	—
New York	27.9	46.3	25.7	37.6	38.9	34.6	26.4	52.9
New York	*34.5*	*46.3*	*19.2*	*42.7*	*39.7*	*53.8*	*6.5*	*42.5*
North Carolina	67.5[1]	0.0[1]	32.5[1]	100.0[1]	54.3[1]	40.4[1]	5.2[1]	57.3[1]
North Carolina	—	—	—	—	*55.9[1]*	*40.4[1]*	*3.7[1]*	*58.0[1]*
North Dakota	—	—	—	—	—	—	—	—
Ohio	44.1	50.4	5.5	46.7	46.3	53.4	0.3	46.4
Oklahoma	—	—	—	—	—	—	—	—
Oregon	—	—	—	—	50.1[1]	49.9[1]	0.0[1]	50.1[1]
Pennsylvania	50.2	47.9	1.9	51.2	37.4	0.0	62.6	100.0
Pennsylvania	—	—	—	—	*47.4*	*0.0*	*52.6*	*100.0*
Rhode Island	35.8[1]	64.2[1]	0.0[1]	35.8[1]	25.7[1]	43.9[1]	30.4[1]	37.0[1]
Rhode Island	—	—	—	—	*25.7[1]*	*74.3[1]*	*0.0[1]*	*25.7[1]*
South Carolina	97.3[2]	0.0[2]	2.7[2]	100.0[2]	59.4[2]	0.0[2]	40.6[2]	100.0[2]
South Dakota	—	—	—	—	—	—	—	—
Tennessee	56.9[1]	0.0[1]	43.1[1]	100.0[1]	50.1[1]	0.0[1]	49.9[1]	100.0[1]
Tennessee	—	—	—	—	*54.4[1]*	*0.0[1]*	*45.6[1]*	*100.0[1]*
Texas	71.2[1]	0.0[1]	28.8[1]	100.0[1]	67.1[1]	0.0[1]	32.9[1]	100.0[1]
Texas	—	—	—	—	*95.1[1]*	*0.0[1]*	*4.9[1]*	*100.0[1]*
Utah	—	—	—	—	—	—	—	—
Vermont	21.5	77.6	0.9	21.7	29.0	71.0	0.0	29.0
Virginia	61.9[1,2]	0.0[1,2]	38.1[1,2]	100.0[1,2]	50.2[1,2]	0.0[1,2]	49.8[1,2]	100.0[1,2]
Virginia	—	—	—	—	*84.3[1,2]*	*0.0[1,2]*	*15.7[1,2]*	*100.0[1,2]*
Washington	—	—	—	—	—	—	—	—
West Virginia	—	—	—	—	—	—	—	—
Wisconsin	44.7	55.3	0.0	44.7	47.4	52.6	0.0	47.4
Wyoming	—	—	—	—	—	—	—	—

Notes: Main entries are calculated from the raw vote values in table series 5-70 to 5-122 for the appropriate years based on candidates who used the sole designation "Democrat" or "Republican" (or their historical antecedents listed in Appendix A) on the ballot. In general, historical antecedents to the Democratic Party were Anti-Federalists, Democratic-Republicans, and Jacksonian Democrats; historical precursors of the Republican party were Federalists, National Republicans, and Whigs. Other = candidates who used third-party names on the ballot or were listed as independent, unidentified, or scatter vote. Bold italicized entries in the table are the author's alternative party coding, which is used when a candidate listed a major party name (Democrat, Republican, or their historical antecedents) on the ballot with other party names or labels. These values are computed from the bold italicized raw vote values in table series 5-70 to 5-122 for the appropriate states and years. For a more detailed explanation of this alternate coding system, see Tables 5-1 and 1-3. —indicates that the state had no data, either because no vote data were found for the state in question or the state had not yet entered the Union. No special House elections are included in the table. The table only lists at-large vote values for states having both at-large and district House races; see Appendix B for these states' district results aggregated to the state level.

[1]Election held in odd-numbered year.
[2]Partial data (less than 100% of the districts reporting).

Sources: Adapted from *United States Congressional Elections, 1788–1997* (1998), *Congressional Quarterly's Guide to U.S. Elections* (1994), ICPSR data sets 0001 and 0075, independent search for state sources by the author, and personal communications with Michael J. Dubin (various dates).

Table 5-35 House Election Results, by State, 1860–1863 (Percentages)

	1860–1861				1862–1863			
State	Democratic	Republican	Other	Democratic % of Two-Party Vote	Democratic	Republican	Other	Democratic % of Two-Party Vote
Alabama	—	—	—	—	—	—	—	—
Alaska	—	—	—	—	—	—	—	—
Arizona	—	—	—	—	—	—	—	—
Arkansas	54.9	0.0	45.1	100.0	—	—	—	—
California	0.0[1]	43.5[1]	56.5[1]	0.0[1]	40.3[1]	59.7[1]	0.0[1]	40.3[1]
California	*56.5[1]*	*43.5[1]*	*0.0[1]*	*56.5[1]*				
Colorado	—	—	—	—	—	—	—	—
Connecticut	49.3[1]	50.7[1]	0.0[1]	49.3[1]	48.6[1]	51.4[1]	0.0[1]	48.6[1]
Delaware	4.8	0.0	95.2	100.0	50.1	49.9	0.0	50.1
Delaware	*51.6*	*0.0*	*48.4*	*100.0*				
Florida	59.9	0.0	40.1	100.0	—	—	—	—
Georgia	—	—	—	—	—	—	—	—
Hawaii	—	—	—	—	—	—	—	—
Idaho	—	—	—	—	—	—	—	—
Illinois	48.1	51.8	0.0	48.1	53.2	46.8	0.0	53.2
Indiana	47.4	52.5	0.1	47.5	52.3	47.7	0.0	52.3
Iowa	44.8	55.2	0.0	44.8	42.9	57.1	0.0	42.9
Kansas	—	—	—	—	6.1	93.9	0.0	6.1
Kentucky	0.0[1]	71.0[1]	29.0[1]	0.0[1]	17.8[1]	0.0[1]	82.2[1]	100.0[1]
Kentucky	—	—	—	—	*99.8[1]*	*0.0[1]*	*0.2[1]*	*100.0[1]*
Louisiana	—	—	—	—	—	—	—	—
Maine	42.8	56.2	1.0	43.3	42.1	54.9	3.0	43.4
Maine	—	—	—	—	*43.6*	*54.9*	*1.5*	*44.3*
Maryland	0.0[1]	63.1[1]	36.9[1]	0.0[1]	20.7[1]	74.6[1]	4.7[1]	21.7[1]
Maryland	*0.0[1]*	*75.7[1]*	*24.3[1]*	*0.0[1]*				
Massachusetts	7.4	61.8	30.8	10.7	2.1	63.5	34.4	3.1
Massachusetts	*29.7*	*61.8*	*8.5*	*32.5*	—	—	—	—
Michigan	42.8	57.0	0.2	42.8	47.4	52.6	0.0	47.4
Minnesota	34.5	63.3	2.2	35.3	41.7	58.3	0.0	41.7
Minnesota	*36.7*	*63.3*	*0.0*	*36.7*				
Mississippi	—	—	—	—	—	—	—	—
Missouri	55.4	7.3	37.2	88.3	43.0	48.5	8.5	47.0
Missouri	—	—	—	—	*48.2*	*48.5*	*3.3*	*49.8*
Montana	—	—	—	—	—	—	—	—
Nebraska	—	—	—	—	—	—	—	—
Nevada	—	—	—	—	—	—	—	—
New Hampshire	46.8[1]	53.2[1]	0.0[1]	46.8[1]	49.6[1]	50.4[1]	0.0[1]	49.6[1]
New Jersey	50.4	49.6	0.0	50.4	56.3	43.7	0.0	56.3
New Mexico	—	—	—	—	—	—	—	—
New York	43.3	53.6	3.2	44.7	50.2	49.2	0.6	50.5
New York	*46.4*	*53.6*	*0.0*	*46.4*	—	—	—	—
North Carolina	—	—	—	—	—	—	—	—
North Dakota	—	—	—	—	—	—	—	—
Ohio	45.1	53.3	1.5	45.8	50.3	48.1	1.6	51.1
Ohio	—	—	—	—	*50.3*	*49.7*	*0.0*	*50.3*
Oklahoma	—	—	—	—	—	—	—	—
Oregon	99.5	0.0	0.5	100.0	34.8	65.2	0.0	34.8
Pennsylvania	43.5	54.2	2.2	44.5	53.2	46.8	0.0	53.2
Pennsylvania	*44.2*	*54.2*	*1.6*	*44.9*	—	—	—	—
Rhode Island	0.0[1]	100.0[1]	0.0[1]	0.0[1]	42.1[1]	57.9[1]	0.0[1]	42.1[1]
South Carolina	—	—	—	—	—	—	—	—
South Dakota	—	—	—	—	—	—	—	—
Tennessee	—	—	—	—	—	—	—	—
Texas	—	—	—	—	—	—	—	—
Utah	—	—	—	—	—	—	—	—
Vermont	22.0	73.8	4.3	22.9	28.1[1]	71.9[1]	0.0[1]	28.1[1]
Vermont	*26.2*	*73.8*	*0.0*	*26.2*	—	—	—	—
Virginia	—	—	—	—	—	—	—	—
Washington	—	—	—	—	—	—	—	—
West Virginia	—	—	—	—	0.0[1]	100.0[1]	0.0[1]	0.0[1]
Wisconsin	43.1	56.9	0.0	43.1	50.9	49.1	0.0	50.9
Wyoming	—	—	—	—	—	—	—	—

Notes: Main entries are calculated from the raw vote values in table series 5-70 to 5-122 for the appropriate years based on candidates who used the sole designation "Democrat" or "Republican" (or their historical antecedents listed in Appendix A) on the ballot. In general, historical antecedents to the Democratic Party were Anti-Federalists, Democratic-Republicans, and Jacksonian Democrats; historical precursors of the Republican party were Federalists, National Republicans, and Whigs. Other = candidates who used third-party names on the ballot or were listed as independent, unidentified, or scatter vote. Bold italicized entries in the table are the author's alternative party coding, which is used when a candidate listed a major party name (Democrat, Republican, or their historical antecedents) on the ballot with other party names or labels. These values are computed from the bold italicized raw vote values in table series 5-70 to 5-122 for the appropriate states and years. For a more detailed explanation of this alternate coding system, see Tables 5-1 and 1-3. —indicates that the state had no data, either because no vote data were found for the state in question or the state had not yet entered the Union. No special House elections are included in the table. The table only lists at-large vote values for states having both at-large and district House races; see Appendix B for these states' district results aggregated to the state level.

[1]Election held in odd-numbered year.

Sources: Adapted from *United States Congressional Elections, 1788–1997* (1998), *Congressional Quarterly's Guide to U.S. Elections* (1994), ICPSR data sets 0001 and 0075, independent search for state sources by the author, and personal communications with Michael J. Dubin (various dates).

Table 5-36 House Election Results, by State, 1864–1867 (Percentages)

State	1864–1865				1866–1867			
	Democratic	Republican	Other	Democratic % of Two-Party Vote	Democratic	Republican	Other	Democratic % of Two-Party Vote
Alabama	—	—	—	—	—	—	—	—
Alaska	—	—	—	—	—	—	—	—
Arizona	—	—	—	—	—	—	—	—
Arkansas	—	—	—	—	—	—	—	—
California	41.0	59.0	0.0	41.0	52.1[1]	47.9[1]	0.0[1]	52.1[1]
Colorado	—	—	—	—	—	—	—	—
Connecticut	42.4[1]	57.6[1]	0.0[1]	42.4[1]	50.7[1]	49.3[1]	0.0[1]	50.7[1]
Delaware	51.5	48.5	0.0	51.5	53.7	46.3	0.0	53.7
Florida	—	—	—	—	—	—	—	—
Georgia	—	—	—	—	—	—	—	—
Hawaii	—	—	—	—	—	—	—	—
Idaho	—	—	—	—	—	—	—	—
Illinois	45.5	54.5	0.0	45.5	42.1	57.9	0.0	42.1
Indiana	47.1	52.9	0.0	47.1	48.1	51.9	0.0	48.1
Iowa	35.7	64.3	0.0	35.7	38.2	61.5	0.3	38.3
Kansas	0.0	100.0	0.0	0.0	0.0	70.1	29.9	0.0
Kentucky	0.0[1]	0.0[1]	100.0[1]	—	68.7[1]	25.6[1]	5.7[1]	72.9[1]
Louisiana	—	—	—	—	—	—	—	—
Maine	41.6	58.4	0.0	41.6	37.8	62.2	0.0	37.8
Maryland	44.1	55.9	0.0	44.1	62.0	38.0	0.0	62.0
Massachusetts	27.8	72.2	0.0	27.8	22.9	76.8	0.4	22.9
Michigan	44.5	55.5	0.0	44.5	41.0	59.0	0.0	41.0
Minnesota	41.1	58.9	0.0	41.1	37.8	62.2	0.0	37.8
Mississippi	—	—	—	—	—	—	—	—
Missouri	27.2	67.0	5.9	28.9	0.0	59.0	41.0	0.0
Missouri	*27.9*	*72.1*	*0.0*	*27.9*	*41.0*	*59.0*	*0.0*	*41.0*
Montana	—	—	—	—	—	—	—	—
Nebraska	—	—	—	—	45.6	54.0	0.3	45.8
Nevada	40.1	59.9	0.0	40.1	45.4	54.6	0.0	45.4
New Hampshire	45.5[1]	53.7[1]	0.8[1]	45.9[1]	47.8[1]	52.2[1]	0.0[1]	47.8[1]
New Jersey	52.3	47.7	0.0	52.3	49.3	50.5	0.1	49.4
New Mexico	—	—	—	—	—	—	—	—
New York	41.2	50.4	8.4	45.0	44.3	51.5	4.2	46.2
New York	*49.5*	*50.4*	*0.0*	*49.5*	*45.3*	*54.7*	*0.0*	*45.3*
North Carolina	—	—	—	—	—	—	—	—
North Dakota	—	—	—	—	—	—	—	—
Ohio	43.8	56.2	0.0	43.8	45.8	54.2	0.0	45.8
Oklahoma	—	—	—	—	—	—	—	—
Oregon	40.9	59.1	0.0	40.9	48.6	51.4	0.0	48.6
Pennsylvania	48.6	49.3	2.1	49.7	49.1	50.9	0.0	49.1
Pennsylvania	*50.7*	*49.3*	*0.0*	*50.7*	—	—	—	—
Rhode Island	13.2[1]	86.2[1]	0.5[1]	13.3[1]	17.3[1]	81.5[1]	1.2[1]	17.5[1]
South Carolina	—	—	—	—	—	—	—	—
South Dakota	—	—	—	—	—	—	—	—
Tennessee	0.0[1]	41.0[1]	59.0[1]	0.0[1]	0.0[1]	76.1[1]	23.9[1]	0.0[1]
Tennessee	—	—	—	—	*0.0[1]*	*76.6[1]*	*23.4[1]*	*0.0[1]*
Texas	—	—	—	—	—	—	—	—
Utah	—	—	—	—	—	—	—	—
Vermont	27.4	72.6	0.0	27.4	23.8	76.2	0.0	23.8
Virginia	—	—	—	—	—	—	—	—
Washington	—	—	—	—	—	—	—	—
West Virginia	0.0	70.0	30.0	0.0	42.0	58.0	0.0	42.0
Wisconsin	44.2	55.8	0.0	44.2	41.3	58.7	0.0	41.3
Wyoming	—	—	—	—	—	—	—	—
Nevada	37.5[2]	62.5[2]	0.0[2]	37.5[2]	—	—	—	—

Notes: Main entries are calculated from the raw vote values in table series 5-70 to 5-122 for the appropriate years based on candidates who used the sole designation "Democrat" or "Republican" (or their historical antecedents listed in Appendix A) on the ballot. In general, historical antecedents to the Democratic Party were Anti-Federalists, Democratic-Republicans, and Jacksonian Democrats; historical precursors of the Republican party were Federalists, National Republicans, and Whigs. Other = candidates who used third-party names on the ballot or were listed as independent, unidentified, or scatter vote. Bold italicized entries in the table are the author's alternative party coding, which is used when a candidate listed a major party name (Democrat, Republican, or their historical antecedents) on the ballot with other party names or labels. These values are computed from the bold italicized raw vote values in table series 5-70 to 5-122 for the appropriate states and years. For a more detailed explanation of this alternate coding system, see Tables 5-1 and 1-3. —indicates that the state had no data, either because no vote data were found for the state in question or the state had not yet entered the Union. No special House elections are included in the table. The table only lists at-large vote values for states having both at-large and district House races; see Appendix B for these states' district results aggregated to the state level.

[1]Election held in odd-numbered year.
[2]1865 election when a state had annual elections in both 1864 and 1865.

Sources: Adapted from *United States Congressional Elections, 1788–1997* (1998), *Congressional Quarterly's Guide to U.S. Elections* (1994), ICPSR data sets 0001 and 0075, independent search for state sources by the author, and personal communications with Michael J. Dubin (various dates).

Table 5-37 House Election Results, by State, 1868–1871 (Percentages)

	1868–1869				1870–1871			
State	Democratic	Republican	Other	Democratic % of Two-Party Vote	Democratic	Republican	Other	Democratic % of Two-Party Vote
Alabama	0.0	91.7	8.3	0.0	51.3	48.7	0.0	51.3
Alaska	—	—	—	—	—	—	—	—
Arizona	—	—	—	—	—	—	—	—
Arkansas	46.4	53.6	0.0	46.4	48.3	51.7	0.0	48.3
California	50.3	49.7	0.0	50.3	47.7[1]	52.3[1]	0.0[1]	47.7[1]
Colorado	—	—	—	—	—	—	—	—
Connecticut	48.7[1]	51.3[1]	0.0[1]	48.7[1]	49.7[1]	50.3[1]	0.0[1]	49.7[1]
Delaware	58.9	41.1	0.0	58.9	55.4	44.6	0.0	55.4
Florida	38.5	56.4	5.1	40.6	48.7	51.3	0.0	48.7
Georgia	44.0	56.0	0.0	44.0	56.3	42.0	1.8	57.3
Georgia	—	—	—	—	*56.7*	*43.3*	*0.0*	*56.7*
Hawaii	—	—	—	—	—	—	—	—
Idaho	—	—	—	—	—	—	—	—
Illinois	44.5	55.5	0.0	44.5	45.8	53.3	0.9	46.2
Indiana	50.1	49.9	0.0	50.1	50.1	49.1	0.9	50.5
Indiana	—	—	—	—	*50.9*	*49.1*	*0.0*	*50.9*
Iowa	39.3	60.7	0.1	39.3	39.2	60.8	0.0	39.2
Kansas	32.3	67.7	0.0	32.3	34.2	65.8	0.0	34.2
Kentucky	75.6	24.2	0.2	75.7	60.1	38.9	0.9	60.7
Kentucky	—	—	—	—	*61.1*	*38.9*	*0.0*	*61.1*
Louisiana	61.0	39.0	0.0	61.0	36.7	63.3	0.0	36.7
Maine	42.9	57.1	0.0	42.9	44.8	54.9	0.3	45.0
Maryland	67.2	32.8	0.0	67.2	57.0	43.0	0.0	57.0
Massachusetts	31.0	68.1	0.9	31.3	36.1	57.1	6.9	38.7
Massachusetts	*31.0*	*69.0*	*0.0*	*31.0*	—	—	—	—
Michigan	44.0	56.0	0.0	44.0	46.5	52.4	1.2	47.0
Minnesota	39.3	44.9	15.7	46.7	44.4	55.6	0.0	44.4
Minnesota	*39.3*	*60.7*	*0.0*	*39.3*				
Mississippi	31.3[1]	65.3[1]	3.4[1]	32.4[1]	—	—	—	—
Missouri	43.1	56.9	0.0	43.1	36.0	34.0	30.0	51.5
Montana	—	—	—	—	—	—	—	—
Nebraska	42.0	58.0	0.0	42.0	39.2	60.8	0.0	39.2
Nevada	46.2	53.8	0.0	46.2	51.2	48.8	0.0	51.2
New Hampshire	47.0[1]	53.0[1]	0.0[1]	47.0[1]	50.5[1]	48.6[1]	0.9[1]	51.0[1]
New Jersey	51.1	48.9	0.0	51.1	48.5	51.1	0.4	48.7
New Jersey	—	—	—	—	*48.9*	*51.1*	*0.0*	*48.9*
New Mexico	—	—	—	—	—	—	—	—
New York	50.4	49.1	0.5	50.7	49.5	45.8	4.7	51.9
New York	*50.6*	*49.1*	*0.3*	*50.8*	*51.8*	*47.8*	*0.4*	*52.0*
North Carolina	0.0[2]	53.6[2]	46.4[2]	0.0[2]	0.0[2]	47.8[2]	52.2[2]	0.0[2]
North Dakota	—	—	—	—	—	—	—	—
Ohio	48.7	51.3	0.0	48.7	48.2	51.4	0.4	48.4
Oklahoma	—	—	—	—	—	—	—	—
Oregon	32.6	67.4	0.0	32.6	50.8	49.2	0.0	50.8
Pennsylvania	49.4	50.6	0.0	49.4	47.9	49.3	2.8	49.3
Pennsylvania	—	—	—	—	*47.9*	*51.7*	*0.4*	*48.1*
Rhode Island	34.7	65.3	0.0	34.7	19.1	78.7	2.2	19.5
South Carolina	42.1	57.6	0.3	42.2	32.4	61.7	5.8	34.5
South Carolina	—	—	—	—	*32.4*	*66.5*	*1.1*	*32.8*
South Dakota	—	—	—	—	—	—	—	—
Tennessee	0.0	100.0	0.0	0.0	61.8	31.4	6.8	66.3
Tennessee	—	—	—	—	*64.7*	*35.3*	*0.0*	*64.7*
Texas	41.5[1]	58.0[1]	0.5[1]	41.7[1]	58.6[1]	41.0[1]	0.4[1]	58.8[1]
Utah	—	—	—	—	—	—	—	—
Vermont	25.5	74.5	0.0	25.5	23.7	76.3	0.0	23.7
Virginia	0.0[1]	46.1[1]	53.9[1]	0.0[1]	—	—	—	—
Washington	—	—	—	—	—	—	—	—
West Virginia	45.0	55.0	0.0	45.0	51.5	48.5	0.0	51.5
Wisconsin	44.3	55.7	0.0	44.3	48.0	52.0	0.0	48.0
Wyoming	—	—	—	—	—	—	—	—
Alabama	42.0[3]	55.6[3]	2.4[3]	43.0[3]	—	—	—	—
Alabama	*42.0[3]*	*58.0[3]*	*0.0[3]*	*42.0[3]*	—	—	—	—

Notes: Main entries are calculated from the raw vote values in table series 5-70 to 5-122 for the appropriate years based on candidates who used the sole designation "Democrat" or "Republican" (or their historical antecedents listed in Appendix A) on the ballot. In general, historical antecedents to the Democratic Party were Anti-Federalists, Democratic-Republicans, and Jacksonian Democrats; historical precursors of the Republican party were Federalists, National Republicans, and Whigs. Other = candidates who used third-party names on the ballot or were listed as independent, unidentified, or scatter vote. Bold italicized entries in the table are the author's alternative party coding, which is used when a candidate listed a major party name (Democrat, Republican, or their historical antecedents) on the ballot with other party names or labels. These values are computed from the bold italicized raw vote values in table series 5-70 to 5-122 for the appropriate states and years. For a more detailed explanation of this alternate coding system, see Tables 5-1 and 1-3. —indicates that the state had no data, either because no vote data were found for the state in question or the state had not yet entered the Union. No special House elections are included in the table. The table only lists at-large vote values for states having both at-large and district House races; see Appendix B for these states' district results aggregated to the state level.

[1] Election held in odd-numbered year.
[2] Partial data (less than 100% of the districts reporting).
[3] 1869 election when a state had annual elections in both 1868 and 1869.

Sources: Adapted from *United States Congressional Elections, 1788–1997* (1998), *Congressional Quarterly's Guide to U.S. Elections* (1994), ICPSR data sets 0001 and 0075, independent search for state sources by the author, and personal communications with Michael J. Dubin (various dates).

Table 5-38 House Election Results, by State, 1872–1875 (Percentages)

State	1872–1873				1874–1875			
	Democratic	Republican	Other	Democratic % of Two-Party Vote	Democratic	Republican	Other	Democratic % of Two-Party Vote
Alabama	47.7	52.3	0.0	47.7	54.1	45.9	0.0	54.1
Alaska	—	—	—	—	—	—	—	—
Arizona	—	—	—	—	—	—	—	—
Arkansas	50.2	49.8	0.0	50.2	64.4	35.6	0.0	64.4
California	48.7	51.3	0.0	48.7	48.0[1]	32.5[1]	19.5[1]	59.6[1]
Colorado	—	—	—	—	—	—	—	—
Connecticut	48.1[1]	50.2[1]	1.7[1]	48.9[1]	50.9[1]	47.1[1]	2.0[1]	51.9[1]
Delaware	—	—	—	—	53.3	46.7	0.0	53.3
Florida	0.0	52.5	47.5	0.0	47.9	52.1	0.0	47.9
Georgia	56.9	42.2	0.9	57.4	67.8	25.4	6.8	72.7
Georgia	*57.8*	*42.2*	*0.0*	*57.8*	*73.8*	*26.2*	*0.1*	*73.8*
Hawaii	—	—	—	—	—	—	—	—
Idaho	—	—	—	—	—	—	—	—
Illinois	44.6	55.2	0.1	44.7	49.5	46.2	4.3	51.7
Illinois	—	—	—	—	*49.5*	*46.9*	*3.6*	*51.4*
Indiana	50.0	50.0	0.0	50.0	50.6	46.7	2.7	52.0
Indiana	—	—	—	—	*50.6*	*46.7*	*2.7*	*52.0*
Iowa	38.5	61.4	0.0	38.5	0.0	56.8	43.2	0.0
Kansas	33.8	66.2	0.0	33.8	12.9	56.1	31.0	18.7
Kentucky	65.6	27.5	6.9	70.5	61.3	21.4	17.3	74.1
Kentucky	*65.6*	*30.7*	*3.7*	*68.2*	*65.9*	*22.4*	*11.7*	*74.6*
Louisiana	46.2	53.8	0.0	46.2	52.7	47.3	0.0	52.7
Maine	42.9	57.1	0.0	42.9	43.5	56.3	0.2	43.6
Maryland	50.3	49.7	0.0	50.3	55.8	44.2	0.0	55.8
Massachusetts	31.7	68.3	0.0	31.7	40.1	48.1	11.8	45.4
Michigan	38.7	60.9	0.4	38.8	41.0	51.6	7.3	44.3
Michigan	*38.7*	*60.9*	*0.3*	*38.9*	*47.2*	*51.6*	*1.2*	*47.7*
Minnesota	38.3	61.7	0.0	38.3	47.0	53.0	0.0	47.0
Mississippi	32.9	64.8	2.3	33.6	53.1[1]	34.7[1]	12.2[1]	60.5[1]
Mississippi	—	—	—	—	*53.1[1]*	*46.9[1]*	*0.0[1]*	*53.1[1]*
Missouri	56.4	42.9	0.6	56.8	64.5	25.8	9.7	71.5
Missouri	*57.0[1]*	*42.9[1]*	*0.0[1]*	*57.0[1]*	—	—	—	—
Montana	—	—	—	—	—	—	—	—
Nebraska	37.8	62.2	0.0	37.8	23.3	62.7	14.0	27.1
Nevada	52.3	47.7	0.0	52.3	48.3	51.7	0.0	48.3
New Hampshire	49.1[1]	49.2[1]	1.7[1]	50.0[1]	49.8[1]	49.4[1]	0.8[1]	50.2[1]
New Jersey	44.7	55.3	0.0	44.7	52.7	47.3	0.0	52.7
New Mexico	—	—	—	—	51.2	44.2	4.6	53.6
New York	47.8	52.2	0.0	47.8	53.8	45.4	0.8	54.2
New York	—	—	—	—	*53.8*	*45.4*	*0.8*	*54.2*
North Carolina	49.1	50.9	0.0	49.1	53.6	38.9	7.5	57.9
North Dakota	—	—	—	—	—	—	—	—
Ohio	50.8	48.9	0.2	50.9	51.5	46.4	2.1	52.6
Ohio	*50.9*	*48.9*	*0.2*	*51.0*	*51.5*	*47.1*	*1.4*	*52.2*
Oklahoma	—	—	—	—	—	—	—	—
Oregon	48.3	51.7	0.0	48.3	38.1	36.9	25.1	50.8
Pennsylvania	46.3	53.5	0.1	46.4	50.3	43.5	6.2	53.6
Pennsylvania	—	—	—	—	*50.3*	*45.0*	*4.7*	*52.8*
Rhode Island	29.8	70.2	0.0	29.8	30.9	69.1	0.0	30.9
South Carolina	0.0	71.2	28.8	0.0	19.3	56.1	24.6	25.7
South Carolina	*0.0*	*99.1*	*0.9*	*0.0*	*19.3*	*77.5*	*3.2*	*20.0*
South Dakota	—	—	—	—	—	—	—	—
Tennessee	35.4	43.9	20.6	44.6	66.4	32.8	0.9	67.0
Tennessee	—	—	—	—	*66.4*	*33.4*	*0.3*	*66.5*
Texas	59.4	40.6	0.0	59.4	78.8	20.7	0.5	79.2
Utah	—	—	—	—	—	—	—	—
Vermont	13.8	80.2	6.0	14.7	19.5	58.2	22.2	25.1
Vermont	—	—	—	—	*19.5*	*80.5*	*0.0*	*19.5*
Virginia	0.0	41.1	58.9	0.0	52.7	43.1	4.2	55.0
Virginia	—	—	—	—	*56.5*	*43.4*	*0.1*	*56.6*
Washington	—	—	—	—	—	—	—	—
West Virginia	25.9	43.5	30.5	37.4	56.7	42.6	0.7	57.1
West Virginia	*55.7*	*43.5*	*0.8*	*56.1*	—	—	—	—
Wisconsin	45.6	54.4	0.0	45.6	0.0	49.9	50.1	0.0
Wisconsin	—	—	—	—	*50.1*	*49.9*	*0.0*	*50.1*
Wyoming	—	—	—	—	—	—	—	—

Notes: Main entries are calculated from the raw vote values in tables series 5-70 to 5-122 for the appropriate years based on candidates who used the sole designation "Democrat" or "Republican" (or their historical antecedents listed in Appendix A) on the ballot. Other = candidates who used third-party names on the ballot or were listed as independent, unidentified, or scatter vote. Bold italicized entries in the table are the author's alternative party coding, which is used when a candidate listed a major party name (Democrat, Republican, or their historical antecedents) on the ballot with other party names or labels. These values are computed from the bold italicized raw vote values in table series 5-70 to 5-122 for the appropriate states and years. For a more detailed explanation of this alternate coding system, see Tables 5-1 and 1-3. —indicates that the state had no data, either because no vote data were found for the state in question or the state had not yet entered the Union. No special House elections are included in the table. The table only lists at-large vote values for states having both at-large and district House races; see Appendix B for these states' district results aggregated to the state level.

[1]Election held in odd-numbered year.

Sources: Adapted from *United States Congressional Elections, 1788–1997* (1998), *Congressional Quarterly's Guide to U.S. Elections* (1994), ICPSR data sets 0001 and 0075, and independent search for state sources by the author.

Table 5-39 House Election Results, by State, 1876–1879 (Percentages)

	1876–1877				1878–1879			
State	Democratic	Republican	Other	Democratic % of Two-Party Vote	Democratic	Republican	Other	Democratic % of Two-Party Vote
Alabama	64.7	19.5	15.8	76.8	62.1	14.9	23.0	80.6
Alabama	*75.9*	*24.1*	*0.0*	*75.9*				
Alaska	—	—	—	—	—	—	—	—
Arizona	—	—	—	—	—	—	—	—
Arkansas	58.1	30.8	11.2	65.4	57.4	27.2	15.4	67.8
Arkansas	*67.7*	*31.0*	*1.3*	*68.6*	*60.8*	*27.2*	*12.0*	*69.1*
California	47.8	52.2	0.0	47.8	30.6[1]	47.6[1]	21.8[1]	39.1[1]
Colorado	48.4	51.6	0.0	48.4	41.9	49.9	8.1	45.6
Connecticut	50.9	48.6	0.5	51.2	46.9	49.6	3.5	48.6
Delaware	54.9	44.1	1.0	55.4	78.1	0.0	21.9	100.0
Florida	50.6	49.4	0.0	50.6	53.5	45.3	1.2	54.1
Florida	—	—	—	—	*53.5*	*46.5*	*0.0*	*53.5*
Georgia	69.8	22.3	7.9	75.8	55.6	6.9	37.5	88.9
Georgia	*77.5*	*22.3*	*0.2*	*77.6*	*86.2*	*6.9*	*6.9*	*92.6*
Hawaii								
Idaho	—	—	—	—	—	—	—	—
Illinois	48.4	48.8	2.8	49.8	38.7	43.2	18.1	47.2
Illinois	*48.4*	*49.9*	*1.7*	*49.2*	—	—	—	—
Indiana	49.2	47.8	2.9	50.7	43.1	42.0	14.9	50.6
Indiana					*47.7*	*44.4*	*8.0*	*51.8*
Iowa	40.5	57.6	1.9	41.3	21.1	50.6	28.3	29.4
Iowa					*33.7*	*50.6*	*15.6*	*40.0*
Kansas	12.8	62.9	24.2	17.0	26.4	54.2	19.4	32.7
Kentucky	59.7	37.1	3.3	61.7	58.7	31.7	9.6	65.0
Kentucky	*62.6*	*37.1*	*0.3*	*62.8*	*63.0*	*31.7*	*5.3*	*66.5*
Louisiana	52.5	47.5	0.0	52.5	66.9	18.7	14.4	78.1
Louisiana					*70.0*	*18.7*	*11.3*	*78.9*
Maine	44.5	55.0	0.4	44.7	16.7	45.2	38.1	26.9
Maine	—	—	—	—	*27.0*	*45.2*	*27.7*	*37.4*
Maryland	55.3	44.7	0.0	55.3	55.8	33.6	10.6	62.5
Maryland	—	—	—	—	*59.1*	*33.6*	*7.3*	*63.8*
Massachusetts	43.3	55.9	0.8	43.6	28.0	53.9	18.1	34.2
Massachusetts	*43.3*	*56.7*	*0.0*	*43.3*	*35.5*	*53.9*	*10.6*	*39.7*
Michigan	31.4	52.3	16.3	37.5	27.6	45.0	27.4	38.0
Michigan	*46.4*	*52.3*	*1.3*	*47.0*	—	—	—	—
Minnesota	42.0	55.6	2.3	43.0	14.4	53.2	32.4	21.3
Minnesota	—	—	—	—	*45.2*	*53.2*	*1.6*	*45.9*
Mississippi	69.1	30.9	0.0	69.1	70.7	16.0	13.4	81.6
Missouri	59.6	39.1	1.3	60.4	51.9	16.8	31.3	75.5
Missouri	*59.6*	*39.6*	*0.7*	*60.1*	*54.9*	*19.5*	*25.6*	*73.8*
Montana	—	—	—	—				
Nebraska	33.3	59.8	6.9	35.8	0.0	56.6	43.4	0.0
Nebraska	—	—	—	—	*43.4*	*56.6*	*0.0*	*43.4*
Nevada	47.7	52.3	0.0	47.7	48.1	51.9	0.0	48.1
New Hampshire	48.6[1]	51.1[1]	0.3[1]	48.8[1]	41.6	50.6	7.8	45.2
New Jersey	52.5	41.8	5.7	55.7	33.4	46.2	20.4	41.9
New Jersey	*58.0*	*41.8*	*0.2*	*58.1*	*40.9*	*46.2*	*12.9*	*46.9*
New Mexico	—	—	—	—	—	—	—	—
New York	50.0	47.5	2.5	51.3	29.8	45.7	24.5	39.5
New York	*51.3*	*48.3*	*0.4*	*51.5*	*43.8*	*47.4*	*8.7*	*48.0*
North Carolina	53.8	46.2	0	53.8	52.6	21.0	26.5	71.5
North Carolina	—	—	—	—	*52.6*	*46.6*	*0.8*	*53.0*
North Dakota								
Ohio	49.1	50.0	0.9	49.6	45.5	47.4	7.1	49.0
Oklahoma	—	—	—	—	—	—	—	—
Oregon	48.1	51.9	0.0	48.1	49.9	46.5	3.5	51.8
Pennsylvania	49.0	50.4	0.6	49.3	38.6	39.4	22.0	49.5
Pennsylvania	—	—	—	—	*40.3*	*45.0*	*14.7*	*47.3*
Rhode Island	39.7	60.1	0.2	39.8	32.1	63.1	4.8	33.7
South Carolina	50.1	49.9	0.0	50.1	72.2	27.8	0.0	72.2
South Dakota					—	—	—	—
Tennessee	61.6	37.5	0.8	62.2	57.1	23.5	19.3	70.8
Tennessee	*61.6*	*38.4*	*0.0*	*61.6*	*65.0*	*23.5*	*11.5*	*73.4*
Texas	70.6	20.2	9.1	77.7	76.7	0.0	23.3	100.0
Texas	*70.6*	*29.4*	*0.0*	*70.6*	—	—	—	—
Utah	—	—	—	—				
Vermont	30.8	69.2	0.0	30.8	26.1	57.3	16.6	31.3
Vermont	—	—	—	—	*26.1*	*73.9*	*0.0*	*26.1*
Virginia	59.3	40.5	0.2	59.4	53.2	21.5	25.3	71.2
Virginia	*59.3*	*40.7*	*0.0*	*59.3*	*58.5*	*21.5*	*19.9*	*73.1*
Washington	—	—	—	—	—	—	—	—
West Virginia	56.7	43.3	0.0	56.7	53.0	38.2	8.8	58.1
Wisconsin	49.1	50.3	0.6	49.4	45.2	48.5	6.3	48.2
Wyoming	—	—	—	—	—	—	—	—

Notes: Main entries are calculated from the raw vote values in tables series 5-70 to 5-122 for the appropriate years based on candidates who used the sole designation "Democrat" or "Republican" (or their historical antecedents listed in Appendix A) on the ballot or were listed as independent, unidentified, or scatter vote. Other = candidates who used third-party names on the ballot or were listed as independent, unidentified, or scatter vote. Bold italicized entries in the table are the author's alternative party coding, which is used when a candidate listed a major party name (Democrat, Republican, or their historical antecedents) on the ballot with other party names or labels. These values are computed from the bold italicized raw vote values in table series 5-70 to 5-122 for the appropriate states and years. For a more detailed explanation of this alternate coding system, see Tables 5-1 and 1-3. —indicates that the state had no data, either because no vote data were found for the state in question or the state had not yet entered the Union. No special House elections are included in the table. The table only lists at-large vote values for states having both at-large and district House races; see Appendix B for these states' district results aggregated to the state level.

[1]Election held in odd-numbered year.

Sources: Adapted from *United States Congressional Elections, 1788–1997* (1998), *Congressional Quarterly's Guide to U.S. Elections* (1994), ICPSR data sets 0001 and 0075, and independent search for state sources by the author.

Table 5-40 House Election Results, by State, 1880–1882 (Percentages)

	1880				1882			
State	Democratic	Republican	Other	Democratic % of Two-Party Vote	Democratic	Republican	Other	Democratic % of Two-Party Vote
Alabama	64.7	24.0	11.3	72.9	63.5	20.0	16.5	76.1
Alabama	*—*	*—*	*—*	*—*	*68.4*	*29.4*	*2.1*	*69.9*
Alaska	—	—	—	—	—	—	—	—
Arizona	—	—	—	—	—	—	—	—
Arkansas	52.5	38.4	9.1	57.7	67.1	32.9	0.0	67.1
Arkansas	*57.9*	*38.4*	*3.7*	*60.1*	*—*	*—*	*—*	*—*
California	24.0	48.8	27.2	33.0	52.9	44.7	2.4	54.2
California	*48.4*	*48.8*	*2.8*	*49.8*	*—*	*—*	*—*	*—*
Colorado	46.0	50.8	3.2	47.5	47.6	50.5	2.0	48.5
Connecticut	48.1	51.1	0.8	48.5	50.4	48.4	1.2	51.0
Delaware	50.8	48.7	0.4	51.1	53.1	46.9	0.0	53.1
Florida	54.8	45.0	0.2	54.9	50.4	42.1	7.4	54.5
Florida	*—*	*—*	*—*	*—*	*50.4*	*49.6*	*0.0*	*50.4*
Georgia	62.3	17.0	20.7	78.6	76.6	23.4	0.0	76.6
Georgia	*83.0*	*17.0*	*0.0*	*83.0*	*—*	*—*	*—*	*—*
Hawaii	—	—	—	—	—	—	—	—
Idaho	—	—	—	—	—	—	—	—
Illinois	45.0	51.3	3.7	46.8	44.7	44.4	10.9	50.1
Illinois	*—*	*—*	*—*	*—*	*50.7*	*44.4*	*4.9*	*53.3*
Indiana	47.9	48.9	3.2	49.5	50.3	47.2	2.5	51.6
Iowa	26.4	56.7	16.8	31.8	36.0	49.0	15.0	42.3
Iowa	*32.0*	*56.7*	*11.2*	*36.1*	*39.9*	*49.0*	*11.0*	*44.9*
Kansas	31.6	60.0	8.3	34.5	39.7	47.6	12.7	45.5
Kentucky	57.6	38.1	4.3	60.2	53.5	41.5	5.0	56.4
Kentucky	*—*	*—*	*—*	*—*	*58.1*	*41.5*	*0.4*	*58.4*
Louisiana	64.9	35.1	0.0	64.9	62.7	29.4	7.9	68.1
Louisiana	*—*	*—*	*—*	*—*	*62.7*	*37.3*	*0.1*	*62.7*
Maine	0.0	50.2	49.8	0.0	0.0	52.7	47.3	0.0
Maine	*49.6*	*50.2*	*0.2*	*49.7*	*45.9*	*52.9*	*1.2*	*46.4*
Maryland	52.9	46.6	0.5	53.2	51.4	47.4	1.2	52.0
Maryland	*—*	*—*	*—*	*—*	*52.4*	*47.4*	*0.2*	*52.5*
Massachusetts	39.8	58.5	1.6	40.5	37.0	50.8	12.3	42.1
Massachusetts	*—*	*—*	*—*	*—*	*46.7*	*50.8*	*2.5*	*47.9*
Michigan	37.2	52.2	10.6	41.6	0.0	50.4	49.6	0.0
Michigan	*—*	*—*	*—*	*—*	*47.4*	*50.4*	*2.1*	*48.5*
Minnesota	37.5	55.5	7.0	40.3	32.0	55.2	12.8	36.7
Minnesota	*37.5*	*60.6*	*1.9*	*38.2*	*32.0*	*63.6*	*4.4*	*33.5*
Mississippi	66.6	21.3	12.1	75.8	60.6	25.9	13.5	70.0
Mississippi	*66.6*	*26.7*	*6.7*	*71.4*	*61.2*	*25.9*	*12.9*	*70.3*
Missouri	56.7	10.2	33.1	84.8	53.0	31.7	15.3	62.5
Missouri	*57.2*	*35.7*	*7.1*	*61.6*	*58.4*	*33.2*	*8.3*	*63.7*
Montana	—	—	—	—	—	—	—	—
Nebraska	28.0	62.4	9.6	31.0	29.2	46.9	23.9	38.4
Nevada	53.4	46.6	0.0	53.4	54.4	45.6	0.0	54.4
New Hampshire	47.4	51.7	0.8	47.8	45.6	53.5	0.9	46.0
New Jersey	49.8	49.0	1.2	50.4	43.2	47.5	9.3	47.6
New Jersey	*—*	*—*	*—*	*—*	*48.6*	*47.5*	*3.9*	*50.6*
New Mexico	—	—	—	—	—	—	—	—
New York	42.5	49.4	8.1	46.2	54.6	42.7	2.7	56.1
New York	*49.1*	*49.4*	*1.4*	*49.9*	*—*	*—*	*—*	*—*
North Carolina	52.5	43.6	3.9	54.6	50.1	0.0	49.9	100.0
North Dakota	—	—	—	—	—	—	—	—
Ohio	47.9	50.9	1.2	48.5	50.4	47.1	2.5	51.7
Oklahoma	—	—	—	—	—	—	—	—
Oregon	47.8	51.4	0.8	48.2	46.0	54.0	0.0	46.0
Pennsylvania	39.5	51.3	9.2	43.5	47.5	43.6	8.9	52.2
Pennsylvania	*45.0*	*52.7*	*2.3*	*46.0*	*—*	*—*	*—*	*—*
Rhode Island	36.7	62.4	0.9	37.1	32.6	67.4	0.0	32.6
South Carolina	65.6	34.1	0.2	65.8	50.5	22.6	26.9	69.1
South Carolina	*—*	*—*	*—*	*—*	*50.5*	*43.8*	*5.6*	*53.6*
South Dakota	—	—	—	—	—	—	—	—
Tennessee	50.9	44.6	4.5	53.3	51.2	39.4	9.4	56.5
Tennessee	*53.9*	*44.6*	*1.5*	*54.7*	*54.8*	*43.4*	*1.8*	*55.8*
Texas	70.7	0.0	29.3	100.0	64.5	17.3	18.2	78.8
Utah	—	—	—	—	—	—	—	—
Vermont	29.8	67.0	3.2	30.8	26.3	71.1	2.7	27.0
Vermont	*29.8*	*67.8*	*2.4*	*30.5*	*—*	*—*	*—*	*—*
Virginia	49.8	25.3	24.8	66.3	47.4	2.2	50.4	95.6
Washington	—	—	—	—	—	—	—	—
West Virginia	51.4	44.1	4.5	53.8	49.4	45.1	5.5	52.3
Wisconsin	43.8	54.2	2.0	44.7	47.8	41.9	10.3	53.3
Wisconsin	*—*	*—*	*—*	*—*	*47.8*	*43.6*	*8.6*	*52.3*
Wyoming	—	—	—	—	—	—	—	—

Notes: Main entries are calculated from the raw vote values in tables series 5-70 to 5-122 for the appropriate years based on candidates who used the sole designation "Democrat" or "Republican" (or their historical antecedents listed in Appendix A) on the ballot. Other = candidates who used third-party names on the ballot or were listed as independent, unidentified, or scatter vote. Bold italicized entries in the table are the author's alternative party coding, which is used when a candidate listed a major party name (Democrat, Republican, or their historical antecedents) on the ballot with other party names or labels. These values are computed from the bold italicized raw vote values in table series 5-70 to 5-122 for the appropriate states and years. For a more detailed explanation of this alternate coding system, see Tables 5-1 and 1-3. —indicates that the state had no data, either because no vote data were found for the state in question or the state had not yet entered the Union. No special House elections are included in the table. The table only lists at-large vote values for states having both at-large and district House races; see Appendix B for these states' district results aggregated to the state level.

Sources: Adapted from *United States Congressional Elections, 1788–1997* (1998), *Congressional Quarterly's Guide to U.S. Elections* (1994), ICPSR data sets 0001 and 0075, and independent search for state sources by the author.

Table 5-41 House Election Results, by State, 1884–1886 (Percentages)

	1884				1886			
State	Democratic	Republican	Other	Democratic % of Two-Party Vote	Democratic	Republican	Other	Democratic % of Two-Party Vote
Alabama	66.1	32.7	1.2	66.9	71.8	25.3	2.9	73.9
Alabama	*66.1*	*33.2*	*0.7*	*66.5*	*71.8*	*28.2*	*0.0*	*71.8*
Alaska	—	—	—	—	—	—	—	—
Arizona	—	—	—	—	—	—	—	—
Arkansas	59.0	41.0	0.0	59.0	66.1	15.4	18.5	81.1
California	46.5	52.0	1.5	47.2	47.3	40.4	12.3	53.9
California	—	—	—	—	*47.3*	*48.4*	*4.3*	*49.4*
Colorado	43.1	53.2	3.7	44.8	46.2	47.6	6.2	49.3
Connecticut	48.5	48.9	2.6	49.8	47.6	46.5	5.8	50.6
Delaware	57.0	43.0	0.0	57.0	62.2	0.0	37.8	100.0
Florida	53.3	46.4	0.4	53.4	58.6	40.6	0.7	59.0
Florida	*53.3*	*46.7*	*0.0*	*53.3*	—	—	—	—
Georgia	73.0	21.7	5.3	77.1	92.5	0.1	7.4	99.9
Georgia	*77.3*	*22.6*	*0.1*	*77.4*	—	—	—	—
Hawaii	—	—	—	—	—	—	—	—
Idaho	—	—	—	—	—	—	—	—
Illinois	44.1	46.8	9.1	48.5	36.7	49.0	14.3	42.8
Illinois	*46.8*	*51.5*	*1.7*	*47.6*	*42.9*	*49.0*	*8.1*	*46.7*
Indiana	50.5	48.4	1.1	51.1	47.3	47.5	5.2	49.9
Indiana	—	—	—	—	*49.4*	*48.3*	*2.3*	*50.6*
Iowa	39.2	52.4	8.4	42.8	37.5	49.9	12.6	43.0
Iowa	*47.6*	*52.4*	*0.0*	*47.6*	*42.3*	*55.1*	*2.6*	*43.5*
Kansas	37.2	59.8	3.0	38.4	40.3	55.0	4.7	42.3
Kansas	—	—	—	—	*40.3*	*56.4*	*3.3*	*41.6*
Kentucky	58.4	38.4	3.2	60.3	53.3	39.9	6.8	57.2
Kentucky	*61.3*	*38.4*	*0.3*	*61.5*	*57.4*	*39.9*	*2.7*	*59.0*
Louisiana	57.3	33.4	9.4	63.2	74.5	24.5	1.0	75.2
Louisiana	*66.6*	*33.4*	*0.0*	*66.6*	*74.5*	*25.3*	*0.2*	*74.6*
Maine	42.3	55.3	2.5	43.3	41.0	53.9	5.1	43.2
Maryland	52.5	46.9	0.6	52.8	55.7	35.4	8.8	61.2
Maryland	—	—	—	—	*60.7*	*35.4*	*3.9*	*63.2*
Massachusetts	38.2	52.2	9.6	42.3	46.9	49.0	4.1	48.9
Michigan	16.2	47.4	36.4	25.5	45.7	48.3	6.1	48.6
Michigan	*48.0*	*47.4*	*4.6*	*50.3*	—	—	—	—
Minnesota	40.9	57.4	1.7	41.6	37.9	58.5	3.7	39.3
Mississippi	73.4	26.6	0.0	73.4	76.1	23.5	0.4	76.4
Missouri	53.7	45.4	0.8	54.2	52.1	41.2	6.7	55.8
Missouri	—	—	—	—	*56.0*	*41.2*	*2.8*	*57.6*
Montana	—	—	—	—	—	—	—	—
Nebraska	45.3	52.7	2.1	46.2	44.4	48.7	6.8	47.7
Nevada	46.9	53.1	0.0	46.9	45.8	54.2	0.0	45.8
New Hampshire	46.1	51.7	2.2	47.2	47.9	49.3	2.8	49.3
New Jersey	49.1	48.0	3.0	50.6	43.8	44.4	11.8	49.6
New Jersey	—	—	—	—	*45.4*	*44.4*	*10.2*	*50.5*
New Mexico	—	—	—	—	—	—	—	—
New York	45.5	44.7	9.7	50.4	41.2	47.4	11.4	46.5
New York	*51.0*	*46.5*	*2.5*	*52.3*	*48.0*	*47.4*	*4.6*	*50.3*
North Carolina	54.1	45.9	0.0	54.1	54.5	21.1	24.3	72.1
North Carolina	—	—	—	—	*58.1*	*28.5*	*13.4*	*67.1*
North Dakota	—	—	—	—	—	—	—	—
Ohio	48.0	50.5	1.5	48.7	47.0	48.5	4.5	49.2
Oklahoma	—	—	—	—	—	—	—	—
Oregon	47.9	52.1	0.0	47.9	46.7	48.2	5.1	49.2
Pennsylvania	44.6	53.2	2.2	45.6	44.9	50.8	4.3	47.0
Rhode Island	37.1	55.7	7.2	40.0	43.6	47.4	8.9	47.9
South Carolina	75.7	22.7	1.5	76.9	84.6	15.3	0.1	84.7
South Dakota	—	—	—	—	—	—	—	—
Tennessee	52.5	46.6	0.9	53.0	54.0	42.7	3.4	55.8
Tennessee	*53.3*	*46.6*	*0.2*	*53.3*	*57.3*	*42.7*	*0.0*	*57.3*
Texas	82.1	13.7	4.2	85.7	74.1	8.0	17.9	90.3
Texas	—	—	—	—	*74.1*	*11.9*	*14.0*	*86.1*
Utah	—	—	—	—	—	—	—	—
Vermont	27.7	71.6	0.7	27.9	28.6	71.0	0.4	28.7
Virginia	50.8	47.0	2.3	51.9	45.5	45.4	9.1	50.1
Virginia	*50.8*	*49.2*	*0.0*	*50.8*	*50.3*	*45.4*	*4.3*	*52.6*
Washington	—	—	—	—	—	—	—	—
West Virginia	51.4	36.1	12.5	58.7	49.6	49.3	1.1	50.2
West Virginia	*51.4*	*48.6*	*0.0*	*51.4*	—	—	—	—
Wisconsin	46.7	42.7	10.6	52.3	40.4	51.1	8.6	44.2
Wisconsin	*46.7*	*50.4*	*2.9*	*48.1*	—	—	—	—
Wyoming	—	—	—	—	—	—	—	—

Notes: Main entries are calculated from the raw vote values in tables series 5-70 to 5-122 for the appropriate years based on candidates who used the sole designation "Democrat" or "Republican" (or their historical antecedents listed in Appendix A) on the ballot. Other = candidates who used third-party names on the ballot or were listed as independent, unidentified, or scatter vote. Bold italicized entries in the table are the author's alternative party coding, which is used when a candidate listed a major party name (Democrat, Republican, or their historical antecedents) on the ballot with other party names or labels. These values are computed from the bold italicized raw vote values in table series 5-70 to 5-122 for the appropriate states and years. For a more detailed explanation of this alternate coding system, see Tables 5-1 and 1-3. —indicates that the state had no data, either because no vote data were found for the state in question or the state had not yet entered the Union. No special House elections are included in the table. The table only lists at-large vote values for states having both at-large and district House races; see Appendix B for these states' district results aggregated to the state level.

Sources: Adapted from *United States Congressional Elections, 1788–1997* (1998), *Congressional Quarterly's Guide to U.S. Elections* (1994), ICPSR data sets 0001 and 0075, and independent search for state sources by the author.

Table 5-42 House Election Results, by State, 1888–1890 (Percentages)

State	1888–1889				1890			
	Democratic	Republican	Other	Democratic % of Two-Party Vote	Democratic	Republican	Other	Democratic % of Two-Party Vote
Alabama	67.9	31.5	0.6	68.3	69.4	20.6	10.0	77.1
Alaska	—	—	—	—	—	—	—	—
Arizona	—	—	—	—	—	—	—	—
Arkansas	57.3	10.9	31.8	84.0	61.9	6.6	31.5	90.3
Arkansas	—	—	—	—	*61.9*	*24.3*	*13.8*	*71.8*
California	46.6	50.8	2.6	47.8	39.3	50.9	9.8	43.6
California	—	—	—	—	*46.3*	*50.9*	*2.8*	*47.6*
Colorado	41.0	55.0	4.0	42.7	41.3	51.3	7.4	44.6
Connecticut	48.4	48.9	2.7	49.7	50.3	47.2	2.4	51.6
Delaware	55.2	43.5	1.3	55.9	50.6	48.7	0.7	51.0
Florida	59.5	40.5	0.0	59.5	65.8	34.2	0.0	65.8
Georgia	73.9	18.2	7.9	80.3	72.6	15.6	11.7	82.3
Georgia	—	—	—	—	*80.5*	*15.6*	*3.8*	*83.7*
Hawaii	—	—	—	—	—	—	—	—
Idaho	—	—	—	—	44.2	55.8	0.0	44.2
Illinois	43.6	49.9	6.5	46.6	50.6	46.1	3.3	52.4
Illinois	*46.6*	*49.9*	*3.5*	*48.3*	—	—	—	—
Indiana	44.5	49.4	6.1	47.4	50.8	45.9	3.3	52.5
Indiana	*48.5*	*49.4*	*2.1*	*49.6*	—	—	—	—
Iowa	41.5	48.7	9.8	46.0	50.1	47.8	2.2	51.2
Iowa	*45.8*	*52.6*	*1.6*	*46.5*	—	—	—	—
Kansas	31.6	55.6	12.8	36.2	9.3	42.2	48.5	18.0
Kentucky	53.5	45.4	1.2	54.1	64.4	28.9	6.7	69.0
Kentucky	—	—	—	—	*64.4*	*34.3*	*1.3*	*65.2*
Louisiana	76.2	23.6	0.2	76.3	80.6	17.3	2.1	82.3
Maine	42.1	55.0	2.9	43.3	40.4	56.6	3.0	41.6
Maryland	50.5	47.5	2.0	51.5	55.0	42.8	2.2	56.2
Massachusetts	40.2	52.6	7.2	43.3	49.0	46.3	4.8	51.4
Massachusetts	*44.1*	*52.6*	*3.3*	*45.6*	*49.0*	*47.6*	*3.5*	*50.7*
Michigan	41.6	50.0	8.4	45.4	47.3	44.8	7.9	51.3
Michigan	*45.4*	*50.0*	*4.6*	*47.6*	—	—	—	—
Minnesota	41.3	53.3	5.5	43.6	29.6	41.7	28.7	41.5
Minnesota	—	—	—	—	*45.5*	*41.7*	*12.8*	*52.2*
Mississippi	76.6	23.3	0.1	76.7	77.6	22.4	0.0	77.6
Missouri	50.6	45.6	3.8	52.6	54.8	39.8	5.4	57.9
Montana	47.8[1]	52.2[1]	0.0[1]	47.8[1]	49.6	48.7	1.8	50.5
Nebraska	40.5	52.5	7.0	43.6	25.9	34.5	39.7	42.9
Nebraska	—	—	—	—	*42.9*	*34.5*	*22.6*	*55.5*
Nevada	45.1	54.9	0.0	45.1	46.5	53.5	0.0	46.5
New Hampshire	48.5	50.0	1.6	49.3	50.2	48.4	1.4	50.9
New Jersey	47.5	48.1	4.3	49.7	51.0	45.6	3.3	52.8
New Jersey	*49.2*	*48.1*	*2.7*	*50.5*	—	—	—	—
New Mexico	—	—	—	—	—	—	—	—
New York	41.2	51.4	7.3	44.5	49.1	43.9	7.0	52.8
New York	*45.5*	*51.4*	*3.0*	*47.0*	*51.8*	*44.1*	*4.1*	*54.0*
North Carolina	53.1	46.8	0.1	53.2	58.4	40.9	0.6	58.8
North Carolina	—	—	—	—	*58.4*	*41.0*	*0.6*	*58.8*
North Dakota	31.6[1]	68.4[1]	0.0[1]	31.6[1]	41.0	59.0	0.0	41.0
Ohio	47.2	49.7	3.1	48.7	47.5	49.0	3.4	49.2
Oklahoma	—	—	—	—	—	—	—	—
Oregon	42.2	54.5	3.3	43.6	41.3	54.8	3.9	43.0
Pennsylvania	43.8	51.2	5.0	46.1	46.6	49.5	3.8	48.5
Pennsylvania	*45.4*	*52.5*	*2.1*	*46.4*	*47.7*	*50.7*	*1.6*	*48.5*
Rhode Island	42.2	54.6	3.2	43.6	50.9	45.9	3.2	52.6
South Carolina	86.4	13.2	0.4	86.8	80.2	17.8	2.0	81.8
South Carolina	*86.4*	*13.3*	*0.3*	*86.7*	*80.2*	*19.8*	*0.0*	*80.2*
South Dakota	29.7[1]	70.3[1]	0.0[1]	29.7[1]	22.7	45.1	32.2	33.5
Tennessee	53.3	45.7	1.0	53.8	53.9	36.1	10.0	59.9
Tennessee	—	—	—	—	*54.0*	*41.6*	*4.4*	*56.5*
Texas	70.5	14.1	15.4	83.3	80.5	18.6	0.8	81.2
Texas	*70.5*	*18.6*	*10.9*	*79.1*	—	—	—	—
Utah	—	—	—	—	—	—	—	—
Vermont	28.4	70.5	1.1	28.7	33.3	66.7	0.0	33.3
Virginia	50.1	49.7	0.2	50.2	66.9	25.7	7.3	72.2
Virginia	*50.2*	*49.7*	*0.1*	*50.2*	*72.3*	*26.2*	*1.5*	*73.4*
Washington	41.8[1]	58.2[1]	0.0[1]	41.8[1]	41.7	53.2	5.1	43.9
West Virginia	49.9	48.8	1.3	50.6	52.0	47.3	0.7	52.3
Wisconsin	33.8	50.8	15.4	39.9	53.7	42.6	3.7	55.8
Wisconsin	*44.3*	*50.8*	*4.9*	*46.6*	—	—	—	—
Wyoming	—	—	—	—	41.8	58.2	0.0	41.8

Notes: Main entries are calculated from the raw vote values in tables series 5-70 to 5-122 for the appropriate years based on candidates who used the sole designation "Democrat" or "Republican" (or their historical antecedents listed in Appendix A) on the ballot. Other = candidates who used third-party names on the ballot or were listed as independent, unidentified, or scatter vote. Bold italicized entries in the table are the author's alternative party coding, which is used when a candidate listed a major party name (Democrat, Republican, or their historical antecedents) on the ballot with other party names or labels. These values are computed from the bold italicized raw vote values in table series 5-70 to 5-122 for the appropriate states and years. For a more detailed explanation of this alternate coding system, see Tables 5-1 and 1-3. —indicates that the state had no data, either because no vote data were found for the state in question or the state had not yet entered the Union. No special House elections are included in the table. The table only lists at-large vote values for states having both at-large and district House races; see Appendix B for these states' district results aggregated to the state level.

[1]Election held in odd-numbered year.

Sources: Adapted from *United States Congressional Elections, 1788–1997* (1998), *Congressional Quarterly's Guide to U.S. Elections* (1994), ICPSR data sets 0001 and 0075, and independent search for state sources by the author.

Table 5-43 House Election Results, by State, 1892–1895 (Percentages)

State	1892				1894–1895			
	Democratic	Republican	Other	Democratic % of Two-Party Vote	Democratic	Republican	Other	Democratic % of Two-Party Vote
Alabama	58.7	4.8	36.5	92.4	57.5	12.1	30.4	82.6
Alabama	*95.1*	*4.8*	*0.1*	*95.2*	—	—	—	—
Alaska	—	—	—	—	—	—	—	—
Arizona	—	—	—	—	—	—	—	—
Arkansas	68.9	11.3	19.8	85.9	71.9	19.9	8.2	78.3
California	40.2	42.0	17.7	48.9	33.3	41.2	25.5	44.7
California	*48.8*	*42.0*	*9.1*	*53.7*	*35.8*	*41.2*	*23.0*	*46.5*
Colorado	2.4	40.2	57.4	5.7	27.8	50.5	21.8	35.5
Colorado	*58.2*	*40.2*	*1.6*	*59.1*				
Connecticut	50.0	47.0	3.0	51.6	41.8	55.2	3.0	43.1
Delaware	50.0	48.7	1.4	50.6	47.5	50.8	1.7	48.3
Florida	86.6	0.0	13.4	100.0	82.9	0.0	17.1	100.0
Georgia	63.4	1.7	34.9	97.4	62.0	0.0	38.0	100.0
Georgia	*63.4*	*4.6*	*31.9*	*93.2*	—	—	—	—
Hawaii	—	—	—	—	—	—	—	—
Idaho	31.1	44.1	24.7	41.4	24.4	43.4	32.3	36.0
Illinois	48.8	45.8	5.4	51.6	36.7	52.6	10.6	41.1
Indiana	47.2	46.1	6.7	50.5	39.1	50.9	10.0	43.5
Indiana	—	—	—	—	*42.7*	*50.9*	*6.4*	*45.6*
Iowa	41.0	49.7	9.3	45.3	20.2	55.0	24.8	26.9
Iowa	*45.7*	*49.7*	*4.6*	*47.9*	*40.1*	*55.0*	*4.9*	*42.2*
Kansas	0.0	48.0	52.0	0.0	8.9	50.4	40.7	15.0
Kansas	*50.7*	*48.0*	*1.3*	*51.4*	—	—	—	—
Kentucky	54.2	37.9	7.9	58.8	47.2	45.1	7.7	51.1
Kentucky	—	—	—	—	*47.2*	*46.6*	*6.3*	*50.3*
Louisiana	74.8	0.0	25.2	100.0	68.1	23.7	8.2	74.2
Louisiana	*81.7*	*18.2*	*0.0*	*81.8*	—	—	—	—
Maine	42.4	51.4	6.2	45.2	28.3	64.4	7.4	30.5
Maine	*43.7*	*51.4*	*4.9*	*45.9*	—	—	—	—
Maryland	53.8	43.3	2.9	55.4	47.3	48.6	4.2	49.3
Massachusetts	44.3	50.2	5.5	46.8	34.8	57.5	7.7	37.7
Massachusetts	*46.8*	*50.2*	*2.9*	*48.2*	*37.5*	*57.9*	*4.6*	*39.3*
Michigan	29.5	47.8	22.6	38.2	27.7	57.4	14.9	32.5
Michigan	*45.2*	*47.8*	*6.9*	*48.6*	*32.0*	*57.4*	*10.6*	*35.8*
Minnesota	37.1	44.5	18.4	45.5	25.6	52.2	22.3	32.9
Mississippi	74.0	1.0	25.0	98.7	68.1	0.4	31.5	99.4
Missouri	50.1	42.7	7.2	54.0	44.2	46.5	9.4	48.7
Montana	41.0	41.4	17.6	49.8	21.0	47.0	32.0	30.9
Nebraska	24.5	42.2	33.3	36.7	9.5	49.5	41.0	16.2
Nebraska	*33.4*	*42.2*	*24.4*	*44.1*	*40.2*	*49.5*	*10.3*	*44.8*
Nevada	3.5	23.2	73.3	13.1	0.0	27.4	72.6	0.0
New Hampshire	48.4	49.6	2.0	49.4	41.0	56.3	2.7	42.2
New Jersey	49.8	47.2	3.0	51.3	38.9	55.3	5.8	41.3
New Mexico	—	—	—	—	—	—	—	—
New York	48.7	46.5	4.8	51.2	39.6	54.5	5.9	42.1
New York	—	—	—	—	*41.4*	*54.5*	*4.1*	*43.2*
North Carolina	49.0	26.0	25.0	65.4	45.7	18.1	36.2	71.6
North Carolina	—	—	—	—	*45.7*	*31.6*	*22.7*	*59.1*
North Dakota	30.5	48.9	20.6	38.4	0.0	55.4	44.6	0.0
Ohio	48.4	47.2	4.4	50.6	36.3	54.1	9.5	40.2
Ohio	*48.4*	*47.2*	*4.4*	*50.6*	—	—	—	—
Oklahoma	—	—	—	—	—	—	—	—
Oregon	33.2	45.7	21.0	42.1	23.0	47.7	29.3	32.5
Pennsylvania	45.4	51.8	2.8	46.7	34.9	0.0	65.1	100.0
Pennsylvania	—	—	—	—	*34.9*	*60.6*	*4.5*	*36.5*
Rhode Island	46.3	49.5	4.2	48.3	35.4	58.9	5.7	37.5
South Carolina	83.0	14.2	2.8	85.4	74.6	22.5	2.9	76.8
South Carolina	—	—	—	—	*76.4*	*22.5*	*1.0*	*77.2*
South Dakota	19.4	46.0	34.7	29.6	10.5	52.8	36.7	16.6
Tennessee	51.5	27.3	21.2	65.4	42.0	38.6	19.4	52.1
Tennessee	*55.8*	*31.7*	*12.6*	*63.8*	*42.0*	*44.4*	*13.6*	*48.7*
Texas	57.7	10.5	31.8	84.6	50.4	10.8	38.8	82.3
Texas	*57.7*	*17.7*	*24.7*	*76.6*	*51.7*	*10.8*	*37.4*	*82.7*
Utah	—	—	—	—	47.5[1]	49.7[1]	2.8[1]	48.9[1]
Vermont	33.2	64.4	2.4	34.0	24.6	75.4	0.0	24.6
Virginia	58.3	13.6	28.1	81.0	52.8	41.4	5.8	56.1
Virginia	*58.3*	*16.7*	*25.1*	*77.8*	—	—	—	—
Washington	34.6	40.0	25.4	46.4	18.9	46.6	34.5	28.9
West Virginia	50.4	47.3	2.4	51.6	44.8	52.7	2.6	45.9
Wisconsin	47.9	46.7	5.4	50.6	32.5	54.4	13.0	37.4
Wisconsin	—	—	—	—	*36.5*	*54.4*	*9.1*	*40.2*
Wyoming	51.3	48.7	0.0	51.3	32.2	52.6	15.2	37.9

Notes: Main entries are calculated from the raw vote values in tables series 5-70 to 5-122 for the appropriate years based on candidates who used the sole designation "Democrat" or "Republican" (or their historical antecedents listed in Appendix A) on the ballot. Other = candidates who used third-party names on the ballot or were listed as independent, unidentified, or scatter vote. Bold italicized entries in the table are the author's alternative party coding, which is used when a candidate listed a major party name (Democrat, Republican, or their historical antecedents) on the ballot with other party names or labels. These values are computed from the bold italicized raw vote values in table series 5-70 to 5-122 for the appropriate states and years. For a more detailed explanation of this alternate coding system, see Tables 5-1 and 1-3. —indicates that the state had no data, either because no vote data were found for the state in question or the state had not yet entered the Union. No special House elections are included in the table. The table only lists at-large vote values for states having both at-large and district House races; see Appendix B for these states' district results aggregated to the state level.

[1]Election held in odd-numbered year.

Sources: Adapted from *United States Congressional Elections, 1788–1997* (1998), *Congressional Quarterly's Guide to U.S. Elections* (1994), ICPSR data sets 0001 and 0075, and independent search for state sources by the author.

Table 5-44 House Election Results, by State, 1896–1898 (Percentages)

	1896				1898			
State	Democratic	Republican	Other	Democratic % of Two-Party Vote	Democratic	Republican	Other	Democratic % of Two-Party Vote
Alabama	56.2	5.0	38.8	91.8	73.3	26.4	0.3	73.5
Alabama	*66.9*	*20.0*	*13.2*	*77.0*	*73.3*	*26.7*	*0.0*	*73.3*
Alaska	—	—	—	—	—	—	—	—
Arizona	—	—	—	—	—	—	—	—
Arkansas	72.4	27.6	0.0	72.4	90.0	10.0	0.0	90.0
California	46.7	46.4	7.0	50.2	46.9	51.0	2.0	47.9
California	—	—	—	—	*47.1*	*51.0*	*1.8*	*48.0*
Colorado	0.0	13.4	86.6	0.0	0.0	12.9	87.1	0.0
Colorado	*84.6*	*13.4*	*2.0*	*86.3*	*66.1*	*31.9*	*2.0*	*67.4*
Connecticut	32.5	62.8	4.8	34.1	42.4	54.8	2.8	43.7
Connecticut	*35.5*	*62.8*	*1.8*	*36.1*	—	—	—	—
Delaware	44.0	20.4	35.6	68.4	45.5	53.1	1.4	46.1
Delaware	*46.4*	*52.2*	*1.3*	*47.1*	—	—	—	—
Florida	69.0	22.3	8.8	75.6	77.8	22.2	0.0	77.8
Florida	*71.7*	*22.3*	*6.0*	*76.3*	—	—	—	—
Georgia	58.5	21.0	20.5	73.5	81.6	10.3	8.2	88.8
Hawaii	—	—	—	—	—	—	—	—
Idaho	47.7	21.0	31.3	69.5	0.0	33.4	66.6	0.0
Idaho	*47.7*	*52.3*	*0.0*	*47.7*	*0.0*	*78.7*	*21.3*	*0.0*
Illinois	42.7	55.6	1.7	43.5	44.7	53.0	2.2	45.8
Illinois	*43.0*	*55.6*	*1.4*	*43.6*	—	—	—	—
Indiana	48.2	50.9	0.9	48.6	48.2	50.1	1.7	49.1
Indiana	*48.3*	*50.9*	*0.8*	*48.7*	—	—	—	—
Iowa	43.7	55.7	0.6	44.0	42.3	55.6	2.1	43.2
Kansas	51.3	48.2	0.5	51.6	46.5	52.5	0.9	47.0
Kentucky	46.8	44.3	8.8	51.4	50.5	43.6	5.8	53.7
Kentucky	*51.3*	*44.3*	*4.4*	*53.6*	*50.5*	*47.9*	*1.6*	*51.3*
Louisiana	66.3	2.6	31.1	96.2	83.3	11.8	4.9	87.6
Louisiana	*66.3*	*22.6*	*11.1*	*74.6*	—	—	—	—
Maine	27.7	67.6	4.7	29.1	31.5	65.6	2.9	32.4
Maine	—	—	—	—	*31.6*	*65.6*	*2.8*	*32.5*
Maryland	43.0	54.5	2.5	44.1	46.6	49.4	4.0	48.5
Maryland	—	—	—	—	*46.9*	*49.4*	*3.8*	*48.7*
Massachusetts	31.3	65.9	2.8	32.2	39.6	56.4	4.0	41.2
Massachusetts	*33.0*	*66.7*	*0.3*	*33.1*	*41.2*	*56.5*	*2.3*	*42.1*
Michigan	45.0	54.6	0.4	45.2	42.5	55.9	1.5	43.2
Minnesota	43.1	55.2	1.6	43.9	41.2	54.8	4.0	42.9
Mississippi	75.5	3.1	21.4	96.0	82.1	3.5	14.5	95.9
Mississippi	*76.7*	*6.6*	*16.8*	*92.1*	*87.1*	*4.8*	*8.0*	*94.8*
Missouri	51.0	45.8	3.2	52.7	51.7	46.4	1.9	52.7
Missouri	—	—	—	—	*51.7*	*46.5*	*1.7*	*52.6*
Montana	0.0	21.9	78.1	0.0	46.9	29.8	23.3	61.2
Montana	*0.0*	*100.0*	*0.0*	*0.0*	*46.9*	*53.1*	*0.0*	*46.9*
Nebraska	52.2	46.2	1.6	53.0	0.0	49.6	50.4	0.0
Nebraska	—	—	—	—	*50.4*	*49.6*	*0.0*	*50.4*
Nevada	66.3	13.6	20.1	83.0	65.0	0.0	35.0	100.0
New Hampshire	33.8	63.7	2.5	34.7	44.0	53.9	2.1	45.0
New Jersey	36.1	54.2	9.7	40.0	46.6	49.7	3.7	48.4
New Jersey	*37.5*	*59.7*	*2.7*	*38.6*	—	—	—	—
New Mexico	—	—	—	—	—	—	—	—
New York	37.7	57.4	4.9	39.6	46.9	49.8	3.3	48.5
New York	*39.7*	*57.4*	*2.8*	*40.9*	*46.9*	*49.8*	*3.3*	*48.5*
North Carolina	44.8	11.6	43.6	79.5	51.6	11.1	37.3	82.2
North Carolina	*44.8*	*54.2*	*1.0*	*45.3*	*51.6*	*43.1*	*5.3*	*54.5*
North Dakota	0.0	54.0	46.0	0.0	0.0	60.9	39.1	0.0
North Dakota	*45.3*	*54.0*	*0.7*	*45.6*	*39.1*	*60.9*	*0.0*	*39.1*
Ohio	47.1	52.2	0.7	47.4	46.2	52.5	1.3	46.8
Oklahoma	—	—	—	—	—	—	—	—
Oregon	16.8	35.7	47.5	32.0	0.0	51.4	48.6	0.0
Oregon	—	—	—	—	*40.9*	*51.4*	*7.6*	*44.3*
Pennsylvania	35.7	61.3	3.0	36.8	37.2	56.6	6.2	39.7
Rhode Island	31.1	63.6	5.3	32.9	34.7	55.9	9.4	38.3
South Carolina	87.4	7.1	5.5	92.5	91.2	8.8	0.0	91.2
South Carolina	*87.4*	*12.6*	*0.0*	*87.4*	—	—	—	—
South Dakota	49.7	49.5	0.9	50.1	0.0	53.9	46.1	0.0
South Dakota	—	—	—	—	*44.9*	*53.9*	*1.2*	*45.5*
Tennessee	49.8	36.9	13.4	57.4	60.3	36.1	3.6	62.5
Tennessee	*53.1*	*41.0*	*5.9*	*56.4*	—	—	—	—
Texas	53.8	19.8	26.4	73.1	62.9	16.9	20.1	78.8
Texas	*55.3*	*22.6*	*22.0*	*71.0*	—	—	—	—
Utah	61.2	0.0	38.8	100.0	52.3	43.5	4.2	54.6
Utah	*61.2*	*35.9*	*2.9*	*63.0*	—	—	—	—

(Table continues)

Table 5-44 (Continued)

| | 1896 | | | | 1898 | | | |
State	Democratic	Republican	Other	Democratic % of Two-Party Vote	Democratic	Republican	Other	Democratic % of Two-Party Vote
Vermont	20.8	78.4	0.9	20.9	26.9	73.1	0.0	26.9
Virginia	53.3	41.2	5.5	56.4	60.8	34.2	5.0	64.0
Virginia	*58.0*	*41.5*	*0.5*	*58.3*	*62.5*	*36.4*	*1.1*	*63.2*
Washington	0.0	42.0	58.0	0.0	0.0	50.9	49.1	0.0
West Virginia	47.5	52.4	0.1	47.5	49.0	50.5	0.6	49.3
Wisconsin	37.8	61.1	1.2	38.2	39.9	56.0	4.2	41.6
Wyoming	49.1	47.9	3.0	50.7	43.0	54.7	2.3	44.0

Notes: Main entries are calculated from the raw vote values in tables series 5-70 to 5-122 for the appropriate years based on candidates who used the sole designation "Democrat" or "Republican" (or their historical antecedents listed in Appendix A) on the ballot. Other = candidates who used third-party names on the ballot or were listed as independent, unidentified, or scatter vote. Bold italicized entries in the table are the author's alternative party coding, which is used when a candidate listed a major party name (Democrat, Republican, or their historical antecedents) on the ballot with other party names or labels. These values are computed from the bold italicized raw vote values in table series 5-70 to 5-122 for the appropriate states and years. For a more detailed explanation of this alternate coding system, see Tables 5-1 and 1-3. —indicates that the state had no data, either because no vote data were found for the state in question or the state had not yet entered the Union. No special House elections are included in the table. The table only lists at-large vote values for states having both at-large and district House races; see Appendix B for these states' district results aggregated to the state level.

Sources: Adapted from *United States Congressional Elections, 1788–1997* (1998), *Congressional Quarterly's Guide to U.S. Elections* (1994), ICPSR data sets 0001 and 0075, and independent search for state sources by the author.

Table 5-45 House Election Results, by State, 1900–1902 (Percentages)

State	1900 Democratic	Republican	Other	Democratic % of Two-Party Vote	1902 Democratic	Republican	Other	Democratic % of Two-Party Vote
Alabama	74.1	23.5	2.4	76.0	76.4	23.3	0.3	76.6
Alabama	*74.1*	*25.7*	*0.2*	*74.2*	*76.4*	*23.4*	*0.3*	*76.6*
Alaska	—	—	—	—	—	—	—	—
Arizona	—	—	—	—	—	—	—	—
Arkansas	66.4	33.6	0.0	66.4	83.3	16.7	0.0	83.3
California	41.2	53.9	4.9	43.3	30.0	52.4	17.6	36.5
California	—	—	—	—	*43.4*	*52.4*	*4.2*	*45.3*
Colorado	0.0	42.7	57.3	0.0	45.6	46.1	8.4	49.7
Colorado	*56.0*	*42.7*	*1.3*	*56.7*	—	—	—	—
Connecticut	41.4	56.7	1.9	42.2	44.3	52.6	3.1	45.8
Delaware	45.5	53.1	1.4	46.2	42.9	21.0	36.1	67.1
Delaware	—	—	—	—	*42.9*	*55.0*	*2.1*	*43.8*
Florida	83.4	16.6	0.0	83.4	100.0	0.0	0.0	100.0
Georgia	79.0	11.0	10.0	87.8	97.9	0.0	2.1	100.0
Hawaii	—	—	—	—	—	—	—	—
Idaho	0.0	48.9	51.1	0.0	41.7	54.3	4.0	43.4
Idaho	*51.1*	*48.9*	*0.0*	*51.1*	—	—	—	—
Illinois	44.9	52.9	2.2	45.9	45.8	49.9	4.3	47.9
Indiana	47.6	50.5	1.9	48.5	46.6	49.8	3.6	48.4
Iowa	40.5	58.0	1.5	41.1	40.4	56.7	3.0	41.6
Kansas	46.7	52.3	1.0	47.2	40.9	56.1	3.0	42.1
Kentucky	50.3	49.4	0.3	50.5	54.0	42.8	3.2	55.8
Louisiana	78.4	21.6	0.0	78.4	84.6	15.4	0.0	84.6
Maine	34.5	62.0	3.5	35.7	36.0	61.1	2.9	37.1
Maine	*34.5*	*62.1*	*3.5*	*35.7*	—	—	—	—
Maryland	46.6	51.4	2.0	47.5	46.4	50.7	2.8	47.8
Maryland	*46.8*	*51.4*	*1.7*	*47.7*	—	—	—	—
Massachusetts	38.6	56.7	4.7	40.5	35.8	49.2	14.9	42.1
Massachusetts	—	—	—	—	*41.1*	*49.2*	*9.7*	*45.5*
Michigan	40.0	57.8	2.2	40.9	39.6	58.1	2.2	40.5
Minnesota	40.2	56.7	3.0	41.5	34.5	60.0	5.6	36.5
Mississippi	92.9	5.0	2.2	94.9	100.0	0.0	0.0	100.0
Missouri	52.6	46.6	0.8	53.0	53.8	45.2	1.0	54.3
Montana	45.8	37.8	16.4	54.8	36.7	46.2	17.1	44.3
Montana	*61.2*	*37.8*	*1.0*	*61.8*	—	—	—	—
Nebraska	0.0	49.7	50.3	0.0	0.0	51.0	49.0	0.0
Nebraska	*48.3*	*49.7*	*2.0*	*49.3*	*46.3*	*51.0*	*2.8*	*47.6*
Nevada	58.8	41.2	0.0	58.8	0.0	46.5	53.5	0.0
Nevada	—	—	—	—	*53.5*	*46.5*	*0.0*	*53.5*
New Hampshire	38.7	59.3	2.0	39.5	39.2	58.0	2.8	40.4
New Jersey	41.4	55.2	3.4	42.9	45.5	50.9	3.6	47.2
New Mexico	—	—	—	—	—	—	—	—
New York	44.1	53.2	2.7	45.3	47.7	48.4	3.8	49.6
New York	—	—	—	—	*47.7*	*48.4*	*3.8*	*49.6*
North Carolina	55.6	38.1	6.3	59.3	68.7	30.1	1.2	69.6
North Carolina	*55.6*	*39.6*	*4.8*	*58.4*	—	—	—	—
North Dakota	37.0	61.0	2.0	37.8	30.2	67.4	2.4	30.9
Ohio	46.6	52.2	1.3	47.2	41.7	54.3	4.0	43.4
Ohio	*46.6*	*52.6*	*0.8*	*47.0*	—	—	—	—
Oklahoma	—	—	—	—	—	—	—	—
Oregon	0.0	52.2	47.8	0.0	36.0	53.2	10.7	40.4
Oregon	*41.3*	*52.2*	*6.5*	*44.2*	—	—	—	—
Pennsylvania	36.5	60.6	2.9	37.6	26.1	38.5	35.5	40.4
Pennsylvania	—	—	—	—	*33.5*	*61.8*	*4.7*	*35.1*
Rhode Island	35.4	58.5	6.1	37.7	47.8	48.4	3.8	49.7
South Carolina	93.8	6.2	0.0	93.8	97.7	2.3	0.0	97.7
South Dakota	0.0	55.9	44.1	0.0	28.3	64.9	6.8	30.3
South Dakota	*42.4*	*55.9*	*1.7*	*43.1*	—	—	—	—
Tennessee	54.1	41.1	4.8	56.8	64.8	35.0	0.2	65.0
Tennessee	—	—	—	—	*64.8*	*35.2*	*0.0*	*64.8*
Texas	74.6	20.2	5.2	78.7	82.6	16.8	0.5	83.1
Utah	49.5	49.7	0.8	49.9	45.0	51.5	3.5	46.6
Vermont	26.1	71.9	2.0	26.6	19.4	76.0	4.6	20.3
Virginia	61.5	36.6	1.9	62.7	67.0	32.0	1.0	67.7
Virginia	—	—	—	—	*67.0*	*32.1*	*0.9*	*67.6*
Washington	42.9	52.3	4.8	45.1	34.0	58.8	7.2	36.6
West Virginia	45.7	53.8	0.5	45.9	46.0	52.2	1.8	46.8
Wisconsin	37.3	59.5	3.3	38.5	38.6	55.0	6.4	41.2
Wyoming	40.8	59.2	0.0	40.8	36.0	64.0	0.0	36.0

Notes: Main entries are calculated from the raw vote values in tables series 5-70 to 5-122 for the appropriate years based on candidates who used the sole designation "Democrat" or "Republican" (or their historical antecedents listed in Appendix A) on the ballot. Other = candidates who used third-party names on the ballot or were listed as independent, unidentified, or scatter vote. Bold italicized entries in the table are the author's alternative party coding, which is used when a candidate listed a major party name (Democrat, Republican, or their historical antecedents) on the ballot with other party names or labels. These values are computed from the bold italicized raw vote values in table series 5-70 to 5-122 for the appropriate states and years. For a more detailed explanation of this alternate coding system, see Tables 5-1 and 1-3. —indicates that the state had no data, either because no vote data were found for the state in question or the state had not yet entered the Union. No special House elections are included in the table. The table only lists at-large vote values for states having both at-large and district House races; see Appendix B for these states' district results aggregated to the state level.

Sources: Adapted from *United States Congressional Elections, 1788–1997* (1998), *Congressional Quarterly's Guide to U.S. Elections* (1994), ICPSR data sets 0001 and 0075, and independent search for state sources by the author.

Table 5-46 House Election Results, by State, 1904–1907 (Percentages)

State	1904				1906–1907			
	Democratic	Republican	Other	Democratic % of Two-Party Vote	Democratic	Republican	Other	Democratic % of Two-Party Vote
Alabama	80.6	19.0	0.4	80.9	90.9	9.1	0.0	90.9
Alaska	—	—	—	—	—	—	—	—
Arizona	—	—	—	—	—	—	—	—
Arkansas	70.4	29.6	0.0	70.4	75.4	24.5	0.1	75.5
California	30.4	56.8	12.8	34.9	34.1	56.0	9.9	37.8
California	*34.3*	*56.8*	*8.9*	*37.7*	*35.2*	*56.0*	*8.8*	*38.6*
Colorado	46.5	50.2	3.3	48.1	39.1	52.2	8.7	42.8
Connecticut	39.4	57.0	3.6	40.8	42.1	54.8	3.1	43.5
Delaware	44.6	53.7	1.7	45.4	44.8	52.8	2.4	45.9
Florida	78.1	18.3	3.5	81.0	89.0	5.1	5.9	94.5
Georgia	82.4	17.2	0.3	82.7	98.7	1.3	0.0	98.7
Hawaii	—	—	—	—	—	—	—	—
Idaho	28.6	63.7	7.7	31.0	33.1	58.6	8.3	36.1
Illinois	32.4	57.5	10.1	36.0	37.8	52.8	9.4	41.7
Illinois	*32.5*	*58.0*	*9.5*	*35.9*	—	—	—	—
Indiana	43.0	52.6	4.4	45.0	47.4	48.5	4.1	49.4
Iowa	33.9	61.9	4.2	35.4	41.6	55.2	3.2	42.9
Kansas	33.8	60.3	5.8	35.9	41.8	54.1	4.1	43.6
Kentucky	51.1	47.6	1.3	51.8	54.0	43.0	3.0	55.7
Louisiana	90.4	8.8	0.8	91.1	87.8	10.6	1.6	89.2
Maine	39.0	59.3	1.7	39.7	45.9	52.5	1.6	46.6
Maryland	47.7	50.0	2.4	48.8	46.4	49.8	3.8	48.2
Maryland	*47.7*	*50.2*	*2.2*	*48.7*	—	—	—	—
Massachusetts	37.0	57.2	5.9	39.3	39.5	56.7	3.8	41.1
Michigan	30.7	66.8	2.5	31.5	25.5	71.0	3.5	26.4
Minnesota	25.8	72.4	1.8	26.3	25.7	67.8	6.5	27.5
Mississippi	99.0	0.2	0.8	99.8	99.1	0.0	0.9	100.0
Missouri	48.2	50.2	1.6	49.0	49.8	48.9	1.4	50.4
Montana	0.0	51.7	48.3	0.0	0.0	0.0	100.0	—
Montana	*42.0*	*51.7*	*6.3*	*44.8*	*40.8*	*50.5*	*8.7*	*44.7*
Nebraska	0.0	55.3	44.7	0.0	6.2	52.7	41.1	10.5
Nebraska	*40.1*	*55.3*	*4.6*	*42.0*	*45.0*	*52.7*	*2.2*	*46.1*
Nevada	0.0	46.5	53.5	0.0	8.8	39.8	51.4	18.1
Nevada	*48.5*	*46.5*	*5.0*	*51.0*	*60.2*	*39.8*	*0.0*	*60.2*
New Hampshire	38.2	59.8	2.0	39.0	39.6	57.9	2.5	40.6
New Jersey	40.2	54.8	5.0	42.3	41.8	48.1	10.1	46.5
New Jersey	—	—	—	—	*47.2*	*48.1*	*4.8*	*49.5*
New Mexico	—	—	—	—	—	—	—	—
New York	42.2	53.7	4.1	44.0	24.6	48.3	27.2	33.7
New York	—	—	—	—	*44.1*	*48.3*	*7.7*	*47.7*
North Carolina	62.3	37.7	0.1	62.3	61.5	38.4	0.1	61.6
North Dakota	23.2	72.8	4.0	24.1	34.8	63.4	1.9	35.4
Ohio	36.0	59.0	5.0	37.9	42.9	52.8	4.3	44.8
Ohio	—	—	—	—	*43.2*	*52.8*	*3.9*	*45.0*
Oklahoma	—	—	—	—	56.0[1]	41.9[1]	2.1[1]	57.2[1]
Oregon	31.9	54.4	13.7	36.9	33.7	55.0	11.3	38.0
Pennsylvania	25.3	66.0	8.7	27.7	22.5	26.4	51.2	46.0
Pennsylvania	*28.9*	*66.0*	*5.1*	*30.5*	*34.6*	*58.5*	*6.9*	*37.2*
Rhode Island	45.4	52.9	1.7	46.2	48.0	50.4	1.6	48.8
South Carolina	95.7	4.3	0.0	95.7	98.4	1.5	0.1	98.5
South Dakota	22.7	70.0	7.3	24.5	27.1	65.0	7.9	29.4
Tennessee	56.2	43.5	0.3	56.4	55.7	40.2	4.1	58.1
Tennessee	—	—	—	—	*55.7*	*43.5*	*0.8*	*56.2*
Texas	82.0	17.3	0.8	82.6	87.1	11.5	1.5	88.4
Texas	—	—	—	—	*87.1*	*11.6*	*1.3*	*88.2*
Utah	36.8	51.8	11.4	41.6	32.1	50.6	17.2	38.8
Vermont	24.6	72.5	2.9	25.3	28.7	69.5	1.7	29.2
Virginia	65.4	33.4	1.2	66.2	64.2	35.5	0.3	64.4
Virginia	*65.4*	*34.0*	*0.6*	*65.8*	—	—	—	—
Washington	25.1	65.5	9.4	27.7	27.7	62.7	9.6	30.7
West Virginia	43.9	53.7	2.4	45.0	42.2	53.8	3.9	44.0
Wisconsin	34.4	57.3	8.2	37.5	36.2	55.0	8.8	39.7
Wisconsin	—	—	—	—	*36.2*	*55.0*	*8.8*	*39.7*
Wyoming	32.2	64.6	3.2	33.3	33.1	62.2	4.8	34.7

Notes: Main entries are calculated from the raw vote values in tables series 5-70 to 5-122 for the appropriate years based on candidates who used the sole designation "Democrat" or "Republican" (or their historical antecedents listed in Appendix A) on the ballot. Other = candidates who used third-party names on the ballot or were listed as independent, unidentified, or scatter vote. Bold italicized entries in the table are the author's alternative party coding, which is used when a candidate listed a major party name (Democrat, Republican, or their historical antecedents) on the ballot with other party names or labels. These values are computed from the bold italicized raw vote values in table series 5-70 to 5-122 for the appropriate states and years. For a more detailed explanation of this alternate coding system, see Tables 5-1 and 1-3. —indicates that the state had no data, either because no vote data were found for the state in question or the state had not yet entered the Union. No special House elections are included in the table. The table only lists at-large vote values for states having both at-large and district House races; see Appendix B for these states' district results aggregated to the state level.

[1] Election held in odd-numbered year.

Sources: Adapted from *United States Congressional Elections, 1788–1997* (1998), *Congressional Quarterly's Guide to U.S. Elections* (1994), ICPSR data sets 0001 and 0075, and independent search for state sources by the author.

Table 5-47 House Election Results, by State, 1908–1911 (Percentages)

State	1908 Democratic	1908 Republican	1908 Other	1908 Democratic % of Two-Party Vote	1910–1911 Democratic	1910–1911 Republican	1910–1911 Other	1910–1911 Democratic % of Two-Party Vote
Alabama	80.7	18.9	0.4	81.0	84.5	15.4	0.1	84.6
Alaska	—	—	—	—	—	—	—	—
Arizona	—	—	—	—	54.0[1]	39.7[1]	6.3[1]	57.7[1]
Arkansas	68.6	31.4	0.0	68.6	77.3	22.7	0.0	77.3
California	36.3	54.4	9.3	40.0	30.8	46.8	22.5	39.7
California	—	—	—	—	*30.8*	*56.2*	*13.0*	*35.4*
Colorado	48.3	46.2	5.5	51.1	47.9	46.1	6.0	51.0
Connecticut	36.8	58.6	4.6	38.6	44.1	47.9	8.0	47.9
Delaware	46.9	50.7	2.4	48.1	46.1	50.9	3.0	47.5
Florida	76.9	16.0	7.1	82.8	82.5	3.7	13.8	95.8
Georgia	99.6	0.4	0.0	99.6	72.8	5.0	22.2	93.6
Georgia	—	—	—	—	*94.8*	*5.0*	*0.2*	*95.0*
Hawaii	—	—	—	—	—	—	—	—
Idaho	39.2	52.0	8.8	42.9	38.0	55.4	6.5	40.7
Illinois	40.1	53.8	6.0	42.7	45.6	47.0	7.4	49.3
Indiana	49.4	47.0	3.6	51.3	50.2	44.7	5.1	52.9
Iowa	42.6	54.7	2.7	43.8	42.0	55.3	2.6	43.2
Kansas	43.6	52.3	4.1	45.5	39.4	55.2	5.4	41.6
Kentucky	50.6	48.2	1.1	51.2	53.4	44.8	1.8	54.4
Louisiana	90.3	7.5	2.2	92.3	90.3	7.6	2.1	92.2
Maine	45.2	52.8	2.0	46.1	50.1	48.0	1.8	51.1
Maryland	50.3	47.4	2.3	51.5	49.7	46.6	3.7	51.6
Massachusetts	35.0	59.0	6.0	37.2	47.8	47.7	4.6	50.1
Massachusetts	—	—	—	—	*50.1*	*47.7*	*2.2*	*51.3*
Michigan	36.3	60.9	2.8	37.3	39.1	56.7	4.1	40.8
Minnesota	28.2	62.9	9.0	30.9	25.4	67.9	6.6	27.3
Mississippi	99.4	0.6	0.0	99.4	99.9	0.0	0.1	100.0
Missouri	49.1	48.8	2.1	50.1	45.5	44.2	10.3	50.7
Missouri	—	—	—	—	*48.9*	*47.5*	*3.6*	*50.7*
Montana	43.2	48.9	7.9	46.9	42.7	49.4	7.9	46.3
Nebraska	7.1	48.8	44.1	12.7	6.8	49.1	44.1	12.1
Nebraska	*49.6*	*48.8*	*1.6*	*50.4*	*48.4*	*49.1*	*2.5*	*49.7*
Nevada	47.3	31.7	21.0	59.8	38.1	49.9	11.9	43.3
New Hampshire	39.2	58.1	2.7	40.3	45.8	52.7	1.6	46.5
New Jersey	44.7	52.3	3.0	46.1	52.4	43.6	3.9	54.6
New Mexico	—	—	—	—	48.4[1]	48.6[1]	3.0[1]	49.9[1]
New York	43.4	50.7	5.9	46.1	37.1	38.6	24.3	49.0
New York	—	—	—	—	*48.9*	*45.7*	*5.3*	*51.7*
North Carolina	56.9	42.9	0.2	57.0	59.8	40.0	0.2	59.9
North Dakota	33.7	65.6	0.7	33.9	32.1	63.9	4.0	33.4
Ohio	44.2	47.7	8.1	48.1	50.3	42.5	7.1	54.2
Ohio	*46.9*	*47.7*	*5.4*	*49.6*	—	—	—	—
Oklahoma	48.5	43.2	8.2	52.9	50.5	39.8	9.8	55.9
Oregon	26.0	61.2	12.8	29.8	33.3	50.3	16.4	39.9
Pennsylvania	35.7	40.8	23.5	46.7	18.1	33.5	48.4	35.1
Pennsylvania	*36.4*	*58.0*	*5.6*	*38.6*	*33.2*	*50.8*	*16.0*	*39.5*
Rhode Island	42.4	54.5	3.1	43.7	46.4	51.5	2.2	47.4
South Carolina	97.4	2.6	0.0	97.4	98.8	1.2	0.1	98.8
South Dakota	34.3	59.9	5.8	36.4	31.6	62.8	5.6	33.5
Tennessee	54.2	45.1	0.7	54.6	63.0	32.1	4.9	66.3
Tennessee	*54.3*	*45.1*	*0.6*	*54.6*	*65.3*	*32.5*	*2.2*	*66.8*
Texas	82.2	16.0	1.8	83.7	87.9	8.3	3.8	91.3
Utah	32.3	51.6	16.1	38.5	32.0	49.5	18.5	39.3
Vermont	24.3	73.4	2.3	24.9	27.6	70.9	1.6	28.0
Virginia	64.5	35.2	0.2	64.7	67.0	31.4	1.6	68.1
Virginia	*64.6*	*35.3*	*0.2*	*64.7*	—	—	—	—
Washington	33.6	64.3	2.2	34.3	32.4	56.6	10.9	36.4
West Virginia	44.1	52.7	3.2	45.6	49.3	45.1	5.6	52.2
Wisconsin	38.1	54.7	7.2	41.1	34.4	52.1	13.5	39.8
Wyoming	36.3	57.1	6.6	38.9	39.5	54.7	5.8	41.9

Notes: Main entries are calculated from the raw vote values in tables series 5-70 to 5-122 for the appropriate years based on candidates who used the sole designation "Democrat" or "Republican" (or their historical antecedents listed in Appendix A) on the ballot. Other = candidates who used third-party names on the ballot or were listed as independent, unidentified, or scatter vote. Bold italicized entries in the table are the author's alternative party coding, which is used when a candidate listed a major party name (Democrat, Republican, or their historical antecedents) on the ballot with other party names or labels. These values are computed from the bold italicized raw vote values in table series 5-70 to 5-122 for the appropriate states and years. For a more detailed explanation of this alternate coding system, see Tables 5-1 and 1-3. —indicates that the state had no data, either because no vote data were found for the state in question or the state had not yet entered the Union. No special House elections are included in the table. The table only lists at-large vote values for states having both at-large and district House races; see Appendix B for these states' district results aggregated to the state level.

[1] Election held in odd-numbered year.

Sources: Adapted from *United States Congressional Elections, 1788–1997* (1998), *Congressional Quarterly's Guide to U.S. Elections* (1994), ICPSR data sets 0001 and 0075, and independent search for state sources by the author.

Table 5-48 House Election Results, by State, 1912–1914 (Percentages)

State	1912 Democratic	1912 Republican	1912 Other	1912 Democratic % of Two-Party Vote	1914 Democratic	1914 Republican	1914 Other	1914 Democratic % of Two-Party Vote
Alabama	87.8	9.6	2.5	90.1	78.0	15.9	6.1	83.0
Alaska	—	—	—	—	—	—	—	—
Arizona	48.4	13.2	38.4	78.6	74.6	17.0	8.4	81.4
Arkansas	77.2	22.8	0.0	77.2	86.5	9.5	4.1	90.1
California	31.6	46.1	22.3	40.6	9.2	23.8	67.0	27.9
California	—	—	—	—	*25.7*	*44.5*	*29.8*	*36.7*
Colorado	43.3	24.0	32.7	64.4	47.8	21.1	31.1	69.3
Colorado	—	—	—	—	*47.8*	*40.4*	*11.9*	*54.2*
Connecticut	40.2	37.0	22.8	52.1	43.1	49.1	7.9	46.7
Delaware	46.2	34.4	19.5	57.3	45.2	50.1	4.6	47.4
Florida	77.4	6.6	16.0	92.1	99.5	0.0	0.5	100.0
Georgia	99.7	0.3	0.0	99.7	99.2	0.0	0.8	100.0
Hawaii	—	—	—	—	—	—	—	—
Idaho	27.8	49.4	22.7	36.0	38.6	44.1	17.2	46.7
Illinois	36.3	27.4	36.3	57.0	40.4	41.8	17.8	49.1
Indiana	45.5	26.0	28.5	63.6	43.8	37.0	19.2	54.2
Iowa	42.6	43.0	14.5	49.8	39.9	52.1	8.0	43.4
Kansas	46.7	45.4	7.8	50.7	40.5	38.9	20.6	51.0
Kentucky	52.6	21.7	25.7	70.8	53.6	38.2	8.2	58.4
Louisiana	95.7	0.0	4.3	100.0	79.6	1.2	19.2	98.5
Maine	47.2	50.7	2.1	48.2	43.0	42.8	14.2	50.2
Maryland	59.7	34.7	5.6	63.3	51.4	44.1	4.6	53.8
Massachusetts	40.2	38.5	21.3	51.1	42.3	46.4	11.4	47.7
Massachusetts	—	—	—	—	*42.3*	*49.8*	*8.0*	*45.9*
Michigan	28.1	34.3	37.6	45.0	34.8	50.8	14.3	40.7
Minnesota	24.9	55.1	20.0	31.1	27.0	56.2	16.7	32.5
Mississippi	99.4	0.0	0.6	100.0	97.0	0.0	3.0	100.0
Missouri	49.2	28.9	21.9	63.0	53.0	40.1	6.8	56.9
Missouri	*49.2*	*32.6*	*18.2*	*60.2*	—	—	—	—
Montana	33.9	30.8	35.3	52.4	45.1	31.9	23.1	58.6
Nebraska	10.5	9.9	79.6	51.4	7.2	10.5	82.4	40.7
Nebraska	*45.6*	*47.5*	*6.9*	*49.0*	*48.1*	*47.4*	*4.5*	*50.3*
Nevada	37.0	37.3	25.7	49.8	37.8	42.0	20.2	47.4
New Hampshire	49.4	42.9	7.6	53.5	43.4	52.3	4.2	45.4
New Jersey	47.3	26.5	26.2	64.1	44.4	46.1	9.5	49.0
New Jersey	*47.3*	*31.4*	*21.2*	*60.1*	*45.0*	*47.0*	*8.0*	*48.9*
New Mexico	45.6	36.8	17.6	55.3	42.7	51.3	6.0	45.4
New York	37.2	26.8	36.0	58.2	30.3	35.4	34.4	46.1
New York	*41.9*	*31.2*	*26.9*	*57.3*	*40.2*	*45.9*	*13.9*	*46.7*
North Carolina	66.2	30.1	3.7	68.8	60.2	39.4	0.4	60.5
North Dakota	30.5	58.8	10.7	34.1	31.7	60.4	7.9	34.4
Ohio	41.6	29.3	29.1	58.7	45.4	45.0	9.6	50.2
Oklahoma	48.5	35.0	16.5	58.1	45.7	30.9	23.5	59.7
Oregon	27.2	32.4	40.5	45.6	28.5	33.0	38.5	46.4
Oregon	*27.2*	*45.3*	*27.6*	*37.5*	*28.5*	*43.2*	*28.3*	*39.7*
Pennsylvania	32.5	0.0	67.5	100.0	26.5	0.0	73.5	100.0
Pennsylvania	*32.5*	*56.1*	*11.4*	*36.6*	*26.5*	*48.4*	*25.1*	*35.3*
Rhode Island	44.9	42.4	12.7	51.5	45.3	50.2	4.6	47.4
South Carolina	99.5	0.2	0.3	99.8	99.1	0.1	0.8	99.9
South Dakota	38.6	55.4	5.9	41.1	39.1	54.6	6.2	41.7
Tennessee	61.3	25.9	12.8	70.3	69.5	22.3	8.2	75.7
Tennessee	*61.3*	*35.9*	*2.8*	*63.1*	*72.2*	*22.3*	*5.5*	*76.4*
Texas	78.4	7.6	14.0	91.2	82.6	5.1	12.3	94.2
Utah	33.2	38.5	28.4	46.3	0.0	48.3	51.7	0.0
Utah	—	—	—	—	*46.7*	*48.3*	*5.0*	*49.1*
Vermont	35.7	58.9	5.4	37.7	22.3	31.3	46.4	41.6
Vermont	—	—	—	—	*22.3*	*60.2*	*17.6*	*27.0*
Virginia	73.5	17.7	8.8	80.6	68.7	27.9	3.4	71.1
Washington	24.1	28.8	47.1	45.5	28.8	38.2	33.0	43.0
West Virginia	42.9	0.0	57.1	100.0	43.4	47.0	9.6	48.0
West Virginia	*42.9*	*49.7*	*7.3*	*46.3*	—	—	—	—
Wisconsin	41.3	46.6	12.1	46.9	37.4	51.6	11.0	42.0
Wyoming	35.7	46.4	17.8	43.5	41.4	51.3	7.2	44.7

Notes: Main entries are calculated from the raw vote values in tables series 5-70 to 5-122 for the appropriate years based on candidates who used the sole designation "Democrat" or "Republican" (or their historical antecedents listed in Appendix A) on the ballot. Other = candidates who used third-party names on the ballot or were listed as independent, unidentified, or scatter vote. Bold italicized entries in the table are the author's alternative party coding, which is used when a candidate listed a major party name (Democrat, Republican, or their historical antecedents) on the ballot with other party names or labels. These values are computed from the bold italicized raw vote values in table series 5-70 to 5-122 for the appropriate states and years. For a more detailed explanation of this alternate coding system, see Tables 5-1 and 1-3. —indicates that the state had no data, either because no vote data were found for the state in question or the state had not yet entered the Union. The table only lists at-large vote values for states having both at-large and district House races; see Appendix B for these states' district results aggregated to the state level.

Sources: Adapted from *United States Congressional Elections, 1788–1997* (1998), *Congressional Quarterly's Guide to U.S. Elections* (1994), ICPSR data sets 0001 and 0075, and independent search for state sources by the author.

Table 5-49 House Election Results, by State, 1916–1918 (Percentages)

| State | 1916 | | | | 1918 | | | |
	Democratic	Republican	Other	Democratic % of Two-Party Vote	Democratic	Republican	Other	Democratic % of Two-Party Vote
Alabama	80.3	19.1	0.6	80.8	85.8	14.2	0.0	85.8
Alaska	—	—	—	—	—	—	—	—
Arizona	65.7	28.5	5.8	69.8	60.4	37.9	1.7	61.4
Arkansas	82.9	17.1	0.0	82.9	100.0	0.0	0.0	100.0
California	22.0	30.2	47.8	42.1	9.9	14.8	75.3	40.0
California	*32.1*	*49.1*	*18.9*	*39.5*	*34.6*	*56.7*	*8.7*	*37.9*
Colorado	50.2	43.5	6.3	53.5	43.6	52.4	4.0	45.4
Connecticut	46.2	50.1	3.6	48.0	46.9	49.7	3.4	48.6
Delaware	47.6	47.3	5.1	50.2	47.6	51.4	1.0	48.1
Florida	77.9	16.3	5.8	82.7	100.0	0.0	0.0	100.0
Georgia	94.3	5.2	0.5	94.8	95.3	4.7	0.0	95.3
Hawaii	—	—	—	—	—	—	—	—
Idaho	43.4	50.3	6.3	46.3	36.8	63.2	0.0	36.8
Illinois	41.5	53.8	4.7	43.6	40.0	55.6	4.4	41.9
Indiana	45.5	48.5	5.9	48.4	44.3	54.1	1.6	45.0
Iowa	39.0	59.0	2.0	39.8	35.0	64.0	1.0	35.3
Kansas	46.0	46.0	7.9	50.0	40.1	56.9	3.0	41.3
Kentucky	52.3	46.5	1.2	52.9	52.2	47.8	0.0	52.2
Louisiana	91.1	0.4	8.5	99.5	100.0	0.0	0.0	100.0
Maine	45.4	53.6	1.1	45.8	44.1	55.9	0.0	44.1
Maryland	48.6	47.0	4.4	50.9	50.9	47.5	1.6	51.7
Massachusetts	39.2	55.8	5.0	41.3	38.2	59.3	2.5	39.2
Michigan	40.0	55.3	4.7	42.0	33.4	65.2	1.4	33.9
Michigan	*42.0*	*55.3*	*2.7*	*43.2*	—	—	—	—
Minnesota	28.6	55.1	16.3	34.1	24.8	65.0	10.2	27.6
Mississippi	97.6	0.0	2.4	100.0	97.8	0.0	2.2	100.0
Missouri	50.9	47.3	1.8	51.8	52.2	46.6	1.2	52.9
Montana	49.6	45.1	5.3	52.3	46.6	45.6	7.8	50.5
Nebraska	0.0	12.7	87.3	0.0	43.6	56.0	0.5	43.8
Nebraska	*47.5*	*49.6*	*3.0*	*48.9*	—	—	—	—
Nevada	40.5	43.6	15.9	48.2	51.3	43.1	5.6	54.3
New Hampshire	46.7	51.6	1.7	47.5	45.7	54.3	0.0	45.7
New Jersey	42.5	51.3	6.2	45.3	45.5	49.6	4.9	47.8
New Mexico	48.9	48.1	3.1	50.4	48.1	50.7	1.2	48.7
New York	15.6	12.7	71.7	55.0	36.1	34.7	29.2	50.9
New York	*41.1*	*52.8*	*6.2*	*43.8*	*42.7*	*48.3*	*9.0*	*46.9*
North Carolina	57.9	42.0	0.1	58.0	60.4	39.6	0.0	60.4
North Dakota	30.1	65.4	4.5	31.5	35.0	65.0	0.0	35.0
Ohio	48.8	48.6	2.6	50.1	43.4	54.7	1.9	44.2
Oklahoma	49.2	34.1	16.7	59.0	55.0	41.3	3.7	57.1
Oregon	4.4	15.9	79.7	21.5	18.5	29.3	52.2	38.6
Oregon	*21.8*	*58.9*	*19.3*	*27.0*	*18.5*	*69.7*	*11.9*	*20.9*
Pennsylvania	37.8	0.0	62.2	100.0	31.5	62.2	6.2	33.6
Pennsylvania	*37.8*	*53.7*	*8.5*	*41.3*	—	—	—	—
Rhode Island	47.9	49.8	2.3	49.0	43.5	54.3	2.2	44.5
South Carolina	98.1	1.8	0.1	98.2	99.3	0.7	0.0	99.3
South Dakota	41.8	54.8	3.4	43.2	39.1	55.9	5.0	41.1
Tennessee	57.4	40.0	2.6	58.9	77.0	22.9	0.1	77.1
Texas	81.8	12.7	5.5	86.5	96.3	3.7	0.0	96.3
Utah	0.0	40.6	59.4	0.0	29.1	42.1	28.8	40.9
Utah	*56.2*	*40.6*	*3.2*	*58.1*	*56.7*	*42.1*	*1.2*	*57.4*
Vermont	25.5	35.3	39.2	42.0	24.8	37.8	37.4	39.6
Vermont	*25.5*	*71.6*	*2.8*	*26.3*	*24.8*	*75.2*	*0.0*	*24.8*
Virginia	67.7	30.5	1.7	68.9	79.8	20.2	0.0	79.8
Washington	42.6	51.4	6.0	45.3	40.4	55.7	3.9	42.0
West Virginia	49.7	50.3	0.0	49.7	46.7	52.4	0.9	47.1
Wisconsin	32.9	57.2	9.9	36.5	22.6	54.5	22.9	29.3
Wyoming	48.0	49.0	3.0	49.5	35.8	64.2	0.0	35.8

Notes: Main entries are calculated from the raw vote values in tables series 5-70 to 5-122 for the appropriate years based on candidates who used the sole designation "Democrat" or "Republican" (or their historical antecedents listed in Appendix A) on the ballot. Other = candidates who used third-party names on the ballot or were listed as independent, unidentified, or scatter vote. Bold italicized entries in the table are the author's alternative party coding, which is used when a candidate listed a major party name (Democrat, Republican, or their historical antecedents) on the ballot with other party names or labels. These values are computed from the bold italicized raw vote values in table series 5-70 to 5-122 for the appropriate states and years. For a more detailed explanation of this alternate coding system, see Tables 5-1 and 1-3. —indicates that the state had no data, either because no vote data were found for the state in question or the state had not yet entered the Union. No special House elections are included in the table. The table only lists at-large vote values for states having both at-large and district House races; see Appendix B for these states' district results aggregated to the state level.

Sources: Adapted from *United States Congressional Elections, 1788–1997* (1998), *Congressional Quarterly's Guide to U.S. Elections* (1994), ICPSR data sets 0001 and 0075, and independent search for state sources by the author.

Table 5-50 House Election Results, by State, 1920–1922 (Percentages)

	1920				1922			
State	Democratic	Republican	Other	Democratic % of Two-Party Vote	Democratic	Republican	Other	Democratic % of Two-Party Vote
Alabama	71.9	27.7	0.4	72.2	81.3	18.7	0.0	81.3
Alaska	—	—	—	—	—	—	—	—
Arizona	57.8	42.2	0.0	57.8	71.8	28.2	0.0	71.8
Arkansas	67.4	32.6	0.0	67.4	87.8	12.2	0.0	87.8
California	7.8	27.6	64.6	22.1	2.9	16.1	81.0	15.3
California	*19.8*	*68.5*	*11.7*	*22.4*	*19.8*	*76.2*	*4.0*	*20.6*
Colorado	39.5	60.5	0.0	39.5	48.1	51.5	0.4	48.3
Connecticut	27.5	62.7	9.8	30.5	45.7	52.6	1.7	46.5
Connecticut	*33.7*	*62.7*	*3.6*	*35.0*	—	—	—	—
Delaware	43.0	55.7	1.3	43.5	53.9	44.9	1.3	54.6
Florida	78.9	17.1	4.1	82.2	87.5	12.4	0.0	87.6
Florida	*78.9*	*18.4*	*2.8*	*81.1*	—	—	—	—
Georgia	61.1	35.8	3.1	63.0	98.0	1.6	0.4	98.4
Hawaii	—	—	—	—	—	—	—	—
Idaho	32.3	61.4	6.3	34.5	27.8	47.4	24.9	37.0
Illinois	27.8	65.6	6.7	29.7	39.7	56.2	4.1	41.4
Indiana	41.2	55.5	3.2	42.6	48.4	50.5	1.0	49.0
Iowa	12.4	84.4	3.2	12.8	38.6	61.0	0.4	38.7
Kansas	36.5	61.7	1.8	37.1	44.5	54.2	1.2	45.1
Kentucky	50.7	48.0	1.3	51.4	55.3	39.2	5.5	58.5
Louisiana	100.0	0.0	0.0	100.0	100.0	0.0	0.0	100.0
Maine	33.3	66.7	0.0	33.3	42.4	57.6	0.0	42.4
Maryland	43.4	50.3	6.3	46.3	49.8	47.8	2.3	51.0
Massachusetts	29.5	66.0	4.5	30.9	42.1	57.7	0.2	42.2
Massachusetts	*31.1*	*66.0*	*2.9*	*32.1*	—	—	—	—
Michigan	22.6	75.4	2.0	23.1	32.7	67.0	0.3	32.8
Minnesota	14.0	59.9	26.1	18.9	21.0	60.5	18.6	25.7
Mississippi	94.1	3.1	2.8	96.9	97.5	2.4	0.1	97.6
Missouri	44.2	54.1	1.7	45.0	50.6	48.8	0.6	50.9
Montana	38.2	61.8	0.0	38.2	50.6	48.9	0.6	50.9
Nebraska	32.3	61.6	6.0	34.4	46.2	47.7	6.1	49.2
Nevada	34.1	48.9	16.9	41.1	57.0	43.0	0.0	57.0
New Hampshire	39.3	60.3	0.4	39.4	51.0	49.0	0.0	51.0
New Jersey	35.3	61.8	2.9	36.3	49.6	49.6	0.7	50.0
New Mexico	46.9	51.9	1.2	47.5	54.0	45.2	0.8	54.4
New York	32.6	56.7	10.7	36.5	42.3	30.0	27.8	58.5
New York	*33.2*	*57.8*	*9.0*	*36.5*	*47.9*	*46.2*	*6.0*	*50.9*
North Carolina	57.7	42.3	0.0	57.7	62.0	38.0	0.0	62.0
North Dakota	11.7	57.3	31.0	17.0	22.9	77.1	0.0	22.9
Ohio	41.2	58.1	0.7	41.5	44.9	53.8	1.3	45.5
Oklahoma	46.9	47.9	5.2	49.5	60.8	38.4	0.9	61.3
Oregon	22.5	33.8	43.7	39.9	29.1	68.3	2.6	29.9
Oregon	*22.5*	*71.7*	*5.8*	*23.9*	—	—	—	—
Pennsylvania	26.0	63.6	10.3	29.0	26.4	24.1	49.5	52.2
Pennsylvania	—	—	—	—	*36.9*	*59.3*	*3.8*	*38.4*
Rhode Island	35.3	63.3	1.4	35.8	52.6	47.4	0.0	52.6
South Carolina	98.0	1.3	0.8	98.7	98.1	1.9	0.0	98.1
South Dakota	21.9	56.8	21.4	27.8	19.5	54.6	25.8	26.4
Tennessee	48.0	49.9	2.0	49.0	64.7	35.3	0.0	64.7
Tennessee	*48.0*	*51.2*	*0.8*	*48.4*	—	—	—	—
Texas	76.8	16.1	7.2	82.7	84.8	15.2	0.0	84.8
Texas	*76.8*	*17.5*	*5.7*	*81.4*	—	—	—	—
Utah	38.9	56.1	5.0	41.0	45.1	51.6	3.3	46.6
Vermont	23.3	38.1	38.7	37.9	35.5	0.0	64.5	100.0
Vermont	*23.3*	*76.7*	*0.0*	*23.3*	*35.5*	*64.5*	*0.0*	*35.5*
Virginia	62.7	35.8	1.5	63.6	67.9	32.0	0.1	68.0
Virginia	*62.7*	*37.2*	*0.2*	*62.8*	—	—	—	—
Washington	16.9	58.3	24.8	22.5	22.6	62.2	15.2	26.7
West Virginia	45.3	54.7	0.0	45.3	51.0	48.5	0.5	51.2
Wisconsin	17.3	68.7	14.0	20.1	2.6	76.5	20.9	3.2
Wisconsin	—	—	—	—	*6.5*	*81.4*	*12.1*	*7.4*
Wyoming	26.5	61.5	12.0	30.1	46.7	53.3	0.0	46.7

Notes: Main entries are calculated from the raw vote values in tables series 5-70 to 5-122 for the appropriate years based on candidates who used the sole designation "Democrat" or "Republican" (or their historical antecedents listed in Appendix A) on the ballot. Other = candidates who used third-party names on the ballot or were listed as independent, unidentified, or scatter vote. Bold italicized entries in the table are the author's alternative party coding, which is used when a candidate listed a major party name (Democrat, Republican, or their historical antecedents) on the ballot with other party names or labels. These values are computed from the bold italicized raw vote values in table series 5-70 to 5-122 for the appropriate states and years. For a more detailed explanation of this alternate coding system, see Tables 5-1 and 1-3. —indicates that the state had no data, either because no vote data were found for the state in question or the state had not yet entered the Union. No special House elections are included in the table. The table only lists at-large vote values for states having both at-large and district House races; see Appendix B for these states' district results aggregated to the state level.

Sources: Adapted from *United States Congressional Elections, 1788–1997* (1998), *Congressional Quarterly's Guide to U.S. Elections* (1994), ICPSR data sets 0001 and 0075, and independent search for state sources by the author.

Table 5-51 House Election Results, by State, 1924–1926 (Percentages)

State	1924				1926			
	Democratic	Republican	Other	Democratic % of Two-Party Vote	Democratic	Republican	Other	Democratic % of Two-Party Vote
Alabama	79.3	20.7	0.0	79.3	84.4	15.6	0.0	84.4
Alaska	—	—	—	—	—	—	—	—
Arizona	82.4	17.6	0.0	82.4	64.1	35.9	0.0	64.1
Arkansas	72.9	27.1	0.0	72.9	85.8	14.2	0.0	85.8
California	8.1	32.3	59.6	20.1	4.9	34.0	61.1	12.7
California	*22.7*	*68.3*	*9.0*	*24.9*	*17.7*	*78.8*	*3.4*	*18.3*
Colorado	43.6	53.1	3.3	45.1	44.8	54.4	0.9	45.1
Connecticut	25.6	65.6	8.8	28.0	35.4	63.7	0.9	35.7
Connecticut	*33.2*	*65.6*	*1.2*	*33.6*	—	—	—	—
Delaware	40.8	58.6	0.6	41.1	43.1	56.9	0.0	43.1
Florida	74.7	22.2	3.1	77.0	76.5	16.9	6.5	81.9
Florida	—	—	—	—	*76.5*	*23.5*	*0.0*	*76.5*
Georgia	97.8	2.2	0.0	97.8	100.0	0.0	0.0	100.0
Hawaii	—	—	—	—	—	—	—	—
Idaho	24.9	57.5	17.6	30.3	18.2	62.9	18.8	22.5
Idaho	—	—	—	—	*23.7*	*62.9*	*13.4*	*27.3*
Illinois	30.3	68.7	1.1	30.6	38.7	60.6	0.7	39.0
Illinois	*30.3*	*68.7*	*1.0*	*30.6*	—	—	—	—
Indiana	43.7	55.3	1.0	44.1	46.8	53.2	0.0	46.8
Iowa	31.3	68.6	0.1	31.3	30.8	69.1	0.1	30.9
Kansas	44.2	54.8	1.0	44.6	40.8	59.1	0.0	40.9
Kentucky	56.0	41.6	2.3	57.4	52.3	47.7	0.0	52.3
Louisiana	100.0	0.0	0.0	100.0	98.4	1.6	0.0	98.4
Maine	39.7	60.3	0.0	39.7	38.3	61.7	0.0	38.3
Maryland	50.8	47.9	1.3	51.5	55.6	43.6	0.8	56.0
Massachusetts	38.6	60.2	1.2	39.1	40.7	54.1	5.2	42.9
Massachusetts	—	—	—	—	*40.7*	*59.3*	*0.0*	*40.7*
Michigan	20.8	79.1	0.1	20.8	21.8	78.1	0.1	21.8
Minnesota	6.6	52.0	41.5	11.2	5.7	58.7	35.6	8.9
Mississippi	99.4	0.6	0.0	99.4	100.0	0.0	0.0	100.0
Missouri	48.6	50.5	1.0	49.0	50.6	49.3	0.1	50.6
Montana	45.8	49.8	4.3	47.9	49.4	48.6	2.0	50.4
Nebraska	45.9	50.1	4.0	47.8	49.6	48.3	2.1	50.7
Nevada	49.6	50.4	0.0	49.6	42.3	57.7	0.0	42.3
New Hampshire	41.7	58.3	0.0	41.7	37.8	62.2	0.0	37.8
New Jersey	36.4	61.7	2.0	37.1	42.9	56.6	0.5	43.1
New Mexico	51.2	47.8	1.0	51.8	51.4	48.3	0.3	51.6
New York	40.5	49.8	9.7	44.8	47.7	44.7	7.6	51.6
New York	*43.4*	*51.8*	*4.8*	*45.6*	*47.7*	*49.2*	*3.1*	*49.2*
North Carolina	61.7	38.3	0.0	61.7	61.3	38.7	0.0	61.3
North Dakota	16.5	66.7	16.7	19.9	17.6	77.9	4.5	18.4
Ohio	41.3	56.7	1.9	42.2	43.6	56.2	0.2	43.7
Oklahoma	56.2	40.4	3.4	58.2	56.4	43.4	0.2	56.5
Oregon	32.6	59.9	7.4	35.3	19.0	71.2	9.8	21.1
Oregon	—	—	—	—	*28.8*	*71.2*	*0.0*	*28.8*
Pennsylvania	10.2	36.1	53.7	22.0	14.1	32.2	53.6	30.5
Pennsylvania	*27.4*	*67.4*	*5.2*	*28.9*	*25.7*	*71.0*	*3.3*	*26.5*
Rhode Island	40.8	59.2	0.0	40.8	41.9	58.1	0.0	41.9
South Carolina	99.5	0.5	0.0	99.5	100.0	0.0	0.0	100.0
South Dakota	19.4	57.3	23.3	25.3	40.4	57.2	2.4	41.4
Tennessee	64.2	33.3	2.5	65.8	70.0	30.0	0.0	70.0
Texas	87.1	12.9	0.0	87.1	97.2	2.8	0.0	97.2
Utah	44.2	55.8	0.0	44.2	38.3	60.8	0.9	38.6
Vermont	20.5	0.0	79.5	100.0	23.9	76.1	0.0	23.9
Vermont	*20.5*	*79.5*	*0.0*	*20.5*	—	—	—	—
Virginia	72.6	27.4	0.0	72.6	68.9	30.4	0.7	69.4
Washington	26.0	64.4	9.7	28.7	29.3	70.5	0.2	29.4
West Virginia	48.2	51.3	0.6	48.5	48.3	51.7	0.0	48.3
Wisconsin	21.8	70.5	7.8	23.6	6.2	79.5	14.3	7.2
Wisconsin	—	—	—	—	*7.6*	*82.9*	*9.5*	*8.4*
Wyoming	39.9	60.1	0.0	39.9	38.7	60.8	0.5	38.9

Notes: Main entries are calculated from the raw vote values in tables series 5-70 to 5-122 for the appropriate years based on candidates who used the sole designation "Democrat" or "Republican" (or their historical antecedents listed in Appendix A) on the ballot. Other = candidates who used third-party names on the ballot or were listed as independent, unidentified, or scatter vote. Bold italicized entries in the table are the author's alternative party coding, which is used when a candidate listed a major party name (Democrat, Republican, or their historical antecedents) on the ballot with other party names or labels. These values are computed from the bold italicized raw vote values in table series 5-70 to 5-122 for the appropriate states and years. For a more detailed explanation of this alternate coding system, see Tables 5-1 and 1-3. —indicates that the state had no data, either because no vote data were found for the state in question or the state had not yet entered the Union. No special House elections are included in the table. The table only lists at-large vote values for states having both at-large and district House races; see Appendix B for these states' district results aggregated to the state level.

Sources: Adapted from *United States Congressional Elections, 1788–1997* (1998), *Congressional Quarterly's Guide to U.S. Elections* (1994), ICPSR data sets 0001 and 0075, and independent search for state sources by the author.

Table 5-52 House Election Results, by State, 1928–1930 (Percentages)

| | 1928 | | | | 1930 | | | |
| | Democratic | Republican | Other | Democratic % of Two-Party Vote | Democratic | Republican | Other | Democratic % of Two-Party Vote |
State								
Alabama	82.2	17.8	0.0	82.2	83.4	16.6	0.0	83.4
Alaska	—	—	—	—	—	—	—	—
Arizona	61.5	38.5	0.0	61.5	100.0	0.0	0.0	100.0
Arkansas	78.7	21.3	0.0	78.7	100.0	0.0	0.0	100.0
California	7.3	26.6	66.1	21.4	5.9	37.8	56.2	13.6
California	*11.5*	*85.0*	*3.5*	*11.9*	*12.0*	*88.0*	*0.0*	*12.0*
Colorado	40.0	59.8	0.3	40.1	46.5	53.1	0.4	46.6
Connecticut	45.4	54.0	0.6	45.7	48.6	50.5	0.8	49.0
Delaware	36.4	63.6	0.0	36.4	0.0	55.7	44.3	0.0
Delaware	*—*	*—*	*—*	*—*	*44.1*	*55.7*	*0.1*	*44.2*
Florida	68.1	31.9	0.0	68.1	87.6	12.3	0.1	87.7
Georgia	100.0	0.0	0.0	100.0	96.6	2.7	0.7	97.3
Hawaii	—	—	—	—	—	—	—	—
Idaho	33.1	66.2	0.7	33.3	36.1	63.9	0.0	36.1
Illinois	40.4	59.0	0.6	40.6	51.4	48.0	0.6	51.7
Indiana	45.4	54.5	0.1	45.4	52.8	47.1	0.1	52.9
Iowa	29.0	71.0	0.0	29.0	39.2	60.7	0.2	39.2
Kansas	36.8	63.2	0.0	36.8	42.9	57.1	0.0	42.9
Kentucky	43.9	56.1	0.0	43.9	52.6	46.3	1.2	53.2
Louisiana	91.2	8.8	0.0	91.2	98.3	1.7	0.0	98.3
Maine	29.8	70.2	0.0	29.8	38.6	61.4	0.0	38.6
Maryland	48.8	50.7	0.5	49.1	59.1	40.7	0.2	59.2
Massachusetts	43.2	52.1	4.6	45.3	45.0	53.5	1.5	45.7
Massachusetts	*47.5*	*52.1*	*0.4*	*47.7*	*—*	*—*	*—*	*—*
Michigan	26.7	73.1	0.2	26.7	23.0	76.2	0.8	23.2
Minnesota	17.9	54.1	28.0	24.9	8.6	54.3	37.0	13.7
Mississippi	100.0	0.0	0.0	100.0	100.0	0.0	0.0	100.0
Missouri	47.9	52.1	0.0	47.9	50.4	49.5	0.1	50.5
Montana	42.7	56.9	0.5	42.9	49.7	48.6	1.6	50.6
Nebraska	44.6	55.4	0.0	44.6	52.1	47.9	0.0	52.1
Nevada	41.4	58.6	0.0	41.4	45.6	54.4	0.0	45.6
New Hampshire	41.1	58.8	0.1	41.2	42.3	57.7	0.0	42.3
New Jersey	39.3	60.6	0.1	39.3	42.9	56.4	0.7	43.2
New Mexico	47.8	52.2	0.0	47.8	55.7	44.0	0.3	55.9
New York	46.1	49.2	4.7	48.4	49.4	43.1	7.5	53.4
New York	*47.2*	*49.2*	*3.6*	*49.0*	*50.7*	*43.1*	*6.2*	*54.0*
North Carolina	55.1	44.9	0.0	55.1	62.8	37.2	0.0	62.8
North Dakota	25.7	74.3	0.0	25.7	28.6	69.4	1.9	29.2
Ohio	39.2	60.7	0.1	39.2	48.5	50.8	0.7	48.8
Oklahoma	50.0	49.6	0.4	50.2	61.9	38.1	0.0	61.9
Oregon	29.1	66.9	3.9	30.3	46.9	51.0	2.1	47.9
Pennsylvania	23.9	31.5	44.6	43.1	21.2	54.1	24.6	28.2
Pennsylvania	*30.4*	*68.8*	*0.8*	*30.6*	*28.1*	*70.8*	*1.1*	*28.4*
Rhode Island	48.7	51.3	0.0	48.7	48.3	51.7	0.0	48.3
South Carolina	100.0	0.0	0.0	100.0	100.0	0.0	0.0	100.0
South Dakota	42.0	57.3	0.7	42.3	32.8	62.6	4.7	34.4
Tennessee	60.5	39.5	0.0	60.5	62.5	19.3	18.3	76.4
Tennessee	*—*	*—*	*—*	*—*	*62.5*	*36.6*	*1.0*	*63.1*
Texas	87.5	12.5	0.0	87.5	84.6	15.4	0.0	84.6
Utah	44.3	55.2	0.5	44.5	40.6	52.3	7.1	43.7
Vermont	28.2	70.5	1.3	28.6	32.6	67.4	0.0	32.6
Virginia	67.5	31.9	0.6	67.9	65.7	32.9	1.4	66.7
Virginia	*—*	*—*	*—*	*—*	*66.1*	*33.8*	*0.1*	*66.2*
Washington	31.5	68.3	0.2	31.6	26.1	71.2	2.8	26.8
West Virginia	45.7	54.3	0.0	45.7	50.6	49.4	0.0	50.6
Wisconsin	26.2	66.7	7.1	28.2	13.4	74.6	12.0	15.2
Wisconsin	*—*	*—*	*—*	*—*	*13.8*	*74.6*	*11.5*	*15.6*
Wyoming	47.8	51.7	0.4	48.0	34.4	65.6	0.0	34.4

Notes: Main entries are calculated from the raw vote values in tables series 5-70 to 5-122 for the appropriate years based on candidates who used the sole designation "Democrat" or "Republican" (or their historical antecedents listed in Appendix A) on the ballot. Other = candidates who used third-party names on the ballot or were listed as independent, unidentified, or scatter vote. Bold italicized entries in the table are the author's alternative party coding, which is used when a candidate listed a major party name (Democrat, Republican, or their historical antecedents) on the ballot with other party names or labels. These values are computed from the bold italicized raw vote values in table series 5-70 to 5-122 for the appropriate states and years. For a more detailed explanation of this alternate coding system, see Tables 5-1 and 1-3. —indicates that the state had no data, either because no vote data were found for the state in question or the state had not yet entered the Union. No special House elections are included in the table. The table only lists at-large vote values for states having both at-large and district House races; see Appendix B for these states' district results aggregated to the state level.

Sources: Adapted from *United States Congressional Elections, 1788–1997* (1998), *Congressional Quarterly's Guide to U.S. Elections* (1994), ICPSR data sets 0001 and 0075, and independent search for state sources by the author.

Table 5-53 House Election Results, by State, 1932–1934 (Percentages)

	1932				1934			
State	Democratic	Republican	Other	Democratic % of Two-Party Vote	Democratic	Republican	Other	Democratic % of Two-Party Vote
Alabama	89.6	9.8	0.6	90.2	90.4	6.2	3.4	93.6
Alaska	—	—	—	—	—	—	—	—
Arizona	70.8	27.9	1.3	71.8	68.6	29.4	1.9	70.0
Arkansas	97.7	2.3	0.0	97.7	92.3	7.3	0.4	92.7
California	41.4	36.7	21.9	53.0	32.9	23.8	43.2	58.0
California	*45.3*	*50.2*	*4.4*	*47.4*	*49.0*	*42.5*	*8.5*	*53.5*
Colorado	54.7	44.7	0.6	55.0	60.0	35.4	4.6	62.9
Connecticut	47.7	48.0	4.3	49.8	48.1	45.2	6.7	51.6
Connecticut	*47.7*	*48.8*	*3.5*	*49.4*	—	—	—	—
Delaware	46.1	43.6	10.3	51.4	46.5	53.1	0.5	46.7
Florida	75.2	24.8	0.0	75.2	100.0	0.0	0.0	100.0
Georgia	94.8	5.2	0.0	94.8	99.5	0.5	0.0	99.5
Hawaii	—	—	—	—	—	—	—	—
Idaho	55.0	42.9	2.1	56.1	61.1	38.7	0.3	61.2
Illinois	53.2	45.1	1.7	54.1	54.8	43.7	1.5	55.7
Indiana	55.0	44.2	0.8	55.4	52.2	47.1	0.7	52.5
Iowa	52.6	46.7	0.7	53.0	53.5	46.5	0.0	53.5
Kansas	49.7	48.7	1.6	50.5	48.6	50.2	1.2	49.2
Kentucky	59.3	40.4	0.4	59.5	54.2	43.9	1.9	55.3
Louisiana	100.0	0.0	0.0	100.0	100.0	0.0	0.0	100.0
Maine	50.3	49.3	0.4	50.5	51.0	49.0	0.0	51.0
Maine	*50.3*	*49.6*	*0.1*	*50.4*	—	—	—	—
Maryland	66.1	33.2	0.7	66.6	58.6	39.6	1.7	59.7
Massachusetts	47.8	51.3	1.0	48.2	46.4	46.6	7.0	49.9
Massachusetts	—	—	—	—	*46.4*	*52.7*	*0.9*	*46.8*
Michigan	48.8	49.1	2.1	49.9	48.7	49.9	1.4	49.4
Minnesota	28.1	29.4	42.5	48.8	25.7	32.5	41.8	44.2
Mississippi	96.5	0.0	3.5	100.0	100.0	0.0	0.0	100.0
Mississippi	*96.5*	*3.5*	*0.0*	*96.5*	—	—	—	—
Missouri	62.0	37.3	0.8	62.5	60.4	39.0	0.5	60.8
Montana	55.2	41.8	3.1	56.9	69.0	30.1	0.9	69.6
Nebraska	54.2	38.3	7.5	58.6	53.3	44.8	1.9	54.4
Nevada	60.8	39.2	0.0	60.8	71.2	28.8	0.0	71.2
New Hampshire	49.1	50.7	0.3	49.2	50.3	49.4	0.2	50.5
New Jersey	48.2	50.0	1.7	49.1	50.9	48.1	1.1	51.4
New Mexico	63.4	35.4	1.3	64.2	51.8	47.7	0.5	52.1
New York	54.0	40.2	5.8	57.4	54.8	39.2	6.0	58.3
North Carolina	69.7	30.3	0.0	69.7	64.9	35.1	0.0	64.9
North Dakota	33.4	66.3	0.3	33.5	31.0	52.3	16.7	37.2
Ohio	51.4	47.3	1.3	52.1	53.6	45.7	0.7	54.0
Oklahoma	72.8	26.7	0.5	73.2	66.8	30.7	2.4	68.5
Oregon	47.3	42.6	10.0	52.6	42.7	46.4	10.9	47.9
Pennsylvania	21.8	14.9	63.2	59.4	38.6	28.8	32.6	57.3
Pennsylvania	*39.8*	*55.2*	*5.0*	*41.9*	*54.4*	*42.4*	*3.2*	*56.2*
Rhode Island	55.1	44.7	0.2	55.2	57.4	42.6	0.0	57.4
South Carolina	98.1	1.9	0.0	98.1	98.9	0.2	0.8	99.8
South Dakota	53.7	44.3	2.0	54.8	57.1	42.1	0.8	57.5
Tennessee	64.0	26.0	10.0	71.1	70.6	25.2	4.2	73.7
Texas	92.6	7.0	0.3	92.9	98.6	1.3	0.1	98.7
Utah	53.6	44.6	1.8	54.6	63.3	35.5	1.2	64.1
Vermont	35.6	64.4	0.0	35.6	42.4	56.9	0.7	42.7
Virginia	56.7	25.4	17.9	69.1	73.4	23.1	3.6	76.1
Washington	59.2	33.7	7.1	63.7	65.6	31.6	2.7	67.5
West Virginia	53.4	46.4	0.2	53.5	55.7	43.9	0.5	55.9
Wisconsin	48.0	44.6	7.4	51.8	31.7	24.3	44.0	56.5
Wisconsin	*48.0*	*45.0*	*7.0*	*51.6*	—	—	—	—
Wyoming	47.7	49.7	2.6	49.0	58.3	41.0	0.7	58.7

Notes: Main entries are calculated from the raw vote values in tables series 5-70 to 5-122 for the appropriate years based on candidates who used the sole designation "Democrat" or "Republican" (or their historical antecedents listed in Appendix A) on the ballot. Other = candidates who used third-party names on the ballot or were listed as independent, unidentified, or scatter vote. Bold italicized entries in the table are the author's alternative party coding, which is used when a candidate listed a major party name (Democrat, Republican, or their historical antecedents) on the ballot with other party names or labels. These values are computed from the bold italicized raw vote values in table series 5-70 to 5-122 for the appropriate states and years. For a more detailed explanation of this alternate coding system, see Tables 5-1 and 1-3. —indicates that the state had no data, either because no vote data were found for the state in question or the state had not yet entered the Union. No special House elections are included in the table. The table only lists at-large vote values for states having both at-large and district House races; see Appendix B for these states' district results aggregated to the state level.

Sources: Adapted from *United States Congressional Elections, 1788–1997* (1998), *Congressional Quarterly's Guide to U.S. Elections* (1994), ICPSR data sets 0001 and 0075, and independent search for state sources by the author.

Table 5-54 House Election Results, by State, 1936–1938 (Percentages)

	1936				1938			
State	Democratic	Republican	Other	Democratic % of Two-Party Vote	Democratic	Republican	Other	Democratic % of Two-Party Vote
Alabama	93.5	6.3	0.2	93.7	92.3	7.7	0.0	92.3
Alaska	—	—	—	—	—	—	—	—
Arizona	77.6	18.7	3.7	80.5	80.3	19.7	0.0	80.3
Arkansas	92.0	8.0	0.0	92.0	100.0	0.0	0.0	100.0
California	33.3	28.8	37.9	53.6	31.4	22.2	46.4	58.6
California	*53.5*	*43.1*	*3.4*	*55.4*	*46.2*	*46.6*	*7.2*	*49.8*
Colorado	61.9	37.1	1.1	62.5	59.0	40.4	0.5	59.3
Connecticut	53.9	41.0	5.1	56.8	39.7	43.1	17.3	48.0
Delaware	51.7	43.9	4.4	54.1	43.3	55.9	0.8	43.6
Delaware	*51.7*	*48.2*	*0.1*	*51.8*	*43.3*	*56.6*	*0.1*	*43.3*
Florida	81.9	18.1	0.0	81.9	95.6	4.4	0.0	95.6
Georgia	94.3	5.7	0.0	94.3	98.8	0.0	1.2	100.0
Hawaii	—	—	—	—	—	—	—	—
Idaho	64.7	35.3	0.0	64.7	53.5	46.5	0.0	53.5
Illinois	55.3	42.1	2.6	56.8	51.5	48.2	0.3	51.6
Indiana	55.9	43.4	0.7	56.3	49.2	50.8	0.0	49.2
Iowa	49.3	48.5	2.2	50.4	43.9	55.6	0.5	44.1
Kansas	47.2	51.5	1.3	47.8	41.0	59.0	0.0	41.0
Kentucky	58.8	40.2	1.0	59.4	59.1	40.9	0.0	59.1
Louisiana	100.0	0.0	0.0	100.0	100.0	0.0	0.0	100.0
Maine	39.6	56.6	3.8	41.2	41.5	58.5	0.0	41.5
Maryland	59.2	39.6	1.2	59.9	59.7	39.5	0.8	60.2
Massachusetts	43.8	47.7	8.5	47.9	46.1	53.8	0.1	46.1
Massachusetts	*45.8*	*49.7*	*4.5*	*48.0*	—	—	—	—
Michigan	52.3	45.1	2.6	53.7	46.1	53.7	0.2	46.2
Michigan	—	—	—	—	*46.2*	*53.7*	*0.1*	*46.3*
Minnesota	17.4	38.5	44.0	31.2	17.7	50.2	32.1	26.1
Mississippi	98.7	1.3	0.0	98.7	100.0	0.0	0.0	100.0
Missouri	60.4	39.5	0.1	60.4	59.3	40.6	0.1	59.3
Montana	64.3	35.3	0.4	64.5	50.2	49.8	0.0	50.2
Nebraska	50.8	46.0	3.1	52.5	45.7	51.9	2.4	46.8
Nevada	58.4	26.8	14.7	68.5	66.4	33.6	0.0	66.4
New Hampshire	47.5	51.8	0.7	47.8	43.7	56.3	0.0	43.7
New Jersey	53.4	45.4	1.2	54.0	47.0	51.9	1.1	47.5
New Mexico	62.9	37.0	0.0	62.9	58.4	41.4	0.2	58.5
New York	57.3	39.5	3.3	59.2	0.0	0.0	100.0	—
New York	—	—	—	—	*52.4*	*44.6*	*3.0*	*54.0*
North Carolina	71.2	28.8	0.0	71.2	66.5	33.5	0.0	66.5
North Dakota	42.7	55.7	1.6	43.4	25.5	70.8	3.7	26.5
Ohio	55.7	44.0	0.3	55.9	47.6	52.4	0.0	47.6
Oklahoma	70.7	28.8	0.5	71.1	68.7	30.9	0.4	69.0
Oregon	47.4	46.6	6.0	50.4	41.4	58.6	0.0	41.4
Pennsylvania	54.4	42.0	3.6	56.5	39.6	50.8	9.6	43.8
Pennsylvania	*55.3*	*42.2*	*2.5*	*56.7*	*46.4*	*52.9*	*0.6*	*46.7*
Rhode Island	49.1	43.9	7.0	52.8	46.3	24.4	29.3	65.4
Rhode Island	—	—	—	—	*46.3*	*53.7*	*0.0*	*46.3*
South Carolina	98.6	0.6	0.8	99.4	99.2	0.7	0.2	99.3
South Carolina	*98.6*	*0.8*	*0.6*	*99.2*	—	—	—	—
South Dakota	50.1	49.9	0.0	50.1	44.2	55.8	0.0	44.2
Tennessee	71.8	27.0	1.3	72.7	64.5	24.2	11.3	72.7
Texas	93.4	6.4	0.3	93.6	98.9	1.0	0.0	99.0
Utah	69.5	30.2	0.2	69.7	61.0	39.0	0.0	61.0
Vermont	40.1	59.2	0.7	40.4	35.4	64.6	0.0	35.4
Virginia	72.4	26.9	0.6	72.9	77.4	20.7	1.9	78.9
Washington	65.9	33.9	0.3	66.0	61.0	38.9	0.1	61.1
West Virginia	60.0	40.0	0.0	60.0	55.1	44.9	0.0	55.1
Wisconsin	28.8	28.1	43.2	50.6	18.2	43.8	38.0	29.4
Wyoming	57.2	42.1	0.8	57.6	47.1	52.9	0.0	47.1

Notes: Main entries are calculated from the raw vote values in tables series 5-70 to 5-122 for the appropriate years based on candidates who used the sole designation "Democrat" or "Republican" (or their historical antecedents listed in Appendix A) on the ballot. Other = candidates who used third-party names on the ballot or were listed as independent, unidentified, or scatter vote. Bold italicized entries in the table are the author's alternative party coding, which is used when a candidate listed a major party name (Democrat, Republican, or their historical antecedents) on the ballot with other party names or labels. These values are computed from the bold italicized raw vote values in table series 5-70 to 5-122 for the appropriate states and years. For a more detailed explanation of this alternate coding system, see Tables 5-1 and 1-3. —indicates that the state had no data, either because no vote data were found for the state in question or the state had not yet entered the Union. No special House elections are included in the table. The table only lists at-large vote values for states having both at-large and district House races; see Appendix B for these states' district results aggregated to the state level.

Sources: Adapted from *United States Congressional Elections, 1788–1997* (1998), *Congressional Quarterly's Guide to U.S. Elections* (1994), ICPSR data sets 0001 and 0075, and independent search for state sources by the author.

Table 5-55 House Election Results, by State, 1940–1942 (Percentages)

	1940				1942			
State	Democratic	Republican	Other	Democratic % of Two-Party Vote	Democratic	Republican	Other	Democratic % of Two-Party Vote
Alabama	94.4	5.5	0.1	94.5	99.5	0.5	0.0	99.5
Alaska	—	—	—	—	—	—	—	—
Arizona	71.1	28.9	0.0	71.1	70.7	28.9	0.5	71.0
Arkansas	95.9	4.1	0.0	95.9	100.0	0.0	0.0	100.0
California	22.8	17.1	60.2	57.1	25.7	22.7	51.6	53.1
California	*42.7*	*53.2*	*4.1*	*44.6*	*47.7*	*49.3*	*3.0*	*49.2*
Colorado	54.5	45.2	0.3	54.7	41.4	58.2	0.4	41.6
Connecticut	52.1	46.7	1.1	52.7	45.3	49.8	4.9	47.7
Delaware	50.6	47.8	1.6	51.4	45.8	53.6	0.7	46.1
Delaware	*52.2*	*47.8*	*0.0*	*52.2*	—	—	—	—
Florida	86.2	13.8	0.0	86.2	100.0	0.0	0.0	100.0
Georgia	71.7	1.9	26.4	97.4	94.3	0.0	5.7	100.0
Georgia	*96.1*	*3.6*	*0.3*	*96.4*	—	—	—	—
Hawaii	—	—	—	—	—	—	—	—
Idaho	53.5	46.5	0.0	53.5	48.8	51.2	0.0	48.8
Illinois	48.8	50.8	0.4	49.0	48.3	51.3	0.4	48.5
Indiana	49.1	50.9	0.0	49.1	44.5	55.5	0.0	44.5
Iowa	45.2	54.7	0.0	45.2	38.0	61.7	0.3	38.1
Kansas	42.3	57.7	0.0	42.3	39.4	60.6	0.0	39.4
Kentucky	62.5	37.5	0.0	62.5	56.4	42.4	1.2	57.1
Louisiana	95.7	4.3	0.0	95.7	100.0	0.0	0.0	100.0
Maine	35.4	64.6	0.0	35.4	30.4	69.6	0.0	30.4
Maryland	60.9	39.1	0.0	60.9	56.3	43.7	0.0	56.3
Massachusetts	47.3	52.4	0.2	47.5	41.0	53.8	5.3	43.2
Massachusetts	—	—	—	—	*46.1*	*53.8*	*0.2*	*46.2*
Michigan	48.8	51.0	0.2	48.9	45.7	53.8	0.5	45.9
Minnesota	21.8	53.1	25.1	29.1	20.6	59.4	20.0	25.7
Minnesota	*21.8*	*53.5*	*24.7*	*29.0*	*20.6*	*59.4*	*20.0*	*25.7*
Mississippi	100.0	0.0	0.0	100.0	100.0	0.0	0.0	100.0
Missouri	52.4	47.6	0.0	52.4	48.4	51.5	0.0	48.4
Montana	54.8	44.7	0.5	55.1	55.0	43.5	1.5	55.9
Nebraska	40.3	55.7	4.0	42.0	34.2	63.8	2.0	34.9
Nevada	64.5	35.5	0.0	64.5	53.6	46.4	0.0	53.6
New Hampshire	48.0	52.0	0.0	48.0	44.9	55.1	0.0	44.9
New Jersey	46.7	52.6	0.7	47.1	45.4	53.9	0.7	45.7
New Mexico	58.8	41.2	0.0	58.8	58.8	41.2	0.0	58.8
New York	0.0	46.9	53.1	0.0	0.0	49.8	50.2	0.0
New York	*53.0*	*46.9*	*0.1*	*53.1*	*48.4*	*49.8*	*1.9*	*49.3*
North Carolina	75.5	24.5	0.0	75.5	72.7	27.3	0.0	72.7
North Dakota	27.1	63.0	9.9	30.0	26.3	47.1	26.6	35.8
North Dakota	—	—	—	—	*26.3*	*73.7*	*0.0*	*26.3*
Ohio	49.4	50.6	0.0	49.4	43.1	56.9	0.0	43.1
Oklahoma	65.7	33.6	0.7	66.1	57.5	42.0	0.5	57.8
Oregon	41.1	57.0	1.9	41.9	41.8	58.2	0.0	41.8
Pennsylvania	51.8	47.7	0.5	52.1	44.4	54.7	0.9	44.8
Rhode Island	55.6	44.4	0.0	55.6	58.2	41.8	0.0	58.2
South Carolina	98.5	1.5	0.0	98.5	100.0	0.0	0.0	100.0
South Dakota	38.9	61.1	0.0	38.9	37.3	62.7	0.0	37.3
Tennessee	67.7	25.8	6.6	72.4	65.4	33.5	1.1	66.1
Texas	96.8	3.2	0.0	96.8	98.8	1.1	0.1	98.9
Utah	60.6	39.4	0.0	60.6	53.1	46.9	0.0	53.1
Vermont	36.2	63.8	0.0	36.2	29.8	70.2	0.0	29.8
Virginia	80.1	19.2	0.7	80.7	85.6	13.3	1.0	86.5
Washington	57.9	42.1	0.0	57.9	52.6	47.3	0.2	52.7
West Virginia	57.5	42.5	0.0	57.5	49.7	50.3	0.0	49.7
Wisconsin	17.4	45.7	37.0	27.6	27.2	46.9	26.0	36.7
Wyoming	53.4	46.5	0.1	53.4	49.3	50.7	0.0	49.3

Notes: Main entries are calculated from the raw vote values in tables series 5-70 to 5-122 for the appropriate years based on candidates who used the sole designation "Democrat" or "Republican" (or their historical antecedents listed in Appendix A) on the ballot. Other = candidates who used third-party names on the ballot or were listed as independent, unidentified, or scatter vote. Bold italicized entries in the table are the author's alternative party coding, which is used when a candidate listed a major party name (Democrat, Republican, or their historical antecedents) on the ballot with other party names or labels. These values are computed from the bold italicized raw vote values in table series 5-70 to 5-122 for the appropriate states and years. For a more detailed explanation of this alternate coding system, see Tables 5-1 and 1-3. —indicates that the state had no data, either because no vote data were found for the state in question or the state had not yet entered the Union. No special House elections are included in the table. The table only lists at-large vote values for states having both at-large and district House races; see Appendix B for these states' district results aggregated to the state level.

Sources: Adapted from *United States Congressional Elections, 1788–1997* (1998), *Congressional Quarterly's Guide to U.S. Elections* (1994), ICPSR data sets 0001 and 0075, and independent search for state sources by the author.

Table 5-56 House Election Results, by State, 1944–1946 (Percentages)

State	1944				1946			
	Democratic	Republican	Other	Democratic % of Two-Party Vote	Democratic	Republican	Other	Democratic % of Two-Party Vote
Alabama	90.2	9.8	0.0	90.2	92.1	7.9	0.0	92.1
Alaska	—	—	—	—	—	—	—	—
Arizona	69.1	30.5	0.4	69.4	66.4	32.8	0.7	66.9
Arkansas	92.4	7.6	0.0	92.4	94.7	4.7	0.6	95.2
Arkansas	—	—	—	—	*94.7*	*5.3*	*0.0*	*94.7*
California	37.9	35.9	26.2	51.3	27.3	33.1	39.5	45.2
California	*50.6*	*49.2*	*0.2*	*50.7*	*47.4*	*51.5*	*1.1*	*47.9*
Colorado	42.6	57.0	0.4	42.8	43.9	55.6	0.6	44.1
Connecticut	51.2	48.0	0.7	51.6	40.9	55.6	3.5	42.4
Delaware	50.3	49.3	0.3	50.5	43.6	56.4	0.0	43.6
Florida	84.7	15.3	0.0	84.7	80.9	19.1	0.0	80.9
Georgia	98.9	0.0	1.1	100.0	87.9	0.0	12.1	100.0
Hawaii	—	—	—	—	—	—	—	—
Idaho	51.5	48.5	0.0	51.5	43.5	56.5	0.0	43.5
Illinois	52.3	47.4	0.3	52.5	44.5	55.1	0.4	44.7
Indiana	46.5	52.9	0.7	46.8	44.2	54.5	1.4	44.8
Iowa	43.2	56.8	0.0	43.2	38.5	61.5	0.0	38.5
Kansas	37.0	63.0	0.0	37.0	40.2	59.2	0.5	40.4
Kentucky	54.5	45.2	0.3	54.7	46.5	53.4	0.1	46.6
Louisiana	100.0	0.0	0.0	100.0	94.7	5.3	0.0	94.7
Maine	29.3	70.7	0.0	29.3	36.6	63.4	0.0	36.6
Maryland	56.4	43.6	0.0	56.4	52.3	47.7	0.0	52.3
Massachusetts	47.0	53.0	0.0	47.0	46.0	53.4	0.6	46.3
Michigan	47.5	52.1	0.4	47.7	38.6	60.8	0.6	38.8
Minnesota	40.8	58.9	0.3	40.9	40.9	58.8	0.3	41.0
Mississippi	96.6	3.4	0.0	96.6	100.0	0.0	0.0	100.0
Missouri	52.5	47.5	0.0	52.5	47.8	52.2	0.0	47.8
Montana	59.9	39.3	0.8	60.4	50.5	49.1	0.4	50.7
Nebraska	32.2	65.4	2.5	33.0	31.9	66.9	1.2	32.3
Nevada	63.1	36.9	0.0	63.1	41.2	58.8	0.0	41.2
New Hampshire	47.4	52.6	0.0	47.4	38.0	62.0	0.0	38.0
New Jersey	46.3	53.1	0.6	46.5	40.1	59.0	0.9	40.5
New Mexico	56.2	43.8	0.0	56.2	52.3	47.7	0.0	52.3
New York	3.7	45.1	51.2	7.6	9.8	51.2	39.0	16.0
New York	*50.7*	*46.1*	*3.2*	*52.3*	*41.2*	*53.9*	*4.9*	*43.3*
North Carolina	69.5	30.5	0.0	69.5	61.3	38.7	0.0	61.3
North Dakota	28.2	50.3	21.4	36.0	28.5	71.5	0.0	28.5
North Dakota	*28.2*	*70.2*	*1.6*	*28.7*	—	—	—	—
Ohio	46.9	53.1	0.0	46.9	40.5	59.5	0.0	40.5
Oklahoma	58.6	41.2	0.2	58.7	58.5	41.5	0.0	58.5
Oregon	38.5	61.5	0.0	38.5	35.2	64.8	0.0	35.2
Pennsylvania	50.0	49.2	0.8	50.4	42.0	57.7	0.3	42.1
Pennsylvania	*50.7*	*49.2*	*0.1*	*50.7*	—	—	—	—
Rhode Island	59.8	40.2	0.0	59.8	54.6	45.1	0.3	54.7
South Carolina	96.5	3.5	0.0	96.5	98.9	0.9	0.2	99.1
South Dakota	34.9	65.1	0.0	34.9	35.7	64.3	0.0	35.7
Tennessee	65.4	33.0	1.6	66.4	65.4	28.4	6.1	69.7
Texas	94.0	6.0	0.0	94.0	95.1	4.9	0.0	95.1
Utah	60.4	39.6	0.0	60.4	48.6	51.4	0.0	48.6
Vermont	37.6	62.4	0.0	37.6	35.7	64.3	0.0	35.7
Virginia	69.8	20.9	9.3	77.0	66.1	32.9	0.9	66.8
Virginia	*73.0*	*23.5*	*3.5*	*75.6*	—	—	—	—
Washington	53.0	46.8	0.2	53.1	41.4	58.3	0.3	41.6
West Virginia	54.2	45.8	0.0	54.2	50.1	49.9	0.0	50.1
Wisconsin	35.2	53.7	11.1	39.5	31.8	62.6	5.7	33.7
Wyoming	44.3	55.7	0.0	44.3	44.0	56.0	0.0	44.0

Notes: Main entries are calculated from the raw vote values in tables series 5-70 to 5-122 for the appropriate years based on candidates who used the sole designation "Democrat" or "Republican" (or their historical antecedents listed in Appendix A) on the ballot. Other = candidates who used third-party names on the ballot or were listed as independent, unidentified, or scatter vote. Bold italicized entries in the table are the author's alternative party coding, which is used when a candidate listed a major party name (Democrat, Republican, or their historical antecedents) on the ballot with other party names or labels. These values are computed from the bold italicized raw vote values in table series 5-70 to 5-122 for the appropriate states and years. For a more detailed explanation of this alternate coding system, see Tables 5-1 and 1-3. —indicates that the state had no data, either because no vote data were found for the state in question or the state had not yet entered the Union. No special House elections are included in the table. The table only lists at-large vote values for states having both at-large and district House races; see Appendix B for these states' district results aggregated to the state level.

Sources: Adapted from *United States Congressional Elections, 1788–1997* (1998), *Congressional Quarterly's Guide to U.S. Elections* (1994), ICPSR data sets 0001 and 0075, and independent search for state sources by the author.

Table 5-57 House Election Results, by State, 1948–1950 (Percentages)

State	1948 Democratic	1948 Republican	1948 Other	1948 Democratic % of Two-Party Vote	1950 Democratic	1950 Republican	1950 Other	1950 Democratic % of Two-Party Vote
Alabama	93.1	6.9	0.0	93.1	99.4	0.6	0.0	99.4
Alaska	—	—	—	—	—	—	—	—
Arizona	60.8	37.7	1.5	61.7	65.0	35.0	0.0	65.0
Arkansas	91.4	8.6	0.0	91.4	100.0	0.0	0.0	100.0
California	16.5	22.0	61.5	43.0	25.2	26.4	48.4	48.8
California	*37.9*	*55.5*	*6.6*	*40.6*	*44.1*	*52.2*	*3.7*	*45.8*
Colorado	54.8	45.2	0.0	54.8	48.4	51.0	0.6	48.7
Connecticut	48.8	49.3	1.9	49.8	48.6	49.4	2.0	49.6
Delaware	49.0	50.6	0.4	49.2	43.3	56.7	0.0	43.3
Florida	84.1	15.9	0.0	84.1	90.4	9.6	0.0	90.4
Georgia	99.9	0.0	0.1	100.0	100.0	0.0	0.0	100.0
Hawaii	—	—	—	—	—	—	—	—
Idaho	49.9	48.6	1.5	50.7	45.6	54.4	0.0	45.6
Illinois	52.0	47.4	0.6	52.3	46.1	53.9	0.0	46.1
Indiana	51.2	47.9	0.9	51.7	45.8	53.6	0.6	46.1
Iowa	45.2	54.5	0.4	45.3	38.7	61.0	0.3	38.8
Iowa	*—*	*—*	*—*	*—*	*38.7*	*61.0*	*0.3*	*38.8*
Kansas	42.5	57.5	0.0	42.5	41.2	58.8	0.0	41.2
Kentucky	56.2	43.3	0.5	56.5	63.0	37.0	0.0	63.0
Louisiana	95.8	4.2	0.0	95.8	100.0	0.0	0.0	100.0
Maine	33.7	66.3	0.0	33.7	42.4	57.6	0.0	42.4
Maryland	54.5	43.2	2.3	55.8	49.5	49.9	0.6	49.8
Massachusetts	50.2	49.8	0.0	50.2	49.5	50.0	0.4	49.7
Michigan	49.5	49.6	0.8	50.0	46.5	53.0	0.5	46.7
Minnesota	49.8	50.2	0.0	49.8	46.5	52.9	0.5	46.8
Mississippi	99.8	0.2	0.0	99.8	94.2	3.3	2.5	96.7
Missouri	58.6	41.1	0.2	58.8	55.8	44.2	0.0	55.8
Montana	57.3	42.4	0.2	57.5	51.4	47.5	1.1	52.0
Nebraska	41.7	58.3	0.0	41.7	37.7	62.3	0.0	37.7
Nevada	50.6	49.4	0.0	50.6	52.8	47.2	0.0	52.8
New Hampshire	42.9	56.4	0.7	43.2	39.3	60.7	0.0	39.3
New Jersey	47.5	50.6	1.9	48.4	43.9	54.7	1.4	44.5
New Mexico	58.3	41.2	0.4	58.6	56.3	43.7	0.0	56.3
New York	6.9	40.6	52.5	14.6	16.9	45.4	37.8	27.1
New York	*14.2*	*40.6*	*45.2*	*26.0*	*46.9*	*46.9*	*6.2*	*50.0*
North Carolina	70.8	28.7	0.4	71.2	70.0	30.0	0.0	70.0
North Dakota	29.7	69.4	0.9	30.0	34.4	65.6	0.0	34.4
Ohio	52.0	48.0	0.0	52.0	46.1	53.9	0.0	46.1
Oklahoma	67.3	32.7	0.0	67.3	59.9	40.1	0.0	59.9
Oregon	29.1	60.3	10.5	32.6	40.3	57.7	2.0	41.1
Oregon	*35.8*	*60.3*	*3.8*	*37.3*	*—*	*—*	*—*	*—*
Pennsylvania	48.8	49.6	1.6	49.5	47.6	52.2	0.1	47.7
Pennsylvania	*48.8*	*51.0*	*0.3*	*48.9*	*—*	*—*	*—*	*—*
Rhode Island	60.8	39.2	0.0	60.8	61.9	38.1	0.0	61.9
South Carolina	95.1	4.9	0.0	95.1	100.0	0.0	0.0	100.0
South Dakota	43.6	56.4	0.0	43.6	39.3	60.7	0.0	39.3
Tennessee	63.1	33.6	3.3	65.3	63.0	29.4	7.7	68.2
Tennessee	*—*	*—*	*—*	*—*	*63.0*	*37.0*	*0.0*	*63.0*
Texas	93.6	6.2	0.2	93.8	90.5	9.5	0.0	90.5
Utah	58.1	41.9	0.0	58.1	52.5	47.5	0.0	52.5
Vermont	39.2	60.7	0.1	39.2	25.6	73.5	1.0	25.8
Virginia	66.6	31.7	1.7	67.7	73.4	24.3	2.3	75.1
Washington	49.2	49.1	1.7	50.1	47.3	52.3	0.4	47.5
West Virginia	58.3	41.7	0.0	58.3	56.6	43.4	0.0	56.6
Wisconsin	42.4	55.9	1.7	43.2	42.4	57.6	0.0	42.4
Wyoming	48.5	51.5	0.0	48.5	45.5	54.5	0.0	45.5

Notes: Main entries are calculated from the raw vote values in tables series 5-70 to 5-122 for the appropriate years based on candidates who used the sole designation "Democrat" or "Republican" (or their historical antecedents listed in Appendix A) on the ballot. Other = candidates who used third-party names on the ballot or were listed as independent, unidentified, or scatter vote. Bold italicized entries in the table are the author's alternative party coding, which is used when a candidate listed a major party name (Democrat, Republican, or their historical antecedents) on the ballot with other party names or labels. These values are computed from the bold italicized raw vote values in table series 5-70 to 5-122 for the appropriate states and years. For a more detailed explanation of this alternate coding system, see Tables 5-1 and 1-3. —indicates that the state had no data, either because no vote data were found for the state in question or the state had not yet entered the Union. No special House elections are included in the table. The table only lists at-large vote values for states having both at-large and district House races; see Appendix B for these states' district results aggregated to the state level.

Sources: Adapted from *United States Congressional Elections, 1788–1997* (1998), *Congressional Quarterly's Guide to U.S. Elections* (1994), *America Votes* (various publication dates), ICPSR data sets 0001 and 0075, and independent search for state sources by the author.

Table 5-58 House Election Results, by State, 1952–1954 (Percentages)

State	1952 Democratic	Republican	Other	Democratic % of Two-Party Vote	1954 Democratic	Republican	Other	Democratic % of Two-Party Vote
Alabama	94.6	5.4	0.0	94.6	96.0	4.0	0.0	96.0
Alaska	—	—	—	—	—	—	—	—
Arizona	51.5	48.5	0.0	51.5	54.3	45.7	0.0	54.3
Arkansas	85.3	14.3	0.3	85.6	100.0	0.0	0.0	100.0
California	26.7	32.3	40.9	45.3	46.3	48.5	5.3	48.8
California	*44.5*	*52.3*	*3.2*	*46.0*	*51.4*	*48.5*	*0.1*	*51.5*
Colorado	44.5	55.3	0.2	44.6	49.9	50.0	0.1	49.9
Connecticut	44.8	55.0	0.3	44.9	48.9	50.9	0.2	49.0
Delaware	48.1	51.9	0.0	48.1	54.9	45.1	0.0	54.9
Florida	74.2	25.8	0.0	74.2	78.2	21.8	0.0	78.2
Georgia	100.0	0.0	0.0	100.0	90.1	8.5	1.5	91.4
Hawaii	—	—	—	—	—	—	—	—
Idaho	40.6	59.4	0.0	40.6	45.5	54.5	0.0	45.5
Illinois	46.0	54.0	0.0	46.0	50.2	49.8	0.0	50.2
Indiana	42.9	56.5	0.6	43.2	47.1	52.5	0.3	47.3
Iowa	33.1	66.7	0.2	33.2	41.5	58.5	0.0	41.5
Kansas	40.6	59.4	0.0	40.6	43.5	56.5	0.0	43.5
Kentucky	52.1	47.8	0.1	52.1	64.7	35.3	0.0	64.7
Louisiana	91.3	8.7	0.0	91.3	96.2	3.8	0.0	96.2
Maine	32.8	66.9	0.3	32.9	45.0	55.0	0.0	45.0
Maine	*33.1*	*66.9*	*0.0*	*33.1*	—	—	—	—
Maryland	48.2	51.8	0.0	48.2	53.7	46.2	0.2	53.7
Massachusetts	46.5	52.9	0.6	46.8	47.4	46.8	5.8	50.3
Massachusetts	—	—	—	—	*53.2*	*46.8*	*0.0*	*53.2*
Michigan	47.3	52.4	0.3	47.5	51.6	48.2	0.2	51.7
Minnesota	46.0	54.0	0.0	46.0	53.0	47.0	0.0	53.0
Mississippi	97.5	2.5	0.0	97.5	100.0	0.0	0.0	100.0
Missouri	52.2	47.8	0.0	52.2	56.2	43.8	0.0	56.2
Montana	43.3	56.4	0.3	43.5	52.1	47.9	0.0	52.1
Nebraska	31.8	68.2	0.0	31.8	38.4	61.6	0.0	38.4
Nevada	49.5	50.5	0.0	49.5	45.5	54.5	0.0	45.5
New Hampshire	36.9	63.1	0.0	36.9	45.3	54.7	0.0	45.3
New Jersey	42.2	56.9	0.9	42.6	48.3	50.6	1.2	48.8
New Mexico	52.0	48.0	0.0	52.0	59.1	40.9	0.0	59.1
New York	12.3	51.0	36.7	19.4	11.8	49.8	38.5	19.1
New York	*44.7*	*52.3*	*3.1*	*46.1*	*48.3*	*49.8*	*1.9*	*49.3*
North Carolina	68.0	32.0	0.0	68.0	64.6	35.4	0.0	64.6
North Dakota	21.6	78.4	0.0	21.6	33.9	66.1	0.0	33.9
Ohio	43.5	54.3	2.2	44.5	44.6	53.7	1.8	45.4
Oklahoma	58.5	41.1	0.4	58.7	64.9	35.1	0.0	64.9
Oregon	38.7	61.3	0.0	38.7	45.5	54.5	0.0	45.5
Pennsylvania	47.6	52.3	0.1	47.7	50.6	49.4	0.0	50.6
Rhode Island	54.1	45.9	0.0	54.1	59.9	40.1	0.0	59.9
South Carolina	98.0	2.0	0.0	98.0	98.7	1.3	0.0	98.7
South Dakota	31.4	68.6	0.0	31.4	40.6	59.4	0.0	40.6
Tennessee	68.5	29.1	2.4	70.2	67.4	32.6	0.0	67.4
Texas	0.0	0.0	100.0	—	88.0	12.0	0.0	88.0
Texas	*100.0*	*0.0*	*0.0*	*100.0*	—	—	—	—
Utah	44.4	55.6	0.0	44.4	44.3	55.7	0.0	44.3
Vermont	28.2	71.8	0.0	28.2	38.6	61.4	0.0	38.6
Virginia	66.7	31.0	2.2	68.3	59.7	37.5	2.8	61.4
Washington	50.5	49.5	0.1	50.5	57.3	42.2	0.5	57.6
West Virginia	53.9	46.1	0.0	53.9	57.5	42.5	0.0	57.5
Wisconsin	38.4	61.6	0.0	38.4	47.5	52.5	0.0	47.5
Wyoming	39.9	60.1	0.0	39.9	43.8	56.2	0.0	43.8

Notes: Main entries are calculated from the raw vote values in tables series 5-70 to 5-122 for the appropriate years based on candidates who used the sole designation "Democrat" or "Republican" (or their historical antecedents listed in Appendix A) on the ballot. Other = candidates who used third-party names on the ballot or were listed as independent, unidentified, or scatter vote. Bold italicized entries in the table are the author's alternative party coding, which is used when a candidate listed a major party name (Democrat, Republican, or their historical antecedents) on the ballot with other party names or labels. These values are computed from the bold italicized raw vote values in table series 5-70 to 5-122 for the appropriate states and years. For a more detailed explanation of this alternate coding system, see Tables 5-1 and 1-3. —indicates that the state had no data, either because no vote data were found for the state in question or the state had not yet entered the Union. No special House elections are included in the table. The table only lists at-large vote values for states having both at-large and district House races; see Appendix B for these states' district results aggregated to the state level.

Sources: Adapted from *United States Congressional Elections, 1788–1997* (1998), *Congressional Quarterly's Guide to U.S. Elections* (1994), *America Votes* (various publication dates), ICPSR data sets 0001 and 0075, and independent search for state sources by the author.

Table 5-59 House Election Results, by State, 1956–1959 (Percentages)

State	1956				1958–1959			
	Democratic	Republican	Other	Democratic % of Two-Party Vote	Democratic	Republican	Other	Democratic % of Two-Party Vote
Alabama	86.5	13.5	0.0	86.5	97.4	2.6	0.0	97.4
Alaska	—	—	—	—	57.4	42.6	0.0	57.4
Arizona	52.4	47.6	0.0	52.4	50.2	49.8	0.0	50.2
Arkansas	90.6	9.4	0.0	90.6	49.0[2]	0.0[2]	51.0[2]	100.0[2]
Arkansas	*—*	*—*	*—*	*—*	*100.0[2]*	*0.0[2]*	*0.0[2]*	*100.0[2]*
California	43.0	47.6	9.4	47.4	45.6	40.0	14.4	53.3
California	*52.4*	*47.6*	*0.0*	*52.4*	*60.0*	*40.0*	*0.0*	*60.0*
Colorado	52.8	47.2	0.0	52.8	58.0	41.8	0.2	58.2
Connecticut	38.5	61.5	0.0	38.5	56.0	44.0	0.0	56.0
Delaware	48.0	52.0	0.0	48.0	50.2	49.8	0.0	50.2
Florida	62.6	37.4	0.0	62.6	71.8	28.2	0.0	71.8
Georgia	88.1	10.0	1.9	89.9	100.0	0.0	0.0	100.0
Hawaii	—	—	—	—	68.2[1]	31.2[1]	0.6[1]	68.6[1]
Idaho	46.4	53.6	0.0	46.4	52.0	48.0	0.0	52.0
Illinois	46.4	53.6	0.0	46.4	54.3	45.5	0.2	54.4
Indiana	44.1	55.7	0.2	44.2	53.6	46.4	0.0	53.6
Iowa	45.6	54.4	0.0	45.6	50.3	49.7	0.0	50.3
Kansas	46.8	53.0	0.2	46.9	50.1	49.4	0.4	50.4
Kentucky	52.2	47.8	0.0	52.2	65.1	34.6	0.3	65.3
Louisiana	85.2	14.8	0.0	85.2	97.7	2.3	0.0	97.7
Maine	48.6	51.4	0.0	48.6	53.2	46.8	0.0	53.2
Maryland	51.3	48.7	0.0	51.3	65.1	34.9	0.0	65.1
Massachusetts	48.6	51.4	0.0	48.6	57.5	42.5	0.0	57.5
Michigan	49.8	50.1	0.1	49.8	53.0	46.8	0.2	53.1
Minnesota	51.3	48.7	0.0	51.3	52.7	47.3	0.0	52.7
Mississippi	100.0	0.0	0.0	100.0	100.0	0.0	0.0	100.0
Missouri	59.7	40.3	0.0	59.7	63.2	36.8	0.0	63.2
Montana	55.6	44.4	0.0	55.6	64.7	35.3	0.0	64.7
Nebraska	40.3	59.2	0.4	40.5	47.0	53.0	0.0	47.0
Nevada	54.2	45.8	0.0	54.2	66.9	33.1	0.0	66.9
New Hampshire	38.7	61.3	0.0	38.7	41.1	58.4	0.4	41.3
New Jersey	40.7	58.3	1.0	41.1	49.2	49.5	1.2	49.8
New Mexico	53.1	46.9	0.0	53.1	63.1	36.9	0.0	63.1
New York	7.4	53.0	39.6	12.3	8.3	47.5	44.3	14.8
New York	*44.6*	*54.4*	*1.0*	*45.1*	*50.0*	*48.6*	*1.3*	*50.7*
North Carolina	69.9	30.1	0.0	69.9	70.8	29.2	0.0	70.8
North Dakota	37.4	62.6	0.0	37.4	50.4	49.6	0.0	50.4
Ohio	42.7	57.3	0.0	42.7	50.8	49.2	0.0	50.8
Oklahoma	59.8	40.2	0.0	59.8	69.7	30.0	0.3	69.9
Oregon	52.9	47.1	0.0	52.9	56.9	43.1	0.0	56.9
Pennsylvania	47.2	52.8	0.0	47.2	51.0	49.0	0.0	51.0
Rhode Island	53.9	46.1	0.0	53.9	63.1	36.8	0.1	63.1
South Carolina	95.3	4.7	0.1	95.3	100.0	0.0	0.0	100.0
South Dakota	50.5	49.5	0.0	50.5	51.4	48.6	0.0	51.4
Tennessee	58.9	41.1	0.0	58.9	74.5	25.0	0.5	74.9
Tennessee	*—*	*—*	*—*	*—*	*75.0*	*25.0*	*0.0*	*75.0*
Texas	98.5	0.0	1.5	100.0	87.6	11.9	0.5	88.1
Utah	41.1	58.9	0.0	41.1	49.2	50.8	0.0	49.2
Vermont	32.9	67.1	0.0	32.9	51.5	48.5	0.0	51.5
Virginia	59.7	40.1	0.2	59.8	73.8	20.0	6.2	78.7
Washington	58.5	41.5	0.0	58.5	46.3	53.3	0.3	46.5
West Virginia	53.1	46.9	0.0	53.1	61.9	38.1	0.0	61.9
Wisconsin	45.8	54.2	0.0	45.8	53.6	46.4	0.0	53.6
Wyoming	41.8	58.2	0.0	41.8	46.4	53.6	0.0	46.4

Notes: Main entries are calculated from the raw vote values in tables series 5-70 to 5-122 for the appropriate years based on candidates who used the sole designation "Democrat" or "Republican" (or their historical antecedents listed in Appendix A) on the ballot. Other = candidates who used third-party names on the ballot or were listed as independent, unidentified, or scatter vote. Bold italicized entries in the table are the author's alternative party coding, which is used when a candidate listed a major party name (Democrat, Republican, or their historical antecedents) on the ballot with other party names or labels. These values are computed from the bold italicized raw vote values in table series 5-70 to 5-122 for the appropriate states and years. For a more detailed explanation of this alternate coding system, see Tables 5-1 and 1-3. —indicates that the state had no data, either because no vote data were found for the state in question or the state had not yet entered the Union. No special House elections are included in the table. The table only lists at-large vote values for states having both at-large and district House races; see Appendix B for these states' district results aggregated to the state level.

[1] Election held in odd-numbered year.
[2] Partial data (less than 100% of the districts reporting).

Sources: Adapted from *United States Congressional Elections, 1788–1997* (1998), *Congressional Quarterly's Guide to U.S. Elections* (1994), *America Votes* (various publication dates), ICPSR data sets 0001 and 0075, and independent search for state sources by the author.

Table 5-60 House Election Results, by State, 1960–1962 (Percentages)

State	1960 Democratic	1960 Republican	1960 Other	1960 Democratic % of Two-Party Vote	1962 Democratic	1962 Republican	1962 Other	1962 Democratic % of Two-Party Vote
Alabama	89.0	11.0	0.0	89.0	63.1	29.9	7.0	67.8
Alaska	56.8	43.2	0.0	56.8	54.5	45.5	0.0	54.5
Arizona	47.6	52.4	0.0	47.6	48.6	51.4	0.0	48.6
Arkansas	82.7[1]	17.3[1]	0.0[1]	82.7[1]	73.7[1]	26.3[1]	0.0[1]	73.7[1]
California	51.6	46.1	2.3	52.8	51.9	48.1	0.0	51.9
California	*53.9*	*46.1*	*0.0*	*53.9*	—	—	—	
Colorado	51.8	48.2	0.0	51.8	47.3	52.7	0.0	47.3
Connecticut	54.0	46.0	0.0	54.0	52.7	47.3	0.0	52.7
Delaware	50.5	49.5	0.0	50.5	52.9	46.9	0.2	53.0
Florida	69.0	31.0	0.0	69.0	62.6	37.4	0.0	62.6
Georgia	95.7	4.2	0.1	95.8	81.7	17.9	0.4	82.1
Georgia	—	—	—	—	*81.7*	*18.1*	*0.2*	*81.9*
Hawaii	74.4	25.6	0.0	74.4	63.6	36.4	0.0	63.6
Idaho	54.8	45.2	0.0	54.8	52.9	47.1	0.0	52.9
Illinois	51.5	48.5	0.0	51.5	49.7	50.3	0.0	49.7
Indiana	48.7	51.3	0.1	48.7	49.1	50.9	0.0	49.1
Iowa	45.9	54.1	0.0	45.9	46.1	53.9	0.0	46.1
Kansas	45.8	54.2	0.0	45.8	39.9	60.1	0.0	39.9
Kentucky	59.1	40.9	0.0	59.1	59.0	40.9	0.1	59.1
Louisiana	85.0	15.0	0.0	85.0	87.7	12.3	0.0	87.7
Maine	43.4	56.5	0.1	43.5	44.6	55.4	0.0	44.6
Maine	*43.5*	*56.5*	*0.0*	*43.5*	—	—	—	
Maryland	59.4	40.6	0.0	59.4	55.7	44.3	0.0	55.7
Massachusetts	61.0	39.0	0.0	61.0	58.2	41.0	0.8	58.7
Michigan	51.0	48.8	0.2	51.1	52.0	47.9	0.2	52.1
Minnesota	50.2	49.5	0.4	50.3	49.8	50.2	0.0	49.8
Mississippi	98.0	2.0	0.0	98.0	97.2	0.0	2.8	100.0
Missouri	57.7	42.3	0.0	57.7	56.4	43.6	0.0	56.4
Montana	50.9	49.1	0.0	50.9	48.0	52.0	0.0	48.0
Nebraska	43.5	56.5	0.0	43.5	36.9	61.1	2.0	37.7
Nevada	57.5	42.5	0.0	57.5	71.6	28.4	0.0	71.6
New Hampshire	41.8	58.2	0.0	41.8	44.9	55.1	0.0	44.9
New Jersey	48.0	51.2	0.8	48.4	50.1	49.2	0.7	50.4
New Mexico	58.6	41.1	0.3	58.8	52.5	47.5	0.0	52.5
New York	14.0	46.5	39.5	23.2	14.6	47.8	37.7	23.4
New York	*51.7*	*46.5*	*1.8*	*52.6*	*50.0*	*48.3*	*1.7*	*50.8*
North Carolina	60.4	39.6	0.0	60.4	58.9	41.1	0.0	58.9
North Dakota	47.1	52.9	0.0	47.1	45.7	54.3	0.0	45.7
Ohio	45.9	54.1	0.0	45.9	39.5	60.5	0.0	39.5
Oklahoma	54.9	45.1	0.0	54.9	61.1	38.9	0.0	61.1
Oregon	51.1	48.9	0.0	51.1	54.3	45.7	0.0	54.3
Pennsylvania	51.6	48.4	0.1	51.6	49.1	50.9	0.0	49.1
Rhode Island	68.5	31.5	0.0	68.5	65.1	34.9	0.0	65.1
South Carolina	100.0	0.0	0.0	100.0	86.0	14.0	0.0	86.0
South Dakota	44.0	56.0	0.0	44.0	40.2	59.8	0.0	40.2
Tennessee	68.5	31.5	0.0	68.5	61.9	35.0	3.0	63.9
Tennessee	—	—	—	—	*61.9*	*36.1*	*2.0*	*63.2*
Texas	82.4	14.6	3.0	85.0	56.1	43.9	0.0	56.1
Utah	50.5	49.5	0.0	50.5	47.2	52.8	0.0	47.2
Vermont	42.8	57.2	0.0	42.8	43.3	56.7	0.0	43.3
Virginia	64.2	31.2	4.6	67.3	59.9	39.9	0.3	60.0
Washington	42.5	57.5	0.0	42.5	38.3	61.7	0.0	38.3
West Virginia	57.1	42.9	0.0	57.1	56.0	44.0	0.0	56.0
Wisconsin	48.9	50.9	0.2	49.0	49.9	50.1	0.0	49.9
Wyoming	47.7	52.3	0.0	47.7	38.6	61.4	0.0	38.6

Notes: Main entries are calculated from the raw vote values in tables series 5-70 to 5-122 for the appropriate years based on candidates who used the sole designation "Democrat" or "Republican" (or their historical antecedents listed in Appendix A) on the ballot. Other = candidates who used third-party names on the ballot or were listed as independent, unidentified, or scatter vote. Bold italicized entries in the table are the author's alternative party coding, which is used when a candidate listed a major party name (Democrat, Republican, or their historical antecedents) on the ballot with other party names or labels. These values are computed from the bold italicized raw vote values in table series 5-70 to 5-122 for the appropriate states and years. For a more detailed explanation of this alternate coding system, see Tables 5-1 and 1-3. —indicates that the state had no data, either because no vote data were found for the state in question or the state had not yet entered the Union. No special House elections are included in the table. The table only lists at-large vote values for states having both at-large and district House races; see Appendix B for these states' district results aggregated to the state level.

[1]Partial data (less than 100% of the districts reporting).

Sources: Adapted from *United States Congressional Elections, 1788–1997* (1998), *Congressional Quarterly's Guide to U.S. Elections* (1994), *America Votes* (various publication dates), ICPSR data sets 0001 and 0075, and independent search for state sources by the author.

Table 5-61 House Election Results, by State, 1964–1966 (Percentages)

	1964				1966			
State	Democratic	Republican	Other	Democratic % of Two-Party Vote	Democratic	Republican	Other	Democratic % of Two-Party Vote
Alabama	48.3	51.4	0.3	48.4	60.8	39.2	0.0	60.8
Alaska	51.5	48.5	0.0	51.5	48.4	51.6	0.0	48.4
Arizona	50.1	49.9	0.0	50.1	43.9	56.1	0.0	43.9
Arkansas	54.7[1]	45.3[1]	0.0[1]	54.7[1]	55.2[1]	44.8[1]	0.0[1]	55.2[1]
California	52.9	47.1	0.0	52.9	46.8	53.1	0.1	46.8
Colorado	58.1	41.8	0.2	58.2	53.0	46.6	0.4	53.2
Connecticut	62.3	37.7	0.0	62.3	54.1	44.2	1.7	55.1
Delaware	56.6	43.4	0.0	56.6	44.2	55.8	0.0	44.2
Florida	70.1	29.7	0.2	70.2	64.6	35.0	0.4	64.8
Georgia	67.3	29.7	3.0	69.4	65.6	34.3	0.1	65.6
Hawaii	61.1	38.9	0.0	61.1	67.7	32.3	0.0	67.7
Idaho	49.3	50.7	0.0	49.3	39.8	60.2	0.0	39.8
Illinois	54.5	45.5	0.0	54.5	45.7	54.3	0.0	45.7
Indiana	52.8	47.2	0.0	52.8	46.5	53.5	0.1	46.5
Iowa	54.6	45.3	0.2	54.6	47.5	52.2	0.3	47.6
Kansas	44.5	55.5	0.0	44.5	36.6	63.1	0.4	36.7
Kentucky	64.8	35.2	0.0	64.8	52.8	47.2	0.0	52.8
Louisiana	71.5	28.5	0.0	71.5	81.8	18.2	0.0	81.8
Maine	55.8	44.2	0.0	55.8	53.5	44.3	2.3	54.7
Maryland	69.4	30.6	0.0	69.4	56.1	43.9	0.0	56.1
Massachusetts	62.3	37.3	0.4	62.5	60.6	39.4	0.0	60.6
Michigan	57.8	42.1	0.1	57.8	48.6	51.4	0.0	48.6
Minnesota	54.4	45.5	0.1	54.5	48.4	51.6	0.0	48.4
Mississippi	90.2	9.8	0.0	90.2	73.9	16.1	10.1	82.1
Missouri	62.5	37.5	0.0	62.5	53.7	46.3	0.0	53.7
Montana	49.3	50.5	0.2	49.4	45.5	54.5	0.0	45.5
Nebraska	48.6	51.4	0.0	48.6	37.9	62.1	0.0	37.9
Nevada	63.3	36.7	0.0	63.3	67.6	32.4	0.0	67.6
New Hampshire	50.7	49.3	0.0	50.7	39.2	60.8	0.1	39.2
New Jersey	54.5	45.1	0.3	54.7	48.7	49.8	1.5	49.4
New Mexico	51.6	48.4	0.0	51.6	50.5	49.5	0.0	50.5
New York	17.9	32.8	49.2	35.3	14.8	31.4	53.8	32.0
New York	***58.0***	***40.2***	***1.9***	***59.1***	***50.1***	***45.3***	***4.6***	***52.6***
North Carolina	60.4	39.6	0.0	60.4	52.9	47.1	0.0	52.9
North Dakota	49.8	50.0	0.3	49.9	40.9	59.1	0.0	40.9
Ohio	52.2	47.8	0.0	52.2	42.8	57.2	0.0	42.8
Oklahoma	63.0	37.0	0.0	63.0	52.4	47.6	0.0	52.4
Oregon	60.1	39.8	0.1	60.2	47.4	52.6	0.0	47.4
Pennsylvania	55.9	44.1	0.0	55.9	47.8	52.2	0.0	47.8
Rhode Island	74.6	25.4	0.0	74.6	61.2	38.7	0.2	61.3
South Carolina	88.5	11.0	0.6	89.0	70.6	29.3	0.1	70.7
South Dakota	42.8	57.2	0.0	42.8	36.2	63.8	0.0	36.2
Tennessee	56.1	40.3	3.6	58.2	47.8	47.9	4.3	50.0
Texas	66.9	32.7	0.4	67.2	82.4	16.4	1.2	83.4
Utah	52.9	47.1	0.0	52.9	36.2	63.8	0.0	36.2
Vermont	43.6	0.0	56.4	100.0	34.4	65.6	0.0	34.4
Vermont	***43.6***	***56.4***	***0.0***	***43.6***	—	—	—	—
Virginia	57.8	32.2	10.0	64.2	57.3	39.3	3.4	59.4
Washington	51.2	48.7	0.0	51.2	50.5	47.9	1.7	51.3
West Virginia	58.4	41.6	0.0	58.4	53.0	47.0	0.0	53.0
Wisconsin	52.1	47.9	0.0	52.1	46.2	53.8	0.0	46.2
Wyoming	50.8	49.2	0.0	50.8	47.7	52.3	0.0	47.7

Notes: Main entries are calculated from the raw vote values in tables series 5-70 to 5-122 for the appropriate years based on candidates who used the sole designation "Democrat" or "Republican" (or their historical antecedents listed in Appendix A) on the ballot. Other = candidates who used third-party names on the ballot or were listed as independent, unidentified, or scatter vote. Bold italicized entries in the table are the author's alternative party coding, which is used when a candidate listed a major party name (Democrat, Republican, or their historical antecedents) on the ballot with other party names or labels. These values are computed from the bold italicized raw vote values in table series 5-70 to 5-122 for the appropriate states and years. For a more detailed explanation of this alternate coding system, see Tables 5-1 and 1-3. —indicates that the state had no data, either because no vote data were found for the state in question or the state had not yet entered the Union. No special House elections are included in the table. The table only lists at-large vote values for states having both at-large and district House races; see Appendix B for these states' district results aggregated to the state level.

[1]Partial data (less than 100% of the districts reporting).

Sources: Adapted from *United States Congressional Elections, 1788–1997* (1998), *Congressional Quarterly's Guide to U.S. Elections* (1994), *America Votes* (various publication dates), ICPSR data sets 0001 and 0075, and independent search for state sources by the author.

Table 5-62 House Election Results, by State, 1968–1970 (Percentages)

State	1968				1970			
	Democratic	Republican	Other	Democratic % of Two-Party Vote	Democratic	Republican	Other	Democratic % of Two-Party Vote
Alabama	60.0	27.2	12.8	68.9	64.0	25.5	10.5	71.5
Alabama	*69.2*	*27.2*	*3.6*	*71.8*	*73.1*	*25.5*	*1.4*	*74.2*
Alaska	45.8	54.2	0.0	45.8	55.1	44.9	0.0	55.1
Arizona	43.8	56.2	0.0	43.8	45.3	54.3	0.3	45.5
Arkansas	47.0[1]	53.0[1]	0.0[1]	47.0[1]	33.3[1]	66.7[1]	0.0[1]	33.3[1]
California	44.1	52.4	3.6	45.7	49.4	49.0	1.6	50.2
California	*44.1*	*54.4*	*1.5*	*44.8*	—	—	—	—
Colorado	46.4	50.3	3.3	48.0	48.7	49.9	1.5	49.4
Connecticut	51.8	47.2	0.9	52.3	49.7	49.0	1.3	50.3
Delaware	41.3	58.7	0.0	41.3	44.6	53.7	1.7	45.3
Florida	57.2	42.8	0.0	57.2	54.5[1]	45.5[1]	0.0[1]	54.5[1]
Georgia	79.5	20.5	0.0	79.5	74.3	25.7	0.0	74.3
Hawaii	66.6	32.4	1.0	67.3	84.7	15.3	0.0	84.7
Idaho	42.0	56.4	1.6	42.7	37.4	61.4	1.2	37.8
Illinois	46.4	53.6	0.0	46.4	51.9	48.1	0.0	51.9
Indiana	46.3	53.7	0.0	46.3	50.9	49.1	0.0	50.9
Iowa	45.8	54.2	0.0	45.8	49.7	49.8	0.5	49.9
Kansas	37.9	62.1	0.0	37.9	42.2	56.6	1.2	42.7
Kentucky	51.0	48.7	0.4	51.2	52.3	47.0	0.7	52.6
Louisiana	81.3	18.7	0.0	81.3	91.0	5.4	3.5	94.4
Maine	56.2	43.8	0.0	56.2	61.5	38.5	0.0	61.5
Maryland	52.5	47.5	0.0	52.5	51.1	48.6	0.3	51.3
Massachusetts	50.2	40.4	9.4	55.4	56.6	39.9	3.5	58.7
Massachusetts	*50.2*	*47.2*	*2.6*	*51.5*	—	—	—	—
Michigan	50.4	49.5	0.1	50.4	51.3	48.4	0.3	51.4
Minnesota	47.7	52.2	0.1	47.7	52.9	46.9	0.2	53.0
Mississippi	92.5	7.5	0.0	92.5	86.2	9.2	4.6	90.3
Missouri	55.8	44.2	0.1	55.8	57.8	41.2	1.0	58.4
Montana	43.5	56.5	0.0	43.5	56.6	43.4	0.0	56.6
Nebraska	39.9	59.2	0.9	40.3	36.7	54.1	9.2	40.4
Nevada	72.1	27.9	0.0	72.1	82.5	17.5	0.0	82.5
New Hampshire	33.2	66.8	0.0	33.2	31.5	68.5	0.0	31.5
New Jersey	47.8	50.6	1.7	48.6	52.3	46.9	0.9	52.7
New Mexico	47.8	51.8	0.5	48.0	45.2	53.4	1.4	45.9
New York	25.3	22.0	52.7	53.4	15.7	13.5	70.8	53.9
New York	*49.0*	*46.0*	*5.0*	*51.6*	*50.0*	*44.9*	*5.1*	*52.6*
North Carolina	54.7	45.3	0.0	54.7	55.3	44.2	0.6	55.6
North Dakota	39.6	58.8	1.6	40.2	41.9	58.1	0.0	41.9
Ohio	39.3	60.7	0.0	39.3	43.5	56.1	0.4	43.7
Oklahoma	54.9	45.1	0.0	54.9	63.5	36.3	0.2	63.6
Oregon	47.0	53.0	0.0	47.0	51.8	48.2	0.0	51.8
Pennsylvania	49.9	44.9	5.1	52.7	53.8	44.6	1.6	54.7
Pennsylvania	*49.9*	*48.7*	*1.3*	*50.6*	—	—	—	—
Rhode Island	60.9	38.6	0.5	61.2	63.9	35.3	0.9	64.4
South Carolina	66.3	32.5	1.2	67.1	72.5	27.1	0.5	72.8
South Dakota	41.4	58.6	0.0	41.4	54.3	45.7	0.0	54.3
Tennessee	48.0	50.2	1.8	48.9	58.6	40.8	0.6	59.0
Texas	71.8	28.2	0.0	71.8	73.0	26.0	0.9	73.7
Utah	35.2	64.8	0.0	35.2	48.9	50.1	1.0	49.4
Vermont	0.0	0.0	100.0	—	29.1	68.0	2.8	30.0
Vermont	*0.0*	*99.9*	*0.1*	*0.0*	—	—	—	—
Virginia	48.9	47.4	3.7	50.8	51.4	45.7	2.9	52.9
Washington	51.8	47.8	0.4	52.0	59.5	39.5	0.9	60.1
West Virginia	61.0	39.0	0.0	61.0	65.2	34.8	0.0	65.2
Wisconsin	45.2	54.6	0.2	45.3	55.8	43.5	0.7	56.2
Wyoming	37.3	62.7	0.0	37.3	50.3	49.7	0.0	50.3

Notes: Main entries are calculated from the raw vote values in tables series 5-70 to 5-122 for the appropriate years based on candidates who used the sole designation "Democrat" or "Republican" (or their historical antecedents listed in Appendix A) on the ballot. Other = candidates who used third-party names on the ballot or were listed as independent, unidentified, or scatter vote. Bold italicized entries in the table are the author's alternative party coding, which is used when a candidate listed a major party name (Democrat, Republican, or their historical antecedents) on the ballot with other party names or labels. These values are computed from the bold italicized raw vote values in table series 5-70 to 5-122 for the appropriate states and years. For a more detailed explanation of this alternate coding system, see Tables 5-1 and 1-3. —indicates that the state had no data, either because no vote data were found for the state in question or the state had not yet entered the Union. No special House elections are included in the table. The table only lists at-large vote values for states having both at-large and district House races; see Appendix B for these states' district results aggregated to the state level.

[1] Partial data (less than 100% of the districts reporting).

Sources: Adapted from *United States Congressional Elections, 1788–1997* (1998), *Congressional Quarterly's Guide to U.S. Elections* (1994), *America Votes* (various publication dates), ICPSR data sets 0001 and 0075, and independent search for state sources by the author.

Table 5-63 House Election Results, by State, 1972–1974 (Percentages)

State	1972 Democratic	1972 Republican	1972 Other	1972 Democratic % of Two-Party Vote	1974 Democratic	1974 Republican	1974 Other	1974 Democratic % of Two-Party Vote
Alabama	55.9	39.4	4.6	58.6	67.0	30.2	2.9	69.0
Alabama	*59.8*	*39.4*	*0.8*	*60.3*	*68.1*	*30.2*	*1.7*	*69.3*
Alaska	56.2	43.8	0.0	56.2	46.2	53.8	0.0	46.2
Arizona	47.8	52.2	0.0	47.8	49.6	48.9	1.5	50.3
Arkansas	22.7[1]	77.3[1]	0.0[1]	22.7[1]	63.1[1]	36.9[1]	0.0[1]	63.1[1]
California	51.9	46.3	1.8	52.8	57.1	40.4	2.5	58.5
Colorado	46.9	52.6	0.5	47.1	52.7	46.4	0.9	53.2
Connecticut	48.7	51.1	0.2	48.8	57.5	40.8	1.7	58.5
Delaware	36.9	62.5	0.6	37.1	39.6	58.5	1.9	40.4
Florida	53.4[1]	46.6[1]	0.0[1]	53.4[1]	44.9[1]	54.7[1]	0.3[1]	45.1[1]
Georgia	71.6	28.4	0.0	71.6	71.6	28.4	0.0	71.6
Hawaii	55.9	44.1	0.0	55.9	61.1	38.9	0.0	61.1
Idaho	35.9	62.3	1.8	36.6	43.0	57.0	0.0	43.0
Illinois	49.0	50.7	0.3	49.1	56.3	42.9	0.8	56.8
Indiana	46.1	53.7	0.1	46.2	55.3	44.5	0.2	55.4
Iowa	51.5	48.3	0.2	51.6	54.0	45.7	0.2	54.2
Kansas	32.0	66.2	1.8	32.5	42.0	53.9	4.2	43.8
Kentucky	50.1	49.5	0.4	50.3	62.6	35.1	2.3	64.1
Louisiana	84.6	12.8	2.6	86.9	72.6[1]	25.6[1]	1.7[1]	73.9[1]
Maine	52.9	47.1	0.0	52.9	39.9	60.1	0.0	39.9
Maryland	52.0	48.0	0.0	52.0	60.3	39.7	0.0	60.3
Massachusetts	57.6	37.4	4.9	60.6	68.8	23.6	7.6	74.4
Michigan	46.9	52.2	0.8	47.3	58.2	40.5	1.4	59.0
Minnesota	53.1	45.0	1.9	54.1	57.8	40.4	1.8	58.9
Mississippi	65.9	31.4	2.7	67.7	51.0	42.8	6.1	54.4
Missouri	59.6	40.2	0.2	59.7	67.0	32.8	0.2	67.1
Montana	60.5	39.5	0.0	60.5	58.6	41.4	0.0	58.6
Nebraska	34.0	66.0	0.0	34.0	47.3	52.7	0.0	47.3
Nevada	47.8	52.2	0.0	47.8	55.8	36.4	7.8	60.5
New Hampshire	29.7	70.3	0.0	29.7	44.1	55.9	0.0	44.1
New Jersey	49.1	50.0	0.9	49.5	59.6	38.1	2.3	61.0
New Mexico	56.3	43.7	0.0	56.3	51.2	47.2	1.6	52.1
New York	25.3	18.5	56.1	57.7	18.1	16.2	65.7	52.8
New York	*50.5*	*45.1*	*4.4*	*52.9*	*57.4*	*39.4*	*3.2*	*59.3*
North Carolina	54.4	45.2	0.5	54.6	64.5	35.2	0.3	64.7
North Dakota	27.1	72.7	0.2	27.2	44.3	55.7	0.0	44.3
Ohio	43.9	54.0	2.1	44.9	47.4	49.5	3.1	48.9
Oklahoma	60.8	38.0	1.3	61.6	58.2	41.1	0.7	58.6
Oregon	55.1	44.9	0.1	55.1	64.1	35.9	0.1	64.1
Pennsylvania	48.7	51.1	0.2	48.8	57.4	42.1	0.5	57.7
Rhode Island	62.7	35.8	1.5	63.7	75.7	24.3	0.0	75.7
South Carolina	52.2	47.8	0.0	52.2	58.3	41.2	0.5	58.6
South Dakota	53.1	46.9	0.0	53.1	38.7	61.3	0.0	38.7
Tennessee	45.8	53.5	0.8	46.1	59.1	40.3	0.5	59.5
Texas	70.4	28.9	0.6	70.9	72.2	27.3	0.5	72.6
Utah	54.9	43.0	2.1	56.1	55.8	39.5	4.7	58.6
Vermont	35.0	65.0	0.0	35.0	40.0	52.9	7.1	43.0
Virginia	49.4	46.4	4.3	51.6	54.8	39.1	6.1	58.4
Washington	65.9	33.7	0.4	66.2	58.5	40.8	0.6	58.9
West Virginia	63.5	36.5	0.0	63.5	69.8	30.2	0.0	69.8
Wisconsin	56.2	42.6	1.2	56.9	58.8	39.7	1.4	59.7
Wyoming	51.7	48.3	0.0	51.7	54.7	45.3	0.0	54.7

Notes: Main entries are calculated from the raw vote values in tables series 5-70 to 5-122 for the appropriate years based on candidates who used the sole designation "Democrat" or "Republican" (or their historical antecedents listed in Appendix A) on the ballot. Other = candidates who used third-party names on the ballot or were listed as independent, unidentified, or scatter vote. Bold italicized entries in the table are the author's alternative party coding, which is used when a candidate listed a major party name (Democrat, Republican, or their historical antecedents) on the ballot with other party names or labels. These values are computed from the bold italicized raw vote values in table series 5-70 to 5-122 for the appropriate states and years. For a more detailed explanation of this alternate coding system, see Tables 5-1 and 1-3. —indicates that the state had no data, either because no vote data were found for the state in question or the state had not yet entered the Union. No special House elections are included in the table. The table only lists at-large vote values for states having both at-large and district House races; see Appendix B for these states' district results aggregated to the state level.

[1]Partial data (less than 100% of the districts reporting).

Sources: Adapted from *United States Congressional Elections, 1788–1997* (1998), *Congressional Quarterly's Guide to U.S. Elections* (1994), *America Votes* (various publication dates), ICPSR data sets 0001 and 0075, and independent search for state sources by the author.

Table 5-64 House Election Results, by State, 1976–1978 (Percentages)

State	1976				1978			
	Democratic	Republican	Other	Democratic % of Two-Party Vote	Democratic	Republican	Other	Democratic % of Two-Party Vote
Alabama	67.8	32.0	0.2	67.9	68.4	30.7	0.9	69.0
Alabama	*67.9*	*32.0*	*0.1*	*68.0*	—	—	—	—
Alaska	28.9	70.8	0.2	29.0	44.4	55.4	0.2	44.5
Arizona	48.8	46.7	4.5	51.1	50.4	44.4	5.2	53.1
Arkansas	77.6[1]	22.4[1]	0.0[1]	77.6[1]	33.4[1]	66.6[1]	0.0[1]	33.4[1]
California	55.6	43.2	1.2	56.3	51.1	47.6	1.3	51.8
Colorado	44.6	52.5	2.9	45.9	47.1	51.2	1.7	47.9
Connecticut	50.6	48.3	1.1	51.1	58.0	41.5	0.5	58.3
Delaware	47.7	51.5	0.8	48.1	41.2	58.2	0.6	41.4
Florida	54.1[1]	45.0[1]	0.9[1]	54.6[1]	58.5[1]	41.5[1]	0.0[1]	58.5[1]
Georgia	74.3	25.7	0.0	74.3	80.2	19.8	0.0	80.2
Hawaii	62.7	26.4	10.9	70.3	80.1	15.9	4.1	83.5
Idaho	47.4	52.6	0.0	47.4	41.4	58.6	0.0	41.4
Illinois	51.5	48.4	0.2	51.6	48.1	51.8	0.1	48.2
Indiana	55.5	44.3	0.2	55.6	51.9	47.0	1.1	52.5
Iowa	57.1	42.4	0.5	57.4	49.7	50.1	0.2	49.8
Kansas	38.3	60.0	1.7	39.0	34.5	65.2	0.3	34.6
Kentucky	61.2	37.8	0.9	61.8	55.5	43.5	1.1	56.1
Louisiana	61.5	35.9	2.5	63.1	50.1[1]	49.9[1]	0.0[1]	50.1[1]
Maine	32.0	66.5	1.5	32.5	38.2	56.5	5.4	40.3
Maryland	60.0	36.0	4.1	62.5	65.4	33.9	0.7	65.9
Massachusetts	64.4	30.8	4.8	67.6	69.0	26.1	4.9	72.6
Michigan	55.3	43.8	0.9	55.8	56.8	42.5	0.7	57.2
Minnesota	58.0	40.7	1.4	58.8	51.1	46.7	2.2	52.2
Mississippi	59.0	40.3	0.7	59.4	48.5	45.5	6.0	51.6
Missouri	56.7	42.6	0.6	57.1	62.5	37.2	0.2	62.7
Montana	56.2	43.8	0.0	56.2	50.6	49.4	0.0	50.6
Nebraska	35.1	64.1	0.9	35.4	37.1	62.8	0.0	37.2
Nevada	77.1	12.1	10.9	86.5	69.5	23.3	7.2	74.9
New Hampshire	53.4	45.8	0.8	53.8	47.3	51.7	0.9	47.8
New Jersey	54.7	43.3	1.9	55.8	54.0	43.3	2.7	55.5
New Mexico	46.2	53.5	0.3	46.3	58.5	41.5	0.0	58.5
New York	18.6	14.6	66.8	56.0	22.9	11.4	65.7	66.7
New York	*58.4*	*39.1*	*2.5*	*59.9*	*51.9*	*45.3*	*2.8*	*53.4*
North Carolina	64.3	35.0	0.7	64.8	59.5	39.8	0.6	59.9
North Dakota	36.0	62.4	1.6	36.5	30.9	67.1	2.1	31.5
Ohio	47.3	49.9	2.8	48.7	46.0	52.9	1.1	46.5
Oklahoma	64.0	34.9	1.2	64.7	56.2	43.8	0.0	56.2
Oregon	64.7	28.3	7.0	69.5	67.2	29.5	3.2	69.5
Pennsylvania	54.4	45.3	0.4	54.6	51.0	48.3	0.7	51.3
Rhode Island	69.7	29.2	1.1	70.5	56.6	43.4	0.0	56.6
South Carolina	64.1	35.7	0.3	64.2	65.6	31.8	2.6	67.4
South Dakota	24.6	75.0	0.4	24.7	47.0	53.0	0.0	47.0
Tennessee	61.9	36.2	1.9	63.1	54.7	42.3	3.1	56.4
Texas	64.7	34.9	0.5	65.0	58.9	40.7	0.4	59.1
Utah	49.0	46.2	4.8	51.5	42.9	54.5	2.6	44.1
Vermont	0.0	67.4	32.6	0.0	19.3	75.3	5.5	20.4
Vermont	*32.6*	*67.4*	*0.1*	*32.6*	—	—	—	—
Virginia	45.5	45.8	8.6	49.8	42.0	56.3	1.7	42.7
Washington	57.4	41.1	1.5	58.3	51.8	46.1	2.1	52.9
West Virginia	67.3	23.7	9.0	74.0	65.7	34.3	0.0	65.7
Wisconsin	60.7	38.8	0.6	61.0	53.0	46.6	0.4	53.2
Wyoming	56.4	43.6	0.0	56.4	41.4	58.6	0.0	41.4

Notes: Main entries are calculated from the raw vote values in tables series 5-70 to 5-122 for the appropriate years based on candidates who used the sole designation "Democrat" or "Republican" (or their historical antecedents listed in Appendix A) on the ballot. Other = candidates who used third-party names on the ballot or were listed as independent, unidentified, or scatter vote. Bold italicized entries in the table are the author's alternative party coding, which is used when a candidate listed a major party name (Democrat, Republican, or their historical antecedents) on the ballot with other party names or labels. These values are computed from the bold italicized raw vote values in table series 5-70 to 5-122 for the appropriate states and years. For a more detailed explanation of this alternate coding system, see Tables 5-1 and 1-3. —indicates that the state had no data, either because no vote data were found for the state in question or the state had not yet entered the Union. No special House elections are included in the table. The table only lists at-large vote values for states having both at-large and district House races; see Appendix B for these states' district results aggregated to the state level.

[1]Partial data (less than 100% of the districts reporting).

Sources: Adapted from *United States Congressional Elections, 1788–1997* (1998), *Congressional Quarterly's Guide to U.S. Elections* (1994), *America Votes* (various publication dates), and independent search for state sources by the author.

Table 5-65 House Election Results, by State, 1980–1982 (Percentages)

	1980				1982			
State	Democratic	Republican	Other	Democratic % of Two-Party Vote	Democratic	Republican	Other	Democratic % of Two-Party Vote
Alabama	62.1	35.0	2.9	63.9	70.4	28.4	1.2	71.3
Alabama	*62.3*	*35.0*	*2.7*	*64.0*	—	—	—	
Alaska	25.8	73.8	0.4	25.9	28.7	70.8	0.4	28.8
Arizona	46.2	50.8	3.0	47.6	42.3	55.5	2.2	43.2
Arkansas	21.0[1]	78.9[1]	0.1[1]	21.0[1]	52.4	47.6	0.0	52.4
California	44.8	51.1	4.1	46.7	50.3	46.6	3.1	51.9
Colorado	44.0	53.9	2.2	44.9	47.4	51.2	1.4	48.0
Connecticut	51.9	47.8	0.3	52.1	53.9	45.3	0.7	54.3
Delaware	37.5	61.8	0.7	37.8	52.4	46.3	1.3	53.1
Florida	58.6[1]	41.2[1]	0.2[1]	58.7[1]	59.3[1]	40.7[1]	0.0[1]	59.3[1]
Georgia	71.9	28.1	0.0	71.9	74.1	24.9	1.0	74.8
Hawaii	85.4	7.1	7.5	92.4	89.6	0.0	10.4	100.0
Idaho	43.9	56.1	0.0	43.9	47.0	53.0	0.0	47.0
Illinois	45.8	54.1	0.1	45.9	57.9	41.7	0.3	58.1
Indiana	49.7	50.2	0.1	49.7	49.1	50.7	0.2	49.2
Iowa	51.1	48.5	0.4	51.3	52.6	47.3	0.1	52.7
Kansas	43.4	55.7	0.9	43.8	45.7	53.0	1.3	46.3
Kentucky	57.8	41.9	0.3	58.0	59.0	40.0	1.0	59.6
Louisiana	100.0[1]	0.0[1]	0.0[1]	100.0[1]	—	—	—	—
Maine	26.9	73.1	0.0	26.9	41.4	57.7	0.9	41.7
Maryland	61.7	38.3	0.0	61.7	68.1	31.9	0.0	68.1
Massachusetts	65.3	33.6	1.1	66.0	68.8	29.7	1.5	69.9
Michigan	52.3	46.2	1.4	53.1	59.4	38.9	1.6	60.4
Minnesota	47.6	51.8	0.6	47.9	54.6	44.4	0.9	55.2
Mississippi	54.3	38.6	7.1	58.4	57.5	40.5	2.1	58.7
Missouri	54.1	45.9	0.0	54.1	57.0	42.8	0.2	57.2
Montana	52.1	47.9	0.0	52.1	52.4	45.0	2.6	53.8
Nebraska	26.8	72.2	1.0	27.1	22.4	77.5	0.2	22.4
Nevada	67.5	25.8	6.7	72.3	48.8	49.5	1.7	49.6
New Hampshire	48.7	51.3	0.0	48.7	42.5	57.3	0.3	42.6
New Jersey	48.0	49.9	2.1	49.0	56.2	42.7	1.1	56.9
New Mexico	43.0	45.9	11.1	48.4	51.4	48.6	0.0	51.4
New York	16.1	9.9	74.0	62.0	20.7	11.4	67.9	64.6
New York	*49.3*	*48.2*	*2.5*	*50.6*	*55.9*	*41.4*	*2.7*	*57.4*
North Carolina	55.5	44.3	0.2	55.6	53.6	43.9	2.5	55.0
North Dakota	56.8	42.6	0.7	57.2	71.6	27.7	0.7	72.1
Ohio	45.3	54.0	0.7	45.6	54.3	43.8	1.9	55.4
Oklahoma	52.6	46.8	0.6	52.9	63.0	36.2	0.8	63.5
Oregon	59.4	39.7	1.0	59.9	56.9	43.0	0.0	57.0
Pennsylvania	47.6	50.0	2.4	48.7	52.7	45.5	1.8	53.6
Rhode Island	55.3	44.7	0.0	55.3	52.2	47.3	0.5	52.5
South Carolina	49.2	48.1	2.7	50.6	53.7	44.9	1.4	54.5
South Dakota	54.3	45.7	0.0	54.3	51.6	48.4	0.0	51.6
Tennessee	50.9	47.5	1.7	51.8	59.4	39.9	0.7	59.8
Texas	59.1	39.5	1.3	59.9	64.8	32.8	2.4	66.4
Utah	39.2	59.4	1.3	39.8	29.6	63.7	6.7	31.7
Vermont	0.0	79.2	20.8	0.0	23.2	69.2	7.6	25.1
Virginia	31.3	64.7	4.0	32.6	47.2	51.7	1.2	47.7
Washington	50.2	48.8	1.1	50.7	52.8	46.2	1.1	53.3
West Virginia	57.0	43.0	0.0	57.0	62.8	37.0	0.1	62.9
Wisconsin	50.2	49.5	0.3	50.4	53.0	46.0	1.0	53.5
Wyoming	31.4	68.6	0.0	31.4	28.9	71.1	0.0	28.9

Notes: Main entries are calculated from the raw vote values in tables series 5-70 to 5-122 for the appropriate years based on candidates who used the sole designation "Democrat" or "Republican" (or their historical antecedents listed in Appendix A) on the ballot. Other = candidates who used third-party names on the ballot or were listed as independent, unidentified, or scatter vote. Bold italicized entries in the table are the author's alternative party coding, which is used when a candidate listed a major party name (Democrat, Republican, or their historical antecedents) on the ballot with other party names or labels. These values are computed from the bold italicized raw vote values in table series 5-70 to 5-122 for the appropriate states and years. For a more detailed explanation of this alternate coding system, see Tables 5-1 and 1-3. —indicates that the state had no data, either because no vote data were found for the state in question or the state had not yet entered the Union. No special House elections are included in the table. The table only lists at-large vote values for states having both at-large and district House races; see Appendix B for these states' district results aggregated to the state level.

[1] Partial data (less than 100% of the districts reporting).

Sources: Adapted from *United States Congressional Elections, 1788–1997* (1998), *Congressional Quarterly's Guide to U.S. Elections* (1994), *America Votes* (various publication dates), ICPSR data sets 0001 and 0075, and independent search for state sources by the author.

Table 5-66 House Election Results, by State, 1984–1986 (Percentages)

	1984				1986			
State	Democratic	Republican	Other	Democratic % of Two-Party Vote	Democratic	Republican	Other	Democratic % of Two-Party Vote
Alabama	71.5	26.8	1.6	72.7	60.8	39.1	0.1	60.9
Alaska	41.7	55.0	3.3	43.1	41.1	56.5	2.5	42.1
Arizona	33.9	63.9	2.2	34.6	32.4	67.2	0.5	32.5
Arkansas	73.7[1]	19.6[1]	6.7[1]	79.0[1]	58.1	40.3	1.6	59.0
California	48.3	49.4	2.3	49.4	52.0	46.2	1.8	52.9
Colorado	34.9	62.5	2.6	35.9	44.2	55.6	0.2	44.3
Connecticut	46.6	53.2	0.2	46.7	55.6	44.3	0.1	55.7
Delaware	58.5	41.4	0.1	58.5	66.2	33.4	0.4	66.4
Florida	51.1[1]	48.9[1]	0.0[1]	51.1[1]	53.9[1]	46.1[1]	0.1[1]	53.9[1]
Georgia	71.7	28.3	0.0	71.7	72.8	27.2	0.0	72.8
Hawaii	82.5	14.7	2.8	84.8	56.4	40.8	2.8	58.1
Idaho	40.7	59.3	0.0	40.7	43.3	55.4	1.3	43.9
Illinois	51.7	48.1	0.2	51.8	53.8	46.2	0.0	53.8
Indiana	46.9	52.6	0.5	47.1	50.7	48.6	0.7	51.0
Iowa	46.9	53.1	0.0	46.9	48.1	51.9	0.0	48.1
Kansas	43.8	54.5	1.7	44.5	39.7	60.3	0.0	39.7
Kentucky	55.3	44.5	0.2	55.4	59.5	40.1	0.4	59.7
Louisiana	—	—	—	—	73.8[1]	26.2[1]	0.0[1]	73.8[1]
Maine	30.0	69.2	0.8	30.2	39.2	59.1	1.7	39.9
Maryland	63.9	35.8	0.3	64.1	62.9	37.1	0.0	62.9
Massachusetts	69.0	30.0	1.0	69.7	79.7	16.7	3.6	82.7
Michigan	53.9	45.4	0.7	54.3	57.7	42.0	0.3	57.9
Minnesota	53.7	45.7	0.6	54.0	59.7	40.0	0.3	59.9
Mississippi	60.2	37.6	2.2	61.5	60.3	39.7	0.0	60.3
Missouri	55.4	44.3	0.3	55.6	57.9	41.9	0.2	58.0
Montana	50.5	48.2	1.3	51.2	54.1	45.9	0.0	54.1
Nebraska	25.8	74.2	0.0	25.8	35.4	64.5	0.1	35.4
Nevada	40.4	57.3	2.2	41.3	47.1	52.0	0.8	47.5
New Hampshire	31.9	67.2	0.9	32.2	35.1	64.9	0.0	35.1
New Jersey	50.4	49.2	0.4	50.6	51.7	47.6	0.8	52.1
New Mexico	40.3	58.9	0.9	40.6	46.4	53.6	0.0	46.4
New York	18.1	9.1	72.8	66.5	23.6	8.6	67.8	73.2
New York	***52.3***	***46.6***	***1.0***	***52.9***	***54.6***	***42.6***	***2.7***	***56.2***
North Carolina	52.4	47.6	0.0	52.4	56.6	43.4	0.0	56.6
North Dakota	78.7	21.3	0.0	78.7	75.5	23.4	1.1	76.3
Ohio	49.3	49.8	0.9	49.7	49.3	50.1	0.6	49.6
Oklahoma	58.1	41.2	0.7	58.5	59.4	40.2	0.5	59.7
Oregon	54.4	45.6	0.0	54.4	56.7	43.3	0.0	56.7
Pennsylvania	54.3	45.3	0.4	54.5	53.3	46.1	0.5	53.6
Rhode Island	50.0	50.0	0.0	50.0	42.4	57.6	0.0	42.4
South Carolina	50.7	47.6	1.7	51.6	63.2	36.5	0.3	63.4
South Dakota	57.4	42.6	0.0	57.4	59.2	40.8	0.0	59.2
Tennessee	55.2	44.8	0.0	55.2	57.6	40.6	1.8	58.6
Texas	57.6	42.3	0.1	57.6	57.0	42.0	1.0	57.6
Utah	34.6	64.5	0.9	35.0	45.9	53.6	0.6	46.1
Vermont	26.7	65.4	7.9	29.0	0.0	89.1	10.9	0.0
Virginia	43.3	54.6	2.1	44.2	52.2	44.7	3.0	53.9
Washington	55.1	44.2	0.6	55.5	59.3	40.7	0.0	59.3
West Virginia	60.9	39.1	0.0	60.9	75.5	24.5	0.0	75.5
Wisconsin	49.8	49.8	0.5	50.0	50.9	48.3	0.7	51.3
Wyoming	24.4	73.6	2.0	24.9	30.5	69.5	0.0	30.5

Notes: Main entries are calculated from the raw vote values in tables series 5-70 to 5-122 for the appropriate years based on candidates who used the sole designation "Democrat" or "Republican" (or their historical antecedents listed in Appendix A) on the ballot. Other = candidates who used third-party names on the ballot or were listed as independent, unidentified, or scatter vote. Bold italicized entries in the table are the author's alternative party coding, which is used when a candidate listed a major party name (Democrat, Republican, or their historical antecedents) on the ballot with other party names or labels. These values are computed from the bold italicized raw vote values in table series 5-70 to 5-122 for the appropriate states and years. For a more detailed explanation of this alternate coding system, see Tables 5-1 and 1-3. —indicates that the state had no data, either because no vote data were found for the state in question or the state had not yet entered the Union. No special House elections are included in the table. The table only lists at-large vote values for states having both at-large and district House races; see Appendix B for these states' district results aggregated to the state level.

[1]Partial data (less than 100% of the districts reporting).

Sources: Adapted from *United States Congressional Elections, 1788–1997* (1998), *Congressional Quarterly's Guide to U.S. Elections* (1994), *America Votes* (various publication dates), ICPSR data sets 0001 and 0075, and independent search for state sources by the author.

Table 5-67 House Election Results, by State, 1988–1990 (Percentages)

State	1988				1990			
	Democratic	Republican	Other	Democratic % of Two-Party Vote	Democratic	Republican	Other	Democratic % of Two-Party Vote
Alabama	61.3	36.7	2.0	62.6	67.9	31.0	1.2	68.7
Alaska	37.3	62.5	0.2	37.3	47.8	51.7	0.5	48.1
Arizona	28.6	68.1	3.3	29.6	35.7	64.3	0.1	35.7
Arkansas	58.3[1]	41.7[1]	0.0[1]	58.3[1]	55.5	44.5	0.0	55.5
California	52.7	44.5	2.8	54.2	49.0	45.9	5.1	51.6
Colorado	49.1	50.7	0.2	49.2	50.3	48.7	1.0	50.8
Connecticut	49.3	50.5	0.3	49.4	47.2	52.6	0.2	47.3
Delaware	67.5	32.5	0.0	67.5	65.5	32.7	1.8	66.7
Florida	47.0[1]	53.0[1]	0.0[1]	47.0[1]	51.0[1]	48.9[1]	0.1[1]	51.0[1]
Georgia	66.7	33.3	0.0	66.7	61.3	38.7	0.0	61.3
Hawaii	65.1	28.5	6.4	69.5	63.3	34.5	2.2	64.7
Idaho	48.7	49.9	1.4	49.4	58.2	41.8	0.0	58.2
Illinois	53.3	46.6	0.1	53.4	53.5	43.8	2.7	55.0
Indiana	51.7	48.3	0.0	51.7	54.9	45.1	0.1	54.9
Iowa	48.8	51.0	0.2	48.9	50.6	48.6	0.8	51.0
Kansas	39.3	60.6	0.0	39.3	50.4	49.6	0.0	50.4
Kentucky	48.4	51.1	0.6	48.6	46.3	52.0	1.7	47.1
Louisiana	43.2[1]	56.8[1]	0.0[1]	43.2[1]	100.0[1]	0.0[1]	0.0[1]	100.0[1]
Maine	49.8	50.2	0.0	49.8	55.0	44.9	0.1	55.0
Maryland	60.0	40.0	0.0	60.0	51.9	47.4	0.7	52.2
Massachusetts	75.4	21.5	3.1	77.8	69.2	27.6	3.1	71.5
Michigan	52.8	46.4	0.8	53.2	54.3	44.8	0.9	54.8
Minnesota	58.3	41.1	0.5	58.7	58.5	41.4	0.1	58.6
Mississippi	66.1	33.5	0.4	66.4	81.2	18.8	0.0	81.2
Missouri	55.5	43.9	0.6	55.8	53.8	46.2	0.0	53.8
Montana	52.9	47.1	0.0	52.9	49.5	50.5	0.0	49.5
Nebraska	35.0	64.9	0.2	35.0	47.2	52.7	0.2	47.2
Nevada	51.4	46.4	2.2	52.6	46.1	48.2	5.7	48.9
New Hampshire	41.0	58.6	0.4	41.2	48.5	51.2	0.2	48.6
New Jersey	48.1	50.9	1.0	48.6	45.8	49.9	4.3	47.9
New Mexico	46.5	52.6	0.9	46.9	40.5	59.5	0.0	40.5
New York	21.8	14.6	63.6	59.9	17.6	19.3	63.1	47.7
New York	***53.6***	***44.3***	***2.1***	***54.7***	***50.0***	***45.4***	***4.6***	***52.4***
North Carolina	55.8	44.2	0.0	55.8	53.5	46.5	0.0	53.5
North Dakota	70.9	28.2	1.0	71.6	65.2	34.8	0.0	65.2
Ohio	50.2	49.8	0.0	50.2	52.9	46.5	0.6	53.2
Oklahoma	52.9	47.1	0.0	52.9	60.6	39.4	0.0	60.6
Oregon	64.9	34.9	0.1	65.0	63.4	32.5	4.1	66.1
Pennsylvania	50.4	41.6	8.0	54.8	45.3	42.9	11.8	51.4
Pennsylvania	***50.4***	***49.3***	***0.2***	***50.6***	***45.3***	***54.5***	***0.2***	***45.4***
Rhode Island	35.9	64.1	0.0	35.9	52.5	47.5	0.0	52.5
South Carolina	55.4	44.3	0.2	55.6	57.2	41.0	1.9	58.2
South Dakota	71.7	28.3	0.0	71.7	67.6	32.4	0.0	67.6
Tennessee	59.9	38.1	2.0	61.1	51.5	40.3	8.2	56.1
Texas	58.6	39.3	2.1	59.9	53.8	45.7	0.5	54.1
Utah	42.7	56.0	1.2	43.3	52.9	43.2	3.9	55.0
Vermont	18.9	41.2	39.9	31.4	3.0	39.5	57.5	7.1
Virginia	42.4	57.0	0.6	42.7	57.5	35.6	6.9	61.7
Washington	57.1	42.9	0.0	57.1	53.0	45.4	1.6	53.9
West Virginia	76.8	23.2	0.0	76.8	67.1	32.9	0.0	67.1
Wisconsin	50.9	49.0	0.1	50.9	47.6	51.9	0.6	47.8
Wyoming	31.8	66.6	1.6	32.3	44.9	55.1	0.0	44.9

Notes: Main entries are calculated from the raw vote values in tables series 5-70 to 5-122 for the appropriate years based on candidates who used the sole desig-nation "Democrat" or "Republican" (or their historical antecedents listed in Appendix A) on the ballot. Other = candidates who used third-party names on the ballot or were listed as independent, unidentified, or scatter vote. Bold italicized entries in the table are the author's alternative party coding, which is used when a candi-date listed a major party name (Democrat, Republican, or their historical antecedents) on the ballot with other party names or labels. These values are computed from the bold italicized raw vote values in table series 5-70 to 5-122 for the appropriate states and years. For a more detailed explanation of this alternate coding system, see Tables 5-1 and 1-3. —indicates that the state had no data, either because no vote data were found for the state in question or the state had not yet entered the Union. No special House elections are included in the table. The table only lists at-large vote values for states having both at-large and district House races; see Appendix B for these states' district results aggregated to the state level.

[1]Partial data (less than 100% of the districts reporting).

Sources: Adapted from *United States Congressional Elections, 1788–1997* (1998), *Congressional Quarterly's Guide to U.S. Elections* (1994), *America Votes* (various pub-lication dates), ICPSR data sets 0001 and 0075, and independent search for state sources by the author.

Table 5-68 House Election Results, by State, 1992–1994 (Percentages)

State	1992				1994			
	Democratic	Republican	Other	Democratic % of Two-Party Vote	Democratic	Republican	Other	Democratic % of Two-Party Vote
Alabama	55.9	40.1	4.0	58.2	49.7	50.1	0.2	49.8
Alaska	42.8	46.8	10.4	47.8	32.7	56.9	10.3	36.5
Arizona	41.3	52.5	6.1	44.0	37.3	59.4	3.4	38.6
Arkansas	59.1	40.2	0.7	59.5	47.4	52.6	0.0	47.4
California	51.7	41.4	6.9	55.5	47.5	48.8	3.7	49.3
Colorado	46.7	51.2	2.0	47.7	34.5	65.1	0.4	34.7
Connecticut	44.9	48.7	6.4	48.0	47.4	48.3	4.4	49.5
Delaware	42.5	55.4	2.1	43.4	26.6	70.7	2.7	27.3
Florida	45.9[1]	51.1[1]	3.0[1]	47.3[1]	40.5[1]	59.4[1]	0.1[1]	40.6[1]
Georgia	54.9	45.1	0.0	54.9	45.5	54.5	0.0	45.5
Hawaii	72.8	22.8	4.5	76.2	61.9	33.8	4.3	64.7
Idaho	47.1	48.8	4.1	49.1	35.0	65.0	0.0	35.0
Illinois	55.4	43.4	1.2	56.1	48.0	51.8	0.2	48.1
Indiana	54.3	45.0	0.7	54.7	43.2	56.6	0.2	43.3
Iowa	39.7	58.7	1.6	40.3	41.7	57.3	1.0	42.1
Kansas	43.4	52.6	4.0	45.2	36.5	63.5	0.0	36.5
Kentucky	53.0	46.9	0.1	53.1	40.3	57.5	2.2	41.2
Louisiana	41.7[1]	58.3[1]	0.0[1]	41.7[1]	45.1[1]	48.5[1]	6.5[1]	48.2[1]
Maine	54.3	41.6	4.1	56.6	46.9	46.6	6.5	50.2
Maryland	52.9	46.6	0.5	53.2	49.2	50.8	0.0	49.2
Massachusetts	58.1	32.8	9.2	63.9	69.0	30.0	1.0	69.7
Michigan	49.3	47.8	3.0	50.8	47.2	51.0	1.8	48.1
Minnesota	51.8	40.9	7.3	55.9	50.6	48.4	1.0	51.1
Mississippi	69.4	28.3	2.3	71.0	57.1	41.3	1.5	58.0
Missouri	54.1	44.1	1.8	55.1	50.6	47.3	2.1	51.7
Montana	50.5	47.0	2.6	51.8	48.7	42.2	9.1	53.5
Nebraska	39.9	60.1	0.0	39.9	35.6	64.0	0.4	35.7
Nevada	49.9	43.5	6.6	53.4	36.6	57.4	6.0	38.9
New Hampshire	52.0	44.4	3.5	53.9	37.7	58.2	4.1	39.3
New Jersey	45.3	50.2	4.5	47.4	43.9	54.4	1.7	44.6
New Mexico	49.1	50.0	0.9	49.5	40.6	57.1	2.3	41.6
New York	20.3	5.6	74.1	78.3	16.9	11.9	71.2	58.8
New York	*51.5*	*45.3*	*3.2*	*53.2*	*48.0*	*48.8*	*3.2*	*49.6*
North Carolina	50.7	47.6	1.6	51.6	42.9	57.1	0.0	42.9
North Dakota	56.8	39.4	3.8	59.0	52.3	45.0	2.7	53.7
Ohio	48.0	47.1	4.9	50.5	40.3	58.4	1.4	40.8
Oklahoma	59.9	39.5	0.6	60.3	38.0	57.3	4.8	39.9
Oregon	59.3	39.8	0.9	59.9	54.2	41.8	4.0	56.5
Pennsylvania	46.9	38.9	14.1	54.7	44.2	45.6	10.1	49.2
Pennsylvania	*46.9*	*51.1*	*1.9*	*47.9*	*44.2*	*54.3*	*1.5*	*44.9*
Rhode Island	48.3	46.7	5.0	50.9	61.3	38.7	0.0	61.3
South Carolina	45.4	52.1	2.5	46.5	36.1	63.6	0.3	36.2
South Dakota	69.1	26.8	4.0	72.0	59.8	36.6	3.5	62.0
Tennessee	51.2	42.7	6.1	54.5	43.4	54.8	1.8	44.2
Texas	49.9	47.8	2.3	51.1	42.1	55.7	2.2	43.0
Utah	45.6	49.8	4.6	47.8	42.8	50.0	7.1	46.1
Vermont	7.9	30.9	61.2	20.4	0.0	46.6	53.4	0.0
Virginia	48.5	48.3	3.2	50.1	39.4	57.1	3.5	40.9
Washington	55.6	41.0	3.4	57.6	49.0	50.6	0.4	49.2
West Virginia	78.1	21.9	0.0	78.1	66.1	33.9	0.0	66.1
Wisconsin	48.3	50.7	1.0	48.8	37.5	61.2	1.2	38.0
Wyoming	39.3	57.8	2.9	40.5	41.3	53.2	5.5	43.7

Notes: Main entries are calculated from the raw vote values in tables series 5-70 to 5-122 for the appropriate years based on candidates who used the sole designation "Democrat" or "Republican" (or their historical antecedents listed in Appendix A) on the ballot. Other = candidates who used third-party names on the ballot or were listed as independent, unidentified, or scatter vote. Bold italicized entries in the table are the author's alternative party coding, which is used when a candidate listed a major party name (Democrat, Republican, or their historical antecedents) on the ballot with other party names or labels. These values are computed from the bold italicized raw vote values in table series 5-70 to 5-122 for the appropriate states and years. For a more detailed explanation of this alternate coding system, see Tables 5-1 and 1-3. —indicates that the state had no data, either because no vote data were found for the state in question or the state had not yet entered the Union. No special House elections are included in the table. The table only lists at-large vote values for states having both at-large and district House races; see Appendix B for these states' district results aggregated to the state level.

[1]Partial data (less than 100% of the districts reporting).

Sources: Adapted from *United States Congressional Elections, 1788–1997* (1998), *Congressional Quarterly's Guide to U.S. Elections* (1994), *America Votes* (various publication dates), ICPSR data sets 0001 and 0075, and independent search for state sources by the author.

Table 5-69 House Election Results, by State, 1996–1998 (Percentages)

State	1996 Democratic	Republican	Other	Democratic % of Two-Party Vote	1998 Democratic	Republican	Other	Democratic % of Two-Party Vote
Alabama	44.7	53.5	1.8	45.5	44.9	54.8	0.3	45.0
Alaska	36.4	59.4	4.2	38.0	34.6	62.6	2.9	35.6
Arizona	38.4	59.0	2.5	39.4	40.5	57.1	2.3	41.5
Arkansas	45.8	52.8	1.4	46.4	32.1[1]	60.9[1]	7.0[1]	34.5[1]
California	49.6	45.3	5.1	52.3	50.6	43.9	5.5	53.5
Colorado	40.8	57.0	2.2	41.7	41.9	56.2	2.0	42.7
Connecticut	55.9	42.3	1.8	56.9	51.9	46.3	1.8	52.9
Delaware	27.5	69.5	3.0	28.3	31.8	66.4	1.8	32.4
Florida	43.4[1]	56.3[1]	0.3[1]	43.6[1]	47.9[1]	46.0[1]	6.2[1]	51.0[1]
Georgia	46.7	53.3	0.0	46.7	36.3	63.7	0.0	36.3
Hawaii	55.5	38.4	6.1	59.1	65.7	30.0	4.3	68.6
Idaho	39.2	58.7	2.1	40.0	44.7	54.0	1.3	45.3
Illinois	54.9	43.9	1.2	55.6	48.7	50.5	0.8	49.1
Indiana	44.9	53.1	2.0	45.8	42.7	54.7	2.6	43.9
Iowa	44.4	54.1	1.5	45.0	37.6	61.3	1.2	38.0
Kansas	40.5	56.4	3.1	41.8	37.4	61.9	0.7	37.7
Kentucky	41.0	59.0	0.0	41.0	41.5	58.0	0.5	41.7
Louisiana	39.7[1]	60.3[1]	0.0[1]	39.7[1]	68.7[1]	31.3[1]	0.0[1]	68.7[1]
Maine	63.2	35.2	1.6	64.2	67.7	30.1	2.2	69.2
Maryland	53.5	46.5	0.0	53.5	53.5	46.5	0.0	53.5
Massachusetts	65.8	32.4	1.8	67.0	75.0	23.7	1.3	76.0
Michigan	52.6	45.4	2.0	53.7	49.2	48.2	2.6	50.5
Minnesota	55.1	41.8	3.1	56.9	53.5	42.3	4.2	55.8
Mississippi	44.0	54.0	2.1	44.9	47.7	42.2	10.1	53.1
Missouri	52.8	39.4	7.9	57.3	50.1	47.6	2.3	51.3
Montana	43.2	52.4	4.4	45.2	44.4	53.0	2.6	45.6
Nebraska	30.9	68.0	1.1	31.2	19.9	74.7	5.5	21.0
Nevada	38.4	55.3	6.3	41.0	19.4	67.1	13.5	22.4
New Hampshire	45.0	50.3	4.7	47.3	39.0	59.8	1.1	39.5
New Jersey	47.9	49.6	2.6	49.1	49.7	47.3	3.0	51.2
New Mexico	49.4	47.6	3.0	51.0	45.8	49.5	4.7	48.1
New York	13.9	3.1	82.9	81.6	15.9	8.8	75.2	64.4
New York	*54.8*	*42.5*	*2.8*	*56.3*	*53.4*	*43.5*	*3.1*	*55.1*
North Carolina	45.2	53.3	1.5	45.9	43.4	53.3	3.3	44.9
North Dakota	55.1	43.2	1.7	56.0	56.2	41.1	2.7	57.8
Ohio	46.3	49.9	3.8	48.1	47.2	51.9	0.8	47.6
Oklahoma	36.5	61.3	2.3	37.3	36.6	62.7	0.7	36.9
Oregon	54.3	41.8	4.0	56.5	57.9	36.8	5.3	61.1
Pennsylvania	51.5	47.2	1.3	52.2	47.7	46.5	5.8	50.6
Pennsylvania	*—*	*—*	*—*	*—*	*47.7*	*50.8*	*1.5*	*48.4*
Rhode Island	66.9	29.9	3.2	69.1	69.5	26.2	4.3	72.7
South Carolina	32.6	64.6	2.8	33.6	38.0	59.6	2.5	38.9
South Dakota	37.0	57.7	5.3	39.1	24.9	75.1	0.0	24.9
Tennessee	48.0	49.8	2.2	49.1	45.1	51.4	3.5	46.8
Texas	44.5	53.4	2.1	45.5	44.2	51.6	4.2	46.1
Utah	39.8	58.2	2.0	40.6	26.9	64.6	8.5	29.4
Vermont	9.4	32.6	58.0	22.3	0.0	32.9	67.1	0.0
Virginia	46.7	50.8	2.5	47.9	44.8	47.2	8.0	48.7
Washington	52.0	46.9	1.1	52.5	52.8	44.1	3.2	54.5
West Virginia	87.8	12.2	0.0	87.8	80.6	8.3	11.1	90.7
Wisconsin	47.1	52.1	0.8	47.5	45.5	52.6	1.9	46.4
Wyoming	40.8	55.2	3.9	42.5	38.7	57.8	3.5	40.1

Notes: Main entries are calculated from the raw vote values in tables series 5-70 to 5-122 for the appropriate years based on candidates who used the sole designation "Democrat" or "Republican" (or their historical antecedents listed in Appendix A) on the ballot. Other = candidates who used third-party names on the ballot or were listed as independent, unidentified, or scatter vote. Bold italicized entries in the table are the author's alternative party coding, which is used when a candidate listed a major party name (Democrat, Republican, or their historical antecedents) on the ballot with other party names or labels. These values are computed from the bold italicized raw vote values in table series 5-70 to 5-122 for the appropriate states and years. For a more detailed explanation of this alternate coding system, see Tables 5-1 and 1-3. —indicates that the state had no data, either because no vote data were found for the state in question or the state had not yet entered the Union. No special House elections are included in the table. The table only lists at-large vote values for states having both at-large and district House races; see Appendix B for these states' district results aggregated to the state level.

[1] Partial data (less than 100% of the districts reporting).

Sources: Adapted from *United States Congressional Elections, 1788–1997* (1998), *America Votes* (various publication dates), and independent search for state sources by the author.

Table 5-70 House Election Results, by State, 1788–1791 (Raw Count)

State	1788–1789				1790–1791			
	Democratic	Republican	Other	Total Vote	Democratic	Republican	Other	Total Vote
Alabama	—	—	—	—	—	—	—	—
Alaska	—	—	—	—	—	—	—	—
Arizona	—	—	—	—	—	—	—	—
Arkansas	—	—	—	—	—	—	—	—
California	—	—	—	—	—	—	—	—
Colorado	—	—	—	—	—	—	—	—
Connecticut	—	—	—	—	0	0	2,969	2,969
Delaware	0[1]	0[1]	2,059[1]	2,059[1]	—	—	—	—
Florida	—	—	—	—	—	—	—	—
Georgia	0[1]	0[1]	2,878[1]	2,878[1]	0[1]	0[1]	1,954[1]	1,954[1]
Hawaii	—	—	—	—	—	—	—	—
Idaho	—	—	—	—	—	—	—	—
Illinois	—	—	—	—	—	—	—	—
Indiana	—	—	—	—	—	—	—	—
Iowa	—	—	—	—	—	—	—	—
Kansas	—	—	—	—	—	—	—	—
Kentucky	—	—	—	—	—	—	—	—
Louisiana	—	—	—	—	—	—	—	—
Maine	—	—	—	—	—	—	—	—
Maryland	2,731[1]	5,154[1]	0[1]	7,885[1]	0	0	17,173	17,173
Massachusetts	0	0	11,509	11,509	0	0	14,235	14,235
Michigan	—	—	—	—	—	—	—	—
Minnesota	—	—	—	—	—	—	—	—
Mississippi	—	—	—	—	—	—	—	—
Missouri	—	—	—	—	—	—	—	—
Montana	—	—	—	—	—	—	—	—
Nebraska	—	—	—	—	—	—	—	—
Nevada	—	—	—	—	—	—	—	—
New Hampshire	0	0	2,374	2,374	0	0	3,585	3,585
New Jersey	0[1]	0[1]	13,811[1]	13,811[1]	0[1]	0[1]	6,435[1]	6,435[1]
New Mexico	—	—	—	—	—	—	—	—
New York	3,531[1,2]	5,845[1,2]	455[1,2]	9,831[1,2]	3,132	7,154	399	10,685
North Carolina	—	—	—	—	2,468[2]	2,907[2]	262[2]	5,637[2]
North Dakota	—	—	—	—	—	—	—	—
Ohio	—	—	—	—	—	—	—	—
Oklahoma	—	—	—	—	—	—	—	—
Oregon	—	—	—	—	—	—	—	—
Pennsylvania	7,417	8,707	0	16,124	0[1,2]	0[1,2]	15,153[1,2]	15,153[1,2]
Rhode Island	—	—	—	—	—	—	—	—
South Carolina	—	—	—	—	—	—	—	—
South Dakota	—	—	—	—	—	—	—	—
Tennessee	—	—	—	—	—	—	—	—
Texas	—	—	—	—	—	—	—	—
Utah	—	—	—	—	—	—	—	—
Vermont	—	—	—	—	0[1,2]	0[1,2]	2,061[1,2]	2,061[1,2]
Virginia	0[1,2]	0[1,2]	4,306[1,2]	4,306[1,2]	0[2]	0[2]	6,097[2]	6,097[2]
Washington	—	—	—	—	—	—	—	—
West Virginia	—	—	—	—	—	—	—	—
Wisconsin	—	—	—	—	—	—	—	—
Wyoming	—	—	—	—	—	—	—	—
North Carolina	—	—	—	—	0[2,3]	0[2,3]	3,166[2,3]	3,166[2,3]

Notes: Entries are raw vote values for candidates who used the sole designation "Democrat" or "Republican" (or their historical antecedents listed in Appendix A) on the ballot. In general, historical antecedents to the Democratic Party were Anti-Federalists, Democratic-Republicans, and Jacksonian Democrats; historical precursors of the Republican Party were Federalists, National Republicans, and Whigs. Other = candidates who used third-party names on the ballot or were listed as independent, unidentified, or scatter vote. —indicates that the state had no data, either because no vote data were found for the state in question or the state had not yet entered the Union. No special House elections are included in the table. The table only lists at-large vote values for states having both at-large and district House races; see Appendix B for these states' district results aggregated to the state level.

[1] Election held in odd-numbered year.
[2] Partial data (less than 100% of the districts reporting).
[3] 1791 election when a state had annual elections in both 1790 and 1791.

Sources: Adapted from *United States Congressional Elections, 1788–1997* (1998), independent search for state sources by the author, and personal communications with Michael J. Dubin (various dates).

Table 5-71 House Election Results, by State, 1792–1795 (Raw Count)

State	1792–1793				1794–1795			
	Democratic	Republican	Other	Total Vote	Democratic	Republican	Other	Total Vote
Alabama	—	—	—	—	—	—	—	—
Alaska	—	—	—	—	—	—	—	—
Arizona	—	—	—	—	—	—	—	—
Arkansas	—	—	—	—	—	—	—	—
California	—	—	—	—	—	—	—	—
Colorado	—	—	—	—	—	—	—	—
Connecticut	0	0	3,303	3,303	0	3,575	0	3,575
Delaware	0	0	4,516	4,516	2,409	2,285	0	4,694
Florida	—	—	—	—	—	—	—	—
Georgia	0	0	5,488	5,488	1,487	1,150	1,143	3,780
Hawaii	—	—	—	—	—	—	—	—
Idaho	—	—	—	—	—	—	—	—
Illinois	—	—	—	—	—	—	—	—
Indiana	—	—	—	—	—	—	—	—
Iowa	—	—	—	—	—	—	—	—
Kansas	—	—	—	—	—	—	—	—
Kentucky	—	—	—	—	—	—	—	—
Louisiana	—	—	—	—	—	—	—	—
Maine	—	—	—	—	—	—	—	—
Maryland	6,696	10,014	23	16,733	6,533	9,533	0	16,066
Massachusetts	—	—	—	—	6,666	9,426	0	16,092
Michigan	—	—	—	—	—	—	—	—
Minnesota	—	—	—	—	—	—	—	—
Mississippi	—	—	—	—	—	—	—	—
Missouri	—	—	—	—	—	—	—	—
Montana	—	—	—	—	—	—	—	—
Nebraska	—	—	—	—	—	—	—	—
Nevada	—	—	—	—	—	—	—	—
New Hampshire	0	0	4,306	4,306	3,175	3,782	0	6,957
New Jersey	0	0	6,993	6,993	0	5,630	3,117	8,747
New Mexico	—	—	—	—	—	—	—	—
New York	11,027[1]	12,951[1]	197[1]	24,175[1]	11,391	12,124	127	23,642
North Carolina	1,160[1,2]	741[1,2]	0[1,2]	1,901[1,2]	1,059[1,2]	514[1,2]	163[1,2]	1,736[1,2]
North Dakota	—	—	—	—	—	—	—	—
Ohio	—	—	—	—	—	—	—	—
Oklahoma	—	—	—	—	—	—	—	—
Oregon	—	—	—	—	—	—	—	—
Pennsylvania	17,372	17,997	0	35,369	8,823[2]	4,017[2]	0[2]	12,840[2]
Rhode Island	—	—	—	—	1,178	1,911	0	3,089
South Carolina	—	—	—	—	0[2]	2,591[2]	1,141[2]	3,732[2]
South Dakota	—	—	—	—	—	—	—	—
Tennessee	—	—	—	—	—	—	—	—
Texas	—	—	—	—	—	—	—	—
Utah	—	—	—	—	—	—	—	—
Vermont	0[1]	0[1]	2,859[1]	2,859[1]	2,899	1,155	664	4,718
Virginia	0[1,2]	0[1,2]	3,546[1,2]	3,546[1,2]	—	—	—	—
Washington	—	—	—	—	—	—	—	—
West Virginia	—	—	—	—	—	—	—	—
Wisconsin	—	—	—	—	—	—	—	—
Wyoming	—	—	—	—	—	—	—	—

Notes: Entries are raw vote values for candidates who used the sole designation "Democrat" or "Republican" (or their historical antecedents listed in Appendix A) on the ballot. In general, historical antecedents to the Democratic Party were Anti-Federalists, Democratic-Republicans, and Jacksonian Democrats; historical precursors of the Republican Party were Federalists, National Republicans, and Whigs. Other = candidates who used third-party names on the ballot or were listed as independent, unidentified, or scatter vote. —indicates that the state had no data, either because no vote data were found for the state in question or the state had not yet entered the Union. No special House elections are included in the table. The table only lists at-large vote values for states having both at-large and district House races; see Appendix B for these states' district results aggregated to the state level.

[1] Election held in odd-numbered year.
[2] Partial data (less than 100% of the districts reporting).

Sources: Adapted from *United States Congressional Elections, 1788–1997* (1998), independent search for state sources by the author, and personal communications with Michael J. Dubin (various dates).

Table 5-72 House Election Results, by State, 1796–1799 (Raw Count)

State	1796–1797				1798–1799			
	Democratic	Republican	Other	Total Vote	Democratic	Republican	Other	Total Vote
Alabama	—	—	—	—	—	—	—	—
Alaska	—	—	—	—	—	—	—	—
Arizona	—	—	—	—	—	—	—	—
Arkansas	—	—	—	—	—	—	—	—
California	—	—	—	—	—	—	—	—
Colorado	—	—	—	—	—	—	—	—
Connecticut	403	2,494	0	2,897	0	4,956	0	4,956
Delaware	1,779	2,292	0	4,071	1,772	2,792	0	4,564
Florida	—	—	—	—	—	—	—	—
Georgia	5,392	3,104	1,745	10,241	3,111	4,055	0	7,166
Hawaii	—	—	—	—	—	—	—	—
Idaho	—	—	—	—	—	—	—	—
Illinois	—	—	—	—	—	—	—	—
Indiana	—	—	—	—	—	—	—	—
Iowa	—	—	—	—	—	—	—	—
Kansas	—	—	—	—	—	—	—	—
Kentucky	—	—	—	—	5,519[1,2]	0[1,2]	4,457[1,2]	9,976[1,2]
Louisiana	—	—	—	—	—	—	—	—
Maine	—	—	—	—	—	—	—	—
Maryland	4,734	7,826	0	12,560	10,718[2]	11,719[2]	0[2]	22,437[2]
Massachusetts	4,799	11,219	1,282	17,300	5,832	15,124	1,903	22,859
Michigan	—	—	—	—	—	—	—	—
Minnesota	—	—	—	—	—	—	—	—
Mississippi	—	—	—	—	—	—	—	—
Missouri	—	—	—	—	—	—	—	—
Montana	—	—	—	—	—	—	—	—
Nebraska	—	—	—	—	—	—	—	—
Nevada	—	—	—	—	—	—	—	—
New Hampshire	978	5,822	491	7,291	167	5,776	1,217	7,160
New Jersey	3,860[1]	7,100[1]	218[1]	11,178[1]	10,035	9,132	0	19,167
New Mexico	—	—	—	—	—	—	—	—
New York	10,255	16,692	227	27,174	16,788	20,035	9	36,832
North Carolina	5,876[2]	5,217[2]	0[2]	11,093[2]	11,787[2]	14,326[2]	0[2]	26,113[2]
North Dakota	—	—	—	—	—	—	—	—
Ohio	—	—	—	—	—	—	—	—
Oklahoma	—	—	—	—	—	—	—	—
Oregon	—	—	—	—	—	—	—	—
Pennsylvania	11,887[2]	11,046[2]	77[2]	23,010[2]	24,567	28,481	0	53,048
Rhode Island	0	3,716	0	3,716	1,415	2,680	0	4,095
South Carolina	4,313	5,435	0	9,748	4,299[2]	5,606[2]	0[2]	9,905[2]
South Dakota	—	—	—	—	—	—	—	—
Tennessee	1,113	0	12	1,125	—	—	—	—
Texas	—	—	—	—	—	—	—	—
Utah	—	—	—	—	—	—	—	—
Vermont	3,095	3,988	320	7,403	3,718	6,402	653	10,773
Virginia	4,883[1,2]	2,206[1,2]	461[1,2]	7,550[1,2]	9,263[1,2]	9,138[1,2]	0[1,2]	18,401[1,2]
Washington	—	—	—	—	—	—	—	—
West Virginia	—	—	—	—	—	—	—	—
Wisconsin	—	—	—	—	—	—	—	—
Wyoming	—	—	—	—	—	—	—	—

Notes: Entries are raw vote values for candidates who used the sole designation "Democrat" or "Republican" (or their historical antecedents listed in Appendix A) on the ballot. In general, historical antecedents to the Democratic Party were Anti-Federalists, Democratic-Republicans, and Jacksonian Democrats; historical precursors of the Republican Party were Federalists, National Republicans, and Whigs. Other = candidates who used third-party names on the ballot or were listed as independent, unidentified, or scatter vote. —indicates that the state had no data, either because no vote data were found for the state in question or the state had not yet entered the Union. No special House elections are included in the table. The table only lists at-large vote values for states having both at-large and district House races; see Appendix B for these states' district results aggregated to the state level.

[1]Election held in odd-numbered year.
[2]Partial data (less than 100% of the districts reporting).

Sources: Adapted from *United States Congressional Elections, 1788–1997* (1998), independent search for state sources by the author, and personal communications with Michael J. Dubin (various dates).

Table 5-73 House Election Results, by State, 1800–1803 (Raw Count)

State	1800–1801				1802–1803			
	Democratic	Republican	Other	Total Vote	Democratic	Republican	Other	Total Vote
Alabama	—	—	—	—	—	—	—	—
Alaska	—	—	—	—	—	—	—	—
Arizona	—	—	—	—	—	—	—	—
Arkansas	—	—	—	—	—	—	—	—
California	—	—	—	—	—	—	—	—
Colorado	—	—	—	—	—	—	—	—
Connecticut	3,012	6,273	0	9,285	0	8,743	0	8,743
Delaware	2,340	2,674	0	5,014	3,421	3,406	0	6,827
Florida	—	—	—	—	—	—	—	—
Georgia	8,616	0	0	8,616	8,138	2,539	0	10,677
Hawaii	—	—	—	—	—	—	—	—
Idaho	—	—	—	—	—	—	—	—
Illinois	—	—	—	—	—	—	—	—
Indiana	—	—	—	—	—	—	—	—
Iowa	—	—	—	—	—	—	—	—
Kansas	—	—	—	—	—	—	—	—
Kentucky	18,124[1]	0[1]	3,752[1]	21,876[1]	14,399[1,2]	238[1,2]	0[1,2]	14,637[1,2]
Louisiana	—	—	—	—	—	—	—	—
Maine	—	—	—	—	—	—	—	—
Maryland	9,272[1]	5,631[1]	0[1]	14,903[1]	12,967[1,2]	7,969[1,2]	0[1,2]	20,936[1,2]
Massachusetts	13,630	15,938	801	30,369	14,887	17,790	147	32,824
Michigan	—	—	—	—	—	—	—	—
Minnesota	—	—	—	—	—	—	—	—
Mississippi	—	—	—	—	—	—	—	—
Missouri	—	—	—	—	—	—	—	—
Montana	—	—	—	—	—	—	—	—
Nebraska	—	—	—	—	—	—	—	—
Nevada	—	—	—	—	—	—	—	—
New Hampshire	1,777	5,472	1,883	9,132	4,104	6,135	1,337	11,576
New Jersey	14,726	14,177	0	28,903	13,907[1]	381[1]	0[1]	14,288[1]
New Mexico	—	—	—	—	—	—	—	—
New York	23,042	23,401	189	46,632	25,946	17,839	1,382	45,167
North Carolina	14,074[2]	15,411[2]	0[2]	29,485[2]	24,592[1,2]	11,040[1,2]	0[1,2]	35,632[1,2]
North Dakota	—	—	—	—	—	—	—	—
Ohio	—	—	—	—	5,531[1]	1,960[1]	0[1]	7,491[1]
Oklahoma	—	—	—	—	—	—	—	—
Oregon	—	—	—	—	—	—	—	—
Pennsylvania	33,852[2]	16,929[2]	0[2]	50,781[2]	44,107[2]	16,717[2]	0[2]	60,824[2]
Rhode Island	2,506	1,243	0	3,749	2,606	1,644	0	4,250
South Carolina	4,363[2]	3,525[2]	0[2]	7,888[2]	4,227[1]	2,324[1]	0[1]	6,551[1]
South Dakota	—	—	—	—	—	—	—	—
Tennessee	9,238[1]	0[1]	0[1]	9,238[1]	9,682[1]	0[1]	0[1]	9,682[1]
Texas	—	—	—	—	—	—	—	—
Utah	—	—	—	—	—	—	—	—
Vermont	5,428	4,891	259	10,578	3,949	5,368	175	9,492
Virginia	1,490[1,2]	938[1,2]	0[1,2]	2,428[1,2]	12,941[1,2]	5,660[1,2]	0[1,2]	18,601[1,2]
Washington	—	—	—	—	—	—	—	—
West Virginia	—	—	—	—	—	—	—	—
Wisconsin	—	—	—	—	—	—	—	—
Wyoming	—	—	—	—	—	—	—	—

Notes: Entries are raw vote values for candidates who used the sole designation "Democrat" or "Republican" (or their historical antecedents listed in Appendix A) on the ballot. In general, historical antecedents to the Democratic Party were Anti-Federalists, Democratic-Republicans, and Jacksonian Democrats; historical precursors of the Republican Party were Federalists, National Republicans, and Whigs. Other = candidates who used third-party names on the ballot or were listed as independent, unidentified, or scatter vote. —indicates that the state had no data, either because no vote data were found for the state in question or the state had not yet entered the Union. No special House elections are included in the table. The table only lists at-large vote values for states having both at-large and district House races; see Appendix B for these states' district results aggregated to the state level.

[1] Election held in odd-numbered year.
[2] Partial data (less than 100% of the districts reporting).

Sources: Adapted from *United States Congressional Elections, 1788–1997* (1998), independent search for state sources by the author, and personal communications with Michael J. Dubin (various dates).

Table 5-74 House Election Results, by State, 1804–1807 (Raw Count)

State	1804–1805				1806–1807			
	Democratic	Republican	Other	Total Vote	Democratic	Republican	Other	Total Vote
Alabama	—	—	—	—	—	—	—	—
Alaska	—	—	—	—	—	—	—	—
Arizona	—	—	—	—	—	—	—	—
Arkansas	—	—	—	—	—	—	—	—
California	—	—	—	—	—	—	—	—
Colorado	—	—	—	—	—	—	—	—
Connecticut	0	9,956	0	9,956	—	—	—	—
Delaware	4,040	4,398	0	8,438	1,212	2,353	323	3,888
Florida	—	—	—	—	—	—	—	—
Georgia	9,903	0	0	9,903	9,336	0	0	9,336
Hawaii	—	—	—	—	—	—	—	—
Idaho	—	—	—	—	—	—	—	—
Illinois	—	—	—	—	—	—	—	—
Indiana	—	—	—	—	—	—	—	—
Iowa	—	—	—	—	—	—	—	—
Kansas	—	—	—	—	—	—	—	—
Kentucky	—	—	—	—	19,203[2]	0[2]	3,261[2]	22,464[2]
Louisiana	—	—	—	—	—	—	—	—
Maine	—	—	—	—	—	—	—	—
Maryland	12,778	4,514	60	17,352	22,243	8,240	353	30,836
Massachusetts	27,815	24,548	466	52,829	20,051	18,300	94	38,445
Michigan	—	—	—	—	—	—	—	—
Minnesota	—	—	—	—	—	—	—	—
Mississippi	—	—	—	—	—	—	—	—
Missouri	—	—	—	—	—	—	—	—
Montana	—	—	—	—	—	—	—	—
Nebraska	—	—	—	—	—	—	—	—
Nevada	—	—	—	—	—	—	—	—
New Hampshire	10,209	10,988	0	21,197	5,773	3,685	719	10,177
New Jersey	13,228	136	0	13,364	14,652	5,789	0	20,441
New Mexico	—	—	—	—	—	—	—	—
New York	43,932	25,385	396	69,713	34,397	20,674	5,446	60,517
New York	—	—	—	—	*34,397*	*23,160*	*2,960*	*60,517*
North Carolina	17,004[2]	6,957[2]	0[2]	23,961[2]	17,826[2]	2,808[2]	133[2]	20,767[2]
North Dakota	—	—	—	—	—	—	—	—
Ohio	4,101	1,718	0	5,819	6,735	0	2,364	9,099
Ohio	—	—	—	—	*6,735*	*2,364*	*0*	*9,099*
Oklahoma	—	—	—	—	—	—	—	—
Oregon	—	—	—	—	—	—	—	—
Pennsylvania	27,574[2]	6,007[2]	2,710[2]	36,291[2]	32,928[2]	5,075[2]	22,497[2]	60,500[2]
Pennsylvania	—	—	—	—	*32,928[2]*	*11,412[2]*	*16,160[2]*	*60,500[2]*
Rhode Island	1,618	0	0	1,618	1,794	1,483	310	3,587
South Carolina	2,259[2]	411[2]	0[2]	2,670[2]	13,463	2,993	0	16,456
South Dakota	—	—	—	—	—	—	—	—
Tennessee	15,346[1]	0[1]	0[1]	15,346[1]	7,424[1,2]	0[1,2]	0[1,2]	7,424[1,2]
Texas	—	—	—	—	—	—	—	—
Utah	—	—	—	—	—	—	—	—
Vermont	8,233	7,195	414	15,842	5,091[2]	5,554[2]	1,174[2]	11,819[2]
Virginia	4,244[1,2]	949[1,2]	0[1,2]	5,193[1,2]	5,411[1,2]	1,034[1,2]	0[1,2]	6,445[1,2]
Washington	—	—	—	—	—	—	—	—
West Virginia	—	—	—	—	—	—	—	—
Wisconsin	—	—	—	—	—	—	—	—
Wyoming	—	—	—	—	—	—	—	—

Notes: Main entries are raw vote values for candidates who used the sole designation "Democrat" or "Republican" (or their historical antecedents listed in Appendix A) on the ballot. In general, historical antecedents to the Democratic Party were Anti-Federalists, Democratic-Republicans, and Jacksonian Democrats; historical precursors of the Republican Party were Federalists, National Republicans, and Whigs. Other = candidates who used third-party names on the ballot or were listed as independent, unidentified, or scatter vote. Bold italicized entries in the table are the author's alternative party coding which is used when a candidate listed a major party name (Democrat, Republican, or their historical antecedents) on the ballot with other party names or labels. For a more detailed explanation of this alternate coding system, see Tables 5-1 and 1-3. —indicates that the state had no data, either because no vote data were found for the state in question or the state had not yet entered the Union. No special House elections are included in the table. The table only lists at-large vote values for states having both at-large and district House races; see Appendix B for these states' district results aggregated to the state level.

[1]Election held in odd-numbered year.
[2]Partial data (less than 100% of the districts reporting).

Sources: Adapted from *United States Congressional Elections, 1788–1997* (1998), independent search for state sources by the author, and personal communications with Michael J. Dubin (various dates).

Table 5-75 House Election Results, by State, 1808–1811 (Raw Count)

State	1808–1809				1810–1811			
	Democratic	Republican	Other	Total Vote	Democratic	Republican	Other	Total Vote
Alabama	—	—	—	—	—	—	—	—
Alaska	—	—	—	—	—	—	—	—
Arizona	—	—	—	—	—	—	—	—
Arkansas	—	—	—	—	—	—	—	—
California	—	—	—	—	—	—	—	—
Colorado	—	—	—	—	—	—	—	—
Connecticut	—	—	—	—	0	4,744	0	4,744
Delaware	2,837	3,242	0	6,079	3,617	3,634	0	7,251
Florida	—	—	—	—	—	—	—	—
Georgia	12,805	4,838	6,240	23,883	17,694	2,591	0	20,285
Hawaii	—	—	—	—	—	—	—	—
Idaho	—	—	—	—	—	—	—	—
Illinois	—	—	—	—	—	—	—	—
Indiana	—	—	—	—	—	—	—	—
Iowa	—	—	—	—	—	—	—	—
Kansas	—	—	—	—	—	—	—	—
Kentucky	—	—	—	—	13,272[2]	0[2]	0[2]	13,272[2]
Louisiana	—	—	—	—	—	—	—	—
Maine	—	—	—	—	—	—	—	—
Maryland	20,242	16,209	0	36,451	13,932	4,753	46	18,731
Massachusetts	32,429	35,895	79	68,403	21,108	22,441	472	44,021
Michigan	—	—	—	—	—	—	—	—
Minnesota	—	—	—	—	—	—	—	—
Mississippi	—	—	—	—	—	—	—	—
Missouri	—	—	—	—	—	—	—	—
Montana	—	—	—	—	—	—	—	—
Nebraska	—	—	—	—	—	—	—	—
Nevada	—	—	—	—	—	—	—	—
New Hampshire	12,271	15,022	0	27,293	11,558	11,473	1,035	24,066
New Jersey	18,705	14,702	0	33,407	13,734	523	0	14,257
New Mexico	—	—	—	—	—	—	—	—
New York	41,290	40,116	1,224	82,630	60,072	48,465	226	108,763
North Carolina	22,398[2]	17,180[2]	0[2]	39,578[2]	23,685[2]	12,596[2]	0[2]	36,281[2]
North Dakota	—	—	—	—	—	—	—	—
Ohio	10,309	4,485	0	14,794	—	—	—	—
Oklahoma	—	—	—	—	—	—	—	—
Oregon	—	—	—	—	—	—	—	—
Pennsylvania	66,080	20,714	23,590	110,384	36,027	16,615	12,138	64,780
Pennsylvania	*66,080*	*44,304*	*0*	*110,384*	*45,430*	*16,615*	*2,735*	*64,780*
Rhode Island	2,911	3,287	0	6,198	3,475	3,648	0	7,123
South Carolina	—	—	—	—	1,650[2]	1,193[2]	0[2]	2,843[2]
South Dakota	—	—	—	—	—	—	—	—
Tennessee	7,793[1,2]	0[1,2]	327[1,2]	8,120[1,2]	14,674[1]	0[1]	5,160[1]	19,834[1]
Texas	—	—	—	—	—	—	—	—
Utah	—	—	—	—	—	—	—	—
Vermont	9,297[2]	10,509[2]	590[2]	20,396[2]	12,584	9,636	459	22,679
Virginia	9,757[1,2]	8,562[1,2]	1,243[1,2]	19,562[1,2]	2,047[1,2]	2,124[1,2]	1,081[1,2]	5,252[1,2]
Virginia	*11,000[1,2]*	*8,562[1,2]*	*0[1,2]*	*19,562[1,2]*	*3,128[1,2]*	*2,124[1,2]*	*0[1,2]*	*5,252[1,2]*
Washington	—	—	—	—	—	—	—	—
West Virginia	—	—	—	—	—	—	—	—
Wisconsin	—	—	—	—	—	—	—	—
Wyoming	—	—	—	—	—	—	—	—

Notes: Main entries are raw vote values for candidates who used the sole designation "Democrat" or "Republican" (or their historical antecedents listed in Appendix A) on the ballot. In general, historical antecedents to the Democratic Party were Anti-Federalists, Democratic-Republicans, and Jacksonian Democrats; historical precursors of the Republican Party were Federalists, National Republicans, and Whigs. Other = candidates who used third-party names on the ballot or were listed as independent, unidentified, or scatter vote. Bold italicized entries in the table are the author's alternative party coding which is used when a candidate listed a major party name (Democrat, Republican, or their historical antecedents) on the ballot with other party names or labels. For a more detailed explanation of this alternate coding system, see Tables 5-1 and 1-3. —indicates that the state had no data, either because no vote data were found for the state in question or the state had not yet entered the Union. No special House elections are included in the table. The table only lists at-large vote values for states having both at-large and district House races; see Appendix B for these states' district results aggregated to the state level.

[1] Election held in odd-numbered year.
[2] Partial data (less than 100% of the districts reporting).

Sources: Adapted from *United States Congressional Elections, 1788–1997* (1998), independent search for state sources by the author, and personal communications with Michael J. Dubin (various dates).

Table 5-76 House Election Results, by State, 1812–1815 (Raw Count)

State	1812–1813				1814–1815			
	Democratic	Republican	Other	Total Vote	Democratic	Republican	Other	Total Vote
Alabama	—	—	—	—	—	—	—	—
Alaska	—	—	—	—	—	—	—	—
Arizona	—	—	—	—	—	—	—	—
Arkansas	—	—	—	—	—	—	—	—
California	—	—	—	—	—	—	—	—
Colorado	—	—	—	—	—	—	—	—
Connecticut	0	10,631	0	10,631	—	—	—	—
Delaware	3,221	4,193	0	7,414	2,547	3,964	0	6,511
Florida	—	—	—	—	—	—	—	—
Georgia	11,881	2,699	0	14,580	16,389	0	0	16,389
Hawaii	—	—	—	—	—	—	—	—
Idaho	—	—	—	—	—	—	—	—
Illinois	—	—	—	—	—	—	—	—
Indiana	—	—	—	—	—	—	—	—
Iowa	—	—	—	—	—	—	—	—
Kansas	—	—	—	—	—	—	—	—
Kentucky	25,470[2]	0[2]	2,871[2]	28,341[2]	11,017[2]	0[2]	2,537[2]	13,554[2]
Louisiana	880	0	1,592	2,472	2,684	242	29	2,955
Maine	—	—	—	—	—	—	—	—
Maryland	21,090	13,074	0	34,164	11,995	20,212	0	32,207
Massachusetts	27,103	42,273	492	69,868	17,909	34,464	932	53,305
Massachusetts	—	—	—	—	*17,909*	*35,289*	*107*	*53,305*
Michigan	—	—	—	—	—	—	—	—
Minnesota	—	—	—	—	—	—	—	—
Mississippi	—	—	—	—	—	—	—	—
Missouri	—	—	—	—	—	—	—	—
Montana	—	—	—	—	—	—	—	—
Nebraska	—	—	—	—	—	—	—	—
Nevada	—	—	—	—	—	—	—	—
New Hampshire	16,066	18,611	0	34,677	16,607	18,130	0	34,737
New Jersey	12,443[1]	13,808[1]	74[1]	26,325[1]	17,859	16,697	0	34,556
New Mexico	—	—	—	—	—	—	—	—
New York	41,874	50,675	1,604	94,153	59,137	51,472	348	110,957
New York	*42,433*	*50,675*	*1,045*	*94,153*	—	—	—	—
North Carolina	16,699[1,2]	20,591[1,2]	0[1,2]	37,290[1,2]	24,884[1,2]	16,971[1,2]	0[1,2]	41,855[1,2]
North Dakota	—	—	—	—	—	—	—	—
Ohio	14,856	4,883	3,205	22,944	8,544[2]	2,806[2]	1,601[2]	12,951[2]
Oklahoma	—	—	—	—	—	—	—	—
Oregon	—	—	—	—	—	—	—	—
Pennsylvania	53,793	36,999	374	91,166	37,668[2]	28,263[2]	0[2]	65,931[2]
Pennsylvania	*54,167*	*36,999*	*0*	*91,166*	—	—	—	—
Rhode Island	3,164	4,454	0	7,618	2,953	3,771	0	6,724
South Carolina	3,160[2]	839[2]	924[2]	4,923[2]	6,972[2]	2,571[2]	0[2]	9,543[2]
South Dakota	—	—	—	—	—	—	—	—
Tennessee	6,169[1,2]	0[1,2]	1,255[1,2]	7,424[1,2]	17,869[1,2]	0[1,2]	5,973[1,2]	23,842[1,2]
Texas	—	—	—	—	—	—	—	—
Utah	—	—	—	—	—	—	—	—
Vermont	16,005	15,745	0	31,750	16,975[2]	17,725[2]	0[2]	34,700[2]
Virginia	9,292[1,2]	6,830[1,2]	936[1,2]	17,058[1,2]	10,192[1,2]	6,964[1,2]	13[1,2]	17,169[1,2]
Virginia	*10,228[1,2]*	*6,830[1,2]*	*0[1,2]*	*17,058[1,2]*	—	—	—	—
Washington	—	—	—	—	—	—	—	—
West Virginia	—	—	—	—	—	—	—	—
Wisconsin	—	—	—	—	—	—	—	—
Wyoming	—	—	—	—	—	—	—	—

Notes: Main entries are raw vote values for candidates who used the sole designation "Democrat" or "Republican" (or their historical antecedents listed in Appendix A) on the ballot. In general, historical antecedents to the Democratic Party were Anti-Federalists, Democratic-Republicans, and Jacksonian Democrats; historical precursors of the Republican Party were Federalists, National Republicans, and Whigs. Other = candidates who used third-party names on the ballot or were listed as independent, unidentified, or scatter vote. Bold italicized entries in the table are the author's alternative party coding which is used when a candidate listed a major party name (Democrat, Republican, or their historical antecedents) on the ballot with other party names or labels. For a more detailed explanation of this alternate coding system, see Tables 5-1 and 1-3. —indicates that the state had no data, either because no vote data were found for the state in question or the state had not yet entered the Union. No special House elections are included in the table. The table only lists at-large vote values for states having both at-large and district House races; see Appendix B for these states' district results aggregated to the state level.

[1]Election held in odd-numbered year.
[2]Partial data (less than 100% of the districts reporting).

Sources: Adapted from *United States Congressional Elections, 1788–1997* (1998), independent search for state sources by the author, and personal communications with Michael J. Dubin (various dates).

Table 5-77 House Election Results, by State, 1816–1819 (Raw Count)

State	1816–1817				1818–1819			
	Democratic	Republican	Other	Total Vote	Democratic	Republican	Other	Total Vote
Alabama	—	—	—	—	8,181[1]	0[1]	7,203[1]	15,384[1]
Alaska	—	—	—	—	—	—	—	—
Arizona	—	—	—	—	—	—	—	—
Arkansas	—	—	—	—	—	—	—	—
California	—	—	—	—	—	—	—	—
Colorado	—	—	—	—	—	—	—	—
Connecticut	0	9,591	0	9,591	4,700	0	4,481	9,181
Connecticut	—	—	—	—	***4,700***	***4,481***	***0***	***9,181***
Delaware	3,534	3,580	0	7,114	3,007	3,098	0	6,105
Florida	—	—	—	—	—	—	—	—
Georgia	10,961	0	7,322	18,283	7,356	0	0	7,356
Hawaii	—	—	—	—	—	—	—	—
Idaho	—	—	—	—	—	—	—	—
Illinois	—	—	—	—	3,978	0	0	3,978
Indiana	5,160	0	1,629	6,789	—	—	—	—
Iowa	—	—	—	—	—	—	—	—
Kansas	—	—	—	—	—	—	—	—
Kentucky	14,765[2]	0[2]	32,232[2]	46,997[2]	12,266[2]	2,663[2]	9,040[2]	23,969[2]
Kentucky	***27,216[2]***	***4,331[2]***	***15,450[2]***	***46,997[2]***	—	—	—	—
Louisiana	2,644	0	0	2,644	3,266	0	872	4,138
Maine	—	—	—	—	—	—	—	—
Maryland	10,013[2]	17,744[2]	86[2]	27,843[2]	10,819[2]	14,627[2]	0[2]	25,446[2]
Massachusetts	18,764	23,869	1,463	44,096	16,748	16,745	861	34,354
Michigan	—	—	—	—	—	—	—	—
Minnesota	—	—	—	—	—	—	—	—
Mississippi	3,225[1]	0[1]	0[1]	3,225[1]	—	—	—	—
Missouri	—	—	—	—	—	—	—	—
Montana	—	—	—	—	—	—	—	—
Nebraska	—	—	—	—	—	—	—	—
Nevada	—	—	—	—	—	—	—	—
New Hampshire	15,571	13,600	100	29,271	13,808[1]	7,093[1]	2,830[1]	23,731[1]
New Jersey	5,690	0	0	5,690	13,949	769	0	14,718
New Mexico	—	—	—	—	—	—	—	—
New York	68,258	55,525	350	124,133	46,394	19,118	14,241	79,753
New York	—	—	—	—	***60,635***	***19,118***	***0***	***79,753***
North Carolina	19,843[1,2]	12,831[1,2]	0[1,2]	32,674[1,2]	19,703[1,2]	10,103[1,2]	0[1,2]	29,806[1,2]
North Dakota	—	—	—	—	—	—	—	—
Ohio	15,285[2]	937[2]	4,678[2]	20,900[2]	34,596	5,819	576	40,991
Oklahoma	—	—	—	—	—	—	—	—
Oregon	—	—	—	—	—	—	—	—
Pennsylvania	30,311[2]	16,583[2]	10,565[2]	57,459[2]	40,051[2]	18,908[2]	8,088[2]	67,047[2]
Pennsylvania	***37,077[2]***	***18,722[2]***	***1,660[2]***	***57,459[2]***	***42,333[2]***	***21,223[2]***	***3,491[2]***	***67,047[2]***
Rhode Island	0	2,239	0	2,239	1,945	0	0	1,945
South Carolina	21,252[2]	4,715[2]	0[2]	25,967[2]	16,765[2]	1,937[2]	0[2]	18,702[2]
South Dakota	—	—	—	—	—	—	—	—
Tennessee	24,234[1]	0[1]	16,659[1]	40,893[1]	25,266[1]	0[1]	21,043[1]	46,309[1]
Texas	—	—	—	—	—	—	—	—
Utah	—	—	—	—	—	—	—	—
Vermont	16,836	13,926	0	30,762	13,635	0	5,438	19,073
Vermont	—	—	—	—	***13,635***	***4,713***	***725***	***19,073***
Virginia	8,858[1,2]	2,873[1,2]	0[1,2]	11,731[1,2]	5,845[1,2]	2,752[1,2]	0[1,2]	8,597[1,2]
Washington	—	—	—	—	—	—	—	—
West Virginia	—	—	—	—	—	—	—	—
Wisconsin	—	—	—	—	—	—	—	—
Wyoming	—	—	—	—	—	—	—	—
Indiana	5,693[3]	0[3]	3,778[3]	9,471[3]	—	—	—	—

Notes: Main entries are raw vote values for candidates who used the sole designation "Democrat" or "Republican" (or their historical antecedents listed in Appendix A) on the ballot. In general, historical antecedents to the Democratic Party were Anti-Federalists, Democratic-Republicans, and Jacksonian Democrats; historical precursors of the Republican Party were Federalists, National Republicans, and Whigs. Other = candidates who used third-party names on the ballot or were listed as independent, unidentified, or scatter vote. Bold italicized entries in the table are the author's alternative party coding which is used when a candidate listed a major party name (Democrat, Republican, or their historical antecedents) on the ballot with other party names or labels. For a more detailed explanation of this alternate coding system, see Tables 5-1 and 1-3. —indicates that the state had no data, either because no vote data were found for the state in question or the state had not yet entered the Union. No special House elections are included in the table. The table only lists at-large vote values for states having both at-large and district House races; see Appendix B for these states' district results aggregated to the state level.

[1]Election held in odd-numbered year.
[2]Partial data (less than 100% of the districts reporting).
[3]1817 election when a state had annual elections in both 1816 and 1817.

Sources: Adapted from *United States Congressional Elections, 1788–1997* (1998), independent search for state sources by the author, and personal communications with Michael J. Dubin (various dates).

Table 5-78 House Election Results, by State, 1820–1823 (Raw Count)

State	1820–1821				1822–1823			
	Democratic	Republican	Other	Total Vote	Democratic	Republican	Other	Total Vote
Alabama	10,996[1]	0[1]	6,027[1]	17,023[1]	2,135[1,2]	0[1,2]	6,498[1,2]	8,633[1,2]
Alaska	—	—	—	—	—	—	—	—
Arizona	—	—	—	—	—	—	—	—
Arkansas	—	—	—	—	—	—	—	—
California	—	—	—	—	—	—	—	—
Colorado	—	—	—	—	—	—	—	—
Connecticut	6,577[1]	464[1]	293[1]	7,334[1]	5,304[1]	0[1]	0[1]	5,304[1]
Delaware	4,029	3,918	0	7,947	3,466	4,110	0	7,576
Florida	—	—	—	—	—	—	—	—
Georgia	10,486	0	5,088	15,574	18,350	0	12,959	31,309
Hawaii	—	—	—	—	—	—	—	—
Idaho	—	—	—	—	—	—	—	—
Illinois	5,322	0	2,358	7,680	4,764	0	3,811	8,575
Indiana	16,331	0	1,623	17,954	0[2]	0[2]	7,204[2]	7,204[2]
Iowa	—	—	—	—	—	—	—	—
Kansas	—	—	—	—	—	—	—	—
Kentucky	2,651[2]	1,686[2]	126[2]	4,463[2]	0[2]	0[2]	23,863[2]	23,863[2]
Louisiana	4,599	0	0	4,599	0[2]	0[2]	1,728[2]	1,728[2]
Maine	5,923	2,185	1,577	9,685	14,951[1]	5,962[1]	5,596[1]	26,509[1]
Maryland	13,318[2]	13,001[2]	0[2]	26,319[2]	21,481	7,181	846	29,508
Massachusetts	9,476	13,986	2,921	26,383	—	—	—	—
Michigan	—	—	—	—	—	—	—	—
Minnesota	—	—	—	—	—	—	—	—
Mississippi	—	—	—	—	0	0	7,469	7,469
Missouri	5,574[2]	0[2]	0[2]	5,574[2]	0	0	9,906	9,906
Montana	—	—	—	—	—	—	—	—
Nebraska	—	—	—	—	—	—	—	—
Nevada	—	—	—	—	—	—	—	—
New Hampshire	9,898	1,616	0	11,514	11,654	0	4,002	15,656
New Jersey	4,701	417	365	5,483	—	—	—	—
New Mexico	—	—	—	—	—	—	—	—
New York	0[1]	0[1]	148,867[1]	148,867[1]	0	0	135,159	135,159
New York	***148,490[1]***	***0[1]***	***377[1]***	***148,867[1]***	***134,481***	***0***	***678***	***135,159***
North Carolina	18,038[1,2]	14,764[1,2]	558[1,2]	33,360[1,2]	26,895[1,2]	14,310[1,2]	0[1,2]	41,205[1,2]
North Dakota	—	—	—	—	—	—	—	—
Ohio	17,839[2]	0[2]	0[2]	17,839[2]	8,860[2]	3,896[2]	38,248[2]	51,004[2]
Oklahoma	—	—	—	—	—	—	—	—
Oregon	—	—	—	—	—	—	—	—
Pennsylvania	76,663	49,950	13,267	139,880	64,095	25,367	16,967	106,429
Pennsylvania	***76,663***	***62,456***	***761***	***139,880***	***80,969***	***25,367***	***93***	***106,429***
Rhode Island	2,891	0	3,563	6,454	1,446	0	0	1,446
South Carolina	6,964[2]	1,161[2]	0[2]	8,125[2]	13,385[1]	1,167[1]	3,516[1]	18,068[1]
South Dakota	—	—	—	—	—	—	—	—
Tennessee	8,587[1,2]	0[1,2]	3,629[1,2]	12,216[1,2]	0[1,2]	0[1,2]	51,472[1,2]	51,472[1,2]
Texas	—	—	—	—	—	—	—	—
Utah	—	—	—	—	—	—	—	—
Vermont	13,033	7,692	557	21,282	17,242	6,772	3,755	27,769
Virginia	9,701[1,2]	2,938[1,2]	333[1,2]	12,972[1,2]	14,450[1,2]	5,458[1,2]	222[1,2]	20,130[1,2]
Washington	—	—	—	—	—	—	—	—
West Virginia	—	—	—	—	—	—	—	—
Wisconsin	—	—	—	—	—	—	—	—
Wyoming	—	—	—	—	—	—	—	—

Notes: Main entries are raw vote values for candidates who used the sole designation "Democrat" or "Republican" (or their historical antecedents listed in Appendix A) on the ballot. In general, historical antecedents to the Democratic Party were Anti-Federalists, Democratic-Republicans, and Jacksonian Democrats; historical precursors of the Republican Party were Federalists, National Republicans, and Whigs. Other = candidates who used third-party names on the ballot or were listed as independent, unidentified, or scatter vote. Bold italicized entries in the table are the author's alternative party coding which is used when a candidate listed a major party name (Democrat, Republican, or their historical antecedents) on the ballot with other party names or labels. For a more detailed explanation of this alternate coding system, see Tables 5-1 and 1-3. —indicates that the state had no data, either because no vote data were found for the state in question or the state had not yet entered the Union. No special House elections are included in the table. The table only lists at-large vote values for states having both at-large and district House races; see Appendix B for these states' district results aggregated to the state level.

[1]Election held in odd-numbered year.
[2]Partial data (less than 100% of the districts reporting).

Sources: Adapted from *United States Congressional Elections, 1788–1997* (1998), independent search for state sources by the author, and personal communications with Michael J. Dubin (various dates).

Table 5-79 House Election Results, by State, 1824–1827 (Raw Count)

	1824–1825				1826–1827			
State	Democratic	Republican	Other	Total Vote	Democratic	Republican	Other	Total Vote
Alabama	4,284[1,2]	0[1,2]	6,187[1,2]	10,471[1,2]	7,078[1,2]	0[1,2]	3,405[1,2]	10,483[1,2]
Alaska	—	—	—	—	—	—	—	—
Arizona	—	—	—	—	—	—	—	—
Arkansas	—	—	—	—	—	—	—	—
California	—	—	—	—	—	—	—	—
Colorado	—	—	—	—	—	—	—	—
Connecticut	6,263[1]	1,293[1]	415[1]	7,971[1]	0[1]	1,304[1]	13,521[1]	14,825[1]
Connecticut					*0[1]*	*13,614[1]*	*1,211[1]*	*14,825[1]*
Delaware	3,163	3,387	0	6,550	3,931	4,630	0	8,561
Florida	—	—	—	—	—	—	—	—
Georgia	10,543	0	0	10,543	20,785	0	13,005	33,790
Hawaii	—	—	—	—	—	—	—	—
Idaho	—	—	—	—	—	—	—	—
Illinois	0	0	12,021	12,021	6,322	5,619	824	12,765
Indiana	8,961[2]	0[2]	10,002[2]	18,963[2]	11,217	18,082	1,763	31,062
Iowa	—	—	—	—	—	—	—	—
Kansas	—	—	—	—	—	—	—	—
Kentucky	11,014[2]	0[2]	5,532[2]	16,546[2]	29,171[1]	17,051[1]	29,328[1]	75,550[1]
Louisiana	—	—	—	—	1,567[2]	1,115[2]	1,671[2]	4,353[2]
Maine	10,403	2,891	3,495	16,789	6,128	8,743	6,592	21,463
Maryland	25,153	15,460	3,217	43,830	8,760	8,607	21,619	38,986
Massachusetts	14,745	15,326	5,845	35,916	0	12,725	8,504	21,229
Michigan	—	—	—	—	—	—	—	—
Minnesota	—	—	—	—	—	—	—	—
Mississippi	5,961	0	0	5,961	3,236	1,451	4,854	9,541
Missouri	9,559	0	1,125	10,684	0	0	10,795	10,795
Montana	—	—	—	—	—	—	—	—
Nebraska	—	—	—	—	—	—	—	—
Nevada	—	—	—	—	—	—	—	—
New Hampshire	11,603	0	5,479	17,082	22,680[1]	0[1]	6,898[1]	29,578[1]
New Jersey	17,706	0	0	17,706	10,166	15,635	642	26,443
New Mexico	—	—	—	—	—	—	—	—
New York	0	0	186,795	186,795	92,939	85,717	1,372	180,028
New York	*184,474*	*0*	*2,321*	*186,795*	—	—	—	—
North Carolina	24,827[1,2]	5,794[1,2]	24,961[1,2]	55,582[1,2]	0[1,2]	5,564[1,2]	38,924[1,2]	44,488[1,2]
North Dakota	—	—	—	—	—	—	—	—
Ohio	0	0	75,723	75,723	17,784	47,335	20,564	85,683
Oklahoma	—	—	—	—	—	—	—	—
Oregon	—	—	—	—	—	—	—	—
Pennsylvania	64,919[2]	17,332[2]	13,130[2]	95,381[2]	46,712[2]	24,117[2]	9,138[2]	79,967[2]
Pennsylvania	*64,919[2]*	*28,305[2]*	*2,157[2]*	*95,381[2]*	*46,712[2]*	*26,980[2]*	*6,275[2]*	*79,967[2]*
Rhode Island	2,932[1]	0[1]	136[1]	3,068[1]	0[1]	2,230[1]	29[1]	2,259[1]
South Carolina	5,220[2]	0[2]	13,000[2]	18,220[2]	2,478[2]	0[2]	2,453[2]	4,931[2]
South Dakota	—	—	—	—	—	—	—	—
Tennessee	0[1,2]	0[1,2]	49,596[1,2]	49,596[1,2]	26,810[1,2]	0[1,2]	46,405[1,2]	73,215[1,2]
Tennessee	—	—	—	—	*26,810[1,2]*	*4,878[1,2]*	*41,527[1,2]*	*73,215[1,2]*
Texas	—	—	—	—	—	—	—	—
Utah	—	—	—	—	—	—	—	—
Vermont	15,336	1,455	5,392	22,183	0	13,586	7,506	21,092
Virginia	0[1,2]	3,938[1,2]	14,294[1,2]	18,232[1,2]	1,583[1,2]	6,368[1,2]	14,621[1,2]	22,572[1,2]
Washington	—	—	—	—	—	—	—	—
West Virginia	—	—	—	—	—	—	—	—
Wisconsin	—	—	—	—	—	—	—	—
Wyoming	—	—	—	—	—	—	—	—

Notes: Main entries are raw vote values for candidates who used the sole designation "Democrat" or "Republican" (or their historical antecedents listed in Appendix A) on the ballot. In general, historical antecedents to the Democratic Party were Anti-Federalists, Democratic-Republicans, and Jacksonian Democrats; historical precursors of the Republican Party were Federalists, National Republicans, and Whigs. Other = candidates who used third-party names on the ballot or were listed as independent, unidentified, or scatter vote. Bold italicized entries in the table are the author's alternative party coding which is used when a candidate listed a major party name (Democrat, Republican, or their historical antecedents) on the ballot with other party names or labels. For a more detailed explanation of this alternate coding system, see Tables 5-1 and 1-3. —indicates that the state had no data, either because no vote data were found for the state in question or the state had not yet entered the Union. No special House elections are included in the table. The table only lists at-large vote values for states having both at-large and district House races; see Appendix B for these states' district results aggregated to the state level.

[1]Election held in odd-numbered year.
[2]Partial data (less than 100% of the districts reporting).

Sources: Adapted from *United States Congressional Elections, 1788–1997* (1998), *Congressional Quarterly's Guide to U.S. Elections* (1994), Inter-university Consortium for Political and Social Research (ICPSR) data sets 0001 and 0075, independent search for state sources by the author, and personal communications with Michael J. Dubin (various dates).

Table 5-80 House Election Results, by State, 1828–1831 (Raw Count)

State	1828–1829				1830–1831			
	Democratic	Republican	Other	Total Vote	Democratic	Republican	Other	Total Vote
Alabama	17,563[1]	3,962[1]	9,629[1]	31,154[1]	18,033[1,2]	4,611[1,2]	0[1,2]	22,644[1,2]
Alaska	—	—	—	—	—	—	—	—
Arizona	—	—	—	—	—	—	—	—
Arkansas	—	—	—	—	—	—	—	—
California	—	—	—	—	—	—	—	—
Colorado	—	—	—	—	—	—	—	—
Connecticut	5,401[1]	8,281[1]	1,299[1]	14,981[1]	5,784[1]	11,950[1]	0[1]	17,734[1]
Delaware	4,347	4,769	0	9,116	3,833	4,267	0	8,100
Florida	—	—	—	—	—	—	—	—
Georgia	16,857	0	31,121	47,978	0	0	55,920	55,920
Georgia	***47,978***	***0***	***0***	***47,978***	***50,772***	***0***	***5,148***	***55,920***
Hawaii	—	—	—	—	—	—	—	—
Idaho	—	—	—	—	—	—	—	—
Illinois	10,447	6,158	0	16,605	13,052[1]	0[1]	11,071[1]	24,123[1]
Indiana	12,778[2]	14,121[2]	0[2]	26,899[2]	27,669[1]	20,260[1]	3,671[1]	51,600[1]
Iowa	—	—	—	—	—	—	—	—
Kansas	—	—	—	—	—	—	—	—
Kentucky	32,511[1,2]	7,753[1,2]	14,761[1,2]	55,025[1,2]	34,178[1,2]	32,401[1,2]	0[1,2]	66,579[1,2]
Louisiana	2,450	3,875	1,134	7,459	0[2]	0[2]	5,086[2]	5,086[2]
Louisiana	—	—	—	—	***0[2]***	***2,442[2]***	***2,644[2]***	***5,086[2]***
Maine	11,178	10,231	6,463	27,872	25,705	23,317	1,209	50,231
Maryland	20,788[1]	18,362[1]	271[1]	39,421[1]	17,424[1]	22,757[1]	266[1]	40,447[1]
Massachusetts	4,272	29,623	1,465	35,360	4,510	22,672	7,343	34,525
Michigan	—	—	—	—	—	—	—	—
Minnesota	—	—	—	—	—	—	—	—
Mississippi	—	—	—	—	8,924	2,756	0	11,680
Missouri	7,868	5,127	0	12,995	7,978[1]	4,835[1]	0[1]	12,813[1]
Montana	—	—	—	—	—	—	—	—
Nebraska	—	—	—	—	—	—	—	—
Nevada	—	—	—	—	—	—	—	—
New Hampshire	21,831[1]	18,284[1]	0[1]	40,115[1]	22,291[1]	18,477[1]	0[1]	40,768[1]
New Jersey	22,014	23,783	0	45,797	14,261	15,268	0	29,529
New Mexico	—	—	—	—	—	—	—	—
New York	141,076	106,499	34,232	281,807	121,495	37,478	91,821	250,794
New York	—	—	—	—	***121,495***	***41,732***	***87,567***	***250,794***
North Carolina	34,587[1,2]	7,870[1,2]	3,304[1,2]	45,761[1,2]	13,513[1,2]	2,872[1,2]	10,731[1,2]	27,116[1,2]
North Dakota	—	—	—	—	—	—	—	—
Ohio	35,305[2]	34,545[2]	2,550[2]	72,400[2]	46,116	49,998	3,383	99,497
Oklahoma	—	—	—	—	—	—	—	—
Oregon	—	—	—	—	—	—	—	—
Pennsylvania	83,229[2]	49,816[2]	13,377[2]	146,422[2]	71,731	29,783	41,229	142,743
Pennsylvania	—	—	—	—	***71,731***	***36,077***	***34,935***	***142,743***
Rhode Island	0[1]	4,328[1]	1,251[1]	5,579[1]	0[1]	2,931[1]	519[1]	3,450[1]
South Carolina	1,808[2]	0[2]	2,554[2]	4,362[2]	0[2]	0[2]	4,093[2]	4,093[2]
South Dakota	—	—	—	—	—	—	—	—
Tennessee	41,530[1,2]	0[1,2]	24,926[1,2]	66,456[1,2]	56,378[1]	16,959[1]	7,040[1]	80,377[1]
Tennessee	***41,530[1,2]***	***6,783[1,2]***	***18,143[1,2]***	***66,456[1,2]***	—	—	—	—
Texas	—	—	—	—	—	—	—	—
Utah	—	—	—	—	—	—	—	—
Vermont	3,747[2]	15,267[2]	2,362[2]	21,376[2]	7,853	12,836	8,475	29,164
Vermont	—	—	—	—	***7,853***	***16,964***	***4,347***	***29,164***
Virginia	5,508[1,2]	3,882[1,2]	6,211[1,2]	15,601[1,2]	10,631[1,2]	13,502[1,2]	5,069[1,2]	29,202[1,2]
Washington	—	—	—	—	—	—	—	—
West Virginia	—	—	—	—	—	—	—	—
Wisconsin	—	—	—	—	—	—	—	—
Wyoming	—	—	—	—	—	—	—	—

Notes: Main entries are raw vote values for candidates who used the sole designation "Democrat" or "Republican" (or their historical antecedents listed in Appendix A) on the ballot. In general, historical antecedents to the Democratic Party were Anti-Federalists, Democratic-Republicans, and Jacksonian Democrats; historical precursors of the Republican Party were Federalists, National Republicans, and Whigs. Other = candidates who used third-party names on the ballot or were listed as independent, unidentified, or scatter vote. Bold italicized entries in the table are the author's alternative party coding which is used when a candidate listed a major party name (Democrat, Republican, or their historical antecedents) on the ballot with other party names or labels. For a more detailed explanation of this alternate coding system, see Tables 5-1 and 1-3. —indicates that the state had no data, either because no vote data were found for the state in question or the state had not yet entered the Union. No special House elections are included in the table. The table only lists at-large vote values for states having both at-large and district House races; see Appendix B for these states' district results aggregated to the state level.

[1]Election held in odd-numbered year.
[2]Partial data (less than 100% of the districts reporting).

Sources: Adapted from *United States Congressional Elections, 1788–1997* (1998), *Congressional Quarterly's Guide to U.S. Elections* (1994), ICPSR data sets 0001 and 0075, independent search for state sources by the author, and personal communications with Michael J. Dubin (various dates).

Table 5-81 House Election Results, by State, 1832–1835 (Raw Count)

State	1832–1833				1834–1835			
	Democratic	Republican	Other	Total Vote	Democratic	Republican	Other	Total Vote
Alabama	14,368[1,2]	2,033[1,2]	5,730[1,2]	22,131[1,2]	9,215[1,2]	0[1,2]	0[1,2]	9,215[1,2]
Alaska	—	—	—	—	—	—	—	—
Arizona	—	—	—	—	—	—	—	—
Arkansas	—	—	—	—	—	—	—	—
California	—	—	—	—	—	—	—	—
Colorado	—	—	—	—	—	—	—	—
Connecticut	7,469[1]	10,121[1]	2,589[1]	20,179[1]	21,286[1]	19,170[1]	413[1]	40,869[1]
Delaware	4,142	4,257	0	8,399	4,626	4,779	0	9,405
Florida	—	—	—	—	—	—	—	—
Georgia	0	0	61,543	61,543	32,934	28,417	0	61,351
Georgia	***61,543***	***0***	***0***	***61,543***	—	—	—	—
Hawaii	—	—	—	—	—	—	—	—
Idaho	—	—	—	—	—	—	—	—
Illinois	18,403	2,078	5,104	25,585	20,334	0	12,143	32,477
Indiana	29,480[1]	3,041[1]	28,667[1]	61,188[1]	38,561[1]	23,095[1]	7,011[1]	68,667[1]
Iowa	—	—	—	—	—	—	—	—
Kansas	—	—	—	—	—	—	—	—
Kentucky	26,214[1,2]	27,197[1,2]	4,724[1,2]	58,135[1,2]	27,123[1,2]	35,920[1,2]	2,572[1,2]	65,615[1,2]
Louisiana	2,800	0	5,081	7,881	945	4,764	3,978	9,687
Louisiana	***2,800***	***5,081***	***0***	***7,881***	—	—	—	—
Maine	26,710[1]	17,191[1]	4,010[1]	47,911[1]	35,998	32,098	598	68,694
Maryland	23,971[1]	23,591[1]	0[1]	47,562[1]	20,774[1,2]	21,467[1,2]	276[1,2]	42,517[1,2]
Massachusetts	6,636[1]	22,391[1]	13,387[1]	42,414[1]	20,785	41,144	7,796	69,725
Massachusetts	***6,636[1]***	***24,559[1]***	***11,219[1]***	***42,414[1]***	—	—	—	—
Michigan	—	—	—	—	7,130[1]	0[1]	302[1]	7,432[1]
Minnesota	—	—	—	—	—	—	—	—
Mississippi	—	—	—	—	9,923[1]	8,293[1]	231[1]	18,447[1]
Missouri	7,060[1]	0[1]	6,193[1]	13,253[1]	10,856[1]	0[1]	12,826[1]	23,682[1]
Missouri	***7,060[1]***	***4,063[1]***	***2,130[1]***	***13,253[1]***	—	—	—	—
Montana	—	—	—	—	—	—	—	—
Nebraska	—	—	—	—	—	—	—	—
Nevada	—	—	—	—	—	—	—	—
New Hampshire	23,141[1]	6,688[1]	1,875[1]	31,704[1]	24,012[1]	14,332[1]	0[1]	38,344[1]
New Jersey	24,278	23,784	0	48,062	27,413	26,413	0	53,826
New Mexico	—	—	—	—	—	—	—	—
New York	166,028	51,830	102,179	320,037	182,502	167,206	0	349,708
North Carolina	21,672[1,2]	11,093[1,2]	12,159[1,2]	44,924[1,2]	22,453[1,2]	34,488[1,2]	3,078[1,2]	60,019[1,2]
North Carolina	—	—	—	—	***22,453[1,2]***	***37,566[1,2]***	***0[1,2]***	***60,019[1,2]***
North Dakota	—	—	—	—	—	—	—	—
Ohio	64,168	60,782	9,428	134,378	65,846	69,345	543	135,734
Oklahoma	—	—	—	—	—	—	—	—
Oregon	—	—	—	—	—	—	—	—
Pennsylvania	88,003	8,202	79,814	176,019	100,047	55,775	28,758	184,580
Pennsylvania	***91,252***	***18,769***	***65,998***	***176,019***	—	—	—	—
Rhode Island	1,904[1]	0[1]	3,162[1]	5,066[1]	3,924[1]	3,776[1]	0[1]	7,700[1]
Rhode Island	***1,904[1]***	***3,162[1]***	***0[1]***	***5,066[1]***	—	—	—	—
South Carolina	0[1,2]	0[1,2]	21,841[1,2]	21,841[1,2]	0[2]	0[2]	25,071[2]	25,071[2]
South Dakota	—	—	—	—	—	—	—	—
Tennessee	27,029[1]	29,736[1]	28,401[1]	85,166[1]	32,256[1]	48,938[1]	4,725[1]	85,919[1]
Tennessee	***30,537[1]***	***29,736[1]***	***24,893[1]***	***85,166[1]***	—	—	—	—
Texas	—	—	—	—	—	—	—	—
Utah	—	—	—	—	—	—	—	—
Vermont	6,249[1]	8,513[1]	8,007[1]	22,769[1]	10,761	14,257	11,223	36,241
Virginia	13,090[1,2]	7,950[1,2]	3,586[1,2]	24,626[1,2]	29,673[1,2]	24,062[1,2]	342[1,2]	54,077[1,2]
Washington	—	—	—	—	—	—	—	—
West Virginia	—	—	—	—	—	—	—	—
Wisconsin	—	—	—	—	—	—	—	—
Wyoming	—	—	—	—	—	—	—	—

Notes: Main entries are raw vote values for candidates who used the sole designation "Democrat" or "Republican" (or their historical antecedents listed in Appendix A) on the ballot. In general, historical antecedents to the Democratic Party were Anti-Federalists, Democratic-Republicans, and Jacksonian Democrats; historical precursors of the Republican Party were Federalists, National Republicans, and Whigs. Other = candidates who used third-party names on the ballot or were listed as independent, unidentified, or scatter vote. Bold italicized entries in the table are the author's alternative party coding which is used when a candidate listed a major party name (Democrat, Republican, or their historical antecedents) on the ballot with other party names or labels. For a more detailed explanation of this alternate coding system, see Tables 5-1 and 1-3. —indicates that the state had no data, either because no vote data were found for the state in question or the state had not yet entered the Union. No special House elections are included in the table. The table only lists at-large vote values for states having both at-large and district House races; see Appendix B for these states' district results aggregated to the state level.

[1]Election held in odd-numbered year.
[2]Partial data (less than 100% of the districts reporting).

Sources: Adapted from *United States Congressional Elections, 1788–1997* (1998), *Congressional Quarterly's Guide to U.S. Elections* (1994), ICPSR data sets 0001 and 0075, independent search for state sources by the author, and personal communications with Michael J. Dubin (various dates).

Table 5-82 House Election Results, by State, 1836–1839 (Raw Count)

State	1836–1837				1838–1839			
	Democratic	Republican	Other	Total Vote	Democratic	Republican	Other	Total Vote
Alabama	16,988[1,2]	11,731[1,2]	0[1,2]	28,719[1,2]	21,673[1,2]	14,130[1,2]	0[1,2]	35,803[1,2]
Alaska	—	—	—	—	—	—	—	—
Arizona	—	—	—	—	—	—	—	—
Arkansas	6,094	2,379	0	8,473	6,722	4,156	0	10,878
California	—	—	—	—	—	—	—	—
Colorado	—	—	—	—	—	—	—	—
Connecticut	23,466[1]	21,303[1]	0[1]	44,769[1]	23,829[1]	26,471[1]	444[1]	50,744[1]
Delaware	4,247	4,705	0	8,952	4,437	4,379	0	8,816
Florida	—	—	—	—	—	—	—	—
Georgia	29,600	29,003	0	58,603	31,270	33,278	0	64,548
Hawaii	—	—	—	—	—	—	—	—
Idaho	—	—	—	—	—	—	—	—
Illinois	27,899	15,939	143	43,981	34,617	23,855	0	58,472
Indiana	28,545[1]	54,111[1]	0[1]	82,656[1]	50,990[1]	49,582[1]	0[1]	100,572[1]
Iowa	—	—	—	—	—	—	—	—
Kansas	—	—	—	—	—	—	—	—
Kentucky	24,105[1,2]	41,295[1,2]	5,136[1,2]	70,536[1,2]	21,445[1,2]	23,142[1,2]	0[1,2]	44,587[1,2]
Louisiana	1,800	4,725	1,268	7,793	3,796	9,090	422	13,308
Maine	26,370	23,341	4,985	54,696	45,591	42,164	224	87,979
Maryland	16,071[1]	23,097[1]	208[1]	39,376[1]	27,553[1]	24,196[1]	2,385[1]	54,134[1]
Massachusetts	31,366	41,891	366	73,623	35,851	50,473	1,275	87,599
Michigan	11,430[1]	10,282[1]	0[1]	21,712[1]	16,255	16,051	0	32,306
Minnesota	—	—	—	—	—	—	—	—
Mississippi	11,203[1]	7,143[1]	0[1]	18,346[1]	18,602[1]	16,215[1]	0[1]	34,817[1]
Missouri	16,468	10,007	280	26,755	23,405	17,193	0	40,598
Montana	—	—	—	—	—	—	—	—
Nebraska	—	—	—	—	—	—	—	—
Nevada	—	—	—	—	—	—	—	—
New Hampshire	21,755[1]	1,341[1]	0[1]	23,096[1]	29,910[1]	23,870[1]	1,768[1]	55,548[1]
New Jersey	25,470	26,006	0	51,476	28,492	28,426	0	56,918
New Mexico	—	—	—	—	—	—	—	—
New York	160,652	132,958	8,914	302,524	181,625	193,417	0	375,042
North Carolina	26,718[1,2]	21,582[1,2]	665[1,2]	48,965[1,2]	32,417[1,2]	30,117[1,2]	0[1,2]	62,534[1,2]
North Dakota	—	—	—	—	—	—	—	—
Ohio	85,272	91,814	102	177,188	103,470	103,242	0	206,712
Oklahoma	—	—	—	—	—	—	—	—
Oregon	—	—	—	—	—	—	—	—
Pennsylvania	91,225	53,558	24,314	169,097	130,409	124,342	0	254,751
Rhode Island	3,261[1]	4,282[1]	72[1]	7,615[1]	3,660[1]	4,050[1]	0[1]	7,710[1]
South Carolina	0[2]	0[2]	2,444[2]	2,444[2]	2,358[2]	3,339[2]	2,329[2]	8,026[2]
South Dakota	—	—	—	—	—	—	—	—
Tennessee	29,995[1]	63,027[1]	0[1]	93,022[1]	49,732[1]	52,311[1]	0[1]	102,043[1]
Texas	—	—	—	—	—	—	—	—
Utah	—	—	—	—	—	—	—	—
Vermont	13,760	18,643	1,540	33,943	18,635	23,842	509	42,986
Virginia	10,803[1,2]	7,450[1,2]	940[1,2]	19,193[1,2]	28,912[1,2]	27,388[1,2]	125[1,2]	56,425[1,2]
Washington	—	—	—	—	—	—	—	—
West Virginia	—	—	—	—	—	—	—	—
Wisconsin	—	—	—	—	—	—	—	—
Wyoming	—	—	—	—	—	—	—	—
Arkansas	2,713[3]	1,636[3]	0[3]	4,349[3]	—	—	—	—

Notes: Entries are raw vote values for candidates who used the sole designation "Democrat" or "Republican" (or their historical antecedents listed in Appendix A) on the ballot. In general, historical antecedents to the Democratic Party were Anti-Federalists, Democratic-Republicans, and Jacksonian Democrats; historical precursors of the Republican Party were Federalists, National Republicans, and Whigs. Other = candidates who used third-party names on the ballot or were listed as independent, unidentified, or scatter vote. —indicates that the state had no data, either because no vote data were found for the state in question or the state had not yet entered the Union. No special House elections are included in the table. The table only lists at-large vote values for states having both at-large and district House races; see Appendix B for these states' district results aggregated to the state level.

[1] Election held in odd-numbered year.
[2] Partial data (less than 100% of the districts reporting).
[3] 1837 election when a state had annual elections in both 1836 and 1837.

Sources: Adapted from *United States Congressional Elections, 1788–1997* (1998), *Congressional Quarterly's Guide to U.S. Elections* (1994), ICPSR data sets 0001 and 0075, independent search for state sources by the author, and personal communications with Michael J. Dubin (various dates).

Table 5-83 House Election Results, by State, 1840–1843 (Raw Count)

State	1840–1841				1842–1843			
	Democratic	Republican	Other	Total Vote	Democratic	Republican	Other	Total Vote
Alabama	23,176[1]	17,449[1]	0[1]	40,625[1]	13,462[1,2]	12,724[1,2]	192[1,2]	26,378[1,2]
Alaska	—	—	—	—	—	—	—	—
Arizona	—	—	—	—	—	—	—	—
Arkansas	7,876	5,788	0	13,664	9,413	5,315	1,686	16,414
California	—	—	—	—	—	—	—	—
Colorado	—	—	—	—	—	—	—	—
Connecticut	21,168[1]	26,800[1]	0[1]	47,968[1]	27,225[1]	25,669[1]	1,609[1]	54,503[1]
Delaware	4,974	5,896	0	10,870	5,456	5,465	0	10,921
Florida	—	—	—	—	—	—	—	—
Georgia	35,572	39,619	0	75,191	35,461	33,580	0	69,041
Hawaii	—	—	—	—	—	—	—	—
Idaho	—	—	—	—	—	—	—	—
Illinois	34,657[1]	27,252[1]	7,722[1]	69,631[1]	49,482[1]	42,288[1]	2,045[1]	93,815[1]
Illinois	*41,778[1]*	*27,252[1]*	*601[1]*	*69,631[1]*	—	—	—	—
Indiana	38,955[1]	49,287[1]	182[1]	88,424[1]	61,280[1]	57,748[1]	876[1]	119,904[1]
Iowa	—	—	—	—	—	—	—	—
Kansas	—	—	—	—	—	—	—	—
Kentucky	9,565[1]	28,413[1]	2,036[1]	40,014[1]	42,623[1]	52,268[1]	7,657[1]	102,548[1]
Louisiana	7,049	9,137	0	16,186	8,143[1]	6,586[1]	0[1]	14,729[1]
Maine	44,540	45,238	498	90,276	31,039[1]	20,867[1]	11,798[1]	63,704[1]
Maryland	15,535[1]	23,791[1]	1,382[1]	40,708[1]				
Massachusetts	52,655	72,041	225	124,921	54,898	53,855	7,066	115,819
Michigan	21,464	22,759	0	44,223	21,242[1]	14,704[1]	2,831[1]	38,777[1]
Minnesota	—	—	—	—	—	—	—	—
Mississippi	19,067[1]	16,601[1]	0[1]	35,668[1]	0[1]	0[1]	38,560[1]	38,560[1]
Mississippi	—	—	—	—	*38,560[1]*	*0[1]*	*0[1]*	*38,560[1]*
Missouri	29,594	21,492	0	51,086	25,658	0	688	26,346
Montana	—	—	—	—	—	—	—	—
Nebraska	—	—	—	—	—	—	—	—
Nevada	—	—	—	—	—	—	—	—
New Hampshire	28,870[1]	20,833[1]	1,266[1]	50,969[1]	22,913[1]	12,901[1]	8,403[1]	44,217[1]
New Jersey	31,138	33,342	68	64,548	19,448[1,2]	23,091[1,2]	5,313[1,2]	47,852[1,2]
New Jersey	—	—	—	—	*19,448[1,2]*	*28,404[1,2]*	*0[1,2]*	*47,852[1,2]*
New Mexico	—	—	—	—	—	—	—	—
New York	214,559	224,021	1,737	440,317	195,886	186,469	7,185	389,540
North Carolina	19,703[1,2]	20,493[1,2]	111[1,2]	40,307[1,2]	26,038[1]	31,462[1]	0[1]	57,500[1]
North Dakota	—	—	—	—	—	—	—	—
Ohio	128,284	145,397	0	273,681	106,834[1]	97,220[1]	14,115[1]	218,169[1]
Ohio	—	—	—	—	*106,834[1]*	*102,264[1]*	*9,071[1]*	*218,169[1]*
Oklahoma	—	—	—	—	—	—	—	—
Oregon	—	—	—	—	—	—	—	—
Pennsylvania	129,817	125,337	113	255,267	103,066[1]	86,441[1]	10,937[1]	200,444[1]
Pennsylvania	—	—	—	—	*104,138[1]*	*86,441[1]*	*9,865[1]*	*200,444[1]*
Rhode Island	0[1]	2,516[1]	246[1]	2,762[1]	4,417[1]	0[1]	7,145[1]	11,562[1]
Rhode Island	—	—	—	—	*4,417[1]*	*7,145[1]*	*0[1]*	*11,562[1]*
South Carolina	7,657[2]	4,530[2]	213[2]	12,400[2]	7,183[1,2]	2,315[1,2]	1,225[1,2]	10,723[1,2]
South Dakota	—	—	—	—	—	—	—	—
Tennessee	30,189[1]	34,597[1]	939[1]	65,725[1]	49,075[1]	55,368[1]	0[1]	104,443[1]
Texas	—	—	—	—	—	—	—	—
Utah	—	—	—	—	—	—	—	—
Vermont	21,655	32,006	110	53,771	20,780[1]	23,992[1]	3,664[1]	48,436[1]
Virginia	9,415[1,2]	9,365[1,2]	3,235[1,2]	22,015[1,2]	17,818[1,2]	16,888[1,2]	0[1,2]	34,706[1,2]
Washington	—	—	—	—	—	—	—	—
West Virginia	—	—	—	—	—	—	—	—
Wisconsin	—	—	—	—	—	—	—	—
Wyoming	—	—	—	—	—	—	—	—

Notes: Main entries are raw vote values for candidates who used the sole designation "Democrat" or "Republican" (or their historical antecedents listed in Appendix A) on the ballot. In general, historical antecedents to the Democratic Party were Anti-Federalists, Democratic-Republicans, and Jacksonian Democrats; historical precursors of the Republican Party were Federalists, National Republicans, and Whigs. Other = candidates who used third-party names on the ballot or were listed as independent, unidentified, or scatter vote. Bold italicized entries in the table are the author's alternative party coding which is used when a candidate listed a major party name (Democrat, Republican, or their historical antecedents) on the ballot with other party names or labels. For a more detailed explanation of this alternate coding system, see Tables 5-1 and 1-3. —indicates that the state had no data, either because no vote data were found for the state in question or the state had not yet entered the Union. No special House elections are included in the table. The table only lists at-large vote values for states having both at-large and district House races; see Appendix B for these states' district results aggregated to the state level.

[1] Election held in odd-numbered year.
[2] Partial data (less than 100% of the districts reporting).

Sources: Adapted from *United States Congressional Elections, 1788–1997* (1998), *Congressional Quarterly's Guide to U.S. Elections* (1994), ICPSR data sets 0001 and 0075, independent search for state sources by the author, and personal communications with Michael J. Dubin (various dates).

Table 5-84 House Election Results, by State, 1844–1847 (Raw Count)

State	1844–1845				1846–1847			
	Democratic	Republican	Other	Total Vote	Democratic	Republican	Other	Total Vote
Alabama	34,180[1,2]	10,066[1,2]	408[1,2]	44,654[1,2]	32,378[1,2]	9,420[1,2]	2,287[1,2]	44,085[1,2]
Alaska	—	—	—	—	—	—	—	—
Arizona	—	—	—	—	—	—	—	—
Arkansas	11,112	7,516	113	18,741	16,426	0	101	16,527
California	—	—	—	—	—	—	—	—
Colorado	—	—	—	—	—	—	—	—
Connecticut	26,199[1]	29,569[1]	2,132[1]	57,900[1]	27,397[1]	30,188[1]	1,827[1]	59,412[1]
Delaware	6,023	6,229	0	12,252	6,007	6,254	0	12,261
Florida	3,608[1]	2,373[1]	0[1]	5,981[1]	2,887	2,990	0	5,877
Georgia	40,377	38,111	0	78,488	30,343	27,350	1,384	59,077
Georgia	—	—	—	—	**31,606**	**27,350**	**121**	**59,077**
Hawaii	—	—	—	—	—	—	—	—
Idaho	—	—	—	—	—	—	—	—
Illinois	62,305	33,485	3,079	98,869	54,364	27,828	17,302	99,494
Illinois	—	—	—	—	**61,432**	**27,828**	**10,234**	**99,494**
Indiana	64,995[1]	58,816[1]	1,769[1]	125,580[1]	67,216[1]	67,459[1]	579[1]	135,254[1]
Iowa	—	—	—	—	8,107	7,308	0	15,415
Kansas	—	—	—	—	—	—	—	—
Kentucky	55,115[1]	55,107[1]	188[1]	110,410[1]	53,949[1]	59,246[1]	8,450[1]	121,645[1]
Kentucky	—	—	—	—	**53,949[1]**	**64,553[1]**	**3,143[1]**	**121,645[1]**
Louisiana	10,176	4,521	0	14,697	9,941[1,2]	9,223[1,2]	345[1,2]	19,509[1,2]
Maine	43,176	39,361	8,999	91,536	32,794	29,654	11,491	73,939
Maryland	21,960	26,877	207	49,044	30,132[1,2]	29,353[1,2]	0[1,2]	59,485[1,2]
Massachusetts	52,827	68,479	10,200	131,506	32,325	54,110	13,730	100,165
Michigan	27,898	24,611	3,147	55,656	23,884	20,904	2,885	47,673
Minnesota	—	—	—	—	—	—	—	—
Mississippi	27,945[1]	18,378[1]	3,150[1]	49,473[1]	28,661[1]	12,526[1]	6,087[1]	47,274[1]
Mississippi	—	—	—	—	**34,694[1]**	**12,526[1]**	**54[1]**	**47,274[1]**
Missouri	36,023	29,225	0	65,248	40,363	25,330	1,572	67,265
Montana	—	—	—	—	—	—	—	—
Nebraska	—	—	—	—	—	—	—	—
Nevada	—	—	—	—	—	—	—	—
New Hampshire	24,904[1]	15,177[1]	13,044[1]	53,125[1]	30,538[1]	21,001[1]	8,368[1]	59,907[1]
New Jersey	30,361	39,145	0	69,506	25,662	28,713	1,431	55,806
New Mexico	—	—	—	—	—	—	—	—
New York	232,430	200,079	50,137	482,646	166,884	187,462	43,668	398,014
New York	**232,430**	**249,285**	**931**	**482,646**	**179,695**	**187,462**	**30,857**	**398,014**
North Carolina	34,107[1]	43,269[1]	0[1]	77,376[1]	22,799[1]	33,856[1]	7,240[1]	63,895[1]
North Carolina	—	—	—	—	**27,014[1]**	**36,881[1]**	**0[1]**	**63,895[1]**
North Dakota	—	—	—	—	—	—	—	—
Ohio	143,950	148,909	8,652	301,511	116,527	113,675	12,930	243,132
Ohio	—	—	—	—	**116,527**	**123,654**	**2,951**	**243,132**
Oklahoma	—	—	—	—	—	—	—	—
Oregon	—	—	—	—	—	—	—	—
Pennsylvania	153,274	139,542	21,912	314,728	91,926	91,607	22,958	206,491
Pennsylvania	—	—	—	—	**96,778**	**91,607**	**18,106**	**206,491**
Rhode Island	0[1]	8,180[1]	3,175[1]	11,355[1]	4,357[1]	5,789[1]	997[1]	11,143[1]
South Carolina	10,316[2]	2,912[2]	0[2]	13,228[2]	—	—	—	—
South Dakota	—	—	—	—	—	—	—	—
Tennessee	55,615[1]	45,849[1]	2,565[1]	104,029[1]	57,994[1]	55,999[1]	58[1]	114,051[1]
Tennessee	**55,615[1]**	**47,947[1]**	**467[1]**	**104,029[1]**	—	—	—	—
Texas	—	—	—	—	2,709	0	4,003	6,712
Utah	—	—	—	—	—	—	—	—
Vermont	19,182	26,831	5,033	51,046	16,637	22,693	6,956	46,286
Virginia	9,446[1,2]	6,843[1,2]	2,320[1,2]	18,609[1,2]	35,176[1,2]	31,030[1,2]	0[1,2]	66,206[1,2]
Washington	—	—	—	—	—	—	—	—
West Virginia	—	—	—	—	—	—	—	—
Wisconsin	—	—	—	—	—	—	—	—
Wyoming	—	—	—	—	—	—	—	—
Iowa	—	—	—	—	10,689[4]	9,859[4]	0[4]	20,548[4]
Maryland	30,731[3]	28,619[3]	1,147[3]	60,497[3]	—	—	—	—

Notes: Main entries are raw vote values for candidates who used the sole designation "Democrat" or "Republican" (or their historical antecedents listed in Appendix A) on the ballot. In general, historical antecedents to the Democratic Party were Anti-Federalists, Democratic-Republicans, and Jacksonian Democrats; historical precursors of the Republican Party were Federalists, National Republicans, and Whigs. Other = candidates who used third-party names on the ballot or were listed as independent, unidentified, or scatter vote. Bold italicized entries in the table are the author's alternative party coding which is used when a candidate listed a major party name (Democrat, Republican, or their historical antecedents) on the ballot with other party names or labels. For a more detailed explanation of this alternate coding system, see Tables 5-1 and 1-3. —indicates that the state had no data, either because no vote data were found for the state in question or the state had not yet entered the Union. No special House elections are included in the table. The table only lists at-large vote values for states having both at-large and district House races; see Appendix B for these states' district results aggregated to the state level.

[1]Election held in odd-numbered year.
[2]Partial data (less than 100% of the districts reporting).
[3]1845 election when a state had annual elections in both 1844 and 1845.
[4]1847 election when a state had annual elections in both 1846 and 1847.

Sources: Adapted from *United States Congressional Elections, 1788–1997* (1998), *Congressional Quarterly's Guide to U.S. Elections* (1994), ICPSR data sets 0001 and 0075, independent search for state sources by the author, and personal communications with Michael J. Dubin (various dates).

Table 5-85 House Election Results, by State, 1848–1851 (Raw Count)

State	1848–1849 Democratic	Republican	Other	Total Vote	1850–1851 Democratic	Republican	Other	Total Vote
Alabama	31,647[1]	32,780[1]	5,975[1]	70,402[1]	0[1,2]	0[1,2]	53,991[1,2]	53,991[1,2]
Alabama	*31,647[1]*	*38,755[1]*	*0[1]*	*70,402[1]*	*31,310[1,2]*	*22,681[1,2]*	*0[1,2]*	*53,991[1,2]*
Alaska	—	—	—	—	—	—	—	—
Arizona	—	—	—	—	—	—	—	—
Arkansas	14,456	9,328	0	23,784	11,965[1]	8,876[1]	0[1]	20,841[1]
California	5,300[1]	0[1]	5,451[1]	10,751[1]	24,473[1]	21,357[1]	0[1]	45,830[1]
Colorado	—	—	—	—	—	—	—	—
Connecticut	20,612[1]	28,023[1]	7,453[1]	56,088[1]	29,984[1]	28,886[1]	1,566[1]	60,436[1]
Connecticut	*27,284[1]*	*28,023[1]*	*781[1]*	*56,088[1]*	—	—	—	—
Delaware	6,026	6,369	0	12,395	6,055	5,926	313	12,294
Florida	3,805	4,382	0	8,187	4,050	4,531	0	8,581
Georgia	38,908	38,651	0	77,559	0[1]	0[1]	93,657[1]	93,657[1]
Hawaii	—	—	—	—	—	—	—	—
Idaho	—	—	—	—	—	—	—	—
Illinois	64,449	34,387	4,760	103,596	59,798	43,204	1,125	104,127
Indiana	69,949[1]	70,504[1]	0[1]	140,453[1]	74,515[1]	60,717[1]	13,316[1]	148,548[1]
Indiana	—	—	—	—	*74,515[1]*	*69,493[1]*	*4,540[1]*	*148,548[1]*
Iowa	12,266	11,489	488	24,243	13,182	11,710	473	25,365
Iowa	—	—	—	—	*13,590*	*11,710*	*65*	*25,365*
Kansas	—	—	—	—	—	—	—	—
Kentucky	41,919[1]	57,248[1]	4,665[1]	103,832[1]	47,446[1]	50,632[1]	3,301[1]	101,379[1]
Kentucky	—	—	—	—	*47,446[1]*	*53,933[1]*	*0[1]*	*101,379[1]*
Louisiana	5,669[1,2]	5,002[1,2]	0[1,2]	10,671[1,2]	18,040[1]	18,322[1]	0.0[1]	36,362[1]
Maine	38,491	32,597	10,671	81,759	39,252	37,058	3,038	79,348
Maryland	25,976[1]	30,699[1]	472[1]	57,147[1]	22,949[1]	22,904[1]	7,845[1]	53,698[1]
Maryland	—	—	—	—	*22,949[1]*	*27,855[1]*	*2,894[1]*	*53,698[1]*
Massachusetts	26,819	53,229	43,538	123,586	34,723	54,968	26,604	116,295
Massachusetts	*26,819*	*64,316*	*32,451*	*123,586*	—	—	—	—
Michigan	31,247	15,832	18,119	65,198	29,259	0	30,906	60,165
Michigan	*31,247*	*29,391*	*4,560*	*65,198*	*29,259*	*30,872*	*34*	*60,165*
Minnesota	—	—	—	—	—	—	—	—
Mississippi	31,732[1]	23,620[1]	0[1]	55,352[1]	0[1]	0[1]	57,792[1]	57,792[1]
Missouri	50,362	31,427	0	81,789	5,878	31,796	40,544	78,218
Missouri	—	—	—	—	*46,422*	*31,796*	*0*	*78,218*
Montana	—	—	—	—	—	—	—	—
Nebraska	—	—	—	—	—	—	—	—
Nevada	—	—	—	—	—	—	—	—
New Hampshire	29,969[1]	15,097[1]	10,520[1]	55,586[1]	27,488[1]	6,150[1]	18,566[1]	52,204[1]
New Hampshire	*29,969[1]*	*22,068[1]*	*3,549[1]*	*55,586[1]*	*27,488[1]*	*22,656[1]*	*2,060[1]*	*52,204[1]*
New Jersey	36,379	36,668	1,459	74,506	39,368	33,319	1,127	73,814
New Mexico	—	—	—	—	—	—	—	—
New York	100,127	217,629	138,013	455,769	207,926	213,082	4,669	425,677
New York	*106,542*	*227,619*	*121,608*	*455,769*	*208,467*	*213,381*	*3,829*	*425,677*
North Carolina	37,458[1]	36,412[1]	1,602[1]	75,472[1]	10,985[1,2]	18,779[1,2]	13,763[1,2]	43,527[1,2]
North Carolina	—	—	—	—	*17,752[1,2]*	*25,379[1,2]*	*396[1,2]*	*43,527[1,2]*
North Dakota	—	—	—	—	—	—	—	—
Ohio	142,344	113,940	30,416	286,700	132,804	105,172	15,855	253,831
Ohio	*143,014*	*121,173*	*22,513*	*286,700*	*138,262*	*105,172*	*10,397*	*253,831*
Oklahoma	—	—	—	—	—	—	—	—
Oregon	—	—	—	—	—	—	—	—
Pennsylvania	155,864	158,266	18,593	332,723	136,826	123,393	18,885	279,104
Pennsylvania	*167,551*	*158,266*	*6,906*	*332,723*	*143,706*	*129,677*	*5,721*	*279,104*
Rhode Island	3,242[1]	5,003[1]	373[1]	8,618[1]	6,763[1]	5,895[1]	154[1]	12,812[1]
South Carolina	21,866[2]	0[2]	10,965[2]	32,831[2]	—	—	—	—
South Carolina	*26,483[2]*	*0[2]*	*6,348[2]*	*32,831[2]*	—	—	—	—
South Dakota	—	—	—	—	—	—	—	—
Tennessee	35,166[1]	31,255[1]	4,062[1]	70,483[1]	42,254[1,2]	47,584[1,2]	5,830[1,2]	95,668[1,2]
Tennessee	—	—	—	—	*48,084[1,2]*	*47,584[1,2]*	*0[1,2]*	*95,668[1,2]*
Texas	15,531[1]	0[1]	4,334[1]	19,865[1]	16,928[1]	0[1]	6,085[1]	23,013[1]
Utah	—	—	—	—	—	—	—	—
Vermont	14,643	20,884	11,373	46,900	9,838	23,895	11,179	44,912
Vermont	*26,016*	*20,884*	*0*	*46,900*	*21,017*	*23,895*	*0*	*44,912*
Virginia	27,430[1,2]	25,636[1,2]	3,127[1,2]	56,193[1,2]	18,219[1,2]	15,738[1,2]	0[1,2]	33,957[1,2]
Virginia	*27,430[1,2]*	*28,446[1,2]*	*317[1,2]*	*56,193[1,2]*	—	—	—	—
Washington	—	—	—	—	—	—	—	—
West Virginia	—	—	—	—	—	—	—	—
Wisconsin	15,872	13,234	9,284	38,390	18,207	5,752	19,031	42,990
Wisconsin	—	—	—	—	*18,207*	*13,264*	*11,519*	*42,990*
Wyoming	—	—	—	—	—	—	—	—

Notes: Main entries are raw vote values for candidates who used the sole designation "Democrat" or "Republican" (or their historical antecedents listed in Appendix A) on the ballot. In general, historical antecedents to the Democratic Party were Anti-Federalists, Democratic-Republicans, and Jacksonian Democrats; historical precursors of the Republican Party were Federalists, National Republicans, and Whigs. Other = candidates who used third-party names on the ballot or were listed as independent, unidentified, or scatter vote. Bold italicized entries in the table are the author's alternative party coding which is used when a candidate listed a major party name (Democrat, Republican, or their historical antecedents) on the ballot with other party names or labels. For a more detailed explanation of this alternate coding system, see Tables 5-1 and 1-3. —indicates that the state had no data, either because no vote data were found for the state in question or the state had not yet entered the Union. No special House elections are included in the table. The table only lists at-large vote values for states having both at-large and district House races; see Appendix B for these states' district results aggregated to the state level.

[1] Election held in odd-numbered year.
[2] Partial data (less than 100% of the districts reporting).

Sources: Adapted from *United States Congressional Elections, 1788–1997* (1998), *Congressional Quarterly's Guide to U.S. Elections* (1994), ICPSR data sets 0001 and 0075, independent search for state sources by the author, and personal communications with Michael J. Dubin (various dates).

Table 5-86 House Election Results, by State, 1852–1855 (Raw Count)

State	1852–1853				1854–1855			
	Democratic	Republican	Other	Total Vote	Democratic	Republican	Other	Total Vote
Alabama	9,582[1,2]	2,769[1,2]	36,407[1,2]	48,758[1,2]	41,108[1]	0[1]	31,685[1]	72,793[1]
Alabama	*32,116[1,2]*	*16,642[1,2]*	*0[1,2]*	*48,758[1,2]*	—	—	—	—
Alaska	—	—	—	—	—	—	—	—
Arizona	—	—	—	—	—	—	—	—
Arkansas	13,186[1]	4,143[1]	0[1]	17,329[1]	24,752	4,842	316	29,910
California	39,736	34,358	0	74,094	0	34,741	46,825	81,566
California	—	—	—	—	*46,825*	*34,741*	*0*	*81,566*
Colorado	—	—	—	—	—	—	—	—
Connecticut	31,605[1]	24,947[1]	3,239[1]	59,791[1]	27,229[1]	0[1]	36,153[1]	63,382[1]
Delaware	6,692	6,630	0	13,322	6,334	0	6,820	13,154
Florida	4,590	4,568	0	9,158	5,638	4,564	0	10,202
Georgia	46,000[1]	40,589[1]	5,099[1]	91,688[1]	56,905[1]	0[1]	45,693[1]	102,598[1]
Hawaii	—	—	—	—	—	—	—	—
Idaho	—	—	—	—	—	—	—	—
Illinois	75,797	62,158	13,379	151,334	60,404	67,884	12,503	140,791
Illinois	*81,734*	*62,158*	*7,442*	*151,334*	*70,244*	*67,884*	*2,663*	*140,791*
Indiana	89,778	76,056	1,518	167,352	87,766	0	102,423	190,189
Iowa	16,823	15,651	0	32,474	21,086	22,466	174	43,726
Kansas	—	—	—	—	—	—	—	—
Kentucky	56,839[1]	61,399[1]	0[1]	118,238[1]	65,845[1]	0[1]	69,687[1]	135,532[1]
Louisiana	—	—	—	—	22,111[1]	0[1]	19,476[1]	41,587[1]
Maine	43,395	40,735	5,170	89,300	31,868	56,903	227	88,998
Maryland	27,456[1]	23,428[1]	20,812[1]	71,696[1]	39,786[1]	0[1]	41,944[1]	81,730[1]
Massachusetts	37,766	57,335	34,208	129,309	10,612	28,838	81,792	121,242
Massachusetts	—	—	—	—	*11,345*	*28,838*	*81,059*	*121,242*
Michigan	41,662	28,287	12,089	82,038	38,247	43,660	0	81,907
Michigan	*41,662*	*37,654*	*2,722*	*82,038*	—	—	—	—
Minnesota	—	—	—	—	—	—	—	—
Mississippi	34,538[1]	29,107[1]	0[1]	63,645[1]	32,718[1]	0[1]	27,575[1]	60,293[1]
Missouri	26,268	35,196	19,698	81,162	13,011	46,074	44,811	103,896
Missouri	*45,966*	*35,196*	*0*	*81,162*	*57,127*	*46,769*	*0*	*103,896*
Montana	—	—	—	—	—	—	—	—
Nebraska	—	—	—	—	—	—	—	—
Nevada	—	—	—	—	—	—	—	—
New Hampshire	28,853[1]	11,909[1]	10,704[1]	51,466[1]	27,090[1]	0[1]	36,874[1]	63,964[1]
New Hampshire	*28,853[1]*	*20,871[1]*	*1,742[1]*	*51,466[1]*	—	—	—	—
New Jersey	44,323	38,270	1,039	83,632	33,852	33,996	10,765	78,613
New Mexico	—	—	—	—	—	—	—	—
New York	245,829	238,933	33,166	517,928	26,701	181,661	250,559	458,921
New York	*245,829*	*249,606*	*22,493*	*517,928*	*218,779*	*217,130*	*23,012*	*458,921*
North Carolina	35,524[1]	32,020[1]	13,554[1]	81,098[1]	45,318[1]	3,756[1]	42,043[1]	91,117[1]
North Carolina	*49,078[1]*	*32,020[1]*	*0[1]*	*81,098[1]*	—	—	—	—
North Dakota	—	—	—	—	—	—	—	—
Ohio	144,063	127,536	24,669	296,268	105,584	0	186,445	292,029
Oklahoma	—	—	—	—	—	—	—	—
Oregon	—	—	—	—	—	—	—	—
Pennsylvania	177,639	136,519	13,450	327,608	160,322	157,617	35,737	353,676
Pennsylvania	—	—	—	—	*177,214*	*168,289*	*8,173*	*353,676*
Rhode Island	9,962[1]	5,392[1]	401[1]	15,755[1]	—	—	—	—
South Carolina	7,580[1,2]	0[1,2]	6,980[1,2]	14,560[1,2]	11,303[2]	0[2]	5,539[2]	16,842[2]
South Dakota	—	—	—	—	—	—	—	—
Tennessee	54,556[1,2]	49,472[1,2]	0[1,2]	104,028[1,2]	61,824[1]	0[1]	64,832[1]	126,656[1]
Texas	30,865[1]	2,326[1]	168[1]	33,359[1]	24,910[1]	0[1]	19,779[1]	44,689[1]
Utah	—	—	—	—	—	—	—	—
Vermont	8,739	21,388	11,870	41,997	12,920	24,868	2,447	40,235
Vermont	*20,609*	*21,388*	*0*	*41,997*	*15,367*	*24,868*	*0*	*40,235*
Virginia	26,869[1,2]	21,200[1,2]	5,295[1,2]	53,364[1,2]	42,916[1,2]	0[1,2]	38,533[1,2]	81,449[1,2]
Virginia	*31,736[1,2]*	*21,200[1,2]*	*428[1,2]*	*53,364[1,2]*	—	—	—	—
Washington	—	—	—	—	—	—	—	—
West Virginia	—	—	—	—	—	—	—	—
Wisconsin	33,832	21,199	9,396	64,427	25,027	32,315	2,072	59,414
Wyoming	—	—	—	—	—	—	—	—

Notes: Main entries are raw vote values for candidates who used the sole designation "Democrat" or "Republican" (or their historical antecedents listed in Appendix A) on the ballot. In general, historical antecedents to the Democratic Party were Anti-Federalists, Democratic-Republicans, and Jacksonian Democrats; historical precursors of the Republican Party were Federalists, National Republicans, and Whigs. Other = candidates who used third-party names on the ballot or were listed as independent, unidentified, or scatter vote. Bold italicized entries in the table are the author's alternative party coding which is used when a candidate listed a major party name (Democrat, Republican, or their historical antecedents) on the ballot with other party names or labels. For a more detailed explanation of this alternate coding system, see Tables 5-1 and 1-3. —indicates that the state had no data, either because no vote data were found for the state in question or the state had not yet entered the Union. No special House elections are included in the table. The table only lists at-large vote values for states having both at-large and district House races; see Appendix B for these states' district results aggregated to the state level.

[1]Election held in odd-numbered year.
[2]Partial data (less than 100% of the districts reporting).

Sources: Adapted from *United States Congressional Elections, 1788–1997* (1998), *Congressional Quarterly's Guide to U.S. Elections* (1994), ICPSR data sets 0001 and 0075, independent search for state sources by the author, and personal communications with Michael J. Dubin (various dates).

Table 5-87 House Election Results, by State, 1856–1859 (Raw Count)

State	1856–1857				1858–1859			
	Democratic	Republican	Other	Total Vote	Democratic	Republican	Other	Total Vote
Alabama	50,104[1]	0[1]	24,224[1]	74,328[1]	30,618[1,2]	0[1,2]	15,222[1,2]	45,840[1,2]
Alabama	*54,060[1]*	*0[1]*	*20,268[1]*	*74,328[1]*	*34,916[1,2]*	*0[1,2]*	*10,924[1,2]*	*45,840[1,2]*
Alaska	—	—	—	—	—	—	—	—
Arizona	—	—	—	—	—	—	—	—
Arkansas	27,234	0	14,862	42,096	34,557	0	9,409	43,966
Arkansas	—	—	—	—	*38,009*	*0*	*5,957*	*43,966*
California	50,892	21,985	35,325	108,202	0[1]	0[1]	98,965[1]	98,965[1]
California	—	—	—	—	*57,508[1]*	*41,457[1]*	*0[1]*	*98,965[1]*
Colorado	—	—	—	—	—	—	—	—
Connecticut	30,834[1]	31,785[1]	0[1]	62,619[1]	38,071[1]	39,731[1]	499[1]	78,301[1]
Delaware	8,111	0	6,360	14,471	7,868	0	7,452	15,320
Florida	6,392	0	5,650	12,042	6,084	0	3,661	9,745
Florida	—	—	—	—	*9,745*	*0*	*0*	*9,745*
Georgia	54,460[1]	0[1]	45,432[1]	99,892[1]	61,104[1]	0[1]	36,836[1]	97,940[1]
Georgia	*66,612[1]*	*0[1]*	*33,280[1]*	*99,892[1]*	—	—	—	—
Hawaii	—	—	—	—	—	—	—	—
Idaho	—	—	—	—	—	—	—	—
Illinois	109,958	118,342	2,231	230,531	122,181	125,668	4,110	251,959
Illinois	—	—	—	—	*126,291*	*125,668*	*0*	*251,959*
Indiana	117,905	111,675	0	229,580	103,205	100,855	12,325	216,385
Indiana	—	—	—	—	*115,530*	*100,855*	*0*	*216,385*
Iowa	32,978	39,950	826	73,754	45,693	49,032	0	94,725
Kansas	—	—	—	—	5,566[1]	7,604[1]	0[1]	13,170[1]
Kentucky	72,681[1]	0[1]	57,539[1]	130,220[1]	76,542[1]	0[1]	64,670[1]	141,212[1]
Louisiana	19,817[1]	0[1]	18,090[1]	37,907[1]	25,638[1]	0[1]	11,812[1]	37,450[1]
Louisiana	*21,962[1]*	*0[1]*	*15,945[1]*	*37,907[1]*	—	—	—	—
Maine	49,988	69,849	0	119,837	52,115	60,584	0	112,699
Maryland	38,252[1]	0[1]	47,237[1]	85,489[1]	28,525[1]	0[1]	46,813[1]	75,338[1]
Massachusetts	33,530	98,716	28,969	161,215	38,912	70,154	7,230	116,296
Massachusetts	*44,124*	*98,716*	*18,375*	*161,215*	—	—	—	—
Michigan	53,425	71,723	0	125,148	55,613	65,789	0	121,402
Minnesota	18,218[1]	17,037[1]	0[1]	35,255[1]	17,666[1]	21,360[1]	0[1]	39,026[1]
Mississippi	27,052[1]	0[1]	10,679[1]	37,731[1]	36,858[1]	0[1]	2,821[1]	39,679[1]
Mississippi	—	—	—	—	*39,234[1]*	*0[1]*	*445[1]*	*39,679[1]*
Missouri	51,941	0	59,502	111,443	73,206	6,631	47,292	127,129
Missouri	*64,772*	*0*	*46,671*	*111,443*	*85,746*	*6,631*	*34,752*	*127,129*
Montana	—	—	—	—	—	—	—	—
Nebraska	—	—	—	—	—	—	—	—
Nevada	—	—	—	—	—	—	—	—
New Hampshire	30,072[1]	33,619[1]	0[1]	63,691[1]	32,949[1]	35,844[1]	0[1]	68,793[1]
New Jersey	47,141	12,356	39,307	98,804	41,500	31,505	22,289	95,294
New Jersey	*47,141*	*43,525*	*8,138*	*98,804*	*60,050*	*31,505*	*3,739*	*95,294*
New Mexico	—	—	—	—	—	—	—	—
New York	165,059	273,448	152,053	590,560	209,380	186,231	141,955	537,566
New York	*203,761*	*273,448*	*113,351*	*590,560*	*213,329*	*289,142*	*35,095*	*537,566*
North Carolina	52,624[1]	0[1]	25,308[1]	77,932[1]	44,453[1]	33,073[1]	4,287[1]	81,813[1]
North Carolina	—	—	—	—	*45,737[1]*	*33,073[1]*	*3,003[1]*	*81,813[1]*
North Dakota	—	—	—	—	—	—	—	—
Ohio	156,654	178,854	19,405	354,913	159,464	184,062	999	344,525
Oklahoma	—	—	—	—	—	—	—	—
Oregon	—	—	—	—	5,646[1]	5,630[1]	0[1]	11,276[1]
Pennsylvania	211,480	201,669	7,856	421,005	138,483	0	231,593	370,076
Pennsylvania	—	—	—	—	*175,520*	*0*	*194,556*	*370,076*
Rhode Island	5,280[1]	9,485[1]	0[1]	14,765[1]	3,257[1]	5,552[1]	3,846[1]	12,655[1]
Rhode Island	—	—	—	—	*3,257[1]*	*9,398[1]*	*0[1]*	*12,655[1]*
South Carolina	12,454[2]	0[2]	342[2]	12,796[2]	7,205[2]	0[2]	4,924[2]	12,129[2]
South Dakota	—	—	—	—	—	—	—	—
Tennessee	70,270[1]	0[1]	53,126[1]	123,396[1]	69,161[1]	0[1]	68,797[1]	137,958[1]
Tennessee	—	—	—	—	*75,005[1]*	*0[1]*	*62,953[1]*	*137,958[1]*
Texas	35,682[1]	0[1]	14,434[1]	50,116[1]	39,185[1]	0[1]	19,174[1]	58,359[1]
Texas	—	—	—	—	*55,501[1]*	*0[1]*	*2,858[1]*	*58,359[1]*
Utah	—	—	—	—	—	—	—	—
Vermont	9,250	33,324	366	42,940	11,667	28,589	0	40,256
Virginia	48,331[1,2]	0[1,2]	29,706[1,2]	78,037[1,2]	44,209[1,2]	0[1,2]	43,943[1,2]	88,152[1,2]
Virginia	—	—	—	—	*74,305[1,2]*	*0[1,2]*	*13,847[1,2]*	*88,152[1,2]*
Washington	—	—	—	—	—	—	—	—
West Virginia	—	—	—	—	—	—	—	—
Wisconsin	53,609	66,315	0	119,924	55,243	61,356	0	116,599
Wyoming	—	—	—	—	—	—	—	—

Notes: Main entries are raw vote values for candidates who used the sole designation "Democrat" or "Republican" (or their historical antecedents listed in Appendix A) on the ballot. In general, historical antecedents to the Democratic Party were Anti-Federalists, Democratic-Republicans, and Jacksonian Democrats; historical precursors of the Republican Party were Federalists, National Republicans, and Whigs. Other = candidates who used third-party names on the ballot or were listed as independent, unidentified, or scatter vote. Bold italicized entries in the table are the author's alternative party coding which is used when a candidate listed a major party name (Democrat, Republican, or their historical antecedents) on the ballot with other party names or labels. For a more detailed explanation of this alternate coding system, see Tables 5-1 and 1-3. —indicates that the state had no data, either because no vote data were found for the state in question or the state had not yet entered the Union. No special House elections are included in the table. The table only lists at-large vote values for states having both at-large and district House races; see Appendix B for these states' district results aggregated to the state level.

[1]Election held in odd-numbered year.

[2]Partial data (less than 100% of the districts reporting).

Sources: Adapted from *United States Congressional Elections, 1788–1997* (1998), *Congressional Quarterly's Guide to U.S. Elections* (1994), ICPSR data sets 0001 and 0075, independent search for state sources by the author, and personal communications with Michael J. Dubin (various dates).

Table 5-88 House Election Results, by State, 1860–1863 (Raw Count)

State	1860–1861				1862–1863			
	Democratic	Republican	Other	Total Vote	Democratic	Republican	Other	Total Vote
Alabama	—	—	—	—	—	—	—	—
Alaska	—	—	—	—	—	—	—	—
Arizona	—	—	—	—	—	—	—	—
Arkansas	33,058	0	27,159	60,217	—	—	—	—
California	0[1]	51,651[1]	67,161[1]	118,812[1]	43,916[1]	65,149[1]	0[1]	109,065[1]
California	*67,161[1]*	*51,651[1]*	*0[1]*	*118,812[1]*				
Colorado	—	—	—	—	—	—	—	—
Connecticut	41,288[1]	42,465[1]	0[1]	83,753[1]	38,880[1]	41,048[1]	0[1]	79,928[1]
Delaware	761	0	15,217	15,978	8,051	8,014	0	16,065
Delaware	*8,246*	*0*	*7,732*	*15,978*				
Florida	7,722	0	5,172	12,894	—	—	—	—
Georgia	—	—	—	—	—	—	—	—
Hawaii	—	—	—	—	—	—	—	—
Idaho	—	—	—	—	—	—	—	—
Illinois	160,832	173,301	159	334,292	136,257	119,819	0	256,076
Indiana	124,259	137,531	308	262,098	128,071	116,739	0	244,810
Iowa	57,446	70,741	0	128,187	49,498	65,842	0	115,340
Kansas	—	—	—	—	930	14,337	0	15,267
Kentucky	0[1]	92,365[1]	37,766[1]	130,131[1]	14,953[1]	0[1]	69,183[1]	84,136[1]
Kentucky	*—*	*—*	*—*	*—*	*83,926[1]*	*0[1]*	*210[1]*	*84,136[1]*
Louisiana	—	—	—	—	—	—	—	—
Maine	52,833	69,286	1,238	123,357	36,131	47,041	2,589	85,761
Maine	*—*	*—*	*—*	*—*	*37,421*	*47,041*	*1,299*	*85,761*
Maryland	0[1]	42,397[1]	24,781[1]	67,178[1]	10,421[1]	37,492[1]	2,346[1]	50,259[1]
Maryland	*0[1]*	*50,821[1]*	*16,357[1]*	*67,178[1]*				
Massachusetts	12,392	103,495	51,559	167,446	2,762	85,053	46,137	133,952
Massachusetts	*49,720*	*103,495*	*14,231*	*167,446*				
Michigan	66,172	88,280	327	154,779	61,404	68,188	0	129,592
Minnesota	12,168	22,333	787	35,288	10,276	14,375	0	24,651
Minnesota	*12,955*	*22,333*	*0*	*35,288*				
Mississippi	—	—	—	—	—	—	—	—
Missouri	86,402	11,453	58,079	155,934	37,192	41,969	7,349	86,510
Missouri	*—*	*—*	*—*	*—*	*41,675*	*41,969*	*2,866*	*86,510*
Montana	—	—	—	—	—	—	—	—
Nebraska	—	—	—	—	—	—	—	—
Nevada	—	—	—	—	—	—	—	—
New Hampshire	31,373[1]	35,596[1]	0[1]	66,969[1]	32,629[1]	33,191[1]	0[1]	65,820[1]
New Jersey	61,452	60,403	0	121,855	60,591	46,964	0	107,555
New Mexico	—	—	—	—	—	—	—	—
New York	289,924	359,067	21,140	670,131	301,707	295,460	3,572	600,739
New York	*310,920*	*359,067*	*144*	*670,131*				
North Carolina	—	—	—	—	—	—	—	—
North Dakota	—	—	—	—	—	—	—	—
Ohio	184,921	218,564	6,268	409,753	182,045	174,379	5,781	362,205
Ohio	*—*	*—*	*—*	*—*	*182,045*	*180,160*	*0*	*362,205*
Oklahoma	—	—	—	—	—	—	—	—
Oregon	4,230	0	20	4,250	3,632	6,800	0	10,432
Pennsylvania	209,637	260,997	10,758	481,392	229,987	202,538	0	432,525
Pennsylvania	*212,871*	*260,997*	*7,524*	*481,392*				
Rhode Island	0[1]	21,951[1]	0[1]	21,951[1]	7,795[1]	10,738[1]	0[1]	18,533[1]
South Carolina	—	—	—	—	—	—	—	—
South Dakota	—	—	—	—	—	—	—	—
Tennessee	—	—	—	—	—	—	—	—
Texas	—	—	—	—	—	—	—	—
Utah	—	—	—	—	—	—	—	—
Vermont	9,272	31,149	1,800	42,221	10,922[1]	27,923[1]	0[1]	38,845[1]
Vermont	*11,072*	*31,149*	*0*	*42,221*				
Virginia	—	—	—	—	—	—	—	—
Washington	—	—	—	—	—	—	—	—
West Virginia	—	—	—	—	0[1]	19,783[1]	0[1]	19,783[1]
Wisconsin	65,502	86,422	0	151,924	64,119	61,829	0	125,948
Wyoming	—	—	—	—	—	—	—	—

Notes: Main entries are raw vote values for candidates who used the sole designation "Democrat" or "Republican" (or their historical antecedents listed in Appendix A) on the ballot. In general, historical antecedents to the Democratic Party were Anti-Federalists, Democratic-Republicans, and Jacksonian Democrats; historical precursors of the Republican Party were Federalists, National Republicans, and Whigs. Other = candidates who used third-party names on the ballot or were listed as independent, unidentified, or scatter vote. Bold italicized entries in the table are the author's alternative party coding which is used when a candidate listed a major party name (Democrat, Republican, or their historical antecedents) on the ballot with other party names or labels. For a more detailed explanation of this alternate coding system, see Tables 5-1 and 1-3. —indicates that the state had no data, either because no vote data were found for the state in question or the state had not yet entered the Union. No special House elections are included in the table. The table only lists at-large vote values for states having both at-large and district House races; see Appendix B for these states' district results aggregated to the state level.

[1] Election held in odd-numbered year.

Sources: Adapted from *United States Congressional Elections, 1788–1997* (1998), *Congressional Quarterly's Guide to U.S. Elections* (1994), ICPSR data sets 0001 and 0075, independent search for state sources by the author, and personal communications with Michael J. Dubin (various dates).

Table 5-89 House Election Results, by State, 1864–1867 (Raw Count)

State	1864–1865				1866–1867			
	Democratic	Republican	Other	Total Vote	Democratic	Republican	Other	Total Vote
Alabama	—	—	—	—	—	—	—	—
Alaska	—	—	—	—	—	—	—	—
Arizona	—	—	—	—	—	—	—	—
Arkansas	—	—	—	—	—	—	—	—
California	43,045	62,039	0	105,084	48,346[1]	44,436[1]	0[1]	92,782[1]
Colorado	—	—	—	—	—	—	—	—
Connecticut	31,015[1]	42,168[1]	0[1]	73,183[1]	47,634[1]	46,240[1]	0[1]	93,874[1]
Delaware	8,762	8,253	0	17,015	9,933	8,553	0	18,486
Florida	—	—	—	—	—	—	—	—
Georgia	—	—	—	—	—	—	—	—
Hawaii	—	—	—	—	—	—	—	—
Idaho	—	—	—	—	—	—	—	—
Illinois	158,784	190,226	0	349,010	147,455	203,045	0	350,500
Indiana	132,305	148,748	0	281,053	155,757	168,302	0	324,059
Iowa	49,362	88,942	0	138,304	56,456	90,930	386	147,772
Kansas	0	20,532	0	20,532	0	19,200	8,206	27,406
Kentucky	0[1]	0[1]	111,683[1]	111,683[1]	77,639[1]	28,874[1]	6,430[1]	112,943[1]
Louisiana	—	—	—	—	—	—	—	—
Maine	46,638	65,502	0	112,140	41,692	68,736	0	110,428
Maryland	31,922	40,448	0	72,370	42,303	25,918	22	68,243
Massachusetts	48,497	125,917	0	174,414	26,721	89,749	463	116,933
Michigan	72,982	91,052	0	164,034	67,347	97,009	0	164,356
Minnesota	17,303	24,839	0	42,142	15,775	25,983	0	41,758
Mississippi	—	—	—	—	—	—	—	—
Missouri	25,967	63,976	5,600	95,543	0	62,377	43,408	105,785
Missouri	*26,662*	*68,881*	*0*	*95,543*	*43,400*	*62,377*	*8*	*105,785*
Montana	—	—	—	—	—	—	—	—
Nebraska	—	—	—	—	4,072	4,820	30	8,922
Nevada	6,552	9,776	0	16,328	4,196	5,047	0	9,243
New Hampshire	30,185[1]	35,583[1]	500[1]	66,268[1]	32,798[1]	35,797[1]	0[1]	68,595[1]
New Jersey	67,608	61,745	0	129,353	63,930	65,473	193	129,596
New Mexico	—	—	—	—	—	—	—	—
New York	294,513	360,593	59,734	714,840	316,022	367,555	29,865	713,442
New York	*353,936*	*360,593*	*311*	*714,840*	*323,236*	*390,182*	*24*	*713,442*
North Carolina	—	—	—	—	—	—	—	—
North Dakota	—	—	—	—	—	—	—	—
Ohio	182,713	234,804	0	417,517	214,401	254,043	0	468,444
Oklahoma	—	—	—	—	—	—	—	—
Oregon	6,056	8,759	0	14,815	9,808	10,362	0	20,170
Pennsylvania	242,122	245,405	10,576	498,103	292,497	303,789	0	596,286
Pennsylvania	*252,698*	*245,405*	*0*	*498,103*	—	—	—	—
Rhode Island	1,286[1]	8,373[1]	53[1]	9,712[1]	1,480[1]	6,980[1]	101[1]	8,561[1]
South Carolina	—	—	—	—	—	—	—	—
South Dakota	—	—	—	—	—	—	—	—
Tennessee	0[1]	24,043[1]	34,579[1]	58,622[1]	0[1]	73,158[1]	22,965[1]	96,123[1]
Tennessee	—	—	—	—	*0[1]*	*73,617[1]*	*22,506[1]*	*96,123[1]*
Texas	—	—	—	—	—	—	—	—
Utah	—	—	—	—	—	—	—	—
Vermont	11,700	30,950	0	42,650	10,366	33,252	0	43,618
Virginia	—	—	—	—	—	—	—	—
Washington	—	—	—	—	—	—	—	—
West Virginia	0	15,307	6,573	21,880	16,885	23,271	0	40,156
Wisconsin	63,490	80,079	0	143,569	55,620	79,170	0	134,790
Wyoming	—	—	—	—	—	—	—	—
Nevada	2,215[2]	3,691[2]	0[2]	5,906[2]	—	—	—	—

Notes: Main entries are raw vote values for candidates who used the sole designation "Democrat" or "Republican" (or their historical antecedents listed in Appendix A) on the ballot. In general, historical antecedents to the Democratic Party were Anti-Federalists, Democratic-Republicans, and Jacksonian Democrats; historical precursors of the Republican Party were Federalists, National Republicans, and Whigs. Other = candidates who used third-party names on the ballot or were listed as independent, unidentified, or scatter vote. Bold italicized entries in the table are the author's alternative party coding which is used when a candidate listed a major party name (Democrat, Republican, or their historical antecedents) on the ballot with other party names or labels. For a more detailed explanation of this alternate coding system, see Tables 5-1 and 1-3. —indicates that the state had no data, either because no vote data were found for the state in question or the state had not yet entered the Union. No special House elections are included in the table. The table only lists at-large vote values for states having both at-large and district House races; see Appendix B for these states' district results aggregated to the state level.

[1] Election held in odd-numbered year.
[2] 1865 election when a state had annual elections in both 1864 and 1865.

Sources: Adapted from *United States Congressional Elections, 1788–1997* (1998), *Congressional Quarterly's Guide to U.S. Elections* (1994), ICPSR data sets 0001 and 0075, independent search for state sources by the author, and personal communications with Michael J. Dubin (various dates).

Table 5-90 House Election Results, by State, 1868–1871 (Raw Count)

State	1868–1869				1870–1871			
	Democratic	Republican	Other	Total Vote	Democratic	Republican	Other	Total Vote
Alabama	0	60,605	5,520	66,125	78,457	74,405	0	152,862
Alaska	—	—	—	—	—	—	—	—
Arizona	—	—	—	—	—	—	—	—
Arkansas	19,085	22,030	0	41,115	25,438	27,278	0	52,716
California	54,548	53,873	0	108,421	57,065[1]	62,539[1]	0[1]	119,604[1]
Colorado	—	—	—	—	—	—	—	—
Connecticut	43,447[1]	45,846[1]	0[1]	89,293[1]	46,718[1]	47,272[1]	0[1]	93,990[1]
Delaware	10,961	7,636	0	18,597	12,434	10,001	0	22,435
Florida	6,653	9,749	877	17,279	11,812	12,439	0	24,251
Georgia	63,991	81,380	0	145,371	95,156	71,028	2,965	169,149
Georgia	*—*	*—*	*—*	*—*	*95,979*	*73,170*	*0*	*169,149*
Hawaii	—	—	—	—	—	—	—	—
Idaho	—	—	—	—	—	—	—	—
Illinois	199,861	249,422	0	449,283	145,191	168,801	2,966	316,958
Indiana	170,880	170,446	0	341,326	157,703	154,581	2,799	315,083
Indiana	*—*	*—*	*—*	*—*	*160,502*	*154,581*	*0*	*315,083*
Iowa	76,242	117,831	149	194,222	63,636	98,636	0	162,272
Kansas	13,969	29,324	0	43,293	20,950	40,368	0	61,318
Kentucky	112,066	35,921	293	148,280	88,945	57,551	1,405	147,901
Kentucky	*—*	*—*	*—*	*—*	*90,350*	*57,551*	*0*	*147,901*
Louisiana	43,120	27,563	0	70,683	38,226	65,992	0	104,218
Maine	56,263	74,926	0	131,189	44,467	54,454	296	99,217
Maryland	61,626	30,079	0	91,705	76,595	57,727	0	134,322
Massachusetts	59,878	131,683	1,811	193,372	49,781	78,721	9,479	137,981
Massachusetts	*59,878*	*133,494*	*0*	*193,372*				
Michigan	99,315	126,166	0	225,481	85,733	96,598	2,176	184,507
Minnesota	28,087	32,088	11,229	71,404	29,395	36,739	0	66,134
Minnesota	*28,087*	*43,317*	*0*	*71,404*				
Mississippi	35,428[1]	73,959[1]	3,847[1]	113,234[1]	—	—	—	—
Missouri	61,975	81,843	0	143,818	63,626	60,022	52,992	176,640
Montana	—	—	—	—	—	—	—	—
Nebraska	6,318	8,724	0	15,042	7,967	12,375	0	20,342
Nevada	5,349	6,230	0	11,579	6,821	6,491	0	13,312
New Hampshire	31,461[1]	35,512[1]	0[1]	66,973[1]	35,098[1]	33,758[1]	623[1]	69,479[1]
New Jersey	83,022	79,467	0	162,489	76,373	80,426	630	157,429
New Jersey	*—*	*—*	*—*	*—*	*77,003*	*80,426*	*0*	*157,429*
New Mexico	—	—	—	—	—	—	—	—
New York	423,564	412,176	4,342	840,082	375,944	348,014	35,862	759,820
New York	*425,323*	*412,176*	*2,583*	*840,082*	*393,409*	*363,291*	*3,120*	*759,820*
North Carolina	0[2]	86,107[2]	74,410[2]	160,517[2]	0[2]	69,776[2]	76,268[2]	146,044[2]
North Dakota	—	—	—	—	—	—	—	—
Ohio	251,048	264,031	0	515,079	205,947	219,341	1,687	426,975
Oklahoma	—	—	—	—	—	—	—	—
Oregon	9,759	20,187	0	29,946	11,588	11,245	0	22,833
Pennsylvania	322,281	329,736	0	652,017	256,334	263,949	14,788	535,071
Pennsylvania	*—*	*—*	*—*	*—*	*256,334*	*276,380*	*2,357*	*535,071*
Rhode Island	6,485	12,206	0	18,691	2,327	9,589	267	12,183
South Carolina	45,186	61,885	356	107,427	39,064	74,317	7,032	120,413
South Carolina	*—*	*—*	*—*	*—*	*39,064*	*80,017*	*1,332*	*120,413*
South Dakota	—	—	—	—	—	—	—	—
Tennessee	0	55,859	0	55,859	74,542	37,873	8,247	120,662
Tennessee	*—*	*—*	*—*	*—*	*78,067*	*42,595*	*0*	*120,662*
Texas	31,588[1]	44,138[1]	381[1]	76,107[1]	62,525[1]	43,771[1]	407[1]	106,703[1]
Utah	—	—	—	—	—	—	—	—
Vermont	13,885	40,511	0	54,396	9,928	31,879	0	41,807
Virginia	0[1]	100,424[1]	117,499[1]	217,923[1]	—	—	—	—
Washington	—	—	—	—	—	—	—	—
West Virginia	22,052	26,931	0	48,983	28,460	26,769	0	55,229
Wisconsin	85,602	107,738	0	193,340	70,638	76,576	0	147,214
Wyoming	—	—	—	—	—	—	—	—
Alabama	48,380[3]	64,031[3]	2,785[3]	115,196[3]	—	—	—	—
Alabama	*48,380[3]*	*66,816[3]*	*0[3]*	*115,196[3]*	*—*	*—*	*—*	*—*

Notes: Main entries are raw vote values for candidates who used the sole designation "Democrat" or "Republican" (or their historical antecedents listed in Appendix A) on the ballot. In general, historical antecedents to the Democratic Party were Anti-Federalists, Democratic-Republicans, and Jacksonian Democrats; historical precursors of the Republican Party were Federalists, National Republicans, and Whigs. Other = candidates who used third-party names on the ballot or were listed as independent, unidentified, or scatter vote. Bold italic entries in the table are the author's alternative party coding which is used when a candidate listed a major party name (Democrat, Republican, or their historical antecedents) on the ballot with other party names or labels. For a more detailed explanation of this alternate coding system, see Tables 5-1 and 1-3. —indicates that the state had no data, either because no vote data were found for the state in question or the state had not yet entered the Union. No special House elections are included in the table. The table only lists at-large vote values for states having both at-large and district House races; see Appendix B for these states' district results aggregated to the state level.

[1] Election held in odd-numbered year.
[2] Partial data (less than 100% of the districts reporting).
[3] 1869 election when a state had annual elections in both 1868 and 1869.

Sources: Adapted from *United States Congressional Elections, 1788–1997* (1998), *Congressional Quarterly's Guide to U.S. Elections* (1994), ICPSR data sets 0001 and 0075, independent search for state sources by the author, and personal communications with Michael J. Dubin (various dates).

Table 5-91 House Election Results, by State, 1872–1875 (Raw Count)

State	1872–1873				1874–1875			
	Democratic	Republican	Other	Total Vote	Democratic	Republican	Other	Total Vote
Alabama	81,561	89,500	0	171,061	106,023	89,909	0	195,932
Alaska	—	—	—	—	—	—	—	—
Arizona	—	—	—	—	—	—	—	—
Arkansas	39,933	39,687	0	79,620	41,175	22,808	0	63,983
California	46,743	49,237	0	95,980	58,688[1]	39,789[1]	23,796[1]	122,273[1]
Colorado	—	—	—	—	—	—	—	—
Connecticut	41,498[1]	43,352[1]	1,432[1]	86,282[1]	51,197[1]	47,418[1]	2,009[1]	100,624[1]
Delaware	—	—	—	—	12,602	11,024	0	23,626
Florida	0	17,537	15,881	33,418	16,796	18,267	0	35,063
Georgia	83,138	61,655	1,293	146,086	85,760	32,180	8,631	126,571
Georgia	*84,431*	*61,655*	*0*	*146,086*	*93,347*	*33,149*	*75*	*126,571*
Hawaii	—	—	—	—	—	—	—	—
Idaho	—	—	—	—	—	—	—	—
Illinois	194,217	240,374	609	435,200	182,060	169,884	15,807	367,751
Illinois	—	—	—	—	*182,060*	*172,301*	*13,390*	*367,751*
Indiana	188,502	188,760	0	377,262	183,172	168,902	9,637	361,711
Indiana	—	—	—	—	*183,201*	*168,902*	*9,608*	*361,711*
Iowa	79,716	127,094	91	206,901	0	104,815	79,816	184,631
Kansas	34,390	67,400	0	101,790	11,225	48,908	27,048	87,181
Kentucky	105,719	44,339	11,084	161,142	76,850	26,873	21,706	125,429
Kentucky	*105,719*	*49,392*	*6,031*	*161,142*	*82,649*	*28,128*	*14,652*	*125,429*
Louisiana	59,130	68,947	0	128,077	76,463	68,505	0	144,968
Maine	54,150	72,094	0	126,244	41,103	53,240	156	94,499
Maryland	67,723	67,024	0	134,747	67,503	53,377	0	120,880
Massachusetts	61,222	131,733	0	192,955	72,976	87,599	21,526	182,101
Michigan	86,160	135,829	883	222,872	88,956	111,965	15,856	216,777
Michigan	*86,355*	*135,829*	*688*	*222,872*	*102,273*	*111,965*	*2,539*	*216,777*
Minnesota	34,386	55,291	0	89,677	43,103	48,637	0	91,740
Mississippi	40,838	80,535	2,859	124,232	83,966[1]	54,845[1]	19,250[1]	158,061[1]
Mississippi	—	—	—	—	*83,966[1]*	*74,095[1]*	*0[1]*	*158,061[1]*
Missouri	155,088	117,961	1,710	274,759	163,609	65,270	24,594	253,473
Missouri	*156,680*	*117,961*	*118*	*274,759*	—	—	—	—
Montana	—	—	—	—	—	—	—	—
Nebraska	10,412	17,124	0	27,536	8,360	22,532	5,046	35,938
Nevada	7,847	7,146	0	14,993	8,627	9,240	0	17,867
New Hampshire	33,131[1]	33,178[1]	1,124[1]	67,433[1]	39,231[1]	38,950[1]	625[1]	78,806[1]
New Jersey	76,308	94,341	0	170,649	95,038	85,455	0	180,493
New Mexico	—	—	—	—	—	—	—	—
New York	400,697	438,456	0	839,153	399,287	345,234	36,022	780,543
New York	—	—	—	—	*419,906*	*354,258*	*6,379*	*780,543*
North Carolina	95,726	99,400	0	195,126	102,317	74,271	14,356	190,944
North Dakota	—	—	—	—	—	—	—	—
Ohio	263,263	253,482	1,263	518,008	238,899	215,123	9,832	463,854
Ohio	*263,479*	*253,482*	*1,047*	*518,008*	*238,899*	*218,550*	*6,405*	*463,854*
Oklahoma	—	—	—	—	—	—	—	—
Oregon	12,317	13,168	0	25,485	9,642	9,340	6,350	25,332
Pennsylvania	311,036	359,485	919	671,440	277,351	239,794	33,939	551,084
Pennsylvania	—	—	—	—	*277,351*	*248,017*	*25,716*	*551,084*
Rhode Island	5,643	13,287	0	18,930	2,092	4,678	0	6,770
South Carolina	0	63,793	25,838	89,631	27,328	79,199	34,770	141,297
South Carolina	*0*	*88,862*	*769*	*89,631*	*27,328*	*109,508*	*4,461*	*141,297*
South Dakota	—	—	—	—	—	—	—	—
Tennessee	65,188	80,825	37,900	183,913	102,574	50,626	1,378	154,578
Tennessee	—	—	—	—	*102,574*	*51,561*	*443*	*154,578*
Texas	69,078	47,125	0	116,203	38,368	10,095	220	48,683
Utah	—	—	—	—	—	—	—	—
Vermont	6,797	39,534	2,943	49,274	8,203	24,437	9,327	41,967
Vermont	—	—	—	—	*8,203*	*33,764*	*0*	*41,967*
Virginia	0	78,371	112,152	190,523	93,956	76,927	7,399	178,282
Virginia	—	—	—	—	*100,716*	*77,371*	*195*	*178,282*
Washington	—	—	—	—	—	—	—	—
West Virginia	11,652	19,544	13,709	44,905	37,823	28,440	434	66,697
West Virginia	*25,013*	*19,544*	*348*	*44,905*	—	—	—	—
Wisconsin	88,055	105,143	0	193,198	0	93,127	93,484	186,611
Wisconsin	—	—	—	—	*93,484*	*93,127*	*0*	*186,611*
Wyoming	—	—	—	—	—	—	—	—

Notes: Main entries are raw vote values for candidates who used the sole designation "Democrat" or "Republican" (or their historical antecedents listed in Appendix A) on the ballot. Other = candidates who used third-party names on the ballot or were listed as independent, unidentified, or scatter vote. Bold italicized entries in the table are the author's alternative party coding, which is used when a candidate listed a major party name (Democrat, Republican, or their historical antecedents) on the ballot with other party names or labels. For a more detailed explanation of this alternate coding system, see Tables 5-1 and 1-3. —indicates that the state had no data, either because no vote data were found for the state in question or the state had not yet entered the Union. No special House elections are included in the table. The table only lists at-large vote values for states having both at-large and district House races; see Appendix B for these states' district results aggregated to the state level.

[1]Election held in odd-numbered year.

Sources: Adapted from *United States Congressional Elections, 1788–1997* (1998), *Congressional Quarterly's Guide to U.S. Elections* (1994), ICPSR data sets 0001 and 0075, and independent search for state sources by the author.

Table 5-92 House Election Results, by State, 1876–1879 (Raw Count)

State	1876–1877 Democratic	Republican	Other	Total Vote	1878–1879 Democratic	Republican	Other	Total Vote
Alabama	102,346	30,918	24,917	158,181	54,775	13,185	20,283	88,243
Alabama	*120,027*	*38,154*	*0*	*158,181*	—	—	—	—
Alaska	—	—	—	—	—	—	—	—
Arizona	—	—	—	—	—	—	—	—
Arkansas	49,688	26,342	9,542	85,572	44,655	21,162	12,007	77,824
Arkansas	*57,965*	*26,522*	*1,085*	*85,572*	*47,294*	*21,162*	*9,368*	*77,824*
California	74,228	81,043	0	155,271	47,915[1]	74,651[1]	34,208[1]	156,774[1]
Colorado	12,584	13,438	0	26,022	12,003	14,294	2,329	28,626
Connecticut	61,797	58,951	643	121,391	48,905	51,763	3,693	104,361
Delaware	13,169	10,592	236	23,997	10,576	0	2,966	13,542
Florida	24,733	24,139	0	48,872	21,169	17,929	464	39,562
Florida	—	—	—	—	*21,169*	*18,393*	*0*	*39,562*
Georgia	120,720	38,573	13,677	172,970	69,788	8,674	47,159	125,621
Georgia	*133,989*	*38,573*	*408*	*172,970*	*108,336*	*8,674*	*8,611*	*125,621*
Hawaii	—	—	—	—	—	—	—	—
Idaho	—	—	—	—	—	—	—	—
Illinois	266,341	268,527	15,273	550,141	174,150	194,470	81,397	450,017
Illinois	*266,341*	*274,518*	*9,282*	*550,141*	—	—	—	—
Indiana	212,619	206,535	12,737	431,891	175,513	171,017	60,837	407,367
Indiana	—	—	—	—	*194,233*	*180,729*	*32,405*	*407,367*
Iowa	118,414	168,289	5,549	292,252	54,996	131,790	73,551	260,337
Iowa	—	—	—	—	*87,836*	*131,790*	*40,711*	*260,337*
Kansas	15,649	76,611	29,535	121,795	36,355	74,714	26,733	137,802
Kentucky	150,901	93,825	8,249	252,975	94,017	50,720	15,419	160,156
Kentucky	*158,441*	*93,825*	*709*	*252,975*	*100,895*	*50,720*	*8,541*	*160,156*
Louisiana	84,388	76,385	0	160,773	78,661	21,997	16,897	117,555
Louisiana	—	—	—	—	*82,327*	*21,997*	*13,231*	*117,555*
Maine	60,514	74,772	550	135,836	20,737	56,296	47,445	124,478
Maine	—	—	—	—	*33,658*	*56,296*	*34,524*	*124,478*
Maryland	89,993	72,627	0	162,620	67,973	40,856	12,884	121,713
Maryland	—	—	—	—	*71,965*	*40,856*	*8,892*	*121,713*
Massachusetts	109,980	142,032	1,955	253,967	70,636	136,116	45,647	252,399
Massachusetts	*109,980*	*143,987*	*0*	*253,967*	*89,548*	*136,116*	*26,735*	*252,399*
Michigan	99,270	165,626	51,508	316,404	77,642	126,461	77,037	281,140
Michigan	*146,802*	*165,626*	*3,976*	*316,404*	—	—	—	—
Minnesota	51,772	68,563	2,879	123,214	14,467	53,298	32,420	100,185
Minnesota	—	—	—	—	*45,241*	*53,298*	*1,646*	*100,185*
Mississippi	113,655	50,917	0	164,572	37,128	8,396	7,026	52,550
Missouri	204,082	133,906	4,290	342,278	167,036	54,214	100,703	321,953
Missouri	*204,082*	*135,643*	*2,553*	*342,278*	*176,763*	*62,789*	*82,401*	*321,953*
Montana	—	—	—	—	—	—	—	—
Nebraska	17,206	30,900	3,579	51,685	0	28,341	21,752	50,093
Nebraska	—	—	—	—	*21,752*	*28,341*	*0*	*50,093*
Nevada	9,330	10,241	0	19,571	9,047	9,747	0	18,794
New Hampshire	37,866[1]	39,771[1]	253[1]	77,890[1]	31,442	38,195	5,855	75,492
New Jersey	115,168	91,579	12,420	219,167	65,328	90,514	39,995	195,837
New Jersey	*127,068*	*91,579*	*520*	*219,167*	*80,051*	*90,514*	*25,272*	*195,837*
New Mexico	—	—	—	—	—	—	—	—
New York	495,373	470,019	24,966	990,358	246,621	377,913	202,973	827,507
New York	*507,909*	*478,597*	*3,852*	*990,358*	*362,573*	*392,567*	*72,367*	*827,507*
North Carolina	121,515	104,534	0	226,049	68,263	27,258	34,374	129,895
North Carolina	—	—	—	—	*68,263*	*60,554*	*1,078*	*129,895*
North Dakota	—	—	—	—	—	—	—	—
Ohio	309,098	314,519	5,869	629,486	266,877	277,875	41,547	586,299
Oklahoma	—	—	—	—	—	—	—	—
Oregon	14,239	15,347	0	29,586	16,744	15,593	1,186	33,523
Pennsylvania	369,226	379,475	4,353	753,054	269,105	274,055	153,294	696,454
Pennsylvania	—	—	—	—	*280,949*	*313,265*	*102,240*	*696,454*
Rhode Island	10,371	15,700	54	26,125	5,872	11,541	886	18,299
South Carolina	91,559	91,143	0	182,702	116,919	45,031	0	161,950
South Dakota	—	—	—	—	—	—	—	—
Tennessee	133,727	81,366	1,841	216,934	83,641	34,413	28,306	146,360
Tennessee	*133,727*	*83,207*	*0*	*216,934*	*95,099*	*34,413*	*16,848*	*146,360*
Texas	102,532	29,378	13,277	145,187	166,958	0	50,603	217,561
Texas	*102,532*	*42,655*	*0*	*145,187*	—	—	—	—
Utah	—	—	—	—	—	—	—	—
Vermont	18,163	40,900	0	59,063	14,359	31,560	9,119	55,038
Vermont	—	—	—	—	*14,359*	*40,679*	*0*	*55,038*
Virginia	139,642	95,440	413	235,495	67,141	27,217	31,960	126,318
Virginia	*139,642*	*95,823*	*30*	*235,495*	*73,957*	*27,217*	*25,144*	*126,318*
Washington	—	—	—	—	—	—	—	—
West Virginia	56,350	43,069	0	99,419	50,318	36,248	8,318	94,884
Wisconsin	125,157	128,231	1,429	254,817	93,253	100,037	13,028	206,318
Wyoming	—	—	—	—	—	—	—	—

Notes: Main entries are raw vote values for candidates who used the sole designation "Democrat" or "Republican" (or their historical antecedents listed in Appendix A) on the ballot. Other = candidates who used third-party names on the ballot or were listed as independent, unidentified, or scatter vote. Bold italicized entries in the table are the author's alternative party coding, which is used when a candidate listed a major party name (Democrat, Republican, or their historical antecedents) on the ballot with other party names or labels. For a more detailed explanation of this alternate coding system, see Tables 5-1 and 1-3. —indicates that the state had no data, either because no vote data were found for the state in question or the state had not yet entered the Union. No special House elections are included in the table. The table only lists at-large vote values for states having both at-large and district House races; see Appendix B for these states' district results aggregated to the state level.

[1] Election held in odd-numbered year.

Sources: Adapted from *United States Congressional Elections, 1788–1997* (1998), *Congressional Quarterly's Guide to U.S. Elections* (1994), ICPSR data sets 0001 and 0075, and independent search for state sources by the author.

Table 5-93 House Election Results, by State, 1880–1882 (Raw Count)

State	1880				1882			
	Democratic	Republican	Other	Total Vote	Democratic	Republican	Other	Total Vote
Alabama	91,421	33,927	15,909	141,257	76,659	24,094	19,891	120,644
Alabama	—	—	—	—	*82,539*	*35,512*	*2,593*	*120,644*
Alaska	—	—	—	—	—	—	—	—
Arizona	—	—	—	—	—	—	—	—
Arkansas	55,438	40,597	9,651	105,686	43,619	21,422	0	65,041
Arkansas	*61,169*	*40,597*	*3,920*	*105,686*	—	—	—	—
California	39,320	79,796	44,486	163,602	87,259	73,647	3,915	164,821
California	*79,184*	*79,796*	*4,622*	*163,602*	—	—	—	—
Colorado	24,476	27,069	1,691	53,236	29,080	30,847	1,195	61,122
Connecticut	63,788	67,695	1,044	132,527	58,004	55,722	1,379	115,105
Delaware	14,966	14,336	132	29,434	16,563	14,640	0	31,203
Florida	28,076	23,035	127	51,238	24,059	20,098	3,547	47,704
Florida	—	—	—	—	*24,059*	*23,645*	*0*	*47,704*
Georgia	92,150	25,060	30,604	147,814	81,443	24,930	0	106,373
Georgia	*122,754*	*25,060*	*0*	*147,814*	—	—	—	—
Hawaii	—	—	—	—	—	—	—	—
Idaho	—	—	—	—	—	—	—	—
Illinois	279,242	317,962	23,149	620,353	235,153	233,799	57,220	526,172
Illinois	—	—	—	—	*266,569*	*233,799*	*25,804*	*526,172*
Indiana	224,750	229,620	15,168	469,538	220,920	207,174	11,187	439,281
Iowa	84,707	181,841	53,924	320,472	103,990	141,795	43,402	289,187
Iowa	*102,618*	*181,841*	*36,013*	*320,472*	*115,463*	*141,795*	*31,929*	*289,187*
Kansas	63,460	120,451	16,714	200,625	83,433	99,866	26,701	210,000
Kentucky	147,918	97,744	11,008	256,670	102,096	79,080	9,533	190,709
Kentucky	—	—	—	—	*110,801*	*79,080*	*828*	*190,709*
Louisiana	66,044	35,691	0	101,735	48,827	22,922	6,133	77,882
Louisiana	—	—	—	—	*48,827*	*29,012*	*43*	*77,882*
Maine	0	73,639	73,163	146,802	0	72,811	65,275	138,086
Maine	*72,799*	*73,639*	*364*	*146,802*	*63,366*	*73,076*	*1,644*	*138,086*
Maryland	91,131	80,313	826	172,270	80,725	74,520	1,864	157,109
Maryland	—	—	—	—	*82,301*	*74,520*	*288*	*157,109*
Massachusetts	111,833	164,280	4,563	280,676	94,860	130,220	31,451	256,531
Massachusetts	—	—	—	—	*119,776*	*130,220*	*6,535*	*256,531*
Michigan	131,122	183,796	37,196	352,114	0	157,519	154,915	312,434
Michigan	—	—	—	—	*148,242*	*157,519*	*6,673*	*312,434*
Minnesota	56,279	83,328	10,497	150,104	46,653	80,564	18,708	145,925
Minnesota	*56,279*	*90,984*	*2,841*	*150,104*	*46,653*	*92,802*	*6,470*	*145,925*
Mississippi	76,125	24,319	13,848	114,292	47,958	20,525	10,719	79,202
Mississippi	*76,125*	*30,512*	*7,655*	*114,292*	*48,479*	*20,525*	*10,198*	*79,202*
Missouri	213,135	38,254	124,287	375,676	194,666	116,659	56,208	367,533
Missouri	*214,905*	*134,075*	*26,696*	*375,676*	*214,753*	*122,164*	*30,616*	*367,533*
Montana	—	—	—	—	—	—	—	—
Nebraska	23,634	52,642	8,133	84,409	25,692	41,283	21,061	88,036
Nevada	9,815	8,578	0	18,393	7,720	6,462	0	14,182
New Hampshire	40,943	44,651	707	86,301	35,091	41,111	673	76,875
New Jersey	122,169	120,114	3,017	245,300	89,017	97,869	19,091	205,977
New Jersey	—	—	—	—	*100,054*	*97,869*	*8,054*	*205,977*
New Mexico	—	—	—	—	—	—	—	—
New York	459,164	533,655	87,060	1,079,879	503,954	394,232	25,281	923,467
New York	*530,758*	*533,655*	*15,466*	*1,079,879*	—	—	—	—
North Carolina	120,479	100,179	8,891	229,549	111,763	0	111,320	223,083
North Dakota	—	—	—	—	—	—	—	—
Ohio	340,562	362,040	8,599	711,201	316,975	296,574	15,786	629,335
Oklahoma	—	—	—	—	—	—	—	—
Oregon	18,181	19,578	300	38,059	19,152	22,517	0	41,669
Pennsylvania	342,036	444,790	79,957	866,783	352,855	323,255	66,038	742,148
Pennsylvania	*389,822*	*456,828*	*20,133*	*866,783*	—	—	—	—
Rhode Island	10,616	18,017	262	28,895	3,322	6,864	0	10,186
South Carolina	116,884	60,796	414	178,094	61,301	27,458	32,640	121,399
South Carolina	—	—	—	—	*61,360*	*53,188*	*6,851*	*121,399*
South Dakota	—	—	—	—	—	—	—	—
Tennessee	119,681	104,818	10,562	235,061	112,426	86,473	20,693	219,592
Tennessee	*126,776*	*104,818*	*3,467*	*235,061*	*120,332*	*95,294*	*3,966*	*219,592*
Texas	176,172	0	72,991	249,163	156,930	42,190	44,249	243,369
Utah	—	—	—	—	—	—	—	—
Vermont	19,660	44,269	2,120	66,049	12,372	33,475	1,255	47,102
Vermont	*19,660*	*44,775*	*1,614*	*66,049*	—	—	—	—
Virginia	96,532	49,094	48,092	193,718	94,184	4,342	99,992	198,518
Washington	—	—	—	—	—	—	—	—
West Virginia	57,114	49,012	5,003	111,129	45,171	41,227	5,006	91,404
Wisconsin	116,062	143,665	5,324	265,051	103,640	90,815	22,413	216,868
Wisconsin	—	—	—	—	*103,640*	*94,606*	*18,622*	*216,868*
Wyoming	—	—	—	—	—	—	—	—

Notes: Main entries are raw vote values for candidates who used the sole designation "Democrat" or "Republican" (or their historical antecedents listed in Appendix A) on the ballot. Other = candidates who used third-party names on the ballot or were listed as independent, unidentified, or scatter vote. Bold italicized entries in the table are the author's alternative party coding, which is used when a candidate listed a major party name (Democrat, Republican, or their historical antecedents) on the ballot with other party names or labels. For a more detailed explanation of this alternate coding system, see Tables 5-1 and 1-3. —indicates that the state had no data, either because no vote data were found for the state in question or the state had not yet entered the Union. No special House elections are included in the table. The table only lists at-large vote values for states having both at-large and district House races; see Appendix B for these states' district results aggregated to the state level.

Sources: Adapted from *United States Congressional Elections, 1788–1997* (1998), *Congressional Quarterly's Guide to U.S. Elections* (1994), ICPSR data sets 0001 and 0075, and independent search for state sources by the author.

Table 5-94   House Election Results, by State, 1884–1886 (Raw Count)

State	1884				1886			
	Democratic	Republican	Other	Total Vote	Democratic	Republican	Other	Total Vote
Alabama	93,404	46,268	1,638	141,310	62,211	21,917	2,535	86,663
Alabama	*93,404*	*46,951*	*955*	*141,310*	*62,211*	*24,436*	*16*	*86,663*
Alaska	—	—	—	—	—	—	—	—
Arizona	—	—	—	—	—	—	—	—
Arkansas	73,491	51,042	0	124,533	36,673	8,549	10,266	55,488
California	90,954	101,572	2,902	195,428	91,710	78,395	23,861	193,966
California					*91,710*	*93,921*	*8,335*	*193,966*
Colorado	28,720	35,446	2,489	66,655	26,929	27,732	3,597	58,258
Connecticut	66,658	67,235	3,593	137,486	58,581	57,234	7,190	123,005
Delaware	17,054	12,878	0	29,932	13,837	0	8,392	22,229
Florida	31,867	27,756	215	59,838	33,383	23,152	420	56,955
Florida	*31,867*	*27,971*	*0*	*59,838*				
Georgia	92,511	27,510	6,666	126,687	25,492	17	2,037	27,546
Georgia	*97,984*	*28,617*	*86*	*126,687*				
Hawaii	—	—	—	—	—	—	—	—
Idaho	—	—	—	—	—	—	—	—
Illinois	299,933	318,194	62,089	680,216	207,078	276,579	80,733	564,390
Illinois	*318,224*	*350,246*	*11,746*	*680,216*	*242,185*	*276,579*	*45,626*	*564,390*
Indiana	248,521	238,233	5,379	492,133	221,680	222,890	24,534	469,104
Indiana					*231,826*	*226,604*	*10,674*	*469,104*
Iowa	147,199	196,980	31,673	375,852	129,527	172,023	43,502	345,052
Iowa	*178,740*	*196,980*	*132*	*375,852*	*146,099*	*189,993*	*8,960*	*345,052*
Kansas	96,624	155,148	7,766	259,538	110,009	150,338	12,815	273,162
Kansas					*110,009*	*154,194*	*8,959*	*273,162*
Kentucky	147,635	97,104	8,101	252,840	111,244	83,258	14,200	208,702
Kentucky	*155,075*	*97,104*	*661*	*252,840*	*119,720*	*83,258*	*5,724*	*208,702*
Louisiana	60,978	35,509	9,971	106,458	63,097	20,793	807	84,697
Louisiana	*70,949*	*35,509*	*0*	*106,458*	*63,097*	*21,450*	*150*	*84,697*
Maine	59,706	78,115	3,474	141,295	52,656	69,126	6,512	128,294
Maryland	96,749	86,360	1,176	184,285	81,386	51,703	12,919	146,008
Maryland					*88,606*	*51,703*	*5,699*	*146,008*
Massachusetts	115,587	157,728	28,883	302,198	114,155	119,100	9,957	243,212
Michigan	64,646	189,282	145,475	399,403	173,376	183,134	22,985	379,495
Michigan	*191,614*	*189,282*	*18,507*	*399,403*				
Minnesota	77,310	108,412	3,219	188,941	81,573	126,000	7,900	215,473
Mississippi	81,932	29,723	0	111,655	35,560	10,998	176	46,734
Missouri	234,673	198,527	3,635	436,835	217,973	172,628	28,172	418,773
Missouri					*234,414*	*172,628*	*11,731*	*418,773*
Montana	—	—	—	—	—	—	—	—
Nebraska	59,990	69,811	2,772	132,573	60,654	66,463	9,339	136,456
Nevada	6,002	6,797	0	12,799	5,670	6,700	0	12,370
New Hampshire	38,085	42,670	1,812	82,567	36,919	37,980	2,174	77,073
New Jersey	127,614	124,800	7,720	260,134	101,264	102,766	27,339	231,369
New Jersey					*104,932*	*102,766*	*23,671*	*231,369*
New Mexico	—	—	—	—	—	—	—	—
New York	514,375	505,312	110,008	1,129,695	383,460	440,915	105,863	930,238
New York	*576,394*	*525,102*	*28,199*	*1,129,695*	*446,237*	*440,915*	*43,086*	*930,238*
North Carolina	140,894	119,448	0	260,342	115,837	44,872	51,710	212,419
North Carolina					*123,496*	*60,552*	*28,371*	*212,419*
North Dakota	—	—	—	—	—	—	—	—
Ohio	374,934	394,578	11,353	780,865	325,639	336,063	31,203	692,905
Oklahoma	—	—	—	—	—	—	—	—
Oregon	23,652	25,699	0	49,351	25,221	26,018	2,753	53,992
Pennsylvania	401,042	478,140	20,155	899,337	367,551	415,166	35,148	817,865
Rhode Island	11,971	17,992	2,313	32,276	7,803	8,485	1,599	17,887
South Carolina	67,804	20,369	1,377	89,550	32,969	5,961	58	38,988
South Dakota	—	—	—	—	—	—	—	—
Tennessee	132,669	117,679	2,298	252,646	125,369	99,164	7,811	232,344
Tennessee	*134,551*	*117,679*	*416*	*252,646*	*133,161*	*99,164*	*19*	*232,344*
Texas	251,128	41,917	12,732	305,777	213,836	23,070	51,642	288,548
Texas					*213,836*	*34,407*	*40,305*	*288,548*
Utah	—	—	—	—	—	—	—	—
Vermont	15,073	38,925	388	54,386	13,831	34,317	214	48,362
Virginia	145,106	134,338	6,451	285,895	102,490	102,145	20,414	225,049
Virginia	*145,106*	*140,789*	*0*	*285,895*	*113,306*	*102,145*	*9,598*	*225,049*
Washington	—	—	—	—	—	—	—	—
West Virginia	67,481	47,439	16,445	131,365	65,194	64,749	1,502	131,445
West Virginia	*67,481*	*63,884*	*0*	*131,365*				
Wisconsin	148,866	136,029	33,738	318,633	114,510	144,757	24,264	283,531
Wisconsin	*148,866*	*160,489*	*9,278*	*318,633*				
Wyoming	—	—	—	—	—	—	—	—

Notes: Main entries are raw vote values for candidates who used the sole designation "Democrat" or "Republican" (or their historical antecedents listed in Appendix A) on the ballot. Other = candidates who used third-party names on the ballot or were listed as independent, unidentified, or scatter vote. Bold italicized entries in the table are the author's alternative party coding, which is used when a candidate listed a major party name (Democrat, Republican, or their historical antecedents) on the ballot with other party names or labels. For a more detailed explanation of this alternate coding system, see Tables 5-1 and 1-3. —indicates that the state had no data, either because no vote data were found for the state in question or the state had not yet entered the Union. No special House elections are included in the table. The table only lists at-large vote values for states having both at-large and district House races; see Appendix B for these states' district results aggregated to the state level.

Sources: Adapted from *United States Congressional Elections, 1788–1997* (1998), *Congressional Quarterly's Guide to U.S. Elections* (1994), ICPSR data sets 0001 and 0075, and independent search for state sources by the author.

Table 5-95 House Election Results, by State, 1888–1890 (Raw Count)

	1888–1889				1890			
State	Democratic	Republican	Other	Total Vote	Democratic	Republican	Other	Total Vote
Alabama	117,673	54,547	1,004	173,224	82,150	24,390	11,849	118,389
Alaska	—	—	—	—	—	—	—	—
Arizona	—	—	—	—	—	—	—	—
Arkansas	89,576	17,011	49,789	156,376	69,768	7,488	35,448	112,704
Arkansas	—	—	—	—	*69,768*	*27,429*	*15,507*	*112,704*
California	116,069	126,646	6,368	249,083	98,872	128,061	24,602	251,535
California	—	—	—	—	*116,361*	*128,061*	*7,113*	*251,535*
Colorado	37,725	50,620	3,664	92,009	34,736	43,118	6,261	84,115
Connecticut	74,340	75,129	4,146	153,615	67,888	63,701	3,250	134,839
Delaware	16,396	12,935	387	29,718	17,848	17,180	257	35,285
Florida	39,836	27,134	0	66,970	29,267	15,209	0	44,476
Georgia	96,046	23,625	10,320	129,991	77,668	16,737	12,547	106,952
Georgia	—	—	—	—	*86,128*	*16,737*	*4,087*	*106,952*
Hawaii	—	—	—	—	—	—	—	—
Idaho	—	—	—	—	8,026	10,130	0	18,156
Illinois	324,865	372,138	48,650	745,653	342,042	311,320	22,263	675,625
Illinois	*347,562*	*372,138*	*25,953*	*745,653*	—	—	—	—
Indiana	238,426	264,365	32,807	535,598	239,204	216,209	15,733	471,146
Indiana	*259,987*	*264,365*	*11,246*	*535,598*	—	—	—	—
Iowa	167,203	196,248	39,424	402,875	194,832	185,785	8,458	389,075
Iowa	*184,384*	*212,090*	*6,401*	*402,875*	—	—	—	—
Kansas	103,629	182,375	41,968	327,972	27,010	122,682	141,013	290,705
Kentucky	182,037	154,413	4,029	340,479	125,485	56,333	13,129	194,947
Kentucky	—	—	—	—	*125,485*	*66,925*	*2,537*	*194,947*
Louisiana	86,435	26,817	244	113,496	59,801	12,873	1,559	74,233
Maine	60,970	79,744	4,204	144,918	45,313	63,489	3,310	112,112
Maryland	106,095	99,975	4,214	210,284	99,848	77,800	3,977	181,625
Massachusetts	137,529	179,841	24,658	342,028	137,079	129,651	13,302	280,032
Massachusetts	*150,917*	*179,841*	*11,270*	*342,028*	*137,079*	*133,189*	*9,764*	*280,032*
Michigan	196,994	236,898	39,954	473,846	186,649	177,021	31,092	394,762
Michigan	*215,090*	*236,898*	*21,858*	*473,846*	—	—	—	—
Minnesota	108,010	139,466	14,310	261,786	69,745	98,316	67,574	235,635
Minnesota	—	—	—	—	*107,249*	*98,316*	*30,070*	*235,635*
Mississippi	88,632	26,904	107	115,643	48,233	13,884	0	62,117
Missouri	261,196	235,668	19,808	516,672	253,736	184,337	25,024	463,097
Montana	18,264[1]	19,912[1]	0[1]	38,176[1]	15,411	15,128	551	31,090
Nebraska	81,838	106,073	14,041	201,952	54,729	72,879	83,891	211,499
Nebraska	—	—	—	—	*90,833*	*72,879*	*47,787*	*211,499*
Nevada	5,682	6,921	0	12,603	5,736	6,610	0	12,346
New Hampshire	43,935	45,271	1,417	90,623	42,870	41,375	1,186	85,431
New Jersey	144,160	146,035	13,155	303,350	128,417	114,808	8,425	251,650
New Jersey	*149,239*	*146,035*	*8,076*	*303,350*	—	—	—	—
New Mexico	—	—	—	—	—	—	—	—
New York	522,012	650,763	92,776	1,265,551	474,215	423,663	67,607	965,485
New York	*576,435*	*650,763*	*38,353*	*1,265,551*	*499,955*	*426,224*	*39,306*	*965,485*
North Carolina	148,344	130,680	239	279,263	149,266	104,599	1,628	255,493
North Carolina	—	—	—	—	*149,266*	*104,771*	*1,456*	*255,493*
North Dakota	12,066[1]	26,077[1]	0[1]	38,143[1]	14,830	21,365	0	36,195
Ohio	395,649	416,520	25,603	837,772	351,528	362,624	25,234	739,386
Oklahoma	—	—	—	—	—	—	—	—
Oregon	25,413	32,820	1,974	60,207	30,263	40,176	2,883	73,322
Pennsylvania	430,914	503,221	48,883	983,018	431,082	457,883	35,449	924,414
Pennsylvania	*446,464*	*515,791*	*20,763*	*983,018*	*441,119*	*468,519*	*14,776*	*924,414*
Rhode Island	17,033	22,032	1,271	40,336	18,706	16,868	1,191	36,765
South Carolina	65,915	10,031	302	76,248	58,805	13,069	1,485	73,359
South Carolina	*65,915*	*10,105*	*228*	*76,248*	*58,805*	*14,554*	*0*	*73,359*
South Dakota	23,229[1]	54,983[1]	0[1]	78,212[1]	17,527	34,856	24,907	77,290
Tennessee	159,506	136,914	3,029	299,449	105,023	70,320	19,517	194,860
Tennessee	—	—	—	—	*105,185*	*81,037*	*8,638*	*194,860*
Texas	239,711	48,063	52,220	339,994	257,393	59,597	2,687	319,677
Texas	*239,711*	*63,379*	*36,904*	*339,994*	—	—	—	—
Utah	—	—	—	—	—	—	—	—
Vermont	19,351	48,111	782	68,244	17,565	35,228	0	52,793
Virginia	151,889	150,579	693	303,161	126,254	48,561	13,811	188,626
Virginia	*152,087*	*150,807*	*267*	*303,161*	*136,435*	*49,351*	*2,840*	*188,626*
Washington	24,492[1]	34,039[1]	0[1]	58,531[1]	22,825	29,153	2,819	54,797
West Virginia	75,484	73,798	1,906	151,188	77,700	70,729	1,088	149,517
Wisconsin	119,405	179,603	54,466	353,474	161,901	128,179	11,134	301,214
Wisconsin	*156,566*	*179,603*	*17,305*	*353,474*	—	—	—	—
Wyoming	—	—	—	—	6,520	9,087	0	15,607

Notes: Main entries are raw vote values for candidates who used the sole designation "Democrat" or "Republican" (or their historical antecedents listed in Appendix A) on the ballot. Other = candidates who used third-party names on the ballot or were listed as independent, unidentified, or scatter vote. Bold italicized entries in the table are the author's alternative party coding, which is used when a candidate listed a major party name (Democrat, Republican, or their historical antecedents) on the ballot with other party names or labels. For a more detailed explanation of this alternate coding system, see Tables 5-1 and 1-3. —indicates that the state had no data, either because no vote data were found for the state in question or the state had not yet entered the Union. No special House elections are included in the table. The table only lists at-large vote values for states having both at-large and district House races; see Appendix B for these states' district results aggregated to the state level.

[1]Election held in odd-numbered year.

Sources: Adapted from *United States Congressional Elections, 1788–1997* (1998), *Congressional Quarterly's Guide to U.S. Elections* (1994), ICPSR data sets 0001 and 0075, and independent search for state sources by the author.

Table 5-96 House Election Results, by State, 1892–1895 (Raw Count)

State	1892				1894–1895			
	Democratic	Republican	Other	Total Vote	Democratic	Republican	Other	Total Vote
Alabama	136,500	11,269	84,782	232,551	73,299	15,473	38,772	127,544
Alabama	***221,109***	***11,269***	***173***	***232,551***	—	—	—	—
Alaska	—	—	—	—	—	—	—	—
Arizona	—	—	—	—	—	—	—	—
Arkansas	94,513	15,451	27,198	137,162	37,584	10,389	4,310	52,283
California	96,747	101,080	42,579	240,406	89,341	110,542	68,570	268,453
California	***117,427***	***101,080***	***21,899***	***240,406***	***96,152***	***110,542***	***61,759***	***268,453***
Colorado	2,240	37,181	53,114	92,535	49,550	90,079	38,877	178,506
Colorado	***53,833***	***37,181***	***1,521***	***92,535***	—	—	—	—
Connecticut	82,004	77,031	4,914	163,949	64,542	85,178	4,589	154,309
Delaware	18,554	18,080	509	37,143	18,492	19,789	651	38,932
Florida	30,781	0	4,775	35,556	21,626	0	4,469	26,095
Georgia	137,197	3,599	75,479	216,275	125,178	0	76,757	201,935
Georgia	***137,197***	***10,046***	***69,032***	***216,275***	—	—	—	—
Hawaii	—	—	—	—	—	—	—	—
Idaho	6,029	8,549	4,789	19,367	5,834	10,383	7,720	23,937
Illinois	425,336	399,307	47,530	872,173	312,837	448,075	90,477	851,389
Indiana	259,190	253,588	36,837	549,615	218,637	284,447	55,973	559,057
Indiana	—	—	—	—	***238,874***	***284,447***	***35,736***	***559,057***
Iowa	181,218	219,214	41,033	441,465	84,791	230,702	104,041	419,534
Iowa	***201,925***	***219,214***	***20,326***	***441,465***	***168,193***	***230,702***	***20,639***	***419,534***
Kansas	0	155,791	168,786	324,577	26,113	147,858	119,327	293,298
Kansas	***164,624***	***155,791***	***4,162***	***324,577***	—	—	—	—
Kentucky	174,359	121,960	25,294	321,613	160,407	153,420	26,319	340,146
Kentucky	—	—	—	—	***160,407***	***158,395***	***21,344***	***340,146***
Louisiana	85,060	0	28,694	113,754	77,650	27,056	9,339	114,045
Louisiana	***92,966***	***20,736***	***52***	***113,754***	—	—	—	—
Maine	54,142	65,637	7,902	127,681	30,502	69,457	7,959	107,918
Maine	***55,758***	***65,637***	***6,286***	***127,681***	—	—	—	—
Maryland	113,931	91,762	6,074	211,767	96,628	99,224	8,521	204,373
Massachusetts	164,782	187,046	20,421	372,249	113,939	188,142	25,066	327,147
Massachusetts	***174,289***	***187,046***	***10,914***	***372,249***	***122,807***	***189,329***	***15,011***	***327,147***
Michigan	137,639	222,783	105,389	465,811	112,893	234,329	60,786	408,008
Michigan	***210,692***	***222,783***	***32,336***	***465,811***	***130,489***	***234,329***	***43,190***	***408,008***
Minnesota	96,432	115,637	47,671	259,740	73,525	149,963	64,021	287,509
Mississippi	37,571	512	12,694	50,777	27,062	165	12,512	39,739
Missouri	266,865	227,652	38,211	532,728	220,217	231,783	46,792	498,792
Montana	17,762	17,934	7,628	43,324	10,369	23,140	15,759	49,268
Nebraska	47,992	82,842	65,429	196,263	18,947	98,241	81,268	198,456
Nebraska	***65,482***	***82,842***	***47,939***	***196,263***	***79,746***	***98,241***	***20,469***	***198,456***
Nevada	345	2,295	7,248	9,888	0	2,774	7,332	10,106
New Hampshire	41,408	42,456	1,689	85,553	33,629	46,146	2,173	81,948
New Jersey	166,796	158,191	9,895	334,882	115,345	163,823	17,048	296,216
New Mexico	—	—	—	—	—	—	—	—
New York	633,621	605,021	61,916	1,300,558	482,676	663,844	71,986	1,218,506
New York	—	—	—	—	***504,199***	***663,844***	***50,463***	***1,218,506***
North Carolina	132,844	70,332	67,699	270,875	126,692	50,182	100,317	277,191
North Carolina	—	—	—	—	***126,692***	***87,624***	***62,875***	***277,191***
North Dakota	11,021	17,695	7,434	36,150	0	21,615	17,382	38,997
Ohio	407,156	397,200	37,215	841,571	274,628	409,245	71,927	755,800
Ohio	***407,230***	***397,200***	***37,141***	***841,571***	—	—	—	—
Oklahoma	—	—	—	—	—	—	—	—
Oregon	25,139	34,588	15,921	75,648	19,803	41,140	25,224	86,167
Pennsylvania	448,714	512,557	27,917	989,188	328,677	0	613,949	942,626
Pennsylvania	—	—	—	—	***328,677***	***571,124***	***42,825***	***942,626***
Rhode Island	23,430	25,088	2,141	50,659	13,619	22,691	2,199	38,509
South Carolina	56,929	9,713	1,943	68,585	47,465	14,322	1,829	63,616
South Carolina	—	—	—	—	***48,628***	***14,322***	***666***	***63,616***
South Dakota	14,218	33,769	25,444	73,431	8,102	40,683	28,255	77,040
Tennessee	132,019	69,934	54,368	256,321	95,750	87,869	44,181	227,800
Tennessee	***142,902***	***81,159***	***32,260***	***256,321***	***95,750***	***101,060***	***30,990***	***227,800***
Texas	238,908	43,646	131,619	414,173	217,880	46,886	167,518	432,284
Texas	***238,908***	***73,108***	***102,157***	***414,173***	***223,660***	***46,886***	***161,738***	***432,284***
Utah	—	—	—	—	19,666[1]	20,563[1]	1,150[1]	41,379[1]
Vermont	18,045	34,995	1,281	54,321	13,645	41,883	0	55,528
Virginia	165,629	38,749	79,817	284,195	113,439	88,846	12,460	214,745
Virginia	***165,629***	***47,343***	***71,223***	***284,195***	—	—	—	—
Washington	30,659	35,434	22,495	88,588	14,602	35,981	26,605	77,188
West Virginia	85,808	80,538	4,051	170,397	76,057	89,518	4,350	169,925
Wisconsin	175,841	171,542	19,913	367,296	119,938	200,517	48,030	368,485
Wisconsin	—	—	—	—	***134,546***	***200,517***	***33,422***	***368,485***
Wyoming	8,855	8,394	0	17,249	6,152	10,068	2,906	19,126

Notes: Main entries are raw vote values for candidates who used the sole designation "Democrat" or "Republican" (or their historical antecedents listed in Appendix A) on the ballot. Other = candidates who used third-party names on the ballot or were listed as independent, unidentified, or scatter vote. Bold italicized entries in the table are the author's alternative party coding, which is used when a candidate listed a major party name (Democrat, Republican, or their historical antecedents) on the ballot with other party names or labels. For a more detailed explanation of this alternate coding system, see Tables 5-1 and 1-3. —indicates that the state had no data, either because no vote data were found for the state in question or the state had not yet entered the Union. No special House elections are included in the table. The table only lists at-large vote values for states having both at-large and district House races; see Appendix B for these states' district results aggregated to the state level.

[1]Election held in odd-numbered year.

Sources: Adapted from *United States Congressional Elections, 1788–1997* (1998), *Congressional Quarterly's Guide to U.S. Elections* (1994), ICPSR data sets 0001 and 0075, and independent search for state sources by the author.

Table 5-97 House Election Results, by State, 1896–1898 (Raw Count)

State	1896				1898			
	Democratic	Republican	Other	Total Vote	Democratic	Republican	Other	Total Vote
Alabama	104,078	9,263	71,969	185,310	66,556	24,000	254	90,810
Alabama	*123,939*	*36,980*	*24,391*	*185,310*	*66,556*	*24,254*	*0*	*90,810*
Alaska	—	—	—	—	—	—	—	—
Arizona	—	—	—	—	—	—	—	—
Arkansas	109,649	41,725	0	151,374	24,473	2,706	0	27,179
California	129,789	128,941	19,366	278,096	128,106	139,382	5,573	273,061
California					*128,700*	*139,382*	*4,979*	*273,061*
Colorado	0	24,010	155,371	179,381	0	18,580	125,908	144,488
Colorado	*151,839*	*24,010*	*3,532*	*179,381*	*95,483*	*46,163*	*2,842*	*144,488*
Connecticut	56,594	109,494	8,288	174,376	63,337	81,747	4,140	149,224
Connecticut	*61,825*	*109,494*	*3,057*	*174,376*	—	—	—	—
Delaware	15,407	7,123	12,465	34,995	15,053	17,566	454	33,073
Delaware	*16,251*	*18,282*	*462*	*34,995*	—	—	—	—
Florida	29,199	9,431	3,715	42,345	25,656	7,316	0	32,972
Florida	*30,355*	*9,431*	*2,559*	*42,345*	—	—	—	—
Georgia	99,816	35,908	34,923	170,647	55,962	7,037	5,613	68,612
Hawaii	—	—	—	—	—	—	—	—
Idaho	13,787	6,054	9,034	28,875	0	13,056	26,036	39,092
Idaho	*13,787*	*15,088*	*0*	*28,875*	*0*	*30,750*	*8,342*	*39,092*
Illinois	461,591	600,667	18,394	1,080,652	390,887	463,298	19,538	873,723
Illinois	*464,354*	*600,667*	*15,631*	*1,080,652*	—	—	—	—
Indiana	303,768	321,250	5,634	630,652	273,097	283,306	9,637	566,040
Indiana	*304,525*	*321,250*	*4,877*	*630,652*	—	—	—	—
Iowa	226,246	287,951	2,940	517,137	177,797	233,456	8,741	419,994
Kansas	168,420	158,147	1,501	328,068	130,801	147,691	2,651	281,143
Kentucky	204,372	193,577	38,636	436,585	138,344	119,461	15,909	273,714
Kentucky	*223,777*	*193,577*	*19,231*	*436,585*	*138,344*	*131,126*	*4,244*	*273,714*
Louisiana	64,509	2,547	30,222	97,278	27,728	3,920	1,627	33,275
Louisiana	*64,509*	*21,940*	*10,829*	*97,278*	—	—	—	—
Maine	34,404	83,947	5,870	124,221	26,366	54,981	2,408	83,755
Maine	—	—	—	—	*26,455*	*54,981*	*2,319*	*83,755*
Maryland	106,832	135,423	6,234	248,489	100,874	106,927	8,699	216,500
Maryland	—	—	—	—	*101,448*	*106,927*	*8,125*	*216,500*
Massachusetts	117,202	246,269	10,462	373,933	123,640	176,262	12,609	312,511
Massachusetts	*123,556*	*249,384*	*993*	*373,933*	*128,640*	*176,674*	*7,197*	*312,511*
Michigan	240,563	291,697	2,180	534,440	176,863	232,535	6,372	415,770
Minnesota	146,574	187,566	5,557	339,697	102,842	136,797	10,034	249,673
Mississippi	50,094	2,082	14,188	66,364	22,412	953	3,948	27,313
Mississippi	*50,873*	*4,353*	*11,138*	*66,364*	*23,802*	*1,316*	*2,195*	*27,313*
Missouri	339,139	304,101	21,437	664,677	285,019	255,796	10,261	551,076
Missouri	—	—	—	—	*285,019*	*256,434*	*9,623*	*551,076*
Montana	0	9,492	33,932	43,424	23,351	14,829	11,607	49,787
Montana	*0*	*43,424*	*0*	*43,424*	*23,351*	*26,436*	*0*	*49,787*
Nebraska	112,998	100,076	3,363	216,437	0	93,509	94,934	188,443
Nebraska	—	—	—	—	*94,884*	*93,509*	*50*	*188,443*
Nevada	6,429	1,319	1,948	9,696	5,766	0	3,111	8,877
New Hampshire	27,805	52,360	2,087	82,252	35,784	43,768	1,689	81,241
New Jersey	133,318	199,977	35,775	369,070	154,658	165,120	12,300	332,078
New Jersey	*138,538*	*220,471*	*10,061*	*369,070*	—	—	—	—
New Mexico	—	—	—	—	—	—	—	—
New York	515,830	785,909	67,564	1,369,303	621,329	658,934	43,801	1,324,064
New York	*544,172*	*786,417*	*38,714*	*1,369,303*	*621,646*	*658,934*	*43,484*	*1,324,064*
North Carolina	146,970	37,971	142,891	327,832	171,070	36,928	123,624	331,622
North Carolina	*146,970*	*177,552*	*3,310*	*327,832*	*171,070*	*143,085*	*17,467*	*331,622*
North Dakota	0	25,233	21,521	46,754	0	27,776	17,844	45,620
North Dakota	*21,172*	*25,233*	*349*	*46,754*	*17,844*	*27,776*	*0*	*45,620*
Ohio	472,986	524,682	7,012	1,004,680	356,169	404,659	9,762	770,590
Oklahoma	—	—	—	—	—	—	—	—
Oregon	15,013	31,972	42,469	89,454	0	42,615	40,260	82,875
Oregon	—	—	—	—	*33,921*	*42,615*	*6,339*	*82,875*
Pennsylvania	413,800	711,246	35,199	1,160,245	350,213	532,898	58,736	941,847
Rhode Island	16,630	33,990	2,809	53,429	13,206	21,309	3,578	38,093
South Carolina	59,930	4,876	3,773	68,579	28,967	2,804	0	31,771
South Carolina	*59,930*	*8,627*	*22*	*68,579*	—	—	—	—
South Dakota	41,125	40,943	723	82,791	0	38,760	33,196	71,956
South Dakota	—	—	—	—	*32,314*	*38,760*	*882*	*71,956*
Tennessee	156,771	116,135	42,187	315,093	106,638	63,923	6,364	176,925
Tennessee	*167,327*	*129,220*	*18,546*	*315,093*	—	—	—	—
Texas	288,036	105,829	141,382	535,247	256,091	68,945	81,990	407,026
Texas	*296,251*	*121,018*	*117,978*	*535,247*	—	—	—	—
Utah	47,456	0	30,092	77,548	35,646	29,603	2,878	68,127
Utah	*47,456*	*27,813*	*2,279*	*77,548*	—	—	—	—
Vermont	13,895	52,464	572	66,931	13,993	38,078	0	52,071
Virginia	160,830	124,228	16,518	301,576	105,554	59,412	8,597	173,563
Virginia	*174,765*	*125,235*	*1,576*	*301,576*	*108,485*	*63,100*	*1,978*	*173,563*
Washington	0	38,196	52,721	90,917	0	39,835	38,479	78,314
West Virginia	94,743	104,544	261	199,548	85,407	87,999	1,003	174,409
Wisconsin	165,327	267,226	5,096	437,649	136,257	191,274	14,246	341,777
Wyoming	10,310	10,044	628	20,982	8,466	10,762	443	19,671

Notes: Main entries are raw vote values for candidates who used the sole designation "Democrat" or "Republican" (or their historical antecedents listed in Appendix A) on the ballot. Other = candidates who used third-party names on the ballot or were listed as independent, unidentified, or scatter vote. Bold italicized entries in the table are the author's alternative party coding, which is used when a candidate listed a major party name (Democrat, Republican, or their historical antecedents) on the ballot with other party names or labels. For a more detailed explanation of this alternate coding system, see Tables 5-1 and 1-3. —indicates that the state had no data, either because no vote data were found for the state in question or the state had not yet entered the Union. No special House elections are included in the table. The table only lists at-large vote values for states having both at-large and district House races; see Appendix B for these states' district results aggregated to the state level.

Sources: Adapted from *United States Congressional Elections, 1788–1997* (1998), *Congressional Quarterly's Guide to U.S. Elections* (1994), ICPSR data sets 0001 and 0075, and independent search for state sources by the author.

Table 5-98 House Election Results, by State, 1900–1902 (Raw Count)

State	1900 Democratic	1900 Republican	1900 Other	1900 Total Vote	1902 Democratic	1902 Republican	1902 Other	1902 Total Vote
Alabama	104,626	33,124	3,440	141,190	69,867	21,315	304	91,486
Alabama	*104,626*	*36,303*	*261*	*141,190*	*69,867*	*21,380*	*239*	*91,486*
Alaska	—	—	—	—	—	—	—	—
Arizona	—	—	—	—	—	—	—	—
Arkansas	84,319	42,650	0	126,969	32,821	6,587	9	39,417
California	120,411	157,440	14,213	292,064	87,432	152,373	51,222	291,027
California					*126,290*	*152,373*	*12,364*	*291,027*
Colorado	0	92,805	124,395	217,200	84,367	85,217	15,463	185,047
Colorado	*121,598*	*92,805*	*2,797*	*217,200*	—	—	—	—
Connecticut	74,989	102,559	3,470	181,018	70,590	83,666	4,932	159,188
Delaware	19,157	22,353	602	42,112	16,396	8,028	13,783	38,207
Delaware					*16,396*	*21,026*	*785*	*38,207*
Florida	26,451	5,254	0	31,705	16,724	0	0	16,724
Georgia	83,504	11,605	10,625	105,734	40,467	0	880	41,347
Hawaii	—	—	—	—	—	—	—	—
Idaho	0	26,860	28,079	54,939	24,878	32,384	2,374	59,636
Idaho	*28,079*	*26,860*	*0*	*54,939*				
Illinois	502,227	591,886	24,673	1,118,786	373,490	406,582	35,340	815,412
Indiana	312,014	330,813	12,534	655,361	273,246	291,459	21,104	585,809
Iowa	212,649	304,302	8,064	525,015	158,849	223,021	11,803	393,673
Kansas	160,980	180,162	3,520	344,662	115,342	158,307	8,332	281,981
Kentucky	232,937	228,676	1,542	463,155	157,471	124,953	9,425	291,849
Louisiana	52,725	14,554	0	67,279	22,218	4,047	0	26,265
Maine	40,485	72,901	4,112	117,498	38,631	65,491	3,098	107,220
Maine	*40,485*	*72,947*	*4,066*	*117,498*	—	—	—	—
Maryland	122,778	135,474	5,359	263,611	91,546	100,054	5,583	197,183
Maryland	*123,492*	*135,546*	*4,573*	*263,611*	—	—	—	—
Massachusetts	151,388	222,299	18,348	392,035	139,703	191,770	58,243	389,716
Massachusetts	—	—	—	—	*160,064*	*191,770*	*37,882*	*389,716*
Michigan	216,664	312,911	11,706	541,281	155,732	228,399	8,760	392,891
Minnesota	127,947	180,356	9,633	317,936	91,291	158,962	14,716	264,969
Mississippi	47,849	2,565	1,110	51,524	18,058	0	0	18,058
Missouri	354,180	313,563	5,405	673,148	274,220	230,649	5,166	510,035
Montana	28,130	23,207	10,056	61,393	19,560	24,626	9,138	53,324
Montana	*37,573*	*23,207*	*613*	*61,393*				
Nebraska	0	113,191	114,571	227,762	0	98,367	94,548	192,915
Nebraska	*110,119*	*113,191*	*4,452*	*227,762*	*89,234*	*98,367*	*5,314*	*192,915*
Nevada	5,975	4,190	0	10,165	0	5,073	5,848	10,921
Nevada	—	—	—	—	*5,848*	*5,073*	*0*	*10,921*
New Hampshire	34,908	53,502	1,817	90,227	30,204	44,629	2,154	76,987
New Jersey	165,370	220,350	13,667	399,387	164,199	183,576	12,907	360,682
New Mexico	—	—	—	—	—	—	—	—
New York	666,943	805,574	40,565	1,513,082	651,067	661,243	52,525	1,364,835
New York	—	—	—	—	*651,325*	*661,243*	*52,267*	*1,364,835*
North Carolina	162,260	111,247	18,260	291,767	135,277	59,166	2,328	196,771
North Carolina	*162,260*	*115,634*	*13,873*	*291,767*				
North Dakota	21,175	34,887	1,119	57,181	14,765	32,986	1,195	48,946
Ohio	479,168	537,026	12,928	1,029,122	337,758	439,765	32,465	809,988
Ohio	*479,168*	*541,265*	*8,689*	*1,029,122*	—	—	—	—
Oklahoma	—	—	—	—	—	—	—	—
Oregon	0	43,300	39,647	82,947	31,811	46,982	9,471	88,264
Oregon	*34,285*	*43,300*	*5,362*	*82,947*				
Pennsylvania	411,552	683,941	32,290	1,127,783	261,193	385,755	355,527	1,002,475
Pennsylvania	—	—	—	—	*335,607*	*619,753*	*47,115*	*1,002,475*
Rhode Island	18,751	30,961	3,231	52,943	27,855	28,215	2,185	58,255
South Carolina	47,929	3,178	0	51,107	31,343	742	5	32,090
South Dakota	0	53,583	42,188	95,771	21,113	48,454	5,057	74,624
South Dakota	*40,560*	*53,583*	*1,628*	*95,771*	—	—	—	—
Tennessee	143,930	109,278	12,712	265,920	98,787	53,303	343	152,433
Tennessee	—	—	—	—	*98,787*	*53,646*	*0*	*152,433*
Texas	307,202	83,291	21,371	411,864	283,196	57,721	1,814	342,731
Utah	45,939	46,180	710	92,829	38,196	43,710	2,938	84,844
Vermont	16,732	46,118	1,305	64,155	8,544	33,539	2,042	44,125
Virginia	165,705	98,728	5,220	269,653	82,526	39,366	1,231	123,123
Virginia	—	—	—	—	*82,526*	*39,514*	*1,083*	*123,123*
Washington	45,448	55,393	5,115	105,956	34,315	59,366	7,240	100,921
West Virginia	100,496	118,223	1,001	219,720	88,350	100,356	3,394	192,100
Wisconsin	163,824	261,537	14,422	439,783	136,859	195,096	22,771	354,726
Wyoming	10,017	14,539	0	24,556	8,892	15,808	0	24,700

Notes: Main entries are raw vote values for candidates who used the sole designation "Democrat" or "Republican" (or their historical antecedents listed in Appendix A) on the ballot. Other = candidates who used third-party names on the ballot or were listed as independent, unidentified, or scatter vote. Bold italicized entries in the table are the author's alternative party coding, which is used when a candidate listed a major party name (Democrat, Republican, or their historical antecedents) on the ballot with other party names or labels. For a more detailed explanation of this alternate coding system, see Tables 5-1 and 1-3. —indicates that the state had no data, either because no vote data were found for the state in question or the state had not yet entered the Union. No special House elections are included in the table. The table only lists at-large vote values for states having both at-large and district House races; see Appendix B for these states' district results aggregated to the state level.

Sources: Adapted from *United States Congressional Elections, 1788–1997* (1998), *Congressional Quarterly's Guide to U.S. Elections* (1994), ICPSR data sets 0001 and 0075, and independent search for state sources by the author.

Table 5-99 House Election Results, by State, 1904–1907 (Raw Count)

	1904				1906–1907			
State	Democratic	Republican	Other	Total Vote	Democratic	Republican	Other	Total Vote
Alabama	82,826	19,551	426	102,803	59,548	5,982	11	65,541
Alaska	—	—	—	—	—	—	—	—
Arizona	—	—	—	—	—	—	—	—
Arkansas	77,460	32,517	0	109,977	38,472	12,511	31	51,014
California	99,775	186,427	41,924	328,126	97,314	159,897	28,120	285,331
California	*112,587*	*186,427*	*29,112*	*328,126*	*100,330*	*159,897*	*25,104*	*285,331*
Colorado	112,373	121,236	7,923	241,532	76,792	102,426	16,994	196,212
Connecticut	75,212	108,918	6,794	190,924	67,747	88,115	5,037	160,899
Delaware	19,552	23,512	750	43,814	17,118	20,210	916	38,244
Florida	25,592	6,010	1,157	32,759	20,419	1,179	1,351	22,949
Georgia	95,979	20,078	396	116,453	32,912	429	3	33,344
Hawaii	—	—	—	—	—	—	—	—
Idaho	20,146	44,813	5,436	70,395	23,818	42,134	5,963	71,915
Illinois	343,125	608,691	107,340	1,059,156	312,082	435,985	77,419	825,486
Illinois	*344,266*	*613,866*	*101,024*	*1,059,156*	—	—	—	—
Indiana	288,706	353,087	29,369	671,162	276,163	282,827	24,078	583,068
Iowa	161,801	295,258	20,221	477,280	168,844	224,341	12,951	406,136
Kansas	105,479	187,983	18,166	311,628	127,715	165,210	12,503	305,428
Kentucky	219,749	204,484	5,387	429,620	155,815	124,044	8,734	288,593
Louisiana	47,388	4,632	412	52,432	32,701	3,962	603	37,266
Maine	50,383	76,519	2,192	129,094	61,196	70,022	2,184	133,402
Maryland	99,180	103,992	4,918	208,090	92,366	99,266	7,523	199,155
Maryland	*99,180*	*104,435*	*4,475*	*208,090*	—	—	—	—
Massachusetts	152,142	235,365	24,125	411,632	159,382	228,536	15,198	403,116
Michigan	158,146	344,043	12,677	514,866	83,432	232,662	11,586	327,680
Minnesota	73,260	205,639	5,252	284,151	64,944	171,349	16,413	252,706
Mississippi	52,797	91	449	53,337	20,100	0	173	20,273
Missouri	304,391	317,003	9,855	631,249	291,276	286,132	7,968	585,376
Montana	0	32,957	30,754	63,711	0	0	56,161	56,161
Montana	*26,729*	*32,957*	*4,025*	*63,711*	*22,894*	*28,368*	*4,899*	*56,161*
Nebraska	0	123,986	100,292	224,278	11,644	98,903	77,000	187,547
Nebraska	*89,959*	*123,986*	*10,333*	*224,278*	*84,449*	*98,903*	*4,195*	*187,547*
Nevada	0	5,301	6,097	11,398	1,251	5,665	7,320	14,236
Nevada	*5,525*	*5,301*	*572*	*11,398*	*8,571*	*5,665*	*0*	*14,236*
New Hampshire	33,328	52,112	1,705	87,145	31,270	45,774	1,990	79,034
New Jersey	173,217	236,218	21,351	430,786	149,860	172,261	36,235	358,356
New Jersey	—	—	—	—	*169,068*	*172,261*	*17,027*	*358,356*
New Mexico	—	—	—	—	—	—	—	—
New York	661,896	841,418	63,581	1,566,895	356,318	700,000	393,956	1,450,274
New York	—	—	—	—	*638,932*	*700,000*	*111,342*	*1,450,274*
North Carolina	130,038	78,693	120	208,851	124,696	77,747	188	202,631
North Dakota	15,622	49,111	2,721	67,454	21,350	38,923	1,151	61,424
Ohio	354,803	581,376	49,389	985,568	330,644	407,698	33,270	771,612
Ohio	—	—	—	—	*333,465*	*407,698*	*30,449*	*771,612*
Oklahoma	—	—	—	—	136,096[1]	101,668[1]	5,083[1]	242,847[1]
Oregon	29,930	51,096	12,880	93,906	31,491	51,435	10,535	93,461
Pennsylvania	279,813	729,760	95,976	1,105,549	215,484	252,892	490,746	959,122
Pennsylvania	*319,647*	*729,760*	*56,142*	*1,105,549*	*331,717*	*561,090*	*66,315*	*959,122*
Rhode Island	28,861	33,662	1,072	63,595	31,439	33,009	1,052	65,500
South Carolina	54,671	2,473	0	57,144	28,874	436	20	29,330
South Dakota	22,692	70,002	7,343	100,037	19,976	48,010	5,831	73,817
Tennessee	128,452	99,439	681	228,572	111,480	80,343	8,270	200,093
Tennessee	—	—	—	—	*111,480*	*87,043*	*1,570*	*200,093*
Texas	204,772	43,124	1,933	249,829	152,885	20,153	2,552	175,590
Texas	—	—	—	—	*152,885*	*20,359*	*2,346*	*175,590*
Utah	37,445	52,675	11,619	101,739	27,021	42,565	14,471	84,057
Vermont	15,934	46,989	1,866	64,789	17,114	41,398	1,017	59,529
Virginia	86,361	44,100	1,559	132,020	55,259	30,558	240	86,057
Virginia	*86,361*	*44,873*	*786*	*132,020*	—	—	—	—
Washington	35,698	93,328	13,384	142,410	31,811	71,921	11,015	114,747
West Virginia	104,896	128,437	5,746	239,079	77,157	98,275	7,199	182,631
Wisconsin	150,376	250,609	36,023	437,008	112,560	170,839	27,451	310,850
Wisconsin	—	—	—	—	*112,560*	*170,893*	*27,397*	*310,850*
Wyoming	9,903	19,862	976	30,741	8,944	16,813	1,292	27,049

Notes: Main entries are raw vote values for candidates who used the sole designation "Democrat" or "Republican" (or their historical antecedents listed in Appendix A) on the ballot. Other = candidates who used third-party names on the ballot or were listed as independent, unidentified, or scatter vote. Bold italicized entries in the table are the author's alternative party coding, which is used when a candidate listed a major party name (Democrat, Republican, or their historical antecedents) on the ballot with other party names or labels. For a more detailed explanation of this alternate coding system, see Tables 5-1 and 1-3. —indicates that the state had no data, either because no vote data were found for the state in question or the state had not yet entered the Union. No special House elections are included in the table. The table only lists at-large vote values for states having both at-large and district House races; see Appendix B for these states' district results aggregated to the state level.

[1]Election held in odd-numbered year.

Sources: Adapted from *United States Congressional Elections, 1788–1997* (1998), *Congressional Quarterly's Guide to U.S. Elections* (1994), ICPSR data sets 0001 and 0075, and independent search for state sources by the author.

Table 5-100 House Election Results, by State, 1908–1911 (Raw Count)

State	1908				1910–1911			
	Democratic	Republican	Other	Total Vote	Democratic	Republican	Other	Total Vote
Alabama	81,629	19,118	359	101,106	82,278	14,976	68	97,322
Alaska	—	—	—	—	—	—	—	—
Arizona	—	—	—	—	11,556[1]	8,485[1]	1,340[1]	21,381[1]
Arkansas	104,861	48,081	0	152,942	31,527	9,236	0	40,763
California	134,699	202,309	34,559	371,567	111,620	169,723	81,605	362,948
California	—	—	—	—	***111,620***	***204,014***	***47,314***	***362,948***
Colorado	126,934	121,265	14,349	262,548	105,700	101,722	13,309	220,731
Connecticut	70,029	111,557	8,662	190,248	73,221	79,585	13,347	166,153
Delaware	22,515	24,314	1,168	47,997	20,281	22,410	1,331	44,022
Florida	30,011	6,254	2,752	39,017	30,995	1,372	5,185	37,552
Georgia	96,226	427	0	96,653	33,308	2,285	10,167	45,760
Georgia	—	—	—	—	***43,361***	***2,285***	***114***	***45,760***
Hawaii	—	—	—	—	—	—	—	—
Idaho	37,605	49,983	8,451	96,039	31,832	46,401	5,463	83,696
Illinois	458,117	614,396	68,705	1,141,218	412,333	424,466	66,774	903,573
Indiana	351,658	334,224	25,949	711,831	312,153	277,636	31,844	621,633
Iowa	198,031	253,826	12,588	464,445	157,504	207,272	9,917	374,693
Kansas	166,452	199,561	15,804	381,817	116,225	162,880	16,044	295,149
Kentucky	242,589	230,988	5,396	478,973	175,574	147,372	6,046	328,992
Louisiana	63,891	5,341	1,523	70,755	46,069	3,874	1,070	51,013
Maine	64,493	75,307	2,801	142,601	70,542	67,563	2,569	140,674
Maryland	106,792	100,611	4,866	212,269	101,663	95,230	7,647	204,540
Massachusetts	147,778	249,206	25,382	422,366	203,619	203,136	19,482	426,237
Massachusetts	—	—	—	—	***213,656***	***203,136***	***9,445***	***426,237***
Michigan	192,437	323,403	14,980	530,820	146,701	212,663	15,523	374,887
Minnesota	87,768	195,812	27,893	311,473	67,474	180,124	17,607	265,205
Mississippi	59,317	384	0	59,701	23,865	0	23	23,888
Missouri	349,047	347,362	14,696	711,105	305,092	296,636	69,011	670,739
Missouri	—	—	—	—	***328,216***	***318,587***	***23,936***	***670,739***
Montana	29,032	32,819	5,318	67,169	28,071	32,519	5,184	65,774
Nebraska	18,781	128,896	116,407	264,084	15,912	115,065	103,491	234,468
Nebraska	***131,027***	***128,896***	***4,161***	***264,084***	***113,505***	***115,065***	***5,898***	***234,468***
Nevada	11,253	7,552	4,996	23,801	7,688	10,066	2,409	20,163
New Hampshire	34,066	50,420	2,317	86,803	37,006	42,580	1,260	80,846
New Jersey	206,808	241,619	13,824	462,251	225,817	187,842	16,901	430,560
New Mexico	—	—	—	—	29,999[1]	30,162[1]	1,845[1]	62,006[1]
New York	707,542	827,619	96,367	1,631,528	527,921	548,825	345,183	1,421,929
New York	—	—	—	—	***695,543***	***650,334***	***76,052***	***1,421,929***
North Carolina	143,840	108,592	422	252,854	141,049	94,430	443	235,922
North Dakota	29,426	57,357	591	87,374	25,880	51,556	3,225	80,661
Ohio	494,235	532,914	90,360	1,117,509	454,224	383,745	64,464	902,433
Ohio	***524,086***	***532,914***	***60,509***	***1,117,509***	—	—	—	—
Oklahoma	122,804	109,413	20,766	252,983	118,348	93,206	22,900	234,454
Oregon	28,706	67,468	14,078	110,252	37,709	56,898	18,603	113,210
Pennsylvania	395,485	451,290	259,800	1,106,575	170,741	315,028	455,829	941,598
Pennsylvania	***403,098***	***641,947***	***61,530***	***1,106,575***	***312,803***	***478,276***	***150,519***	***941,598***
Rhode Island	30,775	39,596	2,270	72,641	31,236	34,664	1,452	67,352
South Carolina	63,732	1,682	0	65,414	30,787	370	18	31,175
South Dakota	38,758	67,582	6,516	112,856	32,655	64,777	5,780	103,212
Tennessee	125,954	104,887	1,518	232,359	142,718	72,700	11,051	226,469
Tennessee	***126,142***	***104,887***	***1,330***	***232,359***	***147,887***	***73,640***	***4,942***	***226,469***
Texas	235,846	46,001	5,027	286,874	182,187	17,260	7,806	207,253
Utah	35,981	57,544	17,927	111,452	32,730	50,614	18,899	102,243
Vermont	14,942	45,058	1,412	61,412	14,441	37,136	837	52,414
Virginia	90,356	49,338	317	140,011	67,570	31,610	1,631	100,811
Virginia	***90,401***	***49,370***	***240***	***140,011***	—	—	—	—
Washington	56,322	107,862	3,666	167,850	44,827	78,291	15,125	138,243
West Virginia	113,579	135,674	8,220	257,473	103,293	94,457	11,834	209,584
Wisconsin	167,277	240,195	31,454	438,926	106,431	161,169	41,727	309,327
Wyoming	13,643	21,431	2,486	37,560	14,659	20,312	2,155	37,126

Notes: Main entries are raw vote values for candidates who used the sole designation "Democrat" or "Republican" (or their historical antecedents listed in Appendix A) on the ballot. Other = candidates who used third-party names on the ballot or were listed as independent, unidentified, or scatter vote. Bold italicized entries in the table are the author's alternative party coding, which is used when a candidate listed a major party name (Democrat, Republican, or their historical antecedents) on the ballot with other party names or labels. For a more detailed explanation of this alternate coding system, see Tables 5-1 and 1-3. —indicates that the state had no data, either because no vote data were found for the state in question or the state had not yet entered the Union. No special House elections are included in the table. The table only lists at-large vote values for states having both at-large and district House races; see Appendix B for these states' district results aggregated to the state level.

[1] Election held in odd-numbered year.

Sources: Adapted from *United States Congressional Elections, 1788–1997* (1998), *Congressional Quarterly's Guide to U.S. Elections* (1994), ICPSR data sets 0001 and 0075, and independent search for state sources by the author.

Table 5-101 House Election Results, by State, 1912–1914 (Raw Count)

State	1912 Democratic	Republican	Other	Total Vote	1914 Democratic	Republican	Other	Total Vote
Alabama	87,519	9,589	2,533	99,641	62,830	12,832	4,885	80,547
Alaska	—	—	—	—				
Arizona	11,389	3,110	9,046	23,545	33,306	7,586	3,773	44,665
Arkansas	89,718	26,453	0	116,171	37,266	4,087	1,747	43,100
California	196,610	287,222	138,946	622,778	78,736	203,824	573,187	855,747
California	—	—	—	—	*220,279*	*380,493*	*254,975*	*855,747*
Colorado	115,143	63,714	86,796	265,653	118,211	52,318	76,977	247,506
Colorado	—	—	—	—	*118,211*	*99,900*	*29,395*	*247,506*
Connecticut	76,148	70,048	43,296	189,492	78,110	89,000	14,245	181,355
Delaware	22,485	16,740	9,482	48,707	20,681	22,922	2,116	45,719
Florida	34,324	2,942	7,093	44,359	23,951	0	125	24,076
Georgia	116,102	356	0	116,458	80,537	0	640	81,177
Hawaii	—	—	—	—				
Idaho	30,172	53,542	24,635	108,349	39,736	45,365	17,717	102,818
Illinois	415,386	313,608	415,502	1,144,496	375,465	388,896	166,055	930,416
Indiana	291,288	166,698	182,841	640,827	275,891	233,140	121,311	630,342
Iowa	182,969	184,776	62,172	429,917	162,982	212,865	32,689	408,536
Kansas	163,926	159,248	27,478	350,652	195,830	188,056	99,747	483,633
Kentucky	210,685	86,975	102,899	400,559	173,374	123,518	26,363	323,255
Louisiana	62,672	0	2,841	65,513	40,545	615	9,750	50,910
Maine	66,894	71,850	2,925	141,669	60,649	60,264	19,986	140,899
Maryland	107,476	62,382	10,070	179,928	111,410	95,586	9,873	216,869
Massachusetts	188,633	180,850	100,103	469,586	189,197	207,623	50,869	447,689
Massachusetts	—	—	—	—	*189,197*	*222,850*	*35,642*	*447,689*
Michigan	152,188	185,657	203,905	541,750	149,762	218,445	61,654	429,861
Minnesota	69,652	154,308	55,905	279,865	87,305	181,482	54,033	322,820
Mississippi	48,797	0	302	49,099	35,830	0	1,124	36,954
Missouri	337,702	198,275	150,170	686,147	318,587	240,897	41,105	600,589
Missouri	*337,702*	*223,341*	*125,104*	*686,147*	—	—	—	—
Montana	25,891	23,505	26,915	76,311	37,011	26,161	18,936	82,108
Nebraska	26,229	24,766	199,299	250,294	16,773	24,441	192,413	233,627
Nebraska	*114,044*	*118,922*	*17,328*	*250,294*	*112,309*	*110,839*	*10,479*	*233,627*
Nevada	7,311	7,380	5,083	19,774	8,031	8,915	4,294	21,240
New Hampshire	40,682	35,324	6,270	82,276	35,241	42,450	3,434	81,125
New Jersey	169,540	94,883	93,721	358,144	173,183	179,930	36,866	389,979
New Jersey	*169,540*	*112,499*	*76,105*	*358,144*	*175,355*	*183,475*	*31,149*	*389,979*
New Mexico	22,139	17,892	8,526	48,557	19,805	23,812	2,805	46,422
New York	575,560	413,604	556,455	1,545,619	408,392	477,172	464,129	1,349,693
New York	*647,635*	*482,874*	*415,110*	*1,545,619*	*542,166*	*619,650*	*187,877*	*1,349,693*
North Carolina	149,569	67,980	8,423	225,972	122,129	79,842	773	202,744
North Dakota	24,341	47,003	8,552	79,896	26,684	50,792	6,655	84,131
Ohio	423,301	297,355	295,872	1,016,528	484,348	480,482	102,710	1,067,540
Oklahoma	121,202	87,409	41,229	249,840	112,161	75,784	57,691	245,636
Oregon	35,285	42,046	52,579	129,910	67,349	77,931	91,092	236,372
Oregon	*35,285*	*58,829*	*35,796*	*129,910*	*67,349*	*102,107*	*66,916*	*236,372*
Pennsylvania	357,562	0	744,044	1,101,606	281,154	0	781,455	1,062,609
Pennsylvania	*357,562*	*618,537*	*125,507*	*1,101,606*	*281,154*	*514,270*	*267,185*	*1,062,609*
Rhode Island	33,626	31,716	9,546	74,888	35,190	39,001	3,562	77,753
South Carolina	49,292	85	153	49,530	33,077	30	269	33,376
South Dakota	44,487	63,809	6,813	115,109	37,842	52,844	6,039	96,725
Tennessee	141,400	59,648	29,472	230,520	149,248	47,932	17,636	214,816
Tennessee	*141,400*	*82,726*	*6,394*	*230,520*	*155,058*	*47,932*	*11,826*	*214,816*
Texas	235,065	22,795	42,083	299,943	173,177	10,605	25,857	209,639
Utah	37,192	43,133	31,834	112,159	0	54,940	58,730	113,670
Utah	—	—	—	—	*53,057*	*54,940*	*5,673*	*113,670*
Vermont	17,422	28,785	2,646	48,853	13,685	19,237	28,544	61,466
Vermont	—	—	—	—	*13,685*	*36,980*	*10,801*	*61,466*
Virginia	99,053	23,856	11,904	134,813	58,320	23,654	2,911	84,885
Washington	73,133	87,613	143,006	303,752	96,652	128,001	110,537	335,190
West Virginia	114,578	0	152,350	266,928	102,223	110,520	22,608	235,351
West Virginia	*114,578*	*132,733*	*19,617*	*266,928*	—	—	—	—
Wisconsin	156,977	177,385	46,090	380,452	115,501	159,370	34,040	308,911
Wyoming	14,720	19,130	7,354	41,204	17,246	21,362	3,001	41,609

Notes: Main entries are raw vote values for candidates who used the sole designation "Democrat" or "Republican" (or their historical antecedents listed in Appendix A) on the ballot. Other = candidates who used third-party names on the ballot or were listed as independent, unidentified, or scatter vote. Bold italicized entries in the table are the author's alternative party coding, which is used when a candidate listed a major party name (Democrat, Republican, or their historical antecedents) on the ballot with other party names or labels. For a more detailed explanation of this alternate coding system, see Tables 5-1 and 1-3. —indicates that the state had no data, either because no vote data were found for the state in question or the state had not yet entered the Union. No special House elections are included in the table. The table only lists at-large vote values for states having both at-large and district House races; see Appendix B for these states' district results aggregated to the state level.

Sources: Adapted from *United States Congressional Elections, 1788–1997* (1998), *Congressional Quarterly's Guide to U.S. Elections* (1994), ICPSR data sets 0001 and 0075, and independent search for state sources by the author.

Table 5-102 House Election Results, by State, 1916–1918 (Raw Count)

State	1916				1918			
	Democratic	Republican	Other	Total Vote	Democratic	Republican	Other	Total Vote
Alabama	98,780	23,515	790	123,085	53,489	8,856	0	62,345
Alaska	—	—	—	—	—	—	—	—
Arizona	34,377	14,907	3,060	52,344	26,805	16,822	754	44,381
Arkansas	143,288	29,626	0	172,914	78,573	0	0	78,573
California	194,126	266,566	421,777	882,469	61,912	92,806	471,704	626,422
California	*282,994*	*433,078*	*166,397*	*882,469*	*216,921*	*355,004*	*54,497*	*626,422*
Colorado	130,589	113,320	16,312	260,221	93,906	112,787	8,626	215,319
Connecticut	98,652	106,930	7,727	213,309	78,373	82,983	5,638	166,994
Delaware	24,395	24,202	2,614	51,211	19,652	21,226	420	41,298
Florida	52,389	10,995	3,906	67,290	31,813	0	0	31,813
Georgia	126,555	6,964	699	134,218	57,274	2,831	0	60,105
Hawaii	—	—	—	—	—	—	—	—
Idaho	55,807	64,648	8,079	128,534	34,499	59,358	0	93,857
Illinois	546,471	707,958	61,201	1,315,630	361,505	501,974	39,980	903,459
Indiana	321,751	342,806	41,825	706,382	251,331	306,807	9,273	567,411
Iowa	186,358	282,179	9,718	478,255	121,994	223,381	3,441	348,816
Kansas	261,589	261,622	45,157	568,368	171,897	244,374	12,837	429,108
Kentucky	266,712	237,106	6,231	510,049	186,214	170,218	0	356,432
Louisiana	78,607	359	7,324	86,290	44,794	0	1	44,795
Maine	68,569	80,998	1,589	151,156	53,775	68,061	0	121,836
Maryland	109,318	105,627	9,823	224,768	81,485	76,077	2,512	160,074
Massachusetts	197,772	281,546	25,424	504,742	150,774	233,809	9,844	394,427
Michigan	257,483	355,298	30,194	642,975	135,987	265,334	5,540	406,861
Michigan	*270,365*	*355,298*	*17,312*	*642,975*	—	—	—	—
Minnesota	108,572	209,611	62,014	380,197	82,619	216,579	33,853	333,051
Mississippi	76,513	0	1,865	78,378	31,599	0	712	32,311
Missouri	396,617	368,832	13,910	779,359	287,840	256,555	6,710	551,105
Montana	84,499	76,932	9,002	170,433	48,356	47,358	8,121	103,835
Nebraska	0	35,871	247,292	283,163	94,538	121,476	1,012	217,026
Nebraska	*134,367*	*140,430*	*8,366*	*283,163*	—	—	—	—
Nevada	13,100	14,106	5,125	32,331	12,670	10,660	1,377	24,707
New Hampshire	39,951	44,122	1,462	85,535	32,045	38,001	0	70,046
New Jersey	186,792	225,858	27,350	440,000	158,899	173,228	17,010	349,137
New Mexico	32,592	32,042	2,050	66,684	22,627	23,862	564	47,053
New York	238,148	194,650	1,094,023	1,526,821	735,530	708,620	595,435	2,039,585
New York	*626,913*	*805,826*	*94,082*	*1,526,821*	*870,236*	*985,960*	*183,389*	*2,039,585*
North Carolina	165,954	120,246	258	286,458	141,807	92,809	0	234,616
North Dakota	29,167	63,329	4,359	96,855	29,405	54,508	0	83,913
Ohio	545,975	543,941	29,101	1,119,017	392,581	495,616	17,344	905,541
Oklahoma	142,031	98,594	48,205	288,830	104,238	78,351	7,041	189,630
Oregon	9,824	35,832	179,194	224,850	26,189	41,589	74,113	141,891
Oregon	*48,925*	*132,421*	*43,504*	*224,850*	*26,189*	*98,834*	*16,868*	*141,891*
Pennsylvania	471,308	0	774,833	1,246,141	276,836	546,373	54,793	878,002
Pennsylvania	*471,308*	*668,571*	*106,262*	*1,246,141*	—	—	—	—
Rhode Island	41,630	43,259	2,041	86,930	34,646	43,225	1,737	79,608
South Carolina	61,869	1,117	87	63,073	25,280	176	0	25,456
South Dakota	52,769	69,243	4,334	126,346	34,165	48,905	4,354	87,424
Tennessee	139,293	97,142	6,252	242,687	92,890	27,620	178	120,688
Texas	298,966	46,467	20,108	365,541	159,032	6,113	0	165,145
Utah	0	57,680	84,456	142,136	25,327	36,612	24,998	86,937
Utah	*79,882*	*57,680*	*4,574*	*142,136*	*49,258*	*36,612*	*1,067*	*86,937*
Vermont	15,955	22,030	24,463	62,448	10,697	16,301	16,145	43,143
Vermont	*15,955*	*44,722*	*1,771*	*62,448*	*10,697*	*32,446*	*0*	*43,143*
Virginia	105,646	47,654	2,711	156,011	33,802	8,555	0	42,357
Washington	152,410	184,117	21,424	357,951	81,350	112,166	7,879	201,395
West Virginia	140,769	142,188	0	282,957	99,917	112,022	1,864	213,803
Wisconsin	137,391	238,537	41,151	417,079	69,043	166,354	70,071	305,468
Wyoming	24,156	24,693	1,521	50,370	14,639	26,244	0	40,883

Notes: Main entries are raw vote values for candidates who used the sole designation "Democrat" or "Republican" (or their historical antecedents listed in Appendix A) on the ballot. Other = candidates who used third-party names on the ballot or were listed as independent, unidentified, or scatter vote. Bold italicized entries in the table are the author's alternative party coding, which is used when a candidate listed a major party name (Democrat, Republican, or their historical antecedents) on the ballot with other party names or labels. For a more detailed explanation of this alternate coding system, see Tables 5-1 and 1-3. —indicates that the state had no data, either because no vote data were found for the state in question or the state had not yet entered the Union. No special House elections are included in the table. The table only lists at-large vote values for states having both at-large and district House races; see Appendix B for these states' district results aggregated to the state level.

Sources: Adapted from *United States Congressional Elections, 1788–1997* (1998), *Congressional Quarterly's Guide to U.S. Elections* (1994), ICPSR data sets 0001 and 0075, and independent search for state sources by the author.

Table 5-103 House Election Results, by State, 1920–1922 (Raw Count)

	1920				1922			
State	Democratic	Republican	Other	Total Vote	Democratic	Republican	Other	Total Vote
Alabama	161,243	62,095	917	224,255	113,610	26,182	0	139,792
Alaska	—	—	—	—				
Arizona	35,397	25,841	0	61,238	37,262	14,601	0	51,863
Arkansas	128,265	61,924	0	190,189	30,374	4,207	0	34,581
California	63,419	224,184	524,187	811,790	22,711	126,123	633,055	781,889
California	*160,693*	*556,025*	*95,072*	*811,790*	*154,615*	*596,084*	*31,190*	*781,889*
Colorado	109,605	167,587	0	277,192	127,751	136,926	959	265,636
Connecticut	99,662	227,635	35,672	362,969	147,760	170,194	5,636	323,590
Connecticut	*122,321*	*227,635*	*13,013*	*362,969*	—	—	—	—
Delaware	40,206	52,145	1,259	93,610	39,126	32,577	908	72,611
Florida	97,082	21,024	5,013	123,119	44,544	6,323	16	50,883
Florida	*97,082*	*22,632*	*3,405*	*123,119*	—	—	—	—
Georgia	170,252	99,890	8,605	278,747	77,071	1,261	347	78,679
Hawaii	—	—	—	—	—	—	—	—
Idaho	44,348	84,296	8,605	137,249	33,647	57,373	30,123	121,143
Illinois	579,799	1,369,673	138,996	2,088,468	666,583	943,684	68,906	1,679,173
Indiana	516,083	695,041	40,549	1,251,673	524,183	546,595	11,310	1,082,088
Iowa	88,857	605,532	22,914	717,303	225,821	357,174	2,595	585,590
Kansas	192,262	325,686	9,484	527,432	233,706	284,687	6,465	524,858
Kentucky	431,913	409,165	11,274	852,352	195,141	138,239	19,478	352,858
Louisiana	92,037	0	15	92,052	44,180	0	18	44,198
Maine	67,515	135,230	0	202,745	74,287	101,064	0	175,351
Maryland	163,920	189,937	23,659	377,516	151,408	145,314	7,137	303,859
Massachusetts	276,217	618,132	42,334	936,683	347,203	475,942	1,568	824,713
Massachusetts	*291,740*	*618,132*	*26,811*	*936,683*	—	—	—	—
Michigan	228,583	761,334	19,842	1,009,759	178,633	365,970	1,730	546,333
Minnesota	104,458	447,297	195,315	747,070	133,482	385,030	118,384	636,896
Mississippi	66,306	2,154	1,988	70,448	66,482	1,621	49	68,152
Missouri	583,378	713,264	22,821	1,319,463	494,376	476,109	6,044	976,529
Montana	66,792	108,215	0	175,007	75,736	73,183	876	149,795
Nebraska	116,512	222,060	21,752	360,324	173,384	179,070	23,087	375,541
Nevada	9,167	13,149	4,554	26,870	15,991	12,084	0	28,075
New Hampshire	60,730	93,326	588	154,644	64,773	62,264	0	127,037
New Jersey	295,260	517,659	24,144	837,063	393,350	393,269	5,652	792,271
New Mexico	49,426	54,672	1,290	105,388	59,254	49,635	871	109,760
New York	881,565	1,535,558	290,849	2,707,972	1,026,100	727,481	674,368	2,427,949
New York	*899,198*	*1,566,205*	*242,569*	*2,707,972*	*1,162,206*	*1,120,920*	*144,823*	*2,427,949*
North Carolina	306,919	225,368	0	532,287	225,921	138,522	0	364,443
North Dakota	24,460	119,788	64,690	208,938	34,506	115,986	0	150,492
Ohio	798,981	1,125,574	13,676	1,938,231	713,974	854,380	21,009	1,589,363
Oklahoma	227,642	232,306	25,150	485,098	285,581	180,203	4,043	469,827
Oregon	44,902	67,539	87,107	199,548	52,479	123,124	4,689	180,292
Oregon	*44,902*	*143,136*	*11,510*	*199,548*	—	—	—	—
Pennsylvania	466,564	1,140,836	185,536	1,792,936	381,326	348,756	716,335	1,446,417
Pennsylvania	—	—	—	—	*533,664*	*857,453*	*55,300*	*1,446,417*
Rhode Island	58,927	105,692	2,417	167,036	81,762	73,688	0	155,450
South Carolina	64,400	834	502	65,736	34,451	679	0	35,130
South Dakota	39,799	103,325	38,932	182,056	31,229	87,277	41,270	159,776
Tennessee	190,153	197,741	8,053	395,947	142,033	77,461	0	219,494
Tennessee	*190,153*	*202,668*	*3,126*	*395,947*	—	—	—	—
Texas	311,565	65,247	29,026	405,838	339,477	60,926	0	400,403
Texas	*311,565*	*70,997*	*23,276*	*405,838*	—	—	—	—
Utah	56,175	80,984	7,214	144,373	53,946	61,779	3,888	119,613
Vermont	20,587	33,670	34,221	88,478	24,989	0	45,362	70,351
Vermont	*20,587*	*67,891*	*0*	*88,478*	*24,989*	*45,340*	*22*	*70,351*
Virginia	154,402	88,286	3,729	246,417	112,906	53,231	97	166,234
Virginia	*154,402*	*91,594*	*421*	*246,417*	—	—	—	—
Washington	63,390	218,655	93,111	375,156	58,882	161,646	39,557	260,085
West Virginia	226,017	273,288	1	499,306	194,525	185,090	1,875	381,490
Wisconsin	107,774	428,825	87,520	624,119	11,585	346,036	94,752	452,373
Wisconsin	—	—	—	—	*29,459*	*368,051*	*54,863*	*452,373*
Wyoming	14,952	34,689	6,780	56,421	27,017	30,885	0	57,902

Notes: Main entries are raw vote values for candidates who used the sole designation "Democrat" or "Republican" (or their historical antecedents listed in Appendix A) on the ballot. Other = candidates who used third-party names on the ballot or were listed as independent, unidentified, or scatter vote. Bold italicized entries in the table are the author's alternative party coding, which is used when a candidate listed a major party name (Democrat, Republican, or their historical antecedents) on the ballot with other party names or labels. For a more detailed explanation of this alternate coding system, see Tables 5-1 and 1-3. —indicates that the state had no data, either because no vote data were found for the state in question or the state had not yet entered the Union. No special House elections are included in the table. The table only lists at-large vote values for states having both at-large and district House races; see Appendix B for these states' district results aggregated to the state level.

Sources: Adapted from *United States Congressional Elections, 1788–1997* (1998), *Congressional Quarterly's Guide to U.S. Elections* (1994), ICPSR data sets 0001 and 0075, and independent search for state sources by the author.

Table 5-104 House Election Results, by State, 1924–1926 (Raw Count)

State	1924				1926			
	Democratic	Republican	Other	Total Vote	Democratic	Republican	Other	Total Vote
Alabama	120,221	31,368	0	151,589	90,366	16,729	0	107,095
Alaska	—	—	—	—	—	—	—	—
Arizona	40,329	8,628	0	48,957	43,725	24,502	0	68,227
Arkansas	99,487	36,899	0	136,386	28,911	4,801	0	33,712
California	80,870	322,320	594,707	997,897	47,046	324,266	583,106	954,418
California	*226,445*	*682,037*	*89,415*	*997,897*	*168,972*	*752,546*	*32,900*	*954,418*
Colorado	139,135	169,546	10,595	319,276	130,377	158,396	2,502	291,275
Connecticut	95,528	245,089	32,738	373,355	106,571	192,082	2,805	301,458
Connecticut	*123,776*	*245,089*	*4,490*	*373,355*				
Delaware	35,943	51,536	519	87,998	29,424	38,909	0	68,333
Florida	72,243	21,525	2,995	96,763	49,495	10,954	4,235	64,684
Florida					*49,495*	*15,189*	*0*	*64,684*
Georgia	154,915	3,500	16	158,431	47,003	0	0	47,003
Hawaii	—	—	—	—	—	—	—	—
Idaho	33,704	77,712	23,736	135,152	20,934	72,210	21,596	114,740
Idaho	—	—	—	—	*27,162*	*72,210*	*15,368*	*114,740*
Illinois	669,555	1,519,021	23,400	2,211,976	631,708	987,968	10,934	1,630,610
Illinois	*669,555*	*1,519,773*	*22,648*	*2,211,976*				
Indiana	544,259	690,066	12,447	1,246,772	480,579	546,605	223	1,027,407
Iowa	258,181	566,978	827	825,986	155,579	348,727	619	504,925
Kansas	262,385	325,550	5,895	593,830	196,084	283,890	187	480,161
Kentucky	389,168	289,123	16,062	694,353	263,307	239,909	0	503,216
Louisiana	93,311	0	0	93,311	53,320	869	3	54,192
Maine	97,855	148,345	0	246,200	66,332	106,707	0	173,039
Maryland	158,272	149,226	4,025	311,523	186,890	146,659	2,549	336,098
Massachusetts	415,710	647,535	13,235	1,076,480	379,424	504,684	48,983	933,091
Massachusetts	—	—	—	—	*379,424*	*553,632*	*35*	*933,091*
Michigan	232,180	882,889	661	1,115,730	122,395	438,653	665	561,713
Minnesota	53,388	422,182	337,035	812,605	37,807	386,448	234,507	658,762
Mississippi	98,548	579	0	99,127	26,917	0	0	26,917
Missouri	620,546	644,762	12,474	1,277,782	499,807	487,173	851	987,831
Montana	72,847	79,202	6,847	158,896	75,833	74,515	3,104	153,452
Nebraska	200,974	219,470	17,644	438,088	193,307	187,963	8,130	389,400
Nevada	12,880	13,107	0	25,987	12,910	17,598	0	30,508
New Hampshire	66,186	92,346	0	158,532	46,887	77,264	0	124,151
New Jersey	353,700	600,352	18,983	973,035	339,937	448,038	3,628	791,603
New Mexico	57,802	53,860	1,126	112,788	55,433	52,075	297	107,805
New York	1,246,391	1,533,374	298,387	3,078,152	1,330,850	1,247,086	211,721	2,789,657
New York	*1,335,228*	*1,595,143*	*147,781*	*3,078,152*	*1,330,850*	*1,372,957*	*85,850*	*2,789,657*
North Carolina	289,754	179,607	0	469,361	220,155	138,762	0	358,917
North Dakota	28,241	113,890	28,558	170,689	25,731	113,856	6,596	146,183
Ohio	769,751	1,055,925	35,902	1,861,578	561,206	722,876	2,396	1,286,478
Oklahoma	283,432	203,869	17,124	504,425	204,335	157,345	864	362,544
Oregon	83,676	153,681	19,002	256,359	39,621	148,266	20,372	208,259
Oregon	—	—	—	—	*59,993*	*148,266*	*0*	*208,259*
Pennsylvania	204,978	725,025	1,078,854	2,008,857	207,821	473,358	787,603	1,468,782
Pennsylvania	*551,102*	*1,353,365*	*104,390*	*2,008,857*	*376,747*	*1,043,281*	*48,754*	*1,468,782*
Rhode Island	84,543	122,775	0	207,318	68,713	95,367	0	164,080
South Carolina	49,238	253	0	49,491	14,322	0	0	14,322
South Dakota	37,973	112,157	45,714	195,844	67,854	96,070	4,077	168,001
Tennessee	144,534	75,113	5,591	225,238	71,851	30,828	0	102,679
Texas	587,437	86,793	0	674,230	230,463	6,563	0	237,026
Utah	65,689	82,771	0	148,460	54,204	86,080	1,262	141,546
Vermont	19,936	0	77,377	97,313	17,282	55,130	14	72,426
Vermont	*19,936*	*77,377*	*0*	*97,313*	—	—	—	—
Virginia	166,708	63,051	0	229,759	74,365	32,801	727	107,893
Washington	90,308	223,883	33,683	347,874	79,434	190,797	526	270,757
West Virginia	270,683	287,992	3,120	561,795	206,284	221,016	163	427,463
Wisconsin	155,982	505,230	55,843	717,055	29,673	382,490	69,053	481,216
Wisconsin	—	—	—	—	*36,431*	*399,167*	*45,618*	*481,216*
Wyoming	28,537	43,026	0	71,563	25,082	39,392	300	64,774

Notes: Main entries are raw vote values for candidates who used the sole designation "Democrat" or "Republican" (or their historical antecedents listed in Appendix A) on the ballot. Other = candidates who used third-party names on the ballot or were listed as independent, unidentified, or scatter vote. Bold italicized entries in the table are the author's alternative party coding, which is used when a candidate listed a major party name (Democrat, Republican, or their historical antecedents) on the ballot with other party names or labels. For a more detailed explanation of this alternate coding system, see Tables 5-1 and 1-3. —indicates that the state had no data, either because no vote data were found for the state in question or the state had not yet entered the Union. No special House elections are included in the table. The table only lists at-large vote values for states having both at-large and district House races; see Appendix B for these states' district results aggregated to the state level.

Sources: Adapted from *United States Congressional Elections, 1788–1997* (1998), *Congressional Quarterly's Guide to U.S. Elections* (1994), ICPSR data sets 0001 and 0075, and independent search for state sources by the author.

Table 5-105 House Election Results, by State, 1928–1930 (Raw Count)

State	1928				1930			
	Democratic	Republican	Other	Total Vote	Democratic	Republican	Other	Total Vote
Alabama	165,023	35,613	0	200,636	165,403	33,030	0	198,433
Alaska	—	—	—	—	—	—	—	—
Arizona	50,231	31,382	0	81,613	52,342	0	0	52,342
Arkansas	157,361	42,581	0	199,942	145,124	0	0	145,124
California	96,210	353,080	876,997	1,326,287	65,156	414,799	616,643	1,096,598
California	*152,591*	*1,127,910*	*45,786*	*1,326,287*	*131,859*	*964,690*	*49*	*1,096,598*
Colorado	141,005	210,838	949	352,792	146,192	167,227	1,224	314,643
Connecticut	250,526	297,651	3,217	551,394	208,202	216,418	3,559	428,179
Delaware	38,045	66,361	0	104,406	0	48,493	38,518	87,011
Delaware	*—*	*—*	*—*	*—*	*38,391*	*48,493*	*127*	*87,011*
Florida	148,528	69,469	17	218,014	84,070	11,819	54	95,943
Georgia	200,188	0	0	200,188	54,563	1,526	369	56,458
Hawaii	—	—	—	—	—	—	—	—
Idaho	48,486	97,006	1,039	146,531	45,659	80,869	0	126,528
Illinois	1,171,520	1,711,651	16,240	2,899,411	1,062,606	991,083	11,747	2,065,436
Indiana	641,498	770,317	2,078	1,413,893	641,406	572,082	899	1,214,387
Iowa	235,327	575,061	0	810,388	207,686	321,706	858	530,250
Kansas	218,182	375,500	0	593,682	242,477	322,775	0	565,252
Kentucky	412,421	526,194	113	938,728	288,354	253,903	6,325	548,582
Louisiana	152,816	14,661	0	167,477	130,086	2,207	0	132,293
Maine	61,890	145,955	0	207,845	55,471	88,070	0	143,541
Maryland	226,116	234,848	2,314	463,278	275,461	189,815	780	466,056
Massachusetts	625,003	753,391	66,849	1,445,243	529,268	629,821	17,496	1,176,585
Massachusetts	*686,700*	*753,391*	*5,152*	*1,445,243*	*—*	*—*	*—*	*—*
Michigan	357,065	979,071	2,452	1,338,588	171,402	567,205	5,822	744,429
Minnesota	174,383	525,511	271,863	971,757	65,490	412,888	281,385	759,763
Mississippi	112,546	0	0	112,546	34,897	0	0	34,897
Missouri	726,050	790,062	187	1,516,299	477,467	468,853	743	947,063
Montana	77,651	103,478	826	181,955	84,604	82,736	2,807	170,147
Nebraska	233,094	289,899	0	522,993	216,405	199,196	0	415,601
Nevada	13,287	18,815	0	32,102	15,343	18,279	0	33,622
New Hampshire	75,843	108,284	186	184,313	52,323	71,506	0	123,829
New Jersey	564,621	870,883	914	1,436,418	425,352	558,925	6,557	990,834
New Mexico	56,045	61,208	0	117,253	65,444	51,655	299	117,398
New York	1,941,034	2,072,853	198,804	4,212,691	1,493,073	1,304,010	228,099	3,025,182
New York	*1,989,414*	*2,072,853*	*150,424*	*4,212,691*	*1,532,413*	*1,304,010*	*188,759*	*3,025,182*
North Carolina	355,360	289,333	0	644,693	334,376	198,310	0	532,686
North Dakota	51,547	149,005	0	200,552	52,284	126,678	3,538	182,500
Ohio	931,103	1,442,859	2,290	2,376,252	910,931	955,686	13,468	1,880,085
Oklahoma	296,574	293,876	2,443	592,893	282,620	173,944	166	456,730
Oregon	85,553	196,539	11,475	293,567	107,187	116,642	4,696	228,525
Pennsylvania	717,653	947,243	1,340,708	3,005,604	428,753	1,092,978	497,576	2,019,307
Pennsylvania	*912,317*	*2,068,355*	*24,932*	*3,005,604*	*567,838*	*1,429,675*	*21,794*	*2,019,307*
Rhode Island	114,454	120,361	0	234,815	105,968	113,354	0	219,322
South Carolina	61,347	0	0	61,347	16,163	0	0	16,163
South Dakota	104,419	142,552	1,744	248,715	55,718	106,429	7,926	170,073
Tennessee	178,476	116,447	0	294,923	123,615	38,099	36,156	197,870
Tennessee	*—*	*—*	*—*	*—*	*123,615*	*72,347*	*1,908*	*197,870*
Texas	568,457	81,283	0	649,740	248,450	45,281	2	293,733
Utah	77,914	97,140	847	175,901	62,828	80,981	10,945	154,754
Vermont	36,451	91,223	1,688	129,362	23,741	49,074	7	72,822
Virginia	206,533	97,686	1,781	306,000	108,308	54,161	2,363	164,832
Virginia	*—*	*—*	*—*	*—*	*109,013*	*55,634*	*185*	*164,832*
Washington	134,910	291,977	823	427,710	75,424	205,937	8,017	289,378
West Virginia	292,061	347,085	115	639,261	271,979	265,857	0	537,836
Wisconsin	234,599	598,077	64,044	896,720	68,130	380,272	61,007	509,409
Wisconsin	*—*	*—*	*—*	*—*	*70,349*	*380,272*	*58,788*	*509,409*
Wyoming	35,972	38,935	333	75,240	23,519	44,890	0	68,409

Notes: Main entries are raw vote values for candidates who used the sole designation "Democrat" or "Republican" (or their historical antecedents listed in Appendix A) on the ballot. Other = candidates who used third-party names on the ballot or were listed as independent, unidentified, or scatter vote. Bold italicized entries in the table are the author's alternative party coding, which is used when a candidate listed a major party name (Democrat, Republican, or their historical antecedents) on the ballot with other party names or labels. For a more detailed explanation of this alternate coding system, see Tables 5-1 and 1-3. —indicates that the state had no data, either because no vote data were found for the state in question or the state had not yet entered the Union. No special House elections are included in the table. The table only lists at-large vote values for states having both at-large and district House races; see Appendix B for these states' district results aggregated to the state level.

Sources: Adapted from *United States Congressional Elections, 1788–1997* (1998), *Congressional Quarterly's Guide to U.S. Elections* (1994), ICPSR data sets 0001 and 0075, and independent search for state sources by the author.

Table 5-106 House Election Results, by State, 1932–1934 (Raw Count)

State	1932				1934			
	Democratic	Republican	Other	Total Vote	Democratic	Republican	Other	Total Vote
Alabama	207,489	22,669	1,476	231,634	149,104	10,200	5,586	164,890
Alaska	—	—	—	—				
Arizona	75,469	29,710	1,405	106,584	65,914	28,283	1,847	96,044
Arkansas	213,189	4,996	0	218,185	129,124	10,158	613	139,895
California	775,870	688,220	410,241	1,874,331	668,282	483,496	876,880	2,028,658
California	*849,270*	*941,668*	*83,393*	*1,874,331*	*993,600*	*862,566*	*172,492*	*2,028,658*
Colorado	234,843	191,903	2,769	429,515	237,491	140,202	18,005	395,698
Connecticut	282,557	284,438	25,781	592,776	265,427	249,146	37,205	551,778
Connecticut	*282,557*	*289,509*	*20,710*	*592,776*	—	—	—	—
Delaware	51,698	48,841	11,557	112,096	45,927	52,468	462	98,857
Florida	186,284	61,300	12	247,596	125,263	0	0	125,263
Georgia	233,915	12,872	44	246,831	52,443	240	0	52,683
Hawaii	—	—	—	—	—	—	—	—
Idaho	100,922	78,838	3,815	183,575	99,770	63,169	437	163,376
Illinois	1,675,274	1,421,221	53,638	3,150,133	1,507,714	1,201,373	41,239	2,750,326
Indiana	850,181	683,517	13,074	1,546,772	759,795	686,598	9,908	1,456,301
Iowa	495,732	439,783	6,135	941,650	443,565	385,862	0	829,427
Kansas	357,154	350,332	11,609	719,095	367,747	380,037	9,450	757,234
Kentucky	575,191	391,868	3,514	970,573	254,584	206,118	8,768	469,470
Louisiana	244,681	0	0	244,681	186,063	0	49	186,112
Maine	118,391	115,963	891	235,245	142,436	136,859	0	279,295
Maine	*118,391*	*116,641*	*213*	*235,245*	—	—	—	—
Maryland	299,954	150,552	3,330	453,836	267,204	180,493	7,933	455,630
Massachusetts	716,971	769,317	14,416	1,500,704	641,349	644,017	96,059	1,381,425
Massachusetts	—	—	—	—	*641,349*	*728,261*	*11,815*	*1,381,425*
Michigan	769,088	773,318	33,626	1,576,032	590,620	605,047	16,859	1,212,526
Minnesota	321,949	337,110	487,741	1,146,800	256,001	323,189	416,415	995,605
Mississippi	129,954	0	4,734	134,688	57,327	0	0	57,327
Mississippi	*129,954*	*4,734*	*0*	*134,688*	—	—	—	—
Missouri	1,013,824	609,268	12,285	1,635,377	797,975	515,268	7,100	1,320,343
Montana	115,262	87,223	6,386	208,871	135,733	59,270	1,736	196,739
Nebraska	296,256	208,954	40,991	546,201	277,028	232,620	9,691	519,339
Nevada	24,979	16,133	0	41,112	29,691	11,992	0	41,683
New Hampshire	94,765	97,802	516	193,083	85,690	84,131	392	170,213
New Jersey	724,572	751,130	26,068	1,501,770	676,016	638,424	13,967	1,328,407
New Mexico	94,764	52,905	1,899	149,568	76,833	70,659	776	148,268
New York	2,363,627	1,756,343	253,763	4,373,733	1,978,670	1,417,271	218,032	3,613,973
North Carolina	492,050	214,022	0	706,072	320,256	173,447	0	493,703
North Dakota	72,659	144,339	690	217,688	85,771	144,605	46,304	276,680
Ohio	1,206,631	1,109,562	31,675	2,347,868	1,061,857	905,233	13,999	1,981,089
Oklahoma	467,644	171,415	3,043	642,102	354,542	162,991	12,823	530,356
Oregon	164,582	148,262	34,790	347,634	121,846	132,441	31,102	285,389
Pennsylvania	607,942	415,686	1,761,590	2,785,218	1,130,389	842,774	953,175	2,926,338
Pennsylvania	*1,109,136*	*1,536,791*	*139,291*	*2,785,218*	*1,591,616*	*1,242,101*	*92,621*	*2,926,338*
Rhode Island	143,652	116,406	626	260,684	140,281	104,278	1	244,560
South Carolina	104,646	1,987	0	106,633	21,921	54	181	22,156
South Dakota	146,886	121,128	5,347	273,361	158,399	116,935	2,259	277,593
Tennessee	217,905	88,686	34,010	340,601	194,312	69,454	11,476	275,242
Texas	794,520	60,360	2,722	857,602	439,685	5,643	555	445,883
Utah	110,176	91,746	3,673	205,595	113,975	63,885	2,117	179,977
Vermont	47,591	86,194	16	133,801	54,967	73,809	949	129,725
Virginia	206,631	92,586	65,308	364,525	108,655	34,178	5,291	148,124
Washington	327,702	186,571	39,265	553,538	314,685	151,655	13,025	479,365
West Virginia	392,924	341,170	1,694	735,788	345,144	272,011	2,792	619,947
Wisconsin	500,710	466,176	77,228	1,044,114	280,367	215,605	389,717	885,689
Wisconsin	*500,710*	*469,809*	*73,595*	*1,044,114*	—	—	—	—
Wyoming	43,056	44,816	2,319	90,191	53,288	37,492	603	91,383

Notes: Main entries are raw vote values for candidates who used the sole designation "Democrat" or "Republican" (or their historical antecedents listed in Appendix A) on the ballot. Other = candidates who used third-party names on the ballot or were listed as independent, unidentified, or scatter vote. Bold italicized entries in the table are the author's alternative party coding, which is used when a candidate listed a major party name (Democrat, Republican, or their historical antecedents) on the ballot with other party names or labels. For a more detailed explanation of this alternate coding system, see Tables 5-1 and 1-3. —indicates that the state had no data, either because no vote data were found for the state in question or the state had not yet entered the Union. No special House elections are included in the table. The table only lists at-large vote values for states having both at-large and district House races; see Appendix B for these states' district results aggregated to the state level.

Sources: Adapted from *United States Congressional Elections, 1788–1997* (1998), *Congressional Quarterly's Guide to U.S. Elections* (1994), ICPSR data sets 0001 and 0075, and independent search for state sources by the author.

Table 5-107 House Election Results, by State, 1936–1938 (Raw Count)

State	1936				1938			
	Democratic	Republican	Other	Total Vote	Democratic	Republican	Other	Total Vote
Alabama	238,558	16,044	450	255,052	114,253	9,573	50	123,876
Alaska	—	—	—	—	—	—	—	—
Arizona	84,343	20,383	4,024	108,750	83,556	20,502	0	104,058
Arkansas	160,305	13,993	0	174,298	143,956	0	0	143,956
California	745,118	645,330	850,047	2,240,495	751,190	530,448	1,107,589	2,389,227
California	*1,199,206*	*965,728*	*75,561*	*2,240,495*	*1,104,772*	*1,112,189*	*172,266*	*2,389,227*
Colorado	283,147	169,765	4,847	457,759	265,297	181,829	2,411	449,537
Connecticut	371,572	282,618	35,322	689,512	250,013	271,329	108,790	630,132
Delaware	65,485	55,664	5,514	126,663	46,989	60,661	921	108,571
Delaware	*65,485*	*61,002*	*176*	*126,663*	*46,989*	*61,477*	*105*	*108,571*
Florida	233,405	51,532	0	284,937	146,356	6,705	0	153,061
Georgia	260,509	15,765	0	276,274	67,252	0	813	68,065
Hawaii	—	—	—	—	—	—	—	—
Idaho	126,179	68,793	0	194,972	95,517	83,167	0	178,684
Illinois	2,062,886	1,568,552	97,412	3,728,850	1,572,870	1,472,638	9,339	3,054,847
Indiana	910,851	706,988	11,277	1,629,116	773,121	799,455	73	1,572,649
Iowa	520,085	510,875	23,404	1,054,364	352,516	445,939	4,182	802,637
Kansas	377,432	412,041	10,377	799,850	302,329	434,692	0	737,021
Kentucky	539,598	368,576	9,473	917,647	315,427	218,331	210	533,968
Louisiana	291,930	0	33	291,963	152,366	0	44	152,410
Maine	119,195	170,431	11,422	301,048	116,774	164,845	0	281,619
Maryland	321,447	215,236	6,698	543,381	290,342	192,168	3,963	486,473
Massachusetts	779,960	848,416	151,914	1,780,290	792,848	925,853	976	1,719,677
Massachusetts	*816,131*	*884,243*	*79,916*	*1,780,290*	—	—	—	—
Michigan	887,874	765,887	44,183	1,697,944	714,017	830,394	2,800	1,547,211
Michigan	—	—	—	—	*714,988*	*830,394*	*1,829*	*1,547,211*
Minnesota	190,367	420,321	480,507	1,091,195	190,036	537,465	343,426	1,070,927
Mississippi	146,511	1,929	0	148,440	35,439	0	0	35,439
Missouri	1,093,138	715,403	2,434	1,810,975	737,851	505,605	1,578	1,245,034
Montana	134,006	73,685	776	208,467	104,825	103,885	0	208,710
Nebraska	289,381	262,155	17,800	569,336	218,116	247,996	11,603	477,715
Nevada	25,575	11,745	6,444	43,764	30,156	15,285	0	45,441
New Hampshire	96,807	105,526	1,403	203,736	79,133	102,140	0	181,273
New Jersey	901,234	766,595	20,412	1,688,241	719,301	794,609	17,211	1,531,121
New Mexico	105,937	62,375	61	168,373	90,608	64,281	268	155,157
New York	3,013,931	2,078,803	171,469	5,264,203	0	0	4,511,005	4,511,005
New York	—	—	—	—	*2,363,463*	*2,011,567*	*135,975*	*4,511,005*
North Carolina	568,482	230,402	0	798,884	318,809	160,458	0	479,267
North Dakota	100,609	131,117	3,850	235,576	55,125	153,106	8,109	216,340
Ohio	1,553,059	1,226,247	8,945	2,788,251	1,068,916	1,177,982	0	2,246,898
Oklahoma	475,567	193,487	3,306	672,360	306,241	137,733	1,850	445,824
Oregon	184,824	181,758	23,358	389,940	151,364	214,571	8	365,943
Pennsylvania	2,215,961	1,708,551	146,087	4,070,599	1,499,632	1,921,793	362,326	3,783,751
Pennsylvania	*2,252,229*	*1,718,625*	*99,745*	*4,070,599*	*1,756,157*	*2,003,483*	*24,111*	*3,783,751*
Rhode Island	149,957	134,180	21,265	305,402	138,892	73,394	87,934	300,220
Rhode Island	—	—	—	—	*138,892*	*161,328*	*0*	*300,220*
South Carolina	113,651	661	937	115,249	45,806	310	74	46,190
South Carolina	*113,651*	*910*	*688*	*115,249*	—	—	—	—
South Dakota	143,378	143,071	0	286,449	121,285	153,140	0	274,425
Tennessee	281,664	105,819	5,070	392,553	170,493	64,062	29,849	264,404
Texas	765,362	52,201	2,110	819,673	362,689	3,815	37	366,541
Utah	149,996	65,270	520	215,786	111,383	71,149	0	182,532
Vermont	56,334	83,091	970	140,395	40,483	73,990	0	114,473
Virginia	233,462	86,840	1,974	322,276	97,531	26,144	2,368	126,043
Washington	425,985	219,024	1,847	646,856	357,686	227,958	849	586,493
West Virginia	495,633	329,833	0	825,466	343,334	279,487	0	622,821
Wisconsin	322,923	315,040	484,692	1,122,655	166,214	399,451	346,637	912,302
Wyoming	56,204	41,362	747	98,313	44,525	49,975	0	94,500

Notes: Main entries are raw vote values for candidates who used the sole designation "Democrat" or "Republican" (or their historical antecedents listed in Appendix A) on the ballot. Other = candidates who used third-party names on the ballot or were listed as independent, unidentified, or scatter vote. Bold italicized entries in the table are the author's alternative party coding, which is used when a candidate listed a major party name (Democrat, Republican, or their historical antecedents) on the ballot with other party names or labels. For a more detailed explanation of this alternate coding system, see Tables 5-1 and 1-3. —indicates that the state had no data, either because no vote data were found for the state in question or the state had not yet entered the Union. No special House elections are included in the table. The table only lists at-large vote values for states having both at-large and district House races; see Appendix B for these states' district results aggregated to the state level.

Sources: Adapted from *United States Congressional Elections, 1788–1997* (1998), *Congressional Quarterly's Guide to U.S. Elections* (1994), ICPSR data sets 0001 and 0075, and independent search for state sources by the author.

Table 5-108 House Election Results, by State, 1940–1942 (Raw Count)

State	1940 Democratic	Republican	Other	Total Vote	1942 Democratic	Republican	Other	Total Vote
Alabama	254,425	14,877	342	269,644	68,724	378	29	69,131
Alaska	—	—	—	—	—	—	—	—
Arizona	99,424	40,360	0	139,784	56,357	23,015	375	79,747
Arkansas	200,324	8,566	0	208,890	98,346	0	0	98,346
California	630,582	473,268	1,666,700	2,770,550	487,700	430,774	980,635	1,899,109
California	*1,183,943*	*1,473,115*	*113,492*	*2,770,550*	*906,614*	*936,042*	*56,453*	*1,899,109*
Colorado	286,104	237,254	1,668	525,026	141,761	199,365	1,270	342,396
Connecticut	407,868	365,851	8,874	782,593	257,941	283,280	27,784	569,005
Delaware	68,205	64,384	2,189	134,778	38,791	45,376	559	84,726
Delaware	*70,394*	*64,384*	*0*	*134,778*				
Florida	327,837	52,411	0	380,248	91,120	0	0	91,120
Georgia	194,533	5,166	71,700	271,399	58,352	0	3,527	61,879
Georgia	*260,783*	*9,817*	*799*	*271,399*	—	—	—	—
Hawaii	—	—	—	—	—	—	—	—
Idaho	123,833	107,803	0	231,636	67,920	71,367	0	139,287
Illinois	1,968,143	2,050,493	14,163	4,032,799	1,395,053	1,481,419	11,160	2,887,632
Indiana	864,576	896,841	200	1,761,617	572,903	713,831	0	1,286,734
Iowa	504,371	610,378	220	1,114,969	252,570	410,472	1,705	664,747
Kansas	333,796	454,866	0	788,662	194,677	299,015	0	493,692
Kentucky	557,992	335,241	0	893,233	193,181	145,391	4,033	342,605
Louisiana	307,102	13,933	9	321,044	84,987	0	0	84,987
Maine	87,286	159,387	0	246,673	48,923	111,918	0	160,841
Maryland	356,667	228,745	6	585,418	189,808	147,628	0	337,436
Massachusetts	925,462	1,024,746	4,530	1,954,738	543,641	713,423	70,178	1,327,242
Massachusetts	—	—	—	—	*611,714*	*713,423*	*2,105*	*1,327,242*
Michigan	969,328	1,013,774	4,256	1,987,358	534,682	629,679	6,333	1,170,694
Minnesota	262,895	640,120	302,738	1,205,753	156,450	452,192	152,632	761,274
Minnesota	*262,895*	*644,608*	*298,250*	*1,205,753*	*156,748*	*452,192*	*152,334*	*761,274*
Mississippi	146,219	0	0	146,219	51,698	0	0	51,698
Missouri	951,656	864,919	154	1,816,729	448,078	476,994	247	925,319
Montana	130,453	106,326	1,196	237,975	93,243	73,654	2,611	169,508
Nebraska	231,873	320,175	23,268	575,316	122,279	228,024	7,266	357,569
Nevada	32,714	18,032	0	50,746	21,100	18,289	0	39,389
New Hampshire	104,694	113,512	0	218,206	70,216	85,999	0	156,215
New Jersey	870,406	979,158	12,876	1,862,440	546,134	648,359	8,962	1,203,455
New Mexico	106,972	75,085	0	182,057	62,320	43,627	0	105,947
New York	0	2,830,517	3,204,698	6,035,215	0	1,967,218	1,986,571	3,953,789
New York	*3,199,019*	*2,830,517*	*5,679*	*6,035,215*	*1,912,114*	*1,967,218*	*74,457*	*3,953,789*
North Carolina	601,972	195,683	0	797,655	228,980	85,847	0	314,827
North Dakota	63,662	148,227	23,399	235,288	47,972	85,936	48,472	182,380
North Dakota	—	—	—	—	*47,972*	*134,408*	*0*	*182,380*
Ohio	1,483,934	1,519,628	0	3,003,562	717,692	945,995	0	1,663,687
Oklahoma	479,433	245,384	4,906	729,723	202,284	147,764	1,679	351,727
Oregon	189,702	263,479	8,721	461,902	115,519	160,904	2	276,425
Pennsylvania	1,993,546	1,834,084	19,984	3,847,614	1,105,992	1,360,664	22,701	2,489,357
Rhode Island	174,862	139,526	0	314,388	137,653	98,951	0	236,604
South Carolina	98,176	1,492	0	99,668	23,356	0	0	23,356
South Dakota	116,144	182,457	0	298,601	66,349	111,762	0	178,111
Tennessee	282,337	107,495	27,325	417,157	102,143	52,367	1,701	156,211
Texas	994,207	33,271	76	1,027,554	275,101	2,949	369	278,419
Utah	149,528	97,353	0	246,881	79,879	70,614	0	150,493
Vermont	50,804	89,637	36	140,477	17,304	40,751	15	58,070
Virginia	253,562	60,731	2,283	316,576	77,087	12,015	912	90,014
Washington	430,442	313,614	230	744,286	225,025	202,332	829	428,186
West Virginia	500,012	370,103	0	870,115	228,549	231,738	0	460,287
Wisconsin	220,520	579,526	469,063	1,269,109	203,537	350,812	194,368	748,717
Wyoming	57,030	49,701	157	106,888	36,892	37,965	0	74,857

Notes: Main entries are raw vote values for candidates who used the sole designation "Democrat" or "Republican" (or their historical antecedents listed in Appendix A) on the ballot. Other = candidates who used third-party names on the ballot or were listed as independent, unidentified, or scatter vote. Bold italicized entries in the table are the author's alternative party coding, which is used when a candidate listed a major party name (Democrat, Republican, or their historical antecedents) on the ballot with other party names or labels. For a more detailed explanation of this alternate coding system, see Tables 5-1 and 1-3. —indicates that the state had no data, either because no vote data were found for the state in question or the state had not yet entered the Union. No special House elections are included in the table. The table only lists at-large vote values for states having both at-large and district House races; see Appendix B for these states' district results aggregated to the state level.

Sources: Adapted from *United States Congressional Elections, 1788–1997* (1998), *Congressional Quarterly's Guide to U.S. Elections* (1994), ICPSR data sets 0001 and 0075, and independent search for state sources by the author.

Table 5-109 House Election Results, by State, 1944–1946 (Raw Count)

State	1944				1946			
	Democratic	Republican	Other	Total Vote	Democratic	Republican	Other	Total Vote
Alabama	200,462	21,876	0	222,338	165,383	14,105	0	179,488
Alaska	—	—	—	—	—	—	—	—
Arizona	88,532	39,035	469	128,036	74,948	37,033	831	112,812
Arkansas	200,700	16,515	0	217,215	143,252	7,186	895	151,333
Arkansas	*—*	*—*	*—*	*—*	*143,252*	*8,081*	*0*	*151,333*
California	1,137,504	1,080,205	787,233	3,004,942	638,387	772,916	923,219	2,334,522
California	*1,519,190*	*1,479,443*	*6,309*	*3,004,942*	*1,105,646*	*1,203,346*	*25,530*	*2,334,522*
Colorado	210,275	281,578	2,009	493,862	145,692	184,429	1,861	331,982
Connecticut	424,146	397,725	5,874	827,745	277,872	377,972	23,922	679,766
Delaware	63,649	62,378	413	126,440	49,105	63,516	0	112,621
Florida	349,570	63,183	0	412,753	151,123	35,640	0	186,763
Georgia	271,976	0	2,929	274,905	141,961	0	19,578	161,539
Hawaii	—	—	—	—	—	—	—	—
Idaho	105,830	99,749	0	205,579	77,740	101,018	0	178,758
Illinois	2,030,755	1,839,518	12,386	3,882,659	1,539,248	1,906,717	12,917	3,458,882
Indiana	767,157	872,721	11,339	1,651,217	588,639	725,622	18,373	1,332,634
Iowa	420,340	552,046	373	972,759	228,039	364,992	0	593,031
Kansas	245,860	418,332	0	664,192	223,173	328,642	3,045	554,860
Kentucky	459,936	381,552	2,355	843,843	271,480	311,502	320	583,302
Louisiana	282,569	0	0	282,569	100,357	5,651	1	106,009
Maine	53,861	129,910	0	183,771	63,860	110,388	0	174,248
Maryland	310,811	240,129	0	550,940	232,498	212,457	0	444,955
Massachusetts	887,957	1,001,682	111	1,889,750	744,765	863,274	9,275	1,617,314
Michigan	1,028,071	1,126,956	8,360	2,163,387	619,318	975,363	10,051	1,604,732
Minnesota	452,945	653,150	3,014	1,109,109	357,758	514,784	2,463	875,005
Mississippi	147,569	5,133	0	152,702	49,957	0	0	49,957
Missouri	798,374	722,889	136	1,521,399	517,980	566,296	0	1,084,276
Montana	118,131	77,513	1,573	197,217	95,982	93,265	841	190,088
Nebraska	165,489	336,400	12,777	514,666	118,800	248,724	4,516	372,040
Nevada	32,648	19,096	0	51,744	20,187	28,859	0	49,046
New Hampshire	102,364	113,448	35	215,847	61,220	99,872	0	161,092
New Jersey	860,326	988,108	11,044	1,859,478	553,964	815,261	12,768	1,381,993
New Mexico	85,244	66,309	0	151,553	66,420	60,519	0	126,939
New York	222,159	2,717,455	3,084,983	6,024,597	459,689	2,412,819	1,839,902	4,712,410
New York	*3,052,178*	*2,780,038*	*192,381*	*6,024,597*	*1,942,166*	*2,540,526*	*229,718*	*4,712,410*
North Carolina	524,274	230,384	0	754,658	277,277	174,945	0	452,222
North Dakota	56,699	101,007	43,023	200,729	41,189	103,205	0	144,394
North Dakota	*56,699*	*140,895*	*3,135*	*200,729*	*—*	*—*	*—*	*—*
Ohio	1,362,843	1,542,422	0	2,905,265	871,660	1,281,864	0	2,153,524
Oklahoma	401,232	282,279	1,049	684,560	287,978	204,163	0	492,141
Oregon	170,264	272,212	0	442,476	117,665	217,005	0	334,670
Pennsylvania	1,855,902	1,827,055	29,673	3,712,630	1,306,723	1,795,552	9,712	3,111,987
Pennsylvania	*1,880,777*	*1,827,055*	*4,798*	*3,712,630*	*—*	*—*	*—*	*—*
Rhode Island	175,368	118,011	102	293,481	148,673	122,887	890	272,450
South Carolina	97,360	3,495	0	100,855	26,067	243	48	26,358
South Dakota	78,850	146,888	0	225,738	58,073	104,731	0	162,804
Tennessee	260,694	131,714	6,224	398,632	126,530	55,031	11,883	193,444
Texas	1,000,010	63,341	0	1,063,351	332,661	16,998	0	349,659
Utah	149,599	98,082	0	247,681	95,486	101,186	0	196,672
Vermont	46,230	76,800	6	123,036	26,056	46,985	25	73,066
Virginia	239,347	71,604	32,029	342,980	167,919	83,638	2,298	253,855
Virginia	*250,366*	*80,623*	*11,991*	*342,980*	*—*	*—*	*—*	*—*
Washington	426,036	375,554	1,503	803,093	267,187	375,715	2,028	644,930
West Virginia	389,738	328,771	0	718,509	269,306	268,051	0	537,357
Wisconsin	408,714	624,833	129,107	1,162,654	312,289	615,287	55,990	983,566
Wyoming	42,569	53,533	0	96,102	34,946	44,512	0	79,458

Notes: Main entries are raw vote values for candidates who used the sole designation "Democrat" or "Republican" (or their historical antecedents listed in Appendix A) on the ballot. Other = candidates who used third-party names on the ballot or were listed as independent, unidentified, or scatter vote. Bold italicized entries in the table are the author's alternative party coding, which is used when a candidate listed a major party name (Democrat, Republican, or their historical antecedents) on the ballot with other party names or labels. For a more detailed explanation of this alternate coding system, see Tables 5-1 and 1-3. —indicates that the state had no data, either because no vote data were found for the state in question or the state had not yet entered the Union. No special House elections are included in the table. The table only lists at-large vote values for states having both at-large and district House races; see Appendix B for these states' district results aggregated to the state level.

Sources: Adapted from *United States Congressional Elections, 1788–1997* (1998), *Congressional Quarterly's Guide to U.S. Elections* (1994), ICPSR data sets 0001 and 0075, and independent search for state sources by the author.

Table 5-110 House Election Results by State, 1948–1950 (Raw Count)

State	1948 Democratic	Republican	Other	Total Vote	1950 Democratic	Republican	Other	Total Vote
Alabama	183,519	13,564	0	197,083	151,212	980	0	152,192
Alaska	—	—	—	—	—	—	—	—
Arizona	96,631	60,004	2,340	158,975	115,517	62,150	0	177,667
Arkansas	229,403	21,629	0	251,032	295,802	0	0	295,802
California	588,615	781,647	2,188,238	3,558,500	845,655	886,713	1,625,336	3,357,704
California	*1,348,098*	*1,974,748*	*235,654*	*3,558,500*	*1,480,639*	*1,754,001*	*123,064*	*3,357,704*
Colorado	272,484	224,927	0	497,411	214,385	225,986	2,521	442,892
Connecticut	429,348	433,311	16,692	879,351	426,485	433,912	17,991	878,388
Delaware	68,909	71,127	499	140,535	56,091	73,313	0	129,404
Florida	295,330	55,803	0	351,133	228,786	24,263	0	253,049
Georgia	365,176	0	234	365,410	289,931	0	77	290,008
Hawaii	—	—	—	—	—	—	—	—
Idaho	105,852	103,094	3,223	212,169	91,295	108,789	0	200,084
Illinois	2,001,650	1,823,266	23,724	3,848,640	1,617,000	1,891,177	1,518	3,509,695
Indiana	836,852	782,346	14,203	1,633,401	727,467	850,357	9,485	1,587,309
Iowa	429,048	517,207	3,489	949,744	317,222	500,426	2,311	819,959
Iowa	—	—	—	—	*317,369*	*500,426*	*2,164*	*819,959*
Kansas	299,478	404,432	0	703,910	248,897	355,849	0	604,746
Kentucky	416,014	320,691	3,822	740,527	307,836	180,778	0	488,614
Louisiana	308,239	13,437	0	321,676	227,075	0	0	227,075
Maine	72,114	141,780	0	213,894	100,731	136,901	0	237,632
Maryland	291,011	230,733	12,172	533,916	283,727	285,957	3,243	572,927
Massachusetts	976,241	970,179	55	1,946,475	920,988	930,280	8,128	1,859,396
Michigan	1,022,761	1,024,507	17,268	2,064,536	838,752	956,497	9,475	1,804,724
Minnesota	588,628	593,088	10	1,181,726	473,710	538,973	5,584	1,018,267
Mississippi	152,285	252	0	152,537	82,696	2,861	2,199	87,756
Missouri	914,886	641,851	3,375	1,560,112	697,542	552,014	594	1,250,150
Montana	122,987	91,061	501	214,549	108,248	99,948	2,331	210,527
Nebraska	191,831	268,620	0	460,451	164,490	271,840	0	436,330
Nevada	29,733	28,972	0	58,705	31,843	28,485	0	60,328
New Hampshire	94,551	124,299	1,513	220,363	72,760	112,487	0	185,247
New Jersey	880,881	937,820	34,812	1,853,513	689,814	859,145	22,304	1,571,263
New Mexico	108,529	76,695	805	186,029	97,187	75,447	0	172,634
New York	415,527	2,432,771	3,149,151	5,997,449	853,389	2,291,370	1,907,130	5,051,889
New York	*854,403*	*2,432,771*	*2,710,275*	*5,997,449*	*2,368,221*	*2,369,182*	*314,486*	*5,051,889*
North Carolina	540,873	219,295	3,345	763,513	365,598	156,602	0	522,200
North Dakota	56,702	132,343	1,758	190,803	62,322	119,047	0	181,369
Ohio	1,455,972	1,342,388	0	2,798,360	1,237,409	1,447,154	0	2,684,563
Oklahoma	457,371	222,390	0	679,761	363,452	243,334	0	606,786
Oregon	143,083	296,387	51,672	491,142	201,096	288,355	10,038	499,489
Oregon	*176,014*	*296,387*	*18,741*	*491,142*	—	—	—	—
Pennsylvania	1,782,985	1,815,625	58,419	3,657,029	1,672,788	1,834,128	4,973	3,511,889
Pennsylvania	*1,782,985*	*1,864,385*	*9,659*	*3,657,029*	—	—	—	—
Rhode Island	193,631	124,881	0	318,512	183,103	112,488	0	295,591
South Carolina	133,732	6,907	0	140,639	50,381	0	19	50,400
South Dakota	104,945	135,775	0	240,720	97,720	150,706	0	248,426
Tennessee	283,231	150,778	14,957	448,966	165,405	77,082	20,121	262,608
Tennessee	—	—	—	—	*165,405*	*97,203*	*0*	*262,608*
Texas	984,944	65,410	1,449	1,051,803	326,128	34,314	0	360,442
Utah	159,411	114,922	0	274,333	138,444	125,403	0	263,847
Vermont	47,767	74,076	125	121,968	22,709	65,248	865	88,822
Virginia	255,176	121,474	6,510	383,160	155,396	51,493	4,941	211,830
Washington	402,505	401,334	13,739	817,578	342,162	378,419	3,024	723,605
West Virginia	442,554	316,077	0	758,631	374,921	287,915	0	662,836
Wisconsin	514,018	676,501	20,649	1,211,168	470,275	639,293	501	1,110,069
Wyoming	47,246	50,218	0	97,464	42,483	50,865	0	93,348

Notes: Main entries are raw vote values for candidates who used the sole designation "Democrat" or "Republican" (or their historical antecedents listed in Appendix A) on the ballot. Other = candidates who used third-party names on the ballot or were listed as independent, unidentified, or scatter vote. Bold italicized entries in the table are the author's alternative party coding, which is used when a candidate listed a major party name (Democrat, Republican, or their historical antecedents) on the ballot with other party names or labels. For a more detailed explanation of this alternate coding system, see Tables 5-1 and 1-3. —indicates that the state had no data, either because no vote data were found for the state in question or the state had not yet entered the Union. No special House elections are included in the table. The table only lists at-large vote values for states having both at-large and district House races; see Appendix B for these states' district results aggregated to the state level.

Sources: Adapted from *United States Congressional Elections, 1788–1997* (1998), *Congressional Quarterly's Guide to U.S. Elections* (1994), *America Votes* (various publication dates), ICPSR data sets 0001 and 0075, and independent search for state sources by the author.

Table 5-111 House Election Results, by State, 1952–1954 (Raw Count)

State	1952 Democratic	Republican	Other	Total Vote	1954 Democratic	Republican	Other	Total Vote
Alabama	324,153	18,673	0	342,826	268,552	11,236	1	279,789
Alaska	—	—	—	—	—	—	—	—
Arizona	127,867	120,533	0	248,400	121,392	102,010	0	223,402
Arkansas	308,838	51,889	1,196	361,923	280,264	4	6	280,274
California	1,219,448	1,474,818	1,865,890	4,560,156	1,791,637	1,876,626	204,812	3,873,075
California	*2,030,549*	*2,382,921*	*146,686*	*4,560,156*	*1,991,169*	*1,876,626*	*5,280*	*3,873,075*
Colorado	269,865	335,394	1,307	606,566	239,565	240,074	415	480,054
Connecticut	489,645	601,238	3,065	1,093,948	455,887	474,585	1,938	932,410
Delaware	81,730	88,285	0	170,015	79,201	65,035	0	144,236
Florida	550,103	191,582	0	741,685	255,150	71,137	0	326,287
Georgia	547,095	0	179	547,274	317,703	29,911	5,129	352,743
Hawaii	—	—	—	—	—	—	—	—
Idaho	107,417	157,181	4	264,602	102,895	123,117	0	226,012
Illinois	2,004,628	2,348,725	5	4,353,358	1,636,443	1,621,278	1	3,257,722
Indiana	830,758	1,093,589	11,216	1,935,563	747,800	833,304	5,527	1,586,631
Iowa	378,763	762,310	1,989	1,143,062	338,931	478,322	0	817,253
Kansas	334,278	489,661	0	823,939	267,531	347,458	0	614,989
Kentucky	495,420	454,802	573	950,795	431,992	236,194	302	668,488
Louisiana	380,242	36,161	0	416,403	208,111	8,212	0	216,323
Maine	76,708	156,727	690	234,125	108,548	132,895	0	241,443
Maine	*77,398*	*156,727*	*0*	*234,125*	—	—	—	—
Maryland	405,225	436,113	0	841,338	342,115	295,426	1,334	638,875
Massachusetts	1,064,454	1,209,742	14,519	2,288,715	844,835	835,165	102,659	1,782,659
Massachusetts	—	—	—	—	*947,494*	*835,165*	*0*	*1,782,659*
Michigan	1,316,374	1,457,342	8,218	2,781,934	1,100,939	1,028,093	4,358	2,133,390
Minnesota	638,773	749,415	0	1,388,188	600,116	531,376	0	1,131,492
Mississippi	234,728	6,024	0	240,752	99,342	0	0	99,342
Missouri	971,199	890,237	0	1,861,436	665,722	519,091	0	1,184,813
Montana	110,882	144,296	888	256,066	117,109	107,478	0	224,587
Nebraska	179,849	386,432	0	566,281	156,343	250,347	0	406,690
Nevada	39,912	40,683	0	80,595	35,318	42,321	0	77,639
New Hampshire	95,119	162,550	0	257,669	86,913	104,905	0	191,818
New Jersey	977,914	1,317,404	20,259	2,315,577	862,382	903,839	20,632	1,786,853
New Mexico	121,477	112,297	0	233,774	111,711	77,151	0	188,862
New York	848,313	3,523,287	2,538,788	6,910,388	588,529	2,489,275	1,924,377	5,002,181
New York	*3,086,262*	*3,613,153*	*210,973*	*6,910,388*	*2,416,963*	*2,489,275*	*95,943*	*5,002,181*
North Carolina	763,388	358,810	0	1,122,198	390,167	214,012	0	604,179
North Dakota	49,829	181,218	0	231,047	64,089	124,845	0	188,934
Ohio	1,471,110	1,836,354	74,821	3,382,285	1,113,334	1,340,847	44,656	2,498,837
Oklahoma	545,713	383,859	3,764	933,336	354,339	191,450	0	545,789
Oregon	257,743	408,349	0	666,092	257,108	307,386	0	564,494
Pennsylvania	2,151,247	2,363,167	3,311	4,517,725	1,871,625	1,824,186	99	3,695,910
Rhode Island	220,461	186,828	0	407,289	195,200	130,859	0	326,059
South Carolina	278,180	5,642	0	283,822	210,624	2,711	0	213,335
South Dakota	90,338	197,137	0	287,475	93,894	137,273	0	231,167
Tennessee	479,641	203,766	16,988	700,395	232,524	112,272	0	344,796
Texas	0	0	1,979,811	1,979,811	555,446	75,472	0	630,918
Texas	*1,979,811*	*0*	*0*	*1,979,811*	—	—	—	—
Utah	144,982	181,841	0	326,823	116,625	146,406	0	263,031
Vermont	43,187	109,871	2	153,060	44,141	70,143	0	114,284
Virginia	298,238	138,604	9,998	446,840	204,433	128,315	9,596	342,344
Washington	515,213	504,783	517	1,020,513	464,045	342,089	3,661	809,795
West Virginia	471,175	403,427	0	874,602	339,958	251,444	0	591,402
Wisconsin	602,521	965,590	0	1,568,111	541,776	598,919	0	1,140,695
Wyoming	50,559	76,161	0	126,720	47,660	61,111	0	108,771

Notes: Main entries are raw vote values for candidates who used the sole designation "Democrat" or "Republican" (or their historical antecedents listed in Appendix A) on the ballot. Other = candidates who used third-party names on the ballot or were listed as independent, unidentified, or scatter vote. Bold italicized entries in the table are the author's alternative party coding, which is used when a candidate listed a major party name (Democrat, Republican, or their historical antecedents) on the ballot with other party names or labels. For a more detailed explanation of this alternate coding system, see Tables 5-1 and 1-3. —indicates that the state had no data, either because no vote data were found for the state in question or the state had not yet entered the Union. No special House elections are included in the table. The table only lists at-large vote values for states having both at-large and district House races; see Appendix B for these states' district results aggregated to the state level.

Sources: Adapted from *United States Congressional Elections, 1788–1997* (1998), *Congressional Quarterly's Guide to U.S. Elections* (1994), *America Votes* (various publication dates), ICPSR data sets 0001 and 0075, and independent search for state sources by the author.

Table 5-112 House Election Results by State, 1956–1959 (Raw Count)

State	1956				1958–1959			
	Democratic	Republican	Other	Total Vote	Democratic	Republican	Other	Total Vote
Alabama	331,137	51,818	0	382,955	231,112	6,050	0	237,162
Alaska	—	—	—	—	27,945	20,699	0	48,644
Arizona	146,915	133,594	0	280,509	139,467	138,099	0	277,566
Arkansas	235,445	24,318	0	259,763	29,483[2]	0[2]	30,739[2]	60,222[2]
Arkansas	*—*	*—*	*—*	*—*	*60,222[2]*	*0[2]*	*0[2]*	*60,222[2]*
California	2,225,027	2,466,620	485,673	5,177,320	2,260,362	1,981,276	711,499	4,953,137
California	*2,710,700*	*2,466,620*	*0*	*5,177,320*	*2,971,861*	*1,981,276*	*0*	*4,953,137*
Colorado	332,051	296,502	1	628,554	309,873	222,971	1,175	534,019
Connecticut	428,709	683,387	0	1,112,096	542,315	425,452	0	967,767
Delaware	84,644	91,538	0	176,182	76,797	76,099	0	152,896
Florida	589,574	352,149	0	941,723	354,942	139,419	0	494,361
Georgia	522,072	58,966	11,232	592,270	158,636	0	2	158,638
Hawaii	—	—	—	—	111,727[1]	51,058[1]	932[1]	163,717[1]
Idaho	120,722	139,712	0	260,434	124,297	114,731	0	239,028
Illinois	1,967,104	2,272,995	1	4,240,100	1,754,248	1,468,590	7,026	3,229,864
Indiana	864,351	1,092,367	4,603	1,961,321	921,795	798,850	819	1,721,464
Iowa	533,641	636,573	0	1,170,214	417,118	412,798	0	829,916
Kansas	387,096	438,868	1,417	827,381	359,763	354,732	3,199	717,694
Kentucky	503,295	461,644	113	965,052	309,771	164,425	1,622	475,818
Louisiana	330,270	57,385	0	387,655	177,963	4,160	1	182,124
Maine	142,041	150,415	0	292,456	146,356	128,606	0	274,962
Maryland	444,418	421,382	0	865,800	463,888	248,238	0	712,126
Massachusetts	1,092,697	1,156,137	672	2,249,506	1,021,174	754,373	671	1,776,218
Michigan	1,490,834	1,500,172	3,668	2,994,674	1,193,696	1,054,854	5,260	2,253,810
Minnesota	712,406	676,104	0	1,388,510	596,257	534,870	0	1,131,127
Mississippi	205,532	0	0	205,532	61,464	0	0	61,464
Missouri	1,011,057	681,724	0	1,692,781	736,877	429,940	0	1,166,817
Montana	146,449	116,755	0	263,204	147,726	80,744	0	228,470
Nebraska	220,372	323,641	2,389	546,402	195,450	220,140	0	415,590
Nevada	51,100	43,154	0	94,254	55,053	27,275	0	82,328
New Hampshire	97,930	155,215	0	253,145	81,263	115,370	868	197,501
New Jersey	972,620	1,391,335	23,447	2,387,402	938,603	944,349	23,500	1,906,452
New Mexico	129,625	114,719	0	244,344	124,924	72,922	0	197,846
New York	510,925	3,646,966	2,728,920	6,886,811	456,109	2,621,500	2,445,307	5,522,916
New York	*3,072,860*	*3,745,821*	*68,130*	*6,886,811*	*2,763,883*	*2,686,818*	*72,215*	*5,522,916*
North Carolina	716,201	309,071	0	1,025,272	431,202	177,651	0	608,853
North Dakota	85,743	143,514	0	229,257	99,562	97,862	0	197,424
Ohio	1,444,705	1,936,662	0	3,381,367	1,581,014	1,529,565	0	3,110,579
Oklahoma	485,321	326,993	401	812,715	369,271	159,168	1,336	529,775
Oregon	380,391	338,303	0	718,694	338,858	256,253	0	595,111
Pennsylvania	2,131,833	2,386,657	289	4,518,779	2,019,994	1,940,666	538	3,961,198
Rhode Island	202,228	173,282	0	375,510	214,931	125,523	188	340,642
South Carolina	249,591	12,278	135	262,004	76,632	0	15	76,647
South Dakota	145,500	142,516	0	288,016	132,693	125,296	0	257,989
Tennessee	401,375	279,903	0	681,278	276,870	92,999	1,934	371,803
Tennessee	*—*	*—*	*—*	*—*	*278,694*	*92,999*	*110*	*371,803*
Texas	1,437,830	0	21,868	1,459,698	673,771	91,287	3,789	768,847
Utah	135,503	193,790	0	329,293	140,948	145,375	0	286,323
Vermont	50,797	103,736	0	154,533	63,131	59,536	0	122,667
Virginia	415,872	279,660	1,253	696,785	318,633	86,211	26,765	431,609
Washington	621,118	439,896	0	1,061,014	406,195	467,678	2,953	876,826
West Virginia	428,264	378,130	0	806,394	380,983	234,804	0	615,787
Wisconsin	696,731	825,305	0	1,522,036	633,152	547,873	0	1,181,025
Wyoming	50,225	69,903	0	120,128	51,886	59,894	0	111,780

Notes: Main entries are raw vote values for candidates who used the sole designation "Democrat" or "Republican" (or their historical antecedents listed in Appendix A) on the ballot. Other = candidates who used third-party names on the ballot or were listed as independent, unidentified, or scatter vote. Bold italicized entries in the table are the author's alternative party coding, which is used when a candidate listed a major party name (Democrat, Republican, or their historical antecedents) on the ballot with other party names or labels. For a more detailed explanation of this alternate coding system, see Tables 5-1 and 1-3. —indicates that the state had no data, either because no vote data were found for the state in question or the state had not yet entered the Union. No special House elections are included in the table. The table only lists at-large vote values for states having both at-large and district House races; see Appendix B for these states' district results aggregated to the state level.

[1] Election held in odd-numbered year.
[2] Partial data (less than 100 percent of the districts reporting).

Sources: Adapted from *United States Congressional Elections, 1788–1997* (1998), *Congressional Quarterly's Guide to U.S. Elections* (1994), *America Votes* (various publication dates), ICPSR data sets 0001 and 0075, and independent search for state sources by the author.

Table 5-113 House Election Results, by State, 1960–1962 (Raw Count)

State	1960 Democratic	Republican	Other	Total Vote	1962 Democratic	Republican	Other	Total Vote
Alabama	389,567	48,117	29	437,713	293,182	138,963	32,446	464,591
Alaska	33,546	25,517	0	59,063	31,953	26,638	0	58,591
Arizona	179,188	197,374	0	376,562	169,632	179,392	0	349,024
Arkansas	57,617[1]	12,054[1]	0[1]	69,671[1]	133,758[1]	47,805[1]	29[1]	181,592[1]
California	3,194,735	2,855,115	142,698	6,192,548	2,891,518	2,679,662	2,166	5,573,346
California	*3,336,709*	*2,855,115*	*724*	*6,192,548*	—	—	—	—
Colorado	370,487	344,792	0	715,279	282,474	314,122	0	596,596
Connecticut	657,680	560,803	0	1,218,483	543,424	487,575	38	1,031,037
Delaware	98,227	96,337	0	194,564	81,166	71,934	256	153,356
Florida	861,261	386,513	0	1,247,774	588,719	351,954	162	940,835
Georgia	549,405	24,369	454	574,228	272,494	59,514	1,363	333,371
Georgia	—	—	—	—	*272,494*	*60,247*	*630*	*333,371*
Hawaii	135,827	46,812	0	182,639	123,649	70,880	0	194,529
Idaho	159,024	131,266	0	290,290	134,574	119,755	0	254,329
Illinois	2,369,523	2,235,048	0	4,604,571	1,802,063	1,822,635	542	3,625,240
Indiana	1,032,683	1,087,942	1,707	2,122,332	878,311	911,596	802	1,790,709
Iowa	563,358	662,864	0	1,226,222	370,362	432,483	0	802,845
Kansas	398,892	471,995	0	870,887	249,556	375,726	0	625,282
Kentucky	539,253	373,773	0	913,026	372,388	258,182	860	631,430
Louisiana	441,533	77,938	0	519,471	303,813	42,419	0	346,232
Maine	177,442	230,834	418	408,694	127,288	158,213	0	285,501
Maine	*177,860*	*230,834*	*0*	*408,694*	—	—	—	—
Maryland	582,315	398,490	0	980,805	388,107	308,792	0	696,899
Massachusetts	1,378,332	880,079	551	2,258,962	1,146,884	808,240	15,358	1,970,482
Michigan	1,638,588	1,567,725	5,110	3,211,423	1,392,221	1,282,082	4,950	2,679,253
Minnesota	759,893	749,770	5,459	1,515,122	599,124	605,054	575	1,204,753
Mississippi	252,741	5,036	0	257,777	157,153	0	4,461	161,614
Missouri	1,062,939	780,432	0	1,843,371	683,877	528,447	0	1,212,324
Montana	138,588	133,624	0	272,212	119,366	129,075	0	248,441
Nebraska	251,931	327,246	0	579,177	164,403	271,777	8,794	444,974
Nevada	59,616	43,986	0	103,602	66,866	26,458	0	93,324
New Hampshire	118,862	165,819	0	284,681	99,449	121,803	0	221,252
New Jersey	1,275,882	1,361,844	21,299	2,659,025	980,509	964,280	14,171	1,958,960
New Mexico	176,514	123,683	851	301,048	128,651	116,262	0	244,913
New York	991,054	3,281,208	2,783,625	7,055,887	810,544	2,655,070	2,094,137	5,559,751
New York	*3,648,347*	*3,281,208*	*126,332*	*7,055,887*	*2,778,105*	*2,686,314*	*95,332*	*5,559,751*
North Carolina	786,983	515,488	0	1,302,471	482,146	336,383	0	818,529
North Dakota	120,773	135,579	0	256,352	98,749	117,533	0	216,282
Ohio	1,766,362	2,080,270	0	3,846,632	1,164,776	1,786,018	0	2,950,794
Oklahoma	459,463	378,131	0	837,594	381,737	242,876	0	624,613
Oregon	389,569	372,187	81	761,837	342,209	288,571	85	630,865
Pennsylvania	2,554,885	2,396,322	2,888	4,954,095	2,135,717	2,217,431	1,059	4,354,207
Rhode Island	268,706	123,532	0	392,238	207,517	111,141	0	318,658
South Carolina	328,326	0	112	328,438	225,714	36,808	32	262,554
South Dakota	132,421	168,583	0	301,004	101,664	151,067	0	252,731
Tennessee	440,103	202,711	5	642,819	375,248	212,362	18,278	605,888
Tennessee	—	—	—	—	*375,248*	*218,672*	*11,968*	*605,888*
Texas	1,680,675	297,239	61,224	2,039,138	870,860	680,839	0	1,551,699
Utah	186,710	182,752	0	369,462	149,620	167,387	0	317,007
Vermont	71,111	94,905	19	166,035	52,535	68,822	0	121,357
Virginia	411,015	199,656	29,320	639,991	268,699	178,913	1,340	448,952
Washington	478,208	646,517	0	1,124,725	337,832	543,318	0	881,150
West Virginia	468,127	352,353	0	820,480	343,274	269,744	0	613,018
Wisconsin	813,217	845,994	3,882	1,663,093	620,317	623,907	107	1,244,331
Wyoming	64,090	70,241	0	134,331	44,985	71,489	0	116,474

Notes: Main entries are raw vote values for candidates who used the sole designation "Democrat" or "Republican" (or their historical antecedents listed in Appendix A) on the ballot. Other = candidates who used third-party names on the ballot or were listed as independent, unidentified, or scatter vote. Bold italicized entries in the table are the author's alternative party coding, which is used when a candidate listed a major party name (Democrat, Republican, or their historical antecedents) on the ballot with other party names or labels. For a more detailed explanation of this alternate coding system, see Tables 5-1 and 1-3. —indicates that the state had no data, either because no vote data were found for the state in question or the state had not yet entered the Union. No special House elections are included in the table. The table only lists at-large vote values for states having both at-large and district House races; see Appendix B for these states' district results aggregated to the state level.

[1]Partial data (less than 100 percent of the districts reporting).

Sources: Adapted from *United States Congressional Elections, 1788–1997* (1998), *Congressional Quarterly's Guide to U.S. Elections* (1994), *America Votes* (various publication dates), ICPSR data sets 0001 and 0075, and independent search for state sources by the author.

Table 5-114 House Election Results, by State, 1964–1966 (Raw Count)

| | 1964 | | | | 1966 | | | |
State	Democratic	Republican	Other	Total Vote	Democratic	Republican	Other	Total Vote
Alabama	297,951	317,160	2,018	617,129	429,770	276,639	0	706,409
Alaska	34,590	32,556	0	67,146	31,867	34,040	0	65,907
Arizona	230,733	230,091	0	460,824	159,945	204,478	0	364,423
Arkansas	71,228[1]	58,884[1]	0[1]	130,112[1]	160,896[1]	130,742[1]	0[1]	291,638[1]
California	3,609,315	3,213,798	586	6,823,699	2,937,862	3,336,943	3,796	6,278,601
Colorado	440,090	316,322	1,183	757,595	339,750	298,472	2,263	640,485
Connecticut	752,983	456,233	163	1,209,379	543,149	443,319	17,149	1,003,617
Delaware	112,361	86,254	76	198,691	72,132	90,961	0	163,093
Florida	991,897	420,856	2,600	1,415,353	680,466	368,976	4,333	1,053,775
Georgia	562,422	248,024	25,078	835,524	557,883	292,150	755	850,788
Hawaii	140,224	89,425	0	229,649	140,880	67,281	0	208,161
Idaho	140,225	144,306	0	284,531	98,794	149,434	0	248,228
Illinois	2,492,433	2,082,167	7	4,574,607	1,707,576	2,027,714	20	3,735,310
Indiana	1,094,999	977,548	734	2,073,281	779,588	897,086	1,363	1,678,037
Iowa	622,844	516,929	1,798	1,141,571	417,740	458,948	2,280	878,968
Kansas	362,162	451,526	0	813,688	241,571	416,610	2,349	660,530
Kentucky	618,489	336,696	0	955,185	357,488	319,636	0	677,124
Louisiana	429,567	171,137	0	600,704	447,006	99,252	0	546,258
Maine	206,126	163,376	0	369,502	167,258	138,460	7,098	312,816
Maryland	683,143	301,250	0	984,393	429,380	336,043	0	765,423
Massachusetts	1,313,448	787,292	7,440	2,108,180	1,098,362	713,144	78	1,811,584
Michigan	1,767,716	1,289,291	2,631	3,059,638	1,150,400	1,216,202	0	2,366,602
Minnesota	826,879	691,118	1,311	1,519,308	590,327	630,049	0	1,220,376
Mississippi	325,950	35,277	0	361,227	282,574	61,514	38,459	382,547
Missouri	1,107,512	664,563	201	1,772,276	561,112	484,098	0	1,045,210
Montana	136,308	139,658	644	276,610	117,431	140,940	0	258,371
Nebraska	272,922	288,153	0	561,075	178,518	292,603	0	471,121
Nevada	82,748	47,989	0	130,737	86,467	41,383	0	127,850
New Hampshire	141,479	137,619	4	279,102	89,588	139,085	142	228,815
New Jersey	1,482,674	1,227,600	9,398	2,719,672	1,020,779	1,045,641	31,571	2,097,991
New Mexico	164,863	154,780	0	319,643	126,984	124,536	0	251,520
New York	1,211,888	2,221,224	3,331,152	6,764,264	814,131	1,733,109	2,965,387	5,512,627
New York	***3,920,002***	***2,718,154***	***126,108***	***6,764,264***	***2,763,837***	***2,494,820***	***253,970***	***5,512,627***
North Carolina	787,902	516,340	0	1,304,242	484,413	432,036	0	916,449
North Dakota	123,959	124,453	659	249,071	80,687	116,812	0	197,499
Ohio	1,872,351	1,716,480	0	3,588,831	1,196,149	1,599,492	0	2,795,641
Oklahoma	529,728	310,563	0	840,291	333,597	302,792	0	636,389
Oregon	461,690	305,682	385	767,757	314,881	349,902	96	664,879
Pennsylvania	2,613,413	2,062,907	0	4,676,320	1,895,621	2,070,037	0	3,965,658
Rhode Island	278,430	94,657	0	373,087	196,957	124,531	534	322,022
South Carolina	395,390	48,970	2,501	446,861	257,153	106,775	345	364,273
South Dakota	123,265	164,448	0	287,713	81,391	143,655	0	225,046
Tennessee	581,011	416,750	37,037	1,034,798	382,296	382,824	34,751	799,871
Texas	1,690,674	826,991	9,190	2,526,855	1,037,344	206,419	14,708	1,258,471
Utah	209,522	186,498	0	396,020	111,261	196,176	0	307,437
Vermont	71,193	0	92,259	163,452	46,643	89,097	8	135,748
Vermont	***71,193***	***92,252***	***7***	***163,452***	*—*	*—*	*—*	*—*
Virginia	536,527	298,888	93,292	928,707	391,538	268,094	23,105	682,737
Washington	613,420	583,765	337	1,197,522	474,021	449,765	15,655	939,441
West Virginia	450,202	320,183	0	770,385	262,023	232,322	0	494,345
Wisconsin	858,858	789,809	164	1,648,831	532,897	620,786	258	1,153,941
Wyoming	70,693	68,482	0	139,175	57,442	62,984	0	120,426

Notes: Main entries are raw vote values for candidates who used the sole designation "Democrat" or "Republican" (or their historical antecedents listed in Appendix A) on the ballot. Other = candidates who used third-party names on the ballot or were listed as independent, unidentified, or scatter vote. Bold italicized entries in the table are the author's alternative party coding, which is used when a candidate listed a major party name (Democrat, Republican, or their historical antecedents) on the ballot with other party names or labels. For a more detailed explanation of this alternate coding system, see Tables 5-1 and 1-3. —indicates that the state had no data, either because no vote data were found for the state in question or the state had not yet entered the Union. No special House elections are included in the table. The table only lists at-large vote values for states having both at-large and district House races; see Appendix B for these states' district results aggregated to the state level.

[1]Partial data (less than 100 percent of the districts reporting).

Sources: Adapted from *United States Congressional Elections, 1788–1997* (1998), *Congressional Quarterly's Guide to U.S. Elections* (1994), *America Votes* (various publication dates), ICPSR data sets 0001 and 0075, and independent search for state sources by the author.

Table 5-115 House Election Results, by State, 1968–1970 (Raw Count)

State	1968 Democratic	Republican	Other	Total Vote	1970 Democratic	Republican	Other	Total Vote
Alabama	546,926	247,438	116,669	911,033	475,095	189,050	77,927	742,072
Alabama	*630,744*	*247,438*	*32,851*	*911,033*	*542,323*	*189,050*	*10,699*	*742,072*
Alaska	36,785	43,577	0	80,362	44,137	35,947	0	80,084
Arizona	202,967	260,663	0	463,630	182,256	218,506	1,357	402,119
Arkansas	139,931[1]	158,055[1]	0[1]	297,986[1]	57,679[1]	115,532[1]	0[1]	173,211[1]
California	3,085,320	3,665,711	250,954	7,001,985	3,124,147	3,095,405	101,842	6,321,394
California	*3,089,104*	*3,808,933*	*103,948*	*7,001,985*	—	—	—	—
Colorado	362,164	392,779	25,499	780,442	310,117	317,696	9,335	637,148
Connecticut	625,278	569,957	11,323	1,206,558	531,523	524,953	14,028	1,070,504
Delaware	82,993	117,827	0	200,820	71,429	86,125	2,759	160,313
Florida	1,011,749	757,907	28	1,769,684	681,393[1]	568,718[1]	0[1]	1,250,111[1]
Georgia	750,538	194,129	166	944,833	653,513	225,632	96	879,241
Hawaii	161,954	78,733	2,432	243,119	176,449	31,764	0	208,213
Idaho	116,258	155,899	4,377	276,534	87,615	143,943	2,759	234,317
Illinois	2,053,892	2,368,310	21	4,422,223	1,814,064	1,680,861	59	3,494,984
Indiana	943,806	1,094,964	366	2,039,136	878,841	848,785	0	1,727,626
Iowa	513,529	608,875	7	1,122,411	387,510	388,428	3,753	779,691
Kansas	309,551	507,733	0	817,284	303,988	407,264	8,419	719,671
Kentucky	440,974	421,010	3,256	865,240	247,585	222,813	3,265	473,663
Louisiana	511,355	117,626	0	628,981	330,464	19,703	12,881	363,048
Maine	215,870	168,347	0	384,217	195,718	122,313	0	318,031
Maryland	535,819	483,829	0	1,019,648	452,549	430,300	2,695	885,544
Massachusetts	1,032,731	830,771	193,466	2,056,968	1,019,657	718,052	62,789	1,800,498
Massachusetts	*1,032,731*	*971,190*	*53,047*	*2,056,968*	—	—	—	—
Michigan	1,532,693	1,506,972	4,014	3,043,679	1,314,448	1,241,474	6,476	2,562,398
Minnesota	731,536	801,209	1,299	1,534,044	709,635	628,583	2,408	1,340,626
Mississippi	415,021	33,683	0	448,704	269,193	28,847	14,317	312,357
Missouri	959,354	760,123	953	1,720,430	692,026	493,557	11,824	1,197,407
Montana	114,726	148,750	0	263,476	141,257	108,140	0	249,397
Nebraska	208,356	309,218	4,597	522,171	164,558	242,507	41,034	448,099
Nevada	104,136	40,209	0	144,345	113,496	24,147	0	137,643
New Hampshire	93,901	188,878	4	282,783	67,256	146,389	0	213,645
New Jersey	1,288,447	1,364,409	45,184	2,698,040	1,098,788	984,728	17,893	2,101,409
New Mexico	147,975	160,374	1,487	309,836	129,116	152,261	3,981	285,358
New York	1,546,144	1,347,554	3,225,222	6,118,920	856,598	734,077	3,855,533	5,446,208
New York	*2,998,439*	*2,812,889*	*307,592*	*6,118,920*	*2,721,338*	*2,447,752*	*277,118*	*5,446,208*
North Carolina	765,065	633,012	0	1,398,077	513,905	410,742	5,301	929,948
North Dakota	94,347	140,076	3,692	238,115	88,104	122,056	0	210,160
Ohio	1,428,021	2,207,658	599	3,636,278	1,323,271	1,706,205	12,535	3,042,011
Oklahoma	444,995	364,866	0	809,861	428,706	245,216	1,534	675,456
Oregon	370,036	417,107	81	787,224	337,998	314,724	268	652,990
Pennsylvania	2,286,363	2,055,950	235,060	4,577,373	1,945,360	1,611,619	56,084	3,613,063
Pennsylvania	*2,286,363*	*2,230,052*	*60,958*	*4,577,373*	—	—	—	—
Rhode Island	221,989	140,896	1,893	364,778	207,987	114,781	2,845	325,613
South Carolina	416,181	203,902	7,749	627,832	309,487	115,531	1,947	426,965
South Dakota	112,421	159,219	0	271,640	127,561	107,422	0	234,983
Tennessee	485,833	507,996	18,574	1,012,403	579,783	403,233	5,682	988,698
Texas	1,720,408	675,574	0	2,395,982	1,339,012	476,824	17,388	1,833,224
Utah	146,213	269,583	0	415,796	182,499	186,818	3,583	372,900
Vermont	0	0	157,133	157,133	44,415	103,806	4,336	152,557
Vermont	*0*	*156,956*	*177*	*157,133*	—	—	—	—
Virginia	621,065	600,893	46,916	1,268,874	465,418	414,275	25,847	905,540
Washington	623,630	576,072	4,379	1,204,081	608,508	403,946	9,670	1,022,124
West Virginia	434,140	277,925	0	712,065	286,006	152,877	0	438,883
Wisconsin	741,661	895,388	3,870	1,640,919	740,485	576,575	8,964	1,326,024
Wyoming	45,950	77,363	0	123,313	58,456	57,848	0	116,304

Notes: Main entries are raw vote values for candidates who used the sole designation "Democrat" or "Republican" (or their historical antecedents listed in Appendix A) on the ballot. Other = candidates who used third-party names on the ballot or were listed as independent, unidentified, or scatter vote. Bold italicized entries in the table are the author's alternative party coding, which is used when a candidate listed a major party name (Democrat, Republican, or their historical antecedents) on the ballot with other party names or labels. For a more detailed explanation of this alternate coding system, see Tables 5-1 and 1-3. —indicates that the state had no data, either because no vote data were found for the state in question or the state had not yet entered the Union. No special House elections are included in the table. The table only lists at-large vote values for states having both at-large and district House races; see Appendix B for these states' district results aggregated to the state level.

[1]Partial data (less than 100 percent of the districts reporting).

Sources: Adapted from *United States Congressional Elections, 1788–1997* (1998), *Congressional Quarterly's Guide to U.S. Elections* (1994), *America Votes* (various publication dates), ICPSR data sets 0001 and 0075, and independent search for state sources by the author.

Table 5-116 House Election Results, by State, 1972–1974 (Raw Count)

	1972				1974			
State	Democratic	Republican	Other	Total Vote	Democratic	Republican	Other	Total Vote
Alabama	544,070	383,623	44,936	972,629	375,976	169,304	16,120	561,400
Alabama	*581,688*	*383,623*	*7,318*	*972,629*	*382,392*	*169,304*	*9,704*	*561,400*
Alaska	53,651	41,750	0	95,401	44,280	51,641	0	95,921
Arizona	284,045	309,862	0	593,907	269,489	266,117	8,217	543,823
Arkansas	42,481[1]	144,571[1]	0[1]	187,052[1]	267,573[1]	156,183[1]	0[1]	423,756[1]
California	4,209,586	3,760,095	146,910	8,116,591	3,343,531	2,369,389	147,342	5,860,262
Colorado	428,259	480,059	4,562	912,880	413,434	364,369	6,737	784,540
Connecticut	657,265	690,839	2,897	1,351,001	620,029	440,207	18,297	1,078,533
Delaware	83,230	141,237	1,384	225,851	63,490	93,826	3,012	160,328
Florida	1,030,817[1]	900,683[1]	10[1]	1,931,510[1]	477,121[1]	580,975[1]	3,524[1]	1,061,620[1]
Georgia	638,826	252,901	79	891,806	588,538	233,769	116	822,423
Hawaii	153,682	121,181	0	274,863	158,468	100,959	0	259,427
Idaho	108,187	187,807	5,560	301,554	107,600	142,678	0	250,278
Illinois	2,146,823	2,223,305	14,895	4,385,023	1,601,152	1,218,921	22,036	2,842,109
Indiana	973,706	1,133,646	2,884	2,110,236	956,675	770,154	4,005	1,730,834
Iowa	616,378	577,425	1,933	1,195,736	488,214	413,230	2,071	903,515
Kansas	280,653	581,900	15,812	878,365	325,400	417,956	32,202	775,558
Kentucky	493,795	487,820	4,362	985,977	425,272	238,637	15,316	679,225
Louisiana	573,977	86,607	17,844	678,428	396,581[1]	140,008[1]	9,453[1]	546,042[1]
Maine	218,543	194,868	0	413,411	140,923	212,357	0	353,280
Maryland	634,077	584,859	0	1,218,936	526,809	347,280	0	874,089
Massachusetts	1,243,753	808,394	106,554	2,158,701	1,168,252	401,300	129,149	1,698,701
Michigan	1,535,707	1,710,177	27,290	3,273,174	1,465,265	1,019,544	34,617	2,519,426
Minnesota	896,854	760,620	32,312	1,689,786	705,139	491,912	21,951	1,219,002
Mississippi	387,389	184,598	16,086	588,073	156,119	130,999	18,791	305,909
Missouri	1,092,405	737,377	2,846	1,832,628	809,719	396,617	2,706	1,209,042
Montana	190,597	124,436	0	315,033	148,984	105,162	0	254,146
Nebraska	193,644	375,065	137	568,846	211,496	236,076	119	447,691
Nevada	86,349	94,113	0	180,462	93,665	61,182	13,119	167,966
New Hampshire	94,255	222,753	26	317,034	96,851	122,678	13	219,542
New Jersey	1,390,819	1,416,485	24,555	2,831,859	1,240,933	794,698	47,926	2,083,557
New Mexico	210,391	163,187	0	373,578	162,095	149,313	4,964	316,372
New York	1,674,240	1,225,219	3,709,969	6,609,428	888,160	792,712	3,213,480	4,894,352
New York	*3,340,862*	*2,980,190*	*288,376*	*6,609,428*	*2,807,472*	*1,929,983*	*156,897*	*4,894,352*
North Carolina	734,627	609,926	6,194	1,350,747	637,833	347,603	2,904	988,340
North Dakota	72,850	195,360	511	268,721	103,504	130,184	0	233,688
Ohio	1,684,303	2,071,010	80,200	3,835,513	1,396,530	1,458,222	90,173	2,944,925
Oklahoma	496,657	310,180	10,244	817,081	294,704	208,243	3,365	506,312
Oregon	479,024	390,138	568	869,730	482,462	270,319	414	753,195
Pennsylvania	2,172,844	2,281,484	8,461	4,462,789	1,937,154	1,421,944	18,179	3,377,277
Rhode Island	243,444	138,786	5,762	387,992	230,047	73,824	0	303,871
South Carolina	328,860	301,695	102	630,657	301,516	212,893	2,803	517,212
South Dakota	159,857	141,135	0	300,992	105,458	167,012	0	272,470
Tennessee	504,782	589,272	8,341	1,102,395	533,402	363,502	4,925	901,829
Texas	2,032,183	835,185	18,581	2,885,949	1,075,346	406,744	6,729	1,488,819
Utah	259,859	203,481	9,728	473,068	230,532	163,066	19,364	412,962
Vermont	65,062	120,924	42	186,028	56,342	74,561	9,996	140,899
Virginia	627,298	589,573	54,117	1,270,988	506,838	361,302	56,046	924,186
Washington	857,621	438,683	5,529	1,301,833	574,055	400,557	6,313	980,925
West Virginia	477,294	274,356	0	751,650	290,146	125,368	0	415,514
Wisconsin	1,012,821	767,139	21,134	1,801,094	703,992	475,292	17,287	1,196,571
Wyoming	75,632	70,667	0	146,299	69,434	57,499	0	126,933

Notes: Main entries are raw vote values for candidates who used the sole designation "Democrat" or "Republican" (or their historical antecedents listed in Appendix A) on the ballot. Other = candidates who used third-party names on the ballot or were listed as independent, unidentified, or scatter vote. Bold italicized entries in the table are the author's alternative party coding, which is used when a candidate listed a major party name (Democrat, Republican, or their historical antecedents) on the ballot with other party names or labels. For a more detailed explanation of this alternate coding system, see Tables 5-1 and 1-3. —indicates that the state had no data, either because no vote data were found for the state in question or the state had not yet entered the Union. No special House elections are included in the table. The table only lists at-large vote values for states having both at-large and district House races; see Appendix B for these states' district results aggregated to the state level.

[1]Partial data (less than 100 percent of the districts reporting).

Sources: Adapted from *United States Congressional Elections, 1788–1997* (1998), *Congressional Quarterly's Guide to U.S. Elections* (1994), *America Votes* (various publication dates), ICPSR data sets 0001 and 0075, and independent search for state sources by the author.

Table 5-117 House Election Results, by State, 1976–1978 (Raw Count)

State	1976 Democratic	Republican	Other	Total Vote	1978 Democratic	Republican	Other	Total Vote
Alabama	667,052	314,970	2,159	984,181	439,564	197,176	5,539	642,279
Alabama	*668,073*	*314,970*	*1,111*	*984,154*	—	—	—	—
Alaska	34,194	83,722	292	118,208	55,176	68,811	200	124,187
Arizona	355,747	340,478	32,777	729,002	261,567	230,573	26,842	518,982
Arkansas	260,997[1]	75,384[1]	8[1]	336,389[1]	97,888[1]	195,371[1]	0[1]	293,259[1]
California	4,144,406	3,220,418	89,204	7,454,028	3,335,212	3,105,933	84,472	6,525,617
Colorado	456,103	536,781	29,361	1,022,245	369,455	402,274	13,446	785,175
Connecticut	681,730	651,250	15,492	1,348,472	592,396	423,474	5,151	1,021,021
Delaware	102,431	110,677	1,691	214,799	64,863	91,689	1,014	157,566
Florida	1,125,782[1]	937,257[1]	19,491[1]	2,082,530[1]	948,045[1]	671,942[1]	0[1]	1,619,987[1]
Georgia	930,621	321,891	578	1,253,090	472,210	116,301	94	588,605
Hawaii	184,166	77,662	31,873	293,701	202,824	40,167	10,378	253,369
Idaho	161,899	180,008	0	341,907	118,012	167,271	0	285,283
Illinois	2,248,614	2,112,868	6,569	4,368,051	1,464,688	1,576,522	2,375	3,043,585
Indiana	1,166,368	931,902	4,868	2,103,138	751,940	680,513	16,410	1,448,863
Iowa	709,435	526,677	6,029	1,242,141	403,365	406,248	1,942	811,555
Kansas	348,621	545,240	15,430	909,291	233,001	440,586	2,353	675,940
Kentucky	605,680	374,086	9,182	988,948	264,798	207,568	5,095	477,461
Louisiana	624,098	364,582	25,657	1,014,337	65,583[1]	65,317[1]	0[1]	130,900[1]
Maine	151,255	314,815	7,143	473,213	141,039	208,730	19,783	369,552
Maryland	789,029	473,316	53,526	1,315,871	604,457	312,974	6,626	924,057
Massachusetts	1,509,521	723,119	112,744	2,345,384	1,249,311	471,755	88,328	1,809,394
Michigan	1,898,241	1,503,114	30,535	3,431,890	1,538,922	1,150,495	18,297	2,707,714
Minnesota	1,039,999	729,577	24,928	1,794,504	779,286	712,270	34,324	1,525,880
Mississippi	375,328	256,608	4,602	636,538	251,558	236,274	31,129	518,961
Missouri	1,080,827	812,238	11,971	1,905,036	966,553	575,578	3,696	1,545,827
Montana	180,459	140,446	0	320,905	143,496	139,859	0	283,355
Nebraska	211,011	385,630	5,171	601,812	183,817	310,919	102	494,838
Nevada	153,998	24,124	21,743	199,865	132,513	44,425	13,705	190,643
New Hampshire	173,598	148,998	2,572	325,168	122,243	133,666	2,407	258,316
New Jersey	1,538,664	1,217,932	54,203	2,810,799	1,043,747	837,783	52,393	1,933,923
New Mexico	185,363	214,718	1,224	401,305	166,471	118,075	136	284,682
New York	1,113,173	875,776	4,001,792	5,990,741	1,000,901	500,639	2,877,488	4,379,028
New York	*3,501,443*	*2,341,925*	*147,373*	*5,990,741*	*2,274,866*	*1,982,507*	*121,655*	*4,379,028*
North Carolina	1,010,630	549,410	11,638	1,571,678	607,324	406,076	6,556	1,019,956
North Dakota	104,263	181,018	4,600	289,881	68,016	147,746	4,586	220,348
Ohio	1,817,528	1,917,324	106,904	3,841,756	1,278,151	1,471,860	29,934	2,779,945
Oklahoma	683,293	372,221	12,410	1,067,924	330,952	258,160	0	589,112
Oregon	599,135	262,514	65,015	926,664	587,445	258,140	28,038	873,623
Pennsylvania	2,410,257	2,006,856	17,132	4,434,245	1,804,598	1,711,318	25,742	3,541,658
Rhode Island	271,127	113,518	4,269	388,914	174,165	133,637	0	307,802
South Carolina	501,943	279,390	2,191	783,524	378,888	183,369	14,944	577,201
South Dakota	72,501	221,188	1,282	294,971	120,199	135,324	0	255,523
Tennessee	775,027	452,877	23,156	1,251,060	580,617	448,825	32,753	1,062,195
Texas	2,368,483	1,277,185	17,747	3,663,415	1,285,348	888,197	8,817	2,182,362
Utah	266,562	251,403	25,866	543,831	162,791	206,520	9,849	379,160
Vermont	0	124,458	60,325	184,783	23,228	90,688	6,586	120,502
Vermont	*60,202*	*124,458*	*123*	*184,783*	—	—	—	—
Virginia	666,082	670,400	126,340	1,462,822	444,049	594,915	17,601	1,056,565
Washington	817,948	585,719	21,935	1,425,602	507,252	450,837	20,475	978,564
West Virginia	446,564	157,062	59,467	663,093	290,927	151,918	0	442,845
Wisconsin	1,190,287	760,740	11,228	1,962,255	768,536	675,953	5,993	1,450,482
Wyoming	85,721	66,147	0	151,868	53,522	75,855	0	129,377

Notes: Main entries are raw vote values for candidates who used the sole designation "Democrat" or "Republican" (or their historical antecedents listed in Appendix A) on the ballot. Other = candidates who used third-party names on the ballot or were listed as independent, unidentified, or scatter vote. Bold italicized entries in the table are the author's alternative party coding, which is used when a candidate listed a major party name (Democrat, Republican, or their historical antecedents) on the ballot with other party names or labels. For a more detailed explanation of this alternate coding system, see Tables 5-1 and 1-3. —indicates that the state had no data, either because no vote data were found for the state in question or the state had not yet entered the Union. No special House elections are included in the table. The table only lists at-large vote values for states having both at-large and district House races; see Appendix B for these states' district results aggregated to the state level.

[1]Partial data (less than 100 percent of the districts reporting).

Sources: Adapted from *United States Congressional Elections, 1788–1997* (1998), *Congressional Quarterly's Guide to U.S. Elections* (1994), *America Votes* (various publication dates), and independent search for state sources by the author.

Table 5-118 House Election Results, by State, 1980–1982 (Raw Count)

State	1980 Democratic	Republican	Other	Total Vote	1982 Democratic	Republican	Other	Total Vote
Alabama	628,133	354,224	29,319	1,011,676	676,584	272,510	11,925	961,019
Alabama	*629,876*	*354,224*	*27,576*	*1,011,676*	—	—	—	—
Alaska	39,922	114,089	607	154,618	52,011	128,274	799	181,084
Arizona	394,275	434,024	25,653	853,952	300,493	394,872	15,646	711,011
Arkansas	42,278[1]	159,148[1]	229[1]	201,655[1]	397,466	361,772	0	759,238
California	3,665,518	4,178,628	335,598	8,179,744	3,815,205	3,536,658	234,694	7,586,557
Colorado	505,654	619,461	24,975	1,150,090	448,295	484,947	13,181	946,423
Connecticut	695,255	640,177	3,813	1,339,245	577,340	485,491	7,844	1,070,675
Delaware	81,227	133,842	1,560	216,629	98,533	87,153	2,378	188,064
Florida	1,813,164[1]	1,275,718[1]	5,480[1]	3,094,362[1]	1,311,342[1]	900,203[1]	49[1]	2,211,594[1]
Georgia	973,540	381,174	87	1,354,801	670,110	225,215	9,132	904,457
Hawaii	239,733	19,819	21,009	280,561	266,851	0	31,064	297,915
Idaho	182,061	233,041	0	415,102	150,996	170,150	0	321,146
Illinois	2,048,658	2,417,747	6,196	4,472,601	2,093,292	1,508,308	11,451	3,613,051
Indiana	1,087,115	1,099,991	2,354	2,189,460	882,378	909,731	3,951	1,796,060
Iowa	642,763	609,478	4,795	1,257,036	528,726	475,356	681	1,004,763
Kansas	404,549	519,874	8,691	933,114	345,507	400,837	10,001	756,345
Kentucky	610,411	442,309	3,372	1,056,092	413,286	280,352	6,684	700,322
Louisiana	162,330[1]	0[1]	0[1]	162,330[1]	—	—	—	—
Maine	137,845	375,073	21	512,939	186,970	260,925	4,246	452,141
Maryland	865,969	537,078	0	1,403,047	742,600	348,561	0	1,091,161
Massachusetts	1,473,289	757,738	25,165	2,256,192	1,300,344	561,091	28,931	1,890,366
Michigan	1,877,335	1,659,101	51,718	3,588,154	1,669,532	1,093,425	45,469	2,808,426
Minnesota	905,793	987,147	11,973	1,904,913	956,321	777,584	16,026	1,749,931
Mississippi	427,773	304,472	56,272	788,517	368,403	259,553	13,176	641,132
Missouri	1,110,060	940,530	0	2,050,590	871,682	653,468	3,266	1,528,416
Montana	176,236	162,305	0	338,541	165,902	142,370	8,267	316,539
Nebraska	167,415	451,328	6,518	625,261	116,107	402,167	807	519,081
Nevada	165,107	63,163	16,317	244,587	114,166	115,863	4,043	234,072
New Hampshire	177,411	186,869	45	364,325	114,187	153,974	757	268,918
New Jersey	1,316,100	1,368,981	56,314	2,741,395	1,206,416	915,472	24,202	2,146,090
New Mexico	175,988	187,474	45,343	408,805	202,802	191,946	158	394,906
New York	906,117	555,570	4,155,679	5,617,366	970,691	532,160	3,178,521	4,681,372
New York	*2,771,427*	*2,706,661*	*139,278*	*5,617,366*	*2,616,753*	*1,940,104*	*124,515*	*4,681,372*
North Carolina	964,493	769,144	3,160	1,736,797	708,279	579,817	32,984	1,321,080
North Dakota	166,437	124,707	1,932	293,076	186,534	72,241	1,724	260,499
Ohio	1,788,410	2,135,669	27,600	3,951,679	1,807,305	1,456,712	62,081	3,326,098
Oklahoma	439,651	391,209	4,722	835,582	539,413	310,186	6,725	856,324
Oregon	656,737	438,738	10,965	1,106,440	577,949	436,754	189	1,014,892
Pennsylvania	2,055,590	2,161,638	103,528	4,320,756	1,910,988	1,651,922	65,808	3,628,718
Rhode Island	213,726	172,901	6	386,633	174,023	157,535	1,624	333,182
South Carolina	408,296	399,039	22,734	830,069	353,111	295,160	9,185	657,456
South Dakota	173,357	146,146	0	319,503	142,122	133,530	0	275,652
Tennessee	663,796	618,876	21,525	1,304,197	697,823	469,527	8,333	1,175,683
Texas	2,405,026	1,608,636	54,873	4,068,535	1,847,048	934,863	67,123	2,849,034
Utah	232,426	351,996	7,913	592,335	144,987	312,003	32,661	489,651
Vermont	0	154,274	40,423	194,697	38,296	114,191	12,464	164,951
Virginia	486,084	1,005,272	61,479	1,552,835	629,656	690,167	15,563	1,335,386
Washington	816,133	792,836	17,276	1,626,245	689,811	603,916	13,772	1,307,499
West Virginia	390,986	294,846	0	685,832	343,236	202,380	787	546,403
Wisconsin	1,071,978	1,055,472	6,878	2,134,328	768,616	667,187	15,123	1,450,926
Wyoming	53,338	116,361	0	169,699	46,041	113,236	0	159,277

Notes: Main entries are raw vote values for candidates who used the sole designation "Democrat" or "Republican" (or their historical antecedents listed in Appendix A) on the ballot. Other = candidates who used third-party names on the ballot or were listed as independent, unidentified, or scatter vote. Bold italicized entries in the table are the author's alternative party coding, which is used when a candidate listed a major party name (Democrat, Republican, or their historical antecedents) on the ballot with other party names or labels. For a more detailed explanation of this alternate coding system, see Tables 5-1 and 1-3. —indicates that the state had no data, either because no vote data were found for the state in question or the state had not yet entered the Union. No special House elections are included in the table. The table only lists at-large vote values for states having both at-large and district House races; see Appendix B for these states' district results aggregated to the state level.

[1]Partial data (less than 100 percent of the districts reporting).

Sources: Adapted from *United States Congressional Elections, 1788–1997* (1998), *Congressional Quarterly's Guide to U.S. Elections* (1994), *America Votes* (various publication dates), and independent search for state sources by the author.

Table 5-119 House Election Results, by State, 1984–1986 (Raw Count)

State	1984 Democratic	Republican	Other	Total Vote	1986 Democratic	Republican	Other	Total Vote
Alabama	821,773	308,182	18,619	1,148,574	678,716	436,357	581	1,115,654
Alaska	86,052	113,582	6,803	206,437	74,053	101,799	4,425	180,277
Arizona	319,560	602,737	20,826	943,123	260,144	539,940	3,646	803,730
Arkansas	341,335[1]	90,841[1]	31,070[1]	463,246[1]	386,672	268,291	10,682	665,645
California	4,327,237	4,423,734	206,712	8,957,683	3,743,542	3,328,119	128,488	7,200,149
Colorado	436,041	779,700	31,893	1,247,634	449,683	566,236	2,338	1,018,257
Connecticut	667,668	761,647	2,973	1,432,288	544,938	433,977	740	979,655
Delaware	142,070	100,650	294	243,014	106,351	53,767	639	160,757
Florida	1,244,688[1]	1,190,776[1]	1,188[1]	2,436,652[1]	1,153,710[1]	986,780[1]	1,561[1]	2,142,051[1]
Georgia	1,090,682	430,143	51	1,520,876	772,986	289,068	274	1,062,328
Hawaii	227,261	40,608	7,737	275,606	186,891	135,054	9,251	331,196
Idaho	164,878	240,202	0	405,080	162,758	208,153	4,848	375,759
Illinois	2,367,383	2,203,506	8,192	4,579,081	1,622,759	1,393,103	1,348	3,017,210
Indiana	1,022,451	1,146,656	11,229	2,180,336	788,419	756,135	10,953	1,555,507
Iowa	595,265	673,343	151	1,268,759	428,022	461,455	118	889,595
Kansas	435,071	541,986	17,268	994,325	312,800	474,570	0	787,370
Kentucky	656,661	528,862	2,199	1,187,722	374,742	252,849	2,205	629,796
Louisiana	—	—	—	—	288,362[1]	102,276[1]	0[1]	390,638[1]
Maine	162,319	374,951	4,268	541,538	165,462	249,030	7,138	421,630
Maryland	954,873	535,915	4,492	1,495,280	668,669	394,393	3	1,063,065
Massachusetts	1,618,131	703,945	23,971	2,346,047	1,198,143	250,385	54,640	1,503,168
Michigan	1,861,442	1,566,919	24,007	3,452,368	1,342,034	977,122	8,020	2,327,176
Minnesota	1,060,800	902,268	12,399	1,975,467	831,715	557,741	3,517	1,392,973
Mississippi	523,161	326,826	18,865	868,852	315,526	208,037	0	523,563
Missouri	1,129,689	903,027	6,861	2,039,577	828,403	599,520	2,204	1,430,127
Montana	187,443	178,726	4,660	370,829	172,084	145,778	0	317,862
Nebraska	167,617	482,121	323	650,061	196,691	358,326	420	555,437
Nevada	109,372	155,166	6,086	270,624	121,263	133,821	2,145	257,229
New Hampshire	119,111	250,602	3,247	372,960	84,475	156,218	54	240,747
New Jersey	1,508,320	1,470,836	12,502	2,991,658	802,762	738,901	11,882	1,553,545
New Mexico	201,131	294,165	4,324	499,620	178,822	206,815	18	385,655
New York	1,126,535	568,000	4,524,257	6,218,792	921,001	336,429	2,646,181	3,903,611
New York	***3,255,244***	***2,898,901***	***64,647***	***6,218,792***	***2,131,745***	***1,664,604***	***107,262***	***3,903,611***
North Carolina	1,130,979	1,026,391	285	2,157,655	890,058	682,447	0	1,572,505
North Dakota	242,968	65,761	0	308,729	216,258	66,989	3,114	286,361
Ohio	2,134,198	2,159,354	38,927	4,332,479	1,512,037	1,536,025	18,710	3,066,772
Oklahoma	645,537	458,053	7,294	1,110,884	430,454	291,098	3,455	725,007
Oregon	655,092	548,201	198	1,203,491	584,763	446,462	319	1,031,544
Pennsylvania	2,531,111	2,111,851	17,160	4,660,122	1,762,935	1,525,803	17,639	3,306,377
Rhode Island	194,942	195,077	0	390,019	129,663	176,000	0	305,663
South Carolina	470,567	441,256	15,779	927,602	453,232	261,489	2,145	716,866
South Dakota	181,401	134,821	0	316,222	171,462	118,261	0	289,723
Tennessee	726,462	589,118	155	1,315,735	636,374	448,987	19,868	1,105,229
Texas	2,695,028	1,981,823	3,534	4,680,385	1,716,978	1,263,413	30,015	3,010,406
Utah	208,223	387,410	5,449	601,082	196,683	229,717	2,395	428,795
Vermont	60,360	148,025	17,912	226,297	0	168,403	20,551	188,954
Virginia	795,009	1,003,211	39,385	1,837,605	544,951	466,747	31,654	1,043,352
Washington	996,950	799,565	11,518	1,808,033	767,678	527,158	0	1,294,836
West Virginia	429,209	275,160	0	704,369	298,956	96,864	0	395,820
Wisconsin	1,033,033	1,032,948	9,397	2,075,378	704,113	668,708	10,320	1,383,141
Wyoming	45,857	138,234	3,813	187,904	48,780	111,007	0	159,787

Notes: Main entries are raw vote values for candidates who used the sole designation "Democrat" or "Republican" (or their historical antecedents listed in Appendix A) on the ballot. Other = candidates who used third-party names on the ballot or were listed as independent, unidentified, or scatter vote. Bold italicized entries in the table are the author's alternative party coding, which is used when a candidate listed a major party name (Democrat, Republican, or their historical antecedents) on the ballot with other party names or labels. For a more detailed explanation of this alternate coding system, see Tables 5-1 and 1-3. —indicates that the state had no data, either because no vote data were found for the state in question or the state had not yet entered the Union. No special House elections are included in the table. The table only lists at-large vote values for states having both at-large and district House races; see Appendix B for these states' district results aggregated to the state level.

[1]Partial data (less than 100 percent of the districts reporting).

Sources: Adapted from *United States Congressional Elections, 1788–1997* (1998), *Congressional Quarterly's Guide to U.S. Elections* (1994), *America Votes* (various publication dates), and independent search for state sources by the author.

Table 5-120 House Election Results, by State, 1988–1990 (Raw Count)

State	1988				1990			
	Democratic	Republican	Other	Total Vote	Democratic	Republican	Other	Total Vote
Alabama	722,200	432,238	23,866	1,178,304	689,987	314,735	12,141	1,016,863
Alaska	71,881	120,595	479	192,955	91,677	99,003	967	191,647
Arizona	321,815	766,111	36,890	1,124,816	344,604	620,906	837	966,347
Arkansas	353,164[1]	252,756[1]	0[1]	605,920[1]	369,194	295,877	0	665,071
California	4,944,646	4,173,715	262,879	9,381,240	3,567,775	3,346,689	372,359	7,286,823
Colorado	645,469	667,091	2,911	1,315,471	503,549	487,326	9,676	1,000,551
Connecticut	660,360	676,817	3,433	1,340,610	489,206	545,751	1,935	1,036,892
Delaware	158,338	76,179	0	234,517	116,274	58,037	3,121	177,432
Florida	1,430,881[1]	1,615,567[1]	594[1]	3,047,042[1]	1,212,978[1]	1,163,084[1]	2,409[1]	2,378,471[1]
Georgia	1,115,343	556,817	18	1,672,178	854,784	538,865	11	1,393,660
Hawaii	221,196	96,848	21,784	339,828	215,777	117,607	7,615	340,999
Idaho	198,284	203,447	5,703	407,434	183,062	131,450	0	314,512
Illinois	2,317,444	2,022,568	3,937	4,343,949	1,646,340	1,349,079	81,748	3,077,167
Indiana	1,096,834	1,023,124	0	2,119,958	830,500	682,593	913	1,514,006
Iowa	580,200	606,647	1,911	1,188,758	400,852	385,003	6,285	792,140
Kansas	366,757	565,308	242	932,307	393,671	387,180	147	780,998
Kentucky	534,313	564,433	6,205	1,104,951	353,439	397,388	12,879	763,706
Louisiana	88,564[1]	116,241[1]	0[1]	204,805[1]	105,853[1]	0[1]	0[1]	105,853[1]
Maine	276,335	278,351	198	554,884	284,421	232,540	433	517,394
Maryland	936,963	624,021	0	1,560,984	565,669	517,386	7,488	1,090,543
Massachusetts	1,787,488	509,360	74,057	2,370,905	1,420,422	566,923	63,826	2,051,171
Michigan	1,824,103	1,604,946	27,344	3,456,393	1,321,449	1,089,299	22,881	2,433,629
Minnesota	1,148,700	809,624	10,766	1,969,090	1,042,201	736,497	2,220	1,780,918
Mississippi	606,715	307,555	3,849	918,119	299,286	69,216	0	368,502
Missouri	1,148,292	909,599	12,295	2,070,186	728,020	624,666	0	1,352,686
Montana	193,347	171,870	0	365,217	157,148	160,286	0	317,434
Nebraska	229,524	425,726	1,028	656,278	276,724	309,106	916	586,746
Nevada	176,927	159,569	7,677	344,173	144,231	150,885	17,945	313,061
New Hampshire	176,300	251,566	1,633	429,499	141,042	148,909	680	290,631
New Jersey	1,336,325	1,411,840	27,939	2,776,104	836,944	910,931	78,649	1,826,524
New Mexico	209,076	236,263	3,839	449,178	145,531	213,803	0	359,334
New York	1,201,622	803,559	3,500,723	5,505,904	644,058	705,548	2,312,282	3,661,888
New York	***2,950,034***	***2,441,140***	***114,730***	***5,505,904***	***1,829,508***	***1,662,206***	***170,174***	***3,661,888***
North Carolina	1,108,311	876,362	0	1,984,673	1,076,340	935,054	0	2,011,394
North Dakota	212,583	84,475	2,924	299,982	152,530	81,443	6	233,979
Ohio	2,086,756	2,067,595	610	4,154,961	1,806,635	1,590,381	21,291	3,418,307
Oklahoma	405,665	361,538	0	767,203	519,047	337,590	0	856,637
Oregon	664,564	357,701	1,331	1,023,596	667,258	342,246	43,197	1,052,701
Pennsylvania	2,117,072	1,744,894	335,202	4,197,168	1,292,717	1,222,036	336,234	2,850,987
Pennsylvania	***2,117,072***	***2,069,885***	***10,211***	***4,197,168***	***1,292,717***	***1,552,475***	***5,795***	***2,850,987***
Rhode Island	140,270	250,724	0	390,994	181,949	164,916	0	346,865
South Carolina	549,652	439,476	2,244	991,372	382,939	274,650	12,450	670,039
South Dakota	223,759	88,157	0	311,916	173,814	83,484	0	257,298
Tennessee	844,210	536,480	28,631	1,409,321	369,294	288,633	58,945	716,872
Texas	2,735,940	1,834,135	99,615	4,669,690	1,763,432	1,498,096	16,730	3,278,258
Utah	260,123	341,056	7,489	608,668	233,821	191,067	17,325	442,213
Vermont	45,330	98,937	95,864	240,131	6,315	82,938	120,603	209,856
Virginia	801,831	1,076,895	12,102	1,890,828	662,800	410,941	79,133	1,152,874
Washington	988,386	742,844	0	1,731,230	696,275	596,407	20,535	1,313,217
West Virginia	436,616	131,963	0	568,579	251,298	123,311	0	374,609
Wisconsin	1,035,249	997,265	2,968	2,035,482	597,332	651,569	7,087	1,255,988
Wyoming	56,527	118,350	2,774	177,651	70,977	87,078	0	158,055

Notes: Main entries are raw vote values for candidates who used the sole designation "Democrat" or "Republican" (or their historical antecedents listed in Appendix A) on the ballot. Other = candidates who used third-party names on the ballot or were listed as independent, unidentified, or scatter vote. Bold italicized entries in the table are the author's alternative party coding, which is used when a candidate listed a major party name (Democrat, Republican, or their historical antecedents) on the ballot with other party names or labels. For a more detailed explanation of this alternate coding system, see Tables 5-1 and 1-3. —indicates that the state had no data, either because no vote data were found for the state in question or the state had not yet entered the Union. No special House elections are included in the table. The table only lists at-large vote values for states having both at-large and district House races; see Appendix B for these states' district results aggregated to the state level.

[1] Partial data (less than 100 percent of the districts reporting).

Sources: Adapted from *United States Congressional Elections, 1788–1997* (1998), *Congressional Quarterly's Guide to U.S. Elections* (1994), *America Votes* (various publication dates), and independent search for state sources by the author.

Table 5-121 House Election Results, by State, 1992–1994 (Raw Count)

State	1992				1994			
	Democratic	Republican	Other	Total Vote	Democratic	Republican	Other	Total Vote
Alabama	895,601	643,150	63,785	1,602,536	554,154	558,437	2,428	1,115,019
Alaska	102,378	111,849	24,889	239,116	68,172	118,537	21,531	208,240
Arizona	582,317	740,047	86,557	1,408,921	409,672	652,831	36,886	1,099,389
Arkansas	525,197	356,900	6,424	888,521	336,123	372,889	0	709,012
California	5,446,965	4,365,155	722,953	10535073	3,959,953	4,070,290	304,504	8,334,747
Colorado	691,479	757,666	30,064	1,479,209	364,391	687,070	4,127	1,055,588
Connecticut	644,424	699,155	91,584	1,435,163	506,272	516,134	46,761	1,069,167
Delaware	117,426	153,037	5,694	276,157	51,803	137,960	5,274	195,037
Florida	2,256,681[1]	2,510,726[1]	147,427[1]	4,914,834[1]	1,155,503[1]	1,693,874[1]	2,415[1]	2,851,792[1]
Georgia	1,214,792	999,182	13	2,213,987	681,051	816,484	1	1,497,536
Hawaii	260,786	81,645	16,000	358,431	219,185	119,514	15,403	354,102
Idaho	222,435	230,766	19,546	472,747	137,762	255,321	0	393,083
Illinois	2,677,685	2,096,717	56,539	4,830,941	1,459,928	1,576,655	7,367	3,043,950
Indiana	1,205,869	998,334	14,773	2,218,976	667,454	875,082	3,403	1,545,939
Iowa	492,843	729,496	20,097	1,242,436	407,309	560,117	9,980	977,406
Kansas	488,386	591,712	44,817	1,124,915	298,269	519,127	356	817,752
Kentucky	721,747	638,166	998	1,360,911	316,037	450,640	17,622	784,299
Louisiana	284,910[1]	398,679[1]	0[1]	683,589[1]	372,503[1]	400,607[1]	53,727[1]	826,837[1]
Maine	363,520	278,258	27,526	669,304	235,988	234,070	32,605	502,663
Maryland	957,952	842,789	8,766	1,809,507	662,312	682,578	183	1,345,073
Massachusetts	1,518,218	856,576	239,443	2,614,237	1,362,572	592,758	20,686	1,976,016
Michigan	1,913,175	1,855,241	115,987	3,884,403	1,418,142	1,532,084	52,848	3,003,074
Minnesota	1,178,072	930,814	166,206	2,275,092	883,905	846,950	17,530	1,748,385
Mississippi	669,582	273,234	22,585	965,401	354,487	256,424	9,408	620,319
Missouri	1,269,486	1,036,268	42,806	2,348,560	893,783	834,456	37,270	1,765,509
Montana	203,711	189,570	10,454	403,735	171,372	148,715	32,055	352,142
Nebraska	283,278	427,398	159	710,835	203,062	365,402	2,299	570,763
Nevada	245,477	213,792	32,680	491,949	137,723	215,971	22,405	376,099
New Hampshire	265,906	227,062	18,070	511,038	116,724	180,138	12,533	309,395
New Jersey	1,354,915	1,503,145	133,679	2,991,739	879,855	1,091,251	34,010	2,005,116
New Mexico	272,607	277,833	5,161	555,601	187,532	263,477	10,595	461,604
New York	1,201,855	332,134	4,390,866	5,924,855	780,324	547,576	3,283,171	4,611,071
New York	***3,050,738***	***2,686,622***	***187,495***	***5,924,855***	***2,213,186***	***2,250,691***	***147,194***	***4,611,071***
North Carolina	1,282,474	1,203,983	40,598	2,527,055	681,064	907,093	33	1,588,190
North Dakota	169,273	117,442	11,183	297,898	123,134	105,988	6,267	235,389
Ohio	2,198,039	2,154,080	224,815	4,576,934	1,327,955	1,925,452	45,107	3,298,514
Oklahoma	764,249	504,133	7,314	1,275,696	368,063	554,800	46,183	969,046
Oregon	824,796	553,101	12,857	1,390,754	646,589	498,628	47,740	1,192,957
Pennsylvania	2,154,372	1,786,710	649,437	4,590,519	1,491,859	1,538,756	340,957	3,371,572
Pennsylvania	***2,154,372***	***2,347,441***	***88,706***	***4,590,519***	***1,491,859***	***1,830,779***	***48,934***	***3,371,572***
Rhode Island	192,542	185,980	19,980	398,502	209,491	132,417	0	341,908
South Carolina	505,887	581,159	28,404	1,115,450	313,043	552,085	2,465	867,593
South Dakota	230,070	89,375	13,457	332,902	183,036	112,054	10,832	305,922
Tennessee	882,973	737,690	105,011	1,725,674	614,512	775,843	26,147	1,416,502
Texas	2,806,044	2,685,973	130,455	5,622,472	1,734,163	2,294,222	91,675	4,120,060
Utah	331,479	362,363	33,442	727,284	216,080	252,300	35,969	504,349
Vermont	22,279	86,901	172,446	281,626	0	98,523	112,926	211,449
Virginia	1,148,470	1,142,649	76,828	2,367,947	752,701	1,089,242	66,811	1,908,754
Washington	1,236,665	911,913	74,580	2,223,158	826,753	853,712	6,620	1,687,085
West Virginia	439,191	123,114	0	562,305	268,901	137,663	0	406,564
Wisconsin	1,153,862	1,210,827	23,241	2,387,930	547,825	893,405	17,837	1,459,067
Wyoming	77,418	113,882	5,677	196,977	81,022	104,426	10,749	196,197

Notes: Main entries are raw vote values for candidates who used the sole designation "Democrat" or "Republican" (or their historical antecedents listed in Appendix A) on the ballot. Other = candidates who used third-party names on the ballot or were listed as independent, unidentified, or scatter vote. Bold italicized entries in the table are the author's alternative party coding, which is used when a candidate listed a major party name (Democrat, Republican, or their historical antecedents) on the ballot with other party names or labels. For a more detailed explanation of this alternate coding system, see Tables 5-1 and 1-3. —indicates that the state had no data, either because no vote data were found for the state in question or the state had not yet entered the Union. No special House elections are included in the table. The table only lists at-large vote values for states having both at-large and district House races; see Appendix B for these states' district results aggregated to the state level.

[1] Partial data (less than 100 percent of the districts reporting).

Sources: Adapted from *United States Congressional Elections, 1788–1997* (1998), *Congressional Quarterly's Guide to U.S. Elections* (1994), *America Votes* (various publication dates), and independent search for state sources by the author.

Table 5-122 House Election Results, by State, 1996–1998 (Raw Count)

State	1996				1998			
	Democratic	Republican	Other	Total Vote	Democratic	Republican	Other	Total Vote
Alabama	656,047	785,513	27,133	1,468,693	545,465	665,625	4,089	1,215,179
Alaska	85,114	138,834	9,752	233,700	77,232	139,676	6,392	223,300
Arizona	521,345	800,917	34,184	1,356,446	406,834	573,651	23,281	1,003,766
Arkansas	395,506	456,033	11,779	863,318	168,528[1]	319,863[1]	36,917[1]	525,308[1]
California	4,706,819	4,291,647	483,059	9,481,525	4,040,164	3,510,494	439,036	7,989,694
Colorado	596,575	832,763	31,911	1,461,249	533,297	715,820	25,032	1,274,149
Connecticut	723,504	547,084	23,747	1,294,335	495,557	442,066	16,836	954,459
Delaware	73,253	185,576	8,007	266,836	57,446	119,811	3,270	180,527
Florida	2,036,620[1]	2,639,567[1]	15,841[1]	4,692,028[1]	580,605[1]	557,825[1]	74,822[1]	1,213,252[1]
Georgia	1,011,190	1,151,993	3	2,163,186	592,004	1,039,711	0	1,631,715
Hawaii	195,910	135,782	21,477	353,169	260,947	119,328	17,167	397,442
Idaho	193,524	289,990	10,512	494,026	169,389	204,568	4,872	378,829
Illinois	2,267,369	1,812,673	47,564	4,127,606	1,565,998	1,624,558	24,706	3,215,262
Indiana	944,469	1,118,533	42,031	2,105,033	673,322	861,951	40,598	1,575,871
Iowa	532,815	649,959	17,984	1,200,758	338,431	551,767	10,503	900,701
Kansas	424,984	591,146	32,748	1,048,878	272,252	450,025	5,171	727,448
Kentucky	507,431	730,739	11	1,238,181	456,218	637,091	5,553	1,098,862
Louisiana	262,184[1]	398,306[1]	0[1]	660,490[1]	213,150[1]	97,044[1]	0[1]	310,194[1]
Maine	379,184	211,210	9,406	599,800	280,537	124,834	9,182	414,553
Maryland	876,658	762,163	424	1,639,245	792,280	689,532	133	1,481,945
Massachusetts	1,585,374	780,729	43,249	2,409,352	1,306,281	412,508	22,964	1,741,753
Michigan	1,945,116	1,678,735	75,716	3,699,567	1,469,111	1,438,283	77,839	2,985,233
Minnesota	1,179,926	895,003	66,446	2,141,375	1,090,488	862,972	86,143	2,039,603
Mississippi	397,410	487,988	18,753	904,151	262,858	232,415	55,644	550,917
Missouri	1,116,201	833,190	166,453	2,115,844	787,655	748,432	36,030	1,572,117
Montana	174,516	211,975	17,935	404,426	147,073	175,748	8,730	331,551
Nebraska	204,432	450,067	7,145	661,644	104,548	392,736	28,675	525,959
Nevada	172,823	248,782	28,180	449,785	79,315	275,163	55,367	409,845
New Hampshire	221,329	246,940	23,054	491,323	124,000	190,170	3,575	317,745
New Jersey	1,351,774	1,398,888	72,497	2,823,159	902,374	858,367	54,748	1,815,489
New Mexico	271,144	260,961	16,250	548,355	228,084	246,127	23,479	497,690
New York	773,946	173,949	4,603,158	5,551,053	680,224	376,014	3,211,122	4,267,360
New York	***3,040,840***	***2,357,553***	***152,660***	***5,551,053***	***2,278,407***	***1,857,572***	***131,381***	***4,267,360***
North Carolina	1,135,731	1,339,515	38,303	2,513,549	827,078	1,014,010	62,678	1,903,766
North Dakota	144,833	113,684	4,493	263,010	119,668	87,511	5,709	212,888
Ohio	2,031,028	2,191,974	165,393	4,388,395	1,593,873	1,752,443	28,625	3,374,941
Oklahoma	430,480	722,998	26,666	1,180,144	314,358	538,194	6,096	858,648
Oregon	724,496	557,525	53,040	1,335,061	631,246	401,501	57,610	1,090,357
Pennsylvania	2,222,863	2,037,508	56,032	4,316,403	1,380,834	1,346,752	168,326	2,895,912
Pennsylvania	—	—	—	—	***1,380,834***	***1,472,161***	***42,917***	***2,895,912***
Rhode Island	240,608	107,657	11,485	359,750	203,705	76,630	12,613	292,948
South Carolina	345,010	682,563	29,811	1,057,384	369,790	580,028	23,858	973,676
South Dakota	119,547	186,393	17,263	323,203	64,433	194,157	0	258,590
Tennessee	856,487	888,546	38,510	1,783,543	412,378	469,551	31,652	913,581
Texas	2,322,729	2,784,875	111,739	5,219,343	1,531,234	1,786,731	143,920	3,461,885
Utah	264,327	386,309	13,179	663,815	126,505	304,256	40,088	470,849
Vermont	23,830	83,021	147,855	254,706	0	70,740	144,393	215,133
Virginia	1,027,020	1,117,187	54,890	2,199,097	514,435	542,216	92,210	1,148,861
Washington	1,129,609	1,020,553	24,099	2,174,261	980,157	818,552	59,339	1,858,048
West Virginia	458,435	63,933	0	522,368	283,272	29,136	38,869	351,277
Wisconsin	1,012,327	1,120,819	17,181	2,150,327	761,821	880,320	31,334	1,673,475
Wyoming	85,724	116,004	8,255	209,983	67,399	100,687	6,133	174,219

Notes: Main entries are raw vote values for candidates who used the sole designation "Democrat" or "Republican" (or their historical antecedents listed in Appendix A) on the ballot. Other = candidates who used third-party names on the ballot or were listed as independent, unidentified, or scatter vote. Bold italicized entries in the table are the author's alternative party coding, which is used when a candidate listed a major party name (Democrat, Republican, or their historical antecedents) on the ballot with other party names or labels. For a more detailed explanation of this alternate coding system, see Tables 5-1 and 1-3. —indicates that the state had no data, either because no vote data were found for the state in question or the state had not yet entered the Union. No special House elections are included in the table. The table only lists at-large vote values for states having both at-large and district House races; see Appendix B for these states' district results aggregated to the state level.

[1] Partial data (less than 100 percent of the districts reporting).

Sources: Adapted from *United States Congressional Elections, 1788–1997* (1998), *America Votes* (various publication dates), and independent search for state sources by the author.

6

The Notoriety of Senate Elections

Notoriety follows Senate elections and U.S. senators. With high stakes and large sums of money spent, Senate elections receive far more national media attention than House races. The contests are often viewed as grand ideological battles between left and right, with any race perhaps tipping the ideological balance of the Senate from liberal to conservative or back again. Many of the people elected are or have become household names—Robert La Follette, Barry Goldwater, Lyndon Johnson, John Kennedy, Ted Kennedy, Henry Cabot Lodge, Huey Long, Joseph McCarthy, Richard Nixon, Margaret Chase Smith, Adlai Stevenson, Robert Taft, and Hillary Rodham Clinton. Many believe that their fame and positions as senators offer unparalleled opportunity to run for president; some, indeed, became president. Next to presidential races, Senate elections are the most visible elections for national office.

Ironically, despite this notoriety, Senate election results tend to follow patterns similar to the more obscure and mundane House races. When one party wins large numbers of seats in the House, they also do so in the Senate. When a party claims majority status in the House, it also typically does so in the Senate. Indeed, this parallel between House and Senate results occurred well before 1913 when the Senate became a popularly elected body. In addition, there are numerous one-party states in Senate elections, as in House and presidential elections. No matter the money, the media, the ideological fight, or the persona of the candidates, outcomes in these states often are foregone conclusions. As the data in the tables of this chapter will make clear, this notoriety has little effect on the underlying party competition in Senate elections.

Part of the notoriety of the Senate was drafted, at least indirectly, into the Constitution. Madison wrote in *Federalist 62* of the "senatorial trust which requires great extent of information and stability of character" (1960, p. 376). This was provided initially in the six-year term given to senators as compared to the two-year term given to representatives. The Framers of the Constitution were also seeking more respected and well-established people to serve in the Senate than in the House. Implicitly, the Framers felt that the tasks assigned to the Senate—ratifying treaties, approving executive appointments, and constituting the jury in impeachment cases—called for politicians of different temperaments and experience than members of the House. John Jay commented further, "as state legislatures, who appoint the senators, will in general be composed of the most enlightened and respectable citizens, there is reason to presume that their attention and their votes will be directed to those men only who have become the most distinguished by their abilities and virtue, and in whom the people perceive just ground for confidence." By contrast, according to Jay, elections by the people, like those for the House, in which "the activity of party zeal, taking advantage of the supineness, the ignorance, and the hopes and fears of the unwary and uninterested, often places men in office by the votes of a small proportion of the electors" (1960, p. 391).

Yet the Framers' calculations about the selection of senators were fundamentally in error. If, according to the Framers' logic, state legislators were not subject to the caprice and passions of voters, the Framers missed the fact that the state lawmakers were surely subject to intense partisan conflicts. This partisanship had two key effects on the selection of senators. First, state partisan divisions guided senatorial choices as much as House elections. Patterns of party strength and organization were determinative in Senate elections. State legislators were not looking for candidates "distinguished by their abilities and virtue" as much as they were intent on selecting a committed partisan. Second, states with competitive parties had difficulties time and time again reaching decisions on who should be sent to the U.S. Senate. Compromise over a high-stakes U.S. Senate seat was troublesome, especially in states where different parties or different wings of the same party held the upper and lower chambers of the state legislature. From 1891 to 1905, forty-five deadlocks in the selection of senators occurred in the legislatures of twenty states. Numerous other deadlocks occurred throughout the nineteenth century (Byrd, 1988, p. 394).

Partly because of these problems and partly because of Progressive demands for direct election of senators, the House of Representatives began routinely passing resolutions for a constitutional amendment for the popular election of senators; the Senate, not unexpectedly, demurred. It was not until 1912 that the Senate approved language for the amendment after continued pressure from the House, insistence from Progressives, and attacks by reform-minded newspapers against the vested interests of senators. "Strictly speaking we have no Senate," wrote an editor for William

Randolph Hearst's *Cosmopolitan* magazine, "only a chamber of butlers for industrialists and financiers" (Byrd, 1988, p. 395). In 1912 six states had direct election of senators, and in 1913 the required number of states ratified the 17th Amendment, which mandated direct election of senators to replace selection of senators by state legislatures

The historical course of Senate elections will be traced in this chapter. These elections provide an intriguing contrast to House elections. Because they begin in the twentieth century, Senate elections are first and foremost stories about the two well-established parties—Democrats and Republicans. Senate elections do not encounter the volatility of party development in the eighteenth and nineteenth centuries that surrounded many House elections. As a part of this contemporary two-party story, Senate elections also reveal state party fortunes. Because Senate races are statewide races, their results clarify the nature of party support in specific states and regions.

This chapter is organized in four parts. First, the dates or classes within which Senate elections take place are presented. Second, an overview is provided of the composition of the Senate and the national results of Senate elections. Third, Senate elections are considered longitudinally as they take place in the twentieth century. Finally, state results for Senate elections are analyzed to examine the extent of one-partyism and two-party competition in the states.

Senate "Classes"

The most important structural characteristic that orders Senate elections are the three classes provided for in the Constitution. As displayed in Table 6-1, only one-third of the Senate is elected every two years, with the two seats from each state falling in different classes. This table shows that the national results for any given Senate election year and, hence, the total composition of the Senate depend heavily on states that have seats up for election in that year. Although the states are divided in roughly equal thirds among the three classes, they are not divided with the same balance by region. Class 2 elections—1918, 1924, 1930, and so on—are dominated by South and Border South states. Since the Democratic Party did well in these states during most of the history of Senate elections, it benefited from having Class 2 elections. As more and more Republicans have been elected to the Senate from the South in the past two decades, they are currently enjoying this same Class 2 advantage. In contrast, states in the Midwest and West regions are more prevalent in Class 3 elections, which have taken place in 1914, 1920, 1926, and so on. With its historically strong base in the Midwest, this gives the Republican Party a Class 3 advantage. Republicans also have a current edge in the West, which, all things being equal, has provided an additional advantage in Class 3 elections from the 1970s to the present. The Class 1 group of elections is the most balanced among the three classes and has no strong bias in favor of either party.

National Patterns of Senate Elections

Table 6-2 provides an overview of the composition of the Senate since 1788. Table 6-3 depicts the national vote for Senate since 1912.[1] In the forty-three Congresses convened since the passage of the 17th Amendment, Democrats have held the Senate majority twenty-eight times and Republicans fifteen times. Majority status has shifted from one party to the other nine times. In comparison, during those same Congresses, Democrats have held the House majority thirty times and Republicans thirteen times; the House majority has shifted seven times (Table 5-3). Since 1914, the majority party has held 57 percent of Senate seats and 59 percent of House seats. As presented in Table 6-3, the majority party (defined by the number of seats held; see Table 6-2) has won 50 percent of the national Senate vote and 52 percent of the national House vote (Table 5-4). There have been three times during popular elections in which the majority party has held the Senate for a considerable time. The Republicans held the Senate for fourteen years from 1918 to 1932; Democrats held it for fourteen years from 1932 to 1946 and for another twenty-six years from 1954 to 1980. As discussed in Chapter 5, a similar, although not identical, pattern exists for the House. The Republicans claimed the House in 1916 and held it until 1930 instead of 1932.[2] The Democrats held the House from 1930 to 1946 but lengthened their stay in the 1954–1994 period. These tables reveal that, on average, when a party becomes the Senate majority, it retains this status for about eight years and House elections tend to follow a similar pattern.

The exception to this was during the late 1940s and early 1950s, when the composition of the Senate was closely competitive. Republicans took the Senate in 1946 with a 51–45 split for the first time since Herbert Hoover was president (1928–1932). Democrats regained the Senate in 1948 (54–42) and held it in 1950 (49–47). Republicans returned to the majority in 1952 (49–47), but the Democrats reciprocated in 1954 (48–47) and retained the advantage in 1956 (49–47). Although largely in the majority since 1954, it was not until the pivotal election of 1958 that the Democrats became a decisive majority in the Senate with 65 seats to the Republicans' 35. During the late 1940s and early 1950s, House majorities were also small, although not as precarious as those in the Senate.

The Senate-House national comparisons indicate that, since the advent of direct Senate elections, there have been four occasions of divided party control of Congress. In 1930 the Republicans held a one-seat majority in the Senate, but the Democrats organized the House after Republican seat vacancies occurred because of deaths and the contesting of one House election. In 1980, 1982, and 1984 Republicans held majority status in the Senate, but Democrats controlled the House. In each instance, though, the Republicans' Senate majority was no more than 8 seats. Overall, Senate results are generally similar to House results. As will become clear later in this chapter, the competitiveness of the two parties in the twentieth century is established in states in such ways that variations between Senate and House elections are not likely to be dramatic.

Since the Constitution provides that only one-third of the Senate is elected every two years, another key measure of Senate two-party competitiveness is the number of seats won by the parties in a specific election (see the first set of columns in Table 6-3). The seats and votes won in Senate races indicate the profound effect certain elections have on the overall composition of the Senate. For instance, contrasting the elections between 1928 and 1942 reveals the vulnerabilities and strengths of the parties in ways that a simple examination of the total composition of the Senate could not (Table 6-2). Republicans won 19 of 32 seats in 1928, 55.1 percent of the vote, and had a commanding Senate majority (56–39), but the Democrats countered in 1930, winning 19 of 32 seats and 51.9 percent of the vote (Table 6-3). In so doing, they nearly took control of the Senate, although the Republicans held a one-seat majority (48–47). In 1932 the Democrats won all but 5 of the 32 seats being contested. Yet by the 1940s Republican strength returned. In 1940 they captured 48.0 percent of the nationwide Senate vote, roughly equal to the 47.4 percent gained by the Democrats (Table 6-3; also Table 6-4). In 1942 the Republicans won 17 seats while the Democrats won only 15. Looking at Table 6-2, it also reveals that certain elections produce party cohorts that, given the longevity of senators' careers, have long-lasting effects on the Senate: the 1920 Republican class gained 10 seats, the 1932 New Deal class of Democrats gained 12, the 1946 Republican class gained 13, the 1958 Democratic class gained 16, and the 1980 Republican class of Ronald Reagan supporters gained 12.

The Historical Development of Senate Elections

Like House and presidential elections, Senate elections fit within critical eras in American political history. As seen in Table 6-2, even during the years in which state legislatures selected senators (1788–1912), the results mimic the popular election transformations seen in the House.

Political Eras Before the Direct Election of Senators

During the Federalist/Democratic-Republican era (1788–1823), clear lines were drawn between the two parties by the election of 1794, when these two parties were formally organized (Dubin, 1998, p. xxv). This resulted in state legislatures choosing Federalist majorities in 1794, 1796, and 1798. When Jefferson won the presidency in 1800, the Democratic-Republicans took the Senate as well as the House. They held proportionally more seats in the Senate than the House during this period, but the Federalists remained a viable minority party, picking up Senate seats in

the 1812–1813 and the 1814–1815 periods as a reaction to the conduct of the War of 1812. (The Federalists also achieved seat gains in the House in the 1812–1813 elections.) While the Federalists were uncompetitive at the presidential level in 1816, they continued to compete for and win state legislative approval for Senate seats in 1816 and 1818, just as they had done in the elections for the House in this period. By 1822–1823, however, only 4 Federalist senators remained out of a total of 48 and the party held just 24 of 213 House seats.

At the outset of the Democratic/National Republican-Whig era in 1824, the Jacksonians held a majority of seats in both houses by 1828 and this advantage continued with only one exception (the 1832–1833 elections) until the Whigs captured Senate and House majorities in 1840 with the resounding victory of their leader, William Henry Harrison, for president.

In contrast, during the Civil War-Reconstruction period (1854–1893) the Senate was slower than the House to react to the growing strength of the Republican Party, which was formed in 1854. In this period, a pattern began in which the partisan direction of the Senate lagged behind that of the House, typically by two years or one election cycle. This was the direct result of the three election classes of the Senate with two-thirds of the Senate membership not involved in any given election cycle. Thus the changes that can be wrought even in elections during periods of crisis are limited by the Senate's compositional inertia. During the 1854–1855 state legislative selections, Democrats actually increased their Senate majority in the 34th Congress by four seats. While Republicans also won some seats in the 1854–1855 Senate selections, the Democrats had earlier done well in 1852 because of the numerous Class 2 Senate elections in the South. This meant that it was more difficult for Republican political strength to erode the base of the Democratic Senate in the same way that it had weakened the House. Thereafter, the Republicans picked up Senate seats until 1860, when they attained a majority in the Senate, which they had achieved earlier in 1858 in the House. During the Civil War-Reconstruction era, Republicans held this Senate majority until 1878 (although losing it in the House in 1874), regained it in the Senate in 1882 (having recaptured it in 1880 in the House), and kept it until 1892, when the Democrats achieved a majority in the Senate (which the Democrats had already done in 1890 in the House).

The Panic of 1893 triggered the conservative Republican/Democratic era (1894–1929) in the Senate as well as the House. So large was the economic shock that Senate changes occurred in the same two-year election cycle as those for the House. The panic led to huge Republican gains in the Senate as state legislatures made selections in 1894 in just the same way voters did in House races. In 1894 the Senate was composed of 44 Republicans and 40 Democrats, the mirror opposite of its composition in 1892, which had been 44 Democrats and 40 Republicans. As noted in Chapter 5, the House in 1892 had 221 Democrats and 130 Republicans, while in 1894 it had 107 Democrats and 245

Republicans. The Republicans held the Senate majority until 1912, when the Democrats took the presidency and the Senate. Democrats had already taken control of the House in 1910. The Democrats kept their Senate majority until 1918, when the Republicans reclaimed a majority that they maintained until the election of 1932. (In the House, Republicans had a one-seat majority in 1916 and lost it in 1930; see note 2.)

During the eighteenth and nineteenth centuries, the lesson for the Framers of the Constitution was that the method of Senate selection had little effect on this body's sensitivity to changing state party fortunes. State legislatures acted much like state voters in making the Senate's composition similar to that of the House. Because of the election classes of the Senate, the political effect often registered two years later than in the House; nevertheless, the direction of partisan change was in each instance the same. The Framers might well have been aghast. State legislatures were open to raging party battles over whom to send to the Senate, which would have stunned the Framers, who were ever suspicious of parties. But, more fundamentally, it did not matter whether "the most enlightened and respectable citizens" in state legislatures or voters, "unwary and uninterested," chose delegates to the U.S. Congress. A state's demographic composition, economic base, and past political direction established partisan patterns—one-party dominant or two-party competitive—to which state legislators and voters alike were connected. Despite the Framers' best laid plans, state politics was still state politics.

Conservative Republican Era and the Direct Election of Senators

The first popular election of senators was held in the midst of the conservative Republican-Democratic era (1894–1929). As a reform measure, direct elections rode a wave of progressivism and were among its major successes. But as practical political exercises, the elections themselves were little affected by the Progressive Movement. The two main parties were too well entrenched nationally, and their organizations and issue directions at the state levels were too well established. While Progressive candidates ran in the Senate elections held in 1912 to 1916, none won except those who also ran as Republicans, and these were only two in number—Hiram Johnson of California and Philander Knox of Pennsylvania. In addition, the Progressives never surmounted the strength of conservatives within the Republican Party, who triggered the Republican landslide in the Senate elections of 1920, giving the party an advantage of twenty-two seats. (Republicans also picked up 59 seats in the House.) This election ushered in conservative Republicanism on a new level.

Still, Senate Republicans were not monolithic. The conservative Republicans generally dominated the Senate and supported Secretary of the Treasury Andrew Mellon's tax measures to lower corporate and personal income taxes. But

a smaller group of progressive Republicans, mostly from the Midwest and West, including Robert La Follette of Wisconsin, William Borah of Idaho, Hiram Johnson of California, and George Norris of Nebraska, often had different policy views. These senators were among the first of the newly elected senators to receive public notoriety beyond the boundaries of their home states. La Follette and Borah had served as appointed senators and were already well known for their fight on behalf of the 17th Amendment. Despite their national visibility, they were not especially effective in stopping the Mellon initiatives, about which Norris commented: "Mr. Mellon himself gets a larger personal reduction than the aggregate of practically all the taxpayers in the state of Nebraska" (Hofstadter, Miller, and Aaron, 1959, p. 448). But the progressive Republicans were able to rout party regulars in farm states, and the resulting divisions in the Republican Party permitted Democratic gains in the 1922 Senate elections.

As shown in Tables 6-5 and 6-6, which examine the Senate vote by region, Democrats improved their standing in New England, increasing their vote share in 1922 by 11 percentage points, in the Mid-Atlantic by 15 percentage points, and in the Midwest by 8 percentage points. For all nonsouthern states, Democrats increased their vote by close to 9 percentage points. Republicans lost 6 seats in 1922 and nearly lost their majority (53 of 96 seats). Democrats also gained 77 seats in the House in 1922. While Republicans recaptured 1 Senate seat in 1924, they lost 6 in 1926 and also lost 10 seats in the House. Republicans held a lone one-seat majority when organizing the Senate after the 1926 election.

Thus, during the 1920s, conservative Republicans controlled the presidency and had majorities in the House and the Senate. While the age of "normalcy" after World War I is typically portrayed as a solely Republican period, this stereotypic image is most accurate at the presidential level. The huge Republican victories for president in 1920, 1924, and 1928, discussed in Chapter 4, were not matched by unquestioned Republican control of the Senate or the House. As shown in Table 6-7, Senate Republicans were strongest during this period in New England and the Midwest despite Democratic vote gains in this region. The Mid-Atlantic, Border South, and West were roughly competitive, while the South remained staunchly Democratic. To be sure, Republicans organized both chambers, but progressive undercurrents in the party and Democratic gains in the 1922 and 1926 midterm elections made running the legislative branches of the party more difficult than controlling the White House.

New Deal Democratic/Republican Era

The election of 1930 proved to be the end of conservative Republicanism in the Senate and the House. The Republicans organized the Senate, but only one vote separated them from the Democrats, who gained 8 seats in the 1930 election. As seen in Tables 6-3 and 6-4, Democrats captured a majority of Senate votes for the first time since direct elections began in 1912. In the solidly Republican Midwest and West, Democrats particularly improved their position with 47 and 46 percent of the vote, respectively (Table 6-5). As shown in Table 6-6, across the regions outside the South, Democrats captured 48 percent of the vote, when they had only received 38 percent of the vote in 1928. This vote shift was completed in 1932 when the Democrats picked up 12 more seats (59D–36R–1). By 1932 their margin outside the South grew to 53 percent of the total vote and they garnered 85 percent of the vote in the South. As shown in Tables 6-2 and 5-6, at the height of the New Deal in 1936 the Democrats held 79 percent of Senate seats and 77 percent of House seats.

But, as the data in these tables also reveal, there was little chance that the Republican Party would collapse or wither away. Although Franklin Roosevelt was elected to an unprecedented third term for president in 1940, partly with the logic that the country should not change leadership in the middle of World War II, voters failed to adopt a similar logic when it came to Congress. In the 1942 midterm elections, Republicans gained 10 Senate seats. Tables 6-5 and 6-6 reveal that in each region of the country, save the South, Republicans captured a majority of Senate votes. Republicans also gained 47 seats in the House.

In the aftermath of the war, Republicans took control of the Senate and House in the 1946 elections. Members of the Republican Senate class of 1946 were not only intensely hostile to Democratic president Harry Truman, but they were also decidedly conservative and well-known public figures. The new Republican conservatives included William Jenner of Indiana, William Knowland of California, George Malone of Nevada, Joseph McCarthy of Wisconsin, Arthur Watkins of Utah, and John Williams of Delaware. They were joined by long-time Democratic southern conservatives—Richard Russell of Georgia, Walter George of Georgia, and Harry Byrd Sr. of Virginia—who helped pass such conservative legislation as the Taft-Hartley Act and tax relief, and who blocked attempts to increase minimum wage and maximum work hour laws.

This coalition reflected the distinct factions in both parties that were built on ideology and geography. The Democrats contended with a rift between conservative southerners and more liberal urban labor Democrats from the industrial portions of the Midwest and Mid-Atlantic regions who advocated pro-labor and civil rights policies. The Republicans were often split between the conservative farm bloc of the Midwest, where Progressivism was increasingly a memory, and a more moderate wing in New England. These party factions continued until the mid-1960s.

The Democratic Party did well in the elections of 1948 with Truman's reelection (see Tables 6-3 and 6-4). The incoming 1948 Democratic Senate class was as liberal and became as prominent and newsworthy as the conservative Republicans from the 1946 class. As columnists Rowland Evans and Robert Novak observed, the Senate class of 1948,

including Clinton Anderson of New Mexico, Paul Douglas of Illinois, Hubert Humphrey of Minnesota, Estes Kefauver of Tennessee, John Pastore of Rhode Island, and Lyndon Johnson of Texas, were "perhaps the most publicized band of freshmen in Senate history [who] consisted of independent personalities whose ambitions, idiosyncrasies, and rivalries were to shape the history of the Senate and the nation for the next decade" (1966, p. 26). These liberal Democrats were pitted against Southern Democrats, who were equally well known and combative, such as Harry Byrd (first elected in 1933), James Eastland of Mississippi (first elected in 1942), John Sparkman of Alabama (first elected in 1946), and John Stennis of Mississippi (first elected in 1947); these men were to prove as tenacious in their long tenure in the Senate as they were their stands against civil rights.

In contrast, *no* Republican won a regular Senate election in the South until 1966, when South Carolina, Tennessee, and Texas elected Strom Thurmond as a newly converted Republican, Howard Baker, and John Tower, respectively.[3] Instead, Republican conservatives held firm in the Midwest—Illinois (Everett Dirksen), Iowa (Thomas Martin), Kansas (Frank Carlson), Nebraska (Carl Curtis), North Dakota (Milton Young), and South Dakota (Karl Mundt). The moderates and liberals of the Republican Party also continued to hold seats in New England and the Mid-Atlantic with candidates like Jacob Javitz of New York, George Aiken of Vermont, and Margaret Chase Smith of Maine.

Table 6-7 shows the regional strengths of the two parties during the New Deal period. New England remained Republican, although not as overwhelmingly as it had been in the earlier period of conservative Republicanism. Republicans claimed 61 percent of Senate seats from New England during the New Deal period, having held 88 percent in the earlier period. Republicans also lost a percentage of seats in the Mid-Atlantic and Midwest but still maintained their majorities in both regions during this period. In contrast, the West and the Border South became heavily Democratic. A very dramatic turnaround occurred in the more populated West, where Democrats took 67 percent of western Senate seats during the New Deal period, when they had only won 49 percent of the seats in the earlier conservative Republican period. The South, of course, displayed its usual Democratic strengths throughout the New Deal period.

Competitive Democratic/Republican Era

In the mid-1960s, the Senate remained overwhelmingly Democratic. The Democrats held comfortable Senate majorities even as the Vietnam War ended the tenure of Democratic president Lyndon Johnson, allowing Richard Nixon to become president. These strong Democratic Senate majorities rested partly on the robust reelection rates for Senate incumbents (see Table 6-9). But the Democrats also captured new seats after President Nixon's resignation and continued their majority in the Senate until 1980, when they lost this advantage. In 1986 they regained the majority only to lose it again in 1994.

While Democrats held what appeared to be comfortable Senate majorities, shifts in competitiveness were occurring in the South and the West. During the New Deal period Republicans did not win any southern Senate races and only won 24 percent of Senate races in the Border South (Table 6-7), but in the current period they have won 39 percent of the races in both the South and Border South. Similarly, while Republicans succeeded in only 33 percent of Senate races in the West during the New Deal era, they were able to capture 56 percent of western Senate seats in the 1966–1998 period.

These shifts in seats, which began slowly in the 1960s, became more obvious in the 1970s and 1980s when Senate majorities (held by either party) fell below 60 seats from the average 65 seats held by the Democrats between 1958 and 1966. This mirrored the growing competition between the two parties in the House (see Chapter 5). In 1980, when the Republicans took control of the Senate, they did so with a minority of votes in all regions except the Border South (Table 6-5). In 1986, when the Democrats regained majority status in the Senate, their strength rested in New England, the Midwest, the South, and the Border South. Reflective of this, during the most recent period New England has become a competitive region rather than one dominated by the Republicans, as it had been in the previous two eras (Table 6-7).

When the Republicans captured the Senate in 1994, the most profound turnaround was in the South. For the first time since the start of direct elections for the Senate, Republicans captured a majority of southern Senate votes: fully 61 percent of the southern vote went to Republican candidates. But evidence of competitiveness has continued since Republicans have not made irreversible gains in the South. In 1996 and especially in 1998, Democrats increased their votes in the South. Having received 37 percent of the southern vote in 1994, they took 45 percent in 1996 and 54 percent in 1998 (Table 6-6).

Overall, this latest period marks competition between the two parties, but less division within the parties than was apparent during the New Deal era. Senate Republicans are more united in their beliefs and votes than they were in the earlier New Deal period. By the early 1990s they have registered some of their highest party unity scores in the Senate since the 1960s. Democrats, too, with many southern Democrats gone, have very high party unity scores (see Mann, Ornstein, and Malbin, 1998, ch. 8).[4] The current period has minimized the internal factions within the parties but increased cross-party conflicts. Inevitably, charges of legislative gridlock and lack of civility stem, in part, from the internal consistencies within the two parties that have fundamentally different policy agendas and methods for achieving them. These charges of gridlock and incivility also have their origins in the national competitiveness of Senate elections.

One-Party States of the Senate

National-level competition does not imply state-level competition. As with the House, much of the competition that appears nationally in analyzing Senate returns disappears in individual states as they select their senators.

To fully understand how states vote for the Senate, party codings must accurately reflect who ran under what party label. This problem is less acute in studying the Senate than in examining the House because of the greater stability of the parties in the twentieth century, the permanence of the official ballot reform, and the greater accuracy in reporting twentieth-century voting returns. Nonetheless, party label questions arise. Table 6-10 shows the states and years when the alternative party codings were used in developing the Senate data files on voting shown in Tables 6-11 through 6-54. As discussed in detail in Chapter 5, the first entries in Tables 6-11 through 6-54 are the conventionally coded voting data; the bold italicized entries below the conventional vote values are the alternative coding values that attempt to more accurately depict the way in which major-party candidates sometimes ran on more than one ticket, were endorsed by more than one party, or used other designations or labels in addition to the party name. As a general rule, conventional coding places the vote of these candidates in the "Other" category, whereas alternative coding assigns the vote values of these candidates to the major party with which they are primarily affiliated (see Chapter 5 for full details). In cases where no alternative coding is provided, there are no multiple party labels or other designations found on the ballot beside these candidate names. One common instance of party coding differences in the Senate occurs in New York, where the Liberal Party frequently endorsed Democratic candidates. The candidates were clearly Democrats and under the alternative coding scheme are coded as such. In the conventional coding system, however, these candidates' vote totals are assigned to the "Other" category since these candidates did not run under the sole designation "Democrat."

Tables 6-11 through 6-54 and also Table 6-7 clarify the extent to which some states maintain strong, local one-party traditions. No matter who runs in Kansas, Maine, New Hampshire, Oregon, Pennsylvania, or Vermont, the winner is likely to be a Republican across the nearly 90 years of Senate elections for these states. Even with the Republican inroads in southern Senate races, Democrats still prevail across the history of Senate elections in all southern states, as well as West Virginia, Hawaii, Rhode Island, Montana, Nevada, and Washington. These one-party profiles for the Senate also largely hold in the House, except Republicans did better in several House races in West Virginia and Montana than they did in Senate races during comparable years (see Tables 5-12 through 5-14). For other states, there are more complicated patterns, but they are often no less entrenched in one-partyism. For instance, New Jersey and California were one-party Republican states in the first two eras but are Democratic states in the most recent period from 1966 to 1998. Arizona, Oklahoma, and Wyoming, which were strongly Democratic during the New Deal era, are now convincingly Republican. A final group of states seem more two-party competitive: New York across all three eras; and, from the New Deal on, Illinois, Indiana, Iowa, Michigan, Minnesota, Ohio, and Colorado.

These state tables also reveal the extent to which Senate elections attract third-party candidacies far more often than House elections in the 1912–1998 period. Also, Senate third-party candidacies receive proportionally far more votes than their counterparts in the House. Still, as Table 6-2 makes clear, running is not necessarily winning. Since 1912 only 37 members of the Senate have been third-party winners.

Conclusion

No matter how much attention specific Senate races receive, no matter who is running—even the son, brother, or wife of a president—Senate elections are actually more predictable than the notoriety they often generate would suggest. Senate elections follow the partisan patterns of numerous other elections and the political trends that sweep across the country. Senate elections, like House elections, are also bound by the rules of incumbency. To only a limited extent do the visibility, popularity, and personal backgrounds of Senate candidates surmount these trends.

Notes

1. The national and regional aggregations of the vote are calculated using the alternative party codings for the statewide Senate vote when they occur. Otherwise, the conventional coding values are used. The alternative party codings are discussed in detail in Chapter 5. Hence, when bold italicized entries appear in Tables 6-11 through 6-54, those data points are used in the calculation of the statewide Senate vote for these particular states and in the subsequent calculations of regional votes, national votes, and the parties' victories in Senate seats. These alternative values do not occur with as much frequency in any given election as the conventionally coded values, which represent the main entries in these tables and are used in the national and regional aggregation process for states not having alternative party codings.

2. Republicans won 217 seats to the Democrats' 216 seats in the 1930 House elections, but the Democrats ended up organizing the House after Republican vacancies occurred through deaths and the successful contesting of one House election result.

3. Tower first won a Senate seat in 1961 in a special election due to a vacancy occurring when Lyndon Johnson assumed the vice presidency.

4. Party unity scores are based on the consistency (or lack thereof) of each party membership's roll-call votes on measures before the Senate. The more a party's membership votes the same way on legislative matters, the higher the party unity scores for that party become.

Table 6-1 Senate Election Classes

	Class 1	Class 2	Class 3
New England			
	Connecticut	Maine	Connecticut
	Maine	Massachusetts	New Hampshire
	Massachusetts	New Hampshire	Vermont
	Rhode Island	Rhode Island	
	Vermont		
Mid-Atlantic			
	Delaware	Delaware	New York
	New Jersey	New Jersey	Pennsylvania
	New York		
	Pennsylvania		
South			
	Florida	Alabama	Alabama
	Mississippi	Arkansas	Arkansas
	Tennessee	Georgia	Florida
	Texas	Louisiana	Georgia
	Virginia	Mississippi	Louisiana
		North Carolina	North Carolina
		South Carolina	South Carolina
		Tennessee	
		Texas	
		Virginia	
Border South			
	Maryland	Kentucky	Kentucky
	West Virginia	Oklahoma	Maryland
		West Virginia	Oklahoma
Midwest			
	Indiana	Illinois	Illinois
	Michigan	Iowa	Indiana
	Minnesota	Kansas	Iowa
	Missouri	Michigan	Kansas
	Nebraska	Minnesota	Missouri
	North Dakota	Nebraska	North Dakota
	Ohio	South Dakota	Ohio
	Wisconsin		South Dakota
			Wisconsin
West			
	Arizona	Alaska	Alaska
	California	Colorado	Arizona
	Hawaii	Idaho	California
	Montana	Montana	Colorado
	Nevada	New Mexico	Hawaii
	New Mexico	Oregon	Idaho
	Utah	Wyoming	Nevada
	Washington		Oregon
	Wyoming		Utah
			Washington

Notes: For the period of direct election of senators, the schedule for the three election classes is as follows: Class 1 Senate elections were held in 1916, 1922, 1928, 1934, 1940, 1946, 1952, 1958, 1964, 1970, 1976, 1982, 1988, 1994, and 2000; Class 2 Senate elections were held in 1918, 1924, 1930, 1936, 1942, 1948, 1954, 1960, 1966, 1972, 1978, 1984, 1990, and 1996; Class 3 Senate elections were held in 1914, 1920, 1926, 1932, 1938, 1944, 1950, 1956, 1962, 1968, 1974, 1980, 1986, 1992, and 1998. Six states also held Senate elections in 1912 and belong in the Class 2 sequence of elections.

The initial year of Senate selection by state legislatures was 1788 (or 1789) according to Article 1, Section 3 of the U.S. Constitution. In that year, all senators for all states were selected by state legislatures to serve staggered terms. Senators in Class 1 would serve two years and then selection for six-year terms would begin in 1790 for those states and follow the progression 1796, 1802, 1808, . . . 2000. Senators in Class 2 would serve for four years and then selection for six-year terms would begin in 1792 for those states and follow the progression 1798, 1804, 1810, . . . 1996. Senators in Class 3 would serve the full six years and then selection for another six-year term would begin in 1794 for those states and follow the progression 1800, 1806, 1812, . . . 1998.

Table 6-2 Political Composition of the Senate, 1788–1998

Election	Congress	Total Composition				Election	Congress	Total Composition			
		Dem.	Rep.	Other	% Dem.			Dem.	Rep.	Other	% Dem.
1788–1789	1st	8	18	0	30.8	1898	56th	26	53	10	29.2
1790–1791	2d	13	16	0	44.8	1900	57th	32	56	2	35.6
1792–1793	3d	14	16	0	46.7	1902	58th	33	57	0	36.7
1794–1795	4th	11	21	0	34.4	1904	59th	32	58	0	35.6
1796–1797	5th	10	22	0	31.3	1906	60th	31	61	0	33.7
1798–1799	6th	10	22	0	31.3	1908	61st	32	60	0	34.8
1800–1801	7th	17	15	0	53.1	1910	62d	44	52	0	45.8
1802–1803	8th	25	9	0	73.5	1912	63d	51	44	1	53.1
1804–1805	9th	27	7	0	79.4	1914	64th	56	40	0	58.3
1806–1807	10th	28	6	0	82.4	1916	65th	54	42	0	56.3
1808–1809	11th	27	7	0	79.4	1918	66th	47	49	0	49.0
1810–1811	12th	30	6	0	83.3	1920	67th	37	59	0	38.5
1812–1813	13th	28	8	0	77.8	1922	68th	42	53	1	43.8
1814–1815	14th	26	12	0	68.4	1924	69th	41	54	1	42.7
1816–1817	15th	30	12	0	71.4	1926	70th	47	48	1	49.0
1818–1819	16th	37	9	0	80.4	1928	71st	39	56	1	40.6
1820–1821	17th	44	4	0	91.7	1930	72d	47	48	1	49.0
1822–1823	18th	44	4	0	91.7	1932	73d	59	36	1	61.5
1824–1825	19th	26	22	0	54.2	1934	74th	69	25	2	71.9
1826–1827	20th	27	21	0	56.3	1936	75th	76	16	4	79.2
1828–1829	21st	25	23	0	52.1	1938	76th	69	23	4	71.9
1830–1831	22d	25	23	0	52.1	1940	77th	66	28	2	68.8
1832–1833	23d	22	26	0	45.8	1942	78th	57	38	1	59.4
1834–1835	24th	26	24	2	50.0	1944	79th	57	38	1	59.4
1836–1837	25th	35	17	0	67.3	1946	80th	45	51	0	46.9
1838–1839	26th	30	22	0	57.7	1948	81st	54	42	0	56.3
1840–1841	27th	22	29	0	43.1	1950	82d	49	47	0	51.0
1842–1843	28th	23	29	0	44.2	1952	83d	47	49	0	49.0
1844–1845	29th	34	22	0	60.7	1954	84th	48	47	1	50.0
1846–1847	30th	38	21	1	63.3	1956	85th	49	47	0	51.0
1848–1849	31st	35	25	2	56.5	1958	86th	65	35	0	65.0
1850–1851	32d	36	23	3	58.1	1960	87th	64	36	0	64.0
1852–1853	33d	38	22	2	61.3	1962	88th	66	34	0	66.0
1854–1855	34th	42	15	5	67.7	1964	89th	68	32	0	68.0
1856–1857	35th	41	20	5	62.1	1966	90th	64	36	0	64.0
1858–1859	36th	38	26	2	57.6	1968	91st	57	43	0	57.0
1860–1861	37th	15	34	0	30.6	1970	92d	54	44	2	54.0
1862–1863	38th	10	37	5	23.8	1972	93d	56	42	2	56.0
1864–1865	39th	11	40	3	20.4	1974	94th	60	38	2	60.0
1866–1867	40th	9	57	0	13.6	1976	95th	61	38	1	61.0
1868–1869	41st	12	62	0	16.2	1978	96th	58	41	1	58.0
1870–1871	42d	18	56	0	24.3	1980	97th	46	53	1	46.0
1872–1873	43d	19	47	7	26.0	1982	98th	46	54	0	46.0
1874–1874	44th	28	46	1	37.3	1984	99th	47	53	0	47.0
1876–1877	45th	35	40	1	46.1	1986	100th	55	45	0	55.0
1878–1879	46th	42	33	1	55.3	1988	101st	55	45	0	55.0
1880	47th	37	37	2	48.7	1990	102d	56	44	0	56.0
1882	48th	36	38	2	47.4	1992	103d	57	43	0	57.0
1884	49th	34	42	0	44.7	1994	104th	48	52	0	48.0
1886	50th	37	39	0	48.7	1996	105th	45	55	0	45.0
1888	51st	37	51	0	42.0	1998	106th	45	55	0	45.0
1890	52d	39	47	2	44.3						
1892	53d	44	40	4	50.0						
1894	54th	40	44	6	44.4						
1896	55th	34	44	12	37.8						

Notes: The column "% Dem." refers to the Democratic percentage of total members in the Senate (not to Democratic percent of major two-party members in the Senate).

The selection process of senators in state legislatures prior to their direct election varied between the even-numbered and odd-numbered year in the two-year election cycles also common to House elections before 1880. After that, selection of senators by state legislatures in an odd-numbered year usually only happened when new states were entering the Union and the particular date of their admission necessitated Senate selection in an odd-numbered year. For direct election of senators, Hawaii had their elections in an odd-numbered year (1959) when they entered the Union. Senate composition numbers, especially prior to direct election of senators, are inconsistent among various sources on the partisan composition of this body. The most reliable source is "Majority and Minority Parties (Party Division in the Senate)" at the Senate History Office and found on the Senate website *www.senate.gov/learning/stat*. Also see the "Years of Service" section for the Senate in *Congressional Quarterly's Guide to U.S. Elections* (1994), pp. 784–811. During this period of legislative selection of senators, there may have been more Senate seats in a given term than shown in this table due to states having missing data, vacant seats, or not reporting their results officially to the state or federal government. The Senate election results since 1914 do not reflect runoffs, seats contested after the election verdict, inaccuracies of other types in reporting party labels or winners, or gubernatorial and legislative proclamations of different winners. For these reasons, these figures on the partisan composition of the Senate may not completely correspond to other reports on the partisan composition of the Senate during this period.

Sources: Adapted from the paper, "Majority and Minority Parties (Party Division in the Senate)" from the Senate History Office and Senate website *www.senate.gov/learning/stat*), total composition from the Clerk of the House of Representatives, *Historical Election Returns,* and *Congressional Quarterly's Guide to U.S. Elections* (1994), pp. 784–811. Discrepancies among these sources were resolved, to the extent possible, by a search of state sources by the author.

Table 6-3 National Results of Senate Elections, 1912–1998

Year	Seats Won Dem.	Rep.	Other	Raw Vote Dem.	Rep.	Other	Total Vote	Percentage Dem.	Rep.	Other	Democratic % of Two-Party Vote
1912	5	1	0	588,552	532,021	208,372	1,328,945	44.29	40.03	15.68	52.52
1914	19	13	0	4,369,156	4,456,558	2,068,156	10,893,870	40.11	40.91	18.98	49.50
1916	16	16	0	5,347,622	5,988,367	689,060	12,025,049	44.47	49.80	5.73	47.17
1918	14	18	0	2,949,345	3,021,493	301,165	6,272,003	47.02	48.17	4.80	49.40
1920	7	25	0	7,375,577	10,577,309	1,557,764	19,510,650	37.80	54.21	7.98	41.08
1922	21	10	1	7,114,494	7,504,600	1,030,972	15,650,066	45.46	47.95	6.59	48.67
1924	12	20	0	6,166,855	7,645,318	716,949	14,529,122	42.44	52.62	4.93	44.65
1926	13	19	0	7,222,971	8,570,397	376,824	16,170,192	44.67	53.00	2.33	45.73
1928	12	19	1	10,646,998	14,347,353	1,051,521	26,045,872	40.88	55.08	4.04	42.60
1930	19	13	0	6,750,996	5,783,617	476,353	13,010,966	51.89	44.45	3.66	53.86
1932	27	5	0	15,637,272	11,354,447	1,530,514	28,522,233	54.82	39.81	5.37	57.93
1934	23	7	2	12,463,210	10,969,496	1,712,328	25,145,034	49.57	43.62	6.81	53.19
1936	24	6	2	11,796,556	8,048,762	1,496,761	21,342,079	55.27	37.71	7.01	59.44
1938	22	10	0	14,424,247	12,932,410	615,189	27,971,846	51.57	46.23	2.20	52.73
1940	21	10	1	16,962,421	17,194,023	1,646,297	35,802,741	47.38	48.02	4.60	49.66
1942	15	17	0	6,330,213	6,693,305	527,649	13,551,167	46.71	49.39	3.89	48.61
1944	22	10	0	18,403,431	16,172,703	189,255	34,765,389	52.94	46.52	0.54	53.23
1946	11	21	0	11,988,304	14,984,371	281,155	27,253,830	43.99	54.98	1.03	44.45
1948	23	9	0	12,750,654	9,663,279	186,337	22,600,270	56.42	42.76	0.82	56.89
1950	15	17	0	15,610,698	16,166,666	403,273	32,180,637	48.51	50.24	1.25	49.13
1952	12	20	0	20,602,942	23,263,955	935,410	44,802,307	45.99	51.93	2.09	46.97
1954	21	10	1	11,435,689	8,838,877	275,386	20,549,952	55.65	43.01	1.34	56.40
1956	17	15	0	22,499,347	21,259,021	94,968	43,853,336	51.31	48.48	0.22	51.42
1958	26	8	0	20,854,861	16,171,640	402,597	37,429,098	55.72	43.21	1.08	56.32
1959	1	1	0	77,647	87,161	0	164,808	47.11	52.89	0.00	47.11
1960	20	13	0	17,638,881	14,014,291	130,457	31,783,629	55.50	44.09	0.41	55.73
1962	23	11	0	19,673,520	19,318,958	193,715	39,186,193	50.21	49.30	0.49	50.45
1964	26	7	0	30,034,984	22,209,269	458,686	52,702,939	56.99	42.14	0.87	57.49
1966	15	18	0	12,357,323	13,170,556	270,092	25,797,971	47.90	51.05	1.05	48.41
1968	18	16	0	25,059,044	24,168,867	1,599,260	50,827,171	49.30	47.55	3.15	50.90
1970	21	10	2	25,371,421	19,509,090	3,647,260	48,527,771	52.28	40.20	7.52	56.53
1972	16	17	0	17,235,409	19,831,998	758,013	37,825,420	45.57	52.43	2.00	46.50
1974	23	11	0	22,637,869	16,421,373	1,878,857	40,938,099	55.30	40.11	4.59	57.96
1976	21	11	1	32,002,771	24,878,982	1,980,723	58,862,476	54.37	42.27	3.37	56.26
1978	14	19	0	14,333,525	13,548,511	505,086	28,387,122	50.49	47.73	1.78	51.41
1980	12	22	0	29,890,042	27,002,551	1,743,087	58,635,680	50.98	46.05	2.97	52.54
1982	20	13	0	28,041,926	22,693,946	859,713	51,595,585	54.35	43.98	1.67	55.27
1984	16	17	0	22,219,681	22,851,333	393,111	45,464,125	48.87	50.26	0.86	49.30
1986	20	14	0	24,290,210	23,487,987	484,272	48,262,469	50.33	48.67	1.00	50.84
1988	19	14	0	35,279,275	31,341,091	811,759	67,432,125	52.32	46.48	1.20	52.96
1990	17	16	0	17,022,004	15,532,598	512,530	33,067,132	51.48	46.97	1.55	52.29
1992	20	14	0	35,184,182	31,870,144	2,929,088	69,983,414	50.28	45.54	4.19	52.47
1994	14	19	0	25,633,008	28,889,442	2,248,701	56,771,151	45.15	50.89	3.96	47.01
1996	13	20	0	23,501,140	24,211,723	1,316,884	49,029,747	47.93	49.38	2.69	49.26
1998	18	16	0	26,924,649	25,718,603	1,155,519	53,798,771	50.05	47.81	2.15	51.15

Notes: Entries are calculated from the raw vote values in Tables 6-33 through 6-54. Whenever bold italicized values occur in Tables 6-33 through 6-54, denoting the author's alternate party coding system, they are used instead of the conventionally coded main entries in these tables in the aggregation process to the national level. See text and Table 6-10 for a more complete discussion of the conventional and alternate party coding systems. Also see Table 1-3 for a similar discussion. Entries in this table are based on candidates who use the designation "Democrat" or "Republican" (or their historical antecedents listed in Appendix A), either solely or with other labels or parties (often minor parties) on the ballot. Other = candidates who use third-party names only on the ballot or are listed as independent or unidentified. Special Senate elections are not included.

Sources: Adapted from the *Congressional Quarterly's Guide to U.S. Elections* (1994), ICPSR data sets 0001 and 0075, *America Votes* (various publication dates), and independent search of state sources by the author. For some party affiliations, the labels were taken from Michael J. Dubin's election archive after verification from the author's data set in Tables 6-33 through 6-54.

Table 6-4 Comparison of National Seats and Votes in Senate Elections, 1912–1998

Election	Congress	Dem. % of Seats Won	Rep. % of Seats Won	Dem. % of Total Votes	Rep. % of Total Votes	Difference Dem. Seats/ Dem. Votes	Difference Rep. Seats/ Rep. Votes
1912	63d	83.33	16.67	44.29	40.03	39.04	−23.96
1914	64th	59.38	40.62	40.11	40.91	19.27	−0.29
1916	65th	50.00	50.00	44.47	49.80	5.33	0.20
1918	66th	43.75	56.25	47.02	48.17	−3.27	8.08
1920	67th	21.88	78.12	37.80	54.21	−15.92	23.91
1922	68th	65.62	31.25	45.46	47.95	20.16	−16.70
1924	69th	37.50	62.50	42.44	52.62	−4.94	9.88
1926	70th	40.62	59.38	44.67	53.00	−4.05	6.38
1928	71st	37.50	59.38	40.88	55.08	−3.38	4.30
1930	72d	59.38	40.62	51.89	44.45	7.49	−3.83
1932	73d	84.38	15.62	54.82	39.81	29.56	−24.19
1934	74th	71.88	21.88	49.57	43.62	22.31	−21.74
1936	75th	75.00	18.75	55.27	37.71	19.73	−18.96
1938	76th	68.75	31.25	51.57	46.23	17.18	−14.98
1940	77th	65.62	31.25	47.38	48.02	18.24	−16.77
1942	78th	46.88	53.12	46.71	49.39	0.17	3.76
1944	79th	68.75	31.25	52.94	46.52	15.81	−15.27
1946	80th	34.38	65.62	43.99	54.98	−9.61	10.64
1948	81st	71.88	28.12	56.42	42.76	15.46	−14.64
1950	82d	46.88	53.12	48.51	50.24	−1.63	2.88
1952	83d	37.50	62.50	45.99	51.93	−8.49	10.57
1954	84th	65.63	31.25	55.65	43.01	9.98	−11.76
1956	85th	53.12	46.88	51.31	48.48	1.81	−1.60
1958	86th	76.47	23.53	55.72	43.21	20.75	−19.68
1960	87th	60.61	39.39	55.50	44.09	5.11	−4.70
1962	88th	67.65	32.35	50.21	49.30	17.44	−16.95
1964	89th	78.79	21.21	56.99	42.14	21.80	−20.93
1966	90th	45.45	54.55	47.90	51.05	−2.45	3.50
1968	91st	52.94	47.06	49.30	47.55	3.64	−0.49
1970	92d	63.64	30.30	52.28	40.20	11.36	−9.90
1972	93d	48.48	51.52	45.57	52.43	2.91	−0.91
1974	94th	67.65	32.35	55.30	40.11	12.35	−7.76
1976	95th	63.64	33.33	54.37	42.27	9.27	−8.94
1978	96th	42.42	57.58	50.49	47.73	−8.07	9.85
1980	97th	35.29	64.71	50.98	46.05	−15.69	18.66
1982	98th	60.61	39.39	54.35	43.98	6.26	−4.59
1984	99th	48.48	51.52	48.87	50.26	−0.39	1.26
1986	100th	58.82	41.18	50.33	48.67	8.49	−7.49
1988	101st	57.58	42.42	52.32	46.48	5.26	−4.06
1990	102d	51.52	48.48	51.48	46.97	0.04	1.51
1992	103d	58.82	41.18	50.28	45.54	8.54	−4.36
1994	104th	42.42	57.58	45.15	50.89	−2.73	6.69
1996	105th	39.39	60.61	47.93	49.38	−8.54	11.23
1998	106th	52.94	47.06	50.05	47.81	2.89	−0.75

Notes: Vote percentage values (columns 5 and 6) are calculated from the raw vote values in Tables 6-33 through 6-54. Whenever bold italicized values occur in Tables 6-33 through 6-54, denoting the author's alternate party coding system, they are used instead of the conventionally coded main entries in these tables in the national aggregation process. See text and Table 6-10 for a more complete discussion of the conventional and alternate party coding systems. Also see Table 1-3 for a similar discussion. Entries in columns 5 and 6 are based on candidates who used the designation "Democrat" or "Republican" (or their historical antecedents listed in Appendix A), either solely or with other labels or parties (often minor parties) on the ballot. Columns 3 and 4 refer to the Democratic and Republican percentage of seats won, respectively, of the total number of seats in the Senate. This information can be derived from vote Tables 6-33 through 6-54 or adapted from the *Congressional Quarterly's Guide to U.S. Elections* (1994) and total composition from the Clerk of the House of Representatives, *Historical Election Returns*. Special Senate elections are also not included.

Sources: Tables 6-33 through 6-54, *Congressional Quarterly's Guide to U.S. Elections* (1994), and total composition from the Clerk of the House of Representatives, *Historical Election Returns*.

Table 6-5 Votes in Senate Elections, by Region, 1912–1998

Year/Region[1]	Raw Vote				Percentage			Democratic % of Two-Party Vote
	Democratic	Republican	Other	Total	Democratic	Republican	Other	
1912 NEng	—	—	—	—	—	—	—	—
1912 South	—	—	—	—	—	—	—	—
1912 MAtl	—	—	—	—	—	—	—	—
1912 BdrS	126,407	83,448	40,876	250,731	50.42	33.28	16.30	60.24
1912 MidW	275,292	324,721	25,785	625,798	43.99	51.89	4.12	45.88
1912 West	186,853	123,852	141,711	452,416	41.30	27.38	31.32	60.14
1914 NEng	139,239	167,233	18,575	325,047	42.84	51.45	5.71	45.43
1914 South	335,329	110,651	34,483	480,463	69.79	23.03	7.18	75.19
1914 MAtl	837,834	1,158,913	473,764	2,470,511	33.91	46.91	19.18	41.96
1914 BdrS	405,646	312,914	86,323	804,883	50.40	38.88	10.72	56.45
1914 MidW	1,937,423	2,014,196	838,324	4,789,943	40.45	42.05	17.50	49.03
1914 West	713,685	692,651	616,687	2,023,023	35.28	34.24	30.48	50.75
1916 NEng	464,377	540,611	29,146	1,034,134	44.90	52.28	2.82	46.21
1916 South	712,525	175,736	26,537	914,798	77.89	19.21	2.90	80.22
1916 MAtl	1,251,498	1,787,405	203,049	3,241,952	38.60	55.13	6.26	41.18
1916 BdrS	248,325	257,905	11,935	518,165	47.92	49.77	2.30	49.05
1916 MidW	1,987,951	2,234,382	272,672	4,495,005	44.23	49.71	6.07	47.08
1916 West	682,946	992,328	145,721	1,820,995	37.50	54.49	8.00	40.77
1918 NEng	331,274	334,987	23,700	689,961	48.01	48.55	3.43	49.72
1918 South	724,773	182,988	3,358	911,119	79.55	20.08	0.37	79.84
1918 MAtl	173,856	200,541	23,263	397,660	43.72	50.43	5.85	46.44
1918 BdrS	387,150	371,201	9,547	767,898	50.42	48.34	1.24	51.05
1918 MidW	1,046,466	1,589,577	203,774	2,839,817	36.85	55.97	7.18	39.70
1918 West	285,826	342,199	37,523	665,548	42.95	51.42	5.64	45.51
1920 NEng	216,439	376,615	17,617	610,671	35.44	61.67	2.88	36.50
1920 South	975,673	396,819	12,218	1,384,710	70.46	28.66	0.88	71.09
1920 MAtl	1,386,172	2,503,378	633,106	4,522,656	30.65	55.35	14.00	35.64
1920 BdrS	836,815	886,946	60,674	1,784,435	46.90	49.70	3.40	48.55
1920 MidW	3,147,032	5,269,380	597,079	9,013,491	34.91	58.46	6.62	37.39
1920 West	813,446	1,144,171	237,070	2,194,687	37.06	52.13	10.80	41.55
1922 NEng	732,975	798,894	63,427	1,595,296	45.95	50.08	3.98	47.85
1922 South	638,322	252,180	6,158	896,660	71.19	28.12	0.69	71.68
1922 MAtl	2,189,386	2,197,245	370,397	4,757,028	46.02	46.19	7.79	49.91
1922 BdrS	359,800	324,627	10,282	694,709	51.79	46.73	1.48	52.57
1922 MidW	2,546,308	3,005,548	408,176	5,960,032	42.72	50.43	6.85	45.86
1922 West	647,703	926,106	172,532	1,746,341	37.09	53.03	9.88	41.16
1924 NEng	796,244	930,218	13,929	1,740,391	45.75	53.45	0.80	46.12
1924 South	1,803,898	476,988	50,340	2,331,226	77.38	20.46	2.16	79.09
1924 MAtl	331,034	660,751	80,206	1,071,991	30.88	61.64	7.48	33.38
1924 BdrS	849,941	1,037,847	23,388	1,911,176	44.47	54.30	1.22	45.02
1924 MidW	1,974,967	3,937,442	490,593	6,403,002	30.84	61.49	7.66	33.40
1924 West	410,771	602,072	58,493	1,071,336	38.34	56.20	5.46	40.56
1926 NEng	174,566	322,966	3,225	500,757	34.86	64.50	0.64	35.09
1926 South	506,081	184,975	13	691,069	73.23	26.77	0.00	73.23
1926 MAtl	1,970,143	2,259,339	118,046	4,347,528	45.32	51.97	2.72	46.58
1926 BdrS	677,714	565,849	5,592	1,249,155	54.25	45.30	0.45	54.50
1926 MidW	2,988,267	3,970,195	144,015	7,102,477	42.07	55.90	2.03	42.94
1926 West	906,200	1,267,073	105,933	2,279,206	39.76	55.59	4.65	41.70
1928 NEng	1,286,177	1,348,386	16,673	2,651,236	48.51	50.86	0.63	48.82
1928 South	1,282,021	321,094	1,429	1,604,544	79.90	20.01	0.09	79.97
1928 MAtl	3,762,779	4,888,137	182,131	8,833,047	42.60	55.34	2.06	43.50
1928 BdrS	532,067	583,490	4,315	1,119,872	47.51	52.10	0.39	47.70
1928 MidW	2,879,455	5,503,965	725,984	9,109,404	31.61	60.42	7.97	34.35
1928 West	904,499	1,702,281	120,989	2,727,769	33.16	62.41	4.44	34.70
1930 NEng	870,471	811,915	17,348	1,699,734	51.21	47.77	1.02	51.74
1930 South	1,386,027	308,364	140,473	1,834,864	75.54	16.81	7.66	81.80
1930 MAtl	440,888	649,406	25,854	1,116,148	39.50	58.18	2.32	40.44
1930 BdrS	935,053	751,196	2,125	1,688,374	55.38	44.49	0.13	55.45
1930 MidW	2,630,450	2,734,031	249,191	5,613,672	46.86	48.70	4.44	49.03
1930 West	488,107	528,705	41,362	1,058,174	46.13	49.96	3.91	48.00
1932 NEng	441,546	459,650	24,175	925,371	47.72	49.67	2.61	49.00
1932 South	1,662,359	296,541	463	1,959,363	84.84	15.13	0.02	84.86
1932 MAtl	3,733,672	3,123,030	465,709	7,322,411	50.99	42.65	6.36	54.45
1932 BdrS	1,294,496	750,985	19,224	2,064,705	62.70	36.37	0.93	63.29
1932 MidW	6,516,696	5,252,652	369,983	12,139,331	53.68	43.27	3.05	55.37
1932 West	1,988,503	1,471,589	650,960	4,111,052	48.37	35.80	15.83	57.47
1934 NEng	1,461,233	1,096,779	83,078	2,641,090	55.33	41.53	3.15	57.12
1934 South	926,136	153,549	9,087	1,088,772	85.06	14.10	0.83	85.78
1934 MAtl	4,372,120	3,337,629	386,921	8,096,670	54.00	41.22	4.78	56.71
1934 BdrS	614,161	479,399	12,123	1,105,683	55.55	43.36	1.10	56.16
1934 MidW	4,324,221	3,489,125	1,075,864	8,889,210	48.65	39.25	12.10	55.34
1934 West	765,339	2,413,015	145,255	3,323,609	23.03	72.60	4.37	24.08
1936 NEng	1,141,523	1,277,325	210,936	2,629,784	43.41	48.57	8.02	47.19
1936 South	3,061,644	438,560	34,535	3,534,739	86.62	12.41	0.98	87.47
1936 MAtl	983,550	792,548	19,922	1,796,020	54.76	44.13	1.11	55.38
1936 BdrS	1,521,995	933,217	17,959	2,473,171	61.54	37.73	0.73	61.99
1936 MidW	4,239,964	3,942,411	1,158,789	9,341,164	45.39	42.20	12.41	51.82
1936 West	847,880	664,701	54,620	1,567,201	54.10	42.41	3.49	56.06

Table 6-5 (Continued)

Year/Region[1]	Raw Vote				Percentage			Democratic % of Two-Party Vote
	Democratic	Republican	Other	Total	Democratic	Republican	Other	
1938 NEng	376,019	445,036	107,598	928,653	40.49	47.92	11.59	45.80
1938 South	962,959	243,129	3,694	1,209,782	79.60	20.10	0.31	79.84
1938 MAtl	4,191,493	4,145,547	61,038	8,398,078	49.91	49.36	0.73	50.28
1938 BdrS	1,011,916	525,253	16,136	1,553,305	65.15	33.82	1.04	65.83
1938 MidW	5,395,796	5,635,118	393,605	11,424,519	47.23	49.32	3.45	48.92
1938 West	2,486,064	1,938,327	33,118	4,457,509	55.77	43.48	0.74	56.19
1940 NEng	1,832,266	1,581,179	39,452	3,452,897	53.06	45.79	1.14	53.68
1940 South	2,030,223	181,841	20,061	2,232,125	90.95	8.15	0.90	91.78
1940 MAtl	6,239,719	5,855,086	53,443	12,148,248	51.36	48.20	0.44	51.59
1940 BdrS	886,652	585,718	10,824	1,483,194	59.78	39.49	0.73	60.22
1940 MidW	4,935,529	6,065,755	1,046,972	12,048,256	40.96	50.35	8.69	44.86
1940 West	1,038,032	2,924,444	475,545	4,438,021	23.39	65.90	10.72	26.20
1942 NEng	908,691	1,021,596	13,163	1,943,450	46.76	52.57	0.68	47.08
1942 South	1,068,765	165,543	26,921	1,261,229	84.74	13.13	2.13	86.59
1942 MAtl	598,173	695,065	14,202	1,307,440	45.75	53.16	1.09	46.25
1942 BdrS	590,656	636,060	1,549	1,228,265	48.09	51.79	0.13	48.15
1942 MidW	2,674,904	3,548,312	465,417	6,688,633	39.99	53.05	6.96	42.98
1942 West	489,024	626,729	6,397	1,122,150	43.58	55.85	0.57	43.83
1944 NEng	579,360	583,391	6,051	1,168,802	49.57	49.91	0.52	49.83
1944 South	1,911,900	438,434	3,351	2,353,685	81.23	18.63	0.14	81.35
1944 MAtl	5,159,311	4,740,440	39,958	9,939,709	51.91	47.69	0.40	52.12
1944 BdrS	1,199,629	903,352	4,469	2,107,450	56.92	42.86	0.21	57.04
1944 MidW	6,607,814	6,756,060	128,247	13,492,121	48.98	50.07	0.95	49.45
1944 West	2,945,417	2,751,026	7,179	5,703,622	51.64	48.23	0.13	51.71
1946 NEng	1,169,765	1,659,788	37,313	2,866,866	40.80	57.90	1.30	41.34
1946 South	849,524	220,274	27,717	1,097,515	77.40	20.07	2.53	79.41
1946 MAtl	4,152,818	5,275,234	47,953	9,476,005	43.82	55.67	0.51	44.05
1946 BdrS	510,383	504,617	0	1,015,000	50.28	49.72	0.00	50.28
1946 MidW	3,439,776	5,171,332	118,132	8,729,240	39.41	59.24	1.35	39.95
1946 West	1,866,038	2,153,126	50,040	4,069,204	45.86	52.91	1.23	46.43
1948 NEng	1,300,516	1,507,925	14,463	2,822,904	46.07	53.42	0.51	46.31
1948 South	3,205,304	896,634	48,248	4,150,186	77.23	21.60	1.16	78.14
1948 MAtl	956,302	1,002,966	51,976	2,011,244	47.55	49.87	2.58	48.81
1948 BdrS	1,285,264	977,479	4,517	2,267,260	56.69	43.11	0.20	56.80
1948 MidW	5,064,859	4,491,832	57,423	9,614,114	52.68	46.72	0.60	53.00
1948 West	938,409	786,443	9,710	1,734,562	54.10	45.34	0.56	54.41
1950 NEng	545,727	584,738	27,106	1,157,571	47.14	50.51	2.34	48.27
1950 South	1,576,013	276,963	38,789	1,891,765	83.31	14.64	2.05	85.05
1950 MAtl	4,326,389	4,187,753	262,903	8,777,045	49.29	47.71	3.00	50.81
1950 BdrS	963,382	889,883	10,639	1,863,904	51.69	47.74	0.57	51.98
1950 MidW	5,621,286	6,723,724	47,902	12,392,912	45.36	54.25	0.39	45.53
1950 West	2,577,901	3,503,605	15,934	6,097,440	42.28	57.46	0.26	42.39
1952 NEng	2,062,767	2,173,830	19,489	4,256,086	48.47	51.08	0.46	48.69
1952 South	3,759,018	153,479	113,149	4,025,646	93.38	3.81	2.81	96.08
1952 MAtl	6,268,929	7,564,770	155,258	13,988,957	44.81	54.08	1.11	45.32
1952 BdrS	876,389	856,377	0	1,732,766	50.58	49.42	0.00	50.58
1952 MidW	6,407,858	7,409,059	83,023	13,899,940	46.10	53.30	0.60	46.38
1952 West	1,227,981	5,106,440	564,491	6,898,912	17.80	74.02	8.18	19.39
1954 NEng	1,301,014	1,351,255	8,206	2,660,475	48.90	50.79	0.31	49.05
1954 South	2,750,088	472,212	175,737	3,398,037	80.93	13.90	5.17	85.35
1954 MAtl	940,669	923,917	50,871	1,915,457	49.11	48.23	2.66	50.45
1954 BdrS	1,094,499	893,027	2,980	1,990,506	54.99	44.86	0.15	55.07
1954 MidW	4,460,032	4,274,041	37,592	8,771,665	50.85	48.73	0.43	51.06
1954 West	889,387	924,425	0	1,813,812	49.03	50.97	0.00	49.03
1956 NEng	622,163	885,553	13,302	1,521,018	40.90	58.22	0.87	41.27
1956 South	3,155,440	485,186	173	3,640,799	86.67	13.33	0.00	86.67
1956 MAtl	5,533,800	5,974,604	12,606	11,521,010	48.03	51.86	0.11	48.08
1956 BdrS	1,379,026	1,351,108	0	2,730,134	50.51	49.49	0.00	50.51
1956 MidW	7,438,107	8,146,292	32,739	15,617,138	47.63	52.16	0.21	47.73
1956 West	4,370,811	4,416,278	36,148	8,823,237	49.54	50.05	0.41	49.74
1958 NEng	2,372,311	1,197,715	13,846	3,583,872	66.19	33.42	0.39	66.45
1958 South	1,668,727	418,253	162,562	2,249,542	74.18	18.59	7.23	79.96
1958 MAtl	5,678,755	5,850,095	97,512	11,626,362	48.84	50.32	0.84	49.26
1958 BdrS	749,015	645,193	0	1,394,208	53.72	46.28	0.00	53.72
1958 MidW	6,184,227	5,065,968	36,962	11,287,157	54.79	44.88	0.33	54.97
1958 West	4,201,826	2,994,416	91,715	7,287,957	57.65	41.09	1.26	58.39
1959 NEng	—	—	—	—	—	—	—	—
1959 South	—	—	—	—	—	—	—	—
1959 MAtl	—	—	—	—	—	—	—	—
1959 BdrS	—	—	—	—	—	—	—	—
1959 MidW	—	—	—	—	—	—	—	—
1959 West	77,647	87,161	0	164,808	47.11	52.89	0.00	47.11
1960 NEng	1,600,133	1,913,375	8,532	3,522,040	45.43	54.33	0.24	45.54
1960 South	5,638,578	1,955,043	49,368	7,642,989	73.77	25.58	0.65	74.25
1960 MAtl	1,247,475	1,582,706	29,339	2,859,520	43.63	55.35	1.03	44.08
1960 BdrS	1,376,761	1,399,668	4,715	2,781,144	49.50	50.33	0.17	49.59
1960 MidW	6,459,402	5,932,196	35,043	12,426,641	51.98	47.74	0.28	52.13
1960 West	1,316,532	1,231,303	3,460	2,551,295	51.60	48.26	0.14	51.67

(Table continues)

Table 6-5 (Continued)

Year/Region[1]	Raw Vote				Percentage			Democratic % of Two-Party Vote
	Democratic	Republican	Other	Total	Democratic	Republican	Other	
1962 NEng	658,100	716,970	0	1,375,070	47.86	52.14	0.00	47.86
1962 South	2,369,757	1,133,159	206	3,503,122	67.65	32.35	0.01	67.65
1962 MAtl	4,527,706	5,407,066	151,820	10,086,592	44.89	53.61	1.51	45.57
1962 BdrS	1,181,053	1,009,745	2,857	2,193,655	53.84	46.03	0.13	53.91
1962 MidW	6,642,304	6,239,647	13,089	12,895,040	51.51	48.39	0.10	51.56
1962 West	4,294,600	4,812,371	25,743	9,132,714	47.02	52.69	0.28	47.16
1964 NEng	3,147,490	1,296,236	7,688	4,451,414	70.71	29.12	0.17	70.83
1964 South	3,967,709	2,366,648	165,581	6,499,938	61.04	36.41	2.55	62.64
1964 MAtl	7,957,337	6,648,976	259,381	14,865,694	53.53	44.73	1.74	54.48
1964 BdrS	1,193,664	648,465	7	1,842,136	64.80	35.20	0.00	64.80
1964 MidW	8,425,926	6,382,451	23,397	14,831,774	56.81	43.03	0.16	56.90
1964 West	5,342,858	4,866,493	2,632	10,211,983	52.32	47.65	0.03	52.33
1966 NEng	1,249,116	1,611,843	11,999	2,872,958	43.48	56.10	0.42	43.66
1966 South	3,933,031	2,661,714	103,350	6,698,095	58.72	39.74	1.54	59.64
1966 MAtl	855,284	1,376,111	63,824	2,295,219	37.26	59.96	2.78	38.33
1966 BdrS	901,561	978,281	0	1,879,842	47.96	52.04	0.00	47.96
1966 MidW	4,325,321	5,357,896	90,285	9,773,502	44.26	54.82	0.92	44.67
1966 West	1,093,010	1,184,711	634	2,278,355	47.97	52.00	0.03	47.99
1968 NEng	771,859	878,772	270	1,650,901	46.75	53.23	0.02	46.76
1968 South	4,632,220	2,646,975	15	7,279,210	63.64	36.36	0.00	63.64
1968 MAtl	4,268,357	5,669,534	1,267,914	11,205,805	38.09	50.59	11.31	42.95
1968 BdrS	1,311,985	1,496,273	177,453	2,985,711	43.94	50.11	5.94	46.72
1968 MidW	7,986,766	8,096,235	36,672	16,119,673	49.55	50.23	0.23	49.66
1968 West	6,087,857	5,381,078	116,936	11,585,871	52.55	46.45	1.01	53.08
1970 NEng	2,063,661	1,493,154	288,126	3,844,941	53.67	38.83	7.49	58.02
1970 South	3,198,044	2,516,287	560,725	6,275,056	50.96	40.10	8.94	55.97
1970 MAtl	5,046,820	4,306,583	2,499,228	11,852,631	42.58	36.33	21.09	53.96
1970 BdrS	806,387	584,618	10,988	1,401,993	57.52	41.70	0.78	57.97
1970 MidW	8,920,310	6,701,660	143,328	15,765,298	56.58	42.51	0.91	57.10
1970 West	5,336,199	3,906,788	144,865	9,387,852	56.84	41.62	1.54	57.73
1972 NEng	1,453,985	2,031,814	43,973	3,529,772	41.19	57.56	1.25	41.71
1972 South	6,201,666	6,074,319	438,261	12,714,246	48.78	47.78	3.45	50.52
1972 MAtl	1,079,579	1,856,698	85,458	3,021,735	35.73	61.44	2.83	36.77
1972 BdrS	1,493,072	1,256,802	24,976	2,774,850	53.81	45.29	0.90	54.30
1972 MidW	5,583,645	6,976,834	136,481	12,696,960	43.98	54.95	1.07	44.45
1972 West	1,423,462	1,635,531	28,864	3,087,857	46.10	52.97	0.93	46.53
1974 NEng	872,373	549,204	29,476	1,451,053	60.12	37.85	2.03	61.37
1974 South	3,795,548	1,589,829	323,496	5,708,873	66.49	27.85	5.67	70.48
1974 MAtl	3,569,902	4,183,505	888,005	8,641,412	41.31	48.41	10.28	46.04
1974 BdrS	1,161,131	1,223,202	31,256	2,415,589	48.07	50.64	1.29	48.70
1974 MidW	7,222,826	4,796,962	258,148	12,277,936	58.83	39.07	2.10	60.09
1974 West	6,016,089	4,078,671	348,476	10,443,236	57.61	39.06	3.34	59.60
1976 NEng	2,833,726	2,026,623	66,792	4,927,141	57.51	41.13	1.36	58.30
1976 South	5,901,096	3,367,487	1,007,446	10,276,029	57.43	32.77	9.80	63.67
1976 MAtl	7,328,766	6,398,534	135,057	13,862,357	52.87	46.16	0.97	53.39
1976 BdrS	1,338,524	530,439	63,395	1,932,358	69.27	27.45	3.28	71.62
1976 MidW	8,641,524	7,213,024	371,320	16,225,868	53.26	44.45	2.29	54.51
1976 West	5,959,135	5,342,875	336,713	11,638,723	51.20	45.91	2.89	52.73
1978 NEng	1,578,112	1,312,684	39,473	2,930,269	53.86	44.80	1.35	54.59
1978 South	4,680,414	3,834,755	278,751	8,793,920	53.22	43.61	3.17	54.97
1978 MAtl	1,176,890	910,679	32,018	2,119,587	55.52	42.96	1.51	56.38
1978 BdrS	1,033,717	667,940	22,741	1,724,398	59.95	38.73	1.32	60.75
1978 MidW	4,702,466	5,110,558	122,608	9,935,632	47.33	51.44	1.23	47.92
1978 West	1,161,926	1,711,895	9,495	2,883,316	40.30	59.37	0.33	40.43
1980 NEng	1,047,600	878,868	13,795	1,940,263	53.99	45.30	0.71	54.38
1980 South	5,069,839	4,763,094	49,263	9,882,196	51.30	48.20	0.50	51.56
1980 MAtl	4,741,052	4,930,056	761,848	10,432,956	45.44	47.25	7.30	49.02
1980 BdrS	1,634,262	1,824,251	32,759	3,491,272	46.81	52.25	0.94	47.25
1980 MidW	9,629,888	8,040,756	248,972	17,919,616	53.74	44.87	1.39	54.50
1980 West	7,767,401	6,565,526	636,450	14,969,377	51.89	43.86	4.25	54.19
1982 NEng	2,272,672	1,770,416	61,791	4,104,879	55.37	43.13	1.51	56.21
1982 South	5,340,941	3,707,229	28,849	9,077,019	58.84	40.84	0.32	59.03
1982 MAtl	5,847,073	4,986,167	123,502	10,956,742	53.37	45.51	1.13	53.97
1982 BdrS	1,094,526	581,244	4,234	1,680,004	65.15	34.60	0.25	65.31
1982 MidW	7,591,524	6,104,881	211,968	13,908,373	54.58	43.89	1.52	55.43
1982 West	5,895,190	5,544,009	429,369	11,868,568	49.67	46.71	3.62	51.53
1984 NEng	1,979,834	1,875,540	5,918	3,861,292	51.27	48.57	0.15	51.35
1984 South	8,260,682	8,665,774	128,232	17,054,688	48.44	50.81	0.75	48.80
1984 MAtl	2,134,475	1,178,201	29,712	3,342,388	63.86	35.25	0.89	64.43
1984 BdrS	1,920,085	1,270,308	22,163	3,212,556	59.77	39.54	0.69	60.18
1984 MidW	6,507,279	7,117,373	174,712	13,799,364	47.16	51.58	1.27	47.76
1984 West	1,417,326	2,744,137	32,374	4,193,837	33.80	65.43	0.77	34.06
1986 NEng	836,043	562,326	19,893	1,418,262	58.95	39.65	1.40	59.79
1986 South	5,556,480	4,695,332	9,821	10,261,633	54.15	45.76	0.10	54.20
1986 MAtl	3,171,435	4,284,734	101,504	7,557,673	41.96	56.69	1.34	42.53
1986 BdrS	1,579,230	1,104,177	176	2,683,583	58.85	41.15	0.01	58.85
1986 MidW	6,823,572	6,144,766	82,158	13,050,496	52.29	47.08	0.63	52.62
1986 West	6,323,450	6,696,652	270,720	13,290,822	47.58	50.39	2.04	48.57

Table 6-5 *(Continued)*

	Raw Vote				Percentage			Democratic % of
Year/Region[1]	Democratic	Republican	Other	Total	Democratic	Republican	Other	Two-Party Vote
1988 NEng	3,086,619	2,047,955	50,659	5,185,233	59.53	39.50	0.98	60.11
1988 South	8,096,845	5,825,364	52,403	13,974,612	57.94	41.69	0.37	58.16
1988 MAtl	7,157,696	6,278,551	202,458	13,638,705	52.48	46.03	1.48	53.27
1988 BdrS	1,410,149	841,101	362	2,251,612	62.63	37.36	0.02	62.64
1988 MidW	8,461,661	8,656,713	137,867	17,256,241	49.04	50.17	0.80	49.43
1988 West	7,066,305	7,691,407	368,010	15,125,722	46.72	50.85	2.43	47.88
1990 NEng	1,839,169	1,640,823	11,995	3,491,987	52.67	46.99	0.34	52.85
1990 South	5,431,732	5,723,639	342,758	11,498,129	47.24	49.78	2.98	48.69
1990 MAtl	1,090,728	983,428	44,450	2,118,606	51.48	46.42	2.10	52.59
1990 BdrS	1,449,894	754,919	0	2,204,813	65.76	34.24	0.00	65.76
1990 MidW	5,709,101	4,459,867	73,548	10,242,516	55.74	43.54	0.72	56.14
1990 West	1,501,380	1,969,922	39,779	3,511,081	42.76	56.11	1.13	43.25
1992 NEng	1,272,313	945,481	87,070	2,304,864	55.20	41.02	3.78	57.37
1992 South	7,225,820	5,092,074	154,523	12,472,417	57.93	40.83	1.24	58.66
1992 MAtl	5,311,166	5,525,119	424,951	11,261,236	47.16	49.06	3.77	49.01
1992 BdrS	2,638,848	1,768,168	60,000	4,467,016	59.07	39.58	1.34	59.88
1992 MidW	9,421,953	9,607,507	782,919	19,812,379	47.56	48.49	3.95	49.51
1992 West	9,314,082	8,931,795	1,419,625	19,665,502	47.36	45.42	7.22	51.05
1994 NEng	2,384,295	1,866,443	77,786	4,328,524	55.08	43.12	1.80	56.09
1994 South	4,601,319	7,633,716	297,020	12,532,055	36.72	60.91	2.37	37.61
1994 MAtl	5,413,063	4,801,331	347,484	10,561,878	51.25	45.46	3.29	52.99
1994 BdrS	1,099,620	690,349	71	1,790,040	61.43	38.57	0.00	61.43
1994 MidW	5,902,645	7,381,800	668,817	13,953,262	42.30	52.90	4.79	44.43
1994 West	6,232,066	6,515,803	857,523	13,605,392	45.81	47.89	6.30	48.89
1996 NEng	2,058,644	1,810,931	149,064	4,018,639	51.23	45.06	3.71	53.20
1996 South	9,163,998	11,098,328	299,894	20,562,220	44.57	53.97	1.46	45.23
1996 MAtl	1,684,793	1,332,905	142,013	3,159,711	53.32	42.18	4.49	55.83
1996 BdrS	1,490,700	1,534,492	60,618	3,085,810	48.31	49.73	1.96	49.28
1996 MidW	7,123,242	5,892,583	458,164	13,473,989	52.87	43.73	3.40	54.73
1996 West	1,979,763	2,542,484	207,131	4,729,378	41.86	53.76	4.38	43.78
1998 NEng	871,756	573,705	47,988	1,493,449	58.37	38.41	3.21	60.31
1998 South	6,301,287	5,236,829	159,681	11,697,797	53.87	44.77	1.37	54.61
1998 MAtl	3,579,904	3,873,168	175,505	7,628,577	46.93	50.77	2.30	48.03
1998 BdrS	1,894,759	1,585,136	32,679	3,512,574	53.94	45.13	0.93	54.45
1998 MidW	6,501,459	7,160,320	214,015	13,875,794	46.85	51.60	1.54	47.59
1998 West	7,775,484	7,289,445	525,651	15,590,580	49.87	46.76	3.37	51.61

Notes: Entries are calculated from the raw vote values in Tables 6-33 through 6-54. Whenever bold italicized values occur in Tables 6-33 through 6-54, denoting the author's alternate party coding system, they are used instead of the conventionally coded main entries in these tables in the aggregation process to the regional level. See text and Table 6-10 for a more complete discussion of the conventional and alternate party coding systems. Also see Table 1-3 for a similar discussion. Entries in this table are, therefore, based on candidates who use the designation "Democrat" or "Republican" (or their historical antecedents listed in Appendix A), either solely or with other labels or parties (often minor parties) on the ballot. Other = candidates who use third-party names only on the ballot or are listed as independent or unidentified. Special Senate elections are not included. —indicates no states had Senate vote data for that region in that year.

[1]Regional categories are adapted from the ICPSR regional codings. In the current analysis, Tennessee is categorized in the South, since it was part of the Confederacy, although the ICPSR treats it as a Border South state. The regional categories are: New England (NEng)—Connecticut, Maine, Massachusetts, New Hampshire, Rhode Island, Vermont; Mid-Atlantic (MAtl)—Delaware, New Jersey, New York, Pennsylvania; South—Alabama, Arkansas, Florida, Georgia, Louisiana, Mississippi, North Carolina, South Carolina, Tennessee, Texas, Virginia; Border South (BdrS)—Maryland, Kentucky, Oklahoma, West Virginia; Midwest (MidW)—Illinois, Indiana, Iowa, Kansas, Michigan, Minnesota, Missouri, Nebraska, North Dakota, Ohio, South Dakota, Wisconsin; West—Alaska, Arizona, California, Colorado, Hawaii, Idaho, Montana, Nevada, New Mexico, Oregon, Utah, Washington, Wyoming.

Sources: Data from Tables 6-33 through 6-54 as adapted from the *Congressional Quarterly's Guide to U.S. Elections* (1994), ICPSR data sets 0001 and 0075, *America Votes* (various publication dates), and independent search of state sources by the author. For some party affiliations, the labels were taken from Michael J. Dubin's election archive after verification by the author.

Table 6-6 Votes in Senate Elections, by Non-South and South, 1912–1998

Year/Region[1]	Regional Raw Vote				Percentage			Democratic % of Two-Party Vote
	Democratic	Republican	Other	Total	Democratic	Republican	Other	
1912 N-S	588,552	532,021	208,372	1,328,945	44.29	40.03	15.68	52.52
1912 S	—	—	—	—	—	—	—	—
1914 N-S	4,033,827	4,345,907	2,033,673	10,413,407	38.74	41.73	19.53	48.14
1914 S	335,329	110,651	34,483	480,463	69.79	23.03	7.18	75.19
1916 N-S	4,635,097	5,812,631	662,523	11,110,251	41.72	52.32	5.96	44.36
1916 S	712,525	175,736	26,537	914,798	77.89	19.21	2.90	80.22
1918 N-S	2,224,572	2,838,505	297,807	5,360,884	41.50	52.95	5.56	43.94
1918 S	724,773	182,988	3,358	911,119	79.55	20.08	0.37	79.84
1920 N-S	6,399,904	10,180,490	1,545,546	18,125,940	35.31	56.17	8.53	38.60
1920 S	975,673	396,819	12,218	1,384,710	70.46	28.66	0.88	71.09
1922 N-S	6,476,172	7,252,420	1,024,814	14,753,406	43.90	49.16	6.95	47.17
1922 S	638,322	252,180	6,158	896,660	71.19	28.12	0.69	71.68
1924 N-S	4,362,957	7,168,330	666,609	12,197,896	35.77	58.77	5.46	37.84
1924 S	1,803,898	476,988	50,340	2,331,226	77.38	20.46	2.16	79.09
1926 N-S	6,716,890	8,385,422	376,811	15,479,123	43.39	54.17	2.43	44.48
1926 S	506,081	184,975	13	691,069	73.23	26.77	0.00	73.23
1928 N-S	9,364,977	14,026,259	1,050,092	24,441,328	38.32	57.39	4.30	40.04
1928 S	1,282,021	321,094	1,429	1,604,544	79.90	20.01	0.09	79.97
1930 N-S	5,364,969	5,475,253	335,880	11,176,102	48.00	48.99	3.01	49.49
1930 S	1,386,027	308,364	140,473	1,834,864	75.54	16.81	7.66	81.80
1932 N-S	13,974,913	11,057,906	1,530,051	26,562,870	52.61	41.63	5.76	55.83
1932 S	1,662,359	296,541	463	1,959,363	84.84	15.13	0.02	84.86
1934 N-S	11,537,074	10,815,947	1,703,241	24,056,262	47.96	44.96	7.08	51.61
1934 S	926,136	153,549	9,087	1,088,772	85.06	14.10	0.83	85.78
1936 N-S	8,734,912	7,610,202	1,462,226	17,807,340	49.05	42.74	8.21	53.44
1936 S	3,061,644	438,560	34,535	3,534,739	86.62	12.41	0.98	87.47
1938 N-S	13,461,288	12,689,281	611,495	26,762,064	50.30	47.42	2.28	51.48
1938 S	962,959	243,129	3,694	1,209,782	79.60	20.10	0.31	79.84
1940 N-S	14,932,198	17,012,182	1,626,236	33,570,616	44.48	50.68	4.84	46.74
1940 S	2,030,223	181,841	20,061	2,232,125	90.95	8.15	0.90	91.78
1942 N-S	5,261,448	6,527,762	500,728	12,289,938	42.81	53.11	4.07	44.63
1942 S	1,068,765	165,543	26,921	1,261,229	84.74	13.13	2.13	86.59
1944 N-S	16,491,531	15,734,269	185,904	32,411,704	50.88	48.55	0.57	51.17
1944 S	1,911,900	438,434	3,351	2,353,685	81.23	18.63	0.14	81.35
1946 N-S	11,138,780	14,764,097	253,438	26,156,315	42.59	56.45	0.97	43.00
1946 S	849,524	220,274	27,717	1,097,515	77.40	20.07	2.53	79.41
1948 N-S	9,545,350	8,766,645	138,089	18,450,084	51.74	47.52	0.75	52.13
1948 S	3,205,304	896,634	48,248	4,150,186	77.23	21.60	1.16	78.14
1950 N-S	14,034,685	15,889,703	364,484	30,288,872	46.34	52.46	1.20	46.90
1950 S	1,576,013	276,963	38,789	1,891,765	83.31	14.64	2.05	85.05
1952 N-S	16,843,924	23,110,476	822,261	40,776,661	41.31	56.68	2.02	42.16
1952 S	3,759,018	153,479	113,149	4,025,646	93.38	3.81	2.81	96.08
1954 N-S	8,685,601	8,366,665	99,649	17,151,915	50.64	48.78	0.58	50.94
1954 S	2,750,088	472,212	175,737	3,398,037	80.93	13.90	5.17	85.35
1956 N-S	19,343,907	20,773,835	94,795	40,212,537	48.10	51.66	0.24	48.22
1956 S	3,155,440	485,186	173	3,640,799	86.67	13.33	0.00	86.67
1958 N-S	19,186,134	15,753,387	240,035	35,179,556	54.54	44.78	0.68	54.91
1958 S	1,668,727	418,253	162,562	2,249,542	74.18	18.59	7.23	79.96
1959 N-S	77,647	87,161	0	164,808	47.11	52.89	0.00	47.11
1959 S	—	—	—	—	—	—	—	—
1960 N-S	12,000,303	12,059,248	81,089	24,140,640	49.71	49.95	0.34	49.88
1960 S	5,638,578	1,955,043	49,368	7,642,989	73.77	25.58	0.65	74.25
1962 N-S	17,303,763	18,185,799	193,509	35,683,071	48.49	50.96	0.54	48.76
1962 S	2,369,757	1,133,159	206	3,503,122	67.65	32.35	0.01	67.65
1964 N-S	26,067,275	19,842,621	293,105	46,203,001	56.42	42.95	0.63	56.78
1964 S	3,967,709	2,366,648	165,581	6,499,938	61.04	36.41	2.55	62.64
1966 N-S	8,424,292	10,508,842	166,742	19,099,876	44.11	55.02	0.87	44.49
1966 S	3,933,031	2,661,714	103,350	6,698,095	58.72	39.74	1.54	59.64
1968 N-S	20,426,824	21,521,892	1,599,245	43,547,961	46.91	49.42	3.67	48.69
1968 S	4,632,220	2,646,975	15	7,279,210	63.64	36.36	0.00	63.64
1970 N-S	22,173,377	16,992,803	3,086,535	42,252,715	52.48	40.22	7.30	56.61
1970 S	3,198,044	2,516,287	560,725	6,275,056	50.96	40.10	8.94	55.97
1972 N-S	11,033,743	13,757,679	319,752	25,111,174	43.94	54.79	1.27	44.51
1972 S	6,201,666	6,074,319	438,261	12,714,246	48.78	47.78	3.45	50.52
1974 N-S	18,842,321	14,831,544	1,555,361	35,229,226	53.48	42.10	4.41	55.96
1974 S	3,795,548	1,589,829	323,496	5,708,873	66.49	27.85	5.67	70.48
1976 N-S	26,101,675	21,511,495	973,277	48,586,447	53.72	44.27	2.00	54.82
1976 S	5,901,096	3,367,487	1,007,446	10,276,029	57.43	32.77	9.80	63.67
1978 N-S	9,653,111	9,713,756	226,335	19,593,202	49.27	49.58	1.16	49.84
1978 S	4,680,414	3,834,755	278,751	8,793,920	53.22	43.61	3.17	54.97

Table 6-6 *(Continued)*

		Raw Vote				Percentage		Democratic % of
Year/Region[1]	Democratic	Republican	Other	Total	Democratic	Republican	Other	Two-Party Vote
1980 N-S	24,820,203	22,239,457	1,693,824	48,753,484	50.91	45.62	3.47	52.74
1980 S	5,069,839	4,763,094	49,263	9,882,196	51.30	48.20	0.50	51.56
1982 N-S	22,700,985	18,986,717	830,864	42,518,566	53.39	44.66	1.95	54.45
1982 S	5,340,941	3,707,229	28,849	9,077,019	58.84	40.84	0.32	59.03
1984 N-S	13,958,999	14,185,559	264,879	28,409,437	49.14	49.93	0.93	49.60
1984 S	8,260,682	8,665,774	128,232	17,054,688	48.44	50.81	0.75	48.80
1986 N-S	18,733,730	18,792,655	474,451	38,000,836	49.30	49.45	1.25	49.92
1986 S	5,556,480	4,695,332	9,821	10,261,633	54.15	45.76	0.10	54.20
1988 N-S	27,182,430	25,515,727	759,356	53,457,513	50.85	47.73	1.42	51.58
1988 S	8,096,845	5,825,364	52,403	13,974,612	57.94	41.69	0.37	58.16
1990 N-S	11,590,272	9,808,959	169,772	21,569,003	53.74	45.48	0.79	54.16
1990 S	5,431,732	5,723,639	342,758	11,498,129	47.24	49.78	2.98	48.69
1992 N-S	27,958,362	26,778,070	2,774,565	57,510,997	48.61	46.56	4.82	51.08
1992 S	7,225,820	5,092,074	154,523	12,472,417	57.93	40.83	1.24	58.66
1994 N-S	21,031,689	21,255,726	1,951,681	44,239,096	47.54	48.05	4.41	49.74
1994 S	4,601,319	7,633,716	297,020	12,532,055	36.72	60.91	2.37	37.61
1996 N-S	14,337,142	13,113,395	1,016,990	28,467,527	50.36	46.06	3.57	52.23
1996 S	9,163,998	11,098,328	299,894	20,562,220	44.57	53.97	1.46	45.23
1998 N-S	20,623,362	20,481,774	995,838	42,100,974	48.99	48.65	2.37	50.17
1998 S	6,301,287	5,236,829	159,681	11,697,797	53.87	44.77	1.37	54.61

Notes: Entries are calculated from the raw vote values in Tables 6-33 through 6-54. Whenever bold italicized values occur in Tables 6-33 through 6-54, denoting the author's alternate party coding system, they are used instead of the conventionally coded main entries in these tables in the aggregation process to the regional level. See text and Table 6-10 for a more complete discussion of the conventional and alternate party coding systems. Also see Table 1-3 for a similar discussion. Entries in this table are based on candidates who use the designation "Democrat" or "Republican" (or their historical antecedents listed in Appendix A), either solely or with other labels or parties (often minor parties) on the ballot. Other = candidates who use third-party names only on the ballot or are listed as independent or unidentified. States with partial Special Senate elections are not included. —indicates no states had Senate vote data for that region in that year.

[1]Regional categories are adapted from the ICPSR, except that in the current analysis Tennessee is categorized in the South since it was part of the Confederacy, whereas the ICPSR codes it as a Border South state. Thus, the South includes Alabama, Arkansas, Florida, Georgia, Louisiana, Mississippi, North Carolina, South Carolina, Tennessee, Texas, and Virginia. All other states make up the non-South.

Sources: Data from Tables 6-33 through 6-54 as adapted from the *Congressional Quarterly's Guide to U.S. Elections* (1994), ICPSR data sets 0001 and 0075, *America Votes* (various publication dates), and independent search of state sources by the author. For some party affiliations, the labels were taken from Michael J. Dubin's election archive after verification by the author.

Table 6-7 Party Victories in Senate Elections by State, in Regions, 1912–1998

	1912–1928	1930–1964	1966–1998	Total Wins	Percent Wins		1912–1928	1930–1964	1966–1998	Total Wins	Percent Wins
NEW ENGLAND						Georgia					
Democratic	4	28	36	68	39.8	Democratic	5	12	10	27	93.1
Republican	28	44	31	103	60.2	Republican	0	0	2	2	6.9
Other	0	0	0	0	0.0	Other	0	0	0	0	0.0
						Louisiana					
Democratic %	12.5	38.9	53.7	—	—	Democratic	5	12	12	29	100.0
Republican %	87.5	61.1	46.3	—	—	Republican	0	0	0	0	0.0
Other %	0.0	0.0	0.0	—	—	Other	0	0	0	0	0.0
Connecticut						Mississippi					
Democratic	0	8	8	16	55.2	Democratic	5	12	5	22	78.6
Republican	6	4	3	13	44.8	Republican	0	0	6	6	21.4
Other	0	0	0	0	0.0	Other	0	0	0	0	0.0
Maine						North Carolina					
Democratic	0	2	5	7	25.0	Democratic	5	12	5	22	75.9
Republican	5	10	6	21	75.0	Republican	0	0	7	7	24.1
Other	0	0	0	0	0.0	Other	0	0	0	0	0.0
Massachusetts						South Carolina					
Democratic	2	6	9	17	60.7	Democratic	5	11	6	22	75.9
Republican	3	6	2	11	39.3	Republican	0	0	6	6	20.7
Other	0	0	0	0	0.0	Other	0	1	0	1	3.4
New Hampshire						Tennessee					
Democratic	0	1	2	3	10.3	Democratic	5	12	5	22	78.6
Republican	5	11	10	26	89.7	Republican	0	0	6	6	21.4
Other	0	0	0	0	0.0	Other	0	0	0	0	0.0
Rhode Island						Texas					
Democratic	2	11	7	20	71.4	Democratic	5	12	3	20	71.4
Republican	3	1	4	8	28.6	Republican	0	0	8	8	28.6
Other	0	0	0	0	0.0	Other	0	0	0	0	0.0
Vermont						Virginia					
Democratic	0	0	5	5	17.2	Democratic	5	12	3	20	71.4
Republican	6	12	6	24	82.8	Republican	0	0	6	6	21.4
Other	0	0	0	0	0.0	Other	0	0	2	2	7.1
MID-ATLANTIC						**BORDER SOUTH**					
Democratic	6	20	19	45	39.5	**Democratic**	11	39	28	78	67.2
Republican	16	28	24	68	59.6	**Republican**	11	9	18	38	32.8
Other	0	0	1	1	0.9	**Other**	0	0	0	0	0.0
Democratic %	27.3	41.7	43.2	—	—	**Democratic %**	50.0	81.3	60.9	—	—
Republican %	72.7	58.3	54.5	—	—	**Republican %**	50.0	23.7	39.1	—	—
Other %	0.0	0.0	2.3	—	—	**Other %**	0.0	0.0	0.0	—	—
Delaware						Kentucky					
Democratic	2	4	5	11	39.3	Democratic	3	9	6	18	62.1
Republican	3	8	6	17	60.7	Republican	2	3	6	11	37.9
Other	0	0	0	0	0.0	Other	0	0	0	0	0.0
New Jersey						Maryland					
Democratic	1	4	9	14	50.0	Democratic	3	8	7	18	62.1
Republican	4	8	2	14	50.0	Republican	3	4	4	11	37.9
Other	0	0	0	0	0.0	Other	0	0	0	0	0.0
New York						Oklahoma					
Democratic	3	7	5	15	51.7	Democratic	4	11	4	19	63.3
Republican	3	5	5	13	44.8	Republican	2	1	8	11	36.7
Other	0	0	1	1	3.4	Other	0	0	0	0	0.0
Pennsylvania						West Virginia					
Democratic	0	5	0	5	17.2	Democratic	1	11	11	23	82.1
Republican	6	7	11	24	82.8	Republican	4	1	0	5	17.9
Other	0	0	0	0	0.0	Other	0	0	0	0	0.0
SOUTH						**MIDWEST**					
Democratic	56	131	76	263	83.5	**Democratic**	12	55	73	140	40.3
Republican	0	0	49	49	15.6	**Republican**	53	84	63	200	57.6
Other	0	1	2	3	1.0	**Other**	2	5	0	7	2.0
Democratic %	100.0	99.2	59.8	—	—	**Democratic %**	17.9	38.2	53.7	—	—
Republican %	0.0	0.0	38.6	—	—	**Republican %**	79.1	58.3	46.3	—	—
Other %	0.0	0.8	1.6	—	—	**Other %**	3.0	3.5	0.0	—	—
Alabama						Illinois					
Democratic	5	12	9	26	89.7	Democratic	0	8	7	15	51.7
Republican	0	0	3	3	10.3	Republican	5	4	5	14	48.3
Other	0	0	0	0	0.0	Other	0	0	0	0	0.0
Arkansas						Indiana					
Democratic	5	12	11	28	96.6	Democratic	2	6	4	12	41.4
Republican	0	0	1	1	3.4	Republican	4	6	7	17	58.6
Other	0	0	0	0	0.0	Other	0	0	0	0	0.0
Florida						Iowa					
Democratic	6	12	7	25	86.2	Democratic	0	4	6	10	34.5
Republican	0	0	4	4	13.8	Republican	5	8	6	19	65.5
Other	0	0	0	0	0.0	Other	0	0	0	0	0.0

Table 6-7 (Continued)

	1912–1928	1930–1964	1966–1998	Total Wins	Percent Wins
Kansas					
Democratic	1	1	0	2	6.7
Republican	5	11	12	28	93.3
Other	0	0	0	0	0.0
Michigan					
Democratic	1	5	8	14	50.0
Republican	4	7	3	14	50.0
Other	0	0	0	0	0.0
Minnesota					
Democratic	0	5	6	11	37.9
Republican	4	5	5	14	48.3
Other	2	2	0	4	13.8
Missouri					
Democratic	4	10	4	18	62.1
Republican	2	2	7	11	37.9
Other	0	0	0	0	0.0
Nebraska					
Democratic	1	1	7	9	32.1
Republican	4	10	4	18	64.3
Other	0	1	0	1	3.6
North Dakota					
Democratic	0	2	8	10	34.5
Republican	6	10	3	19	65.5
Other	0	0	0	0	0.0
Ohio					
Democratic	1	6	7	14	48.3
Republican	5	6	4	15	51.7
Other	0	0	0	0	0.0
South Dakota					
Democratic	1	3	7	11	37.9
Republican	4	9	5	18	62.1
Other	0	0	0	0	0.0
Wisconsin					
Democratic	1	4	9	14	48.3
Republican	5	6	2	13	44.8
Other	0	2	0	2	6.9
WEST					
Democratic	31	94	65	190	54.3
Republican	32	46	82	160	45.7
Other	0	0	0	0	0.0
Democratic %	49.2	67.1	44.2	—	—
Republican %	50.8	32.9	55.8	—	—
Other %	0.0	0.0	0.0	—	—
Alaska					
Democratic	—	4	3	7	43.8
Republican	—	0	9	9	56.3
Other	—	0	0	0	0.0
Arizona					
Democratic	5	9	3	17	58.6
Republican	1	3	8	12	44.4
Other	0	0	0	0	0.0
California					
Democratic	1	4	8	13	44.8
Republican	5	8	3	16	55.2
Other	0	0	0	0	0.0
Colorado					
Democratic	2	7	6	15	50.0
Republican	4	5	6	15	50.0
Other	0	0	0	0	0.0
Hawaii					
Democratic	—	2	10	12	80.0
Republican	—	2	1	3	20.0
Other	—	0	0	0	0.0
Idaho					
Democratic	0	6	2	8	27.6
Republican	5	6	10	21	72.4
Other	0	0	0	0	0.0
Montana					
Democratic	6	11	9	26	89.7
Republican	0	1	2	3	10.3
Other	0	0	0	0	0.0
Nevada					
Democratic	4	10	8	22	75.9
Republican	2	2	3	7	24.1
Other	0	0	0	0	0.0
New Mexico					
Democratic	3	11	5	19	67.9
Republican	2	1	6	9	32.1
Other	0	0	0	0	0.0
Oregon					
Democratic	2	4	1	7	23.3
Republican	4	8	11	23	76.7
Other	0	0	0	0	0.0
Utah					
Democratic	3	7	1	11	37.9
Republican	3	5	10	18	62.1
Other	0	0	0	0	0.0
Washington					
Democratic	2	11	8	21	72.4
Republican	4	1	3	8	27.6
Other	0	0	0	0	0.0
Wyoming					
Democratic	3	8	1	12	42.9
Republican	2	4	10	16	57.1
Other	0	0	0	0	0.0

Notes: These entries reflect winners from the actual vote result and are not adjusted for contested seats, runoffs, inaccuracies of other types in reporting party labels or winners, or gubernatorial and legislative proclamations of different winners. For these reasons, these figures may not completely correspond to other sources such as the most recent reports of the Clerk of the House of Representatives or the Senate History Office. When the author's alternative party coding occurred in the Senate vote data in Tables 6-33 through 6-54 (the bold italicized entries), these party labels were used to designate "Democrat," Republican," and "Other Party" classifications rather than the conventional entries in these tables. See Tables 6-10 and 1-3 for an explanation of these alternative party codings.

Sources: Senate winners, in large part, can be determined from the Senate vote data in Tables 6-33 through 6-54. In general, these vote results are similar to the Senate winners mentioned in *Congressional Quarterly's Guide to U.S. Elections* (1994).

Table 6-8 Party Victories in Senate Elections by Non-South and South, 1912–1998

	1912–1928	1930–1964	1966–1998	Total Wins	1912–1928 Percent Wins	1930–1964 Percent Wins	1966–1998 Percent Wins	1912–1998 Percent Wins
Non-South								
Democrats	64	236	221	521	31.1	52.2	50.2	47.4
Republicans	140	211	218	569	68.0	46.7	49.5	51.8
Other	2	5	1	8	1.0	1.1	0.2	0.7
South								
Democrats	56	131	76	263	100.0	99.2	59.8	83.5
Republicans	0	0	49	49	0.0	0.0	38.6	15.6
Others	0	1	2	3	0.0	0.8	1.6	1.0

Sources: Data from Table 6-7.

Table 6-9 Reelection Rates of Senate Incumbents, 1914–1998

Congress	Years	Seats Subject to Election	Seeking Reelection	%	Reelected	%	Defeated	%
64th	1914	35	24	68.6	22	91.7	2	8.3
65th	1916	35	29	82.9	16	55.2	13	44.8
66th	1918	40	29	72.5	20	69.0	9	31.0
67th	1920	34	30	88.2	18	60.0	12	40.0
68th	1922	36	29	80.6	16	55.2	13	44.8
69th	1924	36	30	83.3	20	66.7	10	33.3
70th	1926	38	33	86.8	21	63.6	12	36.4
71st	1928	37	32	86.5	25	78.1	7	21.9
72d	1930	40	30	75.0	17	56.7	13	43.3
73d	1932	37	32	86.5	18	56.3	14	43.8
74th	1934	38	32	84.2	22	68.8	10	31.3
75th	1936	37	27	73.0	21	77.8	6	22.2
76th	1938	37	31	83.8	22	71.0	9	29.0
77th	1940	36	32	88.9	24	75.0	8	25.0
78th	1942	36	33	91.7	22	66.7	11	33.3
79th	1944	36	30	83.3	21	70.0	9	30.0
80th	1946	40	29	72.5	16	55.2	13	44.8
81st	1948	34	25	73.5	15	60.0	10	40.0
82d	1950	38	32	84.2	22	68.8	10	31.3
83d	1952	36	31	86.1	20	64.5	11	35.5
84th	1954	41	32	78.0	24	75.0	8	25.0
85th	1956	35	29	82.9	25	86.2	4	13.8
86th	1958	37	28	75.7	18	64.3	10	35.7
87th	1960	36	29	80.6	28	96.6	1	3.4
88th	1962	39	35	89.7	29	82.9	6	17.1
89th	1964	35	33	94.3	28	84.8	5	15.2
90th	1966	36	32	88.9	28	87.5	4	12.5
91st	1968	34	28	82.4	20	71.4	8	28.6
92d	1970	34	31	91.2	24	77.4	7	22.6
93d	1972	34	27	79.4	20	74.1	7	25.9
94th	1974	34	27	79.4	23	85.2	4	14.8
95th	1976	33	25	75.8	16	64.0	9	36.0
96th	1978	35	25	71.4	15	60.0	10	40.0
97th	1980	34	29	85.3	16	55.2	13	44.8
98th	1982	33	30	90.9	28	93.3	2	6.7
99th	1984	34	29	85.3	26	89.7	3	10.3
100th	1986	34	28	82.4	21	75.0	7	25.0
101st	1988	33	27	81.8	23	85.2	4	14.8
102d	1990	35	32	91.4	31	96.9	1	3.1
103d	1992	36	28	77.8	24	85.7	4	14.3
104th	1994	33	26	78.8	24	92.3	2	7.7
105th	1996	34	21	61.8	19	90.5	2	9.5
106th	1998	34	29	85.3	26	89.7	3	10.3

Notes: Seats subject to election include special elections. Defeats include those not renominated.

Sources: Adapted from author's data set.

Table 6-10 Alternative Party Coding for Senate Elections, 1912–1998

State	Elections
Alabama	1968(W); 1972(W)
Alaska	
Arizona	
Arkansas	
California	1916(J); 1934(M); 1938(F); 1940(M); 1952(M)
Colorado	
Connecticut	1932(I); 1938(J), 1940(J); 1952(I); 1956(I); 1992(J); 1994(J); 1998(J)
Delaware	1940(W)
Florida	1920(W); 1922(I); 1926(W)
Georgia	
Hawaii	
Idaho	
Illinois	1926(I); 1930(I)
Indiana	
Iowa	1950(W)
Kansas	
Kentucky	
Louisiana	
Maine	1952(I)
Maryland	
Massachusetts	
Michigan	1942(W)
Minnesota	
Mississippi	
Missouri	
Montana	
Nebraska	1916(F); 1924(F)
Nevada	
New Hampshire	
New Jersey	
New Mexico	
New York	1914(J); 1916(F); 1926(I); 1938(J); 1940(J); 1944(J); 1946(J); 1950(J); 1956(J); 1958(J); 1962(J); 1964(J); 1968(J); 1970(J); 1974(J); 1976(J); 1980(J); 1982(J); 1986(J); 1988(J); 1992(J); 1994(J); 1998(J)
North Carolina	
North Dakota	1920(F)1922(F,I); 1926(I); 1944(I)
Ohio	
Oklahoma	
Oregon	
Pennsylvania	1914(J); 1916(J); 1926(J); 1938(J)
Rhode Island	
South Carolina	1944(I)
South Dakota	
Tennessee	
Texas	1952(M)
Utah	1914(F); 1916(F)
Vermont	1914(F); 1926(J); 1964(I); 1968(M); 1974(J); 1976(J)
Virginia	1936(I); 1952(I); 1954(I); 1960(I)
Washington	
West Virginia	
Wisconsin	1922(I); 1926(I); 1928(I); 1938(I)
Wyoming	

Notes: Wing = candidate affiliated with a major party running as a splinter, wing, or factional candidate from that party (e.g., Benton Democrat, Anti-Benton Democrat, Union Democrat). Fusion = candidate of a major party running on a fusion ticket with one or more minor parties (e.g., Democrat-Greenback fusion, Republican-Greenback fusion) or on the "fusion" label itself (if parties in a fusion ticket can be identified). Joint = candidate of a major party also endorsed by a minor party under the latter's own slate of candidates on the ballot (e.g., Liberal Party endorsement of a Democratic candidate in New York under the Liberal Party's own slate of candidates on the ballot). Independent = major party candidate also running as an independent (e.g., using the Independent Democrat label or the Democrat Independent label). Both Major = candidate running on both major party tickets (e.g., listed on both Democratic and Republican tickets on the ballot, as successful crossfiling candidates were in California up to 1960). For a further explanation of these categories, see the text discussion to Tables 1-3 and 5-1.

Sources: *Congressional Quarterly's Guide to U.S. Elections* (1994), *America Votes* (various publication dates), ICPSR data sets 0001 and 0075, the election archive of Michael J. Dubin, and independent search of state sources by the author.

Table 6-11 Senate Election Results, by State, 1912–1914 (Percentages)

State	1912 Democratic	1912 Republican	1912 Other	1912 Democratic % of Two-Party Vote	1914 Democratic	1914 Republican	1914 Other	1914 Democratic % of Two-Party Vote
Alabama	—	—	—	—	78.1	15.2	6.7	83.7
Alaska	—	—	—	—	—	—	—	—
Arizona	—	—	—	—	53.2	18.9	27.8	73.8
Arkansas	—	—	—	—	74.9	25.1	0.0	74.9
California	—	—	—	—	31.6	28.7	39.7	52.4
Colorado	47.3	26.8	25.9	63.9	40.3	39.0	20.7	50.8
Connecticut	—	—	—	—	42.1	49.8	8.2	45.8
Delaware	—	—	—	—	—	—	—	—
Florida	—	—	—	—	99.5	0.0	0.5	100.0
Georgia	—	—	—	—	68.4	0.0	31.6	100.0
Hawaii	—	—	—	—	—	—	—	—
Idaho	—	—	—	—	38.1	43.9	18.0	46.5
Illinois	—	—	—	—	36.8	38.5	24.8	48.9
Indiana	—	—	—	—	42.1	35.1	22.8	54.6
Iowa	—	—	—	—	39.2	48.2	12.6	44.8
Kansas	49.3	43.3	7.4	53.2	34.8	35.5	29.7	49.5
Kentucky	—	—	—	—	51.8	42.6	5.6	54.9
Louisiana	—	—	—	—	—	—	—	—
Maine	—	—	—	—	—	—	—	—
Maryland	—	—	—	—	51.0	43.9	5.1	53.7
Massachusetts	—	—	—	—	—	—	—	—
Michigan	—	—	—	—	—	—	—	—
Minnesota	37.2	62.8	0.0	37.2	—	—	—	—
Mississippi	—	—	—	—	—	—	—	—
Missouri	—	—	—	—	50.4	41.6	8.0	54.8
Montana	41.2	26.7	32.1	60.6	—	—	—	—
Nebraska	—	—	—	—	—	—	—	—
Nevada	—	—	—	—	37.5	37.3	25.3	50.1
New Hampshire	—	—	—	—	44.6	51.7	3.7	46.3
New Jersey	—	—	—	—	—	—	—	—
New Mexico	—	—	—	—	—	—	—	—
New York	—	—	—	—	0.0	47.0	53.0	0.0
New York	—	—	—	—	***42.1***	***47.0***	***10.9***	***47.2***
North Carolina	—	—	—	—	58.1	41.7	0.2	58.2
North Dakota	—	—	—	—	33.9	55.8	10.2	37.8
Ohio	—	—	—	—	39.6	49.2	11.2	44.6
Oklahoma	50.4	33.3	16.3	60.2	48.0	29.4	22.6	62.0
Oregon	30.1	28.8	41.1	51.1	45.5	36.0	18.5	55.9
Pennsylvania	—	—	—	—	24.0	0.0	76.0	100.0
Pennsylvania	—	—	—	—	***24.0***	***46.8***	***29.3***	***33.9***
Rhode Island	—	—	—	—	—	—	—	—
South Carolina	—	—	—	—	99.7	0.0	0.3	100.0
South Dakota	—	—	—	—	48.1	44.6	7.2	51.9
Tennessee	—	—	—	—	—	—	—	—
Texas	—	—	—	—	—	—	—	—
Utah	—	—	—	—	0.0	49.1	50.9	0.0
Utah	—	—	—	—	***46.3***	***49.1***	***4.6***	***48.6***
Vermont	—	—	—	—	0.0	56.0	44.0	0.0
Vermont	—	—	—	—	***42.7***	***56.0***	***1.3***	***43.2***
Virginia	—	—	—	—	—	—	—	—
Washington	—	—	—	—	26.6	37.8	35.6	41.3
West Virginia	—	—	—	—	—	—	—	—
Wisconsin	—	—	—	—	42.5	42.2	15.2	50.2
Wyoming	—	—	—	—	—	—	—	—

Notes: Main entries are calculated from the raw vote values in table series 6-33 through 6-54 for the appropriate years based on candidates who used the sole designation "Democrat" or "Republican" (or their historical antecedents listed in Appendix A) on the ballot. Other = candidates who used third-party names on the ballot or were listed as independent, unidentified, or scatter vote. Bold italicized entries in the table are the author's alternative party coding, which is used when a candidate listed a major party name (Democrat, Republican, or their historical antecedents) on the ballot with other party names or labels. These values are computed from the bold italicized raw vote values in table series 6-33 through 6-54 for the appropriate states and years. For a more detailed explanation of this alternative party coding system, see Tables 6-10 and 1-3. —indicates that the state had no data, either because the state had no Senate election, no vote data were found for the state in question, or the state had not yet entered the Union. No special Senate elections are included in this table.

Sources: *Congressional Quarterly's Guide to U.S. Elections* (1994), ICPSR data sets 0001 and 0075, and independent search of state sources by the author. For some party affiliations, the labels were taken from Michael J. Dubin's election archive after verification by the author.

Table 6-12 Senate Election Results, by State, 1916–1918 (Percentages)

State	1916				1918			
	Democratic	Republican	Other	Democratic % of Two-Party Vote	Democratic	Republican	Other	Democratic % of Two-Party Vote
Alabama	—	—	—	—	100.0	0.0	0.0	100.0
Alaska	—	—	—	—	—	—	—	—
Arizona	55.4	39.4	5.2	58.4	—	—	—	—
Arkansas	—	—	—	—	100.0	0.0	0.0	100.0
California	29.5	0.0	70.5	100.0	—	—	—	—
California	*29.5*	*61.1*	*9.4*	*32.6*	—	—	—	—
Colorado	—	—	—	—	47.9	49.5	2.6	49.2
Connecticut	46.2	50.2	3.6	48.0	—	—	—	—
Delaware	49.7	44.8	5.6	52.6	47.8	51.2	1.0	48.3
Florida	82.9	12.5	4.7	86.9	—	—	—	—
Georgia	—	—	—	—	88.4	11.6	0.0	88.4
Hawaii	—	—	—	—	—	—	—	—
Idaho	—	—	—	—	32.8	67.2	0.0	32.8
Illinois	—	—	—	—	44.9	50.5	4.6	47.1
Indiana	46.1	47.8	6.1	49.1	—	—	—	—
Iowa	—	—	—	—	34.6	65.4	0.0	34.6
Kansas	—	—	—	—	33.7	63.7	2.6	34.6
Kentucky	—	—	—	—	50.8	49.2	0.0	50.8
Louisiana	—	—	—	—	100.0	0.0	0.0	100.0
Maine	46.0	52.8	1.2	46.5	44.4	55.6	0.0	44.4
Maryland	47.6	49.3	3.1	49.1	—	—	—	—
Massachusetts	45.3	51.7	3.0	46.7	49.7	45.1	5.3	52.4
Michigan	39.9	56.3	3.8	41.4	48.5	50.2	1.3	49.1
Minnesota	30.8	48.6	20.6	38.8	0.0	60.1	39.9	0.0
Mississippi	100.0	0.0	0.0	100.0	95.0	0.0	5.0	100.0
Missouri	50.6	47.4	2.0	51.6	—	—	—	—
Montana	51.1	43.4	5.5	54.1	41.1	35.8	23.1	53.4
Nebraska	0.0	0.0	100.0	—	45.5	54.5	0.0	45.5
Nebraska	*50.0*	*45.9*	*4.1*	*52.1*	—	—	—	—
Nevada	38.8	32.3	28.9	54.6	—	—	—	—
New Hampshire	—	—	—	—	46.4	53.6	0.0	46.4
New Jersey	38.9	56.0	5.1	41.0	43.2	50.3	6.4	46.2
New Mexico	51.1	45.8	3.0	52.7	47.5	51.4	1.1	48.0
New York	0.0	54.3	45.7	0.0	—	—	—	—
New York	*39.2*	*54.3*	*6.5*	*41.9*	—	—	—	—
North Carolina	—	—	—	—	60.5	39.5	0.0	60.5
North Dakota	38.2	53.9	7.9	41.5	—	—	—	—
Ohio	49.3	46.2	4.6	51.6	—	—	—	—
Oklahoma	—	—	—	—	55.4	40.7	3.8	57.6
Oregon	—	—	—	—	42.3	54.2	3.5	43.8
Pennsylvania	37.2	0.0	62.8	100.0	—	—	—	—
Pennsylvania	*37.2*	*56.3*	*6.4*	*39.8*	—	—	—	—
Rhode Island	52.9	44.1	2.9	54.5	46.2	51.8	2.0	47.2
South Carolina	—	—	—	—	100.0	0.0	0.0	100.0
South Dakota	—	—	—	—	38.9	55.1	6.0	41.4
Tennessee	54.4	44.8	0.8	54.9	62.2	37.8	0.0	62.2
Texas	81.3	13.1	5.6	86.1	86.7	12.4	0.9	87.5
Utah	0.0	39.9	60.1	0.0	—	—	—	—
Utah	*56.9*	*39.9*	*3.2*	*58.8*	—	—	—	—
Vermont	23.4	74.2	2.3	24.0	—	—	—	—
Virginia	99.9	0.0	0.1	100.0	99.7	0.0	0.3	100.0
Washington	37.1	55.4	7.5	40.1	—	—	—	—
West Virginia	48.2	50.1	1.7	49.0	45.4	53.5	1.1	45.9
Wisconsin	31.9	59.3	8.8	35.0	—	—	—	—
Wyoming	51.5	45.5	3.1	53.1	42.2	57.8	0.0	42.2

Notes: Main entries are calculated from the raw vote values in table series 6-33 through 6-54 for the appropriate years based on candidates who used the sole designation "Democrat" or "Republican" (or their historical antecedents listed in Appendix A) on the ballot. Other = candidates who used third-party names on the ballot or were listed as independent, unidentified, or scatter vote. Bold italicized entries in the table are the author's alternative party coding, which is used when a candidate listed a major party name (Democrat, Republican, or their historical antecedents) on the ballot with other party names or labels. These values are computed from the bold italicized raw vote values in table series 6-33 through 6-54 for the appropriate states and years. For a more detailed explanation of this alternative party coding system, see Tables 6-10 and 1-3. —indicates that the state had no data, either because the state had no Senate election, no vote data were found for the state in question, or the state had not yet entered the Union. No special Senate elections are included in this table.

Sources: *Congressional Quarterly's Guide to U.S. Elections* (1994), ICPSR data sets 0001 and 0075, and independent search of state sources by the author. For some party affiliations, the labels were taken from Michael J. Dubin's election archive after verification by the author.

Table 6-13 Senate Election Results, by State, 1920–1922 (Percentages)

State	1920 Democratic	1920 Republican	1920 Other	1920 Democratic % of Two-Party Vote	1922 Democratic	1922 Republican	1922 Other	1922 Democratic % of Two-Party Vote
Alabama	68.0	31.2	0.9	68.6	—	—	—	—
Alaska	—	—	—	—	—	—	—	—
Arizona	44.8	55.2	0.0	44.8	65.0	35.0	0.0	65.0
Arkansas	65.9	34.1	0.0	65.9	—	—	—	—
California	40.7	49.0	10.3	45.3	23.8	62.2	14.1	27.7
Colorado	39.3	54.5	6.2	41.9	—	—	—	—
Connecticut	36.1	59.4	4.5	37.8	45.5	52.3	2.2	46.5
Delaware	—	—	—	—	49.8	49.4	0.8	50.2
Florida	74.3	20.9	4.8	78.0	88.0	0.0	12.0	100.0
Florida	*74.3*	*23.1*	*2.7*	*76.3*	*88.0*	*11.7*	*0.3*	*88.3*
Georgia	94.9	0.0	5.1	100.0	—	—	—	—
Hawaii	—	—	—	—	—	—	—	—
Idaho	45.9	54.1	0.0	45.9	—	—	—	—
Illinois	26.8	66.8	6.4	28.6	—	—	—	—
Indiana	41.1	54.6	4.3	43.0	50.9	47.8	1.3	51.6
Iowa	37.4	61.4	1.2	37.9	—	—	—	—
Kansas	33.4	64.0	2.6	34.3	—	—	—	—
Kentucky	49.7	50.3	0.0	49.7	—	—	—	—
Louisiana	100.0	0.0	0.0	100.0	—	—	—	—
Maine	—	—	—	—	42.5	57.5	0.0	42.5
Maryland	43.3	47.3	9.5	47.8	52.6	45.6	1.8	53.6
Massachusetts	—	—	—	—	46.7	47.6	5.7	49.6
Michigan	—	—	—	—	50.6	48.3	1.1	51.1
Minnesota	—	—	—	—	17.9	35.0	47.1	33.8
Mississippi	—	—	—	—	93.2	1.9	4.9	98.0
Missouri	44.5	53.7	1.9	45.3	51.9	47.3	0.8	52.3
Montana	—	—	—	—	55.4	43.6	1.0	55.9
Nebraska	—	—	—	—	38.2	56.8	4.9	40.2
Nevada	37.9	42.1	20.0	47.4	62.8	37.2	0.0	62.8
New Hampshire	41.6	57.7	0.6	41.9	—	—	—	—
New Jersey	—	—	—	—	54.9	44.0	1.1	55.5
New Mexico	—	—	—	—	55.2	44.1	0.7	55.6
New York	32.9	52.4	14.7	38.6	52.6	41.0	6.4	56.2
North Carolina	57.5	42.5	0.0	57.5	—	—	—	—
North Dakota	0.0	0.0	100.0	—	0.0	0.0	100.0	—
North Dakota	*40.2*	*59.8*	*0.0*	*40.2*	*47.7*	*52.3*	*0.0*	*47.7*
Ohio	40.8	59.1	0.1	40.8	47.7	50.9	1.4	48.4
Oklahoma	44.6	50.6	4.8	46.9	—	—	—	—
Oregon	43.5	50.7	5.7	46.2	—	—	—	—
Pennsylvania	27.2	59.9	12.9	31.2	29.6	56.0	14.4	34.6
Rhode Island	—	—	—	—	52.2	43.4	4.4	54.6
South Carolina	100.0	0.0	0.0	100.0	—	—	—	—
South Dakota	20.0	50.1	29.9	28.5	—	—	—	—
Tennessee	—	—	—	—	68.0	32.0	0.0	68.0
Texas	—	—	—	—	66.6	33.4	0.0	66.6
Utah	38.6	56.6	4.8	40.5	48.6	48.2	3.2	50.2
Vermont	21.9	78.1	0.0	21.9	32.1	67.9	0.0	32.1
Virginia	—	—	—	—	71.9	26.5	1.6	73.1
Washington	17.8	56.4	25.8	24.0	44.2	42.9	12.8	50.7
West Virginia	—	—	—	—	51.1	47.6	1.3	51.8
Wisconsin	13.2	41.6	45.2	24.1	0.0	80.6	19.4	0.0
Wisconsin	—	—	—	—	*16.6*	*80.6*	*2.8*	*17.1*
Wyoming	—	—	—	—	56.7	42.3	1.0	57.3

Notes: Main entries are calculated from the raw vote values in table series 6-33 through 6-54 for the appropriate years based on candidates who used the sole designation "Democrat" or "Republican" (or their historical antecedents listed in Appendix A) on the ballot. Other = candidates who used third-party names on the ballot or were listed as independent, unidentified, or scatter vote. Bold italicized entries in the table are the author's alternative party coding, which is used when a candidate listed a major party name (Democrat, Republican, or their historical antecedents) on the ballot with other party names or labels. These values are computed from the bold italicized raw vote values in table series 6-33 through 6-54 for the appropriate states and years. For a more detailed explanation of this alternative party coding system, see Tables 6-10 and 1-3. —indicates that the state had no data, either because the state had no Senate election, no vote data were found for the state in question, or the state had not yet entered the Union. No special Senate elections are included in this table.

Sources: *Congressional Quarterly's Guide to U.S. Elections* (1994), ICPSR data sets 0001 and 0075, and independent search of state sources by the author. For some party affiliations, the labels were taken from Michael J. Dubin's election archive after verification by the author.

Table 6-14 Senate Election Results, by State, 1924–1926 (Percentages)

State	1924				1926			
	Democratic	Republican	Other	Democratic % of Two-Party Vote	Democratic	Republican	Other	Democratic % of Two-Party Vote
Alabama	75.2	24.8	0.0	75.2	80.9	19.1	0.0	80.9
Alaska	—	—	—	—	—	—	—	—
Arizona	—	—	—	—	58.3	41.7	0.0	58.3
Arkansas	73.5	26.5	0.0	73.5	82.8	17.2	0.0	82.8
California	—	—	—	—	36.9	63.1	0.0	36.9
Colorado	43.9	50.2	5.9	46.7	46.4	50.2	3.4	48.0
Connecticut	—	—	—	—	35.6	63.3	1.0	36.0
Delaware	0.0	59.4	40.6	0.0	—	—	—	—
Florida	—	—	—	—	77.9	9.4	12.8	89.3
Florida	—	—	—	—	*77.9*	*22.1*	*0.0*	*77.9*
Georgia	100.0	0.0	0.0	100.0	100.0	0.0	0.0	100.0
Hawaii	—	—	—	—	—	—	—	—
Idaho	20.1	79.5	0.4	20.2	25.0	45.4	29.6	35.5
Illinois	35.4	63.5	1.1	35.8	43.1	46.9	10.0	47.9
Illinois	—	—	—	—	*43.3*	*55.6*	*1.1*	*43.8*
Indiana	—	—	—	—	49.0	50.0	1.0	49.5
Iowa	50.0	50.0	0.0	50.0	43.3	56.5	0.2	43.4
Kansas	25.2	70.1	4.7	26.5	34.7	63.6	1.7	35.3
Kentucky	48.4	51.6	0.0	48.4	51.8	48.2	0.0	51.8
Louisiana	100.0	0.0	0.0	100.0	100.0	0.0	0.0	100.0
Maine	39.6	60.4	0.0	39.6	—	—	—	—
Maryland	—	—	—	—	57.6	41.3	1.1	58.3
Massachusetts	48.6	50.3	1.1	49.2	—	—	—	—
Michigan	24.6	74.3	1.1	24.9	—	—	—	—
Minnesota	6.4	46.5	47.1	12.1	—	—	—	—
Mississippi	100.0	0.0	0.0	100.0	—	—	—	—
Missouri	—	—	—	—	51.3	47.7	1.0	51.8
Montana	52.8	42.4	4.8	55.5	—	—	—	—
Nebraska	0.0	62.4	37.6	0.0	—	—	—	—
Nebraska	*37.6*	*62.4*	*0.0*	*37.6*	—	—	—	—
Nevada	—	—	—	—	42.5	55.8	1.7	43.2
New Hampshire	40.2	59.8	0.0	40.2	37.7	62.3	0.0	37.7
New Jersey	33.7	61.8	4.5	35.3	—	—	—	—
New Mexico	49.9	47.4	2.7	51.2	—	—	—	—
New York	—	—	—	—	46.5	42.4	11.1	52.3
New York	—	—	—	—	*46.5*	*50.6*	*3.0*	*47.9*
North Carolina	61.6	38.4	0.0	61.6	60.5	39.5	0.0	60.5
North Dakota	—	—	—	—	8.7	69.6	21.7	11.1
North Dakota	—	—	—	—	*8.7*	*75.9*	*15.4*	*10.3*
Ohio	—	—	—	—	46.6	53.2	0.2	46.7
Oklahoma	35.5	61.7	2.8	36.5	54.8	44.7	0.5	55.1
Oregon	24.7	66.0	9.4	27.2	36.3	39.8	23.9	47.7
Pennsylvania	—	—	—	—	0.0	54.6	45.4	0.0
Pennsylvania	—	—	—	—	*43.1*	*54.6*	*2.2*	*44.1*
Rhode Island	41.8	57.6	0.6	42.0	—	—	—	—
South Carolina	100.0	0.0	0.0	100.0	100.0	0.0	0.0	100.0
South Dakota	34.7	49.1	16.2	41.4	40.5	59.5	0.0	40.5
Tennessee	57.3	42.6	0.1	57.4	—	—	—	—
Texas	85.4	14.6	0.0	85.4	—	—	—	—
Utah	—	—	—	—	37.6	61.5	0.9	37.9
Vermont	—	—	—	—	26.5	0.0	73.5	100.0
Vermont	—	—	—	—	*26.5*	*73.4*	*0.1*	*26.5*
Virginia	73.1	2.7	24.2	96.4	—	—	—	—
Washington	—	—	—	—	47.6	51.3	1.1	48.1
West Virginia	47.7	50.9	1.4	48.4	—	—	—	—
Wisconsin	—	—	—	—	12.2	55.0	32.8	18.1
Wisconsin	—	—	—	—	*12.2*	*75.3*	*12.5*	*13.9*
Wyoming	43.1	53.0	3.9	44.8	—	—	—	—

Notes: Main entries are calculated from the raw vote values in table series 6-33 through 6-54 for the appropriate years based on candidates who used the sole designation "Democrat" or "Republican" (or their historical antecedents listed in Appendix A) on the ballot. Other = candidates who used third-party names on the ballot or were listed as independent, unidentified, or scatter vote. Bold italicized entries in the table are the author's alternative party coding, which is used when a candidate listed a major party name (Democrat, Republican, or their historical antecedents) on the ballot with other party names or labels. These values are computed from the bold italicized raw vote values in table series 6-33 through 6-54 for the appropriate states and years. For a more detailed explanation of this alternative party coding system, see Tables 6-10 and 1-3. —indicates that the state had no data, either because the state had no Senate election, no vote data were found for the state in question, or the state had not yet entered the Union. No special Senate elections are included in this table.

Sources: *Congressional Quarterly's Guide to U.S. Elections* (1994), ICPSR data sets 0001 and 0075, and independent search of state sources by the author. For some party affiliations, the labels were taken from Michael J. Dubin's election archive after verification by the author.

Table 6-15 Senate Election Results, by State, 1928–1930 (Percentages)

State	1928 Democratic	Republican	Other	Democratic % of Two-Party Vote	1930 Democratic	Republican	Other	Democratic % of Two-Party Vote
Alabama	—	—	—	—	59.7	0.0	40.3	100.0
Alaska	—	—	—	—	—	—	—	—
Arizona	54.2	45.8	0.0	54.2	—	—	—	—
Arkansas	—	—	—	—	100.0	0.0	0.0	100.0
California	18.2	74.1	7.7	19.7	—	—	—	—
Colorado	—	—	—	—	55.8	42.7	1.5	56.7
Connecticut	45.6	53.9	0.5	45.8	—	—	—	—
Delaware	39.1	60.9	0.0	39.1	45.4	54.5	0.2	45.4
Florida	68.5	31.5	0.0	68.5	—	—	—	—
Georgia	—	—	—	—	100.0	0.0	0.0	100.0
Hawaii	—	—	—	—	—	—	—	—
Idaho	—	—	—	—	27.6	72.4	0.0	27.6
Illinois	—	—	—	—	64.0	30.7	5.2	67.6
Illinois	—	—	—	—	*64.0*	*35.2*	*0.8*	*64.5*
Indiana	44.1	55.3	0.6	44.4	—	—	—	—
Iowa	—	—	—	—	43.0	56.3	0.7	43.3
Kansas	—	—	—	—	38.9	61.1	0.0	38.9
Kentucky	—	—	—	—	52.1	47.9	0.0	52.1
Louisiana	—	—	—	—	100.0	0.0	0.0	100.0
Maine	30.4	69.6	0.0	30.4	39.1	60.9	0.0	39.1
Maryland	45.2	54.0	0.7	45.6	—	—	—	—
Massachusetts	53.6	45.5	0.9	54.1	54.0	44.7	1.3	54.7
Michigan	27.6	71.8	0.6	27.8	20.9	78.1	0.9	21.1
Minnesota	0.0	33.7	66.3	0.0	36.1	37.6	26.3	49.0
Mississippi	100.0	0.0	0.0	100.0	100.0	0.0	0.0	100.0
Missouri	47.9	51.9	0.2	48.0	—	—	—	—
Montana	53.2	46.8	0.0	53.2	60.3	37.9	1.8	61.4
Nebraska	38.7	61.3	0.0	38.7	39.7	56.8	3.4	41.2
Nevada	59.3	40.7	0.0	59.3	—	—	—	—
New Hampshire	—	—	—	—	41.9	57.9	0.2	42.0
New Jersey	41.8	57.9	0.3	42.0	39.0	58.5	2.5	40.0
New Mexico	42.3	57.7	0.0	42.3	58.6	41.2	0.2	58.7
New York	49.1	47.9	3.0	50.6	—	—	—	—
North Carolina	—	—	—	—	60.6	39.4	0.0	60.6
North Dakota	19.3	79.6	1.0	19.5	—	—	—	—
Ohio	39.1	60.7	0.2	39.1	—	—	—	—
Oklahoma	—	—	—	—	52.3	47.5	0.2	52.4
Oregon	—	—	—	—	27.9	58.1	14.0	32.5
Pennsylvania	34.0	64.4	1.6	34.6	—	—	—	—
Rhode Island	49.3	50.6	0.1	49.4	49.2	50.3	0.5	49.4
South Carolina	—	—	—	—	100.0	0.0	0.0	100.0
South Dakota	—	—	—	—	51.6	48.4	0.0	51.6
Tennessee	59.3	40.7	0.0	59.3	71.3	27.1	1.6	72.5
Texas	81.2	18.7	0.1	81.3	86.9	12.7	0.4	87.2
Utah	55.5	43.9	0.6	55.8	—	—	—	—
Vermont	28.4	71.6	0.0	28.4	—	—	—	—
Virginia	99.8	0.0	0.2	100.0	76.7	0.0	23.3	100.0
Washington	53.4	46.4	0.1	53.5	—	—	—	—
West Virginia	49.2	50.7	0.1	49.3	61.9	37.9	0.2	62.1
Wisconsin	0.0	85.6	14.4	0.0	—	—	—	—
Wisconsin	*0.0*	*96.5*	*3.5*	*0.0*	—	—	—	—
Wyoming	53.5	46.1	0.4	53.7	41.0	59.0	0.0	41.0

Notes: Main entries are calculated from the raw vote values in table series 6-33 through 6-54 for the appropriate years based on candidates who used the sole designation "Democrat" or "Republican" (or their historical antecedents listed in Appendix A) on the ballot. Other = candidates who used third-party names on the ballot or were listed as independent, unidentified, or scatter vote. Bold italicized entries in the table are the author's alternative party coding, which is used when a candidate listed a major party name (Democrat, Republican, or their historical antecedents) on the ballot with other party names or labels. These values are computed from the bold italicized raw vote values in table series 6-33 through 6-54 for the appropriate states and years. For a more detailed explanation of this alternative party coding system, see Tables 6-10 and 1-3. —indicates that the state had no data, either because the state had no Senate election, no vote data were found for the state in question, or the state had not yet entered the Union. No special Senate elections are included in this table.

Sources: *Congressional Quarterly's Guide to U.S. Elections* (1994), ICPSR data sets 0001 and 0075, and independent search of state sources by the author. For some party affiliations, the labels were taken from Michael J. Dubin's election archive after verification by the author.

Table 6-16 Senate Election Results, by State, 1932–1934 (Percentages)

State	1932 Democratic	Republican	Other	Democratic % of Two-Party Vote	1934 Democratic	Republican	Other	Democratic % of Two-Party Vote
Alabama	86.2	13.8	0.0	86.2	—	—	—	—
Alaska	—	—	—	—	—	—	—	—
Arizona	66.7	32.1	1.3	67.5	72.0	25.6	2.3	73.8
Arkansas	89.5	10.5	0.0	89.5	—	—	—	—
California	43.4	30.8	25.8	58.5	0.0	0.0	100.0	—
California	—	—	—	—	*0.0*	*94.5*	*5.5*	*0.0*
Colorado	51.9	45.5	2.6	53.3	—	—	—	—
Connecticut	47.5	46.8	5.7	50.4	48.4	45.1	6.4	51.7
Connecticut	*47.5*	*48.6*	*3.9*	*49.4*	—	—	—	—
Delaware	—	—	—	—	46.2	53.3	0.6	46.4
Florida	99.8	0.0	0.2	100.0	100.0	0.0	0.0	100.0
Georgia	92.8	7.2	0.0	92.8	—	—	—	—
Hawaii	—	—	—	—	—	—	—	—
Idaho	55.7	42.3	2.1	56.8	—	—	—	—
Illinois	52.2	46.0	1.7	53.2	—	—	—	—
Indiana	55.6	42.3	2.2	56.8	51.5	47.5	1.1	52.0
Iowa	54.2	40.2	5.6	57.4	—	—	—	—
Kansas	45.7	42.0	12.3	52.1	—	—	—	—
Kentucky	59.1	40.5	0.3	59.3	—	—	—	—
Louisiana	100.0	0.0	0.0	100.0	—	—	—	—
Maine	—	—	—	—	49.7	50.1	0.2	49.8
Maryland	66.2	31.2	2.6	68.0	56.1	42.0	2.0	57.2
Massachusetts	—	—	—	—	59.4	37.4	3.2	61.4
Michigan	—	—	—	—	47.0	51.3	1.7	47.8
Minnesota	—	—	—	—	29.2	19.8	51.0	59.6
Mississippi	—	—	—	—	100.0	0.0	0.0	100.0
Missouri	63.2	35.9	1.0	63.8	59.5	39.7	0.7	60.0
Montana	—	—	—	—	70.1	29.4	0.4	70.5
Nebraska	—	—	—	—	55.3	42.9	1.8	56.3
Nevada	52.1	47.9	0.0	52.1	64.5	33.4	2.1	65.9
New Hampshire	50.3	49.3	0.4	50.5	—	—	—	—
New Jersey	—	—	—	—	57.9	40.8	1.2	58.6
New Mexico	—	—	—	—	49.4	50.2	0.5	49.6
New York	55.8	38.6	5.7	59.1	55.3	36.9	7.8	60.0
North Carolina	68.3	31.7	0.0	68.3	—	—	—	—
North Dakota	27.4	72.3	0.2	27.5	40.2	58.2	1.5	40.9
Ohio	52.5	45.8	1.7	53.4	59.9	39.4	0.6	60.3
Oklahoma	65.6	33.7	0.7	66.1	—	—	—	—
Oregon	38.9	52.7	8.4	42.4	—	—	—	—
Pennsylvania	43.2	49.3	7.5	46.7	50.8	46.5	2.8	52.2
Rhode Island	—	—	—	—	57.1	42.9	0.0	57.1
South Carolina	98.1	1.9	0.0	98.1	—	—	—	—
South Dakota	44.6	53.8	1.6	45.3	—	—	—	—
Tennessee	—	—	—	—	63.4	35.8	0.8	63.9
Texas	—	—	—	—	96.7	2.8	0.5	97.1
Utah	56.7	41.7	1.6	57.6	53.1	45.4	1.5	53.9
Vermont	44.9	55.1	0.0	44.9	48.4	51.0	0.6	48.7
Virginia	—	—	—	—	76.0	20.9	3.1	78.4
Washington	60.6	32.7	6.7	65.0	60.9	34.0	5.1	64.2
West Virginia	—	—	—	—	55.1	44.4	0.5	55.4
Wisconsin	57.0	36.2	6.8	61.2	24.2	22.8	52.9	51.5
Wyoming	—	—	—	—	56.6	43.0	0.4	56.9

Notes: Main entries are calculated from the raw vote values in table series 6-33 through 6-54 for the appropriate years based on candidates who used the sole designation "Democrat" or "Republican" (or their historical antecedents listed in Appendix A) on the ballot. Other = candidates who used third-party names on the ballot or were listed as independent, unidentified, or scatter vote. Bold italicized entries in the table are the author's alternative party coding, which is used when a candidate listed a major party name (Democrat, Republican, or their historical antecedents) on the ballot with other party names or labels. These values are computed from the bold italicized raw vote values in table series 6-33 through 6-54 for the appropriate states and years. For a more detailed explanation of this alternative party coding system, see Tables 6-10 and 1-3. —indicates that the state had no data, either because the state had no Senate election, no vote data were found for the state in question, or the state had not yet entered the Union. No special Senate elections are included in this table.

Sources: *Congressional Quarterly's Guide to U.S. Elections* (1994), ICPSR data sets 0001 and 0075, and independent search of state sources by the author. For some party affiliations, the labels were taken from Michael J. Dubin's election archive after verification by the author.

Table 6-17 Senate Election Results, by State, 1936–1938 (Percentages)

State	1936 Democratic	Republican	Other	Democratic % of Two-Party Vote	1938 Democratic	Republican	Other	Democratic % of Two-Party Vote
Alabama	87.0	12.2	0.7	87.7	86.4	13.6	0.0	86.4
Alaska	—	—	—	—	—	—	—	—
Arizona	—	—	—	—	76.5	23.5	0.0	76.5
Arkansas	81.8	16.4	1.8	83.3	89.6	10.4	0.0	89.6
California	—	—	—	—	0.0	44.7	55.3	0.0
California	—	—	—	—	**54.4**	**44.7**	**0.9**	**54.9**
Colorado	63.5	35.2	1.3	64.3	58.2	40.2	1.6	59.2
Connecticut	—	—	—	—	0.0	42.9	57.1	0.0
Connecticut	—	—	—	—	**40.0**	**42.9**	**17.1**	**48.3**
Delaware	53.0	41.4	5.6	56.1	—	—	—	—
Florida	—	—	—	—	82.4	17.6	0.0	82.4
Georgia	100.0	0.0	0.0	100.0	95.1	0.0	4.9	100.0
Hawaii	—	—	—	—	—	—	—	—
Idaho	36.6	63.4	0.0	36.6	54.7	44.9	0.5	54.9
Illinois	56.5	40.7	2.8	58.1	51.3	48.3	0.3	51.5
Indiana	—	—	—	—	49.8	49.5	0.6	50.2
Iowa	50.3	47.0	2.7	51.7	49.7	49.4	0.8	50.2
Kansas	48.4	51.0	0.6	48.7	43.8	56.2	0.0	43.8
Kentucky	58.8	39.8	1.4	59.6	62.0	38.0	0.0	62.0
Louisiana	100.0	0.0	0.0	100.0	99.8	0.0	0.2	100.0
Maine	49.3	50.7	0.0	49.3	—	—	—	—
Maryland	—	—	—	—	68.3	29.3	2.4	70.0
Massachusetts	41.0	48.5	10.4	45.8	—	—	—	—
Michigan	53.3	41.8	4.9	56.0	—	—	—	—
Minnesota	0.0	37.8	62.2	0.0	—	—	—	—
Mississippi	100.0	0.0	0.0	100.0	—	—	—	—
Missouri	—	—	—	—	60.7	39.1	0.2	60.8
Montana	55.0	27.1	17.9	67.0	—	—	—	—
Nebraska	18.4	37.8	43.8	32.7	—	—	—	—
Nevada	—	—	—	—	59.0	41.0	0.0	59.0
New Hampshire	47.7	51.9	0.5	47.9	45.8	54.2	0.0	45.8
New Jersey	54.9	44.3	0.8	55.3	—	—	—	—
New Mexico	61.7	38.3	0.0	61.7	—	—	—	—
New York	—	—	—	—	0.0	0.0	100.0	—
New York	—	—	—	—	**54.5**	**44.9**	**0.6**	**54.8**
North Carolina	70.8	29.2	0.0	70.8	63.8	36.2	0.0	63.8
North Dakota	—	—	—	—	7.3	50.1	42.6	12.7
Ohio	—	—	—	—	46.4	53.6	0.0	46.4
Oklahoma	68.0	31.5	0.5	68.3	65.4	33.9	0.7	65.8
Oregon	48.3	49.7	2.0	49.3	45.1	54.9	0.0	45.1
Pennsylvania	—	—	—	—	0.0	54.7	45.3	0.0
Pennsylvania	—	—	—	—	**44.4**	**54.7**	**0.9**	**44.8**
Rhode Island	48.6	44.4	7.0	52.3	—	—	—	—
South Carolina	98.6	1.4	0.0	98.6	98.9	1.1	0.0	98.9
South Dakota	48.8	46.7	4.4	51.1	47.5	52.5	0.0	47.5
Tennessee	76.4	18.8	4.8	80.3	—	—	—	—
Texas	92.6	7.1	0.3	92.9	—	—	—	—
Utah	—	—	—	—	55.8	44.2	0.0	55.8
Vermont	—	—	—	—	34.3	65.7	0.0	34.3
Virginia	91.7	4.7	3.6	95.1	—	—	—	—
Virginia	**91.9**	**4.7**	**3.5**	**95.2**	—	—	—	—
Washington	—	—	—	—	62.6	37.1	0.3	62.8
West Virginia	58.9	40.8	0.2	59.1	—	—	—	—
Wisconsin	—	—	—	—	24.7	47.7	27.6	34.2
Wisconsin	—	—	—	—	**24.7**	**48.4**	**26.8**	**33.8**
Wyoming	53.8	45.4	0.8	54.2	—	—	—	—

Notes: Main entries are calculated from the raw vote values in table series 6-33 through 6-54 for the appropriate years based on candidates who used the sole designation "Democrat" or "Republican" (or their historical antecedents listed in Appendix A) on the ballot. Other = candidates who used third-party names on the ballot or were listed as independent, unidentified, or scatter vote. Bold italicized entries in the table are the author's alternative party coding, which is used when a candidate listed a major party name (Democrat, Republican, or their historical antecedents) on the ballot with other party names or labels. These values are computed from the bold italicized raw vote values in table series 6-33 through 6-54 for the appropriate states and years. For a more detailed explanation of this alternative party coding system, see Tables 6-10 and 1-3. —indicates that the state had no data, either because the state had no Senate election, no vote data were found for the state in question, or the state had not yet entered the Union. No special Senate elections are included in this table.

Sources: *Congressional Quarterly's Guide to U.S. Elections* (1994), ICPSR data sets 0001 and 0075, and independent search of state sources by the author. For some party affiliations, the labels were taken from Michael J. Dubin's election archive after verification by the author.

Table 6-18 Senate Election Results, by State, 1940–1942 (Percentages)

State	1940				1942			
	Democratic	Republican	Other	Democratic % of Two-Party Vote	Democratic	Republican	Other	Democratic % of Two-Party Vote
Alabama	—	—	—	—	100.0	0.0	0.0	100.0
Alaska	—	—	—	—	—	—	—	—
Arizona	71.6	28.0	0.4	71.9	—	—	—	—
Arkansas	—	—	—	—	100.0	0.0	0.0	100.0
California	0.0	0.0	100.0	—	—	—	—	—
California	*0.0*	*82.5*	*17.5*	*0.0*	—	—	—	—
Colorado	—	—	—	—	50.2	49.2	0.6	50.5
Connecticut	53.2	0.0	46.8	100.0	—	—	—	—
Connecticut	*53.2*	*45.7*	*1.1*	*53.8*	—	—	—	—
Delaware	50.6	47.3	2.1	51.7	44.9	54.2	0.9	45.3
Delaware	*52.7*	*47.3*	*0.0*	*52.7*	—	—	—	—
Florida	100.0	0.0	0.0	100.0	—	—	—	—
Georgia	—	—	—	—	96.9	0.0	3.1	100.0
Hawaii	—	—	—	—	—	—	—	—
Idaho	—	—	—	—	48.5	51.5	0.0	48.5
Illinois	—	—	—	—	46.4	53.2	0.3	46.6
Indiana	49.1	50.5	0.4	49.3	—	—	—	—
Iowa	—	—	—	—	41.7	58.0	0.3	41.8
Kansas	—	—	—	—	40.3	57.1	2.6	41.4
Kentucky	—	—	—	—	55.3	44.7	0.0	55.3
Louisiana	—	—	—	—	100.0	0.0	0.0	100.0
Maine	41.3	58.6	0.1	41.3	33.3	66.7	0.0	33.3
Maryland	64.7	33.5	1.8	65.9	—	—	—	—
Massachusetts	55.6	42.8	1.5	56.5	46.6	52.4	1.0	47.1
Michigan	47.0	52.6	0.4	47.2	47.2	49.6	3.3	48.8
Michigan	—	—	—	—	*47.2*	*52.3*	*0.6*	*47.5*
Minnesota	20.6	53.0	26.4	27.9	10.4	47.0	42.6	18.1
Mississippi	100.0	0.0	0.0	100.0	100.0	0.0	0.0	100.0
Missouri	51.2	48.7	0.1	51.2	—	—	—	—
Montana	73.4	26.6	0.0	73.4	49.1	48.4	2.6	50.4
Nebraska	41.5	57.0	1.5	42.1	22.0	49.0	29.0	31.0
Nevada	60.5	39.5	0.0	60.5	—	—	—	—
New Hampshire	—	—	—	—	45.4	54.6	0.0	45.4
New Jersey	44.1	55.1	0.8	44.5	45.8	53.1	1.1	46.3
New Mexico	55.9	44.1	0.0	55.9	59.2	40.8	0.0	59.2
New York	0.0	46.7	53.3	0.0	—	—	—	—
New York	*53.3*	*46.7*	*0.1*	*53.3*	—	—	—	—
North Carolina	—	—	—	—	65.9	34.1	0.0	65.9
North Dakota	26.4	38.1	35.4	41.0	—	—	—	—
Ohio	47.6	52.4	0.0	47.6	—	—	—	—
Oklahoma	—	—	—	—	44.8	54.8	0.4	44.9
Oregon	—	—	—	—	22.9	77.1	0.0	22.9
Pennsylvania	51.8	47.4	0.8	52.2	—	—	—	—
Rhode Island	55.2	44.8	0.0	55.2	58.0	42.0	0.0	58.0
South Carolina	—	—	—	—	100.0	0.0	0.0	100.0
South Dakota	—	—	—	—	41.3	58.7	0.0	41.3
Tennessee	70.8	29.2	0.0	70.8	68.9	21.5	9.6	76.2
Texas	94.3	5.7	0.0	94.3	94.9	4.4	0.7	95.6
Utah	62.8	37.2	0.0	62.8	—	—	—	—
Vermont	33.6	66.4	0.0	33.6	—	—	—	—
Virginia	93.3	0.0	6.7	100.0	91.1	0.0	8.9	100.0
Washington	54.2	45.8	0.0	54.2	—	—	—	—
West Virginia	56.3	43.7	0.0	56.3	44.6	55.4	0.0	44.6
Wisconsin	13.2	41.4	45.4	24.2	—	—	—	—
Wyoming	58.7	41.3	0.0	58.7	45.4	54.6	0.0	45.4

Notes: Main entries are calculated from the raw vote values in table series 6-33 through 6-54 for the appropriate years based on candidates who used the sole designation "Democrat" or "Republican" (or their historical antecedents listed in Appendix A) on the ballot. Other = candidates who used third-party names on the ballot or were listed as independent, unidentified, or scatter vote. Bold italicized entries in the table are the author's alternative party coding, which is used when a candidate listed a major party name (Democrat, Republican, or their historical antecedents) on the ballot with other party names or labels. These values are computed from the bold italicized raw vote values in table series 6-33 through 6-54 for the appropriate states and years. For a more detailed explanation of this alternative party coding system, see Tables 6-10 and 1-3. —indicates that the state had no data, either because the state had no Senate election, no vote data were found for the state in question, or the state had not yet entered the Union. No special Senate elections are included in this table.

Sources: *Congressional Quarterly's Guide to U.S. Elections* (1994), ICPSR data sets 0001 and 0075, and independent search of state sources by the author. For some party affiliations, the labels were taken from Michael J. Dubin's election archive after verification by the author.

Table 6-19 Senate Election Results, by State, 1944–1946 (Percentages)

State	1944 Democratic	1944 Republican	1944 Other	1944 Democratic % of Two-Party Vote	1946 Democratic	1946 Republican	1946 Other	1946 Democratic % of Two-Party Vote
Alabama	81.8	16.9	1.3	82.8	—	—	—	—
Alaska	—	—	—	—	—	—	—	—
Arizona	69.4	30.6	0.0	69.4	69.2	30.1	0.7	69.7
Arkansas	85.1	14.9	0.0	85.1	—	—	—	—
California	52.3	47.7	0.0	52.3	44.2	54.1	1.7	45.0
Colorado	43.3	56.1	0.6	43.6	—	—	—	—
Connecticut	52.0	47.3	0.7	52.4	40.5	55.8	3.7	42.0
Delaware	—	—	—	—	44.8	55.2	0.0	44.8
Florida	71.3	28.7	0.0	71.3	78.6	21.4	0.0	78.6
Georgia	100.0	0.0	0.0	100.0	—	—	—	—
Hawaii	—	—	—	—	—	—	—	—
Idaho	51.1	48.9	0.0	51.1	—	—	—	—
Illinois	52.6	47.1	0.3	52.8	—	—	—	—
Indiana	48.9	50.2	0.9	49.3	43.4	54.9	1.7	44.1
Iowa	48.4	51.3	0.3	48.5	—	—	—	—
Kansas	40.7	57.8	1.5	41.3	—	—	—	—
Kentucky	54.8	44.9	0.3	55.0	—	—	—	—
Louisiana	100.0	0.0	0.0	100.0	—	—	—	—
Maine	—	—	—	—	36.5	63.5	0.0	36.5
Maryland	61.7	38.3	0.0	61.7	50.2	49.8	0.0	50.2
Massachusetts	—	—	—	—	39.7	59.5	0.7	40.0
Michigan	—	—	—	—	32.0	67.1	0.9	32.3
Minnesota	—	—	—	—	39.8	58.9	1.3	40.3
Mississippi	—	—	—	—	100.0	0.0	0.0	100.0
Missouri	49.9	50.0	0.1	49.9	47.1	52.7	0.2	47.2
Montana	—	—	—	—	45.4	53.5	1.1	45.9
Nebraska	—	—	—	—	29.2	70.8	0.0	29.2
Nevada	58.4	41.6	0.0	58.4	44.8	55.2	0.0	44.8
New Hampshire	49.1	50.9	0.0	49.1	—	—	—	—
New Jersey	—	—	—	—	40.1	58.5	1.4	40.7
New Mexico	—	—	—	—	51.5	48.5	0.0	51.5
New York	0.0	46.7	53.3	0.0	0.0	52.6	47.4	0.0
New York	*53.1*	*46.7*	*0.2*	*53.2*	*47.4*	*52.6*	*0.0*	*47.4*
North Carolina	70.3	29.7	0.0	70.3	—	—	—	—
North Dakota	45.2	33.0	21.8	57.8	23.2	53.3	23.5	30.3
North Dakota	*45.2*	*54.2*	*0.6*	*45.5*	—	—	—	—
Ohio	49.7	50.3	0.0	49.7	42.4	57.0	0.6	42.6
Oklahoma	55.6	44.0	0.3	55.8	—	—	—	—
Oregon	39.3	60.7	0.0	39.3	—	—	—	—
Pennsylvania	50.0	49.3	0.7	50.3	39.8	59.3	0.9	40.2
Rhode Island	—	—	—	—	55.1	44.9	0.0	55.1
South Carolina	92.9	3.2	3.9	96.7	—	—	—	—
South Carolina	*96.7*	*3.2*	*0.2*	*96.8*	—	—	—	—
South Dakota	36.1	63.9	0.0	36.1	—	—	—	—
Tennessee	—	—	—	—	66.6	26.2	7.2	71.8
Texas	—	—	—	—	88.5	11.5	0.0	88.5
Utah	59.9	40.1	0.0	59.9	48.8	51.2	0.0	48.8
Vermont	34.2	65.8	0.0	34.2	25.4	74.6	0.0	25.4
Virginia	—	—	—	—	64.8	30.5	4.7	68.0
Washington	55.1	44.4	0.4	55.4	45.2	54.3	0.4	45.4
West Virginia	—	—	—	—	50.3	49.7	0.0	50.3
Wisconsin	42.8	50.5	6.7	45.8	37.4	61.3	1.3	37.9
Wyoming	—	—	—	—	56.2	43.8	0.0	56.2

Notes: Main entries are calculated from the raw vote values in table series 6-33 through 6-54 for the appropriate years based on candidates who used the sole designation "Democrat" or "Republican" (or their historical antecedents listed in Appendix A) on the ballot. Other = candidates who used third-party names on the ballot or were listed as independent, unidentified, or scatter vote. Bold italicized entries in the table are the author's alternative party coding, which is used when a candidate listed a major party name (Democrat, Republican, or their historical antecedents) on the ballot with other party names or labels. These values are computed from the bold italicized raw vote values in table series 6-33 through 6-54 for the appropriate states and years. For a more detailed explanation of this alternative party coding system, see Tables 6-10 and 1-3. —indicates that the state had no data, either because the state had no Senate election, no vote data were found for the state in question, or the state had not yet entered the Union. No special Senate elections are included in this table.

Sources: *Congressional Quarterly's Guide to U.S. Elections* (1994), ICPSR data sets 0001 and 0075, and independent search of state sources by the author. For some party affiliations, the labels were taken from Michael J. Dubin's election archive after verification by the author.

Table 6-20 Senate Election Results, by State, 1948–1950 (Percentages)

State	1948				1950			
	Democratic	Republican	Other	Democratic % of Two-Party Vote	Democratic	Republican	Other	Democratic % of Two-Party Vote
Alabama	84.0	16.0	0.0	84.0	76.5	0.0	23.5	100.0
Alaska	—	—	—	—	—	—	—	—
Arizona	—	—	—	—	62.8	37.2	0.0	62.8
Arkansas	93.3	0.0	6.7	100.0	100.0	0.0	0.0	100.0
California	—	—	—	—	40.8	59.2	0.0	40.8
Colorado	66.8	32.4	0.8	67.4	46.7	53.3	0.0	46.7
Connecticut	—	—	—	—	51.7	46.6	1.7	52.6
Delaware	50.9	48.3	0.9	51.3	—	—	—	—
Florida	—	—	—	—	76.2	23.7	0.1	76.3
Georgia	99.9	0.0	0.1	100.0	100.0	0.0	0.0	100.0
Hawaii	—	—	—	—	—	—	—	—
Idaho	50.0	48.5	1.6	50.7	38.3	61.7	0.0	38.3
Illinois	55.1	44.6	0.3	55.2	45.8	53.9	0.4	45.9
Indiana	—	—	—	—	46.4	52.8	0.8	46.7
Iowa	57.8	41.6	0.6	58.2	44.7	54.8	0.5	44.9
Iowa	—	—	—	—	*44.8*	*54.8*	*0.4*	*45.0*
Kansas	42.7	54.9	2.4	43.7	43.8	54.3	1.9	44.7
Kentucky	51.4	48.3	0.3	51.5	54.2	45.1	0.7	54.6
Louisiana	100.0	0.0	0.0	100.0	87.7	12.3	0.0	87.7
Maine	28.7	71.3	0.0	28.7	—	—	—	—
Maryland	—	—	—	—	46.0	53.0	1.0	46.5
Massachusetts	46.4	52.9	0.6	46.7	—	—	—	—
Michigan	48.5	50.7	0.8	48.9	—	—	—	—
Minnesota	59.8	39.8	0.4	60.0	—	—	—	—
Mississippi	100.0	0.0	0.0	100.0	—	—	—	—
Missouri	—	—	—	—	53.6	46.4	0.1	53.6
Montana	56.6	42.7	0.6	57.0	—	—	—	—
Nebraska	43.3	56.7	0.0	43.3	—	—	—	—
Nevada	—	—	—	—	58.0	42.0	0.0	58.0
New Hampshire	41.2	58.1	0.7	41.5	38.0	55.7	6.3	40.6
New Jersey	47.3	50.0	2.7	48.6	—	—	—	—
New Mexico	57.2	42.4	0.4	57.4	—	—	—	—
New York	—	—	—	—	0.0	45.3	54.7	0.0
New York	—	—	—	—	*50.3*	*45.3*	*4.4*	*52.6*
North Carolina	70.7	28.8	0.5	71.1	68.7	31.3	0.0	68.7
North Dakota	—	—	—	—	32.4	67.6	0.0	32.4
Ohio	—	—	—	—	42.5	57.5	0.0	42.5
Oklahoma	62.3	37.4	0.3	62.5	54.8	45.2	0.0	54.8
Oregon	40.0	60.0	0.0	40.0	23.2	74.8	2.0	23.7
Pennsylvania	—	—	—	—	47.7	51.3	1.0	48.2
Rhode Island	59.3	40.7	0.0	59.3	—	—	—	—
South Carolina	96.4	3.6	0.0	96.4	99.9	0.0	0.1	100.0
South Dakota	40.7	59.3	0.0	40.7	36.1	63.9	0.0	36.1
Tennessee	65.3	33.4	1.2	66.1	—	—	—	—
Texas	66.2	32.9	0.8	66.8	45.8	53.9	0.3	46.0
Utah	—	—	—	—	—	—	—	—
Vermont	—	—	—	—	22.0	78.0	0.0	22.0
Virginia	65.6	30.8	3.6	68.0	—	—	—	—
Washington	—	—	—	—	53.4	46.0	0.6	53.7
West Virginia	57.0	43.0	0.0	57.0	—	—	—	—
Wisconsin	—	—	—	—	46.2	53.3	0.5	46.4
Wyoming	57.1	42.9	0.0	57.1	—	—	—	—

Notes: Main entries are calculated from the raw vote values in table series 6-33 through 6-54 for the appropriate years based on candidates who used the sole designation "Democrat" or "Republican" (or their historical antecedents listed in Appendix A) on the ballot. Other = candidates who used third-party names on the ballot or were listed as independent, unidentified, or scatter vote. Bold italicized entries in the table are the author's alternative party coding, which is used when a candidate listed a major party name (Democrat, Republican, or their historical antecedents) on the ballot with other party names or labels. These values are computed from the bold italicized raw vote values in table series 6-33 through 6-54 for the appropriate states and years. For a more detailed explanation of this alternative party coding system, see Tables 6-10 and 1-3. —indicates that the state had no data, either because the state had no Senate election, no vote data were found for the state in question, or the state had not yet entered the Union. No special Senate elections are included in this table.

Sources: *Congressional Quarterly's Guide to U.S. Elections* (1994), *America Votes* (various publication dates), ICPSR data sets 0001 and 0075, and independent search of state sources by the author. For some party affiliations, the labels were taken from Michael J. Dubin's election archive after verification by the author.

Table 6-21 Senate Election Results, by State, 1952–1954 (Percentages)

| | 1952 | | | | 1954 | | | |
State	Democratic	Republican	Other	Democratic % of Two-Party Vote	Democratic	Republican	Other	Democratic % of Two-Party Vote
Alabama	—	—	—	—	82.5	17.5	0.0	82.5
Alaska	—	—	—	—	—	—	—	—
Arizona	48.7	51.3	0.0	48.7	—	—	—	—
Arkansas	—	—	—	—	100.0	0.0	0.0	100.0
California	0.0	0.0	100.0	—	—	—	—	—
California	*0.0*	*87.7*	*12.3*	*0.0*	—	—	—	—
Colorado	—	—	—	—	48.7	51.3	0.0	48.7
Connecticut	44.4	52.5	3.2	45.8	—	—	—	—
Connecticut	*44.4*	*54.5*	*1.1*	*44.9*	—	—	—	—
Delaware	45.5	54.5	0.0	45.5	56.9	43.1	0.0	56.9
Florida	99.8	0.0	0.2	100.0	—	—	—	—
Georgia	—	—	—	—	100.0	0.0	0.0	100.0
Hawaii	—	—	—	—	—	—	—	—
Idaho	—	—	—	—	37.2	62.8	0.0	37.2
Illinois	—	—	—	—	53.6	46.4	0.0	53.6
Indiana	46.8	52.4	0.7	47.2	—	—	—	—
Iowa	—	—	—	—	47.5	52.2	0.3	47.7
Kansas	—	—	—	—	41.8	56.3	1.8	42.6
Kentucky	—	—	—	—	54.5	45.5	0.0	54.5
Louisiana	—	—	—	—	100.0	0.0	0.0	100.0
Maine	34.9	58.7	6.4	37.3	41.4	58.6	0.0	41.4
Maine	*41.3*	*58.7*	*0.0*	*41.3*	—	—	—	—
Maryland	47.5	52.5	0.0	47.5	—	—	—	—
Massachusetts	51.3	48.3	0.3	51.5	49.0	50.5	0.4	49.2
Michigan	49.0	50.6	0.3	49.2	50.8	48.9	0.3	50.9
Minnesota	42.5	56.6	0.8	42.9	56.4	42.1	1.5	57.2
Mississippi	100.0	0.0	0.0	100.0	95.6	4.4	0.0	95.6
Missouri	54.0	45.9	0.1	54.0	—	—	—	—
Montana	50.7	48.6	0.7	51.1	50.4	49.6	0.0	50.4
Nebraska	27.8	69.1	3.1	28.7	38.9	61.1	0.0	38.9
Nevada	48.3	51.7	0.0	48.3	—	—	—	—
New Hampshire	—	—	—	—	39.8	60.2	0.0	39.8
New Jersey	43.6	55.5	0.9	44.0	48.5	48.7	2.9	49.9
New Mexico	51.1	48.9	0.0	51.1	57.3	42.7	0.0	57.3
New York	43.1	55.2	1.6	43.9	—	—	—	—
North Carolina	—	—	—	—	65.9	34.1	0.0	65.9
North Dakota	23.3	66.3	10.4	26.0	—	—	—	—
Ohio	45.4	54.6	0.0	45.4	—	—	—	—
Oklahoma	—	—	—	—	55.8	43.7	0.5	56.1
Oregon	—	—	—	—	50.2	49.8	0.0	50.2
Pennsylvania	48.0	51.6	0.4	48.2	—	—	—	—
Rhode Island	54.8	45.2	0.0	54.8	59.3	40.7	0.0	59.3
South Carolina	—	—	—	—	36.8	0.0	63.2	100.0
South Dakota	—	—	—	—	42.7	57.3	0.0	42.7
Tennessee	74.2	20.9	4.9	78.0	70.0	30.0	0.0	70.0
Texas	0.0	0.0	100.0	—	84.7	14.8	0.5	85.1
Texas	*100.0*	*0.0*	*0.0*	*100.0*	—	—	—	—
Utah	45.7	54.3	0.0	45.7	—	—	—	—
Vermont	27.7	72.3	0.0	27.7	—	—	—	—
Virginia	73.4	0.0	26.6	100.0	79.9	0.0	20.1	100.0
Virginia	*86.1*	*0.0*	*13.9*	*100.0*	*90.5*	*0.0*	*9.5*	*100.0*
Washington	56.2	43.5	0.2	56.4	—	—	—	—
West Virginia	53.6	46.4	0.0	53.6	54.8	45.2	0.0	54.8
Wisconsin	45.6	54.2	0.2	45.7	—	—	—	—
Wyoming	48.4	51.6	0.0	48.4	51.5	48.5	0.0	51.5

Notes: Main entries are calculated from the raw vote values in table series 6-33 through 6-54 for the appropriate years based on candidates who used the sole designation "Democrat" or "Republican" (or their historical antecedents listed in Appendix A) on the ballot. Other = candidates who used third-party names on the ballot or were listed as independent, unidentified, or scatter vote. Bold italicized entries in the table are the author's alternative party coding, which is used when a candidate listed a major party name (Democrat, Republican, or their historical antecedents) on the ballot with other party names or labels. These values are computed from the bold italicized raw vote values in table series 6-33 through 6-54 for the appropriate states and years. For a more detailed explanation of this alternative party coding system, see Tables 6-10 and 1-3. —indicates that the state had no data, either because the state had no Senate election, no vote data were found for the state in question, or the state had not yet entered the Union. No special Senate elections are included in this table.

Sources: *Congressional Quarterly's Guide to U.S. Elections* (1994), *America Votes* (various publication dates), ICPSR data sets 0001 and 0075, and independent search of state sources by the author. For some party affiliations, the labels were taken from Michael J. Dubin's election archive after verification by the author.

Table 6-22 Senate Election Results, by State, 1956–1959 (Percentages)

State	1956				1958–1959			
	Democratic	Republican	Other	Democratic % of Two-Party Vote	Democratic	Republican	Other	Democratic % of Two-Party Vote
Alabama	100.0	0.0	0.0	100.0	—	—	—	—
Alaska	—	—	—	—	52.6	47.4	0.0	52.6
Arizona	61.4	38.6	0.0	61.4	43.9	56.1	0.0	43.9
Arkansas	83.0	17.0	0.0	83.0	—	—	—	—
California	45.6	54.0	0.4	45.8	57.0	42.9	0.1	57.0
Colorado	50.2	49.8	0.0	50.2	—	—	—	—
Connecticut	43.0	54.8	2.1	44.0	57.3	42.4	0.3	57.5
Connecticut	***43.0***	***55.8***	***1.2***	***43.6***	—	—	—	—
Delaware	—	—	—	—	46.7	53.3	0.0	46.7
Florida	100.0	0.0	0.0	100.0	71.2	28.8	0.0	71.2
Georgia	100.0	0.0	0.0	100.0	—	—	—	—
Hawaii[1]	—	—	—	—	47.1[1]	52.9[1]	0.0[1]	47.1[1]
Idaho	56.2	38.7	5.1	59.2	—	—	—	—
Illinois	45.7	54.1	0.2	45.8	—	—	—	—
Indiana	44.4	55.2	0.4	44.6	56.5	42.4	1.1	57.1
Iowa	46.1	53.9	0.0	46.1	—	—	—	—
Kansas	40.5	57.9	1.6	41.1	—	—	—	—
Kentucky	49.7	50.3	0.0	49.7	—	—	—	—
Louisiana	100.0	0.0	0.0	100.0	—	—	—	—
Maine	—	—	—	—	60.8	39.2	0.0	60.8
Maryland	47.0	53.0	0.0	47.0	49.0	51.0	0.0	49.0
Massachusetts	—	—	—	—	73.2	26.2	0.6	73.6
Michigan	—	—	—	—	53.6	46.1	0.3	53.8
Minnesota	—	—	—	—	52.9	46.6	0.5	53.2
Mississippi	—	—	—	—	100.0	0.0	0.0	100.0
Missouri	56.4	43.6	0.0	56.4	66.5	33.5	0.0	66.5
Montana	—	—	—	—	76.2	23.8	0.0	76.2
Nebraska	—	—	—	—	44.4	55.6	0.0	44.4
Nevada	52.6	47.4	0.0	52.6	57.7	42.3	0.0	57.7
New Hampshire	35.9	64.1	0.0	35.9	—	—	—	—
New Jersey	—	—	—	—	51.4	46.9	1.7	52.3
New Mexico	—	—	—	—	62.7	37.3	0.0	62.7
New York	0.0	53.3	46.7	0.0	0.0	50.7	49.3	0.0
New York	***46.7***	***53.3***	***0.0***	***46.7***	***48.4***	***50.7***	***0.9***	***48.8***
North Carolina	66.6	33.4	0.0	66.6	—	—	—	—
North Dakota	36.0	63.6	0.4	36.1	41.5	57.2	1.3	42.0
Ohio	52.9	47.1	0.0	52.9	52.5	47.5	0.0	52.5
Oklahoma	55.3	44.7	0.0	55.3	—	—	—	—
Oregon	54.2	45.8	0.0	54.2	—	—	—	—
Pennsylvania	50.1	49.7	0.2	50.2	48.4	51.2	0.4	48.6
Rhode Island	—	—	—	—	64.5	35.5	0.0	64.5
South Carolina	82.2	17.8	0.0	82.2	—	—	—	—
South Dakota	49.2	50.8	0.0	49.2	—	—	—	—
Tennessee	—	—	—	—	79.0	19.0	2.0	80.6
Texas	—	—	—	—	74.6	23.6	1.8	75.9
Utah	46.0	54.0	0.0	46.0	38.7	34.8	26.4	52.6
Vermont	33.6	66.4	0.0	33.6	47.8	52.2	0.0	47.8
Virginia	—	—	—	—	69.3	0.0	30.7	100.0
Washington	61.1	38.9	0.0	61.1	67.3	31.4	1.3	68.2
West Virginia	—	—	—	—	59.2	40.8	0.0	59.2
Wisconsin	41.2	58.6	0.2	41.3	57.1	42.7	0.2	57.2
Wyoming	—	—	—	—	50.8	49.2	0.0	50.8

Notes: Main entries are calculated from the raw vote values in table series 6-33 through 6-54 for the appropriate years based on candidates who used the sole designation "Democrat" or "Republican" (or their historical antecedents listed in Appendix A) on the ballot. Other = candidates who used third-party names on the ballot or were listed as independent, unidentified, or scatter vote. Bold italicized entries in the table are the author's alternative party coding, which is used when a candidate listed a major party name (Democrat, Republican, or their historical antecedents) on the ballot with other party names or labels. These values are computed from the bold italicized raw vote values in table series 6-33 through 6-54 for the appropriate states and years. For a more detailed explanation of this alternative party coding system, see Tables 6-10 and 1-3. —indicates that the state had no data, either because the state had no Senate election, no vote data were found for the state in question, or the state had not yet entered the Union. No special Senate elections are included in this table.

[1] The Senate race for Hawaii took place in 1959.

Sources: *Congressional Quarterly's Guide to U.S. Elections* (1994), *America Votes* (various publication dates, ICPSR data sets 0001 and 0075, and independent search of state sources by the author. For some party affiliations, the labels were taken from Michael J. Dubin's election archive after verification by the author.

Table 6-23 Senate Election Results, by State, 1960–1962 (Percentages)

State	1960				1962			
	Democratic	Republican	Other	Democratic % of Two-Party Vote	Democratic	Republican	Other	Democratic % of Two-Party Vote
Alabama	70.2	29.8	0.0	70.2	50.9	49.1	0.0	50.9
Alaska	63.4	36.6	0.0	63.4	58.1	41.9	0.0	58.1
Arizona	—	—	—	—	54.9	45.1	0.0	54.9
Arkansas	99.9	0.0	0.1	100.0	68.7	31.3	0.0	68.7
California	—	—	—	—	43.4	56.3	0.3	43.5
Colorado	46.0	53.5	0.5	46.2	45.6	53.6	0.8	46.0
Connecticut	—	—	—	—	51.3	48.7	0.0	51.3
Delaware	49.3	50.7	0.0	49.3	—	—	—	—
Florida	—	—	—	—	70.0	30.0	0.0	70.0
Georgia	99.9	0.0	0.1	100.0	100.0	0.0	0.0	100.0
Hawaii	—	—	—	—	69.4	30.6	0.0	69.4
Idaho	47.7	52.3	0.0	47.7	54.7	45.3	0.0	54.7
Illinois	54.6	45.2	0.2	54.7	47.1	52.9	0.0	47.1
Indiana	—	—	—	—	50.3	49.7	0.0	50.3
Iowa	48.1	51.9	0.0	48.1	46.6	53.4	0.0	46.6
Kansas	43.8	54.6	1.6	44.5	35.9	62.4	1.6	36.5
Kentucky	40.8	59.2	0.0	40.8	47.2	52.8	0.0	47.2
Louisiana	79.8	20.2	0.0	79.8	75.6	24.4	0.0	75.6
Maine	38.4	61.6	0.0	38.4	—	—	—	—
Maryland	—	—	—	—	62.0	38.0	0.0	62.0
Massachusetts	43.5	56.2	0.4	43.6	—	—	—	—
Michigan	51.7	48.0	0.3	51.9	—	—	—	—
Minnesota	57.5	42.2	0.3	57.7	—	—	—	—
Mississippi	91.8	8.2	0.0	91.8	—	—	—	—
Missouri	—	—	—	—	54.6	45.4	0.0	54.6
Montana	50.7	49.3	0.0	50.7	—	—	—	—
Nebraska	41.1	58.9	0.0	41.1	—	—	—	—
Nevada	—	—	—	—	65.3	34.7	0.0	65.3
New Hampshire	39.7	60.3	0.0	39.7	40.3	59.7	0.0	40.3
New Jersey	43.2	55.7	1.1	43.7	—	—	—	—
New Mexico	63.4	36.6	0.0	63.4	—	—	—	—
New York	—	—	—	—	0.0	57.4	42.6	0.0
New York	—	—	—	—	***40.1***	***57.4***	***2.5***	***41.2***
North Carolina	61.4	38.6	0.0	61.4	60.4	39.6	0.0	60.4
North Dakota	—	—	—	—	39.3	60.7	0.0	39.3
Ohio	—	—	—	—	61.6	38.4	0.0	61.6
Oklahoma	54.8	44.6	0.5	55.1	53.2	46.3	0.4	53.5
Oregon	54.6	45.4	0.0	54.6	54.2	45.8	0.0	54.2
Pennsylvania	—	—	—	—	51.1	48.7	0.2	51.2
Rhode Island	68.9	31.1	0.0	68.9	—	—	—	—
South Carolina	100.0	0.0	0.0	100.0	57.2	42.8	0.0	57.2
South Dakota	47.6	52.4	0.0	47.6	50.1	49.9	0.0	50.1
Tennessee	71.8	28.2	0.0	71.8	—	—	—	—
Texas	58.0	41.1	0.9	58.5	—	—	—	—
Utah	—	—	—	—	47.6	52.4	0.0	47.6
Vermont	—	—	—	—	33.1	66.9	0.0	33.1
Virginia	81.3	0.0	18.7	100.0	—	—	—	—
Virginia	***95.5***	***0.0***	***4.5***	***100.0***	—	—	—	—
Washington	—	—	—	—	52.1	47.3	0.6	52.4
West Virginia	55.3	44.7	0.0	55.3	—	—	—	—
Wisconsin	—	—	—	—	52.6	47.2	0.2	52.7
Wyoming	43.6	56.4	0.0	43.6	—	—	—	—

Notes: Main entries are calculated from the raw vote values in table series 6-33 through 6-54 for the appropriate years based on candidates who used the sole designation "Democrat" or "Republican" (or their historical antecedents listed in Appendix A) on the ballot. Other = candidates who used third-party names on the ballot or were listed as independent, unidentified, or scatter vote. Bold italicized entries in the table are the author's alternative party coding, which is used when a candidate listed a major party name (Democrat, Republican, or their historical antecedents) on the ballot with other party names or labels. These values are computed from the bold italicized raw vote values in table series 6-33 through 6-54 for the appropriate states and years. For a more detailed explanation of this alternative party coding system, see Tables 6-10 and 1-3. —indicates that the state had no data, either because the state had no Senate election, no vote data were found for the state in question, or the state had not yet entered the Union. No special Senate elections are included in this table.

Sources: *Congressional Quarterly's Guide to U.S. Elections* (1994), *America Votes* (various publication dates), ICPSR data sets 0001 and 0075, and independent search of state sources by the author. For some party affiliations, the labels were taken from Michael J. Dubin's election archive after verification by the author.

Table 6-24 Senate Election Results, by State, 1964–1966 (Percentages)

State	1964				1966			
	Democratic	Republican	Other	Democratic % of Two-Party Vote	Democratic	Republican	Other	Democratic % of Two-Party Vote
Alabama	—	—	—	—	60.1	39.0	0.9	60.6
Alaska	—	—	—	—	75.5	24.5	0.0	75.5
Arizona	48.6	51.4	0.0	48.6	—	—	—	—
Arkansas	—	—	—	—	—	—	—	—
California	48.5	51.5	0.0	48.5	—	—	—	—
Colorado	—	—	—	—	41.9	58.0	0.1	42.0
Connecticut	64.7	35.3	0.0	64.7	—	—	—	—
Delaware	48.3	51.7	0.0	48.3	40.9	59.1	0.0	40.9
Florida	64.0	36.0	0.0	64.0	—	—	—	—
Georgia	—	—	—	—	100.0	0.0	0.0	100.0
Hawaii	46.4	53.0	0.6	46.6	—	—	—	—
Idaho	—	—	—	—	44.6	55.4	0.0	44.6
Illinois	—	—	—	—	43.9	54.9	1.2	44.4
Indiana	54.3	45.3	0.3	54.5	—	—	—	—
Iowa	—	—	—	—	37.8	60.9	1.3	38.3
Kansas	—	—	—	—	45.2	52.1	2.7	46.4
Kentucky	—	—	—	—	35.5	64.5	0.0	35.5
Louisiana	—	—	—	—	100.0	0.0	0.0	100.0
Maine	66.6	33.4	0.0	66.6	41.1	58.9	0.0	41.1
Maryland	62.8	37.2	0.0	62.8	—	—	—	—
Massachusetts	74.3	25.4	0.3	74.5	38.7	60.7	0.6	39.0
Michigan	64.4	35.3	0.3	64.6	43.8	55.9	0.3	44.0
Minnesota	60.3	39.3	0.4	60.6	53.9	45.2	0.8	54.4
Mississippi	100.0	0.0	0.0	100.0	65.5	26.8	7.8	71.0
Missouri	66.6	33.4	0.0	66.6	—	—	—	—
Montana	64.5	35.5	0.0	64.5	53.2	46.8	0.0	53.2
Nebraska	38.6	61.4	0.0	38.6	38.8	61.2	0.0	38.8
Nevada	50.0	50.0	0.0	50.0	—	—	—	—
New Hampshire	—	—	—	—	54.0	45.9	0.1	54.1
New Jersey	61.9	37.3	0.8	62.4	37.0	60.0	3.0	38.1
New Mexico	54.7	45.3	0.0	54.7	53.1	46.9	0.0	53.1
New York	0.0	43.4	56.6	0.0	—	—	—	—
New York	*53.5*	*43.4*	*3.1*	*55.2*	—	—	—	—
North Carolina	—	—	—	—	55.6	44.4	0.0	55.6
North Dakota	57.6	42.4	0.0	57.6	—	—	—	—
Ohio	50.2	49.8	—	50.2	—	—	—	—
Oklahoma	—	—	—	—	53.7	46.3	0.0	53.7
Oregon	—	—	—	—	48.2	51.8	0.0	48.2
Pennsylvania	49.1	50.6	0.3	49.3	—	—	—	—
Rhode Island	82.7	17.3	0.0	82.7	67.7	32.3	0.0	67.7
South Carolina	—	—	—	—	37.8	62.2	0.0	37.8
South Dakota	—	—	—	—	33.7	66.3	0.0	33.7
Tennessee	53.6	46.4	0.0	53.6	44.3	55.7	0.0	44.3
Texas	56.2	43.6	0.2	56.3	43.1	56.4	0.5	43.3
Utah	57.3	42.7	0.0	57.3	—	—	—	—
Vermont	46.5	0.0	53.5	100.0	—	—	—	—
Vermont	*46.5*	*53.5*	*0.0*	*46.5*	—	—	—	—
Virginia	63.8	19.0	17.2	77.0	58.6	33.5	7.9	63.6
Washington	72.2	27.8	0.0	72.2	—	—	—	—
West Virginia	67.7	32.3	0.0	67.7	59.5	40.5	0.0	59.5
Wisconsin	53.3	46.6	0.1	53.3	—	—	—	—
Wyoming	54.0	46.0	0.0	54.0	48.2	51.8	0.0	48.2

Notes: Main entries are calculated from the raw vote values in table series 6-33 through 6-54 for the appropriate years based on candidates who used the sole designation "Democrat" or "Republican" (or their historical antecedents listed in Appendix A) on the ballot. Other = candidates who used third-party names on the ballot or were listed as independent, unidentified, or scatter vote. Bold italicized entries in the table are the author's alternative party coding, which is used when a candidate listed a major party name (Democrat, Republican, or their historical antecedents) on the ballot with other party names or labels. These values are computed from the bold italicized raw vote values in table series 6-33 through 6-54 for the appropriate states and years. For a more detailed explanation of this alternative party coding system, see Tables 6-10 and 1-3. —indicates that the state had no data, either because the state had no Senate election, no vote data were found for the state in question, or the state had not yet entered the Union. No special Senate elections are included in this table.

Sources: *Congressional Quarterly's Guide to U.S. Elections* (1994), *America Votes* (various publication dates), ICPSR data sets 0001 and 0075, and independent search of state sources by the author. For some party affiliations, the labels were taken from Michael J. Dubin's election archive after verification by the author.

Table 6-25 Senate Election Results, by State, 1968–1970 (Percentages)

State	1968				1970			
	Democratic	Republican	Other	Democratic % of Two-Party Vote	Democratic	Republican	Other	Democratic % of Two-Party Vote
Alabama	70.0	22.0	8.0	76.0	—	—	—	—
Alabama	*78.0*	*22.0*	*0.0*	*78.0*	—	—	—	—
Alaska	45.1	37.4	17.4	54.7				
Arizona	42.8	57.2	0.0	42.8	44.0	56.0	0.0	44.0
Arkansas	59.1	40.9	0.0	59.1	—	—	—	—
California	51.8	46.9	1.3	52.5	53.9	44.3	1.8	54.9
Colorado	41.4	58.6	0.0	41.4				
Connecticut	54.3	45.7	0.0	54.3	33.8	41.7	24.5	44.7
Delaware	—	—	—	—	40.1	58.8	1.1	40.5
Florida	44.1	55.9	0.0	44.1	53.9	46.1	0.0	53.9
Georgia	77.5	22.5	0.0	77.5	—	—	—	—
Hawaii	83.4	15.0	1.6	84.8	48.4	51.6	0.0	48.4
Idaho	60.3	39.7	0.0	60.3	—	—	—	—
Illinois	46.6	53.0	0.4	46.8	57.4	42.2	0.4	57.6
Indiana	51.7	48.1	0.2	51.8	50.1	49.9	0.0	50.1
Iowa	50.2	49.7	0.1	50.3	—	—	—	—
Kansas	38.7	60.1	1.3	39.2	—	—	—	—
Kentucky	47.6	51.4	1.0	48.1	—	—	—	—
Louisiana	100.0	0.0	0.0	100.0	—	—	—	—
Maine	—	—	—	—	61.7	38.3	0.0	61.7
Maryland	39.1	47.8	13.1	45.0	48.1	50.7	1.1	48.7
Massachusetts	—	—	—	—	62.1	37.0	0.9	62.7
Michigan	—	—	—	—	66.8	32.9	0.3	67.0
Minnesota	—	—	—	—	57.8	41.6	0.6	58.1
Mississippi	—	—	—	—	88.4	0.0	11.6	100.0
Missouri	51.1	48.9	0.0	51.1	51.0	48.1	0.8	51.5
Montana	—	—	—	—	60.5	39.5	0.0	60.5
Nebraska	—	—	—	—	47.4	52.5	0.1	47.5
Nevada	54.8	45.2	0.0	54.8	57.6	41.2	1.2	58.3
New Hampshire	40.7	59.3	0.0	40.7	—	—	—	—
New Jersey	—	—	—	—	54.0	42.2	3.8	56.2
New Mexico	—	—	—	—	52.3	46.6	1.2	52.9
New York	32.7	0.0	67.3	100.0	36.8	0.0	63.2	100.0
New York	*32.7*	*49.7*	*17.6*	*39.7*	*36.8*	*24.3*	*38.9*	*60.2*
North Carolina	60.6	39.4	0.0	60.6	—	—	—	—
North Dakota	33.7	64.6	1.7	34.3	61.3	37.8	0.9	61.8
Ohio	48.5	51.5	0.0	48.5	47.4	49.7	2.9	48.8
Oklahoma	46.2	51.7	2.1	47.2	—	—	—	—
Oregon	49.8	50.2	0.0	49.8	—	—	—	—
Pennsylvania	45.8	51.9	2.3	46.9	45.4	51.4	3.2	46.9
Rhode Island	—	—	—	—	67.5	31.5	1.0	68.2
South Carolina	61.9	38.1	0.0	61.9	—	—	—	—
South Dakota	56.8	43.2	0.0	56.8	—	—	—	—
Tennessee	—	—	—	—	47.4	51.3	1.3	48.0
Texas	—	—	—	—	53.5	46.4	0.1	53.5
Utah	45.8	53.7	0.5	46.1	56.2	42.5	1.4	56.9
Vermont	0.0	0.0	100.0	—	40.2	58.9	0.9	40.6
Vermont	*0.0*	*99.9*	*0.1*	*0.0*	—	—	—	—
Virginia	—	—	—	—	31.2	15.3	53.5	67.0
Washington	64.4	35.3	0.3	64.6	82.4	16.0	1.6	83.7
West Virginia	—	—	—	—	77.6	22.4	0.0	77.6
Wisconsin	61.7	38.3	0.0	61.7	70.8	28.5	0.7	71.3
Wyoming	—	—	—	—	55.8	44.2	0.0	55.8

Notes: Main entries are calculated from the raw vote values in table series 6-33 through 6-54 for the appropriate years based on candidates who used the sole designation "Democrat" or "Republican" (or their historical antecedents listed in Appendix A) on the ballot. Other = candidates who used third-party names on the ballot or were listed as independent, unidentified, or scatter vote. Bold italicized entries in the table are the author's alternative party coding, which is used when a candidate listed a major party name (Democrat, Republican, or their historical antecedents) on the ballot with other party names or labels. These values are computed from the bold italicized raw vote values in table series 6-33 through 6-54 for the appropriate states and years. For a more detailed explanation of this alternative party coding system, see Tables 6-10 and 1-3. —indicates that the state had no data, either because the state had no Senate election, no vote data were found for the state in question, or the state had not yet entered the Union. No special Senate elections are included in this table.

Sources: *Congressional Quarterly's Guide to U.S. Elections* (1994), *America Votes* (various publication dates), ICPSR data sets 0001 and 0075, and independent search of state sources by the author. For some party affiliations, the labels were taken from Michael J. Dubin's election archive after verification by the author.

Table 6-26 Senate Election Results, by State, 1972–1974 (Percentages)

State	1972				1974			
	Democratic	Republican	Other	Democratic % of Two-Party Vote	Democratic	Republican	Other	Democratic % of Two-Party Vote
Alabama	62.3	33.1	4.7	65.3	95.8	0.0	4.2	100.0
Alabama	*65.3*	*33.1*	*1.7*	*66.4*	—	—	—	—
Alaska	22.7	77.3	0.0	22.7	58.3	41.7	0.0	58.3
Arizona	—	—	—	—	41.7	58.3	0.0	41.7
Arkansas	60.9	39.1	0.0	60.9	84.9	15.1	0.0	84.9
California	—	—	—	—	60.5	36.2	3.3	62.6
Colorado	49.4	48.4	2.2	50.5	57.2	39.5	3.3	59.2
Connecticut	—	—	—	—	63.7	34.3	2.0	65.0
Delaware	50.5	49.1	0.4	50.7	—	—	—	—
Florida	—	—	—	—	43.4	40.9	15.7	51.5
Georgia	54.0	46.0	0.0	54.0	71.8	28.2	0.0	71.8
Hawaii	—	—	—	—	82.9	0.0	17.1	100.0
Idaho	45.5	52.3	2.2	46.5	56.1	42.1	1.8	57.1
Illinois	37.3	62.2	0.4	37.5	62.2	37.2	0.6	62.5
Indiana	—	—	—	—	50.7	46.4	2.8	52.2
Iowa	55.1	44.1	0.8	55.5	52.0	47.3	0.7	52.4
Kansas	23.0	71.4	5.5	24.4	49.1	50.9	0.0	49.1
Kentucky	50.9	47.6	1.4	51.7	53.5	44.1	2.4	54.8
Louisiana	55.2	19.1	25.7	74.3	100.0	0.0	0.0	100.0
Maine	53.2	46.8	0.0	53.2	—	—	—	—
Maryland	—	—	—	—	42.7	57.3	0.0	42.7
Massachusetts	34.7	63.5	1.7	35.3	—	—	—	—
Michigan	46.3	52.3	1.4	47.0	—	—	—	—
Minnesota	56.7	42.9	0.5	56.9	—	—	—	—
Mississippi	58.1	38.7	3.2	60.0	—	—	—	—
Missouri	—	—	—	—	60.1	39.3	0.7	60.5
Montana	52.0	48.0	0.0	52.0	—	—	—	—
Nebraska	46.8	53.1	0.1	46.8	—	—	—	—
Nevada	—	—	—	—	46.6	47.0	6.4	49.8
New Hampshire	56.9	43.1	0.0	56.9	49.7	49.7	0.7	50.0
New Jersey	34.5	62.5	3.0	35.6	—	—	—	—
New Mexico	45.9	54.0	0.1	46.0	—	—	—	—
New York	—	—	—	—	38.2	0.0	61.8	100.0
New York	—	—	—	—	*38.2*	*45.3*	*16.5*	*45.8*
North Carolina	46.0	54.0	0.0	46.0	62.1	37.0	0.9	62.7
North Dakota	—	—	—	—	48.3	48.4	3.2	50.0
Ohio	—	—	—	—	64.6	30.7	4.7	67.8
Oklahoma	47.6	51.4	1.0	48.1	48.9	49.4	1.7	49.8
Oregon	46.2	53.7	0.1	46.2	44.2	54.9	0.9	44.6
Pennsylvania	—	—	—	—	45.9	53.0	1.1	46.4
Rhode Island	53.7	45.7	0.6	54.0	—	—	—	—
South Carolina	36.5	63.5	0.0	36.5	69.5	28.6	1.9	70.8
South Dakota	57.0	43.0	0.0	57.0	53.0	47.0	0.0	53.0
Tennessee	37.8	61.5	0.6	38.1	—	—	—	—
Texas	44.3	53.4	2.3	45.3	—	—	—	—
Utah	—	—	—	—	44.1	50.0	5.9	46.9
Vermont	—	—	—	—	0.0	46.4	53.6	0.0
Vermont	—	—	—	—	*49.5*	*46.4*	*4.1*	*51.6*
Virginia	46.1	51.4	2.4	47.3	—	—	—	—
Washington	—	—	—	—	60.7	36.1	3.2	62.7
West Virginia	66.5	33.5	0.0	66.5	—	—	—	—
Wisconsin	—	—	—	—	61.8	35.8	2.5	63.3
Wyoming	28.7	71.3	0.0	28.7	—	—	—	—

Notes: Main entries are calculated from the raw vote values in table series 6-33 through 6-54 for the appropriate years based on candidates who used the sole designation "Democrat" or "Republican" (or their historical antecedents listed in Appendix A) on the ballot. Other = candidates who used third-party names on the ballot or were listed as independent, unidentified, or scatter vote. Bold italicized entries in the table are the author's alternative party coding, which is used when a candidate listed a major party name (Democrat, Republican, or their historical antecedents) on the ballot with other party names or labels. These values are computed from the bold italicized raw vote values in table series 6-33 through 6-54 for the appropriate states and years. For a more detailed explanation of this alternative party coding system, see Tables 6-10 and 1-3. —indicates that the state had no data, either because the state had no Senate election, no vote data were found for the state in question, or the state had not yet entered the Union. No special Senate elections are included in this table.

Sources: *Congressional Quarterly's Guide to U.S. Elections* (1994), *America Votes* (various publication dates), ICPSR data sets 0001 and 0075, and independent search of state sources by the author. For some party affiliations, the labels were taken from Michael J. Dubin's election archive after verification by the author.

Table 6-27 Senate Election Results, by State, 1976–1978 (Percentages)

State	1976				1978			
	Democratic	Republican	Other	Democratic % of Two-Party Vote	Democratic	Republican	Other	Democratic % of Two-Party Vote
Alabama	—	—	—	—	94.0	0.0	6.0	100.0
Alaska	—	—	—	—	24.1	75.6	0.3	24.2
Arizona	54.0	43.3	2.6	55.5	—	—	—	—
Arkansas	—	—	—	—	76.6	16.2	7.2	82.5
California	46.9	50.2	3.0	48.3	—	—	—	—
Colorado	—	—	—	—	40.3	58.7	1.0	40.7
Connecticut	41.2	57.7	1.1	41.7	—	—	—	—
Delaware	43.6	55.8	0.6	43.9	58.0	41.0	1.0	58.6
Florida	63.0	37.0	0.0	63.0	—	—	—	—
Georgia	—	—	—	—	83.1	16.9	0.0	83.1
Hawaii	53.7	40.6	5.6	56.9	—	—	—	—
Idaho	—	—	—	—	31.6	68.4	0.0	31.6
Illinois	—	—	—	—	45.5	53.3	1.2	46.0
Indiana	40.5	58.8	0.8	40.8	—	—	—	—
Iowa	—	—	—	—	47.9	51.1	1.0	48.4
Kansas	—	—	—	—	42.4	53.9	3.7	44.1
Kentucky	—	—	—	—	61.0	36.9	2.2	62.3
Louisiana	—	—	—	—	—	—	—	—
Maine	60.2	39.8	0.0	60.2	33.9	56.6	9.5	37.5
Maryland	56.5	38.8	4.6	59.3	—	—	—	—
Massachusetts	69.3	29.0	1.7	70.5	55.1	44.8	0.1	55.1
Michigan	52.5	46.8	0.7	52.8	52.1	47.9	0.0	52.1
Minnesota	67.5	25.0	7.5	72.9	40.4	56.6	3.1	41.7
Mississippi	100.0	0.0	0.0	100.0	31.8	45.1	23.2	41.3
Missouri	42.5	56.9	0.6	42.7	—	—	—	—
Montana	64.2	35.8	0.0	64.2	55.7	44.3	0.0	55.7
Nebraska	52.5	47.5	0.0	52.5	67.6	32.3	0.1	67.7
Nevada	63.0	31.4	5.6	66.7	—	—	—	—
New Hampshire	—	—	—	—	48.5	50.7	0.8	48.9
New Jersey	60.7	38.0	1.3	61.5	55.3	43.1	1.6	56.2
New Mexico	42.7	56.8	0.5	42.9	46.6	53.4	0.0	46.6
New York	0.0	0.0	100.0	—	—	—	—	—
New York	**54.2**	**44.9**	**1.0**	**54.7**	—	—	—	—
North Carolina	—	—	—	—	45.5	54.5	0.0	45.5
North Dakota	62.1	36.6	1.4	62.9	—	—	—	—
Ohio	49.5	46.5	4.0	51.6	—	—	—	—
Oklahoma	—	—	—	—	65.5	32.9	1.7	66.6
Oregon	—	—	—	—	38.3	61.6	0.1	38.3
Pennsylvania	46.8	52.4	0.8	47.2	—	—	—	—
Rhode Island	42.0	57.7	0.2	42.1	75.1	24.9	0.0	75.1
South Carolina	—	—	—	—	44.4	55.6	0.0	44.4
South Dakota	—	—	—	—	33.2	66.8	0.0	33.2
Tennessee	52.5	47.0	0.5	52.7	40.3	55.5	4.2	42.0
Texas	56.8	42.2	1.0	57.3	49.3	49.8	1.0	49.7
Utah	44.8	53.7	1.5	45.5	—	—	—	—
Vermont	0.0	50.0	50.0	0.0	—	—	—	—
Vermont	**45.3**	**50.0**	**4.7**	**47.6**	—	—	—	—
Virginia	38.3	0.0	61.7	100.0	49.8	50.2	0.0	49.8
Washington	71.8	24.2	3.9	74.8	—	—	—	—
West Virginia	99.9	0.0	0.1	100.0	50.5	49.5	0.0	50.5
Wisconsin	72.2	27.0	0.8	72.8	—	—	—	—
Wyoming	45.4	54.6	0.0	45.4	37.8	62.2	0.0	37.8

Notes: Main entries are calculated from the raw vote values in table series 6-33 through 6-54 for the appropriate years based on candidates who used the sole designation "Democrat" or "Republican" (or their historical antecedents listed in Appendix A) on the ballot. Other = candidates who used third-party names on the ballot or were listed as independent, unidentified, or scatter vote. Bold italicized entries in the table are the author's alternative party coding, which is used when a candidate listed a major party name (Democrat, Republican, or their historical antecedents) on the ballot with other party names or labels. These values are computed from the bold italicized raw vote values in table series 6-33 through 6-54 for the appropriate states and years. For a more detailed explanation of this alternative party coding system, see Tables 6-10 and 1-3. —indicates that the state had no data, either because the state had no Senate election, no vote data were found for the state in question, or the state had not yet entered the Union. No special Senate elections are included in this table.

Sources: *Congressional Quarterly's Guide to U.S. Elections* (1994), *America Votes* (various publication dates), and independent search of state sources by the author. For some party affiliations, the labels were taken from Michael J. Dubin's election archive after verification by the author.

Table 6-28 Senate Election Results, by State, 1980–1982 (Percentages)

State	1980 Democratic	Republican	Other	Democratic % of Two-Party Vote	1982 Democratic	Republican	Other	Democratic % of Two-Party Vote
Alabama	47.1	50.2	2.8	48.4	—	—	—	—
Alaska	45.9	53.7	0.4	46.1	—	—	—	—
Arizona	48.4	49.5	2.2	49.5	56.9	40.3	2.8	58.5
Arkansas	59.1	40.9	0.0	59.1	—	—	—	—
California	56.5	37.1	6.3	60.3	44.8	51.5	3.7	46.5
Colorado	50.3	48.7	1.0	50.8	—	—	—	—
Connecticut	56.3	42.9	0.8	56.8	46.1	50.4	3.6	47.8
Delaware	—	—	—	—	44.2	55.2	0.6	44.5
Florida	48.3	51.7	0.0	48.3	61.7	38.3	0.0	61.7
Georgia	49.1	50.9	0.0	49.1	—	—	—	—
Hawaii	77.9	18.4	3.6	80.9	80.1	17.0	2.9	82.5
Idaho	48.8	49.7	1.5	49.5	—	—	—	—
Illinois	56.0	42.5	1.5	56.9	—	—	—	—
Indiana	46.2	53.8	0.0	46.2	45.6	53.8	0.6	45.9
Iowa	45.5	53.5	1.0	46.0	—	—	—	—
Kansas	36.2	63.8	0.0	36.2	—	—	—	—
Kentucky	65.1	34.9	0.0	65.1	—	—	—	—
Louisiana	—	—	—	—	—	—	—	—
Maine	—	—	—	—	60.9	39.1	0.0	60.9
Maryland	33.8	66.2	0.0	33.8	63.5	36.5	0.0	63.5
Massachusetts	—	—	—	—	60.8	38.3	0.9	61.4
Michigan	—	—	—	—	57.7	40.9	1.4	58.6
Minnesota	—	—	—	—	46.6	52.6	0.8	47.0
Mississippi	—	—	—	—	64.2	35.8	0.0	64.2
Missouri	52.0	47.7	0.3	52.2	49.1	50.9	0.0	49.1
Montana	—	—	—	—	54.5	41.7	3.9	56.7
Nebraska	—	—	—	—	66.6	28.5	4.9	70.0
Nevada	37.4	58.5	4.1	39.0	47.7	50.1	2.2	48.8
New Hampshire	47.9	52.1	0.0	47.9	—	—	—	—
New Jersey	—	—	—	—	50.9	47.8	1.3	51.6
New Mexico	—	—	—	—	53.8	46.2	0.0	53.8
New York	43.5	0.0	56.5	100.0	0.0	0.0	100.0	—
New York	***43.5***	***44.9***	***11.6***	***49.2***	***65.1***	***34.2***	***0.8***	***65.6***
North Carolina	49.4	50.0	0.7	49.7	—	—	—	—
North Dakota	29.0	70.3	0.8	29.2	62.8	34.0	3.2	64.9
Ohio	68.8	28.2	3.0	70.9	56.7	41.1	2.2	57.9
Oklahoma	43.5	53.5	3.0	44.9	—	—	—	—
Oregon	44.0	52.1	3.9	45.8	—	—	—	—
Pennsylvania	48.0	50.5	1.5	48.8	39.2	59.3	1.5	39.8
Rhode Island	—	—	—	—	48.8	51.2	0.0	48.8
South Carolina	70.4	29.6	0.0	70.4	—	—	—	—
South Dakota	39.4	58.2	2.4	40.4	—	—	—	—
Tennessee	—	—	—	—	61.9	38.1	0.0	61.9
Texas	—	—	—	—	58.6	40.5	0.9	59.1
Utah	25.5	73.6	0.9	25.7	41.3	58.3	0.4	41.5
Vermont	49.8	48.5	1.7	50.7	47.2	50.3	2.5	48.4
Virginia	—	—	—	—	48.8	51.2	0.0	48.8
Washington	45.8	54.2	0.0	45.8	69.0	24.3	6.8	74.0
West Virginia	—	—	—	—	68.5	30.8	0.7	69.0
Wisconsin	48.3	50.2	1.5	49.1	63.6	34.1	2.2	65.1
Wyoming	—	—	—	—	43.3	56.7	0.0	43.3

Notes: Main entries are calculated from the raw vote values in table series 6-33 through 6-54 for the appropriate years based on candidates who used the sole designation "Democrat" or "Republican" (or their historical antecedents listed in Appendix A) on the ballot. Other = candidates who used third-party names on the ballot or were listed as independent, unidentified, or scatter vote. Bold italicized entries in the table are the author's alternative party coding, which is used when a candidate listed a major party name (Democrat, Republican, or their historical antecedents) on the ballot with other party names or labels. These values are computed from the bold italicized raw vote values in table series 6-33 through 6-54 for the appropriate states and years. For a more detailed explanation of this alternative party coding system, see Tables 6-10 and 1-3. —indicates that the state had no data, either because the state had no Senate election, no vote data were found for the state in question, or the state had not yet entered the Union. No special Senate elections are included in this table.

Sources: *Congressional Quarterly's Guide to U.S. Elections* (1994), *America Votes* (various publication dates), and independent search of state sources by the author. For some party affiliations, the labels were taken from Michael J. Dubin's election archive after verification by the author.

Table 6-29 Senate Election Results, by State, 1984–1986 (Percentages)

State	1984				1986			
	Democratic	Republican	Other	Democratic % of Two-Party Vote	Democratic	Republican	Other	Democratic % of Two-Party Vote
Alabama	62.8	36.4	0.9	63.3	50.3	49.7	0.0	50.3
Alaska	28.5	71.2	0.3	28.6	44.1	54.0	1.9	44.9
Arizona	—	—	—	—	39.5	60.5	0.0	39.5
Arkansas	57.3	42.7	0.0	57.3	62.3	37.7	0.0	62.3
California	—	—	—	—	49.3	47.9	2.8	50.7
Colorado	34.6	64.2	1.1	35.0	49.9	48.4	1.7	50.8
Connecticut	—	—	—	—	64.8	34.8	0.4	65.0
Delaware	60.1	39.9	0.0	60.1	—	—	—	—
Florida	—	—	—	—	54.7	45.3	0.0	54.7
Georgia	79.9	20.1	0.0	79.9	50.9	49.1	0.0	50.9
Hawaii	—	—	—	—	73.6	26.4	0.0	73.6
Idaho	26.0	72.2	1.8	26.5	48.4	51.6	0.0	48.4
Illinois	50.1	48.2	1.7	50.9	65.1	33.7	1.1	65.9
Indiana	—	—	—	—	38.5	60.6	0.9	38.9
Iowa	55.5	43.7	0.9	56.0	33.6	66.0	0.4	33.7
Kansas	21.2	76.0	2.8	21.8	30.0	70.0	0.0	30.0
Kentucky	49.5	49.9	0.6	49.8	74.4	25.6	0.0	74.4
Louisiana	—	—	—	—	52.8	47.2	0.0	52.8
Maine	25.9	73.3	0.8	26.1	—	—	—	—
Maryland	—	—	—	—	60.7	39.3	0.0	60.7
Massachusetts	55.1	44.9	0.0	55.1	—	—	—	—
Michigan	51.8	47.2	1.1	52.3	—	—	—	—
Minnesota	41.3	58.1	0.6	41.5	—	—	—	—
Mississippi	39.1	60.9	0.0	39.1	—	—	—	—
Missouri	—	—	—	—	47.4	52.6	0.0	47.4
Montana	56.9	40.7	2.4	58.3	—	—	—	—
Nebraska	52.0	48.0	0.0	52.0	—	—	—	—
Nevada	—	—	—	—	50.0	44.5	5.5	52.9
New Hampshire	41.0	58.7	0.3	41.1	32.4	62.9	4.7	34.0
New Jersey	64.2	34.9	1.0	64.8	—	—	—	—
New Mexico	28.1	71.9	0.0	28.1	—	—	—	—
New York	—	—	—	—	41.2	0.0	58.8	100.0
New York	—	—	—	—	***41.2***	***56.9***	***1.9***	***42.0***
North Carolina	47.8	51.7	0.5	48.1	51.8	48.2	0.0	51.8
North Dakota	—	—	—	—	49.8	49.1	1.1	50.4
Ohio	—	—	—	—	62.5	37.5	0.0	62.5
Oklahoma	75.6	23.4	0.9	76.4	44.8	55.2	0.0	44.8
Oregon	33.4	66.6	0.0	33.4	36.0	63.0	1.0	36.4
Pennsylvania	—	—	—	—	42.9	56.4	0.7	43.2
Rhode Island	72.6	27.4	0.0	72.6	—	—	—	—
South Carolina	31.8	66.8	1.4	32.3	63.1	35.6	1.3	63.9
South Dakota	25.5	74.5	0.0	25.5	51.6	48.4	0.0	51.6
Tennessee	60.7	33.8	5.5	64.2	—	—	—	—
Texas	41.4	58.6	0.0	41.4	—	—	—	—
Utah	—	—	—	—	26.6	72.3	1.1	26.9
Vermont	—	—	—	—	63.2	34.5	2.3	64.7
Virginia	29.9	70.1	0.0	29.9	—	—	—	—
Washington	—	—	—	—	50.7	48.7	0.7	51.0
West Virginia	51.8	47.7	0.5	52.1	—	—	—	—
Wisconsin	—	—	—	—	47.4	50.9	1.7	48.2
Wyoming	21.7	78.3	0.0	21.7	—	—	—	—

Notes: Main entries are calculated from the raw vote values in table series 6-33 through 6-54 for the appropriate years based on candidates who used the sole designation "Democrat" or "Republican" (or their historical antecedents listed in Appendix A) on the ballot. Other = candidates who used third-party names on the ballot or were listed as independent, unidentified, or scatter vote. Bold italicized entries in the table are the author's alternative party coding, which is used when a candidate listed a major party name (Democrat, Republican, or their historical antecedents) on the ballot with other party names or labels. These values are computed from the bold italicized raw vote values in table series 6-33 through 6-54 for the appropriate states and years. For a more detailed explanation of this alternative party coding system, see Tables 6-10 and 1-3. —indicates that the state had no data, either because the state had no Senate election, no vote data were found for the state in question, or the state had not yet entered the Union. No special Senate elections are included in this table.

Sources: *Congressional Quarterly's Guide to U.S. Elections* (1994), *America Votes* (various publication dates), and independent search of state sources by the author. For some party affiliations, the labels were taken from Michael J. Dubin's election archive after verification by the author.

Table 6-30 Senate Election Results, by State, 1988–1990 (Percentages)

State	1988 Democratic	Republican	Other	Democratic % of Two-Party Vote	1990 Democratic	Republican	Other	Democratic % of Two-Party Vote
Alabama	—	—	—	—	60.6	39.4	0.0	60.6
Alaska	—	—	—	—	32.2	66.2	1.6	32.7
Arizona	56.7	41.1	2.2	58.0	—	—	—	—
Arkansas	—	—	—	—	99.8	0.0	0.2	100.0
California	44.0	52.8	3.2	45.5	—	—	—	—
Colorado	—	—	—	—	41.7	55.7	2.7	42.8
Connecticut	49.8	49.0	1.2	50.4	—	—	—	—
Delaware	37.9	62.1	0.0	37.9	62.7	35.8	1.5	63.6
Florida	49.6	50.4	0.0	49.6	—	—	—	—
Georgia	—	—	—	—	100.0	0.0	0.0	100.0
Hawaii	76.6	20.7	2.8	78.7	—	—	—	—
Idaho	—	—	—	—	38.7	61.3	0.0	38.7
Illinois	—	—	—	—	65.1	34.9	0.0	65.1
Indiana	31.9	68.1	0.0	31.9	—	—	—	—
Iowa	—	—	—	—	54.5	45.4	0.1	54.5
Kansas	—	—	—	—	26.4	73.6	0.0	26.4
Kentucky	—	—	—	—	47.8	52.2	0.0	47.8
Louisiana	—	—	—	—	—	—	—	—
Maine	81.2	18.8	0.0	81.2	38.6	61.4	0.0	38.6
Maryland	61.8	38.2	0.0	61.8	—	—	—	—
Massachusetts	65.0	33.9	1.1	65.7	57.1	42.9	0.1	57.1
Michigan	60.4	38.5	1.2	61.1	57.5	41.2	1.3	58.2
Minnesota	40.9	56.2	2.9	42.1	50.4	47.8	1.8	51.3
Mississippi	46.1	53.9	0.0	46.1	0.0	100.0	0.0	0.0
Missouri	31.8	67.7	0.5	31.9	—	—	—	—
Montana	48.1	51.9	0.0	48.1	68.1	29.4	2.5	69.9
Nebraska	56.7	41.7	1.6	57.6	58.9	40.9	0.2	59.0
Nevada	50.2	46.1	3.7	52.1	—	—	—	—
New Hampshire	—	—	—	—	31.3	65.1	3.5	32.5
New Jersey	53.6	45.2	1.3	54.2	50.4	47.4	2.2	51.6
New Mexico	63.3	36.7	0.0	63.3	27.1	72.9	0.0	27.1
New York	0.0	0.0	100.0	—	—	—	—	—
New York	***67.0***	***31.1***	***1.9***	***68.3***	—	—	—	—
North Carolina	—	—	—	—	47.4	52.6	0.0	47.4
North Dakota	59.4	39.1	1.5	60.4	—	—	—	—
Ohio	57.0	43.0	0.0	57.0	—	—	—	—
Oklahoma	—	—	—	—	83.2	16.8	0.0	83.2
Oregon	—	—	—	—	46.2	53.7	0.1	46.2
Pennsylvania	32.4	66.5	1.1	32.8	—	—	—	—
Rhode Island	45.4	54.6	0.0	45.4	61.8	38.2	0.0	61.8
South Carolina	—	—	—	—	32.5	64.2	3.3	33.6
South Dakota	—	—	—	—	45.1	52.4	2.5	46.2
Tennessee	65.1	34.5	0.4	65.3	67.7	29.8	2.5	69.4
Texas	59.2	40.0	0.8	59.7	37.4	60.2	2.3	38.3
Utah	31.7	67.1	1.1	32.1	—	—	—	—
Vermont	29.8	68.0	2.3	30.5	—	—	—	—
Virginia	71.2	28.7	0.1	71.3	0.0	80.9	19.1	0.0
Washington	48.9	51.1	0.0	48.9	—	—	—	—
West Virginia	64.8	35.2	0.0	64.8	68.3	31.7	0.0	68.3
Wisconsin	52.1	47.5	0.4	52.3	—	—	—	—
Wyoming	49.6	50.4	0.0	49.6	36.1	63.9	0.0	36.1

Notes: Main entries are calculated from the raw vote values in table series 6-33 through 6-54 for the appropriate years based on candidates who used the sole designation "Democrat" or "Republican" (or their historical antecedents listed in Appendix A) on the ballot. Other = candidates who used third-party names on the ballot or were listed as independent, unidentified, or scatter vote. Bold italicized entries in the table are the author's alternative party coding, which is used when a candidate listed a major party name (Democrat, Republican, or their historical antecedents) on the ballot with other party names or labels. These values are computed from the bold italicized raw vote values in table series 6-33 through 6-54 for the appropriate states and years. For a more detailed explanation of this alternative party coding system, see Tables 6-10 and 1-3. —indicates that the state had no data, either because the state had no Senate election, no vote data were found for the state in question, or the state had not yet entered the Union. No special Senate elections are included in this table.

Sources: *Congressional Quarterly's Guide to U.S. Elections* (1994), *America Votes* (various publication dates), and independent search of state sources by the author. For some party affiliations, the labels were taken from Michael J. Dubin's election archive after verification by the author.

Table 6-31 Senate Election Results, by State, 1992–1994 (Percentages)

	1992				1994			
State	Democratic	Republican	Other	Democratic % of Two-Party Vote	Democratic	Republican	Other	Democratic % of Two-Party Vote
Alabama	64.8	33.1	2.1	66.2	—	—	—	—
Alaska	38.4	53.0	8.5	42.0	—	—	—	—
Arizona	31.6	55.8	12.6	36.1	39.5	53.7	6.8	42.4
Arkansas	60.2	39.8	0.0	60.2	—	—	—	—
California	47.9	43.0	9.1	52.7	46.7	44.8	8.4	51.0
Colorado	51.8	42.7	5.5	54.8	—	—	—	—
Connecticut	0.0	38.1	61.9	0.0	0.0	31.0	69.0	0.0
Connecticut	*58.8*	*38.1*	*3.1*	*60.7*	*67.0*	*31.0*	*2.0*	*68.4*
Delaware	—	—	—	—	42.5	55.8	1.7	43.2
Florida	65.4	34.6	0.0	65.4	29.5	70.5	0.0	29.5
Georgia	49.4	50.6	0.0	49.4	—	—	—	—
Hawaii	57.3	26.9	15.8	68.0	71.8	24.2	4.0	74.8
Idaho	43.5	56.5	0.0	43.5	—	—	—	—
Illinois	53.3	43.1	3.7	55.3	—	—	—	—
Indiana	40.7	57.3	2.0	41.5	30.5	67.4	2.1	31.2
Iowa	27.2	69.6	3.2	28.1	—	—	—	—
Kansas	31.0	62.7	6.3	33.1	—	—	—	—
Kentucky	62.9	35.8	1.3	63.7	—	—	—	—
Louisiana	—	—	—	—	—	—	—	—
Maine	—	—	—	—	36.4	60.2	3.4	37.6
Maryland	71.0	29.0	0.0	71.0	59.1	40.9	0.0	59.1
Massachusetts	—	—	—	—	58.1	41.0	0.9	58.6
Michigan	—	—	—	—	42.7	51.9	5.4	45.2
Minnesota	—	—	—	—	44.1	49.1	6.8	47.3
Mississippi	—	—	—	—	31.2	68.8	0.0	31.2
Missouri	44.9	51.9	3.2	46.4	35.7	59.7	4.6	37.4
Montana	—	—	—	—	37.6	62.4	0.0	37.6
Nebraska	—	—	—	—	54.8	45.0	0.2	54.9
Nevada	51.0	40.2	8.7	55.9	50.9	41.0	8.1	55.4
New Hampshire	45.3	48.1	6.5	48.5	—	—	—	—
New Jersey	—	—	—	—	50.3	47.0	2.7	51.7
New Mexico	—	—	—	—	54.0	46.0	0.0	54.0
New York	0.0	0.0	100.0	—	0.0	0.0	100.0	—
New York	*47.8*	*49.0*	*3.2*	*49.4*	*55.2*	*41.5*	*3.3*	*57.1*
North Carolina	46.3	50.3	3.3	47.9	—	—	—	—
North Dakota	59.0	38.9	2.1	60.3	58.0	42.0	0.0	58.0
Ohio	51.0	42.3	6.7	54.7	39.2	53.4	7.3	42.3
Oklahoma	38.2	58.5	3.3	39.5	—	—	—	—
Oregon	46.5	52.1	1.4	47.1	—	—	—	—
Pennsylvania	46.3	49.1	4.6	48.5	46.9	49.4	3.7	48.7
Rhode Island	—	—	—	—	35.5	64.5	0.0	35.5
South Carolina	50.1	46.9	3.0	51.6	—	—	—	—
South Dakota	64.9	32.5	2.6	66.6	—	—	—	—
Tennessee	—	—	—	—	42.1	56.4	1.6	42.8
Texas	—	—	—	—	38.3	60.8	0.8	38.6
Utah	39.7	55.4	4.9	41.8	28.3	68.8	2.9	29.1
Vermont	54.2	43.3	2.5	55.5	40.6	50.3	9.1	44.6
Virginia	—	—	—	—	45.6	42.9	11.5	51.5
Washington	54.0	46.0	0.0	54.0	44.3	55.7	0.0	44.3
West Virginia	—	—	—	—	69.0	31.0	0.0	69.0
Wisconsin	52.6	46.0	1.4	53.3	58.3	40.7	1.0	58.9
Wyoming	—	—	—	—	39.3	58.9	1.8	40.0

Notes: Main entries are calculated from the raw vote values in table series 6-33 through 6-54 for the appropriate years based on candidates who used the sole designation "Democrat" or "Republican" (or their historical antecedents listed in Appendix A) on the ballot. Other = candidates who used third-party names on the ballot or were listed as independent, unidentified, or scatter vote. Bold italicized entries in the table are the author's alternative party coding, which is used when a candidate listed a major party name (Democrat, Republican, or their historical antecedents) on the ballot with other party names or labels. These values are computed from the bold italicized raw vote values in table series 6-33 through 6-54 for the appropriate states and years. For a more detailed explanation of this alternative party coding system, see Tables 6-10 and 1-3. —indicates that the state had no data, either because the state had no Senate election, no vote data were found for the state in question, or the state had not yet entered the Union. No special Senate elections are included in this table.

Sources: *Congressional Quarterly's Guide to U.S. Elections* (1994), *America Votes* (various publication dates), and independent search of state sources by the author. For some party affiliations, the labels were taken from Michael J. Dubin's election archive after verification by the author.

Table 6-32 Senate Election Results, by State, 1996–1998 (Percentages)

State	1996				1998			
	Democratic	Republican	Other	Democratic % of Two-Party Vote	Democratic	Republican	Other	Democratic % of Two-Party Vote
Alabama	45.5	52.5	2.1	46.4	36.7	63.2	0.1	36.7
Alaska	10.3	76.7	13.0	11.9	19.7	74.5	5.8	20.9
Arizona	—	—	—	—	27.2	68.7	4.1	28.3
Arkansas	47.3	52.7	0.0	47.3	55.1	42.2	2.7	56.6
California	—	—	—	—	53.1	43.0	3.9	55.2
Colorado	46.1	51.1	2.8	47.5	35.0	62.5	2.5	35.9
Connecticut	—	—	—	—	0.0	32.4	67.6	0.0
Connecticut	—	—	—	—	*65.1*	*32.4*	*2.5*	*66.8*
Delaware	60.0	38.1	1.8	61.2	—	—	—	—
Florida	—	—	—	—	62.5	37.5	0.0	62.5
Georgia	48.9	47.5	3.6	50.7	45.2	52.4	2.5	46.3
Hawaii	—	—	—	—	79.2	17.8	3.0	81.6
Idaho	39.9	57.0	3.1	41.2	28.4	69.5	2.1	29.0
Illinois	56.1	40.7	3.2	58.0	47.4	50.3	2.2	48.5
Indiana	—	—	—	—	63.7	34.8	1.5	64.7
Iowa	51.8	46.7	1.5	52.6	30.5	68.4	1.1	30.8
Kansas	34.4	62.0	3.5	35.7	31.6	65.3	3.1	32.6
Kentucky	42.8	55.5	1.7	43.6	49.2	49.7	1.1	49.7
Louisiana	50.2	49.8	0.0	50.2	64.0	31.6	4.3	66.9
Maine	43.9	49.2	6.9	47.1	—	—	—	—
Maryland	—	—	—	—	70.5	29.5	0.0	70.5
Massachusetts	52.2	44.7	3.1	53.9	—	—	—	—
Michigan	58.4	39.9	1.8	59.4	—	—	—	—
Minnesota	50.3	41.3	8.4	54.9	—	—	—	—
Mississippi	27.4	71.0	1.6	27.8	—	—	—	—
Missouri	—	—	—	—	43.8	52.7	3.6	45.4
Montana	49.6	44.7	5.8	52.6	—	—	—	—
Nebraska	41.7	56.1	2.2	42.6	—	—	—	—
Nevada	—	—	—	—	47.9	47.8	4.3	50.1
New Hampshire	46.2	49.2	4.6	48.4	28.2	67.8	4.0	29.4
New Jersey	52.7	42.6	4.7	55.3	—	—	—	—
New Mexico	29.8	64.7	5.5	31.5	—	—	—	—
New York	—	—	—	—	0.0	0.0	100.0	—
New York	—	—	—	—	*54.6*	*44.1*	*1.3*	*55.3*
North Carolina	45.9	52.6	1.4	46.6	51.2	47.0	1.8	52.1
North Dakota	—	—	—	—	63.2	35.2	1.7	64.2
Ohio	—	—	—	—	43.5	56.5	0.0	43.5
Oklahoma	40.1	56.7	3.2	41.4	31.3	66.4	2.3	32.0
Oregon	45.9	49.8	4.3	48.0	61.1	33.8	5.2	64.4
Pennsylvania	—	—	—	—	34.8	61.3	3.9	36.2
Rhode Island	63.5	35.1	1.5	64.4	—	—	—	—
South Carolina	44.0	53.4	2.6	45.2	52.7	45.7	1.6	53.6
South Dakota	51.3	48.7	0.0	51.3	62.1	36.4	1.4	63.1
Tennessee	36.8	61.4	1.8	37.5	—	—	—	—
Texas	43.9	54.8	1.3	44.5	—	—	—	—
Utah	—	—	—	—	33.0	64.0	3.0	34.0
Vermont	—	—	—	—	72.2	22.4	5.3	76.3
Virginia	47.4	52.5	0.1	47.5	—	—	—	—
Washington	—	—	—	—	58.4	41.6	0.0	58.4
West Virginia	76.6	23.4	0.0	76.6	—	—	—	—
Wisconsin	—	—	—	—	50.5	48.4	1.1	51.1
Wyoming	42.2	54.1	3.7	43.8	—	—	—	—

Notes: Main entries are calculated from the raw vote values in table series 6-33 through 6-54 for the appropriate years based on candidates who used the sole designation "Democrat" or "Republican" (or their historical antecedents listed in Appendix A) on the ballot. Other = candidates who used third-party names on the ballot or were listed as independent, unidentified, or scatter vote. Bold italicized entries in the table are the author's alternative party coding, which is used when a candidate listed a major party name (Democrat, Republican, or their historical antecedents) on the ballot with other party names or labels. These values are computed from the bold italicized raw vote values in table series 6-33 through 6-54 for the appropriate states and years. For a more detailed explanation of this alternative party coding system, see Tables 6-10 and 1-3. —indicates that the state had no data, either because the state had no Senate election, no vote data were found for the state in question, or the state had not yet entered the Union. No special Senate elections are included in this table.

Sources: *America Votes* (various publication dates), and independent search of state sources by the author. For some party affiliations, the labels were taken from Michael J. Dubin's election archive after verification by the author.

Table 6-33 Senate Election Results, by State, 1912–1914 (Raw Count)

State	1912				1914			
	Democratic	Republican	Other	Total Vote	Democratic	Republican	Other	Total Vote
Alabama	—	—	—	—	63,338	12,328	5,424	81,090
Alaska	—	—	—	—	—	—	—	—
Arizona	—	—	—	—	25,800	9,182	13,483	48,465
Arkansas	—	—	—	—	33,449	11,222	0	44,671
California	—	—	—	—	279,896	254,159	352,000	886,055
Colorado	118,260	66,949	64,597	249,806	102,037	98,728	52,448	253,213
Connecticut	—	—	—	—	76,081	89,983	14,750	180,814
Delaware	—	—	—	—	—	—	—	—
Florida	—	—	—	—	22,761	0	110	22,871
Georgia	—	—	—	—	61,489	0	28,435	89,924
Hawaii	—	—	—	—	—	—	—	—
Idaho	—	—	—	—	41,266	47,486	19,446	108,198
Illinois	—	—	—	—	373,403	390,661	251,744	1,015,808
Indiana	—	—	—	—	272,249	226,766	147,044	646,059
Iowa	—	—	—	—	167,251	205,832	54,019	427,102
Kansas	172,601	151,647	25,785	350,033	176,929	180,823	151,142	508,894
Kentucky	—	—	—	—	175,999	144,758	18,998	339,755
Louisiana	—	—	—	—	—	—	—	—
Maine	—	—	—	—	—	—	—	—
Maryland	—	—	—	—	110,204	94,864	11,065	216,133
Massachusetts	—	—	—	—	—	—	—	—
Michigan	—	—	—	—	—	—	—	—
Minnesota	102,691	173,074	0	275,765	—	—	—	—
Mississippi	—	—	—	—	—	—	—	—
Missouri	—	—	—	—	311,616	257,054	49,557	618,227
Montana	28,421	18,450	22,161	69,032	—	—	—	—
Nebraska	—	—	—	—	—	—	—	—
Nevada	—	—	—	—	8,078	8,038	5,451	21,567
New Hampshire	—	—	—	—	36,382	42,113	3,033	81,528
New Jersey	—	—	—	—	—	—	—	—
New Mexico	—	—	—	—	—	—	—	—
New York	—	—	—	—	0	639,112	719,573	1,358,685
New York	—	—	—	—	***571,419***	***639,112***	***148,154***	***1,358,685***
North Carolina	—	—	—	—	121,342	87,101	425	208,868
North Dakota	—	—	—	—	29,640	48,732	8,938	87,310
Ohio	—	—	—	—	423,742	526,115	120,312	1,070,169
Oklahoma	126,407	83,448	40,876	250,731	119,443	73,292	56,260	248,995
Oregon	40,172	38,453	54,953	133,578	111,748	88,297	45,535	245,580
Pennsylvania	—	—	—	—	266,415	0	845,411	1,111,826
Pennsylvania	—	—	—	—	***266,415***	***519,801***	***325,610***	***1,111,826***
Rhode Island	—	—	—	—	—	—	—	—
South Carolina	—	—	—	—	32,950	0	89	33,039
South Dakota	—	—	—	—	47,668	44,244	7,184	99,096
Tennessee	—	—	—	—	—	—	—	—
Texas	—	—	—	—	—	—	—	—
Utah	—	—	—	—	0	56,282	58,384	114,666
Utah	—	—	—	—	***53,127***	***56,282***	***5,257***	***114,666***
Vermont	—	—	—	—	0	35,137	27,568	62,705
Vermont	—	—	—	—	***26,776***	***35,137***	***792***	***62,705***
Virginia	—	—	—	—	—	—	—	—
Washington	—	—	—	—	91,733	130,479	123,067	345,279
West Virginia	—	—	—	—	—	—	—	—
Wisconsin	—	—	—	—	134,925	133,969	48,384	317,278
Wyoming	—	—	—	—	—	—	—	—

Notes: Main entries are raw vote values for candidates who used the sole designation "Democrat" or "Republican" (or their historical antecedents listed in Appendix A) on the ballot. Other = candidates who used third-party names on the ballot or were listed as independent, unidentified, or scatter vote. Bold italicized entries in the table are the author's alternative party coding, which is used when a candidate listed a major party name (Democrat, Republican, or their historical antecedents) on the ballot with other party names or labels. For a more detailed explanation of this alternative party coding system, see Tables 6-10 and 1-3. —indicates that the state had no data, either because the state had no Senate election, no vote data were found for the state in question, or the state had not yet entered the Union. No special Senate elections are included in this table.

Sources: *Congressional Quarterly's Guide to U.S. Elections* (1994), ICPSR data sets 0001 and 0075, and independent search of state sources by the author. For some party affiliations, the labels were taken from Michael J. Dubin's election archive after verification by the author.

Table 6-34 Senate Election Results, by State, 1916–1918 (Raw Count)

State	1916				1918			
	Democratic	Republican	Other	Total Vote	Democratic	Republican	Other	Total Vote
Alabama	—	—	—	—	54,880	0	0	54,880
Alaska	—	—	—	—	—	—	—	—
Arizona	29,882	21,261	2,827	53,970	—	—	—	—
Arkansas	—	—	—	—	78,386	0	0	78,386
California	277,852	0	663,104	940,956	—	—	—	—
California	*277,852*	*574,667*	*88,437*	*940,956*	—	—	—	—
Colorado	—	—	—	—	104,347	107,726	5,606	217,679
Connecticut	98,649	107,020	7,675	213,344	—	—	—	—
Delaware	25,434	22,925	2,851	51,210	20,113	21,519	420	42,052
Florida	58,391	8,774	3,304	70,469	—	—	—	—
Georgia	—	—	—	—	53,731	7,078	0	60,809
Hawaii	—	—	—	—	—	—	—	—
Idaho	—	—	—	—	31,018	63,587	0	94,605
Illinois	—	—	—	—	426,943	479,957	43,586	950,486
Indiana	325,588	337,089	42,990	705,667	—	—	—	—
Iowa	—	—	—	—	121,830	230,264	0	352,094
Kansas	—	—	—	—	149,300	281,931	11,423	442,654
Kentucky	—	—	—	—	184,385	178,797	0	363,182
Louisiana	—	—	—	—	44,224	0	0	44,224
Maine	69,486	79,841	1,789	151,116	53,460	66,858	0	120,318
Maryland	109,740	113,662	7,058	230,460	—	—	—	—
Massachusetts	234,238	267,177	15,584	516,999	207,478	188,287	22,077	417,842
Michigan	257,954	364,657	24,667	647,278	212,487	220,054	5,911	438,452
Minnesota	117,541	185,159	78,425	381,125	0	206,687	137,294	343,981
Mississippi	74,290	0	0	74,290	30,055	0	1,569	31,624
Missouri	396,166	371,710	15,616	783,492	—	—	—	—
Montana	85,585	72,753	9,292	167,630	46,160	40,229	26,013	112,402
Nebraska	0	0	286,295	286,295	99,696	119,486	0	219,182
Nebraska	*143,082*	*131,359*	*11,854*	*286,295*	—	—	—	—
Nevada	12,765	10,618	9,507	32,890	—	—	—	—
New Hampshire	—	—	—	—	32,763	37,787	0	70,550
New Jersey	170,019	244,715	22,362	437,096	153,743	179,022	22,843	355,608
New Mexico	34,142	30,622	2,033	66,797	22,470	24,322	531	47,323
New York	0	839,314	705,875	1,545,189	—	—	—	—
New York	*605,933*	*839,314*	*99,942*	*1,545,189*	—	—	—	—
North Carolina	—	—	—	—	143,519	93,707	0	237,226
North Dakota	40,988	57,714	8,472	107,174	—	—	—	—
Ohio	571,488	535,391	53,212	1,160,091	—	—	—	—
Oklahoma	—	—	—	—	105,050	77,188	7,259	189,497
Oregon	—	—	—	—	64,303	82,360	5,373	152,036
Pennsylvania	450,112	0	758,345	1,208,457	—	—	—	—
Pennsylvania	*450,112*	*680,451*	*77,894*	*1,208,457*	—	—	—	—
Rhode Island	47,048	39,211	2,618	88,877	37,573	42,055	1,623	81,251
South Carolina	—	—	—	—	25,792	0	0	25,792
South Dakota	—	—	—	—	36,210	51,198	5,560	92,968
Tennessee	143,718	118,174	2,183	264,075	98,605	59,989	0	158,594
Texas	303,035	48,788	20,938	372,761	155,178	22,214	1,658	179,050
Utah	0	56,862	85,554	142,416	—	—	—	—
Utah	*81,057*	*56,862*	*4,497*	*142,416*	—	—	—	—
Vermont	14,956	47,362	1,480	63,798	—	—	—	—
Virginia	133,091	0	112	133,203	40,403	0	131	40,534
Washington	135,339	202,287	27,563	365,189	—	—	—	—
West Virginia	138,585	144,243	4,877	287,705	97,715	115,216	2,288	215,219
Wisconsin	135,144	251,303	37,436	423,883	—	—	—	—
Wyoming	26,324	23,258	1,565	51,147	17,528	23,975	0	41,503

Notes: Main entries are raw vote values for candidates who used the sole designation "Democrat" or "Republican" (or their historical antecedents listed in Appendix A) on the ballot. Other = candidates who used third-party names on the ballot or were listed as independent, unidentified, or scatter vote. Bold italicized entries in the table are the author's alternative party coding, which is used when a candidate listed a major party name (Democrat, Republican, or their historical antecedents) on the ballot with other party names or labels. For a more detailed explanation of this alternative party coding system, see Tables 6-10 and 1-3. —indicates that the state had no data, either because the state had no Senate election, no vote data were found for the state in question, or the state had not yet entered the Union. No special Senate elections are included in this table.

Sources: *Congressional Quarterly's Guide to U.S. Elections* (1994), ICPSR data sets 0001 and 0075, and independent search of state sources by the author. For some party affiliations, the labels were taken from Michael J. Dubin's election archive after verification by the author.

Table 6-35 Senate Election Results, by State, 1920–1922 (Raw Count)

State	1920 Democratic	1920 Republican	1920 Other	1920 Total Vote	1922 Democratic	1922 Republican	1922 Other	1922 Total Vote
Alabama	155,664	71,334	1,984	228,982	—	—	—	—
Alaska	—	—	—	—				
Arizona	29,169	35,893	0	65,062	39,722	21,358	0	61,080
Arkansas	126,577	65,381	0	191,958	—			
California	371,580	447,835	94,354	913,769	215,748	564,422	127,925	908,095
Colorado	112,890	156,577	17,733	287,200	—	—	—	—
Connecticut	131,824	216,792	16,572	365,188	147,276	169,524	7,106	323,906
Delaware	—	—			37,304	36,979	608	74,891
Florida	98,966	27,914	6,380	133,260	45,707	0	6,243	51,950
Florida	*98,966*	*30,761*	*3,533*	*133,260*	*45,707*	*6,074*	*169*	*51,950*
Georgia	124,630	0	6,700	131,330	—	—	—	—
Hawaii	—				—	—	—	—
Idaho	64,513	75,985	0	140,498	—	—	—	—
Illinois	554,372	1,381,384	131,289	2,067,045	—	—	—	—
Indiana	514,191	681,854	53,522	1,249,567	558,169	524,558	14,635	1,097,362
Iowa	322,015	528,499	9,956	860,470	—	—	—	—
Kansas	170,443	327,072	13,418	510,933	—	—	—	—
Kentucky	449,244	454,226	0	903,470	—	—	—	—
Louisiana	94,944	0	0	94,944	—	—	—	—
Maine	—	—	—	—	74,659	101,026	0	175,685
Maryland	169,200	184,999	37,011	391,210	160,947	139,581	5,387	305,915
Massachusetts	—	—	—	—	406,776	414,130	49,251	870,157
Michigan	—	—	—	—	294,932	281,843	6,195	582,970
Minnesota	—	—	—	—	123,624	241,833	325,372	690,829
Mississippi	—	—	—	—	63,636	1,273	3,362	68,271
Missouri	589,498	711,161	24,860	1,325,519	506,267	462,009	8,089	976,365
Montana	—	—	—	—	88,205	69,464	1,545	159,214
Nebraska	—	—	—	—	148,265	220,350	19,076	387,691
Nevada	10,402	11,550	5,475	27,427	18,201	10,770	0	28,971
New Hampshire	65,035	90,173	1,004	156,212	—	—	—	—
New Jersey	—	—	—	—	451,832	362,699	8,907	823,438
New Mexico	—	—	—	—	60,969	48,721	818	110,508
New York	901,310	1,434,393	403,614	2,739,317	1,276,667	995,421	155,126	2,427,214
North Carolina	310,504	229,343	0	539,847	—	—	—	—
North Dakota	0	0	218,379	218,379	0	0	193,776	193,776
North Dakota	*87,765*	*130,614*	*0*	*218,379*	*92,464*	*101,312*	*0*	*193,776*
Ohio	782,650	1,134,953	2,647	1,920,250	744,558	794,149	21,514	1,560,221
Oklahoma	218,371	247,721	23,663	489,755	—	—	—	—
Oregon	100,124	116,696	13,187	230,007	—	—	—	—
Pennsylvania	484,862	1,068,985	229,492	1,783,339	423,583	802,146	205,756	1,431,485
Rhode Island	—	—			82,889	68,930	7,070	158,889
South Carolina	64,388	0	1	64,389	—	—	—	—
South Dakota	36,833	92,267	55,079	184,179	—	—	—	—
Tennessee	—	—	—	—	151,523	71,199	0	222,722
Texas	—	—	—	—	261,063	130,731	0	391,794
Utah	56,280	82,566	7,012	145,858	58,749	58,188	3,886	120,823
Vermont	19,580	69,650	41	89,271	21,375	45,284	0	66,659
Virginia	—	—	—	—	116,393	42,903	2,627	161,923
Washington	68,488	217,069	99,309	384,866	130,375	126,556	37,746	294,677
West Virginia	—	—	—	—	198,853	185,046	4,895	388,794
Wisconsin	89,265	281,576	306,308	677,149	0	379,494	91,324	470,818
Wisconsin	—	—	—	—	*78,029*	*379,494*	*13,295*	*470,818*
Wyoming	—	—	—	—	35,734	26,627	612	62,973

Notes: Main entries are raw vote values for candidates who used the sole designation "Democrat" or "Republican" (or their historical antecedents listed in Appendix A) on the ballot. Other = candidates who used third-party names on the ballot or were listed as independent, unidentified, or scatter vote. Bold italicized entries in the table are the author's alternative party coding, which is used when a candidate listed a major party name (Democrat, Republican, or their historical antecedents) on the ballot with other party names or labels. For a more detailed explanation of this alternative party coding system, see Tables 6-10 and 1-3. —indicates that the state had no data, either because the state had no Senate election, no vote data were found for the state in question, or the state had not yet entered the Union. No special Senate elections are included in this table.

Sources: *Congressional Quarterly's Guide to U.S. Elections* (1994), ICPSR data sets 0001 and 0075, and independent search of state sources by the author. For some party affiliations, the labels were taken from Michael J. Dubin's election archive after verification by the author.

Table 6-36 Senate Election Results, by State, 1924–1926 (Raw Count)

	1924				1926			
State	Democratic	Republican	Other	Total Vote	Democratic	Republican	Other	Total Vote
Alabama	120,017	39,623	0	159,640	91,843	21,722	0	113,565
Alaska	—	—	—	—	—	—	—	—
Arizona	—	—	—	—	44,591	31,845	0	76,436
Arkansas	100,408	36,163	0	136,571	28,064	5,848	0	33,912
California	—	—	—	—	391,599	670,128	127	1,061,854
Colorado	139,660	159,698	18,811	318,169	138,113	149,585	9,997	297,695
Connecticut	—	—	—	—	107,753	191,401	3,173	302,327
Delaware	0	52,731	36,085	88,816	—	—	—	—
Florida	—	—	—	—	51,054	6,133	8,381	65,568
Florida	—	—	—	—	*51,054*	*14,514*	*0*	*65,568*
Georgia	155,497	0	0	155,497	47,446	0	0	47,446
Hawaii	—	—	—	—	—	—	—	—
Idaho	25,199	99,846	554	125,599	31,285	56,847	37,047	125,179
Illinois	806,702	1,449,180	24,965	2,280,847	774,943	842,273	180,143	1,797,359
Illinois	—	—	—	—	*779,146*	*998,518*	*19,695*	*1,797,359*
Indiana	—	—	—	—	511,454	522,737	10,526	1,044,717
Iowa	446,840	447,594	0	894,434	247,869	323,409	908	572,186
Kansas	154,189	428,494	28,607	611,290	168,446	308,222	8,210	484,878
Kentucky	381,605	406,123	0	787,728	286,997	266,567	0	553,564
Louisiana	94,939	0	0	94,939	54,180	0	13	54,193
Maine	97,428	148,783	0	246,211	—	—	—	—
Maryland	—	—	—	—	195,410	139,995	3,659	339,064
Massachusetts	547,600	566,188	12,738	1,126,526	—	—	—	—
Michigan	284,609	858,934	13,183	1,156,726	—	—	—	—
Minnesota	53,709	388,594	394,260	836,563	—	—	—	—
Mississippi	97,257	0	0	97,257	—	—	—	—
Missouri	—	—	—	—	506,015	470,654	9,817	986,486
Montana	89,681	72,005	8,180	169,866	—	—	—	—
Nebraska	0	274,640	165,370	440,010	—	—	—	—
Nebraska	*165,370*	*274,640*	*0*	*440,010*	—	—	—	—
Nevada	—	—	—	—	13,273	17,430	543	31,246
New Hampshire	63,596	94,432	0	158,028	47,935	79,279	0	127,214
New Jersey	331,034	608,020	44,121	983,175	—	—	—	—
New Mexico	57,355	54,558	3,128	115,041	—	—	—	—
New York	—	—	—	—	1,321,463	1,205,246	316,121	2,842,830
New York	—	—	—	—	*1,321,463*	*1,437,152*	*84,215*	*2,842,830*
North Carolina	295,344	184,493	0	479,837	218,934	142,891	0	361,825
North Dakota	—	—	—	—	13,519	107,921	33,666	155,106
North Dakota	—	—	—	—	*13,519*	*117,659*	*23,928*	*155,106*
Ohio	—	—	—	—	623,221	711,359	2,846	1,337,426
Oklahoma	196,527	341,720	15,637	553,884	195,307	159,287	1,933	356,527
Oregon	65,340	174,672	24,791	264,803	81,301	89,007	53,391	223,699
Pennsylvania	—	—	—	—	0	822,187	682,511	1,504,698
Pennsylvania	—	—	—	—	*648,680*	*822,187*	*33,831*	*1,504,698*
Rhode Island	87,620	120,815	1,191	209,626	—	—	—	—
South Carolina	49,060	0	0	49,060	14,560	0	0	14,560
South Dakota	63,548	90,006	29,578	183,132	71,925	105,756	0	177,681
Tennessee	147,821	109,863	247	257,931	—	—	—	—
Texas	592,057	101,252	0	693,309	—	—	—	—
Utah	—	—	—	—	53,809	88,101	1,315	143,225
Vermont	—	—	—	—	18,878	0	52,338	71,216
Vermont	—	—	—	—	*18,878*	*52,286*	*52*	*71,216*
Virginia	151,498	5,594	50,093	207,185	—	—	—	—
Washington	—	—	—	—	152,229	164,130	3,513	319,872
West Virginia	271,809	290,004	7,751	569,564	—	—	—	—
Wisconsin	—	—	—	—	66,672	300,759	179,207	546,638
Wisconsin	—	—	—	—	*66,672*	*411,881*	*68,085*	*546,638*
Wyoming	33,536	41,293	3,029	77,858	—	—	—	—

Notes: Main entries are raw vote values for candidates who used the sole designation "Democrat" or "Republican" (or their historical antecedents listed in Appendix A) on the ballot. Other = candidates who used third-party names on the ballot or were listed as independent, unidentified, or scatter vote. Bold italicized entries in the table are the author's alternative party coding, which is used when a candidate listed a major party name (Democrat, Republican, or their historical antecedents) on the ballot with other party names or labels. For a more detailed explanation of this alternative party coding system, see Tables 6-10 and 1-3. —indicates that the state had no data, either because the state had no Senate election, no vote data were found for the state in question, or the state had not yet entered the Union. No special Senate elections are included in this table.

Sources: *Congressional Quarterly's Guide to U.S. Elections* (1994), ICPSR data sets 0001 and 0075, and independent search of state sources by the author. For some party affiliations, the labels were taken from Michael J. Dubin's election archive after verification by the author.

Table 6-37 Senate Election Results, by State, 1928–1930 (Raw Count)

State	1928 Democratic	Republican	Other	Total Vote	1930 Democratic	Republican	Other	Total Vote
Alabama	—	—	—	—	150,985	0	101,862	252,847
Alaska	—	—	—	—	—	—	—	—
Arizona	47,013	39,651	0	86,664	—	—	—	—
Arkansas	—	—	—	—	141,806	0	0	141,806
California	282,411	1,148,397	118,988	1,549,796	—	—	—	—
Colorado	—	—	—	—	180,028	137,487	4,833	322,348
Connecticut	251,429	296,958	3,014	551,401	—	—	—	—
Delaware	40,828	63,725	0	104,553	39,881	47,909	135	87,925
Florida	153,816	70,633	2	224,451	—	—	—	—
Georgia	—	—	—	—	55,606	0	1	55,607
Hawaii	—	—	—	—	—	—	—	—
Idaho	—	—	—	—	36,162	94,938	0	131,100
Illinois	—	—	—	—	1,432,216	687,469	117,419	2,237,104
Illinois	—	—	—	—	*1,432,216*	*786,954*	*17,934*	*2,237,104*
Indiana	623,996	782,144	8,300	1,414,440	—	—	—	—
Iowa	—	—	—	—	235,186	307,613	3,715	546,514
Kansas	—	—	—	—	232,161	364,548	0	596,709
Kentucky	—	—	—	—	336,748	309,180	0	645,928
Louisiana	—	—	—	—	130,536	0	24	130,560
Maine	63,429	145,501	0	208,930	56,561	88,262	0	144,823
Maryland	214,447	256,224	3,396	474,067	—	—	—	—
Massachusetts	818,055	693,563	13,335	1,524,953	651,939	539,226	15,871	1,207,036
Michigan	376,592	977,893	7,663	1,362,148	169,757	634,577	7,673	812,007
Minnesota	0	342,992	674,549	1,017,541	282,018	293,626	204,985	780,629
Mississippi	111,210	0	0	111,210	33,953	0	0	33,953
Missouri	726,322	787,499	3,102	1,516,923	—	—	—	—
Montana	103,655	91,185	0	194,840	106,274	66,724	3,163	176,161
Nebraska	204,737	324,014	0	528,751	172,795	247,118	14,884	434,797
Nevada	19,515	13,414	0	32,929	—	—	—	—
New Hampshire	—	—	—	—	52,284	72,225	282	124,791
New Jersey	608,623	841,752	4,252	1,454,627	401,007	601,497	25,719	1,028,223
New Mexico	49,913	68,070	4	117,987	69,356	48,699	254	118,309
New York	2,084,273	2,034,014	128,711	4,246,998	—	—	—	—
North Carolina	—	—	—	—	324,293	210,761	0	535,054
North Dakota	38,856	159,940	2,047	200,843	—	—	—	—
Ohio	908,952	1,412,805	4,448	2,326,205	—	—	—	—
Oklahoma	—	—	—	—	255,838	232,589	832	489,259
Oregon	—	—	—	—	66,028	137,231	33,112	236,371
Pennsylvania	1,029,055	1,948,646	49,168	3,026,869	—	—	—	—
Rhode Island	116,234	119,228	313	235,775	109,687	112,202	1,195	223,084
South Carolina	—	—	—	—	16,213	0	0	16,213
South Dakota	—	—	—	—	106,317	99,595	0	205,912
Tennessee	175,431	120,289	0	295,720	154,071	58,550	3,392	216,013
Texas	566,139	130,172	804	697,115	266,562	39,053	1,100	306,715
Utah	97,436	77,073	998	175,507	—	—	—	—
Vermont	37,030	93,136	11	130,177	—	—	—	—
Virginia	275,425	0	623	276,048	112,002	0	34,094	146,096
Washington	261,524	227,415	666	489,605	—	—	—	—
West Virginia	317,620	327,266	919	645,805	342,467	209,427	1,293	553,187
Wisconsin	0	635,376	107,177	742,553	—	—	—	—
Wisconsin	*0*	*716,678*	*25,875*	*742,553*	—	—	—	—
Wyoming	43,032	37,076	333	80,441	30,259	43,626	0	73,885

Notes: Main entries are raw vote values for candidates who used the sole designation "Democrat" or "Republican" (or their historical antecedents listed in Appendix A) on the ballot. Other = candidates who used third-party names on the ballot or were listed as independent, unidentified, or scatter vote. Bold italicized entries in the table are the author's alternative party coding, which is used when a candidate listed a major party name (Democrat, Republican, or their historical antecedents) on the ballot with other party names or labels. For a more detailed explanation of this alternative party coding system, see Tables 6-10 and 1-3. —indicates that the state had no data, either because the state had no Senate election, no vote data were found for the state in question, or the state had not yet entered the Union. No special Senate elections are included in this table.

Sources: *Congressional Quarterly's Guide to U.S. Elections* (1994), ICPSR data sets 0001 and 0075, and independent search of state sources by the author. For some party affiliations, the labels were taken from Michael J. Dubin's election archive after verification by the author.

Table 6-38 Senate Election Results, by State, 1932–1934 (Raw Count)

State	1932 Democratic	1932 Republican	1932 Other	1932 Total Vote	1934 Democratic	1934 Republican	1934 Other	1934 Total Vote
Alabama	209,614	33,425	1	243,040	—	—	—	—
Alaska	—	—	—	—	—	—	—	—
Arizona	74,310	35,737	1,416	111,463	67,648	24,075	2,197	93,920
Arkansas	183,795	21,597	0	205,392	—	—	—	—
California	943,164	669,676	560,994	2,173,834	0	0	2,058,940	2,058,940
California	*—*	*—*	*—*	*—*	*0*	*1,946,572*	*112,368*	*2,058,940*
Colorado	226,516	198,519	11,304	436,339	—	—	—	—
Connecticut	282,327	278,061	34,014	594,402	265,552	247,623	35,350	548,525
Connecticut	*282,327*	*288,682*	*23,393*	*594,402*	*—*	*—*	*—*	*—*
Delaware	—	—	—	—	45,771	52,829	566	99,166
Florida	204,651	0	459	205,110	131,780	0	0	131,780
Georgia	234,590	18,151	0	252,741	—	—	—	—
Hawaii	—	—	—	—	—	—	—	—
Idaho	103,020	78,225	3,801	185,046	—	—	—	—
Illinois	1,670,466	1,471,841	55,828	3,198,135	—	—	—	—
Indiana	870,053	661,750	33,947	1,565,750	758,801	700,103	15,708	1,474,612
Iowa	538,422	399,929	55,945	994,296	—	—	—	—
Kansas	328,992	302,809	88,607	720,408	—	—	—	—
Kentucky	574,977	393,865	3,291	972,133	—	—	—	—
Louisiana	249,189	0	3	249,192	—	—	—	—
Maine	—	—	—	—	138,573	139,773	422	278,768
Maryland	293,389	138,266	11,413	443,068	264,279	197,643	9,190	471,112
Massachusetts	—	—	—	—	852,776	536,692	46,464	1,435,932
Michigan	—	—	—	—	573,574	626,017	20,143	1,219,734
Minnesota	—	—	—	—	294,757	200,083	514,617	1,009,457
Mississippi	—	—	—	—	51,709	0	0	51,709
Missouri	1,017,046	577,184	15,518	1,609,748	787,110	524,954	9,812	1,321,876
Montana	—	—	—	—	142,823	59,900	903	203,626
Nebraska	—	—	—	—	305,858	237,126	10,171	553,155
Nevada	21,398	19,706	0	41,104	27,581	14,273	901	42,755
New Hampshire	98,766	96,649	761	196,176	—	—	—	—
New Jersey	—	—	—	—	785,971	554,483	16,955	1,357,409
New Mexico	—	—	—	—	74,944	76,228	690	151,862
New York	2,532,905	1,751,186	257,289	4,541,380	2,046,377	1,363,440	288,001	3,697,818
North Carolina	476,048	221,392	0	697,440	—	—	—	—
North Dakota	65,575	172,796	543	238,914	104,477	151,205	3,925	259,607
Ohio	1,290,175	1,126,830	41,987	2,458,992	1,276,206	839,068	13,569	2,128,843
Oklahoma	426,130	218,854	4,520	649,504	—	—	—	—
Oregon	137,237	186,210	29,692	353,139	—	—	—	—
Pennsylvania	1,200,767	1,371,844	208,420	2,781,031	1,494,001	1,366,877	81,399	2,942,277
Rhode Island	—	—	—	—	140,700	105,545	68	246,313
South Carolina	104,472	1,976	0	106,448	—	—	—	—
South Dakota	125,731	151,845	4,516	282,092	—	—	—	—
Tennessee	—	—	—	—	195,430	110,401	2,443	308,274
Texas	—	—	—	—	437,254	12,859	2,146	452,259
Utah	116,909	86,066	3,347	206,322	95,931	82,154	2,707	180,792
Vermont	60,453	74,319	21	134,793	63,632	67,146	774	131,552
Virginia	—	—	—	—	109,963	30,289	4,498	144,750
Washington	365,949	197,450	40,406	603,805	302,606	168,994	25,088	496,688
West Virginia	—	—	—	—	349,882	281,756	2,933	634,571
Wisconsin	610,236	387,668	73,092	1,070,996	223,438	210,569	487,919	921,926
Wyoming	—	—	—	—	53,806	40,819	401	95,026

Notes: Main entries are raw vote values for candidates who used the sole designation "Democrat" or "Republican" (or their historical antecedents listed in Appendix A) on the ballot. Other = candidates who used third-party names on the ballot or were listed as independent, unidentified, or scatter vote. Bold italicized entries in the table are the author's alternative party coding, which is used when a candidate listed a major party name (Democrat, Republican, or their historical antecedents) on the ballot with other party names or labels. For a more detailed explanation of this alternative party coding system, see Tables 6-10 and 1-3. —indicates that the state had no data, either because the state had no Senate election, no vote data were found for the state in question, or the state had not yet entered the Union. No special Senate elections are included in this table.

Sources: *Congressional Quarterly's Guide to U.S. Elections* (1994), ICPSR data sets 0001 and 0075, and independent search of state sources by the author. For some party affiliations, the labels were taken from Michael J. Dubin's election archive after verification by the author.

Table 6-39 Senate Election Results, by State, 1936–1938 (Raw Count)

State	1936 Democratic	Republican	Other	Total Vote	1938 Democratic	Republican	Other	Total Vote
Alabama	239,632	33,698	2,023	275,353	113,413	17,885	0	131,298
Alaska	—	—	—	—				
Arizona	—	—	—	—	82,714	25,378	0	108,092
Arkansas	155,075	30,997	3,425	189,497	122,871	14,240	0	137,111
California	—	—	—	—	0	1,126,240	1,395,902	2,522,142
California					*1,372,314*	*1,126,240*	*23,588*	*2,522,142*
Colorado	299,376	166,308	6,143	471,827	262,806	181,297	7,126	451,229
Connecticut	—	—	—	—	0	270,413	360,020	630,433
Connecticut	—	—	—	—	*252,426*	*270,413*	*107,594*	*630,433*
Delaware	67,136	52,460	7,133	126,729	—	—	—	—
Florida	—	—	—	—	145,757	31,035	0	176,792
Georgia	263,468	0	0	263,468	66,897	0	3,442	70,339
Hawaii	—	—	—	—				
Idaho	74,444	128,723	0	203,167	99,801	81,939	845	182,585
Illinois	2,142,887	1,545,160	106,549	3,794,596	1,638,162	1,542,574	10,707	3,191,443
Indiana	—	—	—	—	788,386	783,189	10,215	1,581,790
Iowa	539,555	503,635	28,526	1,071,716	413,788	410,983	7,068	831,839
Kansas	396,685	417,873	4,810	819,368	326,774	419,532	99	746,405
Kentucky	539,968	365,850	12,509	918,327	346,735	212,266	0	559,001
Louisiana	293,256	0	7	293,263	151,585	0	250	151,835
Maine	153,420	158,068	0	311,488	—	—	—	—
Maryland	—	—	—	—	357,245	153,253	12,740	523,238
Massachusetts	739,751	875,160	188,446	1,803,357	—	—	—	—
Michigan	910,937	714,602	84,025	1,709,564	—	—	—	—
Minnesota	0	402,404	663,363	1,065,767	—	—	—	—
Mississippi	140,570	0	0	140,570	—	—	—	—
Missouri	—	—	—	—	757,587	488,687	2,003	1,248,277
Montana	121,769	60,038	39,655	221,462	—	—	—	—
Nebraska	108,391	223,276	258,700	590,367	—	—	—	—
Nevada	—	—	—	—	27,406	19,078	0	46,484
New Hampshire	99,195	107,923	989	208,107	84,920	100,633	0	185,553
New Jersey	916,414	740,088	12,789	1,669,291	—	—	—	—
New Mexico	104,550	64,817	76	169,443	—	—	—	—
New York	—	—	—	—	0	0	4,583,059	4,583,059
New York	—	—	—	—	*2,497,029*	*2,058,615*	*27,415*	*4,583,059*
North Carolina	564,088	233,000	0	797,088	316,685	179,461	0	496,146
North Dakota	—	—	—	—	19,244	131,907	112,007	263,158
Ohio	—	—	—	—	1,086,815	1,257,412	0	2,344,227
Oklahoma	493,407	229,004	3,510	725,921	307,936	159,734	3,396	471,066
Oregon	193,822	199,332	7,976	401,130	167,135	203,120	6	370,261
Pennsylvania	—	—	—	—	0	2,086,932	1,728,087	3,815,019
Pennsylvania	—	—	—	—	*1,694,464*	*2,086,932*	*33,623*	*3,815,019*
Rhode Island	149,157	136,174	21,501	306,832	—	—	—	—
South Carolina	113,696	1,663	0	115,359	45,751	508	2	46,261
South Dakota	141,509	135,461	12,816	289,786	133,064	146,813	0	279,877
Tennessee	273,298	67,238	17,143	357,679	—	—	—	—
Texas	773,574	59,491	2,731	835,796	—	—	—	—
Utah	—	—	—	—	102,353	81,071	0	183,424
Vermont	—	—	—	—	38,673	73,990	4	112,667
Virginia	244,518	12,473	9,675	266,666	—	—	—	—
Virginia	*244,987*	*12,473*	*9,206*	*266,666*	—	—	—	—
Washington	—	—	—	—	371,535	220,204	1,553	593,292
West Virginia	488,620	338,363	1,940	828,923	—	—	—	—
Wisconsin	—	—	—	—	231,976	446,770	258,757	937,503
Wisconsin	—	—	—	—	*231,976*	*454,021*	*251,506*	*937,503*
Wyoming	53,919	45,483	770	100,172	—	—	—	—

Notes: Main entries are raw vote values for candidates who used the sole designation "Democrat" or "Republican" (or their historical antecedents listed in Appendix A) on the ballot. Other = candidates who used third-party names on the ballot or were listed as independent, unidentified, or scatter vote. Bold italicized entries in the table are the author's alternative party coding, which is used when a candidate listed a major party name (Democrat, Republican, or their historical antecedents) on the ballot with other party names or labels. For a more detailed explanation of this alternative party coding system, see Tables 6-10 and 1-3. —indicates that the state had no data, either because the state had no Senate election, no vote data were found for the state in question, or the state had not yet entered the Union. No special Senate elections are included in this table.

Sources: *Congressional Quarterly's Guide to U.S. Elections* (1994), ICPSR data sets 0001 and 0075, and independent search of state sources by the author. For some party affiliations, the labels were taken from Michael J. Dubin's election archive after verification by the author.

Table 6-40 Senate Election Results, by State, 1940–1942 (Raw Count)

State	1940				1942			
	Democratic	Republican	Other	Total Vote	Democratic	Republican	Other	Total Vote
Alabama	—	—	—	—	69,212	0	4	69,216
Alaska	—	—	—	—	—	—	—	—
Arizona	101,495	39,657	579	141,731	—	—	—	—
Arkansas	—	—	—	—	99,126	0	0	99,126
California	0	0	2,713,865	2,713,865	—	—	—	—
California	*0*	*2,238,899*	*474,966*	*2,713,865*	—	—	—	—
Colorado	—	—	—	—	174,612	170,970	2,014	347,596
Connecticut	416,740	0	367,327	784,067	—	—	—	—
Connecticut	*416,740*	*358,313*	*9,014*	*784,067*	—	—	—	—
Delaware	68,294	63,799	2,786	134,879	38,322	46,210	776	85,308
Delaware	*71,080*	*63,799*	*0*	*134,879*	—	—	—	—
Florida	323,216	0	0	323,216	—	—	—	—
Georgia	—	—	—	—	59,870	0	1,892	61,762
Hawaii	—	—	—	—	—	—	—	—
Idaho	—	—	—	—	68,989	73,353	0	142,342
Illinois	—	—	—	—	1,380,011	1,582,887	10,331	2,973,229
Indiana	864,803	888,070	7,372	1,760,245	—	—	—	—
Iowa	—	—	—	—	295,194	410,333	2,282	707,809
Kansas	—	—	—	—	200,437	284,059	12,863	497,359
Kentucky	—	—	—	—	216,958	175,081	0	392,039
Louisiana	—	—	—	—	85,488	0	0	85,488
Maine	105,740	150,149	305	256,194	55,754	111,520	0	167,274
Maryland	394,239	203,912	10,824	608,975	—	—	—	—
Massachusetts	1,088,838	838,122	30,129	1,957,089	641,042	721,239	13,163	1,375,444
Michigan	939,740	1,053,104	7,499	2,000,343	561,595	589,652	38,719	1,189,966
Michigan	—	—	—	—	*561,595*	*621,825*	*6,546*	*1,189,966*
Minnesota	248,658	641,049	319,892	1,209,599	78,959	356,297	323,196	758,452
Mississippi	143,333	0	0	143,333	51,355	0	0	51,355
Missouri	930,775	886,376	1,865	1,819,016	—	—	—	—
Montana	176,753	63,941	0	240,694	83,673	82,461	4,380	170,514
Nebraska	247,659	340,250	8,982	596,891	83,763	186,207	110,199	380,169
Nevada	31,351	20,488	0	51,839	—	—	—	—
New Hampshire	—	—	—	—	73,656	88,601	0	162,257
New Jersey	823,893	1,029,331	14,551	1,867,775	559,851	648,855	13,426	1,222,132
New Mexico	103,194	81,257	0	184,451	63,301	43,704	0	107,005
New York	0	2,868,852	3,279,722	6,148,574	—	—	—	—
New York	*3,274,766*	*2,868,852*	*4,956*	*6,148,574*	—	—	—	—
North Carolina	—	—	—	—	230,427	119,165	0	349,592
North Dakota	69,847	100,647	93,607	264,101	—	—	—	—
Ohio	1,457,359	1,602,567	0	3,059,926	—	—	—	—
Oklahoma	—	—	—	—	166,653	204,163	1,549	372,365
Oregon	—	—	—	—	63,946	214,755	3	278,704
Pennsylvania	2,069,980	1,893,104	33,936	3,997,020	—	—	—	—
Rhode Island	173,847	141,312	0	315,159	138,239	100,236	0	238,475
South Carolina	—	—	—	—	23,356	0	2	23,358
South Dakota	—	—	—	—	74,945	106,704	0	181,649
Tennessee	295,440	121,790	34	417,264	109,881	34,324	15,317	159,522
Texas	993,974	60,051	406	1,054,431	260,629	12,054	1,975	274,658
Utah	155,499	91,931	0	247,430	—	—	—	—
Vermont	47,101	93,283	4	140,388	—	—	—	—
Virginia	274,260	0	19,621	293,881	79,421	0	7,731	87,152
Washington	404,718	342,589	0	747,307	—	—	—	—
West Virginia	492,413	381,806	0	874,219	207,045	256,816	0	463,861
Wisconsin	176,688	553,692	607,755	1,338,135	—	—	—	—
Wyoming	65,022	45,682	0	110,704	34,503	41,486	0	75,989

Notes: Main entries are raw vote values for candidates who used the sole designation "Democrat" or "Republican" (or their historical antecedents listed in Appendix A) on the ballot. Other = candidates who used third-party names on the ballot or were listed as independent, unidentified, or scatter vote. Bold italicized entries in the table are the author's alternative party coding, which is used when a candidate listed a major party name (Democrat, Republican, or their historical antecedents) on the ballot with other party names or labels. For a more detailed explanation of this alternative party coding system, see Tables 6-10 and 1-3. —indicates that the state had no data, either because the state had no Senate election, no vote data were found for the state in question, or the state had not yet entered the Union. No special Senate elections are included in this table.

Sources: *Congressional Quarterly's Guide to U.S. Elections* (1994), ICPSR data sets 0001 and 0075, and independent search of state sources by the author. For some party affiliations, the labels were taken from Michael J. Dubin's election archive after verification by the author.

Table 6-41 Senate Election Results, by State, 1944–1946 (Raw Count)

State	1944 Democratic	1944 Republican	1944 Other	1944 Total Vote	1946 Democratic	1946 Republican	1946 Other	1946 Total Vote
Alabama	202,604	41,983	3,162	247,749	—	—	—	—
Alaska	—	—	—	—	—	—	—	—
Arizona	90,335	39,891	0	130,226	80,415	35,022	802	116,239
Arkansas	182,529	31,942	0	214,471	—	—	—	—
California	1,728,155	1,576,553	526	3,305,234	1,167,161	1,428,067	44,237	2,639,465
Colorado	214,335	277,410	3,143	494,888	—	—	—	—
Connecticut	430,716	391,748	6,033	828,497	276,424	381,328	25,169	682,921
Delaware	—	—	—	—	50,910	62,603	0	113,513
Florida	335,685	135,258	0	470,943	156,232	42,413	0	198,645
Georgia	272,541	0	4	272,545	—	—	—	—
Hawaii	—	—	—	—	—	—	—	—
Idaho	107,096	102,373	0	209,469	—	—	—	—
Illinois	2,059,023	1,841,793	13,109	3,913,925	—	—	—	—
Indiana	807,766	829,489	14,130	1,651,385	584,288	739,809	23,337	1,347,434
Iowa	494,229	523,963	3,505	1,021,697	—	—	—	—
Kansas	272,053	387,090	10,057	669,200	—	—	—	—
Kentucky	464,053	380,425	2,148	846,626	—	—	—	—
Louisiana	286,365	0	26	286,391	—	—	—	—
Maine	—	—	—	—	63,799	111,215	0	175,014
Maryland	344,725	213,705	0	558,430	237,232	235,000	0	472,232
Massachusetts	—	—	—	—	660,200	989,736	12,127	1,662,063
Michigan	—	—	—	—	517,923	1,085,570	15,227	1,618,720
Minnesota	—	—	—	—	349,520	517,775	11,436	878,731
Mississippi	—	—	—	—	46,747	0	0	46,747
Missouri	777,229	779,029	1,535	1,557,793	511,544	572,556	2,141	1,086,241
Montana	—	—	—	—	86,476	101,901	2,189	190,566
Nebraska	—	—	—	—	111,751	271,208	0	382,959
Nevada	30,595	21,816	0	52,411	22,553	27,801	0	50,354
New Hampshire	106,508	110,549	0	217,057	—	—	—	—
New Jersey	—	—	—	—	548,458	799,808	18,889	1,367,155
New Mexico	—	—	—	—	68,650	64,632	0	133,282
New York	0	2,899,497	3,309,820	6,209,317	0	2,559,365	2,308,112	4,867,477
New York	**3,294,576**	**2,899,497**	**15,244**	**6,209,317**	**2,308,112**	**2,559,365**	**0**	**4,867,477**
North Carolina	533,813	226,037	0	759,850	—	—	—	—
North Dakota	95,102	69,530	45,790	210,422	38,368	88,210	38,804	165,382
North Dakota	**95,102**	**114,126**	**1,194**	**210,422**	—	—	—	—
Ohio	1,483,069	1,500,809	0	2,983,878	947,610	1,275,774	13,885	2,237,269
Oklahoma	390,851	309,222	2,321	702,394	—	—	—	—
Oregon	174,140	269,095	0	443,235	—	—	—	—
Pennsylvania	1,864,735	1,840,943	24,714	3,730,392	1,245,338	1,853,458	29,064	3,127,860
Rhode Island	—	—	—	—	150,748	122,780	0	273,528
South Carolina	94,556	3,214	3,966	101,736	—	—	—	—
South Carolina	**98,363**	**3,214**	**159**	**101,736**	—	—	—	—
South Dakota	82,199	145,248	0	227,447	—	—	—	—
Tennessee	—	—	—	—	145,654	57,237	15,819	218,710
Texas	—	—	—	—	336,931	43,619	0	380,550
Utah	148,748	99,532	0	248,280	96,257	101,142	0	197,399
Vermont	42,136	81,094	18	123,248	18,594	54,729	17	73,340
Virginia	—	—	—	—	163,960	77,005	11,898	252,863
Washington	452,013	364,356	3,510	819,879	298,683	358,847	2,812	660,342
West Virginia	—	—	—	—	273,151	269,617	0	542,768
Wisconsin	537,144	634,513	84,717	1,256,374	378,772	620,430	13,302	1,012,504
Wyoming	—	—	—	—	45,843	35,714	0	81,557

Notes: Main entries are raw vote values for candidates who used the sole designation "Democrat" or "Republican" (or their historical antecedents listed in Appendix A) on the ballot. Other = candidates who used third-party names on the ballot or were listed as independent, unidentified, or scatter vote. Bold italicized entries in the table are the author's alternative party coding, which is used when a candidate listed a major party name (Democrat, Republican, or their historical antecedents) on the ballot with other party names or labels. For a more detailed explanation of this alternative party coding system, see Tables 6-10 and 1-3. —indicates that the state had no data, either because the state had no Senate election, no vote data were found for the state in question, or the state had not yet entered the Union. No special Senate elections are included in this table.

Sources: *Congressional Quarterly's Guide to U.S. Elections* (1994), ICPSR data sets 0001 and 0075, and independent search of state sources by the author. For some party affiliations, the labels were taken from Michael J. Dubin's election archive after verification by the author.

Table 6-42 Senate Election Results, by State, 1948–1950 (Raw Count)

State	1948				1950			
	Democratic	Republican	Other	Total Vote	Democratic	Republican	Other	Total Vote
Alabama	185,534	35,341	0	220,875	125,534	0	38,477	164,011
Alaska	—	—	—	—	—	—	—	—
Arizona	—	—	—	—	116,246	68,846	0	185,092
Arkansas	216,401	0	15,521	231,922	302,582	0	0	302,582
California	—	—	—	—	1,502,507	2,183,454	354	3,686,315
Colorado	340,719	165,069	4,333	510,121	210,442	239,734	0	450,176
Connecticut	—	—	—	—	453,646	409,053	15,128	877,827
Delaware	71,888	68,246	1,228	141,362	—	—	—	—
Florida	—	—	—	—	238,987	74,228	272	313,487
Georgia	362,104	0	400	362,504	261,290	0	3	261,293
Hawaii	—	—	—	—	—	—	—	—
Idaho	107,000	103,868	3,320	214,188	77,180	124,237	0	201,417
Illinois	2,147,754	1,740,026	12,505	3,900,285	1,657,630	1,951,984	13,059	3,622,673
Indiana	—	—	—	—	741,025	844,303	13,396	1,598,724
Iowa	578,226	415,778	6,408	1,000,412	383,766	470,613	4,144	858,523
Iowa	—	—	—	—	*384,337*	*470,613*	*3,573*	*858,523*
Kansas	305,987	393,412	16,943	716,342	271,365	335,880	11,859	619,104
Kentucky	408,256	383,776	2,409	794,441	334,249	278,368	4,496	617,113
Louisiana	330,115	0	9	330,124	220,907	30,931	0	251,838
Maine	64,074	159,182	0	223,256	—	—	—	—
Maryland	—	—	—	—	283,180	326,291	6,143	615,614
Massachusetts	954,398	1,088,475	12,925	2,055,798	—	—	—	—
Michigan	1,000,329	1,045,156	16,612	2,062,097	—	—	—	—
Minnesota	729,494	485,801	4,955	1,220,250	—	—	—	—
Mississippi	151,478	0	0	151,478	—	—	—	—
Missouri	—	—	—	—	685,732	593,139	760	1,279,631
Montana	125,193	94,458	1,352	221,003	—	—	—	—
Nebraska	204,320	267,575	0	471,895	—	—	—	—
Nevada	—	—	—	—	35,829	25,933	0	61,762
New Hampshire	91,760	129,600	1,538	222,898	72,473	106,142	11,958	190,573
New Jersey	884,414	934,720	50,748	1,869,882	—	—	—	—
New Mexico	108,269	80,226	705	189,200	—	—	—	—
New York	—	—	—	—	0	2,367,353	2,861,050	5,228,403
New York	—	—	—	—	*2,632,313*	*2,367,353*	*228,737*	*5,228,403*
North Carolina	540,762	220,307	3,490	764,559	376,473	171,804	0	548,277
North Dakota	—	—	—	—	60,507	126,209	0	186,716
Ohio	—	—	—	—	1,214,459	1,645,643	0	2,860,102
Oklahoma	441,654	265,169	2,108	708,931	345,953	285,224	0	631,177
Oregon	199,275	299,295	0	498,570	116,780	376,510	10,165	503,455
Pennsylvania	—	—	—	—	1,694,076	1,820,400	34,166	3,548,642
Rhode Island	190,284	130,668	0	320,952	—	—	—	—
South Carolina	135,998	5,008	0	141,006	50,240	0	37	50,277
South Dakota	98,749	144,084	0	242,833	90,692	160,670	0	251,362
Tennessee	326,062	166,947	6,129	499,138	—	—	—	—
Texas	702,985	349,665	8,913	1,061,563	—	—	—	—
Utah	—	—	—	—	121,198	142,427	815	264,440
Vermont	—	—	—	—	19,608	69,543	20	89,171
Virginia	253,865	119,366	13,786	387,017	—	—	—	—
Washington	—	—	—	—	397,719	342,464	4,600	744,783
West Virginia	435,354	328,534	0	763,888	—	—	—	—
Wisconsin	—	—	—	—	515,539	595,283	5,255	1,116,077
Wyoming	57,953	43,527	0	101,480	—	—	—	—

Notes: Main entries are raw vote values for candidates who used the sole designation "Democrat" or "Republican" (or their historical antecedents listed in Appendix A) on the ballot. Other = candidates who used third-party names on the ballot or were listed as independent, unidentified, or scatter vote. Bold italicized entries in the table are the author's alternative party coding, which is used when a candidate listed a major party name (Democrat, Republican, or their historical antecedents) on the ballot with other party names or labels. For a more detailed explanation of this alternative party coding system, see Tables 6-10 and 1-3. —indicates that the state had no data, either because the state had no Senate election, no vote data were found for the state in question, or the state had not yet entered the Union. No special Senate elections are included in this table.

Sources: *Congressional Quarterly's Guide to U.S. Elections* (1994), *America Votes* (various publication dates), ICPSR data sets 0001 and 0075, and independent search of state sources by the author. For some party affiliations, the labels were taken from Michael J. Dubin's election archive after verification by the author.

Table 6-43 Senate Election Results, by State, 1952–1954 (Raw Count)

State	1952				1954			
	Democratic	Republican	Other	Total Vote	Democratic	Republican	Other	Total Vote
Alabama	—	—	—	—	259,348	55,110	1	314,459
Alaska	—	—	—	—	—	—	—	—
Arizona	125,338	132,063	0	257,401	—	—	—	—
Arkansas	—	—	—	—	291,058	0	0	291,058
California	0	0	4,542,548	4,542,548	—	—	—	—
California	*0*	*3,982,448*	*560,100*	*4,542,548*	—	—	—	—
Colorado	—	—	—	—	235,686	248,502	0	484,188
Connecticut	485,066	573,854	34,547	1,093,467	—	—	—	—
Connecticut	*485,066*	*596,122*	*12,279*	*1,093,467*	—	—	—	—
Delaware	77,685	93,020	0	170,705	82,511	62,389	0	144,900
Florida	616,665	0	1,135	617,800	—	—	—	—
Georgia	—	—	—	—	333,917	0	19	333,936
Hawaii	—	—	—	—	—	—	—	—
Idaho	—	—	—	—	84,139	142,269	0	226,408
Illinois	—	—	—	—	1,804,338	1,563,683	4	3,368,025
Indiana	911,169	1,020,605	14,344	1,946,118	—	—	—	—
Iowa	—	—	—	—	402,712	442,409	2,234	847,355
Kansas	—	—	—	—	258,575	348,144	11,344	618,063
Kentucky	—	—	—	—	434,109	362,948	0	797,057
Louisiana	—	—	—	—	207,115	0	0	207,115
Maine	82,665	139,205	15,294	237,164	102,075	144,530	0	246,605
Maine	*97,959*	*139,205*	*0*	*237,164*	—	—	—	—
Maryland	406,370	449,823	0	856,193	—	—	—	—
Massachusetts	1,211,984	1,141,247	7,194	2,360,425	927,899	956,605	8,206	1,892,710
Michigan	1,383,416	1,428,352	9,363	2,821,131	1,088,550	1,049,420	6,870	2,144,840
Minnesota	590,011	785,649	11,759	1,387,419	642,193	479,619	17,140	1,138,952
Mississippi	233,919	0	0	233,919	100,848	4,678	0	105,526
Missouri	1,008,523	858,170	1,408	1,868,101	—	—	—	—
Montana	133,109	127,360	1,828	262,297	114,591	112,863	0	227,454
Nebraska	164,660	408,971	18,087	591,718	162,990	255,695	0	418,685
Nevada	39,184	41,906	0	81,090	—	—	—	—
New Hampshire	—	—	—	—	77,386	117,150	0	194,536
New Jersey	1,011,187	1,286,782	20,263	2,318,232	858,158	861,528	50,871	1,770,557
New Mexico	122,543	117,168	0	239,711	111,351	83,071	0	194,422
New York	3,011,511	3,853,934	114,814	6,980,259	—	—	—	—
North Carolina	—	—	—	—	408,312	211,322	0	619,634
North Dakota	55,347	157,907	24,741	237,995	—	—	—	—
Ohio	1,563,330	1,878,961	0	3,442,291	—	—	—	—
Oklahoma	—	—	—	—	335,127	262,013	2,980	600,120
Oregon	—	—	—	—	285,775	283,313	0	569,088
Pennsylvania	2,168,546	2,331,034	20,181	4,519,761	—	—	—	—
Rhode Island	225,128	185,850	0	410,978	193,654	132,970	0	326,624
South Carolina	—	—	—	—	83,525	0	143,707	227,232
South Dakota	—	—	—	—	100,674	135,071	0	235,745
Tennessee	545,432	153,479	36,308	735,219	249,121	106,971	0	356,092
Texas	0	0	1,895,192	1,895,192	539,319	94,131	3,025	636,475
Texas	*1,895,192*	*0*	*0*	*1,895,192*	—	—	—	—
Utah	149,598	177,435	0	327,033	—	—	—	—
Vermont	42,630	111,406	16	154,052	—	—	—	—
Virginia	398,677	0	144,839	543,516	244,844	0	61,666	306,510
Virginia	*467,810*	*0*	*75,706*	*543,516*	*277,525*	*0*	*28,985*	*306,510*
Washington	595,288	460,884	2,563	1,058,735	—	—	—	—
West Virginia	470,019	406,554	0	876,573	325,263	268,066	0	593,329
Wisconsin	731,402	870,444	3,321	1,605,167	—	—	—	—
Wyoming	62,921	67,176	0	130,097	57,845	54,407	0	112,252

Notes: Main entries are raw vote values for candidates who used the sole designation "Democrat" or "Republican" (or their historical antecedents listed in Appendix A) on the ballot. Other = candidates who used third-party names on the ballot or were listed as independent, unidentified, or scatter vote. Bold italicized entries in the table are the author's alternative party coding, which is used when a candidate listed a major party name (Democrat, Republican, or their historical antecedents) on the ballot with other party names or labels. For a more detailed explanation of this alternative party coding system, see Tables 6-10 and 1-3. —indicates that the state had no data, either because the state had no Senate election, no vote data were found for the state in question, or the state had not yet entered the Union. No special Senate elections are included in this table.

Sources: *Congressional Quarterly's Guide to U.S. Elections* (1994), *America Votes* (various publication dates) ICPSR data sets 0001 and 0075, and independent search of state sources by the author. For some party affiliations, the labels were taken from Michael J. Dubin's election archive after verification by the author.

Table 6-44 Senate Election Results, by State, 1956–1959 (Raw Count)

State	1956				1958–1959			
	Democratic	Republican	Other	Total Vote	Democratic	Republican	Other	Total Vote
Alabama	330,182	0	0	330,182	—	—	—	—
Alaska	—	—	—	—	26,063	23,462	0	49,525
Arizona	170,816	107,447	0	278,263	129,030	164,593	0	293,623
Arkansas	331,679	68,016	0	399,695	—	—	—	—
California	2,445,816	2,892,918	22,733	5,361,467	2,927,693	2,204,337	3,191	5,135,221
Colorado	319,872	317,102	0	636,974	—	—	—	—
Connecticut	479,460	610,829	23,497	1,113,786	554,841	410,622	3,043	968,506
Connecticut	*479,460*	*621,028*	*13,298*	*1,113,786*	—	—	—	—
Delaware	—	—	—	—	72,152	82,280	0	154,432
Florida	655,418	0	0	655,418	386,113	155,956	0	542,069
Georgia	541,094	0	173	541,267	—	—	—	—
Hawaii[1]	—	—	—	—	77,647[1]	87,161[1]	0[1]	164,808[1]
Idaho	149,096	102,781	13,415	265,292	—	—	—	—
Illinois	1,949,883	2,307,352	7,595	4,264,830	—	—	—	—
Indiana	871,781	1,084,262	7,943	1,963,986	973,636	731,635	19,327	1,724,598
Iowa	543,156	635,499	0	1,178,655	—	—	—	—
Kansas	333,939	477,822	13,519	825,280	—	—	—	—
Kentucky	499,922	506,903	0	1,006,825	—	—	—	—
Louisiana	335,564	0	0	335,564	—	—	—	—
Maine	—	—	—	—	172,842	111,522	0	284,364
Maryland	419,108	473,059	0	892,167	367,270	382,021	0	749,291
Massachusetts	—	—	—	—	1,362,926	488,318	10,797	1,862,041
Michigan	—	—	—	—	1,216,966	1,046,963	7,715	2,271,644
Minnesota	—	—	—	—	608,847	536,629	5,407	1,150,883
Mississippi	—	—	—	—	61,039	0	0	61,039
Missouri	1,015,936	785,048	0	1,800,984	780,083	393,847	0	1,173,930
Montana	—	—	—	—	174,910	54,573	0	229,483
Nebraska	—	—	—	—	185,152	232,227	0	417,379
Nevada	50,677	45,712	0	96,389	48,732	35,760	0	84,492
New Hampshire	90,519	161,424	0	251,943	—	—	—	—
New Jersey	—	—	—	—	966,832	882,287	32,210	1,881,329
New Mexico	—	—	—	—	127,496	75,827	0	203,323
New York	0	3,723,933	3,267,203	6,991,136	0	2,842,942	2,759,037	5,601,979
New York	*3,265,159*	*3,723,933*	*2,044*	*6,991,136*	*2,709,950*	*2,842,942*	*49,087*	*5,601,979*
North Carolina	731,353	367,475	0	1,098,828	—	—	—	—
North Dakota	87,919	155,305	937	244,161	84,892	117,070	2,673	204,635
Ohio	1,864,589	1,660,910	0	3,525,499	1,652,211	1,497,199	0	3,149,410
Oklahoma	459,996	371,146	0	831,142	—	—	—	—
Oregon	396,849	335,405	0	732,254	—	—	—	—
Pennsylvania	2,268,641	2,250,671	10,562	4,529,874	1,929,821	2,042,586	16,215	3,988,622
Rhode Island	—	—	—	—	222,166	122,353	0	344,519
South Carolina	230,150	49,695	0	279,845	—	—	—	—
South Dakota	143,001	147,621	0	290,622	—	—	—	—
Tennessee	—	—	—	—	317,324	76,371	7,971	401,666
Texas	—	—	—	—	587,030	185,926	14,172	787,128
Utah	152,120	178,261	0	330,381	112,827	101,471	77,013	291,311
Vermont	52,184	103,101	4	155,289	59,536	64,900	6	124,442
Virginia	—	—	—	—	317,221	0	140,419	457,640
Washington	685,565	436,652	0	1,122,217	597,040	278,271	11,511	886,822
West Virginia	—	—	—	—	381,745	263,172	0	644,917
Wisconsin	627,903	892,473	2,745	1,523,121	682,440	510,398	1,840	1,194,678
Wyoming	—	—	—	—	58,035	56,122	0	114,157

Notes: Main entries are raw vote values for candidates who used the sole designation "Democrat" or "Republican" (or their historical antecedents listed in Appendix A) on the ballot. Other = candidates who used third-party names on the ballot or were listed as independent, unidentified, or scatter vote. Bold italicized entries in the table are the author's alternative party coding, which is used when a candidate listed a major party name (Democrat, Republican, or their historical antecedents) on the ballot with other party names or labels. For a more detailed explanation of this alternative party coding system, see Tables 6-10 and 1-3. —indicates that the state had no data, either because the state had no Senate election, no vote data were found for the state in question, or the state had not yet entered the Union. No special Senate elections are included in this table.

[1] The Senate race for Hawaii took place in 1959.

Sources: *Congressional Quarterly's Guide to U.S. Elections* (1994), *America Votes* (various publication dates), ICPSR data sets 0001 and 0075, and independent search of state sources by the author. For some party affiliations, the labels were taken from Michael J. Dubin's election archive after verification by the author.

Table 6-45 Senate Election Results, by State, 1960–1962 (Raw Count)

	1960				1962			
State	Democratic	Republican	Other	Total Vote	Democratic	Republican	Other	Total Vote
Alabama	389,196	164,868	17	554,081	201,937	195,134	8	397,079
Alaska	38,041	21,937	0	59,978	33,827	24,354	0	58,181
Arizona	—	—	—	—	199,217	163,388	0	362,605
Arkansas	377,036	0	449	377,485	214,867	98,013	0	312,880
California	—	—	—	—	2,452,839	3,180,483	14,630	5,647,952
Colorado	334,854	389,428	3,351	727,633	279,586	328,655	5,203	613,444
Connecticut	—	—	—	—	527,522	501,694	0	1,029,216
Delaware	96,090	98,874	0	194,964	—	—	—	—
Florida	—	—	—	—	657,633	281,381	193	939,207
Georgia	576,140	0	355	576,495	306,250	0	0	306,250
Hawaii	—	—	—	—	136,294	60,067	0	196,361
Idaho	139,448	152,648	0	292,096	141,657	117,129	0	258,786
Illinois	2,530,943	2,093,846	8,007	4,632,796	1,748,007	1,961,202	7	3,709,216
Indiana	—	—	—	—	905,491	894,547	0	1,800,038
Iowa	595,119	642,463	0	1,237,582	376,602	431,364	0	807,966
Kansas	388,895	485,499	14,198	888,592	223,630	388,500	10,102	622,232
Kentucky	444,290	644,087	0	1,088,377	387,440	432,648	0	820,088
Louisiana	432,228	109,698	0	541,926	318,838	103,066	0	421,904
Maine	159,809	256,890	0	416,699	—	—	—	—
Maryland	—	—	—	—	439,723	269,131	1	708,855
Massachusetts	1,050,725	1,358,556	8,532	2,417,813	—	—	—	—
Michigan	1,669,179	1,548,873	8,595	3,226,647	—	—	—	—
Minnesota	884,168	648,586	4,085	1,536,839	—	—	—	—
Mississippi	244,341	21,807	0	266,148	—	—	—	—
Missouri	—	—	—	—	666,929	555,330	0	1,222,259
Montana	140,331	136,281	0	276,612	—	—	—	—
Nebraska	245,837	352,748	158	598,743	—	—	—	—
Nevada	—	—	—	—	63,443	33,749	0	97,192
New Hampshire	114,024	173,521	0	287,545	90,444	134,035	0	224,479
New Jersey	1,151,385	1,483,832	29,339	2,664,556	—	—	—	—
New Mexico	190,654	109,897	0	300,551	—	—	—	—
New York	—	—	—	—	0	3,272,417	2,430,700	5,703,117
New York	—	—	—	—	***2,289,323***	***3,272,417***	***141,377***	***5,703,117***
North Carolina	793,521	497,964	0	1,291,485	491,520	321,635	0	813,155
North Dakota	—	—	—	—	88,032	135,705	0	223,737
Ohio	—	—	—	—	1,843,813	1,151,292	0	2,995,105
Oklahoma	474,116	385,646	4,713	864,475	353,890	307,966	2,856	664,712
Oregon	412,757	343,009	109	755,875	344,716	291,587	250	636,553
Pennsylvania	—	—	—	—	2,238,383	2,134,649	10,443	4,383,475
Rhode Island	275,575	124,408	0	399,983	—	—	—	—
South Carolina	330,164	0	102	330,266	178,712	133,930	5	312,647
South Dakota	145,261	160,181	0	305,442	127,458	126,861	0	254,319
Tennessee	594,460	234,053	6	828,519	—	—	—	—
Texas	1,306,605	926,653	20,506	2,253,764	—	—	—	—
Utah	—	—	—	—	151,656	166,755	0	318,411
Vermont	—	—	—	—	40,134	81,241	0	121,375
Virginia	506,169	0	116,651	622,820	—	—	—	—
Virginia	***594,887***	***0***	***27,933***	***622,820***	—	—	—	—
Washington	—	—	—	—	491,365	446,204	5,660	943,229
West Virginia	458,355	369,935	2	828,292	—	—	—	—
Wisconsin	—	—	—	—	662,342	594,846	2,980	1,260,168
Wyoming	60,447	78,103	0	138,550	—	—	—	—

Notes: Main entries are raw vote values for candidates who used the sole designation "Democrat" or "Republican" (or their historical antecedents listed in Appendix A) on the ballot. Other = candidates who used third-party names on the ballot or were listed as independent, unidentified, or scatter vote. Bold italicized entries in the table are the author's alternative party coding, which is used when a candidate listed a major party name (Democrat, Republican, or their historical antecedents) on the ballot with other party names or labels. For a more detailed explanation of this alternative party coding system, see Tables 6-10 and 1-3. —indicates that the state had no data, either because the state had no Senate election, no vote data were found for the state in question, or the state had not yet entered the Union. No special Senate elections are included in this table.

Sources: *Congressional Quarterly's Guide to U.S. Elections* (1994), *America Votes* (various publication dates), ICPSR data sets 0001 and 0075, and independent search of state sources by the author. For some party affiliations, the labels were taken from Michael J. Dubin's election archive after verification by the author.

Table 6-46 Senate Election Results, by State, 1964–1966 (Raw Count)

State	1964				1966			
	Democratic	Republican	Other	Total Vote	Democratic	Republican	Other	Total Vote
Alabama	—	—	—	—	482,138	313,018	7,452	802,608
Alaska	—	—	—	—	49,289	15,961	0	65,250
Arizona	227,712	241,089	0	468,801	—	—	—	—
Arkansas	—	—	—	—	—	—	—	—
California	3,411,912	3,628,555	1,354	7,041,821	—	—	—	—
Colorado	—	—	—	—	266,198	368,307	332	634,837
Connecticut	781,008	426,939	216	1,208,163	—	—	—	—
Delaware	96,850	103,782	71	200,703	67,263	97,268	0	164,531
Florida	997,585	562,212	540	1,560,337	—	—	—	—
Georgia	—	—	—	—	631,002	0	0	631,002
Hawaii	96,789	110,747	1,278	208,814	—	—	—	—
Idaho	—	—	—	—	112,637	139,819	0	252,456
Illinois	—	—	—	—	1,678,147	2,100,449	44,128	3,822,724
Indiana	1,128,505	941,519	6,939	2,076,963	—	—	—	—
Iowa	—	—	—	—	324,114	522,339	11,043	857,496
Kansas	—	—	—	—	303,223	350,077	18,045	671,345
Kentucky	—	—	—	—	266,079	483,805	0	749,884
Louisiana	—	—	—	—	437,695	0	0	437,695
Maine	253,511	127,040	0	380,551	131,136	188,291	108	319,535
Maryland	678,649	402,393	7	1,081,049	—	—	—	—
Massachusetts	1,716,907	587,663	7,458	2,312,028	774,761	1,213,473	11,715	1,999,949
Michigan	1,996,912	1,096,272	8,483	3,101,667	1,069,484	1,363,530	6,351	2,439,365
Minnesota	931,353	605,933	6,304	1,543,590	685,840	574,868	10,718	1,271,426
Mississippi	343,364	0	0	343,364	258,248	105,652	30,641	394,541
Missouri	1,186,666	596,377	0	1,783,043	—	—	—	—
Montana	180,643	99,367	0	280,010	138,166	121,697	0	259,863
Nebraska	217,605	345,772	24	563,401	187,950	296,116	0	484,066
Nevada	67,336	67,288	0	134,624	—	—	—	—
New Hampshire	—	—	—	—	123,888	105,241	176	229,305
New Jersey	1,677,515	1,011,280	20,780	2,709,575	788,021	1,278,843	63,824	2,130,688
New Mexico	178,209	147,562	0	325,771	137,205	120,988	0	258,193
New York	0	3,104,056	4,047,525	7,151,581	—	—	—	—
New York	***3,823,749***	***3,104,056***	***223,776***	***7,151,581***				
North Carolina	—	—	—	—	501,440	400,502	36	901,978
North Dakota	149,264	109,681	0	258,945	—	—	—	—
Ohio	1,923,608	1,906,781	0	3,830,389	—	—	—	—
Oklahoma	—	—	—	—	343,157	295,585	0	638,742
Oregon	—	—	—	—	330,374	354,391	302	685,067
Pennsylvania	2,359,223	2,429,858	14,754	4,803,835	—	—	—	—
Rhode Island	319,607	66,715	0	386,322	219,331	104,838	0	324,169
South Carolina	—	—	—	—	164,955	271,297	0	436,252
South Dakota	—	—	—	—	76,563	150,517	0	227,080
Tennessee	570,542	493,475	1	1,064,018	383,843	483,063	55	866,961
Texas	1,463,958	1,134,337	5,561	2,603,856	643,855	842,501	6,823	1,493,179
Utah	227,822	169,562	0	397,384	—	—	—	—
Vermont	76,457	0	87,893	164,350	—	—	—	—
Vermont	***76,457***	***87,879***	***14***	***164,350***	—	—	—	—
Virginia	592,260	176,624	159,479	928,363	429,855	245,681	58,343	733,879
Washington	875,950	337,138	0	1,213,088	—	—	—	—
West Virginia	515,015	246,072	0	761,087	292,325	198,891	0	491,216
Wisconsin	892,013	780,116	1,647	1,673,776	—	—	—	—
Wyoming	76,485	65,185	0	141,670	59,141	63,548	0	122,689

Notes: Main entries are raw vote values for candidates who used the sole designation "Democrat" or "Republican" (or their historical antecedents listed in Appendix A) on the ballot. Other = candidates who used third-party names on the ballot or were listed as independent, unidentified, or scatter vote. Bold italicized entries in the table are the author's alternative party coding, which is used when a candidate listed a major party name (Democrat, Republican, or their historical antecedents) on the ballot with other party names or labels. For a more detailed explanation of this alternative party coding system, see Tables 6-10 and 1-3. —indicates that the state had no data, either because the state had no Senate election, no vote data were found for the state in question, or the state had not yet entered the Union. No special Senate elections are included in this table.

Sources: *Congressional Quarterly's Guide to U.S. Elections* (1994), *America Votes* (various publication dates), ICPSR data sets 0001 and 0075, and independent search of state sources by the author. For some party affiliations, the labels were taken from Michael J. Dubin's election archive after verification by the author.

Table 6-47 Senate Election Results, by State, 1968–1970 (Raw Count)

| | 1968 | | | | 1970 | | | |
State	Democratic	Republican	Other	Total Vote	Democratic	Republican	Other	Total Vote
Alabama	638,774	201,227	72,699	912,700	—	—	—	—
Alabama	*711,473*	*201,227*	*0*	*912,700*	—	—	—	—
Alaska	36,527	30,286	14,118	80,931	—	—	—	—
Arizona	205,338	274,607	0	479,945	179,512	228,284	0	407,796
Arkansas	349,965	241,739	0	591,704	—	—	—	—
California	3,680,352	3,329,148	92,965	7,102,465	3,496,558	2,877,617	117,982	6,492,157
Colorado	325,584	459,952	0	785,536	—	—	—	—
Connecticut	655,043	551,455	39	1,206,537	368,111	454,721	266,521	1,089,353
Delaware	—	—	—	—	64,740	94,979	1,720	161,439
Florida	892,637	1,131,499	0	2,024,136	902,438	772,817	123	1,675,378
Georgia	885,093	256,796	0	1,141,889	—	—	—	—
Hawaii	189,248	34,008	3,671	226,927	116,597	124,163	0	240,760
Idaho	173,482	114,394	0	287,876	—	—	—	—
Illinois	2,073,242	2,358,947	17,568	4,449,757	2,065,054	1,519,718	14,500	3,599,272
Indiana	1,060,456	988,571	4,091	2,053,118	870,990	866,707	0	1,737,697
Iowa	574,884	568,469	733	1,144,086	—	—	—	—
Kansas	315,911	490,911	10,262	817,084	—	—	—	—
Kentucky	448,960	484,260	9,645	942,865	—	—	—	—
Louisiana	518,586	0	0	518,586	—	—	—	—
Maine	—	—	—	—	199,954	123,906	0	323,860
Maryland	443,367	541,893	148,467	1,133,727	460,422	484,960	10,988	956,370
Massachusetts	—	—	—	—	1,202,856	715,978	16,773	1,935,607
Michigan	—	—	—	—	1,744,672	858,438	7,653	2,610,763
Minnesota	—	—	—	—	788,256	568,025	8,606	1,364,887
Mississippi	—	—	—	—	286,622	0	37,593	324,215
Missouri	887,414	850,544	0	1,737,958	655,431	617,903	10,578	1,283,912
Montana	—	—	—	—	150,060	97,809	0	247,869
Nebraska	—	—	—	—	217,681	240,894	391	458,966
Nevada	83,622	69,068	0	152,690	85,187	60,838	1,743	147,768
New Hampshire	116,816	170,163	10	286,989	—	—	—	—
New Jersey	—	—	—	—	1,157,074	903,026	82,005	2,142,105
New Mexico	—	—	—	—	151,486	135,004	3,416	289,906
New York	2,150,695	0	4,430,892	6,581,587	2,171,232	0	3,733,550	5,904,782
New York	*2,150,695*	*3,269,772*	*1,161,120*	*6,581,587*	*2,171,232*	*1,434,472*	*2,299,078*	*5,904,782*
North Carolina	870,406	566,934	0	1,437,340	—	—	—	—
North Dakota	80,815	154,968	3,993	239,776	134,519	82,996	2,045	219,560
Ohio	1,814,152	1,928,964	5	3,743,121	1,495,262	1,565,682	90,330	3,151,274
Oklahoma	419,658	470,120	19,341	909,119	—	—	—	—
Oregon	405,353	408,646	177	814,176	—	—	—	—
Pennsylvania	2,117,662	2,399,762	106,794	4,624,218	1,653,774	1,874,106	116,425	3,644,305
Rhode Island	—	—	—	—	230,469	107,351	3,402	341,222
South Carolina	404,060	248,780	15	652,855	—	—	—	—
South Dakota	158,961	120,951	0	279,912	—	—	—	—
Tennessee	—	—	—	—	519,858	562,645	14,538	1,097,041
Texas	—	—	—	—	1,194,069	1,035,794	1,808	2,231,671
Utah	192,168	225,075	2,019	419,262	210,207	159,004	5,092	374,303
Vermont	0	0	157,375	157,375	62,271	91,198	1,430	154,899
Vermont	*0*	*157,154*	*221*	*157,375*	—	—	—	—
Virginia	—	—	—	—	295,057	145,031	506,663	946,751
Washington	796,183	435,894	3,986	1,236,063	879,385	170,790	16,632	1,066,807
West Virginia	—	—	—	—	345,965	99,658	0	445,623
Wisconsin	1,020,931	633,910	20	1,654,861	948,445	381,297	9,225	1,338,967
Wyoming	—	—	—	—	67,207	53,279	0	120,486

Notes: Main entries are raw vote values for candidates who used the sole designation "Democrat" or "Republican" (or their historical antecedents listed in Appendix A) on the ballot. Other = candidates who used third-party names on the ballot or were listed as independent, unidentified, or scatter vote. Bold italicized entries in the table are the author's alternative party coding, which is used when a candidate listed a major party name (Democrat, Republican, or their historical antecedents) on the ballot with other party names or labels. For a more detailed explanation of this alternative party coding system, see Tables 6-10 and 1-3. —indicates that the state had no data, either because the state had no Senate election, no vote data were found for the state in question, or the state had not yet entered the Union. No special Senate elections are included in this table.

Sources: *Congressional Quarterly's Guide to U.S. Elections* (1994), *America Votes* (various publication dates), ICPSR data sets 0001 and 0075, and independent search of state sources by the author. For some party affiliations, the labels were taken from Michael J. Dubin's election archive after verification by the author.

Table 6-48 Senate Election Results, by State, 1972–1974 (Raw Count)

State	1972				1974			
	Democratic	Republican	Other	Total Vote	Democratic	Republican	Other	Total Vote
Alabama	654,491	347,523	49,085	1,051,099	501,541	0	21,749	523,290
Alabama	*685,912*	*347,523*	*17,664*	*1,051,099*	—	—	—	—
Alaska	21,791	74,216	0	96,007	54,361	38,914	0	93,275
Arizona	—	—	—	—	229,523	320,396	0	549,919
Arkansas	386,398	248,238	0	634,636	461,056	82,026	0	543,082
California	—	—	—	—	3,693,160	2,210,267	199,005	6,102,432
Colorado	457,545	447,957	20,591	926,093	471,691	325,508	26,967	824,166
Connecticut	—	—	—	—	690,820	372,055	22,043	1,084,918
Delaware	116,006	112,844	978	229,828	—	—	—	—
Florida	—	—	—	—	781,031	736,674	282,834	1,800,539
Georgia	635,970	542,331	407	1,178,708	627,376	246,866	313	874,555
Hawaii	—	—	—	—	207,454	0	42,767	250,221
Idaho	140,913	161,804	6,885	309,602	145,140	109,072	4,635	258,847
Illinois	1,721,031	2,867,078	20,271	4,608,380	1,811,496	1,084,884	18,286	2,914,666
Indiana	—	—	—	—	889,269	814,117	49,592	1,752,978
Iowa	662,637	530,525	10,171	1,203,333	462,947	420,546	6,068	889,561
Kansas	200,764	622,591	48,367	871,722	390,451	403,983	3	794,437
Kentucky	528,550	494,337	14,974	1,037,861	399,406	328,982	17,606	745,994
Louisiana	598,987	206,846	279,071	1,084,904	434,643	0	0	434,643
Maine	224,270	197,040	0	421,310	—	—	—	—
Maryland	—	—	—	—	374,563	503,223	0	877,786
Massachusetts	823,278	1,505,932	41,466	2,370,676	—	—	—	—
Michigan	1,577,178	1,781,065	48,663	3,406,906	—	—	—	—
Minnesota	981,340	742,121	8,192	1,731,653	—	—	—	—
Mississippi	375,102	249,779	20,865	645,746	—	—	—	—
Missouri	—	—	—	—	735,433	480,900	7,970	1,224,303
Montana	163,609	151,316	0	314,925	—	—	—	—
Nebraska	265,922	301,841	817	568,580	—	—	—	—
Nevada	—	—	—	—	78,981	79,605	10,887	169,473
New Hampshire	184,495	139,852	7	324,354	110,924	110,926	1,513	223,363
New Jersey	963,573	1,743,854	84,480	2,791,907	—	—	—	—
New Mexico	173,815	204,253	262	378,330	—	—	—	—
New York	—	—	—	—	1,973,781	0	3,189,819	5,163,600
New York	—	—	—	—	*1,973,781*	*2,340,188*	*849,631*	*5,163,600*
North Carolina	677,293	795,248	0	1,472,541	633,775	377,618	8,974	1,020,367
North Dakota	—	—	—	—	113,931	114,117	7,613	235,661
Ohio	—	—	—	—	1,930,670	918,133	139,148	2,987,951
Oklahoma	478,212	516,934	10,002	1,005,148	387,162	390,997	13,650	791,809
Oregon	425,036	494,671	1,126	920,833	338,591	420,984	6,839	766,414
Pennsylvania	—	—	—	—	1,596,121	1,843,317	38,374	3,477,812
Rhode Island	221,942	188,990	2,500	413,432	—	—	—	—
South Carolina	245,457	426,601	188	672,246	356,126	146,645	9,626	512,397
South Dakota	174,773	131,613	0	306,386	147,929	130,955	0	278,884
Tennessee	440,599	716,539	7,057	1,164,195	—	—	—	—
Texas	1,511,985	1,822,877	79,041	3,413,903	—	—	—	—
Utah	—	—	—	—	185,377	210,299	24,966	420,642
Vermont	—	—	—	—	0	66,223	76,549	142,772
Vermont	—	—	—	—	*70,629*	*66,223*	*5,920*	*142,772*
Virginia	643,963	718,337	33,968	1,396,268	—	—	—	—
Washington	—	—	—	—	611,811	363,626	32,410	1,007,847
West Virginia	486,310	245,531	0	731,841	—	—	—	—
Wisconsin	—	—	—	—	740,700	429,327	29,468	1,199,495
Wyoming	40,753	101,314	0	142,067	—	—	—	—

Notes: Main entries are raw vote values for candidates who used the sole designation "Democrat" or "Republican" (or their historical antecedents listed in Appendix A) on the ballot. Other = candidates who used third-party names on the ballot or were listed as independent, unidentified, or scatter vote. Bold italicized entries in the table are the author's alternative party coding, which is used when a candidate listed a major party name (Democrat, Republican, or their historical antecedents) on the ballot with other party names or labels. For a more detailed explanation of this alternative party coding system, see Tables 6-10 and 1-3. —indicates that the state had no data, either because the state had no Senate election, no vote data were found for the state in question, or the state had not yet entered the Union. No special Senate elections are included in this table.

Sources: *Congressional Quarterly's Guide to U.S. Elections* (1994), *America Votes* (various publication dates), ICPSR data sets 0001 and 0075, and independent search of state sources by the author. For some party affiliations, the labels were taken from Michael J. Dubin's election archive after verification by the author.

Table 6-49 Senate Election Results, by State, 1976–1978 (Raw Count)

State	1976 Democratic	Republican	Other	Total Vote	1978 Democratic	Republican	Other	Total Vote
Alabama	—	—	—	—	547,054	0	34,971	582,025
Alaska	—	—	—	—	29,574	92,783	384	122,741
Arizona	400,334	321,236	19,640	741,210	—	—	—	—
Arkansas	—	—	—	—	399,916	84,722	37,601	522,239
California	3,502,862	3,748,973	220,433	7,472,268	—	—	—	—
Colorado	—	—	—	—	330,247	480,596	8,307	819,150
Connecticut	561,018	785,683	14,965	1,361,666	—	—	—	—
Delaware	98,055	125,502	1,302	224,859	93,930	66,479	1,663	162,072
Florida	1,799,518	1,057,886	130	2,857,534	—	—	—	—
Georgia	—	—	—	—	536,320	108,808	36	645,164
Hawaii	162,305	122,724	17,063	302,092	—	—	—	—
Idaho	—	—	—	—	89,635	194,412	0	284,047
Illinois	—	—	—	—	1,448,187	1,698,711	37,866	3,184,764
Indiana	878,522	1,275,833	16,832	2,171,187	—	—	—	—
Iowa	—	—	—	—	395,066	421,598	7,990	824,654
Kansas	—	—	—	—	317,602	403,354	27,883	748,839
Kentucky	—	—	—	—	290,730	175,766	10,287	476,783
Louisiana	—	—	—	—	—	—	—	—
Maine	292,704	193,489	61	486,254	127,327	212,294	35,551	375,172
Maryland	772,101	530,439	63,028	1,365,568	—	—	—	—
Massachusetts	1,726,657	722,641	41,957	2,491,255	1,093,283	890,584	1,833	1,985,700
Michigan	1,831,031	1,635,087	24,546	3,490,664	1,484,193	1,362,165	272	2,846,630
Minnesota	1,290,736	478,611	142,721	1,912,068	638,375	894,092	48,311	1,580,778
Mississippi	554,433	0	0	554,433	185,454	263,089	135,393	583,936
Missouri	813,571	1,090,067	11,139	1,914,777	—	—	—	—
Montana	206,232	115,213	0	321,445	160,353	127,589	0	287,942
Nebraska	313,809	284,284	221	598,314	334,276	159,806	286	494,368
Nevada	127,295	63,471	11,214	201,980	—	—	—	—
New Hampshire	—	—	—	—	127,945	133,745	2,089	263,779
New Jersey	1,681,140	1,054,508	35,742	2,771,390	1,082,960	844,200	30,355	1,957,515
New Mexico	176,382	234,681	2,078	413,141	160,045	183,442	67	343,554
New York	0	0	6,319,755	6,319,755	—	—	—	—
New York	*3,422,594*	*2,836,633*	*60,528*	*6,319,755*	—	—	—	—
North Carolina	—	—	—	—	516,663	619,151	0	1,135,814
North Dakota	175,772	103,466	3,824	283,062	—	—	—	—
Ohio	1,941,113	1,823,774	155,726	3,920,613	—	—	—	—
Oklahoma	—	—	—	—	493,953	247,857	12,454	754,264
Oregon	—	—	—	—	341,616	550,165	737	892,518
Pennsylvania	2,126,977	2,381,891	37,485	4,546,353	—	—	—	—
Rhode Island	167,665	230,329	912	398,906	229,557	76,061	0	305,618
South Carolina	—	—	—	—	281,119	351,733	0	632,852
South Dakota	—	—	—	—	84,767	170,832	0	255,599
Tennessee	751,180	673,231	7,635	1,432,046	466,228	642,644	48,222	1,157,094
Texas	2,199,956	1,636,370	38,190	3,874,516	1,139,149	1,151,376	22,015	2,312,540
Utah	241,948	290,221	7,939	540,108	—	—	—	—
Vermont	0	94,481	94,579	189,060	—	—	—	—
Vermont	*85,682*	*94,481*	*8,897*	*189,060*	—	—	—	—
Virginia	596,009	0	961,491	1,557,500	608,511	613,232	513	1,222,256
Washington	1,071,219	361,546	58,346	1,491,111	—	—	—	—
West Virginia	566,423	0	367	566,790	249,034	244,317	0	493,351
Wisconsin	1,396,970	521,902	16,311	1,935,183	—	—	—	—
Wyoming	70,558	84,810	0	155,368	50,456	82,908	0	133,364

Notes: Main entries are raw vote values for candidates who used the sole designation "Democrat" or "Republican" (or their historical antecedents listed in Appendix A) on the ballot. Other = candidates who used third-party names on the ballot or were listed as independent, unidentified, or scatter vote. Bold italicized entries in the table are the author's alternative party coding, which is used when a candidate listed a major party name (Democrat, Republican, or their historical antecedents) on the ballot with other party names or labels. For a more detailed explanation of this alternative party coding system, see Tables 6-10 and 1-3. —indicates that the state had no data, either because the state had no Senate election, no vote data were found for the state in question, or the state had not yet entered the Union. No special Senate elections are included in this table.

Sources: *Congressional Quarterly's Guide to U.S. Elections* (1994), *America Votes* (various publication dates), and independent search of state sources by the author. For some party affiliations, the labels were taken from Michael J. Dubin's election archive after verification by the author.

Table 6-50 Senate Election Results, by State, 1980–1982 (Raw Count)

State	1980 Democratic	1980 Republican	1980 Other	1980 Total Vote	1982 Democratic	1982 Republican	1982 Other	1982 Total Vote
Alabama	610,175	650,362	36,220	1,296,757	—	—	—	—
Alaska	72,007	84,159	596	156,762	—	—	—	—
Arizona	422,972	432,371	18,895	874,238	411,970	291,749	20,166	723,885
Arkansas	477,905	330,576	331	808,812	—	—	—	—
California	4,705,399	3,093,426	528,656	8,327,481	3,494,968	4,022,565	288,005	7,805,538
Colorado	590,501	571,295	11,850	1,173,646	—	—	—	—
Connecticut	763,969	581,884	10,222	1,356,075	499,146	545,987	38,480	1,083,613
Delaware	—	—	—	—	84,413	105,357	1,190	190,960
Florida	1,705,409	1,822,460	159	3,528,028	1,637,667	1,015,330	422	2,653,419
Georgia	776,143	803,686	511	1,580,340	—	—	—	—
Hawaii	224,485	53,068	10,453	288,006	245,386	52,071	8,953	306,410
Idaho	214,439	218,701	6,507	439,647	—	—	—	—
Illinois	2,565,302	1,946,296	68,431	4,580,029	—	—	—	—
Indiana	1,015,962	1,182,414	0	2,198,376	828,400	978,301	10,586	1,817,287
Iowa	581,545	683,014	12,475	1,277,034	—	—	—	—
Kansas	340,271	598,686	0	938,957	—	—	—	—
Kentucky	720,861	386,029	0	1,106,890	—	—	—	—
Louisiana	—	—	—	—	—	—	—	—
Maine	—	—	—	—	279,819	179,882	14	459,715
Maryland	435,118	850,970	0	1,286,088	707,356	407,334	0	1,114,690
Massachusetts	—	—	—	—	1,247,084	784,602	19,083	2,050,769
Michigan	—	—	—	—	1,728,793	1,223,288	42,253	2,994,334
Minnesota	—	—	—	—	840,401	949,207	15,067	1,804,675
Mississippi	—	—	—	—	414,099	230,927	0	645,026
Missouri	1,074,859	985,399	6,707	2,066,965	758,629	784,876	16	1,543,521
Montana	—	—	—	—	174,861	133,789	12,412	321,062
Nebraska	—	—	—	—	363,350	155,760	26,537	545,647
Nevada	92,129	144,224	10,083	246,436	114,720	120,377	5,297	240,394
New Hampshire	179,455	195,563	46	375,064	—	—	—	—
New Jersey	—	—	—	—	1,117,549	1,047,626	28,770	2,193,945
New Mexico	—	—	—	—	217,682	187,128	0	404,810
New York	2,618,661	0	3,396,253	6,014,914	0	0	4,967,729	4,967,729
New York	**2,618,661**	**2,699,652**	**696,601**	**6,014,914**	**3,232,146**	**1,696,766**	**38,817**	**4,967,729**
North Carolina	887,653	898,064	11,948	1,797,665	—	—	—	—
North Dakota	86,658	210,347	2,267	299,272	164,873	89,304	8,288	262,465
Ohio	2,770,786	1,137,695	118,822	4,027,303	1,923,767	1,396,790	74,906	3,395,463
Oklahoma	478,283	587,252	32,759	1,098,294	—	—	—	—
Oregon	501,963	594,290	44,241	1,140,494	—	—	—	—
Pennsylvania	2,122,391	2,230,404	65,247	4,418,042	1,412,965	2,136,418	54,725	3,604,108
Rhode Island	—	—	—	—	167,283	175,495	1	342,779
South Carolina	612,554	257,946	94	870,594	—	—	—	—
South Dakota	129,018	190,594	7,866	327,478	—	—	—	—
Tennessee	—	—	—	—	780,113	479,642	30	1,259,785
Texas	—	—	—	—	1,818,223	1,256,759	28,185	3,103,167
Utah	151,454	437,675	5,169	594,298	219,482	309,332	1,988	530,802
Vermont	104,176	101,421	3,527	209,124	79,340	84,450	4,213	168,003
Virginia	—	—	—	—	690,839	724,571	212	1,415,622
Washington	792,052	936,317	0	1,728,369	943,655	332,273	92,548	1,368,476
West Virginia	—	—	—	—	387,170	173,910	4,234	565,314
Wisconsin	1,065,487	1,106,311	32,404	2,204,202	983,311	527,355	34,315	1,544,981
Wyoming	—	—	—	—	72,466	94,725	0	167,191

Notes: Main entries are raw vote values for candidates who used the sole designation "Democrat" or "Republican" (or their historical antecedents listed in Appendix A) on the ballot. Other = candidates who used third-party names on the ballot or were listed as independent, unidentified, or scatter vote. Bold italicized entries in the table are the author's alternative party coding, which is used when a candidate listed a major party name (Democrat, Republican, or their historical antecedents) on the ballot with other party names or labels. For a more detailed explanation of this alternative party coding system, see Tables 6-10 and 1-3. —indicates that the state had no data, either because the state had no Senate election, no vote data were found for the state in question, or the state had not yet entered the Union. No special Senate elections are included in this table.

Sources: *Congressional Quarterly's Guide to U.S. Elections* (1994), *America Votes* (various publication dates), and independent search of state sources by the author. For some party affiliations, the labels were taken from Michael J. Dubin's election archive after verification by the author.

Table 6-51 Senate Election Results, by State, 1984–1986 (Raw Count)

State	1984 Democratic	Republican	Other	Total Vote	1986 Democratic	Republican	Other	Total Vote
Alabama	860,535	498,508	12,195	1,371,238	609,360	602,537	56	1,211,953
Alaska	58,804	146,919	715	206,438	79,727	97,674	3,400	180,801
Arizona	—	—	—	—	340,965	521,850	106	862,921
Arkansas	502,341	373,615	0	875,956	433,122	262,313	52	695,487
California	—	—	—	—	3,646,672	3,541,804	210,073	7,398,549
Colorado	449,327	833,821	14,661	1,297,809	529,449	512,994	18,322	1,060,765
Connecticut	—	—	—	—	632,695	340,438	3,800	976,933
Delaware	147,831	98,101	0	245,932	—	—	—	—
Florida	—	—	—	—	1,877,543	1,552,376	77	3,429,996
Georgia	1,344,104	337,196	44	1,681,344	623,707	601,241	60	1,225,008
Hawaii	—	—	—	—	241,887	86,910	0	328,797
Idaho	105,591	293,193	7,384	406,168	185,066	196,958	0	382,024
Illinois	2,397,303	2,308,039	82,131	4,787,473	2,033,926	1,053,793	35,368	3,123,087
Indiana	—	—	—	—	595,192	936,143	14,228	1,545,563
Iowa	716,883	564,381	11,436	1,292,700	299,406	588,880	3,476	891,762
Kansas	211,664	757,402	27,663	996,729	246,664	576,902	0	823,566
Kentucky	639,721	644,990	7,696	1,292,407	503,775	173,330	175	677,280
Louisiana	—	—	—	—	723,586	646,311	0	1,369,897
Maine	142,626	404,414	4,366	551,406	—	—	—	—
Maryland	—	—	—	—	675,225	437,411	1	1,112,637
Massachusetts	1,392,981	1,136,806	408	2,530,195	—	—	—	—
Michigan	1,915,831	1,745,302	39,805	3,700,938	—	—	—	—
Minnesota	852,844	1,199,926	13,373	2,066,143	—	—	—	—
Mississippi	371,926	580,314	0	952,240	—	—	—	—
Missouri	—	—	—	—	699,624	777,612	91	1,477,327
Montana	215,704	154,308	9,143	379,155	—	—	—	—
Nebraska	332,217	307,147	304	639,668	—	—	—	—
Nevada	—	—	—	—	130,955	116,606	14,371	261,932
New Hampshire	157,447	225,828	1,131	384,406	79,225	154,090	11,482	244,797
New Jersey	1,986,644	1,080,100	29,712	3,096,456	—	—	—	—
New Mexico	141,253	361,371	10	502,634	—	—	—	—
New York	—	—	—	—	1,723,216	0	2,456,231	4,179,447
New York	—	—	—	—	***1,723,216***	***2,378,197***	***78,034***	***4,179,447***
North Carolina	1,070,488	1,156,768	11,795	2,239,051	823,662	767,668	0	1,591,330
North Dakota	—	—	—	—	143,932	141,797	3,269	288,998
Ohio	—	—	—	—	1,949,208	1,171,893	88	3,121,189
Oklahoma	906,131	280,638	11,168	1,197,937	400,230	493,436	0	893,666
Oregon	406,122	808,152	461	1,214,735	375,735	656,317	10,503	1,042,555
Pennsylvania	—	—	—	—	1,448,219	1,906,537	23,470	3,378,226
Rhode Island	286,780	108,492	13	395,285	—	—	—	—
South Carolina	306,982	644,815	13,333	965,130	465,500	262,886	9,576	737,962
South Dakota	80,537	235,176	0	315,713	152,657	143,173	0	295,830
Tennessee	1,000,607	557,016	90,441	1,648,064	—	—	—	—
Texas	2,202,557	3,111,348	273	5,314,178	—	—	—	—
Utah	—	—	—	—	115,523	314,608	4,980	435,111
Vermont	—	—	—	—	124,123	67,798	4,611	196,532
Virginia	601,142	1,406,194	151	2,007,487	—	—	—	—
Washington	—	—	—	—	677,471	650,931	8,965	1,337,367
West Virginia	374,233	344,680	3,299	722,212	—	—	—	—
Wisconsin	—	—	—	—	702,963	754,573	25,638	1,483,174
Wyoming	40,525	146,373	0	186,898	—	—	—	—

Notes: Main entries are raw vote values for candidates who used the sole designation "Democrat" or "Republican" (or their historical antecedents listed in Appendix A) on the ballot. Other = candidates who used third-party names on the ballot or were listed as independent, unidentified, or scatter vote. Bold italicized entries in the table are the author's alternative party coding, which is used when a candidate listed a major party name (Democrat, Republican, or their historical antecedents) on the ballot with other party names or labels. For a more detailed explanation of this alternative party coding system, see Tables 6-10 and 1-3. —indicates that the state had no data, either because the state had no Senate election, no vote data were found for the state in question, or the state had not yet entered the Union. No special Senate elections are included in this table.

Sources: *Congressional Quarterly's Guide to U.S. Elections* (1994), *America Votes* (various publication dates), and independent search of state sources by the author. For some party affiliations, the labels were taken from Michael J. Dubin's election archive after verification by the author.

Table 6-52 Senate Election Results, by State, 1988–1990 (Raw Count)

State	1988				1990			
	Democratic	Republican	Other	Total Vote	Democratic	Republican	Other	Total Vote
Alabama	—	—	—	—	717,814	467,190	559	1,185,563
Alaska	—	—	—	—	61,152	125,806	2,999	189,957
Arizona	660,403	478,060	26,076	1,164,539	—	—	—	—
Arkansas	—	—	—	—	493,910	0	825	494,735
California	4,287,253	5,143,409	312,936	9,743,598	—	—	—	—
Colorado	—	—	—	—	425,746	569,048	27,233	1,022,027
Connecticut	688,499	678,454	16,573	1,383,526	—	—	—	—
Delaware	92,378	151,115	0	243,493	112,918	64,554	2,680	180,152
Florida	2,016,553	2,051,071	585	4,068,209	—	—	—	—
Georgia	—	—	—	—	1,033,439	0	78	1,033,517
Hawaii	247,941	66,987	8,948	323,876	—	—	—	—
Idaho	—	—	—	—	122,295	193,641	0	315,936
Illinois	—	—	—	—	2,115,377	1,135,628	0	3,251,005
Indiana	668,778	1,430,525	0	2,099,303	—	—	—	—
Iowa	—	—	—	—	535,975	446,869	1,089	983,933
Kansas	—	—	—	—	207,491	578,605	139	786,235
Kentucky	—	—	—	—	437,976	478,034	0	916,010
Louisiana	—	—	—	—	—	—	—	—
Maine	452,590	104,758	27	557,375	201,053	319,167	100	520,320
Maryland	999,166	617,537	362	1,617,065	—	—	—	—
Massachusetts	1,693,344	884,267	28,614	2,606,225	1,321,712	992,917	1,583	2,316,212
Michigan	2,116,865	1,348,219	40,901	3,505,985	1,471,753	1,055,695	33,046	2,560,494
Minnesota	856,694	1,176,210	61,049	2,093,953	911,999	864,375	31,671	1,808,045
Mississippi	436,339	510,380	0	946,719	0	274,244	0	274,244
Missouri	660,045	1,407,416	11,414	2,078,875	—	—	—	—
Montana	175,809	189,445	0	365,254	217,563	93,836	7,937	319,336
Nebraska	378,717	278,250	10,893	667,860	349,779	243,013	1,036	593,828
Nevada	175,548	161,336	12,765	349,649	—	—	—	—
New Hampshire	—	—	—	—	91,299	189,792	10,302	291,393
New Jersey	1,599,905	1,349,937	37,792	2,987,634	977,810	918,874	41,770	1,938,454
New Mexico	321,983	186,579	36	508,598	110,033	296,712	193	406,938
New York	0	0	6,040,980	6,040,980	—	—	—	—
New York	***4,048,649***	***1,875,784***	***116,547***	***6,040,980***	—	—	—	—
North Carolina	—	—	—	—	981,573	1,087,331	681	2,069,585
North Dakota	171,899	112,937	4,334	289,170	—	—	—	—
Ohio	2,480,038	1,872,716	151	4,352,905	—	—	—	—
Oklahoma	—	—	—	—	735,684	148,814	0	884,498
Oregon	—	—	—	—	507,743	590,095	1,417	1,099,255
Pennsylvania	1,416,764	2,901,715	48,119	4,366,598	—	—	—	—
Rhode Island	180,717	217,273	6	397,996	225,105	138,947	10	364,062
South Carolina	—	—	—	—	244,112	482,032	24,572	750,716
South Dakota	—	—	—	—	116,727	135,682	6,567	258,976
Tennessee	1,020,061	541,033	6,087	1,567,181	530,898	233,703	19,321	783,922
Texas	3,149,806	2,129,228	44,572	5,323,606	1,429,986	2,302,357	89,814	3,822,157
Utah	203,364	430,089	7,249	640,702	—	—	—	—
Vermont	71,469	163,203	5,439	240,111	—	—	—	—
Virginia	1,474,086	593,652	1,159	2,068,897	0	876,782	206,908	1,083,690
Washington	904,183	944,359	0	1,848,542	—	—	—	—
West Virginia	410,983	223,564	0	634,547	276,234	128,071	0	404,305
Wisconsin	1,128,625	1,030,440	9,125	2,168,190	—	—	—	—
Wyoming	89,821	91,143	0	180,964	56,848	100,784	0	157,632

Notes: Main entries are raw vote values for candidates who used the sole designation "Democrat" or "Republican" (or their historical antecedents listed in Appendix A) on the ballot. Other = candidates who used third-party names on the ballot or were listed as independent, unidentified, or scatter vote. Bold italicized entries in the table are the author's alternative party coding, which is used when a candidate listed a major party name (Democrat, Republican, or their historical antecedents) on the ballot with other party names or labels. For a more detailed explanation of this alternative party coding system, see Tables 6-10 and 1-3. —indicates that the state had no data, either because the state had no Senate election, no vote data were found for the state in question, or the state had not yet entered the Union. No special Senate elections are included in this table.

Sources: *Congressional Quarterly's Guide to U.S. Elections* (1994), *America Votes* (various publication dates), and independent search of state sources by the author. For some party affiliations, the labels were taken from Michael J. Dubin's election archive after verification by the author.

Table 6-53 Senate Election Results, by State, 1992–1994 (Raw Count)

State	1992				1994			
	Democratic	Republican	Other	Total Vote	Democratic	Republican	Other	Total Vote
Alabama	1,022,698	522,015	33,086	1,577,799	—	—	—	—
Alaska	92,065	127,163	20,486	239,714	—	—	—	—
Arizona	436,321	771,395	174,335	1,382,051	442,510	600,999	75,551	1,119,060
Arkansas	553,635	366,373	0	920,008	—	—	—	—
California	5,173,467	4,644,182	982,054	10,799,703	3,979,152	3,817,025	717,912	8,514,089
Colorado	803,725	662,893	85,671	1,552,289	—	—	—	—
Connecticut	0	572,036	928,673	1,500,709	0	334,833	744,934	1,079,767
Connecticut	*882,569*	*572,036*	*46,104*	*1,500,709*	*723,842*	*334,833*	*21,092*	*1,079,767*
Delaware	—	—	—	—	84,554	111,088	3,387	199,029
Florida	3,245,565	1,716,505	220	4,962,290	1,210,412	2,894,726	1,038	4,106,176
Georgia	618,877	635,114	0	1,253,991	—	—	—	—
Hawaii	208,266	97,928	57,468	363,662	256,189	86,320	14,393	356,902
Idaho	208,036	270,468	18	478,522	—	—	—	—
Illinois	2,631,229	2,126,833	181,496	4,939,558	—	—	—	—
Indiana	900,148	1,267,972	43,306	2,211,426	470,799	1,039,625	33,144	1,543,568
Iowa	351,561	899,761	41,172	1,292,494	—	—	—	—
Kansas	349,525	706,246	70,676	1,126,447	—	—	—	—
Kentucky	836,888	476,604	17,366	1,330,858	—	—	—	—
Louisiana	—	—	—	—	—	—	—	—
Maine	—	—	—	—	186,042	308,244	17,447	511,733
Maryland	1,307,610	533,688	437	1,841,735	809,125	559,908	71	1,369,104
Massachusetts	—	—	—	—	1,266,011	894,005	19,948	2,179,964
Michigan	—	—	—	—	1,300,960	1,578,770	163,655	3,043,385
Minnesota	—	—	—	—	781,860	869,653	121,416	1,772,929
Mississippi	—	—	—	—	189,752	418,333	0	608,085
Missouri	1,057,967	1,221,901	75,057	2,354,925	633,697	1,060,149	81,270	1,775,116
Montana	—	—	—	—	131,845	218,542	22	350,409
Nebraska	—	—	—	—	317,297	260,668	1,240	579,205
Nevada	253,150	199,413	43,324	495,887	193,804	156,020	30,706	380,530
New Hampshire	234,982	249,591	33,843	518,416	—	—	—	—
New Jersey	—	—	—	—	1,033,487	966,244	55,156	2,054,887
New Mexico	—	—	—	—	249,989	213,025	182	463,196
New York	0	0	6,458,826	6,458,826	0	0	4,794,601	4,794,601
New York	*3,086,200*	*3,166,994*	*205,632*	*6,458,826*	*2,646,541*	*1,988,308*	*159,752*	*4,794,601*
North Carolina	1,194,015	1,297,892	85,984	2,577,891	—	—	—	—
North Dakota	179,347	118,162	6,448	303,957	137,157	99,390	0	236,547
Ohio	2,444,419	2,028,300	321,234	4,793,953	1,348,213	1,836,556	252,115	3,436,884
Oklahoma	494,350	757,876	42,197	1,294,423	—	—	—	—
Oregon	639,851	717,455	18,727	1,376,033	—	—	—	—
Pennsylvania	2,224,966	2,358,125	219,319	4,802,410	1,648,481	1,735,691	129,189	3,513,361
Rhode Island	—	—	—	—	122,532	222,856	0	345,388
South Carolina	591,030	554,175	35,233	1,180,438	—	—	—	—
South Dakota	217,095	108,733	8,667	334,495	—	—	—	—
Tennessee	—	—	—	—	623,164	834,226	23,001	1,480,391
Texas	—	—	—	—	1,639,615	2,604,218	36,107	4,279,940
Utah	301,228	420,069	37,182	758,479	146,938	357,297	15,088	519,323
Vermont	154,762	123,854	7,123	285,739	85,868	106,505	19,299	211,672
Virginia	—	—	—	—	938,376	882,213	236,874	2,057,463
Washington	1,197,973	1,020,829	360	2,219,162	752,352	947,821	0	1,700,173
West Virginia	—	—	—	—	290,495	130,441	0	420,936
Wisconsin	1,290,662	1,129,599	34,863	2,455,124	912,662	636,989	15,977	1,565,628
Wyoming	—	—	—	—	79,287	118,754	3,669	201,710

Notes: Main entries are raw vote values for candidates who used the sole designation "Democrat" or "Republican" (or their historical antecedents listed in Appendix A) on the ballot. Other = candidates who used third-party names on the ballot or were listed as independent, unidentified, or scatter vote. Bold italicized entries in the table are the author's alternative party coding, which is used when a candidate listed a major party name (Democrat, Republican, or their historical antecedents) on the ballot with other party names or labels. For a more detailed explanation of this alternative party coding system, see Tables 6-10 and 1-3. —indicates that the state had no data, either because the state had no Senate election, no vote data were found for the state in question, or the state had not yet entered the Union. No special Senate elections are included in this table.

Sources: *Congressional Quarterly's Guide to U.S. Elections* (1994), *America Votes* (various publication dates), and independent search of state sources by the author. For some party affiliations, the labels were taken from Michael J. Dubin's election archive after verification by the author.

Table 6-54 Senate Election Results, by State, 1996–1998 (Raw Count)

State	1996				1998			
	Democratic	Republican	Other	Total Vote	Democratic	Republican	Other	Total Vote
Alabama	681,651	786,436	31,306	1,499,393	474,568	817,973	864	1,293,405
Alaska	23,977	177,893	30,046	231,916	43,743	165,227	12,837	221,807
Arizona	—	—	—	—	275,224	696,577	41,479	1,013,280
Arkansas	400,241	445,942	0	846,183	385,878	295,870	18,896	700,644
California	—	—	—	—	4,411,705	3,576,351	326,897	8,314,953
Colorado	677,600	750,325	41,686	1,469,611	464,754	829,370	33,111	1,327,235
Connecticut	—	—	—	—	0	312,177	652,280	964,457
Connecticut	—	—	—	—	***628,306***	***312,177***	***23,974***	***964,457***
Delaware	165,465	105,088	5,052	275,605	—	—	—	—
Florida	—	—	—	—	2,436,407	1,463,755	0	3,900,162
Georgia	1,103,993	1,073,969	81,270	2,259,232	791,904	918,540	43,467	1,753,911
Hawaii	—	—	—	—	315,252	70,964	11,908	398,124
Idaho	198,422	283,532	15,279	497,233	107,375	262,966	7,833	378,174
Illinois	2,384,028	1,728,824	137,870	4,250,722	1,610,496	1,709,041	74,984	3,394,521
Indiana	—	—	—	—	1,012,244	552,732	23,641	1,588,617
Iowa	634,166	571,807	18,081	1,224,054	289,049	648,480	10,378	947,907
Kansas	362,380	652,677	37,243	1,052,300	229,718	474,639	22,879	727,236
Kentucky	560,012	724,794	22,240	1,307,046	563,051	569,817	12,546	1,145,414
Louisiana	852,945	847,157	0	1,700,102	620,502	306,616	42,047	969,165
Maine	266,226	298,422	42,129	606,777	—	—	—	—
Maryland	—	—	—	—	1,062,810	444,637	0	1,507,447
Massachusetts	1,334,345	1,142,837	78,704	2,555,886	—	—	—	—
Michigan	2,195,738	1,500,106	66,731	3,762,575	—	—	—	—
Minnesota	1,098,493	901,282	183,287	2,183,062	—	—	—	—
Mississippi	240,647	624,154	13,861	878,662	—	—	—	—
Missouri	—	—	—	—	690,208	830,625	56,024	1,576,857
Montana	201,935	182,111	23,444	407,490	—	—	—	—
Nebraska	281,904	379,933	14,952	676,789	—	—	—	—
Nevada	—	—	—	—	208,650	208,222	18,918	435,790
New Hampshire	227,397	242,304	22,897	492,598	88,883	213,477	12,596	314,956
New Jersey	1,519,328	1,227,817	136,961	2,884,106	—	—	—	—
New Mexico	164,356	357,171	30,294	551,821	—	—	—	—
New York	—	—	—	—	0	0	4,670,805	4,670,805
New York	—	—	—	—	***2,551,065***	***2,058,988***	***60,752***	***4,670,805***
North Carolina	1,173,875	1,345,833	36,748	2,556,456	1,029,237	945,943	36,963	2,012,143
North Dakota	—	—	—	—	134,747	75,013	3,598	213,358
Ohio	—	—	—	—	1,482,054	1,922,087	210	3,404,351
Oklahoma	474,162	670,610	38,378	1,183,150	268,898	570,682	20,133	859,713
Oregon	624,370	677,336	58,524	1,360,230	682,425	377,739	57,583	1,117,747
Pennsylvania	—	—	—	—	1,028,839	1,814,180	114,753	2,957,772
Rhode Island	230,676	127,368	5,334	363,378	—	—	—	—
South Carolina	510,951	619,859	30,562	1,161,372	562,791	488,132	17,444	1,068,367
South Dakota	166,533	157,954	0	324,487	162,884	95,431	3,796	262,111
Tennessee	654,937	1,091,554	32,173	1,778,664	—	—	—	—
Texas	2,428,776	3,027,680	70,985	5,527,441	—	—	—	—
Utah	—	—	—	—	163,172	316,652	15,085	494,909
Vermont	—	—	—	—	154,567	48,051	11,418	214,036
Virginia	1,115,982	1,235,744	2,989	2,354,715	—	—	—	—
Washington	—	—	—	—	1,103,184	785,377	0	1,888,561
West Virginia	456,526	139,088	0	595,614	—	—	—	—
Wisconsin	—	—	—	—	890,059	852,272	18,505	1,760,836
Wyoming	89,103	114,116	7,858	211,077	—	—	—	—

Notes: Main entries are raw vote values for candidates who used the sole designation "Democrat" or "Republican" (or their historical antecedents listed in Appendix A) on the ballot. Other = candidates who used third-party names on the ballot or were listed as independent, unidentified, or scatter vote. Bold italicized entries in the table are the author's alternative party coding, which is used when a candidate listed a major party name (Democrat, Republican, or their historical antecedents) on the ballot with other party names or labels. For a more detailed explanation of this alternative party coding system, see Tables 6-10 and 1-3. —indicates that the state had no data, either because the state had no Senate election, no vote data were found for the state in question, or the state had not yet entered the Union. No special Senate elections are included in this table.

Sources: *America Votes* (various publication dates), and independent search of state sources by the author. For some party affiliations, the labels were taken from Michael J. Dubin's election archive after verification by the author.

7
The Isolation of Gubernatorial Elections?

Writing of early state governors, James Madison called them "little more than cyphers" in comparison to the "omnipotent" legislatures. Thomas Jefferson lamented about Virginia government: "The judiciary and the executive members were left dependent on the legislature for their subsistence in office and some of them for their continuance in it." Summarizing the governorship in the newly formed states after the American Revolution, political scientist Rowland Egger commented that "the executive apparatus . . . was weak in constitutional stature, confused in lines of authority, and wholly and irresponsibly subservient to the legislative will" (quoted in Sabato, 1978, p. 4).

Such pronouncements were not exaggerations but rather descriptions of an office that was intentionally designed to be weak in response to the perceived excesses of colonial governors serving on behalf of King George III. Whether election was by voters or state legislatures, annual elections were one of the central features of the assailable governorship. Five of the original thirteen states provided for popular election of governors, usually annually, while the remaining eight states designated that the legislature determine the state's chief executive, again mainly at annual intervals. Of these eight states, all later adopted popular election for governor.

Early American governorships thus stood in stark contrast to the presidency as their national counterpart. The two offices revealed distinctly different ways of addressing two key facets of government: popular control and the powers of the executive. While the Framers of the Constitution were reluctant to adopt popular election of presidents, the writers of several of the early state constitutions had no such reluctance. In fact, one of the central strategies adopted by many states, not just in their first constitutions but in changes mandated throughout the nineteenth century, was to isolate the governorship as much as possible from other political offices or partisan trends by having frequent, popular elections in years in which few, if any, other major political offices were being contested.

In contrast, while the Framers gave the presidency fairly well-developed powers as a check on Congress, the writers of state constitutions provided few such powers to state governors, favoring instead "omnipotent" legislatures. Many of the first state governors had limited appointment power, lacked a veto over legislation, and were checked by an executive council appointed by the legislature (Lipson, 1939, pp. 12–15). This lack of powers further isolated governors from the affairs of government, as they were little more than figureheads in many states. Although the Framers of the Constitution worried about the whims and passions of voters, fears concerning the powers of colonial governors overrode any such worries at the state level. The governorship largely began as a democratic office but with few significant powers.

The initial isolation of gubernatorial elections from other American elections is discussed in this chapter. Such isolation has slowly changed so that the governorship has become increasingly more in step with national cycles of elections. Governors' powers have increased over time and become more formidable than when Madison called them "ciphers." But while the isolation has lessened, it has not vanished. The American governorship remains the most popularly constrained office of any major elected official in the United States—warily restricted in term length and reeligibility. The critical question addressed in this chapter is to what extent did these restrictions have an effect on the partisan and competitive nature of races for the top state office.

This chapter is divided into three parts. It begins with an analysis of the legal structures directing state elections for governor. Next, it examines national and regional patterns that emerge in gubernatorial contests. Finally, it presents the statewide votes for governor.

Characteristics of Gubernatorial Elections

Early fears of excessive executive power led states to restrict governorships in four ways: by the method of selection, the length of a term in office, the total number of terms that could be served (that is, term limits), and the timing of elections (that is, the particular years in which gubernatorial elections were held). Table 7-1 records the various combinations of methods of selection, term lengths, term limits, and timing of elections used in the states. In each instance, the table shows how these legal structures varied across the states but what is also important to note is the extent to which these legal structures did not vary much in their intent to reign in the power of the governor, keep the office-holder close to the voters, and isolate the governorship from national political offices and their cycles of election.

Method of Selection

As outlined in early state constitutions, there were three primary ways in which state governors were selected—by majority popular election with legislative intervention if no candidate received a majority vote, by plurality popular election, and by state legislative vote. Table 7-1 denotes that, in the New England states of Connecticut, Massachusetts, New Hampshire, and Rhode Island, governors were directly elected by popular majority vote. The first three states provided for recourse to the legislature if no popular vote majority emerged; Rhode Island sent the matter back to the voters for another election. New York adopted what eventually became the modern method of gubernatorial selection—direct popular election by plurality. The remaining states—Pennsylvania, Delaware, New Jersey, Georgia, Maryland, South Carolina, North Carolina, and Virginia—had the legislature choose the governor. The most common method was by majority joint vote of the upper and lower houses of the legislature. Successive ballots were taken until a majority was reached. Yet individual states varied. Georgia provided for the selection of the governor from the membership of its unicameral assembly. Pennsylvania chose a "president" rather than a "governor," who was selected from among twelve executive councilmen in the state assembly who were popularly elected (Kallenbach and Kallenbach 1977, pp. 1–2).

By the 1860s each of the eight original states that had begun with legislative selection of governor switched to direct popular vote. Pennsylvania in 1790, Delaware in 1792, Georgia in 1825, North Carolina in 1836, Maryland in 1838, New Jersey in 1844, Virginia in 1851, and, finally, South Carolina in 1865 dropped legislative selection in favor of New York's method of direct popular election by plurality. Indeed, South Carolina was the last state in the Union to subscribe to legislative selection of governors.

Among states admitted to the Union after the ratification of the Constitution, Tennessee (1796) and Ohio (1803) followed the New York model and Vermont (1791) followed the New England practice of majority vote with recourse to the legislature. Vermont still requires a majority vote for governor and legislative intervention in the event that no candidate receives a majority; this has happened twenty times, most recently in 1986. Among the remaining new states, all but two—Louisiana and Kentucky—adopted popular election of governors from the beginning. Louisiana first employed a modified popular election plan in which the legislature selected the governor from the two candidates receiving the highest number of popular votes. Louisiana abandoned this in favor of popular plurality election in 1846. In 1792 Kentucky began with electors selecting the governor, but ended this in favor of direct popular election in 1800 (Kallenbach and Kallenbach, 1977). Thus the demand for the democratization of the governor was rapid and consistent across the states, despite the variations in majority or plurality vote requirements that existed in the Federalist and Jacksonian periods. Today only three states

deviate from the plurality vote requirement: Georgia, Mississippi, and Vermont require majority votes, with the first one holding a runoff when a majority is not attained and the latter two allowing the legislature to decide (*Book of the States*, vol. 32, 1999).

Term Length and Term Limits

Two key restrictions on gubernatorial power and central indications of the extent of popular control over such power are the short terms of office and term limits that many governors have. The shortest term appears to have been six months in the initial temporary government plan for Georgia, which was replaced in 1778 with a one-year term. Table 7-1 shows that both term lengths and changes in term lengths vary by region. In the earliest period of the Union, nine of the original thirteen states provided for annual selection of governors.

The New England states were the most consistent region favoring one-year terms. Among the original states, Connecticut, Massachusetts, New Hampshire, and Rhode Island provided for annual elections and Vermont in 1791 and Maine in 1820 followed suit. On the other hand, in the Mid-Atlantic states, New York and Delaware had three-year terms, while Pennsylvania, which began with a one-year term, abandoned it in favor of a three-year term in 1790. Only New Jersey truly had a one-year term in the beginning.[1]

In the South, Georgia, North Carolina, and Virginia began with a one-year term. Georgia changed to two years in 1825 and four years in 1868; North Carolina adopted biennial elections in 1836 and quadrennial elections in 1868; and Virginia moved to quadrennial elections in 1851. Other southern states except for Arkansas, Florida, and Louisiana began with two-year terms that evolved over time to four-year terms. The latter three states had four-year governor terms from the beginning.[2]

Midwestern states typically began with two-year terms, which were then changed to four-year terms. Only Illinois, Indiana, and Missouri adopted quadrennial elections before the twentieth century. Other states changed in the latter half of the 1900s: Ohio (1958), Minnesota (1962), North Dakota (1964), Michigan (1966), Nebraska (1966), Wisconsin (1970), Iowa (1974), Kansas (1974), and South Dakota (1974).[3] In addition, the Far West was partial to four-year terms, but, in this case, most Western states adopted the four-term term at the time of statehood.

Massachusetts was the last state to employ annual elections, which continued until 1920. Beginning in the 1950s, twenty-two states substituted four-year terms for their previous two-year terms. Today, only two states—New Hampshire and Vermont—have two-year gubernatorial election cycles. All other states have four-year cycles.

Although gubernatorial terms have gradually lengthened to match the presidential term and to meet objections by many governors that they spend too much time running for election while in office, many states have attached term limits to these longer election cycles. In the beginning, the thirteen original states were roughly divided about whether restrictions should be placed on a governor's successive years of service. The four New England states (Connecticut, Massachusetts, New Hampshire, and Rhode Island) as well as New York and New Jersey imposed no tenure requirements while the remaining states did. Some states required that governors could serve a certain number of terms, usually two, before stepping down for at least one term. Later, states began to require a maximum number of years of service with no possibility of return. The typical pattern today is a four-year term with a maximum of two consecutive terms. Thirty-eight states have some form of a two consecutive term limit. Virginia permits no successive terms; Utah permits three consecutive terms; and the remaining ten states have no term limits (for a complete discussion of the various changes states made in reeligibility requirements up to 1976, see Kallenbach and Kallenbach, 1977).

Timing of Elections

Another element of the isolation of governors from the patterns of other political offices is the actual times chosen by states to hold gubernatorial elections. In New England the dates for election of governor were timed to town meetings and, therefore, varied considerably, even within a single state across time. Many states also chose to have their gubernatorial elections in odd years, away from the presidential and midterm House election cycles. Even when national law mandated in 1845 that presidential elections be held on the first Tuesday after the first Monday in November of even-numbered years, a number of states held to their odd-numbered year election cycles for governor. It was not until 1872, when a federal law designated the same Tuesday in even-numbered years for elections to the House of Representatives, that states began to change the dates of their elections (Kallenbach, 1966). However, some states continued as a matter of deliberate choice to hold governors' elections outside the national election cycle. While, by 1900, thirty-three of the forty-five states held gubernatorial elections on the first Tuesday after the first Monday of November in presidential election years, several states continued to hold them in the odd-numbered years to avoid the presidential and House races. For instance, even today, Kentucky, Louisiana, Mississippi, New Jersey, and Virginia hold their gubernatorial elections in odd-numbered years preceding presidential election years.

The more customary move for states, however, has been to a four-year election cycle in even-numbered years. But this move has had one particular wrinkle: states have generally opted to hold their gubernatorial elections in midterm rather than presidential years. This is to eliminate any influence the presidential race might have on the gubernatorial contest. Today, only eleven states hold gubernatorial races in presidential election years.

A National View of Gubernatorial Elections

If state constitutions designed governorships to be isolated from national politics, the central question is: Did these designs work? Even given that governor terms are now longer, term limits and elections in the midterm year suggest a continued desire to keep state politics at the state level. But do the partisan patterns present in governors' races instead mimic the patterns found in national politics or are they insulated from them? To begin to address this question, Tables 7-2 through 7-5 present four measures based on the national aggregation of gubernatorial election results: party victories for U.S. governors (Table 7-2), vote percentages received by the parties (presented annually in Table 7-3 and presented over a two-year election cycle in Table 7-4), and party control of statehouses (Table 7-5). Note that the first and fourth measures differ. The first involves the number of gubernatorial races won by a party in a given election year; the fourth counts the number of governorships a party held in a given year, irrespective of whether a state held a gubernatorial election in that year or not. Obviously, not all states held gubernatorial elections in the same year.

Table 7-2 reveals the competitiveness of two-party politics for governor. In examining the entire time frame from 1788 to 1999, the Democratic Party and its historical antecedents, the Democratic-Republicans and the Jacksonian Democrats, have captured 49.4 percent of the governors' contests (for which data are available), and the Republican Party and its historical antecedents (the Federalists, National Republicans, and Whigs) have won 47.4 percent of the gubernatorial elections. Other party candidates have won just 3.2 percent of the races. If only the period since 1854 is examined, when the current Democratic and Republican parties contested elections, then Democrats won 47.5 percent of the races, Republicans took 50.4 percent of the contests, and other candidates won 2.1 percent of the governorships. This suggests not only the highly competitive nature of the gubernatorial races across these two long time frames, but also the extent to which the competition for governor, like that for the national races examined in previous chapters, centers on two main—and only two main—parties. Other party candidates, particularly in the modern period, do not compete very well in gubernatorial races, and this is consistent with their showings in presidential, House, and Senate races.

Another revealing aspect of Table 7-2 is the extent to which the results of even-year and odd-year elections are often quite similar. This similarity is also seen in Table 7-3. Initially, it is important to recognize the sheer number of governors' races in odd years. While House elections in odd years typically involved a substantial minority of states practicing this until 1880 (see Chapter 5), the number of governor elections in odd years often equaled and several times exceeded the number of governor races in even years, although, like the House, the odd-year governors' races tapered off after 1880. However, if the even-year/odd-year election pairs in Table 7-2 are examined (for example,

1792–1793, 1794–1795, and so on), it becomes apparent how party competition for governor viewed at the national level is similar regardless of which year gubernatorial elections were held. From 1788 through 1880 there were twenty-seven pairs of even-odd elections that had similar partisan breakdowns for governor and fifteen that were different if only election pairs with decisive partisan outcomes are considered (that is, election pairs not showing a tied partisan outcome in gubernatorial seats won in one of the two years in any given election pair). If election pairs with tied partisan outcomes are considered, then there are twenty-seven pairs of even-odd elections for governor that had similar partisan breakdowns and twenty that were different.[4] Several of the pairs with different partisan results between even and odd years occurred during the Jeffersonian period—between 1800–1801, 1804–1805, 1806–1807, and 1816–1817—which involved Democratic-Republican states such as Mississippi, Ohio, and Tennessee holding their gubernatorial elections in odd years and thereby accentuating Democratic-Republican strength in those years. Beyond this, though, the political lesson is the extent to which holding gubernatorial elections in odd years does not necessarily achieve different party balances nationally. Of course, candidates running for governor are not really interested in the national party balances between winners and losers since they win and lose in a single state. These separate state vote results for governor in both even- and odd-election years are presented later in this chapter in Tables 7-9 through 7-61. For now, however, the national aggregation of vote results for this race shows that the American governorship is a two-party competitive office that is not isolated from the vote results for president and the House.

Historical Perspective on Gubernatorial Elections

The extent of party competition for governor can also be considered historically (see Tables 7-2 through 7-5). Most significantly, these tables reveal that the six historical eras during which American political parties have competed for national offices are also relevant to the parties' vying for governorships. As discussed in the preceding chapters, these eras are: (1) the Federalist/Democratic-Republican period (1788–1823), (2) the Democratic/National Republican-Whig period (1824–1853), (3) the Civil War and Reconstruction Republican/Democratic period (1854–1893), (4) the conservative Republican/Democratic period (1894–1929), (5) the New Deal Democratic/Republican period (1930–1965), and (6) the competitive Democratic/Republican period (1966 to present).

During the Federalist/Democratic-Republican period, the Federalist Party was successful in winning some gubernatorial elections until 1817, when it declined to only a single victory. The last Federalist candidate for president ran in 1816,[5] while Federalist candidates continued running through 1826 for both the House and governor (see Chapters

4 and 5). Federalists won as many as five statehouses in 1804 at the height of Jeffersonian democracy and consistently won races from 1812 through 1816 during the War of 1812 and its aftermath (see Table 7-2). They also captured a significant percentage of the vote during these years and even during the longer period from 1796 to 1816 (see Table 7-3). But, as can be clearly seen in Table 7-5, the Federalists did less well in controlling statehouses. They held a majority of governorships in only three years during the 1788–1823 period—1788, 1798, and 1800. While they held seven statehouses in 1814, this dwindled thereafter and by 1822 they held only two governorships: Massachusetts and New Jersey. Indeed, as shown in Table 7-6, the strength that the Federalists had in governorships was regionally based in New England and the Mid-Atlantic. This base was similar to that found in House elections (see Chapter 5) and broader than that found in presidential elections, which was concentrated largely in New England alone (see Chapter 4). The Federalists were unable to gain votes in the South and Border South. Thus they had no better luck organizing their party fortunes around governorships than they did around federal offices. Their strength was isolated to two regions and, as Tables 7-9 through 7-17 make clear, it was not in all states in these two regions. The dominance of the Democratic-Republican Party by the early 1820s was a national phenomenon that occurred in virtually all states and across all key elected offices in these states.

In the Democratic/National Republican-Whig era, the National Republicans replaced the Federalists in running for statehouses by the late 1820s. In 1828 they won eight governorships (Table 7-2) and thus held eight statehouses overall in their first year as a formal party (Table 7-5). They were also competitive in votes won during this period, although they never received a majority of the national vote for governor (Tables 7-3 and 7-4). Their successors, the Whigs, fared much better, capturing a majority of statehouses in 1838 and maintaining control over a significant number of them from 1840 through 1850 (Table 7-5). Regionally, Whig candidates for governor, like Whig candidates for the House, ran well in the South and Border South, where the Federalists and National Republicans had failed to make inroads (Tables 7-6 and 7-7). In the 1834–1835 election cycle, southern Whig candidates for governor gained 48 percent of the vote in their first races for the office, while the Democrats averaged 42 percent of the vote. By the election of 1840, when the Whigs took the presidency and the House, their strength was national. They won 10 of 14 governorships, held 13 of 26 statehouses overall, and captured a majority or near majority of the votes for governor in all regions of the country.

However, by 1852, the Whigs began to lose strength in gubernatorial races—they held only four statehouses overall and won elections only in Massachusetts and Vermont in that year. More precisely, Tables 7-3, 7-4, and 7-6 show that the Whigs continued to field relatively strong candidates who garnered more than 40 percent of the total vote, but who, in the final analysis, consistently lost to their Democratic opponents. By 1854–1855, matters worsened for the Whigs. Their support in the South and Border South ended, whereas it had never begun in the West. During this period and also in 1856, candidates began to run as Republicans and on other parties' labels rather than calling themselves Whigs, and the Whig Party's end was at hand. Thus governors' races pinpointed the early erosion of the Whig Party in 1852, before its problems surfaced in House races in 1854 and in the presidential race in 1856 (see Chapters 4 and 5). This shows the ways in which state parties responded to the mounting issue of slavery earlier than is evident in either House or presidential elections. Governorships, then, were not isolated from national politics; instead, they were harbingers of what was going to transpire in national politics. Each state grappled with the issues of slavery, economic growth, and regionalism in different ways, and ultimately these differences could not be resolved.

The Civil War and Reconstruction Republican/Democratic era began in 1854–1855 with victorious Republican candidates for governor in Iowa, Maine, Michigan, New York, and Ohio. Just as the 1854–1855 House election cycle signaled the end of the Whigs and the beginning of the Republican Party and other parties working against the Democrats, governors' races witnessed a similar pattern with Whigs starting to lose strength as early as 1852. Beginning in 1858 Republicans secured a majority of gubernatorial electoral victories in each year until 1874 (except for an electoral tie with Democrats in 1870). In 1862 they gained a majority of the national vote for governor for the first time and also held a majority of all statehouses for the first time (whether elected in that year or not) that they did not relinquish until 1876. Table 7-6 shows that, before the Civil War, Republicans ran best for governor in New England, the Mid-Atlantic, and the Midwest. After the war they did well in all regions, until the 1874–1875 cycle when their support in the South and Border South eroded. While Republicans gained 49 percent of the southern gubernatorial vote in 1872–1873, they captured only 32 percent in 1874–1875. Like House races, the beginnings of the one-party South occurred in 1874–1875 for gubernatorial races—not in 1876 with the Hayes-Tilden presidential contest and the subsequent Compromise of 1876 regarding the removal of Union troops from southern states. The growing split between the voting patterns for governor in the South and the rest of the country is clarified in Table 7-7. After 1874–1875 Republican gubernatorial candidates captured no more than 30 percent of the southern gubernatorial vote until 1960–1961. Outside the South, the 1870s and the 1880s proved to be a very competitive period for the two parties in governors' races, as it was for House and presidential races. However, unlike these two national races, the Democratic Party fared better than the Republican Party in many gubernatorial races. As seen in Table 7-2, the two parties typically won similar numbers of governor races until 1892, when the Democrats won 19 statehouses and the Republicans only won 11. As shown in Table 7-5, the Democrats held a preponderance of statehouses from 1876 to 1894. This advantage was due in part to the South, where Democratic gubernatorial candidates typically won (see Table 7-7). Democrats also did well in the Border South, the Mid-Atlantic, and in some Western states (Table 7-6). Overall, the period after the Civil War reflected a time when governors' races were more local than they had been in the years before the war. The issues fought over in these races tended to be about the state's balance between industrialization and agrarianism and state problems, such as transportation and new forms of communication (Lipson, 1939). While the national races for the presidency and the House tipped slightly in favor of the Republican Party, gubernatorial elections were somewhat removed from this national picture in the postwar period.

However, gubernatorial races were as affected by the events surrounding the Panic of 1893 as were presidential and congressional races. Gubernatorial power shifted in the conservative Republican/Democratic era, which began in 1894. In 1892 Democrats had won 19 gubernatorial contests and the Republicans had won 11; in 1894 the tables turned and Republicans won 20 contests and the Democrats won 8 (Table 7-2). Democrats, who had won 50 percent of the national gubernatorial vote in 1892, only won 39 percent in 1894 (Table 7-3). There was some insulation of governorships from national political trends in 1896, when Democrats were able to win 16 governors' races—the same number won by the Republicans. Thereafter the voting patterns favored the Republicans. The height of Republican strength in this era for president, House, and Senate in 1920 was also matched in gubernatorial elections. Republicans won 29 of 36 governorships in 1920 (Table 7-2) and by 1922 held 34 statehouses overall (Table 7-5).

The emergence of the New Deal era was evident in gubernatorial elections beginning in 1930 when Democrats won 17 of 32 races, having won only 11 statehouses in 1928. This paralleled House and Senate elections in which Democrats took a slight majority in the House and failed to do so by only one seat in the Senate. Democratic strength extended to all regions (Table 7-6), and the party controlled a majority of statehouses in most election years in the 1930–1965 period (Table 7-5). Democratic domination of gubernatorial elections was particularly impressive during the heart of the Democratic realignment from 1930 to 1936. Interestingly, however, Republicans were able to renew their electoral strength in some traditional areas like New England, the Mid-Atlantic, and the Midwest in the mid-to-late 1930s. Still, the dominant political force in gubernatorial elections for much of the 1930–1965 period clearly was the Democratic Party.

The competitive Democratic/Republican era began with a dramatic reversal of Democrats' fortunes in governorships. While Democrats continued to dominate statehouses through 1964–1965, Republicans emerged with 24 of the 35 governorships up for election in 1966, having captured only 8 of 26 in 1964. In the rest of the modern period, Republicans remained competitive in gubernatorial races, winning a substantial number in most years and a majority in 1968,

1980, 1984, 1988, 1994, and 1998 (Table 7-2). In 1968, 1970, 1996, and 1998, the party actually controlled a majority of statehouses (Table 7-5). Beginning in 1980, Republicans made strides in the South in gubernatorial elections and in 1988, for the first time, gained a majority of the votes for governor in the South (Table 7-6). They also continued to do well in the Midwest from 1988 on, although they were not as strongly competitive in the Mid-Atlantic region except in the 1998 election year. The recent election victories of Republicans in the 1990s is believed by some to be a realignment in partisan control of the statehouse. Only time will tell, but what seems obvious at this point is that the 1966–1998 period has witnessed a competitive breakthrough in elections for governor with an increase in Republican successes compared to the previous period in which Democratic realigning forces played a more important role in gubernatorial elections.

Governors of the United States

The remaining tables in this chapter, Tables 7-9 through 7-61, present the state-by-state results of gubernatorial elections from 1788 to 1999. To fully understand these state vote tables, one must realize that the gubernatorial voting data were coded two different ways. As with the House and Senate races, the primary entries in these state vote tables are the percentage of votes received by gubernatorial candidates who used only the label "Democrat" or "Republican" (or their historical antecedents) on the ballot. This is usually referred to as the conventional coding of major-party candidates, which is followed, to a certain extent, by the ICPSR in its coding of the gubernatorial vote. (See ICPSR data set 0075.) Bold italicized vote entries below these conventionally-coded values in Tables 7-9 through 7-61 are designed to more accurately reflect situations where major-party candidates run for governor with other labels, designations, or party names in addition to the major-party label. Table 4-8 shows the five situations where this can occur: major-party candidates running for office (1) who are identified on the ballot as a faction or wing of the major party, (2) who run as a fusion ticket with a minor party, (3) who are endorsed separately on the ballot by a minor party, (4) who are listed as an independent member of the major party, or (5) who are endorsed by both major parties on the ballot. In each case, these are candidates using a major-party label who also have other designations on the ballot. Conventional coding would place these candidates' votes in the "Other" category; the author's alternative coding scheme instead places the votes of these candidates in the column of the major party with which they are affiliated. Thus alternative coding attempts to more accurately capture the partisan nature of the vote for candidates who largely are viewed as major-party candidates but who use other designations or labels on the ballot as well.

Tables 7-9 through 7-61 reveal that, like the national races, most states were predominantly one-party states for governor in several historical periods, the clear exception

being the Democrat/Whig period (for the latter period, see Tables 7-20 through 7-25). As an example, throughout the Federalist/Democratic-Republican period, Pennsylvania was a solidly Democratic state. In each election from 1796 through 1824 the Democratic-Republicans garnered at least a majority of gubernatorial votes in Pennsylvania. In several years Federalists and other parties did not even run candidates against the Democratic-Republicans' choices. In contrast, Massachusetts consistently elected Federalist governors from 1798 through 1822, except in 1808 and 1810. New York was one of the few competitive states for governor during the early Federalist period. Although it typically elected Democratic-Republican governors, the Federalists were quite competitive in the vote for statehouse races (Tables 7-9 through 7-17).

As shown in Tables 7-18 through 7-25, in the Democratic/National Republican-Whig period, what is noteworthy is the keen competition that existed in most states in governor elections from 1834–1835 through the collapse of the Whigs in 1854–1855. Although occasionally there were lopsided victories for one party or the other, in general the two parties fought tight races for governor. It was rare that a candidate won with more than 55 percent of the total vote. The Whigs' appeal to local interests helped to make them far more competitive than the Federalists or National Republicans.

However, as shown in Tables 7-26 through 7-35, the Civil War and its aftermath made states sharply one-party for long periods of time. This was true not only of Democratic governorships in the South, but also of Republican governorships in the Midwest and in New England (especially see Tables 7-30 through 7-35). This one-partyism continued in the conservative Republican-Democratic era (Table 7-35 through 7-44).

Tables 7-45 through 7-53 reveal a temporary suspension of this one-party pattern in 1932, when states with long histories of Republican governors—such as Illinois, Indiana, Iowa, and Michigan in the Midwest, and Massachusetts, Maine, and Rhode Island in New England—elected Democrats to their statehouses. However, this was short-lived as Republican governors were once again soon elected in each of these states. The other pattern of one-partyism is exemplified by the South: states with long traditions of Democratic rule who never deviated in their loyalty to the party of Jefferson and Jackson.

For the most recent period, Tables 7-53 through 7-61 illustrate a return to greater competition, although not to the same degree as experienced in the Democratic/Whig years of the previous century. Most noticeable are southern states who have begun to elect Republican governors but have done so in closely competitive races.

Conclusion

Governors' races, even more than races for the House or Senate, are races about the politics, history, economic conditions, and demographic characteristics of a state.

Governors' races are even less likely to be won or lost on national issues and conditions than are the other races. It is difficult for governors to run on plans to bring about world peace or end nuclear armament, and it is doubtful that gubernatorial candidates who offer plans to revamp major federal programs or end a rising national budget deficit are likely to be taken seriously (although some gubernatorial candidates have indeed offered such plans). The nature of the office, as the chief executive of state government, means that there is a parochial quality to the issues and elections for governor.

This localism, however, should not be confused with a true isolation from national party trends. Throughout the history of American elections there is little evidence that governors have been totally insulated from the throes of national politics. During the pivotal years in American politics, when drastic shifts occurred between parties or one party collapsed and another emerged, these critical realignments have affected races for governor as much as races for national governmental offices. Indeed, notably before the Civil War, changes in party patterns for governor served as a close predictor of the national volatility in the vote yet to come.

Although governorships are not isolated from these major national swings, they do depend heavily on the history of the state, its economy, demography, and past politics during the long stretches when no electoral crisis looms. For many states this political history is wrapped up in one-partyism as the prevailing party has well-established leaders and well-developed ties to key state interests. Thus governor elections maintain a fine balance: they help set state political patterns that are distinct but not isolated from national political questions, controversies, and levels of party competition.

Notes

1. States often had the date of their first gubernatorial election dictated by when the federal government officially admitted them into the Union. However, these states enacted constitutions (or legislation) at the time to ensure that future election dates for governor would be determined according to the preferences of the state rather than circumstances surrounding their admission to statehood. The intent of these constitutional provisions is referred to in the text as the starting date for the election interval and length of term for the gubernatorial office. For example, South Dakota had its first election for state governor for a one-year term in 1889, the year it was admitted to the Union. Once admitted, South Dakota relied on its constitutional provision to have a two-year term for governor starting in 1890 that continued until 1974, when it changed its state law to a four-year term for this office. Obviously, the 1889 election with its one-year term was a temporary expedient to accommodate the fact that statehood was granted in that year and, thus, the state had to quickly select a governor to put in the new statehouse. Thereafter, the state selected its governor according to its constitutional provision that it be a two-year term starting in the even-numbered year of 1890. Other states, however, never bothered to differentiate their election date for governor from their date of admittance to statehood. For example, Alabama held its first election for state governor to serve a two-year term in 1819, the year it was admitted to the Union, and continued with this two-year term for governor with elections in odd-numbered years until the Civil War period. Even though these two states made different decisions on the dates for their gubernatorial elections, their constitutionally imposed starting dates for these elections can be ascertained from Table 7-1 by looking at the pattern of election dates and intervals for the governor's race after each state entered the Union. Similar logic can be employed when determining the constitutional starting dates for the governor's race in the other forty-eight states.

2. See footnote 1.

3. See footnote 1.

4. The author prefers comparisons using gubernatorial data with clear partisan outcomes in adjacent election years to data where ties in partisan outcomes are allowed. In the former, one knows with certainty that in twenty-seven cases the same party won a majority of gubernatorial elections in both election years comprising a two-year election cycle, and that in fifteen cases, different parties were winners in the two election years comprising these election cycles. When adding gubernatorial data with tied partisan outcomes to the data comparisons, these additional election pairings have the potential to change the twenty-seven and fifteen case results above. As it turns out, the addition of tied data to the earlier data comparisons does not change the twenty-seven case result, but it does change the fifteen case result, adding five additional cases, for a total of twenty cases of different election results for governor between the two major parties in adjacent election years. But the meaning of this category has now changed. With the fifteen cases before, it was clear that each major party received a majority of gubernatorial victories in one of the two years comprising a two-year election cycle. But the five additional cases do not indicate this. What they do indicate is that party X won a majority of gubernatorial seats in one election year and tied with party Y in the other year. A tie indicates some weakening of electoral strength of party X, but it does not indicate outright "defeat." Party X has still stayed the course in the sense that it has not allowed party Y to obtain majority status in the second election year. Hence, these five cases present a more mixed picture of the relative strengths of the two major parties rather than a clear-cut picture of one party losing its majority status to its opponent. Seen from this perspective, the twenty-seven versus twenty case comparison does not accurately reflect a national picture of partisan change where one major party has wrested majority power from the other in gubernatorial elections.

5. The Federalists were unable to convene a caucus to nominate an official presidential candidate in 1816, but Rufus King ran as an ad hoc candidate for the party, receiving electoral votes in three states.

Table 7-1 Selection and Terms of American State Governors, 1788–1999

State	Election Year/Selection Method/Term Length/Term Limits
Alabama	1819 (P,2Y); 1865 (P, 3Y); 1868 (P, 2Y); 1902 (P,4Y); 2T
Alaska	1958 (P,4Y); 2T
Arizona	1911 (P, 3Y); 1914 (P,2Y); 1970 (P,4Y); 1990 (MR,4Y); 1994 (P, 4Y) ; 2T
Arkansas	1836 (P,4Y); 1844 (P, 5Y); 1849 (P, 3Y); 1852 (P, 4Y); 1872 (P, 2Y); 1986 (P, 4Y); 2T
California	1849 (P, 2Y); 1863 (P,4Y); 1879 (P, 3Y); 1882 (P, 4Y); 2T
Colorado	1876 (P,2Y);1958 (P,4Y); 2T
Connecticut	1788 (ML,1Y) ; 1876 (M, 2Y); 1902 (P, 2Y); 1950 (P, 4Y); No term limits
Delaware	1789 (L,3Y) ; 1792 (P, 3Y); 1819 (P, 1Y);p 1820 (P, 2Y); 1822 (P, 1Y); 1823 (P, 3Y); 1832 (P, 4Y); 1844 (P, 2Y); 1846 (P, 4Y); 1898 (P, 2Y); 1900 (P, 4Y); 2T
Florida	1845 (P, 3Y); 1848 (P, 4Y); 2T
Georgia	1788 (L, 1Y); 1825 (ML, 2Y); 1868 (ML, 4Y); 1880 (ML, 2Y); 1942 (ML, 4Y); 1994 (MR, 4Y); 2T
Hawaii	1959 (P, 3Y); 1962 (P, 4Y); 2T
Idaho	1890 (P, 2Y); 1946 (P, 4Y); No term limits
Illinois	1818 (P, 4Y); 1846 (P, 2Y); 1848 (P, 4Y); 1976 (P, 2Y); 1978 (P, 4Y); No term limits
Indiana	1816 (P, 3Y); 1852 (P, 4Y); 2T
Iowa	1846 (P, 4Y); 1854 (P, 3Y); 1857 (P, 2Y); 1974 (P, 4Y); 2T
Kansas	1862 (P, 2Y); 1974 (P, 4Y); 2T
Kentucky	1792 (E, 4Y); 1800 (P, 4Y); 1848 (P, 3Y); 1851 (P, 4Y); 2T
Louisiana	1812 (PL, 4Y); 1828 (PL, 3Y); 1834 (PL, 4Y); 1846 (P, 3Y); 1855 (P, 4Y); 1863 (P, 2Y); 1865 (P, 3Y); 1868 (P, 4Y); 1876 (P, 3Y); 1879 (P, 5Y); 1881 (P, 4Y); 1972 (P, 4Y); 1975 (P, 4Y); 2T
Maine	1820 (ML, 1Y); 1880 (P, 2Y); 1958 (P, 4Y); 2T
Maryland	1788 (L, 1Y); 1838 (P, 3Y); 1853 (P, 4Y); 1861 (P, 3Y); 1867 (P, 4Y); 1923 (P, 3Y); 1926 (P, 4Y); 2T
Massachusetts	1788 (ML, 1Y); 1855 (P, 1Y); 1920 (P, 2Y); 1966 (P, 4Y); 2T
Michigan	1835 (P, 2Y); 1966 (P, 4Y); 2T
Minnesota	1857 (P, 2Y); 1962 (P, 4Y); No term limits
Mississippi	1817 (ML, 2Y); 1865 (ML, 3Y); 1868 (ML, 1Y); 1869 (ML, 4Y); 2T
Missouri	1820 (P, 4Y); 1824 (P, 1Y); 1825 (P, 3Y); 1828 (P, 4Y); 1868 (P, 2Y); 1876 (P, 4Y); 2T
Montana	1889 (P, 3Y); 1892 (P, 4Y); 2T
Nebraska	1866 (P, 2Y); 1966 (P, 4Y); 2T
Nevada	1864 (P, 2Y); 1866 (P, 4Y); 2T
New Hampshire	1788 (ML, 1Y); 1880 (P, 2Y); No term limits
New Jersey	1788 (L,1Y); 1844 (P, 3Y); 1949 (P, 4Y) ; 2T
New Mexico	1911 (P, 5Y); 1916 (P, 2Y); 1970 (P, 4Y); 2T
New York	1789 (P, 3Y); 1816 (P, 4Y); 1820 (P, 2Y); 1876 (P, 3Y); 1894 (P, 2Y); 1938 (P, 4Y); No term limits
North Carolina	1788 (L, 1Y); 1836 (P, 2Y); 1864 (P, 1Y); 1866 (P, 2Y); 1868 (P, 4Y); 2T
North Dakota	1889 (P, 1Y); 1890 (P, 2Y); 1964 (P, 4Y); No term limits
Ohio	1803 (P, 2Y); 1807 (P, 1Y); 1808 (P, 2Y); 1850 (P, 1Y); 1851 (P, 2Y); 1905 (P, 3Y); 1908 (P, 2Y); 1958 (P, 4Y); 2T
Oklahoma	1907 (P, 3Y); 1910 (P, 4Y); 2T
Oregon	1858 (P, 4Y); 2T
Pennsylvania	1788 (L, 1Y); 1790 (P, 3Y); 1847 (P, 1Y); 1848 (P, 3Y); 1878 (P, 4Y); 2T
Rhode Island	1790 (MR, 1Y); 1842 (ML, 1Y); 1894 (P, 1Y); 1912 (P, 2Y); 1994 (P, 4Y); 2T
South Carolina	1788 (L, 2Y); 1865 (P, 3Y); 1868 (P, 2Y); 1926 (P, 4Y); 2T
South Dakota	1889 (P, 1Y); 1890 (P, 2Y); 1974 (P, 4Y); 2T
Tennessee	1796 (P, 1Y); 1797 (P, 2Y); 1859 (P, 4Y); 1863 (P, 2Y); 1869 (P, 1Y); 1870 (P, 2Y); 1954 (P, 4Y) ; 2T
Texas	1845 (P, 2Y); 1865 (P, 1Y); 1866 (P, 3Y); 1869 (P, 4Y); 1873 (P, 2Y); 1875 (P, 3Y); 1878 (P, 2Y); 1974 (P, 4Y); No term limits
Utah	1896 (P, 4Y); 3T
Vermont	1791 (ML, 1Y); 1870 (ML, 2Y); No term limits
Virginia	1788 (L, 1Y); 1851 (P, 4Y); 1859 (P, 2Y); 1869 (P, 4Y); 1T
Washington	1889 (P, 3Y); 1892 (P, 4Y); 2T
West Virginia	1863 (P, 1Y); 1864 (P, 2Y); 1872 (P, 4Y); 2T
Wisconsin	1848 (P, 1Y); 1849 (P, 2Y); 1881 (P, 3Y); 1884 (P, 2Y); 1970 (P, 4Y); No term limits
Wyoming	1890 (P, 4Y); 2T

Notes: Election Year = the particular election year for governor in which a change in the term length for governor begins. Selection method = the ways in which governors are elected or selected. The various ways include: P = plurality popular vote of the electorate; MR = majority popular vote of the electorate with a runoff election if no candidate receives a majority of the popular vote; ML = majority popular vote of the electorate with the state legislature making the final choice if no candidate receives a majority of the popular vote; E = electorate votes for electors (usually pledged electors) who, in turn, select the governor (similar to the electoral college system for president); and L = the state legislature selects the governor. Term Length = number of years in a governor's term (or, alternately, the number of years between elections for governor). Term Limits = number of terms that a particular individual can serve as governor according to state law (or, alternately, the number of times that a governor can run for office). 1, 2, and 3T refer to the number of consecutive terms a governor can have before stepping down, according to the current law in each of the fifty states.

To illustrate the use of these definitions: in 1788, selection of the governor in Virginia was decided by the legislature for a one-year term. The legislature selected governors annually in both even- and odd-numbered years (1788, 1789, and so on). In 1851 selection of the governor was by popular plurality vote every four years. The electorate chose governors every four years in odd-numbered years only (1851, 1855, and so on). In 1859 the electorate was asked to vote for governor every two years. The electorate then voted every two years in odd-numbered years (1859, 1861, and so on). Finally, in 1869 Virginia asked its voters to elect a governor every four years, so the electorate voted every four years in odd-numbered years up to the present election for governor in 1997. Currently Virginia has a unique and stringent term limit on governors, allowing governors only to sit for one term and, hence, not succeed themselves at the next election.

Sources: Adapted from *Congressional Quarterly's Guide to U.S. Elections*, (1994); *American State Governors, 1776–1976*, vol. 1 (1977); and *Book of the States*, vol. 32, (1999).

Table 7-2 Election Victories for Governor, 1788–1999

Year	Democrats	Republicans	Others	Year	Democrats	Republicans	Others
1788	0	0	3	1863	1	14	5
1789	1	1	2	1864	0	15	1
1790	2	0	3	1865	2	14	2
1791	2	0	2	1866	1	14	2
1792	4	1	1	1867	4	9	0
1793	3	0	3	1868	4	18	0
1794	1	1	3	1869	0	14	1
1795	1	3	3	1870	9	9	0
1796	3	2	2	1871	4	9	0
1797	2	4	0	1872	4	18	1
1798	1	6	0	1873	5	7	0
1799	3	4	0	1874	12	7	0
1800	2	4	0	1875	5	8	1
1801	4	4	0	1876	13	10	0
1802	2	4	0	1877	4	7	0
1803	3	4	0	1878	7	12	0
1804	3	5	0	1879	3	10	0
1805	5	3	0	1880	11	12	0
1806	1	3	1	1881	1	6	1
1807	7	2	0	1882	16	6	0
1808	7	2	0	1883	4	4	0
1809	2	3	0	1884	13	11	0
1810	6	1	0	1885	3	4	0
1811	4	2	0	1886	12	12	0
1812	1	5	1	1887	3	3	0
1813	2	5	0	1888	12	14	0
1814	2	4	0	1889	7	4	0
1815	2	4	0	1890	15	12	0
1816	4	4	1	1891	6	1	0
1817	5	1	1	1892	19	11	1
1818	4	1	1	1893	2	3	0
1819	5	2	2	1894	8	20	0
1820	10	1	2	1895	1	7	0
1821	8	1	0	1896	16	16	1
1822	10	1	0	1897	1	4	0
1823	10	1	0	1898	11	17	0
1824	8	1	2	1899	2	5	0
1825	9	2	1	1900	14	19	0
1826	7	3	1	1901	1	5	0
1827	8	1	1	1902	9	18	0
1828	3	8	1	1903	4	3	0
1829	7	4	1	1904	13	20	0
1830	4	5	0	1905	2	2	0
1831	6	5	1	1906	11	17	0
1832	9	2	1	1907	4	3	0
1833	7	2	1	1908	15	19	0
1834	5	5	1	1909	1	2	0
1835	8	3	1	1910	16	13	1
1836	7	6	0	1911	5	2	0
1837	6	6	0	1912	20	12	3
1838	6	7	0	1913	3	0	0
1839	7	4	0	1914	15	14	1
1840	4	10	0	1915	3	1	0
1841	8	5	0	1916	17	19	1
1842	8	3	0	1917	1	1	0
1843	7	5	0	1918	10	22	0
1844	6	9	1	1919	3	2	0
1845	7	5	1	1920	7	29	0
1846	7	7	0	1921	1	0	0
1847	9	5	0	1922	20	13	0
1848	5	10	0	1923	3	0	0
1849	13	4	0	1924	14	22	0
1850	9	4	0	1925	2	0	0
1851	10	4	2	1926	13	20	0
1852	12	2	0	1927	1	1	0
1853	14	2	0	1928	11	24	0
1854	3	7	1	1929	1	0	0
1855	8	4	5	1930	17	13	2
1856	6	7	1	1931	3	0	0
1857	8	9	1	1932	29	5	1
1858	3	8	0	1933	1	0	0
1859	9	11	0	1934	25	7	2
1860	5	10	0	1935	2	0	0
1861	1	12	3	1936	28	4	3
1862	2	10	1	1937	2	0	0

Table 7-2 *(Continued)*

Year	Democrats	Republicans	Others	Year	Democrats	Republicans	Others
1938	15	18	0	1973	1	1	0
1939	2	0	0	1974	27	7	1
1940	18	17	0	1975	3	0	0
1941	1	0	0	1976	9	5	0
1942	14	18	1	1977	1	1	0
1943	1	2	0	1978	21	15	0
1944	16	17	0	1979	2	1	0
1945	1	0	0	1980	6	7	0
1946	14	20	0	1981	1	1	0
1947	2	0	0	1982	26	10	0
1948	20	12	0	1983	3	0	0
1949	1	1	0	1984	5	8	0
1950	11	22	0	1985	1	1	0
1951	2	0	0	1986	19	17	0
1952	12	20	0	1987	3	0	0
1953	1	0	0	1988	5	7	0
1954	18	15	0	1989	2	0	0
1955	2	0	0	1990	19	15	2
1956	16	14	0	1991	2	1	0
1957	2	0	0	1992	8	4	0
1958	26	8	0	1993	0	2	0
1959	2	1	0	1994	11	24	1
1960	16	11	0	1995	1	2	0
1961	2	0	0	1996	7	4	0
1962	21	14	0	1997	0	2	0
1963	2	0	0	1998	11	23	2
1964	18	8	0	1999	2	1	0
1965	2	0	0				
1966	11	24	0				
1967	1	1	0				
1968	9	13	0				
1969	0	2	0				
1970	22	13	0				
1971	2	0	0				
1972	12	7	0				

Notes: Entries reflect winners from the actual vote result and are not adjusted for contested seats, runoffs, inaccuracies of other types in reporting party labels or winners, or gubernatorial and legislative proclamations of different winners. For these reasons, the figures may not completely correspond to other reports on gubernatorial winners and losers. The figures also may not completely correspond to the state vote tables for governor in this chapter (Tables 7-9 through 7-61), since winners for governor are usually known in states even when these states do not report any official vote for governor or only report a partial vote for governor. Further, some gubernatorial returns, while reported by the states, were never recovered by this or any other data recovery project.

Parties in Table 7-2 are coded as follows: Republicans = Republican Party since 1854. Federalists, National Republicans, and Whigs are considered historical precursors to the Republican Party in this table. Democrats = Democratic Party since 1830. Anti-Federalists, Democratic-Republicans, and Jackson Democrats are considered historical antecedents to the Democratic Party in this table. Also see Appendix A for a list of the various labels and designations used by historical antecedents of the Republican and Democratic parties. Note that both the Whig Party and the Republican Party fielded candidates for governor in 1854–1855; hence, the winning candidates from both parties are aggregated under the "Republican" column for these years. Other = candidates who use third-party names only on the ballot or are listed as independent or unaffiliated. Odd-numbered year gubernatorial elections were common before 1880 and several states still scheduled governor elections in odd-numbered years after that. Special gubernatorial elections are not included in the table.

Sources: Data adapted from *Congressional Quarterly's Guide to U.S. Elections* (1994); *American State Governors, 1776–1976*, vol. 1 (1977); ICPSR data sets 0001 and 0075; and independent search for state sources by the author. Several pre-1824 party affiliations were obtained from the election archive of Michael J. Dubin. Other party affiliations were obtained from independent searches of state sources when the *American State Governors* volume and the *Congressional Quarterly Guide* disagreed. The author's alternative party coding was used where applicable; see Table 7-8 for states and years when alternative party coding occurred.

Table 7-3 National Results for Gubernatorial Elections, by Election Year, 1788–1999 (Percentages)

Year	Democratic	Republican	Other	Democratic % of Two-Party Vote	Year	Democratic	Republican	Other	Democratic % of Two-Party Vote
1788	25.00	20.75	54.25	54.70	1863	30.28	48.22	21.49	39.65
1789	17.23	14.30	68.47	50.00	1864	31.25	56.51	12.23	35.66
1790	37.43	3.07	59.50	95.40	1865	35.75	47.91	16.34	41.27
1791	48.40	0.00	51.60	100.00	1866	34.33	56.36	9.30	34.36
1792	36.71	24.49	38.80	50.11	1867	44.96	53.36	1.68	44.97
1793	34.62	9.14	56.25	81.73	1868	36.82	60.01	3.16	36.82
1794	0.00	24.29	75.71	0.00	1869	34.28	55.59	10.12	37.29
1795	9.37	40.88	49.74	15.62	1870	45.65	52.81	1.54	46.25
1796	24.19	45.59	30.22	24.19	1871	46.46	52.55	0.98	46.87
1797	47.78	48.53	3.69	47.78	1872	45.35	52.20	2.44	47.69
1798	30.83	65.10	4.08	31.70	1873	40.53	51.24	8.22	41.06
1799	38.38	51.37	10.25	38.46	1874	48.82	48.33	2.84	50.06
1800	37.80	44.03	18.18	54.18	1875	49.16	45.01	5.83	52.01
1801	55.39	42.88	1.73	55.69	1876	49.22	46.58	4.19	51.54
1802	48.64	50.82	0.53	48.82	1877	53.15	41.13	5.71	55.72
1803	61.85	37.77	0.38	61.99	1878	52.47	37.13	10.39	57.86
1804	52.12	47.73	0.14	52.19	1879	42.60	48.26	9.13	46.01
1805	68.39	31.01	0.60	68.62	1880	52.66	41.58	5.75	56.75
1806	53.13	44.39	2.49	54.98	1881	40.62	48.32	11.05	49.01
1807	61.78	31.58	6.64	68.33	1882	53.48	42.50	4.01	55.39
1808	63.15	29.24	7.61	70.45	1883	49.29	49.10	1.60	50.06
1809	46.10	53.28	0.62	46.42	1884	52.93	44.67	2.39	54.10
1810	57.10	42.50	0.40	57.29	1885	54.13	43.49	2.37	55.22
1811	59.84	38.83	1.33	60.79	1886	53.08	40.49	6.42	57.05
1812	40.19	42.70	17.12	50.49	1887	48.17	47.08	4.74	50.55
1813	46.72	52.27	1.02	47.14	1888	53.45	40.84	5.70	57.61
1814	42.53	52.75	4.72	42.96	1889	50.90	46.75	2.34	52.14
1815	44.85	44.40	10.75	54.88	1890	51.89	41.96	6.14	54.77
1816	50.65	31.95	17.39	60.09	1891	49.99	45.18	4.82	52.52
1817	53.86	28.96	17.18	64.45	1892	50.42	37.76	11.81	57.08
1818	64.38	19.97	15.64	76.33	1893	46.84	40.29	12.86	57.15
1819	53.15	14.40	32.46	81.49	1894	38.53	44.06	17.40	47.74
1820	67.95	8.09	23.96	90.41	1895	44.04	46.16	9.79	50.19
1821	73.39	9.58	17.03	90.29	1896	47.88	42.78	9.33	54.10
1822	63.98	17.13	18.89	80.93	1897	44.91	50.82	4.27	46.71
1823	66.96	12.69	20.35	85.99	1898	48.62	44.05	7.33	53.71
1824	56.00	18.52	25.48	77.34	1899	48.63	44.05	7.31	52.79
1825	71.64	22.58	5.79	76.89	1900	52.04	44.60	3.36	54.09
1826	51.14	32.45	16.40	61.52	1901	43.47	52.19	4.33	45.31
1827	72.86	10.55	16.59	88.61	1902	49.22	44.31	6.47	52.02
1828	47.35	41.22	11.42	53.36	1903	53.53	43.10	3.36	55.08
1829	66.34	23.56	10.09	73.73	1904	49.87	45.99	4.13	51.74
1830	50.76	40.19	9.04	56.77	1905	50.92	46.21	2.86	52.32
1831	46.38	34.76	18.86	57.79	1906	51.79	43.29	4.91	54.11
1832	44.43	37.17	18.39	58.74	1907	53.02	41.04	5.93	55.28
1833	55.14	17.09	27.77	76.86	1908	51.53	43.91	4.55	53.90
1834	37.96	44.59	17.44	45.92	1909	49.63	47.26	3.11	51.06
1835	46.25	32.08	21.66	58.22	1910	49.42	43.57	7.00	52.59
1836	46.51	41.04	12.44	55.16	1911	55.86	40.64	3.50	57.98
1837	46.58	43.23	10.19	51.86	1912	47.31	32.82	19.86	58.47
1838	43.89	44.29	11.81	51.80	1913	59.26	20.90	19.83	72.11
1839	49.88	40.77	9.35	55.00	1914	46.21	40.55	13.23	52.50
1840	43.86	52.70	3.43	43.98	1915	59.23	36.05	4.71	62.51
1841	47.70	50.70	1.59	48.43	1916	48.57	46.39	5.03	51.54
1842	47.65	46.68	5.66	49.22	1917	53.22	43.03	3.74	54.76
1843	49.81	45.00	5.18	52.81	1918	48.84	45.10	6.05	51.09
1844	45.32	44.39	10.28	50.63	1919	55.48	41.93	2.58	57.04
1845	51.62	39.22	9.16	58.73	1920	42.58	50.33	7.08	45.19
1846	47.60	46.70	5.69	50.49	1921	66.15	33.62	0.23	66.30
1847	50.70	43.05	6.24	54.39	1922	49.09	45.24	5.66	50.57
1848	48.78	44.99	6.22	51.67	1923	69.74	29.69	0.56	70.05
1849	51.63	37.76	10.60	60.00	1924	47.90	46.86	5.23	49.46
1850	45.36	48.41	6.22	47.68	1925	62.97	36.78	0.24	63.09
1851	49.48	39.09	11.42	53.73	1926	47.44	48.55	4.00	48.48
1852	49.08	43.53	7.38	52.74	1927	73.96	26.04	0.00	73.96
1853	52.52	40.20	7.28	56.39	1928	48.36	50.40	1.23	48.80
1854	41.47	47.13	11.40	46.64	1929	62.78	36.94	0.27	62.95
1855	45.26	21.14	33.60	76.07	1930	48.49	44.58	6.92	51.86
1856	45.65	35.29	19.05	61.90	1931	70.70	28.38	0.91	71.24
1857	50.56	33.30	16.13	64.94	1932	56.16	39.11	4.72	58.46
1858	44.35	41.18	14.46	57.62	1933	73.73	24.24	2.02	75.26
1859	56.00	37.93	6.09	61.64	1934	56.54	37.75	5.70	59.53
1860	49.40	43.76	6.83	55.25	1935	77.22	22.57	0.20	77.34
1861	38.91	48.97	12.12	44.27	1936	56.69	37.81	5.50	58.50
1862	29.79	59.31	10.89	32.28	1937	66.81	31.77	1.42	67.78

Table 7-3 *(Continued)*

Year	Democratic	Republican	Other	Democratic % of Two-Party Vote	Year	Democratic	Republican	Other	Democratic % of Two-Party Vote
1938	53.08	42.41	4.50	54.71	1973	33.20	41.42	25.39	33.70
1939	78.26	21.74	0.00	78.26	1974	56.72	39.86	3.42	58.86
1940	55.69	41.82	2.48	56.40	1975	71.68	27.43	0.89	72.15
1941	80.58	17.88	1.54	81.84	1976	52.89	45.84	1.27	53.53
1942	51.30	45.06	3.63	52.34	1977	49.50	48.86	1.64	50.38
1943	64.33	35.23	0.43	64.54	1978	51.05	45.75	3.20	52.58
1944	52.30	47.17	0.52	52.55	1979	56.71	43.29	0.00	56.71
1945	66.58	31.04	2.38	68.20	1980	50.09	49.28	0.62	50.36
1946	49.88	49.25	0.86	50.19	1981	51.45	47.94	0.62	51.76
1947	77.39	22.47	0.14	77.47	1982	54.75	43.40	1.85	55.80
1948	55.62	43.80	0.57	55.91	1983	57.33	39.76	2.91	59.04
1949	58.78	39.49	1.73	59.86	1984	48.89	50.63	0.47	49.18
1950	52.51	47.02	0.46	52.75	1985	42.26	57.19	0.55	42.42
1951	77.30	22.70	0.00	77.30	1986	50.80	45.00	4.20	52.42
1952	51.48	48.32	0.19	51.57	1987	59.16	40.84	0.00	59.16
1953	54.00	44.47	1.52	54.83	1988	47.52	50.29	2.19	48.58
1954	55.67	43.78	0.54	56.13	1989	55.68	43.49	0.84	56.20
1955	79.01	20.73	0.27	79.16	1990	50.32	44.17	5.50	53.18
1956	53.89	44.60	1.50	54.68	1991	57.83	41.64	0.53	58.08
1957	58.85	40.44	0.70	59.26	1992	52.92	41.94	5.13	55.26
1958	59.48	39.03	1.49	60.66	1993	44.59	53.80	1.62	45.36
1959	69.74	30.18	0.07	69.78	1994	42.95	49.81	7.24	46.61
1960	52.76	46.79	0.44	53.01	1995	43.95	55.92	0.13	44.01
1961	57.10	42.44	0.45	57.34	1996	49.42	48.76	1.82	50.50
1962	54.63	43.95	1.41	55.62	1997	44.19	51.34	4.47	46.35
1963	56.33	43.67	0.00	56.33	1998	42.82	50.64	6.54	45.87
1964	55.23	44.46	0.30	55.39	1999	46.70	49.50	3.80	48.20
1965	52.64	39.39	7.96	57.11					
1966	48.47	49.09	2.43	49.94					
1967	59.13	40.46	0.40	59.33					
1968	52.52	47.11	0.37	52.72					
1969	41.94	56.08	1.98	42.79					
1970	51.64	46.21	2.15	52.91					
1971	63.80	22.17	14.04	76.64					
1972	52.11	45.81	2.08	53.13					

Notes: Main entries are calculated from the two decimal place versions of the vote values in Tables 7-9 through 7-61. Whenever bold italicized values occur in Tables 7-9 through 7-61, denoting the author's alternative party coding system, they are used instead of the conventionally coded main entries in these tables in the aggregation process to the national level for Table 7-3. See text and Table 5-1 for a more complete discussion of the conventional and alternative party coding systems. Also see Table 1-3 in Chapter 1 for a similar discussion. Entries in Table 7-3 are, therefore, based on candidates who use the designation "Democrat" or "Republican" (or their historical antecedents listed in Appendix A), either solely or with other labels or parties (often minor parties) on the ballot. In general, historical antecedents to the Democratic Party were Anti-Federalists, Democratic-Republicans, and Jackson Democrats; historical precursors of the Republican Party were Federalists, National Republicans, and Whigs. Other = candidates who use third-party names only on the ballot or are listed as independent or unidentified. Odd-numbered year gubernatorial elections were common before 1880 and several states still scheduled governor elections in odd-numbered years after that. Special governor elections are not included in this table. Note that both the Whig Party and the Republican Party fielded candidates for governor in 1854–1855; hence, the votes of the winning candidates are aggregated together under the "Republican" column for these years. In this table, each state is weighted equally in getting the national vote result by using state vote percents rather than raw vote counts. In this way, a few highly populated states do not unduly influence the national values in this table. This seems the best strategy for determining national political trends for what is clearly a state, not a national, political office. The reader, however, should note that this strategy is not considered the best strategy to use for national offices such as the presidency, House, and Senate; for these offices, raw votes are generally considered more appropriate to use than vote percents to determine national political trends, as demonstrated in the national vote tables in Chapters 4, 5, and 6.

Sources: Data from Tables 7-9 through 7-61, as adapted from *American State Governors, 1776–1976*, vol. 1 (1977), *Congressional Quarterly's Guide to U.S. Elections* (1994), ICPSR data sets 0001 and 0075, and independent search for state sources by the author. Several pre-1824 party affiliations were obtained from the election archive of Michael J. Dubin. Other party affiliations were obtained from independent searches of state sources when the *American State Governors* volume and the *Congressional Quarterly Guide* disagreed. The author's alternative party coding was used where applicable; see Table 7-8 for states and years when alternative party coding occurred.

Table 7-4 National Results for Gubernatorial Elections, by Two-Year Election Cycle, 1788–1999 (Percentages)

Year	Democratic	Republican	Other	Democratic % of Two-Party Vote	Year	Democratic	Republican	Other	Democratic % of Two-Party Vote
1788–1789	20.34	16.88	62.78	51.57	1898–1899	48.62	44.05	7.32	53.53
1790–1791	41.82	1.84	56.34	96.93	1900–1901	50.73	45.76	3.50	52.74
1792–1793	35.66	16.81	47.53	62.76	1902–1903	50.10	44.06	5.83	52.65
1794–1795	5.86	34.66	59.48	11.72	1904–1905	49.98	46.01	4.00	51.80
1796–1797	34.30	46.85	18.85	34.30	1906–1907	52.03	42.84	5.12	54.35
1798–1799	34.19	58.99	6.82	34.70	1908–1909	51.38	44.18	4.43	53.67
1800–1801	48.99	43.30	7.71	55.14	1910–1911	50.63	43.02	6.34	53.61
1802–1803	54.65	44.89	0.46	54.81	1912–1913	48.30	31.83	19.86	59.61
1804–1805	60.26	39.37	0.37	60.41	1914–1915	47.74	40.02	12.23	53.68
1806–1807	58.45	36.51	5.04	63.20	1916–1917	48.82	46.21	4.96	51.71
1808–1809	56.95	37.98	5.07	61.71	1918–1919	49.74	44.67	5.58	51.89
1810–1811	58.24	40.97	0.79	58.74	1920–1921	43.23	49.87	6.89	45.78
1812–1813	43.45	47.48	9.07	48.70	1922–1923	50.80	43.95	5.24	52.20
1814–1815	43.60	48.90	7.50	48.46	1924–1925	48.69	46.33	4.97	50.17
1816–1817	52.00	30.70	17.30	62.03	1926–1927	48.95	47.27	3.77	49.93
1818–1819	57.80	16.68	25.53	69.37	1928–1929	48.75	50.03	1.21	49.19
1820–1821	70.18	8.70	21.12	90.35	1930–1931	50.39	43.19	6.40	53.52
1822–1823	65.54	14.80	19.65	83.59	1932–1933	56.66	38.69	4.64	58.93
1824–1825	63.82	20.55	15.63	77.09	1934–1935	57.68	36.91	5.40	60.52
1826–1827	61.43	22.08	16.49	75.07	1936–1937	57.23	37.48	5.28	59.00
1828–1829	56.43	32.78	10.79	63.54	1938–1939	54.52	41.23	4.24	56.05
1830–1831	48.26	37.09	14.65	57.35	1940–1941	56.38	41.16	2.45	57.11
1832–1833	49.30	28.04	22.65	66.51	1942–1943	52.38	44.25	3.37	53.36
1834–1835	42.48	37.77	19.74	52.68	1944–1945	52.72	46.70	0.57	53.01
1836–1837	46.54	42.03	11.42	53.67	1946–1947	51.41	47.76	0.82	51.71
1838–1839	46.63	42.68	10.69	53.25	1948–1949	55.80	43.54	0.65	56.14
1840–1841	45.78	51.70	2.51	46.21	1950–1951	53.93	45.63	0.43	54.15
1842–1843	48.73	45.84	5.42	51.02	1952–1953	51.63	48.09	0.27	51.77
1844–1845	48.16	42.07	9.78	56.40	1954–1955	57.00	42.47	0.53	57.44
1846–1847	49.16	44.87	5.96	52.44	1956–1957	54.20	44.34	1.45	54.96
1848–1849	50.29	41.15	8.55	56.10	1958–1959	60.31	38.31	1.38	61.40
1850–1851	47.69	43.13	9.18	51.11	1960–1961	53.05	46.49	0.45	53.31
1852–1853	50.85	41.81	7.33	54.62	1962–1963	54.72	43.94	1.33	55.66
1854–1855	43.69	31.89	24.41	63.89	1964–1965	55.04	44.10	0.85	55.52
1856–1857	48.32	34.21	17.46	63.51	1966–1967	49.05	48.62	2.32	50.45
1858–1859	51.85	39.08	9.06	60.21	1968–1969	51.64	47.86	0.50	51.89
1860–1861	43.86	46.49	9.64	49.76	1970–1971	52.30	44.91	2.79	54.19
1862–1863	30.09	52.59	17.32	36.49	1972–1973	50.31	45.39	4.30	51.28
1864–1865	33.62	51.97	14.40	38.64	1974–1975	57.90	38.88	3.22	59.91
1866–1867	39.13	55.01	5.86	39.15	1976–1977	52.47	46.21	1.32	53.14
1868–1869	35.79	58.22	5.98	37.00	1978–1979	51.49	45.56	2.95	52.89
1870–1871	45.97	52.71	1.31	46.50	1980–1981	50.27	49.10	0.62	50.55
1872–1873	43.70	51.87	4.42	45.42	1982–1983	54.95	43.12	1.93	56.05
1874–1875	48.97	46.92	4.11	50.88	1984–1985	48.01	51.51	0.48	48.28
1876–1877	50.49	44.82	4.68	52.89	1986–1987	51.24	44.79	3.98	52.78
1878–1879	48.46	41.66	9.88	53.04	1988–1989	48.68	49.32	2.00	49.66
1880–1881	49.55	43.32	7.12	54.75	1990–1991	50.90	43.98	5.12	53.55
1882–1883	52.36	44.26	3.37	53.97	1992–1993	51.73	43.64	4.63	53.84
1884–1885	53.21	44.40	2.39	54.36	1994–1995	43.02	50.28	6.69	46.41
1886–1887	52.09	41.82	6.08	55.75	1996–1997	48.61	49.16	2.23	49.86
1888–1889	52.69	42.60	4.70	55.98	1998–1999	43.13	50.54	6.33	46.06
1890–1891	51.50	42.62	5.87	54.31					
1892–1893	49.92	38.11	11.96	57.09					
1894–1895	39.75	44.53	15.71	48.28					
1896–1897	47.49	43.84	8.67	53.13					

Notes: Main entries are calculated from the two decimal place versions of the vote values in Tables 7-9 through 7-61. Whenever bold italicized values occur in Tables 7-9 through 7-61, denoting the author's alternative party coding system, they are used instead of the conventionally coded main entries in these tables in the aggregation process to the national level for Table 7-4. See text and Table 5-1 for a more complete discussion of the conventional and alternative party coding systems. Also see Table 1-3 in Chapter 1 for a similar discussion. Entries in Table 7-4 are, therefore, based on candidates who use the designation "Democrat" or "Republican" (or their historical antecedents listed in Appendix A), either solely or with other labels or parties (often minor parties) on the ballot. In general, historical antecedents to the Democratic Party were Anti-Federalists, Democratic-Republicans, and Jackson Democrats; historical precursors of the Republican Party were Federalists, National Republicans, and Whigs. Other = candidates who use third-party names only on the ballot or are listed as independent or unidentified. Odd-numbered year gubernatorial elections were common before 1880 and several states still scheduled governor elections in odd-numbered years after that. Special governor elections are not included in this table. Note that both the Whig Party and the Republican Party fielded candidates for governor in 1854–1855; hence, the votes of the winning candidates are aggregated together under the "Republican" column for these years. In this table, each state is weighted equally in getting the national vote result by using state vote percents rather than raw vote counts. In this way, a few highly populated states do not unduly influence the national values in this table. This seems the best strategy for determining national political trends for what is clearly a state, not a national, political office. The reader, however, should note that this strategy is not considered the best strategy to use for national offices such as the presidency, House, and Senate; for these offices, raw votes are generally considered more appropriate to use than vote percents to determine national political trends, as demonstrated in the national vote tables in Chapters 4, 5, and 6.

Sources: Data from Tables 7-9 through 7-61, as adapted from *American State Governors, 1776–1976,* vol. 1 (1977), *Congressional Quarterly's Guide to U.S. Elections* (1994), ICPSR data sets 0001 and 0075, and independent search for state sources by the author. Several pre-1824 party affiliations were obtained from the election archive of Michael J. Dubin. Other party affiliations were obtained from independent searches of state sources when the *American State Governors* volume and the *Congressional Quarterly Guide* disagreed. The author's alternative party coding was used where applicable; see Table 7-8 for states and years when alternative party coding occurred.

Table 7-5 Party Control of Statehouses, 1788–1998

Year	Democrats	Republicans	Others	Year	Democrats	Republicans	Others
1788	1	5	6	1898	21	24	0
1790	3	1	4	1900	22	23	0
1792	5	5	5	1902	17	28	0
1794	5	5	5	1904	18	27	0
1796	6	5	5	1906	17	28	0
1798	7	8	1	1908	20	26	0
1800	7	9	0	1910	20	26	0
1802	12	4	0	1912	27	21	0
1804	13	4	0	1914	31	17	0
1806	13	4	0	1916	28	20	0
1808	13	3	1	1918	25	22	1
1810	14	2	1	1920	20	27	1
1812	14	3	1	1922	14	34	0
1814	10	7	1	1924	27	21	0
1816	13	5	1	1926	24	24	0
1818	16	4	1	1928	21	27	0
1820	19	3	1	1930	18	30	0
1822	21	2	1	1932	38	8	2
1824	21	2	1	1934	38	8	2
1826	19	4	1	1936	37	9	2
1828	15	8	1	1938	37	8	3
1830	16	7	1	1940	30	18	0
1832	15	8	1	1942	28	20	0
1834	17	6	1	1944	22	26	0
1836	17	9	0	1946	24	24	0
1838	10	16	0	1948	24	24	0
1840	13	13	0	1950	29	19	0
1842	13	13	0	1952	23	25	0
1844	17	10	0	1954	19	29	0
1846	17	11	1	1956	27	21	0
1848	21	9	0	1958	29	19	0
1850	22	9	0	1960	34	16	0
1852	25	4	2	1962	34	16	0
1854	27	4	0	1964	34	16	0
1856	18	8	5	1966	33	17	0
1858	16	13	3	1968	24	26	0
1860	18	14	1	1970	18	32	0
1862	13	20	1	1972	30	20	0
1864	7	25	4	1974	32	18	0
1866	3	27	6	1976	36	13	1
1868	4	27	6	1978	37	12	1
1870	7	29	1	1980	31	19	0
1872	11	25	1	1982	27	23	0
1874	17	20	0	1984	35	15	0
1876	19	19	0	1986	34	16	0
1878	24	14	0	1988	27	23	0
1880	20	18	0	1990	29	21	0
1882	17	20	1	1992	28	20	2
1884	25	12	1	1994	29	19	2
1886	22	16	0	1996	17	32	1
1888	21	17	0	1998	18	30	2
1890	23	21	0				
1892	26	18	0				
1894	27	16	1				
1896	19	26	0				

Notes: Entries are based on who was governor in each state in the years listed in Table 7-5. Pre-1824 entries are found in a variety of sources: *Biographical Directory of the Governors of the States, 1789–1978*, vol. 1 (1978), *American State Governors, 1776–1976*, vol. 1 (1977), *Congressional Quarterly's Guide to U.S. Elections* (1994), and *The American Governor from Figurehead to Leader* (1939). Discrepancies in these sources were resolved by using the election archive of Michael J. Dubin and independent search of state sources by the author. Entries in the post-1824 period are largely based on the "Governors of the States" section in *Congressional Quarterly's Guide to U.S. Elections* (1994), pp. 639–663, which lists all governors' years of service in office from 1824 to 1994. The author also used Kallenbach and Kallenbach (1977) and independent search of state sources to correct any errors in the Congressional Quarterly source for the post-1824 period. *America Votes* (various publication dates) was used to update the data file through 1998. In cases where two different governors served in a given state in a given year listed in Table 7-5, the governor with the longer term of service in that year was used in the national totals in this table. If three or more different governors served in a given state in a given year listed in Table 7-5, the governor with the longest term of service in that year was used in this table. The governor who served the longest in a year listed in the table was used for Table 7-5 even if he or she was replaced by another governor in an election in that year. In essence, Table 7-5 focuses on determining the governor of record for each state for each year listed in the table according to these guidelines, regardless of whether there was a gubernatorial election in a state in that year or not, and, if there was, regardless of whether the electorate or the state legislature selected the governor.

Sources: *Biographical Directory of the Governors of the United States, 1789–1978*, vol. 1 (1978); *Congressional Quarterly's Guide to U.S. Elections* (1994), especially pp. 639–663; *America State Governors, 1776–1976*, vol. 1 (1977); *The American Governor from Figurehead to Leader* (1939); *America Votes* (various publication dates); the election archive of Michael J. Dubin; and independent search of state sources by the author. The author's alternative party coding system was also used where applicable; see Table 7-8.

Table 7-6 Votes in Gubernatorial Elections by Region, 1788–1999 (Percentages)

Year/Region[1]	Democratic	Republican	Other	Democratic % of Two-Party Vote	Year/Region[1]	Democratic	Republican	Other	Democratic % of Two-Party Vote
1788–1789 NEng	12.50	21.10	66.40	27.35	1814–1815 NEng	38.94	57.14	3.92	39.47
1788–1789 South	—	—	—	—	1814–1815 South	42.80	0.00	57.20	100.00
1788–1789 MAtl	51.70	0.00	48.30	100.00	1814–1815 MAtl	62.59	36.28	1.14	63.31
1788–1789 BdrS	—	—	—	—	1814–1815 BdrS	—	—	—	—
1788–1789 MidW	—	—	—	—	1814–1815 MidW	72.01	27.99	0.00	72.01
1788–1789 West	—	—	—	—	1814–1815 West	—	—	—	—
1790–1791 NEng	29.58	0.00	70.43	100.00	1816–1817 NEng	41.84	47.88	10.28	42.08
1790–1791 South	—	—	—	—	1816–1817 South	54.77	0.00	45.23	100.00
1790–1791 MAtl	90.82	9.18	0.00	90.82	1816–1817 MAtl	51.21	33.06	15.73	66.94
1790–1791 BdrS	—	—	—	—	1816–1817 BdrS	100.00	0.00	0.00	100.00
1790–1791 MidW	—	—	—	—	1816–1817 MidW	75.90	2.61	21.50	97.40
1790–1791 West	—	—	—	—	1816–1817 West	—	—	—	—
1792–1793 NEng	34.30	0.00	65.70	100.00	1818–1819 NEng	44.00	22.91	33.09	66.36
1792–1793 South	—	—	—	—	1818–1819 South	71.80	0.00	28.20	100.00
1792–1793 MAtl	56.90	43.10	0.00	56.90	1818–1819 MAtl	45.44	54.56	0.00	45.44
1792–1793 BdrS	—	—	—	—	1818–1819 BdrS	—	—	—	—
1792–1793 MidW	—	—	—	—	1818–1819 MidW	93.80	0.00	6.20	100.00
1792–1793 West	—	—	—	—	1818–1819 West	—	—	—	—
1794–1795 NEng	0.00	28.63	71.37	0.00	1820–1821 NEng	70.27	12.04	17.68	86.72
1794–1795 South	—	—	—	—	1820–1821 South	53.81	0.00	46.19	100.00
1794–1795 MAtl	23.44	52.73	23.83	23.44	1820–1821 MAtl	84.36	15.63	0.01	84.37
1794–1795 BdrS	—	—	—	—	1820–1821 BdrS	32.80	0.00	67.20	100.00
1794–1795 MidW	—	—	—	—	1820–1821 MidW	99.75	0.00	0.25	100.00
1794–1795 West	—	—	—	—	1820–1821 West	—	—	—	—
1796–1797 NEng	23.89	54.12	21.99	23.89	1822–1823 NEng	65.34	11.77	22.89	85.51
1796–1797 South	—	—	—	—	1822–1823 South	69.34	0.00	30.66	100.00
1796–1797 MAtl	96.74	3.26	0.00	96.74	1822–1823 MAtl	63.63	35.82	0.55	64.18
1796–1797 BdrS	—	—	—	—	1822–1823 BdrS	—	—	—	—
1796–1797 MidW	—	—	—	—	1822–1823 MidW	65.02	12.71	22.27	87.29
1796–1797 West	—	—	—	—	1822–1823 West	—	—	—	—
1798–1799 NEng	12.92	75.65	11.44	13.43	1824–1825 NEng	69.74	16.25	14.01	81.52
1798–1799 South	99.70	0.00	0.30	100.00	1824–1825 South	70.14	0.00	29.86	100.00
1798–1799 MAtl	47.80	50.90	1.30	48.39	1824–1825 MAtl	100.00	0.00	0.00	100.00
1798–1799 BdrS	—	—	—	—	1824–1825 BdrS	59.50	0.00	40.50	100.00
1798–1799 MidW	—	—	—	—	1824–1825 MidW	31.66	68.34	0.00	31.66
1798–1799 West	—	—	—	—	1824–1825 West	—	—	—	—
1800–1801 NEng	42.16	54.39	3.45	43.16	1826–1827 NEng	59.96	23.37	16.67	72.81
1800–1801 South	99.90	0.00	0.10	100.00	1826–1827 South	68.86	0.00	31.14	100.00
1800–1801 MAtl	52.24	47.76	0.00	52.24	1826–1827 MAtl	82.08	17.40	0.52	82.60
1800–1801 BdrS	39.40	0.00	60.60	100.00	1826–1827 BdrS	—	—	—	—
1800–1801 MidW	—	—	—	—	1826–1827 MidW	22.93	66.79	10.27	24.08
1800–1801 West	—	—	—	—	1826–1827 West	—	—	—	—
1802–1803 NEng	40.94	58.44	0.62	41.14	1828–1829 NEng	56.89	37.49	5.61	58.94
1802–1803 South	100.00	0.00	0.00	100.00	1828–1829 South	75.12	19.14	5.74	80.86
1802–1803 MAtl	73.64	26.22	0.14	73.74	1828–1829 MAtl	54.80	19.24	25.95	78.12
1802–1803 BdrS	—	—	—	—	1828–1829 BdrS	49.54	50.46	0.00	49.54
1802–1803 MidW	100.00	0.00	0.00	100.00	1828–1829 MidW	26.84	39.78	33.37	40.29
1802–1803 West	—	—	—	—	1828–1829 West	—	—	—	—
1804–1805 NEng	44.23	55.12	0.65	44.49	1830–1831 NEng	42.48	37.40	20.12	53.58
1804–1805 South	100.00	0.00	0.00	100.00	1830–1831 South	64.13	25.41	10.46	74.35
1804–1805 MAtl	63.26	36.74	0.00	63.26	1830–1831 MAtl	51.65	48.35	0.00	51.65
1804–1805 BdrS	100.00	0.00	0.00	100.00	1830–1831 BdrS	—	—	—	—
1804–1805 MidW	100.00	0.00	0.00	100.00	1830–1831 MidW	43.80	51.56	4.63	45.99
1804–1805 West	—	—	—	—	1830–1831 West	—	—	—	—
1806–1807 NEng	55.87	37.57	6.56	62.04	1832–1833 NEng	39.59	27.52	32.88	62.29
1806–1807 South	—	—	—	—	1832–1833 South	75.51	11.79	12.70	88.21
1806–1807 MAtl	50.58	49.42	0.00	50.58	1832–1833 MAtl	50.90	32.71	16.38	67.27
1806–1807 BdrS	—	—	—	—	1832–1833 BdrS	50.94	49.06	0.00	50.94
1806–1807 MidW	100.00	0.00	0.00	100.00	1832–1833 MidW	51.89	46.16	1.95	52.92
1806–1807 West	—	—	—	—	1832–1833 West	—	—	—	—
1808–1809 NEng	50.08	47.79	2.13	51.79	1834–1835 NEng	36.39	30.83	32.77	56.12
1808–1809 South	—	—	—	—	1834–1835 South	41.68	48.36	9.96	41.70
1808–1809 MAtl	64.52	35.47	0.01	64.52	1834–1835 MAtl	49.37	40.49	10.13	55.33
1808–1809 BdrS	61.30	0.00	38.70	100.00	1834–1835 BdrS	—	—	—	—
1808–1809 MidW	100.00	0.00	0.00	100.00	1834–1835 MidW	56.81	42.23	0.95	57.36
1808–1809 West	—	—	—	—	1834–1835 West	—	—	—	—
1810–1811 NEng	50.43	48.76	0.82	50.84	1836–1837 NEng	38.75	41.05	20.20	48.56
1810–1811 South	—	—	—	—	1836–1837 South	58.90	41.03	0.06	58.94
1810–1811 MAtl	65.15	33.87	0.97	66.06	1836–1837 MAtl	51.27	48.71	0.01	51.28
1810–1811 BdrS	—	—	—	—	1836–1837 BdrS	44.20	55.80	0.00	44.20
1810–1811 MidW	100.00	0.00	0.00	100.00	1836–1837 MidW	48.80	38.98	12.21	60.88
1810–1811 West	—	—	—	—	1836–1837 West	—	—	—	—
1812–1813 NEng	38.74	59.67	1.60	39.36	1838–1839 NEng	40.78	41.94	17.27	49.28
1812–1813 South	50.00	0.00	50.00	100.00	1838–1839 South	54.90	45.04	0.05	54.92
1812–1813 MAtl	48.49	51.51	0.00	48.49	1838–1839 MAtl	49.85	25.69	24.45	74.31
1812–1813 BdrS	70.90	0.00	29.10	100.00	1838–1839 BdrS	50.28	49.72	0.00	50.28
1812–1813 MidW	39.99	60.01	0.00	39.99	1838–1839 MidW	50.10	49.90	0.00	50.10
1812–1813 West	—	—	—	—	1838–1839 West	—	—	—	—

Table 7-6 (Continued)

Year/Region[1]	Democratic	Republican	Other	Democratic % of Two-Party Vote	Year/Region[1]	Democratic	Republican	Other	Democratic % of Two-Party Vote
1840–1841 NEng	40.36	54.52	5.11	41.10	1864–1865 NEng	33.61	65.11	1.27	33.92
1840–1841 South	51.54	48.46	0.00	51.54	1864–1865 South	27.90	21.82	50.28	50.19
1840–1841 MAtl	49.91	49.78	0.30	50.06	1864–1865 MAtl	49.18	50.82	0.00	49.18
1840–1841 BdrS	46.10	53.90	0.00	46.10	1864–1865 BdrS	22.07	77.93	0.00	22.07
1840–1841 MidW	51.59	47.62	0.78	52.04	1864–1865 MidW	38.41	61.54	0.04	38.43
1840–1841 West	—	—	—	—	1864–1865 West	39.99	60.01	0.00	39.99
1842–1843 NEng	46.55	44.62	8.82	50.11	1866–1867 NEng	37.26	62.57	0.16	37.31
1842–1843 South	50.77	49.23	0.00	50.77	1866–1867 South	0.00	40.18	59.82	0.00
1842–1843 MAtl	51.84	46.35	1.80	52.79	1866–1867 MAtl	50.29	49.69	0.02	50.30
1842–1843 BdrS	—	—	—	—	1866–1867 BdrS	63.82	36.18	0.00	63.82
1842–1843 MidW	51.97	45.11	2.91	53.60	1866–1867 MidW	39.38	60.57	0.04	39.40
1842–1843 West	—	—	—	—	1866–1867 West	49.27	50.73	0.00	49.27
1844–1845 NEng	37.71	42.63	19.66	49.48	1868–1869 NEng	39.16	59.56	1.27	39.69
1844–1845 South	61.81	34.07	4.12	65.17	1868–1869 South	20.15	61.40	18.44	22.17
1844–1845 MAtl	49.66	49.36	0.98	50.16	1868–1869 MAtl	50.88	49.12	0.00	50.88
1844–1845 BdrS	48.78	51.22	0.00	48.78	1868–1869 BdrS	45.35	54.65	0.00	45.35
1844–1845 MidW	51.08	45.28	3.63	53.04	1868–1869 MidW	43.46	56.20	0.34	43.62
1844–1845 West	—	—	—	—	1868–1869 West	—	—	—	—
1846–1847 NEng	43.65	45.70	10.64	48.96	1870–1871 NEng	40.59	55.85	3.56	41.94
1846–1847 South	56.55	40.52	2.93	59.28	1870–1871 South	47.20	52.80	0.00	47.20
1846–1847 MAtl	50.64	48.21	1.14	51.25	1870–1871 MAtl	53.16	46.69	0.14	53.23
1846–1847 BdrS	50.47	49.53	0.00	50.47	1870–1871 BdrS	55.41	44.59	0.00	55.41
1846–1847 MidW	52.02	44.53	3.44	53.94	1870–1871 MidW	44.61	55.07	0.31	44.75
1846–1847 West	—	—	—	—	1870–1871 West	51.07	48.93	0.00	51.07
1848–1849 NEng	43.52	47.07	9.40	47.57	1872–1873 NEng	41.84	57.20	0.95	42.31
1848–1849 South	56.19	37.82	5.98	62.17	1872–1873 South	46.79	49.36	3.84	46.80
1848–1849 MAtl	37.52	48.94	13.53	42.18	1872–1873 MAtl	47.04	52.86	0.10	47.08
1848–1849 BdrS	46.58	53.42	0.00	46.58	1872–1873 BdrS	48.45	0.00	51.55	100.00
1848–1849 MidW	58.87	37.17	3.95	61.96	1872–1873 MidW	41.20	53.76	5.04	41.51
1848–1849 West	47.72	0.00	52.28	100.00	1872–1873 West	—	—	—	—
1850–1851 NEng	38.97	47.32	13.70	44.06	1874–1875 NEng	41.65	53.21	5.13	43.75
1850–1851 South	55.34	30.00	14.66	60.33	1874–1875 South	67.85	32.15	0.00	67.85
1850–1851 MAtl	50.64	48.11	1.24	51.27	1874–1875 MAtl	51.63	47.43	0.94	52.11
1850–1851 BdrS	49.91	48.51	1.57	50.70	1874–1875 BdrS	56.20	43.80	0.00	56.19
1850–1851 MidW	52.38	44.84	2.77	53.88	1874–1875 MidW	44.27	52.58	3.14	45.38
1850–1851 West	50.48	49.51	0.01	50.49	1874–1875 West	48.46	34.80	16.73	58.29
1852–1853 NEng	43.71	40.47	15.81	51.59	1876–1877 NEng	41.20	52.79	6.00	43.35
1852–1853 South	57.92	41.94	0.14	58.02	1876–1877 South	66.48	29.99	3.53	69.66
1852–1853 MAtl	51.44	46.69	1.87	52.42	1876–1877 MAtl	51.46	46.59	1.95	52.50
1852–1853 BdrS	52.80	47.20	0.00	52.80	1876–1877 BdrS	56.19	43.47	0.33	56.38
1852–1853 MidW	53.99	40.59	5.41	57.22	1876–1877 MidW	43.23	50.79	5.98	45.83
1852–1853 West	50.97	49.03	0.00	50.97	1876–1877 West	48.47	51.53	0.00	48.47
1854–1855 NEng	35.00	43.62	21.38	47.20	1878–1879 NEng	37.11	52.94	9.94	40.39
1854–1855 South	53.81	6.12	40.06	93.89	1878–1879 South	81.96	12.39	5.65	86.55
1854–1855 MAtl	44.22	46.89	8.88	49.07	1878–1879 MAtl	57.32	30.73	11.94	66.72
1854–1855 BdrS	48.42	0.00	51.58	100.00	1878–1879 BdrS	56.18	39.63	4.18	58.72
1854–1855 MidW	47.02	52.97	0.01	47.03	1878–1879 MidW	33.83	52.34	13.82	38.86
1854–1855 West	47.45	0.00	52.55	100.00	1878–1879 West	41.64	47.87	10.48	46.15
1856–1857 NEng	38.21	51.53	10.25	45.58	1880–1881 NEng	38.97	59.13	1.89	39.66
1856–1857 South	62.52	0.00	37.48	100.00	1880–1881 South	67.70	20.11	12.18	79.47
1856–1857 MAtl	44.72	45.35	9.93	49.79	1880–1881 MAtl	49.53	49.26	1.20	50.13
1856–1857 BdrS	45.07	0.00	54.93	100.00	1880–1881 BdrS	51.31	37.73	10.95	57.62
1856–1857 MidW	50.02	44.00	5.97	55.19	1880–1881 MidW	40.24	52.86	6.89	43.23
1856–1857 West	56.71	22.46	20.83	71.63	1880–1881 West	44.08	53.28	2.63	45.27
1858–1859 NEng	39.04	58.90	2.05	39.81	1882–1883 NEng	44.19	54.60	1.21	44.69
1858–1859 South	70.28	16.90	12.83	83.10	1882–1883 South	70.11	24.63	5.27	74.66
1858–1859 MAtl	47.40	32.08	20.51	65.80	1882–1883 MAtl	52.32	44.78	2.89	52.66
1858–1859 BdrS	53.17	0.00	46.83	100.00	1882–1883 BdrS	56.71	43.29	0.00	56.71
1858–1859 MidW	47.30	52.70	0.00	47.30	1882–1883 MidW	44.22	48.77	7.00	46.23
1858–1859 West	72.43	4.92	22.65	95.08	1882–1883 West	52.17	46.28	1.54	53.03
1860–1861 NEng	36.26	62.31	1.43	36.70	1884–1885 NEng	40.65	55.68	3.66	42.22
1860–1861 South	53.84	15.78	30.39	78.95	1884–1885 South	70.60	28.62	0.78	71.14
1860–1861 MAtl	46.76	53.24	0.00	46.76	1884–1885 MAtl	48.93	47.85	3.22	50.56
1860–1861 BdrS	31.21	68.79	0.00	31.21	1884–1885 BdrS	51.94	48.06	0.00	51.94
1860–1861 MidW	44.98	48.99	6.03	50.22	1884–1885 MidW	46.46	50.41	3.13	47.96
1860–1861 West	53.20	46.80	0.00	53.20	1884–1885 West	46.09	50.73	3.17	47.60
1862–1863 NEng	32.38	64.00	3.61	32.45	1886–1887 NEng	43.56	51.56	4.87	45.79
1862–1863 South	13.91	10.64	75.45	62.76	1886–1887 South	76.74	20.11	3.14	78.92
1862–1863 MAtl	51.46	48.54	0.00	51.46	1886–1887 MAtl	52.06	31.65	16.29	66.05
1862–1863 BdrS	10.19	89.81	0.00	10.19	1886–1887 BdrS	51.39	45.17	3.43	53.22
1862–1863 MidW	34.48	65.52	0.01	34.48	1886–1887 MidW	43.36	50.09	6.54	46.39
1862–1863 West	36.93	63.07	0.00	36.93	1886–1887 West	47.89	46.29	5.81	50.87

(Table continues)

Table 7-6 (Continued)

Year/Region[1]	Democratic	Republican	Other	Democratic % of Two-Party Vote	Year/Region[1]	Democratic	Republican	Other	Democratic % of Two-Party Vote
1888–1889 NEng	44.01	51.80	4.18	46.06	1914–1915 NEng	40.52	50.12	9.35	44.67
1888–1889 South	72.38	20.43	7.18	79.41	1914–1915 South	79.34	14.84	5.81	84.50
1888–1889 MAtl	50.40	47.03	2.56	51.73	1914–1915 MAtl	39.22	50.33	10.45	43.81
1888–1889 BdrS	49.96	50.04	0.00	49.96	1914–1915 BdrS	46.12	45.00	8.87	50.64
1888–1889 MidW	42.88	52.70	4.41	44.87	1914–1915 MidW	41.35	44.72	13.92	47.87
1888–1889 West	45.30	53.51	1.18	45.83	1914–1915 West	39.24	40.36	20.39	47.85
1890–1891 NEng	46.35	49.93	3.71	48.18	1916–1917 NEng	40.09	56.58	3.32	41.44
1890–1891 South	77.46	21.33	1.20	78.24	1916–1917 South	72.63	20.55	6.81	79.02
1890–1891 MAtl	50.19	47.71	2.09	51.28	1916–1917 MAtl	43.11	53.38	3.51	44.64
1890–1891 BdrS	53.18	40.48	6.33	56.73	1916–1917 BdrS	49.54	48.58	1.87	50.49
1890–1891 MidW	42.36	42.95	14.68	49.08	1916–1917 MidW	38.67	56.06	5.26	40.75
1890–1891 West	46.22	51.85	1.92	47.12	1916–1917 West	50.10	44.86	5.03	52.75
1892–1893 NEng	44.74	51.49	3.76	46.52	1918–1919 NEng	42.98	55.60	1.41	43.62
1892–1893 South	67.33	14.80	17.86	82.09	1918–1919 South	88.13	7.53	4.33	92.45
1892–1893 MAtl	49.65	47.38	2.96	51.17	1918–1919 MAtl	43.43	51.21	5.36	45.90
1892–1893 BdrS	49.38	47.07	3.54	51.19	1918–1919 BdrS	49.29	48.47	2.23	50.47
1892–1893 MidW	42.05	46.42	11.52	46.78	1918–1919 MidW	35.79	54.13	10.07	39.10
1892–1893 West	40.55	40.18	19.27	49.62	1918–1919 West	40.28	53.09	6.62	40.82
1894–1895 NEng	35.50	58.91	5.58	37.60	1920–1921 NEng	31.96	66.36	1.67	32.52
1894–1895 South	58.16	11.44	30.39	85.90	1920–1921 South	71.06	25.27	3.66	73.70
1894–1895 MAtl	42.31	54.12	3.56	43.83	1920–1921 MAtl	43.84	50.90	5.25	46.37
1894–1895 BdrS	45.00	50.15	4.84	47.31	1920–1921 BdrS	36.28	47.32	16.40	43.39
1894–1895 MidW	32.78	51.75	15.46	37.27	1920–1921 MidW	34.97	54.77	10.25	38.10
1894–1895 West	30.94	44.85	24.21	38.46	1920–1921 West	36.10	55.51	8.38	38.57
1896–1897 NEng	31.65	63.75	4.60	33.24	1922–1923 NEng	43.86	55.21	0.92	44.29
1896–1897 South	60.73	22.58	16.69	76.02	1922–1923 South	85.06	14.77	0.16	85.19
1896–1897 MAtl	43.21	53.54	3.26	44.67	1922–1923 MAtl	49.04	47.86	3.09	50.62
1896–1897 BdrS	46.44	52.40	1.15	46.99	1922–1923 BdrS	54.55	44.62	0.82	55.01
1896–1897 MidW	43.09	51.21	5.69	43.79	1922–1923 MidW	30.43	54.97	14.59	33.10
1896–1897 West	58.85	31.21	9.94	66.22	1922–1923 West	48.22	46.92	4.85	50.27
1898–1899 NEng	35.02	59.12	5.85	37.19	1924–1925 NEng	37.18	61.86	0.95	37.49
1898–1899 South	74.37	9.47	16.16	89.96	1924–1925 South	79.11	20.89	0.00	79.11
1898–1899 MAtl	43.94	48.98	7.08	47.13	1924–1925 MAtl	47.00	51.29	1.70	47.83
1898–1899 BdrS	50.80	47.17	2.04	51.85	1924–1925 BdrS	45.77	52.96	1.26	46.36
1898–1899 MidW	44.91	51.55	3.54	46.56	1924–1925 MidW	35.99	54.54	9.46	38.47
1898–1899 West	43.90	49.55	6.55	47.00	1924–1925 West	42.38	48.56	9.05	45.46
1900–1901 NEng	35.97	58.89	5.13	37.94	1926–1927 NEng	40.86	58.72	0.41	41.02
1900–1901 South	71.57	23.81	4.62	75.54	1926–1927 South	87.12	12.81	0.06	87.17
1900–1901 MAtl	45.29	52.13	2.57	46.49	1926–1927 MAtl	38.29	58.57	3.14	39.65
1900–1901 BdrS	45.39	53.80	0.81	45.76	1926–1927 BdrS	53.57	45.89	0.53	53.88
1900–1901 MidW	43.92	53.32	2.76	45.15	1926–1927 MidW	31.14	59.87	8.98	32.94
1900–1901 West	53.31	45.13	1.56	54.15	1926–1927 West	42.60	52.34	5.05	44.24
1902–1903 NEng	39.48	49.94	10.57	42.84	1928–1929 NEng	40.25	59.25	0.49	40.47
1902–1903 South	81.23	15.12	3.65	84.19	1928–1929 South	70.89	29.04	0.06	70.93
1902–1903 MAtl	43.16	49.62	7.23	46.43	1928–1929 MAtl	44.15	54.82	1.02	44.66
1902–1903 BdrS	52.07	46.07	1.85	53.06	1928–1929 BdrS	46.10	53.72	0.17	46.18
1902–1903 MidW	39.01	56.39	4.59	40.87	1928–1929 MidW	40.25	56.96	2.78	41.14
1902–1903 West	46.26	48.97	4.77	48.54	1928–1929 West	50.82	48.64	0.53	51.10
1904–1905 NEng	41.62	55.04	3.33	43.09	1930–1931 NEng	44.01	55.23	0.76	44.39
1904–1905 South	76.08	22.44	1.47	77.18	1930–1931 South	81.14	12.35	6.51	87.61
1904–1905 MAtl	44.25	52.33	3.42	45.81	1930–1931 MAtl	53.97	41.21	4.81	56.91
1904–1905 BdrS	47.03	50.77	2.20	48.08	1930–1931 BdrS	56.45	43.00	0.54	56.75
1904–1905 MidW	39.56	54.96	5.47	41.76	1930–1931 MidW	35.02	53.52	11.45	37.75
1904–1905 West	43.34	49.57	7.08	46.50	1930–1931 West	45.80	46.50	7.69	50.05
1906–1907 NEng	42.52	51.72	5.75	44.68	1932–1933 NEng	48.31	50.13	1.55	49.09
1906–1907 South	84.29	14.61	1.11	85.14	1932–1933 South	75.64	20.54	3.81	77.96
1906–1907 MAtl	46.46	50.04	3.50	48.14	1932–1933 MAtl	50.79	46.42	2.78	52.38
1906–1907 BdrS	50.31	46.92	2.76	51.76	1932–1933 BdrS	53.77	45.79	0.43	54.00
1906–1907 MidW	43.16	51.66	5.17	45.33	1932–1933 MidW	49.13	42.51	8.35	52.68
1906–1907 West	42.56	46.54	10.89	47.72	1932–1933 West	57.10	39.86	3.03	58.89
1908–1909 NEng	40.97	54.32	4.70	42.97	1934–1935 NEng	49.71	47.27	3.01	51.29
1908–1909 South	74.65	22.52	2.82	77.08	1934–1935 South	90.63	9.06	0.31	90.92
1908–1909 MAtl	46.21	50.52	3.26	47.77	1934–1935 MAtl	52.29	44.75	2.95	53.98
1908–1909 BdrS	46.09	50.70	3.20	47.62	1934–1935 BdrS	53.67	44.49	1.83	54.69
1908–1909 MidW	46.04	49.67	4.28	48.05	1934–1935 MidW	45.98	43.40	10.61	51.19
1908–1909 West	42.04	49.98	7.97	45.71	1934–1935 West	51.55	40.42	8.02	55.98
1910–1911 NEng	45.85	50.20	3.94	47.74	1936–1937 NEng	46.67	51.09	2.23	47.81
1910–1911 South	78.05	18.43	3.51	81.01	1936–1937 South	86.02	13.57	0.40	86.37
1910–1911 MAtl	38.29	42.51	19.19	44.06	1936–1937 MAtl	51.95	46.69	1.36	52.68
1910–1911 BdrS	50.03	45.28	4.68	52.54	1936–1937 BdrS	59.15	40.84	0.00	59.15
1910–1911 MidW	42.73	50.78	6.48	45.60	1936–1937 MidW	43.64	43.36	12.99	47.16
1910–1911 West	48.61	44.87	6.51	51.91	1936–1937 West	58.70	38.63	2.66	60.28
1912–1913 NEng	40.43	37.73	21.83	52.06	1938–1939 NEng	40.94	53.44	5.62	43.68
1912–1913 South	76.48	14.66	8.85	83.97	1938–1939 South	90.84	7.04	2.12	92.89
1912–1913 MAtl	43.96	37.56	18.48	54.39	1938–1939 MAtl	48.22	51.22	0.56	48.50
1912–1913 BdrS	44.47	47.74	7.80	48.23	1938–1939 BdrS	60.39	38.56	1.05	61.01
1912–1913 MidW	41.49	37.49	21.01	53.02	1938–1939 MidW	37.96	51.93	10.10	39.94
1912–1913 West	33.97	30.84	35.18	52.43	1938–1939 West	50.94	48.44	0.61	51.26

Table 7-6 *(Continued)*

Year/Region[1]	Democratic	Republican	Other	Democratic % of Two-Party Vote	Year/Region[1]	Democratic	Republican	Other	Democratic % of Two-Party Vote
1940–1941 NEng	46.02	53.36	0.61	46.33	1964–1965 NEng	54.97	44.92	0.11	55.02
1940–1941 South	89.17	10.52	0.30	89.44	1964–1965 South	58.68	38.31	3.00	60.39
1940–1941 MAtl	49.49	50.22	0.29	49.64	1964–1965 MAtl	54.37	44.86	0.76	54.81
1940–1941 BdrS	56.38	43.62	0.00	56.38	1964–1965 BdrS	54.91	45.09	0.00	54.91
1940–1941 MidW	43.18	50.23	6.58	44.89	1964–1965 MidW	54.25	45.39	0.35	54.44
1940–1941 West	52.39	47.24	0.36	52.59	1964–1965 West	52.60	47.32	0.07	52.63
1942–1943 NEng	41.82	56.90	1.27	42.42	1966–1967 NEng	48.99	50.87	0.13	49.05
1942–1943 South	93.18	6.22	0.60	93.77	1966–1967 South	61.06	35.70	3.23	64.02
1942–1943 MAtl	41.87	53.65	4.47	43.74	1966–1967 MAtl	42.12	48.35	9.53	46.52
1942–1943 BdrS	51.12	48.52	0.35	51.30	1966–1967 BdrS	44.12	52.12	3.75	45.82
1942–1943 MidW	34.21	55.48	10.30	36.44	1966–1967 MidW	45.11	54.51	0.37	45.30
1942–1943 West	49.46	50.26	0.27	49.60	1966–1967 West	45.50	51.91	2.58	46.72
1944–1945 NEng	45.39	54.17	0.43	45.60	1968–1969 NEng	47.65	52.34	0.01	47.65
1944–1945 South	79.21	20.23	0.56	79.58	1968–1969 South	60.53	39.05	0.42	60.72
1944–1945 MAtl	49.19	50.51	0.29	49.34	1968–1969 MAtl	43.99	55.09	0.93	44.35
1944–1945 BdrS	54.44	45.55	0.00	54.44	1968–1969 BdrS	49.14	50.86	0.00	49.14
1944–1945 MidW	40.61	58.47	0.91	41.00	1968–1969 MidW	49.74	49.89	0.37	49.93
1944–1945 West	53.55	46.20	0.25	53.71	1968–1969 West	51.76	47.23	1.01	52.30
1946–1947 NEng	39.15	59.86	0.98	39.57	1970–1971 NEng	46.06	52.13	1.81	46.94
1946–1947 South	89.34	10.05	0.60	89.82	1970–1971 South	61.91	32.52	5.58	66.93
1946–1947 MAtl	41.73	57.50	0.76	42.05	1970–1971 MAtl	47.75	47.06	5.20	50.21
1946–1947 BdrS	54.82	44.59	0.58	55.14	1970–1971 BdrS	54.90	41.58	3.51	56.83
1946–1947 MidW	38.99	60.23	0.77	39.32	1970–1971 MidW	52.60	46.11	1.30	53.29
1946–1947 West	43.73	55.21	1.05	43.73	1970–1971 West	48.24	50.11	1.65	49.08
1948–1949 NEng	46.51	52.93	0.55	46.80	1972–1973 NEng	48.94	44.01	7.05	52.39
1948–1949 South	81.10	18.44	0.45	81.44	1972–1973 South	45.79	42.82	11.39	46.58
1948–1949 MAtl	50.40	48.93	0.67	50.72	1972–1973 MAtl	58.84	40.02	1.15	59.55
1948–1949 BdrS	57.12	42.88	0.00	57.12	1972–1973 BdrS	45.26	54.74	0.00	45.26
1948–1949 MidW	47.04	52.06	0.89	47.44	1972–1973 MidW	50.16	49.34	0.50	50.40
1948–1949 West	54.70	44.72	0.57	54.99	1972–1973 West	55.54	42.33	2.13	56.51
1950–1951 NEng	45.23	54.23	0.54	45.50	1974–1975 NEng	55.34	36.00	8.66	60.57
1950–1951 South	91.71	8.06	0.22	91.93	1974–1975 South	66.18	32.19	1.63	67.22
1950–1951 MAtl	45.32	51.93	2.76	46.56	1974–1975 MAtl	55.51	43.57	0.93	56.02
1950–1951 BdrS	49.48	50.43	0.09	49.52	1974–1975 BdrS	63.42	36.58	0.00	63.42
1950–1951 MidW	43.30	56.22	0.47	43.51	1974–1975 MidW	51.72	45.06	3.22	53.62
1950–1951 West	43.18	56.77	0.04	43.20	1974–1975 West	55.76	41.42	2.82	57.70
1952–1953 NEng	42.40	57.43	0.16	42.48	1976–1977 NEng	45.87	51.93	2.20	46.84
1952–1953 South	79.98	19.88	0.13	80.06	1976–1977 South	63.81	35.52	0.67	64.20
1952–1953 MAtl	50.53	48.39	1.08	51.11	1976–1977 MAtl	49.09	49.33	1.58	49.94
1952–1953 BdrS	51.54	48.46	0.00	51.54	1976–1977 BdrS	66.17	33.83	0.00	66.17
1952–1953 MidW	42.48	57.14	0.37	42.64	1976–1977 MidW	44.79	54.40	0.81	45.17
1952–1953 West	44.96	54.95	0.08	45.00	1976–1977 West	55.63	42.33	2.04	56.78
1954–1955 NEng	50.34	49.28	0.37	50.53	1978–1979 NEng	50.93	43.52	5.55	54.08
1954–1955 South	87.44	10.77	1.78	89.21	1978–1979 South	59.71	39.88	0.41	59.97
1954–1955 MAtl	51.63	47.78	0.59	51.93	1978–1979 MAtl	48.69	48.88	2.43	49.95
1954–1955 BdrS	54.07	45.74	0.18	54.18	1978–1979 BdrS	60.71	38.94	0.35	60.89
1954–1955 MidW	47.11	52.66	0.22	47.22	1978–1979 MidW	44.32	54.45	1.23	44.91
1954–1955 West	48.93	51.07	0.00	48.93	1978–1979 West	48.66	45.21	6.13	51.19
1956–1957 NEng	49.96	49.96	0.07	50.00	1980–1981 NEng	56.48	41.84	1.67	57.15
1956–1957 South	77.13	21.66	1.20	78.13	1980–1981 South	54.49	45.26	0.25	54.65
1956–1957 MAtl	51.30	48.20	0.50	51.57	1980–1981 MAtl	38.96	60.05	1.00	39.37
1956–1957 BdrS	46.12	53.88	0.00	46.12	1980–1981 BdrS	54.14	45.44	0.41	54.37
1956–1957 MidW	48.14	51.09	0.76	48.50	1980–1981 MidW	45.10	54.65	0.25	45.22
1956–1957 West	49.22	45.98	4.79	51.46	1980–1981 West	51.29	48.58	0.13	51.36
1958–1959 NEng	52.93	46.82	0.24	53.07	1982–1983 NEng	56.32	41.68	1.99	57.54
1958–1959 South	88.07	7.00	4.94	92.38	1982–1983 South	57.86	40.86	1.28	58.62
1958–1959 MAtl	47.75	51.81	0.44	47.96	1982–1983 MAtl	49.50	49.15	1.36	50.18
1958–1959 BdrS	66.08	31.94	1.97	67.64	1982–1983 BdrS	59.52	39.91	0.56	59.84
1958–1959 MidW	53.26	46.46	0.27	53.41	1982–1983 MidW	50.50	48.07	1.43	51.28
1958–1959 West	52.43	46.99	0.57	52.73	1982–1983 West	55.23	41.30	3.46	57.17
1960–1961 NEng	47.88	51.93	0.18	47.97	1984–1985 NEng	41.04	58.42	0.53	41.31
1960–1961 South	66.79	32.79	0.41	67.13	1984–1985 South	54.39	45.50	0.10	54.44
1960–1961 MAtl	51.05	48.50	0.45	51.27	1984–1985 MAtl	36.89	62.56	0.55	37.06
1960–1961 BdrS	53.99	46.01	0.00	53.99	1984–1985 BdrS	46.74	53.26	0.00	46.74
1960–1961 MidW	50.66	48.59	0.74	51.04	1984–1985 MidW	48.61	51.17	0.22	48.72
1960–1961 West	46.58	53.25	0.16	46.66	1984–1985 West	55.81	42.99	1.20	56.65
1962–1963 NEng	52.07	47.86	0.06	52.10	1986–1987 NEng	47.07	44.80	8.13	50.85
1962–1963 South	76.60	18.06	5.33	80.77	1986–1987 South	53.12	46.56	0.32	53.27
1962–1963 MAtl	44.13	54.23	1.64	44.86	1986–1987 MAtl	57.65	40.05	2.30	59.11
1962–1963 BdrS	50.27	49.63	0.10	50.31	1986–1987 BdrS	63.93	33.40	2.67	65.22
1962–1963 MidW	48.25	51.52	0.22	48.36	1986–1987 MidW	47.62	47.50	4.88	48.32
1962–1963 West	50.26	49.12	0.61	50.54	1986–1987 West	50.39	45.27	4.34	52.55

(Table continues)

Table 7-6 *(Continued)*

Year/Region[1]	Democratic	Republican	Other	Democratic % of Two-Party Vote	Year/Region[1]	Democratic	Republican	Other	Democratic % of Two-Party Vote
1988–1989 NEng	47.86	51.53	0.61	48.17	1994–1995 NEng	38.76	44.41	16.83	48.07
1988–1989 South	47.03	52.92	0.06	47.06	1994–1995 South	47.83	51.76	0.41	48.02
1988–1989 MAtl	45.25	53.97	0.79	45.74	1994–1995 MAtl	42.65	47.07	10.29	47.50
1988–1989 BdrS	58.87	41.13	0.00	58.87	1994–1995 BdrS	43.58	48.46	7.95	46.68
1988–1989 MidW	49.27	50.39	0.33	49.39	1994–1995 MidW	39.24	58.68	2.08	40.03
1988–1989 West	48.91	43.28	7.81	52.72	1994–1995 West	44.57	46.11	9.33	49.41
1990–1991 NEng	44.40	45.36	10.24	48.36	1996–1997 NEng	63.85	30.97	5.19	67.50
1990–1991 South	51.30	47.26	1.45	52.01	1996–1997 South	49.28	49.28	1.44	49.98
1990–1991 MAtl	60.41	26.84	12.74	69.51	1996–1997 MAtl	57.66	38.69	3.66	59.47
1990–1991 BdrS	60.64	36.05	3.31	62.75	1996–1997 BdrS	45.80	51.63	2.57	47.01
1990–1991 MidW	45.34	52.81	1.85	46.28	1996–1997 MidW	47.50	51.13	1.37	48.26
1990–1991 West	54.63	38.05	7.32	58.66	1996–1997 West	34.03	65.39	0.57	34.17
1992–1993 NEng	58.73	37.78	3.48	60.77	1998–1999 NEng	43.12	42.60	14.28	49.00
1992–1993 South	46.81	50.75	2.44	48.10	1998–1999 South	42.95	54.89	2.17	43.83
1992–1993 MAtl	56.52	41.04	2.45	57.94	1998–1999 MAtl	32.10	55.86	12.04	36.50
1992–1993 BdrS	56.04	36.58	7.38	60.51	1998–1999 BdrS	52.37	46.83	0.80	52.80
1992–1993 MidW	53.77	45.36	0.87	54.21	1998–1999 MidW	38.94	55.01	6.05	41.55
1992–1993 West	41.35	47.12	11.53	45.44	1998–1999 West	46.47	47.45	6.07	50.22

Notes: Main entries are calculated from the two decimal place versions of the vote values in Tables 7-9 through 7-61. Whenever bold italicized values occur in Tables 7-9 through 7-61, denoting the author's alternative party coding system, they are used instead of the conventionally coded main entries in these tables in the aggregation process to the regional level for Table 7-6. See text and Table 5-1 for a more complete discussion of the conventional and alternative party coding systems. Also see Table 1-3 in Chapter 1 for a similar discussion. Entries in Table 7-6 are, therefore, based on candidates who use the designation "Democrat" or "Republican" (or their historical antecedents listed in Appendix A) either solely or with other labels or parties (often minor parties) on the ballot. In general, historical antecedents to the Democratic Party were Anti-Federalists, Democratic-Republicans, and Jackson Democrats; historical precursors of the Republican Party were Federalists, National Republicans, and Whigs. Other = candidates who use third-party names only on the ballot or are listed as independent or unidentified. Odd-numbered year gubernatorial elections were common before 1880 and several states still scheduled governor elections in odd-numbered years after that. Special governor elections are not included in this table. Note that both the Whig Party and the Republican Party fielded candidates for governor in 1854–1855; hence, the votes of the winning candidates are aggregated together under the "Republican" column for these years. In this table, each state is weighted equally in getting the regional vote result by using state vote percents rather than raw vote counts. In this way, a few highly populated states do not unduly influence the regional values in this table. This seems the best strategy for determining regional political trends for what is clearly a state, not a national, political office. The reader, however, should note that this strategy is not considered the best strategy to use for national offices such as the presidency, House, and Senate; for these offices, raw votes are generally considered more appropriate to use than vote percents to determine regional political trends, as demonstrated in the regional vote tables in Chapters 4, 5, and 6.

[1]Regional categories are adapted from the ICPSR regional codings. In the current analysis, Tennessee is categorized in the South, since it was part of the Confederacy, although the ICPSR treats it as a Border South state. The regional categories are: New England—Connecticut, Maine, Massachusetts, New Hampshire, Rhode Island, Vermont; South—Alabama, Arkansas, Florida, Georgia, Louisiana, Mississippi, North Carolina, South Carolina, Tennessee, Texas, Virginia; Mid-Atlantic—Delaware, New Jersey, New York, Pennsylvania; Border South—Kentucky, Maryland, Oklahoma, West Virginia; Midwest—Illinois, Indiana, Iowa, Kansas, Michigan, Minnesota, Missouri, Nebraska, North Dakota, Ohio, South Dakota, Wisconsin; West—Alaska, Arizona, California, Colorado, Hawaii, Idaho, Montana, Nevada, New Mexico, Oregon, Utah, Washington, Wyoming.

Sources: Data from Tables 7-9 through 7-61, as adapted from *American State Governors, 1776–1976*, vol. 1 (1977), *Congressional Quarterly's Guide to U.S. Elections* (1994), ICPSR data sets 0001 and 0075, and independent search for state sources by the author. Several pre-1824 party affiliations were obtained from the election archive of Michael J. Dubin. Other party affiliations were obtained from independent search of state sources when the *American State Governors* volume and the *Congressional Quarterly Guide* disagreed. The author's alternative party coding was used where applicable; see Table 7-8 for states and years when alternative party coding occurred.

Table 7-7 Votes in Gubernatorial Elections by Non-South and South, 1788–1999 (Percentages)

Year/Region[1]	Democratic	Republican	Other	Democratic % of Two-Party Vote	Year/Region[1]	Democratic	Republican	Other	Democratic % of Two-Party Vote
1788–1789 N-S	20.34	16.88	62.78	51.57	1860–1861 N-S	40.54	56.73	2.73	42.53
1788–1789 S	—	—	—	—	1860–1861 S	53.84	15.78	30.39	78.95
1790–1791 N-S	41.82	1.84	56.34	96.93	1862–1863 N-S	34.44	63.88	1.67	34.47
1790–1791 S	—	—	—	—	1862–1863 S	13.91	10.64	75.45	62.76
1792–1793 N-S	35.66	16.81	47.53	62.76	1864–1865 N-S	35.83	63.57	0.60	35.98
1792–1793 S	—	—	—	—	1864–1865 S	27.90	21.82	50.28	50.19
1794–1795 N-S	5.86	34.66	59.48	11.72	1866–1867 N-S	43.32	56.59	0.08	43.35
1794–1795 S	—	—	—	—	1866–1867 S	0.00	40.18	59.82	0.00
1796–1797 N-S	34.30	46.85	18.85	34.30	1868–1869 N-S	42.41	56.87	0.71	42.71
1796–1797 S	—	—	—	—	1868–1869 S	20.15	61.40	18.44	22.17
1798–1799 N-S	26.00	66.37	8.13	26.54	1870–1871 N-S	45.79	52.70	1.50	46.40
1798–1799 S	99.70	0.00	0.30	100.00	1870–1871 S	47.20	52.80	0.00	47.20
1800–1801 N-S	43.90	47.63	8.47	50.66	1872–1873 N-S	42.28	53.02	4.69	44.78
1800–1801 S	99.90	0.00	0.10	100.00	1872–1873 S	46.79	49.36	3.84	46.80
1802–1803 N-S	50.11	49.38	0.51	50.29	1874–1875 N-S	45.59	49.56	4.84	47.85
1802–1803 S	100.00	0.00	0.00	100.00	1874–1875 S	67.85	32.15	0.00	67.85
1804–1805 N-S	57.20	42.40	0.40	57.36	1876–1877 N-S	43.83	51.00	5.16	45.90
1804–1805 S	100.00	0.00	0.00	100.00	1876–1877 S	66.48	29.99	3.53	69.66
1806–1807 N-S	58.45	36.51	5.04	63.20	1878–1879 N-S	40.72	48.41	10.86	45.31
1806–1807 S	—	—	—	—	1878–1879 S	81.96	12.39	5.65	86.55
1808–1809 N-S	56.95	37.98	5.07	61.71	1880–1881 N-S	40.91	54.38	4.70	42.98
1808–1809 S	—	—	—	—	1880–1881 S	67.70	20.11	12.18	79.47
1810–1811 N-S	58.24	40.99	0.79	58.74	1882–1883 N-S	47.93	49.17	2.89	48.80
1810–1811 S	—	—	—	—	1882–1883 S	70.11	24.63	5.27	74.66
1812–1813 N-S	42.52	54.27	3.22	45.04	1884–1885 N-S	44.51	52.29	3.19	45.97
1812–1813 S	50.00	0.00	50.00	100.00	1884–1885 S	70.60	28.62	0.78	71.14
1814–1815 N-S	43.67	52.97	3.36	44.17	1886–1887 N-S	45.93	47.24	6.82	49.96
1814–1815 S	42.80	0.00	57.20	100.00	1886–1887 S	76.74	20.11	3.14	78.92
1816–1817 N-S	51.49	36.45	12.06	57.28	1888–1889 N-S	44.34	51.98	3.65	46.07
1816–1817 S	54.77	0.00	45.23	100.00	1888–1889 S	72.38	20.43	7.18	79.41
1818–1819 N-S	54.77	20.26	24.96	73.63	1890–1891 N-S	45.94	47.20	6.86	49.18
1818–1819 S	71.80	0.00	28.20	100.00	1890–1891 S	77.46	21.33	1.20	78.24
1820–1821 N-S	73.81	10.63	15.55	88.65	1892–1893 N-S	43.22	47.08	9.69	47.47
1820–1821 S	53.81	0.00	46.19	100.00	1892–1893 S	67.33	14.80	17.86	82.09
1822–1823 N-S	64.91	17.27	17.82	80.51	1894–1895 N-S	35.31	52.51	12.17	39.20
1822–1823 S	69.34	0.00	30.66	100.00	1894–1895 S	58.19	11.44	30.37	85.90
1824–1825 N-S	61.96	26.59	11.45	71.37	1896–1897 N-S	42.77	51.43	5.80	44.96
1824–1825 S	70.14	0.00	29.86	100.00	1896–1897 S	60.73	22.58	16.69	76.02
1826–1827 N-S	59.45	27.96	12.59	67.94	1898–1899 N-S	42.19	52.69	5.11	44.42
1826–1827 S	68.86	0.00	31.14	100.00	1898–1899 S	74.37	9.47	16.16	89.96
1828–1829 N-S	51.24	36.56	12.19	58.45	1900–1901 N-S	43.54	53.34	3.12	44.87
1828–1829 S	75.12	19.14	5.74	80.86	1900–1901 S	71.57	23.81	4.62	75.54
1830–1831 N-S	43.30	40.74	15.96	52.04	1902–1903 N-S	42.04	51.56	6.39	44.47
1830–1831 S	64.13	25.41	10.46	74.35	1902–1903 S	81.23	15.12	3.65	84.19
1832–1833 N-S	43.47	31.65	24.87	61.40	1904–1905 N-S	41.59	53.59	4.81	43.64
1832–1833 S	75.51	11.79	12.70	88.21	1904–1905 S	76.08	22.44	1.47	77.18
1834–1835 N-S	42.72	34.65	22.62	56.34	1906–1907 N-S	43.97	49.90	6.12	46.65
1834–1835 S	41.68	48.36	9.96	41.70	1906–1907 S	84.29	14.61	1.11	85.14
1836–1837 N-S	42.91	42.33	14.76	51.92	1908–1909 N-S	43.89	51.15	4.95	46.15
1836–1837 S	58.90	41.03	0.06	58.94	1908–1909 S	74.65	22.52	2.82	77.08
1838–1839 N-S	43.87	41.89	14.23	52.63	1910–1911 N-S	45.33	47.78	6.89	48.31
1838–1839 S	54.90	45.04	0.05	54.92	1910–1911 S	78.05	18.43	3.51	81.01
1840–1841 N-S	44.40	52.48	3.11	44.94	1912–1913 N-S	40.26	36.73	23.00	52.65
1840–1841 S	51.54	48.46	0.00	51.54	1912–1913 S	76.49	14.66	8.85	83.97
1842–1843 N-S	48.13	44.84	7.02	51.09	1914–1915 N-S	40.97	45.41	13.61	47.07
1842–1843 S	50.77	49.23	0.00	50.77	1914–1915 S	79.34	14.84	5.81	84.50
1844–1845 N-S	42.95	45.11	11.94	50.09	1916–1917 N-S	42.48	53.05	4.46	44.42
1844–1845 S	61.81	34.07	4.12	65.17	1916–1917 S	72.63	20.55	6.81	79.02
1846–1847 N-S	47.14	46.06	6.79	50.58	1918–1919 N-S	40.78	53.34	5.87	42.43
1846–1847 S	56.55	40.52	2.93	59.28	1918–1919 S	88.13	7.53	4.33	92.45
1848–1849 N-S	47.99	42.45	9.55	53.72	1920–1921 N-S	35.28	56.90	7.81	37.80
1848–1849 S	56.19	37.82	5.98	62.17	1920–1921 S	71.06	25.27	3.66	73.70
1850–1851 N-S	45.36	47.12	7.51	48.30	1922–1923 N-S	42.54	50.99	6.46	44.23
1850–1851 S	55.34	30.00	14.66	60.33	1922–1923 S	85.06	14.77	0.16	85.19
1852–1853 N-S	47.96	41.76	10.27	53.23	1924–1925 N-S	39.26	54.22	6.51	41.19
1852–1853 S	57.92	41.94	0.14	58.02	1924–1925 S	79.11	20.89	0.00	79.11
1854–1855 N-S	39.84	41.71	18.45	52.46	1926–1927 N-S	39.41	55.88	4.70	40.62
1854–1855 S	53.81	6.12	40.06	93.89	1926–1927 S	87.12	12.81	0.06	87.17
1856–1857 N-S	43.79	45.15	11.05	52.28	1928–1929 N-S	43.41	55.09	1.49	43.95
1856–1857 S	62.52	0.00	37.48	100.00	1928–1929 S	70.89	29.04	0.06	70.93
1858–1859 N-S	45.44	46.80	7.75	52.24	1930–1931 N-S	44.04	49.57	6.38	46.47
1858–1859 S	70.28	16.90	12.83	83.10	1930–1931 S	81.14	12.35	6.51	87.61

(Table continues)

Table 7-7 *(Continued)*

Year/Region[1]	Democratic	Republican	Other	Democratic % of Two-Party Vote	Year/Region[1]	Democratic	Republican	Other	Democratic % of Two-Party Vote
1932–1933 N-S	51.23	43.88	4.88	53.49	1966–1967 N-S	45.74	52.19	2.06	46.70
1932–1933 S	75.64	20.54	3.81	77.96	1966–1967 S	61.06	35.70	3.23	64.02
1934–1935 N-S	49.74	43.63	6.62	53.18	1968–1969 N-S	49.30	50.18	0.52	49.57
1934–1935 S	90.63	9.06	0.31	90.92	1968–1969 S	60.53	39.05	0.42	60.72
1936–1937 N-S	49.30	44.07	6.62	51.45	1970–1971 N-S	49.65	48.33	2.02	50.68
1936–1937 S	86.02	13.57	0.40	86.37	1970–1971 S	61.91	32.52	5.58	66.93
1938–1939 N-S	45.44	49.77	4.78	46.84	1972–1973 N-S	51.72	46.20	2.09	52.74
1938–1939 S	90.84	7.04	2.12	92.89	1972–1973 S	45.79	42.82	11.39	46.58
1940–1941 N-S	47.02	49.91	3.06	47.87	1974–1975 N-S	55.33	40.95	3.72	57.64
1940–1941 S	89.17	10.52	0.30	89.44	1974–1975 S	66.18	32.19	1.63	67.22
1942–1943 N-S	42.54	53.42	4.03	43.60	1976–1977 N-S	49.85	48.68	1.47	50.58
1942–1943 S	93.18	6.22	0.60	93.77	1976–1977 S	63.81	35.52	0.67	64.20
1944–1945 N-S	45.86	53.56	0.58	46.12	1978–1979 N-S	49.02	47.26	3.72	50.77
1944–1945 S	79.21	20.23	0.56	79.58	1978–1979 S	59.71	39.88	0.41	59.97
1946–1947 N-S	42.25	56.87	0.87	42.51	1980–1981 N-S	49.22	50.06	0.71	49.52
1946–1947 S	89.34	10.05	0.60	89.82	1980–1981 S	54.49	45.26	0.25	54.65
1948–1949 N-S	49.24	50.06	0.69	49.58	1982–1983 N-S	54.08	43.79	2.13	55.28
1948–1949 S	81.10	18.44	0.45	81.44	1982–1983 S	57.86	40.86	1.28	58.62
1950–1951 N-S	44.49	55.02	0.48	44.71	1984–1985 N-S	46.41	53.01	0.58	46.74
1950–1951 S	91.71	8.06	0.22	91.93	1984–1985 S	54.39	45.50	0.10	54.44
1952–1953 N-S	44.01	55.68	0.30	44.15	1986–1987 N-S	50.73	44.31	4.96	52.65
1952–1953 S	79.98	19.88	0.13	80.06	1986–1987 S	53.12	46.56	0.32	53.27
1954–1955 N-S	49.39	50.39	0.21	49.50	1988–1989 N-S	48.96	48.72	2.32	50.10
1954–1955 S	87.44	10.77	1.78	89.21	1988–1989 S	47.03	52.92	0.06	47.06
1956–1957 N-S	48.90	49.58	1.51	49.62	1990–1991 N-S	50.78	42.99	6.22	54.02
1956–1957 S	77.13	21.66	1.20	78.13	1990–1991 S	51.30	47.26	1.45	52.01
1958–1959 N-S	53.83	45.61	0.55	54.18	1992–1993 N-S	52.55	42.45	4.99	54.80
1958–1959 S	88.07	7.00	4.94	92.38	1992–1993 S	46.81	50.75	2.44	48.10
1960–1961 N-S	49.47	50.06	0.46	49.70	1994–1995 N-S	41.58	49.84	8.58	45.93
1960–1961 S	66.79	32.79	0.41	67.13	1994–1995 S	47.83	51.76	0.41	48.02
1962–1963 N-S	49.61	49.98	0.40	49.80	1996–1997 N-S	48.49	49.14	2.37	49.84
1962–1963 S	76.60	18.06	5.33	80.77	1996–1997 S	49.28	49.28	1.44	49.98
1964–1965 N-S	54.05	45.68	0.26	54.19	1998–1999 N-S	43.18	49.24	7.58	46.72
1964–1965 S	58.68	38.31	3.00	60.39	1998–1999 S	42.95	54.89	2.17	43.83

Notes: Main entries are calculated from the two decimal place versions of the vote values in Tables 7-9 through 7-61. Whenever bold italicized values occur in Tables 7-9 through 7-61, denoting the author's alternative party coding system, they are used instead of the conventionally coded main entries in these tables in the aggregation process to the regional level for Table 7-7. See text and Table 5-1 for a more complete discussion of the conventional and alternative party coding systems. Also see Table 1-3 in Chapter 1 for a similar discussion. Entries in Table 7-7 are, therefore, based on candidates who use the designation "Democrat" or "Republican" (or their historical antecedents listed in Appendix A), either solely or with other labels or parties (often minor parties) on the ballot. In general, historical antecedents to the Democratic Party were Anti-Federalists, Democratic-Republicans, and Jackson Democrats; historical precursors of the Republican Party were Federalists, National Republicans, and Whigs. Other = candidates who use third-party names only on the ballot or are listed as independent or unidentified. Odd-numbered year gubernatorial elections were common before 1880 and several states still scheduled governor elections in odd-numbered years after that. Special governor elections are not included in this table. Note that both the Whig Party and the Republican Party fielded candidates for governor in 1854–1855; hence, the votes of the winning candidates are aggregated together under the "Republican" column for these years. —indicates missing data (that is, no states in that region had gubernatorial voting data for that year). In this table, each state is weighted equally in getting the regional vote result by using state vote percents rather than raw vote counts. In this way, a few highly populated states do not unduly influence the regional values in this table. This seems the best strategy for determining regional political trends for what is clearly a state, not a national, political office. The reader, however, should note that this strategy is not considered the best strategy to use for national offices such as the presidency, House, and Senate; for these offices, raw votes are generally considered more appropriate to use than vote percents to determine regional political trends, as demonstrated in the regional vote tables in Chapters 4, 5, and 6.

[1]Regional categories are adapted from the ICPSR regional codings. In the current analysis, Tennessee is categorized in the South, since it was part of the Confederacy, although the ICPSR treats it as a Border South state. Thus, the South includes Alabama, Arkansas, Florida, Georgia, Louisiana, Mississippi, North Carolina, South Carolina, Tennessee, Texas, and Virginia. All other states make up the non-south.

Sources: Data from Tables 7-9 through 7-61, as adapted from *American State Governors, 1776–1976*, vol. 1 (1977), *Congressional Quarterly's Guide to U.S. Elections* (1994), ICPSR data sets 0001 and 0075, and independent search for state sources by the author. Several pre-1824 party affiliations were obtained from the election archive of Michael J. Dubin. Other party affiliations were obtained from independent search of state sources when the *American State Governors* volume and the *Congressional Quarterly Guide* disagreed. The author's alternative party coding was used where applicable; see Table 7-8 for states and years when alternative party coding occurred.

Table 7-8 Alternative Party Codings for Governor, 1788–1999

State	
Alabama	1831(W); 1835(W); 1837(W); 1841(I); 1845(I); 1853(W); 1859(W); 1892(I); 1898(W); 1910(I); 1970(W)
Alaska	
Arizona	1932(W); 1938(I)
Arkansas	1860(I)
California	1849(I); 1859(W); 1861(W); 1867(I); 1898(F); 1906(F); 1918(F); 1946(M)
Colorado	1892(F); 1898(F); 1900(F)
Connecticut	1896(W); 1938(J); 1940(J); 1954(I)
Delaware	1854(F); 1896(W); 1904(W); 1912(F); 1936(I); 1940(W)
Florida	1868(W); 1916(I); 1920(W)
Georgia	1851(W); 1859(W); 1861(W); 1863(W,I); 1880(I); 1882(I); 1940(F); 1966(I)
Hawaii	1982(I)
Idaho	1898(F); 1900(F)
Illinois	1834(I); 1876(F); 1896(W); 1920(W); 1924(I)
Indiana	1825(W); 1828(W); 1872(W,I); 1896(W)
Iowa	1846(W); 1854(W); 1884(W); 1897(W); 1950(W); 1952(W); 1954(W)
Kansas	1890(F); 1892(F); 1894(W,F); 1896(W)
Kentucky	1867(F); 1899(I)
Louisiana	1892(W,I); 1896(F); 1900(F,M)
Maine	1833(W); 1861(W); 1873(W); 1880(F); 1882(F); 1896(W); 1898(W); 1950(W); 1952(I)
Maryland	1861(W)
Massachusetts	1825(M); 1827(W); 1845(W,I); 1848(I); 1856(W); 1860(W); 1878(F); 1879(F); 1882(F); 1883(F); 1896(W); 1897(W); 1906(J); 1907(J); 1910(F); 1911(F)
Michigan	1849(F); 1851(F); 1854(W); 1882(F); 1884(F); 1896(W)
Minnesota	1873(M)
Mississippi	1837(W); 1843(W); 1851(W); 1865(W); 1881(F); 1947(I)
Missouri	1824(W); 1832(W); 1856(W); 1860(W); 1884(W,F); 1896(W)
Montana	1896(F); 1900(I); 1904(F)
Nebraska	1884(F); 1894(W,F); 1896(W,F); 1902(F); 1904(F); 1906(F); 1908(F); 1912(F); 1914(F); 1916(F)
Nevada	1894(W); 1898(W); 1902(F); 1906(F)
New Hampshire	1842(I); 1848(W); 1862(W); 1896(W); 1916(F)
New Jersey	1856(F); 1898(F); 1904(F)
New Mexico	
New York	1807(W); 1810(W); 1820(W); 1824(W); 1826(W); 1850(W); 1854(W,F); 1860(W); 1879(W); 1894(W); 1896(W,F); 1902(W,J); 1906(J); 1914(J); 1916(J); 1918(J); 1936(J); 1938(J); 1946(J); 1950(J); 1954(J); 1958(J); 1962(J); 1970(J); 1974(J); 1978(J); 1982(J); 1986(J); 1990(J); 1994(J)
North Carolina	1866(W); 1960(I)
North Dakota	1892(F); 1900(I); 1918(F,I); 1920(F,I); 1944(I)
Ohio	1875(F); 1897(W)
Oklahoma	
Oregon	
Pennsylvania	1805(M); 1808(W); 1882(I); 1902(J); 1906(J); 1910(J); 1914(J); 1918(J); 1926(J); 1930(J); 1938(J)
Rhode Island	1843(W); 1845(W,F); 1846(W,F); 1853(F); 1855(F); 1856(F); 1860(F); 1863(F); 1877(F); 1878(F); 1879(F); 1880(I); 1883(I); 1938(F)
South Carolina	1872(I); 1874(I) 1890(I); 1896(W); 1916(I)
South Dakota	
Tennessee	1859(W); 1861(W); 1869(W); 1876(W); 1880(W); 1882(W); 1934(F)
Texas	1859(I); 1869(I); 1882(F); 1892(I,M); 1894(W); 1906(W); 1920(W); 1932(W); 1952(M)
Utah	1916(F)
Vermont	1833 (F); 1836(F); 1848(W); 1849(F); 1850(W); 1851(W); 1854(F); 1860(W); 1861(W); 1906(I); 1918(J); 1920(J); 1922(J); 1926(J); 1952(I); 1962(I); 1964(I); 1972(J); 1974(J)
Virginia	1859(W); 1921(W); 1937(I); 1941(I); 1945(I)
Washington	
West Virginia	
Wisconsin	1853(F); 1904(W); 1922(I); 1924(I)
Wyoming	

Notes: Wing = candidate affiliated with a major party running as a splinter, wing, or factional candidate from that party (for example, Benton Democrat, Anti-Benton Democrat, Union Democrat). Fusion = candidate of a major party running on a fusion ticket with one or more minor parties (for example, Democrat-Greenback fusion, Republican-Greenback fusion) or on the "fusion" label itself (if parties in a fusion ticket can be identified). Joint = candidate of a major party also endorsed by a minor party under the latter's own slate of candidates on the ballot (for example, Liberal Party endorsement of a Democratic candidate in New York under the Liberal Party's own slate of candidates on the ballot). Independent = major-party candidate also running as an independent (for example, using the Independent Democrat label or the Democrat Independent label). Both Major = candidate running on both major-party tickets (for example, listed on both Democratic and Republican tickets on the ballot, as successful crossfiling candidates were in California up to 1960).

For a further explanation of these categories, see the notes to Tables 1-3 and 5-1.

Sources: *American State Governors, 1776–1976*, vol. 1 (1977), *Congressional Quarterly's Guide to U.S. Elections* (1994), *America Votes* (various publication dates), ICPSR data sets 0001 and 0075, the election archive of Michael J. Dubin, and independent search for state sources by author.

Table 7-9 Governor Election Results, by State, 1788–1791 (Percentages)

State	1788–1789				1790–1791			
	Democratic	Republican	Other	Democratic % of Two-Party Vote	Democratic	Republican	Other	Democratic % of Two-Party Vote
Alabama	—	—	—	—	—	—	—	—
Alaska	—	—	—	—	—	—	—	—
Arizona	—	—	—	—	—	—	—	—
Arkansas	—	—	—	—	—	—	—	—
California	—	—	—	—	—	—	—	—
Colorado	—	—	—	—	—	—	—	—
Connecticut	—	—	—	—	—	—	—	—
Delaware	—	—	—	—	—	—	—	—
Florida	—	—	—	—	—	—	—	—
Georgia	—	—	—	—	—	—	—	—
Hawaii	—	—	—	—	—	—	—	—
Idaho	—	—	—	—	—	—	—	—
Illinois	—	—	—	—	—	—	—	—
Indiana	—	—	—	—	—	—	—	—
Iowa	—	—	—	—	—	—	—	—
Kansas	—	—	—	—	—	—	—	—
Kentucky	—	—	—	—	—	—	—	—
Louisiana	—	—	—	—	—	—	—	—
Maine	—	—	—	—	—	—	—	—
Maryland	—	—	—	—	—	—	—	—
Massachusetts	0.0	0.0	100.0	—	0.0	0.0	100.0	—
Michigan	—	—	—	—	—	—	—	—
Minnesota	—	—	—	—	—	—	—	—
Mississippi	—	—	—	—	—	—	—	—
Missouri	—	—	—	—	—	—	—	—
Montana	—	—	—	—	—	—	—	—
Nebraska	—	—	—	—	—	—	—	—
Nevada	—	—	—	—	—	—	—	—
New Hampshire	50.0	41.5	8.5	54.7	21.5	0.0	78.5	100.0
New Jersey	—	—	—	—	—	—	—	—
New Mexico	—	—	—	—	—	—	—	—
New York	51.7[1]	0.0[1]	48.3[1]	100.0[1]	—	—	—	—
North Carolina	—	—	—	—	—	—	—	—
North Dakota	—	—	—	—	—	—	—	—
Ohio	—	—	—	—	—	—	—	—
Oklahoma	—	—	—	—	—	—	—	—
Oregon	—	—	—	—	—	—	—	—
Pennsylvania	—	—	—	—	90.8	9.2	0.0	90.8
Rhode Island	—	—	—	—	—	—	—	—
South Carolina	—	—	—	—	—	—	—	—
South Dakota	—	—	—	—	—	—	—	—
Tennessee	—	—	—	—	—	—	—	—
Texas	—	—	—	—	—	—	—	—
Utah	—	—	—	—	—	—	—	—
Vermont	—	—	—	—	—	—	—	—
Virginia	—	—	—	—	—	—	—	—
Washington	—	—	—	—	—	—	—	—
West Virginia	—	—	—	—	—	—	—	—
Wisconsin	—	—	—	—	—	—	—	—
Wyoming	—	—	—	—	—	—	—	—
Massachusetts	0.0[2]	0.0[2]	100.0[2]	—	0.0[3]	0.0[3]	100.0[3]	—
New Hampshire	0.0[2]	42.9[2]	57.1[2]	0[2]	96.8[3]	0.0[3]	3.2[3]	100.0[3]

Notes: Main entries are party vote percentage values for candidates who used the sole designation "Democrat" or "Republican" (or their historical antecedents listed in Appendix A) on the ballot. In general, historical antecedents to the Democratic Party were Anti-Federalists, Democratic-Republicans, and Jackson Democrats; historical precursors of the Republican Party were Federalists, National Republicans, and Whigs. Other = candidates who used third-party names only on the ballot or were listed as independent or unidentified. —indicates that the state had no data, either because the state had no gubernatorial election in that year, no vote data were found for the state in question, or the state had not yet entered the Union. No special gubernatorial elections are included in this table. Odd-numbered year gubernatorial elections were common before 1880 and several states still scheduled governor elections in odd-numbered years after that.

[1]Election held in odd-numbered year.
[2]1789 election when a state had annual elections in both 1788 and 1789.
[3]1791 election when a state had annual elections in both 1790 and 1791.

Sources: Adapted from *American State Governors, 1776–1976),* vol. 1 (1977), *Congressional Quarterly's Guide to U.S. Elections* (1994), and independent search for state sources by the author. Several pre-1824 party affiliations were obtained from the election archive of Michael J. Dubin. Other party affiliations were obtained from independent search of state sources by the author when the *American State Governors* volume and the *Congressional Quarterly Guide* disagreed.

Table 7-10 Governor Election Results, by State, 1792–1795 (Percentages)

State	1792–1793				1794–1795			
	Democratic	Republican	Other	Democratic % of Two-Party Vote	Democratic	Republican	Other	Democratic % of Two-Party Vote
Alabama	—	—	—	—	—	—	—	—
Alaska	—	—	—	—	—	—	—	—
Arizona	—	—	—	—	—	—	—	—
Arkansas	—	—	—	—	—	—	—	—
California	—	—	—	—	—	—	—	—
Colorado	—	—	—	—	—	—	—	—
Connecticut	—	—	—	—	—	—	—	—
Delaware	0.0	48.3	51.7	0.0	0.0[1]	52.3[1]	47.7[1]	0.0[1]
Florida	—	—	—	—	—	—	—	—
Georgia	—	—	—	—	—	—	—	—
Hawaii	—	—	—	—	—	—	—	—
Idaho	—	—	—	—	—	—	—	—
Illinois	—	—	—	—	—	—	—	—
Indiana	—	—	—	—	—	—	—	—
Iowa	—	—	—	—	—	—	—	—
Kansas	—	—	—	—	—	—	—	—
Kentucky	—	—	—	—	—	—	—	—
Louisiana	—	—	—	—	—	—	—	—
Maine	—	—	—	—	—	—	—	—
Maryland	—	—	—	—	—	—	—	—
Massachusetts	0.0	0.0	100.0	—	0.0	0.0	100.0	—
Michigan	—	—	—	—	—	—	—	—
Minnesota	—	—	—	—	—	—	—	—
Mississippi	—	—	—	—	—	—	—	—
Missouri	—	—	—	—	—	—	—	—
Montana	—	—	—	—	—	—	—	—
Nebraska	—	—	—	—	—	—	—	—
Nevada	—	—	—	—	—	—	—	—
New Hampshire	96.5	0.0	3.5	100.0	0.0	72.9	27.1	0.0
New Jersey	—	—	—	—	—	—	—	—
New Mexico	—	—	—	—	—	—	—	—
New York	50.3	49.7	0.0	50.3	46.9[1]	53.1[1]	0.0[1]	46.9[1]
North Carolina	—	—	—	—	—	—	—	—
North Dakota	—	—	—	—	—	—	—	—
Ohio	—	—	—	—	—	—	—	—
Oklahoma	—	—	—	—	—	—	—	—
Oregon	—	—	—	—	—	—	—	—
Pennsylvania	63.5[1]	36.5[1]	0.0[1]	63.5[1]	—	—	—	—
Rhode Island	—	—	—	—	—	—	—	—
South Carolina	—	—	—	—	—	—	—	—
South Dakota	—	—	—	—	—	—	—	—
Tennessee	—	—	—	—	—	—	—	—
Texas	—	—	—	—	—	—	—	—
Utah	—	—	—	—	—	—	—	—
Vermont	0.0[1]	0.0[1]	100.0[1]	—	0.0	0.0	100.0	—
Virginia	—	—	—	—	—	—	—	—
Washington	—	—	—	—	—	—	—	—
West Virginia	—	—	—	—	—	—	—	—
Wisconsin	—	—	—	—	—	—	—	—
Wyoming	—	—	—	—	—	—	—	—
Massachusetts	0.0[2]	0.0[2]	100.0[2]	—	0.0[3]	0.0[3]	100.0[3]	—
New Hampshire	75.0[2]	0.0[2]	25.0[2]	100.0[2]	0.0[3]	98.9[3]	1.1[3]	0.0[3]
Vermont	—	—	—	—	0.0[3]	0.0[3]	100.0[3]	—

Notes: Main entries are party vote percentage values for candidates who used the sole designation "Democrat" or "Republican" (or their historical antecedents listed in Appendix A) on the ballot. In general, historical antecedents to the Democratic Party were Anti-Federalists, Democratic-Republicans, and Jackson Democrats; historical precursors of the Republican Party were Federalists, National Republicans, and Whigs. Other = candidates who used third-party names only on the ballot or were listed as independent or unidentified. —indicates that the state had no data, either because the state had no gubernatorial election in that year, no vote data were found for the state in question, or the state had not yet entered the Union. No special gubernatorial elections are included in this table. Odd-numbered year gubernatorial elections were common before 1880 and several states still scheduled governor elections in odd-numbered years after that.

[1] Election held in odd-numbered year.
[2] 1793 election when a state had annual elections in both 1792 and 1793.
[3] 1795 election when a state had annual elections in both 1794 and 1795.

Sources: Adapted from *American State Governors, 1776–1976,* vol. 1 (1977), *Congressional Quarterly's Guide to U.S. Elections* (1994), and independent search for state sources by the author. Several pre-1824 party affiliations were obtained from the election archive of Michael J. Dubin. Other party affiliations were obtained from independent search of state sources by the author when the *American State Governors* volume and the *Congressional Quarterly Guide* disagreed.

Table 7-11 Governor Election Results, by State, 1796–1799 (Percentages)

State	1796–1797				1798–1799			
	Democratic	Republican	Other	Democratic % of Two-Party Vote	Democratic	Republican	Other	Democratic % of Two-Party Vote
Alabama	—	—	—	—	—	—	—	—
Alaska	—	—	—	—	—	—	—	—
Arizona	—	—	—	—	—	—	—	—
Arkansas	—	—	—	—	—	—	—	—
California	—	—	—	—	—	—	—	—
Colorado	—	—	—	—	—	—	—	—
Connecticut	0.0	64.0	36.0	0.0	—	—	—	—
Delaware	—	—	—	—	43.6	52.5	3.9	45.4
Florida	—	—	—	—	—	—	—	—
Georgia	—	—	—	—	—	—	—	—
Hawaii	—	—	—	—	—	—	—	—
Idaho	—	—	—	—	—	—	—	—
Illinois	—	—	—	—	—	—	—	—
Indiana	—	—	—	—	—	—	—	—
Iowa	—	—	—	—	—	—	—	—
Kansas	—	—	—	—	—	—	—	—
Kentucky	—	—	—	—	—	—	—	—
Louisiana	—	—	—	—	—	—	—	—
Maine	—	—	—	—	—	—	—	—
Maryland	—	—	—	—	—	—	—	—
Massachusetts	0.0	42.6	57.4	0.0	24.8	75.2	0.0	24.8
Michigan	—	—	—	—	—	—	—	—
Minnesota	—	—	—	—	—	—	—	—
Mississippi	—	—	—	—	—	—	—	—
Missouri	—	—	—	—	—	—	—	—
Montana	—	—	—	—	—	—	—	—
Nebraska	—	—	—	—	—	—	—	—
Nevada	—	—	—	—	—	—	—	—
New Hampshire	0.0	72.5	27.5	0.0	9.8	77.3	12.9	11.2
New Jersey	—	—	—	—	—	—	—	—
New Mexico	—	—	—	—	—	—	—	—
New York	—	—	—	—	46.0	54.0	0.0	46.0
North Carolina	—	—	—	—	—	—	—	—
North Dakota	—	—	—	—	—	—	—	—
Ohio	—	—	—	—	—	—	—	—
Oklahoma	—	—	—	—	—	—	—	—
Oregon	—	—	—	—	—	—	—	—
Pennsylvania	96.7	3.3	0.0	96.7	53.8[1]	46.2[1]	0.0[1]	53.8[1]
Rhode Island	100.0[1]	0.0[1]	0.0[1]	100.0[1]	—	—	—	—
South Carolina	—	—	—	—	—	—	—	—
South Dakota	—	—	—	—	—	—	—	—
Tennessee	—	—	—	—	99.7[1]	0.0[1]	0.3[1]	100.0[1]
Texas	—	—	—	—	—	—	—	—
Utah	—	—	—	—	—	—	—	—
Vermont	—	—	—	—	30.0	66.4	3.6	31.1
Virginia	—	—	—	—	—	—	—	—
Washington	—	—	—	—	—	—	—	—
West Virginia	—	—	—	—	—	—	—	—
Wisconsin	—	—	—	—	—	—	—	—
Wyoming	—	—	—	—	—	—	—	—
Massachusetts	43.3[2]	56.7[2]	0.0[2]	43.3[2]	0.0[3]	72.9[3]	27.1[3]	0.0[3]
New Hampshire	0.0[2]	88.9[2]	11.1[2]	0.0[2]	0.0[3]	86.4[3]	13.6[3]	0.0[3]

Notes: Main entries are party vote percentage values for candidates who used the sole designation "Democrat" or "Republican" (or their historical antecedents listed in Appendix A) on the ballot. In general, historical antecedents to the Democratic Party were Anti-Federalists, Democratic-Republicans, and Jackson Democrats; historical precursors of the Republican Party were Federalists, National Republicans, and Whigs. Other = candidates who used third-party names only on the ballot or were listed as independent or unidentified. —indicates that the state had no data, either because the state had no gubernatorial election in that year, no vote data were found for the state in question, or the state had not yet entered the Union. No special gubernatorial elections are included in this table. Odd-numbered year gubernatorial elections were common before 1880 and several states still scheduled governor elections in odd-numbered years after that.

[1] Election held in odd-numbered year.
[2] 1797 election when a state had annual elections in both 1796 and 1797.
[3] 1799 election when a state had annual elections in both 1798 and 1799.

Sources: Adapted from *American State Governors, 1776–1976*, vol. 1 (1977), *Congressional Quarterly's Guide to U.S. Elections* (1994), and independent search for state sources by the author. Several pre-1824 party affiliations were obtained from the election archive of Michael J. Dubin. Other party affiliations were obtained from independent search of state sources by the author when the *American State Governors* volume and the *Congressional Quarterly Guide* disagreed.

Table 7-12 Governor Election Results, by State, 1800–1803 (Percentages)

	1800–1801				1802–1803			
State	Democratic	Republican	Other	Democratic % of Two-Party Vote	Democratic	Republican	Other	Democratic % of Two-Party Vote
Alabama	—	—	—	—	—	—	—	—
Alaska	—	—	—	—	—	—	—	—
Arizona	—	—	—	—	—	—	—	—
Arkansas	—	—	—	—	—	—	—	—
California	—	—	—	—	—	—	—	—
Colorado	—	—	—	—	—	—	—	—
Connecticut	7.9[1]	83.8[1]	8.2[1]	8.6[1]	27.7	69.9	2.4	28.4
Delaware	50.1[1]	49.9[1]	0.0[1]	50.1[1]	—	—	—	—
Florida	—	—	—	—	—	—	—	—
Georgia	—	—	—	—	—	—	—	—
Hawaii	—	—	—	—	—	—	—	—
Idaho	—	—	—	—	—	—	—	—
Illinois	—	—	—	—	—	—	—	—
Indiana	—	—	—	—	—	—	—	—
Iowa	—	—	—	—	—	—	—	—
Kansas	—	—	—	—	—	—	—	—
Kentucky	39.4	0.0	60.6	100.0	—	—	—	—
Louisiana	—	—	—	—	—	—	—	—
Maine	—	—	—	—	—	—	—	—
Maryland	—	—	—	—	—	—	—	—
Massachusetts	43.6	50.3	6.2	46.4	39.2	60.5	0.3	39.3
Michigan	—	—	—	—	—	—	—	—
Minnesota	—	—	—	—	—	—	—	—
Mississippi	—	—	—	—	—	—	—	—
Missouri	—	—	—	—	—	—	—	—
Montana	—	—	—	—	—	—	—	—
Nebraska	—	—	—	—	—	—	—	—
Nevada	—	—	—	—	—	—	—	—
New Hampshire	36.0	61.8	2.2	36.8	45.7	54.1	0.2	45.8
New Jersey	—	—	—	—	—	—	—	—
New Mexico	—	—	—	—	—	—	—	—
New York	54.3[1]	45.7[1]	0.0[1]	54.3[1]	—	—	—	—
North Carolina	—	—	—	—	—	—	—	—
North Dakota	—	—	—	—	—	—	—	—
Ohio	—	—	—	—	100.0[1]	0.0[1]	0.0[1]	100.0[1]
Oklahoma	—	—	—	—	—	—	—	—
Oregon	—	—	—	—	—	—	—	—
Pennsylvania	—	—	—	—	73.6	26.2	0.1	73.7
Rhode Island	100.0[1]	0.0[1]	0.0[1]	100.0[1]	66.3	33.7	0.0	66.3
South Carolina	—	—	—	—	—	—	—	—
South Dakota	—	—	—	—	—	—	—	—
Tennessee	99.9[1]	0.0[1]	0.1[1]	100.0[1]	100.0[1]	0.0[1]	0.0[1]	100.0[1]
Texas	—	—	—	—	—	—	—	—
Utah	—	—	—	—	—	—	—	—
Vermont	32.2	64.0	3.8	33.5	39.3	60.5	0.1	39.4
Virginia	—	—	—	—	—	—	—	—
Washington	—	—	—	—	—	—	—	—
West Virginia	—	—	—	—	—	—	—	—
Wisconsin	—	—	—	—	—	—	—	—
Wyoming	—	—	—	—	—	—	—	—
Connecticut	—	—	—	—	35.0[3]	64.0[3]	1.0[3]	35.3[3]
Massachusetts	43.9[2]	55.3[2]	0.8[2]	44.2[2]	32.0[3]	67.3[3]	0.7[3]	32.3[3]
New Hampshire	31.6[2]	65.5[2]	3.0[2]	32.5[2]	42.3[3]	57.5[3]	0.2[3]	42.4[3]

Notes: Main entries are party vote percentage values for candidates who used the sole designation "Democrat" or "Republican" (or their historical antecedents listed in Appendix A) on the ballot. In general, historical antecedents to the Democratic Party were Anti-Federalists, Democratic-Republicans, and Jackson Democrats; historical precursors of the Republican Party were Federalists, National Republicans, and Whigs. Other = candidates who used third-party names only on the ballot or were listed as independent or unidentified. —indicates that the state had no data, either because the state had no gubernatorial election in that year, no vote data were found for the state in question, or the state had not yet entered the Union. No special gubernatorial elections are included in this table. Odd-numbered year gubernatorial elections were common before 1880 and several states still scheduled governor elections in odd-numbered years after that.

[1] Election held in odd-numbered year.
[2] 1801 election when a state had annual elections in both 1800 and 1801.
[3] 1803 election when a state had annual elections in both 1802 and 1803.

Sources: Adapted from *American State Governors, 1776–1976*, vol. 1 (1977), *Congressional Quarterly's Guide to U.S. Elections* (1994), and independent search for state sources by the author. Several pre-1824 party affiliations were obtained from the election archive of Michael J. Dubin. Other party affiliations were obtained from independent search of state sources by the author when the *American State Governors* volume and the *Congressional Quarterly Guide* disagreed.

Table 7-13 Governor Election Results, by State, 1804–1807 (Percentages)

State	1804–1805				1806–1807			
	Democratic	Republican	Other	Democratic % of Two-Party Vote	Democratic	Republican	Other	Democratic % of Two-Party Vote
Alabama	—	—	—	—	—	—	—	—
Alaska	—	—	—	—	—	—	—	—
Arizona	—	—	—	—	—	—	—	—
Arkansas	—	—	—	—	—	—	—	—
California	—	—	—	—	—	—	—	—
Colorado	—	—	—	—	—	—	—	—
Connecticut	38.2	61.8	0.0	38.2	41.4	58.6	0.0	41.4
Delaware	48.0	52.0	0.0	48.0	48.1[1]	51.9[1]	0.0[1]	48.1[1]
Florida	—	—	—	—	—	—	—	—
Georgia	—	—	—	—	—	—	—	—
Hawaii	—	—	—	—	—	—	—	—
Idaho	—	—	—	—	—	—	—	—
Illinois	—	—	—	—	—	—	—	—
Indiana	—	—	—	—	—	—	—	—
Iowa	—	—	—	—	—	—	—	—
Kansas	—	—	—	—	—	—	—	—
Kentucky	100.0	0.0	0.0	100.0	—	—	—	—
Louisiana	—	—	—	—	—	—	—	—
Maine	—	—	—	—	—	—	—	—
Maryland	—	—	—	—	—	—	—	—
Massachusetts	44.0	55.1	0.9	44.4	49.4	50.2	0.4	49.6
Michigan	—	—	—	—	—	—	—	—
Minnesota	—	—	—	—	—	—	—	—
Mississippi	—	—	—	—	—	—	—	—
Missouri	—	—	—	—	—	—	—	—
Montana	—	—	—	—	—	—	—	—
Nebraska	—	—	—	—	—	—	—	—
Nevada	—	—	—	—	—	—	—	—
New Hampshire	49.5	50.4	0.1	49.5	74.3	15.9	9.8	82.4
New Jersey	—	—	—	—	—	—	—	—
New Mexico	—	—	—	—	—	—	—	—
New York	41.8	58.2	0.0	41.8	53.1[1]	0.0[1]	46.9[1]	100.0[1]
New York	—	—	—	—	***53.1[1]***	***46.9[1]***	***0.0[1]***	***53.1[1]***
North Carolina	—	—	—	—	—	—	—	—
North Dakota	—	—	—	—	—	—	—	—
Ohio	100.0[1]	0.0[1]	0.0[1]	100.0[1]	100.0[1]	0.0[1]	0.0[1]	100.0[1]
Oklahoma	—	—	—	—	—	—	—	—
Oregon	—	—	—	—	—	—	—	—
Pennsylvania	47.1[1]	0.0[1]	52.9[1]	100.0[1]	—	—	—	—
Pennsylvania	***100.0[1]***	***0.0[1]***	***0.0[1]***	***100.0[1]***	—	—	—	—
Rhode Island	—	—	—	—	56.8	43.1	0.2	56.9
South Carolina	—	—	—	—	—	—	—	—
South Dakota	—	—	—	—	—	—	—	—
Tennessee	100.0[1]	0.0[1]	0.0[1]	100.0[1]	—	—	—	—
Texas	—	—	—	—	—	—	—	—
Utah	—	—	—	—	—	—	—	—
Vermont	43.4	56.6	0.0	43.4	43.9	54.1	2.0	44.8
Virginia	—	—	—	—	—	—	—	—
Washington	—	—	—	—	—	—	—	—
West Virginia	—	—	—	—	—	—	—	—
Wisconsin	—	—	—	—	—	—	—	—
Wyoming	—	—	—	—	—	—	—	—
Connecticut	38.1[2]	61.9[2]	0.0[2]	38.1[2]	40.0[3]	60.0[3]	0.0[3]	40.0[3]
Massachusetts	48.6[2]	51.0[2]	0.4[2]	48.8[2]	51.5[3]	48.1[3]	0.4[3]	51.7[3]
New Hampshire	56.6[2]	43.2[2]	0.2[2]	56.7[2]	82.5[3]	0.0[3]	17.5[3]	100.0[3]
Rhode Island	—	—	—	—	65.9[3]	0.0[3]	34.1[3]	100.0[3]
Vermont	35.5[2]	60.9[2]	3.6[2]	36.8[2]	53.2[3]	45.7[3]	1.1[3]	53.8[3]

Notes: Main entries are party vote percentage values for candidates who used the sole designation "Democrat" or "Republican" (or their historical antecedents listed in Appendix A) on the ballot. In general, historical antecedents to the Democratic Party were Anti-Federalists, Democratic-Republicans, and Jackson Democrats; historical precursors of the Republican Party were Federalists, National Republicans, and Whigs. Other = candidates who used third-party names only on the ballot or were listed as independent or unidentified. Bold italicized entries in the table are the author's alternative party coding, which is used when a candidate listed a major-party name (Democrat, Republican, or their historical antecedents) on the ballot with other party names or labels. For a more detailed explanation of this alternative coding system, see Tables 1-3 and 5-1. Also see Table 7-8. —indicates that the state had no data, either because the state had no gubernatorial election in that year, no vote data were found for the state in question, or the state had not yet entered the Union. No special gubernatorial elections are included in this table. Odd-numbered year gubernatorial elections were common before 1880 and several states still scheduled governor elections in odd-numbered years after that.

[1] Election held in odd-numbered year.
[2] 1805 election when a state had annual elections in both 1804 and 1805.
[3] 1807 election when a state had annual elections in both 1806 and 1807.

Sources: Adapted from *American State Governors, 1776–1976*, vol. 1 (1977), *Congressional Quarterly's Guide to U.S. Elections* (1994), and independent search for state sources by the author. Several pre-1824 party affiliations were obtained from the election archive of Michael J. Dubin. Other party affiliations were obtained from independent search of state sources by the author when the *American State Governors* volume and the *Congressional Quarterly Guide* disagreed.

Table 7-14 Governor Election Results, by State, 1808–1811 (Percentages)

State	1808–1809				1810–1811			
	Democratic	Republican	Other	Democratic % of Two-Party Vote	Democratic	Republican	Other	Democratic % of Two-Party Vote
Alabama	—	—	—	—	—	—	—	—
Alaska	—	—	—	—	—	—	—	—
Arizona	—	—	—	—	—	—	—	—
Arkansas	—	—	—	—	—	—	—	—
California	—	—	—	—	—	—	—	—
Colorado	—	—	—	—	—	—	—	—
Connecticut	38.4	61.6	0.0	38.4	34.7	64.5	0.9	34.9
Delaware	—	—	—	—	50.5	49.5	0.0	50.5
Florida	—	—	—	—	—	—	—	—
Georgia	—	—	—	—	—	—	—	—
Hawaii	—	—	—	—	—	—	—	—
Idaho	—	—	—	—	—	—	—	—
Illinois	—	—	—	—	—	—	—	—
Indiana	—	—	—	—	—	—	—	—
Iowa	—	—	—	—	—	—	—	—
Kansas	—	—	—	—	—	—	—	—
Kentucky	61.3	0.0	38.7	100.0	—	—	—	—
Louisiana	—	—	—	—	—	—	—	—
Maine	—	—	—	—	—	—	—	—
Maryland	—	—	—	—	—	—	—	—
Massachusetts	50.8	48.9	0.4	51.0	51.3	48.5	0.2	51.4
Michigan	—	—	—	—	—	—	—	—
Minnesota	—	—	—	—	—	—	—	—
Mississippi	—	—	—	—	—	—	—	—
Missouri	—	—	—	—	—	—	—	—
Montana	—	—	—	—	—	—	—	—
Nebraska	—	—	—	—	—	—	—	—
Nevada	—	—	—	—	—	—	—	—
New Hampshire	79.5	7.9	12.6	90.9	51.7	48.0	0.3	51.8
New Jersey	—	—	—	—	—	—	—	—
New Mexico	—	—	—	—	—	—	—	—
New York	—	—	—	—	54.2	0.0	45.8	100.0
New York	—	—	—	—	**54.2**	**45.8**	**0.0**	**54.2**
North Carolina	—	—	—	—	—	—	—	—
North Dakota	—	—	—	—	—	—	—	—
Ohio	100.0	0.0	0.0	100.0	100.0	0.0	0.0	100.0
Oklahoma	—	—	—	—	—	—	—	—
Oregon	—	—	—	—	—	—	—	—
Pennsylvania	60.9	35.5	3.6	63.2	90.8[1]	6.3[1]	2.9[1]	93.6[1]
Pennsylvania	**64.5**	**35.5**	**0.0**	**64.5**	—	—	—	—
Rhode Island	—	—	—	—	48.1[1]	51.1[1]	0.8[1]	48.4[1]
South Carolina	—	—	—	—	—	—	—	—
South Dakota	—	—	—	—	—	—	—	—
Tennessee	—	—	—	—	—	—	—	—
Texas	—	—	—	—	—	—	—	—
Utah	—	—	—	—	—	—	—	—
Vermont	47.6	50.8	1.6	48.4	57.3	41.2	1.5	58.2
Virginia	—	—	—	—	—	—	—	—
Washington	—	—	—	—	—	—	—	—
West Virginia	—	—	—	—	—	—	—	—
Wisconsin	—	—	—	—	—	—	—	—
Wyoming	—	—	—	—	—	—	—	—
Connecticut	35.8[2]	64.2[2]	0.0[2]	35.8[2]	—	—	—	—
Massachusetts	48.4[2]	51.3[2]	0.3[2]	48.5[2]	51.6[3]	47.8[3]	0.5[3]	51.9[3]
New Hampshire	49.2[2]	50.4[2]	0.4[2]	49.4[2]	54.7[3]	45.1[3]	0.2[3]	54.8[3]
Vermont	51.1[2]	47.2[2]	1.7[2]	52.0[2]	54.0[3]	43.8[3]	2.2[3]	55.2[3]

Notes: Main entries are party vote percentage values for candidates who used the sole designation "Democrat" or "Republican" (or their historical antecedents listed in Appendix A) on the ballot. In general, historical antecedents to the Democratic Party were Anti-Federalists, Democratic-Republicans, and Jackson Democrats; historical precursors of the Republican Party were Federalists, National Republicans, and Whigs. Other = candidates who used third-party names only on the ballot or were listed as independent or unidentified. Bold italicized entries in the table are the author's alternative party coding, which is used when a candidate listed a major-party name (Democrat, Republican, or their historical antecedents) on the ballot with other party names or labels. For a more detailed explanation of this alternative coding system, see Tables 1-3 and 5-1. Also see Table 7-8. —indicates that the state had no data, either because the state had no gubernatorial election in that year, no vote data were found for the state in question, or the state had not yet entered the Union. No special gubernatorial elections are included in this table. Odd-numbered year gubernatorial elections were common before 1880 and several states still scheduled governor elections in odd-numbered years after that.

[1] Election held in odd-numbered year.
[2] 1809 election when a state had annual elections in both 1808 and 1809.
[3] 1811 election when a state had annual elections in both 1810 and 1811.

Sources: Adapted from *American State Governors, 1776–1976*, vol. 1 (1977), *Congressional Quarterly's Guide to U.S. Elections* (1994), and independent search for state sources by the author. Several pre-1824 party affiliations were obtained from the election archive of Michael J. Dubin. Other party affiliations were obtained from independent search of state sources by the author when the *American State Governors* volume and the *Congressional Quarterly Guide* disagreed.

Table 7-15 Governor Election Results, by State, 1812–1815 (Percentages)

State	1812–1813				1814–1815			
	Democratic	Republican	Other	Democratic % of Two-Party Vote	Democratic	Republican	Other	Democratic % of Two-Party Vote
Alabama	—	—	—	—	—	—	—	—
Alaska	—	—	—	—	—	—	—	—
Arizona	—	—	—	—	—	—	—	—
Arkansas	—	—	—	—	—	—	—	—
California	—	—	—	—	—	—	—	—
Colorado	—	—	—	—	—	—	—	—
Connecticut	10.9	86.1	3.0	11.3	20.3	72.9	6.9	21.8
Delaware	44.8[1]	55.2[1]	0.0[1]	44.8[1]	—	—	—	—
Florida	—	—	—	—	—	—	—	—
Georgia	—	—	—	—	—	—	—	—
Hawaii	—	—	—	—	—	—	—	—
Idaho	—	—	—	—	—	—	—	—
Illinois	—	—	—	—	—	—	—	—
Indiana	—	—	—	—	—	—	—	—
Iowa	—	—	—	—	—	—	—	—
Kansas	—	—	—	—	—	—	—	—
Kentucky	70.9	0.0	29.1	100.0	—	—	—	—
Louisiana	0.0	0.0	100.0	—	—	—	—	—
Maine	—	—	—	—	—	—	—	—
Maryland	—	—	—	—	—	—	—	—
Massachusetts	49.3	50.6	0.1	49.3	44.8	55.0	0.2	44.9
Michigan	—	—	—	—	—	—	—	—
Minnesota	—	—	—	—	—	—	—	—
Mississippi	—	—	—	—	—	—	—	—
Missouri	—	—	—	—	—	—	—	—
Montana	—	—	—	—	—	—	—	—
Nebraska	—	—	—	—	—	—	—	—
Nevada	—	—	—	—	—	—	—	—
New Hampshire	48.4	48.8	2.7	49.8	48.7	51.1	0.2	48.8
New Jersey	—	—	—	—	—	—	—	—
New Mexico	—	—	—	—	—	—	—	—
New York	52.2[1]	47.8[1]	0.0[1]	52.2[1]	—	—	—	—
North Carolina	—	—	—	—	—	—	—	—
North Dakota	—	—	—	—	—	—	—	—
Ohio	40.0	60.0	0.0	40.0	72.0	28.0	0.0	72.0
Oklahoma	—	—	—	—	—	—	—	—
Oregon	—	—	—	—	—	—	—	—
Pennsylvania	—	—	—	—	62.6	36.3	1.1	63.3
Rhode Island	48.4	51.5	0.2	48.4	0.0	76.6	23.4	0.0
South Carolina	—	—	—	—	—	—	—	—
South Dakota	—	—	—	—	—	—	—	—
Tennessee	100.0[1]	0.0[1]	0.0[1]	100.0[1]	42.8[1]	0.0[1]	57.2[1]	100.0[1]
Texas	—	—	—	—	—	—	—	—
Utah	—	—	—	—	—	—	—	—
Vermont	53.6	44.6	1.8	54.6	49.3	49.4	1.3	49.9
Virginia	—	—	—	—	—	—	—	—
Washington	—	—	—	—	—	—	—	—
West Virginia	—	—	—	—	—	—	—	—
Wisconsin	—	—	—	—	—	—	—	—
Wyoming	—	—	—	—	—	—	—	—
Connecticut	35.8[2]	59.1[2]	5.1[2]	37.7[2]	35.4[3]	59.3[3]	5.4[3]	37.4[3]
Massachusetts	42.7[2]	56.6[2]	0.7[2]	43.0[2]	46.2[3]	53.6[3]	0.2[3]	46.3[3]
New Hampshire	48.7[2]	50.7[2]	0.6[2]	49.0[2]	49.2[3]	50.7[3]	0.1[3]	49.2[3]
Rhode Island	0.0[2]	100.0[2]	0.0[2]	0.0[2]	43.4[3]	56.6[3]	0.0[3]	43.4[3]
Vermont	49.6[2]	48.7[2]	1.8[2]	50.4[2]	52.1[3]	46.3[3]	1.7[3]	53.0[3]

Notes: Main entries are party vote percentage values for candidates who used the sole designation "Democrat" or "Republican" (or their historical antecedents listed in Appendix A) on the ballot. In general, historical antecedents to the Democratic Party were Anti-Federalists, Democratic-Republicans, and Jackson Democrats; historical precursors of the Republican Party were Federalists, National Republicans, and Whigs. Other = candidates who used third-party names only on the ballot or were listed as independent or unidentified. —indicates that the state had no data, either because the state had no gubernatorial election in that year, no vote data were found for the state in question, or the state had not yet entered the Union. No special gubernatorial elections are included in this table. Odd-numbered year gubernatorial elections were common before 1880 and several states still scheduled governor elections in odd-numbered years after that.

[1] Election held in odd-numbered year.
[2] 1813 election when a state had annual elections in both 1812 and 1813.
[3] 1815 election when a state had annual elections in both 1814 and 1815.

Sources: Adapted from *American State Governors, 1776–1976,* vol. 1 (1977), *Congressional Quarterly's Guide to U.S. Elections* (1994), and independent search for state sources by the author. Several pre-1824 party affiliations were obtained from the election archive of Michael J. Dubin. Other party affiliations were obtained from independent search of state sources by the author when the *American State Governors* volume and the *Congressional Quarterly Guide* disagreed.

Table 7-16 Governor Election Results, by State, 1816–1819 (Percentages)

	1816–1817				*1818–1819*			
State	*Democratic*	*Republican*	*Other*	*Democratic % of Two-Party Vote*	*Democratic*	*Republican*	*Other*	*Democratic % of Two-Party Vote*
Alabama	—	—	—	—	53.9[1]	0.0[1]	46.1[1]	100.0[1]
Alaska	—	—	—	—	—	—	—	—
Arizona	—	—	—	—	—	—	—	—
Arkansas	—	—	—	—	—	—	—	—
California	—	—	—	—	—	—	—	—
Colorado	—	—	—	—	—	—	—	—
Connecticut	0.0	52.3	47.7	0.0	0.0	0.0	100.0	—
Delaware	46.8	53.2	0.0	46.8	45.4[1]	54.6[1]	0.0[1]	45.4[1]
Florida	—	—	—	—	—	—	—	—
Georgia	—	—	—	—	—	—	—	—
Hawaii	—	—	—	—	—	—	—	—
Idaho	—	—	—	—	—	—	—	—
Illinois	—	—	—	—	100.0	0.0	0.0	100.0
Indiana	57.0	0.0	43.0	100.0	81.4[1]	0.0[1]	18.6[1]	100.0[1]
Iowa	—	—	—	—	—	—	—	—
Kansas	—	—	—	—	—	—	—	—
Kentucky	100.0	0.0	0.0	100.0	—	—	—	—
Louisiana	0.0	0.0	100.0	—	—	—	—	—
Maine	—	—	—	—	—	—	—	—
Maryland	—	—	—	—	—	—	—	—
Massachusetts	48.8	51.1	0.1	49.2	42.4	55.7	1.9	43.2
Michigan	—	—	—	—	—	—	—	—
Minnesota	—	—	—	—	—	—	—	—
Mississippi	100.0[1]	0.0[1]	0.0[1]	100.0[1]	61.5[1]	0.0[1]	38.5[1]	100.0[1]
Missouri	—	—	—	—	—	—	—	—
Montana	—	—	—	—	—	—	—	—
Nebraska	—	—	—	—	—	—	—	—
Nevada	—	—	—	—	—	—	—	—
New Hampshire	53.0	46.9	0.2	53.1	59.4	37.7	2.9	61.1
New Jersey	—	—	—	—	—	—	—	—
New Mexico	—	—	—	—	—	—	—	—
New York	54.0	46.0	0.0	54.0	—	—	—	—
North Carolina	—	—	—	—	—	—	—	—
North Dakota	—	—	—	—	—	—	—	—
Ohio	94.8	5.2	0.0	94.8	100.0	0.0	0.0	100.0
Oklahoma	—	—	—	—	—	—	—	—
Oregon	—	—	—	—	—	—	—	—
Pennsylvania	52.8[1]	0.0[1]	47.2[1]	100.0[1]	—	—	—	—
Rhode Island	47.6	52.4	0.0	47.6	53.7	46.3	0.0	53.7
South Carolina	—	—	—	—	—	—	—	—
South Dakota	—	—	—	—	—	—	—	—
Tennessee	64.3[1]	0.0[1]	35.7[1]	100.0[1]	100.0[1]	0.0[1]	0.0[1]	100.0[1]
Texas	—	—	—	—	—	—	—	—
Utah	—	—	—	—	—	—	—	—
Vermont	55.2	44.4	0.3	55.4	95.3	0.0	4.7	100.0
Virginia	—	—	—	—	—	—	—	—
Washington	—	—	—	—	—	—	—	—
West Virginia	—	—	—	—	—	—	—	—
Wisconsin	—	—	—	—	—	—	—	—
Wyoming	—	—	—	—	—	—	—	—
Connecticut	0.0[2]	48.6[2]	51.4[2]	0.0[2]	0.0[3]	0.0[3]	100.0[3]	—
Massachusetts	45.1[2]	54.6[2]	0.2[2]	45.2[2]	44.2[3]	53.7[3]	2.2[3]	45.1[3]
New Hampshire	54.0[2]	44.2[2]	1.8[2]	55.0[2]	56.7[3]	35.7[3]	7.6[3]	61.4[3]
Rhode Island	50.4[2]	49.5[2]	0.0[2]	50.5[2]	0.0[3]	0.0[3]	100.0[3]	—
Vermont	64.3[2]	34.7[2]	1.0[2]	64.9[2]	88.4[3]	0.0[3]	11.6[3]	100.0[3]

Notes: Main entries are party vote percentage values for candidates who used the sole designation "Democrat" or "Republican" (or their historical antecedents listed in Appendix A) on the ballot. In general, historical antecedents to the Democratic Party were Anti-Federalists, Democratic-Republicans, and Jackson Democrats; historical precursors of the Republican Party were Federalists, National Republicans, and Whigs. Other = candidates who used third-party names only on the ballot or were listed as independent or unidentified. —indicates that the state had no data, either because the state had no gubernatorial election in that year, no vote data were found for the state in question, or the state had not yet entered the Union. No special gubernatorial elections are included in this table. Odd-numbered year gubernatorial elections were common before 1880 and several states still scheduled governor elections in odd-numbered years after that.

[1]Election held in odd-numbered year.

[2]1817 election when a state had annual elections in both 1816 and 1817.

[3]1819 election when a state had annual elections in both 1818 and 1819.

Sources: Adapted from *American State Governors, 1776–1976*, vol. 1 (1977), *Congressional Quarterly's Guide to U.S. Elections* (1994), and independent search for state sources by the author. Several pre-1824 party affiliations were obtained from the election archive of Michael J. Dubin. Other party affiliations were obtained from independent search of state sources by the author when the *American State Governors* volume and the *Congressional Quarterly Guide* disagreed.

Table 7-17 Governor Election Results, by State, 1820–1823 (Percentages)

State	1820–1821				1822–1823			
	Democratic	Republican	Other	Democratic % of Two-Party Vote	Democratic	Republican	Other	Democratic % of Two-Party Vote
Alabama	57.4[1]	0.0[1]	42.6[1]	100.0[1]	56.7[1]	0.0[1]	43.3[1]	100.0[1]
Alaska	—	—	—	—	—	—	—	—
Arizona	—	—	—	—	—	—	—	—
Arkansas	—	—	—	—	—	—	—	—
California	—	—	—	—	—	—	—	—
Colorado	—	—	—	—	—	—	—	—
Connecticut	78.4	0.0	21.6	100.0	85.5	0.0	14.5	100.0
Delaware	53.1	46.9	0.0	53.1	50.1	49.9	0.0	50.1
Florida	—	—	—	—	—	—	—	—
Georgia	—	—	—	—	—	—	—	—
Hawaii	—	—	—	—	—	—	—	—
Idaho	—	—	—	—	—	—	—	—
Illinois	—	—	—	—	33.2	0.0	66.8	100.0
Indiana	—	—	—	—	100.0	0.0	0.0	100.0
Iowa	—	—	—	—	—	—	—	—
Kansas	—	—	—	—	—	—	—	—
Kentucky	32.8	0.0	67.2	100.0	—	—	—	—
Louisiana	0.0	0.0	100.0	—	—	—	—	—
Maine	95.3	0.0	4.7	100.0	73.2	26.1	0.7	73.7
Maryland	—	—	—	—	—	—	—	—
Massachusetts	41.1	58.3	0.6	41.4	42.5	57.2	0.4	42.6
Michigan	—	—	—	—	—	—	—	—
Minnesota	—	—	—	—	—	—	—	—
Mississippi	78.8[1]	0.0[1]	21.2[1]	100.0[1]	51.3[1]	0.0[1]	48.7[1]	100.0[1]
Missouri	100.0	0.0	0.0	100.0	—	—	—	—
Montana	—	—	—	—	—	—	—	—
Nebraska	—	—	—	—	—	—	—	—
Nevada	—	—	—	—	—	—	—	—
New Hampshire	89.7	0.0	10.3	100.0	95.6	0.0	4.4	100.0
New Jersey	—	—	—	—	—	—	—	—
New Mexico	—	—	—	—	—	—	—	—
New York	0.0	0.0	100.0	—	97.8	0.0	2.2	100.0
New York	**100.0**	**0.0**	**0.0**	**100.0**	—	—	—	—
North Carolina	—	—	—	—	—	—	—	—
North Dakota	—	—	—	—	—	—	—	—
Ohio	99.5	0.0	0.5	100.0	61.9	38.1	0.0	61.9
Oklahoma	—	—	—	—	—	—	—	—
Oregon	—	—	—	—	—	—	—	—
Pennsylvania	100.0	0.0	0.0	100.0	58.3[1]	41.7[1]	0.0[1]	58.3[1]
Rhode Island	0.0	0.0	100.0	—	0.0	0.0	100.0	—
South Carolina	—	—	—	—	—	—	—	—
South Dakota	—	—	—	—	—	—	—	—
Tennessee	79.0[1]	0.0[1]	21.0[1]	100.0[1]	100.0[1]	0.0[1]	0.0[1]	100.0[1]
Texas	—	—	—	—	—	—	—	—
Utah	—	—	—	—	—	—	—	—
Vermont	93.4	0.0	6.6	100.0	85.6[1]	0.0[1]	14.4[1]	100.0[1]
Virginia	—	—	—	—	—	—	—	—
Washington	—	—	—	—	—	—	—	—
West Virginia	—	—	—	—	—	—	—	—
Wisconsin	—	—	—	—	—	—	—	—
Wyoming	—	—	—	—	—	—	—	—
Connecticut	86.6[2]	0.0[2]	13.4[2]	100.0[2]	88.9[3]	0.0[3]	11.1[3]	100.0[3]
Delaware	—	—	—	—	48.2[3]	51.8[3]	0.0[3]	48.2[3]
Maine	68.7[2]	27.9[2]	3.3[2]	71.1[2]	95.6[3]	0.0[3]	4.4[3]	100.0[3]
Massachusetts	41.3[2]	58.3[2]	0.4[2]	41.5[2]	52.7[3]	46.2[3]	1.2[3]	53.3[3]
New Hampshire	92.4[2]	0.0[2]	7.6[2]	100.0[2]	99.2[3]	0.0[3]	0.8[3]	100.0[3]
Rhode Island	57.6[2]	0.0[2]	42.4[2]	100.0[2]	0.0[3]	0.0[3]	100.0[3]	—
Vermont	98.7[2]	0.0[2]	1.3[2]	100.0[2]	—	—	—	—

Notes: Main entries are party vote percentage values for candidates who used the sole designation "Democrat" or "Republican" (or their historical antecedents listed in Appendix A) on the ballot. In general, historical antecedents to the Democratic Party were Anti-Federalists, Democratic-Republicans, and Jackson Democrats; historical precursors of the Republican Party were Federalists, National Republicans, and Whigs. Other = candidates who used third-party names only on the ballot or were listed as independent or unidentified. Bold italicized entries in the table are the author's alternative party coding, which is used when a candidate listed a major-party name (Democrat, Republican, or their historical antecedents) on the ballot with other party names or labels. For a more detailed explanation of this alternative coding system, see Tables 1-3 and 5-1. Also see Table 7-8. —indicates that the state had no data, either because the state had no gubernatorial election in that year, no vote data were found for the state in question, or the state had not yet entered the Union. No special gubernatorial elections are included in this table. Odd-numbered year gubernatorial elections were common before 1880 and several states still scheduled governor elections in odd-numbered years after that.

[1] Election held in odd-numbered year.
[2] 1821 election when a state had annual elections in both 1820 and 1821.
[3] 1823 election when a state had annual elections in both 1822 and 1823.

Sources: Adapted from *American State Governors, 1776–1976*, vol. 1 (1977), *Congressional Quarterly's Guide to U.S. Elections* (1994), and independent search for state sources by the author. Several pre-1824 party affiliations were obtained from the election archive of Michael J. Dubin. Other party affiliations were obtained from independent search of state sources by the author when the *American State Governors* volume and the *Congressional Quarterly Guide* disagreed.

Table 7-18 Governor Election Results, by State, 1824–1827 (Percentages)

State	1824–1825				1826–1827			
	Democratic	Republican	Other	Democratic % of Two-Party Vote	Democratic	Republican	Other	Democratic % of Two-Party Vote
Alabama	100.0[1]	0.0[1]	0.0[1]	100.0[1]	99.2[1]	0.0[1]	0.8[1]	100.0[1]
Alaska	—	—	—	—	—	—	—	—
Arizona	—	—	—	—	—	—	—	—
Arkansas	—	—	—	—	—	—	—	—
California	—	—	—	—	—	—	—	—
Colorado	—	—	—	—	—	—	—	—
Connecticut	92.1	7.9	0.0	92.1	57.8	42.2	0.0	57.8
Delaware	—	—	—	—	49.4	50.6	0.0	49.4
Florida	—	—	—	—	—	—	—	—
Georgia	50.9[1]	0.0[1]	49.1[1]	100.0[1]	70.6[1]	0.0[1]	29.4[1]	100.0[1]
Hawaii	—	—	—	—	—	—	—	—
Idaho	—	—	—	—	—	—	—	—
Illinois	—	—	—	—	45.9	49.4	4.8	48.2
Indiana	0.0[1]	46.8[1]	53.2[1]	0.0[1]	—	—	—	—
Indiana	**0.0[1]**	**100.0[1]**	**0.0[1]**	**0.0[1]**	—	—	—	—
Iowa	—	—	—	—	—	—	—	—
Kansas	—	—	—	—	—	—	—	—
Kentucky	59.5	0.0	40.5	100.0	—	—	—	—
Louisiana	0.0	0.0	100.0	—	—	—	—	—
Maine	96.8	0.0	3.2	100.0	98.2	0.0	1.8	100.0
Maryland	—	—	—	—	—	—	—	—
Massachusetts	52.9	46.8	0.3	53.1	0.0	96.5	3.5	0.0
Michigan	—	—	—	—	—	—	—	—
Minnesota	—	—	—	—	—	—	—	—
Mississippi	100.0[1]	0.0[1]	0.0[1]	100.0[1]	51.0[1]	0.0[1]	49.0[1]	100.0[1]
Missouri	0.0	57.1	42.9	0.0	—	—	—	—
Missouri	**0.0**	**100.0**	**0.0**	**0.0**	—	—	—	—
Montana	—	—	—	—	—	—	—	—
Nebraska	—	—	—	—	—	—	—	—
Nevada	—	—	—	—	—	—	—	—
New Hampshire	0.0	0.0	100.0	—	0.0	0.0	100.0	—
New Jersey	—	—	—	—	—	—	—	—
New Mexico	—	—	—	—	—	—	—	—
New York	0.0	0.0	100.0	—	0.0	0.0	100.0	—
New York	**100.0**	**0.0**	**0.0**	**100.0**	**100.0**	**0.0**	**0.0**	**100.0**
North Carolina	—	—	—	—	—	—	—	—
North Dakota	—	—	—	—	—	—	—	—
Ohio	51.0	49.0	0.0	51.0	0.0	84.2	15.8	0.0
Oklahoma	—	—	—	—	—	—	—	—
Oregon	—	—	—	—	—	—	—	—
Pennsylvania	—	—	—	—	96.9	1.6	1.6	98.4
Rhode Island	78.0	0.0	22.0	100.0	100.0[1]	0.0[1]	0.0[1]	100.0[1]
South Carolina	—	—	—	—	—	—	—	—
South Dakota	—	—	—	—	—	—	—	—
Tennessee	99.8[1]	0.0[1]	0.2[1]	100.0[1]	54.7[1]	0.0[1]	45.3[1]	100.0[1]
Texas	—	—	—	—	—	—	—	—
Utah	—	—	—	—	—	—	—	—
Vermont	85.8	0.0	14.2	100.0	63.3	0.0	36.7	100.0
Virginia	—	—	—	—	—	—	—	—
Washington	—	—	—	—	—	—	—	—
West Virginia	—	—	—	—	—	—	—	—
Wisconsin	—	—	—	—	—	—	—	—
Wyoming	—	—	—	—	—	—	—	—
Connecticut	70.1[2]	29.9[2]	0.0[2]	70.1[2]	97.5[3]	2.5[3]	0.0[3]	97.5[3]
Maine	93.1[2]	0.0[2]	6.9[2]	100.0[2]	97.6[3]	0.0[3]	2.4[3]	100.0[3]
Massachusetts	0.0[2]	0.0[2]	100.0[2]	—	0.0[3]	74.2[3]	25.8[3]	0.0[3]
Massachusetts	**0.0[2]**	**94.1[2]**	**5.9[2]**	**0.0[2]**	**0.0[3]**	**92.4[3]**	**7.6[3]**	**0.0[3]**
Missouri	75.7[2]	24.3[2]	0.0[2]	75.7[2]	—	—	—	—
Rhode Island	100.0[2]	0.0[2]	0.0[2]	100.0[2]	—	—	—	—
Vermont	98.4[2]	0.0[2]	1.6[2]	100.0[2]	85.2[3]	0.0[3]	14.8[3]	100.0[3]

Notes: Main entries are party vote percentage values for candidates who used the sole designation "Democrat" or "Republican" (or their historical antecedents listed in Appendix A) on the ballot. In general, historical antecedents to the Democratic Party were Anti-Federalists, Democratic-Republicans, and Jackson Democrats; historical precursors of the Republican Party were Federalists, National Republicans, and Whigs. Other = candidates who used third-party names only on the ballot or were listed as independent or unidentified. Bold italicized entries in the table are the author's alternative party coding, which is used when a candidate listed a major-party name (Democrat, Republican, or their historical antecedents) on the ballot with other party names or labels. For a more detailed explanation of this alternative coding system, see Tables 1-3 and 5-1. Also see Table 7-8. —indicates that the state had no data, either because the state had no gubernatorial election in that year, no vote data were found for the state in question, or the state had not yet entered the Union. No special gubernatorial elections are included in this table. Odd-numbered year gubernatorial elections were common before 1880 and several states still scheduled governor elections in odd-numbered years after that.

[1] Election held in odd-numbered year.
[2] 1825 election when a state had annual elections in both 1824 and 1825.
[3] 1827 election when a state had annual elections in both 1826 and 1827.

Sources: Adapted from *American State Governors, 1776–1976*, vol. 1 (1977), *Congressional Quarterly's Guide to U.S. Elections* (1994), ICPSR data sets 0001 and 0075, and independent search for state sources by the author. Party affiliations were obtained from independent search of state sources by the author when the *American State Governors* volume and the *Congressional Quarterly Guide* disagreed.

Table 7-19 Governor Election Results, by State, 1828–1831 (Percentages)

State	1828–1829				1830–1831			
	Democratic	Republican	Other	Democratic % of Two-Party Vote	Democratic	Republican	Other	Democratic % of Two-Party Vote
Alabama	100.0[1]	0.0[1]	0.0[1]	100.0[1]	55.5[1]	32.3[1]	12.2[1]	63.2[1]
Alabama	—	—	—	—	*67.7[1]*	*32.3[1]*	*0.0[1]*	*67.7[1]*
Alaska	—	—	—	—	—	—	—	—
Arizona	—	—	—	—	—	—	—	—
Arkansas	—	—	—	—	—	—	—	—
California	—	—	—	—	—	—	—	—
Colorado	—	—	—	—	—	—	—	—
Connecticut	97.2	0.0	2.8	100.0	95.6	1.4	3.0	98.6
Delaware	—	—	—	—	—	—	—	—
Florida	—	—	—	—	—	—	—	—
Georgia	71.5[1]	0.0[1]	28.5[1]	100.0[1]	0.0[1]	0.0[1]	100.0[1]	—
Georgia	—	—	—	—	*51.7[1]*	*0.0[1]*	*48.3[1]*	*100.0[1]*
Hawaii	—	—	—	—	—	—	—	—
Idaho	—	—	—	—	—	—	—	—
Illinois	—	—	—	—	41.0	59.0	0.0	41.0
Indiana	32.0	28.5	39.5	52.9	40.7[1]	45.6[1]	13.7[1]	47.2[1]
Indiana	*32.0*	*68.0*	*0.0*	*32.0*				
Iowa	—	—	—	—	—	—	—	—
Kansas	—	—	—	—	—	—	—	—
Kentucky	49.5	50.5	0.0	49.5	—	—	—	—
Louisiana	39.6	60.4	0.0	39.6	38.3[1]	61.7[1]	0.0[1]	38.3[1]
Maine	91.6	0.0	8.4	100.0	51.1	48.5	0.4	51.3
Maryland	—	—	—	—	—	—	—	—
Massachusetts	12.9	81.5	5.6	13.7	30.6	65.5	3.9	31.8
Michigan	—	—	—	—	—	—	—	—
Minnesota	—	—	—	—	—	—	—	—
Mississippi	64.6[1]	35.4[1]	0.0[1]	64.6[1]	65.7[1]	30.5[1]	3.8[1]	68.3[1]
Missouri	0.0	0.0	100.0	—	—	—	—	—
Montana	—	—	—	—	—	—	—	—
Nebraska	—	—	—	—	—	—	—	—
Nevada	—	—	—	—	—	—	—	—
New Hampshire	47.3	52.7	0.0	47.3	54.9	45.1	0.0	54.9
New Jersey	—	—	—	—	—	—	—	—
New Mexico	—	—	—	—	—	—	—	—
New York	49.5	38.5	12.1	56.2	51.7	48.3	0.0	51.7
North Carolina	—	—	—	—	—	—	—	—
North Dakota	—	—	—	—	—	—	—	—
Ohio	48.5	51.4	0.1	48.6	49.6	50.1	0.2	49.8
Oklahoma	—	—	—	—	—	—	—	—
Oregon	—	—	—	—	—	—	—	—
Pennsylvania	60.1[1]	0.0[1]	39.9[1]	100.0[1]	—	—	—	—
Rhode Island	100.0	0.0	0.0	100.0	61.9	0.0	38.1	100.0
South Carolina	—	—	—	—	—	—	—	—
South Dakota	—	—	—	—	—	—	—	—
Tennessee	99.8[1]	0.0[1]	0.2[1]	100.0[1]	97.3[1]	2.5[1]	0.2[1]	97.5[1]
Texas	—	—	—	—	—	—	—	—
Utah	—	—	—	—	—	—	—	—
Vermont	0.0	91.8	8.2	0.0	20.5	43.9	35.7	31.8
Virginia	—	—	—	—	—	—	—	—
Washington	—	—	—	—	—	—	—	—
West Virginia	—	—	—	—	—	—	—	—
Wisconsin	—	—	—	—	—	—	—	—
Wyoming	—	—	—	—	—	—	—	—
Connecticut	95.8[2]	0.0[2]	4.2[2]	100.0[2]	1.8[3]	65.4[3]	32.8[3]	2.6[3]
Maine	49.4[2]	50.1[2]	0.5[2]	49.7[2]	56.3[3]	43.5[3]	0.2[3]	56.5[3]
Massachusetts	19.5[2]	71.6[2]	8.9[2]	21.4[2]	20.6[3]	53.9[3]	25.5[3]	27.6[3]
New Hampshire	53.6[2]	46.4[2]	0.0[2]	53.6[2]	55.6[3]	44.2[3]	0.3[3]	55.7[3]
Rhode Island	100.0[2]	0.0[2]	0.0[2]	100.0[2]	43.2[3]	0.0[3]	56.8[3]	100.0[3]
Vermont	15.4[2]	55.7[2]	28.9[2]	21.7[2]	17.8[3]	37.5[3]	44.7[3]	32.2[3]

Notes: Main entries are party vote percentage values for candidates who used the sole designation "Democrat" or "Republican" (or their historical antecedents listed in Appendix A) on the ballot. In general, historical antecedents to the Democratic Party were Anti-Federalists, Democratic-Republicans, and Jackson Democrats; historical precursors of the Republican Party were Federalists, National Republicans, and Whigs. Other = candidates who used third-party names only on the ballot or were listed as independent or unidentified. Bold italicized entries in the table are the author's alternative party coding, which is used when a candidate listed a major-party name (Democrat, Republican, or their historical antecedents) on the ballot with other party names or labels. For a more detailed explanation of this alternative coding system, see Tables 1-3 and 5-1. Also see Table 7-8. —indicates that the state had no data, either because the state had no gubernatorial election in that year, no vote data were found for the state in question, or the state had not yet entered the Union. No special gubernatorial elections are included in this table. Odd-numbered year gubernatorial elections were common before 1880 and several states still scheduled governor elections in odd-numbered years after that.

[1] Election held in odd-numbered year.
[2] 1829 election when a state had annual elections in both 1828 and 1829.
[3] 1831 election when a state had annual elections in both 1830 and 1831.

Sources: Adapted from *American State Governors, 1776–1976*, vol. 1 (1977), *Congressional Quarterly's Guide to U.S. Elections* (1994), ICPSR data sets 0001 and 0075, and independent search for state sources by the author. Party affiliations were obtained from independent search of state sources by the author when the *American State Governors* volume and the *Congressional Quarterly Guide* disagreed.

Table 7-20 Governor Election Results, by State, 1832–1835 (Percentages)

State	1832–1833 Democratic	Republican	Other	Democratic % of Two-Party Vote	1834–1835 Democratic	Republican	Other	Democratic % of Two-Party Vote
Alabama	100.0[1]	0.0[1]	0.0[1]	100.0[1]	64.8[1]	0.0[1]	35.2[1]	100.0[1]
Alabama	—	—	—	—	*64.8[1]*	*35.0[1]*	*0.2[1]*	*64.9[1]*
Alaska	—	—	—	—	—	—	—	—
Arizona	—	—	—	—	—	—	—	—
Arkansas	—	—	—	—	—	—	—	—
California	—	—	—	—	—	—	—	—
Colorado	—	—	—	—	—	—	—	—
Connecticut	26.2	70.3	3.5	27.2	42.9	49.8	7.3	46.2
Delaware	50.3	49.6	0.1	50.3	—	—	—	—
Florida	—	—	—	—	—	—	—	—
Georgia	0.0[1]	0.0[1]	100.0[1]	—	52.3[1]	47.7[1]	0.0[1]	52.3[1]
Georgia	*51.4[1]*	*0.0[1]*	*48.6[1]*	*100.0[1]*	—	—	—	—
Hawaii	—	—	—	—	—	—	—	—
Idaho	—	—	—	—	—	—	—	—
Illinois	—	—	—	—	31.2	52.9	15.9	37.1
Illinois	—	—	—	—	*44.4*	*52.9*	*2.8*	*45.6*
Indiana	—	—	—	—	42.6	57.4	0.0	42.6
Iowa	—	—	—	—	—	—	—	—
Kansas	—	—	—	—	—	—	—	—
Kentucky	50.9	49.1	0.0	50.9	—	—	—	—
Louisiana	—	—	—	—	42.4	57.6	0.0	42.4
Maine	52.8	45.6	1.6	53.6	52.1	46.3	1.6	52.9
Maryland	—	—	—	—	—	—	—	—
Massachusetts	23.7	52.9	23.5	30.9	24.8	58.1	17.1	29.9
Michigan	—	—	—	—	89.2[1]	9.8[1]	1.0[1]	90.1[1]
Minnesota	—	—	—	—	—	—	—	—
Mississippi	52.9[1]	47.1[1]	0.0[1]	52.9[1]	48.9[1]	51.1[1]	0.0[1]	48.9[1]
Missouri	50.9	0.0	49.1	100.0	—	—	—	—
Missouri	*50.9*	*45.2*	*3.9*	*52.9*	—	—	—	—
Montana	—	—	—	—	—	—	—	—
Nebraska	—	—	—	—	—	—	—	—
Nevada	—	—	—	—	—	—	—	—
New Hampshire	62.3	0.0	37.7	100.0	63.4[1]	0.0[1]	36.6[1]	100.0[1]
New Jersey	—	—	—	—	—	—	—	—
New Mexico	—	—	—	—	—	—	—	—
New York	51.5	48.5	0.0	51.5	51.8	48.2	0.0	51.8
North Carolina	—	—	—	—	—	—	—	—
North Dakota	—	—	—	—	—	—	—	—
Ohio	52.9	47.1	0.0	52.9	51.2	48.8	0.0	51.2
Oklahoma	—	—	—	—	—	—	—	—
Oregon	—	—	—	—	—	—	—	—
Pennsylvania	50.9	0.0	49.1	100.0	46.9[1]	32.8[1]	20.3[1]	58.8[1]
Rhode Island	40.8	0.0	59.2	100.0	0.0	0.0	100.0	—
South Carolina	—	—	—	—	—	—	—	—
South Dakota	—	—	—	—	—	—	—	—
Tennessee	97.8[1]	0.0[1]	2.2[1]	100.0[1]	0.0[1]	50.4[1]	49.6[1]	0.0[1]
Texas	—	—	—	—	—	—	—	—
Utah	—	—	—	—	—	—	—	—
Vermont	20.0	37.7	42.3	34.6	27.5	26.9	45.6	50.6
Virginia	—	—	—	—	—	—	—	—
Washington	—	—	—	—	—	—	—	—
West Virginia	—	—	—	—	—	—	—	—
Wisconsin	—	—	—	—	—	—	—	—
Wyoming	—	—	—	—	—	—	—	—
Connecticut	41.5[2]	42.3[2]	16.2[2]	49.5[2]	51.5[3]	47.3[3]	1.1[3]	52.1[3]
Maine	52.1[2]	36.7[2]	11.2[2]	58.7[2]	61.3[3]	37.3[3]	1.4[3]	62.2[3]
Maine	*58.2[2]*	*36.7[2]*	*5.1[2]*	*61.4[2]*	—	—	—	—
Massachusetts	24.8[2]	40.3[2]	34.9[2]	38.1[2]	38.9[3]	57.9[3]	3.3[3]	40.2[3]
New Hampshire	84.5[2]	0.0[2]	15.5[2]	100.0[2]	—	—	—	—
Rhode Island	0.0[2]	0.0[2]	100.0[2]	—	0.0[3]	0.0[3]	100.0[3]	—
Vermont	0.0[2]	0.0[2]	100.0[2]	—	37.9[3]	15.6[3]	46.5[3]	70.9[3]
Vermont	*40.3[2]*	*4.5[2]*	*55.2[2]*	*89.9[2]*	—	—	—	—

Notes: Main entries are party vote percentage values for candidates who used the sole designation "Democrat" or "Republican" (or their historical antecedents listed in Appendix A) on the ballot. In general, historical antecedents to the Democratic Party were Anti-Federalists, Democratic-Republicans, and Jackson Democrats; historical precursors of the Republican Party were Federalists, National Republicans, and Whigs. Other = candidates who used third-party names only on the ballot or were listed as independent or unidentified. Bold italicized entries in the table are the author's alternative party coding, which is used when a candidate listed a major-party name (Democrat, Republican, or their historical antecedents) on the ballot with other party names or labels. For a more detailed explanation of this alternative coding system, see Tables 1-3 and 5-1. Also see Table 7-8. —indicates that the state had no data, either because the state had no gubernatorial election in that year, no vote data were found for the state in question, or the state had not yet entered the Union. No special gubernatorial elections are included in this table. Odd-numbered year gubernatorial elections were common before 1880 and several states still scheduled governor elections in odd-numbered years after that.

[1] Election held in odd-numbered year.
[2] 1833 election when a state had annual elections in both 1832 and 1833.
[3] 1835 election when a state had annual elections in both 1834 and 1835.

Sources: Adapted from *American State Governors, 1776–1976*, vol. 1 (1977), *Congressional Quarterly's Guide to U.S. Elections* (1994), ICPSR data sets 0001 and 0075, and independent search for state sources by the author. Party affiliations were obtained from independent search of state sources by the author when the *American State Governors* volume and the *Congressional Quarterly Guide* disagreed.

Table 7-21 Governor Election Results, by State, 1836–1839 (Percentages)

State	1836–1837				1838–1839			
	Democratic	Republican	Other	Democratic % of Two-Party Vote	Democratic	Republican	Other	Democratic % of Two-Party Vote
Alabama	53.7[1]	0.0[1]	46.3[1]	100.0[1]	89.9[1]	10.0[1]	0.0[1]	90.0[1]
Alabama	*100.0[1]*	*0.0[1]*	*0.0[1]*	*100.0[1]*	—	—	—	—
Alaska	—	—	—	—	—	—	—	—
Arizona	—	—	—	—	—	—	—	—
Arkansas	62.2	37.5	0.3	62.4	—	—	—	—
California	—	—	—	—	—	—	—	—
Colorado	—	—	—	—	—	—	—	—
Connecticut	53.6	45.8	0.6	53.9	42.9	54.1	3.0	44.2
Delaware	47.7	52.3	0.0	47.7	—	—	—	—
Florida	—	—	—	—	—	—	—	—
Georgia	—	—	—	—	51.4[1]	48.6[1]	0.0[1]	51.4[1]
Hawaii	—	—	—	—	—	—	—	—
Idaho	—	—	—	—	—	—	—	—
Illinois	—	—	—	—	50.8	49.2	0.0	50.8
Indiana	44.5[1]	55.5[1]	0.0[1]	44.5[1]	—	—	—	—
Iowa	—	—	—	—	—	—	—	—
Kansas	—	—	—	—	—	—	—	—
Kentucky	44.2	55.8	0.0	44.2	—	—	—	—
Louisiana	—	—	—	—	47.2	52.8	0.0	47.2
Maine	58.2	41.5	0.3	58.4	51.6	47.9	0.5	51.9
Maryland	—	—	—	—	50.3	49.7	0.0	50.3
Massachusetts	45.9	53.8	0.3	46.1	44.5	55.0	0.5	44.7
Michigan	50.2[1]	48.8[1]	1.0[1]	50.7[1]	48.2[1]	51.8[1]	0.0[1]	48.2[1]
Minnesota	—	—	—	—	—	—	—	—
Mississippi	46.4[1]	0.0[1]	53.6[1]	100.0[1]	54.3[1]	45.7[1]	0.0[1]	54.3[1]
Mississippi	*46.4[1]*	*53.6[1]*	*0.0[1]*	*46.4[1]*	—	—	—	—
Missouri	52.3	0.0	47.7	100.0	—	—	—	—
Montana	—	—	—	—	—	—	—	—
Nebraska	—	—	—	—	—	—	—	—
Nevada	—	—	—	—	—	—	—	—
New Hampshire	—	—	—	—	52.7	46.9	0.4	52.9
New Jersey	—	—	—	—	—	—	—	—
New Mexico	—	—	—	—	—	—	—	—
New York	54.9	45.1	0.0	54.9	48.6	51.4	0.0	48.6
North Carolina	46.8	53.2	0.0	46.8	35.6	64.2	0.2	35.7
North Dakota	—	—	—	—	—	—	—	—
Ohio	48.3	51.6	0.1	48.3	51.4	48.6	0.0	51.4
Oklahoma	—	—	—	—	—	—	—	—
Oregon	—	—	—	—	—	—	—	—
Pennsylvania	—	—	—	—	51.1	0.0	48.9	100.0
Rhode Island	0.0	0.0	100.0	—	0.0	0.0	100.0	—
South Carolina	—	—	—	—	—	—	—	—
South Dakota	—	—	—	—	—	—	—	—
Tennessee	39.1[1]	60.9[1]	0.0[1]	39.1[1]	51.0[1]	49.0[1]	0.0[1]	51.0[1]
Texas	—	—	—	—	—	—	—	—
Utah	—	—	—	—	—	—	—	—
Vermont	44.2	0.0	55.8	100.0	44.0	56.0	0.0	44.0
Vermont	*44.2*	*55.8*	*0.0*	*44.2*	—	—	—	—
Virginia	—	—	—	—	—	—	—	—
Washington	—	—	—	—	—	—	—	—
West Virginia	—	—	—	—	—	—	—	—
Wisconsin	—	—	—	—	—	—	—	—
Wyoming	—	—	—	—	—	—	—	—
Connecticut	52.5[2]	47.5[2]	0.0[2]	52.5[2]	46.5[3]	51.4[3]	2.1[3]	47.5[3]
Maine	49.4[2]	50.1[2]	0.4[2]	49.6[2]	53.8[3]	45.9[3]	0.3[3]	54.0[3]
Massachusetts	39.4[2]	60.3[2]	0.3[2]	39.5[2]	50.0[3]	49.7[3]	0.3[3]	50.2[3]
New Hampshire	—	—	—	—	55.9[3]	43.9[3]	0.2[3]	56.0[3]
Rhode Island	0.0[2]	0.0[2]	100.0[2]	—	0.0[3]	0.0[3]	100.0[3]	—
Vermont	44.3[2]	55.7[2]	0.0[2]	44.3[2]	47.5[3]	52.5[3]	0.0[3]	47.5[3]

Notes: Main entries are party vote percentage values for candidates who used the sole designation "Democrat" or "Republican" (or their historical antecedents listed in Appendix A) on the ballot. In general, historical antecedents to the Democratic Party were Anti-Federalists, Democratic-Republicans, and Jackson Democrats; historical precursors of the Republican Party were Federalists, National Republicans, and Whigs. Other = candidates who used third-party names only on the ballot or were listed as independent or unidentified. Bold italicized entries in the table are the author's alternative party coding, which is used when a candidate listed a major-party name (Democrat, Republican, or their historical antecedents) on the ballot with other party names or labels. For a more detailed explanation of this alternative coding system, see Tables 1-3 and 5-1. Also see Table 7-8. —indicates that the state had no data, either because the state had no gubernatorial election in that year, no vote data were found for the state in question, or the state had not yet entered the Union. No special gubernatorial elections are included in this table. Odd-numbered year gubernatorial elections were common before 1880 and several states still scheduled governor elections in odd-numbered years after that.

[1]Election held in odd-numbered year.
[2]1837 election when a state had annual elections in both 1836 and 1837.
[3]1839 election when a state had annual elections in both 1838 and 1839.

Sources: Adapted from *American State Governors, 1776–1976*, vol. 1 (1977), *Congressional Quarterly's Guide to U.S. Elections* (1994), ICPSR data sets 0001 and 0075, and independent search for state sources by the author. Party affiliations were obtained from independent search of state sources by the author when the *American State Governors* volume and the *Congressional Quarterly Guide* disagreed.

Table 7-22 Governor Election Results, by State, 1840–1843 (Percentages)

	1840–1841				1842–1843			
State	Democratic	Republican	Other	Democratic % of Two-Party Vote	Democratic	Republican	Other	Democratic % of Two-Party Vote
Alabama	58.3[1]	0.0[1]	41.7[1]	100.0[1]	—	—	—	—
Alabama	*58.3[1]*	*41.7[1]*	*0.0[1]*	*58.3[1]*	—	—	—	—
Alaska	—	—	—	—	—	—	—	—
Arizona	—	—	—	—	—	—	—	—
Arkansas	—	—	—	—	—	—	—	—
California	—	—	—	—	—	—	—	—
Colorado	—	—	—	—	—	—	—	—
Connecticut	45.8	54.0	0.2	45.9	49.9	46.2	3.9	51.9
Delaware	46.2	53.8	0.0	46.2	—	—	—	—
Florida	—	—	—	—	—	—	—	—
Georgia	52.7[1]	47.3[1]	0.0[1]	52.7[1]	47.7[1]	52.3[1]	0.0[1]	47.7[1]
Hawaii	—	—	—	—	—	—	—	—
Idaho	—	—	—	—	—	—	—	—
Illinois	—	—	—	—	53.8	45.2	1.0	54.4
Indiana	46.3	53.7	0.0	46.3	50.2[1]	48.4[1]	1.4[1]	50.9[1]
Iowa	—	—	—	—	—	—	—	—
Kansas	—	—	—	—	—	—	—	—
Kentucky	41.6	58.4	0.0	41.6	—	—	—	—
Louisiana	—	—	—	—	54.2	45.8	0.0	54.2
Maine	49.9	50.0	0.1	50.0	56.9	37.3	5.8	60.4
Maryland	50.6[1]	49.4[1]	0.0[1]	50.6[1]	—	—	—	—
Massachusetts	43.3	55.7	1.0	43.8	47.9	46.6	5.6	50.7
Michigan	55.8[1]	41.1[1]	3.1[1]	57.6[1]	54.6[1]	38.3[1]	7.1[1]	58.7[1]
Minnesota	—	—	—	—	—	—	—	—
Mississippi	53.2[1]	46.8[1]	0.0[1]	53.2[1]	0.0[1]	43.7[1]	56.3[1]	0.0[1]
Mississippi	—	—	—	—	*56.3[1]*	*43.7[1]*	*0.0[1]*	*56.3[1]*
Missouri	57.2	42.8	0.0	57.2	—	—	—	—
Montana	—	—	—	—	—	—	—	—
Nebraska	—	—	—	—	—	—	—	—
Nevada	—	—	—	—	—	—	—	—
New Hampshire	58.1	40.8	1.1	58.7	55.8	25.7	18.5	68.5
New Hampshire	—	—	—	—	*68.2*	*25.7*	*6.1*	*72.6*
New Jersey	—	—	—	—	—	—	—	—
New Mexico	—	—	—	—	—	—	—	—
New York	49.1	50.3	0.6	49.4	51.8	46.4	1.8	52.8
North Carolina	45.0	55.0	0.0	45.0	46.9	53.1	0.0	46.9
North Dakota	—	—	—	—	—	—	—	—
Ohio	47.1	52.9	0.0	47.1	49.3	48.6	2.1	50.4
Oklahoma	—	—	—	—	—	—	—	—
Oregon	—	—	—	—	—	—	—	—
Pennsylvania	54.4[1]	45.3[1]	0.3[1]	54.6[1]	—	—	—	—
Rhode Island	0.0	58.4	41.6	0.0	0.0	67.9	32.1	0.0
South Carolina	—	—	—	—	—	—	—	—
South Dakota	—	—	—	—	—	—	—	—
Tennessee	48.5[1]	51.5[1]	0.0[1]	48.5[1]	48.7[1]	51.3[1]	0.0[1]	48.7[1]
Texas	—	—	—	—	—	—	—	—
Utah	—	—	—	—	—	—	—	—
Vermont	40.6	59.4	0.0	40.6	45.2	50.9	4.0	47.0
Virginia	—	—	—	—	—	—	—	—
Washington	—	—	—	—	—	—	—	—
West Virginia	—	—	—	—	—	—	—	—
Wisconsin	—	—	—	—	—	—	—	—
Wyoming	—	—	—	—	—	—	—	—
Connecticut	44.0[2]	56.0[2]	0.0[2]	44.0[2]	50.1[3]	46.4[3]	3.5[3]	51.9[3]
Maine	55.0[2]	42.7[2]	2.3[2]	56.3[2]	55.4[3]	34.6[3]	10.0[3]	61.6[3]
Massachusetts	46.3[2]	50.4[2]	3.3[2]	47.9[2]	44.7[3]	47.7[3]	7.5[3]	48.4[3]
New Hampshire	56.7[2]	40.8[2]	2.5[2]	58.2[2]	51.7[3]	28.2[3]	20.1[3]	64.7[3]
Rhode Island	0.0[2]	97.7[2]	2.3[2]	0.0[2]	44.7[3]	0.0[3]	55.3[3]	100.0[3]
Rhode Island	—	—	—	—	*44.7[1]*	*55.3[1]*	*0.0[1]*	*44.7[1]*
Vermont	44.6[2]	48.5[2]	6.9[2]	47.9[2]	43.8[3]	48.7[3]	7.5[3]	47.3[3]

Notes: Main entries are party vote percentage values for candidates who used the sole designation "Democrat" or "Republican" (or their historical antecedents listed in Appendix A) on the ballot. In general, historical antecedents to the Democratic Party were Anti-Federalists, Democratic-Republicans, and Jackson Democrats; historical precursors of the Republican Party were Federalists, National Republicans, and Whigs. Other = candidates who used third-party names only on the ballot or were listed as independent or unidentified. Bold italicized entries in the table are the author's alternative party coding, which is used when a candidate listed a major-party name (Democrat, Republican, or their historical antecedents) on the ballot with other party names or labels. For a more detailed explanation of this alternative coding system, see Tables 1-3 and 5-1. Also see Table 7-8. —indicates that the state had no data, either because the state had no gubernatorial election in that year, no vote data were found for the state in question, or the state had not yet entered the Union. No special gubernatorial elections are included in this table. Odd-numbered year gubernatorial elections were common before 1880 and several states still scheduled governor elections in odd-numbered years after that.

[1] Election held in odd-numbered year.
[2] 1841 election when a state had annual elections in both 1840 and 1841.
[3] 1843 election when a state had annual elections in both 1842 and 1843.

Sources: Adapted from *American State Governors, 1776–1976*, vol. 1 (1977), *Congressional Quarterly's Guide to U.S. Elections* (1994), ICPSR data sets 0001 and 0075, and independent search for state sources by the author. Party affiliations were obtained from independent search of state sources by the author when the *American State Governors* volume and the *Congressional Quarterly Guide* disagreed.

Table 7-23 Governor Election Results, by State, 1844–1847 (Percentages)

	1844–1845				*1846–1847*			
State	*Democratic*	*Republican*	*Other*	*Democratic % of Two-Party Vote*	*Democratic*	*Republican*	*Other*	*Democratic % of Two-Party Vote*
Alabama	45.3[1]	1.2[1]	53.5[1]	97.5[1]	55.7[1]	44.3[1]	0.0[1]	55.7[1]
Alabama	***97.4[1]***	***1.2[1]***	***1.5[1]***	***98.8[1]***	—	—	—	—
Alaska	—	—	—	—	—	—	—	—
Arizona	—	—	—	—	—	—	—	—
Arkansas	47.6	38.9	13.5	55.0	—	—	—	—
California	—	—	—	—	—	—	—	—
Colorado	—	—	—	—	—	—	—	—
Connecticut	47.3	49.4	3.3	48.9	47.5	48.6	3.8	49.4
Delaware	49.8	50.2	0.0	49.8	50.6	49.4	0.0	50.6
Florida	55.1[1]	44.9[1]	0.0[1]	55.1[1]	—	—	—	—
Georgia	48.9[1]	51.1[1]	0.0[1]	48.9[1]	50.8[1]	49.2[1]	0.0[1]	50.8[1]
Hawaii	—	—	—	—	—	—	—	—
Idaho	—	—	—	—	—	—	—	—
Illinois	—	—	—	—	58.2	36.7	5.1	61.3
Indiana	—	—	—	—	50.7	47.5	1.8	51.6
Iowa	—	—	—	—	0.0	49.2	50.8	0.0
Iowa	—	—	—	—	***50.8***	***49.2***	***0.0***	***50.8***
Kansas	—	—	—	—	—	—	—	—
Kentucky	48.0	52.0	0.0	48.0	—	—	—	—
Louisiana	—	—	—	—	53.1	44.2	2.7	54.6
Maine	51.1	42.0	7.0	54.9	46.9	40.2	13.0	53.8
Maryland	49.6	50.4	0.0	49.6	50.5[1]	49.5[1]	0.0[1]	50.5[1]
Massachusetts	40.8	51.8	7.4	44.0	32.6	53.8	13.6	37.7
Michigan	50.8[1]	41.2[1]	7.9[1]	55.2[1]	53.1[1]	41.0[1]	5.9[1]	56.5[1]
Minnesota	—	—	—	—	—	—	—	—
Mississippi	64.8[1]	35.2[1]	0.0[1]	64.8[1]	—	—	—	—
Missouri	54.1	45.9	0.0	54.1	—	—	—	—
Montana	—	—	—	—	—	—	—	—
Nebraska	—	—	—	—	—	—	—	—
Nevada	—	—	—	—	—	—	—	—
New Hampshire	53.6	30.3	16.2	63.9	48.6	32.0	19.5	60.3
New Jersey	49.1	50.9	0.0	49.1	51.9[1]	48.1[1]	0.0[1]	51.9[1]
New Mexico	—	—	—	—	—	—	—	—
New York	49.5	47.4	3.1	51.1	49.3	50.7	0.0	49.3
North Carolina	48.1	51.9	0.0	48.1	45.0	55.0	0.0	45.0
North Dakota	—	—	—	—	—	—	—	—
Ohio	48.3	48.7	3.0	49.8	47.3	48.3	4.4	49.5
Oklahoma	—	—	—	—	—	—	—	—
Oregon	—	—	—	—	—	—	—	—
Pennsylvania	50.3	48.9	0.8	50.7	50.8[1]	44.6[1]	4.6[1]	53.3[1]
Rhode Island	0.0	0.0	100.0	—	0.0	0.0	100.0	—
Rhode Island	—	—	—	—	***49.2***	***49.8***	***1.0***	***49.7***
South Carolina	—	—	—	—	—	—	—	—
South Dakota	—	—	—	—	—	—	—	—
Tennessee	50.6[1]	49.4[1]	0.0[1]	50.6[1]	49.6[1]	50.4[1]	0.0[1]	49.6[1]
Texas	82.0[1]	0.0[1]	18.0[1]	100.0[1]	85.1[1]	0.0[1]	14.9[1]	100.0[1]
Utah	—	—	—	—	—	—	—	—
Vermont	38.2	51.5	10.3	42.5	36.7	48.5	14.8	43.1
Virginia	—	—	—	—	—	—	—	—
Washington	—	—	—	—	—	—	—	—
West Virginia	—	—	—	—	—	—	—	—
Wisconsin	—	—	—	—	—	—	—	—
Wyoming	—	—	—	—	—	—	—	—
Connecticut	45.3[2]	51.0[2]	3.7[2]	47.1[2]	45.9[3]	50.5[3]	3.6[3]	47.6[3]
Maine	50.7[2]	40.2[2]	9.0[2]	55.8[2]	51.3[3]	37.2[3]	11.5[3]	57.9[3]
Massachusetts	35.3[2]	48.8[2]	15.9[2]	42.0[2]	37.4[3]	51.0[3]	11.6[3]	42.3[3]
Massachusetts	***35.7[2]***	***48.8[2]***	***15.6[2]***	***42.3[2]***	—	—	—	—
New Hampshire	51.3[2]	0.0[2]	48.7[2]	100.0[2]	50.9[3]	34.9[3]	14.2[3]	59.3[3]
Rhode Island	0.0[2]	0.0[2]	100.0[2]	—	38.2[3]	55.3[3]	6.5[3]	40.8[3]
Rhode Island	***0.0[2]***	***99.6[2]***	***0.4[2]***	***0.0[2]***	—	—	—	—
Vermont	38.5[2]	47.2[2]	14.3[2]	44.9[2]	38.8[3]	46.6[3]	14.6[3]	45.4[3]

Notes: Main entries are party vote percentage values for candidates who used the sole designation "Democrat" or "Republican" (or their historical antecedents listed in Appendix A) on the ballot. In general, historical antecedents to the Democratic Party were Anti-Federalists, Democratic-Republicans, and Jackson Democrats; historical precursors of the Republican Party were Federalists, National Republicans, and Whigs. Other = candidates who used third-party names only on the ballot or were listed as independent or unidentified. Bold italicized entries in the table are the author's alternative party coding, which is used when a candidate listed a major-party name (Democrat, Republican, or their historical antecedents) on the ballot with other party names or labels. For a more detailed explanation of this alternative coding system, see Tables 1-3 and 5-1. Also see Table 7-8. —indicates that the state had no data, either because the state had no gubernatorial election in that year, no vote data were found for the state in question, or the state had not yet entered the Union. No special gubernatorial elections are included in this table. Odd-numbered year gubernatorial elections were common before 1880 and several states still scheduled governor elections in odd-numbered years after that.

[1]Election held in odd-numbered year.

[2]1845 election when a state had annual elections in both 1844 and 1845.

[3]1847 election when a state had annual elections in both 1846 and 1847.

Sources: Adapted from *American State Governors, 1776–1976*, vol. 1 (1977), *Congressional Quarterly's Guide to U.S. Elections* (1994), ICPSR data sets 0001 and 0075, and independent search for state sources by the author. Party affiliations were obtained from independent search of state sources by the author when the *American State Governors* volume and the *Congressional Quarterly Guide* disagreed.

Table 7-24 Governor Election Results, by State, 1848–1851 (Percentages)

State	1848–1849				1850–1851			
	Democratic	Republican	Other	Democratic % of Two-Party Vote	Democratic	Republican	Other	Democratic % of Two-Party Vote
Alabama	98.1[1]	0.0[1]	1.9[1]	100.0[1]	86.5[1]	12.8[1]	0.7[1]	87.1[1]
Alaska	—	—	—	—	—	—	—	—
Arizona	—	—	—	—	—	—	—	—
Arkansas	50.5[1]	49.5[1]	0.0[1]	50.5[1]	—	—	—	—
California	0.0[1]	0.0[1]	100.0[1]	—	50.5[1]	49.5[1]	0.0[1]	50.5[1]
California	*47.7[1]*	*0.0[1]*	*52.3[1]*	*100.0[1]*	—	—	—	—
Colorado	—	—	—	—	—	—	—	—
Connecticut	46.8	50.4	2.8	48.1	48.3	46.9	4.8	50.7
Delaware	—	—	—	—	48.3	48.1	3.7	50.1
Florida	46.7	53.3	0.0	46.7	—	—	—	—
Georgia	51.8[1]	48.2[1]	0.0[1]	51.8[1]	0.0[1]	0.0[1]	100.0[1]	—
Georgia	—	—	—	—	*0.0[1]*	*40.3[1]*	*59.7[1]*	*0.0[1]*
Hawaii	—	—	—	—	—	—	—	—
Idaho	—	—	—	—	—	—	—	—
Illinois	86.8	0.0	13.2	100.0	—	—	—	—
Indiana	52.3[1]	45.6[1]	2.1[1]	53.4[1]	—	—	—	—
Iowa	—	—	—	—	52.9	44.8	2.3	54.2
Kansas	—	—	—	—	—	—	—	—
Kentucky	46.6	53.4	0.0	46.6	48.8[1]	48.1[1]	3.1[1]	50.4[1]
Louisiana	51.5[1]	48.5[1]	0.0[1]	51.5[1]	—	—	—	—
Maine	47.0	37.9	15.1	55.4	51.0	40.0	9.0	56.1
Maryland	—	—	—	—	51.0	49.0	0.0	51.0
Massachusetts	20.4	49.7	29.9	29.1	29.7	46.8	23.5	38.8
Massachusetts	*20.8*	*49.7*	*29.5*	*29.5*	—	—	—	—
Michigan	54.0[1]	0.0[1]	46.0[1]	100.0[1]	58.3[1]	0.0[1]	41.7[1]	100.0[1]
Michigan	*54.0[1]*	*45.7[1]*	*0.3[1]*	*54.2[1]*	*58.3[1]*	*41.3[1]*	*0.4[1]*	*58.5[1]*
Minnesota	—	—	—	—	—	—	—	—
Mississippi	59.0[1]	41.0[1]	0.0[1]	59.0[1]	0.0[1]	0.0[1]	100.0[1]	—
Mississippi	—	—	—	—	*100.0[1]*	*0.0[1]*	*0.0[1]*	*100.0[1]*
Missouri	59.0	41.0	0.0	59.0	—	—	—	—
Montana	—	—	—	—	—	—	—	—
Nebraska	—	—	—	—	—	—	—	—
Nevada	—	—	—	—	—	—	—	—
New Hampshire	52.4	0.0	47.6	100.0	55.1	33.0	11.9	62.5
New Hampshire	*52.4*	*46.9*	*0.8*	*52.8*	—	—	—	—
New Jersey	—	—	—	—	53.8	46.2	0.0	53.8
New Mexico	—	—	—	—	—	—	—	—
New York	25.1	47.9	27.0	34.4	49.6	0.0	50.4	100.0
New York	—	—	—	—	*49.6*	*49.6*	*0.8*	*50.0*
North Carolina	49.5	50.5	0.0	49.5	51.6	48.4	0.0	51.6
North Dakota	—	—	—	—	—	—	—	—
Ohio	49.8	49.9	0.3	49.9	49.7	45.2	5.2	52.4
Oklahoma	—	—	—	—	—	—	—	—
Oregon	—	—	—	—	—	—	—	—
Pennsylvania	50.0	50.0	0.0	50.0	50.9[1]	48.6[1]	0.5[1]	51.2[1]
Rhode Island	37.5	58.0	4.5	39.3	0.0	80.2	19.8	0.0
South Carolina	—	—	—	—	—	—	—	—
South Dakota	—	—	—	—	—	—	—	—
Tennessee	50.6[1]	49.4[1]	0.0[1]	50.6[1]	49.3[1]	50.7[1]	0.0[1]	49.3[1]
Texas	48.0[1]	0.0[1]	52.0[1]	100.0[1]	47.0[1]	10.8[1]	42.2[1]	81.3[1]
Utah	—	—	—	—	—	—	—	—
Vermont	0.0	43.7	56.3	0.0	0.0	51.3	48.7	0.0
Vermont	*56.2*	*43.7*	*0.1*	*56.3*	*48.7*	*51.3*	*0.1*	*48.7*
Virginia	—	—	—	—	53.0[1]	47.0[1]	0.0[1]	53.0[1]
Washington	—	—	—	—	—	—	—	—
West Virginia	—	—	—	—	—	—	—	—
Wisconsin	57.6	42.4	0.0	57.6	49.4[1]	50.6[1]	0.0[1]	49.4[1]
Wyoming	—	—	—	—	—	—	—	—
Connecticut	44.9[2]	48.8[2]	6.3[2]	47.9[2]	49.0[3]	46.9[3]	4.1[3]	51.1[3]
Maine	50.8[2]	38.3[2]	10.9[2]	57.0[2]	—	—	—	—
Massachusetts	27.4[2]	49.3[2]	23.2[2]	35.7[2]	32.0[3]	46.9[3]	21.0[3]	40.6[3]
New Hampshire	53.6[2]	33.4[2]	13.0[2]	61.6[2]	47.1[3]	31.7[3]	21.2[3]	59.8[3]
Ohio	—	—	—	—	51.6[3]	42.4[3]	6.0[3]	54.9[3]
Rhode Island	34.4[2]	59.0[2]	6.6[2]	36.8[2]	52.6[3]	45.9[3]	1.5[3]	53.4[3]
Vermont	6.3[2]	49.6[2]	44.1[2]	11.3[2]	0.0[3]	51.0[3]	49.0[3]	0.0[3]
Vermont	*50.4[2]*	*49.6[2]*	*0.1[2]*	*50.4[2]*	*15.2[3]*	*51.0[3]*	*33.8[3]*	*22.9[3]*
Wisconsin	52.6[2]	35.6[2]	11.8[2]	59.6[2]	—	—	—	—

Notes: Main entries are party vote percentage values for candidates who used the sole designation "Democrat" or "Republican" (or their historical antecedents listed in Appendix A) on the ballot. In general, historical antecedents to the Democratic Party were Anti-Federalists, Democratic-Republicans, and Jackson Democrats; historical precursors of the Republican Party were Federalists, National Republicans, and Whigs. Other = candidates who used third-party names only on the ballot or were listed as independent or unidentified. Bold italicized entries in the table are the author's alternative party coding, which is used when a candidate listed a major-party name (Democrat, Republican, or their historical antecedents) on the ballot with other party names or labels. For a more detailed explanation of this alternative coding system, see Tables 1-3 and 5-1. Also see Table 7-8. —indicates that the state had no data, either because the state had no gubernatorial election in that year, no vote data were found for the state in question, or the state had not yet entered the Union. No special gubernatorial elections are included in this table. Odd-numbered year gubernatorial elections were common before 1880 and several states still scheduled governor elections in odd-numbered years after that.

[1]Election held in odd-numbered year.
[2]1849 election when a state had annual elections in both 1848 and 1849.
[3]1851 election when a state had annual elections in both 1850 and 1851.

Sources: Adapted from *American State Governors, 1776–1976*, vol. 1 (1977), *Congressional Quarterly's Guide to U.S. Elections* (1994), ICPSR data sets 0001 and 0075, and independent search for state sources by the author. Party affiliations were obtained from independent search of state sources by the author when the *American State Governors* volume and the *Congressional Quarterly Guide* disagreed.

Table 7-25 Governor Election Results, by State, 1852–1855 (Percentages)

State	1852–1853				1854–1855			
	Democratic	Republican	Other	Democratic % of Two-Party Vote	Democratic	Republican	Other	Democratic % of Two-Party Vote
Alabama	65.0[1]	20.0[1]	15.0[1]	76.5[1]	57.2[1]	0.0[1]	42.8[1]	100.0[1]
Alabama	*80.0[1]*	*20.0[1]*	*0.0[1]*	*80.0[1]*	—	—	—	—
Alaska	—	—	—	—	—	—	—	—
Arizona	—	—	—	—	—	—	—	—
Arkansas	55.2	44.8	0.0	55.2	—	—	—	—
California	51.0[1]	49.0[1]	0.0[1]	51.0[1]	47.5[1]	0.0[1]	52.5[1]	100.0[1]
Colorado	—	—	—	—	—	—	—	—
Connecticut	50.4	45.0	4.6	52.8	48.6	33.2	18.2	59.5
Delaware	—	—	—	—	47.4	0.0	52.6	100.0
Delaware	—	—	—	—	*47.4*	*52.6*	*0.0*	*47.4*
Florida	51.6	48.4	0.0	51.6	—	—	—	—
Georgia	50.3[1]	49.7[1]	0.0[1]	50.3[1]	52.1[1]	0.0[1]	47.9[1]	100.0[1]
Hawaii	—	—	—	—	—	—	—	—
Idaho	—	—	—	—	—	—	—	—
Illinois	52.4	41.8	5.9	55.6	—	—	—	—
Indiana	54.7	43.3	1.9	55.8	—	—	—	—
Iowa	—	—	—	—	0.0	52.4	47.6	0.0
Iowa	—	—	—	—	*47.6*	*52.4*	*0.0*	*47.6*
Kansas	—	—	—	—	—	—	—	—
Kentucky	—	—	—	—	48.4[1]	0.0[1]	51.6[1]	100.0[1]
Louisiana	53.0	47.0	0.0	53.0	53.5[1]	0.0[1]	46.5[1]	100.0[1]
Maine	44.3	31.0	24.7	58.8	31.2	65.0	3.8	32.5
Maryland	52.8[1]	47.2[1]	0.0[1]	52.8[1]	—	—	—	—
Massachusetts	28.0	45.0	27.0	38.4	10.6	20.9	68.5	33.5
Michigan	51.3	41.6	7.1	55.2	0.0	53.0	47.0	0.0
Michigan	—	—	—	—	*47.0*	*53.0*	*0.0*	*47.0*
Minnesota	—	—	—	—	—	—	—	—
Mississippi	54.0[1]	46.0[1]	0.0[1]	54.0[1]	54.2[1]	0.0[1]	45.8[1]	100.0[1]
Missouri	58.7	41.3	0.0	58.7	—	—	—	—
Montana	—	—	—	—	—	—	—	—
Nebraska	—	—	—	—	—	—	—	—
Nevada	—	—	—	—	—	—	—	—
New Hampshire	50.9	32.9	16.2	60.8	51.3	29.4	19.3	63.6
New Jersey	52.6[1]	47.4[1]	0.0[1]	52.6[1]	—	—	—	—
New Mexico	—	—	—	—	—	—	—	—
New York	50.3	46.0	3.7	52.2	0.0	0.0	100.0	—
New York	—	—	—	—	*40.6*	*33.4*	*26.1*	*54.8*
North Carolina	53.0	47.0	0.0	53.0	51.1	48.9	0.0	51.1
North Dakota	—	—	—	—	—	—	—	—
Ohio	52.1[1]	30.3[1]	17.6[1]	63.2[1]	43.4[1]	56.6[1]	0.0[1]	43.4[1]
Oklahoma	—	—	—	—	—	—	—	—
Oregon	—	—	—	—	—	—	—	—
Pennsylvania	—	—	—	—	44.8	54.6	0.6	45.0
Rhode Island	51.2	48.8	0.0	51.2	41.6	58.4	0.0	41.6
South Carolina	—	—	—	—	—	—	—	—
South Dakota	—	—	—	—	—	—	—	—
Tennessee	50.9[1]	49.1[1]	0.0[1]	50.9[1]	50.8[1]	0.0[1]	49.2[1]	100.0[1]
Texas	73.3[1]	25.4[1]	1.3[1]	74.3[1]	58.4[1]	0.0[1]	41.6[1]	100.0[1]
Utah	—	—	—	—	—	—	—	—
Vermont	31.1	49.3	19.6	38.7	33.9	63.7	2.4	34.8
Vermont	—	—	—	—	*36.0*	*63.7*	*0.3*	*36.1*
Virginia	—	—	—	—	53.2[1]	0.0[1]	46.8[1]	100.0[1]
Washington	—	—	—	—	—	—	—	—
West Virginia	—	—	—	—	—	—	—	—
Wisconsin	54.7[1]	6.0[1]	39.3[1]	90.2[1]	50.1[1]	49.9[1]	0.0[1]	50.1[1]
Wisconsin	*54.7[1]*	*45.3[1]*	*0.0[1]*	*54.7[1]*	—	—	—	—
Wyoming	—	—	—	—	—	—	—	—
Connecticut	51.0[2]	34.2[2]	14.8[2]	59.9[2]	42.3[3]	14.2[3]	43.5[3]	74.9[3]
Maine	43.3[2]	32.7[2]	24.0[2]	57.0[2]	43.7[3]	56.2[3]	0.1[3]	43.8[3]
Massachusetts	27.2[2]	45.9[2]	26.9[2]	37.2[2]	25.4[3]	36.7[3]	37.9[3]	41.0[3]
New Hampshire	54.7[2]	31.1[2]	14.2[2]	63.7[2]	41.8[3]	5.3[3]	52.9[3]	88.7[3]
Rhode Island	54.2[2]	43.0[2]	2.9[2]	55.8[2]	18.0[3]	0.0[3]	82.0[3]	100.0[3]
Rhode Island	*54.2[2]*	*45.8[2]*	*0.1[2]*	*54.2[2]*	*18.0[3]*	*81.5[3]*	*0.5[3]*	*18.1[3]*
Vermont	38.2[2]	44.1[2]	17.8[2]	46.4[2]	29.4[3]	59.0[3]	11.6[3]	33.3[3]

Notes: Main entries are party vote percentage values for candidates who used the sole designation "Democrat" or "Republican" (or their historical antecedents listed in Appendix A) on the ballot. In general, historical antecedents to the Democratic Party were Anti-Federalists, Democratic-Republicans, and Jackson Democrats; historical precursors of the Republican Party were Federalists, National Republicans, and Whigs. Other = candidates who used third-party names only on the ballot or were listed as independent or unidentified. Bold italicized entries in the table are the author's alternative party coding, which is used when a candidate listed a major-party name (Democrat, Republican, or their historical antecedents) on the ballot with other party names or labels. For a more detailed explanation of this alternative coding system, see Tables 1-3 and 5-1. Also see Table 7-8. —indicates that the state had no data, either because the state had no gubernatorial election in that year, no vote data were found for the state in question, or the state had not yet entered the Union. No special gubernatorial elections are included in this table. Odd-numbered year gubernatorial elections were common before 1880 and several states still scheduled governor elections in odd-numbered years after that.

[1]Election held in odd-numbered year.
[2]1853 election when a state had annual elections in both 1852 and 1853.
[3]1855 election when a state had annual elections in both 1854 and 1855.

Sources: Adapted from *American State Governors, 1776–1976*, vol. 1 (1977), *Congressional Quarterly's Guide to U.S. Elections* (1994), ICPSR data sets 0001 and 0075, and independent search for state sources by the author. Party affiliations were obtained from independent search of state sources by the author when the *American State Governors* volume and the *Congressional Quarterly Guide* disagreed.

Table 7-26 Governor Election Results, by State, 1856–1859 (Percentages)

	1856–1857				1858–1859			
State	Democratic	Republican	Other	Democratic % of Two-Party Vote	Democratic	Republican	Other	Democratic % of Two-Party Vote
Alabama	94.5[1]	0.0[1]	5.5[1]	100.0[1]	72.4[1]	0.0[1]	27.6[1]	100.0[1]
Alabama	—	—	—	—	*100.0[1]*	*0.0[1]*	*0.0[1]*	*100.0[1]*
Alaska	—	—	—	—	—	—	—	—
Arizona	—	—	—	—	—	—	—	—
Arkansas	64.6	0.0	35.4	100.0	—	—	—	—
California	56.7[1]	22.5[1]	20.8[1]	71.6[1]	59.7[1]	9.8[1]	30.5[1]	85.9[1]
California	—	—	—	—	*90.2[1]*	*9.8[1]*	*0.0[1]*	*90.2[1]*
Colorado	—	—	—	—	—	—	—	—
Connecticut	49.0	12.0	39.0	80.4	47.8	51.8	0.4	48.0
Delaware	—	—	—	—	50.7	0.0	49.3	100.0
Florida	51.3	0.0	48.7	100.0	—	—	—	—
Georgia	55.1[1]	0.0[1]	44.9[1]	100.0[1]	60.2[1]	0.0[1]	39.8[1]	100.0[1]
Georgia	—	—	—	—	*60.2[1]*	*39.8[1]*	*0.0[1]*	*60.2[1]*
Hawaii	—	—	—	—	—	—	—	—
Idaho	—	—	—	—	—	—	—	—
Illinois	45.0	47.0	8.0	48.9	—	—	—	—
Indiana	51.3	48.7	0.0	51.3	—	—	—	—
Iowa	47.7[1]	50.9[1]	1.3[1]	48.4[1]	48.6[1]	51.4[1]	0.0[1]	48.6[1]
Kansas	—	—	—	—	—	—	—	—
Kentucky	—	—	—	—	53.2[1]	0.0[1]	46.8[1]	100.0[1]
Louisiana	—	—	—	—	62.0[1]	0.0[1]	38.0[1]	100.0[1]
Maine	37.1	62.9	0.0	37.1	46.5	53.5	0.0	46.5
Maryland	45.1[1]	0.0[1]	54.9[1]	100.0[1]	—	—	—	—
Massachusetts	25.5	4.5	70.0	85.0	32.1	57.6	10.3	35.8
Massachusetts	*25.5*	*70.1*	*4.4*	*26.7*	—	—	—	—
Michigan	43.1	56.9	0.0	43.1	46.2	53.8	0.0	46.2
Minnesota	50.3[1]	49.7[1]	0.0[1]	50.3[1]	45.2[1]	54.8[1]	0.0[1]	45.2[1]
Mississippi	66.0[1]	0.0[1]	34.0[1]	100.0[1]	76.8[1]	0.0[1]	23.2[1]	100.0[1]
Missouri	40.8	0.0	59.2	100.0	—	—	—	—
Missouri	*64.8*	*0.0*	*35.2*	*100.0*	—	—	—	—
Montana	—	—	—	—	—	—	—	—
Nebraska	—	—	—	—	—	—	—	—
Nevada	—	—	—	—	—	—	—	—
New Hampshire	48.0	3.5	48.4	93.1	46.5	53.4	0.1	46.5
New Jersey	48.7	0.0	51.3	100.0	49.2[1]	50.8[1]	0.0[1]	49.2[1]
New Jersey	*48.7*	*51.3*	*0.0*	*48.7*	—	—	—	—
New Mexico	—	—	—	—	—	—	—	—
New York	33.4	44.5	22.0	42.9	42.3	45.5	12.2	48.2
North Carolina	56.2	0.0	43.8	100.0	58.5	0.0	41.5	100.0
North Dakota	—	—	—	—	—	—	—	—
Ohio	48.2[1]	48.6[1]	3.2[1]	49.8[1]	48.1[1]	51.9[1]	0.0[1]	48.1[1]
Oklahoma	—	—	—	—	—	—	—	—
Oregon	—	—	—	—	54.7	0.0	45.3	100.0
Pennsylvania	52.0[1]	40.2[1]	7.8[1]	56.4[1]	—	—	—	—
Rhode Island	41.6	0.0	58.4	100.0	31.0	69.0	0.0	31.0
Rhode Island	*41.6*	*58.3*	*0.2*	*41.6*	—	—	—	—
South Carolina	—	—	—	—	—	—	—	—
South Dakota	—	—	—	—	—	—	—	—
Tennessee	54.4[1]	0.0[1]	45.6[1]	100.0[1]	52.8[1]	0.0[1]	47.2[1]	100.0[1]
Tennessee	—	—	—	—	*52.8[1]*	*47.2[1]*	*0.0[1]*	*52.8[1]*
Texas	57.9[1]	0.0[1]	42.1[1]	100.0[1]	43.1[1]	0.0[1]	56.9[1]	100.0[1]
Texas	—	—	—	—	*100.0[1]*	*0.0[1]*	*0.0[1]*	*100.0[1]*
Utah	—	—	—	—	—	—	—	—
Vermont	25.1	74.3	0.6	25.3	31.5	68.5	0.0	31.5
Virginia	—	—	—	—	51.9[1]	0.0[1]	48.1[1]	100.0[1]
Virginia	—	—	—	—	*51.9[1]*	*48.1[1]*	*0.0[1]*	*51.9[1]*
Washington	—	—	—	—	—	—	—	—
West Virginia	—	—	—	—	—	—	—	—
Wisconsin	49.7[1]	50.3[1]	0.0[1]	49.7[1]	48.4[1]	51.6[1]	0.0[1]	48.4[1]
Wyoming	—	—	—	—	—	—	—	—
Connecticut	49.5[2]	50.4[2]	0.1[2]	49.6[2]	48.7[3]	51.1[3]	0.2[3]	48.8[3]
Maine	44.0[2]	56.0[2]	0.0[2]	44.0[2]	44.2[3]	55.8[3]	0.0[3]	44.2[3]
Massachusetts	24.3[2]	46.6[2]	29.1[2]	34.3[2]	32.5[3]	54.0[3]	13.5[3]	37.5[3]
New Hampshire	47.4[2]	51.9[2]	0.7[2]	47.7[2]	47.5[3]	52.5[3]	0.0[3]	47.5[3]
Rhode Island	34.7[2]	65.3[2]	0.0[2]	34.7[2]	28.6[3]	71.3[3]	0.1[3]	28.6[3]
Vermont	32.2[2]	67.1[2]	0.7[2]	32.4[2]	31.6[3]	68.4[3]	0.0[3]	31.6[3]

Notes: Main entries are party vote percentage values for candidates who used the sole designation "Democrat" or "Republican" (or their historical antecedents listed in Appendix A) on the ballot. In general, historical antecedents to the Democratic Party were Anti-Federalists, Democratic-Republicans, and Jackson Democrats; historical precursors of the Republican Party were Federalists, National Republicans, and Whigs. Other = candidates who used third-party names only on the ballot or were listed as independent or unidentified. Bold italicized entries in the table are the author's alternative party coding, which is used when a candidate listed a major-party name (Democrat, Republican, or their historical antecedents) on the ballot with other party names or labels. For a more detailed explanation of this alternative coding system, see Tables 1-3 and 5-1. Also see Table 7-8. —indicates that the state had no data, either because the state had no gubernatorial election in that year, no vote data were found for the state in question, or the state had not yet entered the Union. No special gubernatorial elections are included in this table. Odd-numbered year gubernatorial elections were common before 1880 and several states still scheduled governor elections in odd-numbered years after that.

[1] Election held in odd-numbered year.
[2] 1857 election when a state had annual elections in both 1856 and 1857.
[3] 1859 election when a state had annual elections in both 1858 and 1859.

Sources: Adapted from *American State Governors, 1776–1976*, vol. 1 (1977), *Congressional Quarterly's Guide to U.S. Elections* (1994), ICPSR data sets 0001 and 0075, and independent search for state sources by the author. Party affiliations were obtained from independent search of state sources by the author when the *American State Governors* volume and the *Congressional Quarterly Guide* disagreed.

Table 7-27 Governor Election Results, by State, 1860–1863 (Percentages)

	1860–1861				1862–1863			
State	Democratic	Republican	Other	Democratic % of Two-Party Vote	Democratic	Republican	Other	Democratic % of Two-Party Vote
Alabama	57.5[1]	42.3[1]	0.2[1]	57.6[1]	25.5[1]	74.5[1]	0.0[1]	25.5[1]
Alaska	—	—	—	—	—	—	—	—
Arizona	—	—	—	—	—	—	—	—
Arkansas	47.5	0.0	52.5	100.0	—	—	—	—
Arkansas	*100.0*	*0.0*	*0.0*	*100.0*	—	—	—	—
California	0.0[1]	46.8[1]	53.2[1]	0.0[1]	41.0[1]	59.0[1]	0.0[1]	41.0[1]
California	*53.2[1]*	*46.8[1]*	*0.0[1]*	*53.2[1]*	—	—	—	—
Colorado	—	—	—	—	—	—	—	—
Connecticut	49.7	50.3	0.0	49.7	43.5	56.5	0.0	43.5
Delaware	—	—	—	—	49.7	50.3	0.0	49.7
Florida	57.1	0.0	42.9	100.0	—	—	—	—
Georgia	58.6[1]	0.0[1]	41.4[1]	100.0[1]	0.0[1]	0.0[1]	100.0[1]	—
Georgia	*100.0[1]*	*0.0[1]*	*0.0[1]*	*100.0[1]*	*71.9[1]*	*0.0[1]*	*28.1[1]*	*100.0[1]*
Hawaii	—	—	—	—	—	—	—	—
Idaho	—	—	—	—	—	—	—	—
Illinois	47.3	51.2	1.5	48.1	—	—	—	—
Indiana	48.1	51.9	0.0	48.1	—	—	—	—
Iowa	39.8[1]	55.5[1]	4.7[1]	41.8[1]	39.5[1]	60.5[1]	0.0[1]	39.5[1]
Kansas	—	—	—	—	0.0	100.0	0.0	0.0
Kentucky	—	—	—	—	20.4[1]	79.6[1]	0.0[1]	20.4[1]
Louisiana	—	—	—	—	0.0[1]	0.0[1]	100.0[1]	—
Maine	42.1	56.5	1.4	42.7	46.7	53.3	0.0	46.7
Maryland	0.0[1]	68.8[1]	31.2[1]	0.0[1]	—	—	—	—
Maryland	*31.2[1]*	*68.8[1]*	*0.0[1]*	*31.2[1]*	—	—	—	—
Massachusetts	20.8	61.6	17.6	25.2	0.0	59.5	40.5	0.0
Massachusetts	*24.3*	*61.6*	*14.1*	*28.3*	—	—	—	—
Michigan	43.3	56.7	0.0	43.3	47.5	52.5	0.0	47.5
Minnesota	39.1[1]	60.9[1]	0.0[1]	39.1[1]	39.4[1]	60.6[1]	0.0[1]	39.4[1]
Mississippi	0.0[1]	0.0[1]	100.0[1]	—	0.0[1]	0.0[1]	100.0[1]	—
Missouri	46.9	3.9	49.2	92.4	—	—	—	—
Missouri	*54.1*	*3.9*	*42.0*	*93.3*	—	—	—	—
Montana	—	—	—	—	—	—	—	—
Nebraska	—	—	—	—	—	—	—	—
Nevada	—	—	—	—	—	—	—	—
New Hampshire	46.9	53.1	0.0	46.9	45.8	51.5	2.7	47.1
New Hampshire	—	—	—	—	*48.5*	*51.5*	*0.0*	*48.5*
New Jersey	—	—	—	—	56.8	43.2	0.0	56.8
New Mexico	—	—	—	—	—	—	—	—
New York	43.8	53.2	2.9	45.2	50.9	49.1	0.0	50.9
New York	*46.8*	*53.2*	*0.0*	*46.8*	—	—	—	—
North Carolina	52.7	47.3	0.0	52.7	0.0	0.0	100.0	—
North Dakota	—	—	—	—	—	—	—	—
Ohio	42.3[1]	57.7[1]	0.0[1]	42.3[1]	39.4[1]	60.6[1]	0.0[1]	39.4[1]
Oklahoma	—	—	—	—	—	—	—	—
Oregon	—	—	—	—	32.9	67.1	0.0	32.9
Pennsylvania	46.7	53.3	0.0	46.7	48.5[1]	51.5[1]	0.0[1]	48.5[1]
Rhode Island	0.0	46.6	53.4	0.0	0.0	99.4	0.6	0.0
Rhode Island	*52.8*	*46.6*	*0.6*	*53.2*	—	—	—	—
South Carolina	—	—	—	—	—	—	—	—
South Dakota	—	—	—	—	—	—	—	—
Tennessee	0.0[1]	36.6[1]	63.4[1]	0.0[1]	0.0[1]	0.0[1]	100.0[1]	—
Tennessee	*63.4[1]*	*36.6[1]*	*0.0[1]*	*63.4[1]*	—	—	—	—
Texas	0.0[1]	0.0[1]	100.0[1]	—	0.0[1]	0.0[1]	100.0[1]	—
Utah	—	—	—	—	—	—	—	—
Vermont	24.6	70.9	4.4	25.8	11.0	88.5	0.6	11.0
Vermont	*29.1*	*70.9*	*0.0*	*29.1*	—	—	—	—
Virginia	—	—	—	—	—	—	—	—
Washington	—	—	—	—	—	—	—	—
West Virginia	—	—	—	—	0.0[1]	100.0[1]	0.0[1]	0.0[1]
Wisconsin	45.8[1]	54.2[1]	0.0[1]	45.8[1]	41.2[1]	58.8[1]	0.0[1]	41.2[1]
Wyoming	—	—	—	—	—	—	—	—
Connecticut	48.8[2]	51.2[2]	0.0[2]	48.8[2]	48.3[3]	51.6[3]	0.1[3]	48.3[3]
Maine	21.6[2]	58.7[2]	19.8[2]	26.9[2]	42.6[3]	57.4[3]	0.0[3]	42.6[3]
Maine	*41.3[2]*	*58.7[2]*	*0.0[2]*	*41.3[2]*	—	—	—	—
Massachusetts	32.1[2]	67.1[2]	0.8[2]	32.4[2]	29.3[3]	70.6[3]	0.1[3]	29.3[3]
New Hampshire	46.9[2]	52.9[2]	0.3[2]	47.0[2]	49.6[3]	50.4[3]	0.0[3]	49.6[3]
Rhode Island	0.0[2]	100.0[2]	0.0[2]	0.0[2]	0.0[3]	58.0[3]	42.0[3]	0.0[3]
Rhode Island	—	—	—	—	*40.4[3]*	*58.0[3]*	*1.6[3]*	*41.0[3]*
Vermont	0.0[2]	78.8[2]	21.2[2]	0.0[2]	28.8[3]	71.2[3]	0.0[3]	28.8[3]
Vermont	*21.2[2]*	*78.8[2]*	*0.0[2]*	*21.2[2]*	—	—	—	—

Notes: Main entries are party vote percentage values for candidates who used the sole designation "Democrat" or "Republican" (or their historical antecedents listed in Appendix A) on the ballot. In general, historical antecedents to the Democratic Party were Anti-Federalists, Democratic-Republicans, and Jackson Democrats; historical precursors of the Republican Party were Federalists, National Republicans, and Whigs. Other = candidates who used third-party names only on the ballot or were listed as independent or unidentified. Bold italicized entries in the table are the author's alternative party coding, which is used when a candidate listed a major-party name (Democrat, Republican, or their historical antecedents) on the ballot with other party names or labels. For a more detailed explanation of this alternative coding system, see Tables 1-3 and 5-1. Also see Table 7-8. —indicates that the state had no data, either because the state had no gubernatorial election in that year, no vote data were found for the state in question, or the state had not yet entered the Union. No special gubernatorial elections are included in this table. Odd-numbered year gubernatorial elections were common before 1880 and several states still scheduled governor elections in odd-numbered years after that.

[1]Election held in odd-numbered year.
[2]1861 election when a state had annual elections in both 1860 and 1861.
[3]1863 election when a state had annual elections in both 1862 and 1863.

Sources: Adapted from *American State Governors, 1776–1976*, vol. 1 (1977), *Congressional Quarterly's Guide to U.S. Elections* (1994), ICPSR data sets 0001 and 0075, and independent search for state sources by the author. Party affiliations were obtained from independent search of state sources by the author when the *American State Governors* volume and the *Congressional Quarterly Guide* disagreed.

Table 7-28 Governor Election Results, by State, 1864–1867 (Percentages)

State	1864–1865				1866–1867			
	Democratic	Republican	Other	Democratic % of Two-Party Vote	Democratic	Republican	Other	Democratic % of Two-Party Vote
Alabama	35.9[1]	64.0[1]	0.1[1]	36.0[1]	—	—	—	—
Alaska	—	—	—	—	—	—	—	—
Arizona	—	—	—	—	—	—	—	—
Arkansas	—	—	—	—	54.0[1]	43.7[1]	2.3[1]	55.3[1]
California	—	—	—	—	54.0[1]	46.0[1]	0.0[1]	54.0[1]
California	—	—	—	—	*54.0[1]*	*46.0[1]*	*0.0[1]*	*54.0[1]*
Colorado	—	—	—	—	—	—	—	—
Connecticut	46.2	53.8	0.0	46.2	49.7	50.3	0.0	49.7
Delaware	—	—	—	—	53.3	46.7	0.0	53.3
Florida	99.9[1]	0.0[1]	0.1[1]	100.0[1]	—	—	—	—
Georgia	—	—	—	—	—	—	—	—
Hawaii	—	—	—	—	—	—	—	—
Idaho	—	—	—	—	—	—	—	—
Illinois	45.5	54.5	0.0	45.5	—	—	—	—
Indiana	46.3	53.7	0.0	46.3	—	—	—	—
Iowa	43.3[1]	56.4[1]	0.3[1]	43.4[1]	41.1[1]	58.9[1]	0.0[1]	41.1[1]
Kansas	0.0	100.0	0.0	0.0	0.0	100.0	0.0	0.0
Kentucky	—	—	—	—	65.7[1]	24.7[1]	9.6[1]	72.7[1]
Kentucky	—	—	—	—	*75.3[1]*	*24.7[1]*	*0.0[1]*	*75.3[1]*
Louisiana	0.0	0.0	100.0	—	—	—	—	—
Maine	41.4	58.6	0.0	41.4	37.6	62.4	0.0	37.6
Maryland	44.1	55.9	0.0	44.1	74.3[1]	25.7[1]	0.0[1]	74.3[1]
Massachusetts	28.2	71.8	0.0	28.2	22.5	77.5	0.1	22.5
Michigan	44.9	55.1	0.0	44.9	41.4	58.6	0.0	41.4
Minnesota	44.4[1]	55.6[1]	0.0[1]	44.4[1]	45.8[1]	54.2[1]	0.0[1]	45.8[1]
Mississippi	42.5[1]	34.7[1]	22.8[1]	55.1[1]	—	—	—	—
Mississippi	*65.0[1]*	*34.7[1]*	*0.3[1]*	*65.2[1]*	—	—	—	—
Missouri	29.7	70.3	0.0	29.7	—	—	—	—
Montana	—	—	—	—	—	—	—	—
Nebraska	—	—	—	—	49.4	50.4	0.3	49.5
Nevada	40.0	60.0	0.0	40.0	44.5	55.5	0.0	44.5
New Hampshire	45.9	54.1	0.0	45.9	46.5	53.5	0.0	46.5
New Jersey	48.9[1]	51.1[1]	0.0[1]	48.9[1]	—	—	—	—
New Mexico	—	—	—	—	—	—	—	—
New York	49.4	50.6	0.0	49.4	49.0	50.9	0.1	49.0
North Carolina	0.0	0.0	100.0	—	0.0	0.0	100.0	0.0
North Carolina	—	—	—	—	*0.0*	*23.8*	*76.2*	*0.0*
North Dakota	—	—	—	—	—	—	—	—
Ohio	46.4[1]	53.5[1]	0.1[1]	46.4[1]	49.7[1]	50.3[1]	0.0[1]	49.7[1]
Oklahoma	—	—	—	—	—	—	—	—
Oregon	—	—	—	—	49.3	50.7	0.0	49.3
Pennsylvania	—	—	—	—	48.6	51.4	0.0	48.6
Rhode Island	41.7	50.4	7.9	45.2	25.2	73.3	1.5	25.6
South Carolina	0.0[1]	0.0[1]	100.0[1]	—	—	—	—	—
South Dakota	—	—	—	—	—	—	—	—
Tennessee	0.0[1]	99.8[1]	0.2[1]	0.0[1]	0.0[1]	76.8[1]	23.2[1]	0.0[1]
Texas	0.0[1]	19.7[1]	80.3[1]	0.0[1]	0.0	19.9	80.1	0.0
Utah	—	—	—	—	—	—	—	—
Vermont	28.2	71.8	0.0	28.2	24.9	75.1	0.0	24.9
Virginia	—	—	—	—	—	—	—	—
Washington	—	—	—	—	—	—	—	—
West Virginia	0.0	100.0	0.0	0.0	41.9	58.1	0.0	41.9
Wisconsin	45.3[1]	54.7[1]	0.0[1]	45.3[1]	48.3[1]	51.7[1]	0.0[1]	48.3[1]
Wyoming	—	—	—	—	—	—	—	—
Connecticut	42.5[2]	57.5[2]	0.0[2]	42.5[2]	50.5[3]	49.5[3]	0.0[3]	50.5[3]
Louisiana	78.2[2]	0.0[2]	21.8[2]	100.0[2]	—	—	—	—
Maine	36.7[2]	63.3[2]	0.0[2]	36.7[2]	44.3[3]	55.6[3]	0.1[3]	44.3[3]
Massachusetts	23.3[2]	76.6[2]	0.2[2]	23.3[2]	41.7[3]	58.3[3]	0.0[3]	41.7[3]
New Hampshire	45.0[2]	54.9[2]	0.1[2]	45.1[2]	47.6[3]	52.2[3]	0.2[3]	47.7[3]
North Carolina	0.0[2]	0.0[2]	100.0[2]	—	—	—	—	—
Rhode Island	0.0[2]	93.0[2]	7.0[2]	—	30.1[3]	69.9[3]	0.0[3]	30.1[3]
Vermont	24.3[2]	75.7[2]	0.0[2]	24.3[2]	26.6[3]	73.3[3]	0.1[3]	26.6[3]

Notes: Main entries are party vote percentage values for candidates who used the sole designation "Democrat" or "Republican" (or their historical antecedents listed in Appendix A) on the ballot. In general, historical antecedents to the Democratic Party were Anti-Federalists, Democratic-Republicans, and Jackson Democrats; historical precursors of the Republican Party were Federalists, National Republicans, and Whigs. Other = candidates who used third-party names only on the ballot or were listed as independent or unidentified. Bold italicized entries in the table are the author's alternative party coding, which is used when a candidate listed a major-party name (Democrat, Republican, or their historical antecedents) on the ballot with other party names or labels. For a more detailed explanation of this alternative coding system, see Tables 1-3 and 5-1. Also see Table 7-8. —indicates that the state had no data, either because the state had no gubernatorial election in that year, no vote data were found for the state in question, or the state had not yet entered the Union. No special gubernatorial elections are included in this table. Odd-numbered year gubernatorial elections were common before 1880 and several states still scheduled governor elections in odd-numbered years after that.

[1] Election held in odd-numbered year.
[2] 1865 election when a state had annual elections in both 1864 and 1865.
[3] 1867 election when a state had annual elections in both 1866 and 1867.

Sources: Adapted from *American State Governors, 1776–1976*, vol. 1 (1977), *Congressional Quarterly's Guide to U.S. Elections* (1994), ICPSR data sets 0001 and 0075, and independent search for state sources by the author. Party affiliations were obtained from independent search of state sources by the author when the *American State Governors* volume and the *Congressional Quarterly Guide* disagreed.

Table 7-29 Governor Election Results, by State, 1868–1871 (Percentages)

State	1868–1869				1870–1871			
	Democratic	Republican	Other	Democratic % of Two-Party Vote	Democratic	Republican	Other	Democratic % of Two-Party Vote
Alabama	0.0	100.0	0.0	0.0	50.5	49.5	0.0	50.5
Alaska	—	—	—	—	—	—	—	—
Arizona	—	—	—	—	—	—	—	—
Arkansas	—	—	—	—	—	—	—	—
California	—	—	—	—	47.9[1]	52.1[1]	0.0[1]	47.9[1]
Colorado	—	—	—	—	—	—	—	—
Connecticut	50.9	49.1	0.0	50.9	50.5	49.5	0.0	50.5
Delaware	—	—	—	—	55.7	44.3	0.0	55.7
Florida	31.7	59.1	9.2	34.9	35.6	64.4	0.0	35.6
Florida	*31.7*	*68.3*	*0.0*	*31.7*	—	—	—	—
Georgia	47.9	52.1	0.0	47.9	—	—	—	—
Hawaii	—	—	—	—	—	—	—	—
Idaho	—	—	—	—	—	—	—	—
Illinois	44.5	55.5	0.0	44.5	—	—	—	—
Indiana	49.9	50.1	0.0	49.9	—	—	—	—
Iowa	37.1[1]	62.9[1]	0.0[1]	37.1[1]	38.4[1]	61.6[1]	0.0[1]	38.4[1]
Kansas	31.8	68.2	0.0	31.8	33.5	66.4	0.2	33.5
Kentucky	—	—	—	—	58.6[1]	41.4[1]	0.0[1]	58.6[1]
Louisiana	37.2	62.8	0.0	37.2	—	—	—	—
Maine	42.7	57.3	0.0	42.7	45.8	54.1	0.0	45.8
Maryland	—	—	—	—	55.7[1]	44.3[1]	0.0[1]	55.7[1]
Massachusetts	32.4	67.6	0.0	32.4	32.3	53.0	14.7	37.9
Michigan	43.2	56.8	0.0	43.2	44.8	53.8	1.5	45.4
Minnesota	46.4[1]	50.4[1]	3.2[1]	47.9[1]	40.1[1]	59.9[1]	0.0[1]	40.1[1]
Mississippi	52.6	47.4	0.0	52.6	—	—	—	—
Missouri	43.3	56.7	0.0	43.3	62.3	37.7	0.0	62.3
Montana	—	—	—	—	—	—	—	—
Nebraska	42.5	57.5	0.0	42.5	43.7	56.3	0.0	43.7
Nevada	—	—	—	—	53.9	46.1	0.0	53.9
New Hampshire	48.4	51.6	0.0	48.4	36.5	51.0	12.5	41.8
New Jersey	51.4	48.6	0.0	51.4	51.9[1]	48.1[1]	0.0[1]	51.9[1]
New Mexico	—	—	—	—	—	—	—	—
New York	51.6	48.4	0.0	51.6	51.9	47.6	0.4	52.2
North Carolina	0.0	55.5	44.5	0.0	—	—	—	—
North Dakota	—	—	—	—	—	—	—	—
Ohio	49.1[1]	50.7[1]	0.2[1]	49.2[1]	47.4[1]	51.7[1]	0.9[1]	47.8[1]
Oklahoma	—	—	—	—	—	—	—	—
Oregon	—	—	—	—	51.4	48.6	0.0	51.4
Pennsylvania	49.6[1]	50.4[1]	0.0[1]	49.6[1]	—	—	—	—
Rhode Island	36.3	63.7	0.0	36.3	37.5	62.5	0.0	37.5
South Carolina	0.0	75.0	25.0	0.0	37.7	62.3	0.0	37.7
South Dakota	—	—	—	—	—	—	—	—
Tennessee	0.0[1]	0.0[1]	100.0[1]	—	65.0	35.0	0.0	65.0
Tennessee	*0.0[1]*	*100.0[1]*	*0.0[1]*	*0.0[1]*	—	—	—	—
Texas	46.8[1]	47.8[1]	5.4[1]	49.5[1]	—	—	—	—
Texas	*52.2[1]*	*47.8[1]*	*0.0[1]*	*52.2[1]*	—	—	—	—
Utah	—	—	—	—	—	—	—	—
Vermont	26.4	73.6	0.0	26.4	26.5	73.5	0.0	26.5
Virginia	0.0[1]	0.0[1]	100.0[1]	—	—	—	—	—
Washington	—	—	—	—	—	—	—	—
West Virginia	45.4	54.6	0.0	45.4	51.9	48.1	0.0	51.9
Wisconsin	46.8[1]	53.2[1]	0.0[1]	46.8[1]	46.8[1]	53.2[1]	0.0[1]	46.8[1]
Wyoming	—	—	—	—	—	—	—	—
Connecticut	49.8[2]	50.2[2]	0.0[2]	49.8[2]	49.9[3]	50.1[3]	0.0[3]	49.9[3]
Maine	41.4[2]	53.3[2]	5.3[2]	43.7[2]	44.9[3]	55.1[3]	0.0[3]	44.9[3]
Massachusetts	36.6[2]	53.5[2]	9.9[2]	40.6[2]	34.9[3]	54.9[3]	10.2[3]	38.8[3]
Mississippi	0.0[2]	66.7[2]	33.3[2]	0.0[2]	—	—	—	—
New Hampshire	47.2[2]	52.8[2]	0.0[2]	47.2[2]	49.8[3]	48.6[3]	1.6[3]	50.6[3]
Rhode Island	31.5[2]	68.5[2]	0.0[2]	31.5[2]	37.8[3]	62.2[3]	0.0[3]	37.8[3]
Vermont	26.5[2]	73.5[2]	0.0[2]	26.5[2]	—	—	—	—

Notes: Main entries are party vote percentage values for candidates who used the sole designation "Democrat" or "Republican" (or their historical antecedents listed in Appendix A) on the ballot. In general, historical antecedents to the Democratic Party were Anti-Federalists, Democratic-Republicans, and Jackson Democrats; historical precursors of the Republican Party were Federalists, National Republicans, and Whigs. Other = candidates who used third-party names only on the ballot or were listed as independent or unidentified. Bold italicized entries in the table are the author's alternative party coding, which is used when a candidate listed a major-party name (Democrat, Republican, or their historical antecedents) on the ballot with other party names or labels. For a more detailed explanation of this alternative coding system, see Tables 1-3 and 5-1. Also see Table 7-8. —indicates that the state had no data, either because the state had no gubernatorial election in that year, no vote data were found for the state in question, or the state had not yet entered the Union. No special gubernatorial elections are included in this table. Odd-numbered year gubernatorial elections were common before 1880 and several states still scheduled governor elections in odd-numbered years after that.

[1]Election held in odd-numbered year.
[2]1869 election when a state had annual elections in both 1868 and 1869.
[3]1871 election when a state had annual elections in both 1870 and 1871.

Sources: Adapted from *American State Governors, 1776–1976*, vol. 1 (1977), *Congressional Quarterly's Guide to U.S. Elections* (1994), ICPSR data sets 0001 and 0075, and independent search for state sources by the author. Party affiliations were obtained from independent search of state sources by the author when the *American State Governors* volume and the *Congressional Quarterly Guide* disagreed.

Table 7-30 Governor Election Results, by State, 1872–1875 (Percentages)

State	1872–1873				1874–1875			
	Democratic	Republican	Other	Democratic % of Two-Party Vote	Democratic	Republican	Other	Democratic % of Two-Party Vote
Alabama	47.5	52.5	0.0	47.5	53.3	46.7	0.0	53.3
Alaska	—	—	—	—	—	—	—	—
Arizona	—	—	—	—	—	—	—	—
Arkansas	48.2	51.8	0.0	48.2	100.0	0.0	0.0	100.0
California	—	—	—	—	50.0[1]	25.5[1]	24.5[1]	66.3[1]
Colorado	—	—	—	—	—	—	—	—
Connecticut	47.9	50.0	2.1	48.9	53.9	46.1	0.0	53.9
Delaware	—	—	—	—	52.6	47.4	0.0	52.6
Florida	47.6	52.4	0.0	47.6	—	—	—	—
Georgia	69.2	30.8	0.0	69.2	—	—	—	—
Hawaii	—	—	—	—	—	—	—	—
Idaho	—	—	—	—	—	—	—	—
Illinois	45.1	54.4	0.5	45.3	—	—	—	—
Indiana	50.1	49.8	0.1	50.2	—	—	—	—
Indiana	*50.2*	*49.8*	*0.0*	*50.2*	—	—	—	—
Iowa	0.0[1]	56.0[1]	44.0[1]	0.0[1]	42.6[1]	57.0[1]	0.4[1]	42.8[1]
Kansas	34.2	65.8	0.0	34.2	40.8	56.4	2.8	42.0
Kentucky	—	—	—	—	58.3[1]	41.7[1]	0.0[1]	58.3[1]
Louisiana	42.6	57.4	0.0	42.6	—	—	—	—
Maine	43.5	56.5	0.0	43.5	44.0	53.4	2.5	45.2
Maryland	—	—	—	—	54.1[1]	45.9[1]	0.0[1]	54.1[1]
Massachusetts	30.8	69.1	0.1	30.8	51.8	48.0	0.2	51.9
Michigan	37.0	63.0	0.0	37.0	47.8	50.5	1.8	48.6
Minnesota	0.0[1]	52.9[1]	47.1[1]	0.0[1]	41.9[1]	53.6[1]	4.5[1]	43.9[1]
Minnesota	*45.8[1]*	*52.9[1]*	*1.3[1]*	*46.4[1]*	—	—	—	—
Mississippi	0.0[1]	58.1[1]	41.9[1]	0.0[1]	—	—	—	—
Missouri	56.3	43.7	0.0	56.3	57.2	42.8	0.0	57.2
Montana	—	—	—	—	—	—	—	—
Nebraska	40.4	59.6	0.0	40.4	24.9	59.9	15.3	29.3
Nevada	—	—	—	—	57.1	42.9	0.0	57.1
New Hampshire	47.9	50.8	1.3	48.6	49.6	47.5	2.9	51.1
New Jersey	—	—	—	—	53.6	46.4	0.0	53.6
New Mexico	—	—	—	—	—	—	—	—
New York	46.8	53.2	0.0	46.8	52.4	46.0	1.6	53.2
North Carolina	49.5	50.5	0.0	49.5	—	—	—	—
North Dakota	—	—	—	—	—	—	—	—
Ohio	47.8[1]	47.6[1]	4.5[1]	50.1[1]	0.0[1]	50.2[1]	49.8[1]	0.0[1]
Ohio	—	—	—	—	*49.3[1]*	*50.2[1]*	*0.4[1]*	*49.5[1]*
Oklahoma	—	—	—	—	—	—	—	—
Oregon	—	—	—	—	38.2	36.1	25.7	51.5
Pennsylvania	47.3	52.5	0.2	47.4	47.9[1]	49.9[1]	2.2[1]	49.0[1]
Rhode Island	46.4	53.6	0.0	46.4	11.3	87.5	1.3	11.4
South Carolina	0.0	65.4	34.6	0.0	0.0	53.9	46.1	0.0
South Carolina	*34.2*	*65.4*	*0.3*	*34.4*	*46.1*	*53.9*	*0.0*	*46.1*
South Dakota	—	—	—	—	—	—	—	—
Tennessee	53.7	46.3	0.0	53.7	64.9	35.1	0.0	64.9
Texas	66.0[1]	34.0[1]	0.0[1]	66.0[1]	75.0[1]	25.0[1]	0.0[1]	75.0[1]
Utah	—	—	—	—	—	—	—	—
Vermont	28.4	71.6	0.0	28.4	28.3	71.7	0.0	28.3
Virginia	56.2[1]	43.8[1]	0.0[1]	56.2[1]	—	—	—	—
Washington	—	—	—	—	—	—	—	—
West Virginia	48.4	0.0	51.6	100.0	—	—	—	—
Wisconsin	55.2[1]	44.8[1]	0.0[1]	55.2[1]	49.8[1]	50.2[1]	0.0[1]	49.8[1]
Wyoming	—	—	—	—	—	—	—	—
Connecticut	51.9[2]	45.2[2]	2.9[2]	53.4[2]	53.2[3]	43.9[3]	2.9[3]	54.8[3]
Maine	40.7[2]	55.9[2]	3.4[2]	42.1[2]	48.2[3]	51.7[3]	0.1[3]	48.2[3]
Maine	*43.3[2]*	*55.9[2]*	*0.8[2]*	*43.7[2]*	—	—	—	—
Massachusetts	44.9[2]	54.5[2]	0.6[2]	45.1[2]	45.2[3]	48.3[3]	6.5[3]	48.4[3]
New Hampshire	47.2[2]	50.2[2]	2.6[2]	48.5[2]	49.4[3]	49.6[3]	1.0[3]	49.9[3]
Rhode Island	28.2[2]	71.8[2]	0.0[2]	28.2[2]	23.2[3]	37.6[3]	39.2[3]	38.2[3]

Notes: Main entries are party vote percentage values for candidates who used the sole designation "Democrat" or "Republican" (or their historical antecedents listed in Appendix A) on the ballot. In general, historical antecedents to the Democratic Party were Anti-Federalists, Democratic-Republicans, and Jackson Democrats; historical precursors of the Republican Party were Federalists, National Republicans, and Whigs. Other = candidates who used third-party names only on the ballot or were listed as independent or unidentified. Bold italicized entries in the table are the author's alternative party coding, which is used when a candidate listed a major-party name (Democrat, Republican, or their historical antecedents) on the ballot with other party names or labels. For a more detailed explanation of this alternative coding system, see Tables 1-3 and 5-1. Also see Table 7-8. —indicates that the state had no data, either because the state had no gubernatorial election in that year, no vote data were found for the state in question, or the state had not yet entered the Union. No special gubernatorial elections are included in this table. Odd-numbered year gubernatorial elections were common before 1880 and several states still scheduled governor elections in odd-numbered years after that.

[1] Election held in odd-numbered year.
[2] 1873 election when a state had annual elections in both 1872 and 1873.
[3] 1875 election when a state had annual elections in both 1874 and 1875.

Sources: Adapted from *American State Governors, 1776–1976*, vol. 1 (1977), *Congressional Quarterly's Guide to U.S. Elections* (1994), ICPSR data sets 0001 and 0075, and independent search for state sources by the author. Party affiliations were obtained from independent search of state sources by the author when the *American State Governors* volume and the *Congressional Quarterly Guide* disagreed.

Table 7-31 Governor Election Results, by State, 1876–1879 (Percentages)

State	1876–1877				1878–1879			
	Democratic	Republican	Other	Democratic % of Two-Party Vote	Democratic	Republican	Other	Democratic % of Two-Party Vote
Alabama	63.4	36.6	0.0	63.4	100.0	0.0	0.0	100.0
Alaska	—	—	—	—	—	—	—	—
Arizona	—	—	—	—	—	—	—	—
Arkansas	65.6	34.1	0.3	65.8	100.0	0.0	0.0	100.0
California	—	—	—	—	29.7[1]	42.4[1]	27.8[1]	41.2[1]
Colorado	48.5	51.5	0.0	48.5	40.3	50.0	9.7	44.6
Connecticut	50.8	48.0	1.1	51.4	44.3	46.7	9.0	48.7
Delaware	—	—	—	—	79.1	0.0	20.9	100.0
Florida	50.5	49.5	0.0	50.5	—	—	—	—
Georgia	76.2	23.8	0.0	76.2	—	—	—	—
Hawaii	—	—	—	—	—	—	—	—
Idaho	—	—	—	—	—	—	—	—
Illinois	0.0	50.6	49.4	0.0	—	—	—	—
Illinois	*49.4*	*50.6*	*0.1*	*49.4*	—	—	—	—
Indiana	49.1	47.9	3.0	50.6	—	—	—	—
Iowa	32.3[1]	49.4[1]	18.3[1]	39.5[1]	29.3[1]	53.9[1]	16.8[1]	35.2[1]
Kansas	37.9	56.8	5.3	40.0	26.9	53.5	19.6	33.5
Kentucky	—	—	—	—	55.4[1]	36.2[1]	8.4[1]	60.5[1]
Louisiana	52.5	47.5	0.0	52.5	64.6[1]	35.4[1]	0.0[1]	64.6[1]
Maine	44.2	55.4	0.4	44.3	22.4	44.8	32.8	33.3
Maryland	—	—	—	—	56.9[1]	43.1[1]	0.0[1]	56.9[1]
Massachusetts	41.6	53.6	4.8	43.7	4.0	52.6	43.5	7.0
Massachusetts	—	—	—	—	*46.7*	*52.6*	*0.8*	*47.0*
Michigan	44.9	52.3	2.9	46.2	28.2	45.4	26.4	38.3
Minnesota	39.7[1]	57.9[1]	2.4[1]	40.7[1]	39.3[1]	54.0[1]	6.7[1]	42.1[1]
Mississippi	98.8[1]	1.2[1]	0.0[1]	98.8[1]	—	—	—	—
Missouri	57.0	42.2	0.8	57.5	—	—	—	—
Montana	—	—	—	—	—	—	—	—
Nebraska	33.0	61.2	5.9	35.0	25.8	56.0	18.2	31.5
Nevada	—	—	—	—	48.6	51.4	0.0	48.6
New Hampshire	47.5	52.0	0.5	47.7	48.7	50.6	0.7	49.0
New Jersey	51.7[1]	44.9[1]	3.4[1]	53.5[1]	—	—	—	—
New Mexico	—	—	—	—	—	—	—	—
New York	51.3	48.3	0.5	51.5	41.9[1]	46.7[1]	11.4[1]	47.3[1]
New York	—	—	—	—	*50.6[1]*	*46.7[1]*	*2.8[1]*	*52.0[1]*
North Carolina	52.8	47.2	0.0	52.8	—	—	—	—
North Dakota	—	—	—	—	—	—	—	—
Ohio	48.9[1]	44.9[1]	6.2[1]	52.2[1]	47.7[1]	50.3[1]	2.1[1]	48.7[1]
Oklahoma	—	—	—	—	—	—	—	—
Oregon	—	—	—	—	47.9	47.7	4.4	50.1
Pennsylvania	—	—	—	—	42.3	45.5	12.2	48.2
Rhode Island	18.9	45.6	35.5	29.3	38.8	0.0	61.2	100.0
Rhode Island	—	—	—	—	*38.8*	*58.1*	*3.1*	*40.0*
South Carolina	50.3	49.7	0.0	50.3	99.8	0.0	0.2	100.0
South Dakota	—	—	—	—	—	—	—	—
Tennessee	58.7	5.2	36.0	91.8	60.3	29.2	10.5	67.4
Tennessee	*58.7*	*6.3*	*35.0*	*90.4*	—	—	—	—
Texas	—	—	—	—	67.1	9.7	23.2	87.4
Utah	—	—	—	—	—	—	—	—
Vermont	31.9	68.0	0.1	31.9	29.8	64.3	5.9	31.6
Virginia	95.9[1]	4.1[1]	0.0[1]	95.9[1]	—	—	—	—
Washington	—	—	—	—	—	—	—	—
West Virginia	56.2	43.5	0.3	56.4	—	—	—	—
Wisconsin	40.2[1]	44.9[1]	14.9[1]	47.2[1]	39.7[1]	53.2[1]	7.1[1]	42.7[1]
Wyoming	—	—	—	—	—	—	—	—
Maine	42.2[2]	52.5[2]	5.3[2]	44.5[2]	15.6[3]	49.5[3]	34.9[3]	23.9[3]
Massachusetts	39.7[2]	49.5[2]	10.9[2]	44.5[2]	4.1[3]	50.4[3]	45.5[3]	7.5[3]
Massachusetts	—	—	—	—	*48.9[3]*	*50.4[3]*	*0.7[3]*	*49.3[3]*
New Hampshire	47.2[2]	52.3[2]	0.5[2]	47.4[2]	41.0[3]	50.3[3]	8.8[3]	44.9[3]
Rhode Island	48.2[2]	0.0[2]	51.8[2]	100.0[2]	35.2[3]	0.0[3]	64.8[3]	100.0[3]
Rhode Island	*48.2[2]*	*50.9[2]*	*0.9[2]*	*48.6[2]*	*35.2[3]*	*62.1[3]*	*2.7[3]*	*36.2[3]*

Notes: Main entries are party vote percentage values for candidates who used the sole designation "Democrat" or "Republican" (or their historical antecedents listed in Appendix A) on the ballot. In general, historical antecedents to the Democratic Party were Anti-Federalists, Democratic-Republicans, and Jackson Democrats; historical precursors of the Republican Party were Federalists, National Republicans, and Whigs. Other = candidates who used third-party names only on the ballot or were listed as independent or unidentified. Bold italicized entries in the table are the author's alternative party coding, which is used when a candidate listed a major-party name (Democrat, Republican, or their historical antecedents) on the ballot with other party names or labels. For a more detailed explanation of this alternative coding system, see Tables 1-3 and 5-1. Also see Table 7-8. —indicates that the state had no data, either because the state had no gubernatorial election in that year, no vote data were found for the state in question, or the state had not yet entered the Union. No special gubernatorial elections are included in this table. Odd-numbered year gubernatorial elections were common before 1880 and several states still scheduled governor elections in odd-numbered years after that.

[1] Election held in odd-numbered year.
[2] 1877 election when a state had annual elections in both 1876 and 1877.
[3] 1879 election when a state had annual elections in both 1878 and 1879.

Sources: Adapted from *American State Governors, 1776–1976*, vol. 1 (1977), *Congressional Quarterly's Guide to U.S. Elections* (1994), ICPSR data sets 0001 and 0075, and independent search for state sources by the author. Party affiliations were obtained from independent search of state sources by the author when the *American State Governors* volume and the *Congressional Quarterly Guide* disagreed.

Table 7-32 Governor Election Results, by State, 1880–1883 (Percentages)

	1880–1881				1882–1883			
State	Democratic	Republican	Other	Democratic % of Two-Party Vote	Democratic	Republican	Other	Democratic % of Two-Party Vote
Alabama	76.1	0.0	23.9	100.0	68.7	31.3	0.0	68.7
Alaska	—	—	—	—	—	—	—	—
Arizona	—	—	—	—	—	—	—	—
Arkansas	72.8	0.0	27.2	100.0	59.6	33.5	6.9	64.0
California	—	—	—	—	55.1	40.8	4.1	57.4
Colorado	44.1	53.3	2.6	45.3	51.1	46.9	2.0	52.1
Connecticut	48.4	50.5	1.1	48.9	51.0	47.4	1.5	51.8
Delaware	—	—	—	—	53.1	46.9	0.0	53.1
Florida	54.9	45.1	0.0	54.9	—	—	—	—
Georgia	64.9	0.0	35.1	100.0	70.6	0.0	29.4	100.0
Georgia	***100.0***	***0.0***	***0.0***	***100.0***	***100.0***	***0.0***	***0.0***	***100.0***
Hawaii	—	—	—	—	—	—	—	—
Idaho	—	—	—	—	—	—	—	—
Illinois	44.5	50.4	5.1	46.9	—	—	—	—
Indiana	47.7	49.2	3.2	49.2	—	—	—	—
Iowa	31.2[1]	56.7[1]	12.1[1]	35.5[1]	42.8[1]	50.1[1]	7.1[1]	46.0[1]
Kansas	32.0	57.9	10.1	35.6	46.4	41.9	11.7	45.5
Kentucky	—	—	—	—	60.0[1]	40.0[1]	0.0[1]	60.0[1]
Louisiana	—	—	—	—	—	—	—	—
Maine	0.0	49.8	50.2	0.0	46.2	52.4	1.5	46.9
Maine	***49.9***	***49.8***	***0.4***	***50.1***	***46.2***	***52.6***	***1.3***	***46.8***
Maryland	—	—	—	—	53.5[1]	46.5[1]	0.0[1]	53.5[1]
Massachusetts	39.5	58.4	2.1	40.3	0.0	46.8	53.2	0.0
Massachusetts	—	—	—	—	***52.3***	***46.8***	***0.9***	***52.8***
Michigan	39.4	51.3	9.3	43.5	0.0	48.0	52.0	0.0
Michigan	—	—	—	—	***49.5***	***48.0***	***2.5***	***50.8***
Minnesota	36.4[1]	63.6[1]	0.0[1]	36.4[1]	44.6[1]	55.4[1]	0.0[1]	44.6[1]
Mississippi	59.6[1]	0.0[1]	40.4[1]	100.0[1]	—	—	—	—
Mississippi	***59.6[1]***	***40.4[1]***	***0.0[1]***	***59.6[1]***	—	—	—	—
Missouri	52.2	38.6	9.1	57.5	—	—	—	—
Montana	—	—	—	—	—	—	—	—
Nebraska	32.3	63.2	4.5	33.8	32.1	48.8	19.1	39.6
Nevada	—	—	—	—	54.3	45.7	0.0	54.3
New Hampshire	47.4	51.6	1.1	47.9	48.4	50.4	1.2	49.0
New Jersey	49.5	49.3	1.2	50.1	49.9[1]	46.7[1]	3.4[1]	51.7[1]
New Mexico	—	—	—	—	—	—	—	—
New York	—	—	—	—	58.5	37.3	4.2	56.1
North Carolina	51.3	48.7	0.0	51.3	—	—	—	—
North Dakota	—	—	—	—	—	—	—	—
Ohio	46.2[1]	50.1[1]	3.7[1]	48.0[1]	50.1[1]	48.3[1]	1.6[1]	50.9[1]
Oklahoma	—	—	—	—	—	—	—	—
Oregon	—	—	—	—	48.3	51.7	0.0	48.3
Pennsylvania	—	—	—	—	47.8	42.4	9.8	53.0
Pennsylvania	—	—	—	—	***47.8***	***48.3***	***3.9***	***49.8***
Rhode Island	32.6	44.8	22.6	42.1	34.2	64.8	1.0	34.6
Rhode Island	***32.6***	***67.0***	***0.4***	***32.8***	—	—	—	—
South Carolina	96.4	0.0	3.6	100.0	79.5	0.0	20.5	100.0
South Dakota	—	—	—	—	—	—	—	—
Tennessee	0.0	42.6	57.4	0.0	0.0	41.0	59.0	0.0
Tennessee	***56.0***	***42.6***	***1.5***	***56.8***	***54.9***	***41.0***	***4.1***	***57.2***
Texas	62.9	24.4	12.8	72.1	58.0	0.0	42.0	100.0
Texas	—	—	—	—	***58.0***	***41.9***	***0.1***	***58.1***
Utah	—	—	—	—	—	—	—	—
Vermont	30.1	67.7	2.2	30.7	27.9	69.1	3.0	28.8
Virginia	47.0[1]	0.0[1]	53.0[1]	100.0[1]	—	—	—	—
Washington	—	—	—	—	—	—	—	—
West Virginia	51.3	37.7	11.0	57.6	—	—	—	—
Wisconsin	40.6[1]	47.6[1]	11.8[1]	46.1[1]	—	—	—	—
Wyoming	—	—	—	—	—	—	—	—
Massachusetts	34.6[2]	61.2[2]	4.2[2]	36.1[2]	0.0[3]	51.3[3]	48.7[3]	0.0[3]
Massachusetts	—	—	—	—	***48.1[3]***	***51.3[3]***	***0.7[3]***	***48.4[3]***
Rhode Island	29.4[2]	67.0[2]	3.7[2]	30.5[2]	42.5[3]	54.5[3]	3.0[3]	43.8[3]
Rhode Island	—	—	—	—	***45.4[3]***	***54.5[3]***	***0.1[3]***	***45.5[3]***

Notes: Main entries are party vote percentage values for candidates who used the sole designation "Democrat" or "Republican" (or their historical antecedents listed in Appendix A) on the ballot. In general, historical antecedents to the Democratic Party were Anti-Federalists, Democratic-Republicans, and Jackson Democrats; historical precursors of the Republican Party were Federalists, National Republicans, and Whigs. Other = candidates who used third-party names only on the ballot or were listed as independent or unidentified. Bold italicized entries in the table are the author's alternative party coding, which is used when a candidate listed a major-party name (Democrat, Republican, or their historical antecedents) on the ballot with other party names or labels. For a more detailed explanation of this alternative coding system, see Tables 1-3 and 5-1. Also see Table 7-8. —indicates that the state had no data, either because the state had no gubernatorial election in that year, no vote data were found for the state in question, or the state had not yet entered the Union. No special gubernatorial elections are included in this table. Odd-numbered year gubernatorial elections were common before 1880 and several states still scheduled governor elections in odd-numbered years after that.

[1] Election held in odd-numbered year.
[2] 1881 election when a state had annual elections in both 1880 and 1881.
[3] 1883 election when a state had annual elections in both 1882 and 1883.

Sources: Adapted from *American State Governors, 1776–1976,* vol. 1 (1977), *Congressional Quarterly's Guide to U.S. Elections* (1994), ICPSR data sets 0001 and 0075, and independent search for state sources by the author. Party affiliations were obtained from independent search of state sources by the author when the *American State Governors* volume and the *Congressional Quarterly Guide* disagreed.

Table 7-33 Governor Election Results, by State, 1884–1887 (Percentages)

State	1884–1885				1886–1887			
	Democratic	Republican	Other	Democratic % of Two-Party Vote	Democratic	Republican	Other	Democratic % of Two-Party Vote
Alabama	99.7	0.0	0.3	100.0	79.4	20.1	0.4	79.8
Alaska	—	—	—	—	—	—	—	—
Arizona	—	—	—	—	—	—	—	—
Arkansas	64.6	35.4	0.0	64.6	55.3	33.0	11.7	62.6
California	—	—	—	—	43.4	43.1	13.5	50.2
Colorado	46.1	50.7	3.2	47.6	49.7	45.6	4.8	52.2
Connecticut	49.3	48.1	2.6	50.6	47.7	46.2	6.1	50.8
Delaware	—	—	—	—	63.6	0.6	35.7	99.0
Florida	53.5	46.5	0.0	53.5	—	—	—	—
Georgia	—	—	—	—	99.2	0.0	0.8	100.0
Hawaii	—	—	—	—	—	—	—	—
Idaho	—	—	—	—	—	—	—	—
Illinois	47.5	49.6	2.9	48.9	—	—	—	—
Indiana	49.5	48.0	2.5	50.8	—	—	—	—
Iowa	48.7[1]	50.8[1]	0.5[1]	49.0[1]	45.4[1]	50.1[1]	4.4[1]	47.5[1]
Kansas	40.8	55.3	3.8	42.5	42.3	54.7	3.0	43.6
Kentucky	—	—	—	—	50.7[1]	44.8[1]	4.5[1]	53.1[1]
Louisiana	67.1	32.9	0.0	67.1	—	—	—	—
Maine	41.5	55.4	3.0	42.8	43.1	53.7	3.1	44.5
Maryland	—	—	—	—	52.1[1]	45.6[1]	2.3[1]	53.3[1]
Massachusetts	36.8	52.4	10.8	41.2	46.3	50.2	3.5	48.0
Michigan	0.0	47.7	52.3	0.0	45.7	47.7	6.6	49.0
Michigan	*46.7*	*47.7*	*5.7*	*49.5*				
Minnesota	—	—	—	—	47.4	48.5	4.1	49.4
Mississippi	100.0[1]	0.0[1]	0.0[1]	100.0[1]	—	—	—	—
Missouri	50.0	0.0	50.0	100.0	—	—	—	—
Missouri	*50.0*	*47.6*	*2.4*	*51.3*	—	—	—	—
Montana	—	—	—	—	—	—	—	—
Nebraska	0.0	54.5	45.5	0.0	37.9	55.2	7.0	40.7
Nebraska	*43.2*	*54.5*	*2.3*	*44.2*	—	—	—	—
Nevada	—	—	—	—	47.6	52.4	0.0	47.6
New Hampshire	46.9	50.3	2.8	48.2	48.2	48.9	2.9	49.7
New Jersey	—	—	—	—	47.4	44.0	8.6	51.9
New Mexico	—	—	—	—	—	—	—	—
New York	48.9[1]	47.9[1]	3.2[1]	50.6[1]	—	—	—	—
North Carolina	53.8	46.1	0.1	53.8	—	—	—	—
North Dakota	—	—	—	—	—	—	—	—
Ohio	46.8[1]	49.1[1]	4.1[1]	48.8[1]	44.8[1]	47.9[1]	7.3[1]	48.3[1]
Oklahoma	—	—	—	—	—	—	—	—
Oregon	—	—	—	—	50.9	44.1	5.0	53.6
Pennsylvania	—	—	—	—	45.1	50.3	4.6	47.3
Rhode Island	37.6	62.4	0.1	37.6	37.0	53.4	9.6	40.9
South Carolina	100.0	0.0	0.0	100.0	100.0	0.0	0.0	100.0
South Dakota	—	—	—	—	—	—	—	—
Tennessee	51.3	48.7	0.0	51.3	53.5	46.5	0.0	53.5
Texas	63.2	29.4	7.4	68.2	73.0	21.1	5.9	77.6
Utah	—	—	—	—	—	—	—	—
Vermont	31.4	67.3	1.3	31.8	30.1	66.0	3.9	31.3
Virginia	52.8[1]	47.2[1]	0.0[1]	52.8[1]	—	—	—	—
Washington	—	—	—	—	—	—	—	—
West Virginia	51.9	48.1	0.0	51.9	—	—	—	—
Wisconsin	45.0	51.0	4.0	46.9	40.0	46.5	13.5	46.2
Wyoming	—	—	—	—	—	—	—	—
Massachusetts	43.1[2]	53.5[2]	3.4[2]	44.6[2]	44.5[3]	51.1[3]	4.4[3]	46.5[3]
Rhode Island	38.6[2]	56.0[2]	5.4[2]	40.8[2]	51.5[3]	43.0[3]	5.5[3]	54.5[3]

Notes: Main entries are party vote percentage values for candidates who used the sole designation "Democrat" or "Republican" (or their historical antecedents listed in Appendix A) on the ballot. In general, historical antecedents to the Democratic Party were Anti-Federalists, Democratic-Republicans, and Jackson Democrats; historical precursors of the Republican Party were Federalists, National Republicans, and Whigs. Other = candidates who used third-party names only on the ballot or were listed as independent or unidentified. Bold italicized entries in the table are the author's alternative party coding, which is used when a candidate listed a major-party name (Democrat, Republican, or their historical antecedents) on the ballot with other party names or labels. For a more detailed explanation of this alternative coding system, see Tables 1-3 and 5-1. Also see Table 7-8. —indicates that the state had no data, either because the state had no gubernatorial election in that year, no vote data were found for the state in question, or the state had not yet entered the Union. No special gubernatorial elections are included in this table. Odd-numbered year gubernatorial elections were common before 1880 and several states still scheduled governor elections in odd-numbered years after that.

[1] Election held in odd-numbered year.
[2] 1885 election when a state had annual elections in both 1884 and 1885.
[3] 1887 election when a state had annual elections in both 1886 and 1887.

Sources: Adapted from *American State Governors, 1776–1976*, vol. 1 (1977), *Congressional Quarterly's Guide to U.S. Elections* (1994), ICPSR data sets 0001 and 0075, and independent search for state sources by the author. Party affiliations were obtained from independent search of state sources by the author when the *American State Governors* volume and the *Congressional Quarterly Guide* disagreed.

Table 7-34 Governor Election Results, by State, 1888–1891 (Percentages)

State	1888–1889				1890–1891			
	Democratic	Republican	Other	Democratic % of Two-Party Vote	Democratic	Republican	Other	Democratic % of Two-Party Vote
Alabama	77.6	22.2	0.2	77.7	76.1	23.1	0.8	76.7
Alaska	—	—	—	—	—	—	—	—
Arizona	—	—	—	—	—	—	—	—
Arkansas	54.1	0.0	45.9	100.0	55.5	44.5	0.0	55.5
California	—	—	—	—	46.4	49.6	4.0	48.4
Colorado	42.6	53.8	3.5	44.2	42.4	50.1	7.5	45.8
Connecticut	48.9	47.9	3.2	50.5	50.0	47.3	2.7	51.4
Delaware	—	—	—	—	50.4	48.9	0.7	50.8
Florida	60.4	39.6	0.0	60.4	—	—	—	—
Georgia	100.0	0.0	0.0	100.0	100.0	0.0	0.0	100.0
Hawaii	—	—	—	—	—	—	—	—
Idaho	—	—	—	—	43.6	56.4	0.0	43.6
Illinois	47.5	49.1	3.4	49.1	—	—	—	—
Indiana	48.6	49.0	2.4	49.8	—	—	—	—
Iowa	49.9[1]	48.1[1]	2.0[1]	50.9[1]	49.4[1]	47.4[1]	3.2[1]	51.0[1]
Kansas	32.5	54.7	12.8	37.3	0.0	39.1	60.9	0.0
Kansas	—	—	—	—	**_60.5_**	**_39.1_**	**_0.4_**	**_60.8_**
Kentucky	—	—	—	—	49.9[1]	40.1[1]	10.0[1]	55.4[1]
Louisiana	72.5	27.5	0.0	72.5	—	—	—	—
Maine	42.2	54.6	3.2	43.6	39.8	56.4	3.8	41.4
Maryland	—	—	—	—	56.5[1]	40.8[1]	2.7[1]	58.1[1]
Massachusetts	44.5	52.7	2.8	45.8	49.2	46.0	4.8	51.7
Michigan	45.6	49.2	5.2	48.1	46.2	43.3	10.5	51.6
Minnesota	42.1	51.3	6.6	45.1	35.6	36.6	27.8	49.3
Mississippi	100.0[1]	0.0[1]	0.0[1]	100.0[1]	—	—	—	—
Missouri	49.4	46.8	3.8	51.3	—	—	—	—
Montana	51.0[1]	49.0[1]	0.0[1]	51.0[1]	—	—	—	—
Nebraska	42.1	51.3	6.6	45.1	33.3	32.2	34.5	50.9
Nevada	—	—	—	—	46.7	53.3	0.0	46.7
New Hampshire	48.8	49.4	1.8	49.7	49.1	49.3	1.6	49.9
New Jersey	51.4[1]	46.1[1]	2.5[1]	52.7[1]	—	—	—	—
New Mexico	—	—	—	—	—	—	—	—
New York	49.4	48.0	2.6	50.7	50.1[1]	46.0[1]	3.9[1]	52.1[1]
North Carolina	52.0	46.9	1.1	52.5	—	—	—	—
North Dakota	33.4[1]	66.6[1]	0.0[1]	33.4[1]	34.6	52.2	13.2	39.8
Ohio	48.9[1]	47.5[1]	3.6[1]	50.7[1]	45.9[1]	48.6[1]	5.5[1]	48.6[1]
Oklahoma	—	—	—	—	—	—	—	—
Oregon	—	—	—	—	53.5	46.5	0.0	53.5
Pennsylvania	—	—	—	—	50.0	48.2	1.8	50.9
Rhode Island	44.3	52.3	3.4	45.8	48.8	45.1	6.1	52.0
South Carolina	100.0	0.0	0.0	100.0	79.8	0.0	20.2	100.0
South Carolina	—	—	—	—	**_99.8_**	**_0.0_**	**_0.2_**	**_100.0_**
South Dakota	30.6[1]	69.4[1]	0.0[1]	30.6[1]	23.8	44.5	31.7	34.9
Tennessee	51.8	45.9	2.3	53.0	56.6	37.9	5.5	59.9
Texas	70.8	0.0	29.2	100.0	76.7	22.5	0.8	77.3
Utah	—	—	—	—	—	—	—	—
Vermont	28.1	69.9	2.0	28.7	35.8	62.1	2.2	36.6
Virginia	57.2[1]	42.5[1]	0.3[1]	57.4[1]	—	—	—	—
Washington	42.3[1]	57.7[1]	0.0[1]	42.3[1]	—	—	—	—
West Virginia	50.0	50.0	0.0	50.0	—	—	—	—
Wisconsin	43.8	49.5	6.7	46.9	51.9	42.7	5.4	54.8
Wyoming	—	—	—	—	44.6	55.4	0.0	44.6
Massachusetts	45.8[2]	48.4[2]	5.8[2]	48.6[2]	49.1[3]	47.1[3]	3.8[3]	51.0[3]
Rhode Island	49.4[2]	39.1[2]	11.5[2]	55.8[2]	48.9[3]	46.2[3]	4.9[3]	51.4[3]

Notes: Main entries are party vote percentage values for candidates who used the sole designation "Democrat" or "Republican" (or their historical antecedents listed in Appendix A) on the ballot. In general, historical antecedents to the Democratic Party were Anti-Federalists, Democratic-Republicans, and Jackson Democrats; historical precursors of the Republican Party were Federalists, National Republicans, and Whigs. Other = candidates who used third-party names only on the ballot or were listed as independent or unidentified. Bold italicized entries in the table are the author's alternative party coding, which is used when a candidate listed a major-party name (Democrat, Republican, or their historical antecedents) on the ballot with other party names or labels. For a more detailed explanation of this alternative coding system, see Tables 1-3 and 5-1. Also see Table 7-8. —indicates that the state had no data, either because the state had no gubernatorial election in that year, no vote data were found for the state in question, or the state had not yet entered the Union. No special gubernatorial elections are included in this table. Odd-numbered year gubernatorial elections were common before 1880 and several states still scheduled governor elections in odd-numbered years after that.

[1] Election held in odd-numbered year.
[2] 1889 election when a state had annual elections in both 1888 and 1889.
[3] 1891 election when a state had annual elections in both 1890 and 1891.

Sources: Adapted from *American State Governors, 1776–1976*, vol. 1 (1977), *Congressional Quarterly's Guide to U.S. Elections* (1994), ICPSR data sets 0001 and 0075, and independent search for state sources by the author. Party affiliations were obtained from independent search of state sources by the author when the *American State Governors* volume and the *Congressional Quarterly Guide* disagreed.

Table 7-35 Governor Election Results, by State, 1892–1895 (Percentages)

State	1892–1893 Democratic	Republican	Other	Democratic % of Two-Party Vote	1894–1895 Democratic	Republican	Other	Democratic % of Two-Party Vote
Alabama	52.2	0.0	47.8	100.0	57.1	0.0	42.9	100.0
Alabama	*99.8*	*0.0*	*0.2*	*100.0*	—	—	—	—
Alaska	—	—	—	—	—	—	—	—
Arizona	—	—	—	—	—	—	—	—
Arkansas	57.7	21.5	20.8	72.8	59.1	20.6	20.3	74.1
California	—	—	—	—	39.3	38.9	21.7	50.3
Colorado	9.6	41.8	48.6	18.7	4.6	52.0	43.4	8.2
Colorado	*56.3*	*41.8*	*1.9*	*57.4*	—	—	—	—
Connecticut	50.3	46.6	3.1	51.9	42.8	54.2	3.0	44.1
Delaware	—	—	—	—	47.7	50.8	1.5	48.4
Florida	78.7	0.0	21.3	100.0	—	—	—	—
Georgia	66.7	0.0	33.3	100.0	55.6	0.0	44.4	100.0
Hawaii	—	—	—	—	—	—	—	—
Idaho	33.7	40.7	25.6	45.3	28.7	41.5	29.8	40.9
Illinois	48.7	46.1	5.1	51.4	—	—	—	—
Indiana	47.5	46.2	6.3	50.7	—	—	—	—
Iowa	42.0[1]	49.7[1]	8.3[1]	45.8[1]	37.2[1]	52.0[1]	10.8[1]	41.7[1]
Kansas	0.0	48.7	51.3	0.0	48.6	49.5	50.5	0.0
Kansas	*50.0*	*48.7*	*1.3*	*50.7*	*48.6*	*49.5*	*1.8*	*49.5*
Kentucky	—	—	—	—	45.8[1]	48.3[1]	5.9[1]	48.7[1]
Louisiana	26.4	16.6	57.0	61.3	—	—	—	—
Louisiana	*70.9*	*23.6*	*5.5*	*75.0*	—	—	—	—
Maine	42.5	52.1	5.4	44.9	28.2	64.3	7.5	30.5
Maryland	—	—	—	—	44.2[1]	52.0[1]	3.8[1]	45.9[1]
Massachusetts	49.0	48.4	2.6	50.3	37.0	56.5	6.6	39.6
Michigan	43.8	47.2	9.0	48.1	31.4	56.9	11.7	35.5
Minnesota	37.0	42.7	20.4	46.4	18.1	49.9	32.0	26.6
Mississippi	—	—	—	—	72.1[1]	0.0[1]	27.9[1]	100.0[1]
Missouri	49.0	43.5	7.5	53.0	—	—	—	—
Montana	40.0	41.2	18.9	49.3	—	—	—	—
Nebraska	22.4	39.7	37.9	36.0	0.0	46.4	53.6	0.0
Nebraska	—	—	—	—	*51.4*	*46.4*	*2.3*	*52.6*
Nevada	—	—	—	—	6.5	36.9	56.7	14.9
Nevada	—	—	—	—	*56.3*	*36.9*	*6.8*	*60.4*
New Hampshire	47.7	50.2	2.2	48.7	40.9	56.0	3.1	42.2
New Jersey	49.7	47.4	3.0	51.2	43.6[1]	52.3[1]	4.1[1]	45.5[1]
New Mexico	—	—	—	—	—	—	—	—
New York	—	—	—	—	40.8	53.1	6.1	43.4
New York	—	—	—	—	*42.9*	*53.1*	*4.0*	*44.7*
North Carolina	48.3	33.8	17.9	58.8	—	—	—	—
North Dakota	0.0	47.6	52.4	0.0	19.2	55.8	25.0	25.7
North Dakota	*52.4*	*47.6*	*0.0*	*52.4*	—	—	—	—
Ohio	42.8[1]	52.6[1]	4.6[1]	44.8[1]	40.0[1]	51.0[1]	9.0[1]	43.9[1]
Oklahoma	—	—	—	—	—	—	—	—
Oregon	—	—	—	—	20.5	47.2	32.3	30.3
Pennsylvania	—	—	—	—	35.0	60.3	4.7	36.7
Rhode Island	46.5	50.2	3.3	48.1	41.3	53.2	5.5	43.7
South Carolina	99.9	0.0	0.1	100.0	69.6	0.0	30.4	100.0
South Dakota	21.1	47.2	31.7	30.9	11.3	52.0	36.8	17.8
Tennessee	47.9	38.1	14.0	55.7	44.9	45.2	9.9	49.8
Texas	43.7	30.7	25.6	58.8	48.9	12.9	38.3	79.2
Texas	*43.7*	*31.0*	*25.3*	*58.6*	*48.9*	*14.3*	*36.8*	*77.3*
Utah	—	—	—	—	—	—	—	—
Vermont	32.2	65.2	2.6	33.1	24.4	73.6	2.1	24.9
Virginia	59.7[1]	0.0[1]	40.3[1]	100.0[1]	—	—	—	—
Washington	32.2	37.0	30.8	46.5	—	—	—	—
West Virginia	49.4	47.1	3.5	51.2	—	—	—	—
Wisconsin	47.9	45.9	6.2	51.1	37.9	52.3	9.8	42.0
Wyoming	—	—	—	—	36.1	52.6	11.3	40.7
Massachusetts	43.0[2]	52.8[2]	4.2[2]	44.9[2]	37.1[3]	56.8[3]	6.2[3]	39.5[3]
Rhode Island	46.7[2]	46.3[2]	6.9[2]	50.2[2]	32.4[3]	56.9[3]	10.7[3]	36.3[3]

Notes: Main entries are party vote percentage values for candidates who used the sole designation "Democrat" or "Republican" (or their historical antecedents listed in Appendix A) on the ballot. In general, historical antecedents to the Democratic Party were Anti-Federalists, Democratic-Republicans, and Jackson Democrats; historical precursors of the Republican Party were Federalists, National Republicans, and Whigs. Other = candidates who used third-party names only on the ballot or were listed as independent or unidentified. Bold italicized entries in the table are the author's alternative party coding, which is used when a candidate listed a major-party name (Democrat, Republican, or their historical antecedents) on the ballot with other party names or labels. For a more detailed explanation of this alternative coding system, see Tables 1-3 and 5-1. Also see Table 7-8. —indicates that the state had no data, either because the state had no gubernatorial election in that year, no vote data were found for the state in question, or the state had not yet entered the Union. No special gubernatorial elections are included in this table. Odd-numbered year gubernatorial elections were common before 1880 and several states still scheduled governor elections in odd-numbered years after that.

[1] Election held in odd-numbered year.
[2] 1893 election when a state had annual elections in both 1892 and 1893.
[3] 1895 election when a state had annual elections in both 1894 and 1895.

Sources: Adapted from *American State Governors, 1776–1976,* vol. 1 (1977), *Congressional Quarterly's Guide to U.S. Elections* (1994), ICPSR data sets 0001 and 0075, and independent search for state sources by the author. Party affiliations were obtained from independent search of state sources by the author when the *American State Governors* volume and the *Congressional Quarterly Guide* disagreed.

Table 7-36 Governor Election Results, by State, 1896–1899 (Percentages)

State	1896–1897				1898–1899			
	Democratic	Republican	Other	Democratic % of Two-Party Vote	Democratic	Republican	Other	Democratic % of Two-Party Vote
Alabama	59.0	0.0	41.0	100.0	67.0	0.0	33.0	100.0
Alabama	—	—	—	—	*67.0*	*1.9*	*31.1*	*97.2*
Alaska								
Arizona	—	—	—	—	—	—	—	—
Arkansas	64.3	25.3	10.5	71.8	67.3	24.6	8.1	73.2
California	—	—	—	—	45.0	0.0	55.0	100.0
California	—	—	—	—	*45.0*	*51.7*	*3.3*	*46.6*
Colorado	46.2	12.7	41.1	78.5	0.0	34.1	65.9	0.0
Colorado	—	—	—	—	*62.8*	*34.1*	*3.0*	*64.8*
Connecticut	32.5	62.5	5.0	34.2	42.9	54.2	2.9	44.2
Connecticut	*35.7*	*62.5*	*1.8*	*36.3*	—	—	—	—
Delaware	44.2	31.4	24.4	58.5	—	—	—	—
Delaware	*44.2*	*51.8*	*4.0*	*46.0*	—	—	—	—
Florida	66.5	20.3	13.2	76.6	—	—	—	—
Georgia	58.9	0.0	41.1	100.0	69.7	0.0	30.3	100.0
Hawaii								
Idaho	0.0	22.4	77.6	0.0	0.0	34.7	65.3	0.0
Idaho	*76.8*	*22.4*	*0.8*	*77.4*	*48.8*	*34.7*	*16.5*	*58.5*
Illinois	43.7	54.1	2.2	44.7	—	—	—	—
Illinois	*44.5*	*54.1*	*1.4*	*45.1*	—	—	—	—
Indiana	46.8	50.9	2.3	47.9	—	—	—	—
Indiana	*47.2*	*50.9*	*1.9*	*48.1*	—	—	—	—
Iowa	44.5[1]	51.3[1]	4.3[1]	46.4[1]	42.3[1]	55.3[1]	2.4[1]	43.4[1]
Iowa	*45.4*[1]	*51.3*[1]	*3.3*[1]	*47.0*[1]	—	—	—	—
Kansas	50.5	48.3	1.2	51.1	46.5	51.8	1.6	47.3
Kansas	*50.8*	*48.3*	*0.9*	*51.2*	—	—	—	—
Kentucky	—	—	—	—	47.5[1]	48.0[1]	4.5[1]	49.7[1]
Kentucky	—	—	—	—	*50.5*[1]	*48.0*[1]	*1.5*[1]	*51.2*[1]
Louisiana	56.9	0.0	43.1	100.0	—	—	—	—
Louisiana	*56.9*	*43.0*	*0.1*	*57.0*	—	—	—	—
Maine	27.8	66.9	5.3	29.4	33.2	62.9	3.9	34.6
Maine	*28.3*	*66.9*	*4.9*	*29.7*	*33.6*	*62.9*	*3.5*	*34.8*
Maryland	—	—	—	—	51.1[1]	46.3[1]	2.6[1]	52.5[1]
Massachusetts	26.9	67.1	6.0	28.6	34.0	60.2	5.9	36.1
Massachusetts	*30.6*	*67.1*	*2.3*	*31.3*	—	—	—	—
Michigan	42.5	56.0	1.5	43.1	39.9	57.8	2.3	40.9
Michigan	*42.8*	*56.0*	*1.1*	*43.3*	—	—	—	—
Minnesota	48.1	49.2	2.7	49.4	52.3	44.3	3.5	54.1
Mississippi	—	—	—	—	87.4[1]	0.0[1]	12.6[1]	100.0[1]
Missouri	52.9	46.4	0.8	53.3	—	—	—	—
Missouri	*53.1*	*46.4*	*0.5*	*53.4*	—	—	—	—
Montana	71.0	0.0	29.0	100.0	—	—	—	—
Montana	*71.0*	*29.0*	*0.0*	*71.0*	—	—	—	—
Nebraska	55.1	43.5	1.4	55.9	50.2	48.8	1.0	50.7
Nebraska	*55.5*	*43.5*	*1.0*	*56.1*	—	—	—	—
Nevada	—	—	—	—	20.6	35.5	44.0	36.7
Nevada	—	—	—	—	*20.6*	*71.1*	*8.3*	*22.4*
New Hampshire	36.0	61.4	2.6	36.9	43.2	54.2	2.5	44.4
New Hampshire	*36.3*	*61.4*	*2.3*	*37.1*	—	—	—	—
New Jersey	—	—	—	—	0.0	48.9	51.1	0.0
New Jersey	—	—	—	—	*47.3*	*48.9*	*3.8*	*49.1*
New Mexico	—	—	—	—	—	—	—	—
New York	40.3	55.3	4.4	42.2	47.7	49.0	3.3	49.3
New York	*42.2*	*55.3*	*2.5*	*43.3*	—	—	—	—
North Carolina	43.9	46.5	9.6	48.5	—	—	—	—
North Dakota	44.4	55.6	0.0	44.4	41.7	58.3	0.0	41.7
Ohio	47.0[1]	50.3[1]	2.7[1]	48.3[1]	40.5[1]	45.9[1]	13.5[1]	46.9[1]
Ohio	*47.2*[1]	*50.3*[1]	*2.5*[1]	*48.4*[1]	—	—	—	—
Oklahoma	—	—	—	—	—	—	—	—
Oregon	—	—	—	—	40.8	53.2	6.0	43.4
Pennsylvania	—	—	—	—	36.9	49.0	14.1	42.9
Rhode Island	33.8	56.4	9.8	37.5	30.9	57.7	11.4	34.8
South Carolina	89.1	0.0	10.9	100.0	100.0	0.0	0.0	100.0
South Carolina	*89.1*	*10.8*	*0.1*	*89.2*	—	—	—	—
South Dakota	0.0	49.4	50.6	0.0	49.6	49.2	1.2	50.2
Tennessee	48.8	46.6	4.6	51.1	57.9	39.8	2.3	59.3
Texas	55.3	0.0	44.7	100.0	71.2	0.0	28.8	100.0
Utah	44.7	50.3	5.0	47.1	—	—	—	—
Vermont	21.3	76.4	2.4	21.8	27.0	71.0	2.0	27.6
Virginia	64.6[1]	33.2[1]	2.2[1]	66.0[1]	—	—	—	—
Washington	55.5	41.7	2.8	57.1	—	—	—	—
West Virginia	46.4	52.4	1.2	47.0	—	—	—	—
Wisconsin	38.1	59.7	2.2	39.0	41.1	52.6	6.3	43.9
Wyoming	—	—	—	—	45.4	52.4	2.2	46.4
Massachusetts	29.5[2]	61.2[2]	9.3[2]	32.5[2]	34.7[3]	56.5[3]	8.8[3]	38.1[3]
Massachusetts	*34.6*[2]	*61.2*[2]	*4.2*[2]	*36.1*[2]	—	—	—	—
Rhode Island	32.7[2]	58.1[2]	9.2[2]	36.0[2]	33.9[3]	56.4[3]	9.8[3]	37.5[3]

Notes: Main entries are party vote percentage values for candidates who used the sole designation "Democrat" or "Republican" (or their historical antecedents listed in Appendix A) on the ballot. In general, historical antecedents to the Democratic Party were Anti-Federalists, Democratic-Republicans, and Jackson Democrats; historical precursors of the Republican Party were Federalists, National Republicans, and Whigs. Other = candidates who used third-party names only on the ballot or

(Notes continue)

Table 7-36 *(Continued)*

were listed as independent or unidentified. Bold italicized entries in the table are the author's alternative party coding, which is used when a candidate listed a major-party name (Democrat, Republican, or their historical antecedents) on the ballot with other party names or labels. For a more detailed explanation of this alternative coding system, see Tables 1-3 and 5-1. Also see Table 7-8. —indicates that the state had no data, either because the state had no gubernatorial election in that year, no vote data were found for the state in question, or the state had not yet entered the Union. No special gubernatorial elections are included in this table. Odd-numbered year gubernatorial elections were common before 1880 and several states still scheduled governor elections in odd-numbered years after that.

[1] Election held in odd-numbered year.
[2] 1897 election when a state had annual elections in both 1896 and 1897.
[3] 1899 election when a state had annual elections in both 1898 and 1899.

Sources: Adapted from *American State Governors, 1776–1976,* vol. 1 (1977), *Congressional Quarterly's Guide to U.S. Elections* (1994), ICPSR data sets 0001 and 0075, and independent search for state sources by the author. Party affiliations were obtained from independent search of state sources by the author when the *American State Governors* volume and the *Congressional Quarterly Guide* disagreed.

Table 7-37 Governor Election Results, by State, 1900–1903 (Percentages)

State	1900–1901				1902–1903			
	Democratic	Republican	Other	Democratic % of Two-Party Vote	Democratic	Republican	Other	Democratic % of Two-Party Vote
Alabama	71.0	17.4	11.6	80.3	73.7	26.3	0.0	73.7
Alaska	—	—	—	—	—	—	—	—
Arizona	—	—	—	—	—	—	—	—
Arkansas	66.7	30.6	2.7	68.5	64.6	24.4	11.0	72.6
California	—	—	—	—	47.2	48.1	4.7	49.6
Colorado	0.0	43.5	56.5	0.0	43.2	46.9	9.8	47.9
Colorado	*53.8*	*43.5*	*2.7*	*55.3*	—	—	—	—
Connecticut	45.1	53.0	1.9	45.9	43.4	53.4	3.2	44.8
Delaware	44.9	53.6	1.5	45.6	—	—	—	—
Florida	82.0	18.0	0.0	82.0	—	—	—	—
Georgia	78.6	0.0	21.4	100.0	93.6	0.0	6.4	100.0
Hawaii	—	—	—	—	—	—	—	—
Idaho	0.0	48.0	52.0	0.0	43.2	52.9	3.9	44.9
Idaho	*52.0*	*48.0*	*0.0*	*52.0*	—	—	—	—
Illinois	46.1	51.5	2.5	47.2	—	—	—	—
Indiana	46.7	50.5	2.8	48.0	—	—	—	—
Iowa	36.8[1]	58.1[1]	5.1[1]	38.8[1]	38.2[1]	57.1[1]	4.6[1]	40.1[1]
Kansas	47.0	51.9	1.1	47.5	40.8	55.5	3.8	42.4
Kentucky	—	—	—	—	52.1[1]	46.2[1]	1.7[1]	53.0[1]
Louisiana	78.3	3.2	18.5	96.1	—	—	—	—
Louisiana	*78.3*	*21.7*	*0.0*	*78.3*	—	—	—	—
Maine	34.0	62.3	3.7	35.3	34.7	59.5	5.8	36.8
Maryland	—	—	—	—	52.0[1]	46.0[1]	2.0[1]	53.1[1]
Massachusetts	33.7	59.1	7.3	36.3	39.9	49.2	10.9	44.8
Michigan	41.3	55.8	3.0	42.5	43.3	52.5	4.2	45.2
Minnesota	48.0	48.7	3.4	49.6	36.7	57.5	5.8	38.9
Mississippi	—	—	—	—	100.0[1]	0.0[1]	0.0[1]	100.0[1]
Missouri	51.2	46.5	2.4	52.4	—	—	—	—
Montana	49.2	35.6	15.2	58.1	—	—	—	—
Montana	*63.6*	*35.6*	*0.8*	*64.2*	—	—	—	—
Nebraska	48.5	48.9	2.6	49.8	0.0	49.7	50.3	0.0
Nebraska	—	—	—	—	*46.9*	*49.7*	*3.4*	*48.6*
Nevada	—	—	—	—	0.0	42.2	57.8	0.0
Nevada	—	—	—	—	*57.8*	*42.2*	*0.0*	*57.8*
New Hampshire	38.5	59.4	2.1	39.3	42.7	53.2	4.1	44.6
New Jersey	46.1[1]	50.9[1]	3.0[1]	47.6[1]	—	—	—	—
New Mexico	—	—	—	—	—	—	—	—
New York	44.8	52.0	3.2	46.3	0.0	48.1	51.9	0.0
New York	—	—	—	—	*47.5*	*48.1*	*4.5*	*49.7*
North Carolina	59.6	40.3	0.1	59.6	—	—	—	—
North Dakota	0.0	59.2	40.8	0.0	34.8	62.7	2.5	35.7
North Dakota	*38.7*	*59.2*	*2.1*	*39.5*	—	—	—	—
Ohio	44.5[1]	52.7[1]	2.8[1]	45.8[1]	41.8[1]	54.9[1]	3.3[1]	43.2[1]
Oklahoma	—	—	—	—	—	—	—	—
Oregon	—	—	—	—	46.2	45.9	7.9	50.1
Pennsylvania	—	—	—	—	0.0	0.0	100.0	—
Pennsylvania	—	—	—	—	*38.9*	*51.1*	*10.0*	*43.2*
Rhode Island	35.9	54.3	9.8	39.8	54.0	41.0	5.0	56.8
South Carolina	100.0	0.0	0.0	100.0	100.0	0.0	0.0	100.0
South Dakota	42.0	56.3	1.7	42.7	28.7	64.7	6.5	30.7
Tennessee	53.9	44.3	1.8	54.9	61.8	36.8	1.4	62.6
Texas	67.6	25.1	7.3	72.9	74.9	18.3	6.8	80.4
Utah	48.3	51.7	0.0	48.3	—	—	—	—
Vermont	25.5	72.2	2.3	26.1	10.5	45.6	43.9	18.8
Virginia	58.2[1]	40.6[1]	1.2[1]	58.9[1]	—	—	—	—
Washington	48.9	46.8	4.3	51.1	—	—	—	—
West Virginia	45.4	53.8	0.8	45.8	—	—	—	—
Wisconsin	36.4	59.8	3.8	37.8	39.9	52.9	7.2	43.0
Wyoming	—	—	—	—	40.0	57.8	2.2	40.9
Massachusetts	35.2[2]	57.3[2]	7.5[2]	38.1[2]	41.3[3]	50.4[3]	8.3[3]	45.0[3]
Rhode Island	39.9[2]	53.6[2]	6.4[2]	42.7[2]	49.3[3]	47.2[3]	3.5[3]	51.1[3]

Notes: Main entries are party vote percentage values for candidates who used the sole designation "Democrat" or "Republican" (or their historical antecedents listed in Appendix A) on the ballot. In general, historical antecedents to the Democratic Party were Anti-Federalists, Democratic-Republicans, and Jackson Democrats; historical precursors of the Republican Party were Federalists, National Republicans, and Whigs. Other = candidates who used third-party names only on the ballot or were listed as independent or unidentified. Bold italicized entries in the table are the author's alternative party coding, which is used when a candidate listed a major-party name (Democrat, Republican, or their historical antecedents) on the ballot with other party names or labels. For a more detailed explanation of this alternative coding system, see Tables 1-3 and 5-1. Also see Table 7-8. —indicates that the state had no data, either because the state had no gubernatorial election in that year, no vote data were found for the state in question, or the state had not yet entered the Union. No special gubernatorial elections are included in this table. Odd-numbered year gubernatorial elections were common before 1880 and several states still scheduled governor elections in odd-numbered years after that.

[1] Election held in odd-numbered year.
[2] 1901 election when a state had annual elections in both 1900 and 1901.
[3] 1903 election when a state had annual elections in both 1902 and 1903.

Sources: Adapted from *American State Governors, 1776–1976*, vol. 1 (1977), *Congressional Quarterly's Guide to U.S. Elections* (1994), ICPSR data sets 0001 and 0075, and independent search for state sources by the author. Party affiliations were obtained from independent search of state sources by the author when the *American State Governors* volume and the *Congressional Quarterly Guide* disagreed.

Table 7-38 Governor Election Results, by State, 1904–1907 (Percentages)

	1904–1905				1906–1907			
State	Democratic	Republican	Other	Democratic % of Two-Party Vote	Democratic	Republican	Other	Democratic % of Two-Party Vote
Alabama	—	—	—	—	85.5	13.9	0.6	86.0
Alaska	—	—	—	—	—	—	—	—
Arizona	—	—	—	—	—	—	—	—
Arkansas	61.0	36.4	2.6	62.6	69.1	27.3	3.6	71.7
California	—	—	—	—	0.0	40.4	59.6	0.0
California	—	—	—	—	*37.7*	*40.4*	*21.9*	*48.3*
Colorado	50.6	46.8	2.6	52.0	36.6	45.6	17.8	44.6
Connecticut	41.5	54.9	3.6	43.0	42.1	54.8	3.1	43.4
Delaware	45.1	51.4	3.5	46.7	—	—	—	—
Delaware	*45.1*	*53.2*	*1.6*	*45.9*	—	—	—	—
Florida	79.2	17.4	3.5	82.0	—	—	—	—
Georgia	100.0	0.0	0.0	100.0	99.9	0.0	0.1	100.0
Hawaii	—	—	—	—	—	—	—	—
Idaho	34.0	58.7	7.3	36.7	40.1	52.2	7.7	43.5
Illinois	31.2	59.1	9.7	34.6	—	—	—	—
Indiana	41.0	53.5	5.5	43.4	—	—	—	—
Iowa	—	—	—	—	45.3	50.2	4.5	47.5
Kansas	36.3	57.9	5.8	38.5	47.6	48.2	4.2	49.6
Kentucky	—	—	—	—	46.9[1]	51.2[1]	2.0[1]	47.8[1]
Louisiana	89.0	11.0	0.0	89.0	—	—	—	—
Maine	38.1	58.5	3.4	39.5	46.0	52.0	2.0	46.9
Maryland	—	—	—	—	50.7[1]	46.8[1]	2.5[1]	52.0[1]
Massachusetts	52.1	44.1	3.7	54.2	0.0	52.0	48.0	0.0
Massachusetts	—	—	—	—	*44.9*	*52.0*	*3.1*	*46.4*
Michigan	42.6	54.1	3.3	44.1	34.8	60.9	4.3	36.4
Minnesota	48.7	46.1	5.2	51.4	60.9	34.8	4.3	63.7
Mississippi	—	—	—	—	100.0[1]	0.0[1]	0.0[1]	100.0[1]
Missouri	50.7	46.1	3.2	52.4	—	—	—	—
Montana	0.0	41.0	59.0	0.0	—	—	—	—
Montana	*53.8*	*41.0*	*5.2*	*56.8*	—	—	—	—
Nebraska	0.0	49.7	50.3	0.0	0.0	51.3	48.7	0.0
Nebraska	*45.6*	*49.7*	*4.7*	*47.9*	*44.5*	*51.3*	*4.3*	*46.5*
Nevada	—	—	—	—	0.0	36.0	64.0	0.0
Nevada	—	—	—	—	*58.5*	*36.0*	*5.5*	*62.0*
New Hampshire	40.1	57.8	2.1	40.9	46.2	49.8	4.0	48.1
New Jersey	41.6	53.5	4.9	43.7	47.3[1]	49.3[1]	3.5[1]	48.9[1]
New Jersey	*42.3*	*53.5*	*4.2*	*44.2*	—	—	—	—
New Mexico	—	—	—	—	—	—	—	—
New York	45.3	50.3	4.4	47.4	0.0	50.5	49.5	0.0
New York	—	—	—	—	*46.6*	*50.5*	*2.9*	*48.0*
North Carolina	61.7	38.1	0.2	61.8	—	—	—	—
North Dakota	24.7	70.7	4.6	25.9	53.2	45.3	1.5	54.0
Ohio	50.5[1]	46.0[1]	3.5[1]	52.4[1]	—	—	—	—
Oklahoma	—	—	—	—	53.4[1]	42.8[1]	3.8[1]	55.5[1]
Oregon	—	—	—	—	47.6	45.0	7.4	51.4
Pennsylvania	—	—	—	—	0.0	0.0	100.0	0.0
Pennsylvania	—	—	—	—	*45.5*	*50.3*	*4.2*	*47.5*
Rhode Island	47.7	48.9	3.4	49.4	49.9	47.9	2.2	51.0
South Carolina	100.0	0.0	0.0	100.0	99.9	0.0	0.1	100.0
South Dakota	24.7	68.3	7.1	26.5	26.7	65.3	8.0	29.0
Tennessee	55.7	43.8	0.5	56.0	54.4	45.2	0.4	54.7
Texas	73.6	20.3	6.2	78.4	81.2	12.9	5.9	86.3
Texas	—	—	—	—	*81.2*	*15.9*	*3.0*	*83.7*
Utah	37.4	50.0	12.6	42.8	—	—	—	—
Vermont	24.9	72.2	2.9	25.6	0.0	60.0	40.0	0.0
Vermont	—	—	—	—	*38.2*	*60.0*	*1.8*	*38.9*
Virginia	64.5[1]	35.1[1]	0.4[1]	64.8[1]	—	—	—	—
Washington	40.9	51.3	7.8	44.3	—	—	—	—
West Virginia	47.0	50.8	2.2	48.1	—	—	—	—
Wisconsin	39.2	50.6	10.2	43.7	32.3	57.4	10.3	36.0
Wisconsin	*39.2*	*53.2*	*7.5*	*42.4*	—	—	—	—
Wyoming	—	—	—	—	34.8	60.2	5.0	36.7
Massachusetts	44.7[2]	50.5[2]	4.8[2]	47.0[2]	0.0[3]	50.3[3]	49.7[3]	0.0[3]
Massachusetts					*22.6[3]*	*50.3[3]*	*27.1[3]*	*31.0[3]*
Rhode Island	44.0[2]	53.3[2]	2.8[2]	45.2[2]	50.4[3]	46.9[3]	2.7[3]	51.8[3]

Notes: Main entries are party vote percentage values for candidates who used the sole designation "Democrat" or "Republican" (or their historical antecedents listed in Appendix A) on the ballot. In general, historical antecedents to the Democratic Party were Anti-Federalists, Democratic-Republicans, and Jackson Democrats; historical precursors of the Republican Party were Federalists, National Republicans, and Whigs. Other = candidates who used third-party names only on the ballot or were listed as independent or unidentified. Bold italicized entries in the table are the author's alternative party coding, which is used when a candidate listed a major-party name (Democrat, Republican, or their historical antecedents) on the ballot with other party names or labels. For a more detailed explanation of this alternative coding system, see Tables 1-3 and 5-1. Also see Table 7-8. —indicates that the state had no data, either because the state had no gubernatorial election in that year, no vote data were found for the state in question, or the state had not yet entered the Union. No special gubernatorial elections are included in this table. Odd-numbered year gubernatorial elections were common before 1880 and several states still scheduled governor elections in odd-numbered years after that.

[1] Election held in odd-numbered year.
[2] 1905 election when a state had annual elections in both 1904 and 1905.
[3] 1907 election when a state had annual elections in both 1906 and 1907.

Sources: Adapted from *American State Governors, 1776–1976*, vol. 1 (1977), *Congressional Quarterly's Guide to U.S. Elections* (1994), ICPSR data sets 0001 and 0075, and independent search for state sources by the author. Party affiliations were obtained from independent search of state sources by the author when the *American State Governors* volume and the *Congressional Quarterly Guide* disagreed.

Table 7-39 Governor Election Results, by State, 1908–1911 (Percentages)

	1908–1909				1910–1911			
State	Democratic	Republican	Other	Democratic % of Two-Party Vote	Democratic	Republican	Other	Democratic % of Two-Party Vote
Alabama	—	—	—	—	78.7	19.5	1.9	80.2
Alabama	—	—	—	—	*78.7*	*20.3*	*1.0*	*79.5*
Alaska	—	—	—	—	—	—	—	—
Arizona	—	—	—	—	51.5[1]	42.4[1]	6.1[1]	54.8[1]
Arkansas	68.1	27.7	4.3	71.1	67.4	26.5	6.1	71.8
California	—	—	—	—	40.1	45.9	13.9	46.6
Colorado	49.4	45.2	5.4	52.2	54.0	46.0	0.0	54.0
Connecticut	43.5	51.9	4.6	45.6	46.5	44.2	9.3	51.2
Delaware	47.6	52.0	0.5	47.8	—	—	—	—
Florida	78.8	15.4	5.8	83.7	—	—	—	—
Georgia	90.5	0.0	9.5	100.0	—	—	—	—
Hawaii	—	—	—	—	—	—	—	—
Idaho	41.6	49.6	8.8	45.6	47.4	46.4	6.2	50.6
Illinois	45.6	47.6	6.7	48.9	—	—	—	—
Indiana	48.9	46.9	4.2	51.1	—	—	—	—
Iowa	41.8	54.6	3.6	43.4	45.4	49.8	4.8	47.7
Kansas	43.3	52.5	4.2	45.2	44.8	49.8	5.4	47.4
Kentucky	—	—	—	—	53.7[1]	46.3[1]	0.0[1]	53.7[1]
Louisiana	87.1	11.1	1.8	88.7	—	—	—	—
Maine	46.5	51.5	2.0	47.4	52.0	45.9	2.1	53.1
Maryland	—	—	—	—	47.9[1]	49.3[1]	2.9[1]	49.3[1]
Massachusetts	38.0	51.6	10.4	42.4	0.0	44.0	56.0	0.0
Massachusetts	—	—	—	—	*52.0*	*44.0*	*3.9*	*54.2*
Michigan	46.6	48.4	5.0	49.1	41.6	52.9	5.5	44.1
Minnesota	52.2	43.8	4.0	54.3	35.2	55.7	9.0	38.7
Mississippi	—	—	—	—	95.2[1]	0.0[1]	4.8[1]	100.0[1]
Missouri	47.5	49.7	2.8	48.9	—	—	—	—
Montana	47.3	45.2	7.5	51.2	—	—	—	—
Nebraska	0.0	47.3	52.7	0.0	45.5	51.9	2.7	46.7
Nebraska	*49.9*	*47.3*	*2.8*	*51.4*	—	—	—	—
Nevada	—	—	—	—	42.7	50.6	6.8	45.7
New Hampshire	46.7	50.4	2.9	48.1	44.8	53.4	1.8	45.7
New Jersey	—	—	—	—	53.9	42.6	3.5	55.9
New Mexico	—	—	—	—	51.0[1]	46.1[1]	2.9[1]	52.6[1]
New York	44.8	49.1	6.1	47.7	48.0	43.3	8.7	52.6
North Carolina	57.3	42.6	0.1	57.4	—	—	—	—
North Dakota	51.1	48.4	0.5	51.3	50.0	47.4	2.7	51.3
Ohio	49.2	47.5	3.3	50.9	51.6	40.8	7.7	55.9
Oklahoma	—	—	—	—	48.6	40.2	11.2	54.7
Oregon	—	—	—	—	46.6	41.4	12.0	52.9
Pennsylvania	—	—	—	—	13.0	0.0	87.0	100.0
Pennsylvania	—	—	—	—	*13.0*	*41.6*	*45.4*	*23.7*
Rhode Island	42.7	52.6	4.7	44.8	47.9	49.6	2.5	49.1
South Carolina	100.0	0.0	0.0	100.0	99.8	0.0	0.2	100.0
South Dakota	39.4	55.3	5.3	41.6	35.9	58.4	5.7	38.1
Tennessee	53.7	45.7	0.6	54.0	47.5	51.9	0.6	47.8
Texas	72.9	24.2	2.9	75.1	79.8	12.0	8.2	87.0
Utah	38.8	47.5	13.8	45.0	—	—	—	—
Vermont	24.8	70.8	4.4	25.9	31.7	64.2	4.1	33.1
Virginia	63.4[1]	36.1[1]	0.5[1]	63.7[1]	—	—	—	—
Washington	33.0	62.6	4.4	34.5	—	—	—	—
West Virginia	46.1	50.7	3.2	47.6	—	—	—	—
Wisconsin	36.9	54.0	9.1	40.6	34.6	50.6	14.8	40.6
Wyoming	—	—	—	—	55.6	40.2	4.2	58.1
Massachusetts	46.6[2]	48.6[2]	4.8[2]	48.9[2]	0.0[3]	47.0[3]	53.0[3]	0.0[3]
Massachusetts	—	—	—	—	*48.8[3]*	*47.0[3]*	*4.2[3]*	*51.0[3]*
Rhode Island	38.9[2]	57.0[2]	4.1[2]	40.6[2]	43.0[3]	53.4[3]	3.7[3]	44.6[3]

Notes: Main entries are party vote percentage values for candidates who used the sole designation "Democrat" or "Republican" (or their historical antecedents listed in Appendix A) on the ballot. In general, historical antecedents to the Democratic Party were Anti-Federalists, Democratic-Republicans, and Jackson Democrats; historical precursors of the Republican Party were Federalists, National Republicans, and Whigs. Other = candidates who used third-party names only on the ballot or were listed as independent or unidentified. Bold italicized entries in the table are the author's alternative party coding, which is used when a candidate listed a major-party name (Democrat, Republican, or their historical antecedents) on the ballot with other party names or labels. For a more detailed explanation of this alternative coding system, see Tables 1-3 and 5-1. Also see Table 7-8. —indicates that the state had no data, either because the state had no gubernatorial election in that year, no vote data were found for the state in question, or the state had not yet entered the Union. No special gubernatorial elections are included in this table. Odd-numbered year gubernatorial elections were common before 1880 and several states still scheduled governor elections in odd-numbered years after that.

[1] Election held in odd-numbered year.
[2] 1909 election when a state had annual elections in both 1908 and 1909.
[3] 1911 election when a state had annual elections in both 1910 and 1911.

Sources: Adapted from *American State Governors, 1776–1976*, vol. 1 (1977), *Congressional Quarterly's Guide to U.S. Elections* (1994), ICPSR data sets 0001 and 0075, and independent search for state sources by the author. Party affiliations were obtained from independent search of state sources by the author when the *American State Governors* volume and the *Congressional Quarterly Guide* disagreed.

Table 7-40 Governor Election Results, by State, 1912–1915 (Percentages)

State	1912–1913				1914–1915			
	Democratic	Republican	Other	Democratic % of Two-Party Vote	Democratic	Republican	Other	Democratic % of Two-Party Vote
Alabama	—	—	—	—	78.7	15.1	6.2	83.9
Alaska	—	—	—	—	—	—	—	—
Arizona	—	—	—	—	49.5	34.5	16.0	58.9
Arkansas	64.7	27.4	7.9	70.3	69.5	22.8	7.7	75.3
California	—	—	—	—	12.5	29.4	58.1	29.9
Colorado	42.9	23.7	33.4	64.4	34.2	48.7	17.2	41.3
Connecticut	41.1	35.5	23.4	53.7	40.8	50.4	8.8	44.7
Delaware	44.3	0.0	55.7	100.0	—	—	—	—
Delaware	*44.3*	*47.0*	*8.7*	*48.5*	—	—	—	—
Florida	80.2	5.5	14.3	93.5	—	—	—	—
Georgia	—	—	—	—	—	—	—	—
Hawaii	—	—	—	—	—	—	—	—
Idaho	32.2	33.2	34.5	49.2	44.1	37.4	18.5	54.1
Illinois	38.1	27.4	34.5	58.2	—	—	—	—
Indiana	43.0	22.1	35.0	66.0	—	—	—	—
Iowa	39.6	39.9	20.5	49.8	42.9	49.3	7.8	46.5
Kansas	46.6	46.5	6.9	50.0	30.6	39.7	29.7	43.6
Kentucky	—	—	—	—	49.1[1]	49.0[1]	2.0[1]	50.1[1]
Louisiana	89.5	8.8	1.7	91.1	—	—	—	—
Maine	47.7	50.0	2.3	48.8	43.8	41.6	14.6	51.3
Maryland	—	—	—	—	49.6[1]	48.2[1]	2.2[1]	50.7[1]
Massachusetts	40.6	30.2	29.2	57.4	45.9	43.4	10.7	51.4
Michigan	35.3	31.0	33.7	53.3	48.2	40.0	11.8	54.6
Minnesota	31.3	40.7	28.0	43.5	45.5	41.9	12.6	52.1
Mississippi	—	—	—	—	92.6[1]	0.0[1]	7.4[1]	100.0[1]
Missouri	48.2	31.2	20.6	60.7	—	—	—	—
Montana	31.7	28.7	39.6	52.5	—	—	—	—
Nebraska	0.0	0.0	100.0	—	0.0	42.4	57.6	0.0
Nebraska	*49.3*	*45.3*	*5.4*	*52.1*	*50.4*	*42.4*	*7.2*	*54.3*
Nevada	—	—	—	—	44.7	39.6	15.7	53.0
New Hampshire	41.1	39.0	19.9	51.3	40.0	55.2	4.8	42.0
New Jersey	46.1[1]	37.4[1]	16.5[1]	55.2[1]	—	—	—	—
New Mexico	—	—	—	—	—	—	—	—
New York	41.5	28.3	30.2	59.4	0.0	47.7	52.3	0.0
New York	—	—	—	—	*37.6*	*47.7*	*14.7*	*44.1*
North Carolina	61.4	17.9	20.8	77.5	—	—	—	—
North Dakota	36.0	45.5	18.5	44.2	38.9	49.6	11.5	44.0
Ohio	42.4	26.3	31.3	61.7	43.7	46.3	9.9	48.6
Oklahoma	—	—	—	—	39.7	37.8	22.5	51.2
Oregon	—	—	—	—	38.1	48.8	13.1	43.9
Pennsylvania	—	—	—	—	0.0	0.0	100.0	—
Pennsylvania	—	—	—	—	*40.8*	*53.0*	*6.2*	*43.5*
Rhode Island	41.9	43.7	14.4	48.9	41.3	53.8	4.9	43.4
South Carolina	99.5	0.0	0.5	100.0	99.8	0.0	0.2	100.0
South Dakota	45.7	48.5	5.8	48.5	35.2	50.1	14.7	41.3
Tennessee	46.9	50.2	2.9	48.3	53.6	45.8	0.6	53.9
Texas	77.8	7.6	14.6	91.0	82.0	5.3	12.7	93.9
Utah	32.4	38.2	29.4	45.9	—	—	—	—
Vermont	30.8	40.5	28.7	43.3	26.1	59.5	14.4	30.5
Virginia	91.9[1]	0.0[1]	8.1[1]	100.0[1]	—	—	—	—
Washington	30.6	30.4	39.1	50.2	—	—	—	—
West Virginia	44.5	47.7	7.8	48.2	—	—	—	—
Wisconsin	42.5	45.6	11.9	48.3	36.7	43.3	20.0	45.9
Wyoming	—	—	—	—	51.6	44.2	4.2	53.9
Massachusetts	39.8[2]	25.3[2]	34.9[2]	61.1[2]	45.7[3]	47.0[3]	7.3[3]	49.3[3]

Notes: Main entries are party vote percentage values for candidates who used the sole designation "Democrat" or "Republican" (or their historical antecedents listed in Appendix A) on the ballot. In general, historical antecedents to the Democratic Party were Anti-Federalists, Democratic-Republicans, and Jackson Democrats; historical precursors of the Republican Party were Federalists, National Republicans, and Whigs. Other = candidates who used third-party names only on the ballot or were listed as independent or unidentified. Bold italicized entries in the table are the author's alternative party coding, which is used when a candidate listed a major-party name (Democrat, Republican, or their historical antecedents) on the ballot with other party names or labels. For a more detailed explanation of this alternative coding system, see Tables 1-3 and 5-1. Also see Table 7-8. —indicates that the state had no data, either because the state had no gubernatorial election in that year, no vote data were found for the state in question, or the state had not yet entered the Union. No special gubernatorial elections are included in this table. Odd-numbered year gubernatorial elections were common before 1880 and several states still scheduled governor elections in odd-numbered years after that.

[1] Election held in odd-numbered year.
[2] 1913 election when a state had annual elections in both 1912 and 1913.
[3] 1915 election when a state had annual elections in both 1914 and 1915.

Sources: Adapted from *American State Governors, 1776–1976*, vol. 1 (1977), *Congressional Quarterly's Guide to U.S. Elections* (1994), ICPSR data sets 0001 and 0075, and independent search for state sources by the author. Party affiliations were obtained from independent search of state sources by the author when the *American State Governors* volume and the *Congressional Quarterly Guide* disagreed.

Table 7-41 Governor Election Results, by State, 1916–1919 (Percentages)

State	1916–1917				1918–1919			
	Democratic	Republican	Other	Democratic % of Two-Party Vote	Democratic	Republican	Other	Democratic % of Two-Party Vote
Alabama	—	—	—	—	80.2	0.0	19.8	100.0
Alaska	—	—	—	—	—	—	—	—
Arizona	47.9	48.0	4.1	50.0	49.2	49.9	0.9	49.7
Arkansas	69.5	25.0	5.5	73.5	93.4	0.0	6.6	100.0
California	—	—	—	—	0.0	0.0	100.0	—
California	*—*	*—*	*—*	*—*	*0.0*	*56.3*	*43.7*	*0.0*
Colorado	53.3	41.3	5.4	56.3	46.5	51.1	2.4	47.6
Connecticut	45.3	51.1	3.6	47.0	45.9	50.7	3.4	47.5
Delaware	47.0	52.1	1.0	47.4	—	—	—	—
Florida	36.6	12.5	50.9	74.6	—	—	—	—
Florida	*84.3*	*12.5*	*3.2*	*87.1*	*—*	*—*	*—*	*—*
Georgia	—	—	—	—	100.0	0.0	0.0	100.0
Hawaii	—	—	—	—	—	—	—	—
Idaho	47.5	47.1	5.4	50.2	40.1	59.9	0.0	40.1
Illinois	42.1	52.7	5.2	44.4	—	—	—	—
Indiana	46.0	47.8	6.2	49.0	—	—	—	—
Iowa	36.4	61.0	2.6	37.3	46.9	50.6	2.5	48.1
Kansas	33.0	60.8	6.2	35.2	30.7	66.4	2.9	31.6
Kentucky	—	—	—	—	45.3[1]	53.8[1]	0.9[1]	45.7[1]
Louisiana	62.5	0.0	37.5	100.0	—	—	—	—
Maine	44.9	54.0	1.1	45.4	47.7	52.3	0.0	47.7
Maryland	—	—	—	—	49.1[1]	49.0[1]	1.9[1]	50.0[1]
Massachusetts	43.7	52.5	3.9	45.4	46.8	50.9	2.3	47.9
Michigan	40.6	55.8	3.6	42.1	36.4	61.4	2.2	37.2
Minnesota	23.8	62.9	13.2	27.5	20.8	45.0	34.2	31.6
Mississippi	—	—	—	—	96.9[1]	0.0[1]	3.1[1]	100.0[1]
Missouri	48.6	48.4	3.0	50.1	—	—	—	—
Montana	49.4	44.1	6.5	52.8	—	—	—	—
Nebraska	0.0	0.0	100.0	—	44.0	54.5	1.5	44.7
Nebraska	*49.3*	*47.0*	*3.8*	*51.2*	*—*	*—*	*—*	*—*
Nevada	—	—	—	—	52.1	47.9	0.0	52.1
New Hampshire	45.1	0.0	54.9	100.0	45.9	54.1	0.0	45.9
New Hampshire	*45.1*	*53.2*	*1.7*	*45.8*	*—*	*—*	*—*	*—*
New Jersey	39.8	55.4	4.7	41.8	49.2[1]	45.9[1]	4.9[1]	51.7[1]
New Mexico	49.4	47.4	3.2	51.0	47.7	50.5	1.8	48.6
New York	42.5	0.0	57.5	100.0	47.4	0.0	52.6	100.0
New York	*42.5*	*52.6*	*4.9*	*44.7*	*47.4*	*46.7*	*6.0*	*50.4*
North Carolina	58.1	41.7	0.2	58.3	—	—	—	—
North Dakota	18.4	79.2	2.4	18.8	0.0	0.0	100.0	—
North Dakota	*—*	*—*	*—*	*—*	*40.3*	*59.7*	*0.0*	*40.3*
Ohio	48.4	47.8	3.8	50.3	50.6	49.4	0.0	50.6
Oklahoma	—	—	—	—	53.5	42.6	3.8	55.7
Oregon	—	—	—	—	42.8	53.0	4.2	44.7
Pennsylvania	—	—	—	—	0.0	0.0	100.0	—
Pennsylvania	*—*	*—*	*—*	*—*	*33.7*	*61.1*	*5.2*	*35.6*
Rhode Island	40.8	55.9	3.3	42.2	44.8	53.1	2.1	45.8
South Carolina	97.9	0.0	2.1	100.0	100.0	0.0	0.0	100.0
South Carolina	*99.6*	*0.0*	*0.4*	*100.0*	*—*	*—*	*—*	*—*
South Dakota	39.3	56.6	4.0	41.0	18.6	53.2	28.2	25.9
Tennessee	55.0	44.2	0.8	55.5	62.4	37.6	0.0	62.4
Texas	80.5	13.3	6.2	85.8	84.0	15.1	0.9	84.8
Utah	0.0	41.8	58.2	0.0	—	—	—	—
Utah	*55.1*	*41.8*	*3.1*	*56.9*	*—*	*—*	*—*	*—*
Vermont	26.0	71.1	3.0	26.7	0.0	67.2	32.8	0.0
Vermont	*—*	*—*	*—*	*—*	*32.8*	*67.2*	*0.0*	*32.8*
Virginia	71.5[1]	27.8[1]	0.8[1]	72.0[1]	—	—	—	—
Washington	48.1	44.4	7.5	52.0	—	—	—	—
West Virginia	49.5	48.6	1.9	50.5	—	—	—	—
Wisconsin	38.1	52.7	9.2	41.9	34.0	47.0	19.1	41.9
Wyoming	—	—	—	—	43.9	56.1	0.0	43.9
Massachusetts	35.0[2]	58.3[2]	6.7[2]	37.5[2]	37.0[3]	60.9[3]	2.1[3]	37.7[3]

Notes: Main entries are party vote percentage values for candidates who used the sole designation "Democrat" or "Republican" (or their historical antecedents listed in Appendix A) on the ballot. In general, historical antecedents to the Democratic Party were Anti-Federalists, Democratic-Republicans, and Jackson Democrats; historical precursors of the Republican Party were Federalists, National Republicans, and Whigs. Other = candidates who used third-party names only on the ballot or were listed as independent or unidentified. Bold italicized entries in the table are the author's alternative party coding, which is used when a candidate listed a major-party name (Democrat, Republican, or their historical antecedents) on the ballot with other party names or labels. For a more detailed explanation of this alternative coding system, see Tables 1-3 and 5-1. Also see Table 7-8. —indicates that the state had no data, either because the state had no gubernatorial election in that year, no vote data were found for the state in question, or the state had not yet entered the Union. No special gubernatorial elections are included in this table. Odd-numbered year gubernatorial elections were common before 1880 and several states still scheduled governor elections in odd-numbered years after that.

[1] Election held in odd-numbered year.
[2] 1917 election when a state had annual elections in both 1916 and 1917.
[3] 1919 election when a state had annual elections in both 1918 and 1919.

Sources: Adapted from *American State Governors, 1776–1976*, vol. 1 (1977), *Congressional Quarterly's Guide to U.S. Elections* (1994), ICPSR data sets 0001 and 0075, and independent search for state sources by the author. Party affiliations were obtained from independent search of state sources by the author when the *American State Governors* volume and the *Congressional Quarterly Guide* disagreed.

Table 7-42 Governor Election Results, by State, 1920–1923 (Percentages)

State	1920–1921 Democratic	Republican	Other	Democratic % of Two-Party Vote	1922–1923 Democratic	Republican	Other	Democratic % of Two-Party Vote
Alabama	—	—	—	—	77.6	21.3	1.2	78.5
Alaska	—	—	—	—	—	—	—	—
Arizona	45.9	54.1	0.0	45.9	54.9	45.1	0.0	54.9
Arkansas	65.0	24.4	10.6	72.7	78.1	21.9	0.0	78.1
California	—	—	—	—	36.0	59.7	4.3	37.6
Colorado	37.1	59.6	3.4	38.4	49.6	48.3	2.1	50.7
Connecticut	32.8	63.0	4.2	34.2	45.7	52.4	1.9	46.6
Delaware	43.7	55.2	1.1	44.2	—	—	—	—
Florida	77.9	17.9	4.2	81.3	—	—	—	—
Florida	*77.9*	*19.9*	*2.2*	*79.6*	—	—	—	—
Georgia	—	—	—	—	100.0	0.0	0.0	100.0
Hawaii	—	—	—	—	—	—	—	—
Idaho	26.9	53.0	20.1	33.7	28.8	39.5	31.7	42.1
Illinois	34.6	58.9	6.5	37.0	—	—	—	—
Illinois	*34.6*	*59.2*	*6.2*	*36.9*	—	—	—	—
Indiana	41.2	54.6	4.2	43.0	—	—	—	—
Iowa	38.6	58.7	2.7	39.7	29.5	70.5	0.0	29.5
Kansas	39.3	58.4	2.3	40.2	50.9	47.4	1.7	51.8
Kentucky	—	—	—	—	53.3[1]	45.8[1]	0.9[1]	53.8[1]
Louisiana	97.5	2.5	0.0	97.5	—	—	—	—
Maine	34.1	65.9	0.0	34.1	42.0	58.0	0.0	42.0
Maryland	—	—	—	—	56.0[1]	43.3[1]	0.8[1]	56.4[1]
Massachusetts	30.2	67.0	2.8	31.1	45.4	52.2	2.3	46.5
Michigan	29.3	66.4	4.2	30.6	37.4	61.2	1.4	37.9
Minnesota	10.4	53.1	36.6	16.4	11.7	45.2	43.1	20.5
Mississippi	—	—	—	—	100.0[1]	0.0[1]	0.0[1]	100.0[1]
Missouri	43.6	54.3	2.1	44.6	—	—	—	—
Montana	40.3	59.7	0.0	40.3	—	—	—	—
Nebraska	34.5	40.4	25.1	46.0	54.6	42.0	3.4	56.6
Nevada	—	—	—	—	53.9	46.1	0.0	53.9
New Hampshire	39.7	59.6	0.7	40.0	53.3	46.7	0.0	53.3
New Jersey	—	—	—	—	52.2	46.8	1.0	52.7
New Mexico	47.8	51.3	0.9	48.3	54.6	44.7	0.8	55.0
New York	44.0	46.6	9.4	48.6	55.2	40.0	4.8	58.0
North Carolina	57.2	42.8	0.0	57.2	—	—	—	—
North Dakota	0.0	0.0	100.0	—	0.0	57.6	42.4	0.0
North Dakota	*49.0*	*51.0*	*0.0*	*49.0*	—	—	—	—
Ohio	45.9	51.9	2.2	46.9	50.5	49.5	0.0	50.5
Oklahoma	—	—	—	—	54.4	44.8	0.8	54.9
Oregon	—	—	—	—	57.4	42.6	0.0	57.4
Pennsylvania	—	—	—	—	39.7	56.8	3.5	41.2
Rhode Island	33.2	64.6	2.2	33.9	51.7	47.2	1.1	52.3
South Carolina	100.0	0.0	0.0	100.0	100.0	0.0	0.0	100.0
South Dakota	17.3	56.3	26.3	23.5	28.7	45.0	26.2	39.0
Tennessee	44.6	54.9	0.5	44.8	57.9	42.1	0.0	57.9
Texas	60.2	18.7	21.2	76.3	81.9	18.1	0.0	81.9
Texas	*60.2*	*24.1*	*15.8*	*71.4*	—	—	—	—
Utah	38.2	58.2	3.6	39.7	—	—	—	—
Vermont	21.8	0.0	78.2	100.0	25.0	0.0	75.0	100.0
Vermont	*21.8*	*78.0*	*0.2*	*21.8*	*25.0*	*74.8*	*0.2*	*25.0*
Virginia	66.2[1]	31.2[1]	2.6[1]	67.9[1]	—	—	—	—
Virginia	*66.2[1]*	*33.6[1]*	*0.2[1]*	*66.3[1]*	—	—	—	—
Washington	16.5	52.7	30.7	23.9	—	—	—	—
West Virginia	36.3	47.3	16.4	43.4	—	—	—	—
Wisconsin	35.8	53.0	11.2	40.3	0.0	76.4	23.6	0.0
Wisconsin	—	—	—	—	*10.6*	*76.4*	*13.0*	*12.2*
Wyoming	—	—	—	—	50.6	49.4	0.0	50.6

Notes: Main entries are party vote percentage values for candidates who used the sole designation "Democrat" or "Republican" (or their historical antecedents listed in Appendix A) on the ballot. In general, historical antecedents to the Democratic Party were Anti-Federalists, Democratic-Republicans, and Jackson Democrats; historical precursors of the Republican Party were Federalists, National Republicans, and Whigs. Other = candidates who used third-party names only on the ballot or were listed as independent or unidentified. Bold italicized entries in the table are the author's alternative party coding, which is used when a candidate listed a major-party name (Democrat, Republican, or their historical antecedents) on the ballot with other party names or labels. For a more detailed explanation of this alternative coding system, see Tables 1-3 and 5-1. Also see Table 7-8. —indicates that the state had no data, either because the state had no gubernatorial election in that year, no vote data were found for the state in question, or the state had not yet entered the Union. No special gubernatorial elections are included in this table. Odd-numbered year gubernatorial elections were common before 1880 and several states still scheduled governor elections in odd-numbered years after that.

[1]Election held in odd-numbered year.

Sources: Adapted from *American State Governors, 1776–1976*, vol. 1 (1977), *Congressional Quarterly's Guide to U.S. Elections* (1994), ICPSR data sets 0001 and 0075, and independent search for state sources by the author. Party affiliations were obtained from independent search of state sources by the author when the *American State Governors* volume and the *Congressional Quarterly Guide* disagreed.

Table 7-43 Governor Election Results, by State, 1924–1927 (Percentages)

State	1924–1925				1926–1927			
	Democratic	Republican	Other	Democratic % of Two-Party Vote	Democratic	Republican	Other	Democratic % of Two-Party Vote
Alabama	—	—	—	—	81.2	18.8	0.0	81.2
Alaska	—	—	—	—	—	—	—	—
Arizona	50.5	49.5	0.0	50.5	50.3	49.7	0.0	50.3
Arkansas	79.8	20.2	0.0	79.8	76.4	23.6	0.0	76.4
California	—	—	—	—	24.7	71.2	4.1	25.7
Colorado	44.0	51.9	4.0	45.9	59.8	38.1	2.1	61.1
Connecticut	31.9	66.2	1.9	32.5	35.4	63.6	1.1	35.7
Delaware	39.2	59.6	1.2	39.6	—	—	—	—
Florida	82.8	17.2	0.0	82.8	—	—	—	—
Georgia	100.0	0.0	0.0	100.0	100.0	0.0	0.0	100.0
Hawaii	—	—	—	—	—	—	—	—
Idaho	16.8	43.9	39.3	27.7	20.6	51.0	28.4	28.7
Illinois	42.4	56.7	0.9	42.8	—	—	—	—
Illinois	*42.4*	*56.8*	*0.8*	*42.8*	—	—	—	—
Indiana	46.3	52.9	0.8	46.7	—	—	—	—
Iowa	27.3	72.7	0.0	27.3	28.4	71.3	0.3	28.5
Kansas	27.7	49.0	23.3	36.1	35.3	63.3	1.4	35.8
Kentucky	—	—	—	—	47.9[1]	52.1[1]	0.0[1]	47.9[1]
Louisiana	97.9	2.1	0.0	97.9	—	—	—	—
Maine	42.8	57.2	0.0	42.8	44.5	55.5	0.0	44.5
Maryland	—	—	—	—	57.9	41.4	0.7	58.3
Massachusetts	42.2	56.0	1.8	43.0	40.2	58.8	1.0	40.6
Michigan	29.6	68.8	1.6	30.1	36.0	63.4	0.6	36.2
Minnesota	5.9	48.7	45.4	10.8	5.4	56.5	38.1	8.8
Mississippi	—	—	—	—	100.0[1]	0.0[1]	0.0[1]	100.0[1]
Missouri	48.9	49.4	1.7	49.8	—	—	—	—
Montana	51.0	42.6	6.4	54.5	—	—	—	—
Nebraska	41.0	51.1	7.9	44.5	49.0	49.8	1.2	49.6
Nevada	—	—	—	—	47.0	53.0	0.0	47.0
New Hampshire	46.1	53.9	0.0	46.1	40.3	59.7	0.0	40.3
New Jersey	51.9[1]	47.6[1]	0.5[1]	52.1[1]	—	—	—	—
New Mexico	48.8	48.6	2.5	50.1	48.1	51.6	0.3	48.3
New York	50.0	46.6	3.4	51.7	52.3	43.8	3.9	54.4
North Carolina	61.3	38.7	0.0	61.3	—	—	—	—
North Dakota	46.1	53.9	0.0	46.1	15.2	81.7	3.1	15.6
Ohio	54.0	45.0	1.0	54.6	50.5	49.0	0.5	50.8
Oklahoma	—	—	—	—	54.9	44.2	0.9	55.4
Oregon	—	—	—	—	41.4	53.1	5.5	43.8
Pennsylvania	—	—	—	—	0.0	73.3	26.7	0.0
Pennsylvania	—	—	—	—	*24.3*	*73.3*	*2.4*	*24.9*
Rhode Island	41.0	58.6	0.4	41.2	45.7	53.9	0.4	45.9
South Carolina	100.0	0.0	0.0	100.0	100.0	0.0	0.0	100.0
South Dakota	22.9	53.9	23.2	29.8	47.4	40.3	12.3	54.0
Tennessee	57.2	42.8	0.0	57.2	64.7	35.2	0.1	64.8
Texas	58.9	41.1	0.0	58.9	87.5	12.2	0.3	87.8
Utah	53.0	47.0	0.0	53.0	—	—	—	—
Vermont	19.2	79.2	1.6	19.5	0.0	60.9	39.1	0.0
Vermont	—	—	—	—	*39.1*	*60.9*	*0.0*	*39.1*
Virginia	74.1[1]	25.9[1]	0.0[1]	74.1[1]	—	—	—	—
Washington	32.4	56.4	11.2	36.5	—	—	—	—
West Virginia	45.8	53.0	1.3	46.4	—	—	—	—
Wisconsin	39.9	51.8	8.4	43.5	13.1	63.5	23.4	17.1
Wisconsin	*39.9*	*52.3*	*7.9*	*43.3*	—	—	—	—
Wyoming	—	—	—	—	49.0	50.9	0.1	49.0

Notes: Main entries are party vote percentage values for candidates who used the sole designation "Democrat" or "Republican" (or their historical antecedents listed in Appendix A) on the ballot. In general, historical antecedents to the Democratic Party were Anti-Federalists, Democratic-Republicans, and Jackson Democrats; historical precursors of the Republican Party were Federalists, National Republicans, and Whigs. Other = candidates who used third-party names only on the ballot or were listed as independent or unidentified. Bold italicized entries in the table are the author's alternative party coding, which is used when a candidate listed a major-party name (Democrat, Republican, or their historical antecedents) on the ballot with other party names or labels. For a more detailed explanation of this alternative coding system, see Tables 1-3 and 5-1. Also see Table 7-8. —indicates that the state had no data, either because the state had no gubernatorial election in that year, no vote data were found for the state in question, or the state had not yet entered the Union. No special gubernatorial elections are included in this table. Odd-numbered year gubernatorial elections were common before 1880 and several states still scheduled governor elections in odd-numbered years after that.

[1] Election held in odd-numbered year.

Sources: Adapted from *American State Governors, 1776–1976*, vol. 1 (1977), *Congressional Quarterly's Guide to U.S. Elections* (1994), ICPSR data sets 0001 and 0075, and independent search for state sources by the author. Party affiliations were obtained from independent search of state sources by the author when the *American State Governors* volume and the *Congressional Quarterly Guide* disagreed.

Table 7-44 Governor Election Results, by State, 1928–1931 (Percentages)

State	1928–1929 Democratic	Republican	Other	Democratic % of Two-Party Vote	1930–1931 Democratic	Republican	Other	Democratic % of Two-Party Vote
Alabama	—	—	—	—	61.8	0.0	38.2	100.0
Alaska	—	—	—	—	—	—	—	—
Arizona	48.2	51.7	0.1	48.2	51.4	48.6	0.0	51.4
Arkansas	77.3	22.7	0.0	77.3	81.2	18.8	0.0	81.2
California	—	—	—	—	24.1	72.2	3.7	25.0
Colorado	61.9	37.1	1.0	62.5	60.4	38.1	1.5	61.3
Connecticut	45.6	53.6	0.8	46.0	49.9	48.6	1.4	50.6
Delaware	38.8	61.2	0.0	38.8	—	—	—	—
Florida	61.0	39.0	0.0	61.0	—	—	—	—
Georgia	—	—	—	—	—	—	—	—
Hawaii	—	—	—	—	—	—	—	—
Idaho	41.6	57.8	0.6	41.8	56.0	44.0	0.0	56.0
Illinois	42.7	56.8	0.6	42.9	—	—	—	—
Indiana	48.1	51.3	0.7	48.4	—	—	—	—
Iowa	37.2	62.8	0.0	37.2	33.6	65.7	0.7	33.8
Kansas	33.2	65.6	1.2	33.6	35.0	34.9	30.1	50.0
Kentucky	—	—	—	—	54.3[1]	45.4[1]	0.3[1]	54.4[1]
Louisiana	96.1	3.9	0.0	96.1	—	—	—	—
Maine	30.7	69.3	0.0	30.7	44.9	55.1	0.0	44.9
Maryland	—	—	—	—	56.0	42.8	1.3	56.7
Massachusetts	48.8	50.1	1.1	49.4	49.5	48.2	2.3	50.7
Michigan	29.4	69.9	0.6	29.6	42.0	56.9	1.1	42.5
Minnesota	21.4	55.0	23.6	28.0	3.7	36.3	60.0	9.1
Mississippi	—	—	—	—	100.0[1]	0.0[1]	0.0[1]	100.0[1]
Missouri	48.2	51.6	0.2	48.3	—	—	—	—
Montana	58.6	41.0	0.4	58.9	—	—	—	—
Nebraska	42.6	57.0	0.4	42.8	50.7	49.3	0.0	50.7
Nevada	—	—	—	—	46.8	53.2	0.0	46.8
New Hampshire	42.3	57.5	0.2	42.4	41.8	58.0	0.2	41.9
New Jersey	44.7	54.9	0.4	44.9	57.8[1]	39.7[1]	2.4[1]	59.3[1]
New Mexico	44.3	55.6	0.1	44.3	53.2	46.6	0.2	53.3
New York	49.0	48.4	2.7	50.3	56.1	33.1	10.8	62.9
North Carolina	55.6	44.4	0.0	55.6	—	—	—	—
North Dakota	43.2	56.5	0.4	43.3	23.2	73.6	3.2	24.0
Ohio	44.7	54.8	0.5	44.9	52.8	47.2	0.0	52.8
Oklahoma	—	—	—	—	59.1	40.8	0.1	59.1
Oregon	—	—	—	—	25.1	18.8	56.1	57.1
Pennsylvania	—	—	—	—	0.0	0.0	100.0	—
Pennsylvania	—	—	—	—	***48.0***	***50.8***	***1.3***	***48.6***
Rhode Island	48.1	51.6	0.3	48.3	48.9	50.5	0.5	49.2
South Carolina	—	—	—	—	100.0	0.0	0.0	100.0
South Dakota	52.5	46.9	0.6	52.8	46.2	53.0	0.8	46.6
Tennessee	61.1	38.9	0.0	61.1	63.8	35.6	0.5	64.2
Texas	82.4	17.4	0.1	82.5	80.0	19.7	0.3	80.3
Utah	58.5	41.1	0.4	58.7	—	—	—	—
Vermont	26.0	73.5	0.5	26.1	28.9	71.0	0.1	29.0
Virginia	62.8[1]	36.9[1]	0.3[1]	63.0[1]	—	—	—	—
Washington	42.7	56.2	1.1	43.2	—	—	—	—
West Virginia	46.1	53.7	0.2	46.2	—	—	—	—
Wisconsin	39.9	55.4	4.7	41.9	28.0	64.8	7.2	30.2
Wyoming	—	—	—	—	49.4	50.6	0.0	49.4

Notes: Main entries are party vote percentage values for candidates who used the sole designation "Democrat" or "Republican" (or their historical antecedents listed in Appendix A) on the ballot. In general, historical antecedents to the Democratic Party were Anti-Federalists, Democratic-Republicans, and Jackson Democrats; historical precursors of the Republican Party were Federalists, National Republicans, and Whigs. Other = candidates who used third-party names only on the ballot or were listed as independent or unidentified. Bold italicized entries in the table are the author's alternative party coding, which is used when a candidate listed a major-party name (Democrat, Republican, or their historical antecedents) on the ballot with other party names or labels. For a more detailed explanation of this alternative coding system, see Tables 1-3 and 5-1. Also see Table 7-8. —indicates that the state had no data, either because the state had no gubernatorial election in that year, no vote data were found for the state in question, or the state had not yet entered the Union. No special gubernatorial elections are included in this table. Odd-numbered year gubernatorial elections were common before 1880 and several states still scheduled governor elections in odd-numbered years after that.

[1] Election held in odd-numbered year.

Sources: Adapted from *American State Governors, 1776–1976*, vol. 1 (1977), *Congressional Quarterly's Guide to U.S. Elections* (1994), ICPSR data sets 0001 and 0075, and independent search for state sources by the author. Party affiliations were obtained from independent search of state sources by the author when the *American State Governors* volume and the *Congressional Quarterly Guide* disagreed.

Table 7-45 Governor Election Results, by State, 1932–1935 (Percentages)

State	1932–1933 Democratic	Republican	Other	Democratic % of Two-Party Vote	1934–1935 Democratic	Republican	Other	Democratic % of Two-Party Vote
Alabama	—	—	—	—	86.9	12.7	0.4	87.3
Alaska	—	—	—	—	—	—	—	—
Arizona	63.2	35.4	1.4	64.1	59.7	38.2	2.2	61.0
Arizona	*63.7*	*35.4*	*0.9*	*64.3*	—	—	—	—
Arkansas	90.4	8.9	0.7	91.0	89.2	9.4	1.4	90.5
California	—	—	—	—	37.8	48.9	13.4	43.6
Colorado	57.2	40.8	2.0	58.4	58.1	39.9	2.0	59.3
Connecticut	49.0	47.1	3.9	51.0	46.7	45.2	8.1	50.8
Delaware	44.9	54.2	0.9	45.3	—	—	—	—
Florida	66.6	33.4	0.0	66.6	—	—	—	—
Georgia	100.0	0.0	0.0	100.0	100.0	0.0	0.0	100.0
Hawaii	—	—	—	—	—	—	—	—
Idaho	61.7	36.4	1.8	62.9	54.6	44.3	1.2	55.2
Illinois	57.6	40.7	1.7	58.6	—	—	—	—
Indiana	55.0	42.8	2.2	56.3	—	—	—	—
Iowa	52.8	47.2	0.0	52.8	54.3	45.7	0.0	54.3
Kansas	34.1	34.8	31.1	49.5	45.6	53.5	0.9	46.0
Kentucky	—	—	—	—	54.5[1]	45.1[1]	0.4[1]	54.7[1]
Louisiana	99.9	0.0	0.1	100.0	—	—	—	—
Maine	50.3	49.3	0.5	50.5	54.0	45.9	0.1	54.0
Maryland	—	—	—	—	48.3	49.5	2.2	49.4
Massachusetts	52.8	45.0	2.2	54.0	49.7	42.3	8.0	54.0
Michigan	54.9	43.1	2.0	56.0	45.8	52.4	1.8	46.7
Minnesota	16.4	32.3	51.2	33.7	16.8	37.7	45.5	30.9
Mississippi	—	—	—	—	100.0[1]	0.0[1]	0.0[1]	100.0[1]
Missouri	60.2	39.1	0.7	60.6	—	—	—	—
Montana	48.5	46.7	4.8	50.9	—	—	—	—
Nebraska	52.5	46.3	1.2	53.2	50.8	47.7	1.4	51.6
Nevada	—	—	—	—	53.9	34.5	11.5	61.0
New Hampshire	45.4	54.2	0.4	45.6	49.2	50.5	0.3	49.3
New Jersey	—	—	—	—	49.0	49.9	1.1	49.5
New Mexico	54.8	44.2	1.0	55.4	51.9	47.6	0.5	52.2
New York	56.7	38.6	4.7	59.5	57.8	36.6	5.6	61.2
North Carolina	70.1	29.9	0.0	70.1	—	—	—	—
North Dakota	45.0	54.7	0.3	45.1	53.0	46.6	0.4	53.2
Ohio	52.8	44.9	2.3	54.1	51.1	48.1	0.7	51.5
Oklahoma	—	—	—	—	58.2	38.8	2.9	60.0
Oregon	—	—	—	—	38.6	28.7	32.7	57.3
Pennsylvania	—	—	—	—	50.0	47.8	2.2	51.1
Rhode Island	55.2	43.5	1.3	55.9	56.6	42.4	0.9	57.2
South Carolina	—	—	—	—	100.0	0.0	0.0	100.0
South Dakota	55.6	42.4	2.0	56.7	58.6	40.7	0.7	59.0
Tennessee	42.8	29.8	27.5	58.9	61.8	0.0	38.2	100.0
Tennessee	—	—	—	—	*61.8*	*38.2*	*0.0*	*61.8*
Texas	61.6	38.1	0.4	61.8	96.4	3.1	0.5	96.9
Texas	*61.7*	*38.1*	*0.3*	*61.8*	—	—	—	—
Utah	56.4	41.8	1.8	57.5	—	—	—	—
Vermont	37.2	61.7	1.1	37.6	42.1	57.3	0.6	42.4
Virginia	73.7[1]	24.2[1]	2.0[1]	75.3[1]	—	—	—	—
Washington	57.3	33.8	8.9	62.9	—	—	—	—
West Virginia	53.8	45.8	0.4	54.0	—	—	—	—
Wisconsin	52.5	41.9	5.6	55.6	37.7	18.1	44.2	67.5
Wyoming	—	—	—	—	57.9	41.4	0.7	58.3

Notes: Main entries are party vote percentage values for candidates who used the sole designation "Democrat" or "Republican" (or their historical antecedents listed in Appendix A) on the ballot. In general, historical antecedents to the Democratic Party were Anti-Federalists, Democratic-Republicans, and Jackson Democrats; historical precursors of the Republican Party were Federalists, National Republicans, and Whigs. Other = candidates who used third-party names only on the ballot or were listed as independent or unidentified. Bold italicized entries in the table are the author's alternative party coding, which is used when a candidate listed a major-party name (Democrat, Republican, or their historical antecedents) on the ballot with other party names or labels. For a more detailed explanation of this alternative coding system, see Tables 1-3 and 5-1. Also see Table 7-8. —indicates that the state had no data, either because the state had no gubernatorial election in that year, no vote data were found for the state in question, or the state had not yet entered the Union. No special gubernatorial elections are included in this table. Odd-numbered year gubernatorial elections were common before 1880 and several states still scheduled governor elections in odd-numbered years after that.

[1] Election held in odd-numbered year.

Sources: Adapted from *American State Governors, 1776–1976*, vol. 1 (1977), *Congressional Quarterly's Guide to U.S. Elections* (1994), ICPSR data sets 0001 and 0075, and independent search for state sources by the author. Party affiliations were obtained from independent search of state sources by the author when the *American State Governors* volume and the *Congressional Quarterly Guide* disagreed.

Table 7-46 Governor Election Results, by State, 1936–1939 (Percentages)

State	1936–1937 Democratic	Republican	Other	Democratic % of Two-Party Vote	1938–1939 Democratic	Republican	Other	Democratic % of Two-Party Vote
Alabama	—	—	—	—	87.4	12.5	0.2	87.5
Alaska	—	—	—	—	—	—	—	—
Arizona	70.7	29.1	0.2	70.8	68.6	27.3	4.1	71.5
Arizona	—	—	—	—	*72.7*	*27.3*	*0.0*	*72.7*
Arkansas	84.9	14.7	0.4	85.2	86.3	4.9	8.8	94.6
California	—	—	—	—	52.5	44.2	3.3	54.3
Colorado	54.6	43.6	1.8	55.6	43.7	55.8	0.5	43.9
Connecticut	55.3	41.1	3.6	57.4	36.0	0.0	64.0	100.0
Connecticut	—	—	—	—	*36.0*	*36.4*	*27.6*	*49.7*
Delaware	51.6	41.6	6.8	55.4	—	—	—	—
Delaware	*51.6*	*48.2*	*0.2*	*51.7*	—	—	—	—
Florida	80.9	19.1	0.0	80.9	—	—	—	—
Georgia	99.7	0.0	0.3	100.0	94.3	0.0	5.7	100.0
Hawaii	—	—	—	—	—	—	—	—
Idaho	57.2	41.5	1.3	58.0	41.9	57.3	0.8	42.2
Illinois	53.1	43.2	3.6	55.1	—	—	—	—
Indiana	55.4	44.3	0.3	55.5	—	—	—	—
Iowa	48.7	48.4	2.9	50.1	45.7	52.7	1.6	46.4
Kansas	51.1	48.5	0.4	51.3	45.1	52.1	2.8	46.4
Kentucky	—	—	—	—	56.5[1]	43.5[1]	0.0[1]	56.5[1]
Louisiana	100.0	0.0	0.0	100.0	—	—	—	—
Maine	42.1	56.0	1.9	42.9	47.0	52.9	0.1	47.1
Maryland	—	—	—	—	54.6	42.9	2.5	56.0
Massachusetts	47.6	46.1	6.3	50.8	45.0	53.3	1.7	45.7
Michigan	51.0	48.2	0.8	51.4	47.0	52.8	0.3	47.1
Minnesota	0.0	38.6	61.4	0.0	5.8	59.9	34.3	8.8
Mississippi	—	—	—	—	100.0[1]	0.0[1]	0.0[1]	100.0[1]
Missouri	57.1	42.5	0.4	57.3	—	—	—	—
Montana	51.0	48.1	0.9	51.4	—	—	—	—
Nebraska	55.9	43.1	1.0	56.4	44.0	40.6	15.4	52.0
Nevada	—	—	—	—	61.9	38.1	0.0	61.9
New Hampshire	42.6	56.6	0.8	43.0	42.8	57.1	0.1	42.8
New Jersey	50.8[1]	47.8[1]	1.4[1]	51.6[1]	—	—	—	—
New Mexico	57.2	42.8	0.0	57.2	52.2	47.6	0.2	52.3
New York	0.0	44.1	55.9	0.0	0.0	0.0	100.0	—
New York	*53.5*	*44.1*	*2.5*	*54.8*	*50.4*	*49.0*	*0.6*	*50.7*
North Carolina	66.7	33.3	0.0	66.7	—	—	—	—
North Dakota	29.3	34.7	36.0	45.8	52.5	47.5	0.0	52.5
Ohio	52.0	47.7	0.3	52.1	47.6	52.4	0.0	47.6
Oklahoma	—	—	—	—	70.0	29.3	0.7	70.5
Oregon	—	—	—	—	42.6	57.4	0.0	42.6
Pennsylvania	—	—	—	—	0.0	53.4	46.6	0.0
Pennsylvania	—	—	—	—	*46.1*	*53.4*	*0.5*	*46.3*
Rhode Island	53.7	45.8	0.5	53.9	41.6	0.0	58.4	100.0
Rhode Island	—	—	—	—	*41.6*	*54.2*	*4.2*	*43.5*
South Carolina	—	—	—	—	99.4	0.6	0.0	99.4
South Dakota	48.4	51.6	0.0	48.4	46.0	54.0	0.0	46.0
Tennessee	80.4	18.7	0.9	81.1	71.7	28.3	0.0	71.7
Texas	92.9	7.0	0.2	93.0	96.8	3.0	0.1	96.9
Utah	50.9	37.2	11.8	57.8	—	—	—	—
Vermont	38.8	60.9	0.3	38.9	33.2	66.8	0.0	33.2
Virginia	82.8[1]	0.0[1]	17.2[1]	100.0[1]	—	—	—	—
Virginia	*82.8[1]*	*15.8[1]*	*1.4[1]*	*84.0[1]*	—	—	—	—
Washington	69.4	28.1	2.5	71.2	—	—	—	—
West Virginia	59.2	40.8	0.0	59.2	—	—	—	—
Wisconsin	21.7	29.4	48.9	42.5	8.0	55.4	36.6	12.6
Wyoming	—	—	—	—	40.2	59.8	0.0	40.2

Notes: Main entries are party vote percentage values for candidates who used the sole designation "Democrat" or "Republican" (or their historical antecedents listed in Appendix A) on the ballot. In general, historical antecedents to the Democratic Party were Anti-Federalists, Democratic-Republicans, and Jackson Democrats; historical precursors of the Republican Party were Federalists, National Republicans, and Whigs. Other = candidates who used third-party names only on the ballot or were listed as independent or unidentified. Bold italicized entries in the table are the author's alternative party coding, which is used when a candidate listed a major-party name (Democrat, Republican, or their historical antecedents) on the ballot with other party names or labels. For a more detailed explanation of this alternative coding system, see Tables 1-3 and 5-1. Also see Table 7-8. —indicates that the state had no data, either because the state had no gubernatorial election in that year, no vote data were found for the state in question, or the state had not yet entered the Union. No special gubernatorial elections are included in this table. Odd-numbered year gubernatorial elections were common before 1880 and several states still scheduled governor elections in odd-numbered years after that.

[1] Election held in odd-numbered year.

Sources: Adapted from *American State Governors, 1776–1976*, vol. 1 (1977), *Congressional Quarterly's Guide to U.S. Elections* (1994), ICPSR data sets 0001 and 0075, and independent search for state sources by the author. Party affiliations were obtained from independent search of state sources by the author when the *American State Governors* volume and the *Congressional Quarterly Guide* disagreed.

Table 7-47 Governor Election Results, by State, 1940–1943 (Percentages)

State	1940–1941				1942–1943			
	Democratic	Republican	Other	Democratic % of Two-Party Vote	Democratic	Republican	Other	Democratic % of Two-Party Vote
Alabama	—	—	—	—	89.0	10.5	0.5	89.4
Alaska	—	—	—	—	—	—	—	—
Arizona	65.5	33.8	0.7	66.0	72.5	26.9	0.6	72.9
Arkansas	91.4	8.2	0.4	91.7	100.0	0.0	0.0	100.0
California	—	—	—	—	41.8	57.1	1.2	42.3
Colorado	45.0	54.4	0.7	45.3	43.4	56.2	0.4	43.6
Connecticut	49.5	0.0	50.5	100.0	44.4	48.9	6.7	47.6
Connecticut	**49.5**	**47.8**	**2.7**	**50.9**	—	—	—	—
Delaware	45.4	52.4	2.2	46.4	—	—	—	—
Delaware	**47.6**	**52.4**	**0.0**	**47.6**	—	—	—	—
Florida	100.0	0.0	0.0	100.0	—	—	—	—
Georgia	0.0	0.0	100.0	—	96.3	0.0	3.7	100.0
Georgia	**99.6**	**0.0**	**0.4**	**100.0**	—	—	—	—
Hawaii	—	—	—	—	—	—	—	—
Idaho	50.5	49.5	0.0	50.5	49.8	50.2	0.0	49.8
Illinois	46.7	52.9	0.3	46.9	—	—	—	—
Indiana	49.9	49.7	0.4	50.1	—	—	—	—
Iowa	47.1	52.7	0.2	47.2	37.0	62.7	0.3	37.1
Kansas	49.6	49.6	0.8	50.0	41.8	56.7	1.6	42.4
Kentucky	—	—	—	—	48.9[1]	50.5[1]	0.6[1]	49.2[1]
Louisiana	99.4	0.6	0.0	99.4	33.2	66.8	0.0	33.2
Maine	36.1	63.8	0.1	36.1	52.6	47.4	0.0	52.6
Maryland	—	—	—	—	45.0	54.1	0.9	45.4
Massachusetts	49.5	49.7	0.8	49.9	46.7	52.6	0.7	47.0
Michigan	53.1	46.6	0.4	53.2	—	—	—	—
Minnesota	11.1	52.1	36.8	17.6	9.5	51.6	38.9	15.5
Mississippi	—	—	—	—	100.0[1]	0.0[1]	0.0[1]	100.0[1]
Missouri	49.9	50.1	0.1	49.9	—	—	—	—
Montana	48.6	50.7	0.7	49.0	—	—	—	—
Nebraska	39.1	60.9	0.0	39.1	25.2	74.8	0.0	25.2
Nevada	—	—	—	—	60.3	39.7	0.0	60.3
New Hampshire	49.3	50.7	0.0	49.3	47.8	52.2	0.0	47.8
New Jersey	51.4	48.0	0.6	51.7	44.1[1]	55.2[1]	0.7[1]	44.4[1]
New Mexico	55.6	44.4	0.0	55.6	54.5	45.5	0.0	54.5
New York	—	—	—	—	36.4	52.1	11.5	41.1
North Carolina	75.7	24.3	0.0	75.7	—	—	—	—
North Dakota	63.1	36.9	0.0	63.1	57.6	42.4	0.0	57.6
Ohio	44.5	55.5	0.0	44.5	39.5	60.5	0.0	39.5
Oklahoma	—	—	—	—	51.9	47.6	0.5	52.1
Oregon	—	—	—	—	22.1	77.9	0.0	22.1
Pennsylvania	—	—	—	—	45.1	53.7	1.2	45.7
Rhode Island	55.8	44.1	0.1	55.9	58.5	41.5	0.0	58.5
South Carolina	—	—	—	—	100.0	0.0	0.0	100.0
South Dakota	44.9	55.1	0.0	44.9	38.5	61.5	0.0	38.5
Tennessee	72.1	27.9	0.0	72.1	70.2	29.8	0.0	70.2
Texas	94.7	5.3	0.0	94.7	96.8	3.2	0.0	96.8
Utah	52.1	47.7	0.2	52.2	—	—	—	—
Vermont	36.0	64.0	0.0	36.0	22.1	77.9	0.0	22.1
Virginia	80.6[1]	0.0[1]	19.4[1]	100.0[1]	—	—	—	—
Virginia	**80.6[1]**	**17.9[1]**	**1.5[1]**	**81.8[1]**	—	—	—	—
Washington	49.5	50.2	0.3	49.6	—	—	—	—
West Virginia	56.4	43.6	0.0	56.4	—	—	—	—
Wisconsin	19.3	40.7	40.0	32.2	12.3	36.5	51.3	25.2
Wyoming	—	—	—	—	51.3	48.7	0.0	51.3

Notes: Main entries are party vote percentage values for candidates who used the sole designation "Democrat" or "Republican" (or their historical antecedents listed in Appendix A) on the ballot. In general, historical antecedents to the Democratic Party were Anti-Federalists, Democratic-Republicans, and Jackson Democrats; historical precursors of the Republican Party were Federalists, National Republicans, and Whigs. Other = candidates who used third-party names only on the ballot or were listed as independent or unidentified. Bold italicized entries in the table are the author's alternative party coding, which is used when a candidate listed a major-party name (Democrat, Republican, or their historical antecedents) on the ballot with other party names or labels. For a more detailed explanation of this alternative coding system, see Tables 1-3 and 5-1. Also see Table 7-8. —indicates that the state had no data, either because the state had no gubernatorial election in that year, no vote data were found for the state in question, or the state had not yet entered the Union. No special gubernatorial elections are included in this table. Odd-numbered year gubernatorial elections were common before 1880 and several states still scheduled governor elections in odd-numbered years after that.

[1] Election held in odd-numbered year.

Sources: Adapted from *American State Governors, 1776–1976*, vol. 1 (1977), *Congressional Quarterly's Guide to U.S. Elections* (1994), ICPSR data sets 0001 and 0075, and independent search for state sources by the author. Party affiliations were obtained from independent search of state sources by the author when the *American State Governors* volume and the *Congressional Quarterly Guide* disagreed.

Table 7-48 Governor Election Results, by State, 1944–1947 (Percentages)

State	1944–1945 Democratic	Republican	Other	Democratic % of Two-Party Vote	1946–1947 Democratic	Republican	Other	Democratic % of Two-Party Vote
Alabama	—	—	—	—	88.7	11.3	0.0	88.7
Alaska	—	—	—	—	—	—	—	—
Arizona	77.9	21.2	0.9	78.6	60.1	39.9	0.0	60.1
Arkansas	86.0	14.0	0.0	86.0	84.1	15.9	0.0	84.1
California	—	—	—	—	0.0	0.0	100.0	—
California	—	—	—	—	**0.0**	**91.6**	**8.4**	**0.0**
Colorado	47.6	52.4	0.0	47.6	52.1	47.9	0.0	52.1
Connecticut	47.4	50.5	2.2	48.4	40.4	54.4	5.2	42.6
Delaware	49.2	50.5	0.3	49.3	—	—	—	—
Florida	78.9	21.1	0.0	78.9	—	—	—	—
Georgia	—	—	—	—	98.5	0.0	1.5	100.0
Hawaii	—	—	—	—	—	—	—	—
Idaho	52.6	47.4	0.0	52.6	43.6	56.4	0.0	43.6
Illinois	48.9	50.8	0.3	49.1	—	—	—	—
Indiana	48.2	51.0	0.8	48.6	—	—	—	—
Iowa	43.6	56.0	0.4	43.8	42.1	57.4	0.5	42.3
Kansas	32.8	65.7	1.4	33.3	44.0	53.5	2.5	45.1
Kentucky	—	—	—	—	57.2[1]	42.5[1]	0.3[1]	57.4[1]
Louisiana	100.0[1]	0.0	0.0	100.0	—	—	—	—
Maine	29.7	70.3	0.0	29.7	38.7	61.3	0.0	38.7
Maryland	—	—	—	—	54.7	45.3	0.0	54.7
Massachusetts	53.6	45.9	0.4	53.9	45.3	54.1	0.6	45.6
Michigan	44.8	54.7	0.5	45.0	38.7	60.3	1.0	39.1
Minnesota	38.3	61.1	0.6	38.6	39.7	59.0	1.3	40.2
Mississippi	—	—	—	—	97.5[1]	0.0[1]	2.5[1]	100.0[1]
Mississippi	—	—	—	—	**97.5[1]**	**2.5[1]**	**0.0[1]**	**97.5[1]**
Missouri	50.9	49.0	0.1	51.0	—	—	—	—
Montana	43.2	56.4	0.5	43.4	—	—	—	—
Nebraska	23.9	76.1	0.0	23.9	34.5	65.5	0.0	34.5
Nevada	—	—	—	—	57.4	42.6	0.0	57.4
New Hampshire	46.9	53.1	0.0	46.9	36.9	63.1	0.0	36.9
New Jersey	—	—	—	—	41.4	57.1	1.5	42.1
New Mexico	51.8	48.2	0.0	51.8	52.8	47.2	0.0	52.8
New York	—	—	—	—	0.0	56.9	43.1	0.0
New York	—	—	—	—	**43.1**	**56.9**	**0.0**	**43.1**
North Carolina	69.6	30.4	0.0	69.6	—	—	—	—
North Dakota	28.9	52.0	19.1	35.7	31.1	68.9	0.0	31.1
North Dakota	**28.9**	**70.8**	**0.3**	**29.0**	—	—	—	—
Ohio	51.8	48.2	0.0	51.8	48.9	50.6	0.5	49.1
Oklahoma	—	—	—	—	52.5	46.0	1.5	53.3
Oregon	—	—	—	—	30.9	69.1	0.0	30.9
Pennsylvania	—	—	—	—	40.7	58.5	0.8	41.0
Rhode Island	60.6	39.4	0.0	60.6	54.1	45.9	0.0	54.1
South Carolina	—	—	—	—	100.0	0.0	0.0	100.0
South Dakota	34.5	65.5	0.0	34.5	32.8	67.2	0.0	32.8
Tennessee	62.5	36.0	1.5	63.5	65.3	31.9	2.7	67.2
Texas	90.9	9.1	0.0	90.9	91.2	8.8	0.0	91.2
Utah	50.2	49.8	0.0	50.2	—	—	—	—
Vermont	34.1	65.9	0.0	34.1	19.6	80.3	0.1	19.6
Virginia	66.6[1]	0.0[1]	33.4[1]	100.0[1]	—	—	—	—
Virginia	**66.6[1]**	**31.0[1]**	**2.4[1]**	**68.2[1]**	—	—	—	—
Washington	51.5	48.1	0.4	51.7	—	—	—	—
West Virginia	54.4	45.6	0.0	54.4	—	—	—	—
Wisconsin	40.6	52.8	6.5	43.5	39.1	59.8	1.1	39.5
Wyoming	—	—	—	—	52.9	47.1	0.0	52.9

Notes: Main entries are party vote percentage values for candidates who used the sole designation "Democrat" or "Republican" (or their historical antecedents listed in Appendix A) on the ballot. In general, historical antecedents to the Democratic Party were Anti-Federalists, Democratic-Republicans, and Jackson Democrats; historical precursors of the Republican Party were Federalists, National Republicans, and Whigs. Other = candidates who used third-party names only on the ballot or were listed as independent or unidentified. Bold italicized entries in the table are the author's alternative party coding, which is used when a candidate listed a major-party name (Democrat, Republican, or their historical antecedents) on the ballot with other party names or labels. For a more detailed explanation of this alternative coding system, see Tables 1-3 and 5-1. Also see Table 7-8. —indicates that the state had no data, either because the state had no gubernatorial election in that year, no vote data were found for the state in question, or the state had not yet entered the Union. No special gubernatorial elections are included in this table. Odd-numbered year gubernatorial elections were common before 1880 and several states still scheduled governor elections in odd-numbered years after that.

[1] Election held in odd-numbered year.

Sources: Adapted from *American State Governors, 1776–1976*, vol. 1 (1977), *Congressional Quarterly's Guide to U.S. Elections* (1994), ICPSR data sets 0001 and 0075, and independent search for state sources by the author. Party affiliations were obtained from independent search of state sources by the author when the *American State Governors* volume and the *Congressional Quarterly Guide* disagreed.

Table 7-49 Governor Election Results, by State, 1948–1951 (Percentages)

State	1948–1949 Democratic	Republican	Other	Democratic % of Two-Party Vote	1950–1951 Democratic	Republican	Other	Democratic % of Two-Party Vote
Alabama	—	—	—	—	91.1	8.9	0.0	91.1
Alaska	—	—	—	—	—	—	—	—
Arizona	59.2	40.1	0.8	59.6	49.2	50.8	0.0	49.2
Arkansas	89.2	10.8	0.0	89.2	84.1	15.9	0.0	84.1
California	—	—	—	—	35.1	64.9	0.0	35.1
Colorado	66.3	33.7	0.0	66.3	47.2	52.4	0.3	47.4
Connecticut	49.3	49.0	1.7	50.2	47.7	49.7	2.6	49.0
Delaware	53.7	46.3	0.0	53.7	—	—	—	—
Florida	83.4	16.6	0.0	83.4	—	—	—	—
Georgia	—	—	—	—	98.4	0.0	1.6	100.0
Hawaii	—	—	—	—	—	—	—	—
Idaho	—	—	—	—	47.4	52.6	0.0	47.4
Illinois	57.1	42.6	0.3	57.3	—	—	—	—
Indiana	53.6	45.1	1.3	54.3	—	—	—	—
Iowa	43.7	55.7	0.6	44.0	40.5	59.1	0.4	40.7
Iowa	—	—	—	—	*40.6*	*59.1*	*0.3*	*40.7*
Kansas	40.4	57.0	2.6	41.5	44.5	53.8	1.7	45.3
Kentucky	—	—	—	—	54.6[1]	45.4[1]	0.0[1]	54.6[1]
Louisiana	100.0	0.0	0.0	100.0	—	—	—	—
Maine	34.4	65.6	0.0	34.4	39.1	60.5	0.4	39.3
Maine	—	—	—	—	*39.5*	*60.5*	*0.0*	*39.5*
Maryland	—	—	—	—	42.7	57.3	0.0	42.7
Massachusetts	59.0	40.5	0.5	59.3	56.3	43.1	0.6	56.6
Michigan	53.4	45.7	0.9	53.9	49.8	49.7	0.5	50.0
Minnesota	45.1	53.1	1.8	45.9	38.3	60.7	1.0	38.7
Mississippi	—	—	—	—	100.0[1]	0.0[1]	0.0[1]	100.0[1]
Missouri	57.0	42.8	0.3	57.1	—	—	—	—
Montana	55.7	43.9	0.4	56.0	—	—	—	—
Nebraska	39.9	60.1	0.0	39.9	45.1	54.9	0.0	45.1
Nevada	—	—	—	—	42.4	57.6	0.0	42.4
New Hampshire	47.3	52.2	0.5	47.5	43.0	57.0	0.0	43.0
New Jersey	47.1[1]	51.5[1]	1.3[1]	47.8[1]	—	—	—	—
New Mexico	54.7	45.3	0.0	54.7	46.3	53.7	0.0	46.3
New York	—	—	—	—	0.0	53.1	46.9	0.0
New York	—	—	—	—	*42.3*	*53.1*	*4.6*	*44.3*
North Carolina	73.2	26.4	0.4	73.5	—	—	—	—
North Dakota	37.5	61.3	1.2	38.0	33.7	66.3	0.0	33.7
Ohio	53.7	46.3	0.0	53.7	52.6	47.4	0.0	52.6
Oklahoma	—	—	—	—	51.1	48.6	0.3	51.3
Oregon	—	—	—	—	33.9	66.1	0.0	33.9
Pennsylvania	—	—	—	—	48.3	50.7	1.0	48.8
Rhode Island	61.2	38.4	0.4	61.4	59.3	40.7	0.0	59.3
South Carolina	—	—	—	—	100.0	0.0	0.0	100.0
South Dakota	38.9	61.1	0.0	38.9	39.1	60.9	0.0	39.1
Tennessee	66.9	33.1	0.0	66.9	78.1	21.9	0.0	78.1
Texas	84.7	14.7	0.6	85.2	90.2	9.8	0.0	90.2
Utah	45.0	55.0	0.0	45.0	—	—	—	—
Vermont	27.9	71.9	0.2	28.0	25.5	74.5	0.0	25.5
Virginia	70.4[1]	27.4[1]	2.1[1]	72.0[1]	—	—	—	—
Washington	47.2	50.5	2.3	48.3	—	—	—	—
West Virginia	57.1	42.9	0.0	57.1	—	—	—	—
Wisconsin	44.1	54.1	1.8	44.9	46.2	53.2	0.6	46.4
Wyoming	—	—	—	—	43.9	56.1	0.0	43.9

Notes: Main entries are party vote percentage values for candidates who used the sole designation "Democrat" or "Republican" (or their historical antecedents listed in Appendix A) on the ballot. In general, historical antecedents to the Democratic Party were Anti-Federalists, Democratic-Republicans, and Jackson Democrats; historical precursors of the Republican Party were Federalists, National Republicans, and Whigs. Other = candidates who used third-party names only on the ballot or were listed as independent or unidentified. Bold italicized entries in the table are the author's alternative party coding, which is used when a candidate listed a major-party name (Democrat, Republican, or their historical antecedents) on the ballot with other party names or labels. For a more detailed explanation of this alternative coding system, see Tables 1-3 and 5-1. Also see Table 7-8. —indicates that the state had no data, either because the state had no gubernatorial election in that year, no vote data were found for the state in question, or the state had not yet entered the Union. No special gubernatorial elections are included in this table. Odd-numbered year gubernatorial elections were common before 1880 and several states still scheduled governor elections in odd-numbered years after that.

[1] Election held in odd-numbered year.

Sources: Adapted from *American State Governors, 1776–1976*, vol. 1 (1977), *Congressional Quarterly's Guide to U.S. Elections* (1994), *America Votes* (various publication dates), ICPSR data sets 0001 and 0075, and independent search for state sources by the author. Party affiliations were obtained from independent search of state sources by the author when the *American State Governors* volume and the *Congressional Quarterly Guide* disagreed.

Table 7-50 Governor Election Results, by State, 1952–1955 (Percentages)

State	1952–1953				1954–1955			
	Democratic	Republican	Other	Democratic % of Two-Party Vote	Democratic	Republican	Other	Democratic % of Two-Party Vote
Alabama	—	—	—	—	73.4	26.6	0.0	73.4
Alaska	—	—	—	—	—	—	—	—
Arizona	39.8	60.2	0.0	39.8	52.5	47.5	0.0	52.5
Arkansas	87.4	12.6	0.0	87.4	62.1	37.9	0.0	62.1
California	—	—	—	—	43.2	56.8	0.0	43.2
Colorado	42.4	57.1	0.5	42.6	53.6	46.4	0.0	53.6
Connecticut	—	—	—	—	49.5	49.2	1.3	50.2
Connecticut	—	—	—	—	***49.5***	***49.3***	***1.2***	***50.1***
Delaware	47.9	52.1	0.0	47.9	—	—	—	—
Florida	74.8	25.2	0.0	74.8	—	—	—	—
Georgia	—	—	—	—	100.0	0.0	0.0	100.0
Hawaii	—	—	—	—	—	—	—	—
Idaho	—	—	—	—	45.8	54.2	0.0	45.8
Illinois	47.3	52.5	0.2	47.4	—	—	—	—
Indiana	43.6	55.7	0.7	43.9	—	—	—	—
Iowa	47.8	51.9	0.3	47.9	48.3	51.4	0.3	48.5
Iowa	***47.8***	***52.0***	***0.2***	***47.9***	***48.3***	***51.7***	***0.0***	***48.3***
Kansas	41.7	56.3	2.0	42.5	46.0	53.0	1.1	46.5
Kentucky	—	—	—	—	58.0[1]	41.5[1]	0.5[1]	58.3[1]
Louisiana	96.0	4.0	0.0	96.0	—	—	—	—
Maine	33.4	52.1	14.5	39.1	54.5	45.5	0.0	54.5
Maine	***33.4***	***66.6***	***0.0***	***33.4***				
Maryland	—	—	—	—	45.5	54.5	0.0	45.5
Massachusetts	49.3	49.9	0.8	49.7	47.8	51.8	0.4	48.0
Michigan	50.0	49.7	0.4	50.2	55.6	44.1	0.3	55.8
Minnesota	44.0	55.3	0.7	44.3	52.7	46.8	0.5	53.0
Mississippi	—	—	—	—	100.0[1]	0.0[1]	0.0[1]	100.0[1]
Missouri	52.5	47.4	0.1	52.6	—	—	—	—
Montana	49.0	51.0	0.0	49.0	—	—	—	—
Nebraska	38.6	61.4	0.0	38.6	39.7	60.3	0.0	39.7
Nevada	—	—	—	—	46.9	53.1	0.0	46.9
New Hampshire	36.9	63.1	0.0	36.9	44.9	55.1	0.0	44.9
New Jersey	53.2[1]	44.7[1]	2.2[1]	54.3[1]	—	—	—	—
New Mexico	46.2	53.8	0.0	46.2	57.0	43.0	0.0	57.0
New York	—	—	—	—	0.0	49.4	50.6	0.0
New York	—	—	—	—	***49.6***	***49.4***	***1.0***	***50.1***
North Carolina	67.5	32.5	0.0	67.5	—	—	—	—
North Dakota	21.3	78.7	0.0	21.3	35.8	64.2	0.0	35.8
Ohio	55.9	44.1	0.0	55.9	54.1	45.9	0.0	54.1
Oklahoma	—	—	—	—	58.7	41.3	0.0	58.7
Oregon	—	—	—	—	43.1	56.9	0.0	43.1
Pennsylvania	—	—	—	—	53.7	46.2	0.2	53.8
Rhode Island	52.6	47.4	0.0	52.6	57.7	41.7	0.6	58.0
South Carolina	—	—	—	—	100.0	0.0	0.0	100.0
South Dakota	29.8	70.2	0.0	29.8	43.3	56.7	0.0	43.3
Tennessee	79.4	20.6	0.0	79.4	87.2	0.5	12.3	99.4
Texas	0.0	0.0	100.0	—	89.4	10.4	0.2	89.6
Texas	***100.0***	***0.0***	***0.0***	***100.0***	—	—	—	—
Utah	44.9	55.1	0.0	44.9	—	—	—	—
Vermont	39.8	51.9	8.3	43.4	47.7	52.3	0.0	47.7
Vermont	***39.8***	***60.2***	***0.0***	***39.8***	—	—	—	—
Virginia	54.8[1]	44.3[1]	0.9[1]	55.3[1]	—	—	—	—
Washington	47.4	52.6	0.0	47.4	—	—	—	—
West Virginia	51.5	48.5	0.0	51.5	—	—	—	—
Wisconsin	37.3	62.5	0.2	37.4	48.4	51.5	0.1	48.5
Wyoming	—	—	—	—	49.5	50.5	0.0	49.5

Notes: Main entries are party vote percentage values for candidates who used the sole designation "Democrat" or "Republican" (or their historical antecedents listed in Appendix A) on the ballot. In general, historical antecedents to the Democratic Party were Anti-Federalists, Democratic-Republicans, and Jackson Democrats; historical precursors of the Republican Party were Federalists, National Republicans, and Whigs. Other = candidates who used third-party names only on the ballot or were listed as independent or unidentified. Bold italicized entries in the table are the author's alternative party coding, which is used when a candidate listed a major-party name (Democrat, Republican, or their historical antecedents) on the ballot with other party names or labels. For a more detailed explanation of this alternative coding system, see Tables 1-3 and 5-1. Also see Table 7-8. —indicates that the state had no data, either because the state had no gubernatorial election in that year, no vote data were found for the state in question, or the state had not yet entered the Union. No special gubernatorial elections are included in this table. Odd-numbered year gubernatorial elections were common before 1880 and several states still scheduled governor elections in odd-numbered years after that.

[1]Election held in odd-numbered year.

Sources: Adapted from *American State Governors, 1776–1976*, vol. 1 (1977), *Congressional Quarterly's Guide to U.S. Elections* (1994), *America Votes* (various publication dates), ICPSR data sets 0001 and 0075, and independent search for state sources by the author. Party affiliations were obtained from independent search of state sources by the author when the *American State Governors* volume and the *Congressional Quarterly Guide* disagreed.

Table 7-51 Governor Election Results, by State, 1956–1959 (Percentages)

State	1956–1957				1958–1959			
	Democratic	Republican	Other	Democratic % of Two-Party Vote	Democratic	Republican	Other	Democratic % of Two-Party Vote
Alabama	—	—	—	—	88.4	11.2	0.3	88.7
Alaska	—	—	—	—	59.6	39.4	1.0	60.2
Arizona	59.5	40.5	0.0	59.5	44.9	55.1	0.0	44.9
Arkansas	80.6	19.4	0.0	80.6	82.5	17.5	0.0	82.5
California	—	—	—	—	59.7	40.2	0.1	59.8
Colorado	51.3	48.7	0.0	51.3	58.4	41.6	0.0	58.4
Connecticut	—	—	—	—	62.3	37.0	0.7	62.7
Delaware	48.0	52.0	0.0	48.0	—	—	—	—
Florida	73.7	26.3	0.0	73.7	—	—	—	—
Georgia	—	—	—	—	100.0	0.0	0.0	100.0
Hawaii	—	—	—	—	48.7[1]	51.1[1]	0.2[1]	48.8[1]
Idaho	—	—	—	—	49.0	51.0	0.0	49.0
Illinois	49.5	50.3	0.2	49.6	—	—	—	—
Indiana	44.0	55.6	0.4	44.2	—	—	—	—
Iowa	51.2	48.8	0.0	51.2	54.1	45.9	0.0	54.1
Kansas	55.5	42.1	2.4	56.8	56.5	42.5	1.0	57.0
Kentucky	—	—	—	—	60.6[1]	39.4[1]	0.0[1]	60.6[1]
Louisiana	100.0	0.0	0.0	100.0	—	—	—	—
Maine	59.2	40.8	0.0	59.2	52.0	48.0	0.0	52.0
Maryland	—	—	—	—	63.6	36.4	0.0	63.6
Massachusetts	52.8	46.9	0.4	53.0	56.2	43.1	0.7	56.6
Michigan	54.7	45.1	0.2	54.8	53.0	46.6	0.4	53.2
Minnesota	51.4	48.2	0.4	51.6	56.8	42.3	0.9	57.3
Mississippi	—	—	—	—	100.0[1]	0.0[1]	0.0[1]	100.0[1]
Missouri	52.1	47.9	0.0	52.1	—	—	—	—
Montana	48.6	51.4	0.0	48.6	—	—	—	—
Nebraska	40.2	54.3	5.6	42.5	50.2	49.8	0.0	50.2
Nevada	—	—	—	—	59.9	40.1	0.0	59.9
New Hampshire	45.3	54.7	0.0	45.3	48.3	51.7	0.0	48.3
New Jersey	54.6[1]	44.5[1]	1.0[1]	55.1[1]	—	—	—	—
New Mexico	47.8	52.2	0.0	47.8	50.5	49.5	0.0	50.5
New York	—	—	—	—	0.0	54.7	45.3	0.0
New York	—	—	—	—	***44.7***	***54.7***	***0.6***	***45.0***
North Carolina	67.0	33.0	0.0	67.0	—	—	—	—
North Dakota	41.5	58.5	0.0	41.5	46.9	53.1	0.0	46.9
Ohio	44.0	56.0	0.0	44.0	56.9	43.1	0.0	56.9
Oklahoma	—	—	—	—	74.1	20.0	5.9	78.8
Oregon	—	—	—	—	44.7	55.3	0.0	44.7
Pennsylvania	—	—	—	—	50.8	48.9	0.3	51.0
Rhode Island	50.1	49.9	0.0	50.1	49.1	50.9	0.0	49.1
South Carolina	—	—	—	—	100.0	0.0	0.0	100.0
South Dakota	45.6	54.4	0.0	45.6	51.4	48.6	0.0	51.4
Tennessee	—	—	—	—	57.5	8.3	34.2	87.4
Texas	78.4	14.8	6.8	84.1	88.1	11.9	0.0	88.1
Utah	33.4	38.2	28.4	46.7	—	—	—	—
Vermont	42.5	57.5	0.0	42.5	49.7	50.3	0.0	49.7
Virginia	63.2[1]	36.4[1]	0.4[1]	63.4[1]	—	—	—	—
Washington	54.6	45.0	0.4	54.8	—	—	—	—
West Virginia	46.1	53.9	0.0	46.1	—	—	—	—
Wisconsin	48.1	51.9	0.0	48.1	53.6	46.3	0.1	53.7
Wyoming	—	—	—	—	48.9	46.6	4.4	51.2

Notes: Main entries are party vote percentage values for candidates who used the sole designation "Democrat" or "Republican" (or their historical antecedents listed in Appendix A) on the ballot. In general, historical antecedents to the Democratic Party were Anti-Federalists, Democratic-Republicans, and Jackson Democrats; historical precursors of the Republican Party were Federalists, National Republicans, and Whigs. Other = candidates who used third-party names only on the ballot or were listed as independent or unidentified. Bold italicized entries in the table are the author's alternative party coding, which is used when a candidate listed a major-party name (Democrat, Republican, or their historical antecedents) on the ballot with other party names or labels. For a more detailed explanation of this alternative coding system, see Tables 1-3 and 5-1. Also see Table 7-8. —indicates that the state had no data, either because the state had no gubernatorial election in that year, no vote data were found for the state in question, or the state had not yet entered the Union. No special gubernatorial elections are included in this table. Odd-numbered year gubernatorial elections were common before 1880 and several states still scheduled governor elections in odd-numbered years after that.

[1] Election held in odd-numbered year.

Sources: Adapted from *American State Governors, 1776–1976*, vol. 1 (1977), *Congressional Quarterly's Guide to U.S. Elections* (1994), *America Votes* (various publication dates), ICPSR data sets 0001 and 0075, and independent search for state sources by the author. Party affiliations were obtained from independent search of state sources by the author when the *American State Governors* volume and the *Congressional Quarterly Guide* disagreed.

Table 7-52 Governor Election Results, by State, 1960–1963 (Percentages)

State	1960–1961				1962–1963			
	Democratic	Republican	Other	Democratic % of Two-Party Vote	Democratic	Republican	Other	Democratic % of Two-Party Vote
Alabama	—	—	—	—	96.3	0.0	3.7	100.0
Alaska	—	—	—	—	52.3	47.7	0.0	52.3
Arizona	40.7	59.3	0.0	40.7	45.2	54.8	0.0	45.2
Arkansas	69.2	30.8	0.0	69.2	73.3	26.7	0.0	73.3
California	—	—	—	—	51.9	46.8	1.3	52.6
Colorado	—	—	—	—	42.6	56.7	0.7	42.9
Connecticut	—	—	—	—	53.2	46.8	0.0	53.2
Delaware	51.7	48.3	0.0	51.7	—	—	—	—
Florida	59.8	40.2	0.0	59.8	—	—	—	—
Georgia	—	—	—	—	99.9	0.0	0.1	100.0
Hawaii	—	—	—	—	58.3	41.7	0.0	58.3
Idaho	—	—	—	—	45.4	54.6	0.0	45.4
Illinois	55.5	44.3	0.2	55.6	—	—	—	—
Indiana	50.4	49.3	0.3	50.5	—	—	—	—
Iowa	47.9	52.1	0.0	47.9	52.6	47.4	0.0	52.6
Kansas	43.6	55.5	1.0	44.0	45.6	53.4	1.0	46.0
Kentucky	—	—	—	—	50.7[1]	49.3[1]	0.0[1]	50.7[1]
Louisiana	80.5	17.0	2.5	82.6	—	—	—	—
Maine	—	—	—	—	49.9	50.1	0.0	49.9
Maryland	—	—	—	—	55.6	44.4	0.0	55.6
Massachusetts	46.8	52.5	0.7	47.1	49.9	49.7	0.4	50.1
Michigan	50.5	49.2	0.3	50.6	48.4	51.4	0.2	48.5
Minnesota	49.1	50.6	0.4	49.3	49.7	49.7	0.6	50.0
Mississippi	—	—	—	—	61.9[1]	38.1[1]	0.0[1]	61.9[1]
Missouri	58.0	42.0	0.0	58.0	—	—	—	—
Montana	44.9	55.1	0.0	44.9	—	—	—	—
Nebraska	52.0	48.0	0.0	52.0	52.2	47.8	0.0	52.2
Nevada	—	—	—	—	66.8	33.2	0.0	66.8
New Hampshire	44.5	55.5	0.0	44.5	58.9	41.1	0.0	58.9
New Jersey	50.4[1]	48.7[1]	0.9[1]	50.8[1]				
New Mexico	49.7	50.3	0.0	49.7	53.0	47.0	0.0	53.0
New York	—	—	—	—	0.0	53.1	46.9	0.0
New York					***44.0***	***53.1***	***3.0***	***45.3***
North Carolina	54.4	45.5	0.1	54.5	—	—	—	—
North Carolina	***54.5***	***45.5***	***0.0***	***54.5***				
North Dakota	49.4	44.5	6.1	52.6	50.4	49.6	0.0	50.4
Ohio	—	—	—	—	41.1	58.9	0.0	41.1
Oklahoma	—	—	—	—	44.4	55.3	0.3	44.6
Oregon	—	—	—	—	41.6	54.2	4.2	43.4
Pennsylvania	—	—	—	—	44.3	55.4	0.3	44.4
Rhode Island	56.6	43.4	0.0	56.6	49.9	50.1	0.0	49.9
South Carolina	—	—	—	—	100.0	0.0	0.0	100.0
South Dakota	49.3	50.7	0.0	49.3	43.9	56.1	0.0	43.9
Tennessee	—	—	—	—	50.8	16.1	33.1	76.0
Texas	72.8	27.2	0.0	72.8	54.0	45.6	0.5	54.2
Utah	47.3	52.7	0.0	47.3	—	—	—	—
Vermont	43.6	56.4	0.0	43.6	0.0	49.4	50.6	0.0
Vermont					***50.6***	***49.4***	***0.0***	***50.6***
Virginia	63.8[1]	36.1[1]	0.0[1]	63.9[1]	—	—	—	—
Washington	50.3	48.9	0.8	50.7	—	—	—	—
West Virginia	54.0	46.0	0.0	54.0	—	—	—	—
Wisconsin	51.6	48.4	0.0	51.6	50.4	49.4	0.2	50.5
Wyoming	—	—	—	—	45.5	54.5	0.0	45.5

Notes: Main entries are party vote percentage values for candidates who used the sole designation "Democrat" or "Republican" (or their historical antecedents listed in Appendix A) on the ballot. In general, historical antecedents to the Democratic Party were Anti-Federalists, Democratic-Republicans, and Jackson Democrats; historical precursors of the Republican Party were Federalists, National Republicans, and Whigs. Other = candidates who used third-party names only on the ballot or were listed as independent or unidentified. Bold italicized entries in the table are the author's alternative party coding, which is used when a candidate listed a major-party name (Democrat, Republican, or their historical antecedents) on the ballot with other party names or labels. For a more detailed explanation of this alternative coding system, see Tables 1-3 and 5-1. Also see Table 7-8. —indicates that the state had no data, either because the state had no gubernatorial election in that year, no vote data were found for the state in question, or the state had not yet entered the Union. No special gubernatorial elections are included in this table. Odd-numbered year gubernatorial elections were common before 1880 and several states still scheduled governor elections in odd-numbered years after that.

[1]Election held in odd-numbered year.

Sources: Adapted from *American State Governors, 1776–1976*, vol. 1 (1977), *Congressional Quarterly's Guide to U.S. Elections* (1994), *America Votes* (various publication dates), ICPSR data sets 0001 and 0075, and independent search for state sources by the author. Party affiliations were obtained from independent search of state sources by the author when the *American State Governors* volume and the *Congressional Quarterly Guide* disagreed.

Table 7-53 Governor Election Results, by State, 1964–1967 (Percentages)

	1964–1965				1966–1967			
State	Democratic	Republican	Other	Democratic % of Two-Party Vote	Democratic	Republican	Other	Democratic % of Two-Party Vote
Alabama	—	—	—	—	63.4	31.0	5.6	67.2
Alaska	—	—	—	—	48.4	50.0	1.6	49.2
Arizona	53.2	46.8	0.0	53.2	46.2	53.8	0.0	46.2
Arkansas	57.0	43.0	0.0	57.0	45.6	54.4	0.0	45.6
California	—	—	—	—	42.3	57.6	0.2	42.3
Colorado	—	—	—	—	43.5	54.0	2.5	44.6
Connecticut	—	—	—	—	55.7	44.3	0.0	55.7
Delaware	51.4	48.6	0.0	51.4	—	—	—	—
Florida	56.1	41.3	2.6	57.6	44.9	55.1	0.0	44.9
Georgia	—	—	—	—	47.4	47.8	4.8	49.8
Georgia	—	—	—	—	*52.2*	*47.8*	*0.0*	*52.2*
Hawaii	—	—	—	—	51.1	48.9	0.0	51.1
Idaho	—	—	—	—	37.1	41.4	21.5	47.3
Illinois	51.9	48.1	0.0	51.9	—	—	—	—
Indiana	56.2	43.5	0.3	56.4	—	—	—	—
Iowa	68.0	31.3	0.7	68.5	55.3	44.2	0.5	55.6
Kansas	47.1	50.9	2.1	48.1	54.8	43.9	1.2	55.5
Kentucky	—	—	—	—	48.0[1]	51.2[1]	0.8[1]	48.4[1]
Louisiana	60.7	38.5	0.8	61.2	—	—	—	—
Maine	—	—	—	—	53.1	46.9	0.0	53.1
Maryland	—	—	—	—	40.6	49.5	9.9	45.1
Massachusetts	49.3	50.3	0.4	49.5	36.9	62.6	0.5	37.1
Michigan	43.7	55.9	0.4	43.9	39.1	60.5	0.3	39.3
Minnesota	—	—	—	—	46.9	52.6	0.5	47.2
Mississippi	—	—	—	—	70.3[1]	29.7[1]	0.0[1]	70.3[1]
Missouri	62.1	37.9	0.0	62.1	—	—	—	—
Montana	48.7	51.3	0.0	48.7	—	—	—	—
Nebraska	60.0	40.0	0.0	60.0	38.5	61.5	0.0	38.5
Nevada	—	—	—	—	47.8	52.2	0.0	47.8
New Hampshire	66.8	33.2	0.0	66.8	53.9	45.9	0.2	54.0
New Jersey	57.4[1]	41.1[1]	1.5[1]	58.3[1]	—	—	—	—
New Mexico	60.2	39.8	0.0	60.2	48.3	51.7	0.0	48.3
New York	—	—	—	—	38.1	44.6	17.3	46.1
North Carolina	56.6	43.4	0.0	56.6	—	—	—	—
North Dakota	55.7	44.3	0.0	55.7	—	—	—	—
Ohio	—	—	—	—	37.8	62.2	0.0	37.8
Oklahoma	—	—	—	—	43.8	55.7	0.6	44.0
Oregon	—	—	—	—	44.7	55.3	0.1	44.7
Pennsylvania	—	—	—	—	46.1	52.1	1.8	47.0
Rhode Island	38.9	61.1	0.0	38.9	36.7	63.3	0.0	36.7
South Carolina	—	—	—	—	58.2	41.8	0.0	58.2
South Dakota	48.3	51.7	0.0	48.3	42.3	57.7	0.0	42.3
Tennessee	—	—	—	—	81.2	0.0	18.8	100.0
Texas	73.8	26.0	0.2	73.9	72.8	25.8	1.4	73.8
Utah	57.0	43.0	0.0	57.0	—	—	—	—
Vermont	64.9	0.0	35.1	100.0	57.7	42.3	0.0	57.7
Vermont	*64.9*	*35.1*	*0.0*	*64.9*	—	—	—	—
Virginia	47.9[1]	37.7[1]	14.4[1]	55.9[1]	—	—	—	—
Washington	43.9	55.8	0.3	44.0	—	—	—	—
West Virginia	54.9	45.1	0.0	54.9	—	—	—	—
Wisconsin	49.4	50.6	0.0	49.4	46.1	53.5	0.4	46.3
Wyoming	—	—	—	—	45.7	54.3	0.0	45.7

Notes: Main entries are party vote percentage values for candidates who used the sole designation "Democrat" or "Republican" (or their historical antecedents listed in Appendix A) on the ballot. In general, historical antecedents to the Democratic Party were Anti-Federalists, Democratic-Republicans, and Jackson Democrats; historical precursors of the Republican Party were Federalists, National Republicans, and Whigs. Other = candidates who used third-party names only on the ballot or were listed as independent or unidentified. Bold italicized entries in the table are the author's alternative party coding, which is used when a candidate listed a major-party name (Democrat, Republican, or their historical antecedents) on the ballot with other party names or labels. For a more detailed explanation of this alternative coding system, see Tables 1-3 and 5-1. Also see Table 7-8. —indicates that the state had no data, either because the state had no gubernatorial election in that year, no vote data were found for the state in question, or the state had not yet entered the Union. No special gubernatorial elections are included in this table. Odd-numbered year gubernatorial elections were common before 1880 and several states still scheduled governor elections in odd-numbered years after that.

[1] Election held in odd-numbered year.

Sources: Adapted from *American State Governors, 1776–1976*, vol. 1 (1977), *Congressional Quarterly's Guide to U.S. Elections* (1994), *America Votes* (various publication dates), ICPSR data sets 0001 and 0075, and independent search for state sources by the author. Party affiliations were obtained from independent search of state sources by the author when the *American State Governors* volume and the *Congressional Quarterly Guide* disagreed.

Table 7-54 Governor Election Results, by State, 1968–1971 (Percentages)

State	1968–1969				1970–1971			
	Democratic	Republican	Other	Democratic % of Two-Party Vote	Democratic	Republican	Other	Democratic % of Two-Party Vote
Alabama	—	—	—	—	74.5	0.0	25.5	100.0
Alabama	—	—	—	—	*89.2*	*0.0*	*10.8*	*100.0*
Alaska	—	—	—	—	52.4	46.1	1.5	53.2
Arizona	42.2	57.8	0.0	42.2	49.1	50.9	0.0	49.1
Arkansas	47.6	52.4	0.0	47.6	61.7	32.4	5.9	65.6
California	—	—	—	—	45.1	52.8	2.0	46.1
Colorado	—	—	—	—	45.2	52.5	2.3	46.3
Connecticut	—	—	—	—	46.2	53.8	0.0	46.2
Delaware	49.5	50.5	0.0	49.5	—	—	—	—
Florida	—	—	—	—	56.9	43.1	0.0	56.9
Georgia	—	—	—	—	59.3	40.6	0.1	59.3
Hawaii	—	—	—	—	57.6	42.4	0.0	57.6
Idaho	—	—	—	—	52.2	47.8	0.0	52.2
Illinois	48.4	51.2	0.4	48.6	—	—	—	—
Indiana	47.1	52.7	0.2	47.2	—	—	—	—
Iowa	45.9	54.1	0.1	45.9	46.6	51.0	2.4	47.8
Kansas	51.9	47.6	0.5	52.1	54.3	44.7	1.0	54.8
Kentucky	—	—	—	—	50.6[1]	44.3[1]	5.1[1]	53.3[1]
Louisiana	100.0	0.0	0.0	100.0	—	—	—	—
Maine	—	—	—	—	50.1	49.9	0.0	50.1
Maryland	—	—	—	—	65.7	32.3	2.0	67.0
Massachusetts	—	—	—	—	42.8	56.7	0.5	43.0
Michigan	—	—	—	—	48.7	50.4	0.9	49.2
Minnesota	—	—	—	—	54.0	45.5	0.4	54.3
Mississippi	—	—	—	—	77.0[1]	0.0[1]	23.0[1]	100.0[1]
Missouri	60.7	39.3	0.0	60.7	—	—	—	—
Montana	54.1	41.9	4.0	56.4	—	—	—	—
Nebraska	—	—	—	—	53.8	43.8	2.4	55.2
Nevada	—	—	—	—	48.1	43.8	8.1	52.3
New Hampshire	47.5	52.5	0.0	47.5	44.1	46.0	9.9	49.0
New Jersey	38.5[1]	59.7[1]	1.9[1]	39.2[1]	—	—	—	—
New Mexico	49.5	50.5	0.0	49.5	51.3	46.4	2.4	52.5
New York	—	—	—	—	0.0	0.0	100.0	—
New York	—	—	—	—	*40.3*	*52.4*	*7.3*	*43.5*
North Carolina	52.7	47.3	0.0	52.7	—	—	—	—
North Dakota	54.8	43.7	1.5	55.6	—	—	—	—
Ohio	—	—	—	—	54.2	43.4	2.4	55.5
Oklahoma	—	—	—	—	48.4	48.1	3.5	50.2
Oregon	—	—	—	—	44.2	55.6	0.2	44.3
Pennsylvania	—	—	—	—	55.2	41.7	3.1	57.0
Rhode Island	51.0	49.0	0.0	51.0	50.1	49.5	0.4	50.3
South Carolina	—	—	—	—	51.7	45.6	2.7	53.1
South Dakota	42.3	57.7	0.0	42.3	54.8	45.2	0.0	54.8
Tennessee	—	—	—	—	46.0	52.0	2.1	46.9
Texas	57.0	43.0	0.0	57.0	53.6	46.4	0.0	53.6
Utah	68.7	31.3	0.0	68.7	—	—	—	—
Vermont	44.5	55.5	0.0	44.5	43.0	57.0	0.0	43.0
Virginia	45.4[1]	52.5[1]	2.1[1]	46.4[1]	—	—	—	—
Washington	44.3	54.7	1.0	44.7	—	—	—	—
West Virginia	49.1	50.9	0.0	49.1	—	—	—	—
Wisconsin	46.8	52.9	0.3	47.0	54.2	44.9	0.9	54.7
Wyoming	—	—	—	—	37.2	62.8	0.0	37.2

Notes: Main entries are party vote percentage values for candidates who used the sole designation "Democrat" or "Republican" (or their historical antecedents listed in Appendix A) on the ballot. In general, historical antecedents to the Democratic Party were Anti-Federalists, Democratic-Republicans, and Jackson Democrats; historical precursors of the Republican Party were Federalists, National Republicans, and Whigs. Other = candidates who used third-party names only on the ballot or were listed as independent or unidentified. Bold italicized entries in the table are the author's alternative party coding, which is used when a candidate listed a major-party name (Democrat, Republican, or their historical antecedents) on the ballot with other party names or labels. For a more detailed explanation of this alternative coding system, see Tables 1-3 and 5-1. Also see Table 7-8. —indicates that the state had no data, either because the state had no gubernatorial election in that year, no vote data were found for the state in question, or the state had not yet entered the Union. No special gubernatorial elections are included in this table. Odd-numbered year gubernatorial elections were common before 1880 and several states still scheduled governor elections in odd-numbered years after that.

[1]Election held in odd-numbered year.

Sources: Adapted from *American State Governors, 1776–1976*, vol. 1 (1977), *Congressional Quarterly's Guide to U.S. Elections* (1994), *America Votes* (various publication dates), ICPSR data sets 0001 and 0075, and independent search for state sources by the author. Party affiliations were obtained from independent search of state sources by the author when the *American State Governors* volume and the *Congressional Quarterly Guide* disagreed.

Table 7-55 Governor Election Results, by State, 1972–1975 (Percentages)

State	1972–1973				1974–1975			
	Democratic	Republican	Other	Democratic % of Two-Party Vote	Democratic	Republican	Other	Democratic % of Two-Party Vote
Alabama	—	—	—	—	83.2	14.8	2.1	84.9
Alaska	—	—	—	—	47.4	47.7	5.0	49.8
Arizona	—	—	—	—	50.4	49.6	0.0	50.4
Arkansas	75.4	24.6	0.0	75.4	65.6	34.4	0.0	65.6
California	—	—	—	—	50.1	47.3	2.6	51.5
Colorado	—	—	—	—	53.2	45.7	1.1	53.8
Connecticut	—	—	—	—	58.4	39.9	1.7	59.4
Delaware	51.3	47.9	0.8	51.7	—	—	—	—
Florida	—	—	—	—	61.2	38.8	0.0	61.2
Georgia	—	—	—	—	69.1	30.9	0.1	69.1
Hawaii	—	—	—	—	54.6	45.4	0.0	54.6
Idaho	—	—	—	—	70.9	26.5	2.6	72.8
Illinois	50.7	49.0	0.3	50.8	—	—	—	—
Indiana	42.5	56.8	0.8	42.8	—	—	—	—
Iowa	40.3	58.4	1.3	40.8	41.0	58.1	0.9	41.4
Kansas	62.0	37.1	1.0	62.6	49.0	49.5	1.5	49.8
Kentucky	—	—	—	—	62.8[1]	37.2[1]	0.0[1]	62.8[1]
Louisiana	57.2	42.8	0.0	57.2	100.0[1]	0.0[1]	0.0[1]	100.0[1]
Maine	—	—	—	—	36.3	23.1	40.5	61.1
Maryland	—	—	—	—	63.5	36.5	0.0	63.5
Massachusetts	—	—	—	—	53.5	42.3	4.2	55.9
Michigan	—	—	—	—	46.8	51.1	2.2	47.8
Minnesota	—	—	—	—	62.8	29.3	7.9	68.2
Mississippi	—	—	—	—	52.2[1]	45.1[1]	2.7[1]	53.6[1]
Missouri	44.6	55.2	0.2	44.7	—	—	—	—
Montana	54.1	45.9	0.0	54.1	—	—	—	—
Nebraska	—	—	—	—	59.2	35.4	5.4	62.6
Nevada	—	—	—	—	67.4	17.1	15.5	79.8
New Hampshire	39.0	41.4	19.6	48.5	48.8	51.1	0.1	48.8
New Jersey	66.4[1]	32.1[1]	1.5[1]	67.4[1]	—	—	—	—
New Mexico	—	—	—	—	49.9	48.8	1.3	50.6
New York	—	—	—	—	0.0	0.0	100.0	—
New York	—	—	—	—	***57.2***	***41.9***	***0.9***	***57.7***
North Carolina	48.5	51.0	0.6	48.7	—	—	—	—
North Dakota	51.0	49.0	0.0	51.0	—	—	—	—
Ohio	—	—	—	—	48.2	48.6	3.1	49.8
Oklahoma	—	—	—	—	63.9	36.1	0.0	63.9
Oregon	—	—	—	—	57.7	42.1	0.1	57.8
Pennsylvania	—	—	—	—	53.8	45.2	1.0	54.3
Rhode Island	52.6	47.1	0.4	52.8	78.5	21.5	0.0	78.5
South Carolina	—	—	—	—	47.6	50.9	1.6	48.3
South Dakota	60.0	40.0	0.0	60.0	53.6	46.4	0.0	53.6
Tennessee	—	—	—	—	55.4	43.8	0.8	55.9
Texas	47.9	45.0	7.1	51.6	61.4	31.1	7.5	66.4
Utah	69.7	30.3	0.0	69.7	—	—	—	—
Vermont	0.0	43.6	56.4	0.0	0.0	38.0	62.0	0.0
Vermont	***55.2***	***43.6***	***1.2***	***55.9***	***56.6***	***38.0***	***5.4***	***59.8***
Virginia	0.0[1]	50.7[1]	49.3[1]	0.0[1]	—	—	—	—
Washington	42.8	50.8	6.4	45.7	—	—	—	—
West Virginia	45.3	54.7	0.0	45.3	—	—	—	—
Wisconsin	—	—	—	—	53.2	42.1	4.8	55.8
Wyoming	—	—	—	—	55.9	44.1	0.0	55.9

Notes: Main entries are party vote percentage values for candidates who used the sole designation "Democrat" or "Republican" (or their historical antecedents listed in Appendix A) on the ballot. In general, historical antecedents to the Democratic Party were Anti-Federalists, Democratic-Republicans, and Jackson Democrats; historical precursors of the Republican Party were Federalists, National Republicans, and Whigs. Other = candidates who used third-party names only on the ballot or were listed as independent or unidentified. Bold italicized entries in the table are the author's alternative party coding, which is used when a candidate listed a major-party name (Democrat, Republican, or their historical antecedents) on the ballot with other party names or labels. For a more detailed explanation of this alternative coding system, see Tables 1-3 and 5-1. Also see Table 7-8. —indicates that the state had no data, either because the state had no gubernatorial election in that year, no vote data were found for the state in question, or the state had not yet entered the Union. No special gubernatorial elections are included in this table. Odd-numbered year gubernatorial elections were common before 1880 and several states still scheduled governor elections in odd-numbered years after that.

[1]Election held in odd-numbered year.

Sources: Adapted from *American State Governors, 1776–1976*, vol. 1 (1977), *Congressional Quarterly's Guide to U.S. Elections* (1994), *America Votes* (various publication dates), ICPSR data sets 0001 and 0075, and independent search for state sources by the author. Party affiliations were obtained from independent search of state sources by the author when the *American State Governors* volume and the *Congressional Quarterly Guide* disagreed.

Table 7-56 Governor Election Results, by State, 1976–1979 (Percentages)

State	1976–1977				1978–1979			
	Democratic	Republican	Other	Democratic % of Two-Party Vote	Democratic	Republican	Other	Democratic % of Two-Party Vote
Alabama	—	—	—	—	72.6	25.9	1.5	73.7
Alaska	—	—	—	—	20.2	39.1	40.7	34.1
Arizona	—	—	—	—	52.5	44.8	2.8	54.0
Arkansas	83.2	16.7	0.1	83.3	63.4	36.6	0.0	63.4
California	—	—	—	—	56.0	36.5	7.5	60.6
Colorado	—	—	—	—	58.7	38.5	2.7	60.4
Connecticut	—	—	—	—	59.1	40.7	0.1	59.2
Delaware	42.5	56.9	0.7	42.8	—	—	—	—
Florida	—	—	—	—	55.6	44.4	0.0	55.6
Georgia	—	—	—	—	80.6	19.3	0.1	80.7
Hawaii	—	—	—	—	54.5	44.3	1.3	55.2
Idaho	—	—	—	—	58.8	39.6	1.7	59.8
Illinois	34.7	64.7	0.6	34.9	40.1	59.0	0.9	40.5
Indiana	42.6	56.8	0.5	42.9	—	—	—	—
Iowa	—	—	—	—	41.0	58.3	0.7	41.3
Kansas	—	—	—	—	49.4	47.3	3.3	51.1
Kentucky	—	—	—	—	59.4[1]	40.6[1]	0.0[1]	59.4[1]
Louisiana	—	—	—	—	49.7[1]	50.3[1]	0.0[1]	49.7[1]
Maine	—	—	—	—	47.7	34.3	18.1	58.2
Maryland	—	—	—	—	71.0	29.0	0.0	71.0
Massachusetts	—	—	—	—	52.5	47.2	0.3	52.7
Michigan	—	—	—	—	43.2	56.8	0.1	43.2
Minnesota	—	—	—	—	45.3	52.3	2.4	46.4
Mississippi	—	—	—	—	61.1[1]	38.9[1]	0.0[1]	61.1[1]
Missouri	50.2	49.6	0.2	50.3	—	—	—	—
Montana	61.7	36.6	1.7	62.8	—	—	—	—
Nebraska	—	—	—	—	44.0	55.9	0.0	44.0
Nevada	—	—	—	—	39.7	56.2	4.2	41.4
New Hampshire	42.3	57.7	0.0	42.3	49.4	45.4	5.2	52.1
New Jersey	55.7[1]	41.8[1]	2.5[1]	57.1[1]	—	—	—	—
New Mexico	—	—	—	—	50.5	49.4	0.1	50.6
New York	—	—	—	—	0.0	0.0	100.0	—
New York	—	—	—	—	***50.9***	***45.2***	***3.8***	***53.0***
North Carolina	65.0	33.9	1.1	65.7	—	—	—	—
North Dakota	51.6	46.5	1.9	52.6	—	—	—	—
Ohio	—	—	—	—	47.6	49.3	3.0	49.1
Oklahoma	—	—	—	—	51.7	47.2	1.0	52.3
Oregon	—	—	—	—	44.9	54.7	0.4	45.1
Pennsylvania	—	—	—	—	46.4	52.5	1.0	46.9
Rhode Island	54.8	44.7	0.5	55.1	62.8	30.7	6.5	67.1
South Carolina	—	—	—	—	61.4	37.8	0.9	61.9
South Dakota	—	—	—	—	43.4	56.6	0.0	43.4
Tennessee	—	—	—	—	44.0	55.6	0.4	44.2
Texas	—	—	—	—	49.2	50.0	0.8	49.6
Utah	52.0	46.0	2.0	53.1	—	—	—	—
Vermont	40.5	53.4	6.1	43.1	34.1	62.8	3.1	35.2
Virginia	43.3[1]	55.9[1]	0.8[1]	43.6[1]	—	—	—	—
Washington	53.1	44.4	2.4	54.5	—	—	—	—
West Virginia	66.2	33.8	0.0	66.2	—	—	—	—
Wisconsin	—	—	—	—	44.9	54.4	0.7	45.2
Wyoming	—	—	—	—	50.9	49.1	0.0	50.9

Notes: Main entries are party vote percentage values for candidates who used the sole designation "Democrat" or "Republican" (or their historical antecedents listed in Appendix A) on the ballot. In general, historical antecedents to the Democratic Party were Anti-Federalists, Democratic-Republicans, and Jackson Democrats; historical precursors of the Republican Party were Federalists, National Republicans, and Whigs. Other = candidates who used third-party names only on the ballot or were listed as independent or unidentified. Bold italicized entries in the table are the author's alternative party coding, which is used when a candidate listed a major-party name (Democrat, Republican, or their historical antecedents) on the ballot with other party names or labels. For a more detailed explanation of this alternative coding system, see Tables 1-3 and 5-1. Also see Table 7-8. —indicates that the state had no data, either because the state had no gubernatorial election in that year, no vote data were found for the state in question, or the state had not yet entered the Union. No special gubernatorial elections are included in this table. Odd-numbered year gubernatorial elections were common before 1880 and several states still scheduled governor elections in odd-numbered years after that.

[1] Election held in odd-numbered year.

Sources: Adapted from *Congressional Quarterly's Guide to U.S. Elections* (1994), *America Votes* (various publication dates), and independent search for state sources by the author.

Table 7-57 Governor Election Results, by State, 1980–1983 (Percentages)

State	1980–1981				1982–1983			
	Democratic	Republican	Other	Democratic % of Two-Party Vote	Democratic	Republican	Other	Democratic % of Two-Party Vote
Alabama	—	—	—	—	57.6	39.1	3.3	59.6
Alaska	—	—	—	—	46.1	37.1	16.8	55.4
Arizona	—	—	—	—	62.5	32.5	5.1	65.8
Arkansas	48.1	51.9	0.0	48.1	54.7	45.3	0.0	54.7
California	—	—	—	—	48.1	49.3	2.6	49.4
Colorado	—	—	—	—	65.7	31.7	2.7	67.5
Connecticut	—	—	—	—	53.3	45.9	0.8	53.7
Delaware	28.5	70.6	0.8	28.8	—	—	—	—
Florida	—	—	—	—	64.7	35.3	0.0	64.7
Georgia	—	—	—	—	62.8	37.2	0.0	62.8
Hawaii	—	—	—	—	45.2	26.1	28.6	63.4
Hawaii	—	—	—	—	*73.9*	*26.1*	*0.0*	*73.9*
Idaho	—	—	—	—	50.6	49.4	0.0	50.6
Illinois	—	—	—	—	49.3	49.4	1.3	49.9
Indiana	41.9	57.7	0.4	42.1	—	—	—	—
Iowa	—	—	—	—	46.5	52.8	0.6	46.8
Kansas	—	—	—	—	53.2	44.5	2.4	54.5
Kentucky	—	—	—	—	54.5[1]	44.1[1]	1.4[1]	55.3[1]
Louisiana	—	—	—	—	62.4[1]	36.3[1]	1.3[1]	63.2[1]
Maine	—	—	—	—	61.1	37.6	1.4	61.9
Maryland	—	—	—	—	62.0	38.0	0.0	62.0
Massachusetts	—	—	—	—	59.5	36.6	4.0	61.9
Michigan	—	—	—	—	51.4	45.1	3.6	53.3
Minnesota	—	—	—	—	58.6	40.0	1.4	59.4
Mississippi	—	—	—	—	55.1[1]	38.9[1]	6.0[1]	58.6[1]
Missouri	47.0	52.6	0.3	47.2	—	—	—	—
Montana	55.4	44.6	0.0	55.4	—	—	—	—
Nebraska	—	—	—	—	50.6	49.3	0.1	50.7
Nevada	—	—	—	—	53.4	41.8	4.8	56.1
New Hampshire	59.0	40.7	0.4	59.2	46.8	51.4	1.7	47.6
New Jersey	49.4[1]	49.5[1]	1.2[1]	50.0[1]	—	—	—	—
New Mexico	—	—	—	—	53.0	47.0	0.0	53.0
New York	—	—	—	—	0.0	0.0	100.0	—
New York	—	—	—	—	*50.9*	*47.5*	*1.6*	*51.7*
North Carolina	61.9	37.4	0.7	62.3	—	—	—	—
North Dakota	46.4	53.6	0.0	46.4	—	—	—	—
Ohio	—	—	—	—	59.0	38.8	2.1	60.3
Oklahoma	—	—	—	—	62.1	37.6	0.3	62.3
Oregon	—	—	—	—	35.9	61.4	2.7	36.9
Pennsylvania	—	—	—	—	48.1	50.8	1.1	48.6
Rhode Island	73.7	26.3	0.0	73.7	73.3	23.6	3.1	75.6
South Carolina	—	—	—	—	69.8	30.2	0.0	69.8
South Dakota	—	—	—	—	29.1	70.9	0.0	29.1
Tennessee	—	—	—	—	40.4	59.6	0.0	40.4
Texas	—	—	—	—	53.2	45.9	0.9	53.7
Utah	55.2	44.4	0.4	55.4	—	—	—	—
Vermont	36.8	58.6	4.7	38.6	44.0	55.0	1.0	44.4
Virginia	53.5[1]	46.4[1]	0.1[1]	53.6[1]	—	—	—	—
Washington	43.3	56.7	0.0	43.3	—	—	—	—
West Virginia	54.1	45.4	0.4	54.4	—	—	—	—
Wisconsin	—	—	—	—	56.7	41.9	1.3	57.5
Wyoming	—	—	—	—	63.1	36.9	0.0	63.1

Notes: Main entries are party vote percentage values for candidates who used the sole designation "Democrat" or "Republican" (or their historical antecedents listed in Appendix A) on the ballot. In general, historical antecedents to the Democratic Party were Anti-Federalists, Democratic-Republicans, and Jackson Democrats; historical precursors of the Republican Party were Federalists, National Republicans, and Whigs. Other = candidates who used third-party names only on the ballot or were listed as independent or unidentified. Bold italicized entries in the table are the author's alternative party coding, which is used when a candidate listed a major-party name (Democrat, Republican, or their historical antecedents) on the ballot with other party names or labels. For a more detailed explanation of this alternative coding system, see Tables 1-3 and 5-1. Also see Table 7-8. —indicates that the state had no data, either because the state had no gubernatorial election in that year, no vote data were found for the state in question, or the state had not yet entered the Union. No special gubernatorial elections are included in this table. Odd-numbered year gubernatorial elections were common before 1880 and several states still scheduled governor elections in odd-numbered years after that.

[1] Election held in odd-numbered year.

Sources: Adapted from *Congressional Quarterly's Guide to U.S. Elections* (1994), *America Votes* (various publication dates), and independent search for state sources by the author.

Table 7-58 Governor Election Results, by State, 1984–1987 (Percentages)

| | 1984–1985 | | | | 1986–1987 | | | |
State	Democratic	Republican	Other	Democratic % of Two-Party Vote	Democratic	Republican	Other	Democratic % of Two-Party Vote
Alabama	—	—	—	—	43.5	56.3	0.2	43.6
Alaska	—	—	—	—	47.3	42.6	10.1	52.6
Arizona	—	—	—	—	34.5	39.7	25.9	46.5
Arkansas	62.6	37.4	0.0	62.6	63.9	36.1	0.0	63.9
California	—	—	—	—	37.4	60.5	2.1	38.2
Colorado	—	—	—	—	58.2	41.0	0.8	58.7
Connecticut	—	—	—	—	57.9	41.1	1.0	58.5
Delaware	44.5	55.5	0.0	44.5	—	—	—	—
Florida	—	—	—	—	45.4	54.6	0.0	45.4
Georgia	—	—	—	—	70.5	29.5	0.0	70.5
Hawaii	—	—	—	—	52.0	48.0	0.0	52.0
Idaho	—	—	—	—	49.9	49.0	1.1	50.5
Illinois	—	—	—	—	6.6	52.7	40.7	11.2
Indiana	47.2	52.2	0.7	47.5	—	—	—	—
Iowa	—	—	—	—	48.0	51.9	0.1	48.0
Kansas	—	—	—	—	48.1	51.9	0.0	48.1
Kentucky	—	—	—	—	64.9[1]	35.1[1]	0.0[1]	64.9[1]
Louisiana	—	—	—	—	—	—	—	—
Maine	—	—	—	—	30.2	39.9	29.9	43.1
Maryland	—	—	—	—	82.4	17.6	0.0	82.4
Massachusetts	—	—	—	—	68.7	31.2	0.1	68.8
Michigan	—	—	—	—	68.1	31.4	0.5	68.4
Minnesota	—	—	—	—	55.8	42.9	1.4	56.6
Mississippi	—	—	—	—	53.4[1]	46.6[1]	0.0[1]	53.4[1]
Missouri	43.3	56.7	0.0	43.3	—	—	—	—
Montana	70.3	26.4	3.3	72.7	—	—	—	—
Nebraska	—	—	—	—	47.0	52.9	0.2	47.1
Nevada	—	—	—	—	71.9	25.0	3.1	74.2
New Hampshire	33.1	66.8	0.1	33.1	46.3	53.7	0.1	46.3
New Jersey	29.3[1]	69.6[1]	1.1[1]	29.6[1]	—	—	—	—
New Mexico	—	—	—	—	47.0	53.0	0.0	47.0
New York	—	—	—	—	0.0	0.0	100.0	—
New York	—	—	—	—	*64.6*	*31.8*	*3.6*	*67.1*
North Carolina	45.4	54.3	0.3	45.6	—	—	—	—
North Dakota	55.3	44.7	0.0	55.3	—	—	—	—
Ohio	—	—	—	—	60.6	39.4	0.0	60.6
Oklahoma	—	—	—	—	44.5	47.5	8.0	48.4
Oregon	—	—	—	—	51.9	47.8	0.3	52.0
Pennsylvania	—	—	—	—	50.7	48.3	1.0	51.2
Rhode Island	40.0	60.0	0.0	40.0	32.4	64.7	2.9	33.4
South Carolina	—	—	—	—	47.9	51.0	1.0	48.4
South Dakota	—	—	—	—	48.2	51.8	0.0	48.2
Tennessee	—	—	—	—	54.3	45.7	0.0	54.3
Texas	—	—	—	—	46.0	52.7	1.3	46.6
Utah	43.8	55.9	0.3	43.9	—	—	—	—
Vermont	50.0	48.5	1.5	50.8	47.0	38.2	14.8	55.1
Virginia	55.2[1]	44.8[1]	0.0[1]	55.2[1]	—	—	—	—
Washington	53.3	46.7	0.0	53.3	—	—	—	—
West Virginia	46.7	53.3	0.0	46.7	—	—	—	—
Wisconsin	—	—	—	—	46.2	52.7	1.1	46.7
Wyoming	—	—	—	—	54.0	46.0	0.0	54.0

Notes: Main entries are party vote percentage values for candidates who used the sole designation "Democrat" or "Republican" (or their historical antecedents listed in Appendix A) on the ballot. In general, historical antecedents to the Democratic Party were Anti-Federalists, Democratic-Republicans, and Jackson Democrats; historical precursors of the Republican Party were Federalists, National Republicans, and Whigs. Other = candidates who used third-party names only on the ballot or were listed as independent or unidentified. Bold italicized entries in the table are the author's alternative party coding, which is used when a candidate listed a major-party name (Democrat, Republican, or their historical antecedents) on the ballot with other party names or labels. For a more detailed explanation of this alternative coding system, see Tables 1-3 and 5-1. Also see Table 7-8. —indicates that the state had no data, either because the state had no gubernatorial election in that year, no vote data were found for the state in question, or the state had not yet entered the Union. No special gubernatorial elections are included in this table. Odd-numbered year gubernatorial elections were common before 1880 and several states still scheduled governor elections in odd-numbered years after that.

[1] Election held in odd-numbered year.

Sources: Adapted from *Congressional Quarterly's Guide to U.S. Elections* (1994), *America Votes* (various publication dates), and independent search for state sources by the author.

Table 7-59 Governor Election Results, by State, 1988–1991 (Percentages)

State	1988–1989				1990–1991			
	Democratic	Republican	Other	Democratic % of Two-Party Vote	Democratic	Republican	Other	Democratic % of Two-Party Vote
Alabama	—	—	—	—	47.9	52.1	0.1	47.9
Alaska	—	—	—	—	30.9	26.2	42.9	54.1
Arizona	—	—	—	—	49.2	49.6	1.2	49.8
Arkansas	—	—	—	—	57.5	42.5	0.0	57.5
California	—	—	—	—	45.8	49.2	5.0	48.2
Colorado	—	—	—	—	61.9	35.4	2.7	63.6
Connecticut	—	—	—	—	20.7	37.5	41.8	35.6
Delaware	29.3	70.7	0.0	29.3	—	—	—	—
Florida	—	—	—	—	56.5	43.5	0.0	56.5
Georgia	—	—	—	—	52.9	44.5	2.6	54.3
Hawaii	—	—	—	—	59.8	38.6	1.6	60.8
Idaho	—	—	—	—	68.2	31.8	0.0	68.2
Illinois	—	—	—	—	48.2	50.7	1.1	48.7
Indiana	53.2	46.8	0.0	53.2	—	—	—	—
Iowa	—	—	—	—	38.9	60.6	0.5	39.1
Kansas	—	—	—	—	48.6	42.6	8.8	53.3
Kentucky	—	—	—	—	64.7[1]	35.3[1]	0.0[1]	64.7[1]
Louisiana	—	—	—	—	61.2[1]	38.8[1]	0.0[1]	61.2[1]
Maine	—	—	—	—	44.0	46.7	9.3	48.6
Maryland	—	—	—	—	59.8	40.2	0.0	59.8
Massachusetts	—	—	—	—	46.9	50.2	2.9	48.3
Michigan	—	—	—	—	49.1	49.8	1.2	49.7
Minnesota	—	—	—	—	46.3	49.6	4.1	48.3
Mississippi	—	—	—	—	47.6[1]	50.8[1]	1.6[1]	48.4[1]
Missouri	34.8	64.2	1.0	35.1	—	—	—	—
Montana	46.1	51.9	1.9	47.0	—	—	—	—
Nebraska	—	—	—	—	49.9	49.2	0.9	50.3
Nevada	—	—	—	—	64.8	29.9	5.3	68.5
New Hampshire	39.0	60.4	0.5	39.2	34.6	60.2	5.2	36.4
New Jersey	61.2[1]	37.2[1]	1.6[1]	62.2[1]	—	—	—	—
New Mexico	—	—	—	—	54.6	45.2	0.2	54.7
New York	—	—	—	—	0.0	21.3	78.7	0.0
New York	—	—	—	—	***53.2***	***21.3***	***25.5***	***71.4***
North Carolina	43.9	56.1	0.0	43.9	—	—	—	—
North Dakota	59.9	40.1	0.0	59.9	—	—	—	—
Ohio	—	—	—	—	44.3	55.7	0.0	44.3
Oklahoma	—	—	—	—	57.4	32.7	9.9	63.7
Oregon	—	—	—	—	45.7	40.0	14.3	53.4
Pennsylvania	—	—	—	—	67.7	32.3	0.0	67.7
Rhode Island	49.2	50.8	0.0	49.2	74.2	25.8	0.0	74.2
South Carolina	—	—	—	—	27.9	69.5	2.6	28.6
South Dakota	—	—	—	—	41.1	58.9	0.0	41.1
Tennessee	—	—	—	—	60.8	36.6	2.6	62.4
Texas	—	—	—	—	49.5	46.9	3.6	51.3
Utah	38.4	40.1	21.5	48.9	—	—	—	—
Vermont	55.4	43.3	1.3	56.1	46.0	51.8	2.2	47.1
Virginia	50.1[1]	49.8[1]	0.1[1]	50.2[1]	—	—	—	—
Washington	62.2	37.8	0.0	62.2	—	—	—	—
West Virginia	58.9	41.1	0.0	58.9	—	—	—	—
Wisconsin	—	—	—	—	41.8	58.2	0.1	41.8
Wyoming	—	—	—	—	65.4	34.6	0.0	65.4

Notes: Main entries are party vote percentage values for candidates who used the sole designation "Democrat" or "Republican" (or their historical antecedents listed in Appendix A) on the ballot. In general, historical antecedents to the Democratic Party were Anti-Federalists, Democratic-Republicans, and Jackson Democrats; historical precursors of the Republican Party were Federalists, National Republicans, and Whigs. Other = candidates who used third-party names only on the ballot or were listed as independent or unidentified. Bold italicized entries in the table are the author's alternative party coding, which is used when a candidate listed a major-party name (Democrat, Republican, or their historical antecedents) on the ballot with other party names or labels. For a more detailed explanation of this alternative coding system, see Tables 1-3 and 5-1. Also see Table 7-8. —indicates that the state had no data, either because the state had no gubernatorial election in that year, no vote data were found for the state in question, or the state had not yet entered the Union. No special gubernatorial elections are included in this table. Odd-numbered year gubernatorial elections were common before 1880 and several states still scheduled governor elections in odd-numbered years after that.

[1] Election held in odd-numbered year.

Sources: Adapted from *Congressional Quarterly's Guide to U.S. Elections* (1994), *America Votes* (various publication dates), and independent search for state sources by the author.

Table 7-60 Governor Election Results, by State, 1992–1995 (Percentages)

State	1992–1993 Democratic	1992–1993 Republican	1992–1993 Other	1992–1993 Democratic % of Two-Party Vote	1994–1995 Democratic	1994–1995 Republican	1994–1995 Other	1994–1995 Democratic % of Two-Party Vote
Alabama	—	—	—	—	49.4	50.3	0.2	49.6
Alaska	—	—	—	—	41.1	40.8	18.1	50.2
Arizona	—	—	—	—	44.3	52.5	3.1	45.8
Arkansas	—	—	—	—	59.8	40.2	0.0	59.8
California	—	—	—	—	40.6	55.2	4.2	42.4
Colorado	—	—	—	—	55.5	38.7	5.8	58.9
Connecticut	—	—	—	—	32.7	36.2	31.1	47.5
Delaware	64.7	32.7	2.5	66.4	—	—	—	—
Florida	—	—	—	—	50.8	49.2	0.0	50.8
Georgia	—	—	—	—	51.1	48.9	0.0	51.1
Hawaii	—	—	—	—	36.6	29.2	34.2	55.6
Idaho	—	—	—	—	43.9	52.3	3.8	45.6
Illinois	—	—	—	—	34.4	63.9	1.7	35.0
Indiana	62.0	36.9	1.1	62.7	—	—	—	—
Iowa	—	—	—	—	41.6	56.8	1.6	42.3
Kansas	—	—	—	—	35.9	64.1	0.0	35.9
Kentucky	—	—	—	—	50.9[1]	48.7[1]	0.4[1]	51.1[1]
Louisiana	—	—	—	—	36.5[1]	63.5[1]	0.0[1]	36.5[1]
Maine	—	—	—	—	33.8	23.1	43.1	59.4
Maryland	—	—	—	—	50.2	49.8	0.0	50.2
Massachusetts	—	—	—	—	28.3	70.9	0.9	28.5
Michigan	—	—	—	—	38.5	61.5	0.1	38.5
Minnesota	—	—	—	—	33.4	62.0	4.7	35.0
Mississippi	—	—	—	—	44.4[1]	55.6[1]	0.0[1]	44.4[1]
Missouri	58.7	41.3	0.0	58.7	—	—	—	—
Montana	48.7	51.3	0.0	48.7	—	—	—	—
Nebraska	—	—	—	—	73.0	25.6	1.4	74.1
Nevada	—	—	—	—	52.7	41.3	6.0	56.0
New Hampshire	40.0	56.0	4.0	41.6	25.6	69.9	4.5	26.8
New Jersey	48.3[1]	49.3[1]	2.4[1]	49.5[1]	—	—	—	—
New Mexico	—	—	—	—	39.9	49.8	10.3	44.5
New York	—	—	—	—	0.0	0.0	100.0	—
New York	—	—	—	—	*45.4*	*48.7*	*5.9*	*48.2*
North Carolina	52.7	43.2	4.1	55.0	—	—	—	—
North Dakota	40.6	57.9	1.5	41.3	—	—	—	—
Ohio	—	—	—	—	25.0	71.8	3.3	25.8
Oklahoma	—	—	—	—	29.6	46.9	23.5	38.7
Oregon	—	—	—	—	50.9	42.4	6.6	54.6
Pennsylvania	—	—	—	—	39.9	45.4	14.7	46.8
Rhode Island	61.5	34.3	4.2	64.2	43.5	47.4	9.1	47.9
South Carolina	—	—	—	—	47.9	50.4	1.7	48.7
South Dakota	—	—	—	—	40.5	55.4	4.1	42.3
Tennessee	—	—	—	—	44.7	54.3	1.1	45.1
Texas	—	—	—	—	45.9	53.5	0.6	46.2
Utah	23.2	42.2	34.6	35.5	—	—	—	—
Vermont	74.7	23.0	2.2	76.4	68.7	19.0	12.3	78.3
Virginia	40.9[1]	58.3[1]	0.8[1]	41.2[1]	—	—	—	—
Washington	52.2	47.8	0.0	52.2	—	—	—	—
West Virginia	56.0	36.6	7.4	60.5	—	—	—	—
Wisconsin	—	—	—	—	30.9	67.2	1.9	31.5
Wyoming	—	—	—	—	40.2	58.7	1.1	40.6

Notes: Main entries are party vote percentage values for candidates who used the sole designation "Democrat" or "Republican" (or their historical antecedents listed in Appendix A) on the ballot. In general, historical antecedents to the Democratic Party were Anti-Federalists, Democratic-Republicans, and Jackson Democrats; historical precursors of the Republican Party were Federalists, National Republicans, and Whigs. Other = candidates who used third-party names only on the ballot or were listed as independent or unidentified. Bold italicized entries in the table are the author's alternative party coding, which is used when a candidate listed a major-party name (Democrat, Republican, or their historical antecedents) on the ballot with other party names or labels. For a more detailed explanation of this alternative coding system, see Tables 1-3 and 5-1. Also see Table 7-8. —indicates that the state had no data, either because the state had no gubernatorial election in that year, no vote data were found for the state in question, or the state had not yet entered the Union. No special gubernatorial elections are included in this table. Odd-numbered year gubernatorial elections were common before 1880 and several states still scheduled governor elections in odd-numbered years after that.

[1] Election held in odd-numbered year.

Sources: Adapted from *Congressional Quarterly's Guide to U.S. Elections* (1994), *America Votes* (various publication dates), and independent search for state sources by the author.

Table 7-61 Governor Election Results, by State, 1996–1999 (Percentages)

State	1996–1997				1998–1999			
	Democratic	Republican	Other	Democratic % of Two-Party Vote	Democratic	Republican	Other	Democratic % of Two-Party Vote
Alabama	—	—	—	—	57.7	42.1	0.2	57.8
Alaska	—	—	—	—	51.3	17.9	30.9	74.2
Arizona	—	—	—	—	35.5	60.9	3.5	36.8
Arkansas	—	—	—	—	38.7	59.8	1.6	39.3
California	—	—	—	—	58.0	38.4	3.7	60.2
Colorado	—	—	—	—	48.4	49.1	2.5	49.7
Connecticut	—	—	—	—	35.4	62.9	1.7	36.0
Delaware	69.5	30.5	0.0	69.5	—	—	—	—
Florida	—	—	—	—	44.7	55.3	0.0	44.7
Georgia	—	—	—	—	52.5	44.1	3.4	54.4
Hawaii	—	—	—	—	50.1	48.8	1.1	50.7
Idaho	—	—	—	—	29.1	67.7	3.2	30.0
Illinois	—	—	—	—	47.5	51.0	1.5	48.2
Indiana	51.5	46.8	1.7	52.4	—	—	—	—
Iowa	—	—	—	—	52.3	46.5	1.2	52.9
Kansas	—	—	—	—	22.7	73.4	4.0	23.6
Kentucky	—	—	—	—	61.0[1]	37.8[1]	1.2[1]	61.8[1]
Louisiana	—	—	—	—	29.5[1]	62.2[1]	8.3[1]	32.2[1]
Maine	—	—	—	—	12.0	18.9	69.1	38.8
Maryland	—	—	—	—	55.2	44.8	0.0	55.2
Massachusetts	—	—	—	—	47.4	50.8	1.8	48.3
Michigan	—	—	—	—	37.8	62.2	0.0	37.8
Minnesota	—	—	—	—	28.1	34.3	37.6	45.0
Mississippi	—	—	—	—	49.6[1]	48.5[1]	1.9[1]	50.6[1]
Missouri	57.2	40.4	2.4	58.6	—	—	—	—
Montana	20.8	79.2	0.0	20.8	—	—	—	—
Nebraska	—	—	—	—	46.0	53.9	0.1	46.0
Nevada	—	—	—	—	42.0	51.6	6.3	44.9
New Hampshire	57.2	39.5	3.3	59.1	66.1	30.9	3.0	68.2
New Jersey	45.8[1]	46.9[1]	7.3[1]	49.4[1]	—	—	—	—
New Mexico	—	—	—	—	45.5	54.5	0.0	45.5
New York	—	—	—	—	33.2	54.3	12.5	37.9
North Carolina	56.0	42.8	1.3	56.7	—	—	—	—
North Dakota	33.8	66.2	0.0	33.8	—	—	—	—
Ohio	—	—	—	—	44.7	50.0	5.3	47.2
Oklahoma	—	—	—	—	40.9	57.9	1.2	41.4
Oregon	—	—	—	—	64.4	30.0	5.6	68.2
Pennsylvania	—	—	—	—	31.0	57.4	11.6	35.1
Rhode Island	—	—	—	—	42.1	51.0	6.9	45.3
South Carolina	—	—	—	—	53.2	45.2	1.6	54.1
South Dakota	—	—	—	—	32.9	64.0	3.1	33.9
Tennessee	—	—	—	—	29.5	68.6	1.9	30.0
Texas	—	—	—	—	31.2	68.2	0.6	31.4
Utah	23.3	75.0	1.7	23.7	—	—	—	—
Vermont	70.5	22.4	7.1	75.9	55.7	41.1	3.2	57.5
Virginia	42.6[1]	55.8[1]	1.6[1]	43.3[1]	—	—	—	—
Washington	58.0	42.0	0.0	58.0	—	—	—	—
West Virginia	45.8	51.6	2.6	47.0	—	—	—	—
Wisconsin	—	—	—	—	38.7	59.7	1.6	39.3
Wyoming	—	—	—	—	40.5	55.6	3.9	42.1

Notes: Main entries are party vote percentage values for candidates who used the sole designation "Democrat" or "Republican" (or their historical antecedents listed in Appendix A) on the ballot. In general, historical antecedents to the Democratic Party were Anti-Federalists, Democratic-Republicans, and Jackson Democrats; historical precursors of the Republican Party were Federalists, National Republicans, and Whigs. Other = candidates who used third-party names only on the ballot or were listed as independent or unidentified. —indicates that the state had no data, either because the state had no gubernatorial election in that year, no vote data were found for the state in question, or the state had not yet entered the Union. No special gubernatorial elections are included in this table. Odd-numbered year gubernatorial elections were common before 1880 and several states still scheduled governor elections in odd-numbered years after that.

[1] Election held in odd-numbered year.

Sources: Adapted from *America Votes* (various publication dates) and independent search for state sources by the author.

8

Party Winners and Losers Across Multiple Elections

Party competition is an important component of democratic government. Political scientist Robert Dahl refers to the notion of public contestation, which involves political parties competing for support as they vie for public office and opponents of elected officials running against these incumbents and replacing them in office at least some of the time (Dahl, 1971, p. 4). Without public contestation, citizens have little choice in their elected officials and the level of democracy deteriorates. Part of this degree of contestation or competition rests on how often the "ins" go out, not simply whether it is possible for a change in elected officials. Dahl writes about the "right to oppose" the government and its officials. But if the right to oppose is available, yet no one successfully opposes officials from a single, dominant party over long periods of time, then ultimately this limits contestation and democracy.

In this chapter party competition in the United States is compared in races for president, House, Senate, and governor. Two features of American party competition have been presented in previous chapters. First, competition revolves around two, and typically only two, parties. Minor parties and minor candidates do not fare well in any of the offices examined in this or the previous chapters. Second, competition is bifurcated. The two parties often look highly competitive when races are examined at the national level, but this national picture belies the one-partyism found in many states across most races. While a few states are historically competitive, most are not. True, opposition party candidates have the "right" to oppose elected officials from the dominant party in a given state, but such a right is not likely to successfully bring them to office, unless demographic changes occur in the state, state issues are inadequately handled by the prevailing party over a prolonged period of time, or issue positions taken by major candidates shift over equally extensive periods of time.

This chapter is divided into three parts. First, party competition is considered nationally. Second, party competition is discussed historically, using regional breakdowns to more fully examine the historical periods of partisanship. Finally party competition is analyzed at the state level.

Measures of Party Competition

This chapter offers four measures of party competition: Democratic percent of the major two-party vote, the margin

of victory for the winning party, a party competition index devised by Paul David (1972), and a composite competition index of several races. The first measure is self-explanatory; it involves how well the Democratic Party fared in a given race in a given election year relative to its nearest major-party rival. The Democratic Party is chosen as the basis for comparison because it and its main historical antecedent, the Democratic-Republicans, have had more historical continuity than their opponents.

The second measure involves the absolute value of the difference between the Democratic percent of the major two-party vote and the Republican percent. Hence, the absolute value is [D percent minus R percent]. This indicates, literally, by how much a candidate won a race. Hence, if the Democratic candidate gained 60 percent of the vote and the Republican candidate had 40 percent, the margin of victory is 20 percentage points, indicating that the Democrat had a rather convincing win over the Republican. When aggregated to a higher level of analysis, say to the region or nation, the margin-of-victory measure indicates by how much a party's candidates for a specific office won. In general, the smaller the number, the more competitive the race is. This measure does not denote the direction of partisanship—whether the level of competition favors the Democrats or the Republicans. However, in combination with the Democratic percent of major two-party vote in a given year, it is easy to ascertain which party is favored by the size of the victory margin.

The third measure—Paul David's party competition index—takes this margin-of-victory measure and subtracts it from 100. Thus, when the party competition index is 0, the race is uncompetitive; when the index is 100, the race is perfectly competitive. Although David presented values for this index for the 1870–1970 time frame, the data he used to calculate these values were drawn from the Inter-university Consortium for Political and Social Research, a far less accurate data collection than the data presented here. The tables in this chapter adopt the David index as a useful measure, but correct and update the data upon which this measure is calculated.

The final measure is a composite competition index, which is the average of the David index values for the number of races held in a given election year across the possible array of presidential, House, Senate, and gubernatorial contests. Obviously, in presidential election years, the composite competition index potentially involves an average of values for all four races after 1912 (when voters began directly electing senators) and potentially involves three races before this. In midterm years the composite index is potentially based on values for three races after 1912 and two races before this. This measure provides a barometer of the parties' overall competitiveness or lack thereof at a particular level of analysis, whether state, region, or nation. It takes into account situations in which there may be a long-standing incumbent, which discourages competition in one race while reflecting a possibly highly competitive situation in another race or races. The higher the value of this measure, the more competition occurs across these various races.

National Party Competition

Tables 8-1 and 8-2 present the national composite competition index annually and biennially, respectively, from 1788 to 1999. Tables 8-3 and 8-4 offer the other three measures of national party competition (Democratic percent of major two-party vote, margin of victory, and David's party competition index) for presidential, House, senatorial, and gubernatorial races annually and biennially, respectively, from 1788 to 1999. Tables 8-1 and 8-2 reveal that, when viewed together, major elected offices are quite competitive at the national level. On average, from 1794 (when parties were formally established) to 1999, the composite competition index is 69.3 percent for annual election years in Table 8-1 and 70.9 percent for biennial election cycles in Table 8-2. For all these races in the eighteenth and nineteenth centuries (1794–1899), the index is 66.4 percent; for these races in the twentieth century, it is 75.6 percent. There are some years in which competition clearly falls well below these various mean values. Notably, as the Federalists began to disappear (from 1816 through 1827), the composite index in Table 8-2 averages 30.3 percent, indicating that the races for president, House, and governor during this period were very uncompetitive. But after this period there are only two election cycles in which this index in Table 8-2 goes below 50 percent—the 1854–1855 and 1856–1857 cycles when the index is 47.8 and 49.1 percent, respectively. Still, this is far higher than the 30.3 value for the latter part of the Federalist/Democratic-Republican period. Even during the periods when one party dominated the presidency, such as the 1920s for the Republicans and the 1930s for the Democrats, it is clear that the two major parties remained highly competitive overall. For instance, in 1920—the best year for Republican candidates of *any* election year—the composite competition index calculated nationally is 67.0 percent, suggesting that the Democratic Party was far from being eliminated in politics. Democrats continued to be competitive, despite the fact that Republicans achieved many victories in 1920. Similarly, in 1932 the composite index score is 72.4 percent, showing that Republicans continued to compete against

Democrats at the onset of the New Deal with some degree of competitive success.

Thus the composite competition index tables underscore two basic points. First, at the national level, contestation is alive and well in American elections. Dahl's notion of the right to compete is complemented by the degree to which candidates can and do compete for the several major governmental offices examined. Second, however, it should be kept in mind that these composite competition values are not designed to pinpoint who wins and who loses. It is conceivable that, even with high composite competition scores, one party usually loses, although competing admirably. Of course, these composite competition values do not provide any detail regarding which races keep overall competition high and which tend to dampen it.

Tables 8-3 and 8-4 are helpful in this regard. Table 8-3 shows that, in general, the governorship is the least competitive of the races (when specifically examining the party competition index column) in the late eighteenth century and throughout the nineteenth century, especially in even-numbered election years. The average gubernatorial competition index score in Table 8-4 is 64.1 percent from 1794 to 1899, in contrast to 67.6 for the House and 68.1 for the presidency. However, this changes in the twentieth century as House races are less competitive than gubernatorial races. The party competition index value from 1900 to 1999 was 74.8 percent for House races and 77.6 for gubernatorial contests. This pattern fits well with research that points to the evolution and expansion of the governorship in power, responsibility, and visibility during the Progressive Era (Lipson, 1939). It is also consistent with the rise in the strength of incumbency that becomes a key to congressional elections as both houses professionalize and members make careers of serving on Capitol Hill (King and Gelman, 1991). Presidential races are highly competitive across the entire sweep of history, although more in the twentieth century than before. Since 1900 the competition index for president has been 77.7 percent. Senate races have been less competitive with an index score of 73.8 percent.

The numbers in these four tables would please Dahl, who would point to the notions of contestation and polyarchy as alive and well in the American case (Dahl, 1971). While American elections may not offer as much rotation in office as they do in competition, nonetheless, applying Dahl's logic, there is much to applaud regarding the extent of competitiveness in our country. Still, the tables of the preceding chapters have alerted researchers to be conservative with such claims since the national aggregation of results depends on regional and state results, which often look quite different.

Regions and Competition

The regional tables provide a clear understanding of the emergence of one-partyism in certain areas of the country. Perhaps the most striking early pattern of one-partyism is in the South. As shown in Tables 8-5 and 8-7, Democratic-Republicans and then Democrats dominated the South from 1794 through the 1950s. These tables reveal that the mean composite competition index score from 1794 through 1960 was 38.7 percent. It has only been since the early 1960s that southern races have gained in competitiveness—on average a composite competition score of 75.1 percent. Table 8-5 shows that no other region was as uncompetitive as early and with such long-lasting consequences as the South. Even during the period of two-party competition between the Democrats and the Whigs from 1834 to 1853, the Whigs continually did better in regions other than the South. The average composite competition index value for the South during these years was 77.1 percent, while it was 85.4 percent for the rest of the nation. Table 8-5 also shows the collapse of whatever southern competitiveness existed in this era by 1854–1855, when the composite competition index dropped from a relatively strong 79.2 percent in the 1852–1853 election cycle to 13.8 percent in this next election cycle.

Tables 8-6 and 8-8 make clear that this one-partyism in the South emerged initially in races for governor and continued to be strongest in gubernatorial elections across time. As early as 1798–1799 the Democratic-Republicans captured southern governorships with 100 percent of the vote (as seen in the margin of victory column in Table 8-8). They continued to do well in governors' races until the Whigs began to stake claims in several southern states (see Chapter 7). But even during these years (1834–1853) Democrats continually received 57 percent of the major two-party vote in the South while achieving 51 percent in the rest of the country (Table 8-8). The Democrats' grip on southern governorships became stronger again in 1874, and this continued for nearly one hundred years until 1972–1973 when, for the first time since 1872, Democrats received less than 50 percent of the two-party vote for governor. Table 8-6 reveals that, by comparison, there was generally more two-party competition in presidential and House races in the South (although, again, Democratic candidates tended to win these races). These particular voting patterns reveal one way that one-partyism can develop in a region of the country, in this case leading to the development of the "Solid South."

As shown in Table 8-5, the Mid-Atlantic is arguably the most competitive region historically. The composite competition index is very high and relatively stable throughout the entire time period from 1794 to 1999. Table 8-6 indicates that the Mid-Atlantic was competitive for all major races, with usually small margins of victory for the winners. This is largely because of the competitiveness of Pennsylvania and more especially New York, two key states making up the region. Their competitiveness for the several offices considered here will become clearer in later tables on the state vote (Tables 8-36 through 8-140). Competition in the West and Border South, although not as strong as in the Mid-Atlantic, is also noteworthy (see Tables 8-5 and 8-6).

Competition in the Midwest is much more subdued than in the Mid-Atlantic. A quick survey of Table 8-6 shows

that the margins of victory for political races in the Midwest are larger than in the Mid-Atlantic. Overall, as the Democratic percent of the major two-party vote reveals in Table 8-6, Democrats did relatively well in the Midwest until the Civil War years. Whereas Democrats had won nearly 50 percent of the two-party vote in races in the 1860–1861 elections, they captured only 38 percent of this vote in the 1864–1865 races. Republicans, then, continued to hold an average of about 58 percent of the two-party vote in each of the races considered here until 1932, when the Democrats gained a majority of this vote in all four races for president, House, Senate, and governor (Table 8-6). Still, as observed in several of the earlier chapters, this New Deal transformation is largely limited to the Midwest, which soon returned to its Republican pattern by 1938, with Republicans basically controlling the midwestern states until 1982. Thereafter, there is some return to the Democrats, and, hence, to some competition in this region, principally in House races. What this suggests is that Democratic House incumbents are often holding their seats in the face of Republican trends in the Midwest in more recent times. Incumbency thus is to some extent surmounting party (Jacobson, 1983).

These regional tables present a more sobering look at American party competition than is offered in the rosier picture shown in the national tables. The Mid-Atlantic, Border South, and West are fairly competitive regions across the several offices studied. In stark contrast, however, within the first few elections held under the Constitution, southern states had already become one-party dominant and largely stayed that way. The Midwest also tended to be one-party through much of America's electoral history, especially since the Civil War. Despite some recent Democratic intrusions, the Midwest generally still continues to favor the Republican Party. The South, however, in recent decades has seen more dramatic political changes, as Republicans have made significant inroads in breaking up the once "Solid South." The focus here is on the behavioral patterns of each region in the country. Analysis of these regional patterns suggests the degree to which public contestation for key national and state offices varies by area of the country. In some regions, public contestation is strong; in others, it is far less vigorous.

Competition Within the States

The difficulty with viewing American elected offices at the national level is that *none* of these political races are decided at that level. Not even presidential elections are national elections, although they yield one national winner. Relying too much on national results can be misleading. It is difficult to judge the degree of party competition at the national level without judging, at the same time, the competition that exists at the state and district levels where races are actually contested and decided. Also, it is somewhat misleading to consider regional results. No election is actually decided at the regional level either, so these aggregated patterns can distort state decisions. The remaining set of tables examines competition measures at the state level. For example, Tables 8-9 through 8-35 present composite competition values by state for election years from 1788 to 1999. These are perhaps some of the most valuable indicators of state politics and state party competition. They call attention to how some states have long been competitive. For instance, New York and Ohio consistently had some of the highest composite competition scores of any state. But, at the same time, these tables also reveal that states like Georgia and Mississippi posted low competition scores until the mid-1960s.

The composite competition index tables permit an assessment of the historical development of party competition for individual states across all races. Four additional sets of tables permit analyses of these historical changes in individual states by election contest: Tables 8-36 through 8-53 examine state competition in presidential races, Tables 8-54 through 8-89 do so for House races, Tables 8-90 through 8-104 present individual state competition for Senate elections, and Tables 8-105 through 8-140 offer this for gubernatorial contests. Together these tables present the most complete and accurate account of state-level party competition presently available.

These tables offer new insights into the first era of electoral politics—the Federalist/Democratic-Republican period from 1788 to 1823. It is clear in examining the composite index values in Tables 8-9 through 8-13 that some states—Delaware, Maryland, New York, and Vermont—had quite healthy competition between the Federalists and Democratic-Republicans, despite the national weakness of the Federalist Party. At the same time, these tables also reveal when this early two-party competition collapsed in individual states. In Delaware, House races (Tables 8-54 through 8-59) and gubernatorial races (Tables 8-105 through 8-110) were keenly competitive throughout this period. For Maryland, this competition was more notable at the presidential level (Tables 8-36 through 8-38) than at the congressional level, where the state favored the Democratic-Republicans for Congress by 1800. New York was competitive at the congressional level until 1818 (Table 8-59) and at the gubernatorial level until 1820 (Table 8-110), when the Democratic-Republicans secured victories in both races that were sustained in the next several election cycles. In Vermont, the Federalists were competitive in both House and gubernatorial elections until their support collapsed in 1818 (Tables 8-59, 8-110). In contrast to these competitive states, the competition tables also reveal the extent to which other states such as Kentucky and Tennessee were always strongholds for the Democratic-Republicans throughout this period in all election contests.

These state competition tables also permit an assessment of the second era of electoral politics—the Democratic/National Republican-Whig period from 1824 through 1853. The most revealing aspect of the composite scores in Tables 8-13 through 8-17 is how competition increased across this period as first the National Republicans and then the Whigs fielded candidates against the Democrats. For most states the nadir of competition during this period was the election of 1824 when Jefferson's Democratic-Republican Party was splintering apart, and only three of twenty-two states (14 percent) had composite values of 90 percent or more, indicating that elections were competitive in few political arenas (Table 8-13). Competition increased after 1824 when the National Republican and then the Whig Party were formed to compete against Andrew Jackson's new Democratic Party. It hit a high point in the election of 1840 when 60 percent of the states (15 of the 25 states) had composite competition values at 90 percent (Table 8-15). Thereafter, competition tapered off somewhat in several states during the early 1850s as the Whigs and Democrats became more entrenched in specific states. In the election of 1852, 57 percent of the states (17 of the 30 states) had composite competition values at 90 percent or more and, in 1854, only 38 percent (8 of 21 states) did (see Table 8-17).

The subsequent tables for presidential, House, and gubernatorial races by state show no particular pattern among political offices for this decline in competition in 1852, but discernible patterns are evident by 1854. These tables show that this decline in competition was the result of fewer states having competitive races for both House and governor—where competitive races are defined as those in which the Democratic percentage of two-party vote ranged between 45 percent and 55 percent (or, alternately, the Republican percentage of two-party vote ranged between 45 percent and 55 percent). In 1840, for example, 43 percent of states (10 of 23 states) had Democratic votes for the House in the 45–55 percent range while, in 1854, only 25 percent of states (7 of 28 states) did, according to Tables 8-62 and 8-65. Also, in 1840, 54 percent of states (14 of 26 states) had Democratic votes for governor in this competitive voting range whereas only 24 percent of states (7 of 29 states) followed suit in 1854, as a comparison of Tables 8-113 and 8-116 indicates. In each case, competition declines as the nation approaches the crucial period leading to the Civil War.

Competition tables also provide a revealing look at the third political period—the Civil War era and its aftermath. This period began, not surprisingly, with the presidential election year of 1856 showing erratic competition across the states and significant declines in competition from the waning years of the previous era. For example, as shown in Table 8-17, only four of thirty states—Illinois, Indiana, Pennsylvania, and Wisconsin—revealed higher political competition in the elections of 1856 than in 1852. Among the states in 1856, only five—Illinois, Indiana, Iowa, Ohio, and Pennsylvania—had composite competition values of 90 percent or more. Competition returned for some states, albeit somewhat slowly, during the Civil War years and the immediate postwar years. By 1880, competition became more stable but did not return to prewar levels: 45 percent of the states (17 of 38 states), including the two southern states of Florida and North Carolina, had composite competition values of 90 percent or above (Table 8-20). By the end of this era, in the 1892 elections, 45 percent of states (20 of 44 states) still had composite values of 90 percent or more (Table 8-22).

The subsequent state competition tables reveal that the races for president and House were roughly similar in their degree of competitiveness between 1880 and 1892. In 1880, 47 percent of states (18 of 38 states) had their Democratic percentage of two-party vote in the range between 45 and 55 percent for president (Table 8-43); in 1892, 45 percent of states (20 of 44 states) were in this voting range for the presidential election (Table 8-44). In 1880, 50 percent of the states (19 of 38 states) had House races in the 45–55 percent range (Table 8-69), and 52 percent of states were in this range in the 1892 House elections (twenty-three of forty-four states as seen in Table 8-71). Competition in gubernatorial elections, however, sharply increased from 1880, during which 35 percent of states (11 of 31 states as shown in Table 8-120) fell in the competitive 45–55 percent voting range, to 1892 when 53 percent of the states (19 of 36 states) were in this range (Table 8-122). This occurred despite southern states like Alabama, Florida, Georgia, South Carolina, and Virginia being completely uncompetitive in their gubernatorial races (Table 8-122).

The composite tables reveal the sharp drop in competitiveness in numerous states during the fourth Republican/ Democratic era from 1894 through 1929, an era which saw the Republican Party rise to new heights of power. This era began with 30 percent of states (13 of 45 states) with composite competition values of 90 percent or higher in the first presidential election year of this period (Table 8-22). After World War I, this level of competition dropped precipitously. In 1920, for example, only 10 percent of states (5 of 48 states) had a composite value of 90 percent or more (Table 8-25). This resulted from only 6 percent of states (3 of 48 states) having presidential races in which the Democrats received 45–55 percent of the two-party vote (Table 8-47), 15 percent of states with House races in this competitive voting range (7 of 48 states, as shown in Table 8-76), and 17 percent of states (6 of 36 states) with gubernatorial races in this voting range (Table 8-127). The most competitive races were for the Senate in which 25 percent of these races (8 of 32 states with Senate elections in 1920) fell in this competitive voting range (Table 8-91). Yet this was dramatically lower than the 52 percent of states (16 of 31 states) being competitive in the first Senate elections after enactment of the 17th Amendment (Table 8-90). Of course, the 1920 elections have been recorded in history as a supreme triumph for the Republican Party electorally—the party achieved one of the greatest victories in its history for the presidency and followed suit with very impressive wins in the House and gubernatorial races.

The composite tables show that the early years of the fifth New Deal era from 1930 to 1965 continued this uncompetitive pattern. In 1930 only 19 percent of states (9 of 48 states) had composite competition values of 90 percent or more, and in 1932 this number increased to only 25 percent of states (12 of 48 states). (See Tables 8-26 and 8-27.) Yet at the end of World War II, competition heightened as 44

percent of states (21 of 48 states) had composite competition scores of at least 90 percent in the presidential election year of 1944 (Table 8-28). As late as 1962, 21 states still had composite competition scores of 90 percent or greater, although, in 1964, this figure drops back to 8 states because of the massive Democratic victories in that year. In 1962 these high composite competition scores resulted from 45 percent of the states with House races giving the Democratic Party 45–55 percent of the two-party vote; 50 percent of the Senate races being similarly competitive; and 57 percent of the gubernatorial races also falling in this 45–55 percent voting range. In 1964, 41 percent of states had House races in the 45–55 percent Democratic range, 39 percent of states had Senate races in this competitive voting range, and 32 percent of states had gubernatorial races in this voting range, which helps to explain the drop-off in competition in that year (Tables 8-83, 8-98, 8-134). The presidential election in 1964 dramatically dampened competition. The Democratic candidate, Lyndon Johnson, won a landslide victory that saw only 16 percent of the states (8 of 50 states) showing any semblance of competition when voting on the presidential race (Table 8-50).

The composite tables reveal that, in the final competitive Democratic/Republican era from 1966 to the present, the more competitive vote scenario of the later New Deal years continues. In the first presidential election year in this era, 42 percent of states (21 of 50 states) had composite competition values of 90 percent or more (Table 8-31). By 1996, 38 percent of states (19 of 50 states) still had composite competition values of 90 percent or more (Tables 8-35). This 38 percent rate in 1996 resulted from 22 states (44 percent) having presidential races in which the Democrats received between 45 and 55 percent of the two-party vote; 20 states (40 percent) having House races in this competitive range; and 16 states (48 percent) having Senate races that also were relatively competitive. Only the governor's race does not contribute to the generally high competition rate in this particular year: only 3 states—or 23 percent of the states with gubernatorial races—were competitive in 1996. (See Tables 8-53, 8-88, 8-104, 8-139.)

In general, what seems to typify this last era is the similarity in competition levels not only across successive election years but also across different types of political races in the same year. While many pundits have been quick to lament the decline of party competition in modern American politics (for example, see Burnham, 1969), these tables go a long way toward dispelling such views.

Conclusion

The degree to which public contestation in American elections exists depends in large measure on the state in which these elections are held. In some states, Dahl's (1971) vision of polyarchy is obvious and long-standing. In other states, the picture is murkier. In the Midwest the competition picture is one of similitude across a long time span: races are more competitive here than they have been in the South, but Republicans still win more races than Democrats in this region and this pattern has continued since the Civil War. In southern states, after almost two centuries of one-partyism, political change has only recently occurred as levels of competition have increased.

But which part of the southern picture is more crucial—the nearly two hundred years of one-partyism or the South's recent break from this in the last forty years? Certainly both parts of the picture are critical to understanding the nature of partisan competition in the United States. What they suggest is that in certain states there are deep-rooted political traditions, economic patterns, and demographic identities that change slowly. If the party that holds most of the offices in such states is able to adapt to these rather slow changes, it is likely to remain in power. In other states, where population characteristics and economic growth are more fast paced, competition is likely to be keener and these competitive patterns are likely to feed on themselves. This political lesson extends far beyond the regional voting patterns of the South. Viable parties continue to be viable by adapting to changing circumstances. Parties that have historically been unsuccessful in a state have considerable difficulty making inroads on established political power unless circumstances radically change. Political party strength is like a self-fulfilling prophecy. Dahl wrote that in the United States an "election is a critical technique for insuring that governmental leaders will be relatively responsive to non-leaders" (1956, p. 125). The data in this chapter suggest that Dahl was overly optimistic about the extent to which this technique is successful in all states and the degree to which public contestation adequately exists across America.

Table 8-1 National Composite Competition Index, by Election Year, 1788–1999

Year	Composite Competition Index	Year	Composite Competition Index	Year	Composite Competition Index	Year	Composite Competition Index
1788	45.7	1843	85.7	1898	70.8	1953	90.4
1789	23.1	1844	91.0	1899	74.9	1954	74.1
1790	26.4	1845	69.9	1900	76.9	1955	41.7
1791	0.0	1846	84.6	1901	84.7	1956	78.6
1792	39.7	1847	85.4	1902	72.4	1957	81.5
1793	55.0	1848	86.3	1903	77.5	1958	75.5
1794	60.9	1849	74.1	1904	68.2	1959	58.8
1795	31.3	1850	88.3	1905	87.5	1960	82.5
1796	44.7	1851	76.4	1906	72.0	1961	85.3
1797	39.3	1852	88.6	1907	76.7	1962	81.6
1798	64.3	1853	80.3	1908	76.1	1963	87.4
1799	23.1	1854	75.1	1909	83.9	1964	78.8
1800	70.6	1855	19.5	1910	76.0	1965	85.8
1801	43.7	1856	51.2	1911	80.5	1966	81.7
1802	70.6	1857	44.7	1912	70.8	1967	78.1
1803	38.8	1858	60.2	1913	55.8	1968	82.9
1804	52.8	1859	55.2	1914	75.4	1969	85.6
1805	41.8	1860	58.1	1915	74.3	1970	82.0
1806	67.0	1861	65.6	1916	77.4	1971	46.7
1807	57.4	1862	73.2	1917	65.5	1972	79.3
1808	68.9	1863	63.7	1918	67.5	1973	32.6
1809	90.9	1864	76.3	1919	72.7	1974	79.2
1810	69.2	1865	55.5	1920	67.0	1975	55.7
1811	64.3	1866	74.7	1921	67.4	1976	81.4
1812	68.8	1867	71.1	1922	72.1	1977	86.5
1813	71.0	1868	77.4	1923	59.9	1978	80.5
1814	66.9	1869	73.0	1924	63.3	1979	86.1
1815	74.4	1870	84.7	1925	73.8	1980	82.8
1816	42.3	1871	89.8	1926	66.0	1981	96.4
1817	31.8	1872	80.0	1927	47.9	1982	81.0
1818	40.7	1873	75.7	1928	73.2	1983	81.9
1819	29.6	1874	77.4	1929	74.0	1984	77.7
1820	19.9	1875	88.5	1930	66.7	1985	74.4
1821	12.8	1876	84.0	1931	57.5	1986	81.2
1822	31.1	1877	76.8	1932	72.5	1987	81.7
1823	26.6	1878	68.1	1933	49.4	1988	82.6
1824	31.9	1879	81.3	1934	72.5	1989	87.6
1825	11.0	1880	79.6	1935	45.3	1990	78.7
1826	48.5	1881	68.3	1936	67.7	1991	81.7
1827	6.1	1882	79.4	1937	64.4	1992	85.5
1828	61.2	1883	92.1	1938	68.8	1993	90.7
1829	40.6	1884	84.2	1939	43.5	1994	81.9
1830	65.3	1885	79.9	1940	72.8	1995	86.5
1831	52.7	1886	76.9	1941	36.4	1996	83.3
1832	60.6	1887	93.8	1942	65.7	1997	92.7
1833	56.2	1888	80.9	1943	62.4	1998	77.7
1834	81.7	1889	79.3	1944	75.8	1999	79.9
1835	62.6	1890	79.9	1945	63.6		
1836	85.7	1891	94.2	1946	71.4		
1837	76.5	1892	72.5	1947	45.1		
1838	87.4	1893	74.1	1948	75.6		
1839	90.2	1894	64.7	1949	75.8		
1840	88.2	1895	75.4	1950	71.7		
1841	79.8	1896	70.2	1951	45.4		
1842	79.9	1897	80.6	1952	76.1		

Notes: The national composite competition index is the mean of all state values for the party competition index devised by Paul David (1972) for all races in a given election year among the following set of races: president, House, Senate, and governor. The state values for these races are presented in Tables 8-36 through 8-53 for president, Tables 8-54 through 8-89 for House, Tables 8-90 through 8-104 for Senate, and Tables 8-105 through 8-140 for governor. David's competition index is defined as 100 − the absolute difference between the Democratic and Republican percentage of two-party vote for each of the four races mentioned here. The values for Democratic and Republican percent of two-party vote for president, House, Senate, and governor used in the computations to get the David party competition values in Tables 8-36 through 8-140 are taken from the state vote tables for these races in Chapters 4, 5, 6, and 7, respectively. The author's alternative party coding in Chapters 4–7 is used whenever it occurs in place of the conventional party coding for vote data in computing David's party competition index. Zero (0) percent on David's competition index represents a complete absence of two-party competition for that election year, whereas a score of 100 percent indicates perfect competition between the two major parties. The Democratic Party is defined as the Anti-Federalists, Democratic-Republicans, and Jackson Democrats prior to 1830 when the "Democratic Party" as such was established. The Republican Party is defined as the Federalists, National Republicans, and Whigs prior to the establishment of the "Republican Party" in the 1850s. See Appendix A for an explanation of the historical antecedents of the current Democratic and Republican parties. No special elections for any of the four races are used in the calculations, nor are partial voting data reported for any of the four races in any of the states.

Sources: Tables 8-36 through 8-140. Specifically, state party competition values in Tables 8-36 through 8-140 for the presidential, House, Senate, and gubernatorial races are aggregated across states to the national level for each year to obtain the national composite competition averages shown in Table 8-1.

Table 8-2 National Composite Competition Index, by Two-Year Election Cycle, 1788–1999

Year	Composite Competition Index	Year	Composite Competition Index	Year	Composite Competition Index	Year	Composite Competition Index
1788–1789	37.2	1848–1849	82.3	1908–1909	76.3	1968–1969	82.9
1790–1791	19.8	1850–1851	82.1	1910–1911	76.4	1970–1971	81.4
1792–1793	44.3	1852–1853	86.1	1912–1913	70.5	1972–1973	78.7
1794–1795	54.6	1854–1855	47.8	1914–1915	75.4	1974–1975	78.6
1796–1797	43.7	1856–1857	49.1	1916–1917	77.3	1976–1977	81.5
1798–1799	55.6	1858–1859	57.4	1918–1919	67.8	1978–1979	80.7
1800–1801	60.3	1860–1861	59.9	1920–1921	67.0	1980–1981	83.0
1802–1803	58.1	1862–1863	68.9	1922–1923	71.7	1982–1983	81.1
1804–1805	50.2	1864–1865	70.8	1924–1925	63.4	1984–1985	77.6
1806–1807	63.6	1866–1867	73.0	1926–1927	65.7	1986–1987	81.2
1808–1809	72.1	1868–1869	76.6	1928–1929	73.2	1988–1989	82.7
1810–1811	68.0	1870–1871	86.0	1930–1931	66.5	1990–1991	78.8
1812–1813	69.4	1872–1873	79.5	1932–1933	72.4	1992–1993	85.6
1814–1815	68.9	1874–1875	80.3	1934–1935	72.0	1994–1995	82.0
1816–1817	39.4	1876–1877	83.2	1936–1937	67.6	1996–1997	83.4
1818–1819	36.3	1878–1879	70.7	1938–1939	68.4	1998–1999	78.1
1820–1821	18.1	1880–1881	78.8	1940–1941	72.5		
1822–1823	29.2	1882–1883	80.9	1942–1943	65.6		
1824–1825	26.6	1884–1885	83.9	1944–1945	75.7		
1826–1827	32.3	1886–1887	78.4	1946–1947	70.9		
1828–1829	55.5	1888–1889	80.8	1948–1949	75.6		
1830–1831	58.8	1890–1891	81.1	1950–1951	71.3		
1832–1833	59.3	1892–1893	72.5	1952–1953	76.2		
1834–1835	72.4	1894–1895	65.8	1954–1955	73.6		
1836–1837	83.2	1896–1897	70.6	1956–1957	78.6		
1838–1839	88.5	1898–1899	71.2	1958–1959	75.1		
1840–1841	85.6	1900–1901	77.2	1960–1961	82.5		
1842–1843	83.4	1902–1903	72.9	1962–1963	81.7		
1844–1845	84.7	1904–1905	68.8	1964–1965	78.9		
1846–1847	85.0	1906–1907	72.4	1966–1967	81.7		

Notes: The national composite competition index is the mean of all state values for the party competition index devised by Paul David (1972) for all races in a given two-year election cycle among the following set of races: president, House, Senate, and governor. The state values for these races are presented in Tables 8-36 through 8-53 for president, Tables 8-54 through 8-89 for House, Tables 8-90 through 8-104 for Senate, and Tables 8-105 through 8-140 for governor. David's competition index is defined as 100 − the absolute difference between the Democratic and Republican percentage of two-party vote for each of the four races mentioned here. The values for Democratic and Republican percent of two-party vote for president, House, Senate, and governor used in the computations to get the David party competition values in Tables 8-36 through 8-140 are taken from the state vote tables for these races in Chapters 4, 5, 6, and 7, respectively. The author's alternative party coding in Chapters 4–7 is used whenever it occurs in place of the conventional party coding for vote data in computing David's party competition index. Zero (0) percent on David's competition index represents a complete absence of two-party competition for that election cycle, whereas a score of 100 percent indicates perfect competition between the two major parties. The Democratic Party is defined as the Anti-Federalists, Democratic-Republicans, and Jackson Democrats prior to 1830 when the "Democratic Party" as such was established. The Republican Party is defined as the Federalists, National Republicans, and Whigs prior to the establishment of the "Republican Party" in the 1850s. See Appendix A for a complete explanation of the historical antecedents of the current Democratic and Republican parties. No special elections for any of the four races are used in the calculations for Table 8-2 nor are partial voting data for any of the four races in any of the states.

Sources: Tables 8-36 through 8-140. Specifically, state party competition values in Tables 8-36 through 8-140 for the presidential, House, Senate, and gubernatorial races are aggregated across states to the national level for each two-year election cycle to obtain the national composite competition averages shown in Table 8-2.

Table 8-3 National Competition Measures, by Election Year, 1788–1999

Year	Democratic % of Two-Party Vote	Margin of Victory	Party Competition Index	Year	Democratic % of Two-Party Vote	Margin of Victory	Party Competition Index
1788				**1811**			
President	7.6	84.7	15.3	House	100.0	100.0	0.0
House	46.0	8.0	92.0	Governor	60.8	22.8	77.2
Governor	54.7	9.4	90.6	**1812**			
1789				President	53.4	24.9	75.1
House	34.6	30.8	69.2	House	53.7	35.4	64.6
Governor	50.0	100.0	0.0	Governor	50.5	30.2	69.8
1790				**1813**			
House	30.4	39.2	60.8	House	47.4	5.2	94.8
Governor	95.4	90.8	9.2	Governor	47.1	32.0	68.0
1791				**1814**			
House	—	—	—	House	55.4	32.3	67.7
Governor	100.0	100.0	0.0	Governor	43.0	34.3	65.7
1792				**1815**			
President	0.0	100.0	0.0	House	—	—	—
House	44.6	10.8	89.2	Governor	54.9	25.6	74.4
Governor	50.1	66.9	33.1	**1816**			
1793				President	87.9	75.7	24.3
House	46.0	8.0	92.0	House	59.7	58.1	41.9
Governor	81.8	63.5	36.5	Governor	60.1	42.7	57.3
1794				**1817**			
House	39.3	33.0	67.0	House	100.0	100.0	0.0
Governor	0.0	100.0	0.0	Governor	64.5	56.3	43.7
1795				**1818**			
House	—	—	—	House	80.1	60.5	39.5
Governor	15.6	68.7	31.3	Governor	76.3	57.2	42.8
1796				**1819**			
President	32.8	35.2	64.8	House	88.7	77.4	22.6
House	39.0	45.1	54.9	Governor	81.5	67.7	32.3
Governor	24.2	98.4	1.6	**1820**			
1797				President	93.7	93.4	6.6
House	35.2	29.6	70.4	House	80.0	63.2	36.8
Governor	47.8	71.1	28.9	Governor	90.4	83.9	16.1
1798				**1821**			
House	32.8	35.3	64.7	House	97.8	95.6	4.4
Governor	31.7	36.6	63.4	Governor	90.3	84.4	15.6
1799				**1822**			
House	—	—	—	House	85.4	72.7	27.3
Governor	38.5	76.9	23.1	Governor	80.9	65.1	34.9
1800				**1823**			
President	60.3	20.7	79.3	House	87.8	75.7	24.3
House	52.2	26.9	73.1	Governor	86.0	72.7	27.3
Governor	54.2	41.7	58.4	**1824**			
1801				President	52.6	62.6	37.4
House	87.4	74.8	25.2	House	84.4	69.9	30.1
Governor	55.7	48.3	51.7	Governor	77.4	76.9	23.1
1802				**1825**			
House	46.9	29.7	70.3	House	91.5	82.9	17.1
Governor	48.8	29.0	71.0	Governor	76.9	90.1	9.9
1803				**1826**			
House	83.9	67.8	32.2	House	43.0	38.7	61.3
Governor	62.0	56.0	44.0	Governor	61.5	68.6	31.4
1804				**1827**			
President	82.8	65.6	34.5	House	40.8	81.6	18.5
House	64.5	48.6	51.4	Governor	88.6	99.4	0.6
Governor	52.2	24.2	75.8	**1828**			
1805				President	56.9	36.8	63.2
House	100.0	100.0	0.0	House	53.3	30.1	69.9
Governor	68.6	52.3	47.7	Governor	53.4	50.1	49.9
1806				**1829**			
House	66.2	38.9	61.1	House	45.7	39.8	60.2
Governor	55.0	21.4	78.6	Governor	73.7	68.3	31.7
1807				**1830**			
House	—	—	—	House	56.2	35.6	64.4
Governor	68.3	42.6	57.4	Governor	56.8	33.8	66.2
1808				**1831**			
President	66.0	35.7	64.3	House	53.5	43.9	56.1
House	55.1	15.6	84.4	Governor	57.8	49.6	50.4
Governor	70.5	48.5	51.5	**1832**			
1809				President	65.4	40.1	59.9
House	—	—	—	House	67.0	41.5	58.5
Governor	46.4	9.2	90.8	Governor	58.7	36.6	63.4
1810				**1833**			
House	58.2	35.7	64.3	House	53.7	30.0	70.0
Governor	57.3	23.2	76.8	Governor	76.9	59.2	40.8

Table 8-3 *(Continued)*

Year	Democratic % of Two-Party Vote	Margin of Victory	Party Competition Index	Year	Democratic % of Two-Party Vote	Margin of Victory	Party Competition Index
1834				**1856**			
House	51.4	24.1	75.9	President	71.1	57.7	42.3
Governor	45.9	11.1	88.9	House	58.2	36.5	63.5
1835				Governor	61.9	45.2	54.8
House	65.4	35.9	64.1	**1857**			
Governor	58.2	38.6	61.4	House	83.4	72.2	27.8
1836				Governor	64.9	43.1	56.9
President	52.1	11.0	89.0	**1858**			
House	52.1	17.1	82.9	House	62.7	40.1	59.9
Governor	55.2	18.6	81.4	Governor	57.6	39.3	60.7
1837				**1859**			
House	52.6	27.1	72.9	House	71.8	54.1	45.9
Governor	51.8	20.0	80.0	Governor	61.6	37.7	62.3
1838				**1860**			
House	49.6	10.1	89.9	President	59.3	50.5	49.5
Governor	51.8	15.5	84.5	House	57.8	37.4	62.6
1839				Governor	55.3	29.3	70.7
House	50.9	5.5	94.5	**1861**			
Governor	55.0	12.7	87.3	House	25.4	53.5	46.5
1840				Governor	44.3	31.1	68.9
President	46.5	10.8	89.2	**1862**			
House	48.3	8.5	91.5	House	42.9	18.3	81.7
Governor	44.0	16.9	83.1	Governor	32.3	38.0	62.0
1841				**1863**			
House	42.9	25.9	74.1	House	41.3	42.4	57.6
Governor	48.4	15.9	84.1	Governor	39.7	33.2	66.8
1842				**1864**			
House	61.2	22.3	77.7	President	42.2	19.6	80.4
Governor	49.2	18.8	81.2	House	37.9	25.0	75.0
1843				Governor	35.7	28.7	71.3
House	54.8	17.2	82.8	**1865**			
Governor	52.8	10.4	89.6	House	27.8	44.4	55.6
1844				Governor	41.3	44.6	55.4
President	51.3	8.9	91.1	**1866**			
House	51.9	11.7	88.3	House	41.0	21.0	79.0
Governor	50.6	6.7	93.3	Governor	34.4	32.0	68.0
1845				**1867**			
House	48.2	19.9	80.1	House	40.2	36.8	63.2
Governor	58.7	38.0	62.0	Governor	45.0	25.5	74.5
1846				**1868**			
House	57.3	21.4	78.6	President	45.9	18.8	81.2
Governor	50.5	8.5	91.5	House	42.7	23.0	77.0
1847				Governor	36.8	27.5	72.5
House	51.5	12.8	87.2	**1869**			
Governor	54.4	15.7	84.3	House	35.3	29.4	70.6
1848				Governor	37.3	26.0	74.0
President	48.8	11.6	88.4	**1870**			
House	51.0	13.0	87.0	House	46.4	14.5	85.5
Governor	51.7	18.3	81.7	Governor	46.3	16.6	83.4
1849				**1871**			
House	57.5	24.5	75.5	House	51.8	6.2	93.8
Governor	60.0	27.0	73.0	Governor	46.9	11.4	88.6
1850				**1872**			
House	51.8	9.1	90.9	President	42.5	17.7	82.3
Governor	47.7	14.6	85.4	House	41.4	23.4	76.6
1851				Governor	47.7	18.4	81.6
House	56.3	16.0	84.0	**1873**			
Governor	53.7	28.1	71.9	House	49.5	1.1	98.9
1852				Governor	41.1	28.2	71.8
President	55.3	13.2	86.8	**1874**			
House	52.5	8.0	92.0	House	49.4	23.5	76.5
Governor	52.7	11.6	88.4	Governor	50.1	21.0	79.0
1853				**1875**			
House	61.8	24.3	75.7	House	53.7	7.4	92.6
Governor	56.4	16.9	83.1	Governor	52.0	12.7	87.3
1854				**1876**			
House	58.5	30.9	69.1	President	50.9	14.2	85.8
Governor	46.6	16.4	83.6	House	52.0	16.7	83.3
1855				Governor	51.5	17.7	82.3
House	99.3	98.6	1.4	**1877**			
Governor	76.1	68.7	31.3	House	48.8	2.4	97.6
				Governor	55.7	25.1	74.9

(Table continues)

Table 8-3 *(Continued)*

Year	Democratic % of Two-Party Vote	Margin of Victory	Party Competition Index	Year	Democratic % of Two-Party Vote	Margin of Victory	Party Competition Index
1878				1904			
House	56.9	28.8	71.2	President	44.2	36.1	63.9
Governor	57.9	38.0	62.0	House	48.5	31.5	68.5
1879				Governor	51.7	26.4	73.6
House	39.1	21.8	78.2	1905			
Governor	46.0	18.4	81.6	Governor	52.4	12.5	87.5
1880				1906			
President	50.6	15.7	84.3	House	52.0	30.2	69.8
House	52.6	19.3	80.7	Governor	54.1	24.3	75.7
Governor	56.8	30.0	70.0	1907			
1881				House	57.2	14.4	85.6
Governor	49.0	31.8	68.2	Governor	55.3	23.3	76.7
1882				1908			
House	55.1	20.2	79.8	President	49.1	23.5	76.5
Governor	55.4	21.3	78.7	House	51.9	26.6	73.4
1883				Governor	53.9	20.7	79.3
Governor	50.1	7.9	92.1	1909			
1884				Governor	51.1	16.1	83.9
President	50.6	13.4	86.6	1910			
House	52.6	15.6	84.4	House	54.3	27.1	72.9
Governor	54.1	20.2	79.8	Governor	52.6	19.2	80.8
1885				1911			
Governor	55.2	20.1	79.9	House	53.8	7.8	92.2
1886				Governor	58.0	19.5	80.5
House	56.9	22.3	77.7	1912[1]			
Governor	57.1	24.4	75.6	President	67.2	35.6	64.4
1887				House	59.2	29.7	70.3
Governor	50.5	6.2	93.8	Senate	54.4	17.3	82.7
1888				Governor	58.5	21.1	78.9
President	51.8	15.5	84.5	1913			
House	53.3	17.9	82.1	Governor	72.1	44.2	55.8
Governor	57.6	26.1	73.9	1914			
1889				House	56.8	28.2	71.8
House	37.7	24.6	75.4	Senate	56.8	22.8	77.2
Governor	52.1	20.7	79.3	Governor	52.5	20.6	79.4
1890				1915			
House	54.6	20.4	79.6	Governor	62.5	25.8	74.3
Governor	54.8	19.8	80.2	1916			
1891				President	57.5	20.4	79.6
Governor	52.5	5.8	94.2	House	54.7	24.9	75.1
1892				Senate	52.7	22.3	77.7
President	47.7	33.0	67.0	Governor	51.5	22.7	77.3
House	56.5	24.9	75.1	1917			
Governor	57.1	23.5	76.5	Governor	54.8	34.5	65.5
1893				1918			
Governor	57.1	25.9	74.1	House	53.9	32.3	67.7
1894				Senate	58.1	35.4	64.6
House	46.4	35.4	64.6	Governor	51.1	29.8	70.2
Governor	47.7	35.2	64.8	1919			
1895				Governor	57.0	27.3	72.7
House	48.9	2.2	97.8	1920			
Governor	50.2	24.6	75.4	President	41.9	33.4	66.6
1896				House	44.1	36.1	63.9
President	53.5	27.9	72.1	Senate	48.2	30.9	69.1
House	50.1	29.3	70.7	Governor	45.2	30.0	70.0
Governor	54.1	33.1	66.9	1921			
1897				Governor	66.3	32.6	67.4
Governor	46.7	19.4	80.6	1922			
1898				House	52.9	31.3	68.7
House	52.8	29.0	71.0	Senate	52.8	21.8	78.2
Governor	53.7	29.4	70.6	Governor	50.6	29.0	71.0
1899				1923			
Governor	52.8	25.1	74.9	Governor	70.1	40.1	59.9
1900				1924			
President	50.5	21.7	78.3	President	40.8	40.7	59.3
House	52.4	23.4	76.6	House	49.3	35.9	64.1
Governor	54.1	24.7	75.3	Senate	52.0	40.6	59.4
1901				Governor	49.5	29.1	70.9
Governor	45.3	15.3	84.7	1925			
1902				Governor	63.1	26.2	73.8
House	53.2	28.4	71.6	1926			
Governor	52.0	26.2	73.8	House	49.4	36.6	63.4
1903				Senate	51.6	31.5	68.5
Governor	55.1	22.5	77.5	Governor	48.5	32.7	67.3

Table 8-3 *(Continued)*

Year	Democratic % of Two-Party Vote	Margin of Victory	Party Competition Index	Year	Democratic % of Two-Party Vote	Margin of Victory	Party Competition Index
1927				1950			
Governor	74.0	52.1	47.9	House	57.1	28.3	71.7
1928				Senate	55.2	30.2	69.8
President	43.6	22.6	77.4	Governor	52.7	26.4	73.6
House	48.8	31.8	68.2	1951			
Senate	46.5	31.2	68.8	Governor	77.3	54.6	45.4
Governor	48.8	21.5	78.5	1952			
1929				President	44.0	17.0	83.0
Governor	63.0	26.0	74.0	House	53.5	28.3	71.7
1930				Senate	52.2	27.0	73.0
House	53.1	34.3	65.7	Governor	51.6	25.0	75.0
Senate	60.8	39.0	61.0	1953			
Governor	51.9	26.1	73.9	Governor	54.8	9.6	90.4
1931				1954			
Governor	71.2	42.5	57.5	House	57.8	24.9	75.1
1932				Senate	62.2	32.1	67.9
President	64.1	30.0	70.0	Governor	56.1	21.2	78.8
House	61.5	27.0	73.0	1955			
Senate	62.6	30.6	69.4	Governor	79.2	58.3	41.7
Governor	58.5	21.9	78.1	1956			
1933				President	43.2	19.0	81.0
Governor	75.3	50.6	49.4	House	55.8	22.7	77.3
1934				Senate	57.4	27.0	73.0
House	63.6	30.3	69.7	Governor	54.7	17.3	82.7
Senate	59.4	27.2	72.8	1957			
Governor	59.5	24.0	76.0	Governor	59.3	18.5	81.5
1935				1958			
Governor	77.4	54.7	45.3	House	61.8	25.3	74.7
1936				Senate	60.1	23.8	76.2
President	66.2	33.6	66.4	Governor	60.7	24.0	76.0
House	63.4	30.9	69.1	1959			
Senate	63.6	38.3	61.7	Senate	47.1	5.8	94.2
Governor	58.5	27.1	72.9	Governor	69.8	41.2	58.8
1937				1960			
Governor	67.8	35.6	64.4	President	49.4	8.7	91.3
1938				House	58.0	21.4	78.6
House	59.2	31.9	68.1	Senate	60.1	29.4	70.6
Senate	59.8	31.7	68.3	Governor	53.0	12.2	87.8
Governor	54.7	29.8	70.2	1961			
1939				Governor	57.4	14.7	85.3
Governor	78.3	56.5	43.5	1962			
1940				House	55.0	18.3	81.7
President	59.4	22.1	77.9	Senate	54.3	18.3	81.7
House	59.2	30.6	69.4	Governor	55.6	18.5	81.5
Senate	56.2	31.3	68.7	1963			
Governor	56.4	25.9	74.1	Governor	56.3	12.6	87.4
1941				1964			
Governor	81.8	63.6	36.4	President	58.9	26.2	73.8
1942				House	58.2	18.2	81.8
House	56.9	31.8	68.2	Senate	59.8	22.5	77.5
Senate	59.5	38.7	61.3	Governor	55.4	15.3	84.7
Governor	52.3	33.6	66.4	1965			
1943				Governor	57.1	14.2	85.8
Governor	64.5	37.6	62.4	1966			
1944				House	52.3	17.0	83.0
President	57.1	18.6	81.4	Senate	52.2	23.3	76.7
House	57.4	28.9	71.1	Governor	49.9	15.4	84.6
Senate	58.3	25.1	74.9	1967			
Governor	52.6	24.7	75.3	Governor	59.4	21.9	78.1
1945				1968			
Governor	68.2	36.4	63.6	President	48.7	13.0	87.0
1946				House	51.1	19.5	80.5
House	53.5	29.7	70.3	Senate	52.8	22.0	78.0
Senate	49.7	24.3	75.7	Governor	52.7	13.5	86.5
Governor	50.2	31.2	68.8	1969			
1947				Governor	42.8	14.4	85.6
Governor	77.5	54.9	45.1	1970			
1948				House	56.2	20.4	79.6
President	54.0	16.1	83.9	Senate	57.6	20.2	79.8
House	57.8	27.2	72.8	Governor	52.9	12.5	87.5
Senate	61.8	32.2	67.8	1971			
Governor	55.9	24.8	75.2	Governor	76.7	53.3	46.7
1949							
Governor	59.9	24.2	75.8				*(Table continues)*

Table 8-3 (Continued)

Year	Democratic % of Two-Party Vote	Margin of Victory	Party Competition Index	Year	Democratic % of Two-Party Vote	Margin of Victory	Party Competition Index
1972				**1986**			
President	36.8	29.0	71.0	House	52.9	20.5	79.5
House	52.4	16.8	83.2	Senate	50.6	17.8	82.2
Senate	48.4	17.7	82.3	Governor	52.4	17.5	82.5
Governor	53.1	13.3	86.7	**1987**			
1973				Governor	59.2	18.3	81.7
Governor	33.7	67.4	32.6	**1988**			
1974				President	45.7	14.0	86.0
House	56.8	19.6	80.4	House	53.1	18.2	81.8
Senate	60.0	24.0	76.0	Senate	53.2	21.9	78.1
Governor	58.9	19.4	80.6	Governor	48.6	16.3	83.7
1975				**1989**			
Governor	72.1	44.3	55.7	Governor	56.2	12.4	87.6
1976				**1990**			
President	50.6	10.2	89.8	House	54.1	16.1	83.9
House	55.6	22.3	77.7	Senate	50.3	33.7	66.3
Senate	59.1	25.7	74.3	Governor	53.2	17.1	82.9
Governor	53.5	19.7	80.3	**1991**			
1977				Governor	58.1	18.3	81.7
Governor	50.4	13.5	86.5	**1992**			
1978				President	52.5	12.0	88.0
House	53.5	19.2	80.8	House	52.9	13.7	86.3
Senate	51.8	23.4	76.6	Senate	51.9	16.8	83.2
Governor	52.6	16.3	83.7	Governor	55.3	21.5	78.5
1979				**1993**			
Governor	56.7	13.9	86.1	Governor	45.4	9.3	90.7
1980				**1994**			
President	43.7	17.1	82.9	House	45.4	17.4	82.6
House	49.9	18.4	81.6	Senate	47.6	19.6	80.4
Senate	49.8	15.5	84.5	Governor	46.6	17.8	82.2
Governor	50.4	17.8	82.2	**1995**			
1981				Governor	44.0	13.5	86.5
Governor	51.8	3.6	96.4	**1996**			
1982				President	53.7	14.7	85.3
House	53.8	19.8	80.2	House	48.2	16.7	83.3
Senate	56.4	18.8	81.2	Senate	47.5	16.1	83.9
Governor	55.8	17.9	82.1	Governor	50.5	28.2	71.8
1983				**1997**			
Governor	59.0	18.1	81.9	Governor	46.3	7.3	92.7
1984				**1998**			
President	39.7	23.4	76.6	House	46.6	21.8	78.2
House	50.8	19.3	80.7	Senate	49.8	25.5	74.5
Senate	46.4	27.8	72.2	Governor	45.9	19.7	80.3
Governor	49.2	15.4	84.6	**1999**			
1985				Governor	48.2	20.1	79.9
Governor	42.4	25.6	74.4				

Notes: The Democratic percent of two-party vote is the national average of the state Democratic percent of two-party vote values for president shown in Tables 8-36 through 8-53, for House shown in Tables 8-54 through 8-89, for Senate shown in Tables 8-90 through 8-104, and for governor shown in Table 8-105 through 8-140 for a given election year. (These same values can be found in the state vote tables in Chapters 4, 5, 6, and 7, respectively.) The Democratic vote values are different from the national vote tables presented in Chapters 4–6 since the former are based on voter percentage values and the latter on raw vote numbers. Margin of victory is the national average of the state margin of victory values for president, House, Senate, and governor found in Tables 8-36 through 8-140 for a given election year. Margin of victory is defined as the absolute difference between the Democratic and Republican percent of the two-party vote for each of these separate races in a given election year. Averaging these percent values (instead of the raw vote numbers on which they are based) is purposely done in order that each state is weighted equally in determining the national result for margin of victory. Paul David's (1972) party competition index is the national average of the state party competition values for president, House, Senate, and governor found in Tables 8-36 through 8-140 for a given election year. It is defined as 100 − the margin of victory or, alternately, as 100 − the absolute difference between the Democratic and Republican percent of two-party vote for each political race in a given election year. The values for Democratic and Republican percent of two-party vote for president, House, Senate, and governor used in the computations to get the David party competition values in Tables 8-36 through 8-140 are taken from the state vote tables for these races in Chapters 4, 5, 6, and 7, respectively. The author's alternative party coding in Chapters 4–7 is used whenever it occurs in place of the conventional party coding for vote data in computing David's party competition index. Zero (0) percent on David's competition index represents a complete absence of two-party competition for that year, whereas a score of 100 percent indicates perfect competition between the two major parties. The Democratic Party is defined as the Anti-Federalists, Democratic-Republicans, and Jackson Democrats prior to 1830 when the "Democratic Party" as such was established. The Republican Party is defined as the Federalists, National Republicans, and Whigs prior to the establishment of the "Republican Party" in the 1850s. See Appendix A for an explanation of the historical antecedents of the current Democratic and Republican parties. No special elections for any of the four races are used in the calculations, nor are partial voting data reported for any of the four races in any of the states. Because of rounding, margin of victory and competition values when added together, may equal 100.1 or 99.9 percent instead of 100.0 percent in some instances.

[1]Voters began directly electing senators in 1912.

Sources: Tables 8-36 through 8-140. Specifically, state Democratic percent values of the two-party vote for each race in Tables 8-36 through 8-140 are aggregated in any given year to obtain the national Democratic percent of two-party vote for each race in that year. National margin of victory values and national party competition values are obtained in the same manner from Tables 8-36 through 8-140 for each political race.

Table 8-4 National Competition Measures, by Two-Year Election Cycle, 1788–1999

Year	Democratic % of Two-Party Vote	Margin of Victory	Party Competition Index	Year	Democratic % of Two-Party Vote	Margin of Victory	Party Competition Index
1788–1789				1824–1825			
President	7.6	84.7	15.3	President	52.6	62.6	37.4
House	40.3	19.4	80.6	House	85.5	71.9	28.1
Governor	51.6	69.8	30.2	Governor	77.1	84.2	15.8
1790–1791				1826–1827			
President	—	—	—	President	—	—	—
House	30.4	39.2	60.8	House	42.5	49.4	50.6
Governor	96.9	93.9	6.1	Governor	75.1	84.0	16.0
1792–1793				1828–1829			
President	0.0	100.0	0.0	President	56.9	36.8	63.2
House	45.1	9.9	90.1	House	50.6	33.6	66.4
Governor	62.8	65.5	34.5	Governor	63.5	59.2	40.8
1794–1795				1830–1831			
President	—	—	—	President	—	—	—
House	39.3	33.0	67.0	House	55.0	39.3	60.7
Governor	11.7	76.6	23.4	Governor	57.4	42.8	57.2
1796–1797				1832–1833			
President	32.8	35.2	64.8	President	65.4	40.1	59.9
House	38.7	43.8	56.2	House	59.6	35.1	64.9
Governor	34.3	86.7	13.3	Governor	66.5	46.3	53.7
1798–1799				1834–1835			
President	—	—	—	President	—	—	—
House	32.8	35.3	64.7	House	57.3	29.1	70.9
Governor	34.7	54.5	45.5	Governor	52.7	26.2	73.8
1800–1801				1836–1837			
President	60.3	20.7	79.3	President	52.1	11.0	89.0
House	61.0	38.9	61.1	House	52.3	21.2	78.8
Governor	55.1	45.9	54.1	Governor	53.7	19.2	80.8
1802–1803				1838–1839			
President	—	—	—	President	—	—	—
House	59.2	42.4	57.6	House	50.0	8.6	91.4
Governor	54.8	41.3	58.7	Governor	53.3	14.2	85.8
1804–1805				1840–1841			
President	82.8	65.6	34.5	President	46.5	10.8	89.2
House	67.5	52.9	47.1	House	45.9	16.1	83.9
Governor	60.4	38.2	61.8	Governor	46.2	16.4	83.6
1806–1807				1842–1843			
President	—	—	—	President	—	—	—
House	66.2	38.9	61.1	House	56.6	18.7	81.3
Governor	63.2	34.5	65.5	Governor	51.0	14.6	85.4
1808–1809				1844–1845			
President	66.0	35.7	64.3	President	51.3	8.9	91.1
House	55.1	15.6	84.4	House	50.4	15.0	85.0
Governor	61.7	34.2	65.8	Governor	54.4	21.2	78.8
1810–1811				1846–1847			
President	—	—	—	President	—	—	—
House	61.7	41.0	59.0	House	55.2	18.3	81.7
Governor	58.7	23.0	77.0	Governor	52.4	12.1	87.9
1812–1813				1848–1849			
President	53.4	24.9	75.1	President	48.8	11.6	88.4
House	53.2	33.1	66.9	House	53.8	18.0	82.0
Governor	48.7	31.2	68.8	Governor	56.1	22.9	77.1
1814–1815				1850–1851			
President	—	—	—	President	—	—	—
House	55.4	32.3	67.7	House	53.7	12.0	88.0
Governor	48.5	30.2	69.8	Governor	51.1	22.3	77.7
1816–1817				1852–1853			
President	87.9	75.7	24.3	President	55.3	13.2	86.8
House	68.4	67.1	32.9	House	56.1	14.3	85.7
Governor	62.0	48.8	51.2	Governor	54.6	14.3	85.7
1818–1819				1854–1855			
President	—	—	—	President	—	—	—
House	82.0	64.1	35.9	House	74.5	57.5	42.5
Governor	79.3	63.2	36.8	Governor	63.9	47.1	52.9
1820–1821				1856–1857			
President	93.7	93.4	6.6	President	71.1	57.7	42.3
House	83.6	69.7	30.3	House	69.1	52.0	48.0
Governor	90.4	84.1	15.9	Governor	63.5	44.1	55.9
1822–1823				1858–1859			
President	—	—	—	President	—	—	—
House	86.0	73.4	26.6	House	67.1	46.9	53.1
Governor	83.6	69.1	30.9	Governor	60.2	38.3	61.7

(Table continues)

Table 8-4 (Continued)

Year	Democratic % of Two-Party Vote	Margin of Victory	Party Competition Index	Year	Democratic % of Two-Party Vote	Margin of Victory	Party Competition Index
1860–1861				**1898–1899**			
President	59.3	50.5	49.5	President	—	—	—
House	49.7	41.4	58.6	House	52.8	29.0	71.0
Governor	49.8	30.2	69.8	Governor	53.5	28.6	71.4
1862–1863				**1900–1901**			
President	—	—	—	President	50.5	21.7	78.3
House	42.4	26.4	73.6	House	52.4	23.4	76.6
Governor	36.5	35.2	64.8	Governor	52.7	23.3	76.7
1864–1865				**1902–1903**			
President	42.2	19.6	80.4	President	—	—	—
House	36.0	28.7	71.3	House	53.2	28.4	71.6
Governor	38.6	37.1	62.9	Governor	52.6	25.4	74.6
1866–1867				**1904–1905**			
President	—	—	—	President	44.2	36.1	63.9
House	40.8	24.5	75.5	House	48.5	31.5	68.5
Governor	39.2	29.1	70.9	Governor	51.8	24.9	75.1
1868–1869				**1906–1907**			
President	45.9	18.8	81.2	President	—	—	—
House	41.5	24.1	75.9	House	52.1	29.9	70.1
Governor	37.0	27.0	73.0	Governor	54.4	24.1	75.9
1870–1871				**1908–1909**			
President	—	—	—	President	49.1	23.5	76.5
House	47.0	13.5	86.5	House	51.9	26.6	73.4
Governor	46.5	14.5	85.5	Governor	53.7	20.4	79.6
1872–1873				**1910–1911**			
President	42.5	17.7	82.3	President	—	—	—
House	41.8	22.2	77.8	House	54.3	26.3	73.7
Governor	45.4	21.8	78.2	Governor	53.6	19.2	80.8
1874–1875				**1912–1913**[1]			
President	—	—	—	President	67.2	35.6	64.4
House	49.9	21.8	78.2	House	59.2	29.7	70.3
Governor	50.9	17.5	82.5	Senate	54.4	17.3	82.7
1876–1877				Governor	59.6	23.1	76.9
President	50.9	14.2	85.8	**1914–1915**			
House	51.9	16.3	83.7	President	—	—	—
Governor	52.9	20.1	79.9	House	56.8	28.2	71.8
1878–1879				Senate	56.8	22.8	77.2
President	—	—	—	Governor	53.7	21.2	78.8
House	56.4	28.6	71.4	**1916–1917**			
Governor	53.0	30.0	70.0	President	57.5	20.4	79.6
1880–1881				House	54.7	24.9	75.1
President	50.6	15.7	84.3	Senate	52.7	22.3	77.7
House	52.6	19.3	80.7	Governor	51.7	23.3	76.7
Governor	54.8	30.5	69.5	**1918–1919**			
1882–1883				President	—	—	—
President	—	—	—	House	53.9	32.3	67.7
House	55.1	20.2	79.8	Senate	58.1	35.4	64.6
Governor	54.0	17.7	82.3	Governor	51.9	29.5	70.5
1884–1885				**1920–1921**			
President	50.6	13.4	86.6	President	41.9	33.4	66.6
House	52.6	15.6	84.4	House	44.1	36.1	63.9
Governor	54.4	20.1	79.9	Senate	48.2	30.9	69.1
1886–1887				Governor	45.8	30.1	69.9
President	—	—	—	**1922–1923**			
House	56.9	22.3	77.7	President	—	—	—
Governor	55.8	20.8	79.2	House	52.9	31.3	68.7
1888–1889				Senate	52.8	21.8	78.2
President	51.8	15.5	84.5	Governor	52.2	29.9	70.1
House	51.9	18.5	81.5	**1924–1925**			
Governor	56.0	24.5	75.5	President	40.8	40.7	59.3
1890–1891				House	49.3	35.9	64.1
President	—	—	—	Senate	52.0	40.6	59.4
House	54.6	20.4	79.6	Governor	50.2	28.9	71.1
Governor	54.3	16.9	83.1	**1926–1927**			
1892–1893				President	—	—	—
President	47.7	33.0	67.0	House	49.4	36.6	63.4
House	56.5	24.9	75.1	Senate	51.6	31.5	68.5
Governor	57.1	23.9	76.1	Governor	49.9	33.8	66.2
1894–1895				**1928–1929**			
President	—	—	—	President	43.6	22.6	77.4
House	46.5	34.6	65.4	House	48.8	31.8	68.2
Governor	48.3	32.9	67.1	Senate	46.5	31.2	68.8
1896–1897				Governor	49.2	21.6	78.4
President	53.5	27.9	72.1				
House	50.1	29.3	70.7				
Governor	53.1	31.3	68.7				

Table 8-4 (Continued)

Year	Democratic % of Two-Party Vote	Margin of Victory	Party Competition Index	Year	Democratic % of Two-Party Vote	Margin of Victory	Party Competition Index
1930–1931				**1960–1961**			
President	—	—	—	President	49.4	8.7	91.3
House	53.1	34.3	65.7	House	58.0	21.4	78.6
Senate	60.8	39.0	61.0	Senate	60.1	29.4	70.6
Governor	53.5	27.5	72.5	Governor	53.3	12.4	87.6
1932–1933				**1962–1963**			
President	64.1	30.0	70.0	President	—	—	—
House	61.5	27.0	73.0	House	55.0	18.3	81.7
Senate	62.6	30.6	69.4	Senate	54.3	18.3	81.7
Governor	58.9	22.7	77.3	Governor	55.7	18.2	81.8
1934–1935				**1964–1965**			
President	—	—	—	President	58.9	26.2	73.8
House	63.6	30.3	69.7	House	58.2	18.2	81.8
Senate	59.4	27.2	72.8	Senate	59.8	22.5	77.5
Governor	60.5	25.7	74.3	Governor	55.5	15.2	84.8
1936–1937				**1966–1967**			
President	66.2	33.6	66.4	President	—	—	—
House	63.4	30.9	69.1	House	52.3	17.0	83.0
Senate	63.6	38.3	61.7	Senate	52.2	23.3	76.7
Governor	59.0	27.6	72.4	Governor	50.5	15.8	84.2
1938–1939				**1968–1969**			
President	—	—	—	President	48.7	13.0	87.0
House	59.2	31.9	68.1	House	51.1	19.5	80.5
Senate	59.8	31.7	68.3	Senate	52.8	22.0	78.0
Governor	56.0	31.3	68.7	Governor	51.9	13.6	86.4
1940–1941				**1970–1971**			
President	59.4	22.1	77.9	President	—	—	—
House	59.2	30.6	69.4	House	56.2	20.4	79.6
Senate	56.2	31.3	68.7	Senate	57.6	20.2	79.8
Governor	57.1	27.0	73.0	Governor	54.2	14.7	85.3
1942–1943				**1972–1973**			
President	—	—	—	President	36.8	29.0	71.0
House	56.9	31.8	68.2	House	52.4	16.8	83.2
Senate	59.5	38.7	61.3	Senate	48.4	17.7	82.3
Governor	53.4	34.0	66.0	Governor	51.3	18.4	81.6
1944–1945				**1974–1975**			
President	57.1	18.6	81.4	President	—	—	—
House	57.4	28.9	71.1	House	56.8	19.6	80.4
Senate	58.3	25.1	74.9	Senate	60.0	24.0	76.0
Governor	53.0	25.0	75.0	Governor	59.9	21.3	78.7
1946–1947				**1976–1977**			
President	—	—	—	President	50.6	10.2	89.8
House	53.5	29.7	70.3	House	55.6	22.3	77.7
Senate	49.7	24.3	75.7	Senate	59.1	25.7	74.3
Governor	51.7	32.5	67.5	Governor	53.1	18.9	81.1
1948–1949				**1978–1979**			
President	54.0	16.1	83.9	President	—	—	—
House	57.8	27.2	72.8	House	53.5	19.2	80.8
Senate	61.8	32.2	67.8	Senate	51.8	23.4	76.6
Governor	56.1	24.7	75.3	Governor	52.9	16.1	83.9
1950–1951				**1980–1981**			
President	—	—	—	President	43.7	17.1	82.9
House	57.1	28.3	71.7	House	49.9	18.4	81.6
Senate	55.2	30.2	69.8	Senate	49.8	15.5	84.5
Governor	54.2	28.0	72.0	Governor	50.6	15.9	84.1
1952–1953				**1982–1983**			
President	44.0	17.0	83.0	President	—	—	—
House	53.5	28.3	71.7	House	53.8	19.8	80.2
Senate	52.2	27.0	73.0	Senate	56.4	18.8	81.2
Governor	51.8	24.0	76.0	Governor	56.0	17.9	82.1
1954–1955				**1984–1985**			
President	—	—	—	President	39.7	23.4	76.6
House	57.8	24.9	75.1	House	50.8	19.3	80.7
Senate	62.2	32.1	67.9	Senate	46.4	27.8	72.2
Governor	57.4	23.3	76.7	Governor	48.3	16.8	83.2
1956–1957				**1986–1987**			
President	43.2	19.0	81.0	President	—	—	—
House	55.8	22.7	77.3	House	52.9	20.5	79.5
Senate	57.4	27.0	73.0	Senate	50.6	17.8	82.2
Governor	55.0	17.4	82.6	Governor	52.8	17.6	82.4
1958–1959				**1988–1989**			
President	—	—	—	President	45.7	14.0	86.0
House	62.0	25.6	74.4	House	53.1	18.2	81.8
Senate	59.8	23.3	76.7	Senate	53.2	21.9	78.1
Governor	61.4	25.4	74.6	Governor	49.7	15.7	84.3

(Table continues)

Table 8-4 *(Continued)*

Year	Democratic % of Two-Party Vote	Margin of Victory	Party Competition Index	Year	Democratic % of Two-Party Vote	Margin of Victory	Party Competition Index
1990–1991				1996–1997			
President	—	—	—	President	53.7	14.7	85.3
House	54.1	16.1	83.9	House	48.2	16.7	83.3
Senate	50.3	33.7	66.3	Senate	47.5	16.1	83.9
Governor	53.6	17.2	82.8	Governor	49.9	25.0	75.0
1992–1993				1998–1999			
President	52.5	12.0	88.0	President	—	—	—
House	52.9	13.7	86.3	House	46.6	21.8	78.2
Senate	51.9	16.8	83.2	Senate	49.8	25.5	74.5
Governor	53.9	19.8	80.2	Governor	46.1	19.8	80.2
1994–1995							
President	—	—	—				
House	45.4	17.4	82.6				
Senate	47.6	19.6	80.4				
Governor	46.4	17.4	82.6				

Notes: The Democratic percent of two-party vote is the national average of the state Democratic percent of two-party vote values for president shown in Tables 8-36 through 8-53, for House shown in Tables 8-54 through 8-89, for Senate shown in Tables 8-90 through 8-104, and for governor shown in Table 8-105 through 8-140 for a given two-year election year. (These same values can be found in the state vote tables in Chapters 4, 5, 6, and 7, respectively.) The Democratic vote values are different from the national vote tables presented in Chapters 4–6 since the former are based on voter percentage values and the latter on raw vote numbers. Margin of victory is the national average of the state margin of victory values for president, House, Senate, and governor found in Tables 8-36 through 8-140 for a given election year. Margin of victory is defined as the absolute difference between the Democratic and Republican percent of the two-party vote for each of these separate races in a given election year. Averaging these percent values (instead of the raw vote numbers on which they are based) is purposely done in order that each state is weighted equally in determining the national result for margin of victory. Paul David's (1972) party competition index is the national average of the state party competition values for president, House, Senate, and governor found in Tables 8-36 through 8-140 for a given election year. It is defined as 100 − the margin of victory or, alternately, as 100 − the absolute difference between the Democratic and Republican percent of two-party vote for each political race in a given election year. The values for Democratic and Republican percent of two-party vote for president, House, Senate, and governor used in the computations to get the David party competition values in Tables 8-36 through 8-140 are taken from the state vote tables for these races in Chapters 4, 5, 6, and 7, respectively. The author's alternative party coding in Chapters 4–7 is used whenever it occurs in place of the conventional party coding for vote data in computing David's party competition index. Zero (0) percent on David's competition index represents a complete absence of two-party competition for that election cycle, whereas a score of 100 percent indicates perfect competition between the two major parties. The Democratic Party is defined as the Anti-Federalists, Democratic-Republicans, and Jackson Democrats prior to 1830 when the "Democratic Party" as such was established. The Republican Party is defined as the Federalists, National Republicans, and Whigs prior to the establishment of the "Republican Party" in the 1850s. See Appendix A for an explanation of the historical antecedents of the current Democratic and Republican parties. No special elections for any of the four races are used in the calculations, nor are partial voting data reported for any of the four races in any of the states. Because of rounding, margin of victory and competition values when added together may equal 100.1 or 99.9 percent instead of 100.0 percent in some instances.

[1]Voters began directly electing senators in 1912.

Sources: Tables 8-36 through 8-140. Specifically, state Democratic percent values of the two-party vote for each race in Tables 8-36 through 8-140 are aggregated in any given two-year election cycle to obtain the national Democratic percent of two-party vote for each race for that cycle as shown in Table 8-4. National margin of victory values and national party competition values are obtained in the same manner from Tables 8-36 through 8-140 for each political race.

Table 8-5 Composite Competition Index, by Region, by Two-Year Election Cycle, 1788–1999

Year/Region[1]	Composite Competition Index	Year/Region[1]	Composite Competition Index	Year/Region[1]	Composite Competition Index	Year/Region[1]	Composite Competition Index
1788–1789		1810–1811		1832–1833		1854–1855	
NEng	22.7	NEng	84.7	NEng	62.6	NEng	58.3
South	—	South	12.8	South	30.7	South	13.8
MAtl	46.0	MAtl	64.8	MAtl	69.9	MAtl	81.7
BdrS	57.5	BdrS	50.8	BdrS	97.1	BdrS	0.0
MidW	—	MidW	0.0	MidW	64.7	MidW	76.5
West	—	West	—	West	—	West	42.6
1790–1791		1812–1813		1834–1835		1856–1857	
NEng	0.0	NEng	57.7	NEng	78.0	NEng	69.9
South	—	South	12.3	South	71.6	South	0.0
MAtl	39.6	MAtl	87.7	MAtl	90.4	MAtl	74.2
BdrS	—	BdrS	58.3	BdrS	—	BdrS	0.3
MidW	—	MidW	63.7	MidW	51.8	MidW	81.2
West	—	West	—	West	—	West	57.7
1792–1793		1814–1815		1836–1837		1858–1859	
NEng	0.0	NEng	79.1	NEng	83.4	NEng	79.0
South	—	South	5.5	South	78.1	South	22.1
MAtl	72.5	MAtl	85.3	MAtl	92.5	MAtl	49.8
BdrS	40.1	BdrS	74.4	BdrS	89.4	BdrS	0.0
MidW	—	MidW	56.0	MidW	81.4	MidW	87.9
West	—	West	—	West	—	West	50.8
1794–1795		1816–1817		1838–1839		1860–1861	
NEng	43.9	NEng	64.2	NEng	92.0	NEng	69.3
South	87.2	South	1.6	South	81.4	South	15.2
MAtl	57.6	MAtl	46.9	MAtl	81.8	MAtl	71.3
BdrS	81.4	BdrS	29.1	BdrS	96.5	BdrS	25.6
MidW	—	MidW	8.1	MidW	94.5	MidW	80.1
West	—	West	—	West	—	West	73.4
1796–1797		1818–1819		1840–1841		1862–1863	
NEng	24.2	NEng	61.8	NEng	76.6	NEng	67.2
South	53.8	South	0.0	South	90.0	South	25.5
MAtl	67.9	MAtl	62.0	MAtl	95.4	MAtl	95.1
BdrS	85.5	BdrS	—	BdrS	79.2	BdrS	16.8
MidW	—	MidW	5.8	MidW	90.0	MidW	78.4
West	—	West	—	West	—	West	74.5
1798–1799		1820–1821		1842–1843		1864–1865	
NEng	33.8	NEng	24.4	NEng	81.4	NEng	69.3
South	43.4	South	0.0	South	82.6	South	20.2
MAtl	90.3	MAtl	33.2	MAtl	95.7	MAtl	97.3
BdrS	—	BdrS	7.8	BdrS	89.8	BdrS	55.7
MidW	—	MidW	0.0	MidW	82.2	MidW	76.1
West	—	West	—	West	—	West	81.8
1800–1801		1822–1823		1844–1845		1866–1867	
NEng	66.7	NEng	24.6	NEng	75.4	NEng	71.8
South	11.4	South	3.2	South	80.4	South	0.0
MAtl	96.4	MAtl	59.8	MAtl	97.2	MAtl	95.5
BdrS	43.2	BdrS	50.2	BdrS	95.5	BdrS	66.5
MidW	—	MidW	19.1	MidW	91.6	MidW	77.3
West	—	West	—	West	—	West	93.9
1802–1803		1824–1825		1846–1847		1868–1869	
NEng	71.3	NEng	17.3	NEng	87.0	NEng	76.7
South	29.7	South	18.7	South	68.8	South	58.6
MAtl	59.8	MAtl	35.4	MAtl	96.8	MAtl	95.0
BdrS	—	BdrS	44.0	BdrS	95.0	BdrS	70.6
MidW	26.2	MidW	44.4	MidW	89.9	MidW	85.1
West	—	West	—	West	—	West	90.8
1804–1805		1826–1827		1848–1849		1870–1871	
NEng	72.4	NEng	11.5	NEng	82.2	NEng	80.6
South	0.0	South	10.3	South	81.9	South	82.1
MAtl	45.2	MAtl	61.4	MAtl	88.3	MAtl	94.2
BdrS	34.2	BdrS	86.5	BdrS	90.0	BdrS	88.1
MidW	28.1	MidW	64.4	MidW	86.2	MidW	86.4
West	—	West	—	West	0.0	West	96.1
1806–1807		1828–1829		1850–1851		1872–1873	
NEng	71.2	NEng	45.3	NEng	81.5	NEng	76.7
South	18.2	South	36.5	South	57.4	South	75.8
MAtl	79.0	MAtl	78.1	MAtl	96.8	MAtl	91.3
BdrS	54.0	BdrS	95.3	BdrS	95.3	BdrS	77.1
MidW	26.0	MidW	77.8	MidW	90.1	MidW	80.6
West	—	West	—	West	96.1	West	90.0
1808–1809		1830–1831		1852–1853		1874–1875	
NEng	86.1	NEng	53.6	NEng	84.7	NEng	81.8
South	32.0	South	37.9	South	79.2	South	70.3
MAtl	80.4	MAtl	81.2	MAtl	95.1	MAtl	94.1
BdrS	54.1	BdrS	86.8	BdrS	94.6	BdrS	80.0
MidW	36.5	MidW	76.0	MidW	88.4	MidW	79.1
West	—	West	—	West	94.9	West	87.7

(Table continues)

Table 8-5 (Continued)

Year/Region[1]	Composite Competition Index	Year/Region[1]	Composite Competition Index	Year/Region[1]	Composite Competition Index	Year/Region[1]	Composite Competition Index
1876–1877		**1898–1899**		**1920–1921**		**1942–1943**	
NEng	85.5	NEng	75.1	NEng	65.4	NEng	80.8
South	72.4	South	34.2	South	50.9	South	13.0
MAtl	93.7	MAtl	92.6	MAtl	73.2	MAtl	90.8
BdrS	83.8	BdrS	97.2	BdrS	93.6	BdrS	91.4
MidW	86.0	MidW	90.5	MidW	65.9	MidW	75.0
West	96.3	West	66.2	West	75.0	West	84.9
1878–1879		**1900–1901**		**1922–1923**		**1944–1945**	
NEng	79.3	NEng	74.3	NEng	86.3	NEng	85.7
South	41.5	South	52.4	South	33.0	South	34.8
MAtl	68.1	MAtl	87.7	MAtl	88.4	MAtl	96.3
BdrS	77.7	BdrS	94.4	BdrS	90.6	BdrS	88.7
MidW	81.3	MidW	87.8	MidW	72.1	MidW	86.6
West	91.3	West	87.7	West	82.2	West	86.4
1880–1881		**1902–1903**		**1924–1925**		**1946–1947**	
NEng	82.1	NEng	80.8	NEng	71.4	NEng	77.9
South	61.1	South	31.5	South	39.5	South	27.0
MAtl	97.5	MAtl	89.5	MAtl	69.3	MAtl	85.2
BdrS	87.7	BdrS	93.1	BdrS	91.9	BdrS	93.3
MidW	82.6	MidW	82.3	MidW	64.4	MidW	77.5
West	95.9	West	88.6	West	73.2	West	83.5
1882–1883		**1904–1905**		**1926–1927**		**1948–1949**	
NEng	85.3	NEng	77.1	NEng	75.3	NEng	83.1
South	55.4	South	46.0	South	27.6	South	37.4
MAtl	94.2	MAtl	83.2	MAtl	81.1	MAtl	93.1
BdrS	89.3	BdrS	94.8	BdrS	90.5	BdrS	84.2
MidW	89.0	MidW	71.1	MidW	67.8	MidW	89.0
West	92.6	West	74.0	West	79.5	West	88.5
1884–1885		**1906–1907**		**1928–1929**		**1950–1951**	
NEng	84.1	NEng	86.0	NEng	81.3	NEng	79.5
South	69.2	South	31.8	South	53.5	South	19.1
MAtl	94.0	MAtl	92.8	MAtl	81.4	MAtl	93.6
BdrS	91.9	BdrS	92.3	BdrS	89.1	BdrS	88.8
MidW	92.2	MidW	80.4	MidW	72.7	MidW	85.5
West	92.4	West	80.5	West	78.9	West	86.1
1886–1887		**1908–1909**		**1930–1931**		**1952–1953**	
NEng	89.0	NEng	78.1	NEng	87.0	NEng	81.0
South	48.9	South	47.2	South	23.0	South	46.5
MAtl	69.3	MAtl	88.6	MAtl	83.0	MAtl	91.6
BdrS	88.5	BdrS	95.3	BdrS	87.7	BdrS	93.4
MidW	91.4	MidW	87.6	MidW	75.0	MidW	80.0
West	96.3	West	83.7	West	76.2	West	85.6
1888–1889		**1910–1911**		**1932–1933**		**1954–1955**	
NEng	87.2	NEng	90.1	NEng	92.2	NEng	89.2
South	57.1	South	32.9	South	30.4	South	23.9
MAtl	94.4	MAtl	84.5	MAtl	90.6	MAtl	95.4
BdrS	96.5	BdrS	93.4	BdrS	74.8	BdrS	84.5
MidW	90.4	MidW	85.4	MidW	85.0	MidW	88.3
West	89.5	West	87.2	West	81.0	West	91.3
1890–1891		**1912–1913**		**1934–1935**		**1956–1957**	
NEng	91.4	NEng	90.6	NEng	92.1	NEng	80.1
South	49.7	South	27.1	South	19.6	South	48.9
MAtl	96.3	MAtl	82.3	MAtl	89.7	MAtl	88.7
BdrS	85.1	BdrS	77.2	BdrS	85.0	BdrS	91.2
MidW	87.3	MidW	82.0	MidW	87.6	MidW	87.5
West	91.0	West	80.3	West	75.6	West	87.9
1892–1893		**1914–1915**		**1936–1937**		**1958–1959**	
NEng	90.5	NEng	88.1	NEng	89.7	NEng	85.6
South	38.7	South	26.3	South	25.6	South	22.4
MAtl	96.5	MAtl	86.8	MAtl	88.5	MAtl	96.7
BdrS	91.5	BdrS	90.7	BdrS	75.6	BdrS	72.1
MidW	84.1	MidW	89.6	MidW	82.9	MidW	91.2
West	70.5	West	85.2	West	72.6	West	85.6
1894–1895		**1916–1917**		**1938–1939**		**1960–1961**	
NEng	74.0	NEng	86.4	NEng	86.9	NEng	82.9
South	37.5	South	37.7	South	18.0	South	56.0
MAtl	86.2	MAtl	88.8	MAtl	92.3	MAtl	96.5
BdrS	95.8	BdrS	94.0	BdrS	75.2	BdrS	87.8
MidW	69.8	MidW	87.1	MidW	80.8	MidW	92.4
West	65.4	West	87.5	West	81.3	West	91.2
1896–1897		**1918–1919**		**1940–1941**		**1962–1963**	
NEng	61.6	NEng	86.8	NEng	87.8	NEng	88.7
South	54.8	South	18.6	South	24.9	South	52.3
MAtl	82.5	MAtl	89.9	MAtl	94.3	MAtl	93.7
BdrS	93.0	BdrS	92.7	BdrS	80.6	BdrS	87.6
MidW	88.7	MidW	76.3	MidW	86.1	MidW	90.9
West	60.0	West	82.3	West	81.4	West	86.9

Table 8-5 *(Continued)*

Year/Region[1]	Composite Competition Index	Year/Region[1]	Composite Competition Index	Year/Region[1]	Composite Competition Index	Year/Region[1]	Composite Competition Index
1964–1965		**1974–1975**		**1984–1985**		**1994–1995**	
NEng	69.3	NEng	78.1	NEng	76.6	NEng	71.9
South	68.9	South	61.7	South	77.0	South	86.2
MAtl	83.3	MAtl	85.7	MAtl	84.1	MAtl	88.9
BdrS	70.0	BdrS	78.9	BdrS	77.8	BdrS	83.0
MidW	85.4	MidW	86.1	MidW	82.5	MidW	79.9
West	86.3	West	82.7	West	72.0	West	83.8
1966–1967		**1976–1977**		**1986–1987**		**1996–1997**	
NEng	81.7	NEng	82.5	NEng	69.8	NEng	75.0
South	64.6	South	73.8	South	84.3	South	90.4
MAtl	90.2	MAtl	90.1	MAtl	84.6	MAtl	82.1
BdrS	89.1	BdrS	68.8	BdrS	70.6	BdrS	73.9
MidW	85.6	MidW	85.8	MidW	82.5	MidW	86.4
West	88.8	West	83.2	West	85.3	West	82.4
1968–1969		**1978–1979**		**1988–1989**		**1998–1999**	
NEng	76.5	NEng	77.9	NEng	80.8	NEng	66.4
South	72.7	South	73.3	South	81.4	South	83.7
MAtl	92.5	MAtl	90.1	MAtl	82.1	MAtl	82.1
BdrS	87.4	BdrS	78.8	BdrS	78.3	BdrS	68.1
MidW	88.4	MidW	86.6	MidW	84.9	MidW	81.3
West	84.3	West	81.1	West	84.1	West	75.6
1970–1971		**1980–1981**		**1990–1991**			
NEng	82.4	NEng	79.3	NEng	77.3		
South	62.3	South	88.0	South	68.2		
MAtl	88.6	MAtl	91.3	MAtl	80.0		
BdrS	81.8	BdrS	81.0	BdrS	75.1		
MidW	88.9	MidW	85.1	MidW	87.5		
West	85.1	West	77.3	West	82.0		
1972–1973		**1982–1983**		**1992–1993**			
NEng	83.3	NEng	81.7	NEng	81.2		
South	68.8	South	79.1	South	89.3		
MAtl	84.4	MAtl	88.6	MAtl	90.8		
BdrS	77.5	BdrS	74.2	BdrS	74.7		
MidW	82.4	MidW	84.0	MidW	85.3		
West	80.6	West	79.1	West	87.3		

Notes: The regional composite competition index is the mean of all state values for the party competition index devised by Paul David (1972) for all races in a given two-year election cycle in a given region among the following set of races: president, House, Senate, and governor. The state values for these races are presented in Tables 8-36 through 8-53 for president, Tables 8-54 through 8-89 for House, Tables 8-90 through 8-104 for Senate, and Tables 8-105 through 8-140 for governor. David's competition index is defined as 100 − the absolute difference between the Democratic and Republican percentage of two-party vote for each of the four races mentioned here. The values for Democratic and Republican percent of two-party vote for president, House, Senate, and governor used in the computations to get the David party competition values in Tables 8-36 through 8-140 are taken from the state vote tables for these races in Chapters 4, 5, 6, and 7, respectively. The author's alternative party coding in Chapters 4–7 is used whenever it occurs in place of the conventional party coding for vote data in computing David's party competition index. Zero (0) percent on David's competition index represents a complete absence of two-party competition for that election cycle in that region, whereas a score of 100 percent indicates perfect competition between the two major parties in that region. The Democratic Party is defined as the Anti-Federalists, Democratic-Republicans, and Jackson Democrats prior to 1830 when the "Democratic Party" as such was established. The Republican Party is defined as the Federalists, National Republicans, and Whigs prior to the establishment of the "Republican Party" in the 1850s. See Appendix A for an explanation of the historical antecedents of the current Democratic and Republican parties. No special elections for any of the four races are used in the calculations, nor are partial voting data reported for any of the four races in any of the states. —indicates no data available.

[1]The regional categorizations are adapted from the ICPSR regional codings. In the current analysis, Tennessee is categorized in the South since it was part of the Confederacy, although the ICPSR treats it as a Border South state. The regional categories are: New England—Connecticut, Maine, Massachusetts, New Hampshire, Rhode Island, Vermont; Mid-Atlantic—Delaware, New Jersey, New York, Pennsylvania; South—Alabama, Arkansas, Florida, Georgia, Louisiana, Mississippi, North Carolina, South Carolina, Tennessee, Texas, Virginia; Border South—Kentucky, Maryland, Oklahoma, West Virginia; Midwest—Illinois, Indiana, Iowa, Kansas, Michigan, Minnesota, Missouri, Nebraska, North Dakota, Ohio, South Dakota, Wisconsin; West—Alaska, Arizona, California, Colorado, Hawaii, Idaho, Montana, Nevada, New Mexico, Oregon, Utah, Washington, Wyoming.

Sources: Tables 8-36 through 8-140. Specifically, state party competition values in Tables 8-36 through 8-140 for the presidential, House, Senate, and gubernatorial races are aggregated across states in a given region for each two-year election cycle to obtain the regional composite competition averages shown for that cycle.

Table 8-6 Competition Measures by Region, by Two-Year Election Cycle, 1788–1999

Year/Region[1]	Democratic % of Two-Party Vote	Margin of Victory	Party Competition Index	Year/Region[1]	Democratic % of Two-Party Vote	Margin of Victory	Party Competition Index
1788–1789				**South**			
New England				President	—	—	—
President	0.0	100.0	0.0	House	56.4	12.8	87.2
House	—	—	—	Governor	—	—	—
Governor	27.4	54.7	45.3	*Mid-Atlantic*			
South				President	—	—	—
President	—	—	—	House	33.2	35.3	64.7
House	—	—	—	Governor	23.5	53.1	46.9
Governor	—	—	—	*Border South*			
Mid-Atlantic				President	—	—	—
President	—	—	—	House	40.7	18.6	81.4
House	46.0	8.0	92.0	Governor	—	—	—
Governor	100.0	100.0	0.0	*Midwest*			
Border South				President	—	—	—
President	22.9	54.2	45.8	House	—	—	—
House	34.6	30.8	69.2	Governor	—	—	—
Governor	—	—	—	*West*			
Midwest				President	—	—	—
President	—	—	—	House	—	—	—
House	—	—	—	Governor	—	—	—
Governor	—	—	—	**1796–1797**			
West				*New England*			
President	—	—	—	President	0.0	100.0	0.0
House	—	—	—	House	20.4	59.2	40.8
Governor	—	—	—	Governor	23.9	85.6	14.4
1790–1791				*South*			
New England				President	—	—	—
President	—	—	—	House	69.2	46.2	53.8
House	—	—	—	Governor	—	—	—
Governor	100.0	100.0	0.0	*Mid-Atlantic*			
South				President	50.6	1.2	98.8
President	—	—	—	House	39.0	22.0	78.0
House	—	—	—	Governor	96.7	93.4	6.6
Governor	—	—	—	*Border South*			
Mid-Atlantic				President	47.8	4.4	95.6
President	—	—	—	House	37.7	24.6	75.4
House	30.4	39.2	60.8	Governor	—	—	—
Governor	90.8	81.6	18.4	*Midwest*			
Border South				President	—	—	—
President	—	—	—	House	—	—	—
House	—	—	—	Governor	—	—	—
Governor	—	—	—	*West*			
Midwest				President	—	—	—
President	—	—	—	House	—	—	—
House	—	—	—	Governor	—	—	—
Governor	—	—	—	**1798–1799**			
West				*New England*			
President	—	—	—	President	—	—	—
House	—	—	—	House	20.4	59.2	40.8
Governor	—	—	—	Governor	13.4	73.2	26.8
1792–1793				*South*			
New England				President	—	—	—
President	0.0	100.0	0.0	House	43.4	13.2	86.8
House	—	—	—	Governor	100.0	100.0	0.0
Governor	100.0	100.0	0.0	*Mid-Atlantic*			
South				President	—	—	—
President	—	—	—	House	45.8	10.8	89.2
House	—	—	—	Governor	48.4	8.3	91.7
Governor	—	—	—	*Border South*			
Mid-Atlantic				President	—	—	—
President	—	—	—	House	—	—	—
House	47.6	4.9	95.1	Governor	—	—	—
Governor	37.9	42.5	57.5	*Midwest*			
Border South				President	—	—	—
President	0.0	100.0	0.0	House	—	—	—
House	40.1	19.8	80.2	Governor	—	—	—
Governor	—	—	—	*West*			
Midwest				President	—	—	—
President	—	—	—	House	—	—	—
House	—	—	—	Governor	—	—	—
Governor	—	—	—	**1800–1801**			
West				*New England*			
President	—	—	—	President	52.2	4.4	95.6
House	—	—	—	House	44.5	26.6	73.4
Governor	—	—	—	Governor	43.1	42.3	57.7
1794–1795				*South*			
New England				President	77.3	54.6	45.4
President	—	—	—	House	100.0	100.0	0.0
House	39.3	38.6	61.4	Governor	100.0	100.0	0.0
Governor	0.0	100.0	0.0				

Table 8-6 *(Continued)*

Year/Region[1]	Democratic % of Two-Party Vote	Margin of Victory	Party Competition Index	Year/Region[1]	Democratic % of Two-Party Vote	Margin of Victory	Party Competition Index
Mid-Atlantic				**Border South**			
President	—	—	—	President	—	—	—
House	49.1	3.1	96.9	House	73.0	46.0	54.0
Governor	52.2	4.4	95.6	Governor	—	—	—
Border South				**Midwest**			
President	51.5	3.0	97.0	President	—	—	—
House	81.1	62.2	37.8	House	74.0	48.0	52.0
Governor	100.0	100.0	0.0	Governor	100.0	100.0	0.0
Midwest				**West**			
President	—	—	—	President	—	—	—
House	—	—	—	House	—	—	—
Governor	—	—	—	Governor	—	—	—
West				**1808–1809**			
President	—	—	—	**New England**			
House	—	—	—	President	46.8	6.5	93.5
Governor	—	—	—	House	46.5	7.0	93.0
1802–1803				Governor	51.8	18.3	81.7
New England				**South**			
President	—	—	—	President	95.4	90.8	9.2
House	37.9	33.3	66.7	House	72.6	45.2	54.8
Governor	41.2	25.9	74.2	Governor	—	—	—
South				**Mid-Atlantic**			
President	—	—	—	President	67.1	34.1	65.9
House	80.2	60.5	39.5	House	53.3	10.0	90.0
Governor	100.0	100.0	0.0	Governor	64.5	29.0	71.0
Mid-Atlantic				**Border South**			
President	—	—	—	President	63.4	26.8	73.2
House	68.9	37.8	62.2	House	55.5	11.0	89.0
Governor	73.7	47.4	52.6	Governor	100.0	100.0	0.0
Border South				**Midwest**			
President	—	—	—	President	75.6	51.2	48.8
House	—	—	—	House	69.7	39.4	60.6
Governor	—	—	—	Governor	100.0	100.0	0.0
Midwest				**West**			
President	—	—	—	President	—	—	—
House	73.8	47.6	52.4	House	—	—	—
Governor	100.0	100.0	0.0	Governor	—	—	—
West				**1810–1811**			
President	—	—	—	**New England**			
House	—	—	—	President	—	—	—
Governor	—	—	—	House	40.8	23.8	76.2
1804–1805				Governor	50.8	10.0	90.0
New England				**South**			
President	68.5	36.9	63.1	President	—	—	—
House	50.9	43.3	56.7	House	93.6	87.2	12.8
Governor	44.5	14.4	85.6	Governor	—	—	—
South				**Mid-Atlantic**			
President	100.0	100.0	0.0	President	—	—	—
House	100.0	100.0	0.0	House	68.7	37.5	62.5
Governor	100.0	100.0	0.0	Governor	66.1	32.2	67.8
Mid-Atlantic				**Border South**			
President	97.4	94.7	5.3	President	—	—	—
House	70.1	43.0	57.0	House	74.6	49.2	50.8
Governor	63.3	40.1	59.9	Governor	—	—	—
Border South				**Midwest**			
President	74.8	49.6	50.4	President	—	—	—
House	73.9	47.8	52.2	House	—	—	—
Governor	100.0	100.0	0.0	Governor	100.0	100.0	0.0
Midwest				**West**			
President	87.3	74.6	25.4	President	—	—	—
House	70.5	41.0	59.0	House	—	—	—
Governor	100.0	100.0	0.0	Governor	—	—	—
West				**1812–1813**			
President	—	—	—	**New England**			
House	—	—	—	President	39.4	21.1	78.9
Governor	—	—	—	House	35.5	29.4	70.6
1806–1807				Governor	39.4	23.3	76.7
New England				**South**			
President	—	—	—	President	72.9	45.8	54.2
House	56.0	12.0	88.0	House	90.8	81.5	18.5
Governor	62.1	33.8	66.2	Governor	100.0	100.0	0.0
South				**Mid-Atlantic**			
President	—	—	—	President	62.6	25.2	74.8
House	90.9	81.8	18.2	House	49.0	11.5	88.5
Governor	—	—	—	Governor	48.5	7.4	92.6
Mid-Atlantic				**Border South**			
President	—	—	—	President	50.8	1.6	98.4
House	55.2	31.7	68.3	House	61.7	23.4	76.6
Governor	50.6	5.0	95.0	Governor	100.0	100.0	0.0

(Table continues)

Table 8-6 (Continued)

Year/Region[1]	Democratic % of Two-Party Vote	Margin of Victory	Party Competition Index	Year/Region[1]	Democratic % of Two-Party Vote	Margin of Victory	Party Competition Index
Midwest				West			
President	69.2	38.4	61.6	President	—	—	—
House	75.3	50.6	49.4	House	—	—	—
Governor	40.0	20.0	80.0	Governor	—	—	—
West				1820–1821			
President	—	—	—	New England			
House	—	—	—	President	86.4	87.2	12.8
Governor	—	—	—	House	76.0	58.3	41.7
1814–1815				Governor	86.7	79.7	20.3
New England				South			
President	—	—	—	President	100.0	100.0	0.0
House	41.8	16.4	83.6	House	100.0	100.0	0.0
Governor	39.5	22.3	77.7	Governor	100.0	100.0	0.0
South				Mid-Atlantic			
President	—	—	—	President	100.0	100.0	0.0
House	95.9	91.7	8.3	House	74.4	48.9	51.1
Governor	100.0	100.0	0.0	Governor	84.4	68.7	31.3
Mid-Atlantic				Border South			
President	—	—	—	President	92.2	84.4	15.6
House	48.1	10.7	89.3	House	—	—	—
Governor	63.3	26.6	73.4	Governor	100.0	100.0	0.0
Border South				Midwest			
President	—	—	—	President	100.0	100.0	0.0
House	37.2	25.6	74.4	House	100.0	100.0	0.0
Governor	—	—	—	Governor	100.0	100.0	0.0
Midwest				West			
President	—	—	—	President	—	—	—
House	—	—	—	House	—	—	—
Governor	72.0	44.0	56.0	Governor	—	—	—
West				1822–1823			
President	—	—	—	New England			
House	—	—	—	President	—	—	—
Governor	—	—	—	House	88.7	77.3	22.7
1816–1817				Governor	85.5	74.3	25.7
New England				South			
President	76.7	53.3	46.7	President	—	—	—
House	30.4	45.6	54.4	House	96.0	92.0	8.0
Governor	42.1	27.4	72.6	Governor	100.0	100.0	0.0
South				Mid-Atlantic			
President	96.9	93.7	6.3	President	—	—	—
House	100.0	100.0	0.0	House	73.9	53.6	46.4
Governor	100.0	100.0	0.0	Governor	64.2	30.1	69.9
Mid-Atlantic				Border South			
President	100.0	100.0	0.0	President	—	—	—
House	68.3	36.9	63.1	House	74.9	49.8	50.2
Governor	66.9	38.1	61.9	Governor	—	—	—
Border South				Midwest			
President	70.9	41.8	58.2	President	—	—	—
House	—	—	—	House	100.0	100.0	0.0
Governor	100.0	100.0	0.0	Governor	87.3	74.6	25.4
Midwest				West			
President	84.9	69.8	30.2	President	—	—	—
House	100.0	100.0	0.0	House	—	—	—
Governor	97.4	94.8	5.2	Governor	—	—	—
West				1824–1825			
President	—	—	—	New England			
House	—	—	—	President	0.0	100.0	0.0
Governor	—	—	—	House	83.6	67.8	32.2
1818–1819				Governor	81.5	83.1	16.9
New England				South			
President	—	—	—	President	78.1	59.0	41.0
House	68.3	36.6	63.4	House	100.0	100.0	0.0
Governor	66.4	39.4	60.6	Governor	100.0	100.0	0.0
South				Mid-Atlantic			
President	—	—	—	President	71.1	42.2	57.8
House	100.0	100.0	0.0	House	82.8	67.8	32.2
Governor	100.0	100.0	0.0	Governor	100.0	100.0	0.0
Mid-Atlantic				Border South			
President	—	—	—	President	74.9	50.2	49.8
House	73.4	47.7	52.3	House	61.9	23.8	76.2
Governor	45.4	9.2	90.8	Governor	100.0	100.0	0.0
Border South				Midwest			
President	—	—	—	President	66.1	36.6	63.4
House	—	—	—	House	100.0	100.0	0.0
Governor	—	—	—	Governor	31.7	63.4	36.6
Midwest				West			
President	—	—	—	President	—	—	—
House	92.8	85.6	14.4	House	—	—	—
Governor	100.0	100.0	0.0	Governor	—	—	—

Table 8-6 *(Continued)*

Year/Region[1]	Democratic % of Two-Party Vote	Margin of Victory	Party Competition Index
1826–1827			
New England			
President	—	—	—
House	23.5	86.3	13.7
Governor	72.8	90.1	9.9
South			
President	—	—	—
House	84.5	69.0	31.0
Governor	100.0	100.0	0.0
Mid-Atlantic			
President	—	—	—
House	45.8	11.1	88.9
Governor	82.6	66.0	34.0
Border South			
President	—	—	—
House	56.8	13.5	86.5
Governor	—	—	—
Midwest			
President	—	—	—
House	39.5	24.9	75.1
Governor	24.1	51.8	48.2
West			
President	—	—	—
House	—	—	—
Governor	—	—	—
1828–1829			
New England			
President	29.3	41.5	58.5
House	31.7	41.8	58.2
Governor	59.0	66.6	33.4
South			
President	79.7	59.5	40.5
House	73.4	61.9	38.1
Governor	80.8	70.0	30.0
Mid-Atlantic			
President	55.3	13.5	86.5
House	50.9	7.5	92.5
Governor	78.1	56.2	43.8
Border South			
President	52.6	5.8	94.2
House	53.1	6.2	93.8
Governor	49.5	1.0	99.0
Midwest			
President	61.5	23.0	77.0
House	61.7	23.4	76.6
Governor	40.3	19.4	80.6
West			
President	—	—	—
House	—	—	—
Governor	—	—	—
1830–1831			
New England			
President	—	—	—
House	31.3	42.1	57.9
Governor	53.6	48.5	51.5
South			
President	—	—	—
House	84.4	68.9	31.1
Governor	74.4	58.1	41.9
Mid-Atlantic			
President	—	—	—
House	59.1	22.6	77.4
Governor	51.7	3.4	96.6
Border South			
President	—	—	—
House	43.4	13.2	86.8
Governor	—	—	—
Midwest			
President	—	—	—
House	67.0	36.0	64.0
Governor	46.0	8.0	92.0
West			
President	—	—	—
House	—	—	—
Governor	—	—	—
1832–1833			
New England			
President	44.0	20.2	79.8
House	47.0	31.6	68.4
Governor	62.3	49.9	50.1

Year/Region[1]	Democratic % of Two-Party Vote	Margin of Victory	Party Competition Index
South			
President	88.1	76.3	23.7
House	62.1	43.5	56.5
Governor	88.2	76.5	23.5
Mid-Atlantic			
President	62.9	26.8	73.3
House	64.7	30.1	69.9
Governor	67.3	34.5	65.5
Border South			
President	47.8	4.5	95.5
House	50.4	0.8	99.2
Governor	50.9	1.8	98.2
Midwest			
President	68.8	37.6	62.4
House	73.9	47.7	52.3
Governor	52.9	5.8	94.2
West			
President	—	—	—
House	—	—	—
Governor	—	—	—
1834–1835			
New England			
President	—	—	—
House	49.3	14.2	85.8
Governor	56.1	27.2	72.8
South			
President	—	—	—
House	41.1	26.0	74.0
Governor	41.7	30.4	69.6
Mid-Atlantic			
President	—	—	—
House	54.1	9.0	91.0
Governor	55.3	10.6	89.4
Border South			
President	—	—	—
House	—	—	—
Governor	—	—	—
Midwest			
President	—	—	—
House	82.2	65.5	34.5
Governor	57.4	26.5	73.5
West			
President	—	—	—
House	—	—	—
Governor	—	—	—
1836–1837			
New England			
President	53.9	17.9	82.1
House	54.7	23.7	76.3
Governor	48.6	10.3	89.7
South			
President	52.8	10.4	89.6
House	50.9	28.7	71.3
Governor	58.9	32.0	68.0
Mid-Atlantic			
President	50.5	4.8	95.2
House	53.7	10.4	89.6
Governor	51.3	7.2	92.8
Border South			
President	46.8	6.3	93.7
House	41.0	18.0	82.0
Governor	44.2	11.6	88.4
Midwest			
President	52.2	10.5	89.5
House	52.2	18.3	81.7
Governor	60.9	29.0	71.0
West			
President	—	—	—
House	—	—	—
Governor	—	—	—
1838–1839			
New England			
President	—	—	—
House	48.0	9.1	90.9
Governor	49.3	7.4	92.6
South			
President	—	—	—
House	48.4	15.4	84.6
Governor	54.9	21.3	78.7

(Table continues)

Table 8-6 *(Continued)*

Year/Region[1]	Democratic % of Two-Party Vote	Margin of Victory	Party Competition Index	Year/Region[1]	Democratic % of Two-Party Vote	Margin of Victory	Party Competition Index
Mid-Atlantic				Border South			
President	—	—	—	President	46.8	6.5	93.5
House	50.0	1.6	98.4	House	48.9	4.5	95.5
Governor	74.3	51.4	48.6	Governor	48.8	2.4	97.6
Border South				Midwest			
President	—	—	—	President	53.3	7.4	92.6
House	53.2	6.4	93.6	House	55.0	10.6	89.4
Governor	50.3	0.6	99.4	Governor	53.0	6.3	93.7
Midwest				West			
President	—	—	—	President	—	—	—
House	53.6	7.2	92.8	House	—	—	—
Governor	50.1	2.7	97.3	Governor	—	—	—
West				**1846–1847**			
President	—	—	—	New England			
House	—	—	—	President	—	—	—
Governor	—	—	—	House	47.0	13.9	86.1
1840–1841				Governor	48.9	12.5	87.5
New England				South			
President	44.3	15.1	84.9	President	—	—	—
House	39.1	27.3	72.7	House	67.1	39.0	61.0
Governor	41.1	25.5	74.5	Governor	59.3	22.2	77.8
South				Mid-Atlantic			
President	47.4	10.9	89.1	President	—	—	—
House	50.9	10.2	89.8	House	49.1	3.1	96.9
Governor	51.5	8.3	91.7	Governor	51.3	3.2	96.8
Mid-Atlantic				Border South			
President	47.9	4.3	95.7	President	—	—	—
House	48.5	4.0	96.0	House	45.5	9.0	91.0
Governor	50.1	6.0	94.0	Governor	50.5	1.0	99.0
Border South				Midwest			
President	41.0	18.0	82.0	President	—	—	—
House	32.4	35.3	64.7	House	55.2	11.3	88.7
Governor	46.1	9.0	91.0	Governor	53.9	8.3	91.7
Midwest				West			
President	49.1	8.0	92.0	President	—	—	—
House	51.6	11.6	88.4	House	—	—	—
Governor	52.1	10.7	89.3	Governor	—	—	—
West				**1848–1849**			
President	—	—	—	New England			
House	—	—	—	President	44.9	22.6	77.4
Governor	—	—	—	House	47.5	16.4	83.6
1842–1843				Governor	47.6	16.0	84.0
New England				South			
President	—	—	—	President	50.5	9.4	90.6
House	51.7	13.7	86.3	House	57.9	20.1	79.9
Governor	50.1	21.1	78.9	Governor	62.2	26.0	74.0
South				Mid-Atlantic			
President	—	—	—	President	44.6	10.9	89.1
House	60.5	26.1	73.9	House	45.4	10.5	89.5
Governor	50.8	6.9	93.1	Governor	42.2	15.6	84.4
Mid-Atlantic				Border South			
President	—	—	—	President	45.2	9.7	90.3
House	51.9	3.9	96.1	House	44.1	11.9	88.1
Governor	52.8	5.6	94.4	Governor	46.6	6.8	93.2
Border South				Midwest			
President	—	—	—	President	53.2	6.4	93.6
House	44.9	10.2	89.8	House	55.5	11.1	88.9
Governor	—	—	—	Governor	62.0	24.0	76.0
Midwest				West			
President	—	—	—	President	—	—	—
House	63.1	26.2	73.8	House	100.0	100.0	0.0
Governor	53.6	7.2	92.8	Governor	100.0	100.0	0.0
West				**1850–1851**			
President	—	—	—	New England			
House	—	—	—	President	—	—	—
Governor	—	—	—	House	49.3	8.3	91.7
1844–1845				Governor	44.1	24.1	75.9
New England				South			
President	48.2	15.1	84.9	President	—	—	—
House	41.1	27.4	72.6	House	63.6	30.3	69.7
Governor	49.5	28.2	71.8	Governor	60.3	49.6	50.4
South				Mid-Atlantic			
President	54.1	9.3	90.7	President	—	—	—
House	57.0	17.3	82.7	House	51.7	4.0	96.0
Governor	65.2	31.8	68.2	Governor	51.3	2.6	97.4
Mid-Atlantic				Border South			
President	49.9	1.5	98.5	President	—	—	—
House	48.4	5.5	94.5	House	46.0	8.0	92.0
Governor	50.2	1.5	98.5	Governor	50.7	1.4	98.6

Table 8-6 (Continued)

Year/Region[1]	Democratic % of Two-Party Vote	Margin of Victory	Party Competition Index	Year/Region[1]	Democratic % of Two-Party Vote	Margin of Victory	Party Competition Index
Midwest				**West**			
President	—	—	—	President	72.0	44.0	56.0
House	55.2	11.1	88.9	House	69.8	39.6	60.4
Governor	53.9	8.2	91.8	Governor	71.6	43.2	56.8
West				**1858–1859**			
President	—	—	—	**New England**			
House	53.4	6.8	93.2	President	—	—	—
Governor	50.5	1.0	99.0	House	38.9	22.2	77.8
1852–1853				Governor	39.8	20.4	79.6
New England				**South**			
President	51.6	14.6	85.4	President	—	—	—
House	53.2	13.9	86.1	House	94.8	89.5	10.5
Governor	51.6	16.3	83.7	Governor	83.1	66.2	33.8
South				**Mid-Atlantic**			
President	59.9	20.0	80.0	President	—	—	—
House	64.5	29.0	71.0	House	77.0	61.6	38.4
Governor	58.0	16.1	83.9	Governor	65.8	35.1	64.9
Mid-Atlantic				**Border South**			
President	52.2	4.5	95.5	President	—	—	—
House	52.5	5.4	94.6	House	100.0	100.0	0.0
Governor	52.4	4.8	95.2	Governor	100.0	100.0	0.0
Border South				**Midwest**			
President	50.8	4.9	95.1	President	—	—	—
House	51.1	5.9	94.1	House	52.4	15.8	84.2
Governor	52.8	5.6	94.4	Governor	47.3	5.4	94.6
Midwest				**West**			
President	55.3	10.5	89.5	President	—	—	—
House	55.2	10.4	89.6	House	54.1	8.2	91.8
Governor	57.2	14.4	85.6	Governor	95.1	90.2	9.8
West				**1860–1861**			
President	53.1	6.2	93.8	**New England**			
House	53.6	7.2	92.8	President	30.4	39.2	60.8
Governor	51.0	2.0	98.0	House	33.0	34.0	66.0
1854–1855				Governor	36.7	27.6	72.4
New England				**South**			
President	—	—	—	President	98.8	97.7	2.3
House	60.5	59.1	40.9	House	100.0	100.0	0.0
Governor	47.2	34.5	65.5	Governor	79.0	57.9	42.1
South				**Mid-Atlantic**			
President	—	—	—	President	31.5	39.0	61.0
House	92.4	84.7	15.3	House	60.4	29.5	70.5
Governor	93.9	87.8	12.2	Governor	46.8	6.5	93.5
Mid-Atlantic				**Border South**			
President	—	—	—	President	83.6	67.2	32.8
House	62.9	25.8	74.2	House	0.0	100.0	0.0
Governor	49.1	8.3	91.7	Governor	31.2	37.6	62.4
Border South				**Midwest**			
President	—	—	—	President	47.6	18.6	81.4
House	100.0	100.0	0.0	House	49.6	19.9	80.1
Governor	100.0	100.0	0.0	Governor	50.2	21.2	78.8
Midwest				**West**			
President	—	—	—	President	46.6	6.8	93.2
House	63.5	33.5	66.5	House	78.3	56.5	43.5
Governor	47.0	6.1	93.9	Governor	53.2	6.4	93.6
West				**1862–1863**			
President	—	—	—	**New England**			
House	57.4	14.8	85.2	President	—	—	—
Governor	100.0	100.0	0.0	House	36.0	28.1	71.9
1856–1857				Governor	32.4	35.1	64.9
New England				**South**			
President	35.4	29.2	70.8	President	—	—	—
House	37.8	24.5	75.5	House	—	—	—
Governor	45.6	33.4	66.6	Governor	62.8	74.5	25.5
South				**Mid-Atlantic**			
President	100.0	100.0	0.0	President	—	—	—
House	100.0	100.0	0.0	House	52.5	5.1	94.9
Governor	100.0	100.0	0.0	Governor	51.5	4.7	95.3
Mid-Atlantic				**Border South**			
President	65.3	39.0	61.0	President	—	—	—
House	61.5	30.2	69.8	House	40.6	85.5	14.5
Governor	49.8	8.0	92.0	Governor	10.2	79.6	20.4
Border South				**Midwest**			
President	99.7	99.3	0.7	President	—	—	—
House	100.0	100.0	0.0	House	43.8	15.3	84.7
Governor	100.0	100.0	0.0	Governor	34.5	31.0	69.0
Midwest				**West**			
President	55.3	22.5	77.5	President	—	—	—
House	53.8	18.9	81.1	House	37.6	24.9	75.1
Governor	55.2	15.4	84.6	Governor	37.0	26.1	73.9

(Table continues)

Table 8-6 (Continued)

Year/Region[1]	Democratic % of Two-Party Vote	Margin of Victory	Party Competition Index	Year/Region[1]	Democratic % of Two-Party Vote	Margin of Victory	Party Competition Index
1864–1865				South			
New England				President	—	—	—
President	37.7	24.5	75.5	House	49.8	16.2	83.8
House	33.1	33.9	66.1	Governor	47.2	21.1	78.9
Governor	33.9	32.2	67.8	Mid-Atlantic			
South				President	—	—	—
President	—	—	—	House	51.1	5.2	94.8
House	0.0	100.0	0.0	Governor	53.3	6.5	93.5
Governor	50.2	76.4	23.6	Border South			
Mid-Atlantic				President	—	—	—
President	50.6	3.3	96.7	House	56.5	13.1	86.9
House	51.0	2.5	97.5	Governor	55.4	10.8	89.2
Governor	49.2	1.7	98.3	Midwest			
Border South				President	—	—	—
President	48.8	28.7	71.3	House	44.9	11.2	88.8
House	22.1	55.9	44.1	Governor	44.8	16.6	83.4
Governor	22.1	55.9	44.1	West			
Midwest				President	—	—	—
President	39.0	22.0	78.0	House	49.9	2.9	97.1
House	36.6	26.7	73.3	Governor	51.1	4.9	95.1
Governor	38.4	23.1	76.9	**1872–1873**			
West				New England			
President	42.6	14.9	85.1	President	34.2	31.6	68.4
House	39.9	20.2	79.8	House	36.3	27.3	72.7
Governor	40.0	20.0	80.0	Governor	42.3	16.6	83.4
1866–1867				South			
New England				President	45.8	14.2	85.8
President	—	—	—	House	35.3	35.7	64.3
House	33.4	33.6	66.4	Governor	46.8	22.8	77.2
Governor	37.3	25.5	74.5	Mid-Atlantic			
South				President	44.5	11.1	88.9
President	—	—	—	House	46.3	7.4	92.6
House	0.0	100.0	0.0	Governor	47.1	5.8	94.2
Governor	0.0	100.0	0.0	Border South			
Mid-Atlantic				President	50.3	3.7	96.3
President	—	—	—	House	58.2	16.4	83.6
House	49.4	5.0	95.0	Governor	100.0	100.0	0.0
Governor	50.3	3.8	96.2	Midwest			
Border South				President	41.0	20.5	79.5
President	—	—	—	House	43.6	16.1	83.9
House	59.0	28.6	71.4	Governor	41.5	21.7	78.3
Governor	63.8	38.5	61.5	West			
Midwest				President	41.7	16.5	83.5
President	—	—	—	House	49.8	3.5	96.5
House	38.1	23.8	76.2	Governor	—	—	—
Governor	39.4	21.2	78.8	**1874–1875**			
West				New England			
President	—	—	—	President	—	—	—
House	48.7	5.4	94.6	House	40.3	20.9	79.1
Governor	49.3	6.8	93.2	Governor	43.8	16.7	83.3
1868–1869				South			
New England				President	—	—	—
President	36.0	28.1	71.9	House	56.9	25.5	74.5
House	38.3	23.4	76.6	Governor	67.9	38.8	61.2
Governor	39.7	20.9	79.1	Mid-Atlantic			
South				President	—	—	—
President	50.0	19.9	80.1	House	53.3	6.5	93.5
House	31.8	40.3	59.7	Governor	52.1	5.2	94.8
Governor	22.2	57.6	42.4	Border South			
Mid-Atlantic				President	—	—	—
President	52.1	6.3	93.7	House	62.5	25.0	75.0
House	52.6	5.7	94.3	Governor	56.2	12.4	87.6
Governor	50.9	2.3	97.7	Midwest			
Border South				President	—	—	—
President	61.0	33.7	66.3	House	41.8	27.3	72.7
House	62.6	31.9	68.1	Governor	45.4	12.8	87.2
Governor	45.4	9.2	90.8	West			
Midwest				President	—	—	—
President	41.3	17.4	82.6	House	52.9	8.1	91.9
House	42.8	14.5	85.5	Governor	58.3	16.6	83.4
Governor	43.6	12.8	87.2	**1876–1877**			
West				New England			
President	48.3	4.0	96.0	President	42.7	15.4	84.6
House	43.0	14.3	85.7	House	43.1	14.6	85.4
Governor	—	—	—	Governor	43.3	13.9	86.1
1870–1871				South			
New England				President	59.1	19.3	80.7
President	—	—	—	House	62.7	25.4	74.6
House	37.9	24.8	75.2	Governor	69.7	39.3	60.7
Governor	42.0	16.4	83.6				

Table 8-6 *(Continued)*

Year/Region[1]	Democratic % of Two-Party Vote	Margin of Victory	Party Competition Index	Year/Region[1]	Democratic % of Two-Party Vote	Margin of Victory	Party Competition Index
Mid-Atlantic				Border South			
President	52.1	5.5	94.5	President	—	—	—
House	53.6	7.8	92.2	House	54.4	8.8	91.2
Governor	52.5	5.0	95.0	Governor	56.8	13.5	86.5
Border South				Midwest			
President	58.5	17.0	83.0	President	—	—	—
House	58.3	16.5	83.5	House	48.3	12.4	87.6
Governor	56.4	12.8	87.2	Governor	46.2	8.7	91.3
Midwest				West			
President	44.9	13.8	86.2	President	—	—	—
House	44.3	15.7	84.3	House	50.8	7.1	92.9
Governor	45.8	12.5	87.5	Governor	53.0	7.7	92.3
West				**1884–1885**			
President	48.2	3.6	96.4	New England			
House	48.0	4.0	96.0	President	42.6	15.2	84.8
Governor	48.5	3.0	97.0	House	41.7	16.5	83.5
1878–1879				Governor	42.2	15.9	84.1
New England				South			
President	—	—	—	President	60.4	20.8	79.2
House	38.5	23.1	76.9	House	65.2	30.4	69.6
Governor	40.4	19.2	80.8	Governor	71.1	42.3	57.7
South				Mid-Atlantic			
President	—	—	—	President	50.8	6.0	94.0
House	75.3	50.5	49.5	House	51.4	7.1	92.9
Governor	86.6	73.1	26.9	Governor	50.6	1.2	98.8
Mid-Atlantic				Border South			
President	—	—	—	President	53.6	7.3	92.7
House	60.6	28.9	71.1	House	55.2	10.5	89.5
Governor	66.7	35.9	64.1	Governor	51.9	3.8	96.2
Border South				Midwest			
President	—	—	—	President	45.6	10.6	89.4
House	62.8	25.6	74.4	House	47.4	7.5	92.5
Governor	58.7	17.4	82.6	Governor	48.0	5.0	95.0
Midwest				West			
President	—	—	—	President	45.4	9.2	90.8
House	47.0	16.2	83.8	House	46.7	6.6	93.4
Governor	38.9	22.3	77.7	Governor	47.6	4.8	95.2
West				**1886–1887**			
President	—	—	—	New England			
House	46.2	9.5	90.5	President	—	—	—
Governor	46.1	7.8	92.2	House	44.8	10.9	89.1
1880–1881				Governor	45.8	11.1	88.9
New England				South			
President	41.6	16.8	83.2	President	—	—	—
House	42.4	15.3	84.7	House	73.7	47.4	52.6
Governor	39.7	20.7	79.3	Governor	78.9	57.8	42.2
South				Mid-Atlantic			
President	61.8	23.6	76.4	President	—	—	—
House	68.1	36.1	63.9	House	62.0	26.9	73.1
Governor	79.5	58.9	41.1	Governor	66.1	35.7	64.3
Mid-Atlantic				Border South			
President	49.8	2.7	97.3	President	—	—	—
House	49.4	2.8	97.2	House	57.5	14.9	85.1
Governor	50.1	0.2	99.8	Governor	53.2	6.4	93.6
Border South				Midwest			
President	56.0	12.1	87.9	President	—	—	—
House	55.7	11.5	88.5	House	46.9	9.5	90.5
Governor	57.6	15.2	84.8	Governor	46.4	7.2	92.8
Midwest				West			
President	42.7	17.7	82.3	President	—	—	—
House	43.3	18.1	81.9	House	48.4	3.1	96.9
Governor	43.3	16.5	83.5	Governor	50.9	4.2	95.8
West				**1888–1889**			
President	49.7	2.9	97.1	New England			
House	49.7	4.0	96.0	President	42.7	14.7	85.3
Governor	45.3	9.4	90.6	House	43.4	13.3	86.7
1882–1883				Governor	46.1	11.0	89.0
New England				South			
President	—	—	—	President	65.1	30.2	69.8
House	41.8	17.0	83.0	House	69.8	39.7	60.3
Governor	44.7	12.9	87.1	Governor	79.4	58.8	41.2
South				Mid-Atlantic			
President	—	—	—	President	50.6	5.9	94.1
House	71.0	42.0	58.0	House	50.0	6.5	93.5
Governor	74.7	49.3	50.7	Governor	51.7	3.4	96.6
Mid-Atlantic				Border South			
President	—	—	—	President	52.0	3.9	96.1
House	53.0	6.0	94.0	House	52.1	4.1	95.9
Governor	52.7	5.6	94.4	Governor	50.0	0.0	100.0

(Table continues)

Table 8-6 (Continued)

Year/Region[1]	Democratic % of Two-Party Vote	Margin of Victory	Party Competition Index	Year/Region[1]	Democratic % of Two-Party Vote	Margin of Victory	Party Competition Index
Midwest				West			
President	46.1	8.9	91.1	President	—	—	—
House	43.7	13.4	86.6	House	33.0	34.0	66.0
Governor	44.9	11.2	88.8	Governor	38.5	30.2	69.8
West				**1896–1897**			
President	44.4	11.2	88.8	New England			
House	44.8	10.4	89.6	President	27.3	45.4	54.6
Governor	45.8	9.7	90.3	House	31.1	37.7	62.3
1890–1891				Governor	33.2	33.6	66.4
New England				South			
President	—	—	—	President	69.6	39.2	60.8
House	46.8	10.3	89.7	House	71.3	44.3	55.7
Governor	48.2	7.4	92.6	Governor	76.0	52.6	47.4
South				Mid-Atlantic			
President	—	—	—	President	40.0	20.0	80.0
House	73.5	47.0	53.0	House	40.8	18.3	81.7
Governor	78.2	56.5	43.5	Governor	44.7	10.7	89.3
Mid-Atlantic				Border South			
President	—	—	—	President	46.8	6.3	93.7
House	51.6	4.6	95.4	House	48.4	8.0	92.0
Governor	51.3	2.5	97.5	Governor	47.0	6.0	94.0
Border South				Midwest			
President	—	—	—	President	46.8	9.5	90.5
House	57.9	15.8	84.2	House	47.0	8.5	91.5
Governor	56.8	13.5	86.5	Governor	43.8	16.0	84.0
Midwest				West			
President	—	—	—	President	68.5	37.7	62.3
House	47.5	14.5	85.5	House	45.9	45.2	54.8
Governor	49.1	10.3	89.7	Governor	66.2	34.8	65.2
West				**1898–1899**			
President	—	—	—	New England			
House	45.3	9.7	90.3	President	—	—	—
Governor	47.1	8.1	91.9	House	38.1	23.8	76.2
1892–1893				Governor	37.2	25.6	74.4
New England				South			
President	44.5	12.1	87.9	President	—	—	—
House	46.2	8.6	91.4	House	78.4	56.8	43.2
Governor	46.5	8.2	91.8	Governor	90.0	79.9	20.1
South				Mid-Atlantic			
President	76.0	52.0	48.0	President	—	—	—
House	84.0	68.0	32.0	House	45.7	8.6	91.4
Governor	82.1	64.2	35.8	Governor	47.1	5.8	94.2
Mid-Atlantic				Border South			
President	50.4	4.0	96.0	President	—	—	—
House	50.0	3.2	96.8	House	49.8	2.2	97.8
Governor	51.2	2.4	97.6	Governor	51.9	3.7	96.3
Border South				Midwest			
President	54.3	8.5	91.5	President	—	—	—
House	55.3	10.5	89.5	House	45.6	9.8	90.2
Governor	51.2	2.4	97.6	Governor	46.6	9.1	90.9
Midwest				West			
President	36.6	29.2	70.8	President	—	—	—
House	46.9	9.1	90.9	House	45.0	42.0	58.0
Governor	46.8	9.6	90.4	Governor	47.0	21.5	78.5
West				**1900–1901**			
President	24.0	51.9	48.1	New England			
House	44.6	17.8	82.2	President	36.2	27.6	72.4
Governor	49.6	8.1	91.9	House	37.0	25.9	74.1
1894–1895				Governor	37.9	24.1	75.9
New England				South			
President	—	—	—	President	70.1	40.2	59.8
House	36.2	27.6	72.4	House	76.0	51.9	48.1
Governor	37.6	24.8	75.2	Governor	75.5	51.1	48.9
South				Mid-Atlantic			
President	—	—	—	President	42.7	14.6	85.4
House	78.0	56.5	43.5	House	43.0	14.0	86.0
Governor	85.9	71.9	28.1	Governor	46.5	7.0	93.0
Mid-Atlantic				Border South			
President	—	—	—	President	47.8	5.6	94.4
House	42.3	15.3	84.7	House	48.0	4.6	95.4
Governor	43.8	12.3	87.7	Governor	45.8	8.4	91.6
Border South				Midwest			
President	—	—	—	President	43.5	14.0	86.0
House	48.5	3.4	96.6	House	44.5	12.0	88.0
Governor	47.3	5.4	94.6	Governor	45.1	10.5	89.5
Midwest				West			
President	—	—	—	President	49.9	13.8	86.2
House	33.6	32.8	67.2	House	50.2	12.2	87.8
Governor	37.3	26.6	73.4	Governor	54.2	9.7	90.3

Table 8-6 (Continued)

Year/Region[1]	Democratic % of Two-Party Vote	Margin of Victory	Party Competition Index	Year/Region[1]	Democratic % of Two-Party Vote	Margin of Victory	Party Competition Index
1902–1903				South			
New England				President	72.2	44.3	55.7
President	—	—	—	House	80.1	60.2	39.8
House	39.8	20.4	79.6	Governor	77.1	54.2	45.8
Governor	42.8	18.3	81.7	Mid-Atlantic			
South				President	42.2	15.6	84.4
President	—	—	—	House	44.7	10.5	89.5
House	84.3	68.6	31.4	Governor	47.8	4.5	95.5
Governor	84.2	68.4	31.6	Border South			
Mid-Atlantic				President	49.5	4.4	95.6
President	—	—	—	House	50.3	5.0	95.0
House	43.9	12.1	87.9	Governor	47.6	4.8	95.2
Governor	46.5	7.1	92.9	Midwest			
Border South				President	42.5	15.3	84.7
President	—	—	—	House	42.8	15.1	84.9
House	50.1	7.5	92.5	Governor	48.1	6.9	93.1
Governor	53.1	6.1	93.9	West			
Midwest				President	42.6	15.6	84.4
President	—	—	—	House	42.5	19.9	80.1
House	42.1	17.3	82.7	Governor	45.7	11.3	88.7
Governor	40.9	18.3	81.7	**1910–1911**			
West				New England			
President	—	—	—	President	—	—	—
House	44.0	13.6	86.4	House	45.4	10.9	89.1
Governor	48.5	8.2	91.8	Governor	47.8	9.2	90.8
1904–1905				South			
New England				President	—	—	—
President	34.0	32.0	68.0	House	84.5	69.1	30.9
House	38.4	23.2	76.8	Governor	81.0	63.5	36.5
Governor	43.1	15.9	84.1	Mid-Atlantic			
South				President	—	—	—
President	74.9	49.9	50.1	House	48.3	9.6	90.4
House	79.0	57.9	42.1	Governor	44.1	23.2	76.8
Governor	77.2	54.4	45.6	Border South			
Mid-Atlantic				President	—	—	—
President	39.5	21.0	79.0	House	53.5	7.1	92.9
House	40.6	18.9	81.1	Governor	52.6	6.1	93.9
Governor	45.8	8.3	91.7	Midwest			
Border South				President	—	—	—
President	48.2	5.5	94.5	House	43.0	16.5	83.5
House	48.5	5.4	94.6	Governor	45.6	12.0	88.0
Governor	48.1	3.8	96.2	West			
Midwest				President	—	—	—
President	31.1	37.8	62.2	House	43.8	15.6	84.4
House	35.4	29.2	70.8	Governor	51.9	7.7	92.3
Governor	41.8	18.7	81.3	**1912–1913[2]**			
West				New England			
President	31.8	36.5	63.5	President	52.3	11.5	88.5
House	39.1	22.2	77.8	House	49.0	7.4	92.6
Governor	46.5	14.0	86.0	Senate	—	—	—
1906–1907				Governor	52.1	9.3	90.7
New England				South			
President	—	—	—	President	87.0	73.9	26.1
House	41.6	16.7	83.3	House	87.5	75.0	25.0
Governor	44.7	12.0	88.0	Senate	—	—	—
South				Governor	84.0	68.8	31.2
President	—	—	—	Mid-Atlantic			
House	83.4	66.9	33.1	President	60.9	21.7	78.3
Governor	85.2	70.3	29.7	House	52.8	19.0	81.0
Mid-Atlantic				Senate	—	—	—
President	—	—	—	Governor	54.4	10.7	89.3
House	45.1	9.8	90.2	Border South			
Governor	48.1	3.7	96.3	President	64.0	28.0	72.0
Border South				House	59.6	23.0	77.0
President	—	—	—	Senate	60.2	20.4	79.6
House	51.3	10.3	89.7	Governor	48.2	3.6	96.4
Governor	51.8	6.5	93.5	Midwest			
Midwest				President	63.8	27.7	72.3
President	—	—	—	House	48.9	15.5	84.5
House	39.8	20.5	79.5	Senate	45.2	16.0	84.0
Governor	45.3	18.2	81.8	Governor	53.0	11.3	88.7
West				West			
President	—	—	—	President	62.7	26.7	73.3
House	40.5	23.5	76.5	House	50.0	18.5	81.5
Governor	47.8	13.4	86.6	Senate	58.5	17.1	82.9
1908–1909				Governor	52.4	8.8	91.2
New England							
President	34.4	31.2	68.8				
House	38.5	23.1	76.9				
Governor	43.0	14.1	85.9				

(Table continues)

Table 8-6 *(Continued)*

Year/Region[1]	Democratic % of Two-Party Vote	Margin of Victory	Party Competition Index
1914–1915			
New England			
President	—	—	—
House	43.8	12.6	87.4
Senate	45.1	9.8	90.2
Governor	44.7	12.2	87.8
South			
President	—	—	—
House	88.5	77.0	23.0
Senate	86.1	72.3	27.7
Governor	84.5	69.0	31.0
Mid-Atlantic			
President	—	—	—
House	44.6	10.8	89.2
Senate	40.6	18.9	81.1
Governor	43.8	12.4	87.6
Border South			
President	—	—	—
House	55.0	12.0	88.0
Senate	56.9	13.7	86.3
Governor	50.7	1.3	98.7
Midwest			
President	—	—	—
House	45.5	13.1	86.9
Senate	48.6	8.0	92.0
Governor	47.9	9.1	90.9
West			
President	—	—	—
House	49.7	16.6	83.4
Senate	52.4	11.6	88.4
Governor	47.9	15.7	84.3
1916–1917			
New England			
President	46.3	7.4	92.6
House	43.0	14.0	86.0
Senate	43.9	15.7	84.3
Governor	41.4	17.1	82.9
South			
President	78.9	57.8	42.2
House	82.8	65.7	34.3
Senate	85.6	71.2	28.8
Governor	79.0	58.0	42.0
Mid-Atlantic			
President	45.4	9.1	90.9
House	45.2	9.9	90.1
Senate	43.8	15.0	85.0
Governor	44.6	10.7	89.3
Border South			
President	54.2	8.9	91.1
House	53.1	6.5	93.5
Senate	49.1	1.9	98.1
Governor	50.5	1.0	99.0
Midwest			
President	49.7	6.4	93.6
House	43.4	13.8	86.2
Senate	45.1	12.4	87.6
Governor	40.7	19.1	80.9
West			
President	56.5	13.5	86.5
House	49.1	14.2	85.8
Senate	50.6	14.8	85.2
Governor	52.7	5.5	94.5
1918–1919			
New England			
President	—	—	—
House	41.2	17.7	82.3
Senate	47.6	7.2	92.8
Governor	43.6	12.8	87.2
South			
President	—	—	—
House	90.4	80.7	19.3
Senate	89.9	79.7	20.3
Governor	92.5	84.9	15.1
Mid-Atlantic			
President	—	—	—
House	44.1	11.8	88.2
Senate	47.3	5.5	94.5
Governor	45.9	11.0	89.0

Year/Region[1]	Democratic % of Two-Party Vote	Margin of Victory	Party Competition Index
Border South			
President	—	—	—
House	52.0	7.0	93.0
Senate	51.4	8.3	91.7
Governor	50.5	6.7	93.3
Midwest			
President	—	—	—
House	39.3	22.4	77.6
Senate	36.0	27.9	72.1
Governor	39.1	22.1	77.9
West			
President	—	—	—
House	44.6	19.3	80.7
Senate	44.9	12.5	87.5
Governor	40.8	19.4	80.6
1920–1921			
New England			
President	31.8	36.4	63.6
House	33.2	33.7	66.3
Senate	33.9	32.3	67.7
Governor	32.5	35.0	65.0
South			
President	68.6	37.8	62.2
House	75.4	51.4	48.6
Senate	81.2	62.4	37.6
Governor	73.7	50.0	50.0
Mid-Atlantic			
President	32.8	34.4	65.7
House	36.3	27.4	72.7
Senate	34.9	30.2	69.8
Governor	46.4	7.2	92.8
Border South			
President	46.1	8.0	92.0
House	48.1	5.1	94.9
Senate	48.1	3.7	96.3
Governor	43.4	13.2	86.8
Midwest			
President	29.4	41.2	58.8
House	29.2	41.7	58.3
Senate	35.9	28.3	71.7
Governor	38.1	23.8	76.2
West			
President	36.2	27.6	72.4
House	36.2	30.4	69.6
Senate	42.0	16.0	84.0
Governor	38.6	22.8	77.2
1922–1923			
New England			
President	—	—	—
House	45.0	12.3	87.7
Senate	45.1	13.6	86.4
Governor	44.3	15.2	84.8
South			
President	—	—	—
House	84.6	69.1	30.9
Senate	78.8	57.6	42.4
Governor	85.2	70.4	29.6
Mid-Atlantic			
President	—	—	—
House	48.5	8.5	91.5
Senate	49.1	13.6	86.4
Governor	50.6	13.0	87.0
Border South			
President	—	—	—
House	55.5	11.0	89.0
Senate	52.7	5.4	94.6
Governor	55.0	10.1	89.9
Midwest			
President	—	—	—
House	36.2	27.8	72.2
Senate	42.8	17.0	83.0
Governor	33.1	37.7	62.3
West			
President	—	—	—
House	44.5	23.3	76.7
Senate	53.2	17.5	82.5
Governor	50.3	10.7	89.3

Table 8-6 (Continued)

Year/Region[1]	Democratic % of Two-Party Vote	Margin of Victory	Party Competition Index
1924–1925			
New England			
President	29.0	42.0	58.0
House	35.9	28.2	71.8
Senate	42.8	14.5	85.5
Governor	37.5	25.0	75.0
South			
President	74.1	48.3	51.7
House	83.0	66.0	34.0
Senate	85.0	69.9	30.1
Governor	79.1	58.2	41.8
Mid-Atlantic			
President	31.6	36.8	63.2
House	38.2	23.7	76.4
Senate	17.7	64.7	35.3
Governor	47.8	9.5	90.5
Border South			
President	49.1	4.8	95.2
House	53.9	9.3	90.7
Senate	44.4	11.1	88.9
Governor	46.4	7.2	92.8
Midwest			
President	26.1	47.8	52.2
House	32.5	34.9	65.1
Senate	32.6	34.8	65.2
Governor	38.5	24.5	75.5
West			
President	30.4	39.1	60.9
House	43.6	25.1	74.9
Senate	40.9	22.6	77.4
Governor	45.5	13.7	86.3
1926–1927			
New England			
President	—	—	—
House	36.4	27.2	72.8
Senate	33.4	33.2	66.8
Governor	41.0	18.0	82.0
South			
President	—	—	—
House	85.7	71.5	28.5
Senate	86.0	72.0	28.0
Governor	87.2	74.3	25.7
Mid-Atlantic			
President	—	—	—
House	40.5	19.0	81.0
Senate	46.0	8.0	92.0
Governor	39.7	29.5	70.5
Border South			
President	—	—	—
House	53.3	8.2	91.8
Senate	55.1	10.1	89.9
Governor	53.9	10.5	89.5
Midwest			
President	—	—	—
House	33.5	33.5	66.5
Senate	37.2	26.3	73.7
Governor	32.9	36.3	63.7
West			
President	—	—	—
House	39.5	26.8	73.2
Senate	44.5	15.2	84.8
Governor	44.2	17.2	82.8
1928–1929			
New England			
President	42.0	16.5	83.5
House	40.3	19.4	80.6
Senate	41.6	20.0	80.0
Governor	40.5	19.0	81.0
South			
President	58.4	26.0	74.0
House	81.0	62.0	38.0
Senate	81.8	63.6	36.4
Governor	70.9	41.9	58.1
Mid-Atlantic			
President	39.2	21.5	78.5
House	38.8	22.4	77.6
Senate	41.6	17.5	82.5
Governor	44.7	11.1	88.9

Year/Region[1]	Democratic % of Two-Party Vote	Margin of Victory	Party Competition Index
Border South			
President	40.1	19.9	80.1
House	47.2	5.7	94.3
Senate	47.5	5.1	94.9
Governor	46.2	7.6	92.4
Midwest			
President	38.6	22.8	77.2
House	35.9	28.1	71.9
Senate	27.2	45.6	54.4
Governor	41.1	18.6	81.4
West			
President	38.2	23.6	76.4
House	39.4	25.4	74.6
Senate	49.0	16.9	83.1
Governor	51.1	15.0	85.0
1930–1931			
New England			
President	—	—	—
House	42.8	14.5	85.5
Senate	46.3	12.1	87.9
Governor	44.4	12.1	87.9
South			
President	—	—	—
House	85.8	71.5	28.5
Senate	92.0	84.1	15.9
Governor	87.6	75.2	24.8
Mid-Atlantic			
President	—	—	—
House	42.5	19.1	80.9
Senate	42.7	14.6	85.4
Governor	56.9	15.7	84.3
Border South			
President	—	—	—
House	56.2	12.5	87.5
Senate	55.5	11.1	88.9
Governor	56.7	13.5	86.5
Midwest			
President	—	—	—
House	37.8	26.7	73.3
Senate	44.2	20.7	79.3
Governor	37.7	26.1	73.9
West			
President	—	—	—
House	45.4	29.7	70.3
Senate	46.3	25.2	74.8
Governor	50.0	14.5	85.5
1932–1933			
New England			
President	48.7	8.1	91.9
House	48.0	7.7	92.3
Senate	48.3	4.1	95.9
Governor	49.1	9.4	90.6
South			
President	83.9	67.9	32.1
House	86.8	73.7	26.3
Senate	90.7	81.4	18.6
Governor	78.0	55.9	44.1
Mid-Atlantic			
President	50.9	5.9	94.1
House	50.0	8.9	91.1
Senate	52.9	12.4	87.6
Governor	52.4	14.2	85.8
Border South			
President	62.7	25.5	74.5
House	63.2	26.4	73.6
Senate	64.5	28.9	71.1
Governor	54.0	8.0	92.0
Midwest			
President	60.5	21.1	78.9
House	52.1	10.1	89.9
Senate	52.3	16.7	83.3
Governor	52.7	12.6	87.4
West			
President	62.0	24.0	76.0
House	57.5	16.2	83.8
Senate	56.7	17.1	82.9
Governor	58.9	17.8	82.2

(Table continues)

Table 8-6 (Continued)

Year/Region[1]	Democratic % of Two-Party Vote	Margin of Victory	Party Competition Index	Year/Region[1]	Democratic % of Two-Party Vote	Margin of Victory	Party Competition Index
1934–1935				**Midwest**			
New England				President	—	—	—
President	—	—	—	House	42.7	18.3	81.7
House	50.0	7.0	93.0	Senate	44.1	17.4	82.6
Senate	53.7	8.7	91.3	Governor	39.9	22.1	77.9
Governor	51.3	8.1	91.9	**West**			
South				President	—	—	—
President	—	—	—	House	57.1	18.5	81.5
House	90.8	81.6	18.4	Senate	58.5	19.5	80.5
Senate	87.9	75.8	24.2	Governor	51.3	18.1	81.9
Governor	90.9	81.9	18.1	**1940–1941**			
Mid-Atlantic				**New England**			
President	—	—	—	President	51.8	7.7	92.3
House	53.1	9.6	90.4	House	45.9	13.7	86.3
Senate	54.3	12.2	87.8	Senate	48.1	16.2	83.8
Governor	53.9	8.5	91.5	Governor	46.4	11.8	88.2
Border South				**South**			
President	—	—	—	President	81.1	62.1	37.9
House	59.9	19.7	80.3	House	90.2	80.5	19.5
Senate	56.3	12.6	87.4	Senate	93.0	86.0	14.0
Governor	54.7	10.2	89.8	Governor	89.4	78.9	21.1
Midwest				**Mid-Atlantic**			
President	—	—	—	President	53.0	5.9	94.1
House	52.1	10.8	89.2	House	51.1	5.1	94.9
Senate	53.6	12.8	87.2	Senate	50.7	6.8	93.2
Governor	51.2	14.1	85.9	Governor	49.7	4.1	95.9
West				**Border South**			
President	—	—	—	President	57.8	15.5	84.5
House	61.7	24.2	75.8	House	61.8	23.5	76.5
Senate	54.4	33.9	66.1	Senate	61.1	22.2	77.8
Governor	56.0	15.2	84.8	Governor	56.4	12.8	87.2
1936–1937				**Midwest**			
New England				President	48.2	6.5	93.5
President	51.1	11.5	88.5	House	42.0	16.8	83.2
House	47.8	10.7	89.3	Senate	41.3	18.0	82.0
Senate	48.8	4.6	95.4	Governor	44.9	15.7	84.3
Governor	47.8	12.4	87.6	**West**			
South				President	57.2	15.0	85.0
President	83.4	66.9	33.1	House	56.0	16.9	83.1
House	88.2	76.4	23.6	Senate	54.7	34.3	65.7
Senate	90.9	81.8	18.2	Governor	52.6	8.7	91.3
Governor	86.4	72.7	27.3	**1942–1943**			
Mid-Atlantic				**New England**			
President	58.4	16.7	83.3	President	—	—	—
House	55.4	10.8	89.2	House	42.9	19.7	80.3
Senate	55.7	11.4	88.6	Senate	46.0	16.1	83.9
Governor	52.7	5.4	94.6	Governor	42.4	20.8	79.2
Border South				**South**			
President	62.5	25.0	75.0	President	—	—	—
House	62.6	25.2	74.8	House	93.1	86.1	13.9
Senate	62.3	24.7	75.3	Senate	93.8	87.5	12.5
Governor	59.2	18.4	81.6	Governor	93.8	87.5	12.5
Midwest				**Mid-Atlantic**			
President	60.5	21.0	79.0	President	—	—	—
House	50.8	10.7	89.3	House	46.5	7.0	93.0
Senate	42.6	24.4	75.6	Senate	45.8	8.4	91.6
Governor	47.2	15.4	84.6	Governor	43.7	12.5	87.5
West				**Border South**			
President	67.7	35.3	64.7	President	—	—	—
House	63.9	27.8	72.2	House	55.2	10.7	89.3
Senate	55.5	20.4	79.6	Senate	48.3	10.5	89.5
Governor	60.3	20.6	79.4	Governor	51.3	3.7	96.3
1938–1939				**Midwest**			
New England				President	—	—	—
President	—	—	—	House	39.1	21.9	78.1
House	43.5	13.0	87.0	Senate	38.2	23.5	76.5
Senate	42.8	14.4	85.6	Governor	36.4	30.5	69.5
Governor	43.7	12.7	87.3	**West**			
South				President	—	—	—
President	—	—	—	House	52.3	11.7	88.3
House	91.3	82.6	17.4	Senate	46.2	14.4	85.6
Senate	88.7	77.5	22.5	Governor	49.6	20.3	79.7
Governor	92.9	85.7	14.3	**1944–1945**			
Mid-Atlantic				**New England**			
President	—	—	—	President	51.1	8.7	91.3
House	47.9	8.2	91.8	House	45.5	16.7	83.3
Senate	49.8	10.0	90.0	Senate	45.2	12.7	87.3
Governor	48.5	4.4	95.6	Governor	45.6	18.5	81.5
Border South				**South**			
President	—	—	—	President	76.7	53.5	46.5
House	60.9	21.7	78.3	House	87.8	75.6	24.4
Senate	65.9	31.9	68.1	Senate	86.6	73.2	26.8
Governor	61.0	22.0	78.0	Governor	79.6	59.2	40.8

Table 8-6 *(Continued)*

Year/Region[1]	Democratic % of Two-Party Vote	Margin of Victory	Party Competition Index	Year/Region[1]	Democratic % of Two-Party Vote	Margin of Victory	Party Competition Index
Mid-Atlantic				1950–1951			
President	52.3	4.6	95.4	New England			
House	50.0	3.5	96.5	President	—	—	—
Senate	51.8	3.5	96.5	House	44.8	18.4	81.6
Governor	49.3	1.4	98.6	Senate	38.4	26.7	73.3
Border South				Governor	45.5	19.6	80.4
President	54.3	8.5	91.5	South			
House	56.0	12.0	88.0	President	—	—	—
Senate	57.5	15.0	85.0	House	89.6	79.1	20.9
Governor	54.4	8.8	91.2	Senate	90.4	80.8	19.2
Midwest				Governor	91.9	83.9	16.1
President	47.4	7.4	92.6	Mid-Atlantic			
House	42.0	17.7	82.3	President	—	—	—
Senate	46.5	8.2	91.8	House	46.4	7.3	92.8
Governor	41.0	18.9	81.1	Senate	50.4	4.4	95.6
West				Governor	46.6	6.9	93.1
President	54.2	10.1	89.9	Border South			
House	53.7	16.2	83.8	President	—	—	—
Senate	53.7	15.9	84.1	House	57.3	14.8	85.2
Governor	53.7	12.5	87.5	Senate	52.0	8.6	91.4
1946–1947				Governor	49.5	8.8	91.2
New England				Midwest			
President	—	—	—	President	—	—	—
House	42.3	18.6	81.4	House	43.4	15.0	85.0
Senate	39.8	24.5	75.5	Senate	43.7	14.2	85.8
Governor	39.6	23.6	76.4	Governor	43.5	14.1	85.9
South				West			
President	—	—	—	President	—	—	—
House	86.8	73.5	26.5	House	50.3	9.9	90.1
Senate	81.4	62.8	37.2	Senate	46.3	19.7	80.3
Governor	89.8	79.6	20.4	Governor	43.2	13.6	86.4
Mid-Atlantic				1952–1953			
President	—	—	—	New England			
House	42.4	15.2	84.8	President	40.0	20.0	80.0
Senate	43.3	13.5	86.5	House	40.7	21.4	78.6
Governor	42.1	15.9	84.1	Senate	44.0	17.0	83.0
Border South				Governor	42.5	17.1	82.9
President	—	—	—	South			
House	51.9	7.1	92.9	President	54.0	13.3	86.7
Senate	50.3	0.5	99.5	House	86.2	72.3	27.7
Governor	55.1	10.3	89.7	Senate	95.6	91.2	8.8
Midwest				Governor	80.1	60.1	39.9
President	—	—	—	Mid-Atlantic			
House	38.9	22.2	77.8	President	45.4	9.2	90.8
Senate	38.0	24.0	76.0	House	46.1	7.7	92.3
Governor	39.3	21.4	78.6	Senate	45.4	9.2	90.8
West				Governor	51.1	6.4	93.6
President	—	—	—	Border South			
House	46.9	13.4	86.6	President	47.9	6.1	93.9
Senate	50.9	11.9	88.1	House	53.2	8.3	91.7
Governor	43.7	25.2	74.8	Senate	50.6	6.1	93.9
1948–1949				Governor	51.5	3.0	97.0
New England				Midwest			
President	48.4	12.5	87.5	President	38.6	22.9	77.1
House	46.2	15.0	85.0	House	39.7	21.3	78.7
Senate	44.1	21.2	78.8	Senate	42.4	17.2	82.8
Governor	46.8	20.3	79.7	Governor	42.7	17.6	82.4
South				West			
President	62.7	43.6	56.4	President	40.4	19.2	80.8
House	87.0	74.1	25.9	House	45.6	10.3	89.7
Senate	85.2	70.5	29.5	Senate	43.7	16.9	83.1
Governor	81.5	62.9	37.1	Governor	45.0	10.0	90.0
Mid-Atlantic				1954–1955			
President	48.7	2.7	97.3	New England			
House	43.1	13.7	86.3	President	—	—	—
Senate	50.0	2.7	97.3	House	48.5	11.7	88.3
Governor	50.8	5.9	94.1	Senate	47.4	14.5	85.5
Border South				Governor	50.5	7.3	92.7
President	56.9	14.4	85.6	South			
House	59.5	18.9	81.1	President	—	—	—
Senate	57.0	14.0	86.0	House	85.6	71.3	28.7
Governor	57.1	14.2	85.8	Senate	89.9	79.8	20.2
Midwest				Governor	89.2	78.4	21.6
President	50.4	6.4	93.6	Mid-Atlantic			
House	46.7	11.4	88.6	President	—	—	—
Senate	50.0	13.4	86.6	House	50.9	3.7	96.3
Governor	47.4	13.9	86.1	Senate	53.4	7.0	93.0
West				Governor	52.0	3.9	96.1
President	53.0	6.7	93.3				
House	51.7	11.9	88.1				
Senate	54.9	16.5	83.5				
Governor	55.0	14.4	85.6				

(Table continues)

Table 8-6 *(Continued)*

Year/Region[1]	Democratic % of Two-Party Vote	Margin of Victory	Party Competition Index	Year/Region[1]	Democratic % of Two-Party Vote	Margin of Victory	Party Competition Index
Border South				**South**			
President	—	—	—	President	54.0	10.9	89.1
House	60.2	20.4	79.6	House	81.8	63.6	36.4
Senate	55.1	10.3	89.7	Senate	83.4	66.7	33.3
Governor	54.2	14.3	85.7	Governor	67.1	34.3	65.7
Midwest				**Mid-Atlantic**			
President	—	—	—	President	51.3	2.5	97.5
House	45.8	12.2	87.8	House	50.8	3.1	96.9
Senate	47.7	11.4	88.6	Senate	46.5	7.0	93.0
Governor	47.2	11.3	88.7	Governor	51.3	2.5	97.5
West				**Border South**			
President	—	—	—	President	48.4	9.5	90.5
House	49.9	9.1	90.9	House	57.6	15.2	84.8
Senate	49.2	7.8	92.2	Senate	50.4	13.1	86.9
Governor	48.9	8.6	91.4	Governor	54.0	8.0	92.0
1956–1957				**Midwest**			
New England				President	45.7	9.3	90.7
President	34.9	30.2	69.8	House	48.4	6.8	93.2
House	43.5	15.5	84.5	Senate	49.4	9.4	90.6
Senate	37.7	24.6	75.4	Governor	51.0	5.5	94.5
Governor	50.0	9.8	90.2	**West**			
South				President	47.8	4.9	95.1
President	53.1	17.1	82.9	House	53.7	11.2	88.8
House	81.7	63.4	36.6	Senate	52.8	12.7	87.3
Senate	90.3	80.5	19.5	Governor	46.7	7.2	92.8
Governor	78.1	56.3	43.7	**1962–1963**			
Mid-Atlantic				**New England**			
President	40.4	19.3	80.7	President	—	—	—
House	45.3	9.3	90.7	House	51.6	14.6	85.4
Senate	48.5	3.5	96.5	Senate	41.6	18.6	81.4
Governor	51.6	7.1	92.9	Governor	52.1	4.3	95.7
Border South				**South**			
President	44.1	11.9	88.1	President	—	—	—
House	54.1	8.1	91.9	House	72.4	44.8	55.2
Senate	50.7	5.7	94.3	Senate	69.0	37.9	62.1
Governor	46.1	7.8	92.2	Governor	80.8	61.5	38.5
Midwest				**Mid-Atlantic**			
President	40.6	18.8	81.2	President	—	—	—
House	46.7	10.4	89.6	House	50.8	2.5	97.5
Senate	45.9	12.2	87.8	Senate	46.2	10.0	90.0
Governor	48.5	8.5	91.5	Governor	44.8	10.3	89.7
West				**Border South**			
President	41.3	17.4	82.6	President	—	—	—
House	51.0	9.6	90.4	House	58.0	16.0	84.0
Senate	53.8	11.7	88.3	Senate	54.2	12.2	87.8
Governor	51.5	7.5	92.5	Governor	50.3	7.8	92.2
1958–1959				**Midwest**			
New England				President	—	—	—
President	—	—	—	House	46.3	10.1	89.9
House	53.8	13.3	86.7	Senate	48.8	11.1	88.9
Senate	60.8	23.4	76.6	Governor	48.4	5.8	94.2
Governor	53.1	8.1	91.9	**West**			
South				President	—	—	—
President	—	—	—	House	51.5	12.8	87.2
House	88.0	75.9	24.1	Senate	54.6	14.4	85.6
Senate	85.5	71.1	28.9	Governor	50.5	12.1	87.9
Governor	92.4	84.8	15.2	**1964–1965**			
Mid-Atlantic				**New England**			
President	—	—	—	President	70.7	41.4	58.6
House	50.4	1.1	98.9	House	58.3	20.8	79.2
Senate	49.1	4.1	95.9	Senate	67.0	36.8	63.2
Governor	48.0	6.0	94.0	Governor	55.0	21.6	78.4
Border South				**South**			
President	—	—	—	President	43.6	26.0	74.0
House	65.6	31.1	68.9	House	68.9	38.4	61.6
Senate	54.1	10.2	89.8	Senate	70.2	40.4	59.6
Governor	67.7	35.3	64.7	Governor	60.4	20.7	79.3
Midwest				**Mid-Atlantic**			
President	—	—	—	President	65.3	30.5	69.5
House	52.6	6.1	93.9	House	56.6	13.2	86.9
Senate	53.3	13.5	86.5	Senate	53.8	10.0	90.0
Governor	53.4	8.2	91.8	Governor	54.9	9.7	90.3
West				**Border South**			
President	—	—	—	President	67.8	35.5	64.5
House	56.9	16.3	83.7	House	63.9	27.8	72.2
Senate	56.9	17.4	82.6	Senate	65.3	30.5	69.5
Governor	52.7	10.5	89.5	Governor	54.9	9.8	90.2
1960–1961				**Midwest**			
New England				President	59.9	19.7	80.3
President	51.5	15.6	84.4	House	52.2	9.2	90.8
House	51.9	18.5	81.5	Senate	55.8	17.2	82.8
Senate	47.7	23.6	76.4	Governor	54.4	13.0	87.0
Governor	47.9	10.7	89.3				

Table 8-6 (Continued)

Year/Region[1]	Democratic % of Two-Party Vote	Margin of Victory	Party Competition Index	Year/Region[1]	Democratic % of Two-Party Vote	Margin of Victory	Party Competition Index
West				**Mid-Atlantic**			
President	60.1	20.3	79.7	President	—	—	—
House	54.0	8.5	91.5	House	51.3	7.3	92.7
Senate	55.2	13.1	86.9	Senate	51.0	14.5	85.5
Governor	52.6	11.1	88.9	Governor	50.3	13.5	86.5
1966–1967				**Border South**			
New England				President	—	—	—
President	—	—	—	House	58.2	16.3	83.7
House	50.9	19.4	80.6	Senate	63.2	28.9	71.1
Senate	50.5	20.8	79.2	Governor	56.8	13.7	86.3
Governor	49.1	15.6	84.4	**Midwest**			
South				President	—	—	—
President	—	—	—	House	49.6	9.6	90.4
House	67.2	34.3	65.7	Senate	57.1	15.8	84.2
Senate	64.0	39.0	61.0	Governor	53.3	8.1	91.9
Governor	64.0	32.8	67.2	**West**			
Mid-Atlantic				President	—	—	—
President	—	—	—	House	55.3	17.4	82.6
House	48.5	5.6	94.4	Senate	57.3	17.9	82.1
Senate	39.5	21.0	79.0	Governor	49.1	9.0	91.0
Governor	46.6	6.9	93.1	**1972–1973**			
Border South				**New England**			
President	—	—	—	President	42.1	18.8	81.2
House	53.6	7.1	92.9	House	48.4	21.2	78.8
Senate	49.6	18.5	81.5	Senate	49.9	14.4	85.6
Governor	45.8	8.3	91.7	Governor	52.4	6.8	93.2
Midwest				**South**			
President	—	—	—	President	28.4	43.3	56.7
House	44.3	12.7	87.3	House	62.4	26.6	73.4
Senate	42.9	16.8	83.2	Senate	52.9	20.5	79.5
Governor	45.3	14.9	85.1	Governor	46.6	34.2	65.8
West				**Mid-Atlantic**			
President	—	—	—	President	39.6	20.9	79.1
House	49.7	13.0	87.0	House	47.1	8.7	91.3
Senate	52.1	13.9	86.1	Senate	43.2	15.1	84.9
Governor	46.7	7.0	93.0	Governor	59.6	19.1	80.9
1968–1969				**Border South**			
New England				President	42.5	37.6	62.4
President	55.4	16.9	83.1	House	56.9	13.7	86.3
House	42.4	29.3	70.7	Senate	55.4	13.4	86.6
Senate	31.7	42.4	57.6	Governor	45.3	9.4	90.6
Governor	47.7	6.0	94.0	**Midwest**			
South				President	39.1	21.8	78.2
President	48.8	11.7	88.3	House	46.4	15.7	84.3
House	67.6	35.6	64.4	Senate	46.4	18.2	81.8
Senate	68.7	40.9	59.1	Governor	50.4	13.2	86.8
Governor	60.7	26.3	73.7	**West**			
Mid-Atlantic				President	36.3	27.3	72.7
President	50.4	4.0	96.0	House	53.1	12.5	87.5
House	48.0	6.1	93.9	Senate	41.8	17.8	82.2
Senate	43.3	13.4	86.6	Governor	56.5	18.7	81.3
Governor	44.4	11.3	88.7	**1974–1975**			
Border South				**New England**			
President	54.8	20.6	79.4	President	—	—	—
House	54.9	9.8	90.2	House	55.9	27.2	72.8
Senate	46.8	6.5	93.5	Senate	55.5	11.1	88.9
Governor	49.1	1.8	98.2	Governor	60.6	22.0	78.0
Midwest				**South**			
President	45.8	11.9	88.1	President	—	—	—
House	44.7	12.6	87.4	House	63.6	27.3	72.7
Senate	48.9	11.8	88.2	Senate	77.4	54.8	45.2
Governor	49.9	9.3	90.7	Governor	67.2	35.2	64.8
West				**Mid-Atlantic**			
President	45.1	13.4	86.6	President	—	—	—
House	48.3	16.2	83.8	House	54.6	18.8	81.2
Senate	55.2	18.3	81.7	Senate	46.1	7.8	92.2
Governor	52.3	15.5	84.5	Governor	56.0	12.0	88.0
1970–1971				**Border South**			
New England				President	—	—	—
President	—	—	—	House	63.2	26.4	73.6
House	49.4	24.5	75.5	Senate	49.1	8.2	91.8
Senate	55.6	22.9	77.1	Governor	63.4	26.8	73.2
Governor	46.9	6.4	93.6	**Midwest**			
South				President	—	—	—
President	—	—	—	House	52.8	14.7	85.3
House	71.9	43.8	56.2	Senate	56.8	13.9	86.1
Senate	64.5	30.6	69.4	Governor	53.6	12.9	87.1
Governor	66.9	35.4	64.6				

(Table continues)

Table 8-6 (Continued)

Year/Region[1]	Democratic % of Two-Party Vote	Margin of Victory	Party Competition Index
West			
President	—	—	—
House	55.4	14.1	85.9
Senate	58.3	23.4	76.6
Governor	57.7	15.5	84.5
1976–1977			
New England			
President	49.9	9.4	90.6
House	51.4	26.0	74.0
Senate	52.4	19.7	80.3
Governor	46.8	13.1	86.9
South			
President	55.9	12.1	87.9
House	63.5	27.1	72.9
Senate	74.6	49.2	50.8
Governor	64.2	36.9	63.1
Mid-Atlantic			
President	51.3	3.7	96.3
House	54.6	11.1	88.9
Senate	51.8	12.5	87.5
Governor	50.0	14.3	85.7
Border South			
President	59.5	19.4	80.6
House	65.8	31.5	68.5
Senate	79.7	59.3	40.7
Governor	66.2	32.4	67.6
Midwest			
President	48.6	5.9	94.1
House	48.5	18.8	81.2
Senate	56.1	20.5	79.5
Governor	45.2	12.5	87.5
West			
President	44.5	11.5	88.5
House	55.7	21.2	78.8
Senate	55.6	19.1	80.9
Governor	56.8	13.6	86.4
1978–1979			
New England			
President	—	—	—
House	49.3	26.3	73.7
Senate	54.2	21.9	78.1
Governor	54.1	18.0	82.0
South			
President	—	—	—
House	60.8	25.2	74.8
Senate	59.8	31.8	68.2
Governor	60.0	22.9	77.1
Mid-Atlantic			
President	—	—	—
House	50.4	9.4	90.6
Senate	57.4	14.8	85.2
Governor	50.0	6.1	93.9
Border South			
President	—	—	—
House	61.0	22.0	78.0
Senate	59.8	19.6	80.4
Governor	60.9	21.8	78.2
Midwest			
President	—	—	—
House	47.7	13.8	86.2
Senate	47.6	16.1	83.9
Governor	44.9	10.7	89.3
West			
President	—	—	—
House	54.9	19.3	80.7
Senate	39.3	24.7	75.3
Governor	51.2	14.2	85.8
1980–1981			
New England			
President	46.3	11.5	88.5
House	41.5	32.6	67.4
Senate	51.8	6.4	93.6
Governor	57.2	29.5	70.5
South			
President	48.0	6.8	93.2
House	55.6	19.9	80.1
Senate	54.2	11.3	88.7
Governor	54.7	11.9	88.1
Mid-Atlantic			
President	46.5	7.0	93.0
House	46.5	7.6	92.4
Senate	49.0	2.0	98.0
Governor	39.4	21.2	78.8

Year/Region[1]	Democratic % of Two-Party Vote	Margin of Victory	Party Competition Index
Border South			
President	54.9	21.2	78.8
House	57.4	14.8	85.2
Senate	47.9	24.3	75.7
Governor	54.4	8.8	91.2
Midwest			
President	41.2	18.4	81.6
House	48.4	10.1	89.9
Senate	47.5	18.4	81.6
Governor	45.2	9.5	90.5
West			
President	35.9	28.6	71.4
House	50.5	22.9	77.1
Senate	49.3	18.1	81.9
Governor	51.4	11.7	88.3
1982–1983			
New England			
President	—	—	—
House	47.7	22.4	77.6
Senate	53.5	10.9	89.1
Governor	57.5	20.4	79.6
South			
President	—	—	—
House	60.1	21.2	78.8
Senate	59.1	19.2	80.8
Governor	58.6	21.5	78.5
Mid-Atlantic			
President	—	—	—
House	55.3	10.5	89.5
Senate	50.4	16.5	83.5
Governor	50.2	3.1	96.9
Border South			
President	—	—	—
House	63.5	27.0	73.0
Senate	66.3	32.5	67.5
Governor	59.9	19.7	80.3
Midwest			
President	—	—	—
House	52.8	16.4	83.6
Senate	57.3	18.6	81.4
Governor	51.3	13.3	86.7
West			
President	—	—	—
House	49.6	21.6	78.4
Senate	56.2	21.2	78.8
Governor	57.2	19.8	80.2
1984–1985			
New England			
President	41.2	17.6	82.4
House	43.0	27.2	72.8
Senate	48.7	30.2	69.8
Governor	41.3	18.5	81.5
South			
President	38.0	24.1	75.9
House	58.4	19.6	80.4
Senate	50.6	27.5	72.5
Governor	54.5	14.8	85.2
Mid-Atlantic			
President	43.0	14.1	85.9
House	54.1	8.2	91.8
Senate	62.5	24.9	75.1
Governor	37.1	25.9	74.1
Border South			
President	49.7	29.5	70.5
House	59.7	19.4	80.6
Senate	59.4	19.1	80.9
Governor	46.7	6.6	93.4
Midwest			
President	39.8	20.5	79.5
House	51.3	14.6	85.4
Senate	42.9	20.7	79.3
Governor	48.7	9.7	90.3
West			
President	35.7	28.6	71.4
House	45.5	23.1	76.9
Senate	33.1	38.6	61.4
Governor	56.6	21.4	78.6
1986–1987			
New England			
President	—	—	—
House	42.6	40.3	59.7
Senate	54.6	30.5	69.5
Governor	50.9	19.9	80.1

Table 8-6 (Continued)

Year/Region[1]	Democratic % of Two-Party Vote	Margin of Victory	Party Competition Index	Year/Region[1]	Democratic % of Two-Party Vote	Margin of Victory	Party Competition Index
South				Midwest			
President	—	—	—	President	—	—	—
House	60.3	20.7	79.3	House	55.0	11.6	88.4
Senate	55.2	10.5	89.5	Senate	51.5	18.7	81.3
Governor	53.3	14.5	85.5	Governor	46.3	9.0	91.0
Mid-Atlantic				West			
President	—	—	—	President	—	—	—
House	57.1	14.1	85.9	House	51.4	12.7	87.3
Senate	42.6	14.8	85.2	Senate	41.9	27.5	72.5
Governor	59.2	18.3	81.7	Governor	58.7	18.1	81.9
Border South				1992–1993			
President	—	—	—	New England			
House	64.5	28.9	71.1	President	57.5	15.1	84.9
Senate	60.0	26.9	73.1	House	48.9	19.0	81.0
Governor	65.2	32.6	67.4	Senate	54.9	11.8	88.2
Midwest				Governor	60.7	32.7	67.3
President	—	—	—	South			
House	53.4	15.8	84.2	President	49.6	6.4	93.6
Senate	47.6	18.3	81.7	House	55.3	12.1	87.9
Governor	48.3	19.2	80.8	Senate	56.8	15.4	84.6
West				Governor	48.1	13.8	86.2
President	—	—	—	Mid-Atlantic			
House	47.3	15.0	85.0	President	55.4	10.8	89.2
Senate	47.5	16.6	83.4	House	48.0	7.2	92.8
Governor	52.6	12.5	87.5	Senate	49.0	2.1	97.9
1988–1989				Governor	58.0	16.9	83.1
New England				Border South			
President	47.8	11.1	88.9	President	60.5	25.6	74.4
House	47.6	23.4	76.6	House	61.2	22.4	77.6
Senate	54.6	28.6	71.4	Senate	58.1	30.1	69.9
Governor	48.2	11.8	88.2	Governor	60.5	21.0	79.0
South				Midwest			
President	41.0	18.1	81.9	President	50.5	10.6	89.4
House	58.9	21.4	78.6	House	52.4	13.3	86.7
Senate	58.4	20.2	79.8	Senate	48.8	20.2	79.8
Governor	47.1	6.3	93.7	Governor	54.2	20.1	79.9
Mid-Atlantic				West			
President	47.0	8.2	91.8	President	50.4	11.7	88.3
House	55.4	12.1	87.9	House	52.4	12.0	88.0
Senate	48.3	25.9	74.1	Senate	49.6	15.0	85.0
Governor	45.8	32.9	67.1	Governor	45.5	12.0	88.0
Border South				1994–1995			
President	54.4	21.4	78.6	New England			
House	59.6	20.5	79.5	President	—	—	—
Senate	63.3	26.6	73.4	House	45.0	30.8	69.2
Governor	58.9	17.8	82.2	Senate	48.9	23.7	76.3
Midwest				Governor	48.1	29.0	71.0
President	46.7	10.0	90.0	South			
House	53.4	15.7	84.3	President	—	—	—
Senate	49.3	20.6	79.4	House	45.3	12.9	87.1
Governor	49.4	18.7	81.3	Senate	38.7	23.8	76.2
West				Governor	48.0	9.2	90.8
President	43.9	14.6	85.4	Mid-Atlantic			
House	49.2	17.4	82.6	President	—	—	—
Senate	52.9	17.3	82.7	House	41.6	16.8	83.2
Governor	52.7	10.9	89.1	Senate	50.2	8.5	91.5
1990–1991				Governor	47.5	5.0	95.0
New England				Border South			
President	—	—	—	President	—	—	—
House	47.0	25.3	74.7	House	49.1	17.9	82.1
Senate	47.5	23.9	76.1	Senate	64.1	28.1	71.9
Governor	48.4	19.4	80.6	Governor	46.7	8.4	91.6
South				Midwest			
President	—	—	—	President	—	—	—
House	61.1	22.3	77.7	House	45.9	14.3	85.7
Senate	49.9	57.9	42.1	Senate	46.9	17.1	82.9
Governor	52.0	15.2	84.8	Governor	40.0	30.6	69.4
Mid-Atlantic				West			
President	—	—	—	President	—	—	—
House	53.1	12.9	87.1	House	45.3	17.1	82.9
Senate	57.6	15.2	84.8	Senate	47.6	20.4	79.6
Governor	69.6	39.1	60.9	Governor	49.4	11.3	88.7
Border South				1996–1997			
President	—	—	—	New England			
House	56.8	16.4	83.6	President	63.2	26.5	73.5
Senate	66.4	35.8	64.2	House	54.5	29.2	70.8
Governor	62.7	25.5	74.5	Senate	53.5	11.4	88.6
				Governor	67.5	35.0	65.0

(Table continues)

Table 8-6 (Continued)

Year/Region[1]	Democratic % of Two-Party Vote	Margin of Victory	Party Competition Index	Year/Region[1]	Democratic % of Two-Party Vote	Margin of Victory	Party Competition Index
South				South			
President	50.4	6.7	93.3	President	—	—	—
House	45.1	9.9	90.1	House	45.0	11.6	88.4
Senate	44.4	11.6	88.4	Senate	53.5	16.8	83.2
Governor	50.0	13.4	86.6	Governor	43.8	19.8	80.2
Mid-Atlantic				Mid-Atlantic			
President	60.0	19.9	80.1	President	—	—	—
House	46.5	15.5	84.5	House	46.8	12.7	87.3
Senate	58.3	16.5	83.5	Senate	45.8	19.1	80.9
Governor	59.5	20.1	79.9	Governor	36.5	27.0	73.0
Border South				Border South			
President	60.6	24.8	75.2	President	—	—	—
House	54.9	31.5	68.5	House	55.7	32.8	67.2
Senate	53.9	27.7	72.3	Senate	50.7	25.9	74.1
Governor	47.0	6.0	94.0	Governor	52.8	17.1	82.9
Midwest				Midwest			
President	51.3	12.4	87.6	President	—	—	—
House	48.2	13.5	86.5	House	43.7	17.8	82.2
Senate	50.6	13.7	86.3	Senate	49.3	20.5	79.5
Governor	48.3	18.1	81.9	Governor	41.5	18.2	81.8
West				West			
President	49.7	12.7	87.3	President	—	—	—
House	46.1	14.3	85.7	House	45.3	21.1	78.9
Senate	39.5	22.5	77.5	Senate	45.8	32.3	67.7
Governor	34.2	42.3	57.7	Governor	50.2	20.9	79.1
1998–1999							
New England							
President	—	—	—				
House	51.7	43.8	56.2				
Senate	57.5	42.5	57.5				
Governor	49.0	19.1	80.9				

Notes: The Democratic percent of two-party vote values are the regional averages of the state Democratic percent of two-party vote values for president shown in Tables 8-36 through 8-53, for House shown in Tables 8-54 through 8-89, for Senate shown in Tables 8-90 through 8-104, and for governor shown in Table 8-105 through 8-140 for a given two-year election cycle. (These same values can be found in the state vote tables in Chapters 4, 5, 6, and 7, respectively.) The Democratic vote values are different from the national vote tables presented in Chapters 4–6 since the former are based on voter percentage values and the latter on raw vote numbers. Margin of victory values are the regional averages of the state margin of victory values for president, House, Senate, and governor found in Tables 8-36 through 8-140 for two-year election cycles. Margin of victory is defined as the absolute difference between the Democratic and Republican percent of the two-party vote for each of these separate races in a given election year. Averaging these percent values (instead of the raw vote numbers on which they are based) is purposely done in order that each state is weighted equally in determining the regional result for margin of victory. Paul David's (1972) party competition index values are the regional averages of the state party competition values for president, House, Senate, and governor found in Tables 8-36 through 8-140 for a given election year. David's index is defined as 100 − the margin of victory or, alternately, as 100 − the absolute difference between the Democratic and Republican percent of two-party vote for each political race in a given election year. The values for Democratic and Republican percent of two-party vote for president, House, Senate, and governor used in the computations to get the David party competition values in Tables 8-36 through 8-140 are taken from the state vote tables for these races in Chapters 4, 5, 6, and 7, respectively. The author's alternative party coding in Chapters 4–7 is used whenever it occurs in place of the conventional party coding for vote data in computing David's party competition index. Zero (0) percent on David's competition index represents a complete absence of two-party competition for a given region for that election cycle, whereas a score of 100 percent indicates perfect competition between the two major parties for that region in that election cycle. The Democratic Party is defined as the Anti-Federalists, Democratic-Republicans, and Jackson Democrats prior to 1830 when the "Democratic Party" as such was established. The Republican Party is defined as the Federalists, National Republicans, and Whigs prior to the establishment of the "Republican Party" in the 1850's. See Appendix A for an explanation of the historical antecedents of the current Democratic and Republican parties. No special elections for any of the four races are used in the calculations, nor are partial voting data reported for any of the four races in any of the states. Because of rounding, margin of victory and competition values when added together may equal 100.1 or 99.9 percent instead of 100.0 percent in some instances. —indicates no data available.

[1]The regional categorizations are adapted from the ICPSR regional codings. In the current analysis, Tennessee is categorized in the South since it was part of the Confederacy, although the ICPSR treats it as a Border South state. The regional categories are: New England—Connecticut, Maine, Massachusetts, New Hampshire, Rhode Island, Vermont; Mid-Atlantic—Delaware, New Jersey, New York, Pennsylvania; South—Alabama, Arkansas, Florida, Georgia, Louisiana, Mississippi, North Carolina, South Carolina, Tennessee, Texas, Virginia; Border South—Kentucky, Maryland, Oklahoma, West Virginia; Midwest—Illinois, Indiana, Iowa, Kansas, Michigan, Minnesota, Missouri, Nebraska, North Dakota, Ohio, South Dakota, Wisconsin; West—Alaska, Arizona, California, Colorado, Hawaii, Idaho, Montana, Nevada, New Mexico, Oregon, Utah, Washington, Wyoming.
[2]Voters began directly electing senators in 1912.

Sources: Tables 8-36 through 8-140. Specifically, state Democratic percent values of the two-party vote for each race in Tables 8-36 through 8-140 are aggregated across states in each given region for each two-year election cycle to obtain the regional Democratic percent of two-party vote averages for each race. Regional margin of victory values and regional party competition values are obtained in the same manner from Tables 8-36 through 8-140 for each political race.

Table 8-7 Composite Competition Index for Non-South and South, by Two-Year Election Cycle, 1788–1999

Year/Region[1]	Composite Competition Index	Year/Region[1]	Composite Competition Index	Year/Region[1]	Composite Competition Index	Year/Region[1]	Composite Competition Index
1788–1789		1844–1845		1900–1901		1956–1957	
Non-South	37.2	Non-South	86.6	Non-South	85.5	Non-South	86.9
South	—	South	80.4	South	52.4	South	48.9
1790–1791		1846–1847		1902–1903		1958–1959	
Non-South	19.8	Non-South	90.2	Non-South	85.1	Non-South	87.2
South	—	South	68.8	South	31.5	South	22.4
1792–1793		1848–1849		1904–1905		1960–1961	
Non-South	44.3	Non-South	82.5	Non-South	76.2	Non-South	90.5
South	—	South	81.9	South	46.0	South	56.0
1794–1795		1850–1851		1906–1907		1962–1963	
Non-South	52.0	Non-South	88.7	Non-South	84.2	Non-South	89.1
South	87.2	South	57.4	South	31.8	South	52.3
1796–1797		1852–1853		1908–1909		1964–1965	
Non-South	42.2	Non-South	88.9	Non-South	85.5	Non-South	81.4
South	53.8	South	79.2	South	47.2	South	68.9
1798–1799		1854–1855		1910–1911		1966–1967	
Non-South	57.0	Non-South	62.2	Non-South	87.6	Non-South	86.7
South	43.4	South	13.8	South	32.9	South	64.6
1800–1801		1856–1857		1912–1913		1968–1969	
Non-South	69.2	Non-South	68.8	Non-South	82.6	Non-South	85.6
South	11.4	South	0.0	South	27.1	South	72.7
1802–1803		1858–1859		1914–1915		1970–1971	
Non-South	64.1	Non-South	69.7	Non-South	87.9	Non-South	85.8
South	29.7	South	22.1	South	26.3	South	62.3
1804–1805		1860–1861		1916–1917		1972–1973	
Non-South	56.9	Non-South	72.1	Non-South	87.8	Non-South	81.6
South	0.0	South	15.2	South	37.7	South	68.8
1806–1807		1862–1863		1918–1919		1974–1975	
Non-South	68.0	Non-South	70.6	Non-South	83.2	Non-South	82.9
South	18.2	South	25.5	South	18.6	South	61.7
1808–1809		1864–1865		1920–1921		1976–1977	
Non-South	75.1	Non-South	75.5	Non-South	71.8	Non-South	83.3
South	32.0	South	20.2	South	50.9	South	73.8
1810–1811		1866–1867		1922–1923		1978–1979	
Non-South	73.0	Non-South	78.5	Non-South	81.3	Non-South	82.5
South	12.8	South	0.0	South	33.0	South	73.3
1812–1813		1868–1869		1924–1925		1980–1981	
Non-South	74.7	Non-South	83.1	Non-South	71.2	Non-South	81.8
South	12.3	South	58.6	South	39.5	South	88.0
1814–1815		1870–1871		1926–1927		1982–1983	
Non-South	78.9	Non-South	86.9	Non-South	76.3	Non-South	81.5
South	5.5	South	82.1	South	27.6	South	79.1
1816–1817		1872–1873		1928–1929		1984–1985	
Non-South	48.9	Non-South	81.1	Non-South	78.4	Non-South	77.8
South	1.6	South	75.8	South	53.5	South	77.0
1818–1819		1874–1875		1930–1931		1986–1987	
Non-South	48.5	Non-South	83.2	Non-South	79.8	Non-South	80.4
South	0.0	South	70.3	South	23.0	South	84.3
1820–1821		1876–1877		1932–1933		1988–1989	
Non-South	21.8	Non-South	87.7	Non-South	84.6	Non-South	82.9
South	0.0	South	72.4	South	30.4	South	81.4
1822–1823		1878–1879		1934–1935		1990–1991	
Non-South	35.2	Non-South	80.1	Non-South	85.0	Non-South	81.9
South	3.2	South	41.5	South	19.6	South	68.2
1824–1825		1880–1881		1936–1937		1992–1993	
Non-South	28.8	Non-South	86.3	Non-South	81.1	Non-South	84.7
South	18.7	South	61.1	South	25.6	South	89.3
1826–1827		1882–1883		1938–1939		1994–1995	
Non-South	37.0	Non-South	89.4	Non-South	82.4	Non-South	81.0
South	10.3	South	55.4	South	18.0	South	86.2
1828–1829		1884–1885		1940–1941		1996–1997	
Non-South	62.1	Non-South	90.2	Non-South	85.5	Non-South	81.4
South	36.5	South	69.2	South	24.9	South	90.4
1830–1831		1886–1887		1942–1943		1998–1999	
Non-South	64.2	Non-South	88.2	Non-South	82.3	Non-South	76.3
South	37.9	South	48.9	South	13.0	South	83.7
1832–1833		1888–1889		1944–1945			
Non-South	67.6	Non-South	90.5	Non-South	87.4	*(Notes continue)*	
South	30.7	South	57.1	South	34.8		
1834–1835		1890–1891		1946–1947			
Non-South	72.6	Non-South	89.9	Non-South	81.8		
South	71.6	South	49.7	South	27.0		
1836–1837		1892–1893		1948–1949			
Non-South	85.2	Non-South	84.3	Non-South	87.7		
South	78.1	South	38.7	South	37.4		
1838–1839		1894–1895		1950–1951			
Non-South	91.0	Non-South	74.0	Non-South	85.8		
South	81.4	South	37.5	South	19.1		
1840–1841		1896–1897		1952–1953			
Non-South	84.1	Non-South	75.8	Non-South	84.2		
South	90.0	South	54.8	South	46.5		
1842–1843		1898–1899		1954–1955			
Non-South	83.7	Non-South	81.9	Non-South	89.6		
South	82.6	South	34.2	South	23.9		

Table 8-7 *(Continued)*

Notes: The regional composite competition index is the mean of all state values for the party competition index devised by Paul David (1972) for all races in a given two-year election cycle in a given region among the following set of races: president, House, Senate, and governor. The state values for these races are presented in Tables 8-36 through 8-53 for president, Tables 8-54 through 8-89 for House, Tables 8-90 through 8-104 for Senate, and Tables 8-105 through 8-140 for governor. David's competition index is defined as 100 − the absolute difference between the Democratic and Republican percentage of two-party vote for each of the four races mentioned here. The values for Democratic and Republican percent of two-party vote for president, House, Senate, and governor used in the computations to get the David party competition values in Tables 8-36 through 8-140 are taken from the state vote tables for these races in Chapters 4, 5, 6, and 7, respectively. The author's alternative party coding in Chapters 4–7 is used whenever it occurs in place of the conventional party coding for vote data in computing David's party competition index. Zero (0) percent on David's competition index represents a complete absence of two-party competition for that election cycle in that region, whereas a score of 100 percent indicates perfect competition between the two major parties in that region. The Democratic Party is defined as the Anti-Federalists, Democratic-Republicans, and Jackson Democrats prior to 1830 when the "Democratic Party" as such was established. The Republican Party is defined as the Federalists, National Republicans, and Whigs prior to the establishment of the "Republican Party" in the 1850s. See Appendix A for an explanation of the historical antecedents of the current Democratic and Republican parties. No special elections for any of the four races are used in the calculations, nor are partial voting data reported for any of the four races in any of the states. —indicates no data available.

[1]Regional categorization follows that of the ICPSR except that in the current analysis Tennessee is categorized in the South since it was part of the Confederacy, whereas the ICPSR codes it as a Border South state. Thus, the South includes Alabama, Arkansas, Florida, Georgia, Louisiana, Mississippi, North Carolina, South Carolina, Tennessee, Texas, and Virginia. All other states make up the non-South.

Sources: Tables 8-36 through 8-140. Specifically, state party competition values in Tables 8-36 through 8-140 for the presidential, House, Senate, and gubernatorial races are aggregated across states in a given region for each two-year election cycle to obtain the regional composite competition averages shown for that cycle.

Table 8-8 Competition Measures for Non-South and South, by Two-Year Election Cycle, 1788–1999

Year/Region[1]	Democratic % of Two-Party Vote	Margin of Victory	Party Competition Index	Year/Region[1]	Democratic % of Two-Party Vote	Margin of Victory	Party Competition Index
1788–1789				**1806–1807**			
Non-South				Non-South			
President	7.6	84.7	15.3	President	—	—	—
House	40.3	19.4	80.6	House	60.1	28.1	71.9
Governor	51.6	69.8	30.2	Governor	63.2	34.5	65.5
South				South			
President	—	—	—	President	—	—	—
House	—	—	—	House	90.9	81.8	18.2
Governor	—	—	—	Governor	—	—	—
1790–1791				**1808–1809**			
Non-South				Non-South			
President	—	—	—	President	61.1	26.5	73.5
House	30.4	39.2	60.8	House	53.1	12.4	87.6
Governor	96.9	93.9	6.1	Governor	61.7	34.2	65.8
South				South			
President	—	—	—	President	95.4	90.8	9.2
House	—	—	—	House	72.6	45.2	54.8
Governor	—	—	—	Governor	—	—	—
1792–1793				**1810–1811**			
Non-South				Non-South			
President	0.0	100.0	0.0	President	—	—	—
House	45.1	9.9	90.1	House	55.3	31.8	68.2
Governor	62.8	65.5	34.5	Governor	58.7	23.0	77.0
South				South			
President	—	—	—	President	—	—	—
House	—	—	—	House	93.6	87.2	12.8
Governor	—	—	—	Governor	—	—	—
1794–1795				**1812–1813**			
Non-South				Non-South			
President	—	—	—	President	50.2	21.4	78.6
House	37.4	35.2	64.8	House	46.4	24.3	75.7
Governor	11.7	76.5	23.5	Governor	45.0	26.3	73.7
South				South			
President	—	—	—	President	72.9	45.8	54.2
House	56.4	12.8	87.2	House	90.8	81.5	18.5
Governor	—	—	—	Governor	100.0	100.0	0.0
1796–1797				**1814–1815**			
Non-South				Non-South			
President	32.8	35.2	64.8	President	—	—	—
House	28.5	43.0	57.0	House	43.8	15.3	84.7
Governor	34.3	86.7	13.3	Governor	44.2	24.4	75.6
South				South			
President	—	—	—	President	—	—	—
House	69.2	46.2	53.8	House	95.9	91.7	8.3
Governor	—	—	—	Governor	100.0	100.0	0.0
1798–1799				**1816–1817**			
Non-South				Non-South			
President	—	—	—	President	84.9	69.7	30.3
House	31.7	37.7	62.3	House	55.7	53.9	46.1
Governor	26.5	48.8	51.2	Governor	57.3	42.4	57.6
South				South			
President	—	—	—	President	96.9	93.7	6.3
House	43.4	13.2	86.8	House	100.0	100.0	0.0
Governor	100.0	100.0	0.0	Governor	100.0	100.0	0.0
1800–1801				**1818–1819**			
Non-South				Non-South			
President	51.9	3.7	96.3	President	—	—	—
House	53.2	26.6	73.4	House	74.7	49.7	50.3
Governor	50.6	40.5	59.5	Governor	73.6	53.2	46.8
South				South			
President	77.3	54.6	45.4	President	—	—	—
House	100.0	100.0	0.0	House	100.0	100.0	0.0
Governor	100.0	100.0	0.0	Governor	100.0	100.0	0.0
1802–1803				**1820–1821**			
Non-South				Non-South			
President	—	—	—	President	92.4	92.0	8.0
House	52.2	36.4	63.6	House	79.5	62.1	37.9
Governor	50.3	35.4	64.6	Governor	88.7	81.3	18.7
South				South			
President	—	—	—	President	100.0	100.0	0.0
House	80.2	60.5	39.5	House	100.0	100.0	0.0
Governor	100.0	100.0	0.0	Governor	100.0	100.0	0.0
1804–1805				**1822–1823**			
Non-South				Non-South			
President	80.3	60.6	39.4	President	—	—	—
House	60.9	43.4	56.6	House	84.0	69.7	30.3
Governor	57.4	33.5	66.5	Governor	80.5	63.3	36.7
South				South			
President	100.0	100.0	0.0	President	—	—	—
House	100.0	100.0	0.0	House	96.0	92.0	8.0
Governor	100.0	100.0	0.0	Governor	100.0	100.0	0.0

(Table continues)

Table 8-8 (Continued)

Year/Region[1]	Democratic % of Two-Party Vote	Margin of Victory	Party Competition Index	Year/Region[1]	Democratic % of Two-Party Vote	Margin of Victory	Party Competition Index
1824–1825				**1842–1843**			
Non-South				Non-South			
President	42.8	64.0	36.0	President	—	—	—
House	82.9	66.7	33.3	House	55.1	15.7	84.3
Governor	71.4	80.2	19.8	Governor	51.1	16.9	83.1
South				South			
President	78.1	59.0	41.0	President	—	—	—
House	100.0	100.0	0.0	House	60.5	26.1	73.9
Governor	100.0	100.0	0.0	Governor	50.8	6.9	93.1
1826–1827				**1844–1845**			
Non-South				Non-South			
President	—	—	—	President	49.9	8.6	91.4
House	36.5	46.6	53.4	House	47.9	14.1	85.9
Governor	68.0	79.4	20.6	Governor	50.1	17.0	83.0
South				South			
President	—	—	—	President	54.1	9.3	90.7
House	84.5	69.0	31.0	House	57.0	17.3	82.7
Governor	100.0	100.0	0.0	Governor	65.2	31.8	68.2
1828–1829				**1846–1847**			
Non-South				Non-South			
President	46.2	26.2	73.8	President	—	—	—
House	44.4	25.9	74.1	House	51.7	8.3	91.7
Governor	58.5	56.0	44.0	Governor	48.3	13.9	86.1
South				South			
President	79.7	59.5	40.5	President	—	—	—
House	73.4	61.9	38.1	House	63.6	30.3	69.7
Governor	80.8	70.0	30.0	Governor	63.0	55.0	45.0
1830–1831				**1848–1849**			
Non-South				Non-South			
President	—	—	—	President	47.9	12.8	87.2
House	49.1	33.4	66.6	House	52.2	17.1	82.9
Governor	52.0	38.1	61.9	Governor	53.7	21.7	78.3
South				South			
President	—	—	—	President	50.5	9.4	90.6
House	84.4	68.9	31.1	House	57.9	20.1	79.9
Governor	74.4	58.1	41.9	Governor	62.2	26.0	74.0
1832–1833				**1850–1851**			
Non-South				Non-South			
President	55.4	24.2	75.8	President	—	—	—
House	59.1	33.4	66.6	House	51.7	8.3	91.7
Governor	61.4	39.2	60.8	Governor	48.3	13.9	86.1
South				South			
President	88.1	76.3	23.7	President	—	—	—
House	62.1	43.5	56.5	House	63.6	30.3	69.7
Governor	88.2	76.5	23.5	Governor	60.3	49.6	50.4
1834–1835				**1852–1853**			
Non-South				Non-South			
President	—	—	—	President	53.0	9.7	90.3
House	61.6	29.9	70.1	House	53.6	9.8	90.2
Governor	56.3	24.8	75.2	Governor	53.2	13.6	86.4
South				South			
President	—	—	—	President	59.9	20.0	80.0
House	41.1	26.0	74.0	House	64.5	29.0	71.0
Governor	41.7	30.4	69.6	Governor	58.0	16.1	83.9
1836–1837				**1854–1855**			
Non-South				Non-South			
President	51.8	11.3	88.7	President	—	—	—
House	52.8	18.3	81.7	House	66.1	44.6	55.4
Governor	51.9	14.9	85.1	Governor	52.5	31.6	68.4
South				South			
President	52.8	10.4	89.6	President	—	—	—
House	50.9	28.7	71.3	House	92.4	84.7	15.3
Governor	58.9	32.0	68.0	Governor	93.9	87.8	12.2
1838–1839				**1856–1857**			
Non-South				Non-South			
President	—	—	—	President	56.6	36.6	63.4
House	50.6	6.5	93.5	House	55.8	31.4	68.6
Governor	53.3	14.2	85.8	Governor	52.3	26.9	73.1
South				South			
President	—	—	—	President	100.0	100.0	0.0
House	48.4	15.4	84.6	House	100.0	100.0	0.0
Governor	54.9	21.3	78.7	Governor	100.0	100.0	0.0
1840–1841				**1858–1859**			
Non-South				Non-South			
President	46.1	10.8	89.2	President	—	—	—
House	44.2	18.1	81.9	House	57.5	32.1	67.9
Governor	44.9	18.3	81.7	Governor	52.2	28.6	71.4
South				South			
President	47.4	10.9	89.1	President	—	—	—
House	50.9	10.2	89.8	House	94.8	89.5	10.5
Governor	51.5	8.3	91.7	Governor	83.1	66.2	33.8

Table 8-8 *(Continued)*

Year/Region[1]	Democratic % of Two-Party Vote	Margin of Victory	Party Competition Index	Year/Region[1]	Democratic % of Two-Party Vote	Margin of Victory	Party Competition Index
1860–1861				1878–1879			
Non-South				Non-South			
President	43.2	31.3	68.7	President	—	—	—
House	45.2	36.1	63.9	House	48.7	19.7	80.3
Governor	42.5	23.3	76.7	Governor	45.3	20.1	79.9
South				South			
President	98.8	97.7	2.3	President	—	—	—
House	100.0	100.0	0.0	House	75.3	50.5	49.5
Governor	79.0	57.9	42.1	Governor	86.6	73.1	26.9
1862–1863				1880–1881			
Non-South				Non-South			
President	—	—	—	President	46.0	12.5	87.5
House	42.4	26.4	73.6	House	46.3	12.4	87.6
Governor	34.5	32.2	67.8	Governor	43.0	16.9	83.1
South				South			
President	—	—	—	President	61.8	23.6	76.4
House	—	—	—	House	68.1	36.1	63.9
Governor	62.8	74.5	25.5	Governor	79.5	58.9	41.1
1864–1865				1882–1883			
Non-South				Non-South			
President	42.2	19.6	80.4	President	—	—	—
House	37.4	25.9	74.1	House	48.6	11.3	88.7
Governor	36.0	28.1	71.9	Governor	48.8	9.8	90.2
South				South			
President	—	—	—	President	—	—	—
House	0.0	100.0	0.0	House	71.0	42.0	58.0
Governor	50.2	76.4	23.6	Governor	74.7	49.3	50.7
1866–1867				1884–1885			
Non-South				Non-South			
President	—	—	—	President	46.6	10.4	89.6
House	42.4	21.6	78.4	House	47.5	9.6	90.4
Governor	43.3	21.5	78.5	Governor	46.0	9.1	90.9
South				South			
President	—	—	—	President	60.4	20.8	79.2
House	0.0	100.0	0.0	House	65.2	30.4	69.6
Governor	0.0	100.0	0.0	Governor	71.1	42.3	57.7
1868–1869				1886–1887			
Non-South				Non-South			
President	44.8	18.5	81.5	President	—	—	—
House	45.6	17.2	82.8	House	50.1	12.0	88.0
Governor	42.7	15.2	84.8	Governor	50.0	11.5	88.5
South				South			
President	50.0	19.9	80.1	President	—	—	—
House	31.8	40.3	59.7	House	73.7	47.4	52.6
Governor	22.2	57.6	42.4	Governor	78.9	57.8	42.2
1870–1871				1888–1889			
Non-South				Non-South			
President	—	—	—	President	46.4	9.5	90.5
House	46.2	12.7	87.3	House	45.5	11.0	89.0
Governor	46.4	13.6	86.4	Governor	46.1	10.0	90.0
South				South			
President	—	—	—	President	65.1	30.2	69.8
House	49.8	16.2	83.8	House	69.8	39.7	60.3
Governor	47.2	21.1	78.9	Governor	79.4	58.8	41.2
1872–1873				1890–1891			
Non-South				Non-South			
President	41.1	19.2	80.8	President	—	—	—
House	44.7	16.3	83.7	House	48.3	11.5	88.5
Governor	44.8	21.3	78.7	Governor	49.2	8.4	91.6
South				South			
President	45.8	14.2	85.8	President	—	—	—
House	35.3	35.7	64.3	House	73.5	47.0	53.0
Governor	46.8	22.8	77.2	Governor	78.2	56.5	43.5
1874–1875				1892–1893			
Non-South				Non-South			
President	—	—	—	President	38.3	26.7	73.3
House	46.9	20.2	79.8	House	47.4	10.5	89.5
Governor	47.9	13.6	86.4	Governor	47.5	8.4	91.6
South				South			
President	—	—	—	President	76.0	52.0	48.0
House	56.9	25.5	74.5	House	84.0	68.0	32.0
Governor	67.9	38.8	61.2	Governor	82.1	64.2	35.8
1876–1877				1894–1895			
Non-South				Non-South			
President	47.4	12.1	87.9	President	—	—	—
House	47.5	12.7	87.3	House	36.2	27.6	72.4
Governor	45.9	12.1	87.9	Governor	39.2	23.4	76.6
South				South			
President	59.1	19.3	80.7	President	—	—	—
House	62.7	25.4	74.6	House	78.0	56.5	43.5
Governor	69.7	39.3	60.7	Governor	85.9	71.9	28.1

(Table continues)

Table 8-8 (Continued)

Year/Region[1]	Democratic % of Two-Party Vote	Margin of Victory	Party Competition Index	Year/Region[1]	Democratic % of Two-Party Vote	Margin of Victory	Party Competition Index
1896–1897				**1914–1915**			
Non-South				Non-South			
President	48.3	24.3	75.7	President	—	—	—
House	43.3	24.5	75.5	House	47.4	13.7	86.3
Governor	44.9	23.6	76.4	Senate	49.7	10.9	89.1
South				Governor	47.1	10.9	89.1
President	69.6	39.2	60.8	South			
House	71.3	44.3	55.7	President	—	—	—
Governor	76.0	52.6	47.4	House	88.5	77.0	23.0
1898–1899				Senate	86.1	72.3	27.7
Non-South				Governor	84.5	69.0	31.0
President	—	—	—	**1916–1917**			
House	44.5	20.0	80.0	Non-South			
Governor	44.4	15.7	84.3	President	51.2	9.2	90.8
South				House	46.3	12.8	87.2
President	—	—	—	Senate	46.6	13.3	86.7
House	78.4	56.8	43.2	Governor	44.4	14.0	86.0
Governor	90.0	79.9	20.1	South			
1900–1901				President	78.9	57.8	42.2
Non-South				House	82.8	65.7	34.3
President	44.2	15.7	84.3	Senate	85.6	71.2	28.8
House	44.8	14.1	85.9	Governor	79.0	58.0	42.0
Governor	44.9	13.7	86.3	**1918–1919**			
South				Non-South			
President	70.1	40.2	59.8	President	—	—	—
House	76.0	51.9	48.1	House	43.1	17.9	82.1
Governor	75.5	51.1	48.9	Senate	43.7	15.2	84.8
1902–1903				Governor	42.4	16.5	83.5
Non-South				South			
President	—	—	—	President	—	—	—
House	43.1	15.4	84.6	House	90.4	80.7	19.3
Governor	44.5	14.3	85.7	Senate	89.9	79.7	20.3
South				Governor	92.5	84.9	15.1
President	—	—	—	**1920–1921**			
House	84.3	68.6	31.4	Non-South			
Governor	84.2	68.4	31.6	President	34.0	32.1	67.9
1904–1905				House	34.7	31.5	68.5
Non-South				Senate	39.0	22.0	78.0
President	34.3	31.6	68.4	Governor	37.8	24.4	75.6
House	38.7	23.0	77.0	South			
Governor	43.7	15.4	84.6	President	68.6	37.8	62.2
South				House	75.4	51.4	48.6
President	74.9	49.9	50.1	Senate	81.2	62.4	37.6
House	79.0	57.9	42.1	Governor	73.7	50.0	50.0
Governor	77.2	54.4	45.6	**1922–1923**			
1906–1907				Non-South			
Non-South				President	—	—	—
President	—	—	—	House	43.5	20.1	79.9
House	42.2	18.3	81.7	Senate	47.9	15.1	84.9
Governor	46.7	12.6	87.4	Governor	44.2	20.2	79.8
South				South			
President	—	—	—	President	—	—	—
House	83.4	66.9	33.1	House	84.6	69.1	30.9
Governor	85.2	70.3	29.7	Senate	78.8	57.6	42.4
1908–1909				Governor	85.2	70.4	29.6
Non-South				**1924–1925**			
President	41.9	16.9	83.1	Non-South			
House	43.0	16.0	84.0	President	30.9	38.5	61.5
Governor	46.1	9.5	90.5	House	39.3	26.9	73.1
South				Senate	37.0	27.3	72.7
President	72.2	44.3	55.7	Governor	41.2	19.9	80.1
House	80.1	60.2	39.8	South			
Governor	77.1	54.2	45.8	President	74.1	48.3	51.7
1910–1911				House	83.0	66.0	34.0
Non-South				Senate	85.0	69.9	30.1
President	—	—	—	Governor	79.1	58.2	41.8
House	45.3	13.6	86.4	**1926–1927**			
Governor	48.3	10.7	89.3	Non-South			
South				President	—	—	—
President	—	—	—	House	38.6	26.2	73.8
House	84.5	69.1	30.9	Senate	41.9	20.2	79.8
Governor	81.0	63.5	36.5	Governor	40.6	23.7	76.3
1912–1913[2]				South			
Non-South				President	—	—	—
President	61.3	24.2	75.8	House	85.7	71.5	28.5
House	50.8	16.3	83.7	Senate	86.0	72.0	28.0
Senate	54.4	17.3	82.7	Governor	87.2	74.3	25.7
Governor	52.7	10.0	90.0	**1928–1929**			
South				Non-South			
President	87.0	73.9	26.1	President	39.3	21.6	78.4
House	87.5	75.0	25.0	House	39.2	22.9	77.1
Senate	—	—	—	Senate	39.9	25.2	74.8
Governor	84.0	68.8	31.2	Governor	43.9	16.7	83.3

Table 8-8 (Continued)

Year/Region[1]	Democratic % of Two-Party Vote	Margin of Victory	Party Competition Index	Year/Region[1]	Democratic % of Two-Party Vote	Margin of Victory	Party Competition Index
South				1944–1945			
President	58.4	26.0	74.0	Non-South			
House	81.0	62.0	38.0	President	51.3	8.2	91.8
Senate	81.8	63.6	36.4	House	48.4	15.0	85.0
Governor	70.9	41.9	58.1	Senate	50.4	11.6	88.4
1930–1931				Governor	46.1	16.1	83.9
Non-South				South			
President	—	—	—	President	76.7	53.5	46.5
House	43.4	23.3	76.7	House	87.8	75.6	24.4
Senate	46.6	18.5	81.5	Senate	86.6	73.2	26.8
Governor	46.5	17.6	82.4	Governor	79.6	59.2	40.8
South				1946–1947			
President	—	—	—	Non-South			
House	85.8	71.5	28.5	President	—	—	—
Senate	92.0	84.1	15.9	House	43.6	16.6	83.4
Governor	87.6	75.2	24.8	Senate	43.8	17.2	82.8
1932–1933				Governor	42.5	21.2	78.8
Non-South				South			
President	58.2	18.7	81.3	President	—	—	—
House	54.0	13.2	86.8	House	86.8	73.5	26.5
Senate	54.7	16.4	83.6	Senate	81.4	62.8	37.2
Governor	53.5	13.2	86.8	Governor	89.8	79.6	20.4
South				1948–1949			
President	83.9	67.9	32.1	Non-South			
House	86.8	73.7	26.3	President	51.4	7.9	92.1
Senate	90.7	81.4	18.6	House	49.1	13.2	86.8
Governor	78.0	55.9	44.1	Senate	51.2	14.8	85.2
1934–1935				Governor	49.6	14.9	85.1
Non-South				South			
President	—	—	—	President	62.7	43.6	56.4
House	55.6	15.0	85.0	House	87.0	74.1	25.9
Senate	54.1	18.2	81.8	Senate	85.2	70.5	29.5
Governor	53.2	12.2	87.8	Governor	81.5	62.9	37.1
South				1950–1951			
President	—	—	—	Non-South			
House	90.8	81.6	18.4	President	—	—	—
Senate	87.9	75.8	24.2	House	47.5	13.2	86.8
Governor	90.9	81.9	18.1	Senate	45.4	16.0	84.0
1936–1937				Governor	44.7	14.1	85.9
Non-South				South			
President	61.1	23.7	76.3	President	—	—	—
House	56.0	17.4	82.6	House	89.6	79.1	20.9
Senate	51.1	18.6	81.4	Senate	90.4	80.8	19.2
Governor	51.5	15.1	84.9	Governor	91.9	83.9	16.1
South				1952–1953			
President	83.4	66.9	33.1	Non-South			
House	88.2	76.4	23.6	President	41.1	18.0	82.0
Senate	90.9	81.8	18.2	House	43.8	15.2	84.8
Governor	86.4	72.7	27.3	Senate	44.1	15.1	84.9
1938–1939				Governor	44.1	14.3	85.7
Non-South				South			
President	—	—	—	President	54.0	13.3	86.7
House	49.6	16.8	83.2	House	86.2	72.3	27.7
Senate	51.6	18.9	81.1	Senate	95.6	91.2	8.8
Governor	46.8	17.7	82.3	Governor	80.1	60.1	39.9
South				1954–1955			
President	—	—	—	Non-South			
House	91.3	82.6	17.4	President	—	—	—
Senate	88.7	77.5	22.5	House	49.6	11.2	88.8
Governor	92.9	85.7	14.3	Senate	49.6	10.4	89.6
1940–1941				Governor	49.5	9.5	90.5
Non-South				South			
President	53.0	10.1	89.9	President	—	—	—
House	49.9	15.8	84.2	House	85.6	71.3	28.7
Senate	49.4	21.2	78.8	Senate	89.9	79.8	20.2
Governor	47.9	12.2	87.8	Governor	89.2	78.4	21.6
South				1956–1957			
President	81.1	62.1	37.9	Non-South			
House	90.2	80.5	19.5	President	40.2	19.6	80.4
Senate	93.0	86.0	14.0	House	48.1	10.6	89.4
Governor	89.4	78.9	21.2	Senate	48.2	12.1	87.9
1942–1943				Governor	49.6	8.4	91.6
Non-South				South			
President	—	—	—	President	53.1	17.1	82.9
House	46.2	15.7	84.3	House	81.7	63.4	36.6
Senate	43.9	16.5	83.5	Senate	90.3	80.5	19.5
Governor	43.6	21.0	79.0	Governor	78.1	56.3	43.7
South				1958–1959			
President	—	—	—	Non-South			
House	93.1	86.1	13.9	President	—	—	—
Senate	93.8	87.5	12.5	House	55.3	12.7	87.3
Governor	93.8	87.5	12.5	Senate	55.3	15.0	85.0
				Governor	54.2	11.5	88.5

(Table continues)

Table 8-8 (Continued)

Year/Region[1]	Democratic % of Two-Party Vote	Margin of Victory	Party Competition Index	Year/Region[1]	Democratic % of Two-Party Vote	Margin of Victory	Party Competition Index
South				1974–1975			
President	—	—	—	Non-South			
House	88.0	75.9	24.1	President	—	—	—
Senate	85.5	71.1	28.9	House	55.4	18.0	82.0
Governor	92.4	84.8	15.2	Senate	55.5	16.0	84.0
1960–1961				Governor	57.6	17.0	83.0
Non-South				South			
President	48.1	8.1	91.9	President	—	—	—
House	51.9	10.5	89.5	House	63.6	27.3	72.7
Senate	50.0	13.2	86.8	Senate	77.4	54.8	45.2
Governor	49.7	6.6	93.4	Governor	67.2	35.2	64.8
South				1976–1977			
President	54.0	10.9	89.1	Non-South			
House	81.8	63.6	36.4	President	49.1	9.7	90.3
Senate	83.4	66.7	33.3	House	53.7	21.2	78.8
Governor	67.1	34.3	65.7	Senate	56.4	21.6	78.5
1962–1963				Governor	50.6	14.7	85.3
Non-South				South			
President	—	—	—	President	55.9	12.1	87.9
House	50.5	11.5	88.5	House	63.5	27.1	72.9
Senate	50.5	13.2	86.8	Senate	74.6	49.2	50.8
Governor	49.8	8.1	91.9	Governor	64.2	36.9	63.1
South				1978–1979			
President	—	—	—	Non-South			
House	72.4	44.8	55.2	President	—	—	—
Senate	69.0	37.9	62.1	House	52.0	18.0	82.0
Governor	80.8	61.5	38.5	Senate	48.6	20.1	79.9
1964–1965				Governor	50.8	14.1	85.9
Non-South				South			
President	63.1	26.2	73.8	President	—	—	—
House	55.4	13.1	86.9	House	60.8	25.2	74.8
Senate	58.0	19.3	80.7	Senate	59.8	31.8	68.2
Governor	54.2	13.7	86.3	Governor	60.0	22.9	77.1
South				1980–1981			
President	43.6	26.0	74.0	Non-South			
House	68.9	38.4	61.6	President	42.5	19.9	80.1
Senate	70.2	40.4	59.6	House	48.7	18.0	82.0
Governor	60.4	20.7	79.3	Senate	48.8	16.4	83.6
1966–1967				Governor	49.5	17.0	83.0
Non-South				South			
President	—	—	—	President	48.0	6.8	93.2
House	48.5	12.5	87.5	House	55.6	19.9	80.1
Senate	47.6	17.2	82.8	Senate	54.2	11.3	88.7
Governor	46.7	11.1	88.9	Governor	54.7	11.9	88.1
South				1982–1983			
President	—	—	—	Non-South			
House	67.2	34.3	65.7	President	—	—	—
Senate	64.0	39.0	61.0	House	52.3	19.5	80.5
Governor	64.0	32.8	67.2	Senate	55.9	18.8	81.2
1968–1969				Governor	55.3	16.9	83.1
Non-South				South			
President	48.6	13.4	86.6	President	—	—	—
House	46.9	15.4	84.6	House	60.1	21.2	78.8
Senate	48.7	17.1	82.9	Senate	59.1	19.2	80.8
Governor	49.6	10.2	89.8	Governor	58.6	21.5	78.5
South				1984–1985			
President	48.8	11.7	88.3	Non-South			
House	67.6	35.6	64.4	President	40.2	23.2	76.8
Senate	68.7	40.9	59.1	House	49.2	19.2	80.8
Governor	60.7	26.3	73.7	Senate	44.8	28.0	72.0
1970–1971				Governor	46.7	17.2	82.8
Non-South				South			
President	—	—	—	President	38.0	24.1	75.9
House	52.5	15.0	85.0	House	58.4	19.6	80.4
Senate	56.5	18.4	81.6	Senate	50.6	27.5	72.5
Governor	50.7	9.0	91.0	Governor	54.5	14.8	85.2
South				1986–1987			
President	—	—	—	Non-South			
House	71.9	43.8	56.2	President	—	—	—
Senate	64.5	30.6	69.4	House	51.2	20.5	79.5
Governor	66.9	35.4	64.6	Senate	49.4	19.7	80.3
1972–1973				Governor	52.7	18.4	81.6
Non-South				South			
President	39.1	25.0	75.0	President	—	—	—
House	50.1	14.6	85.4	House	60.3	20.7	79.3
Senate	46.5	16.5	83.5	Senate	55.2	10.5	89.5
Governor	52.7	13.5	86.5	Governor	53.3	14.5	85.5
South				1988–1989			
President	28.4	43.3	56.7	Non-South			
House	62.4	26.6	73.4	President	46.9	12.9	87.1
Senate	52.9	20.5	79.5	House	51.9	17.6	82.4
Governor	46.6	34.2	65.8	Senate	52.3	22.2	77.8
				Governor	50.1	17.3	82.7

Table 8-8 (Continued)

Year/Region[1]	Democratic % of Two-Party Vote	Margin of Victory	Party Competition Index	Year/Region[1]	Democratic % of Two-Party Vote	Margin of Victory	Party Competition Index
South				South			
President	41.0	18.1	81.9	President	—	—	—
House	58.9	21.4	78.6	House	45.3	12.9	87.1
Senate	58.4	20.2	79.8	Senate	38.7	23.8	76.2
Governor	47.1	6.3	93.7	Governor	48.0	9.2	90.8
1990–1991				1996–1997			
Non-South				Non-South			
President	—	—	—	President	54.6	16.9	83.1
House	52.5	14.7	85.3	House	49.0	18.2	81.8
Senate	50.4	24.2	75.8	Senate	48.8	18.0	82.0
Governor	54.0	17.8	82.2	Governor	49.8	27.1	72.9
South				South			
President	—	—	—	President	50.4	6.7	93.3
House	61.1	22.3	77.7	House	45.1	9.9	90.1
Senate	49.9	57.9	42.1	Senate	44.4	11.6	88.4
Governor	52.0	15.2	84.8	Governor	50.0	13.4	86.6
1992–1993				1998–1999			
Non-South				Non-South			
President	53.3	13.5	86.5	President	—	—	—
House	52.3	14.1	85.9	House	47.0	23.9	76.1
Senate	50.8	17.1	82.9	Senate	48.8	27.8	72.2
Governor	54.8	20.8	79.2	Governor	46.7	19.7	80.3
South				South			
President	49.6	6.4	93.6	President	—	—	—
House	55.3	12.1	87.9	House	45.0	11.6	88.4
Senate	56.8	15.4	84.6	Senate	53.5	16.8	83.2
Governor	48.1	13.8	86.2	Governor	43.8	19.8	80.2
1994–1995							
Non-South							
President	—	—	—				
House	45.4	18.4	81.6				
Senate	49.2	18.9	81.1				
Governor	45.9	19.9	80.1				

Notes: The Democratic percent of two-party vote values are the regional averages of the state Democratic percent of two-party vote values for president shown in Tables 8-36 through 8-53, for House shown in Tables 8-54 through 8-89, for Senate shown in Tables 8-90 through 8-104, and for governor shown in Table 8-105 through 8-140 for a given two-year election cycle. (These same values can be found in the state vote tables in Chapters 4, 5, 6, and 7, respectively.) The Democratic vote values are different from the national vote tables presented in Chapters 4–6 since the former are based on voter percentage values and the latter on raw vote numbers. Margin of victory values are the regional averages of the state margin of victory values for president, House, Senate, and governor found in Tables 8-36 through 8-140 for two-year election cycles. Margin of victory is defined as the absolute difference between the Democratic and Republican percent of the two-party vote for each of these separate races in a given two-year election cycle. Averaging these percent values (instead of the raw vote numbers on which they are based) is purposely done in order that each state is weighted equally in determining the regional result for margin of victory. Paul David's (1972) party competition index values are the regional averages of the state party competition values for president, House, Senate, and governor found in Tables 8-36 through 8-140 for a given election year. David's index is defined as 100 − the margin of victory or, alternately, as 100 − the absolute difference between the Democratic and Republican percent of two-party vote for each political race in a given election year. The values for Democratic and Republican percent of two-party vote for president, House, Senate, and governor used in the computations to get the David party competition values in Tables 8-36 through 8-140 are taken from the state vote tables for these races in Chapters 4, 5, 6, and 7, respectively. The author's alternative party coding in Chapters 4–7 is used whenever it occurs in place of the conventional party coding for vote data in computing David's party competition index. Zero (0) percent on David's competition index represents a complete absence of two-party competition for a given region for that election cycle, whereas a score of 100 percent indicates perfect competition between the two major parties for that region in that election cycle. The Democratic Party is defined as the Anti-Federalists, Democratic-Republicans, and Jackson Democrats prior to 1830 when the "Democratic Party" as such was established. The Republican Party is defined as the Federalists, National Republicans, and Whigs prior to the establishment of the "Republican Party" in the 1850s. See Appendix A for an explanation of the historical antecedents of the current Democratic and Republican parties. No special elections for any of the four races are used in the calculations, nor are partial voting data reported for any of the four races in any of the states. Because of rounding, margin of victory and competition values when added together may equal 100.1 or 99.9 percent instead of 100.0 percent in some instances.

[1]Regional categorization follows that of the ICPSR except that in the current analysis Tennessee is categorized in the South since it was part of the Confederacy, whereas the ICPSR codes it as a Border South state. Thus, the South includes Alabama, Arkansas, Florida, Georgia, Louisiana, Mississippi, North Carolina, South Carolina, Tennessee, Texas and Virginia. All other states make up the non-South.

[2]Voters began directly electing senators in 1912.

Sources: Tables 8-36 through 8-140. Specifically, state Democratic percent values of the two-party vote for each race in Tables 8-36 through 8-140 are aggregated across states in each region in each two-year election cycle to obtain the regional Democratic percent of two-party vote averages for each race. Regional margin of victory values and regional party competition values are obtained in the same manner from Tables 8-36 through 8-140 for each political race.

Table 8-9 Composite Competition Index, by State, by Election Year, 1788–1795 (Percentages)

State	1788	1789	1790	1791	1792	1793	1794	1795
Alabama	—	—	—	—	—	—	—	—
Alaska	—	—	—	—	—	—	—	—
Arizona	—	—	—	—	—	—	—	—
Arkansas	—	—	—	—	—	—	—	—
California	—	—	—	—	—	—	—	—
Colorado	—	—	—	—	—	—	—	—
Connecticut	—	—	—	—	—	—	0.0	—
Delaware	—	—	—	—	0.0	—	97.4	0.0
Dist. of Columbia	—	—	—	—	—	—	—	—
Florida	—	—	—	—	—	—	—	—
Georgia	—	—	—	—	—	—	87.2	—
Hawaii	—	—	—	—	—	—	—	—
Idaho	—	—	—	—	—	—	—	—
Illinois	—	—	—	—	—	—	—	—
Indiana	—	—	—	—	—	—	—	—
Iowa	—	—	—	—	—	—	—	—
Kansas	—	—	—	—	—	—	—	—
Kentucky	—	—	—	—	—	—	—	—
Louisiana	—	—	—	—	—	—	—	—
Maine	—	—	—	—	—	—	—	—
Maryland	45.8	69.2	—	—	40.1	—	81.4	—
Massachusetts	0.0	—	—	—	—	—	82.8	—
Michigan	—	—	—	—	—	—	—	—
Minnesota	—	—	—	—	—	—	—	—
Mississippi	—	—	—	—	—	—	—	—
Missouri	—	—	—	—	—	—	—	—
Montana	—	—	—	—	—	—	—	—
Nebraska	—	—	—	—	—	—	—	—
Nevada	—	—	—	—	—	—	—	—
New Hampshire	45.3	0.0	0.0	0.0	0.0	0.0	45.6	0.0
New Jersey	—	—	—	—	—	—	0.0	—
New Mexico	—	—	—	—	—	—	—	—
New York	—	0.0	60.8	—	99.4	92.0	96.8	93.8
North Carolina	—	—	—	—	—	—	—	—
North Dakota	—	—	—	—	—	—	—	—
Ohio	—	—	—	—	—	—	—	—
Oklahoma	—	—	—	—	—	—	—	—
Oregon	—	—	—	—	—	—	—	—
Pennsylvania	92.0	—	18.4	—	98.2	73.0	—	—
Rhode Island	—	—	—	—	—	—	76.2	—
South Carolina	—	—	—	—	—	—	—	—
South Dakota	—	—	—	—	—	—	—	—
Tennessee	—	—	—	—	—	—	—	—
Texas	—	—	—	—	—	—	—	—
Utah	—	—	—	—	—	—	—	—
Vermont	—	—	—	—	—	—	57.0	—
Virginia	—	—	—	—	—	—	—	—
Washington	—	—	—	—	—	—	—	—
West Virginia	—	—	—	—	—	—	—	—
Wisconsin	—	—	—	—	—	—	—	—
Wyoming	—	—	—	—	—	—	—	—

Notes: The composite competition index value for each state is the mean of a state's values for the party competition index devised by Paul David (1972) for all races held in a given election year among the following set of races: president, House, Senate, and governor. David's party competition index is defined as 100 − the absolute difference between the Democratic and Republican percentage of two-party vote for each of the races mentioned here. Zero (0) percent on David's index represents a complete absence of two-party competition for that election year, whereas a score of 100 percent indicates perfect competition between the two major parties. A state can only receive a composite index score of 0 if all races held in that state in a given election year are 100–0 vote splits between the two major parties. Conversely, a state can only receive a composite competition score of 100 if all races held in that state in a given election year are 50–50 vote splits between the two major parties. A state's overall value on the composite competition index for a given election year is obtained by averaging that state's party competition values for president (in Tables 8-36 through 8-53), House (in Tables 8-54 through 8-89), Senate (in Tables 8-90 through 8-104), and governor (in Tables 8-105 through 8-140). For example, in 1788 New Hampshire's party competition values were 0 percent for president (Table 8-36) and 90.6 percent for governor (Table 8-105). There were no election data available for the presidential race. Hence, New Hampshire's composite competition score in 1788 was 45.3 percent (90.6 ÷ 2) as shown in Table 8-9. In 1996 Illinois's party competition values were 80.8 percent for president (Table 8-53), 88.8 percent for House (Table 8-88), and 84.0 percent for Senate (Table 8-104). There was no race for governor in 1996. Thus Illinois's composite competition score in 1996 was 84.5 percent (253.6 ÷ 3) as shown in Table 8-35. The values for Democratic and Republican percent of two-party vote for president, House, Senate, and governor used to get the party competition values for these races in Tables 8-36 through 8-140 are taken from the state vote tables in Chapters 4, 5, 6, and 7, respectively (where the Republican vote percent is obtained by subtracting the Democratic vote percent from 100 for each race). The author's alternative party coding in these tables in Chapters 4–7 is used whenever it occurs in place of the conventional party coding of voting data. The Democratic Party is defined as the Anti-Federalists, Federalists, and Jackson Democrats prior to 1830 when the "Democratic Party" as such was established. The Republican Party is defined as the Federalists, National Republicans, and Whigs prior to the establishment of the "Republican Party" in the 1850s. See Appendix A for an explanation of the historical antecedents of the current Democratic and Republican parties. No special elections for any of the four races are used in the calculations, nor are partial voting data reported for any of the four races in any of the states. —indicates that the state had no data, either because no vote data were found for the state in question or the state had not yet entered the Union. Data for the District of Columbia are included from 1964 to the present, after being granted the right to elect presidential electors by the 23rd Amendment.

Sources: Tables 8-36 through 8-140. Specifically, state party competition values in Tables 8-36 through 8-140 for the presidential, House, Senate, and gubernatorial races are aggregated for each election year separately in order to obtain each state's average composite competition values for the election years shown in Tables 8-9 through 8-35.

Table 8-10 Composite Competition Index, by State, by Election Year, 1796–1803 (Percentages)

State	1796	1797	1798	1799	1800	1801	1802	1803
Alabama	—	—	—	—	—	—	—	—
Alaska	—	—	—	—	—	—	—	—
Arizona	—	—	—	—	—	—	—	—
Arkansas	—	—	—	—	—	—	—	—
California	—	—	—	—	—	—	—	—
Colorado	—	—	—	—	—	—	—	—
Connecticut	13.9	—	0.0	—	64.8	17.2	28.4	70.6
Delaware	87.4	—	84.2	—	93.4	99.8	99.8	—
Dist. of Columbia	—	—	—	—	—	—	—	—
Florida	—	—	—	—	—	—	—	—
Georgia	73.0	—	86.8	—	0.0	—	47.6	—
Hawaii	—	—	—	—	—	—	—	—
Idaho	—	—	—	—	—	—	—	—
Illinois	—	—	—	—	—	—	—	—
Indiana	—	—	—	—	—	—	—	—
Iowa	—	—	—	—	—	—	—	—
Kansas	—	—	—	—	—	—	—	—
Kentucky	—	—	—	—	0.0	0.0	—	—
Louisiana	—	—	—	—	—	—	—	—
Maine	—	—	—	—	—	—	—	—
Maryland	85.5	—	—	—	97.0	75.6	—	—
Massachusetts	30.0	86.6	52.6	0.0	92.5	88.4	84.9	64.6
Michigan	—	—	—	—	—	—	—	—
Minnesota	—	—	—	—	—	—	—	—
Mississippi	—	—	—	—	—	—	—	—
Missouri	—	—	—	—	—	—	—	—
Montana	—	—	—	—	—	—	—	—
Nebraska	—	—	—	—	—	—	—	—
Nevada	—	—	—	—	—	—	—	—
New Hampshire	9.6	0.0	14.0	0.0	61.3	65.0	85.9	84.8
New Jersey	—	70.4	95.2	—	98.2	—	—	5.4
New Mexico	—	—	—	—	—	—	—	—
New York	76.2	—	91.6	—	99.2	91.4	81.4	—
North Carolina	—	—	—	—	—	—	—	—
North Dakota	—	—	—	—	—	—	—	—
Ohio	—	—	—	—	—	—	—	26.2
Oklahoma	—	—	—	—	—	—	—	—
Oregon	—	—	—	—	—	—	—	—
Pennsylvania	52.7	—	92.6	92.4	—	—	52.6	—
Rhode Island	0.0	0.0	69.2	—	81.0	0.0	72.4	—
South Carolina	88.4	—	—	—	—	—	—	71.0
South Dakota	—	—	—	—	—	—	—	—
Tennessee	0.0	—	—	0.0	—	0.0	—	0.0
Texas	—	—	—	—	—	—	—	—
Utah	—	—	—	—	—	—	—	—
Vermont	87.4	—	67.8	—	80.9	—	81.8	—
Virginia	—	—	—	—	45.4	—	—	—
Washington	—	—	—	—	—	—	—	—
West Virginia	—	—	—	—	—	—	—	—
Wisconsin	—	—	—	—	—	—	—	—
Wyoming	—	—	—	—	—	—	—	—

Notes: The composite competition index value for each state is the mean of a state's values for the party competition index devised by Paul David (1972) for all races held in a given election year among the following set of races: president, House, Senate, and governor. David's party competition index is defined as 100 − the absolute difference between the Democratic and Republican percentage of two-party vote for each of the races mentioned here. Zero (0) percent on David's index represents a complete absence of two-party competition for that election year, whereas a score of 100 percent indicates perfect competition between the two major parties. A state can only receive a composite index score of 0 if all races held in that state in a given election year are 100–0 vote splits between the two major parties. Conversely, a state can only receive a composite competition score of 100 if all races held in that state in a given election year are 50–50 vote splits between the two major parties. A state's overall value on the composite competition index for a given election year is obtained by averaging that state's party competition values for president (in Tables 8-36 through 8-53), House (in Tables 8-54 through 8-89), Senate (in Tables 8-90 through 8-104), and governor (in Tables 8-105 through 8-140). For example, in 1788 New Hampshire's party competition values were 0 percent for president (Table 8-36) and 90.6 percent for governor (Table 8-105). There were no election data available for the presidential race. Hence, New Hampshire's party competition score in 1788 was 45.3 percent (90.6 ÷ 2) as shown in Table 8-9. In 1996 Illinois's party competition values were 80.8 percent for president (Table 8-53), 88.8 percent for House (Table 8-88), and 84.0 percent for Senate (Table 8-104). There was no race for governor in 1996. Thus Illinois's composite competition score in 1996 was 84.5 percent (253.6 ÷ 3) as shown in Table 8-35. The values for Democratic and Republican percent of two-party vote for president, House, Senate, and governor used to get the party competition values for these races in Tables 8-36 through 8-140 are taken from the state vote tables in Chapters 4, 5, 6, and 7, respectively (where the Republican vote percent is obtained by subtracting the Democratic vote percent from 100 for each race). The author's alternative party coding in these tables in Chapters 4–7 is used whenever it occurs in place of the conventional party coding of voting data. The Democratic Party is defined as the Anti-Federalists, Federalists, and Jackson Democrats prior to 1830 when the "Democratic Party" as such was established. The Republican Party is defined as the Federalists, National Republicans, and Whigs prior to the establishment of the "Republican Party" in the 1850s. See Appendix A for an explanation of the historical antecedents of the current Democratic and Republican parties. No special elections for any of the four races are used in the calculations, nor are partial voting data reported for any of the four races in any of the states. —indicates that the state had no data, either because no vote data were found for the state in question or the state had not yet entered the Union. Data for the District of Columbia are included from 1964 to the present, after being granted the right to elect presidential electors by the 23rd Amendment.

Sources: Tables 8-36 through 8-140. Specifically, state party competition values in Tables 8-36 through 8-140 for the presidential, House, Senate, and gubernatorial races are aggregated for each election year separately in order to obtain each state's average composite competition values for the election years shown in Tables 8-9 through 8-35.

Table 8-11 Composite Competition Index, by State, by Election Year, 1804–1811 (Percentages)

State	1804	1805	1806	1807	1808	1809	1810	1811
Alabama	—	—	—	—	—	—	—	—
Alaska	—	—	—	—	—	—	—	—
Arizona	—	—	—	—	—	—	—	—
Arkansas	—	—	—	—	—	—	—	—
California	—	—	—	—	—	—	—	—
Colorado	—	—	—	—	—	—	—	—
Connecticut	38.2	76.2	82.8	80.0	76.8	71.6	34.9	—
Delaware	95.9	—	68.0	96.2	93.4	—	99.4	—
Dist. of Columbia	—	—	—	—	—	—	—	—
Florida	—	—	—	—	—	—	—	—
Georgia	0.0	—	0.0	—	54.8	—	25.6	—
Hawaii	—	—	—	—	—	—	—	—
Idaho	—	—	—	—	—	—	—	—
Illinois	—	—	—	—	—	—	—	—
Indiana	—	—	—	—	—	—	—	—
Iowa	—	—	—	—	—	—	—	—
Kansas	—	—	—	—	—	—	—	—
Kentucky	0.0	—	—	—	0.0	—	—	—
Louisiana	—	—	—	—	—	—	—	—
Maine	—	—	—	—	—	—	—	—
Maryland	51.3	—	54.0	—	81.1	—	50.8	—
Massachusetts	92.0	97.6	97.3	96.6	96.5	97.0	97.1	96.2
Michigan	—	—	—	—	—	—	—	—
Minnesota	—	—	—	—	—	—	—	—
Mississippi	—	—	—	—	—	—	—	—
Missouri	—	—	—	—	—	—	—	—
Montana	—	—	—	—	—	—	—	—
Nebraska	—	—	—	—	—	—	—	—
Nevada	—	—	—	—	—	—	—	—
New Hampshire	97.1	86.6	56.6	0.0	67.8	98.8	98.0	90.4
New Jersey	1.0	—	56.6	—	88.3	—	7.4	—
New Mexico	—	—	—	—	—	—	—	—
New York	78.4	—	80.4	93.8	98.6	—	90.5	—
North Carolina	—	—	—	—	—	—	—	—
North Dakota	—	—	—	—	—	—	—	—
Ohio	42.2	0.0	52.0	0.0	36.5	—	0.0	—
Oklahoma	—	—	—	—	—	—	—	—
Oregon	—	—	—	—	—	—	—	—
Pennsylvania	10.6	0.0	—	—	64.8	—	53.6	12.8
Rhode Island	0.0	—	88.4	0.0	92.9	—	97.6	96.8
South Carolina	—	—	36.4	—	—	—	—	—
South Dakota	—	—	—	—	—	—	—	—
Tennessee	—	0.0	—	—	—	—	—	0.0
Texas	—	—	—	—	—	—	—	—
Utah	—	—	—	—	—	—	—	—
Vermont	90.0	73.6	89.6	92.4	96.8	96.0	85.2	89.6
Virginia	0.0	—	—	—	9.2	—	—	—
Washington	—	—	—	—	—	—	—	—
West Virginia	—	—	—	—	—	—	—	—
Wisconsin	—	—	—	—	—	—	—	—
Wyoming	—	—	—	—	—	—	—	—

Notes: The composite competition index value for each state is the mean of a state's values for the party competition index devised by Paul David (1972) for all races held in a given election year among the following set of races: president, House, Senate, and governor. David's party competition index is defined as 100 − the absolute difference between the Democratic and Republican percentage of two-party vote for each of the races mentioned here. Zero (0) percent on David's index represents a complete absence of two-party competition for that election year, whereas a score of 100 percent indicates perfect competition between the two major parties. A state can only receive a composite index score of 0 if all races held in that state in a given election year are 100–0 vote splits between the two major parties. Conversely, a state can only receive a composite competition score of 100 if all races held in that state in a given election year are 50–50 vote splits between the two major parties. A state's overall value on the composite competition index for a given election year is obtained by averaging that state's party competition values for president (in Tables 8-36 through 8-53), House (in Tables 8-54 through 8-89), Senate (in Tables 8-90 through 8-104), and governor (in Tables 8-105 through 8-140). For example, in 1788 New Hampshire's party competition values were 0 percent for president (Table 8-36) and 90.6 percent for governor (Table 8-105). There were no election data available for the presidential race. Hence, New Hampshire's composite competition score in 1788 was 45.3 percent (90.6 ÷ 2) as shown in Table 8-9. In 1996 Illinois's party competition values were 80.8 percent for president (Table 8-53), 88.8 percent for House (Table 8-88), and 84.0 percent for Senate (Table 8-104). There was no race for governor in 1996. Thus Illinois's composite competition score in 1996 was 84.5 percent (253.6 ÷ 3) as shown in Table 8-35. The values for Democratic and Republican percent of two-party vote for president, House, Senate, and governor used to get the party competition values for these races in Tables 8-36 through 8-140 are taken from the state vote tables in Chapters 4, 5, 6, and 7, respectively (where the Republican vote percent is obtained by subtracting the Democratic vote percent from 100 for each race). The author's alternative party coding in these tables in Chapters 4–7 is used whenever it occurs in place of the conventional party coding of voting data. The Democratic Party is defined as the Anti-Federalists, Federalists, and Jackson Democrats prior to 1830 when the "Democratic Party" as such was established. The Republican Party is defined as the Federalists, National Republicans, and Whigs prior to the establishment of the "Republican Party" in the 1850s. See Appendix A for an explanation of the historical antecedents of the current Democratic and Republican parties. No special elections for any of the four races are used in the calculations, nor are partial voting data reported for any of the four races in any of the states. —indicates that the state had no data, either because no vote data were found for the state in question or the state had not yet entered the Union. Data for the District of Columbia are included from 1964 to the present, after being granted the right to elect presidential electors by the 23rd Amendment.

Sources: Tables 8-36 through 8-140. Specifically, state party competition values in Tables 8-36 through 8-140 for the presidential, House, Senate, and gubernatorial races are aggregated for each election year separately in order to obtain each state's average composite competition values for the election years shown in Tables 8-9 through 8-35.

Table 8-12 Composite Competition Index, by State, by Election Year, 1812–1819 (Percentages)

State	1812	1813	1814	1815	1816	1817	1818	1819
Alabama	—	—	—	—	—	—	—	0.0
Alaska	—	—	—	—	—	—	—	—
Arizona	—	—	—	—	—	—	—	—
Arkansas	—	—	—	—	—	—	—	—
California	—	—	—	—	—	—	—	—
Colorado	—	—	—	—	—	—	—	—
Connecticut	11.3	75.4	43.6	74.8	0.0	0.0	97.6	—
Delaware	86.8	89.6	78.2	—	96.5	—	98.6	90.8
Dist. of Columbia	—	—	—	—	—	—	—	—
Florida	—	—	—	—	—	—	—	—
Georgia	37.0	—	0.0	—	0.0	—	0.0	—
Hawaii	—	—	—	—	—	—	—	—
Idaho	—	—	—	—	—	—	—	—
Illinois	—	—	—	—	—	—	0.0	—
Indiana	—	—	—	—	0.0	0.0	—	0.0
Iowa	—	—	—	—	—	—	—	—
Kansas	—	—	—	—	—	—	—	—
Kentucky	0.0	—	—	—	0.0	—	—	—
Louisiana	0.0	—	16.6	—	0.0	—	0.0	—
Maine	—	—	—	—	—	—	—	—
Maryland	87.5	—	74.4	—	58.2	—	—	—
Massachusetts	83.3	86.0	78.6	92.6	93.2	90.4	93.2	90.2
Michigan	—	—	—	—	—	—	—	—
Minnesota	—	—	—	—	—	—	—	—
Mississippi	—	—	—	—	—	0.0	—	0.0
Missouri	—	—	—	—	—	—	—	—
Montana	—	—	—	—	—	—	—	—
Nebraska	—	—	—	—	—	—	—	—
Nevada	—	—	—	—	—	—	—	—
New Hampshire	95.8	98.0	96.6	98.4	93.5	90.0	77.8	72.5
New Jersey	—	94.8	96.6	—	0.0	—	10.4	—
New Mexico	—	—	—	—	—	—	—	—
New York	91.2	95.6	93.0	—	90.9	—	48.0	—
North Carolina	—	—	—	—	12.6	—	—	—
North Dakota	—	—	—	—	—	—	—	—
Ohio	63.7	—	56.0	—	20.3	—	14.4	—
Oklahoma	—	—	—	—	—	—	—	—
Oregon	—	—	—	—	—	—	—	—
Pennsylvania	78.0	—	73.4	—	0.0	0.0	—	—
Rhode Island	82.7	0.0	43.9	86.8	31.7	99.0	46.3	—
South Carolina	—	—	—	—	—	—	—	—
South Dakota	—	—	—	—	—	—	—	—
Tennessee	—	0.0	—	0.0	—	0.0	—	0.0
Texas	—	—	—	—	—	—	—	—
Utah	—	—	—	—	—	—	—	—
Vermont	95.0	99.2	99.8	94.0	89.9	70.2	25.7	0.0
Virginia	54.2	—	—	—	0.0	—	—	—
Washington	—	—	—	—	—	—	—	—
West Virginia	—	—	—	—	—	—	—	—
Wisconsin	—	—	—	—	—	—	—	—
Wyoming	—	—	—	—	—	—	—	—

Notes: The composite competition index value for each state is the mean of a state's values for the party competition index devised by Paul David (1972) for all races held in a given election year among the following set of races: president, House, Senate, and governor. David's party competition index is defined as 100 − the absolute difference between the Democratic and Republican percentage of two-party vote for each of the races mentioned here. Zero (0) percent on David's index represents a complete absence of two-party competition for that election year, whereas a score of 100 percent indicates perfect competition between the two major parties. A state can only receive a composite index score of 0 if all races held in that state in a given election year are 100–0 vote splits between the two major parties. Conversely, a state can only receive a composite competition score of 100 if all races held in that state in a given election year are 50–50 vote splits between the two major parties. A state's overall value on the composite competition index for a given election year is obtained by averaging that state's party competition values for president (in Tables 8-36 through 8-53), House (in Tables 8-54 through 8-89), Senate (in Tables 8-90 through 8-104), and governor (in Tables 8-105 through 8-140). For example, in 1788 New Hampshire's party competition values were 0 percent for president (Table 8-36) and 90.6 percent for governor (Table 8-105). There were no election data available for the presidential race. Hence, New Hampshire's composite competition score in 1788 was 45.3 percent (90.6 ÷ 2) as shown in Table 8-9. In 1996 Illinois's party competition values were 80.8 percent for president (Table 8-53), 88.8 percent for House (Table 8-88), and 84.0 percent for Senate (Table 8-104). There was no race for governor in 1996. Thus Illinois's composite competition score in 1996 was 84.5 percent (253.6 ÷ 3) as shown in Table 8-35. The values for Democratic and Republican percent of two-party vote for president, House, Senate, and governor used to get the party competition values for these races in Tables 8-36 through 8-140 are taken from the state vote tables in Chapters 4, 5, 6, and 7, respectively (where the Republican vote percent is obtained by subtracting the Democratic vote percent from 100 for each race). The author's alternative party coding in these tables in Chapters 4–7 is used whenever it occurs in place of the conventional party coding of voting data. The Democratic Party is defined as the Anti-Federalists, Federalists, and Jackson Democrats prior to 1830 when the "Democratic Party" as such was established. The Republican Party is defined as the Federalists, National Republicans, and Whigs prior to the establishment of the "Republican Party" in the 1850s. See Appendix A for an explanation of the historical antecedents of the current Democratic and Republican parties. No special elections for any of the four races are used in the calculations, nor are partial voting data reported for any of the four races in any of the states. —indicates that the state had no data, either because no vote data were found for the state in question or the state had not yet entered the Union. Data for the District of Columbia are included from 1964 to the present, after being granted the right to elect presidential electors by the 23rd Amendment.

Sources: Tables 8-36 through 8-140. Specifically, state party competition values in Tables 8-36 through 8-140 for the presidential, House, Senate, and gubernatorial races are aggregated for each election year separately in order to obtain each state's average composite competition values for the election years shown in Tables 8-9 through 8-35.

Table 8-13 Composite Competition Index, by State, by Election Year, 1820–1827 (Percentages)

State	1820	1821	1822	1823	1824	1825	1826	1827
Alabama	—	0.0	—	0.0	40.8	0.0	—	0.0
Alaska	—	—	—	—	—	—	—	—
Arizona	—	—	—	—	—	—	—	—
Arkansas	—	—	—	—	—	—	—	—
California	—	—	—	—	—	—	—	—
Colorado	—	—	—	—	—	—	—	—
Connecticut	0.0	6.6	0.0	0.0	7.9	47.0	84.4	2.5
Delaware	96.2	—	95.6	96.4	96.6	—	95.3	—
Dist. of Columbia	—	—	—	—	—	—	—	—
Florida	—	—	—	—	—	—	—	—
Georgia	0.0	—	0.0	—	0.0	0.0	0.0	0.0
Hawaii	—	—	—	—	—	—	—	—
Idaho	—	—	—	—	—	—	—	—
Illinois	0.0	—	0.0	—	91.2	—	95.3	—
Indiana	0.0	—	0.0	—	58.4	0.0	76.6	—
Iowa	—	—	—	—	—	—	—	—
Kansas	—	—	—	—	—	—	—	—
Kentucky	0.0	—	—	—	0.0	—	—	73.8
Louisiana	0.0	—	—	—	—	—	—	—
Maine	17.9	57.8	52.6	28.5	14.5	0.0	41.2	0.0
Maryland	15.6	—	50.2	—	87.9	—	99.2	—
Massachusetts	75.9	83.0	85.2	93.4	63.9	0.0	0.0	0.0
Michigan	—	—	—	—	—	—	—	—
Minnesota	—	—	—	—	—	—	—	—
Mississippi	—	0.0	—	0.0	34.6	0.0	62.0	0.0
Missouri	0.0	—	—	—	8.0	48.6	—	—
Montana	—	—	—	—	—	—	—	—
Nebraska	—	—	—	—	—	—	—	—
Nevada	—	—	—	—	—	—	—	—
New Hampshire	9.3	0.0	0.0	0.0	0.0	—	—	0.0
New Jersey	8.1	—	—	—	44.6	—	78.8	—
New Mexico	—	—	—	—	—	—	—	—
New York	0.0	0.0	0.0	—	0.0	—	48.0	—
North Carolina	0.0	—	—	—	0.0	—	—	—
North Dakota	—	—	—	—	—	—	—	—
Ohio	0.0	—	76.2	—	88.9	—	27.3	—
Oklahoma	—	—	—	—	—	—	—	—
Oregon	—	—	—	—	—	—	—	—
Pennsylvania	29.9	—	47.8	83.4	26.4	—	3.2	—
Rhode Island	0.0	0.0	0.0	—	0.0	0.0	—	0.0
South Carolina	—	—	—	16.0	—	—	—	—
South Dakota	—	—	—	—	—	—	—	—
Tennessee	—	0.0	—	0.0	2.2	0.0	—	0.0
Texas	—	—	—	—	—	—	—	—
Utah	—	—	—	—	—	—	—	—
Vermont	37.1	0.0	56.4	0.0	8.7	0.0	0.0	0.0
Virginia	0.0	—	—	—	93.0	—	—	—
Washington	—	—	—	—	—	—	—	—
West Virginia	—	—	—	—	—	—	—	—
Wisconsin	—	—	—	—	—	—	—	—
Wyoming	—	—	—	—	—	—	—	—

Notes: The composite competition index value for each state is the mean of a state's values for the party competition index devised by Paul David (1972) for all races held in a given election year among the following set of races: president, House, Senate, and governor. David's party competition index is defined as 100 − the absolute difference between the Democratic and Republican percentage of two-party vote for each of the races mentioned here. Zero (0) percent on David's index represents a complete absence of two-party competition for that election year, whereas a score of 100 percent indicates perfect competition between the two major parties. A state can only receive a composite index score of 0 if all races held in that state in a given election year are 100–0 vote splits between the two major parties. Conversely, a state can only receive a composite competition score of 100 if all races held in a given election year are 50–50 vote splits between the two major parties. A state's overall value on the composite competition index for a given election year is obtained by averaging that state's party competition values for president (in Tables 8-36 through 8-53), House (in Tables 8-54 through 8-89), Senate (in Tables 8-90 through 8-104), and governor (in Tables 8-105 through 8-140). For example, in 1788 New Hampshire's party competition values were 0 percent for president (Table 8-36) and 90.6 percent for governor (Table 8-105). There were no election data available for the presidential race. Hence, New Hampshire's composite competition score in 1788 was 45.3 percent (90.6 ÷ 2) as shown in Table 8-9. In 1996 Illinois's party competition values were 80.8 percent for president (Table 8-53), 88.8 percent for House (Table 8-88), and 84.0 percent for Senate (Table 8-104). There was no race for governor in 1996. Thus Illinois's composite competition score in 1996 was 84.5 percent (253.6 ÷ 3) as shown in Table 8-35. The values for Democratic and Republican percent of two-party vote for president, House, Senate, and governor used to get the party competition values for these races in Tables 8-36 through 8-140 are taken from the state vote tables in Chapters 4, 5, 6, and 7, respectively (where the Republican vote percent is obtained by subtracting the Democratic vote percent from 100 for each race). The author's alternative party coding in these tables in Chapters 4–7 is used whenever it occurs in place of the conventional party coding of voting data. The Democratic Party is defined as the Anti-Federalists, Federalists, and Jackson Democrats prior to 1830 when the "Democratic Party" as such was established. The Republican Party is defined as the Federalists, National Republicans, and Whigs prior to the establishment of the "Republican Party" in the 1850s. See Appendix A for an explanation of the historical antecedents of the current Democratic and Republican parties. No special elections for any of the four races are used in the calculations, nor are partial voting data reported for any of the four races in any of the states. —indicates that the state had no data, either because no vote data were found for the state in question or the state had not yet entered the Union. Data for the District of Columbia are included from 1964 to the present, after being granted the right to elect presidential electors by the 23rd Amendment.

Sources: Tables 8-36 through 8-140. Specifically, state party competition values in Tables 8-36 through 8-140 for the presidential, House, Senate, and gubernatorial races are aggregated for each election year separately in order to obtain each state's average composite competition values for the election years shown in Tables 8-9 through 8-35.

Table 8-14 Composite Competition Index, by State, by Election Year, 1828–1835 (Percentages)

State	1828	1829	1830	1831	1832	1833	1834	1835
Alabama	20.2	18.4	—	64.6	0.0	0.0	—	70.2
Alaska	—	—	—	—	—	—	—	—
Arizona	—	—	—	—	—	—	—	—
Arkansas	—	—	—	—	—	—	—	—
California	—	—	—	—	—	—	—	—
Colorado	—	—	—	—	—	—	—	—
Connecticut	24.3	39.5	2.8	35.2	65.5	92.0	92.4	95.3
Delaware	95.4	—	94.6	—	98.7	—	98.4	—
Dist. of Columbia	—	—	—	—	—	—	—	—
Florida	—	—	—	—	—	—	—	—
Georgia	3.2	0.0	0.0	0.0	0.0	0.0	92.6	95.4
Hawaii	—	—	—	—	—	—	—	—
Idaho	—	—	—	—	—	—	—	—
Illinois	69.9	—	82.0	0.0	41.7	—	45.6	—
Indiana	75.4	—	—	89.5	89.2	18.8	85.2	75.0
Iowa	—	—	—	—	—	—	—	—
Kansas	—	—	—	—	—	—	—	—
Kentucky	94.0	—	—	—	94.6	—	—	—
Louisiana	83.5	—	—	76.6	73.8	—	59.0	—
Maine	58.6	99.4	96.3	87.0	91.0	77.8	94.2	75.6
Maryland	99.4	93.8	—	86.8	100.0	99.2	—	—
Massachusetts	28.7	42.8	48.4	55.2	61.3	59.4	63.5	80.4
Michigan	—	—	—	—	—	—	—	9.9
Minnesota	—	—	—	—	—	—	—	—
Mississippi	37.8	70.8	47.2	63.4	0.0	94.2	—	94.4
Missouri	68.9	—	—	75.4	47.1	73.0	—	0.0
Montana	—	—	—	—	—	—	—	—
Nebraska	—	—	—	—	—	—	—	—
Nevada	—	—	—	—	—	—	—	—
New Hampshire	93.2	92.0	90.2	89.6	43.2	22.4	—	37.4
New Jersey	96.0	—	96.6	—	99.1	—	98.2	—
New Mexico	—	—	—	—	—	—	—	—
New York	90.3	—	73.9	—	80.1	—	96.0	—
North Carolina	53.8	—	—	—	30.4	—	—	—
North Dakota	—	—	—	—	—	—	—	—
Ohio	97.0	—	97.8	—	96.1	—	97.5	—
Oklahoma	—	—	—	—	—	—	—	—
Oregon	—	—	—	—	—	—	—	—
Pennsylvania	66.6	0.0	67.0	—	11.4	—	71.6	82.4
Rhode Island	22.9	0.0	0.0	0.0	41.7	75.2	—	98.0
South Carolina	—	—	—	—	—	—	—	—
South Dakota	—	—	—	—	—	—	—	—
Tennessee	9.6	0.0	—	25.6	9.2	49.3	—	39.7
Texas	—	—	—	—	—	—	—	—
Utah	—	—	—	—	—	—	—	—
Vermont	25.5	43.4	63.4	64.4	75.9	52.4	92.4	58.2
Virginia	62.0	—	—	—	50.0	—	—	—
Washington	—	—	—	—	—	—	—	—
West Virginia	—	—	—	—	—	—	—	—
Wisconsin	—	—	—	—	—	—	—	—
Wyoming	—	—	—	—	—	—	—	—

Notes: The composite competition index value for each state is the mean of a state's values for the party competition index devised by Paul David (1972) for all races held in a given election year among the following set of races: president, House, Senate, and governor. David's party competition index is defined as 100 − the absolute difference between the Democratic and Republican percentage of two-party vote for each of the races mentioned here. Zero (0) percent on David's index represents a complete absence of two-party competition for that election year, whereas a score of 100 percent indicates perfect competition between the two major parties. A state can only receive a composite index score of 0 if all races held in that state in a given election year are 100–0 vote splits between the two major parties. Conversely, a state can only receive a composite competition score of 100 if all races held in that state in a given election year are 50–50 vote splits between the two major parties. A state's overall value on the composite competition index for a given election year is obtained by averaging that state's party competition values for president (in Tables 8-36 through 8-53), House (in Tables 8-54 through 8-89), Senate (in Tables 8-90 through 8-104), and governor (in Tables 8-105 through 8-140). For example, in 1788 New Hampshire's party competition values were 0 percent for president (Table 8-36) and 90.6 percent for governor (Table 8-105). There were no election data available for the presidential race. Hence, New Hampshire's composite competition score in 1788 was 45.3 percent (90.6 ÷ 2) as shown in Table 8-9. In 1996 Illinois's party competition values were 80.8 percent for president (Table 8-53), 88.8 percent for House (Table 8-88), and 84.0 percent for Senate (Table 8-104). There was no race for governor in 1996. Thus Illinois's composite competition score in 1996 was 84.5 percent (253.6 ÷ 3) as shown in Table 8-35. The values for Democratic and Republican percent of two-party vote for president, House, Senate, and governor used to get the party competition values for these races in Tables 8-36 through 8-140 are taken from the state vote tables in Chapters 4, 5, 6, and 7, respectively (where the Republican vote percent is obtained by subtracting the Democratic vote percent from 100 for each race). The author's alternative party coding in these tables in Chapters 4–7 is used whenever it occurs in place of the conventional party coding of voting data. The Democratic Party is defined as the Anti-Federalists, Federalists, and Jackson Democrats prior to 1830 when the "Democratic Party" as such was established. The Republican Party is defined as the Federalists, National Republicans, and Whigs prior to the establishment of the "Republican Party" in the 1850s. See Appendix A for an explanation of the historical antecedents of the current Democratic and Republican parties. No special elections for any of the four races are used in the calculations, nor are partial voting data reported for any of the four races in any of the states. —indicates that the state had no data, either because no vote data were found for the state in question or the state had not yet entered the Union. Data for the District of Columbia are included from 1964 to the present, after being granted the right to elect presidential electors by the 23rd Amendment.

Sources: Tables 8-36 through 8-140. Specifically, state party competition values in Tables 8-36 through 8-140 for the presidential, House, Senate, and gubernatorial races are aggregated for each election year separately in order to obtain each state's average composite competition values for the election years shown in Tables 8-9 through 8-35.

Table 8-15 Composite Competition Index, by State, by Election Year, 1836–1843 (Percentages)

State	1836	1837	1838	1839	1840	1841	1842	1843
Alabama	89.4	0.0	—	20.0	91.2	84.7	—	—
Alaska	—	—	—	—	—	—	—	—
Arizona	—	—	—	—	—	—	—	—
Arkansas	67.7	75.2	76.4	—	86.0	—	72.2	—
California	—	—	—	—	—	—	—	—
Colorado	—	—	—	—	—	—	—	—
Connecticut	95.5	95.1	88.4	94.9	90.3	88.1	96.2	96.6
Delaware	94.5	—	99.4	—	91.3	—	100.0	—
Dist. of Columbia	—	—	—	—	—	—	—	—
Florida	—	—	—	—	—	—	—	—
Georgia	97.7	—	96.8	97.2	91.5	94.6	97.2	95.4
Hawaii	—	—	—	—	—	—	—	—
Idaho	—	—	—	—	—	—	—	—
Illinois	81.7	—	90.0	—	98.0	79.0	91.2	92.2
Indiana	89.0	79.0	—	98.6	90.5	88.2	—	97.6
Iowa	—	—	—	—	—	—	—	—
Kansas	—	—	—	—	—	—	—	—
Kentucky	91.6	—	—	—	77.4	50.4	—	89.8
Louisiana	75.9	—	76.7	—	83.8	—	91.6	89.4
Maine	85.3	99.2	96.1	92.0	99.6	87.4	79.2	78.6
Maryland	92.6	82.0	99.4	93.6	92.4	88.9	—	—
Massachusetts	89.1	79.0	86.2	99.6	85.2	95.8	98.8	96.8
Michigan	92.0	96.7	99.4	96.4	96.4	84.8	—	82.2
Minnesota	—	—	—	—	—	—	—	—
Mississippi	97.4	85.3	—	92.3	93.2	93.3	—	43.7
Missouri	51.9	—	84.6	—	85.5	—	0.0	—
Montana	—	—	—	—	—	—	—	—
Nebraska	—	—	—	—	—	—	—	—
Nevada	—	—	—	—	—	—	—	—
New Hampshire	50.0	11.6	94.2	88.4	85.8	83.7	54.8	71.3
New Jersey	99.0	—	99.8	—	96.5	—	—	—
New Mexico	—	—	—	—	—	—	—	—
New York	90.5	—	97.0	—	97.9	—	96.0	—
North Carolina	93.7	—	71.4	—	87.3	—	93.8	90.6
North Dakota	—	—	—	—	—	—	—	—
Ohio	96.3	—	98.5	—	93.1	—	99.2	97.8
Oklahoma	—	—	—	—	—	—	—	—
Oregon	—	—	—	—	—	—	—	—
Pennsylvania	85.8	—	48.8	—	99.0	90.8	—	90.8
Rhode Island	95.6	86.4	—	95.0	38.5	0.0	0.0	82.9
South Carolina	—	—	—	—	—	—	—	—
South Dakota	—	—	—	—	—	—	—	—
Tennessee	84.2	71.3	—	97.7	88.6	95.1	—	95.7
Texas	—	—	—	—	—	—	—	—
Utah	—	—	—	—	—	—	—	—
Vermont	84.5	88.6	87.9	95.0	77.8	95.8	94.0	93.7
Virginia	86.8	—	—	—	98.8	—	—	—
Washington	—	—	—	—	—	—	—	—
West Virginia	—	—	—	—	—	—	—	—
Wisconsin	—	—	—	—	—	—	—	—
Wyoming	—	—	—	—	—	—	—	—

Notes: The composite competition index value for each state is the mean of a state's values for the party competition index devised by Paul David (1972) for all races held in a given election year among the following set of races: president, House, Senate, and governor. David's party competition index is defined as 100 − the absolute difference between the Democratic and Republican percentage of two-party vote for each of the races mentioned here. Zero (0) percent on David's index represents a complete absence of two-party competition for that election year, whereas a score of 100 percent indicates perfect competition between the two major parties. A state can only receive a composite index score of 0 if all races held in that state in a given election year are 100–0 vote splits between the two major parties. Conversely, a state can only receive a composite competition score of 100 if all races held in that state in a given election year are 50–50 vote splits between the two major parties. A state's overall value on the composite competition index for a given election year is obtained by averaging that state's party competition values for president (in Tables 8-36 through 8-53), House (in Tables 8-54 through 8-89), Senate (in Tables 8-90 through 8-104), and governor (in Tables 8-105 through 8-140). For example, in 1788 New Hampshire's party competition values were 0 percent for president (Table 8-36) and 90.6 percent for governor (Table 8-105). There were no election data available for the presidential race. Hence, New Hampshire's composite competition score in 1788 was 45.3 percent (90.6 ÷ 2) as shown in Table 8-9. In 1996 Illinois's party competition values were 80.8 percent for president (Table 8-53), 88.8 percent for House (Table 8-88), and 84.0 percent for Senate (Table 8-104). There was no race for governor in 1996. Thus Illinois's composite competition score in 1996 was 84.5 percent (253.6 ÷ 3) as shown in Table 8-35. The values for Democratic and Republican percent of two-party vote for president, House, Senate, and governor used to get the party competition values for these races in Tables 8-36 through 8-140 are taken from the state vote tables in Chapters 4, 5, 6, and 7, respectively (where the Republican vote percent is obtained by subtracting the Democratic vote percent from 100 for each race). The author's alternative party coding in these tables in Chapters 4–7 is used whenever it occurs in place of the conventional party coding of voting data. The Democratic Party is defined as the Anti-Federalists, Federalists, and Jackson Democrats prior to 1830 when the "Democratic Party" as such was established. The Republican Party is defined as the Federalists, National Republicans, and Whigs prior to the establishment of the "Republican Party" in the 1850s. See Appendix A for an explanation of the historical antecedents of the current Democratic and Republican parties. No special elections for any of the four races are used in the calculations, nor are partial voting data reported for any of the four races in any of the states. —indicates that the state had no data, either because no vote data were found for the state in question or the state had not yet entered the Union. Data for the District of Columbia are included from 1964 to the present, after being granted the right to elect presidential electors by the 23rd Amendment.

Sources: Tables 8-36 through 8-140. Specifically, state party competition values in Tables 8-36 through 8-140 for the presidential, House, Senate, and gubernatorial races are aggregated for each election year separately in order to obtain each state's average composite competition values for the election years shown in Tables 8-9 through 8-35.

Table 8-16 Composite Competition Index, by State, by Election Year, 1844–1851 (Percentages)

State	1844	1845	1846	1847	1848	1849	1850	1851
Alabama	82.0	2.4	—	88.6	98.8	45.0	—	25.8
Alaska	—	—	—	—	—	—	—	—
Arizona	—	—	—	—	—	—	—	—
Arkansas	81.5	—	0.0	—	84.1	99.0	—	85.2
California	—	—	—	—	—	0.0	—	96.1
Colorado	—	—	—	—	—	—	—	—
Connecticut	96.5	94.1	98.8	95.2	95.3	97.2	98.6	98.0
Delaware	98.5	—	98.4	—	96.5	—	99.4	—
Dist. of Columbia	—	—	—	—	—	—	—	—
Florida	—	84.6	98.2	—	90.7	—	94.4	—
Georgia	97.4	97.8	92.8	98.4	98.3	96.4	—	0.0
Hawaii	—	—	—	—	—	—	—	—
Idaho	—	—	—	—	—	—	—	—
Illinois	78.8	—	69.9	—	55.6	—	83.8	—
Indiana	98.4	95.0	96.8	99.8	96.6	96.4	—	96.6
Iowa	—	—	96.6	96.0	95.3	—	92.1	—
Kansas	—	—	—	—	—	—	—	—
Kentucky	93.9	100.0	—	91.0	89.1	84.6	—	96.4
Louisiana	79.5	—	90.8	—	90.8	97.0	—	99.2
Maine	90.5	88.4	93.7	84.2	91.5	86.0	92.5	—
Maryland	94.8	96.4	—	99.0	95.6	91.6	98.0	90.4
Massachusetts	87.8	84.6	75.1	84.6	63.7	71.4	77.5	81.2
Michigan	93.5	89.6	93.4	87.0	92.3	91.6	97.4	83.0
Minnesota	—	—	—	—	—	—	—	—
Mississippi	85.2	74.9	—	53.0	98.8	83.7	—	0.0
Missouri	89.1	—	77.2	—	82.9	—	81.4	—
Montana	—	—	—	—	—	—	—	—
Nebraska	—	—	—	—	—	—	—	—
Nevada	—	—	—	—	—	—	—	—
New Hampshire	75.8	37.9	79.4	81.4	81.9	80.8	75.0	85.4
New Jersey	94.9	—	94.4	96.2	97.8	—	92.0	—
New Mexico	—	—	—	—	—	—	—	—
New York	97.8	—	98.2	—	67.1	—	99.4	—
North Carolina	95.7	88.2	90.0	84.6	94.3	98.6	96.8	—
North Dakota	—	—	—	—	—	—	—	—
Ohio	98.7	—	98.0	—	95.4	—	90.8	90.2
Oklahoma	—	—	—	—	—	—	—	—
Oregon	—	—	—	—	—	—	—	—
Pennsylvania	97.4	—	97.2	93.4	97.8	—	94.8	97.6
Rhode Island	79.8	0.0	99.4	83.7	74.3	76.1	0.0	93.2
South Carolina	—	—	—	—	—	—	—	—
South Dakota	—	—	—	—	—	—	—	—
Tennessee	99.8	95.7	—	98.7	95.0	96.5	—	98.6
Texas	—	0.0	0.0	0.0	62.4	0.0	—	18.7
Utah	—	—	—	—	—	—	—	—
Vermont	83.0	89.8	85.4	90.8	80.2	99.2	95.5	45.8
Virginia	94.0	—	—	—	98.4	—	—	94.0
Washington	—	—	—	—	—	—	—	—
West Virginia	—	—	—	—	—	—	—	—
Wisconsin	—	—	—	—	90.5	80.8	84.2	98.8
Wyoming	—	—	—	—	—	—	—	—

Notes: The composite competition index value for each state is the mean of a state's values for the party competition index devised by Paul David (1972) for all races held in a given election year among the following set of races: president, House, Senate, and governor. David's party competition index is defined as 100 − the absolute difference between the Democratic and Republican percentage of two-party vote for each of the races mentioned here. Zero (0) percent on David's index represents a complete absence of two-party competition for that election year, whereas a score of 100 percent indicates perfect competition between the two major parties. A state can only receive a composite index score of 0 if all races held in that state in a given election year are 100–0 vote splits between the two major parties. Conversely, a state can only receive a composite competition score of 100 if all races held in that state in a given election year are 50–50 vote splits between the two major parties. A state's overall value on the composite competition index for a given election year is obtained by averaging that state's party competition values for president (in Tables 8-36 through 8-53), House (in Tables 8-54 through 8-89), Senate (in Tables 8-90 through 8-104), and governor (in Tables 8-105 through 8-140). For example, in 1788 New Hampshire's party competition values were 0 percent for president (Table 8-36) and 90.6 percent for governor (Table 8-105). There were no election data available for the presidential race. Hence, New Hampshire's composite competition score in 1788 was 45.3 percent (90.6 ÷ 2) as shown in Table 8-9. In 1996 Illinois's party competition values were 80.8 percent for president (Table 8-53), 88.8 percent for House (Table 8-88), and 84.0 percent for Senate (Table 8-104). There was no race for governor in 1996. Thus Illinois's composite competition score in 1996 was 84.5 percent (253.6 ÷ 3) as shown in Table 8-35. The values for Democratic and Republican percent of two-party vote for president, House, Senate, and governor used to get the party competition values for these races in Tables 8-36 through 8-140 are taken from the state vote tables in Chapters 4, 5, 6, and 7, respectively (where the Republican vote percent is obtained by subtracting the Democratic vote percent from 100 for each race). The author's alternative party coding in these tables in Chapters 4–7 is used whenever it occurs in place of the conventional party coding of voting data. The Democratic Party is defined as the Anti-Federalists, Federalists, and Jackson Democrats prior to 1830 when the "Democratic Party" as such was established. The Republican Party is defined as the Federalists, National Republicans, and Whigs prior to the establishment of the "Republican Party" in the 1850s. See Appendix A for an explanation of the historical antecedents of the current Democratic and Republican parties. No special elections for any of the four races are used in the calculations, nor are partial voting data reported for any of the four races in any of the states. —indicates that the state had no data, either because no vote data were found for the state in question or the state had not yet entered the Union. Data for the District of Columbia are included from 1964 to the present, after being granted the right to elect presidential electors by the 23rd Amendment.

Sources: Tables 8-36 through 8-140. Specifically, state party competition values in Tables 8-36 through 8-140 for the presidential, House, Senate, and gubernatorial races are aggregated for each election year separately in order to obtain each state's average composite competition values for the election years shown in Tables 8-9 through 8-35.

Table 8-17 Composite Competition Index, by State, by Election Year, 1852–1859 (Percentages)

State	1852	1853	1854	1855	1856	1857	1858	1859
Alabama	71.8	40.0	—	0.0	0.0	0.0	—	0.0
Alaska	—	—	—	—	—	—	—	—
Arizona	—	—	—	—	—	—	—	—
Arkansas	82.6	47.8	32.8	—	0.0	—	0.0	—
California	93.3	98.0	85.2	0.0	58.2	56.8	—	51.7
Colorado	—	—	—	—	—	—	—	—
Connecticut	94.9	84.2	81.0	25.1	64.7	98.8	96.0	97.7
Delaware	99.7	—	47.4	—	3.7	—	0.0	—
Dist. of Columbia	—	—	—	—	—	—	—	—
Florida	92.2	—	89.4	—	0.0	—	0.0	—
Georgia	58.2	96.6	—	0.0	0.0	0.0	—	39.8
Hawaii	—	—	—	—	—	—	—	—
Idaho	—	—	—	—	—	—	—	—
Illinois	88.1	—	98.2	—	96.5	—	99.8	—
Indiana	90.7	—	0.0	—	94.4	—	93.2	—
Iowa	95.4	—	96.0	—	90.7	96.8	96.4	97.2
Kansas	—	—	—	—	—	—	—	84.6
Kentucky	96.8	96.2	—	0.0	0.0	0.0	—	0.0
Louisiana	95.1	—	—	0.0	0.0	0.0	—	0.0
Maine	89.0	86.0	68.4	87.6	77.1	88.0	92.7	88.4
Maryland	93.4	93.2	—	0.0	1.4	0.0	—	0.0
Massachusetts	82.6	74.4	61.7	82.0	56.1	68.6	71.5	75.0
Michigan	91.3	—	93.7	—	85.3	—	92.0	—
Minnesota	—	—	—	—	—	98.0	—	90.5
Mississippi	79.0	91.7	—	0.0	0.0	0.0	—	0.0
Missouri	85.5	—	90.0	—	0.0	—	14.4	—
Montana	—	—	—	—	—	—	—	—
Nebraska	—	—	—	—	—	—	—	—
Nevada	—	—	—	—	—	—	—	—
New Hampshire	74.4	78.3	72.8	11.3	52.9	94.9	93.0	95.4
New Jersey	92.8	94.8	99.8	—	89.5	—	68.8	98.4
New Mexico	—	—	—	—	—	—	—	—
New York	96.5	—	95.0	—	84.7	—	90.7	—
North Carolina	96.5	79.0	97.8	15.4	0.0	0.0	0.0	84.0
North Dakota	—	—	—	—	—	—	—	—
Ohio	94.4	73.6	0.0	86.8	94.4	99.6	92.8	96.2
Oklahoma	—	—	—	—	—	—	—	—
Oregon	—	—	—	—	—	—	0.0	99.8
Pennsylvania	90.9	—	93.7	—	91.1	87.2	0.0	—
Rhode Island	95.4	80.9	83.2	36.2	78.4	70.5	62.0	54.3
South Carolina	—	—	—	—	—	—	—	—
South Dakota	—	—	—	—	—	—	—	—
Tennessee	98.6	98.2	—	0.0	0.0	0.0	—	47.2
Texas	53.0	32.7	—	0.0	0.0	0.0	—	0.0
Utah	—	—	—	—	—	—	—	—
Vermont	83.2	92.8	74.3	66.6	45.4	64.8	60.5	63.2
Virginia	88.6	—	—	0.0	0.0	—	—	96.2
Washington	—	—	—	—	—	—	—	—
West Virginia	—	—	—	—	—	—	—	—
Wisconsin	78.3	90.6	87.2	99.8	88.8	99.4	94.8	96.8
Wyoming	—	—	—	—	—	—	—	—

Notes: The composite competition index value for each state is the mean of a state's values for the party competition index devised by Paul David (1972) for all races held in a given election year among the following set of races: president, House, Senate, and governor. David's party competition index is defined as 100 − the absolute difference between the Democratic and Republican percentage of two-party vote for each of the races mentioned here. Zero (0) percent on David's index represents a complete absence of two-party competition for that election year, whereas a score of 100 percent indicates perfect competition between the two major parties. A state can only receive a composite index score of 0 if all races held in that state in a given election year are 100–0 vote splits between the two major parties. Conversely, a state can only receive a composite competition score of 100 if all races held in that state in a given election year are 50–50 vote splits between the two major parties. A state's overall value on the composite competition index for a given election year is obtained by averaging that state's party competition values for president (in Tables 8-36 through 8-53), House (in Tables 8-54 through 8-89), Senate (in Tables 8-90 through 8-104), and governor (in Tables 8-105 through 8-140). For example, in 1788 New Hampshire's party competition values were 0 percent for president (Table 8-36) and 90.6 percent for governor (Table 8-105). There were no election data available for the presidential race. Hence, New Hampshire's composite competition score in 1788 was 45.3 percent (90.6 ÷ 2) as shown in Table 8-9. In 1996 Illinois's party competition values were 80.8 percent for president (Table 8-53), 88.8 percent for House (Table 8-88), and 84.0 percent for Senate (Table 8-104). There was no race for governor in 1996. Thus Illinois's composite competition score in 1996 was 84.5 percent (253.6 ÷ 3) as shown in Table 8-35. The values for Democratic and Republican percent of two-party vote for president, House, Senate, and governor used to get the party competition values for these races in Tables 8-36 through 8-140 are taken from the state vote tables in Chapters 4, 5, 6, and 7, respectively (where the Republican vote percent is obtained by subtracting the Democratic vote percent from 100 for each race). The author's alternative party coding in these tables in Chapters 4–7 is used whenever it occurs in place of the conventional party coding of voting data. The Democratic Party is defined as the Anti-Federalists, Federalists, and Jackson Democrats prior to 1830 when the "Democratic Party" as such was established. The Republican Party is defined as the Federalists, National Republicans, and Whigs prior to the establishment of the "Republican Party" in the 1850s. See Appendix A for an explanation of the historical antecedents of the current Democratic and Republican parties. No special elections for any of the four races are used in the calculations, nor are partial voting data reported for any of the four races in any of the states. —indicates that the state had no data, either because no vote data were found for the state in question or the state had not yet entered the Union. Data for the District of Columbia are included from 1964 to the present, after being granted the right to elect presidential electors by the 23rd Amendment.

Sources: Tables 8-36 through 8-140. Specifically, state party competition values in Tables 8-9 through 8-140 for the presidential, House, Senate, and gubernatorial races are aggregated for each election year separately in order to obtain each state's average composite competition values for the election years shown in Tables 8-9 through 8-35.

Table 8-18 Composite Competition Index, by State, by Election Year, 1860–1867 (Percentages)

State	1860	1861	1862	1863	1864	1865	1866	1867
Alabama	0.0	84.8	—	51.0	—	72.0	—	—
Alaska	—	—	—	—	—	—	—	—
Arizona	—	—	—	—	—	—	—	—
Arkansas	0.0	—	—	—	—	—	—	—
California	99.0	90.3	—	81.3	82.4	—	—	93.9
Colorado	—	—	—	—	—	—	—	—
Connecticut	75.9	98.1	87.0	96.9	94.8	84.9	99.4	98.8
Delaware	21.8	—	99.6	—	96.7	—	93.0	—
Dist. of Columbia	—	—	—	—	—	—	—	—
Florida	0.0	—	—	—	—	0.0	—	—
Georgia	0.0	0.0	—	0.0	—	—	—	—
Hawaii	—	—	—	—	—	—	—	—
Idaho	—	—	—	—	—	—	—	—
Illinois	96.3	—	93.6	—	91.1	—	84.2	—
Indiana	94.0	—	95.4	—	93.3	—	96.2	—
Iowa	89.0	83.6	85.8	79.0	72.6	86.8	76.6	82.2
Kansas	—	—	6.1	—	12.2	—	0.0	—
Kentucky	10.0	0.0	—	20.4	60.4	—	—	51.8
Louisiana	0.0	—	—	—	—	100.0	—	—
Maine	78.7	82.6	91.0	85.2	82.6	73.4	75.4	88.6
Maryland	55.6	31.2	—	43.4	88.7	—	76.0	51.4
Massachusetts	56.8	64.8	3.1	58.6	55.9	46.6	45.4	83.4
Michigan	85.7	—	94.9	—	89.5	—	82.4	—
Minnesota	71.8	78.2	83.4	78.8	82.1	88.8	75.6	91.6
Mississippi	0.0	—	—	—	—	69.6	—	—
Missouri	27.3	—	99.6	—	58.6	—	82.0	—
Montana	—	—	—	—	—	—	—	—
Nebraska	—	—	—	—	—	—	95.3	—
Nevada	—	—	—	—	80.2	75.0	89.9	—
New Hampshire	87.7	93.8	97.0	99.2	93.3	91.0	93.0	95.5
New Jersey	97.7	—	86.9	—	94.9	97.8	98.8	—
New Mexico	—	—	—	—	—	—	—	—
New York	93.0	—	98.6	—	98.9	—	94.3	—
North Carolina	47.3	—	—	—	—	—	0.0	—
North Dakota	—	—	—	—	—	—	—	—
Ohio	90.5	84.6	99.4	78.8	87.4	92.8	91.6	99.4
Oklahoma	—	—	—	—	—	—	—	—
Oregon	43.7	—	67.7	—	87.0	—	97.9	—
Pennsylvania	65.0	—	93.6	97.0	97.7	—	97.7	—
Rhode Island	85.4	0.0	0.0	83.1	83.0	13.3	51.2	47.6
South Carolina	—	—	—	—	—	—	—	—
South Dakota	—	—	—	—	—	—	—	—
Tennessee	0.0	73.2	—	—	—	0.0	—	0.0
Texas	—	—	—	—	—	0.0	0.0	—
Utah	—	—	—	—	—	—	—	—
Vermont	50.5	42.4	22.0	56.9	53.0	48.6	48.7	53.2
Virginia	20.8	—	—	—	—	—	—	—
Washington	—	—	—	—	—	—	—	—
West Virginia	—	—	—	0.0	21.2	—	83.9	—
Wisconsin	86.1	91.6	98.2	82.4	88.3	90.6	82.6	96.6
Wyoming	—	—	—	—	—	—	—	—

Notes: The composite competition index value for each state is the mean of a state's values for the party competition index devised by Paul David (1972) for all races held in a given election year among the following set of races: president, House, Senate, and governor. David's party competition index is defined as 100 − the absolute difference between the Democratic and Republican percentage of two-party vote for each of the races mentioned here. Zero (0) percent on David's index represents a complete absence of two-party competition for that election year, whereas a score of 100 percent indicates perfect competition between the two major parties. A state can only receive a composite index score of 0 if all races held in that state in a given election year are 100–0 vote splits between the two major parties. Conversely, a state can only receive a composite competition score of 100 if all races held in that state in a given election year are 50–50 vote splits between the two major parties. A state's overall value on the composite competition index for a given election year is obtained by averaging that state's party competition values for president (in Tables 8-36 through 8-53), House (in Tables 8-54 through 8-89), Senate (in Tables 8-90 through 8-104), and governor (in Tables 8-105 through 8-140). For example, in 1788 New Hampshire's party competition values were 0 percent for president (Table 8-36) and 90.6 percent for governor (Table 8-105). There was no election data available for the presidential race. Hence, New Hampshire's composite competition in 1788 was 45.3 percent (90.6 ÷ 2) as shown in Table 8-9. In 1996 Illinois's party competition values were 80.8 percent for president (Table 8-53), 88.8 percent for House (Table 8-88), and 84.0 percent for Senate (Table 8-104). There was no race for governor in 1996. Thus Illinois's composite competition score in 1996 was 84.5 percent (253.6 ÷ 3) as shown in Table 8-35. The values for Democratic and Republican percent of two-party vote for president, House, Senate, and governor used to get the party competition values for these races in Tables 8-36 through 8-140 are taken from the state vote tables in Chapters 4, 5, 6, and 7, respectively (where the Republican vote percent is obtained by subtracting the Democratic vote percent from 100 for each race). The author's alternative party coding in these tables in Chapters 4–7 is used whenever it occurs in place of the conventional party coding of voting data. The Democratic Party is defined as the Anti-Federalists, Federalists, and Jackson Democrats prior to 1830 when the "Democratic Party" as such was established. The Republican Party is defined as the Federalists, National Republicans, and Whigs prior to the establishment of the "Republican Party" in the 1850s. See Appendix A for an explanation of the historical antecedents of the current Democratic and Republican parties. No special elections for any of the four races are used in the calculations, nor are partial voting data reported for any of the four races in any of the states. —indicates that the state had no data, either because no vote data were found for the state in question or the state had not yet entered the Union. Data for the District of Columbia are included from 1964 to the present, after being granted the right to elect presidential electors by the 23rd Amendment.

Sources: Tables 8-36 through 8-140. Specifically, state party competition values in Tables 8-36 through 8-140 for the presidential, House, Senate, and gubernatorial races are aggregated for each election year separately in order to obtain each state's average composite competition values for the election years shown in Tables 8-9 through 8-35.

Table 8-19 Composite Competition Index, by State, by Election Year, 1868–1875 (Percentages)

State	1868	1869	1870	1871	1872	1873	1874	1875
Alabama	32.5	84.0	98.2	—	94.7	—	92.6	—
Alaska	—	—	—	—	—	—	—	—
Arizona	—	—	—	—	—	—	—	—
Arkansas	92.7	—	96.6	—	97.2	—	35.6	—
California	99.5	—	—	95.6	91.7	—	—	74.1
Colorado								
Connecticut	97.6	98.5	99.0	99.6	96.5	95.5	92.2	93.3
Delaware	82.1	—	88.9	—	95.6	—	94.1	—
Dist. of Columbia	—	—	—	—	—	—	—	—
Florida	72.3	—	84.3	—	62.7	—	95.8	—
Georgia	85.1	—	86.6	—	78.7	—	52.4	—
Hawaii	—	—	—	—	—	—	—	—
Idaho	—	—	—	—	—	—	—	—
Illinois	88.9	—	92.4	—	88.9	—	97.2	—
Indiana	98.9	—	98.2	—	97.7	—	96.0	—
Iowa	77.4	74.2	78.4	76.8	73.6	0.0	0.0	85.6
Kansas	63.5	—	67.7	—	67.3	—	60.7	—
Kentucky	49.8	—	77.8	82.8	78.8	—	50.8	83.4
Louisiana	70.3	—	73.4	—	88.7	—	94.6	—
Maine	82.1	87.4	90.8	89.8	79.0	87.4	88.8	96.4
Maryland	65.6	—	86.0	88.6	99.4	—	88.4	91.8
Massachusetts	62.4	81.2	76.6	77.6	62.1	90.2	93.5	96.8
Michigan	86.8	—	92.4	—	74.7	—	96.3	—
Minnesota	78.5	95.8	88.8	80.2	76.8	92.8	94.0	87.8
Mississippi	94.8	32.4	—	—	70.1	0.0	—	93.8
Missouri	86.3	—	86.2	—	87.1	—	71.3	—
Montana	—	—	—	—	—	—	—	—
Nebraska	80.4	—	82.9	—	71.7	—	56.4	—
Nevada	90.8	—	94.9	—	90.3	—	91.2	—
New Hampshire	93.2	94.2	83.6	98.4	94.4	98.5	97.8	99.7
New Jersey	97.7	—	97.8	96.2	90.2	—	93.7	—
New Mexico	—	—	—	—	—	—	—	—
New York	98.0	—	95.8	—	94.3	—	92.6	—
North Carolina	46.6	—	—	—	94.1	—	84.2	—
North Dakota	—	—	—	—	—	—	—	—
Ohio	94.7	98.4	96.8	95.6	95.4	99.8	95.6	99.0
Oklahoma	—	—	—	—	—	—	—	—
Oregon	82.2	—	97.8	—	87.9	—	97.7	—
Pennsylvania	97.2	99.2	96.2	—	87.7	—	94.4	98.0
Rhode Island	69.5	63.0	57.0	75.6	69.5	56.4	42.3	76.4
South Carolina	56.2	—	70.5	—	38.9	—	66.1	—
South Dakota	—	—	—	—	—	—	—	—
Tennessee	31.6	0.0	70.3	—	92.5	—	68.6	—
Texas	—	89.5	—	82.4	82.1	68.0	41.6	50.0
Utah	—	—	—	—	—	—	—	—
Vermont	48.9	53.0	50.2	—	42.6	—	47.8	—
Virginia	—	0.0	—	—	49.5	87.6	86.8	—
Washington	—	—	—	—	—	—	—	—
West Virginia	87.7	—	96.6	—	61.1	—	85.8	—
Wisconsin	88.0	93.6	96.0	93.6	90.7	89.6	99.8	99.6
Wyoming	—	—	—	—	—	—	—	—

Notes: The composite competition index value for each state is the mean of a state's values for the party competition index devised by Paul David (1972) for all races held in a given election year among the following set of races: president, House, Senate, and governor. David's party competition index is defined as 100 − the absolute difference between the Democratic and Republican percentage of two-party vote for each of the races mentioned here. Zero (0) percent on David's index represents a complete absence of two-party competition for that election year, whereas a score of 100 percent indicates perfect competition between the two major parties. A state can only receive a composite index score of 0 if all races held in that state in a given election year are 100–0 vote splits between the two major parties. Conversely, a state can only receive a composite competition score of 100 if all races held in that state in a given election year are 50–50 vote splits between the two major parties. A state's overall value on the composite competition index for a given election year is obtained by averaging that state's party competition values for president (in Tables 8-36 through 8-53), House (in Tables 8-54 through 8-89), Senate (in Tables 8-90 through 8-104), and governor (in Tables 8-105 through 8-140). For example, in 1788 New Hampshire's party competition values were 0 percent for president (Table 8-36) and 90.6 percent for governor (Table 8-105). There were no election data available for the presidential race. Hence, New Hampshire's composite competition score in 1788 was 45.3 percent (90.6 ÷ 2) as shown in Table 8-9. In 1996 Illinois's party competition values were 80.8 percent for president (Table 8-53), 88.8 percent for House (Table 8-88), and 84.0 percent for Senate (Table 8-104). There was no race for governor in 1996. Thus Illinois's composite competition score in 1996 was 84.5 percent (253.6 ÷ 3) as shown in Table 8-35. The values for Democratic and Republican percent of two-party vote for president, House, Senate, and governor used to get the party competition values for these races in Tables 8-36 through 8-140 are taken from the state vote tables in Chapters 4, 5, 6, and 7, respectively (where the Republican vote percent is obtained by subtracting the Democratic vote percent from 100 for each race). The author's alternative party coding in these tables in Chapters 4–7 is used whenever it occurs in place of the conventional party coding of voting data. The Democratic Party is defined as the Anti-Federalists, Federalists, and Jackson Democrats prior to 1830 when the "Democratic Party" as such was established. The Republican Party is defined as the Federalists, National Republicans, and Whigs prior to the establishment of the "Republican Party" in the 1850s. See Appendix A for an explanation of the historical antecedents of the current Democratic and Republican parties. No special elections for any of the four races are used in the calculations, nor are partial voting data reported for any of the four races in any of the states. —indicates that the state had no data, either because no vote data were found for the state in question or the state had not yet entered the Union. Data for the District of Columbia are included from 1964 to the present, after being granted the right to elect presidential electors by the 23rd Amendment.

Sources: Tables 8-36 through 8-140. Specifically, state party competition values in Tables 8-36 through 8-140 for the presidential, House, Senate, and gubernatorial races are aggregated for each election year separately in order to obtain each state's average composite competition values for the election years shown in Tables 8-9 through 8-35.

Table 8-20 Composite Competition Index, by State, by Election Year, 1876–1883 (Percentages)

State	1876	1877	1878	1879	1880	1881	1882	1883
Alabama	67.1	—	19.4	—	43.5	—	61.4	—
Alaska	—	—	—	—	—	—	—	—
Arizona	—	—	—	—	—	—	—	—
Arkansas	70.4	—	30.9	—	53.8	—	68.9	—
California	96.9	—	—	80.3	99.8	—	88.4	—
Colorado	96.9	—	90.2	—	93.4	—	96.4	—
Connecticut	97.5	—	97.3	—	97.6	—	97.2	—
Delaware	89.2	—	0.0	—	97.1	—	93.8	—
Dist. of Columbia	—	—	—	—	—	—	—	—
Florida	98.6	—	93.0	—	90.7	—	99.2	—
Georgia	49.5	—	14.8	—	34.4	—	23.4	—
Hawaii	—	—	—	—	—	—	—	—
Idaho	—	—	—	—	—	—	—	—
Illinois	97.9	—	94.4	—	93.5	—	93.4	—
Indiana	98.7	—	96.4	—	98.7	—	96.8	—
Iowa	80.9	79.0	80.0	70.4	72.6	71.0	89.8	92.0
Kansas	59.7	—	66.2	—	68.7	—	91.0	—
Kentucky	75.1	—	67.0	79.0	81.5	—	83.2	80.0
Louisiana	95.6	—	42.2	70.8	72.6	—	74.6	—
Maine	88.0	89.0	70.7	47.8	97.6	—	93.2	—
Maryland	88.7	—	72.4	86.2	92.4	—	95.0	93.0
Massachusetts	86.0	89.0	86.7	98.6	80.8	72.2	95.1	96.8
Michigan	92.7	—	76.3	—	84.4	—	97.7	—
Minnesota	83.1	81.4	91.8	84.2	74.4	72.8	67.0	89.2
Mississippi	62.8	2.4	36.8	—	60.1	80.8	59.4	—
Missouri	82.8	—	52.4	—	82.2	—	72.6	—
Montana	—	—	—	—	—	—	—	—
Nebraska	70.7	—	74.9	—	66.0	—	78.0	—
Nevada	95.0	—	96.7	—	94.2	—	91.3	—
New Hampshire	95.8	96.2	94.2	89.8	95.5	—	95.0	—
New Jersey	89.1	93.0	93.8	—	99.4	—	98.8	96.6
New Mexico	—	—	—	—	—	—	—	—
New York	96.9	—	96.0	96.0	98.9	—	87.8	—
North Carolina	93.2	—	94.0	—	94.9	—	0.0	—
North Dakota	—	—	—	—	—	—	—	—
Ohio	99.0	95.6	98.0	97.4	96.1	96.0	96.6	98.2
Oklahoma	—	—	—	—	—	—	—	—
Oregon	96.3	—	98.1	—	97.4	—	94.3	—
Pennsylvania	98.1	—	95.5	—	93.8	—	97.6	—
Rhode Island	73.0	97.2	73.7	72.4	71.4	61.0	67.2	91.0
South Carolina	99.6	—	27.8	—	45.7	—	46.4	—
South Dakota	—	—	—	—	—	—	—	—
Tennessee	58.8	—	59.2	—	89.3	—	87.0	—
Texas	59.1	—	12.6	—	34.9	—	63.1	—
Utah	—	—	—	—	—	—	—	—
Vermont	62.8	—	57.7	—	59.9	—	55.8	—
Virginia	81.1	8.2	53.8	—	73.2	0.0	8.8	—
Washington	—	—	—	—	—	—	—	—
West Virginia	86.3	—	83.8	—	88.8	—	95.4	—
Wisconsin	98.2	94.4	96.4	85.4	89.0	92.2	95.4	—
Wyoming	—	—	—	—	—	—	—	—

Notes: The composite competition index value for each state is the mean of a state's values for the party competition index devised by Paul David (1972) for all races held in a given election year among the following set of races: president, House, Senate, and governor. David's party competition index is defined as 100 − the absolute difference between the Democratic and Republican percentage of two-party vote for each of the races mentioned here. Zero (0) percent on David's index represents a complete absence of two-party competition for that election year, whereas a score of 100 percent indicates perfect competition between the two major parties. A state can only receive a composite index score of 0 if all races held in that state in a given election year are 100–0 vote splits between the two major parties. Conversely, a state can only receive a composite competition score of 100 if all races held in that state in a given election year are 50–50 vote splits between the two major parties. A state's overall value on the composite competition index for a given election year is obtained by averaging that state's party competition values for president (in Tables 8-36 through 8-53), House (in Tables 8-54 through 8-89), Senate (in Tables 8-90 through 8-104), and governor (in Tables 8-105 through 8-140). For example, in 1788 New Hampshire's party competition values were 0 percent for president (Table 8-36) and 90.6 percent for governor (Table 8-105). There were no election data available for the presidential race. Hence, New Hampshire's composite competition score in 1788 was 45.3 percent (90.6 ÷ 2) as shown in Table 8-9. In 1996 Illinois's party competition values were 80.8 percent for president (Table 8-53), 88.8 percent for House (Table 8-88), and 84.0 percent for Senate (Table 8-104). There was no race for governor in 1996. Thus Illinois's composite competition score in 1996 was 84.5 percent (253.6 ÷ 3) as shown in Table 8-35. The values for Democratic and Republican percent of two-party vote for president, House, Senate, and governor used to get the party competition values for these races in Tables 8-36 through 8-140 are taken from the state vote tables in Chapters 4, 5, 6, and 7, respectively (where the Republican vote percent is obtained by subtracting the Democratic vote percent from 100 for each race). The author's alternative party coding in these tables in Chapters 4–7 is used whenever it occurs in place of the conventional party coding of voting data. The Democratic Party is defined as the Anti-Federalists, Federalists, and Jackson Democrats prior to 1830 when the "Democratic Party" as such was established. The Republican Party is defined as the Federalists, National Republicans, and Whigs prior to the establishment of the "Republican Party" in the 1850s. See Appendix A for an explanation of the historical antecedents of the current Democratic and Republican parties. No special elections for any of the four races are used in the calculations, nor are partial voting data reported for any of the four races in any of the states. —indicates that the state had no data, either because no vote data were found for the state in question or the state had not yet entered the Union. Data for the District of Columbia are included from 1964 to the present, after being granted the right to elect presidential electors by the 23rd Amendment.

Sources: Tables 8-36 through 8-140. Specifically, state party competition values in Tables 8-36 through 8-140 for the presidential, House, Senate, and gubernatorial races are aggregated for each election year separately in order to obtain each state's average composite competition values for the election years shown in Tables 8-9 through 8-35.

Table 8-21 Composite Competition Index, by State, by Election Year, 1884–1891 (Percentages)

State	1884	1885	1886	1887	1888	1889	1890	1891
Alabama	48.4	—	48.4	—	57.9	—	46.2	—
Alaska	—	—	—	—	—	—	—	—
Arizona	—	—	—	—	—	—	—	—
Arkansas	78.5	—	56.3	—	38.0	—	72.7	—
California	93.8	—	99.2	—	96.3	—	96.0	—
Colorado	90.5	—	97.1	—	86.3	—	90.4	—
Connecticut	99.1	—	98.6	—	99.4	—	97.0	—
Delaware	86.3	—	1.0	—	88.2	—	98.2	—
Dist. of Columbia	—	—	—	—	—	—	—	—
Florida	93.4	—	82.0	—	80.1	—	68.4	—
Georgia	56.5	—	0.1	—	32.3	—	16.3	—
Hawaii	—	—	—	—	—	—	—	—
Idaho	—	—	—	—	—	—	87.8	—
Illinois	96.4	—	93.4	—	97.3	—	95.2	—
Indiana	98.3	—	98.8	—	99.5	—	95.0	—
Iowa	95.0	98.0	87.0	95.0	92.4	98.2	97.6	98.0
Kansas	78.5	—	85.2	—	73.0	—	57.2	—
Kentucky	82.2	—	82.0	93.8	91.7	—	69.6	89.2
Louisiana	72.5	—	50.8	—	51.8	—	35.4	—
Maine	85.3	—	87.7	—	85.0	—	83.0	—
Maryland	94.2	—	73.6	93.4	97.0	—	87.6	83.8
Massachusetts	86.0	89.2	96.9	93.0	91.1	97.2	97.6	98.0
Michigan	95.3	—	97.6	—	95.5	—	97.1	—
Minnesota	80.2	—	88.7	—	87.3	—	97.1	—
Mississippi	62.3	0.0	47.2	—	49.3	0.0	44.8	—
Missouri	93.8	—	84.8	—	95.7	—	84.2	—
Montana	—	—	—	—	—	96.8	99.0	—
Nebraska	87.9	—	88.4	—	87.5	—	93.6	—
Nevada	90.6	—	93.4	—	87.4	—	93.2	—
New Hampshire	95.3	—	99.0	—	98.5	—	99.0	—
New Jersey	98.5	—	97.6	—	98.3	94.6	94.4	—
New Mexico	—	—	—	—	—	—	—	—
New York	97.7	98.8	99.4	—	97.1	—	92.0	95.8
North Carolina	92.5	—	65.8	—	94.7	—	82.4	—
North Dakota	—	—	—	—	—	65.0	80.8	—
Ohio	96.6	97.6	98.4	96.6	97.4	98.6	98.4	97.2
Oklahoma	—	—	—	—	—	—	—	—
Oregon	95.7	—	95.6	—	87.9	—	89.5	—
Pennsylvania	91.1	—	94.3	—	92.3	—	97.6	—
Rhode Island	78.0	81.6	88.8	91.0	89.2	88.4	95.4	97.2
South Carolina	31.2	—	15.3	—	20.4	—	19.8	—
South Dakota	—	—	—	—	—	60.3	68.4	—
Tennessee	95.7	—	89.2	—	93.3	—	83.6	—
Texas	50.1	—	36.3	—	32.3	—	41.5	—
Utah	—	—	—	—	—	—	—	—
Vermont	60.1	—	60.0	—	56.3	—	69.9	—
Virginia	98.1	94.4	94.8	—	99.5	85.2	53.2	—
Washington	—	—	—	—	—	84.1	87.8	—
West Virginia	96.7	—	99.6	—	99.5	—	95.4	—
Wisconsin	95.1	—	90.4	—	93.5	—	89.4	—
Wyoming	—	—	—	—	—	—	86.4	—

Notes: The composite competition index value for each state is the mean of a state's values for the party competition index devised by Paul David (1972) for all races held in a given election year among the following set of races: president, House, Senate, and governor. David's party competition index is defined as 100 − the absolute difference between the Democratic and Republican percentage of two-party vote for each of the races mentioned here. Zero (0) percent on David's index represents a complete absence of two-party competition for that election year, whereas a score of 100 percent indicates perfect competition between the two major parties. A state can only receive a composite index score of 0 if all races held in that state in a given election year are 100–0 vote splits between the two major parties. Conversely, a state can only receive a composite competition score of 100 if all races held in that state in a given election year are 50–50 vote splits between the two major parties. A state's overall value on the composite competition index for a given election year is obtained by averaging that state's party competition values for president (in Tables 8-36 through 8-53), House (in Tables 8-54 through 8-89), Senate (in Tables 8-90 through 8-104), and governor (in Tables 8-105 through 8-140). For example, in 1788 New Hampshire's party competition values were 0 percent for president (Table 8-36) and 90.6 percent for governor (Table 8-105). There were no election data available for the presidential race. Hence, New Hampshire's composite competition score in 1788 was 45.3 percent (90.6 ÷ 2) as shown in Table 8-9. In 1996 Illinois's party competition values were 80.8 percent for president (Table 8-53), 88.8 percent for House (Table 8-88), and 84.0 percent for Senate (Table 8-104). There was no race for governor in 1996. Thus Illinois's composite competition score in 1996 was 84.5 percent (253.6 ÷ 3) as shown in Table 8-35. The values for Democratic and Republican percent of two-party vote for president, House, Senate, and governor used to get the party competition values for these races in Tables 8-36 through 8-140 are taken from the state vote tables in Chapters 4, 5, 6, and 7, respectively (where the Republican vote percent is obtained by subtracting the Democratic vote percent from 100 for each race). The author's alternative party coding in these tables in Chapters 4–7 is used whenever it occurs in place of the conventional party coding of voting data. The Democratic Party is defined as the Anti-Federalists, Federalists, and Jackson Democrats prior to 1830 when the "Democratic Party" as such was established. The Republican Party is defined as the Federalists, National Republicans, and Whigs prior to the establishment of the "Republican Party" in the 1850s. See Appendix A for an explanation of the historical antecedents of the current Democratic and Republican parties. No special elections for any of the four races are used in the calculations, nor are partial voting data reported for any of the four races in any of the states. —indicates that the state had no data, either because no vote data were found for the state in question or the state had not yet entered the Union. Data for the District of Columbia are included from 1964 to the present, after being granted the right to elect presidential electors by the 23rd Amendment.

Sources: Tables 8-36 through 8-140. Specifically, state party competition values in Tables 8-36 through 8-140 for the presidential, House, Senate, and gubernatorial races are aggregated for each election year separately in order to obtain each state's average composite competition values for the election years shown in Tables 8-9 through 8-35.

Table 8-22 Composite Competition Index, by State, by Election Year, 1892–1899 (Percentages)

State	1892	1893	1894	1895	1896	1897	1898	1899
Alabama	7.3	—	17.4	—	35.3	—	29.5	—
Alaska	—	—	—	—	—	—	—	—
Arizona	—	—	—	—	—	—	—	—
Arkansas	50.8	—	47.6	—	54.1	—	36.8	—
California	96.3	—	96.2	—	99.5	—	94.6	—
Colorado	55.7	—	43.7	—	32.8	—	67.8	—
Connecticut	96.5	—	87.2	—	70.9	—	87.9	—
Delaware	98.7	—	96.7	—	91.9	—	92.2	—
Dist. of Columbia	—	—	—	—	—	—	—	—
Florida	0.0	—	0.0	—	48.5	—	44.4	—
Georgia	22.7	—	0.0	—	43.5	—	11.2	—
Hawaii	—	—	—	—	—	—	—	—
Idaho	57.8	—	76.9	—	61.2	—	41.5	—
Illinois	96.9	—	82.2	—	88.1	—	91.6	—
Indiana	98.7	—	91.2	—	96.9	—	98.2	—
Iowa	95.1	91.6	84.4	83.4	87.6	94.0	86.4	86.8
Kansas	65.3	—	64.5	—	96.8	—	94.3	—
Kentucky	84.8	—	99.4	97.4	96.4	—	97.4	97.6
Louisiana	44.5	—	51.6	—	60.4	—	24.8	—
Maine	89.4	—	61.0	—	59.3	—	67.3	—
Maryland	89.5	—	98.6	91.8	87.3	—	97.4	95.0
Massachusetts	96.3	89.8	78.9	79.0	61.2	72.2	78.2	76.2
Michigan	96.2	—	71.3	—	88.8	—	84.1	—
Minnesota	91.3	—	59.5	—	90.1	—	88.8	—
Mississippi	4.7	—	1.2	0.0	15.0	—	10.4	0.0
Missouri	92.6	—	97.4	—	93.0	—	94.8	—
Montana	98.3	—	61.8	—	32.5	—	93.8	—
Nebraska	68.2	—	92.2	—	92.1	—	98.9	—
Nevada	33.1	—	39.6	—	35.8	—	22.4	—
New Hampshire	97.4	—	84.4	—	66.1	—	89.4	—
New Jersey	96.8	—	82.6	91.0	76.3	—	97.5	—
New Mexico	—	—	—	—	—	—	—	—
New York	97.0	—	87.9	—	82.9	—	97.8	—
North Carolina	79.2	—	81.8	—	93.9	—	91.0	—
North Dakota	57.3	—	25.7	—	89.3	—	80.8	—
Ohio	99.3	89.6	80.4	87.8	95.0	96.8	93.6	93.8
Oklahoma	—	—	—	—	—	—	—	—
Oregon	71.0	—	62.8	—	81.0	—	87.7	—
Pennsylvania	93.4	—	73.2	—	74.1	—	82.6	—
Rhode Island	95.9	99.6	81.2	72.6	65.5	72.0	73.1	75.0
South Carolina	22.8	—	22.8	—	24.7	—	8.8	—
South Dakota	53.9	—	34.4	—	66.5	—	95.3	—
Tennessee	81.9	—	98.5	—	93.1	—	78.2	—
Texas	58.5	—	40.0	—	39.8	—	21.2	—
Utah	—	—	—	97.8	67.6	—	90.8	—
Vermont	64.8	—	49.5	—	39.7	—	54.5	—
Virginia	63.0	0.0	87.8	—	88.4	68.0	73.6	—
Washington	91.9	—	57.8	—	56.8	—	0.0	—
West Virginia	97.3	—	91.8	—	94.5	—	98.6	—
Wisconsin	98.3	—	82.2	—	76.9	—	85.5	—
Wyoming	48.7	—	78.6	—	97.4	—	90.4	—

Notes: The composite competition index value for each state is the mean of a state's values for the party competition index devised by Paul David (1972) for all races held in a given election year among the following set of races: president, House, Senate, and governor. David's party competition index is defined as 100 − the absolute difference between the Democratic and Republican percentage of two-party vote for each of the races mentioned here. Zero (0) percent on David's index represents a complete absence of two-party competition for that election year, whereas a score of 100 percent indicates perfect competition between the two major parties. A state can only receive a composite index score of 0 if all races held in that state in a given election year are 100–0 vote splits between the two major parties. Conversely, a state can only receive a composite competition score of 100 if all races held in that state in a given election year are 50–50 vote splits between the two major parties. A state's overall value on the composite competition index for a given election year is obtained by averaging that state's party competition values for president (in Tables 8-36 through 8-53), House (in Tables 8-54 through 8-89), Senate (in Tables 8-90 through 8-104), and governor (in Tables 8-105 through 8-140). For example, in 1788 New Hampshire's party competition values were 0 percent for president (Table 8-36) and 90.6 percent for governor (Table 8-105). There was no election data available for the presidential race. Hence, New Hampshire's composite competition score in 1788 was 45.3 percent (90.6 ÷ 2) as shown in Table 8-9. In 1996 Illinois's party competition values were 80.8 percent for president (Table 8-53), 88.8 percent for House (Table 8-88), and 84.0 percent for Senate (Table 8-104). There was no race for governor in 1996. Thus Illinois's composite competition score in 1996 was 84.5 percent (253.6 ÷ 3) as shown in Table 8-35. The values for Democratic and Republican percent of two-party vote for president, House, Senate, and governor used to get the party competition values for these races in Tables 8-36 through 8-140 are taken from the state vote tables in Chapters 4, 5, 6, and 7, respectively (where the Republican vote percent is obtained by subtracting the Democratic vote percent from 100 for each race). The author's alternative party coding in these tables in Chapters 4–7 is used whenever it occurs in place of the conventional party coding of voting data. The Democratic Party is defined as the Anti-Federalists, Federalists, and Jackson Democrats prior to 1830 when the "Democratic Party" as such was established. The Republican Party is defined as the Federalists, National Republicans, and Whigs prior to the establishment of the "Republican Party" in the 1850s. See Appendix A for an explanation of the historical antecedents of the current Democratic and Republican parties. No special elections for any of the four races are used in the calculations, nor are partial voting data reported for any of the four races in any of the states. —indicates that the state had no data, either because no vote data were found for the state in question or the state had not yet entered the Union. Data for the District of Columbia are included from 1964 to the present, after being granted the right to elect presidential electors by the 23rd Amendment.

Sources: Tables 8-36 through 8-140. Specifically, state party competition values in Tables 8-36 through 8-140 for the presidential, House, Senate, and gubernatorial races are aggregated for each election year separately in order to obtain each state's average composite competition values for the election years shown in Tables 8-9 through 8-35.

Table 8-23 Composite Competition Index, by State, by Election Year, 1900–1907 (Percentages)

State	1900	1901	1902	1903	1904	1905	1906	1907
Alabama	54.6	—	49.7	—	41.1	—	23.1	—
Alaska	—	—	—	—	—	—	—	—
Arizona	—	—	—	—	—	—	—	—
Arkansas	67.1	—	44.1	—	72.7	—	52.8	—
California	86.4	—	94.9	—	68.0	—	86.9	—
Colorado	87.3	—	97.6	—	92.5	—	87.4	—
Connecticut	86.7	—	90.6	—	82.3	—	86.9	—
Delaware	91.6	—	87.6	—	90.8	—	91.8	—
Dist. of Columbia	—	—	—	—	—	—	—	—
Florida	36.8	—	0.0	—	40.6	—	11.0	—
Georgia	27.9	—	0.0	—	26.4	—	1.3	—
Hawaii	—	—	—	—	—	—	—	—
Idaho	96.6	—	88.3	—	63.7	—	79.6	—
Illinois	92.5	—	95.8	—	69.7	—	83.4	—
Indiana	96.3	—	96.8	—	87.4	—	98.8	—
Iowa	81.6	77.6	83.2	80.2	68.0	—	90.4	—
Kansas	94.2	—	84.5	—	68.8	—	93.2	—
Kentucky	98.6	—	88.4	94.0	96.8	—	88.6	95.6
Louisiana	42.9	—	30.8	—	19.8	—	21.6	—
Maine	71.3	—	73.9	—	72.6	—	93.5	—
Maryland	95.0	—	95.6	93.8	98.7	—	96.4	96.0
Massachusetts	77.7	76.2	90.3	90.0	82.8	94.0	87.5	62.0
Michigan	82.3	—	85.7	—	68.4	—	62.8	—
Minnesota	85.5	—	75.4	—	63.5	—	63.8	—
Mississippi	15.0	—	0.0	0.0	6.0	—	0.0	0.0
Missouri	94.5	—	91.4	—	96.4	—	99.2	—
Montana	76.3	—	88.6	—	84.7	—	89.4	—
Nebraska	98.3	—	96.2	—	78.3	—	92.6	—
Nevada	79.0	—	88.7	—	85.7	—	77.8	—
New Hampshire	78.7	—	85.0	—	79.0	—	88.7	—
New Jersey	85.5	95.2	94.4	—	84.5	—	99.0	97.8
New Mexico	—	—	—	—	—	—	—	—
New York	91.2	—	99.3	—	90.5	—	95.7	—
North Carolina	85.1	—	60.8	—	77.2	—	76.8	—
North Dakota	75.8	—	66.6	—	47.5	—	81.4	—
Ohio	93.6	91.6	86.8	86.4	74.4	95.2	90.0	—
Oklahoma	—	—	—	—	—	—	—	87.3
Oregon	85.7	—	90.3	—	59.2	—	86.6	—
Pennsylvania	74.9	—	78.3	—	59.2	—	84.7	—
Rhode Island	76.3	85.4	92.9	97.8	88.7	90.4	97.8	96.4
South Carolina	8.8	—	2.3	—	5.9	—	1.5	—
South Dakota	85.2	—	61.0	—	49.6	—	58.4	—
Tennessee	89.5	—	72.6	—	88.1	—	89.1	—
Texas	54.2	—	36.5	—	41.7	—	28.1	—
Utah	98.0	—	93.2	—	79.5	—	77.6	—
Vermont	50.6	—	39.1	—	46.9	—	68.1	—
Virginia	81.5	82.2	64.8	—	71.6	70.4	71.2	—
Washington	91.9	—	73.2	—	62.5	—	61.4	—
West Virginia	91.3	—	93.6	—	90.9	—	88.0	—
Wisconsin	75.9	—	84.2	—	73.7	—	75.7	—
Wyoming	82.0	—	76.9	—	63.7	—	71.4	—

Notes: The composite competition index value for each state is the mean of a state's values for the party competition index devised by Paul David (1972) for all races held in a given election year among the following set of races: president, House, Senate, and governor. David's party competition index is defined as 100 − the absolute difference between the Democratic and Republican percentage of two-party vote for each of the races mentioned here. Zero (0) percent on David's index represents a complete absence of two-party competition for that election year, whereas a score of 100 percent indicates perfect competition between the two major parties. A state can only receive a composite index score of 0 if all races held in that state in a given election year are 100–0 vote splits between the two major parties. Conversely, a state can only receive a composite competition score of 100 if all races held in a given election year are 50–50 vote splits between the two major parties. A state's overall value on the composite competition index for a given election year is obtained by averaging that state's party competition values for president (in Tables 8-36 through 8-53), House (in Tables 8-54 through 8-89), Senate (in Tables 8-90 through 8-104), and governor (in Tables 8-105 through 8-140). For example, in 1788 New Hampshire's party competition values were 0 percent for president (Table 8-36) and 90.6 percent for governor (Table 8-105). There were no election data available for the presidential race. Hence, New Hampshire's composite competition score in 1788 was 45.3 percent (90.6 ÷ 2) as shown in Table 8-9. In 1996 Illinois's party competition values were 80.8 percent for president (Table 8-53), 88.8 percent for House (Table 8-88), and 84.0 percent for Senate (Table 8-104). There was no race for governor in 1996. Thus Illinois's composite competition score in 1996 was 84.5 percent (253.6 ÷ 3) as shown in Table 8-35. The values for Democratic and Republican percent of two-party vote for president, House, Senate, and governor used to get the party competition values for these races in Tables 8-36 through 8-140 are taken from the state vote tables in Chapters 4, 5, 6, and 7, respectively (where the Republican vote percent is obtained by subtracting the Democratic vote percent from 100 for each race). The author's alternative party coding in these tables in Chapters 4–7 is used whenever it occurs in place of the conventional party coding of voting data. The Democratic Party is defined as the Anti-Federalists, Federalists, and Jackson Democrats prior to 1830 when the "Democratic Party" as such was established. The Republican Party is defined as the Federalists, National Republicans, and Whigs prior to the establishment of the "Republican Party" in the 1850s. See Appendix A for an explanation of the historical antecedents of the current Democratic and Republican parties. No special elections for any of the four races are used in the calculations, nor are partial voting data reported for any of the four races in any of the states. —indicates that the state had no data, either because no vote data were found for the state in question or the state had not yet entered the Union. Data for the District of Columbia are included from 1964 to the present, after being granted the right to elect presidential electors by the 23rd Amendment.

Sources: Tables 8-36 through 8-140. Specifically, state party competition values in Tables 8-36 through 8-140 for the presidential, House, Senate, and gubernatorial races are aggregated for each election year separately in order to obtain each state's average composite competition values for the election years shown in Tables 8-9 through 8-35.

Table 8-24 Composite Competition Index, by State, by Election Year, 1908–1915 (Percentages)

State	1908	1909	1910	1911	1912	1913	1914	1915
Alabama	44.6	—	35.9	—	20.5	—	32.9	—
Alaska	—	—	—	—	—	—	—	—
Arizona	—	—	—	87.5	43.8	—	57.3	—
Arkansas	66.5	—	50.9	—	53.1	—	39.8	—
California	77.3	—	82.0	—	41.9	—	76.1	—
Colorado	97.4	—	95.0	—	70.6	—	90.9	—
Connecticut	81.3	—	96.7	—	94.7	—	91.5	—
Delaware	95.2	—	95.0	—	88.4	—	94.8	—
Dist. of Columbia	—	—	—	—	—	—	—	—
Florida	39.3	—	8.4	—	16.8	—	0.0	—
Georgia	24.5	—	10.0	—	5.6	—	0.0	—
Hawaii	—	—	—	—	—	—	—	—
Idaho	86.1	—	90.1	—	89.6	—	92.7	—
Illinois	88.9	—	98.6	—	82.2	—	98.0	—
Indiana	97.9	—	94.2	—	70.2	—	91.2	—
Iowa	86.3	—	90.9	—	92.6	—	89.8	—
Kansas	90.5	—	89.0	—	90.2	—	94.7	—
Kentucky	97.9	—	91.2	92.6	63.7	—	86.7	99.8
Louisiana	20.9	—	15.6	—	9.9	—	3.0	—
Maine	85.4	—	95.8	—	87.5	—	98.5	—
Maryland	98.4	—	96.8	98.6	69.5	—	92.5	98.6
Massachusetts	77.7	97.8	94.5	98.0	92.5	77.8	94.5	98.6
Michigan	80.5	—	84.9	—	94.3	—	86.1	—
Minnesota	74.9	—	66.0	—	74.8	—	80.4	—
Mississippi	7.3	—	0.0	0.0	2.6	—	0.0	0.0
Missouri	99.2	—	98.6	—	78.5	—	88.3	—
Montana	95.5	—	92.6	—	87.2	—	82.8	—
Nebraska	98.3	—	96.4	—	86.7	—	95.4	—
Nevada	89.2	—	89.0	—	78.4	—	96.2	—
New Hampshire	84.8	—	92.2	—	95.9	—	89.1	—
New Jersey	86.9	—	89.5	—	73.2	89.6	97.8	—
New Mexico	—	—	—	97.3	90.3	—	90.8	—
New York	91.5	—	95.7	—	82.9	—	92.0	—
North Carolina	87.5	—	80.2	—	47.0	—	81.3	—
North Dakota	79.3	—	82.1	—	81.4	—	77.5	—
Ohio	97.0	—	89.9	—	79.5	—	95.3	—
Oklahoma	94.5	—	89.4	—	83.3	—	84.7	—
Oregon	67.5	—	87.0	—	85.9	—	85.1	—
Pennsylvania	76.2	—	63.2	—	77.5	—	75.1	—
Rhode Island	83.0	81.2	96.5	89.2	96.7	—	90.8	—
South Carolina	5.7	—	1.2	—	0.9	—	0.1	—
South Dakota	76.9	—	71.6	—	59.7	—	87.4	—
Tennessee	91.9	—	81.0	—	77.7	—	69.7	—
Texas	42.9	—	21.7	—	19.5	—	11.9	—
Utah	83.1	—	78.6	—	92.5	—	97.7	—
Vermont	48.9	—	61.1	—	80.5	—	67.1	—
Virginia	74.1	72.6	63.8	—	39.9	0.0	57.8	—
Washington	69.5	—	72.8	—	93.4	—	84.3	—
West Virginia	91.9	—	95.6	—	85.3	—	96.0	—
Wisconsin	81.3	—	80.4	—	93.0	—	91.8	—
Wyoming	80.6	—	83.8	—	92.2	—	90.8	—

Notes: The composite competition index value for each state is the mean of a state's values for the party competition index devised by Paul David (1972) for all races held in a given election year among the following set of races: president, House, Senate, and governor. David's party competition index is defined as 100 − the absolute difference between the Democratic and Republican percentage of two-party vote for each of the races mentioned here. Zero (0) percent on David's index represents a complete absence of two-party competition for that election year, whereas a score of 100 percent indicates perfect competition between the two major parties. A state can only receive a composite index score of 0 if all races held in that state in a given election year are 100–0 vote splits between the two major parties. Conversely, a state can only receive a composite competition score of 100 if all races held in that state in a given election year are 50–50 vote splits between the two major parties. A state's overall value on the composite competition index for a given election year is obtained by averaging that state's party competition values for president (in Tables 8-36 through 8-53), House (in Tables 8-54 through 8-89), Senate (in Tables 8-90 through 8-104), and governor (in Tables 8-105 through 8-140). For example, in 1788 New Hampshire's party competition values were 0 percent for president (Table 8-36) and 90.6 percent for governor (Table 8-105). There were no election data available for the presidential race. Hence, New Hampshire's composite competition score in 1788 was 45.3 percent (90.6 ÷ 2) as shown in Table 8-9. In 1996 Illinois's party competition values were 80.8 percent for president (Table 8-53), 88.8 percent for House (Table 8-88), and 84.0 percent for Senate (Table 8-104). There was no race for governor in 1996. Thus Illinois's composite competition score in 1996 was 84.5 percent (253.6 ÷ 3) as shown in Table 8-35. The values for Democratic and Republican percent of two-party vote for president, House, Senate, and governor used to get the party competition values for these races in Tables 8-36 through 8-140 are taken from the state vote tables in Chapters 4, 5, 6, and 7, respectively (where the Republican vote percent is obtained by subtracting the Democratic vote percent from 100 for each race). The author's alternative party coding in these tables in Chapters 4–7 is used whenever it occurs in place of the conventional party coding of voting data. The Democratic Party is defined as the Anti-Federalists, Federalists, and Jackson Democrats prior to 1830 when the "Democratic Party" as such was established. The Republican Party is defined as the Federalists, National Republicans, and Whigs prior to the establishment of the "Republican Party" in the 1850s. See Appendix A for an explanation of the historical antecedents of the current Democratic and Republican parties. No special elections for any of the four races are used in the calculations, nor are partial voting data reported for any of the four races in any of the states. —indicates that the state had no data, either because no vote data were found for the state in question or the state had not yet entered the Union. Data for the District of Columbia are included from 1964 to the present, after being granted the right to elect presidential electors by the 23rd Amendment.

Sources: Tables 8-36 through 8-140. Specifically, state party competition values in Tables 8-36 through 8-140 for the presidential, House, Senate, and gubernatorial races are aggregated for each election year separately in order to obtain each state's average composite competition values for the election years shown in Tables 8-9 through 8-35.

Table 8-25 Composite Competition Index, by State, by Election Year, 1916–1923 (Percentages)

State	1916	1917	1918	1919	1920	1921	1922	1923
Alabama	41.6	—	9.5	—	61.1	—	40.2	—
Alaska	—	—	—	—	—	—	—	—
Arizona	80.0	—	88.3	—	88.7	—	72.2	—
Arkansas	49.3	—	0.0	—	67.3	—	34.1	—
California	81.3	—	37.9	—	63.0	—	57.3	—
Colorado	84.4	—	94.8	—	78.8	—	97.6	—
Connecticut	95.7	—	96.1	—	70.8	—	93.1	—
Delaware	96.7	—	96.4	—	87.1	—	95.2	—
Dist. of Columbia	—	—	—	—	—	—	—	—
Florida	32.0	—	0.0	—	48.1	—	24.1	—
Georgia	13.3	—	10.9	—	43.9	—	1.6	—
Hawaii	—	—	—	—	—	—	—	—
Idaho	93.5	—	73.1	—	74.0	—	79.1	—
Illinois	88.8	—	89.0	—	61.3	—	82.8	—
Indiana	98.0	—	90.0	—	85.5	—	97.4	—
Iowa	80.9	—	78.7	—	58.4	—	68.2	—
Kansas	88.1	—	71.7	—	72.5	—	93.3	—
Kentucky	94.4	—	97.0	91.4	98.7	—	83.0	92.4
Louisiana	5.3	—	0.0	—	16.5	—	0.0	—
Maine	92.9	—	90.8	—	65.1	—	84.6	—
Maryland	96.1	—	96.6	100.0	91.6	—	95.4	87.2
Massachusetts	90.7	75.0	89.8	75.4	61.4	—	92.2	—
Michigan	86.2	—	80.1	—	51.4	—	79.7	—
Minnesota	75.2	—	39.5	—	37.9	—	53.3	—
Mississippi	3.3	—	0.0	0.0	17.4	—	4.4	0.0
Missouri	97.3	—	94.2	—	89.5	—	96.8	—
Montana	90.3	—	96.1	—	75.3	—	93.2	—
Nebraska	94.1	—	89.3	—	75.3	—	88.5	—
Nevada	89.5	—	93.6	—	84.9	—	84.2	—
New Hampshire	95.5	—	92.0	—	80.5	—	95.7	—
New Jersey	86.1	—	94.0	96.6	65.9	—	94.5	—
New Mexico	96.9	—	96.9	—	93.7	—	90.0	—
New York	88.4	—	96.5	—	76.6	—	89.9	—
North Carolina	83.7	—	79.1	—	85.4	—	76.0	—
North Dakota	70.5	—	75.3	—	62.6	—	47.1	—
Ohio	97.0	—	93.6	—	84.5	—	95.6	—
Oklahoma	80.6	—	86.4	—	95.6	—	83.8	—
Oregon	75.6	—	72.9	—	70.6	—	72.5	—
Pennsylvania	82.5	—	69.2	—	59.6	—	76.1	—
Rhode Island	92.1	—	91.7	—	69.1	—	93.7	—
South Carolina	2.8	—	0.5	—	2.6	—	1.9	—
South Dakota	88.1	—	72.3	—	52.2	—	65.4	—
Tennessee	86.9	—	65.5	—	94.5	—	72.9	—
Texas	30.0	—	20.9	—	50.5	—	44.5	—
Utah	82.7	—	85.2	—	81.1	—	96.4	—
Vermont	56.6	—	57.6	—	45.3	—	61.7	—
Virginia	42.2	56.0	20.2	—	75.4	67.4	58.9	—
Washington	90.6	—	84.0	—	48.9	—	76.0	—
West Virginia	98.9	—	93.0	—	88.4	—	97.0	—
Wisconsin	79.9	—	71.2	—	51.5	—	24.5	—
Wyoming	93.1	—	81.3	—	63.3	—	92.5	—

Notes: The composite competition index value for each state is the mean of a state's values for the party competition index devised by Paul David (1972) for all races held in a given election year among the following set of races: president, House, Senate, and governor. David's party competition index is defined as 100 − the absolute difference between the Democratic and Republican percentage of two-party vote for each of the races mentioned here. Zero (0) percent on David's index represents a complete absence of two-party competition for that election year, whereas a score of 100 percent indicates perfect competition between the two major parties. A state can only receive a composite index score of 0 if all races held in that state in a given election year are 100–0 vote splits between the two major parties. Conversely, a state can only receive a composite competition score of 100 if all races held in that state in a given election year are 50–50 vote splits between the two major parties. A state's overall value on the composite competition index for a given election year is obtained by averaging that state's party competition values for president (in Tables 8-36 through 8-53), House (in Tables 8-54 through 8-89), Senate (in Tables 8-90 through 8-104), and governor (in Tables 8-105 through 8-140). For example, in 1788 New Hampshire's party competition values were 0 percent for president (Table 8-36) and 90.6 percent for governor (Table 8-105). There were no election data available for the presidential race. Hence, New Hampshire's composite competition score in 1788 was 45.3 percent (90.6 ÷ 2) as shown in Table 8-9. In 1996 Illinois's party competition values were 80.8 percent for president (Table 8-53), 88.8 percent for House (Table 8-88), and 84.0 percent for Senate (Table 8-104). There was no race for governor in 1996. Thus Illinois's composite competition score in 1996 was 84.5 percent (253.6 ÷ 3) as shown in Table 8-35. The values for Democratic and Republican percent of two-party vote for president, House, Senate, and governor used to get the party competition values for these races in Tables 8-36 through 8-140 are taken from the state vote tables in Chapters 4, 5, 6, and 7, respectively (where the Republican vote percent is obtained by subtracting the Democratic vote percent from 100 for each race). The author's alternative party coding in these tables in Chapters 4–7 is used whenever it occurs in place of the conventional party coding of voting data. The Democratic Party is defined as the Anti-Federalists, Federalists, and Jackson Democrats prior to 1830 when the "Democratic Party" as such was established. The Republican Party is defined as the Federalists, National Republicans, and Whigs prior to the establishment of the "Republican Party" in the 1850s. See Appendix A for an explanation of the historical antecedents of the current Democratic and Republican parties. No special elections for any of the four races are used in the calculations, nor are partial voting data reported for any of the four races in any of the states. —indicates that the state had no data, either because no vote data were found for the state in question or the state had not yet entered the Union. Data for the District of Columbia are included from 1964 to the present, after being granted the right to elect presidential electors by the 23rd Amendment.

Sources: Tables 8-36 through 8-140. Specifically, state party competition values in Tables 8-36 through 8-140 for the presidential, House, Senate, and gubernatorial races are aggregated for each election year separately in order to obtain each state's average composite competition values for the election years shown in Tables 8-9 through 8-35.

Table 8-26 Composite Competition Index, by State, by Election Year, 1924–1931 (Percentages)

State	1924	1925	1926	1927	1928	1929	1930	1931
Alabama	48.7	—	35.7	—	66.4	—	11.1	—
Alaska	—	—	—	—	—	—	—	—
Arizona	75.5	—	84.9	—	87.4	—	48.6	—
Arkansas	53.1	—	36.7	—	55.7	—	12.5	—
California	37.5	—	53.9	—	44.1	—	37.0	—
Colorado	82.8	—	88.0	—	74.7	—	85.7	—
Connecticut	64.7	—	71.6	—	91.7	—	98.4	—
Delaware	59.8	—	86.2	—	74.1	—	89.6	—
Dist. of Columbia	—	—	—	—	—	—	—	—
Florida	48.8	—	45.6	—	71.8	—	24.6	—
Georgia	11.0	—	0.0	—	44.0	—	2.7	—
Hawaii	—	—	—	—	—	—	—	—
Idaho	51.9	—	61.0	—	73.5	—	71.8	—
Illinois	68.8	—	82.8	—	84.1	—	83.8	—
Indiana	88.0	—	96.3	—	89.1	—	94.2	—
Iowa	65.8	—	68.5	—	69.3	—	77.5	—
Kansas	67.5	—	74.7	—	65.1	—	87.9	—
Kentucky	93.1	—	95.9	95.8	84.5	—	94.7	91.2
Louisiana	11.5	—	1.6	—	24.3	—	1.7	—
Maine	72.7	—	82.8	—	61.0	—	81.7	—
Maryland	96.2	—	84.9	—	91.5	—	84.1	—
Massachusetts	79.9	—	81.3	—	96.3	—	93.5	—
Michigan	45.3	—	58.0	—	56.6	—	57.9	—
Minnesota	22.9	—	17.7	—	47.2	—	47.9	—
Mississippi	5.6	—	0.0	0.0	11.9	—	0.0	0.0
Missouri	97.2	—	97.6	—	94.3	—	99.0	—
Montana	84.6	—	99.2	—	85.9	—	88.0	—
Nebraska	84.2	—	98.9	—	81.3	—	92.3	—
Nevada	84.1	—	88.3	—	83.7	—	92.4	—
New Hampshire	82.4	—	77.2	—	83.2	—	84.1	—
New Jersey	68.7	95.8	86.2	—	83.1	—	83.2	81.4
New Mexico	96.9	—	96.7	—	87.7	—	88.1	—
New York	85.5	—	95.1	—	98.5	—	83.1	—
North Carolina	77.8	—	78.2	—	89.6	—	76.6	—
North Dakota	52.5	—	29.5	—	66.7	—	53.2	—
Ohio	77.7	—	93.1	—	79.0	—	96.0	—
Oklahoma	83.5	—	88.7	—	85.5	—	84.4	—
Oregon	63.1	—	80.2	—	65.0	—	82.2	—
Pennsylvania	51.5	—	63.7	—	66.3	—	77.0	—
Rhode Island	80.9	—	87.8	—	98.1	—	97.9	—
South Carolina	1.4	—	0.0	—	8.5	—	0.0	—
South Dakota	58.9	—	85.3	—	85.9	—	86.3	—
Tennessee	82.4	—	65.2	—	81.9	—	66.8	—
Texas	45.0	—	15.0	—	48.4	—	31.9	—
Utah	86.0	—	76.5	—	88.0	—	87.4	—
Vermont	37.8	—	59.7	—	58.1	—	61.6	—
Virginia	43.6	51.8	61.2	—	52.1	74.0	33.8	—
Washington	54.3	—	77.5	—	76.6	—	53.6	—
West Virginia	95.2	—	96.6	—	91.3	—	87.3	—
Wisconsin	56.5	—	26.3	—	57.7	—	45.8	—
Wyoming	72.1	—	87.9	—	86.7	—	83.2	—

Notes: The composite competition index value for each state is the mean of a state's values for the party competition index devised by Paul David (1972) for all races held in a given election year among the following set of races: president, House, Senate, and governor. David's party competition index is defined as 100 − the absolute difference between the Democratic and Republican percentage of two-party vote for each of the races mentioned here. Zero (0) percent on David's index represents a complete absence of two-party competition for that election year, whereas a score of 100 percent indicates perfect competition between the two major parties. A state can only receive a composite index score of 0 if all races held in that state in a given election year are 100–0 vote splits between the two major parties. Conversely, a state can only receive a composite competition score of 100 if all races held in that state in a given election year are 50–50 vote splits between the two major parties. A state's overall value on the composite competition index for a given election year is obtained by averaging that state's party competition values for president (in Tables 8-36 through 8-53), House (in Tables 8-54 through 8-89), Senate (in Tables 8-90 through 8-104), and governor (in Tables 8-105 through 8-140). For example, in 1788 New Hampshire's party competition values were 0 percent for president (Table 8-36) and 90.6 percent for governor (Table 8-105). There were no election data available for the presidential race. Hence, New Hampshire's composite competition score in 1788 was 45.3 percent (90.6 ÷ 2) as shown in Table 8-9. In 1996 Illinois's party competition values were 80.8 percent for president (Table 8-53), 88.8 percent for House (Table 8-88), and 84.0 percent for Senate (Table 8-104). There was no race for governor in 1996. Thus Illinois's composite competition score in 1996 was 84.5 percent (253.6 ÷ 3) as shown in Table 8-35. The values for Democratic and Republican percent of two-party vote for president, House, Senate, and governor used to get the party competition values for these races in Tables 8-36 through 8-140 are taken from the state vote tables in Chapters 4, 5, 6, and 7, respectively (where the Republican vote percent is obtained by subtracting the Democratic vote percent from 100 for each race). The author's alternative party coding in these tables in Chapters 4–7 is used whenever it occurs in place of the conventional party coding of voting data. The Democratic Party is defined as the Anti-Federalists, Federalists, and Jackson Democrats prior to 1830 when the "Democratic Party" as such was established. The Republican Party is defined as the Federalists, National Republicans, and Whigs prior to the establishment of the "Republican Party" in the 1850s. See Appendix A for an explanation of the historical antecedents of the current Democratic and Republican parties. No special elections for any of the four races are used in the calculations, nor are partial voting data reported for any of the four races in any of the states. —indicates that the state had no data, either because no vote data were found for the state in question or the state had not yet entered the Union. Data for the District of Columbia are included from 1964 to the present, after being granted the right to elect presidential electors by the 23rd Amendment.

Sources: Tables 8-36 through 8-140. Specifically, state party competition values in Tables 8-36 through 8-140 for the presidential, House, Senate, and gubernatorial races are aggregated for each election year separately in order to obtain each state's average composite competition values for the election years shown in Tables 8-9 through 8-35.

Table 8-27 Composite Competition Index, by State, by Election Year, 1932–1939 (Percentages)

State	1932	1933	1934	1935	1936	1937	1938	1939
Alabama	25.3	—	19.1	—	21.0	—	22.5	—
Alaska	—	—	—	—	—	—	—	—
Arizona	63.9	—	63.5	—	51.0	—	47.0	—
Arkansas	17.3	—	16.8	—	28.7	—	10.5	—
California	85.3	—	60.1	—	76.7	—	93.7	—
Colorado	88.2	—	77.8	—	77.9	—	83.6	—
Connecticut	98.6	—	97.3	—	85.3	—	97.3	—
Delaware	95.1	—	93.1	—	92.8	—	86.6	—
Dist. of Columbia	—	—	—	—	—	—	—	—
Florida	41.7	—	0.0	—	40.7	—	22.0	—
Georgia	10.1	—	0.5	—	9.1	—	0.0	—
Hawaii	—	—	—	—	—	—	—	—
Idaho	81.8	—	83.6	—	74.2	—	89.2	—
Illinois	88.7	—	88.6	—	85.4	—	96.9	—
Indiana	87.8	—	95.5	—	87.1	—	99.0	—
Iowa	88.9	—	92.2	—	95.9	—	93.5	—
Kansas	96.1	—	95.2	—	95.7	—	87.5	—
Kentucky	81.1	—	89.4	90.6	81.1	—	78.9	87.0
Louisiana	3.5	—	0.0	—	5.6	—	0.0	—
Maine	95.1	—	96.5	—	88.1	—	88.6	—
Maryland	68.2	—	88.3	—	77.4	—	75.9	—
Massachusetts	94.7	—	87.6	—	94.0	—	91.8	—
Michigan	93.2	—	95.9	—	89.9	—	93.4	—
Minnesota	80.1	—	77.0	—	32.3	—	34.9	—
Mississippi	7.1	—	0.0	0.0	2.7	—	0.0	0.0
Missouri	74.3	—	79.2	—	80.6	—	79.9	—
Montana	86.8	—	59.9	—	72.8	—	99.6	—
Nebraska	82.7	—	91.8	—	82.7	—	94.8	—
Nevada	78.5	—	67.9	—	58.7	—	75.1	—
New Hampshire	96.8	—	98.8	—	93.9	—	88.2	—
New Jersey	98.1	—	93.0	—	87.1	96.8	95.0	—
New Mexico	77.8	—	96.9	—	77.5	—	89.2	—
New York	83.7	—	80.3	—	83.9	—	93.7	—
North Carolina	60.7	—	70.2	—	59.0	—	69.7	—
North Dakota	67.4	—	83.3	—	80.0	—	57.8	—
Ohio	94.5	—	89.5	—	87.5	—	94.4	—
Oklahoma	58.3	—	71.5	—	62.3	—	63.1	—
Oregon	85.8	—	90.6	—	86.9	—	86.1	—
Pennsylvania	90.5	—	93.7	—	85.1	—	91.9	—
Rhode Island	88.6	—	85.5	—	92.1	—	89.8	—
South Carolina	3.8	—	0.2	—	2.4	—	1.6	—
South Dakota	84.4	—	83.5	—	95.6	—	91.8	—
Tennessee	68.5	—	67.1	—	48.4	—	55.6	—
Texas	37.7	—	4.9	—	16.5	—	4.1	—
Utah	86.2	—	82.0	—	68.4	—	83.2	—
Vermont	79.9	—	89.2	—	81.8	—	68.6	—
Virginia	61.4	49.4	45.5	—	40.9	32.0	42.2	—
Washington	72.8	—	68.3	—	62.5	—	76.1	—
West Virginia	91.6	—	88.7	—	80.5	—	89.8	—
Wisconsin	82.3	—	83.0	—	82.7	—	50.5	—
Wyoming	91.1	—	84.1	—	84.3	—	87.3	—

Notes: The composite competition index value for each state is the mean of a state's values for the party competition index devised by Paul David (1972) for all races held in a given election year among the following set of races: president, House, Senate, and governor. David's party competition index is defined as 100 − the absolute difference between the Democratic and Republican percentage of two-party vote for each of the races mentioned here. Zero (0) percent on David's index represents a complete absence of two-party competition for that election year, whereas a score of 100 percent indicates perfect competition between the two major parties. A state can only receive a composite index score of 0 if all races held in that state in a given election year are 100–0 vote splits between the two major parties. Conversely, a state can only receive a composite competition score of 100 if all races held in that state in a given election year are 50–50 vote splits between the two major parties. A state's overall value on the composite competition index for a given election year is obtained by averaging that state's party competition values for president (in Tables 8-36 through 8-53), House (in Tables 8-54 through 8-89), Senate (in Tables 8-90 through 8-104), and governor (in Tables 8-105 through 8-140). For example, in 1788 New Hampshire's party competition values were 0 percent for president (Table 8-36) and 90.6 percent for governor (Table 8-105). There were no election data available for the presidential race. Hence, New Hampshire's composite competition score in 1788 was 45.3 percent (90.6 ÷ 2) as shown in Table 8-9. In 1996 Illinois's party competition values were 80.8 percent for president (Table 8-53), 88.8 percent for House (Table 8-88), and 84.0 percent for Senate (Table 8-104). There was no race for governor in 1996. Thus Illinois's composite competition score in 1996 was 84.5 percent (253.6 ÷ 3) as shown in Table 8-35. The values for Democratic and Republican percent of two-party vote for president, House, Senate, and governor used to get the party competition values for these races in Tables 8-36 through 8-140 are taken from the state vote tables in Chapters 4, 5, 6, and 7, respectively (where the Republican vote percent is obtained by subtracting the Democratic vote percent from 100 for each race). The author's alternative party coding in these tables in Chapters 4–7 is used whenever it occurs in place of the conventional party coding of voting data. The Democratic Party is defined as the Anti-Federalists, Federalists, and Jackson Democrats prior to 1830 when the "Democratic Party" as such was established. The Republican Party is defined as the Federalists, National Republicans, and Whigs prior to the establishment of the "Republican Party" in the 1850s. See Appendix A for an explanation of the historical antecedents of the current Democratic and Republican parties. No special elections for any of the four races are used in the calculations, nor are partial voting data reported for any of the four races in any of the states. —indicates that the state had no data, either because no vote data were found for the state in question or the state had not yet entered the Union. Data for the District of Columbia are included from 1964 to the present, after being granted the right to elect presidential electors by the 23rd Amendment.

Sources: Tables 8-36 through 8-140. Specifically, state party competition values in Tables 8-36 through 8-140 for the presidential, House, Senate, and gubernatorial races are aggregated for each election year separately in order to obtain each state's average composite competition values for the election years shown in Tables 8-9 through 8-35.

Table 8-28 Composite Competition Index, by State, by Election Year, 1940–1947 (Percentages)

State	1940	1941	1942	1943	1944	1945	1946	1947
Alabama	19.9	—	7.4	—	30.2	—	19.2	—
Alaska	—	—	—	—	—	—	—	—
Arizona	63.6	—	56.1	—	61.8	—	68.9	—
Arkansas	22.3	—	0.0	—	33.2	—	21.2	—
California	57.7	—	91.5	—	93.5	—	61.9	—
Colorado	92.9	—	89.8	—	90.3	—	92.0	—
Connecticut	94.5	—	95.3	—	95.9	—	84.7	—
Delaware	93.9	—	91.4	—	96.1	—	88.4	—
Dist. of Columbia	—	—	—	—	—	—	—	—
Florida	19.9	—	0.0	—	47.4	—	40.5	—
Georgia	12.3	—	0.0	—	12.2	—	0.0	—
Hawaii	—	—	—	—	—	—	—	—
Idaho	94.3	—	98.1	—	96.6	—	87.1	—
Illinois	96.5	—	95.1	—	96.1	—	89.4	—
Indiana	98.8	—	89.0	—	95.9	—	88.9	—
Iowa	93.5	—	78.0	—	91.6	—	80.8	—
Kansas	90.0	—	82.1	—	75.5	—	85.5	—
Kentucky	79.9	—	87.6	98.4	90.5	—	93.2	85.2
Louisiana	12.7	—	0.0	—	9.7	—	10.6	—
Maine	80.8	—	64.6	—	71.0	—	74.5	—
Maryland	76.3	—	91.1	—	86.7	—	95.2	—
Massachusetts	93.8	—	92.5	—	93.5	—	87.9	—
Michigan	96.4	—	93.6	—	94.8	—	73.5	—
Minnesota	61.3	—	39.5	—	84.5	—	81.0	—
Mississippi	2.8	—	0.0	0.0	9.8	—	0.0	5.0
Missouri	96.9	—	96.8	—	97.5	—	95.0	—
Montana	80.6	—	93.7	—	85.5	—	95.2	—
Nebraska	83.0	—	60.7	—	65.5	—	64.0	—
Nevada	76.6	—	86.1	—	82.6	—	85.7	—
New Hampshire	96.1	—	92.1	—	95.6	—	74.9	—
New Jersey	94.1	—	92.0	88.8	95.8	—	82.2	—
New Mexico	86.5	—	85.0	—	92.3	—	95.6	—
New York	94.5	—	90.4	—	94.7	—	89.2	—
North Carolina	49.9	—	61.4	—	62.0	—	77.4	—
North Dakota	76.2	—	68.7	—	74.5	—	59.9	—
Ohio	94.6	—	82.6	—	97.3	—	88.1	—
Oklahoma	76.3	—	90.0	—	86.5	—	88.2	—
Oregon	87.8	—	57.9	—	83.5	—	66.1	—
Pennsylvania	94.8	—	90.5	—	98.4	—	82.2	—
Rhode Island	88.3	—	83.5	—	80.6	—	90.7	—
South Carolina	5.9	—	0.0	—	7.7	—	0.9	—
South Dakota	84.3	—	78.1	—	73.6	—	68.5	—
Tennessee	58.6	—	58.3	—	73.0	—	60.9	—
Texas	16.6	—	5.8	—	22.7	—	16.8	—
Utah	81.0	—	93.8	—	84.5	—	97.4	—
Vermont	75.5	—	51.9	—	74.4	—	53.8	—
Virginia	34.0	36.4	13.5	—	61.9	63.6	65.2	—
Washington	89.3	—	94.6	—	91.2	—	87.0	—
West Virginia	86.4	—	94.3	—	91.0	—	99.6	—
Wisconsin	66.6	—	61.9	—	88.9	—	74.1	—
Wyoming	89.9	—	95.6	—	93.1	—	89.9	—

Notes: The composite competition index value for each state is the mean of a state's values for the party competition index devised by Paul David (1972) for all races held in a given election year among the following set of races: president, House, Senate, and governor. David's party competition index is defined as 100 − the absolute difference between the Democratic and Republican percentage of two-party vote for each of the races mentioned here. Zero (0) percent on David's index represents a complete absence of two-party competition for that election year, whereas a score of 100 percent indicates perfect competition between the two major parties. A state can only receive a composite index score of 0 if all races held in that state in a given election year are 100–0 vote splits between the two major parties. Conversely, a state can only receive a composite competition score of 100 if all races held in that state in a given election year are 50–50 vote splits between the two major parties. A state's overall value on the composite competition index for a given election year is obtained by averaging that state's party competition values for president (in Tables 8-36 through 8-53), House (in Tables 8-54 through 8-89), Senate (in Tables 8-90 through 8-104), and governor (in Tables 8-105 through 8-140). For example, in 1788 New Hampshire's party competition values were 0 percent for president (Table 8-36) and 90.6 percent for governor (Table 8-105). There were no election data available for the presidential race. Hence, New Hampshire's composite competition score in 1788 was 45.3 percent (90.6 ÷ 2) as shown in Table 8-9. In 1996 Illinois's party competition values were 80.8 percent for president (Table 8-53), 88.8 percent for House (Table 8-88), and 84.0 percent for Senate (Table 8-104). There was no race for governor in 1996. Thus Illinois's composite competition score in 1996 was 84.5 percent (253.6 ÷ 3) as shown in Table 8-35. The values for Democratic and Republican percent of two-party vote for president, House, Senate, and governor used to get the party competition values for these races in Tables 8-36 through 8-140 are taken from the state vote tables in Chapters 4, 5, 6, and 7, respectively (where the Republican vote percent is obtained by subtracting the Democratic vote percent from 100 for each race). The author's alternative party coding in these tables in Chapters 4–7 is used whenever it occurs in place of the conventional party coding of voting data. The Democratic Party is defined as the Anti-Federalists, Federalists, and Jackson Democrats prior to 1830 when the "Democratic Party" as such was established. The Republican Party is defined as the Federalists, National Republicans, and Whigs prior to the establishment of the "Republican Party" in the 1850s. See Appendix A for an explanation of the historical antecedents of the current Democratic and Republican parties. No special elections for any of the four races are used in the calculations, nor are partial voting data reported for any of the four races in any of the states. —indicates that the state had no data, either because no vote data were found for the state in question or the state had not yet entered the Union. Data for the District of Columbia are included from 1964 to the present, after being granted the right to elect presidential electors by the 23rd Amendment.

Sources: Tables 8-36 through 8-140. Specifically, state party competition values in Tables 8-36 through 8-140 for the presidential, House, Senate, and gubernatorial races are aggregated for each election year separately in order to obtain each state's average composite competition values for the election years shown in Tables 8-9 through 8-35.

Table 8-29 Composite Competition Index, by State, by Election Year, 1948–1955 (Percentages)

State	1948	1949	1950	1951	1952	1953	1954	1955
Alabama	15.3	—	6.3	—	40.6	—	32.1	—
Alaska	—	—	—	—	—	—	—	—
Arizona	82.4	—	80.9	—	89.4	—	93.2	—
Arkansas	22.4	—	10.6	—	47.3	—	25.3	—
California	90.4	—	81.1	—	59.4	—	91.7	—
Colorado	79.4	—	95.2	—	84.3	—	96.7	—
Connecticut	99.2	—	97.3	—	89.3	—	98.9	—
Delaware	96.8	—	86.6	—	94.8	—	88.2	—
Dist. of Columbia	—	—	—	—	—	—	—	—
Florida	48.9	—	33.3	—	48.0	—	43.6	—
Georgia	15.4	—	0.0	—	30.3	—	5.7	—
Hawaii	—	—	—	—	—	—	—	—
Idaho	98.1	—	87.5	—	75.1	—	85.7	—
Illinois	92.4	—	92.0	—	92.3	—	96.2	—
Indiana	95.7	—	92.8	—	87.9	—	94.6	—
Iowa	89.9	—	83.0	—	77.9	—	91.7	—
Kansas	86.6	—	87.5	—	75.9	—	88.4	—
Kentucky	89.5	—	82.4	90.8	97.9	—	80.8	83.4
Louisiana	19.5	—	12.3	—	39.9	—	3.8	—
Maine	69.8	—	81.9	—	70.8	—	87.9	—
Maryland	93.5	—	92.7	—	93.3	—	91.8	—
Massachusetts	90.7	—	93.1	—	95.3	—	96.0	—
Michigan	97.1	—	96.7	—	95.4	—	94.4	—
Minnesota	88.4	—	85.5	—	88.8	—	91.2	—
Mississippi	13.9	—	6.6	0.0	28.1	—	4.4	0.0
Missouri	83.9	—	90.6	—	95.2	—	87.6	—
Montana	87.2	—	96.0	—	90.9	—	97.5	—
Nebraska	85.4	—	82.8	—	64.9	—	78.0	—
Nevada	97.8	—	87.7	—	90.9	—	92.4	—
New Hampshire	89.7	—	81.9	—	75.3	—	86.7	—
New Jersey	96.5	95.6	89.0	—	86.1	91.4	98.7	—
New Mexico	86.2	—	90.0	—	93.8	—	84.4	—
New York	75.5	—	94.5	—	89.3	—	99.2	—
North Carolina	60.1	—	61.3	—	73.7	—	69.5	—
North Dakota	75.6	—	67.0	—	48.8	—	69.7	—
Ohio	96.1	—	90.7	—	88.6	—	91.3	—
Oklahoma	71.7	—	89.3	—	86.7	—	80.2	—
Oregon	83.7	—	65.8	—	77.8	—	92.3	—
Pennsylvania	96.9	—	96.5	—	95.3	—	95.6	—
Rhode Island	80.2	—	78.8	—	93.8	—	81.9	—
South Carolina	14.7	—	0.0	—	51.3	—	0.9	—
South Dakota	85.4	—	76.3	—	61.3	—	84.4	—
Tennessee	72.3	—	58.9	—	61.1	—	42.1	—
Texas	40.6	—	19.3	—	23.4	—	24.9	—
Utah	88.3	—	93.5	—	88.1	—	88.6	—
Vermont	69.8	—	48.9	—	62.0	—	86.3	—
Virginia	73.6	56.0	49.8	—	50.1	89.4	38.6	—
Washington	95.3	—	93.8	—	92.8	—	84.8	—
West Virginia	85.0	—	86.8	—	94.6	—	87.7	—
Wisconsin	90.5	—	90.1	—	80.2	—	96.0	—
Wyoming	92.8	—	89.4	—	83.7	—	94.5	—

Notes: The composite competition index value for each state is the mean of a state's values for the party competition index devised by Paul David (1972) for all races held in a given election year among the following set of races: president, House, Senate, and governor. David's party competition index is defined as 100 − the absolute difference between the Democratic and Republican percentage of two-party vote for each of the races mentioned here. Zero (0) percent on David's index represents a complete absence of two-party competition for that election year, whereas a score of 100 percent indicates perfect competition between the two major parties. A state can only receive a composite index score of 0 if all races held in that state in a given election year are 100–0 vote splits between the two major parties. Conversely, a state can only receive a composite competition score of 100 if all races held in that state in a given election year are 50–50 vote splits between the two major parties. A state's overall value on the composite competition index for a given election year is obtained by averaging that state's party competition values for president (in Tables 8-36 through 8-53), House (in Tables 8-54 through 8-89), Senate (in Tables 8-90 through 8-104), and governor (in Tables 8-105 through 8-140). For example, in 1788 New Hampshire's party competition values were 0 percent for president (Table 8-36) and 90.6 percent for governor (Table 8-105). There were no election data available for the presidential race. Hence, New Hampshire's composite competition score in 1788 was 45.3 percent (90.6 ÷ 2) as shown in Table 8-9. In 1996 Illinois's party competition values were 80.8 percent for president (Table 8-53), 88.8 percent for House (Table 8-88), and 84.0 percent for Senate (Table 8-104). There was no race for governor in 1996. Thus Illinois's composite competition score in 1996 was 84.5 percent (253.6 ÷ 3) as shown in Table 8-35. The values for Democratic and Republican percent of two-party vote for president, House, Senate, and governor used to get the party competition values for these races in Tables 8-36 through 8-140 are taken from the state vote tables in Chapters 4, 5, 6, and 7, respectively (where the Republican vote percent is obtained by subtracting the Democratic vote percent from 100 for each race). The author's alternative party coding in these tables in Chapters 4–7 is used whenever it occurs in place of the conventional party coding of voting data. The Democratic Party is defined as the Anti-Federalists, Federalists, and Jackson Democrats prior to 1830 when the "Democratic Party" as such was established. The Republican Party is defined as the Federalists, National Republicans, and Whigs prior to the establishment of the "Republican Party" in the 1850s. See Appendix A for an explanation of the historical antecedents of the current Democratic and Republican parties. No special elections for any of the four races are used in the calculations, nor are partial voting data reported for any of the four races in any of the states. —indicates that the state had no data, either because no vote data were found for the state in question or the state had not yet entered the Union. Data for the District of Columbia are included from 1964 to the present, after being granted the right to elect presidential electors by the 23rd Amendment.

Sources: Tables 8-36 through 8-140. Specifically, state party competition values in Tables 8-36 through 8-140 for the presidential, House, Senate, and gubernatorial races are aggregated for each election year separately in order to obtain each state's average composite competition values for the election years shown in Tables 8-9 through 8-35.

Table 8-30 Composite Competition Index, by State, by Election Year, 1956–1963 (Percentages)

State	1956	1957	1958	1959	1960	1961	1962	1963
Alabama	36.4	—	13.9	—	55.4	—	54.2	—
Alaska	—	—	86.5	—	85.9	—	90.1	—
Arizona	82.8	—	92.4	—	88.5	—	92.6	—
Arkansas	46.2	—	35.0	—	51.3	—	58.0	—
California	91.9	—	82.1	—	95.8	—	92.7	—
Colorado	92.6	—	83.4	—	93.0	—	90.8	—
Connecticut	78.9	—	82.5	—	92.3	—	95.2	—
Delaware	93.8	—	96.5	—	98.2	—	94.0	—
Dist. of Columbia	—	—	—	—	—	—	—	—
Florida	53.2	—	57.0	—	79.8	—	67.4	—
Georgia	29.0	—	0.0	—	27.7	—	12.1	—
Hawaii	—	—	—	84.9	75.6	—	72.5	—
Idaho	84.0	—	97.0	—	92.7	—	91.9	—
Illinois	91.1	—	91.2	—	94.1	—	96.8	—
Indiana	86.5	—	89.3	—	95.3	—	98.8	—
Iowa	90.6	—	95.6	—	92.6	—	93.4	—
Kansas	82.8	—	92.6	—	86.8	—	81.6	—
Kentucky	95.3	—	69.4	78.8	85.4	—	88.1	98.6
Louisiana	28.7	—	4.6	—	44.4	—	36.7	—
Maine	79.0	—	89.3	—	83.3	—	94.5	—
Maryland	90.5	—	80.2	—	87.0	—	84.5	—
Massachusetts	90.7	—	74.9	—	84.6	—	91.2	—
Michigan	92.8	—	93.3	—	97.7	—	96.4	—
Minnesota	95.5	—	91.2	—	95.3	—	99.8	—
Mississippi	29.6	—	0.0	0.0	33.7	—	0.0	76.2
Missouri	90.9	—	70.3	—	89.3	—	89.0	—
Montana	90.6	—	59.1	—	96.0	—	96.0	—
Nebraska	78.3	—	94.1	—	85.3	—	85.5	—
Nevada	90.1	—	77.0	—	91.3	—	64.2	—
New Hampshire	76.9	—	89.6	—	86.3	—	84.2	—
New Jersey	75.7	89.8	97.5	—	94.5	98.4	99.2	—
New Mexico	91.1	—	82.5	—	88.6	—	94.5	—
New York	87.0	—	95.4	—	94.8	—	90.5	—
North Carolina	72.9	—	58.4	—	85.8	—	80.7	—
North Dakota	76.6	—	92.3	—	92.7	—	89.7	—
Ohio	86.4	—	93.2	—	92.6	—	79.3	—
Oklahoma	86.5	—	51.3	—	87.3	—	86.7	—
Oregon	91.8	—	87.8	—	94.5	—	89.9	—
Pennsylvania	93.6	—	97.7	—	97.2	—	94.9	—
Rhode Island	91.8	—	81.0	—	71.2	—	84.8	—
South Carolina	38.8	—	0.0	—	32.5	—	37.9	—
South Dakota	92.9	—	97.2	—	91.4	—	89.3	—
Tennessee	90.8	—	38.0	—	70.7	—	60.8	—
Texas	40.1	—	31.9	—	66.4	—	89.7	—
Utah	84.6	—	96.6	—	94.7	—	94.8	—
Vermont	68.4	—	97.3	—	85.2	—	83.9	—
Virginia	81.1	73.2	21.3	—	53.3	72.2	80.0	—
Washington	85.7	—	78.3	—	93.7	—	85.9	—
West Virginia	92.6	—	78.9	—	90.4	—	88.0	—
Wisconsin	86.7	—	90.3	—	97.0	—	97.8	—
Wyoming	81.7	—	96.3	—	90.9	—	84.1	—

Notes: The composite competition index value for each state is the mean of a state's values for the party competition index devised by Paul David (1972) for all races held in a given election year among the following set of races: president, House, Senate, and governor. David's party competition index is defined as 100 − the absolute difference between the Democratic and Republican percentage of two-party vote for each of the races mentioned here. Zero (0) percent on David's index represents a complete absence of two-party competition for that election year, whereas a score of 100 percent indicates perfect competition between the two major parties. A state can only receive a composite index score of 0 if all races held in that state in a given election year are 100–0 vote splits between the two major parties. Conversely, a state can only receive a composite competition score of 100 if all races held in that state in a given election year are 50–50 vote splits between the two major parties. A state's overall value on the composite competition index for a given election year is obtained by averaging that state's party competition values for president (in Tables 8-36 through 8-53), House (in Tables 8-54 through 8-89), Senate (in Tables 8-90 through 8-104), and governor (in Tables 8-105 through 8-140). For example, in 1788 New Hampshire's party competition values were 0 percent for president (Table 8-36) and 90.6 percent for governor (Table 8-105). There were no election data available for the presidential race. Hence, New Hampshire's composite competition score in 1788 was 45.3 percent (90.6 ÷ 2) as shown in Table 8-9. In 1996 Illinois's party competition values were 80.8 percent for president (Table 8-53), 88.8 percent for House (Table 8-88), and 84.0 percent for Senate (Table 8-104). There was no race for governor in 1996. Thus Illinois's composite competition score in 1996 was 84.5 percent (253.6 ÷ 3) as shown in Table 8-35. The values for Democratic and Republican percent of two-party vote for president, House, Senate, and governor used to get the party competition values for these races in Tables 8-36 through 8-140 are taken from the state vote tables in Chapters 4, 5, 6, and 7, respectively (where the Republican vote percent is obtained by subtracting the Democratic vote percent from 100 for each race). The author's alternative party coding in these tables in Chapters 4–7 is used whenever it occurs in place of the conventional party coding of voting data. The Democratic Party is defined as the Anti-Federalists, Federalists, and Jackson Democrats prior to 1830 when the "Democratic Party" as such was established. The Republican Party is defined as the Federalists, National Republicans, and Whigs prior to the establishment of the "Republican Party" in the 1850s. See Appendix A for an explanation of the historical antecedents of the current Democratic and Republican parties. No special elections for any of the four races are used in the calculations, nor are partial voting data reported for any of the four races in any of the states. —indicates that the state had no data, either because no vote data were found for the state in question or the state had not yet entered the Union. Data for the District of Columbia are included from 1964 to the present, after being granted the right to elect presidential electors by the 23rd Amendment.

Sources: Tables 8-36 through 8-140. Specifically, state party competition values in Tables 8-36 through 8-140 for the presidential, House, Senate, and gubernatorial races are aggregated for each election year separately in order to obtain each state's average composite competition values for the election years shown in Tables 8-9 through 8-35.

Table 8-31 Composite Competition Index, by State, by Election Year, 1964–1971 (Percentages)

State	1964	1965	1966	1967	1968	1969	1970	1971
Alabama	48.4	—	74.3	—	62.0	—	25.8	—
Alaska	82.6	—	81.4	—	93.1	—	91.7	—
Arizona	97.4	—	90.1	—	83.9	—	92.4	—
Arkansas	86.6	—	91.2	—	92.1	—	68.8	—
California	90.9	—	89.1	—	93.7	—	94.0	—
Colorado	80.2	—	88.9	—	89.6	—	95.7	—
Connecticut	70.1	—	89.2	—	93.7	—	93.7	—
Delaware	89.6	—	85.1	—	92.5	—	85.8	—
Dist. of Columbia	29.0	—	—	—	36.4	—	—	—
Florida	78.6	—	80.1	—	86.8	—	89.2	—
Georgia	76.5	—	54.8	—	59.9	—	66.4	—
Hawaii	71.1	—	81.2	—	58.1	—	70.7	—
Idaho	98.4	—	87.8	—	78.3	—	85.6	—
Illinois	89.4	—	90.1	—	95.1	—	90.5	—
Indiana	90.1	—	93.0	—	92.4	—	99.0	—
Iowa	76.6	—	86.9	—	92.4	—	97.7	—
Kansas	92.0	—	85.1	—	81.9	—	87.9	—
Kentucky	71.0	—	82.7	96.8	95.4	—	94.8	93.4
Louisiana	73.7	—	18.2	—	32.1	—	11.2	—
Maine	72.5	—	88.9	—	87.6	—	84.5	—
Maryland	68.2	—	89.0	—	94.3	—	86.9	—
Massachusetts	68.0	—	77.0	—	82.8	—	81.1	—
Michigan	77.4	—	87.9	—	95.8	—	87.2	—
Minnesota	80.7	—	94.1	—	91.1	—	89.7	—
Mississippi	15.1	—	46.9	59.4	44.5	—	9.7	0.0
Missouri	72.4	—	92.6	—	90.9	—	90.1	—
Montana	87.2	—	92.3	—	88.1	—	82.9	—
Nebraska	87.3	—	76.8	—	75.0	—	88.5	—
Nevada	85.4	—	80.2	—	78.9	—	71.3	—
New Hampshire	79.1	—	87.4	—	83.6	—	80.5	—
New Jersey	77.9	83.4	87.5	—	97.4	78.4	91.1	—
New Mexico	87.1	—	96.5	—	93.9	—	93.7	—
New York	78.0	—	93.5	—	90.1	—	87.1	—
North Carolina	84.5	—	91.5	—	87.3	—	88.8	—
North Dakota	89.3	—	81.8	—	79.8	—	80.1	—
Ohio	89.8	—	80.6	—	91.0	—	91.3	—
Oklahoma	81.3	—	91.9	—	88.3	—	86.2	—
Oregon	75.9	—	93.5	—	95.7	—	92.5	—
Pennsylvania	85.5	—	94.8	—	96.3	—	90.1	—
Rhode Island	50.4	—	71.8	—	80.7	—	78.1	—
South Carolina	52.1	—	72.6	—	76.5	—	74.1	—
South Dakota	90.3	—	74.8	—	85.5	—	90.9	—
Tennessee	88.5	—	62.9	—	91.5	—	90.6	—
Texas	69.6	—	57.4	—	80.3	—	79.5	—
Utah	89.1	—	72.4	—	76.1	—	92.5	—
Vermont	79.5	—	76.7	—	44.9	—	75.7	—
Virginia	70.1	88.2	77.0	—	92.0	92.8	80.1	—
Washington	79.1	—	97.4	—	88.5	—	56.2	—
West Virginia	75.5	—	87.5	—	88.8	—	57.2	—
Wisconsin	90.9	—	92.5	—	89.3	—	78.5	—
Wyoming	92.4	—	94.4	—	76.2	—	87.4	—

Notes: The composite competition index value for each state is the mean of a state's values for the party competition index devised by Paul David (1972) for all races held in a given election year among the following set of races: president, House, Senate, and governor. David's party competition index is defined as 100 − the absolute difference between the Democratic and Republican percentage of two-party vote for each of the races mentioned here. Zero (0) percent on David's index represents a complete absence of two-party competition for that election year, whereas a score of 100 percent indicates perfect competition between the two major parties. A state can only receive a composite index score of 0 if all races held in that state in a given election year are 100–0 vote splits between the two major parties. Conversely, a state can only receive a composite competition score of 100 if all races held in that state in a given election year are 50–50 vote splits between the two major parties. A state's overall value on the composite competition index for a given election year is obtained by averaging that state's party competition values for president (in Tables 8-36 through 8-53), House (in Tables 8-54 through 8-89), Senate (in Tables 8-90 through 8-104), and governor (in Tables 8-105 through 8-140). For example, in 1788 New Hampshire's party competition values were 0 percent for president (Table 8-36) and 90.6 percent for governor (Table 8-105). There were no election data available for the presidential race. Hence, New Hampshire's composite competition score in 1788 was 45.3 percent (90.6 ÷ 2) as shown in Table 8-9. In 1996 Illinois's party competition values were 80.8 percent for president (Table 8-53), 88.8 percent for House (Table 8-88), and 84.0 percent for Senate (Table 8-104). There was no race for governor in 1996. Thus Illinois's composite competition score in 1996 was 84.5 percent (253.6 ÷ 3) as shown in Table 8-35. The values for Democratic and Republican percent of two-party vote for president, House, Senate, and governor used to get the party competition values for these races in Tables 8-36 through 8-140 are taken from the state vote tables in Chapters 4, 5, 6, and 7, respectively (where the Republican vote percent is obtained by subtracting the Democratic vote percent from 100 for each race). The author's alternative party coding in these tables in Chapters 4–7 is used whenever it occurs in place of the conventional party coding of voting data. The Democratic Party is defined as the Anti-Federalists, Federalists, and Jackson Democrats prior to 1830 when the "Democratic Party" as such was established. The Republican Party is defined as the Federalists, National Republicans, and Whigs prior to the establishment of the "Republican Party" in the 1850s. See Appendix A for an explanation of the historical antecedents of the current Democratic and Republican parties. No special elections for any of the four races are used in the calculations, nor are partial voting data reported for any of the four races in any of the states. —indicates that the state had no data, either because no vote data were found for the state in question or the state had not yet entered the Union. Data for the District of Columbia are included from 1964 to the present, after being granted the right to elect presidential electors by the 23rd Amendment.

Sources: Tables 8-36 through 8-140. Specifically, state party competition values in Tables 8-36 through 8-140 for the presidential, House, Senate, and gubernatorial races are aggregated for each election year separately in order to obtain each state's average composite competition values for the election years shown in Tables 8-9 through 8-35.

Table 8-32   Composite Competition Index, by State, by Election Year, 1972–1979 (Percentages)

State	1972	1973	1974	1975	1976	1977	1978	1979
Alabama	66.3	—	30.5	—	75.3	—	38.2	—
Alaska	69.2	—	91.8	—	67.1	—	68.5	—
Arizona	80.8	—	94.0	—	89.9	—	92.9	—
Arkansas	63.0	—	49.5	—	51.7	—	54.1	—
California	90.2	—	84.9	—	94.1	—	87.6	—
Colorado	88.1	—	89.2	—	90.0	—	85.5	—
Connecticut	89.5	—	78.1	—	92.0	—	82.5	—
Delaware	87.2	—	80.8	—	91.1	—	82.8	—
Dist. of Columbia	43.2	—	—	—	33.6	—	—	—
Florida	55.8	—	87.3	—	84.3	—	88.8	—
Georgia	66.1	—	58.3	—	58.8	—	37.3	—
Hawaii	81.6	—	56.2	—	81.0	—	61.3	—
Idaho	74.6	—	75.4	—	85.7	—	75.5	—
Illinois	88.3	—	80.7	—	88.2	—	89.8	—
Indiana	81.7	—	92.4	—	87.2	—	95.0	—
Iowa	87.5	—	89.9	—	92.1	—	93.0	—
Kansas	62.4	—	95.1	—	85.1	—	85.1	—
Kentucky	88.9	—	81.1	74.4	84.5	—	81.6	81.2
Louisiana	56.0	—	0.0	0.0	83.9	—	—	99.4
Maine	88.3	—	78.8	—	81.3	—	79.7	—
Maryland	85.9	—	79.3	—	83.5	—	63.1	—
Massachusetts	80.1	—	69.7	—	69.2	—	79.7	—
Michigan	91.3	—	88.8	—	92.5	—	89.3	—
Minnesota	90.8	—	72.9	—	74.5	—	90.6	—
Mississippi	61.6	—	91.2	92.8	59.7	—	89.7	77.8
Missouri	81.8	—	72.4	—	91.8	—	74.6	—
Montana	86.5	—	82.8	—	81.5	—	93.7	—
Nebraska	73.5	—	84.7	—	81.5	—	75.7	—
Nevada	84.1	—	73.0	—	63.0	—	66.5	—
New Hampshire	78.3	—	95.3	—	88.5	—	96.4	—
New Jersey	81.7	65.2	78.0	—	87.7	85.8	88.3	—
New Mexico	84.8	—	97.3	—	92.0	—	91.7	—
New York	88.4	—	85.9	—	88.8	—	93.6	—
North Carolina	84.8	—	72.6	—	75.9	—	85.6	—
North Dakota	75.2	—	94.3	—	84.0	—	63.0	—
Ohio	83.9	—	87.3	—	98.0	—	95.6	—
Oklahoma	74.1	—	84.9	—	84.7	—	83.3	—
Oregon	90.5	—	81.8	—	80.4	—	75.9	—
Pennsylvania	88.6	—	89.6	—	94.1	—	95.6	—
Rhode Island	88.2	—	45.8	—	80.4	—	67.5	—
South Carolina	74.9	—	79.3	—	79.2	—	76.7	—
South Dakota	87.8	—	88.1	—	74.0	—	82.4	—
Tennessee	76.5	—	84.6	—	85.1	—	86.5	—
Texas	78.1	—	61.0	—	84.1	—	93.5	—
Utah	68.2	—	88.3	—	88.0	—	88.2	—
Vermont	77.3	—	87.7	—	83.8	—	55.6	—
Virginia	84.3	0.0	83.2	—	66.1	87.2	92.5	—
Washington	79.9	—	78.4	—	80.2	—	94.2	—
West Virginia	75.9	—	60.4	—	50.9	—	83.8	—
Wisconsin	88.1	—	80.8	—	76.9	—	92.0	—
Wyoming	71.7	—	89.4	—	86.1	—	85.5	—

Notes: The composite competition index value for each state is the mean of a state's values for the party competition index devised by Paul David (1972) for all races held in a given election year among the following set of races: president, House, Senate, and governor. David's party competition index is defined as 100 − the absolute difference between the Democratic and Republican percentage of two-party vote for each of the races mentioned here. Zero (0) percent on David's index represents a complete absence of two-party competition for that election year, whereas a score of 100 percent indicates perfect competition between the two major parties. A state can only receive a composite index score of 0 if all races held in that state in a given election year are 100–0 vote splits between the two major parties. Conversely, a state can only receive a composite competition score of 100 if all races held in that state in a given election year are 50–50 vote splits between the two major parties. A state's overall value on the composite competition index for a given election year is obtained by averaging that state's party competition values for president (in Tables 8-36 through 8-53), House (in Tables 8-54 through 8-89), Senate (in Tables 8-90 through 8-104), and governor (in Tables 8-105 through 8-140). For example, in 1788 New Hampshire's party competition values were 0 percent for president (Table 8-36) and 90.6 percent for governor (Table 8-105). There were no election data available for the presidential race. Hence, New Hampshire's composite competition score in 1788 was 45.3 percent (90.6 ÷ 2) as shown in Table 8-9. In 1996 Illinois's party competition values were 80.8 percent for president (Table 8-53), 88.8 percent for House (Table 8-88), and 84.0 percent for Senate (Table 8-104). There was no race for governor in 1996. Thus Illinois's composite competition score in 1996 was 84.5 percent (253.6 ÷ 3) as shown in Table 8-35. The values for Democratic and Republican percent of two-party vote for president, House, Senate, and governor used to get the party competition values for these races in Tables 8-36 through 8-140 are taken from the state vote tables in Chapters 4, 5, 6, and 7, respectively (where the Republican vote percent is obtained by subtracting the Democratic vote percent from 100 for each race). The author's alternative party coding in these tables in Chapters 4–7 is used whenever it occurs in place of the conventional party coding of voting data. The Democratic Party is defined as the Anti-Federalists, Federalists, and Jackson Democrats prior to 1830 when the "Democratic Party" as such was established. The Republican Party is defined as the Federalists, National Republicans, and Whigs prior to the establishment of the "Republican Party" in the 1850s. See Appendix A for an explanation of the historical antecedents of the current Democratic and Republican parties. No special elections for any of the four races are used in the calculations, nor are partial voting data reported for any of the four races in any of the states. —indicates that the state had no data, either because no vote data were found for the state in question or the state had not yet entered the Union. Data for the District of Columbia are included from 1964 to the present, after being granted the right to elect presidential electors by the 23rd Amendment.

Sources: Tables 8-36 through 8-140. Specifically, state party competition values in Tables 8-36 through 8-140 for the presidential, House, Senate, and gubernatorial races are aggregated for each election year separately in order to obtain each state's average composite competition values for the election years shown in Tables 8-9 through 8-35.

Table 8-33 Composite Competition Index, by State, by Election Year, 1980–1987 (Percentages)

State	1980	1981	1982	1983	1984	1985	1986	1987
Alabama	89.1	—	69.1	—	68.5	—	88.3	—
Alaska	69.8	—	73.4	—	68.4	—	89.6	—
Arizona	85.9	—	79.3	—	67.5	—	79.0	—
Arkansas	92.5	—	92.9	—	79.3	—	76.5	—
California	84.6	—	96.0	—	91.2	—	89.7	—
Colorado	86.8	—	80.5	—	71.0	—	89.9	—
Connecticut	90.3	—	93.2	—	85.7	—	80.5	—
Delaware	76.9	—	91.4	—	83.0	—	67.2	—
Dist. of Columbia	30.4	—	—	—	27.8	—	—	—
Florida	89.2	—	73.6	—	69.4	—	90.7	—
Georgia	79.7	—	62.4	—	58.8	—	70.5	—
Hawaii	50.4	—	29.1	—	59.5	—	77.5	—
Idaho	80.6	—	96.4	—	62.6	—	94.5	—
Illinois	89.8	—	91.8	—	93.9	—	61.0	—
Indiana	89.1	—	95.1	—	88.3	—	87.9	—
Iowa	91.7	—	94.1	—	91.5	—	86.5	—
Kansas	77.7	—	91.8	—	66.2	—	78.5	—
Kentucky	84.1	—	80.8	89.4	89.3	—	65.9	70.2
Louisiana	94.4	—	—	73.6	77.2	—	94.4	—
Maine	75.0	—	79.3	—	63.5	—	83.0	—
Maryland	80.3	—	70.9	—	83.1	—	62.7	—
Massachusetts	83.9	—	71.2	—	82.5	—	48.5	—
Michigan	93.4	—	85.1	—	89.3	—	73.7	—
Minnesota	95.7	—	88.3	—	91.6	—	83.5	—
Mississippi	90.9	—	77.1	82.8	76.9	—	79.4	93.2
Missouri	93.7	—	91.9	—	85.1	—	89.4	—
Montana	85.9	—	89.5	—	78.3	—	91.8	—
Nebraska	55.5	—	67.8	—	68.5	—	82.5	—
Nevada	64.5	—	94.9	—	74.0	—	80.3	—
New Hampshire	85.2	—	90.2	—	68.8	—	76.9	—
New Jersey	91.6	100.0	91.5	—	82.7	59.2	95.8	—
New Mexico	88.5	—	94.5	—	72.3	—	93.4	—
New York	98.1	—	83.5	—	93.1	—	79.1	—
North Carolina	90.4	—	90.0	—	89.6	—	91.6	—
North Dakota	73.7	—	63.0	—	66.9	—	73.3	—
Ohio	79.3	—	84.3	—	90.2	—	84.3	—
Oklahoma	85.7	—	74.2	—	64.0	—	89.0	—
Oregon	86.9	—	79.9	—	81.9	—	85.1	—
Pennsylvania	95.7	—	89.9	—	91.8	—	92.3	—
Rhode Island	76.5	—	80.5	—	82.8	—	75.8	—
South Carolina	85.5	—	75.7	—	77.7	—	80.7	—
South Dakota	80.3	—	77.5	—	69.9	—	91.6	—
Tennessee	98.1	—	79.1	—	81.6	—	87.1	—
Texas	82.9	—	80.5	—	80.0	—	89.0	—
Utah	66.1	—	73.2	—	69.2	—	73.0	—
Vermont	67.2	—	78.6	—	79.7	—	53.5	—
Virginia	75.8	92.8	96.5	—	74.3	89.6	92.2	—
Washington	90.7	—	72.7	—	89.7	—	89.7	—
West Virginia	90.8	—	68.1	—	89.2	—	49.0	—
Wisconsin	97.4	—	82.6	—	95.4	—	95.7	—
Wyoming	62.3	—	72.7	—	50.1	—	76.5	—

Notes: The composite competition index value for each state is the mean of a state's values for the party competition index devised by Paul David (1972) for all races held in a given election year among the following set of races: president, House, Senate, and governor. David's party competition index is defined as 100 − the absolute difference between the Democratic and Republican percentage of two-party vote for each of the races mentioned here. Zero (0) percent on David's index represents a complete absence of two-party competition for that election year, whereas a score of 100 percent indicates perfect competition between the two major parties. A state can only receive a composite index score of 0 if all races held in that state in a given election year are 100–0 vote splits between the two major parties. Conversely, a state can only receive a composite competition score of 100 if all races held in that state in a given election year are 50–50 vote splits between the two major parties. A state's overall value on the composite competition index for a given election year is obtained by averaging that state's party competition values for president (in Tables 8-36 through 8-53), House (in Tables 8-54 through 8-89), Senate (in Tables 8-90 through 8-104), and governor (in Tables 8-105 through 8-140). For example, in 1788 New Hampshire's party competition values were 0 percent for president (Table 8-36) and 90.6 percent for governor (Table 8-105). There was no election data available for the presidential race. Hence, New Hampshire's composite competition score in 1788 was 45.3 percent (90.6 ÷ 2) as shown in Table 8-9. In 1996 Illinois's party competition values were 80.8 percent for president (Table 8-53), 88.8 percent for House (Table 8-88), and 84.0 percent for Senate (Table 8-104). There was no race for governor in 1996. Thus Illinois's composite competition score in 1996 was 84.5 percent (253.6 ÷ 3) as shown in Table 8-35. The values for Democratic and Republican percent of two-party vote for president, House, Senate, and governor used to get the party competition values for these races in Tables 8-36 through 8-140 are taken from the state vote tables in Chapters 4, 5, 6, and 7, respectively (where the Republican vote percent is obtained by subtracting the Democratic vote percent from 100 for each race). The author's alternative party coding in these tables in Chapters 4–7 is used whenever it occurs in place of the conventional party coding of voting data. The Democratic Party is defined as the Anti-Federalists, Federalists, and Jackson Democrats prior to 1830 when the "Democratic Party" as such was established. The Republican Party is defined as the Federalists, National Republicans, and Whigs prior to the establishment of the "Republican Party" in the 1850s. See Appendix A for an explanation of the historical antecedents of the current Democratic and Republican parties. No special elections for any of the four races are used in the calculations, nor are partial voting data reported for any of the four races in any of the states. —indicates that the state had no data, either because no vote data were found for the state in question or the state had not yet entered the Union. Data for the District of Columbia are included from 1964 to the present, after being granted the right to elect presidential electors by the 23rd Amendment.

Sources: Tables 8-36 through 8-140. Specifically, state party competition values in Tables 8-36 through 8-140 for the presidential, House, Senate, and gubernatorial races are aggregated for each election year separately in order to obtain each state's average composite competition values for the election years shown in Tables 8-9 through 8-35.

Table 8-34 Composite Competition Index, by State, by Election Year, 1988–1995 (Percentages)

State	1988	1989	1990	1991	1992	1993	1994	1995
Alabama	77.7	—	79.1	—	81.2	—	99.4	—
Alaska	75.1	—	84.5	—	88.8	—	86.3	—
Arizona	73.9	—	85.5	—	85.9	—	84.5	—
Arkansas	85.6	—	58.0	—	80.2	—	87.6	—
California	93.0	—	96.6	—	88.9	—	93.8	—
Colorado	95.2	—	85.6	—	93.4	—	75.8	—
Connecticut	97.6	—	82.9	—	88.8	—	85.7	—
Delaware	71.8	—	69.7	—	81.2	—	70.5	—
Dist. of Columbia	29.6	—	—	—	19.4	—	—	—
Florida	88.3	—	87.0	—	83.4	—	78.7	—
Georgia	73.1	—	56.3	—	96.1	—	94.4	—
Hawaii	64.7	—	74.5	—	66.1	—	69.9	—
Idaho	86.1	—	74.9	—	88.6	—	80.6	—
Illinois	95.6	—	85.7	—	86.7	—	83.1	—
Indiana	83.5	—	90.2	—	85.2	—	74.5	—
Iowa	93.8	—	89.1	—	76.5	—	84.4	—
Kansas	82.6	—	81.8	—	83.2	—	72.4	—
Kentucky	92.7	—	94.9	70.6	87.5	—	82.4	97.8
Louisiana	89.6	—	—	77.6	94.6	—	—	73.0
Maine	75.2	—	88.1	—	87.3	—	85.3	—
Maryland	84.5	—	88.0	—	78.3	—	93.3	—
Massachusetts	68.3	—	79.8	—	74.0	—	66.8	—
Michigan	87.8	—	91.1	—	94.6	—	87.9	—
Minnesota	86.5	—	92.3	—	86.4	—	87.5	—
Mississippi	79.5	—	18.8	96.8	74.1	—	73.2	88.8
Missouri	79.6	—	92.4	—	88.1	—	85.7	—
Montana	94.6	—	79.6	—	96.8	—	84.1	—
Nebraska	77.9	—	91.9	—	78.6	—	71.1	—
Nevada	89.7	—	80.4	—	92.6	—	85.0	—
New Hampshire	78.1	—	78.3	—	92.7	—	66.1	—
New Jersey	91.7	75.6	96.3	—	96.0	99.0	92.9	—
New Mexico	87.4	—	75.3	—	94.4	—	88.1	—
New York	83.3	—	76.2	—	91.1	—	93.8	—
North Carolina	86.6	—	93.9	—	95.4	—	85.8	—
North Dakota	75.8	—	69.6	—	82.1	—	88.3	—
Ohio	91.5	—	91.1	—	95.7	—	72.6	—
Oklahoma	88.7	—	61.7	—	82.4	—	78.6	—
Oregon	82.6	—	84.5	—	87.1	—	88.9	—
Pennsylvania	87.3	—	77.7	—	93.9	—	93.6	—
Rhode Island	87.3	—	74.3	—	82.1	—	81.4	—
South Carolina	82.3	—	69.3	—	93.5	—	84.9	—
South Dakota	75.1	—	79.8	—	72.7	—	80.3	—
Tennessee	76.9	—	74.7	—	92.9	—	88.1	—
Texas	82.7	—	88.6	—	96.7	—	85.2	—
Utah	78.4	—	90.0	—	80.7	—	75.2	—
Vermont	77.0	—	54.2	—	64.1	—	44.2	—
Virginia	74.0	99.6	38.3	—	97.3	82.4	89.4	—
Washington	89.4	—	92.2	—	89.3	—	93.5	—
West Virginia	73.6	—	64.6	—	69.1	—	64.9	—
Wisconsin	96.7	—	89.6	—	95.1	—	73.7	—
Wyoming	80.3	—	77.1	—	86.7	—	82.9	—

Notes: The composite competition index value for each state is the mean of a state's values for the party competition index devised by Paul David (1972) for all races held in a given election year among the following set of races: president, House, Senate, and governor. David's party competition index is defined as 100 − the absolute difference between the Democratic and Republican percentage of two-party vote for each of the races mentioned here. Zero (0) percent on David's index represents a complete absence of two-party competition for that election year, whereas a score of 100 percent indicates perfect competition between the two major parties. A state can only receive a composite index score of 0 if all races held in that state in a given election year are 100–0 vote splits between the two major parties. Conversely, a state can only receive a composite competition score of 100 if all races held in that state in a given election year are 50–50 vote splits between the two major parties. A state's overall value on the composite competition index for a given election year is obtained by averaging that state's party competition values for president (in Tables 8-36 through 8-53), House (in Tables 8-54 through 8-89), Senate (in Tables 8-90 through 8-104), and governor (in Tables 8-105 through 8-140). For example, in 1788 New Hampshire's party competition values were 0 percent for president (Table 8-36) and 90.6 percent for governor (Table 8-105). There were no election data available for the presidential race. Hence, New Hampshire's composite competition score in 1788 was 45.3 percent (90.6 ÷ 2) as shown in Table 8-9. In 1996 Illinois's party competition values were 80.8 percent for president (Table 8-53), 88.8 percent for House (Table 8-88), and 84.0 percent for Senate (Table 8-104). There was no race for governor in 1996. Thus Illinois's composite competition score in 1996 was 84.5 percent (253.6 ÷ 3) as shown in Table 8-35. The values for Democratic and Republican percent of two-party vote for president, House, Senate, and governor used to get the party competition values for these races in Tables 8-36 through 8-140 are taken from the state vote tables in Chapters 4, 5, 6, and 7, respectively (where the Republican vote percent is obtained by subtracting the Democratic vote percent from 100 for each race). The author's alternative party coding in these tables in Chapters 4–7 is used whenever it occurs in place of the conventional party coding of voting data. The Democratic Party is defined as the Anti-Federalists, Federalists, and Jackson Democrats prior to 1830 when the "Democratic Party" as such was established. The Republican Party is defined as the Federalists, National Republicans, and Whigs prior to the establishment of the "Republican Party" in the 1850s. See Appendix A for an explanation of the historical antecedents of the current Democratic and Republican parties. No special elections for any of the four races are used in the calculations, nor are partial voting data reported for any of the four races in any of the states. —indicates that the state had no data, either because no vote data were found for the state in question or the state had not yet entered the Union. Data for the District of Columbia are included from 1964 to the present, after being granted the right to elect presidential electors by the 23rd Amendment.

Sources: Tables 8-36 through 8-140. Specifically, state party competition values in Tables 8-36 through 8-140 for the presidential, House, Senate, and gubernatorial races are aggregated for each election year separately in order to obtain each state's average composite competition values for the election years shown in Tables 8-9 through 8-35.

Table 8-35 Composite Competition Index, by State, by Election Year, 1996–1999

State	1996	1997	1998	1999
Alabama	92.1	—	82.6	—
Alaska	59.7	—	54.9	—
Arizona	88.2	—	71.1	—
Arkansas	89.5	—	82.7	—
California	90.5	—	87.4	—
Colorado	92.3	—	85.5	—
Connecticut	82.7	—	77.5	—
Delaware	69.5	—	64.8	—
Dist. of Columbia	19.8	—	—	—
Florida	93.6	—	82.2	—
Georgia	96.9	—	85.5	—
Hawaii	76.6	—	66.1	—
Idaho	80.3	—	69.5	—
Illinois	84.5	—	97.2	—
Indiana	93.5	—	79.2	—
Iowa	91.1	—	77.3	—
Kansas	78.3	—	62.6	—
Kentucky	89.4	—	91.4	76.4
Louisiana	93.2	—	66.2	64.4
Maine	80.1	—	69.6	—
Maryland	87.9	—	80.5	—
Massachusetts	73.7	—	72.3	—
Michigan	86.4	—	87.3	—
Minnesota	85.9	—	89.2	—
Mississippi	80.0	—	93.8	98.8
Missouri	87.1	—	94.1	—
Montana	80.9	—	91.2	—
Nebraska	75.5	—	67.0	—
Nevada	90.4	—	78.1	—
New Hampshire	90.5	—	67.1	—
New Jersey	89.2	98.8	97.6	—
New Mexico	84.3	—	93.6	—
New York	77.7	—	85.0	—
North Carolina	91.6	—	92.8	—
North Dakota	82.6	—	78.0	—
Ohio	94.5	—	92.2	—
Oklahoma	82.9	—	73.5	—
Oregon	91.2	—	70.9	—
Pennsylvania	92.6	—	79.8	—
Rhode Island	65.0	—	72.6	—
South Carolina	83.8	—	87.5	—
South Dakota	90.6	—	63.8	—
Tennessee	90.2	—	76.8	—
Texas	91.5	—	77.5	—
Utah	68.2	—	63.4	—
Vermont	55.5	—	44.1	—
Virginia	96.2	86.6	97.4	—
Washington	88.2	—	87.1	—
West Virginia	62.1	—	18.6	—
Wisconsin	91.6	—	89.7	—
Wyoming	85.9	—	82.2	—

Notes: The composite competition index value for each state is the mean of a state's values for the party competition index devised by Paul David (1972) for all races held in a given election year among the following set of races: president, House, Senate, and governor. David's party competition index is defined as 100 − the absolute difference between the Democratic and Republican percentage of two-party vote for each of the races mentioned here. Zero (0) percent on David's index represents a complete absence of two-party competition for that election year, whereas a score of 100 percent indicates perfect competition between the two major parties. A state can only receive a composite index score of 0 if all races held in that state in a given election year are 100–0 vote splits between the two major parties. Conversely, a state can only receive a composite competition score of 100 if all races held in that state in a given election year are 50–50 vote splits between the two major parties. A state's overall value on the composite competition index for a given election year is obtained by averaging that state's party competition values for president (in Tables 8-36 through 8-53), House (in Tables 8-54 through 8-89), Senate (in Tables 8-90 through 8-104), and governor (in Tables 8-105 through 8-140). For example, in 1788 New Hampshire's party competition values were 0 percent for president (Table 8-36) and 90.6 percent for governor (Table 8-105). There were no election data available for the presidential race. Hence, New Hampshire's composite competition score in 1788 was 45.3 percent (90.6 ÷ 2) as shown in Table 8-9. In 1996 Illinois's party competition values were 80.8 percent for president (Table 8-53), 88.8 percent for House (Table 8-88), and 84.0 percent for Senate (Table 8-104). There was no race for governor in 1996. Thus Illinois's composite competition score in 1996 was 84.5 percent (253.6 ÷ 3) as shown in Table 8-35. The values for Democratic and Republican percent of two-party vote for president, House, Senate, and governor used to get the party competition values for these races in Tables 8-36 through 8-140 are taken from the state vote tables in Chapters 4, 5, 6, and 7, respectively (where the Republican vote percent is obtained by subtracting the Democratic vote percent from 100 for each race). The author's alternative party coding in these tables in Chapters 4–7 is used whenever it occurs in place of the conventional party coding of voting data. The Democratic Party is defined as the Anti-Federalists, Federalists, and Jackson Democrats prior to 1830 when the "Democratic Party" as such was established. The Republican Party is defined as the Federalists, National Republicans, and Whigs prior to the establishment of the "Republican Party" in the 1850s. See Appendix A for an explanation of the historical antecedents of the current Democratic and Republican parties. No special elections for any of the four races are used in the calculations, nor are partial voting data reported for any of the four races in any of the states. —indicates that the state had no data, either because no vote data were found for the state in question or the state had not yet entered the Union. Data for the District of Columbia are included from 1964 to the present, after being granted the right to elect presidential electors by the 23rd Amendment.

Sources: Tables 8-36 through 8-140. Specifically, state party competition values in Tables 8-36 through 8-140 for the presidential, House, Senate, and gubernatorial races are aggregated for each election year separately in order to obtain each state's average composite competition values for the election years shown in Tables 8-9 through 8-35.

Table 8-36 Presidential Competition Measures, by State, by Election Year, 1788–1796 (Percentages)

State	1788 Democratic % of Two-Party Vote	1788 Margin of Victory	1788 Party Competition Index	1792 Democratic % of Two-Party Vote	1792 Margin of Victory	1792 Party Competition Index	1796 Democratic % of Two-Party Vote	1796 Margin of Victory	1796 Party Competition Index
Alabama	—	—	—	—	—	—	—	—	—
Alaska	—	—	—	—	—	—	—	—	—
Arizona	—	—	—	—	—	—	—	—	—
Arkansas	—	—	—	—	—	—	—	—	—
California	—	—	—	—	—	—	—	—	—
Colorado	—	—	—	—	—	—	—	—	—
Connecticut	—	—	—	—	—	—	—	—	—
Delaware	—	—	—	—	—	—	—	—	—
Dist. of Columbia	—	—	—	—	—	—	—	—	—
Florida	—	—	—	—	—	—	—	—	—
Georgia	—	—	—	—	—	—	—	—	—
Hawaii	—	—	—	—	—	—	—	—	—
Idaho	—	—	—	—	—	—	—	—	—
Illinois	—	—	—	—	—	—	—	—	—
Indiana	—	—	—	—	—	—	—	—	—
Iowa	—	—	—	—	—	—	—	—	—
Kansas	—	—	—	—	—	—	—	—	—
Kentucky	—	—	—	—	—	—	—	—	—
Louisiana	—	—	—	—	—	—	—	—	—
Maine	—	—	—	—	—	—	—	—	—
Maryland	22.9	54.2	45.8	—	—	—	47.8	4.4	95.6
Massachusetts	0.0	100.0	0.0	—	—	—	—	—	—
Michigan	—	—	—	—	—	—	—	—	—
Minnesota	—	—	—	—	—	—	—	—	—
Mississippi	—	—	—	—	—	—	—	—	—
Missouri	—	—	—	—	—	—	—	—	—
Montana	—	—	—	—	—	—	—	—	—
Nebraska	—	—	—	—	—	—	—	—	—
Nevada	—	—	—	—	—	—	—	—	—
New Hampshire	0.0	100.0	0.0	0.0	100.0	0.0	0.0	100.0	0.0
New Jersey	—	—	—	—	—	—	—	—	—
New Mexico	—	—	—	—	—	—	—	—	—
New York	—	—	—	—	—	—	—	—	—
North Carolina	—	—	—	—	—	—	—	—	—
North Dakota	—	—	—	—	—	—	—	—	—
Ohio	—	—	—	—	—	—	—	—	—
Oklahoma	—	—	—	—	—	—	—	—	—
Oregon	—	—	—	—	—	—	—	—	—
Pennsylvania	—	—	—	—	—	—	50.6	1.2	98.8
Rhode Island	—	—	—	—	—	—	—	—	—
South Carolina	—	—	—	—	—	—	—	—	—
South Dakota	—	—	—	—	—	—	—	—	—
Tennessee	—	—	—	—	—	—	—	—	—
Texas	—	—	—	—	—	—	—	—	—
Utah	—	—	—	—	—	—	—	—	—
Vermont	—	—	—	—	—	—	—	—	—
Virginia	—	—	—	—	—	—	—	—	—
Washington	—	—	—	—	—	—	—	—	—
West Virginia	—	—	—	—	—	—	—	—	—
Wisconsin	—	—	—	—	—	—	—	—	—
Wyoming	—	—	—	—	—	—	—	—	—

Notes: The first entries are the Democratic percent of two-party vote values for each state for the presidential race. The second entries are the margin of victory values for each state for the presidential race, where margin of victory is defined as the absolute difference between the Democratic percent and the Republican percent of the two-party vote for president. The third entries are the party competition index values for each state for the presidential race, where the competition index devised by Paul David (1972) is defined as (100 − the margin of victory) or, alternatively, as (100 − the absolute difference between the Democratic and Republican percent of two-party vote for president). The values for Democratic and Republican percent of two-party vote for president are taken from the state vote tables in Chapter 4. Zero (0) percent on David's index represents a complete absence of two-party competition for that election year, whereas a score of 100 percent indicates perfect competition between the two major parties. A state can only receive a party competition score of 0 if it has a 100–0 vote split for president. Conversely, a state can only receive a score of 100 if it has a 50–50 vote split for president. For example, if Maryland in 1788 reported a 22.9 percent Democratic vote for president of its two-party vote, then its Republican vote for president would be 77.1 percent. The absolute difference between the two figures is the margin of victory, or 54.2 percent. 100 percent − 54.2 percent would equal 45.8 percent on David's party competition scale, indicating little competition in the presidential race in Maryland in 1788. The two-party vote percent values used to derive the margin of victory and party competition figures are initially found in the state vote tables in Chapter 4. The author's alternative party coding in these tables is used whenever it occurs instead of the conventional party coding of voting data. The Democratic Party is defined here as the Anti-Federalists, Democratic-Republicans, and Jackson Democrats prior to 1830 when the "Democratic Party" as such was established. The Republican Party is defined as the Federalists, National Republicans, and Whigs prior to the establishment of the "Republican Party" in the 1850s. See Appendix A for an explanation of the historical antecedents of the current Democratic and Republican parties. States reporting only partial voting returns for president are not included in the calculations for the years in which this occurred. —indicates that the state had no data, either because no vote data were found for the state in question or the state had not yet entered the Union. Data for the District of Columbia are included from 1964 to the present, after being granted the right to elect presidential electors by the 23rd Amendment.

Sources: State vote tables for president in Chapter 4.

Table 8-37 Presidential Competition Measures, by State, by Election Year, 1800–1808 (Percentages)

State	1800 Democratic % of Two-Party Vote	1800 Margin of Victory	1800 Party Competition Index	1804 Democratic % of Two-Party Vote	1804 Margin of Victory	1804 Party Competition Index	1808 Democratic % of Two-Party Vote	1808 Margin of Victory	1808 Party Competition Index
Alabama	—	—	—	—	—	—	—	—	—
Alaska	—	—	—	—	—	—	—	—	—
Arizona	—	—	—	—	—	—	—	—	—
Arkansas	—	—	—	—	—	—	—	—	—
California	—	—	—	—	—	—	—	—	—
Colorado	—	—	—	—	—	—	—	—	—
Connecticut	—	—	—	—	—	—	—	—	—
Delaware	—	—	—	—	—	—	—	—	—
Dist. of Columbia	—	—	—	—	—	—	—	—	—
Florida	—	—	—	—	—	—	—	—	—
Georgia	—	—	—	—	—	—	—	—	—
Hawaii	—	—	—	—	—	—	—	—	—
Idaho	—	—	—	—	—	—	—	—	—
Illinois	—	—	—	—	—	—	—	—	—
Indiana	—	—	—	—	—	—	—	—	—
Iowa	—	—	—	—	—	—	—	—	—
Kansas	—	—	—	—	—	—	—	—	—
Kentucky	—	—	—	—	—	—	—	—	—
Louisiana	—	—	—	—	—	—	—	—	—
Maine	—	—	—	—	—	—	—	—	—
Maryland	51.5	3.0	97.0	74.8	49.6	50.4	63.4	26.8	73.2
Massachusetts	—	—	—	53.3	6.6	93.4	—	—	—
Michigan	—	—	—	—	—	—	—	—	—
Minnesota	—	—	—	—	—	—	—	—	—
Mississippi	—	—	—	—	—	—	—	—	—
Missouri	—	—	—	—	—	—	—	—	—
Montana	—	—	—	—	—	—	—	—	—
Nebraska	—	—	—	—	—	—	—	—	—
Nevada	—	—	—	—	—	—	—	—	—
New Hampshire	—	—	—	52.1	4.2	95.8	47.6	4.8	95.2
New Jersey	—	—	—	100.0	100.0	0.0	55.7	11.4	88.6
New Mexico	—	—	—	—	—	—	—	—	—
New York	—	—	—	—	—	—	—	—	—
North Carolina	—	—	—	—	—	—	—	—	—
North Dakota	—	—	—	—	—	—	—	—	—
Ohio	—	—	—	87.3	74.6	25.4	75.6	51.2	48.8
Oklahoma	—	—	—	—	—	—	—	—	—
Oregon	—	—	—	—	—	—	—	—	—
Pennsylvania	—	—	—	94.7	89.4	10.6	78.4	56.8	43.2
Rhode Island	52.2	4.4	95.6	100.0	100.0	0.0	45.9	8.2	91.8
South Carolina	—	—	—	—	—	—	—	—	—
South Dakota	—	—	—	—	—	—	—	—	—
Tennessee	—	—	—	—	—	—	—	—	—
Texas	—	—	—	—	—	—	—	—	—
Utah	—	—	—	—	—	—	—	—	—
Vermont	—	—	—	—	—	—	—	—	—
Virginia	77.3	54.6	45.4	100.0	100.0	0.0	95.4	90.8	9.2
Washington	—	—	—	—	—	—	—	—	—
West Virginia	—	—	—	—	—	—	—	—	—
Wisconsin	—	—	—	—	—	—	—	—	—
Wyoming	—	—	—	—	—	—	—	—	—

Notes: The first entries are the Democratic percent of two-party vote values for each state for the presidential race. The second entries are the margin of victory values for each state for the presidential race, where margin of victory is defined as the absolute difference between the Democratic percent and the Republican percent of the two-party vote for president. The third entries are the party competition index values for each state for the presidential race, where the competition index devised by Paul David (1972) is defined as (100 − the margin of victory) or, alternatively, as (100 − the absolute difference between the Democratic and Republican percent of two-party vote for president). The values for Democratic and Republican percent of two-party vote for president are taken from the state vote tables in Chapter 4. Zero (0) percent on David's index represents a complete absence of two-party competition for that election year, whereas a score of 100 percent indicates perfect competition between the two major parties. A state can only receive a party competition score of 0 if it has a 100–0 vote split for president. Conversely, a state can only receive a score of 100 if it has a 50–50 vote split for president. For example, if Maryland in 1788 reported a 22.9 percent Democratic vote for president of its two-party vote, then its Republican vote for president would be 77.1 percent. The absolute difference between the two figures is the margin of victory, or 54.2 percent. 100 percent − 54.2 percent would equal 45.8 percent on David's party competition scale, indicating little competition in the presidential race in Maryland in 1788. The two-party vote percent values used to derive the margin of victory and party competition figures are initially found in the state vote tables in Chapter 4. The author's alternative party coding in these tables is used whenever it occurs instead of the conventional party coding of voting data. The Democratic Party is defined here as the Anti-Federalists, Democratic-Republicans, and Jackson Democrats prior to 1830 when the "Democratic Party" as such was established. The Republican Party is defined as the Federalists, National Republicans, and Whigs prior to the establishment of the "Republican Party" in the 1850s. See Appendix A for an explanation of the historical antecedents of the current Democratic and Republican parties. States reporting only partial voting returns for president are not included in the calculations for the years in which this occurred. —indicates that the state had no data, either because no vote data were found for the state in question or the state had not yet entered the Union. Data for the District of Columbia are included from 1964 to the present, after being granted the right to elect presidential electors by the 23rd Amendment.

Sources: State vote tables for president in Chapter 4.

Table 8-38 Presidential Competition Measures, by State, by Election Year, 1812–1820 (Percentages)

State	1812 Democratic % of Two-Party Vote	1812 Margin of Victory	1812 Party Competition Index	1816 Democratic % of Two-Party Vote	1816 Margin of Victory	1816 Party Competition Index	1820 Democratic % of Two-Party Vote	1820 Margin of Victory	1820 Party Competition Index
Alabama	—	—	—	—	—	—	—	—	—
Alaska	—	—	—	—	—	—	—	—	—
Arizona	—	—	—	—	—	—	—	—	—
Arkansas	—	—	—	—	—	—	—	—	—
California	—	—	—	—	—	—	—	—	—
Colorado	—	—	—	—	—	—	—	—	—
Connecticut	—	—	—	—	—	—	100.0	100.0	0.0
Delaware	—	—	—	—	—	—	—	—	—
Dist. of Columbia	—	—	—	—	—	—	—	—	—
Florida	—	—	—	—	—	—	—	—	—
Georgia	—	—	—	—	—	—	—	—	—
Hawaii	—	—	—	—	—	—	—	—	—
Idaho	—	—	—	—	—	—	—	—	—
Illinois	—	—	—	—	—	—	100.0	100.0	0.0
Indiana	—	—	—	—	—	—	—	—	—
Iowa	—	—	—	—	—	—	—	—	—
Kansas	—	—	—	—	—	—	—	—	—
Kentucky	—	—	—	—	—	—	—	—	—
Louisiana	—	—	—	—	—	—	—	—	—
Maine	—	—	—	—	—	—	100.0	100.0	0.0
Maryland	50.8	1.6	98.4	70.9	41.8	58.2	92.2	84.4	15.6
Massachusetts	36.6	26.8	73.2	—	—	—	32.0	36.0	64.0
Michigan	—	—	—	—	—	—	—	—	—
Minnesota	—	—	—	—	—	—	—	—	—
Mississippi	—	—	—	—	—	—	—	—	—
Missouri	—	—	—	—	—	—	—	—	—
Montana	—	—	—	—	—	—	—	—	—
Nebraska	—	—	—	—	—	—	—	—	—
Nevada	—	—	—	—	—	—	—	—	—
New Hampshire	47.6	4.8	95.2	53.3	6.6	93.4	100.0	100.0	0.0
New Jersey	—	—	—	100.0	100.0	0.0	100.0	100.0	0.0
New Mexico	—	—	—	—	—	—	—	—	—
New York	—	—	—	—	—	—	—	—	—
North Carolina	—	—	—	93.7	87.4	12.6	100.0	100.0	0.0
North Dakota	—	—	—	—	—	—	—	—	—
Ohio	69.2	38.4	61.6	84.9	69.8	30.2	100.0	100.0	0.0
Oklahoma	—	—	—	—	—	—	—	—	—
Oregon	—	—	—	—	—	—	—	—	—
Pennsylvania	62.6	25.2	74.8	100.0	100.0	0.0	100.0	100.0	0.0
Rhode Island	34.1	31.8	68.2	100.0	100.0	0.0	100.0	100.0	0.0
South Carolina	—	—	—	—	—	—	—	—	—
South Dakota	—	—	—	—	—	—	—	—	—
Tennessee	—	—	—	—	—	—	—	—	—
Texas	—	—	—	—	—	—	—	—	—
Utah	—	—	—	—	—	—	—	—	—
Vermont	—	—	—	—	—	—	—	—	—
Virginia	72.9	45.8	54.2	100.0	100.0	0.0	100.0	100.0	0.0
Washington	—	—	—	—	—	—	—	—	—
West Virginia	—	—	—	—	—	—	—	—	—
Wisconsin	—	—	—	—	—	—	—	—	—
Wyoming	—	—	—	—	—	—	—	—	—

Notes: The first entries are the Democratic percent of two-party vote values for each state for the presidential race. The second entries are the margin of victory values for each state for the presidential race, where margin of victory is defined as the absolute difference between the Democratic percent and the Republican percent of the two-party vote for president. The third entries are the party competition index values for each state for the presidential race, where the competition index devised by Paul David (1972) is defined as (100 − the margin of victory) or, alternatively, as (100 − the absolute difference between the Democratic and Republican percent of two-party vote for president). The values for Democratic and Republican percent of two-party vote for president are taken from the state vote tables in Chapter 4. Zero (0) percent on David's index represents a complete absence of two-party competition for that election year, whereas a score of 100 percent indicates perfect competition between the two major parties. A state can only receive a party competition score of 0 if it has a 100–0 vote split for president. Conversely, a state can only receive a score of 100 if it has a 50–50 vote split for president. For example, if Maryland in 1788 reported a 22.9 percent Democratic vote for president of its two-party vote, then its Republican vote for president would be 77.1 percent. The absolute difference between the two figures is the margin of victory, or 54.2 percent. 100 percent − 54.2 percent would equal 45.8 percent on David's party competition scale, indicating little competition in the presidential race in Maryland in 1788. The two-party vote percent values used to derive the margin of victory and party competition figures are initially found in the state vote tables in Chapter 4. The author's alternative party coding in these tables is used whenever it occurs instead of the conventional party coding of voting data. The Democratic Party is defined here as the Anti-Federalists, Democratic-Republicans, and Jackson Democrats prior to 1830 when the "Democratic Party" as such was established. The Republican Party is defined as the Federalists, National Republicans, and Whigs prior to the establishment of the "Republican Party" in the 1850s. See Appendix A for an explanation of the historical antecedents of the current Democratic and Republican parties. States reporting only partial voting returns for president are not included in the calculations for the years in which this occurred. —indicates that the state had no data, either because no vote data were found for the state in question or the state had not yet entered the Union. Data for the District of Columbia are included from 1964 to the present, after being granted the right to elect presidential electors by the 23rd Amendment.

Sources: State vote tables for president in Chapter 4.

Table 8-39 Presidential Competition Measures, by State, by Election Year, 1824–1832 (Percentages)

State	1824 Democratic % of Two-Party Vote	1824 Margin of Victory	1824 Party Competition Index	1828 Democratic % of Two-Party Vote	1828 Margin of Victory	1828 Party Competition Index	1832 Democratic % of Two-Party Vote	1832 Margin of Victory	1832 Party Competition Index
Alabama	79.6	59.2	40.8	89.9	79.8	20.2	100.0	100.0	0.0
Alaska	—	—	—	—	—	—	—	—	—
Arizona	—	—	—	—	—	—	—	—	—
Arkansas	—	—	—	—	—	—	—	—	—
California	—	—	—	—	—	—	—	—	—
Colorado	—	—	—	—	—	—	—	—	—
Connecticut	0.0	100.0	0.0	24.3	51.4	48.6	38.3	23.4	76.6
Delaware	—	—	—	—	—	—	49.0	2.0	98.0
Dist. of Columbia	—	—	—	—	—	—	—	—	—
Florida	—	—	—	—	—	—	—	—	—
Georgia	—	—	—	96.8	93.6	6.4	100.0	100.0	0.0
Hawaii	—	—	—	—	—	—	—	—	—
Idaho	—	—	—	—	—	—	—	—	—
Illinois	45.6	8.8	91.2	67.2	34.4	65.6	68.4	36.8	63.2
Indiana	70.8	41.6	58.4	56.6	13.2	86.8	55.4	10.8	89.2
Iowa	—	—	—	—	—	—	—	—	—
Kansas	—	—	—	—	—	—	—	—	—
Kentucky	100.0	100.0	0.0	55.5	11.0	89.0	45.5	9.0	91.0
Louisiana	—	—	—	53.0	6.0	94.0	61.7	23.4	76.6
Maine	0.0	100.0	0.0	40.1	19.8	80.2	55.4	10.8	89.2
Maryland	49.8	0.4	99.6	49.7	0.6	99.4	50.0	0.0	100.0
Massachusetts	0.0	100.0	0.0	16.8	66.4	33.6	30.4	39.2	60.8
Michigan	—	—	—	—	—	—	—	—	—
Minnesota	—	—	—	—	—	—	—	—	—
Mississippi	65.4	30.8	69.2	81.1	62.2	37.8	100.0	100.0	0.0
Missouri	88.0	76.0	24.0	70.6	41.2	58.8	100.0	100.0	0.0
Montana	—	—	—	—	—	—	—	—	—
Nebraska	—	—	—	—	—	—	—	—	—
Nevada	—	—	—	—	—	—	—	—	—
New Hampshire	0.0	100.0	0.0	45.9	8.2	91.8	56.8	13.6	86.4
New Jersey	55.4	10.8	89.2	47.9	4.2	95.8	50.4	0.8	99.2
New Mexico	—	—	—	—	—	—	—	—	—
New York	—	—	—	51.4	2.8	97.2	52.1	4.2	95.8
North Carolina	100.0	100.0	0.0	73.1	46.2	53.8	84.8	69.6	30.4
North Dakota	—	—	—	—	—	—	—	—	—
Ohio	60.1	20.2	79.8	51.6	3.2	96.8	51.5	3.0	97.0
Oklahoma	—	—	—	—	—	—	—	—	—
Oregon	—	—	—	—	—	—	—	—	—
Pennsylvania	86.8	73.6	26.4	66.7	33.4	66.6	100.0	100.0	0.0
Rhode Island	0.0	100.0	0.0	22.9	54.2	45.8	41.7	16.6	83.4
South Carolina	—	—	—	—	—	—	—	—	—
South Dakota	—	—	—	—	—	—	—	—	—
Tennessee	98.9	97.8	2.2	95.2	90.4	9.6	95.4	90.8	9.2
Texas	—	—	—	—	—	—	—	—	—
Utah	—	—	—	—	—	—	—	—	—
Vermont	—	—	—	25.5	49.0	51.0	41.3	17.4	82.6
Virginia	46.5	7.0	93.0	69.0	38.0	62.0	75.0	50.0	50.0
Washington	—	—	—	—	—	—	—	—	—
West Virginia	—	—	—	—	—	—	—	—	—
Wisconsin	—	—	—	—	—	—	—	—	—
Wyoming	—	—	—	—	—	—	—	—	—

Notes: The first entries are the Democratic percent of two-party vote values for each state for the presidential race. The second entries are the margin of victory values for each state for the presidential race, where margin of victory is defined as the absolute difference between the Democratic percent and the Republican percent of the two-party vote for president. The third entries are the party competition index values for each state for the presidential race, where the competition index devised by Paul David (1972) is defined as (100 − the margin of victory) or, alternatively, as (100 − the absolute difference between the Democratic and Republican percent of two-party vote for president). The values for Democratic and Republican percent of two-party vote for president are taken from the state vote tables in Chapter 4. Zero (0) percent on David's index represents a complete absence of two-party competition for that election year, whereas a score of 100 percent indicates perfect competition between the two major parties. A state can only receive a party competition score of 0 if it has a 100–0 vote split for president. Conversely, a state can only receive a score of 100 if it has a 50–50 vote split for president. For example, if Maryland in 1788 reported a 22.9 percent Democratic vote for president of its two-party vote, then its Republican vote for president would be 77.1 percent. The absolute difference between the two figures is the margin of victory, or 54.2 percent. 100 percent − 54.2 percent would equal 45.8 percent on David's party competition scale, indicating little competition in the presidential race in Maryland in 1788. The two-party vote percent values used to derive the margin of victory and party competition figures are initially found in the state vote tables in Chapter 4. The author's alternative party coding in these tables is used whenever it occurs instead of the conventional party coding of voting data. The Democratic Party is defined here as the Anti-Federalists, Democratic-Republicans, and Jackson Democrats prior to 1830 when the "Democratic Party" as such was established. The Republican Party is defined as the Federalists, National Republicans, and Whigs prior to the establishment of the "Republican Party" in the 1850s. See Appendix A for an explanation of the historical antecedents of the current Democratic and Republican parties. States reporting only partial voting returns for president are not included in the calculations for the years in which this occurred. —indicates that the state had no data, either because no vote data were found for the state in question or the state had not yet entered the Union. Data for the District of Columbia are included from 1964 to the present, after being granted the right to elect presidential electors by the 23rd Amendment.

Sources: State vote tables for president in Chapter 4.

Table 8-40 Presidential Competition Measures, by State, by Election Year, 1836–1844 (Percentages)

State	1836 Democratic % of Two-Party Vote	1836 Margin of Victory	1836 Party Competition Index	1840 Democratic % of Two-Party Vote	1840 Margin of Victory	1840 Party Competition Index	1844 Democratic % of Two-Party Vote	1844 Margin of Victory	1844 Party Competition Index
Alabama	55.3	10.6	89.4	54.4	8.8	91.2	59.0	18.0	82.0
Alaska	—	—	—	—	—	—	—	—	—
Arizona	—	—	—	—	—	—	—	—	—
Arkansas	64.1	28.2	71.8	56.4	12.8	87.2	63.0	26.0	74.0
California	—	—	—	—	—	—	—	—	—
Colorado	—	—	—	—	—	—	—	—	—
Connecticut	50.6	1.2	98.8	44.4	11.2	88.8	47.6	4.8	95.2
Delaware	46.7	6.6	93.4	44.9	10.2	89.8	48.8	2.4	97.6
Dist. of Columbia	—	—	—	—	—	—	—	—	—
Florida	—	—	—	—	—	—	—	—	—
Georgia	48.2	3.6	96.4	44.2	11.6	88.4	51.2	2.4	97.6
Hawaii	—	—	—	—	—	—	—	—	—
Idaho	—	—	—	—	—	—	—	—	—
Illinois	54.7	9.4	90.6	51.0	2.0	98.0	56.2	12.4	87.6
Indiana	44.5	11.0	89.0	44.2	11.6	88.4	50.8	1.6	98.4
Iowa	—	—	—	—	—	—	—	—	—
Kansas	—	—	—	—	—	—	—	—	—
Kentucky	47.4	5.2	94.8	35.8	28.4	71.6	45.9	8.2	91.8
Louisiana	51.7	3.4	96.6	40.3	19.4	80.6	51.3	2.6	97.4
Maine	60.7	21.4	78.6	49.8	0.4	99.6	57.1	14.2	85.8
Maryland	46.3	7.4	92.6	46.2	7.6	92.4	47.6	4.8	95.2
Massachusetts	44.8	10.4	89.6	41.8	16.4	83.6	44.2	11.6	88.4
Michigan	54.0	8.0	92.0	47.9	4.2	95.8	53.4	6.8	93.2
Minnesota	—	—	—	—	—	—	—	—	—
Mississippi	51.3	2.6	97.4	46.6	6.8	93.2	57.4	14.8	85.2
Missouri	60.0	20.0	80.0	56.6	13.2	86.8	57.0	14.0	86.0
Montana	—	—	—	—	—	—	—	—	—
Nebraska	—	—	—	—	—	—	—	—	—
Nevada	—	—	—	—	—	—	—	—	—
New Hampshire	75.0	50.0	50.0	55.5	11.0	89.0	60.3	20.6	79.4
New Jersey	49.5	1.0	99.0	48.2	3.6	96.4	49.5	1.0	99.0
New Mexico	—	—	—	—	—	—	—	—	—
New York	54.6	9.2	90.8	48.5	3.0	97.0	50.5	1.0	99.0
North Carolina	53.1	6.2	93.8	42.3	15.4	84.6	47.6	4.8	95.2
North Dakota	—	—	—	—	—	—	—	—	—
Ohio	47.9	4.2	95.8	45.6	8.8	91.2	49.0	2.0	98.0
Oklahoma	—	—	—	—	—	—	—	—	—
Oregon	—	—	—	—	—	—	—	—	—
Pennsylvania	51.2	2.4	97.6	49.9	0.2	99.8	50.9	1.8	98.2
Rhode Island	52.2	4.4	95.6	38.5	23.0	77.0	39.9	20.2	79.8
South Carolina	—	—	—	—	—	—	—	—	—
South Dakota	—	—	—	—	—	—	—	—	—
Tennessee	42.1	15.8	84.2	44.3	11.4	88.6	49.9	0.2	99.8
Texas	—	—	—	—	—	—	—	—	—
Utah	—	—	—	—	—	—	—	—	—
Vermont	40.1	19.8	80.2	35.7	28.6	71.4	40.3	19.4	80.6
Virginia	56.6	13.2	86.8	50.6	1.2	98.8	53.0	6.0	94.0
Washington	—	—	—	—	—	—	—	—	—
West Virginia	—	—	—	—	—	—	—	—	—
Wisconsin	—	—	—	—	—	—	—	—	—
Wyoming	—	—	—	—	—	—	—	—	—

Notes: The first entries are the Democratic percent of two-party vote values for each state for the presidential race. The second entries are the margin of victory values for each state for the presidential race, where margin of victory is defined as the absolute difference between the Democratic percent and the Republican percent of the two-party vote for president. The third entries are the party competition index values for each state for the presidential race, where the competition index devised by Paul David (1972) is defined as (100 − the margin of victory) or, alternatively, as (100 − the absolute difference between the Democratic and Republican percent of two-party vote for president). The values for Democratic and Republican percent of two-party vote for president are taken from the state vote tables in Chapter 4. Zero (0) percent on David's index represents a complete absence of two-party competition for that election year, whereas a score of 100 percent indicates perfect competition between the two major parties. A state can only receive a party competition score of 0 if it has a 100–0 vote split for president. Conversely, a state can only receive a score of 100 if it has a 50–50 vote split for president. For example, if Maryland in 1788 reported a 22.9 percent Democratic vote for president of its two-party vote, then its Republican vote for president would be 77.1 percent. The absolute difference between the two figures is the margin of victory, or 54.2 percent. 100 percent − 54.2 percent would equal 45.8 percent on David's party competition scale, indicating little competition in the presidential race in Maryland in 1788. The two-party vote percent values used to derive the margin of victory and party competition figures are initially found in the state vote tables in Chapter 4. The author's alternative party coding in these tables is used whenever it occurs instead of the conventional party coding of voting data. The Democratic Party is defined here as the Anti-Federalists, Democratic-Republicans, and Jackson Democrats prior to 1830 when the "Democratic Party" as such was established. The Republican Party is defined as the Federalists, National Republicans, and Whigs prior to the establishment of the "Republican Party" in the 1850s. See Appendix A for an explanation of the historical antecedents of the current Democratic and Republican parties. States reporting only partial voting returns for president are not included in the calculations for the years in which this occurred. —indicates that the state had no data, either because no vote data were found for the state in question or the state had not yet entered the Union. Data for the District of Columbia are included from 1964 to the present, after being granted the right to elect presidential electors by the 23rd Amendment.

Sources: State vote tables for president in Chapter 4.

Table 8-41 Presidential Competition Measures, by State, by Election Year, 1848–1856 (Percentages)

| | 1848 | | | 1852 | | | 1856 | | |
State	Democratic % of Two-Party Vote	Margin of Victory	Party Competition Index	Democratic % of Two-Party Vote	Margin of Victory	Party Competition Index	Democratic % of Two-Party Vote	Margin of Victory	Party Competition Index
Alabama	50.6	1.2	98.8	64.1	28.2	71.8	100.0	100.0	0.0
Alaska	—	—	—	—	—	—	—	—	—
Arizona	—	—	—	—	—	—	—	—	—
Arkansas	55.1	10.2	89.8	62.2	24.4	75.6	100.0	100.0	0.0
California	—	—	—	53.1	6.2	93.8	72.0	44.0	56.0
Colorado	—	—	—	—	—	—	—	—	—
Connecticut	47.2	5.6	94.4	52.3	4.6	95.4	45.1	9.8	90.2
Delaware	47.9	4.2	95.8	50.1	0.2	99.8	96.3	92.6	7.4
Dist. of Columbia	—	—	—	—	—	—	—	—	—
Florida	42.8	14.4	85.6	60.0	20.0	80.0	100.0	100.0	0.0
Georgia	48.5	3.0	97.0	70.9	41.8	58.2	100.0	100.0	0.0
Hawaii	—	—	—	—	—	—	—	—	—
Idaho	—	—	—	—	—	—	—	—	—
Illinois	51.4	2.8	97.2	55.4	10.8	89.2	52.3	4.6	95.4
Indiana	51.7	3.4	96.6	54.1	8.2	91.8	55.7	11.4	88.6
Iowa	53.1	6.2	93.8	52.8	5.6	94.4	45.5	9.0	91.0
Kansas	—	—	—	—	—	—	—	—	—
Kentucky	42.5	15.0	85.0	48.4	3.2	96.8	100.0	100.0	0.0
Louisiana	45.4	9.2	90.8	51.9	3.8	96.2	100.0	100.0	0.0
Maine	53.3	6.6	93.4	56.1	12.2	87.8	36.8	26.4	73.6
Maryland	47.8	4.4	95.6	53.3	6.6	93.4	99.3	98.6	1.4
Massachusetts	36.6	26.8	73.2	45.8	8.4	91.6	26.6	46.8	53.2
Michigan	56.2	12.4	87.6	55.3	10.6	89.4	42.1	15.8	84.2
Minnesota	—	—	—	—	—	—	—	—	—
Mississippi	50.6	1.2	98.8	60.5	21.0	79.0	100.0	100.0	0.0
Missouri	55.1	10.2	89.8	56.4	12.8	87.2	100.0	100.0	0.0
Montana	—	—	—	—	—	—	—	—	—
Nebraska	—	—	—	—	—	—	—	—	—
Nevada	—	—	—	—	—	—	—	—	—
New Hampshire	65.3	30.6	69.4	64.8	29.6	70.4	46.0	8.0	92.0
New Jersey	48.0	4.0	96.0	53.5	7.0	93.0	62.4	24.8	75.2
New Mexico	—	—	—	—	—	—	—	—	—
New York	34.3	31.4	68.6	52.7	5.4	94.6	41.5	17.0	83.0
North Carolina	44.8	10.4	89.6	50.5	1.0	99.0	100.0	100.0	0.0
North Dakota	—	—	—	—	—	—	—	—	—
Ohio	52.7	5.4	94.6	52.6	5.2	94.8	47.7	4.6	95.4
Oklahoma	—	—	—	—	—	—	—	—	—
Oregon	—	—	—	—	—	—	—	—	—
Pennsylvania	48.1	3.8	96.2	52.6	5.2	94.8	60.9	21.8	78.2
Rhode Island	35.0	30.0	70.0	53.4	6.8	93.2	36.8	26.4	73.6
South Carolina	—	—	—	—	—	—	—	—	—
South Dakota	—	—	—	—	—	—	—	—	—
Tennessee	47.5	5.0	95.0	49.3	1.4	98.6	100.0	100.0	0.0
Texas	68.8	37.6	62.4	73.5	47.0	53.0	100.0	100.0	0.0
Utah	—	—	—	—	—	—	—	—	—
Vermont	32.1	35.8	64.2	37.0	26.0	74.0	21.1	57.8	42.2
Virginia	50.8	1.6	98.4	55.7	11.4	88.6	100.0	100.0	0.0
Washington	—	—	—	—	—	—	—	—	—
West Virginia	—	—	—	—	—	—	—	—	—
Wisconsin	52.2	4.4	95.6	60.2	20.4	79.6	44.1	11.8	88.2
Wyoming	—	—	—	—	—	—	—	—	—

Notes: The first entries are the Democratic percent of two-party vote values for each state for the presidential race. The second entries are the margin of victory values for each state for the presidential race, where margin of victory is defined as the absolute difference between the Democratic percent and the Republican percent of the two-party vote for president. The third entries are the party competition index values for each state for the presidential race, where the competition index devised by Paul David (1972) is defined as (100 − the margin of victory) or, alternatively, as (100 − the absolute difference between the Democratic and Republican percent of two-party vote for president). The values for Democratic and Republican percent of two-party vote for president are taken from the state vote tables in Chapter 4. Zero (0) percent on David's index represents a complete absence of two-party competition for that election year, whereas a score of 100 percent indicates perfect competition between the two major parties. A state can only receive a party competition score of 0 if it has a 100–0 vote split for president. Conversely, a state can only receive a score of 100 if it has a 50–50 vote split for president. For example, if Maryland in 1788 reported a 22.9 percent Democratic vote for president of its two-party vote, then its Republican vote for president would be 77.1 percent. The absolute difference between the two figures is the margin of victory, or 54.2 percent. 100 percent − 54.2 percent would equal 45.8 percent on David's party competition scale, indicating little competition in the presidential race in Maryland in 1788. The two-party vote percent values used to derive the margin of victory and party competition figures are initially found in the state vote tables in Chapter 4. The author's alternative party coding in these tables is used whenever it occurs instead of the conventional party coding of voting data. The Democratic Party is defined here as the Anti-Federalists, Democratic-Republicans, and Jackson Democrats prior to 1830 when the "Democratic Party" as such was established. The Republican Party is defined as the Federalists, National Republicans, and Whigs prior to the establishment of the "Republican Party" in the 1850s. See Appendix A for an explanation of the historical antecedents of the current Democratic and Republican parties. States reporting only partial voting returns for president are not included in the calculations for the years in which this occurred. —indicates that the state had no data, either because no vote data were found for the state in question or the state had not yet entered the Union. Data for the District of Columbia are included from 1964 to the present, after being granted the right to elect presidential electors by the 23rd Amendment.

Sources: State vote tables for president in Chapter 4.

Table 8-42 Presidential Competition Measures, by State, by Election Year, 1860–1868 (Percentages)

State	1860			1864			1868		
	Democratic % of Two-Party Vote	Margin of Victory	Party Competition Index	Democratic % of Two-Party Vote	Margin of Victory	Party Competition Index	Democratic % of Two-Party Vote	Margin of Victory	Party Competition Index
Alabama	100.0	100.0	0.0	—	—	—	48.7	2.6	97.4
Alaska	—	—	—	—	—	—	—	—	—
Arizona	—	—	—	—	—	—	—	—	—
Arkansas	100.0	100.0	0.0	—	—	—	46.3	7.4	92.6
California	49.5	1.0	99.0	41.4	17.2	82.8	49.8	0.4	99.6
Colorado	—	—	—	—	—	—	—	—	—
Connecticut	26.2	47.6	52.4	48.6	2.8	97.2	48.5	3.0	97.0
Delaware	21.8	56.4	43.6	51.8	3.6	96.4	59.0	18.0	82.0
Dist. of Columbia	—	—	—	—	—	—	—	—	—
Florida	100.0	100.0	0.0	—	—	—	—	—	—
Georgia	100.0	100.0	0.0	—	—	—	64.3	28.6	71.4
Hawaii	—	—	—	—	—	—	—	—	—
Idaho	—	—	—	—	—	—	—	—	—
Illinois	48.2	3.6	96.4	45.6	8.8	91.2	44.3	11.4	88.6
Indiana	45.4	9.2	90.8	46.5	7.0	93.0	48.6	2.8	97.2
Iowa	44.2	11.6	88.4	36.9	26.2	73.8	38.1	23.8	76.2
Kansas	—	—	—	18.3	63.4	36.6	31.2	37.6	62.4
Kentucky	95.0	90.0	10.0	69.8	39.6	60.4	74.5	49.0	51.0
Louisiana	100.0	100.0	0.0	—	—	—	70.7	41.4	58.6
Maine	32.1	35.8	64.2	40.9	18.2	81.8	37.6	24.8	75.2
Maryland	72.2	44.4	55.6	44.9	10.2	89.8	67.2	34.4	65.6
Massachusetts	24.4	51.2	48.8	27.8	44.4	55.6	30.2	39.6	60.4
Michigan	42.4	15.2	84.8	44.9	10.2	89.8	43.0	14.0	86.0
Minnesota	35.1	29.8	70.2	41.0	18.0	82.0	39.2	21.6	78.4
Mississippi	100.0	100.0	0.0	—	—	—	—	—	—
Missouri	77.5	55.0	45.0	30.3	39.4	60.6	43.0	14.0	86.0
Montana	—	—	—	—	—	—	—	—	—
Nebraska	—	—	—	—	—	—	36.1	27.8	72.2
Nevada	—	—	—	40.2	19.6	80.4	44.6	10.8	89.2
New Hampshire	40.8	18.4	81.6	47.4	5.2	94.8	44.8	10.4	89.6
New Jersey	51.9	3.8	96.2	52.8	5.6	94.4	50.9	1.8	98.2
New Mexico	—	—	—	—	—	—	—	—	—
New York	46.3	7.4	92.6	49.5	1.0	99.0	50.6	1.2	98.8
North Carolina	100.0	100.0	0.0	—	—	—	46.6	6.8	93.2
North Dakota	—	—	—	—	—	—	—	—	—
Ohio	44.7	10.6	89.4	43.6	12.8	87.2	46.0	8.0	92.0
Oklahoma	—	—	—	—	—	—	—	—	—
Oregon	43.7	12.6	87.4	46.1	7.8	92.2	50.4	0.8	99.2
Pennsylvania	5.9	88.2	11.8	48.4	3.2	96.8	47.8	4.4	95.6
Rhode Island	38.6	22.8	77.2	37.8	24.4	75.6	33.3	33.4	66.6
South Carolina	—	—	—	—	—	—	42.1	15.8	84.2
South Dakota	—	—	—	—	—	—	—	—	—
Tennessee	100.0	100.0	0.0	—	—	—	31.6	36.8	63.2
Texas	—	—	—	—	—	—	—	—	—
Utah	—	—	—	—	—	—	—	—	—
Vermont	20.4	59.2	40.8	23.9	52.2	47.8	21.4	57.2	42.8
Virginia	89.6	79.2	20.8	—	—	—	—	—	—
Washington	—	—	—	—	—	—	—	—	—
West Virginia	—	—	—	31.8	36.4	63.6	41.2	17.6	82.4
Wisconsin	43.0	14.0	86.0	44.1	11.8	88.2	43.7	12.6	87.4
Wyoming	—	—	—	—	—	—	—	—	—

Notes: The first entries are the Democratic percent of two-party vote values for each state for the presidential race. The second entries are the margin of victory values for each state for the presidential race, where margin of victory is defined as the absolute difference between the Democratic percent and the Republican percent of the two-party vote for president. The third entries are the party competition index values for each state for the presidential race, where the competition index devised by Paul David (1972) is defined as (100 − the margin of victory) or, alternatively, as (100 − the absolute difference between the Democratic and Republican percent of two-party vote for president). The values for Democratic and Republican percent of two-party vote for president are taken from the state vote tables in Chapter 4. Zero (0) percent on David's index represents a complete absence of two-party competition for that election year, whereas a score of 100 percent indicates perfect competition between the two major parties. A state can only receive a party competition score of 0 if it has a 100–0 vote split for president. Conversely, a state can only receive a score of 100 if it has a 50–50 vote split for president. For example, if Maryland in 1788 reported a 22.9 percent Democratic vote for president of its two-party vote, then its Republican vote for president would be 77.1 percent. The absolute difference between the two figures is the margin of victory, or 54.2 percent. 100 percent − 54.2 percent would equal 45.8 percent on David's party competition scale, indicating little competition in the presidential race in Maryland in 1788. The two-party vote percent values used to derive the margin of victory and party competition figures are found in Chapter 4. The author's alternative party coding in these tables is used whenever it occurs instead of the conventional party coding of voting data. The Democratic Party is defined here as the Anti-Federalists, Democratic-Republicans, and Jackson Democrats prior to 1830 when the "Democratic Party" as such was established. The Republican Party is defined as the Federalists, National Republicans, and Whigs prior to the establishment of the "Republican Party" in the 1850s. See Appendix A for an explanation of the historical antecedents of the current Democratic and Republican parties. States reporting only partial voting returns for president are not included in the calculations for the years in which this occurred. —indicates that the state had no data, either because no vote data were found for the state in question or the state had not yet entered the Union. Data for the District of Columbia are included from 1964 to the present, after being granted the right to elect presidential electors by the 23rd Amendment.

Sources: State vote tables for president in Chapter 4.

Table 8-43 Presidential Competition Measures, by State, by Election Year, 1872–1880 (Percentages)

State	1872 Democratic % of Two-Party Vote	1872 Margin of Victory	1872 Party Competition Index	1876 Democratic % of Two-Party Vote	1876 Margin of Victory	1876 Party Competition Index	1880 Democratic % of Two-Party Vote	1880 Margin of Victory	1880 Party Competition Index
Alabama	46.8	6.4	93.6	60.0	20.0	80.0	61.8	23.6	76.4
Alaska	—	—	—	—	—	—	—	—	—
Arizona	—	—	—	—	—	—	—	—	—
Arkansas	47.8	4.4	95.6	60.0	20.0	80.0	59.2	18.4	81.6
California	43.0	14.0	86.0	49.1	1.8	98.2	50.0	0.0	100.0
Colorado	—	—	—	—	—	—	47.3	5.4	94.6
Connecticut	47.6	4.8	95.2	51.2	2.4	97.6	49.0	2.0	98.0
Delaware	47.8	4.4	95.6	55.4	10.8	89.2	51.8	3.6	96.4
Dist. of Columbia	—	—	—	—	—	—	—	—	—
Florida	46.5	7.0	93.0	49.0	2.0	98.0	54.2	8.4	91.6
Georgia	55.0	10.0	90.0	72.0	44.0	56.0	65.4	30.8	69.2
Hawaii	—	—	—	—	—	—	—	—	—
Idaho	—	—	—	—	—	—	—	—	—
Illinois	43.3	13.4	86.6	48.2	3.6	96.4	46.6	6.8	93.2
Indiana	46.8	6.4	93.6	50.7	1.4	98.6	49.3	1.4	98.6
Iowa	35.1	29.8	70.2	39.6	20.8	79.2	36.5	27.0	73.0
Kansas	33.0	34.0	66.0	32.6	34.8	65.2	33.0	34.0	66.0
Kentucky	53.0	6.0	94.0	62.1	24.2	75.8	58.3	16.6	83.4
Louisiana	44.3	11.4	88.6	48.4	3.2	96.8	62.5	25.0	75.0
Maine	32.1	35.8	64.2	43.0	14.0	86.0	46.8	6.4	93.6
Maryland	50.3	0.6	99.4	56.0	12.0	88.0	54.4	8.8	91.2
Massachusetts	30.7	38.6	61.4	42.0	16.0	84.0	40.4	19.2	80.8
Michigan	36.2	27.6	72.4	45.9	8.2	91.8	41.5	17.0	83.0
Minnesota	38.5	23.0	77.0	40.1	19.8	80.2	36.2	27.6	72.4
Mississippi	36.5	27.0	73.0	68.1	36.2	63.8	68.5	37.0	63.0
Missouri	56.0	12.0	88.0	58.2	16.4	83.6	57.6	15.2	84.8
Montana	—	—	—	—	—	—	—	—	—
Nebraska	29.3	41.4	58.6	35.2	29.6	70.4	34.2	31.6	68.4
Nevada	42.6	14.8	85.2	47.3	5.4	94.6	52.4	4.8	95.2
New Hampshire	45.8	8.4	91.6	48.1	3.8	96.2	47.6	4.8	95.2
New Jersey	45.5	9.0	91.0	52.8	5.6	94.4	50.4	0.8	99.2
New Mexico	—	—	—	—	—	—	—	—	—
New York	46.8	6.4	93.6	51.6	3.2	96.8	49.0	2.0	98.0
North Carolina	42.5	15.0	85.0	53.6	7.2	92.8	51.8	3.6	96.4
North Dakota	—	—	—	—	—	—	—	—	—
Ohio	46.4	7.2	92.8	49.4	1.2	98.8	47.6	4.8	95.2
Oklahoma	—	—	—	—	—	—	—	—	—
Oregon	39.6	20.8	79.2	48.2	3.6	96.4	49.2	1.6	98.4
Pennsylvania	37.8	24.4	75.6	48.8	2.4	97.6	47.8	4.4	95.6
Rhode Island	28.1	43.8	56.2	40.4	19.2	80.8	37.2	25.6	74.4
South Carolina	23.9	52.2	47.8	49.8	0.4	99.6	65.7	31.4	68.6
South Dakota	—	—	—	—	—	—	—	—	—
Tennessee	52.2	4.4	95.6	59.8	19.6	80.4	54.6	9.2	90.8
Texas	58.5	17.0	83.0	70.3	40.6	59.4	75.6	51.2	48.8
Utah	—	—	—	—	—	—	—	—	—
Vermont	20.8	58.4	41.6	31.5	37.0	63.0	28.7	42.6	57.4
Virginia	49.5	1.0	99.0	59.6	19.2	80.8	60.5	21.0	79.0
Washington	—	—	—	—	—	—	—	—	—
West Virginia	47.7	4.6	95.4	57.4	14.8	85.2	55.4	10.8	89.2
Wisconsin	45.1	9.8	90.2	48.8	2.4	97.6	44.3	11.4	88.6
Wyoming	—	—	—	—	—	—	—	—	—

Notes: The first entries are the Democratic percent of two-party vote values for each state for the presidential race. The second entries are the margin of victory values for each state for the presidential race, where margin of victory is defined as the absolute difference between the Democratic percent and the Republican percent of the two-party vote for president. The third entries are the party competition index values for each state for the presidential race, where the competition index devised by Paul David (1972) is defined as (100 − the margin of victory) or, alternatively, as (100 − the absolute difference between the Democratic and Republican percent of two-party vote for president). The values for Democratic and Republican percent of two-party vote for president are taken from the state vote tables in Chapter 4. Zero (0) percent on David's index represents a complete absence of two-party competition for that election year, whereas a score of 100 percent indicates perfect competition between the two major parties. A state can only receive a party competition score of 0 if it has a 100–0 vote split for president. Conversely, a state can only receive a score of 100 if it has a 50–50 vote split for president. For example, if Maryland in 1788 reported a 22.9 percent Democratic vote for president of its two-party vote, then its Republican vote for president would be 77.1 percent. The absolute difference between the two figures is the margin of victory, or 54.2 percent. 100 percent − 54.2 percent would equal 45.8 percent on David's party competition scale, indicating little competition in the presidential race in Maryland in 1788. The two-party vote percent values used to derive the margin of victory and party competition figures are initially found in the state vote tables in Chapter 4. The author's alternative party coding in these tables is used whenever it occurs instead of the conventional party coding of voting data. The Democratic Party is defined here as the Anti-Federalists, Democratic-Republicans, and Jackson Democrats prior to 1830 when the "Democratic Party" as such was established. The Republican Party is defined as the Federalists, National Republicans, and Whigs prior to the establishment of the "Republican Party" in the 1850s. See Appendix A for an explanation of the historical antecedents of the current Democratic and Republican parties. States reporting only partial voting returns for president are not included in the calculations for the years in which this occurred. —indicates that the state had no data, either because no vote data were found for the state in question or the state had not yet entered the Union. Data for the District of Columbia are included from 1964 to the present, after being granted the right to elect presidential electors by the 23rd Amendment.

Sources: State vote tables for president in Chapter 4.

Table 8-44 Presidential Competition Measures, by State, by Election Year, 1884–1892 (Percentages)

	1884			1888			1892		
State	Democratic % of Two-Party Vote	Margin of Victory	Party Competition Index	Democratic % of Two-Party Vote	Margin of Victory	Party Competition Index	Democratic % of Two-Party Vote	Margin of Victory	Party Competition Index
Alabama	60.9	21.8	78.2	67.2	34.4	65.6	93.8	87.6	12.4
Alaska	—	—	—	—	—	—	—	—	—
Arizona	—	—	—	—	—	—	—	—	—
Arkansas	58.7	17.4	82.6	59.0	18.0	82.0	65.1	30.2	69.8
California	46.6	6.8	93.2	48.5	3.0	97.0	50.0	0.0	100.0
Colorado	43.4	13.2	86.8	42.5	15.0	85.0	0.0	100.0	0.0
Connecticut	50.5	1.0	99.0	50.1	0.2	99.8	51.7	3.4	96.6
Delaware	56.7	13.4	86.6	55.9	11.8	88.2	50.7	1.4	98.6
Dist. of Columbia	—	—	—	—	—	—	—	—	—
Florida	53.1	6.2	93.8	59.9	19.8	80.2	100.0	100.0	0.0
Georgia	66.1	32.2	67.8	71.3	42.6	57.4	72.8	45.6	54.4
Hawaii	—	—	—	—	—	—	0.0	100.0	0.0
Idaho	—	—	—	—	—	—	51.6	3.2	96.8
Illinois	48.1	3.8	96.2	48.5	3.0	97.0	51.6	3.2	96.8
Indiana	50.7	1.4	98.6	49.8	0.4	99.6	50.7	1.4	98.6
Iowa	47.4	5.2	94.8	45.9	8.2	91.8	47.2	5.6	94.4
Kansas	36.9	26.2	73.8	36.0	28.0	72.0	0.0	100.0	0.0
Kentucky	56.3	12.6	87.4	54.2	8.4	91.6	56.4	12.8	87.2
Louisiana	57.5	15.0	85.0	73.5	47.0	53.0	76.5	53.0	47.0
Maine	41.9	16.2	83.8	40.6	18.8	81.2	43.3	13.4	86.6
Maryland	53.0	6.0	94.0	51.5	3.0	97.0	55.1	10.2	89.8
Massachusetts	45.5	9.0	91.0	45.2	9.6	90.4	46.6	6.8	93.2
Michigan	43.7	12.6	87.4	47.5	5.0	95.0	47.6	4.8	95.2
Minnesota	38.6	22.8	77.2	42.3	15.4	84.6	45.0	10.0	90.0
Mississippi	64.3	28.6	71.4	74.0	48.0	52.0	96.6	93.2	6.8
Missouri	53.8	7.6	92.4	52.6	5.2	94.8	54.1	8.2	91.8
Montana	—	—	—	—	—	—	48.4	3.2	96.8
Nebraska	41.4	17.2	82.8	42.6	14.8	85.2	22.2	55.6	44.4
Nevada	43.7	12.6	87.4	42.3	15.4	84.6	20.0	60.0	40.0
New Hampshire	47.5	5.0	95.0	48.7	2.6	97.4	48.0	4.0	96.0
New Jersey	50.9	1.8	98.2	51.2	2.4	97.6	52.3	4.6	95.4
New Mexico	—	—	—	—	—	—	—	—	—
New York	50.0	0.0	100.0	49.4	1.2	98.8	51.8	3.6	96.4
North Carolina	53.3	6.6	93.4	52.3	4.6	95.4	57.0	14.0	86.0
North Dakota	—	—	—	—	—	—	0.0	100.0	0.0
Ohio	47.9	4.2	95.8	48.7	2.6	97.4	49.9	0.2	99.8
Oklahoma	—	—	—	—	—	—	—	—	—
Oregon	47.8	4.4	95.6	44.3	11.4	88.6	28.9	42.2	57.8
Pennsylvania	45.5	9.0	91.0	45.9	8.2	91.8	46.7	6.6	93.4
Rhode Island	39.4	21.2	78.8	44.4	11.2	88.8	47.4	5.2	94.8
South Carolina	76.3	52.6	47.4	82.7	65.4	34.6	80.4	60.8	39.2
South Dakota	—	—	—	—	—	—	20.4	59.2	40.8
Tennessee	51.9	3.8	96.2	53.3	6.6	93.4	57.6	15.2	84.8
Texas	71.0	42.0	58.0	72.4	44.8	55.2	77.0	54.0	46.0
Utah	—	—	—	—	—	—	—	—	—
Vermont	30.5	39.0	61.0	27.1	45.8	54.2	30.1	39.8	60.2
Virginia	51.1	2.2	97.8	50.3	0.6	99.4	59.2	18.4	81.6
Washington	—	—	—	—	—	—	45.0	10.0	90.0
West Virginia	51.6	3.2	96.8	50.2	0.4	99.6	51.3	2.6	97.4
Wisconsin	47.6	4.8	95.2	46.8	6.4	93.6	50.9	1.8	98.2
Wyoming	—	—	—	—	—	—	0.0	100.0	0.0

Notes: The first entries are the Democratic percent of two-party vote values for each state for the presidential race. The second entries are the margin of victory values for each state for the presidential race, where margin of victory is defined as the absolute difference between the Democratic percent and the Republican percent of the two-party vote for president. The third entries are the party competition index values for each state for the presidential race, where the competition index devised by Paul David (1972) is defined as (100 − the margin of victory) or, alternatively, as (100 − the absolute difference between the Democratic and Republican percent of two-party vote for president). The values for Democratic and Republican percent of two-party vote for president are taken from the state vote tables in Chapter 4. Zero (0) percent on David's index represents a complete absence of two-party competition for that election year, whereas a score of 100 percent indicates perfect competition between the two major parties. A state can only receive a party competition score of 0 if it has a 100–0 vote split for president. Conversely, a state can only receive a score of 100 if it has a 50–50 vote split for president. For example, if Maryland in 1788 reported a 22.9 percent Democratic vote for president of its two-party vote, then its Republican vote for president would be 77.1 percent. The absolute difference between the two figures is the margin of victory, or 54.2 percent. 100 percent − 54.2 percent would equal 45.8 percent on David's party competition scale, indicating little competition in the presidential race in Maryland in 1788. The two-party vote percent values used to derive the margin of victory and party competition figures are initially found in the state vote tables in Chapter 4. The author's alternative party coding in these tables is used whenever it occurs instead of the conventional party coding of voting data. The Democratic Party is defined here as the Anti-Federalists, Democratic-Republicans, and Jackson Democrats prior to 1830 when the "Democratic Party" as such was established. The Republican Party is defined as the Federalists, National Republicans, and Whigs prior to the establishment of the "Republican Party" in the 1850s. See Appendix A for an explanation of the historical antecedents of the current Democratic and Republican parties. States reporting only partial voting returns for president are not included in the calculations for the years in which this occurred. —indicates that the state had no data, either because no vote data were found for the state in question or the state had not yet entered the Union. Data for the District of Columbia are included from 1964 to the present, after being granted the right to elect presidential electors by the 23rd Amendment.

Sources: State vote tables for president in Chapter 4.

Table 8-45 Presidential Competition Measures, by State, by Election Year, 1896–1904 (Percentages)

	1896			1900			1904		
State	Democratic % of Two-Party Vote	Margin of Victory	Party Competition Index	Democratic % of Two-Party Vote	Margin of Victory	Party Competition Index	Democratic % of Two-Party Vote	Margin of Victory	Party Competition Index
Alabama	70.1	40.2	59.8	63.6	27.2	72.8	78.0	56.0	44.0
Alaska	—	—	—	—	—	—	—	—	—
Arizona	—	—	—	—	—	—	—	—	—
Arkansas	74.6	49.2	50.8	64.5	29.0	71.0	57.9	15.8	84.2
California	49.7	0.6	99.4	43.1	13.8	86.2	30.3	39.4	60.6
Colorado	86.0	72.0	28.0	57.0	14.0	86.0	42.6	14.8	85.2
Connecticut	34.0	32.0	68.0	41.9	16.2	83.8	39.6	20.8	79.2
Delaware	44.8	10.4	89.6	45.6	8.8	91.2	44.9	10.2	89.8
Dist. of Columbia	—	—	—	—	—	—	—	—	—
Florida	74.4	48.8	51.2	79.4	58.8	41.2	76.1	52.2	47.8
Georgia	61.3	22.6	77.4	70.3	40.6	59.4	77.7	55.4	44.6
Hawaii	—	—	—	—	—	—	—	—	—
Idaho	78.5	57.0	43.0	52.0	4.0	96.0	27.9	44.2	55.8
Illinois	43.4	13.2	86.8	45.7	8.6	91.4	34.1	31.8	68.2
Indiana	48.6	2.8	97.2	47.9	4.2	95.8	42.7	14.6	85.4
Iowa	43.6	12.8	87.2	40.5	19.0	81.0	32.6	34.8	65.2
Kansas	52.0	4.0	96.0	46.6	6.8	93.2	28.8	42.4	57.6
Kentucky	50.0	0.0	100.0	50.9	1.8	98.2	51.4	2.8	97.2
Louisiana	77.8	55.6	44.4	79.0	58.0	42.0	90.2	80.4	19.6
Maine	30.1	39.8	60.2	36.0	28.0	72.0	29.7	40.6	59.4
Maryland	43.2	13.6	86.4	47.3	5.4	94.6	50.0	0.0	100.0
Massachusetts	27.4	45.2	54.8	39.7	20.6	79.4	39.1	21.8	78.2
Michigan	44.7	10.6	89.4	40.1	19.8	80.2	27.0	46.0	54.0
Minnesota	41.9	16.2	83.8	37.2	25.6	74.4	20.3	59.4	40.6
Mississippi	92.9	85.8	14.2	90.1	80.2	19.8	94.2	88.4	11.6
Missouri	54.4	8.8	91.2	52.8	5.6	94.4	48.0	4.0	96.0
Montana	80.2	60.4	39.6	59.5	19.0	81.0	39.1	21.8	78.2
Nebraska	52.7	5.4	94.6	48.3	3.4	96.6	27.6	44.8	55.2
Nevada	81.2	62.4	37.6	62.2	24.4	75.6	36.7	26.6	73.4
New Hampshire	27.4	45.2	54.8	39.3	21.4	78.6	38.6	22.8	77.2
New Jersey	37.7	24.6	75.4	42.6	14.8	85.2	40.2	19.6	80.4
New Mexico	—	—	—	—	—	—	—	—	—
New York	40.2	19.6	80.4	45.2	9.6	90.4	44.3	11.4	88.6
North Carolina	52.9	5.8	94.2	54.3	8.6	91.4	60.1	20.2	79.8
North Dakota	44.0	12.0	88.0	36.4	27.2	72.8	21.3	57.4	42.6
Ohio	47.6	4.8	95.2	46.6	6.8	93.2	36.5	27.0	73.0
Oklahoma	—	—	—	—	—	—	—	—	—
Oregon	49.0	2.0	98.0	41.5	17.0	83.0	22.3	55.4	44.6
Pennsylvania	37.3	25.4	74.6	37.3	25.4	74.6	28.7	42.6	57.4
Rhode Island	27.9	44.2	55.8	37.0	26.0	74.0	37.4	25.2	74.8
South Carolina	86.3	72.6	27.4	93.0	86.0	14.0	95.4	90.8	9.2
South Dakota	50.1	0.2	99.8	42.0	16.0	84.0	23.4	53.2	46.8
Tennessee	52.9	5.8	94.2	54.1	8.2	91.8	55.5	11.0	89.0
Texas	69.3	38.6	61.4	67.1	34.2	65.8	76.5	53.0	47.0
Utah	82.7	65.4	34.6	48.8	2.4	97.6	34.9	30.2	69.8
Vermont	16.9	66.2	33.8	23.2	53.6	46.4	19.5	61.0	39.0
Virginia	53.3	6.6	93.4	55.8	11.6	88.4	62.6	25.2	74.8
Washington	57.7	15.4	84.6	43.8	12.4	87.6	21.7	56.6	43.4
West Virginia	47.3	5.4	94.6	45.2	9.6	90.4	43.2	13.6	86.4
Wisconsin	38.2	23.6	76.4	37.5	25.0	75.0	30.7	38.6	61.4
Wyoming	51.9	3.8	96.2	41.2	17.6	82.4	30.4	39.2	60.8

Notes: The first entries are the Democratic percent of two-party vote values for each state for the presidential race. The second entries are the margin of victory values for each state for the presidential race, where margin of victory is defined as the absolute difference between the Democratic percent and the Republican percent of the two-party vote for president. The third entries are the party competition index values for each state for the presidential race, where the competition index devised by Paul David (1972) is defined as (100 − the margin of victory) or, alternatively, as (100 − the absolute difference between the Democratic and Republican percent of two-party vote for president). The values for Democratic and Republican percent of two-party vote for president are taken from the state vote tables in Chapter 4. Zero (0) percent on David's index represents a complete absence of two-party competition for that election year, whereas a score of 100 percent indicates perfect competition between the two major parties. A state can only receive a party competition score of 0 if it has a 100–0 vote split for president. Conversely, a state can only receive a score of 100 if it has a 50–50 vote split for president. For example, if Maryland in 1788 reported a 22.9 percent Democratic vote for president of its two-party vote, then its Republican vote for president would be 77.1 percent. The absolute difference between the two figures is the margin of victory, or 54.2 percent. 100 percent − 54.2 percent would equal 45.8 percent on David's party competition scale, indicating little competition in the presidential race in Maryland in 1788. The two-party vote percent values used to derive the margin of victory and party competition figures are initially found in the state vote tables in Chapter 4. The author's alternative party coding in these tables is used whenever it occurs instead of the conventional party coding of voting data. The Democratic Party is defined here as the Anti-Federalists, Democratic-Republicans, and Jackson Democrats prior to 1830 when the "Democratic Party" as such was established. The Republican Party is defined as the Federalists, National Republicans, and Whigs prior to the establishment of the "Republican Party" in the 1850s. See Appendix A for an explanation of the historical antecedents of the current Democratic and Republican parties. States reporting only partial voting returns for president are not included in the calculations for the years in which this occurred. —indicates that the state had no data, either because no vote data were found for the state in question or the state had not yet entered the Union. Data for the District of Columbia are included from 1964 to the present, after being granted the right to elect presidential electors by the 23rd Amendment.

Sources: State vote tables for president in Chapter 4.

Table 8-46 Presidential Competition Measures, by State, by Election Year, 1908–1916 (Percentages)

	1908			1912			1916		
State	Democratic % of Two-Party Vote	Margin of Victory	Party Competition Index	Democratic % of Two-Party Vote	Margin of Victory	Party Competition Index	Democratic % of Two-Party Vote	Margin of Victory	Party Competition Index
Alabama	74.4	48.8	51.2	89.4	78.8	21.2	77.6	55.2	44.8
Alaska	—	—	—	—	—	—	—	—	—
Arizona	—	—	—	77.6	55.2	44.8	61.8	23.6	76.4
Arkansas	60.6	21.2	78.8	72.9	45.8	54.2	69.7	39.4	60.6
California	37.3	25.4	74.6	98.7	97.4	2.6	50.2	0.4	99.6
Colorado	50.6	1.2	98.8	66.1	32.2	67.8	63.6	27.2	72.8
Connecticut	37.7	24.6	75.4	52.2	4.4	95.6	48.4	3.2	96.8
Delaware	46.9	6.2	93.8	58.6	17.2	82.8	48.8	2.4	97.6
Dist. of Columbia	—	—	—	—	—	—	—	—	—
Florida	74.5	49.0	51.0	89.2	78.4	21.6	79.3	58.6	41.4
Georgia	63.6	27.2	72.8	94.7	89.4	10.6	91.9	83.8	16.2
Hawaii	—	—	—	—	—	—	—	—	—
Idaho	40.7	18.6	81.4	50.8	1.6	98.4	55.9	11.8	88.2
Illinois	41.7	16.6	83.4	61.5	23.0	77.0	45.2	9.6	90.4
Indiana	49.2	1.6	98.4	65.1	30.2	69.8	49.5	1.0	99.0
Iowa	42.2	15.6	84.4	60.7	21.4	78.6	44.2	11.6	88.4
Kansas	45.0	10.0	90.0	65.7	31.4	68.6	53.1	6.2	93.8
Kentucky	50.9	1.8	98.2	65.5	31.0	69.0	52.7	5.4	94.6
Louisiana	87.6	75.2	24.8	94.1	88.2	11.8	92.5	85.0	15.0
Maine	34.6	30.8	69.2	65.8	31.6	68.4	48.0	4.0	96.0
Maryland	49.9	0.2	99.8	67.2	34.4	65.6	54.1	8.2	91.8
Massachusetts	36.9	26.2	73.8	52.7	5.4	94.6	48.0	4.0	96.0
Michigan	34.4	31.2	68.8	49.8	0.4	99.6	45.7	8.6	91.4
Minnesota	35.8	28.4	71.6	62.3	24.6	75.4	49.9	0.2	99.8
Mississippi	93.3	86.6	13.4	97.4	94.8	5.2	95.0	90.0	10.0
Missouri	50.0	0.0	100.0	61.4	22.8	77.2	51.9	3.8	96.2
Montana	47.6	4.8	95.2	60.2	20.4	79.6	60.2	20.4	79.6
Nebraska	50.8	1.6	98.4	66.8	33.6	66.4	57.4	14.8	85.2
Nevada	51.0	2.0	98.0	71.4	42.8	57.2	59.4	18.8	81.2
New Hampshire	38.8	22.4	77.6	51.3	2.6	97.4	50.0	0.0	100.0
New Jersey	40.8	18.4	81.6	66.7	33.4	66.6	44.0	12.0	88.0
New Mexico	—	—	—	54.4	8.8	91.2	52.0	4.0	96.0
New York	43.4	13.2	86.8	59.0	18.0	82.0	46.3	7.4	92.6
North Carolina	54.4	8.8	91.2	83.2	66.4	33.6	58.2	16.4	83.6
North Dakota	36.3	27.4	72.6	56.2	12.4	87.6	50.8	1.6	98.4
Ohio	46.8	6.4	93.6	60.4	20.8	79.2	54.0	8.0	92.0
Oklahoma	52.6	5.2	94.8	56.8	13.6	86.4	60.4	20.8	79.2
Oregon	37.7	24.6	75.4	57.6	15.2	84.8	48.6	2.8	97.2
Pennsylvania	37.6	24.8	75.2	59.1	18.2	81.8	42.6	14.8	85.2
Rhode Island	36.0	28.0	72.0	52.3	4.6	95.4	47.4	5.2	94.8
South Carolina	94.0	88.0	12.0	98.9	97.8	2.2	97.6	95.2	4.8
South Dakota	37.4	25.2	74.8	100.0	100.0	0.0	48.0	4.0	96.0
Tennessee	53.5	7.0	93.0	68.7	37.4	62.6	56.9	13.8	86.2
Texas	76.8	53.6	46.4	88.5	77.0	23.0	81.6	63.2	36.8
Utah	41.1	17.8	82.2	46.5	7.0	93.0	60.9	21.8	78.2
Vermont	22.5	55.0	45.0	39.7	20.6	79.4	36.1	27.8	72.2
Virginia	61.2	22.4	77.6	79.5	59.0	41.0	67.8	35.6	64.4
Washington	35.5	29.0	71.0	55.2	10.4	89.6	52.3	4.6	95.4
West Virginia	44.7	10.6	89.4	66.6	33.2	66.8	49.5	1.0	99.0
Wisconsin	40.2	19.6	80.4	55.7	11.4	88.6	46.4	7.2	92.8
Wyoming	41.7	16.6	83.4	51.3	2.6	97.4	56.7	13.4	86.6

Notes: The first entries are the Democratic percent of two-party vote values for each state for the presidential race. The second entries are the margin of victory values for each state for the presidential race, where margin of victory is defined as the absolute difference between the Democratic percent and the Republican percent of two-party vote for president. The third entries are the party competition index values for each state for the presidential race, where the competition index devised by Paul David (1972) is defined as (100 − the margin of victory) or, alternatively, as (100 − the absolute difference between the Democratic and Republican percent of two-party vote for president). The values for Democratic and Republican percent of two-party vote for president are taken from the state vote tables in Chapter 4. Zero (0) percent on David's index represents a complete absence of two-party competition for that election year, whereas a score of 100 percent indicates perfect competition between the two major parties. A state can only receive a party competition score of 0 if it has a 100–0 vote split for president. Conversely, a state can only receive a score of 100 if it has a 50–50 vote split for president. For example, if Maryland in 1788 reported a 22.9 percent Democratic vote for president of its two-party vote, then its Republican vote for president would be 77.1 percent. The absolute difference between the two figures is the margin of victory, or 54.2 percent. 100 percent − 54.2 percent would equal 45.8 percent on David's party competition scale, indicating little competition in the presidential race in Maryland in 1788. The two-party vote percent values used to derive the margin of victory and party competition figures are initially found in the state vote tables in Chapter 4. The author's alternative party coding in these tables is used whenever it occurs instead of the conventional party coding of voting data. The Democratic Party is defined here as the Anti-Federalists, Democratic-Republicans, and Jackson Democrats prior to 1830 when the "Democratic Party" as such was established. The Republican Party is defined as the Federalists, National Republicans, and Whigs prior to the establishment of the "Republican Party" in the 1850s. See Appendix A for an explanation of the historical antecedents of the current Democratic and Republican parties. States reporting only partial voting returns for president are not included in the calculations for the years in which this occurred. —indicates that the state had no data, either because no vote data were found for the state in question or the state had not yet entered the Union. Data for the District of Columbia are included from 1964 to the present, after being granted the right to elect presidential electors by the 23rd Amendment.

Sources: State vote tables for president in Chapter 4.

Table 8-47 Presidential Competition Measures, by State, by Election Year, 1920–1928 (Percentages)

State	1920 Democratic % of Two-Party Vote	1920 Margin of Victory	1920 Party Competition Index	1924 Democratic % of Two-Party Vote	1924 Margin of Victory	1924 Party Competition Index	1928 Democratic % of Two-Party Vote	1928 Margin of Victory	1928 Party Competition Index
Alabama	67.6	35.2	64.8	72.5	45.0	55.0	51.4	2.8	97.2
Alaska	—	—	—	—	—	—	—	—	—
Arizona	44.4	11.2	88.8	46.2	7.6	92.4	42.3	15.4	84.6
Arkansas	59.5	19.0	81.0	67.6	35.2	64.8	60.5	21.0	79.0
California	26.8	46.4	53.6	12.6	74.8	25.2	34.6	30.8	69.2
Colorado	37.7	24.6	75.4	27.8	44.4	55.6	34.4	31.2	68.8
Connecticut	34.5	31.0	69.0	30.9	38.2	61.8	45.9	8.2	91.8
Delaware	43.0	14.0	86.0	38.9	22.2	77.8	33.9	32.2	67.8
Dist. of Columbia	—	—	—	—	—	—	—	—	—
Florida	66.9	33.8	66.2	67.0	34.0	66.0	41.1	17.8	82.2
Georgia	71.2	42.4	57.6	80.3	60.6	39.4	56.0	12.0	88.0
Hawaii	—	—	—	—	—	—	—	—	—
Idaho	33.9	32.2	67.8	25.5	49.0	51.0	35.2	29.6	70.4
Illinois	27.3	45.4	54.6	28.4	43.2	56.8	42.6	14.8	85.2
Indiana	42.3	15.4	84.6	41.2	17.6	82.4	39.9	20.2	79.8
Iowa	26.4	47.2	52.8	23.0	54.0	46.0	37.8	24.4	75.6
Kansas	33.4	33.2	66.8	27.7	44.6	55.4	27.3	45.4	54.6
Kentucky	50.2	0.4	99.6	48.6	2.8	97.2	40.6	18.8	81.2
Louisiana	69.4	38.8	61.2	79.1	58.2	41.8	76.3	52.6	47.4
Maine	30.2	39.6	60.4	23.3	53.4	46.6	31.1	37.8	62.2
Maryland	43.3	13.4	86.6	47.7	4.6	95.4	42.6	14.8	85.2
Massachusetts	28.9	42.2	57.8	28.5	43.0	57.0	50.5	1.0	99.0
Michigan	23.4	53.2	46.8	14.8	70.4	29.6	29.1	41.8	58.2
Minnesota	21.6	56.8	43.2	11.7	76.6	23.4	41.4	17.2	82.8
Mississippi	85.7	71.4	28.6	92.2	84.4	15.6	82.2	64.4	35.6
Missouri	44.1	11.8	88.2	47.0	6.0	94.0	44.3	11.4	88.6
Montana	34.4	31.2	68.8	31.3	37.4	62.6	41.0	18.0	82.0
Nebraska	32.6	34.8	65.2	38.5	23.0	77.0	36.4	27.2	72.8
Nevada	38.9	22.2	77.8	34.5	31.0	69.0	43.5	13.0	87.0
New Hampshire	39.7	20.6	79.4	36.7	26.6	73.4	41.2	17.6	82.4
New Jersey	29.6	40.8	59.2	30.6	38.8	61.2	40.0	20.0	80.0
New Mexico	44.7	10.6	89.4	47.0	6.0	94.0	40.9	18.2	81.8
New York	29.5	41.0	59.0	34.3	31.4	68.6	48.8	2.4	97.6
North Carolina	56.7	13.4	86.6	59.8	19.6	80.4	45.1	9.8	90.2
North Dakota	18.9	62.2	37.8	12.7	74.6	25.4	44.8	10.4	89.6
Ohio	39.8	20.4	79.6	28.9	42.2	57.8	34.7	30.6	69.4
Oklahoma	47.0	6.0	94.0	53.1	6.2	93.8	35.7	28.6	71.4
Oregon	35.8	28.4	71.6	32.2	35.6	64.4	34.7	30.6	69.4
Pennsylvania	29.2	41.6	58.4	22.6	54.8	45.2	34.2	31.6	68.4
Rhode Island	33.9	32.2	67.8	37.9	24.2	75.8	50.3	0.6	99.4
South Carolina	96.1	92.2	7.8	97.8	95.6	4.4	91.5	83.0	17.0
South Dakota	24.5	51.0	49.0	21.2	57.6	42.4	39.4	21.2	78.8
Tennessee	48.5	3.0	97.0	54.9	9.8	90.2	44.6	10.8	89.2
Texas	71.5	43.0	57.0	78.7	57.4	42.6	48.1	3.8	96.2
Utah	41.0	18.0	82.0	37.8	24.4	75.6	46.1	7.8	92.2
Vermont	23.5	53.0	47.0	16.7	66.6	33.4	33.0	34.0	66.0
Virginia	61.8	23.6	76.4	65.6	31.2	68.8	46.0	8.0	92.0
Washington	27.4	45.2	54.8	16.3	67.4	32.6	31.8	36.4	63.6
West Virginia	43.9	12.2	87.8	47.1	5.8	94.2	41.3	17.4	82.6
Wisconsin	18.5	63.0	37.0	17.9	64.2	35.8	45.3	9.4	90.6
Wyoming	33.2	33.6	66.4	23.5	53.0	47.0	35.7	28.6	71.4

Notes: The first entries are the Democratic percent of two-party vote values for each state for the presidential race. The second entries are the margin of victory values for each state for the presidential race, where margin of victory is defined as the absolute difference between the Democratic percent and the Republican percent of the two-party vote for president. The third entries are the party competition index values for each state for the presidential race, where the competition index devised by Paul David (1972) is defined as (100 − the margin of victory) or, alternatively, as (100 − the absolute difference between the Democratic and Republican percent of two-party vote for president). The values for Democratic and Republican percent of two-party vote for president are taken from the state vote tables in Chapter 4. Zero (0) percent on David's index represents a complete absence of two-party competition for that election year, whereas a score of 100 percent indicates perfect competition between the two major parties. A state can only receive a party competition score of 0 if it has a 100–0 vote split for president. Conversely, a state can only receive a score of 100 if it has a 50–50 vote split for president. For example, if Maryland in 1788 reported a 22.9 percent Democratic vote for president of its two-party vote, then its Republican vote for president would be 77.1 percent. The absolute difference between the two figures is the margin of victory, or 54.2 percent. 100 percent − 54.2 percent would equal 45.8 percent on David's party competition scale, indicating little competition in the presidential race in Maryland in 1788. The two-party vote percent values used to derive the margin of victory and party competition figures are initially found in the state vote tables in Chapter 4. The author's alternative party coding in these tables is used whenever it occurs instead of the conventional party coding of voting data. The Democratic Party is defined here as the Anti-Federalists, Democratic-Republicans, and Jackson Democrats prior to 1830 when the "Democratic Party" as such was established. The Republican Party is defined as the Federalists, National Republicans, and Whigs prior to the establishment of the "Republican Party" in the 1850s. See Appendix A for an explanation of the historical antecedents of the current Democratic and Republican parties. States reporting only partial voting returns for president are not included in the calculations for the years in which this occurred. —indicates that the state had no data, either because no vote data were found for the state in question or the state had not yet entered the Union. Data for the District of Columbia are included from 1964 to the present, after being granted the right to elect presidential electors by the 23rd Amendment.

Sources: State vote tables for president in Chapter 4.

Table 8-48 Presidential Competition Measures, by State, by Election Year, 1932–1940 (Percentages)

State	1932 Democratic % of Two-Party Vote	1932 Margin of Victory	1932 Party Competition Index	1936 Democratic % of Two-Party Vote	1936 Margin of Victory	1936 Party Competition Index	1940 Democratic % of Two-Party Vote	1940 Margin of Victory	1940 Party Competition Index
Alabama	85.7	71.4	28.6	87.1	74.2	25.8	85.6	71.2	28.8
Alaska	—	—	—	—	—	—	—	—	—
Arizona	68.7	37.4	62.6	72.2	44.4	55.6	63.8	27.6	72.4
Arkansas	87.2	74.4	25.6	82.1	64.2	35.8	78.9	57.8	42.2
California	61.0	22.0	78.0	67.9	35.8	64.2	58.1	16.2	83.8
Colorado	57.0	14.0	86.0	61.9	23.8	76.2	48.7	2.6	97.4
Connecticut	49.4	1.2	98.8	57.8	15.6	84.4	53.6	7.2	92.8
Delaware	48.8	2.4	97.6	54.9	9.8	90.2	54.8	9.6	90.4
Dist. of Columbia	—	—	—	—	—	—	—	—	—
Florida	74.9	49.8	50.2	76.1	52.2	47.8	74.0	48.0	52.0
Georgia	92.2	84.4	15.6	87.4	74.8	25.2	85.1	70.2	29.8
Hawaii	—	—	—	—	—	—	—	—	—
Idaho	60.6	21.2	78.8	65.5	31.0	69.0	54.5	9.0	91.0
Illinois	56.8	13.6	86.4	59.2	18.4	81.6	51.2	2.4	97.6
Indiana	56.0	12.0	88.0	57.5	15.0	85.0	49.3	1.4	98.6
Iowa	59.1	18.2	81.8	56.0	12.0	88.0	47.8	4.4	95.6
Kansas	54.8	9.6	90.4	53.9	7.8	92.2	42.7	14.6	85.4
Kentucky	59.5	19.0	81.0	59.4	18.8	81.2	57.6	15.2	84.8
Louisiana	93.0	86.0	14.0	88.8	77.6	22.4	85.9	71.8	28.2
Maine	43.6	12.8	87.2	42.8	14.4	85.6	48.8	2.4	97.6
Maryland	63.1	26.2	73.8	62.7	25.4	74.6	58.8	17.6	82.4
Massachusetts	52.1	4.2	95.8	55.1	10.2	89.8	53.4	6.8	93.2
Michigan	54.1	8.2	91.8	59.2	18.4	81.6	49.8	0.4	99.6
Minnesota	62.3	24.6	75.4	66.6	33.2	66.8	51.9	3.8	96.2
Mississippi	96.4	92.8	7.2	97.2	94.4	5.6	95.8	91.6	8.4
Missouri	64.5	29.0	71.0	61.4	22.8	77.2	52.4	4.8	95.2
Montana	62.0	24.0	76.0	71.5	43.0	57.0	59.4	18.8	81.2
Nebraska	64.1	28.2	71.8	58.4	16.8	83.2	42.8	14.4	85.6
Nevada	69.4	38.8	61.2	72.8	45.6	54.4	60.1	20.2	79.8
New Hampshire	49.3	1.4	98.6	50.9	1.8	98.2	53.2	6.4	93.6
New Jersey	51.0	2.0	98.0	60.1	20.2	79.8	51.8	3.6	96.4
New Mexico	63.7	27.4	72.6	63.2	26.4	73.6	56.7	13.4	86.6
New York	56.7	13.4	86.6	60.2	20.4	79.6	51.8	3.6	96.4
North Carolina	70.5	41.0	59.0	73.4	46.8	53.2	74.0	48.0	52.0
North Dakota	71.3	42.6	57.4	69.2	38.4	61.6	44.5	11.0	89.0
Ohio	51.5	3.0	97.0	60.8	21.6	78.4	52.2	4.4	95.6
Oklahoma	73.3	46.6	53.4	67.2	34.4	65.6	57.6	15.2	84.8
Oregon	61.1	22.2	77.8	68.5	37.0	63.0	54.1	8.2	91.8
Pennsylvania	47.1	5.8	94.2	58.2	16.4	83.6	53.5	7.0	93.0
Rhode Island	56.0	12.0	88.0	56.8	13.6	86.4	56.8	13.6	86.4
South Carolina	98.1	96.2	3.8	98.6	97.2	2.8	95.6	91.2	8.8
South Dakota	64.9	29.8	70.2	56.0	12.0	88.0	42.6	14.8	85.2
Tennessee	67.2	34.4	65.6	69.1	38.2	61.8	67.5	35.0	65.0
Texas	88.7	77.4	22.6	87.6	75.2	24.8	81.1	62.2	37.8
Utah	57.9	15.8	84.2	69.9	39.8	60.2	62.4	24.8	75.2
Vermont	41.6	16.8	83.2	43.4	13.2	86.8	45.1	9.8	90.2
Virginia	69.5	39.0	61.0	70.5	41.0	59.0	68.3	36.6	63.4
Washington	62.9	25.8	74.2	69.0	38.0	62.0	58.9	17.8	82.2
West Virginia	55.1	10.2	89.8	60.7	21.4	78.6	57.1	14.2	85.8
Wisconsin	67.0	34.0	66.0	67.8	35.6	64.4	50.9	1.8	98.2
Wyoming	57.9	15.8	84.2	61.8	23.6	76.4	53.0	6.0	94.0

Notes: The first entries are the Democratic percent of two-party vote values for each state for the presidential race. The second entries are the margin of victory values for each state for the presidential race, where margin of victory is defined as the absolute difference between the Democratic percent and the Republican percent of the two-party vote for president. The third entries are the party competition index values for each state for the presidential race, where the competition index devised by Paul David (1972) is defined as (100 − the margin of victory) or, alternatively, as (100 − the absolute difference between the Democratic and Republican percent of two-party vote for president). The values for Democratic and Republican percent of two-party vote for president are taken from the state vote tables in Chapter 4. Zero (0) percent on David's index represents a complete absence of two-party competition for that election year, whereas a score of 100 percent indicates perfect competition between the two major parties. A state can only receive a party competition score of 0 if it has a 100–0 vote split for president. Conversely, a state can only receive a score of 100 if it has a 50–50 vote split for president. For example, if Maryland in 1788 reported a 22.9 percent Democratic vote for president of its two-party vote, then its Republican vote for president would be 77.1 percent. The absolute difference between the two figures is the margin of victory, or 54.2 percent. 100 percent − 54.2 percent would equal 45.8 percent on David's party competition scale, indicating little competition in the presidential race in Maryland in 1788. The two-party vote percent values used to derive the margin of victory and party competition figures are initially found in the state vote tables in Chapter 4. The author's alternative party coding in these tables is used whenever it occurs instead of the conventional party coding of voting data. The Democratic Party is defined here as the Anti-Federalists, Democratic-Republicans, and Jackson Democrats prior to 1830 when the "Democratic Party" as such was established. The Republican Party is defined as the Federalists, National Republicans, and Whigs prior to the establishment of the "Republican Party" in the 1850s. See Appendix A for an explanation of the historical antecedents of the current Democratic and Republican parties. States reporting only partial voting returns for president are not included in the calculations for the years in which this occurred. —indicates that the state had no data, either because no vote data were found for the state in question or the state had not yet entered the Union. Data for the District of Columbia are included from 1964 to the present, after being granted the right to elect presidential electors by the 23rd Amendment.

Sources: State vote tables for president in Chapter 4.

Table 8-49 Presidential Competition Measures, by State, by Election Year, 1944–1952 (Percentages)

	1944			1948			1952		
State	Democratic % of Two-Party Vote	Margin of Victory	Party Competition Index	Democratic % of Two-Party Vote	Margin of Victory	Party Competition Index	Democratic % of Two-Party Vote	Margin of Victory	Party Competition Index
Alabama	81.7	63.4	36.6	0.0	100.0	0.0	64.8	29.6	70.4
Alaska	—	—	—						
Arizona	59.0	18.0	82.0	55.1	10.2	89.8	41.7	16.6	83.4
Arkansas	70.1	40.2	59.8	74.6	49.2	50.8	56.1	12.2	87.8
California	56.8	13.6	86.4	50.2	0.4	99.6	43.1	13.8	86.2
Colorado	46.6	6.8	93.2	52.7	5.4	94.6	39.3	21.4	78.6
Connecticut	52.7	5.4	94.6	49.2	1.6	98.4	44.1	11.8	88.2
Delaware	54.6	9.2	90.8	49.4	1.2	98.8	48.1	3.8	96.2
Dist. of Columbia	—	—	—	—	—	—			
Florida	70.3	40.6	59.4	59.2	18.4	81.6	45.0	10.0	90.0
Georgia	81.7	63.4	36.6	76.9	53.8	46.2	69.7	39.4	60.6
Hawaii	—	—	—						
Idaho	51.7	3.4	96.6	51.4	2.8	97.2	34.5	31.0	69.0
Illinois	51.7	3.4	96.6	50.4	0.8	99.2	45.0	10.0	90.0
Indiana	47.1	5.8	94.2	49.6	0.8	99.2	41.4	17.2	82.8
Iowa	47.7	4.6	95.4	51.4	2.8	97.2	35.8	28.4	71.6
Kansas	39.4	21.2	78.8	45.4	9.2	90.8	30.7	38.6	61.4
Kentucky	54.6	9.2	90.8	57.8	15.6	84.4	50.0	0.0	100.0
Louisiana	80.6	61.2	38.8	65.2	30.4	69.6	52.9	5.8	94.2
Maine	47.5	5.0	95.0	42.7	14.6	85.4	33.8	32.4	67.6
Maryland	51.9	3.8	96.2	49.3	1.4	98.6	44.2	11.6	88.4
Massachusetts	52.9	5.8	94.2	55.9	11.8	88.2	45.6	8.8	91.2
Michigan	50.5	1.0	99.0	49.1	1.8	98.2	44.2	11.6	88.4
Minnesota	52.8	5.6	94.4	58.9	17.8	82.2	44.4	11.2	88.8
Mississippi	93.6	87.2	12.8	79.4	58.8	41.2	60.4	20.8	79.2
Missouri	51.5	3.0	97.0	58.3	16.6	83.4	49.2	1.6	98.4
Montana	54.7	9.4	90.6	55.2	10.4	89.6	40.3	19.4	80.6
Nebraska	41.4	17.2	82.8	45.8	8.4	91.6	30.8	38.4	61.6
Nevada	54.6	9.2	90.8	51.6	3.2	96.8	38.6	22.8	77.2
New Hampshire	52.1	4.2	95.8	47.1	5.8	94.2	39.1	21.8	78.2
New Jersey	50.7	1.4	98.6	47.7	4.6	95.4	42.5	15.0	85.0
New Mexico	53.5	7.0	93.0	56.8	13.6	86.4	44.4	11.2	88.8
New York	52.5	5.0	95.0	49.5	1.0	99.0	44.0	12.0	88.0
North Carolina	66.7	33.4	66.6	64.0	28.0	72.0	53.9	7.8	92.2
North Dakota	45.8	8.4	91.6	45.4	9.2	90.8	28.6	42.8	57.2
Ohio	49.8	0.4	99.6	50.1	0.2	99.8	43.2	13.6	86.4
Oklahoma	55.7	11.4	88.6	62.7	25.4	74.6	45.4	9.2	90.8
Oregon	52.5	5.0	95.0	48.2	3.6	96.4	39.1	21.8	78.2
Pennsylvania	51.4	2.8	97.2	48.0	4.0	96.0	47.0	6.0	94.0
Rhode Island	58.7	17.4	82.6	58.2	16.4	83.6	49.1	1.8	98.2
South Carolina	95.2	90.4	9.6	86.5	73.0	27.0	50.7	1.4	98.6
South Dakota	41.7	16.6	83.4	47.6	4.8	95.2	30.7	38.6	61.4
Tennessee	60.6	21.2	78.8	57.1	14.2	85.8	49.9	0.2	99.8
Texas	81.1	62.2	37.8	73.1	46.2	53.8	46.8	6.4	93.6
Utah	60.5	21.0	79.0	54.5	9.0	91.0	41.1	17.8	82.2
Vermont	42.9	14.2	85.8	37.5	25.0	75.0	28.3	43.4	56.6
Virginia	62.5	25.0	75.0	53.9	7.8	92.2	43.5	13.0	87.0
Washington	57.4	14.8	85.2	55.2	10.4	89.6	45.1	9.8	90.2
West Virginia	54.9	9.8	90.2	57.6	15.2	84.8	51.9	3.8	96.2
Wisconsin	49.1	1.8	98.2	52.3	4.6	95.4	38.8	22.4	77.6
Wyoming	48.8	2.4	97.6	52.2	4.4	95.6	37.2	25.6	74.4

Notes: The first entries are the Democratic percent of two-party vote values for each state for the presidential race. The second entries are the margin of victory values for each state for the presidential race, where margin of victory is defined as the absolute difference between the Democratic percent and the Republican percent of the two-party vote for president. The third entries are the party competition index values for each state for the presidential race, where the competition index devised by Paul David (1972) is defined as (100 − the margin of victory) or, alternatively, as (100 − the absolute difference between the Democratic and the Republican percent of two-party vote for president). The values for Democratic and Republican percent of two-party vote for president are taken from the state vote tables in Chapter 4. Zero (0) percent on David's index represents a complete absence of two-party competition for that election year, whereas a score of 100 percent indicates perfect competition between the two major parties. A state can only receive a party competition score of 0 if it has a 100–0 vote split for president. Conversely, a state can only receive a score of 100 if it has a 50–50 vote split for president. For example, if Maryland in 1788 reported a 22.9 percent Democratic vote for president of its two-party vote, then its Republican vote for president would be 77.1 percent. The absolute difference between the two figures is the margin of victory, or 54.2 percent. 100 percent − 54.2 percent would equal 45.8 percent on David's party competition scale, indicating little competition in the presidential race in Maryland in 1788. The two-party vote percent values used to derive the margin of victory and party competition figures are initially found in Chapter 4. The author's alternative party coding in these tables is used whenever it occurs instead of the conventional party coding of voting data. The Democratic Party is defined here as the Anti-Federalists, Democratic-Republicans, and Jackson Democrats prior to 1830 when the "Democratic Party" as such was established. The Republican Party is defined as the Federalists, National Republicans, and Whigs prior to the establishment of the "Republican Party" in the 1850s. See Appendix A for an explanation of the historical antecedents of the current Democratic and Republican parties. States reporting only partial voting returns for president are not included in the calculations for the years in which this occurred. —indicates that the state had no data, either because no vote data were found for the state in question or the state had not yet entered the Union. Data for the District of Columbia are included from 1964 to the present, after being granted the right to elect presidential electors by the 23rd Amendment.

Sources: State vote tables for president in Chapter 4.

Table 8-50 Presidential Competition Measures, by State, by Election Year, 1956–1964 (Percentages)

	1956			1960			1964		
State	Democratic % of Two-Party Vote	Margin of Victory	Party Competition Index	Democratic % of Two-Party Vote	Margin of Victory	Party Competition Index	Democratic % of Two-Party Vote	Margin of Victory	Party Competition Index
Alabama	58.9	17.8	82.2	57.7	15.4	84.6	0.0	100.0	0.0
Alaska	—	—	—	49.1	1.8	98.2	65.9	31.8	68.2
Arizona	38.9	22.2	77.8	44.4	11.2	88.8	49.5	1.0	99.0
Arkansas	53.4	6.8	93.2	53.8	7.6	92.4	56.4	12.8	87.2
California	44.4	11.2	88.8	49.7	0.6	99.4	59.2	18.4	81.6
Colorado	39.5	21.0	79.0	45.1	9.8	90.2	61.6	23.2	76.8
Connecticut	36.3	27.4	72.6	53.7	7.4	92.6	67.9	35.8	64.2
Delaware	44.7	10.6	89.4	50.8	1.6	98.4	61.1	22.2	77.8
Dist. of Columbia	—	—	—	—	—	—	85.5	71.0	29.0
Florida	42.7	14.6	85.4	48.5	3.0	97.0	51.1	2.2	97.8
Georgia	66.6	33.2	66.8	62.6	25.2	74.8	45.9	8.2	91.8
Hawaii	—	—	—	50.0	0.0	100.0	78.8	57.6	42.4
Idaho	38.8	22.4	77.6	46.2	7.6	92.4	50.9	1.8	98.2
Illinois	40.4	19.2	80.8	50.1	0.2	99.8	59.5	19.0	81.0
Indiana	39.9	20.2	79.8	44.8	10.4	89.6	56.2	12.4	87.6
Iowa	40.8	18.4	81.6	43.3	13.4	86.6	62.0	24.0	76.0
Kansas	34.3	31.4	68.6	39.3	21.4	78.6	54.6	9.2	90.8
Kentucky	45.4	9.2	90.8	46.4	7.2	92.8	64.2	28.4	71.6
Louisiana	42.6	14.8	85.2	63.8	27.6	72.4	43.2	13.6	86.4
Maine	29.1	41.8	58.2	43.0	14.0	86.0	68.8	37.6	62.4
Maryland	40.0	20.0	80.0	53.6	7.2	92.8	65.5	31.0	69.0
Massachusetts	40.5	19.0	81.0	60.4	20.8	79.2	76.5	53.0	47.0
Michigan	44.2	11.6	88.4	51.0	2.0	98.0	66.8	33.6	66.4
Minnesota	46.2	7.6	92.4	50.7	1.4	98.6	63.9	27.8	72.2
Mississippi	70.4	40.8	59.2	59.6	19.2	80.8	12.9	74.2	25.8
Missouri	50.1	0.2	99.8	50.3	0.6	99.4	64.0	28.0	72.0
Montana	42.9	14.2	85.8	48.7	2.6	97.4	59.2	18.4	81.6
Nebraska	34.5	31.0	69.0	37.9	24.2	75.8	52.6	5.2	94.8
Nevada	42.0	16.0	84.0	51.2	2.4	97.6	58.6	17.2	82.8
New Hampshire	33.9	32.2	67.8	46.6	6.8	93.2	63.9	27.8	72.2
New Jersey	34.6	30.8	69.2	50.4	0.8	99.2	66.0	32.0	68.0
New Mexico	42.0	16.0	84.0	50.4	0.8	99.2	59.4	18.8	81.2
New York	38.7	22.6	77.4	52.6	5.2	94.8	68.7	37.4	62.6
North Carolina	50.7	1.4	98.6	52.1	4.2	95.8	56.2	12.4	87.6
North Dakota	38.2	23.6	76.4	44.5	11.0	89.0	58.1	16.2	83.8
Ohio	38.9	22.2	77.8	46.7	6.6	93.4	62.9	25.8	74.2
Oklahoma	44.9	10.2	89.8	41.0	18.0	82.0	55.7	11.4	88.6
Oregon	44.8	10.4	89.6	47.4	5.2	94.8	63.9	27.8	72.2
Pennsylvania	43.4	13.2	86.8	51.2	2.4	97.6	65.2	30.4	69.6
Rhode Island	41.7	16.6	83.4	63.6	27.2	72.8	80.9	61.8	38.2
South Carolina	64.3	28.6	71.4	51.2	2.4	97.6	41.1	17.8	82.2
South Dakota	41.6	16.8	83.2	41.8	16.4	83.6	55.6	11.2	88.8
Tennessee	49.7	0.6	99.4	46.4	7.2	92.8	55.5	11.0	89.0
Texas	44.3	11.4	88.6	51.0	2.0	98.0	63.4	26.8	73.2
Utah	35.4	29.2	70.8	45.2	9.6	90.4	54.7	9.4	90.6
Vermont	27.8	44.4	55.6	41.4	17.2	82.8	66.3	32.6	67.4
Virginia	40.9	18.2	81.8	47.2	5.6	94.4	53.7	7.4	92.6
Washington	45.7	8.6	91.4	48.8	2.4	97.6	62.4	24.8	75.2
West Virginia	45.9	8.2	91.8	52.7	5.4	94.6	67.9	35.8	64.2
Wisconsin	38.1	23.8	76.2	48.1	3.8	96.2	62.2	24.4	75.6
Wyoming	39.9	20.2	79.8	45.0	10.0	90.0	56.6	13.2	86.8

Notes: The first entries are the Democratic percent of two-party vote values for each state for the presidential race. The second entries are the margin of victory values for each state for the presidential race, where margin of victory is defined as the absolute difference between the Democratic percent and the Republican percent of the two-party vote for president. The third entries are the party competition index values for each state for the presidential race, where the competition index devised by Paul David (1972) is defined as (100 − the margin of victory) or, alternatively, as (100 − the absolute difference between the Democratic and Republican percent of two-party vote for president). The values for Democratic and Republican percent of two-party vote for president are taken from the state vote tables in Chapter 4. Zero (0) percent on David's index represents a complete absence of two-party competition for that election year, whereas a score of 100 percent indicates perfect competition between the two major parties. A state can only receive a party competition score of 0 if it has a 100–0 vote split for president. Conversely, a state can only receive a score of 100 if it has a 50–50 vote split for president. For example, if Maryland in 1788 reported a 22.9 percent Democratic vote for president of its two-party vote, then its Republican vote for president would be 77.1 percent. The absolute difference between the two figures is the margin of victory, or 54.2 percent. 100 percent − 54.2 percent would equal 45.8 percent on David's party competition scale, indicating little competition in the presidential race in Maryland in 1788. The two-party vote percent values used to derive the margin of victory and party competition figures are initially found in the state vote tables in Chapter 4. The author's alternative party coding in these tables is used whenever it occurs instead of the conventional party coding of voting data. The Democratic Party is defined here as the Anti-Federalists, Democratic-Republicans, and Jackson Democrats prior to 1830 when the "Democratic Party" as such was established. The Republican Party is defined as the Federalists, National Republicans, and Whigs prior to the establishment of the "Republican Party" in the 1850s. See Appendix A for an explanation of the historical antecedents of the current Democratic and Republican parties. States reporting only partial voting returns for president are not included in the calculations for the years in which this occurred. —indicates that the state had no data, either because no vote data were found for the state in question or the state had not yet entered the Union. Data for the District of Columbia are included from 1964 to the present, after being granted the right to elect presidential electors by the 23rd Amendment.

Sources: State vote tables for president in Chapter 4.

Table 8-51 Presidential Competition Measures, by State, by Election Year, 1968–1976 (Percentages)

State	1968 Democratic % of Two-Party Vote	1968 Margin of Victory	1968 Party Competition Index	1972 Democratic % of Two-Party Vote	1972 Margin of Victory	1972 Party Competition Index	1976 Democratic % of Two-Party Vote	1976 Margin of Victory	1976 Party Competition Index
Alabama	57.2	14.4	85.6	26.1	47.8	52.2	56.7	13.4	86.6
Alaska	48.5	3.0	97.0	37.3	25.4	74.6	38.1	23.8	76.2
Arizona	39.0	22.0	78.0	33.0	34.0	66.0	41.4	17.2	82.8
Arkansas	49.7	0.6	99.4	30.8	38.4	61.6	65.0	30.0	70.0
California	48.3	3.4	96.6	43.0	14.0	86.0	49.1	1.8	98.2
Colorado	45.0	10.0	90.0	35.6	28.8	71.2	44.1	11.8	88.2
Connecticut	52.8	5.6	94.4	40.7	18.6	81.4	47.4	5.2	94.8
Delaware	48.0	4.0	96.0	39.7	20.6	79.4	52.7	5.4	94.6
Dist. of Columbia	81.8	63.6	36.4	78.4	56.8	43.2	83.2	66.4	33.6
Florida	43.3	13.4	86.6	27.9	44.2	55.8	52.7	5.4	94.6
Georgia	46.8	6.4	93.6	24.7	50.6	49.4	66.9	33.8	66.2
Hawaii	60.7	21.4	78.6	37.5	25.0	75.0	51.3	2.6	97.4
Idaho	35.1	29.8	70.2	28.8	42.4	57.6	38.3	23.4	76.6
Illinois	48.4	3.2	96.8	40.7	18.6	81.4	49.0	2.0	98.0
Indiana	43.0	14.0	86.0	33.5	33.0	67.0	46.2	7.6	92.4
Iowa	43.5	13.0	87.0	41.3	17.4	82.6	49.5	1.0	99.0
Kansas	38.8	22.4	77.6	30.4	39.2	60.8	46.1	7.8	92.2
Kentucky	46.2	7.6	92.4	35.4	29.2	70.8	53.7	7.4	92.6
Louisiana	54.6	9.2	90.8	30.3	39.4	60.6	53.0	6.0	94.0
Maine	56.2	12.4	87.6	38.5	23.0	77.0	49.6	0.8	99.2
Maryland	51.0	2.0	98.0	37.9	24.2	75.8	53.0	6.0	94.0
Massachusetts	65.7	31.4	68.6	54.5	9.0	91.0	58.1	16.2	83.8
Michigan	53.8	7.6	92.4	42.7	14.6	85.4	47.3	5.4	94.6
Minnesota	56.6	13.2	86.8	47.2	5.6	94.4	56.6	13.2	86.8
Mississippi	63.0	26.0	74.0	20.1	59.8	40.2	51.0	2.0	98.0
Missouri	49.4	1.2	98.8	37.7	24.6	75.4	51.8	3.6	96.4
Montana	45.1	9.8	90.2	39.5	21.0	79.0	46.2	7.6	92.4
Nebraska	34.7	30.6	69.4	29.5	41.0	59.0	39.4	21.2	78.8
Nevada	45.3	9.4	90.6	36.3	27.4	72.6	47.7	4.6	95.4
New Hampshire	45.7	8.6	91.4	35.3	29.4	70.6	44.3	11.4	88.6
New Jersey	48.8	2.4	97.6	37.4	25.2	74.8	48.9	2.2	97.8
New Mexico	43.4	13.2	86.8	37.5	25.0	75.0	48.8	2.4	97.6
New York	52.9	5.8	94.2	41.3	17.4	82.6	52.2	4.4	95.6
North Carolina	42.5	15.0	85.0	29.4	41.2	58.8	55.6	11.2	88.8
North Dakota	40.6	18.8	81.2	36.6	26.8	73.2	47.0	6.0	94.0
Ohio	48.7	2.6	97.4	39.0	22.0	78.0	50.1	0.2	99.8
Oklahoma	40.1	19.8	80.2	24.6	50.8	49.2	49.4	1.2	98.8
Oregon	46.8	6.4	93.6	44.7	10.6	89.4	49.9	0.2	99.8
Pennsylvania	51.9	3.8	96.2	39.8	20.4	79.6	51.4	2.8	97.2
Rhode Island	66.8	33.6	66.4	46.9	6.2	93.8	55.7	11.4	88.6
South Carolina	43.7	12.6	87.4	28.1	43.8	56.2	56.6	13.2	86.8
South Dakota	44.1	11.8	88.2	45.7	8.6	91.4	49.3	1.4	98.6
Tennessee	42.6	14.8	85.2	30.5	39.0	61.0	56.6	13.2	86.8
Texas	50.8	1.6	98.4	33.4	33.2	66.8	51.6	3.2	96.8
Utah	39.6	20.8	79.2	28.1	43.8	56.2	35.0	30.0	70.0
Vermont	45.2	9.6	90.4	36.8	26.4	73.6	44.2	11.6	88.4
Virginia	42.8	14.4	85.6	30.7	38.6	61.4	49.3	1.4	98.6
Washington	51.1	2.2	97.8	40.4	19.2	80.8	48.0	4.0	96.0
West Virginia	54.9	9.8	90.2	36.4	27.2	72.8	58.1	16.2	83.8
Wisconsin	48.0	4.0	96.0	45.0	10.0	90.0	50.9	1.8	98.2
Wyoming	38.9	22.2	77.8	30.6	38.8	61.2	40.2	19.6	80.4

Notes: The first entries are the Democratic percent of two-party vote values for each state for the presidential race. The second entries are the margin of victory values for each state for the presidential race, where margin of victory is defined as the absolute difference between the Democratic percent and the Republican percent of the two-party vote for president. The third entries are the party competition index values for each state for the presidential race, where the competition index devised by Paul David (1972) is defined as (100 − the margin of victory) or, alternatively, as (100 − the absolute difference between the Democratic and Republican percent of two-party vote for president). The values for Democratic and Republican percent of two-party vote for president are taken from the state vote tables in Chapter 4. Zero (0) percent on David's index represents a complete absence of two-party competition for that election year, whereas a score of 100 percent indicates perfect competition between the two major parties. A state can only receive a party competition score of 0 if it has a 100–0 vote split for president. Conversely, a state can only receive a score of 100 if it has a 50–50 vote split for president. For example, if Maryland in 1788 reported a 22.9 percent Democratic vote for president of its two-party vote, then its Republican vote for president would be 77.1 percent. The absolute difference between the two figures is the margin of victory, or 54.2 percent. 100 percent − 54.2 percent would equal 45.8 percent on David's party competition scale, indicating little competition in the presidential race in Maryland in 1788. The two-party vote percent values used to derive the margin of victory and party competition figures are initially found in the state vote tables in Chapter 4. The author's alternative party coding in these tables is used whenever it occurs instead of the conventional party coding of voting data. The Democratic Party is defined here as the Anti-Federalists, Democratic-Republicans, and Jackson Democrats prior to 1830 when the "Democratic Party" as such was established. The Republican Party is defined as the Federalists, National Republicans, and Whigs prior to the establishment of the "Republican Party" in the 1850s. See Appendix A for an explanation of the historical antecedents of the current Democratic and Republican parties. States reporting only partial voting returns for president are not included in the calculations for the years in which this occurred. —indicates that the state had no data, either because no vote data were found for the state in question or the state had not yet entered the Union. Data for the District of Columbia are included from 1964 to the present, after being granted the right to elect presidential electors by the 23rd Amendment.

Sources: State vote tables for president in Chapter 4.

Table 8-52 Presidential Competition Measures, by State, by Election Year, 1980–1988 (Percentages)

	1980			1984			1988		
State	Democratic % of Two-Party Vote	Margin of Victory	Party Competition Index	Democratic % of Two-Party Vote	Margin of Victory	Party Competition Index	Democratic % of Two-Party Vote	Margin of Victory	Party Competition Index
Alabama	49.3	1.4	98.6	38.7	22.6	77.4	40.3	19.4	80.6
Alaska	32.7	34.6	65.4	30.9	38.2	61.8	37.8	24.4	75.6
Arizona	31.8	36.4	63.6	32.9	34.2	65.8	39.3	21.4	78.6
Arkansas	49.7	0.6	99.4	38.8	22.4	77.6	42.8	14.4	85.6
California	40.5	19.0	81.0	41.8	16.4	83.6	48.2	3.6	96.4
Colorado	36.1	27.8	72.2	35.6	28.8	71.2	46.0	8.0	92.0
Connecticut	44.4	11.2	88.8	39.0	22.0	78.0	47.4	5.2	94.8
Delaware	48.7	2.6	97.4	40.0	20.0	80.0	43.8	12.4	87.6
Dist. of Columbia	84.8	69.6	30.4	86.1	72.2	27.8	85.2	70.4	29.6
Florida	40.9	18.2	81.8	34.7	30.6	69.4	38.7	22.6	77.4
Georgia	57.7	15.4	84.6	39.8	20.4	79.6	39.8	20.4	79.6
Hawaii	51.1	2.2	97.8	44.3	11.4	88.6	54.8	9.6	90.4
Idaho	27.5	45.0	55.0	26.7	46.6	53.4	36.7	26.6	73.4
Illinois	45.7	8.6	91.4	43.5	13.0	87.0	49.0	2.0	98.0
Indiana	40.2	19.6	80.4	37.9	24.2	75.8	39.9	20.2	79.8
Iowa	42.9	14.2	85.8	46.3	7.4	92.6	55.1	10.2	89.8
Kansas	36.5	27.0	73.0	33.0	34.0	66.0	43.3	13.4	86.6
Kentucky	49.2	1.6	98.4	39.6	20.8	79.2	44.1	11.8	88.2
Louisiana	47.2	5.6	94.4	38.6	22.8	77.2	44.8	10.4	89.6
Maine	48.1	3.8	96.2	38.9	22.2	77.8	44.2	11.6	88.4
Maryland	51.6	3.2	96.8	47.2	5.6	94.4	48.5	3.0	97.0
Massachusetts	49.9	0.2	99.8	48.6	2.8	97.2	54.0	8.0	92.0
Michigan	46.5	7.0	93.0	40.5	19.0	81.0	46.0	8.0	92.0
Minnesota	52.2	4.4	95.6	50.1	0.2	99.8	53.6	7.2	92.8
Mississippi	49.3	1.4	98.6	37.7	24.6	75.4	39.5	21.0	79.0
Missouri	46.4	7.2	92.8	40.0	20.0	80.0	48.0	4.0	96.0
Montana	36.3	27.4	72.6	38.7	22.6	77.4	47.0	6.0	94.0
Nebraska	28.4	43.2	56.8	29.0	42.0	58.0	39.4	21.2	78.8
Nevada	30.1	39.8	60.2	32.7	34.6	65.4	39.2	21.6	78.4
New Hampshire	32.9	34.2	65.8	31.1	37.8	62.2	36.8	26.4	73.6
New Jersey	42.6	14.8	85.2	39.5	21.0	79.0	43.1	13.8	86.2
New Mexico	40.1	19.8	80.2	39.7	20.6	79.4	47.5	5.0	95.0
New York	48.5	3.0	97.0	46.0	8.0	92.0	52.1	4.2	95.8
North Carolina	48.9	2.2	97.8	38.0	24.0	76.0	41.8	16.4	83.6
North Dakota	29.0	42.0	58.0	34.3	31.4	68.6	43.4	13.2	86.8
Ohio	44.3	11.4	88.6	40.5	19.0	81.0	44.5	11.0	89.0
Oklahoma	36.6	26.8	73.2	30.9	38.2	61.8	41.6	16.8	83.2
Oregon	44.4	11.2	88.8	43.9	12.2	87.8	52.4	4.8	95.2
Pennsylvania	46.1	7.8	92.2	46.3	7.4	92.6	48.8	2.4	97.6
Rhode Island	56.2	12.4	87.6	48.2	3.6	96.4	55.9	11.8	88.2
South Carolina	49.3	1.4	98.6	35.9	28.2	71.8	37.9	24.2	75.8
South Dakota	34.4	31.2	68.8	36.7	26.6	73.4	46.8	6.4	93.6
Tennessee	49.9	0.2	99.8	41.8	16.4	83.6	41.8	16.4	83.6
Texas	42.8	14.4	85.6	36.2	27.6	72.4	43.7	12.6	87.4
Utah	22.0	56.0	44.0	24.9	50.2	49.8	32.6	34.8	65.2
Vermont	46.4	7.2	92.8	41.3	17.4	82.6	48.2	3.6	96.4
Virginia	43.2	13.6	86.4	37.3	25.4	74.6	39.6	20.8	79.2
Washington	42.9	14.2	85.8	43.4	13.2	86.8	50.8	1.6	98.4
West Virginia	52.4	4.8	95.2	44.7	10.6	89.4	52.4	4.8	95.2
Wisconsin	47.4	5.2	94.8	45.4	9.2	90.8	51.8	3.6	96.4
Wyoming	30.9	38.2	61.8	28.6	42.8	57.2	38.6	22.8	77.2

Notes: The first entries are the Democratic percent of two-party vote values for each state for the presidential race. The second entries are the margin of victory values for each state for the presidential race, where margin of victory is defined as the absolute difference between the Democratic percent and the Republican percent of the two-party vote for president. The third entries are the party competition index values for each state for the presidential race, where the competition index devised by Paul David (1972) is defined as (100 − the margin of victory) or, alternatively, as (100 − the absolute difference between the Democratic and Republican percent of two-party vote for president). The values for Democratic and Republican percent of two-party vote for president are taken from the state vote tables in Chapter 4. Zero (0) percent on David's index represents a complete absence of two-party competition for that election year, whereas a score of 100 percent indicates perfect competition between the two major parties. A state can only receive a party competition score of 0 if it has a 100–0 vote split for president. Conversely, a state can only receive a score of 100 if it has a 50–50 vote split for president. For example, if Maryland in 1788 reported a 22.9 percent Democratic vote for president of its two-party vote, then its Republican vote for president would be 77.1 percent. The absolute difference between the two figures is the margin of victory, or 54.2 percent. 100 percent − 54.2 percent would equal 45.8 percent on David's party competition scale, indicating little competition in the presidential race in Maryland in 1788. The two-party vote percent values used to derive the margin of victory and party competition figures are initially found in the state vote tables in Chapter 4. The author's alternative party coding in these tables is used whenever it occurs instead of the conventional party coding of voting data. The Democratic Party is defined here as the Anti-Federalists, Democratic-Republicans, and Jackson Democrats prior to 1830 when the "Democratic Party" as such was established. The Republican Party is defined as the Federalists, National Republicans, and Whigs prior to the establishment of the "Republican Party" in the 1850s. See Appendix A for an explanation of the historical antecedents of the current Democratic and Republican parties. States reporting only partial voting returns for president are not included in the calculations for the years in which this occurred. —indicates that the state had no data, either because no vote data were found for the state in question or the state had not yet entered the Union. Data for the District of Columbia are included from 1964 to the present, after being granted the right to elect presidential electors by the 23rd Amendment.

Sources: State vote tables for president in Chapter 4.

Table 8-53 Presidential Competition Measures, by State, by Election Year, 1992–1996 (Percentages)

	1992			1996		
State	Democratic % of Two-Party Vote	Margin of Victory	Party Competition Index	Democratic % of Two-Party Vote	Margin of Victory	Party Competition Index
Alabama	46.2	7.6	92.4	46.3	7.4	92.6
Alaska	43.4	13.2	86.8	39.6	20.8	79.2
Arizona	48.7	2.6	97.4	51.2	2.4	97.6
Arkansas	60.0	20.0	80.0	59.4	18.8	81.2
California	58.5	17.0	83.0	57.2	14.4	85.6
Colorado	52.8	5.6	94.4	49.2	1.6	98.4
Connecticut	54.1	8.2	91.8	60.4	20.8	79.2
Delaware	55.2	10.4	89.6	58.6	17.2	82.8
Dist. of Columbia	90.3	80.6	19.4	90.1	80.2	19.8
Florida	48.8	2.4	97.6	53.2	6.4	93.6
Georgia	50.3	0.6	99.4	49.4	1.2	98.8
Hawaii	56.7	13.4	86.6	64.3	28.6	71.4
Idaho	40.3	19.4	80.6	39.2	21.6	78.4
Illinois	58.6	17.2	82.8	59.6	19.2	80.8
Indiana	46.2	7.6	92.4	46.9	6.2	93.8
Iowa	53.7	7.4	92.6	55.7	11.4	88.6
Kansas	46.5	7.0	93.0	39.9	20.2	79.8
Kentucky	51.9	3.8	96.2	50.5	1.0	99.0
Louisiana	52.7	5.4	94.6	56.6	13.2	86.8
Maine	56.1	12.2	87.8	62.7	25.4	74.6
Maryland	58.3	16.6	83.4	58.6	17.2	82.8
Massachusetts	62.1	24.2	75.8	68.6	37.2	62.8
Michigan	54.6	9.2	90.8	57.3	14.6	85.4
Minnesota	57.7	15.4	84.6	59.4	18.8	81.2
Mississippi	45.1	9.8	90.2	47.3	5.4	94.6
Missouri	56.5	13.0	87.0	53.5	7.0	93.0
Montana	51.7	3.4	96.6	48.3	3.4	96.6
Nebraska	38.7	22.6	77.4	39.4	21.2	78.8
Nevada	51.8	3.6	96.4	50.6	1.2	98.8
New Hampshire	50.8	1.6	98.4	55.6	11.2	88.8
New Jersey	51.4	2.8	97.2	60.0	20.0	80.0
New Mexico	55.1	10.2	89.8	54.0	8.0	92.0
New York	59.5	19.0	81.0	66.0	32.0	68.0
North Carolina	49.5	1.0	99.0	47.5	5.0	95.0
North Dakota	42.1	15.8	84.2	46.1	7.8	92.2
Ohio	51.2	2.4	97.6	53.6	7.2	92.8
Oklahoma	44.4	11.2	88.8	45.6	8.8	91.2
Oregon	56.6	13.2	86.8	54.7	9.4	90.6
Pennsylvania	55.5	11.0	89.0	55.2	10.4	89.6
Rhode Island	61.8	23.6	76.4	69.0	38.0	62.0
South Carolina	45.4	9.2	90.8	46.9	6.2	93.8
South Dakota	47.7	4.6	95.4	48.1	3.8	96.2
Tennessee	52.6	5.2	94.8	51.3	2.6	97.4
Texas	47.8	4.4	95.6	47.3	5.4	94.6
Utah	36.2	27.6	72.4	38.0	24.0	76.0
Vermont	60.3	20.6	79.4	63.2	26.4	73.6
Virginia	47.4	5.2	94.8	48.9	2.2	97.8
Washington	57.6	15.2	84.8	57.2	14.4	85.6
West Virginia	57.8	15.6	84.4	58.4	16.8	83.2
Wisconsin	52.8	5.6	94.4	55.9	11.8	88.2
Wyoming	46.2	7.6	92.4	42.5	15.0	85.0

Notes: The first entries are the Democratic percent of two-party vote values for each state for the presidential race. The second entries are the margin of victory values for each state for the presidential race, where margin of victory is defined as the absolute difference between the Democratic percent and the Republican percent of the two-party vote for president. The third entries are the party competition index values for each state for the presidential race, where the competition index devised by Paul David (1972) is defined as (100 − the margin of victory) or, alternatively, as (100 − the absolute difference between the Democratic and Republican percent of two-party vote for president). The values for Democratic and Republican percent of two-party vote for president are taken from the state vote tables in Chapter 4. Zero (0) percent on David's index represents a complete absence of two-party competition for that election year, whereas a score of 100 percent indicates perfect competition between the two major parties. A state can only receive a party competition score of 0 if it has a 100–0 vote split for president. Conversely, a state can only receive a score of 100 if it has a 50–50 vote split for president. For example, if Maryland in 1788 reported a 22.9 percent Democratic vote for president of its two-party vote, then its Republican vote for president would be 77.1 percent. The absolute difference between the two figures is the margin of victory, or 54.2 percent. 100 percent − 54.2 percent would equal 45.8 percent on David's party competition scale, indicating little competition in the presidential race in Maryland in 1788. The two-party vote percent values used to derive the margin of victory and party competition figures are initially found in the state vote tables in Chapter 4. The author's alternative party coding in these tables is used whenever it occurs instead of the conventional party coding of voting data. The Democratic Party is defined here as the Anti-Federalists, Democratic-Republicans, and Jackson Democrats prior to 1830 when the "Democratic Party" as such was established. The Republican Party is defined as the Federalists, National Republicans, and Whigs prior to the establishment of the "Republican Party" in the 1850s. See Appendix A for an explanation of the historical antecedents of the current Democratic and Republican parties. States reporting only partial voting returns for president are not included in the calculations for the years in which this occurred. —indicates that the state had no data, either because no vote data were found for the state in question or the state had not yet entered the Union. Data for the District of Columbia are included from 1964 to the present, after being granted the right to elect presidential electors by the 23rd Amendment.

Sources: State vote tables for president in Chapter 4.

Table 8-54 House Competition Measures, by State, by Two-Year Election Cycle, 1788–1793 (Percentages)

State	1788–1789			1790–1791			1792–1793		
	Democratic % of Two-Party Vote	Margin of Victory	Party Competition Index	Democratic % of Two-Party Vote	Margin of Victory	Party Competition Index	Democratic % of Two-Party Vote	Margin of Victory	Party Competition Index
Alabama	—	—	—	—	—	—	—	—	—
Alaska	—	—	—	—	—	—	—	—	—
Arizona	—	—	—	—	—	—	—	—	—
Arkansas	—	—	—	—	—	—	—	—	—
California	—	—	—	—	—	—	—	—	—
Colorado	—	—	—	—	—	—	—	—	—
Connecticut	—	—	—	—	—	—	—	—	—
Delaware	—	—	—	—	—	—	—	—	—
Florida	—	—	—	—	—	—	—	—	—
Georgia	—	—	—	—	—	—	—	—	—
Hawaii	—	—	—	—	—	—	—	—	—
Idaho	—	—	—	—	—	—	—	—	—
Illinois	—	—	—	—	—	—	—	—	—
Indiana	—	—	—	—	—	—	—	—	—
Iowa	—	—	—	—	—	—	—	—	—
Kansas	—	—	—	—	—	—	—	—	—
Kentucky	—	—	—	—	—	—	—	—	—
Louisiana	—	—	—	—	—	—	—	—	—
Maine	—	—	—	—	—	—	—	—	—
Maryland	34.6[1]	30.8[1]	69.2[1]	—	—	—	40.1	19.8	80.2
Massachusetts	—	—	—	—	—	—	—	—	—
Michigan	—	—	—	—	—	—	—	—	—
Minnesota	—	—	—	—	—	—	—	—	—
Mississippi	—	—	—	—	—	—	—	—	—
Missouri	—	—	—	—	—	—	—	—	—
Montana	—	—	—	—	—	—	—	—	—
Nebraska	—	—	—	—	—	—	—	—	—
Nevada	—	—	—	—	—	—	—	—	—
New Hampshire	—	—	—	—	—	—	—	—	—
New Jersey	—	—	—	—	—	—	—	—	—
New Mexico	—	—	—	—	—	—	—	—	—
New York	—	—	—	30.4	39.2	60.8	46.0[1]	8.0[1]	92.0[1]
North Carolina	—	—	—	—	—	—	—	—	—
North Dakota	—	—	—	—	—	—	—	—	—
Ohio	—	—	—	—	—	—	—	—	—
Oklahoma	—	—	—	—	—	—	—	—	—
Oregon	—	—	—	—	—	—	—	—	—
Pennsylvania	46.0	8.0	92.0	—	—	—	49.1	1.8	98.2
Rhode Island	—	—	—	—	—	—	—	—	—
South Carolina	—	—	—	—	—	—	—	—	—
South Dakota	—	—	—	—	—	—	—	—	—
Tennessee	—	—	—	—	—	—	—	—	—
Texas	—	—	—	—	—	—	—	—	—
Utah	—	—	—	—	—	—	—	—	—
Vermont	—	—	—	—	—	—	—	—	—
Virginia	—	—	—	—	—	—	—	—	—
Washington	—	—	—	—	—	—	—	—	—
West Virginia	—	—	—	—	—	—	—	—	—
Wisconsin	—	—	—	—	—	—	—	—	—
Wyoming	—	—	—	—	—	—	—	—	—

Notes: The first entries are the Democratic percent of two-party vote values for each state for the House race. The second entries are the margin of victory values for each state for the House race, where margin of victory is defined as the absolute difference between the Democratic percent and the Republican percent of the two-party vote for the House. The third entries are the party competition index values for each state for the House race, where the competition index devised by Paul David (1972) is defined as (100 − the margin of victory) or, alternatively, as (100 − the absolute difference between the Democratic and Republican percent of two-party vote for the House). The values for Democratic and Republican percent of two-party vote for the House are taken from the state vote tables in Chapter 5. Zero (0) percent on David's index represents a complete absence of two-party competition for that election year, whereas a score of 100 percent indicates perfect competition between the two major parties. A state can only receive a party competition score of 0 if it has a 100–0 vote split in all House races in the state. Conversely, a state can only receive a score of 100 if it has a 50–50 vote split in all House races in the state. For example, if Pennsylvania in 1788 cast an average of 46.0 percent Democratic vote for all House races in the state of its two-party vote, then its average Republican vote for House would be 54.0 percent. The absolute difference between the two figures is the margin of victory, or 8 percent; 100 percent − 8 percent would equal 92 percent on David's party competition scale, indicating very competitive contests in House races in Pennsylvania in 1788. The two-party vote percent values used to derive the margin of victory and party competition figures are initially found in the state vote tables in Chapter 5. The author's alternative party coding in these tables is used whenever it occurs instead of the conventional party coding of voting data. The Democratic Party is defined here as the Anti-Federalists, Democratic-Republicans, and Jackson Democrats prior to 1830 when the "Democratic Party" as such was established. The Republican Party is defined as the Federalists, National Republicans, and Whigs prior to the establishment of the "Republican Party" in the 1850s. See Appendix A for an explanation of the historical antecedents of the current Democratic and Republican parties. States reporting only partial voting returns for House races are not included in the calculations for the years in which this occurred. —indicates that the state had no data, either because no vote data were found for the state in question or the state had not yet entered the Union.

[1]Election held in an odd-numbered year.

Sources: State vote tables for House in Chapter 5.

Table 8-55 House Competition Measures, by State, by Two-Year Election Cycle, 1794–1799 (Percentages)

State	1794–1795 Democratic % of Two-Party Vote	1794–1795 Margin of Victory	1794–1795 Party Competition Index	1796–1797 Democratic % of Two-Party Vote	1796–1797 Margin of Victory	1796–1797 Party Competition Index	1798–1799 Democratic % of Two-Party Vote	1798–1799 Margin of Victory	1798–1799 Party Competition Index
Alabama	—	—	—	—	—	—	—	—	—
Alaska	—	—	—	—	—	—	—	—	—
Arizona	—	—	—	—	—	—	—	—	—
Arkansas	—	—	—	—	—	—	—	—	—
California	—	—	—	—	—	—	—	—	—
Colorado	—	—	—	—	—	—	—	—	—
Connecticut	0.0	100.0	0.0	13.9	72.2	27.8	0.0	100.0	0.0
Delaware	51.3	2.6	97.4	43.7	12.6	87.4	38.8	22.4	77.6
Florida	—	—	—	—	—	—	—	—	—
Georgia	56.4	12.8	87.2	63.5	27.0	73.0	43.4	13.2	86.8
Hawaii	—	—	—	—	—	—	—	—	—
Idaho	—	—	—	—	—	—	—	—	—
Illinois	—	—	—	—	—	—	—	—	—
Indiana	—	—	—	—	—	—	—	—	—
Iowa	—	—	—	—	—	—	—	—	—
Kansas	—	—	—	—	—	—	—	—	—
Kentucky	—	—	—	—	—	—	—	—	—
Louisiana	—	—	—	—	—	—	—	—	—
Maine	—	—	—	—	—	—	—	—	—
Maryland	40.7	18.6	81.4	37.7	24.6	75.4	—	—	—
Massachusetts	41.4	17.2	82.8	30.0	40.0	60.0	27.8	44.4	55.6
Michigan	—	—	—	—	—	—	—	—	—
Minnesota	—	—	—	—	—	—	—	—	—
Mississippi	—	—	—	—	—	—	—	—	—
Missouri	—	—	—	—	—	—	—	—	—
Montana	—	—	—	—	—	—	—	—	—
Nebraska	—	—	—	—	—	—	—	—	—
Nevada	—	—	—	—	—	—	—	—	—
New Hampshire	45.6	8.8	91.2	14.4	71.2	28.8	2.8	94.4	5.6
New Jersey	0.0	100.0	0.0	35.2 [1]	29.6 [1]	70.4 [1]	52.4	4.8	95.2
New Mexico	—	—	—	—	—	—	—	—	—
New York	48.4	3.2	96.8	38.1	23.8	76.2	45.6	8.8	91.2
North Carolina	—	—	—	—	—	—	—	—	—
North Dakota	—	—	—	—	—	—	—	—	—
Ohio	—	—	—	—	—	—	—	—	—
Oklahoma	—	—	—	—	—	—	—	—	—
Oregon	—	—	—	—	—	—	—	—	—
Pennsylvania	—	—	—	—	—	—	46.3	7.4	92.6
Rhode Island	38.1	23.8	76.2	0.0	100.0	0.0	34.6	30.8	69.2
South Carolina	—	—	—	44.2	11.6	88.4	—	—	—
South Dakota	—	—	—	—	—	—	—	—	—
Tennessee	—	—	—	100.0	100.0	0.0	—	—	—
Texas	—	—	—	—	—	—	—	—	—
Utah	—	—	—	—	—	—	—	—	—
Vermont	71.5	43.0	57.0	43.7	12.6	87.4	36.7	26.6	73.4
Virginia	—	—	—	—	—	—	—	—	—
Washington	—	—	—	—	—	—	—	—	—
West Virginia	—	—	—	—	—	—	—	—	—
Wisconsin	—	—	—	—	—	—	—	—	—
Wyoming	—	—	—	—	—	—	—	—	—

Notes: The first entries are the Democratic percent of two-party vote values for each state for the House race. The second entries are the margin of victory values for each state for the House race, where margin of victory is defined as the absolute difference between the Democratic percent and the Republican percent of the two-party vote for the House. The third entries are the party competition index values for each state for the House race, where the competition index devised by Paul David (1972) is defined as (100 − the margin of victory) or, alternatively, as (100 − the absolute difference between the Democratic and Republican percent of two-party vote for the House). The values for Democratic and Republican percent of two-party vote for the House are taken from the state vote tables in Chapter 5. Zero (0) percent on David's index represents a complete absence of two-party competition for that election year, whereas a score of 100 percent indicates perfect competition between the two major parties. A state can only receive a party competition score of 0 if it has a 100–0 vote split in all House races in the state. Conversely, a state can only receive a score of 100 if it has a 50–50 vote split in all House races in the state. For example, if Pennsylvania in 1788 cast an average of 46.0 percent Democratic vote for all House races in the state of its two-party vote, then its average Republican vote for House would be 54.0 percent. The absolute difference between the two figures is the margin of victory, or 8 percent; 100 percent − 8 percent would equal 92 percent on David's party competition scale, indicating very competitive contests in House races in Pennsylvania in 1788. The two-party vote percent values used to derive the margin of victory and party competition figures are initially found in the state vote tables in Chapter 5. The author's alternative party coding in these tables is used whenever it occurs instead of the conventional party coding of voting data. The Democratic Party is defined here as the Anti-Federalists, Democratic-Republicans, and Jackson Democrats prior to 1830 when the "Democratic Party" as such was established. The Republican Party is defined as the Federalists, National Republicans, and Whigs prior to the establishment of the "Republican Party" in the 1850s. See Appendix A for an explanation of the historical antecedents of the current Democratic and Republican parties. States reporting only partial voting returns for House races are not included in the calculations for the years in which this occurred. —indicates that the state had no data, either because no vote data were found for the state in question or the state had not yet entered the Union.

[1] Election held in an odd-numbered year.

Sources: State vote tables for House in Chapter 5.

Table 8-56 House Competition Measures, by State, by Two-Year Election Cycle, 1800–1805 (Percentages)

State	1800–1801			1802–1803			1804–1805		
	Democratic % of Two-Party Vote	Margin of Victory	Party Competition Index	Democratic % of Two-Party Vote	Margin of Victory	Party Competition Index	Democratic % of Two-Party Vote	Margin of Victory	Party Competition Index
Alabama	—	—	—	—	—	—	—	—	—
Alaska	—	—	—	—	—	—	—	—	—
Arizona	—	—	—	—	—	—	—	—	—
Arkansas	—	—	—	—	—	—	—	—	—
California	—	—	—	—	—	—	—	—	—
Colorado	—	—	—	—	—	—	—	—	—
Connecticut	32.4	35.2	64.8	0.0	100.0	0.0	0.0	100.0	0.0
Delaware	46.7	6.6	93.4	50.1	0.2	99.8	47.9	4.2	95.8
Florida	—	—	—	—	—	—	—	—	—
Georgia	100.0	100.0	0.0	76.2	52.4	47.6	100.0	100.0	0.0
Hawaii	—	—	—	—	—	—	—	—	—
Idaho	—	—	—	—	—	—	—	—	—
Illinois	—	—	—	—	—	—	—	—	—
Indiana	—	—	—	—	—	—	—	—	—
Iowa	—	—	—	—	—	—	—	—	—
Kansas	—	—	—	—	—	—	—	—	—
Kentucky	100.0 [1]	100.0 [1]	0.0 [1]	—	—	—	—	—	—
Louisiana	—	—	—	—	—	—	—	—	—
Maine	—	—	—	—	—	—	—	—	—
Maryland	62.2 [1]	24.4 [1]	75.6 [1]	—	—	—	73.9	47.8	52.2
Massachusetts	46.1	7.8	92.2	45.6	8.8	91.2	53.1	6.2	93.8
Michigan	—	—	—	—	—	—	—	—	—
Minnesota	—	—	—	—	—	—	—	—	—
Mississippi	—	—	—	—	—	—	—	—	—
Missouri	—	—	—	—	—	—	—	—	—
Montana	—	—	—	—	—	—	—	—	—
Nebraska	—	—	—	—	—	—	—	—	—
Nevada	—	—	—	—	—	—	—	—	—
New Hampshire	24.5	51.0	49.0	40.1	19.8	80.2	48.2	3.6	96.4
New Jersey	50.9	1.8	98.2	97.3 [1]	94.6 [1]	5.4 [1]	99.0	98.0	2.0
New Mexico	—	—	—	—	—	—	—	—	—
New York	49.6	0.8	99.2	59.3	18.6	81.4	63.4	26.8	73.2
North Carolina	—	—	—	—	—	—	—	—	—
North Dakota	—	—	—	—	—	—	—	—	—
Ohio	—	—	—	73.8 [1]	47.6 [1]	52.4 [1]	70.5	41.0	59.0
Oklahoma	—	—	—	—	—	—	—	—	—
Oregon	—	—	—	—	—	—	—	—	—
Pennsylvania	—	—	—	—	—	—	—	—	—
Rhode Island	66.8	33.6	66.4	61.3	22.6	77.4	100.0	100.0	0.0
South Carolina	—	—	—	64.5 [1]	29.0 [1]	71.0 [1]	—	—	—
South Dakota	—	—	—	—	—	—	—	—	—
Tennessee	100.0 [1]	100.0 [1]	0.0 [1]	100.0 [1]	100.0 [1]	0.0 [1]	100.0 [1]	100.0 [1]	0.0 [1]
Texas	—	—	—	—	—	—	—	—	—
Utah	—	—	—	—	—	—	—	—	—
Vermont	52.6	5.2	94.8	42.4	15.2	84.8	53.4	6.8	93.2
Virginia	—	—	—	—	—	—	—	—	—
Washington	—	—	—	—	—	—	—	—	—
West Virginia	—	—	—	—	—	—	—	—	—
Wisconsin	—	—	—	—	—	—	—	—	—
Wyoming	—	—	—	—	—	—	—	—	—

Notes: The first entries are the Democratic percent of two-party vote values for each state for the House race. The second entries are the margin of victory values for each state for the House race, where margin of victory is defined as the absolute difference between the Democratic percent and the Republican percent of the two-party vote for the House. The third entries are the party competition index values for each state for the House race, where the competition index devised by Paul David (1972) is defined as (100 − the margin of victory) or, alternatively, as (100 − the absolute difference between the Democratic and Republican percent of two-party vote for the House). The values for Democratic and Republican percent of two-party vote for the House are taken from the state vote tables in Chapter 5. Zero (0) percent on David's index represents a complete absence of two-party competition for that election year, whereas a score of 100 percent indicates perfect competition between the two major parties. A state can only receive a party competition score of 0 if it has a 100–0 vote split in all House races in the state. Conversely, a state can only receive a score of 100 if it has a 50–50 vote split in all House races in the state. For example, if Pennsylvania in 1788 cast an average of 46.0 percent Democratic vote for all House races in the state of its two-party vote, then its average Republican vote for House would be 54.0 percent. The absolute difference between the two figures is the margin of victory, or 8 percent; 100 percent − 8 percent would equal 92 percent on David's party competition scale, indicating very competitive contests in House races in Pennsylvania in 1788. The two-party vote percent values used to derive the margin of victory and party competition figures are initially found in the state vote tables in Chapter 5. The Democratic Party is defined here as the Anti-Federalists, Democratic-Republicans, and Jackson Democrats prior to 1830 when the "Democratic Party" as such was established. The Republican Party is defined as the Federalists, National Republicans, and Whigs prior to the establishment of the "Republican Party" in the 1850s. See Appendix A for an explanation of the historical antecedents of the current Democratic and Republican parties. States reporting only partial voting returns for House races are not included in the calculations for the years in which this occurred. —indicates that the state had no data, either because no vote data were found for the state in question or the state had not yet entered the Union.

[1] Election held in an odd-numbered year.

Sources: State vote tables for House in Chapter 5.

Table 8-57 House Competition Measures, by State, by Two-Year Election Cycle, 1806–1811 (Percentages)

	1806–1807			1808–1809			1810–1811		
State	Democratic % of Two-Party Vote	Margin of Victory	Party Competition Index	Democratic % of Two-Party Vote	Margin of Victory	Party Competition Index	Democratic % of Two-Party Vote	Margin of Victory	Party Competition Index
Alabama	—	—	—	—	—	—	—	—	—
Alaska	—	—	—	—	—	—	—	—	—
Arizona	—	—	—	—	—	—	—	—	—
Arkansas	—	—	—	—	—	—	—	—	—
California	—	—	—	—	—	—	—	—	—
Colorado	—	—	—	—	—	—	—	—	—
Connecticut	—	—	—	—	—	—	0.0	100.0	0.0
Delaware	34.0	32.0	68.0	46.7	6.6	93.4	49.9	0.2	99.8
Florida	—	—	—	—	—	—	—	—	—
Georgia	100.0	100.0	0.0	72.6	45.2	54.8	87.2	74.4	25.6
Hawaii	—	—	—	—	—	—	—	—	—
Idaho	—	—	—	—	—	—	—	—	—
Illinois	—	—	—	—	—	—	—	—	—
Indiana	—	—	—	—	—	—	—	—	—
Iowa	—	—	—	—	—	—	—	—	—
Kansas	—	—	—	—	—	—	—	—	—
Kentucky	—	—	—	—	—	—	—	—	—
Louisiana	—	—	—	—	—	—	—	—	—
Maine	—	—	—	—	—	—	—	—	—
Maryland	73.0	46.0	54.0	55.5	11.0	89.0	74.6	49.2	50.8
Massachusetts	52.3	4.6	95.4	47.5	5.0	95.0	48.5	3.0	97.0
Michigan	—	—	—	—	—	—	—	—	—
Minnesota	—	—	—	—	—	—	—	—	—
Mississippi	—	—	—	—	—	—	—	—	—
Missouri	—	—	—	—	—	—	—	—	—
Montana	—	—	—	—	—	—	—	—	—
Nebraska	—	—	—	—	—	—	—	—	—
Nevada	—	—	—	—	—	—	—	—	—
New Hampshire	61.0	22.0	78.0	45.0	10.0	90.0	50.2	0.4	99.6
New Jersey	71.7	43.4	56.6	56.0	12.0	88.0	96.3	92.6	7.4
New Mexico	—	—	—	—	—	—	—	—	—
New York	59.8	19.6	80.4	50.7	1.4	98.6	55.3	10.6	89.4
North Carolina	—	—	—	—	—	—	—	—	—
North Dakota	—	—	—	—	—	—	—	—	—
Ohio	74.0	48.0	52.0	69.7	39.4	60.6	—	—	—
Oklahoma	—	—	—	—	—	—	—	—	—
Oregon	—	—	—	—	—	—	—	—	—
Pennsylvania	—	—	—	59.9	19.8	80.2	73.2	46.4	53.6
Rhode Island	54.7	9.4	90.6	47.0	6.0	94.0	48.8	2.4	97.6
South Carolina	81.8	63.6	36.4	—	—	—	—	—	—
South Dakota	—	—	—	—	—	—	—	—	—
Tennessee	—	—	—	—	—	—	100.0[1]	100.0[1]	0.0[1]
Texas	—	—	—	—	—	—	—	—	—
Utah	—	—	—	—	—	—	—	—	—
Vermont	—	—	—	—	—	—	56.6	13.2	86.8
Virginia	—	—	—	—	—	—	—	—	—
Washington	—	—	—	—	—	—	—	—	—
West Virginia	—	—	—	—	—	—	—	—	—
Wisconsin	—	—	—	—	—	—	—	—	—
Wyoming	—	—	—	—	—	—	—	—	—

Notes: The first entries are the Democratic percent of two-party vote values for each state for the House race. The second entries are the margin of victory values for each state for the House race, where margin of victory is defined as the absolute difference between the Democratic percent and the Republican percent of the two-party vote for the House. The third entries are the party competition index values for each state for the House race, where the competition index devised by Paul David (1972) is defined as (100 − the margin of victory) or, alternatively, as (100 − the absolute difference between the Democratic and Republican percent of two-party vote for the House). The values for Democratic and Republican percent of two-party vote for the House are taken from the state vote tables in Chapter 5. Zero (0) percent on David's index represents a complete absence of two-party competition for that election year, whereas a score of 100 percent indicates perfect competition between the two major parties. A state can only receive a party competition score of 0 if it has a 100–0 vote split in all House races in the state. Conversely, a state can only receive a score of 100 if it has a 50–50 vote split in all House races in the state. For example, if Pennsylvania in 1788 cast an average of 46.0 percent Democratic vote for all House races in the state of its two-party vote, then its average Republican vote for House would be 54.0 percent. The absolute difference between the two figures is the margin of victory, or 8 percent; 100 percent − 8 percent would equal 92 percent on David's party competition scale, indicating very competitive contests in House races in Pennsylvania in 1788. The two-party vote percent values used to derive the margin of victory and party competition figures are initially found in the state vote tables in Chapter 5. The author's alternative party coding in these tables is used whenever it occurs instead of the conventional party coding of voting data. The Democratic Party is defined here as the Anti-Federalists, Democratic-Republicans, and Jackson Democrats prior to 1830 when the "Democratic Party" as such was established. The Republican Party is defined as the Federalists, National Republicans, and Whigs prior to the establishment of the "Republican Party" in the 1850s. See Appendix A for an explanation of the historical antecedents of the current Democratic and Republican parties. States reporting only partial voting returns for House races are not included in the calculations for the years in which this occurred. —indicates that the state had no data, either because no vote data were found for the state in question or the state had not yet entered the Union.

[1] Election held in an odd-numbered year.

Sources: State vote tables for House in Chapter 5.

Table 8-58 House Competition Measures, by State, by Two-Year Election Cycle, 1812–1817 (Percentages)

	1812–1813			1814–1815			1816–1817		
State	Democratic % of Two-Party Vote	Margin of Victory	Party Competition Index	Democratic % of Two-Party Vote	Margin of Victory	Party Competition Index	Democratic % of Two-Party Vote	Margin of Victory	Party Competition Index
Alabama	—	—	—	—	—	—	—	—	—
Alaska	—	—	—	—	—	—	—	—	—
Arizona	—	—	—	—	—	—	—	—	—
Arkansas	—	—	—	—	—	—	—	—	—
California	—	—	—	—	—	—	—	—	—
Colorado	—	—	—	—	—	—	—	—	—
Connecticut	0.0	100.0	0.0	—	—	—	0.0	100.0	0.0
Delaware	43.4	13.2	86.8	39.1	21.8	78.2	49.7	0.6	99.4
Florida	—	—	—	—	—	—	—	—	—
Georgia	81.5	63.0	37.0	100.0	100.0	0.0	100.0	100.0	0.0
Hawaii	—	—	—	—	—	—	—	—	—
Idaho	—	—	—	—	—	—	—	—	—
Illinois	—	—	—	—	—	—	—	—	—
Indiana	—	—	—	—	—	—	100.0	100.0	0.0
Iowa	—	—	—	—	—	—	—	—	—
Kansas	—	—	—	—	—	—	—	—	—
Kentucky	—	—	—	—	—	—	—	—	—
Louisiana	100.0	100.0	0.0	91.7	83.4	16.6	100.0	100.0	0.0
Maine	—	—	—	—	—	—	—	—	—
Maryland	61.7	23.4	76.6	37.2	25.6	74.4	—	—	—
Massachusetts	39.1	21.8	78.2	33.7	32.6	67.4	44.0	12.0	88.0
Michigan	—	—	—	—	—	—	—	—	—
Minnesota	—	—	—	—	—	—	—	—	—
Mississippi	—	—	—	—	—	—	100.0 [1]	100.0 [1]	0.0 [1]
Missouri	—	—	—	—	—	—	—	—	—
Montana	—	—	—	—	—	—	—	—	—
Nebraska	—	—	—	—	—	—	—	—	—
Nevada	—	—	—	—	—	—	—	—	—
New Hampshire	46.3	7.4	92.6	47.8	4.4	95.6	53.4	6.8	93.2
New Jersey	47.4 [1]	5.2 [1]	94.8 [1]	51.7	3.4	96.6	100.0	100.0	0.0
New Mexico	—	—	—	—	—	—	—	—	—
New York	45.6	8.8	91.2	53.5	7.0	93.0	55.1	10.2	89.8
North Carolina	—	—	—	—	—	—	—	—	—
North Dakota	—	—	—	—	—	—	—	—	—
Ohio	75.3	50.6	49.4	—	—	—	—	—	—
Oklahoma	—	—	—	—	—	—	—	—	—
Oregon	—	—	—	—	—	—	—	—	—
Pennsylvania	59.4	18.8	81.2	—	—	—	—	—	—
Rhode Island	41.5	17.0	83.0	43.9	12.2	87.8	0.0	100.0	0.0
South Carolina	—	—	—	—	—	—	—	—	—
South Dakota	—	—	—	—	—	—	—	—	—
Tennessee	—	—	—	—	—	—	100.0 [1]	100.0 [1]	0.0 [1]
Texas	—	—	—	—	—	—	—	—	—
Utah	—	—	—	—	—	—	—	—	—
Vermont	50.4	0.8	99.2	—	—	—	54.7	9.4	90.6
Virginia	—	—	—	—	—	—	—	—	—
Washington	—	—	—	—	—	—	—	—	—
West Virginia	—	—	—	—	—	—	—	—	—
Wisconsin	—	—	—	—	—	—	—	—	—
Wyoming	—	—	—	—	—	—	—	—	—
Indiana	—	—	—	—	—	—	100.0 [2]	100.0 [2]	0.0 [2]

Notes: The first entries are the Democratic percent of two-party vote values for each state for the House race. The second entries are the margin of victory values for each state for the House race, where margin of victory is defined as the absolute difference between the Democratic percent and the Republican percent of the two-party vote for the House. The third entries are the party competition index values for each state for the House race, where the competition index devised by Paul David (1972) is defined as (100 − the margin of victory) or, alternatively, as (100 − the absolute difference between the Democratic and Republican percent of two-party vote for the House). The values for Democratic and Republican percent of two-party vote for the House are taken from the state vote tables in Chapter 5. Zero (0) percent on David's index represents a complete absence of two-party competition for that election year, whereas a score of 100 percent indicates perfect competition between the two major parties. A state can only receive a party competition score of 0 if it has a 100–0 vote split in all House races in the state. Conversely, a state can only receive a score of 100 if it has a 50–50 vote split in all House races in the state. For example, if Pennsylvania in 1788 cast an average of 46.0 percent Democratic vote for all House races in the state of its two-party vote, then its average Republican vote for House would be 54.0 percent. The absolute difference between the two figures is the margin of victory, or 8 percent; 100 percent − 8 percent would equal 92 percent on David's party competition scale, indicating very competitive contests in House races in Pennsylvania in 1788. The two-party vote percent values used to derive the margin of victory and party competition figures are initially found in the state vote tables in Chapter 5. The author's alternative party coding in these tables is used whenever it occurs instead of the conventional party coding of voting data. The Democratic Party is defined here as the Anti-Federalists, Democratic-Republicans, and Jackson Democrats prior to 1830 when the "Democratic Party" as such was established. The Republican Party is defined as the Federalists, National Republicans, and Whigs prior to the establishment of the "Republican Party" in the 1850s. See Appendix A for an explanation of the historical antecedents of the current Democratic and Republican parties. States reporting only partial voting returns for House races are not included in the calculations for the years in which this occurred. —indicates that the state had no data, either because no vote data were found for the state in question or the state had not yet entered the Union.

[1] Election held in an odd-numbered year.
[2] 1817 election when state had annual elections in both 1816 and 1817.

Sources: State vote tables for House in Chapter 5.

Table 8-59 House Competition Measures, by State, by Two-Year Election Cycle, 1818–1823 (Percentages)

	1818–1819			1820–1821			1822–1823		
State	Democratic % of Two-Party Vote	Margin of Victory	Party Competition Index	Democratic % of Two-Party Vote	Margin of Victory	Party Competition Index	Democratic % of Two-Party Vote	Margin of Victory	Party Competition Index
Alabama	100.0 [1]	100.0 [1]	0.0 [1]	100.0 [1]	100.0 [1]	0.0 [1]	—	—	—
Alaska	—	—	—	—	—	—	—	—	—
Arizona	—	—	—	—	—	—	—	—	—
Arkansas	—	—	—	—	—	—	—	—	—
California	—	—	—	—	—	—	—	—	—
Colorado	—	—	—	—	—	—	—	—	—
Connecticut	51.2	2.4	97.6	93.4 [1]	86.8 [1]	13.2 [1]	100.0 [1]	100.0 [1]	0.0 [1]
Delaware	49.3	1.4	98.6	50.7	1.4	98.6	45.7	8.6	91.4
Florida	—	—	—	—	—	—	—	—	—
Georgia	100.0	100.0	0.0	100.0	100.0	0.0	100.0	100.0	0.0
Hawaii	—	—	—	—	—	—	—	—	—
Idaho	—	—	—	—	—	—	—	—	—
Illinois	100.0	100.0	0.0	100.0	100.0	0.0	100.0	100.0	0.0
Indiana	—	—	—	100.0	100.0	0.0	—	—	—
Iowa	—	—	—	—	—	—	—	—	—
Kansas	—	—	—	—	—	—	—	—	—
Kentucky	—	—	—	—	—	—	—	—	—
Louisiana	100.0	100.0	0.0	100.0	100.0	0.0	—	—	—
Maine	—	—	—	73.1	46.2	53.8	71.5 [1]	43.0 [1]	57.0 [1]
Maryland	—	—	—	—	—	—	74.9	49.8	50.2
Massachusetts	50.0	0.0	100.0	40.4	19.2	80.8	—	—	—
Michigan	—	—	—	—	—	—	—	—	—
Minnesota	—	—	—	—	—	—	—	—	—
Mississippi	—	—	—	—	—	—	—	—	—
Missouri	—	—	—	—	—	—	—	—	—
Montana	—	—	—	—	—	—	—	—	—
Nebraska	—	—	—	—	—	—	—	—	—
Nevada	—	—	—	—	—	—	—	—	—
New Hampshire	66.1 [1]	32.2 [1]	67.8 [1]	86.0	72.0	28.0	100.0	100.0	0.0
New Jersey	94.8	89.6	10.4	91.9	83.8	16.2	—	—	—
New Mexico	—	—	—	—	—	—	—	—	—
New York	76.0	52.0	48.0	100.0 [1]	100.0 [1]	0.0 [1]	100.0	100.0	0.0
North Carolina	—	—	—	—	—	—	—	—	—
North Dakota	—	—	—	—	—	—	—	—	—
Ohio	85.6	71.2	28.8	—	—	—	—	—	—
Oklahoma	—	—	—	—	—	—	—	—	—
Oregon	—	—	—	—	—	—	—	—	—
Pennsylvania	—	—	—	55.1	10.2	89.8	76.1	52.2	47.8
Rhode Island	100.0	100.0	0.0	100.0	100.0	0.0	100.0	100.0	0.0
South Carolina	—	—	—	—	—	—	92.0 [1]	84.0 [1]	16.0 [1]
South Dakota	—	—	—	—	—	—	—	—	—
Tennessee	100.0 [1]	100.0 [1]	0.0 [1]	—	—	—	—	—	—
Texas	—	—	—	—	—	—	—	—	—
Utah	—	—	—	—	—	—	—	—	—
Vermont	74.3	48.6	51.4	62.9	25.8	74.2	71.8	43.6	56.4
Virginia	—	—	—	—	—	—	—	—	—
Washington	—	—	—	—	—	—	—	—	—
West Virginia	—	—	—	—	—	—	—	—	—
Wisconsin	—	—	—	—	—	—	—	—	—
Wyoming	—	—	—	—	—	—	—	—	—

Notes: The first entries are the Democratic percent of two-party vote values for each state for the House race. The second entries are the margin of victory values for each state for the House race, where margin of victory is defined as the absolute difference between the Democratic percent and the Republican percent of the two-party vote for the House. The third entries are the party competition index values for each state for the House race, where the competition index devised by Paul David (1972) is defined as (100 − the margin of victory) or, alternatively, as (100 − the absolute difference between the Democratic and Republican percent of two-party vote for the House). The values for Democratic and Republican percent of two-party vote for the House are taken from the state vote tables in Chapter 5. Zero (0) percent on David's index represents a complete absence of two-party competition for that election year, whereas a score of 100 percent indicates perfect competition between the two parties. A state can only receive a party competition score of 0 if it has a 100–0 vote split in all House races in the state. Conversely, a state can only receive a score of 100 if it has a 50–50 vote split in all House races in the state. For example, if Pennsylvania in 1788 cast an average of 46.0 percent Democratic vote for all House races in the state of its two-party vote, then its average Republican vote for House would be 54.0 percent. The absolute difference between the two figures is the margin of victory, or 8 percent; 100 percent − 8 percent would equal 92 percent on David's party competition scale, indicating very competitive contests in House races in Pennsylvania in 1788. The two-party vote percent values used to derive the margin of victory and party competition figures are initially found in the state vote tables in Chapter 5. The author's alternative party coding in these tables is used whenever it occurs instead of the conventional party coding of voting data. The Democratic Party is defined here as the Anti-Federalists, Democratic-Republicans, and Jackson Democrats prior to 1830 when the "Democratic Party" as such was established. The Republican Party is defined as the Federalists, National Republicans, and Whigs prior to the establishment of the "Republican Party" in the 1850s. See Appendix A for an explanation of the historical antecedents of the current Democratic and Republican parties. States reporting only partial voting returns for House races are not included in the calculations for the years in which this occurred. —indicates that the state had no data, either because no vote data were found for the state in question or the state had not yet entered the Union.

[1] Election held in an odd-numbered year.

Sources: State vote tables for House in Chapter 5.

Table 8-60 House Competition Measures, by State, by Two-Year Election Cycle, 1824–1829 (Percentages)

State	1824–1825 Democratic % of Two-Party Vote	Margin of Victory	Party Competition Index	1826–1827 Democratic % of Two-Party Vote	Margin of Victory	Party Competition Index	1828–1829 Democratic % of Two-Party Vote	Margin of Victory	Party Competition Index
Alabama	—	—	—	—	—	—	81.6[1]	63.2[1]	36.8[1]
Alaska	—	—	—	—	—	—	—	—	—
Arizona	—	—	—	—	—	—	—	—	—
Arkansas	—	—	—	—	—	—	—	—	—
California	—	—	—	—	—	—	—	—	—
Colorado	—	—	—	—	—	—	—	—	—
Connecticut	82.9[1]	65.8[1]	34.2[1]	0.0[1]	100.0[1]	0.0[1]	39.5[1]	21.0[1]	79.0[1]
Delaware	48.3	3.4	96.6	45.9	8.2	91.8	47.7	4.6	95.4
Florida	—	—	—	—	—	—	—	—	—
Georgia	100.0	100.0	0.0	100.0	100.0	0.0	100.0	100.0	0.0
Hawaii	—	—	—	—	—	—	—	—	—
Idaho	—	—	—	—	—	—	—	—	—
Illinois	—	—	—	52.9	5.8	94.2	62.9	25.8	74.2
Indiana	—	—	—	38.3	23.4	76.6	—	—	—
Iowa	—	—	—	—	—	—	—	—	—
Kansas	—	—	—	—	—	—	—	—	—
Kentucky	—	—	—	63.1[1]	26.2[1]	73.8[1]	—	—	—
Louisiana	—	—	—	—	—	—	38.7	22.6	77.4
Maine	78.3	56.6	43.4	41.2	17.6	82.4	52.2	4.4	95.6
Maryland	61.9	23.8	76.2	50.4	0.8	99.2	53.1[1]	6.2[1]	93.8[1]
Massachusetts	49.0	2.0	98.0	0.0	100.0	0.0	12.6	74.8	25.2
Michigan	—	—	—	—	—	—	—	—	—
Minnesota	—	—	—	—	—	—	—	—	—
Mississippi	100.0	100.0	0.0	69.0	38.0	62.0	—	—	—
Missouri	100.0	100.0	0.0	—	—	—	60.5	21.0	79.0
Montana	—	—	—	—	—	—	—	—	—
Nebraska	—	—	—	—	—	—	—	—	—
Nevada	—	—	—	—	—	—	—	—	—
New Hampshire	100.0	100.0	0.0	100.0[1]	100.0[1]	0.0[1]	54.4[1]	8.8[1]	91.2[1]
New Jersey	100.0	100.0	0.0	39.4	21.2	78.8	48.1	3.8	96.2
New Mexico	—	—	—	—	—	—	—	—	—
New York	100.0	100.0	0.0	52.0	4.0	96.0	57.0	14.0	86.0
North Carolina	—	—	—	—	—	—	—	—	—
North Dakota	—	—	—	—	—	—	—	—	—
Ohio	—	—	—	27.3	45.4	54.6	—	—	—
Oklahoma	—	—	—	—	—	—	—	—	—
Oregon	—	—	—	—	—	—	—	—	—
Pennsylvania	—	—	—	—	—	—	—	—	—
Rhode Island	100.0[1]	100.0[1]	0.0[1]	0.0[1]	100.0[1]	0.0[1]	0.0[1]	100.0[1]	0.0[1]
South Carolina	—	—	—	—	—	—	—	—	—
South Dakota	—	—	—	—	—	—	—	—	—
Tennessee	—	—	—	—	—	—	—	—	—
Texas	—	—	—	—	—	—	—	—	—
Utah	—	—	—	—	—	—	—	—	—
Vermont	91.3	82.6	17.4	0.0	100.0	0.0	—	—	—
Virginia	—	—	—	—	—	—	—	—	—
Washington	—	—	—	—	—	—	—	—	—
West Virginia	—	—	—	—	—	—	—	—	—
Wisconsin	—	—	—	—	—	—	—	—	—
Wyoming	—	—	—	—	—	—	—	—	—

Notes: The first entries are the Democratic percent of two-party vote values for each state for the House race. The second entries are the margin of victory values for each state for the House race, where margin of victory is defined as the absolute difference between the Democratic percent and the Republican percent of the two-party vote for the House. The third entries are the party competition index values for each state for the House race, where the competition index devised by Paul David (1972) is defined as (100 − the margin of victory) or, alternatively, as (100 − the absolute difference between the Democratic and Republican percent of two-party vote for the House). The values for Democratic and Republican percent of two-party vote for the House are taken from the state vote tables in Chapter 5. Zero (0) percent on David's index represents a complete absence of two-party competition for that election year, whereas a score of 100 percent indicates perfect competition between the two major parties. A state can only receive a party competition score of 0 if it has a 100–0 vote split in all House races in the state. Conversely, a state can only receive a score of 100 if it has a 50–50 vote split in all House races in the state. For example, if Pennsylvania in 1788 cast an average of 46.0 percent Democratic vote for all House races in the state of its two-party vote, then its average Republican vote for House would be 54.0 percent. The absolute difference between the two figures is the margin of victory, or 8 percent; 100 percent − 8 percent would equal 92 percent on David's party competition scale, indicating very competitive contests in House races in Pennsylvania in 1788. The two-party vote percent values used to derive the margin of victory and party competition figures are initially found in the state vote tables in Chapter 5. The author's alternative party coding in these tables is used whenever it occurs instead of the conventional party coding of voting data. The Democratic Party is defined here as the Anti-Federalists, Democratic-Republicans, and Jackson Democrats prior to 1830 when the "Democratic Party" as such was established. The Republican Party is defined as the Federalists, National Republicans, and Whigs prior to the establishment of the "Republican Party" in the 1850s. See Appendix A for an explanation of the historical antecedents of the current Democratic and Republican parties. States reporting only partial voting returns for House races are not included in the calculations for the years in which this occurred. —indicates that the state had no data, either because no vote data were found for the state in question or the state had not yet entered the Union.

[1]Election held in an odd-numbered year.

Sources: State vote tables for House in Chapter 5.

Table 8-61 House Competition Measures, by State, by Two-Year Election Cycle, 1830–1835 (Percentages)

State	1830–1831			1832–1833			1834–1835		
	Democratic % of Two-Party Vote	Margin of Victory	Party Competition Index	Democratic % of Two-Party Vote	Margin of Victory	Party Competition Index	Democratic % of Two-Party Vote	Margin of Victory	Party Competition Index
Alabama	—	—	—	—	—	—	—	—	—
Alaska	—	—	—	—	—	—	—	—	—
Arizona	—	—	—	—	—	—	—	—	—
Arkansas	—	—	—	—	—	—	—	—	—
California	—	—	—	—	—	—	—	—	—
Colorado	—	—	—	—	—	—	—	—	—
Connecticut	32.6[1]	34.8[1]	65.2[1]	42.5[1]	15.0[1]	85.0[1]	52.6[1]	5.2[1]	94.8[1]
Delaware	47.3	5.4	94.6	49.3	1.4	98.6	49.2	1.6	98.4
Florida	—	—	—	—	—	—	—	—	—
Georgia	100.0	100.0	0.0	100.0	100.0	0.0	53.7	7.4	92.6
Hawaii	—	—	—	—	—	—	—	—	—
Idaho	—	—	—	—	—	—	—	—	—
Illinois	100.0[1]	100.0[1]	0.0[1]	89.9	79.8	20.2	100.0	100.0	0.0
Indiana	57.7[1]	15.4[1]	84.6[1]	90.6[1]	81.2[1]	18.8[1]	62.5[1]	25.0[1]	75.0[1]
Iowa	—	—	—	—	—	—	—	—	—
Kansas	—	—	—	—	—	—	—	—	—
Kentucky	—	—	—	—	—	—	—	—	—
Louisiana	—	—	—	35.5	29.0	71.0	16.6	66.8	33.2
Maine	52.4	4.8	95.2	60.8[1]	21.6[1]	78.4[1]	52.9	5.8	94.2
Maryland	43.4[1]	13.2[1]	86.8[1]	50.4[1]	0.8[1]	99.2[1]	—	—	—
Massachusetts	16.6	66.8	33.2	21.3[1]	57.4[1]	42.6[1]	33.6	32.8	67.2
Michigan	—	—	—	—	—	—	100.0[1]	100.0[1]	0.0[1]
Minnesota	—	—	—	—	—	—	—	—	—
Mississippi	76.4	52.8	47.2	—	—	—	54.5[1]	9.0[1]	91.0[1]
Missouri	62.3[1]	24.6[1]	75.4[1]	63.5[1]	27.0[1]	73.0[1]	100.0[1]	100.0[1]	0.0[1]
Montana	—	—	—	—	—	—	—	—	—
Nebraska	—	—	—	—	—	—	—	—	—
Nevada	—	—	—	—	—	—	—	—	—
New Hampshire	54.7[1]	9.4[1]	90.6[1]	77.6[1]	55.2[1]	44.8[1]	62.6[1]	25.2[1]	74.8[1]
New Jersey	48.3	3.4	96.6	50.5	1.0	99.0	50.9	1.8	98.2
New Mexico	—	—	—	—	—	—	—	—	—
New York	74.4	48.8	51.2	76.2	52.4	47.6	52.2	4.4	95.6
North Carolina	—	—	—	—	—	—	—	—	—
North Dakota	—	—	—	—	—	—	—	—	—
Ohio	48.0	4.0	96.0	51.4	2.8	97.2	48.7	2.6	97.4
Oklahoma	—	—	—	—	—	—	—	—	—
Oregon	—	—	—	—	—	—	—	—	—
Pennsylvania	66.5	33.0	67.0	82.9	65.8	34.2	64.2	28.4	71.6
Rhode Island	0.0[1]	100.0[1]	0.0[1]	37.6[1]	24.8[1]	75.2[1]	51.0[1]	2.0[1]	98.0[1]
South Carolina	—	—	—	—	—	—	—	—	—
South Dakota	—	—	—	—	—	—	—	—	—
Tennessee	76.9[1]	53.8[1]	46.2[1]	50.7[1]	1.4[1]	98.6[1]	39.7[1]	20.6[1]	79.4[1]
Texas	—	—	—	—	—	—	—	—	—
Utah	—	—	—	—	—	—	—	—	—
Vermont	31.6	36.8	63.2	42.3[1]	15.4[1]	84.6[1]	43.0	14.0	86.0
Virginia	—	—	—	—	—	—	—	—	—
Washington	—	—	—	—	—	—	—	—	—
West Virginia	—	—	—	—	—	—	—	—	—
Wisconsin	—	—	—	—	—	—	—	—	—
Wyoming	—	—	—	—	—	—	—	—	—

Notes: The first entries are the Democratic percent of two-party vote values for each state for the House race. The second entries are the margin of victory values for each state for the House race, where margin of victory is defined as the absolute difference between the Democratic percent and the Republican percent of the two-party vote for the House. The third entries are the party competition index values for each state for the House race, where the competition index devised by Paul David (1972) is defined as (100 − the margin of victory) or, alternatively, as (100 − the absolute difference between the Democratic and Republican percent of two-party vote for the House). The values for Democratic and Republican percent of two-party vote for the House are taken from the state vote tables in Chapter 5. Zero (0) percent on David's index represents a complete absence of two-party competition for that election year, whereas a score of 100 percent indicates perfect competition between the two major parties. A state can only receive a party competition score of 0 if it has a 100–0 vote split in all House races in the state. Conversely, a state can only receive a score of 100 if it has a 50–50 vote split in all House races in the state. For example, if Pennsylvania in 1788 cast an average of 46.0 percent Democratic vote for all House races in the state of its two-party vote, then its average Republican vote for House would be 54.0 percent. The absolute difference between the two figures is the margin of victory, or 8 percent; 100 percent − 8 percent would equal 92 percent on David's party competition scale, indicating very competitive contests in House races in Pennsylvania in 1788. The two-party vote percent values used to derive the margin of victory and party competition figures are initially found in the state vote tables in Chapter 5. The author's alternative party coding in these tables is used whenever it occurs instead of the conventional party coding of voting data. The Democratic Party is defined here as the Anti-Federalists, Democratic-Republicans, and Jackson Democrats prior to 1830 when the "Democratic Party" as such was established. The Republican Party is defined as the Federalists, National Republicans, and Whigs prior to the establishment of the "Republican Party" in the 1850s. See Appendix A for an explanation of the historical antecedents of the current Democratic and Republican parties. States reporting only partial voting returns for House races are not included in the calculations for the years in which this occurred. —indicates that the state had no data, either because no vote data were found for the state in question or the state had not yet entered the Union.

[1]Election held in an odd-numbered year.

Sources: State vote tables for House in Chapter 5.

Table 8-62 House Competition Measures, by State, by Two-Year Election Cycle, 1836–1841 (Percentages)

	1836–1837			*1838–1839*			*1840–1841*		
State	*Democratic % of Two-Party Vote*	*Margin of Victory*	*Party Competition Index*	*Democratic % of Two-Party Vote*	*Margin of Victory*	*Party Competition Index*	*Democratic % of Two-Party Vote*	*Margin of Victory*	*Party Competition Index*
Alabama	—	—	—	—	—	—	57.0[1]	14.0[1]	86.0[1]
Alaska	—	—	—	—	—	—	—	—	—
Arizona	—	—	—	—	—	—	—	—	—
Arkansas	71.9	43.8	56.2	61.8	23.6	76.4	57.6	15.2	84.8
California	—	—	—	—	—	—	—	—	—
Colorado	—	—	—	—	—	—	—	—	—
Connecticut	52.4[1]	4.8[1]	95.2[1]	47.4[1]	5.2[1]	94.8[1]	44.1[1]	11.8[1]	88.2[1]
Delaware	47.4	5.2	94.8	50.3	0.6	99.4	45.8	8.4	91.6
Florida	—	—	—	—	—	—	—	—	—
Georgia	50.5	1.0	99.0	48.4	3.2	96.8	47.3	5.4	94.6
Hawaii	—	—	—	—	—	—	—	—	—
Idaho	—	—	—	—	—	—	—	—	—
Illinois	63.6	27.2	72.8	59.2	18.4	81.6	60.5[1]	21.0[1]	79.0[1]
Indiana	34.5[1]	31.0[1]	69.0[1]	50.7[1]	1.4[1]	98.6[1]	44.1[1]	11.8[1]	88.2[1]
Iowa	—	—	—	—	—	—	—	—	—
Kansas	—	—	—	—	—	—	—	—	—
Kentucky	—	—	—	—	—	—	25.2[1]	49.6[1]	50.4[1]
Louisiana	27.6	44.8	55.2	29.5	41.0	59.0	43.5	13.0	87.0
Maine	53.0	6.0	94.0	52.0	4.0	96.0	49.6	0.8	99.2
Maryland	41.0[1]	18.0[1]	82.0[1]	53.2[1]	6.4[1]	93.6[1]	39.5[1]	21.0[1]	79.0[1]
Massachusetts	42.8	14.4	85.6	41.5	17.0	83.0	42.2	15.6	84.4
Michigan	52.6[1]	5.2[1]	94.8[1]	50.3	0.6	99.4	48.5	3.0	97.0
Minnesota	—	—	—	—	—	—	—	—	—
Mississippi	61.1[1]	22.2[1]	77.8[1]	53.4[1]	6.8[1]	93.2[1]	53.5[1]	7.0[1]	93.0[1]
Missouri	62.2	24.4	75.6	57.7	15.4	84.6	57.9	15.8	84.2
Montana	—	—	—	—	—	—	—	—	—
Nebraska	—	—	—	—	—	—	—	—	—
Nevada	—	—	—	—	—	—	—	—	—
New Hampshire	94.2[1]	88.4[1]	11.6[1]	55.6[1]	11.2[1]	88.8[1]	58.1[1]	16.2[1]	83.8[1]
New Jersey	49.5	1.0	99.0	50.1	0.2	99.8	48.3	3.4	96.6
New Mexico	—	—	—	—	—	—	—	—	—
New York	54.7	9.4	90.6	48.4	3.2	96.8	48.9	2.2	97.8
North Carolina	—	—	—	—	—	—	—	—	—
North Dakota	—	—	—	—	—	—	—	—	—
Ohio	48.2	3.6	96.4	50.1	0.2	99.8	46.9	6.2	93.8
Oklahoma	—	—	—	—	—	—	—	—	—
Oregon	—	—	—	—	—	—	—	—	—
Pennsylvania	63.0	26.0	74.0	51.2	2.4	97.6	50.9	1.8	98.2
Rhode Island	43.2[1]	13.6[1]	86.4[1]	47.5[1]	5.0[1]	95.0[1]	0.0[1]	100.0[1]	0.0[1]
South Carolina	—	—	—	—	—	—	—	—	—
South Dakota	—	—	—	—	—	—	—	—	—
Tennessee	32.2[1]	35.6[1]	64.4[1]	48.7[1]	2.6[1]	97.4[1]	46.6[1]	6.8[1]	93.2[1]
Texas	—	—	—	—	—	—	—	—	—
Utah	—	—	—	—	—	—	—	—	—
Vermont	42.5	15.0	85.0	43.9	12.2	87.8	40.4	19.2	80.8
Virginia	—	—	—	—	—	—	—	—	—
Washington	—	—	—	—	—	—	—	—	—
West Virginia	—	—	—	—	—	—	—	—	—
Wisconsin	—	—	—	—	—	—	—	—	—
Wyoming	—	—	—	—	—	—	—	—	—
Arkansas	62.4[2]	24.8[2]	75.2[2]	—	—	—	—	—	—

Notes: The first entries are the Democratic percent of two-party vote values for each state for the House race. The second entries are the margin of victory values for each state for the House race, where margin of victory is defined as the absolute difference between the Democratic percent and the Republican percent of the two-party vote for the House. The third entries are the party competition index values for each state for the House race, where the competition index devised by Paul David (1972) is defined as (100 − the margin of victory) or, alternatively, as (100 − the absolute difference between the Democratic and Republican percent of two-party vote for the House). The values for Democratic and Republican percent of two-party vote for the House are taken from the state vote tables in Chapter 5. Zero (0) percent on David's index represents a complete absence of two-party competition for that election year, whereas a score of 100 percent indicates perfect competition between the two major parties. A state can only receive a party competition score of 0 if it has a 100–0 vote split in all House races in the state. Conversely, a state can only receive a score of 100 if it has a 50–50 vote split in all House races in the state. For example, if Pennsylvania in 1788 cast an average of 46.0 percent Democratic vote for all House races in the state of its two-party vote, then its average Republican vote for House would be 54.0 percent. The absolute difference between the two figures is the margin of victory, or 8 percent; 100 percent − 8 percent would equal 92 percent on David's party competition scale, indicating very competitive contests in House races in Pennsylvania in 1788. The two-party vote percent values used to derive the margin of victory and party competition figures are initially found in the state vote tables in Chapter 5. The author's alternative party coding in these tables is used whenever it occurs instead of the conventional party coding of voting data. The Democratic Party is defined here as the Anti-Federalists, Democratic-Republicans, and Jackson Democrats prior to 1830 when the "Democratic Party" as such was established. The Republican Party is defined as the Federalists, National Republicans, and Whigs prior to the establishment of the "Republican Party" in the 1850s. See Appendix A for an explanation of the historical antecedents of the current Democratic and Republican parties. States reporting only partial voting returns for House races are not included in the calculations for the years in which this occurred. —indicates that the state had no data, either because no vote data were found for the state in question or the state had not yet entered the Union.

[1] Election held in an odd-numbered year.

[2] 1837 election when state had annual elections in both 1836 and 1837.

Sources: State vote tables for House in Chapter 5.

Table 8-63 House Competition Measures, by State, by Two-Year Election Cycle, 1842–1847 (Percentages)

	1842–1843			1844–1845			1846–1847		
State	Democratic % of Two-Party Vote	Margin of Victory	Party Competition Index	Democratic % of Two-Party Vote	Margin of Victory	Party Competition Index	Democratic % of Two-Party Vote	Margin of Victory	Party Competition Index
Alabama	—	—	—	—	—	—	—	—	—
Alaska	—	—	—	—	—	—	—	—	—
Arizona	—	—	—	—	—	—	—	—	—
Arkansas	63.9	27.8	72.2	59.7	19.4	80.6	100.0	100.0	0.0
California	—	—	—	—	—	—	—	—	—
Colorado	—	—	—	—	—	—	—	—	—
Connecticut	51.5[1]	3.0[1]	97.0[1]	47.0[1]	6.0[1]	94.0[1]	47.6[1]	4.8[1]	95.2[1]
Delaware	50.0	0.0	100.0	49.2	1.6	98.4	49.0	2.0	98.0
Florida	—	—	—	60.3[1]	20.6[1]	79.4[1]	49.1	1.8	98.2
Georgia	51.4	2.8	97.2	51.4	2.8	97.2	53.6	7.2	92.8
Hawaii	—	—	—	—	—	—	—	—	—
Idaho	—	—	—	—	—	—	—	—	—
Illinois	53.9[1]	7.8[1]	92.2[1]	65.0	30.0	70.0	68.8	37.6	62.4
Indiana	51.5[1]	3.0[1]	97.0[1]	52.5[1]	5.0[1]	95.0[1]	49.9[1]	0.2[1]	99.8[1]
Iowa	—	—	—	—	—	—	52.6	5.2	94.8
Kansas	—	—	—	—	—	—	—	—	—
Kentucky	44.9[1]	10.2[1]	89.8[1]	50.0[1]	0.0[1]	100.0[1]	45.5[1]	9.0[1]	91.0[1]
Louisiana	55.3[1]	10.6[1]	89.4[1]	69.2	38.4	61.6	—	—	—
Maine	59.8[1]	19.6[1]	80.4[1]	52.3	4.6	95.4	52.5	5.0	95.0
Maryland	—	—	—	45.0	10.0	90.0	—	—	—
Massachusetts	50.5	1.0	99.0	43.5	13.0	87.0	37.4	25.2	74.8
Michigan	59.1[1]	18.2[1]	81.8[1]	53.1	6.2	93.8	53.3	6.6	93.4
Minnesota	—	—	—	—	—	—	—	—	—
Mississippi	100.0[1]	100.0[1]	0.0[1]	60.3[1]	20.6[1]	79.4[1]	73.5[1]	47.0[1]	53.0[1]
Missouri	100.0	100.0	0.0	55.2	10.4	89.6	61.4	22.8	77.2
Montana	—	—	—	—	—	—	—	—	—
Nebraska	—	—	—	—	—	—	—	—	—
Nevada	—	—	—	—	—	—	—	—	—
New Hampshire	64.0[1]	28.0[1]	72.0[1]	62.1[1]	24.2[1]	75.8[1]	59.3[1]	18.6[1]	81.4[1]
New Jersey	—	—	—	43.7	12.6	87.4	47.2	5.6	94.4
New Mexico	—	—	—	—	—	—	—	—	—
New York	51.2	2.4	97.6	48.3	3.4	96.6	48.9	2.2	97.8
North Carolina	45.3[1]	9.4[1]	90.6[1]	44.1[1]	11.8[1]	88.2[1]	42.3[1]	15.4[1]	84.6[1]
North Dakota	—	—	—	—	—	—	—	—	—
Ohio	51.1[1]	2.2[1]	97.8[1]	49.2	1.6	98.4	48.5	3.0	97.0
Oklahoma	—	—	—	—	—	—	—	—	—
Oregon	—	—	—	—	—	—	—	—	—
Pennsylvania	54.6[1]	9.2[1]	90.8[1]	52.3	4.6	95.4	51.4	2.8	97.2
Rhode Island	38.2[1]	23.6[1]	76.4[1]	0.0[1]	100.0[1]	0.0[1]	42.9[1]	14.2[1]	85.8[1]
South Carolina	—	—	—	—	—	—	—	—	—
South Dakota	—	—	—	—	—	—	—	—	—
Tennessee	47.0[1]	6.0[1]	94.0[1]	53.7[1]	7.4[1]	92.6[1]	50.9[1]	1.8[1]	98.2[1]
Texas	—	—	—	—	—	—	100.0	100.0	0.0
Utah	—	—	—	—	—	—	—	—	—
Vermont	46.4[1]	7.2[1]	92.8[1]	41.7	16.6	83.4	42.3	15.4	84.6
Virginia	—	—	—	—	—	—	—	—	—
Washington	—	—	—	—	—	—	—	—	—
West Virginia	—	—	—	—	—	—	—	—	—
Wisconsin	—	—	—	—	—	—	—	—	—
Wyoming	—	—	—	—	—	—	—	—	—
Maryland	—	—	—	51.8[2]	3.6[2]	96.4[2]	—	—	—
Iowa	—	—	—	—	—	—	52.0[3]	4.0[3]	96.0[3]

Notes: The first entries are the Democratic percent of two-party vote values for each state for the House race. The second entries are the margin of victory values for each state for the House race, where margin of victory is defined as the absolute difference between the Democratic percent and the Republican percent of the two-party vote for the House. The third entries are the party competition index values for each state for the House race, where the competition index devised by Paul David (1972) is defined as (100 − the margin of victory) or, alternatively, as (100 − the absolute difference between the Democratic and Republican percent of two-party vote for the House). The values for Democratic and Republican percent of two-party vote for the House are taken from the state vote tables in Chapter 5. Zero (0) percent on David's index represents a complete absence of two-party competition for that election year, whereas a score of 100 percent indicates perfect competition between the two major parties. A state can only receive a party competition score of 0 if it has a 100–0 vote split in all House races in the state. Conversely, a state can only receive a score of 100 if it has a 50–50 vote split in all House races in the state. For example, if Pennsylvania in 1788 cast an average of 46.0 percent Democratic vote for all House races in the state of its two-party vote, then its average Republican vote for House would be 54.0 percent. The absolute difference between the two figures is the margin of victory, or 8 percent; 100 percent − 8 percent would equal 92 percent on David's party competition scale, indicating very competitive contests in House races in Pennsylvania in 1788. The two-party vote percent values used to derive the margin of victory and party competition figures are initially found in the state vote tables in Chapter 5. The author's alternative party coding in these tables is used whenever it occurs instead of the conventional party coding of voting data. The Democratic Party is defined here as the Anti-Federalists, Democratic-Republicans, and Jackson Democrats prior to 1830 when the "Democratic Party" as such was established. The Republican Party is defined as the Federalists, National Republicans, and Whigs prior to the establishment of the "Republican Party" in the 1850s. See Appendix A for an explanation of the historical antecedents of the current Democratic and Republican parties. States reporting only partial voting returns for House races are not included in the calculations for the years in which this occurred. —indicates that the state had no data, either because no vote data were found for the state in question or the state had not yet entered the Union.

[1] Election held in an odd-numbered year.
[2] 1845 election when state had annual elections in both 1844 and 1845.
[3] 1847 election when state had annual elections in both 1846 and 1847.

Sources: State vote tables for House in Chapter 5.

Table 8-64 House Competition Measures, by State, by Two-Year Election Cycle, 1848–1853 (Percentages)

State	1848–1849			1850–1851			1852–1853		
	Democratic % of Two-Party Vote	Margin of Victory	Party Competition Index	Democratic % of Two-Party Vote	Margin of Victory	Party Competition Index	Democratic % of Two-Party Vote	Margin of Victory	Party Competition Index
Alabama	45.0[1]	10.0[1]	90.0[1]	—	—	—	—	—	—
Alaska	—	—	—	—	—	—	—	—	—
Arizona	—	—	—	—	—	—	—	—	—
Arkansas	60.8	21.6	78.4	57.4[1]	14.8[1]	85.2[1]	76.1[1]	52.2[1]	47.8[1]
California	100.0[1]	100.0[1]	0.0[1]	53.4[1]	6.8[1]	93.2[1]	53.6	7.2	92.8
Colorado	—	—	—	—	—	—	—	—	—
Connecticut	49.3[1]	1.4[1]	98.6[1]	50.9[1]	1.8[1]	98.2[1]	55.9[1]	11.8[1]	88.2[1]
Delaware	48.6	2.8	97.2	50.5	1.0	99.0	50.2	0.4	99.6
Florida	46.5	7.0	93.0	47.2	5.6	94.4	50.1	0.2	99.8
Georgia	50.2	0.4	99.6	—	—	—	53.1[1]	6.2[1]	93.8[1]
Hawaii	—	—	—	—	—	—	—	—	—
Idaho	—	—	—	—	—	—	—	—	—
Illinois	65.2	30.4	69.6	58.1	16.2	83.8	56.8	13.6	86.4
Indiana	49.8[1]	0.4[1]	99.6[1]	51.7[1]	3.4[1]	96.6[1]	54.1	8.2	91.8
Iowa	51.6	3.2	96.8	53.7	7.4	92.6	51.8	3.6	96.4
Kansas	—	—	—	—	—	—	—	—	—
Kentucky	42.3[1]	15.4[1]	84.6[1]	46.8[1]	6.4[1]	93.6[1]	48.1[1]	3.8[1]	96.2[1]
Louisiana	—	—	—	49.6[1]	0.8[1]	99.2[1]	—	—	—
Maine	54.1	8.2	91.8	51.4	2.8	97.2	51.6	3.2	96.8
Maryland	45.8[1]	8.4[1]	91.6[1]	45.2[1]	9.6[1]	90.4[1]	54.0[1]	8.0[1]	92.0[1]
Massachusetts	29.4	41.2	58.8	38.7	22.6	77.4	39.7	20.6	79.4
Michigan	51.5	3.0	97.0	48.7	2.6	97.4	52.5	5.0	95.0
Minnesota	—	—	—	—	—	—	—	—	—
Mississippi	57.3[1]	14.6[1]	85.4[1]	—	—	—	54.3[1]	8.6[1]	91.4[1]
Missouri	61.6	23.2	76.8	59.3	18.6	81.4	56.6	13.2	86.8
Montana	—	—	—	—	—	—	—	—	—
Nebraska	—	—	—	—	—	—	—	—	—
Nevada	—	—	—	—	—	—	—	—	—
New Hampshire	57.6[1]	15.2[1]	84.8[1]	54.8[1]	9.6[1]	90.4[1]	58.0[1]	16.0[1]	84.0[1]
New Jersey	49.8	0.4	99.6	54.2	8.4	91.6	53.7	7.4	92.6
New Mexico	—	—	—	—	—	—	—	—	—
New York	31.9	36.2	63.8	49.4	1.2	98.8	49.6	0.8	99.2
North Carolina	50.7[1]	1.4[1]	98.6[1]	—	—	—	60.5[1]	21.0[1]	79.0[1]
North Dakota	—	—	—	—	—	—	—	—	—
Ohio	54.1	8.2	91.8	56.8	13.6	86.4	53.0	6.0	94.0
Oklahoma	—	—	—	—	—	—	—	—	—
Oregon	—	—	—	—	—	—	—	—	—
Pennsylvania	51.4	2.8	97.2	52.6	5.2	94.8	56.5	13.0	87.0
Rhode Island	39.3[1]	21.4[1]	78.6[1]	53.4[1]	6.8[1]	93.2[1]	64.9[1]	29.8[1]	70.2[1]
South Carolina	—	—	—	—	—	—	—	—	—
South Dakota	—	—	—	—	—	—	—	—	—
Tennessee	52.9[1]	5.8[1]	94.2[1]	—	—	—	—	—	—
Texas	100.0[1]	100.0[1]	0.0[1]	100.0[1]	100.0[1]	0.0[1]	93.0[1]	86.0[1]	14.0[1]
Utah	—	—	—	—	—	—	—	—	—
Vermont	55.5	11.0	89.0	46.8	6.4	93.6	49.1	1.8	98.2
Virginia	—	—	—	—	—	—	—	—	—
Washington	—	—	—	—	—	—	—	—	—
West Virginia	—	—	—	—	—	—	—	—	—
Wisconsin	54.5	9.0	91.0	57.9	15.8	84.2	61.5	23.0	77.0
Wyoming	—	—	—	—	—	—	—	—	—

Notes: The first entries are the Democratic percent of two-party vote values for each state for the House race. The second entries are the margin of victory values for each state for the House race, where margin of victory is defined as the absolute difference between the Democratic percent and the Republican percent of the two-party vote for the House. The third entries are the party competition index values for each state for the House race, where the competition index devised by Paul David (1972) is defined as (100 − the margin of victory) or, alternatively, as (100 − the absolute difference between the Democratic and Republican percent of two-party vote for the House). The values for Democratic and Republican percent of two-party vote for the House are taken from the state vote tables in Chapter 5. Zero (0) percent on David's index represents a complete absence of two-party competition for that election year, whereas a score of 100 percent indicates perfect competition between the two major parties. A state can only receive a party competition score of 0 if it has a 100–0 vote split in all House races in the state. Conversely, a state can only receive a score of 100 if it has a 50–50 vote split in all House races in the state. For example, if Pennsylvania in 1788 cast an average of 46.0 percent Democratic vote for all House races in the state of its two-party vote, then its average Republican vote for House would be 54.0 percent. The absolute difference between the two figures is the margin of victory, or 8 percent; 100 percent − 8 percent would equal 92 percent on David's party competition scale, indicating very competitive contests in House races in Pennsylvania in 1788. The two-party vote percent values used to derive the margin of victory and party competition figures are initially found in the state vote tables in Chapter 5. The author's alternative party coding in these tables is used whenever it occurs instead of the conventional party coding of voting data. The Democratic Party is defined here as the Anti-Federalists, Democratic-Republicans, and Jackson Democrats prior to 1830 when the "Democratic Party" as such was established. The Republican Party is defined as the Federalists, National Republicans, and Whigs prior to the establishment of the "Republican Party" in the 1850s. See Appendix A for an explanation of the historical antecedents of the current Democratic and Republican parties. States reporting only partial voting returns for House races are not included in the calculations for the years in which this occurred. —indicates that the state had no data, either because no vote data were found for the state in question or the state had not yet entered the Union.

[1]Election held in an odd-numbered year.

Sources: State vote tables for House in Chapter 5.

Table 8-65 House Competition Measures, by State, by Two-Year Election Cycle, 1854–1859 (Percentages)

State	1854–1855 Democratic % of Two-Party Vote	Margin of Victory	Party Competition Index	1856–1857 Democratic % of Two-Party Vote	Margin of Victory	Party Competition Index	1858–1859 Democratic % of Two-Party Vote	Margin of Victory	Party Competition Index
Alabama	100.0[1]	100.0[1]	0.0[1]	100.0[1]	100.0[1]	0.0[1]	—	—	—
Alaska	—	—	—	—	—	—	—	—	—
Arizona	—	—	—	—	—	—	—	—	—
Arkansas	83.6	67.2	32.8	100.0	100.0	0.0	100.0	100.0	0.0
California	57.4	14.8	85.2	69.8	39.6	60.4	58.1[1]	16.2[1]	83.8[1]
Colorado	—	—	—	—	—	—	—	—	—
Connecticut	100.0[1]	100.0[1]	0.0[1]	49.2[1]	1.6[1]	98.4[1]	48.9[1]	2.2[1]	97.8[1]
Delaware	100.0	100.0	0.0	100.0	100.0	0.0	100.0	100.0	0.0
Florida	55.3	10.6	89.4	100.0	100.0	0.0	100.0	100.0	0.0
Georgia	100.0[1]	100.0[1]	0.0[1]	100.0[1]	100.0[1]	0.0[1]	100.0[1]	100.0[1]	0.0[1]
Hawaii	—	—	—	—	—	—	—	—	—
Idaho	—	—	—	—	—	—	—	—	—
Illinois	50.9	1.8	98.2	48.2	3.6	96.4	50.1	0.2	99.8
Indiana	100.0	100.0	0.0	51.4	2.8	97.2	53.4	6.8	93.2
Iowa	48.4	3.2	96.8	45.2	9.6	90.4	48.2	3.6	96.4
Kansas	—	—	—	—	—	—	42.3[1]	15.4[1]	84.6[1]
Kentucky	100.0[1]	100.0[1]	0.0[1]	100.0[1]	100.0[1]	0.0[1]	100.0[1]	100.0[1]	0.0[1]
Louisiana	100.0[1]	100.0[1]	0.0[1]	100.0[1]	100.0[1]	0.0[1]	100.0[1]	100.0[1]	0.0[1]
Maine	35.9	28.2	71.8	41.7	16.6	83.4	46.2	7.6	92.4
Maryland	100.0[1]	100.0[1]	0.0[1]	100.0[1]	100.0[1]	0.0[1]	100.0[1]	100.0[1]	0.0[1]
Massachusetts	28.2	43.6	56.4	30.9	38.2	61.8	35.7	28.6	71.4
Michigan	46.7	6.6	93.4	42.7	14.6	85.4	45.8	8.4	91.6
Minnesota	—	—	—	51.7[1]	3.4[1]	96.6[1]	45.3[1]	9.4[1]	90.6[1]
Mississippi	100.0[1]	100.0[1]	0.0[1]	100.0[1]	100.0[1]	0.0[1]	100.0[1]	100.0[1]	0.0[1]
Missouri	55.0	10.0	90.0	100.0	100.0	0.0	92.8	85.6	14.4
Montana	—	—	—	—	—	—	—	—	—
Nebraska	—	—	—	—	—	—	—	—	—
Nevada	—	—	—	—	—	—	—	—	—
New Hampshire	100.0[1]	100.0[1]	0.0[1]	47.2[1]	5.6[1]	94.4[1]	47.9[1]	4.2[1]	95.8[1]
New Jersey	49.9	0.2	99.8	52.0	4.0	96.0	65.6	31.2	68.8
New Mexico	—	—	—	—	—	—	—	—	—
New York	50.2	0.4	99.6	42.7	14.6	85.4	42.5	15.0	85.0
North Carolina	92.3[1]	84.6[1]	15.4[1]	100.0[1]	100.0[1]	0.0[1]	58.0[1]	16.0[1]	84.0[1]
North Dakota	—	—	—	—	—	—	—	—	—
Ohio	100.0	100.0	0.0	46.7	6.6	93.4	46.4	7.2	92.8
Oklahoma	—	—	—	—	—	—	—	—	—
Oregon	—	—	—	—	—	—	50.1[1]	0.2[1]	99.8[1]
Pennsylvania	51.3	2.6	97.4	51.2	2.4	97.6	100.0	100.0	0.0
Rhode Island	—	—	—	35.8[1]	28.4[1]	71.6[1]	25.7[1]	48.6[1]	51.4[1]
South Carolina	—	—	—	—	—	—	—	—	—
South Dakota	—	—	—	—	—	—	—	—	—
Tennessee	100.0[1]	100.0[1]	0.0[1]	100.0[1]	100.0[1]	0.0[1]	100.0[1]	100.0[1]	0.0[1]
Texas	100.0[1]	100.0[1]	0.0[1]	100.0[1]	100.0[1]	0.0[1]	100.0[1]	100.0[1]	0.0[1]
Utah	—	—	—	—	—	—	—	—	—
Vermont	38.2	23.6	76.4	21.7	56.6	43.4	29.0	42.0	58.0
Virginia	—	—	—	—	—	—	—	—	—
Washington	—	—	—	—	—	—	—	—	—
West Virginia	—	—	—	—	—	—	—	—	—
Wisconsin	43.6	12.8	87.2	44.7	10.6	89.4	47.4	5.2	94.8
Wyoming	—	—	—	—	—	—	—	—	—

Notes: The first entries are the Democratic percent of two-party vote values for each state for the House race. The second entries are the margin of victory values for each state for the House race, where margin of victory is defined as the absolute difference between the Democratic percent and the Republican percent of the two-party vote for the House. The third entries are the party competition index values for each state for the House race, where the competition index devised by Paul David (1972) is defined as (100 − the margin of victory) or, alternatively, as (100 − the absolute difference between the Democratic and Republican percent of two-party vote for the House). The values for Democratic and Republican percent of two-party vote for the House are taken from the state vote tables in Chapter 5. Zero (0) percent on David's index represents a complete absence of two-party competition for that election year, whereas a score of 100 percent indicates perfect competition between the two major parties. A state can only receive a party competition score of 0 if it has a 100–0 vote split in all House races in the state. Conversely, a state can only receive a score of 100 if it has a 50–50 vote split in all House races in the state. For example, if Pennsylvania in 1788 cast an average of 46.0 percent Democratic vote for all House races in the state of its two-party vote, then its average Republican vote for House would be 54.0 percent. The absolute difference between the two figures is the margin of victory, or 8 percent; 100 percent − 8 percent would equal 92 percent on David's party competition scale, indicating very competitive contests in House races in Pennsylvania in 1788. The two-party vote percent values used to derive the margin of victory and party competition figures are initially found in the state vote tables in Chapter 5. The author's alternative party coding in these tables is used whenever it occurs instead of the conventional party coding of voting data. The Democratic Party is defined here as the Anti-Federalists, Democratic-Republicans, and Jackson Democrats prior to 1830 when the "Democratic Party" as such was established. The Republican Party is defined as the Federalists, National Republicans, and Whigs prior to the establishment of the "Republican Party" in the 1850s. See Appendix A for an explanation of the historical antecedents of the current Democratic and Republican parties. States reporting only partial voting returns for House races are not included in the calculations for the years in which this occurred. —indicates that the state had no data, either because no vote data were found for the state in question or the state had not yet entered the Union.

[1]Election held in an odd-numbered year.

Sources: State vote tables for House in Chapter 5.

Table 8-66 House Competition Measures, by State, by Two-Year Election Cycle, 1860–1865 (Percentages)

	1860–1861			1862–1863			1864–1865		
State	Democratic % of Two-Party Vote	Margin of Victory	Party Competition Index	Democratic % of Two-Party Vote	Margin of Victory	Party Competition Index	Democratic % of Two-Party Vote	Margin of Victory	Party Competition Index
Alabama	—	—	—	—	—	—	—	—	—
Alaska	—	—	—	—	—	—	—	—	—
Arizona	—	—	—	—	—	—	—	—	—
Arkansas	100.0	100.0	0.0	—	—	—	—	—	—
California	56.5[1]	13.0[1]	87.0[1]	40.3[1]	19.4[1]	80.6[1]	41.0	18.0	82.0
Colorado	—	—	—	—	—	—	—	—	—
Connecticut	49.3[1]	1.4[1]	98.6[1]	48.6[1]	2.8[1]	97.2[1]	42.4[1]	15.2[1]	84.8[1]
Delaware	100.0	100.0	0.0	50.1	0.2	99.8	51.5	3.0	97.0
Florida	100.0	100.0	0.0	—	—	—	—	—	—
Georgia	—	—	—	—	—	—	—	—	—
Hawaii	—	—	—	—	—	—	—	—	—
Idaho	—	—	—	—	—	—	—	—	—
Illinois	48.1	3.8	96.2	53.2	6.4	93.6	45.5	9.0	91.0
Indiana	47.5	5.0	95.0	52.3	4.6	95.4	47.1	5.8	94.2
Iowa	44.8	10.4	89.6	42.9	14.2	85.8	35.7	28.6	71.4
Kansas	—	—	—	6.1	87.8	12.2	0.0	100.0	0.0
Kentucky	0.0[1]	100.0[1]	0.0[1]	100.0[1]	100.0[1]	0.0[1]	—	—	—
Louisiana	—	—	—	—	—	—	—	—	—
Maine	43.3	13.4	86.6	44.3	11.4	88.6	41.6	16.8	83.2
Maryland	0.0[1]	100.0[1]	0.0[1]	21.7[1]	56.6[1]	43.4[1]	44.1	11.8	88.2
Massachusetts	32.5	35.0	65.0	3.1	93.8	6.2	27.8	44.4	55.6
Michigan	42.8	14.4	85.6	47.4	5.2	94.8	44.5	11.0	89.0
Minnesota	36.7	26.6	73.4	41.7	16.6	83.4	41.1	17.8	82.2
Mississippi	—	—	—	—	—	—	—	—	—
Missouri	88.3	76.6	23.4	49.8	0.4	99.6	27.9	44.2	55.8
Montana	—	—	—	—	—	—	—	—	—
Nebraska	—	—	—	—	—	—	—	—	—
Nevada	—	—	—	—	—	—	40.1	19.8	80.2
New Hampshire	46.8[1]	6.4[1]	93.6[1]	49.6[1]	0.8[1]	99.2[1]	45.9[1]	8.2[1]	91.8[1]
New Jersey	50.4	0.8	99.2	56.3	12.6	87.4	52.3	4.6	95.4
New Mexico	—	—	—	—	—	—	—	—	—
New York	46.4	7.2	92.8	50.5	1.0	99.0	49.5	1.0	99.0
North Carolina	—	—	—	—	—	—	—	—	—
North Dakota	—	—	—	—	—	—	—	—	—
Ohio	45.8	8.4	91.6	50.3	0.6	99.4	43.8	12.4	87.6
Oklahoma	—	—	—	—	—	—	—	—	—
Oregon	100.0	100.0	0.0	34.8	30.4	69.6	40.9	18.2	81.8
Pennsylvania	44.9	10.2	89.8	53.2	6.4	93.6	50.7	1.4	98.6
Rhode Island	0.0[1]	100.0[1]	0.0[1]	42.1[1]	15.8[1]	84.2[1]	13.3[1]	73.4[1]	26.6[1]
South Carolina	—	—	—	—	—	—	—	—	—
South Dakota	—	—	—	—	—	—	—	—	—
Tennessee	—	—	—	—	—	—	0.0[1]	100.0[1]	0.0[1]
Texas	—	—	—	—	—	—	—	—	—
Utah	—	—	—	—	—	—	—	—	—
Vermont	26.2	47.6	52.4	28.1[1]	43.8[1]	56.2[1]	27.4	45.2	54.8
Virginia	—	—	—	—	—	—	—	—	—
Washington	—	—	—	—	—	—	—	—	—
West Virginia	—	—	—	0.0[1]	100.0[1]	0.0[1]	0.0	100.0	0.0
Wisconsin	43.1	13.8	86.2	50.9	1.8	98.2	44.2	11.6	88.4
Wyoming	—	—	—	—	—	—	—	—	—
Nevada	—	—	—	—	—	—	37.5[2]	25.0[2]	75.0[2]

Notes: The first entries are the Democratic percent of two-party vote values for each state for the House race. The second entries are the margin of victory values for each state for the House race, where margin of victory is defined as the absolute difference between the Democratic percent and the Republican percent of the two-party vote for the House. The third entries are the party competition index values for each state for the House race, where the competition index devised by Paul David (1972) is defined as (100 − the margin of victory) or, alternatively, as (100 − the absolute difference between the Democratic and Republican percent of two-party vote for the House). The values for Democratic and Republican percent of two-party vote for the House are taken from the state vote tables in Chapter 5. Zero (0) percent on David's index represents a complete absence of two-party competition for that election year, whereas a score of 100 percent indicates perfect competition between the two major parties. A state can only receive a party competition score of 0 if it has a 100–0 vote split in all House races in the state. Conversely, a state can only receive a score of 100 if it has a 50–50 vote split in all House races in the state. For example, if Pennsylvania in 1788 cast an average of 46.0 percent Democratic vote for all House races in the state of its two-party vote, then its average Republican vote for House would be 54.0 percent. The absolute difference between the two figures is the margin of victory, or 8 percent; 100 percent − 8 percent would equal 92 percent on David's party competition scale, indicating very competitive contests in House races in Pennsylvania in 1788. The two-party vote percent values used to derive the margin of victory and party competition figures are initially found in the state vote tables in Chapter 5. The author's alternative party coding in these tables is used whenever it occurs instead of the conventional party coding of voting data. The Democratic Party is defined here as the Anti-Federalists, Democratic-Republicans, and Jackson Democrats prior to 1830 when the "Democratic Party" as such was established. The Republican Party is defined as the Federalists, National Republicans, and Whigs prior to the establishment of the "Republican Party" in the 1850s. See Appendix A for an explanation of the historical antecedents of the current Democratic and Republican parties. States reporting only partial voting returns for House races are not included in the calculations for the years in which this occurred. —indicates that the state had no data, either because no vote data were found for the state in question or the state had not yet entered the Union.

[1] Election held in an odd-numbered year.
[2] 1865 election when state had annual elections in both 1864 and 1865.

Sources: State vote tables for House in Chapter 5.

Table 8-67 House Competition Measures, by State, by Two-Year Election Cycle, 1866–1871 (Percentages)

| | 1866–1867 | | | 1868–1869 | | | 1870–1871 | | |
| | Democratic % of Two-Party Vote | Margin of Victory | Party Competition Index | Democratic % of Two-Party Vote | Margin of Victory | Party Competition Index | Democratic % of Two-Party Vote | Margin of Victory | Party Competition Index |
State									
Alabama	—	—	—	0.0	100.0	0.0	51.3	2.6	97.4
Alaska	—	—	—	—	—	—	—	—	—
Arizona	—	—	—	—	—	—	—	—	—
Arkansas	—	—	—	46.4	7.2	92.8	48.3	3.4	96.6
California	52.1[1]	4.2[1]	95.8[1]	50.3	0.6	99.4	47.7[1]	4.6[1]	95.4[1]
Colorado	—	—	—	—	—	—	—	—	—
Connecticut	50.7[1]	1.4[1]	98.6[1]	48.7[1]	2.6[1]	97.4[1]	49.7[1]	0.6[1]	99.4[1]
Delaware	53.7	7.4	92.6	58.9	17.8	82.2	55.4	10.8	89.2
Florida	—	—	—	40.6	18.8	81.2	48.7	2.6	97.4
Georgia	—	—	—	44.0	12.0	88.0	56.7	13.4	86.6
Hawaii	—	—	—	—	—	—	—	—	—
Idaho	—	—	—	—	—	—	—	—	—
Illinois	42.1	15.8	84.2	44.5	11.0	89.0	46.2	7.6	92.4
Indiana	48.1	3.8	96.2	50.1	0.2	99.8	50.9	1.8	98.2
Iowa	38.3	23.4	76.6	39.3	21.4	78.6	39.2	21.6	78.4
Kansas	0.0	100.0	0.0	32.3	35.4	64.6	34.2	31.6	68.4
Kentucky	72.9[1]	45.8[1]	54.2[1]	75.7	51.4	48.6	61.1	22.2	77.8
Louisiana	—	—	—	61.0	22.0	78.0	36.7	26.6	73.4
Maine	37.8	24.4	75.6	42.9	14.2	85.8	45.0	10.0	90.0
Maryland	62.0	24.0	76.0	67.2	34.4	65.6	57.0	14.0	86.0
Massachusetts	22.9	54.2	45.8	31.0	38.0	62.0	38.7	22.6	77.4
Michigan	41.0	18.0	82.0	44.0	12.0	88.0	47.0	6.0	94.0
Minnesota	37.8	24.4	75.6	39.3	21.4	78.6	44.4	11.2	88.8
Mississippi	—	—	—	32.4[1]	35.2[1]	64.8[1]	—	—	—
Missouri	41.0	18.0	82.0	43.1	13.8	86.2	51.5	3.0	97.0
Montana	—	—	—	—	—	—	—	—	—
Nebraska	45.8	8.4	91.6	42.0	16.0	84.0	39.2	21.6	78.4
Nevada	45.4	9.2	90.8	46.2	7.6	92.4	51.2	2.4	97.6
New Hampshire	47.8[1]	4.4[1]	95.6[1]	47.0[1]	6.0[1]	94.0[1]	51.0[1]	2.0[1]	98.0[1]
New Jersey	49.4	1.2	98.8	51.1	2.2	97.8	48.9	2.2	97.8
New Mexico	—	—	—	—	—	—	—	—	—
New York	45.3	9.4	90.6	50.8	1.6	98.4	52.0	4.0	96.0
North Carolina	—	—	—	—	—	—	—	—	—
North Dakota	—	—	—	—	—	—	—	—	—
Ohio	45.8	8.4	91.6	48.7	2.6	97.4	48.4	3.2	96.8
Oklahoma	—	—	—	—	—	—	—	—	—
Oregon	48.6	2.8	97.2	32.6	34.8	65.2	50.8	1.6	98.4
Pennsylvania	49.1	1.8	98.2	49.4	1.2	98.8	48.1	3.8	96.2
Rhode Island	17.5[1]	65.0[1]	35.0[1]	34.7	30.6	69.4	19.5	61.0	39.0
South Carolina	—	—	—	42.2	15.6	84.4	32.8	34.4	65.6
South Dakota	—	—	—	—	—	—	—	—	—
Tennessee	0.0[1]	100.0[1]	0.0[1]	0.0	100.0	0.0	64.7	29.4	70.6
Texas	—	—	—	41.7[1]	16.6[1]	83.4[1]	58.8[1]	17.6[1]	82.4[1]
Utah	—	—	—	—	—	—	—	—	—
Vermont	23.8	52.4	47.6	25.5	49.0	51.0	23.7	52.6	47.4
Virginia	—	—	—	0.0[1]	100.0[1]	0.0[1]	—	—	—
Washington	—	—	—	—	—	—	—	—	—
West Virginia	42.0	16.0	84.0	45.0	10.0	90.0	51.5	3.0	97.0
Wisconsin	41.3	17.4	82.6	44.3	11.4	88.6	48.0	4.0	96.0
Wyoming	—	—	—	—	—	—	—	—	—
Alabama	—	—	—	42.0[2]	16.0[2]	84.0[2]	—	—	—

Notes: The first entries are the Democratic percent of two-party vote values for each state for the House race. The second entries are the margin of victory values for each state for the House race, where margin of victory is defined as the absolute difference between the Democratic percent and the Republican percent of the two-party vote for the House. The third entries are the party competition index values for each state for the House race, where the competition index devised by Paul David (1972) is defined as (100 − the margin of victory) or, alternatively, as (100 − the absolute difference between the Democratic and Republican percent of two-party vote for the House). The values for Democratic and Republican percent of two-party vote for the House are taken from the state vote tables in Chapter 5. Zero (0) percent on David's index represents a complete absence of two-party competition for that election year, whereas a score of 100 percent indicates perfect competition between the two major parties. A state can only receive a party competition score of 0 if it has a 100–0 vote split in all House races in the state. Conversely, a state can only receive a score of 100 if it has a 50–50 vote split in all House races in the state. For example, if Pennsylvania in 1788 cast an average of 46.0 percent Democratic vote for all House races in the state, then its average Republican vote for House would be 54.0 percent. The absolute difference between the two figures is the margin of victory, or 8 percent; 100 percent − 8 percent would equal 92 percent on David's party competition scale, indicating very competitive contests in House races in Pennsylvania in 1788. The two-party vote percent values used to derive the margin of victory and party competition figures are initially found in the state vote tables in Chapter 5. The author's alternative party coding in these tables is used whenever it occurs instead of the conventional party coding of voting data. The Democratic Party is defined here as the Anti-Federalists, Democratic-Republicans, and Jackson Democrats prior to 1830 when the "Democratic Party" as such was established. The Republican Party is defined as the Federalists, National Republicans, and Whigs prior to the establishment of the "Republican Party" in the 1850s. See Appendix A for an explanation of the historical antecedents of the current Democratic and Republican parties. States reporting only partial voting returns for House races are not included in the calculations for the years in which this occurred. —indicates that the state had no data, either because no vote data were found for the state in question or the state had not yet entered the Union.

[1]Election held in an odd-numbered year.
[2]1869 election when state had annual elections in both 1868 and 1869.

Sources: State vote tables for House in Chapter 5.

Table 8-68 House Competition Measures, by State, by Two-Year Election Cycle, 1872–1877 (Percentages)

	1872–1873			*1874–1875*			*1876–1877*		
State	*Democratic % of Two-Party Vote*	*Margin of Victory*	*Party Competition Index*	*Democratic % of Two-Party Vote*	*Margin of Victory*	*Party Competition Index*	*Democratic % of Two-Party Vote*	*Margin of Victory*	*Party Competition Index*
Alabama	47.7	4.6	95.4	54.1	8.2	91.8	75.9	51.8	48.2
Alaska	—	—	—	—	—	—	—	—	—
Arizona	—	—	—	—	—	—	—	—	—
Arkansas	50.2	0.4	99.6	64.4	28.8	71.2	68.6	37.2	62.8
California	48.7	2.6	97.4	59.6 [1]	19.2 [1]	80.8 [1]	47.8	4.4	95.6
Colorado	—	—	—	—	—	—	48.4	3.2	96.8
Connecticut	48.9 [1]	2.2 [1]	97.8 [1]	51.9 [1]	3.8 [1]	96.2 [1]	51.2	2.4	97.6
Delaware	—	—	—	53.3	6.6	93.4	55.4	10.8	89.2
Florida	0.0	100.0	0.0	47.9	4.2	95.8	50.6	1.2	98.8
Georgia	57.8	15.6	84.4	73.8	47.6	52.4	77.6	55.2	44.8
Hawaii	—	—	—	—	—	—	—	—	—
Idaho	—	—	—	—	—	—	—	—	—
Illinois	44.7	10.6	89.4	51.4	2.8	97.2	49.2	1.6	98.4
Indiana	50.0	0.0	100.0	52.0	4.0	96.0	50.7	1.4	98.6
Iowa	38.5	23.0	77.0	0.0	100.0	0.0	41.3	17.4	82.6
Kansas	33.8	32.4	67.6	18.7	62.6	37.4	17.0	66.0	34.0
Kentucky	68.2	36.4	63.6	74.6	49.2	50.8	62.8	25.6	74.4
Louisiana	46.2	7.6	92.4	52.7	5.4	94.6	52.5	5.0	95.0
Maine	42.9	14.2	85.8	43.6	12.8	87.2	44.7	10.6	89.4
Maryland	50.3	0.6	99.4	55.8	11.6	88.4	55.3	10.6	89.4
Massachusetts	31.7	36.6	63.4	45.4	9.2	90.8	43.3	13.4	86.6
Michigan	38.9	22.2	77.8	47.7	4.6	95.4	47.0	6.0	94.0
Minnesota	38.3	23.4	76.6	47.0	6.0	94.0	43.0	14.0	86.0
Mississippi	33.6	32.8	67.2	53.1 [1]	6.2 [1]	93.8 [1]	69.1	38.2	61.8
Missouri	57.0	14.0	86.0	71.5	43.0	57.0	60.1	20.2	79.8
Montana	—	—	—	—	—	—	—	—	—
Nebraska	37.8	24.4	75.6	27.1	45.8	54.2	35.8	28.4	71.6
Nevada	52.3	4.6	95.4	48.3	3.4	96.6	47.7	4.6	95.4
New Hampshire	50.0 [1]	0.0 [1]	100.0 [1]	50.2 [1]	0.4 [1]	99.6 [1]	48.8 [1]	2.4 [1]	97.6 [1]
New Jersey	44.7	10.6	89.4	52.7	5.4	94.6	58.1	16.2	83.8
New Mexico	—	—	—	—	—	—	—	—	—
New York	47.8	4.4	95.6	54.2	8.4	91.6	51.5	3.0	97.0
North Carolina	49.1	1.8	98.2	57.9	15.8	84.2	53.8	7.6	92.4
North Dakota	—	—	—	—	—	—	—	—	—
Ohio	51.0	2.0	98.0	52.2	4.4	95.6	49.6	0.8	99.2
Oklahoma	—	—	—	—	—	—	—	—	—
Oregon	48.3	3.4	96.6	50.8	1.6	98.4	48.1	3.8	96.2
Pennsylvania	46.4	7.2	92.8	52.8	5.6	94.4	49.3	1.4	98.6
Rhode Island	29.8	40.4	59.6	30.9	38.2	61.8	39.8	20.4	79.6
South Carolina	0.0	100.0	0.0	20.0	60.0	40.0	50.1	0.2	99.8
South Dakota	—	—	—	—	—	—	—	—	—
Tennessee	44.6	10.8	89.2	66.5	33.0	67.0	61.6	23.2	76.8
Texas	59.4	18.8	81.2	79.2	58.4	41.6	70.6	41.2	58.8
Utah	—	—	—	—	—	—	—	—	—
Vermont	14.7	70.6	29.4	19.5	61.0	39.0	30.8	38.4	61.6
Virginia	0.0	100.0	0.0	56.6	13.2	86.8	59.3	18.6	81.4
Washington	—	—	—	—	—	—	—	—	—
West Virginia	56.1	12.2	87.8	57.1	14.2	85.8	56.7	13.4	86.6
Wisconsin	45.6	8.8	91.2	50.1	0.2	99.8	49.4	1.2	98.8
Wyoming	—	—	—	—	—	—	—	—	—

Notes: The first entries are the Democratic percent of two-party vote values for each state for the House race. The second entries are the margin of victory values for each state for the House race, where margin of victory is defined as the absolute difference between the Democratic percent and the Republican percent of the two-party vote for the House. The third entries are the party competition index values for each state for the House race, where the competition index devised by Paul David (1972) is defined as (100 − the margin of victory) or, alternatively, as (100 − the absolute difference between the Democratic and Republican percent of two-party vote for the House). The values for Democratic and Republican percent of two-party vote for the House are taken from the state vote tables in Chapter 5. Zero (0) percent on David's index represents a complete absence of two-party competition for that election year, whereas a score of 100 percent indicates perfect competition between the two major parties. A state can only receive a party competition score of 0 if it has a 100–0 vote split in all House races in the state. Conversely, a state can only receive a score of 100 if it has a 50–50 vote split in all House races in the state. For example, if Pennsylvania in 1788 cast an average of 46.0 percent Democratic vote for all House races in the state of its two-party vote, then its average Republican vote for House would be 54.0 percent. The absolute difference between the two figures is the margin of victory, or 8 percent; 100 percent − 8 percent would equal 92 percent on David's party competition scale, indicating very competitive contests in House races in Pennsylvania in 1788. The two-party vote percent values used to derive the margin of victory and party competition figures are initially found in the state vote tables in Chapter 5. The author's alternative party coding in these tables is used whenever it occurs instead of the conventional party coding of voting data. The Democratic Party is defined here as the Anti-Federalists, Democratic-Republicans, and Jackson Democrats prior to 1830 when the "Democratic Party" as such was established. The Republican Party is defined as the Federalists, National Republicans, and Whigs prior to the establishment of the "Republican Party" in the 1850s. See Appendix A for an explanation of the historical antecedents of the current Democratic and Republican parties. States reporting only partial voting returns for House races are not included in the calculations for the years in which this occurred. —indicates that the state had no data, either because no vote data were found for the state in question or the state had not yet entered the Union.

[1] Election held in an odd-numbered year.

Sources: State vote tables for House in Chapter 5.

Table 8-69 House Competition Measures by State, by Two-Year Election Cycle, 1878–1882 (Percentages)

	1878–1879			1880			1882		
State	Democratic % of Two-Party Vote	Margin of Victory	Party Competition Index	Democratic % of Two-Party Vote	Margin of Victory	Party Competition Index	Democratic % of Two-Party Vote	Margin of Victory	Party Competition Index
Alabama	80.6	61.2	38.8	72.9	45.8	54.2	69.9	39.8	60.2
Alaska	—	—	—	—	—	—	—	—	—
Arizona	—	—	—	—	—	—	—	—	—
Arkansas	69.1	38.2	61.8	60.1	20.2	79.8	67.1	34.2	65.8
California	39.1[1]	21.8[1]	78.2[1]	49.8	0.4	99.6	54.2	8.4	91.6
Colorado	45.6	8.8	91.2	47.5	5.0	95.0	48.5	3.0	97.0
Connecticut	48.6	2.8	97.2	48.5	3.0	97.0	51.0	2.0	98.0
Delaware	100.0	100.0	0.0	51.1	2.2	97.8	53.1	6.2	93.8
Florida	53.5	7.0	93.0	54.9	9.8	90.2	50.4	0.8	99.2
Georgia	92.6	85.2	14.8	83.0	66.0	34.0	76.6	53.2	46.8
Hawaii	—	—	—	—	—	—	—	—	—
Idaho	—	—	—	—	—	—	—	—	—
Illinois	47.2	5.6	94.4	46.8	6.4	93.6	53.3	6.6	93.4
Indiana	51.8	3.6	96.4	49.5	1.0	99.0	51.6	3.2	96.8
Iowa	40.0	20.0	80.0	36.1	27.8	72.2	44.9	10.2	89.8
Kansas	32.7	34.6	65.4	34.5	31.0	69.0	45.5	9.0	91.0
Kentucky	66.5	33.0	67.0	60.2	20.4	79.6	58.4	16.8	83.2
Louisiana	78.9	57.8	42.2	64.9	29.8	70.2	62.7	25.4	74.6
Maine	37.4	25.2	74.8	49.7	0.6	99.4	46.4	7.2	92.8
Maryland	63.8	27.6	72.4	53.2	6.4	93.6	52.5	5.0	95.0
Massachusetts	39.7	20.6	79.4	40.5	19.0	81.0	47.9	4.2	95.8
Michigan	38.0	24.0	76.0	41.6	16.8	83.2	48.5	3.0	97.0
Minnesota	45.9	8.2	91.8	38.2	23.6	76.4	33.5	33.0	67.0
Mississippi	81.6	63.2	36.8	71.4	42.8	57.2	70.3	40.6	59.4
Missouri	73.8	47.6	52.4	61.6	23.2	76.8	63.7	27.4	72.6
Montana	—	—	—	—	—	—	—	—	—
Nebraska	43.4	13.2	86.8	31.0	38.0	62.0	38.4	23.2	76.8
Nevada	48.1	3.8	96.2	53.4	6.8	93.2	54.4	8.8	91.2
New Hampshire	45.2	9.6	90.4	47.8	4.4	95.6	46.0	8.0	92.0
New Jersey	46.9	6.2	93.8	50.4	0.8	99.2	50.6	1.2	98.8
New Mexico	—	—	—	—	—	—	—	—	—
New York	48.0	4.0	96.0	49.9	0.2	99.8	56.1	12.2	87.8
North Carolina	53.0	6.0	94.0	54.6	9.2	90.8	100.0	100.0	0.0
North Dakota	—	—	—	—	—	—	—	—	—
Ohio	49.0	2.0	98.0	48.5	3.0	97.0	51.7	3.4	96.6
Oklahoma	—	—	—	—	—	—	—	—	—
Oregon	51.8	3.6	96.4	48.2	3.6	96.4	46.0	8.0	92.0
Pennsylvania	47.3	5.4	94.6	46.0	8.0	92.0	52.2	4.4	95.6
Rhode Island	33.7	32.6	67.4	37.1	25.8	74.2	32.6	34.8	65.2
South Carolina	72.2	44.4	55.6	65.8	31.6	68.4	53.6	7.2	92.8
South Dakota	—	—	—	—	—	—	—	—	—
Tennessee	73.4	46.8	53.2	54.7	9.4	90.6	55.8	11.6	88.4
Texas	100.0	100.0	0.0	100.0	100.0	0.0	78.8	57.6	42.4
Utah	—	—	—	—	—	—	—	—	—
Vermont	26.1	47.8	52.2	30.5	39.0	61.0	27.0	46.0	54.0
Virginia	73.1	46.2	53.8	66.3	32.6	67.4	95.6	91.2	8.8
Washington	—	—	—	—	—	—	—	—	—
West Virginia	58.1	16.2	83.8	53.8	7.6	92.4	52.3	4.6	95.4
Wisconsin	48.2	3.6	96.4	44.7	10.6	89.4	52.3	4.6	95.4
Wyoming	—	—	—	—	—	—	—	—	—

Notes: The first entries are the Democratic percent of two-party vote values for each state for the House race. The second entries are the margin of victory values for each state for the House race, where margin of victory is defined as the absolute difference between the Democratic percent and the Republican percent of the two-party vote for the House. The third entries are the party competition index values for each state for the House race, where the competition index devised by Paul David (1972) is defined as (100 − the margin of victory) or, alternatively, as (100 − the absolute difference between the Democratic and Republican percent of two-party vote for the House). The values for Democratic and Republican percent of two-party vote for the House are taken from the state vote tables in Chapter 5. Zero (0) percent on David's index represents a complete absence of two-party competition for that election year, whereas a score of 100 percent indicates perfect competition between the two major parties. A state can only receive a party competition score of 0 if it has a 100–0 vote split in all House races in the state. Conversely, a state can only receive a score of 100 if it has a 50–50 vote split in all House races in the state. For example, if Pennsylvania in 1788 cast an average of 46.0 percent Democratic vote for all House races in the state of its two-party vote, then its average Republican vote for House would be 54.0 percent. The absolute difference between the two figures is the margin of victory, or 8 percent; 100 percent − 8 percent would equal 92 percent on David's party competition scale, indicating very competitive contests in House races in Pennsylvania in 1788. The two-party vote percent values used to derive the margin of victory and party competition figures are initially found in the state vote tables in Chapter 5. The author's alternative party coding in these tables is used whenever it occurs instead of the conventional party coding of voting data. The Democratic Party is defined here as the Anti-Federalists, Democratic-Republicans, and Jackson Democrats prior to 1830 when the "Democratic Party" as such was established. The Republican Party is defined as the Federalists, National Republicans, and Whigs prior to the establishment of the "Republican Party" in the 1850s. See Appendix A for an explanation of the historical antecedents of the current Democratic and Republican parties. States reporting only partial voting returns for House races are not included in the calculations for the years in which this occurred. The tendency of some states to have House elections in odd-numbered years largely disappeared after 1880. —indicates that the state had no data, either because no vote data were found for the state in question or the state had not yet entered the Union.

[1]Election held in an odd-numbered year.

Sources: State vote tables for House in Chapter 5.

Table 8-70 House Competition Measures, by State, by Two-Year Election Cycle, 1884–1889 (Percentages)

	1884			1886			1888–1889		
State	Democratic % of Two-Party Vote	Margin of Victory	Party Competition Index	Democratic % of Two-Party Vote	Margin of Victory	Party Competition Index	Democratic % of Two-Party Vote	Margin of Victory	Party Competition Index
Alabama	66.5	33.0	67.0	71.8	43.6	56.4	68.3	36.6	63.4
Alaska	—	—	—	—	—	—	—	—	—
Arizona	—	—	—	—	—	—	—	—	—
Arkansas	59.0	18.0	82.0	81.1	62.2	37.8	84.0	68.0	32.0
California	47.2	5.6	94.4	49.4	1.2	98.8	47.8	4.4	95.6
Colorado	44.8	10.4	89.6	49.3	1.4	98.6	42.7	14.6	85.4
Connecticut	49.8	0.4	99.6	50.6	1.2	98.8	49.7	0.6	99.4
Delaware	57.0	14.0	86.0	100.0	100.0	0.0	55.9	11.8	88.2
Florida	53.3	6.6	93.4	59.0	18.0	82.0	59.5	19.0	81.0
Georgia	77.4	54.8	45.2	99.9	99.8	0.2	80.3	60.6	39.4
Hawaii	—	—	—	—	—	—	—	—	—
Idaho	—	—	—	—	—	—	—	—	—
Illinois	47.6	4.8	95.2	46.7	6.6	93.4	48.3	3.4	96.6
Indiana	51.1	2.2	97.8	50.6	1.2	98.8	49.6	0.8	99.2
Iowa	47.6	4.8	95.2	43.5	13.0	87.0	46.5	7.0	93.0
Kansas	38.4	23.2	76.8	41.6	16.8	83.2	36.2	27.6	72.4
Kentucky	61.5	23.0	77.0	59.0	18.0	82.0	54.1	8.2	91.8
Louisiana	66.6	33.2	66.8	74.6	49.2	50.8	76.3	52.6	47.4
Maine	43.3	13.4	86.6	43.2	13.6	86.4	43.3	13.4	86.6
Maryland	52.8	5.6	94.4	63.2	26.4	73.6	51.5	3.0	97.0
Massachusetts	42.3	15.4	84.6	48.9	2.2	97.8	45.6	8.8	91.2
Michigan	50.3	0.6	99.4	48.6	2.8	97.2	47.6	4.8	95.2
Minnesota	41.6	16.8	83.2	39.3	21.4	78.6	43.6	12.8	87.2
Mississippi	73.4	46.8	53.2	76.4	52.8	47.2	76.7	53.4	46.6
Missouri	54.2	8.4	91.6	57.6	15.2	84.8	52.6	5.2	94.8
Montana	—	—	—	—	—	—	47.8[1]	4.4[1]	95.6[1]
Nebraska	46.2	7.6	92.4	47.7	4.6	95.4	43.6	12.8	87.2
Nevada	46.9	6.2	93.8	45.8	8.4	91.6	45.1	9.8	90.2
New Hampshire	47.2	5.6	94.4	49.3	1.4	98.6	49.3	1.4	98.6
New Jersey	50.6	1.2	98.8	50.5	1.0	99.0	50.5	1.0	99.0
New Mexico	—	—	—	—	—	—	47.0	6.0	94.0
New York	52.3	4.6	95.4	50.3	0.6	99.4	53.2	6.4	93.6
North Carolina	54.1	8.2	91.8	67.1	34.2	65.8	53.2	6.4	93.6
North Dakota	—	—	—	—	—	—	31.6[1]	36.8[1]	63.2[1]
Ohio	48.7	2.6	97.4	49.2	1.6	98.4	48.7	2.6	97.4
Oklahoma	—	—	—	—	—	—	—	—	—
Oregon	47.9	4.2	95.8	49.2	1.6	98.4	43.6	12.8	87.2
Pennsylvania	45.6	8.8	91.2	47.0	6.0	94.0	46.4	7.2	92.8
Rhode Island	40.0	20.0	80.0	47.9	4.2	95.8	43.6	12.8	87.2
South Carolina	76.9	53.8	46.2	84.7	69.4	30.6	86.7	73.4	26.6
South Dakota	—	—	—	—	—	—	29.7[1]	40.6[1]	59.4[1]
Tennessee	53.3	6.6	93.4	57.3	14.6	85.4	53.8	7.6	92.4
Texas	85.7	71.4	28.6	86.1	72.2	27.8	79.1	58.2	41.8
Utah	—	—	—	—	—	—	—	—	—
Vermont	27.9	44.2	55.8	28.7	42.6	57.4	28.7	42.6	57.4
Virginia	50.8	1.6	98.4	52.6	5.2	94.8	50.2	0.4	99.6
Washington	—	—	—	—	—	—	41.8[1]	16.4[1]	83.6[1]
West Virginia	51.4	2.8	97.2	50.2	0.4	99.6	50.6	1.2	98.8
Wisconsin	48.1	3.8	96.2	44.2	11.6	88.4	46.6	6.8	93.2
Wyoming	—	—	—	—	—	—	—	—	—

Notes: The first entries are the Democratic percent of two-party vote values for each state for the House race. The second entries are the margin of victory values for each state for the House race, where margin of victory is defined as the absolute difference between the Democratic percent and the Republican percent of the two-party vote for the House. The third entries are the party competition index values for each state for the House race, where the competition index devised by Paul David (1972) is defined as (100 − the margin of victory) or, alternatively, as (100 − the absolute difference between the Democratic and Republican percent of two-party vote for the House). The values for Democratic and Republican percent of two-party vote for the House are taken from the state vote tables in Chapter 5. Zero (0) percent on David's index represents a complete absence of two-party competition for that election year, whereas a score of 100 percent indicates perfect competition between the two major parties. A state can only receive a party competition score of 0 if it has a 100–0 vote split in all House races in the state. Conversely, a state can only receive a score of 100 if it has a 50–50 vote split in all House races in the state. For example, if Pennsylvania in 1788 cast an average of 46.0 percent Democratic vote for all House races in the state of its two-party vote, then its average Republican vote for House would be 54.0 percent. The absolute difference between the two figures is the margin of victory, or 8 percent; 100 percent − 8 percent would equal 92 percent on David's party competition scale, indicating very competitive contests in House races in Pennsylvania in 1788. The two-party vote percent values used to derive the margin of victory and party competition figures are initially found in the state vote tables in Chapter 5. The author's alternative party coding in these tables is used whenever it occurs instead of the conventional party coding of voting data. The Democratic Party is defined here as the Anti-Federalists, Democratic-Republicans, and Jackson Democrats prior to 1830 when the "Democratic Party" as such was established. The Republican Party is defined as the Federalists, National Republicans, and Whigs prior to the establishment of the "Republican Party" in the 1850s. See Appendix A for an explanation of the historical antecedents of the current Democratic and Republican parties. States reporting only partial voting returns for House races are not included in the calculations for the years in which this occurred. —indicates that the state had no data, either because no vote data were found for the state in question or the state had not yet entered the Union.

[1]Election held in an odd-numbered year.

Sources: State vote tables for House in Chapter 5.

Table 8-71 House Competition Measures, by State, by Two-Year Election Cycle, 1890–1895 (Percentages)

| | 1890 | | | 1892 | | | 1894–1895 | | |
State	Democratic % of Two-Party Vote	Margin of Victory	Party Competition Index	Democratic % of Two-Party Vote	Margin of Victory	Party Competition Index	Democratic % of Two-Party Vote	Margin of Victory	Party Competition Index
Alabama	77.1	54.2	45.8	95.2	90.4	9.6	82.6	65.2	34.8
Alaska	—	—	—	—	—	—	—	—	—
Arizona	—	—	—	—	—	—	—	—	—
Arkansas	71.8	43.6	56.4	85.9	71.8	28.2	78.3	56.6	43.4
California	47.6	4.8	95.2	53.7	7.4	92.6	46.5	7.0	93.0
Colorado	44.6	10.8	89.2	59.1	18.2	81.8	35.5	29.0	71.0
Connecticut	51.6	3.2	96.8	51.6	3.2	96.8	43.1	13.8	86.2
Delaware	51.0	2.0	98.0	50.6	1.2	98.8	48.3	3.4	96.6
Florida	65.8	31.6	68.4	100.0	100.0	0.0	100.0	100.0	0.0
Georgia	83.7	67.4	32.6	93.2	86.4	13.6	100.0	100.0	0.0
Hawaii	—	—	—	—	—	—	—	—	—
Idaho	44.2	11.6	88.4	41.4	17.2	82.8	36.0	28.0	72.0
Illinois	52.4	4.8	95.2	51.6	3.2	96.8	41.1	17.8	82.2
Indiana	52.5	5.0	95.0	50.5	1.0	99.0	45.6	8.8	91.2
Iowa	51.2	2.4	97.6	47.9	4.2	95.8	42.2	15.6	84.4
Kansas	18.0	64.0	36.0	51.4	2.8	97.2	15.0	70.0	30.0
Kentucky	65.2	30.4	69.6	58.8	17.6	82.4	50.3	0.6	99.4
Louisiana	82.3	64.6	35.4	81.8	63.6	36.4	74.2	48.4	51.6
Maine	41.6	16.8	83.2	45.9	8.2	91.8	30.5	39.0	61.0
Maryland	56.2	12.4	87.6	55.4	10.8	89.2	49.3	1.4	98.6
Massachusetts	50.7	1.4	98.6	48.2	3.6	96.4	39.3	21.4	78.6
Michigan	51.3	2.6	97.4	48.6	2.8	97.2	35.8	28.4	71.6
Minnesota	52.2	4.4	95.6	45.5	9.0	91.0	32.9	34.2	65.8
Mississippi	77.6	55.2	44.8	98.7	97.4	2.6	99.4	98.8	1.2
Missouri	57.9	15.8	84.2	54.0	8.0	92.0	48.7	2.6	97.4
Montana	50.5	1.0	99.0	49.8	0.4	99.6	30.9	38.2	61.8
Nebraska	55.5	11.0	89.0	44.1	11.8	88.2	44.8	10.4	89.6
Nevada	46.5	7.0	93.0	13.1	73.8	26.2	0.0	100.0	0.0
New Hampshire	50.9	1.8	98.2	49.4	1.2	98.8	42.2	15.6	84.4
New Jersey	52.8	5.6	94.4	51.3	2.6	97.4	41.3	17.4	82.6
New Mexico	—	—	—	—	—	—	—	—	—
New York	54.0	8.0	92.0	51.2	2.4	97.6	43.2	13.6	86.4
North Carolina	58.8	17.6	82.4	65.4	30.8	69.2	59.1	18.2	81.8
North Dakota	41.0	18.0	82.0	38.4	23.2	76.8	0.0	100.0	0.0
Ohio	49.2	1.6	98.4	50.6	1.2	98.8	40.2	19.6	80.4
Oklahoma	—	—	—	—	—	—	—	—	—
Oregon	43.0	14.0	86.0	42.1	15.8	84.2	32.5	35.0	65.0
Pennsylvania	48.5	3.0	97.0	46.7	6.6	93.4	36.5	27.0	73.0
Rhode Island	52.6	5.2	94.8	48.3	3.4	96.6	37.5	25.0	75.0
South Carolina	80.2	60.4	39.6	85.4	70.8	29.2	77.2	54.4	45.6
South Dakota	33.5	33.0	67.0	29.6	40.8	59.2	16.6	66.8	33.2
Tennessee	56.5	13.0	87.0	63.8	27.6	72.4	48.7	2.6	97.4
Texas	81.2	62.4	37.6	76.6	53.2	46.8	82.7	65.4	34.6
Utah	—	—	—	—	—	—	48.9[1]	2.2[1]	97.8[1]
Vermont	33.3	33.4	66.6	34.0	32.0	68.0	24.6	50.8	49.2
Virginia	73.4	46.8	53.2	77.8	55.6	44.4	56.1	12.2	87.8
Washington	43.9	12.2	87.8	46.4	7.2	92.8	28.9	42.2	57.8
West Virginia	52.3	4.6	95.4	51.6	3.2	96.8	45.9	8.2	91.8
Wisconsin	55.8	11.6	88.4	50.6	1.2	98.8	40.2	19.6	80.4
Wyoming	41.8	16.4	83.6	51.3	2.6	97.4	37.9	24.2	75.8

Notes: The first entries are the Democratic percent of two-party vote values for each state for the House race. The second entries are the margin of victory values for each state for the House race, where margin of victory is defined as the absolute difference between the Democratic percent and the Republican percent of the two-party vote for the House. The third entries are the party competition index values for each state for the House race, where the competition index devised by Paul David (1972) is defined as (100 − the margin of victory) or, alternatively, as (100 − the absolute difference between the Democratic and Republican percent of two-party vote for the House). The values for Democratic and Republican percent of two-party vote for the House are taken from the state vote tables in Chapter 5. Zero (0) percent on David's index represents a complete absence of two-party competition for that election year, whereas a score of 100 percent indicates perfect competition between the two major parties. A state can only receive a party competition score of 0 if it has a 100–0 vote split in all House races in the state. Conversely, a state can only receive a score of 100 if it has a 50–50 vote split in all House races in the state. For example, if Pennsylvania in 1788 cast an average of 46.0 percent Democratic vote for all House races in the state of its two-party vote, then its average Republican vote for House would be 54.0 percent. The absolute difference between the two figures is the margin of victory, or 8 percent; 100 percent − 8 percent would equal 92 percent on David's party competition scale, indicating very competitive contests in House races in Pennsylvania in 1788. The two-party vote percent values used to derive the margin of victory and party competition figures are initially found in the state vote tables in Chapter 5. The author's alternative party coding in these tables is used whenever it occurs instead of the conventional party coding of voting data. The Democratic Party is defined here as the Anti-Federalists, Democratic-Republicans, and Jackson Democrats prior to 1830 when the "Democratic Party" as such was established. The Republican Party is defined as the Federalists, National Republicans, and Whigs prior to the establishment of the "Republican Party" in the 1850s. See Appendix A for an explanation of the historical antecedents of the current Democratic and Republican parties. States reporting only partial voting returns for House races are not included in the calculations for the years in which this occurred. —indicates that the state had no data, either because no vote data were found for the state in question or the state had not yet entered the Union.

[1] Election held in an odd-numbered year.

Sources: State vote tables for House in Chapter 5.

Table 8-72 House Competition Measures, by State, by Election Year, 1896–1900 (Percentages)

| | 1896 | | | 1898 | | | 1900 | | |
| | Democratic % of Two-Party Vote | Margin of Victory | Party Competition Index | Democratic % of Two-Party Vote | Margin of Victory | Party Competition Index | Democratic % of Two-Party Vote | Margin of Victory | Party Competition Index |
State									
Alabama	77.0	54.0	46.0	73.3	46.6	53.4	74.2	48.4	51.6
Alaska	—	—	—	—	—	—	—	—	—
Arizona	—	—	—	—	—	—	—	—	—
Arkansas	72.4	44.8	55.2	90.0	80.0	20.0	66.4	32.8	67.2
California	50.2	0.4	99.6	48.0	4.0	96.0	43.3	13.4	86.6
Colorado	86.3	72.6	27.4	67.4	34.8	65.2	56.7	13.4	86.6
Connecticut	36.1	27.8	72.2	43.7	12.6	87.4	42.2	15.6	84.4
Delaware	47.1	5.8	94.2	46.1	7.8	92.2	46.2	7.6	92.4
Florida	76.3	52.6	47.4	77.8	55.6	44.4	83.4	66.8	33.2
Georgia	73.5	47.0	53.0	88.8	77.6	22.4	87.8	75.6	24.4
Hawaii	—	—	—	—	—	—	—	—	—
Idaho	47.7	4.6	95.4	0.0	100.0	0.0	51.1	2.2	97.8
Illinois	43.6	12.8	87.2	45.8	8.4	91.6	45.9	8.2	91.8
Indiana	48.7	2.6	97.4	49.1	1.8	98.2	48.5	3.0	97.0
Iowa	44.0	12.0	88.0	43.2	13.6	86.4	41.1	17.8	82.2
Kansas	51.6	3.2	96.8	47.0	6.0	94.0	47.2	5.6	94.4
Kentucky	53.6	7.2	92.8	51.3	2.6	97.4	50.5	1.0	99.0
Louisiana	74.6	49.2	50.8	87.6	75.2	24.8	78.4	56.8	43.2
Maine	29.1	41.8	58.2	32.5	35.0	65.0	35.7	28.6	71.4
Maryland	44.1	11.8	88.2	48.7	2.6	97.4	47.7	4.6	95.4
Massachusetts	33.1	33.8	66.2	42.1	15.8	84.2	40.5	19.0	81.0
Michigan	45.2	9.6	90.4	43.2	13.6	86.4	40.9	18.2	81.8
Minnesota	43.9	12.2	87.8	42.9	14.2	85.8	41.5	17.0	83.0
Mississippi	92.1	84.2	15.8	94.8	89.6	10.4	94.9	89.8	10.2
Missouri	52.7	5.4	94.6	52.6	5.2	94.8	53.0	6.0	94.0
Montana	0.0	100.0	0.0	46.9	6.2	93.8	61.8	23.6	76.4
Nebraska	53.0	6.0	94.0	50.4	0.8	99.2	49.3	1.4	98.6
Nevada	83.0	66.0	34.0	100.0	100.0	0.0	58.8	17.6	82.4
New Hampshire	34.7	30.6	69.4	45.0	10.0	90.0	39.5	21.0	79.0
New Jersey	38.6	22.8	77.2	48.4	3.2	96.8	42.9	14.2	85.8
New Mexico	—	—	—	—	—	—	—	—	—
New York	40.9	18.2	81.8	48.5	3.0	97.0	45.3	9.4	90.6
North Carolina	45.3	9.4	90.6	54.5	9.0	91.0	58.4	16.8	83.2
North Dakota	45.6	8.8	91.2	39.1	21.8	78.2	37.8	24.4	75.6
Ohio	47.4	5.2	94.8	46.8	6.4	93.6	47.0	6.0	94.0
Oklahoma	—	—	—	—	—	—	—	—	—
Oregon	32.0	36.0	64.0	44.3	11.4	88.6	44.2	11.6	88.4
Pennsylvania	36.8	26.4	73.6	39.7	20.6	79.4	37.6	24.8	75.2
Rhode Island	32.9	34.2	65.8	38.3	23.4	76.6	37.7	24.6	75.4
South Carolina	87.4	74.8	25.2	91.2	82.4	17.6	93.8	87.6	12.4
South Dakota	50.1	0.2	99.8	45.5	9.0	91.0	43.1	13.8	86.2
Tennessee	56.4	12.8	87.2	62.5	25.0	75.0	56.8	13.6	86.4
Texas	71.0	42.0	58.0	78.8	57.6	42.4	78.7	57.4	42.6
Utah	63.0	26.0	74.0	54.6	9.2	90.8	49.9	0.2	99.8
Vermont	20.9	58.2	41.8	26.9	46.2	53.8	26.6	46.8	53.2
Virginia	58.3	16.6	83.4	63.2	26.4	73.6	62.7	25.4	74.6
Washington	0.0	100.0	0.0	0.0	100.0	0.0	45.1	9.8	90.2
West Virginia	47.5	5.0	95.0	49.3	1.4	98.6	45.9	8.2	91.8
Wisconsin	38.2	23.6	76.4	41.6	16.8	83.2	38.5	23.0	77.0
Wyoming	50.7	1.4	98.6	44.0	12.0	88.0	40.8	18.4	81.6

Notes: The first entries are the Democratic percent of two-party vote values for each state for the House race. The second entries are the margin of victory values for each state for the House race, where margin of victory is defined as the absolute difference between the Democratic percent and the Republican percent of the two-party vote for the House. The third entries are the party competition index values for each state for the House race, where the competition index devised by Paul David (1972) is defined as (100 − the margin of victory) or, alternatively, as (100 − the absolute difference between the Democratic and Republican percent of two-party vote for the House). The values for Democratic and Republican percent of two-party vote for the House are taken from the state vote tables in Chapter 5. Zero (0) percent on David's index represents a complete absence of two-party competition for that election year, whereas a score of 100 percent indicates perfect competition between the two major parties. A state can only receive a party competition score of 0 if it has a 100–0 vote split in all House races in the state. Conversely, a state can only receive a score of 100 if it has a 50–50 vote split in all House races in the state. For example, if Pennsylvania in 1788 cast an average of 46.0 percent Democratic vote for all House races in the state of its two-party vote, then its average Republican vote for House would be 54.0 percent. The absolute difference between the two figures is the margin of victory, or 8 percent; 100 percent − 8 percent would equal 92 percent on David's party competition scale, indicating very competitive contests in House races in Pennsylvania in 1788. The two-party vote percent values used to derive the margin of victory and party competition figures are initially found in the state vote tables in Chapter 5. The author's alternative party coding in these tables is used whenever it occurs instead of the conventional party coding of voting data. The Democratic Party is defined here as the Anti-Federalists, Democratic-Republicans, and Jackson Democrats prior to 1830 when the "Democratic Party" as such was established. The Republican Party is defined as the Federalists, National Republicans, and Whigs prior to the establishment of the "Republican Party" in the 1850s. See Appendix A for an explanation of the historical antecedents of the current Democratic and Republican parties. States reporting only partial voting returns for House races are not included in the calculations for the years in which this occurred. —indicates that the state had no data, either because no vote data were found for the state in question or the state had not yet entered the Union.

Sources: State vote tables for House in Chapter 5.

Table 8-73 House Competition Measures, by State, by Two-Year Election Cycle, 1902–1907 (Percentages)

	1902			1904			1906–1907		
State	Democratic % of Two-Party Vote	Margin of Victory	Party Competition Index	Democratic % of Two-Party Vote	Margin of Victory	Party Competition Index	Democratic % of Two-Party Vote	Margin of Victory	Party Competition Index
Alabama	76.6	53.2	46.8	80.9	61.8	38.2	90.9	81.8	18.2
Alaska	—	—	—	—	—	—	—	—	—
Arizona	—	—	—	—	—	—	—	—	—
Arkansas	83.3	66.6	33.4	70.4	40.8	59.2	75.5	51.0	49.0
California	45.3	9.4	90.6	37.7	24.6	75.4	38.6	22.8	77.2
Colorado	49.7	0.6	99.4	48.1	3.8	96.2	42.8	14.4	85.6
Connecticut	45.8	8.4	91.6	40.8	18.4	81.6	43.5	13.0	87.0
Delaware	43.8	12.4	87.6	45.4	9.2	90.8	45.9	8.2	91.8
Florida	100.0	100.0	0.0	81.0	62.0	38.0	94.5	89.0	11.0
Georgia	100.0	100.0	0.0	82.7	65.4	34.6	98.7	97.4	2.6
Hawaii	—	—	—	—	—	—	—	—	—
Idaho	43.4	13.2	86.8	31.0	38.0	62.0	36.1	27.8	72.2
Illinois	47.9	4.2	95.8	35.9	28.2	71.8	41.7	16.6	83.4
Indiana	48.4	3.2	96.8	45.0	10.0	90.0	49.4	1.2	98.8
Iowa	41.6	16.8	83.2	35.4	29.2	70.8	42.9	14.2	85.8
Kansas	42.1	15.8	84.2	35.9	28.2	71.8	43.6	12.8	87.2
Kentucky	55.8	11.6	88.4	51.8	3.6	96.4	55.7	11.4	88.6
Louisiana	84.6	69.2	30.8	91.1	82.2	17.8	89.2	78.4	21.6
Maine	37.1	25.8	74.2	39.7	20.6	79.4	46.6	6.8	93.2
Maryland	47.8	4.4	95.6	48.7	2.6	97.4	48.2	3.6	96.4
Massachusetts	45.5	9.0	91.0	39.3	21.4	78.6	41.1	17.8	82.2
Michigan	40.5	19.0	81.0	31.5	37.0	63.0	26.4	47.2	52.8
Minnesota	36.5	27.0	73.0	26.3	47.4	52.6	27.5	45.0	55.0
Mississippi	100.0	100.0	0.0	99.8	99.6	0.4	100.0	100.0	0.0
Missouri	54.3	8.6	91.4	49.0	2.0	98.0	50.4	0.8	99.2
Montana	44.3	11.4	88.6	44.8	10.4	89.6	44.7	10.6	89.4
Nebraska	47.6	4.8	95.2	42.0	16.0	84.0	46.1	7.8	92.2
Nevada	53.5	7.0	93.0	51.0	2.0	98.0	60.2	20.4	79.6
New Hampshire	40.4	19.2	80.8	39.0	22.0	78.0	40.6	18.8	81.2
New Jersey	47.2	5.6	94.4	42.3	15.4	84.6	49.5	1.0	99.0
New Mexico	—	—	—	—	—	—	—	—	—
New York	49.6	0.8	99.2	44.0	12.0	88.0	47.7	4.6	95.4
North Carolina	69.6	39.2	60.8	62.3	24.6	75.4	61.6	23.2	76.8
North Dakota	30.9	38.2	61.8	24.1	51.8	48.2	35.4	29.2	70.8
Ohio	43.4	13.2	86.8	37.9	24.2	75.8	45.0	10.0	90.0
Oklahoma	—	—	—	—	—	—	57.2[1]	14.4[1]	85.6[1]
Oregon	40.4	19.2	80.8	36.9	26.2	73.8	38.0	24.0	76.0
Pennsylvania	35.1	29.8	70.2	30.5	39.0	61.0	37.2	25.6	74.4
Rhode Island	49.7	0.6	99.4	46.2	7.6	92.4	48.8	2.4	97.6
South Carolina	97.7	95.4	4.6	95.7	91.4	8.6	98.5	97.0	3.0
South Dakota	30.3	39.4	60.6	24.5	51.0	49.0	29.4	41.2	58.8
Tennessee	64.8	29.6	70.4	56.4	12.8	87.2	56.2	12.4	87.6
Texas	83.1	66.2	33.8	82.6	65.2	34.8	88.2	76.4	23.6
Utah	46.6	6.8	93.2	41.6	16.8	83.2	38.8	22.4	77.6
Vermont	20.3	59.4	40.6	25.3	49.4	50.6	29.2	41.6	58.4
Virginia	67.6	35.2	64.8	65.8	31.6	68.4	64.4	28.8	71.2
Washington	36.6	26.8	73.2	27.7	44.6	55.4	30.7	38.6	61.4
West Virginia	46.8	6.4	93.6	45.0	10.0	90.0	44.0	12.0	88.0
Wisconsin	41.2	17.6	82.4	37.5	25.0	75.0	39.7	20.6	79.4
Wyoming	36.0	28.0	72.0	33.3	33.4	66.6	34.7	30.6	69.4

Notes: The first entries are the Democratic percent of two-party vote values for each state for the House race. The second entries are the margin of victory values for each state for the House race, where margin of victory is defined as the absolute difference between the Democratic percent and the Republican percent of the two-party vote for the House. The third entries are the party competition index values for each state for the House race, where the competition index devised by Paul David (1972) is defined as (100 − the margin of victory) or, alternatively, as (100 − the absolute difference between the Democratic and Republican percent of two-party vote for the House). The values for Democratic and Republican percent of two-party vote for the House are taken from the state vote tables in Chapter 5. Zero (0) percent on David's index represents a complete absence of two-party competition for that election year, whereas a score of 100 percent indicates perfect competition between the two major parties. A state can only receive a party competition score of 0 if it has a 100–0 vote split in all House races in the state. Conversely, a state can only receive a score of 100 if it has a 50–50 vote split in all House races in the state. For example, if Pennsylvania in 1788 cast an average of 46.0 percent Democratic vote for all House races in the state of its two-party vote, then its average Republican vote for House would be 54.0 percent. The absolute difference between the two figures is the margin of victory, or 8 percent; 100 percent − 8 percent would equal 92 percent on David's party competition scale, indicating very competitive contests in House races in Pennsylvania in 1788. The two-party vote percent values used to derive the margin of victory and party competition figures are initially found in the state vote tables in Chapter 5. The author's alternative party coding in these tables is used whenever it occurs instead of the conventional party coding of voting data. The Democratic Party is defined here as the Anti-Federalists, Democratic-Republicans, and Jackson Democrats prior to 1830 when the "Democratic Party" as such was established. The Republican Party is defined as the Federalists, National Republicans, and Whigs prior to the establishment of the "Republican Party" in the 1850s. See Appendix A for an explanation of the historical antecedents of the current Democratic and Republican parties. States reporting only partial voting returns for House races are not included in the calculations for the years in which this occurred. —indicates that the state had no data, either because no vote data were found for the state in question or the state had not yet entered the Union.

[1] Election held in an odd-numbered year.

Sources: State vote tables for House in Chapter 5.

Table 8-74 House Competition Measures, by State, by Two-Year Election Cycle, 1908–1912 (Percentages)

	1908			1910–1911			1912		
State	Democratic % of Two-Party Vote	Margin of Victory	Party Competition Index	Democratic % of Two-Party Vote	Margin of Victory	Party Competition Index	Democratic % of Two-Party Vote	Margin of Victory	Party Competition Index
Alabama	81.0	62.0	38.0	84.6	69.2	30.8	90.1	80.2	19.8
Alaska	—	—	—	—	—	—	—	—	—
Arizona	—	—	—	57.7[1]	15.4[1]	84.6[1]	78.6	57.2	42.8
Arkansas	68.6	37.2	62.8	77.3	54.6	45.4	77.2	54.4	45.6
California	40.0	20.0	80.0	35.4	29.2	70.8	40.6	18.8	81.2
Colorado	51.1	2.2	97.8	51.0	2.0	98.0	64.4	28.8	71.2
Connecticut	38.6	22.8	77.2	47.9	4.2	95.8	52.1	4.2	95.8
Delaware	48.1	3.8	96.2	47.5	5.0	95.0	57.3	14.6	85.4
Florida	82.8	65.6	34.4	95.8	91.6	8.4	92.1	84.2	15.8
Georgia	99.6	99.2	0.8	95.0	90.0	10.0	99.7	99.4	0.6
Hawaii	—	—	—	—	—	—	—	—	—
Idaho	42.9	14.2	85.8	40.7	18.6	81.4	36.0	28.0	72.0
Illinois	42.7	14.6	85.4	49.3	1.4	98.6	57.0	14.0	86.0
Indiana	51.3	2.6	97.4	52.9	5.8	94.2	63.6	27.2	72.8
Iowa	43.8	12.4	87.6	43.2	13.6	86.4	49.8	0.4	99.6
Kansas	45.5	9.0	91.0	41.6	16.8	83.2	50.7	1.4	98.6
Kentucky	51.2	2.4	97.6	54.4	8.8	91.2	70.8	41.6	58.4
Louisiana	92.3	84.6	15.4	92.2	84.4	15.6	100.0	100.0	0.0
Maine	46.1	7.8	92.2	51.1	2.2	97.8	48.2	3.6	96.4
Maryland	51.5	3.0	97.0	51.6	3.2	96.8	63.3	26.6	73.4
Massachusetts	37.2	25.6	74.4	51.3	2.6	97.4	51.1	2.2	97.8
Michigan	37.3	25.4	74.6	40.8	18.4	81.6	45.0	10.0	90.0
Minnesota	30.9	38.2	61.8	27.3	45.4	54.6	31.1	37.8	62.2
Mississippi	99.4	98.8	1.2	100.0	100.0	0.0	100.0	100.0	0.0
Missouri	50.1	0.2	99.8	50.7	1.4	98.6	60.2	20.4	79.6
Montana	46.9	6.2	93.8	46.3	7.4	92.6	52.4	4.8	95.2
Nebraska	50.4	0.8	99.2	49.7	0.6	99.4	49.0	2.0	98.0
Nevada	59.8	19.6	80.4	43.3	13.4	86.6	49.8	0.4	99.6
New Hampshire	40.3	19.4	80.6	46.5	7.0	93.0	53.5	7.0	93.0
New Jersey	46.1	7.8	92.2	54.6	9.2	90.8	60.1	20.2	79.8
New Mexico	—	—	—	49.9[1]	0.2[1]	99.8[1]	55.3	10.6	89.4
New York	46.1	7.8	92.2	51.7	3.4	96.6	57.3	14.6	85.4
North Carolina	57.0	14.0	86.0	59.9	19.8	80.2	68.8	37.6	62.4
North Dakota	33.9	32.2	67.8	33.4	33.2	66.8	34.1	31.8	68.2
Ohio	49.6	0.8	99.2	54.2	8.4	91.6	58.7	17.4	82.6
Oklahoma	52.9	5.8	94.2	55.9	11.8	88.2	58.1	16.2	83.8
Oregon	29.8	40.4	59.6	39.9	20.2	79.8	37.5	25.0	75.0
Pennsylvania	38.6	22.8	77.2	39.5	21.0	79.0	36.6	26.8	73.2
Rhode Island	43.7	12.6	87.4	47.4	5.2	94.8	51.5	3.0	97.0
South Carolina	97.4	94.8	5.2	98.8	97.6	2.4	99.8	99.6	0.4
South Dakota	36.4	27.2	72.8	33.5	33.0	67.0	41.1	17.8	82.2
Tennessee	54.6	9.2	90.8	66.8	33.6	66.4	63.1	26.2	73.8
Texas	83.7	67.4	32.6	91.3	82.6	17.4	91.2	82.4	17.6
Utah	38.5	23.0	77.0	39.3	21.4	78.6	46.3	7.4	92.6
Vermont	24.9	50.2	49.8	28.0	44.0	56.0	37.7	24.6	75.4
Virginia	64.7	29.4	70.6	68.1	36.2	63.8	80.6	61.2	38.8
Washington	34.3	31.4	68.6	36.4	27.2	72.8	45.5	9.0	91.0
West Virginia	45.6	8.8	91.2	52.2	4.4	95.6	46.3	7.4	92.6
Wisconsin	41.1	17.8	82.2	39.8	20.4	79.6	46.9	6.2	93.8
Wyoming	38.9	22.2	77.8	41.9	16.2	83.8	43.5	13.0	87.0

Notes: The first entries are the Democratic percent of two-party vote values for each state for the House race. The second entries are the margin of victory values for each state for the House race, where margin of victory is defined as the absolute difference between the Democratic percent and the Republican percent of the two-party vote for the House. The third entries are the party competition index values for each state for the House race, where the competition index devised by Paul David (1972) is defined as (100 − the margin of victory) or, alternatively, as (100 − the absolute difference between the Democratic and Republican percent of two-party vote for the House). The values for Democratic and Republican percent of two-party vote for the House are taken from the state vote tables in Chapter 5. Zero (0) percent on David's index represents a complete absence of two-party competition for that election year, whereas a score of 100 percent indicates perfect competition between the two major parties. A state can only receive a party competition score of 0 if it has a 100–0 vote split in all House races in the state. Conversely, a state can only receive a score of 100 if it has a 50–50 vote split in all House races in the state. For example, if Pennsylvania in 1788 cast an average of 46.0 percent Democratic vote for all House races in the state of its two-party vote, then its average Republican vote for House would be 54.0 percent. The absolute difference between the two figures is the margin of victory, or 8 percent; 100 percent − 8 percent would equal 92 percent on David's party competition scale, indicating very competitive contests in House races in Pennsylvania in 1788. The two-party vote percent values used to derive the margin of victory and party competition figures are initially found in the state vote tables in Chapter 5. The author's alternative party coding in these tables is used whenever it occurs instead of the conventional party coding of voting data. The Democratic Party is defined here as the Anti-Federalists, Democratic-Republicans, and Jackson Democrats prior to 1830 when the "Democratic Party" as such was established. The Republican Party is defined as the Federalists, National Republicans, and Whigs prior to the establishment of the "Republican Party" in the 1850s. See Appendix A for an explanation of the historical antecedents of the current Democratic and Republican parties. States reporting only partial voting returns for House races are not included in the calculations for the years in which this occurred. —indicates that the state had no data, either because no vote data were found for the state in question or the state had not yet entered the Union.

[1] Election held in an odd-numbered year.

Sources: State vote tables for House in Chapter 5.

Table 8-75 House Competition Measures, by State, by Election Year, 1914–1918 (Percentages)

State	1914 Democratic % of Two-Party Vote	1914 Margin of Victory	1914 Party Competition Index	1916 Democratic % of Two-Party Vote	1916 Margin of Victory	1916 Party Competition Index	1918 Democratic % of Two-Party Vote	1918 Margin of Victory	1918 Party Competition Index
Alabama	83.0	66.0	34.0	80.8	61.6	38.4	85.8	71.6	28.4
Alaska	—	—	—	—	—	—	—	—	—
Arizona	81.4	62.8	37.2	69.8	39.6	60.4	61.4	22.8	77.2
Arkansas	90.1	80.2	19.8	82.9	65.8	34.2	100.0	100.0	0.0
California	36.7	26.6	73.4	39.5	21.0	79.0	37.9	24.2	75.8
Colorado	54.2	8.4	91.6	53.5	7.0	93.0	45.4	9.2	90.8
Connecticut	46.7	6.6	93.4	48.0	4.0	96.0	48.6	2.8	97.2
Delaware	47.4	5.2	94.8	50.2	0.4	99.6	48.1	3.8	96.2
Florida	100.0	100.0	0.0	82.7	65.4	34.6	100.0	100.0	0.0
Georgia	100.0	100.0	0.0	94.8	89.6	10.4	95.3	90.6	9.4
Hawaii	—	—	—	—	—	—	—	—	—
Idaho	46.7	6.6	93.4	46.3	7.4	92.6	36.8	26.4	73.6
Illinois	49.1	1.8	98.2	43.6	12.8	87.2	41.9	16.2	83.8
Indiana	54.2	8.4	91.6	48.4	3.2	96.8	45.0	10.0	90.0
Iowa	43.4	13.2	86.8	39.8	20.4	79.6	35.3	29.4	70.6
Kansas	51.0	2.0	98.0	50.0	0.0	100.0	41.3	17.4	82.6
Kentucky	58.4	16.8	83.2	52.9	5.8	94.2	52.2	4.4	95.6
Louisiana	98.5	97.0	3.0	99.5	99.0	1.0	100.0	100.0	0.0
Maine	50.2	0.4	99.6	45.8	8.4	91.6	44.1	11.8	88.2
Maryland	53.8	7.6	92.4	50.9	1.8	98.2	51.7	3.4	96.6
Massachusetts	45.9	8.2	91.8	41.3	17.4	82.6	39.2	21.6	78.4
Michigan	40.7	18.6	81.4	43.2	13.6	86.4	33.9	32.2	67.8
Minnesota	32.5	35.0	65.0	34.1	31.8	68.2	27.6	44.8	55.2
Mississippi	100.0	100.0	0.0	100.0	100.0	0.0	100.0	100.0	0.0
Missouri	56.9	13.8	86.2	51.8	3.6	96.4	52.9	5.8	94.2
Montana	58.6	17.2	82.8	52.3	4.6	95.4	50.5	1.0	99.0
Nebraska	50.3	0.6	99.4	48.9	2.2	97.8	43.8	12.4	87.6
Nevada	47.4	5.2	94.8	48.2	3.6	96.4	54.3	8.6	91.4
New Hampshire	45.4	9.2	90.8	47.5	5.0	95.0	45.7	8.6	91.4
New Jersey	48.9	2.2	97.8	45.3	9.4	90.6	47.8	4.4	95.6
New Mexico	45.4	9.2	90.8	50.4	0.8	99.2	48.7	2.6	97.4
New York	46.7	6.6	93.4	43.8	12.4	87.6	46.9	6.2	93.8
North Carolina	60.5	21.0	79.0	58.0	16.0	84.0	60.4	20.8	79.2
North Dakota	34.4	31.2	68.8	31.5	37.0	63.0	35.0	30.0	70.0
Ohio	50.2	0.4	99.6	50.1	0.2	99.8	44.2	11.6	88.4
Oklahoma	59.7	19.4	80.6	59.0	18.0	82.0	57.1	14.2	85.8
Oregon	39.7	20.6	79.4	27.0	46.0	54.0	20.9	58.2	41.8
Pennsylvania	35.3	29.4	70.6	41.3	17.4	82.6	33.6	32.8	67.2
Rhode Island	47.4	5.2	94.8	49.0	2.0	98.0	44.5	11.0	89.0
South Carolina	99.9	99.8	0.2	98.2	96.4	3.6	99.3	98.6	1.4
South Dakota	41.7	16.6	83.4	43.2	13.6	86.4	41.1	17.8	82.2
Tennessee	76.4	52.8	47.2	58.9	17.8	82.2	77.1	54.2	45.8
Texas	94.2	88.4	11.6	86.5	73.0	27.0	96.3	92.6	7.4
Utah	49.1	1.8	98.2	58.1	16.2	83.8	57.4	14.8	85.2
Vermont	27.0	46.0	54.0	26.3	47.4	52.6	24.8	50.4	49.6
Virginia	71.1	42.2	57.8	68.9	37.8	62.2	79.8	59.6	40.4
Washington	43.0	14.0	86.0	45.3	9.4	90.6	42.0	16.0	84.0
West Virginia	48.0	4.0	96.0	49.7	0.6	99.4	47.1	5.8	94.2
Wisconsin	42.0	16.0	84.0	36.5	27.0	73.0	29.3	41.4	58.6
Wyoming	44.7	10.6	89.4	49.5	1.0	99.0	35.8	28.4	71.6

Notes: The first entries are the Democratic percent of two-party vote values for each state for the House race. The second entries are the margin of victory values for each state for the House race, where margin of victory is defined as the absolute difference between the Democratic percent and the Republican percent of the two-party vote for the House. The third entries are the party competition index values for each state for the House race, where the competition index devised by Paul David (1972) is defined as (100 − the margin of victory) or, alternatively, as (100 − the absolute difference between the Democratic and Republican percent of two-party vote for the House). The values for Democratic and Republican percent of two-party vote for the House are taken from the state vote tables in Chapter 5. Zero (0) percent on David's index represents a complete absence of two-party competition for that election year, whereas a score of 100 percent indicates perfect competition between the two major parties. A state can only receive a party competition score of 0 if it has a 100–0 vote split in all House races in the state. Conversely, a state can only receive a score of 100 if it has a 50–50 vote split in all House races in the state. For example, if Pennsylvania in 1788 cast an average of 46.0 percent Democratic vote for all House races in the state of its two-party vote, then its average Republican vote for House would be 54.0 percent. The absolute difference between the two figures is the margin of victory, or 8 percent; 100 percent − 8 percent would equal 92 percent on David's party competition scale, indicating very competitive contests in House races in Pennsylvania in 1788. The two-party vote percent values used to derive the margin of victory and party competition figures are initially found in the state vote tables in Chapter 5. The author's alternative party coding in these tables is used whenever it occurs instead of the conventional party coding of voting data. The Democratic Party is defined here as the Anti-Federalists, Democratic-Republicans, and Jackson Democrats prior to 1830 when the "Democratic Party" as such was established. The Republican Party is defined as the Federalists, National Republicans, and Whigs prior to the establishment of the "Republican Party" in the 1850s. See Appendix A for an explanation of the historical antecedents of the current Democratic and Republican parties. States reporting only partial voting returns for House races are not included in the calculations for the years in which this occurred. —indicates that the state had no data, either because no vote data were found for the state in question or the state had not yet entered the Union.

Sources: State vote tables for House in Chapter 5.

Table 8-76 House Competition Measures, by State, by Election Year, 1920–1924 (Percentages)

	1920			1922			1924		
State	Democratic % of Two-Party Vote	Margin of Victory	Party Competition Index	Democratic % of Two-Party Vote	Margin of Victory	Party Competition Index	Democratic % of Two-Party Vote	Margin of Victory	Party Competition Index
Alabama	72.2	44.4	55.6	81.3	62.6	37.4	79.3	58.6	41.4
Alaska	—	—	—	—	—	—	—	—	—
Arizona	57.8	15.6	84.4	71.8	43.6	56.4	82.4	64.8	35.2
Arkansas	67.4	34.8	65.2	87.8	75.6	24.4	72.9	45.8	54.2
California	22.4	55.2	44.8	20.6	58.8	41.2	24.9	50.2	49.8
Colorado	39.5	21.0	79.0	48.3	3.4	96.6	45.1	9.8	90.2
Connecticut	35.0	30.0	70.0	46.5	7.0	93.0	33.6	32.8	67.2
Delaware	43.5	13.0	87.0	54.6	9.2	90.8	41.1	17.8	82.2
Florida	81.1	62.2	37.8	87.6	75.2	24.8	77.0	54.0	46.0
Georgia	63.0	26.0	74.0	98.4	96.8	3.2	97.8	95.6	4.4
Hawaii	—	—	—	—	—	—	—	—	—
Idaho	34.5	31.0	69.0	37.0	26.0	74.0	30.3	39.4	60.6
Illinois	29.7	40.6	59.4	41.4	17.2	82.8	30.6	38.8	61.2
Indiana	42.6	14.8	85.2	49.0	2.0	98.0	44.1	11.8	88.2
Iowa	12.8	74.4	25.6	38.7	22.6	77.4	31.3	37.4	62.6
Kansas	37.1	25.8	74.2	45.1	9.8	90.2	44.6	10.8	89.2
Kentucky	51.4	2.8	97.2	58.5	17.0	83.0	57.4	14.8	85.2
Louisiana	100.0	100.0	0.0	100.0	100.0	0.0	100.0	100.0	0.0
Maine	33.3	33.4	66.6	42.4	15.2	84.8	39.7	20.6	79.4
Maryland	46.3	7.4	92.6	51.0	2.0	98.0	51.5	3.0	97.0
Massachusetts	32.1	35.8	64.2	42.2	15.6	84.4	39.1	21.8	78.2
Michigan	23.1	53.8	46.2	32.8	34.4	65.6	20.8	58.4	41.6
Minnesota	18.9	62.2	37.8	25.7	48.6	51.4	11.2	77.6	22.4
Mississippi	96.9	93.8	6.2	97.6	95.2	4.8	99.4	98.8	1.2
Missouri	45.0	10.0	90.0	50.9	1.8	98.2	49.0	2.0	98.0
Montana	38.2	23.6	76.4	50.9	1.8	98.2	47.9	4.2	95.8
Nebraska	34.4	31.2	68.8	49.2	1.6	98.4	47.8	4.4	95.6
Nevada	41.1	17.8	82.2	57.0	14.0	86.0	49.6	0.8	99.2
New Hampshire	39.4	21.2	78.8	51.0	2.0	98.0	41.7	16.6	83.4
New Jersey	36.3	27.4	72.6	50.0	0.0	100.0	37.1	25.8	74.2
New Mexico	47.5	5.0	95.0	54.4	8.8	91.2	51.8	3.6	96.4
New York	36.5	27.0	73.0	50.9	1.8	98.2	45.6	8.8	91.2
North Carolina	57.7	15.4	84.6	62.0	24.0	76.0	61.7	23.4	76.6
North Dakota	17.0	66.0	34.0	22.9	54.2	45.8	19.9	60.2	39.8
Ohio	41.5	17.0	83.0	45.5	9.0	91.0	42.2	15.6	84.4
Oklahoma	49.5	1.0	99.0	61.3	22.6	77.4	58.2	16.4	83.6
Oregon	23.9	52.2	47.8	29.9	40.2	59.8	35.3	29.4	70.6
Pennsylvania	29.0	42.0	58.0	38.4	23.2	76.8	28.9	42.2	57.8
Rhode Island	35.8	28.4	71.6	52.6	5.2	94.8	40.8	18.4	81.6
South Carolina	98.7	97.4	2.6	98.1	96.2	3.8	99.5	99.0	1.0
South Dakota	27.8	44.4	55.6	26.4	47.2	52.8	25.3	49.4	50.6
Tennessee	48.4	3.2	96.8	64.7	29.4	70.6	65.8	31.6	68.4
Texas	81.4	62.8	37.2	84.8	69.6	30.4	87.1	74.2	25.8
Utah	41.0	18.0	82.0	46.6	6.8	93.2	44.2	11.6	88.4
Vermont	23.3	53.4	46.6	35.5	29.0	71.0	20.5	59.0	41.0
Virginia	62.8	25.6	74.4	68.0	36.0	64.0	72.6	45.2	54.8
Washington	22.5	55.0	45.0	26.7	46.6	53.4	28.7	42.6	57.4
West Virginia	45.3	9.4	90.6	51.2	2.4	97.6	48.5	3.0	97.0
Wisconsin	20.1	59.8	40.2	7.4	85.2	14.8	23.6	52.8	47.2
Wyoming	30.1	39.8	60.2	46.7	6.6	93.4	39.9	20.2	79.8

Notes: The first entries are the Democratic percent of two-party vote values for each state for the House race. The second entries are the margin of victory values for each state for the House race, where margin of victory is defined as the absolute difference between the Democratic percent and the Republican percent of the two-party vote for the House. The third entries are the party competition index values for each state for the House race, where the competition index devised by Paul David (1972) is defined as (100 − the margin of victory) or, alternatively, as (100 − the absolute difference between the Democratic and Republican percent of two-party vote for the House). The values for Democratic and Republican percent of two-party vote for the House are taken from the state vote tables in Chapter 5. Zero (0) percent on David's index represents a complete absence of two-party competition for that election year, whereas a score of 100 percent indicates perfect competition between the two major parties. A state can only receive a party competition score of 0 if it has a 100–0 vote split in all House races in the state. Conversely, a state can only receive a score of 100 if it has a 50–50 vote split in all House races in the state. For example, if Pennsylvania in 1788 cast an average of 46.0 percent Democratic vote for all House races in the state of its two-party vote, then its average Republican vote for House would be 54.0 percent. The absolute difference between the two figures is the margin of victory, or 8 percent; 100 percent − 8 percent would equal 92 percent on David's party competition scale, indicating very competitive contests in House races in Pennsylvania in 1788. The two-party vote percent values used to derive the margin of victory and party competition figures are initially found in the state vote tables in Chapter 5. The author's alternative party coding in these tables is used whenever it occurs instead of the conventional party coding of voting data. The Democratic Party is defined here as the Anti-Federalists, Democratic-Republicans, and Jackson Democrats prior to 1830 when the "Democratic Party" as such was established. The Republican Party is defined as the Federalists, National Republicans, and Whigs prior to the establishment of the "Republican Party" in the 1850s. See Appendix A for an explanation of the historical antecedents of the current Democratic and Republican parties. States reporting only partial voting returns for House races are not included in the calculations for the years in which this occurred. —indicates that the state had no data, either because no vote data were found for the state in question or the state had not yet entered the Union.

Sources: State vote tables for House in Chapter 5.

Table 8-77 House Competition Measures, by State, by Election Year, 1926–1930 (Percentage)

State	1926 Democratic % of Two-Party Vote	1926 Margin of Victory	1926 Party Competition Index	1928 Democratic % of Two-Party Vote	1928 Margin of Victory	1928 Party Competition Index	1930 Democratic % of Two-Party Vote	1930 Margin of Victory	1930 Party Competition Index
Alabama	84.4	68.8	31.2	82.2	64.4	35.6	83.4	66.8	33.2
Alaska	—	—	—	—	—	—	—	—	—
Arizona	64.1	28.2	71.8	61.5	23.0	77.0	100.0	100.0	0.0
Arkansas	85.8	71.6	28.4	78.7	57.4	42.6	100.0	100.0	0.0
California	18.3	63.4	36.6	11.9	76.2	23.8	12.0	76.0	24.0
Colorado	45.1	9.8	90.2	40.1	19.8	80.2	46.6	6.8	93.2
Connecticut	35.7	28.6	71.4	45.7	8.6	91.4	49.0	2.0	98.0
Delaware	43.1	13.8	86.2	36.4	27.2	72.8	44.2	11.6	88.4
Florida	76.5	53.0	47.0	68.1	36.2	63.8	87.7	75.4	24.6
Georgia	100.0	100.0	0.0	100.0	100.0	0.0	97.3	94.6	5.4
Hawaii	—	—	—	—	—	—	—	—	—
Idaho	27.3	45.4	54.6	33.3	33.4	66.6	36.1	27.8	72.2
Illinois	39.0	22.0	78.0	40.6	18.8	81.2	51.7	3.4	96.6
Indiana	46.8	6.4	93.6	45.4	9.2	90.8	52.9	5.8	94.2
Iowa	30.9	38.2	61.8	29.0	42.0	58.0	39.2	21.6	78.4
Kansas	40.9	18.2	81.8	36.8	26.4	73.6	42.9	14.2	85.8
Kentucky	52.3	4.6	95.4	43.9	12.2	87.8	53.2	6.4	93.6
Louisiana	98.4	96.8	3.2	91.2	82.4	17.6	98.3	96.6	3.4
Maine	38.3	23.4	76.6	29.8	40.4	59.6	38.6	22.8	77.2
Maryland	56.0	12.0	88.0	49.1	1.8	98.2	59.2	18.4	81.6
Massachusetts	40.7	18.6	81.4	47.7	4.6	95.4	45.7	8.6	91.4
Michigan	21.8	56.4	43.6	26.7	46.6	53.4	23.2	53.6	46.4
Minnesota	8.9	82.2	17.8	24.9	50.2	49.8	13.7	72.6	27.4
Mississippi	100.0	100.0	0.0	100.0	100.0	0.0	100.0	100.0	0.0
Missouri	50.6	1.2	98.8	47.9	4.2	95.8	50.5	1.0	99.0
Montana	50.4	0.8	99.2	42.9	14.2	85.8	50.6	1.2	98.8
Nebraska	50.7	1.4	98.6	44.6	10.8	89.2	52.1	4.2	95.8
Nevada	42.3	15.4	84.6	41.4	17.2	82.8	45.6	8.8	91.2
New Hampshire	37.8	24.4	75.6	41.2	17.6	82.4	42.3	15.4	84.6
New Jersey	43.1	13.8	86.2	39.3	21.4	78.6	43.2	13.6	86.4
New Mexico	51.6	3.2	96.8	47.8	4.4	95.6	55.9	11.8	88.2
New York	49.2	1.6	98.4	49.0	2.0	98.0	54.0	8.0	92.0
North Carolina	61.3	22.6	77.4	55.1	10.2	89.8	62.8	25.6	74.4
North Dakota	18.4	63.2	36.8	25.7	48.6	51.4	29.2	41.6	58.4
Ohio	43.7	12.6	87.4	39.2	21.6	78.4	48.8	2.4	97.6
Oklahoma	56.5	13.0	87.0	50.2	0.4	99.6	61.9	23.8	76.2
Oregon	28.8	42.4	57.6	30.3	39.4	60.6	47.9	4.2	95.8
Pennsylvania	26.5	47.0	53.0	30.6	38.8	61.2	28.4	43.2	56.8
Rhode Island	41.9	16.2	83.8	48.7	2.6	97.4	48.3	3.4	96.6
South Carolina	100.0	100.0	0.0	100.0	100.0	0.0	100.0	100.0	0.0
South Dakota	41.4	17.2	82.8	42.3	15.4	84.6	34.4	31.2	68.8
Tennessee	70.0	40.0	60.0	60.5	21.0	79.0	63.1	26.2	73.8
Texas	97.2	94.4	5.6	87.5	75.0	25.0	84.6	69.2	30.8
Utah	38.6	22.8	77.2	44.5	11.0	89.0	43.7	12.6	87.4
Vermont	23.9	52.2	47.8	28.6	42.8	57.2	32.6	34.8	65.2
Virginia	69.4	38.8	61.2	67.9	35.8	64.2	66.2	32.4	67.6
Washington	29.4	41.2	58.8	31.6	36.8	63.2	26.8	46.4	53.6
West Virginia	48.3	3.4	96.6	45.7	8.6	91.4	50.6	1.2	98.8
Wisconsin	8.4	83.2	16.8	28.2	43.6	56.4	15.6	68.8	31.2
Wyoming	38.9	22.2	77.8	48.0	4.0	96.0	34.4	31.2	68.8

Notes: The first entries are the Democratic percent of two-party vote values for each state for the House race. The second entries are the margin of victory values for each state for the House race, where margin of victory is defined as the absolute difference between the Democratic percent and the Republican percent of the two-party vote for the House. The third entries are the party competition index values for each state for the House race, where the competition index devised by Paul David (1972) is defined as (100 − the margin of victory) or, alternatively, as (100 − the absolute difference between the Democratic and Republican percent of two-party vote for the House). The values for Democratic and Republican percent of two-party vote for the House are taken from the state vote tables in Chapter 5. Zero (0) percent on David's index represents a complete absence of two-party competition for that election year, whereas a score of 100 percent indicates perfect competition between the two major parties. A state can only receive a party competition score of 0 if it has a 100–0 vote split in all House races in the state. Conversely, a state can only receive a score of 100 if it has a 50–50 vote split in all House races in the state. For example, if Pennsylvania in 1788 cast an average of 46.0 percent Democratic vote for all House races in the state of its two-party vote, then its average Republican vote for House would be 54.0 percent. The absolute difference between the two figures is the margin of victory, or 8 percent; 100 percent − 8 percent would equal 92 percent on David's party competition scale, indicating very competitive contests in House races in Pennsylvania in 1788. The two-party vote percent values used to derive the margin of victory and party competition figures are initially found in the state vote tables in Chapter 5. The author's alternative party coding in these tables is used whenever it occurs instead of the conventional party coding of voting data. The Democratic Party is defined here as the Anti-Federalists, Democratic-Republicans, and Jackson Democrats prior to 1830 when the "Democratic Party" as such was established. The Republican Party is defined as the Federalists, National Republicans, and Whigs prior to the establishment of the "Republican Party" in the 1850s. See Appendix A for an explanation of the historical antecedents of the current Democratic and Republican parties. States reporting only partial voting returns for House races are not included in the calculations for the years in which this occurred. —indicates that the state had no data, either because no vote data were found for the state in question or the state had not yet entered the Union.

Sources: State vote tables for House in Chapter 5.

Table 8-78 House Competition Measures, by State, by Election Year, 1932–1936 (Percentages)

	1932			1934			1936		
State	Democratic % of Two-Party Vote	Margin of Victory	Party Competition Index	Democratic % of Two-Party Vote	Margin of Victory	Party Competition Index	Democratic % of Two-Party Vote	Margin of Victory	Party Competition Index
Alabama	90.2	80.4	19.6	93.6	87.2	12.8	93.7	87.4	12.6
Alaska	—	—	—	—	—	—	—	—	—
Arizona	71.8	43.6	56.4	70.0	40.0	60.0	80.5	61.0	39.0
Arkansas	97.7	95.4	4.6	92.7	85.4	14.6	92.0	84.0	16.0
California	47.4	5.2	94.8	53.5	7.0	93.0	55.4	10.8	89.2
Colorado	55.0	10.0	90.0	62.9	25.8	74.2	62.5	25.0	75.0
Connecticut	49.4	1.2	98.8	51.6	3.2	96.8	56.8	13.6	86.4
Delaware	51.4	2.8	97.2	46.7	6.6	93.4	51.8	3.6	96.4
Florida	75.2	50.4	49.6	100.0	100.0	0.0	81.9	63.8	36.2
Georgia	94.8	89.6	10.4	99.5	99.0	1.0	94.3	88.6	11.4
Hawaii	—	—	—	—	—	—	—	—	—
Idaho	56.1	12.2	87.8	61.2	22.4	77.6	64.7	29.4	70.6
Illinois	54.1	8.2	91.8	55.7	11.4	88.6	56.8	13.6	86.4
Indiana	55.4	10.8	89.2	52.5	5.0	95.0	56.3	12.6	87.4
Iowa	53.0	6.0	94.0	53.5	7.0	93.0	50.4	0.8	99.2
Kansas	50.5	1.0	99.0	49.2	1.6	98.4	47.8	4.4	95.6
Kentucky	59.5	19.0	81.0	55.3	10.6	89.4	59.4	18.8	81.2
Louisiana	100.0	100.0	0.0	100.0	100.0	0.0	100.0	100.0	0.0
Maine	50.4	0.8	99.2	51.0	2.0	98.0	41.2	17.6	82.4
Maryland	66.6	33.2	66.8	59.7	19.4	80.6	59.9	19.8	80.2
Massachusetts	48.2	3.6	96.4	46.8	6.4	93.6	48.0	4.0	96.0
Michigan	49.9	0.2	99.8	49.4	1.2	98.8	53.7	7.4	92.6
Minnesota	48.8	2.4	97.6	44.2	11.6	88.4	31.2	37.6	62.4
Mississippi	96.5	93.0	7.0	100.0	100.0	0.0	98.7	97.4	2.6
Missouri	62.5	25.0	75.0	60.8	21.6	78.4	60.4	20.8	79.2
Montana	56.9	13.8	86.2	69.6	39.2	60.8	64.5	29.0	71.0
Nebraska	58.6	17.2	82.8	54.4	8.8	91.2	52.5	5.0	95.0
Nevada	60.8	21.6	78.4	71.2	42.4	57.6	68.5	37.0	63.0
New Hampshire	49.2	1.6	98.4	50.5	1.0	99.0	47.8	4.4	95.6
New Jersey	49.1	1.8	98.2	51.4	2.8	97.2	54.0	8.0	92.0
New Mexico	64.2	28.4	71.6	52.1	4.2	95.8	62.9	25.8	74.2
New York	57.4	14.8	85.2	58.3	16.6	83.4	59.2	18.4	81.6
North Carolina	69.7	39.4	60.6	64.9	29.8	70.2	71.2	42.4	57.6
North Dakota	33.5	33.0	67.0	37.2	25.6	74.4	43.4	13.2	86.8
Ohio	52.1	4.2	95.8	54.0	8.0	92.0	55.9	11.8	88.2
Oklahoma	73.2	46.4	53.6	68.5	37.0	63.0	71.1	42.2	57.8
Oregon	52.6	5.2	94.8	47.9	4.2	95.8	50.4	0.8	99.2
Pennsylvania	41.9	16.2	83.8	56.2	12.4	87.6	56.7	13.4	86.6
Rhode Island	55.2	10.4	89.6	57.4	14.8	85.2	52.8	5.6	94.4
South Carolina	98.1	96.2	3.8	99.8	99.6	0.4	99.2	98.4	1.6
South Dakota	54.8	9.6	90.4	57.5	15.0	85.0	50.1	0.2	99.8
Tennessee	71.1	42.2	57.8	73.7	47.4	52.6	72.7	45.4	54.6
Texas	92.9	85.8	14.2	98.7	97.4	2.6	93.6	87.2	12.8
Utah	54.6	9.2	90.8	64.1	28.2	71.8	69.7	39.4	60.6
Vermont	35.6	28.8	71.2	42.7	14.6	85.4	40.4	19.2	80.8
Virginia	69.1	38.2	61.8	76.1	52.2	47.8	72.9	45.8	54.2
Washington	63.7	27.4	72.6	67.5	35.0	65.0	66.0	32.0	68.0
West Virginia	53.5	7.0	93.0	55.9	11.8	88.2	60.0	20.0	80.0
Wisconsin	51.6	3.2	96.8	56.5	13.0	87.0	50.6	1.2	98.8
Wyoming	49.0	2.0	98.0	58.7	17.4	82.6	57.6	15.2	84.8

Notes: The first entries are the Democratic percent of two-party vote values for each state for the House race. The second entries are the margin of victory values for each state for the House race, where margin of victory is defined as the absolute difference between the Democratic percent and the Republican percent of the two-party vote for the House. The third entries are the party competition index values for each state for the House race, where the competition index devised by Paul David (1972) is defined as (100 − the margin of victory) or, alternatively, as (100 − the absolute difference between the Democratic and Republican percent of two-party vote for the House). The values for Democratic and Republican percent of two-party vote for the House are taken from the state vote tables in Chapter 5. Zero (0) percent on David's index represents a complete absence of two-party competition for that election year, whereas a score of 100 percent indicates perfect competition between the two major parties. A state can only receive a party competition score of 0 if it has a 100–0 vote split in all House races in the state. Conversely, a state can only receive a score of 100 if it has a 50–50 vote split in all House races in the state. For example, if Pennsylvania in 1788 cast an average of 46.0 percent Democratic vote for all House races in the state of its two-party vote, then its average Republican vote for House would be 54.0 percent. The absolute difference between the two figures is the margin of victory, or 8 percent; 100 percent − 8 percent would equal 92 percent on David's party competition scale, indicating very competitive contests in House races in Pennsylvania in 1788. The two-party vote percent values used to derive the margin of victory and party competition figures are initially found in the state vote tables in Chapter 5. The author's alternative party coding in these tables is used whenever it occurs instead of the conventional party coding of voting data. The Democratic Party is defined here as the Anti-Federalists, Democratic-Republicans, and Jackson Democrats prior to 1830 when the "Democratic Party" as such was established. The Republican Party is defined as the Federalists, National Republicans, and Whigs prior to the establishment of the "Republican Party" in the 1850s. See Appendix A for an explanation of the historical antecedents of the current Democratic and Republican parties. States reporting only partial voting returns for House races are not included in the calculations for the years in which this occurred. —indicates that the state had no data, either because no vote data were found for the state in question or the state had not yet entered the Union.

Sources: State vote tables for House in Chapter 5.

Table 8-79 House Competition Measures, by State, by Election Year, 1938–1942 (Percentages)

| | 1938 | | | 1940 | | | 1942 | | |
State	Democratic % of Two-Party Vote	Margin of Victory	Party Competition Index	Democratic % of Two-Party Vote	Margin of Victory	Party Competition Index	Democratic % of Two-Party Vote	Margin of Victory	Party Competition Index
Alabama	92.3	84.6	15.4	94.5	89.0	11.0	99.5	99.0	1.0
Alaska	—	—	—	—	—	—	—	—	—
Arizona	80.3	60.6	39.4	71.1	42.2	57.8	71.0	42.0	58.0
Arkansas	100.0	100.0	0.0	95.9	91.8	8.2	100.0	100.0	0.0
California	49.8	0.4	99.6	44.6	10.8	89.2	49.2	1.6	98.4
Colorado	59.3	18.6	81.4	54.7	9.4	90.6	41.6	16.8	83.2
Connecticut	48.0	4.0	96.0	52.7	5.4	94.6	47.7	4.6	95.4
Delaware	43.3	13.4	86.6	52.2	4.4	95.6	46.1	7.8	92.2
Florida	95.6	91.2	8.8	86.2	72.4	27.6	100.0	100.0	0.0
Georgia	100.0	100.0	0.0	96.4	92.8	7.2	100.0	100.0	0.0
Hawaii	—	—	—	—	—	—	—	—	—
Idaho	53.5	7.0	93.0	53.5	7.0	93.0	48.8	2.4	97.6
Illinois	51.6	3.2	96.8	49.0	2.0	98.0	48.5	3.0	97.0
Indiana	49.2	1.6	98.4	49.1	1.8	98.2	44.5	11.0	89.0
Iowa	44.1	11.8	88.2	45.2	9.6	90.4	38.1	23.8	76.2
Kansas	41.0	18.0	82.0	42.3	15.4	84.6	39.4	21.2	78.8
Kentucky	59.1	18.2	81.8	62.5	25.0	75.0	57.1	14.2	85.8
Louisiana	100.0	100.0	0.0	95.7	91.4	8.6	100.0	100.0	0.0
Maine	41.5	17.0	83.0	35.4	29.2	70.8	30.4	39.2	60.8
Maryland	60.2	20.4	79.6	60.9	21.8	78.2	56.3	12.6	87.4
Massachusetts	46.1	7.8	92.2	47.5	5.0	95.0	46.2	7.6	92.4
Michigan	46.3	7.4	92.6	48.9	2.2	97.8	45.9	8.2	91.8
Minnesota	26.1	47.8	52.2	29.0	42.0	58.0	25.7	48.6	51.4
Mississippi	100.0	100.0	0.0	100.0	100.0	0.0	100.0	100.0	0.0
Missouri	59.3	18.6	81.4	52.4	4.8	95.2	48.4	3.2	96.8
Montana	50.2	0.4	99.6	55.1	10.2	89.8	55.9	11.8	88.2
Nebraska	46.8	6.4	93.6	42.0	16.0	84.0	34.9	30.2	69.8
Nevada	66.4	32.8	67.2	64.5	29.0	71.0	53.6	7.2	92.8
New Hampshire	43.7	12.6	87.4	48.0	4.0	96.0	44.9	10.2	89.8
New Jersey	47.5	5.0	95.0	47.1	5.8	94.2	45.7	8.6	91.4
New Mexico	58.5	17.0	83.0	58.8	17.6	82.4	58.8	17.6	82.4
New York	54.0	8.0	92.0	53.1	6.2	93.8	49.3	1.4	98.6
North Carolina	66.5	33.0	67.0	75.5	51.0	49.0	72.7	45.4	54.6
North Dakota	26.5	47.0	53.0	30.0	40.0	60.0	26.3	47.4	52.6
Ohio	47.6	4.8	95.2	49.4	1.2	98.8	43.1	13.8	86.2
Oklahoma	69.0	38.0	62.0	66.1	32.2	67.8	57.8	15.6	84.4
Oregon	41.4	17.2	82.8	41.9	16.2	83.8	41.8	16.4	83.6
Pennsylvania	46.7	6.6	93.4	52.1	4.2	95.8	44.8	10.4	89.6
Rhode Island	46.3	7.4	92.6	55.6	11.2	88.8	58.2	16.4	83.6
South Carolina	99.3	98.6	1.4	98.5	97.0	3.0	100.0	100.0	0.0
South Dakota	44.2	11.6	88.4	38.9	22.2	77.8	37.3	25.4	74.6
Tennessee	72.7	45.4	54.6	72.4	44.8	55.2	66.1	32.2	67.8
Texas	99.0	98.0	2.0	96.8	93.6	6.4	98.9	97.8	2.2
Utah	61.0	22.0	78.0	60.6	21.2	78.8	53.1	6.2	93.8
Vermont	35.4	29.2	70.8	36.2	27.6	72.4	29.8	40.4	59.6
Virginia	78.9	57.8	42.2	80.7	61.4	38.6	86.5	73.0	27.0
Washington	61.1	22.2	77.8	57.9	15.8	84.2	52.7	5.4	94.6
West Virginia	55.1	10.2	89.8	57.5	15.0	85.0	49.7	0.6	99.4
Wisconsin	29.4	41.2	58.8	27.6	44.8	55.2	36.7	26.6	73.4
Wyoming	47.1	5.8	94.2	53.4	6.8	93.2	49.3	1.4	98.6

Notes: The first entries are the Democratic percent of two-party vote values for each state for the House race. The second entries are the margin of victory values for each state for the House race, where margin of victory is defined as the absolute difference between the Democratic percent and the Republican percent of the two-party vote for the House. The third entries are the party competition index values for each state for the House race, where the competition index devised by Paul David (1972) is defined as (100 − the margin of victory) or, alternatively, as (100 − the absolute difference between the Democratic and Republican percent of two-party vote for the House). The values for Democratic and Republican percent of two-party vote for the House are taken from the state vote tables in Chapter 5. Zero (0) percent on David's index represents a complete absence of two-party competition for that election year, whereas a score of 100 percent indicates perfect competition between the two major parties. A state can only receive a party competition score of 0 if it has a 100–0 vote split in all House races in the state. Conversely, a state can only receive a score of 100 if it has a 50–50 vote split in all House races in the state. For example, if Pennsylvania in 1788 cast an average of 46.0 percent Democratic vote for all House races in the state of its two-party vote, then its average Republican vote for House would be 54.0 percent. The absolute difference between the two figures is the margin of victory, or 8 percent; 100 percent − 8 percent would equal 92 percent on David's party competition scale, indicating very competitive contests in House races in Pennsylvania in 1788. The two-party vote percent values used to derive the margin of victory and party competition figures are initially found in the state vote tables in Chapter 5. The author's alternative party coding in these tables is used whenever it occurs instead of the conventional party coding of voting data. The Democratic Party is defined here as the Anti-Federalists, Democratic-Republicans, and Jackson Democrats prior to 1830 when the "Democratic Party" as such was established. The Republican Party is defined as the Federalists, National Republicans, and Whigs prior to the establishment of the "Republican Party" in the 1850s. See Appendix A for an explanation of the historical antecedents of the current Democratic and Republican parties. States reporting only partial voting returns for House races are not included in the calculations for the years in which this occurred. —indicates that the state had no data, either because no vote data were found for the state in question or the state had not yet entered the Union.

Sources: State vote tables for House in Chapter 5.

Table 8-80 House Competition Measures, by State, by Election Year, 1944–1948

	1944			1946			1948		
State	Democratic % of Two-Party Vote	Margin of Victory	Party Competition Index	Democratic % of Two-Party Vote	Margin of Victory	Party Competition Index	Democratic % of Two-Party Vote	Margin of Victory	Party Competition Index
Alabama	90.2	80.4	19.6	92.1	84.2	15.8	93.1	86.2	13.8
Alaska	—	—	—	—	—	—	—	—	—
Arizona	69.4	38.8	61.2	66.9	33.8	66.2	61.7	23.4	76.6
Arkansas	92.4	84.8	15.2	94.7	89.4	10.6	91.4	82.8	17.2
California	50.7	1.4	98.6	47.9	4.2	95.8	40.6	18.8	81.2
Colorado	42.8	14.4	85.6	44.1	11.8	88.2	54.8	9.6	90.4
Connecticut	51.6	3.2	96.8	42.4	15.2	84.8	49.8	0.4	99.6
Delaware	50.5	1.0	99.0	43.6	12.8	87.2	49.2	1.6	98.4
Florida	84.7	69.4	30.6	80.9	61.8	38.2	84.1	68.2	31.8
Georgia	100.0	100.0	0.0	100.0	100.0	0.0	100.0	100.0	0.0
Hawaii	—	—	—	—	—	—	—	—	—
Idaho	51.5	3.0	97.0	43.5	13.0	87.0	50.7	1.4	98.6
Illinois	52.5	5.0	95.0	44.7	10.6	89.4	52.3	4.6	95.4
Indiana	46.8	6.4	93.6	44.8	10.4	89.6	51.7	3.4	96.6
Iowa	43.2	13.6	86.4	38.5	23.0	77.0	45.3	9.4	90.6
Kansas	37.0	26.0	74.0	40.4	19.2	80.8	42.5	15.0	85.0
Kentucky	54.7	9.4	90.6	46.6	6.8	93.2	56.5	13.0	87.0
Louisiana	100.0	100.0	0.0	94.7	89.4	10.6	95.8	91.6	8.4
Maine	29.3	41.4	58.6	36.6	26.8	73.2	33.7	32.6	67.4
Maryland	56.4	12.8	87.2	52.3	4.6	95.4	55.8	11.6	88.4
Massachusetts	47.0	6.0	94.0	46.3	7.4	92.6	50.2	0.4	99.6
Michigan	47.7	4.6	95.4	38.8	22.4	77.6	50.0	0.0	100.0
Minnesota	40.9	18.2	81.8	41.0	18.0	82.0	49.8	0.4	99.6
Mississippi	96.6	93.2	6.8	100.0	100.0	0.0	99.8	99.6	0.4
Missouri	52.5	5.0	95.0	47.8	4.4	95.6	58.8	17.6	82.4
Montana	60.4	20.8	79.2	50.7	1.4	98.6	57.5	15.0	85.0
Nebraska	33.0	34.0	66.0	32.3	35.4	64.6	41.7	16.6	83.4
Nevada	63.1	26.2	73.8	41.2	17.6	82.4	50.6	1.2	98.8
New Hampshire	47.4	5.2	94.8	38.0	24.0	76.0	43.2	13.6	86.4
New Jersey	46.5	7.0	93.0	40.5	19.0	81.0	48.4	3.2	96.8
New Mexico	56.2	12.4	87.6	52.3	4.6	95.4	58.6	17.2	82.8
New York	52.3	4.6	95.4	43.3	13.4	86.6	26.0	48.0	52.0
North Carolina	69.5	39.0	61.0	61.3	22.6	77.4	71.2	42.4	57.6
North Dakota	28.7	42.6	57.4	28.5	43.0	57.0	30.0	40.0	60.0
Ohio	46.9	6.2	93.8	40.5	19.0	81.0	52.0	4.0	96.0
Oklahoma	58.7	17.4	82.6	58.5	17.0	83.0	67.3	34.6	65.4
Oregon	38.5	23.0	77.0	35.2	29.6	70.4	37.3	25.4	74.6
Pennsylvania	50.7	1.4	98.6	42.1	15.8	84.2	48.9	2.2	97.8
Rhode Island	59.8	19.6	80.4	54.7	9.4	90.6	60.8	21.6	78.4
South Carolina	96.5	93.0	7.0	99.1	98.2	·1.8	95.1	90.2	9.8
South Dakota	34.9	30.2	69.8	35.7	28.6	71.4	43.6	12.8	87.2
Tennessee	66.4	32.8	67.2	69.7	39.4	60.6	65.3	30.6	69.4
Texas	94.0	88.0	12.0	95.1	90.2	9.8	93.8	87.6	12.4
Utah	60.4	20.8	79.2	48.6	2.8	97.2	58.1	16.2	83.8
Vermont	37.6	24.8	75.2	35.7	28.6	71.4	39.2	21.6	78.4
Virginia	75.6	51.2	48.8	66.8	33.6	66.4	67.7	35.4	64.6
Washington	53.1	6.2	93.8	41.6	16.8	83.2	50.1	0.2	99.8
West Virginia	54.2	8.4	91.6	50.1	0.2	99.8	58.3	16.6	83.4
Wisconsin	39.5	21.0	79.0	33.7	32.6	67.4	43.2	13.6	86.4
Wyoming	44.3	11.4	88.6	44.0	12.0	88.0	48.5	3.0	97.0

Notes: The first entries are the Democratic percent of two-party vote values for each state for the House race. The second entries are the margin of victory values for each state for the House race, where margin of victory is defined as the absolute difference between the Democratic percent and the Republican percent of the two-party vote for the House. The third entries are the party competition index values for each state for the House race, where the competition index devised by Paul David (1972) is defined as (100 − the margin of victory) or, alternatively, as (100 − the absolute difference between the Democratic and Republican percent of two-party vote for the House). The values for Democratic and Republican percent of two-party vote for the House are taken from the state vote tables in Chapter 5. Zero (0) percent on David's index represents a complete absence of two-party competition for that election year, whereas a score of 100 percent indicates perfect competition between the two major parties. A state can only receive a party competition score of 0 if it has a 100–0 vote split in all House races in the state. Conversely, a state can only receive a score of 100 if it has a 50–50 vote split in all House races in the state. For example, if Pennsylvania in 1788 cast an average of 46.0 percent Democratic vote for all House races in the state of its two-party vote, then its average Republican vote for House would be 54.0 percent. The absolute difference between the two figures is the margin of victory, or 8 percent; 100 percent − 8 percent would equal 92 percent on David's party competition scale, indicating very competitive contests in House races in Pennsylvania in 1788. The two-party vote percent values used to derive the margin of victory and party competition figures are initially found in the state vote tables in Chapter 5. The author's alternative party coding in these tables is used whenever it occurs instead of the conventional party coding of voting data. The Democratic Party is defined here as the Anti-Federalists, Democratic-Republicans, and Jackson Democrats prior to 1830 when the "Democratic Party" as such was established. The Republican Party is defined as the Federalists, National Republicans, and Whigs prior to the establishment of the "Republican Party" in the 1850s. See Appendix A for an explanation of the historical antecedents of the current Democratic and Republican parties. States reporting only partial voting returns for House races are not included in the calculations for the years in which this occurred. —indicates that the state had no data, either because no vote data were found for the state in question or the state had not yet entered the Union.

Sources: State vote tables for House in Chapter 5.

Table 8-81 House Competition Measures, by State, by Election Year, 1950–1954 (Percentages)

State	1950 Democratic % of Two-Party Vote	1950 Margin of Victory	1950 Party Competition Index	1952 Democratic % of Two-Party Vote	1952 Margin of Victory	1952 Party Competition Index	1954 Democratic % of Two-Party Vote	1954 Margin of Victory	1954 Party Competition Index
Alabama	99.4	98.8	1.2	94.6	89.2	10.8	96.0	92.0	8.0
Alaska	—	—	—	—	—	—	—	—	—
Arizona	65.0	30.0	70.0	51.5	3.0	97.0	54.3	8.6	91.4
Arkansas	100.0	100.0	0.0	85.6	71.2	28.8	100.0	100.0	0.0
California	45.8	8.4	91.6	46.0	8.0	92.0	51.5	3.0	97.0
Colorado	48.7	2.6	97.4	44.6	10.8	89.2	49.9	0.2	99.8
Connecticut	49.6	0.8	99.2	44.9	10.2	89.8	49.0	2.0	98.0
Delaware	43.3	13.4	86.6	48.1	3.8	96.2	54.9	9.8	90.2
Florida	90.4	80.8	19.2	74.2	48.4	51.6	78.2	56.4	43.6
Georgia	100.0	100.0	0.0	100.0	100.0	0.0	91.4	82.8	17.2
Hawaii	—	—	—	—	—	—	—	—	—
Idaho	45.6	8.8	91.2	40.6	18.8	81.2	45.5	9.0	91.0
Illinois	46.1	7.8	92.2	46.0	8.0	92.0	50.2	0.4	99.6
Indiana	46.1	7.8	92.2	43.2	13.6	86.4	47.3	5.4	94.6
Iowa	38.8	22.4	77.6	33.2	33.6	66.4	41.5	17.0	83.0
Kansas	41.2	17.6	82.4	40.6	18.8	81.2	43.5	13.0	87.0
Kentucky	63.0	26.0	74.0	52.1	4.2	95.8	64.7	29.4	70.6
Louisiana	100.0	100.0	0.0	91.3	82.6	17.4	96.2	92.4	7.6
Maine	42.4	15.2	84.8	33.1	33.8	66.2	45.0	10.0	90.0
Maryland	49.8	0.4	99.6	48.2	3.6	96.4	53.7	7.4	92.6
Massachusetts	49.7	0.6	99.4	46.8	6.4	93.6	53.2	6.4	93.6
Michigan	46.7	6.6	93.4	47.5	5.0	95.0	51.7	3.4	96.6
Minnesota	46.8	6.4	93.6	46.0	8.0	92.0	53.0	6.0	94.0
Mississippi	96.7	93.4	6.6	97.5	95.0	5.0	100.0	100.0	0.0
Missouri	55.8	11.6	88.4	52.2	4.4	95.6	56.2	12.4	87.6
Montana	52.0	4.0	96.0	43.5	13.0	87.0	52.1	4.2	95.8
Nebraska	37.7	24.6	75.4	31.8	36.4	63.6	38.4	23.2	76.8
Nevada	52.8	5.6	94.4	49.5	1.0	99.0	45.5	9.0	91.0
New Hampshire	39.3	21.4	78.6	36.9	26.2	73.8	45.3	9.4	90.6
New Jersey	44.5	11.0	89.0	42.6	14.8	85.2	48.8	2.4	97.6
New Mexico	56.3	12.6	87.4	52.0	4.0	96.0	59.1	18.2	81.8
New York	50.0	0.0	100.0	46.1	7.8	92.2	49.3	1.4	98.6
North Carolina	70.0	40.0	60.0	68.0	36.0	64.0	64.6	29.2	70.8
North Dakota	34.4	31.2	68.8	21.6	56.8	43.2	33.9	32.2	67.8
Ohio	46.1	7.8	92.2	44.5	11.0	89.0	45.4	9.2	90.8
Oklahoma	59.9	19.8	80.2	58.7	17.4	82.6	64.9	29.8	70.2
Oregon	41.1	17.8	82.2	38.7	22.6	77.4	45.5	9.0	91.0
Pennsylvania	47.7	4.6	95.4	47.7	4.6	95.4	50.6	1.2	98.8
Rhode Island	61.9	23.8	76.2	54.1	8.2	91.8	59.9	19.8	80.2
South Carolina	100.0	100.0	0.0	98.0	96.0	4.0	98.7	97.4	2.6
South Dakota	39.3	21.4	78.6	31.4	37.2	62.8	40.6	18.8	81.2
Tennessee	63.0	26.0	74.0	70.2	40.4	59.6	67.4	34.8	65.2
Texas	90.5	81.0	19.0	100.0	100.0	0.0	88.0	76.0	24.0
Utah	52.5	5.0	95.0	44.4	11.2	88.8	44.3	11.4	88.6
Vermont	25.8	48.4	51.6	28.2	43.6	56.4	38.6	22.8	77.2
Virginia	75.1	50.2	49.8	68.3	36.6	63.4	61.4	22.8	77.2
Washington	47.5	5.0	95.0	50.5	1.0	99.0	57.6	15.2	84.8
West Virginia	56.6	13.2	86.8	53.9	7.8	92.2	57.5	15.0	85.0
Wisconsin	42.4	15.2	84.8	38.4	23.2	76.8	47.5	5.0	95.0
Wyoming	45.5	9.0	91.0	39.9	20.2	79.8	43.8	12.4	87.6

Notes: The first entries are the Democratic percent of two-party vote values for each state for the House race. The second entries are the margin of victory values for each state for the House race, where margin of victory is defined as the absolute difference between the Democratic percent and the Republican percent of the two-party vote for the House. The third entries are the party competition index values for each state for the House race, where the competition index devised by Paul David (1972) is defined as (100 − the margin of victory) or, alternatively, as (100 − the absolute difference between the Democratic and Republican percent of two-party vote for the House). The values for Democratic and Republican percent of two-party vote for the House are taken from the state vote tables in Chapter 5. Zero (0) percent on David's index represents a complete absence of two-party competition for that election year, whereas a score of 100 percent indicates perfect competition between the two major parties. A state can only receive a party competition score of 0 if it has a 100–0 vote split in all House races in the state. Conversely, a state can only receive a score of 100 if it has a 50–50 vote split in all House races in the state. For example, if Pennsylvania in 1788 cast an average of 46.0 percent Democratic vote for all House races in the state of its two-party vote, then its average Republican vote for House would be 54.0 percent. The absolute difference between the two figures is the margin of victory, or 8 percent; 100 percent − 8 percent would equal 92 percent on David's party competition scale, indicating very competitive contests in House races in Pennsylvania in 1788. The two-party vote percent values used to derive the margin of victory and party competition figures are initially found in the state vote tables in Chapter 5. The author's alternative party coding in these tables is used whenever it occurs instead of the conventional party coding of voting data. The Democratic Party is defined here as the Anti-Federalists, Democratic-Republicans, and Jackson Democrats prior to 1830 when the "Democratic Party" as such was established. The Republican Party is defined as the Federalists, National Republicans, and Whigs prior to the establishment of the "Republican Party" in the 1850s. See Appendix A for an explanation of the historical antecedents of the current Democratic and Republican parties. States reporting only partial voting returns for House races are not included in the calculations for the years in which this occurred. —indicates that the state had no data, either because no vote data were found for the state in question or the state had not yet entered the Union.

Sources: State vote tables for House in Chapter 5.

Table 8-82 House Competition Measures, by State, by Two-Year Election Cycle, 1956–1960 (Percentages)

	1956			1958–1959			1960		
State	Democratic % of Two-Party Vote	Margin of Victory	Party Competition Index	Democratic % of Two-Party Vote	Margin of Victory	Party Competition Index	Democratic % of Two-Party Vote	Margin of Victory	Party Competition Index
Alabama	86.5	73.0	27.0	97.4	94.8	5.2	89.0	78.0	22.0
Alaska	—	—	—	57.4	14.8	85.2	56.8	13.6	86.4
Arizona	52.4	4.8	95.2	50.2	0.4	99.6	47.6	4.8	95.2
Arkansas	90.6	81.2	18.8	—	—	—	—	—	—
California	52.4	4.8	95.2	60.0	20.0	80.0	53.9	7.8	92.2
Colorado	52.8	5.6	94.4	58.2	16.4	83.6	51.8	3.6	96.4
Connecticut	38.5	23.0	77.0	56.0	12.0	88.0	54.0	8.0	92.0
Delaware	48.0	4.0	96.0	50.2	0.4	99.6	50.5	1.0	99.0
Florida	62.6	25.2	74.8	71.8	43.6	56.4	69.0	38.0	62.0
Georgia	89.9	79.8	20.2	100.0	100.0	0.0	95.8	91.6	8.4
Hawaii	—	—	—	68.6[1]	37.2[1]	62.8[1]	74.4	48.8	51.2
Idaho	46.4	7.2	92.8	52.0	4.0	96.0	54.8	9.6	90.4
Illinois	46.4	7.2	92.8	54.4	8.8	91.2	51.5	3.0	97.0
Indiana	44.2	11.6	88.4	53.6	7.2	92.8	48.7	2.6	97.4
Iowa	45.6	8.8	91.2	50.3	0.6	99.4	45.9	8.2	91.8
Kansas	46.9	6.2	93.8	50.4	0.8	99.2	45.8	8.4	91.6
Kentucky	52.2	4.4	95.6	65.3	30.6	69.4	59.1	18.2	81.8
Louisiana	85.2	70.4	29.6	97.7	95.4	4.6	85.0	70.0	30.0
Maine	48.6	2.8	97.2	53.2	6.4	93.6	43.5	13.0	87.0
Maryland	51.3	2.6	97.4	65.1	30.2	69.8	59.4	18.8	81.2
Massachusetts	48.6	2.8	97.2	57.5	15.0	85.0	61.0	22.0	78.0
Michigan	49.8	0.4	99.6	53.1	6.2	93.8	51.1	2.2	97.8
Minnesota	51.3	2.6	97.4	52.7	5.4	94.6	50.3	0.6	99.4
Mississippi	100.0	100.0	0.0	100.0	100.0	0.0	98.0	96.0	4.0
Missouri	59.7	19.4	80.6	63.2	26.4	73.6	57.7	15.4	84.6
Montana	55.6	11.2	88.8	64.7	29.4	70.6	50.9	1.8	98.2
Nebraska	40.5	19.0	81.0	47.0	6.0	94.0	43.5	13.0	87.0
Nevada	54.2	8.4	91.6	66.9	33.8	66.2	57.5	15.0	85.0
New Hampshire	38.7	22.6	77.4	41.3	17.4	82.6	41.8	16.4	83.6
New Jersey	41.1	17.8	82.2	49.8	0.4	99.6	48.4	3.2	96.8
New Mexico	53.1	6.2	93.8	63.1	26.2	73.8	58.8	17.6	82.4
New York	45.1	9.8	90.2	50.7	1.4	98.6	52.6	5.2	94.8
North Carolina	69.9	39.8	60.2	70.8	41.6	58.4	60.4	20.8	79.2
North Dakota	37.4	25.2	74.8	50.4	0.8	99.2	47.1	5.8	94.2
Ohio	42.7	14.6	85.4	50.8	1.6	98.4	45.9	8.2	91.8
Oklahoma	59.8	19.6	80.4	69.9	39.8	60.2	54.9	9.8	90.2
Oregon	52.9	5.8	94.2	56.9	13.8	86.2	51.1	2.2	97.8
Pennsylvania	47.2	5.6	94.4	51.0	2.0	98.0	51.6	3.2	96.8
Rhode Island	53.9	7.8	92.2	63.1	26.2	73.8	68.5	37.0	63.0
South Carolina	95.3	90.6	9.4	100.0	100.0	0.0	100.0	100.0	0.0
South Dakota	50.5	1.0	99.0	51.4	2.8	97.2	44.0	12.0	88.0
Tennessee	58.9	17.8	82.2	75.0	50.0	50.0	68.5	37.0	63.0
Texas	100.0	100.0	0.0	88.1	76.2	23.8	85.0	70.0	30.0
Utah	41.1	17.8	82.2	49.2	1.6	98.4	50.5	1.0	99.0
Vermont	32.9	34.2	65.8	51.5	3.0	97.0	42.8	14.4	85.6
Virginia	59.8	19.6	80.4	78.7	57.4	42.6	67.3	34.6	65.4
Washington	58.5	17.0	83.0	46.5	7.0	93.0	42.5	15.0	85.0
West Virginia	53.1	6.2	93.8	61.9	23.8	76.2	57.1	14.2	85.8
Wisconsin	45.8	8.4	91.6	53.6	7.2	92.8	49.0	2.0	98.0
Wyoming	41.8	16.4	83.6	46.4	7.2	92.8	47.7	4.6	95.4

Notes: The first entries are the Democratic percent of two-party vote values for each state for the House race. The second entries are the margin of victory values for each state for the House race, where margin of victory is defined as the absolute difference between the Democratic percent and the Republican percent of the two-party vote for the House. The third entries are the party competition index values for each state for the House race, where the competition index devised by Paul David (1972) is defined as (100 − the margin of victory) or, alternatively, as (100 − the absolute difference between the Democratic and Republican percent of two-party vote for the House). The values for Democratic and Republican percent of two-party vote for the House are taken from the state vote tables in Chapter 5. Zero (0) percent on David's index represents a complete absence of two-party competition for that election year, whereas a score of 100 percent indicates perfect competition between the two major parties. A state can only receive a party competition score of 0 if it has a 100–0 vote split in all House races in the state. Conversely, a state can only receive a score of 100 if it has a 50–50 vote split in all House races in the state. For example, if Pennsylvania in 1788 cast an average of 46.0 percent Democratic vote for all House races in the state of its two-party vote, then its average Republican vote for House would be 54.0 percent. The absolute difference between the two figures is the margin of victory, or 8 percent; 100 percent − 8 percent would equal 92 percent on David's party competition scale, indicating very competitive contests in House races in Pennsylvania in 1788. The two-party vote percent values used to derive the margin of victory and party competition figures are initially found in the state vote tables in Chapter 5. The author's alternative party coding in these tables is used whenever it occurs instead of the conventional party coding of voting data. The Democratic Party is defined here as the Anti-Federalists, Democratic-Republicans, and Jackson Democrats prior to 1830 when the "Democratic Party" as such was established. The Republican Party is defined as the Federalists, National Republicans, and Whigs prior to the establishment of the "Republican Party" in the 1850s. See Appendix A for an explanation of the historical antecedents of the current Democratic and Republican parties. States reporting only partial voting returns for House races are not included in the calculations for the years in which this occurred. —indicates that the state had no data, either because no vote data were found for the state in question or the state had not yet entered the Union.

[1] Election held in an odd-numbered year.

Sources: State vote tables for House in Chapter 5.

Table 8-83 House Competition Measures, by State, by Election Year, 1962–1966 (Percentages)

	1962			1964			1966		
State	Democratic % of Two-Party Vote	Margin of Victory	Party Competition Index	Democratic % of Two-Party Vote	Margin of Victory	Party Competition Index	Democratic % of Two-Party Vote	Margin of Victory	Party Competition Index
Alabama	67.8	35.6	64.4	48.4	3.2	96.8	60.8	21.6	78.4
Alaska	54.5	9.0	91.0	51.5	3.0	97.0	48.4	3.2	96.8
Arizona	48.6	2.8	97.2	50.1	0.2	99.8	43.9	12.2	87.8
Arkansas	—	—	—	—	—	—	—	—	—
California	51.9	3.8	96.2	52.9	5.8	94.2	46.8	6.4	93.6
Colorado	47.3	5.4	94.6	58.2	16.4	83.6	53.2	6.4	93.6
Connecticut	52.7	5.4	94.6	62.3	24.6	75.4	55.1	10.2	89.8
Delaware	53.0	6.0	94.0	56.6	13.2	86.8	44.2	11.6	88.4
Florida	62.6	25.2	74.8	70.2	40.4	59.6	64.8	29.6	70.4
Georgia	81.9	63.8	36.2	69.4	38.8	61.2	65.6	31.2	68.8
Hawaii	63.6	27.2	72.8	61.1	22.2	77.8	67.7	35.4	64.6
Idaho	52.9	5.8	94.2	49.3	1.4	98.6	39.8	20.4	79.6
Illinois	49.7	0.6	99.4	54.5	9.0	91.0	45.7	8.6	91.4
Indiana	49.1	1.8	98.2	52.8	5.6	94.4	46.5	7.0	93.0
Iowa	46.1	7.8	92.2	54.6	9.2	90.8	47.6	4.8	95.2
Kansas	39.9	20.2	79.8	44.5	11.0	89.0	36.7	26.6	73.4
Kentucky	59.1	18.2	81.8	64.8	29.6	70.4	52.8	5.6	94.4
Louisiana	87.7	75.4	24.6	71.5	43.0	57.0	81.8	63.6	36.4
Maine	44.6	10.8	89.2	55.8	11.6	88.4	54.7	9.4	90.6
Maryland	55.7	11.4	88.6	69.4	38.8	61.2	56.1	12.2	87.8
Massachusetts	58.7	17.4	82.6	62.5	25.0	75.0	60.6	21.2	78.8
Michigan	52.1	4.2	95.8	57.8	15.6	84.4	48.6	2.8	97.2
Minnesota	49.8	0.4	99.6	54.5	9.0	91.0	48.4	3.2	96.8
Mississippi	100.0	100.0	0.0	90.2	80.4	19.6	82.1	64.2	35.8
Missouri	56.4	12.8	87.2	62.5	25.0	75.0	53.7	7.4	92.6
Montana	48.0	4.0	96.0	49.4	1.2	98.8	45.5	9.0	91.0
Nebraska	37.7	24.6	75.4	48.6	2.8	97.2	37.9	24.2	75.8
Nevada	71.6	43.2	56.8	63.3	26.6	73.4	67.6	35.2	64.8
New Hampshire	44.9	10.2	89.8	50.7	1.4	98.6	39.2	21.6	78.4
New Jersey	50.4	0.8	99.2	54.7	9.4	90.6	49.4	1.2	98.8
New Mexico	52.5	5.0	95.0	51.6	3.2	96.8	50.5	1.0	99.0
New York	50.8	1.6	98.4	59.1	18.2	81.8	52.6	5.2	94.8
North Carolina	58.9	17.8	82.2	60.4	20.8	79.2	52.9	5.8	94.2
North Dakota	45.7	8.6	91.4	49.9	0.2	99.8	40.9	18.2	81.8
Ohio	39.5	21.0	79.0	52.2	4.4	95.6	42.8	14.4	85.6
Oklahoma	61.1	22.2	77.8	63.0	26.0	74.0	52.4	4.8	95.2
Oregon	54.3	8.6	91.4	60.2	20.4	79.6	47.4	5.2	94.8
Pennsylvania	49.1	1.8	98.2	55.9	11.8	88.2	47.8	4.4	95.6
Rhode Island	65.1	30.2	69.8	74.6	49.2	50.8	61.3	22.6	77.4
South Carolina	86.0	72.0	28.0	89.0	78.0	22.0	70.7	41.4	58.6
South Dakota	40.2	19.6	80.4	42.8	14.4	85.6	36.2	27.6	72.4
Tennessee	63.2	26.4	73.6	58.2	16.4	83.6	50.0	0.0	100.0
Texas	56.1	12.2	87.8	67.2	34.4	65.6	83.4	66.8	33.2
Utah	47.2	5.6	94.4	52.9	5.8	94.2	36.2	27.6	72.4
Vermont	43.3	13.4	86.6	43.6	12.8	87.2	34.4	31.2	68.8
Virginia	60.0	20.0	80.0	64.2	28.4	71.6	59.4	18.8	81.2
Washington	38.3	23.4	76.6	51.2	2.4	97.6	51.3	2.6	97.4
West Virginia	56.0	12.0	88.0	58.4	16.8	83.2	53.0	6.0	94.0
Wisconsin	49.9	0.2	99.8	52.1	4.2	95.8	46.2	7.6	92.4
Wyoming	38.6	22.8	77.2	50.8	1.6	98.4	47.7	4.6	95.4

Notes: The first entries are the Democratic percent of two-party vote values for each state for the House race. The second entries are the margin of victory values for each state for the House race, where margin of victory is defined as the absolute difference between the Democratic percent and the Republican percent of the two-party vote for the House. The third entries are the party competition index values for each state for the House race, where the competition index devised by Paul David (1972) is defined as (100 − the margin of victory) or, alternatively, as (100 − the absolute difference between the Democratic and Republican percent of two-party vote for the House). The values for Democratic and Republican percent of two-party vote for the House are taken from the state vote tables in Chapter 5. Zero (0) percent on David's index represents a complete absence of two-party competition for that election year, whereas a score of 100 percent indicates perfect competition between the two major parties. A state can only receive a party competition score of 0 if it has a 100–0 vote split in all House races in the state. Conversely, a state can only receive a score of 100 if it has a 50–50 vote split in all House races in the state. For example, if Pennsylvania in 1788 cast an average of 46.0 percent Democratic vote for all House races in the state of its two-party vote, then its average Republican vote for House would be 54.0 percent. The absolute difference between the two figures is the margin of victory, or 8 percent; 100 percent − 8 percent would equal 92 percent on David's party competition scale, indicating very competitive contests in House races in Pennsylvania in 1788. The two-party vote percent values used to derive the margin of victory and party competition figures are initially found in the state vote tables in Chapter 5. The author's alternative party coding in these tables is used whenever it occurs instead of the conventional party coding of voting data. The Democratic Party is defined here as the Anti-Federalists, Democratic-Republicans, and Jackson Democrats prior to 1830 when the "Democratic Party" as such was established. The Republican Party is defined as the Federalists, National Republicans, and Whigs prior to the establishment of the "Republican Party" in the 1850s. See Appendix A for an explanation of the historical antecedents of the current Democratic and Republican parties. States reporting only partial voting returns for House races are not included in the calculations for the years in which this occurred. —indicates that the state had no data because no vote data were found.

Sources: State vote tables for House in Chapter 5.

Table 8-84 House Competition Measures, by State, by Election Year, 1968–1972 (Percentages)

State	1968 Democratic % of Two-Party Vote	1968 Margin of Victory	1968 Party Competition Index	1970 Democratic % of Two-Party Vote	1970 Margin of Victory	1970 Party Competition Index	1972 Democratic % of Two-Party Vote	1972 Margin of Victory	1972 Party Competition Index
Alabama	71.8	43.6	56.4	74.2	48.4	51.6	60.3	20.6	79.4
Alaska	45.8	8.4	91.6	55.1	10.2	89.8	56.2	12.4	87.6
Arizona	43.8	12.4	87.6	45.5	9.0	91.0	47.8	4.4	95.6
Arkansas	—	—	—	—	—	—	—	—	—
California	44.8	10.4	89.6	50.2	0.4	99.6	52.8	5.6	94.4
Colorado	48.0	4.0	96.0	49.4	1.2	98.8	47.1	5.8	94.2
Connecticut	52.3	4.6	95.4	50.3	0.6	99.4	48.8	2.4	97.6
Delaware	41.3	17.4	82.6	45.3	9.4	90.6	37.1	25.8	74.2
Florida	57.2	14.4	85.6	—	—	—	—	—	—
Georgia	79.5	59.0	41.0	74.3	48.6	51.4	71.6	43.2	56.8
Hawaii	67.3	34.6	65.4	84.7	69.4	30.6	55.9	11.8	88.2
Idaho	42.7	14.6	85.4	37.8	24.4	75.6	36.6	26.8	73.2
Illinois	46.4	7.2	92.8	51.9	3.8	96.2	49.1	1.8	98.2
Indiana	46.3	7.4	92.6	50.9	1.8	98.2	46.2	7.6	92.4
Iowa	45.8	8.4	91.6	49.9	0.2	99.8	51.6	3.2	96.8
Kansas	37.9	24.2	75.8	42.7	14.6	85.4	32.5	35.0	65.0
Kentucky	51.2	2.4	97.6	52.6	5.2	94.8	50.3	0.6	99.4
Louisiana	81.3	62.6	37.4	94.4	88.8	11.2	86.9	73.8	26.2
Maine	56.2	12.4	87.6	61.5	23.0	77.0	52.9	5.8	94.2
Maryland	52.5	5.0	95.0	51.3	2.6	97.4	52.0	4.0	96.0
Massachusetts	51.5	3.0	97.0	58.7	17.4	82.6	60.6	21.2	78.8
Michigan	50.4	0.8	99.2	51.4	2.8	97.2	47.3	5.4	94.6
Minnesota	47.7	4.6	95.4	53.0	6.0	94.0	54.1	8.2	91.8
Mississippi	92.5	85.0	15.0	90.3	80.6	19.4	67.7	35.4	64.6
Missouri	55.8	11.6	88.4	58.4	16.8	83.2	59.7	19.4	80.6
Montana	43.5	13.0	87.0	56.6	13.2	86.8	60.5	21.0	79.0
Nebraska	40.3	19.4	80.6	40.4	19.2	80.8	34.0	32.0	68.0
Nevada	72.1	44.2	55.8	82.5	65.0	35.0	47.8	4.4	95.6
New Hampshire	33.2	33.6	66.4	31.5	37.0	63.0	29.7	40.6	59.4
New Jersey	48.6	2.8	97.2	52.7	5.4	94.6	49.5	1.0	99.0
New Mexico	48.0	4.0	96.0	45.9	8.2	91.8	56.3	12.6	87.4
New York	51.6	3.2	96.8	52.6	5.2	94.8	52.9	5.8	94.2
North Carolina	54.7	9.4	90.6	55.6	11.2	88.8	54.6	9.2	90.8
North Dakota	40.2	19.6	80.4	41.9	16.2	83.8	27.2	45.6	54.4
Ohio	39.3	21.4	78.6	43.7	12.6	87.4	44.9	10.2	89.8
Oklahoma	54.9	9.8	90.2	63.6	27.2	72.8	61.6	23.2	76.8
Oregon	47.0	6.0	94.0	51.8	3.6	96.4	55.1	10.2	89.8
Pennsylvania	50.6	1.2	98.8	54.7	9.4	90.6	48.8	2.4	97.6
Rhode Island	61.2	22.4	77.6	64.4	28.8	71.2	63.7	27.4	72.6
South Carolina	67.1	34.2	65.8	72.8	45.6	54.4	52.2	4.4	95.6
South Dakota	41.4	17.2	82.8	54.3	8.6	91.4	53.1	6.2	93.8
Tennessee	48.9	2.2	97.8	59.0	18.0	82.0	46.1	7.8	92.2
Texas	71.8	43.6	56.4	73.7	47.4	52.6	70.9	41.8	58.2
Utah	35.2	29.6	70.4	49.4	1.2	98.8	56.1	12.2	87.8
Vermont	0.0	100.0	0.0	30.0	40.0	60.0	35.0	30.0	70.0
Virginia	50.8	1.6	98.4	52.9	5.8	94.2	51.6	3.2	96.8
Washington	52.0	4.0	96.0	60.1	20.2	79.8	66.2	32.4	67.6
West Virginia	61.0	22.0	78.0	65.2	30.4	69.6	63.5	27.0	73.0
Wisconsin	45.3	9.4	90.6	56.2	12.4	87.6	56.9	13.8	86.2
Wyoming	37.3	25.4	74.6	50.3	0.6	99.4	51.7	3.4	96.6

Notes: The first entries are the Democratic percent of two-party vote values for each state for the House race. The second entries are the margin of victory values for each state for the House race, where margin of victory is defined as the absolute difference between the Democratic percent and the Republican percent of the two-party vote for the House. The third entries are the party competition index values for each state for the House race, where the competition index devised by Paul David (1972) is defined as (100 − the margin of victory) or, alternatively, as (100 − the absolute difference between the Democratic and Republican percent of two-party vote for the House). The values for Democratic and Republican percent of two-party vote for the House are taken from the state vote tables in Chapter 5. Zero (0) percent on David's index represents a complete absence of two-party competition for that election year, whereas a score of 100 percent indicates perfect competition between the two major parties. A state can only receive a party competition score of 0 if it has a 100–0 vote split in all House races in the state. Conversely, a state can only receive a score of 100 if it has a 50–50 vote split in all House races in the state. For example, if Pennsylvania in 1788 cast an average of 46.0 percent Democratic vote for all House races in the state of its two-party vote, then its average Republican vote for House would be 54.0 percent. The absolute difference between the two figures is the margin of victory, or 8 percent; 100 percent − 8 percent would equal 92 percent on David's party competition scale, indicating very competitive contests in House races in Pennsylvania in 1788. The two-party vote percent values used to derive the margin of victory and party competition figures are initially found in the state vote tables in Chapter 5. The author's alternative party coding in these tables is used whenever it occurs instead of the conventional party coding of voting data. The Democratic Party is defined here as the Anti-Federalists, Democratic-Republicans, and Jackson Democrats prior to 1830 when the "Democratic Party" as such was established. The Republican Party is defined as the Federalists, National Republicans, and Whigs prior to the establishment of the "Republican Party" in the 1850s. See Appendix A for an explanation of the historical antecedents of the current Democratic and Republican parties. States reporting only partial voting returns for House races are not included in the calculations for the years in which this occurred. —indicates that the state had no data because no vote data were found.

Sources: State vote tables for House in Chapter 5.

Table 8-85 House Competition Measures, by State, by Election Year, 1974–1978 (Percentages)

State	1974 Democratic % of Two-Party Vote	1974 Margin of Victory	1974 Party Competition Index	1976 Democratic % of Two-Party Vote	1976 Margin of Victory	1976 Party Competition Index	1978 Democratic % of Two-Party Vote	1978 Margin of Victory	1978 Party Competition Index
Alabama	69.3	38.6	61.4	68.0	36.0	64.0	69.0	38.0	62.0
Alaska	46.2	7.6	92.4	29.0	42.0	58.0	44.5	11.0	89.0
Arizona	50.3	0.6	99.4	51.1	2.2	97.8	53.1	6.2	93.8
Arkansas	—	—	—	—	—	—	—	—	—
California	58.5	17.0	83.0	56.3	12.6	87.4	51.8	3.6	96.4
Colorado	53.2	6.4	93.6	45.9	8.2	91.8	47.9	4.2	95.8
Connecticut	58.5	17.0	83.0	51.1	2.2	97.8	58.3	16.6	83.4
Delaware	40.4	19.2	80.8	48.1	3.8	96.2	41.4	17.2	82.8
Florida	—	—	—	—	—	—	—	—	—
Georgia	71.6	43.2	56.8	74.3	48.6	51.4	80.2	60.4	39.6
Hawaii	61.1	22.2	77.8	70.3	40.6	59.4	83.5	67.0	33.0
Idaho	43.0	14.0	86.0	47.4	5.2	94.8	41.4	17.2	82.8
Illinois	56.8	13.6	86.4	51.6	3.2	96.8	48.2	3.6	96.4
Indiana	55.4	10.8	89.2	55.6	11.2	88.8	52.5	5.0	95.0
Iowa	54.2	8.4	91.6	57.4	14.8	85.2	49.8	0.4	99.6
Kansas	43.8	12.4	87.6	39.0	22.0	78.0	34.6	30.8	69.2
Kentucky	64.1	28.2	71.8	61.8	23.6	76.4	56.1	12.2	87.8
Louisiana	—	—	—	63.1	26.2	73.8	—	—	—
Maine	39.9	20.2	79.8	32.5	35.0	65.0	40.3	19.4	80.6
Maryland	60.3	20.6	79.4	62.5	25.0	75.0	65.9	31.8	68.2
Massachusetts	74.4	48.8	51.2	67.6	35.2	64.8	72.6	45.2	54.8
Michigan	59.0	18.0	82.0	55.8	11.6	88.4	57.2	14.4	85.6
Minnesota	58.9	17.8	82.2	58.8	17.6	82.4	52.2	4.4	95.6
Mississippi	54.4	8.8	91.2	59.4	18.8	81.2	51.6	3.2	96.8
Missouri	67.1	34.2	65.8	57.1	14.2	85.8	62.7	25.4	74.6
Montana	58.6	17.2	82.8	56.2	12.4	87.6	50.6	1.2	98.8
Nebraska	47.3	5.4	94.6	35.4	29.2	70.8	37.2	25.6	74.4
Nevada	60.5	21.0	79.0	86.5	73.0	27.0	74.9	49.8	50.2
New Hampshire	44.1	11.8	88.2	53.8	7.6	92.4	47.8	4.4	95.6
New Jersey	61.0	22.0	78.0	55.8	11.6	88.4	55.5	11.0	89.0
New Mexico	52.1	4.2	95.8	46.3	7.4	92.6	58.5	17.0	83.0
New York	59.3	18.6	81.4	59.9	19.8	80.2	53.4	6.8	93.2
North Carolina	64.7	29.4	70.6	64.8	29.6	70.4	59.9	19.8	80.2
North Dakota	44.3	11.4	88.6	36.5	27.0	73.0	31.5	37.0	63.0
Ohio	48.9	2.2	97.8	48.7	2.6	97.4	46.5	7.0	93.0
Oklahoma	58.6	17.2	82.8	64.7	29.4	70.6	56.2	12.4	87.6
Oregon	64.1	28.2	71.8	69.5	39.0	61.0	69.5	39.0	61.0
Pennsylvania	57.7	15.4	84.6	54.6	9.2	90.8	51.3	2.6	97.4
Rhode Island	75.7	51.4	48.6	70.5	41.0	59.0	56.6	13.2	86.8
South Carolina	58.6	17.2	82.8	64.2	28.4	71.6	67.4	34.8	65.2
South Dakota	38.7	22.6	77.4	24.7	50.6	49.4	47.0	6.0	94.0
Tennessee	59.5	19.0	81.0	63.1	26.2	73.8	56.4	12.8	87.2
Texas	72.6	45.2	54.8	65.0	30.0	70.0	59.1	18.2	81.8
Utah	58.6	17.2	82.8	51.5	3.0	97.0	44.1	11.8	88.2
Vermont	43.0	14.0	86.0	32.6	34.8	65.2	20.4	59.2	40.8
Virginia	58.4	16.8	83.2	49.8	0.4	99.6	42.7	14.6	85.4
Washington	58.9	17.8	82.2	58.3	16.6	83.4	52.9	5.8	94.2
West Virginia	69.8	39.6	60.4	74.0	48.0	52.0	65.7	31.4	68.6
Wisconsin	59.7	19.4	80.6	61.0	22.0	78.0	53.2	6.4	93.6
Wyoming	54.7	9.4	90.6	56.4	12.8	87.2	41.4	17.2	82.8

Notes: The first entries are the Democratic percent of two-party vote values for each state for the House race. The second entries are the margin of victory values for each state for the House race, where margin of victory is defined as the absolute difference between the Democratic percent and the Republican percent of the two-party vote for the House. The third entries are the party competition index values for each state for the House race, where the competition index devised by Paul David (1972) is defined as (100 − the margin of victory) or, alternatively, as (100 − the absolute difference between the Democratic and Republican percent of two-party vote for the House). The values for Democratic and Republican percent of two-party vote for the House are taken from the state vote tables in Chapter 5. Zero (0) percent on David's index represents a complete absence of two-party competition for that election year, whereas a score of 100 percent indicates perfect competition between the two parties. A state can only receive a party competition score of 0 if it has a 100–0 vote split in all House races in the state. Conversely, a state can only receive a score of 100 if it has a 50–50 vote split in all House races in the state. For example, if Pennsylvania in 1788 cast an average of 46.0 percent Democratic vote for all House races in the state of its two-party vote, then its average Republican vote for House would be 54.0 percent. The absolute difference between the two figures is the margin of victory, or 8 percent; 100 percent − 8 percent would equal 92 percent on David's party competition scale, indicating very competitive contests in House races in Pennsylvania in 1788. The two-party vote percent values used to derive the margin of victory and party competition figures are initially found in the state vote tables in Chapter 5. The author's alternative party coding in these tables is used whenever it occurs instead of the conventional party coding of voting data. The Democratic Party is defined here as the Anti-Federalists, Democratic-Republicans, and Jackson Democrats prior to 1830 when the "Democratic Party" as such was established. The Republican Party is defined as the Federalists, National Republicans, and Whigs prior to the establishment of the "Republican Party" in the 1850s. See Appendix A for an explanation of the historical antecedents of the current Democratic and Republican parties. States reporting only partial voting returns for House races are not included in the calculations for the years in which this occurred. —indicates that the state had no data because no vote data were found.

Sources: State vote tables for House in Chapter 5.

Table 8-86 House Competition Measures, by State, by Election Year, 1980–1984 (Percentages)

	1980			1982			1984		
State	Democratic % of Two-Party Vote	Margin of Victory	Party Competition Index	Democratic % of Two-Party Vote	Margin of Victory	Party Competition Index	Democratic % of Two-Party Vote	Margin of Victory	Party Competition Index
Alabama	64.0	28.0	72.0	71.3	42.6	57.4	72.7	45.4	54.6
Alaska	25.9	48.2	51.8	28.8	42.4	57.6	43.1	13.8	86.2
Arizona	47.6	4.8	95.2	43.2	13.6	86.4	34.6	30.8	69.2
Arkansas	—	—	—	52.4	4.8	95.2	—	—	—
California	46.7	6.6	93.4	51.9	3.8	96.2	49.4	1.2	98.8
Colorado	44.9	10.2	89.8	48.0	4.0	96.0	35.9	28.2	71.8
Connecticut	52.1	4.2	95.8	54.3	8.6	91.4	46.7	6.6	93.4
Delaware	37.8	24.4	75.6	53.1	6.2	93.8	58.5	17.0	83.0
Florida	—	—	—	—	—	—	—	—	—
Georgia	71.9	43.8	56.2	74.8	49.6	50.4	71.7	43.4	56.6
Hawaii	92.4	84.8	15.2	100.0	100.0	0.0	84.8	69.6	30.4
Idaho	43.9	12.2	87.8	47.0	6.0	94.0	40.7	18.6	81.4
Illinois	45.9	8.2	91.8	58.1	16.2	83.8	51.8	3.6	96.4
Indiana	49.7	0.6	99.4	49.2	1.6	98.4	47.1	5.8	94.2
Iowa	51.3	2.6	97.4	52.7	5.4	94.6	46.9	6.2	93.8
Kansas	43.8	12.4	87.6	46.3	7.4	92.6	44.5	11.0	89.0
Kentucky	58.0	16.0	84.0	59.6	19.2	80.8	55.4	10.8	89.2
Louisiana	—	—	—	—	—	—	—	—	—
Maine	26.9	46.2	53.8	41.7	16.6	83.4	30.2	39.6	60.4
Maryland	61.7	23.4	76.6	68.1	36.2	63.8	64.1	28.2	71.8
Massachusetts	66.0	32.0	68.0	69.9	39.8	60.2	69.7	39.4	60.6
Michigan	53.1	6.2	93.8	60.4	20.8	79.2	54.3	8.6	91.4
Minnesota	47.9	4.2	95.8	55.2	10.4	89.6	54.0	8.0	92.0
Mississippi	58.4	16.8	83.2	58.7	17.4	82.6	61.5	23.0	77.0
Missouri	54.1	8.2	91.8	57.2	14.4	85.6	55.6	11.2	88.8
Montana	52.1	4.2	95.8	53.8	7.6	92.4	51.2	2.4	97.6
Nebraska	27.1	45.8	54.2	22.4	55.2	44.8	25.8	48.4	51.6
Nevada	72.3	44.6	55.4	49.6	0.8	99.2	41.3	17.4	82.6
New Hampshire	48.7	2.6	97.4	42.6	14.8	85.2	32.2	35.6	64.4
New Jersey	49.0	2.0	98.0	56.9	13.8	86.2	50.6	1.2	98.8
New Mexico	48.4	3.2	96.8	51.4	2.8	97.2	40.6	18.8	81.2
New York	50.6	1.2	98.8	57.4	14.8	85.2	52.9	5.8	94.2
North Carolina	55.6	11.2	88.8	55.0	10.0	90.0	52.4	4.8	95.2
North Dakota	57.2	14.4	85.6	72.1	44.2	55.8	78.7	57.4	42.6
Ohio	45.6	8.8	91.2	55.4	10.8	89.2	49.7	0.6	99.4
Oklahoma	52.9	5.8	94.2	63.5	27.0	73.0	58.5	17.0	83.0
Oregon	59.9	19.8	80.2	57.0	14.0	86.0	54.4	8.8	91.2
Pennsylvania	48.7	2.6	97.4	53.6	7.2	92.8	54.5	9.0	91.0
Rhode Island	55.3	10.6	89.4	52.5	5.0	95.0	50.0	0.0	100.0
South Carolina	50.6	1.2	98.8	54.5	9.0	91.0	51.6	3.2	96.8
South Dakota	54.3	8.6	91.4	51.6	3.2	96.8	57.4	14.8	85.2
Tennessee	51.8	3.6	96.4	59.8	19.6	80.4	55.2	10.4	89.6
Texas	59.9	19.8	80.2	66.4	32.8	67.2	57.6	15.2	84.8
Utah	39.8	20.4	79.6	31.7	36.6	63.4	35.0	30.0	70.0
Vermont	0.0	100.0	0.0	25.1	49.8	50.2	29.0	42.0	58.0
Virginia	32.6	34.8	65.2	47.7	4.6	95.4	44.2	11.6	88.4
Washington	50.7	1.4	98.6	53.3	6.6	93.4	55.5	11.0	89.0
West Virginia	57.0	14.0	86.0	62.9	25.8	74.2	60.9	21.8	78.2
Wisconsin	50.4	0.8	99.2	53.5	7.0	93.0	50.0	0.0	100.0
Wyoming	31.4	37.2	62.8	28.9	42.2	57.8	24.9	50.2	49.8

Notes: The first entries are the Democratic percent of two-party vote values for each state for the House race. The second entries are the margin of victory values for each state for the House race, where margin of victory is defined as the absolute difference between the Democratic percent and the Republican percent of the two-party vote for the House. The third entries are the party competition index values for each state for the House race, where the competition index devised by Paul David (1972) is defined as (100 − the margin of victory) or, alternatively, as (100 − the absolute difference between the Democratic and Republican percent of two-party vote for the House). The values for Democratic and Republican percent of two-party vote for the House are taken from the state vote tables in Chapter 5. Zero (0) percent on David's index represents a complete absence of two-party competition for that election year, whereas a score of 100 percent indicates perfect competition between the two major parties. A state can only receive a party competition score of 0 if it has a 100–0 vote split in all House races in the state. Conversely, a state can only receive a score of 100 if it has a 50–50 vote split in all House races in the state. For example, if Pennsylvania in 1788 cast an average of 46.0 percent Democratic vote for all House races in the state of its two-party vote, then its average Republican vote for House would be 54.0 percent. The absolute difference between the two figures is the margin of victory, or 8 percent; 100 percent − 8 percent would equal 92 percent on David's party competition scale, indicating very competitive contests in House races in Pennsylvania in 1788. The two-party vote percent values used to derive the margin of victory and party competition figures are initially found in the state vote tables in Chapter 5. The author's alternative party coding in these tables is used whenever it occurs instead of the conventional party coding of voting data. The Democratic Party is defined here as the Anti-Federalists, Democratic-Republicans, and Jackson Democrats prior to 1830 when the "Democratic Party" as such was established. The Republican Party is defined as the Federalists, National Republicans, and Whigs prior to the establishment of the "Republican Party" in the 1850s. See Appendix A for an explanation of the historical antecedents of the current Democratic and Republican parties. States reporting only partial voting returns for House races are not included in the calculations for the years in which this occurred. —indicates that the state had no data because no vote data were found.

Sources: State vote tables for House in Chapter 5.

Table 8-87 House Competition Measures, by State, by Election Year, 1986–1990 (Percentages)

State	1986 Democratic % of Two-Party Vote	1986 Margin of Victory	1986 Party Competition Index	1988 Democratic % of Two-Party Vote	1988 Margin of Victory	1988 Party Competition Index	1990 Democratic % of Two-Party Vote	1990 Margin of Victory	1990 Party Competition Index
Alabama	60.9	21.8	78.2	62.6	25.2	74.8	68.7	37.4	62.6
Alaska	42.1	15.8	84.2	37.3	25.4	74.6	48.1	3.8	96.2
Arizona	32.5	35.0	65.0	29.6	40.8	59.2	35.7	28.6	71.4
Arkansas	59.0	18.0	82.0	—	—	—	55.5	11.0	89.0
California	52.9	5.8	94.2	54.2	8.4	91.6	51.6	3.2	96.8
Colorado	44.3	11.4	88.6	49.2	1.6	98.4	50.8	1.6	98.4
Connecticut	55.7	11.4	88.6	49.4	1.2	98.8	47.3	5.4	94.6
Delaware	66.4	32.8	67.2	67.5	35.0	65.0	66.7	33.4	66.6
Florida	—	—	—	—	—	—	—	—	—
Georgia	72.8	45.6	54.4	66.7	33.4	66.6	61.3	22.6	77.4
Hawaii	58.1	16.2	83.8	69.5	39.0	61.0	64.7	29.4	70.6
Idaho	43.9	12.2	87.8	49.4	1.2	98.8	58.2	16.4	83.6
Illinois	53.8	7.6	92.4	53.4	6.8	93.2	55.0	10.0	90.0
Indiana	51.0	2.0	98.0	51.7	3.4	96.6	54.9	9.8	90.2
Iowa	48.1	3.8	96.2	48.9	2.2	97.8	51.0	2.0	98.0
Kansas	39.7	20.6	79.4	39.3	21.4	78.6	50.4	0.8	99.2
Kentucky	59.7	19.4	80.6	48.6	2.8	97.2	47.1	5.8	94.2
Louisiana	—	—	—	—	—	—	—	—	—
Maine	39.9	20.2	79.8	49.8	0.4	99.6	55.0	10.0	90.0
Maryland	62.9	25.8	74.2	60.0	20.0	80.0	52.2	4.4	95.6
Massachusetts	82.7	65.4	34.6	77.8	55.6	44.4	71.5	43.0	57.0
Michigan	57.9	15.8	84.2	53.2	6.4	93.6	54.8	9.6	90.4
Minnesota	59.9	19.8	80.2	58.7	17.4	82.6	58.6	17.2	82.8
Mississippi	60.3	20.6	79.4	66.4	32.8	67.2	81.2	62.4	37.6
Missouri	58.0	16.0	84.0	55.8	11.6	88.4	53.8	7.6	92.4
Montana	54.1	8.2	91.8	52.9	5.8	94.2	49.5	1.0	99.0
Nebraska	35.4	29.2	70.8	35.0	30.0	70.0	47.2	5.6	94.4
Nevada	47.5	5.0	95.0	52.6	5.2	94.8	48.9	2.2	97.8
New Hampshire	35.1	29.8	70.2	41.2	17.6	82.4	48.6	2.8	97.2
New Jersey	52.1	4.2	95.8	48.6	2.8	97.2	47.9	4.2	95.8
New Mexico	46.4	7.2	92.8	46.9	6.2	93.8	40.5	19.0	81.0
New York	56.2	12.4	87.6	54.7	9.4	90.6	52.4	4.8	95.2
North Carolina	56.6	13.2	86.8	55.8	11.6	88.4	53.5	7.0	93.0
North Dakota	76.3	52.6	47.4	71.6	43.2	56.8	65.2	30.4	69.6
Ohio	49.6	0.8	99.2	50.2	0.4	99.6	53.2	6.4	93.6
Oklahoma	59.7	19.4	80.6	52.9	5.8	94.2	60.6	21.2	78.8
Oregon	56.7	13.4	86.6	65.0	30.0	70.0	66.1	32.2	67.8
Pennsylvania	53.6	7.2	92.8	50.6	1.2	98.8	45.4	9.2	90.8
Rhode Island	42.4	15.2	84.8	35.9	28.2	71.8	52.5	5.0	95.0
South Carolina	63.4	26.8	73.2	55.6	11.2	88.8	58.2	16.4	83.6
South Dakota	59.2	18.4	81.6	71.7	43.4	56.6	67.6	35.2	64.8
Tennessee	58.6	17.2	82.8	61.1	22.2	77.8	56.1	12.2	87.8
Texas	57.6	15.2	84.8	59.9	19.8	80.2	54.1	8.2	91.8
Utah	46.1	7.8	92.2	43.3	13.4	86.6	55.0	10.0	90.0
Vermont	0.0	100.0	0.0	31.4	37.2	62.8	7.1	85.8	14.2
Virginia	53.9	7.8	92.2	42.7	14.6	85.4	61.7	23.4	76.6
Washington	59.3	18.6	81.4	57.1	14.2	85.8	53.9	7.8	92.2
West Virginia	75.5	51.0	49.0	76.8	53.6	46.4	67.1	34.2	65.8
Wisconsin	51.3	2.6	97.4	50.9	1.8	98.2	47.8	4.4	95.6
Wyoming	30.5	39.0	61.0	32.3	35.4	64.6	44.9	10.2	89.8

Notes: The first entries are the Democratic percent of two-party vote values for each state for the House race. The second entries are the margin of victory values for each state for the House race, where margin of victory is defined as the absolute difference between the Democratic percent and the Republican percent of the two-party vote for the House. The third entries are the party competition index values for each state for the House race, where the competition index devised by Paul David (1972) is defined as (100 − the margin of victory) or, alternatively, as (100 − the absolute difference between the Democratic and Republican percent of two-party vote for the House). The values for Democratic and Republican percent of two-party vote for the House are taken from the state vote tables in Chapter 5. Zero (0) percent on David's index represents a complete absence of two-party competition for that election year, whereas a score of 100 percent indicates perfect competition between the two major parties. A state can only receive a party competition score of 0 if it has a 100–0 vote split in all House races in the state. Conversely, a state can only receive a score of 100 if it has a 50–50 vote split in all House races in the state. For example, if Pennsylvania in 1788 cast an average of 46.0 percent Democratic vote for all House races in the state of its two-party vote, then its average Republican vote for House would be 54.0 percent. The absolute difference between the two figures is the margin of victory, or 8 percent; 100 percent − 8 percent would equal 92 percent on David's party competition scale, indicating very competitive contests in House races in Pennsylvania in 1788. The two-party vote percent values used to derive the margin of victory and party competition figures are initially found in the state vote tables in Chapter 5. The author's alternative party coding in these tables is used whenever it occurs instead of the conventional party coding of voting data. The Democratic Party is defined here as the Anti-Federalists, Democratic-Republicans, and Jackson Democrats prior to 1830 when the "Democratic Party" as such was established. The Republican Party is defined as the Federalists, National Republicans, and Whigs prior to the establishment of the "Republican Party" in the 1850s. See Appendix A for an explanation of the historical antecedents of the current Democratic and Republican parties. States reporting only partial voting returns for House races are not included in the calculations for the years in which this occurred. —indicates that the state had no data because no vote data were found.

Sources: State vote tables for House in Chapter 5.

Table 8-88 House Competition Measures, by State, by Election Year, 1992–1996 (Percentages)

State	1992			1994			1996		
	Democratic % of Two-Party Vote	Margin of Victory	Party Competition Index	Democratic % of Two-Party Vote	Margin of Victory	Party Competition Index	Democratic % of Two-Party Vote	Margin of Victory	Party Competition Index
Alabama	58.2	16.4	83.6	49.8	0.4	99.6	45.5	9.0	91.0
Alaska	47.8	4.4	95.6	36.5	27.0	73.0	38.0	24.0	76.0
Arizona	44.0	12.0	88.0	38.6	22.8	77.2	39.4	21.2	78.8
Arkansas	59.5	19.0	81.0	47.4	5.2	94.8	46.4	7.2	92.8
California	55.5	11.0	89.0	49.3	1.4	98.6	52.3	4.6	95.4
Colorado	47.7	4.6	95.4	34.7	30.6	69.4	41.7	16.6	83.4
Connecticut	48.0	4.0	96.0	49.5	1.0	99.0	56.9	13.8	86.2
Delaware	43.4	13.2	86.8	27.3	45.4	54.6	28.3	43.4	56.6
Florida	—	—	—	—	—	—	—	—	—
Georgia	54.9	9.8	90.2	45.5	9.0	91.0	46.7	6.6	93.4
Hawaii	76.2	52.4	47.6	64.7	29.4	70.6	59.1	18.2	81.8
Idaho	49.1	1.8	98.2	35.0	30.0	70.0	40.0	20.0	80.0
Illinois	56.1	12.2	87.8	48.1	3.8	96.2	55.6	11.2	88.8
Indiana	54.7	9.4	90.6	43.3	13.4	86.6	45.8	8.4	91.6
Iowa	40.3	19.4	80.6	42.1	15.8	84.2	45.0	10.0	90.0
Kansas	45.2	9.6	90.4	36.5	27.0	73.0	41.8	16.4	83.6
Kentucky	53.1	6.2	93.8	41.2	17.6	82.4	41.0	18.0	82.0
Louisiana	—	—	—	—	—	—	—	—	—
Maine	56.6	13.2	86.8	50.2	0.4	99.6	64.2	28.4	71.6
Maryland	53.2	6.4	93.6	49.2	1.6	98.4	53.5	7.0	93.0
Massachusetts	63.9	27.8	72.2	69.7	39.4	60.6	67.0	34.0	66.0
Michigan	50.8	1.6	98.4	48.1	3.8	96.2	53.7	7.4	92.6
Minnesota	55.9	11.8	88.2	51.1	2.2	97.8	56.9	13.8	86.2
Mississippi	71.0	42.0	58.0	58.0	16.0	84.0	44.9	10.2	89.8
Missouri	55.1	10.2	89.8	51.7	3.4	96.6	57.3	14.6	85.4
Montana	51.8	3.6	96.4	53.5	7.0	93.0	45.2	9.6	90.4
Nebraska	39.9	20.2	79.8	35.7	28.6	71.4	31.2	37.6	62.4
Nevada	53.4	6.8	93.2	38.9	22.2	77.8	41.0	18.0	82.0
New Hampshire	53.9	7.8	92.2	39.3	21.4	78.6	47.3	5.4	94.6
New Jersey	47.4	5.2	94.8	44.6	10.8	89.2	49.1	1.8	98.2
New Mexico	49.5	1.0	99.0	41.6	16.8	83.2	51.0	2.0	98.0
New York	53.2	6.4	93.6	49.6	0.8	99.2	56.3	12.6	87.4
North Carolina	51.6	3.2	96.8	42.9	14.2	85.8	45.9	8.2	91.8
North Dakota	59.0	18.0	82.0	53.7	7.4	92.6	56.0	12.0	88.0
Ohio	50.5	1.0	99.0	40.8	18.4	81.6	48.1	3.8	96.2
Oklahoma	60.3	20.6	79.4	39.9	20.2	79.8	37.3	25.4	74.6
Oregon	59.9	19.8	80.2	56.5	13.0	87.0	56.5	13.0	87.0
Pennsylvania	47.9	4.2	95.8	44.9	10.2	89.8	52.2	4.4	95.6
Rhode Island	50.9	1.8	98.2	61.3	22.6	77.4	69.1	38.2	61.8
South Carolina	46.5	7.0	93.0	36.2	27.6	72.4	33.6	32.8	67.2
South Dakota	72.0	44.0	56.0	62.0	24.0	76.0	39.1	21.8	78.2
Tennessee	54.5	9.0	91.0	44.2	11.6	88.4	49.1	1.8	98.2
Texas	51.1	2.2	97.8	43.0	14.0	86.0	45.5	9.0	91.0
Utah	47.8	4.4	95.6	46.1	7.8	92.2	40.6	18.8	81.2
Vermont	20.4	59.2	40.8	0.0	100.0	0.0	22.3	55.4	44.6
Virginia	50.1	0.2	99.8	40.9	18.2	81.8	47.9	4.2	95.8
Washington	57.6	15.2	84.8	49.2	1.6	98.4	52.5	5.0	95.0
West Virginia	78.1	56.2	43.8	66.1	32.2	67.8	87.8	75.6	24.4
Wisconsin	48.8	2.4	97.6	38.0	24.0	76.0	47.5	5.0	95.0
Wyoming	40.5	19.0	81.0	43.7	12.6	87.4	42.5	15.0	85.0

Notes: The first entries are the Democratic percent of two-party vote values for each state for the House race. The second entries are the margin of victory values for each state for the House race, where margin of victory is defined as the absolute difference between the Democratic percent and the Republican percent of the two-party vote for the House. The third entries are the party competition index values for each state for the House race, where the competition index devised by Paul David (1972) is defined as (100 − the margin of victory) or, alternatively, as (100 − the absolute difference between the Democratic and Republican percent of two-party vote for the House). The values for Democratic and Republican percent of two-party vote for the House are taken from the state vote tables in Chapter 5. Zero (0) percent on David's index represents a complete absence of two-party competition for that election year, whereas a score of 100 percent indicates perfect competition between the two major parties. A state can only receive a party competition score of 0 if it has a 100–0 vote split in all House races in the state. Conversely, a state can only receive a score of 100 if it has a 50–50 vote split in all House races in the state. For example, if Pennsylvania in 1788 cast an average of 46.0 percent Democratic vote for all House races in the state of its two-party vote, then its average Republican vote for House would be 54.0 percent. The absolute difference between the two figures is the margin of victory, or 8 percent; 100 percent − 8 percent would equal 92 percent on David's party competition scale, indicating very competitive contests in House races in Pennsylvania in 1788. The two-party vote percent values used to derive the margin of victory and party competition figures are initially found in the state vote tables in Chapter 5. The author's alternative party coding in these tables is used whenever it occurs instead of the conventional party coding of voting data. The Democratic Party is defined here as the Anti-Federalists, Democratic-Republicans, and Jackson Democrats prior to 1830 when the "Democratic Party" as such was established. The Republican Party is defined as the Federalists, National Republicans, and Whigs prior to the establishment of the "Republican Party" in the 1850s. See Appendix A for an explanation of the historical antecedents of the current Democratic and Republican parties. States reporting only partial voting returns for House races are not included in the calculations for the years in which this occurred. —indicates that the state had no data because no vote data were found.

Sources: State vote tables for House in Chapter 5.

Table 8-89 House Competition Measures, by State, by Election Year, 1998 (Percentages)

	1998				1998		
State	Democratic % of Two-Party Vote	Margin of Victory	Party Competition Index	State	Democratic % of Two-Party Vote	Margin of Victory	Party Competition Index
Alabama	45.0	10.0	90.0	Montana	45.6	8.8	91.2
Alaska	35.6	28.8	71.2	Nebraska	21.0	58.0	42.0
Arizona	41.5	17.0	83.0	Nevada	22.4	55.2	44.8
Arkansas	—	—	—	New Hampshire	39.5	21.0	79.0
California	53.5	7.0	93.0	New Jersey	51.2	2.4	97.6
Colorado	42.7	14.6	85.4	New Mexico	48.1	3.8	96.2
Connecticut	52.9	5.8	94.2	New York	55.1	10.2	89.8
Delaware	32.4	35.2	64.8	North Carolina	44.9	10.2	89.8
Florida	—	—	—	North Dakota	57.8	15.6	84.4
Georgia	36.3	27.4	72.6	Ohio	47.6	4.8	95.2
Hawaii	68.6	37.2	62.8	Oklahoma	36.9	26.2	73.8
Idaho	45.3	9.4	90.6	Oregon	61.1	22.2	77.8
Illinois	49.1	1.8	98.2	Pennsylvania	48.4	3.2	96.8
Indiana	43.9	12.2	87.8	Rhode Island	72.7	45.4	54.6
Iowa	38.0	24.0	76.0	South Carolina	38.9	22.2	77.8
Kansas	37.7	24.6	75.4	South Dakota	24.9	50.2	49.8
Kentucky	41.7	16.6	83.4	Tennessee	46.8	6.4	93.6
Louisiana	—	—	—	Texas	46.1	7.8	92.2
Maine	69.2	38.4	61.6	Utah	29.4	41.2	58.8
Maryland	53.5	7.0	93.0	Vermont	0.0	100.0	0.0
Massachusetts	76.0	52.0	48.0	Virginia	48.7	2.6	97.4
Michigan	50.5	1.0	99.0	Washington	54.5	9.0	91.0
Minnesota	55.8	11.6	88.4	West Virginia	90.7	81.4	18.6
Mississippi	53.1	6.2	93.8	Wisconsin	46.4	7.2	92.8
Missouri	51.3	2.6	97.4	Wyoming	40.1	19.8	80.2

Notes: The first entries are the Democratic percent of two-party vote values for each state for the House race. The second entries are the margin of victory values for each state for the House race, where margin of victory is defined as the absolute difference between the Democratic percent and the Republican percent of the two-party vote for the House. The third entries are the party competition index values for each state for the House race, where the competition index devised by Paul David (1972) is defined as (100 − the margin of victory) or, alternatively, as (100 − the absolute difference between the Democratic and Republican percent of two-party vote for the House). The values for Democratic and Republican percent of two-party vote for the House are taken from the state vote tables in Chapter 5. Zero (0) percent on David's index represents a complete absence of two-party competition for that election year, whereas a score of 100 percent indicates perfect competition between the two major parties. A state can only receive a party competition score of 0 if it has a 100–0 vote split in all House races in the state. Conversely, a state can only receive a score of 100 if it has a 50–50 vote split in all House races in the state. For example, if Pennsylvania in 1788 cast an average of 46.0 percent Democratic vote for all House races in the state of its two-party vote, then its average Republican vote for House would be 54.0 percent. The absolute difference between the two figures is the margin of victory, or 8 percent; 100 percent − 8 percent would equal 92 percent on David's party competition scale, indicating very competitive contests in House races in Pennsylvania in 1788. The two-party vote percent values used to derive the margin of victory and party competition figures are initially found in the state vote tables in Chapter 5. The author's alternative party coding in these tables is used whenever it occurs instead of the conventional party coding of voting data. The Democratic Party is defined here as the Anti-Federalists, Democratic-Republicans, and Jackson Democrats prior to 1830 when the "Democratic Party" as such was established. The Republican Party is defined as the Federalists, National Republicans, and Whigs prior to the establishment of the "Republican Party" in the 1850s. See Appendix A for an explanation of the historical antecedents of the current Democratic and Republican parties. States reporting only partial voting returns for House races are not included in the calculations for the years in which this occurred. —indicates that the state had no data because no vote data were found.

Sources: State vote tables for House in Chapter 5.

Table 8-90 Senate Competition Measures, by State, by Election Year, 1912–1916 (Percentages)

State	1912			1914			1916		
	Democratic % of Two-Party Vote	Margin of Victory	Party Competition Index	Democratic % of Two-Party Vote	Margin of Victory	Party Competition Index	Democratic % of Two-Party Vote	Margin of Victory	Party Competition Index
Alabama	—	—	—	83.7	67.4	32.6	—	—	—
Alaska	—	—	—	—	—	—	—	—	—
Arizona	—	—	—	73.8	47.6	52.4	58.4	16.8	83.2
Arkansas	—	—	—	74.9	49.8	50.2	—	—	—
California	—	—	—	52.4	4.8	95.2	32.6	34.8	65.2
Colorado	63.9	27.8	72.2	50.8	1.6	98.4	—	—	—
Connecticut	—	—	—	45.8	8.4	91.6	48.0	4.0	96.0
Delaware	—	—	—	—	—	—	52.6	5.2	94.8
Florida	—	—	—	100.0	100.0	0.0	86.9	73.8	26.2
Georgia	—	—	—	100.0	100.0	0.0	—	—	—
Hawaii	—	—	—	—	—	—	—	—	—
Idaho	—	—	—	46.5	7.0	93.0	—	—	—
Illinois	—	—	—	48.9	2.2	97.8	—	—	—
Indiana	—	—	—	54.6	9.2	90.8	49.1	1.8	98.2
Iowa	—	—	—	44.8	10.4	89.6	—	—	—
Kansas	53.2	6.4	93.6	49.5	1.0	99.0	—	—	—
Kentucky	—	—	—	54.9	9.8	90.2	—	—	—
Louisiana	—	—	—	—	—	—	—	—	—
Maine	—	—	—	—	—	—	46.5	7.0	93.0
Maryland	—	—	—	53.7	7.4	92.6	49.1	1.8	98.2
Massachusetts	—	—	—	—	—	—	46.7	6.6	93.4
Michigan	—	—	—	—	—	—	41.4	17.2	82.8
Minnesota	37.2	25.6	74.4	—	—	—	38.8	22.4	77.6
Mississippi	—	—	—	—	—	—	100.0	100.0	0.0
Missouri	—	—	—	54.8	9.6	90.4	51.6	3.2	96.8
Montana	60.6	21.2	78.8	—	—	—	54.1	8.2	91.8
Nebraska	—	—	—	—	—	—	52.1	4.2	95.8
Nevada	—	—	—	50.1	0.2	99.8	54.6	9.2	90.8
New Hampshire	—	—	—	46.3	7.4	92.6	—	—	—
New Jersey	—	—	—	—	—	—	41.0	18.0	82.0
New Mexico	—	—	—	—	—	—	52.7	5.4	94.6
New York	—	—	—	47.2	5.6	94.4	41.9	16.2	83.8
North Carolina	—	—	—	58.2	16.4	83.6	—	—	—
North Dakota	—	—	—	37.8	24.4	75.6	41.5	17.0	83.0
Ohio	—	—	—	44.6	10.8	89.2	51.6	3.2	96.8
Oklahoma	60.2	20.4	79.6	62.0	24.0	76.0	—	—	—
Oregon	51.1	2.2	97.8	55.9	11.8	88.2	—	—	—
Pennsylvania	—	—	—	33.9	32.2	67.8	39.8	20.4	79.6
Rhode Island	—	—	—	—	—	—	54.5	9.0	91.0
South Carolina	—	—	—	100.0	100.0	0.0	—	—	—
South Dakota	—	—	—	51.9	3.8	96.2	—	—	—
Tennessee	—	—	—	—	—	—	54.9	9.8	90.2
Texas	—	—	—	—	—	—	86.1	72.2	27.8
Utah	—	—	—	48.6	2.8	97.2	58.8	17.6	82.4
Vermont	—	—	—	43.2	13.6	86.4	24.0	52.0	48.0
Virginia	—	—	—	—	—	—	100.0	100.0	0.0
Washington	—	—	—	41.3	17.4	82.6	40.1	19.8	80.2
West Virginia	—	—	—	—	—	—	49.0	2.0	98.0
Wisconsin	—	—	—	50.2	0.4	99.6	35.0	30.0	70.0
Wyoming	—	—	—	—	—	—	53.1	6.2	93.8

Notes: The first entries are the Democratic percent of two-party vote values for each state for the Senate race. The second entries are the margin of victory values for each state for the Senate race, where margin of victory is defined as the absolute difference between the Democratic percent and the Republican percent of the two-party vote for the Senate. The third entries are the party competition index values for each state for the Senate race, where the competition index devised by Paul David (1972) is defined as (100 − the margin of victory) or, alternatively, as (100 − the absolute difference between the Democratic and Republican percent of two-party vote for the Senate). The values for Democratic and Republican percent of two-party vote for the Senate are taken from the state vote tables in Chapter 6. Zero (0) percent on David's index represents a complete absence of two-party competition for that election year, whereas a score of 100 percent indicates perfect competition between the two major parties. A state can only receive a party competition score of 0 if it has 100–0 vote split for the Senate. Conversely, a state can only get a score of 100 if it has a 50–50 vote split for Senate. For example, if Alabama in 1914 reported an 83.7 percent Democratic vote for the Senate of its two-party vote, then its Republican vote for Senate would be 16.3 percent. The absolute difference between the two figures is the margin of victory, or 67.4 percent; 100 percent − 67.4 percent would equal 32.6 percent on David's party competition scale, indicating very little competition in the Senate race in Alabama in 1914. The two-party vote percent values used to derive the margin of victory and party competition figures are initially found in the state vote tables in Chapter 6. The author's alternative party coding in these tables is used whenever it occurs instead of the conventional party coding of voting data. The Democratic Party is defined here as the Anti-Federalists, Democratic-Republicans, and Jackson Democrats prior to 1830 when the "Democratic Party" as such was established. The Republican Party is defined as the Federalists, National Republicans, and Whigs prior to the establishment of the "Republican Party" in the 1850s. See Appendix A for an explanation of the historical antecedents of the current Democratic and Republican parties. States reporting only partial voting returns for Senate races are not included in the calculations for the years in which this occurred. —indicates that the state had no data, either because the state had no Senate election, no vote data were found for the state in question, or the state had not yet entered the Union.

Sources: State vote tables for Senate in Chapter 6.

Table 8-91 Senate Competition Measures, by State, by Election Year, 1918–1922 (Percentages)

	1918			1920			1922		
State	Democratic % of Two-Party Vote	Margin of Victory	Party Competition Index	Democratic % of Two-Party Vote	Margin of Victory	Party Competition Index	Democratic % of Two-Party Vote	Margin of Victory	Party Competition Index
Alabama	100.0	100.0	0.0	68.6	37.2	62.8	—	—	—
Alaska	—	—	—	—	—	—	—	—	—
Arizona	—	—	—	44.8	10.4	89.6	65.0	30.0	70.0
Arkansas	100.0	100.0	0.0	65.9	31.8	68.2	—	—	—
California	—	—	—	45.3	9.4	90.6	27.7	44.6	55.4
Colorado	49.2	1.6	98.4	41.9	16.2	83.8	—	—	—
Connecticut	—	—	—	37.8	24.4	75.6	46.5	7.0	93.0
Delaware	48.3	3.4	96.6	—	—	—	50.2	0.4	99.6
Florida	—	—	—	76.3	52.6	47.4	88.3	76.6	23.4
Georgia	88.4	76.8	23.2	100.0	100.0	0.0	—	—	—
Hawaii	—	—	—	—	—	—	—	—	—
Idaho	32.8	34.4	65.6	45.9	8.2	91.8	—	—	—
Illinois	47.1	5.8	94.2	28.6	42.8	57.2	—	—	—
Indiana	—	—	—	43.0	14.0	86.0	51.6	3.2	96.8
Iowa	34.6	30.8	69.2	37.9	24.2	75.8	—	—	—
Kansas	34.6	30.8	69.2	34.3	31.4	68.6	—	—	—
Kentucky	50.8	1.6	98.4	49.7	0.6	99.4	—	—	—
Louisiana	100.0	100.0	0.0	100.0	100.0	0.0	—	—	—
Maine	44.4	11.2	88.8	—	—	—	42.5	15.0	85.0
Maryland	—	—	—	47.8	4.4	95.6	53.6	7.2	92.8
Massachusetts	52.4	4.8	95.2	—	—	—	49.6	0.8	99.2
Michigan	49.1	1.8	98.2	—	—	—	51.1	2.2	97.8
Minnesota	0.0	100.0	0.0	—	—	—	33.8	32.4	67.6
Mississippi	100.0	100.0	0.0	—	—	—	98.0	96.0	4.0
Missouri	—	—	—	45.3	9.4	90.6	52.3	4.6	95.4
Montana	53.4	6.8	93.2	—	—	—	55.9	11.8	88.2
Nebraska	45.5	9.0	91.0	—	—	—	40.2	19.6	80.4
Nevada	—	—	—	47.4	5.2	94.8	62.8	25.6	74.4
New Hampshire	46.4	7.2	92.8	41.9	16.2	83.8	—	—	—
New Jersey	46.2	7.6	92.4	—	—	—	55.5	11.0	89.0
New Mexico	48.0	4.0	96.0	—	—	—	55.6	11.2	88.8
New York	—	—	—	38.6	22.8	77.2	56.2	12.4	87.6
North Carolina	60.5	21.0	79.0	57.5	15.0	85.0	—	—	—
North Dakota	—	—	—	40.2	19.6	80.4	47.7	4.6	95.4
Ohio	—	—	—	40.8	18.4	81.6	48.4	3.2	96.8
Oklahoma	57.6	15.2	84.8	46.9	6.2	93.8	—	—	—
Oregon	43.8	12.4	87.6	46.2	7.6	92.4	—	—	—
Pennsylvania	—	—	—	31.2	37.6	62.4	34.6	30.8	69.2
Rhode Island	47.2	5.6	94.4	—	—	—	54.6	9.2	90.8
South Carolina	100.0	100.0	0.0	100.0	100.0	0.0	—	—	—
South Dakota	41.4	17.2	82.8	28.5	43.0	57.0	—	—	—
Tennessee	62.2	24.4	75.6	—	—	—	68.0	36.0	64.0
Texas	87.5	75.0	25.0	—	—	—	66.6	33.2	66.8
Utah	—	—	—	40.5	19.0	81.0	50.2	0.4	99.6
Vermont	—	—	—	21.9	56.2	43.8	32.1	35.8	64.2
Virginia	100.0	100.0	0.0	—	—	—	73.1	46.2	53.8
Washington	—	—	—	24.0	52.0	48.0	50.7	1.4	98.6
West Virginia	45.9	8.2	91.8	—	—	—	51.8	3.6	96.4
Wisconsin	—	—	—	24.1	51.8	48.2	17.1	65.8	34.2
Wyoming	42.2	15.6	84.4	—	—	—	57.3	14.6	85.4

Notes: The first entries are the Democratic percent of two-party vote values for each state for the Senate race. The second entries are the margin of victory values for each state for the Senate race, where margin of victory is defined as the absolute difference between the Democratic percent and the Republican percent of the two-party vote for the Senate. The third entries are the party competition index values for each state for the Senate race, where the competition index devised by Paul David (1972) is defined as (100 − the margin of victory) or, alternatively, as (100 − the absolute difference between the Democratic and Republican percent of two-party vote for the Senate). The values for Democratic and Republican percent of two-party vote for the Senate are taken from the state vote tables in Chapter 6. Zero (0) percent on David's index represents a complete absence of two-party competition for that election year, whereas a score of 100 percent indicates perfect competition between the two major parties. A state can only receive a party competition score of 0 if it has 100–0 vote split for the Senate. Conversely, a state can only get a score of 100 if it has a 50–50 vote split for Senate. For example, if Alabama in 1914 reported an 83.7 percent Democratic vote for the Senate or its two-party vote, then its Republican vote for Senate would be 16.3 percent. The absolute difference between the two figures is the margin of victory, or 67.4 percent; 100 percent − 67.4 percent would equal 32.6 percent on David's party competition scale, indicating very little competition in the Senate race in Alabama in 1914. The two-party vote percent values used to derive the margin of victory and party competition figures are initially found in the state vote tables in Chapter 6. The author's alternative party coding in these tables is used whenever it occurs instead of the conventional party coding of voting data. The Democratic Party is defined here as the Anti-Federalists, Democratic-Republicans, and Jackson Democrats prior to 1830 when the "Democratic Party" as such was established. The Republican Party is defined as the Federalists, National Republicans, and Whigs prior to the establishment of the "Republican Party" in the 1850s. See Appendix A for an explanation of the historical antecedents of the current Democratic and Republican parties. States reporting only partial voting returns for Senate races are not included in the calculations for the years in which this occurred. —indicates that the state had no data, either because the state had no Senate election, no vote data were found for the state in question, or the state had not yet entered the Union.

Sources: State vote tables for Senate in Chapter 6.

Table 8-92 Senate Competition Measures, by State, by Election Year, 1924–1928 (Percentages)

	1924			1926			1928		
State	Democratic % of Two-Party Vote	Margin of Victory	Party Competition Index	Democratic % of Two-Party Vote	Margin of Victory	Party Competition Index	Democratic % of Two-Party Vote	Margin of Victory	Party Competition Index
Alabama	75.2	50.4	49.6	80.9	61.8	38.2	—	—	—
Alaska	—	—	—	—	—	—	—	—	—
Arizona	—	—	—	58.3	16.6	83.4	54.2	8.4	91.6
Arkansas	73.5	47.0	53.0	82.8	65.6	34.4	—	—	—
California	—	—	—	36.9	26.2	73.8	19.7	60.6	39.4
Colorado	46.7	6.6	93.4	48.0	4.0	96.0	—	—	—
Connecticut	—	—	—	36.0	28.0	72.0	45.8	8.4	91.6
Delaware	0.0	100.0	0.0	—	—	—	39.1	21.8	78.2
Florida	—	—	—	77.9	55.8	44.2	68.5	37.0	63.0
Georgia	100.0	100.0	0.0	100.0	100.0	0.0	—	—	—
Hawaii	—	—	—	—	—	—	—	—	—
Idaho	20.2	59.6	40.4	35.5	29.0	71.0	—	—	—
Illinois	35.8	28.4	71.6	43.8	12.4	87.6	—	—	—
Indiana	—	—	—	49.5	1.0	99.0	44.4	11.2	88.8
Iowa	50.0	0.0	100.0	43.4	13.2	86.8	—	—	—
Kansas	26.5	47.0	53.0	35.3	29.4	70.6	—	—	—
Kentucky	48.4	3.2	96.8	51.8	3.6	96.4	—	—	—
Louisiana	100.0	100.0	0.0	100.0	100.0	0.0	—	—	—
Maine	39.6	20.8	79.2	—	—	—	30.4	39.2	60.8
Maryland	—	—	—	58.3	16.6	83.4	45.6	8.8	91.2
Massachusetts	49.2	1.6	98.4	—	—	—	54.1	8.2	91.8
Michigan	24.9	50.2	49.8	—	—	—	27.8	44.4	55.6
Minnesota	12.1	75.8	24.2	—	—	—	0.0	100.0	0.0
Mississippi	100.0	100.0	0.0	—	—	—	100.0	100.0	0.0
Missouri	—	—	—	51.8	3.6	96.4	48.0	4.0	96.0
Montana	55.5	11.0	89.0	—	—	—	53.2	6.4	93.6
Nebraska	37.6	24.8	75.2	—	—	—	38.7	22.6	77.4
Nevada	—	—	—	43.2	13.6	86.4	59.3	18.6	81.4
New Hampshire	40.2	19.6	80.4	37.7	24.6	75.4	—	—	—
New Jersey	35.3	29.4	70.6	—	—	—	42.0	16.0	84.0
New Mexico	51.2	2.4	97.6	—	—	—	42.3	15.4	84.6
New York	—	—	—	47.9	4.2	95.8	50.6	1.2	98.8
North Carolina	61.6	23.2	76.8	60.5	21.0	79.0	—	—	—
North Dakota	—	—	—	10.3	79.4	20.6	19.5	61.0	39.0
Ohio	—	—	—	46.7	6.6	93.4	39.1	21.8	78.2
Oklahoma	36.5	27.0	73.0	55.1	10.2	89.8	—	—	—
Oregon	27.2	45.6	54.4	47.7	4.6	95.4	—	—	—
Pennsylvania	—	—	—	44.1	11.8	88.2	34.6	30.8	69.2
Rhode Island	42.0	16.0	84.0	—	—	—	49.4	1.2	98.8
South Carolina	100.0	100.0	0.0	100.0	100.0	0.0	—	—	—
South Dakota	41.4	17.2	82.8	40.5	19.0	81.0	—	—	—
Tennessee	57.4	14.8	85.2	—	—	—	59.3	18.6	81.4
Texas	85.4	70.8	29.2	—	—	—	81.3	62.6	37.4
Utah	—	—	—	37.9	24.2	75.8	55.8	11.6	88.4
Vermont	—	—	—	26.5	47.0	53.0	28.4	43.2	56.8
Virginia	96.4	92.8	7.2	—	—	—	100.0	100.0	0.0
Washington	—	—	—	48.1	3.8	96.2	53.5	7.0	93.0
West Virginia	48.4	3.2	96.8	—	—	—	49.3	1.4	98.6
Wisconsin	—	—	—	13.9	72.2	27.8	0.0	100.0	0.0
Wyoming	44.8	10.4	89.6	—	—	—	53.7	7.4	92.6

Notes: The first entries are the Democratic percent of two-party vote values for each state for the Senate race. The second entries are the margin of victory values for each state for the Senate race, where margin of victory is defined as the absolute difference between the Democratic percent and the Republican percent of the two-party vote for the Senate. The third entries are the party competition index values for each state for the Senate race, where the competition index devised by Paul David (1972) is defined as (100 − the margin of victory) or, alternatively, as (100 − the absolute difference between the Democratic and Republican percent of two-party vote for the Senate). The values for Democratic and Republican percent of two-party vote for the Senate are taken from the state vote tables in Chapter 6. Zero (0) percent on David's index represents a complete absence of two-party competition for that election year, whereas a score of 100 percent indicates perfect competition between the two major parties. A state can only receive a party competition score of 0 if it has 100–0 vote split for the Senate. Conversely, a state can only get a score of 100 if it has a 50–50 vote split for Senate. For example, if Alabama in 1914 reported an 83.7 percent Democratic vote for the Senate of its two-party vote, then its Republican vote for Senate would be 16.3 percent. The absolute difference between the two figures is the margin of victory, or 67.4 percent; 100 percent − 67.4 percent would equal 32.6 percent on David's party competition scale, indicating very little competition in the Senate race in Alabama in 1914. The two-party vote percent values used to derive the margin of victory and party competition figures are initially found in the state vote tables in Chapter 6. The author's alternative party coding in these tables is used whenever it occurs instead of the conventional party coding of voting data. The Democratic Party is defined here as the Anti-Federalists, Democratic-Republicans, and Jackson Democrats prior to 1830 when the "Democratic Party" as such was established. The Republican Party is defined as the Federalists, National Republicans, and Whigs prior to the establishment of the "Republican Party" in the 1850s. See Appendix A for an explanation of the historical antecedents of the current Democratic and Republican parties. States reporting only partial voting returns for Senate races are not included in the calculations for the years in which this occurred. —indicates that the state had no data, either because the state had no Senate election, no vote data were found for the state in question, or the state had not yet entered the Union.

Sources: State vote tables for Senate in Chapter 6.

Table 8-93 Senate Competition Measures, by State, by Election Year, 1930–1934 (Percentages)

State	1930 Democratic % of Two-Party Vote	Margin of Victory	Party Competition Index	1932 Democratic % of Two-Party Vote	Margin of Victory	Party Competition Index	1934 Democratic % of Two-Party Vote	Margin of Victory	Party Competition Index
Alabama	100.0	100.0	0.0	86.2	72.4	27.6	—	—	—
Alaska	—	—	—	—	—	—	—	—	—
Arizona	—	—	—	67.5	35.0	65.0	73.8	47.6	52.4
Arkansas	100.0	100.0	0.0	89.5	79.0	21.0	—	—	—
California	—	—	—	58.5	17.0	83.0	0.0	100.0	0.0
Colorado	56.7	13.4	86.6	53.3	6.6	93.4	—	—	—
Connecticut	—	—	—	49.4	1.2	98.8	51.7	3.4	96.6
Delaware	45.4	9.2	90.8	—	—	—	46.4	7.2	92.8
Florida	—	—	—	100.0	100.0	0.0	100.0	100.0	0.0
Georgia	100.0	100.0	0.0	92.8	85.6	14.4	—	—	—
Hawaii	—	—	—	—	—	—	—	—	—
Idaho	27.6	44.8	55.2	56.8	13.6	86.4	—	—	—
Illinois	64.5	29.0	71.0	53.2	6.4	93.6	—	—	—
Indiana	—	—	—	56.8	13.6	86.4	52.0	4.0	96.0
Iowa	43.3	13.4	86.6	57.4	14.8	85.2	—	—	—
Kansas	38.9	22.2	77.8	52.1	4.2	95.8	—	—	—
Kentucky	52.1	4.2	95.8	59.3	18.6	81.4	—	—	—
Louisiana	100.0	100.0	0.0	100.0	100.0	0.0	—	—	—
Maine	39.1	21.8	78.2	—	—	—	49.8	0.4	99.6
Maryland	—	—	—	68.0	36.0	64.0	57.2	14.4	85.6
Massachusetts	54.7	9.4	90.6	—	—	—	61.4	22.8	77.2
Michigan	21.1	57.8	42.2	—	—	—	47.8	4.4	95.6
Minnesota	49.0	2.0	98.0	—	—	—	59.6	19.2	80.8
Mississippi	100.0	100.0	0.0	—	—	—	100.0	100.0	0.0
Missouri	—	—	—	63.8	27.6	72.4	60.0	20.0	80.0
Montana	61.4	22.8	77.2	—	—	—	70.5	41.0	59.0
Nebraska	41.2	17.6	82.4	—	—	—	56.3	12.6	87.4
Nevada	—	—	—	52.1	4.2	95.8	65.9	31.8	68.2
New Hampshire	42.0	16.0	84.0	50.5	1.0	99.0	—	—	—
New Jersey	40.0	20.0	80.0	—	—	—	58.6	17.2	82.8
New Mexico	58.7	17.4	82.6	—	—	—	49.6	0.8	99.2
New York	—	—	—	59.1	18.2	81.8	60.0	20.0	80.0
North Carolina	60.6	21.2	78.8	68.3	36.6	63.4	—	—	—
North Dakota	—	—	—	27.5	45.0	55.0	40.9	18.2	81.8
Ohio	—	—	—	53.4	6.8	93.2	60.3	20.6	79.4
Oklahoma	52.4	4.8	95.2	66.1	32.2	67.8	—	—	—
Oregon	32.5	35.0	65.0	42.4	15.2	84.8	—	—	—
Pennsylvania	—	—	—	46.7	6.6	93.4	52.2	4.4	95.6
Rhode Island	49.4	1.2	98.8	—	—	—	57.1	14.2	85.8
South Carolina	100.0	100.0	0.0	98.1	96.2	3.8	—	—	—
South Dakota	51.6	3.2	96.8	45.3	9.4	90.6	—	—	—
Tennessee	72.5	45.0	55.0	—	—	—	63.9	27.8	72.2
Texas	87.2	74.4	25.6	—	—	—	97.1	94.2	5.8
Utah	—	—	—	57.6	15.2	84.8	53.9	7.8	92.2
Vermont	—	—	—	44.9	10.2	89.8	48.7	2.6	97.4
Virginia	100.0	100.0	0.0	—	—	—	78.4	56.8	43.2
Washington	—	—	—	65.0	30.0	70.0	64.2	28.4	71.6
West Virginia	62.1	24.2	75.8	—	—	—	55.4	10.8	89.2
Wisconsin	—	—	—	61.2	22.4	77.6	51.5	3.0	97.0
Wyoming	41.0	18.0	82.0	—	—	—	56.9	13.8	86.2

Notes: The first entries are the Democratic percent of two-party vote values for each state for the Senate race. The second entries are the margin of victory values for each state for the Senate race, where margin of victory is defined as the absolute difference between the Democratic percent and the Republican percent of the two-party vote for the Senate. The third entries are the party competition index values for each state for the Senate race, where the competition index devised by Paul David (1972) is defined as (100 − the margin of victory) or, alternatively, as (100 − the absolute difference between the Democratic and Republican percent of two-party vote for the Senate). The values for Democratic and Republican percent of two-party vote for the Senate are taken from the state vote tables in Chapter 6. Zero (0) percent on David's index represents a complete absence of two-party competition for that election year, whereas a score of 100 percent indicates perfect competition between the two major parties. A state can only receive a party competition score of 0 if it has 100–0 vote split for the Senate. Conversely, a state can only get a score of 100 if it has a 50–50 vote split for Senate. For example, if Alabama in 1914 reported an 83.7 percent Democratic vote for the Senate of its two-party vote, then its Republican vote for Senate would be 16.3 percent. The absolute difference between the two figures is the margin of victory, or 67.4 percent; 100 percent − 67.4 percent would equal 32.6 percent on David's party competition scale, indicating very little competition in the Senate race in Alabama in 1914. The two-party vote percent values used to derive the margin of victory and party competition figures are initially found in the state vote tables in Chapter 6. The author's alternative party coding in these tables is used whenever it occurs instead of the conventional party coding of voting data. The Democratic Party is defined here as the Anti-Federalists, Democratic-Republicans, and Jackson Democrats prior to 1830 when the "Democratic Party" as such was established. The Republican Party is defined as the Federalists, National Republicans, and Whigs prior to the establishment of the "Republican Party" in the 1850s. See Appendix A for an explanation of the historical antecedents of the current Democratic and Republican parties. States reporting only partial voting returns for Senate races are not included in the calculations for the years in which this occurred. —indicates that the state had no data, either because the state had no Senate election, no vote data were found for the state in question, or the state had not yet entered the Union.

Sources: State vote tables for Senate in Chapter 6.

Table 8-94 Senate Competition Measures, by State, by Election Year, 1936–1940 (Percentages)

State	1936 Democratic % of Two-Party Vote	1936 Margin of Victory	1936 Party Competition Index	1938 Democratic % of Two-Party Vote	1938 Margin of Victory	1938 Party Competition Index	1940 Democratic % of Two-Party Vote	1940 Margin of Victory	1940 Party Competition Index
Alabama	87.7	75.4	24.6	86.4	72.8	27.2	—	—	—
Alaska	—	—	—	—	—	—	—	—	—
Arizona	—	—	—	76.5	53.0	47.0	71.9	43.8	56.2
Arkansas	83.3	66.6	33.4	89.6	79.2	20.8	—	—	—
California	—	—	—	54.9	9.8	90.2	0.0	100.0	0.0
Colorado	64.3	28.6	71.4	59.2	18.4	81.6	—	—	—
Connecticut	—	—	—	48.3	3.4	96.6	53.8	7.6	92.4
Delaware	56.1	12.2	87.8	—	—	—	52.7	5.4	94.6
Florida	—	—	—	82.4	64.8	35.2	100.0	100.0	0.0
Georgia	100.0	100.0	0.0	100.0	100.0	0.0	—	—	—
Hawaii	—	—	—	—	—	—	—	—	—
Idaho	36.6	26.8	73.2	54.9	9.8	90.2	—	—	—
Illinois	58.1	16.2	83.8	51.5	3.0	97.0	—	—	—
Indiana	—	—	—	50.2	0.4	99.6	49.3	1.4	98.6
Iowa	51.7	3.4	96.6	50.2	0.4	99.6	—	—	—
Kansas	48.7	2.6	97.4	43.8	12.4	87.6	—	—	—
Kentucky	59.6	19.2	80.8	62.0	24.0	76.0	—	—	—
Louisiana	100.0	100.0	0.0	100.0	100.0	0.0	—	—	—
Maine	49.3	1.4	98.6	—	—	—	41.3	17.4	82.6
Maryland	—	—	—	70.0	40.0	60.0	65.9	31.8	68.2
Massachusetts	45.8	8.4	91.6	—	—	—	56.5	13.0	87.0
Michigan	56.0	12.0	88.0	—	—	—	47.2	5.6	94.4
Minnesota	0.0	100.0	0.0	—	—	—	27.9	44.2	55.8
Mississippi	100.0	100.0	0.0	—	—	—	100.0	100.0	0.0
Missouri	—	—	—	60.8	21.6	78.4	51.2	2.4	97.6
Montana	67.0	34.0	66.0	—	—	—	73.4	46.8	53.2
Nebraska	32.7	34.6	65.4	—	—	—	42.1	15.8	84.2
Nevada	—	—	—	59.0	18.0	82.0	60.5	21.0	79.0
New Hampshire	47.9	4.2	95.8	45.8	8.4	91.6	—	—	—
New Jersey	55.3	10.6	89.4	—	—	—	44.5	11.0	89.0
New Mexico	61.7	23.4	76.6	—	—	—	55.9	11.8	88.2
New York	—	—	—	54.8	9.6	90.4	53.3	6.6	93.4
North Carolina	70.8	41.6	58.4	63.8	27.6	72.4	—	—	—
North Dakota	—	—	—	12.7	74.6	25.4	41.0	18.0	82.0
Ohio	—	—	—	46.4	7.2	92.8	47.6	4.8	95.2
Oklahoma	68.3	36.6	63.4	65.8	31.6	68.4	—	—	—
Oregon	49.3	1.4	98.6	45.1	9.8	90.2	—	—	—
Pennsylvania	—	—	—	44.8	10.4	89.6	52.2	4.4	95.6
Rhode Island	52.3	4.6	95.4	—	—	—	55.2	10.4	89.6
South Carolina	98.6	97.2	2.8	98.9	97.8	2.2	—	—	—
South Dakota	51.1	2.2	97.8	47.5	5.0	95.0	—	—	—
Tennessee	80.3	60.6	39.4	—	—	—	70.8	41.6	58.4
Texas	92.9	85.8	14.2	—	—	—	94.3	88.6	11.4
Utah	—	—	—	55.8	11.6	88.4	62.8	25.6	74.4
Vermont	—	—	—	34.3	31.4	68.6	33.6	32.8	67.2
Virginia	95.2	90.4	9.6	—	—	—	100.0	100.0	0.0
Washington	—	—	—	62.8	25.6	74.4	54.2	8.4	91.6
West Virginia	59.1	18.2	81.8	—	—	—	56.3	12.6	87.4
Wisconsin	—	—	—	33.8	32.4	67.6	24.2	51.6	48.4
Wyoming	54.2	8.4	91.6	—	—	—	58.7	17.4	82.6

Notes: The first entries are the Democratic percent of two-party vote values for each state for the Senate race. The second entries are the margin of victory values for each state for the Senate race, where margin of victory is defined as the absolute difference between the Democratic percent and the Republican percent of the two-party vote for the Senate. The third entries are the party competition index values for each state for the Senate race, where the competition index devised by Paul David (1972) is defined as (100 − the margin of victory) or, alternatively, as (100 − the absolute difference between the Democratic and Republican percent of two-party vote for the Senate). The values for Democratic and Republican percent of two-party vote for the Senate are taken from the state vote tables in Chapter 6. Zero (0) percent on David's index represents a complete absence of two-party competition for that election year, whereas a score of 100 percent indicates perfect competition between the two major parties. A state can only receive a party competition score of 0 if it has 100–0 vote split for the Senate. Conversely, a state can only get a score of 100 if it has a 50–50 vote split for Senate. For example, if Alabama in 1914 reported an 83.7 percent Democratic vote for the Senate of its two-party vote, then its Republican vote for Senate would be 16.3 percent. The absolute difference between the two figures is the margin of victory, or 67.4 percent; 100 percent − 67.4 percent would equal 32.6 percent on David's party competition scale, indicating very little competition in the Senate race in Alabama in 1914. The two-party vote percent values used to derive the margin of victory and party competition figures are initially found in the state vote tables in Chapter 6. The author's alternative party coding in these tables is used whenever it occurs instead of the conventional party coding of voting data. The Democratic Party is defined here as the Anti-Federalists, Democratic-Republicans, and Jackson Democrats prior to 1830 when the "Democratic Party" as such was established. The Republican Party is defined as the Federalists, National Republicans, and Whigs prior to the establishment of the "Republican Party" in the 1850s. See Appendix A for an explanation of the historical antecedents of the current Democratic and Republican parties. States reporting only partial voting returns for Senate races are not included in the calculations for the years in which this occurred. —indicates that the state had no data, either because the state had no Senate election, no vote data were found for the state in question, or the state had not yet entered the Union.

Sources: State vote tables for Senate in Chapter 6.

Table 8-95 Senate Competition Measures, by State, by Election Year, 1942–1946 (Percentages)

	1942			1944			1946		
State	Democratic % of Two-Party Vote	Margin of Victory	Party Competition Index	Democratic % of Two-Party Vote	Margin of Victory	Party Competition Index	Democratic % of Two-Party Vote	Margin of Victory	Party Competition Index
Alabama	100.0	100.0	0.0	82.8	65.6	34.4	—	—	—
Alaska	—	—	—	—	—	—	—	—	—
Arizona	—	—	—	69.4	38.8	61.2	69.7	39.4	60.6
Arkansas	100.0	100.0	0.0	85.1	70.2	29.8	—	—	—
California	—	—	—	52.3	4.6	95.4	45.0	10.0	90.0
Colorado	50.5	1.0	99.0	43.6	12.8	87.2	—	—	—
Connecticut	—	—	—	52.4	4.8	95.2	42.0	16.0	84.0
Delaware	45.3	9.4	90.6	—	—	—	44.8	10.4	89.6
Florida	—	—	—	71.3	42.6	57.4	78.6	57.2	42.8
Georgia	100.0	100.0	0.0	100.0	100.0	0.0	—	—	—
Hawaii	—	—	—	—	—	—	—	—	—
Idaho	48.5	3.0	97.0	51.1	2.2	97.8	—	—	—
Illinois	46.6	6.8	93.2	52.8	5.6	94.4	—	—	—
Indiana	—	—	—	49.3	1.4	98.6	44.1	11.8	88.2
Iowa	41.8	16.4	83.6	48.5	3.0	97.0	—	—	—
Kansas	41.4	17.2	82.8	41.3	17.4	82.6	—	—	—
Kentucky	55.3	10.6	89.4	55.0	10.0	90.0	—	—	—
Louisiana	100.0	100.0	0.0	100.0	100.0	0.0	—	—	—
Maine	33.3	33.4	66.6	—	—	—	36.5	27.0	73.0
Maryland	—	—	—	61.7	23.4	76.6	50.2	0.4	99.6
Massachusetts	47.1	5.8	94.2	—	—	—	40.0	20.0	80.0
Michigan	47.5	5.0	95.0	—	—	—	32.3	35.4	64.6
Minnesota	18.1	63.8	36.2	—	—	—	40.3	19.4	80.6
Mississippi	100.0	100.0	0.0	—	—	—	100.0	100.0	0.0
Missouri	—	—	—	49.9	0.2	99.8	47.2	5.6	94.4
Montana	50.4	0.8	99.2	—	—	—	45.9	8.2	91.8
Nebraska	31.0	38.0	62.0	—	—	—	29.2	41.6	58.4
Nevada	—	—	—	58.4	16.8	83.2	44.8	10.4	89.6
New Hampshire	45.4	9.2	90.8	49.1	1.8	98.2	—	—	—
New Jersey	46.3	7.4	92.6	—	—	—	40.7	18.6	81.4
New Mexico	59.2	18.4	81.6	—	—	—	51.5	3.0	97.0
New York	—	—	—	53.2	6.4	93.6	47.4	5.2	94.8
North Carolina	65.9	31.8	68.2	70.3	40.6	59.4	—	—	—
North Dakota	—	—	—	45.5	9.0	91.0	30.3	39.4	60.6
Ohio	—	—	—	49.7	0.6	99.4	42.6	14.8	85.2
Oklahoma	44.9	10.2	89.8	55.8	11.6	88.4	—	—	—
Oregon	22.9	54.2	45.8	39.3	21.4	78.6	—	—	—
Pennsylvania	—	—	—	50.3	0.6	99.4	40.2	19.6	80.4
Rhode Island	58.0	16.0	84.0	—	—	—	55.1	10.2	89.8
South Carolina	100.0	100.0	0.0	96.8	93.6	6.4	—	—	—
South Dakota	41.3	17.4	82.6	36.1	27.8	72.2	—	—	—
Tennessee	76.2	52.4	47.6	—	—	—	71.8	43.6	56.4
Texas	95.6	91.2	8.8	—	—	—	88.5	77.0	23.0
Utah	—	—	—	59.9	19.8	80.2	48.8	2.4	97.6
Vermont	—	—	—	34.2	31.6	68.4	25.4	49.2	50.8
Virginia	100.0	100.0	0.0	—	—	—	68.0	36.0	64.0
Washington	—	—	—	55.4	10.8	89.2	45.4	9.2	90.8
West Virginia	44.6	10.8	89.2	—	—	—	50.3	0.6	99.4
Wisconsin	—	—	—	45.8	8.4	91.6	37.9	24.2	75.8
Wyoming	45.4	9.2	90.8	—	—	—	56.2	12.4	87.6

Notes: The first entries are the Democratic percent of two-party vote values for each state for the Senate race. The second entries are the margin of victory values for each state for the Senate race, where margin of victory is defined as the absolute difference between the Democratic percent and the Republican percent of the two-party vote for the Senate. The third entries are the party competition index values for each state for the Senate race, where the competition index devised by Paul David (1972) is defined as (100 − the margin of victory) or, alternatively, as (100 − the absolute difference between the Democratic and Republican percent of two-party vote for the Senate). The values for Democratic and Republican percent of two-party vote for the Senate are taken from the state vote tables in Chapter 6. Zero (0) percent on David's index represents a complete absence of two-party competition for that election year, whereas a score of 100 percent indicates perfect competition between the two major parties. A state can only receive a party competition score of 0 if it has 100–0 vote split for the Senate. Conversely, a state can only get a score of 100 if it has a 50–50 vote split for Senate. For example, if Alabama in 1914 reported an 83.7 percent Democratic vote for the Senate of its two-party vote, then its Republican vote for Senate would be 16.3 percent. The absolute difference between the two figures is the margin of victory, or 67.4 percent; 100 percent − 67.4 percent would equal 32.6 percent on David's party competition scale, indicating very little competition in the Senate race in Alabama in 1914. The two-party vote percent values used to derive the margin of victory and party competition figures are initially found in the state vote tables in Chapter 6. The author's alternative party coding in these tables is used whenever it occurs instead of the conventional party coding of voting data. The Democratic Party is defined here as the Anti-Federalists, Democratic-Republicans, and Jackson Democrats prior to 1830 when the "Democratic Party" as such was established. The Republican Party is defined as the Federalists, National Republicans, and Whigs prior to the establishment of the "Republican Party" in the 1850s. See Appendix A for an explanation of the historical antecedents of the current Democratic and Republican parties. States reporting only partial voting returns for Senate races are not included in the calculations for the years in which this occurred. —indicates that the state had no data, either because the state had no Senate election, no vote data were found for the state in question, or the state had not yet entered the Union.

Sources: State vote tables for Senate in Chapter 6.

Table 8-96 Senate Competition Measures, by State, by Election Year, 1948–1952 (Percentages)

State	1948 Democratic % of Two-Party Vote	Margin of Victory	Party Competition Index	1950 Democratic % of Two-Party Vote	Margin of Victory	Party Competition Index	1952 Democratic % of Two-Party Vote	Margin of Victory	Party Competition Index
Alabama	84.0	68.0	32.0	100.0	100.0	0.0	—	—	—
Alaska	—	—	—	—	—	—	—	—	—
Arizona	—	—	—	62.8	25.6	74.4	48.7	2.6	97.4
Arkansas	100.0	100.0	0.0	100.0	100.0	0.0	—	—	—
California	—	—	—	40.8	18.4	81.6	0.0	100.0	0.0
Colorado	67.4	34.8	65.2	46.7	6.6	93.4	—	—	—
Connecticut	—	—	—	52.6	5.2	94.8	44.9	10.2	89.8
Delaware	51.3	2.6	97.4	—	—	—	45.5	9.0	91.0
Florida	—	—	—	76.3	52.6	47.4	100.0	100.0	0.0
Georgia	100.0	100.0	0.0	100.0	100.0	0.0	—	—	—
Hawaii	—	—	—	—	—	—	—	—	—
Idaho	50.7	1.4	98.6	38.3	23.4	76.6	—	—	—
Illinois	55.2	10.4	89.6	45.9	8.2	91.8	—	—	—
Indiana	—	—	—	46.7	6.6	93.4	47.2	5.6	94.4
Iowa	58.2	16.4	83.6	45.0	10.0	90.0	—	—	—
Kansas	43.7	12.6	87.4	44.7	10.6	89.4	—	—	—
Kentucky	51.5	3.0	97.0	54.6	9.2	90.8	—	—	—
Louisiana	100.0	100.0	0.0	87.7	75.4	24.6	—	—	—
Maine	28.7	42.6	57.4	—	—	—	41.3	17.4	82.6
Maryland	—	—	—	46.5	7.0	93.0	47.5	5.0	95.0
Massachusetts	46.7	6.6	93.4	—	—	—	51.5	3.0	97.0
Michigan	48.9	2.2	97.8	—	—	—	49.2	1.6	98.4
Minnesota	60.0	20.0	80.0	—	—	—	42.9	14.2	85.8
Mississippi	100.0	100.0	0.0	—	—	—	100.0	100.0	0.0
Missouri	—	—	—	53.6	7.2	92.8	54.0	8.0	92.0
Montana	57.0	14.0	86.0	—	—	—	51.1	2.2	97.8
Nebraska	43.3	13.4	86.6	—	—	—	28.7	42.6	57.4
Nevada	—	—	—	58.0	16.0	84.0	48.3	3.4	96.6
New Hampshire	41.5	17.0	83.0	40.6	18.8	81.2	—	—	—
New Jersey	48.6	2.8	97.2	—	—	—	44.0	12.0	88.0
New Mexico	57.4	14.8	85.2	—	—	—	51.1	2.2	97.8
New York	—	—	—	52.6	5.2	94.8	43.9	12.2	87.8
North Carolina	71.1	42.2	57.8	68.7	37.4	62.6	—	—	—
North Dakota	—	—	—	32.4	35.2	64.8	26.0	48.0	52.0
Ohio	—	—	—	42.5	15.0	85.0	45.4	9.2	90.8
Oklahoma	62.5	25.0	75.0	54.8	9.6	90.4	—	—	—
Oregon	40.0	20.0	80.0	23.7	52.6	47.4	—	—	—
Pennsylvania	—	—	—	48.2	3.6	96.4	48.2	3.6	96.4
Rhode Island	59.3	18.6	81.4	—	—	—	54.8	9.6	90.4
South Carolina	96.4	92.8	7.2	100.0	100.0	0.0	—	—	—
South Dakota	40.7	18.6	81.4	36.1	27.8	72.2	—	—	—
Tennessee	66.1	32.2	67.8	—	—	—	78.0	56.0	44.0
Texas	66.8	33.6	66.4	—	—	—	100.0	100.0	0.0
Utah	—	—	—	46.0	8.0	92.0	45.7	8.6	91.4
Vermont	—	—	—	22.0	56.0	44.0	27.7	44.6	55.4
Virginia	68.0	36.0	64.0	—	—	—	100.0	100.0	0.0
Washington	—	—	—	53.7	7.4	92.6	56.4	12.8	87.2
West Virginia	57.0	14.0	86.0	—	—	—	53.6	7.2	92.8
Wisconsin	—	—	—	46.4	7.2	92.8	45.7	8.6	91.4
Wyoming	57.1	14.2	85.8	—	—	—	48.4	3.2	96.8

Notes: The first entries are the Democratic percent of two-party vote values for each state for the Senate race. The second entries are the margin of victory values for each state for the Senate race, where margin of victory is defined as the absolute difference between the Democratic percent and the Republican percent of the two-party vote for the Senate. The third entries are the party competition index values for each state for the Senate race, where the competition index devised by Paul David (1972) is defined as (100 − the margin of victory) or, alternatively, as (100 − the absolute difference between the Democratic and Republican percent of two-party vote for the Senate). The values for Democratic and Republican percent of two-party vote for the Senate are taken from the state vote tables in Chapter 6. Zero (0) percent on David's index represents a complete absence of two-party competition for that election year, whereas a score of 100 percent indicates perfect competition between the two major parties. A state can only receive a party competition score of 0 if it has a 100–0 vote split for the Senate. Conversely, a state can only get a score of 100 if it has a 50–50 vote split for Senate. For example, if Alabama in 1914 reported an 83.7 percent Democratic vote for the Senate of its two-party vote, then its Republican vote for Senate would be 16.3 percent. The absolute difference between the two figures is the margin of victory, or 67.4 percent; 100 percent − 67.4 percent would equal 32.6 percent on David's party competition scale, indicating very little competition in the Senate race in Alabama in 1914. The two-party vote percent values used to derive the margin of victory and party competition figures are initially found in the state vote tables in Chapter 6. The author's alternative party coding in these tables is used whenever it occurs instead of the conventional party coding of voting data. The Democratic Party is defined here as the Anti-Federalists, Democratic-Republicans, and Jackson Democrats prior to 1830 when the "Democratic Party" as such was established. The Republican Party is defined as the Federalists, National Republicans, and Whigs prior to the establishment of the "Republican Party" in the 1850s. See Appendix A for an explanation of the historical antecedents of the current Democratic and Republican parties. States reporting only partial voting returns for Senate races are not included in the calculations for the years in which this occurred. —indicates that the state had no data, either because the state had no Senate election, no vote data were found for the state in question, or the state had not yet entered the Union.

Sources: State vote tables for Senate in Chapter 6.

Table 8-97 Senate Competition Measures, by State, by Election Year, 1954–1959 (Percentages)

State	1954 Democratic % of Two-Party Vote	1954 Margin of Victory	1954 Party Competition Index	1956 Democratic % of Two-Party Vote	1956 Margin of Victory	1956 Party Competition Index	1958–1959 Democratic % of Two-Party Vote	1958–1959 Margin of Victory	1958–1959 Party Competition Index
Alabama	82.5	65.0	35.0	100.0	100.0	0.0	—	—	—
Alaska	—	—	—	—	—	—	52.6	5.2	94.8
Arizona	—	—	—	61.4	22.8	77.2	43.9	12.2	87.8
Arkansas	100.0	100.0	0.0	83.0	66.0	34.0	—	—	—
California	—	—	—	45.8	8.4	91.6	57.0	14.0	86.0
Colorado	48.7	2.6	97.4	50.2	0.4	99.6	—	—	—
Connecticut	—	—	—	43.6	12.8	87.2	57.5	15.0	85.0
Delaware	56.9	13.8	86.2	—	—	—	46.7	6.6	93.4
Florida	—	—	—	100.0	100.0	0.0	71.2	42.4	57.6
Georgia	100.0	100.0	0.0	100.0	100.0	0.0	—	—	—
Hawaii	—	—	—	—	—	—	47.1[1]	5.8[1]	94.2[1]
Idaho	37.2	25.6	74.4	59.2	18.4	81.6	—	—	—
Illinois	53.6	7.2	92.8	45.8	8.4	91.6	—	—	—
Indiana	—	—	—	44.6	10.8	89.2	57.1	14.2	85.8
Iowa	47.7	4.6	95.4	46.1	7.8	92.2	—	—	—
Kansas	42.6	14.8	85.2	41.1	17.8	82.2	—	—	—
Kentucky	54.5	9.0	91.0	49.7	0.6	99.4	—	—	—
Louisiana	100.0	100.0	0.0	100.0	100.0	0.0	—	—	—
Maine	41.4	17.2	82.8	—	—	—	60.8	21.6	78.4
Maryland	—	—	—	47.0	6.0	94.0	49.0	2.0	98.0
Massachusetts	49.2	1.6	98.4	—	—	—	73.6	47.2	52.8
Michigan	50.9	1.8	98.2	—	—	—	53.8	7.6	92.4
Minnesota	57.2	14.4	85.6	—	—	—	53.2	6.4	93.6
Mississippi	95.6	91.2	8.8	—	—	—	100.0	100.0	0.0
Missouri	—	—	—	56.4	12.8	87.2	66.5	33.0	67.0
Montana	50.4	0.8	99.2	—	—	—	76.2	52.4	47.6
Nebraska	38.9	22.2	77.8	—	—	—	44.4	11.2	88.8
Nevada	—	—	—	52.6	5.2	94.8	57.7	15.4	84.6
New Hampshire	39.8	20.4	79.6	35.9	28.2	71.8	—	—	—
New Jersey	49.9	0.2	99.8	—	—	—	52.3	4.6	95.4
New Mexico	57.3	14.6	85.4	—	—	—	62.7	25.4	74.6
New York	—	—	—	46.7	6.6	93.4	48.8	2.4	97.6
North Carolina	65.9	31.8	68.2	66.6	33.2	66.8	—	—	—
North Dakota	—	—	—	36.1	27.8	72.2	42.0	16.0	84.0
Ohio	—	—	—	52.9	5.8	94.2	52.5	5.0	95.0
Oklahoma	56.1	12.2	87.8	55.3	10.6	89.4	—	—	—
Oregon	50.2	0.4	99.6	54.2	8.4	91.6	—	—	—
Pennsylvania	—	—	—	50.2	0.4	99.6	48.6	2.8	97.2
Rhode Island	59.3	18.6	81.4	—	—	—	64.5	29.0	71.0
South Carolina	100.0	100.0	0.0	82.2	64.4	35.6	—	—	—
South Dakota	42.7	14.6	85.4	49.2	1.6	98.4	—	—	—
Tennessee	70.0	40.0	60.0	—	—	—	80.6	61.2	38.8
Texas	85.1	70.2	29.8	—	—	—	75.9	51.8	48.2
Utah	—	—	—	46.0	8.0	92.0	52.6	5.2	94.8
Vermont	—	—	—	33.6	32.8	67.2	47.8	4.4	95.6
Virginia	100.0	100.0	0.0	—	—	—	100.0	100.0	0.0
Washington	—	—	—	61.1	22.2	77.8	68.2	36.4	63.6
West Virginia	54.8	9.6	90.4	—	—	—	59.2	18.4	81.6
Wisconsin	—	—	—	41.3	17.4	82.6	57.2	14.4	85.6
Wyoming	51.5	3.0	97.0	—	—	—	50.8	1.6	98.4

Notes: The first entries are the Democratic percent of two-party vote values for each state for the Senate race. The second entries are the margin of victory values for each state for the Senate race, where margin of victory is defined as the absolute difference between the Democratic percent and the Republican percent of the two-party vote for the Senate. The third entries are the party competition index values for each state for the Senate race, where the competition index devised by Paul David (1972) is defined as (100 − the margin of victory) or, alternatively, as (100 − the absolute difference between the Democratic and Republican percent of two-party vote for the Senate). The values for Democratic and Republican percent of two-party vote for the Senate are taken from the state vote tables in Chapter 6. Zero (0) percent on David's index represents a complete absence of two-party competition for that election year, whereas a score of 100 percent indicates perfect competition between the two major parties. A state can only receive a party competition score of 0 if it has 100–0 vote split for the Senate. Conversely, a state can only get a score of 100 if it has a 50–50 vote split for Senate. For example, if Alabama in 1914 reported an 83.7 percent Democratic vote for the Senate of its two-party vote, then its Republican vote for Senate would be 16.3 percent. The absolute difference between the two figures is the margin of victory, or 67.4 percent; 100 percent − 67.4 percent would equal 32.6 percent on David's party competition scale, indicating very little competition in the Senate race in Alabama in 1914. The two-party vote percent values used to derive the margin of victory and party competition figures are initially found in the state vote tables in Chapter 6. The author's alternative party coding in these tables is used whenever it occurs instead of the conventional party coding of voting data. The Democratic Party is defined here as the Anti-Federalists, Democratic-Republicans, and Jackson Democrats prior to 1830 when the "Democratic Party" as such was established. The Republican Party is defined as the Federalists, National Republicans, and Whigs prior to the establishment of the "Republican Party" in the 1850s. See Appendix A for an explanation of the historical antecedents of the current Democratic and Republican parties. States reporting only partial voting returns for Senate races are not included in the calculations for the years in which this occurred. —indicates that the state had no data, either because the state had no Senate election, no vote data were found for the state in question, or the state had not yet entered the Union.

[1]Election held in odd-numbered year.

Sources: State vote tables for Senate in Chapter 6.

Table 8-98 Senate Competition Measures, by State, by Election Year, 1960–1964 (Percentages)

| | 1960 | | | 1962 | | | 1964 | | |
| | Democratic % of Two-Party Vote | Margin of Victory | Party Competition Index | Democratic % of Two-Party Vote | Margin of Victory | Party Competition Index | Democratic % of Two-Party Vote | Margin of Victory | Party Competition Index |
State									
Alabama	70.2	40.4	59.6	50.9	1.8	98.2	—	—	—
Alaska	63.4	26.8	73.2	58.1	16.2	83.8	—	—	—
Arizona	—	—	—	54.9	9.8	90.2	48.6	2.8	97.2
Arkansas	100.0	100.0	0.0	68.7	37.4	62.6	—	—	—
California	—	—	—	43.5	13.0	87.0	48.5	3.0	97.0
Colorado	46.2	7.6	92.4	46.0	8.0	92.0	—	—	—
Connecticut	—	—	—	51.3	2.6	97.4	64.7	29.4	70.6
Delaware	49.3	1.4	98.6	—	—	—	48.3	3.4	96.6
Florida	—	—	—	70.0	40.0	60.0	64.0	28.0	72.0
Georgia	100.0	100.0	0.0	100.0	100.0	0.0	—	—	—
Hawaii	—	—	—	69.4	38.8	61.2	46.6	6.8	93.2
Idaho	47.7	4.6	95.4	54.7	9.4	90.6	—	—	—
Illinois	54.7	9.4	90.6	47.1	5.8	94.2	—	—	—
Indiana	—	—	—	50.3	0.6	99.4	54.5	9.0	91.0
Iowa	48.1	3.8	96.2	46.6	6.8	93.2	—	—	—
Kansas	44.5	11.0	89.0	36.5	27.0	73.0	—	—	—
Kentucky	40.8	18.4	81.6	47.2	5.6	94.4	—	—	—
Louisiana	79.8	59.6	40.4	75.6	51.2	48.8	—	—	—
Maine	38.4	23.2	76.8	—	—	—	66.6	33.2	66.8
Maryland	—	—	—	62.0	24.0	76.0	62.8	25.6	74.4
Massachusetts	43.6	12.8	87.2	—	—	—	74.5	49.0	51.0
Michigan	51.9	3.8	96.2	—	—	—	64.6	29.2	70.8
Minnesota	57.7	15.4	84.6	—	—	—	60.6	21.2	78.8
Mississippi	91.8	83.6	16.4	—	—	—	100.0	100.0	0.0
Missouri	—	—	—	54.6	9.2	90.8	66.6	33.2	66.8
Montana	50.7	1.4	98.6	—	—	—	64.5	29.0	71.0
Nebraska	41.1	17.8	82.2	—	—	—	38.6	22.8	77.2
Nevada	—	—	—	65.3	30.6	69.4	50.0	0.0	100.0
New Hampshire	39.7	20.6	79.4	40.3	19.4	80.6	—	—	—
New Jersey	43.7	12.6	87.4	—	—	—	62.4	24.8	75.2
New Mexico	63.4	26.8	73.2	—	—	—	54.7	9.4	90.6
New York	—	—	—	41.2	17.6	82.4	55.2	10.4	89.6
North Carolina	61.4	22.8	77.2	60.4	20.8	79.2	—	—	—
North Dakota	—	—	—	39.3	21.4	78.6	57.6	15.2	84.8
Ohio	—	—	—	61.6	23.2	76.8	50.2	0.4	99.6
Oklahoma	55.1	10.2	89.8	53.5	7.0	93.0	—	—	—
Oregon	54.6	9.2	90.8	54.2	8.4	91.6	—	—	—
Pennsylvania	—	—	—	51.2	2.4	97.6	49.3	1.4	98.6
Rhode Island	68.9	37.8	62.2	—	—	—	82.7	65.4	34.6
South Carolina	100.0	100.0	0.0	57.2	14.4	85.6	—	—	—
South Dakota	47.6	4.8	95.2	50.1	0.2	99.8	—	—	—
Tennessee	71.8	43.6	56.4	—	—	—	53.6	7.2	92.8
Texas	58.5	17.0	83.0	—	—	—	56.3	12.6	87.4
Utah	—	—	—	47.6	4.8	95.2	57.3	14.6	85.4
Vermont	—	—	—	33.1	33.8	66.2	46.5	7.0	93.0
Virginia	100.0	100.0	0.0	—	—	—	77.0	54.0	46.0
Washington	—	—	—	52.4	4.8	95.2	72.2	44.4	55.6
West Virginia	55.3	10.6	89.4	—	—	—	67.7	35.4	64.6
Wisconsin	—	—	—	52.7	5.4	94.6	53.3	6.6	93.4
Wyoming	43.6	12.8	87.2	—	—	—	54.0	8.0	92.0

Notes: The first entries are the Democratic percent of two-party vote values for each state for the Senate race. The second entries are the margin of victory values for each state for the Senate race, where margin of victory is defined as the absolute difference between the Democratic percent and the Republican percent of the two-party vote for the Senate. The third entries are the party competition index values for each state for the Senate race, where the competition index devised by Paul David (1972) is defined as (100 − the margin of victory) or, alternatively, as (100 − the absolute difference between the Democratic and Republican percent of two-party vote for the Senate). The values for Democratic and Republican percent of two-party vote for the Senate are taken from the state vote tables in Chapter 6. Zero (0) percent on David's index represents a complete absence of two-party competition for that election year, whereas a score of 100 percent indicates perfect competition between the two major parties. A state can only receive a party competition score of 0 if it has 100–0 vote split for the Senate. Conversely, a state can only get a score of 100 if it has a 50–50 vote split for Senate. For example, if Alabama in 1914 reported an 83.7 percent Democratic vote for the Senate of its two-party vote, then its Republican vote for Senate would be 16.3 percent. The absolute difference between the two figures is the margin of victory, or 67.4 percent; 100 percent − 67.4 percent would equal 32.6 percent on David's party competition scale, indicating very little competition in the Senate race in Alabama in 1914. The two-party vote percent values used to derive the margin of victory and party competition figures are initially found in the state vote tables in Chapter 6. The author's alternative party coding in these tables is used whenever it occurs instead of the conventional party coding of voting data. The Democratic Party is defined here as the Anti-Federalists, Democratic-Republicans, and Jackson Democrats prior to 1830 when the "Democratic Party" as such was established. The Republican Party is defined as the Federalists, National Republicans, and Whigs prior to the establishment of the "Republican Party" in the 1850s. See Appendix A for an explanation of the historical antecedents of the current Democratic and Republican parties. States reporting only partial voting returns for Senate races are not included in the calculations for the years in which this occurred. —indicates that the state had no data, either because the state had no Senate election or no vote data were found for the state in question.

Sources: State vote tables for Senate in Chapter 6.

Table 8-99 Senate Competition Measures, by State, by Election Year, 1966–1970 (Percentages)

State	1966 Democratic % of Two-Party Vote	Margin of Victory	Party Competition Index	1968 Democratic % of Two-Party Vote	Margin of Victory	Party Competition Index	1970 Democratic % of Two-Party Vote	Margin of Victory	Party Competition Index
Alabama	60.6	21.2	78.8	78.0	56.0	44.0	—	—	—
Alaska	75.5	51.0	49.0	54.7	9.4	90.6	—	—	—
Arizona	—	—	—	42.8	14.4	85.6	44.0	12.0	88.0
Arkansas	—	—	—	59.1	18.2	81.8	—	—	—
California	—	—	—	52.5	5.0	95.0	54.9	9.8	90.2
Colorado	42.0	16.0	84.0	41.4	17.2	82.8	—	—	—
Connecticut	—	—	—	54.3	8.6	91.4	44.7	10.6	89.4
Delaware	40.9	18.2	81.8	—	—	—	40.5	19.0	81.0
Florida	—	—	—	44.1	11.8	88.2	53.9	7.8	92.2
Georgia	100.0	100.0	0.0	77.5	55.0	45.0	—	—	—
Hawaii	—	—	—	84.8	69.6	30.4	48.4	3.2	96.8
Idaho	44.6	10.8	89.2	60.3	20.6	79.4	—	—	—
Illinois	44.4	11.2	88.8	46.8	6.4	93.6	57.6	15.2	84.8
Indiana	—	—	—	51.8	3.6	96.4	50.1	0.2	99.8
Iowa	38.3	23.4	76.6	50.3	0.6	99.4	—	—	—
Kansas	46.4	7.2	92.8	39.2	21.6	78.4	—	—	—
Kentucky	35.5	29.0	71.0	48.1	3.8	96.2	—	—	—
Louisiana	100.0	100.0	0.0	100.0	100.0	0.0	—	—	—
Maine	41.1	17.8	82.2	—	—	—	61.7	23.4	76.6
Maryland	—	—	—	45.0	10.0	90.0	48.7	2.6	97.4
Massachusetts	39.0	22.0	78.0	—	—	—	62.7	25.4	74.6
Michigan	44.0	12.0	88.0	—	—	—	67.0	34.0	66.0
Minnesota	54.4	8.8	91.2	—	—	—	58.1	16.2	83.8
Mississippi	71.0	42.0	58.0	—	—	—	100.0	100.0	0.0
Missouri	—	—	—	51.1	2.2	97.8	51.5	3.0	97.0
Montana	53.2	6.4	93.6	—	—	—	60.5	21.0	79.0
Nebraska	38.8	22.4	77.6	—	—	—	47.5	5.0	95.0
Nevada	—	—	—	54.8	9.6	90.4	58.3	16.6	83.4
New Hampshire	54.1	8.2	91.8	40.7	18.6	81.4	—	—	—
New Jersey	38.1	23.8	76.2	—	—	—	56.2	12.4	87.6
New Mexico	53.1	6.2	93.8	—	—	—	52.9	5.8	94.2
New York	—	—	—	39.7	20.6	79.4	60.2	20.4	79.6
North Carolina	55.6	11.2	88.8	60.6	21.2	78.8	—	—	—
North Dakota	—	—	—	34.3	31.4	68.6	61.8	23.6	76.4
Ohio	—	—	—	48.5	3.0	97.0	48.8	2.4	97.6
Oklahoma	53.7	7.4	92.6	47.2	5.6	94.4	—	—	—
Oregon	48.2	3.6	96.4	49.8	0.4	99.6	—	—	—
Pennsylvania	—	—	—	46.9	6.2	93.8	46.9	6.2	93.8
Rhode Island	67.7	35.4	64.6	—	—	—	68.2	36.4	63.6
South Carolina	37.8	24.4	75.6	61.9	23.8	76.2	—	—	—
South Dakota	33.7	32.6	67.4	56.8	13.6	86.4	—	—	—
Tennessee	44.3	11.4	88.6	—	—	—	48.0	4.0	96.0
Texas	43.3	13.4	86.6	—	—	—	53.5	7.0	93.0
Utah	—	—	—	46.1	7.8	92.2	56.9	13.8	86.2
Vermont	—	—	—	0.0	100.0	0.0	40.6	18.8	81.2
Virginia	63.6	27.2	72.8	—	—	—	67.0	34.0	66.0
Washington	—	—	—	64.6	29.2	70.8	83.7	67.4	32.6
West Virginia	59.5	19.0	81.0	—	—	—	77.6	55.2	44.8
Wisconsin	—	—	—	61.7	23.4	76.6	71.3	42.6	57.4
Wyoming	48.2	3.6	96.4	—	—	—	55.8	11.6	88.4

Notes: The first entries are the Democratic percent of two-party vote values for each state for the Senate race. The second entries are the margin of victory values for each state for the Senate race, where margin of victory is defined as the absolute difference between the Democratic percent and the Republican percent of the two-party vote for the Senate. The third entries are the party competition index values for each state for the Senate race, where the competition index devised by Paul David (1972) is defined as (100 − the margin of victory) or, alternatively, as (100 − the absolute difference between the Democratic and Republican percent of two-party vote for the Senate. The values for Democratic and Republican percent of two-party vote for the Senate are taken from the state vote tables in Chapter 6. Zero (0) percent on David's index represents a complete absence of two-party competition for that election year, whereas a score of 100 percent indicates perfect competition between the two major parties. A state can only receive a party competition score of 0 if it has 100–0 vote split for the Senate. Conversely, a state can only get a score of 100 if it has a 50–50 vote split for Senate. For example, if Alabama in 1914 reported an 83.7 percent Democratic vote for the Senate of its two-party vote, then its Republican vote for Senate would be 16.3 percent. The absolute difference between the two figures is the margin of victory, or 67.4 percent; 100 percent − 67.4 percent would equal 32.6 percent on David's party competition scale, indicating very little competition in the Senate race in Alabama in 1914. The two-party vote percent values used to derive the margin of victory and party competition figures are initially found in the state vote tables in Chapter 6. The author's alternative party coding in these tables is used whenever it occurs instead of the conventional party coding of voting data. The Democratic Party is defined here as the Anti-Federalists, Democratic-Republicans, and Jackson Democrats prior to 1830 when the "Democratic Party" as such was established. The Republican Party is defined as the Federalists, National Republicans, and Whigs prior to the establishment of the "Republican Party" in the 1850s. See Appendix A for an explanation of the historical antecedents of the current Democratic and Republican parties. States reporting only partial voting returns for Senate races are not included in the calculations for the years in which this occurred. —indicates that the state had no data, either because the state had no Senate election or no vote data were found for the state in question.

Sources: State vote tables for Senate in Chapter 6.

Table 8-100 Senate Competition Measures, by State, by Election Year, 1972–1976 (Percentages)

State	1972			1974			1976		
	Democratic % of Two-Party Vote	Margin of Victory	Party Competition Index	Democratic % of Two-Party Vote	Margin of Victory	Party Competition Index	Democratic % of Two-Party Vote	Margin of Victory	Party Competition Index
Alabama	66.4	32.8	67.2	100.0	100.0	0.0	—	—	—
Alaska	22.7	54.6	45.4	58.3	16.6	83.4	—	—	—
Arizona	—	—	—	41.7	16.6	83.4	55.5	11.0	89.0
Arkansas	60.9	21.8	78.2	84.9	69.8	30.2	—	—	—
California	—	—	—	62.6	25.2	74.8	48.3	3.4	96.6
Colorado	50.5	1.0	99.0	59.2	18.4	81.6	—	—	—
Connecticut	—	—	—	65.0	30.0	70.0	41.7	16.6	83.4
Delaware	50.7	1.4	98.6	—	—	—	43.9	12.2	87.8
Florida	—	—	—	51.5	3.0	97.0	63.0	26.0	74.0
Georgia	54.0	8.0	92.0	71.8	43.6	56.4	—	—	—
Hawaii	—	—	—	100.0	100.0	0.0	56.9	13.8	86.2
Idaho	46.5	7.0	93.0	57.1	14.2	85.8	—	—	—
Illinois	37.5	25.0	75.0	62.5	25.0	75.0	—	—	—
Indiana	—	—	—	52.2	4.4	95.6	40.8	18.4	81.6
Iowa	55.5	11.0	89.0	52.4	4.8	95.2	—	—	—
Kansas	24.4	51.2	48.8	49.1	1.8	98.2	—	—	—
Kentucky	51.7	3.4	96.6	54.8	9.6	90.4	—	—	—
Louisiana	74.3	48.6	51.4	100.0	100.0	0.0	—	—	—
Maine	53.2	6.4	93.6	—	—	—	60.2	20.4	79.6
Maryland	—	—	—	42.7	14.6	85.4	59.3	18.6	81.4
Massachusetts	35.3	29.4	70.6	—	—	—	70.5	41.0	59.0
Michigan	47.0	6.0	94.0	—	—	—	52.8	5.6	94.4
Minnesota	56.9	13.8	86.2	—	—	—	72.9	45.8	54.2
Mississippi	60.0	20.0	80.0	—	—	—	100.0	100.0	0.0
Missouri	—	—	—	60.5	21.0	79.0	42.7	14.6	85.4
Montana	52.0	4.0	96.0	—	—	—	64.2	28.4	71.6
Nebraska	46.8	6.4	93.6	—	—	—	52.5	5.0	95.0
Nevada	—	—	—	49.8	0.4	99.6	66.7	33.4	66.6
New Hampshire	56.9	13.8	86.2	50.0	0.0	100.0	—	—	—
New Jersey	35.6	28.8	71.2	—	—	—	61.5	23.0	77.0
New Mexico	46.0	8.0	92.0	—	—	—	42.9	14.2	85.8
New York	—	—	—	45.8	8.4	91.6	54.7	9.4	90.6
North Carolina	46.0	8.0	92.0	62.7	25.4	74.6	—	—	—
North Dakota	—	—	—	50.0	0.0	100.0	62.9	25.8	74.2
Ohio	—	—	—	67.8	35.6	64.4	51.6	3.2	96.8
Oklahoma	48.1	3.8	96.2	49.8	0.4	99.6	—	—	—
Oregon	46.2	7.6	92.4	44.6	10.8	89.2	—	—	—
Pennsylvania	—	—	—	46.4	7.2	92.8	47.2	5.6	94.4
Rhode Island	54.0	8.0	92.0	—	—	—	42.1	15.8	84.2
South Carolina	36.5	27.0	73.0	70.8	41.6	58.4	—	—	—
South Dakota	57.0	14.0	86.0	53.0	6.0	94.0	—	—	—
Tennessee	38.1	23.8	76.2	—	—	—	52.7	5.4	94.6
Texas	45.3	9.4	90.6	—	—	—	57.3	14.6	85.4
Utah	—	—	—	46.9	6.2	93.8	45.5	9.0	91.0
Vermont	—	—	—	51.6	3.2	96.8	47.6	4.8	95.2
Virginia	47.3	5.4	94.6	—	—	—	100.0	100.0	0.0
Washington	—	—	—	62.7	25.4	74.6	74.8	49.6	50.4
West Virginia	66.5	33.0	67.0	—	—	—	100.0	100.0	0.0
Wisconsin	—	—	—	63.3	26.6	73.4	72.8	45.6	54.4
Wyoming	28.7	42.6	57.4	—	—	—	45.4	9.2	90.8

Notes: The first entries are the Democratic percent of two-party vote values for each state for the Senate race. The second entries are the margin of victory values for each state for the Senate race, where margin of victory is defined as the absolute difference between the Democratic percent and the Republican percent of the two-party vote for the Senate. The third entries are the party competition index values for each state for the Senate race, where the competition index devised by Paul David (1972) is defined as (100 − the margin of victory) or, alternatively, as (100 − the absolute difference between the Democratic and Republican percent of two-party vote for the Senate). The values for Democratic and Republican percent of two-party vote for the Senate are taken from the state vote tables in Chapter 6. Zero (0) percent on David's index represents a complete absence of two-party competition for that election year, whereas a score of 100 percent indicates perfect competition between the two major parties. A state can only receive a party competition score of 0 if it has 100–0 vote split for the Senate. Conversely, a state can only get a score of 100 if it has a 50–50 vote split for Senate. For example, if Alabama in 1914 reported an 83.7 percent Democratic vote for the Senate of its two-party vote, then its Republican vote for Senate would be 16.3 percent. The absolute difference between the two figures is the margin of victory, or 67.4 percent; 100 percent − 67.4 percent would equal 32.6 percent on David's party competition scale, indicating very little competition in the Senate race in Alabama in 1914. The two-party vote percent values used to derive the margin of victory and party competition figures are initially found in the state vote tables in Chapter 6. The author's alternative party coding in these tables is used whenever it occurs instead of the conventional party coding of voting data. The Democratic Party is defined here as the Anti-Federalists, Democratic-Republicans, and Jackson Democrats prior to 1830 when the "Democratic Party" as such was established. The Republican Party is defined as the Federalists, National Republicans, and Whigs prior to the establishment of the "Republican Party" in the 1850s. See Appendix A for an explanation of the historical antecedents of the current Democratic and Republican parties. States reporting only partial voting returns for Senate races are not included in the calculations for the years in which this occurred. —indicates that the state had no data, either because the state had no Senate election or no vote data were found for the state in question.

Sources: State vote tables for Senate in Chapter 6.

Table 8-101 Senate Competition Measures, by State, by Election Year, 1978–1982 (Percentages)

	1978			1980			1982		
State	Democratic % of Two-Party Vote	Margin of Victory	Party Competition Index	Democratic % of Two-Party Vote	Margin of Victory	Party Competition Index	Democratic % of Two-Party Vote	Margin of Victory	Party Competition Index
Alabama	100.0	100.0	0.0	48.4	3.2	96.8	—	—	—
Alaska	24.2	51.6	48.4	46.1	7.8	92.2	—	—	—
Arizona	—	—	—	49.5	1.0	99.0	58.5	17.0	83.0
Arkansas	82.5	65.0	35.0	59.1	18.2	81.8	—	—	—
California	—	—	—	60.3	20.6	79.4	46.5	7.0	93.0
Colorado	40.7	18.6	81.4	50.8	1.6	98.4	—	—	—
Connecticut	—	—	—	56.8	13.6	86.4	47.8	4.4	95.6
Delaware	58.6	17.2	82.8	—	—	—	44.5	11.0	89.0
Florida	—	—	—	48.3	3.4	96.6	61.7	23.4	76.6
Georgia	83.1	66.2	33.8	49.1	1.8	98.2	—	—	—
Hawaii	—	—	—	80.9	61.8	38.2	82.5	65.0	35.0
Idaho	31.6	36.8	63.2	49.5	1.0	99.0	—	—	—
Illinois	46.0	8.0	92.0	56.9	13.8	86.2	—	—	—
Indiana	—	—	—	46.2	7.6	92.4	45.9	8.2	91.8
Iowa	48.4	3.2	96.8	46.0	8.0	92.0	—	—	—
Kansas	44.1	11.8	88.2	36.2	27.6	72.4	—	—	—
Kentucky	62.3	24.6	75.4	65.1	30.2	69.8	—	—	—
Louisiana	—	—	—	—	—	—	—	—	—
Maine	37.5	25.0	75.0	—	—	—	60.9	21.8	78.2
Maryland	—	—	—	33.8	32.4	67.6	63.5	27.0	73.0
Massachusetts	55.1	10.2	89.8	—	—	—	61.4	22.8	77.2
Michigan	52.1	4.2	95.8	—	—	—	58.6	17.2	82.8
Minnesota	41.7	16.6	83.4	—	—	—	47.0	6.0	94.0
Mississippi	41.3	17.4	82.6	—	—	—	64.2	28.4	71.6
Missouri	—	—	—	52.2	4.4	95.6	49.1	1.8	98.2
Montana	55.7	11.4	88.6	—	—	—	56.7	13.4	86.6
Nebraska	67.7	35.4	64.6	—	—	—	70.0	40.0	60.0
Nevada	—	—	—	39.0	22.0	78.0	48.8	2.4	97.6
New Hampshire	48.9	2.2	97.8	47.9	4.2	95.8	—	—	—
New Jersey	56.2	12.4	87.6	—	—	—	51.6	3.2	96.8
New Mexico	46.6	6.8	93.2	—	—	—	53.8	7.6	92.4
New York	—	—	—	49.2	1.6	98.4	65.6	31.2	68.8
North Carolina	45.5	9.0	91.0	49.7	0.6	99.4	—	—	—
North Dakota	—	—	—	29.2	41.6	58.4	64.9	29.8	70.2
Ohio	—	—	—	70.9	41.8	58.2	57.9	15.8	84.2
Oklahoma	66.6	33.2	66.8	44.9	10.2	89.8	—	—	—
Oregon	38.3	23.4	76.6	45.8	8.4	91.6	—	—	—
Pennsylvania	—	—	—	48.8	2.4	97.6	39.8	20.4	79.6
Rhode Island	75.1	50.2	49.8	—	—	—	48.8	2.4	97.6
South Carolina	44.4	11.2	88.8	70.4	40.8	59.2	—	—	—
South Dakota	33.2	33.6	66.4	40.4	19.2	80.8	—	—	—
Tennessee	42.0	16.0	84.0	—	—	—	61.9	23.8	76.2
Texas	49.7	0.6	99.4	—	—	—	59.1	18.2	81.8
Utah	—	—	—	25.7	48.6	51.4	41.5	17.0	83.0
Vermont	—	—	—	50.7	1.4	98.6	48.4	3.2	96.8
Virginia	49.8	0.4	99.6	—	—	—	48.8	2.4	97.6
Washington	—	—	—	45.8	8.4	91.6	74.0	48.0	52.0
West Virginia	50.5	1.0	99.0	—	—	—	69.0	38.0	62.0
Wisconsin	—	—	—	49.1	1.8	98.2	65.1	30.2	69.8
Wyoming	37.8	24.4	75.6	—	—	—	43.3	13.4	86.6

Notes: The first entries are the Democratic percent of two-party vote values for each state for the Senate race. The second entries are the margin of victory values for each state for the Senate race, where margin of victory is defined as the absolute difference between the Democratic percent and the Republican percent of the two-party vote for the Senate. The third entries are the party competition index values for each state for the Senate race, where the competition index devised by Paul David (1972) is defined as (100 − the margin of victory) or, alternatively, as (100 − the absolute difference between the Democratic and Republican percent of two-party vote for the Senate). The values for Democratic and Republican percent of two-party vote for the Senate are taken from the state vote tables in Chapter 6. Zero (0) percent on David's index represents a complete absence of two-party competition for that election year, whereas a score of 100 percent indicates perfect competition between the two major parties. A state can only receive a party competition score of 0 if it has 100–0 vote split for the Senate. Conversely, a state can only get a score of 100 if it has a 50–50 vote split for Senate. For example, if Alabama in 1914 reported an 83.7 percent Democratic vote for the Senate of its two-party vote, then its Republican vote for Senate would be 16.3 percent. The absolute difference between the two figures is the margin of victory, or 67.4 percent; 100 percent − 67.4 percent would equal 32.6 percent on David's party competition scale, indicating very little competition in the Senate race in Alabama in 1914. The two-party vote percent values used to derive the margin of victory and party competition figures are initially found in the state vote tables in Chapter 6. The author's alternative party coding in these tables is used whenever it occurs instead of the conventional party coding of voting data. The Democratic Party is defined here as the Anti-Federalists, Democratic-Republicans, and Jackson Democrats prior to 1830 when the "Democratic Party" as such was established. The Republican Party is defined as the Federalists, National Republicans, and Whigs prior to the establishment of the "Republican Party" in the 1850s. See Appendix A for an explanation of the historical antecedents of the current Democratic and Republican parties. States reporting only partial voting returns for Senate races are not included in the calculations for the years in which this occurred. —indicates that the state had no data, either because the state had no Senate election or no vote data were found for the state in question.

Sources: State vote tables for Senate in Chapter 6.

Table 8-102 Senate Competition Measures, by State, by Election Year, 1984–1988 (Percentages)

State	1984 Democratic % of Two-Party Vote	1984 Margin of Victory	1984 Party Competition Index	1986 Democratic % of Two-Party Vote	1986 Margin of Victory	1986 Party Competition Index	1988 Democratic % of Two-Party Vote	1988 Margin of Victory	1988 Party Competition Index
Alabama	63.3	26.6	73.4	50.3	0.6	99.4	—	—	—
Alaska	28.6	42.8	57.2	44.9	10.2	89.8	—	—	—
Arizona	—	—	—	39.5	21.0	79.0	58.0	16.0	84.0
Arkansas	57.3	14.6	85.4	62.3	24.6	75.4	—	—	—
California	—	—	—	50.7	1.4	98.6	45.5	9.0	91.0
Colorado	35.0	30.0	70.0	50.8	1.6	98.4	—	—	—
Connecticut	—	—	—	65.0	30.0	70.0	50.4	0.8	99.2
Delaware	60.1	20.2	79.8	—	—	—	37.9	24.2	75.8
Florida	—	—	—	54.7	9.4	90.6	49.6	0.8	99.2
Georgia	79.9	59.8	40.2	50.9	1.8	98.2	—	—	—
Hawaii	—	—	—	73.6	47.2	52.8	78.7	57.4	42.6
Idaho	26.5	47.0	53.0	48.4	3.2	96.8	—	—	—
Illinois	50.9	1.8	98.2	65.9	31.8	68.2	—	—	—
Indiana	—	—	—	38.9	22.2	77.8	31.9	36.2	63.8
Iowa	56.0	12.0	88.0	33.7	32.6	67.4	—	—	—
Kansas	21.8	56.4	43.6	30.0	40.0	60.0	—	—	—
Kentucky	49.8	0.4	99.6	74.4	48.8	51.2	—	—	—
Louisiana	—	—	—	52.8	5.6	94.4	—	—	—
Maine	26.1	47.8	52.2	—	—	—	81.2	62.4	37.6
Maryland	—	—	—	60.7	21.4	78.6	61.8	23.6	76.4
Massachusetts	55.1	10.2	89.8	—	—	—	65.7	31.4	68.6
Michigan	52.3	4.6	95.4	—	—	—	61.1	22.2	77.8
Minnesota	41.5	17.0	83.0	—	—	—	42.1	15.8	84.2
Mississippi	39.1	21.8	78.2	—	—	—	46.1	7.8	92.2
Missouri	—	—	—	47.4	5.2	94.8	31.9	36.2	63.8
Montana	58.3	16.6	83.4	—	—	—	48.1	3.8	96.2
Nebraska	52.0	4.0	96.0	—	—	—	57.6	15.2	84.8
Nevada	—	—	—	52.9	5.8	94.2	52.1	4.2	95.8
New Hampshire	41.1	17.8	82.2	34.0	32.0	68.0	—	—	—
New Jersey	64.8	29.6	70.4	—	—	—	54.2	8.4	91.6
New Mexico	28.1	43.8	56.2	—	—	—	63.3	26.6	73.4
New York	—	—	—	42.0	16.0	84.0	68.3	36.6	63.4
North Carolina	48.1	3.8	96.2	51.8	3.6	96.4	—	—	—
North Dakota	—	—	—	50.4	0.8	99.2	60.4	20.8	79.2
Ohio	—	—	—	62.5	25.0	75.0	57.0	14.0	86.0
Oklahoma	76.4	52.8	47.2	44.8	10.4	89.6	—	—	—
Oregon	33.4	33.2	66.8	36.4	27.2	72.8	—	—	—
Pennsylvania	—	—	—	43.2	13.6	86.4	32.8	34.4	65.6
Rhode Island	72.6	45.2	54.8	—	—	—	45.4	9.2	90.8
South Carolina	32.3	35.4	64.6	63.9	27.8	72.2	—	—	—
South Dakota	25.5	49.0	51.0	51.6	3.2	96.8	—	—	—
Tennessee	64.2	28.4	71.6	—	—	—	65.3	30.6	69.4
Texas	41.4	17.2	82.8	—	—	—	59.7	19.4	80.6
Utah	—	—	—	26.9	46.2	53.8	32.1	35.8	64.2
Vermont	—	—	—	64.7	29.4	70.6	30.5	39.0	61.0
Virginia	29.9	40.2	59.8	—	—	—	71.3	42.6	57.4
Washington	—	—	—	51.0	2.0	98.0	48.9	2.2	97.8
West Virginia	52.1	4.2	95.8	—	—	—	64.8	29.6	70.4
Wisconsin	—	—	—	48.2	3.6	96.4	52.3	4.6	95.4
Wyoming	21.7	56.6	43.4	—	—	—	49.6	0.8	99.2

Notes: The first entries are the Democratic percent of two-party vote values for each state for the Senate race. The second entries are the margin of victory values for each state for the Senate race, where margin of victory is defined as the absolute difference between the Democratic percent and the Republican percent of the two-party vote for the Senate. The third entries are the party competition index values for each state for the Senate race, where the competition index devised by Paul David (1972) is defined as (100 − the margin of victory) or, alternatively, as (100 − the absolute difference between the Democratic and Republican percent of two-party vote for the Senate). The values for Democratic and Republican percent of two-party vote for the Senate are taken from the state vote tables in Chapter 6. Zero (0) percent on David's index represents a complete absence of two-party competition for that election year, whereas a score of 100 percent indicates perfect competition between the two major parties. Conversely, a state can only receive a party competition score of 0 if it has 100–0 vote split for the Senate. For example, if Alabama in 1914 reported an 83.7 percent Democratic vote for the Senate of its two-party vote, then its Republican vote for Senate would be 16.3 percent. The absolute difference between the two figures is the margin of victory, or 67.4 percent; 100 percent − 67.4 percent would equal 32.6 percent on David's party competition scale, indicating very little competition in the Senate race in Alabama in 1914. The two-party vote percent values used to derive the margin of victory and party competition figures are initially found in the state vote tables in Chapter 6. The author's alternative party coding in these tables is used whenever it occurs instead of the conventional party coding of voting data. The Democratic Party is defined here as the Anti-Federalists, Democratic-Republicans, and Jackson Democrats prior to 1830 when the "Democratic Party" as such was established. The Republican Party is defined as the Federalists, National Republicans, and Whigs prior to the establishment of the "Republican Party" in the 1850s. See Appendix A for an explanation of the historical antecedents of the current Democratic and Republican parties. States reporting only partial voting returns for Senate races are not included in the calculations for the years in which this occurred. —indicates that the state had no data, either because the state had no Senate election or no vote data were found for the state in question.

Sources: State vote tables for Senate in Chapter 6.

Table 8-103 Senate Competition Measures, by State, by Election Year, 1990–1994 (Percentages)

	1990			1992			1994		
State	Democratic % of Two-Party Vote	Margin of Victory	Party Competition Index	Democratic % of Two-Party Vote	Margin of Victory	Party Competition Index	Democratic % of Two-Party Vote	Margin of Victory	Party Competition Index
Alabama	60.6	21.2	78.8	66.2	32.4	67.6	—	—	—
Alaska	32.7	34.6	65.4	42.0	16.0	84.0	—	—	—
Arizona	—	—	—	36.1	27.8	72.2	42.4	15.2	84.8
Arkansas	100.0	100.0	0.0	60.2	20.4	79.6	—	—	—
California	—	—	—	52.7	5.4	94.6	51.0	2.0	98.0
Colorado	42.8	14.4	85.6	54.8	9.6	90.4	—	—	—
Connecticut	—	—	—	60.7	21.4	78.6	68.4	36.8	63.2
Delaware	63.6	27.2	72.8	—	—	—	43.2	13.6	86.4
Florida	—	—	—	65.4	30.8	69.2	29.5	41.0	59.0
Georgia	100.0	100.0	0.0	49.4	1.2	98.8	—	—	—
Hawaii	—	—	—	68.0	36.0	64.0	74.8	49.6	50.4
Idaho	38.7	22.6	77.4	43.5	13.0	87.0	—	—	—
Illinois	65.1	30.2	69.8	55.3	10.6	89.4	—	—	—
Indiana	—	—	—	41.5	17.0	83.0	31.2	37.6	62.4
Iowa	54.5	9.0	91.0	28.1	43.8	56.2	—	—	—
Kansas	26.4	47.2	52.8	33.1	33.8	66.2	—	—	—
Kentucky	47.8	4.4	95.6	63.7	27.4	72.6	—	—	—
Louisiana	—	—	—	—	—	—	—	—	—
Maine	38.6	22.8	77.2	—	—	—	37.6	24.8	75.2
Maryland	—	—	—	71.0	42.0	58.0	59.1	18.2	81.8
Massachusetts	57.1	14.2	85.8	—	—	—	58.6	17.2	82.8
Michigan	58.2	16.4	83.6	—	—	—	45.2	9.6	90.4
Minnesota	51.3	2.6	97.4	—	—	—	47.3	5.4	94.6
Mississippi	0.0	100.0	0.0	—	—	—	31.2	37.6	62.4
Missouri	—	—	—	46.4	7.2	92.8	37.4	25.2	74.8
Montana	69.9	39.8	60.2	—	—	—	37.6	24.8	75.2
Nebraska	59.0	18.0	82.0	—	—	—	54.9	9.8	90.2
Nevada	—	—	—	55.9	11.8	88.2	55.4	10.8	89.2
New Hampshire	32.5	35.0	65.0	48.5	3.0	97.0	—	—	—
New Jersey	51.6	3.2	96.8	—	—	—	51.7	3.4	96.6
New Mexico	27.1	45.8	54.2	49.4	1.2	98.8	54.0	8.0	92.0
New York	—	—	—	49.4	1.2	98.8	57.1	14.2	85.8
North Carolina	47.4	5.2	94.8	47.9	4.2	95.8	—	—	—
North Dakota	—	—	—	60.3	20.6	79.4	58.0	16.0	84.0
Ohio	—	—	—	54.7	9.4	90.6	42.3	15.4	84.6
Oklahoma	83.2	66.4	33.6	39.5	21.0	79.0	—	—	—
Oregon	46.2	7.6	92.4	47.1	5.8	94.2	—	—	—
Pennsylvania	—	—	—	48.5	3.0	97.0	48.7	2.6	97.4
Rhode Island	61.8	23.6	76.4	—	—	—	35.5	29.0	71.0
South Carolina	33.6	32.8	67.2	51.6	3.2	96.8	—	—	—
South Dakota	46.2	7.6	92.4	66.6	33.2	66.8	—	—	—
Tennessee	69.4	38.8	61.2	—	—	—	42.8	14.4	85.6
Texas	38.3	23.4	76.6	—	—	—	38.6	22.8	77.2
Utah	—	—	—	41.8	16.4	83.6	29.1	41.8	58.2
Vermont	—	—	—	55.5	11.0	89.0	44.6	10.8	89.2
Virginia	0.0	100.0	0.0	—	—	—	51.5	3.0	97.0
Washington	—	—	—	54.0	8.0	92.0	44.3	11.4	88.6
West Virginia	68.3	36.6	63.4	—	—	—	69.0	38.0	62.0
Wisconsin	—	—	—	53.3	6.6	93.4	58.9	17.8	82.2
Wyoming	36.1	27.8	72.2	—	—	—	40.0	20.0	80.0

Notes: The first entries are the Democratic percent of two-party vote values for each state for the Senate race. The second entries are the margin of victory values for each state for the Senate race, where margin of victory is defined as the absolute difference between the Democratic percent and the Republican percent of the two-party vote for the Senate. The third entries are the party competition index values for each state for the Senate race, where the competition index devised by Paul David (1972) is defined as (100 − the margin of victory) or, alternatively, as (100 − the absolute difference between the Democratic and Republican percent of two-party vote for the Senate). The values for Democratic and Republican percent of two-party vote for the Senate are taken from the state vote tables in Chapter 6. Zero (0) percent on David's index represents a complete absence of two-party competition for that election year, whereas a score of 100 percent indicates perfect competition between the two major parties. A state can only receive a party competition score of 0 if it has 100–0 vote split for the Senate. Conversely, a state can only get a score of 100 if it has a 50–50 vote split for Senate. For example, if Alabama in 1914 reported an 83.7 percent Democratic vote for the Senate of its two-party vote, then its Republican vote for Senate would be 16.3 percent. The absolute difference between the two figures is the margin of victory, or 67.4 percent; 100 percent − 67.4 percent would equal 32.6 percent on David's party competition scale, indicating very little competition in the Senate race in Alabama in 1914. The two-party vote percent values used to derive the margin of victory and party competition figures are initially found in the state vote tables in Chapter 6. The author's alternative party coding in these tables is used whenever it occurs instead of the conventional party coding of voting data. The Democratic Party is defined here as the Anti-Federalists, Democratic-Republicans, and Jackson Democrats prior to 1830 when the "Democratic Party" as such was established. The Republican Party is defined as the Federalists, National Republicans, and Whigs prior to the establishment of the "Republican Party" in the 1850s. See Appendix A for an explanation of the historical antecedents of the current Democratic and Republican parties. States reporting only partial voting returns for Senate races are not included in the calculations for the years in which this occurred. —indicates that the state had no data, either because the state had no Senate election or no vote data were found for the state in question.

Sources: State vote tables for Senate in Chapter 6.

Table 8-104 Senate Competition Measures, by State, by Election Year, 1996–1998 (Percentages)

State	1996			1998		
	Democratic % of Two-Party Vote	Margin of Victory	Party Competition Index	Democratic % of Two-Party Vote	Margin of Victory	Party Competition Index
Alabama	46.4	7.2	92.8	36.7	26.6	73.4
Alaska	11.9	76.2	23.8	20.9	58.2	41.8
Arizona	—	—	—	28.3	43.4	56.6
Arkansas	47.3	5.4	94.6	56.6	13.2	86.8
California	—	—	—	55.2	10.4	89.6
Colorado	47.5	5.0	95.0	35.9	28.2	71.8
Connecticut	—	—	—	66.8	33.6	66.4
Delaware	61.2	22.4	77.6	—	—	—
Florida	—	—	—	62.5	25.0	75.0
Georgia	50.7	1.4	98.6	46.3	7.4	92.6
Hawaii	—	—	—	81.6	63.2	36.8
Idaho	41.2	17.6	82.4	29.0	42.0	58.0
Illinois	58.0	16.0	84.0	48.5	3.0	97.0
Indiana	—	—	—	64.7	29.4	70.6
Iowa	52.6	5.2	94.8	30.8	38.4	61.6
Kansas	35.7	28.6	71.4	32.6	34.8	65.2
Kentucky	43.6	12.8	87.2	49.7	0.6	99.4
Louisiana	50.2	0.4	99.6	66.9	33.8	66.2
Maine	47.1	5.8	94.2	—	—	—
Maryland	—	—	—	70.5	41.0	59.0
Massachusetts	53.9	7.8	92.2	—	—	—
Michigan	59.4	18.8	81.2	—	—	—
Minnesota	54.9	9.8	90.2	—	—	—
Mississippi	27.8	44.4	55.6	—	—	—
Missouri	—	—	—	45.4	9.2	90.8
Montana	52.6	5.2	94.8	—	—	—
Nebraska	42.6	14.8	85.2	—	—	—
Nevada	—	—	—	50.1	0.2	99.8
New Hampshire	48.4	3.2	96.8	29.4	41.2	58.8
New Jersey	55.3	10.6	89.4	—	—	—
New Mexico	31.5	37.0	63.0	—	—	—
New York	—	—	—	55.3	10.6	89.4
North Carolina	46.6	6.8	93.2	52.1	4.2	95.8
North Dakota	—	—	—	64.2	28.4	71.6
Ohio	—	—	—	43.5	13.0	87.0
Oklahoma	41.4	17.2	82.8	32.0	36.0	64.0
Oregon	48.0	4.0	96.0	64.4	28.8	71.2
Pennsylvania	—	—	—	36.2	27.6	72.4
Rhode Island	64.4	28.8	71.2	—	—	—
South Carolina	45.2	9.6	90.4	53.6	7.2	92.8
South Dakota	51.3	2.6	97.4	63.1	26.2	73.8
Tennessee	37.5	25.0	75.0	—	—	—
Texas	44.5	11.0	89.0	—	—	—
Utah	—	—	—	34.0	32.0	68.0
Vermont	—	—	—	76.3	52.6	47.4
Virginia	47.5	5.0	95.0	—	—	—
Washington	—	—	—	58.4	16.8	83.2
West Virginia	76.6	53.2	46.8	—	—	—
Wisconsin	—	—	—	51.1	2.2	97.8
Wyoming	43.8	12.4	87.6	—	—	—

Notes: The first entries are the Democratic percent of two-party vote values for each state for the Senate race. The second entries are the margin of victory values for each state for the Senate race, where margin of victory is defined as the absolute difference between the Democratic percent and the Republican percent of the two-party vote for the Senate. The third entries are the party competition index values for each state for the Senate race, where the competition index devised by Paul David (1972) is defined as (100 − the margin of victory) or, alternatively, as (100 − the absolute difference between the Democratic and Republican percent of two-party vote for the Senate). The values for Democratic and Republican percent of two-party vote for the Senate are taken from the state vote tables in Chapter 6. Zero (0) percent on David's index represents a complete absence of two-party competition for that election year, whereas a score of 100 percent indicates perfect competition between the two major parties. A state can only receive a party competition score of 0 if it has 100–0 vote split for the Senate. Conversely, a state can only get a score of 100 if it has a 50–50 vote split for Senate. For example, if Alabama in 1914 reported an 83.7 percent Democratic vote for the Senate of its two-party vote, then its Republican vote for Senate would be 16.3 percent. The absolute difference between the two figures is the margin of victory, or 67.4 percent; 100 percent − 67.4 percent would equal 32.6 percent on David's party competition scale, indicating very little competition in the Senate race in Alabama in 1914. The two-party vote percent values used to derive the margin of victory and party competition figures are initially found in the state vote tables in Chapter 6. The author's alternative party coding in these tables is used whenever it occurs instead of the conventional party coding of voting data. The Democratic Party is defined here as the Anti-Federalists, Democratic-Republicans, and Jackson Democrats prior to 1830 when the "Democratic Party" as such was established. The Republican Party is defined as the Federalists, National Republicans, and Whigs prior to the establishment of the "Republican Party" in the 1850s. See Appendix A for an explanation of the historical antecedents of the current Democratic and Republican parties. States reporting only partial voting returns for Senate races are not included in the calculations for the years in which this occurred. —indicates that the state had no data, either because the state had no Senate election or no vote data were found for the state in question.

Sources: State vote tables for Senate in Chapter 6.

Table 8-105 Governor Competition Measures, by State, by Two-Year Election Cycle, 1788–1793 (Percentages)

	1788–1789			1790–1791			1792–1793		
State	Democratic % of Two-Party Vote	Margin of Victory	Party Competition Index	Democratic % of Two-Party Vote	Margin of Victory	Party Competition Index	Democratic % of Two-Party Vote	Margin of Victory	Party Competition Index
Alabama	—	—	—	—	—	—	—	—	—
Alaska	—	—	—	—	—	—	—	—	—
Arizona	—	—	—	—	—	—	—	—	—
Arkansas	—	—	—	—	—	—	—	—	—
California	—	—	—	—	—	—	—	—	—
Colorado	—	—	—	—	—	—	—	—	—
Connecticut	—	—	—	—	—	—	—	—	—
Delaware	—	—	—	—	—	—	0.0	100.0	0.0
Florida	—	—	—	—	—	—	—	—	—
Georgia	—	—	—	—	—	—	—	—	—
Hawaii	—	—	—	—	—	—	—	—	—
Idaho	—	—	—	—	—	—	—	—	—
Illinois	—	—	—	—	—	—	—	—	—
Indiana	—	—	—	—	—	—	—	—	—
Iowa	—	—	—	—	—	—	—	—	—
Kansas	—	—	—	—	—	—	—	—	—
Kentucky	—	—	—	—	—	—	—	—	—
Louisiana	—	—	—	—	—	—	—	—	—
Maine	—	—	—	—	—	—	—	—	—
Maryland	—	—	—	—	—	—	—	—	—
Massachusetts	—	—	—	—	—	—	—	—	—
Michigan	—	—	—	—	—	—	—	—	—
Minnesota	—	—	—	—	—	—	—	—	—
Mississippi	—	—	—	—	—	—	—	—	—
Missouri	—	—	—	—	—	—	—	—	—
Montana	—	—	—	—	—	—	—	—	—
Nebraska	—	—	—	—	—	—	—	—	—
Nevada	—	—	—	—	—	—	—	—	—
New Hampshire	54.7	9.4	90.6	100.0	100.0	0.0	100.0	100.0	0.0
New Jersey	—	—	—	—	—	—	—	—	—
New Mexico	—	—	—	—	—	—	—	—	—
New York	100.0[1]	100.0[1]	0.0[1]	—	—	—	50.3	0.6	99.4
North Carolina	—	—	—	—	—	—	—	—	—
North Dakota	—	—	—	—	—	—	—	—	—
Ohio	—	—	—	—	—	—	—	—	—
Oklahoma	—	—	—	—	—	—	—	—	—
Oregon	—	—	—	—	—	—	—	—	—
Pennsylvania	—	—	—	0.0	100.0	0.0	63.5[1]	27.0[1]	73.0[1]
Rhode Island	—	—	—	—	—	—	—	—	—
South Carolina	—	—	—	—	—	—	—	—	—
South Dakota	—	—	—	—	—	—	—	—	—
Tennessee	—	—	—	—	—	—	—	—	—
Texas	—	—	—	—	—	—	—	—	—
Utah	—	—	—	—	—	—	—	—	—
Vermont	—	—	—	—	—	—	—	—	—
Virginia	—	—	—	—	—	—	—	—	—
Washington	—	—	—	—	—	—	—	—	—
West Virginia	—	—	—	—	—	—	—	—	—
Wisconsin	—	—	—	—	—	—	—	—	—
Wyoming	—	—	—	—	—	—	—	—	—
New Hampshire	0.0[2]	100.0[2]	0.0[2]	100.0[3]	100.0[3]	0.0[3]	100.0[4]	100.0[4]	0.0[4]

Notes: The first entries are the Democratic percent of two-party vote values for each state for the gubernatorial race. The second entries are the margin of victory values for each state for the gubernatorial race, where margin of victory is defined as the absolute difference between the Democratic percent and the Republican percent of the two-party vote for governor. The third entries are the party competition index values for each state for the gubernatorial race, where the competition index devised by Paul David (1972) is defined as (100 − the margin of victory) or, alternatively, as (100 − the absolute difference between the Democratic and Republican percent of two-party vote for governor). The values for Democratic and Republican percent of two-party vote for governor are taken from the state vote tables in Chapter 7. Zero (0) percent on David's index represents a complete absence of two-party competition for that election year, whereas a score of 100 percent indicates perfect competition between the two major parties. A state can only receive a party competition score of 0 if it has a 100–0 vote split in the governor's race. Conversely, a state can only receive a score of 100 if it has a 50–50 vote split in the governor's race. For example, if New Hampshire in 1788 reported a 54.7 percent Democratic vote for governor of its two-party vote, then its Republican vote for governor would be 45.3 percent. The absolute difference between the two figures is the margin of victory, or 9.4 percent; 100 percent − 9.4 percent would equal 90.6 percent on David's party competition scale, indicating a very competitive contest for governor in New Hampshire in 1788. The two-party vote percent values used to derive the margin of victory and party competition figures are initially found in the state vote tables in Chapter 7. The author's alternative party coding in these tables is used whenever it occurs instead of the conventional party coding of voting data. The Democratic Party is defined here as the Anti-Federalists, Democratic-Republicans, and Jackson Democrats prior to 1830 when the "Democratic Party" in as such was established. The Republican Party is defined as the Federalists, National Republicans and Whigs prior to the establishment of the "Republican Party" in the 1850s. See Appendix A for an explanation of the historical antecedents of the current Democratic and Republican parties. States reporting only partial voting returns for governor's races are not included in the calculations for the years in which this occurred. —indicates that the state had no data, either because the state had no gubernatorial election, no vote data were found for the state in question, or the state had not yet entered the Union.

[1] Election held in odd-numbered year.
[2] 1789 election when state had annual elections in both 1788 and 1789.
[3] 1791 election when state had annual elections in both 1790 and 1791.
[4] 1793 election when state had annual elections in both 1792 and 1793.

Sources: State vote tables for governor in Chapter 7.

Table 8-106 Governor Competition Measures, by State, by Two-Year Election Cycle, 1794–1799 (Percentages)

	1794–1795			1796–1797			1798–1799		
State	Democratic % of Two-Party Vote	Margin of Victory	Party Competition Index	Democratic % of Two-Party Vote	Margin of Victory	Party Competition Index	Democratic % of Two-Party Vote	Margin of Victory	Party Competition Index
Alabama	—	—	—	—	—	—	—	—	—
Alaska	—	—	—	—	—	—	—	—	—
Arizona	—	—	—	—	—	—	—	—	—
Arkansas	—	—	—	—	—	—	—	—	—
California	—	—	—	—	—	—	—	—	—
Colorado	—	—	—	—	—	—	—	—	—
Connecticut	—	—	—	0.0	100.0	0.0	—	—	—
Delaware	0.0[1]	100.0[1]	0.0[1]	—	—	—	45.4	9.2	90.8
Florida	—	—	—	—	—	—	—	—	—
Georgia	—	—	—	—	—	—	—	—	—
Hawaii	—	—	—	—	—	—	—	—	—
Idaho	—	—	—	—	—	—	—	—	—
Illinois	—	—	—	—	—	—	—	—	—
Indiana	—	—	—	—	—	—	—	—	—
Iowa	—	—	—	—	—	—	—	—	—
Kansas	—	—	—	—	—	—	—	—	—
Kentucky	—	—	—	—	—	—	—	—	—
Louisiana	—	—	—	—	—	—	—	—	—
Maine	—	—	—	—	—	—	—	—	—
Maryland	—	—	—	—	—	—	—	—	—
Massachusetts	—	—	—	0.0	100.0	0.0	24.8	50.4	49.6
Michigan	—	—	—	—	—	—	—	—	—
Minnesota	—	—	—	—	—	—	—	—	—
Mississippi	—	—	—	—	—	—	—	—	—
Missouri	—	—	—	—	—	—	—	—	—
Montana	—	—	—	—	—	—	—	—	—
Nebraska	—	—	—	—	—	—	—	—	—
Nevada	—	—	—	—	—	—	—	—	—
New Hampshire	0.0	100.0	0.0	0.0	100.0	0.0	11.2	77.6	22.4
New Jersey	—	—	—	—	—	—	—	—	—
New Mexico	—	—	—	—	—	—	—	—	—
New York	46.9[1]	6.2[1]	93.8[1]	—	—	—	46.0	8.0	92.0
North Carolina	—	—	—	—	—	—	—	—	—
North Dakota	—	—	—	—	—	—	—	—	—
Ohio	—	—	—	—	—	—	—	—	—
Oklahoma	—	—	—	—	—	—	—	—	—
Oregon	—	—	—	—	—	—	—	—	—
Pennsylvania	—	—	—	96.7	93.4	6.6	53.8[1]	7.6[1]	92.4[1]
Rhode Island	—	—	—	100.0[1]	100.0[1]	0.0[1]	—	—	—
South Carolina	—	—	—	—	—	—	—	—	—
South Dakota	—	—	—	—	—	—	100.0[1]	100.0[1]	0.0[1]
Tennessee	—	—	—	—	—	—	—	—	—
Texas	—	—	—	—	—	—	—	—	—
Utah	—	—	—	—	—	—	31.1	37.8	62.2
Vermont	—	—	—	—	—	—	—	—	—
Virginia	—	—	—	—	—	—	—	—	—
Washington	—	—	—	—	—	—	—	—	—
West Virginia	—	—	—	—	—	—	—	—	—
Wisconsin	—	—	—	—	—	—	—	—	—
Wyoming	—	—	—	—	—	—	—	—	—
Massachusetts	—	—	—	43.3[3]	13.4[3]	86.6[3]	0.0[4]	100.0[4]	0.0[4]
New Hampshire	0.0[2]	100.0[2]	0.0[2]	0.0[3]	100.0[3]	0.0[3]	0.0[4]	100.0[4]	0.0[4]

Notes: The first entries are the Democratic percent of two-party vote values for each state for the gubernatorial race. The second entries are the margin of victory values for each state for the gubernatorial race, where margin of victory is defined as the absolute difference between the Democratic percent and the Republican percent of the two-party vote for governor. The third entries are the party competition index values for each state for the gubernatorial race, where the competition index devised by Paul David (1972) is defined as (100 − the margin of victory) or, alternatively, as (100 − the absolute difference between the Democratic and Republican percent of two-party vote for governor). The values for Democratic and Republican percent of two-party vote for governor are taken from the state vote tables in Chapter 7. Zero (0) percent on David's index represents a complete absence of two-party competition for that election year, whereas a score of 100 percent indicates perfect competition between the two major parties. A state can only receive a party competition score of 0 if it has a 100–0 vote split in the governor's race. Conversely, a state can only receive a score of 100 if it has a 50–50 vote split in the governor's race. For example, if New Hampshire in 1788 reported a 54.7 percent Democratic vote for governor of its two-party vote, then its Republican vote for governor would be 45.3 percent. The absolute difference between the two figures is the margin of victory, or 9.4 percent; 100 percent − 9.4 percent would equal 90.6 percent on David's party competition scale, indicating a very competitive contest for governor in New Hampshire in 1788. The two-party vote percent values used to derive the margin of victory and party competition figures are initially found in the state vote tables in Chapter 7. The author's alternative party coding in these tables is used whenever it occurs instead of the conventional party coding of voting data. The Democratic Party is defined here as the Anti-Federalists, Democratic-Republicans, and Jackson Democrats prior to 1830 when the "Democratic Party" in as such was established. The Republican Party is defined as the Federalists, National Republicans and Whigs prior to the establishment of the "Republican Party" in the 1850s. See Appendix A for an explanation of the historical antecedents of the current Democratic and Republican parties. States reporting only partial voting returns for governor's races are not included in the calculations for the years in which this occurred. —indicates that the state had no data, either because the state had no gubernatorial election, no vote data were found for the state in question, or the state had not yet entered the Union.

[1] Election held in odd-numbered year.
[2] 1795 election when state had annual elections in both 1794 and 1795.
[3] 1797 election when state had annual elections in both 1796 and 1797.
[4] 1799 election when state had annual elections in both 1798 and 1799.

Sources: State vote tables for governor in Chapter 7.

Table 8-107 Governor Competition Measures, by State, by Two-Year Election Cycle, 1800–1805 (Percentages)

State	1800–1801 Democratic % of Two-Party Vote	Margin of Victory	Party Competition Index	1802–1803 Democratic % of Two-Party Vote	Margin of Victory	Party Competition Index	1804–1805 Democratic % of Two-Party Vote	Margin of Victory	Party Competition Index
Alabama	—	—	—	—	—	—	—	—	—
Alaska	—	—	—	—	—	—	—	—	—
Arizona	—	—	—	—	—	—	—	—	—
Arkansas	—	—	—	—	—	—	—	—	—
California	—	—	—	—	—	—	—	—	—
Colorado	—	—	—	—	—	—	—	—	—
Connecticut	8.6[1]	82.8[1]	17.2[1]	28.4	43.2	56.8	38.2	23.6	76.4
Delaware	50.1[1]	0.2[1]	99.8[1]	—	—	—	48.0	4.0	96.0
Florida	—	—	—	—	—	—	—	—	—
Georgia	—	—	—	—	—	—	—	—	—
Hawaii	—	—	—	—	—	—	—	—	—
Idaho	—	—	—	—	—	—	—	—	—
Illinois	—	—	—	—	—	—	—	—	—
Indiana	—	—	—	—	—	—	—	—	—
Iowa	—	—	—	—	—	—	—	—	—
Kansas	—	—	—	—	—	—	—	—	—
Kentucky	100.0	100.0	0.0	—	—	—	100.0	100.0	0.0
Louisiana	—	—	—	—	—	—	—	—	—
Maine	—	—	—	—	—	—	—	—	—
Maryland	—	—	—	—	—	—	—	—	—
Massachusetts	46.4	7.2	92.8	39.3	21.4	78.6	44.4	11.2	88.8
Michigan	—	—	—	—	—	—	—	—	—
Minnesota	—	—	—	—	—	—	—	—	—
Mississippi	—	—	—	—	—	—	—	—	—
Missouri	—	—	—	—	—	—	—	—	—
Montana	—	—	—	—	—	—	—	—	—
Nebraska	—	—	—	—	—	—	—	—	—
Nevada	—	—	—	—	—	—	—	—	—
New Hampshire	36.8	26.4	73.6	45.8	8.4	91.6	49.5	1.0	99.0
New Jersey	—	—	—	—	—	—	—	—	—
New Mexico	—	—	—	—	—	—	—	—	—
New York	54.3[1]	8.6[1]	91.4[1]	—	—	—	41.8	16.4	83.6
North Carolina	—	—	—	—	—	—	—	—	—
North Dakota	—	—	—	—	—	—	—	—	—
Ohio	—	—	—	100.0[1]	100.0[1]	0.0[1]	100.0[1]	100.0[1]	0.0[1]
Oklahoma	—	—	—	—	—	—	—	—	—
Oregon	—	—	—	—	—	—	—	—	—
Pennsylvania	—	—	—	73.7	47.4	52.6	100.0[1]	100.0[1]	0.0[1]
Rhode Island	100.0[1]	100.0[1]	0.0[1]	66.3	32.6	67.4	—	—	—
South Carolina	—	—	—	—	—	—	—	—	—
South Dakota	—	—	—	—	—	—	—	—	—
Tennessee	100.0[1]	100.0[1]	0.0[1]	100.0[1]	100.0[1]	0.0[1]	100.0[1]	100.0[1]	0.0[1]
Texas	—	—	—	—	—	—	—	—	—
Utah	—	—	—	—	—	—	—	—	—
Vermont	33.5	33.0	67.0	39.4	21.2	78.8	43.4	13.2	86.8
Virginia	—	—	—	—	—	—	—	—	—
Washington	—	—	—	—	—	—	—	—	—
West Virginia	—	—	—	—	—	—	—	—	—
Wisconsin	—	—	—	—	—	—	—	—	—
Wyoming	—	—	—	—	—	—	—	—	—
Connecticut	—	—	—	35.3[3]	29.4[3]	70.6[3]	38.1[4]	23.8[4]	76.2[4]
Massachusetts	44.2[2]	11.6[2]	88.4[2]	32.3[3]	35.4[3]	64.6[3]	48.8[4]	2.4[4]	97.6[4]
New Hampshire	32.5[2]	35.0[2]	65.0[2]	42.4[3]	15.2[3]	84.8[3]	56.7[4]	13.4[4]	86.6[4]
Vermont	—	—	—	—	—	—	36.8[4]	26.4[4]	73.6[4]

Notes: The first entries are the Democratic percent of two-party vote values for each state for the gubernatorial race. The second entries are the margin of victory values for each state for the gubernatorial race, where margin of victory is defined as the absolute difference between the Democratic percent and the Republican percent of the two-party vote for governor. The third entries are the party competition index values for each state for the gubernatorial race, where the competition index devised by Paul David (1972) is defined as (100 − the margin of victory) or, alternatively, as (100 − the absolute difference between the Democratic and Republican percent of two-party vote for governor). The values for Democratic and Republican percent of two-party vote for governor are taken from the state vote tables in Chapter 7. Zero (0) percent on David's index represents a complete absence of two-party competition for that election year, whereas a score of 100 percent indicates perfect competition between the two major parties. A state can only receive a party competition score of 0 if it has a 100–0 vote split in the governor's race. Conversely, a state can only receive a score of 100 if it has a 50–50 vote split in the governor's race. For example, if New Hampshire in 1788 reported a 54.7 percent Democratic vote for governor of its two-party vote, then its Republican vote for governor would be 45.3 percent. The absolute difference between the two figures is the margin of victory, or 9.4 percent; 100 percent − 9.4 percent would equal 90.6 percent on David's party competition scale, indicating a very competitive contest for governor in New Hampshire in 1788. The two-party vote percent values used to derive the margin of victory and party competition figures are initially found in the state vote tables in Chapter 7. The author's alternative party coding in these tables is used whenever it occurs instead of the conventional party coding of voting data. The Democratic Party is defined here as the Anti-Federalists, Democratic-Republicans, and Jackson Democrats prior to 1830 when the "Democratic Party" in as such was established. The Republican Party is defined as the Federalists, National Republicans and Whigs prior to the establishment of the "Republican Party" in the 1850s. See Appendix A for an explanation of the historical antecedents of the current Democratic and Republican parties. States reporting only partial voting returns for governor's races are not included in the calculations for the years in which this occurred. —indicates that the state had no data, either because the state had no gubernatorial election, no vote data were found for the state in question, or the state had not yet entered the Union.

[1] Election held in odd-numbered year.
[2] 1801 election when state had annual elections in both 1800 and 1801.
[3] 1803 election when state had annual elections in both 1802 and 1803.
[4] 1805 election when state had annual elections in both 1804 and 1805.

Sources: State vote tables for governor in Chapter 7.

Table 8-108 Governor Competition Measures, by State, by Two-Year Election Cycle, 1806–1811 (Percentages)

	1806–1807			1808–1809			1810–1811		
State	Democratic % of Two-Party Vote	Margin of Victory	Party Competition Index	Democratic % of Two-Party Vote	Margin of Victory	Party Competition Index	Democratic % of Two-Party Vote	Margin of Victory	Party Competition Index
Alabama	—	—	—	—	—	—	—	—	—
Alaska	—	—	—	—	—	—	—	—	—
Arizona	—	—	—	—	—	—	—	—	—
Arkansas	—	—	—	—	—	—	—	—	—
California	—	—	—	—	—	—	—	—	—
Colorado	—	—	—	—	—	—	—	—	—
Connecticut	41.4	17.2	82.8	38.4	23.2	76.8	34.9	30.2	69.8
Delaware	48.1[1]	3.8[1]	96.2[1]	—	—	—	50.5	1.0	99.0
Florida	—	—	—	—	—	—	—	—	—
Georgia	—	—	—	—	—	—	—	—	—
Hawaii	—	—	—	—	—	—	—	—	—
Idaho	—	—	—	—	—	—	—	—	—
Illinois	—	—	—	—	—	—	—	—	—
Indiana	—	—	—	—	—	—	—	—	—
Iowa	—	—	—	—	—	—	—	—	—
Kansas	—	—	—	—	—	—	—	—	—
Kentucky	—	—	—	100.0	100.0	0.0	—	—	—
Louisiana	—	—	—	—	—	—	—	—	—
Maine	—	—	—	—	—	—	—	—	—
Maryland	—	—	—	—	—	—	—	—	—
Massachusetts	49.6	0.8	99.2	51.0	2.0	98.0	51.4	2.8	97.2
Michigan	—	—	—	—	—	—	—	—	—
Minnesota	—	—	—	—	—	—	—	—	—
Mississippi	—	—	—	—	—	—	—	—	—
Missouri	—	—	—	—	—	—	—	—	—
Montana	—	—	—	—	—	—	—	—	—
Nebraska	—	—	—	—	—	—	—	—	—
Nevada	—	—	—	—	—	—	—	—	—
New Hampshire	82.4	64.8	35.2	90.9	81.8	18.2	51.8	3.6	96.4
New Jersey	—	—	—	—	—	—	—	—	—
New Mexico	—	—	—	—	—	—	—	—	—
New York	53.1[1]	6.2[1]	93.8[1]	—	—	—	54.2	8.4	91.6
North Carolina	—	—	—	—	—	—	—	—	—
North Dakota	—	—	—	—	—	—	—	—	—
Ohio	100.0[1]	100.0[1]	0.0[1]	100.0	100.0	0.0	100.0	100.0	0.0
Oklahoma	—	—	—	—	—	—	—	—	—
Oregon	—	—	—	—	—	—	—	—	—
Pennsylvania	—	—	—	64.5	29.0	71.0	93.6[1]	87.2[1]	12.8[1]
Rhode Island	56.9	13.8	86.2	—	—	—	48.4[1]	3.2[1]	96.8[1]
South Carolina	—	—	—	—	—	—	—	—	—
South Dakota	—	—	—	—	—	—	—	—	—
Tennessee	—	—	—	—	—	—	—	—	—
Texas	—	—	—	—	—	—	—	—	—
Utah	—	—	—	—	—	—	—	—	—
Vermont	44.8	10.4	89.6	48.4	3.2	96.8	58.2	16.4	83.6
Virginia	—	—	—	—	—	—	—	—	—
Washington	—	—	—	—	—	—	—	—	—
West Virginia	—	—	—	—	—	—	—	—	—
Wisconsin	—	—	—	—	—	—	—	—	—
Wyoming	—	—	—	—	—	—	—	—	—
Connecticut	40.0[2]	20.0[2]	80.0[2]	35.8[3]	28.4[3]	71.6[3]	—	—	—
Massachusetts	51.7[2]	3.4[2]	96.6[2]	48.5[3]	3.0[3]	97.0[3]	51.9[4]	3.8[4]	96.2[4]
New Hampshire	100.0[2]	100.0[2]	0.0[2]	49.4[3]	1.2[3]	98.8[3]	54.8[4]	9.6[4]	90.4[4]
Rhode Island	100.0[2]	100.0[2]	0.0[2]	—	—	—	—	—	—
Vermont	53.8[2]	7.6[2]	92.4[2]	52.0[3]	4.0[3]	96.0[3]	55.2[4]	10.4[4]	89.6[4]

Notes: The first entries are the Democratic percent of two-party vote values for each state for the gubernatorial race. The second entries are the margin of victory values for each state for the gubernatorial race, where margin of victory is defined as the absolute difference between the Democratic percent and the Republican percent of the two-party vote for governor. The third entries are the party competition index values for each state for the gubernatorial race, where the competition index devised by Paul David (1972) is defined as (100 − the margin of victory) or, alternatively, as (100 − the absolute difference between the Democratic and Republican percent of two-party vote for governor). The values for Democratic and Republican percent of two-party vote for governor are taken from the state vote tables in Chapter 7. Zero (0) percent on David's index represents a complete absence of two-party competition for that election year, whereas a score of 100 per-cent indicates perfect competition between the two major parties. A state can only receive a party competition score of 0 if it has a 100–0 vote split in the governor's race. Conversely, a state can only receive a score of 100 if it has a 50–50 vote split in the governor's race. For example, if New Hampshire in 1788 reported a 54.7 percent Democratic vote for governor of its two-party vote, then its Republican vote for governor would be 45.3 percent. The absolute difference between the two figures is the margin of victory, or 9.4 percent; 100 percent − 9.4 percent would equal 90.6 percent on David's party competition scale, indicating a very competitive contest for governor in New Hampshire in 1788. The two-party vote percent values used to derive the margin of victory and party competition figures are initially found in the state vote tables in Chapter 7. The author's alternative party coding in these tables is used whenever it occurs instead of the conventional party coding of voting data. The Democratic Party is defined here as the Anti-Federalists, Democratic-Republicans, and Jackson Democrats prior to 1830 when the "Democratic Party" as such was established. The Republican Party is defined as the Federalists, National Republicans, and Whigs prior to the establishment of the "Republican Party" in the 1850s. See Appendix A for an explanation of the historical antecedents of the current Democratic and Republican parties. States reporting only partial voting returns for governor's races are not included in the calculations for the years in which this occurred. —indicates that the state had no data, either because the state had no gubernatorial election, no vote data were found for the state in question, or the state had not yet entered the Union.

[1]Election held in odd-numbered year.
[2]1807 election when state had annual elections in both 1806 and 1807.
[3]1809 election when state had annual elections in both 1808 and 1809.
[4]1811 election when state had annual elections in both 1810 and 1811.

Sources: State vote tables for governor in Chapter 7.

Table 8-109 Governor Competition Measures, by State, by Two-Year Election Cycle, 1812–1817 (Percentages)

| | 1812–1813 | | | 1814–1815 | | | 1816–1817 | | |
	Democratic % of Two-Party Vote	Margin of Victory	Party Competition Index	Democratic % of Two-Party Vote	Margin of Victory	Party Competition Index	Democratic % of Two-Party Vote	Margin of Victory	Party Competition Index
State									
Alabama	—	—	—	—	—	—	—	—	—
Alaska	—	—	—	—	—	—	—	—	—
Arizona	—	—	—	—	—	—	—	—	—
Arkansas	—	—	—	—	—	—	—	—	—
California	—	—	—	—	—	—	—	—	—
Colorado	—	—	—	—	—	—	—	—	—
Connecticut	11.3	77.4	22.6	21.8	56.4	43.6	0.0	100.0	0.0
Delaware	44.8[1]	10.4[1]	89.6[1]	—	—	—	46.8	6.4	93.6
Florida	—	—	—	—	—	—	—	—	—
Georgia	—	—	—	—	—	—	—	—	—
Hawaii	—	—	—	—	—	—	—	—	—
Idaho	—	—	—	—	—	—	—	—	—
Illinois	—	—	—	—	—	—	—	—	—
Indiana	—	—	—	—	—	—	100.0	100.0	0.0
Iowa	—	—	—	—	—	—	—	—	—
Kansas	—	—	—	—	—	—	—	—	—
Kentucky	100.0	100.0	0.0	—	—	—	100.0	100.0	0.0
Louisiana	—	—	—	—	—	—	—	—	—
Maine	—	—	—	—	—	—	—	—	—
Maryland	—	—	—	—	—	—	—	—	—
Massachusetts	49.3	1.4	98.6	44.9	10.2	89.8	49.2	1.6	98.4
Michigan	—	—	—	—	—	—	—	—	—
Minnesota	—	—	—	—	—	—	—	—	—
Mississippi	—	—	—	—	—	—	100.0[1]	100.0[1]	0.0[1]
Missouri	—	—	—	—	—	—	—	—	—
Montana	—	—	—	—	—	—	—	—	—
Nebraska	—	—	—	—	—	—	—	—	—
Nevada	—	—	—	—	—	—	—	—	—
New Hampshire	49.8	0.4	99.6	48.8	2.4	97.6	53.1	6.2	93.8
New Jersey	—	—	—	—	—	—	—	—	—
New Mexico	—	—	—	—	—	—	—	—	—
New York	52.2[1]	4.4[1]	95.6[1]	—	—	—	54.0	8.0	92.0
North Carolina	—	—	—	—	—	—	—	—	—
North Dakota	—	—	—	—	—	—	—	—	—
Ohio	40.0	20.0	80.0	72.0	44.0	56.0	94.8	89.6	10.4
Oklahoma	—	—	—	—	—	—	—	—	—
Oregon	—	—	—	—	—	—	—	—	—
Pennsylvania	—	—	—	63.3	26.6	73.4	100.0[1]	100.0[1]	0.0[1]
Rhode Island	48.4	3.2	96.8	0.0	100.0	0.0	47.6	4.8	95.2
South Carolina	—	—	—	—	—	—	—	—	—
South Dakota	—	—	—	—	—	—	—	—	—
Tennessee	100.0[1]	100.0[1]	0.0[1]	100.0[1]	100.0[1]	0.0[1]	100.0[1]	100.0[1]	0.0[1]
Texas	—	—	—	—	—	—	—	—	—
Utah	—	—	—	—	—	—	—	—	—
Vermont	54.6	9.2	90.8	49.9	0.2	99.8	55.4	10.8	89.2
Virginia	—	—	—	—	—	—	—	—	—
Washington	—	—	—	—	—	—	—	—	—
West Virginia	—	—	—	—	—	—	—	—	—
Wisconsin	—	—	—	—	—	—	—	—	—
Wyoming	—	—	—	—	—	—	—	—	—
Connecticut	37.7[2]	24.6[2]	75.4[2]	37.4[3]	25.2[3]	74.8[3]	0.0[4]	100.0[4]	0.0[4]
Massachusetts	43.0[2]	14.0[2]	86.0[2]	46.3[3]	7.4[3]	92.6[3]	45.2[4]	9.6[4]	90.4[4]
New Hampshire	49.0[2]	2.0[2]	98.0[2]	49.2[3]	1.6[3]	98.4[3]	55.0[4]	10.0[4]	90.0[4]
Rhode Island	0.0[2]	100.0[2]	0.0[2]	43.4[3]	13.2[3]	86.8[3]	50.5[4]	1.0[4]	99.0[4]
Vermont	50.4[2]	0.8[2]	99.2[2]	53.0[3]	6.0[3]	94.0[3]	64.9[4]	29.8[4]	70.2[4]

Notes: The first entries are the Democratic percent of two-party vote values for each state for the gubernatorial race. The second entries are the margin of victory values for each state for the gubernatorial race, where margin of victory is defined as the absolute difference between the Democratic percent and the Republican percent of the two-party vote. The third entries are the party competition index values for each state for the gubernatorial race, where the competition index devised by Paul David (1972) is defined as (100 − the margin of victory) or, alternatively, as (100 − the absolute difference between the Democratic and Republican percent of two-party vote for governor). The values for Democratic and Republican percent of two-party vote for governor are taken from the state vote tables in Chapter 7. Zero (0) percent on David's index represents a complete absence of two-party competition for that election year, whereas a score of 100 percent indicates perfect competition between the two major parties. A state can only receive a party competition score of 0 if it has a 100–0 vote split in the governor's race. Conversely, a state can only receive a score of 100 if it has a 50–50 vote split in the governor's race. For example, if New Hampshire in 1788 reported a 54.7 percent Democratic vote for governor of its two-party vote, then its Republican vote for governor would be 45.3 percent. The absolute difference between the two figures is the margin of victory, or 9.4 percent; 100 percent − 9.4 percent would equal 90.6 percent on David's party competition scale, indicating a very competitive contest for governor in New Hampshire in 1788. The two-party vote percent values used to derive the margin of victory and party competition figures are initially found in the state vote tables in Chapter 7. The author's alternative party coding in these tables is used whenever it occurs instead of the conventional party coding of voting data. The Democratic Party is defined here as the Anti-Federalists, Democratic-Republicans, and Jackson Democrats prior to 1830 when the "Democratic Party" as such was established. The Republican Party is defined as the Federalists, National Republicans, and Whigs prior to the establishment of the "Republican Party" in the 1850s. See Appendix A for an explanation of the historical antecedents of the current Democratic and Republican parties. States reporting only partial voting returns for governor's races are not included in the calculations for the years in which this occurred. —indicates that the state had no data, either because the state had no gubernatorial election, no vote data were found for the state in question, or the state had not yet entered the Union.

[1]Election held in odd-numbered year.
[2]1813 election when state had annual elections in both 1812 and 1813.
[3]1815 election when state had annual elections in both 1814 and 1815.
[4]1817 election when state had annual elections in both 1816 and 1817.

Sources: State vote tables for governor in Chapter 7.

Table 8-110 Governor Competition Measures, by State, by Two-Year Election Cycle, 1818–1823 (Percentages)

State	1818–1819			1820–1821			1822–1823		
	Democratic % of Two-Party Vote	Margin of Victory	Party Competition Index	Democratic % of Two-Party Vote	Margin of Victory	Party Competition Index	Democratic % of Two-Party Vote	Margin of Victory	Party Competition Index
Alabama	100.0[1]	100.0[1]	0.0[1]	100.0[1]	100.0[1]	0.0[1]	100.0[1]	100.0[1]	0.0[1]
Alaska	—	—	—	—	—	—	—	—	—
Arizona	—	—	—	—	—	—	—	—	—
Arkansas	—	—	—	—	—	—	—	—	—
California	—	—	—	—	—	—	—	—	—
Colorado	—	—	—	—	—	—	—	—	—
Connecticut	—	—	—	100.0	100.0	0.0	100.0	100.0	0.0
Delaware	45.4[1]	9.2[1]	90.8[1]	53.1	6.2	93.8	50.1	0.2	99.8
Florida	—	—	—	—	—	—	—	—	—
Georgia	—	—	—	—	—	—	—	—	—
Hawaii	—	—	—	—	—	—	—	—	—
Idaho	—	—	—	—	—	—	—	—	—
Illinois	100.0	100.0	0.0	—	—	—	100.0	100.0	0.0
Indiana	100.0[1]	100.0[1]	0.0[1]	—	—	—	100.0	100.0	0.0
Iowa	—	—	—	—	—	—	—	—	—
Kansas	—	—	—	—	—	—	—	—	—
Kentucky	—	—	—	100.0	100.0	0.0	—	—	—
Louisiana	—	—	—	100.0	100.0	0.0	73.7	47.4	52.6
Maine	—	—	—	—	—	—	—	—	—
Maryland	—	—	—	—	—	—	—	—	—
Massachusetts	43.2	13.6	86.4	41.4	17.2	82.8	42.6	14.8	85.2
Michigan	—	—	—	—	—	—	—	—	—
Minnesota	—	—	—	—	—	—	—	—	—
Mississippi	100.0[1]	100.0[1]	0.0[1]	100.0[1]	100.0[1]	0.0[1]	100.0[1]	100.0[1]	0.0[1]
Missouri	—	—	—	100.0	100.0	0.0	—	—	—
Montana	—	—	—	—	—	—	—	—	—
Nebraska	—	—	—	—	—	—	—	—	—
Nevada	—	—	—	—	—	—	—	—	—
New Hampshire	61.1	22.2	77.8	100.0	100.0	0.0	100.0	100.0	0.0
New Jersey	—	—	—	—	—	—	—	—	—
New Mexico	—	—	—	—	—	—	—	—	—
New York	—	—	—	100.0	100.0	0.0	100.0	100.0	0.0
North Carolina	—	—	—	—	—	—	—	—	—
North Dakota	—	—	—	—	—	—	—	—	—
Ohio	100.0	100.0	0.0	100.0	100.0	0.0	61.9	23.8	76.2
Oklahoma	—	—	—	—	—	—	—	—	—
Oregon	—	—	—	—	—	—	—	—	—
Pennsylvania	—	—	—	100.0	100.0	0.0	58.3[1]	16.6[1]	83.4[1]
Rhode Island	53.7	7.4	92.6	100.0[1]	100.0[1]	0.0[1]	—	—	—
South Carolina	—	—	—	—	—	—	—	—	—
South Dakota	—	—	—	—	—	—	—	—	—
Tennessee	100.0[1]	100.0[1]	0.0[1]	100.0[1]	100.0[1]	0.0[1]	100.0[1]	100.0[1]	0.0[1]
Texas	—	—	—	—	—	—	—	—	—
Utah	—	—	—	—	—	—	—	—	—
Vermont	100.0	100.0	0.0	100.0	100.0	0.0	100.0[1]	100.0[1]	0.0[1]
Virginia	—	—	—	—	—	—	—	—	—
Washington	—	—	—	—	—	—	—	—	—
West Virginia	—	—	—	—	—	—	—	—	—
Wisconsin	—	—	—	—	—	—	—	—	—
Wyoming	—	—	—	—	—	—	—	—	—
Connecticut	—	—	—	100.0[3]	100.0[3]	0.0[3]	100.0[4]	100.0[4]	0.0[4]
Delaware	—	—	—	—	—	—	48.2[4]	3.6[4]	96.4[4]
Maine	—	—	—	71.1[3]	42.2[3]	57.8[3]	100.0[4]	100.0[4]	0.0[4]
Massachusetts	45.1[2]	9.8[2]	90.2[2]	41.5[3]	17.0[3]	83.0[3]	53.3[4]	6.6[4]	93.4[4]
New Hampshire	61.4[2]	22.8[2]	77.2[2]	100.0[3]	100.0[3]	0.0[3]	100.0[4]	100.0[4]	0.0[4]
Vermont	100.0[2]	100.0[2]	0.0[2]	100.0[3]	100.0[3]	0.0[3]	—	—	—

Notes: The first entries are the Democratic percent of two-party vote values for each state for the gubernatorial race. The second entries are the margin of victory values for each state for the gubernatorial race, where margin of victory is defined as the absolute difference between the Democratic percent and the Republican percent of the two-party vote for governor. The third entries are the party competition index values for each state for the gubernatorial race, where the competition index devised by Paul David (1972) is defined as (100 − the margin of victory) or, alternatively, as (100 − the absolute difference between the Democratic and Republican percent of two-party vote for governor). The values for Democratic and Republican percent of two-party vote for governor are taken from the state vote tables in Chapter 7. Zero (0) percent on David's index represents a complete absence of two-party competition for that election year, whereas a score of 100 percent indicates perfect competition between the two major parties. A state can only receive a party competition score of 0 if it has a 100–0 vote split in the governor's race. Conversely, a state can only receive a score of 100 if it has a 50–50 vote split in the governor's race. For example, if New Hampshire in 1788 reported a 54.7 percent Democratic vote for governor of its two-party vote, then its Republican vote for governor would be 45.3 percent. The absolute difference between the two figures is the margin of victory, or 9.4 percent; 100 percent − 9.4 percent would equal 90.6 percent on David's party competition scale, indicating a very competitive contest for governor in New Hampshire in 1788. The two-party vote percent values used to derive the margin of victory and party competition figures are initially found in the state vote tables in Chapter 7. The author's alternative party coding in these tables is used whenever it occurs instead of the conventional party coding of voting data. The Democratic Party is defined here as the Anti-Federalists, Democratic-Republicans, and Jackson Democrats prior to 1830 when the "Democratic Party" as such was established. The Republican Party is defined as the Federalists, National Republicans, and Whigs prior to the establishment of the "Republican Party" in the 1850s. See Appendix A for an explanation of the historical antecedents of the current Democratic and Republican parties. States reporting only partial voting returns for governor's races are not included in the calculations for the years in which this occurred. —indicates that the state had no data, either because the state had no gubernatorial election, no vote data were found for the state in question, or the state had not yet entered the Union.

[1] Election held in odd-numbered year.
[2] 1819 election when state had annual elections in both 1818 and 1819.
[3] 1821 election when state had annual elections in both 1820 and 1821.
[4] 1823 election when state had annual elections in both 1822 and 1823.

Sources: State vote tables for governor in Chapter 7.

Table 8-111 Governor Competition Measures, by State, by Two-Year Election Cycle, 1824–1829 (Percentages)

State	1824–1825			1826–1827			1828–1829		
	Democratic % of Two-Party Vote	Margin of Victory	Party Competition Index	Democratic % of Two-Party Vote	Margin of Victory	Party Competition Index	Democratic % of Two-Party Vote	Margin of Victory	Party Competition Index
Alabama	100.0[1]	100.0[1]	0.0[1]	100.0[1]	100.0[1]	0.0[1]	100.0[1]	100.0[1]	0.0[1]
Alaska	—	—	—	—	—	—	—	—	—
Arizona	—	—	—	—	—	—	—	—	—
Arkansas	—	—	—	—	—	—	—	—	—
California	—	—	—	—	—	—	—	—	—
Colorado	—	—	—	—	—	—	—	—	—
Connecticut	92.1	84.2	15.8	57.8	15.6	84.4	100.0	100.0	0.0
Delaware	—	—	—	49.4	1.2	98.8	—	—	—
Florida	—	—	—	—	—	—	—	—	—
Georgia	100.0[1]	100.0[1]	0.0[1]	100.0[1]	100.0[1]	0.0[1]	100.0[1]	100.0[1]	0.0[1]
Hawaii	—	—	—	—	—	—	—	—	—
Idaho	—	—	—	—	—	—	—	—	—
Illinois	—	—	—	48.2	3.6	96.4	—	—	—
Indiana	0.0[1]	100.0[1]	0.0[1]	—	—	—	32.0	36.0	64.0
Iowa	—	—	—	—	—	—	—	—	—
Kansas	—	—	—	—	—	—	—	—	—
Kentucky	100.0	100.0	0.0	—	—	—	49.5	1.0	99.0
Louisiana	—	—	—	—	—	—	39.6	20.8	79.2
Maine	100.0	100.0	0.0	100.0	100.0	0.0	100.0	100.0	0.0
Maryland	—	—	—	—	—	—	—	—	—
Massachusetts	53.1	6.2	93.8	0.0	100.0	0.0	13.7	72.6	27.4
Michigan	—	—	—	—	—	—	—	—	—
Minnesota	—	—	—	—	—	—	—	—	—
Mississippi	100.0[1]	100.0[1]	0.0[1]	100.0[1]	100.0[1]	0.0[1]	64.6[1]	29.2[1]	70.8[1]
Missouri	0.0	100.0	0.0	—	—	—	—	—	—
Montana	—	—	—	—	—	—	—	—	—
Nebraska	—	—	—	—	—	—	—	—	—
Nevada	—	—	—	—	—	—	—	—	—
New Hampshire	—	—	—	—	—	—	47.3	5.4	94.6
New Jersey	—	—	—	—	—	—	—	—	—
New Mexico	—	—	—	—	—	—	—	—	—
New York	100.0	100.0	0.0	100.0	100.0	0.0	56.2	12.4	87.6
North Carolina	—	—	—	—	—	—	—	—	—
North Dakota	—	—	—	—	—	—	—	—	—
Ohio	51.0	2.0	98.0	0.0	100.0	0.0	48.6	2.8	97.2
Oklahoma	—	—	—	—	—	—	—	—	—
Oregon	—	—	—	—	—	—	—	—	—
Pennsylvania	—	—	—	98.4	96.8	3.2	100.0[1]	100.0[1]	0.0[1]
Rhode Island	100.0	100.0	0.0	100.0[1]	100.0[1]	0.0[1]	100.0	100.0	0.0
South Carolina	—	—	—	—	—	—	—	—	—
South Dakota	—	—	—	—	—	—	—	—	—
Tennessee	100.0[1]	100.0[1]	0.0[1]	100.0[1]	100.0[1]	0.0[1]	100.0[1]	100.0[1]	0.0[1]
Texas	—	—	—	—	—	—	—	—	—
Utah	—	—	—	—	—	—	—	—	—
Vermont	100.0	100.0	0.0	100.0	100.0	0.0	0.0	100.0	0.0
Virginia	—	—	—	—	—	—	—	—	—
Washington	—	—	—	—	—	—	—	—	—
West Virginia	—	—	—	—	—	—	—	—	—
Wisconsin	—	—	—	—	—	—	—	—	—
Wyoming	—	—	—	—	—	—	—	—	—
Connecticut	70.1[2]	40.2[2]	59.8[2]	97.5[3]	95.0[3]	5.0[3]	100.0[4]	100.0[4]	0.0[4]
Maine	100.0[2]	100.0[2]	0.0[2]	100.0[3]	100.0[3]	0.0[3]	49.7[4]	0.6[4]	99.4[4]
Massachusetts	0.0[2]	100.0[2]	0.0[2]	0.0[3]	100.0[3]	0.0[3]	21.4[4]	57.2[4]	42.8[4]
Missouri	75.7[2]	51.4[2]	48.6[2]	—	—	—	—	—	—
New Hampshire	—	—	—	—	—	—	53.6[4]	7.2[4]	92.8[4]
Rhode Island	100.0[2]	100.0[2]	0.0[2]	—	—	—	100.0[4]	100.0[4]	0.0[4]
Vermont	100.0[2]	100.0[2]	0.0[2]	100.0[3]	100.0[3]	0.0[3]	21.7[4]	56.6[4]	43.4[4]

Notes: The first entries are the Democratic percent of two-party vote values for each state for the gubernatorial race. The second entries are the margin of victory values for each state for the gubernatorial race, where margin of victory is defined as the absolute difference between the Democratic percent and the Republican percent of the two-party vote for governor. The third entries are the party competition index values for each state for the gubernatorial race, where the competition index devised by Paul David (1972) is defined as (100 − the margin of victory) or, alternatively, as (100 − the absolute difference between the Democratic and Republican percent of two-party vote for governor). The values for Democratic and Republican percent of two-party vote for governor are taken from the state vote tables in Chapter 7. Zero (0) percent on David's index represents a complete absence of two-party competition for that election year, whereas a score of 100 percent indicates perfect competition between the two major parties. A state can only receive a party competition score of 0 if it has a 100–0 vote split in the governor's race. Conversely, a state can only receive a score of 100 if it has a 50–50 vote split in the governor's race. For example, if New Hampshire in 1788 reported a 54.7 percent Democratic vote for governor of its two-party vote, then its Republican vote for governor would be 45.3 percent. The absolute difference between the two figures is the margin of victory, or 9.4 percent; 100 percent − 9.4 percent would equal 90.6 percent on David's party competition scale, indicating a very competitive contest for governor in New Hampshire in 1788. The two-party vote percent values used to derive the margin of victory and party competition figures are initially found in the state vote tables in Chapter 7. The author's alternative party coding in these tables is used whenever it occurs instead of the conventional party coding of voting data. The Democratic Party is defined here as the Anti-Federalists, Democratic-Republicans, and Jackson Democrats prior to 1830 when the "Democratic Party" as such was established. The Republican Party is defined as the Federalists, National Republicans, and Whigs prior to the establishment of the "Republican Party" in the 1850s. See Appendix A for an explanation of the historical antecedents of the current Democratic and Republican parties. States reporting only partial voting returns for governor's races are not included in the calculations for the years in which this occurred. —indicates that the state had no data, either because the state had no gubernatorial election, no vote data were found for the state in question, or the state had not yet entered the Union.

[1]Election held in odd-numbered year.
[2]1825 election when state had annual elections in both 1824 and 1825.
[3]1827 election when state had annual elections in both 1826 and 1827.
[4]1829 election when state had annual elections in both 1828 and 1829.

Sources: State vote tables for governor in Chapter 7.

Table 8-112 Governor Competition Measures, by State, by Two-Year Election Cycle, 1830–1835 (Percentages)

	1830–1831			1832–1833			1834–1835		
State	Democratic % of Two-Party Vote	Margin of Victory	Party Competition Index	Democratic % of Two-Party Vote	Margin of Victory	Party Competition Index	Democratic % of Two-Party Vote	Margin of Victory	Party Competition Index
Alabama	67.7[1]	35.4[1]	64.6[1]	100.0[1]	100.0[1]	0.0[1]	64.9[1]	29.8[1]	70.2[1]
Alaska	—	—	—	—	—	—	—	—	—
Arizona	—	—	—	—	—	—	—	—	—
Arkansas	—	—	—	—	—	—	—	—	—
California	—	—	—	—	—	—	—	—	—
Colorado	—	—	—	—	—	—	—	—	—
Connecticut	98.6	97.2	2.8	27.2	45.6	54.4	46.2	7.6	92.4
Delaware	—	—	—	50.3	0.6	99.4	—	—	—
Florida	—	—	—	—	—	—	—	—	—
Georgia	100.0[1]	100.0[1]	0.0[1]	100.0[1]	100.0[1]	0.0[1]	52.3[1]	4.6[1]	95.4[1]
Hawaii	—	—	—	—	—	—	—	—	—
Idaho	—	—	—	—	—	—	—	—	—
Illinois	41.0	18.0	82.0	—	—	—	45.6	8.8	91.2
Indiana	47.2[1]	5.6[1]	94.4[1]	—	—	—	42.6	14.8	85.2
Iowa	—	—	—	—	—	—	—	—	—
Kansas	—	—	—	—	—	—	—	—	—
Kentucky	—	—	—	50.9	1.8	98.2	42.4	15.2	84.8
Louisiana	38.3[1]	23.4[1]	76.6[1]	—	—	—	52.9	5.8	94.2
Maine	51.3	2.6	97.4	53.6	7.2	92.8	—	—	—
Maryland	—	—	—	—	—	—	—	—	—
Massachusetts	31.8	36.4	63.6	30.9	38.2	61.8	29.9	40.2	59.8
Michigan	—	—	—	—	—	—	90.1[1]	80.2[1]	19.8[1]
Minnesota	—	—	—	—	—	—	—	—	—
Mississippi	68.3[1]	36.6[1]	63.4[1]	52.9[1]	5.8[1]	94.2[1]	48.9[1]	2.2[1]	97.8[1]
Missouri	—	—	—	52.9	5.8	94.2	—	—	—
Montana	—	—	—	—	—	—	—	—	—
Nebraska	—	—	—	—	—	—	—	—	—
Nevada	—	—	—	—	—	—	—	—	—
New Hampshire	54.9	9.8	90.2	100.0	100.0	0.0	100.0[1]	100.0[1]	0.0[1]
New Jersey	—	—	—	—	—	—	—	—	—
New Mexico	—	—	—	—	—	—	—	—	—
New York	51.7	3.4	96.6	51.5	3.0	97.0	51.8	3.6	96.4
North Carolina	—	—	—	—	—	—	—	—	—
North Dakota	—	—	—	—	—	—	—	—	—
Ohio	49.8	0.4	99.6	52.9	5.8	94.2	51.2	2.4	97.6
Oklahoma	—	—	—	—	—	—	—	—	—
Oregon	—	—	—	—	—	—	—	—	—
Pennsylvania	—	—	—	100.0	100.0	0.0	58.8[1]	17.6[1]	82.4[1]
Rhode Island	100.0	100.0	0.0	100.0	100.0	0.0	—	—	—
South Carolina	—	—	—	—	—	—	—	—	—
South Dakota	—	—	—	—	—	—	—	—	—
Tennessee	97.5[1]	95.0[1]	5.0[1]	100.0[1]	100.0[1]	0.0[1]	0.0[1]	100.0[1]	0.0[1]
Texas	—	—	—	—	—	—	—	—	—
Utah	—	—	—	—	—	—	—	—	—
Vermont	31.8	36.4	63.6	34.6	30.8	69.2	50.6	1.2	98.8
Virginia	—	—	—	—	—	—	—	—	—
Washington	—	—	—	—	—	—	—	—	—
West Virginia	—	—	—	—	—	—	—	—	—
Wisconsin	—	—	—	—	—	—	—	—	—
Wyoming	—	—	—	—	—	—	—	—	—
Connecticut	2.6[2]	94.8[2]	5.2[2]	49.5[3]	1.0[3]	99.0[3]	52.1[4]	4.2[4]	95.8[4]
Maine	56.5[2]	13.0[2]	87.0[2]	61.4[3]	22.8[3]	77.2[3]	62.2[4]	24.4[4]	75.6[4]
Massachusetts	27.6[2]	44.8[2]	55.2[2]	38.1[3]	23.8[3]	76.2[3]	40.2[4]	19.6[4]	80.4[4]
New Hampshire	55.7[2]	11.4[2]	88.6[2]	100.0[3]	100.0[3]	0.0[3]	—	—	—
Rhode Island	100.0[2]	100.0[2]	0.0[2]	89.9[3]	79.8[3]	20.2[3]	70.9[4]	41.8[4]	58.2[4]
Vermont	32.2[2]	35.6[2]	64.4[2]						

Notes: The first entries are the Democratic percent of two-party vote values for each state for the gubernatorial race. The second entries are the margin of victory values for each state for the gubernatorial race, where margin of victory is defined as the absolute difference between the Democratic percent and the Republican percent of the two-party vote for governor. The third entries are the party competition index values for each state for the gubernatorial race, where the competition index devised by Paul David (1972) is defined as (100 − the margin of victory) or, alternatively, as (100 − the absolute difference between the Democratic and Republican percent of two-party vote for governor). The values for Democratic and Republican percent of two-party vote for governor are taken from the state vote tables in Chapter 7. Zero (0) percent on David's index represents a complete absence of two-party competition for that election year, whereas a score of 100 percent indicates perfect competition between the two major parties. A state can only receive a party competition score of 0 if it has a 100–0 vote split in the governor's race. Conversely, a state can only receive a score of 100 if it has a 50–50 vote split in the governor's race. For example, if New Hampshire in 1788 reported a 54.7 percent Democratic vote for governor of its two-party vote, then its Republican vote for governor would be 45.3 percent. The absolute difference between the two figures is the margin of victory, or 9.4 percent; 100 percent − 9.4 percent would equal 90.6 percent on David's party competition scale, indicating a very competitive contest for governor in New Hampshire in 1788. The two-party vote percent values used to derive the margin of victory and party competition figures are initially found in the state vote tables in Chapter 7. The author's alternative party coding in these tables is used whenever it occurs instead of the conventional party coding of voting data. The Democratic Party is defined here as the Anti-Federalists, Democratic-Republicans, and Jackson Democrats prior to 1830 when the "Democratic Party" as such was established. The Republican Party is defined as the Federalists, National Republicans, and Whigs prior to the establishment of the "Republican Party" in the 1850s. See Appendix A for an explanation of the historical antecedents of the current Democratic and Republican parties. States reporting only partial voting returns for governor's races are not included in the calculations for the years in which this occurred. —indicates that the state had no data, either because the state had no gubernatorial election, no vote data were found for the state in question, or the state had not yet entered the Union.

[1] Election held in odd-numbered year.
[2] 1831 election when state had annual elections in both 1830 and 1831.
[3] 1823 election when state had annual elections in both 1822 and 1823.
[4] 1835 election when state had annual elections in both 1834 and 1835.

Sources: State vote tables for governor in Chapter 7.

Table 8-113 Governor Competition Measures, by State, by Two-Year Election Cycle, 1836–1841 (Percentages)

	1836–1837			1838–1839			1840–1841		
State	Democratic % of Two-Party Vote	Margin of Victory	Party Competition Index	Democratic % of Two-Party Vote	Margin of Victory	Party Competition Index	Democratic % of Two-Party Vote	Margin of Victory	Party Competition Index
Alabama	100.0[1]	100.0[1]	0.0[1]	90.0[1]	80.0[1]	20.0[1]	58.3[1]	16.6[1]	83.4[1]
Alaska	—	—	—	—	—	—	—	—	—
Arizona	—	—	—	—	—	—	—	—	—
Arkansas	62.4	24.8	75.2	—	—	—	—	—	—
California	—	—	—	—	—	—	—	—	—
Colorado	—	—	—	—	—	—	—	—	—
Connecticut	53.9	7.8	92.2	44.2	11.6	88.4	45.9	8.2	91.8
Delaware	47.7	4.6	95.4	—	—	—	46.2	7.6	92.4
Florida	—	—	—	—	—	—	—	—	—
Georgia	—	—	—	51.4[1]	2.8[1]	97.2[1]	52.7[1]	5.4[1]	94.6[1]
Hawaii	—	—	—	—	—	—	—	—	—
Idaho	—	—	—	—	—	—	—	—	—
Illinois	—	—	—	50.8	1.6	98.4	—	—	—
Indiana	44.5[1]	11.0[1]	89.0[1]	—	—	—	46.3	7.4	92.6
Iowa	—	—	—	—	—	—	—	—	—
Kansas	—	—	—	—	—	—	—	—	—
Kentucky	44.2	11.6	88.4	—	—	—	41.6	16.8	83.2
Louisiana	—	—	—	47.2	5.6	94.4	—	—	—
Maine	58.4	16.8	83.2	51.9	3.8	96.2	50.0	0.0	100.0
Maryland	—	—	—	50.3	0.6	99.4	50.6[1]	1.2[1]	98.8[1]
Massachusetts	46.1	7.8	92.2	44.7	10.6	89.4	43.8	12.4	87.6
Michigan	50.7[1]	1.4[1]	98.6[1]	48.2[1]	3.6[1]	96.4[1]	57.6[1]	15.2[1]	84.8[1]
Minnesota	—	—	—	—	—	—	—	—	—
Mississippi	46.4[1]	7.2[1]	92.8[1]	54.3[1]	8.6[1]	91.4[1]	53.2[1]	6.4[1]	93.6[1]
Missouri	100.0	100.0	0.0	—	—	—	57.2	14.4	85.6
Montana	—	—	—	—	—	—	—	—	—
Nebraska	—	—	—	—	—	—	—	—	—
Nevada	—	—	—	—	—	—	—	—	—
New Hampshire	—	—	—	52.9	5.8	94.2	58.7	17.4	82.6
New Jersey	—	—	—	—	—	—	—	—	—
New Mexico	—	—	—	—	—	—	—	—	—
New York	54.9	9.8	90.2	48.6	2.8	97.2	49.4	1.2	98.8
North Carolina	46.8	6.4	93.6	35.7	28.6	71.4	45.0	10.0	90.0
North Dakota	—	—	—	—	—	—	—	—	—
Ohio	48.3	3.4	96.6	51.4	2.8	97.2	47.1	5.8	94.2
Oklahoma	—	—	—	—	—	—	—	—	—
Oregon	—	—	—	—	—	—	—	—	—
Pennsylvania	—	—	—	100.0	100.0	0.0	54.6[1]	9.2[1]	90.8[1]
Rhode Island	—	—	—	—	—	—	0.0	100.0	0.0
South Carolina	—	—	—	—	—	—	—	—	—
South Dakota	—	—	—	—	—	—	—	—	—
Tennessee	39.1[1]	21.8[1]	78.2[1]	51.0[1]	2.0[1]	98.0[1]	48.5[1]	3.0[1]	97.0[1]
Texas	—	—	—	—	—	—	—	—	—
Utah	—	—	—	—	—	—	—	—	—
Vermont	44.2	11.6	88.4	44.0	12.0	88.0	40.6	18.8	81.2
Virginia	—	—	—	—	—	—	—	—	—
Washington	—	—	—	—	—	—	—	—	—
West Virginia	—	—	—	—	—	—	—	—	—
Wisconsin	—	—	—	—	—	—	—	—	—
Wyoming	—	—	—	—	—	—	—	—	—
Connecticut	52.5[2]	5.0[2]	95.0[2]	47.5[3]	5.0[3]	95.0[3]	44.0[4]	12.0[4]	88.0[4]
Maine	49.6[2]	0.8[2]	99.2[2]	54.0[3]	8.0[3]	92.0[3]	56.3[4]	12.6[4]	87.4[4]
Massachusetts	39.5[2]	21.0[2]	79.0[2]	50.2[3]	0.4[3]	99.6[3]	47.9[4]	4.2[4]	95.8[4]
New Hampshire	—	—	—	56.0[3]	12.0[3]	88.0[3]	58.2[4]	16.4[4]	83.6[4]
Rhode Island	—	—	—	—	—	—	0.0[4]	100.0[4]	0.0[4]
Vermont	44.3[2]	11.4[2]	88.6[2]	47.5[3]	5.0[3]	95.0[3]	47.9[4]	4.2[4]	95.8[4]

Notes: The first entries are the Democratic percent of two-party vote values for each state for the gubernatorial race. The second entries are the margin of victory values for each state for the gubernatorial race, where margin of victory is defined as the absolute difference between the Democratic percent and the Republican percent of the two-party vote for governor. The third entries are the party competition index values for each state for the gubernatorial race, where the competition index devised by Paul David (1972) is defined as (100 − the margin of victory) or, alternatively, as (100 − the absolute difference between the Democratic and Republican percent of two-party vote for governor). The values for Democratic and Republican percent of two-party vote for governor are taken from the state vote tables in Chapter 7. Zero (0) percent on David's index represents a complete absence of two-party competition for that election year, whereas a score of 100 percent indicates perfect competition between the two major parties. A state can only receive a party competition score of 0 if it has a 100–0 vote split in the governor's race. Conversely, a state can only receive a score of 100 if it has a 50–50 vote split in the governor's race. For example, if New Hampshire in 1788 reported a 54.7 percent Democratic vote for governor of its two-party vote, then its Republican vote for governor would be 45.3 percent. The absolute difference between the two figures is the margin of victory, or 9.4 percent; 100 percent − 9.4 percent would equal 90.6 percent on David's party competition scale, indicating a very competitive contest for governor in New Hampshire in 1788. The two-party vote percent values used to derive the margin of victory and party competition figures are initially found in the state vote tables in Chapter 7. The author's alternative party coding in these tables is used whenever it occurs instead of the conventional party coding of voting data. The Democratic Party is defined here as the Anti-Federalists, Democratic-Republicans, and Jackson Democrats prior to 1830 when the "Democratic Party" as such was established. The Republican Party is defined as the Federalists, National Republicans, and Whigs prior to the establishment of the "Republican Party" in the 1850s. See Appendix A for an explanation of the historical antecedents of the current Democratic and Republican parties. States reporting only partial voting returns for governor's races are not included in the calculations for the years in which this occurred. —indicates that the state had no data, either because the state had no gubernatorial election, no vote data were found for the state in question, or the state had not yet entered the Union.

[1]Election held in odd-numbered year.
[2]1837 election when state had annual elections in both 1836 and 1837.
[3]1839 election when state had annual elections in both 1838 and 1839.
[4]1841 election when state had annual elections in both 1840 and 1841.

Sources: State vote tables for governor in Chapter 7.

Table 8-114 Governor Competition Measures, by State, by Two-Year Election Cycle, 1842–1847 (Percentages)

State	1842–1843			1844–1845			1846–1847		
	Democratic % of Two-Party Vote	Margin of Victory	Party Competition Index	Democratic % of Two-Party Vote	Margin of Victory	Party Competition Index	Democratic % of Two-Party Vote	Margin of Victory	Party Competition Index
Alabama	—	—	—	98.8[1]	97.6[1]	2.4[1]	55.7[1]	11.4[1]	88.6[1]
Alaska	—	—	—	—	—	—	—	—	—
Arizona	—	—	—	—	—	—	—	—	—
Arkansas	—	—	—	55.0	10.0	90.0	—	—	—
California	—	—	—	—	—	—	—	—	—
Colorado	—	—	—	—	—	—	—	—	—
Connecticut	51.9	3.8	96.2	48.9	2.2	97.8	49.4	1.2	98.8
Delaware	—	—	—	49.8	0.4	99.6	50.6	1.2	98.8
Florida	—	—	—	55.1[1]	10.2[1]	89.8[1]	—	—	—
Georgia	47.7[1]	4.6[1]	95.4[1]	48.9[1]	2.2[1]	97.8[1]	50.8[1]	1.6[1]	98.4[1]
Hawaii	—	—	—	—	—	—	—	—	—
Idaho	—	—	—	—	—	—	—	—	—
Illinois	54.4	8.8	91.2	—	—	—	61.3	22.6	77.4
Indiana	50.9[1]	1.8[1]	98.2[1]	—	—	—	51.6	3.2	96.8
Iowa	—	—	—	—	—	—	50.8	1.6	98.4
Kansas	—	—	—	—	—	—	—	—	—
Kentucky	—	—	—	48.0	4.0	96.0	—	—	—
Louisiana	54.2	8.4	91.6	—	—	—	54.6	9.2	90.8
Maine	60.4	20.8	79.2	54.9	9.8	90.2	53.8	7.6	92.4
Maryland	—	—	—	49.6	0.8	99.2	50.5[1]	1.0[1]	99.0[1]
Massachusetts	50.7	1.4	98.6	44.0	12.0	88.0	37.7	24.6	75.4
Michigan	58.7[1]	17.4[1]	82.6[1]	55.2[1]	10.4[1]	89.6[1]	56.5[1]	13.0[1]	87.0[1]
Minnesota	—	—	—	—	—	—	—	—	—
Mississippi	56.3[1]	12.6[1]	87.4[1]	64.8[1]	29.6[1]	70.4[1]	—	—	—
Missouri	—	—	—	54.1	8.2	91.8	—	—	—
Montana	—	—	—	—	—	—	—	—	—
Nebraska	—	—	—	—	—	—	—	—	—
Nevada	—	—	—	—	—	—	—	—	—
New Hampshire	72.6	45.2	54.8	63.9	27.8	72.2	60.3	20.6	79.4
New Jersey	—	—	—	49.1	1.8	98.2	51.9[1]	3.8[1]	96.2[1]
New Mexico	—	—	—	—	—	—	—	—	—
New York	52.8	5.6	94.4	51.1	2.2	97.8	49.3	1.4	98.6
North Carolina	46.9	6.2	93.8	48.1	3.8	96.2	45.0	10.0	90.0
North Dakota	—	—	—	—	—	—	—	—	—
Ohio	50.4	0.8	99.2	49.8	0.4	99.6	49.5	1.0	99.0
Oklahoma	—	—	—	—	—	—	—	—	—
Oregon	—	—	—	—	—	—	—	—	—
Pennsylvania	—	—	—	50.7	1.4	98.6	53.3[1]	6.6[1]	93.4[1]
Rhode Island	0.0	100.0	0.0	—	—	—	49.7	0.6	99.4
South Carolina	—	—	—	—	—	—	—	—	—
South Dakota	—	—	—	—	—	—	—	—	—
Tennessee	48.7[1]	2.6[1]	97.4[1]	50.6[1]	1.2[1]	98.8[1]	49.6[1]	0.8[1]	99.2[1]
Texas	—	—	—	100.0[1]	100.0[1]	0.0[1]	100.0[1]	100.0[1]	0.0[1]
Utah	—	—	—	—	—	—	—	—	—
Vermont	47.0	6.0	94.0	42.5	15.0	85.0	43.1	13.8	86.2
Virginia	—	—	—	—	—	—	—	—	—
Washington	—	—	—	—	—	—	—	—	—
West Virginia	—	—	—	—	—	—	—	—	—
Wisconsin	—	—	—	—	—	—	—	—	—
Wyoming	—	—	—	—	—	—	—	—	—
Connecticut	51.9[2]	3.8[2]	96.2[2]	47.1[3]	5.8[3]	94.2[3]	47.6[4]	4.8[4]	95.2[4]
Maine	61.6[2]	23.2[2]	76.8[2]	55.8[3]	11.6[3]	88.4[3]	57.9[4]	15.8[4]	84.2[4]
Massachusetts	48.4[2]	3.2[2]	96.8[2]	42.0[3]	16.0[3]	84.0[3]	42.3[4]	15.4[4]	84.6[4]
New Hampshire	64.7[2]	29.4[2]	70.6[2]	100.0[3]	100.0[3]	0.0[3]	59.3[4]	18.6[4]	81.4[4]
Rhode Island	44.7[2]	10.6[2]	89.4[2]	0.0[3]	100.0[3]	0.0[3]	—	—	—
Vermont	47.3[2]	5.4[2]	94.6[2]	44.9[3]	10.2[3]	89.8[3]	45.4[4]	9.2[4]	90.8[4]

Notes: The first entries are the Democratic percent of two-party vote values for each state for the gubernatorial race. The second entries are the margin of victory values for each state for the gubernatorial race, where margin of victory is defined as the absolute difference between the Democratic percent and the Republican percent of the two-party vote for governor. The third entries are the party competition index values for each state for the gubernatorial race, where the competition index devised by Paul David (1972) is defined as (100 − the margin of victory) or, alternatively, as (100 − the absolute difference between the Democratic and Republican percent of two-party vote for governor). The values for Democratic and Republican percent of two-party vote for governor are taken from the state vote tables in Chapter 7. Zero (0) percent on David's index represents a complete absence of two-party competition for that election year, whereas a score of 100 percent indicates perfect competition between the two major parties. A state can only receive a party competition score of 0 if it has a 100–0 vote split in the governor's race. Conversely, a state can only receive a score of 100 if it has a 50–50 vote split in the governor's race. For example, if New Hampshire in 1788 reported a 54.7 percent Democratic vote for governor of its two-party vote, then its Republican vote for governor would be 45.3 percent. The absolute difference between the two figures is the margin of victory, or 9.4 percent; 100 percent − 9.4 percent would equal 90.6 percent on David's party competition scale, indicating a very competitive contest for governor in New Hampshire in 1788. The two-party vote percent values used to derive the margin of victory and party competition figures are initially found in the state vote tables in Chapter 7. The author's alternative party coding in these tables is used whenever it occurs instead of the conventional party coding of voting data. The Democratic Party is defined here as the Anti-Federalists, Democratic-Republicans, and Jackson Democrats prior to 1830 when the "Democratic Party" as such was established. The Republican Party is defined as the Federalists, National Republicans, and Whigs prior to the establishment of the "Republican Party" in the 1850s. See Appendix A for an explanation of the historical antecedents of the current Democratic and Republican parties. States reporting only partial voting returns for governor's races are not included in the calculations for the years in which this occurred. —indicates that the state had no data, either because the state had no gubernatorial election, no vote data were found for the state in question, or the state had not yet entered the Union.

[1] Election held in odd-numbered year.
[2] 1843 election when state had annual elections in both 1842 and 1843.
[3] 1845 election when state had annual elections in both 1844 and 1845.
[4] 1847 election when state had annual elections in both 1846 and 1847.

Sources: State vote tables for governor in Chapter 7.

Table 8-115 Governor Competition Measures, by State, by Two-Year Election Cycle, 1848–1853 (Percentages)

State	1848–1849 Democratic % of Two-Party Vote	Margin of Victory	Party Competition Index	1850–1851 Democratic % of Two-Party Vote	Margin of Victory	Party Competition Index	1852–1853 Democratic % of Two-Party Vote	Margin of Victory	Party Competition Index
Alabama	100.0[1]	100.0[1]	0.0[1]	87.1[1]	74.2[1]	25.8[1]	80.0[1]	60.0[1]	40.0[1]
Alaska	—	—	—	—	—	—	—	—	—
Arizona	—	—	—	—	—	—	—	—	—
Arkansas	50.5[1]	1.0[1]	99.0[1]	—	—	—	55.2	10.4	89.6
California	100.0[1]	100.0[1]	0.0[1]	50.5[1]	1.0[1]	99.0[1]	51.0[1]	2.0[1]	98.0[1]
Colorado	—	—	—	—	—	—	—	—	—
Connecticut	48.1	3.8	96.2	50.7	1.4	98.6	52.8	5.6	94.4
Delaware	—	—	—	50.1	0.2	99.8	—	—	—
Florida	46.7	6.6	93.4	—	—	—	51.6	3.2	96.8
Georgia	51.8[1]	3.6[1]	96.4[1]	0.0[1]	100.0[1]	0.0[1]	50.3[1]	0.6[1]	99.4[1]
Hawaii	—	—	—	—	—	—	—	—	—
Idaho	—	—	—	—	—	—	—	—	—
Illinois	100.0	100.0	0.0	—	—	—	55.6	11.2	88.8
Indiana	53.4[1]	6.8[1]	93.2[1]	—	—	—	55.8	11.6	88.4
Iowa	—	—	—	54.2	8.4	91.6	—	—	—
Kansas	—	—	—	—	—	—	—	—	—
Kentucky	46.6	6.8	93.2	50.4[1]	0.8[1]	99.2[1]	—	—	—
Louisiana	51.5[1]	3.0[1]	97.0[1]	—	—	—	53.0	6.0	94.0
Maine	55.4	10.8	89.2	56.1	12.2	87.8	58.8	17.6	82.4
Maryland	—	—	—	51.0	2.0	98.0	52.8[1]	5.6[1]	94.4[1]
Massachusetts	29.5	41.0	59.0	38.8	22.4	77.6	38.4	23.2	76.8
Michigan	54.2[1]	8.4[1]	91.6[1]	58.5[1]	17.0[1]	83.0[1]	55.2	10.4	89.6
Minnesota	—	—	—	—	—	—	—	—	—
Mississippi	59.0[1]	18.0[1]	82.0[1]	100.0[1]	100.0[1]	0.0[1]	54.0[1]	8.0[1]	92.0[1]
Missouri	59.0	18.0	82.0	—	—	—	58.7	17.4	82.6
Montana	—	—	—	—	—	—	—	—	—
Nebraska	—	—	—	—	—	—	—	—	—
Nevada	—	—	—	—	—	—	—	—	—
New Hampshire	52.8	5.6	94.4	62.5	25.0	75.0	60.8	21.6	78.4
New Jersey	—	—	—	53.8	7.6	92.4	52.6[1]	5.2[1]	94.8[1]
New Mexico	—	—	—	—	—	—	—	—	—
New York	34.4	31.2	68.8	50.0	0.0	100.0	52.2	4.4	95.6
North Carolina	49.5	1.0	99.0	51.6	3.2	96.8	53.0	6.0	94.0
North Dakota	—	—	—	—	—	—	—	—	—
Ohio	49.9	0.2	99.8	52.4	4.8	95.2	63.2[1]	26.4[1]	73.6[1]
Oklahoma	—	—	—	—	—	—	—	—	—
Oregon	—	—	—	—	—	—	—	—	—
Pennsylvania	50.0	0.0	100.0	51.2[1]	2.4[1]	97.6[1]	—	—	—
Rhode Island	39.3	21.4	78.6	0.0	100.0	0.0	51.2	2.4	97.6
South Carolina	—	—	—	—	—	—	—	—	—
South Dakota	—	—	—	—	—	—	—	—	—
Tennessee	50.6[1]	1.2[1]	98.8[1]	49.3[1]	1.4[1]	98.6[1]	50.9[1]	1.8[1]	98.2[1]
Texas	100.0[1]	100.0[1]	0.0[1]	81.3[1]	62.6[1]	37.4[1]	74.3[1]	48.6[1]	51.4[1]
Utah	—	—	—	—	—	—	—	—	—
Vermont	56.3	12.6	87.4	48.7	2.6	97.4	38.7	22.6	77.4
Virginia	—	—	—	53.0[1]	6.0[1]	94.0[1]	—	—	—
Washington	—	—	—	—	—	—	—	—	—
West Virginia	—	—	—	—	—	—	—	—	—
Wisconsin	57.6	15.2	84.8	49.4[1]	1.2[1]	98.8[1]	54.7[1]	9.4[1]	90.6[1]
Wyoming	—	—	—	—	—	—	—	—	—
Connecticut	47.9[2]	4.2[2]	95.8[2]	51.1[3]	2.2[3]	97.8[3]	59.9[4]	19.8[4]	80.2[4]
Maine	57.0[2]	14.0[2]	86.0[2]	—	—	—	57.0[4]	14.0[4]	86.0[4]
Massachusetts	35.7[2]	28.6[2]	71.4[2]	40.6[3]	18.8[3]	81.2[3]	37.2[4]	25.6[4]	74.4[4]
New Hampshire	61.6[2]	23.2[2]	76.8[2]	59.8[3]	19.6[3]	80.4[3]	63.7[4]	27.4[4]	72.6[4]
Ohio	—	—	—	54.9[3]	9.8[3]	90.2[3]			
Rhode Island	36.8[2]	26.4[2]	73.6[2]	53.4[3]	6.8[3]	93.2[3]	54.2[4]	8.4[4]	91.6[4]
Vermont	50.4[2]	0.8[2]	99.2[2]	22.9[3]	54.2[3]	45.8[3]	46.4[4]	7.2[4]	92.8[4]
Wisconsin	59.6[2]	19.2[2]	80.8[2]						

Notes: The first entries are the Democratic percent of two-party vote values for each state for the gubernatorial race. The second entries are the margin of victory values for each state for the gubernatorial race, where margin of victory is defined as the absolute difference between the Democratic percent and the Republican percent of the two-party vote for governor. The third entries are the party competition index values for each state for the gubernatorial race, where the competition index devised by Paul David (1972) is defined as (100 − the margin of victory) or, alternatively, as (100 − the absolute difference between the Democratic and Republican percent of two-party vote for governor). The values for Democratic and Republican percent of two-party vote for governor are taken from the state vote tables in Chapter 7. Zero (0) percent on David's index represents a complete absence of two-party competition for that election year, whereas a score of 100 percent indicates perfect competition between the two major parties. A state can only receive a party competition score of 0 if it has a 100–0 vote split in the governor's race. Conversely, a state can only receive a score of 100 if it has a 50–50 vote split in the governor's race. For example, if New Hampshire in 1788 reported a 54.7 percent Democratic vote for governor of its two-party vote, then its Republican vote for governor would be 45.3 percent. The absolute difference between the two figures is the margin of victory, or 9.4 percent; 100 percent − 9.4 percent would equal 90.6 percent on David's party competition scale, indicating a very competitive contest for governor in New Hampshire in 1788. The two-party vote percent values used to derive the margin of victory and party competition figures are initially found in the state vote tables in Chapter 7. The author's alternative party coding in these tables is used whenever it occurs instead of the conventional party coding of voting data. The Democratic Party is defined here as the Anti-Federalists, Democratic-Republicans, and Jackson Democrats prior to 1830 when the "Democratic Party" as such was established. The Republican Party is defined as the Federalists, National Republicans, and Whigs prior to the establishment of the "Republican Party" in the 1850s. See Appendix A for an explanation of the historical antecedents of the current Democratic and Republican parties. States reporting only partial voting returns for governor's races are not included in the calculations for the years in which this occurred. —indicates that the state had no data, either because the state had no gubernatorial election, no vote data were found for the state in question, or the state had not yet entered the Union.

[1]Election held in odd-numbered year.
[2]1849 election when state had annual elections in both 1848 and 1849.
[3]1851 election when state had annual elections in both 1850 and 1851.
[4]1853 election when state had annual elections in both 1852 and 1853.

Sources: State vote tables for governor in Chapter 7.

Table 8-116 Governor Competition Measures, by State, by Two-Year Election Cycle, 1854–1859 (Percentages)

State	1854–1855 Democratic % of Two-Party Vote	Margin of Victory	Party Competition Index	1856–1857 Democratic % of Two-Party Vote	Margin of Victory	Party Competition Index	1858–1859 Democratic % of Two-Party Vote	Margin of Victory	Party Competition Index
Alabama	100.0[1]	100.0[1]	0.0[1]	100.0[1]	100.0[1]	0.0[1]	100.0[1]	100.0[1]	0.0[1]
Alaska	—	—	—	—	—	—	—	—	—
Arizona	—	—	—	—	—	—	—	—	—
Arkansas	—	—	—	100.0	100.0	0.0	—	—	—
California	100.0[1]	100.0[1]	0.0[1]	71.6[1]	43.2[1]	56.8[1]	90.2[1]	80.4[1]	19.6[1]
Colorado	—	—	—	—	—	—	—	—	—
Connecticut	59.5	19.0	81.0	80.4	60.8	39.2	48.0	4.0	96.0
Delaware	47.4	5.2	94.8	—	—	—	100.0	100.0	0.0
Florida	—	—	—	100.0	100.0	0.0	—	—	—
Georgia	100.0[1]	100.0[1]	0.0[1]	100.0[1]	100.0[1]	0.0[1]	60.2[1]	20.4[1]	79.6[1]
Hawaii	—	—	—	—	—	—	—	—	—
Idaho	—	—	—	—	—	—	—	—	—
Illinois	—	—	—	48.9	2.2	97.8	—	—	—
Indiana	—	—	—	51.3	2.6	97.4	—	—	—
Iowa	47.6	4.8	95.2	48.4[1]	3.2[1]	96.8[1]	48.6[1]	2.8[1]	97.2[1]
Kansas	—	—	—	—	—	—	—	—	—
Kentucky	100.0[1]	100.0[1]	0.0[1]	—	—	—	100.0[1]	100.0[1]	0.0[1]
Louisiana	100.0[1]	100.0[1]	0.0[1]	—	—	—	100.0[1]	100.0[1]	0.0[1]
Maine	32.5	35.0	65.0	37.1	25.8	74.2	46.5	7.0	93.0
Maryland	—	—	—	100.0[1]	100.0[1]	0.0[1]	—	—	—
Massachusetts	33.5	33.0	67.0	26.7	46.6	53.4	35.8	28.4	71.6
Michigan	47.0	6.0	94.0	43.1	13.8	86.2	46.2	7.6	92.4
Minnesota	—	—	—	50.3[1]	0.6[1]	99.4[1]	45.2[1]	9.6[1]	90.4[1]
Mississippi	100.0[1]	100.0[1]	0.0[1]	100.0[1]	100.0[1]	0.0[1]	100.0[1]	100.0[1]	0.0[1]
Missouri	—	—	—	100.0	100.0	0.0	—	—	—
Montana	—	—	—	—	—	—	—	—	—
Nebraska	—	—	—	—	—	—	—	—	—
Nevada	—	—	—	—	—	—	—	—	—
New Hampshire	63.6	27.2	72.8	93.1	86.2	13.8	46.5	7.0	93.0
New Jersey	—	—	—	48.7	2.6	97.4	49.2[1]	1.6[1]	98.4[1]
New Mexico	—	—	—	—	—	—	—	—	—
New York	54.8	9.6	90.4	42.9	14.2	85.8	48.2	3.6	96.4
North Carolina	51.1	2.2	97.8	100.0	100.0	0.0	100.0	100.0	0.0
North Dakota	—	—	—	—	—	—	—	—	—
Ohio	43.4[1]	13.2[1]	86.8[1]	49.8[1]	0.4[1]	99.6[1]	48.1[1]	3.8[1]	96.2[1]
Oklahoma	—	—	—	—	—	—	—	—	—
Oregon	—	—	—	—	—	—	100.0	100.0	0.0
Pennsylvania	45.0	10.0	90.0	56.4[1]	12.8[1]	87.2[1]	—	—	—
Rhode Island	41.6	16.8	83.2	41.6	16.8	83.2	31.0	38.0	62.0
South Carolina	—	—	—	—	—	—	—	—	—
South Dakota	—	—	—	—	—	—	—	—	—
Tennessee	100.0[1]	100.0[1]	0.0[1]	100.0[1]	100.0[1]	0.0[1]	52.8[1]	5.6[1]	94.4[1]
Texas	100.0[1]	100.0[1]	0.0[1]	100.0[1]	100.0[1]	0.0[1]	100.0[1]	100.0[1]	0.0[1]
Utah	—	—	—	—	—	—	—	—	—
Vermont	36.1	27.8	72.2	25.3	49.4	50.6	31.5	37.0	63.0
Virginia	100.0[1]	100.0[1]	0.0[1]	—	—	—	51.9[1]	3.8[1]	96.2[1]
Washington	—	—	—	—	—	—	—	—	—
West Virginia	—	—	—	—	—	—	—	—	—
Wisconsin	50.1[1]	0.2[1]	99.8[1]	49.7[1]	0.6[1]	99.4[1]	48.4[1]	3.2[1]	96.8[1]
Wyoming	—	—	—	—	—	—	—	—	—
Connecticut	74.9[2]	49.8[2]	50.2[2]	49.6[3]	0.8[3]	99.2[3]	48.8[4]	2.4[4]	97.6[4]
Maine	43.8[2]	12.4[2]	87.6[2]	44.0[3]	12.0[3]	88.0[3]	44.2[4]	11.6[4]	88.4[4]
Massachusetts	41.0[2]	18.0[2]	82.0[2]	34.3[3]	31.4[3]	68.6[3]	37.5[4]	25.0[4]	75.0[4]
New Hampshire	88.7[2]	77.4[2]	22.6[2]	47.7[3]	4.6[3]	95.4[3]	47.5[4]	5.0[4]	95.0[4]
Rhode Island	18.1[2]	63.8[2]	36.2[2]	34.7[3]	30.6[3]	69.4[3]	28.6[4]	42.8[4]	57.2[4]
Vermont	33.3[2]	33.4[2]	66.6[2]	32.4[3]	35.2[3]	64.8[3]	31.6[4]	36.8[4]	63.2[4]

Notes: The first entries are the Democratic percent of two-party vote values for each state for the gubernatorial race. The second entries are the margin of victory values for each state for the gubernatorial race, where margin of victory is defined as the absolute difference between the Democratic percent and the Republican percent of the two-party vote for governor. The third entries are the party competition index values for each state for the gubernatorial race, where the competition index devised by Paul David (1972) is defined as (100 − the margin of victory) or, alternatively, as (100 − the absolute difference between the Democratic and Republican percent of two-party vote for governor). The values for Democratic and Republican percent of two-party vote for governor are taken from the state vote tables in Chapter 7. Zero (0) percent on David's index represents a complete absence of two-party competition for that election year, whereas a score of 100 percent indicates perfect competition between the two major parties. A state can only receive a party competition score of 0 if it has a 100–0 vote split in the governor's race. Conversely, a state can only receive a score of 100 if it has a 50–50 vote split in the governor's race. For example, if New Hampshire in 1788 reported a 54.7 percent Democratic vote for governor of its two-party vote, then its Republican vote for governor would be 45.3 percent. The absolute difference between the two figures is the margin of victory, or 9.4 percent; 100 percent − 9.4 percent would equal 90.6 percent on David's party competition scale, indicating a very competitive contest for governor in New Hampshire in 1788. The two-party vote percent values used to derive the margin of victory and party competition figures are initially found in the state vote tables in Chapter 7. The author's alternative party coding in these tables is used whenever it occurs instead of the conventional party coding of voting data. The Democratic Party is defined here as the Anti-Federalists, Democratic-Republicans, and Jackson Democrats prior to 1830 when the "Democratic Party" as such was established. The Republican Party is defined as the Federalists, National Republicans, and Whigs prior to the establishment of the "Republican Party" in the 1850s. See Appendix A for an explanation of the historical antecedents of the current Democratic and Republican parties. States reporting only partial voting returns for governor's races are not included in the calculations for the years in which this occurred. —indicates that the state had no data, either because the state had no gubernatorial election, no vote data were found for the state in question, or the state had not yet entered the Union.

[1]Election held in odd-numbered year.
[2]1855 election when state had annual elections in both 1854 and 1855.
[3]1857 election when state had annual elections in both 1856 and 1857.
[4]1859 election when state had annual elections in both 1858 and 1859.

Sources: State vote tables for governor in Chapter 7.

Table 8-117 Governor Competition Measures, by State, by Two-Year Election Cycle, 1860–1865 (Percentages)

	1860–1861			1862–1863			1864–1865		
State	Democratic % of Two-Party Vote	Margin of Victory	Party Competition Index	Democratic % of Two-Party Vote	Margin of Victory	Party Competition Index	Democratic % of Two-Party Vote	Margin of Victory	Party Competition Index
Alabama	57.6[1]	15.2[1]	84.8[1]	25.5[1]	49.0[1]	51.0[1]	36.0[1]	28.0[1]	72.0[1]
Alaska	—	—	—	—	—	—	—	—	—
Arizona	—	—	—	—	—	—	—	—	—
Arkansas	100.0	100.0	0.0	—	—	—	—	—	—
California	53.2[1]	6.4[1]	93.6[1]	41.0[1]	18.0[1]	82.0[1]	—	—	—
Colorado	—	—	—	—	—	—	—	—	—
Connecticut	49.7	0.6	99.4	43.5	13.0	87.0	46.2	7.6	92.4
Delaware	—	—	—	49.7	0.6	99.4	—	—	—
Florida	100.0	100.0	0.0	—	—	—	100.0[1]	100.0[1]	0.0[1]
Georgia	100.0[1]	100.0[1]	0.0[1]	100.0[1]	100.0[1]	0.0[1]	—	—	—
Hawaii	—	—	—	—	—	—	—	—	—
Idaho	—	—	—	—	—	—	—	—	—
Illinois	48.1	3.8	96.2	—	—	—	45.5	9.0	91.0
Indiana	48.1	3.8	96.2	—	—	—	46.3	7.4	92.6
Iowa	41.8[1]	16.4[1]	83.6[1]	39.5[1]	21.0[1]	79.0[1]	43.4[1]	13.2[1]	86.8[1]
Kansas	—	—	—	0.0	100.0	0.0	0.0	100.0	0.0
Kentucky	—	—	—	20.4[1]	59.2[1]	40.8[1]	—	—	—
Louisiana	—	—	—	—	—	—	100.0[1]	100.0[1]	0.0[1]
Maine	42.7	14.6	85.4	46.7	6.6	93.4	41.4	17.2	82.8
Maryland	31.2[1]	37.6[1]	62.4[1]	—	—	—	44.1	11.8	88.2
Massachusetts	28.3	43.4	56.6	0.0	100.0	0.0	28.2	43.6	56.4
Michigan	43.3	13.4	86.6	47.5	5.0	95.0	44.9	10.2	89.8
Minnesota	39.1[1]	21.8[1]	78.2[1]	39.4[1]	21.2[1]	78.8[1]	44.4[1]	11.2[1]	88.8[1]
Mississippi	—	—	—	—	—	—	65.2[1]	30.4[1]	69.6[1]
Missouri	93.3	86.6	13.4	—	—	—	29.7	40.6	59.4
Montana	—	—	—	—	—	—	—	—	—
Nebraska	—	—	—	—	—	—	—	—	—
Nevada	—	—	—	—	—	—	40.0	20.0	80.0
New Hampshire	46.9	6.2	93.8	48.5	3.0	97.0	45.9	8.2	91.8
New Jersey	—	—	—	56.8	13.6	86.4	48.9[1]	2.2[1]	97.8[1]
New Mexico	—	—	—	—	—	—	—	—	—
New York	46.8	6.4	93.6	50.9	1.8	98.2	49.4	1.2	98.8
North Carolina	52.7	5.4	94.6	—	—	—	—	—	—
North Dakota	—	—	—	—	—	—	—	—	—
Ohio	42.3[1]	15.4[1]	84.6[1]	39.4[1]	21.2[1]	78.8[1]	46.4[1]	7.2[1]	92.8[1]
Oklahoma	—	—	—	—	—	—	—	—	—
Oregon	—	—	—	32.9	34.2	65.8	—	—	—
Pennsylvania	46.7	6.6	93.4	48.5[1]	3.0[1]	97.0[1]	—	—	—
Rhode Island	53.2	6.4	93.6	0.0	100.0	0.0	45.2	9.6	90.4
South Carolina	—	—	—	—	—	—	—	—	—
South Dakota	—	—	—	—	—	—	—	—	—
Tennessee	63.4[1]	26.8[1]	73.2[1]	—	—	—	0.0[1]	100.0[1]	0.0[1]
Texas	—	—	—	—	—	—	0.0[1]	100.0[1]	0.0[1]
Utah	—	—	—	—	—	—	—	—	—
Vermont	29.1	41.8	58.2	11.0	78.0	22.0	28.2	43.6	56.4
Virginia	—	—	—	—	—	—	—	—	—
Washington	—	—	—	—	—	—	—	—	—
West Virginia	—	—	—	0.0[1]	100.0[1]	0.0[1]	0.0	100.0	0.0
Wisconsin	45.8[1]	8.4[1]	91.6[1]	41.2[1]	17.6[1]	82.4[1]	45.3[1]	9.4[1]	90.6[1]
Wyoming	—	—	—	—	—	—	—	—	—
Connecticut	48.8[2]	2.4[2]	97.6[2]	48.3[3]	3.4[3]	96.6[3]	42.5[4]	15.0[4]	85.0[4]
Louisiana	—	—	—	—	—	—	100.0[4]	100.0[4]	0.0[4]
Maine	41.3[2]	17.4[2]	82.6[2]	42.6[3]	14.8[3]	85.2[3]	36.7[4]	26.6[4]	73.4[4]
Massachusetts	32.4[2]	35.2[2]	64.8[2]	29.3[3]	41.4[3]	58.6[3]	23.3[4]	53.4[4]	46.6[4]
New Hampshire	47.0[2]	6.0[2]	94.0[2]	49.6[3]	0.8[3]	99.2[3]	45.1[4]	9.8[4]	90.2[4]
Rhode Island	0.0[2]	100.0[2]	0.0[2]	41.0[3]	18.0[3]	82.0[3]	0.0[4]	100.0[4]	0.0[4]
Vermont	21.2[2]	57.6[2]	42.4[2]	28.8[3]	42.4[3]	57.6[3]	24.3[4]	51.4[4]	48.6[4]

Notes: The first entries are the Democratic percent of two-party vote values for each state for the gubernatorial race. The second entries are the margin of victory values for each state for the gubernatorial race, where margin of victory is defined as the absolute difference between the Democratic percent and the Republican percent of the two-party vote for governor. The third entries are the party competition index values for each state for the gubernatorial race, where the competition index devised by Paul David (1972) is defined as (100 − the margin of victory) or, alternatively, as (100 − the absolute difference between the Democratic and Republican percent of two-party vote for governor). The values for Democratic and Republican percent of two-party vote for governor are taken from the state vote tables in Chapter 7. Zero (0) percent on David's index represents a complete absence of two-party competition for that election year, whereas a score of 100 percent indicates perfect competition between the two major parties. A state can only receive a party competition score of 0 if it has a 100–0 vote split in the governor's race. Conversely, a state can only receive a score of 100 if it has a 50–50 vote split in the governor's race. For example, if New Hampshire in 1788 reported a 54.7 percent Democratic vote for governor of its two-party vote, then its Republican vote for governor would be 45.3 percent. The absolute difference between the two figures is the margin of victory, or 9.4 percent; 100 percent − 9.4 percent would equal 90.6 percent on David's party competition scale, indicating a very competitive contest for governor in New Hampshire in 1788. The two-party vote percent values used to derive the margin of victory and party competition figures are initially found in the state vote tables in Chapter 7. The author's alternative party coding in these tables is used whenever it occurs instead of the conventional party coding of voting data. The Democratic Party is defined here as the Anti-Federalists, Democratic-Republicans, and Jackson Democrats prior to 1830 when the "Democratic Party" as such was established. The Republican Party is defined as the Federalists, National Republicans, and Whigs prior to the establishment of the "Republican Party" in the 1850s. See Appendix A for an explanation of the historical antecedents of the current Democratic and Republican parties. States reporting only partial voting returns for governor's races are not included in the calculations for the years in which this occurred. —indicates that the state had no data, either because the state had no gubernatorial election, no vote data were found for the state in question, or the state had not yet entered the Union.

[1]Election held in odd-numbered year.
[2]1861 election when state had annual elections in both 1860 and 1861.
[3]1863 election when state had annual elections in both 1862 and 1863.
[4]1865 election when state had annual elections in both 1864 and 1865.

Sources: State vote tables for governor in Chapter 7.

Table 8-118 Governor Competition Measures, by State, by Two-Year Election Cycle, 1866–1871 (Percentages)

State	1866–1867 Democratic % of Two-Party Vote	Margin of Victory	Party Competition Index	1868–1869 Democratic % of Two-Party Vote	Margin of Victory	Party Competition Index	1870–1871 Democratic % of Two-Party Vote	Margin of Victory	Party Competition Index
Alabama	—	—	—	0.0	100.0	0.0	50.5	1.0	99.0
Alaska	—	—	—	—	—	—	—	—	—
Arizona	—	—	—	—	—	—	—	—	—
Arkansas	—	—	—	—	—	—	—	—	—
California	54.0[1]	8.0[1]	92.0[1]	—	—	—	47.9[1]	4.2[1]	95.8[1]
Colorado	—	—	—	—	—	—	—	—	—
Connecticut	49.7	0.6	99.4	50.9	1.8	98.2	50.5	1.0	99.0
Delaware	53.3	6.6	93.4	—	—	—	55.7	11.4	88.6
Florida	—	—	—	31.7	36.6	63.4	35.6	28.8	71.2
Georgia	—	—	—	47.9	4.2	95.8	—	—	—
Hawaii	—	—	—	—	—	—	—	—	—
Idaho	—	—	—	—	—	—	—	—	—
Illinois	—	—	—	44.5	11.0	89.0	—	—	—
Indiana	—	—	—	49.9	0.2	99.8	—	—	—
Iowa	41.1[1]	17.8[1]	82.2[1]	37.1[1]	25.8[1]	74.2[1]	38.4[1]	23.2[1]	76.8[1]
Kansas	0.0	100.0	0.0	31.8	36.4	63.6	33.5	33.0	67.0
Kentucky	75.3[1]	50.6[1]	49.4[1]	—	—	—	58.6[1]	17.2[1]	82.8[1]
Louisiana	—	—	—	37.2	25.6	74.4	—	—	—
Maine	37.6	24.8	75.2	42.7	14.6	85.4	45.8	8.4	91.6
Maryland	74.3[1]	48.6[1]	51.4[1]	—	—	—	55.7[1]	11.4[1]	88.6[1]
Massachusetts	22.5	55.0	45.0	32.4	35.2	64.8	37.9	24.2	75.8
Michigan	41.4	17.2	82.8	43.2	13.6	86.4	45.4	9.2	90.8
Minnesota	45.8[1]	8.4[1]	91.6[1]	47.9[1]	4.2[1]	95.8[1]	40.1[1]	19.8[1]	80.2[1]
Mississippi	—	—	—	52.6	5.2	94.8	—	—	—
Missouri	—	—	—	43.3	13.4	86.6	62.3	24.6	75.4
Montana	—	—	—	—	—	—	—	—	—
Nebraska	49.5	1.0	99.0	42.5	15.0	85.0	43.7	12.6	87.4
Nevada	44.5	11.0	89.0	—	—	—	53.9	7.8	92.2
New Hampshire	46.5	7.0	93.0	48.4	3.2	96.8	41.8	16.4	83.6
New Jersey	—	—	—	51.4	2.8	97.2	51.9[1]	3.8[1]	96.2[1]
New Mexico	—	—	—	—	—	—	—	—	—
New York	49.0	2.0	98.0	51.6	3.2	96.8	52.2	4.4	95.6
North Carolina	0.0	100.0	0.0	0.0	100.0	0.0	—	—	—
North Dakota	—	—	—	—	—	—	—	—	—
Ohio	49.7[1]	0.6[1]	99.4[1]	49.2[1]	1.6[1]	98.4[1]	47.8[1]	4.4[1]	95.6[1]
Oklahoma	—	—	—	—	—	—	—	—	—
Oregon	49.3	1.4	98.6	—	—	—	51.4	2.8	97.2
Pennsylvania	48.6	2.8	97.2	49.6[1]	0.8[1]	99.2[1]	—	—	—
Rhode Island	25.6	48.8	51.2	36.3	27.4	72.6	37.5	25.0	75.0
South Carolina	—	—	—	0.0	100.0	0.0	37.7	24.6	75.4
South Dakota	—	—	—	—	—	—	—	—	—
Tennessee	0.0[1]	100.0[1]	0.0[1]	0.0[1]	100.0[1]	0.0[1]	65.0	30.0	70.0
Texas	0.0	100.0	0.0	52.2[1]	4.4[1]	95.6[1]	—	—	—
Utah	—	—	—	—	—	—	—	—	—
Vermont	24.9	50.2	49.8	26.4	47.2	52.8	26.5	47.0	53.0
Virginia	—	—	—	—	—	—	—	—	—
Washington	—	—	—	—	—	—	—	—	—
West Virginia	41.9	16.2	83.8	45.4	9.2	90.8	51.9	3.8	96.2
Wisconsin	48.3[1]	3.4[1]	96.6[1]	46.8[1]	6.4[1]	93.6[1]	46.8[1]	6.4[1]	93.6[1]
Wyoming	—	—	—	—	—	—	—	—	—
Connecticut	50.5[2]	1.0[2]	99.0[2]	49.8[3]	0.4[3]	99.6[3]	49.9[4]	0.2[4]	99.8[4]
Maine	44.3[2]	11.4[2]	88.6[2]	43.7[3]	12.6[3]	87.4[3]	44.9[4]	10.2[4]	89.8[4]
Massachusetts	41.7[2]	16.6[2]	83.4[2]	40.6[3]	18.8[3]	81.2[3]	38.8[4]	22.4[4]	77.6[4]
Mississippi	—	—	—	0.0[3]	100.0[3]	0.0[3]	—	—	—
New Hampshire	47.7[2]	4.6[2]	95.4[2]	47.2[3]	5.6[3]	94.4[3]	50.6[4]	1.2[4]	98.8[4]
Rhode Island	30.1[2]	39.8[2]	60.2[2]	31.5[3]	37.0[3]	63.0[3]	37.8[4]	24.4[4]	75.6[4]
Vermont	26.6[2]	46.8[2]	53.2[2]	26.5[3]	47.0[3]	53.0[3]	—	—	—

Notes: The first entries are the Democratic percent of two-party vote values for each state for the gubernatorial race. The second entries are the margin of victory values for each state for the gubernatorial race, where margin of victory is defined as the absolute difference between the Democratic percent and the Republican percent of the two-party vote for governor. The third entries are the party competition index values for each state for the gubernatorial race, where the competition index devised by Paul David (1972) is defined as (100 − the margin of victory) or, alternatively, as (100 − the absolute difference between the Democratic and Republican percent of two-party vote for governor). The values for Democratic and Republican percent of two-party vote for governor are taken from the state vote tables in Chapter 7. Zero (0) percent on David's index represents a complete absence of two-party competition for that election year, whereas a score of 100 percent indicates perfect competition between the two major parties. A state can only receive a party competition score of 0 if it has a 100–0 vote split in the governor's race. Conversely, a state can only receive a score of 100 if it has a 50–50 vote split in the governor's race. For example, if New Hampshire in 1788 reported a 54.7 percent Democratic vote for governor of its two-party vote, then its Republican vote for governor would be 45.3 percent. The absolute difference between the two figures is the margin of victory, or 9.4 percent; 100 percent − 9.4 percent would equal 90.6 percent on David's party competition scale, indicating a very competitive contest for governor in New Hampshire in 1788. The two-party vote percent values used to derive the margin of victory and party competition figures are initially found in the state vote tables in Chapter 7. The author's alternative party coding in these tables is used whenever it occurs instead of the conventional party coding of voting data. The Democratic Party is defined here as the Anti-Federalists, Democratic-Republicans, and Jackson Democrats prior to 1830 when the "Democratic Party" as such was established. The Republican Party is defined as the Federalists, National Republicans, and Whigs prior to the establishment of the "Republican Party" in the 1850s. See Appendix A for an explanation of the historical antecedents of the current Democratic and Republican parties. States reporting only partial voting returns for governor's races are not included in the calculations for the years in which this occurred. —indicates that the state had no data, either because the state had no gubernatorial election, no vote data were found for the state in question, or the state had not yet entered the Union.

[1] Election held in odd-numbered year.
[2] 1867 election when state had annual elections in both 1866 and 1867.
[3] 1869 election when state had annual elections in both 1868 and 1869.
[4] 1871 election when state had annual elections in both 1870 and 1871.

Sources: State vote tables for governor in Chapter 7.

Table 8-119 Governor Competition Measures, by State, by Two-Year Election Cycle, 1872–1877 (Percentages)

State	1872–1873 Democratic % of Two-Party Vote	Margin of Victory	Party Competition Index	1874–1875 Democratic % of Two-Party Vote	Margin of Victory	Party Competition Index	1876–1877 Democratic % of Two-Party Vote	Margin of Victory	Party Competition Index
Alabama	47.5	5.0	95.0	53.3	6.6	93.4	63.4	26.8	73.2
Alaska	—	—	—	—	—	—	—	—	—
Arizona	—	—	—	—	—	—	—	—	—
Arkansas	48.2	3.6	96.4	100.0	100.0	0.0	65.8	31.6	68.4
California	—	—	—	66.3[1]	32.6[1]	67.4[1]	—	—	—
Colorado	—	—	—	—	—	—	48.5	3.0	97.0
Connecticut	48.9	2.2	97.8	53.9	7.8	92.2	51.4	2.8	97.2
Delaware	—	—	—	52.6	5.2	94.8	—	—	—
Florida	47.6	4.8	95.2	—	—	—	50.5	1.0	99.0
Georgia	69.2	38.4	61.6	—	—	—	76.2	52.4	47.6
Hawaii	—	—	—	—	—	—	—	—	—
Idaho	—	—	—	—	—	—	—	—	—
Illinois	45.3	9.4	90.6	—	—	—	49.4	1.2	98.8
Indiana	50.2	0.4	99.6	—	—	—	50.6	1.2	98.8
Iowa	0.0[1]	100.0[1]	0.0[1]	42.8[1]	14.4[1]	85.6[1]	39.5[1]	21.0[1]	79.0[1]
Kansas	34.2	31.6	68.4	42.0	16.0	84.0	40.0	20.0	80.0
Kentucky	—	—	—	58.3[1]	16.6[1]	83.4[1]	—	—	—
Louisiana	42.6	14.8	85.2	—	—	—	52.5	5.0	95.0
Maine	43.5	13.0	87.0	45.2	9.6	90.4	44.3	11.4	88.6
Maryland	—	—	—	54.1[1]	8.2[1]	91.8[1]	—	—	—
Massachusetts	30.8	38.4	61.6	51.9	3.8	96.2	43.7	12.6	87.4
Michigan	37.0	26.0	74.0	48.6	2.8	97.2	46.2	7.6	92.4
Minnesota	46.4[1]	7.2[1]	92.8[1]	43.9[1]	12.2[1]	87.8[1]	40.7[1]	18.6[1]	81.4[1]
Mississippi	0.0[1]	100.0[1]	0.0[1]	—	—	—	98.8[1]	97.6[1]	2.4[1]
Missouri	56.3	12.6	87.4	57.2	14.4	85.6	57.5	15.0	85.0
Montana	—	—	—	—	—	—	—	—	—
Nebraska	40.4	19.2	80.8	29.3	41.4	58.6	35.0	30.0	70.0
Nevada	—	—	—	57.1	14.2	85.8	—	—	—
New Hampshire	48.6	2.8	97.2	51.1	2.2	97.8	47.7	4.6	95.4
New Jersey	—	—	—	53.6	7.2	92.8	53.5[1]	7.0[1]	93.0[1]
New Mexico	—	—	—	—	—	—	—	—	—
New York	46.8	6.4	93.6	53.2	6.4	93.6	51.5	3.0	97.0
North Carolina	49.5	1.0	99.0	—	—	—	52.8	5.6	94.4
North Dakota	—	—	—	—	—	—	—	—	—
Ohio	50.1[1]	0.2[1]	99.8[1]	49.5[1]	1.0[1]	99.0[1]	52.2[1]	4.4[1]	95.6[1]
Oklahoma	—	—	—	—	—	—	—	—	—
Oregon	—	—	—	51.5	3.0	97.0	—	—	—
Pennsylvania	47.4	5.2	94.8	49.0[1]	2.0[1]	98.0[1]	—	—	—
Rhode Island	46.4	7.2	92.8	11.4	77.2	22.8	29.3	41.4	58.6
South Carolina	34.4	31.2	68.8	46.1	7.8	92.2	50.3	0.6	99.4
South Dakota	—	—	—	—	—	—	—	—	—
Tennessee	53.7	7.4	92.6	64.9	29.8	70.2	90.4	80.8	19.2
Texas	66.0[1]	32.0[1]	68.0[1]	75.0[1]	50.0[1]	50.0[1]	—	—	—
Utah	—	—	—	—	—	—	—	—	—
Vermont	28.4	43.2	56.8	28.3	43.4	56.6	31.9	36.2	63.8
Virginia	56.2[1]	12.4[1]	87.6[1]	—	—	—	95.9[1]	91.8[1]	8.2[1]
Washington	—	—	—	—	—	—	—	—	—
West Virginia	100.0	100.0	0.0	—	—	—	56.4	12.8	87.2
Wisconsin	55.2[1]	10.4[1]	89.6[1]	49.8[1]	0.4[1]	99.6[1]	47.2[1]	5.6[1]	94.4[1]
Wyoming	—	—	—	—	—	—	—	—	—
Connecticut	53.4[2]	6.8[2]	93.2[2]	54.8[3]	9.6[3]	90.4[3]	—	—	—
Maine	43.7[2]	12.6[2]	87.4[2]	48.2[3]	3.6[3]	96.4[3]	44.5[4]	11.0[4]	89.0[4]
Massachusetts	45.1[2]	9.8[2]	90.2[2]	48.4[3]	3.2[3]	96.8[3]	44.5[4]	11.0[4]	89.0[4]
New Hampshire	48.5[2]	3.0[2]	97.0[2]	49.9[3]	0.2[3]	99.8[3]	47.4[4]	5.2[4]	94.8[4]
Rhode Island	28.2[2]	43.6[2]	56.4[2]	38.2[3]	23.6[3]	76.4[3]	48.6[4]	2.8[4]	97.2[4]

Notes: The first entries are the Democratic percent of two-party vote values for each state for the gubernatorial race. The second entries are the margin of victory values for each state for the gubernatorial race, where margin of victory is defined as the absolute difference between the Democratic percent and the Republican percent of the two-party vote for governor. The third entries are the party competition index values for each state for the gubernatorial race, where the competition index devised by Paul David (1972) is defined as (100 − the margin of victory) or, alternatively, as (100 − the absolute difference between the Democratic and Republican percent of two-party vote for governor). The values for Democratic and Republican percent of two-party vote for governor are taken from the state vote tables in Chapter 7. Zero (0) percent on David's index represents a complete absence of two-party competition for that election year, whereas a score of 100 percent indicates perfect competition between the two major parties. A state can only receive a party competition score of 0 if it has a 100–0 vote split in the governor's race. Conversely, a state can only receive a score of 100 if it has a 50–50 vote split in the governor's race. For example, if New Hampshire in 1788 reported a 54.7 percent Democratic vote for governor of its two-party vote, then its Republican vote for governor would be 45.3 percent. The absolute difference between the two figures is the margin of victory, or 9.4 percent; 100 percent − 9.4 percent would equal 90.6 percent on David's party competition scale, indicating a very competitive contest for governor in New Hampshire in 1788. The two-party vote percent values used to derive the margin of victory and party competition figures are initially found in the state vote tables in Chapter 7. The author's alternative party coding in these tables is used whenever it occurs instead of the conventional party coding of voting data. The Democratic Party is defined here as the Anti-Federalists, Democratic-Republicans, and Jackson Democrats prior to 1830 when the "Democratic Party" as such was established. The Republican Party is defined as the Federalists, National Republicans, and Whigs prior to the establishment of the "Republican Party" in the 1850s. See Appendix A for an explanation of the historical antecedents of the current Democratic and Republican parties. States reporting only partial voting returns for governor's races are not included in the calculations for the years in which this occurred. —indicates that the state had no data, either because the state had no gubernatorial election, no vote data were found for the state in question, or the state had not yet entered the Union.

[1] Election held in odd-numbered year.
[2] 1873 election when state had annual elections in both 1872 and 1873.
[3] 1875 election when state had annual elections in both 1874 and 1875.
[4] 1877 election when state had annual elections in both 1876 and 1877.

Sources: State vote tables for governor in Chapter 7.

Table 8-120 Governor Competition Measures, by State, by Two-Year Election Cycle, 1878–1883 (Percentages)

	1878–1879			1880–1881			1882–1883		
State	Democratic % of Two-Party Vote	Margin of Victory	Party Competition Index	Democratic % of Two-Party Vote	Margin of Victory	Party Competition Index	Democratic % of Two-Party Vote	Margin of Victory	Party Competition Index
Alabama	100.0	100.0	0.0	100.0	100.0	0.0	68.7	37.4	62.6
Alaska	—	—	—	—	—	—	—	—	—
Arizona	—	—	—	—	—	—	—	—	—
Arkansas	100.0	100.0	0.0	100.0	100.0	0.0	64.0	28.0	72.0
California	41.2[1]	17.6[1]	82.4[1]	—	—	—	57.4	14.8	85.2
Colorado	44.6	10.8	89.2	45.3	9.4	90.6	52.1	4.2	95.8
Connecticut	48.7	2.6	97.4	48.9	2.2	97.8	51.8	3.6	96.4
Delaware	100.0	100.0	0.0	—	—	—	53.1	6.2	93.8
Florida	—	—	—	54.9	9.8	90.2	—	—	—
Georgia	—	—	—	100.0	100.0	0.0	100.0	100.0	0.0
Hawaii	—	—	—	—	—	—	—	—	—
Idaho	—	—	—	—	—	—	—	—	—
Illinois	—	—	—	46.9	6.2	93.8	—	—	—
Indiana	—	—	—	49.2	1.6	98.4	—	—	—
Iowa	35.2[1]	29.6[1]	70.4[1]	35.5[1]	29.0[1]	71.0[1]	46.0[1]	8.0[1]	92.0[1]
Kansas	33.5	33.0	67.0	35.6	28.8	71.2	45.5	9.0	91.0
Kentucky	60.5[1]	21.0[1]	79.0[1]	—	—	—	60.0[1]	20.0[1]	80.0[1]
Louisiana	64.6[1]	29.2[1]	70.8[1]	—	—	—	—	—	—
Maine	33.3	33.4	66.6	50.1	0.2	99.8	46.8	6.4	93.6
Maryland	56.9[1]	13.8[1]	86.2[1]	—	—	—	53.5[1]	7.0[1]	93.0[1]
Massachusetts	47.0	6.0	94.0	40.3	19.4	80.6	52.8	5.6	94.4
Michigan	38.3	23.4	76.6	43.5	13.0	87.0	50.8	1.6	98.4
Minnesota	42.1[1]	15.8[1]	84.2[1]	36.4[1]	27.2[1]	72.8[1]	44.6[1]	10.8[1]	89.2[1]
Mississippi	—	—	—	59.6[1]	19.2[1]	80.8[1]	—	—	—
Missouri	—	—	—	57.5	15.0	85.0	—	—	—
Montana	—	—	—	—	—	—	—	—	—
Nebraska	31.5	37.0	63.0	33.8	32.4	67.6	39.6	20.8	79.2
Nevada	48.6	2.8	97.2	—	—	—	54.3	8.6	91.4
New Hampshire	49.0	2.0	98.0	47.9	4.2	95.8	49.0	2.0	98.0
New Jersey	—	—	—	50.1	0.2	99.8	51.7[1]	3.4[1]	96.6[1]
New Mexico	—	—	—	—	—	—	—	—	—
New York	52.0[1]	4.0[1]	96.0[1]	—	—	—	56.1	12.2	87.8
North Carolina	—	—	—	51.3	2.6	97.4	—	—	—
North Dakota	—	—	—	—	—	—	—	—	—
Ohio	48.7[1]	2.6[1]	97.4[1]	48.0[1]	4.0[1]	96.0[1]	50.9[1]	1.8[1]	98.2[1]
Oklahoma	—	—	—	—	—	—	—	—	—
Oregon	50.1	0.2	99.8	—	—	—	48.3	3.4	96.6
Pennsylvania	48.2	3.6	96.4	—	—	—	49.8	0.4	99.6
Rhode Island	40.0	20.0	80.0	32.8	34.4	65.6	34.6	30.8	69.2
South Carolina	100.0	100.0	0.0	100.0	100.0	0.0	100.0	100.0	0.0
South Dakota	—	—	—	—	—	—	—	—	—
Tennessee	67.4	34.8	65.2	56.8	13.6	86.4	57.2	14.4	85.6
Texas	87.4	74.8	25.2	72.1	44.2	55.8	58.1	16.2	83.8
Utah	—	—	—	—	—	—	—	—	—
Vermont	31.6	36.8	63.2	30.7	38.6	61.4	28.8	42.4	57.6
Virginia	—	—	—	100.0[1]	100.0[1]	0.0[1]	—	—	—
Washington	—	—	—	—	—	—	—	—	—
West Virginia	—	—	—	57.6	15.2	84.8	—	—	—
Wisconsin	42.7[1]	14.6[1]	85.4[1]	46.1[1]	7.8[1]	92.2[1]	—	—	—
Wyoming	—	—	—	—	—	—	—	—	—
Maine	23.9[2]	52.2[2]	47.8[2]	—	—	—	—	—	—
Massachusetts	49.3[2]	1.4[2]	98.6[2]	36.1[3]	27.8[3]	72.2[3]	48.4[4]	3.2[4]	96.8[4]
New Hampshire	44.9[2]	10.2[2]	89.8[2]	—	—	—	—	—	—
Rhode Island	36.2[2]	27.6[2]	72.4[2]	30.5[3]	39.0[3]	61.0[3]	45.5[4]	9.0[4]	91.0[4]

Notes: The first entries are the Democratic percent of two-party vote values for each state for the gubernatorial race. The second entries are the margin of victory values for each state for the gubernatorial race, where margin of victory is defined as the absolute difference between the Democratic percent and the Republican percent of the two-party vote for governor. The third entries are the party competition index values for each state for the gubernatorial race, where the competition index devised by Paul David (1972) is defined as (100 − the margin of victory) or, alternatively, as (100 − the absolute difference between the Democratic and Republican percent of two-party vote for governor). The values for Democratic and Republican percent of two-party vote for governor are taken from the state vote tables in Chapter 7. Zero (0) percent on David's index represents a complete absence of two-party competition for that election year, whereas a score of 100 percent indicates perfect competition between the two major parties. A state can only receive a party competition score of 0 if it has a 100–0 vote split in the governor's race. Conversely, a state can only receive a score of 100 if it has a 50–50 vote split in the governor's race. For example, if New Hampshire in 1788 reported a 54.7 percent Democratic vote for governor of its two-party vote, then its Republican vote for governor would be 45.3 percent. The absolute difference between the two figures is the margin of victory, or 9.4 percent; 100 percent − 9.4 percent would equal 90.6 percent on David's party competition scale, indicating a very competitive contest for governor in New Hampshire in 1788. The two-party vote percent values used to derive the margin of victory and party competition figures are initially found in the state vote tables in Chapter 7. The author's alternative party coding in these tables is used whenever it occurs instead of the conventional party coding of voting data. The Democratic Party is defined here as the Anti-Federalists, Democratic-Republicans, and Jackson Democrats prior to 1830 when the "Democratic Party" as such was established. The Republican Party is defined as the Federalists, National Republicans, and Whigs prior to the establishment of the "Republican Party" in the 1850s. See Appendix A for an explanation of the historical antecedents of the current Democratic and Republican parties. States reporting only partial voting returns for governor's races are not included in the calculations for the years in which this occurred. —indicates that the state had no data, either because the state had no gubernatorial election, no vote data were found for the state in question, or the state had not yet entered the Union.

[1] Election held in odd-numbered year.
[2] 1879 election when state had annual elections in both 1878 and 1879.
[3] 1881 election when state had annual elections in both 1880 and 1881.
[4] 1883 election when state had annual elections in both 1882 and 1883.

Sources: State vote tables for governor in Chapter 7.

Table 8-121 Governor Competition Measures, by State, by Election Year, 1884–1889 (Percentages)

	1884–1885			1886–1887			1888–1889		
State	Democratic % of Two-Party Vote	Margin of Victory	Party Competition Index	Democratic % of Two-Party Vote	Margin of Victory	Party Competition Index	Democratic % of Two-Party Vote	Margin of Victory	Party Competition Index
Alabama	100.0	100.0	0.0	79.8	59.6	40.4	77.7	55.4	44.6
Alaska	—	—	—	—	—	—	—	—	—
Arizona	—	—	—	—	—	—	—	—	—
Arkansas	64.6	29.2	70.8	62.6	25.2	74.8	100.0	100.0	0.0
California	—	—	—	50.2	0.4	99.6	—	—	—
Colorado	47.6	4.8	95.2	52.2	4.4	95.6	44.2	11.6	88.4
Connecticut	50.6	1.2	98.8	50.8	1.6	98.4	50.5	1.0	99.0
Delaware	—	—	—	99.0	98.0	2.0	—	—	—
Florida	53.5	7.0	93.0	—	—	—	60.4	20.8	79.2
Georgia	—	—	—	100.0	100.0	0.0	100.0	100.0	0.0
Hawaii	—	—	—	—	—	—	—	—	—
Idaho	—	—	—	—	—	—	—	—	—
Illinois	48.9	2.2	97.8	—	—	—	49.1	1.8	98.2
Indiana	50.8	1.6	98.4	—	—	—	49.8	0.4	99.6
Iowa	49.0[1]	2.0[1]	98.0[1]	47.5[1]	5.0[1]	95.0[1]	50.9[1]	1.8[1]	98.2[1]
Kansas	42.5	15.0	85.0	43.6	12.8	87.2	37.3	25.4	74.6
Kentucky	—	—	—	53.1[1]	6.2[1]	93.8[1]	—	—	—
Louisiana	67.1	34.2	65.8	—	—	—	72.5	45.0	55.0
Maine	42.8	14.4	85.6	44.5	11.0	89.0	43.6	12.8	87.2
Maryland	—	—	—	53.3[1]	6.6[1]	93.4[1]	—	—	—
Massachusetts	41.2	17.6	82.4	48.0	4.0	96.0	45.8	8.4	91.6
Michigan	49.5	1.0	99.0	49.0	2.0	98.0	48.1	3.8	96.2
Minnesota	—	—	—	49.4	1.2	98.8	45.1	9.8	90.2
Mississippi	100.0[1]	100.0[1]	0.0[1]	—	—	—	100.0[1]	100.0[1]	0.0[1]
Missouri	51.3	2.6	97.4	—	—	—	51.3	2.6	97.4
Montana	—	—	—	—	—	—	51.0[1]	2.0[1]	98.0[1]
Nebraska	44.2	11.6	88.4	40.7	18.6	81.4	45.1	9.8	90.2
Nevada	—	—	—	47.6	4.8	95.2	—	—	—
New Hampshire	48.2	3.6	96.4	49.7	0.6	99.4	49.7	0.6	99.4
New Jersey	—	—	—	51.9	3.8	96.2	52.7[1]	5.4[1]	94.6[1]
New Mexico	—	—	—	—	—	—	—	—	—
New York	50.6[1]	1.2[1]	98.8[1]	—	—	—	50.7	1.4	98.6
North Carolina	53.8	7.6	92.4	—	—	—	52.5	5.0	95.0
North Dakota	—	—	—	—	—	—	33.4[1]	33.2[1]	66.8[1]
Ohio	48.8[1]	2.4[1]	97.6[1]	48.3[1]	3.4[1]	96.6[1]	50.7[1]	1.4[1]	98.6[1]
Oklahoma	—	—	—	—	—	—	—	—	—
Oregon	—	—	—	53.6	7.2	92.8	—	—	—
Pennsylvania	—	—	—	47.3	5.4	94.6	—	—	—
Rhode Island	37.6	24.8	75.2	40.9	18.2	81.8	45.8	8.4	91.6
South Carolina	100.0	100.0	0.0	100.0	100.0	0.0	100.0	100.0	0.0
South Dakota	—	—	—	—	—	—	30.6[1]	38.8[1]	61.2[1]
Tennessee	51.3	2.6	97.4	53.5	7.0	93.0	53.0	6.0	94.0
Texas	68.2	36.4	63.6	77.6	55.2	44.8	100.0	100.0	0.0
Utah	—	—	—	—	—	—	—	—	—
Vermont	31.8	36.4	63.6	31.3	37.4	62.6	28.7	42.6	57.4
Virginia	52.8[1]	5.6[1]	94.4[1]	—	—	—	57.4[1]	14.8[1]	85.2[1]
Washington	—	—	—	—	—	—	42.3[1]	15.4[1]	84.6[1]
West Virginia	51.9	3.8	96.2	—	—	—	50.0	0.0	100.0
Wisconsin	46.9	6.2	93.8	46.2	7.6	92.4	46.9	6.2	93.8
Wyoming	—	—	—	—	—	—	—	—	—
Massachusetts	44.6[2]	10.8[2]	89.2[2]	46.5[3]	7.0[3]	93.0[3]	48.6[4]	2.8[4]	97.2[4]
Rhode Island	40.8[2]	18.4[2]	81.6[2]	54.5[3]	9.0[3]	91.0[3]	55.8[4]	11.6[4]	88.4[4]

Notes: The first entries are the Democratic percent of two-party vote values for each state for the gubernatorial race. The second entries are the margin of victory values for each state for the gubernatorial race, where margin of victory is defined as the absolute difference between the Democratic percent and the Republican percent of the two-party vote for governor. The third entries are the party competition index values for each state for the gubernatorial race, where the competition index devised by Paul David (1972) is defined as (100 − the margin of victory) or, alternatively, as (100 − the absolute difference between the Democratic and Republican percent of two-party vote for governor). The values for Democratic and Republican percent of two-party vote for governor are taken from the state vote tables in Chapter 7. Zero (0) percent on David's index represents a complete absence of two-party competition for that election year, whereas a score of 100 percent indicates perfect competition between the two major parties. A state can only receive a party competition score of 0 if it has a 100–0 vote split in the governor's race. Conversely, a state can only receive a score of 100 if it has a 50–50 vote split in the governor's race. For example, if New Hampshire in 1788 reported a 54.7 percent Democratic vote for governor of its two-party vote, then its Republican vote for governor would be 45.3 percent. The absolute difference between the two figures is the margin of victory, or 9.4 percent; 100 percent − 9.4 percent would equal 90.6 percent on David's party competition scale, indicating a very competitive contest for governor in New Hampshire in 1788. The two-party vote percent values used to derive the margin of victory and party competition figures are initially found in the state vote tables in Chapter 7. The author's alternative party coding in these tables is used whenever it occurs instead of the conventional party coding of voting data. The Democratic Party is defined here as the Anti-Federalists, Democratic-Republicans, and Jackson Democrats prior to 1830 when the "Democratic Party" as such was established. The Republican Party is defined as the Federalists, National Republicans, and Whigs prior to the establishment of the "Republican Party" in the 1850s. See Appendix A for an explanation of the historical antecedents of the current Democratic and Republican parties. States reporting only partial voting returns for governor's races are not included in the calculations for the years in which this occurred. —indicates that the state had no data, either because the state had no gubernatorial election, no vote data were found for the state in question, or the state had not yet entered the Union.

[1] Election held in odd-numbered year.
[2] 1885 election when state had annual elections in both 1884 and 1885.
[3] 1887 election when state had annual elections in both 1886 and 1887.
[4] 1889 election when state had annual elections in both 1888 and 1889.

Sources: State vote tables for governor in Chapter 7.

Table 8-122 Governor Competition Measures, by State, by Two-Year Election Cycle, 1890–1895 (Percentages)

State	1890–1891 Democratic % of Two-Party Vote	1890–1891 Margin of Victory	1890–1891 Party Competition Index	1892–1893 Democratic % of Two-Party Vote	1892–1893 Margin of Victory	1892–1893 Party Competition Index	1894–1895 Democratic % of Two-Party Vote	1894–1895 Margin of Victory	1894–1895 Party Competition Index
Alabama	76.7	53.4	46.6	100.0	100.0	0.0	100.0	100.0	0.0
Alaska	—	—	—	—	—	—	—	—	—
Arizona	—	—	—	—	—	—	—	—	—
Arkansas	55.5	11.0	89.0	72.8	45.6	54.4	74.1	48.2	51.8
California	48.4	3.2	96.8	—	—	—	50.3	0.6	99.4
Colorado	45.8	8.4	91.6	57.4	14.8	85.2	8.2	83.6	16.4
Connecticut	51.4	2.8	97.2	51.9	3.8	96.2	44.1	11.8	88.2
Delaware	50.8	1.6	98.4	—	—	—	48.4	3.2	96.8
Florida	—	—	—	100.0	100.0	0.0	—	—	—
Georgia	100.0	100.0	0.0	100.0	100.0	0.0	100.0	100.0	0.0
Hawaii	—	—	—	—	—	—	—	—	—
Idaho	43.6	12.8	87.2	45.3	9.4	90.6	40.9	18.2	81.8
Illinois	—	—	—	51.4	2.8	97.2	—	—	—
Indiana	—	—	—	50.7	1.4	98.6	—	—	—
Iowa	51.0[1]	2.0[1]	98.0[1]	45.8[1]	8.4[1]	91.6[1]	41.7[1]	16.6[1]	83.4[1]
Kansas	60.8	21.6	78.4	50.7	1.4	98.6	49.5	1.0	99.0
Kentucky	55.4[1]	10.8[1]	89.2[1]	—	—	—	48.7[1]	2.6[1]	97.4[1]
Louisiana	—	—	—	75.0	50.0	50.0	—	—	—
Maine	41.4	17.2	82.8	44.9	10.2	89.8	30.5	39.0	61.0
Maryland	58.1[1]	16.2[1]	83.8[1]	—	—	—	45.9[1]	8.2[1]	91.8[1]
Massachusetts	51.7	3.4	96.6	50.3	0.6	99.4	39.6	20.8	79.2
Michigan	51.6	3.2	96.8	48.1	3.8	96.2	35.5	29.0	71.0
Minnesota	49.3	1.4	98.6	46.4	7.2	92.8	26.6	46.8	53.2
Mississippi	—	—	—	—	—	—	100.0[1]	100.0[1]	0.0[1]
Missouri	—	—	—	53.0	6.0	94.0	—	—	—
Montana	—	—	—	49.3	1.4	98.6	52.6	5.2	94.8
Nebraska	50.9	1.8	98.2	36.0	28.0	72.0	60.4	20.8	79.2
Nevada	46.7	6.6	93.4	—	—	—	42.2	15.6	84.4
New Hampshire	49.9	0.2	99.8	48.7	2.6	97.4	45.5[1]	9.0[1]	91.0[1]
New Jersey	—	—	—	51.2	2.4	97.6	44.7	10.6	89.4
New Mexico	—	—	—	—	—	—	—	—	—
New York	52.1[1]	4.2[1]	95.8[1]	—	—	—	44.7	10.6	89.4
North Carolina	—	—	—	58.8	17.6	82.4	—	—	—
North Dakota	39.8	20.4	79.6	52.4	4.8	95.2	25.7	48.6	51.4
Ohio	48.6[1]	2.8[1]	97.2[1]	44.8[1]	10.4[1]	89.6[1]	43.9[1]	12.2[1]	87.8[1]
Oklahoma	—	—	—	—	—	—	—	—	—
Oregon	53.5	7.0	93.0	—	—	—	30.3	39.4	60.6
Pennsylvania	50.9	1.8	98.2	—	—	—	36.7	26.6	73.4
Rhode Island	52.0	4.0	96.0	48.1	3.8	96.2	43.7	12.6	87.4
South Carolina	100.0	100.0	0.0	100.0	100.0	0.0	100.0	100.0	0.0
South Dakota	34.9	30.2	69.8	30.9	38.2	61.8	17.8	64.4	35.6
Tennessee	59.9	19.8	80.2	55.7	11.4	88.6	49.8	0.4	99.6
Texas	77.3	54.6	45.4	58.6	17.2	82.8	77.3	54.6	45.4
Utah	—	—	—	—	—	—	—	—	—
Vermont	36.6	26.8	73.2	33.1	33.8	66.2	24.9	50.2	49.8
Virginia	—	—	—	100.0[1]	100.0[1]	0.0[1]	—	—	—
Washington	—	—	—	46.5	7.0	93.0	—	—	—
West Virginia	—	—	—	51.2	2.4	97.6	—	—	—
Wisconsin	54.8	9.6	90.4	51.1	2.2	97.8	42.0	16.0	84.0
Wyoming	44.6	10.8	89.2	—	—	—	40.7	18.6	81.4
Massachusetts	51.0[2]	2.0[2]	98.0[2]	44.9[3]	10.2[3]	89.8[3]	39.5[4]	21.0[4]	79.0[4]
Rhode Island	51.4[2]	2.8[2]	97.2[2]	50.2[3]	0.4[3]	99.6[3]	36.3[4]	27.4[4]	72.6[4]

Notes: The first entries are the Democratic percent of two-party vote values for each state for the gubernatorial race. The second entries are the margin of victory values for each state for the gubernatorial race, where margin of victory is defined as the absolute difference between the Democratic percent and the Republican percent of the two-party vote for governor. The third entries are the party competition index values for each state for the gubernatorial race, where the competition index devised by Paul David (1972) is defined as (100 − the margin of victory) or, alternatively, as (100 − the absolute difference between the Democratic and Republican percent of two-party vote for governor). The values for Democratic and Republican percent of two-party vote for governor are taken from the state vote tables in Chapter 7. Zero (0) percent on David's index represents a complete absence of two-party competition for that election year, whereas a score of 100 percent indicates perfect competition between the two major parties. A state can only receive a party competition score of 0 if it has a 100–0 vote split in the governor's race. Conversely, a state can only receive a score of 100 if it has a 50–50 vote split in the governor's race. For example, if New Hampshire in 1788 reported a 54.7 percent Democratic vote for governor of its two-party vote, then its Republican vote for governor would be 45.3 percent. The absolute difference between the two figures is the margin of victory, or 9.4 percent; 100 percent − 9.4 percent would equal 90.6 percent on David's party competition scale, indicating a very competitive contest for governor in New Hampshire in 1788. The two-party vote percent values used to derive the margin of victory and party competition figures are initially found in the state vote tables in Chapter 7. The author's alternative party coding in these tables is used whenever it occurs instead of the conventional party coding of voting data. The Democratic Party is defined here as the Anti-Federalists, Democratic-Republicans, and Jackson Democrats prior to 1830 when the "Democratic Party" as such was established. The Republican Party is defined as the Federalists, National Republicans, and Whigs prior to the establishment of the "Republican Party" in the 1850s. See Appendix A for an explanation of the historical antecedents of the current Democratic and Republican parties. States reporting only partial voting returns for governor's races are not included in the calculations for the years in which this occurred. —indicates that the state had no data, either because the state had no gubernatorial election, no vote data were found for the state in question, or the state had not yet entered the Union.

[1] Election held in odd-numbered year.
[2] 1891 election when state had annual elections in both 1890 and 1891.
[3] 1893 election when state had annual elections in both 1892 and 1893.
[4] 1895 election when state had annual elections in both 1894 and 1895.

Sources: State vote tables for governor in Chapter 7.

Table 8-123 Governor Competition Measures, by State, by Two-Year Election Cycle, 1896–1901 (Percentages)

State	1896–1897			1898–1899			1900–1901		
	Democratic % of Two-Party Vote	Margin of Victory	Party Competition Index	Democratic % of Two-Party Vote	Margin of Victory	Party Competition Index	Democratic % of Two-Party Vote	Margin of Victory	Party Competition Index
Alabama	100.0	100.0	0.0	97.2	94.4	5.6	80.3	60.6	39.4
Alaska	—	—	—	—	—	—	—	—	—
Arizona	—	—	—	—	—	—	—	—	—
Arkansas	71.8	43.6	56.4	73.2	46.4	53.6	68.5	37.0	63.0
California	—	—	—	46.6	6.8	93.2	—	—	—
Colorado	78.5	57.0	43.0	64.8	29.6	70.4	55.3	10.6	89.4
Connecticut	36.3	27.4	72.6	44.2	11.6	88.4	45.9	8.2	91.8
Delaware	46.0	8.0	92.0	—	—	—	45.6	8.8	91.2
Florida	76.6	53.2	46.8	—	—	—	82.0	64.0	36.0
Georgia	100.0	100.0	0.0	100.0	100.0	0.0	100.0	100.0	0.0
Hawaii	—	—	—	—	—	—	—	—	—
Idaho	77.4	54.8	45.2	58.5	17.0	83.0	52.0	4.0	96.0
Illinois	45.1	9.8	90.2	—	—	—	47.2	5.6	94.4
Indiana	48.1	3.8	96.2	—	—	—	48.0	4.0	96.0
Iowa	47.0[1]	6.0[1]	94.0[1]	43.4[1]	13.2[1]	86.8[1]	38.8[1]	22.4[1]	77.6[1]
Kansas	51.2	2.4	97.6	47.3	5.4	94.6	47.5	5.0	95.0
Kentucky	—	—	—	51.2[1]	2.4[1]	97.6[1]	—	—	—
Louisiana	57.0	14.0	86.0	—	—	—	78.3	56.6	43.4
Maine	29.7	40.6	59.4	34.8	30.4	69.6	35.3	29.4	70.6
Maryland	—	—	—	52.5[1]	5.0[1]	95.0[1]	—	—	—
Massachusetts	31.3	37.4	62.6	36.1	27.8	72.2	36.3	27.4	72.6
Michigan	43.3	13.4	86.6	40.9	18.2	81.8	42.5	15.0	85.0
Minnesota	49.4	1.2	98.8	54.1	8.2	91.8	49.6	0.8	99.2
Mississippi	—	—	—	100.0[1]	100.0[1]	0.0[1]	—	—	—
Missouri	53.4	6.8	93.2	—	—	—	52.4	4.8	95.2
Montana	71.0	42.0	58.0	—	—	—	64.2	28.4	71.6
Nebraska	56.1	12.2	87.8	50.7	1.4	98.6	49.8	0.4	99.6
Nevada	—	—	—	22.4	55.2	44.8	—	—	—
New Hampshire	37.1	25.8	74.2	44.4	11.2	88.8	39.3	21.4	78.6
New Jersey	—	—	—	49.1	1.8	98.2	47.6[1]	4.8[1]	95.2[1]
New Mexico	—	—	—	—	—	—	—	—	—
New York	43.3	13.4	86.6	49.3	1.4	98.6	46.3	7.4	92.6
North Carolina	48.5	3.0	97.0	—	—	—	59.6	19.2	80.8
North Dakota	44.4	11.2	88.8	41.7	16.6	83.4	39.5	21.0	79.0
Ohio	48.4[1]	3.2[1]	96.8[1]	46.9[1]	6.2[1]	93.8[1]	45.8[1]	8.4[1]	91.6[1]
Oklahoma	—	—	—	—	—	—	—	—	—
Oregon	—	—	—	43.4	13.2	86.8	—	—	—
Pennsylvania	—	—	—	42.9	14.2	85.8	—	—	—
Rhode Island	37.5	25.0	75.0	34.8	30.4	69.6	39.8	20.4	79.6
South Carolina	89.2	78.4	21.6	100.0	100.0	0.0	100.0	100.0	0.0
South Dakota	0.0	100.0	0.0	50.2	0.4	99.6	42.7	14.6	85.4
Tennessee	51.1	2.2	97.8	59.3	18.6	81.4	54.9	9.8	90.2
Texas	100.0	100.0	0.0	100.0	100.0	0.0	72.9	45.8	54.2
Utah	47.1	5.8	94.2	—	—	—	48.3	3.4	96.6
Vermont	21.8	56.4	43.6	27.6	44.8	55.2	26.1	47.8	52.2
Virginia	66.0[1]	32.0[1]	68.0[1]	—	—	—	58.9[1]	17.8[1]	82.2[1]
Washington	57.1	14.2	85.8	—	—	—	51.1	2.2	97.8
West Virginia	47.0	6.0	94.0	—	—	—	45.8	8.4	91.6
Wisconsin	39.0	22.0	78.0	43.9	12.2	87.8	37.8	24.4	75.6
Wyoming	—	—	—	46.4	7.2	92.8	—	—	—
Massachusetts	36.1[2]	27.8[2]	72.2[2]	38.1[3]	23.8[3]	76.2[3]	38.1[4]	23.8[4]	76.2[4]
Rhode Island	36.0[2]	28.0[2]	72.0[2]	37.5[3]	25.0[3]	75.0[3]	42.7[4]	14.6[4]	85.4[4]

Notes: The first entries are the Democratic percent of two-party vote values for each state for the gubernatorial race. The second entries are the margin of victory values for each state for the gubernatorial race, where margin of victory is defined as the absolute difference between the Democratic percent and the Republican percent of the two-party vote for governor. The third entries are the party competition index values for each state for the gubernatorial race, where the competition index devised by Paul David (1972) is defined as (100 − the margin of victory) or, alternatively, as (100 − the absolute difference between the Democratic and Republican percent of two-party vote for governor). The values for Democratic and Republican percent of two-party vote for governor are taken from the state vote tables in Chapter 7. Zero (0) percent on David's index represents a complete absence of two-party competition for that election year, whereas a score of 100 percent indicates perfect competition between the two major parties. A state can only receive a party competition score of 0 if it has a 100–0 vote split in the governor's race. Conversely, a state can only receive a score of 100 if it has a 50–50 vote split in the governor's race. For example, if New Hampshire in 1788 reported a 54.7 percent Democratic vote for governor of its two-party vote, then its Republican vote for governor would be 45.3 percent. The absolute difference between the two figures is the margin of victory, or 9.4 percent; 100 percent − 9.4 percent would equal 90.6 percent on David's party competition scale, indicating a very competitive contest for governor in New Hampshire in 1788. The two-party vote percent values used to derive the margin of victory and party competition figures are initially found in the state vote tables in Chapter 7. The author's alternative party coding in these tables is used whenever it occurs instead of the conventional party coding of voting data. The Democratic Party is defined here as the Anti-Federalists, Democratic-Republicans, and Jackson Democrats prior to 1830 when the "Democratic Party" as such was established. The Republican Party is defined as the Federalists, National Republicans, and Whigs prior to the establishment of the "Republican Party" in the 1850s. See Appendix A for an explanation of the historical antecedents of the current Democratic and Republican parties. States reporting only partial voting returns for governor's races are not included in the calculations for the years in which this occurred. —indicates that the state had no data, either because the state had no gubernatorial election, no vote data were found for the state in question, or the state had not yet entered the Union.

[1] Election held in odd-numbered year.
[2] 1897 election when state had annual elections in both 1896 and 1897.
[3] 1899 election when state had annual elections in both 1898 and 1899.
[4] 1901 election when state had annual elections in both 1900 and 1901.

Sources: State vote tables for governor in Chapter 7.

Table 8-124 Governor Competition Measures, by State, by Two-Year Election Cycle, 1902–1907 (Percentages)

| | 1902–1903 | | | 1904–1905 | | | 1906–1907 | | |
State	Democratic % of Two-Party Vote	Margin of Victory	Party Competition Index	Democratic % of Two-Party Vote	Margin of Victory	Party Competition Index	Democratic % of Two-Party Vote	Margin of Victory	Party Competition Index
Alabama	73.7	47.4	52.6	—	—	—	86.0	72.0	28.0
Alaska	—	—	—	—	—	—	—	—	—
Arizona	—	—	—	—	—	—	—	—	—
Arkansas	72.6	45.2	54.8	62.6	25.2	74.8	71.7	43.4	56.6
California	49.6	0.8	99.2	—	—	—	48.3	3.4	96.6
Colorado	47.9	4.2	95.8	52.0	4.0	96.0	44.6	10.8	89.2
Connecticut	44.8	10.4	89.6	43.0	14.0	86.0	43.4	13.2	86.8
Delaware	—	—	—	45.9	8.2	91.8	—	—	—
Florida	—	—	—	82.0	64.0	36.0	—	—	—
Georgia	100.0	100.0	0.0	100.0	100.0	0.0	100.0	100.0	0.0
Hawaii	—	—	—	—	—	—	—	—	—
Idaho	44.9	10.2	89.8	36.7	26.6	73.4	43.5	13.0	87.0
Illinois	—	—	—	34.6	30.8	69.2	—	—	—
Indiana	—	—	—	43.4	13.2	86.8	—	—	—
Iowa	40.1[1]	19.8[1]	80.2[1]	—	—	—	47.5	5.0	95.0
Kansas	42.4	15.2	84.8	38.5	23.0	77.0	49.6	0.8	99.2
Kentucky	53.0[1]	6.0[1]	94.0[1]	—	—	—	47.8[1]	4.4[1]	95.6[1]
Louisiana	—	—	—	89.0	78.0	22.0	—	—	—
Maine	36.8	26.4	73.6	39.5	21.0	79.0	46.9	6.2	93.8
Maryland	53.1[1]	6.2[1]	93.8[1]	—	—	—	52.0[1]	4.0[1]	96.0[1]
Massachusetts	44.8	10.4	89.6	54.2	8.4	91.6	46.4	7.2	92.8
Michigan	45.2	9.6	90.4	44.1	11.8	88.2	36.4	27.2	72.8
Minnesota	38.9	22.2	77.8	51.4	2.8	97.2	63.7	27.4	72.6
Mississippi	100.0[1]	100.0[1]	0.0[1]	—	—	—	100.0[1]	100.0[1]	0.0[1]
Missouri	—	—	—	52.4	4.8	95.2	—	—	—
Montana	—	—	—	56.8	13.6	86.4	—	—	—
Nebraska	48.6	2.8	97.2	47.9	4.2	95.8	46.5	7.0	93.0
Nevada	57.8	15.6	84.4	—	—	—	62.0	24.0	76.0
New Hampshire	44.6	10.8	89.2	40.9	18.2	81.8	48.1	3.8	96.2
New Jersey	—	—	—	44.2	11.6	88.4	48.9[1]	2.2[1]	97.8[1]
New Mexico	—	—	—	—	—	—	—	—	—
New York	49.7	0.6	99.4	47.4	5.2	94.8	48.0	4.0	96.0
North Carolina	—	—	—	61.8	23.6	76.4	—	—	—
North Dakota	35.7	28.6	71.4	25.9	48.2	51.8	54.0	8.0	92.0
Ohio	43.2[1]	13.6[1]	86.4[1]	52.4[1]	4.8[1]	95.2[1]	—	—	—
Oklahoma	—	—	—	—	—	—	55.5[1]	11.0[1]	89.0[1]
Oregon	50.1	0.2	99.8	—	—	—	51.4	2.8	97.2
Pennsylvania	43.2	13.6	86.4	—	—	—	47.5	5.0	95.0
Rhode Island	56.8	13.6	86.4	49.4	1.2	98.8	51.0	2.0	98.0
South Carolina	100.0	100.0	0.0	100.0	100.0	0.0	100.0	100.0	0.0
South Dakota	30.7	38.6	61.4	26.5	47.0	53.0	29.0	42.0	58.0
Tennessee	62.6	25.2	74.8	56.0	12.0	88.0	54.7	9.4	90.6
Texas	80.4	60.8	39.2	78.4	56.8	43.2	83.7	67.4	32.6
Utah	—	—	—	42.8	14.4	85.6	—	—	—
Vermont	18.8	62.4	37.6	25.6	48.8	51.2	38.9	22.2	77.8
Virginia	—	—	—	64.8[1]	29.6[1]	70.4[1]	—	—	—
Washington	—	—	—	44.3	11.4	88.6	—	—	—
West Virginia	—	—	—	48.1	3.8	96.2	—	—	—
Wisconsin	43.0	14.0	86.0	42.4	15.2	84.8	36.0	28.0	72.0
Wyoming	40.9	18.2	81.8	—	—	—	36.7	26.6	73.4
Massachusetts	45.0[2]	10.0[2]	90.0[2]	47.0[3]	6.0[3]	94.0[3]	31.0[4]	38.0[4]	62.0[4]
Rhode Island	51.1[2]	2.2[2]	97.8[2]	45.2[3]	9.6[3]	90.4[3]	51.8[4]	3.6[4]	96.4[4]

Notes: The first entries are the Democratic percent of two-party vote values for each state for the gubernatorial race. The second entries are the margin of victory values for each state for the gubernatorial race, where margin of victory is defined as the absolute difference between the Democratic percent and the Republican percent of the two-party vote for governor. The third entries are the party competition index values for each state for the gubernatorial race, where the competition index devised by Paul David (1972) is defined as (100 − the margin of victory) or, alternatively, as (100 − the absolute difference between the Democratic and Republican percent of two-party vote for governor). The values for Democratic and Republican percent of two-party vote for governor are taken from the state vote tables in Chapter 7. Zero (0) percent on David's index represents a complete absence of two-party competition for that election year, whereas a score of 100 percent indicates perfect competition between the two major parties. A state can only receive a party competition score of 0 if it has a 100–0 vote split in the governor's race. Conversely, a state can only receive a score of 100 if it has a 50–50 vote split in the governor's race. For example, if New Hampshire in 1788 reported a 54.7 percent Democratic vote for governor of its two-party vote, then its Republican vote for governor would be 45.3 percent. The absolute difference between the two figures is the margin of victory, or 9.4 percent; 100 percent − 9.4 percent would equal 90.6 percent on David's party competition scale, indicating a very competitive contest for governor in New Hampshire in 1788. The two-party vote percent values used to derive the margin of victory and party competition figures are initially found in the state vote tables in Chapter 7. The author's alternative party coding in these tables is used whenever it occurs instead of the conventional party coding of voting data. The Democratic Party is defined here as the Anti-Federalists, Democratic-Republicans, and Jackson Democrats prior to 1830 when the "Democratic Party" as such was established. The Republican Party is defined as the Federalists, National Republicans, and Whigs prior to the establishment of the "Republican Party" in the 1850s. See Appendix A for an explanation of the historical antecedents of the current Democratic and Republican parties. States reporting only partial voting returns for governor's races are not included in the calculations for the years in which this occurred. —indicates that the state had no data, either because the state had no gubernatorial election, no vote data were found for the state in question, or the state had not yet entered the Union.

[1] Election held in odd-numbered year.
[2] 1903 election when state had annual elections in both 1902 and 1903.
[3] 1905 election when state had annual elections in both 1904 and 1905.
[4] 1907 election when state had annual elections in both 1906 and 1907.

Sources: State vote tables for governor in Chapter 7.

Table 8-125 Governor Competition Measures, by State, by Two-Year Election Cycle, 1908–1913 (Percentages)

State	1908–1909 Democratic % of Two-Party Vote	Margin of Victory	Party Competition Index	1910–1911 Democratic % of Two-Party Vote	Margin of Victory	Party Competition Index	1912–1913 Democratic % of Two-Party Vote	Margin of Victory	Party Competition Index
Alabama	—	—	—	79.5	59.0	41.0	—	—	—
Alaska	—	—	—	—	—	—	—	—	—
Arizona	—	—	—	54.8[1]	9.6[1]	90.4[1]	—	—	—
Arkansas	71.1	42.2	57.8	71.8	43.6	56.4	70.3	40.6	59.4
California	—	—	—	46.6	6.8	93.2	—	—	—
Colorado	52.2	4.4	95.6	54.0	8.0	92.0	64.4	28.8	71.2
Connecticut	45.6	8.8	91.2	51.2	2.4	97.6	53.7	7.4	92.6
Delaware	47.8	4.4	95.6	—	—	—	48.5	3.0	97.0
Florida	83.7	67.4	32.6	—	—	—	93.5	87.0	13.0
Georgia	100.0	100.0	0.0	—	—	—	—	—	—
Hawaii	—	—	—	—	—	—	—	—	—
Idaho	45.6	8.8	91.2	50.6	1.2	98.8	49.2	1.6	98.4
Illinois	48.9	2.2	97.8	—	—	—	58.2	16.4	83.6
Indiana	51.1	2.2	97.8	—	—	—	66.0	32.0	68.0
Iowa	43.4	13.2	86.8	47.7	4.6	95.4	49.8	0.4	99.6
Kansas	45.2	9.6	90.4	47.4	5.2	94.8	50.0	0.0	100.0
Kentucky	—	—	—	53.7[1]	7.4[1]	92.6[1]	—	—	—
Louisiana	88.7	77.4	22.6	—	—	—	91.1	82.2	17.8
Maine	47.4	5.2	94.8	53.1	6.2	93.8	48.8	2.4	97.6
Maryland	—	—	—	49.3[1]	1.4[1]	98.6[1]	—	—	—
Massachusetts	42.4	15.2	84.8	54.2	8.4	91.6	57.4	14.8	85.2
Michigan	49.1	1.8	98.2	44.1	11.8	88.2	53.3	6.6	93.4
Minnesota	54.3	8.6	91.4	38.7	22.6	77.4	43.5	13.0	87.0
Mississippi	—	—	—	100.0[1]	100.0[1]	0.0[1]	—	—	—
Missouri	48.9	2.2	97.8	—	—	—	60.7	21.4	78.6
Montana	51.2	2.4	97.6	—	—	—	52.5	5.0	95.0
Nebraska	51.4	2.8	97.2	46.7	6.6	93.4	52.1	4.2	95.8
Nevada	—	—	—	45.7	8.6	91.4	—	—	—
New Hampshire	48.1	3.8	96.2	45.7	8.6	91.4	51.3	2.6	97.4
New Jersey	—	—	—	55.9	11.8	88.2	55.2[1]	10.4[1]	89.6[1]
New Mexico	—	—	—	52.6[1]	5.2[1]	94.8[1]	—	—	—
New York	47.7	4.6	95.4	52.6	5.2	94.8	59.4	18.8	81.2
North Carolina	57.4	14.8	85.2	—	—	—	77.5	55.0	45.0
North Dakota	51.3	2.6	97.4	51.3	2.6	97.4	44.2	11.6	88.4
Ohio	50.9	1.8	98.2	55.9	11.8	88.2	61.7	23.4	76.6
Oklahoma	—	—	—	54.7	9.4	90.6	—	—	—
Oregon	—	—	—	52.9	5.8	94.2	—	—	—
Pennsylvania	—	—	—	23.7	52.6	47.4	—	—	—
Rhode Island	44.8	10.4	89.6	49.1	1.8	98.2	48.9	2.2	97.8
South Carolina	100.0	100.0	0.0	100.0	100.0	0.0	100.0	100.0	0.0
South Dakota	41.6	16.8	83.2	38.1	23.8	76.2	48.5	3.0	97.0
Tennessee	54.0	8.0	92.0	47.8	4.4	95.6	48.3	3.4	96.6
Texas	75.1	50.2	49.8	87.0	74.0	26.0	91.0	82.0	18.0
Utah	45.0	10.0	90.0	—	—	—	45.9	8.2	91.8
Vermont	25.9	48.2	51.8	33.1	33.8	66.2	43.3	13.4	86.6
Virginia	63.7[1]	27.4[1]	72.6[1]	—	—	—	100.0[1]	100.0[1]	0.0[1]
Washington	34.5	31.0	69.0	—	—	—	50.2	0.4	99.6
West Virginia	47.6	4.8	95.2	—	—	—	48.2	3.6	96.4
Wisconsin	40.6	18.8	81.2	40.6	18.8	81.2	48.3	3.4	96.6
Wyoming	—	—	—	58.1	16.2	83.8	—	—	—
Massachusetts	48.9[2]	2.2[2]	97.8[2]	51.0[3]	2.0[3]	98.0[3]	61.1[4]	22.2[4]	77.8[4]
Rhode Island	40.6[2]	18.8[2]	81.2[2]	44.6[3]	10.8[3]	89.2[3]	—	—	—

Notes: The first entries are the Democratic percent of two-party vote values for each state for the gubernatorial race. The second entries are the margin of victory values for each state for the gubernatorial race, where margin of victory is defined as the absolute difference between the Democratic percent and the Republican percent of the two-party vote for governor. The third entries are the party competition index values for each state for the gubernatorial race, where the competition index devised by Paul David (1972) is defined as (100 − the margin of victory) or, alternatively, as (100 − the absolute difference between the Democratic and Republican percent of two-party vote for governor). The values for Democratic and Republican percent of two-party vote for governor are taken from the state vote tables in Chapter 7. Zero (0) percent on David's index represents a complete absence of two-party competition for that election year, whereas a score of 100 percent indicates perfect competition between the two major parties. A state can only receive a party competition score of 0 if it has a 100–0 vote split in the governor's race. Conversely, a state can only receive a score of 100 if it has a 50–50 vote split in the governor's race. For example, if New Hampshire in 1788 reported a 54.7 percent Democratic vote for governor of its two-party vote, then its Republican vote for governor would be 45.3 percent. The absolute difference between the two figures is the margin of victory, or 9.4 percent; 100 percent − 9.4 percent would equal 90.6 percent on David's party competition scale, indicating a very competitive contest for governor in New Hampshire in 1788. The two-party vote percent values used to derive the margin of victory and party competition figures are initially found in the state vote tables in Chapter 7. The author's alternative party coding in these tables is used whenever it occurs instead of the conventional party coding of voting data. The Democratic Party is defined here as the Anti-Federalists, Democratic-Republicans, and Jackson Democrats prior to 1830 when the "Democratic Party" as such was established. The Republican Party is defined as the Federalists, National Republicans, and Whigs prior to the establishment of the "Republican Party" in the 1850s. See Appendix A for an explanation of the historical antecedents of the current Democratic and Republican parties. States reporting only partial voting returns for governor's races are not included in the calculations for the years in which this occurred. —indicates that the state had no data, either because the state had no gubernatorial election, no vote data were found for the state in question, or the state had not yet entered the Union.

[1] Election held in odd-numbered year.
[2] 1909 election when state had annual elections in both 1908 and 1909.
[3] 1911 election when state had annual elections in both 1910 and 1911.
[4] 1913 election when state had annual elections in both 1912 and 1913.

Sources: State vote tables for governor in Chapter 7.

Table 8-126 Governor Competition Measures, by State, by Two-Year Election Cycle, 1914–1919 (Percentages)

State	1914–1915 Democratic % of Two-Party Vote	1914–1915 Margin of Victory	1914–1915 Party Competition Index	1916–1917 Democratic % of Two-Party Vote	1916–1917 Margin of Victory	1916–1917 Party Competition Index	1918–1919 Democratic % of Two-Party Vote	1918–1919 Margin of Victory	1918–1919 Party Competition Index
Alabama	83.9	67.8	32.2	—	—	—	100.0	100.0	0.0
Alaska	—	—	—	—	—	—	—	—	—
Arizona	58.9	17.8	82.2	50.0	0.0	100.0	49.7	0.6	99.4
Arkansas	75.3	50.6	49.4	73.5	47.0	53.0	100.0	100.0	0.0
California	29.9	40.2	59.8	—	—	—	0.0	100.0	0.0
Colorado	41.3	17.4	82.6	56.3	12.6	87.4	47.6	4.8	95.2
Connecticut	44.7	10.6	89.4	47.0	6.0	94.0	47.5	5.0	95.0
Delaware	—	—	—	47.4	5.2	94.8	—	—	—
Florida	—	—	—	87.1	74.2	25.8	—	—	—
Georgia	—	—	—	—	—	—	100.0	100.0	0.0
Hawaii	—	—	—	—	—	—	—	—	—
Idaho	54.1	8.2	91.8	50.2	0.4	99.6	40.1	19.8	80.2
Illinois	—	—	—	44.4	11.2	88.8	—	—	—
Indiana	—	—	—	49.0	2.0	98.0	—	—	—
Iowa	46.5	7.0	93.0	37.3	25.4	74.6	48.1	3.8	96.2
Kansas	43.6	12.8	87.2	35.2	29.6	70.4	31.6	36.8	63.2
Kentucky	50.1[1]	0.2[1]	99.8[1]	—	—	—	45.7[1]	8.6[1]	91.4[1]
Louisiana	—	—	—	100.0	100.0	0.0	—	—	—
Maine	51.3	2.6	97.4	45.4	9.2	90.8	47.7	4.6	95.4
Maryland	50.7[1]	1.4[1]	98.6[1]	—	—	—	50.0[1]	0.0[1]	100.0[1]
Massachusetts	51.4	2.8	97.2	45.4	9.2	90.8	47.9	4.2	95.8
Michigan	54.6	9.2	90.8	42.1	15.8	84.2	37.2	25.6	74.4
Minnesota	52.1	4.2	95.8	27.5	45.0	55.0	31.6	36.8	63.2
Mississippi	100.0[1]	100.0[1]	0.0[1]	—	—	—	100.0[1]	100.0[1]	0.0[1]
Missouri	—	—	—	50.1	0.2	99.8	—	—	—
Montana	—	—	—	52.8	5.6	94.4	—	—	—
Nebraska	54.3	8.6	91.4	51.2	2.4	97.6	44.7	10.6	89.4
Nevada	53.0	6.0	94.0	—	—	—	52.1	4.2	95.8
New Hampshire	42.0	16.0	84.0	45.8	8.4	91.6	45.9	8.2	91.8
New Jersey	—	—	—	41.8	16.4	83.6	51.7[1]	3.4[1]	96.6[1]
New Mexico	—	—	—	51.0	2.0	98.0	48.6	2.8	97.2
New York	44.1	11.8	88.2	44.7	10.6	89.4	50.4	0.8	99.2
North Carolina	—	—	—	58.3	16.6	83.4	—	—	—
North Dakota	44.0	12.0	88.0	18.8	62.4	37.6	40.3	19.4	80.6
Ohio	48.6	2.8	97.2	50.3	0.6	99.4	50.6	1.2	98.8
Oklahoma	51.2	2.4	97.6	—	—	—	55.7	11.4	88.6
Oregon	43.9	12.2	87.8	—	—	—	44.7	10.6	89.4
Pennsylvania	43.5	13.0	87.0	—	—	—	35.6	28.8	71.2
Rhode Island	43.4	13.2	86.8	42.2	15.6	84.4	45.8	8.4	91.6
South Carolina	100.0	100.0	0.0	100.0	100.0	0.0	100.0	100.0	0.0
South Dakota	41.3	17.4	82.6	41.0	18.0	82.0	25.9	48.2	51.8
Tennessee	53.9	7.8	92.2	55.5	11.0	89.0	62.4	24.8	75.2
Texas	93.9	87.8	12.2	85.8	71.6	28.4	84.8	69.6	30.4
Utah	—	—	—	56.9	13.8	86.2	—	—	—
Vermont	30.5	39.0	61.0	26.7	46.6	53.4	32.8	34.4	65.6
Virginia	—	—	—	72.0[1]	44.0[1]	56.0[1]	—	—	—
Washington	—	—	—	52.0	4.0	96.0	—	—	—
West Virginia	—	—	—	50.5	1.0	99.0	—	—	—
Wisconsin	45.9	8.2	91.8	41.9	16.2	83.8	41.9	16.2	83.8
Wyoming	53.9	7.8	92.2	—	—	—	43.9	12.2	87.8
Massachusetts	49.3[2]	1.4[2]	98.6[2]	37.5[3]	25.0[3]	75.0[3]	37.7[4]	24.6[4]	75.4[4]

Notes: The first entries are the Democratic percent of two-party vote values for each state for the gubernatorial race. The second entries are the margin of victory values for each state for the gubernatorial race, where margin of victory is defined as the absolute difference between the Democratic percent and the Republican percent of the two-party vote for governor. The third entries are the party competition index values for each state for the gubernatorial race, where the competition index devised by Paul David (1972) is defined as (100 − the margin of victory) or, alternatively, as (100 − the absolute difference between the Democratic and Republican percent of two-party vote for governor). The values for Democratic and Republican percent of two-party vote for governor are taken from the state vote tables in Chapter 7. Zero (0) percent on David's index represents a complete absence of two-party competition for that election year, whereas a score of 100 percent indicates perfect competition between the two major parties. A state can only receive a party competition score of 0 if it has a 100–0 vote split in the governor's race. Conversely, a state can only receive a score of 100 if it has a 50–50 vote split in the governor's race. For example, if New Hampshire in 1788 reported a 54.7 percent Democratic vote for governor of its two-party vote, then its Republican vote for governor would be 45.3 percent. The absolute difference between the two figures is the margin of victory, or 9.4 percent; 100 percent − 9.4 percent would equal 90.6 percent on David's party competition scale, indicating a very competitive contest for governor in New Hampshire in 1788. The two-party vote percent values used to derive the margin of victory and party competition figures are initially found in the state vote tables in Chapter 7. The author's alternative party coding used in these tables is used whenever it occurs instead of the conventional party coding of voting data. The Democratic Party is defined here as the Anti-Federalists, Democratic-Republicans, and Jackson Democrats prior to 1830 when the "Democratic Party" as such was established. The Republican Party is defined as the Federalists, National Republicans, and Whigs prior to the establishment of the "Republican Party" in the 1850s. See Appendix A for an explanation of the historical antecedents of the current Democratic and Republican parties. States reporting only partial voting returns for governor's races are not included in the calculations for the years in which this occurred. —indicates that the state had no data, either because the state had no gubernatorial election, no vote data were found for the state in question, or the state had not yet entered the Union.

[1] Election held in odd-numbered year.
[2] 1915 election when state had annual elections in both 1914 and 1915.
[3] 1917 election when state had annual elections in both 1916 and 1917.
[4] 1919 election when state had annual elections in both 1918 and 1919.

Sources: State vote tables for governor in Chapter 7.

Table 8-127 Governor Competition Measures, by State, by Two-Year Election Cycle, 1920–1925 (Percentages)

	1920–1921			1922–1923			1924–1925		
State	Democratic % of Two-Party Vote	Margin of Victory	Party Competition Index	Democratic % of Two-Party Vote	Margin of Victory	Party Competition Index	Democratic % of Two-Party Vote	Margin of Victory	Party Competition Index
Alabama	—	—	—	78.5	57.0	43.0	—	—	—
Alaska	—	—	—	—	—	—	—	—	—
Arizona	45.9	8.2	91.8	54.9	9.8	90.2	50.5	1.0	99.0
Arkansas	72.7	45.4	54.6	78.1	56.2	43.8	79.8	59.6	40.4
California	—	—	—	37.6	24.8	75.2	—	—	—
Colorado	38.4	23.2	76.8	50.7	1.4	98.6	45.9	8.2	91.8
Connecticut	34.2	31.6	68.4	46.6	6.8	93.2	32.5	35.0	65.0
Delaware	44.2	11.6	88.4	—	—	—	39.6	20.8	79.2
Florida	79.6	59.2	40.8	—	—	—	82.8	65.6	34.4
Georgia	—	—	—	100.0	100.0	0.0	100.0	100.0	0.0
Hawaii	—	—	—	—	—	—	—	—	—
Idaho	33.7	32.6	67.4	42.1	15.8	84.2	27.7	44.6	55.4
Illinois	36.9	26.2	73.8	—	—	—	42.8	14.4	85.6
Indiana	43.0	14.0	86.0	—	—	—	46.7	6.6	93.4
Iowa	39.7	20.6	79.4	29.5	41.0	59.0	27.3	45.4	54.6
Kansas	40.2	19.6	80.4	51.8	3.6	96.4	36.1	27.8	72.2
Kentucky	—	—	—	53.8[1]	7.6[1]	92.4[1]	—	—	—
Louisiana	97.5	95.0	5.0	—	—	—	97.9	95.8	4.2
Maine	34.1	31.8	68.2	42.0	16.0	84.0	42.8	14.4	85.6
Maryland	—	—	—	56.4[1]	12.8[1]	87.2[1]	—	—	—
Massachusetts	31.1	37.8	62.2	46.5	7.0	93.0	43.0	14.0	86.0
Michigan	30.6	38.8	61.2	37.9	24.2	75.8	30.1	39.8	60.2
Minnesota	16.4	67.2	32.8	20.5	59.0	41.0	10.8	78.4	21.6
Mississippi	—	—	—	100.0[1]	100.0[1]	0.0[1]	—	—	—
Missouri	44.6	10.8	89.2	—	—	—	49.8	0.4	99.6
Montana	40.3	19.4	80.6	—	—	—	54.5	9.0	91.0
Nebraska	46.0	8.0	92.0	56.6	13.2	86.8	44.5	11.0	89.0
Nevada	—	—	—	53.9	7.8	92.2	—	—	—
New Hampshire	40.0	20.0	80.0	53.3	6.6	93.4	46.1	7.8	92.2
New Jersey	—	—	—	52.7	5.4	94.6	52.1[1]	4.2[1]	95.8[1]
New Mexico	48.3	3.4	96.6	55.0	10.0	90.0	50.1	0.2	99.8
New York	48.6	2.8	97.2	58.0	16.0	84.0	51.7	3.4	96.6
North Carolina	57.2	14.4	85.6	—	—	—	61.3	22.6	77.4
North Dakota	49.0	2.0	98.0	0.0	100.0	0.0	46.1	7.8	92.2
Ohio	46.9	6.2	93.8	50.5	1.0	99.0	54.6	9.2	90.8
Oklahoma	—	—	—	54.9	9.8	90.2	—	—	—
Oregon	—	—	—	57.4	14.8	85.2	—	—	—
Pennsylvania	—	—	—	41.2	17.6	82.4	—	—	—
Rhode Island	33.9	32.2	67.8	52.3	4.6	95.4	41.2	17.6	82.4
South Carolina	100.0	100.0	0.0	100.0	100.0	0.0	100.0	100.0	0.0
South Dakota	23.5	53.0	47.0	39.0	22.0	78.0	29.8	40.4	59.6
Tennessee	44.8	10.4	89.6	57.9	15.8	84.2	57.2	14.4	85.6
Texas	71.4	42.8	57.2	81.9	63.8	36.2	58.9	17.8	82.2
Utah	39.7	20.6	79.4	—	—	—	53.0	6.0	94.0
Vermont	21.8	56.4	43.6	25.0	50.0	50.0	19.5	61.0	39.0
Virginia	66.3[1]	32.6[1]	67.4[1]	—	—	—	74.1[1]	48.2[1]	51.8[1]
Washington	23.9	52.2	47.8	—	—	—	36.5	27.0	73.0
West Virginia	43.4	13.2	86.8	—	—	—	46.4	7.2	92.8
Wisconsin	40.3	19.4	80.6	12.2	75.6	24.4	43.3	13.4	86.6
Wyoming	—	—	—	50.6	1.2	98.8	—	—	—

Notes: The first entries are the Democratic percent of two-party vote values for each state for the gubernatorial race. The second entries are the margin of victory values for each state for the gubernatorial race, where margin of victory is defined as the absolute difference between the Democratic percent and the Republican percent of the two-party vote for governor. The third entries are the party competition index values for each state for the gubernatorial race, where the competition index devised by Paul David (1972) is defined as (100 − the margin of victory) or, alternatively, as (100 − the absolute difference between the Democratic and Republican percent of two-party vote for governor). The values for Democratic and Republican percent of two-party vote for governor are taken from the state vote tables in Chapter 7. Zero (0) percent on David's index represents a complete absence of two-party competition for that election year, whereas a score of 100 percent indicates perfect competition between the two major parties. A state can only receive a party competition score of 0 if it has a 100–0 vote split in the governor's race. Conversely, a state can only receive a score of 100 if it has a 50–50 vote split in the governor's race. For example, if New Hampshire in 1788 reported a 54.7 percent Democratic vote for governor of its two-party vote, then its Republican vote for governor would be 45.3 percent. The absolute difference between the two figures is the margin of victory, or 9.4 percent; 100 percent − 9.4 percent would equal 90.6 percent on David's party competition scale, indicating a very competitive contest for governor in New Hampshire in 1788. The two-party vote percent values used to derive the margin of victory and party competition figures are initially found in the state vote tables in Chapter 7. The author's alternative party coding in these tables is used whenever it occurs instead of the conventional party coding of voting data. The Democratic Party is defined here as the Anti-Federalists, Democratic-Republicans, and Jackson Democrats prior to 1830 when the "Democratic Party" as such was established. The Republican Party is defined as the Federalists, National Republicans, and Whigs prior to the establishment of the "Republican Party" in the 1850s. See Appendix A for an explanation of the historical antecedents of the current Democratic and Republican parties. States reporting only partial voting returns for governor's races are not included in the calculations for the years in which this occurred. —indicates that the state had no data, either because the state had no gubernatorial election, no vote data were found for the state in question, or the state had not yet entered the Union.

[1] Election held in odd-numbered year.

Sources: State vote tables for governor in Chapter 7.

Table 8-128 Governor Competition Measures, by State, by Two-Year Election Cycle, 1926–1931 (Percentages)

	1926–1927			1928–1929			1930–1931		
State	Democratic % of Two-Party Vote	Margin of Victory	Party Competition Index	Democratic % of Two-Party Vote	Margin of Victory	Party Competition Index	Democratic % of Two-Party Vote	Margin of Victory	Party Competition Index
Alabama	81.2	62.4	37.6	—	—	—	100.0	100.0	0.0
Alaska	—	—	—	—	—	—	—	—	—
Arizona	50.3	0.6	99.4	48.2	3.6	96.4	51.4	2.8	97.2
Arkansas	76.4	52.8	47.2	77.3	54.6	45.4	81.2	62.4	37.6
California	25.7	48.6	51.4	—	—	—	25.0	50.0	50.0
Colorado	61.1	22.2	77.8	62.5	25.0	75.0	61.3	22.6	77.4
Connecticut	35.7	28.6	71.4	46.0	8.0	92.0	50.6	1.2	98.8
Delaware	—	—	—	38.8	22.4	77.6	—	—	—
Florida	—	—	—	61.0	22.0	78.0	—	—	—
Georgia	100.0	100.0	0.0	—	—	—	—	—	—
Hawaii	—	—	—	—	—	—	—	—	—
Idaho	28.7	42.6	57.4	41.8	16.4	83.6	56.0	12.0	88.0
Illinois	—	—	—	42.9	14.2	85.8	—	—	—
Indiana	—	—	—	48.4	3.2	96.8	—	—	—
Iowa	28.5	43.0	57.0	37.2	25.6	74.4	33.8	32.4	67.6
Kansas	35.8	28.4	71.6	33.6	32.8	67.2	50.0	0.0	100.0
Kentucky	47.9[1]	4.2[1]	95.8[1]	—	—	—	54.4[1]	8.8[1]	91.2[1]
Louisiana	—	—	—	96.1	92.2	7.8	—	—	—
Maine	44.5	11.0	89.0	30.7	38.6	61.4	44.9	10.2	89.8
Maryland	58.3	16.6	83.4	—	—	—	56.7	13.4	86.6
Massachusetts	40.6	18.8	81.2	49.4	1.2	98.8	50.7	1.4	98.6
Michigan	36.2	27.6	72.4	29.6	40.8	59.2	42.5	15.0	85.0
Minnesota	8.8	82.4	17.6	28.0	44.0	56.0	9.1	81.8	18.2
Mississippi	100.0[1]	100.0[1]	0.0[1]	—	—	—	100.0[1]	100.0[1]	0.0[1]
Missouri	—	—	—	48.3	3.4	96.6	—	—	—
Montana	—	—	—	58.9	17.8	82.2	—	—	—
Nebraska	49.6	0.8	99.2	42.8	14.4	85.6	50.7	1.4	98.6
Nevada	47.0	6.0	94.0	—	—	—	46.8	6.4	93.6
New Hampshire	40.3	19.4	80.6	42.4	15.2	84.8	41.9	16.2	83.8
New Jersey	—	—	—	44.9	10.2	89.8	59.3[1]	18.6[1]	81.4[1]
New Mexico	48.3	3.4	96.6	44.3	11.4	88.6	53.3	6.6	93.4
New York	54.4	8.8	91.2	50.3	0.6	99.4	62.9	25.8	74.2
North Carolina	—	—	—	55.6	11.2	88.8	—	—	—
North Dakota	15.6	68.8	31.2	43.3	13.4	86.6	24.0	52.0	48.0
Ohio	50.8	1.6	98.4	44.9	10.2	89.8	52.8	5.6	94.4
Oklahoma	55.4	10.8	89.2	—	—	—	59.1	18.2	81.8
Oregon	43.8	12.4	87.6	—	—	—	57.1	14.2	85.8
Pennsylvania	24.9	50.2	49.8	—	—	—	48.6	2.8	97.2
Rhode Island	45.9	8.2	91.8	48.3	3.4	96.6	49.2	1.6	98.4
South Carolina	100.0	100.0	0.0	—	—	—	100.0	100.0	0.0
South Dakota	54.0	8.0	92.0	52.8	5.6	94.4	46.6	6.8	93.2
Tennessee	64.8	29.6	70.4	61.1	22.2	77.8	64.2	28.4	71.6
Texas	87.8	75.6	24.4	82.5	65.0	35.0	80.3	60.6	39.4
Utah	—	—	—	58.7	17.4	82.6	—	—	—
Vermont	39.1	21.8	78.2	26.1	47.8	52.2	29.0	42.0	58.0
Virginia	—	—	—	63.0[1]	26.0[1]	74.0[1]	—	—	—
Washington	—	—	—	43.2	13.6	86.4	—	—	—
West Virginia	—	—	—	46.2	7.6	92.4	—	—	—
Wisconsin	17.1	65.8	34.2	41.9	16.2	83.8	30.2	39.6	60.4
Wyoming	49.0	2.0	98.0	—	—	—	49.4	1.2	98.8

Notes: The first entries are the Democratic percent of two-party vote values for each state for the gubernatorial race. The second entries are the margin of victory values for each state for the gubernatorial race, where margin of victory is defined as the absolute difference between the Democratic percent and the Republican percent of the two-party vote for governor. The third entries are the party competition index values for each state for the gubernatorial race, where the competition index devised by Paul David (1972) is defined as (100 − the margin of victory) or, alternatively, as (100 − the absolute difference between the Democratic and Republican percent of two-party vote for governor). The values for Democratic and Republican percent of two-party vote for governor are taken from the state vote tables in Chapter 7. Zero (0) percent on David's index represents a complete absence of two-party competition for that election year, whereas a score of 100 percent indicates perfect competition between the two major parties. A state can only receive a party competition score of 0 if it has a 100–0 vote split in the governor's race. Conversely, a state can only receive a score of 100 if it has a 50–50 vote split in the governor's race. For example, if New Hampshire in 1788 reported a 54.7 percent Democratic vote for governor of its two-party vote, then its Republican vote for governor would be 45.3 percent. The absolute difference between the two figures is the margin of victory, or 9.4 percent; 100 percent − 9.4 percent would equal 90.6 percent on David's party competition scale, indicating a very competitive contest for governor in New Hampshire in 1788. The two-party vote percent values used to derive the margin of victory and party competition figures are initially found in the state vote tables in Chapter 7. The author's alternative party coding in these tables is used whenever it occurs instead of the conventional party coding of voting data. The Democratic Party is defined here as the Anti-Federalists, Democratic-Republicans, and Jackson Democrats prior to 1830 when the "Democratic Party" as such was established. The Republican Party is defined as the Federalists, National Republicans, and Whigs prior to the establishment of the "Republican Party" in the 1850s. See Appendix A for an explanation of the historical antecedents of the current Democratic and Republican parties. States reporting only partial voting returns for governor's races are not included in the calculations for the years in which this occurred. —indicates that the state had no data, either because the state had no gubernatorial election, no vote data were found for the state in question, or the state had not yet entered the Union.

[1] Election held in odd-numbered year.

Sources: State vote tables for governor in Chapter 7.

Table 8-129 Governor Competition Measures, by State, by Two-Year Election Cycle, 1932–1937 (Percentages)

State	1932–1933 Democratic % of Two-Party Vote	Margin of Victory	Party Competition Index	1934–1935 Democratic % of Two-Party Vote	Margin of Victory	Party Competition Index	1936–1937 Democratic % of Two-Party Vote	Margin of Victory	Party Competition Index
Alabama	—	—	—	87.3	74.6	25.4	—	—	—
Alaska	—	—	—	—	—	—	—	—	—
Arizona	64.3	28.6	71.4	61.0	22.0	78.0	70.8	41.6	58.4
Arkansas	91.0	82.0	18.0	90.5	81.0	19.0	85.2	70.4	29.6
California	—	—	—	43.6	12.8	87.2	—	—	—
Colorado	58.4	16.8	83.2	59.3	18.6	81.4	55.6	11.2	88.8
Connecticut	51.0	2.0	98.0	50.8	1.6	98.4	57.4	14.8	85.2
Delaware	45.3	9.4	90.6	—	—	—	51.7	3.4	96.6
Florida	66.6	33.2	66.8	—	—	—	80.9	61.8	38.2
Georgia	100.0	100.0	0.0	100.0	100.0	0.0	100.0	100.0	0.0
Hawaii	—	—	—	—	—	—	—	—	—
Idaho	62.9	25.8	74.2	55.2	10.4	89.6	58.0	16.0	84.0
Illinois	58.6	17.2	82.8	—	—	—	55.1	10.2	89.8
Indiana	56.3	12.6	87.4	—	—	—	55.5	11.0	89.0
Iowa	52.8	5.6	94.4	54.3	8.6	91.4	50.1	0.2	99.8
Kansas	49.5	1.0	99.0	46.0	8.0	92.0	51.3	2.6	97.4
Kentucky	—	—	—	54.7 [1]	9.4 [1]	90.6 [1]	—	—	—
Louisiana	100.0	100.0	0.0	—	—	—	100.0	100.0	0.0
Maine	50.5	1.0	99.0	54.0	8.0	92.0	42.9	14.2	85.8
Maryland	—	—	—	49.4	1.2	98.8	—	—	—
Massachusetts	54.0	8.0	92.0	54.0	8.0	92.0	50.8	1.6	98.4
Michigan	56.0	12.0	88.0	46.7	6.6	93.4	51.4	2.8	97.2
Minnesota	33.7	32.6	67.4	30.9	38.2	61.8	0.0	100.0	0.0
Mississippi	—	—	—	100.0 [1]	100.0 [1]	0.0 [1]	—	—	—
Missouri	60.6	21.2	78.8	—	—	—	57.3	14.6	85.4
Montana	50.9	1.8	98.2	—	—	—	51.4	2.8	97.2
Nebraska	53.2	6.4	93.6	51.6	3.2	96.8	56.4	12.8	87.2
Nevada	—	—	—	61.0	22.0	78.0	—	—	—
New Hampshire	45.6	8.8	91.2	49.3	1.4	98.6	43.0	14.0	86.0
New Jersey	—	—	—	49.5	1.0	99.0	51.6 [1]	3.2 [1]	96.8 [1]
New Mexico	55.4	10.8	89.2	52.2	4.4	95.6	57.2	14.4	85.6
New York	59.5	19.0	81.0	61.2	22.4	77.6	54.8	9.6	90.4
North Carolina	70.1	40.2	59.8	—	—	—	66.7	33.4	66.6
North Dakota	45.1	9.8	90.2	53.2	6.4	93.6	45.8	8.4	91.6
Ohio	54.1	8.2	91.8	51.5	3.0	97.0	52.1	4.2	95.8
Oklahoma	—	—	—	60.0	20.0	80.0	—	—	—
Oregon	—	—	—	57.3	14.6	85.4	—	—	—
Pennsylvania	—	—	—	51.1	2.2	97.8	—	—	—
Rhode Island	55.9	11.8	88.2	57.2	14.4	85.6	53.9	7.8	92.2
South Carolina	—	—	—	100.0	100.0	0.0	—	—	—
South Dakota	56.7	13.4	86.6	59.0	18.0	82.0	48.4	3.2	96.8
Tennessee	58.9	17.8	82.2	61.8	23.6	76.4	81.1	62.2	37.8
Texas	61.8	23.6	76.4	96.9	93.8	6.2	93.0	86.0	14.0
Utah	57.5	15.0	85.0	—	—	—	57.8	15.6	84.4
Vermont	37.6	24.8	75.2	42.4	15.2	84.8	38.9	22.2	77.8
Virginia	75.3 [1]	50.6 [1]	49.4 [1]	—	—	—	84.0 [1]	68.0 [1]	32.0 [1]
Washington	62.9	25.8	74.2	—	—	—	71.2	42.4	57.6
West Virginia	54.0	8.0	92.0	—	—	—	59.2	18.4	81.6
Wisconsin	55.6	11.2	88.8	67.5	35.0	65.0	42.5	15.0	85.0
Wyoming	—	—	—	58.3	16.6	83.4	—	—	—

Notes: The first entries are the Democratic percent of two-party vote values for each state for the gubernatorial race. The second entries are the margin of victory values for each state for the gubernatorial race, where margin of victory is defined as the absolute difference between the Democratic percent and the Republican percent of the two-party vote for governor. The third entries are the party competition index values for each state for the gubernatorial race, where the competition index devised by Paul David (1972) is defined as (100 − the margin of victory) or, alternatively, as (100 − the absolute difference between the Democratic and Republican percent of the two-party vote for governor). The values for Democratic and Republican percent of two-party vote for governor are taken from the state vote tables in Chapter 7. Zero (0) percent on David's index represents a complete absence of two-party competition for that election year, whereas a score of 100 percent indicates perfect competition between the two major parties. A state can only receive a party competition score of 0 if it has a 100–0 vote split in the governor's race. Conversely, a state can only receive a score of 100 if it has a 50–50 vote split in the governor's race. For example, if New Hampshire in 1788 reported a 54.7 percent Democratic vote for governor of its two-party vote, then its Republican vote for governor would be 45.3 percent. The absolute difference between the two figures is the margin of victory, or 9.4 percent; 100 percent − 9.4 percent would equal 90.6 percent on David's party competition scale, indicating a very competitive contest for governor in New Hampshire in 1788. The two-party vote percent values used to derive the margin of victory and party competition figures are initially found in the state vote tables in Chapter 7. The author's alternative party coding in these tables is used whenever it occurs instead of the conventional party coding of voting data. The Democratic Party is defined here as the Anti-Federalists, Democratic-Republicans, and Jackson Democrats prior to 1830 when the "Democratic Party" as such was established. The Republican Party is defined as the Federalists, National Republicans, and Whigs prior to the establishment of the "Republican Party" in the 1850s. See Appendix A for an explanation of the historical antecedents of the current Democratic and Republican parties. States reporting only partial voting returns for governor's races are not included in the calculations for the years in which this occurred. —indicates that the state had no data, either because the state had no gubernatorial election, no vote data were found for the state in question, or the state had not yet entered the Union.

[1] Election held in odd-numbered year.

Sources: State vote tables for governor in Chapter 7.

Table 8-130 Governor Competition Measures, by State, by Two-Year Election Cycle, 1938–1943 (Percentages)

| | 1938–1939 | | | 1940–1941 | | | 1942–1943 | | |
| | Democratic % of Two-Party Vote | Margin of Victory | Party Competition Index | Democratic % of Two-Party Vote | Margin of Victory | Party Competition Index | Democratic % of Two-Party Vote | Margin of Victory | Party Competition Index |
State									
Alabama	87.5	75.0	25.0	—	—	—	89.4	78.8	21.2
Alaska	—	—	—	—	—	—	—	—	—
Arizona	72.7	45.4	54.6	66.0	32.0	68.0	72.9	45.8	54.2
Arkansas	94.6	89.2	10.8	91.7	83.4	16.6	100.0	100.0	0.0
California	54.3	8.6	91.4	—	—	—	42.3	15.4	84.6
Colorado	43.9	12.2	87.8	45.3	9.4	90.6	43.6	12.8	87.2
Connecticut	49.7	0.6	99.4	50.9	1.8	98.2	47.6	4.8	95.2
Delaware	—	—	—	47.6	4.8	95.2	—	—	—
Florida	—	—	—	100.0	100.0	0.0	—	—	—
Georgia	100.0	100.0	0.0	100.0	100.0	0.0	100.0	100.0	0.0
Hawaii	—	—	—	—	—	—	—	—	—
Idaho	42.2	15.6	84.4	50.5	1.0	99.0	49.8	0.4	99.6
Illinois	—	—	—	46.9	6.2	93.8	—	—	—
Indiana	—	—	—	50.1	0.2	99.8	—	—	—
Iowa	46.4	7.2	92.8	47.2	5.6	94.4	37.1	25.8	74.2
Kansas	46.4	7.2	92.8	50.0	0.0	100.0	42.4	15.2	84.8
Kentucky	56.5[1]	13.0[1]	87.0[1]	—	—	—	49.2[1]	1.6[1]	98.4[1]
Louisiana	—	—	—	99.4	98.8	1.2	—	—	—
Maine	47.1	5.8	94.2	36.1	27.8	72.2	33.2	33.6	66.4
Maryland	56.0	12.0	88.0	—	—	—	52.6	5.2	94.8
Massachusetts	45.7	8.6	91.4	49.9	0.2	99.8	45.4	9.2	90.8
Michigan	47.1	5.8	94.2	53.2	6.4	93.6	47.0	6.0	94.0
Minnesota	8.8	82.4	17.6	17.6	64.8	35.2	15.5	69.0	31.0
Mississippi	100.0[1]	100.0[1]	0.0[1]	—	—	—	100.0[1]	100.0[1]	0.0[1]
Missouri	—	—	—	49.9	0.2	99.8	—	—	—
Montana	—	—	—	49.0	2.0	98.0	—	—	—
Nebraska	52.0	4.0	96.0	39.1	21.8	78.2	25.2	49.6	50.4
Nevada	61.9	23.8	76.2	—	—	—	60.3	20.6	79.4
New Hampshire	42.8	14.4	85.6	49.3	1.4	98.6	47.8	4.4	95.6
New Jersey	—	—	—	51.7	3.4	96.6	44.4[1]	11.2[1]	88.8[1]
New Mexico	52.3	4.6	95.4	55.6	11.2	88.8	54.5	9.0	91.0
New York	50.7	1.4	98.6	—	—	—	41.1	17.8	82.2
North Carolina	—	—	—	75.7	51.4	48.6	—	—	—
North Dakota	52.5	5.0	95.0	63.1	26.2	73.8	57.6	15.2	84.8
Ohio	47.6	4.8	95.2	44.5	11.0	89.0	39.5	21.0	79.0
Oklahoma	70.5	41.0	59.0	—	—	—	52.1	4.2	95.8
Oregon	42.6	14.8	85.2	—	—	—	22.1	55.8	44.2
Pennsylvania	46.3	7.4	92.6	—	—	—	45.7	8.6	91.4
Rhode Island	43.5	13.0	87.0	55.9	11.8	88.2	58.5	17.0	83.0
South Carolina	99.4	98.8	1.2	—	—	—	100.0	100.0	0.0
South Dakota	46.0	8.0	92.0	44.9	10.2	89.8	38.5	23.0	77.0
Tennessee	71.7	43.4	56.6	72.1	44.2	55.8	70.2	40.4	59.6
Texas	96.9	93.8	6.2	94.7	89.4	10.6	96.8	93.6	6.4
Utah	—	—	—	52.2	4.4	95.6	—	—	—
Vermont	33.2	33.6	66.4	36.0	28.0	72.0	22.1	55.8	44.2
Virginia	—	—	—	81.8[1]	63.6[1]	36.4[1]	—	—	—
Washington	—	—	—	49.6	0.8	99.2	—	—	—
West Virginia	—	—	—	56.4	12.8	87.2	—	—	—
Wisconsin	12.6	74.8	25.2	32.2	35.6	64.4	25.2	49.6	50.4
Wyoming	40.2	19.6	80.4	—	—	—	51.3	2.6	97.4

Notes: The first entries are the Democratic percent of two-party vote values for each state for the gubernatorial race. The second entries are the margin of victory values for each state for the gubernatorial race, where margin of victory is defined as the absolute difference between the Democratic percent and the Republican percent of the two-party vote for governor. The third entries are the party competition index values for each state for the gubernatorial race, where the competition index devised by Paul David (1972) is defined as (100 − the margin of victory) or, alternatively, as (100 − the absolute difference between the Democratic and Republican percent of two-party vote for governor). The values for Democratic and Republican percent of two-party vote for governor are taken from the state vote tables in Chapter 7. Zero (0) percent on David's index represents a complete absence of two-party competition for that election year, whereas a score of 100 percent indicates perfect competition between the two major parties. A state can only receive a party competition score of 0 if it has a 100–0 vote split in the governor's race. Conversely, a state can only receive a score of 100 if it has a 50–50 vote split in the governor's race. For example, if New Hampshire in 1788 reported a 54.7 percent Democratic vote for governor of its two-party vote, then its Republican vote for governor would be 45.3 percent. The absolute difference between the two figures is the margin of victory, or 9.4 percent; 100 percent − 9.4 percent would equal 90.6 percent on David's party competition scale, indicating a very competitive contest for governor in New Hampshire in 1788. The two-party vote percent values used to derive the margin of victory and party competition figures are initially found in the state vote tables in Chapter 7. The author's alternative party coding in these tables is used whenever it occurs instead of the conventional party coding of voting data. The Democratic Party is defined here as the Anti-Federalists, Democratic-Republicans, and Jackson Democrats prior to 1830 when the "Democratic Party" as such was established. The Republican Party is defined as the Federalists, National Republicans, and Whigs prior to the establishment of the "Republican Party" in the 1850s. See Appendix A for an explanation of the historical antecedents of the current Democratic and Republican parties. States reporting only partial voting returns for governor's races are not included in the calculations for the years in which this occurred. —indicates that the state had no data, either because the state had no gubernatorial election, no vote data were found for the state in question, or the state had not yet entered the Union.

[1] Election held in odd-numbered year.

Sources: State vote tables for governor in Chapter 7.

Table 8-131 Governor Competition Measures, by State, by Two-Year Election Cycle, 1944–1949 (Percentages)

	1944–1945			1946–1947			1948–1949		
State	Democratic % of Two-Party Vote	Margin of Victory	Party Competition Index	Democratic % of Two-Party Vote	Margin of Victory	Party Competition Index	Democratic % of Two-Party Vote	Margin of Victory	Party Competition Index
Alabama	—	—	—	88.7	77.4	22.6	—	—	—
Alaska	—	—	—	—	—	—	—	—	—
Arizona	78.6	57.2	42.8	60.1	20.2	79.8	59.6	19.2	80.8
Arkansas	86.0	72.0	28.0	84.1	68.2	31.8	89.2	78.4	21.6
California	—	—	—	0.0	100.0	0.0	—	—	—
Colorado	47.6	4.8	95.2	52.1	4.2	95.8	66.3	32.6	67.4
Connecticut	48.4	3.2	96.8	42.6	14.8	85.2	50.2	0.4	99.6
Delaware	49.3	1.4	98.6	—	—	—	53.7	7.4	92.6
Florida	78.9	57.8	42.2	—	—	—	83.4	66.8	33.2
Georgia	—	—	—	100.0	100.0	0.0	—	—	—
Hawaii	—	—	—	—	—	—	—	—	—
Idaho	52.6	5.2	94.8	43.6	12.8	87.2	—	—	—
Illinois	49.1	1.8	98.2	—	—	—	57.3	14.6	85.4
Indiana	48.6	2.8	97.2	—	—	—	54.3	8.6	91.4
Iowa	43.8	12.4	87.6	42.3	15.4	84.6	44.0	12.0	88.0
Kansas	33.3	33.4	66.6	45.1	9.8	90.2	41.5	17.0	83.0
Kentucky	—	—	—	57.4[1]	14.8[1]	85.2[1]	—	—	—
Louisiana	100.0	100.0	0.0	—	—	—	100.0	100.0	0.0
Maine	29.7	40.6	59.4	38.7	22.6	77.4	34.4	31.2	68.8
Maryland	—	—	—	54.7	9.4	90.6	—	—	—
Massachusetts	53.9	7.8	92.2	45.6	8.8	91.2	59.3	18.6	81.4
Michigan	45.0	10.0	90.0	39.1	21.8	78.2	53.9	7.8	92.2
Minnesota	38.6	22.8	77.2	40.2	19.6	80.4	45.9	8.2	91.8
Mississippi	—	—	—	97.5[1]	95.0[1]	5.0[1]	—	—	—
Missouri	51.0	2.0	98.0	—	—	—	57.1	14.2	85.8
Montana	43.4	13.2	86.8	—	—	—	56.0	12.0	88.0
Nebraska	23.9	52.2	47.8	34.5	31.0	69.0	39.9	20.2	79.8
Nevada	—	—	—	57.4	14.8	85.2	—	—	—
New Hampshire	46.9	6.2	93.8	36.9	26.2	73.8	47.5	5.0	95.0
New Jersey	—	—	—	42.1	15.8	84.2	47.8[1]	4.4[1]	95.6[1]
New Mexico	51.8	3.6	96.4	52.8	5.6	94.4	54.7	9.4	90.6
New York	—	—	—	43.1	13.8	86.2	—	—	—
North Carolina	69.6	39.2	60.8	—	—	—	73.5	47.0	53.0
North Dakota	29.0	42.0	58.0	31.1	37.8	62.2	38.0	24.0	76.0
Ohio	51.8	3.6	96.4	49.1	1.8	98.2	53.7	7.4	92.6
Oklahoma	—	—	—	53.3	6.6	93.4	—	—	—
Oregon	—	—	—	30.9	38.2	61.8	—	—	—
Pennsylvania	—	—	—	41.0	18.0	82.0	—	—	—
Rhode Island	60.6	21.2	78.8	54.1	8.2	91.8	61.4	22.8	77.2
South Carolina	—	—	—	100.0	100.0	0.0	—	—	—
South Dakota	34.5	31.0	69.0	32.8	34.4	65.6	38.9	22.2	77.8
Tennessee	63.5	27.0	73.0	67.2	34.4	65.6	66.9	33.8	66.2
Texas	90.9	81.8	18.2	91.2	82.4	17.6	85.2	70.4	29.6
Utah	50.2	0.4	99.6	—	—	—	45.0	10.0	90.0
Vermont	34.1	31.8	68.2	19.6	60.8	39.2	28.0	44.0	56.0
Virginia	68.2[1]	36.4[1]	63.6[1]	—	—	—	72.0[1]	44.0[1]	56.0[1]
Washington	51.7	3.4	96.6	—	—	—	48.3	3.4	96.6
West Virginia	54.4	8.8	91.2	—	—	—	57.1	14.2	85.8
Wisconsin	43.5	13.0	87.0	39.5	21.0	79.0	44.9	10.2	89.8
Wyoming	—	—	—	52.9	5.8	94.2	—	—	—

Notes: The first entries are the Democratic percent of two-party vote values for each state for the gubernatorial race. The second entries are the margin of victory values for each state for the gubernatorial race, where margin of victory is defined as the absolute difference between the Democratic percent and the Republican percent of the two-party vote for governor. The third entries are the party competition index values for each state for the gubernatorial race, where the competition index devised by Paul David (1972) is defined as (100 − the margin of victory) or, alternatively, as (100 − the absolute difference between the Democratic and Republican percent of two-party vote for governor). The values for Democratic and Republican percent of two-party vote for governor are taken from the state vote tables in Chapter 7. Zero (0) percent on David's index represents a complete absence of two-party competition for that election year, whereas a score of 100 percent indicates perfect competition between the two major parties. A state can only receive a party competition score of 0 if it has a 100–0 vote split in the governor's race. Conversely, a state can only receive a score of 100 if it has a 50–50 vote split in the governor's race. For example, if New Hampshire in 1788 reported a 54.7 percent Democratic vote for governor of its two-party vote, then its Republican vote for governor would be 45.3 percent. The absolute difference between the two figures is the margin of victory, or 9.4 percent; 100 percent − 9.4 percent would equal 90.6 percent on David's party competition scale, indicating a very competitive contest for governor in New Hampshire in 1788. The two-party vote percent values used to derive the margin of victory and party competition figures are initially found in the state vote tables in Chapter 7. The author's alternative party coding in these tables is used whenever it occurs instead of the conventional party coding of voting data. The Democratic Party is defined here as the Anti-Federalists, Democratic-Republicans, and Jackson Democrats prior to 1830 when the "Democratic Party" as such was established. The Republican Party is defined as the Federalists, National Republicans, and Whigs prior to the establishment of the "Republican Party" in the 1850s. See Appendix A for an explanation of the historical antecedents of the current Democratic and Republican parties. States reporting only partial voting returns for governor's races are not included in the calculations for the years in which this occurred. —indicates that the state had no data, either because the state had no gubernatorial election, no vote data were found for the state in question, or the state had not yet entered the Union.

[1] Election held in odd-numbered year.

Sources: State vote tables for governor in Chapter 7.

Table 8-132 Governor Competition Measures, by State, by Two-Year Election Cycle, 1950–1955 (Percentages)

	1950–1951			1952–1953			1954–1955		
State	Democratic % of Two-Party Vote	Margin of Victory	Party Competition Index	Democratic % of Two-Party Vote	Margin of Victory	Party Competition Index	Democratic % of Two-Party Vote	Margin of Victory	Party Competition Index
Alabama	91.1	82.2	17.8	—	—	—	73.4	46.8	53.2
Alaska	—	—	—	—	—	—	—	—	—
Arizona	49.2	1.6	98.4	39.8	20.4	79.6	52.5	5.0	95.0
Arkansas	84.1	68.2	31.8	87.4	74.8	25.2	62.1	24.2	75.8
California	35.1	29.8	70.2	—	—	—	43.2	13.6	86.4
Colorado	47.4	5.2	94.8	42.6	14.8	85.2	53.6	7.2	92.8
Connecticut	49.0	2.0	98.0	—	—	—	50.1	0.2	99.8
Delaware	—	—	—	47.9	4.2	95.8	—	—	—
Florida	—	—	—	74.8	49.6	50.4	—	—	—
Georgia	100.0	100.0	0.0	—	—	—	100.0	100.0	0.0
Hawaii	—	—	—	—	—	—	—	—	—
Idaho	47.4	5.2	94.8	—	—	—	45.8	8.4	91.6
Illinois	—	—	—	47.4	5.2	94.8	—	—	—
Indiana	—	—	—	43.9	12.2	87.8	—	—	—
Iowa	40.7	18.6	81.4	47.9	4.2	95.8	48.3	3.4	96.6
Kansas	45.3	9.4	90.6	42.5	15.0	85.0	46.5	7.0	93.0
Kentucky	54.6[1]	9.2[1]	90.8[1]	—	—	—	58.3[1]	16.6[1]	83.4[1]
Louisiana	—	—	—	96.0	92.0	8.0	—	—	—
Maine	39.5	21.0	79.0	33.4	33.2	66.8	54.5	9.0	91.0
Maryland	42.7	14.6	85.4	—	—	—	45.5	9.0	91.0
Massachusetts	56.6	13.2	86.8	49.7	0.6	99.4	48.0	4.0	96.0
Michigan	50.0	0.0	100.0	50.2	0.4	99.6	55.8	11.6	88.4
Minnesota	38.7	22.6	77.4	44.3	11.4	88.6	53.0	6.0	94.0
Mississippi	100.0[1]	100.0[1]	0.0[1]	—	—	—	100.0[1]	100.0[1]	0.0[1]
Missouri	—	—	—	52.6	5.2	94.8	—	—	—
Montana	—	—	—	49.0	2.0	98.0	—	—	—
Nebraska	45.1	9.8	90.2	38.6	22.8	77.2	39.7	20.6	79.4
Nevada	42.4	15.2	84.8	—	—	—	46.9	6.2	93.8
New Hampshire	43.0	14.0	86.0	36.9	26.2	73.8	44.9	10.2	89.8
New Jersey	—	—	—	54.3[1]	8.6[1]	91.4[1]	—	—	—
New Mexico	46.3	7.4	92.6	46.2	7.6	92.4	57.0	14.0	86.0
New York	44.3	11.4	88.6	—	—	—	50.1	0.2	99.8
North Carolina	—	—	—	67.5	35.0	65.0	—	—	—
North Dakota	33.7	32.6	67.4	21.3	57.4	42.6	35.8	28.4	71.6
Ohio	52.6	5.2	94.8	55.9	11.8	88.2	54.1	8.2	91.8
Oklahoma	51.3	2.6	97.4	—	—	—	58.7	17.4	82.6
Oregon	33.9	32.2	67.8	—	—	—	43.1	13.8	86.2
Pennsylvania	48.8	2.4	97.6	—	—	—	53.8	7.6	92.4
Rhode Island	59.3	18.6	81.4	52.6	5.2	94.8	58.0	16.0	84.0
South Carolina	100.0	100.0	0.0	—	—	—	100.0	100.0	0.0
South Dakota	39.1	21.8	78.2	29.8	40.4	59.6	43.3	13.4	86.6
Tennessee	78.1	56.2	43.8	79.4	58.8	41.2	99.4	98.8	1.2
Texas	90.2	80.4	19.6	100.0	100.0	0.0	89.6	79.2	20.8
Utah	—	—	—	44.9	10.2	89.8	—	—	—
Vermont	25.5	49.0	51.0	39.8	20.4	79.6	47.7	4.6	95.4
Virginia	—	—	—	55.3[1]	10.6[1]	89.4[1]	—	—	—
Washington	—	—	—	47.4	5.2	94.8	—	—	—
West Virginia	—	—	—	51.5	3.0	97.0	—	—	—
Wisconsin	46.4	7.2	92.8	37.4	25.2	74.8	48.5	3.0	97.0
Wyoming	43.9	12.2	87.8	—	—	—	49.5	1.0	99.0

Notes: The first entries are the Democratic percent of two-party vote values for each state for the gubernatorial race. The second entries are the margin of victory values for each state for the gubernatorial race, where margin of victory is defined as the absolute difference between the Democratic percent and the Republican percent of the two-party vote for governor. The third entries are the party competition index values for each state for the gubernatorial race, where the competition index devised by Paul David (1972) is defined as (100 − the margin of victory) or, alternatively, as (100 − the absolute difference between the Democratic and Republican percent of two-party vote for governor). The values for Democratic and Republican percent of two-party vote for governor are taken from the state vote tables in Chapter 7. Zero (0) percent on David's index represents a complete absence of two-party competition for that election year, whereas a score of 100 percent indicates perfect competition between the two major parties. A state can only receive a party competition score of 0 if it has a 100–0 vote split in the governor's race. Conversely, a state can only receive a score of 100 if it has a 50–50 vote split in the governor's race. For example, if New Hampshire in 1788 reported a 54.7 percent Democratic vote for governor of its two-party vote, then its Republican vote for governor would be 45.3 percent. The absolute difference between the two figures is the margin of victory, or 9.4 percent; 100 percent − 9.4 percent would equal 90.6 percent on David's party competition scale, indicating a very competitive contest for governor in New Hampshire in 1788. The two-party vote percent values used to derive the margin of victory and party competition figures are initially found in the state vote tables in Chapter 7. The author's alternative party coding in these tables is used whenever it occurs instead of the conventional party coding of voting data. The Democratic Party is defined here as the Anti-Federalists, Democratic-Republicans, and Jackson Democrats prior to 1830 when the "Democratic Party" as such was established. The Republican Party is defined as the Federalists, National Republicans, and Whigs prior to the establishment of the "Republican Party" in the 1850s. See Appendix A for an explanation of the historical antecedents of the current Democratic and Republican parties. States reporting only partial voting returns for governor's races are not included in the calculations for the years in which this occurred. —indicates that the state had no data, either because the state had no gubernatorial election, no vote data were found for the state in question, or the state had not yet entered the Union.

[1] Election held in odd-numbered year.

Sources: State vote tables for governor in Chapter 7.

Table 8-133 Governor Competition Measures, by State, by Two-Year Election Cycle, 1956–1961 (Percentages)

	1956–1957			1958–1959			1960–1961		
State	Democratic % of Two-Party Vote	Margin of Victory	Party Competition Index	Democratic % of Two-Party Vote	Margin of Victory	Party Competition Index	Democratic % of Two-Party Vote	Margin of Victory	Party Competition Index
Alabama	—	—	—	88.7	77.4	22.6	—	—	—
Alaska	—	—	—	60.2	20.4	79.6	—	—	—
Arizona	59.5	19.0	81.0	44.9	10.2	89.8	40.7	18.6	81.4
Arkansas	80.6	61.2	38.8	82.5	65.0	35.0	69.2	38.4	61.6
California	—	—	—	59.8	19.6	80.4	—	—	—
Colorado	51.3	2.6	97.4	58.4	16.8	83.2	—	—	—
Connecticut	—	—	—	62.7	25.4	74.6	—	—	—
Delaware	48.0	4.0	96.0	—	—	—	51.7	3.4	96.6
Florida	73.7	47.4	52.6	—	—	—	59.8	19.6	80.4
Georgia	—	—	—	100.0	100.0	0.0	—	—	—
Hawaii	—	—	—	48.8[1]	2.4[1]	97.6[1]	—	—	—
Idaho	—	—	—	49.0	2.0	98.0	—	—	—
Illinois	49.6	0.8	99.2	—	—	—	55.6	11.2	88.8
Indiana	44.2	11.6	88.4	—	—	—	50.5	1.0	99.0
Iowa	51.2	2.4	97.6	54.1	8.2	91.8	47.9	4.2	95.8
Kansas	56.8	13.6	86.4	57.0	14.0	86.0	44.0	12.0	88.0
Kentucky	—	—	—	60.6[1]	21.2[1]	78.8[1]	—	—	—
Louisiana	100.0	100.0	0.0	—	—	—	82.6	65.2	34.8
Maine	59.2	18.4	81.6	52.0	4.0	96.0	—	—	—
Maryland	—	—	—	63.6	27.2	72.8	—	—	—
Massachusetts	53.0	6.0	94.0	56.6	13.2	86.8	47.1	5.8	94.2
Michigan	54.8	9.6	90.4	53.2	6.4	93.6	50.6	1.2	98.8
Minnesota	51.6	3.2	96.8	57.3	14.6	85.4	49.3	1.4	98.6
Mississippi	—	—	—	100.0[1]	100.0[1]	0.0[1]	—	—	—
Missouri	52.1	4.2	95.8	—	—	—	58.0	16.0	84.0
Montana	48.6	2.8	97.2	—	—	—	44.9	10.2	89.8
Nebraska	42.5	15.0	85.0	50.2	0.4	99.6	52.0	4.0	96.0
Nevada	—	—	—	59.9	19.8	80.2	—	—	—
New Hampshire	45.3	9.4	90.6	48.3	3.4	96.6	44.5	11.0	89.0
New Jersey	55.1[1]	10.2[1]	89.8[1]	—	—	—	50.8[1]	1.6[1]	98.4[1]
New Mexico	47.8	4.4	95.6	50.5	1.0	99.0	49.7	0.6	99.4
New York	—	—	—	45.0	10.0	90.0	—	—	—
North Carolina	67.0	34.0	66.0	—	—	—	54.5	9.0	91.0
North Dakota	41.5	17.0	83.0	46.9	6.2	93.8	52.6	5.2	94.8
Ohio	44.0	12.0	88.0	56.9	13.8	86.2	—	—	—
Oklahoma	—	—	—	78.8	57.6	42.4	—	—	—
Oregon	—	—	—	44.7	10.6	89.4	—	—	—
Pennsylvania	—	—	—	51.0	2.0	98.0	—	—	—
Rhode Island	50.1	0.2	99.8	49.1	1.8	98.2	56.6	13.2	86.8
South Carolina	—	—	—	100.0	100.0	0.0	—	—	—
South Dakota	45.6	8.8	91.2	51.4	2.8	97.2	49.3	1.4	98.6
Tennessee	—	—	—	87.4	74.8	25.2	—	—	—
Texas	84.1	68.2	31.8	88.1	76.2	23.8	72.8	45.6	54.4
Utah	46.7	6.6	93.4	—	—	—	47.3	5.4	94.6
Vermont	42.5	15.0	85.0	49.7	0.6	99.4	43.6	12.8	87.2
Virginia	63.4[1]	26.8[1]	73.2[1]	—	—	—	63.9[1]	27.8[1]	72.2[1]
Washington	54.8	9.6	90.4	—	—	—	50.7	1.4	98.6
West Virginia	46.1	7.8	92.2	—	—	—	54.0	8.0	92.0
Wisconsin	48.1	3.8	96.2	53.7	7.4	92.6	51.6	3.2	96.8
Wyoming	—	—	—	51.2	2.4	97.6	—	—	—

Notes: The first entries are the Democratic percent of two-party vote values for each state for the gubernatorial race. The second entries are the margin of victory values for each state for the gubernatorial race, where margin of victory is defined as the absolute difference between the Democratic percent and the Republican percent of the two-party vote for governor. The third entries are the party competition index values for each state for the gubernatorial race, where the competition index devised by Paul David (1972) is defined as (100 − the margin of victory) or, alternatively, as (100 − the absolute difference between the Democratic and Republican percent of two-party vote for governor). The values for Democratic and Republican percent of two-party vote for governor are taken from the state vote tables in Chapter 7. Zero (0) percent on David's index represents a complete absence of two-party competition for that election year, whereas a score of 100 per-cent indicates perfect competition between the two major parties. A state can only receive a party competition score of 0 if it has a 100–0 vote split in the governor's race. Conversely, a state can only receive a score of 100 if it has a 50–50 vote split in the governor's race. For example, if New Hampshire in 1788 reported a 54.7 percent Democratic vote for governor of its two-party vote, then its Republican vote for governor would be 45.3 percent. The absolute difference between the two figures is the margin of victory, or 9.4 percent; 100 percent − 9.4 percent would equal 90.6 percent on David's party competition scale, indicating a very competi-tive contest for governor in New Hampshire in 1788. The two-party vote percent values used to derive the margin of victory and party competition figures are initially found in the state vote tables in Chapter 7. The author's alternative party coding in these tables is used whenever it occurs instead of the conventional party coding of voting data. The Democratic Party is defined here as the Anti-Federalists, Democratic-Republicans, and Jackson Democrats prior to 1830 when the "Democratic Party" as such was established. The Republican Party is defined as the Federalists, National Republicans, and Whigs prior to the establishment of the "Republican Party" in the 1850s. See Appendix A for an explanation of the historical antecedents of the current Democratic and Republican parties. States reporting only partial voting returns for governor's races are not included in the calculations for the years in which this occurred. —indicates that the state had no data, either because the state had no gubernatorial election, no vote data were found for the state in question, or the state had not yet entered the Union.

[1] Election held in odd-numbered year.

Sources: State vote tables for governor in Chapter 7.

Table 8-134 Governor Competition Measures, by State, by Two-Year Election Cycle, 1962–1967 (Percentages)

State	1962–1963 Democratic % of Two-Party Vote	Margin of Victory	Party Competition Index	1964–1965 Democratic % of Two-Party Vote	Margin of Victory	Party Competition Index	1966–1967 Democratic % of Two-Party Vote	Margin of Victory	Party Competition Index
Alabama	100.0	100.0	0.0	—	—	—	67.2	34.4	65.6
Alaska	52.3	4.6	95.4	—	—	—	49.2	1.6	98.4
Arizona	45.2	9.6	90.4	53.2	6.4	93.6	46.2	7.6	92.4
Arkansas	73.3	46.6	53.4	57.0	14.0	86.0	45.6	8.8	91.2
California	52.6	5.2	94.8	—	—	—	42.3	15.4	84.6
Colorado	42.9	14.2	85.8	—	—	—	44.6	10.8	89.2
Connecticut	53.2	6.4	93.6	—	—	—	55.7	11.4	88.6
Delaware	—	—	—	51.4	2.8	97.2	—	—	—
Florida	—	—	—	57.6	15.2	84.8	44.9	10.2	89.8
Georgia	100.0	100.0	0.0	—	—	—	52.2	4.4	95.6
Hawaii	58.3	16.6	83.4	—	—	—	51.1	2.2	97.8
Idaho	45.4	9.2	90.8	—	—	—	47.3	5.4	94.6
Illinois	—	—	—	51.9	3.8	96.2	—	—	—
Indiana	—	—	—	56.4	12.8	87.2	—	—	—
Iowa	52.6	5.2	94.8	68.5	37.0	63.0	55.6	11.2	88.8
Kansas	46.0	8.0	92.0	48.1	3.8	96.2	55.5	11.0	89.0
Kentucky	50.7[1]	1.4[1]	98.6[1]	—	—	—	48.4[1]	3.2[1]	96.8[1]
Louisiana	—	—	—	61.2	22.4	77.6	—	—	—
Maine	49.9	0.2	99.8	—	—	—	53.1	6.2	93.8
Maryland	55.6	11.2	88.8	—	—	—	45.1	9.8	90.2
Massachusetts	50.1	0.2	99.8	49.5	1.0	99.0	37.1	25.8	74.2
Michigan	48.5	3.0	97.0	43.9	12.2	87.8	39.3	21.4	78.6
Minnesota	50.0	0.0	100.0	—	—	—	47.2	5.6	94.4
Mississippi	61.9[1]	23.8[1]	76.2[1]	—	—	—	70.3[1]	40.6[1]	59.4[1]
Missouri	—	—	—	62.1	24.2	75.8	—	—	—
Montana	—	—	—	48.7	2.6	97.4	—	—	—
Nebraska	52.2	4.4	95.6	60.0	20.0	80.0	38.5	23.0	77.0
Nevada	66.8	33.6	66.4	—	—	—	47.8	4.4	95.6
New Hampshire	58.9	17.8	82.2	66.8	33.6	66.4	54.0	8.0	92.0
New Jersey	—	—	—	58.3[1]	16.6[1]	83.4[1]	—	—	—
New Mexico	53.0	6.0	94.0	60.2	20.4	79.6	48.3	3.4	96.6
New York	45.3	9.4	90.6	—	—	—	46.1	7.8	92.2
North Carolina	—	—	—	56.6	13.2	86.8	—	—	—
North Dakota	50.4	0.8	99.2	55.7	11.4	88.6	—	—	—
Ohio	41.1	17.8	82.2	—	—	—	37.8	24.4	75.6
Oklahoma	44.6	10.8	89.2	—	—	—	44.0	12.0	88.0
Oregon	43.4	13.2	86.8	—	—	—	44.7	10.6	89.4
Pennsylvania	44.4	11.2	88.8	—	—	—	47.0	6.0	94.0
Rhode Island	49.9	0.2	99.8	38.9	22.2	77.8	36.7	26.6	73.4
South Carolina	100.0	100.0	0.0	—	—	—	58.2	16.4	83.6
South Dakota	43.9	12.2	87.8	48.3	3.4	96.6	42.3	15.4	84.6
Tennessee	76.0	52.0	48.0	—	—	—	100.0	100.0	0.0
Texas	54.2	8.4	91.6	73.9	47.8	52.2	73.8	47.6	52.4
Utah	—	—	—	57.0	14.0	86.0	—	—	—
Vermont	50.6	1.2	98.8	64.9	29.8	70.2	57.7	15.4	84.6
Virginia	—	—	—	55.9[1]	11.8[1]	88.2[1]	—	—	—
Washington	—	—	—	44.0	12.0	88.0	—	—	—
West Virginia	—	—	—	54.9	9.8	90.2	—	—	—
Wisconsin	50.5	1.0	99.0	49.4	1.2	98.8	46.3	7.4	92.6
Wyoming	45.5	9.0	91.0	—	—	—	45.7	8.6	91.4

Notes: The first entries are the Democratic percent of two-party vote values for each state for the gubernatorial race. The second entries are the margin of victory values for each state for the gubernatorial race, where margin of victory is defined as the absolute difference between the Democratic percent and the Republican percent of the two-party vote for governor. The third entries are the party competition index values for each state for the gubernatorial race, where the competition index devised by Paul David (1972) is defined as (100 − the margin of victory) or, alternatively, as (100 − the absolute difference between the Democratic and Republican percent of two-party vote for governor). The values for Democratic and Republican percent of two-party vote for governor are taken from the state vote tables in Chapter 7. Zero (0) percent on David's index represents a complete absence of two-party competition for that election year, whereas a score of 100 percent indicates perfect competition between the two major parties. A state can only receive a party competition score of 0 if it has a 100–0 vote split in the governor's race. Conversely, a state can only receive a score of 100 if it has a 50–50 vote split in the governor's race. For example, if New Hampshire in 1788 reported a 54.7 percent Democratic vote for governor of its two-party vote, then its Republican vote for governor would be 45.3 percent. The absolute difference between the two figures is the margin of victory, or 9.4 percent; 100 percent − 9.4 percent would equal 90.6 percent on David's party competition scale, indicating a very competitive contest for governor in New Hampshire in 1788. The two-party vote percent values used to derive the margin of victory and party competition figures are initially found in the state vote tables in Chapter 7. The author's alternative party coding in these tables is used whenever it occurs instead of the conventional party coding of voting data. The Democratic Party is defined here as the Anti-Federalists, Democratic-Republicans, and Jackson Democrats prior to 1830 when the "Democratic Party" as such was established. The Republican Party is defined as the Federalists, National Republicans, and Whigs prior to the establishment of the "Republican Party" in the 1850s. See Appendix A for an explanation of the historical antecedents of the current Democratic and Republican parties. States reporting only partial voting returns for governor's races are not included in the calculations for the years in which this occurred. —indicates that the state had no data, either because the state had no gubernatorial election or no vote data were found.

Sources: State vote tables for governor in Chapter 7.

Table 8-135 Governor Competition Measures, by Two-Year Election Cycle, by State, 1968–1973 (Percentages)

	1968–1969			1970–1971			1972–1973		
State	Democratic % of Two-Party Vote	Margin of Victory	Party Competition Index	Democratic % of Two-Party Vote	Margin of Victory	Party Competition Index	Democratic % of Two-Party Vote	Margin of Victory	Party Competition Index
Alabama	—	—	—	100.0	100.0	0.0	—	—	—
Alaska	—	—	—	53.2	6.4	93.6	—	—	—
Arizona	42.2	15.6	84.4	49.1	1.8	98.2	—	—	—
Arkansas	47.6	4.8	95.2	65.6	31.2	68.8	75.4	50.8	49.2
California	—	—	—	46.1	7.8	92.2	—	—	—
Colorado	—	—	—	46.3	7.4	92.6	—	—	—
Connecticut	—	—	—	46.2	7.6	92.4	—	—	—
Delaware	49.5	1.0	99.0	—	—	—	51.7	3.4	96.6
Florida	—	—	—	56.9	13.8	86.2	—	—	—
Georgia	—	—	—	59.3	18.6	81.4	—	—	—
Hawaii	—	—	—	57.6	15.2	84.8	—	—	—
Idaho	—	—	—	52.2	4.4	95.6	—	—	—
Illinois	48.6	2.8	97.2	—	—	—	50.8	1.6	98.4
Indiana	47.2	5.6	94.4	—	—	—	42.8	14.4	85.6
Iowa	45.9	8.2	91.8	47.8	4.4	95.6	40.8	18.4	81.6
Kansas	52.1	4.2	95.8	54.8	9.6	90.4	62.6	25.2	74.8
Kentucky	—	—	—	53.3[1]	6.6[1]	93.4[1]	—	—	—
Louisiana	100.0	100.0	0.0	—	—	—	57.2	14.4	85.6
Maine	—	—	—	50.1	0.2	99.8	—	—	—
Maryland	—	—	—	67.0	34.0	66.0	—	—	—
Massachusetts	—	—	—	43.0	14.0	86.0	—	—	—
Michigan	—	—	—	49.2	1.6	98.4	—	—	—
Minnesota	—	—	—	54.3	8.6	91.4	—	—	—
Mississippi	—	—	—	100.0[1]	100.0[1]	0.0[1]	—	—	—
Missouri	60.7	21.4	78.6	—	—	—	44.7	10.6	89.4
Montana	56.4	12.8	87.2	—	—	—	54.1	8.2	91.8
Nebraska	—	—	—	55.2	10.4	89.6	—	—	—
Nevada	—	—	—	52.3	4.6	95.4	—	—	—
New Hampshire	47.5	5.0	95.0	49.0	2.0	98.0	48.5	3.0	97.0
New Jersey	39.2[1]	21.6[1]	78.4[1]	—	—	—	67.4[1]	34.8[1]	65.2[1]
New Mexico	49.5	1.0	99.0	52.5	5.0	95.0	—	—	—
New York	—	—	—	43.5	13.0	87.0	—	—	—
North Carolina	52.7	5.4	94.6	—	—	—	48.7	2.6	97.4
North Dakota	55.6	11.2	88.8	—	—	—	51.0	2.0	98.0
Ohio	—	—	—	55.5	11.0	89.0	—	—	—
Oklahoma	—	—	—	50.2	0.4	99.6	—	—	—
Oregon	—	—	—	44.3	11.4	88.6	—	—	—
Pennsylvania	—	—	—	57.0	14.0	86.0	—	—	—
Rhode Island	51.0	2.0	98.0	50.3	0.6	99.4	52.8	5.6	94.4
South Carolina	—	—	—	53.1	6.2	93.8	—	—	—
South Dakota	42.3	15.4	84.6	54.8	9.6	90.4	60.0	20.0	80.0
Tennessee	—	—	—	46.9	6.2	93.8	—	—	—
Texas	57.0	14.0	86.0	53.6	7.2	92.8	51.6	3.2	96.8
Utah	68.7	37.4	62.6	—	—	—	69.7	39.4	60.6
Vermont	44.5	11.0	89.0	43.0	14.0	86.0	55.9	11.8	88.2
Virginia	46.4[1]	7.2[1]	92.8[1]	—	—	—	0.0[1]	100.0[1]	0.0[1]
Washington	44.7	10.6	89.4	—	—	—	45.7	8.6	91.4
West Virginia	49.1	1.8	98.2	—	—	—	45.3	9.4	90.6
Wisconsin	47.0	6.0	94.0	54.7	9.4	90.6	—	—	—
Wyoming	—	—	—	37.2	25.6	74.4	—	—	—

Notes: The first entries are the Democratic percent of two-party vote values for each state for the gubernatorial race. The second entries are the margin of victory values for each state for the gubernatorial race, where margin of victory is defined as the absolute difference between the Democratic percent and the Republican percent of the two-party vote for governor. The third entries are the party competition index values for each state for the gubernatorial race, where the competition index devised by Paul David (1972) is defined as (100 − the margin of victory) or, alternatively, as (100 − the absolute difference between the Democratic and Republican percent of two-party vote for governor). The values for Democratic and Republican percent of two-party vote for governor are taken from the state vote tables in Chapter 7. Zero (0) percent on David's index represents a complete absence of two-party competition for that election year, whereas a score of 100 percent indicates perfect competition between the two major parties. A state can only receive a party competition score of 0 if it has a 100–0 vote split in the governor's race. Conversely, a state can only receive a score of 100 if it has a 50–50 vote split in the governor's race. For example, if New Hampshire in 1788 reported a 54.7 percent Democratic vote for governor of its two-party vote, then its Republican vote for governor would be 45.3 percent. The absolute difference between the two figures is the margin of victory, or 9.4 percent; 100 percent − 9.4 percent would equal 90.6 percent on David's party competition scale, indicating a very competitive contest for governor in New Hampshire in 1788. The two-party vote percent values used to derive the margin of victory and party competition figures are initially found in the state vote tables in Chapter 7. The author's alternative party coding in these tables is used whenever it occurs instead of the conventional party coding of voting data. The Democratic Party is defined here as the Anti-Federalists, Democratic-Republicans, and Jackson Democrats prior to 1830 when the "Democratic Party" as such was established. The Republican Party is defined as the Federalists, National Republicans, and Whigs prior to the establishment of the "Republican Party" in the 1850s. See Appendix A for an explanation of the historical antecedents of the current Democratic and Republican parties. States reporting only partial voting returns for governor's races are not included in the calculations for the years in which this occurred. —indicates that the state had no data, either because the state had no gubernatorial election or no vote data were found.

[1] Election held in odd-numbered year.

Sources: State vote tables for governor in Chapter 7.

Table 8-136 Governor Competition Measures, by State, by Two-Year Election Cycle, 1974–1979 (Percentages)

	1974–1975			1976–1977			1978–1979		
State	Democratic % of Two-Party Vote	Margin of Victory	Party Competition Index	Democratic % of Two-Party Vote	Margin of Victory	Party Competition Index	Democratic % of Two-Party Vote	Margin of Victory	Party Competition Index
Alabama	84.9	69.8	30.2	—	—	—	73.7	47.4	52.6
Alaska	49.8	0.4	99.6	—	—	—	34.1	31.8	68.2
Arizona	50.4	0.8	99.2	—	—	—	54.0	8.0	92.0
Arkansas	65.6	31.2	68.8	83.3	66.6	33.4	63.4	26.8	73.2
California	51.5	3.0	97.0	—	—	—	60.6	21.2	78.8
Colorado	53.8	7.6	92.4	—	—	—	60.4	20.8	79.2
Connecticut	59.4	18.8	81.2	—	—	—	59.2	18.4	81.6
Delaware	—	—	—	42.8	14.4	85.6	—	—	—
Florida	61.2	22.4	77.6	—	—	—	55.6	11.2	88.8
Georgia	69.1	38.2	61.8	—	—	—	80.7	61.4	38.6
Hawaii	54.6	9.2	90.8	—	—	—	55.2	10.4	89.6
Idaho	72.8	45.6	54.4	—	—	—	59.8	19.6	80.4
Illinois	—	—	—	34.9	30.2	69.8	40.5	19.0	81.0
Indiana	—	—	—	42.9	14.2	85.8	—	—	—
Iowa	41.4	17.2	82.8	—	—	—	41.3	17.4	82.6
Kansas	49.8	0.4	99.6	—	—	—	51.1	2.2	97.8
Kentucky	62.8[1]	25.6[1]	74.4[1]	—	—	—	59.4[1]	18.8[1]	81.2[1]
Louisiana	100.0[1]	100.0[1]	0.0[1]	—	—	—	49.7[1]	0.6[1]	99.4[1]
Maine	61.1	22.2	77.8	—	—	—	58.2	16.4	83.6
Maryland	63.5	27.0	73.0	—	—	—	71.0	42.0	58.0
Massachusetts	55.9	11.8	88.2	—	—	—	52.7	5.4	94.6
Michigan	47.8	4.4	95.6	—	—	—	43.2	13.6	86.4
Minnesota	68.2	36.4	63.6	—	—	—	46.4	7.2	92.8
Mississippi	53.6[1]	7.2[1]	92.8[1]	—	—	—	61.1[1]	22.2[1]	77.8[1]
Missouri	—	—	—	50.3	0.6	99.4	—	—	—
Montana	—	—	—	62.8	25.6	74.4	—	—	—
Nebraska	62.6	25.2	74.8	—	—	—	44.0	12.0	88.0
Nevada	79.8	59.6	40.4	—	—	—	41.4	17.2	82.8
New Hampshire	48.8	2.4	97.6	42.3	15.4	84.6	52.1	4.2	95.8
New Jersey	—	—	—	57.1[1]	14.2[1]	85.8[1]	—	—	—
New Mexico	50.6	1.2	98.8	—	—	—	50.6	1.2	98.8
New York	57.7	15.4	84.6	—	—	—	53.0	6.0	94.0
North Carolina	—	—	—	65.7	31.4	68.6	—	—	—
North Dakota	—	—	—	52.6	5.2	94.8	—	—	—
Ohio	49.8	0.4	99.6	—	—	—	49.1	1.8	98.2
Oklahoma	63.9	27.8	72.2	—	—	—	52.3	4.6	95.4
Oregon	57.8	15.6	84.4	—	—	—	45.1	9.8	90.2
Pennsylvania	54.3	8.6	91.4	—	—	—	46.9	6.2	93.8
Rhode Island	78.5	57.0	43.0	55.1	10.2	89.8	67.1	34.2	65.8
South Carolina	48.3	3.4	96.6	—	—	—	61.9	23.8	76.2
South Dakota	53.6	7.2	92.8	—	—	—	43.4	13.2	86.8
Tennessee	55.9	11.8	88.2	—	—	—	44.2	11.6	88.4
Texas	66.4	32.8	67.2	—	—	—	49.6	0.8	99.2
Utah	—	—	—	53.1	6.2	93.8	—	—	—
Vermont	59.8	19.6	80.4	43.1	13.8	86.2	35.2	29.6	70.4
Virginia	—	—	—	43.6[1]	12.8[1]	87.2[1]	—	—	—
Washington	—	—	—	54.5	9.0	91.0	—	—	—
West Virginia	—	—	—	66.2	32.4	67.6	—	—	—
Wisconsin	55.8	11.6	88.4	—	—	—	45.2	9.6	90.4
Wyoming	55.9	11.8	88.2	—	—	—	50.9	1.8	98.2

Notes: The first entries are the Democratic percent of two-party vote values for each state for the gubernatorial race. The second entries are the margin of victory values for each state for the gubernatorial race, where margin of victory is defined as the absolute difference between the Democratic percent and the Republican percent of the two-party vote for governor. The third entries are the party competition index values for each state for the gubernatorial race, where the competition index devised by Paul David (1972) is defined as (100 − the margin of victory) or, alternatively, as (100 − the absolute difference between the Democratic and Republican percent of the two-party vote for governor). The values for Democratic and Republican percent of two-party vote for governor are taken from the state vote tables in Chapter 7. Zero (0) percent on David's index represents a complete absence of two-party competition for that election year, whereas a score of 100 per-cent indicates perfect competition between the two major parties. A state can only receive a party competition score of 0 if it has a 100–0 vote split in the governor's race. Conversely, a state can only receive a score of 100 if it has a 50–50 vote split in the governor's race. For example, if New Hampshire in 1788 reported a 54.7 percent Democratic vote for governor of its two-party vote, then its Republican vote for governor would be 45.3 percent. The absolute difference between the two figures is the margin of victory, or 9.4 percent; 100 percent − 9.4 percent would equal 90.6 percent on David's party competition scale, indicating a very competi-tive contest for governor in New Hampshire in 1788. The two-party vote percent values used to derive the margin of victory and party competition figures are initially found in the state vote tables in Chapter 7. The author's alternative party coding in these tables is used whenever it occurs instead of the conventional party coding of voting data. The Democratic Party is defined here as the Anti-Federalists, Democratic-Republicans, and Jackson Democrats prior to 1830 when the "Democratic Party" as such was established. The Republican Party is defined as the Federalists, National Republicans, and Whigs prior to the establishment of the "Republican Party" in the 1850s. See Appendix A for an explanation of the historical antecedents of the current Democratic and Republican parties. States reporting only partial voting returns for governor's races are not included in the calculations for the years in which this occurred. —indicates that the state had no data, either because the state had no gubernatorial election or no vote data were found.

[1] Election held in odd-numbered year.

Sources: State vote tables for governor in Chapter 7.

Table 8-137 Governor Competition Measures, by State, by Two-Year Election Cycle, 1980–1985 (Percentages)

	1980–1981			1982–1983			1984–1985		
State	Democratic % of Two-Party Vote	Margin of Victory	Party Competition Index	Democratic % of Two-Party Vote	Margin of Victory	Party Competition Index	Democratic % of Two-Party Vote	Margin of Victory	Party Competition Index
Alabama	—	—	—	59.6	19.2	80.8	—	—	—
Alaska	—	—	—	55.4	10.8	89.2	—	—	—
Arizona	—	—	—	65.8	31.6	68.4	—	—	—
Arkansas	48.1	3.8	96.2	54.7	9.4	90.6	62.6	25.2	74.8
California	—	—	—	49.4	1.2	98.8	—	—	—
Colorado	—	—	—	67.5	35.0	65.0	—	—	—
Connecticut	—	—	—	53.7	7.4	92.6	—	—	—
Delaware	28.8	42.4	57.6	—	—	—	44.5	11.0	89.0
Florida	—	—	—	64.7	29.4	70.6	—	—	—
Georgia	—	—	—	62.8	25.6	74.4	—	—	—
Hawaii	—	—	—	73.9	47.8	52.2	—	—	—
Idaho	—	—	—	50.6	1.2	98.8	—	—	—
Illinois	—	—	—	49.9	0.2	99.8	—	—	—
Indiana	42.1	15.8	84.2	—	—	—	47.5	5.0	95.0
Iowa	—	—	—	46.8	6.4	93.6	—	—	—
Kansas	—	—	—	54.5	9.0	91.0	—	—	—
Kentucky	—	—	—	55.3[1]	10.6[1]	89.4[1]	—	—	—
Louisiana	—	—	—	63.2[1]	26.4[1]	73.6[1]	—	—	—
Maine	—	—	—	61.9	23.8	76.2	—	—	—
Maryland	—	—	—	62.0	24.0	76.0	—	—	—
Massachusetts	—	—	—	61.9	23.8	76.2	—	—	—
Michigan	—	—	—	53.3	6.6	93.4	—	—	—
Minnesota	—	—	—	59.4	18.8	81.2	—	—	—
Mississippi	—	—	—	58.6[1]	17.2[1]	82.8[1]	—	—	—
Missouri	47.2	5.6	94.4	—	—	—	43.3	13.4	86.6
Montana	55.4	10.8	89.2	—	—	—	72.7	45.4	54.6
Nebraska	—	—	—	50.7	1.4	98.6	—	—	—
Nevada	—	—	—	56.1	12.2	87.8	—	—	—
New Hampshire	59.2	18.4	81.6	47.6	4.8	95.2	33.1	33.8	66.2
New Jersey	50.0[1]	0.0[1]	100.0[1]	—	—	—	29.6[1]	40.8[1]	59.2[1]
New Mexico	—	—	—	53.0	6.0	94.0	—	—	—
New York	—	—	—	51.7	3.4	96.6	—	—	—
North Carolina	62.3	24.6	75.4	—	—	—	45.6	8.8	91.2
North Dakota	46.4	7.2	92.8	—	—	—	55.3	10.6	89.4
Ohio	—	—	—	60.3	20.6	79.4	—	—	—
Oklahoma	—	—	—	62.3	24.6	75.4	—	—	—
Oregon	—	—	—	36.9	26.2	73.8	—	—	—
Pennsylvania	—	—	—	48.6	2.8	97.2	—	—	—
Rhode Island	73.7	47.4	52.6	75.6	51.2	48.8	40.0	20.0	80.0
South Carolina	—	—	—	69.8	39.6	60.4	—	—	—
South Dakota	—	—	—	29.1	41.8	58.2	—	—	—
Tennessee	—	—	—	40.4	19.2	80.8	—	—	—
Texas	—	—	—	53.7	7.4	92.6	—	—	—
Utah	55.4	10.8	89.2	—	—	—	43.9	12.2	87.8
Vermont	38.6	22.8	77.2	44.4	11.2	88.8	50.8	1.6	98.4
Virginia	53.6[1]	7.2[1]	92.8[1]	—	—	—	55.2[1]	10.4[1]	89.6[1]
Washington	43.3	13.4	86.6	—	—	—	53.3	6.6	93.4
West Virginia	54.4	8.8	91.2	—	—	—	46.7	6.6	93.4
Wisconsin	—	—	—	57.5	15.0	85.0	—	—	—
Wyoming	—	—	—	63.1	26.2	73.8	—	—	—

Notes: The first entries are the Democratic percent of two-party vote values for each state for the gubernatorial race. The second entries are the margin of victory values for each state for the gubernatorial race, where margin of victory is defined as the absolute difference between the Democratic percent and the Republican percent of the two-party vote for governor. The third entries are the party competition index values for each state for the gubernatorial race, where the competition index devised by Paul David (1972) is defined as (100 − the margin of victory) or, alternatively, as (100 − the absolute difference between the Democratic and Republican percent of two-party vote for governor). The values for Democratic and Republican percent of two-party vote for governor are taken from the state vote tables in Chapter 7. Zero (0) percent on David's index represents a complete absence of two-party competition for that election year, whereas a score of 100 percent indicates perfect competition between the two major parties. A state can only receive a party competition score of 0 if it has a 100–0 vote split in the governor's race. Conversely, a state can only receive a score of 100 if it has a 50–50 vote split in the governor's race. For example, if New Hampshire in 1788 reported a 54.7 percent Democratic vote for governor of its two-party vote, then its Republican vote for governor would be 45.3 percent. The absolute difference between the two figures is the margin of victory, or 9.4 percent; 100 percent − 9.4 percent would equal 90.6 percent on David's party competition scale, indicating a very competitive contest for governor in New Hampshire in 1788. The two-party vote percent values used to derive the margin of victory and party competition figures are initially found in the state vote tables in Chapter 7. The author's alternative party coding in these tables is used whenever it occurs instead of the conventional party coding of voting data. The Democratic Party is defined here as the Anti-Federalists, Democratic-Republicans, and Jackson Democrats prior to 1830 when the "Democratic Party" as such was established. The Republican Party is defined as the Federalists, National Republicans, and Whigs prior to the establishment of the "Republican Party" in the 1850s. See Appendix A for an explanation of the historical antecedents of the current Democratic and Republican parties. States reporting only partial voting returns for governor's races are not included in the calculations for the years in which this occurred. —indicates that the state had no data, either because the state had no gubernatorial election or no vote data were found.

[1] Election held in odd-numbered year.

Sources: State vote tables for governor in Chapter 7.

Table 8-138 Governor Competition Measures, by State, by Two-Year Election Cycle, 1986–1991 (Percentages)

State	1986–1987			1988–1989			1990–1991		
	Democratic % of Two-Party Vote	Margin of Victory	Party Competition Index	Democratic % of Two-Party Vote	Margin of Victory	Party Competition Index	Democratic % of Two-Party Vote	Margin of Victory	Party Competition Index
Alabama	43.6	12.8	87.2	—	—	—	47.9	4.2	95.8
Alaska	52.6	5.2	94.8	—	—	—	54.1	8.2	91.8
Arizona	46.5	7.0	93.0	—	—	—	49.8	0.4	99.6
Arkansas	63.9	27.8	72.2	—	—	—	57.5	15.0	85.0
California	38.2	23.6	76.4	—	—	—	48.2	3.6	96.4
Colorado	58.7	17.4	82.6	—	—	—	63.6	27.2	72.8
Connecticut	58.5	17.0	83.0	—	—	—	35.6	28.8	71.2
Delaware	—	—	—	29.3	41.4	58.6	—	—	—
Florida	45.4	9.2	90.8	—	—	—	56.5	13.0	87.0
Georgia	70.5	41.0	59.0	—	—	—	54.3	8.6	91.4
Hawaii	52.0	4.0	96.0	—	—	—	60.8	21.6	78.4
Idaho	50.5	1.0	99.0	—	—	—	68.2	36.4	63.6
Illinois	11.2	77.6	22.4	—	—	—	48.7	2.6	97.4
Indiana	—	—	—	53.2	6.4	93.6	—	—	—
Iowa	48.0	4.0	96.0	—	—	—	39.1	21.8	78.2
Kansas	48.1	3.8	96.2	—	—	—	53.3	6.6	93.4
Kentucky	64.9[1]	29.8[1]	70.2[1]	—	—	—	64.7[1]	29.4[1]	70.6[1]
Louisiana	—	—	—	—	—	—	61.2[1]	22.4[1]	77.6[1]
Maine	43.1	13.8	86.2	—	—	—	48.6	2.8	97.2
Maryland	82.4	64.8	35.2	—	—	—	59.8	19.6	80.4
Massachusetts	68.8	37.6	62.4	—	—	—	48.3	3.4	96.6
Michigan	68.4	36.8	63.2	—	—	—	49.7	0.6	99.4
Minnesota	56.6	13.2	86.8	—	—	—	48.3	3.4	96.6
Mississippi	53.4[1]	6.8[1]	93.2[1]	—	—	—	48.4[1]	3.2[1]	96.8[1]
Missouri	—	—	—	35.1	29.8	70.2	—	—	—
Montana	—	—	—	47.0	6.0	94.0	50.3	0.6	99.4
Nebraska	47.1	5.8	94.2	—	—	—	68.5	37.0	63.0
Nevada	74.2	48.4	51.6	—	—	—	36.4	27.2	72.8
New Hampshire	46.3	7.4	92.6	39.2	21.6	78.4	—	—	—
New Jersey	—	—	—	62.2[1]	24.4[1]	75.6[1]	—	—	—
New Mexico	47.0	6.0	94.0	—	—	—	54.7	9.4	90.6
New York	67.1	34.2	65.8	—	—	—	71.4	42.8	57.2
North Carolina	—	—	—	43.9	12.2	87.8	—	—	—
North Dakota	—	—	—	59.9	19.8	80.2	—	—	—
Ohio	60.6	21.2	78.8	—	—	—	44.3	11.4	88.6
Oklahoma	48.4	3.2	96.8	—	—	—	63.7	27.4	72.6
Oregon	52.0	4.0	96.0	—	—	—	53.4	6.8	93.2
Pennsylvania	51.2	2.4	97.6	—	—	—	67.7	35.4	64.6
Rhode Island	33.4	33.2	66.8	49.2	1.6	98.4	74.2	48.4	51.6
South Carolina	48.4	3.2	96.8	—	—	—	28.6	42.8	57.2
South Dakota	48.2	3.6	96.4	—	—	—	41.1	17.8	82.2
Tennessee	54.3	8.6	91.4	—	—	—	62.4	24.8	75.2
Texas	46.6	6.8	93.2	—	—	—	51.3	2.6	97.4
Utah	—	—	—	48.9	2.2	97.8	—	—	—
Vermont	55.1	10.2	89.8	56.1	12.2	87.8	47.1	5.8	94.2
Virginia	—	—	—	50.2[1]	0.4[1]	99.6[1]	—	—	—
Washington	—	—	—	62.2	24.4	75.6	—	—	—
West Virginia	—	—	—	58.9	17.8	82.2	—	—	—
Wisconsin	46.7	6.6	93.4	—	—	—	41.8	16.4	83.6
Wyoming	54.0	8.0	92.0	—	—	—	65.4	30.8	69.2

Notes: The first entries are the Democratic percent of two-party vote values for each state for the gubernatorial race. The second entries are the margin of victory values for each state for the gubernatorial race, where margin of victory is defined as the absolute difference between the Democratic percent and the Republican percent of the two-party vote for governor. The third entries are the party competition index values for each state for the gubernatorial race, where the competition index devised by Paul David (1972) is defined as (100 − the margin of victory) or, alternatively, as (100 − the absolute difference between the Democratic and Republican percent of two-party vote for governor). The values for Democratic and Republican percent of two-party vote for governor are taken from the state vote tables in Chapter 7. Zero (0) percent on David's index represents a complete absence of two-party competition for that election year, whereas a score of 100 percent indicates perfect competition between the two major parties. A state can only receive a party competition score of 0 if it has a 100–0 vote split in the governor's race. Conversely, a state can only receive a score of 100 if it has a 50–50 vote split in the governor's race. For example, if New Hampshire in 1788 reported a 54.7 percent Democratic vote for governor of its two-party vote, then its Republican vote for governor would be 45.3 percent. The absolute difference between the two figures is the margin of victory, or 9.4 percent; 100 percent − 9.4 percent would equal 90.6 percent on David's party competition scale, indicating a very competitive contest for governor in New Hampshire in 1788. The two-party vote percent values used to derive the margin of victory and party competition figures are initially found in the state vote tables in Chapter 7. The author's alternative party coding in these tables is used whenever it occurs instead of the conventional party coding of voting data. The Democratic Party is defined here as the Anti-Federalists, Democratic-Republicans, and Jackson Democrats prior to 1830 when the "Democratic Party" as such was established. The Republican Party is defined as the Federalists, National Republicans, and Whigs prior to the establishment of the "Republican Party" in the 1850s. See Appendix A for an explanation of the historical antecedents of the current Democratic and Republican parties. States reporting only partial voting returns for governor's races are not included in the calculations for the years in which this occurred. —indicates that the state had no data, either because the state had no gubernatorial election or no vote data were found.

[1] Election held in odd-numbered year.

Sources: State vote tables for governor in Chapter 7.

Table 8-139 Governor Competition Measures, by State, by Two-Year Election Cycle, 1992–1997 (Percentages)

	1992–1993			1994–1995			1996–1997		
State	Democratic % of Two-Party Vote	Margin of Victory	Party Competition Index	Democratic % of Two-Party Vote	Margin of Victory	Party Competition Index	Democratic % of Two-Party Vote	Margin of Victory	Party Competition Index
Alabama	—	—	—	49.6	0.8	99.2	—	—	—
Alaska	—	—	—	50.2	0.4	99.6	—	—	—
Arizona	—	—	—	45.8	8.4	91.6	—	—	—
Arkansas	—	—	—	59.8	19.6	80.4	—	—	—
California	—	—	—	42.4	15.2	84.8	—	—	—
Colorado	—	—	—	58.9	17.8	82.2	—	—	—
Connecticut	—	—	—	47.5	5.0	95.0	—	—	—
Delaware	66.4	32.8	67.2	—	—	—	69.5	39.0	61.0
Florida	—	—	—	50.8	1.6	98.4	—	—	—
Georgia	—	—	—	51.1	2.2	97.8	—	—	—
Hawaii	—	—	—	55.6	11.2	88.8	—	—	—
Idaho	—	—	—	45.6	8.8	91.2	—	—	—
Illinois	—	—	—	35.0	30.0	70.0	—	—	—
Indiana	62.7	25.4	74.6	—	—	—	52.4	4.8	95.2
Iowa	—	—	—	42.3	15.4	84.6	—	—	—
Kansas	—	—	—	35.9	28.2	71.8	—	—	—
Kentucky	—	—	—	51.1[1]	2.2[1]	97.8[1]	—	—	—
Louisiana	—	—	—	36.5[1]	27.0[1]	73.0[1]	—	—	—
Maine	—	—	—	59.4	18.8	81.2	—	—	—
Maryland	—	—	—	50.2	0.4	99.6	—	—	—
Massachusetts	—	—	—	28.5	43.0	57.0	—	—	—
Michigan	—	—	—	38.5	23.0	77.0	—	—	—
Minnesota	—	—	—	35.0	30.0	70.0	—	—	—
Mississippi	—	—	—	44.4[1]	11.2[1]	88.8[1]	—	—	—
Missouri	58.7	17.4	82.6	—	—	—	58.6	17.2	82.8
Montana	48.7	2.6	97.4	—	—	—	20.8	58.4	41.6
Nebraska	—	—	—	74.1	48.2	51.8	—	—	—
Nevada	—	—	—	56.0	12.0	88.0	—	—	—
New Hampshire	41.6	16.8	83.2	26.8	46.4	53.6	59.1	18.2	81.8
New Jersey	49.5[1]	1.0[1]	99.0[1]	—	—	—	49.4[1]	1.2[1]	98.8[1]
New Mexico	—	—	—	44.5	11.0	89.0	—	—	—
New York	—	—	—	48.2	3.6	96.4	—	—	—
North Carolina	55.0	10.0	90.0	—	—	—	56.7	13.4	86.6
North Dakota	41.3	17.4	82.6	—	—	—	33.8	32.4	67.6
Ohio	—	—	—	25.8	48.4	51.6	—	—	—
Oklahoma	—	—	—	38.7	22.6	77.4	—	—	—
Oregon	—	—	—	54.6	9.2	90.8	—	—	—
Pennsylvania	—	—	—	46.8	6.4	93.6	—	—	—
Rhode Island	64.2	28.4	71.6	47.9	4.2	95.8	—	—	—
South Carolina	—	—	—	48.7	2.6	97.4	—	—	—
South Dakota	—	—	—	42.3	15.4	84.6	—	—	—
Tennessee	—	—	—	45.1	9.8	90.2	—	—	—
Texas	—	—	—	46.2	7.6	92.4	—	—	—
Utah	35.5	29.0	71.0	—	—	—	23.7	52.6	47.4
Vermont	76.4	52.8	47.2	78.3	56.6	43.4	75.9	51.8	48.2
Virginia	41.2[1]	17.6[1]	82.4[1]	—	—	—	43.3[1]	13.4[1]	86.6[1]
Washington	52.2	4.4	95.6	—	—	—	58.0	16.0	84.0
West Virginia	60.5	21.0	79.0	—	—	—	47.0	6.0	94.0
Wisconsin	—	—	—	31.5	37.0	63.0	—	—	—
Wyoming	—	—	—	40.6	18.8	81.2	—	—	—

Notes: The first entries are the Democratic percent of two-party vote values for each state for the gubernatorial race. The second entries are the margin of victory values for each state for the gubernatorial race, where margin of victory is defined as the absolute difference between the Democratic percent and the Republican percent of the two-party vote for governor. The third entries are the party competition index values for each state for the gubernatorial race, where the competition index devised by Paul David (1972) is defined as (100 − the margin of victory) or, alternatively, as (100 − the absolute difference between the Democratic and Republican percent of two-party vote for governor). The values for Democratic and Republican percent of two-party vote for governor are taken from the state vote tables in Chapter 7. Zero (0) percent on David's index represents a complete absence of two-party competition for that election year, whereas a score of 100 percent indicates perfect competition between the two major parties. A state can only receive a party competition score of 0 if it has a 100–0 vote split in the governor's race. Conversely, a state can only receive a score of 100 if it has a 50–50 vote split in the governor's race. For example, if New Hampshire in 1788 reported a 54.7 percent Democratic vote for governor of its two-party vote, then its Republican vote for governor would be 45.3 percent. The absolute difference between the two figures is the margin of victory, or 9.4 percent; 100 percent − 9.4 percent would equal 90.6 percent on David's party competition scale, indicating a very competitive contest for governor in New Hampshire in 1788. The two-party vote percent values used to derive the margin of victory and party competition figures are initially found in the state vote tables in Chapter 7. The author's alternative party coding in these tables is used whenever it occurs instead of the conventional party coding of voting data. The Democratic Party is defined here as the Anti-Federalists, Democratic-Republicans, and Jackson Democrats prior to 1830 when the "Democratic Party" as such was established. The Republican Party is defined as the Federalists, National Republicans, and Whigs prior to the establishment of the "Republican Party" in the 1850s. See Appendix A for an explanation of the historical antecedents of the current Democratic and Republican parties. States reporting only partial voting returns for governor's races are not included in the calculations for the years in which this occurred. —indicates that the state had no data, either because the state had no gubernatorial election or no vote data were found.

[1]Election held in odd-numbered year.

Sources: State vote tables for governor in Chapter 7.

Table 8-140 Governor Competition Measures, by State, by Two-Year Election Cycle, 1998–1999 (Percentages)

State	1998–1999		
	Democratic % of Two-Party Vote	Margin of Victory	Party Competition Index
Alabama	57.8	15.6	84.4
Alaska	74.2	48.4	51.6
Arizona	36.8	26.4	73.6
Arkansas	39.3	21.4	78.6
California	60.2	20.4	79.6
Colorado	49.7	0.6	99.4
Connecticut	36.0	28.0	72.0
Delaware	—	—	—
Florida	44.7	10.6	89.4
Georgia	54.4	8.8	91.2
Hawaii	50.7	1.4	98.6
Idaho	30.0	40.0	60.0
Illinois	48.2	3.6	96.4
Indiana	—	—	—
Iowa	52.9	5.8	94.2
Kansas	23.6	52.8	47.2
Kentucky	61.8[1]	23.6[1]	76.4[1]
Louisiana	32.2[1]	35.6[1]	64.4[1]
Maine	38.8	22.4	77.6
Maryland	55.2	10.4	89.6
Massachusetts	48.3	3.4	96.6
Michigan	37.8	24.4	75.6
Minnesota	45.0	10.0	90.0
Mississippi	50.6[1]	1.2[1]	98.8[1]
Missouri	—	—	—
Montana	—	—	—
Nebraska	46.0	8.0	92.0
Nevada	44.9	10.2	89.8
New Hampshire	68.2	36.4	63.6
New Jersey	—	—	—
New Mexico	45.5	9.0	91.0
New York	37.9	24.2	75.8
North Carolina	—	—	—
North Dakota	—	—	—
Ohio	47.2	5.6	94.4
Oklahoma	41.4	17.2	82.8
Oregon	68.2	36.4	63.6
Pennsylvania	35.1	29.8	70.2
Rhode Island	45.3	9.4	90.6
South Carolina	54.1	8.2	91.8
South Dakota	33.9	32.2	67.8
Tennessee	30.0	40.0	60.0
Texas	31.4	37.2	62.8
Utah	—	—	—
Vermont	57.5	15.0	85.0
Virginia	—	—	—
Washington	—	—	—
West Virginia	—	—	—
Wisconsin	39.3	21.4	78.6
Wyoming	42.1	15.8	84.2

Notes: The first entries are the Democratic percent of two-party vote values for each state for the gubernatorial race. The second entries are the margin of victory values for each state for the gubernatorial race, where margin of victory is defined as the absolute difference between the Democratic percent and the Republican percent of the two-party vote for governor. The third entries are the party competition index values for each state for the gubernatorial race, where the competition index devised by Paul David (1972) is defined as (100 − the margin of victory) or, alternatively, as (100 − the absolute difference between the Democratic and Republican percent of two-party vote for governor). The values for Democratic and Republican percent of two-party vote for governor are taken from the state vote tables in Chapter 7. Zero (0) percent on David's index represents a complete absence of two-party competition for that election year, whereas a score of 100 percent indicates perfect competition between the two major parties. A state can only receive a party competition score of 0 if it has a 100–0 vote split in the governor's race. Conversely, a state can only receive a score of 100 if it has a 50–50 vote split in the governor's race. For example, if New Hampshire in 1788 reported a 54.7 percent Democratic vote for governor of its two-party vote, then its Republican vote for governor would be 45.3 percent. The absolute difference between the two figures is the margin of victory, or 9.4 percent; 100 percent − 9.4 percent would equal 90.6 percent on David's party competition scale, indicating a very competitive contest for governor in New Hampshire in 1788. The two-party vote percent values used to derive the margin of victory and party competition figures are initially found in the state vote tables in Chapter 7. The author's alternative party coding in these tables is used whenever it occurs instead of the conventional party coding of voting data. The Democratic Party is defined here as the Anti-Federalists, Democratic-Republicans, and Jackson Democrats prior to 1830 when the "Democratic Party" as such was established. The Republican Party is defined as the Federalists, National Republicans, and Whigs prior to the establishment of the "Republican Party" in the 1850s. See Appendix A for an explanation of the historical antecedents of the current Democratic and Republican parties. States reporting only partial voting returns for governor's races are not included in the calculations for the years in which this occurred. —indicates that the state had no data, either because the state had no gubernatorial election or no vote data were found.

[1] Election held in odd-numbered year.

Sources: State vote tables for governor in Chapter 7.

Appendix A
Major-Party Labels

This book employs two different systems for coding the major-party labels of candidates found on state ballots. The first system is called "conventional coding" and only allows candidates to be coded as Democrats or Republicans if they use the labels "Democrat" or "Republican" on the state ballot in isolation of any other labels, designations, or party names. If candidates use any other label, designation, or party name in addition to Democrat or Republican, they are coded as "Other" rather than as Democrats or Republicans. For example, if Joe Smith is running for governor on the "Democrat" label alone, he is coded as a Democrat. If, instead, he is running on the label "Benton Democrat," "Democrat-Greenback," or "Independent Democrat," he is then coded as "Other."

The second coding system used in the book is the author's "alternative" system for coding the major-party labels of candidates found on state ballots. Under this system, if candidates use the label "Democrat" or "Republican" on a state ballot in combination with other labels, designations, or party names, they are coded as Democrats or Republicans rather than as Other. Tables 1-3 and 5-1 in the text explain this alternative coding system in detail. For example, if Joe Smith is running on the label "Benton Democrat," he is coded in the alternative system as a Democrat. Conventional coding would code him as Other. (Of course, if candidates are running solely on the "Democrat" or "Republican" label, they are coded as Democrats or Republicans in the same manner as under conventional coding.) The author believes this alternative party coding system more accurately depicts the partisan and competitive nature of a political contest than the conventional coding system since it considers a person to be a candidate of a major party rather than "Other" if that candidate uses a major-party label on the state ballot in conjunction with other designations or labels.

The current Democratic and Republican parties were established formally in 1830 and 1854, respectively. Prior to that time, the two major parties used different party names. Historians generally consider the historical forerunners of the Democratic Party to be the Anti-Federalists, Democratic-Republicans, and Jackson Democrats. They generally consider the historical precursors of the Republican Party to be the Federalists, National Republicans, and Whigs. The conventional and alternative coding systems treat these party names in exactly the same way in the coding procedure as they do the labels "Democrat" and "Republican" discussed above. For example, if a candidate is running solely on the "Anti-Federalist," " Democratic-Republican," or "Jackson Democrat" label, he is coded as a Democrat under conventional coding. If he instead is running as a "Clinton Democratic-Republican," he is coded as Other under conventional coding and as a Democrat under the author's alternative coding scheme.

Even though these two coding systems seem easy to use, three complications emerge that require additional decisions to be made before they can be employed. The first complication is that political parties were not formally established before 1794. Prior to that time, candidates did not use party labels on ballots but were generally known in political circles to have "tendencies," such as Jim Brown having an "anti-federalist tendency" and Jack Jones having a "federalist tendency." Following Dubin's logic (1998, p. xxv), the author has coded these "tendencies" prior to 1794 as Democrat and Republican, respectively, if sufficient evidence exists in the historical record to indicate which tendency a particular candidate had. If no such evidence exists, the candidate would be coded Other.

The second complication is more important and also more pervasive. History prior to 1830 for the Democrats and prior to 1854 for the Republicans records the fact that the two major parties used a variety of labels or designations besides the major-party name to refer to the major party alone and no others, a practice that was less frequent after these dates for the two major parties. Usually these additional designations or names referred to the founders of the early parties (Thomas Jefferson for the Democratic-Republican Party, Andrew Jackson for the Democratic Party, John Quincy Adams for the National Republican Party, and so on), paying homage to these party founders by including their names in the party label on the ballot. For example, Democrats in the early days might call themselves "Jefferson Democratic-Republicans," "Jefferson Democrats," "Jefferson Republicans," or simply "Jefferson." While a term like "Jefferson Republican" might seem confusing since it is coded here as a Democrat, it actually refers to the Democratic-Republican Party that Jefferson founded. (To complicate matters further, Jefferson often referred to his "Democratic-Republican" Party as simply "Republican.") Some Jeffersonians even called themselves

"Old Republicans." Followers of Andrew Jackson often called themselves "Jackson Democrats," "Jackson Republicans," or simply "Jackson." Followers of John Quincy Adams, who initially was a member of the Democratic-Republican Party before founding the National Republican Party, often called themselves "Adams Democratic-Republicans," "Adams Democrats," "Adams Republicans," or simply "Adams" or "Adams Administration" after he captured the presidency in the controversial election of 1824.

Indeed, the presidential election of 1824 is a history lesson that bears repeating here to better understand the various designations and labels that the followers of Andrew Jackson and John Quincy Adams used in the 1820s. This includes the political developments leading to the formation of the Democratic Party in 1830 and the National Republican Party by 1828, the latter a forerunner of the Whig Party of the 1830s and eventually the Republican Party in 1854. In 1824 only one party existed to contest elections at most levels of government: Jefferson's Democratic-Republican Party. The earlier Federalist Party had largely withered away, a consequence of its elitist proclivities and, hence, its failure to develop a grass-roots party organization. (The Anti-Federalists had already been replaced by Jefferson's party by the mid-1790s.) This period of one-partyism, mainly in the 1816–1824 period, was unique in American history. Except for this period, America has essentially had a two-party system contesting political offices. With only one party existing in 1824, all four candidates contesting the presidential election in that year ran under the "Democratic-Republican" label, including Andrew Jackson and John Quincy Adams who, even then, had fundamentally different political ideologies and philosophies on how to run the federal government. These ideological differences were compounded by personal animosity when Jackson, who received more popular votes than Adams and the other two candidates but not a sufficient number to win the electoral college, saw the House of Representatives reject his candidacy and instead select Adams as president—the only time in American history when the House of Representatives has been called upon, under the constitution, to select a president when no majority vote was obtained by any candidate in the electoral college.

This crucial presidential election led to the split of the Democratic-Republican Party into two factions that, in essence, revived the two-party system in America. The followers of John Quincy Adams initially represented the "Republican" wing of the Democratic-Republican Party and soon would establish a new party called the National Republican Party. Before this party was established, the followers of Adams would simply call themselves "Adams," "Administration" loyalists, "Adams Democratic-Republicans," "Adams Republicans," or even "Adams Democrats." The followers of Andrew Jackson would initially represent the "Democratic" faction of the Democratic-Republican Party and, by 1830, would form the Democrat Party. Prior to 1830 they would call themselves simply "Jackson," "Jackson Democratic-Republicans," "Jackson Democrats," or even "Jackson Republicans." In 1828 Jackson had his

revenge by defeating his nemesis, John Quincy Adams, who sought reelection to the presidency under the new National Republican party label. Jackson then defeated Henry Clay in the 1832 presidential contest. Henry Clay, also a National Republican, was a supporter of Adams and a former member of his cabinet who had engineered the "deal" in 1824 in the House of Representatives to make Adams president. With these two losses by the National Republican Party, the party became vulnerable and was replaced by the Whig Party in the early 1830s. The Whig Party, in turn, was replaced by the Republican Party in the 1850s, largely due to the Whigs' failure to adequately address the slavery question.

In essence, all these various labels would be considered major-party labels alone and would be coded as Democrat or Republican under the conventional coding system, since they refer only to the major parties themselves rather than to other parties, factions, or tendencies. In such cases, the author's alternative system of coding does not need to be used.

A third coding complication remains. Even after the establishment of the Democratic and Republican parties, some candidates used other labels or designations that actually referred to only the major parties. One example occurred around the time of the Civil War. During this period, politicians sometimes used the label "Union" to denote their intention to preserve the Union. These were Republicans simply using a different label on the ballot. (Note that the use of the label "Union" with other labels attached to it would not necessarily lead to the same conclusion, such as the use of the "Constitutional Union" label, which clearly represented a third-party movement.) Examples of the tendency to use other labels to refer to only the major parties also occurred after the Civil War. They involved the rare instances when a presidential candidate used other designations on the ballot in addition to the major-party name, prompting his followers contesting lower offices on the ballot to often follow suit. In 1872 the Democratic Party candidate, Horace Greeley, also used the "Liberal Republican" label on the ballot to denote unity with a faction that had split from the Republican Party. He was defeated by the incumbent Republican candidate, Ulysses S. Grant, in his bid for the White House. In 1896 William Jennings Bryan, the Democratic Party candidate, also used the label "People's" or "Populists" with the major-party name on the ballot to denote alliance with the Populist political movement that he, himself, had been associated with prior to 1896. Followers of Bryan contesting lower offices on the ballot often followed suit by using such labels as "Democratic-Populists," "Democratic-People's," or even "Bryan Democrats," a trend that continued until 1900 when Bryan was again the Democratic Party's nominee for president. In both the Greeley and Bryan cases, candidates using these designations would be coded Democrat under conventional coding, since they were following the definition of the party label established by the leader of their party who was contesting the presidency. In these situations, the alternative coding system is not needed.

A last variant of this tendency occurs when the official Democrat or Republican Party in a particular state uses the major-party label with other designations rather than simply using the major-party name alone. Such cases are extremely rare, although Minnesota, for example, engages in this practice. In 1944 the Farmers Labor Party merged with the official Democratic Party, and since then the official Democratic Party in Minnesota has been called the "Democratic Farmers Labor Party." In 1976 the official Republican Party in Minnesota started calling itself the "Independent Republican Party" and uses this term to the present day. Conventional coding is used in these highly unique cases to designate these parties as Democrat and Republican, respectively. Alternative coding is not needed.

Table A-1 lists all the party labels that are considered major-party labels for coding candidates' party affiliations and, hence, their vote for the presidential, House, Senate, and gubernatorial races in this book. These labels cover the entire time period of American elections (1788–1999). The explanation for why only these labels are considered to be major-party labels is given in this appendix and in relevant sections in Chapters 4–7 of this book. If any of the labels listed in Table A-1 are used by candidates on the ballot, they are coded as major-party labels: either Democrat or Republican under the conventional coding system. Table A-1 lists whether these labels are considered a Democratic or Republican major-party label. The party labels listed in Table A-1 must be the only designation beside candidates' names on the ballot. If other labels, designations, or party names are used by candidates *in addition* to the party labels listed in Table A-1, then conventional coding designates these candidates as Other instead of as major-party candidates. However, the author's alternative coding system categorizes these same candidates as major-party candidates with whichever party, Democrat or Republican, is denoted for these major-party labels in Table A-1. For example, if candidate X was listed as a "Federalist," "National Republican," "Whig," "Republican," or even as "Adams," "Adams Republican," or "Union" (during the Civil War period) on the ballot, conventional coding designates this candidate as Republican, and the alternative coding system is not needed. However, if candidate X was listed as a "Secessionist Whig" or a "Republican-Greenback," then that candidate is coded as Other under the conventional coding system and as a Republican under the author's alternative coding system.

What seems to be a substantial list of major-party labels and a complicated set of decision rules in coding actually follows a simple logic. People know that the historical antecedents of the Democratic Party are the Anti-Federalists, Democratic-Republicans, and Jackson Democrats. Other party labels referring solely to the historical antecedents of the Democratic Party largely used the names of the founders of the party—Jefferson and Jackson—either by themselves or in association with the major-party label. People also know that the historical antecedents of the Republican Party are the Federalists, National Republicans, and Whigs. Other party labels referring solely to the historical antecedents of the Republican Party largely used the name of one of the founders of an earlier version of this party—John Quincy Adams—either by itself or in association with the major-party label. Significantly, the founders of these parties occupied the most powerful and prestigious office in the land: the presidency. Most of the remaining labels used to refer to the major parties alone were also associated with the presidency—specifically with the presidential election campaign. In these cases, the major-party candidate for president leading the party ticket opted to use other labels alongside the major-party label on the ballot, prompting other members of his party running for office to follow suit. The few remaining examples in American history of other labels or designations used to refer solely to the major parties cannot be explained by the power and prestige of occupying the presidency or the publicity and impact of the presidential campaign preceding it. In these rare cases, political events (for example, the impending Civil War) or political idiosyncrasies in a given state (for example, Minnesota) seem to provide a different explanation.

The alert reader will note that the discussion of the author's alternative coding system in Chapter 1 (especially see Table 1-3) indicates that candidates running on fusion tickets (for example, Democrat-Greenback) will always be coded Other under conventional coding and with the major party involved in the fusion ticket under alternative coding (for example, Democrat for the Democrat-Greenback fusion example here), and yet this rule in coding fusion tickets is violated in the two instances discussed above when Greeley and Bryan were campaigning for president. Even though these were unique situations in American electoral history, this alone does not justify treating them as exceptions to a more general rule of coding. What justifies treating them as exceptions to the general rule on coding fusion candidates is that they were their party's leader at the time, contesting the most powerful office in America. They defined the Democratic ticket at the national level as a fusion ticket, sending a clear signal to their followers to also run as candidates for political office on this fusion label. Hence, these two presidential candidates and their followers who used the fusion label are coded under their major party (Democrat) in conventional coding and no alternative coding is required. The only other exception in Table A-1 to the general rules of coding set forth in this book is the case of John Quincy Adams in the presidential election of 1824. Although technically listed as a Democratic-Republican candidate, most historians have regarded his candidacy, and his ensuing efforts to establish the National Republican Party, as defining him as a "Republican" to his supporters, even as early as 1824. The author has followed this logic, coding him as Republican in 1824 under the conventional coding system.

Table A-1 Major-Party Labels Used on State Ballots, 1788–1999

Major Party Label Used on Ballot	Applicable Time Period	Democratic/Republican Equivalency
Adams	Mainly 1820s	Republican
Adams Administration	Mainly 1820s	Republican
Adams Democrat	Mainly 1820s	Republican
Adams Democratic-Republican	Mainly 1820s	Republican
Adams Republican	Mainly 1820s	Republican
Administration	Mainly 1820s	Republican
Anti-Federalist	Mainly 1780s and 1790s	Democrat
Bryan Democrat	1896–1900	Democrat
Cass Democrat	1848 only	Democrat
Democrat	1788–present	Democrat
Democrat-Liberal Republican	1872 only	Democrat
Democrat-(National) Silver	1896–1900	Democrat
Democrat-People's	1896–1900	Democrat
Democrat-Populist	1896–1900	Democrat
Democrat-Populist-Silver	1896–1900	Democrat
Democratic Farmer Labor	Minnesota, 1944–present	Democrat
Democratic Party of the U.S.	Michigan, 1896–1898	Democrat
Democratic-Republican	Mainly pre-1830	Democrat
Douglas Democrat	1860 only	Democrat
Federalist	Mainly pre-1830	Republican
Independent Republican	Minnesota, 1976–present	Republican
Jackson	Mainly 1820s to 1840s	Democrat
Jackson Democrat	Mainly 1820s to 1840s	Democrat
Jackson Democratic-Republican	Mainly 1820s to 1830s	Democrat
Jackson Republican	Mainly 1820s to 1840s	Democrat
Jefferson	Mainly pre-1830	Democrat
Jefferson Democrat	Mainly pre-1830	Democrat
Jefferson Democratic-Republican	Mainly pre-1830	Democrat
Jefferson Republican	Mainly pre-1830	Democrat
Liberal Republican	1872 only	Democrat
Liberal Republican-Democrat	1872 only	Democrat
National Republican	Mainly 1820s and 1830s	Republican
Old Republican	Mainly pre-1830	Republican
Republican	1854–present	Republican
Union	circa Civil War period	Republican
Union Republican	circa Civil War period	Republican
Whig	Mainly 1830s to 1850s	Republican

Notes: Table A-1 includes all the party labels used on state ballots in the 1788–1999 period considered by the author to be referring to the two major political parties in America at any particular time during its history. Candidates using one of these labels, with no further designations or names, are considered to be major-party candidates under the conventional coding system discussed in the text. Major Party Label = actual party labels used by the two major parties on state ballots. Applicable Time Period = approximate time period a given party label was used on state ballots to refer to one of America's two major political parties. (If one of these labels was used by a candidate outside of the time period specified in Table A-1, this label usually was not referring to one of the two major political parties. Detailed research on a case-by-case basis was the only way to determine how to code candidates' use of these labels outside the time periods given for these labels in Table A-1.) Democratic/Republican Equivalency = assignment by the author of each party label in Table A-1 to the Democratic or Republican vote categories used throughout the data tables in this book, according to whether a given label represented a historical antecedent of the Democratic or Republican party, or represented a name change for either major party dictated by the presidential candidates of the party, the party's current occupant in the White House, or the proclamations of the official party organization.

Sources: See the sources listed in the state vote tables in Chapters 4, 5, 6, and 7 for the presidential, House, Senate, and gubernatorial races, respectively.

Appendix B
Additional House Election Data

Several states in America's electoral history used a combined system of district and at-large elections for selecting members to the U.S. House of Representatives. In the state vote tables in Chapter 5 (table series 5-17 through 5-122), the at-large vote results are presented at the state level for these states. In this appendix, district-level results are instead used to obtain state-level vote values for these states.

An example illustrates the difference between these two ways of calculating the House vote. In 1872 the state of Alabama used a combined system of district and at-large elections to select members to the House of Representatives. Aggregating the House voting results for the six districts in the state produces state totals of 80,152 Democratic votes, 78,747 Republican votes, and 7,024 Other votes, for a total of 165,923 votes cast. Computing percentage values from these raw vote totals gives us 48.3 percent Democratic of total vote, 47.5 percent Republican of total vote, and 4.2 percent Other of total vote for the House at the state level. The Democratic percent of major two-party vote is 50.4. At the same time, Alabama had at-large (statewide) elections for two additional House seats. Using the methodological rules discussed in Chapter 5 to determine the at-large vote result, the Democratic vote is 81,561, the Republican vote is 89,500, and the Other vote is 0, for a total of 171,061 votes cast (as shown in Table 5-91). The corresponding vote percentages are 54.1 percent Democratic of total vote, 45.9 percent Republican of total vote, and 0 percent Other of total vote (as shown in Table 5-38). The Democratic percent of major two-party vote is 54.1 percent.

The researcher must decide which set of figures is the best representation of Alabama's House vote at the state level: the district results aggregated to the state level or the at-large election results. While the total votes in the two instances vary little (165,923 versus 171,061), the partisan breakdowns of the vote vary considerably. For example, the Democratic percent of major two-party vote for the district vote aggregated to the state level is 50.4 percent, but the corresponding value is 54.1 percent when using at-large election results. As another example, the Other percent of total vote using district election data is 4.2 percent at the state level, while it is 0 percent using at-large election data. The difference between these two values is the direct result of the fact that no Other Party candidates contested the two at-large House seats in Alabama in 1872.

The author believes that at-large election races represent the "purest" expression of a state-level vote result for the House of Representatives, but other researchers believe that district-level competition must be the base for any determination of state-level voting results for the House. Certainly, the use of the latter set of voting results (as shown in Table B-1) for states having these combination systems for electing House members corresponds to the vote results shown in the state vote tables in Chapter 5 for the vast majority of the states who used only a district system for electing House members. In any event, the researcher is given both sets of vote results in this book and, hence, the flexibility of using either, just as the author provided, in another context, the flexibility for the researcher to choose between two different versions of coding the major-party vote for the political races in this volume (the conventional and alternative coding schemes).

Table B-1 State House Vote Based Only on District Results for States Having Combination Systems for Selecting Members to the House of Representatives (Combination Systems of District and At-Large Elections), 1788–1998

State	Year	Democratic Raw Vote	Republican Raw Vote	Other Raw Vote	Total Raw Vote	Democratic %	Republican %	Other %	Democratic % of Two-Party Vote
Alabama	1872	80,152	78,747	7,024	165,923	48.31	47.46	4.23	50.44
Alabama	*1872*	*80,152*	*85,771*	*0*	*165,923*	*48.31*	*51.69*	*0.00*	*48.31*
Alabama	1874	102,944	94,792	0	197,736	52.06	47.94	0.00	52.06
Alabama	1912	90,958	8,372	8,980	108,310	83.98	7.73	8.29	91.57
Alabama	1914	64,141	19,416	1,167	84,724	75.71	22.92	1.38	76.76
Arkansas	1872	37,831	40,072	0	77,903	48.56	51.44	0.00	48.56
Arkansas	1882	43,706	21,092	0	64,798	67.45	32.55	0.00	67.45
California	1882	87,874	71,953	3,471	163,298	53.81	44.06	2.13	54.98
Colorado	1902	41,440	86,194	56,762	184,396	22.47	46.74	30.78	32.47
Colorado	*1902*	*86,674*	*86,194*	*11,528*	*184,396*	*47.00*	*46.74*	*6.25*	*50.14*
Colorado	1904	108,576	124,041	8,100	240,717	45.11	51.53	3.36	46.68
Colorado	1906	77,916	102,418	16,597	196,931	39.57	52.01	8.43	43.21
Colorado	1908	126,457	122,150	8,127	256,734	49.26	47.58	3.17	50.87
Colorado	1910	100,659	94,972	27,568	223,199	45.10	42.55	12.35	51.45
Colorado	1912	117,775	65,877	77,489	261,141	45.10	25.23	29.67	64.13
Connecticut	1902	67,746	86,827	4,787	159,360	42.51	54.48	3.00	43.83
Connecticut	1904	73,375	110,558	6,692	190,625	38.49	58.00	3.51	39.89
Connecticut	1906	66,598	89,538	4,718	160,854	41.40	55.66	2.93	42.65
Connecticut	1908	71,040	110,690	7,825	189,555	37.48	58.39	4.13	39.09
Connecticut	1910	76,193	77,337	12,659	166,189	45.85	46.54	7.62	49.63
Connecticut	1932	282,021	285,208	22,696	589,925	47.81	48.35	3.85	49.72
Connecticut	*1932*	*282,091*	*290,277*	*17,627*	*589,995*	*47.81*	*49.20*	*2.99*	*49.28*
Connecticut	1934	188,139	249,696	110,203	548,038	34.33	45.56	20.11	42.97
Connecticut	*1934*	*262,923*	*249,696*	*35,419*	*548,038*	*47.98*	*45.56*	*6.46*	*51.29*
Connecticut	1936	371,202	280,615	31,442	683,259	54.33	41.07	4.60	56.95
Connecticut	1938	249,882	101,312	272,695	623,889	40.05	16.24	43.71	71.15
Connecticut	*1938*	*249,882*	*274,043*	*99,964*	*623,889*	*40.05*	*43.92*	*16.02*	*47.69*
Connecticut	1940	320,123	198,113	262,363	780,601	41.01	25.38	33.61	61.77
Connecticut	*1940*	*411,315*	*364,171*	*5,115*	*780,601*	*52.69*	*46.65*	*0.66*	*53.04*
Connecticut	1942	260,382	282,665	17,088	560,135	46.49	50.46	3.05	47.95
Connecticut	1944	420,505	402,163	2,448	825,116	50.96	48.74	0.30	51.11
Connecticut	1946	281,709	374,545	18,245	674,499	41.77	55.53	2.70	42.93
Connecticut	1948	432,508	432,051	9,829	874,388	49.46	49.41	1.12	50.03
Connecticut	1950	435,606	425,156	12,959	873,721	49.86	48.66	1.48	50.61
Connecticut	1952	504,257	586,922	1,618	1,092,797	46.14	53.71	0.15	46.21
Connecticut	1954	457,654	472,677	5,413	935,744	48.91	50.51	0.58	49.19
Connecticut	1956	437,424	673,507	2,746	1,113,677	39.28	60.48	0.25	39.37
Connecticut	*1956*	*437,424*	*674,799*	*1,454*	*1,113,677*	*39.28*	*60.59*	*0.13*	*39.33*
Connecticut	1958	519,185	449,130	0	968,315	53.62	46.38	0.00	53.62
Connecticut	1960	649,877	566,246	2,350	1,218,473	53.34	46.47	0.19	53.44
Connecticut	1962	556,907	473,659	1,674	1,032,240	53.95	45.89	0.16	54.04
Connecticut	*1962*	*556,907*	*475,333*	*0*	*1,032,240*	*53.95*	*46.05*	*0.00*	*53.95*
Florida	1912	36,092	2,465	5,757	44,314	81.45	5.56	12.99	93.61
Florida	1932	197,903	19,010	0	216,913	91.24	8.76	0.00	91.24
Florida	1934	131,817	0	0	131,817	100.00	0.00	0.00	100.00
Florida	1942	94,459	12,631	0	107,090	88.21	11.79	0.00	88.21
Georgia	1882	69,168	14,455	24,800	108,423	63.79	13.33	22.87	82.71
Georgia	*1882*	*91,829*	*14,455*	*2,139*	*108,423*	*84.70*	*13.33*	*1.97*	*86.40*
Illinois	1862	136,981	109,955	744	247,680	55.31	44.39	0.30	55.47
Illinois	1864	158,373	189,730	0	348,103	45.50	54.50	0.00	45.50
Illinois	1866	147,605	201,859	133	349,597	42.22	57.74	0.04	42.24
Illinois	1868	200,679	247,663	212	448,554	44.74	55.21	0.05	44.76
Illinois	1870	148,611	156,571	8,718	313,900	47.34	49.88	2.78	48.70
Illinois	1912	428,511	362,761	303,681	1,094,953	39.14	33.13	27.73	54.15
Illinois	1914	391,454	417,978	159,295	968,727	40.41	43.15	16.44	48.36
Illinois	1916	552,225	696,318	54,067	1,302,610	42.39	53.46	4.15	44.23
Illinois	1918	339,376	497,857	35,125	872,358	38.90	57.07	4.03	40.54
Illinois	1920	585,521	1,349,867	99,828	2,035,216	28.77	66.33	4.91	30.25
Illinois	1922	744,545	910,335	54,955	1,709,835	43.54	53.24	3.21	44.99
Illinois	1924	747,449	1,467,805	46,194	2,261,448	33.05	64.91	2.04	33.74
Illinois	*1924*	*747,449*	*1,481,394*	*32,605*	*2,261,448*	*33.05*	*65.51*	*1.44*	*33.54*
Illinois	1926	699,292	969,787	1,800	1,670,879	41.85	58.04	0.11	41.90
Illinois	1928	1,212,916	1,603,978	6,465	2,823,359	42.96	56.81	0.23	43.06
Illinois	*1928*	*1,212,916*	*1,604,151*	*6,292*	*2,823,359*	*42.96*	*56.82*	*0.22*	*43.06*
Illinois	1930	1,020,319	1,002,947	5,787	2,029,053	50.29	49.43	0.29	50.43
Illinois	1932	1,728,587	1,369,666	57,150	3,155,403	54.78	43.41	1.81	55.79
Illinois	1934	1,538,326	1,208,456	1,619	2,748,401	55.97	43.97	0.06	56.00
Illinois	1936	2,061,002	1,635,734	34,796	3,731,532	55.23	43.84	0.93	55.75
Illinois	1938	1,575,621	1,526,607	2,201	3,104,429	50.75	49.18	0.07	50.79
Illinois	1940	1,955,148	2,053,262	442	4,008,852	48.77	51.22	0.01	48.78
Illinois	1942	1,314,996	1,567,846	0	2,882,842	45.61	54.39	0.00	45.61
Illinois	1944	1,933,888	1,939,543	1,414	3,874,845	49.91	50.05	0.04	49.93
Illinois	1946	1,500,635	1,946,276	0	3,446,911	43.54	56.46	0.00	43.54
Indiana	1872	187,804	188,829	0	376,633	49.86	50.14	0.00	49.86
Kansas	1882	38,144	100,943	32,882	171,969	22.18	58.70	19.12	27.42

(Table continues)

Table B-1 (Continued)

State	Year	Democratic Raw Vote	Republican Raw Vote	Other Raw Vote	Total Raw Vote	Democratic %	Republican %	Other %	Democratic % of Two-Party Vote
Kansas	1892	2,030	158,004	162,019	322,053	0.63	49.06	50.31	1.27
Kansas	*1892*	*105,260*	*158,004*	*59,789*	*322,053*	*32.68*	*49.06*	*18.25*	*39.98*
Kansas	1894	15,743	150,013	118,736	284,492	5.53	52.73	41.74	9.50
Kansas	*1894*	*57,046*	*150,013*	*77,433*	*284,492*	*20.05*	*52.73*	*27.22*	*27.55*
Kansas	1896	166,524	159,699	1,547	327,770	50.81	48.72	0.47	51.05
Kansas	*1896*	*168,071*	*159,699*	*0*	*327,770*	*51.28*	*48.72*	*0.00*	*51.28*
Kansas	1898	118,036	148,275	14,732	281,043	42.00	52.76	5.24	44.32
Kansas	1900	147,569	180,989	15,334	343,892	42.91	52.63	4.46	44.91
Kansas	1902	118,137	158,465	3,917	280,519	42.11	56.49	1.40	42.71
Kansas	1904	68,892	185,484	55,691	310,067	22.22	59.82	17.96	27.08
Kansas	*1904*	*112,851*	*185,484*	*11,732*	*310,067*	*36.40*	*59.82*	*3.78*	*37.83*
Maryland	1962	403,239	315,533	0	718,772	56.10	43.90	0.00	56.10
Maryland	1964	636,445	375,746	0	1,012,191	62.88	37.12	0.00	62.88
Massachusetts	1792	0	17,312	34,629	51,941	0.00	33.33	66.67	0.00
Michigan	1912	164,115	190,673	179,001	533,789	30.75	35.72	33.53	46.26
Michigan	1962	1,377,814	1,297,259	0	2,675,073	51.51	48.49	0.00	51.51
Minnesota	1912	76,001	178,943	55,579	310,523	24.48	57.63	17.90	29.81
Mississippi	1853	32,333	21,920	0	54,253	59.60	40.40	0.00	59.60
New York	1872	391,589	432,869	8,099	832,557	47.03	51.99	0.97	47.50
New York	*1872*	*399,688*	*432,869*	*0*	*832,557*	*48.01*	*51.99*	*0.00*	*48.01*
New York	1882	454,053	371,819	40,682	866,554	52.40	42.91	4.69	54.98
New York	*1882*	*469,787*	*371,819*	*24,948*	*866,554*	*54.21*	*42.91*	*2.88*	*55.82*
New York	1932	2,387,621	1,323,896	712,704	4,424,221	53.97	29.92	16.11	64.33
New York	*1932*	*2,387,621*	*1,785,365*	*251,235*	*4,424,221*	*53.97*	*40.35*	*5.68*	*57.22*
New York	1934	1,592,456	735,234	1,321,920	3,649,610	43.63	20.15	36.22	68.41
New York	*1934*	*1,955,981*	*1,484,586*	*209,043*	*3,649,610*	*53.59*	*40.68*	*5.73*	*56.85*
New York	1936	2,541,979	2,098,152	668,611	5,308,742	47.88	39.52	12.59	54.78
New York	1936	2,945,877	2,115,364	247,501	5,308,742	55.49	39.85	4.66	58.20
New York	1938	870,919	1,618,747	1,997,593	4,487,259	19.41	36.07	44.52	34.98
New York	*1938*	*2,095,394*	*2,116,841*	*275,024*	*4,487,259*	*46.70*	*47.17*	*6.13*	*49.75*
New York	1940	2,206,058	2,780,187	1,091,582	6,077,827	36.30	45.74	17.96	44.24
New York	*1940*	*2,926,449*	*2,805,441*	*345,937*	*6,077,827*	*48.15*	*46.16*	*5.69*	*51.06*
New York	1942	527,008	1,810,423	1,537,839	3,875,270	13.60	46.72	39.68	22.55
New York	*1942*	*1,835,625*	*1,967,286*	*72,359*	*3,875,270*	*47.37*	*50.77*	*1.87*	*48.27*
Ohio	1912	458,461	302,056	210,263	970,780	47.23	31.11	21.66	60.28
Ohio	1932	1,293,936	1,168,955	16,498	2,479,389	52.19	47.15	0.67	52.54
Ohio	1934	1,094,685	974,370	16,842	2,085,897	52.48	46.71	0.81	52.91
Ohio	1936	1,560,270	1,201,623	74,937	2,836,830	55.00	42.36	2.64	56.49
Ohio	1938	1,105,305	1,203,539	4,614	2,313,458	47.78	52.02	0.20	47.87
Ohio	1940	1,559,859	1,515,928	2,527	3,078,314	50.67	49.25	0.08	50.71
Ohio	1942	766,499	960,649	8,033	1,735,181	44.17	55.36	0.46	44.38
Ohio	1944	1,392,534	1,560,467	1,360	2,954,361	47.13	52.82	0.05	47.16
Ohio	1946	943,878	1,262,164	10,705	2,216,747	42.58	56.94	0.48	42.79
Ohio	1948	1,469,758	1,337,499	1,273	2,808,530	52.33	47.62	0.05	52.36
Ohio	1950	1,257,468	1,450,968	58,270	2,766,706	45.45	52.44	2.11	46.43
Ohio	1962	1,318,741	1,676,274	5,595	3,000,610	43.95	55.86	0.19	44.03
Ohio	1964	1,886,763	1,845,598	0	3,732,361	50.55	49.45	0.00	50.55
Oklahoma	1912	122,974	87,676	41,402	252,052	48.79	34.78	16.43	58.38
Oklahoma	1932	462,132	186,599	5,049	653,780	70.69	28.54	0.77	71.24
Oklahoma	1934	370,602	169,603	13,274	553,479	66.96	30.64	2.40	68.60
Oklahoma	1936	474,260	218,400	1,529	694,189	68.32	31.46	0.22	68.47
Oklahoma	1938	320,759	146,070	1,428	468,257	68.50	31.19	0.30	68.71
Oklahoma	1940	508,197	255,201	2,643	766,041	66.34	33.31	0.35	66.57
Pennsylvania	1882	334,777	313,069	83,630	731,476	45.77	42.80	11.43	51.68
Pennsylvania	*1882*	*365,156*	*345,652*	*20,668*	*731,476*	*49.92*	*47.25*	*2.83*	*51.37*
Pennsylvania	1884	358,581	470,622	43,500	872,703	41.09	53.93	4.98	43.24
Pennsylvania	*1884*	*389,950*	*473,324*	*9,429*	*872,703*	*44.68*	*54.24*	*1.08*	*45.17*
Pennsylvania	1886	363,393	379,991	41,772	785,156	46.28	48.40	5.32	48.88
Pennsylvania	*1886*	*363,393*	*384,957*	*36,806*	*785,156*	*46.28*	*49.03*	*4.69*	*48.56*
Pennsylvania	1892	445,423	502,751	39,349	987,523	45.11	50.91	3.98	46.98
Pennsylvania	*1892*	*460,939*	*503,680*	*22,904*	*987,523*	*46.68*	*51.00*	*2.32*	*47.78*
Pennsylvania	1894	329,497	548,311	60,806	938,614	35.10	58.42	6.48	37.54
Pennsylvania	*1894*	*329,497*	*574,982*	*34,135*	*938,614*	*35.10*	*61.26*	*3.64*	*36.43*
Pennsylvania	1896	388,355	643,581	98,663	1,130,599	34.35	56.92	8.73	37.63
Pennsylvania	*1896*	*407,803*	*671,966*	*50,830*	*1,130,599*	*36.07*	*59.43*	*4.50*	*37.77*
Pennsylvania	1898	333,005	499,459	105,791	938,255	35.49	53.23	11.28	40.00
Pennsylvania	*1898*	*357,840*	*499,459*	*80,956*	*938,255*	*38.14*	*53.23*	*8.63*	*41.74*
Pennsylvania	1900	377,183	677,333	64,114	1,118,630	33.72	60.55	5.73	35.77
Pennsylvania	*1900*	*400,928*	*677,333*	*40,369*	*1,118,630*	*35.84*	*60.55*	*3.61*	*37.18*
Pennsylvania	1912	191,486	41,609	886,074	1,119,169	17.11	3.72	79.17	82.15
Pennsylvania	*1912*	*398,587*	*465,544*	*255,038*	*1,119,169*	*35.61*	*41.60*	*22.79*	*46.13*
Pennsylvania	1914	188,365	295,127	614,728	1,098,220	17.15	26.87	55.97	38.96
Pennsylvania	*1914*	*343,234*	*559,924*	*195,062*	*1,098,220*	*31.25*	*50.98*	*17.76*	*38.00*
Pennsylvania	1916	306,467	198,902	735,356	1,240,725	24.70	16.03	59.27	60.64
Pennsylvania	*1916*	*472,589*	*696,034*	*72,102*	*1,240,725*	*38.09*	*56.10*	*5.81*	*40.44*

Table B-1 (Continued)

State	Year	Democratic Raw Vote	Republican Raw Vote	Other Raw Vote	Total Raw Vote	Democratic %	Republican %	Other %	Democratic % of Two-Party Vote
Pennsylvania	1918	131,906	156,976	592,839	881,721	14.96	17.80	67.24	45.66
Pennsylvania	*1918*	*315,090*	*535,043*	*31,588*	*881,721*	*35.74*	*60.68*	*3.58*	*37.06*
Pennsylvania	1920	377,231	438,580	985,400	1,801,211	20.94	24.35	54.71	46.24
Pennsylvania	*1920*	*580,237*	*1,092,054*	*128,920*	*1,801,211*	*32.21*	*60.63*	*7.16*	*34.70*
Pennsylvania	1942	1,132,418	1,351,254	25,106	2,508,778	45.14	53.86	1.00	45.59
Pennsylvania	*1942*	*1,152,758*	*1,351,254*	*4,766*	*2,508,778*	*45.95*	*53.86*	*0.19*	*46.04*
South Carolina	1868	45,186	61,885	356	107,427	42.06	57.61	0.33	42.20
South Carolina	1870	39,064	74,317	17,032	130,413	29.95	56.99	13.06	34.45
South Carolina	*1870*	*39,064*	*90,017*	*1,332*	*130,413*	*29.95*	*69.02*	*1.02*	*30.26*
South Carolina	1872	20,522	76,043	577	97,142	21.13	78.28	0.59	21.25
Tennessee	1872	87,729	81,767	9,150	178,646	49.11	45.77	5.12	51.76
Texas	1872	70,080	51,259	0	121,339	57.76	42.24	0.00	57.76
Texas	1912	242,146	5,842	9,634	257,622	93.99	2.27	3.74	97.64
Texas	1914	177,303	7,303	13,225	197,831	89.62	3.69	6.68	96.04
Texas	1916	303,871	40,760	17,472	362,103	83.92	11.26	4.83	88.17
Texas	1932	774,373	36,385	8	810,766	95.51	4.49	0.00	95.51
Texas	1952	1,697,195	22,108	0	1,719,303	98.71	1.29	0.00	98.71
Texas	1954	540,171	80,527	481	621,179	86.96	12.96	0.08	87.03
Texas	1956	1,465,069	238,760	3,619	1,707,448	85.80	13.98	0.21	85.99
Texas	1962	1,014,147	489,860	0	1,504,007	67.43	32.57	0.00	67.43
Texas	1964	1,797,298	819,890	0	2,617,188	68.67	31.33	0.00	68.67
Virginia	1869	0	85,018	132,040	217,058	0.00	39.17	60.83	0.00
Virginia	*1869*	*0*	*91,541*	*125,517*	*217,058*	*0.00*	*42.17*	*57.83*	*0.00*
Virginia	1870	4,591	78,025	93,374	175,990	2.61	44.33	53.06	5.56
Virginia	*1870*	*8,608*	*83,318*	*84,064*	*175,990*	*4.89*	*47.34*	*47.77*	*9.36*
Virginia	1882	93,587	4,397	101,126	199,110	47.00	2.21	50.79	95.51
Washington	1912	74,911	95,798	127,566	298,275	25.11	32.12	42.77	43.88
Washington	1952	440,938	574,194	1,347	1,016,479	43.38	56.49	0.13	43.44
Washington	1954	353,761	462,061	0	815,822	43.36	56.64	0.00	43.36
Washington	1956	477,617	584,276	0	1,061,893	44.98	55.02	0.00	44.98
West Virginia	1912	119,862	0	145,858	265,720	45.11	0.00	54.89	100.00
West Virginia	*1912*	*119,862*	*127,682*	*18,176*	*265,720*	*45.11*	*48.05*	*6.84*	*48.42*
West Virginia	1914	106,042	107,747	21,913	235,702	44.99	45.71	9.30	49.60

Notes: The only states listed in this table are those having combination systems of district and at-large elections to select members to the U.S. House of Representatives. Only the district House results are used to produce the state-level voting entries in this table. The at-large vote results for these states are given in the relevant tables in Chapter 5. The raw vote entries in the current table are obtained by aggregating district House votes to the state level for these states. The percentage vote entries in the current table are calculated from these raw vote entries. See the notes to Tables 5-21 and 5-74 for an explanation of what constitutes a "Democratic," "Republican," and "Other" vote under the conventional and alternative coding systems. Also see Tables 1-3 and 5-1 for a more detailed explanation of these coding systems. Bold italicized entries in the current table represent the alternative coding system. All other entries represent the conventional coding system.

Sources: See Table 5-4.

Bibliography

Abramson, Paul. "Generational Change and the Decline of Party Identification in America: 1952–1974." *American Political Science Review* 70 (1976): 469–478.

Allen, Howard, and Kay Allen. "Vote Fraud and Data Validity." In *Analyzing Electoral History,* edited by Jerome Clubb, William Flanigan, and Nancy Zingale, 153–193. Beverly Hills, Calif.: Sage Publications, 1981.

Austin, Erik, and Jerome Clubb. *Political Facts of the United States Since 1789.* New York: Columbia University Press, 1986.

Barber, James. *Presidential Character.* Englewood Cliffs, N.J.: Prentice-Hall, 1972.

Beard, Charles. *An Economic Interpretation of the Constitution of the United States.* New York: Macmillan, 1935. Originally published in 1913.

Becker, Carl. *The Declaration of Independence: A Study in the History of Political Ideas.* New York: Harcourt, Brace, 1922.

Brady, David. *Critical Elections and Congressional Policy Making.* Stanford, Calif.: Stanford University Press, 1988.

Burnham, Walter. *Presidential Ballots, 1836–1892.* Baltimore: Johns Hopkins University Press, 1955.

———. "The Changing Shape of the American Political Universe." *American Political Science Review* 59 (1965): 7–28.

———. "The End of Party Politics." *Transaction* 7 (1969): 12–22.

———. *Critical Elections and the Mainsprings of American Politics.* New York: W. W. Norton and Co., 1970.

———. "Election and Politics." In *Historical Statistics of the United States, Colonial Times to 1970,* 1067–1072. Washington, D.C.: U.S. Government Printing Office, 1975.

Byrd, Robert. *The Senate 1789–1989: Addresses on the History of the United States Senate.* Washington, D.C.: U.S. Government Printing Office, 1988.

Campbell, Angus. "Surge and Decline: A Study of Electoral Change." *Public Opinion Quarterly* 24 (1960): 397–418.

Campbell, Angus, Philip Converse, Warren Miller, and Donald Stokes. *The American Voter.* New York: John Wiley and Sons, 1960.

Campbell, James. *The Presidential Pulse of Congressional Elections.* Lexington: University Press of Kentucky, 1993.

Clerk of the House of Representatives. *History of the House of Representatives.* Washington, D.C.: U.S. Government Printing Office, 1998.

———. *Historical Election Returns.* Washington, D.C.: U.S. Government Printing Office, various dates.

———. *Report of the Clerk of the House of Representatives.* Washington, D.C.: U.S. Government Printing Office, various dates.

Codes of the 50 States. Published by state governments or by private publishers under state contract, various dates.

Congressional Quarterly. *Congressional Quarterly's Guide to U.S. Elections.* 3d ed. Washington, D.C.: CQ Press, 1994; 4th ed., 2001.

———. *CQ Weekly,* formerly *Congressional Quarterly Weekly Report.* Washington, D.C. Various dates.

Constitutions of the 50 States. Published by state governments or by private publishers under state contract, various dates.

Converse, Philip. "Change in the American Electorate." In *The Human Meaning of Social Change,* edited by Angus Campbell and Philip Converse, 263–337. New York: Russell Sage Foundation, 1972.

Converse, Philip, Warren Miller, Jerrold Rusk, and Arthur Wolfe. "Continuity and Change in American Politics: Parties and Issues in the 1968 Election." *American Political Science Review* 63 (1969): 1083–1105.

Council of State Governments. *Book of the States.* Lexington, Ky.: Author, various dates.

Cox, Edward. *State and National Voting in Federal Elections, 1910–1970.* Hamden, Conn.: Archon Publishing, 1972.

Dahl, Robert. *A Preface to Democratic Theory.* Chicago: University of Chicago Press, 1956.

———. *Polyarchy: Participation and Opposition.* New Haven, Conn.: Yale University Press, 1971.

David, Paul. *Party Strength in the United States, 1872–1970.* Charlottesville: University Press of Virginia, 1972.

Den Boer, Gordon, ed. *The Documentary History of the First Federal Elections, 1788–1790.* Madison: University of Wisconsin Press, 1986.

Dinkin, Robert. *Voting in Provincial America.* Westport, Conn.: Greenwood Press, 1978.

———. *Voting in Revolutionary America.* Westport, Conn.: Greenwood Press, 1982.

Downs, Anthony. *An Economic Theory of Democracy.* New York: Harper and Row, 1957.

Dubin, Michael. *United States Congressional Elections, 1788–1997.* Jefferson, N.C.: McFarland and Co., 1998.

———. Communications to the author, various dates.

———. Election archive of historical voting returns, various dates.

Evans, Eldon. *A History of the Australian Ballot System in the United States.* Chicago: University of Chicago Press, 1917.

Evans, Rowland, and Robert Novak. *Lyndon Johnson: The Exercise of Power, A Political Biography.* New York: New American Library, 1966.

Ewing, Cortez. *Congressional Elections, 1896–1944.* Norman: University of Oklahoma Press, 1947.

Fredman, L. *The Australian Ballot: The Story of an American Reform.* East Lansing: Michigan State University Press, 1968.

Gimpel, James. *National Elections and the Autonomy of American State Party Systems.* Pittsburgh: University of Pittsburgh Press, 1993.

Hoadley, John. *Origins of American Political Parties, 1789–1803.* Lexington: University of Kentucky Press, 1986.

Hofstadter, Richard, William Miller, and Daniel Aaron. *The American Republic Since 1865.* Vol. 2. Englewood Cliffs, N.J.: Prentice-Hall, 1959.

Holt, Michael. *The Rise and Fall of the American Whig Party.* New York: Oxford University Press, 1999.

Inter-university Consortium for Political and Social Research. Data Set 0003: "Historical, Demographic, Economic, and Social Data: The United States, 1790–1970." Compiled by ICPSR staff, University of Michigan, no date.

———. Data Set 0001: "United States Historical Election Returns, 1824–1968." Compiled by the ICPSR staff under the supervision of Howard Allen and Jerome Clubb, University of Michigan, no date.

———. Data Set 0019: "State-Level Presidential Election Data for the United States, 1824–1972." Compiled by Walter Burnham, Jerome Clubb, and William Flanigan, University of Michigan, no date.

———. Data Set 0075: "State-Level Congressional, Gubernatorial, and Senatorial Election Data for the United States, 1824–1973." Compiled by Walter Burnham, Jerome Clubb, and William Flanigan, University of Michigan, no date.

Jacobson, Gary. *The Politics of Congressional Elections.* Boston: Little, Brown, and Co., 1983.

Jensen, Richard. *The Winning of the Midwest: Social and Political Conflict, 1888–1896.* Chicago: University of Chicago Press, 1971.

Kallenbach, Joseph. *The American Chief Executive.* New York: Harper and Row, 1966.

Kallenbach, Joseph, and Jessamine Kallenbach. *American State Governors, 1776–1976.* 3 vols. Dobbs Ferry, N.Y.: Oceana Publishing, 1977.

Key, V. O., Jr. *Southern Politics.* New York: Alfred Knopf, 1949.

———. *American State Politics.* New York: Alfred Knopf, 1956.

King, Gary, and Andrew Gelman. "Systemic Consequences of the Incumbency Advantage in the U.S. House of Representatives." *American Journal of Political Science* 35 (1991): 110–138.

Kleppner, Paul. *The Cross of Culture: A Social Analysis of Midwestern Politics, 1850–1900.* New York: The Free Press, 1970.

———. "Were Women to Blame? Female Suffrage and Voter Turnout." *Journal of Interdisciplinary History* 12 (1982a): 621–643.

———. *Who Voted?* New York: Praeger, 1982b.

Kousser, J. Morgan. *The Shaping of Southern Politics.* New Haven, Conn.: Yale University Press, 1974.

Lane, Robert *Political Life.* Glencoe, Illinois: The Free Press, 1959.

Lipson, Leslie. *The American Governor from Figurehead to Leader.* Chicago: University of Chicago Press, 1939.

Madison, James, John Jay, and Alexander Hamilton. *The Federalist Papers.* New York: New Mentor Books, 1960.

Mann, Thomas, Norman Ornstein, and Michael Malbin. *Vital Statistics on Congress, 1997–1998.* Washington, D.C.: Congressional Quarterly Press, 1998.

McCulloch, Albert. *Suffrage and Its Problems.* Baltimore: Worwich and York, 1929.

McGovney, Dudley. *The American Suffrage Medley.* Chicago: University of Chicago Press, 1949.

McKinley, Albert. *The Suffrage Franchise in the Thirteen English Colonies in America.* Philadelphia: Ginn and Co., 1905.

Norpoth, Helmut, and Jerrold Rusk. "Partisan Dealignment in the American Electorate: Itemizing the Deductions Since 1964." *American Political Science Review* 76 (1982): 522–537.

Petersen, Svend. *A Statistical History of the American Presidential Elections.* New York: Frederick Ungar, 1963.

Porter, Kirk. *A History of Suffrage in the United States.* Chicago: University of Chicago Press, 1918.

Przeworski, Adam, and John Sprague. "Concepts in Search of Explicit Formulation: A Study in Measurement." *Midwest Journal of Political Science* 15 (1971): 183–218.

Ragsdale, Lyn. "Institutional Autonomy and Divided Government." Paper presented at the annual meeting of the American Political Science Association, San Francisco, 1996.

———. *Vital Statistics on the Presidency,* rev. ed. Washington, D.C.: Congressional Quarterly Press, 1998.

Robinson, Edgar. *The Presidential Vote, 1896–1932.* Stanford: Stanford University Press, 1934.

Roscoe, Douglas. "Ticket Splitting in American Elections: Voters, Candidates, and the Political Environment." Ph.D. dissertation, Loyola University, Chicago, 2001.

Rubin, Richard. *Press, Party and Presidency.* New York: W. W. Norton, 1981.

Rusk, Jerrold. "The Effect of the Australian Ballot Reform on Split Ticket Voting: 1876–1908." *American Political Science Review* 64 (1970): 1220–1238.

———. "Communications to the Editor." *American Political Science Review* 65 (1971): 1153–1157.

———. "The American Electoral Universe: Speculation and Evidence." *American Political Science Review* 68 (1974): 1028–1057.

———. "Political Participation: A Review Essay." *American Political Science Review* 70 (1976): 583–591.

Rusk, Jerrold, and John Stucker. "The Effect of the Southern System of Election Laws on Voting Participation: A Reply to V. O. Key, Jr." Paper presented at the Mathematical Social Science Board's Conference on the History of Popular Voting Behavior, Cornell University, June 11–13, 1973. In *The History of American Voting Behavior,* edited by Joel Silbey, Allan Bogue, and William Flanigan, 198–250. Princeton: Princeton University Press, 1978.

———. "Measuring Patterns of Electoral Participation in the United States." *Micropolitics* 3 (1984): 465–498.

———. "Legal-Institutional Factors and Voting Participation: The Impact of Women's Suffrage on Voter Turnout." In *Political Participation and American Democracy,* edited by William Crotty. Westport, Conn.: Greenwood Press, 1991.

Rusk, Jerrold, and Herbert Weisberg. "Perceptions of Presidential Candidates: Implications for Electoral Change." *Midwest Journal of Political Science* 16 (1972): 388–411.

Sabato, Larry. *Goodbye to Good-Time Charlie: The American Governorship Transformed.* Washington, D.C.: Congressional Quarterly Press, 1978.

Scammon, Richard. *America at the Polls. 1920–1964.* Washington, D.C.: Elections Research Center, 1965.

———. *America Votes.* Biennial, 1952–1998. Vols. 1–18 published by the Elections Research Center, Washington D.C.; vols. 19–23 published by Congressional Quarterly Press, Washington, D.C.

Schlesinger, Arthur, and Fred Israel, eds. *History of American Presidential Elections, 1789–1968.* 4 vols. New York: Chelsea House, 1971.

Seymour, Charles, and Donald Frary. *How the World Votes.* 2 vols. Springfield, Ill.: C. A. Nichols, 1918.

Sobel, Robert, ed. *Biographical Directory of the Governors of the United States, 1789–1978.* 4 vols. Westport, Conn.: Meckler Publishing, 1978.

Statutes of the 50 States. Published by state governments or by private publishers under state contract, various dates.

Stucker, John. "The Impact of Woman Suffrage on Patterns of Voter Participation." Ph.D. dissertation, University of Michigan, 1973.

Turner, Frederick Jackson. *The Frontier in American History.* New York: Henry Holt, 1920. Original paper presented in 1893.

U.S. Bureau of the Census. *Decennial Censuses, 1790–1990.* Washington, D.C.: U.S. Government Printing Office, various dates.

————. *Statistical Abstract of the United States.* Washington, D.C.: U.S. Government Printing Office, various dates.

————. *Series P Pamphlets on Voting Eligibility.* Washington, D.C.: U.S. Government Printing Office, various dates.

U.S. Civil War Center. *Statistical Summary of America's Major Wars.* Website for U.S. Civil War Center, 2001. Available at www.cwc.lsu.edu.

U.S. Department of Commerce. *Historical Statistics of the United States, Colonial Times to 1970.* Washington, D.C.: U.S. Government Printing Office, 1975.

————. *Votes Cast in Presidential and Congressional Elections, 1928–1944.* Washington, D.C.: U.S. Government Printing Office, 1945.

U.S. Congress. *Biographical Directory of the United States Congress, 1774–1978.* Washington, D.C.: U.S. Government Printing Office, 1989.

————. *Congressional Directory.* Washington, D.C.: U.S. Government Printing Office, various dates.

U.S. House of Representatives. Available at www.house.gov.

U.S. Senate. "Majority and Minority Parties: Party Divisions in the Senate." Available at www.senate.gov.

Verba, Sidney, and Norman Nie. *Participation in America: Political Democracy and Social Equality.* New York: Harper and Row, 1972.

Weisberg, Herbert, and Jerrold Rusk. "Dimensions of Candidate Evaluation." *American Political Science Review* 64 (1970): 1167–1185.

Wigmore, J. *The Australian Ballot System as Embodied in the Legislation of Various Countries.* 2nd ed. Boston: Boston Book Company, 1889.

Williamson, Chilton. *American Suffrage from Property to Democracy, 1760–1860.* Princeton: Princeton University Press, 1960.

Wolfinger, Raymond, and Steven Rosenstone. *Who Votes?* New Haven, Conn.: Yale University Press, 1980.

Index

Adams, John, 119, 122
Adams, John Quincy, 120, 123, 129, 210
Agricultural issues, 126
Alabama
    admission to the Union, 204
    elections and political issues, 128–129, 208, 209, 210, 514
    governorships, 440n1
    voting requirements, 15–16, 17
Alaska, 128, 202
Aliens. *See* Immigrants and immigration
Allen, Howard, 3
American Antiquarian Society, 6
American Independent Party, 122
American Labor Party, 7
American Party, 200, 205, 206
American Revolution, 13
Anderson, John, 122
Anti-Federalist Party, 120, 199
Anti-Mason Party, 123, 205, 212n7
Arizona, 128, 210, 374
Arkansas
    admission to the Union, 205
    elections and political issues, 127, 128, 209, 210
    governors, 435
    voting requirements, 17
Austin, Erik, 3
Australia, 5, 45
Australian secret ballot. *See* Ballots

Ballots
    Australian secret ballot, 4, 5, 6, 45, 212n2
    early ballots, 5, 45, 46, 212n2
Bank of the U.S., 122, 123, 205
Beard, Charles, 13, 16
Becker, Carl, 13
Bell, John, 122, 125
Benton, Thomas Hart, 199
Blackstone, William, 13, 14
Border South, U.S. *See* South, U.S.
Bourgeoisie, 14
Breckinridge, John, 122, 125, 130n4
Bryan, William Jennings, 125, 126, 129, 201, 207
Buchanan, James, 125, 206
Bullmoose Progressive Party, 200
Burnham, Walter Dean, 3, 45, 47, 199
Bush, George H. W., 118
Bush, George W., 120

Calhoun, John C., 123
California
    admission to the Union, 124, 205
    Democratic Party, 209
    elections and political issues, 7, 129, 201, 211, 374
    Republican Party, 208, 209, 210
Candidates
    dual major-party endorsement, 200–201
    incumbents, 209, 261, 388, 511, 512
    independent, 7, 42–43, 200
    joint endorsements, 200
    state definition of qualifications, 13
    third-party candidacies, 375
Carpetbaggers, 15, 17, 41–42
Carter, Jimmy, 118
Cass, Lewis, 199
Celler, Emanuel, 7
Census, U.S., 37, 38, 39, 40
Citizenship and residency
    barriers to voting, 13
    voting requirements, 16–17, 25–32, 38, 39
City Fusion Party, 7
Civil War and Reconstruction
    15th Amendment to the Constitution, 17
    Civil War–Reconstruction era, 38, 42–44, 124–125, 128, 205–207, 371
    elections and campaigns, 124–125, 128, 205–207, 371
    governorships and, 437, 438, 439
    Hayes, Rutherford, and Compromise of 1876, 15, 17, 42, 206
    party competition, 513
    Reconstruction, 17, 38, 39, 42–43, 124–125, 128, 371, 437, 438
    suffrage and voting, 39, 40, 43–44
Clay, Henry, 120, 123, 124, 129
Cleveland, Grover, 121, 130n7, 207
Clinton, Bill, 118, 127
Clinton, De Witt, 199
Clubb, Jerome, 3, 199
Colonial period, U.S., 13–14, 16, 22, 38
Colorado, 19, 128, 210, 374–375
Competitiveness and competitive eras. *See* Political parties
Compromise of 1850, 205
Compromise of 1876, 15, 17, 125, 206. *See also* Missouri Compromises
Confederacy, 17–18, 39–40. *See also individual states*
Congress, U.S., 123, 124–125, 511. *See also* House of Representatives, U.S.; Senate, U.S.

Congressional Directory, 6, 199
Congressional Quarterly (CQ), 3
Congressional Quarterly's Guide to U.S. Elections, 3, 200, 201
Connecticut
    constitution, 13, 16
    elections and political issues, 119, 127, 128, 208
    governors, 435, 436
    voting requirements, 14, 16, 18
Conservatism, 126
Constitution, U.S., 18, 119, 120, 198, 369–370
    15th Amendment, 13, 17, 19, 36, 39, 40
    17th Amendment, 36, 47, 121, 369–370, 514
    19th Amendment, 13, 19, 36, 40, 42, 44, 47
    24th Amendment, 13, 18, 36
    26th Amendment, 19, 36, 40
Constitutional Union Party, 122, 125
Constitutions, state, 435
Coolidge, Calvin, 126, 128
Corruption, 5–6
Crawford, William, 120, 123

Dahl, Robert, 13, 510, 511, 514, 515
Daily News Almanac, 6
Data. *See* Political science
David index, 510–511
David, Paul, 510
Declaration of Independence, 41
Delaware
    constitution, 13
    elections and political issues, 119, 127, 128, 202, 210, 513
    governors, 435
    voting requirements, 14, 15
Democracy, 119
Democratic eras, 38–40, 43, 124–125, 372–374
Democratic Party. *See also* South, U.S.
    antecedents of, 199
    Bourbon Democrats, 17, 18
    discrepancies in data sets, 9–11
    as dominant party, 38–39, 118, 121, 123, 125–129, 203, 370
    election issues, 42, 120
    governorships, 436, 437, 438, 439
    Jackson, Andrew, and, 41
    Jacksonian Democratic Party, 120, 123, 124, 199, 203, 204–205
    New Deal, 208–209, 372–373
    party competition and, 510–515
    party unity scores, 374, 375n4
    post–Civil War period, 206
    precursors to, 120
    pre-Roosevelt, Franklin D., 38
    Solid South, 125, 209, 210, 512
    stability of, 211
    suffrage issues, 17, 39
    vision of America, 207
    white primaries, 18
Democratic-Republican Party
    elections and political issues, 119, 120, 203
    factions in, 199
    Federalist/Democratic-Republican era, 38, 41, 43, 123, 204, 371, 437, 513
    party competition, 511, 513
    presidential candidates, 123–124
Dixiecrats. *See* States' Rights Democratic Party

Douglas, Stephen, 125, 130n4
Dred Scott v. Sanford (1857), 124–125
Dubin, Michael J., 3, 118, 199, 201
Dunn v. Blumstein (1972), 15

Early Republic era, 41, 43
East, U.S., 16, 123, 127, 128. *See also* New England
Economic issues, 126, 207. *See also* Property issues
Egger, Rowland, 434
Eisenhower, Dwight D., 121, 126, 130n5, 373
Elections. *See also* Candidates; Voters and voting issues
    comparison of national seats and votes, 222–223
    competitive, 510
    cross-filing, 7
    data accuracy and availability, 1–12, 118–119, 202
    election results, 217–221, 262–368, 390–433
    electoral college, 119–120
    gubernatorial, 434–509
    historical development of, 122–127, 371–374
    House elections, 198–368
    legal structures, 202
    midterm, 47, 211
    odd- and even-numbered years, 48, 202
    party codings, 12, 199–202
    party victories by state, 238–259
    presidential, Senate and House compared, 203, 369
    primaries, 18, 19, 46
    regional effects, 224–237, 260
    results, 132–197, 199
    role in democratic government, 13
    Senate elections, 369–433
    southern system, 18, 19
Elections—specific
    1788, 118–119, 122, 199
    1790, 199
    1792, 122
    1794, 204, 371
    1796, 122, 204, 371
    1798, 204, 371, 512
    1800, 119, 122, 204, 210, 371, 513
    1804, 437
    1808, 204, 439
    1810, 439
    1812, 41, 200, 204, 371, 437
    1814, 371
    1816, 41, 43, 122, 123, 204, 371, 437
    1817, 437
    1818, 123, 204, 371, 513
    1820, 41, 43, 119, 122, 123, 204, 208, 371, 513
    1822, 123, 204, 437
    1824, 4, 41, 43, 119, 120, 122, 123, 204, 371, 513
    1826, 123, 204
    1828, 41, 43, 119, 121, 123, 204, 210, 437
    1830, 205
    1832, 41, 121, 123, 205
    1834, 41, 205, 212, 437, 439
    1836, 41, 43, 119, 123–124, 212
    1838, 437
    1840, 41, 42, 43, 47, 124, 129, 437, 513
    1842, 46, 205
    1844, 124, 129
    1846, 205

1848, 44, 124, 129
1852, 205, 437, 513
1854, 121, 205, 206, 371, 438, 439, 513
1856, 120, 122, 124, 125, 129, 206, 438, 513
1858, 206, 371, 438
1860, 41, 42, 44, 47, 120, 122, 124, 125, 129, 203, 206, 371
1862, 438
1868, 119, 128, 130*n*5
1870, 438
1872, 4, 126, 128, 130*n*5, 438
1874, 4, 206, 371, 438
1876, 42, 120, 125, 129, 130*nn*5, 7, 206, 438
1878, 371
1880, 129, 130*n*7, 206, 371, 513, 514
1882, 206, 371
1884, 129
1888, 120, 129, 130*n*7, 206
1890, 206
1892, 122, 125, 207, 211, 371, 438, 513–514
1894, 203, 207, 211, 371, 438
1896, 4, 42, 126, 128, 129, 201, 203, 207, 438
1900, 128, 129, 130*n*1, 207
1904, 128
1908, 129
1910, 207, 372
1912, 120, 122, 128, 130*n*1, 207, 372, 373
1916, 42, 44, 47, 208, 370
1918, 47, 370, 372
1920, 42, 44, 47, 128, 130*n*5, 208, 371, 438, 511, 514
1922, 47, 438
1924, 122, 128
1928, 42, 130*n*5, 208, 371, 373, 438
1930, 208, 212, 370, 371, 372, 375*n*2, 438, 514
1932, 42, 47, 126, 204, 208, 211, 212, 370–373, 439, 511, 512, 514
1934, 47
1936, 126, 208, 373, 438
1938, 7, 208, 438, 512
1940, 126, 371, 373
1942, 208, 371, 373
1944, 126, 514
1946, 208, 370, 371, 373
1948, 42, 122, 126, 370, 373
1950, 370
1952, 126, 130*n*5, 208, 370, 373
1954, 209, 370
1956, 126, 130*n*5, 208, 370
1958, 209, 370, 371
1960, 126, 130*n*5, 208, 438
1962, 208, 514
1964, 127, 209, 514
1966, 209, 373, 438, 514
1968, 44, 120, 122, 127, 129, 439
1970, 439
1972, 15, 44, 119, 209, 512
1974, 209
1976, 126, 129, 209
1978, 209
1980, 122, 127, 209, 370, 371, 373, 374, 439
1982, 209, 370, 512
1984, 127, 370, 439
1986, 373, 374, 435

1988, 127, 438, 439
1990, 209
1992, 44, 118, 122, 127, 209, 210
1994, 209, 210, 370, 373, 374, 439
1996, 44, 118, 122, 127, 209, 210, 374, 439, 514
1998, 47, 209, 210, 374, 439
2000, 120, 209
Electoral college. *See* Electors and electoral college
Electoral history, U.S., 1
Electorates. *See* Elections; Voters and voting issues
Electors and electoral college
    effects of, 129
    meeting of 1789, 119
    methods of choosing, 131
    qualifications, 13
    voters and voting, 127, 132–133
Eligibility. *See* Voters and voting issues
Employment issues, 45, 207
England, 13, 15, 22
Ethnic issues. *See* Racial and minority issues
Evans, Rowland, 373
Evening Journal Almanac, 6

Federal government. *See* Government
Federalism, 13
Federalist Papers, 369
Federalist Party
    elections and political issues, 119, 122–123, 126–127, 440*n*5
    Federalist/Democratic-Republican era, 38, 41, 43, 123, 203, 204, 371, 437, 513
    governorships, 437, 439
    party competition, 511, 513
    presidential candidates, 120
    Republican Party and, 199
Fillmore, Millard, 206
Flanigan, William, 3, 199
Florida
    admission to the Union, 205
    Clinton, Bill, 127
    governor term, 435
    party competitiveness, 128, 513, 514
    Republican Party in, 125, 209, 210
Ford, Gerald, 129
Franchise. *See* Voters and voting issues
Free Soil Party, 200, 205
Fremont, John C., 125, 206
Fusion Party, 205

Garfield, James A., 121
George III, King of England, 434
Georgia
    constitution, 13
    elections and political issues, 119, 127, 128, 205, 209, 210, 513, 514
    governors, 435
    voting requirements, 14, 15, 17
Gerry, Eldridge, 198
Gold standard, 207
Gore, Al, 120
Government
    distrust of, 43
    federal government, 19, 20

participation in, 13
  role of, 126, 127
Governors
  characteristics of gubernatorial elections, 434–435, 436
  election results by state, 456–509
  historical perspective on gubernatorial elections, 437–440
  national view of gubernatorial elections, 436–437
  one-partyism, 512
  party codings, 445
  party competition, 511, 513, 514, 518–526, 530–548, 551–557, 654–689
  party control of statehouses, 447
  power of, 511
  regional voting, 448–454
  state results of U.S. governors, 439, 442–446
  term length and term limits, 435–436, 441
Grant, Ulysses S., 121, 128, 130n5
Great Depression, 42, 126, 212
Great Society, 126
Greeley, Horace, 126
Greenback Party, 200
Guinn v. U.S. (1915), 18

Hamilton, Alexander, 122
Harding, Warren G., 125, 126, 208
Harrison, Benjamin, 120, 121
Harrison, William Henry, 42, 43, 123–124, 205, 371
Hawaii, 129, 202, 374
Hayes, Rutherford B.
  Compromise of 1876, 15, 17, 42, 206
  election of, 120, 121, 125, 130n5
Hoover, Herbert, 126, 130n5, 208
House of Representatives, U.S. *See also* Elections
  constitutional issues, 13
  data discrepancies and coding, 3–5, 9–11, 198–202
  elections, 198–368
  expansion of, 204
  legal structure of elections, 202–203
  methods of apportioning seats, 214
  national party patterns, 370
  one-party states, 210–211
  party competition, 513, 514, 518–526, 530–548, 551–557, 603–638
  political composition of, 215–216
  political eras and, 38, 203–210
  presidential elections, 119, 120, 123, 125, 203
  representatives, 369
  state as unit of analysis, 2
  surge and decline theory, 47
  voters and voting issues, 46–47, 48, 53–55, 76–107
Humphrey, Hubert, 127

ICPSR. *See* Inter-university Consortium for Political and Social Research
Idaho, 18–19, 128
Illinois
  admission to the Union, 204
  Democratic Party, 208, 209, 212
  elections and political issues, 129, 513
  governor elections, 435
  party competitiveness, 210–211, 374–375

party regionalism, 128
  Republican Party, 373
Immigrants and immigration, 16, 18, 19, 39, 40, 46
Incumbents. *See* Candidates
Independent candidates. *See* Candidates
Indiana
  admission to the Union, 204
  Democratic Party, 128, 208, 209, 212
  election of 1828, 129
  elections and political issues, 513
  governor elections, 435
  party competitiveness, 374–375
Inter-university Consortium for Political and Social Research (ICPSR), 2–3, 4, 6, 7, 8, 9–11, 118, 198, 439, 510
Iowa
  admission to the Union, 205
  elections and political issues, 513
  governor elections, 435
  party competitiveness, 128, 374–375
  Republican Party, 208, 210, 373, 438

Jackson, Andrew
  election of 1824, 41, 120
  election of 1828, 129, 204
  election of 1836, 123–124
  elections and political issues, 121
  Whig Party, 205, 513
Jacksonian era
  Jacksonian/National Republican–Whig era, 38, 39, 41, 122, 123–124, 203, 204–205, 371
  opposition to Jacksonian Democratic Party, 38
  patronage during, 5
  voter turnout, 43
Jay, John, 369
Jefferson, Thomas, 119, 122, 124, 371, 434, 513
Jeffersonian period, 122, 127, 128, 437
Jensen, Richard, 45, 46
Johnson, Lyndon B., 118, 126–127, 373, 375n3, 514
Johnson (Lyndon B.) administration, 209. *See also* Great Society

Kansas, 210, 373, 374, 435
Kansas-Nebraska Act (1854), 124, 125, 200, 205, 206, 211
Kennedy, John F., 118
Kennedy (John F.) administration, 209
Kentucky
  Democratic Party, 210
  elections and political issues, 127, 129
  governor elections, 435, 436
  party competitiveness, 513
  Whig Party, 128
Key, V. O., 127
King, Rufus, 122, 440n5
Kleppner, Paul, 19, 45
Know-Nothing Party, 18, 205

Lampi, Philip, 3, 199
Legal issues, 119–120
Legislation and laws
  grandfather and old soldier clauses, 18, 35
  November presidential elections, 16
  southern system of election laws, 18

suffrage laws, 1, 19, 46
  voters and voting issues, 14, 44, 45
Legislatures, 435
Liberal Party, 374
Library of Congress, 3, 6
Lincoln, Abraham, 38, 121, 125
Literacy tests, 13, 17–18, 34–35, 41
Louisiana
  admission to the Union, 204
  elections and political issues, 125, 127, 128, 129, 209, 210
  governors, 435, 436
  voting requirements, 14, 17–18

Madison, James, 41, 122, 200, 369, 434
Maine
  admission to the Union, 204
  elections and political issues, 119, 128, 129, 210, 374
  governors, 438
Maryland
  constitution, 13
  elections and political issues, 119, 127, 128, 211, 513
  governors, 435
  voting requirements, 14
Masons, 212n7
Massachusetts
  constitution, 13
  elections and political issues, 119, 127, 128, 204, 205, 210
  governors, 435, 436, 437, 439
  introduction of Australian secret ballot, 5
  voting requirements, 14, 15, 18
Massachusetts Antiquarian Society, 3
McKinley, William, 121, 126, 130n1, 207
Michigan, 128, 205, 208, 209, 211, 374–375, 435, 438
Mid-Atlantic states
  Federalist Party, 204, 437
  governor elections, 435, 439
  party competitiveness, 206–207, 512
  Republican Party, 373, 438
  Whig Party, 205
Midwest, U.S. See West and Midwest, U.S.
Miller, George, 201
Minnesota, 205, 210, 374–375, 435
Mississippi
  admission to the Union, 204
  elections and political issues, 128–129, 208, 209, 210, 513
  governors, 435, 436
  voting requirements, 14, 17
Missouri
  admission to the Union, 204
  elections and political issues, 7, 128, 210, 212
  governors, 435
  slavery, 130n3
Missouri Compromises (1820, 1850), 124, 130n3, 205
Mobilization. See Voters and voting issues
Monroe, James, 122, 208
Montana, 128, 202, 374

Nationalism, 205
National Republican Party
  factions, 199
  Federalist Party and, 210

Jacksonian/National Republican–Whig era, 38, 39, 41,
    123–124, 203, 204–205, 371
  governorships, 437, 439
  party competition, 513
  presidential candidates, 120
Native American Party, 18
Nebraska, 124, 128, 208, 210, 373, 435
Nevada, 128, 374
New Deal and New Deal era. See also Roosevelt, Franklin D.
  Democratic Party, 128–129, 373
  governor elections, 437, 438
  New Deal era, 42, 44, 203, 208, 372–373
  party competition, 374, 511, 512, 514
  political parties and, 20
  voters and voting issues, 40, 44, 126–127
New England
  Democratic Party, 127, 128, 209, 374
  Federalist Party, 122, 204
  governors, 435, 436, 437, 438
  party competitiveness, 123
  Republican Party, 125, 127, 128, 206, 207, 208, 373
  voters and voting issues, 18
  Whig Party, 124
New Hampshire
  constitution, 13
  elections and political issues, 119, 127, 128, 210, 374
  governors, 435, 436
  voting requirements, 15
New Jersey
  constitution, 13
  elections and political issues, 119, 127, 128, 129, 202, 203,
    207, 209, 211, 374
  governors, 435, 436, 437
  Republican Party, 208
  voting requirements, 14
New Mexico, 124, 128, 205
New York
  constitution, 13
  elections and political issues, 7, 127, 128, 129, 200, 205, 207,
    208, 209, 211, 374, 512, 513
  governors, 435, 436, 438, 439
  Liberal Party, 374
  voting requirements, 14
  women's suffrage, 18–19
New York Public Library, 3
Nixon, Richard, 40, 118, 121, 127, 129, 130n5, 374
North Carolina
  constitution, 13
  elections and political issues, 127, 128–129, 205,
    209, 513
  governors, 435
  Republican Party, 125
  voting requirements, 14, 17–18
North Dakota, 202, 210, 373, 435
North, U.S., 40, 44
Novak, Robert, 373

Ohio
  admission to the Union, 204
  elections and political issues, 127, 128, 129, 202, 205, 207,
    208, 209, 210–211, 212, 374–375, 513

governors, 435, 438
  voting requirements, 14
Oklahoma, 17, 18, 128, 210, 374
O'Neill, Thomas "Tip," 211
Oregon, 128, 205, 210, 374
Oregon v. Mitchell (1970), 18

Panic of 1893, 207, 211, 371, 438
Patronage and spoils, 5, 41, 46, 124
Pendleton Act of 1883, 20
Pennsylvania
  constitution, 13
  elections and political issues, 119, 127, 128, 129, 200, 205,
    208, 210, 374, 512, 513
  governors, 435, 439
  joint party endorsements, 7
  voting requirements, 14, 15
People's Party, 205
Personal Liberty Party, 200
Pierce, Franklin, 205
Political eras, 38, 48, 122–127
  Civil War–Reconstruction era, 38, 41–42, 43–44, 124–125,
    128, 205–207, 371
  Democratic eras, 38–39, 124–125, 372–374
  Early Republic era, 41, 43
  Federalist/Democratic-Republican era, 38, 41, 43, 123, 204,
    371, 437, 513
  House of Representatives and, 38, 203–210
  Jacksonian era, 5, 38, 39, 41, 43, 122, 204–205, 210
  Jacksonian/National Republican–Whig era, 38, 39, 41,
    123–124, 203, 204–205, 371
  New Deal era, 42, 44, 203, 208, 372–373
  Reform era, 207–208
  Republican eras, 44, 122, 124–125, 372–374
  Senate and, 371–374
Political Facts of the United States Since 1789 (Austin and
  Chubb), 3, 199
Political issues
  elections, 369
  golden age, 43, 45, 46, 47
  governorships, 436
  historical eras, 38, 48, 122–127
  partisanship, 369, 377
  political machines, 41, 45
  presidential elections, 118, 119
  realignments, 198
  socioeconomic status, 13–14
  state versus county politics, 1
  television, 42
  voter turnout, 19, 45, 46
Political parties. *See also* Independent candidates; *individual parties*
  analysis of party codings, 7–8, 12
  candidate endorsements, 200
  Civil War and, 206
  coding schemes, 199–201
  corruption, 5
  election issues, 5–6, 20, 45, 119–130, 134–142, 144–197, 198,
    203, 369
  end to, 45
  factions, 199–200
  fusion and joint parties, 7, 200

historical eras, 122–127
  issues, 126
  modern period, 208–210
  New Deal and, 208
  one-party state politics, 210–211, 374–375, 510, 511–512
  party labels, 6
  public contestation, 510, 511
  strength and development of, 19, 20, 38, 198
  third- and minor-party issues, 121–122, 510
  two-party system, 38, 120–121, 125, 204, 510
  two-stage dynamic, 212
  voter mobilization and turnout, 38, 41, 45, 46
Political parties—competition
  Civil War and Reconstruction Republican/Democratic era, 125
  Democratic/National Republican–Whig era, 124
  Democratic-Republican era, 373–374
  Federalist/Democratic-Republican era, 123
  governor elections, 436–437, 438, 439
  measures of competition, 130n6, 510–511
  national party competition, 511, 516–526
  regions and competition, 511–512, 527–548
  state party competition, 512–514
  two-party competition, 121, 127–129, 370–371
Political science, 1, 2–5, 6–7
Polk, James K., 129
Poll taxes. *See* Taxation issues
Population, 40
Populist movement, 126
Populist Party, 122, 125, 126, 207
Presidents and presidential elections
  data prior to 1824 election, 3
  data problems, 2–3
  elections, 118–130, 131–197, 434, 512
  mandates and strength, 120, 121, 132
  party competition, 511, 513, 514, 518–526, 530–548,
    551–557, 585–602
  political parties, 120–129, 212n5
  reelection, 121
  voters and voting issues, 46–48, 50–52, 55, 57, 58–75
Primaries. *See* Elections
Progressive movement and era election reforms, 16
  fusion party tickets, 200
  government role, 126
  power of governors, 511
  reforms, 40
  Republican Party and, 207
  voting requirements, 18
Progressive Party, 122, 126
Prohibition, 18
Property issues, 13–14, 22–24, 38, 39
Pullman strike of 1894, 207

Racial and minority issues. *See also* Compromise of 1876
  in post–Civil War South, 125
  voting rights, 13, 14, 17, 18, 19, 33, 39, 40, 41
Radical Republican period, 122
Reagan, Ronald, 118, 121, 127
Reconstruction. *See* Civil War and Reconstruction
Reconstruction Acts of 1867, 17, 19, 40
Reform era, 207–208
Reforms
  19th century, 6, 49

ballot, 45
civil service, 19, 46
political parties, 46, 49
Progressive movement, 16
women's suffrage, 46
Regional issues. *See also individual regions*
elections, 123, 124, 125
party competition, 511–512
voters and voting, 135–142
Religion and religious issues, 45
Republican eras, 40, 43, 44, 122, 124–125, 372–374
Republican Party. *See also* South, U.S.
discrepancies in data sets, 9–11
as dominant party, 38–39, 118, 121, 125–127, 128–129, 203, 204–210, 370
election issues, 120, 122, 125
emergence of, 41
governorships, 436, 438–439
party competition and, 510–515
party unity scores, 374, 375n4
pre– and post–Civil War, 38, 41–42, 206, 371
precursors to, 120
Revolution of 1994, 210
in the Senate, 370
slavery and, 206
stability of, 211
suffrage issues, 39, 40
vision of America, 207
Residency requirements. *See* Citizenship and residency
Revolutionary War, 20, 22, 41
Rhode Island
constitution, 13
elections and political issues, 127, 128, 205, 374
governors, 435, 436
voting requirements, 14, 15
Roosevelt, Franklin D., 20, 38, 46, 121, 126, 208, 373. *See also* New Deal and New Deal era
Roosevelt, Theodore, 126, 130n2, 207

Senate, U.S. *See also* Constitution, U.S.
direct election of, 372
election classes, 370–371, 373, 376
elections, 47, 369–433
national party patterns of elections, 370–371, 378–379
one-party states, 374–375
partisan composition, 377
party competition, 511, 514, 518–526, 539–548, 554–557, 639–653
political eras, 371–374
regional issues, 380–387
terms, 369, 370
voters and voting issues, 47–48, 55–57, 108–117
Sherman, Roger, 198
Sherman Silver Purchase Act of 1890, 207
Slavery, 44, 124–125, 130n3, 200, 205, 206, 212
Smith v. Allwright (1944), 18
South Carolina
elections and political issues, 119, 125, 127, 128–129, 209, 210, 373, 514
governors, 435
succession of, 125
voting requirements, 14, 17

South Carolina v. Katzenbach (1966), 18
South Dakota, 210, 373, 435, 440n1
Southern Democratic Party, 122
South, U.S. *See also individual states*
alien voting movement, 16
Democratic Party, 206, 207, 208, 209, 373, 374, 512
Federalists in, 204
governorships, 437, 438, 439
Jacksonians, 205
literacy requirements, 17
one-partyism, 511–512, 515
party competition, 512, 515, 549–557
political issues, 122–124, 125, 126, 127, 128, 130n4
poll taxes, 17
post–Civil War period, 15, 41–42
racial issues, 19
Republican Party, 130n5, 209, 210, 373, 374, 512
Senate classes, 370
"Solid Democratic South," 16, 18, 42, 126
southern system of election laws, 18, 19
voters and voting issues, 39–40, 41, 44–45, 50–56, 139–141
Whigs, 205, 212
Spoils system. *See* Patronage and spoils
State Historical Society of Wisconsin, 6
States. *See also* Political parties; *individual states*
ballots and balloting processes, 5, 6
constitutions, 13, 21
definition of electorate, 13, 14
election issues and results, 4–5, 119, 122, 129, 144–197, 262–368, 390–433
gubernatorial elections, 434–509
importance as unit of analysis, 2
inclusiveness in government, 13
legislatures, 434
nullification of states' rights, 123
party competition, 512–515, 558–689
party politics, 210–211, 212, 238–240, 510
political issues, 2, 127–129, 211–212, 515
Senate and senators, 372
suffrage, 19
trends, 2
vote count errors, 3–5
voter and voting issues, 13–20, 48, 58–117
States' Rights Democratic Party, 122, 126
Statistical and measure issues
analysis of party codings, 7–8, 12, 199–202, 213, 374, 389, 439, 445
data errors, 198–199, 202
measures of voting participation, 37–38
standard deviation, 4
vote count errors, 3–5
Stevenson, Adlai, 126
Stucker, John, 38
Suffrage and franchise. *See* Voters and voting issues
Supreme Court, U.S., 15, 18, 124–125

Taft, William Howard, 130n2, 207
Taxation issues
poll taxes, 13, 14–15, 17, 18, 33–34, 41
voting requirements, 14, 22–24, 38, 39
Taylor, Zachary, 129, 199
Television, 42

Tennessee
  elections and political issues, 127, 128, 205, 373, 513
  governors, 435
  Republican Party, 125
  voting requirements, 14
Texas
  admission to the Union, 205
  elections and political issues, 209, 210, 373
  constitution, 16–17
  Republican Party, 125, 210
  voting requirements, 17
Thurmond, Strom, 122, 126
Tilden, Samuel J., 120, 125, 130n7, 206
Tower, John, 373, 375n3
Truman, Harry S., 42, 126, 373
Turner, Frederick Jackson, 16
Turnout. *See* Voters and voting issues

Understanding clause, 17
Union Party, 205
United States Congressional Elections, 1788–1997 (Dubin), 3, 200, 201
Utah, 19, 124, 128, 205, 210, 436

Van Buren, Martin, 124, 129
Vermont
  constitution, 13
  elections and political issues, 127, 128, 202, 205, 210, 374, 513
  governors, 435, 437
  joint party endorsements, 7
Vietnam War, 40, 43, 126–127, 373
Virginia
  constitution, 13
  elections and political issues, 119, 127, 128–129, 205, 514
  governors, 435, 436
  Republican Party, 125
  voting requirements, 14, 17
Voters and voting issues. *See also* Elections; Legislation and laws
  coding, 200
  corruption and, 5–6, 45, 46
  districting, 202
  economic and class issues, 46
  eligibility and eligibility index, 37–38, 41, 44, 50, 58–63
  errors and problems, 1–5, 43, 44, 47, 48, 118
  historical background, 38–44, 45–46, 48–49
  legal-institutional theory of voting, 14, 18, 45
  measures of, 37–38, 44, 47, 48
  mobilization, 37, 41–44, 46, 48, 51, 53, 55, 64–69, 76–91, 108–112
  participation and turnout, 1, 2, 18, 19, 37–49, 52, 54, 55–57, 70–75, 92–107, 113–117
  patterns of, 46–48
  political issues, 6–8, 45, 127
  popular vote and electoral vote connection, 120, 132

  presidential elections, 119, 132–141
  regional effects, 44–45
  results, 132–197
  split-ticket, 5, 45
  suffrage, franchise, and eligibility, 13–20, 22–36, 37, 39–41, 44
  surge and decline theory, 47, 48
  vote shifts, 129, 143
Voting Rights Acts of 1965 and 1970, 15, 18

Wallace, George, 122, 127
War of 1812, 41, 43, 200, 204, 371
Washington, George, 122
Washington State, 128, 210, 211, 374
Webster, Daniel, 123–124
Welfare, social
  control of vote, 5
  federal government and, 20
  political parties and, 46
West and Midwest, U.S.
  Democratic Party, 208, 209, 372–373, 374, 512
  democratic values, 16
  elections and political issues, 123, 125, 127, 128, 206–207, 512, 514–515
  governors, 435, 438
  one-partyism, 512
  Republican Party, 208, 373, 512
  Senate classes, 370
  Whig Party, 212
  women's suffrage, 18–19, 40
West Virginia, 128, 374
Whig Party
  fusion tickets, 200
  governorships, 437–438, 439
  Jacksonian/National Republican–Whig era, 38, 39, 41, 122, 123–124, 203, 204–205, 371
  National Republican Party, 210
  party competition, 129, 513
  presidential candidates, 120
  regionalism, 128, 212
  Republican Party, 125, 199
  in the South, 512
Whig/Tribune Almanac, 6
Whiskey Rebellion, 122
White, Hugh, 123–124
Wilson, Woodrow, 20, 46, 120, 125, 126, 207–208
Wisconsin
  admission to the Union, 205
  elections and political issues, 128, 208, 513
  governors, 435
  voting requirements, 16
Women's suffrage, 13, 14, 18–19, 36, 40, 44, 46, 49
World Almanac, 6
World War I, 208, 514
World War II, 42, 44, 118, 126, 373, 514
Wyoming, 19, 42, 128, 202, 374